W9-CAF-587

P9-CFM-602

From the Nation's Leading Social Studies Educator

Adventures in Time and Place

ENHANCE YOUR TEACHING AND HAVE MORE FUN HELPING YOUR STUDENTS TO BECOME 21ST CENTURY CITIZENS & GEOGRAPHY-LITERATE EXPLORERS & HISTORY-SMART ADVENTURERS

GRADE 2

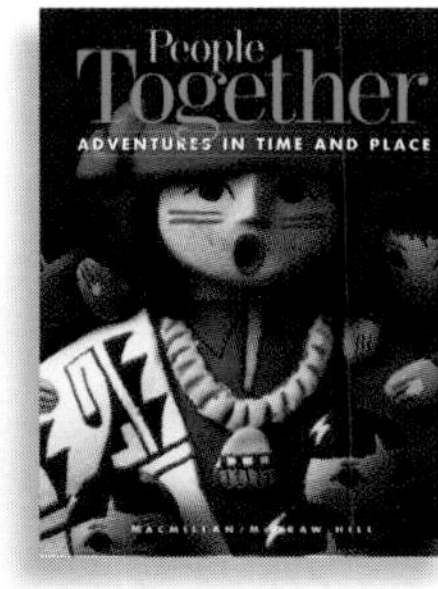

GRADE 1

MyWorld

ADVENTURES IN TIME AND PLACE

GRADE 3

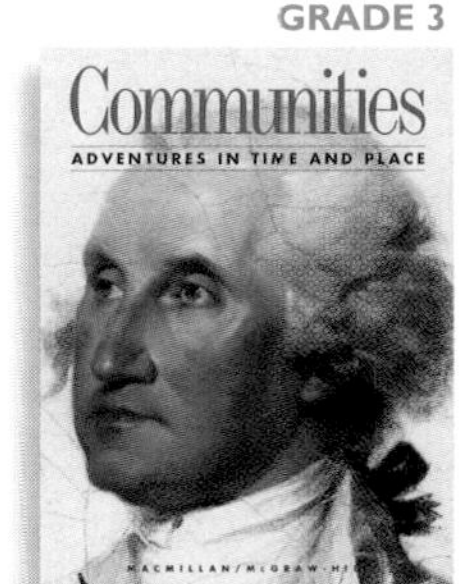

GRADE 4

Regions

ADVENTURES IN TIME AND PLACE

GRADE K

GRADE 6/7

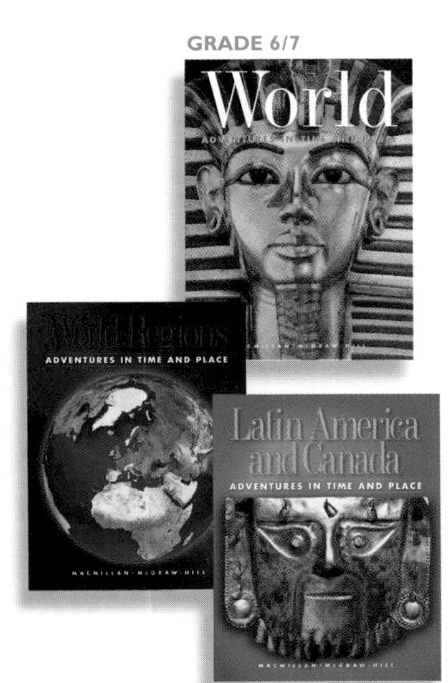

GRADE 5

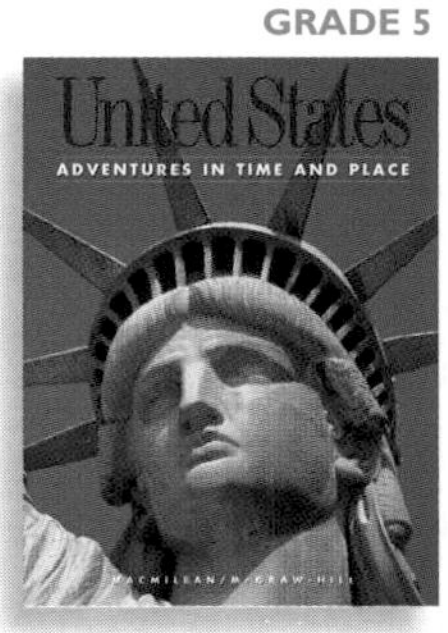

MACMILLAN / McGRAW-HILL

Macmillan McGraw-Hill invites you to experience

Adventures in

COMPONENTS FROM GRADES 1-2
(SAMPLE SHOWN FROM GRADE 1)

ANTHOLOGY MyWorld ADVENTURES IN TIME AND PLACE

ASSESSMENT BOOK MyWorld ADVENTURES IN TIME AND PLACE

TAAS STRATEGIES AND PRACTICE MyWorld ADVENTURES IN TIME AND PLACE

OUTLINE MAPS MyWorld ADVENTURES IN TIME AND PLACE

PRACTICE BOOK MyWorld ADVENTURES IN TIME AND PLACE

PROJECT BOOK MyWorld ADVENTURES IN TIME AND PLACE

UNIT 1 THEME BIG BOOK WHERE WE LIVE MyWorld ADVENTURES IN TIME AND PLACE

UNIT 2 THEME BIG BOOK WE BELONG MyWorld

UNIT 3 THEME BIG BOOK PEOPLE AT WORK

UNIT 4 THEME BIG BOOK OUR WORLD

TEACHER'S *MULTIMEDIA* EDITION MyWorld ADVENTURES IN TIME AND PLACE MACMILLAN/McGRAW-HILL

MyWorld ADVENTURES IN TIME AND PLACE MACMILLAN/McGRAW-HILL

ADVENTURES IN TIME AND PLACE GEO Big Book

MY WORLD ADVENTURES IN TIME AND PLACE STICKERS MACMILLAN/McGRAW-HILL

GEO ADVENTURES Daily Geography Activities My World

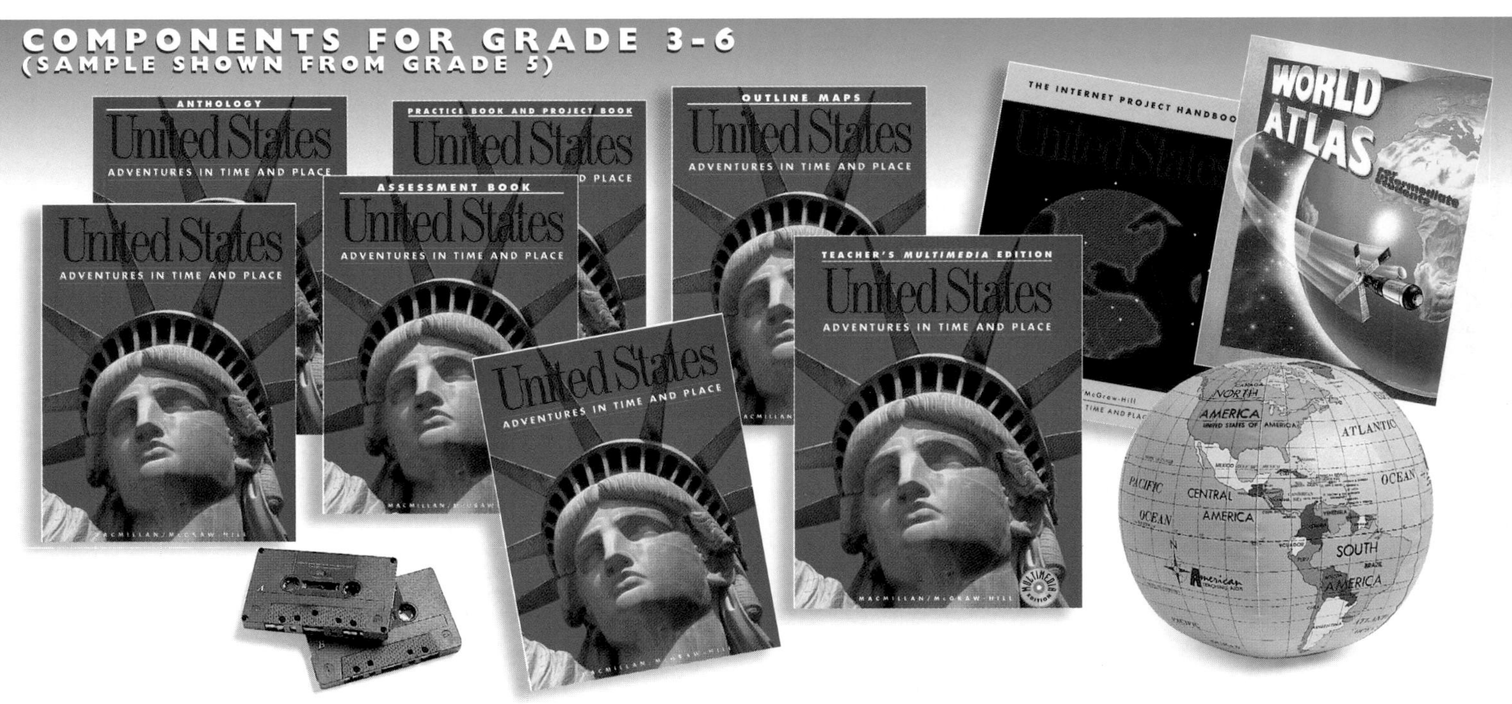

Choices in easy-to-use materials

GRADES 1–2

You have these options to choose from:

- Teach with Big Books
- Teach with Pupil Edition
- Teach with a combination

Use the same manageable Teacher's Edition, whichever approach you use. Choose the activities that meet your needs, in your setting, to fit your classroom style!

6 theme big books for group instruction

A Teacher's Multimedia Edition to support your approach

A Pupil Edition for individual teaching

Activities provide options for hands-on learning

Choices help you meet your needs and reach your goals

AT EVERY GRADE

The rich content is supported by hands-on activites and brought to life through motivating primary sources and diverse perspectives. Your teaching is supported with a 3-Step Lesson Plan — **1 PREPARE, 2 TEACH, 3 CLOSE** — easy to use and easy to manage.

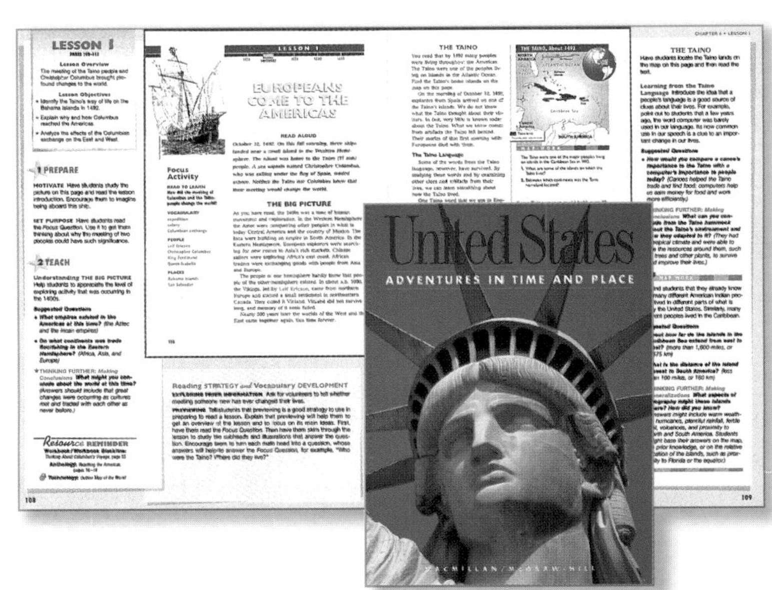

Program Philosophy

Each and every one of the educators, authors, editors, and designers who created Macmillan/McGraw-Hill's Adventures in Time and Place share a deep commitment to provide

- **rich, relevant content** in all areas of social studies, at every grade level.
- **geographic literacy skills** for all students, created in partnership with the National Geographic Society.
- **easy-to-use teaching materials** with choices to suit different student learning styles and diversity in teaching styles.

Program Authorship

National Geographic Society, the world's premier authority on

NATIONAL GEOGRAPHIC SOCIETY

geography and geography education, joins the same team that created the best-selling Macmillan/McGraw-Hill Social Studies Program THE WORLD AROUND US to bring you a brand new program... Adventures in Time and Place.

DR. BARRY BEYER
George Mason University
Fairfax, VA

DR. JAMES BANKS
University of Washington
Seattle, WA

JEAN CRAVEN
Albuquerque Public Schools
Albuquerque, NM

DR. GLORIA CONTRERAS
University of North Texas
Denton, TX

DR. MARY MCFARLAND
Parkway Public Schools
Creve Coeur, MO

DR. WALTER PARKER
University of Washington
Seattle, WA

DR. GLORIA LADSON-BILLINGS
University of Wisconsin-Madison
Madison, WI

Adventures in Rich, Relevant Content

1 Active Citizenship is taught through skill lessons, interactive activities and concrete examples.

- Citizenship and Thinking Skills lessons help form the ideas, and thought processes needed by citizens of the 21st century.
- "Making a Difference" introduces everyday people who practice good citizenship in their communities.

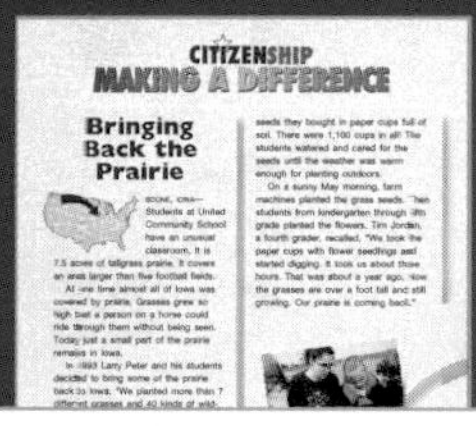
CITIZENSHIP
MAKING A DIFFERENCE
Bringing Back the Prairie

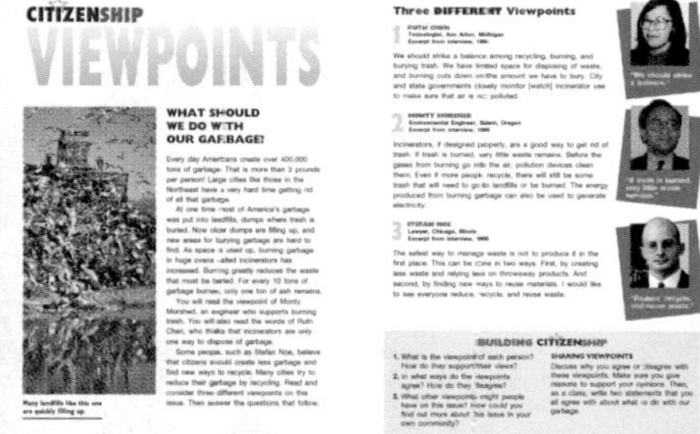
CITIZENSHIP
VIEWPOINTS
WHAT SHOULD WE DO WITH OUR GARBAGE?
Three DIFFERENT Viewpoints
BUILDING CITIZENSHIP

FROM GRADE 4 PUPIL EDITION

- "Viewpoints" in grades 3–7 provide chances for students to discover and appreciate many different points of view — and to learn to handle differences.

2 Geographic Literacy for all students is assured through the co-authorship of the National Geographic Society.

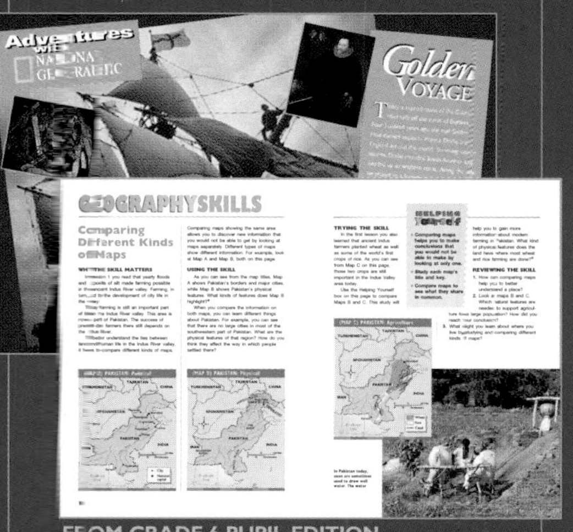
Adventures with National Geographic
Golden Voyage
GEOGRAPHY SKILLS
Comparing Different Kinds of Maps

FROM GRADE 6 PUPIL EDITION

- Geography's impact on history is emphasized to teach students the connection between them.
- Geography's five fundamental themes are the focus of skill lessons and features that support the ties among past and present people, places and events.
- Map skills are developed systematically for use in real life situations and for standardized test-taking.

3 History lessons link past and present in ways that make sense for all students — at all grade levels.

- More solid content at grades 1 and 2, with a narrative style that puts the "story" back in history, and lets you teach real history at primary grade levels.
- "Many Voices" from meaningful primary sources and literature are integrated in text features to bring history alive in words and pictures.
- Historical figures of many backgrounds, both famous and ordinary, provide reflections on our past from diverse perspectives.

FROM GRADE 3 PUPIL EDITION

Legacy
LINKING PAST AND PRESENT
A Family Reunion

Poor Richard's Almanac

Choices for assessment and accountability

Adventures in Time and Place provides a variety of methods to check both students' recall of factual information and their application of that knowledge. It's your choice:

- Standardized Test Format
- Written Response Format
- Performance Assessments with Scoring Rubrics

There's a way to get an accurate assessment — a real grade — for every child, whichever approach you use for evaluation.

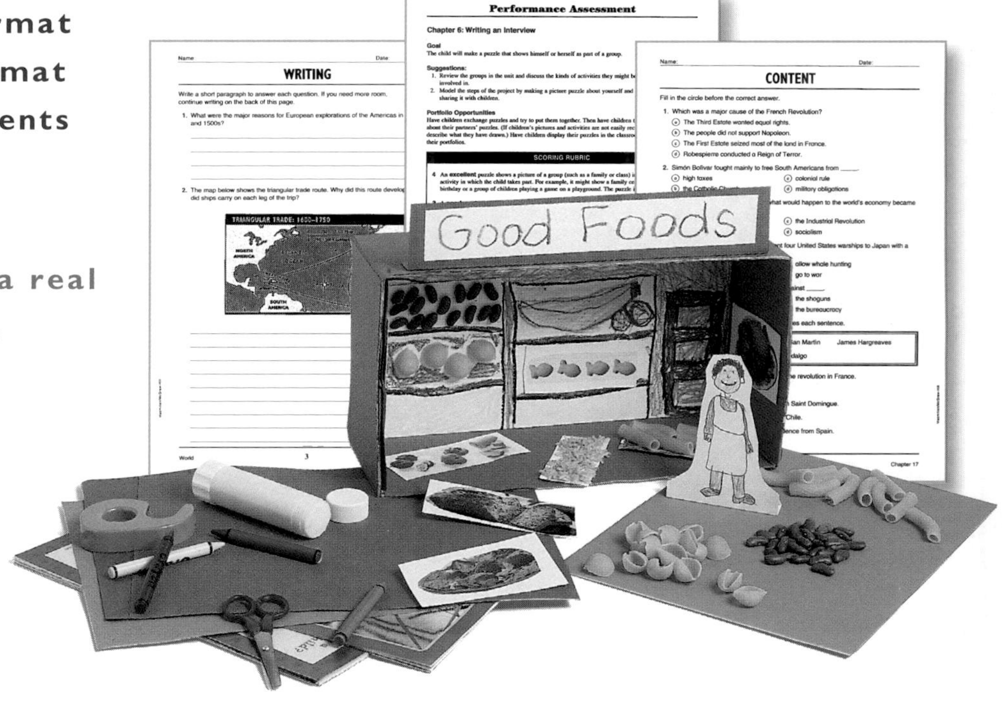

Choices in technology support

Multimedia technology options, correlated directly to the program, are easy extensions at your fingertips. You have the widest variety of choices available to meet your needs.

• Videodiscs • CD-ROM • Videotapes

Barcoded lessons on videodisc make enriching your teaching a breeze. These same lessons are also available on videotape to add to your flexibility. And best of all, it's all at point-of-use in your Teacher's Edition.

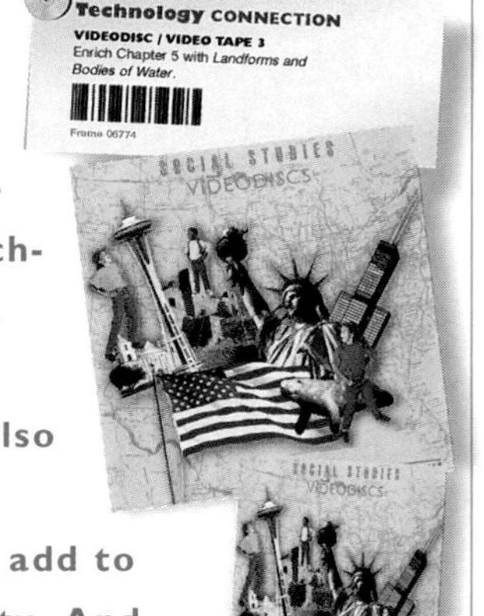

CD-ROM technology adds sight-and-sound power through an enhanced atlas and searchable database. The correlation to the program's lessons and activities make this a useful research tool for all students.

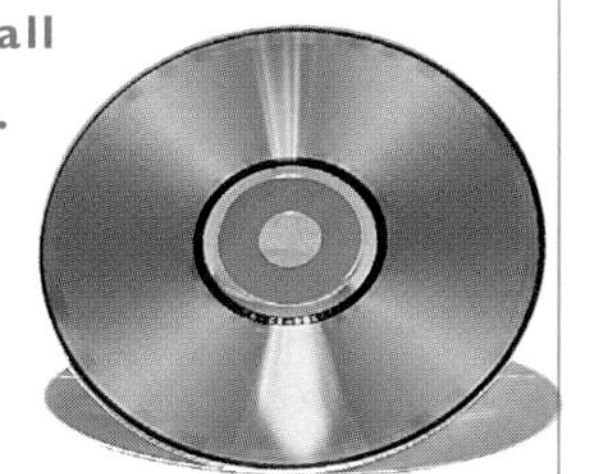

National Geographic Technology is now available through Macmillan McGraw-Hill to support your teaching. Direct correlations of these resources in Adventures in Time and Place ensure that you have the options to support all your students' needs and your teaching style.

the excitement of their new Social Studies Program

Time and Place

HAPPY HOLIDAYSAURUS!
by BERNARD MOST

HOMEPLACE
by Anne Shelby
illustrations by Wendy Anderson Halperin

As the Crow Flies
A FIRST BOOK OF MAPS

AMERICA THE BEAUTIFUL

Johanna Hurwitz
New Shoes for Silvia
Illustrated by Jerry Pinkney

UNIT FOUR
Our World

WORLD ATLAS for primary students
MACMILLAN/McGRAW-HILL

NATIONAL GEOGRAPHIC
Look at Your World
What does this place have that other places don't have?
How do you get to school in the morning?
What makes the beach a fun place to be?
What do people do to help plants grow?
How does this boy know where he is?
ADVENTURES IN TIME AND PLACE

Happy Birthday, Martin Luther King

ONE AFTERNOON
by Yumi Heo

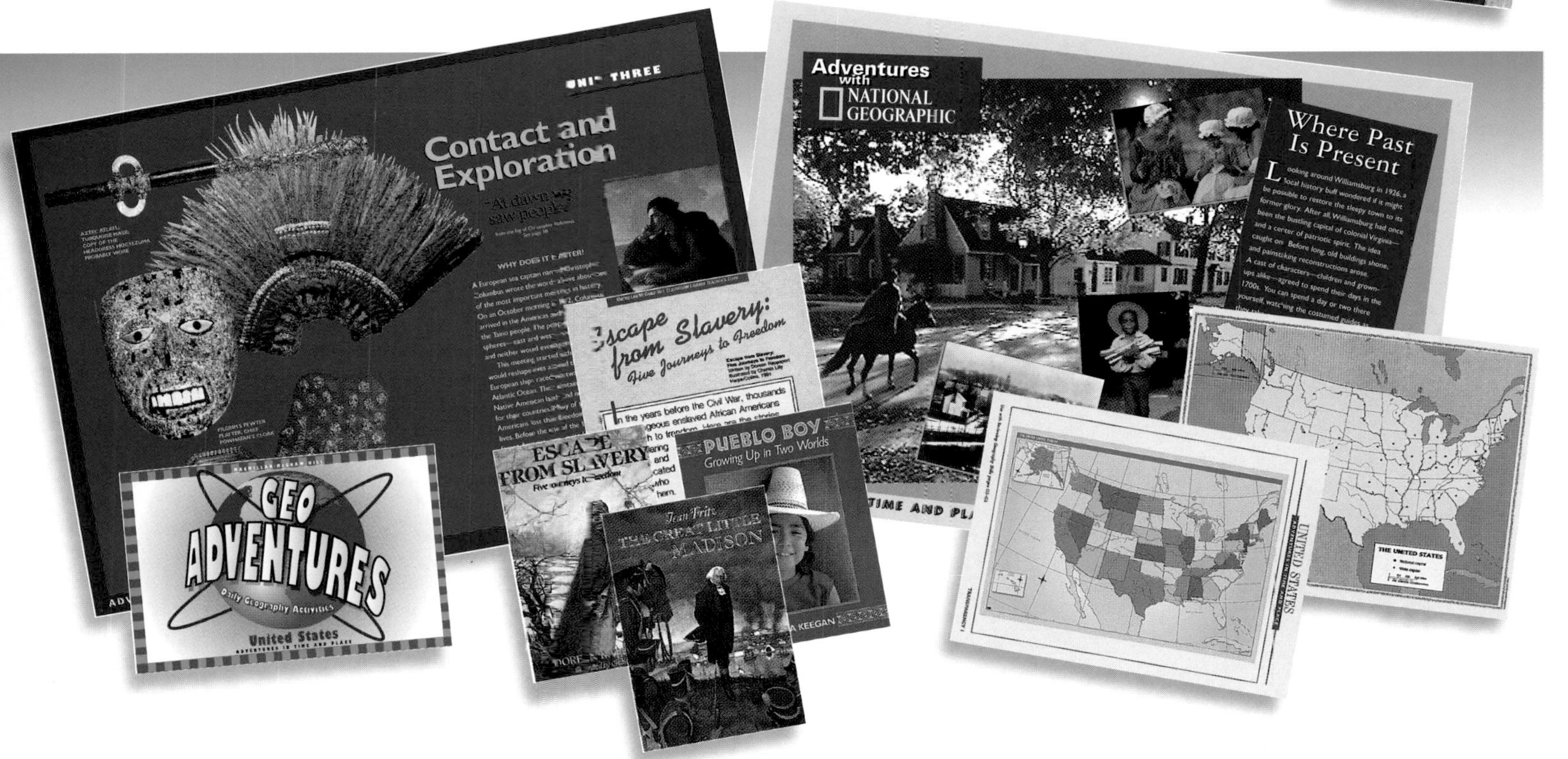

Designed for teacher-friendly classroom management

COMPONENTS CHART

	K HERE I AM	1 MY WORLD	2 PEOPLE TOGETHER	3 COMMUNITIES	4 REGIONS	5 UNITED STATES	6/7 WORLD	6/7 LATIN AMERICA AND CANADA	6/7 WORLD REGIONS
PUPIL EDITION		✔	✔	✔	✔	✔	✔	✔	✔
PUPIL EDITION ON CASSETTE		✔	✔	✔	✔	✔	✔		✔
TEACHER'S MULTIMEDIA EDITION	✔	✔	✔	✔	✔	✔	✔	✔	✔
COLOR MAP TRANSPARENCIES		✔	✔	✔	✔	✔	✔	✔	✔
GRAPHIC ORGANIZERS				✔	✔	✔	✔	✔	✔
THEME BIG BOOKS	✔	✔	✔						
STICKERS FOR THEME BIG BOOKS	✔	✔	✔						
LITERATURE BIG BOOKS	✔	✔	✔						
GEO BIG BOOK	✔	✔	✔	✔					
PRACTICE BOOK		✔	✔	✔	✔	✔	✔	✔	✔
PROJECT BOOK	✔	✔	✔	✔					
GEOADVENTURES/ DAILY GEOGRAPHY ACTIVITIES		✔	✔	✔	✔	✔	✔	✔	✔
FLOOR MAP	✔	✔	✔	✔					
DESK MAPS	✔	✔	✔	✔	✔	✔	✔	✔	✔
OUTLINE MAPS		✔	✔	✔	✔	✔	✔	✔	✔
INFLATABLE GLOBE	✔	✔	✔	✔	✔	✔	✔	✔	✔
STUDENT ATLAS		✔	✔	✔	✔	✔	✔	✔	✔
SOURCES, STORIES AND SONGS/ READ ALOUD ANTHOLOGY	✔	✔	✔	✔	✔	✔	✔	✔	✔
SOURCES, STORIES AND SONGS CASSETTE	✔	✔	✔	✔	✔	✔	✔	✔	✔
CLASSROOM LIBRARY TRADE BOOKS	✔	✔	✔	✔	✔	✔	✔		
CLASSROOM LIBRARY TEACHER'S GUIDES	✔	✔	✔	✔	✔	✔	✔		
POSTERS	✔	✔	✔	✔	✔	✔	✔		✔
UNIT TESTS		✔	✔	✔	✔	✔	✔	✔	✔
CHAPTER TESTS				✔	✔	✔	✔	✔	✔
PERFORMANCE ASSESSMENT	✔	✔	✔	✔	✔	✔	✔	✔	✔
VIDEODISCS	✔	✔	✔	✔	✔	✔	✔		✔
VIDEOTAPES	✔	✔	✔	✔	✔	✔	✔		✔
CD-ROM		✔	✔	✔	✔	✔	✔	✔	✔
INTERNET PROJECT HANDBOOK				✔	✔	✔	✔	✔	✔

Adventures in Time and Place...

COME ALONG AND BRING YOUR STUDENTS TO JOIN IN ON THE ADVENTURE!

World Regions

ADVENTURES IN TIME AND PLACE

James A. Banks

Barry K. Beyer

Gloria Contreras

Jean Craven

Gloria Ladson-Billings

Mary A. McFarland

Walter C. Parker

FROM SPACE, THE EARTH LOOKS LIKE A BEAUTIFUL BLUE MARBLE. A CLOSER LOOK, HOWEVER, REVEALS THOUSANDS OF UNIQUE LANDFORMS AND BODIES OF WATER. EARTH IS HOME TO MANY MILLIONS OF PEOPLE WHO LIVE IN DIVERSE CULTURES. AS YOU READ, YOU WILL DISCOVER WHAT MAKES EACH REGION OF OUR WORLD SPECIAL.

New York Farmington

PROGRAM AUTHORS

Dr. James A. Banks
Professor of Education and Director of the Center for Multicultural Education
University of Washington
Seattle, Washington

Dr. Barry K. Beyer
Professor Emeritus, Graduate School of Education
George Mason University
Fairfax, Virginia

Dr. Gloria Contreras
Professor of Education
University of North Texas
Denton, Texas

Jean Craven
District Coordinator of Curriculum Development
Albuquerque Public Schools
Albuquerque, New Mexico

Dr. Gloria Ladson-Billings
Professor of Education
University of Wisconsin
Madison, Wisconsin

Dr. Mary A. McFarland
Instructional Coordinator of Social Studies, K-12 and Director of Staff Development
Parkway School District
Chesterfield, Missouri

Dr. Walter C. Parker
Professor and Program Chair for Social Studies Education
University of Washington
Seattle, Washington

NATIONAL GEOGRAPHIC SOCIETY
Washington, D.C.

CONTENT CONSULTANTS

Virginia Arnold
Former Professor of Reading, Language Arts, and Children's Literature
Virginia Commonwealth University
Richmond, Virginia

Yvonne Beamer
Writer and Curriculum Developer
Resource Specialist, Native American Education Program
New York, New York

Joyce Buckner
School Principal, Boyde Elementary
Omaha Public Schools
Omaha, Nebraska

Sheilah Clarke-Ekong
Assistant Professor, Department of Anthropology and Research Associate, Center for International Studies
University of Missouri, St. Louis
St. Louis, Missouri

Walter Enloe
Associate Professor
Hamline University
St. Paul, Minnesota

Helen P. Gillotte
Associate Professor of English
San Francisco State University
San Francisco, California

Margaret Lippert
Literature Consultant and Storyteller
North Bend, Washington

Narcita Medina
Reading Specialist
Middle School 135
New York, New York

Harlan Rimmerman
Assistant Superintendent
Fort Levenworth School District
Kansas City, Missouri

Joseph B. Rubin
Director of Reading and Language Arts
Fort Worth Independent School District
Fort Worth, Texas

Clifford E. Trafzer
Professor of History and Ethnic Studies
University of California
Riverside, California

Nancy Winter
Former Member of the Executive Board of the National Council for Geographic Education
Social Studies Consultant
Clark University
Worcester, Massachusetts

GRADE-LEVEL CONSULTANTS

John Allega
Seventh Grade Teacher
Whitin Intermediate School
Uxbridge, Massachusetts

Sister Judith Coreil
Former Assistant Director
National Catholic Education Association
Washington, D.C.

Nadine Kaufman
Principal and Seventh Grade Teacher
St. Francis Xavier School
Lake Station, Indiana

Linda Kuhlman
Seventh Grade Teacher
Trinity Lutheran School
Portland, Oregon

Mary Male
Seventh Grade Teacher
Sacred Heart School
Bethlehem, Pennsylvania

LEGACY WRITERS

Elza Dinwiddie Boyd
New York, New York

Blake Eskin
New York, New York

Carrie Evento
Waterford, Connecticut

Eric Kimmel
Portland, Oregon

Cheryl Haldane
Austin, Texas

Argentina Palacios
Fresh Meadows, New York

CONTRIBUTING WRITERS

Spencer Finch
Brooklyn, New York

Paula Franklin
New York, New York

Diana Reische
Pelham, New York

Linda Scher
Raleigh, North Carolina

Acknowledgments
The publisher gratefully acknowledges permission to reprint the following copyrighted material: Excerpt from "The Talking Cat" from THE TALKING CAT AND OTHER STORIES OF FRENCH CANADA by Natalie Savage Carlson. Illustrated by Roger Duvoisin. Copyright © 1952 by Natalie Savage Carlson. Reprinted by permission of Harper & Row, Publishers, Inc. Excerpt from A STORY-A STORY by Gail E. Haley. Copyright © 1970 by Gail E. Haley. Reprinted by permission of the Macmillan Publishing Company. Excerpt from ROOTS by Alex Haley. Copyright © 1976 by Alex Haley. Reprinted by permission ofBantam Doubleday Dell Publishing Group, Inc. Excerpt from SUNDIATA: AN EPIC OF OLD MALI by D.T. Niane, translated by G.D. Pickett. Copyright © 1960 by Presence Africaine. Reprinted with permission. Simon & Schuster, Inc. for "The Role of the Griot" by D'jimo Kouyate. Copyright © 1989 by D'jimo Kouyate. Reprinted by permission of the publisher. Excerpt from "It's Time for Less Perilous Energy Sources" from The Los Angeles Times, May 1, 1986. Reprinted by permission. Excerpt from "France Stands By Nuclear Power" from

continued on page 677

Macmillan/McGraw-Hill
A Division of The ***McGraw-Hill*** *Companies*

Macmillan/McGraw-Hill
1221 Avenue of the Americas
New York, New York 10020

Printed in the United States of America

ISBN 0-02-147339-0

1 2 3 4 5 6 7 8 9 RRW 03 02 01 00 99 98 97

CONTENTS

iii

v

vii

UNIT SEVEN Southern and Eastern Asia 486

UNIT EIGHT *The Pacific* 578

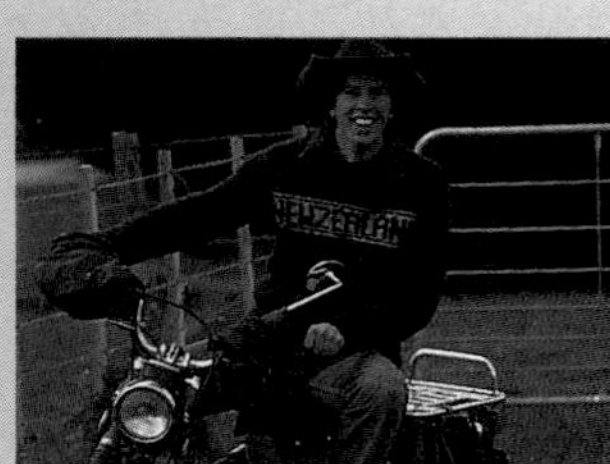

x

REFERENCE SECTION

FEATURES

BUILDING CITIZINSHIP

Making a Difference

Viewpoints

LEGACIES

SONGS

BUILDING SKILLS

Thinking / Reading

Geography

Study / Time

CHARTS, GRAPHS, DIAGRAMS, & TIME LINES

MAPS

xiii

Your Textbook at a Glance
pages 2-3

INTRODUCING THE TEXTBOOK

Discussing the Table of Contents Have students turn to the Table of Contents beginning on page iii. Explain that these pages list the titles and first pages of units and chapters as well as the titles and first pages of other sections.

Ask students:

- **What is the title of Chapter 2?** (''The United States'')
- **How many chapters are there in Unit 4?** (three)

Discussing the Geography Skills Review Have students turn to *Reviewing Geography Skills* on pages 4–13. Explain that this section helps them to review map skills.

Ask students:

- **What information is reviewed on page 5?** (continents, oceans, hemispheres)

Discussing Legacies Have students turn to a *Legacy* lesson, such as the one on pages 74–77. Explain that these lessons give additional information about the ways of life of people in different regions of the world.

Discussing the Five Themes of Geography Have students turn to page 4. Explain that they will be learning about five themes geographers use to study the earth and everything on it.

Discussing the *Read to Learn* Have students turn to a lesson opener, such as the one on page 233. Explain that each lesson begins with a section called *Read to Learn*. This section tells what students will learn in the lesson.

Ask students:

- **What are the names of the sections of *Read to Learn*?** *(Key Vocabulary, Key People, Key Places, Read Aloud, Read for Purpose)*

YOUR TEXTBOOK at a glance

Your textbook contains many special features that will help you read, understand, and remember the people, geography, and history of the world.

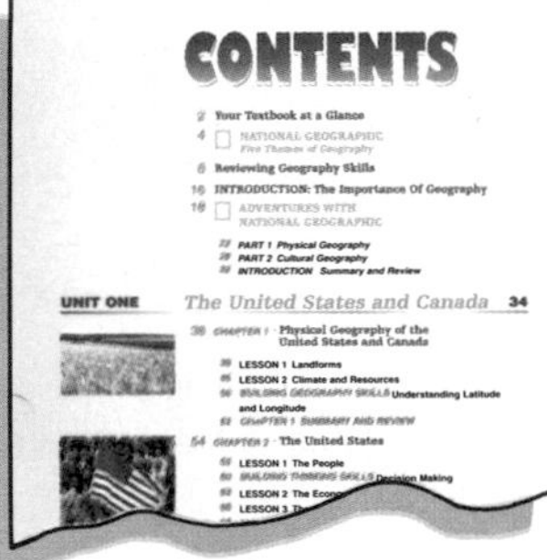

TABLE OF CONTENTS
Lists all parts of your book and tells you where to find them

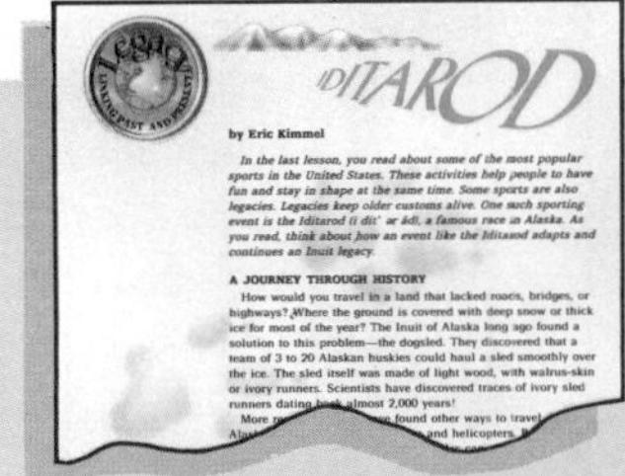

LEGACIES
Lessons which give you a deeper insight into the literature and cultures of the regions you are studying

Reviewing
GEOGRAPHY SKILLS
Using Globes

REVIEWING GEOGRAPHY SKILLS
Reviews skills that will help you use the maps in your book

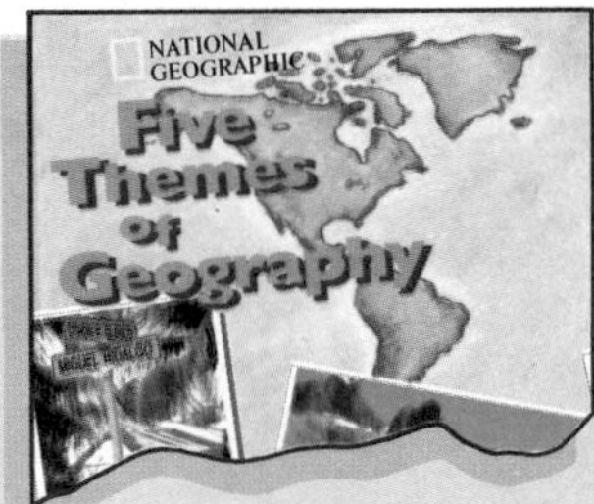

FIVE THEMES OF GEOGRAPHY
Introduces important themes of geography that will help you to compare, to contrast, and to understand the regions and people you will be studying

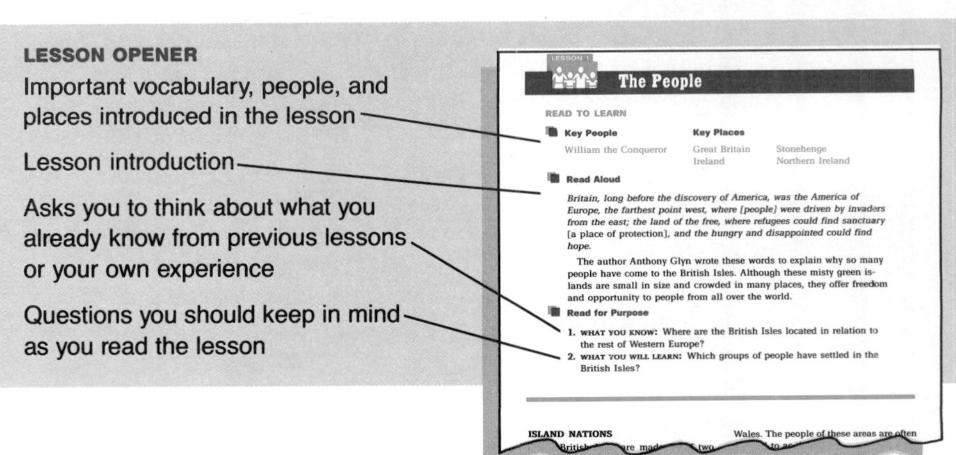

LESSON OPENER
Important vocabulary, people, and places introduced in the lesson

Lesson introduction

Asks you to think about what you already know from previous lessons or your own experience

Questions you should keep in mind as you read the lesson

2

ADDITIONAL FEATURES OF THE TEXTBOOK

Building Citizenship Tell students that other important parts of their textbook are the pages called *Building Citizenship.* There are two types of citizenship features in the textbook: *Making a Difference* and *Viewpoints.* Have students turn to page 69 and pages 84–85 for examples of each.

Skills Lessons Tell students that the textbook also has skills lessons that help them to learn important skills needed for comprehending social studies and other subjects. Examples of skills lessons are: Geography (pages 50-51), Thinking (pages 126-127), and Study and Research (page 253).

REFERENCE SECTION

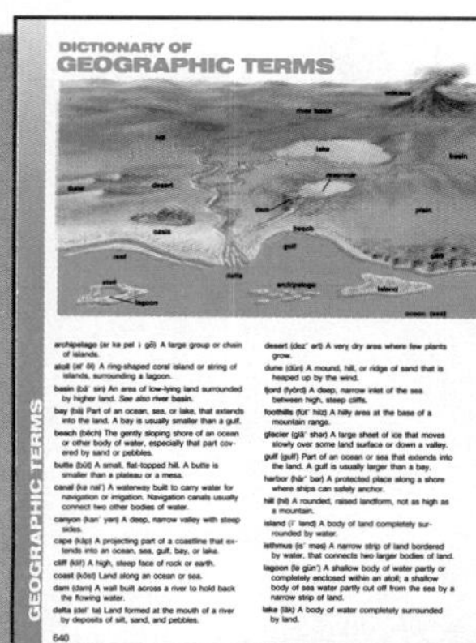

DICTIONARY OF GEOGRAPHIC TERMS
Definition and pronunciation of major geographic features

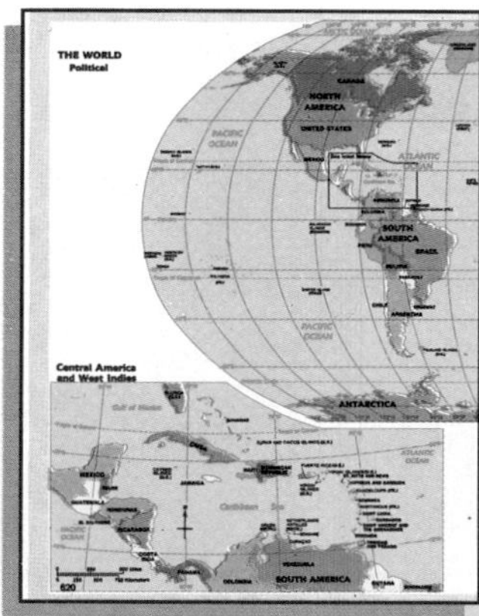

ATLAS
Maps of the eight culture regions of the world, plus a special overlay map showing population and land use

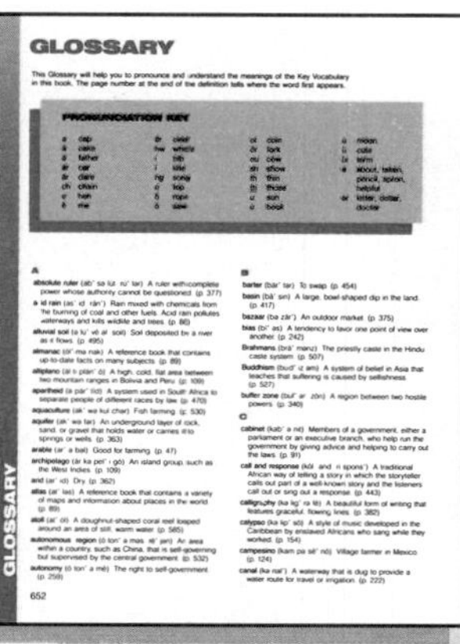

GLOSSARY
Definition and pronunciation of all Key Vocabulary and page where each is introduced

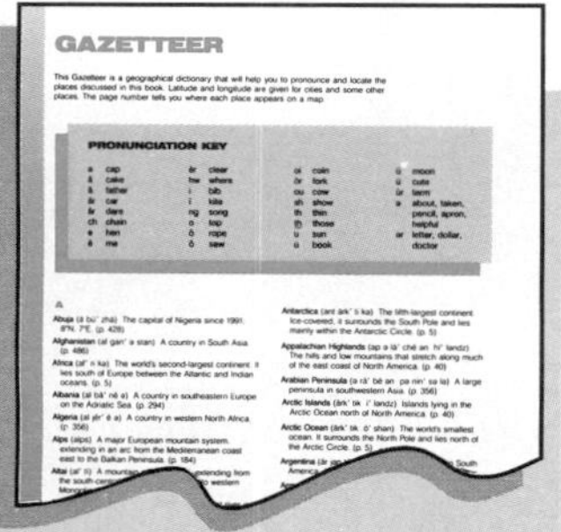

GAZETTEER
Location and pronunciation of major places discussed in your book and page where each is shown on a map

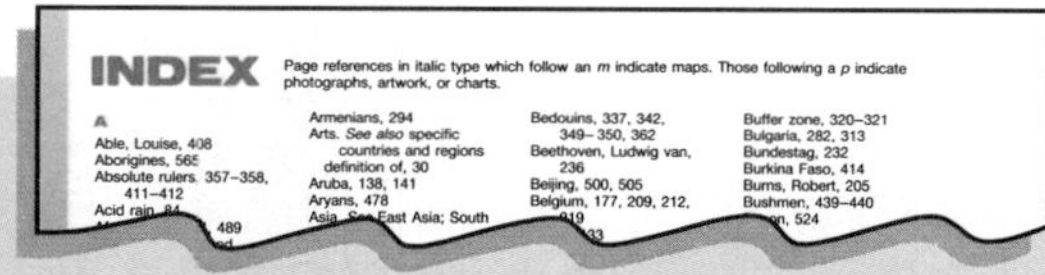

INDEX
Alphabetical list of important people, places, events, and subjects in your book and pages where information is found

3

Discussing the *Atlas* and Other Maps Have students skim the maps in their textbooks. Then ask them to turn to the *Atlas* on pages 620–643.

Ask students:

- **Which pages of the *Atlas* have a map of Latin America?** (pages 624–625)

Discussing the *Dictionary of Geographic Terms* Have students turn to pages 644-645. Explain that this section gives the meanings of geographic terms.

Ask students:

- **What does the drawing show?** (the appearance of various geographical features)
- **What other information is found in this section?** (definitions and pronunciations of geographic terms)

Discussing the *Gazetter* Have students turn to pages 646-655. Ask them to study the section and then to explain what the section is about.

Ask students:

- **What is the *Gazetteer*?** (a section that tells where places are located, how to pronounce the names of the places, and where to find them on a map in the text)

Discussing the *Glossary* Have students turn to pages 656-663.

Ask students:

- **What information does the *Glossary* have?** (definitions of *Key Vocabulary* terms and the page on which each term is first mentioned)

Discussing the *Index* Have students turn to pages 664-674.

Ask students:

- **For what would you use the *Index*?** (to find the places in the textbook with information about a particular subject)

ADDITIONAL FEATURES OF THE TEXTBOOK

Unit Opener This section introduces a unit. Have students turn to pages 34–37 and point out to them the various components of the unit opener: a globe, photographs, and statistical charts for countries.

Chapter Opener This section introduces a chapter. Have students preview the Chapter 1 Opener on page 38 as an example.

Chapter Summary and Review Have students turn to pages 52–53 in their textbooks and tell them that this is a *Chapter Summary and Review.* These pages contain an illustrated section that summarizes information, such as *Ideas to Remember,* and another section that reviews information, such as *Reviewing Vocabulary.*

Unit Summary and Review Have students turn to pages 98–99 to look at a sample *Unit Summary and Review.* Explain that these pages summarize and review the important information learned in each unit.

NATIONAL GEOGRAPHIC

FIVE THEMES OF GEOGRAPHY
pages 4–5

Lesson Overview Geographers use five basic themes to study the earth and everything on it.

Lesson Objectives

- Define *geography*.
- Recognize and describe the five fundamental themes of geography.

PREPARE

Motivate Have volunteers share their understanding of the word *geography*. Help students understand that geography is the study of all the regions of Earth, the physical characteristics of the regions, the people, and how all these things work together.

Set Purpose Explain that the five themes will help students gather, classify, and understand information about geography.

TEACH

Discussing Geography Allow students time to examine the pictures and their captions.

Begin an explanation and discussion of the five themes:

- *Region:* an area with common features that set it apart from other areas
- *Human-Environment Interaction:* how the environment influences and is influenced by people
- *Location:* finding either the exact or the relative location of a place
- *Place:* comparing the natural and human-made features of different areas
- *Movement:* how people, goods, and ideas have moved around the world

NATIONAL GEOGRAPHIC

Five Themes of Geography

Location
How do these people know where they are in Mexico?

Region
What are some things that make South America a unique area?

BACKGROUND INFORMATION

The Five Themes and the National Geography Standards To help educators organize and convey geographic knowledge, the five themes of geography were introduced in 1984. A more comprehensive instructional framework—the National Geography Standards—was published in 1994.

How do the themes and the standards relate to each other? The themes are content organizers; they provide a framework for structuring and focusing lessons in geography. The standards identify the specific subject matter, skills, and perspectives that students should master. The themes flow all through the standards and can be used in teaching any of the material specified in the standards.

To order a copy of *Geography for Life: National Geography Standards 1994*, contact: National Geographic Society, P.O. Box 98171, Washington, D.C., 20013-8171.

Human-Environment Interaction
How are these people in Africa making use of the environment?

Place
What makes London, England, different from other places?

Movement
What is one way people can travel from place to place in Southeast Asia?

5

Suggested Questions

- **Describe some of the street signs in your neighborhood. How do they help you and visitors find your way through the community?** (Students' responses should include specific information about signs and community.)
- **Think of two landmarks in your community. How would you compare them?** (Students' responses should indicate specific differences in construction, historical significance, and location.)
- **What types of wildlife make your region unique?** (Accept appropriate responses.)
- **How do local landforms and bodies of water affect transportation in your region? Describe types of water transportation in your region.** (Accept appropriate responses.)
- **Name three ways people use the environment in your community.** (Students' responses should reflect specific information.)

3 CLOSE

Summarizing Students should understand how geography encompasses all the regions of the world. They should also recognize how the five themes can help increase their knowledge of the world.

Evaluating Tell students to suppose that they have visited each place on these two pages. Have them write a postcard that answers the question in each caption.

BACKGROUND INFORMATION

Developing Geography Skills Use these activities to reinforce what students have learned about geography.

- Ask students to list one site that they would like to visit in each of the regions mentioned. Then have students locate these places on their *Atlas* maps.
- Invite students to research and describe the natural features and resources that would be found in the places they have chosen.
- Have students determine which area shown here is closest to their community, which place is farthest from their community, and which two of the regions shown are closest to one another.
- Have students choose two destinations and describe how they might travel to each from their own community.

REVIEWING GEOGRAPHY SKILLS
pages 6–15

USING GLOBES

Lesson Theme Globes are valuable because they accurately show shapes, sizes, locations, directions, and distances on the earth.

Lesson Objectives

- Identify and locate the earth's seven continents and four oceans.
- Explain how the earth is divided into hemispheres by the equator and the prime meridian.
- Identify and locate the four hemispheres.

Lesson Resources

Practice Book: *Using Globes,* page 1
Outline Maps: *The World, The Western Hemisphere, The Eastern Hemisphere, The Northern Hemisphere, The Southern Hemisphere*
Transparency Map: 3

PREPARE

Motivate Have students examine the illustrations on pages 6–8 and relate each illustration to the heading that indicates the topic.

Set Purpose Tell students that learning to use maps and globes will help them get the most out of the course they are now starting.

TEACH

Reviewing Globes Using the classroom globe, have students identify the continents and the oceans. Then have them locate and identify the United States and its neighbors to the north and south—Canada and Mexico.

Ask students:

- **Why is a globe a good model of the earth?** (because it is the same shape as the earth)

Reviewing GEOGRAPHY SKILLS

Using Globes

Key Vocabulary

geography	hemisphere
region	equator
continent	prime meridian

In social studies this year, you will be learning about the lands and peoples of the different parts of the world. You will discover that maps and globes can often help you to better understand what you read. Maps and globes are the "tools" you will use in your studies. They can help you answer questions about locations of countries and cities, oceans and rivers, mountains and deserts. They show the shapes and sizes of places on the earth. Maps and globes can also help you to make comparisons and determine distances and directions between places in the world.

Since ancient times, people have used maps and globes to study **geography**. Geography is the study of the earth and everything on it. In this book you will learn a great deal about different kinds of geography. You will also learn about tools such as maps and globes.

Look at your classroom globe. Globes are especially valuable tools for learning about the earth. Globes are models, or small copies, of the earth, and they provide very accurate information. Looking at a globe is a lot like looking at the earth from a point in outer space. On a globe shapes and relative sizes are shown correctly. Directions and relative distances are also shown correctly.

Maps are drawings on flat surfaces of all or part of the earth. Maps have some advantages that globes do not. Maps can be folded or rolled. They can be carried and stored easily. A map can show the

BACKGROUND INFORMATION

Suggestions for Using the Section This section contains three parts.

- Using Globes, pages 6–8
- Using Maps, pages 9–11
- Different Kinds of Maps, pages 12–15

Reviewing Geography Skills is intended to help students review their knowledge of geography and of skills learned in previous years of study. It also allows you to evaluate students' knowledge and to determine how much class time, if any, is needed to review these concepts. The Practice Book, found in the Teacher's Resource Center, will also help in evaluation and review. You may want students to return to this section throughout the year to refresh their memories.

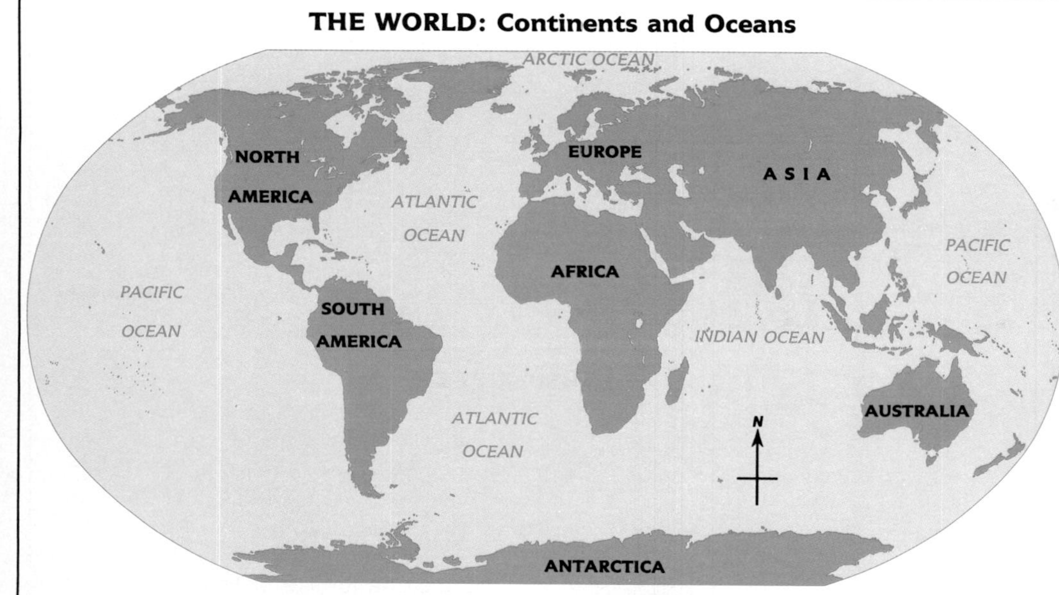

world so that it can be seen all at once. On a globe only half the world can be seen at a time. You will be using maps as you read this book.

You will see that most of the maps in this book focus on different **regions**. A region is an area with common geographic or cultural features that set it apart from other areas. Geographers divide the world into regions to make it easier to study.

Continents and Oceans

The surface of the earth is made up of land and water. Globes show the parts of the earth's surface that are land and the parts that are water. Large bodies of land are called **continents**. You may know that there are seven continents on the earth: North America, South America, Europe, Asia, Africa, Australia, and Antarctica. Find these continents on the map of the world on this page.

As the map shows, most of the continents are separated, or nearly separated, from one another by water. If you look carefully at a globe, you will see that most of the water on the earth's surface is part of a single, large connected body of water. This body of water, which covers more than half the earth, is divided into smaller parts, called oceans. You may know that the earth has four oceans: the Atlantic, the Pacific, the Indian, and the Arctic. Find these oceans on the map above.

Hemispheres

Do you know what a **hemisphere** is? If you break down the word into its parts, you can see what it means. A sphere is a round object, such as the earth. *Hemi* is a Greek word that means "half." Thus, the word *hemisphere* means "half a sphere." Geographers use the term *hemisphere* to refer to half of the earth.

By turning a globe or moving around it, you can see that the earth can be divided into an almost endless number of hemispheres. In order to simplify, geographers divide the earth in two ways.

7

Reviewing Continents and Oceans
Discuss the meanings of these terms.

Ask students:

- **What two kinds of surfaces cover the earth?** (land, water)
- **What are the large masses of land and the large masses of water called?** (continents, oceans)
- **How many continents are there?** (seven)
- **How many oceans?** (four)

EXTENDING MAP SKILLS

Refer to the globe on page 6 and the world map on this page.

Ask students:

- **On which continent do we live? Which other continent lies in our part of the world?** (Students should identify North America and South America.)
- **Which three oceans surround these two continents?** (Arctic, Pacific, Atlantic)
- **Which continent lies farthest south on the globe?** (Antarctica)
- **Which continents lie west and northwest of Australia?** (Africa, Asia)
- **Which ocean separates these three continents?** (Indian)
- **Which continent lies near both Africa and Asia?** (Europe)

Reviewing Hemispheres Discuss the meaning of *hemisphere.*

Ask students:

- **To geographers, what is a hemisphere?** (one half of the earth)

BACKGROUND INFORMATION

About Globes

- Globes may be the most accurate scale models of the earth, but they generally do not reflect two important features—a flattening at the two poles and a slight bulge south of the equator.
- Despite all their advantages, most globes are inconvenient to carry around for reference. Today, however, there is a way to overcome this drawback—the inflatable globe.
- Perhaps the most famous globe in the United States was the two-ton, revolving aluminum model, 12 feet (3.66 m) in diameter, that was constructed for exhibition in New York City's *Daily News* Building.

Discussing Hemispheres Continue discussing the hemispheres.

Ask students:

- **What is the equator?** (an imaginary line around the earth halfway between the North Pole and the South Pole)
- **Which hemispheres does the equator separate?** (the Northern Hemisphere and the Southern Hemisphere)
- **What other imaginary line divides the earth into hemispheres? How does it differ from the equator?** (The prime meridian divides the earth between east and west instead of between north and south.)

EXTENDING MAP SKILLS

Refer to the four hemispheres.

Ask students:

- **Which continents lie entirely in the Northern Hemisphere?** (Asia, Europe, North America)
- **Which two continents lie entirely in the Southern Hemisphere?** (Australia, Antarctica)
- **Which two continents lie entirely in the Western Hemisphere?** (North America, South America)

CLOSE

Summarizing Students have reviewed the globe, the continents, the oceans, and the hemispheres.

Evaluating Use the review questions (answers given below) to assess students' understanding.

1. a large body of land
2. half of a globe
3. equator
4. prime meridian
5. They show distances, shapes, and directions.

Independent Practice

Practice Book: page 1

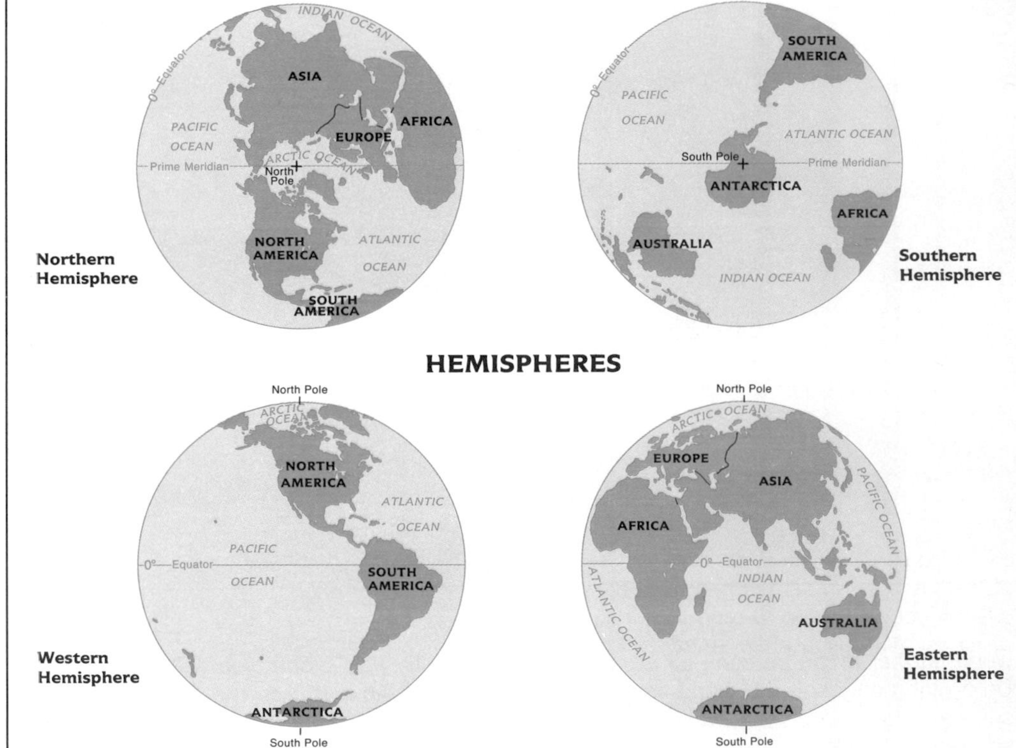

One division is made along an imaginary line called the **equator**. The equator circles the earth halfway between the North Pole and the South Pole. As you can see from the maps above, it runs through South America and Africa. The equator divides the earth into the Northern Hemisphere and the Southern Hemisphere. The Northern Hemisphere is the part of the earth you would see if you were looking at the earth from a point in space directly above the North Pole. The Southern Hemisphere is the part of the earth you would see if you were looking at it from a point in space directly above the South Pole.

The earth can also be divided into the Eastern Hemisphere and the Western Hemisphere. These hemispheres are separated by another imaginary line around the earth. This line is known as the **prime meridian**. You will learn about the prime meridian on pages 50–51.

One way in which you can identify the hemispheres is by learning the names of the continents they contain. As you can see from the maps of the hemispheres on this page, most of the earth's landmasses are found in the Northern Hemisphere. Name the continents of the Eastern Hemisphere and the Western Hemisphere. *

1. What is a continent?
2. What is a hemisphere?
3. Which imaginary line separates the Northern and Southern hemispheres?
4. Which imaginary line separates the Eastern and Western hemispheres?
5. How can using globes help you learn about the earth?

8

* Africa, Antarctica, Asia, Australia, Europe; Antarctica, North America, South America

MEETING INDIVIDUAL NEEDS

Reteaching (easy) On an outline map of the world, which can be found in the Teacher's Resource Center, have students label the continents and the oceans, the equator, the prime meridian, and the four hemispheres.

Extension (average) Have students use a globe or a globe projection of the world and trace the equator around it. Ask them to make a list of the countries and the continents that the equator crosses.

Enrichment (challenging) Have students use an almanac or encyclopedia as a research tool. Ask them to create a chart comparing the areas of land and water in the Northern Hemisphere with those in the Southern Hemisphere, and those in the Eastern Hemisphere with those in the Western Hemisphere.

Using Maps

Key Vocabulary

cardinal directions
intermediate directions
scale
symbol
map key

While globes are the most accurate representations of the earth, maps are usually much more useful. Your book includes more than 100 maps. Some show the entire world, and others show only a part of the world.

In order to use maps effectively, you must know how to "read" them. Information on maps is presented in a special "language." The "language" of maps allows mapmakers to show a great deal of information in a small space. In this section you will learn to read the language of maps. When you understand this language, you will be able to read the maps in this book and the other maps you will find in books and magazines.

BRAZIL

Directions

You already know that there are four cardinal directions—north, south, east, and west. North is the direction toward the North Pole. If you face north, south is directly behind you, east is to your right, and west is to your left. The letters *N*, *S*, *E*, and *W* are often used to stand for the cardinal directions.

There are also the four intermediate directions. *Intermediate* means "between." The intermediate directions are the directions halfway between the cardinal directions. Northeast (*NE*), for example, is the intermediate direction halfway between north and east. The other intermediate directions are northwest (*NW*), southeast (*SE*), and southwest (*SW*).

Most maps are drawn so that north is toward the top of the map. Many maps have a north pointer that shows which way north is on the map. If you know where north is, you can easily find all the other directions. Look at the map of Brazil on this page. In what direction is Belém from Manaus? As you can see from the map, Belém lies east of Manaus.

Scale

All maps are smaller than the part of the earth they show. For this reason a short distance on a map stands for a much greater real distance on the earth.

The scale, or relative size, of a map will tell you how much smaller map distances are than real distances. The scale of a map can be shown in a few ways. On the maps in this book, scale is shown by lines, called line scales. Each map has two line scales, one for miles and the other for kilometers. Find the line scales on the map on this page.

USING MAPS

Lesson Theme Map keys help us to interpret maps.

Lesson Objectives

- Find cardinal and intermediate directions on maps.
- Use scales to measure distances.
- Interpret symbols in map keys.

Lesson Resources

Practice Book: *Distance and Direction on a Map,* page 2; *Using Map Symbols,* pages 3–4
Outline Map: *The World*
Transparency Maps: 4, 5

1 PREPARE

Motivate Discuss the advantages of being able to read maps.

Set Purpose Have students read the first two paragraphs. Ask them to guess three uses of the "language" of maps.

2 TEACH

Reviewing Directions

Ask students:

- **How does knowing where north is help you find other directions?** (Other directions have a fixed relation to north.)

EXTENDING MAP SKILLS

Use this map to assess students' ability to work with directions. Name two places and ask students in which direction they would travel to go from one place to another.

Reviewing Scale

Ask students:

- **What does a map's scale tell us?** (the relation between real distances and the distances as they are shown on the map)

CURRICULUM CONNECTION

Language Arts Call attention to the two types of direction—*cardinal* and *intermediate.*

- Have students brainstorm to suggest different meanings of *cardinal.* Students may define *cardinal* as a kind of red bird or an official of the Roman Catholic Church. Have them look up the word in the dictionary to find out why it is used in connection with direction. (Help them to identify the core meaning—"chief" or "major.")
- Write *intermediate* on the chalkboard. Have students analyze the word with the help of the dictionary. (Help them to identify the word's core meaning—"in between.")

Working with Scale Continue discussing map scale.

Ask students:

- **Why is map scale useful?** (We can use it to determine the size of areas and the distances between places.)
- **Why can 1 inch (2.5 cm) on a map represent a different distance on another map?** (Maps may be drawn to different scales to show more or less detail.)

EXTENDING MAP SKILLS

Refer students to the two maps of New Zealand.

Ask students:

- **Which of these maps gives more information about New Zealand? Why?** (Map B; It shows New Zealand in larger scale, thus providing room to identify more places.)
- **What kinds of additional details does the larger-scale map give?** (mountain peaks, more cities and places, more names of bodies of water)

After students answer the questions about distance in their textbooks, ask some additional questions, using the formula "How far is Place A from Place B?" Such questions provide additional practice. Have students use the maps in this section as well as other maps in their textbooks.

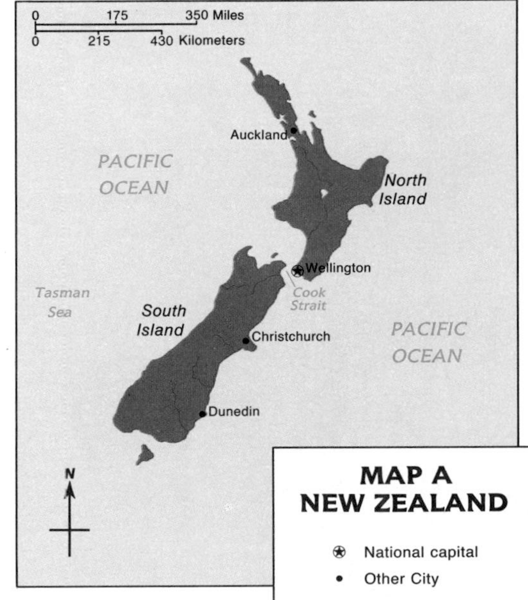

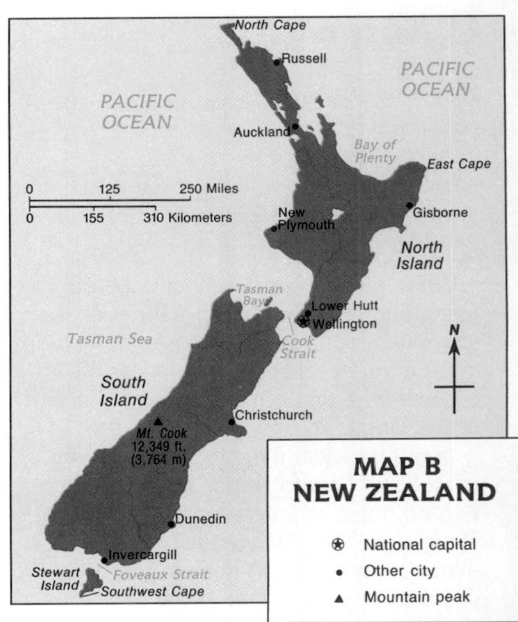

Now find the line scales on **Map A** of New Zealand on this page. The top line shows how many miles on the earth are represented by one inch on the map. The bottom line shows how many kilometers on the earth are represented by two centimeters on the map. How many miles on the earth does one inch on the map represent? How many kilometers do two centimeters represent? How many kilometers does one centimeter represent?*

Suppose you want to know the distance between the cities of Auckland and Dunedin. Use a ruler to measure the map distance in inches between the two cities. Then multiply the number of inches by 350 to find the real distance in miles. To get the number of kilometers between Auckland and Dunedin, multiply the number of centimeters by 215 to find the real distance in kilometers. What is the approximate distance between the cities of Auckland and Dunedin in miles? What is the approximate distance between the cities in kilometers?**

10 *350 mi; 430 km; 215
**1.5 in × 350 mi = 525 mi; 4 cm × 215 km = 860 km

Now look at **Map B** on this page. It shows the same area shown on **Map A**. The shape of New Zealand is the same on both maps, but New Zealand appears larger on **Map B**. You know, of course, that New Zealand has not changed in size. What has changed is the scale of the map. One inch on **Map B** stands for a fewer number of miles than one inch stands for on **Map A**.

Use the line scale and a ruler to determine the distance between Auckland and Dunedin on **Map B** as you did on **Map A**. What is the distance in miles and in kilometers? If you measured and figured correctly, your answers will be the same as they were before, because the distance remains the same no matter which map you use.

The scale of **Map B** is larger than that of **Map A**. More details, that is, more information, can be shown on large-scale maps than on small-scale maps. Which things shown on **Map B** are *not* shown on **Map A**?*

*more cities and places, a mountain, names of islands, names of bodies of water

CURRICULUM CONNECTION

Math To reinforce the idea that scale is a ratio between different sizes, have students make a scale model of their classroom. Ask them to measure the room in either feet or meters and to project a scale of either 1 inch = 1 foot or 3 centimeters = 1 meter. Have students compute what the dimensions of their scale model should be and then make the model out of posterboard.

Art Have students look at maps in various sources—textbooks, atlases, encyclopedias—to form an idea of the many kinds of details for which map symbols are used. Have each student draw a symbol for some piece of information on a map and present it to the class. Ask students to guess what each drawing symbolizes.

Symbols

Information on maps can be shown by **symbols**. A symbol is anything that stands for something else. Common map symbols are dots, squares, circles, triangles, lines, letters, and numbers. Color is a special symbol on maps. It is often used to show differences in height above sea level, rainfall, weather patterns, and plant life. Different colors are often used to distinguish one state or country from another. Blue is a commonly used symbol for water.

Some symbols look like the things they stand for. Others suggest the things they stand for. For example, a tiny drawing of an airplane may be a symbol for an airport. A small drawing of a tree may be a symbol for a forest or a small drawing of a fish may be a symbol for the fishing industry.

To find out what the symbols used on a map mean, you must look at the **map key**. The map key explains what each symbol stands for. It is important to check the map key on each map you use. A symbol that stands for one thing on one map may stand for a completely different thing on another map.

Look at the two maps on this page and check each map key. After studying the maps and their symbols, answer the following questions.

1. Where on maps is north usually shown?
2. In which direction would you travel going from Nairobi to Mount Kenya? From Nairobi to Mount Kilimanjaro?
3. Do both maps on this page have the same scale?
4. What does the color purple stand for on the map of Madagascar? What does the color orange stand for on the same map?
5. Which symbol is used to show cities?
6. Why do you think it is important to understand the different kinds of symbols that are used on maps?

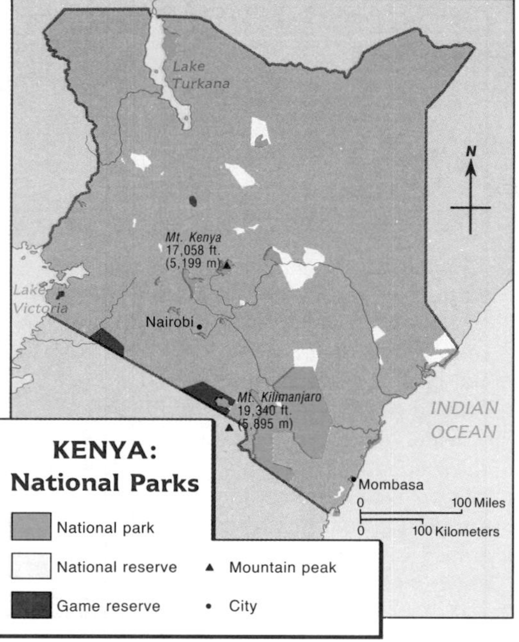

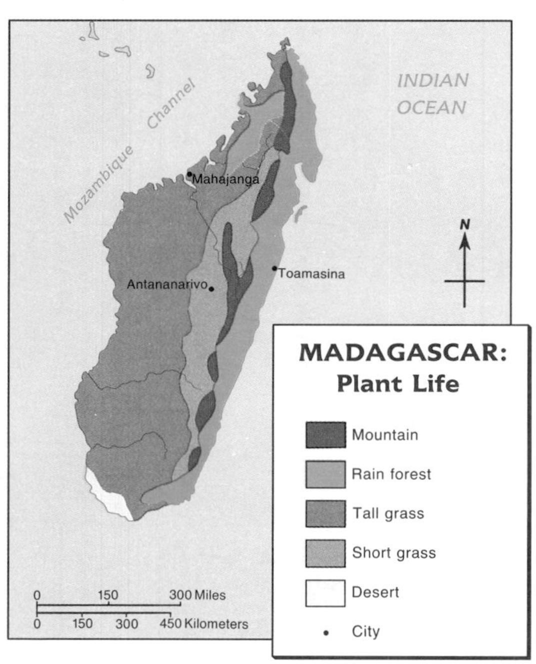

11

Reviewing Symbols

Ask students:

- **Why are symbols used on maps?** (to fit many details into a small space)
- **How does the map key help you understand map symbols?** (It "decodes" them.)

EXTENDING MAP SKILLS

Refer the class to the maps of Kenya and Madagascar.

Ask students:

- **What type of symbol is used most on these maps?** (color)
- **If these maps had no map key, what problems might a reader have in using them?** (Without a map key the reader would not be able to figure out what each of these maps shows.)

3 CLOSE

Summarizing Students have reviewed the crucial role that directions, scale, symbols, and map keys play in conveying the information shown on a map. Display a wall map and have students call out the types of information maps provide—for example, distance between places, capital cities. Then have students identify the device or symbol they would use to find particular information.

Evaluating Use the review questions (answers given below) to assess students' understanding.

1. North is toward the top of both maps; it is shown by the north pointer.
2. northeast; southeast
3. No.
4. mountains; short grass
5. dot
6. Symbols help us understand the information on a map.

Independent Practice
Practice Book: pages 2–4

MEETING INDIVIDUAL NEEDS

Reteaching (easy) Give students a simple map and call on them to identify the compass rose (or north pointer), scale, and key and to answer one question concerning each.

Extension (average) Have students draw a map of their state showing the capital, major cities, their community, their county seat, three points of interest, a compass rose or north pointer, a scale, and a key. Have them write three statements about their maps that involve direction, scale, and the key.

Enrichment (challenging) Have students draw the outline of an imaginary island. Have them add three places, symbols for crops, and locations where the crops grow, as well as a compass rose, a scale, and a map key. Have students write questions that involve all the symbols and then exchange papers and answer each other's questions.

DIFFERENT KINDS OF MAPS

Lesson Theme Different kinds of maps provide different types of information.

Lesson Objectives

- Differentiate among varieties of maps and their purposes.
- Interpret physical, political, and distribution maps.
- Use a grid map.

Lesson Resources

Practice Book: *Touring Paris,* page 5; *Using a Distribution Map,* page 6
Transparency Maps: 6, 7

PREPARE

Motivate Have students skim pages 12–15 and comment on differences among the maps.

Set Purpose Have students examine each map's key to see the kinds of maps they will be reviewing in this lesson.

TEACH

Reviewing Political Maps

Ask students:

- **What kinds of information do political maps show?** (national borders, capitals, cities)

EXTENDING MAP SKILLS

Discuss the political map of the Middle East.

Ask students:

- **How does the map show which area belongs to each country?** (by the use of boundary lines, colors, country names)
- **How can you tell which countries are part of the Middle East?** (They have distinct colors and labels.)

Different Kinds of Maps

Key Vocabulary

political map
physical map
landform map
grid map
distribution map

People study maps to understand the earth. The variety of information that can be shown on a map is endless. In order to keep things clear, most maps have a special purpose. Maps can be grouped according to the kind of information they provide. For example, **political maps** show countries, capitals, and other important political features. **Physical maps** show the natural features of the earth. For example, on physical maps you can find mountains, plains, lakes, rivers, deserts, and other kinds of land found on the earth.

Special-purpose maps provide information about particular subjects. The focus of a special-purpose map may be population, rainfall, language, or religion. No matter what you want to know about the world, there is sure to be a map for your purpose. As you read this book, think about the purpose of each of the maps that you come across.

Political Maps

This book has many different kinds of maps. In every unit you will find at least one political map. Political maps show political divisions such as countries and states. Political maps may also show national and state capitals and other important cities in countries.

The map on this page shows the countries of the Middle East. It is a political map. As you see, this map shows such political features as national boundaries,

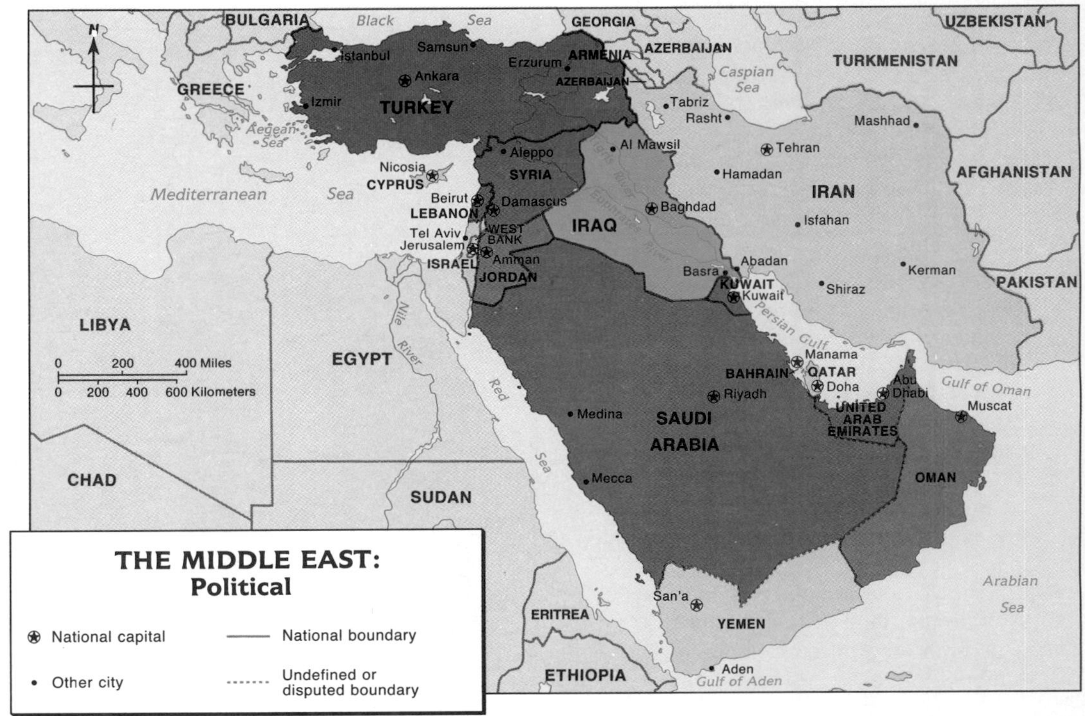

12

BACKGROUND INFORMATION

About Making Maps Students may not be aware of how difficult it was in the past to chart places that had never been mapped before. Encourage students to picture early explorers sailing along shores they had never seen, trying to estimate distances, following inlets to track their shapes, trying to gauge the direction of rivers' twists and turns, and so on. Help students to contrast these early methods with the advantages afforded by the aerial photography available to mapmakers today. Finely tuned measuring devices that are part of satellite photography also help mapmakers in their quest for accuracy.

capitals, and other cities. Note that each country is shown in a special color. Also note that the land lying outside of the Middle East is shown in the same shade of gray. The map shows that some of the national boundaries are disputed, or uncertain. These boundaries appear as dotted lines on the map. Use the map to identify the capital of Turkey. Name the countries that border Syria.

Physical Maps

Physical maps emphasize the natural features of the earth. The earth's physical features include continents, oceans, islands, lakes, rivers, mountains, plains, and deserts. Some physical maps also show some political features, such as national boundaries and the names of cities and countries.

Landform maps are physical maps that show how the earth's surface varies from place to place. Landform maps use color to show the parts of the earth that are mountains, hills, plateaus, and plains. You may wish to use the Dictionary of Geographic Terms on pages 644–645 to help you picture some of these landforms. Some landform maps use shading to give a better idea of relief, or variation in height above sea level.

Look at the map of Scandinavia on this page. Check the key to see which colors are used to show mountains, hills, plateaus, and plains. Which country, Norway or Sweden, is more mountainous? Which part of Finland is mostly plains? Which country has plateaus? Find Denmark on the map. What kind of landform does Denmark have?

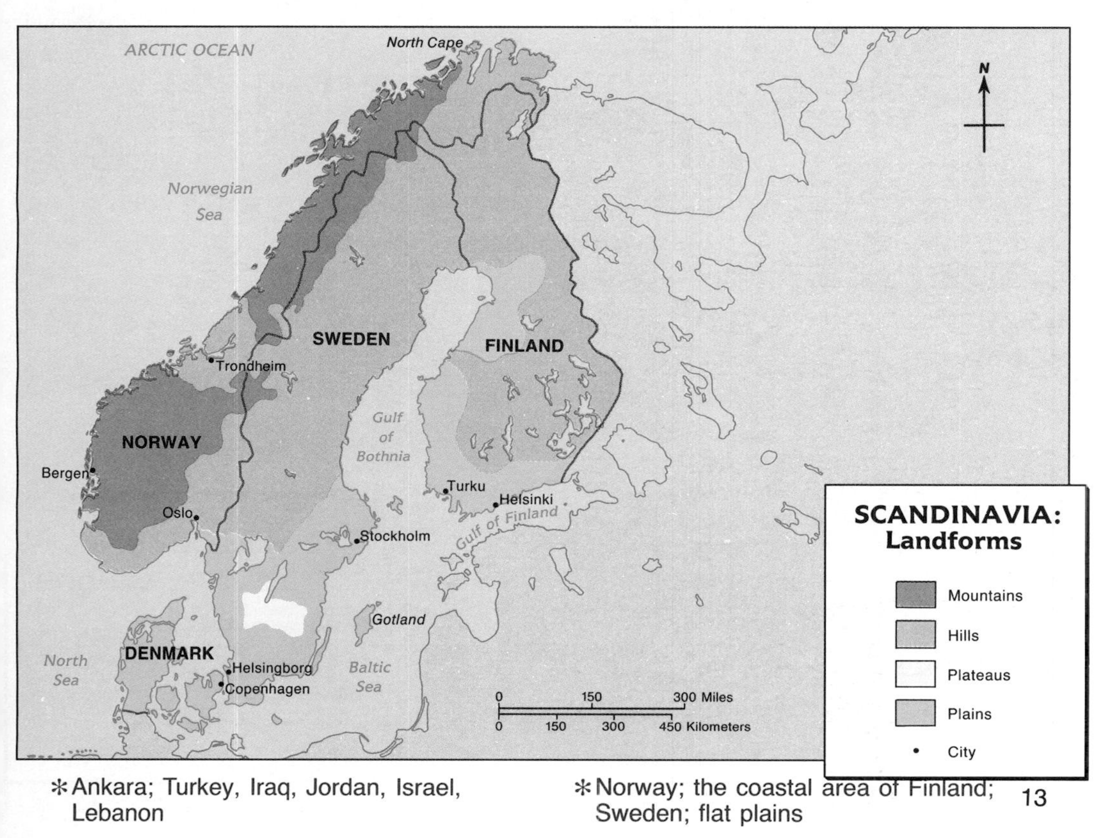

*Ankara; Turkey, Iraq, Jordan, Israel, Lebanon

*Norway; the coastal area of Finland; Sweden; flat plains

13

Reviewing Physical Maps

Ask students:

- **What do physical maps show that simple political maps do not?** (the earth's surface features, such as hills and plains)
- **How do they show these features?** (by the use of colors and shading)
- **What kinds of features might be found on both political and physical maps?** (Possible answers include: national boundaries, oceans, rivers, scales, keys.)
- **What is a landform map?** (a physical map that shows where the earth's surface is covered by mountains, hills, plateaus, plains, and other landforms)

EXTENDING MAP SKILLS

Refer to the map on this page.

Ask students:

- **Which map key symbols must you figure out to understand this map?** (the color used for each kind of landform)
- **Which landforms are shown?** (mountains, hills, plateaus, plains)
- **What other physical feature is indicated in the map key?** (cities)
- **Which countries' landforms are shown on this map?** (Norway, Sweden, Denmark, Finland)
- **Which parts of Scandinavia are mountainous?** (Norway, northwestern Sweden)
- **What kinds of landforms surround the Gulf of Bothnia?** (plains and hills)
- **How would you describe the land surface of North Cape?** (hilly and mountainous)
- **What kinds of landforms are found in southern Sweden?** (plains and plateaus)
- **Which nation is almost completely made up of plains?** (Denmark)

BUILDING CITIZENSHIP

Learning More About Our Country Often newspapers and magazines include maps of the United States in comments, explanations, or advertisements. Have students find such maps, clip them out, and put together a collection of them. These maps will be useful at times when you want students to understand the range of information that maps convey. Encourage students to interpret various maps. Working with such maps may provide the bonus of enhancing students' knowledge of their country.

Reviewing the Use of a Grid Map

Ask students:

- **How does a map grid "organize" a map?** (by dividing it into sections that can be located by letter and number)
- **How does this aid in finding locations?** (An index of place names can tell in which section on the map each can be found.)

Have students locate and name the park in grid A-1 (Regent's Park).

EXTENDING MAP SKILLS

Refer students to the map on this page. Have them draw up a list of the places they might want to visit in London. List the places named below and have students enter the grid letter and number next to each.

- Regent's Park (A–1)
- Westminster Abbey (C–2)
- The British Museum (B–2)
- The Tower of London (C–4)

Reviewing Distribution Maps

Ask students:

- **What does it mean when something is "distributed"? What kinds of things can distribution maps show?** (Help students to recognize the idea that some places—like cities— may have many people, while other places—like deserts— may have few people.)

Point out other uses for distribution maps. They can show areas with different amounts of rainfall or areas where people speak different languages or practice different religions.

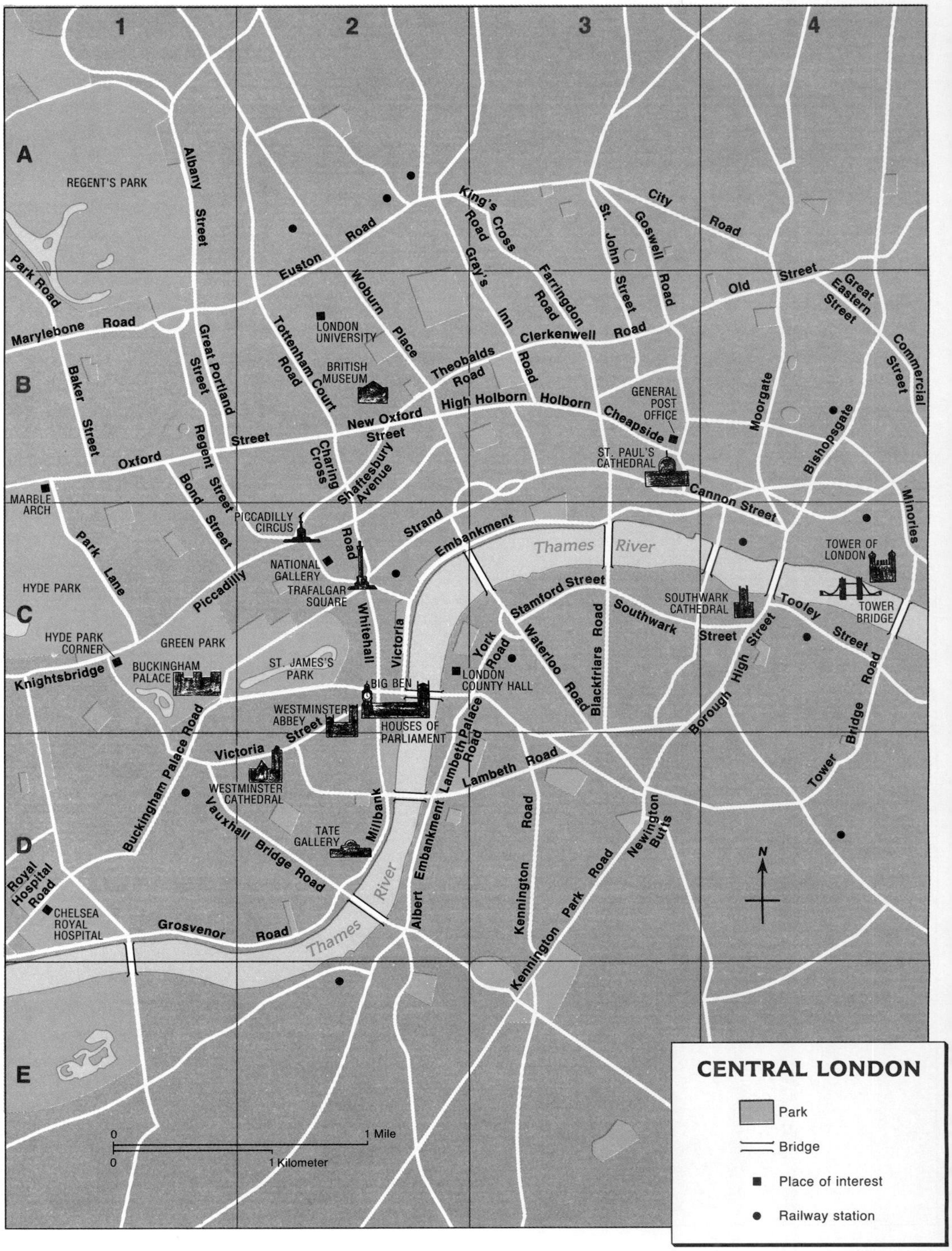

CENTRAL LONDON

Park

Bridge

■ Place of interest

● Railway station

14

BACKGROUND INFORMATION

About Geography Skills in the United States In studies over the past several years, United States citizens have scored well below citizens of many other modern countries in their knowledge of geography. Point out that some college freshmen of the United States could not locate their own state on a map and that other United States citizens could not locate the United States. Encourage students to identify ways that they can learn more about the geography of their state, their country, and the world around them and in so doing help themselves, as well as improve our country's standing in tests of geographical awareness.

Using a Grid Map

One kind of special-purpose map is a city map. Imagine that you are about to take a trip to London, the capital city of England. Imagine that you have only a few days to spend in this important city and that you do not know anything about its geography. How will you be able to find your way around London?

Those who have made the journey to London before suggest that you pick up a good city map. As the map on the opposite page shows, London's streets dart off in many directions. If you do not want to get lost, you will need to use this city map carefully.

City maps are special-purpose maps because they have a unique purpose: they help people find their way around a city. A good city map is also a **grid map**. For example, the map of London shows the central part of the city. This map has a number–letter grid that makes it easy to find places. Each square on the map can be identified by its letter and number. For example, St. Paul's Cathedral is found in square B–3. Find this place of interest on the map. Give the letter and number of the square in which Buckingham Palace is shown on the map.*

Distribution Maps

Some maps show how such things as population, rainfall, language, and religion are distributed in different parts of the world. These kinds of maps are called **distribution maps**

The map on this page shows the distribution of population in India. Different colors are used to show the parts of India in which there are few people per square mile (or square kilometer) and in which there are many people per square mile (or square kilometer). Look at the map key. It shows different population categories. Which color shows areas where there are more than 500 people per square mile (200 people per square kilometer)?**

*C1
**red

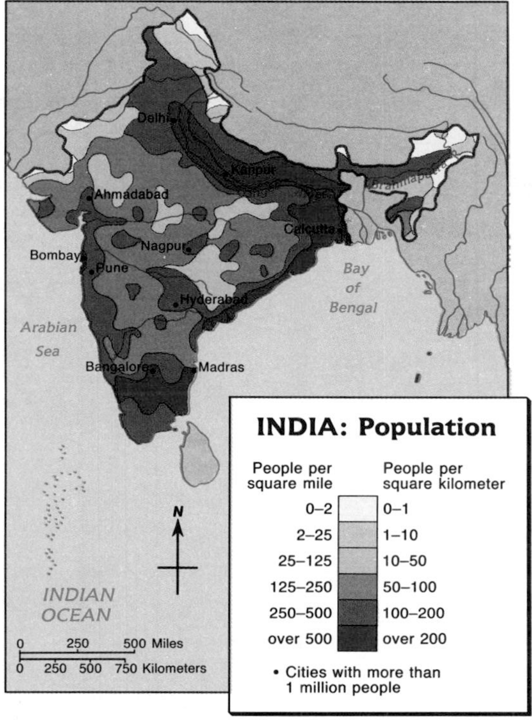

Which parts of India have more than 500 people per square mile (200 people per square kilometer)? Where are there two or fewer people per square mile (one or fewer people per square kilometer)?*

1. What are some of the things commonly shown on political maps?
2. What are some of the things commonly shown on physical maps?
3. What is a distribution map? Explain how distribution is shown on the map on this page.
4. What is a grid map?
5. In which grid on the map of Central London on page 12 are each of the following sites located? St. Paul's Cathedral; General Post Office; London University; St. James's Park; Parliament; Victoria Street.
6. How can a grid map help you find your way around a city?

*the north, the east coast, the south; the extreme north, the east, the west

EXTENDING MAP SKILLS

Refer to the map on this page.

Ask students:

- **What kind of map is this?** (a population distribution map)
- **How are differences in population shown?** (by color)
- **Which color is used to show the least populated areas?** (yellow)
- **Which part of India is the least populated?** (the northwest)
- **In general, are the seacoasts or the interior areas more heavily populated?** (seacoasts)

3 CLOSE

Summarizing Students have reviewed the uses of political, physical, and distribution maps and have investigated how map grids help locate places on maps. Refer students to other distribution maps in the textbook, and have them identify briefly what each shows and the devices used to show that information.

Evaluating Use the review questions (answers given below) to assess students' understanding.

1. boundaries between countries, capitals, important cities
2. natural features of the earth—bodies of land and their surfaces and bodies of water
3. a map that shows how some feature is spread out over an area; by showing how population is spread out over India
4. a map divided into lettered and numbered sections that aid in finding locations
5. St. Paul's—B–3; General Post Office—B–3; London University—B-2; St. James's Park—C–2; Parliament—C–2; Victoria Street—C–1, D–1, D–2, C–2
6. by pinpointing places

Independent Practice
Practice Book: pages 5–6

MEETING INDIVIDUAL NEEDS

Reteaching (easy) Have students draw a map of their state, add to it the names of cities, and place a grid over it. Then have them tell the location of three cities by giving the grid letter and number.

Extension (average) Have students research their state in an encyclopedia and then draw a map showing the distribution of some feature in the state—population, state parks, or state universities, for example.

Enrichment (challenging) Have students do the research necessary to draw a political/physical map of their state. Have them include a map key to explain landform differentiations.

INTRODUCTION
pages 16–17

USING THE INTRODUCTION

Discussing the Photograph To give students an insight into the many different regions and cultures that exist on Earth, invite them to examine the aerial photograph of the globe. Have them choose a spot and imagine what they might find there.

Thinking About the Importance of Geography Have students examine the four photographs on page 17. Tell them that these pictures represent the enormous variety of geography and cultures that they will explore throughout this book.

Hong Kong, Asia Discuss with students how geography can influence the development of an economy.

Suggested Question

- **How do you know that Hong Kong is a major business center?** (shipping traffic in the harbor, skyscrapers, other office buildings)
- *THINKING FURTHER:* **Besides international trade, what other industries would develop in a harbor city?** (fishing, tourism, water recreation)

Tunisia, Africa The Sahara Desert covers 40% of the nation of Tunisia. The entire Sahara is about 1,000 miles wide and 3,500 miles long.

Suggested Questions

- **What means of transportation is shown in the photo?** (camel)
- **How is this man's clothing well-suited to the desert environment?** (It provides protection from the hot sun and the desert sands.)

Introduction

THE IMPORTANCE OF GEOGRAPHY

Earth is a big place. With the population at nearly 6 billion people and growing, there is still room for us all. People live in many different regions and have many different cultures. Still, we all share some basic similarities. In this book you will read about many of these similarities and differences—in geography, in culture, and in lifestyle—which combine to form the great tapestry that is life on Earth.

BACKGROUND INFORMATION

About the Photograph Explain that the photograph of the globe was taken by a camera mounted on a satellite.

- Satellite photography is often used by weather reporting services such as the National Weather Service. The NWS analyzes such photographs to track the paths of weather systems and storms. This can help to warn people about the approach of dangerous weather.
- Satellite photographs are also used by scientists and environmentalists to identify problems and changes in the earth's upper atmosphere.

Hong Kong
ASIA

City lights sparkle across the calm waters of Hong Kong Harbor. Harbors such as this one are important for international trade.

Tunisia
AFRICA

For thousands of years, people have enjoyed rich cultures in even the most difficult places, like the Sahara Desert in North Africa.

United States
NORTH AMERICA

The harvesting of wheat has been a vital part of culture since ancient times. Modern machinery, such as the combine, enables us to feed more people than ever before.

Brazil
SOUTH AMERICA

This beautiful native of the rain forest, the toucan, reminds us of the importance of our natural environments.

17

United States, North America Help students recognize that agriculture is a major industry in the United States. Point out the wheat-farming regions of the United States.

Suggested Questions

- **How do the machines in the photograph make it possible to feed more people?** (They are more efficient and harvest more wheat in less time.)
- *THINKING FURTHER:* **What products are produced from wheat?** (flour, cereals, bread products, animal feed)

Brazil, South America In addition to its importance as a natural habitat, the Brazilian rain forest is also the source of many products, such as rubber, medicines, vegetable oils, nuts, and wood.

Suggested Questions

- **How might the lumber industry affect the toucan in the picture?** (If trees are cut down, the bird would lose its source of shelter and food.)
- **Why is the preservation of the rain forest important to the earth?** (The plants help clean the air and provide shelter and food for wildlife; careful use of natural resources ensures continued benefits for humans.)

BACKGROUND INFORMATION

More About the Photographs

- Students may be interested to know that the Sahara was once fertile farmland. Over thousands of years, climatic changes caused the land to become arid, thus forcing farmers to abandon their lands.
- Point out that the rain forests of Brazil are being destroyed by logging, mining, and agricultural interests. By 1997, more than 40% of Brazil's rain forests had been destroyed.

NATIONAL GEOGRAPHIC
Adventures
pages 18–19

Introducing
Around the Western Hemisphere

Exploring Prior Knowledge Have students study the photographs on these pages. Ask students to share what they know about the images they see.

Links to the Book Point out that these pictures show places from different regions of the Western Hemisphere. Let students know that as they continue through this book, they will meet and learn about people and places from these regions.

Around the Western Hemisphere Refer students to the large photo showing the Mayan ruins at Palenque, Mexico. Tell them that archaeologists and historians are able to learn much about a culture by studying ruins such as these. For example, artifacts collected at Palenque and other Mayan sites indicate that the Maya placed great value on lineage, sustaining royal bloodlines over long periods.

Ask students if we share a similar value in modern American culture. Do any of these photos indicate otherwise? Point out the photo of Mount Rushmore, which may indicate to future historians our admiration for the achievements of four American presidents.

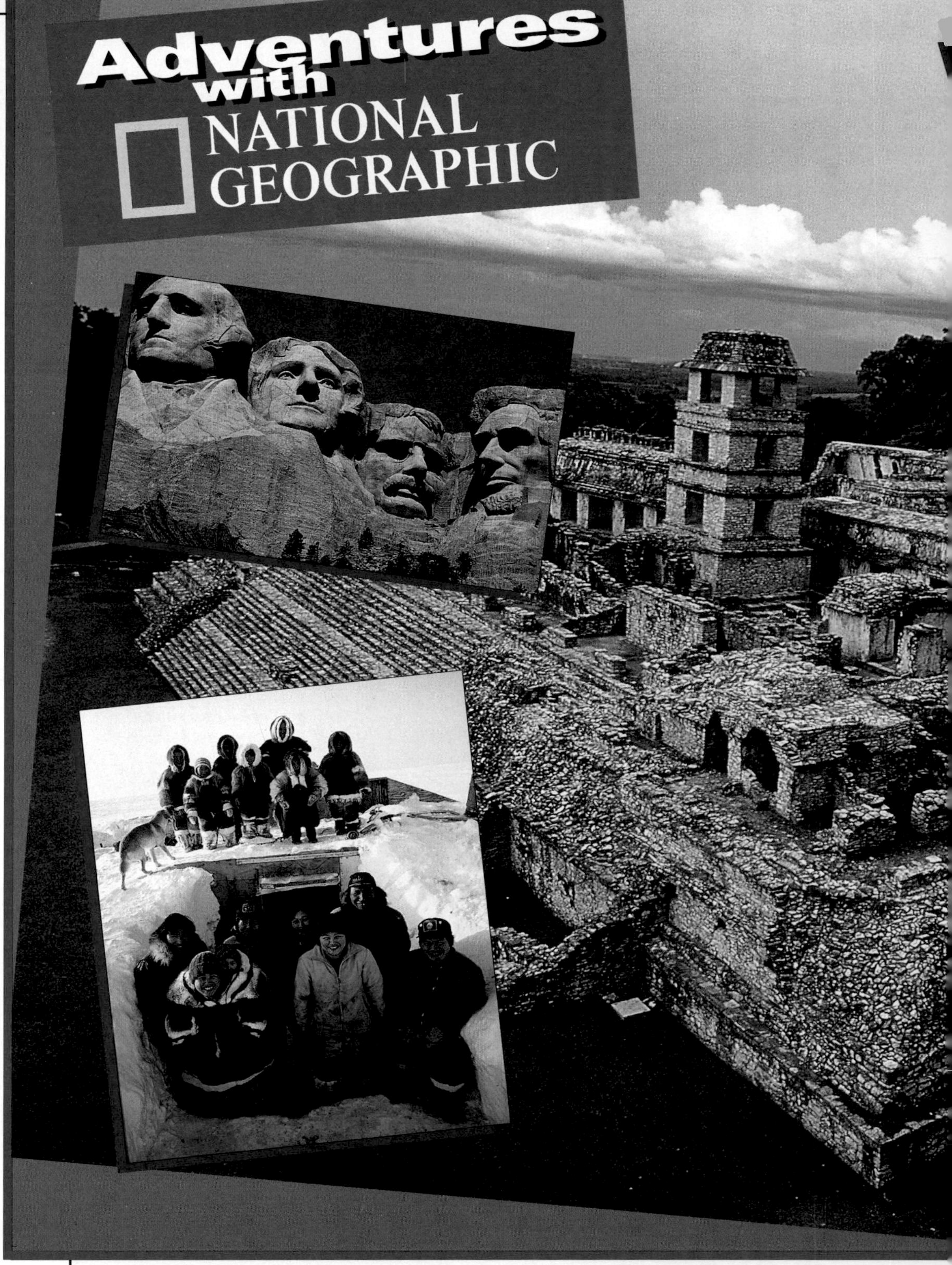

BACKGROUND INFORMATION

More About the Photographs

- The ruins at Palenque are located in Chiapas, and were once covered by dense tropical jungle. They represent the structures of the classic Maya period (A.D. 300–900), and are covered with carved figures and hieroglyphics.
- At Mount Rushmore in South Dakota, the massive carved heads of four U.S. presidents—Washington, Jefferson, Lincoln, and Theodore Roosevelt—are a national memorial. Each head is 50–70 feet high and was carved by the American sculptor Gutzon Borglum.
- Named after William Baffin, who arrived there in 1616, Baffin Island in northeastern Canada is the fifth largest island in the world. Its arctic climate supports an amazing variety of birds and aquatic life such as narwhals, walruses, and harp seals.

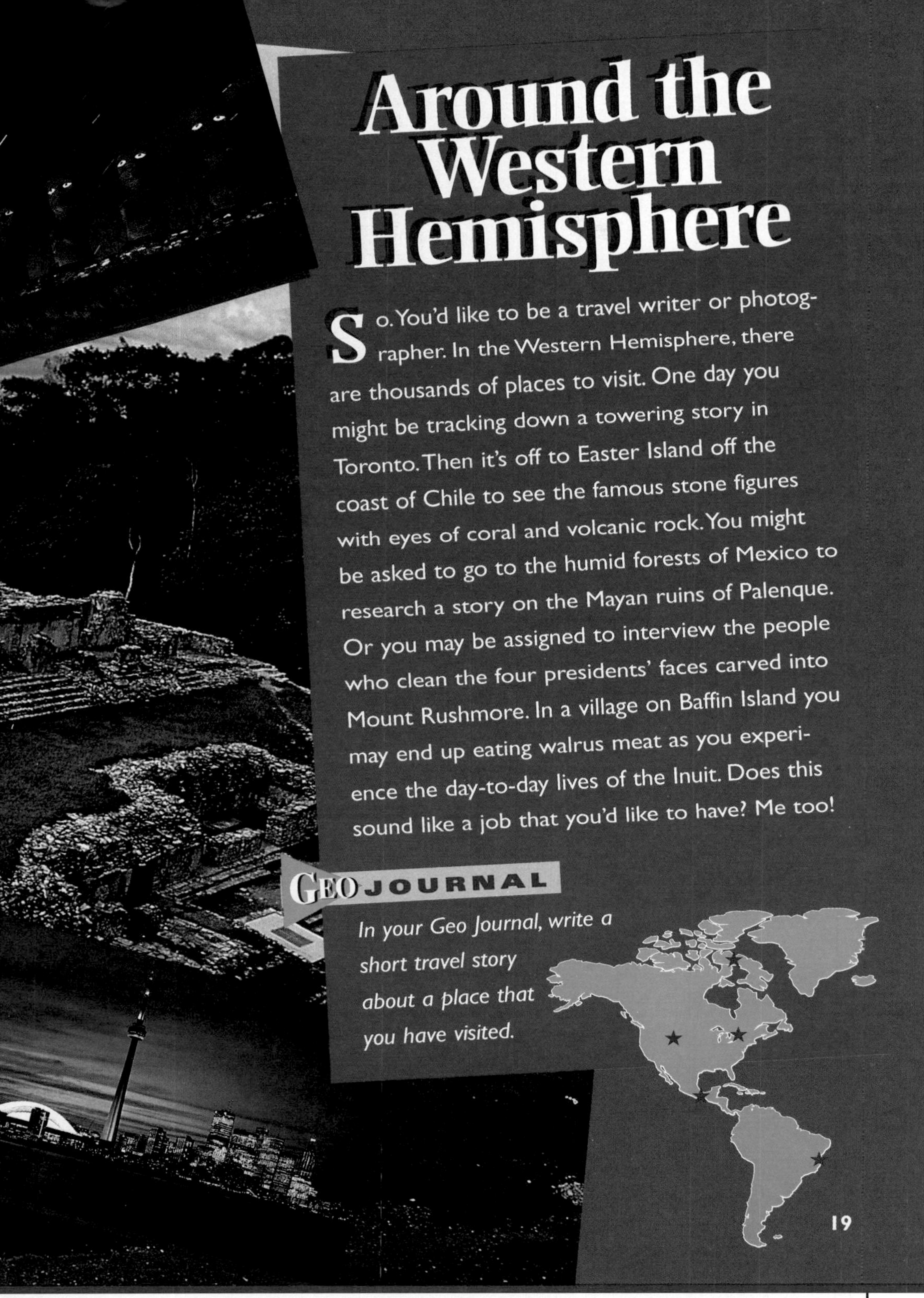

Help students realize that each of these pictures shows an important landmark or structure. Prompt a discussion with questions such as the following: *Which of these sites are historical? Which are modern? Which represent the culture of a place? What does each of these sites say about the culture that created it?*

Have students brainstorm a list of places in their community that visitors may enjoy seeing. Encourage students to tell why these places are special to the community.

Using the Geo Journal Tell students that they may write about either a place they have traveled to or their own region from the perspective of a recent visitor.

Before students begin their travel story, have them write a list of the characteristics of the place they have chosen. Suggest that they include information about the local people, their customs, and landmarks or other special places of interest.

BACKGROUND INFORMATION

More About the Photographs

- Toronto's CN Tower, at 1815 feet, is one of the tallest free standing structures in the world. It was completed in 1976 and functions as an observation and communications tower.
- Easter Island, formed from three extinct volcanoes, is located 2,300 miles west of Chile. The massive heads, called megaliths, were carved of soft volcanic rock and stand 10–40 feet high. Of approximately 600 original carvings, only 100 remain.

NATIONAL GEOGRAPHIC
Adventures
pages 20–21

Introducing
Around the Eastern Hemisphere

Exploring Prior Knowledge Have students examine the photographs on these pages. Ask volunteers to share information they have about any of these locations.

Links to the Book Point out that each picture is from a different region of the Eastern Hemisphere. Let students know that as they explore this book, they will encounter more people and places from each of these regions.

Around the Eastern Hemisphere Have students examine the text and photos on these pages. Tell them that each photo shows a particular structure which is widely perceived to be representative of the culture that produced it.

The Great Wall of China, for example, was begun in 221 B.C., but was not completed in its final form until nearly A.D. 1600. It reflects the great age and continuity of the world's most enduring culture. Similarly, the Great Sphinx of Giza has become synonymous with the majesty and mystery of Africa's ancient Egyptian culture.

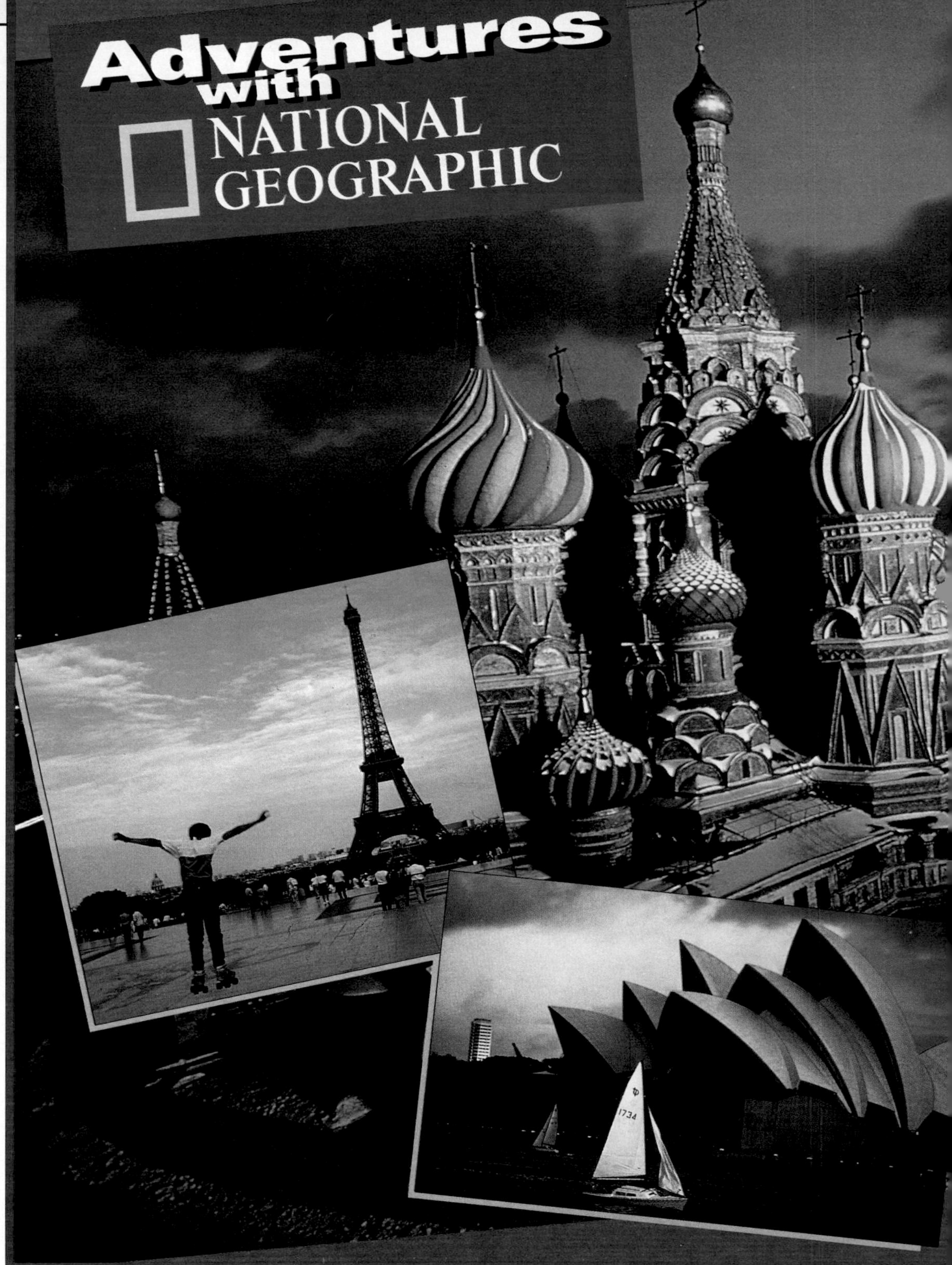

BACKGROUND INFORMATION

More About the Photographs

- The Eiffel Tower was created by civil engineer Alexandre Gustave Eiffel for the Paris World's Fair in 1889. The 984-foot structure was built from over 7000 tons of iron. It has three observation decks.
- Built in 1973, the Sydney Opera House sits on a point of land that juts into Port Jackson. Sydney will be the site of the Summer Olympic Games in the year 2000.
- The Great Sphinx of Giza—the most famous of the sphinxes—dates from the 26th century B.C. The face is most likely that of Pharaoh Khafre. The statue stands 66 feet high and 240 feet long.
- The 1500-mile Great Wall of China runs westward from Jinwangdao to Gaodai, and south from Beijing to Handan. The average height is 25 feet, and watchtowers are located 200 yards apart.

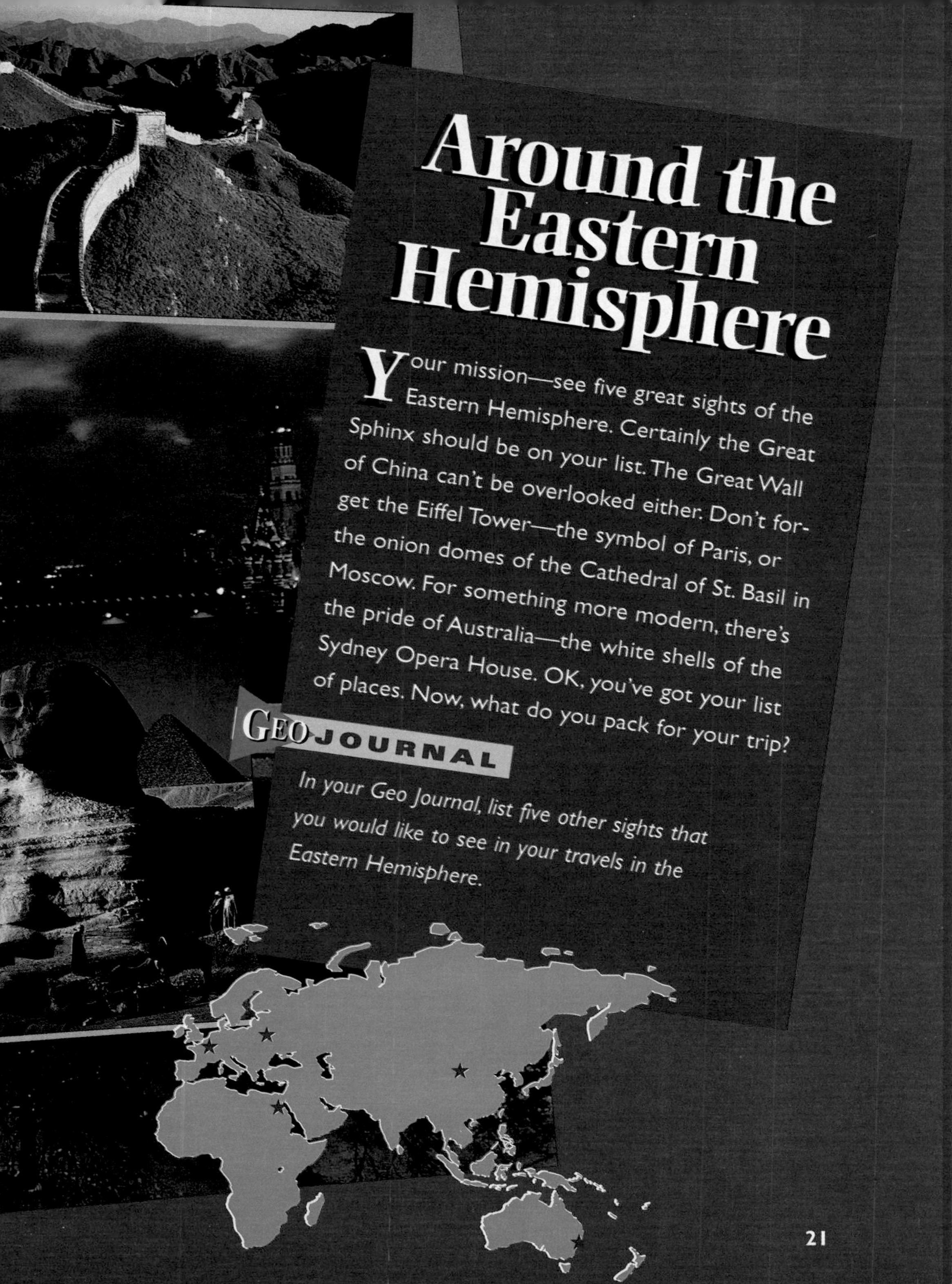

Help students to realize that each of these pictures shows a symbol for a different country. Begin a discussion of the significance of each of the structures shown here. Prompt the discussion with questions such as, *Which of these symbols are religious? Which represent cultural aspects of the country? Which show great technological skill?*

Challenge students to think of cultural landmarks that represent their own community or state. For example, the Golden Gate Bridge is a symbol of San Francisco, and the Empire State Building is a symbol of New York City. Then have students think of symbols that represent the United States. Initiate a class discussion about why these became such strong symbols.

Using the Geo Journal Before students begin a list of additional sites, have them work in pairs to construct a list of some other countries in the Eastern Hemisphere. Suggest that they check an encyclopedia, travel guide, or some other resource to find possible points of interest in their chosen countries. If students already have a particular site in mind, encourage them to locate it on the appropriate *Atlas* map.

CURRICULUM CONNECTION

Art and Architecture Tell students that the Eiffel Tower was originally built for a world's fair. Have them find out about other structures that remained after world's fairs closed and which later became important on their own.

Students should work in small groups to prepare an illustrated report about the structures they have researched. They may also enjoy creating three-dimensional models of the structures.

PART 1
pages 22–27

Lesson Theme Landforms, climate, and natural resources are the main parts of physical geography.

Lesson Objective

- Describe landforms, climate, and natural resources.

Lesson Resources

Outline Map: *The World*
Transparency Maps: 1–3

PREPARE

Motivate Have students close their eyes while you read the *Read Aloud* section. Ask for a student volunteer to draw a picture of foothills on the chalkboard. Have students guess how high the Andes are; then have them use the elevation map on page 108 to find the actual height. (Mt. Aconcagua in the Andes is 22,834 feet [6,960 m].) Help students to calculate that the plane was about one third of the way up an Andes peak.

Set Purpose Use the *What You Know* question to discuss the land nearby. Ask the *What You Will Learn* question to stress that physical geography includes more than just land.

TEACH

Studying the Land Discuss students' ideas of the meaning of physical geography.

Discussing Environments

Ask students:

- **What is an environment?** (all the surroundings of a place)
- **What are some parts of a natural environment?** (land, water, weather, plants, animals)

PART

1 Physical Geography

READ TO LEARN

Key Vocabulary

physical geography
environment
landform
climate
tropical climate
temperate climate
polar climate
elevation
natural resources
vegetation
fossil fuel

Read Aloud

Five, six, seven thousand feet and we turned eastward over the broad valley of the Juncal River and toward the mountains. We gained on them. At first they looked like colossal gobs of sponge cake sprinkled with a thin coating of powdered sugar. . . .The great gobs of sponge cake were not the Andes at all. They were only the foothills of the Andes. We hadn't started to climb.

This is how one writer described an airplane trip over the Andes mountains. Mountains are just one part of the amazingly different kinds of physical geography in the world.

Read for Purpose

1. **WHAT YOU KNOW:** What have people done over the years to change the land where you live?
2. **WHAT YOU WILL LEARN:** Why is it important to study physical geography?

STUDYING THE LAND

In this book you will study the regions of the earth. When you start to study each region, the first chapter you will read will be about the physical geography of that region. As you may guess, **physical geography** is the study of the earth's surface. On the next few pages you will read in more detail about what is included in the study of physical geography.

ENVIRONMENTS

Every place on earth has its own special kind of physical geography. The earth has many different **environments**. An environment is made up of all of the surroundings of a place. It includes the land and the water, the weather patterns, and all the plants and animals that live in a place.

Physical geographers study the characteristics of all of the earth's environments. A physical geographer, for example, may study a mountain environment to determine how high the mountains are or how easy they are to travel through. Physical geographers also may study how such natural conditions affect things like rainfall and transportation.

WHAT YOU KNOW: Responses could include a variety of activities, from planting different crops to building large cities.

READING STRATEGY AND VOCABULARY DEVELOPMENT

Using Prior Knowledge The purpose of this strategy is to have students identify information they know about a topic before they read. Reinforce the strategy of using prior knowledge to think about the topic of a lesson. Explain to students that the things they already know about a subject could help them in studying this lesson. Brainstorm with students the information they know about geography. Develop this information into a semantic map. After students have read the lesson, return to the map and categorize the information by physical geography, landforms, climate, and natural resources. Then have students add to or refine the information on the map.

LANDFORMS

Did you know that people can live on only a small part of the earth? More than 70 percent of our planet is covered with water. The 30 percent of the surface that is dry land is divided into different types of **landforms**, or physical features. Mountains, hills, plains, and plateaus are different kinds of landforms. Landforms vary greatly in size and shape.

If you look at pages 644–645 in the back of your book, you will find a Dictionary of Geographic Terms. This dictionary shows many of the earth's landforms and gives a definition of each. As you read this book, refer to this dictionary to read about each landform and to see what it looks like.

As you have read, geographers are very interested in studying landforms and how they affect the ways people live. Landforms are one of the most important parts of physical geography that you will study in this book.

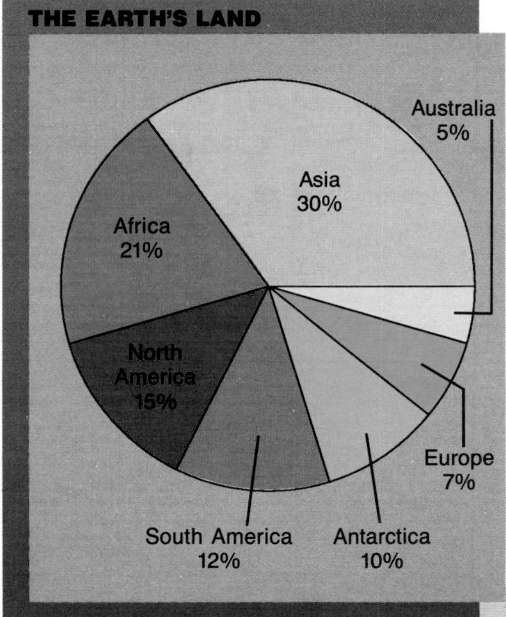

GRAPH SKILL: The land surface of the earth is divided into seven continents. Which is the largest? Which is the smallest?

CLIMATE

Climate is another important part of physical geography that you will study. Climate is the kind of weather a place has over a long period of time. Climate includes seasonal temperatures, the amount of precipitation (pri sip i tā′ shən), and wind patterns in a place. Precipitation is rain, snow, hail, sleet, and any other form of water that falls to the earth.

The climate where you live affects your everyday life. Think of your community and of places nearby. Do they almost always have cold winters? Are the summers long or short? Does it rain all year or only part of the year?

The answers to the above questions will help you to understand why climate is important to our lives. It affects how we live and work. It also affects the kinds of houses that we build and the types of clothes that we wear. Finally, climate has a great effect on the kinds of crops, if any, that we grow in a region.

There are many different climates on the earth. Let's look at some of them.

THE EFFECT OF THE SUN

Do you know why some places on earth are warmer or colder than others? One important reason is the sun. Some places on the earth receive more of the sun's rays than other places receive. Because of the tilt of the earth as it revolves around the sun, places near the equator receive more direct rays of the sun than do places farther away from the equator. This helps to explain why places near the equator are warm most of the time, while the North and South poles tend to be very cold.

GRAPH SKILL: Asia; Australia

Introducing Landforms Be sure students realize how large the percentage of the earth that is covered with water is. Point out that 70 percent is more than twice 30 percent.

Ask students:

- **How is the earth's surface divided between water and dry land?** (70 percent is water; 30 percent is dry land.)
- **What are some types of landforms?** (mountains, hills, valleys, plains, plateaus)

You may wish to point out to students the definitions of some important terms in the *Dictionary of Geographic Terms* on pages 644–645.

EXTENDING GRAPH SKILLS

Have students study the circle graph on this page.

Ask students:

- **What does the circle represent?** (100 percent of the land surface of the earth)
- **Name the continents by size in descending order.** (Asia, Africa, North America, South America, Antarctica, Europe, Australia)

Introducing Climate

Ask students:

- **What is climate?** (the kind of weather a place has over a long period of time)
- **What makes up the climate of a place?** (seasonal temperatures, amount of precipitation, wind patterns)
- **What is precipitation?** (any form of water that falls to the earth)
- **Which things in our lives are controlled by climate?** (how we live and work, the type of houses and clothes we have, and the kinds of crops we grow)

Understanding the Effect of the Sun Be sure students understand how the sun affects temperatures on earth.

CURRICULUM CONNECTION

Math Help students see some of the mathematical relationships in the circle graph on this page. Encourage them to look at relationships in any circle graph. Use the following samples.

- Asia and Africa each has more than one fifth, or 20 percent, of the earth's land.
- Together Australia, Antarctica, and North America are equal in land surface to Asia.
- North America has half the land surface of Asia.

Have students come up with other such relationships, using the information in the circle graph.

EXTENDING MAP SKILLS

Give students time to study the two climate maps on this page. Ask them to try to match the map colors with the map legend.

Ask students:

- **How many types of climates are shown on the top map?** (12)
- **How many of these climates have cold winters?** (four)
- **How many of these climates have mild winters?** (three)
- **How many of these climates vary with elevation?** (one)
- **How many of these climates vary with latitude?** (two)
- **How many of these climates are warm all year?** (two)
- **Name two countries in each of the world climate zones shown in the lower map.** (Answers will vary.)
- **In which climate zone is Central America?** (tropical zone/low latitudes)
- **In which climate zone is most of Europe?** (temperate zone/middle latitudes)
- *THINKING FURTHER:* **Which four world areas seem to have the largest amount of land covered by one climate?** (northern North America and northern Asia; west-central Asia; northern Africa; Antarctica)

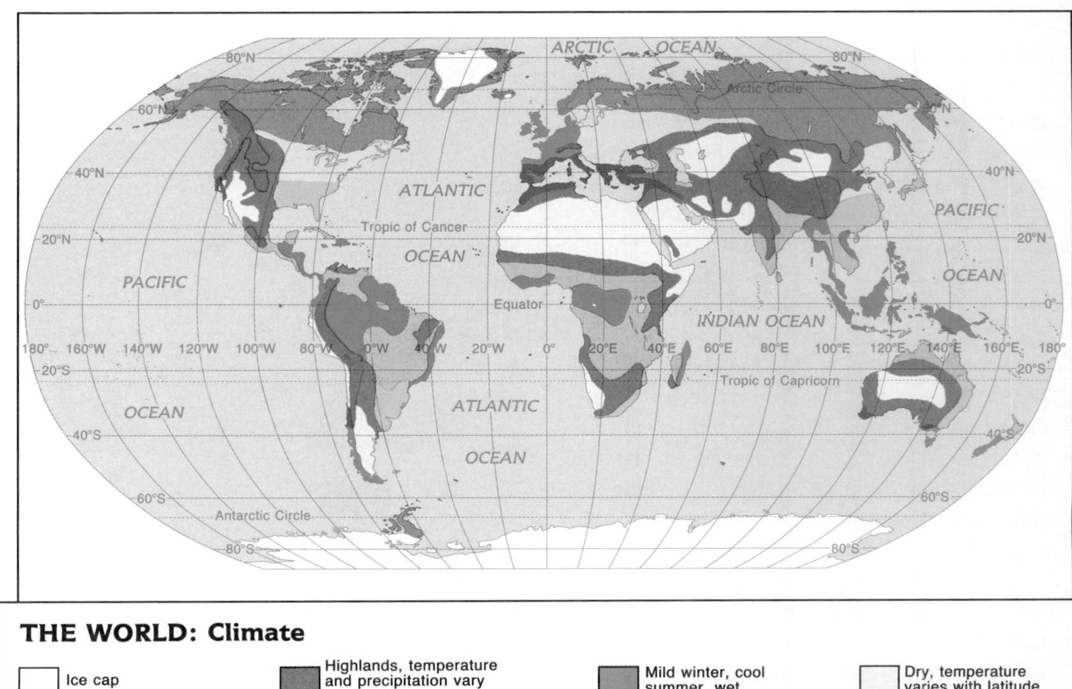

THE WORLD: Climate

- Ice cap
- Very cold winter, cold summer, dry
- Very cold winter, cool summer, wet
- Highlands, temperature and precipitation vary with elevation
- Semi-dry, temperature varies with latitude
- Cold winter, hot or warm summer, wet
- Mild winter, cool summer, wet
- Mild or warm winter, hot summer, wet
- Mild, wet winter; hot, dry summer
- Dry, temperature varies with latitude
- Warm all year, wet with one dry season
- Warm and wet all year

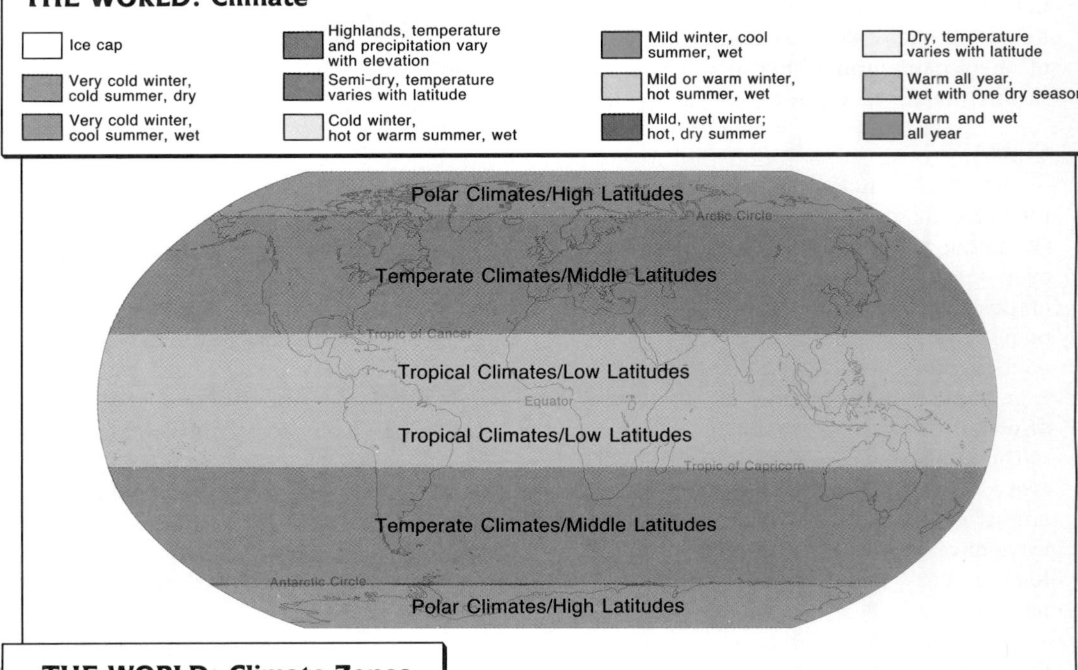

THE WORLD: Climate Zones

MAP SKILL: How many different types of climate are found in Africa? In which climate zone is most of Africa located?

24 MAP SKILL: Six; tropical zones/low latitudes

BACKGROUND INFORMATION

The Tilt of the Earth on Its Axis A common misconception is that the distance of the earth from the sun determines the amount of heat that reaches the earth. In the Northern Hemisphere just the opposite happens.

- During winter in the Northern Hemisphere the earth is closest to the sun; the earth is farthest from the sun in the summer.
- The tilt of the earth on its axis makes the sun's rays hit the earth's surface at a greater or lesser angle; this angle controls the amount of heat during different seasons of the year.

5 FUNDAMENTAL THEMES OF GEOGRAPHY

Location The Tropic of Cancer and the Tropic of Capricorn are called sun lines. This means that in the lands between these lines you can see the sun directly overhead about noon and that the lands between these lines are in the tropical climate zone. In places located north or south of these sun lines, you can never see the sun directly overhead.

- Have students use the map on this page to find the latitude of the Tropic of Cancer (23.5°N) and the Tropic of Capricorn (23.5°S).

CLIMATE ZONES

Look at the two maps on page 24. They show some of the different climate areas of the world.

Find the equator on the map at the bottom of the page. Now locate the area to the north and south of the equator—from the Tropic of Cancer to the Tropic of Capricorn. This area receives the most direct rays of the sun. Occasionally, temperatures here reach as high as 130°F. (54°C)! This is called the **tropical climate** zone. The word *tropical* comes from an ancient Greek word meaning "turning to the sun."

North and south of the tropics are the **temperate climate** zones. Places in the temperate climate zones have weather that changes considerably during four distinct seasons. Places located in these zones usually do not experience extremely high or low temperatures, or extremely large or small amounts of precipitation.

Some places on earth are always cold. The **polar climate** zones, which are located north and south of the temperate zones, receive only the most indirect rays of the sun. As a result, the polar zones are the coldest areas of the earth.

OTHER INFLUENCES ON CLIMATE

Look again at the map on the top of page 24. It shows that even though the world is divided into different climate zones, climates are not always the same within these zones. Why is this true?

In addition to heat from the sun's rays, other factors also affect climate. One of them is winds. Winds are currents, or masses, of air that blow around the earth. As the sun heats the earth, masses of air grow warmer and expand. When the warm air rises, it pushes out cold air. You may have seen a weather report on television that showed a cold front or a warm front coming to the area where you live. A front is air that is expanding or being pushed out of one area into another one.

Winds also carry moisture in the form of water vapor, which is tiny drops of water. The warm air that rises carries water vapor. The amount of moisture in the air determines the amount of precipitation that falls in a place.

Another factor that affects climate is **elevation**, or height above sea level. Areas with high elevations are cooler because temperatures become lower as the land grows higher. You will read more about how and why this happens in Unit 2.

Finally, distance from the ocean and the size and shape of landforms in a region also affect climate. You will read more about these factors throughout this book.

NATURAL RESOURCES

You have now looked at two of the important parts of physical geography, landforms and climate. The third important part is **natural resources**. Natural resources are the materials found in nature that people can use, such as water, air, soil, or animals.

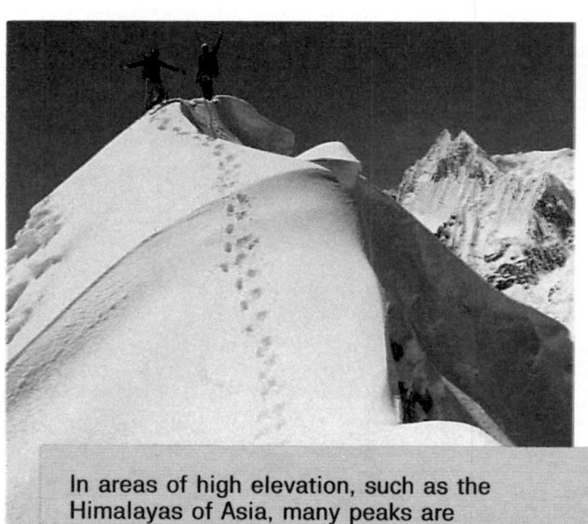

In areas of high elevation, such as the Himalayas of Asia, many peaks are covered with snow all year.

25

Introducing Climate Zones Make sure students can readily locate the equator, the Tropic of Cancer, and the Tropic of Capricorn on the maps on page 24.

Ask students:

- **What is the name of the area between the Tropic of Cancer and the Tropic of Capricorn?** (the tropical climate zone)
- **What characterizes the climate in the tropical climate zone?** (It has the most direct rays of the sun and is warm year-round.)
- **Where are the temperate climate zones?** (north and south of the tropical climate zone)
- **Describe the climate in the temperate climate zones.** (It has seasonal changes with moderate temperatures and moderate amounts of precipitation.)
- **Which zones are north and south of the temperate zones?** (the polar climate zones)
- **What characterizes the climate in the polar zones?** (They receive very indirect rays of the sun and are the coldest areas of the earth.)

Analyzing Other Influences on Climate Emphasize to students that the simple climate zones shown on the map at the bottom of page 24 become the complicated patterns shown on the climate map at the top of the page because of four other climate influences.

Ask students:

- **What are winds?** (masses of air that blow around the earth)
- **What is a front?** (air that is expanding or being pushed out of one area into another)
- **What do winds affect in addition to temperature and pressure?** (the amount of water vapor that can fall as precipitation)
- **Which three factors, in addition to the wind, affect climate?** (elevation, distance from the ocean, size and shape of landforms)

Defining *Natural Resources* Be sure students understand what natural resources are.

BACKGROUND INFORMATION

Convection Simply stated, the rule of convection is: Hot materials expand and rise and cold materials condense and fall.

- *Wind Systems:* Air heated near the equator rises and flows toward the poles, where it cools and falls back, then flows toward the equator.
- *Water Cycle:* Rising hot air picks up moisture; the air cools aloft and drops its water vapor as precipitation, which makes crops grow.
- *Ocean Currents:* When surface ocean water is heated by the sun, it expands. As it moves into cooler areas, it cools; as it cools, it falls downward. This expansion and descent constitutes the flow of ocean water known as ocean currents.
- *Plate Tectonics:* Magma, heated by the earth's core, rises to the surface, cools, and descends, moving the earth's crustal plates.

Discussing Natural Resources
Discuss the natural resources of your area. Have students name the important parts of physical geography (landforms, climate, natural resources).

Looking at Vegetation
Ask students:

- **What is vegetation?** (different kinds of plants, such as trees, flowers, and grasses)
- **What are the main types of vegetation areas?** (forest, grassland, desert, and tundra)
- **What are the chief characteristics of forests?** (The main vegetation is trees. They require much water. They exist in many climate zones.)
- **What are the characteristics of grasslands?** (They are covered with many types of grasses, they require less water than forests, they are found in most temperate zones.)
- **Which characteristics describe deserts?** (dry areas, little plant life)
- **What is a tundra?** (a polar-zone plain with a permanently frozen subsurface and low plants and mosses)

EXTENDING MAP SKILLS
Have students study the vegetation map on this page.

Ask students:

- **How many kinds of vegetation areas are represented on this map?** (9)
- **How many kinds of forests are shown? What are their names?** (4; Deciduous, Evergreen, Tropical Rain Forest, Mediterranean and Scrub Forest)
- **Which continents have the largest desert areas?** (Africa, Asia, Australia)
- **Which continents have the largest evergreen forest areas?** (North America, Europe, and Asia)

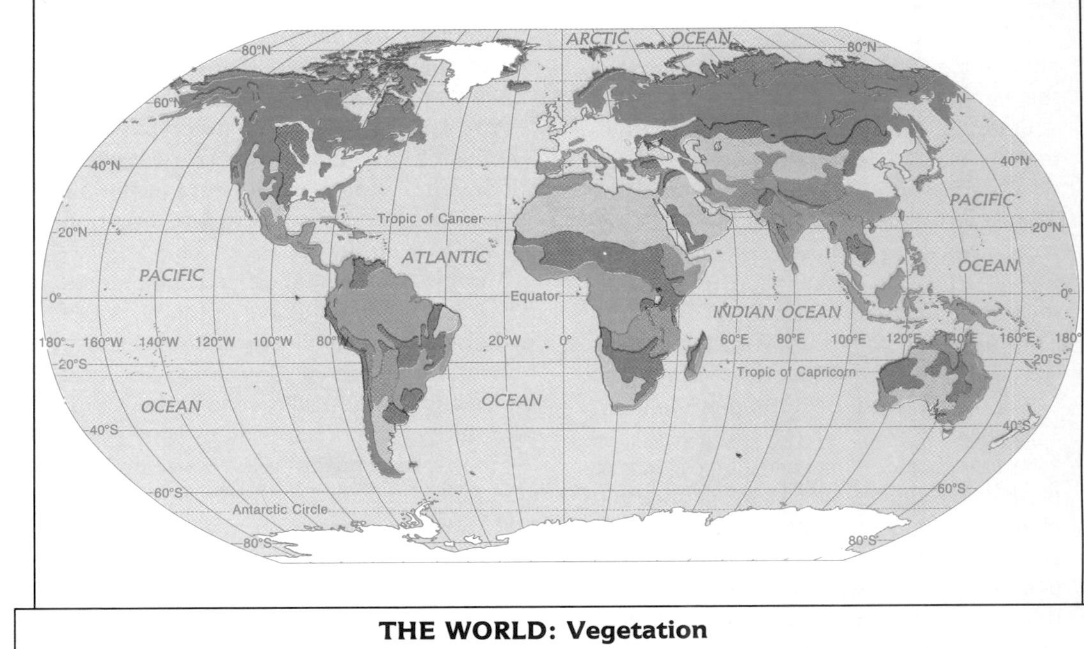

MAP SKILL: In which part of the world is the vegetation mainly tundra? What kinds of vegetation are found on the continent of Antarctica at the South Pole?

Different parts of the world have natural resources in uneven amounts. What are some of the important natural resources of your area?

VEGETATION
Plants are one kind of natural resource. Trees, flowers, and grasses are all part of the vegetation, or plant life, that grows in an area. The main types of vegetation areas in the world are forest, grassland, desert, and tundra.

A forest is a place in which trees are the main type of vegetation. Forests require large amounts of water and are found in many climate zones.

Grasslands may be covered with many types of grasses. Grasses do not require as much water as trees and are found in most parts of the temperate zones.

Deserts are dry areas that have little plant life. Only plants that can live for long periods with little water can survive there.

A tundra is a type of plain found in polar zones. Although tundras have soil that is permanently frozen under the surface, the surface is warm enough to allow tiny plants and mosses to live.

26

MAP SKILL: Tundra is found in the north, near the North Pole; Antarctica has little or no vegetation.

CURRICULUM CONNECTION
Math Not all of the 30 percent of the earth that is land can grow vegetation. Land that can be farmed for crops is called arable land. Help students to recognize the difference between the amount of land on earth and the percentage of that land that is arable. Each continent has only a certain percentage of land that is arable. Have students set up a chart to fill in as they study this book. Have them make seven columns, one labeled for each continent. As they study each unit, have students list under each continent the percentage of the world's land (see circle graph on page 23) and the percentage of the arable land that are found in that continent. When the chart is completed, students will be able to calculate how much of the total amount of the earth's land is arable.

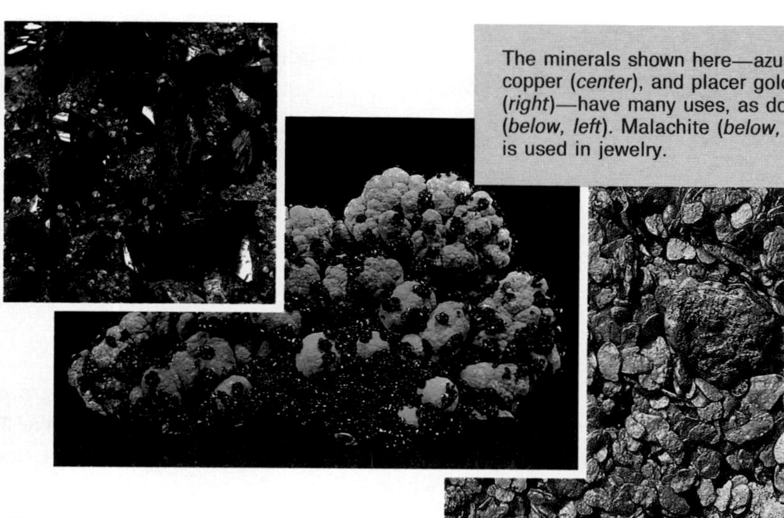

The minerals shown here—azurite (*left*), copper (*center*), and placer gold (*right*)—have many uses, as does hematite (*below, left*). Malachite (*below, right*) is used in jewelry.

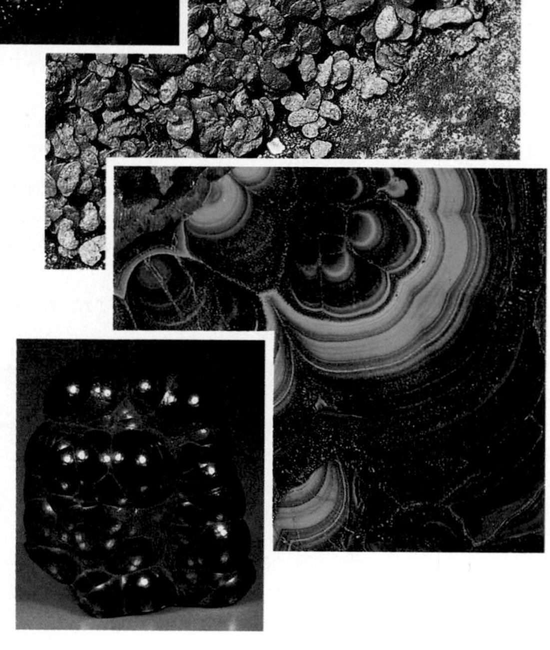

MINERALS AND FOSSIL FUELS

Other natural resources besides various kinds of vegetation are also found in the earth. Minerals are substances in nature that are not animals or plants. Some minerals are metals. Iron, copper, and gold are among the metals that people have used since very early times. Other minerals are nonmetals, such as table salt.

Coal, natural gas, and petroleum are **fossil fuels**, the remains of animals and plants that died thousands of years ago. Fossil fuels are important sources of energy used today for heating, lighting, and the running of machinery.

LANDFORMS, CLIMATE, NATURAL RESOURCES

In this section you have learned about the study of physical geography. You have read that there are three important parts of physical geography: landforms, climate, and natural resources. In this book there are chapters on the physical geography of each of the world's regions. As you read each chapter on physical geography, notice that it is divided into two lessons: one lesson on landforms and one lesson on climate and resources.

Check Your Reading

1. Give some examples of the earth's landforms.
2. What is climate?
3. Why is it important to study the physical geography of the earth?
4. THINKING SKILL: List three questions you could ask to find out what kind of environment a place has.

THINKING SKILL: Asking Questions

Introducing Minerals and Fossil Fuels Help students to distinguish between natural resources that are living things, such as vegetation and animals, and other substances in nature, such as minerals and fossil fuels.

Ask students:

- **What are minerals?** (substances in nature that are not animals or plants)
- **What are fossil fuels?** (remains of animals and plants that died thousands of years ago; Examples are coal, natural gas, and petroleum.)
- **Why are fossil fuels important today?** (They are the major sources of energy for heat, light, and the running of machinery.)

Applying the Lesson Have students write a paragraph describing the physical geography where they live, including landforms, climate, and natural resources.

3 CLOSE

Summarizing Students have learned how landforms, climate, and natural resources shape the physical geography of a place. Ask which they think has been the most dominant in shaping the physical geography of their community.

Evaluating Ask students to write definitions for each of the ten *Key Vocabulary* words on page 22.

Answers to Check Your Reading

1. mountains, valleys, plains, plateaus, hills, and so on
2. the kind of weather a place has over a long period of time
3. to understand how it shapes human lives and provides the resources to sustain life
4. Possible questions include: Which landforms make up this place? What is the climate like? Which plants and animals grow in this place?

MEETING INDIVIDUAL NEEDS

Reteaching (easy) Have each student make a set of definition cards for the *Key Vocabulary* words and for definitions of other words found in this lesson. Allow pairs of students to quiz each other, using the cards.

Extension (average) Divide the class into three groups to make models of the physical geography of their community. Each group should focus on one of the three important parts of physical geography. Provide the groups with oaktag, glue, clay, and other construction materials.

Enrichment (challenging) As a cooperative project have the class work together to research and draw a mural-sized time line showing the changes in the physical geography of their community that have occurred in the last 100 years.

PART 2
pages 28–31

Lesson Theme People, economy, government, and arts and recreation are all part of cultural geography.

Lesson Objective

- Define *culture* by describing its four main parts: people, economy, government, and arts and recreation.

Lesson Resources

Outline Map: *The World*
Transparency Maps: 1–3

PREPARE

Motivate Read the *Read Aloud* section to the class. Discuss with students why Chinese people would talk about a job in terms of rice or a rice bowl. (The purpose of a job is to sustain people with food, and rice is the most important food in China.)

Set Purpose Ask the *What You Know* question and have students make their own individual lists. Explain that even young people in our culture have experience with many kinds of social organizations. Use the *What You Will Learn* question to explain to students that human culture is a complex topic.

TEACH

Introducing Culture Stress that cultures are the same in many ways and yet different in other ways.

Ask students:

- **What do cultural geographers study?** (how people adapt to their environment to build their own special culture)

PART

2 Cultural Geography

READ TO LEARN

Key Vocabulary

cultural geography
culture
ethnic group
custom

Read Aloud

The Chinese often talk about success in terms of food. "Having grains to chew" is an expression indicating a person has a job. If you "have an iron rice bowl" you have a very secure job. If you "have a porcelain rice bowl" you have an insecure job, while saying "the rice bowl is broken" means you are unemployed.

All of the peoples of the world find ways to express what is important to them and to their way of life. Studying these different ways through cultural geography will help you to understand what is special about people everywhere.

Read for Purpose

1. **WHAT YOU KNOW:** What are some of the groups you belong to besides your family?
2. **WHAT YOU WILL LEARN:** What are the main parts of culture?

CULTURE

As you can tell from its name, an important part of cultural geography is **culture**. Culture is the way of life of a group of people. Just as there are many environments, there are many cultures. Cultural geographers study how people use their environment to build their own special culture.

Cultural geography shows how people are alike and how they are different. All people, for example, have a way of greeting one another. However, people in different cultures greet one another in different ways. People in the United States shake hands when they meet, the Japanese bow, and the French kiss both cheeks.

WHAT MAKES UP CULTURE?

Culture includes all the ways in which people relate to one another. Social organizations, rules and governments, values, beliefs, languages, arts, and even sports and hobbies are all parts of culture.

In this book you will read about many cultures. In each unit, after you read a chapter about the physical geography of a region, you will read chapters about the cultural geography of each part of that region. These chapters will be divided into four lessons. Each lesson will cover one part of cultural geography. These parts are: people, economy, government, and arts and recreation. Let's look at them.

WHAT YOU KNOW: Students should think about the clubs, sports teams, religious groups, and other organizations they belong to.

READING STRATEGY AND VOCABULARY DEVELOPMENT

Using Prior Knowledge On a chart list the parts of cultural geography discussed in this lesson (people, economy, government, arts and recreation). Have students skim the lesson, looking at headings, charts, photographs, and maps to remind them of information they may already know about cultural geography. Brainstorm information from students in order to fill in the chart. After students have read the lesson, have them add to or modify the chart.

PEOPLE

One place to start studying a culture is to study the people in it and the groups they form. To understand a people, you need to know about their **ethnic groups**, languages, family structure, religions, and **customs**. An ethnic group is a group of people who share a language, history, and/or place of origin. Customs are the practices from the past that people continue to observe.

The family is the most important group in a culture. Geographers study families because they show how cultures provide for people's physical and emotional needs. Families provide food and shelter, raise children, teach values, and give love, affection, and a sense of purpose.

Studying language is another key to understanding culture. There are many different languages in the world. However, most languages belong to one of a few large language families. A language family is a group of languages that are similar to one another.

In addition to language, religion also helps to hold families and cultures together. For many people religion offers answers to important questions about how people should act in life and what will happen after they die. Thus religion strongly influences the way many people think and act. You will read more about many different religions as you study the cultural geography of the world.

ECONOMY

In Part 1 you read about the earth's environment. People all over the world have had to change their environments in order to earn a living. One way in which people have adapted their environments is by finding uses for their natural resources. For example, people may cut down trees to sell. This wood is bought by different people to make a variety of products. All the ways in which people use their resources in order to earn a living are known as economic systems.

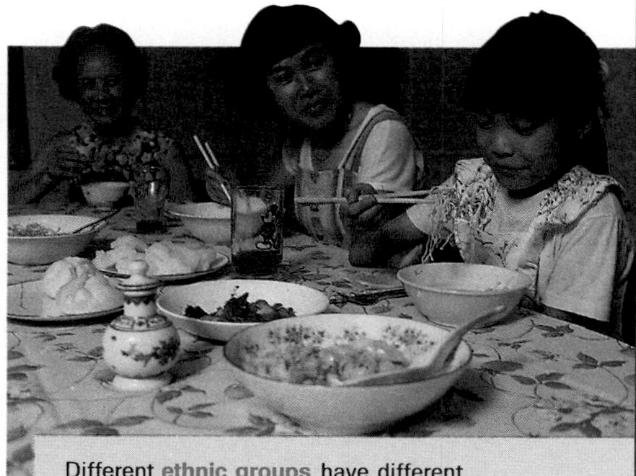

Different **ethnic groups** have different **customs**. These Chinese Americans sometimes use chopsticks to eat their food.

There are many kinds of economic systems because people respond to basic economic questions differently. Who or what determines what people will produce? How do goods get from one place to another? How should goods be shared?

Understanding the answers to these questions will help to explain differences in economic systems. In the United States, for example, individuals decide what and how much to produce. Most property is owned privately, by individuals or corporations, and goods are produced by privately owned businesses. By contrast, in China the government owns much of the property and most large factories.

In this book you will read about many of the economic systems in the world. As you read about them, think about how they answer the economic questions.

GOVERNMENT

In the different regions of the world people have found different ways to rule and

Discussing What Makes Up Culture

Ask students:

- **What makes up culture?** (all the ways in which people relate to one another from social organizations to governments, including values, beliefs, languages, arts, sports and hobbies)
- **Which four parts of cultural geography are covered in this text?** (people, economy, government, arts and recreation)

Studying People Help students to recognize that people belong to different ethnic groups and have different languages, religions, and customs.

Ask students:

- **What is an ethnic group?** (a group of people who share a language, history, and/or place of origin)
- **What are customs?** (practices from the past that people continue to observe)
- **Why is the family the most important group in any culture?** (because it provides for the physical and emotional needs of people)
- **What is a language family?** (a group of languages that are similar to one another)
- **Why is religion important to many people?** (It unites families and cultures and offers answers to basic questions about how people should act in life and what will happen after they die.)

Discussing Economies Point out to students that different nations often solve the problem of making money in different ways.

Ask students:

- **What is an economic system?** (a way of using resources to earn a living)
- **Why are there many kinds of economic systems?** (because people respond to basic economic problems differently)

Discussing Government Discuss students' ideas about types of governments.

BUILDING CITIZENSHIP

Evaluating Changes in Knowledge and Attitude A before-and-after art exercise often reveals to what degree students have increased their understanding of another culture or group. Have students do this exercise before telling them what they will study next.

- Hand out drawing paper and colored pens, pencils, or crayons.
- Have students put their names on the back of the paper.
- Tell students that you are going to say a word and that you then want them to draw the first thing that comes into their minds.
- Say the name of the country, culture, or group to be studied.
- Collect and save the drawings until the unit of study is over; then repeat the same exercise. Pass the first drawings back to students so that they can compare their own responses. Discuss any differences.

EXTENDING CHART SKILLS

Emphasize that this chart shows which foods feed most of the world's peoples.

Ask students:

- **How many major farm products are grown in the world?** (seven)
- **What are the major farm products of the world?** (wheat, rice, corn, potatoes, soybeans, coffee, cacao)
- **Which farm products are grown in the United States?** (wheat, corn, potatoes, soybeans)

Introducing Government

Ask students:

- **Why were governments first developed?** (for organization or defense or to solve an environmental problem)
- **What are some questions that you could ask yourself when you study about a government of today?** (How are the government leaders chosen? What responsibilities does the government have? How does it share power?)

Introducing Arts and Recreation
Help students to understand that arts and recreation reveal a culture's values.

Introducing Culture Regions

Ask students:

- **What is a culture region?** (an area of the world in which people use their environment in similar ways and have a common culture)
- **What are the main ways that cultural geographers study how cultures vary?** (They look at: [1] environments and how resources have been used; [2] how people have changed the land; and [3] which ethnic groups, religions, economic and political systems, and arts and recreation exist in the region.)
- **Why do cultural geographers study culture regions?** (to discover how cultures vary)

MAJOR FARM PRODUCTS OF THE WORLD

Product	Major Producing Nations	Major Uses
Wheat	China, Russia, Ukraine, United States, India, France, Canada	Bread, breakfast foods, macaroni products, livestock feed
Rice	Vietnam, Thailand, Cambodia, Myanmar, Japan	Food
Corn	United States, China, Brazil, Mexico	Flour, starch, cooking oil, livestock feed
Potatoes	Russia, China, Poland, United States, India	Food
Soybeans	United States, Brazil, Argentina, China	Bean sprouts, tofu, soy sauce, livestock feed
Coffee	Brazil, Colombia, Indonesia, Côte d'Ivoire, Ethiopia	Beverage
Cacao	Côte d'Ivoire, Brazil, Ghana, Malaysia, Indonesia	Chocolate, cocoa butter, cocoa powder

CHART SKILL: What do wheat, corn, and soybeans have in common?

govern themselves. Long ago most governments developed from the need of a people to organize or defend themselves or to solve an environmental problem. Today almost all of the world's governments have many purposes.

When reading about one of the world's governments, ask yourself: How is the government and its leaders chosen? What responsibilities does it have? How does it share power? What rights do the people have? You will read in this book that, as with economic questions, different countries choose to answer these questions differently. In some governments people have a voice in running their country. Other governments are controlled by one person.

ARTS AND RECREATION

Studying the arts of a region also helps us to understand its culture. There are many different kinds of artists. For example, some paint beautiful pictures, some make sculptures, some write stories or poetry, and some compose and perform works of music and dance.

Leisure activities may also be special to a particular people. In Japan, for example, many people enjoy origami (ôr i gä′ mē), or the art of folding paper into the forms of animals, flowers, and other shapes.

CULTURE REGIONS

Geographers divide the world into culture regions. These are areas of the world in which people use their environment in similar ways and have developed a common culture.

Cultural geographers study culture regions to discover how cultures vary from place to place. First they study environments to determine what resources are available and how people have used them. Geographers look to see how people have changed the land. Have people built canals? What kinds of crops have farmers planted? Have people built many cities?

Cultural geographers also compare and contrast cultures of different regions. They identify the different kinds of ethnic groups, religions, economic and political

CHART SKILL: They are all used as livestock feed; produced in U.S. and China.

BACKGROUND INFORMATION

Why We Study Arts and Recreation Scientists tell us that, more than any other species, humans spend a large part of their life cycle at play. Most other species lose their ability to play when they become adults. The ability of people to play past childhood is a measure of human intelligence. By studying the way that the people of a certain culture express themselves during their leisure time, we are tapping into some of the most creative parts of a culture.

THE WORLD: Culture Regions

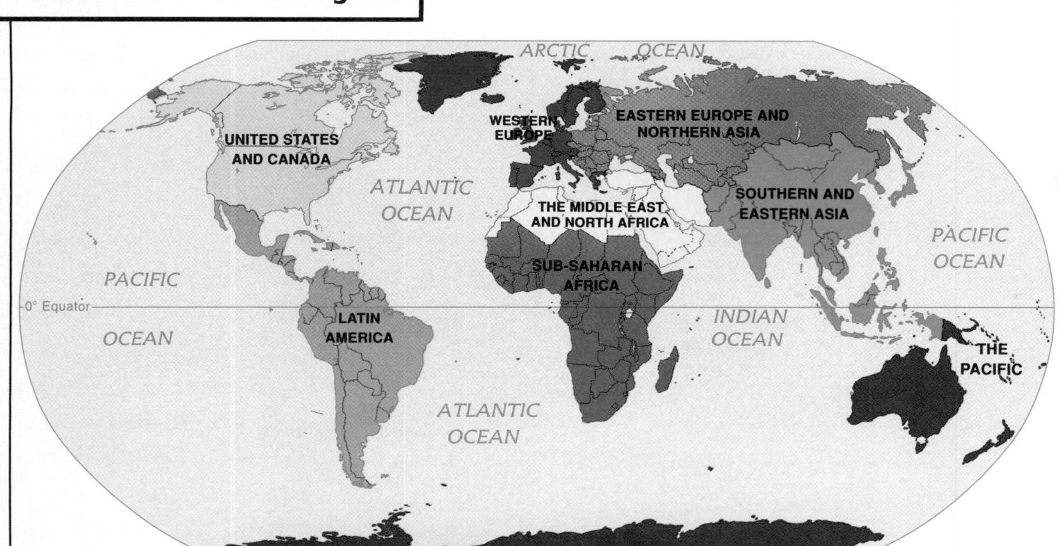

MAP SKILL: In this book you will study the world's eight culture regions. Which region contains South America? Which region contains countries in both Europe and Asia?

systems, and arts and types of recreation in the regions of the world. Such comparisons help geographers to identify what makes each culture region distinctive, or different from others.

EIGHT WORLD REGIONS

As a result of their studies, many geographers divide the world into eight major culture regions. In this book each of these regions will be studied as a separate unit. They are:

1. The United States and Canada
2. Latin America
3. Western Europe
4. Eastern Europe and Northern Asia
5. The Middle East and North Africa
6. Sub-Saharan Africa
7. Southern and Eastern Asia
8. The Pacific

In Part 1 you learned about physical geography. In each of the units listed above you will read a chapter about the physical geography of the region. Then you will read chapters about that region's cultural geography. As you read, compare each region to the others you have studied. How are they similar? How are they different? By the end of the book you will have found out what the world's cultures have in common, as well as the many ways in which they are different.

Check Your Reading

1. What is culture?
2. In which culture region do you live?
3. What are the four major parts of cultural geography?
4. THINKING SKILL: Look at the list of regions on this page. Classify the regions into two or more groups, and explain why you divided them the way you did.

MAP SKILL: Latin America; Eastern Europe and Northern Asia

THINKING SKILL: Classifying

31

EXTENDING MAP SKILLS

Have students study the map on this page. Help them to identify and locate the eight world culture regions.

Ask students:

- **Which subject was chosen to define the regions shown on this map?** (culture)
- **Which culture regions are spread across two continents?** (Latin America, the Middle East and North Africa, Eastern Europe and Northern Asia, and the Pacific)
- **How many cultural regions does Africa have?** (two, Sub-Saharan Africa and the Middle East and North Africa)
- **Would a map showing world language regions look the same as this map?** (No, but in some areas it might match somewhat.)

Applying the Lesson Have students identify the four major parts of cultural geography. Then have them create a chart about the culture of their community, using these four categories.

CLOSE

Summarizing Students have learned the four major parts of cultural geography. Discuss which parts they judge to be most important.

Evaluating Have students draw up a list of questions they would ask when studying the four major parts of cultural geography.

Answers to Check Your Reading

1. the way of life of a group of people
2. the United States and Canada
3. people, economy, government, and arts and recreation
4. Possible answers include: Western and Eastern hemispheres; Northern and Southern hemispheres.

MEETING INDIVIDUAL NEEDS

Reteaching (easy) Have students make posters about the four parts of culture: people, economy, government, and arts and recreation.

Extension (average) Give students outline maps of the world, found in the Teacher's Resource Center. Have them color and label the world culture regions using the map on this page as a guide. Using a classroom wall map, quiz students about the location of the eight world culture regions.

Enrichment (challenging) Divide the class into groups for cooperative learning. Have each group make a large cardboard jigsaw puzzle of the "Culture Regions" map on this page. Have students take turns putting the puzzles together.

INTRODUCTION REVIEW
pages 32–33

USING THE INTRODUCTION SUMMARY AND REVIEW

The Importance of Geography
These questions may be used for review.

- **What is geography? What are its two parts?** (the study of the earth; physical geography and cultural geography)
- **Which five things affect climate?** (sun, wind, elevation, distance from the ocean, size and shape of a landform)
- **What is culture? What are its four parts?** (the way of life of a group of people; people, economy, government, arts and recreation)

Ideas to Remember
- **What is physical geography?** (the study of the earth's environment)
- **What do many cultural geographers study?** (the people, economies, governments, and arts and recreations of the world's culture regions)

INTRODUCTION • SUMMARY

THE IMPORTANCE OF GEOGRAPHY

■ Physical geography is the study of the earth's surface

■ The environment includes: land, water, climates, plants, animals

■ Climate is affected by: sun, winds, elevation, distance from the ocean, size and shape of the landform

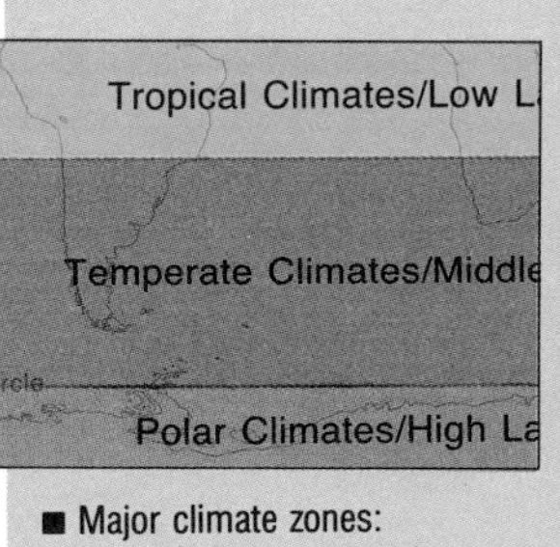

■ Major climate zones: tropical, temperate, polar

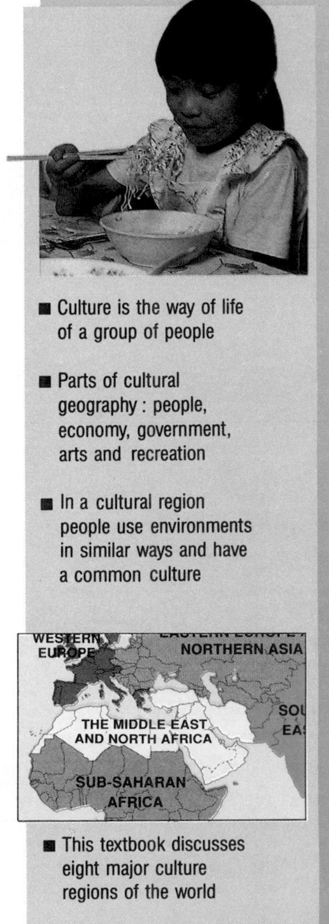

■ Culture is the way of life of a group of people

■ Parts of cultural geography: people, economy, government, arts and recreation

■ In a cultural region people use environments in similar ways and have a common culture

■ This textbook discusses eight major culture regions of the world

IDEAS TO REMEMBER

■ Physical geography is the study of the earth's environments.
■ Many cultural geographers study the people, economies, governments, and arts and recreations of the world's eight culture regions.

32

INTRODUCTION ▪ REVIEW

REVIEWING VOCABULARY

vegetation	polar climate
environment	fossil fuel
cultural geography	landform
custom	culture
physical geography	ethnic group

Number a sheet of paper from 1 to 10. Beside each number write the word or term from the list above that best matches the definition.

1. Physical features of the earth's surface
2. The weather pattern north and south of the temperate zones
3. Trees, flowers, and grasses
4. All the surroundings of a place
5. The energy source from the remains of plants and animals that died thousands of years ago
6. A practice from the past that people continue to observe
7. A group of people who share a language, history, or place of origin
8. The way of life of a group of people including their beliefs, customs, roles, and ways of relating to each other
9. The study of the earth's people and their ways of life
10. The study of all the different kinds of land that make up our planet

REVIEWING FACTS

1. List two ways in which exploration of our world continues today.
2. How does elevation affect climate?
3. Why do geographers study the physical characteristics of places?
4. Explain why the existence of vast amounts of fertile farmland is an example of a relationship within a place.
5. Why do geographers divide the world into regions?
6. How does the sun affect climate?
7. List the major natural resources of the earth. Why are they important to the well-being of people?
8. What do cultural geographers study about ethnic groups to determine what makes them alike or different?
9. Which three questions could you ask to help find out what kind of an economic system a people have?
10. What are some of the ways in which governments may differ from one another?

WRITING ABOUT MAIN IDEAS

1. **Writing a List:** List four of the world's culture regions that are located nearest to the one in which you live.
2. **Writing a Paragraph:** Write a paragraph explaining why it is important to study the world's eight culture regions. Name the regions in your paragraph.
3. **Writing About Perspectives:** Imagine that you are visiting a place that has a very different climate from the place where you live. What place did you choose? Write a letter to someone back home. In it, describe the differences in temperatures, precipitation, and winds between the two places.

33

Answers to Reviewing Vocabulary

1. landform
2. polar climate
3. vegetation
4. environment
5. fossil fuel
6. custom
7. ethnic group
8. culture
9. cultural geography
10. physical geography

Answers to Reviewing Facts

1. ocean, space
2. Areas with high elevations are cooler because temperatures decrease with elevation, or height above sea level.
3. so they can compare places
4. It shows both the physical and cultural geography of the area.
5. to study the different parts of the earth more closely
6. It affects how hot or cold a place is due to the amount of the sun's rays that each place receives.
7. water, air, soil, animals, vegetation, minerals, fossil fuels; People need natural resources to meet their basic needs.
8. their languages, family structures, religions, and customs
9. Possible questions include: Who or what determines what people will produce? How do goods get from one place to another? How should goods be shared?
10. how leaders are chosen, responsibilities of government, how power is shared, rights people have

Suggestions for Writing About Main Ideas

1. Students' answers will depend on whether they live in the region of the United States and Canada or the region of the Pacific.
2. Students' answers might include: to understand how people around the world live, to find out what the world's cultures have in common and how they differ. The world's eight culture regions are listed on page 31.
3. Discuss students' reasons for their responses. You may wish to discuss students' ideas on other ways to divide the earth into culture regions.

UNIT 1

ORGANIZER

THE UNITED STATES AND CANADA text pages 34–99

UNIT THEME

Two of the world's largest countries, the United States and Canada, share most of the North American continent, many similar landforms, and the world's longest friendly national border.

UNIT RESOURCES

- Practice Book: pp. 7–22
- Anthology: Part 1
- Anthology Cassette
- Outline Maps: 1, 8–12
- Transparency Maps: 1–2, 8
- Unit 1 Poster
- Desk Maps
- Internet Project Handbook
- Geo Adventures Pad
- Pupil Edition on Cassette
- Transparency: Graphic Organizer
- **Technology:** *Adventures CD-ROM*
- Assessment Book, Chapter Tests: 1, 2, 3

Internet CONNECTION

The Home Page at **http://www.mmhschool.com** and the **Internet Project Handbook** contain on-line student activities related to this unit.

UNIT PLANNING GUIDE

CHAPTER	SUGGESTED PACING	THEMES
1 **PHYSICAL GEOGRAPHY OF THE UNITED STATES AND CANADA** pages 38–53	4 days	The United States and Canada share regions rich in natural resources while each has regions with unique landforms and climates.
2 **THE UNITED STATES** pages 54–79	7 days	Freedom forms the American way of life, driving a highly developed economy, shaping the republic, and fostering creative arts.
3 **CANADA** pages 80–97	6 days	People of diverse origins have conquered Canada's cold climate to develop a leading world economy under parliamentary rule.

UNIT PROJECTS

Writing a Rap Song/Poem Discuss with students how regions have characteristics based on landforms, climate, resources, population, land use, and economic activities. Ask them to choose a region of the United States or Canada and write a rap song/poem that describes its characteristics and can be said/sung to a strong rhythm.

Oral Reports Have students choose places from regions in the United States or Canada other than the one in which they live. They should research their chosen places and then report to the class on the physical and human characteristics that make those places interesting.

Cooperative Learning: Making Mobiles Many educators believe that the cooperative learning approach works very well in racially and ethnically diverse classes by reducing tension and promoting friendliness and good citizenship. Divide the class into five groups. Each group is to design a mobile about the United States and Canada showing one of these aspects: physical geography, people, economy, government, or arts and sports. Throughout the school year reassign students to different groups and reward groups for their cooperative efforts.

Field Trip Have students research grain production and use in the United States and Canada and its role in the raising of livestock. Make a class visit to the butcher's area of a supermarket to learn how meat is transported and prepared.

BULLETIN BOARD IDEAS

Making Your Own Bulletin Board Help students to create a bulletin board display about the seven regions of North America. Student groups may map the regions, then illustrate the geographical and cultural features of each region. Invite a discussion of the similarities and differences among the regions.

Using the Unit Poster As an alternative to the bulletin board activity, display the Unit 1 Poster, which shows an enlarged version of the Unit Opener globe on pages 34–35.

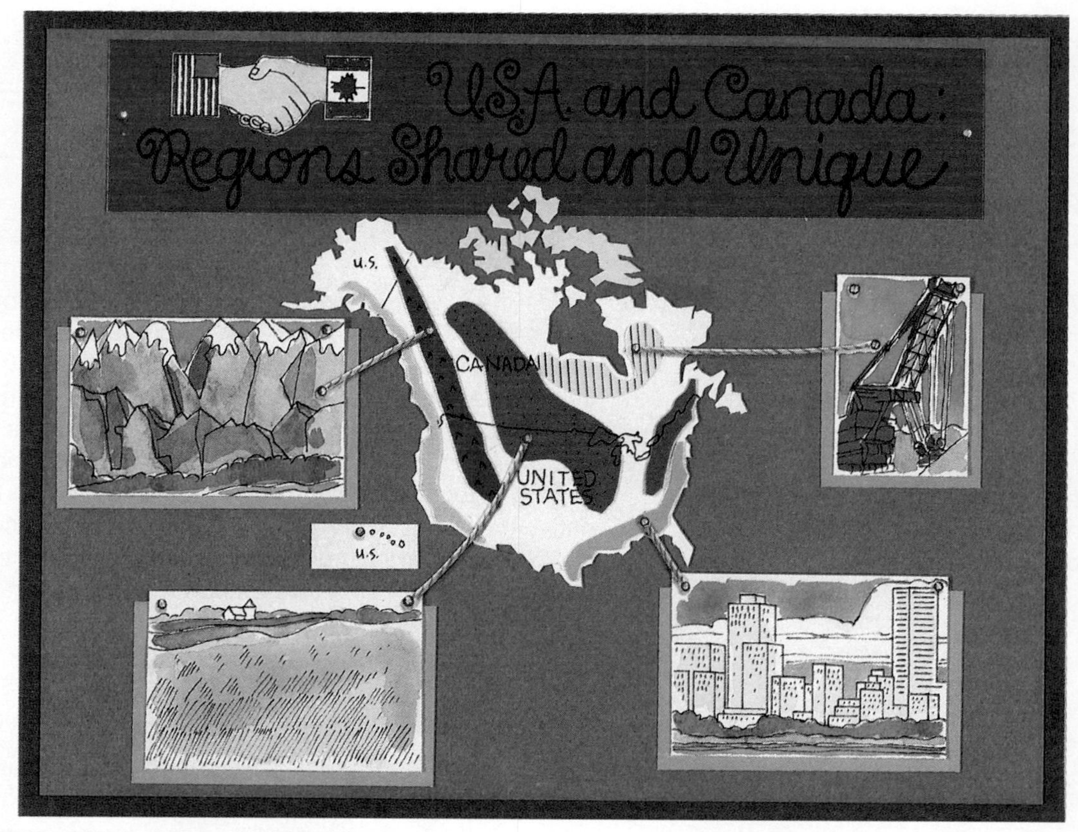

UNIT BIBLIOGRAPHY

For descriptions and additional resources, see the Annotated Bibliography beginning on page T-1 in the back of the book.

For the Teacher

Books

Gordon, Patricia, and Snow, Reed C. *Kids Learn America: Bringing Geography to Life With People, Places, and History.* Charlotte, VT: Williamson Publishing Company, 1992.

Wartik, Nancy. *The French Canadians.* New York: Chelsea House Publishers, 1989.

Read-Alouds

Cohn, Amy, ed. *From Sea to Shining Sea: A Treasury of American Folklore and Folk Songs.* New York: Scholastic Inc., 1993.

Martin, Eva. *Tales of the Far North.* New York: Dial Press, 1987

Technology Multimedia

Canada: Land of Diversity. 2 Videos. Society For Visual Education. Toll Free: 1-800-829-1900

■ *STV North America.* Interactive Videodisc. National Geographic. Toll Free: 1-800-541-5513.

■ *ZipZapMap! Canada.* National Geographic. Toll Free: 1-800-368-2728.

■ *ZipZapMap! USA.* National Geographic. Toll Free: 1-800-368-2728.

Free Materials

For information on the Province of Ontario, send to: Management Board Secretariat; Citizens' Inquiry Bureau; Room zm1-52; MacDonald Block; 900 Bay Street; Toronto, Ontario, Canada. M7A IN3.

For the Student

■ Carlson, Natalie Savage. *The Talking Cat and Other Stories of French Canada.* New York: Harper & Row Publishers, Inc., 1952. **(Average)**

Harrison, Ted. *O Canada.* New York: Ticknor and Fields, 1993. **(Easy)**

Hicks, Roger. *The Big Book of America: A Young Person's Guide to the United States of America.* Philadelphia, PA: Running Press, 1994. **(Average)**

Kalman, Bobbie. *Canada: The Culture.* New York: Crabtree Publishing Company, 1993. **(Easy)**

Kalman, Bobbie. *Canada: The People.* New York: Crabtree Publishing Company, 1993. **(Easy)**

Katz, William Loren. *A History of Multicultural America: The Great Migrations 1800s–1912.* Austin, TX: Raintree Steck-Vaughn, 1993. **(Challenging)**

LeVert, Suzanne. *Northwest Territories.* New York: Chelsea House Publishers, 1992. **(Easy)**

O'Dell, Scott. *Black Star, Bright Dawn.* Boston: Houghton Mifflin, 1988. **(Average)**

■ Wilder, Laura Ingalls. *On the Way Home: The Diary of a Trip from South Dakota to Mansfield, Missouri, in 1894.* New York: Harper & Row, Publishers, 1962. **(Challenging)**

■ Books excerpted in the Anthology

■ National Geographic selection

UNIT 1
ORGANIZER

TEACHER EXCHANGE

Planning an Ethnic Heritage Fair

Thanks to:
Marie Luke
St. Robert's School
Shorewood, Wisconsin

Materials
poster paper and art supplies, resource books, tape recorders or record players

Instructions
1. After discussing the information in Chapter 2, Lesson 1 on the diversity of ethnic groups in the United States, help students to plan an ethnic fair.
2. Divide the class into groups, each group representing a nation or region from which Americans have originally come. (Remember to include Native Americans and the land area that is now the United States.) If students research their own cultural heritage, make sure that a variety of countries are represented.
3. Have each group prepare fact sheets and reports on its country's or area's geography, government, traditions, and so on. Then have each group develop a display that includes flags (or other symbols), money or other forms of barter, native dress, music (including anthems), and special foods.
4. Help students to plan a fair and invite parents, the community, and members of other classes to visit. Have students greet visitors and answer questions.

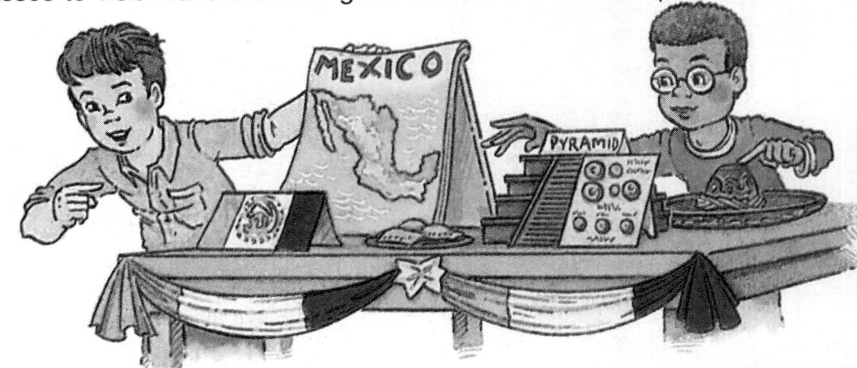

Taking Public Opinion Polls

Thanks to:
Mary Jo Hagey
Holy Spirit Central School
Norway, Michigan

Materials
chart and graph paper, examples of public opinion poll data, articles analyzing polls

Instructions
1. Hold a class discussion about the variety and effects of public opinion polls in this country. Encourage students to bring in articles in which data from polls are used; discuss the influence of polls upon voting or local action.
2. Ask pairs of students to select a topic and design a few questions for a classroom or schoolwide poll. Guide students in deciding whether questions will be answered with a *yes* or a *no* or by discussion, and whom they should include in their surveys.
3. Have each pair conduct interviews, chart or graph the results, and present the data to the class.
4. Have the class discuss the survey procedures, results, and presentations. Then ask students to decide whether the kinds of answers that were desired were given and if the results can be interpreted in more than one way.

TECHNOLOGY CENTER

Enriching with Multimedia

RESOURCE: ***Internet Project Handbook***

Look at the ***Internet Project Handbook*** for student projects related to this unit or have students go on-line at http://www.mmhschool.com, Macmillan/McGraw-Hill's Home School page on the World Wide Web.

RESOURCE: ***Adventures CD-ROM***

Enrich Unit 1 with the *Investigate* and *Explore* activities on the Adventures CD-ROM.

SCHOOL-TO-HOME

Nations of Similarity

- In this unit, students will have the opportunity to learn about two of the world's largest countries, which share more than a continent and a border. Throughout the unit, actively make comparisons between Canada and the United States, noting the similarities and differences in aspects of their physical geography, people, economy, government, arts, and recreation. With students, create a chart which will organize elements the two nations have in common.
- Students and their families can complete the chart at home. You might suggest that they expand the chart, noting current news issues and events shared by both nations, or that they add any personal data or fun facts they discover while working together.

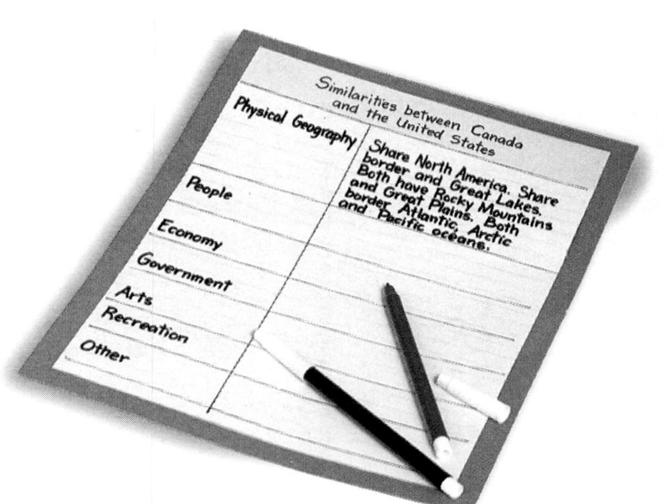

SECOND-LANGUAGE SUPPORT

While these activities are designed especially for students needing second-language support, they are meant to be shared by all students in the class.

Chapter 1, Lesson 1 ■ Physical Geography of the United States and Canada

Explain to students that this lesson discusses the seven geographic regions of the United States and Canada. Assign one region to each of seven heterogeneous groups of students. Have groups read their sections of the lesson and then look in magazines for representative geographic photos and illustrations. Assemble a class illustrated map.

Chapter 2, Lesson 4 ■ The United States

To reinforce the concepts of *arts* and *recreation,* have pairs of students prepare short dramatic presentations of recreational activities Americans enjoy.

Chapter 3, Lesson 4 ■ Canada

To help students needing second-language support understand recreational activities in other countries, have students create posters or other art projects illustrating Canadian recreational activities. Possible subjects include: Indian crafts, landscapes, rodeo, or the indoor lake at the West Edmonton Mall.

Chapter 1, Lesson 1

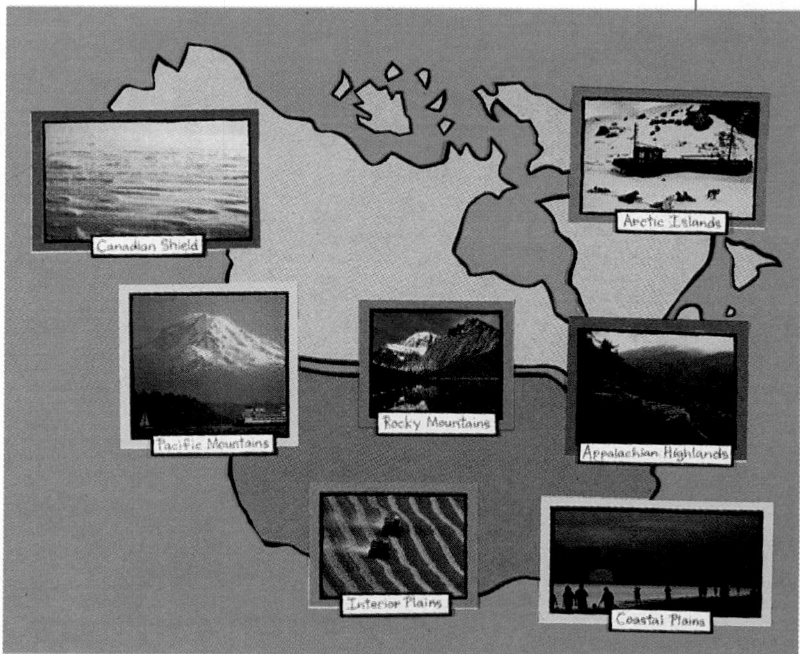

UNIT 1

pages 34–99

USING THE UNIT OPENER

Introducing the Unit Have students look at the unit title and silently read the *Where We Are* section on the facing page.

Ask students:

- **What is the title of the unit?** ("The United States and Canada")
- **What does the map show about the extent of these two countries?** (They cover most of North America.)
- **What are some things that you will learn about in Unit 1?** (landforms, climates, natural resources, people, economies, governments, arts, and recreation of the United States and Canada)

EXTENDING MAP SKILLS

Point out that the United States and Canada cover more than three fourths of North America, and that Mexico and the Central American nations are also in North America.

Ask students:

- **What aspects of physical geography are shown on this map?** (the relative locations of the countries shown, mountains, oceans, rivers)

ONGOING UNIT PROJECT

Planning for Assessment Tell students that in this unit they will be learning about the geography and culture of the United States and Canada. Explain to them that when they finish the unit they will have an opportunity to demonstrate what they have learned by pretending that they are news broadcasters giving reports from different places in the United States and Canada. Students should think about what information they would like to include in their broadcasts as they read the unit. Each student should then write a script. If possible, plan to tape students' broadcasts with a video camera or audiocassette recorder.

Note: For information on executing this unit project, please see the Unit Review, page 99.

Goal: Students' work should show they understand that the United States and Canada share many similarities, but also have differences.

Signs of Success: Tell students that an adequate broadcast should include weather, sports, and business reports, as well as reports on local cultural events. An excellent broadcast would also include a report on one current issue that affects both Canada and the United States.

THE UNITED STATES AND CANADA

WHERE WE ARE

You are about to begin an adventure that will take you all over the world around us. You will start your journey at home, in the region that consists of the United States and its neighbor to the north, Canada. As the map shows, these two countries cover a large part of the Western Hemisphere.

As you read about the landforms, climate, natural resources, people, economies, governments, and arts and recreation of the United States and Canada, think about how you would describe the region to a person from another land. Knowing what makes the part of the world in which you live special will help you to compare it with the other regions you will visit on your journey.

35

Continue the discussion.

Ask students:

- **What north-south physical features do you notice immediately as you look at this map?** (two north-south mountain ranges running down the western side of the continent, another mountain range on the eastern side, and a large river almost in the center of the continent)
- **Where is your hometown located on this map?** (Have students point to the approximate location of their hometown on the map on pages 34 and 35.)
- **Why is it difficult to pinpoint your hometown on this map?** (The map scale is too small and the map is not labeled in detail.)
- **Why must the scale of this map remain small?** (A large-scale map of North America showing our home states with all their towns would be too big to fit in the book.)

Thinking About Geography Remind students that to understand geography they must pull together, or synthesize, many sets of facts. Geography includes the study of the physical factors of the land, plants, animals, resources, and the climate of the earth. It also includes the human or cultural ways in which people use the physical world to adapt to the places in which they live. Suggest to students that geographers use three questions to synthesize this physical and cultural information and to give it meaning. Geographers ask:

- What precisely does the question "Where?" mean? Does it mean "Where is a place in terms of another place?" or does it mean "Where is a place in terms of latitude and longitude?"
- Why are human settlements located where they are?
- Why is this information important?

Encourage students to ask themselves these questions throughout their study of regions in this book.

5 FUNDAMENTAL THEMES OF GEOGRAPHY

Location The United States and Canada have been separated from the rest of the world because of their relative locations. This was true especially before air travel began. The Atlantic Ocean to the east and the Pacific Ocean on the west have helped to isolate North America.

- This location apart from the rest of the world has also made some Americans "isolationists." They think that the United States can remain uninvolved with the rest of the world.
- Today our relative location can give us an economic advantage. Historically, European-Atlantic countries, such as Great Britain, have led world trade; today Pacific Rim countries, such as Japan, are participating in world trade so successfully that some economists predict that the Pacific Rim countries will soon lead the world economy. We have an advantage because we have coastal ports on both oceans.

EXTENDING TABLE SKILLS

Help students to analyze the statistics in the tables, or the boxes containing information, on these two pages.

Ask students:

- **What is the capital of the United States? Of Canada?** (*United States*—Washington, D.C.; *Canada*—Ottawa)
- **How are the languages of the United States and Canada the same? How are they different?** (English is spoken in both countries; Canada is a bilingual country—French is its other major language—but the United States has only one predominant language.)
- **How do the populations of the two countries compare?** (The population of the United States is almost ten times larger than Canada's population.)
- **How do the land areas of the two countries compare?** (They are both almost 4,000,000 square miles, or 10,000,000 sq km; however, Canada is the larger of the two.)
- **What are the leading exports of the United States? Of Canada?** (*United States*—machinery and transportation equipment; *Canada*—automotive products)
- **In what ways are the two countries similar?** (In both countries English is a major language; both countries are large; both countries export types of machinery.)
- *THINKING FURTHER:* **According to the figures in these tables, what is the most dramatic difference between the United States and Canada?** (the large difference in size of population)

DAY • LIFE TODAY • LIFE TODAY • LIFE TODAY • LIFE TODAY • LIFE TODAY • LIFE TODAY • LIFE T

THE UNITED STATES AND CANADA

UNITED STATES

Capital ★
Washington, D.C.

Major language: English
Population: 260.8 million
Area: 3,623,420 sq mi; 9,384,658 sq km
Leading exports: machinery and transportation equipment

BACKGROUND INFORMATION

United States Symbols Famous American symbols are shown above.

- In 1782 the American bald eagle was chosen as a symbol of strength on the Great Seal of the United States. Benjamin Franklin good-humoredly had suggested the less predatory turkey.
- The Grand Canyon of the Colorado River, in northwestern Arizona, is one of the world's most spectacular natural wonders. This immense canyon was formed over millions of years by erosion caused by the running waters of the Colorado River, rain, frost, and wind.

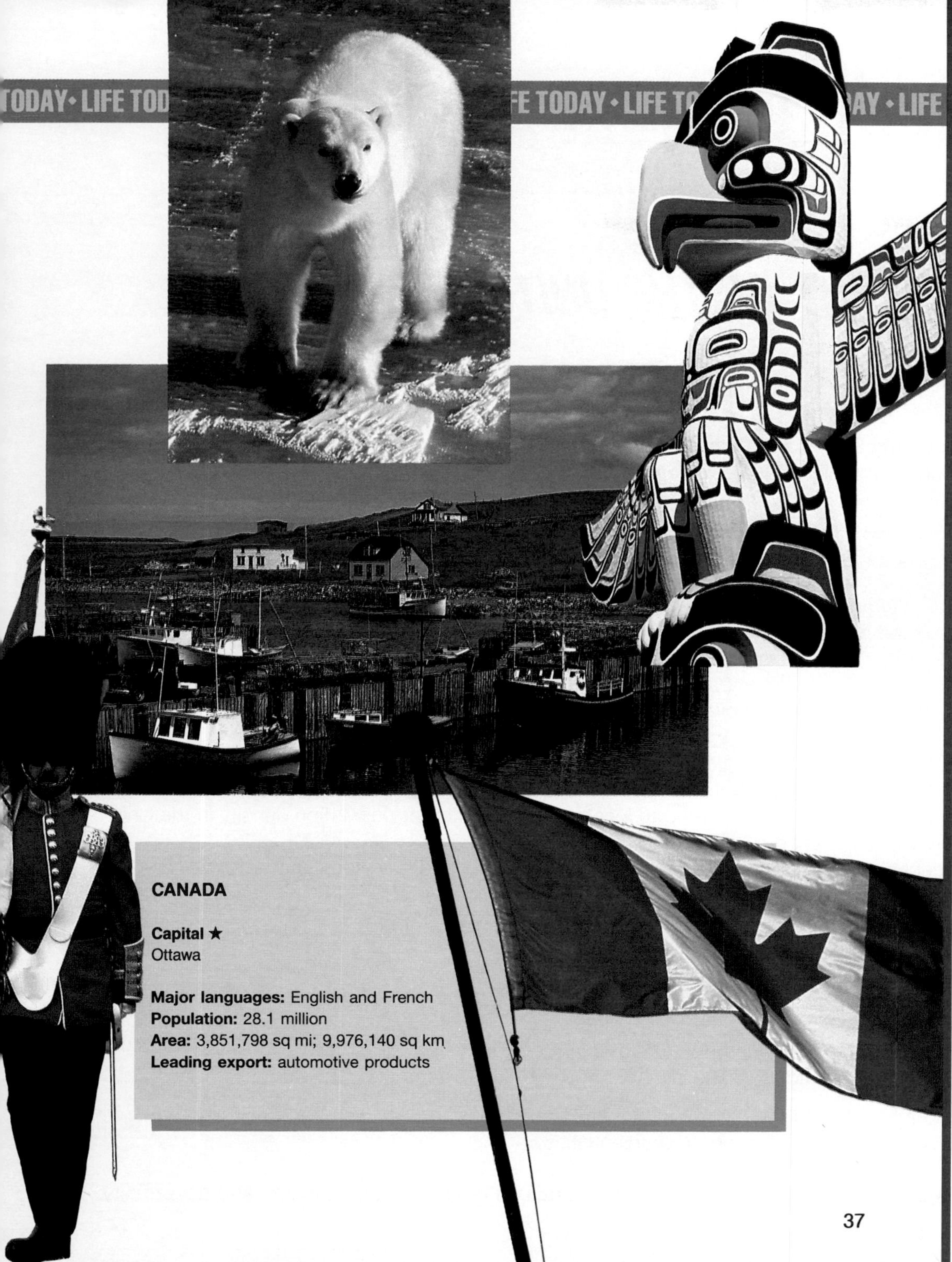

Discussing the Photographs Ask students how many symbols on these pages they can identify. (See Background Information below.) Have students volunteer their own reactions to the American symbols on the facing page. Help students to recognize that these symbols show pride in the United States, including its traditions and history.

Comparing Illustrations Compare the photos on page 36 with the pictures of Canada on page 37. Ask students why they think these pictures were chosen to symbolize Canada and what overall message the pictures seem to portray about what Canadians value. Help students to see that the symbols show the closeness of the Canadians to their environment and how they value nature, the outdoors, and the Indian heritage of their country.

Comparing Flags Help students to recognize the symbols in the flags of the United States and Canada.

Ask students:

- **What do the red and white stripes of the American flag stand for?** (the thirteen original colonies of the United States)
- **How many stars are on the flag of the United States, and what do they stand for?** (50 stars; one for each state)
- **Do you think the United States flag could ever change? When?** (It could. Every time a new state is admitted to the Union, another star is added to the American flag to represent that state.)
- **What is the figure on the Canadian flag?** (a red maple leaf)

BACKGROUND INFORMATION

Discussing the Photographs These images of Canada illustrate the value that many Canadians place on nature both for its own sake and for the sake of the resources it provides for their country.

- Unlike most other land mammals of Canada's far northern tundra, polar bears do not migrate south for the winter. They hibernate in snow caves on the tundra during the long winters.
- Totem poles are important religious symbols to the western Indians of Canada and are erected to honor the animal from which the Indians believe their tribe has descended. Important animal spirits, such as the raven and the bear, are depicted on the poles.
- Fishing is one of the vital human-environment interactions in Canada. It adds to the profits of the economy and provides subsistence for the Indian and Inuit populations.

CHAPTER 1
ORGANIZER

PHYSICAL GEOGRAPHY OF THE UNITED STATES AND CANADA text pages 38–53

CHAPTER THEME The United States and Canada share regions rich in natural resources while each has regions with unique landforms and climates.

CHAPTER OBJECTIVES

CONTENT

- Identify and describe the seven geographic regions of the United States and Canada.
- List the major natural resources of the United States and Canada.
- Describe the effects of latitude and elevation on climate.
- Define *arable* and compare the amount of arable land in the United States and Canada.
- Define *hydroelectric power* and list the advantages and disadvantages of using it.

SKILLS

Geography
- Interpret an elevation map of the United States and Canada.
- Use a population density map to locate areas of different population density in the United States and Canada.
- Identify different climate regions on a climate map of the United States and Canada.
- Interpret a land use map of the United States and Canada.
- Interpret a map showing latitude and longitude.

Study and Research
- Interpret a diagram of the Continental Divide.

Thinking
- Make inferences based on the statement of a settler.
- Compare and contrast the climates of the United States and Canada.

Reading and Writing
- Write a description of two Canadian cities.

CITIZENSHIP VALUES

- Appreciate the importance of abundant natural resources to prosperity and opportunity.

TEACHER OPTIONS

READING STRATEGY: Previewing Strategies to help students read and remember the main ideas of the lesson.
Lesson 1: p. 39 Lesson 2: p. 45

MEETING INDIVIDUAL NEEDS Activities for reteaching, extension, and enrichment.
Lesson 1: p. 44 Geography Skills: p. 51
Lesson 2: p. 49

GEO ADVENTURES ACTIVITIES PAD Daily activities to assess students' understanding of geography skills.

CURRICULUM CONNECTION Activities to help integrate other subject areas with Social Studies.
Language Arts: p. 41

PUPIL EDITION ON CASSETTE Language support for students who have difficulty reading or who will benefit from listening to the Pupil Edition on Cassette as they read.

SECOND-LANGUAGE SUPPORT Activities and suggestions for second-language learners.
Lesson 1: p. 1

CHAPTER PLANNING GUIDE

LESSON	SUGGESTED PACING	THEMES	TEACHER SUPPORT MATERIALS: TEACHER'S RESOURCE CENTER
1 LANDFORMS pages 39–44	1 day	The seven physical regions of the United States and Canada present a great variety of landforms.	Practice Book p. 7 ■ Anthology pp. 2, 3, 4 **Technology:** *Adventures CD-ROM* Transparency Map: 2
2 CLIMATE AND RESOURCES pages 45–49	1 day	The United States and Canada prosper in farming and industry due to an abundance of natural resources, a temperate climate, and waterways that serve their interiors.	Practice Book p. 8 ■ Anthology pp. 4, 20–21 **Technology:** *Adventures CD-ROM*
BUILDING GEOGRAPHY SKILLS Understanding Latitude and Longitude pages 50–51	1 day	A global grid of latitude and longitude helps us to locate places on earth.	Practice Book p. 9 Transparency Map 8 Outline Map p. 1 Desk Maps
CHAPTER SUMMARY AND REVIEW pages 52–53	1 day	Chapter content, skills, and vocabulary are reviewed and evaluated.	Practice Book p. 10 Transparency: Graphic Organizer Assessment Book, Chapter 1 Test

Technology CONNECTION

Lesson 1
ADVENTURES CD-ROM
Have students find the climate Movies in *Explore.*

Lesson 2
ADVENTURES CD-ROM
Using *Paint* and *Stamps,* have students make a map of their own state showing major industries.

CHAPTER 1
pages 38–53

USING THE CHAPTER OPENER

Discussing the Photograph Use the photograph to help students gain a sense of the plains as a symbol of the physical variety and agricultural abundance found in North America.

Ask students:

- **Which words would you use to describe this place?** (*flat, sunny, abundant, fertile*)
- **What can you tell about the people who live here?** (They have knowledge of farming methods; they grow wheat.)

Reading/Listening to the Primary Source Ask students to look at the photograph while you read the quotation aloud. (You might ask students to make some inferences about the meaning of the word *aromatic*.)

Ask students:

- **What might make up the "dry aromatic odor" Willa Cather wrote about?** (dust in the air, the smell of ripening crops, sagebrush, and fragrant bushes)
- **Which aromas from natural environments are you familiar with and where do you find them?** (sea air on coastal plains, pine-scented woods on hills or mountains, musty swamps, and so on)
- **In what ways are the "great grass plains" the "bright edges of the world"?** (There are brilliant sunrises and sunsets; the horizon dominates the view; the frontier sweeps westward.)
- *THINKING FURTHER:* **Why do you think this picture was chosen to symbolize a chapter on the physical variety and agricultural abundance of the United States and Canada?** (The plains represent just one of the many physical regions of the United States and Canada. Agricultural abundance is one aspect of the economies of both nations.)

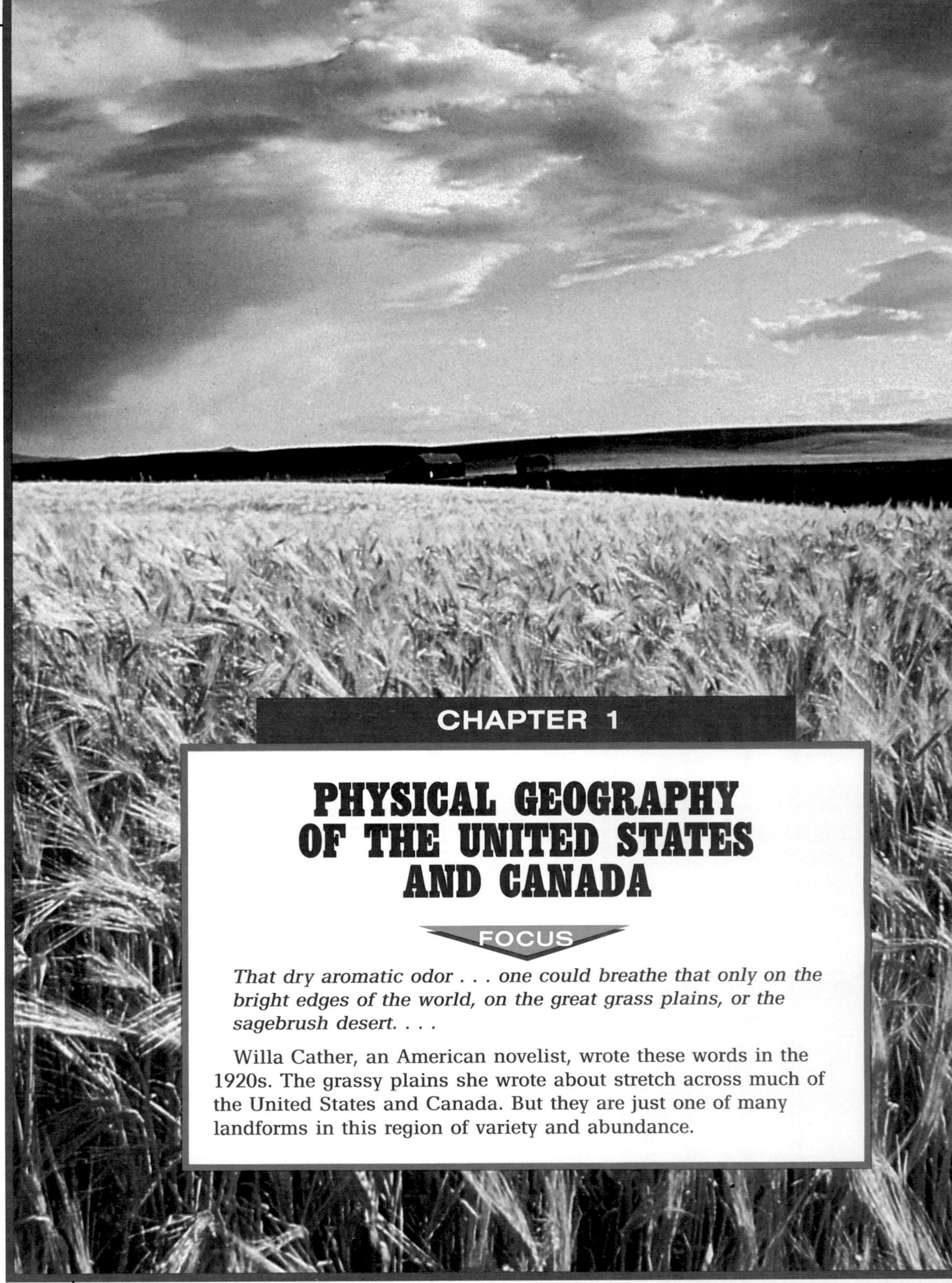

CHAPTER 1

PHYSICAL GEOGRAPHY OF THE UNITED STATES AND CANADA

FOCUS

That dry aromatic odor . . . one could breathe that only on the bright edges of the world, on the great grass plains, or the sagebrush desert. . . .

Willa Cather, an American novelist, wrote these words in the 1920s. The grassy plains she wrote about stretch across much of the United States and Canada. But they are just one of many landforms in this region of variety and abundance.

BACKGROUND INFORMATION

About the Photograph Use the photograph to help students focus on the physical variety and agricultural abundance of North America.

- The photograph shows a wheat field in the Great Plains part of the state of Montana, a leading U.S. grain grower.
- The United States and Canada, along with Russia and China, are the world's main wheat-producing nations.
- In the 1870s Russian settlers introduced wheat well-suited to the Great Plains; it could withstand heat, cold, and drought. By the early 1900s farmers were producing millions of bushels of "Russian" wheat.
- Wheat is used to make bread, pasta, and many kinds of breakfast foods. Parts of the wheat plant are used to make feed for livestock.

LESSON 1

Landforms

READ TO LEARN

Key Vocabulary

erosion
Continental Divide
population density
permafrost

Key Places

Appalachian Highlands
Interior Plains
Rocky Mountains
Pacific Mountains
Coastal Plains
Canadian Shield
Arctic Islands

Read Aloud

I think I shall never forget the scenery in the Santa Cruz Mountains. To me the most beautiful spot in our journey of thousands of miles was found among the stately pines on the mountaintop where a natural fountain poured its crystal waters into a granite basin . . .

These thoughts come from the diary of Susan Parrish, a young pioneer who traveled west across the United States with her family in 1850. Just as Willa Cather was struck by the beauty of the plains, Susan Parrish was excited by the mountains of the West.

Read for Purpose

1. **WHAT YOU KNOW:** What are the main geographic features of the area in which you live?
2. **WHAT YOU WILL LEARN:** What are the physical regions of the United States and Canada?

SEVEN GEOGRAPHIC REGIONS

People like Susan Parrish who travel through the United States and Canada come across many different landforms. Geographers group these landforms into seven physical regions. These regions are shown on the map of the United States and Canada on page 40.

The United States and Canada share four of these regions: the Appalachian Highlands, the Interior Plains, the Rocky Mountains, and the Pacific Mountains. One region, the Coastal Plains, is found only in the United States. The two remaining regions, the Canadian Shield and the Arctic Islands, are located almost entirely in Canada.

APPALACHIAN HIGHLANDS

Suppose you lived hundreds of years ago, before there were airplanes, trains, and cars. You are hiking across the land, starting in the East. Your first challenge is to cross the Appalachian Mountains. They are in the **Appalachian Highlands** region, which stretches from the southeastern part of the United States to Canada's Newfoundland Island.

Even though this region is called "highlands," the mountains here are not that

WHAT YOU KNOW: Students should think about the various geographic features of their community, such as mountains, hills, lakes, rivers, and oceans.

39

LESSON 1
pages 39–44

Lesson Theme The seven physical regions of the U.S. and Canada present a great variety of landforms.

Lesson Objectives

- Locate and describe the seven physical regions of the United States and Canada.
- Recognize that the western part of North America has higher elevations than does the eastern part.
- Describe the Continental Divide.
- Relate United States and Canadian population densities to elevation and location.

1 PREPARE

Motivate Ask students to close their eyes while you or a student reads the opening passage aloud. Discuss what the class visualized as it listened to the *Read Aloud*.

Set Purpose Have students use the *What You Know* question to list the geographic features of your area. Then have the class decide what kind of physical region they have just described.

2 TEACH

Comparing Regions Display the physical Transparency Map of the World. Explain that there are many different kinds of regions. In this chapter, regions are discussed in terms of their physical features.

Discussing the Appalachian Highlands Have students locate the Appalachian Highlands region on the map on page 40.

READING STRATEGY AND VOCABULARY DEVELOPMENT

Previewing The purpose of this strategy is to help students develop a method for reading lessons that have a social studies content. Brainstorm with students about the ways in which they get ready for school, prepare for a test, or prepare for participation in an athletic event. Suggest that getting ready to read social studies lessons is an important part of developing their comprehension. Develop a class previewing guide, including all sources of information in the lesson. (See the sample below.)

PREVIEWING GUIDE

Title	Key Vocabulary	Questions	Headings	Illustrations

EXTENDING MAP SKILLS

Use the elevation map on this page to locate the regions described in this lesson.

Ask students:

- **Which geographic features does this map show besides land and water?** (elevation and the names of major landforms)
- **How is elevation shown on the map?** (by various colors)
- **Which four regions do the United States and Canada share?** (the Appalachian Highlands, the Interior Plains, the Rocky Mountains, the Pacific Mountains)
- **Which region is found only in the United States?** (the Coastal Plains)
- **Which regions are unique to Canada?** (the Canadian Shield, the Arctic Islands)
- **What is the range of elevation in the eastern part of North America?** (0 feet, or sea level, to 7,000 feet [2,000 m] above sea level)
- **What is the range of elevation in the western part of North America?** (282 feet [89 m] below sea level at Death Valley to 20,320 feet [6,194 m] above sea level at Mount McKinley)
- *THINKING FURTHER:* **How do the overall elevations in the western part of North America compare with those in the eastern part?** (Overall elevations are higher in the West and lower in the East.)

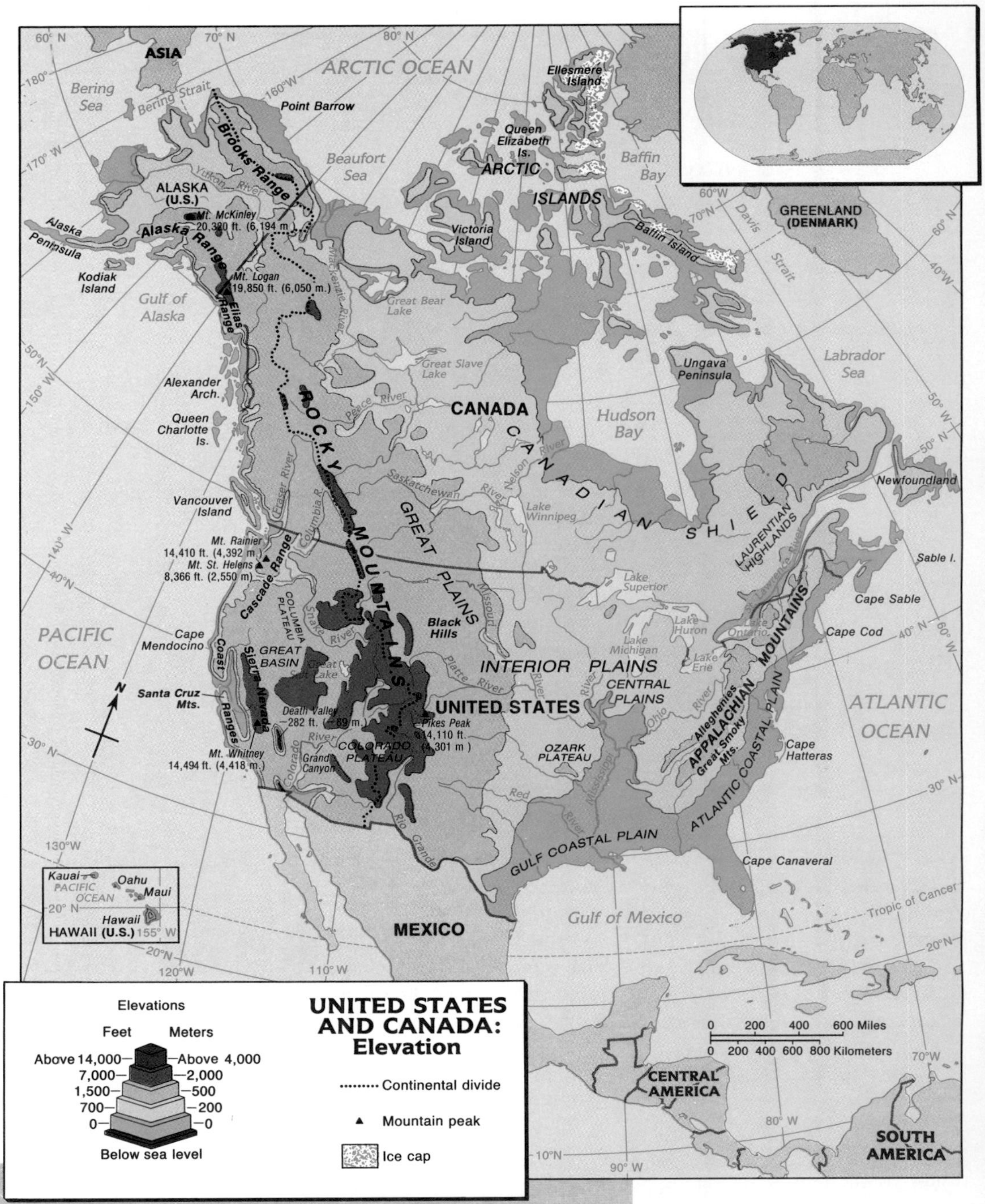

UNITED STATES AND CANADA: Elevation

MAP SKILL: The land of the United States and Canada varies greatly in elevation. What is the approximate elevation of the Black Hills?

MAP SKILL: 1500–7000 feet (500–2000 m)

5 FUNDAMENTAL THEMES OF GEOGRAPHY

Regions The five fundamental themes of geography are defined in the beginning of the textbook. This lesson offers a good opportunity to introduce one of geography's five fundamental themes—regions. Geographers divide the world into regions to organize their study of how people use the earth. Help students to recognize that regions may be defined in terms of both cultural characteristics (human activities) and physical geography. Then provide these two models.

- This textbook is organized according to cultural regions. Have students skim the Table of Contents and list the eight world cultural regions. Then discuss with them which clues the Table of Contents provides to identify the defining characteristics of each region.
- This chapter introduces the idea of physical regions—specifically the seven geographic regions of North America. Have students skim the lesson and then list these regions. After they have read the lesson, ask them to write down some defining characteristics next to each region's name.

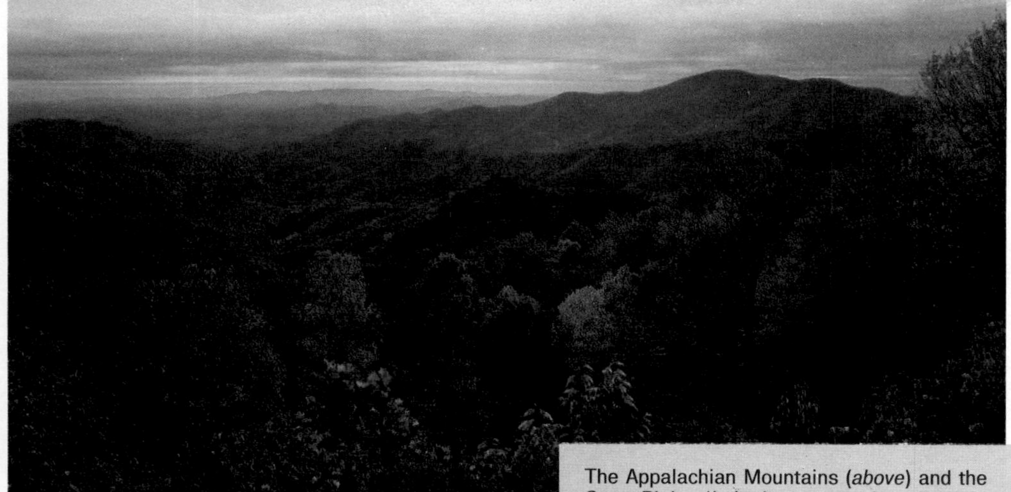

The Appalachian Mountains (*above*) and the Great Plains (*below*) are examples of two major landforms found in the United States.

high. None of them reaches 7,000 feet (2,134 m). This is because the mountains are very old—about 500 million years old. As a result, they have been exposed to **erosion** over a long period of time. Erosion is the gradual wearing down of the earth's surface by water or wind.

In Canada the Appalachian Highlands end in Newfoundland. There the highlands meet the Atlantic Ocean and continue underwater. This makes the offshore waters dangerous in this area. Find Sable Island, off the coast of Nova Scotia, on the map on the opposite page. Sable Island is called the "graveyard of the Atlantic" because so many ships have been wrecked in its shallow waters.

INTERIOR PLAINS

After crossing the Appalachian Mountains, you enter a completely different region, called the **Interior Plains**. The Interior Plains extend through much of the central part of the United States and Canada.

Look at this region on the map on page 40. It is mostly flat land with rich soil. Most of the land is a prairie, an area of gently rolling grassland with few trees. As you travel west, the land gradually rises.

For centuries, people gathered plants and hunted animals on the Interior Plains. They also recognized that the Interior Plains offered good land for farming, and they planted crops there.

The western part of the Interior Plains, called the Great Plains, is drier than the rest of the region. The Great Plains are almost treeless, and you can see for miles in all directions.

ROCKY MOUNTAINS

From the flatlands of the Interior Plains, your westward journey would take you to the **Rocky Mountains**. These mountains stretch along most of the western part of North America.

Discussing the Photographs Help students understand the impact of elevation on land use by drawing their attention to the photographs on this page. (The upper photograph shows the Appalachian Highlands in North Carolina; the lower photograph shows a wheat field in the Interior Plains.)

Ask students:

- **What kind of human activity do you think might take place in the Appalachian Highlands of North Carolina?** (The abundance of trees might lead to lumbering; dense forests might also contain animals for hunting, trails for hiking, and campgrounds for camping.)
- **In which region might the wheat field be located?** (in the Interior Plains, where flat land is used for large-scale farming)

Discussing the Interior Plains Have students locate the plains on the map on page 40.

Ask students:

- **How are the plains divided geographically?** (The Central Plains are located around the Great Lakes; the Great Plains are in the western part of the Interior Plains.)

Looking at the Rocky Mountains Have students locate the Rocky Mountains on the map on page 40.

BACKGROUND INFORMATION

About the Great Plains

- The Great Plains are about 2,500 miles (4,000 km) from north to south and about 600 miles (960 km) from east to west. The Plains extend from the southwestern United States deep into Canada.
- Where the Great Plains begin and end cannot be determined exactly. Many geographers have said that the Great Plains begin at the hundredth meridian of longitude because the areas west of the line receive less than 20 inches (50.8 cm) of rainfall annually.

CURRICULUM CONNECTION

Language Arts Have students read the first four chapters of *Prairie Songs* by Pam Conrad. Ask them to imagine a brief episode not directly dealt with by the book's author, such as a conversation between Dr. and Mrs. Berryman about their new home on the prairie and their new neighbors. Have each student write his or her concept of this episode in the form of a dramatic scene. Have the students form groups and act out these scenes for the rest of the class. After each presentation, have the students in the audience ask questions to which the actors must respond as if they were the characters they have just represented.

Discussing the Rocky Mountains Discuss the location of the Rocky Mountains and refer students to the photograph at the top of this page.

Ask students:

- **How are the Rockies different from the Appalachians?** (The Rockies are newer mountains and are more rugged; they have not been worn down by erosion as have the Appalachians. The Rockies are also higher than the Appalachians.)

EXTENDING DIAGRAM SKILLS

Have students locate the Continental Divide on the diagram.

Ask students:

- **What function does the Continental Divide serve?** (It separates rivers flowing eastward from those flowing westward.)
- *THINKING FURTHER:* **If the Continental Divide was not labeled on a map or diagram, how could you locate it?** (You would have to find the sources of the rivers flowing east and of those flowing west; the land between these sources would be the Continental Divide.)

Locating the Grand Canyon Have students read the definition of *canyon* on this page. Then have them locate the Grand Canyon on the map on page 40.

Ask students:

- **Which river created the Grand Canyon?** (the Colorado River)
- **How deep is the Grand Canyon?** (almost 1 mile, or 1.6 km)

Identifying the Pacific Mountains Region Discuss the region west of the Grand Canyon. Again, refer students to the map on page 40.

Ask students:

- **Where is the Pacific Mountains region located?** (between the Rockies and the Pacific Ocean)

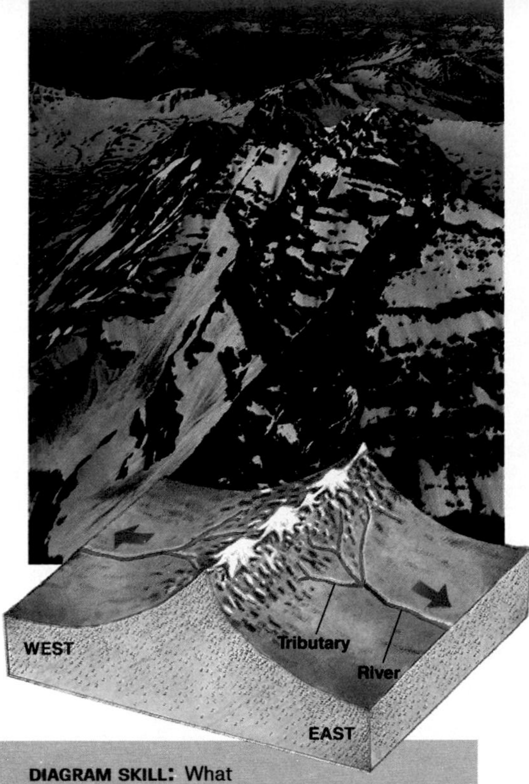

DIAGRAM SKILL: What does the Continental Divide do?

Look at the photograph above. Note that the Rockies are higher and more rugged than the Appalachians of the East. Many of the Rockies are over 10,000 feet (3,048 m) high. Unlike the Appalachians, the Rockies are young mountains — about 130 million years old. They have not been as worn down by erosion.

The summits, or peaks, of the Rockies form an imaginary line known as the **Continental Divide**. Sometimes called the "backbone of North America," the Continental Divide separates rivers flowing eastward and westward. Rivers west of the Continental Divide flow toward the Pacific Ocean. Those on the east flow toward the Atlantic Ocean or Gulf of Mexico.

As you descend west from the summits of the Rockies, you pass through plateaus, canyons, and deserts. A plateau is an area of flat land that rises above the land around it. A canyon is just the opposite—a deep valley with steep sides.

The Grand Canyon in Arizona is one of the most famous canyons in the world. Over a period of about 6 million years, water from the Colorado River carved out the Grand Canyon. Today, from the floor of the canyon you can gaze at walls that rise upward for almost a mile (1.6 km). Brilliant colors glow on the canyon walls as the light changes.

PACIFIC MOUNTAINS

The Grand Canyon is beautiful, but you continue your journey into the **Pacific Mountains** region. Here, between the Rockies and the Pacific Ocean, you find both rich, rolling land and high mountains, such as the Cascade Range. Find this landform on the map on page 40.

Like the Appalachian Highlands, the Pacific Mountains extend into the ocean. Several peaks rise above the Pacific Ocean to form islands, such as Canada's Vancouver Island and Queen Charlotte Islands. The highest peak is Mount McKinley, which reaches 20,320 feet (6,194 m).

The Cascade Range has many active volcanoes, such as Mount St. Helens, which last erupted in 1980. Its ashes drifted across much of the United States.

COASTAL PLAINS

You have reached the West Coast of North America, and your journey has ended. Although you have visited many regions of the United States and Canada, you have missed some. For example, you have yet to visit the **Coastal Plains**, which are in the United States.

The Coastal Plains are divided into two parts. One part is the Atlantic Coastal

 DIAGRAM SKILL: separates rivers flowing eastward and westward

BUILDING CITIZENSHIP

The Role of National Parks About the Grand Canyon, President Theodore Roosevelt asked Americans to "keep this greatest wonder of nature as it is now." Today the Grand Canyon belongs to all Americans as a part of the National Park System of the United States. The national parks serve many purposes. Some protect wilderness areas, some provide camping and hiking lands, and others protect special locations where historic events took place. Today many of the national parks are deteriorating as a result of overuse. Have students discuss ways of dealing with this problem. For example, park managers at Inyo National Forest in California limit access to some parts of the forest to 50 campers a day. Campers are chosen by lottery.

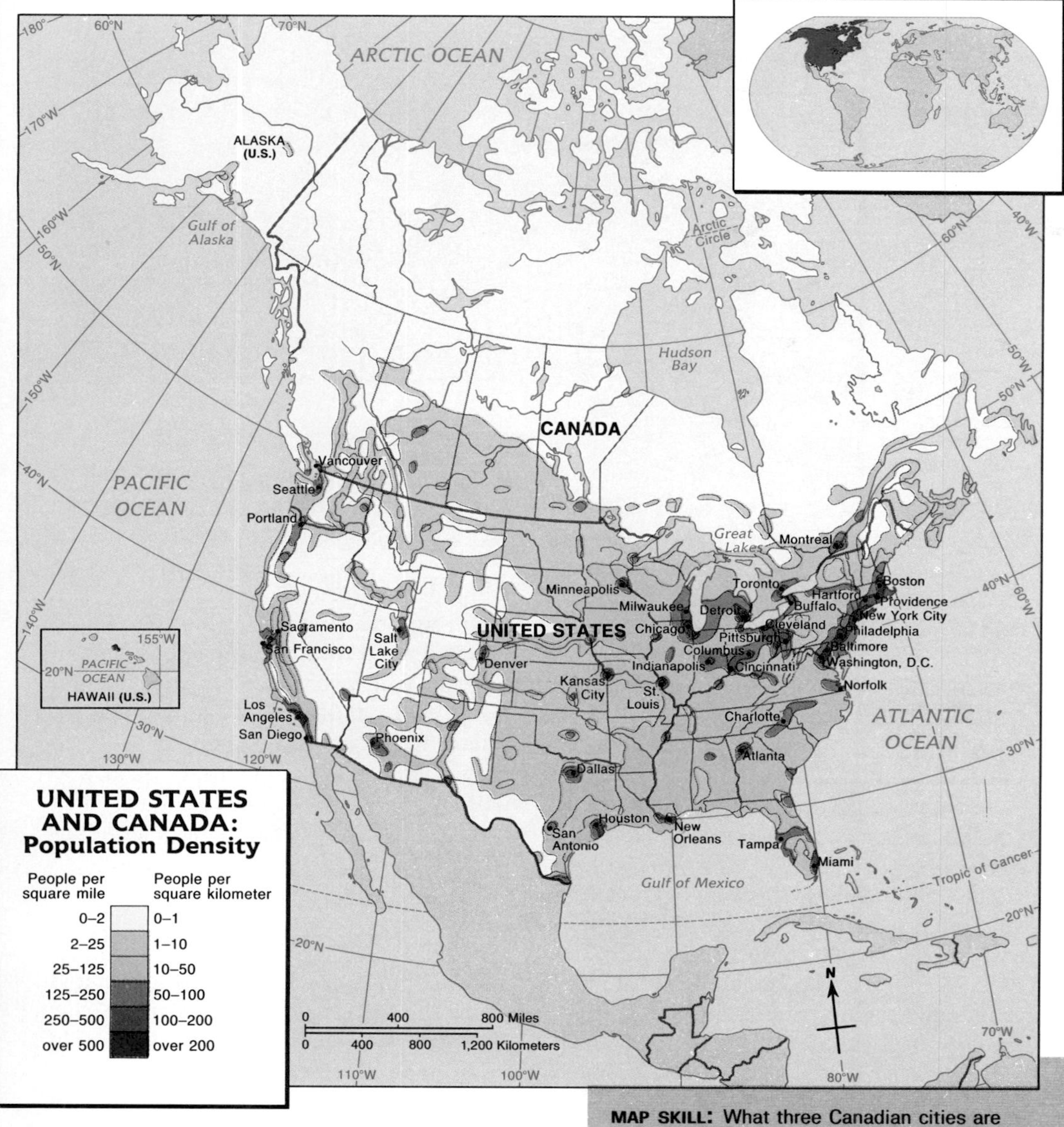

MAP SKILL: What three Canadian cities are shown above?

Plain, which borders the Atlantic Ocean. The other part is the broad Gulf Coastal Plain, which borders the Gulf of Mexico.

Many people today live in the Coastal Plains. Look at the map above. It shows the **population density** of the United States and Canada. Population density is the number of people per square mile (or per square kilometer) in a given land area. As the map shows, the Coastal Plains include some of the most heavily populated areas of the United States today. This is

MAP SKILL: Vancouver, Toronto, and Montreal

Locating the Coastal Plains Have students read the last section at the bottom of page 42.

Ask students:

- **How are the Coastal Plains divided?** (into two parts: the Atlantic Coastal Plain bordering the Atlantic Ocean, the Gulf Coastal Plain bordering the Gulf of Mexico)

EXTENDING MAP SKILLS

Have students study the population-density map on this page.

Ask students:

- **What does a population-density map show?** (the number of people per square mile, or per square kilometer, in a given area)
- **Which geographic regions of the United States are the most densely populated according to the maps on pages 40 and 43?** (the Coastal Plains, the Interior Plains)
- **Which geographic regions are the least densely populated?** (the Great Plains, the Rocky Mountains region, northern Canada)
- **In which part of Canada do most Canadians live?** (along the Canada/United States border)
- *THINKING FURTHER:* **Near which physical feature are most heavily populated cities located? Why?** (bodies of water; Water has long enabled people to transport goods.)

BACKGROUND INFORMATION

The North American Plate North America has natural features that can be traced back 250 million years. At that time in the earth's history, only one supercontinent existed—Pangaea.

- When Pangaea broke up into smaller continents, the eastern edge of what became the North American continent broke away from what are today Europe and Africa. Magma, or molten rock, formed the floor of the Atlantic Ocean.
- According to geologists the continents, including North America, sit on adjoining, moving plates. The plates are the North American Plate, the South American Plate, the African Plate, the Eurasian Plate, the Indo-Australian Plate, the Pacific Plate, the Nazca Plate, and the Antarctic Plate.

Discussing the Canadian Shield and the Arctic Islands Have students read page 44.

Ask students:

- **What are the far northern regions of Canada called?** (the Canadian Shield, the Arctic Islands)
- **Which geographic features can be found in Baffin Island and Ellesmere Island?** (mountains and glaciers)

Applying the Lesson Have students make a list of all the natural resources from their region that are used in their school or homes.

3 CLOSE

Summarizing Students have learned that the seven physical regions of the United States and Canada present a variety of landforms.

Evaluating Use the *Check Your Reading* questions (answers given below) to assess students' understanding.

Answers to Check Your Reading

1. the Appalachian Highlands, the Interior Plains, the Rocky Mountains, the Pacific Mountains
2. Canadian Shield; Arctic Islands
3. Appalachian Highlands—low, rounded mountains; Interior Plains—mostly flat, treeless in Great Plains; Rocky Mountains—high peaks; Pacific Mountains—rich farmland and high mountains; Coastal Plains—borders Atlantic Ocean and Gulf of Mexico; Canadian Shield—low hills, lakes, and forests; Arctic Islands—treeless plains called tundra
4. The Rocky Mountains at the Continental Divide; "first water running west" means she had just crossed the Continental Divide, where water begins its descent to the Pacific Ocean.

Independent Practice
Practice Book: page 7

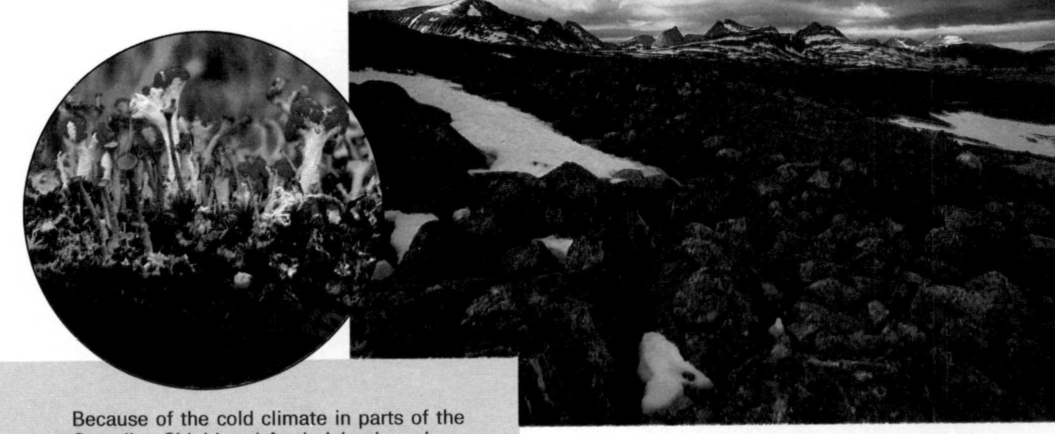

Because of the cold climate in parts of the Canadian Shield and Arctic Islands, only simple plant life such as that shown at left can live.

because some major port cities—such as New Orleans, New York City, and Boston—are here. Can you name some other major coastal cities?*

CANADIAN SHIELD AND ARCTIC ISLANDS

There are two more regions to visit. In those far northern regions of Canada, the **Canadian Shield** and the **Arctic Islands**, you would expect to encounter a cold climate.

The Canadian Shield covers half of Canada. It has a landscape of low hills, lakes, and forests. Look again at the map on page 43. Why do you think a visitor to the Canadian Shield said that this region was "nothin' but miles and miles of miles and miles"?

North of the Canadian Shield are the Arctic Islands. Of the larger islands in this area, Victoria Island is very flat. Baffin Island and Ellesmere Island are marked by mountains and glaciers. A glacier is a large body of ice that moves slowly over the land.

The land of the Arctic Islands is tundra. This treeless plain has a thin layer of topsoil under which the soil is permanently frozen. The frozen layer of soil is called **permafrost**. Only simple plant life, such as mosses and small woody plants, can survive in the permafrost of the tundra.

VARIED LANDS

During your travels across the United States and to the far northern reaches of Canada, you have visited all kinds of land, from wide plains to huge mountains. These two large countries offer a great variety of landforms. In the next lesson, you will learn how climate and resources also help to make this a region of great abundance.

Check Your Reading

1. What four physical regions are shared by the United States and Canada?
2. What two regions are located only in Canada?
3. Identify a major physical feature of each of the seven regions of Canada and the United States.
4. THINKING SKILL: The following words are taken from a traveler's journal: "We . . . stopped for the night, using water that . . . was the first water running west. . . . " What region do you think she was describing? Explain your answer.

THINKING SKILL: Drawing Conclusions

*Providence, Baltimore, Washington, D.C., Norfolk, Tampa, Miami, San Diego, Los Angeles, San Francisco

MEETING INDIVIDUAL NEEDS

Reteaching (easy) Have students draw the shapes of the seven physical regions. Have them cut these shapes out and then glue each on a matching piece of cardboard to create a puzzle of North America. Divide the class into two teams to compete in identifying the regions and putting the puzzle together.

Extension (average) Have students, using the elevation map on page 40 as a model, draw a cross-section diagram of Canada along the 50th parallel from Newfoundland to Vancouver Island. Students should label each physical region and indicate its elevation in feet or meters.

Enrichment (challenging) Divide the class into seven groups and assign each group a region of the United States and Canada. Have the groups prepare travelogues about their region, noting such characteristics as elevation, land use, and population density.

LESSON 2

Climate and Resources

Key Vocabulary

temperate timberline
arable hydroelectric power

Key Places

Great Lakes
St. Lawrence Seaway

Read Aloud

The Seneca Indians of eastern North America believe that once, long ago, Sky Woman, who lived high above the land, had a daughter who went to live on the earth. Years later, the daughter died. For many days afterward, Sky Woman's grandson, Good Mind, watered the earth above his mother's grave. Soon plants began to grow. From her body came corn and squash. From her hands came beans, looking like fingers. From her feet came potatoes, which look like large toes.

Today, most people in the United States and Canada have other explanations for the abundance of their land. But they still rely on the many resources it provides.

Read for Purpose

1. WHAT YOU KNOW: What are some of the natural resources of the area in which you live?
2. WHAT YOU WILL LEARN: What are the climate regions and the major natural resources of the United States and Canada?

A TEMPERATE CLIMATE

For humans, health depends greatly on body temperature. When a person's body temperature is too high or too low, he or she is likely to be sick. As with the human body, the health of the United States and Canada depends on temperatures that are neither too hot nor too cold. For instance, a sudden frost can destroy an orange crop in Florida. A long heat wave can destroy a corn crop in Iowa.

Too much or too little precipitation is also dangerous for many reasons. For example, if the Cascade Mountains do not receive enough rain, the forests there dry out. The chances of forest fires increase. What are some other examples of extreme weather that can cause damage? *

Generally, the regions of the United States have a temperate climate. That means they are neither too hot nor too cold. Although temperate areas have few extremes in weather, their climates do change from place to place.

In general, as you go farther south in North America, the summers are longer and hotter and the winters are shorter and milder. As you go farther north, the summers are shorter and milder and the win-

WHAT YOU KNOW: Possible answers include: water, forests, and farmland.

* Some other examples are floods, hurricanes, and tornadoes.

45

LESSON 2

pages 45–49

Lesson Theme The United States and Canada prosper in farming and industry due to an abundance of natural resources, a temperate climate, and waterways that serve their interiors.

Lesson Objectives

- Describe how the interaction of a temperate climate and fertile soil has benefited the United States and Canada.
- Locate the vital waterways of the United States and Canada.
- List factors that build the economic strength of the United States and Canada.

PREPARE

Motivate Read the *Read Aloud* section and ask if students know of other beliefs similar to this.

Set Purpose Pose the *What You Will Learn* question and tell students that they will read about why North America is a land of abundance.

TEACH

Discussing Temperate Climate Help students understand the meaning of the word *temperate*.

Ask students:

- **What do you think the word *temperate* means?** (moderate; not extreme)
- **What kind of climate generally exists in the regions of the United States?** (a temperate climate; that is, one that is neither too hot nor too cold)

READING STRATEGY AND VOCABULARY DEVELOPMENT

Previewing Using a class previewing guide (summarized on page 39), have students preview the lesson, reviewing each step of the previewing process as they proceed. Then remind them that the *Key Vocabulary* is a particularly important source of information for previewing. Explain that *Key Vocabulary* terms are defined in this textbook when they first appear in the lesson in order to help readers understand the words' meanings. Point out to students that the text also provides a phonetic respelling, or pronunciation, for difficult words. Tell them that sometimes being able to pronounce a word will help them to remember it. Have students locate the first appearance of each vocabulary word or term in the lesson. Ask them to pronounce the words and read the definitions.

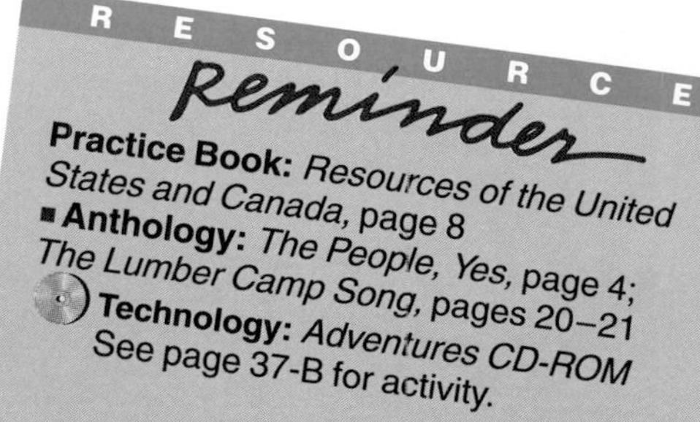

RESOURCE Reminder

Practice Book: *Resources of the United States and Canada*, page 8

Anthology: *The People, Yes*, page 4; *The Lumber Camp Song*, pages 20–21

Technology: Adventures CD-ROM
See page 37-B for activity.

Discussing Climate Continue the discussion from the previous page.

Ask students:

- **Besides its position in either the north or the south, what determines the climate of a place?** (its elevation)
- *THINKING FURTHER:* **Why is farming a major industry in California's lowland valleys but not in higher places like Mount Whitney?** (Farming at high elevations is difficult due to cooler temperatures; only certain kinds of crops can flourish at high elevations.)

EXTENDING MAP SKILLS

Have students examine the climate map and the map key on this page.

Ask students:

- **Where in Canada is the climate most temperate?** (in its southern part and around the Great Lakes)
- **How would you describe the climate of most of Canada?** (short, cool summers; long, cold winters)
- **Where in North America would you find warm, humid summers and mild, rainy winters?** (in the Atlantic Coastal Plain and the Gulf Coastal Plain)
- *THINKING FURTHER:* **Where in North America would economic activity be most limited as a result of climate?** (In the far northern parts of Alaska and of Canada and in extremely dry, hot areas of the United States)

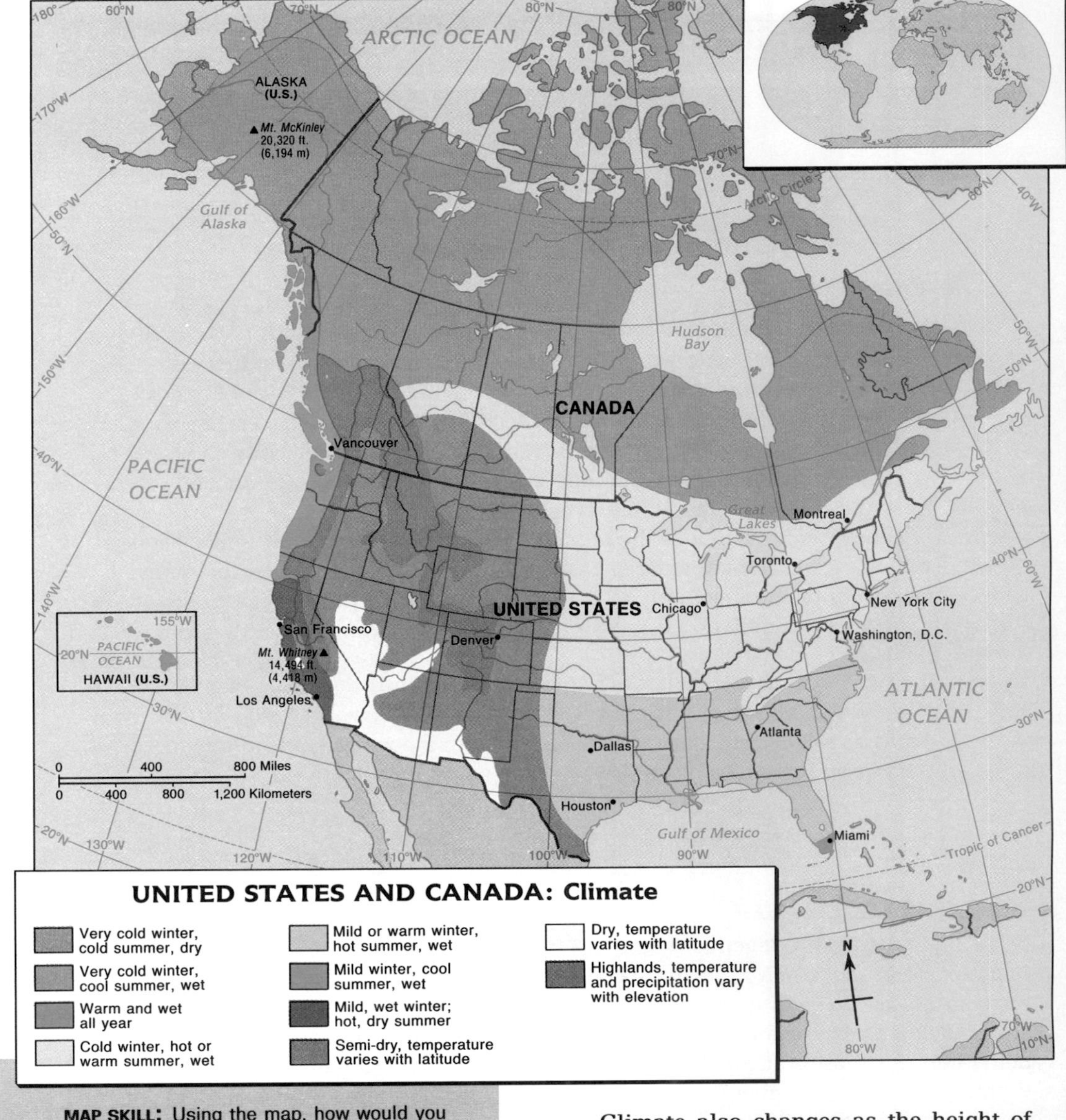

MAP SKILL: Using the map, how would you describe the climate of the area around Washington, D.C.?

ters are longer and colder. Look at the climate map of the United States and Canada above. What are some of the ways in which temperate climates differ?*

*in temperature in summer and winter and in the amount of precipitation

Climate also changes as the height of the land changes. The higher the land, the colder the temperature. In California's Pacific Mountain region, for instance, the peak of Mount Whitney is 14,494 feet (4,418 m) above sea level. It is so high that the peak is snow-capped all year. In contrast, the climate is much warmer in

MAP SKILL: cold winter, hot or warm summer, wet

46

BACKGROUND INFORMATION

Climate You may want to give students this mnemonic to help them recall the three factors that control climate.

LEN

L Latitude (the most important climate factor)
E Elevation (For every 1,000-foot [300-m] rise, air cools 3°F., or 2°C.)
N Nearness to water (Water heats up and cools down more slowly than land.)

FUNDAMENTAL THEMES OF GEOGRAPHY

Location The location of a place can be expressed in two ways.

- *Absolute location* is found by using latitude and longitude coordinates. It is expressed in measurement that pinpoints an exact spot on the earth's surface.
- *Relative location* is not so exact. It is expressed as a place's location in relation to another place.

Use the climate map on this page to show how both ways of expressing location can help us understand a place's climate. Two factors affecting climate are a place's latitude (an absolute location) and its distance from the ocean (a relative location).

California's sunny lowland valleys, where farming is a major industry.

Not all parts of the United States and Canada have temperate climates. Look again at the climate map. What other climates are found in these two nations? ✻

SOIL AND CROPS

The United States grows more food than any other nation. This abundance is helped by the region's temperate climate, rich soil, and good water supply.

About half of the land in the United States is **arable** (ar′ ə bəl), or good for farming. Major farming areas are found in the Interior Plains and the valleys of the Pacific Mountains and the Coastal Plains. Among the wide variety of crops grown in these areas are cotton, wheat, and corn.

Since much of Canada is cold and rocky, only about 5 percent of its land is arable. Yet Canadians make the most of what arable land they have. As one farmer from the Interior Plains says:

> *We farm as a family. On our farm three of our sons are farmers. . . . Wheat is our main crop, but we grow barley if the price is right, and the boys like to grow flax.*

Many Canadian farmers feel they must grow those crops that they know will sell for high prices.

FORESTS

Forests cover about one third of the land in the United States and Canada. As a result, lumbering is an important economic activity in both countries.

In the Pacific Mountains region and the southern part of the Canadian Shield, broad forests are filled with evergreen trees such as pine and fir. Along the highways in these regions, you often see huge truckloads of lumber.

A long **timberline** divides the northern part of the Canadian Shield from the southern part. A timberline is the elevation above which, because of the cold climate at high elevations, trees cannot grow. Only small plants are able to live above the timberline.

WATERWAYS

Many important waterways are located in the United States and in Canada. Both countries share the five **Great Lakes**, the largest freshwater lakes in the world. The Great Lakes are connected to the Atlantic Ocean by a system of rivers and canals

Forests are a major resource of the United States and Canada. Can you find the **timberline** in the photo at left?

✻Some places are very cold in both winter and summer, and some places are warm and wet all year.

47

Understanding the Interaction of Climate, Soil, and Crops Focus students' attention on the two physical factors that control plant growth: climate and soil.

Ask students:

- **Which physical features allow the United States to grow more food than any other nation?** (a temperate climate, rich soil, enough rainfall)
- **What percentage of the land in the United States is capable of supporting farming as compared to Canada?** (Fifty percent of the land in the United States is arable as compared to 5 percent in Canada.)
- **Where are the major farming areas of the United States?** (the Interior Plains, the valleys of the Pacific Mountains, the Coastal Plains)
- *THINKING FURTHER:* **Read the quotation on this page. Why do you think farming might be practiced as a family business?** (The work of running a farm can be divided up among family members; farms can be handed down from one generation to another.)

Measuring the Percentage of Forestlands Help students to compare the percentage of forestlands in both countries and to locate major commercial lumbering forests.

Ask students:

- **What percentage of the land in North America is covered by forests?** (33 percent in both the United States and Canada)
- **Name two evergreen trees found in the United States and Canada. In which parts of both countries are they logged?** (pine, fir; the Pacific Mountains in the United States and the southern part of the Canadian Shield in Canada)

Identifying Important Waterways Have students read the section on waterways on this page.

Ask students:

- **Which important waterways are shared by the United States and Canada?** (four of the Great Lakes, the St. Lawrence Seaway)

BACKGROUND INFORMATION

Deforestation and Reforestation Forests are endangered worldwide. For example, the loss of large sections of forest in Brazil in Latin America and in Nepal in Asia has caused soil erosion, flooding, and the destruction of animal habitats. When more trees are cut than are planted, *deforestation* takes place.

- Acid rain in Canada is another cause of deforestation. American factories near the Canadian border burn high-sulfur coal and release the resulting acid into the air. This pollution is blown by winds into Canada where it falls on the trees as rain.
- Replacing cut-down forests by planting seedlings is called *reforestation.* Reforestation efforts are made by both the United States and Canada. Both countries replant commercially logged forests with seedlings.

Discussing Waterways Continue the discussion from the previous page.

Ask students:

- **Which rivers in Canada and the United States are important transportation routes?** (the Columbia, Mississippi, Mackenzie, Nelson, and Frazier rivers)

EXTENDING MAP SKILLS

Refer students to the map on this page. Help students define the words in the map key. For example, *manufacturing* means "making products in factories"; *livestock raising* means "raising animals for meat and for dairy products."

Ask students:

- **Which land uses are employed in Canada but not in the United States?** (All uses are employed in both.)
- **Where in the United States does mining take place?** (Except for the Northwest, mining is done throughout the United States. Most mining takes place in the West)
- *THINKING FURTHER:* **Where does most manufacturing take place? Why?** (near bodies of water; for ease of transporting products to markets)

Discussing Hydroelectric Power and Mining Help students understand how both hydroelectric power and mining have led to the development of the economies of North America.

Ask students:

- **What is hydroelectric power?** (electrical power generated by rapidly moving water)
- **For what is hydroelectric power used?** (to provide energy for a region's homes and factories)
- **Which minerals are found in the United States and Canada?** (coal, oil, copper, nickel)

called the St. Lawrence Seaway. Large ships are able to sail hundreds of miles inland on the seaway. Trace the routes that ships take on the map of the St. Lawrence Seaway on page 49.

Both the United States and Canada have many rivers that can be sailed far inland. The two nations share the Columbia River in the West. The Mississippi River in the United States, as well as the Mackenzie, Fraser, and other rivers in Canada, are all important transportation routes.

MAP SKILL: What is much of the land used for in the central part of the United States?

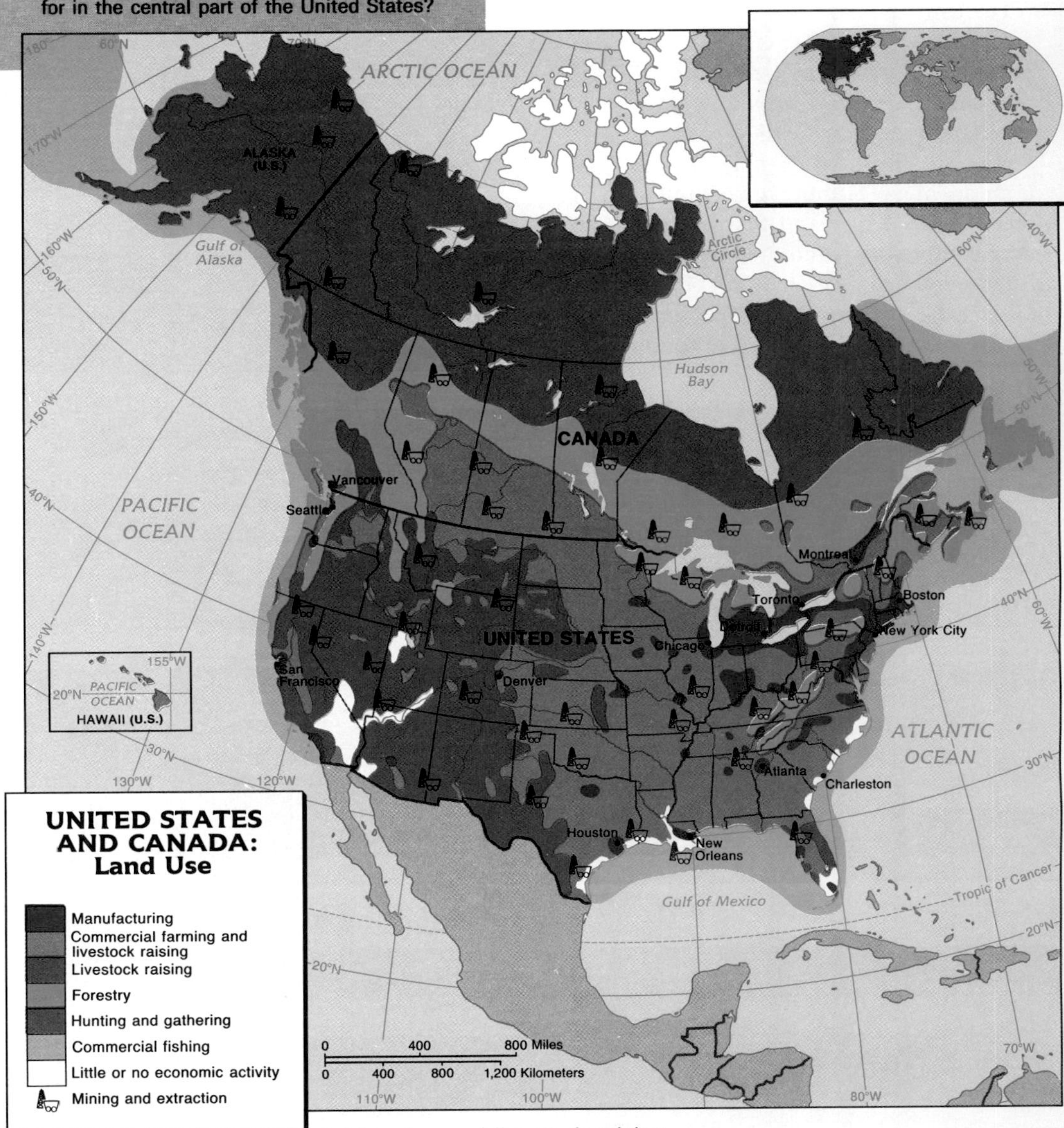

MAP SKILL: commercial farming and livestock raising

48

BACKGROUND INFORMATION

Multicultural Perspectives The brown area on the map above shows where North Americans make their living from hunting and gathering. Hunting and gathering is a way of life for people around the world, including the Inuit of Alaska, the Fulani of western Africa, and the Bedouins of the Arabian Peninsula. In the past historians usually called hunters and gatherers nomads, which means "people who wander for pasture" in Greek. But *nomad* conjured up the image of people wandering aimlessly looking for food—an image that is inaccurate. Hunters and gatherers move about in a well-defined area for well-defined reasons, such as following animals and seeking edible plants and water. Today historians are more selective with their usage of the word *nomad*. Ask students why people who make their living as hunters and gatherers might dislike the label "nomads."

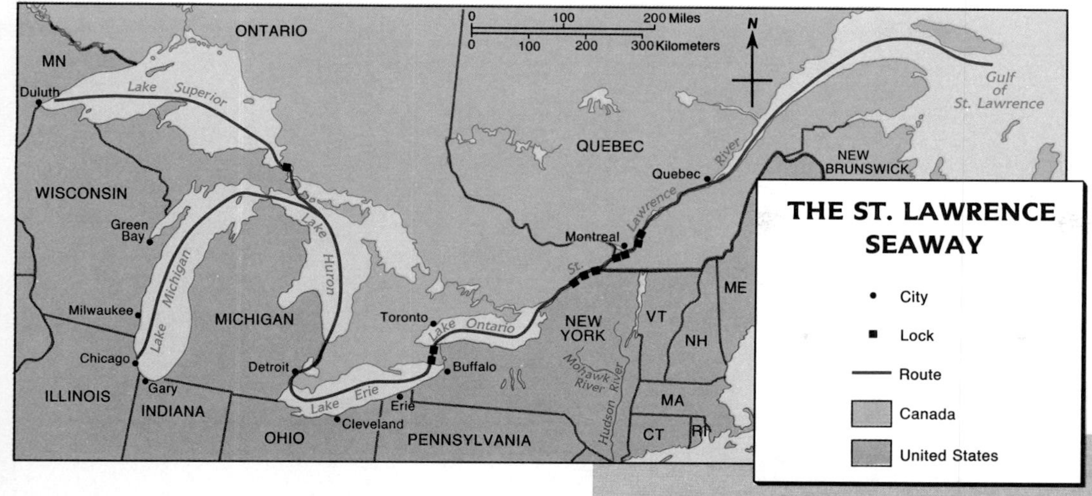

MAP SKILL: How does the St. Lawrence Seaway help the United States and Canada?

HYDROELECTRIC POWER

People in the United States and Canada use many rivers to produce **hydroelectric** (hī drō i lek' trik) **power**. Hydroelectric power is electricity that is generated, or produced, by the force of rapidly moving water.

An advantage of hydroelectric power over other sources of energy is that it does not pollute the air. However, dams built for hydroelectric power block rivers, thus harming underwater life. For example, some fish need to migrate from place to place. Therefore, dams need to be planned and built carefully.

MINERALS AND MINING

A Canadian miner wrote that "rich nickel and copper deposits were actually found by accident" in his country about 100 years ago. Railroad workers who were blasting rock found ore in it. This started, he said, a "real land rush" in which miners "swarmed in and began to dig."

Both the United States and Canada have large reserves of valuable minerals. A look at the map on page 48 shows you the major mining areas of this region.

In recent times those coal and oil reserves that were easy to reach have nearly all been mined. However, new mining and drilling techniques are now making it possible to mine hard-to-reach reserves.

A LAND OF ABUNDANCE

The United States and Canada are very fortunate. As you have read, they form a region that has a temperate climate, abundant natural resources, and several rivers that can be sailed far inland. These factors allow the two nations to feed their people and to have many different kinds of industry.

Check Your Reading

1. Why are temperate climates important to the United States and Canada?
2. Why is only 5 percent of Canada's land arable?
3. Describe the major resources of the United States and Canada.
4. **THINKING SKILL:** How are the climates of the United States similar to those of Canada? How are they different?

MAP SKILL: by allowing ships to sail far inland from the Atlantic Ocean

THINKING SKILL: Compare and Contrast

EXTENDING MAP SKILLS

Have students examine the map on this page.

Ask students:

- **Name some places connected by the St. Lawrence Seaway.** (Quebec and Montreal, the Great Lakes and the Atlantic Ocean)

Applying the Lesson Have the class cut out pictures from magazines to create a collage depicting the physical variety and agricultural abundance in North America.

3 CLOSE

Summarizing Students have read that climate, natural resources, and transportation routes give the United States and Canada success in farming and industry.

Evaluating Use the *Check Your Reading* questions (answers given below) to assess students' understanding.

Answers to Check Your Reading

1. Temperate climates help farmers produce a wide variety of crops.
2. Much of Canada is too cold, too rocky, and too mountainous for farming.
3. Natural resources include arable land for the United States, various metals and minerals and water power for both the United States and Canada.
4. Winters tend to be longer and colder in the northern parts of both countries; summers are longer and warmer in the southern parts of both countries; more of Canada experiences longer periods of cold than does the United States.

Independent Practice
Practice Book: page 8

MEETING INDIVIDUAL NEEDS

Reteaching (easy) Have students look at the three maps in this lesson and write a paragraph about the most important thing they learned from each.

Extension (average) Divide the class into eight groups. Assign each group one of the categories from the map key on page 48. Have students gather newspaper or magazine articles about their category and have them put together a small newspaper on the topic.

Enrichment (challenging) Have students work together in groups to redesign the river systems of the United States and Canada so that the Mississippi River is a west-east or east-west system and Canadian rivers flow south. Each group should report on specific changes in human-environment interactions, human movement, regional concerns, and the location of cities.

SKILLS LESSON
pages 50–51

Lesson Theme A global grid of latitude and longitude helps us to locate places on earth.

Lesson Objectives
- Explain why we need a global grid of latitude and longitude.
- Locate places on a globe or map, using latitude and longitude.
- Identify the latitude and longitude of places on a globe or map.

PREPARE

Motivate Read the introduction aloud to the class. You may wish to display Transparency Map 8 and have students compare the globe that shows latitude and the globe that shows longitude on this page. Suggest that lines of latitude look like a ladder and that, at the poles, lines of longitude look like the spokes of a wheel.

Set Purpose Tell students they will learn that we need lines of latitude and longitude on globes and maps to pinpoint exact location of a place.

TEACH

Identifying Latitude and Longitude Make sure that students understand the differences between lines of latitude and lines of longitude.

Ask students:

- **Why is it that lines of latitude never meet?** (They are parallel.)
- **Why isn't the longitude of the prime meridian indicated as either east or west?** (It is the beginning point of measure. If you traveled 180° in either direction, you would be in the same location—0°, or the prime meridian.)

RESOURCE Reminder

Practice Book: *Using Latitude and Longitude, page 9*
Outline Map: *The World*
Transparency Map: 8
Desk Map: *The World, Political*

BUILDING SKILLS
GEOGRAPHY SKILLS

Understanding Latitude and Longitude

Key Vocabulary

latitude	prime meridian
longitude	meridian
parallel	global grid

As you have already seen, this book contains many maps. Have you noticed the system of lines drawn on many of them? The lines that extend east and west are called lines of latitude. The lines that extend north and south are called lines of longitude.

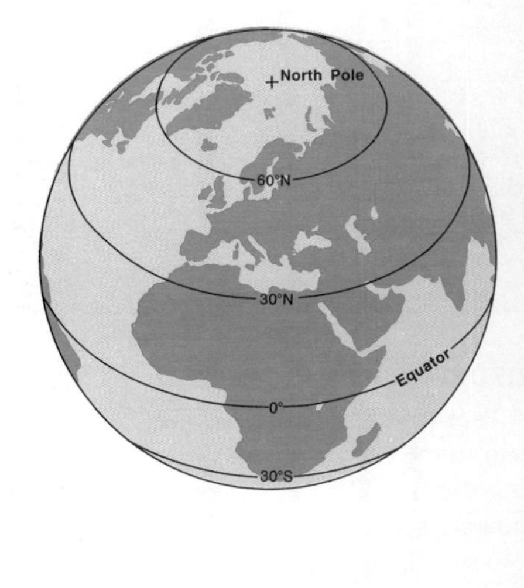

LINES OF LATITUDE

Using Latitude

The equator is the starting line for measuring latitude. Latitude is distance, measured in degrees (°), north or south of the equator. The latitude of the equator is 0°. Lines of latitude north of the equator are labeled *N* for "north." Those south of the equator are labeled *S* for "south."

Look at the lines of latitude on the Lines of Latitude map on this page. These lines are also called parallels. Lines of latitude are always the same distance apart, or parallel. If you follow any two lines of latitude, you will see that they never meet.

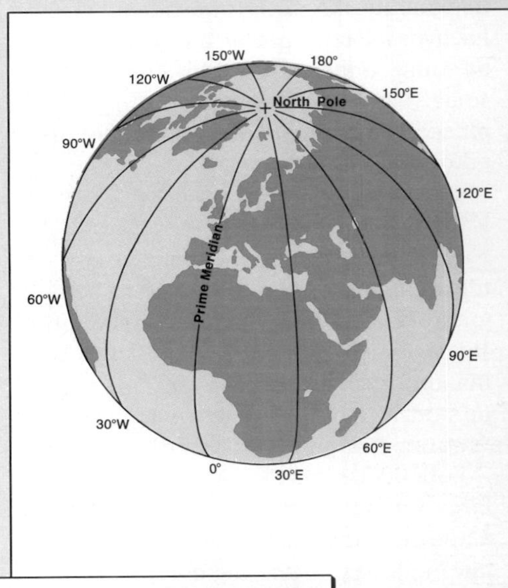

LINES OF LONGITUDE

Using Longitude

The prime meridian is the starting line for measuring longitude. All lines of longitude are called meridians. Longitude is distance, measured in degrees, east or west of the prime meridian. The longitude

50

FUNDAMENTAL THEMES OF GEOGRAPHY

Location Absolute location can be pinpointed with extreme accuracy because lines of latitude and longitude are measured with degrees (°), which are divided further into minutes (′) and seconds (″). A point called a coordinate can be measured where the imaginary lines of latitude and longitude cross. A coordinate is designated by a number, a degree sign, and a letter indicating direction.

Students can work with latitude and longitude in two ways. When given a coordinate, they can find a place by tracing a parallel and a meridian, as directed in this lesson in "Finding Places on a Map." When given only the name of a place, they must reverse the steps to find its coordinate.

GLOBAL GRID

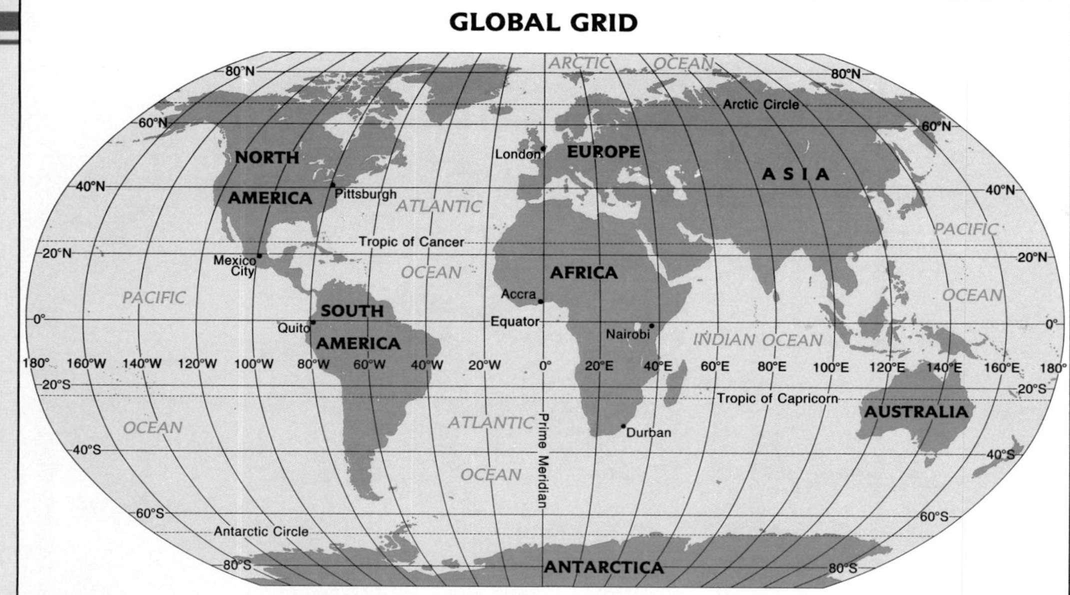

of the prime meridian is 0°. Meridians that lie east of the prime meridian are labeled *E*. Those west of the prime meridian are labeled *W*. If you traveled 180° eastward, you would be in the same place as you would be if you traveled westward 180°. Since 180°E and 180°W signify the same location, the line marking this longitude is not labeled *E* or *W*.

Look at the Lines of Longitude map. Notice how all meridians meet at the North Pole. They meet at the South Pole too. Distances between meridians increase as you move from the poles toward the equator. Meridians are farthest apart at the equator.

Finding Places on a Map

Together, lines of latitude and longitude make up the global grid. The global grid helps us to locate places on maps and globes. You can find any place on earth if you know its latitude and longitude. For example, suppose you know that Pittsburgh, Pennsylvania, is located at approximately 40°N, 80°W. To find Pittsburgh on the map, first put your finger on the point where the equator and the prime meridian cross. Now move your finger north to the parallel labeled 40°N. Next move your finger west along this parallel to the point where it crosses the meridian, labeled 80°W. You have located Pittsburgh.

Reviewing the Skill

1. What are parallels and meridians? How do they help you to understand latitude and longitude?
2. Which city on the Global Grid map is located at approximately 20°N, 100°W?
3. Which South American city shown on the map is located very close to the equator?
4. At what longitude is Accra, Africa?
5. Why is it important to understand how to use latitude and longitude?

51

Examining How to Find Places on a Map Help students to locate Pittsburgh by following the steps in the text. Explain to them that they can find the latitude and longitude of a particular place by reversing the steps. Help the students to calculate the latitude and longitude of a particular city. Tell students to put their fingers on the point where the equator and the prime meridian cross. Then have them move their fingers east or west away from the prime meridian toward the chosen city and record the number of degrees as *E* or *W*. Next have them move their fingers north or south on the longitude line for the chosen city and note the number of degrees *N* or *S*. Have students practice finding the latitude and longitude of several cities in this way.

Applying the Skill Divide the class into two groups. Have each group choose three places that appear on the world map in the *Atlas* and write the latitude and longitude of each place on a sheet of paper. Have the groups exchange papers and identify the places chosen.

CLOSE

Summarizing Students have learned that we can locate places on a map by using a global grid.

Answers to Reviewing the Skill

1. Parallels, or lines of latitude, measure distances north or south of the equator. Meridians, or lines of longitude, measure distances east or west of the prime meridian. Together they make a global grid that helps us to locate places on earth.
2. Mexico City
3. Quito
4. 0°, or the prime meridian
5. Understanding how to use latitude and longitude enables us to locate places on earth.

Independent Practice
Practice Book: page 9

MEETING INDIVIDUAL NEEDS

Reteaching (easy) Have students work in pairs to locate places in the United States, using latitude and longitude. Use the *Atlas* map of the United States on page 622. Have one student give the latitude and longitude of a place. Then have the other student identify the place.

Extension (average) Have students use the map of Europe in the *Atlas* on page 626 to find the latitude and longitude of various cities.

Enrichment (challenging) Give each student a copy of an outline map of the world (or, alternatively, give 12 groups of students the desk maps of the world) that are available in the Teacher's Resource Center. Have students use the *Atlas* map of the United States on page 622 to indicate the latitude and longitude ranges for (1) the contiguous United States, (2) Hawaii, and (3) Alaska. Then have them write a paragraph titled "Interesting Latitudes and Longitudes in the United States."

CHAPTER 1 REVIEW
pages 52–53

USING THE CHAPTER SUMMARY AND REVIEW

Physical Geography These questions may be used for review.

- **What are the seven physical regions of Canada and the United States?** (Appalachian Highlands, Rocky Mountains, Pacific Mountains, Interior Plains, Coastal Plains, Canadian Shield, Arctic Islands)
- **In general, what type of climate does the United States have?** (temperate)
- **What are the major natural resources of Canada and the United States?** (arable land, forests, navigable rivers, minerals)

Ideas to Remember

- **Which landforms divide the United States and Canada into seven physical regions?** (mountains and plains)
- **How does the temperate climate of this region help its people meet their needs?** (It helps farmers to produce a variety of crops.)

Answers to Reviewing Vocabulary

1. timberline
2. erosion
3. arable
4. Continental Divide
5. permafrost

Answers to Reviewing Facts

1. Appalachian Highlands, Rocky Mountains, Pacific Mountains, Interior Plains, Coastal Plains, Canadian Shield, Arctic Islands; Canadian Shield and Arctic Islands; Coastal Plains
2. They are younger and have not yet been worn down by erosion.
3. They are opposites—a plateau is an area of flat land that rises above the land around it, while a canyon is a deep valley with steep sides; carved out by the water from the Colorado River.

CHAPTER 1 • SUMMARY

UNITED STATES AND CANADA: PHYSICAL GEOGRAPHY

LANDFORMS

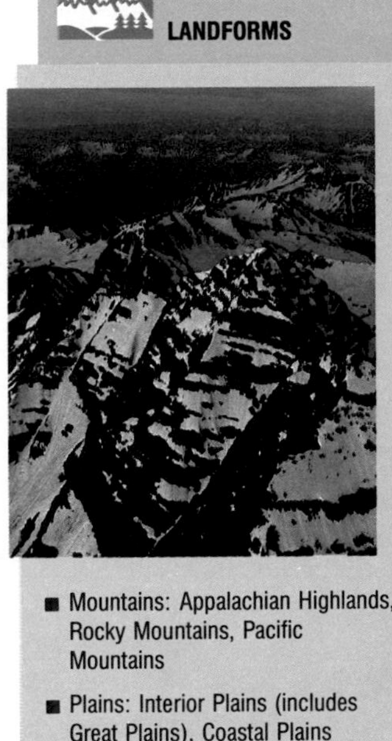

- Mountains: Appalachian Highlands, Rocky Mountains, Pacific Mountains
- Plains: Interior Plains (includes Great Plains), Coastal Plains

- Northern Canada: Canadian Shield and Arctic Islands

CLIMATE

- Temperate climate: few extremes in weather

- Temperatures: Colder in mountains, warmer in lowlands

NATURAL RESOURCES

- Arable land: 50 percent of land in United States, only 5 percent in Canada

- United States grows more food than any other nation
- Forests cover one third of United States and Canada

- Waterways: Great Lakes, St. Lawrence Seaway, Mississippi River, Columbia River

IDEAS TO REMEMBER

- Mountains, plains, and other landforms divide the United States and Canada into seven physical regions.
- A temperate climate and abundant natural resources combine to provide this area with most of its needs.

52

ENRICHMENT ACTIVITY

Making a Relief Map **Materials:** modeling clay, outline map

1. Tell students that they are going to construct a relief map of the United States and Canada. Have them discuss the major natural features (they should include the major mountain ranges—the Pacific, the Rockies, and the Appalachians—the Interior Plains; the Great Lakes; and the Mississippi River).
2. Begin with a large outline map of the area as a guide. Divide the class into groups and assign each a part of the area to model.
3. Have the groups assemble their parts within the outline to construct the full relief map. Save the relief map for comparison of regions to be studied later.

CHAPTER 1 • REVIEW

REVIEWING VOCABULARY

arable
Continental Divide
erosion
permafrost
timberline

Number a sheet of paper from 1 to 5. Beside each number write the word or term from the list above that best matches each statement.

1. Harsh conditions resulting from a cold climate at high elevation keep trees from growing beyond this boundary.
2. This wearing-away process explains why the Appalachian Mountains are low and rounded compared with other mountain chains.
3. This term refers to land that is good for farming.
4. In North America this long line of mountain peaks divides rivers flowing eastward from those flowing westward.
5. In arctic regions this layer of permanently frozen soil allows only small plants and mosses to grow.

REVIEWING FACTS

1. Name the seven geographic regions of the United States and Canada. Which of the regions are found only in Canada? Which region is found only in the United States?
2. Why are the Rocky Mountains higher and more rugged than the Appalachian Mountains?
3. What is the difference between a *plateau* and a *canyon*? How was the Grand Canyon formed?
4. Name the two coastal plains in the United States. Why are these regions among the most heavily populated areas in the United States?
5. What is meant by the term *temperate climate*? In what ways does a temperate climate differ from an arctic or a tropical climate?
6. How does climate change as one moves north? As one moves south? How does altitude affect climate?
7. What are three reasons that the United States grows more food than any other country in the world?
8. How does the location of the Great Lakes and of the St. Lawrence Seaway encourage trade and transportation for both Canada and the United States?
9. Why is hydroelectric power cleaner than other forms of power generation?
10. Why do minerals, such as gold or oil, attract people to a place?

WRITING ABOUT MAIN IDEAS

1. **Writing an Outline:** Write an outline of the major physical regions of North America. Under each region list its important characteristics.
2. **Writing About Perspectives:** People in one country may view their country differently. Choose two cities of Canada and write descriptions of Canada as someone living in each city might see it.

BUILDING SKILLS: UNDERSTANDING LATITUDE AND LONGITUDE

1. What are lines of latitude and lines of longitude?
2. Which lines run north and south? Which lines run east and west?
3. Explain how the lines of latitude and lines of longitude are numbered.
4. What are the names of the lines at 0° latitude and 0° longitude?
5. How do lines of latitude and lines of longitude help you to read a map?

4. Atlantic Coastal Plain and Gulf Coastal Plain; Most of the major port cities are located in this region.
5. neither too hot nor too cold; Arctic and tropical climates are extremes—one very cold, the other very hot.
6. Summers are shorter and milder and winters are longer and colder; summers are longer and hotter and winters are shorter and milder; the higher the land, the colder the temperature.
7. temperate climate, rich soil, good water supply
8. Inland sailing from the ocean is possible, which allows shipping for trade and transportation.
9. It does not pollute the air.
10. Minerals are a valuable resource that can bring wealth and attract industry.

Suggestions for Writing About Main Ideas

1. Outlines should include the seven physical regions of North America: Appalachian Highlands, Rocky Mountains, Pacific Mountains, Interior Plains, Coastal Plains, Canadian Shield, Arctic Islands.
2. Have students use the maps in this chapter to locate two Canadian cities and extrapolate information about them.

Answers to Building Skills: Understanding Latitude and Longitude

1. imaginary lines that help us locate places on maps and globes
2. lines of longitude; lines of latitude
3. Lines of latitude are measured in degrees north or south of the equator. Lines of longitude are numbered in degrees east or west of the prime meridian.
4. equator; prime meridian
5. They create a global grid that tells us how far north or south of the equator or how far east or west of the prime meridian a place is.

Chapter Review and Test
Practice Book: *Vocabulary Review,* page 10
Transparency: *Graphic Organizer*
Assessment Book: *Chapter 1 Test*

MAKING CONNECTIONS

Comparing and Contrasting Use the Matrix Chart Graphic Organizer Transparency, filling in only the underlined headings. Have students fill in each column with geographic features of the United States and Canada. *Ask:* How is the physical geography of the United States and Canada alike? Different?

	Regions	Climate	Natural Resources
United States	Appalachian Highlands, Interior Plains, Rocky Mountains, Pacific Mountains, Coastal Plains	generally temperate, cold year-round (Alaska), warm and wet year-round (Hawaii)	50% arable land, forests, waterways, minerals
Canada	Appalachian Highlands, Interior Plains, Rocky Mountains, Pacific Mountains, Canadian Shield, Arctic Islands (tundra)	generally temperate in south, cold in north	5% arable land, forests, waterways, minerals

CHAPTER 2

ORGANIZER

THE UNITED STATES text pages 54–79

CHAPTER THEME In the United States freedom permits a highly developed economy, shapes the republic, and fosters the creative arts.

CHAPTER OBJECTIVES

CONTENT

- Describe the first people to live in what is now the United States.
- Define *immigrant* and identify the freedoms that have traditionally attracted millions of people to the United States.
- Describe the various ethnic groups that make up the population of the United States.
- Explain why the United States is known as a developed economy.
- Define the terms *capitalism* and *free enterprise.*
- Describe how the people of the United States govern themselves.
- Name the three branches of government and describe the function of each.
- Outline the functions and duties of state and local governments.
- Describe the major arts, leisure activities, and sports of the United States.
- Explain the link between a modern sporting event and traditional skills and customs.

SKILLS

Geography

- Interpret a political map of the United States.

Study and Research

- Analyze a graph showing the different types of jobs in the United States.

Thinking

- Classify ten freedoms enjoyed by Americans into four different categories.
- Compare and contrast nations with high and low standards of living.
- Make decisions following a step-by-step procedure.

Reading and Writing

- Write an essay explaining the meaning of the phrase "pursuit of happiness."

CITIZENSHIP VALUES

- Appreciate the contributions of outstanding people to our freedoms.
- Appreciate American democracy and the institutions that sustain it.

TEACHER OPTIONS

READING STRATEGY: Previewing and Questioning Strategies to help students read and remember the main ideas of the lesson.

Lesson 1: p. 55 Lesson 4: p. 70
Lesson 2: p. 62 Legacy: p. 74
Lesson 3: p. 66

MEETING INDIVIDUAL NEEDS Activities for reteaching, extension, and enrichment.

Lesson 1: p. 59 Lesson 4: p. 73
Lesson 2: p. 65 Legacy: p. 77
Lesson 3: p. 69

GEO ADVENTURES ACTIVITIES PAD Daily activities to assess students' understanding of geography skills.

CURRICULUM CONNECTION Activities to help integrate other subject areas with Social Studies.

Language Arts: pp. 63, 76 Math: p. 72
Drama: p. 68

PUPIL EDITION ON CASSETTE Language support for students who have difficulty reading or who will benefit from listening to the Pupil Edition on Cassette as they read.

SECOND-LANGUAGE SUPPORT Activities and suggestions for second-language learners.

Lesson 3: p. 4

CHAPTER PLANNING GUIDE

LESSON	SUGGESTED PACING	THEMES	TEACHER SUPPORT MATERIALS: TEACHER'S RESOURCE CENTER
1 THE PEOPLE pages 55–59	1 day	Americans have a diverse ethnic background and have come to this country from many different areas of the world for a variety of reasons.	Practice Book p. 11 ■ Anthology pp. 5–6, 7–8, 9–11, 12–13, 14–15 Outline Map p. 11 Desk Maps **Technology:** *Adventures CD-ROM*
BUILDING THINKING SKILLS Decision Making pages 60–61	1 day	Making good decisions involves defining goal(s) and choosing from a number of alternatives the one that will best achieve the goal(s).	Practice Book p. 12
2 THE ECONOMY pages 62–65	1 day	In the American capitalist system a developed economy exists in which people start businesses and there are many different kinds of high-technology jobs for workers.	Practice Book p. 13 **Technology:** *Adventures CD-ROM*
3 THE GOVERNMENT pages 66–69	1 day	The Constitution of the United States created a representative democracy in which power is divided among different branches of government and in which citizens have certain rights and responsibilities.	Practice Book p. 14 **Technology:** *Adventures CD-ROM*
4 ARTS AND RECREATION pages 70–73	1 day	Americans enjoy freedom of expression in the arts and in many forms of recreation.	Practice Book p. 15
LEGACY Iditarod pages 74–77	1 day	The Iditarod is a special sporting event that helps keep traditional skills and customs alive.	Outline Maps pp. 4, 6
CHAPTER SUMMARY AND REVIEW pages 78–79	1 day	Chapter content, skills, and vocabulary are reviewed and evaluated.	Practice Book p. 16 Transparency: Graphic Organizer Assessment Book, Chapter 2 Test

Technology CONNECTION

Lesson 1
ADVENTURES CD-ROM
Have students learn about immigration history in *Movies,* U.S.

Lesson 2
ADVENTURES CD-ROM
Using *Paint* and *Stamps,* have students make a map of their own state showing major industries.

Lesson 3
ADVENTURES CD-ROM
Students can discover the *Infographic* on the National Mall in *Explore.*

CHAPTER 2
pages 54–79

USING THE CHAPTER OPENER

Discussing the Photograph Suggest to students that the people in the picture may be immigrants who are being sworn in as citizens of the United States. Tell students that the oath that immigrants take during the naturalization ceremony is longer and more detailed than the Pledge of Allegiance quoted in the passage under the photograph. As part of this oath, new citizens must promise to defend the Constitution of the United States against all enemies, to renounce their allegiance to their native countries, and to give up any titles of nobility that they may possess.

Ask students:

- **How do you think these people are feeling?** (Possible answers include: solemn, proud, hopeful)
- **In which situations have you been asked to pledge allegiance to the flag?** (Possible answers include: at school assemblies, at scout meeting, at camp)
- *THINKING FURTHER:* **Why do you think people who are already citizens of the United States are asked from time to time to pledge their allegiance?** (Encourage students to realize that the ceremony of pledging allegiance may intensify people's feelings of unity and remind them of the advantages of citizenship in the United States.)

Reading/Listening to the Primary Source Ask students to read or recite in unison the Pledge of Allegiance. Encourage them to imagine how the words of the pledge might affect an immigrant who had come to the United States as a refugee from political oppression. Ask them which words they think might be especially meaningful to such a person. (For example, students might suggest the words *with liberty and justice for all*.)

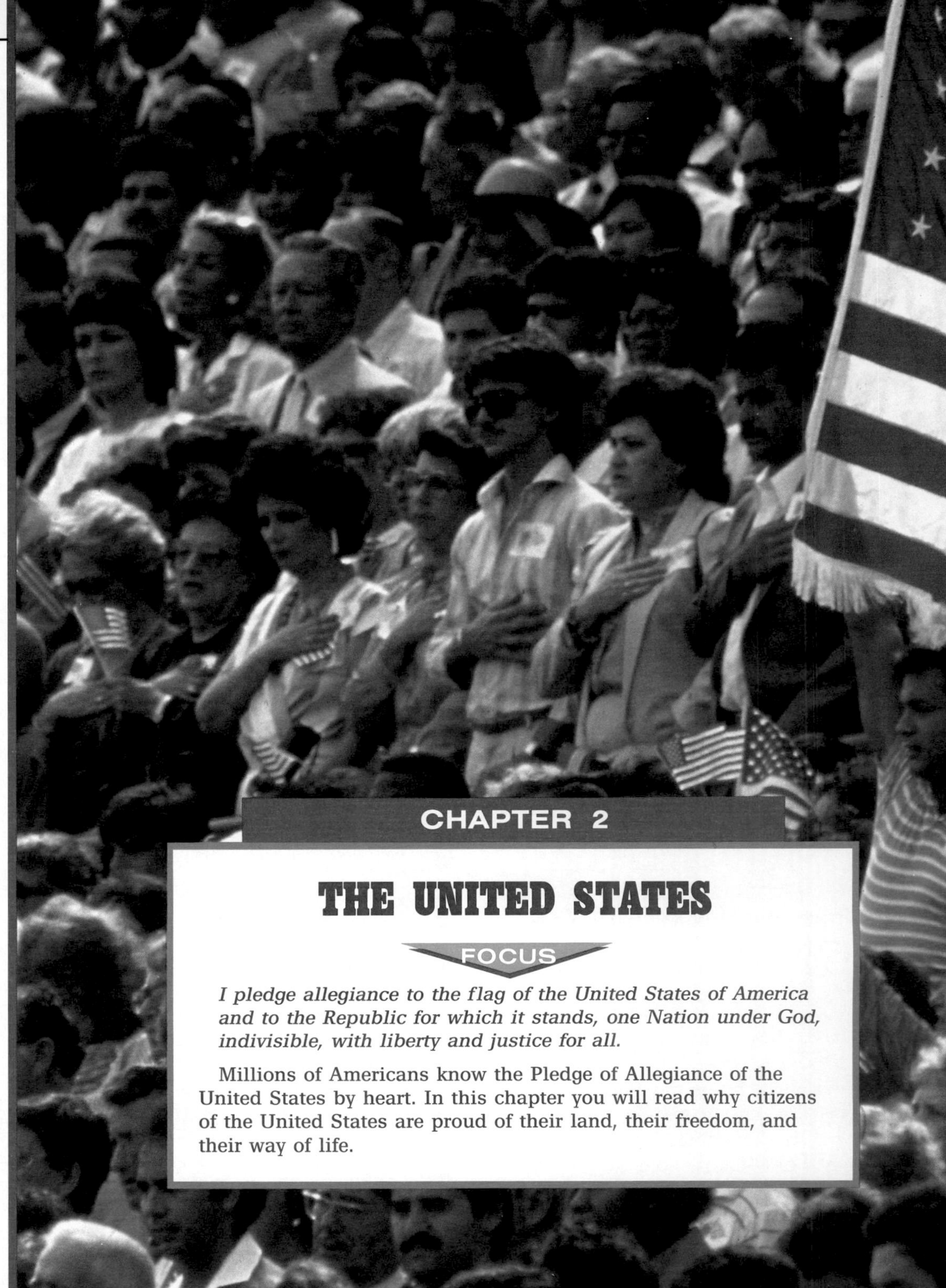

CHAPTER 2

THE UNITED STATES

FOCUS

I pledge allegiance to the flag of the United States of America and to the Republic for which it stands, one Nation under God, indivisible, with liberty and justice for all.

Millions of Americans know the Pledge of Allegiance of the United States by heart. In this chapter you will read why citizens of the United States are proud of their land, their freedom, and their way of life.

BACKGROUND INFORMATION

About the Pledge of Allegiance This pledge first appeared in the September 1892 issue of a Boston magazine, *The Youth's Companion.*

- For many years two members of the magazine's staff, James B. Upham and Francis Bellamy, each claimed to have written the pledge.
- It was not until 47 years later, in 1939, that the United States Flag Association finally acknowledged Francis Bellamy as the authentic author of the pledge.
- Make sure that students understand the difficult words in the pledge. You may want to ask them to rephrase the pledge in simpler language.

LESSON 1

The People

READ TO LEARN

Key Vocabulary

immigrant, discrimination, prejudice, megalopolis

Key Places

San Francisco

Read Aloud

It took us 12 days to cross the sea, and we thought we should die, but at last the voyage was over, and we came up and saw the beautiful bay and the big woman with the . . . lamp that is lighted at night in her hand.

These words were written in 1902 by Sadie Frowne, a garment worker in New York. Her joy at seeing the Statue of Liberty—of arriving in the United States—has been echoed in the words and thoughts of countless numbers of people coming to the United States to start a new life.

Read for Purpose

1. **WHAT YOU KNOW:** Do you know people who have come to the United States from other lands?
2. **WHAT YOU WILL LEARN:** Why have people from many different ethnic groups settled in the United States?

A FAMILY REUNION

It's the second Sunday in July, and in Dundee, Ohio, it's time for the annual Walter family reunion. More than 60 people, from 9 to 87 years old, have gathered at the schoolhouse. Many members of the Walter family live in Ohio. However, many others come all the way from Florida, California, and Massachusetts to be with the rest of the family.

Everyone sits down to a big dinner. First Glen Walter, who is the oldest, says a prayer. Then everyone starts to eat. The Walters have met in this way for 70 years.

Everyone at today's reunion is related to Remus and Abigail Walter, who ran a big farm near Dundee in the late 1800s. The Walter family traces its roots back to the Netherlands in Europe. In about 1780 a Dutch ancestor named Christian Walter sailed to the United States with his two brothers. They wanted a chance to better their lives, and they did so, buying land and turning it into successful farms.

PEOPLE FROM MANY LANDS

Like the Walters, people from all over the world have come to the United States. Many hoped to improve their lives.

They did not reach an empty land. For thousands of years, Indians had lived on this land and developed its resources. Many different Indian groups lived throughout North America and South America. They were the first people who lived in what is now the United States.

WHAT YOU KNOW: As they think about this question, students should be reminded that people are constantly immigrating to the United States.

LESSON 1
pages 55–59

Lesson Theme Americans have a diverse ethnic background and have come to this country from many different areas of the world for a variety of reasons.

Lesson Objectives

- Identify the origins of the people of the United States.
- Identify ethnic groups and their problems in America.
- Describe where Americans live today.

PREPARE

Motivate Have a student read the passage aloud. Briefly discuss Sadie Frowne's sea voyage and compare it to travel today.

Set Purpose Ask the *What You Know* question and have students tell if they know of immigrants in their family or neighborhood. Tell students they will learn the answer to the *What You Will Learn* question as they read the lesson.

TEACH

Locating a Family Reunion Have students consider how American families may be so spread out that a family reunion often entails travel over great distances.

Discussing People from Many Lands Have students read the section on immigrants on this page.

Ask students:

- **What are some of the places immigrants have come from?** (the Netherlands, South Korea, Lebanon, and so on)

READING STRATEGY AND VOCABULARY DEVELOPMENT

Previewing and Questioning Have students continue the previewing strategy initiated in Chapter 1. Ask students to change the headings in this lesson into questions to use as guides to reading. Examples of possible questions derived from the headings are:

Heading	Sample Question
A Family Reunion	Who attended a family reunion in Dundee, Ohio?
Immigrants from Many Lands	Where do today's immigrants come from?
The Search for Freedom	When did great numbers of immigrants come to America?
Ethnic Groups	What is an ethnic group?

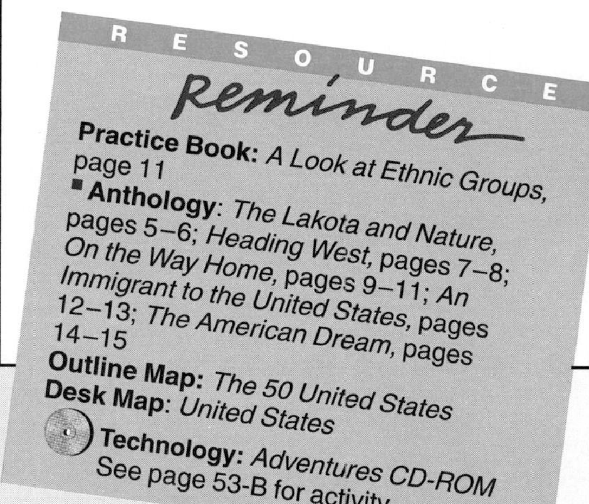

RESOURCE Reminder

Practice Book: *A Look at Ethnic Groups,* page 11

Anthology: *The Lakota and Nature,* pages 5–6; *Heading West,* pages 7–8; *On the Way Home,* pages 9–11; *An Immigrant to the United States,* pages 12–13; *The American Dream,* pages 14–15

Outline Map: *The 50 United States*

Desk Map: *United States*

Technology: *Adventures CD-ROM* See page 53-B for activity.

Discussing People from Many Lands Continue the discussion from the previous page. Help students examine the reasons that people came to the United States.

Ask students:

- **Who were the first people to live in America, and where did they come from?** (American Indians; Asia)

The Search for Freedom

Ask students:

- **When did immigrants first start coming to America in large numbers? Where did most of them come from?** (in the 1800s; from Europe)
- **What caused Europeans to leave their countries?** (They were seeking economic, religious, and political freedom.)

EXTENDING GRAPH SKILLS

Refer to the bar graph on this page to help students understand the results of immigration to the United States, in terms of population.

Ask students:

- **From which three places do the greatest number of immigrants come?** (Germany, Latin America, and Asia)
- **How many immigrants have come to the United States from Africa? Asia?** (under one million; more than 7 million)
- *THINKING FURTHER:* **What does this graph tell you about the American people?** (The American population includes many different ethnic groups.)

People like the Walters family, who arrived much later, are descendants of **immigrants**. An immigrant is a person who moves to a country other than the one where he or she was born. Most people now living in the United States are either immigrants or descendants of immigrants.

Not all of the people who reached the Western Hemisphere came voluntarily. Starting in the 1600s, millions of Africans were shipped to the Americas, where they were enslaved. Slavery in the United States ended after the Civil War. Those who had been enslaved were now free.

THE SEARCH FOR FREEDOM

Freedom attracted many immigrants to the United States. In the 1800s, great numbers of people immigrated to America from Europe. The main reason they came can be summed up in one word: *freedom*.

Many came for economic freedom—the opportunity to make a good living. Others came for religious freedom—the right to worship as they wished. Still others wanted political freedom—the right to have a say in the government of their country and be protected by its laws.

GRAPH SKILL: Has Latin America or Asia sent more **immigrants** to the United States?

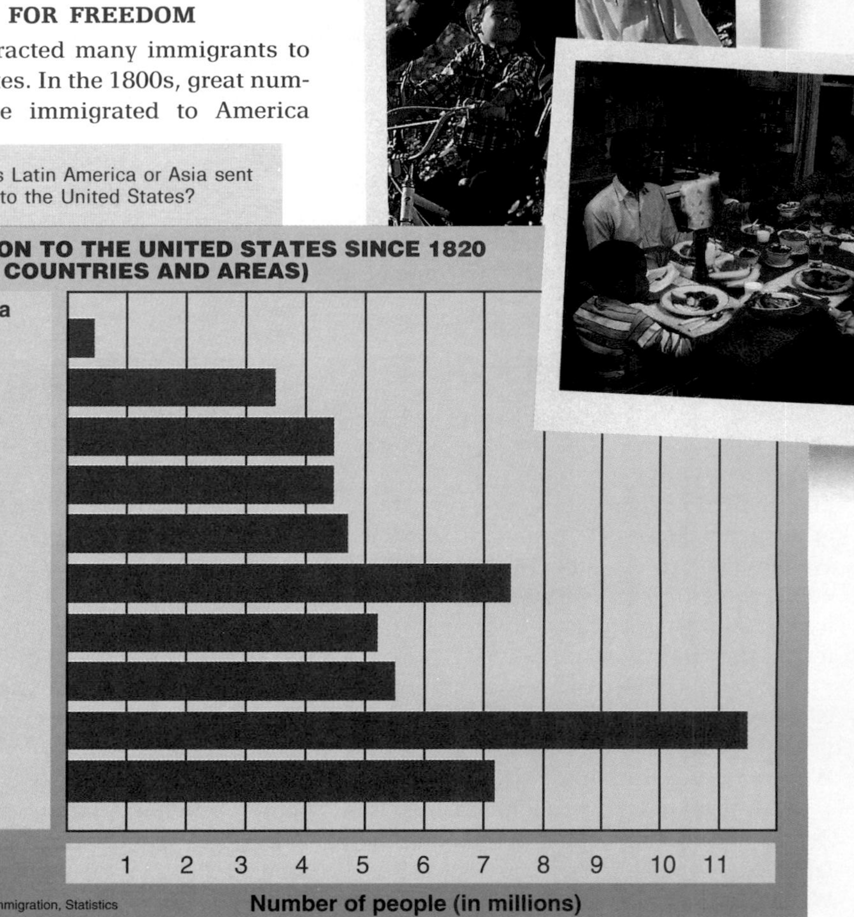

GRAPH SKILL: Latin America

BUILDING CITIZENSHIP

Interviewing to Learn About Our Families' Pasts Encourage students to investigate their family backgrounds. Prepare a questionnaire that students can use to conduct interviews with members of their families. Have students pose the following questions: Are my ancestors originally from the area that is now the United States? If so, what part of the United States are they from? If not, when did they come to this country? Which countries or areas of the world did they come from? Why and how did they come? How has our family changed over the years? Are there any photos or drawings of my ancestors I could show? Have students compile a list of their ancestors' homelands and, if applicable, immigration routes. Then mount a world map on the wall and use colored strings or ribbons to show all the movement to and within the United States by previous generations. Tack students' photos and drawings around the outside of the map.

Today immigrants continue to come to the United States for the same reasons. As one Cuban American explained:

When I came here from my country, I was living in New Jersey. . . . Very cold apartment, eight windows with no heat . . . It doesn't matter. . . . I was so happy to be here. The most important thing we were looking for was freedom. When you lose it once, you really know what freedom is.

ETHNIC GROUPS

During the early history of the United States most immigrants came to the country from Europe. Today, however, immigrants come from many parts of the world. Look at the graph on page 56. It shows where immigrants to the United States have come from. According to the graph, what areas have been the three largest sources of immigration to the United States since 1820? ❇

Today the largest groups of immigrants come from Asia and Latin America—especially from Mexico. Spanish-speaking Americans from Latin America, called Hispanics, are the fastest-growing ethnic group in the United States today. An ethnic group is a group of people who share common roots, customs, and traditions.

The Spanish were the first Europeans to arrive in what is now the United States. Beginning in the 1500s, they began settlements in Florida and parts of the Southwest. Many Hispanics in the United States are descended from both Indians and Spanish people. They come from Latin America—from Mexico, Central America, South America, and from the Caribbean Islands.

Not all of America's ethnic groups came voluntarily. A few Africans immigrated to the United States in the 1600s, but soon after millions of Africans were forced to come to the Americas and were enslaved.

❇ Germany, Latin America, and Asia

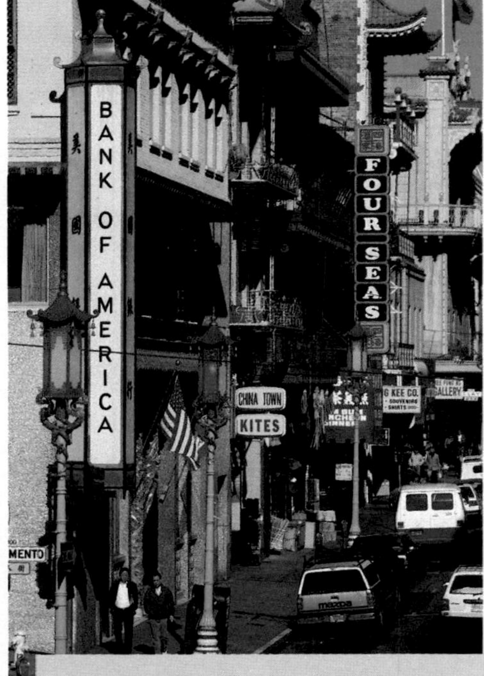

The influence of Chinese Americans can be clearly seen in the Chinatown neighborhood of San Francisco.

Slavery ended in 1865. However, African Americans have had to continue their struggle for certain rights, such as the freedom to vote and to live where they choose.

ETHNIC NEIGHBORHOODS

Many ethnic groups have left their marks on the American landscape and culture. Look at the photograph of Chinatown in San Francisco above. Note that many of the signs are in Chinese.

In addition to Chinatown, San Francisco has several other neighborhoods in which most of the residents are from a single ethnic group. The United States has many ethnic neighborhoods, but most American neighborhoods have people from many different ethnic groups living side by side.

Discussing Ethnic Groups Make sure students understand that the groups who immigrate change over time. Use this section to discuss that topic.

Ask students:

- **Where do large groups of immigrants to the United States come from today?** (Asia and Latin America)
- **Which group represents the fastest-growing ethnic group in the United States?** (Hispanics)
- **Where are these new immigrants coming from?** (Mexico, Central America, the Caribbean, South America)
- **How did most ancestors of African Americans come to America?** (they were enslaved and forced to come)

Understanding Ethnic Neighborhoods Discuss with students how and why people form ethnic neighborhoods.

Ask students:

- **What is an ethnic neighborhood?** (a place where people speak the same language, practice similar customs, and are often of the same background)
- **Why do you think immigrants move into ethnic neighborhoods?** (They may feel more at home in a place where people speak their language and practice their customs.)

BACKGROUND INFORMATION

Multicultural Perspectives Ethnic neighborhoods enrich life in cities throughout the United States. Within their borders are self-contained worlds that reflect the cultural values of their residents. Ask students what sights, smells, and sounds make their own neighborhood special.

Discussing Prejudice and Discrimination Help students to see the difference between a legitimate dislike of an individual based on personal experience and unfair, negative prejudging without facts.

Ask students:

- **What is the key difference between prejudice and discrimination?** (Prejudice is opinion, discrimination is action.)
- **Some people have unfavorable opinions or stereotyped ideas of young people. Have you ever been a victim of prejudice or discrimination that was based on your age?** (Lead the discussion to an expression of empathy for victims of prejudice.)
- **Is there any way you could change your age? Is there any way a member of an ethnic group could change having been born into that group?** (Student responses should establish the innocence of victims of prejudice.)
- *THINKING FURTHER:* **Where does prejudice come from?** (Ignorance; Prejudice is often taught in the family and reinforced by groups within the society.)

EXTENDING MAP SKILLS

Use the map on this page to locate the major cities from Boston to Washington, D.C., near the Atlantic Coast.

Ask students:

- **Name the largest cities located along the Atlantic Coast.** (Boston; Providence; Hartford; New York; Trenton; Philadelphia; Dover; Annapolis; Washington, D.C.)
- *THINKING FURTHER:* **Why do you think that the area that these cities form is called a megalopolis?** (This area is so crowded with cities and suburbs that it looks like one vast city.)

From Farms to Cities Help students understand that the United States is a highly urbanized nation.

Ethnic groups do not always live together peacefully. **Prejudice** (prej′ ə dis) and **discrimination** (di skrim ə nā′ shən) are problems that most ethnic groups have faced at some time in their history. Prejudice is one person or group's unfavorable opinion of another group that is formed unfairly, without knowing all the facts. Discrimination is the unfair treatment of a person or a group of people by another person or group. Today an ethnic group may still sometimes meet with prejudice and discrimination. However, laws have been passed to protect people in the United States against unfair treatment in jobs, housing, transportation, education, and other areas of life.

FROM FARMS TO CITIES

Most ethnic neighborhoods are in cities. When the Walter family you read about at

MAP SKILL: As you know, the United States is divided into 50 states. What state is in the northwest corner, south of Canada?

THE UNITED STATES: Political

National capital · State capital · Other city

58 MAP SKILL: Washington

BACKGROUND INFORMATION

Megalopolises in the United States These large concentrations of urban-suburban sprawl developed most rapidly after World War II.

- Airplane pilots see the most dramatic proof of a megalopolis when they fly over one at night. The lighted structures and streets below indicate how one city flows into another.
- Three major megalopolises have been given nicknames. The megalopolis on the East Coast from Boston, Massachusetts, to Washington, D.C., is referred to as BOSWASH.
- In the north-central United States, from Chicago, Illinois, to Pittsburgh, Pennsylvania, there's a megalopolis called CHIPITS.
- On the West Coast the megalopolis from San Francisco to San Diego is referred to as SANSAN.

the beginning of the lesson came to the United States in the 1700s, most people in the United States lived on farms. Today less than one fourth of the people live in rural areas—that is, on farms or in towns with only a few thousand people. Each year, the number of farms gets smaller.

A LARGE POPULATION

Geographers can learn a lot about a country by studying its population. About 260 million people live in the United States. The country covers about 3.5 million square miles (9.1 million sq km), so it has an average of about 71 persons per square mile (27 per sq km). Each of these square miles could contain about 400 city blocks. That means that if people were spread out evenly across the nation, there would be one person every 5.6 blocks in the United States.

The United States has many areas where people live closely together. Often, people live in one city and work in another. At the beginning of the 1900s many people in the United States began moving to suburbs, the residential communities surrounding large cities. Today many suburbs have grown into towns and cities. Some places are so crowded that the entire area looks like one vast city. The name for such an area is a **megalopolis** (meg ə lop′ ə lis). The United States has megalopolises on the East and West coasts. Look at the map on page 58. Where are many cities close together? ✻

ONE LAND, MANY PEOPLE

The people of the United States come from many different lands. Some lived here for centuries. Others immigrated to enjoy economic, religious, and political freedom. Still others were forced to come. Today, people of many backgrounds live throughout the land.

✻On the Atlantic and Pacific coasts

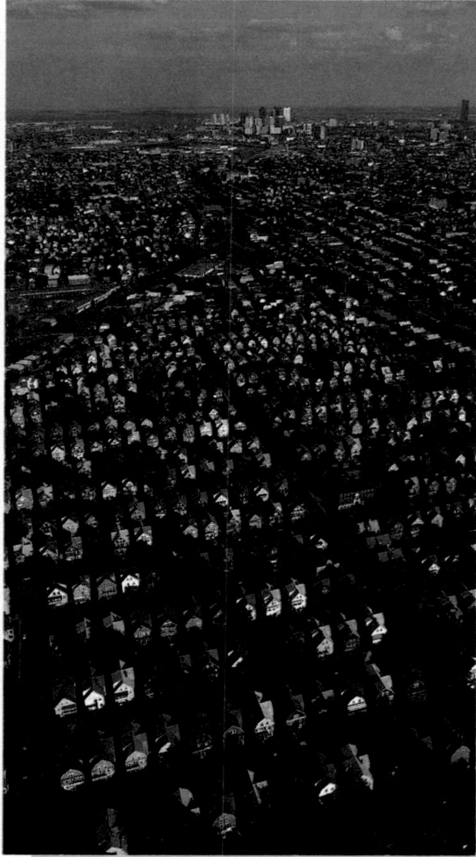

This photograph of Boston, Massachusetts, shows the city and the suburbs that have grown up around it.

Check Your Reading

1. What is an ethnic group?
2. Approximately what fraction of Americans lives in rural areas?
3. From what you have read in this lesson, how would you describe the origins of the people of the United States?
4. **THINKING SKILL:** List at least 10 freedoms Americans enjoy. Then group them by category: economic, political, and religious.

THINKING SKILL: Classifying

Analyzing America's Large Population

Ask students:

- **Where do most of America's 260 million people live?** (in cities and surrounding suburbs)
- **What is a megalopolis?** (a large area containing so many cities and surrounding suburbs that it appears to be one huge city)

Applying the Lesson Have students find their state on the map on page 58 and then read page 59. Have them determine if they live in a rural, suburban, or urban area. Then have students refer to the population-density map on page 43 to test their hypotheses.

CLOSE

Summarizing Students have learned that the movement of freedom-seeking people to the United States has produced a population of great ethnic and racial variety.

Evaluating Use these questions to assess students' understanding.

- **How is the United States a land of variety in terms of its population?** (People from many different parts of the world live here.)
- **What kinds of freedom do immigrants find in this country?** (personal, political, religious, economic)

Answers to Check Your Reading

1. people who share common roots, traditions, customs
2. Approximately one fourth live in rural areas.
3. Native Americans were here for thousands of years before other ethnic groups arrived; Americans today come from many lands.
4. *economic:* own property, make a profit; *political:* election, speech, assembly, petition, press; *religious:* worship, conscience

Independent Practice
Practice Book: page 11

MEETING INDIVIDUAL NEEDS

Reteaching (easy) Have students use an outline map or desk map of the United States to make a map and map key that show the nation's five largest cities and three megalopolises.

Extension (average) Ask students to review the regions of the United States. Have them imagine that they are writing a letter to a friend in a foreign country whose family is thinking about immigrating to the United States. Tell them to choose a region and describe its characteristics and why their friend's family might like to live there.

Enrichment (challenging) Have students work in groups to research the history of Ellis Island and of the immigration and naturalization procedures of the 1890s. Have them role-play the steps an immigrant would have taken to become a citizen in 1890.

SKILLS LESSON
pages 60–61

Lesson Theme Making good decisions involves defining the goal(s) and choosing from a number of alternatives the one that will best achieve the goal(s).

Lesson Objective
- Identify and apply a procedure that leads to making good decisions.

1 PREPARE

Motivate Before students read the introductory paragraph, ask them to recall some choices they made today (which clothes to wear, what to eat for breakfast or pack for lunch). Have students discuss important choices they have had to make recently, such as which courses to take or which clubs to join. Ask students for other words that mean the same as *choosing* and write them on the chalkboard. (*deciding, selecting*) Discuss why some decisions are more difficult to make than others. (too many options, negative outcomes) Then ask a volunteer to read the passage.

Set Purpose Tell students that in this lesson they will learn one way to make good decisions.

2 TEACH

Trying the Skill Have students read about a decision Carlos Martinez has to make and then have them answer the questions that follow the passage. (Answers can be found at the bottom of the next page.) Tell students that if they have trouble answering the questions, they may refer to the *Helping Yourself* section on the next page. This feature appears in all thinking skills lessons.

RESOURCE Reminder
Practice Book: *Immigrating to the United States*, page 12

BUILDING SKILLS
THINKING SKILLS

Decision Making

Every day you make many small decisions, like what to wear and what to eat. Some days you may also make big decisions that affect you and others around you. Decision making means selecting from a number of alternatives, or options, one option that will help you to achieve your goal. In this lesson you will learn one way to make good decisions.

Trying the Skill

In the last lesson you read about people who came from other countries to the United States. Here is a story about someone who is deciding whether or not to return to the country of his origin for his vacation.

Carlos Martinez is a 13-year-old boy who lives in New York City. Carlos and his family moved to New York from Honduras three years ago. The school year is nearly over, and Carlos has to decide how to spend his summer. His parents have told him he has two options. He can either stay at home and help in his father's grocery store or visit his grandparents in Honduras. Carlos enjoys helping in his father's store, but he would like to spend his summer outside the city, which gets very hot during the summer. He misses his grandparents in Honduras but does not want to be so far from his parents and friends.

Carlos's friend Eddy suggests another alternative. Eddy is spending the summer in the country with his family. He invites Carlos to spend one month with him on his family's farm in the country. Carlos thinks he would enjoy living on a farm. He wants to be away from the city but not too far from his family. He wonders, however, what it would be like living with Eddy's family.

1. What is Carlos's goal?
2. Which alternatives is he considering?
3. What do you think Carlos should do?

60

BUILDING CITIZENSHIP

Decision Making in a Democracy Ask students to bring in newspaper articles telling about important issues facing legislators in their town, city, state, or country. The articles can describe social, economic, environmental, political, or cultural issues of any kind. Have students imagine that they are legislators, select one of the issues, and tell how they would go about making a decision.

HELPING YOURSELF

The steps on the left can help you to make better decisions. The examples on the right apply these steps to Carlos's decision.

One Way to Make a Decision	Example
1. Identify and clearly define the goal(s) you wish to achieve.	Carlos's goal is to spend an enjoyable summer away from the city.
2. Identify all possible alternatives (options) by which you can achieve your goal(s).	Carlos can stay home, spend the summer with his grandparents, or visit Eddy on his family's farm in the country.
3. Predict the likely outcomes (consequences), both immediate and long range, of each alternative.	If Carlos stays home, he will spend the summer in the city. If he goes to Honduras, he might miss his family and friends. If Carlos visits Eddy, he will probably enjoy himself in the country.
4. Evaluate each outcome by determining whether it will benefit or harm you or others.	If Carlos does not enjoy the city during the summer, he will probably be unhappy if he stays home. If he goes to Honduras, he will probably miss his family and friends. If he goes to Eddy's farm, he will probably enjoy himself. However, he might miss his parents or have trouble adjusting to another family's way of life.
5. Choose the best alternative.	Which alternative did you choose?

Applying the Skill

Now apply what you have learned about the decision-making process. Read the following story.

Sam had always wanted to have a dog. One day he found a dog on the street. He called the animal shelter and looked in the newspaper for reports of lost dogs. When he could not find the dog's owner, he decided to keep the dog.

Then Sam saw a lost-dog sign with the dog's picture on it. Sam could call the phone number on the sign. But then he would miss his new pet. Or he could keep the dog and try to forget that he saw the sign. But then the owner of the dog would never get his pet back.

1. What was Sam's goal?
   a. to have a dog
   b. to return a lost dog
   c. to get a dog from an animal shelter
2. Which alternative did Sam probably not consider?
   a. returning the dog to its owner
   b. keeping the dog
   c. returning the dog and going to the animal shelter for a new dog
3. What do you think Sam should do? Explain your answer.

Reviewing the Skill

1. What does the term *decision making* mean?
2. What are some important steps to follow when you make a decision?
3. Why should you think of as many options as possible before making a choice?

61

Thinking About Thinking To help students identify the decision-making process that they used, ask them these questions: How did you decide what Carlos should do? What did you do first? Why? What did you do next? Why? List students' answers on the chalkboard.

Helping Yourself Point out that this section outlines one step-by-step decision-making procedure. Discuss how each step is carried out in the example. Call on students to compare the steps on the chalkboard with those listed in this section to identify the most helpful ones.

Applying the Skill Tell students to read the story and answer the questions about Sam. (See answers below.) Suggest that to answer question 3, students should fill in a chart with these headings: "Goal," "Options," "Possible Results." Tell them to evaluate each result as beneficial (+) or harmful (−) and then choose the "best" option for Sam.

3 CLOSE

Reviewing the Skill On the chalkboard next to the list of synonyms for *choosing,* list synonyms for *alternatives (choices, options).* Call on a student to use these words to explain the term *decision making.* Use questions 2 and 3 as a starting point for students to explain in their own words what they could do in the future to make better decisions and to cite situations outside school in which they would use this skill.

Independent Practice
Practice Book: page 12

ANSWERS TO SKILLS QUESTIONS

Applying the Skill

1. a.
2. c
3. Check to see that students have cited reasons for the alternative they selected.

Reviewing the Skill

1. Decision making is choosing from a number of alternatives one that will help you to achieve a goal.
2. Identify and clearly define your goal(s). Identify alternatives by which you can reach your goal(s). Predict and evaluate the likely immediate and long-term outcomes of each alternative. Choose the best alternative.
3. Considering all possible options gives you a broader range of choices.

LESSON 2
pages 62–65

Lesson Theme In the American capitalist system a developed economy exists in which people start businesses and there are many different kinds of high-technology jobs for workers.

Lesson Objectives
- Explain how a free-enterprise system works.
- List American imports and exports.
- Describe a developed economy.

1 PREPARE

Motivate Have a student read the *Read Aloud* to the class. Then poll the class to find out how many students have started their own businesses, such as a lemonade stand or a baby-sitting service. Tell them their efforts have made them part of the free-enterprise system. Explain to students that in this lesson they will read about the free-enterprise system and the American economy.

Set Purpose List on the chalkboard students' answers to the *What You Know* question. Then have students estimate how many people in their community hold each job on the list. Pose the *What You Will Learn* question, and tell students they will read about the things that contribute to the developed economy of the United States.

2 TEACH

Analyzing Free Enterprise Help students examine the essential elements of free enterprise.

Ask students:

- **What does *free enterprise* mean?** (the freedom to own property and run a business largely free from government control)

LESSON 2

The Economy

READ TO LEARN

Key Vocabulary

capitalism	import
free enterprise	developed economy
export	technology

Read Aloud

I took care of three cats for a few days. The cats' owners told other people. Now I've taken care of two dogs, five cats, a bird, and a gerbil. I earned $88. Doing a good job helps people notice you.

This account was written by a 12-year-old student from Gastonia, North Carolina. In this lesson you will learn why the student's pet-care business is a good example of how the economy of the United States works.

Read for Purpose

1. WHAT YOU KNOW: What are some jobs done by people in your community?
2. WHAT YOU WILL LEARN: Why is the economy of the United States known as a developed economy?

FREE ENTERPRISE

The United States has an economic system known as **capitalism**. In a capitalist system businesses are owned by individuals or groups of individuals rather than by the government. An important part of the capitalist system is **free enterprise**, the freedom to own property and run a business largely free of government control.

The pet-care business you read about in the Read Aloud is an example of the free enterprise system in practice. The student, like all Americans, is free to run a business with the goal of making a profit.

American businesspeople are also free to decide what to sell and what prices to charge. Consumers are free to buy whatever they can afford. However, in a free enterprise system, businesspeople must make sure there is a demand for things they want to sell and to price them carefully. If the price is too high, people will not get any business. If the price is too low, people cannot make a profit. By figuring out the right price, the student above can make more than $2,000 a year!

HOW AMERICANS EARN A LIVING

What kinds of jobs do people perform within a free enterprise system? Look at the graph on page 63. It shows the jobs in which most workers in the United States are employed.

WHAT YOU KNOW: Students should be encouraged to think about different jobs in areas such as services, manufacturing, and trade.

READING STRATEGY AND VOCABULARY DEVELOPMENT

Previewing and Questioning Review the previewing strategy with the class. Then plan a group activity in which students will work together to develop purpose-setting questions using the subtitles in Lesson 2: "Free Enterprise," "How Americans Earn a Living," "Foreign Trade," "A Developed Economy," and "Economic Opportunity."

Introduce the activity by developing a general question using the name of Lesson 2, "The Economy." Or you may want to use the *What You Will Learn* question. Suggest to students that their questions should relate to this general question.

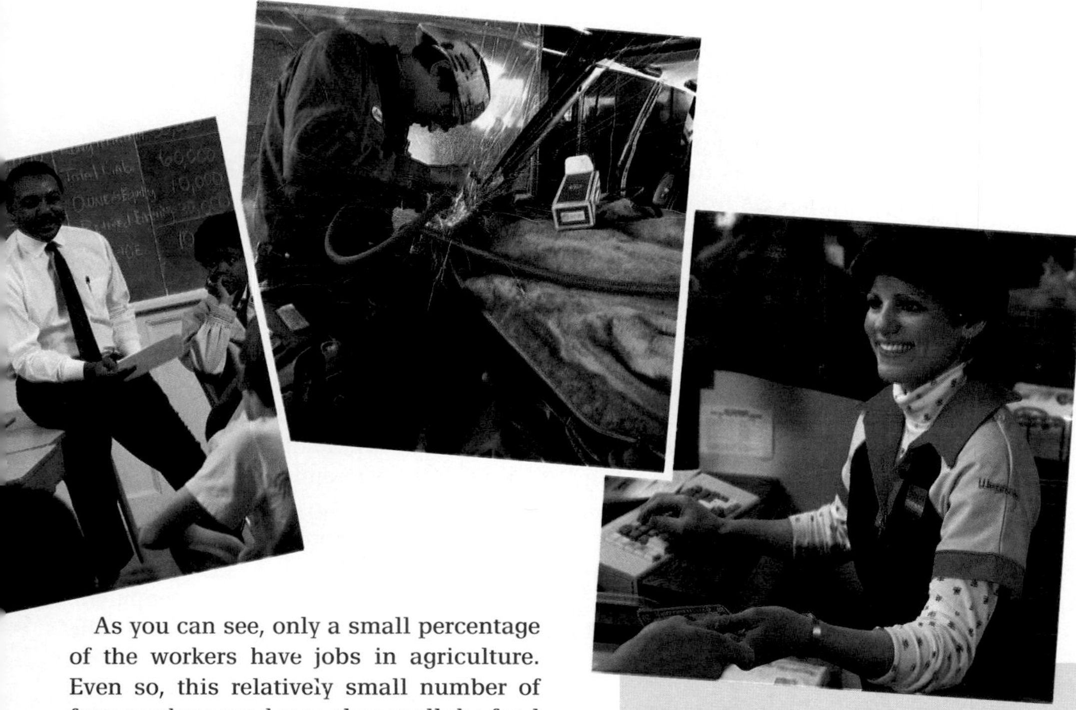

As you can see, only a small percentage of the workers have jobs in agriculture. Even so, this relatively small number of farm workers produces almost all the food the nation needs. Many United States farms are large, and farmers use huge machines to harvest their crops. These crops are sold all over the United States and the world.

The graph also shows that about 20 percent of the nation's workers have jobs in manufacturing and mining. Products that are manufactured include machinery, plastics, and chemicals.

How would you describe the pet-care business you read about on page 62? It is not farming, nor is it the manufacturing of a product. Neither is it trade, which is the business of buying and selling things. It is a type of economic activity called a service. That is, the worker helps people, or serves them, rather than makes or sells a product.

Service workers include government workers, secretaries, teachers, doctors, and lawyers. What other service jobs can you name?

GRAPH SKILL: What are the three largest categories of jobs found in the United States? How are they shown above?

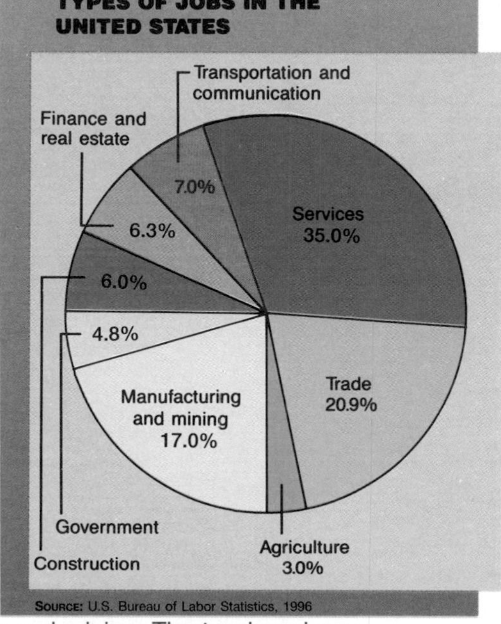

GRAPH SKILL: Services, trade, and manufacturing and mining. The teacher shown at left is a service worker, the welder in the middle works in manufacturing, and the cashier at right works in trade.

63

Analyzing Free Enterprise Continue the discussion from the previous page.

Ask students:

- **What are some things businesspeople have to be aware of when running a business?** (knowing what consumers will buy, pricing a product appropriately, knowing when to recognize a drop in demand)
- **What is the ultimate goal of a businessperson in a free-enterprise system?** (to make a profit)
- *THINKING FURTHER:* **What kinds of controls do you think the government should have in a free-enterprise system?** (Possible answers include: setting standards to ensure the purity of foods and the safety of products; passing laws to prevent one company from controlling a single industry or service.)

Knowing How Americans Earn a Living Students should be aware of the variety of occupations available in our free-enterprise system. Have them read the section starting at the bottom of page 62.

EXTENDING GRAPH SKILLS

Have students study the circle graph on this page.

Ask students:

- **What does the whole circle represent?** (types of jobs in the United States)
- **In which category are most workers employed?** (service jobs)
- **Which area employs the smallest number of workers?** (agriculture)
- *THINKING FURTHER:* **Why are only 3 percent of American workers needed to grow enough food to feed the whole nation?** (because farm machinery helps harvest crops and transportation systems help distribute food products)

CURRICULUM CONNECTION

Language Arts Divide the class into groups and challenge each group to design a new product for the American consumer market. Have each group follow these four steps: (1) brainstorming to decide on a new product; (2) filling out a Production Process sheet to answer the questions: *Which raw materials will be needed to make the product? Which countries will the materials be imported from? What steps will be followed in the factory to process the raw materials into a finished product?* (3) filling out a Marketing Decisions sheet to answer the questions: *What kinds of stores will sell this item? How much will it cost the consumer? What will its name be?* and (4) designing an advertising campaign for the new product, including one poster to be displayed on a bus and a script for one TV commercial.

Understanding Foreign Trade Help students recognize how the United States is tied to the rest of the world by foreign trade.

Ask students:

- **What are some United States exports?** (transportation equipment, machinery, chemicals, food)
- **What are some United States imports?** (petroleum, automobiles, clothing, food)
- *THINKING FURTHER:* **Why do you think the United States imports food when it also exports food?** (Surplus grain is exported; some foods like coffee and bananas are difficult to grow here, so they are imported.)

Analyzing a Developed Economy

Ask students:

- **What are the characteristics of a developed economy?** (Many different economic activities; most jobs are in manufacturing and service industries; workers use advanced technology.)
- **What are some examples of advanced technology?** (computers, automation, robots)
- *THINKING FURTHER:* **How do many factory workers guide machines today?** (by using computers)

EXTENDING MAP SKILLS

Have students study the map on page 65.

Ask students:

- **What symbols are used to represent various forms of advanced technologies?** (*aerospace:* a spaceship; *electronics:* a robot; *scientific equipment:* a microscope; *computers:* a computer; *nuclear research:* an atom)
- *THINKING FURTHER:* **What can you conclude from the location of advanced technology centers in the United States?** (The use of advanced technology has spread throughout the country.)

FOREIGN TRADE

Did you ever notice all the different places from around the world the products you buy come from? People in the United States buy and sell products from foreign nations as well as those from their own country.

The United States is one of the largest traders of goods in the world. People in the United States send many **exports** overseas. An export is any item sold to another nation. The leading exports are transportation equipment, machinery, chemicals, and different kinds of food.

The United States also receives **imports** such as petroleum, automobiles, clothing, food, and other goods. An import is an item bought from another nation.

Look at the chart below. What does it tell you about United States exports and imports since 1965?*

A DEVELOPED ECONOMY

Many people in the United States have a comfortable way of life. The reason for this is that the United States has a **developed economy**. A developed economy is an economy that has many different economic activities, not just one or two. Most of the jobs in a developed economy are in the manufacturing and service industries rather than in agriculture.

Developed economies also make use of advanced **technology**. Technology is the methods, tools, and machinery that are used to meet human needs. Advanced technology, such as robots and computers, offers people new jobs. It also changes the way that many Americans do their work.

Today, for example, many factories are being automated. That means that machines controlled by other machines make

GRAPH SKILL: This chart shows United States imports and exports since 1965. Was the value of United States imports or exports greater in 1985?

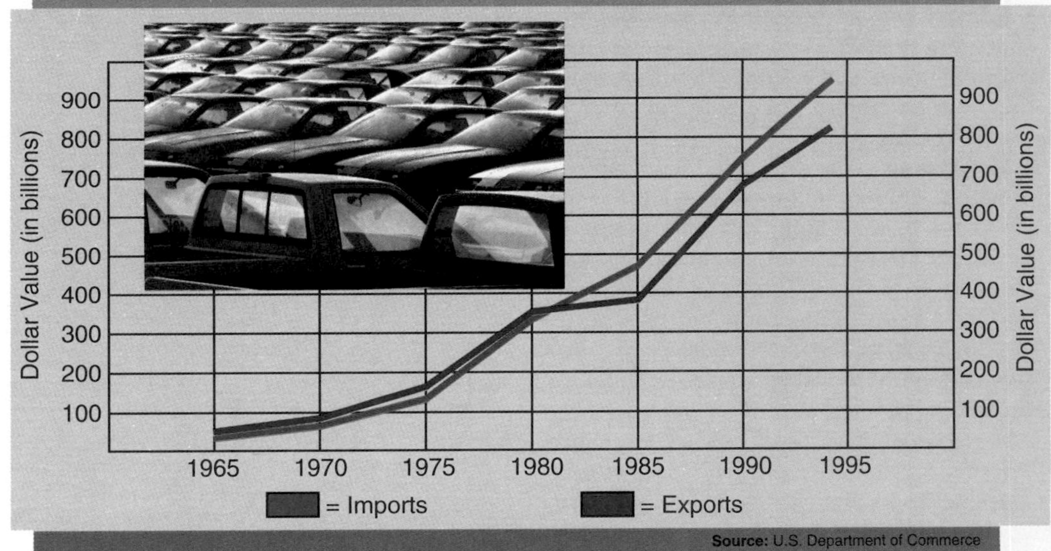

64 GRAPH SKILL: imports

*Both have greatly increased, particularly imports.

BACKGROUND INFORMATION

Foreign Trade and Current Events Students may have questions about trade stories in the newspapers. Extend their understanding of trade balances with this information.

- The difference between net imports and net exports can be a trade surplus or a trade deficit. A trade surplus exists when the value of imports is less than the value of exports. If a nation imports more than it exports, it has a trade deficit.
- In years of surplus grain production in the United States, the government purchases the excess grain to help stabilize grain prices so that American farmers can make a profit. Much grain is sold to foreign countries, such as Russia and China.

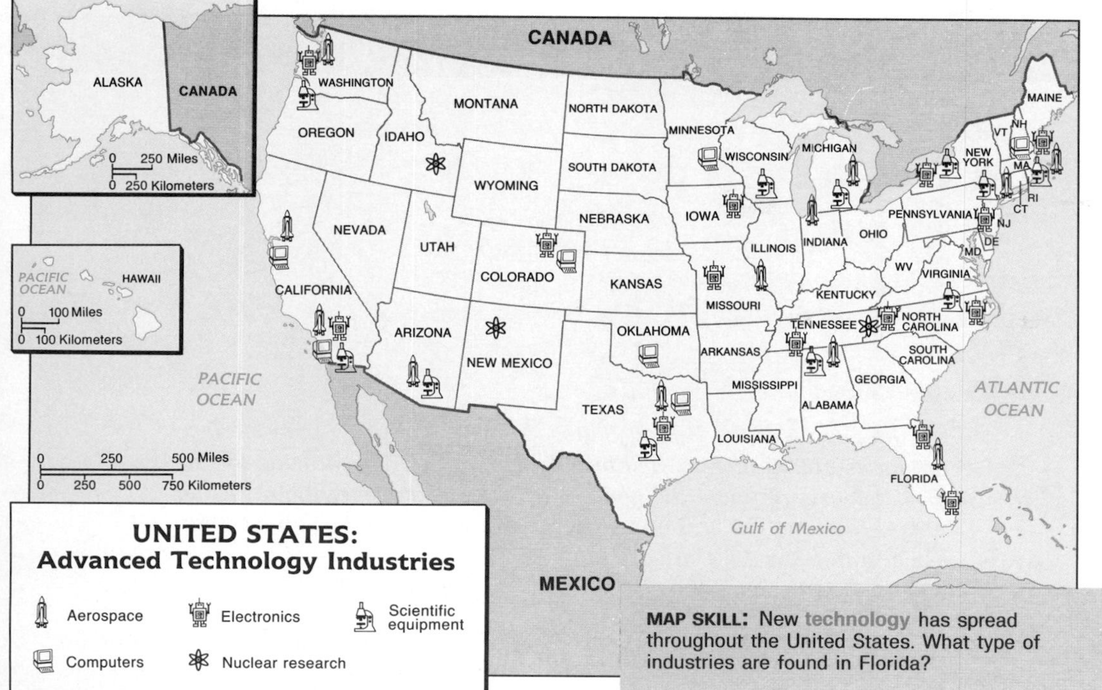

MAP SKILL: New technology has spread throughout the United States. What type of industries are found in Florida?

the products. In the past many automated machines were run from one large control room. Increasingly, though, workers are guiding the machines from computers at their desks. What do workers who must learn to use computers think of the change? According to one factory worker:

> *I used to be afraid I couldn't learn to use a computer. Now, I use one every day and I get more work out also. Our technology keeps changing and we have to change along with it.*

Look at the map above. It shows some of the industries that make use of the latest technology. As the map shows, there are advanced technology industries throughout the United States.

ECONOMIC OPPORTUNITY

People in the United States seek economic opportunity under the system known as free enterprise, or capitalism. Today, as you have read, most workers in the United States are service workers, and fewer work in manufacturing and agriculture. The United States has a developed economy, which means that it involves many different economic activities and makes use of advanced technology.

Check Your Reading

1. Define *technology*. How might you use technology during a normal day?
2. List the characteristics of a developed economy.
3. What are the three main areas of employment in the United States?
4. **THINKING SKILL:** Suppose you wanted to start your own small business. What three questions could you ask to learn how to go about it?

MAP SKILL: aerospace, electronics
THINKING SKILL: Asking Questions

65

Applying the Lesson Have students make a list of some of the foods and pieces of equipment found in their homes. Have them include on their lists the nations in which these things were produced. Which nation leads each list?

CLOSE

Summarizing Students have learned that Americans have used the free-enterprise system to build a developed economy based on trade with many other nations.

Evaluating Use these questions to assess students' understanding.

- **Under a free enterprise system who or what has most of the control of the nation's businesses?** (individuals or groups of individuals)
- **What is an export?** (any item sold to another nation)
- **What does the word *technology* mean?** (the methods, tools, and machinery that are used to meet human needs)

Answers to Check Your Reading

1. the methods, tools, and machinery used to meet human needs; computers at school or home; microwave ovens
2. It is based on more than one or two economic activities; most jobs are in service industries; advanced technology is used by workers.
3. services, trade, manufacturing, mining
4. Where is there a need for my service or product? How should I advertise the service or product? How much are people willing to pay for my service or product?

Independent Practice
Practice Book: page 13

MEETING INDIVIDUAL NEEDS

Reteaching (easy) Have students make illustrated flashcards containing definitions and pictures of the *Key Vocabulary* words. Have students use the cards to quiz one another in a team competition.

Extension (average) Ask students what kinds of jobs they would like to have in the American economy. Have them write a paragraph in which they give the reasons for their choices.

Enrichment (challenging) Divide the class into seven groups. Each group will represent one of these countries: the United States, Japan, Nigeria, Germany, China, Egypt, and Hungary. Have each group research their country's current trade situation. Then have students present their findings in a group report or chart display in which their country's trade surplus or trade deficit is explained.

LESSON 3

pages 66–69

Lesson Theme The Constitution of the United States created a representative democracy in which power is divided among different branches of government and in which citizens have certain rights and responsibilities.

Lesson Objectives
- Explain the system of checks and balances in the United States government.
- Describe how the federal system is organized.
- Identify the duties of an American citizen.

PREPARE

Motivate Read aloud the Preamble and define words and phrases such as *union, domestic tranquility,* and *posterity.* Remind students that the Preamble states the goals of the American people in forming a government.

Set Purpose Read aloud the *What You Will Learn* question and tell students that they will find the answer to this question as they read the lesson.

TEACH

Understanding a Republic and the Role of Its Citizens Discuss why a large population would make a direct democracy difficult to achieve.

Ask students:

- **What is a democracy?** (a system of government in which citizens make the decisions)

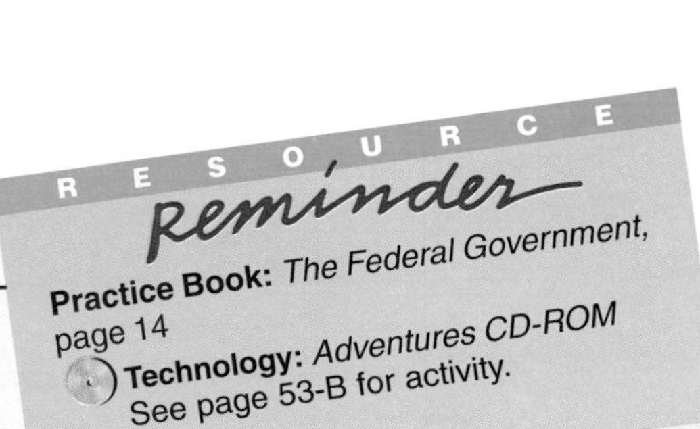

Practice Book: *The Federal Government,* page 14

Technology: *Adventures CD-ROM* See page 53-B for activity.

LESSON 3

The Government

READ TO LEARN

Key Vocabulary

democracy
republic
checks and balances
federal system
executive branch
legislative branch
judicial branch

Read Aloud

We the people of the United States, in order to form a more perfect union, establish justice, insure domestic tranquility, provide for the common defense, promote the general welfare, and secure the blessings of liberty to ourselves and our posterity, do ordain and establish this Constitution for the United States of America.

These words form the Preamble, or introduction, to the Constitution of the United States. For more than 200 years the Constitution has served as the plan for the nation's government.

Read for Purpose

1. **WHAT YOU KNOW:** Which do you think is the most important of the ideas in the Preamble?
2. **WHAT YOU WILL LEARN:** How do the people of the United States govern themselves?

A REPUBLIC

The government of the United States is a form of **democracy**. A democracy is a government in which decisions are made by citizens. However, the United States has too many people to allow everyone to have a direct say in government. So the writers of the Constitution made the United States a representative democracy, or a **republic**. In a republic voters elect officials to represent them in government.

When the Constitution was being written in 1787, Americans did not know what kind of government they would have. Right after the Constitution was written, one of its writers, Benjamin Franklin, was asked, "What kind of government have you given us?" He answered, "A republic, madam, if you can keep it."

THE RESPONSIBILITIES OF CITIZENS

How have Americans kept their republic? One way has been through participation in government. It is the responsibility of every United States citizen 18 years and over to vote for their government representatives. You may be too young now to vote in elections for government leaders. But

WHAT YOU KNOW: Students may need some help in interpreting the various ideas of the Preamble.

READING STRATEGY AND VOCABULARY DEVELOPMENT

Previewing and Questions Review the Reading Strategies from the previous lessons of this chapter. Suggest to students that the *Key Vocabulary* in Lesson 3 also can be used to generate purpose-setting questions. Brainstorm some questions using this vocabulary. Some questions might be: *What is a democracy? What is the purpose of checks and balances?* Then have students skim the lesson to see if they can find sentences that define or explain the *Key Vocabulary* words.

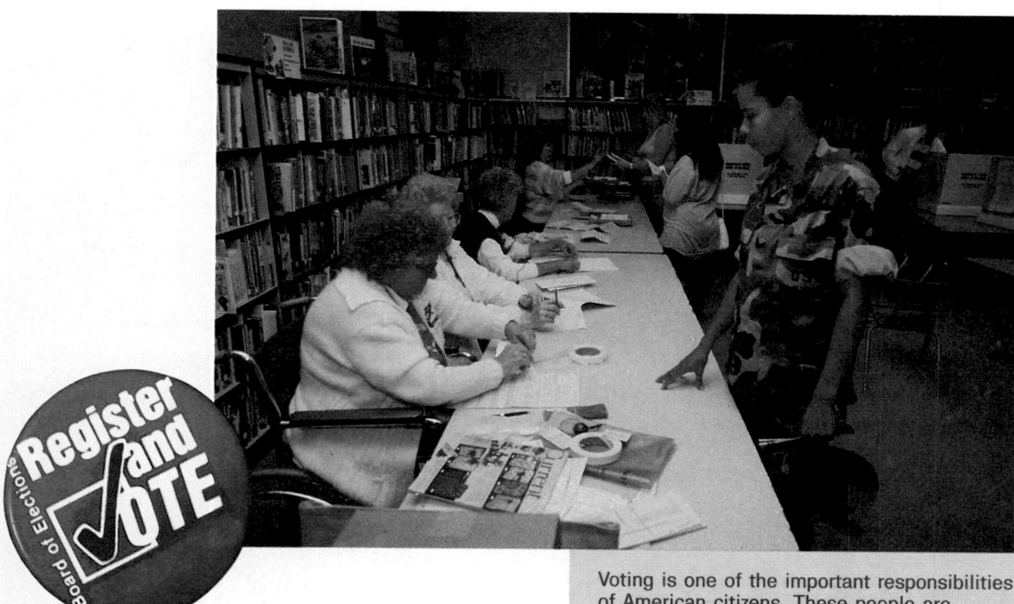

Voting is one of the important responsibilities of American citizens. These people are registering to vote.

every time you vote for a class leader, you are practicing to become a responsible citizen.

Citizens of the United States have many other responsibilities, including obeying the laws and helping to solve problems in their own communities.

LIMITED POWER

The writers of the Constitution had lived under a powerful British king. Not surprisingly, after the United States gained its independence, its citizens wanted to make sure their new government did not become too powerful. One way to ensure this was to divide the powers of government.

A look at the organization of the United States government shows how this is done in our country. The national government is divided into three branches, or parts. The division of the government into three branches ensures that no one branch will hold too much power. The system by which each branch limits the power of the others is known as the system of **checks and balances**

Checks and balances are built into our system of government. Voters in the United States elect a President, a Vice President, and members of Congress. The President names judges to the Supreme Court but must gain congressional approval. Congress can propose that a bill become law. However, the President has the power to veto, or refuse to sign, the bill. If the President does not sign the bill, it usually does not become a law.

The Constitution also divides power between the national government and local governments. This division of power is called a **federal system**. The national government is sometimes called the federal government. It is responsible for tasks that concern the entire nation. Running the armed forces is one example. What are some other federal tasks?*

*Some other examples are: running the treasury, regulating trade with foreign countries, operating the national parks.

Discussing a Republic and the Role of Its Citizens Continue the discussion from the previous page.

Ask students:

- **What kind of democracy is the United States?** (a representative democracy)
- **What have Americans done to keep their republic?** (They have participated in government through voting; they have supported and obeyed laws; they have solved problems in their communities.)

Understanding How Power Is Limited Have students read the section on this page to understand the system of checks and balances.

Ask students:

- **How many branches are there in our national government?** (three)
- **Why did the writers of the Constitution divide the government into three branches?** (They wanted to ensure that no one person or group had too much power.)
- **How do the different branches keep one another from gaining too much power?** (by a system of checks and balances)
- **In what other way is governmental power divided in the United States? What is this system called?** (among the national government and local governments; a federal system)
- *THINKING FURTHER:* **How is the power of the President checked by Congress?** (One example is the right of the Senate to approve presidential choices for the Supreme Court.)

BACKGROUND INFORMATION

The Rule of Law vs. the Rule of Man Among the great achievements of the Constitution of the United States was that historically it helped to shift power from the rule of the man to the rule of law and that it guaranteed citizens' rights and defined their responsibilities.

- The rule of man gives the power to govern to one person or to a small group that can make rules as they please. They often govern by force.
- In the Middle Ages, European monarchs ruled in the belief that their power came from God. This philosophy came to be known as the divine right of kings.
- Under the rule of law, the people make the laws. No person is above the law.

EXTENDING DIAGRAM SKILLS

Examine the diagram on this page and discuss the function of each branch of government.

Ask students:

- **What are the names of the three branches of government?** (executive, legislative, judicial)
- **What are the tasks of each branch?** (The legislative branch makes laws; the judicial branch judges the laws to make sure they are constitutional; the executive branch carries out the laws, creates programs, makes treaties, and heads the armed forces.)
- *THINKING FURTHER:* **How is the legislative branch divided?** (It is divided into two houses: the House of Representatives and the Senate.)

Discussing State and Local Government Ask students to read the section at the bottom of page 68.

Ask students:

- **At what other levels are decisions made in our government?** (at state and local levels)
- **What kinds of decisions are made by state governments?** (Possible answers include: how much money to spend on education, what kinds of mass transportation are needed.)
- **How is local government organized?** (Usually a council makes the laws and a mayor or manager carries them out.)

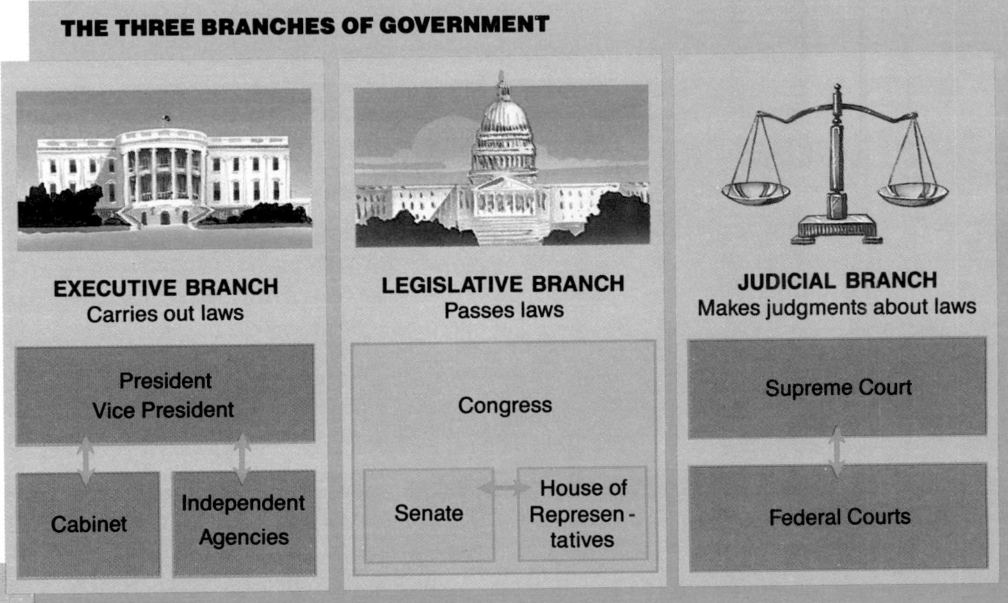

CHART SKILL: What are the three important parts of the executive branch?

THE NATIONAL GOVERNMENT

Look at the chart above. What are the names of the three branches of the national government? One branch is the **executive branch**, which is responsible for carrying out the laws of the United States. The President is head of the executive branch. Among the many duties of the President are creating programs to improve the welfare of the nation, heading the armed forces, and making treaties.

The executive branch includes the Cabinet, which consists of the heads of several federal departments to help the President. One Cabinet member heads the Department of the Treasury. It prints money, collects federal taxes, and pays federal bills.

The second branch of government, the **legislative branch**, is called Congress. Congress makes laws for the nation and decides how much money the government can spend. Congress is made up of two houses, the House of Representatives and the Senate. Each of the 50 states of the United States sends a number of representatives to the House, depending upon the size of the state's population. The Senate has 100 senators, 2 from each state.

The **judicial branch** is the third branch of government. The judicial branch interprets the nation's laws. That is, it makes sure that the laws are faithful to the law of the land as set down in the Constitution. This branch is headed by the Supreme Court, which has nine judges.

STATE AND LOCAL GOVERNMENTS

The national government does not make all the decisions in the United States. Some decisions, such as those concerning the enforcement of local laws, neighborhood schools, or garbage collection, are made by state and local governments.

68 CHART SKILL: the President and Vice President, the Cabinet, and independent agencies

CURRICULUM CONNECTION

Drama To help students understand the Preamble phrase "to promote the General Welfare," present the play *Plain Jane* by Marc Kornblatt. The play can be acted out by the class. Class discussion after the play should focus on the motives for and effects of Jane Addams's project. Questions to pose after the play include:

- *Why did she start this project?* (to promote the general welfare; because of her empathy for the poor, her sense of Christian charity, and her belief in the value of work)
- *What did Addams achieve by starting Hull House?* (To answer this, have the class gather more facts about Addams's work.)

MEETING INDIVIDUAL NEEDS

Reteaching (easy) Have students work in groups to discuss and list all the responsibilities of a good citizen. Ask each group to draw a mural depicting citizens carrying out each duty.

Extension (average) Have students research the lawmaking process. Ask them to draw flowcharts showing "How a Bill Becomes a Law."

Enrichment (challenging) Ask students to think about freedom of speech as guaranteed in the Bill of Rights of the United States Constitution. Have students write an essay discussing the famous quote, "I disagree with what you say, but I will defend to the death your right to say it."

The people of each of the 50 states elect their state governments. Each state has an executive branch (headed by a governor), a judicial branch, and a legislative branch. Among the many decisions made by state governments are how much money to spend on public education or what kind of mass transportation is needed.

Citizens of cities and towns elect a council of people to make local laws. Usually the citizens also elect or appoint a mayor or city manager to lead the city. This official chooses others to help govern the city.

State and local governments make many decisions every day. Who are some of your state and local representatives? What are some of the major issues that are important in your community?

A GOVERNMENT OF THE PEOPLE

The plan of government of the United States, called the Constitution, created a representative democracy. It also created a federal system in which power is divided between the national and local governments. In the national and state governments, power is divided among three branches of government. This division into the executive, legislative, and judicial branches is called the system of checks and balances. It ensures that no one branch becomes too powerful.

Check Your Reading

1. What is a republic?
2. Name the three branches of the United States federal government.
3. What are the three levels of government that operate in the United States?
4. **THINKING SKILL:** Look at the chart on page 68. What are two things it shows about the way the United States government is organized?

THINKING SKILL: Observing

CITIZENSHIP MAKING A DIFFERENCE

PHOTOGRAPHS of the HOMELESS

While Matthew Rothman was a college student in Providence, Rhode Island, he became interested in photography. Matthew started taking photographs of homeless people on the streets of Providence. Matthew soon met and became friendly with many of the people who lived on the streets. He photographed the shelters where homeless people slept and the soup kitchens where they ate.

Matthew wanted to help other people become aware of the problem of homelessness. One of his professors told him about a bill that had been proposed in the Rhode Island legislature. If the bill were to pass, the state government would provide $1 million for services to the homeless.

Next Matthew met with the sponsors of the bill. He arranged to exhibit his photographs in the Rhode Island Senate building, where the state senators would see them. The legislators remarked on the effect the photographs had on them.

With Matthew's help the bill was passed into law. Matthew had used his talents—his skill with a camera and his sense of caring—to make a difference in the lives of others.

69

Applying the Lesson Have students gather news articles about the actions of the federal, state, and local government. Then have them prepare a bulletin board to display the most important news articles.

3 CLOSE

Summarizing Students have read that the United States government is based on a constitution that provides for a federal system of government, a system of checks and balances at the national level, and the participation of citizens in the governmental process.

Evaluating Use these questions to assess students' understanding.

- **How is the power of the national government limited?** (by the division of the government into three parts and by the system of checks and balances)
- **What is the role of our federal government?** (to take care of tasks which concern the entire nation such as running the armed forces, running the treasury, regulating foreign trade, operating the post office)
- **How is the structure of state governments like that of the federal government?** (each state has executive, legislative, and judicial branches)

Answers to Check Your Reading

1. a form of government in which voters elect officials to represent them
2. *executive*—President; *legislative*—Congress; *judicial*—Supreme Court
3. *federal level*—executive, legislative, and judicial branches; *state level*—executive, legislative, and judicial branches; *local level*—council; mayor or manager
4. three branches; each with different duties.

Independent Practice
Practice Book: page 14

BUILDING CITIZENSHIP

Making a Difference Have students read the feature about Matthew Rothman. Discuss why Matthew's action (putting photographs of homeless people where Rhode Island senators could see them) showed good citizenship. Help students to understand how Matthew used ingenuity to attain his goal. Ask students to list the usual ways people influence legislators (such as writing petitions and holding demonstrations). Have students study a problem in their own neighborhoods and then write proposals for solving it.

LESSON 4
pages 70–73

Lesson Theme Americans enjoy freedom of expression in the arts and in many forms of recreation.

Lesson Objectives
- Describe how freedom of expression affects the arts.
- Identify the ways in which Americans pursue happiness in their recreational activities.
- Tell why many Americans make physical fitness a goal.

PREPARE

Motivate Have a student read the *Read Aloud* to the class. Discuss the kinds of freedom referred to either directly or indirectly in the passage. Ask students if any of them have ever skied. Did they have similar feelings of freedom?

Set Purpose Use students' responses to the *What You Know* question to begin a master list titled: "The Ways in Which People Relax." Post the list in the classroom and add to it throughout the school year. Read the *What You Will Learn* question and tell students that in this lesson they will read more about the ways in which Americans express themselves and have fun.

TEACH

Looking at the Arts in the United States Help students appreciate the wide range of arts practiced in the United States and the advantage of being an artist in a free society.

Ask students:

- **What are some types of artists found in the United States?** (dancers, painters, writers, poets, musicians, singers, sculptors)

Practice Book: *Freedom and the Arts,* page 15

LESSON 4

Arts and Recreation

READ TO LEARN

Key Vocabulary

freedom of expression

Read Aloud

I was around 10 years old the first time I went skiing. . . . I pointed the skis straight down and somehow still had control. Snow flew everywhere. I loved the feeling of going so fast without being in some kind of vehicle.

These words were written by Shane Gregory, a young man who is training to be a professional dancer. Like other Americans Shane works hard. But he also enjoys relaxing in his spare time, and skiing is one of the things he does to relax. Through sports like skiing and other kinds of recreational activities, Americans make the most of their leisure time.

Read for Purpose

1. **WHAT YOU KNOW:** What do you do to relax in your spare time?
2. **WHAT YOU WILL LEARN:** What are the major arts, leisure activities, and sports of the United States?

THE ARTS IN THE UNITED STATES

The United States is proud of its arts, which are known throughout the world. Dancers, painters, writers, musicians, and other artists from many nations come to the United States to study and work.

What makes the arts of the United States so well known? There are many reasons. But one of the most important reasons is that all artists in the United States have freedom of expression. As you have read, freedom is an important American value.

Freedom of expression means that artists in the United States are free to describe all aspects of American life. Given this freedom, American artists often use their art to help people to understand important facts about their nation. The United States shows a willingness to look at its sorrows and problems as well as its successes and strengths. Knowing about their country's weaknesses can help the people of a nation to improve them.

Freedom of expression has been important to many different artists in the United States. Look at the song on the next page. What do you think its composer, Woody Guthrie, was trying to say about the United States? ✻

Artists in other fields also use their freedom of expression to communicate their ideas. The Alvin Ailey American Dance Theater, for example, is known for works that often explore African American themes set to folk music or jazz. The company and its dancers are highly regarded

WHAT YOU KNOW: Students should compare their different interests.

✻ Students should be encouraged to think about the meaning of lines like "This land was made for you and me."

READING STRATEGY AND VOCABULARY DEVELOPMENT

Previewing and Questioning Review the previewing strategies from the previous lessons. Indicate that most textbook lessons start with an introduction that states the purpose of the lesson and end with a summary section. Have students silently read the *Read Aloud* section on this page and the final section called "The Pursuit of Happiness" on page 73.

Discussing the Arts in the United States Continue the discussion from the previous page.

Ask students:

- **For American artists, what does *freedom of expression mean?*** (They are free to express all aspects of their lives.)
- **Why is this freedom valuable to the nation?** (The arts show both the good and the bad in American life, thus allowing us to evaluate and improve things.)
- *THINKING FURTHER:* **What kinds of artistic institutions help people in your community participate in the arts?** (Students might mention rock, rap, and jazz bands; orchestras; theater groups; dance companies; museums; craft centers; and community centers.)

Discussing the Song Have students read the song's lyrics. If possible, have a student who knows the song teach the others to sing it or teach them yourself. Stress to students that this song is a song about freedom.

Ask students:

- **What do you think Woody Guthrie meant by the line "This land was made for you and me"?** (One answer might be that all the people in the United States are represented by the government.)
- **Why do you think Woody Guthrie talks so much about travel in this song?** (One answer might be that thinking of travel helps us see that all the different parts of America belong to Americans.)
- *THINKING FURTHER:* **Who do you think needs to hear this song?** (people who discriminate unfairly against groups of other people)

FUNDAMENTAL THEMES OF GEOGRAPHY

Description of Place To understand a place we learn about its physical characteristics, such as landforms, water bodies, climate, and resources, and about its human characteristics, such as population patterns, economy, and language. This lesson discusses the human characteristics of art and recreation in relation to the United States. Introduce the theme "description of place" by asking students:

- *What type of art is characteristic of the Southwest?* (Navajo rugs and jewelry, for example)
- *The Kentucky Derby is a famous American recreational event of what place?* (Louisville, Kentucky)

Ask students to give other descriptions of art and of recreation that characterize places in the United States.

Defining What Americans Do for Fun Tell students that Americans have a good deal of free time as a result of their technologically developed economy.

Ask students:

- **How do many Americans spend their free time?** (reading, watching television and movies, participating in or watching sports events, enjoying hobbies)
- **How do you spend your free time?** (Students may respond by naming reading, sports, hobbies, club activities, and so on.)

Discussing American Sports Have students examine the variety of sports in the United States.

Ask students:

- **Which sports were invented in the United States?** (baseball, basketball, football)
- **What are some of the sports Americans watch on television?** (baseball, basketball, football, ice hockey, golf, bowling, tennis, and so on)
- **What are the Olympic games and who takes part in them?** (an international sporting event held every four years in a different country; athletes)
- **What is a fitness sport?** (one that builds good health)
- **What are some fitness sports that are popular in the United States?** (weightlifting, hiking, bicycling)
- *THINKING FURTHER:* **In what ways do Americans use the environment to lead a healthy life?** (Americans use the environment in healthful recreational activities, such as swimming, walking, and jogging.)

Applying the Lesson Have students make a list of their favorite leisure-time activities for each season of the year. Ask them to tell what they have learned from each activity.

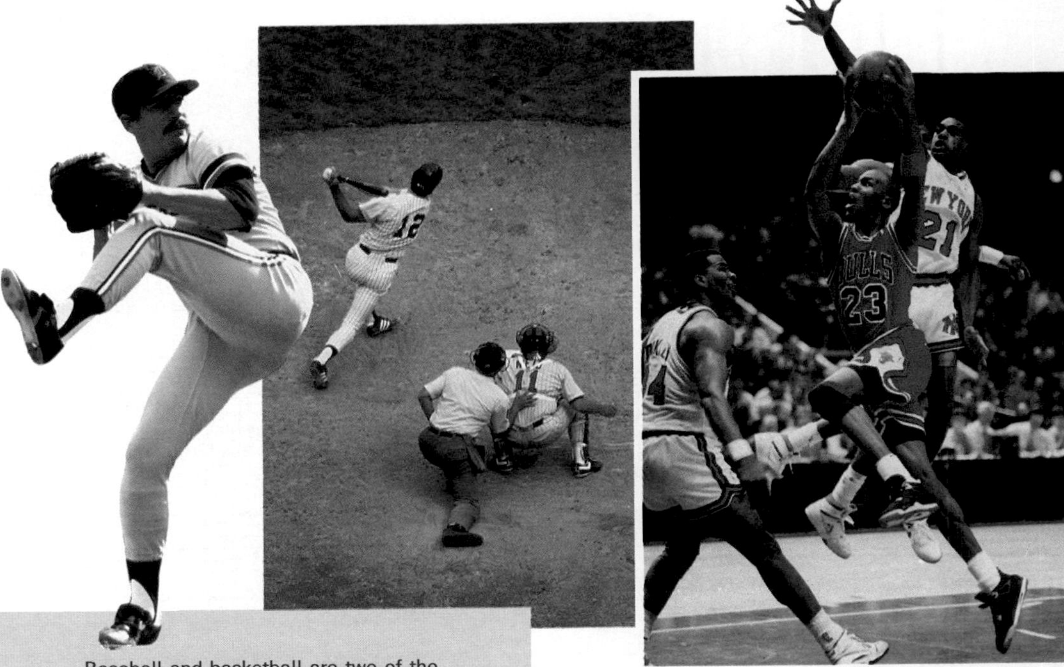

Baseball and basketball are two of the popular spectator sports enjoyed by people in the United States.

all over the world in the field of dance. Like so many other artists, they explore what it means to be an American.

WHAT PEOPLE DO FOR FUN

Many people in the United States have hours of free time after work or school every day. People use this time to enjoy many different hobbies and pastimes. The hobbies are as different as doll collecting, model building, quilting, stamp collecting, and photography.

In the United States, people are fond of reading, going to movies, and watching special events, such as rodeos and circuses. The skills seen in a rodeo include steer wrestling, lassoing, and horse taming. These were the same skills needed by the cowhands of the West during the 1800s. Circuses have been popular for hundreds of years. Clowns, acrobats, and trained animals are some of the many kinds of performers that work in circuses.

SPORTS IN THE UNITED STATES

Do you have a favorite sport? Many of the sports popular in the United States were invented by North Americans. Baseball, football, and basketball are three examples. Baseball, often referred to as "the national pastime," is based on an earlier English game called rounders. Football also developed from an English sport, rugby. Basketball may have been invented by a Canadian living in Massachusetts.

People follow both professional and amateur sports, many of which they watch on television. Besides baseball, football, and basketball, professional sports include ice hockey, golf, bowling, and tennis. Do you play on any teams? Many schools and other organizations support amateur athletics.

72

CURRICULUM CONNECTION

Math To avoid heart attacks and live a long, healthy life, Americans have been told that they should regularly, over the course of a lifetime, burn up 2,000 calories a week in physical activity. Everything counts—walking to school or work, mowing the lawn, and so on. Have students calculate some weekly totals, using these figures for the calories expended in one hour of activity.

Physical Activity	Calories	Physical Activity	Calories
Walking (3 mph)	230	Walking (briskly, 4 mph)	350
Cycling (leisurely)	270	Bicycle racing	680
Swimming (slow crawl)	480	Swimming (fast crawl)	630
Running (4 mph)	550	Running (6 mph)	1,030

People love to enjoy the outdoors in the national, state, and local parks of the United States.

Many of the best amateur athletes train hard for the Summer and Winter Olympics. The Olympics are held in a different country every four years. Athletes also take part in special contests, such as the Iditarod, which you will read about on pages 74–77.

Most people know that a good diet and exercise are important for a long and happy life. As a result, fitness sports such as weightlifting, bicycling, jogging, hiking, and swimming are very popular.

People in the United States also like to explore the outdoors. Throughout the country, large areas of land have been set aside as national, state, and local parks. Many families visit the nation's parks each summer to hike, picnic, camp, and enjoy the natural beauty of their country.

"THE PURSUIT OF HAPPINESS"

The Declaration of Independence says that one of the "inalienable rights" all citizens have is the right to the "pursuit of happiness." As you have read, the people of the United States pursue happiness in many different ways.

The arts are one important way. Freedom of expression guarantees that many different art forms flourish in the United States.

People in the United States also watch and participate in many different sports. Freedom of choice and expression makes for a rich and varied artistic and recreational life in the United States.

Check Your Reading

1. Name three recreational activities enjoyed in the United States.
2. Name three different kinds of physical activities that Americans take part in.
3. Why is freedom of expression important to different artists in the United States?
4. **THINKING SKILL:** Sort the activities mentioned in this lesson into at least three groups.

THINKING SKILL: Classifying

3 CLOSE

Summarizing Students have read that Americans are free to express themselves through the arts and that Americans relax through participation in a wide variety of recreational activities and sports.

Evaluating Use these questions to assess students' understanding.

- **What role do the arts play in American life?** (They allow individuals to freely express their views of life and of the environment. The arts also enrich the lives of Americans.)
- **How do Americans try to stay fit?** (by participation in various fitness sports)
- **In what ways have Americans shown their inventiveness through sports?** (They have invented new games like baseball and football, and have perfected techniques and equipment.)

Answers to Check Your Reading

1. Answers will vary, but responses will probably focus on participation sports, hobbies, camping and hiking, singing, and so on.
2. swimming, bicycling, jogging, hiking, exercise, weightlifting.
3. because the arts and other forms of recreation give Americans opportunities to exercise their freedom to express themselves
4. hobbies, the arts, sports

Independent Practice
Practice Book: page 15

MEETING INDIVIDUAL NEEDS

Reteaching (easy) Ask students to think about their favorite recreational activity. Then have them each write a paragraph about all the ways that recreation fosters intellectual and physical expression.

Extension (average) Have students interview their parents or an older friend or relative to discover which arts, forms of recreation, games, and sports were current in their youth. Have students focus on those activities that are not practiced today. Then have them write a comparative essay titled "How Fun Changes Through the Years."

Enrichment (challenging) Have students work in groups to research and prepare a television script titled "Can We Keep On Breaking Sports Records?" Each group should focus on the role of sports medicine and sports technology in helping athletes to break records in their chosen sport. Have a member from each group read its script to the class.

LEGACY
pages 74–77

Lesson Theme The Iditarod is a special sporting event that helps to keep traditional skills and customs alive.

Lesson Objectives

- Identify the Inuit roots of the Iditarod Trail Sled Dog Race.
- Explain why the Iditarod is a unique race that requires endurance as well as courage.
- Describe the experiences of one Iditarod racer, Susan Butcher.

1 PREPARE

Motivate Ask students to name a few of the most rigorous sporting events in the United States today. (Examples might include: marathoning, high-diving.) Then have them discuss why people enjoy taking part in such challenging sports.

Set Purpose Focus students' attention with the following question. What are some sporting events that make use of traditional skills and equipment? (Encourage students to describe any traditional sports they may have seen, such as running, javelin or discus throwing, or horse racing.) Direct students to read the introductory section. Ask them to think about the concluding suggestion as they read the lesson.

2 TEACH

Understanding the Concept of Legacies Have students discuss the definition of a legacy. Then ask students why they think the Iditarod is held today. (Possible answers include: People enjoy using a means of transport—the dogsled—that has existed for thousands of years.)

Discussing the Location of the Iditarod Have students look at the Outline Maps of the Western Hemisphere and Northern Hemisphere. Have them find Alaska.

RESOURCE *Reminder*

Outline Maps: *Western Hemisphere, Northern Hemisphere*

IDITAROD

by Eric Kimmel

In the last lesson, you read about some of the most popular sports in the United States. These activities help people to have fun and stay in shape at the same time. Some sports are also legacies. Legacies keep older customs alive. One such sporting event is the Iditarod (ī dit' ər äd), a famous race in Alaska. As you read, think about how an event like the Iditarod adapts and continues an Inuit legacy.

A JOURNEY THROUGH HISTORY

How would you travel in a land that lacked roads, bridges, or highways? Where the ground is covered with deep snow or thick ice for most of the year? The Inuit of Alaska long ago found a solution to this problem—the dogsled. They discovered that a team of 3 to 20 Alaskan huskies could haul a sled smoothly over the ice. The sled itself was made of light wood, with walrus-skin or ivory runners. Scientists have discovered traces of ivory sled runners dating back almost 2,000 years!

More recently, people have found other ways to travel during Alaska's winters, including planes and helicopters. Roads now connect most communities. Snowmobiles can go where cars can't. But meanwhile, the Iditarod Trail Sled Dog Race has become an Alaskan tradition.

The original Iditarod Trail was blazed by thousands of people during the early 1900s. Most of these people were searching for gold, which had been discovered in Alaska in the late 1800s. Many traveled to the gold rush town of Iditarod, which gave the trail its name.

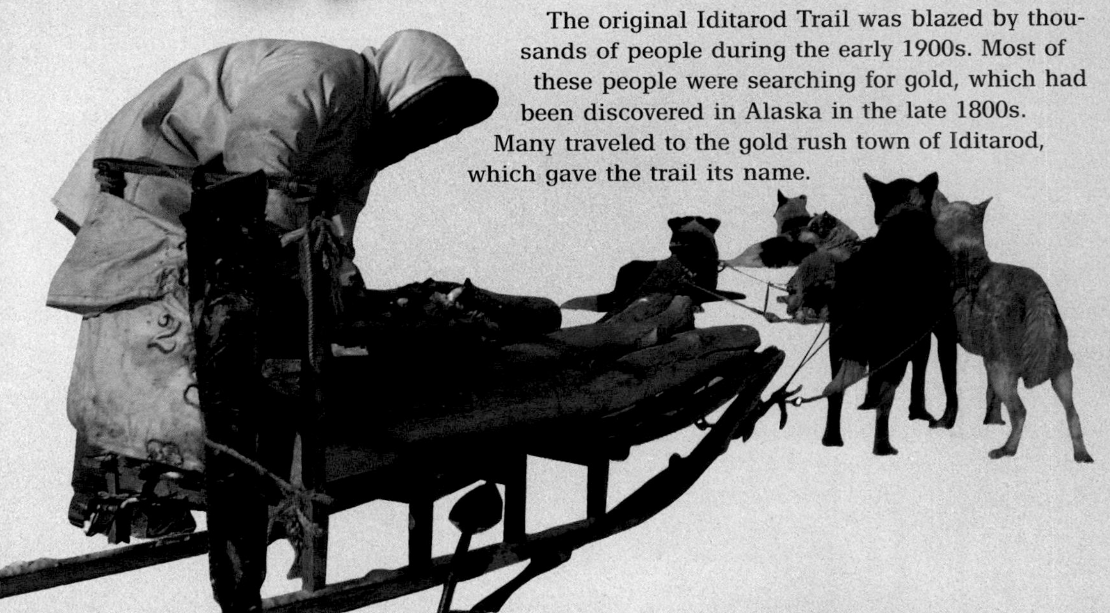

READING STRATEGY AND VOCABULARY DEVELOPMENT

Previewing and Questioning Review the previewing strategies presented in the previous lessons. Then plan a group activity in which students will work together to develop purpose-setting questions, using the following subtitles in the lesson: "A Journey Through History," "A Unique Race," "A Test of Endurance," "A Champion Dogsledder," and "The Real Champions."

Introduce the activity by developing a general question, using the title of the lesson, "Iditarod." Or you may want to use the question that concludes the lesson. Suggest to students that their questions should relate to this general question.

The trail became famous for another reason in 1925, when an illness called diphtheria (dif thîr′ ē ə) struck the town of Nome. A serum, or medicine, existed to fight this deadly illness. But how could the isolated community get the serum in time? A relay of dogsled teams rushed the precious medicine over hundreds of miles, saving many lives. In fact, several of the original "serum runners" were honored at Iditarod races during the 1970s.

In a sense, then, the Iditarod racers of today journey not only through Alaska's landscape, but through its history. "We travel through the country," says Jon Van Zyle, who has raced the Iditarod several times. "We're part of the past, and it's very much part of the race."

IDITAROD

Iditarod Sled Race

Original Iditarod Trail

A UNIQUE RACE

No other race of any kind matches the Iditarod as a test of skill and endurance. The race begins in Anchorage on the first weekend of every March. As you can see from the map on this page, the trail takes the racers over many different kinds of terrain. They cross icy tundra, frozen rivers, towering mountain ranges, dense forests, and a windswept seacoast. The dogsled teams fight their way through areas with names like Rainy Pass and Hell's Gate. After covering 1,049 miles (1,688 km), they finally reach Nome about 2 weeks later!

The man or woman driving the dog team is called a "musher"—a term that comes from *marcher* (mär shā′), a French word meaning "to march." In fact, the musher often cries out "Mush! Mush!" to urge the dogs on.

Each musher begins the race with between 7 and 20 huskies. The specific makeup of the team is important, since dogs cannot be added or switched once the race starts. If a dog weakens or becomes ill, however, it can be dropped off at checkpoints along the way.

75

Understanding the Background of the Iditarod Continue the discussion.

Ask students:

- **Why did the Inuit first use dogsleds as a means of transportation?** (Dogsledding was the only way to get across the rugged, frozen terrain of the Alaskan countryside.)
- **What were two previous uses of the Iditarod Trail?** (It was used by people traveling northwest during the Gold Rush and for transporting medicine during a diphtheria epidemic.)

Describing a Unique Race Tell students that they will be reading about why the Iditarod is unlike any other race in the world.

Ask students:

- **What makes the Iditarod such a unique sporting event?** (Racers have to cross many different kinds of terrain during approximately two weeks of icy cold Alaskan weather.)
- *THINKING FURTHER:* **Why do you think that racers are willing to undergo such difficult conditions?** (Possible answers include: for the feeling of accomplishment, because of a love of the environment.)

BACKGROUND INFORMATION

About Dogsledding The history of dogsledding dates back thousands of years. At first, people built sledges, or sleds, by lashing logs together. These sledges were used to haul cargo over both snow and bare ground. Later people found that the sleds would move more easily if slats called runners were fastened beneath the logs. The slats could be made of wood, walrus skin, or ivory.

Alaskan sleds today are built to withstand the toughest winter travel. The most common type is called the Nome sledge—a long, narrow sled with basketlike sides. Pulled by a good team of dogs, a Nome sledge can transport about 1,000 pounds (450 kg) of cargo.

Riding a dogsled is a unique experience. Have the class comment on the following description written by an Alaskan park ranger:

> *[Dogsledding] is swift and natural. No barrier of metal or glass gets between you and the landscape. The cold stings the cheeks, and crumbs of ice form around the nostrils. Yet instead of being discomforted by this, you are invigorated. . . . You are at peace with yourself and happy, energetically happy. At last you have room to expand. And though you are no more than a speck on the landscape, you feel as big as the space around you.*

Discussing a Test of Endurance
Point out to students that the Iditarod involves unique difficulties and hardships.

Ask students:

- **Name three skills that mushers must make use of during the race.** (Mushers must know how to build a fire, care for their dogs, and adapt to the rugged terrain and constantly changing weather.)

Discussing a Champion Dogsledder
Remind students that Susan Butcher is only one of many Iditarod racers. Point out that the 1995 Iditarod was won by a musher named Doug Swigley, who set a record time of 9 days, 2 hours, and 42 minutes.

Ask students:

- **Describe two situations in which Susan Butcher showed both courage and endurance.** (when a blizzard destroyed much of the trail and when a moose attacked her team of dogs)
- *THINKING FURTHER:* **What kinds of study and training do you think are needed to become a champion dogsledder?** (Possible answers include: increasing one's physical endurance; learning about the training and care of dogs; learning to survive in the wilderness.)

A TEST OF ENDURANCE

Day in and day out, the mushers drive their teams over the snow and ice. Some of the time, the musher rides on the back of the sled runners. Often, though, he or she will jump off to help the dogs tug the sled over a rough patch of ground.

Some mushers stop each evening. Unpacking a portable stove, they build a fire, feed the dogs, and curl up in a cold-weather sleeping bag. Other mushers press on through the night. Sooner or later, however, every team must rest, and the rules specify at least one 24-hour stopover for each musher.

There's no such thing as an Iditarod "rain date"—the race continues no matter what the weather is like. This can make things very hard for the musher and the dog team. Take the case of Iditarod veteran Susan Butcher. During the 1982 race, a blizzard wiped out much of the trail, and Butcher's dogsled crashed into a tree. Then she was stranded for several days by a fierce storm, with winds blowing at 80 miles (129 km) per hour!

Butcher faced even worse problems during the 1985 Iditarod, when an enraged moose attacked her team. It killed 2 dogs and injured 13 others. Butcher tried to drive the moose away, but it might have killed her, too, if another musher hadn't come along and helped her.

76

CURRICULUM CONNECTION

Language Arts Writers have long been fascinated by the relationships between humans and animals. Jack London is an American writer who is best known for his stories depicting the struggles of men and dogs against the forces of nature.

London wrote two great animal novels. In *The Call of the Wild* he tells the story of Buck, a dog that is stolen from a comfortable home and forced to survive as an Alaskan sled dog. In *White Fang* London reverses the story. He describes a wolf that is transformed from a savage beast into a loyal domestic animal through the power of a human master's love and kindness.

BACKGROUND INFORMATION

Multicultural Perspectives Although participants in the Iditarod include people of all backgrounds, the Inuit have always played an important role. Isaac Okleasik, an Inuit from Teller, Alaska, won an unofficial running of the race in 1967. Another Inuit named Herbert Nayokpuk finished in the top five in several Iditarods during the 1970s and 1980s. Nayokpuk, who had been an ivory carver since boyhood, applied this traditional Inuit skill to the Iditarod. Instead of using modern brass snaps to attach his dogs to the sled, he used carved ivory toggles. He also experimented with traditional ivory sled runners.

Have students discuss how Nayokpuk has kept an Inuit legacy alive.

A CHAMPION DOGSLEDDER

If anyone is capable of handling the problems you just read about, it's Susan Butcher. Winner of the 1986, 1987, 1988, and 1990 Iditarods, Butcher long held the Iditarod speed record: 11 days, 1 hour, 53 minutes, and 23 seconds. She also held records in several other dogsled races. How did this Massachusetts-born woman end up as one of the world's champion dogsledders?

Butcher moved to Fairbanks, Alaska, in 1975. Then she moved to rural Alaska to learn to be a musher. She took along three sled dogs, a sack of flour, two cats, a slab of bacon, and a jar of peanut butter! After a period of study and training, Butcher's dream came true in 1978 when she raced in the Iditarod for the first time.

"THE REAL CHAMPIONS"

Being a musher requires amazing skill and endurance. But according to Butcher, the dogs are the real champions. In fact, training and caring for the sled dogs is a tradition in itself. Butcher cares for her Alaskan huskies from the moment they are born. She talks to them, pets them, and plays with them. When the pups turn four-and-a-half months old, their training begins. Butcher teaches the unruly pups to work together. They pull a small sled at first and then move up to a larger one.

By the time they are ready for competition, the huskies pull as a team. Butcher never uses force to encourage them. Her dogs run because they love her, she says, and love what they are doing. As Susan Butcher knows, that combination is hard to beat.

The dogs also save lives. Butcher, her lead dog Tekla, and 14 other huskies were making a training run across a frozen river in 1977. Tekla kept trying to stray off the trail. Butcher couldn't understand why. Her lead husky had never disobeyed her before. Soon she decided to let Tekla go where she wanted. Moments after the team pulled aside, the trail collapsed into the river. "That day I learned that the wilderness is their domain," Butcher later said. "The dogs know more about it than I do, and I'm better off trusting their instincts."

How does the Iditarod race of Alaska keep an Inuit legacy alive?

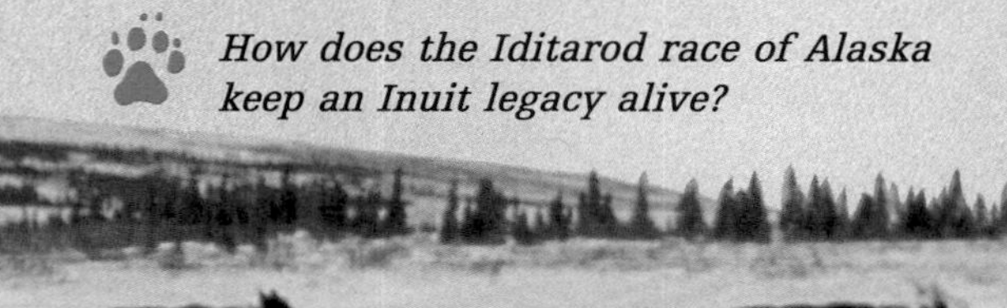

Discussing the Real Champions Tell students that animals are often an important part of a sporting event. Point out that the official Iditarod rules mandate a high standard of care for the dogs. Veterinarians examine the teams at each checkpoint, and straw bedding is required for them at each rest stop. Mushers are also required to carry an extra pair of snow booties for each animal.

Ask students:

- **How does a musher like Susan Butcher train her dogs?** (At first she simply pets and plays with the animals. Later she teaches them how to work together, and how to become strong and self-reliant.)
- *THINKING FURTHER:* **In which other sports do animals play a major role?** (Possible answers include: thoroughbred racing, hunting, and polo.)

Applying the Lesson Have students imagine that they are going to interview Susan Butcher. Then ask them to write three questions they would ask her.

3 CLOSE

Summarizing Students have read about the Iditarod Trail Sled Dog Race. They have learned that the race involves traditional skills and customs. They have also learned how it has become an Alaskan legacy.

Evaluating Assess students' understanding of the lesson by asking them the question at the bottom of the pupil page. (Possible answers include: The Iditarod keeps the Inuit custom of dogsled travel alive, as well as Inuit methods of adapting to a harsh environment.)

MEETING INDIVIDUAL NEEDS

Reteaching (easy) Have students design a poster announcing the next running of the Iditarod. Suggest that the poster include the date of the race, its location, and some of the possible problems that the mushers might face.

Extension (average) Have students write a newspaper article describing an imaginary Iditarod. Before the class begins, you might want to review the major parts of a news article. After students have finished, have them read their articles to the rest of the class.

Enrichment (challenging) Ask students to read any short story by Jack London that deals with the relationship between humans and animals. After they have finished, have students write a book report describing the story they selected.

CHAPTER 2 REVIEW

pages 78–79

USING THE CHAPTER SUMMARY AND REVIEW

Cultural Geography These questions may be used for review.

- **Why have people from different ethnic groups come to the United States?** (in search of freedom and opportunity; Africans were forced)
- **Describe the economic system of the United States.** (It is a capitalist system in which businesses are owned by individuals or groups of individuals rather than by the government. Free enterprise, or the freedom to own property and run a business, is an important part of this system.)
- **What form of democracy is the government of the United States?** (a representative democracy, or a republic, in which voters elect officials to represent them in government)

Ideas to Remember

- **What is the makeup of the population of the United States?** (a mixture of various ethnic groups)
- **What is a developed economy?** (an economy that has many different economic activities and makes use of advanced technology)
- **Why is power divided between national and state governments in the United States?** (to keep the federal government from becoming too powerful)
- **What does freedom of expression mean to artists in the United States?** (that they are free to express themselves in many different ways)

Answers to Reviewing Vocabulary

1. capitalism
2. federal system
3. discrimination
4. developed economy
5. megalopolis
6. republic
7. immigrant
8. technology

CHAPTER 2 • SUMMARY

THE UNITED STATES: CULTURAL GEOGRAPHY

PEOPLE

- Many different ethnic groups in the United States today

- People from many lands came to the United States searching for freedom and opportunity

- Hispanics: fastest growing ethnic group

ECONOMY

- Capitalist system: freedom and economic opportunity

- Free enterprise: freedom to own property and run a business

- Large foreign trade: exports and imports
- Developed economy: many different economic activities, advanced technology

GOVERNMENT

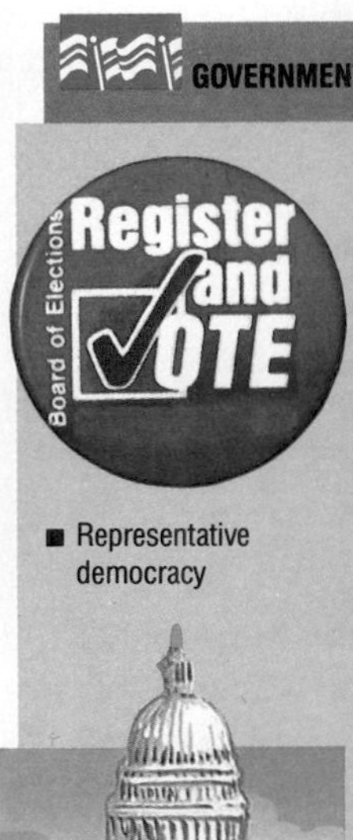

- Representative democracy
- Three branches: executive, legislative, and judicial
- Federal republic: divides power between national and local governments

ARTS AND RECREATION

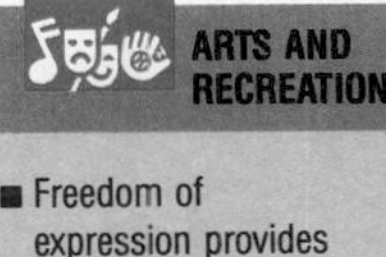

- Freedom of expression provides opportunities for artists

- Americans enjoy hobbies: reading, movies, sports

- Exploring the outdoors: Americans enjoy national, state, and local parks

IDEAS TO REMEMBER

- The population of the United States is made up of a mixture of many different ethnic groups.
- The developed economy of the United States, with its advanced technology, employs many workers in services, manufacturing, trade, and other fields.
- The United States is a federal republic with elected representatives and with power divided between national and state governments.
- Freedom of expression provides artists in the United States with opportunities to express themselves in many different ways.

78

ENRICHMENT ACTIVITY

Making a Class Tape **Materials:** tape recorder, tape

1. Refer students to the sheet music for "This Land Is Your Land" on page 71, and have them sing the song. Tell students that they are going to make their own tape recording of songs that express their feelings about the U.S. Call for suggestions of songs they might include (for example, "America the Beautiful," Bruce Springsteen's "Born in the U.S.A.," their state song, folk songs, and rap songs with relevant social commentary).
2. Divide the class into groups, and make each group responsible for learning and rehearsing one song.
3. Have the groups perform and record their songs in the order that they think is best, possibly ending their tape with an all-class rendition of "This Land Is Your Land."

CHAPTER 2 • REVIEW

REVIEWING VOCABULARY

capitalism
checks and balances
democracy
developed economy
discrimination
federal system
immigrant
megalopolis
republic
technology

Number a sheet of paper from 1 to 10. Beside each number write the word or term from the list above that best completes each sentence.

1. _____ is an economic system in which businesses and factories are owned by individuals or private groups.
2. In a _____ governmental power is divided between the national government and state and local governments.
3. _____ is the unfair treatment of a person or a group of people because of race, class, ethnic origin, or other factors.
4. A country that employs many people in a variety of manufacturing and service jobs is said to have a _____.
5. A large area of interconnected cities, suburbs, and towns is called a _____.
6. A _____ is a type of democracy in which citizens elect people to represent them in government.
7. An _____ is a person who moves to a country other than the country in which he or she was born.
8. _____ refers to any method, machine, or tool that is used to meet human needs.
9. By dividing power among three branches of government, the framers of the Constitution established a system of _____ to limit governmental power.
10. A _____ is a form of government in which decisions are made by citizens.

REVIEWING FACTS

1. Why is the United States a land of many people? From where are the largest numbers of immigrants to the United States coming today?
2. How have the living patterns of Americans changed since the 1700s?
3. List three economic freedoms that Americans enjoy under the free enterprise system of the United States.
4. Name the two houses of Congress. What is the function of each house?
5. What is meant by the phrase "freedom of expression"? List three ways this freedom is practiced in the United States.

WRITING ABOUT MAIN IDEAS

1. **Writing a Pamphlet:** Write a pamphlet for foreign visitors entitled "Democracy in Action: How the United States Government Works."
2. **Writing an Essay:** Write a short essay explaining the meaning of the phrase "the pursuit of happiness." How do you exercise this right in your own life?
3. **Writing About Perspectives:** Citizens in the United States have the right to vote, a right many other people in the world do not have. Yet many citizens do not vote. Write a paragraph giving your point of view about why people do or do not vote.

BUILDING SKILLS: DECISION MAKING

1. What is another word or phrase that means *decision making*?
2. Write a set of instructions for a student who is not familiar with the steps to making a decision.
3. Why is it important to consider many alternatives when making a decision?

79

9. checks and balances
10. democracy

Answers to Reviewing Facts

1. because it has so many different ethnic groups; Asia and Latin America
2. More people live in urban rather than in rural areas.
3. to own property, to run a business, to import or export goods
4. House of Representatives and Senate; to make laws for the nation and to decide how much money the government can spend
5. the freedom of a person to describe all aspects of American life and to communicate his or her ideas; Possible answers include: in artwork, books, plays.

Suggestions for Writing About Main Ideas

1. Students' pamphlets should include information on what a democracy is, the responsibilities of citizens, and the branches of government and their powers.
2. Students should stress that Americans have the right to do what they want as long as it is within the law.
3. Students should be aware that a general sense of apathy and hopelessness keeps many people from voting.

Answers to Building Skills: Decision Making

1. selecting from a number of alternatives, or options
2. Identify and define the goal; identify all possible alternative means of achieving the goal; predict immediate and long-range outcomes of each alternative; evaluate the advantages and disadvantages of each outcome.
3. In order to make the right decision you must first know all of your options; otherwise you may not make the best possible decision.

Chapter Review and Test

Practice Book: *Vocabulary Review*, page 16
Transparency: *Graphic Organizer*
Assessment Book: *Chapter 2 Test*

MAKING CONNECTIONS

Supporting Main Ideas Use the Main Idea Table Graphic Organizer Transparency, writing in only the underlined copy. In the legs of the table, have students add details that support the main idea. *Ask:* What are some of the factors that contribute to the United States's strength as a nation?

MAIN IDEA: The United States is a democratic republic that has a diverse population, a developed economy, and a desire to foster the creative arts.

People	Economy	Government	Arts & Recreation
People from many different ethnic groups live in the United States.	The American economic system is based on free enterprise.	The Constitution created a representative democracy and a system of checks and balances.	Americans enjoy freedom of expression and choice in arts and recreation.

CHAPTER 3 ORGANIZER

CANADA text pages 80–97

CHAPTER THEME

People of diverse origins have conquered Canada's cold climate to develop a leading world economy under parliamentary rule.

CHAPTER OBJECTIVES

CONTENT

- Explain why Canada is often described as a mosaic of peoples and cultures.
- Identify the Inuit and describe their origins.
- Define *separatism* and explain how it affects Canadian politics.
- Explain why most Canadians live in a narrow belt along the United States border.
- Describe how the Canadian economy depends on the country's natural resources.
- Define *acid rain* and describe its impact on Canada's lakes, rivers, and forests.
- Describe how Canada's parliamentary democracy is organized, and explain the basis of the country's membership in the Commonwealth of Nations.
- Compare and contrast the structure of Canadian democracy with that of the United States.
- Explain why Canada has maintained more of its British heritage than the United States.
- Describe how the arts and recreation of Canada reflect the country's cultures.

SKILLS

Geography
- Use a map to locate regions with coal deposits, petroleum, and natural gas in Canada.
- Locate deposits of lead, zinc, and nickel on a natural resources map of Canada.

Thinking
- Make business decisions about locating a mine on Canada's north coast.
- Arrange information in sequential order.

Reading and Writing
- Write a paragraph describing how the present form of Canadian government reflects Canada's British heritage.
- Write a help wanted ad for mining jobs in northern Canada.

CITIZENSHIP VALUES

- Appreciate the many different forms that democracy can take.

TEACHER OPTIONS

READING STRATEGY: Skimming and Scanning Strategies to help students read and remember the main ideas of the lesson.
Lesson 1: p. 81
Lesson 2: p. 86
Lesson 3: p. 90
Lesson 4: p. 93

MEETING INDIVIDUAL NEEDS Activities for reteaching, extension, and enrichment.
Lesson 1: p. 83
Lesson 2: p. 88
Study and Research Skills: p. 89
Lesson 3: p. 92
Lesson 4: p. 95

GEO ADVENTURES ACTIVITIES PAD Daily activities to assess students' understanding of geography skills.

CURRICULUM CONNECTION Activities to help integrate other subject areas with Social Studies.
Music: p. 91

PUPIL EDITION ON CASSETTE Language support for students who have difficulty reading or who will benefit from listening to the Pupil Edition on Cassette as they read.

SECOND-LANGUAGE SUPPORT Activities and suggestions for second-language learners.
Lesson 4: p. 6

CHAPTER PLANNING GUIDE

LESSON	SUGGESTED PACING	THEMES	TEACHER SUPPORT MATERIALS: TEACHER'S RESOURCE CENTER
1 THE PEOPLE pages 81–85	1 day	Canada, the second-largest nation in the world, is composed of a mosaic of people, most of whom live within 100 miles (160 km) of the United States border.	Practice Book p. 17 ■ Anthology pp. 17–18, 19, 22–23, 31–32 Outline Map p. 12
2 THE ECONOMY pages 86–88	1 day	Mining as well as farming and manufacturing make Canada a world economic leader.	Practice Book p. 18 **Technology:** *Adventures CD-ROM*
BUILDING STUDY AND RESEARCH SKILLS Using the Library page 89	1 day	Books containing factual information can be found in the reference section of the library.	Practice Book p. 19
3 THE GOVERNMENT pages 90–92	1 day	Canada is a parliamentary democracy with an elected head of government. As a member of the Commonwealth of Nations, Canada recognizes Great Britain's monarch as its nominal leader.	Practice Book p. 20 ■ Anthology pp. 29–30
4 ARTS AND RECREATION pages 93–95	1 day	The Canadian environment and the country's varied cultures have enriched the arts and recreation of Canada.	Practice Book p. 21 ■ Anthology pp. 24–28 **Technology:** *Adventures CD-ROM*
CHAPTER SUMMARY AND REVIEW pages 96–97	1 day	Chapter content, skills, and vocabulary are reviewed and evaluated.	Practice Book p. 22 Transparency: Graphic Organizer Assessment Book, Chapter 3 Test

Technology CONNECTION

Lesson 2
ADVENTURES CD-ROM
Have students make a resources map of Canada using *Build* and *Paint.*

Lesson 4
ADVENTURES CD-ROM
Have students listen to some Canadian French in *Investigate, Sounds.*

CHAPTER 3
pages 80–97

USING THE CHAPTER OPENER

Discussing the Photograph Tell students that the horsemen wearing red in the picture are police officers. Partly because they wear dashing uniforms and partly because they are responsible for keeping order in the still-rugged Yukon and Northwest Territories, these police officers are considered by many to have some of the glamour often associated with the cowhands of the Old West in the United States.

Ask students:

- **How do you think the prospect of wearing such a uniform might make a young person feel about joining the Mounties?** (Possible answers include: It probably would make him or her feel that joining the Mounties is like joining a special group.)
- *THINKING FURTHER:* **What kinds of skills do you think Mounties need to have?** (horseback riding, police skills)

Reading/Listening to the Primary Source Have students read the passage. Ask them to volunteer ideas about some of the duties of a Mountie. Encourage students to speculate about how the Mounties might differ from the police officers of the United States. Ask them if they think that a picture of a police officer might be chosen as a symbol of the United States, and have them explain their answers.

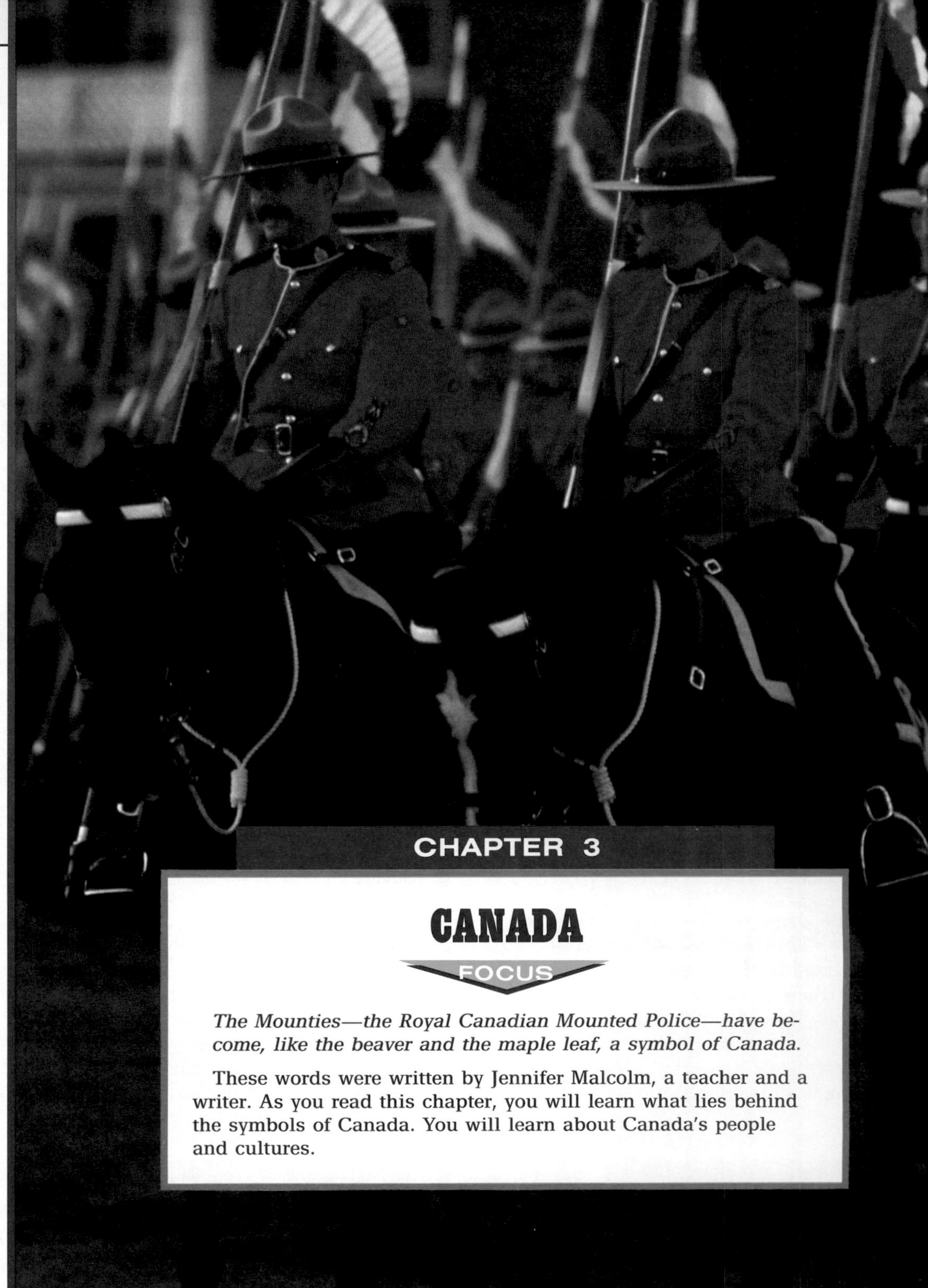

CHAPTER 3

CANADA

FOCUS

The Mounties—the Royal Canadian Mounted Police—have become, like the beaver and the maple leaf, a symbol of Canada.

These words were written by Jennifer Malcolm, a teacher and a writer. As you read this chapter, you will learn what lies behind the symbols of Canada. You will learn about Canada's people and cultures.

BACKGROUND INFORMATION

About the Photograph The Royal Canadian Mounted Police force was founded in 1873.

- To join the Royal Canadian Mounted Police force, a candidate must be a Canadian citizen or British subject between the ages of 18 and 30, at least 5 feet 8 inches (170 cm) tall, and in good physical condition.
- The Mounties are not appointed to the northern posts. Only those who volunteer to do so serve in those rugged territories. Their many duties include the prevention of smuggling and drug trafficking, the tracking of criminals, and the performance of rescue work.
- The modern Mountie's horsemanship is usually reserved for ceremonies. Besides using such familiar means of travel as cars, planes, and boats, Mounties also use snowmobiles and dogsleds.

LESSON 1

The People

READ TO LEARN

Key Vocabulary

mosaic province Roman Catholicism separatism

Read Aloud

The working language here in Hull is mainly French. About 75 percent of the people speak it, I guess. . . . It bothers a lot of French Canadians that they have to be the ones who are bilingual [speak two languages] *rather than the other way around. This doesn't bother me. . . . I have always spoken both languages* [French and English] *and I don't remember learning either.*

These thoughts on language in Canada come from Francine Letellier, a librarian. Both English and French are commonly spoken among the people of Canada. Knowing both languages is required for many jobs in the country.

Read for Purpose

1. WHAT YOU KNOW: What vast landform covers half of Canada?
2. WHAT YOU WILL LEARN: Why is it often said that Canada is a "mosaic" of people and cultures?

THE CANADA MOSAIC

Canada was colonized mainly by people from France and Great Britain. For this reason Canada has two official languages, English and French. But Canada has many other groups of people in addition to the British and the French. In fact, Canadians like to describe their country as a mosaic (mō zā′ ik). A mosaic is a pattern or picture made up of many small pieces of stone or glass. Like a mosaic, Canada's groups of people keep separate identities while forming parts of the whole.

THE INDIANS AND THE INUIT

Indians, the first people to live in North America, were the first Canadians. Most archaeologists believe that the first Indians came from Asia more than 40,000 years ago. They were expert hunters and farmers who built villages in the area that is now southern Canada. Today Indians live throughout the nation.

The Inuit (in′ ü it) are another Canadian group descended from Asians. The Inuit often live in their own communities in the north, where they hunt for a living.

The Inuit came to Canada about 6,000 years ago. Peter Green, an Inuit representative, explains that the name of the group is important: "We used to be called *Eskimos*, but that is an Indian word, not our own. *Inuit* simply means 'the people,' and is the name we call ourselves."

WHAT YOU KNOW: This question refers to material covered in Chapter 1, Lesson 1; the Canadian Shield.

LESSON 1
pages 81–83

Lesson Theme Canada, the second-largest nation in the world, is composed of a mosaic of people, most of whom live within 100 miles (160 km) of the United States border.

Lesson Objectives
- Describe Canada's major cultures.
- Explain why Canada has two official languages.
- Explain the reasons for the location of most of Canada's population.

1 PREPARE

Motivate Read the *Read Aloud* passage to the class. Tell the class they will read about how Canada came to have two official languages.

Set Purpose Use the *What You Know* question to help students recall the population centers of Canada. Students will learn the answers to the *What You Will Learn* question as they read the lesson.

2 TEACH

Identifying the Canadian Mosaic Help students identify Canada's mosaic of cultures.

Ask students:

- **What is meant by the word *mosaic*?** (a picture made up of many small pieces of glass)
- **How is Canada like a mosaic?** (Canada is made up of many different groups of people who maintain their separate identities but still form one nation.)

Discussing the Indians and the Inuit Point out that the Indians and the Inuit were two of the first groups of people known to have lived in Canada.

READING STRATEGY AND VOCABULARY DEVELOPMENT

Skimming and Scanning The purpose of this strategy is to introduce students to a way of varying their reading rates to match specific purposes. Explain to students that effective readers vary their reading rate depending upon the purpose for reading. Skimming is a way of surveying content quickly. Have students practice skimming by looking through Lesson 1 to find the *Key Vocabulary* words. Students will notice that these words appear in boldface, or heavy, dark type. Phonetic respellings, or pronunciations, often follow difficult or unusual words.

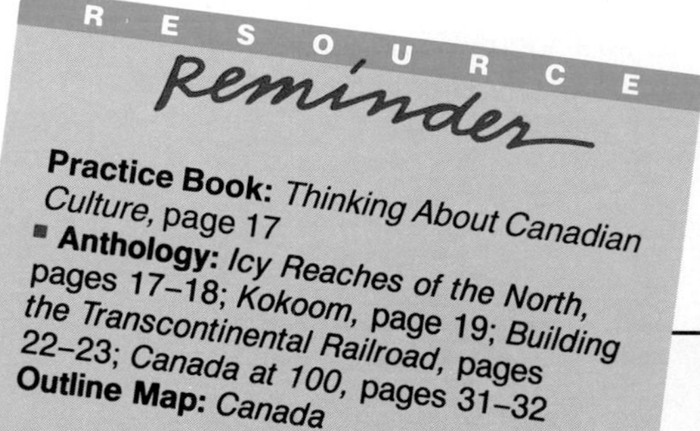

Discussing Groups That Arrived Later Have students analyze the ethnic makeup of Canada.

Ask students:

- **When did Europeans first begin to settle in Canada?** (in the 1600s)
- **Who are Canada's largest groups of people?** (British Canadians, French Canadians)

EXTENDING MAP SKILLS

Have students examine the map on this page.

Ask students:

- **What does the map show?** (Canada's provinces and territories)
- **Is Quebec Province in the eastern or western part of Canada?** (eastern)
- **According to this map, which is the southernmost city in Canada?** (Toronto, Ontario)

Discussing Canada and the United States Have students examine relations between these two nations.

Ask students:

- **A Canadian once said that having the United States as a neighbor was a little like sleeping next to an elephant. What do you think the Canadian meant?** (Like a person sleeping next to an elephant, Canada is affected by every action of the United States.)
- **In which part of Canada do most Canadians live?** (in a narrow belt below the Canadian Shield; all of this belt is within 100 miles [160 km] of the Canada-United States border)
- **Why do some Canadians feel threatened by their proximity to the United States?** (They fear the replacement of their own Canadian cultural identity and values by those of the United States.)

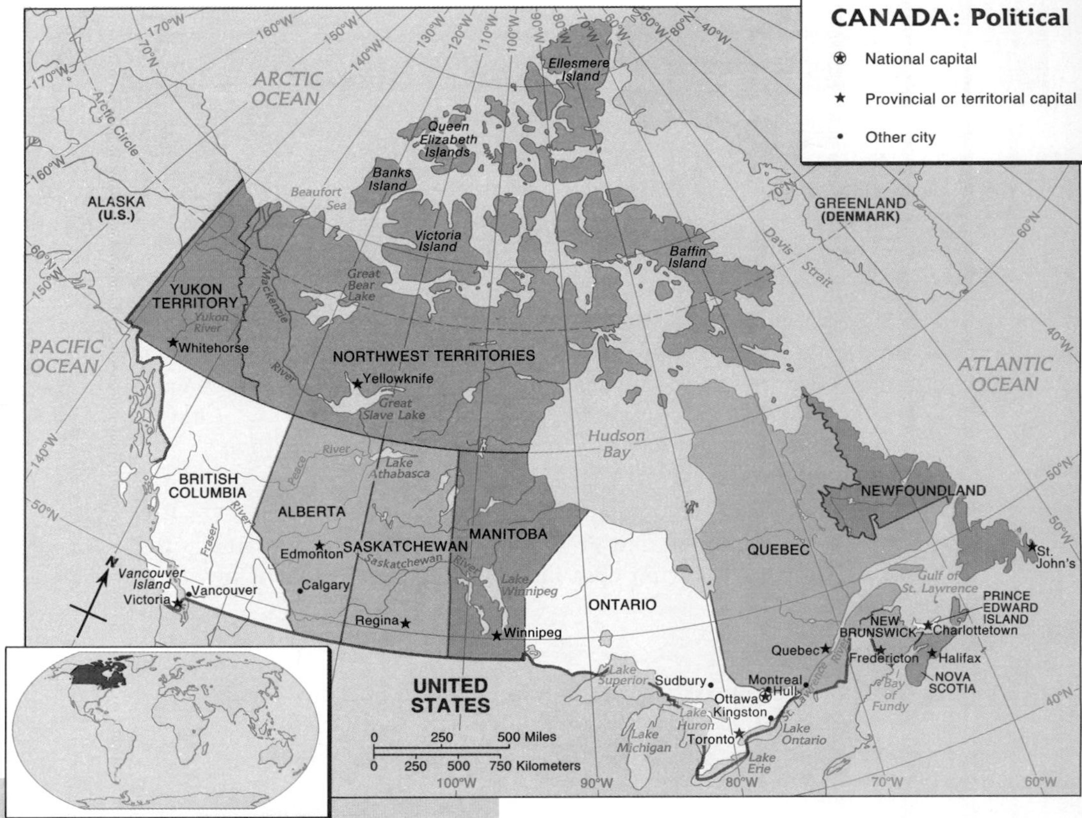

MAP SKILL: Canada is divided into separate areas that are called provinces. What is the capital of the province of Alberta?

LATER GROUPS

In the 1600s, large numbers of Europeans began settling in Canada. As in the United States, the Europeans colonized Canada mainly from east to west. The French were the first Europeans to settle in Canada. They were followed by the British and then by immigrants from other lands.

Today British Canadians are the largest group in Canada. They make up about 40 percent of Canada's 28 million people. Another 27 percent belong to the second-largest group, the French Canadians. French Canadians are the majority in the province of Quebec. A province is a self-governing area within a nation, similar to a state in the United States. In New Brunswick, French Canadians make up almost half the population. Find Quebec and New Brunswick on the map on this page.

A CULTURAL MIX

Canada also has two main cultural traditions—French Canadian and British. British traditions are strong almost everywhere in Canada except in Quebec and New Brunswick. British Canadians are mostly of the Protestant faith, speak and write English, and follow many British customs.

82

MAP SKILL: Edmonton

BACKGROUND INFORMATION

Plans for Nunavut In 1993, the Canadian government agreed to grant the Inuit political control and land rights over a fifth of Canada. The new territory would be carved out of the eastern part of the Northwest Territories and would measure 136,000 square miles (350,000 sq km). According to the agreement, the Inuit will gain limited economic rights over mineral and other resource development and a cash settlement amounting to more than $1 billion over 14 years. For the Inuit, the agreement marks a victory in the battle for political and economic rights that began centuries ago when the Europeans first reached their homeland. Appropriately, the new territory will be known as *Nunavut,* an Inuit term meaning "our land."

As a minority, French Canadians have fought to keep their French way of life—French language, **Roman Catholicism** and French customs. Roman Catholicism is the branch of Christianity that is headed by the pope in Rome.

In the 1960s some French Canadians believed their way of life was in danger. They felt they had to break away from Canada in order to preserve their culture. This kind of movement is called **separatism**. In 1995 the people of Quebec voted on whether or not to remain part of Canada. After a heated debate Quebec elected to stay a Canadian province. You will read more about this issue on pages 84–85.

CANADA AND THE UNITED STATES

Some Canadians also worry about what they see as a different threat to their way of life. This threat comes from across the border—from the United States. According to one Canadian:

> *We are already inundated with American magazines and televison shows that don't reflect Canadian opinions and values. We have much in common with Americans but not enough to justify merging our thinking.*

One reason for the great influence of the United States is that most Canadians live close to the United States–Canadian border. Although Canada is the world's second-largest nation in area, much of it is made up of land that is difficult to live on.

Almost three fourths of all Canadians live in a narrow belt below the Canadian Shield. All of this belt is within 100 miles (160 km) of the United States border. It has Canada's most fertile land and its warmest climates. According to the Canadian writer Pierre Berton:

> *The Shield and the wilderness bear down upon us, a crushing weight, squeezing us like toothpaste along the border.*

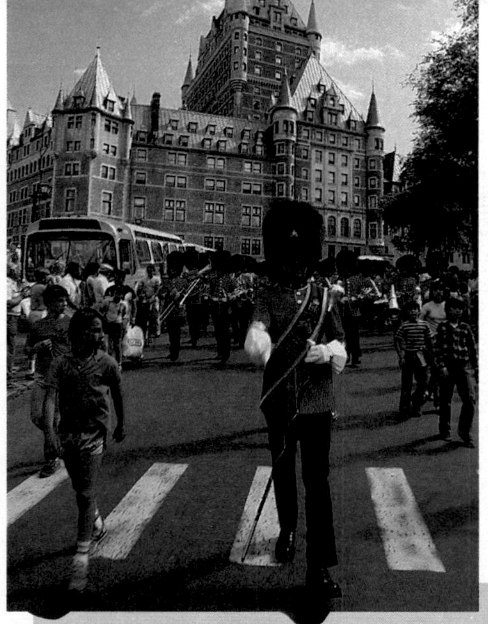

Traditional parades like this one in Quebec City show the influence of British culture in Canada.

THE CULTURES OF CANADA

Canada, as you have read, is a mosaic of different groups that live together in this vast country. The earliest, and now the smallest, of these groups are the Indians and the Inuit. The British Canadians and the French Canadians are the two largest groups of people in the country today. Most of them live in a narrow belt of land bordering the United States.

Check Your Reading

1. What two languages are commonly spoken in Canada?
2. Why do the Inuit not want to be called "Eskimos"?
3. What are some of the important groups in the "mosaic" of Canada?
4. **THINKING SKILL:** What causes nearly three fourths of all Canadians to live close to the United States border? Give at least two causes.

THINKING SKILL: Cause and Effect

83

Applying the Lesson Encourage students to name one Canadian place or ethnic group they would like to know more about. Have students make a list of the steps they would take to learn more about that place or group.

3 CLOSE

Summarizing Students have learned about the mosaic of cultures that make up Canada. Most of these different groups live in close proximity to the United States and, as a result, they worry about the United States' influence on Canadian life.

Evaluating Use these questions to assess students' understanding.

- **In what way is Canada bilingual?** (Two official languages—English and French—are recognized.)
- **Which Canadian ethnic groups date from thousands of years ago, and which have arrived more recently?** (Indians and Inuit; European immigrants arrived in the seventeenth to early twentieth centuries.)
- **Why do Canadians worry about their proximity to the United States?** (They are concerned about the influence of such a powerful neighbor.)

Answers to Check Your Reading

1. English and French
2. Eskimo is an Indian name; their name for themselves is *Inuit*, or "the people."
3. English, French, Indian, Inuit
4. Much of the land is difficult to live on; the most fertile land in Canada exists in a narrow belt south of the Canadian Shield.

Independent Practice
Practice Book: page 17

MEETING INDIVIDUAL NEEDS

Reteaching (easy) Have students fill in the political outline map of Canada found in the Teacher's Resource Center. Students should label the names of provinces and territories. Have students use a color pencil or felt marker to fill in the 100-mile (160-km) area of dense population along the United States border. Have them use different color markers to fill in the Arctic Circle and the Canadian Shield.

Extension (average) Have students design posters showing the cultural mosaic of Canada. Students should include the names of specific ethnic groups and choose an appropriate poster title. Display student posters.

Enrichment (challenging) Divide the class into five groups to research the Canadian Indians, English, French, the Inuit, and other immigrant groups.

CHAPTER 3

CITIZENSHIP Viewpoints

pages 84–85

Lesson Objective

- Analyze three points of view on the effects of biculturalism in Canada.

Identifying the Issue Help students see that genuine differences of opinion can arise on issues of language and culture in a country.

Suggested Question

- ***What does biculturalism mean in Canada?*** *(There are two major cultures, one English and one French, that are part of Canadian life.)*

Discussing Three Different Viewpoints Have students read the viewpoints on page 85.

LUCIEN BOUCHARD

Suggested Questions

- ***What does Bouchard say that most people in Quebec want?*** *(They want to control their own laws, collect their own taxes, and sign their own treaties.)*
- ***Why does Bouchard feel that the people in Quebec are increasingly vulnerable?*** *(Because they are increasingly a minority in Canada.)*

MARCEL HAMELIN

Suggested Questions

- ***According to Hamelin, should policies of bilingualism and biculturalism be stonger or weaker?*** *(They should be stronger.)*
- ***Why does Hamelin believe that the University of Ottawa is a small version of what an ideal Canada should be?*** *(Because it fosters understanding and respect between people of various cultures.)*

PAMELA PAUL

Suggested Questions

- **Why does Paul believe the policy of biculturalism is a misnomer?** (Because it portrays an inaccurate picture of the history of Canada.)

CITIZENSHIP VIEWPOINTS

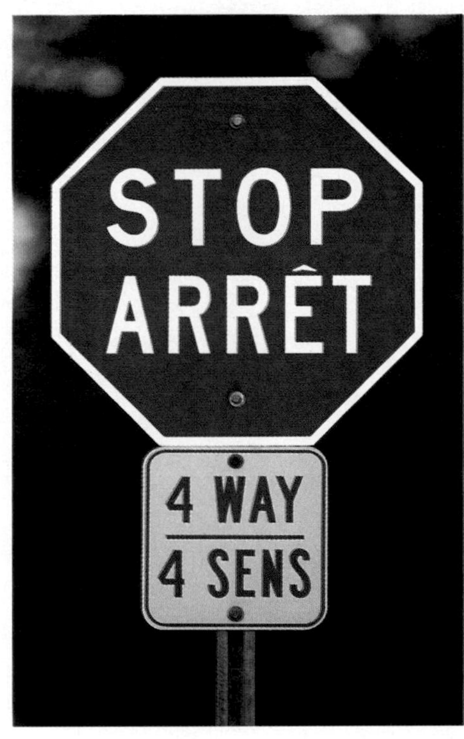

Street signs such as this one are examples of Canada's official biculturalism policy.

WHAT ARE THE EFFECTS OF BICULTURALISM IN CANADA?

One of the things that makes Canada a unique country is its long history of biculturalism. This means that there are officially two major cultures, one French and one English, that are both part of Canadian life. Biculturalism is most apparent in the fact that many Canadians speak both French and English. Others, however, speak only one of these languages.

Most of the people who live in the province of Québec are French-speaking and known as French Canadians. Most of the people who live in the other provinces of Canada are English-speaking and known as British Canadians. Some people, such as Lucien Bouchard, feel that French Canadians must separate from the rest of Canada to preserve their culture. Other Canadians, like Marcel Hamelin, believe that two cultures and two languages help make Canada unique. Pamela Paul holds a different viewpoint completely. She feels that a discussion of biculturalism in Canada ignores the first Canadians—Native Americans.

Consider these three viewpoints on the issue and then answer the questions that follow.

84

BACKGROUND INFORMATION

The tradition of biculturalism in Canada goes back to the exploration of North America by French and English sailors in the 16th century. As settlers and trappers came from Britain and France, both languages were used for communication. During the French and Indian War, these two cultures clashed in a conflict that ended with the British ruling most of North America. Following the war, however, the British allowed the French settlers in Quebec to keep their culture, including their language.

Today the policy of biculturalism is most evident in government activities and publications. The Canadian government provides services in both languages, French and English. This service is quite expensive, since everything has to be printed twice—it comes to a cost of about 3 cents per citizen per day. In spite of the policy of bilingualism, the vast majority of people remain unilingual, with a majority in Quebec being French-speaking and a majority in every other province being English-speaking.

Three **DIFFERENT** Viewpoints

1 LUCIEN BOUCHARD
President, Parti Québécois, Québec
Excerpt from interview, 1996

A very large majority of us [in Québec] want to control our own laws, collect our own taxes, sign our own treaties. Which is the definition of sovereignty. The vast majority of Canadians, however, are convinced that Quebeckers do not form a distinct people. Since we are increasingly a minority, we're increasingly vulnerable to the English-speaking majority. . . . That is why Québec sovereignty is now the only way to ensure that two distinct people will thrive, side by side.

"... Québec sovereignty is now the only way ..."

2 MARCEL HAMELIN
Rector, University of Ottawa, Ottawa, Ontario
Excerpt from interview, 1996

I strongly believe that Canada needs to maintain its attitude of openness towards all cultures. We have to make sure we maintain and even strengthen our policies in such distinct areas as bilingualism [and] biculturalism. Our campus is a [small version] of what an ideal Canada should be: a place that fosters mutual understanding and respect between people of various cultures.

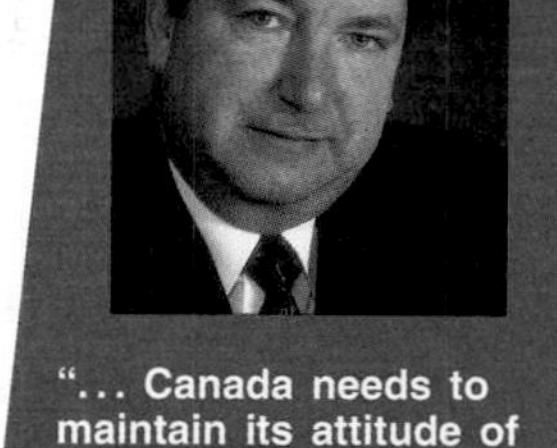

"... Canada needs to maintain its attitude of openness ..."

3 PAMELA PAUL
Executive Director, The Alliance Tribal Council, Delta, British Columbia
Excerpt from interview, 1996

I feel that the policy of biculturalism in Canada is a misnomer [incorrect phrase]. Because the term *biculturalism* is often used to describe the two founding nations of Canada, it portrays an inaccurate history of Canada and implies that only two nations of people, French and English, existed at the time of Confederation. In fact, at the time of contact, there were 57–60 distinct tribes of Native people living in the area now called Canada. Biculturalism does not provide for recognition nor the appreciation of . . . the original inhabitants of Canada, the Native people.

"... the policy of biculturalism in Canada is a misnomer."

BUILDING CITIZENSHIP

1. What is the viewpoint of each person? How does each support his or her views?
2. In what ways are some of the viewpoints alike? In what ways are they different?
3. What other viewpoints might people have on this issue? How might people in other countries feel about this issue?

SHARING VIEWPOINTS

Discuss what you agree or disagree with about each of these viewpoints. Discuss why you think each speaker might feel as he or she does. Then, as a class, write a statement that all of you can agree with on this issue.

■ **According to Paul, how many distinct groups of Native Americans were living in Canada at the time of Confederation?** (57–60)

EVALUATE
Answers to Citizenship Viewpoints

1. Bouchard believes that the only way for two cultures to survive is for Quebec to become sovereign, or independent. Hamelin uses the example of his university to argue that it is a good thing for Canada. Paul thinks that the policy of biculturalism ignores the contributions of people from other cultures, such as Native Americans.
2. Bouchard and Hamelin both think biculturalism is a positive thing, but they employ different arguments to promote it. Bouchard thinks the two cultures should become more separate, Hamelin feels they should work together more closely. Paul feels that biculturalism is a bad thing, since it ignores other cultures in Canada.
3. Some Canadians might feel that English should be the main language and culture of Canada, since English-speakers are the majority. Other ethnic minorities might feel that biculturalism ignores their cultural contribution. People in other countries might admire Canada's cultural diversity.

Sharing Viewpoints Ask students to try to find a link between each of the speakers' jobs and their opinions. On a map, show the different locations of each of the speakers. Statements the three might agree on include: **1.** Biculturalism is an important part of Canada's heritage. **2.** The voice of each Canadian deserves to be heard in Canada.

Debating Viewpoints Discuss with students how engaging in debate can help to clarify viewpoints and resolve conflicts. As an extension, have groups of students adopt the viewpoints of each of the speakers and present that opinion to the class. Other students can then ask each group questions about Canadian biculturalism to spur debate. See if the groups can work together to find a compromise situation on the issue.

CITIZENSHIP

Understanding Government The issue of biculturalism continues to be a hot topic in Canadian politics. Although the separatists of Quebec have failed so far in their effort to become an independent nation, strong separatist feelings remain there. Meanwhile, Canada continues to become an increasingly multicultural country, as immigrants arrive from different countries and Native people raise their voices and gain more rights. In fact, the government recently started a new department, the Ministry of Multiculturalism, to handle matters dealing with multiculturalism.

- Have students research recent developments in the government of Canada. Two good sources on the internet are www.canada.gc.ca/ (the home page of the Federal government) and www.gouv.qc.ca/(the home page of the provincial government of Quebec).
- Have students research bilingualism in different communities in the United States, such as among Native American groups and in areas with large Hispanic populations.

LESSON 2
pages 86–88

Lesson Theme Mining as well as farming and manufacturing make Canada a world economic leader.

Lesson Objectives
- List Canada's major natural resources.
- Describe how Canada is a leader in farming and manufacturing.
- Describe Canada's trade with other nations.
- Describe the problem of acid rain.

PREPARE

Motivate After reading the *Read Aloud* passage to the class, ask students why mining is an important industry in Canada.

Set Purpose Use the *What You Know* question to explain that Canada, like the United States, has an economy based on free enterprise. Students will learn the answer to the *What You Will Learn* question as they read the lesson.

TEACH

Discussing Mining in Canada Students should recognize that much of Canada's economy is devoted to mining.

Ask students:

- **What is the most profitable industry in Canada?** (mining)
- **Which fossil fuels are produced in Canada?** (coal, petroleum, natural gas)

LESSON 2

The Economy

READ TO LEARN

Key Vocabulary

fossil fuel acid rain NAFTA tariff

Read Aloud

Today mining is big business in Canada. There are more than 300 operating mines across the country and the various companies that own them employ 7 percent of all working Canadians. From these mines about 60 different commodities are [taken out], including nickel, copper, gold, silver, platinum, coal, and iron.

These words were written by Robin Rose, a driller in a mine in Sudbury, in southeastern Ontario. They help to explain why mining is so important to the economy of Canada. Many of the nation's industries are based on obtaining raw materials or using them to make goods.

Read for Purpose

1. WHAT YOU KNOW: What is a free enterprise economy?
2. WHAT YOU WILL LEARN: In what ways does the Canadian economy depend on the country's natural resources?

MINING

Canada, like the United States, has a developed economy. More than in many other countries with developed economies, Canada's wealth comes from its natural resources.

The most profitable industry in Canada is mining. The nation's abundant mineral resources make it one of the world's largest producers of minerals. In 1990 it was the third-largest exporter of minerals after the United States and the Soviet Union.

Canada has the world's largest nickel mine, near Sudbury, Ontario. The Sullivan Mine, in Kimberley, British Columbia, is the world's largest source of lead, zinc, and silver. Canada is also a leading producer of fossil fuels—coal, petroleum, and natural gas.

THE POLARIS MINE

Many of Canada's most valuable resources are located in areas where the climate is extremely cold. How do people live and work there?

In one mine, far beneath the Arctic ice and snow, electric lights burn 24 hours a day. Heavy machinery drills through the permafrost and scoops out tons of ore that contain lead and zinc. This is the Polaris Mine, located on desolate Cornwallis Island, in far northern Canada.

Here, north of the Arctic Circle, more than 200 men and women work to mine lead and zinc. Because of ice on the Arctic Ocean, the sea route to the Polaris Mine is open fewer than 50 days a year. During this time, a year's worth of ore from the mine is shipped out.

WHAT YOU KNOW: This question refers to material covered in Chapter 2, Lesson 2; a system in which people are free to own property and run businesses largely free of government control.

READING STRATEGY AND VOCABULARY DEVELOPMENT

Scanning Review the skimming strategy from Lesson 1. Suggest to students that scanning is another reading strategy they will use to find specific information. Begin the scanning strategy by having students find the *Key Vocabulary* terms in Lesson 2. Have them read the exact definitions provided in the text. Then have students scan the text to find the answers to the questions in the *Check Your Reading* section on page 88.

The Polaris Mine is located in one of Canada's most remote regions. But it produces shiploads of lead and zinc every year.

The workers have learned to live with this schedule and with many other features of life in the frozen north. In the winter it is dark 24 hours a day. It is so cold that door handles break off in people's hands. Motors must be left running from October to May so that they do not freeze.

The Polaris Mine is expensive to run. However, the ore is of high quality—much richer than ores mined farther south. Therefore, the mine can make a big profit. The maps on page 88 show where some of Canada's minerals are located.

FARMING

Canadians also make use of resources other than minerals. Farmland is one of these resources. As you read in Chapter 1, only about 5 percent of Canada's land is arable.

In some areas, such as Quebec, small plots of land are farmed using traditional methods of agriculture. However, most of the nation's farmers depend on modern technology to run large farms. They use giant machines to plant and harvest their crops.

Large-scale farming is carried out mainly on the flat expanses of the Interior Plains. So much wheat is grown there that Canada is one of the world's leading wheat exporters. Canada also produces corn, oats, barley, and dairy products.

MANUFACTURING

Canada is one of the world's leading manufacturing nations. Canadian industries use the products from its mines, forests, and farms to produce many different goods. With its huge forests, Canada is the world's leading producer of newsprint, the inexpensive paper on which newspapers are printed.

The center of Canadian manufacturing is called the "Golden Horseshoe." This is the urban area along Lake Ontario that has the city of Toronto near its center. Many cars and metal products are made here.

FOREIGN TRADE

Canada exports more natural resources than most nations. About 25 percent of Canada's total exports consist of natural resources. In comparison, natural resources make up only about 10 percent of United States exports. Canada's leading exports are minerals such as zinc, petroleum, natural gas, and steel. Canada is also the world's leading exporter of fish and forest products.

Because Canada produces many more goods than it can use, it depends upon other nations to buy them. This can cause problems. For example, the United States

87

Describing the Polaris Mine Have students describe the workings of the Polaris Mine.

Ask students:

- **Where is the Polaris Mine located?** (north of the Arctic Circle on Cornwallis Island)
- **What are some disadvantages of working in the Arctic?** (isolation, extreme cold, long periods of darkness in the winter, the expense of bringing in supplies)
- *THINKING FURTHER:* **How have Polaris Mine workers solved the problems of working in the harsh environment of the Arctic?** (They leave mine lights on continuously and, during the coldest months, let motors run continuously.)

Discussing Farming in Canada As students read this section, help them to understand how Canadian farmers make productive use of their arable farmland.

Ask students:

- **How much of Canada's land is arable?** (about 5 percent)
- **How do methods of farming vary within Canada?** (Some farmers use traditional methods on smaller farms; others use the latest technology to farm vast expanses of land.)

Learning About Manufacturing and Foreign Trade Have students read the last two sections on page 87.

Ask students:

- **How does the Canadian manufacturing industry make use of the nation's abundant natural resources?** (by manufacturing products using raw materials from Canada's mines, forests, and farms)
- **Who is Canada's main trading partner?** (the United States)
- *THINKING FURTHER:* **How is Canada dependent economically on other nations?** (Canada depends on other nations to buy its surplus natural resources and manufactured products.)

5 FUNDAMENTAL THEMES OF GEOGRAPHY

Human-Environment Interaction People interact with their environment wherever they go. Whether building settlements, seeking resources, or growing crops, people modify the environment and adapt to it as their culture grows and changes. Canadians have interacted strongly with their environment as they built a strong economy based on natural resources. Have students scan Lesson 2. Then have them make a list of Canada's major economic activities and the natural resources these activities are based on (mining—fossil fuels and minerals; farming—soil; lumbering—trees; manufacturing—all of the previously mentioned resources). Ask students to think further about the impact these activities might have had and continue to have on the natural environment of Canada.

The Problem of Acid Rain Discuss the threat posed by acid rain.

EXTENDING MAP SKILLS

Ask students to examine the three maps on this page.

Ask students:

- **What do the maps show?** (the location of Canadian coal, lead, zinc, silver, and petroleum and natural gas deposits)

Applying the Lesson Have students make a chart of Canada in which they list the following: percentage of arable land, percentage of work force in mining, leading exports, percentage of exports that are natural resources, and percentage of exports sold to the United States.

CLOSE

Summarizing Students have learned that Canada's developed economy is the result of mining, farming, and manufacturing.

Evaluating Use the *Check Your Reading* questions (answers given below) to assess students' understanding.

Answers to Check Your Reading

1. Situated in the far North, it is cold, dark, and isolated much of the year. It is 10 times richer in ore than southern mines.
2. Seventy-five percent goes to the United States.
3. They are 25 percent of total exports; Canada leads the world in the export of forest and fish products.
4. Movement stops when waterways are icebound; extreme cold; shipping supplies to the north coast is expensive; isolation.

Independent Practice
Practice Book: page 18

0 500 Miles
0 750 Kilometers
N

CANADA: Coal

Extensive coal field
Small coal field

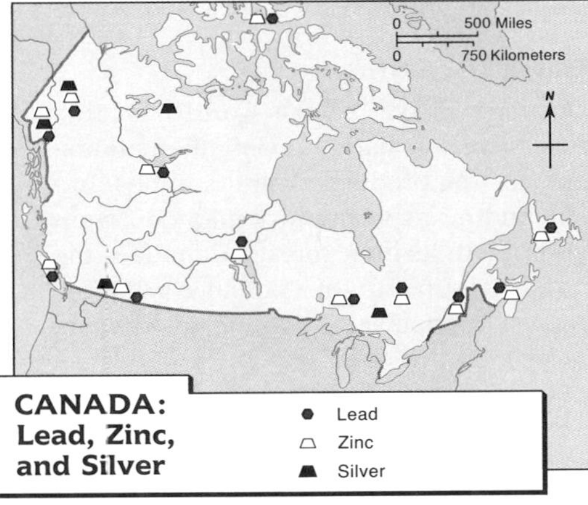

CANADA: Lead, Zinc, and Silver

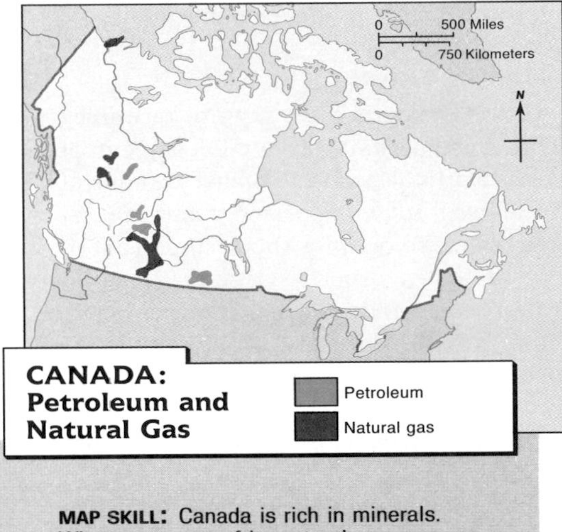

CANADA: Petroleum and Natural Gas

MAP SKILL: Canada is rich in minerals. Where are most of its natural gas reserves located?

MAP SKILL: in the southwest part of the country

is Canada's major trading partner. But this partnership is not balanced. About 20 percent of American exports go to Canada, while about 75 percent of Canada's exports are sold to the United States.

In 1994 the United States, Canada, and Mexico began the North American Free Trade Agreement, or **NAFTA**. Under that agreement, most goods traded between the nations will not be subject to **tariffs**. A tariff is a tax on goods. NAFTA's goal is increased trade among the three nations.

ACID RAIN

Factories in both the United States and Canada cause pollution. But a great deal of the **acid rain** in Canada comes from the United States. Acid rain is rain mixed with chemicals from the burning of coal and other fuels. Acid rain pollutes lakes and other waterways, killing fish and other water life. It also damages trees and buildings. For this reason both countries have cooperated to control acid rain.

A WORLD ECONOMIC LEADER

Canada has one of the world's leading economies. You have read that much of the nation's wealth comes from its abundant natural resources. Mining is the most important industry in Canada. Agriculture, forestry, fishing, and manufacturing also are important to the Canadian economy.

Check Your Reading

1. What is unusual about the Polaris Mine?
2. To which nation do most of Canada's exports go?
3. Explain why natural resources are so important to Canada's economy.
4. **THINKING SKILL:** Suppose a Canadian firm wants to develop a mine in far northern Canada. What are some of the difficulties it must consider?

THINKING SKILL: Decision Making

MEETING INDIVIDUAL NEEDS

Reteaching (easy) Have students list the natural resources of Canada and classify them using these categories: energy sources, metals, vegetation products, products from the sea.

Extension (average) Divide the class into groups and have each group research a resource discussed in this lesson (nickel, lead, zinc, copper, platinum, silver, iron). Ask each group to name the commercial products made from its assigned resource.

Enrichment (challenging) Have students research and write a report on acid rain and the environmental damage it causes. Students should include a status report on recent talks between Canada and the United States aimed at solving the problem. A good source on the topic is the book *Acid Rain* by Robert Anderson (San Diego, CA: Greenhaven Press, Inc. 1994).

BUILDING SKILLS
STUDY AND RESEARCH SKILLS

Using the Library

Key Vocabulary

reference
dictionary
encyclopedia
almanac
atlas

As you read about the regions of the world, you may want to learn more about certain subjects. For example, you may want answers to such questions as: How do the Inuit live today? What is it like to live near the Arctic Circle?

Reference Books

You can find information about many subjects in a library. The reference section is a good place to begin looking. Here you will find reference books, or books that are sources of information. Dictionaries, encyclopedias, almanacs, and atlases are reference books that are useful for research.

A dictionary provides the meanings of words and indicates their pronunciation. An encyclopedia has information about many subjects written in the form of articles. An almanac is published every year and contains up-to-date facts on many subjects. When you want to locate a certain place on a map, use an atlas.

Finding Books

You may also want to find informational books that are not in the reference section. As you may know, a card catalog or a computer is used to tell you where these books are located. Each book is listed three different ways—by author, by title, and by subject. The card in the catalog or entry in the computer lists the author's last name, followed by the first name. Each card or entry has a call number to help you to find the book you are looking for.

Reviewing the Skill

1. Name four kinds of reference books.
2. Which reference book would you use to find out how to pronounce *mosaic*?
3. How would you go about finding a book on the Arctic Circle?
4. Why is it important to know how to use the library?

89

SKILLS LESSON
page 89

Lesson Theme Books containing factual information can be found in the reference section of the library.

Lesson Objectives

- Describe four kinds of reference books.
- Identify how to locate informational books in the library.

1 PREPARE

Motivate Have students identify all the places in the library where they would look for factual information.

2 TEACH

Discussing Reference Books

Ask students:

- **In which three ways are books listed in the card catalog?** (by author, title, and subject)

Applying the Skill Have students list four questions about their hometowns. Then have them identify the reference book they would use to find each answer.

3 CLOSE

Summarizing Students should realize the library is a source for factual information.

Answers to Reviewing the Skill

1. dictionary, encyclopedia, almanac, and atlas
2. a dictionary
3. look under the subject listing in the card catalog or computer.
4. It makes finding books and information easier and more efficient.

MEETING INDIVIDUAL NEEDS

Reteaching (easy) Prepare a list of topics that students could find in the card catalog of a library. Pair students to test each other on whether they would look under a title card, subject card, or author card to find each topic on the list.

Extension (average) Have students visit the school library or a community library to draw a floor plan showing where the reference section, card catalog, and computer are located.

Enrichment (challenging) Have students research the history of how the Dewey Decimal System became the organizational plan for American libraries. Have each student write a short essay on the advantages and disadvantages of this library system.

LESSON 3
pages 90–92

Lesson Theme Canada is a parliamentary democracy with an elected head of government. As a member of the Commonwealth of Nations, Canada recognizes Britain's monarch as its nominal leader.

Lesson Objectives
- Describe Canada's parliamentary democracy.
- Describe the prime minister's and governor general's roles in Canada's parliamentary democracy.
- Explain Canada's role as a member of the Commonwealth of Nations.

PREPARE

Motivate Have a student read the *Read Aloud* passage to the class. Discuss the role of Members of Parliament (or MPs) in Canada's representative democracy.

Set Purpose Ask the *What You Know* question and discuss why a direct democracy is not practical in a huge nation with a complex social and economic life. Tell students they will learn the answer to *What You Will Learn* as they read the lesson.

TEACH

Examining Canada's Government Help students focus on the role of Great Britain in shaping Canada's representative democracy.

Ask students:

- **In what way is the government of Canada like the government of the United States?** (Both are representative democracies in which voters elect people to represent them.)

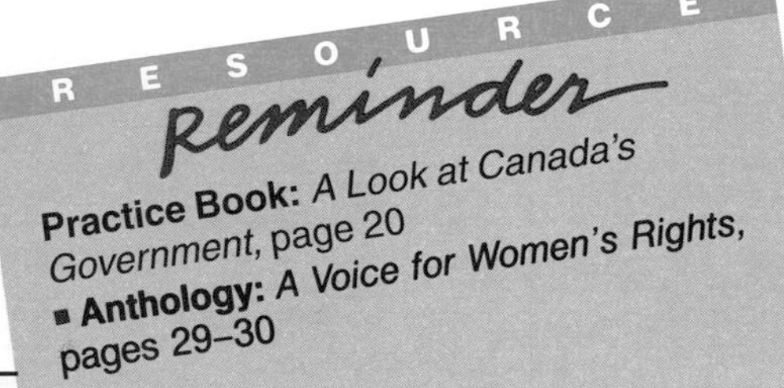

Practice Book: *A Look at Canada's Government,* page 20
- **Anthology:** *A Voice for Women's Rights,* pages 29–30

LESSON 3

The Government

READ TO LEARN

Key Vocabulary

parliamentary democracy
prime minister
cabinet
Commonwealth of Nations
monarchy

Read Aloud

A Member of Parliament's function is to represent his political party and [the people who elect him] at the federal level, to gain for them whatever aid and support he can.

This is how John Crosbie, a member of the Canadian Parliament, explained how the people who serve in Canada's national legislature view their roles. They believe that it is their duty to aid and support the people who voted them into office. In Canada, as in the United States, this belief is the foundation of representative government.

Read for Purpose

1. **WHAT YOU KNOW:** What is a representative democracy?
2. **WHAT YOU WILL LEARN:** How is Canada's parliamentary democracy organized, and how does it fit within the Commonwealth of Nations?

CANADA'S GOVERNMENT

In 1988, after they were criticized for "betraying the people," important members of the Canadian government suddenly resigned. Why did this happen? The Canadian government was trying to win approval of a trade treaty with the United States. There were bitter debates between Canada's political parties. These debates were televised both in French and in English. Opponents of the treaty kept criticizing it, and it appeared that people were losing confidence in the government. When that happens in Canada, the government leaders resign. New elections are then held.

Like the United States, Canada has a representative government in which the voters elect the people they wish to represent them at both the national and local levels. However, the Canadian government has kept more of its British heritage than has the United States.

Great Britain governed Canada as a colony for about a century. Canada won the right to govern itself in 1867, but it did not win full independence from British rule until 1982. Canada's government is still much like Great Britain's. You will read more about the government of Great Britain in Chapter 9.

WHAT YOU KNOW: a government in which people elect representatives to serve them in the government

READING STRATEGY AND VOCABULARY DEVELOPMENT

Skimming and Scanning Review the skimming and scanning strategies from the previous lessons. Relate the use of skimming and scanning to the information students learned in the skills lesson about using a library. Have students read Lesson 3. Then have them work in groups to scan the text to answer the *What You Will Learn* question in the *Read Aloud* section on this page.

PARLIAMENTARY DEMOCRACY

Canada is a **parliamentary democracy**. The country has a national legislature called Parliament, which meets in Ottawa, the national capital. The Canadian Parliament is made up of the House of Commons and the Senate. Representatives of the lower house, the House of Commons, are elected. Members of the upper house, the Senate, are appointed by the governor general, whom you will read about later in this lesson.

The leader of Canada's national government is the **prime minister**. A prime minister is the leader of the political party that has a majority of members in the House of Commons. A majority is more than half the total number.

You have read that in the United States the President heads the executive branch of government. In Canada the prime minister heads both the executive and the legislative branches of government. The two branches are not separate in Canada as they are in the United States. The prime minister governs with the help of the **cabinet**. The cabinet is made up of the prime minister and about 30 members of the House of Commons. The cabinet members advise the prime minister and help him or her carry out the law.

The prime minister depends on the support of Parliament to stay in office. Without support from Parliament, the prime minister must resign, as Canada's prime minister did after the events you read about at the beginning of this lesson. In any parliamentary democracy, the prime minister and Parliament must work together to govern the country.

The representatives to the Canadian Parliament meet in Ottawa, the capital of Canada.

Discussing Canada's Government
Continue the discussion from the previous page.

Ask students:

- **Why is Canada's government so similar to Great Britain's?** (Great Britain ruled Canada as a colony for about a century.)
- **What is the name given to Canada's legislature or lawmaking body?** (Parliament)
- **What are the two houses of the Canadian legislature?** (the House of Commons and the Senate)
- **What is the name given to the head of Canada's government?** (prime minister)
- **How do the roles of the United States President and the Canadian prime minister differ?** (In the United States the President heads the executive branch; in Canada the prime minister is the leader of both the executive *and* the legislative branches.)
- **Who comprises the cabinet in Canada?** (the prime minister and about 30 members of the House of Commons)
- *THINKING FURTHER:* **What happens if the prime minister loses the support of Parliament?** (He or she must resign, and new parliamentary elections are held.)

CURRICULUM CONNECTION

Music Suggest that students explore Canadian and American patriotic songs. Give students copies of the words of two songs. One should be the Canadian national anthem "O Canada"; the other, "Columbia, the Gem of the Ocean." Have students analyze the wording of both songs to find identical words, such as *home, free, patriot,* and *allegiance.*

BACKGROUND INFORMATION

Multicultural Perspectives Canada, a former British colony, is only one of several nations around the world that gained its blueprint for democracy from Britain. Today other former colonies of Britain have also adopted its system of parliamentary democracy and made it their own. These include the nations of Jamaica, Malaysia, Australia, Papua New Guinea, and India. In India the equivalent of the House of Commons is called *Lok Sabha,* or ''House of the People,'' and the equivalent of the Senate is called *Rajya Sabha,* or ''Council of States.'' Ask students why they think the system of parliamentary democracy has appealed to people around the world.

Discussing the Commonwealth of Nations Help students understand the Commonwealth of Nations.

Ask students:

- **What is the shared background of the members of the Commonwealth of Nations?** (They were once ruled by Great Britain.)
- *THINKING FURTHER:* **What is the difference between a governor general and a prime minister in Canada?** (The governor general is a leader in name only; the prime minister has actual power.)

Applying the Lesson Have students draw a diagram of the Canadian government organization showing that the executive and legislative functions are united in the function of the prime minister.

3 CLOSE

Summarizing Students have read that Canada is a parliamentary democracy like Great Britain. As members of the Commonwealth of Nations, Canadians maintain their ties to Great Britain.

Answers to Check Your Reading

1. The British monarch is considered the head of the government and the governor general represents this person.
2. If Parliament shows a lack of support for the prime minister and his or her government, the prime minister must resign.
3. a government elected by citizens in which the legislative and executive powers are combined in one branch and in which the leader of the majority party is the leader of the government
4. What did Canada and Great Britain disagree about? Did Canada go to war with Great Britain to gain independence? If it didn't go to war, how did Canada gain its independence?

Independent Practice
Practice Book: page 20

The members of the British royal family are still treated with great respect in Canada.

Canada is one of the members of the **Commonwealth of Nations**. This is a group of independent nations once ruled by Great Britain. Commonwealth nations think of the British monarch—the king or queen—as the head of their governments. A **monarchy** is any government headed by a hereditary ruler, such as a king or queen. However, in Canada the British monarch is leader in name only.

In Canada the British monarch is represented by an official called the governor general. The governor general has little power. For the most part, this official approves decisions made by Parliament and the prime minister. For example, the prime minister recommends people to serve in the Senate, and the governor general officially appoints them.

CANADA'S PARLIAMENTARY DEMOCRACY

You have read that Canada's government is a democracy in which people choose their representatives. They elect the members of the House of Commons, the lower house of Parliament. The members of the upper house, the Senate, are appointed.

Canada inherited a parliamentary democracy from Great Britain. In a parliamentary democracy the legislative and executive functions are not separate, as they are in the United States. The prime minister leads both the executive and legislative branches.

Check Your Reading

1. How does Canada have elements of a monarchy in its government?
2. Why is the prime minister and his or her government sometimes forced to resign in Canada?
3. What is a parliamentary democracy?
4. **THINKING SKILL:** What three questions could you ask to learn how Canada won its independence from Great Britain?

THINKING SKILL: Asking Questions

MEETING INDIVIDUAL NEEDS

Reteaching (easy) Have students use the text to list the following Canadian government positions: prime minister, member of House of Commons, senator, cabinet member, and governor general. Ask students to define the duties of each position.

Extension (average) Have students imagine they live in a Canadian city being visited by the British monarch. Have them write a letter to a friend in the United States describing their thoughts and feelings about the royal visit.

Enrichment (challenging) Have students research the Commonwealth of Nations to: (1) learn the present extent of the British Empire; (2) learn important dates in Canada's transition from colony to Commonwealth member; and (3) list the advantages of membership in the Commonwealth.

Arts and Recreation

READ TO LEARN

Key Places

Edmonton, Alberta

Read Aloud

Once in another time, my friends, a great change came into Tante Odette's life although she was already an old woman . . . It all happened because of a change that came over [her cat] Chouchou . . . As Tante Odette worked at her loom every evening, Chouchou would lie on the little rug by the stove and stare at her with his big green eyes. "If only you could talk, what company you would be for me." Suddenly . . . a thump, thump . . . came from the door. . . .

In this French Canadian folktale, called "The Tale of the Talking Cat," the knock at the door was a woodsman named Pierre Leblanc. Tante Odette refused him entry. Suddenly her cat miraculously began to speak and told her to let him in. How could this be? Leblanc had used ventriloquism, the ability to throw his voice, to get his way. The story warned, "If you must follow the advice of a talking cat, be sure you know who is doing the talking for him." Folktales are just one part of Canada's cultural heritage.

Read for Purpose

1. WHAT YOU KNOW: What is distinctive about the arts of the United States?
2. WHAT YOU WILL LEARN: What do the arts and recreation of Canada tell you about Canada and its people?

LOVE OF THE OUTDOORS

Canada has many traditional arts. The Inuit, American Indians, French Canadians, and British Canadians are just a few of the groups whose artistic traditions go back hundreds of years in Canada. Inuit sculpture in soapstone, a soft soapy-feeling stone, American Indian masks and poems, and folktales such as "The Tale of the Talking Cat" are well known throughout the world.

Even though the arts of different groups may differ, many of them deal with the same topics. One such topic is nature and the beauty of the Canadian land. Canada, as you know, is a land of beautiful mountains, forests, and rivers. Canadian writings, paintings, and songs often describe the country's landscape. From Canada's artists we know Canadians have a great love of the outdoors.

WHAT YOU KNOW: This question refers to material covered in Chapter 2, Lesson 4; the arts of the United States often reflect the freedom of expression that artists in the United States have.

LESSON 4

pages 93–95

Lesson Theme The Canadian environment and the country's varied cultures have enriched the arts and recreation of Canada.

Lesson Objectives
- Describe the forms of traditional and ethnic art in Canada.
- Describe the modern recreational activities of the Canadian people.
- List the kinds of sports activities available in Canada.

PREPARE

Motivate Have a student read the *Read Aloud* and the explanation at the end of the passage to the class. Ask students if they can recall similar folktales that give wise advice.

Set Purpose Use the *What You Know* question to recall the degree of freedom of expression in the United States. Tell students they will learn the answer to the *What You Will Learn* question as they read the lesson.

TEACH

Discussing Canadians' Love of the Outdoors Have students analyze the influence of the outdoors on Canadian forms of expression.

Ask students:

- **What is a traditional art?** (an art whose practice has been handed down from generation to generation)
- **What are some of the traditional arts in Canada?** (soapstone sculpting, mask carving, storytelling)

READING STRATEGY AND VOCABULARY DEVELOPMENT

Skimming and Scanning Have students work in groups to preview Lesson 4. Ask each group to develop questions using the lesson headings. After the class has read the lesson, have each group ask its questions. The responding group should scan the text to provide evidence to support its answers.

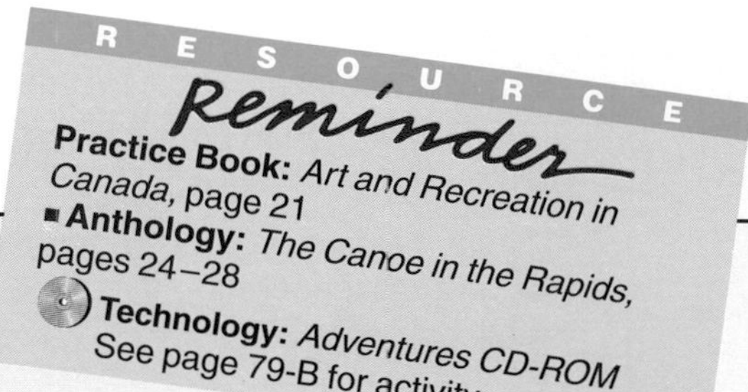
RESOURCE *Reminder*

Practice Book: *Art and Recreation in Canada*, page 21

Anthology: *The Canoe in the Rapids*, pages 24–28

Technology: *Adventures CD-ROM* See page 79-B for activity.

Discussing Ethnic Identity Help students realize the ways in which Canada's cultural identity influences artistic expression.

Ask students:

- **What is meant by ethnic identity?** (the feeling of belonging to a cultural group with its own traditions and customs)
- **Why do ethnic groups in Canada express themselves through the arts?** (to keep their cultures alive and to show what it's like to live in Canada)

Identifying Canadian Sports and Other Amusements Have students focus on the role of Canadians in sports.

Ask students:

- **Which present-day professional sport was invented by Canadian soldiers?** (ice hockey)
- **What other sports are popular in Canada?** (rodeos, skiing)
- **What is the Calgary Stampede and where is it held?** (an agricultural fair and rodeo; Calgary, Alberta)
- **How have Canadians managed to provide recreation and entertainment in their cold environment?** (They have moved some sports indoors and built huge shopping centers indoors or underground.)
- *THINKING FURTHER:* **How did Canadians show creativity when developing sports?** (Soldiers used boots with blades attached, field hockey sticks, and a lacrosse ball when inventing ice hockey.)

ETHNIC IDENTITY

Another topic that interests Canadians is ethnic identity. Because Canada is a mosaic of cultures, groups often are concerned with keeping their cultures alive or learning to live with other ethnic groups. A Canadian television program or a modern dance, for example, may show what it is like to be a French Canadian in British Canada. Programs may also show an Inuit or Indian in European Canada or a Canadian in a culture that is dominated by the United States.

SPORTS AND OTHER AMUSEMENTS

The Canadian interest in nature is expressed not only in the arts but also in sports and other amusements. Canadians excel in many sports.

According to one story, on Christmas Day in 1855 soldiers at Kingston, Ontario, were bored. So they tied blades to their boots and took to the ice with field hockey sticks and an old lacrosse ball. This was the beginning of Canada's national sport, ice hockey. Today ice hockey is played all over the world. Canadian players are included on many of the world's professional hockey teams.

Canadian sports fans like baseball and basketball, too. It was probably a Canadian living in Massachusetts—James Naismith—who invented the game of basketball, using a soccer ball and two peach baskets that he nailed to a wall in a gym.

Ice hockey is sometimes called the national sport of Canada. Rodeo and skiing are also popular sports in Canada.

94

BACKGROUND INFORMATION

Inuit Art The Inuit believed that the spirits of the animals they hunted felt honored if their images were carved beautifully.

- The Inuit learned to carve lifelike stone and ivory sculptures of animals.
- Today, art objects made by the Inuit are certified by the Canadian government and are sold with registration numbers that attest to their authenticity.
- The Inuit elders pass down the techniques of their art to the next generation in traditional teacher-student relationships.

5 FUNDAMENTAL THEMES OF GEOGRAPHY

Description of Place The arts, sports, and amusements of Canada mark it as a place with a wide variety of cultural expressions reflecting Canada's mosaic of people. One important expression is the Canadian passion for ice hockey, a sport that conforms to the physical characteristics of a cold, icy land. As students read the lesson, ask them to cite another example of the creative way Canadians respond to their cold environment. (vast indoor and underground shopping malls)

Water sports and other amusements, in addition to stores and restaurants, are found at the West Edmonton Mall.

A Canadian sports event that draws thousands of spectators to Alberta every year is the Calgary Stampede. This ten-day spectacle is a combination agricultural fair and rodeo, with Indian displays and stage shows.

Because of Canada's cold climate, many recreational activities in the country take place indoors. Even in warmer areas of Canada, cities are built with the cold winter in mind. Canada has the world's largest indoor shopping mall, the West Edmonton Mall in Edmonton, Alberta. Edmonton is the northernmost of Canada's major cities. The West Edmonton Mall is the size of 108 football fields. It boasts 800 stores, an indoor lake, and the world's largest parking lot. Farther south, Montreal has a huge underground shopping mall. It includes restaurants and many different kinds of stores. Advanced technology and vast energy resources make it possible for such malls to remain lighted and warm, even in the coldest weather.

CULTURAL TRADITIONS

Canada has a variety of cultural traditions. Within these traditions, Canada's artists often express their concern for the environment, for ethnic identity, and with what it means to be a Canadian today.

For recreation, many Canadians love being outdoors. Canadian athletes excel in many different sports and are supported by avid fans.

Check Your Reading

1. What are some of the traditional arts of Canada?
2. What is Canada's national sport?
3. How do the arts in Canada reflect the people's love for the outdoors?
4. THINKING SKILL: What do you think the activities shown in the photographs on page 94 say about the arts and recreation of Canada?

THINKING SKILL: Observing

95

Applying the Lesson Have students write short descriptions of what they might see at the Calgary Stampede. (farm animals, crops, a rodeo, Indian arts, stage shows; an aspect of Canada's varied culture)

3 CLOSE

Summarizing Students have read that Canadians value their ethnic identity and also love the outdoors. These two factors are seen in their art and in their forms of recreation.

Evaluating Use these questions to assess students' understanding.

- **How do their arts and forms of recreation show Canadians' adaptation to the cold environment?** (Their arts reflect the beauty of the northern environment; they have used technology to design indoor recreation facilities, and have created sports like ice hockey to take advantage of the cold climate.)
- **How have Canadians been creative in developing new forms of recreation?** (They have designed new sports and have built indoor malls containing lakes and rinks.)
- **What are some examples of ethnic or traditional Canadian art?** (folktales, soapstone carvings, carved masks)

Answers to Check Your Reading

1. soapstone sculpting, making of American Indian masks, creation of poems and folktales
2. ice hockey
3. Nature themes are often the subject matter.
4. The activities shown in these pictures reflect the Canadians' love of the outdoors.

Independent Practice
Practice Book: page 21

MEETING INDIVIDUAL NEEDS

Reteaching (easy) Ask students to choose the Canadian art or form of recreation they are most interested in and write a paragraph giving at least two reasons for their choice.

Extension (average) Ask students to reread the *Read Aloud* passage on page 93. Then have them conduct library research to discover other Canadian folktales and compare the tales' messages with the message of the tale on page 93. Discuss the history of the folktales and the wisdom gained from them.

Enrichment (challenging) Inuit carvings are renowned for their lifelike animal poses. Have students research Inuit stone and ivory sculptures. Ask them to write a paragraph about the forms Inuit sculptures have taken over thousands of years.

CHAPTER 3 REVIEW

pages 96–97

USING THE CHAPTER SUMMARY AND REVIEW

Cultural Geography These questions may be used for review.

- **What are the three main cultural groups that make up the Canadian mosaic?** (American Indian, French, British)
- **Which four industries are important to Canada's developed economy?** (mining, farming, fishing, manufacturing)
- **How does a parliamentary democracy differ from the representative democracy of the United States?** (The legislative and executive functions in a parliamentary democracy are not separate as they are in the representative democracy of the United States.)
- **What are some of the cultures reflected in Canadian traditional arts?** (Inuit, American Indian, French Canadian, and British Canadian, to name a few)

Ideas to Remember

- **Why is Canada called a mosaic?** (Canada's groups of people keep their separate identities while forming parts of the whole.)
- **Which natural resources are important to Canada's economy?** (minerals and fossil fuels)
- **Who leads Canada's national government?** (the prime minister)
- **What do Canada's arts and recreational activities revolve around?** (nature, ethnic identity)

Answers to Reviewing Vocabulary

1.–3. True.
4. Unlike the President of the United States, the Canadian prime minister heads the executive and the legislative branches of government.
5. True.
6. A province is a self-governing area within a nation.
7. True.
8. True.

CHAPTER 3 ▪ SUMMARY

IDEAS TO REMEMBER

- Canada is a "mosaic" of different ethnic groups living together.
- Canada's natural wealth has made it a leading world economic power.
- Canada's system of government is a parliamentary democracy, with an elected parliament and a prime minister.
- Many of the arts and popular recreational activities of Canada reflect a love of the outdoors.

96

ENRICHMENT ACTIVITY

Making a Ring-and-Pin Toss **Materials:** 21-inch sticks; shower curtain rings or rings cut from salt or oatmeal boxes

1. In the last part of this chapter, students learned how varied cultures have enriched the arts and recreation of Canada. Tell the class that a popular recreation among some Canadian Indians is the ring-and-pin toss. On the chalkboard, draw a sketch of the equipment that is used—a length of string tied at one end to the top of a stick, and at the other to a ring.
2. Tell students (or groups of students) to follow the diagram on the chalkboard to make their own ring-and-pin tosses.
3. Explain that a player holds the stick in his or her hand (with the ring dangling at the end of the string) and tries to move the stick so that the ring lands over it.

CHAPTER 3 • REVIEW

REVIEWING VOCABULARY

Each of the following statements contains an underlined vocabulary word or term. Number a sheet of paper from 1 to 10. Beside each number write whether each of the following statements is true or false. If the statement is true, write "true." If it is false, rewrite the sentence using the vocabulary word or term correctly.

1. Acid rain, or rain mixed with certain forms of air pollution, has caused great damage to Canada's lakes and rivers.
2. A monarchy is a government that is headed by a king or queen, or by another hereditary ruler.
3. Canadians describe their country as a mosaic because of the many different groups of people living there.
4. Like the United States President, the Canadian prime minister heads only the executive branch of government.
5. Canada is one of many countries that belongs to the Commonwealth of Nations.
6. A province is an area that is ruled by a monarch.
7. Canada is a parliamentary democracy in which the Prime Minister and the Parliament work closely together.
8. Separatism, or the desire to break away from a larger country, has been a powerful political force in Quebec.
9. Canada is a leading producer of fossil fuels such as lead, zinc, and silver.
10. The Canadian cabinet is a group of business and labor leaders who recommend legislation in the Parliament.

REVIEWING FACTS

1. Name two things that many Canadians feel are threats to their country.
2. In which part of Canada do most Canadians live? Why?
3. Only a small percentage of Canada's land is good for farming, yet agriculture is one of Canada's most important industries. Explain why.
4. Name two ways in which the governments of Canada and the United States are similar. In what two ways are they different?
5. What is one way in which people in Canadian cities adapt to harsh northern winters? How do Canada's vast natural resources help its people to do this?

WRITING ABOUT MAIN IDEAS

1. **Writing a Help Wanted Ad:** Imagine that you are the director of the Polaris Mine in extreme northern Canada. How would you interest people in coming to the Arctic to work? Write a help wanted ad for mining jobs in your company.
2. **Writing a Paragraph:** Write a paragraph describing how the present form of Canadian government reflects the country's British heritage.
3. **Writing About Perspectives:** Imagine that you are an Indian who must learn French and English as well as your own language. Write a letter to a friend telling how you feel about having to speak three languages.

BUILDING SKILLS: USING THE LIBRARY

1. Name four kinds of reference books.
2. Which reference book would you use to find out how to pronounce *monarchy*?
3. What kind of information is found in an atlas?
4. Why is it important to know how to use the library?

9. Canada is a leading producer of fossil fuels such as coal, petroleum, and natural gas.
10. The cabinet is a group of about 30 members of the House of Commons who advise the prime minister.

Answers to Reviewing Facts

1. American influences and pollution
2. a narrow belt below the Canadian Shield; It has Canada's most fertile land and warmest climate.
3. Modern technology helps farmers produce more from their land.
4. Both are representative governments whose citizens elect people to represent them; both guarantee civil rights. Canada has a constitutional monarch; executive and legislative branches are not separate in Canada, since Canada has a parliamentary democracy.
5. Possible answers include: wearing warm clothing, staying where there is heat; there is an abundance of fossil fuels.

Suggestions for Writing About Main Ideas

1. Ads should highlight positive aspects of working in the Polaris Mine.
2. Students should mention Canada's parliamentary democracy and the role of the governor-general.
3. Students might say they feel the situation is unfair because Canadians of European background are not required to learn Indian languages.

Answers to Building Skills: Using the Library

1. dictionaries, encyclopedias, almanacs, atlases
2. dictionary
3. the location of places
4. so you can find information about many different subjects

Chapter Review and Test
Practice Book: *Vocabulary Review,* page 22
Transparency: *Graphic Organizer*
Assessment Book: *Chapter 3 Test*

MAKING CONNECTIONS

Organizing Information Use the Main Idea Map Graphic Organizer Transparency, writing in only the underlined headings. Have students fill in words or phrases about Canada that relate to each heading. *Ask:* What are some of the factors that make up the cultural geography of Canada?

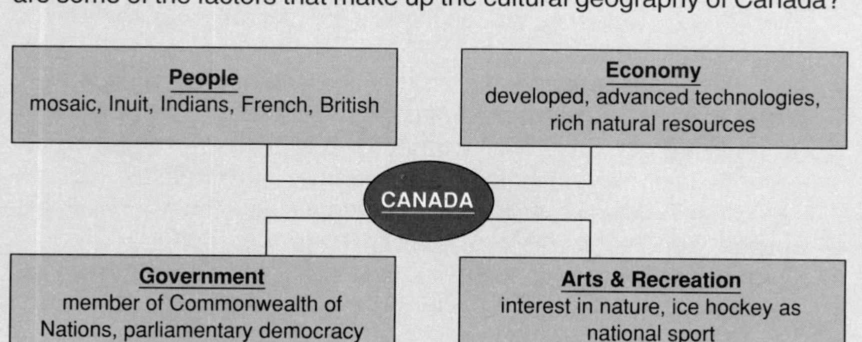

UNIT 1 REVIEW
pages 98–99

USING THE UNIT SUMMARY AND REVIEW

Physical Geography These questions may be used for review.

- **What are the major mountain and plains areas of the United States?** (*Mountains:* Appalachian Highlands, Rocky Mountains, Pacific Mountains; *Plains:* Interior and Coastal plains)
- **Where does the temperature of the region tend to be warmer?** (in the lowlands)
- **How much land in the United States is suitable for farming? In Canada?** (50 percent; 5 percent)

Cultural Geography

- **When was the region first inhabited?** (more than 40,000 years ago)
- **What is a threat to the environment of the region?** (acid rain)
- **What form of democracy does the United States have? What form does Canada have?** (representative democracy; parliamentary democracy)
- **Which freedom allows artists to express their opinions?** (freedom of expression)

Answers to Reviewing Vocabulary

1. timberline
2. prime minister
3. cabinet
4. capitalism
5. republic

UNIT 1 ▪ SUMMARY

UNITED STATES AND CANADA: PHYSICAL GEOGRAPHY

LANDFORMS

- Mountains (Appalachian Highlands, Rocky Mountains, Pacific Mountains) and Plains (Interior Plains, Coastal Plains)

- Northern Canada: Canadian Shield and Arctic Islands

CLIMATE

- Temperate climate: few extremes in weather
- Temperatures: colder in mountains and north, warmer in lowlands and south

NATURAL RESOURCES

- Arable land: 50 percent of land in Unites States, only 5 percent in Canada
- United States grows more food than any other nation
- Forests cover one third of United States and Canada
- Waterways: Great Lakes, St. Lawrence Seaway, Mississippi River, Columbia River

UNITED STATES AND CANADA: CULTURAL GEOGRAPHY

PEOPLE

- Indians came to the region more than 40,000 years ago
- Inuit came to Canada about 6,000 years ago, still alive in the north today
- In the United States, many different ethnic groups; in Canada, most people are of British or French descent
- Hispanics are fastest-growing ethnic group in the United States today
- Immigrants came from many lands searching for opportunity

ECONOMY

- Developed economies: many different economic activities, advanced technology
- Capitalist system: freedom and economic opportunity
- Free enterprise: freedom to own property and run a business
- Foreign trade: extensive in both countries, especially with each other
- Acid rain: threatens the environment of Canada and the United States

GOVERNMENT

- Democratic government: representative democracy in the United States, parliamentary democracy in Canada
- United States: power divided between national and local governments, federal government divided into three branches (executive, legislative, judicial)
- Canada: House of Commons elected, Senate appointed; prime minister leads government

ARTS AND RECREATION

- Freedom of expression provides opportunities for artists

- Popular sports: baseball, football, basketball, ice hockey, skiing, and many others
- People use leisure time for hobbies: reading, movies, sports

98

ENRICHMENT ACTIVITY

Creating a Picture Atlas **Materials:** construction paper, paints or markers, pencils, yarn

1. Tell students that they are going to create illustrated maps that, when bound together, will become a picture atlas of the United States and Canada.
2. Divide the class into groups, and assign each group a subregion, such as Western Canada and Alaska.
3. Have each group draw an illustrated map of their area, showing important cities, rivers, landmarks, resources, and products. (Groups may use their texts as well as other reference sources—for example, National Geographic's *Picture Atlas of Our World,* 1993.)
4. Have students make a cover for their atlas and bind it with yarn. Save the atlas for comparison to regions that will be studied later.

UNIT 1 • REVIEW

REVIEWING VOCABULARY

cabinet
capitalism
prime minister
republic
timberline

Number a sheet of paper from 1 to 5. Beside each number write the word or term from the list above that best matches each statement.

1. Trees cannot grow above this line because of high elevation or cold climate.
2. This head of state depends on the support of Parliament to remain in office.
3. Canada's prime minister governs with the help of this group of advisers.
4. In this type of economic system, an individual may establish his or her own business largely free of government control.
5. The United States is an example of this form of democracy in which citizens elect people to represent them in government.

WRITING ABOUT THE UNIT

1. **Writing a Myth:** The Seneca used the myth of Sky Woman to explain how the land became fruitful. Write a myth of your own explaining a natural event you have read about, such as the eruption of Mount St. Helens or the creation of the Rocky Mountains.
2. **Writing an Essay:** Many people throughout the world have marveled at the strength of democracy in the United States. Write an essay entitled "Why Democracy Works in the United States."
3. **Writing About Perspectives:** Write a "letter to the editor" expressing your opinion for or against Quebec's independence.

ACTIVITIES

1. **Constructing a Chart:** Use almanacs, encyclopedias, and atlases to find the following geographical data about both Canada and the United States: capital, area (in square miles and kilometers), population, and gross national product. Then make a chart comparing the data.
2. **Making a List:** Make a list of states that border on a province, territory, or body of water in Canada. Next to each state on the list, write the province, territory, or body of water on which it borders.
3. **Working Together to Research Canadian-American Issues:** Work in groups to find information on the current issues affecting both the United States and Canada. Use newspapers and magazines to find articles about acid rain, trade policies, or United States influence on Canada. Then present summaries of the issues to the class.

LINKING PAST, PRESENT, AND FUTURE

During the past, large segments of our nation's population have been employed in farming and in manufacturing. Today increasing numbers of people are employed in services. In which of these industries do you think you will be employed in the future? Is your prediction related to the results reflected by today's trends in industry and employment?

99

Suggestions for Writing About the Unit

1. Students' myths should be about an actual event that has occurred.
2. Students' essays might focus on the role of citizens in our democracy, the system of checks and balances, or the federal system.
3. Students should give reasons for their opinions.

Suggestions for Activities

1. Students should use the most current almanac to find current population and gross national product statistics. You may wish to have students list additional information to compare, such as highest and lowest points, largest bodies of water, number of states or provinces, and so on.
2. Alaska—Yukon Territory; Washington—British Columbia; Montana—Alberta and Saskatchewan; Idaho—Alberta; North Dakota—Saskatchewan and Manitoba; Minnesota—Manitoba, Ontario, Lake Superior; Wisconsin—Lake Superior; Michigan—Lakes Superior and Huron, Ontario; Ohio—Lake Erie; Pennsylvania—Lake Erie; New York—Lakes Erie and Ontario, Ontario, Quebec, St. Lawrence River; Vermont—Quebec; New Hampshire—Quebec; Maine—Quebec, New Brunswick
3. This activity lends itself to a cooperative learning approach. You may wish to have students prepare collages on the issues they research.

Suggestions for Linking Past, Present, and Future Students should state the industry they predict and why they chose that industry. For example, students may say they will be employed in the service industry. Their prediction may be based on our growing population and the fact that the service industry is growing.

PERFORMANCE ASSESSMENT

Demonstrating Understanding Remind students that at the beginning of this unit they were told to imagine that they were news broadcasters giving reports from various places in the United States and Canada. Ask each student to choose one part of the United States or Canada he or she would like to represent—for example, a city in Canada or a Native American rural community in the southwestern United States. Students' broadcasts should represent the geography and culture of the places they choose. Remind them of the standards that will be applied to their broadcasts, which were outlined in the Unit Opener on page 35. For additional performance assessment information, see page T41 in the *Assessment Book*.

For the Portfolio: Include students' scripts and tapes, along with your anecdotal record or observational checklist.

UNIT 2 ORGANIZER

LATIN AMERICA text pages 100–177

UNIT THEME

Latin America covers a vast area with little arable land, developing economies, and unstable governments, but with a rich mix of cultures from the blending of Indian, European, and African backgrounds.

UNIT RESOURCES

- Practice Book: pp. 23–44
- Anthology: Part 2
- Anthology Cassette
- Outline Maps: 3, 4, 13–16
- Transparency Maps: 1–2, 9
- Unit 2 Poster
- Desk Maps
- Internet Project Handbook
- Geo Adventures Pad
- Pupil Edition on Cassette
- Transparency: Graphic Organizer
- **Technology:** *Adventures CD-ROM*
- Assessment Book, Chapter Tests: 4, 5, 6, 7

Internet CONNECTION

The Home Page at **http://www.mmhschool.com** and the **Internet Project Handbook** contain on-line student activities related to this unit.

UNIT PLANNING GUIDE

CHAPTER	SUGGESTED PACING	THEMES
4 PHYSICAL GEOGRAPHY OF LATIN AMERICA pages 106–117	4 days	A wide variety of elevations and climates is found in Latin America, but there is little farmland, and natural resources are distributed unevenly.
5 MEXICO pages 118–139	7 days	Characterized by a mestizo culture that is an Indian and European mix, Mexico faces economic problems in spite of oil revenues and population growth.
6 CENTRAL AMERICA AND THE CARIBBEAN pages 140–157	6 days	Lacking natural resources, the countries of Central America and the Caribbean rely on the industries of agriculture and tourism.
7 SOUTH AMERICA pages 158–175	6 days	South America is a continent that has people from many cultures, countries with developing economies, and a history of unstable governments.

UNIT PROJECTS

Writing a Travel Brochure Tell students to imagine that they are taking a trip through one subregion of Latin America. Have them find out more about the area and then write a travel brochure about that part of Latin America.

Oral Reports Ask students to imagine that they are the leaders of an environmental expedition to the Amazon rain forest to conduct one of the research projects described in the Cooperative Learning section in the next column of this page. Have them write and deliver an inspirational speech that they would make to expedition members before entering the rain forest.

Cooperative Learning: Planning a Research Project Divide the class into groups of five to plan an environmental research project on the Amazon rain forest. Its purpose will be to find out how to develop businesses based on gathering nuts, fruits, and leaves from the rain forest instead of burning it to make farmland.

Field Trip Visit an exhibition or a museum collection of Latin American art. Have students analyze the themes, colors, and common forms in Latin American art and the ways in which these elements reflect life in Latin America today. After the trip have students share their perceptions.

BULLETIN BOARD IDEAS

Making Your Own Bulletin Board As the class studies Latin America, ask students to collect or draw pictures that depict the contributions of various peoples to Latin American culture. Have them label and post their illustrations to make a bulletin board display titled "Latin America: A Cultural Blend." Encourage students to share some information on the topics they illustrate with the class.

Using the Unit Poster As an alternative to the bulletin board activity, display the Unit 2 Poster, which shows an enlarged version of the Unit Opener globe and photographs on pages 100–101.

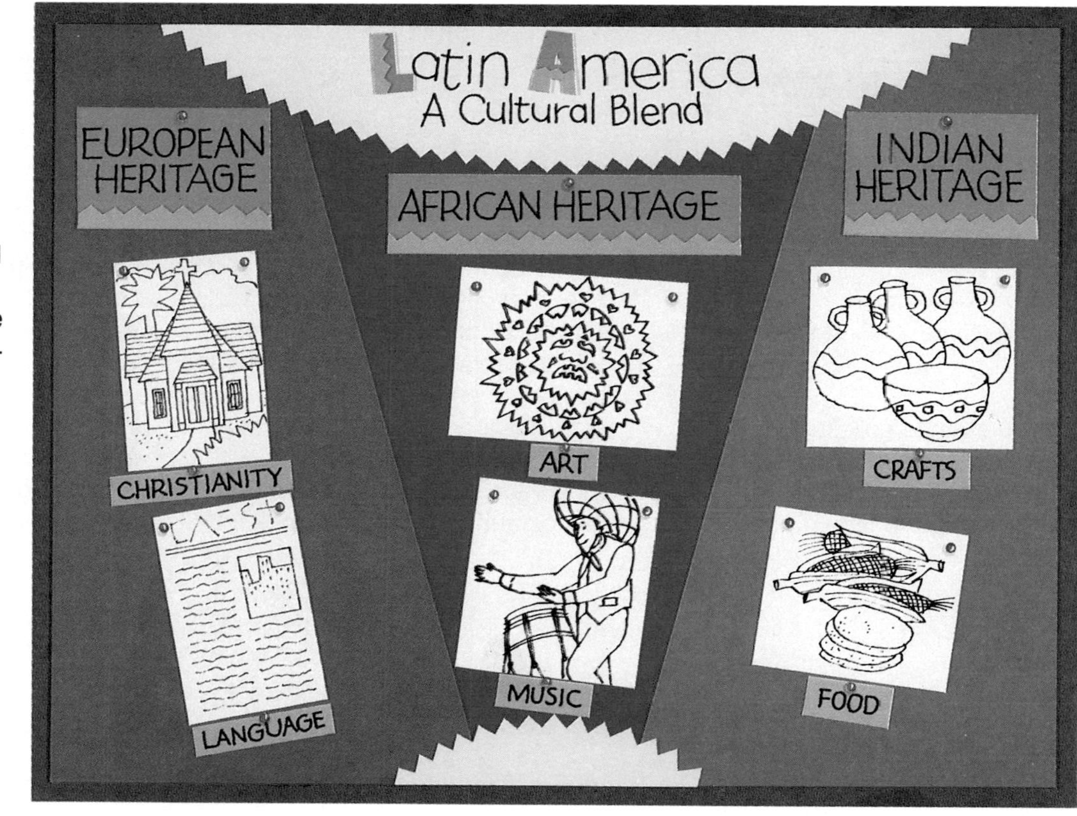

UNIT BIBLIOGRAPHY

For descriptions and additional resources, see the Annotated Bibliography beginning on page T-1 in the back of the book.

For the Teacher

Books

Machado, Ana Marie. *Exploration Into Latin America.* Columbus, OH: Silver Burdett Press, 1996.

Morrison, Marion. *Central America.* Austin, TX: Raintree Steck-Vaughn, 1993.

Read-Alouds

Carlson, Lori M., and Cynthia L. Ventura, ed. *Where Angels Glide at Dawn: New Stories From Latin America.* New York: J. B. Lippincott, 1993.

Turenne Des Pres, Francois. *Children of Yayoute.* New York: Universe Publishing, 1994.

Technology Multimedia

The Amazon Trail. CD-ROM. MECC. Toll Free: 1-800-215-0368.

Central America and the West Indies. 5 Videos. Society For Visual Education. Toll Free: 1-800-829-1900.

■ *Mexico.* Video. National Geographic. Toll Free: 1-800-368-2728.

■ *South America.* Video. National Geographic. Toll Free: 1-800-368-2728.

Free Materials

For information on the Panama Canal, send to: Panama Canal Commission; Office of Public Affairs; Unit 2300; APO, AA 34011-2300.

For the Student

■ Ada, Alma Flor. *The Gold Coin.* New York: Atheneum, 1991. **(Average)**

Ancona, George. *The Piñata Maker/El Piñatero.* San Diego, CA: Harcourt Brace, 1994. **(Easy)**

Bachelis, Faren Maree. *The Central Americans.* New York: Chelsea House Publishers, 1990 **(Average)**

Lewis, Richard. *All of You was Singing.* New York: Atheneum, 1991. **(Easy)**

■ Montejo, Victor. *The Bird Who Cleans the World and Other Mayan Fables.* Willimantic, CT: Curbstone Press, 1991. **(Average)**

Robb, Patricia. *We Live in Brazil.* New York: The Bookwright Press, 1985. **(Easy)**

Stein, R. Conrad. *Mexico.* Chicago, IL: Childrens Press, 1992. **(Challenging)**

■ Books excerpted in Anthology

■ National Geographic selection

UNIT 2
ORGANIZER

TEACHER EXCHANGE

Collecting Stamps

Thanks to:
Judith Witt
District 1-R School
Grand Island, Nebraska

Materials
canceled stamps collected by students, binders or albums, stamp collectors' tabs for sticking stamps to album pages

Instructions

1. Have the class begin an ongoing project in which each student puts together a stamp collection.
2. Have students contact friends and relatives to help them save stamps. Suggest other sources of finding stamps, such as advertising in the school newsletter or local paper and visiting local stamp shows.
3. Ask students to sort stamps by categories, such as subject matter, state, country, and so on. Have them use an album page for each category and label each page. Tell them that using a binder or album to which pages can be added is a good way for them to display their growing collections.
4. Encourage students to find out the locations of countries represented by their stamps and to research people and events commemorated on the stamps.

Illustrating Climate Regions

Thanks to:
Carolyn Claiborne
South Middle School
Downey, California

Materials
large pieces of construction paper or poster paper, glue, scissors, markers

Instructions

1. Have students review the meaning of *climate* and the various climates they have studied. Assign different climate regions to groups of two or three students.
2. Ask the groups to draw pictures and to write brief explanations about their climate regions. Have them include information about the location, seasons, precipitation, and temperature of the regions as well as other facts that interest them.
3. Have each group design a colorful poster to display its work. After students have mounted their pictures and information, have the groups title their posters.

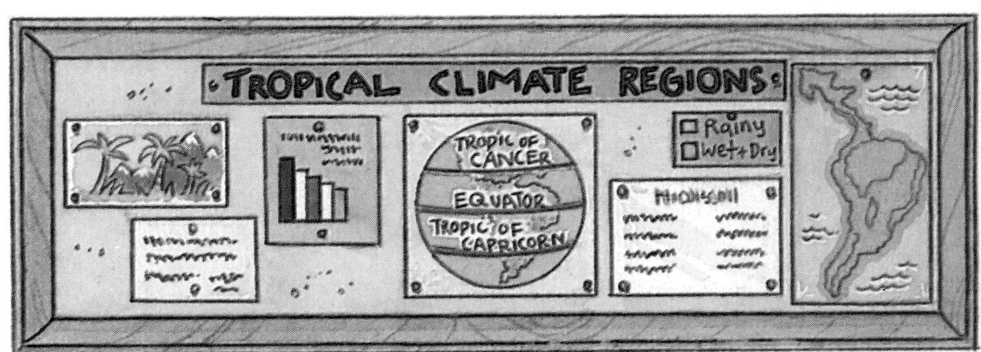

TECHNOLOGY CENTER

Enriching with Multimedia

RESOURCE: ***Internet Project Handbook***

Look at the ***Internet Project Handbook*** for student projects related to this unit or have students go on-line at http://www.mmhschool.com, Macmillan/McGraw-Hill's Home School page on the World Wide Web.

RESOURCE: ***Adventures CD-ROM***

Enrich Unit 2 with the *Travel* and *Explore* activities on the Adventures CD-ROM.

SCHOOL-TO-HOME

Exploring Ancient Civilizations

- Throughout this unit, students will have an opportunity to learn about three early Indian civilizations in Latin America: the Maya, the Aztec, and the Inca. The Maya used a system of writing called hieroglyphics. *Codices,* or written records, were used by the Aztecs to record their religion and history. Have the class brainstorm a list of words and ideas related to the unit. Then encourage students to record these words in their own codices.
- To make a codex, have students cut a sheet of drawing paper in half vertically and then slightly overlap and glue the edges of the pieces together. Then have them accordion-fold the strip into equal sections. Students and their families can invent picture symbols to illustrate the class-generated list. Encourage students to share their completed codices with the class.

SECOND-LANGUAGE SUPPORT

While these activities are designed especially for students needing second-language support, they are meant to be shared by all students in the class.

Chapter 4, Lesson 1 ■ Physical Geography of Latin America

After the class has read and discussed the lesson, create visual and textual clues for students needing second-language support. Organize the class into several heterogeneous groups and assign each group a portion of the lesson. Have each group reread and discuss its section and agree on a representative symbol to be placed on a class map.

Chapter 5, Lesson 2 ■ Mexico

To make sure all students grasp the material, conduct a guided class reading of pages 123 to 125. Create a Semantic Map on the chalkboard with "Mexico's Problems" as its center. Have students volunteer words and phrases for spokes, such as *subsistence farming, pollution, overpopulation.*

Chapter 6, Lesson 2 ■ Central America and the Caribbean

Second-language students may have trouble with lesson-end economics questions. Working in small groups to write a short lesson-based play will provide a relaxed atmosphere in which to discuss the lesson. Assign each group a section of the lesson. Have students present their plays to the class.

Chapter 7, Lesson 2 ■ South America

Student comprehension of South American industries will be enhanced by working in small groups to create collages as visual summaries of what they have read. Supply magazines, tourist brochures, glue, and posterboard.

Chapter 5, Lesson 2

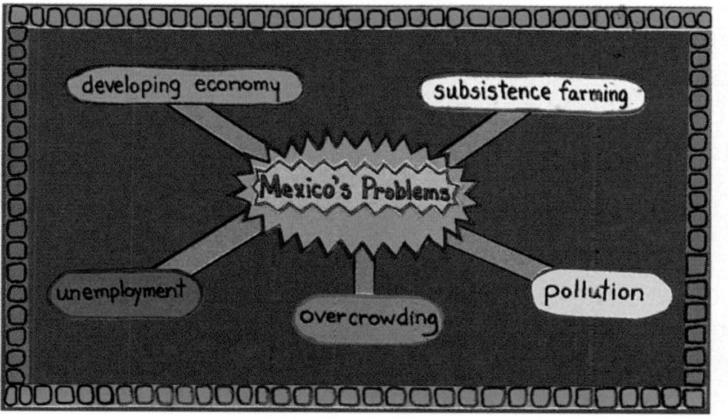

UNIT 2

pages 100–177

USING THE UNIT OPENER

Introducing the Unit Display the Unit 2 Poster. Have students look at the unit title and silently read the *Where We Are* section on the facing page.

Ask students:

- **In which direction is Latin America from the region that we studied in the last unit?** (south)
- **Which three areas are labeled on the maps of Latin America?** (Mexico, Central America and the Caribbean, South America)
- **According to the map, what are two geographical features that characterize Latin America?** (mountains and rivers)

EXTENDING MAP SKILLS

Help students recognize the three uniquely shaped areas that make up Latin America.

Ask students:

- **What are the two key lines of latitude and longitude that you used on this map to locate the hemispheres in which Latin America is located?** (0° latitude, or the equator, and 0° longitude, or the prime meridian)
- **Which major bodies of water surround Latin America?** (the Gulf of Mexico and the Atlantic and Pacific oceans)

APHY • GEOGRAPHY • GEOGRAPHY

NORTH AMERICA
Gulf of Mexico
Tropic of Cancer
MEXICO
CENTRAL AMERICA AND THE CARIBBEAN
ATLANTIC OCEAN
Equator
SOUTH AMERICA
PACIFIC OCEAN
Tropic of Capricorn
South Pole
30°N 15°N 0° 15°S 30°S 45°S 60°S
135°W 120°W 105°W 90°W 75°W 45°W 30°W

100

ONGOING UNIT PROJECT

Planning for Assessment Tell students that they will have many opportunities to learn about Latin America in this unit. Explain that when they finish this unit, they will have a chance to demonstrate what they have learned by making a map of Latin America. Students should think about the information they would like to include on their maps as they read the unit. So that students can see what they have learned by the time they finish this unit, have them try to draw a map of Latin America now, without using their books. Have students save these maps. Tell them that they will make new maps at the end of the unit. For information on completing this unit project, see page 177.

Goal: Students' work should show a knowledge of the geographical features that characterize Latin America.

Signs of Success: Assure students that they will not be assessed on their drawing ability. An adequate map should show the borders of the countries of Latin America and correctly label the countries, important geographic features, and major cities. An excellent map would also include information about land use and products.

HY • GEOGRAPHY • GEOGRAPHY • GEOGRAPHY • GEOGRAPHY • GEOGRAPHY • GEOGRA

AFRICA

LATIN AMERICA

WHERE WE ARE

In Unit 2 your journey through the world around us continues, south of the United States, to the part of the world known as Latin America. This region includes not only the entire continent of South America, but also Mexico and the countries of Central America and the Caribbean Sea.

On your journey through Latin America you will visit a land of high mountain peaks and vast river valleys. You will meet people like Alfredo Rios Perez, who lives and works in Mexico City. As you read about Latin America, think about how it compares to the region in which you live. What makes Latin America unique?

101

Using a Map to Make Predictions Tell students to look carefully at Latin America's location relative to the latitude and longitude lines and to the Tropic of Cancer and the Tropic of Capricorn.

Ask students:

- **Within which longitude lines drawn on the map does Latin America fit?** (30°W and 120°W)
- **Within which latitude lines shown on the map does Latin America almost fit?** (30°N and 45°S)
- **Where is Latin America in relation to the Tropic of Cancer and the Tropic of Capricorn?** (Most of the region is located between these two lines of latitude.)
- **Where is most of South America located in relation to the equator?** (Most of South America is located south of the equator.)
- *THINKING FURTHER:* **What predictions can you make about the climates of Latin America based on latitude, longitude, and its relative location to the Tropic of Cancer and the Tropic of Capricorn?** (Students should relate latitude, which includes the equator, the Tropic of Cancer, and the Tropic of Capricorn, to the amount of sunshine and heat in Latin America. Students should be able to predict that those areas that are located between the Tropic of Cancer and the Tropic of Capricorn will have direct sunlight and therefore a great deal of heat, while those areas north of the Tropic of Cancer and south of the Tropic of Capricorn will have less direct sunlight and therefore less heat. Students should recognize that east-west longitude lines do not affect climate. They should predict warm semitropical and tropical climates for Latin America.)

CURRICULUM CONNECTION

Music One of the outstanding cultural contributions of Latin America to the world is "Latin music." Discuss types of Latin music with which students may be familiar, such as tangos, rumbas, congas, calypsos, and reggae. Allow students to bring in tapes or CDs of Latin music to play for the class. Examples might be Gloria Estefan or Tito Puente.

Introducing the Tables Explain to students that the tables at the beginning of each unit list information about the countries in the region that is to be studied. Point out that the countries are listed alphabetically in the tables.

EXTENDING TABLE SKILLS

Have students skim the four-page table on Latin America. Then encourage students to identify the kinds of information that are given about each country.

Ask students:

- **What are the four categories of information in the tables?** (major language, population, size or area, leading exports)
- **How many countries are presented in this table?** (35)
- **How many major languages are spoken in this region?** (twelve)
- **Which language is most common in the countries in this table?** (Spanish)
- **Which is the second most common language?** (English)
- **Which country has the largest population?** (Brazil)
- **Which country has the largest area?** (Brazil)
- **Which country has two capitals? What are they?** (Bolivia; the judicial capital of Sucre and the administrative capital of La Paz)
- **Which symbol is shown for each country?** (flag)

LATIN AMERICA

BARBADOS
Capital ★ Bridgetown
Major language: English
Population: 0.3 million
Area: 166 sq mi; 430 sq km
Leading export: sugar

ANTIGUA AND BARBUDA
Capital ★ St. Johns
Major language: English
Population: 0.1 million
Area: 170 sq mi; 440 sq km
Leading export: clothing

BELIZE
Capital ★ Belmopan
Major languages: English and Spanish
Population: 0.2 million
Area: 8,865 sq mi; 22,960 sq km
Leading export: sugar

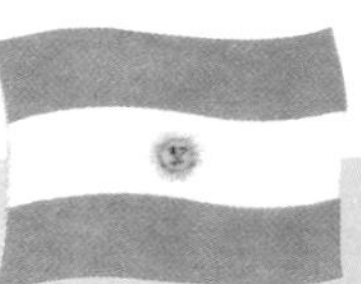

ARGENTINA
Capital ★ Buenos Aires
Major language: Spanish
Population: 33.9 million
Area: 1,068,299 sq mi; 2,766,890 sq km
Leading exports: meats and corn

BOLIVIA
Capital ★ Sucre (judicial) and La Paz (administrative)
Major languages: Spanish, Quechua, and Aymará
Population: 7.7 million
Area: 424,163 sq mi; 1,098,580 sq km
Leading exports: tin and copper

BAHAMAS
Capital ★ Nassau
Major language: English
Population: 0.3 million
Area: 5,382 sq mi; 13,940 sq km
Leading export: lobster

BRAZIL
Capital ★ Brasília
Major language: Portuguese
Population: 153.7 million
Area: 3,286,480 sq mi; 8,511,970 sq km
Leading exports: iron ore and coffee

BUILDING CITIZENSHIP

Flags Flags represent loyalty to a group or nation. The first known flags were banners carried by the Egyptians in war. Colors on flags are thought to symbolize certain qualities, such as red for courage and blue for peace. Assign each student a Latin American flag. Have students find out the history of the flag and the meaning of its symbols and colors. Assign one student the flag of the United Nations to research as a symbol of world citizenship. Have students prepare written reports about their assigned flags and draw sketches that show their layouts and symbols.

CHILE
Capital ★ Santiago

Major language: Spanish
Population: 14 million
Area: 292,259 sq mi; 756,950 sq km
Leading export: copper

DOMINICA
Capital ★ Roseau

Major language: English
Population: 0.1 million
Area: 290 sq mi; 750 sq km
Leading export: bananas

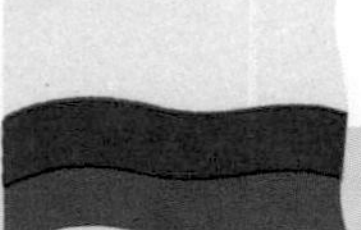

COLOMBIA
Capital ★ Bogotá

Major language: Spanish
Population: 35.6 million
Area: 439,734 sq mi; 1,138,910 sq km
Leading export: coffee

DOMINICAN REPUBLIC
Capital ★ Santo Domingo

Major language: Spanish
Population: 7.8 million
Area: 18,816 sq mi; 48,730 sq km
Leading export: sugar

COSTA RICA
Capital ★ San Jośe

Major language: Spanish
Population: 3.3 million
Area: 19,652 sq mi; 50,900 sq km
Leading export: coffee

ECUADOR
Capital ★ Quito

Major languages: Spanish and Quechua
Population: 10.8 million
Area: 109,483 sq mi; 283,560 sq km
Leading export: oil

CUBA
Capital ★ Havana

Major language: Spanish
Population: 11.1 million
Area: 42,803 sq mi; 110,860 sq km
Leading export: sugar

EL SALVADOR
Capital ★ San Salvador

Major language: Spanish
Population: 5.8 million
Area: 8,124 sq mi; 21,040 sq km
Leading export: coffee

Continue the discussion.

Ask students:

- **What is the most common leading export from Latin American countries?** (coffee)
- **What is the second most common leading export from this region?** (sugar)
- **What are the leading minerals exported from Latin America?** (tin, copper, iron ore, bauxite)
- **Which Latin American product that is processed from a mineral is a leading export?** (aluminum)
- **How many Latin American countries have oil or oil products as one of their leading exports? Which countries are they?** (five; Ecuador, Mexico, Trinidad and Tobago, Venezuela)
- **Which countries have a fish product as their leading export?** (French Guiana has shrimp and the Bahamas have lobster.)
- **Which two countries export livestock?** (Argentina and Uruguay)

BACKGROUND INFORMATION

Copper Paraguay, Bolivia, Chile, and Peru mine copper. It is one of the important minerals exported from Latin America.

- Copper was probably the first metal to be used by humans. Fused with zinc to form bronze, copper was used to make body armor, swords, and statues. Today it is commonly used for copper wire and water pipes.
- Chuquicamata, in Chile's Atacama Desert, is one of the world's largest open-pit mines. Chuquicamata is so huge, in fact, that it is visible from outer space. Chile is the world's largest producer of copper.

Bauxite Most of the world's bauxite is found in semitropical or tropical areas. Sixty percent of the bauxite mined has alumina extracted from it to make aluminum. Other uses for bauxite include:

- the production of abrasives such as emery;
- the making of quick-hardening cement;
- the production of refractories, or materials that can endure high temperatures;
- paper making;
- oil refining;
- water purification.

Understanding How to Use Tables of Statistics Help students identify the kinds of questions that give meaning to the set of statistics found in the tables on pages 102–105. Have students share their ideas by asking them what questions they might ask about the information in these tables. List the questions on the chalkboard, and have the class help you put them in a logical order. Stress to students that they should seek both common and unique elements in the statistics. Tell them the following questions could be asked about these tables.

- What is the subject of the table?
- What types of information are presented in the table?
- What types of information can be totaled?
- Which countries share similar statistical information?
- Which countries have sharply differing statistical information?
- Which categories of statistical information can be compared?
- What happens when similar categories are ranked?
- What might be some reasons for a low figure in the case of a statistical category such as population?

LIFE TODAY • LIFE TODAY • LIFE TODAY • LIFE TODAY • LIFE TODAY • LIFE TODAY • LIFE TODAY

FRENCH GUIANA

Capital ★ Cayenne

Major languages: French and Creole
Population: 0.1 million
Area: 35,135 sq mi; 91,000 sq km
Leading export: shrimp

HONDURAS

Capital ★ Tegucigalpa

Major language: Spanish
Population: 5.3 million
Area: 43,277 sq mi; 112,090 sq km
Leading export: coffee

GRENADA

Capital ★ St. George's

Major language: English
Population: 0.1 million
Area: 131 sq mi; 340 sq km
Leading export: nutmeg

JAMAICA

Capital ★ Kingston

Major languages: English and Jamaican Creole
Population: 2.6 million
Area: 4,243 sq mi; 10,990 sq km
Leading export: aluminum

GUATEMALA

Capital ★ Guatemala City

Major language: Spanish
Population: 10.7 million
Area: 42,042 sq mi; 108,890 sq km
Leading export: coffee

MEXICO

Capital ★ Mexico City

Major language: Spanish
Population: 92.2 million
Area: 761,604 sq mi; 1,972,550 sq km
Leading exports: oil and cotton

GUYANA

Capital ★ Georgetown

Major languages: English, Hindi, and Urdu
Population: 0.8 million
Area: 83,000 sq mi; 214,970 sq km
Leading exports: sugar and bauxite

NICARAGUA

Capital ★ Managua

Major language: Spanish
Population: 4.1 million
Area: 49,998 sq mi; 129,494 sq km
Leading exports: cotton and coffee

HAITI

Capital ★ Port-au-Prince

Major languages: French and French Creole
Population: 6.5 million
Area: 10,714 sq mi; 27,750 sq km
Leading export: coffee

PANAMA

Capital ★ Panama City

Major languages: Spanish and English
Population: 2.6 million
Area: 30,193 sq mi; 78,200 sq km
Leading export: bananas

104

BUILDING CITIZENSHIP

Learning About Your State Have students create a table of statistics about their state. Discuss the various categories that they could include in their tables. List students' ideas on the chalkboard. Then have students choose five categories that they feel should be included on their tables and research the statistics. When students have finished, have them compare the statistics that they felt were important enough to include on their tables. Compile one major class table.

• LIFE TODAY • LIFE TODAY • LIFE TODAY • LIFE TODAY • LIFE TODAY • LIFE TODAY • LIFE TODAY

PARAGUAY
Capital ★ Asunción
Major languages: Spanish and Guaraní
Population: 5.2 million
Area: 157,047 sq mi; 406,750 sq km
Leading exports: cotton, timber, and coffee

ST. VINCENT AND THE GRENADINES
Capital ★ Kingstown
Major language: English
Population: 0.1 million
Area: 131 sq mi; 340 sq km
Leading export: bananas

PERU
Capital ★ Lima
Major languages: Spanish, Quechua, and Aymará
Population: 23.7 million
Area: 496,225 sq mi; 1,285,220 sq km
Leading exports: oil and copper

SURINAME
Capital ★ Paramaribo
Major languages: Dutch, English, and Hindi
Population: 0.4 million
Area: 63,039 sq mi; 163,270 sq km
Leading exports: bauxite and aluminum, rice, and bananas

PUERTO RICO
Capital ★ San Juan
Major languages: Spanish and English
Population: 3.5 million
Area: 3,515 sq mi; 9,104 sq km
Leading exports: chemicals

TRINIDAD AND TOBAGO
Capital ★ Port-of-Spain
Major language: English
Population: 1.3 million
Area: 1,980 sq mi; 5,130 sq km
Leading export: oil

ST. KITTS AND NEVIS
Capital ★ Basseterre
Major language: English
Population: 40,000
Area: 139 sq mi; 360 sq km
Leading export: sugar

URUGUAY
Capital ★ Montevideo
Major language: Spanish
Population: 3.2 million
Area: 68,039 sq mi; 175,220 sq km
Leading exports: meat and wool

ST. LUCIA
Capital ★ Castries
Major languages: English and French patois
Population: 0.2 million
Area: 239 sq mi; 620 sq km
Leading export: bananas

VENEZUELA
Capital ★ Caracas
Major language: Spanish
Population: 20.6 million
Area: 352,143 sq mi; 912,050 sq km
Leading export: oil

105

Analyzing How to Make Figures in a Table Meaningful Help students see that using a table is like a detective game. They should not only read the statistics in the table but also think about how they can make connections between them and about what they mean. Use the following information to help students understand these connections. Ask them which clue they can find in the numbers in this table of Latin American nations that might help them to guess which nations are islands. (Tell students that one possible way is to find all the populations of around 1 million or less.) Have students refer to the Atlas map on page 624 to check their success rate. They should have identified nine island nations. Expect some errors. Jamaica, Puerto Rico, and Cuba are islands they might have missed, and French Guiana, Guyana, Suriname, and Belize are mainland nations with populations of less than one million that they might have mistaken for islands. Point out to students that they might have come closer to the correct answer if they had also considered the areas of these nations. Explain to students that this effort to give meaning to the figures helps them to start classifying these nations, but it is not intended to be perfectly accurate. The point of the exercise is to "work the numbers" for their significance. Discuss other questions that students could ask in order to make connections between the statistics and what they mean.

BACKGROUND INFORMATION

Creole and Nahuatl

- Creole is a mixture of French and African languages. It is a major language in French Guiana and in Haiti.
- Nahuatl is one of the major languages of Mexico. The ancient Toltecs and Aztecs of Mexico spoke Nahuatl.
- One million Mexicans still speak Nahuatl.
- Certain English words came from the Nahuatl language that the Spanish used in Mexico. Some English words with ancient Nahuatl origins are *tomato*, *avocado*, *chili*, *coyote*, *chocolate*, and *Mexico*.

CHAPTER 4
ORGANIZER

PHYSICAL GEOGRAPHY OF LATIN AMERICA

text pages 106–117

CHAPTER THEME

A wide variety of elevations and climates is found in Latin America, but there is little farmland, and natural resources are distributed unevenly.

CHAPTER OBJECTIVES

CONTENT

- Name the major landforms of Latin America and describe how they separate people.
- Identify the four main regions that make up Latin America.
- Explain why the region is called Latin America.
- Define *archipelago* and name the three main archipelagos of the West Indies.
- Identify the three main river systems of South America.
- Describe the major climate zones and natural resources of Latin America.
- Define *rain forest* and identify the largest rain forest in Latin America.
- Explain why only 5 percent of the land in Latin America can be farmed.
- Name and describe the two largest plains in Latin America.
- Discuss the impact of excessive development in the Amazon region.

SKILLS

Geography
- Interpret an elevation map of Latin America.
- Interpret a land use map of Latin America.
- Use a climate map to identify different climate zones in Latin America.
- Explain the relationship between latitude, altitude, and climate using a map.

Study and Research
- Interpret a diagram about mountain climates.

Thinking
- Make inferences about Brazil's rivers.

Reading and Writing
- Write a brochure describing a tour of the Amazon rain forest.

CITIZENSHIP VALUES

- Appreciate the importance of natural resources to the welfare of a people.

TEACHER OPTIONS

READING STRATEGY: Note Taking   Strategies to help students read and remember the main ideas of the lesson.
Lesson 1: p. 107   Lesson 2: p. 111

MEETING INDIVIDUAL NEEDS   Activities for reteaching, extension, and enrichment.
Lesson 1: p. 110   Geography Skills: p. 115
Lesson 2: p. 114

GEO ADVENTURES ACTIVITIES PAD   Daily activities to assess students' understanding of geography skills.

CURRICULUM CONNECTION   Activities to help integrate other subject areas with Social Studies.
Math: p. 109   Science: p. 113

PUPIL EDITION ON CASSETTE   Language support for students who have difficulty reading or who will benefit from listening to the Pupil Edition on Cassette as they read.

SECOND-LANGUAGE SUPPORT   Activities and suggestions for second-language learners.
Lesson 1: p. 7

CHAPTER PLANNING GUIDE

LESSON	SUGGESTED PACING	THEMES	TEACHER SUPPORT MATERIALS: TEACHER'S RESOURCE CENTER
1 LANDFORMS pages 107–110	1 day	High mountains, tropical forests, and mighty river systems make travel and farming difficult in Latin America.	Practice Book p. 23 Outline Map p. 13 **Technology:** *Adventures CD-ROM*
2 CLIMATE AND RESOURCES pages 111–114	1 day	Latin America has a wide range of elevations and climate conditions, limited land to support farming, and a random pattern of rich natural resources.	Practice Book p. 24 Outline Map p. 13 **Technology:** *Adventures CD-ROM*
BUILDING GEOGRAPHY SKILLS Relating Latitude, Elevation, and Climate page 115	1 day	Latitude and elevation affect climate.	Practice Book p. 25 Outline Map p. 4 Transparency Map 2
CHAPTER SUMMARY AND REVIEW pages 116–117	1 day	Chapter content, skills, and vocabulary are reviewed and evaluated.	Practice Book p. 26 Transparency: Graphic Organizer Assessment Book, Chapter 4 Test

Technology CONNECTION

Lesson 1
ADVENTURES CD-ROM
Have students *Travel* to a Latin American country of their choice in *Travel.*

Lesson 2
ADVENTURES CD-ROM
Students can find a movie on the rain forest in *Investigate, South America.*

CHAPTER 4

pages 106–117

USING THE CHAPTER OPENER

Discussing the Photograph Encourage students to think about the factors that contribute to the richness of the fields pictured here. Help them to understand that the physical characteristics of this place (such as nearness to the equator) and the human characteristics (such as hard-working farmers) both contribute to the richness of the fields.

Ask students:

- **What are the physical characteristics of this place?** (steep slopes, green fields, a river, tropical climate)
- **What are the human characteristics of this place?** (The organized planting of the fields demonstrates the farmers' skill and the necessity for workers.)

Reading/Listening to the Primary Source Ask students to look at the photograph while you read the quotation in the *Focus* section aloud.

Ask students:

- **Where is the speaker located?** (high over the scene in the photograph)
- **What does the speaker mean by "emerald pile carpets"?** (green, thick crops)
- **What do you see as you are looking down at this place that you would not see if you were walking in it?** (geometric pattern of fields, contrast between landforms, vast size of area)

CHAPTER 4

PHYSICAL GEOGRAPHY OF LATIN AMERICA

FOCUS

I've never seen anything to compare with the richness and beauty of the land over which we've been flying. The patterning of fields covering all but the steepest slopes with those emerald pile carpets is fantastic.

Selden Rodman, the author of many books about Latin America, used these words to describe the view he had from his plane as he flew over the mountain valleys of South America. The "richness and beauty of the land" is just one of the qualities of this region.

BACKGROUND INFORMATION

About the Photograph This photo was taken in the Sacred Valley of the Incas on the Vilcanota River. The valley is near Pisac on the Pacific coast of Peru. Pisac is the Cuzco area. Cuzco was the Incan capital.

FUNDAMENTAL THEMES OF GEOGRAPHY

Location Also near Cuzco is the ancient Incan military outpost of Machu Picchu. Perched between two peaks in Peru, Machu Picchu was never seen by Spanish explorers. Machu Picchu is a breathtaking example of Incan technology—gardens terraced on the steepest slopes imaginable and irrigated by stone aqueducts. Even more impressive than the buildings of Machu Picchu are the Incan coastal highways, which are made of stone. The highways extend across most of the length of the Andes.

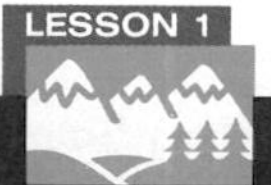

LESSON 1

Landforms

READ TO LEARN

Key Vocabulary

archipelago
altiplano
river system

Key Places

Central America
Caribbean Islands
Mexico
South America
Andes Mountains
Amazon River
Río de la Plata
Orinoco River

Read Aloud

In 1911 Hiram Bingham, an American explorer, discovered Machu Picchu (mäch' ü pēk' chü)—the "Lost City" of the ancient Inca Indians—deep in the Andes Mountains of Peru. The city Hiram Bingham saw consisted of several massive stone buildings on a lonely strip surrounded by steep cliffs. Today people visit Machu Picchu by train. They continue to be amazed at finding massive stone buildings in such an isolated area. But even today, many Latin Americans live in isolation, separated from each other by major landforms.

Read for Purpose

1. WHAT YOU KNOW: Where is Latin America located?
2. WHAT YOU WILL LEARN: What are the major landforms of Latin America, and how do they separate people?

LATIN AMERICA

The region of Latin America is vast in size and includes land on two continents. Central America, the Caribbean Islands, and Mexico—all of which are located in North America—are part of the region. All of the countries located on the continent of South America are also part of the region of Latin America.

Latin America gets its name from Latin, the language of ancient Rome. Languages that developed from Latin are spoken by many people today. These "Latin languages" include Spanish and Portuguese. When Spain and Portugal conquered large parts of the Western Hemisphere in the 1500s, they started colonies there. The colonies formed a large region where either Spanish or Portuguese became the official language. This region came to be called Latin America.

HIGH MOUNTAINS AND LONG RIVERS

After the Spanish conqueror Hernando Cortés captured Mexico from the Aztecs in the 1500s, he was asked to describe its landscape. Cortés took a piece of paper, crumpled it up, and tossed it onto a table, saying, "This is a map of Mexico." This dramatic description applies to most parts of the region of Latin America.

Look at the map on page 108. It shows that two contrasting physical features

WHAT YOU KNOW: in North America and South America, which are both in the Western Hemisphere

LESSON 1
pages 107–110

Lesson Theme High mountains, tropical forests, and mighty river systems make travel and farming difficult in Latin America.

Lesson Objectives

- Identify the area known as Latin America.
- Describe the mountains and rivers of Latin America.
- Explain the origin of the islands of the Caribbean.

1 PREPARE

Motivate Read the lesson title and the *Read Aloud* section to the class. Discuss students' ideas on why Machu Picchu is known as the "Lost City."

Set Purpose Use the *What You Know* question to review the location of Latin America relative to North America. Tell students that in this lesson they will learn about the landforms of Latin America. Have students use the *Atlas* map of Latin America on page 625 to point out the major landforms in the region.

2 TEACH

Defining Latin America Help students to understand the colonial background of this region.

Ask students:

- **Why is this region called Latin America?** (The region was settled by the Spanish and Portuguese, who spoke Latin languages.)

READING STRATEGY AND VOCABULARY DEVELOPMENT

Note Taking The purpose of this strategy is to help students paraphrase important information they need to remember from their reading. Explain to students that note taking is a strategy that involves two steps: (1) reading and selecting important information, and (2) paraphrasing and recording the information. Point out to students that they can select important information by reading the section headings, topic sentences of the sections, captions, and lesson questions. Tell students that once they determine what is important, they should take notes. To be sure students understand the information, stress that their notes should be written in their own words rather than copied from the text. Help students to take notes on the section titled "Latin America." Then have students work in groups to prepare notes for the remainder of the lesson.

RESOURCE Reminder

Practice Book: *Using Maps*, page 23
Outline Map: *Latin America*
Technology: *Adventures CD-ROM*
See page 105-B for activity.

EXTENDING MAP SKILLS

Discuss Latin America's location. Use the map on this page to help students visualize the decrease in the elevation of Latin America as you travel from west to east.

Ask students:

- **What is the highest peak in the Andes?** (Mt. Aconcagua at 22,834 feet, or 6,960 meters)
- **How does the elevation of South America change as you travel from the mouth of the Amazon River to southeastern Peru?** (For most of this area the elevation remains at 0 feet, or 0 meters, until you reach the Andes. There the elevation ranges from 1,500 to over 14,000 feet, or 500 to 4,000 meters.)
- **What is the elevation of the Brazilian Highlands?** (1,500–7,000 feet, or 500–2,000 meters)
- **Which has a higher elevation, Patagonia or the Llanos?** (Patagonia)
- **What is the highest point in Ecuador?** (Chimborazo at 20,561 feet, or 6,267 meters)

Describing the Mountains and Rivers Help students describe the various land and water features of Latin America.

Ask students:

- **Why do people live near volcanoes?** (The ash deposits from the eruptions make the soil very fertile.)
- **What is impressive about the sizes of the mountains and rivers of Latin America?** (The Andes are the longest mountain chain in the world; the Amazon is the second-longest river in the world.)
- **How do these physical features influence the South American continent?** (These features affect the climate, limit land available for farming, separate people, and are barriers to trade and transportation.)

dominate the Latin American landscape. They are high, rugged mountains and vast river valleys. These two features wind their way through most of Latin America.

The **Andes Mountains** of South America are more than 4,000 miles (6,437 km) long. They are the longest mountain chain in the world.

The mountains contain many volcanoes. When they erupt, the volcanoes can cause great damage. Yet people still live close to them because the ash from the eruptions makes the soil fertile.

One of the most famous Latin American volcanoes, Popocatépetl (pō pō kä tā′ pə təl), is in southern Mexico. According to an Indian legend, Popocatépetl, "Smoking Mountain," and the nearby volcano Ixtaccihuatl (ēs tä sē′ wät əl), "Sleeping Woman," were once a prince and princess. After the two were forbidden to marry, the princess died of a broken heart. Now when Smoking Mountain rumbles, the Indians say the prince mourns his sweetheart.

The **Amazon River** in South America is 3,900 miles (6,275 km) long. It is the world's second longest river, after the Nile River in Africa. The Amazon flows eastward across almost all of the northern part of South America.

The Andes Mountains and the Amazon River Valley have a great influence on the South American continent. They affect the climate and limit the land that can be

MAP SKILL: High, rugged mountains run along the western coasts of Mexico, Central America, and South America. In which nations are the highest elevations located?

108 **MAP SKILL:** Peru, Bolivia, Chile, Argentina, Ecuador, Colombia

BACKGROUND INFORMATION

What Made the Longest Mountain Chain? The force of the collision of the Pacific plate against the American plate caused the Andes Mountains to rise.

- Subduction, or the sliding of the Pacific plate under the American plate, causes the Andes to be volcanic.
- As the Pacific plate subducts, magma pressure is built up under the Andes and thereby fuels volcanoes.
- The sliding of the plate also created a deep underwater trench along the western coast of South America, which provides cool, nutrient-rich waters for excellent fish growth along the Pacific coast.

farmed. They also separate people and form barriers to trade and transportation.

ISLANDS OF THE CARIBBEAN

Most of the islands of the Caribbean Sea are also part of Latin America's mountain system. They are contained in a large circle of mountains under the sea whose peaks rise above the water. The mountain tops form the **archipelago** (är kə pel′ i gō), or island group, known as the Caribbean Islands or West Indies. They are divided into smaller archipelagos called the Greater Antilles (an til′ ēz), Lesser Antilles, and Netherlands Antilles. Find these island groups on the map on page 108.

The Bahamas are among the few islands in the area that are not mountain peaks. The Bahamas are coral islands. They were formed by layers of tiny sea animals.

THE ANDES

The Andes Mountains stretch along most of western South America. They are higher and more rugged than the mountains of Mexico and Central America. The highest peaks of the Andes are on the border between Argentina and Chile. There, peaks reach over 20,000 feet (6,000 m) above sea level.

Maria Yupanqui (ū pän′ kē) of Argentina lives in the Andes. She explains that because the mountains are so high, there "is less oxygen up here than at sea level." The weather is hot during the day, but the elevation makes it "very cold at night."

Look at the population density map on page 110. It shows that many people live in the Andes today. This area is more crowded than the lowlands in the middle of the continent. One crowded Andean area is the **altiplano** (äl ti plän′ ō). The altiplano is a high, cold, flat area between two mountain ranges in Bolivia and Peru. Lake Titicaca, the highest navigable lake in the world, is on the altiplano.

Popocatépetl, a volcano in Mexico, is North America's fifth-highest peak. It gives off smoke but has had no major eruption since 1702.

GREAT RIVER SYSTEMS

South America's continental divide is on the west coast, in the Andes Mountains. From the eastern peaks of the Andes, many rivers flow thousands of miles east to the ocean. No other continent has so many long rivers flowing in one direction.

In other parts of Latin America, though, rivers are short, with many waterfalls and rocks. As a result, ships cannot travel along them for long distances. South America is the only part of Latin America that has long, navigable rivers.

South America has three large **river systems**: the Amazon, the **Río de la Plata**, and the **Orinoco River**. A river system, or river basin, is the land drained by a river and its tributaries. This land is often shaped like a bowl. One of the world's greatest river systems, the Amazon flows through an area about three fourths the size of the United States.

Latin America's second-largest river system is the Río de la Plata. Made up mainly of the Paraná and Uruguay rivers,

Identifying the Islands of the Caribbean Emphasize that the Caribbean Islands are made up of mountain peaks and coral islands.

Ask students:

- **What special geographic term is used for an island group?** (an archipelago)
- **What is another name for the Caribbean Islands?** (the West Indies)
- **How were the Bahamas formed?** (Layers of tiny sea animals formed coral islands.)

Understanding the Andes Help students understand the effects the Andes have on humans.

Ask students:

- **How do the Andes compare to the mountains of Mexico and Central America?** (They are higher and more rugged than Mexican and Central American mountains.)
- **Where are the Andes the highest?** (They are highest on the border between Argentina and Chile.)
- **Why is it difficult to live on high mountains?** (There is less oxygen; it is cold at night so human bodies must adapt.)
- *THINKING FURTHER:* **How do you think the people who live on the altiplano make their living?** (Students may guess that since the altiplano is flat and has a good water source, its inhabitants probably farm.)

Discussing Great River Systems Help students to trace the three large river systems of Latin America on the map on page 108.

Ask students:

- **What is unique about the effect of the continental divide on the Andes?** (More rivers flow east from there than on any other continent.)
- **How do South American rivers compare to those in other parts of Latin America?** (South America is the only part of Latin America that has long, navigable rivers.)

CURRICULUM CONNECTION

Math Have three teams of volunteers research and make comparisons between Latin American waterways and United States waterways. Allow them to present their findings to the class in the form of visual displays. One team should find the figures for the height of the highest waterfall in the world, Angel Falls, Venezuela (3,212 feet [979 m]) and compare it to the height of Upper Yosemite Falls (1,430 feet [436 m]) and Niagara Falls (167 feet [51 m]). The second team should research the height of Lake Titicaca at 12,507 feet (3,812 m) and compare it to one of the Great Lakes, Lake Superior, at 600 feet (183 m). The third group should find out about the largest lake in Latin America, Lake Maracaibo, Venezuela, with a water surface area of 6,300 square miles (16,380 sq km) and compare it to Lake Superior at 31,810 square miles (82,708 sq km).

EXTENDING MAP SKILLS

Have students study the population density map on page 110.

Ask students:

- **In general, where are the most dense areas and least dense areas of population in South America?** (For the most part, the most dense areas are along the coast and the least dense are inland.)
- **Which major city in Brazil is the furthest inland?** (Brasília)
- *THINKING FURTHER:* **Compare this population density map with the one of the United States on page 43. How do the population densities in the Rocky Mountain and Andes Mountain areas compare?** (Population density is higher in the Andes.)

Applying the Lesson Have students list the major land and water features of Latin America and name similar features in the United States.

CLOSE

Summarizing Students have learned that Mexico, South America, Central America, and the Caribbean Islands make up the region called Latin America. Have students review how travel is hindered by the great physical features of Latin America.

Evaluating Use the *Check Your Reading* questions (answers below) to assess students' understanding.

Answers to Check Your Reading

1. Mexico, Central America, Caribbean Islands, South America
2. Amazon, Río de la Plata, Orinoco
3. Amazon River Valley, Andes Range
4. Brazil has mountains on three sides; water flows from the mountains into the Amazon.

Independent Practice
Practice Book: page 23

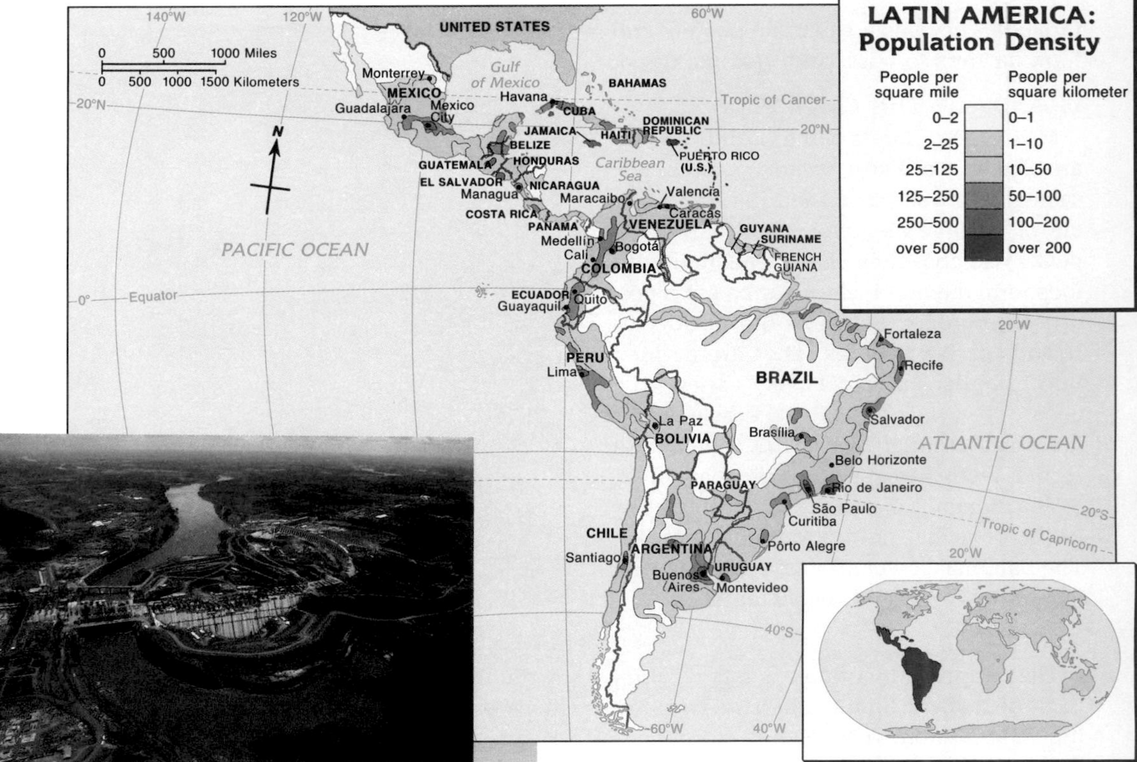

MAP SKILL: The Itaipu Dam provides energy for southern Brazil's most crowded areas. Name two cities that are located in these crowded areas.

it flows through east-central South America. The Río de la Plata system is a major transportation route for southeastern South America. The Itaipu (ē tī′ pü) Dam, the world's largest hydroelectric project, is on a tributary of the Río de la Plata.

The third large river system in Latin America is the Orinoco. In the north, the Orinoco's tributaries flow mainly across Venezuela and eastern Colombia.

MOUNTAINS AND TROPICAL LOWLANDS

Latin America is made up of Mexico, Central America, the Caribbean Islands, and South America. This region is dominated by its high mountains and the Amazon River Valley. Latin America has three great river systems—the Amazon, the Río de la Plata, and the Orinoco. High mountains and tropical forests make farming difficult and form barriers to travel.

Check Your Reading

1. What are the main parts of the Latin American region?
2. Name the three major river systems of Latin America.
3. What are the two main features of the physical geography of Latin America?
4. **THINKING SKILL:** Look at the map on page 108. Why do you think Brazil has so many rivers that flow into the Amazon River? Explain.

MAP SKILL: São Paulo, Rio de Janeiro

THINKING SKILL: Observing

MEETING INDIVIDUAL NEEDS

Reteaching (easy) Give students the outline map of Latin America, which can be found in the Teacher's Resource Center. Then have them label the following on the map: Mexico, Central America, Caribbean Islands, South America, Andes Mountains, and the Amazon River.

Extension (average) Have students construct a clay or plaster relief map of Latin America and include such natural features as the Andes, Amazon Basin, Brazilian Highlands, and Caribbean Islands.

Enrichment (challenging) Divide the class into three groups and ask them to draw cross-sectional diagrams of the elevations across Latin America. One group should do a cross section along the 20°N line of latitude; the second should do a cross section along the equator; and the third, a cross section along the 20°S latitude line. Have the groups mark the elevation ranges on the right and left edges of their diagrams.

LESSON 2

Climate and Resources

READ TO LEARN

Key Vocabulary

rain forest

Read Aloud

The land animals here have all fled or died. . . . We are looking for tree animals like . . . anteaters and felines.

These words were spoken by a member of an animal rescue mission in Brazil. Every day this mission sends boats into a part of the Amazon River Valley that is being flooded by water to form a reservoir. Some scientists question whether it was wise to begin developing this area because of its poor soil and difficult climate.

Read for Purpose

1. **WHAT YOU KNOW:** What are Latin America's most important landforms?
2. **WHAT YOU WILL LEARN:** What are the major climates and resources of Latin America?

EL DORADO

Latin America is rich in natural resources. Before the Europeans arrived, Indians created beautiful objects of gold and jewels.

Stories of precious metals and jewels drew many Europeans seeking to become rich from American treasure. They heard tales about a land where gold was lying around for anyone to pick up. This legendary kingdom was called *El Dorado,* the Spanish words for "the golden one."

No treasure hunter ever found the legendary El Dorado. However, conquerors found and took gold, silver, tin, emeralds, and other resources. Today new resources are being discovered. Mexico and Venezuela have huge petroleum reserves. Mexico also has considerable reserves of natural gas. However, mineral resources are often not easy to find. As one author has written:

> *Although nature has blessed the region in great abundance . . . it has jealously hidden the keys to this treasure house. Much of this wealth [cannot be reached] because of the barriers of jungles, mountains, and rivers.*

UNEVEN DISTRIBUTION OF RESOURCES

Latin America's natural resources are unevenly spread around. A number of countries, especially in Central America and the Caribbean Islands, have few minerals, or none at all.

Some Latin American nations have large ore deposits but lack other resources needed to use them for industry. Brazil, for example, has iron ore but no coal to turn

WHAT YOU KNOW: This question refers to information in Lesson 1; mountains and rivers.

LESSON 2
pages 111–114

Lesson Theme Latin America has a wide range of elevations and climate conditions, limited land to support farming, and a random pattern of rich natural resources.

Lesson Objectives
- Describe the pattern of land use in Latin America.
- Explain the distribution of Latin America's natural resources.
- Explain the climate zones of Latin America's mountains.

1 PREPARE

Motivate Read the *Read Aloud* section to the class. Discuss the problems that arise when people begin to develop the land.

Set Purpose Use the *What You Will Learn* question to discuss what kinds of resources might be found with each kind of landform.

2 TEACH

Discussing El Dorado Make sure students understand that El Dorado was only a legendary city.

Ask students:

- **What are the main barriers to finding the mineral riches of Latin America today?** (difficulty in traveling through rain forests and across mountains and rivers)

Identifying Uneven Distribution of Resources Help students to see that resources are distributed unevenly throughout Latin America.

READING STRATEGY AND VOCABULARY DEVELOPMENT

Note Taking Have students preview the lesson. Review the note-taking strategy introduced in the last lesson: reading and selecting important information and then paraphrasing and recording the information. Have students take notes as they read the lesson. Remind them to put the important ideas of the lesson into their own words. When students have finished, have them compare the information they selected.

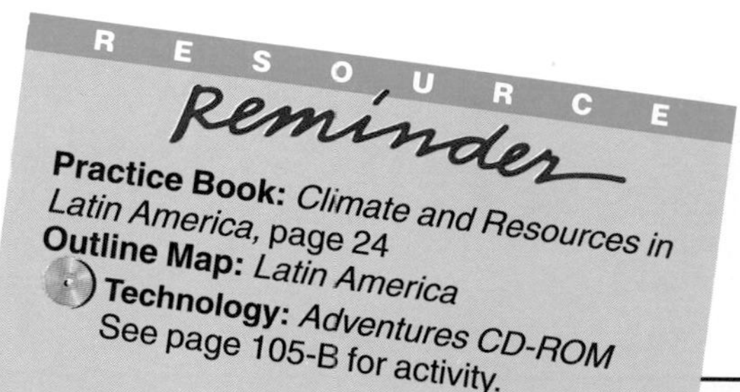

RESOURCE Reminder

Practice Book: *Climate and Resources in Latin America,* page 24

Outline Map: *Latin America*

Technology: *Adventures CD-ROM*

See page 105-B for activity.

Understanding Agriculture Make sure students realize that little land is arable in South America.

Ask students:

- **What percent of South America is arable?** (about 5 percent)
- **What are two reasons for land not being suitable for farming in South America?** (mountains, too much or too little rain)
- **Where is there good farmland in Latin America**? (Caribbean Islands, mountain valleys, and some lowland plains)

Identifying Grasslands Help students to understand what percent of the continent of South America is grassland. Be sure they understand what grasslands are.

Ask students:

- **How do the Chaco and the Pampas differ?** (The Chaco, located in northern Argentina, is smaller in area than the Pampas and has harsh land and thorn bushes. The Pampas, located in southern Argentina, is larger in area than the Chaco, is green, and has fertile land.)

EXTENDING MAP SKILLS

Have students look at the map on this page, and direct their attention to the various types of land use throughout Latin America.

Ask students:

- **Which three types of land use are the most prevalent throughout Latin America?** (forestry, with farming, hunting, and gathering; livestock raising; commercial fishing)
- **Which part of Latin America has the most tourism?** (the Caribbean Islands)

the iron into steel. So Brazil must import coal in order to make steel.

AGRICULTURE

As the map on this page shows, very little land in Latin America is good for farming. In South America only about 5 percent of the land can be farmed. That's an area slightly smaller than the nation of Bolivia. The main reasons for the lack of arable land are the mountains and the fact that there is too much or too little rain in many areas. The daily rain in the rain forests, for example, washes away the nutrients in the soil.

Some of the best farmland in Latin America is found in the islands of the Caribbean. Other good farmland is in mountain valleys and in some lowlands.

GRASSLANDS

From Buenos Aires, Argentina, south almost to Patagonia are miles and miles of flat grasslands. They are Latin America's largest plains. In the north the plain is called the Chaco and is about 200,000 square miles (518,000 sq km) in area. In the south the plain is called the Pampas and is almost 300,000 square miles (777,000 sq km) in area.

The Chaco is a harsh land covered with thorn bushes, but the Pampas is green and gentle. In the Pampas the summers are long, the winters are mild, and the soil is fertile. It is both a cattle range and one of the world's great producers of grain.

MAP SKILL: Only the largest manufacturing centers are shown on the map. Which countries have manufacturing centers inland?

MAP SKILL: Mexico, Colombia, Argentina, Venezuela, Brazil

BACKGROUND INFORMATION

Multicultural Perspectives There are many viewpoints on the future of the Amazon rain forest. Chico Mendes, a tapper of rubber trees, represented one view. *Let's use the forest rationally without destroying it. The tappers, the Indians . . . have been occupying the forest for more than a hundred years and have never menaced it. We [can] commercialize and industrialize the products that the forest generously yields us.* Another Brazilian, Julio Cesar, gets angry when people from other countries protest Brazil's development of its forest. *We don't want to be the backyard of anyone anymore. When my mother was a kid even the butter came from the Netherlands. You have all these hundreds of species of hummingbirds, and you're miserable. You can't buy a car or dignity with hummingbirds . . .*

Ask students why people have different views about this issue.

FORESTS

Trees are one of Latin America's most valuable resources. About two fifths of Latin America is covered with trees. Most of these trees are in the rain forest of the Amazon River Valley. One writer has written that there "even the trees war with each other for a place in the soil and the sun . . . ." Among the many kinds of trees in the tropical rain forest are hardwood trees, such as rosewood and mahogany.

Now much of the Amazon forest is being cleared for dams, roads, farms, and factories. Some people, however, say that too much is being cleared. You can read about this issue on pages 168–169.

THREE CLIMATE ZONES

Most of Latin America is in the tropics. So you might expect the region to have a warm climate. Yet, as you can see from the map on page 114, the region has several different climates. Latin America is mountainous. The high elevation in the mountains causes them to be cooler than you might think.

Latin America has three different climate zones in the mountains. The diagram on this page shows you these zones and the crops that grow in each one. Look at the diagram and find the *tierra caliente* (tē âr′ ə käl ē en′ tā), meaning "hot land." This lowland tropic zone is hot all year.

The second climate zone is the higher *tierra templada* (tē âr′ ə tem plä′ də), or "temperate land." The Central Plateau of Mexico and many of Latin America's highland plateaus and valleys are in this mild climate zone. As you might expect, the tierra templada is the most heavily populated part of Latin America.

The *tierra fría* (tē âr′ ə frē′ ə), Latin America's "cold land," is the highest climate zone. It is made up of land above 6,000 feet (1,800 m). Even in the tropics,

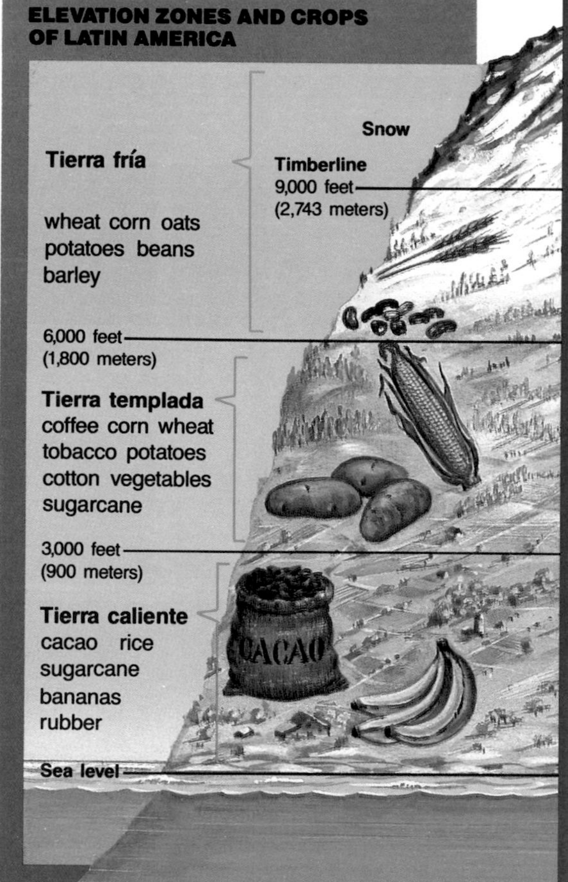

DIAGRAM SKILL: Which climate zone has mild temperatures, average rainfall, and crops that do not need much heat and moisture?

high peaks such as Mount Aconcagua (ak ən kä′ gwə) in Argentina are snowcapped all year. Mount Aconcagua is 22,831 feet (6,959 m) above sea level.

RAINFALL

Latin America has the largest rainy area in the world—the Amazon River Valley. It rains almost every day here. You can see this wet area on the map on page 114.

Throughout Latin America the amount of rainfall varies, depending on whether

DIAGRAM SKILL: tierra templada

113

Discussing Forests Make sure students realize that trees are a valuable Latin American resource.

Ask students:

- **How much of Latin America is forest?** (two fifths)
- **What are some of the many kinds of trees in Latin America?** (hardwoods like rosewood and mahogany)

Identifying Three Climate Zones Make sure students understand that the higher the elevation, the cooler the climate.

Ask students:

- **What besides latitude greatly influences climates of the Latin American region?** (elevation)
- **How does the climate change as you travel up a mountain?** (The climate becomes cooler the higher you go.)
- *THINKING FURTHER:* **Why is the *tierra templada* the most heavily populated area?** (It has a mild climate and plateaus and valleys for farming.)

EXTENDING DIAGRAM SKILLS

Help students to identify food crops versus nonfood crops.

Ask students:

- **Which nonfood crop is grown in the *tierra caliente*?** (rubber)
- **What crops are grown in the *tierra fría*?** (potatoes, barley, wheat, beans, corn, oats)
- **In which zone is the timberline?** (*tierra fría*)
- **In which zone is the greatest variety of crops grown?** (*tierra templada*)

Discussing Rainfall Help students identify the extremes of wet and dry lands in Latin America.

Ask students:

- **What is the largest rainy area in the world?** (the Amazon basin)

CURRICULUM CONNECTION

Science Have students interested in scientific research look up the effects of rain shadow (the dry area on the leeward side of a mountain). Ask students to provide illustrated charts for the class on how mountains affect rainfall. Tell students that the key elements they should draw and label on the rain shadow charts include: a wind off an ocean hitting a mountain (in this case, the easterlies off the Atlantic crossing the Amazon basin); the wet, rising wind, cooling and then dropping rain on the mountain; a falling, warming air mass drying the other side of the mountain (the rain shadow), picking up moisture as it descends. This makes land on the leeward side of the mountain very dry.

Identifying Effects of Rainfall Continue discussing rainfall.

Ask students:

- **Where is there too much rain in Latin America?** (Mosquito Coast of Nicaragua and Honduras)

EXTENDING MAP SKILLS

Help students interpret the map key and identify various climatic conditions in Latin America. Discuss why the range in climate is so great.

Applying the Lesson Encourage students to name one place in Latin America that they would like to know more about. Then have them make a list of the things they would like to learn.

CLOSE

Summarizing Students have learned that Latin America is a region of varied climates, elevations, and natural resources. It has little farmland. Have students review each of these characteristics.

Evaluating Use the *Check Your Reading* questions (answers given below) to assess students' understanding of the lesson.

Answers to Check Your Reading

1. grassy plains lying in northern and southern Argentina
2. waterpower, trees, iron ore, petroleum, natural gas, gold, silver, tin, emeralds
3. *tierra caliente* (hot), *tierra templada* (temperate), *tierra fría* (cold)
4. a great effect; Though Latin America straddles the equator, its climate includes temperate-to-cold areas as you travel up the mountains.

Independent Practice
Practice Book: page 24

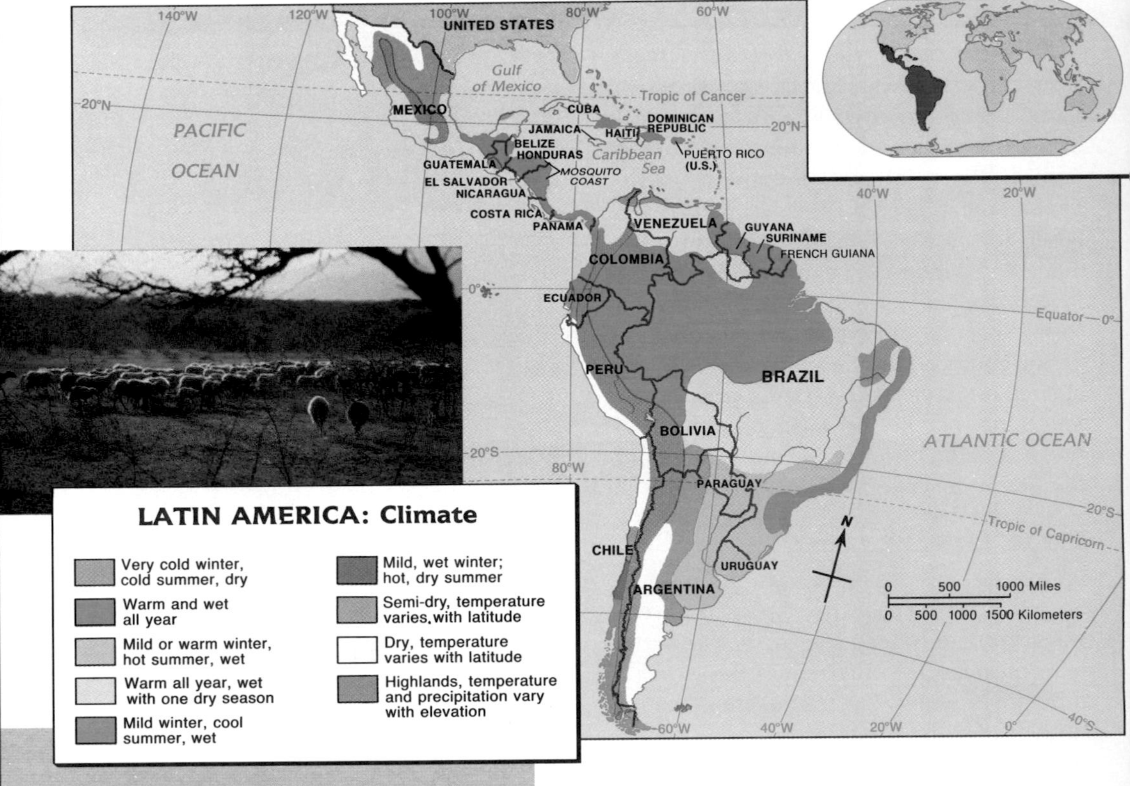

MAP SKILL: Name a part of Latin America in which a semidry climate is found.

rain-bearing winds blow onshore and where they hit the mountains. The heaviest rains fall along the eastern part of the region. Some places have too much rain. Along the Mosquito Coast of Nicaragua and Honduras, more than 200 inches (500 cm) of rain can fall in a year.

Latin America also has the driest place in the world, the Atacama Desert of Chile. Imagine having to "travel overland by mule and afoot across . . . burning flats where it hasn't rained for a thousand years." This is what miners traveling here in the 1800s experienced. They said that nothing grew or moved there.

DIFFERENT CLIMATES AND RESOURCES

Although most of Latin America is in the tropics, the high elevation of its mountains form hot, temperate, and cold climate zones. Latin America also has areas of high rainfall and of low rainfall. The region is rich in natural resources. However, many resources are difficult to reach or are unevenly distributed.

Check Your Reading

1. What are the Chaco and the Pampas?
2. What are some important natural resources found in Latin America?
3. Name Latin America's climate zones.
4. **THINKING SKILL:** What effect do Latin America's mountains have on the climate of the region?

114 MAP SKILL: Central Chile, northern and southwestern Argentina, northeastern Brazil, northern Venezuela, northeastern Colombia, western Ecuador, northern Mexico, and the northern coast of the Yucatán Peninsula.

THINKING S
Cause anc

MEETING INDIVIDUAL NEEDS

Reteaching (easy) Have students draw a pie chart to show how much of the land in Latin America is arable. Tell them to use the information they know about landforms and elevation in Latin America to write an appropriate label for the 95 percent of the land that cannot be farmed (for example, "Too High" or "Too Dry").

Extension (average) Give each student a copy of the outline map of Latin America, found in the Teacher's Resource Center, and have them label the climate regions and natural resources.

Enrichment (challenging) Have students work in groups to gather information about the history and use of one of Latin America's natural resources. Each group should illustrate its findings on posterboard for presentation to the class.

BUILDING SKILLS
GEOGRAPHY SKILLS

Relating Latitude, Elevation, and Climate

Key Vocabulary
low latitudes
middle latitudes
high latitudes

In the last lesson you read about Latin America's climate. You learned that although most of Latin America lies in a tropical zone, the region has a wide variety of different climates. In fact, there are three different climate zones in Latin America. In order to understand the reasons for this fact, it is important to know how latitude, elevation, and climate are related to each other.

How Latitude Affects Climate

You may recall that the amount of heat received by any location on earth depends on its latitude. Regions near the equator generally have the hottest temperatures because they receive more of the sun's rays all year long. These areas are said to be located in the **low latitudes**. Regions farther from the equator have generally cooler temperatures and experience changing seasons throughout the year. These milder areas are said to be in the **middle latitudes**. The lands around the North and South poles are the coldest places on earth because they receive less direct sunlight. These areas, which are covered by snow and ice, are in the **high latitudes**. In general, the latitude of an area tells us a great deal about the temperatures found there.

How Elevation Affects Climate

Imagine you are in Ecuador, which is located on the equator in South America. In the lowlands of Ecuador temperatures are very warm. In the mountains, however, temperatures are much colder. Higher elevation means lower temperatures. In fact, for each 1,000-foot (300-m) increase in elevation, the temperature drops about 3.6°F. (2°C).

You have read that the higher elevations in Latin America are called the *tierra friá*, or "cold land." Only a few crops grow in the higher elevations of the *tierra friá*, where temperatures are very cold. In fact, if you were to climb to the top of one of Ecuador's higher mountains, you would most likely find snow, ice, and freezing temperatures.

Latitude and Elevation

Climate is affected by many factors: Latitude and elevation are two of the most important. Much of Latin America lies in the low and middle latitudes and therefore has a warm climate. But because of variations in elevation, some mountainous regions in Latin America are very cold.

Reviewing the Skill

1. How does latitude affect climate?
2. In which latitudes are temperatures coldest? In which are they hottest?
3. How does elevation affect climate?
4. Why are some regions of Latin America very cold?
5. Why is it important to understand the relationships among latitude, elevation, and climate?

115

SKILLS LESSON
page 115

Lesson Theme Latitude and elevation affect climate.

Lesson Objective
- Explain how latitude and elevation affect climate.

PREPARE

Motivate Review with students the climates discussed in the last lesson.

Set Purpose Tell students they will read about the effects of elevation and latitude on climate. You may project Transparency Map 2 so that students can get a sense of the elevation and latitude of a given area.

2 TEACH

Identifying Latitude's Effect on Climate Help students understand the effect of latitude on climate.

Discussing Elevation's Effect on Climate Discuss why elevated land in the low latitudes may be cold.

Applying the Skill On an outline map of the Western Hemisphere, have students label the low, middle, and high latitudes.

CLOSE

Summarizing Students have learned that latitude and elevation affect climate.

Answers to Reviewing the Skill

1. The amount of heat received by any location depends on its latitude.
2. high; low
3. Higher elevation means lower temperatures.
4. They are in a location with a high elevation.
5. Climate is affected by latitude and elevation.

MEETING INDIVIDUAL NEEDS

Reteaching (easy) Give students drawing paper. Have them draw and label three scenes that show the climates in the low, middle, and high latitudes.

Extension (average) Have students draw a picture of how natural plant productivity changes from the bottom to the top of a mountain: a tropical rain forest at the bottom; pines halfway up; low scrub; then snow at the top. Have them mark the mountain with 1,000-foot (300-m) elevation lines and indicate the drop in temperature for each 1,000 feet (300 m).

Enrichment (challenging) Have students do further research about how the sun's rays strike the earth. Have them make visual displays showing how the sun's rays strike the earth during different seasons of the year in the low, middle, and high latitudes.

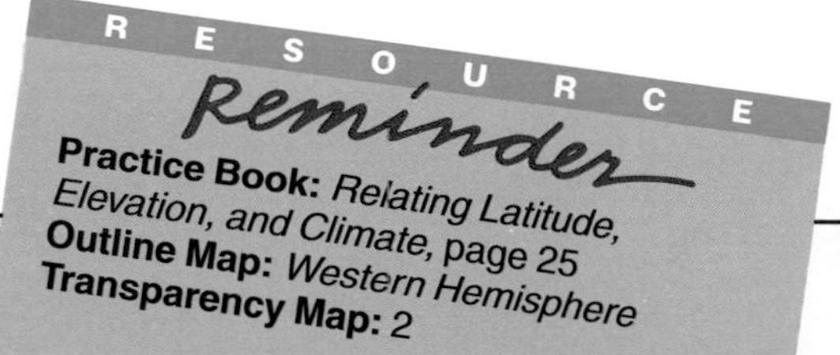

RESOURCE Reminder

Practice Book: *Relating Latitude, Elevation, and Climate*, page 25
Outline Map: *Western Hemisphere*
Transparency Map: 2

CHAPTER 4 REVIEW
pages 116–117

USING THE CHAPTER SUMMARY AND REVIEW

Physical Geography These questions may be used for review.

- **What are the major landforms of Latin America?** (high mountains, vast river systems, volcanoes, islands)
- **Where would you find the *tierra caliente, tierra templada,* and *tierra fría* climate zones?** (in the mountains of Latin America)
- **Which Latin American countries have large petroleum reserves?** (Mexico and Venezuela)

Ideas to Remember

- **Which landforms divide Latin America?** (high mountains and vast rivers)
- **What are the major natural resources of Latin America?** (petroleum, gold, silver, tin, other minerals)

Answers to Reviewing Vocabulary

1. True.
2. A rain forest is a tropical area of dense trees where rain falls almost every day.
3. A river system is the land drained by a river and its tributaries.
4. True.
5. The Caribbean Islands are an example of an archipelago.

Answers to Reviewing Facts

1. Central America, Caribbean Islands, Mexico
2. Its name comes from Latin, the language of ancient Rome; Spanish and Portuguese.
3. the Andes
4. climate, limits on land that can be farmed, separation of people, and barriers to trade and transportation
5. the Amazon River

CHAPTER 4 • SUMMARY

LATIN AMERICA: PHYSICAL GEOGRAPHY

LANDFORMS

- High mountains: Andes

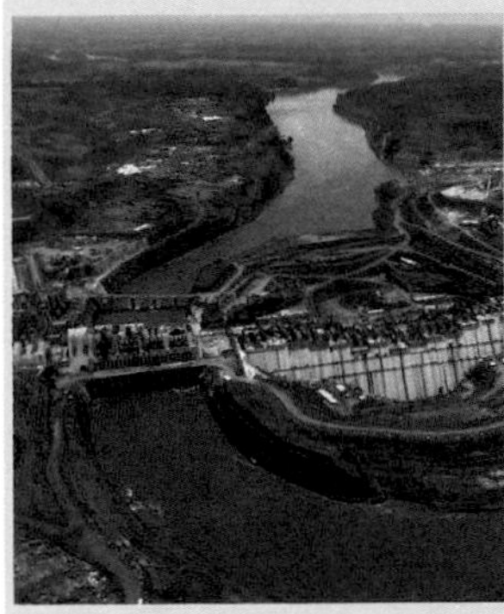

- Vast river systems: Amazon, Río de la Plata, Orinoco

- Volcanoes: Popocatépetl
- Caribbean Islands: formed into archipelagos

CLIMATE

- Three climate zones:
  - a) Tierra caliente ("hot land")
  - b) Tierra templada ("temperate land")
  - c) Tierra fría ("cold land")

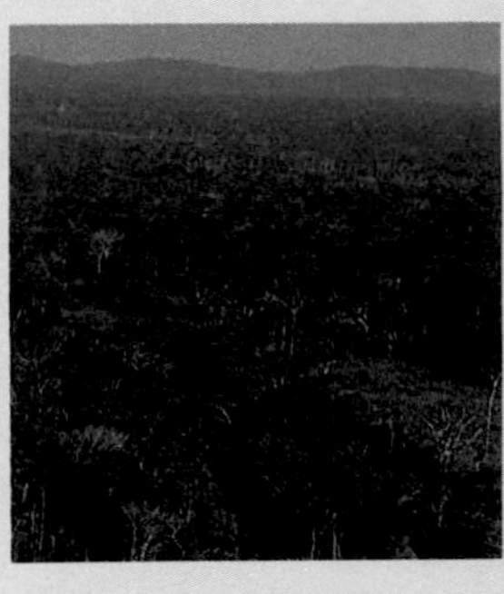

- Largest rainy place in the world: Amazon River Valley
- Driest place in the world: Atacama Desert

NATURAL RESOURCES

- Gold, silver, tin, and other minerals

- Mexico and Venezuela: huge petroleum reserves
- Uneven distribution: some countries have many resources, some have few

IDEAS TO REMEMBER

- High mountains and vast rivers dominate the Latin American continent.
- Latin America has a variety of natural resources and, because of its mountains, three different climate zones.

116

ENRICHMENT ACTIVITY

Making Island Models **Materials:** modeling clay (various colors), clear plastic containers

1. Refer the class to the description of the Caribbean Islands on page 109. Tell students that there are three different types of islands in the Caribbean. The Bahamas are coral islands, the Greater Antilles are continental islands, and the Lesser Antilles are volcanic islands. Tell students that they are going to make models showing the formation of each type of island.
2. Divide the class into three groups, and assign each group one of the three types of islands. Refer them to an encyclopedia to gather the information they need.
3. Have students mold the clay to make their models. Have them put the models in the clear plastic containers. Then have them add water to show the sea covering the island bases.

CHAPTER 4 • REVIEW

REVIEWING VOCABULARY

Each of the following statements contains an underlined vocabulary word or term. Number a sheet of paper from 1 to 5. Beside each number write whether each of the following statements is true or false. If the statement is true, write "true." If it is false, rewrite the sentence using the vocabulary word or term correctly.

1. The islands of the West Indies are an example of an archipelago.
2. The land drained by a major river and its tributaries is called a rain forest.
3. A river system is a tropical area of dense trees where rain falls almost every day.
4. The altiplano is a high, flat region that has a cold climate and the world's highest navigable lake.
5. The Andes Mountains are an example of an archipelago.

REVIEWING FACTS

1. Which of the four main areas of Latin America are part of North America?
2. Why is this region called Latin America? What are the two main European languages spoken by people in Latin America today?
3. Which mountain system is the largest in Latin America?
4. Name three effects that the Andes Mountains have on the continent of South America.
5. What is the name of the second longest river in the world?
6. In which part of South America are the Andes Mountains located? Between which two countries are the chain's highest peaks found?
7. Why are temperatures very low in some Andean regions even though these mountains are located in the tropics?
8. Which region in South America is among the wettest in the world? Which region is among the driest in the world?
9. What does *El Dorado* mean? How did El Dorado affect the exploration and settlement of Latin America?
10. Name two reasons that only a small percentage of land in Latin America is suitable for farming.

WRITING ABOUT MAIN IDEAS

1. **Writing a Paragraph:** Look again at the diagram of mountain climates on page 113. Write a paragraph describing the changes in climate from the lowlands to the mountains.
2. **Writing a Travel Brochure:** Imagine that you will be leading a tour of the Amazon rain forest. Describe in several paragraphs the sights and sounds the tourists will see.
3. **Writing About Perspectives:** Imagine that you are moving from the *tierra caliente* to the *tierra fría*. Write a letter to a friend describing some of the changes you have to make in the way you live.

BUILDING SKILLS: RELATING LATITUDE, ELEVATION, AND CLIMATE

1. How do latitude and elevation affect climate?
2. What are the three climate zones of Latin America?
3. Why does Latin America have more than one climate zone?
4. Why is it important to understand how latitude and elevation affect climate?

6. most of western South America; Argentina and Chile
7. The higher elevations cause the mountain regions to be cold.
8. along the Mosquito Coast of Nicaragua and Honduras; the Atacama Desert of Chile
9. "the golden one"; Many came to Latin America looking for the treasures of El Dorado about which they had heard.
10. mountains and too much or too little rain

Suggestions for Writing About Main Ideas

1. Students' paragraphs should focus on the drop in temperature as the elevation rises.
2. Students' brochures will vary, but should include: the hot and humid climate, the many types of vegetation and wildlife, and the possibility that something exciting might happen, such as encounters with animals or meeting the people of the region.
3. Students' letters should mention the difficulty of adjusting from life in a hot climate to life in a very cold climate.

Answers to Building Skills: Relating Latitude, Elevation, and Climate

1. The latitudes closest to the equator have the hottest temperatures; those farther from the equator have cooler temperatures. The higher the elevation, the lower the temperature.
2. low, middle, and high latitudes
3. because of its mountains
4. It helps us to know what climate to expect at different elevations and latitudes.

Chapter Review and Test

Practice Book: *Vocabulary Review,* page 26

Transparency: *Graphic Organizer*

Assessment Book: *Chapter 5 Test*

MAKING CONNECTIONS

Organizing Information Use the Main Idea Map Graphic Organizer Transparency, filling in only the underlined main ideas. Have students complete the map by filling in supporting details about Latin America's physical geography. *Ask:* How has geography affected the growth and development of South America?

Latin America is a land of varied physical geography, with a limited amount of arable land and uneven mineral deposits.

High mountains and river valleys dominate the landscape.
Andes Mountains, Amazon, Río de la Plata, Orinoco river systems

Mountain climates vary with elevation.
tierra fría, tierra templada, tierra caliente

Resources are unevenly distributed.
mineral deposits unevenly distributed
only 5% of land is arable
vegetation varies from rain forest to desert

CHAPTER 5
ORGANIZER

MEXICO text pages 118–139

CHAPTER THEME

Characterized by a mestizo culture that is an Indian and European mix, Mexico faces population growth and economic problems in spite of oil revenues.

CHAPTER OBJECTIVES

CONTENT

- Define *civilization* and identify the two major Indian civilizations of early Mexico.
- Describe the effects of the Spanish conquest on the culture and people of Mexico.
- List the major features of Mexico's developing economy.
- List positive and negative effects of improvements in living conditions in Mexico.
- Identify the PRI and describe its role in Mexican politics in the twentieth century.
- Describe how Mexico's arts and amusements reflect its different cultures.

SKILLS

Geography
- Identify Indian civilizations on a historical map of Mexico.
- Interpret a political map of Mexico.

Study and Research
- Use a table to identify the world's largest metropolitan areas.

Thinking
- Compare and contrast families in the United States and Mexico.
- Ask focused questions about a particular topic.

Reading and Writing
- Write a letter from the viewpoint of a Mexican campesino.

CITIZENSHIP VALUES

- Appreciate the fact that individuals have the ability to contribute to the well-being of the society in which they live.
- Appreciate the contributions of art to a people's identity.

TEACHER OPTIONS

READING STRATEGY: Previewing and Predicting
Strategies to help students read and remember the main ideas of the lesson.

Lesson 1: p. 119 Lesson 4: p. 131
Lesson 2: p. 123 Legacy: p. 134
Lesson 3: p. 128

MEETING INDIVIDUAL NEEDS Activities for reteaching, extension, and enrichment.

Lesson 1: p. 122 Lesson 4: p. 133
Lesson 2: p. 125 Legacy: p. 137
Lesson 3: p. 130

GEO ADVENTURES ACTIVITIES PAD Daily activities to assess students' understanding of geography skills.

CURRICULUM CONNECTION Activities to help integrate other subject areas with Social Studies.

Science: p. 126 Art: p. 132
Math: p. 129 Language Arts: p. 132

PUPIL EDITION ON CASSETTE Language support for students who have difficulty reading or who will benefit from listening to the Pupil Edition on Cassette as they read.

SECOND-LANGUAGE SUPPORT Activities and suggestions for second-language learners.

Lesson 2: p. 9

CHAPTER PLANNING GUIDE

LESSON	SUGGESTED PACING	THEMES	TEACHER'S RESOURCE CENTER
1 THE PEOPLE pages 119–122	1 day	The culture of Mexico is a blend of the early Indian and Spanish civilizations.	Practice Book p. 27 ■ Anthology Outline Map p. 14
2 THE ECONOMY pages 123–125	1 day	Mexico's limited farmland, expanding population, and partial industrialization pose continuing challenges for the country's economy.	Practice Book p. 28 **Technology:** *Adventures CD-ROM*
BUILDING THINKING SKILLS Determining the Accuracy of Information pages 126–127	1 day	To determine the accuracy of information, you need to know the source of the information and whether or not the source is credible.	Practice Book p. 29
3 THE GOVERNMENT pages 128–130	1 day	At the center of Mexico's democratic government are strong presidential powers and a powerful political party.	Practice Book p. 30 **Technology:** *Adventures CD-ROM*
4 ARTS AND RECREATION pages 131–133	1 day	Mexican arts and amusements reflect Indian, mestizo, and Spanish influences.	Practice Book p. 31 **Technology:** *Adventures CD-ROM*
LEGACY Mexican Murals pages 134–137	1 day	The tradition of mural painting dates back in Mexico to the days of the Aztecs and the Mayas.	■ Anthology
CHAPTER SUMMARY AND REVIEW pages 138–139	1 day	Chapter content, skills, and vocabulary are reviewed and evaluated.	Practice Book p. 32 Transparency: Graphic Organizer Assessment Book, Chapter 5 Test

Technology CONNECTION

Lesson 2
ADVENTURES CD-ROM
Have students make a natural resources map using stamps in *Build* and *Paint.*

Lesson 3
ADVENTURES CD-ROM
Have students look at information on Mexico under *Symbols* in *Investigate.*

Lesson 4
ADVENTURES CD-ROM
Explore Mexico's media elements.

CHAPTER 5
pages 118–139

USING THE CHAPTER OPENER

Discussing the Photograph Suggest to students that the young women in the picture seem to be dressed up for a special occasion. Point out to students that the clothes worn by these women are traditional Mexican finery.

Ask students:

- **What kind of holiday do you think these women are celebrating?** (Possible answers include: a national holiday, a religious holiday.)
- **How do we Americans dress for the Fourth of July?** (Possible answers include: We may choose to wear clothes that have the colors red, white, and blue, but mainly we dress in ordinary, everyday clothing.)
- *THINKING FURTHER:* **Why do you think many Mexicans wear traditional dress to celebrate a special occasion?** (Possible answers include: It's their way of expressing their love for their country and their ethnic heritage.)

Reading/Listening to the Primary Source Have students read the passage under the picture. Help them to appreciate that Mexican festivals are usually religious rather than patriotic in nature, but that they also serve as a means for Mexicans to celebrate their sense of unity with other Mexicans and with their past.

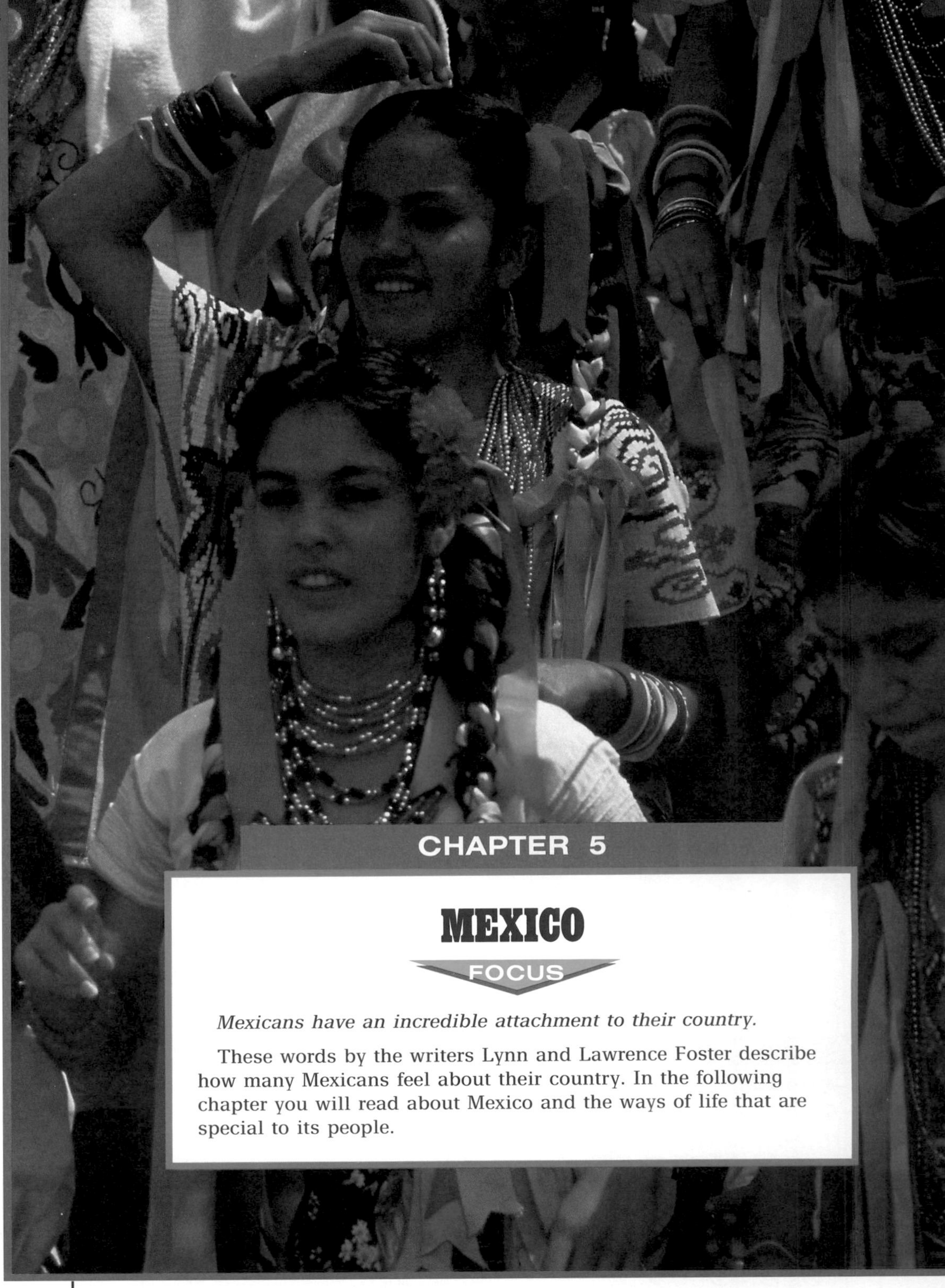

CHAPTER 5

MEXICO

FOCUS

Mexicans have an incredible attachment to their country.

These words by the writers Lynn and Lawrence Foster describe how many Mexicans feel about their country. In the following chapter you will read about Mexico and the ways of life that are special to its people.

BACKGROUND INFORMATION

About Christmas in Mexico In Mexico the most important fiestas occur during the Christmas season, which lasts for 22 days.

- This period is filled with such activities as dancing, singing, parades, and fireworks.
- The highlight of these activities is the piñata celebration. The piñata is a colorfully decorated container filled with candy. The children are blindfolded and then given long sticks with which to break the container. When the container is broken, candy comes showering down, and the children scramble to get their share.
- Gifts are exchanged not on Christmas Day but on Epiphany on January 6.

The People

READ TO LEARN

Key Vocabulary
civilization
mestizo
extended family

Key People
Hernando Cortés

Key Places
Tenochtitlán
Mexico City

Read Aloud

Have you ever eaten a taco? The outside is a corn-flour pancake called a tortilla (tôr tē′ yə). The tortilla is fried and folded around a filling that often includes pieces of beef or chicken. The tortilla pancake is Indian, a product of thousands of years of growing corn. The filling for the taco comes from animals like cattle and chickens. These animals were brought to Mexico by the Spanish. The tasty food that results is neither Spanish nor Indian. It is Mexican.

Read for Purpose

1. WHAT YOU KNOW: Who were the first people known to have lived in North America?
2. WHAT YOU WILL LEARN: In what ways is Mexico a blend of cultures?

EARLY INDIAN CIVILIZATIONS

As you may remember from Chapter 2, the first peoples in North America were Indians. The first peoples in Latin America were also Indians. Thousands of years ago Indian groups in Mexico created civilizations (siv ə li zā′ shənz). A civilization is a culture that has developed systems of government, religion, and learning.

Among the earliest Indian civilizations was that of the Mayas (mä′ yəz). About 1,500 years ago these skilled farmers and mathematicians built stone temples and palaces in the rain forests of the Yucatán Peninsula. The Mayas were also splendid craftworkers, decorating their buildings with both fine paintings and sculptures.

During the 1200s the Mexica, whom the Spanish called the Aztecs, settled in Mexico's high Central Plateau. Their capital city was called Tenochtitlán (te nôch tē tlän′). It stood where Mexico City, the capital of Mexico, stands today.

THE ARRIVAL OF THE SPANISH

The Spanish military leader Hernando Cortés reached Mexico in 1519. He was amazed at the wealth and beauty of Tenochtitlán, which he called "the most beautiful city in the world." Yet Cortés and his followers destroyed the city in order to defeat the Aztecs. Although the Aztecs fought bravely, their weapons were no match for Spanish horses and guns and the help of the Aztecs' enemies who aided the Spanish.

LESSON 1
pages 119–122

Lesson Theme The culture of Mexico is a blend of the early Indian and Spanish civilizations.

Lesson Objectives
- Identify the ancient Indian civilizations of Mexico.
- Describe how the Spanish influence affected Mexico.
- Describe the role of religion in Mexican life.

PREPARE

Motivate Read the *Read Aloud* section to the class. Have students discuss other foods that are of Mexican origin.

Set Purpose Use the *What You Know* question to review the story of the Indian habitation of North America. Use the *What You Will Learn* question to prepare students to learn how Spanish and Indian influences have blended in Mexico.

TEACH

Identifying Indian Civilizations Help students to appreciate the heights that early Indian civilizations reached.

Ask students:

- **What were some skills of the Mayas?** (farming, mathematics, stone building, crafts, painting, and sculpting)

Discussing the Arrival of the Spanish Discuss students' ideas on why the Spanish destroyed Tenochtitlán.

READING STRATEGY AND VOCABULARY DEVELOPMENT

Previewing and Predicting Review with students the previewing strategy that they learned in Chapter 1. Then have students discuss ways that both they and other people make predictions. Predicting is an important reading strategy to help students relate their own knowledge to the content of the text. Tell students that by learning to predict, they can become more effective readers. Tell them that when they are reading, they should think about the author's purpose and try to predict the information they will find. Ask students to preview the lesson and make predictions about the information they think might be covered under each section heading. After students have read the lesson, have them compare and evaluate their predictions.

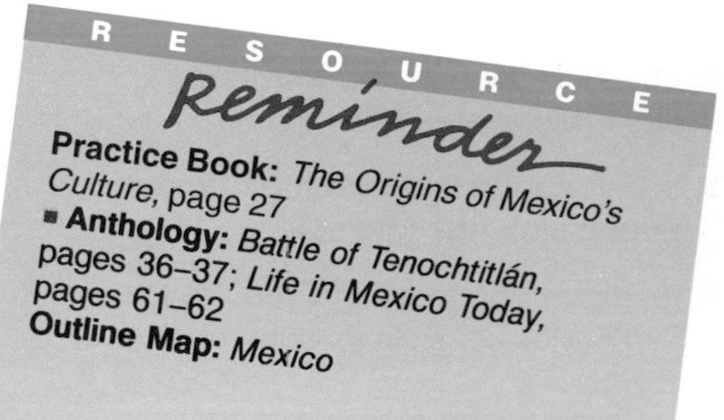

Explaining the Arrival of the Spanish Help students to recognize how the defeat of the Aztecs changed Mexican culture.

Ask students:

- **What effects did defeat have on the Indians?** (The Indians lost their land; they were forced to work in Spanish mines and on ranches and farms; they were forced to convert to Christianity; thousands of Indians died from diseases brought by Europeans; Indian ways were blended with Spanish ways to create the Mexican culture.)

You may wish to have students compare the changes in American Indian culture after the arrival of Europeans in the United States with the changes forced on the Indians in Mexico after the Spanish arrived.

Understanding Mexicans Today Help students consider the cultural makeup of Mexico.

Ask students:

- **What is the official language of Mexico?** (Spanish)
- *THINKING FURTHER:* **Why do you think Spanish rather than an Indian language became the official language?** (Students' answers should note the control that the Spanish exerted over the Indians after the Spanish arrived in Mexico; the fact that only 29 percent of the population is of pure Indian ancestry; and the fact that there is more than one Indian language.)

EXTENDING MAP SKILLS

Have students compare the map on this page with the one on page 122 to find the areas in which the Aztecs and Mayas lived.

Ask students:

- **In which country did the Aztecs live?** (Mexico)
- **Which group lived on the Yucatan Peninsula?** (the Mayas)
- **In which countries did the Mayas live?** (Mexico, Belize, Guatemala)

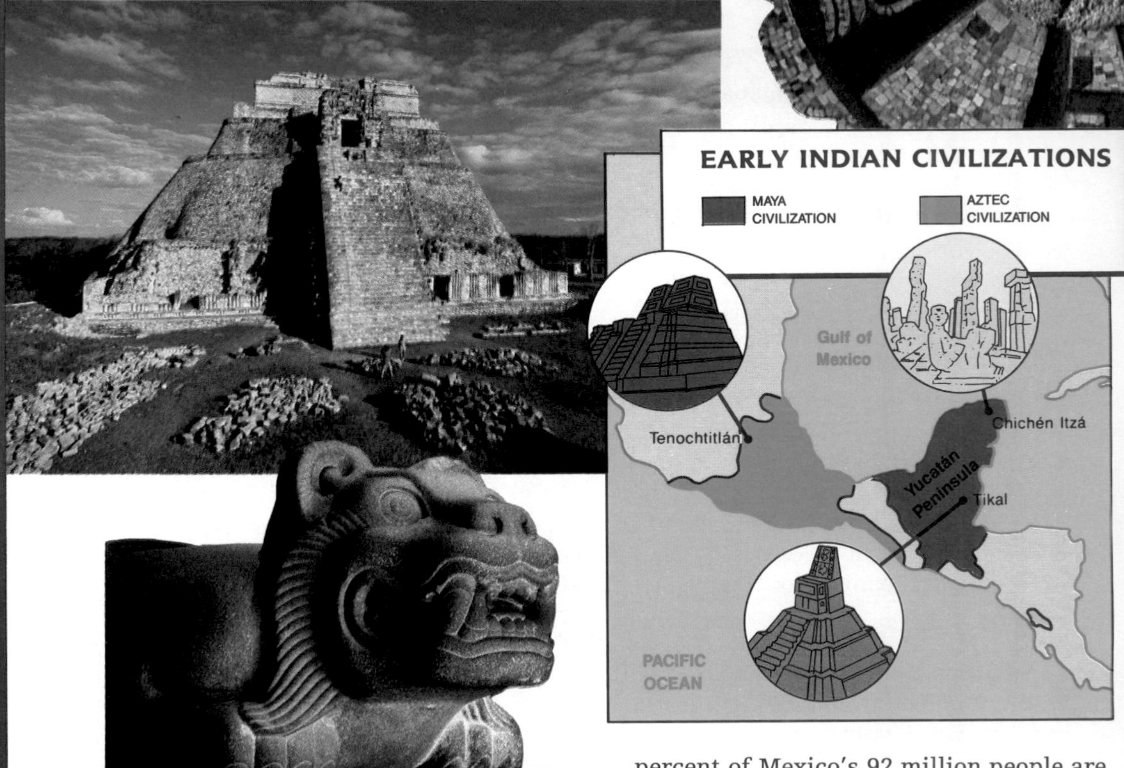

MAP SKILL: Which of the two civilizations shown on the map extended onto the Yucatán Peninsula? Near which bodies of water were the Mayas located?

The Spanish conquest of Mexico in 1521 changed the history and culture of the country. The Indians lost control of their land and their lives. They were forced to work on Spanish farms and ranches and in mines. Thousands of Indians died from diseases brought by Europeans. Many Indians also had to convert, or change their religion, to Christianity. As a result, the way of life of Mexico's people became a mixture of the Spanish and Indian cultures.

MEXICANS TODAY

Today most of the people of Mexico are a blend of Indian and Spanish. About 55 percent of Mexico's 92 million people are considered to be **mestizos** (mes tē′ zōz). That is, they are of mixed Indian and Spanish ancestry. Another 29 percent are Indian. Most of the rest are of Spanish ancestry. Some of Mexico's people have come from other European countries as well as from Africa, Asia, and North and South America.

Spanish is the official language of Mexico. However, some Mexicans speak one of about 50 Indian languages, including the Aztec and Mayan languages. And like American English, Mexican Spanish has adopted some words from different Indian languages.

RELIGION

The Spanish who conquered Mexico were Roman Catholics and wanted to convert the Indians to Christianity. The Indians had followed traditional religions,

MAP SKILL: Mayan civilization; Gulf of Mexico, Pacific Ocean

FUNDAMENTAL THEMES OF GEOGRAPHY

Description of Place Why did Cortés call Tenochtitlán the most beautiful city in the world? Its physical characteristics included canals crisscrossing the city and great causeways connecting it to the mainland. Aqueducts carried water from the springs of Chapultepec. Huge temples and pyramids encircled broad plazas, and spotlessly clean markets thrived. Flowers cascaded from roof gardens. Human characteristics were shown by a skillfully organized system of trading that brought goods from all of Central Mexico. Fresh seafood from the Gulf Coast and rare fruits, vegetables, spices, aromatic woods, and exotic flowers were brought regularly from the tropics for the Aztec priests and nobles.

which included worship of nature gods such as the gods of rain, thunder, and agriculture. The Spanish destroyed the temples to these gods.

Today more than 90 percent of all Mexicans are Roman Catholic, and most villages have a Catholic Church. In Mexico there are also many shrines, or holy places named for a special religious figure.

Mexico has a patron saint, the Virgin of Guadalupe (gwäd ä lü' pā), for the entire country. The shrine of the Virgin of Guadalupe is located near Mexico City. The shrine of Guadalupe is devoted to Mary, the mother of Jesus.

Leobardo Lopez, a photographer at the shrine, tells the story of its origin.

> *In 1531, it is said that the Virgin [Mary] appeared to a young Indian boy named Juan Diego, and asked him to build a church in her memory. . . . To convince the priests of her wishes, Juan was to go to the hills of "El Tepayac" and pick all the roses he could find there. . . . When he returned to the town [and took] the flowers from his shirt, . . . the image of the Virgin [was] printed on Juan's shirt.*

The shrine was built where Juan Diego said Mary appeared to him. About 6 million people visit the shrine every year.

HOLIDAYS

Many Mexican cities and towns celebrate religious holidays with a *fiesta,* or festival. Fiestas often involve costumes and traditions kept alive from the time of the Aztecs.

Mexico also celebrates holidays that mark important days in its history. September 16 is Mexico's Independence Day. It marks the beginning of a struggle against Spanish rule. Cinco de Mayo, May 5, celebrates an important battle in 1862 when a Mexican army defended the city of Puebla from French invaders.

Fiestas may be celebrated with traditional music and dance (*above*). Revolution Day in Mexico is often marked with a modern parade (*below*).

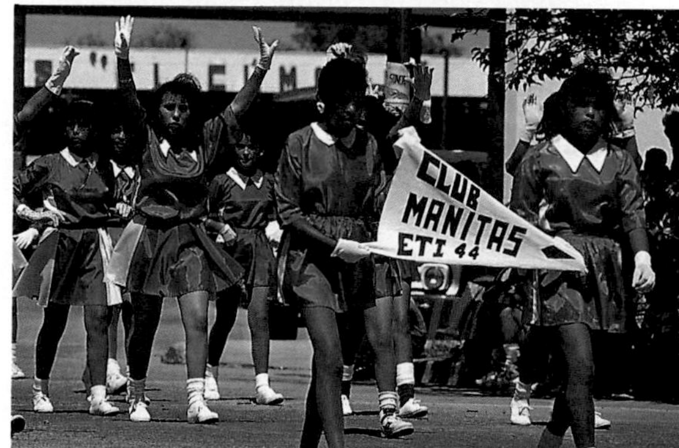

Understanding Religion in Mexico Help students become aware of the effects of religious unity in Mexico.

Ask students:

- **Why did the Spanish destroy the Indian temples?** (to stop the Indians from worshipping nature gods and to convert them to Catholicism)
- **What is the story of the most famous shrine in Mexico?** (Our Lady of Guadalupe was built on the site where Mary was said to have appeared to a young Indian boy.)

Examining Fiestas Encourage students to discuss festivals they may have attended. Help students to develop the idea that a fiesta is more than just a party.

Ask students:

- **In what ways is a fiesta different from a picnic?** (Focus of a fiesta is often religious; it lasts a long time, usually ten days, and includes food, dance, and songs.)

BUILDING CITIZENSHIP

What Unifies a Country? The Virgin of Guadalupe plays a special role for Mexicans in unifying their country. She is the patron saint of the nation, and her shrine is considered by Catholics to be one of the most holy places in the Americas. Pope John Paul II said mass at the shrine in 1979. The Virgin's name was a rallying cry for Mexicans when they began to fight for freedom from Spain. First called out by Father Miguel Hidalgo in the village of Dolores northwest of Mexico City, the *Grito de Dolores* (Cry of Dolores) is: "Long live Mexico! Long live independence! Long live the Virgin of Guadalupe!" Discuss with students the slogans or symbols that unify the United States. (the flag, Statue of Liberty, the President)

EXTENDING MAP SKILLS

Ask students:

- **Which river forms part of the border between Mexico and the United States?** (the Rio Grande)
- **Which region is east of the Gulf of California?** (Sonora)

Looking at Families Discuss extended families and the role of godparents in Mexico.

Applying the Lesson Have students list the ways in which our culture has been influenced by the Spanish and Indian cultures of Mexico.

CLOSE

Summarizing Students have learned that Mexican culture is a blend of Indian and Spanish ways.

Evaluating Use the *Check Your Reading* questions (answers given below) to assess students' understanding.

Answers to Check Your Reading

1. people of mixed Indian and Spanish ancestry
2. Most Spanish settlers were Roman Catholic and the Spanish sent many Roman Catholic priests to convert the Indians.
3. Independence Day, Cinco de Mayo
4. *Differences:* more extended families in Mexico; more Mexican people have godparents. *Similarities:* Parents head the family; family works and plays together.

Independent Practice
Practice Book: page 27

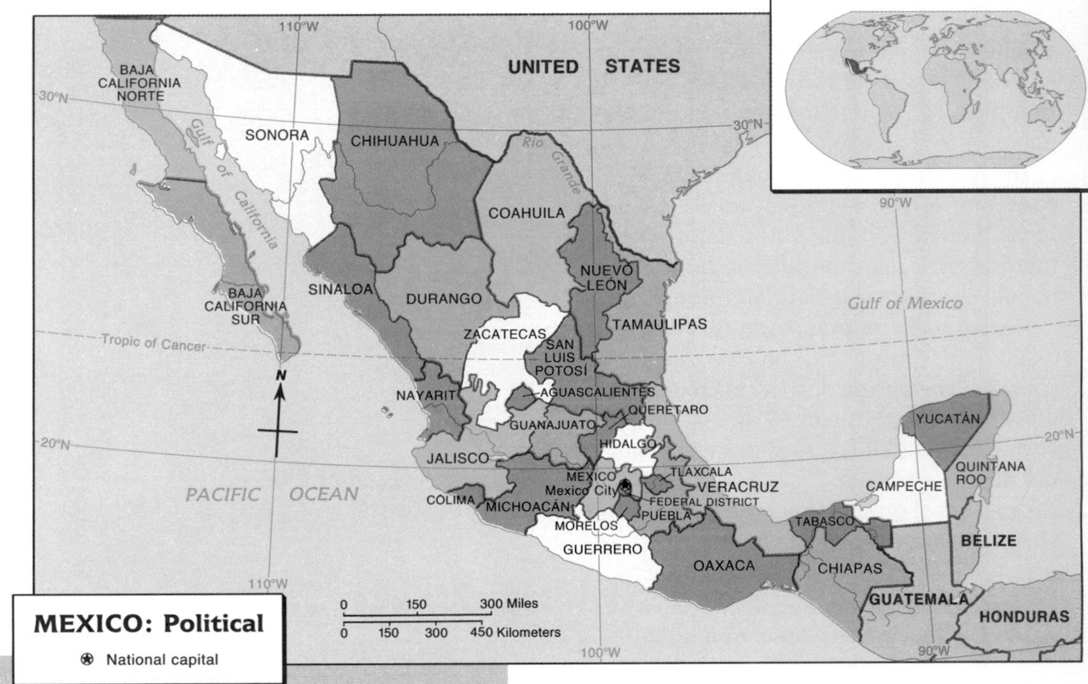

MEXICO: Political
⊛ National capital

MAP SKILL: Find the national capital of Mexico. At about what latitude and longitude is the capital located?

FAMILIES

Family life is important to most Mexicans. Often people live with or near their **extended families.** An extended family includes parents, children, and other family members, such as aunts, uncles, grandparents, and cousins. When family members leave a rural area to find work elsewhere, they often go to stay with their extended families.

Godparents are an important part of a Mexican family. As in many countries, a godparent is an adult sponsor who promises to oversee a child's religious upbringing. In Mexico, godparents are like a second set of parents to whom children may turn for help.

 MAP SKILL: about 19°N latitude, 99°W longitude

A BLEND OF INDIAN AND SPANISH

You have read that Indians were the first settlers of Mexico and that Indian groups such as the Mayas and Aztecs developed civilizations. Mexico's culture changed after the Spanish conquered Mexico in the 1500s and introduced Spanish ways of life. Today most Mexicans are Catholics and mestizos.

Check Your Reading

1. Who are the mestizos?
2. Why are most present-day Mexicans Roman Catholics?
3. What are some important holidays people in Mexico celebrate?
4. **THINKING SKILL:** List some ways in which families in the United States are different from families in Mexico. How are they similar?

THINKING SKILL: Compare and Contrast

MEETING INDIVIDUAL NEEDS

Reteaching (easy) Give each student a copy of the outline map of Mexico from the Teacher's Resource Center. Have them label the five largest Mexican cities, the Rio Grande, the Pacific Ocean, the Gulf of California, and the Gulf of Mexico.

Extension (average) Divide the class into groups. Provide each group with a number of travel magazines and brochures. Have students select pictures of Mexico to cut out and sort to make a two-part collage: one part to be labeled "Modern Mexico," the other, "Historic Mexico."

Enrichment (challenging) Have students research the story of the Mexican flag. Have each student draw the flag on an 8½" x 11" sheet of paper. Have students write a short paragraph below the flag explaining its meaning. Display the flags with the title "Honoring Mexico's Heritage."

LESSON 2

The Economy

READ TO LEARN

Key Vocabulary

metropolitan area
campesino
subsistence farming
commercial farming
developing economy
petrochemical

Read Aloud

I left home maybe six months ago. Why? To better myself!

As Alfredo Rios Perez speaks these words, he proudly straightens his mud-spattered hard hat. He works on a construction project in Mexico City. But he was born in a village to the north. When he worked on a farm, he earned about six dollars a week. Now he makes six times as much—enough to bring his wife and three children to the capital.

Read for Purpose

1. WHAT YOU KNOW: Why do workers sometimes move to different places to work?
2. WHAT YOU WILL LEARN: What are the major features of Mexico's developing economy?

MEXICO CITY—A SPRAWLING GIANT

Alfredo Rios Perez is only one of about 1,000 Mexicans who move to Mexico City every day. Besides being the nation's capital, Mexico City is also the economic and cultural center of the nation.

Mexico City is a bustling, modern city. Among its high buildings is the 44-story Latin America Tower—the tallest skyscraper in Latin America. Mexico City's subway riders travel for the world's cheapest fare. A ride costs one peso, which is less than one United States cent. City leaders encourage people to take the subway because more than 2 million automobiles are used in the city daily.

No other city in Mexico offers more opportunities than Mexico City does. As a result, the constant movement of people to the city caused its population to reach 24 million by the mid-1990s. The table on page 124 shows that Mexico City is one of the largest **metropolitan areas** in the world. A metropolitan area includes a large city and all of its surrounding suburbs and towns.

AGRICULTURE

Outside the large cities most Mexicans farm for a living. Their lives are similar to those described by Rosa Valdepeñas, a teacher in Tlaxcala, east of Mexico City:

> *Most of my pupils' parents are farmers with small plots of land and very low incomes. After school, many of my pupils spend the afternoon helping their parents farm the land.*

WHAT YOU KNOW: Encourage students to think about the different jobs that may be available in specific geographic areas, such as jobs in manufacturing and in the professions.

LESSON 2
pages 123–125

Lesson Theme Mexico's limited farmland, expanding population, and partial industrialization pose continuing challenges for the country's economy.

Lesson Objectives
- Describe the role of Mexico City in Mexican life today.
- Explain the two types of Mexican agriculture.
- Describe the developing economy of Mexico and its relation to population growth.

1 PREPARE

Motivate Read the *Read Aloud* section to the class and discuss how job opportunities control movement of families. Tell students that the same economic force, the need for a job, that brought Alfredo Rios Perez to Mexico City draws rural people everywhere in the world into metropolitan areas.

Set Purpose Use the *What You Know* question to further discuss ways in which families are affected by job moves. Use the *What You Will Learn* question to help students suggest factors that aid in the industrialization of a nation's economy.

2 TEACH

Describing Mexico City Make sure students recognize the dual nature of Mexico City as both the cultural and economic heart of Mexico.

Ask students:

- **Why does Mexico City's modern subway system cost so little to ride?** (The government wants people to ride the subway, not drive cars, to cut down air pollution.)

READING STRATEGY AND VOCABULARY DEVELOPMENT

Previewing and Predicting Review with students the steps in predicting: previewing the lesson, thinking about what you know about the topic of the lesson and then making predictions about what the author will discuss, and confirming predictions through reading. Have students work in groups and make predictions about what living and working in Mexico might be like. Some students may have visited Mexico, and their predictions may be more accurate. Point out that the more information you have about a topic, the more accurate your predictions are apt to be. After they read the lesson, have students compare and evaluate their predictions.

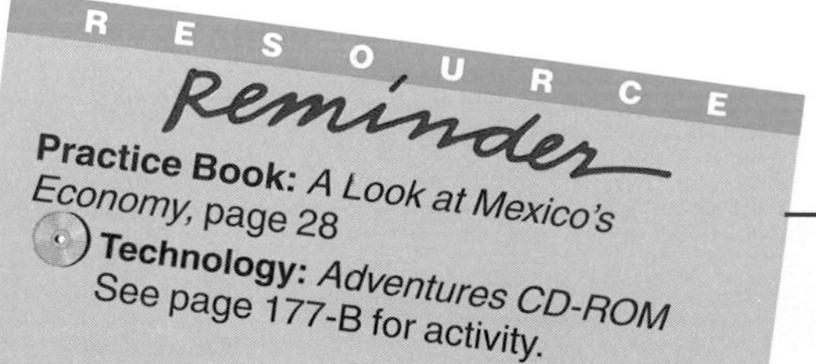

RESOURCE *Reminder*

Practice Book: *A Look at Mexico's Economy*, page 28

Technology: *Adventures CD-ROM* See page 177-B for activity.

EXTENDING CHART SKILLS

Define an urban area and refer students to the chart on this page.

Ask students:

- **What kind of information is given about each urban area?** (total population)
- **Which is the most populated area? The least populated?** (Tokyo-Yokohama, Japan; Buenos Aires, Argentina)
- **What are the large urban areas in Latin America?** (Mexico City, Mexico; São Paulo, Brazil; Buenos Aires, Argentina; Rio de Janeiro, Brazil)

Understanding Agriculture Help students to compare subsistence farming with commercial farming.

Ask students:

- **Who are campesinos?** (village farmers who do subsistence farming)
- *THINKING FURTHER:* **How do subsistence farming and commercial farming help Mexico?** (Subsistence farming feeds the nation; commercial farming brings profits with which to purchase other goods or services.)

Discussing Industrialization and a Growing Population Point out to students that a burgeoning population slows the industrialization of Mexico's economy since the number of people who need jobs is greater than the number of jobs that are available.

Ask students:

- **What resources does Mexico have today on which to build industries?** (silver, gold, petroleum, coal, iron, and zinc)
- **How have improved living conditions caused a problem in Mexico?** (People live longer and have larger families so the population has doubled in ten years, leaving one third of the population unemployed.)

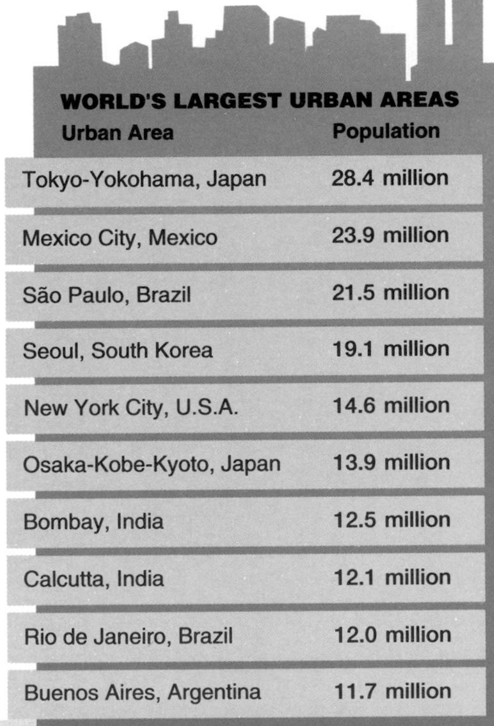

WORLD'S LARGEST URBAN AREAS

Urban Area	Population
Tokyo-Yokohama, Japan	28.4 million
Mexico City, Mexico	23.9 million
São Paulo, Brazil	21.5 million
Seoul, South Korea	19.1 million
New York City, U.S.A.	14.6 million
Osaka-Kobe-Kyoto, Japan	13.9 million
Bombay, India	12.5 million
Calcutta, India	12.1 million
Rio de Janeiro, Brazil	12.0 million
Buenos Aires, Argentina	11.7 million

SOURCE: 1995 Information Please Almanac

CHART SKILL: How many of the large urban areas listed in the chart are located in Latin America? Name them.

124 CHART SKILL: 4; Mexico City, São Paulo, Buenos Aires, Rio de Janeiro

These village farmers, or **campesinos** (käm pə sē′ nōz), grow just enough corn, beans, and squash for their families. Farming of this type is called **subsistence farming**. Without surplus, or extra, food, subsistence farmers have little to trade at markets. Moreover, the little money they earn is often just enough to buy other kinds of food. As a result, large trade centers have not developed in Mexico's poor farming areas.

Only 11 percent of Mexico's land can be farmed. Besides the campesinos, the other people who own this land cultivate mainly sugarcane, cotton, and tropical fruits on large farms. This type of farming in which all the crops are grown for sale is called **commercial farming**. Many commercial crops are exported to other nations.

INDUSTRIALIZATION

Mexico is working to increase its mineral manufacturing industries. Mexico has great amounts of silver and gold—the treasure that may have been behind the legend of El Dorado that you read about earlier. For centuries about one third of the world's silver came from Mexico's mines. This ore was not used in Mexico to develop the nation's businesses and factories but went instead to other countries. Partly for this reason, Mexico today has a **developing economy**. A developing economy is one that is only partly industrialized.

Mexico also has other minerals—coal, iron, zinc, and petroleum. Large deposits of petroleum, discovered in the 1970s, helped Mexico's economy. The discovery of oil has created new industries, like the **petrochemical** industry. Petrochemicals are chemicals, like ammonia and benzene, that are made from petroleum. Mexico has the largest petrochemical industry in Latin America.

BACKGROUND INFORMATION

Peasant Farmers of Mexico The legacy of Spanish colonial days has left land ownership a problem for Mexico. Before the 1920s a few privileged Spanish families owned most of Mexico in the form of huge estates called *haciendas*. Peasants who worked the fields were paid almost nothing. When the Mexican Constitution was passed, the government split up the huge haciendas into smaller pieces. These were called *ejidos*. Organized around a village and the adjoining farmlands, an ejido is owned jointly by the campesinos who live there. Almost half of all Mexican farmers are members of ejidos. Meanwhile, many other Mexicans still seek farmland.

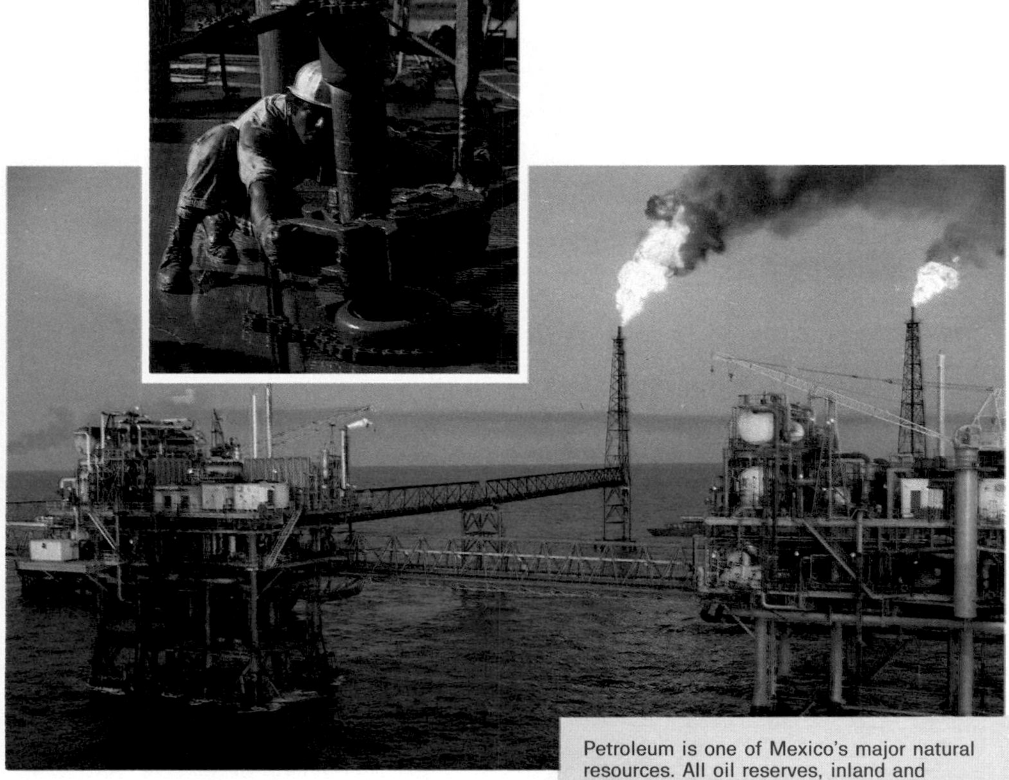

Petroleum is one of Mexico's major natural resources. All oil reserves, inland and offshore, are developed by PEMEX, the state-owned oil company of Mexico.

THE GROWING POPULATION

Despite its new industries, Mexico's economic growth slowed in the 1980s. The main reason for this was that as Mexico became industrialized, the nation's living conditions and the health of its population improved. People began to live longer and have larger families. As a result, the population doubled between 1972 and 1982. Today Mexico's population is growing twice as rapidly as that of the United States and faster than the nation's ability to provide jobs. In 1995, Mexico's economy verged on total collapse. With a loan from the U.S., Mexico is slowly recovering.

CHALLENGES FOR THE FUTURE

Mexico, as you have read, has a developing economy that is partially industrialized. Most of its industry is concentrated in Mexico City and a few other cities. Because it has poor farmland and a rapidly growing population, Mexico finds it difficult to provide jobs, goods, and services for all of its people.

Check Your Reading

1. Why is Mexico's economy called a developing economy?
2. Why is Mexico City important?
3. What is the difference between subsistence farming and commercial farming?
4. THINKING SKILL: What factors might you consider if you were trying to decide whether or not to move to a large city in Mexico?

THINKING SKILL: Decision Making

125

Applying the Lesson Have students construct a chart to show the factors in the Mexican economy that aid industrialization versus those that hamper economic development. Then discuss what Mexico needs so that it can develop further.

3 CLOSE

Summarizing Students have learned that a lack of jobs characterizes Mexico's partly industrialized economy, which is further hampered by insufficient farmland and an expanding population. Have students discuss possible solutions to Mexico's industrial problems.

Evaluating Use these questions to assess students' understanding.

- **Which Mexican city offers the most job opportunities?** (Mexico City)
- **Which form of farming do you think is more important in Mexico?** (Students should give reasons for their answers.)
- **How has industrialization helped the people of Mexico?** (economic growth, improved living conditions, better health care)

Answers to Check Your Reading

1. because it is only partly industrialized
2. It is Mexico's capital city and the economic and cultural center of Mexico.
3. The goal of subsistence farming is family survival. The goal of commercial farming is to make a cash profit.
4. Possible answers include: if the family is able to stay together, the kinds of jobs available, the types of housing available.

Independent Practice
Practice Book: page 28

MEETING INDIVIDUAL NEEDS

Reteaching (easy) Have students prepare a chart to compare Mexico City with their own town or city. Have them compare locations, populations, land areas, land use, and physical environments.

Extension (average) Have students research the rate of population growth for the United States and Mexico. Then have them draw charts depicting the population growth of the United States versus that of Mexico.

Enrichment (challenging) Have students research and construct charts comparing the United States, Canada, and Mexico. Have them compare unemployment, foods exported, goods exported, and petroleum income. Students can make posters of the charts for display.

SKILLS LESSON
pages 126–127

Lesson Theme Determining the accuracy of information involves determining the credibility of the source.

Lesson Objective
- Describe and use a method to determine the accuracy of information.

PREPARE

Motivate Ask students to name sources of information that they have and use every day (television, newspapers, friends, family, books, magazines). Ask students if they think these sources provide accurate information. Write the word *accurate* on the chalkboard and ask for other words that have almost the same meaning. (*right, correct*)

Have students read the introductory paragraph. Call on students to describe *accurate information.* Discuss with students why and when it is important to determine if information is accurate. (You need accurate information to make good decisions, form opinions, write reports.)

Set Purpose Tell students that in this lesson they will learn one way to determine the accuracy of information.

TEACH

Trying the Skill Have students read the information about Mexico's school enrollment and write down the questions that follow. Tell students to refer to the *Helping Yourself* section on the next page if they have trouble answering the questions.

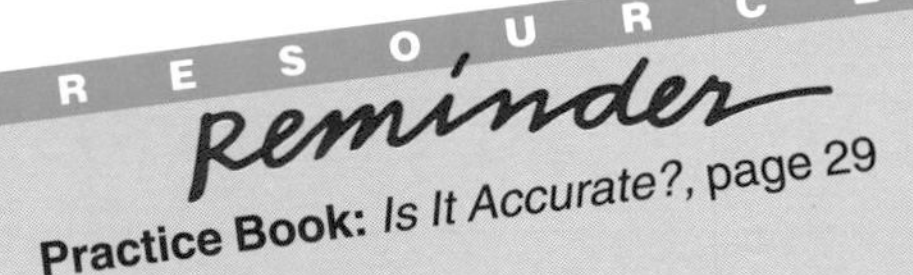

BUILDING SKILLS
THINKING SKILLS

Determining the Accuracy of Information

Suppose a friend shows you a baseball card and tells you that it is worth $6.35. The card is one of your favorites. Your friend offers to sell it to you, telling you it will increase in value each year. Before you buy the card, wouldn't you want to know if your friend is giving you accurate information? You need accurate information to make good decisions. Information that is accurate is free of errors. Therefore, when you check information for errors, you are determining the accuracy of that information.

Trying the Skill

Suppose you were to read the following in a magazine article about Mexico dated January 1995.

> According to Mexico's Minister of Public Education, there has been a dramatic increase in public school enrollment since the 1950s. Enrollment in secondary schools today is over five times higher than it was in 1955. About 90 percent of children ages 6–14 are now attending primary schools. A major effort is being made to promote education in rural areas.

1. Do you think the above information is accurate? Why?
2. What could you do to determine the accuracy of the information given?

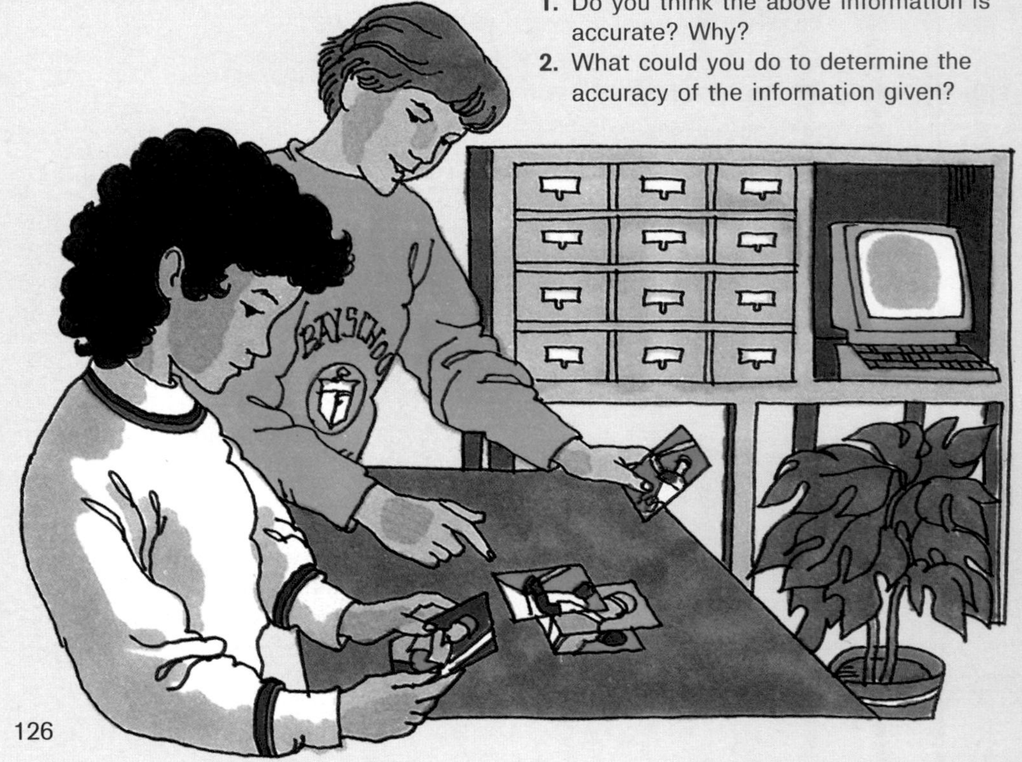

126

CURRICULUM CONNECTION

Science Ask students to scan their science textbooks for an experiment that interests them. Have them read about the experiment and the scientific principle that the experiment illustrates. Ask students to explain how they would go about verifying the accuracy of the experiment.

HELPING YOURSELF

The steps on the left can help you to determine the accuracy of information. The examples on the right show how these steps can be used to evaluate the information about education in Mexico.

One Way to Determine the Accuracy of Information	Example
1. Identify the source of the information.	The source is Mexico's Minister of Public Education.
2. Determine the credibility, or believability, of the source by asking the following questions. • Is the author or speaker an expert or well informed about the topic? • Does the author or speaker have anything to gain by giving inaccurate information?	The speaker is the Minister of Public Education and is therefore likely to be well informed about the topic. The speaker appears to have nothing to gain by giving inaccurate information.
3. Determine if the information is current.	The article was written in 1995, so the education figures provided for "today" are current.
4. Compare the information with similar information in other sources.	Checking the same information in other sources helps you to determine its accuracy. In this case, you might look for information in current world almanacs and encyclopedias. If all the sources agree, the information is probably accurate.

Applying the Skill

Now apply what you have learned. Determine the accuracy of the following information from a book about Mexico written in 1979. The author of the book is a geography professor who has taught at a university in Mexico City for 20 years.

Since 1950 economic growth has been steady in Mexico. Oil and gas reserves were discovered in 1975, making Mexico self-sufficient in petroleum. Tourism is at a record high. The Mexican stock market is on an upswing.

1. Is the information presented accurate? How can you tell?
2. Is the source of the information a credible source? How do you know that the source is credible?
3. What are two sources you might check to determine the accuracy of the information above?

Reviewing the Skill

1. What does the word *accuracy* mean?
2. What are three things you can do to determine the accuracy of information?
3. Why is it important to determine whether or not information is accurate?

Thinking About Thinking Call on several students to read their answers aloud. Focus on question 2. *Ask:* What did you do first? Why? Next? Why? and so on. List each student's answers on the chalkboard and have the class identify key steps common to all lists.

Helping Yourself Tell students that this section presents one useful method for determining accuracy. Call on students to compare the steps in the chart with those on the chalkboard to draw up a composite list of helpful steps.

Applying the Skill Tell students that they will now have a chance to apply what they have learned. Have them read this section and answer the questions that follow. (See answers below.) Remind students that they may refer to the steps outlined in *Helping Yourself* and on the chalkboard.

CLOSE

Reviewing the Skill Use answers to question 1 to add synonyms to those listed on the chalkboard for *accuracy.* Use questions 2 and 3 as a starting point for students to explain in their own words how they would go about determining the accuracy of information they hear and read and to describe situations outside of school when they would use this skill.

Independent Practice
Practice Book: page 29

ANSWERS TO SKILLS QUESTIONS

Applying the Skill

1. Some of the information is inaccurate because it is out-of-date.
2. The source of the information is a geography professor who has taught in Mexico City for 20 years. The professor is well informed and so is a credible source.
3. Other sources to check include: articles in current newspapers, current magazines such as *National Geographic*, current encyclopedias and almanacs, and reports issued by the Mexican government.

Reviewing the Skill

1. *Accuracy* means "the state of being up-to-date and being free of errors or mistakes."
2. Identify the source of the information and determine its credibility. Check that the information is current. Look up the information in other sources.
3. Having inaccurate information can lead you to make mistakes or poor decisions. For example, if the baseball card was worth less than your friend said, you would pay more money than it was worth.

LESSON 3
pages 128–130

Lesson Theme At the center of Mexico's democratic government are strong presidential powers and a powerful political party.

Lesson Objectives
- Identify the type of rule in Mexico.
- Describe the role of the president compared with that of the legislature of Mexico.
- Identify the political parties in Mexico and how they may change in the future.

PREPARE

Motivate Ask students what time periods are mentioned in the *Read Aloud* section. (present, future) Have students discuss which time period is more important for a president to plan for—the present or the future.

Set Purpose Pose the *What You Know* question. Then have students review the key branches of government in a federal republic as you list them on the chalkboard. Read the *What You Will Learn* question and write students' answers on the chalkboard. Review their list after they have read the lesson. Have students make any necessary changes or additions to the list.

TEACH

Discussing a Strong President Help students to understand how a long period of political turmoil caused Mexicans to develop a government with a strong leader.

LESSON 3

The Government

READ TO LEARN

Key People

Carlos Salinas de Gotari Ernesto Zedillo

Read Aloud

I take office at a complicated moment, between . . . the necessity to build for the future and the urgency of immediate achievements. . . . I am determined to move ahead with a democratic reform, and I have invited political parties to join me. . . .

Carlos Salinas de Gortari spoke these words when he was sworn in as president of Mexico in 1988, after the most troubled election in modern Mexican history. Like many other Mexican leaders before him, he faced the prospect of turmoil in the country he was to lead.

Read for Purpose

1. **WHAT YOU KNOW:** What is a federal republic?
2. **WHAT YOU WILL LEARN:** How is Mexico's representative democracy different from that of the United States?

A STRONG PRESIDENT

Mexico gained its independence from Spain in 1821. However, independence did not bring stability to the country. Instead a series of strong leaders, usually from the military, ruled Mexico. Finally in 1910, a popular revolution swept across Mexico. When it was over, Mexicans wrote a constitution that guaranteed basic rights for all of its citizens. Today Mexicans are proud of what they accomplished in their popular revolution.

Mexico's constitution made the country a representative democracy. However, its government is a little different from the governments of the United States and Canada in that it provides for strong leadership by one person.

The Mexican constitution gives its president more power than the Constitution of the United States gives to the President of the United States. The president of Mexico can remove local officials from office and change laws with the approval of the Senate. However, the Mexican president can be elected for only one six-year term.

The Mexican constitution also established a legislature of two houses. One house, the Chamber of Deputies, passes laws and is responsible for elections. The second house, the Senate, approves or disapproves treaties and presidential appointments. Mexico also has a federal system of government. This means that its 31 states control many local affairs. A Supreme Court interprets laws.

128 WHAT YOU KNOW: This question refers to information in Chapter 2, Lesson 3; a system in which voters elect officials to represent them in government and in which power is divided between national and local governments.

READING STRATEGY AND VOCABULARY DEVELOPMENT

Previewing and Predicting By now students should be familiar with the strategies for previewing and predicting. Have students preview the lesson and then, as a class, make predictions. Have them make a chart, divided into two columns, comparing the United States government and the Mexican government. In one column of the chart have students list information about the United States government. Then ask students to predict how the Mexican government might be alike or different. Have students write their predictions in the second column. After they have read the lesson, have students evaluate their predictions.

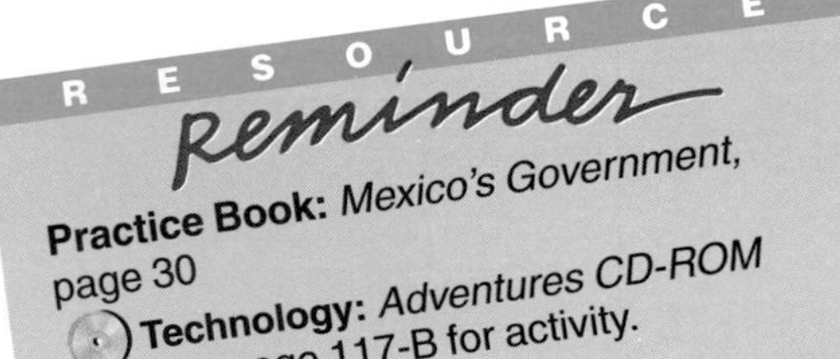

Practice Book: *Mexico's Government,* page 30

Technology: *Adventures CD-ROM* See page 117-B for activity.

LEADERSHIP BY ONE PARTY

Unlike the United States, Mexico has only one strong political party, the Party of Institutional Revolution (PRI). It was formed in 1929 to include many interests—labor, agriculture, professional people, and the military. The reason for this union was to prevent different groups from clashing and causing unrest.

For about 60 years the PRI won elections easily. In the 1988 election, however, the PRI was losing until the last minute. After it was declared the winner by less than 1 percent, Carlos Salinas de Gortari became president. But some people believed that the party had really lost the election. Critics said the PRI had "fixed" the returns to make the party win.

A CHANGING GOVERNMENT

In the next presidential election, held in 1994, PRI candidate Luis Colosio was assassinated at a political rally. The new candidate, Ernesto Zedillo, was elected a few months later.

Zedillo faced many of the same problems of his predecessor, including an increasingly unstable economy. Although Mexico was a part of the North American Free Trade Agreement, or NAFTA, early in 1995, Mexico's economy verged on total collapse. As you have read, Mexico was able to avoid disaster with help from its trading partner to the north, the United States. Even so, many Mexicans cannot find work, and Zedillo and the PRI are often criticized.

Critics of the PRI today say it is time to make the government more directly responsible to the people and to allow parties to air their differences in public. They say that Mexico "needs [several] political parties . . . to express those divisions—of class, of racial background, of politics."

Many Mexicans took part in the 1994 presidential election. Ernesto Zedillo (*below*), who won, was the candidate of the PRI. The party's emblem is shown above.

INTERNATIONAL COOPERATION

Despite its party troubles, Mexico has one of the most stable governments in Latin America. This enables Mexico to be very active in international affairs.

Describing a Strong President Continue the discussion of the president and legislature of Mexico.

Ask students:

- **In what ways does Mexico's representative democracy give more power to its president than does the United States' but less opportunity for that power to grow?** (Mexico's president can remove local officials and change laws with Senate consent but is allowed only one term in office.)
- **How does the basic process of lawmaking in Mexico differ from that of the United States Congress?** (In Mexico only one house passes laws; in the United States Congress both houses have this duty.)
- **What are two ways in which the structure of the Mexican government and the United States government are the same?** (Both have a federal system and a Supreme Court.)

Understanding Leadership by One Party Help students to realize that after 100 years of internal fighting in Mexico, the unification of the people into one political party has given the country stability.

Ask students:

- **Why did so many different kinds of groups and levels of society join to make the PRI?** (Forming the PRI prevented different groups from clashing, thus helping Mexico to unite as one nation.)
- **What advantages might having several political parties give Mexico today?** (Issues might be discussed more openly and more fully; people of different classes, politics, and racial backgrounds could be represented.)

Discussing Mexico's Changing Government In early 1997, Mexico repaid, with interest, its debt to the United States. This repayment and steady economic growth are a result of a strict austerity program instituted by Mexican President Zedillo. Discuss with students the current state of Mexico's government and economy.

CURRICULUM CONNECTION

Math Have students calculate the length of time that Mexicans fought for a written constitution, from the call for independence by Father Hidalgo in 1810 to the adoption of the Mexican constitution in 1917. Have students also calculate the number of years that American colonists fought and worked for a constitution, from the shots at Lexington and Concord in 1775 to the adoption of the United States Constitution in 1789. Have them draw time lines of these two nations' struggles for rights. Discuss how much longer the Mexicans had to fight for independence and a constitution than did the American colonists. Tell students that the lengthier 107-year Mexican struggle is the reason that Mexicans today still call themselves revolutionaries. Americans received their constitution after only 14 years and today do not think of themselves as revolutionaries.

Applying the Lesson Have students debate the pros and cons of having only one political party.

3 CLOSE

Summarize Students have learned that Mexico's representative democracy is based on a strong executive branch of government. Have students explain the current political party in Mexico and compare it with the kinds of political parties some Mexicans think they should have in Mexico today.

Evaluating Use the *Check Your Reading* questions (answers given below) to assess students' understanding.

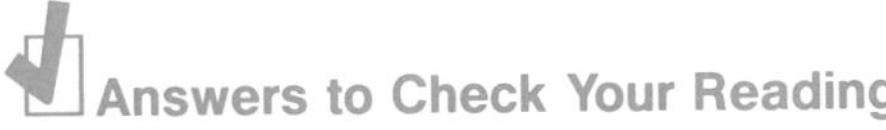

Answers to Check Your Reading

1. Mexico's president has more power over lawmaking and can be in office only one term.
2. It has two branches: the Chamber of Deputies passes laws and runs elections; the Senate approves treaties and presidential appointments.
3. One party, the Party of Institutional Revolution, has held power since 1929 as a union of many interests—labor, agriculture, professional people, and the military. For 60 years they easily won elections, but they won the 1988 election by less than 1 percent of the vote.
4. *executive*: (with Senate approval) remove local officials from office, change laws, and make appointments; *legislative*: pass laws; approve treaties, appointments, changes in the law, and removal of local officials

Independent Practice
Practice Book: page 30

The Organization of American States Building and its emblem are in Washington, D.C.

One of the Latin American organizations in which Mexico is very active is the Organization of American States (OAS). The main goals of the OAS are to improve the lives of Latin American people and to keep peace in the Western Hemisphere. Mexico has also been a strong supporter of the United Nations (UN), the world's largest international organization. The UN was formed in 1945 to keep peace among nations and to help poor people.

OVER 70 YEARS OF DEMOCRACY

Mexico's government combines strong presidential leadership with democracy. Until 1988 one party, the PRI, easily won elections in Mexico. Since then, critics of the government have said that it is time for a multiparty system to be formed in Mexico.

Check Your Reading

1. List two ways in which the presidency of Mexico is different from the presidency of the United States.
2. Describe Mexico's legislature.
3. Briefly describe the political party system of Mexico.
4. **THINKING SKILL:** Classify the powers of the Mexican government into its executive and legislative branches.

THINKING SKILL: Classifying

MEETING INDIVIDUAL NEEDS

Reteaching (easy) Ask students to draw a chart that shows the branches of government in Mexico and their powers and the branches of the United States government and their powers.

Extension (average) Ask students to research the life stories of Mexican presidents. Ask them to choose three Mexican presidents and then write a short paragraph about each.

Enrichment (challenging) Ask students to research Mexico's role in international affairs. Have them write an essay on Mexico's contributions to the OAS and the UN.

LESSON 4

Arts and Recreation

READ TO LEARN

Key Vocabulary

mural

Key People

Diego Rivera
José Orozco

Read Aloud

La Cucaracha, La Cucaracha,
Just the same as you and I,
He got the jitters, the sweets, and bitters,
Lived and loved and said "Goodbye."

This is the last chorus from "La Cucaracha," or "The Mexican Cockroach Song." It was a favorite marching song of the Mexican revolutionaries in 1910. Today it is still one of the most popular Mexican songs.

Read for Purpose

1. WHAT YOU KNOW: What songs express the way people in the United States feel about their country?
2. WHAT YOU WILL LEARN: How are Mexico's arts and amusements the products of different cultures?

1910 AND THE ARTS

You read in Lesson 3 that the Mexican Revolution, which changed the country into a republic, began in 1910. After the revolution, Mexicans started to think of themselves as one people. Indians, mestizos, and Mexicans of Spanish ancestry had fought together. They had succeeded in creating a government that guarantees people's rights. One writer explains:

> *The 1910 Revolution was the revolution of the campesinos. Before this time they were a forgotten people. But the campesinos gave their hearts and their lives to create a new Mexico. Now let their voices be heard!*

The people's pride in their achievement inspired Mexico's artists. They began to explore what it meant to be Mexican.

INDIAN AND MESTIZO CULTURES

A number of artists explored their Indian heritage. Well-known composers, such as Carlos Chávez, began to use Indian melodies in their music.

The mestizo heritage was also explored. Two Mexican painters are identified with the mestizo art of their country. They are Diego Rivera (dyā′ gō ri ver′ ə) and José Orozco (hō sā′ ō rô′ skō). Both artists painted large murals, or works of art on building walls.

With simple lines and bold colors Rivera and Orozco captured the spirit of Mexico—both the past sufferings and the hopes for the future. Their murals are among the first and best works of modern Mexican art. Every year thousands of people visit Mexico City, Guadalajara, and

WHAT YOU KNOW: Encourage students to think of the national anthem and other patriotic songs of the United States.

LESSON 4
pages 131–133

Lesson Theme Mexican arts and amusements reflect Indian, mestizo, and Spanish influences.

Lesson Objectives

- Explain the impact of post-1910 Mexican pride on the arts.
- Explain the blend of Indian, mestizo, and Spanish cultures in Mexican arts and sports.

1 PREPARE

Motivate Ask for a volunteer to sing the *Read Aloud* in a "rap" style. Discuss students' ideas of what this song is about.

Set Purpose Use students' answers to the *What You Know* question to point out the expression of patriotism and love of country in songs like "America, the Beautiful," "God Bless America," and "This Is My Country." Use the *What You Will Learn* question to challenge students to look for ways in which a blend of cultures produced Mexican arts and sports.

2 TEACH

Discussing 1910 and the Arts Help students to recognize the great sense of pride in things Mexican that arose after the Mexican Revolution.

Ask students:

- **Why did the new constitutional government mean so much to the ordinary people? How did this affect the arts?** (They were proud of their part in fighting for rights for the people and were thus proud to be one people—Mexican; this pride spurred artists to create a new Mexican style.)

Identifying Indian and Mestizo Cultures Help students to identify the three cultures reflected in Mexican arts and crafts.

READING STRATEGY AND VOCABULARY DEVELOPMENT

Previewing and Predicting Students should now be able to make their own predictions. Have students make predictions about Mexican arts and recreation based on a comparison with arts and recreation in the United States. (Refer to Chapter 2 for information on the United States.) Use students' predictions for a class discussion or for writing a compare/contrast paragraph.

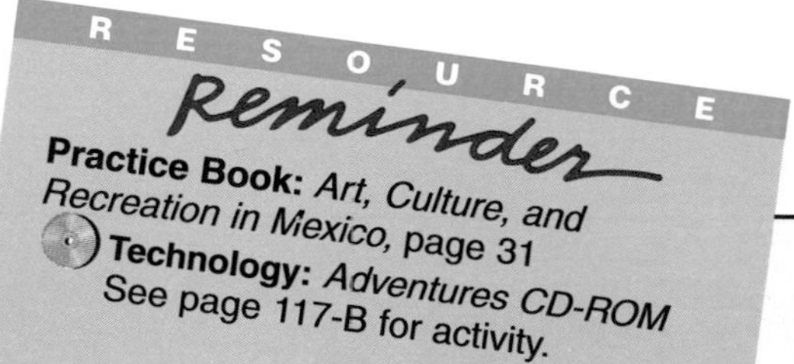

Discussing the Photograph Have students examine the photograph of the mural on this page. Ask them to discuss what a mural is and what it stands for. Have students discuss murals they have seen and what those murals stand for.

Discussing Mexican Crafts Tell students that craft skills are handed down from one generation to the next. Have students think of skills that American families hand down from generation to generation.

Ask students:

- **How did the Mexican government help mestizo craftspeople?** (Awards given helped to keep the craft skills alive, gave people income, and enabled craftspeople to make goods for export.)

Discussing Sports Stress sports as a continuing part of Mexican life.

Ask students:

- **What makes handball different from the other favorite Mexican sports?** (Ancient Indians played a game similar to handball 1,000 years ago in Mexico.)
- **The riding skills used in Mexico today are a blend of which two cultures?** (Spanish and Indian)

Applying the Lesson Have students review the lesson and create a three-column chart on which they list the arts and amusements that are Indian, Spanish, and mestizo. Have students discuss the photos and visuals in the lesson to see how they show these three influences.

Among Mexico's famous art works is the mural *Mexico Through the Centuries* by Diego Rivera. It highlights Mexico's fight for land and freedom. Craftworkers like the weaver below also create works of art.

Cuernavaca (kwâr nə väk′ ə) to see the beautiful murals painted by these artists.

CRAFTS

After the Mexican Revolution the Mexican government began to support traditional Mexican crafts. It gave craftworkers awards and helped them export their best works. In so doing, Mexico hoped to maintain its traditions, give people income, and produce goods for export.

Today craftworkers produce a wide variety of colorful and well-made products, including pottery, woven goods, jewelry, and objects made of wood, reeds, bark, and cactus. Usually each town specializes in a particular craft, such as silvermaking or goldmaking. Craft skills are handed down from one generation to the next.

Celestino Bautista, who lives in the state of Oaxaca (wä häk′ ə) learned to weave when he was young. He says, "My father taught me to weave when I was 11, and now my youngest son, José, is that age, and I am teaching him the same skills."

CURRICULUM CONNECTION

Art Have students look in newspapers and in art and decorating magazines for articles on different Mexican crafts and on the craftsworkers. Then have students create a bulletin board display using articles about the crafts and the craftsworkers, and pictures showing some examples of their work.

Language Arts Have students research the history of rodeos in Mexico and prepare a short report on the topic. Have them include a drawing of what they think a Mexican rodeo would look like.

SPORTS

Among the favorite sports in Mexico are baseball, soccer, and jai alai (hī′ lī), which is a form of handball. Mexicans have long played handball. Paintings more than 1,000 years old show that Indians of that time played a game like handball. The game was part of a religious ceremony. Losers of the game sometimes lost their freedom and wealth, and even their lives.

Many Mexicans are skilled horseback riders. The Spanish brought horses to the Americas in the 1500s. But the riding skills used in Mexico today are both Spanish and Indian. Luis Bernal, a welder, describes a Mexican rodeo.

> *Horsemen wearing richly embroidered costumes, topped by massive sombreros with specially shaped brims, perform spectacular feats of riding as they lasso young bulls and wild horses.*

BLENDING THE TRADITIONAL AND THE MODERN

Almost everything in Mexico—from the people themselves to the arts and amusements they enjoy—reflects a blend of different cultures. Writers, painters, and craftworkers have combined Indian and Spanish traditions to create a distinctive Mexican style.

Check Your Reading

1. What are two popular sports in Mexico?
2. What is a mural? How are Mexico's cultures combined in its murals?
3. How did the 1910 Revolution affect the arts in Mexico?
4. THINKING SKILL: Look at the mural *Mexico Through the Centuries* by Diego Rivera on page 132. What does this mural tell you about the people of Mexico and the blend of cultures in the country?

THINKING SKILL: Observing

CITIZENSHIP MAKING A DIFFERENCE

PRESERVING FOLK ART

Maria Teresa Pomar was born soon after the Mexican Revolution. At that time artists and composers were creating new ways to work, and traditional craftsworkers were being encouraged by the government to develop their skills.

Maria, whose father was a famous musician, learned at a young age to appreciate the work of artists. In time she became especially interested in the traditional crafts of Mexico.

Later Maria visited Mexican craftsworkers all over the country. After years of travel and study she became an expert on Mexico's traditional crafts. By examining a piece of art, Maria could identify the person who had made it.

In 1976 Maria was asked to manage the National Museum of Folk Arts in Mexico City. Later she opened museums throughout Mexico to further spread the traditions of Mexican crafts.

In 1985 the president of Mexico awarded Maria the Gamio Prize, one of Mexico's highest honors. On behalf of all Mexicans he honored her hard work to preserve the history and protect the future of traditional Mexican art.

3 CLOSE

Summarizing Tell students that they have learned that Mexican arts and leisure activities are created from a rich blend of Indian, mestizo, and Spanish cultural themes and skills. Have students explain how the feelings of Mexican citizens after 1910 resulted in a Mexican art style.

Evaluating Use these questions to assess students' understanding.

- **What Mexican art draws tourists to Mexico City, Guadalajara, and Cuernavaca?** (the mestizo murals of Rivera and Orozco)
- **What role do crafts play in Mexican towns?** (Towns specialize in certain crafts and become known for them.)

Answers to Check Your Reading

1. baseball, soccer, jai alai
2. Murals are works of art on building walls; Mexico's Indian and mestizo heritages are expressed in the murals of artists such as Diego Rivera and José Orozco.
3. It united the ordinary people and gave them pride, which inspired Mexico's artists to design Mexican themes.
4. Students' answers should focus on the blending of the cultures in Mexico and on the Mexican fight for freedom.

Independent Practice
Practice Book: page 31

MEETING INDIVIDUAL NEEDS

Reteaching (easy) Divide the class into groups and give each group a long sheet of butcher paper. Have groups discuss, plan, and draw a mural titled "Mexican Arts, Crafts, and Sports Today."

Extension (average) Have students research the National Museum of Anthropology in Mexico City. Have students write a description of which art in that museum they would like to see.

Enrichment (challenging) Have students research and write a short history of Mexico's Indian art, including comparative descriptions of Toltec, Mixtec, Zapotec, Mayan, and Aztec art.

BUILDING CITIZENSHIP

Preserving Mexico's Folk Art Have students read about Mexico's folk art in the *Making a Difference* feature. Help students understand what folk art is. Help them to give examples of American folk art. Discuss the special thing Maria did for her country and why it is important. Have students list the things they can do to preserve the history of American folk art and protect its future.

LEGACY
pages 134–137

Lesson Theme In Mexico the legacy of mural painting dates back to the days of the Aztec and Mayan civilizations. Blending Indian and European styles of art, modern muralists have taught the people of Mexico about their rich past.

Lesson Objectives
- Describe how muralists combine the artistic traditions of the Indian and European ancestors of modern Mexicans.
- Explain how murals provide a means of communicating beliefs about Mexican history and about life in Mexico today.
- Describe the ancient Mayan murals of Bonampak.
- Discuss the work of Dr. Atl and of Diego Rivera.

1 PREPARE

Motivate Ask students if they have ever seen an outdoor mural. Have them discuss why an artist might want to paint a large outdoor mural rather than a painting that will be housed in a home or a museum.

Set Purpose Focus students' attention with the following question. How do artists such as painters or songwriters communicate beliefs or feelings about the world? (Encourage students to think of popular music or art that conveys particular beliefs or feelings.) Have students read the introduction. Ask them to think about the concluding suggestion while they read the rest of the lesson.

2 TEACH

Understanding the Concept of Legacies Review the definition of a legacy. Ask students to name forms of art that are legacies. (kinds of music, theater, painting, sculpture)

Discussing an Artist and Teacher Make sure that students can point out Mexico on the political map of Latin America.

RESOURCE *Reminder*
- **Anthology:** *Life in Mexico Today,* pages 61–62

MEXICAN MURALS

by Argentina Palacios

Long ago the great ancient civilizations of Mexico created spectacular buildings and beautiful works of art. Among the most impressive artwork they left behind were beautiful murals painted on the walls of stone buildings. You can still see these beautiful ancient murals in Mexico today.

As you read in Lesson 4, modern Mexican artists are still painting murals such as this one by Diego Rivera. Mural painting is a Mexican tradition that is centuries old. The artists of modern Mexico paint murals that combine the artistic traditions of their Indian and European ancestors. As you read this lesson, think about how the legacy of mural painting connects past, present, and future generations in Mexico.

AN ARTIST AND TEACHER

It was the early 1900s, and Dr. Atl (ot′ əl) had just come home from a trip through Europe and Eastern Asia. He was returning to his position as a teacher at San Carlos Academy, a school of fine arts in Mexico City. Dr. Atl was an expert on art, architecture, and volcanoes, as well as a fine painter of portraits and landscape scenes. When he was born, he had been given the name Gerardo Murillo (mü rē′ yō). He had changed his name to Dr. Atl in honor of the Aztecs—his Indian ancestors who had created one of Mexico's great civilizations. *Atl* means "water" in the Aztec language.

READING STRATEGY AND VOCABULARY DEVELOPMENT

Previewing and Predicting Students should now be able to make predictions about the content of this lesson. Have them preview the subheadings and photos in order to make predictions about the lesson content and why mural painting has become an important artistic legacy in Mexico. Discuss with students how skimming a lesson and predicting its content can increase their reading comprehension.

During his travels through Europe, Dr. Atl had been particularly impressed by the murals of a great Italian artist, Michelangelo. He described these murals in detail to his students. Dr. Atl believed that painting murals could provide a perfect way to honor the artistic traditions of the Indian and European ancestors of modern Mexicans. Some of his students were to become the finest muralists in Mexico.

MEXICO'S ANCIENT MURALS

Dr. Atl was drawn to murals because he knew that mural painting has a long history. Beautiful murals had been painted by the artists of the Aztecs, the Mayas, and Mexico's other Indian civilizations. Perhaps the most beautiful ancient murals in Mexico are found in the Mayan city of Bonampak (bō näm päk'), located in the present-day Mexican state of Chiapas. In fact, the name *Bonampak* means "painted wall" in the Mayan language.

The Bonampak murals were painted in about A.D. 700 but their existence was unknown in modern times until 1946. The largest of them is divided into three parts, each showing a different stage of warfare. One part shows a battle scene in which soldiers dressed in scary headdresses attack their enemies with knives and long spears.

PUBLIC ART

Dr. Atl and many of his students believed that murals painted in public places are a powerful way of communicating ideas to the Mexican people. They wanted to produce art that would be enjoyed in public by all Mexicans, not just by collectors in their own homes. Many of the muralists also hoped to teach Mexicans about their history. In many of their murals and other paintings,

135

Discussing Dr. Atl Continue the discussion. You may wish to show the class photos of Michelangelo's Sistine Chapel murals, which inspired Dr. Atl.

Ask students:

- **Who was Dr. Atl?** (a teacher in Mexico City, an expert in many fields, and a fine painter)
- **Why did Dr. Atl change his name from Gerardo Murillo?** (to honor his Aztec ancestors; *Atl* means "water" in the Aztec language.)
- **Why was Dr. Atl so interested in mural painting?** (He saw it as a way to honor the traditions of the Indian and European ancestors of modern Mexicans.)

Discussing Mexico's Ancient Murals Tell students that many Mayas and other Indians still live in Mexico. You may wish to have them read *Life in Mexico Today* on pages 61–62 in the anthology.

Ask students:

- **What does the name *Bonampak* mean in the Mayan language?** ("painted wall")
- **What do the Bonampak murals show?** (The largest of the murals is divided into three parts showing different stages of warfare. This photo shows a detail from a great battle scene.)

Discussing Public Art Ask students what they think is meant by the term *public art*.

Ask students:

- **Why did Dr. Atl think that art should be shown in public places?** (He believed that art in public places was a powerful means of communicating ideas.)

BACKGROUND INFORMATION

Multicultural Perspectives Long before Mayan artists painted the Bonampak murals, prehistoric people were painting caves with images of animals. In a later Legacy lesson, students will read about traditional forms of Australian Aborigine painting that go back thousands of years. In ancient Egypt, murals painted on the walls of tombs showed the people and possessions that were important to the pharaoh or the distinguished person who was buried there.

The murals that so impressed Dr. Atl were those he saw on a trip through Europe. In ancient Rome, artists decorated some homes with murals showing gardens and architecture as well as gods and mythical heroes. In the late 1200s and early 1300s the great Italian artist, Giotto, painted many beautiful murals in churches. His works, many of which still survive, provide vivid and dramatic representations of biblical scenes. Later, during the 1400s and 1500s, artists like Michelangelo and Raphael painted some of Italy's most beautiful murals. Spain's most famous muralist, El Greco, was influenced by the work of Michelangelo. El Greco's paintings are full of elongated forms, vivid color, and dramatic motion.

Ask students why murals have appealed to people in so many different parts of the world.

Thinking About Public Art Continue the discussion. Ask students why art in public places reaches a wider audience than most other art.

Ask students:

- **What is a mosaic mural?** (a mural made by fitting together colored pieces of stone, glass, or other hard materials)
- *THINKING FURTHER:* **How would you feel if you discovered the mural shown here during a walk through Mexico City?** (Encourage students to think about how outdoor murals enrich people's lives.)

Discussing Diego Rivera Tell students that like Dr. Atl, Rivera traveled to Europe to study the murals of Michelangelo and other European artists.

Ask students:

- **Why did Diego Rivera consider his murals to be "visual books"?** (because they could teach people about Mexico's past; because they could make people care more about the welfare of Mexico's surviving Indians)
- **How was the design of Rivera's house, *Anahuacalli,* similar to his murals?** (In both, he combined traditional and modern styles.)
- **What is shown in Rivera's mural called "The History of Mexico"?** (Mexico's great Indian civilizations, their conquest by the Spanish, and the history of modern Mexico)

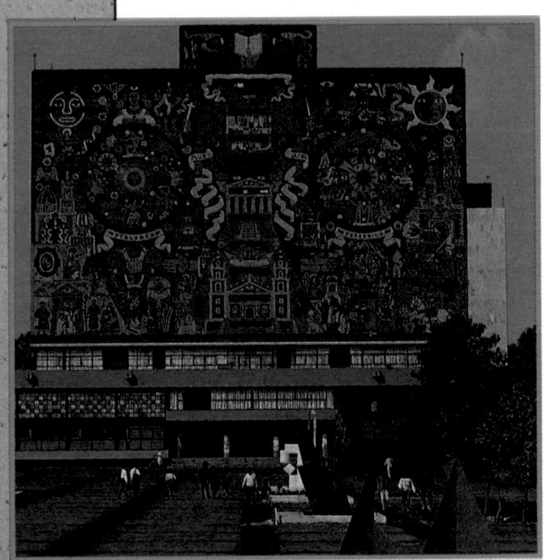

they used symbols and images that were directly drawn from the murals of the Aztecs, the Mayas, and other Mexican civilizations.

Dr. Atl and his followers were aided by supporters in the Mexican government who made it possible for the artists to paint on walls in public places. Sometimes, as in this photograph, the artists covered the walls of buildings with mosaic (mō zā′ ik) murals. A mosaic is a picture or design made by fitting together colored pieces of stone, glass, or other hard materials.

DIEGO RIVERA

One of Mexico's greatest muralists and most famous artists was Diego Rivera. From an early age, Rivera displayed great artistic ability. He started taking art classes when he was 10 years old and at age 16 became a student of Dr. Atl. Rivera was fascinated by Mexico's ancient Indian civilizations. He saw his mural paintings as "visual books" that could teach people Mexican history. He also hoped that his murals would make people care more about the welfare of Mexico's surviving Indians.

Rivera put together a large collection of ancient Indian art objects. More than once he made himself nearly penniless after purchasing a prized and expensive piece of art. Toward the end of his life, Rivera built a large house that displayed designs based on Aztec and Mayan architecture. He called the house *Anahuacalli* (än ä hwä kä′ yē), which is a combination of two Aztec words. *Anahuac* is the Aztec name for the valley where Mexico City is located, and *calli* is the Aztec word for "house." Rivera combined traditional and modern styles in this house, just as he did in his mural paintings.

One of Rivera's most famous murals shows over 1,000 years of Mexican history. The huge mural, called "The History of Mexico," covers more than 1,900 square feet (176 sq m). It is located on a wall above a large staircase in the Palacio Nacional, a

136

BACKGROUND INFORMATION

About Diego Rivera After World War I, life in Mexico changed dramatically. Cities grew, factories were built, labor unions developed, and strikes became common. In his murals Diego Rivera helped to record and encourage these changes. As a member of the art movement known as Social Realism, Rivera created many paintings that dealt with the problems that Mexico was facing. Despite his controversial stand on many issues, in general the Mexican government supported Rivera's art and paid him to paint murals on the walls of schools and government buildings.

CURRICULUM CONNECTION

Art Point out to the class that artists often use murals to show their concern about social issues, such as war, discrimination, and poverty. Have students discuss something they would like to see changed in their school or community. Then have them draw or paint a mural illustrating the issue and how it might be solved. Encourage students to include several scenes in their mural. For example, the problem of litter might be illustrated in one scene. Other scenes might show people cleaning up the litter and the clean streets and parks that result from such an effort.

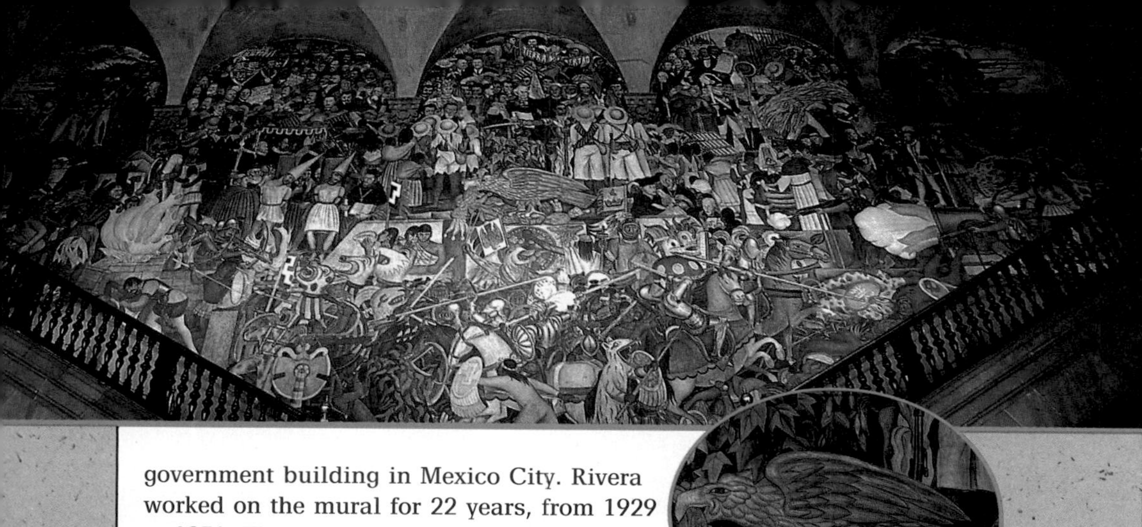

government building in Mexico City. Rivera worked on the mural for 22 years, from 1929 to 1951. The mural shows Mexico's great Indian civilizations, their conquest by the Spanish, and the history of modern Mexico. Some experts consider Rivera's mural one of the most dramatic historical paintings in the world.

In the center of Rivera's huge mural is a large golden eagle. The image of the eagle is based on an Aztec sculpture and is a symbol of modern Mexico. Another large part of the mural shows Aztec rulers, gods, and ways of life. Underneath the golden eagle, Rivera painted Aztecs fighting Spanish invaders. He was reminding Mexicans that the time of the Aztec Empire was an important part of their history.

A LEGACY FOR THE PEOPLE

You may know that many artists in the United States have also painted murals in public places. Art in public places becomes a part of people's lives. People see mural art on their way to work and school and at other times during the day.

Mural painting is a legacy in Mexico that goes back centuries to the time of the great Mayan and Aztec civilizations. Like the artists of Mexico's great Indian civilizations, Mexico's modern mural painters have created large works of art that can be seen by everyone. The legacy of mural painting teaches Mexicans of today about their past. It also adds to their enjoyment of the world in which they live.

How does the legacy of mural painting connect past, present, and future generations in Mexico?

Discussing Rivera's Art Continue the discussion. Focus on Rivera's mural called "The History of Mexico," which is shown on this page.

Ask students:

- **How does Rivera's mural remind viewers that the Aztec era was an important part of Mexican history?** (In the center of the mural is a large golden eagle, an Aztec symbol that has become the symbol of modern Mexico. The mural also shows Aztec rulers, gods, and ways of life.)
- *THINKING FURTHER:* **What was Rivera's point of view about the role of art in modern Mexico?** (that it should serve as a tool for educating the people of Mexico)

Discussing a Legacy for the People Help students to understand the role of mural painting both in Mexico and the United States.

Ask students:

- **How does art in public places become part of people's lives?** (People see mural art on their way to work and school and at other times during the day.)

Applying the Lesson Have students discuss how murals might be used in their community. Ask them to think about what useful lessons or beliefs these "visual books" could illustrate and the best places for them to be painted.

3 CLOSE

Summarizing Students have read about the legacy of mural painting in Mexico. By combining the artistic traditions of their Indian and European ancestors, modern mural painters help to teach Mexicans of today about their past. Murals also can provide a way for artists to comment on the modern world.

Evaluating Assess students' understanding of the lesson by asking them the question at the bottom of the pupil page. (Make sure students understand that murals are a lasting way of communicating ideas and beliefs and preserve a record of Mexican history.)

MEETING INDIVIDUAL NEEDS

Reteaching (easy) Have students imagine that they are Dr. Atl or Diego Rivera. Ask them to write a paragraph in their own words describing the role of mural painting in modern Mexico.

Extension (average) Have students find or provide them with pictures of Michelangelo's famous murals on the ceiling and walls of the Sistine Chapel in Rome. Ask students to write a paragraph describing why they think these murals inspired Dr. Atl and Diego Rivera.

Enrichment (challenging) Along with Diego Rivera, José Clemente Orozco and David Alfaro Siqueiros are considered to be Mexico's greatest mural painters. Have students report on one of these artists and the contribution he made to Mexican art.

CHAPTER 5 REVIEW
pages 138–139

USING THE CHAPTER SUMMARY AND REVIEW

Cultural Geography These questions may be used for review.

- **Which group of people did the Spanish encounter when they arrived in Mexico?** (the Aztecs)
- **How do the campesinos survive?** (by subsistence farming)
- **What type of government does Mexico have?** (a representative democracy)
- **What role does tradition play in Mexican crafts?** (Traditional craft skills are handed down from one generation to the next.)

Ideas to Remember

- **How did Spanish ways become a part of the culture of Mexico?** (The Spanish introduced their ways into the Indian way of life when they conquered Mexico, thus creating a blend of cultures.)
- **What kind of economy does Mexico have?** (a developed economy that is partially industrialized)
- **By what authority does the president have power in Mexico?** (the constitution)
- **Which cultures are reflected in Mexican arts, crafts, and sports?** (Spanish and Indian)

Answers to Reviewing Vocabulary

1. petrochemical
2. mural
3. extended family
4. civilization
5. subsistence farming
6. mestizo
7. metropolitan area
8. developing economy
9. campesino
10. commercial farming

CHAPTER 5 ▪ SUMMARY

MEXICO: CULTURAL GEOGRAPHY

PEOPLE

- First people: Indians (Mayan civilization, Aztec civilization)
- Spanish conquerors came in 1500s: Hernando Cortés
- Today: blend of Indian and Spanish cultures

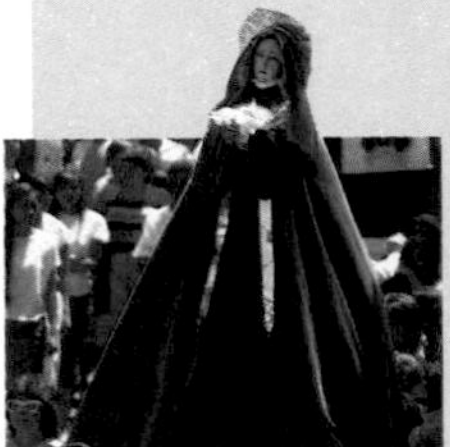

- Religion: mostly Roman Catholic
- Extended families

ECONOMY

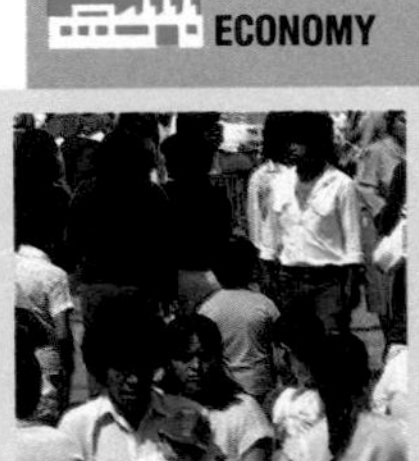

- Mexico City: world's second largest metropolitan area

- Outside cities: campesinos (village farmers) live by subsistence farming
- Developing economy
- Rapidly growing population

GOVERNMENT

- Representative democracy, with strong leadership by president

- Until recently, only one strong political party: PRI

ARTS AND RECREATION

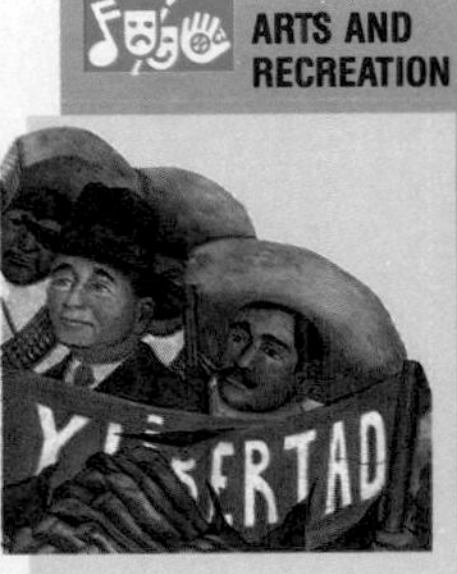

- Important painters: Diego Rivera, José Orozco

- Crafts: traditional, handed down from generation to generation
- Sports: baseball, soccer, jai alai, horseback riding

IDEAS TO REMEMBER

- The culture of Mexico is a blend of the Spanish and the Indian.
- Mexico, one of the fastest-growing countries in the world, has a developing economy that is only partly industrialized.
- The Mexican constitution provides for a representative democracy, but with strong leadership by the president.
- The Spanish and Indian cultures are both reflected in the arts, crafts, and sports of Mexico.

ENRICHMENT ACTIVITY

Making Foods of Ancient Mexico **Materials:** hot plates, a water heater, soft corn tortillas, kidney beans, avocados, mild tomato and chili pepper salsa, instant hot chocolate (Use tortilla chips, bean dip, and salsa if you cannot heat food.)

1. Tell the class that they are going to have a feast of foods enjoyed by the Aztecs and Mayas of ancient Mexico.
2. Have students bring in the different items of food. Warm up the beans and tortillas and prepare the hot chocolate. Slice the avocados and set them out with the other foods. Have students roll or fold the various foods in the tortillas.
3. Discuss that all the food items students used in this activity were originally unknown to Europeans and that modern Mexican cuisine combines food indigenous to the Americas with foods that the Aztecs and Mayas did not have, such as beef and cheese.

CHAPTER 5 • REVIEW

REVIEWING VOCABULARY

subsistence farming	extended family
campesino	mestizo
civilization	metropolitan area
commercial farming	petrochemical
developing economy	mural

Number a sheet of paper from 1 to 10. Beside each number write the word or term from the list above that best matches the definition.

1. A product developed from petroleum
2. Large work of art painted on building walls
3. A family that includes aunts, uncles, cousins, and grandparents
4. A culture that has developed systems of government, religion, and learning
5. A form of agriculture that produces only enough food for a family's immediate needs
6. A person of mixed Spanish and Indian ancestry
7. A large city and the smaller towns surrounding it
8. An economy that is still in the process of becoming industrialized
9. A farmer in a Mexican village
10. A form of agriculture in which crops are raised for profit and sometimes for export

REVIEWING FACTS

1. List three ways in which the Spanish conquest changed the people and the culture of Mexico.
2. What is the relationship between rural poverty and the tremendous growth of Mexico City?
3. How did improvements in health and living conditions affect Mexico's population growth?
4. How has the public attitude toward the PRI changed?
5. How has the Mexican government contributed to the arts in Mexico?

WRITING ABOUT MAIN IDEAS

1. **Writing a Time Line:** Write a time line showing important events in the history of Mexico from the Mayan civilization to the national elections in 1994.
2. **Writing a Brief Biography:** Diego Rivera and José Orozco painted murals that expressed the Mexican culture. Choose one of the artists and write a brief biography that also explains how his art reflected the Mexican experience.
3. **Writing About Perspectives:** Imagine that you are a Mexican campesino deciding whether to move to a city or remain on the farm. Make your decision. Then write a letter to a friend explaining the reasons for your choice. In your letter, tell both the advantages and the drawbacks of your decision.

BUILDING SKILLS: DETERMINING THE ACCURACY OF INFORMATION

1. What does the word *accuracy* mean?
2. Name three steps you can take to determine the accuracy of information.
3. What questions can you ask to determine the credibility of a source?
4. When would it be helpful to know how to determine the accuracy of information?

Answers to Reviewing Facts

1. The Indians lost control of their land and their lives; they were made to work on Spanish farms, ranches, and in mines; they had to convert to Christianity.
2. Because of the poverty in rural areas many Mexicans are moving to Mexico City, causing tremendous growth in population.
3. Mexicans are living longer, thus increasing Mexico's population.
4. People seem ready to make a change and want the government to be more directly responsible to them.
5. The Mexican government gave awards to craftworkers and helped them export their best work.

Suggestions for Writing About Main Ideas

1. You may wish to have students work in groups to create pictorial time lines.
2. Students should be encouraged to use encyclopedias, as well as to read books about these people, in order to find source material for their reports.
3. Students should mention the advantages and drawbacks of living in a Mexican city.

Answers to Building Skills: Determining Accuracy

1. free from errors
2. Accept any three of the following: identify the source of the information; determine the credibility, or believability, of the source; check to see if the information is current; compare the information with similar information from other sources.
3. Is the author or speaker an expert or a person who is well informed on the topic? Does the author or speaker have anything to gain by giving inaccurate information?
4. when a decision must be made on the basis of that information

Chapter Review and Test
Practice Book: *Vocabulary Review,* page 32
Transparency: *Graphic Organizer*
Assessment Book: *Chapter 5 Test*

MAKING CONNECTIONS

Recognizing Cause and Effect Use the Cause and Effect Diagram Graphic Organizer Transparency, filling in only the underlined sentences. For Diagram 1, have students write three effects of the cause stated. For Diagram 2, have students write three causes of the effects stated. Ask: How has Mexico's history shaped the lives of its people?

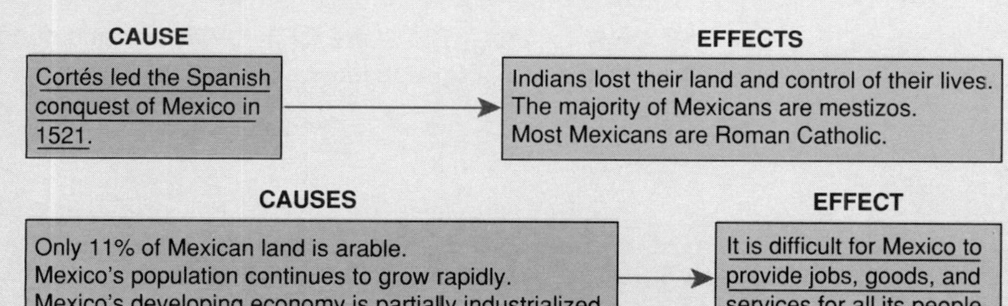

CHAPTER 6
ORGANIZER

CENTRAL AMERICA AND THE CARIBBEAN text pages 140–157

CHAPTER THEME

Lacking natural resources, the countries of Central America and the Caribbean rely on the industries of agriculture and tourism.

CHAPTER OBJECTIVES

CONTENT

- Name the "three streams of people" who make up the main population of Central America and the Caribbean.
- Explain why most Central American and Caribbean economies are limited in what they can produce.
- Describe the importance of tourism to the economies of the Caribbean Islands.
- Identify the different types of government in Central America and the Caribbean.
- Define *socialism* and *communism* and apply these terms to Cuba.
- Define *dictator* and explain why dictators have often seized power in Central America and the Caribbean.
- Outline the artistic achievements and major forms of entertainment in Central America and the Caribbean.

SKILLS

Geography
- Interpret a political map of Central America.
- Use a product map to identify the major agricultural products of the Caribbean.
- Interpret a map showing the Panama Canal.

Thinking
- Analyze a quotation about the effects of colonialism in Central America and the Caribbean.
- Classify the governments of five Caribbean nations into various categories.
- Analyze two contrasting points of view.

Reading and Writing
- Write a travel article about the Caribbean Islands.
- Write a paragraph describing everyday life in a Central American or Caribbean country.

CITIZENSHIP VALUES

- Appreciate the value of the free and open debate of public issues.

TEACHER OPTIONS

READING STRATEGY: Outlining Strategies to help students read and remember the main ideas of the lesson.

Lesson 1: p. 141 Lesson 3: p. 149
Lesson 2: p. 145 Lesson 4: p. 154

MEETING INDIVIDUAL NEEDS Activities for reteaching, extension, and enrichment.

Lesson 1: p. 144 Lesson 3: p. 151
Lesson 2: p. 147 Lesson 4: p. 155
Geography Skills:
p. 148

GEO ADVENTURES ACTIVITIES PAD Daily activities to assess students' understanding of geography skills.

CURRICULUM CONNECTION Activities to help integrate other subject areas with Social Studies.

Language Arts:
p. 143

PUPIL EDITION ON CASSETTE Language support for students who have difficulty reading or who will benefit from listening to the Pupil Edition on Cassette as they read.

SECOND-LANGUAGE SUPPORT Activities and suggestions for second-language learners.

Lesson 2: p. 11

CHAPTER PLANNING GUIDE

LESSON	SUGGESTED PACING	THEMES	
1 THE PEOPLE pages 141–144	1 day	Because it is a crossroads of human migrations from Asia, Europe, and Africa, Central America and the Caribbean is a region with a rich blend of peoples and customs.	Practice Book p. 33 ■ Anthology pp. 16, 34–35, 48–52 Outline Map p. 3 Desk Maps
2 THE ECONOMY pages 145–147	1 day	The economies of the developing countries of Central America and the Caribbean are hampered by a lack of natural resources and depend mainly on agricultural products and tourism.	Practice Book p. 34 Outline Map p. 15 **Technology:** *Adventures CD-ROM*
BUILDING GEOGRAPHY SKILLS Understanding Transportation Routes page 148	1 day	The Pan-American Highway affects the movement of people, goods, and ideas throughout Latin America.	Practice Book p. 35 Outline Map p. 13 Transparency Map 9
3 THE GOVERNMENT pages 149–153	1 day	Governments take many forms in Central America and the Caribbean, with democracies constantly threatened and often lost to dictatorships.	Practice Book p. 36 ■ Anthology pp. 46–47, 63–64 **Technology:** *Adventures CD-ROM*
4 ARTS AND RECREATION pages 154–155	1 day	The blend of cultures in Central America and the Caribbean has created distinctive music. The people enjoy sports, especially soccer and baseball.	Practice Book p. 37 **Technology:** *Adventures CD-ROM*
CHAPTER SUMMARY AND REVIEW pages 156–157	1 day	Chapter content, skills, and vocabulary are reviewed and evaluated.	Practice Book p. 38 Transparency: Graphic Organizer Assessment Book, Chapter 6 Test

Technology CONNECTION

Lesson 2
ADVENTURES CD-ROM
Have students *Travel* to and *Explore* the island nation of Cuba.

Lesson 3
ADVENTURES CD-ROM
Have students *Travel* to Haiti and Puerto Rico.

Lesson 4
ADVENTURES CD-ROM
Explore Jamaica's media elements in *Investigate.*

CHAPTER 6
pages 140–157

USING THE CHAPTER OPENER

Discussing the Photograph Tell students that this is a photograph of a painting by the Jamaican-born artist Leonard Morris. Ask students what they think is eye-catching about the painting. (Students may remark on the contrasting colors and on the different types of people.) Suggest to students that the figures seem to be in some kind of parade or pageant celebrating the variety of the human race.

Ask students:

- **What does a society with a mixture of skin colors indicate?** (a society with many ethnic migrations)
- *THINKING FURTHER:* **What would the world be like if all the people looked and acted the same?** (Most students will probably agree that such a world would be at best very boring.)

Reading/Listening to the Primary Source Ask a student to read the passage under the picture to the class.

Ask students:

- **Which word in the quotation expresses the artist's opinion that although people are all individuals, they share many important qualities?** (*family*)

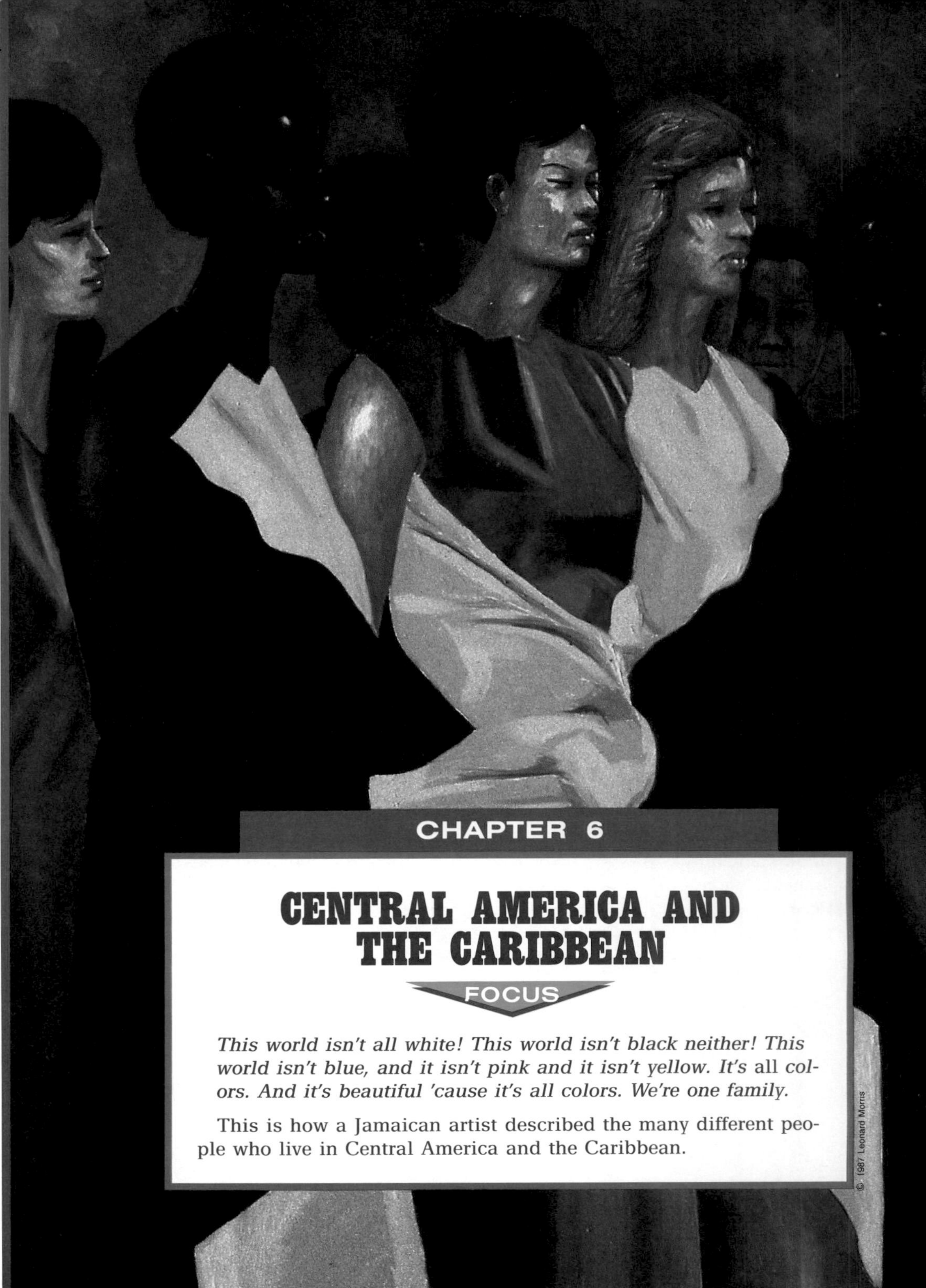

CHAPTER 6

CENTRAL AMERICA AND THE CARIBBEAN

FOCUS

This world isn't all white! This world isn't black neither! This world isn't blue, and it isn't pink and it isn't yellow. It's all colors. And it's beautiful 'cause it's all colors. We're one family.

This is how a Jamaican artist described the many different people who live in Central America and the Caribbean.

BACKGROUND INFORMATION

About Haiti Haiti illustrates one way in which the people of the Caribbean areas have intertwined different cultures. Since Haiti was once a colony of African slaves ruled by French plantation owners, the present language of the people is Creole, a language with both African and French roots. The lifestyles of most Haitians combine African and European influences.

- Haitian farmers often live in thatched huts and work their land with tools similar to those found in West Africa.
- Many Haitians practice both Catholicism and voodoo, an African folk religion.
- Another example of the Haitians' combination of the two cultures is their celebration of the European festival Mardi Gras with music and dances that have traditional African rhythms.

The People

READ TO LEARN

Key Vocabulary
Maroon
sect

Key Places
Guatemala
Belize
Costa Rica
Montego Bay

Read Aloud

Looking at Central America and the Caribbean is like looking through a kaleidoscope. Every time you glance into the tube you see a different pattern of people.

A kaleidoscope is a tube in which a new colored design forms whenever the tube is turned. As the journalist who wrote the observation above says, the people of Central America and the Caribbean form an ever-changing kaleidoscope.

Read for Purpose

1. WHAT YOU KNOW: Who are the mestizo people?
2. WHAT YOU WILL LEARN: How are the people of Central America and the Caribbean like a kaleidoscope?

LATIN AMERICA'S KALEIDOSCOPE

Central America and the Caribbean form the southernmost part of North America. Central America is a thin ribbon of land that connects Mexico to the continent of South America. The Caribbean Islands are scattered throughout the Caribbean Sea between North America and South America. The entire area is made up mainly of mountains and volcanoes.

This area is one of the most ethnically diverse in the world. According to one writer, "Three streams of people flowed from the Eastern Hemisphere to create one of the most amazing blending of peoples that history has ever seen." These streams of people were the Indians, the Europeans, and the Africans.

THE FIRST STREAM OF PEOPLE

Indians were the first peoples to live in Central America and the Caribbean. In addition to several small groups of Indians who lived in the Caribbean, the Mayan civilization extended beyond Mexico to what is now **Guatemala**, **Belize** (be lēz′), and western Honduras. Find these places on the map on page 142.

Today many of the people living in these areas, especially in Guatemala, are descendants of the Mayas. In fact, Guatemala is the only nation in Central America where most of the people are Indian.

As in Mexico, the Indians of Guatemala often live in small mountain villages. Many Indians prefer to live with their own people, speak their own language, and

WHAT YOU KNOW: This question refers to information in Chapter 5, Lesson 1; people of mixed Indian and Spanish ancestry.

LESSON 1
pages 141–144

Lesson Theme Because it is a crossroads of human migrations from Asia, Europe, and Africa, Central America and the Caribbean is a region with a rich blend of cultures.

Lesson Objectives
- Explain the three main streams of people to Central America and the Caribbean.
- Describe the languages, religions, and traditions of Central America and the Caribbean.

PREPARE

Motivate Have students read the *Read Aloud* section. Have students discuss and compare the three models used so far to denote multiethnic populations: United States salad bowl; Canadian mosaic; Central American and Caribbean kaleidoscope.

Set Purpose Review the *What You Know* question to emphasize the definition of *mestizo*. Use the *What You Will Learn* question to help students understand that the movement of people with many cultural backgrounds to Central America and the Caribbean has resulted in the human kaleidoscope of that region.

TEACH

Locating Latin America's Kaleidoscope Use a world map to help students trace the origin of people from the Eastern Hemisphere.

Understanding the First Stream of Settlers Discuss the early settlers of Central America and the Caribbean.

READING STRATEGY AND VOCABULARY DEVELOPMENT

Outlining The purpose of this strategy is to help students use a graphic organizer to recall information. Review with students the note-taking strategy that they learned in Chapter 4. Suggest to students that another strategy for remembering and organizing information is outlining. Before they write an outline, students must first read and select the main idea and supporting details for each lesson section. Tell students that they can use the section headings as the outline headings and the main ideas of the sections as the subheadings. Tell students that they can use sentences, phrases, individual words, or a combination of these for the headings of an outline. Together with the class, develop an outline of this lesson and write it on the chalkboard.

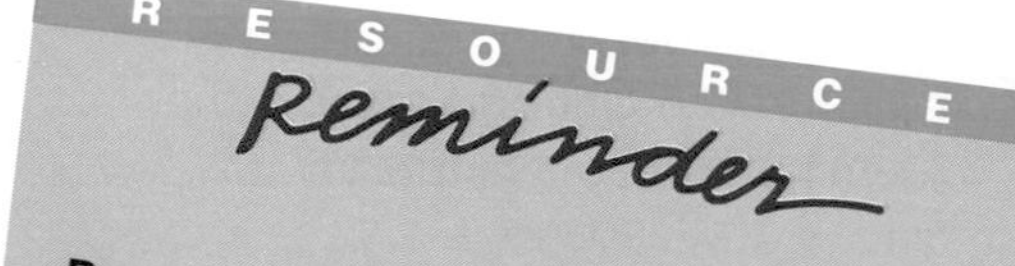

Practice Book: *The Origins of Latin American Cultures*, page 33
▪ **Anthology:** *Child of the Americas*, page 16; *From Mouse to Bat*, pages 34–35; *The Gold Coin*, pages 48–52
Outline Map: *The World*
Desk Map: *The World, Political*

Discussing the First Stream Continue discussing the first stream of settlers to Central America and the Caribbean.

Ask students:

- **How would you describe the lifestyle of the Indian in Guatemala today?** (isolated in small villages, following traditional Indian ways)
- **What was the focus of the traditional Indian religion?** (nature)
- *THINKING FURTHER:* **What is one way in which Mexican Indians follow the customs of their group?** (They continue to observe their traditional religion.)

Describing the Second Stream Emphasize the dominance of the Spanish settlers during this stream.

Ask students:

- **What was the Spanish pattern of settlement when they arrived in Central America?** (They settled areas that were rich in natural resources and had mild climates and avoided mountains and poor land.)
- **What other Europeans took control of islands in the Caribbean?** (the British, French, and Dutch)

EXTENDING MAP SKILLS

Have students use the scale on this map to measure the distance between various island chains.

Ask students:

- **What are the the countries of Central America?** (Belize, Guatemala, El Salvador, Honduras, Nicaragua, Costa Rica, Panama)
- **Using the scale, estimate the distance between Belmopan and Panama City.** (almost 900 miles [1,350 km] by air)
- **Which Caribbean island group is closest to the United States?** (the Bahamas) **Which is farthest?** (Trinidad and Tobago)

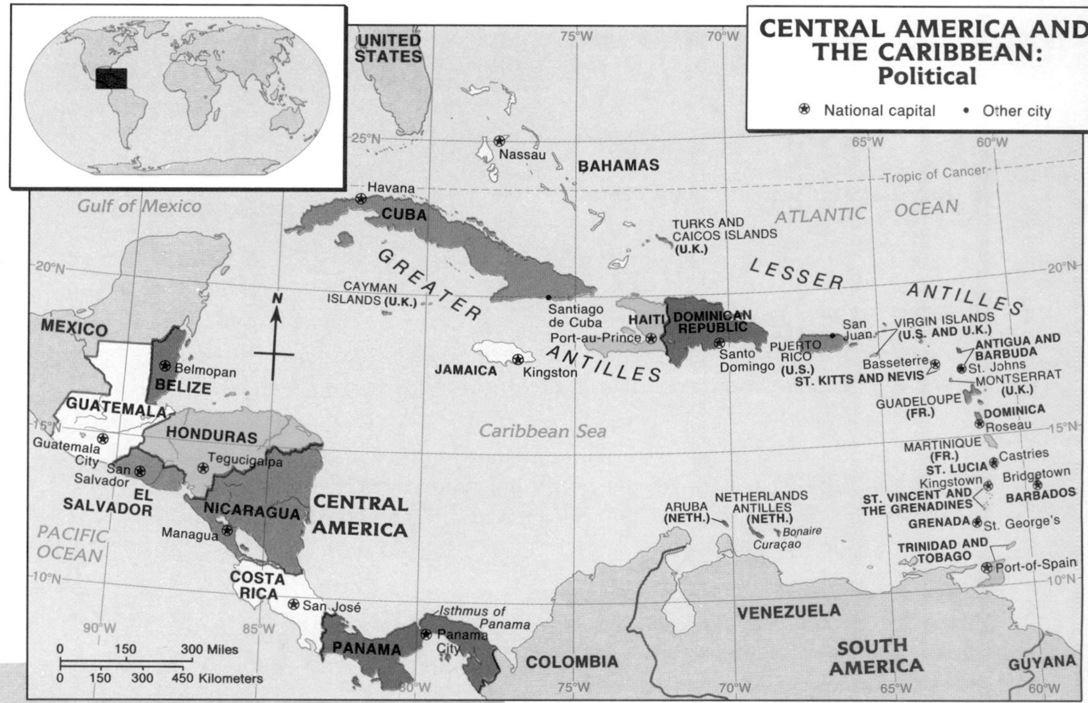

MAP SKILL: Which three countries are on the two largest Caribbean Islands?

follow the customs of their group. They often observe both their traditional religion and Roman Catholicism, which was brought by Europeans. For example, some Mayas continue to worship *mams*, spirits who live in the "wind, the rain, the lakes, the rivers, and the mountains. . . ."

THE SECOND STREAM

Led by the Spanish, the Europeans were the second stream of people to settle Central America and the Caribbean. The Spanish claimed vast areas of the Americas after Christopher Columbus arrived in 1492. However, they settled only in areas rich in natural resources. If an area was mountainous and poor, few Spanish people stayed there.

However, in Costa Rica, with its mild climate and few Indians, many Spanish people came to live and divided the land among themselves. As a result, Costa Rica's present population is mainly of Spanish ancestry. In other parts of Central America, most people are of mixed Spanish and Indian origin.

The Spanish were the dominant force in Central America and the Caribbean, but sometimes they lost control of their holdings. In the 1600s the British, French, and Dutch gained control of some Caribbean Islands. These islands were mainly in the Lesser Antilles and the Netherlands Antilles. Find these islands on the map above.

THE THIRD STREAM

After the Europeans arrived, thousands of Indians were killed. This lack of people was a problem for the British and French,

 MAP SKILL: Cuba, Haiti, Dominican Republic

BACKGROUND INFORMATION

Multicultural Perspectives The belief of the Mayas and many other peoples that inanimate objects and forces have souls or spirits is called animism. Animism has been an important belief shared by many civilizations around the world. For example, people from many different cultures have worshipped a sun god or goddess.

- The ancient Egyptians called the sun Raò and believed that their pharaohs were descended from him.
- The ancient Japanese believed that the sun was a goddess named Amaterasu. According to tradition, Japan's first emperor was one of her decendants.
- The ancient Greeks believed that the sun was a god called Helios who drove his chariot across the sky each day.

Ask students why the sun was so important to all of these peoples.

a problem for the British and French, who wanted to start sugarcane, tobacco, and other plantations there. They solved this problem by bringing captured Africans to the plantations to work as slaves. These Africans were the third stream of people to come to Latin America.

South of **Montego Bay** in northwestern Jamaica is a dry, rugged, hilly land called "Cockpit Country," or "Look Behind Country." Find Montego Bay, Jamaica, on the map on page 142.

Cockpit Country is the home of the descendants of the **Maroons**. "Maroon" comes from the Spanish *cimarrones* (sē mä rrō' nes), which means "peak dwellers." The Maroons were enslaved Africans who escaped from the Spanish, set up their own communities, and later fought the British, who tried to conquer them, for more than 100 years.

East Indians, people whose ancestors came from India, Pakistan, and other countries of southern Asia, also live in the Caribbean region. Forty percent of the population of Trinidad and Tobago is of East Indian descent.

Smaller numbers of people came from other Asian countries. It is not unusual to find people who are part Asian and part African or European.

ONE CARIBBEAN PEOPLE

The combination of historical events, customs, and different ethnic groups makes the individual Caribbean Islands unique. Jamaica has many British customs because it was long a colony of Great Britain. Its population, however, includes many different ethnic groups. In addition to people of African ancestry, Jamaica is made up of people of British, Chinese, and East Indian origin. This mixture of peoples is the reason that Jamaica took as its motto, "Out of many, one people."

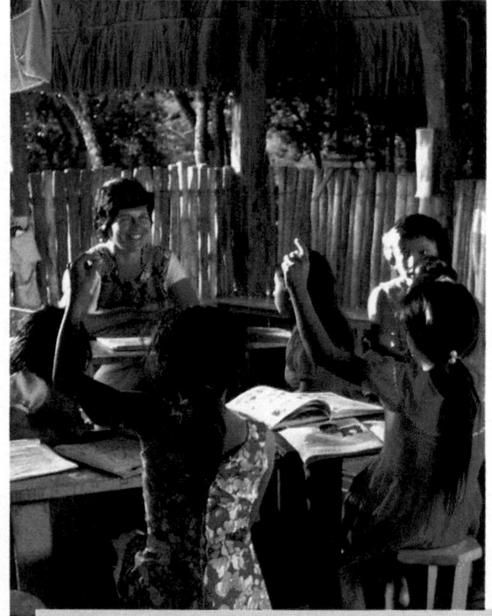

Like children in the United States, children of all the different ethnic groups of Central America and the Caribbean attend school to learn the skills they need.

LANGUAGE

If you traveled through Central America and the Caribbean, what differences would you expect to find? As you might expect, you would hear French spoken if you visited the French Caribbean island of Martinique (mär ti nēk'). People in the areas long held by Spain—Cuba, the Dominican Republic, and Puerto Rico—speak Spanish.

In general, the people of Central America and the Caribbean speak the languages of the Europeans who colonized their countries. An exception is Haiti, where many people speak Creole, a mixture of French and African languages. In the Netherlands Antilles, Papiamento, a language that combines Dutch, English, and Spanish, is used.

Discussing the Third Stream

Ask students:

- **Why was a third stream of people deliberately introduced into the Caribbean Islands?** (The British and French needed labor for plantations.)
- **Who were the Maroons?** (slaves who escaped from the Spanish and set up their own communities)
- *THINKING FURTHER:* **What key historical difference can be seen between the first stream of people settling this region and the second and third streams of people?** (The first stream lived and thrived in the Americas for thousands of years before people arrived from other parts of the world. The second and third streams are, on a historical scale, very new to this region.)

Recognizing One Caribbean People Stress that Jamaica is an example of a society made up of a mix of many ethnic groups. Have students explain Jamaica's motto. ("Out of many, one people" refers to Jamaican ethnic groups, including those of African, British, Chinese, and East Indian ancestry.)

Identifying Language

Ask students:

- **What determines the language in each country of Central America and the Caribbean?** (its colonial background)
- **Which new languages grew from the mixture of peoples?** (Creole resulted from a French and African mix in Haiti; Papiamento resulted from a mix of Dutch, English, and Spanish in the Netherlands Antilles.)

CURRICULUM CONNECTION

Language Arts Have student groups apply the Jamaican motto, "Out of many, one people," to the United States, Canada, Mexico, and Jamaica. Divide the class into four groups. Assign each group one of these four countries. Have the groups review the lessons already covered and list which ethnic groups make up the populations of their countries. Each group should write and present a short skit to show how "Out of many, one people" applies to their assigned nation.

Discussing Religion Reinforce students' understanding of the additional effects of colonization by having them consider religions. Discuss the religions found in Central America and the Caribbean.

Applying the Lesson Have students make a two-column chart with the headings "Central America" and "The Caribbean Islands." Using their text and the map on page 142, students should list the names of the countries, islands, or island groups that make up the two areas of this region.

CLOSE

Summarizing Students have learned of the three migrations of people to Central America and the Caribbean, which produced the varied languages, religions, and customs found in this area today. Have students review the three groups of migrants.

Evaluating Use these questions to assess students' understanding.

- **In what order did the various groups of people live in this area?** (the Indians, the Spanish and other Europeans, the Africans and Asians)
- **How is the ethnic makeup of Guatemala and of Costa Rica similar and yet different?** (They are probably the two least "mixed" populations in this area. Guatemala is predominantly Indian; Costa Rica is mainly European.)

Answers to Check Your Reading

1. from the European countries that colonized this area
2. They are descendants of Africans who were enslaved and brought to the Caribbean Islands.
3. They mix and change like the shapes in a kaleidoscope.
4. Students will probably answer: Yes, it affected the language, heritage, and religion of the populations.

Independent Practice
Practice Book: page 33

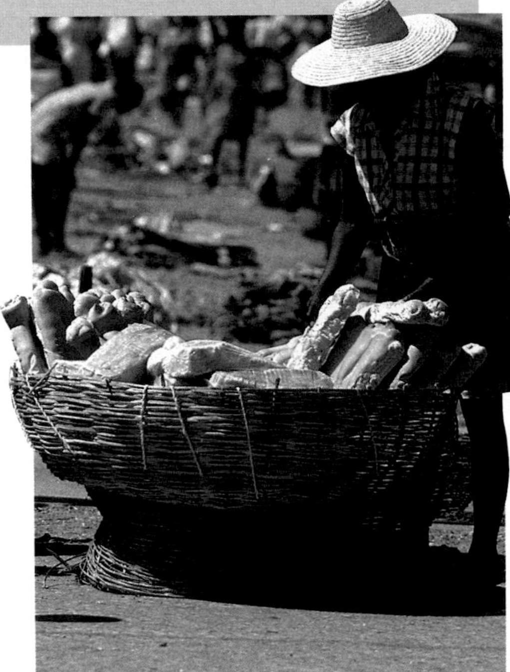

Haiti has been independent of France since 1804. Yet many signs of French culture remain. In Port-au-Prince, the capital, French bread is sold in the market at the harbor.

RELIGION

The major religions of Central America and the Caribbean were also determined by the colonists who settled there. Most of the colonists were Roman Catholics and Protestants. The Caribbean Islands also have several religious **sects**. A sect is a religious group that is outside the mainstream of large, organized religions. Rastafari, one of the newest sects, is the fastest-growing one in Jamaica. Rastafarians honor the last emperor of Ethiopia, Haile Selassie (hī′ lē sə · las′ ē), whom they call Ras Tafari, as a god.

A BLENDING OF PEOPLE AND TRADITIONS

The area that is made up of Central America and the Caribbean is one of the most ethnically diverse in the world. Indians were its first settlers. Then came the Spanish, followed by the British, French, and Dutch. These colonists brought enslaved Africans to the area. In Central America and the Caribbean, the African, the European, and the Indian cultures blended to form new cultures.

Check Your Reading

1. Where did most of the languages and religions in Central America and the Caribbean come from?
2. Why are there many people of African ancestry in the Caribbean Islands?
3. How are the people and culture of Central America and the Caribbean like a kaleidoscope?
4. **THINKING SKILL:** Do you think the following statement is correct?: "Colonialism changed the historical path of Central America and the Caribbean Islands." Give evidence to support your answer.

THINKING SKILL: Evaluating Information

MEETING INDIVIDUAL NEEDS

Reteaching (easy) Give each student a copy of an outline map of the world (or alternatively, give 12 groups of students the desk maps of the world), which can be found in the Teacher's Resource Center. Have them make a legend and show on the map the three streams of people who made their homes in Central America and the Caribbean.

Extension (average) Have students choose one country or one island in Central America and the Caribbean and gather information about its ethnic makeup, customs, religions, languages, and festivals. Have students present the information on posters decorated with drawings or magazine pictures.

Enrichment (challenging) Have students construct a crossword puzzle using words from Lesson 1. Tell them to write an accurate definition for each word in the puzzle.

LESSON 2

The Economy

READ TO LEARN

Key Vocabulary

plantation
one-crop economy
dictator
communism

Key People

Fidel Castro

Key Places

Barbados
Cuba

Read Aloud

If God wills and my wife's health improves, we'll soon move to our new house.

Andres Ramirez expresses the hope of many people in Central America and the Caribbean—the hope of raising their standard of living. Ramirez raises corn and beans on his farm in southern Honduras. He also works on a nearby sugarcane plantation to earn extra money. Ramirez lived with his in-laws for years before he could save enough money to buy material to build his home.

Read for Purpose

1. WHAT YOU KNOW: What is commercial farming?
2. WHAT YOU WILL LEARN: Why are most Central American and Caribbean economies limited in what they can produce?

PLANTATION AGRICULTURE

The story of Andres Ramirez is typical of thousands of families in Central America and the Caribbean. Most of the countries in this area do not have developed economies. More than half the people farm small plots of land that do not produce much food because of the poor quality of the soil.

As in the rest of Latin America, the best land in the area is used for plantations. These are large farms that grow crops for sale. Central America and the Caribbean have more plantations than do most areas of the world. About 15 percent of the world's coffee is grown in this area, as is about 10 percent of the world's bananas. Other fruits, sugarcane, cacao, and spices are also grown in abundance on plantations in the area.

Most economies of Central America and the Caribbean are one-crop economies. That is, countries often depend on a single crop for income. Over half of Panama's exports are bananas, for example, and sugar makes up over 75 percent of the exports of the Caribbean Island country of St. Kitts-Nevis.

Depending heavily on one crop is risky for a nation. If world prices for that crop fall, or a natural disaster strikes, nations may lose money or the main cash crop they export. In addition, many businesses could close and thousands of people could lose their jobs.

WHAT YOU KNOW: This question refers to information in Chapter 5, Lesson 2; raising crops mainly for sale on large farms.

LESSON 2
pages 145–147

Lesson Theme The economies of the developing countries of Central America and the Caribbean are hampered by a lack of natural resources and depend mainly on agricultural products and tourism.

Lesson Objectives

- Explain the advantages and disadvantages of one-crop economies.
- Describe the relationship between available natural resources and the developing economies of Central America and the Caribbean.
- Describe the changes that communism brought to the people of Cuba.

PREPARE

Motivate Have a student read the *Read Aloud* section and discuss why Andres Ramirez works at two jobs to achieve his hopes and goals. Discuss how, increasingly, many people in the United States are doing the same thing.

Set Purpose Use the *What You Know* question to introduce the plantation system of farming and the *What You Will Learn* question to emphasize the limited natural resources of this region.

TEACH

Discussing Plantation Agriculture Help students understand how growing only one crop can make it difficult for individuals to feed their families and can create instability in a nation's economy.

READING STRATEGY AND VOCABULARY DEVELOPMENT

Outlining Review the steps in making an outline. Stress the idea that an outline is a way of organizing important information in a lesson. Have students work in groups to develop outlines of this lesson. Remind them that they can use the section headings of the lesson as outline headings. When students have finished, have them compare their outlines and discuss any differences.

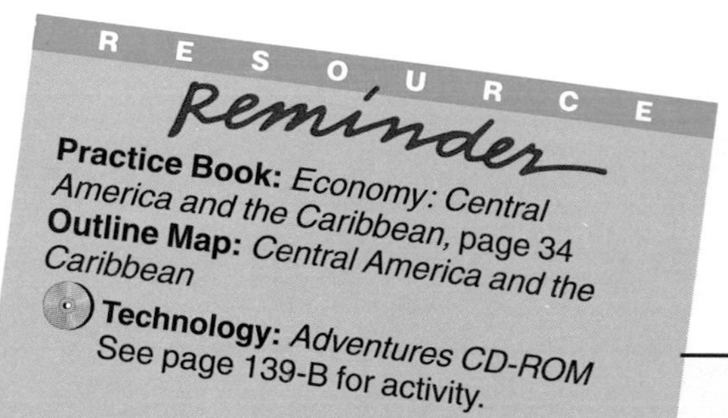

Understanding Manufacturing Make sure students realize that manufacturing in this region is based on the processing of agricultural products because very few mineral resources exist in this area.

Ask students:

- **What mineral resources are there on the Caribbean Islands?** (bauxite in Jamaica; oil in Trinidad)

Recognizing the Importance of Tourism Help students realize that while tourism brings money to the area, it provides mainly unskilled jobs that do not help develop the economy.

EXTENDING MAP SKILLS

Emphasize that the map on this page shows a predominance of plantation crops.

Ask students:

- **Are there any products that are grown on all the islands?** (No.)
- **Which products are nonfood products?** (cotton, tobacco)
- **Which country grows the greatest variety of products?** (Dominican Republic)

Discussing a Revolution in Cuba Help students to understand that under communism the lives of many black and mestizo Cubans have improved, but the Cuban economy remains weak.

Ask students:

- **Which country in this area turned to a socialistic economic system called communism?** (Cuba)
- **How successful an economy has the centrally controlled government been able to build?** (a one-crop economy, based on sugar, that is shaky and was hurt by the breakup of the Soviet Union.

MANUFACTURING

One reason that the economies of Central America and the Caribbean depend on agriculture is that they are poor in minerals. Many of the nations in this part of the world do not have coal or other minerals needed for manufacturing. Moreover, most manufacturing jobs are related to agriculture. Costa Rica, Guatemala, and Puerto Rico, for example, are the most industrialized areas of Central America. Yet most of their factories process food and beverages.

Jamaica is one of the few Caribbean nations that has a large mining industry. Bauxite, a mineral used in making aluminum, is mined in Jamaica. Other places with valuable resources and industries are Trinidad, which has oil, and the islands of Curaçao (kyu̇r′ ə sō) and Aruba, which refine petroleum imported from Venezuela.

TOURISM

Tourism is the major industry of the Caribbean Islands. According to a resident of **Barbados**, one of the most beautiful of the area's islands: "God made the world. Then He said, 'I must have somewhere for Myself—a place to rest.' So He made Barbados."

Barbados has few natural resources. However, it has one of the strongest economies in the Caribbean. Most people there work in tourism and earn more money than people in other parts of the Caribbean. Barbados is very small, only 21 miles (33 km) long and 14 miles (22.4 km) wide. Yet the island is dotted with almost 140 tourist hotels and many golf courses.

MAP SKILL: What products do Cuba and the Dominican Republic both produce? Where is nutmeg grown?

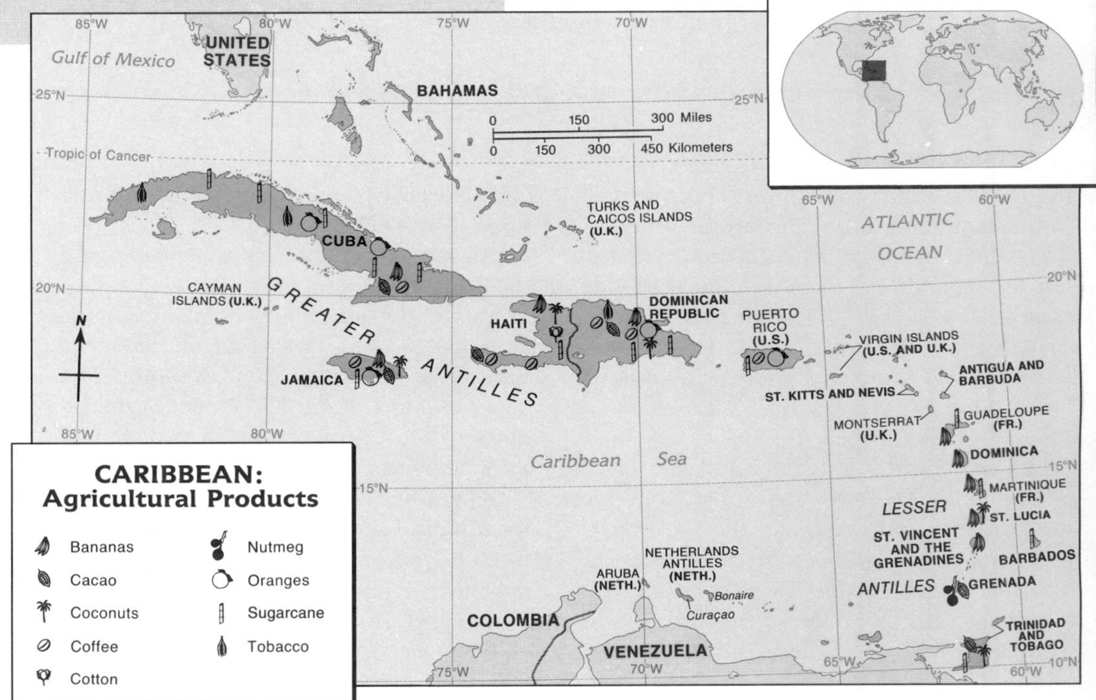

146

BUILDING CITIZENSHIP

Learning About Our State Students have learned about the importance of tourism to the Caribbean. Discuss the importance of tourism to the economy of your state. Have students write to the Department of Tourism in your state to find out about places to visit. Students can then plan an imaginary one- or two-week vacation to these places.

Although the nations of the area welcome tourism, they seek new industries. Tourism helps economies by giving jobs mainly to unskilled workers. A healthy nation also needs jobs for skilled workers.

A REVOLUTION IN CUBA

The region's leaders have made many attempts to solve economic problems in Central America and the Caribbean. In Cuba, for example, a revolution brought in a completely new kind of government.

In 1959 Fidel Castro led a revolution in Cuba and overthrew the Cuban dictator. A dictator is a ruler who has total control over a country.

Castro said he wanted all Cubans to have an equal share in their country. So he set up a system called communism. You will read more about communism in Chapter 15.

Under communism, the government controls the economy and way of life. Castro's government seized private property from most foreigners and wealthy citizens and redistributed it.

Did the Cuban revolution solve the nation's problems? Most people think of Castro as another dictator. Although health care, schooling, and other services are free, the Cuban economy remains weak. The map on the opposite page shows that Cuba grows several crops, but sugar makes up most of Cuba's exports.

For many years, the Soviet Union helped support Cuba. But the breakup of the Soviet Union greatly reduced Eastern European support. Tough trade restrictions begun by the United States in 1992 have caused further economic difficulties for the Cuban people. In 1994, over 30,000 Cuban refugees left for the United States. The island nation is now on its own more than ever before.

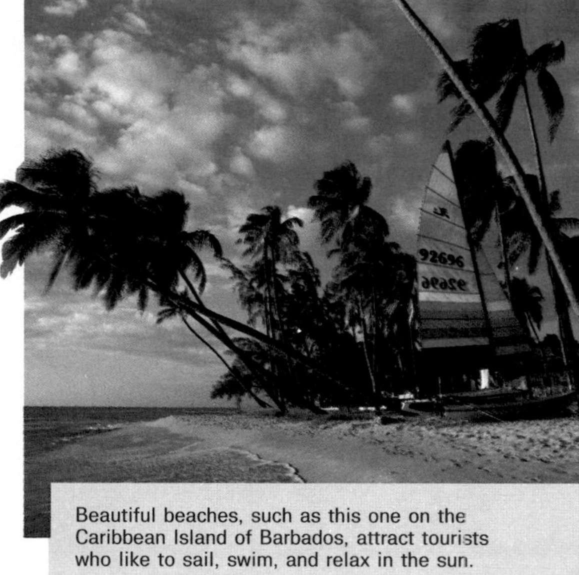

Beautiful beaches, such as this one on the Caribbean Island of Barbados, attract tourists who like to sail, swim, and relax in the sun.

LIMITED CHOICES

Central America and the Caribbean Islands have limited natural resources. So the people make use of the resources they have. Usually, this means good farmland, as well as warm weather and sandy beaches that draw tourists. Jamaica has bauxite and Trinidad has some petroleum. Still, the economies of most countries are developing ones.

Check Your Reading

1. Why is it risky to have a one-crop economy?
2. Why do so many Caribbean islands depend upon tourism?
3. What is a dictator?
4. THINKING SKILL: List some of the questions you would ask if you were planning to start a business in a Central American or Caribbean nation.

THINKING SKILL: Asking Questions

Applying the Lesson Have students go to the grocery store or supermarket and look at the crates of fruits and vegetables to find the names of the nations from which the fruits and vegetables came. Discuss why these agricultural products are available in winter. (because of the subtropical and tropical climates of Central America and the Caribbean)

3 CLOSE

Summarizing Students have learned that Central America and the Caribbean have developing economies that are limited because of few mineral resources. Discuss how the tropical environment makes it possible for people to live on much smaller incomes than is possible in much of the United States. For example, no winter clothes are needed, and there is a year-round sunny climate for home gardens.

Evaluating Use the *Check Your Reading* questions (answers given below) to assess students' understanding.

Answers to Check Your Reading

1. World price changes, natural disasters, and political events can lower profits in the whole economy.
2. They have few resources, and they are assured of income from tourism.
3. A dictator is a ruler who has total control over a country.
4. Possible questions include: Is it a centrally planned economy or a free-enterprise economy? What transportation systems exist to get raw materials in and products out? Is a trained labor force available? What resources are available?

Independent Practice
Practice Book: page 34

MEETING INDIVIDUAL NEEDS

Reteaching (easy) Have students plan a Caribbean vacation by collecting travel brochures and choosing places to visit. Provide outline maps of Central America and the Caribbean found in the Teacher's Resource Center on which students can trace their trip. Have them write a paragraph telling what they plan to see and do on their trip.

Extension (average) Have students find Caribbean travel ads in newspapers or magazines and analyze the physical and human characteristics of the Caribbean that are used in them. Discuss with students the vision of the Caribbean that the ads are trying to sell.

Enrichment (challenging) Have students research the production and income records for Central America and the Caribbean over the past five years for petroleum, agriculture, and minerals. Have students decide which of these activities seems to be growing.

SKILLS LESSON

page 148

Lesson Theme The Pan-American Highway affects the movement of people, goods, and ideas throughout Latin America.

Lesson Objective

- Describe the role of the Pan-American Highway.

PREPARE

Motivate Have students check the meaning of *pan* in the dictionary.

Set Purpose Tell students they will learn how the Pan-American Highway connects the nations of Latin America. You may wish to project Transparency Map 9 so that students can see the main routes of the Pan-American Highway.

TEACH

Discussing the Pan-American Highway Help students understand the importance of this highway as a lifeline for the movement of goods.

Applying the Skill Have students review Chapters 5 and 6 and list goods that might be transported over the Pan-American Highway.

CLOSE

Summarizing Students should understand how dependent Latin American nations are on the highway.

Answers to Reviewing the Skill

1. Puerto Montt, Chile
2. 5,300 miles (8,529 km)
3. Accept all Central and South American countries, except Belize.
4. It provides transportation routes throughout Latin America.

RESOURCE Reminder

Practice Book: *The Pan-American Highway*, page 35
Outline Map: *Latin America*
Transparency Map: 9

BUILDING SKILLS
GEOGRAPHY SKILLS

Understanding Transportation Routes

Today the nations of the world are connected by transportation routes that make trade and travel direct and convenient. Air and water routes, railroads, and highways crisscross the earth, bringing countries closer together than ever before.

Countries in Central America and the Caribbean depend heavily on trade with other countries in Latin America. For people in these countries, it is very important that goods move quickly from one country to another. The Pan-American Highway is one transportation route that has been developed to meet the needs of people in Latin America.

THE PAN-AMERICAN HIGHWAY

Main Route
National capital
Other city

The Pan-American Highway

The Pan-American Highway extends from the United States-Mexico border in the north to the southern tip of Chile in the south. It also connects the east and west coasts of South America, linking many major cities. The entire highway system with its interconnecting routes is about 45,000 miles (72,000 km) long.

The Pan-American Highway is of great importance to the Latin American economy because it provides routes for the transportation of raw materials, agricultural products, and other goods. The highway cuts through dense jungles, passes through scorching deserts, and crosses some of the highest mountains in the world—areas that are otherwise difficult to reach.

The map on this page shows the main routes of the Pan-American Highway. Find Rio de Janeiro, located on the east coast of Brazil. Imagine how important the highway is to people in this city. Without it they would have to depend on air or water transportation for many goods and products. Which other major cities are connected by this highway?

Reviewing the Skill

1. What is the southernmost city on the Pan-American Highway?
2. What is the approximate distance along the Pan-American Highway between Laredo, Texas, and Puerto Montt, Chile?
3. Name five countries the Pan-American Highway passes through.
4. Why is the Pan-American Highway an important transportation route?

MEETING INDIVIDUAL NEEDS

Reteaching (easy) Give students the outline map of Latin America, and have them draw the Pan-American Highway with appropriate labels for countries and major bodies of water.

Extension (average) On the outline map of Latin America found in the Teacher's Resource Center, have students indicate the goods transported on the Pan-American Highway from various countries.

Enrichment (challenging) Divide the class into four groups, each to research topics on the building of the Pan-American Highway. Assign topics such as: "Technical Difficulties"; "Who Paid How Much to Build the Highway?"; "Who Were the People Who Worked to Build the Highway?"; "A Time Line of the Construction of the Pan-American Highway"; and "Interesting Stories About the Building of the Pan-American Highway."

The Government

READ TO LEARN

Key Vocabulary
commonwealth

Key People
François Duvalier
Jean-Bertrand Aristide

Key Places
Haiti
Puerto Rico
Panama Canal

Read Aloud

Who would not give his life for the land in which he was born?

The man who wrote these words, José Martí (hō sā′ mär tē′), did just that. A Cuban patriot and poet, Martí died in 1895 fighting to free Cuba from Spain. Other Cubans carried on the struggle, and they won their freedom a few years later. Then another struggle began—to keep the freedom they had won.

Read for Purpose

1. WHAT YOU KNOW: How would you describe the people of Central America and the Caribbean?
2. WHAT YOU WILL LEARN: What types of government do the nations of Central America and the Caribbean have?

COLONIES AND OVERSEAS AREAS

As you read in Lesson 1, all of Central America and the Caribbean was once divided into European colonies. Today only a few colonies are left. Great Britain has five colonies—more than any other nation. They are Montserrat, the British Virgin Islands, the Turks and Caicos (kā′ kəs) Islands, the Cayman Islands, and Bermuda. The people who live in the colonies are citizens of Great Britain and have a voice in their own government.

Some parts of the Caribbean are also "overseas areas" of European countries. An overseas area is a place that is part of a nation far away across the ocean. The island of Martinique, for example, is an overseas area of France. Aruba is part of the Netherlands.

REPUBLICS AND DICTATORSHIPS

Almost all of the 21 nations of Central America and the Caribbean have constitutions that give them representative governments. Some of these governments are true republics. However, unrest and economic problems have made it difficult for others to govern themselves as republics. In some nations, dictators have taken advantage of political divisions to seize power. Some dictators rule for 20 or 30 years. Long-term rule by one leader is common in many countries of the region.

THE LEADERS AND THE PEOPLE

Dictators often take power when there is a wide gap between the ordinary people and their leaders. In Haiti, for example, most of the people were, and are, descen-

WHAT YOU KNOW: This question refers to information in Lesson 1; a blend of people of Indian, European, and African descent.

LESSON 3

pages 149–151

Lesson Theme Governments take many forms in Central America and the Caribbean, with democratic representation constantly threatened and often lost to dictatorship.

Lesson Objectives

- Explain the various types of governments in Central America and the Caribbean.
- Describe United States interests in the Central American and Caribbean nations.

PREPARE

Motivate Read the *Read Aloud* section to the class. Discuss Patrick Henry's quote, "Give me liberty or give me death," to find the similarity between the Americans' fight and José Martí's freedom fight.

Set Purpose Use the *What You Know* question to establish that the people of this region are of many mixed origins and that they want freedom and a say in their governments. Have students list all the types of government they know. At the end of this lesson, have students compare the list with what they learn about the governments in this region.

TEACH

Identifying Colonies and Overseas Areas Use the map in Lesson 1 on page 142 to locate Britain's colonies and the overseas areas of France and the Netherlands.

Discussing Republics and Dictatorships Help students to understand how a country with a constitution can still have a dictatorial government.

READING STRATEGY AND VOCABULARY DEVELOPMENT

Outlining Have students work in pairs to outline this lesson. Encourage students to include more details in their outlines than they have previously included. If students are having difficulty with outlining, you may wish to provide them with a partial outline that they can complete.

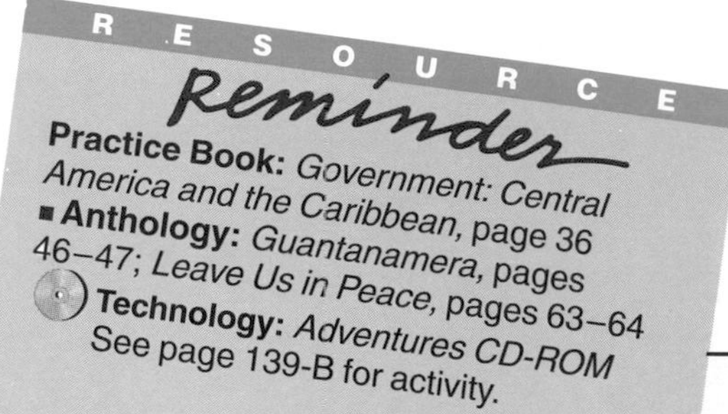
RESOURCE *Reminder*

Practice Book: *Government: Central America and the Caribbean*, page 36
Anthology: *Guantanamera*, pages 46–47; *Leave Us in Peace*, pages 63–64
Technology: *Adventures CD-ROM* See page 139-B for activity.

Understanding the Relationship Between the Leaders and the People Help students to recognize that colonies often cannot achieve democratic government. Discuss the conditions that led to dictators seizing power.

Identifying United States Interests Stress the proximity of the region to the United States and the fact that it includes an American commonwealth. Discuss the degree to which Puerto Rico is democratic. You might wish to have students read the *Viewpoints* on pages 152–153 at this time.

Discussing the Panama Canal Emphasize how the Panama Canal saved time for the people and companies of the United States as well as those of European and South American countries when they were traveling or shipping goods between the East and West coasts.

EXTENDING MAP SKILLS

Ask students:

- **Using the compass rose for the map on page 151, name the direction in which the Panama Canal runs.** (northwest to southeast)
- **Name the body of water that forms part of the canal.** (Gatun Lake)

Haiti's dictator François Duvalier (*above*) ruled from 1957 until his death in 1971. Unlike Duvalier, who was elected, Fidel Castro of Cuba (*below*) took power through revolution.

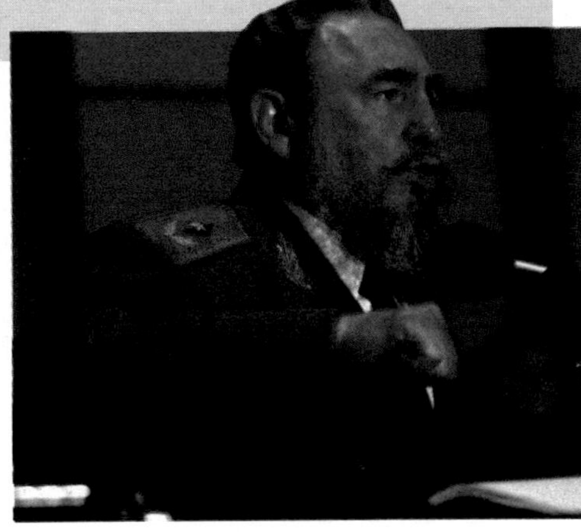

dants of enslaved Africans. The rulers, however, were French or people of mixed blood. Most Haitians spoke Creole, while the rulers spoke French.

In an election in 1957, Francois Duvalier (fran swä′ dü val yā′), called "Papa Doc," was elected president of Haiti. The people hoped he would lead a democratic government. But Duvalier was not only another dictator, he stripped the people of much of their remaining wealth. When Haitians forced the Duvalier family to flee the country in 1986, Haiti was one of the poorest nations in the world.

One leader says about the future:

> *Haiti needs peace and good leadership. Everyone wants democracy, but after so many dictators, Haiti has to go slowly to find the right way.*

Since 1986, Haiti has had several changes of government. In late 1990, Jean-Bertrand Aristide was elected president in the first free elections ever held in Haiti. He was forced out in a revolt a year later, but regained his office in 1994 with the help of the United States.

UNITED STATES INTERESTS

The United States watches events in the Caribbean closely because the area is very near to its borders. At various times in the past, the United States has sent troops or advisers to most of the Central American nations, as well as to Cuba, Haiti, the Dominican Republic, and Grenada.

The United States also has possessions in the Caribbean. One of the most important is Puerto Rico. This is how one Puerto Rican describes his life:

> *I have two names. When I am in Puerto Rico my name is Federico, and I speak Spanish. When I am in New York my name is Freddy, and I speak English. My last name is Ramirez in both places.*

Many Puerto Ricans live like Ramirez. They move back and forth between their island home and the United States. Puerto Rico is part of the United States. However, it is not a state, but a self-governing territory known as a commonwealth.

Puerto Ricans choose their own governor and legislators. They also elect a nonvoting representative to the United States Congress. Many Puerto Ricans like living

FUNDAMENTAL THEMES OF GEOGRAPHY

Location The Panama Canal is an excellent example of the importance of the relative location of a place. Have students find out how many miles the trip from New York to San Francisco by ship would be if they sailed south around the tip of South America (slightly more than 13,000 miles; or 20,917 km) and how many miles the same trip through the canal would be (5,200 miles; or 8,367 km). Have students discuss the advantages that the canal has offered other nations of the world. (For example, the convenience of the canal's location for European ships going to western Canada.)

MAP SKILL: The Panama Canal is the main route for goods shipped between the Atlantic and Pacific coasts of the Americas. In what directions would you sail to go from northeastern Nicaragua to southwestern Colombia?

in a commonwealth. Others want the island to become a state of the United States or else to have it become completely independent. Both sides feel that their alternative would help Puerto Rico economically. In an election on this issue in 1993, however, Puerto Ricans voted to remain a commonwealth.

PANAMA CANAL

Another reason the United States is interested in Central America and the Caribbean is the **Panama Canal**. Find the canal on the map on this page. The United States built the canal from 1903 to 1914 to provide a direct water route between the Pacific and Atlantic oceans.

The United States controlled the canal for a long time. In 1978, the United States and Panama signed a treaty that turned the ownership of the Panama Canal Zone over to Panama. Panama will have complete control of the canal by the year 2000.

VARIETIES OF GOVERNMENT

The countries of Central America and the Caribbean have many types of government. These include republics, dictatorships, colonies, overseas areas, and commonwealths. Many nations in the region suffer from economic and social unrest.

Check Your Reading

1. Describe the kind of leader that François Duvalier was.
2. Why has the United States been so active in Central America and the Caribbean?
3. What bodies of water does the Panama Canal connect?
4. **THINKING SKILL:** Classify the following countries into three or more categories, based on their governments: Bermuda, Martinique, Cuba, Puerto Rico.

MAP SKILL: southeast to the canal, southeast through the canal, southeast to the coast to Colombia

THINKING SKILL: Classifying

151

Applying the Lesson Have students make lists classifying the nations of this region as dictatorships, republics, colonial governments, overseas areas, or commonwealths.

CLOSE

Summarizing Students have learned that due to unrest and socioeconomic problems, dictatorships are common in Central America and the Caribbean, as are a variety of other types of government. Have students discuss the conditions that lead to dictatorships.

Evaluating Use these questions to assess students' understanding.

- **What factor in the past history of Haiti led to its government's becoming a dictatorship?** (The ordinary people were of African or Creole backgrounds, while the leaders were French or of mixed origins.)
- **What is Puerto Rico's relationship to the United States?** (It is a self-governing commonwealth.)
- **How long did it take to build the Panama Canal?** (11 years)

Answers to Check Your Reading

1. a dictator who stripped Haiti of its remaining wealth, leaving it one of the poorest nations in the world
2. because the region is close to the United States border, and the U.S. commonwealth of Puerto Rico and the Panama Canal are there
3. the Pacific and Atlantic oceans
4. *dictatorships:* Cuba, *colonial government:* Bermuda; *overseas area:* Martinique; *commonwealth:* Puerto Rico

Independent Practice
Practice Book: page 36

MEETING INDIVIDUAL NEEDS

Reteaching (easy) Have students write an essay on the subject "Why the United States Needs to Be a Good Neighbor to Central America and the Caribbean."

Extension (average) Have students draw a cartoon showing the kinds of conditions within Central American and Caribbean countries that have led to a dictator's taking power. Have students discuss what safeguards exist in the American form of government to help prevent a leader from taking such power.

Enrichment (challenging) Have students define the term "Banana Republic." Then challenge them to find historical information about the nations to which this term is applied. Have them write a comparison titled "The 'Banana Republics' Then and Now."

CHAPTER 6

CITIZENSHIP

Viewpoints

pages 152–153

Lesson Objective

- Analyze how people from three different countries in the Western Hemisphere view trade with Cuba.

Identifying the Issue Help students to see that international trade policies can be influenced by political as well as by economic interests.

Suggested Questions

- ***Why are trade restrictions on Cuba an issue that can cause conflict between the United States and its neighbors?*** *(Many nations disagree with the United States that trade restrictions are the best way to influence Cuba.)*

Discussing Three Different Viewpoints Give students time to read the viewpoints on these pages.

CHRISTON ARCHER

Suggested Questions

- ***What does Archer say the positive benefits of trade with Cuba have been so far?*** *(It has shown Cubans models of democratic government, promoted the spread of new ideas, increased interaction between peoples, and has led the Cuban government to change some economic policies.)*
- ***What does he predict a result of trade will be in the future?*** *(The Cuban government will make changes, perhaps moving towards more democratic government.)*

ROSITA JARA

Suggested Questions

- ***Why does Jara say other countries should not use their trade policies to influence Cuba?*** *(She says it is not the business of other countries to interfere in the operations of the Cuban government.)*
- ***Who does she say should decide how Cuba is governed?*** *(The Cuban people.)*

CITIZENSHIP VIEWPOINTS

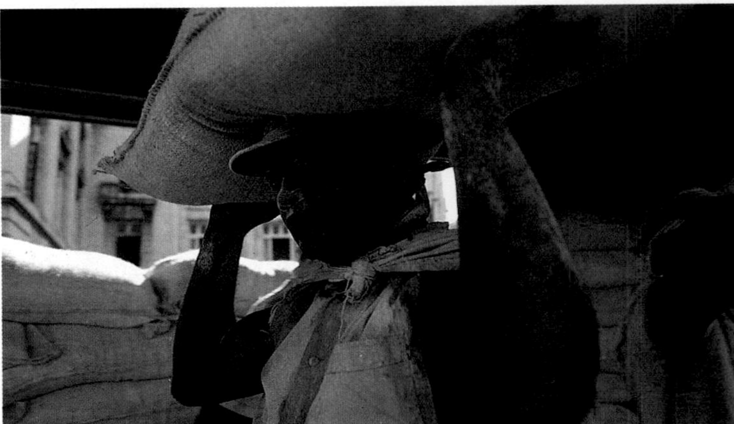

This Cuban dock worker is loading sacks of flour at Havana harbor.

WHAT IS THE FUTURE OF TRADE WITH CUBA?

Nations have always used their trade policies not only to achieve economic goals, but for political aims as well. Nations sometimes limit trade with other countries to express opposition to a particular form of government, or to express their anger about the way a government treats its citizens. For more than 30 years, the United States has limited trade with Cuba to express its opposition to the communist government of Fidel Castro. In recent times, the United States has also called for other nations to restrict trade with Cuba.

Those who oppose trade restrictions argue that limiting trade hurts the Cuban people, but does little to influence the government. Some, such as Christon Archer, believe that free trade would actually encourage democracy. Others, like Rosita Jara, say that Cubans should decide for themselves how they will be governed.

Ninoska Perez-Castellón and others argue that trade restrictions are the best way to pressure the Cuban government to change. Many Cuban Americans believe that trade restrictions will one day force Cuba to pay for property seized by Castro's government during the Cuban revolution. Consider three viewpoints on this issue.

152

BACKGROUND INFORMATION

About Cuba Today The U.S. has had trade restrictions, or sanctions, against Cuba since the early 1960s. These sanctions prohibit the shipment of American goods to Cuba and the sale of Cuban goods in the U.S.

Relations between the United States and Cuba worsened after Castro developed close ties with the Soviet Union and confiscated property belonging to American companies and individuals.

Cuba has one of the highest literacy rates in all of Latin America and its health care system is recognized as one of the best among the less-industrialized nations.

After Castro's overthrow of the Cuban dictator Fulgencio Batista in 1959, many Cubans fled to the United States and settled in southern Florida. Hope of returning to Cuba still inspires many Cuban exiles and Cuban Americans to work for Castro's overthrow.

Three **DIFFERENT** Viewpoints

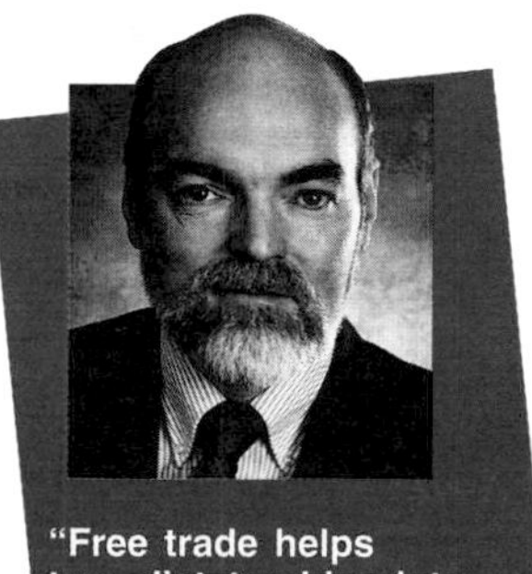

"Free trade helps turn dictatorships into democracies."

1 CHRISTON ARCHER
Professor of History, Calgary, Canada
Excerpt from interview, 1996

Free trade helps turn dictatorships into democracies. The more we can show the Cuban people how democracy works, the more we can influence them. The movement of people and businesses opens Cuba to new ideas, helps advance education, and even gets Cubans on computers and the Internet. Good, solid investment has already helped shake Cuba loose from rather backward economic policies. It will slowly lead to political change, too.

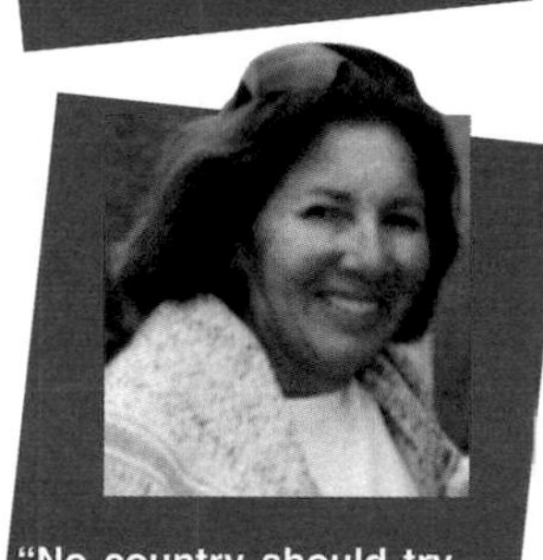

"No country should try to influence another country through trade."

2 ROSITA JARA
Farm manager, Santiago, Chile
Excerpt from interview, 1996

Each country has the right to its own form of government. No country should try to influence another country through trade. If Cubans are satisfied with their country the way it is, why should another country try to change that? The people of Cuba do want change, but they want to do it at their own pace and in their own way. Right now in Cuba everybody has access to education and health care without any problems. This is much better than in the past.

"The way to oust dictators ... is through economic or trade restrictions."

3 NINOSKA PEREZ-CASTELLÓN
Radio commentator, Miami, Florida
Excerpt from interview, 1996

The way to oust dictators in a peaceful manner is through economic or trade restrictions. The Castro government has been in power for over 37 years and must come to an end. Human rights abuses have put thousands of Cubans in prison. Trade restrictions should be imposed by the U.S. and other countries. Once trade links and vital funds are cut off, the Cuban government will have difficulty staying in power. After democracy is established the U.S. and other countries can renew relations.

BUILDING CITIZENSHIP

1. What is the viewpoint of each person?
2. In what ways are some of the viewpoints alike? In what ways are they different?
3. What other viewpoints might people have on this issue?

SHARING VIEWPOINTS

Discuss what you agree with or disagree with about these viewpoints. Discuss why you think each speaker might feel as he or she does. Then, as a class, write three statements that all of you can agree with about international trade with Cuba.

NINOSKA PEREZ-CASTELLÓN

Suggested Questions

- ***What does Perez-Castellón believe trade restrictions will accomplish in Cuba?*** *(She believes they will lead to the fall of the Castro government.)*
- ***What reasons does she give for favoring trade restrictions?*** *(She points to lack of democratic government and human rights abuses by the Castro government.)*

EVALUATE
Answers to Citizenship Viewpoints

1. Archer opposes trade restrictions, believing that greater openness will lead to political change. Jara also opposes trade restrictions because she believes other countries should not try to influence Cuba's domestic policies. Perez-Castellón believes trade restrictions are the best way to bring down the Castro government and a return to democracy.
2. All viewpoints suggest that some political change is needed in Cuba. Archer and Perez-Castellón want to see democracy restored, but favor different approaches to achieving this goal. Archer and Jara oppose trade restrictions, while Perez-Castellón strongly favors them and, unlike Archer, does not want any interaction with Cuba until the fall of Castro's government.
3. Other viewpoints might include allowing limited trade, including such humanitarian items as medical supplies, or proposing reduction of trade restrictions in exchange for making steps towards multiparty government.

Sharing Viewpoints Three agreed-upon statements might include: **1.** The trade policies of other countries can have an impact on Cuba. **2.** Political change is needed in Cuba. **3.** Restricting trade hurts the Cuban economy.

Debating Viewpoints Have students debate the pros and cons of using trade restrictions to influence political affairs.

CITIZENSHIP

Using Current Events Trade sanctions have been used by the international community through the United Nations to bring an end to apartheid and a white-minority government in South Africa. In 1990, the U.N. imposed a ban on all trade with Iraq after Iraq refused to disclose and destroy machinery used to make weapons of mass destruction. Some argue that trade sanctions are most effective when undertaken by a body like the United Nations, when broad international agreement exists. Ask student volunteers to research the differences in the trade sanctions placed on South Africa, Iraq, and Cuba, the reasons for the sanctions in each case, their effectiveness, and the degree of support for these restrictions in the United States and other nations.

LESSON 4
pages 154–155

Lesson Theme The blend of cultures in Central America and the Caribbean has created distinctive music. The people enjoy sports, especially soccer and baseball.

Lesson Objectives
- Describe the new forms of music that have developed in Central America and the Caribbean.
- Explain the pastimes of this region.

PREPARE

Motivate Have a student read the *Read Aloud* section aloud. Ask students for their interpretations of what this folktale might mean.

Set Purpose Use the *What You Know* question to reinforce the idea of the rich backgrounds for development of new cultural forms. Tell students to keep the *What You Will Learn* question in mind as they read the lesson.

TEACH

Discussing Music Have students explain how the inventions of the steel drum and calypso music show a high level of creativity.

Looking at Sports

Ask students:

- **What shows the fervor of the people of Central America and the Caribbean for baseball?** (A disproportionate percentage of people from this area play professional baseball.)
- *THINKING FURTHER:* **Why do you think one area produces so many excellent baseball players?** (Students might note that economic opportunity is a strong motivation.)

LESSON 4

Arts and Recreation

READ TO LEARN

Key Vocabulary
calypso
reggae

Key Places
Dominican Republic
San Pedro de Macorís

Read Aloud

A favorite Haitian folktale says that many of the island's pigeons were flying to New York. A turtle wanted to go, too, but he had no wings. Feeling sorry for the turtle, a pigeon said "Turtle, I'll take you with me. I'll hold one end of a piece of wood in my mouth and you hold on to the other end. But do not let go, or you'll fall into the water." As they flew over the shore, the turtle saw a group of animals waving good-bye. He was so pleased, he called out the one English word he knew, "Bye-bye!" He fell into the sea. For that reason, according to the tale, there are many pigeons in New York, but turtles are still in Haiti.

Read for Purpose

1. **WHAT YOU KNOW:** What group of people first lived in Central America and the Caribbean?
2. **WHAT YOU WILL LEARN:** What are the artistic achievements and main entertainments of Central America and the Caribbean?

MUSIC

Have you ever heard a steel drum? This musical instrument was developed in Trinidad in the 1930s. An inventor—nobody knows who—took an oil drum, sliced off the end, and hammered the other end into sections that produced different tones. Melodies are played by hitting these sections of the drum with mallets, or wooden hammers. With drums of different sizes, steel bands can play any form of music.

One style of music associated with steel bands is **calypso**. Calypso developed from music that enslaved Africans sang while they worked.

Another form of music that developed in the Caribbean is **reggae** (reg′ ā). Reggae mixes American pop music and calypso rhythms. Reggae music is popular in many parts of the world.

SPORTS

Sports are popular in the area, and soccer is one of the favorites. So, too, is baseball. The nations in which baseball is played most frequently are Nicaragua, Cuba, and especially the **Dominican Republic**. Over 200 Dominicans also play on major and minor league teams in the United States. Remarkably, half of this number come from just one town, **San Pedro de Macorís** (mä kô rēs′), which is in the southeastern part of the nation. This

154 WHAT YOU KNOW: This question refers to information in Lesson 1; Indians.

READING STRATEGY AND VOCABULARY DEVELOPMENT

Outlining Review the steps in making an outline. Have students work independently or in pairs to create an outline of this lesson. Then have them discuss the differences and similarities among the outlines. You may wish to have students create an outline comparing and contrasting the cultural life in Mexico and Central America.

city of about 110,000 people has about 200 teams. According to one of the townspeople, "Baseball is in the blood here."

Many of the people in San Pedro de Macorís have few possessions. Nevertheless, the baseball-crazy youngsters of this area often make bats out of palm leaves and balls out of wadded socks.

CREATIVITY AND TRADITION

Indian, Spanish, African, and other ethnic traditions have blended in Central America and the Caribbean to create unique forms of art. Steel-drum bands, calypso and reggae singers, and many other artists perform music. Sports like soccer and baseball are very popular.

Check Your Reading

1. What are calypso and reggae?
2. What is the town of San Pedro de Macorís famous for?
3. What are three popular pastimes in Central America and the Caribbean?
4. THINKING SKILL: What are three questions you could ask to learn more about the arts and entertainment in Central America and the Caribbean?

THINKING SKILL: Asking Questions

Calypso music is often played by steel drum bands (*above left*). Bob Marley was the most popular reggae musician of his time (*above right*). Baseball is a popular sport in the Caribbean (*below*).

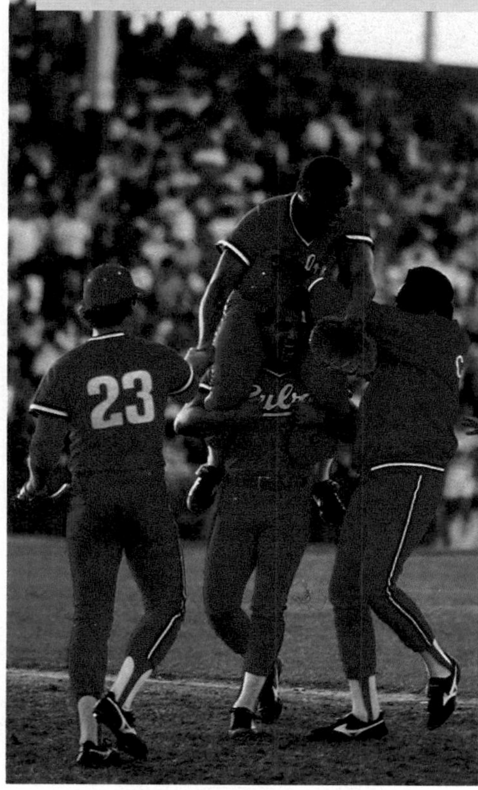

Applying the Lesson Have students skim newspapers to find the names of calypso performers or baseball or soccer players from Central America and the Caribbean who might be performing in the United States.

3 CLOSE

Summarizing Students have learned that creative art forms have come from the varied peoples of Central America and the Caribbean and that sports are important to them. Have students list the art forms and sports that are important to the people of our country.

Evaluating Use the *Check Your Reading* questions (answers given below) to assess students' understanding.

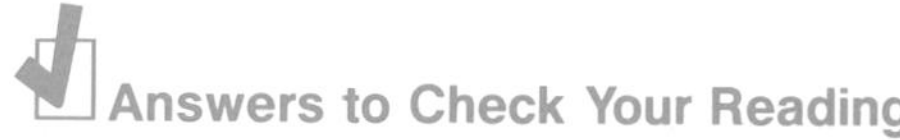

Answers to Check Your Reading

1. Calypso is a style of music that developed from songs sung by enslaved Africans as they worked; Reggae is a mixture of American pop music and calypso rhythms.
2. It is a town of 110,000 people with 200 baseball teams, and more than 100 players in the minor and major leagues in the United States come from it.
3. playing steel drums, baseball, soccer
4. Possible questions include: What special musical instruments are used there? Who are the best calypso singers? How many major league baseball players in the United States are from this region?

Independent Practice
Practice Book: page 37

MEETING INDIVIDUAL NEEDS

Reteaching (easy) Have students write a paragraph about the cultural achievement in Central America and the Caribbean that they find most interesting. Ask them to tell why it interests them.

Extension (average) Ask students to gather more information about the invention of the steel drum and how to play a steel drum. Have them write a paragraph describing their findings. Have them make an illustration of a steel drum band on art paper. Mount the paragraphs at the bottom of their pictures for display.

Enrichment (challenging) Encourage students to bring in reggae songs. Discuss their meanings. Have students try writing their own verses for the songs.

CHAPTER 6 REVIEW
pages 156–157

USING THE CHAPTER SUMMARY AND REVIEW

Cultural Geography These questions may be used for review.

- **Which groups of people were part of the three streams of settlers in Central America and the Caribbean?** (Indians, Europeans, Africans and Asians)
- **Why is it dangerous for a country to rely on a one-crop economy?** (If world prices fall, or a natural disaster strikes, the country may lose money and its main cash crop.)
- **What type of government does Puerto Rico have?** (a commonwealth)
- **Which sports are popular in Central America and the Caribbean?** (soccer and baseball)

Ideas to Remember

- **Which cultures have blended to create the present-day culture in Central America and the Caribbean?** (Indian, European, African, Asian)
- **On which two industries does the economy of this region depend?** (agriculture and tourism)
- **What types of government are found in this region?** (republics, colonies, dictatorships, commonwealths)
- **What are two unique art forms that resulted from the blending of Indian, Spanish, and African traditions?** (calypso and steel-drum bands)

Answers to Reviewing Vocabulary

1. True.
2. Calypso is a style of music started by African slaves in the Caribbean.
3. True.
4. A dictator is a ruler who has total control over a country and usually rules by force.
5. True.

CHAPTER 6 • SUMMARY

CENTRAL AMERICA AND THE CARIBBEAN: CULTURAL GEOGRAPHY

PEOPLE

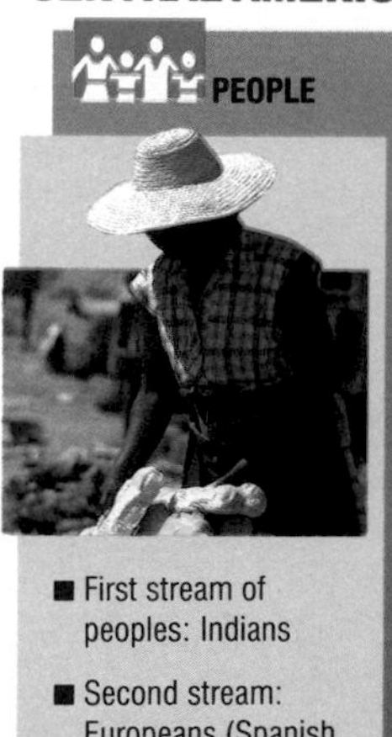

- First stream of peoples: Indians
- Second stream: Europeans (Spanish, British, French, and Dutch)
- Third and fourth streams: Africans and Asians

- Today: blend of Indian, European, African, and Asian people
- Religion: Roman Catholic and Protestant

ECONOMY

- Plantations: coffee, bananas, sugarcane, spices
- Most countries have one-crop economies

- Caribbean's major industry: tourism
- Cuba: communist system led by Fidel Castro

GOVERNMENT

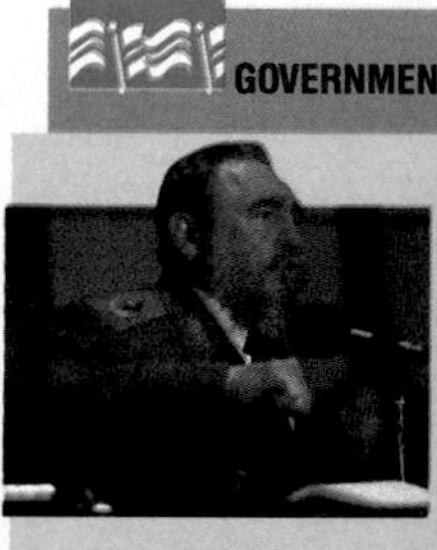

- Dictatorship: Cuba
- Only a few European colonies left

- United States interests: Puerto Rico and the Panama Canal

ARTS AND RECREATION

- Popular forms of music: calypso, reggae, and steel drum bands

- Sports: baseball and soccer very popular

IDEAS TO REMEMBER

- The population of the Caribbean and Central America is ethnically diverse.
- The region, which has limited economic resources, depends largely on agriculture and tourism.
- Many types of government are found in the region, including republics, colonies, dictatorships, and commonwealths.
- Unique forms of music and art have evolved from the mixed cultural traditions of Central America and the Caribbean.

156

ENRICHMENT ACTIVITY

Creating Commemorative Coins **Materials:** 3-inch diameter posterboard circles, pens

1. Remind the class that they probably see commemorative coins advertised on TV. Such coins are often keepsakes issued by nations to honor an important event or aspect of national life. Discuss the information included on such a coin—country, year, wording, and pictures. Tell students that they are going to design their own coins to honor the countries of Central America and the Caribbean.
2. Assign each of the 22 Central American and Caribbean nations listed on pages 102–105 to one or more students.
3. Tell students to research their country, choose something about it to celebrate, and create a two-sided design for a commemorative coin on a piece of paper. Have them transfer their design to the posterboard "coin" for class display.

CHAPTER 6 • REVIEW

REVIEWING VOCABULARY

Each of the following statements contains an underlined vocabulary word. Number a sheet of paper from 1 to 5. Beside each number write whether each of the following statements is true or false. If the statement is true, write "true." If it is false, rewrite the sentence using the vocabulary word correctly.

1. Plantations are large farms on which crops are grown for sale.
2. Calypso is a type of fruit that is grown for export in Central America and the Caribbean Islands.
3. Puerto Rico is a self-governing territory known as a commonwealth.
4. Although a dictator has many powers, he or she must act within the limits of a constitution and a legislature.
5. A sect is a religious group whose beliefs and practices are outside those of mainstream religions.

REVIEWING FACTS

1. Why is it important for countries to develop more than one industry?
2. Why is the United States watchful of developments in the Caribbean Islands?
3. What conditions have enabled dictators to take control of several countries in Central America and the Caribbean?
4. Which island is the United States' most important possession in the Caribbean Islands?
5. Which Central American country has given the world an unusually large number of baseball players?

WRITING ABOUT MAIN IDEAS

1. **Writing a Paragraph:** Write an opening paragraph for a travel article about the Caribbean Islands. Tell why the Caribbean is a particularly attractive area for tourists to visit.
2. **Writing a Summary:** Think about the three groups of people who settled the Caribbean Islands and Central America. Choose one of these groups and write a summary about them. Describe the group's development from their arrival in the area through the present.
3. **Writing About Perspectives:** Imagine that you live in more than one place like Federico (Freddy) Ramirez, who is mentioned on page 150. One place you live is your town in the United States. The other place is a country you choose in the Caribbean or Central America. Name the country. Then write one paragraph describing your life in each place. In a final paragraph, write about the differences between each place.

BUILDING SKILLS: UNDERSTANDING TRANSPORTATION ROUTES

1. Name three different kinds of transportation routes.
2. What geographical feature makes land transportation difficult in the countries of Central America?
3. Which continents does the Pan-American Highway connect?
4. Why is it helpful to understand transportation routes?

157

Answers to Reviewing Facts

1. A country should develop more than one industry to avoid the disaster that would result should its only industry fail.
2. because the Caribbean is close to the borders of the United States
3. Economic and social problems and quarrels among political groups enable dictators to take power in this region.
4. Puerto Rico
5. the Dominican Republic

Suggestions for Writing About Main Ideas

1. Students' articles should stress the positive aspects that would draw people to the area. If you wish, ask students to create brochures that include pictures that highlight their articles.
2. Students' summaries should be about the Indian, European, or African groups who settled the region.
3. Students' essays should include geographical and cultural factors that would affect their everyday lives, such as climate, language, food, and so on.

Answers to Building Skills: Understanding Transportation Routes

1. air, water, and land transportation
2. mountains
3. North America and South America
4. Possible answers include: Transportation routes show how easy or difficult it is to move goods, which helps us to understand the problems the economy of a country may face.

Chapter Review and Test

Practice Book: *Vocabulary Review,* page 38
Transparency: *Graphic Organizer*
Assessment Book: *Chapter 6 Test*

MAKING CONNECTIONS

Supporting Main Ideas Use the Main Idea Table Graphic Organizer Transparency, writing in only the underlined copy. Have students fill in supporting details about the people, economy, government, and culture of the region in the table "legs." Have them fill in subjects by listing specific names or examples in the table "feet." *Ask:* How has the lack of natural resources affected Central America and the Caribbean?

MAIN IDEA: Central America and the Caribbean is a region of mostly weak economies, varied forms of governments, and a blend of people and cultures.

one-crop economies, limited natural resources	republics, commonwealths, dictatorships	people of Indian, African, European, Asian ancestry	unique forms of art and music
bananas, sugarcane	Fidel Castro, François Duvalier	Mayas, Spanish, Maroons	reggae, calypso

CHAPTER 7
ORGANIZER

SOUTH AMERICA text pages 158–175

CHAPTER THEME South America is a continent that has people from many cultures, countries with developing economies, and a history of unstable governments.

CHAPTER OBJECTIVES

CONTENT

- Describe how the ethnic groups of South America have shaped life on the continent.
- List some of the ways in which South American nations are trying to develop their economies.
- Explain why thousands of Brazilians are moving to the Amazon rain forest.
- Describe how overdependence on one product can hurt a nation's economy.
- Explain why South America has been troubled by frequent political change and social unrest.
- Explain why caudillos came to power in many South American nations following independence.
- Define *junta* and explain why juntas have been common in South America.
- Describe the major events in the political career of Juan Perón and his impact on Argentina.
- Describe how the arts in South America reflect the continent's many ethnic groups.

SKILLS

Geography
- Interpret a political map of South America.

Thinking
- Draw conclusions about the impact of Juan Perón on the political life of Argentina.
- Distinguish fact from opinion in an issue affecting South America.
- Analyze two contrasting points of view.

Reading and Writing
- Write about life in Argentina under military rule.

CITIZENSHIP VALUES

- Appreciate the importance of keeping the armed forces and the government separate.

TEACHER OPTIONS

READING STRATEGY: Summarizing Strategies to help students read and remember the main ideas of the lesson.
Lesson 1: p. 159 Lesson 3: p. 170
Lesson 2: p. 164 Lesson 4: p. 172

MEETING INDIVIDUAL NEEDS Activities for reteaching, extension, and enrichment.
Lesson 1: p. 161 Lesson 3: p. 171
Lesson 2: p. 167 Lesson 4: p. 173

GEO ADVENTURES ACTIVITIES PAD Daily activities to assess students' understanding of geography skills.

CURRICULUM CONNECTION Activities to help integrate other subject areas with Social Studies.
Literature: p. 160 Art: p. 162
Science: p. 160 Math: p. 165

PUPIL EDITION ON CASSETTE Language support for students who have difficulty reading or who will benefit from listening to the Pupil Edition on Cassette as they read.

SECOND-LANGUAGE SUPPORT Activities and suggestions for second-language learners.
Lesson 2: p. 13

CHAPTER PLANNING GUIDE

LESSON	SUGGESTED PACING	THEMES	
1 THE PEOPLE pages 159–161	1 day	The largest part of the Latin American region is the continent of South America, which is inhabited by people from a variety of ethnic groups.	Practice Book p. 39 ■ Anthology pp. 38–40 **Technology:** *Adventures CD-ROM*
BUILDING THINKING SKILLS Distinguishing Facts from Opinions pages 162–163	1 day	Distinguishing fact from opinion means telling the difference between information that can be proved true and personal beliefs that cannot be proved true.	Practice Book p. 40
2 THE ECONOMY pages 164–169	1 day	The developing economies of South America are based on limited farmland and attempts to develop a wider range of mining and manufacturing.	Practice Book p. 41 ■ Anthology pp. 53, 56–57
3 THE GOVERNMENT pages 170–171	1 day	Although most countries in South America are guaranteed a democratic government by their constitutions, dictatorial governments are common.	Practice Book p. 42 ■ Anthology pp. 58–60 Outline Map p. 16 **Technology:** *Adventures CD-ROM*
4 ARTS AND RECREATION pages 172–173	1 day	South Americans celebrate their heritage and share their culture through their literature, the arts, sports, and music.	Practice Book p. 43 ■ Anthology pp. 54–55 **Technology:** *Adventures CD-ROM*
CHAPTER SUMMARY AND REVIEW pages 174–175	1 day	Chapter content, skills, and vocabulary are reviewed and evaluated.	Practice Book p. 44 Transparency: Graphic Organizer Assessment Book, Chapter 7 Test

Technology CONNECTION

Lesson 1
ADVENTURES CD-ROM
Have students *Travel* to and *Explore* Argentina and Uruguay on the CD-ROM.

Lesson 3
ADVENTURES CD-ROM
Have students *Explore* Argentina.

Lesson 4
ADVENTURES CD-ROM
Have students make a map of Argentina showing the capital city, using *Build* and *Paint.*

CHAPTER 7
pages 158–175

USING THE CHAPTER OPENER

Discussing the Photograph Tell students that the man in the picture is a gaucho, or Argentine cowhand.

Ask students:

- **What qualities do you associate with American cowhands?** (Possible answers include: bravery, adventurousness, self-reliance.)
- **Why might Argentine cowhands have the same qualities?** (Like American cowhands, they do dangerous work in a lonely and rugged terrain.)
- *THINKING FURTHER:* **Why do you think this picture was chosen to represent the chapter on South America?** (Possible answers include: to show that people in this land, as in other lands, are both different from and similar to people in the United States.)

Reading/Listening to the Primary Source Have students read the passage under the picture. Encourage them to guess why this picture has been used to illustrate this quotation. Tell them that reading about Argentina's population in this chapter will help them to appreciate the idea that many different peoples have settled South America.

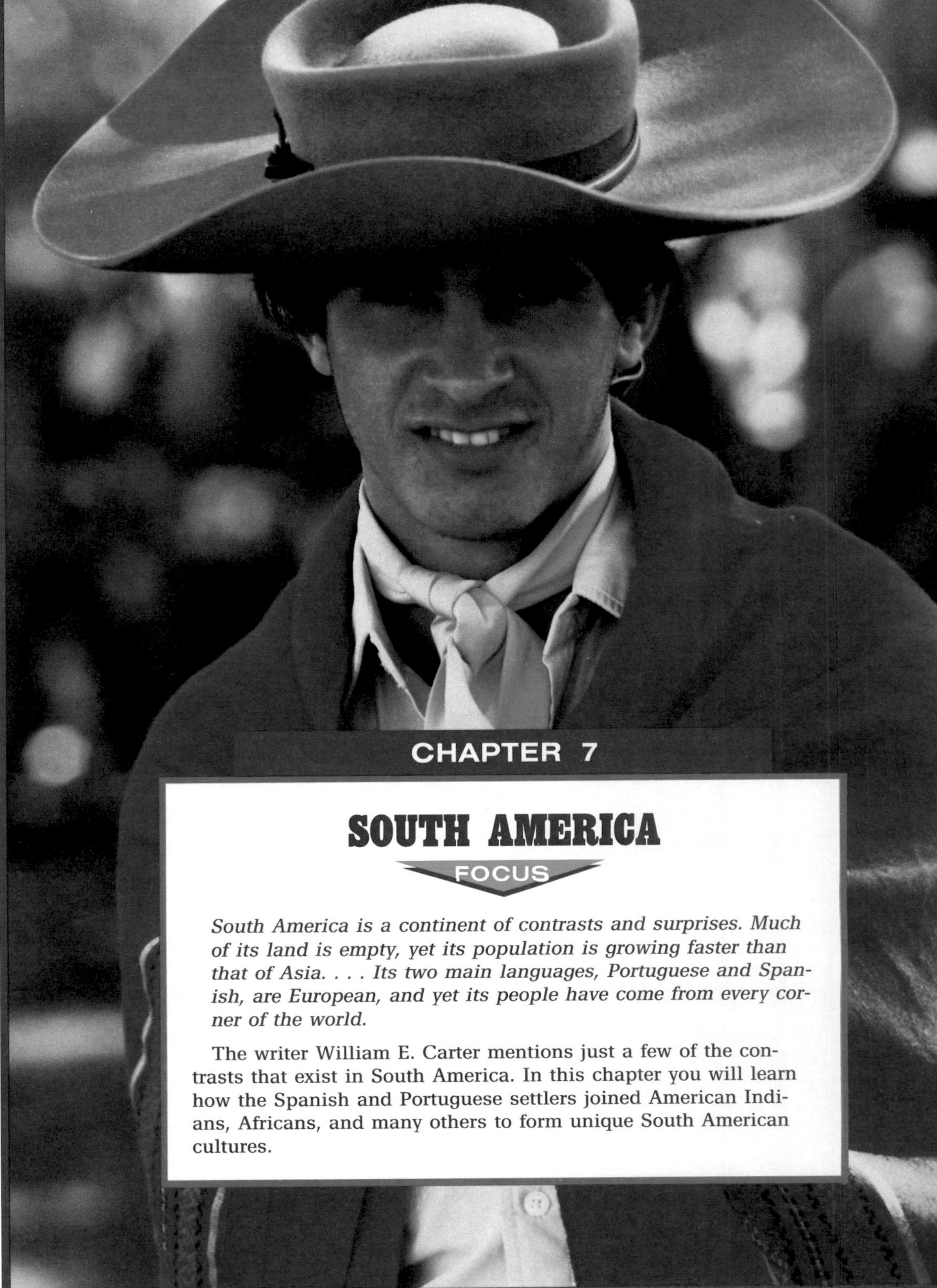

CHAPTER 7

SOUTH AMERICA

FOCUS

South America is a continent of contrasts and surprises. Much of its land is empty, yet its population is growing faster than that of Asia. . . . Its two main languages, Portuguese and Spanish, are European, and yet its people have come from every corner of the world.

The writer William E. Carter mentions just a few of the contrasts that exist in South America. In this chapter you will learn how the Spanish and Portuguese settlers joined American Indians, Africans, and many others to form unique South American cultures.

BACKGROUND INFORMATION

About the Photograph Gauchos, like the cowhands of the western United States, are popularly seen as people who perform a hard and dangerous job with skill and dash. Although the fencing in and farming of pasture land has reduced the numbers of gauchos and cowhands and although mechanization of ranch work has altered their roles, members of both these groups continue to be seen as romantic figures.

- Gauchos not only contribute to their nation's culture by serving as folk heroes but also contribute to the culture as creative and performing artists.
- Besides making up songs and folktales as some of our cowhands do, gauchos form traveling theaters, or *dramas criollas*, and bring their plays, music, and dances to people living in isolated places.

LESSON 1

The People

READ TO LEARN

Key Vocabulary

gaucho

Key Places

Argentina
Uruguay
Pampas

Read Aloud

October 12 is an important day for us [South Americans]. *North Americans call this holiday Columbus Day, but we call it* El Día de la Raza, *the "Day of the Race." It was the beginning of Latin America.*

In South America, October 12 is set aside to celebrate the birth of the new "race" of mestizos that formed after the coming of the Europeans. South Americans are proud of the many people and traditions that have blended to make their culture unique.

Read for Purpose

1. WHAT YOU KNOW: What is the meaning of the term *Latin America*?
2. WHAT YOU WILL LEARN: How have the ethnic groups of South America shaped life on the continent?

INDIAN HERITAGE

The continent of South America is the largest part of Latin America. South America is a little smaller in size than the United States and Canada together.

The population of South America consists of people of many different ethnic groups. As in other parts of Latin America, Indians were the first people in South America. By the 1300s, an Indian people called the Incas had created a great civilization in the Andes Mountains. Some stone buildings the Incas built long ago are still standing.

Today many Indians live in the Andean nations of Peru, Bolivia, and Ecuador. About half of the people who live in Bolivia and Peru and about a quarter of the people in Ecuador are Indians.

EUROPEANS

South America also has many European immigrants—more than the rest of Latin America. In fact, almost all of the people of Argentina and Uruguay are European or of European ancestry. Juan Roberts of Patagonia, in Argentina, is Welsh. His story is similar to that of many Europeans whose ancestors left their homelands to seek a better life.

I'm a direct descendant of one of the 153 Welsh people who landed . . . in 1865. They were poor people who were escaping from the crowded mining valleys. . . .

Between 1857 and 1930 more than 6 million immigrants entered Argentina alone. Today both Argentina and Uruguay have many Italian, Spanish, French, English, and German people.

WHAT YOU KNOW: This question refers to information in Chapter 4, Lesson 1; that part of the Western Hemisphere where most of the people speak Latin languages (Mexico, Central America and the Caribbean, South America).

LESSON 1

pages 159–161

Lesson Theme The largest part of the Latin American region is the continent of South America, which is inhabited by people from a variety of ethnic groups.

Lesson Objectives

- Identify the three major ethnic groups of South America.
- Identify the various religions of South America.

PREPARE

Motivate Read the *Read Aloud* section to the class. Tell students that Columbus Day may mean different things to different U.S. citizens. Have students discuss ways they think South Americans might feel about El Día de la Raza.

Set Purpose Have a student answer the *What You Know* question. Based on what they have already learned about ethnic groups in the rest of Latin America, have students answer the *What You Will Learn* question.

TEACH

Locating the Indian and European Populations Use the *Atlas* map of Latin America to help students identify the chief locations of the people of Indian and European ancestry.

Ask students:

- **Which early Indian people built a great civilization in the Andes Mountains?** (the Incas)
- **Why did some Europeans leave their homelands for South America?** (to escape the crowded mining valleys and to find a better way of life)

READING STRATEGY AND VOCABULARY DEVELOPMENT

Summarizing The purpose of this strategy is to encourage students to use their notes or outlines to create a summary of the lesson in their own words. Review the note-taking and outlining strategies. Emphasize to students the importance of paraphrasing information in their own words. Tell students that to summarize, they must first make notes and then develop a one-sentence summary for each section of the lesson. After they read the lesson, help the class summarize the first section. Then have students make notes on the remaining sections. Help students develop a class summary of the lesson.

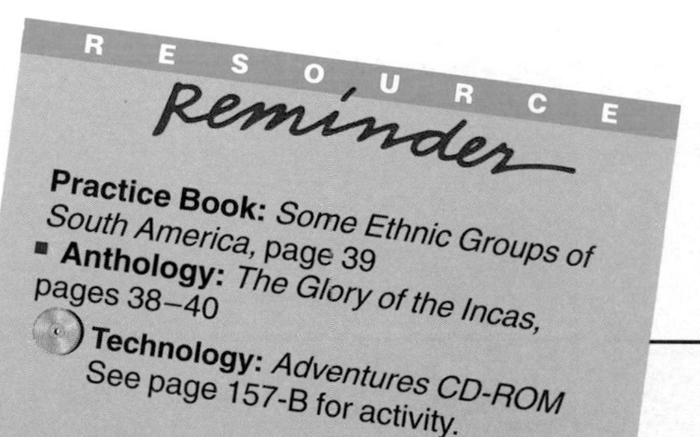

RESOURCE Reminder

Practice Book: *Some Ethnic Groups of South America,* page 39

Anthology: *The Glory of the Incas,* pages 38–40

Technology: *Adventures CD-ROM* See page 157-B for activity.

EXTENDING MAP SKILLS

Give students time to study the political map of South America.

Ask students:

- **How many independent nations are there in South America?** (Twelve—French Guiana is not an independent nation.)
- **Which inland country borders Chile?** (Bolivia)
- **Which cities are on the mouth of the Río de la Plata?** (Buenos Aires, Montevideo)
- **How many nations are there within 10° of the equator?** (8)
- **Which countries are entirely north of the equator?** (Venezuela, Guyana, Suriname, French Guiana)
- **Which is the largest nation?** (Brazil)
- **Which is the smallest independent nation?** (Suriname—French Guiana is not an independent nation.)
- **Which waterway divides Chile?** (Strait of Magellan)
- **Which country borders Central America?** (Colombia)
- **Which cities are on the Tropic of Capricorn?** (São Paulo, Antofagasta)
- **In which countries is Lake Titicaca?** (Peru and Bolivia)

Identifying the Gauchos Review for students who the mestizos are. Then help students locate the Pampas of Argentina on the map.

Ask students:

- **Who are the gauchos?** (cowhands who roam the Pampas herding cattle)

Have students draw comparisons between the gauchos and the cowhands of the American West.

SOUTH AMERICA: Political

⊛ National capital • Other city

MAP SKILL: South America has only two countries that do not have coast lines. What are these two countries? What are their capital cities? Which countries do not share a border with Brazil?

MAP SKILL: Paraguay, Bolivia; Asunción, La Paz and Sucre; Ecuador and Chile

CURRICULUM CONNECTION

Literature Have students compare gauchos with North American cowhands by reading various books about each subject. Tell students to compare and contrast lifestyles, work, and geographical locations. After they have finished reading, let students create posters showing similarities and differences.

Science The Galapagos Islands are world famous for unusual fauna and flora. Have each student research one unusual species found on the islands and present their findings in a brief presentation to the class. Have students provide visuals if possible.

South America has many different peoples and ways of life. Buenos Aires, Argentina (*left*), for example, has many European-style cafés. In Peru (*right*), Indians follow traditional ways.

GAUCHOS

The population of Paraguay, Venezuela, Chile, and Ecuador consists mainly of mestizos. Perhaps the best known of South America's mestizo groups are the gauchos of the Pampas. The Pampas is Argentina's vast inland plain. The gauchos are cowhands who roam the Pampas herding cattle. Life changed for the gauchos after the Pampas was fenced in. Nevertheless, the gaucho spirit remains alive today.

> *To be a gaucho is to belong to a big fraternity where there is a code of honor and friendship. After a hard day's work, gauchos still meet around an open fire . . . and express our feelings through music and song.*

RELIGION

As you might expect from a continent that was ruled by Spain and Portugal, many South Americans are Roman Catholics. Guyana, a British colony until 1966, has many Protestants. So does Suriname, which was a Dutch colony until 1975. Yet about half the people in Suriname are East Indian. Many of them are Hindus. The Hindu religion is discussed in Chapter 25.

South America also has different religious sects. Some sects, such as candomblé (kan dōm blā'), follow African beliefs and practices. One spiritual leader explains that believers "call on the gods and spirits of Africa." During ceremonies, she says, they "beat drums, chant, dance, and meditate as our ancestors did."

PEOPLE FROM ALL OVER THE WORLD

South America is made up of many different ethnic groups. Indians, Europeans, and Africans are the largest of these groups. Their different ways of life form the cultures of present-day South America.

 Check Your Reading

1. Name two countries in South America made up largely of Europeans and their descendants.
2. Where did the Incas build their civilization?
3. Name three ethnic groups found in South America today.
4. **THINKING SKILL:** How are South America's people similar to people in the rest of Latin America? How do they differ?

THINKING SKILL: Compare and Contrast

161

Discussing Religion Help students recognize that the religions in South America have been influenced by Europeans, East Indians, and Africans. Have students list the religious groups in South America. (Roman Catholics, Protestants, Hindus, Candomblés) Explain to students what a sect is.

Applying the Lesson Have students label and color the outline map of South America to show countries and locations of ethnic groups.

 3 CLOSE

Summarizing Tell students they have learned that South America is a continent of many nations and many kinds of people. Have students identify the countries of South America and the various religions.

Evaluating Use these questions to assess students' understanding.

- **What are the major ethnic groups of South America?** (Indians, Europeans, Africans)
- **What are the three main religious groups found in South America?** (Roman Catholic, Protestant, Hindu)

 **Answers to Check Your Reading**

1. Argentina, Uruguay
2. in the Andes Mountains
3. Indians, Europeans, mestizos
4. They are both a blend of origins. More people in South America are directly descended from Europeans.

Independent Practice
Practice Book: page 39

MEETING INDIVIDUAL NEEDS

Reteaching (easy) Have students create a scrapbook or collage of South American people, using their own drawings, postcards, magazines, and travel brochures. Have students attach a short written explanation of the ethnic groups illustrated.

Extension (average) Have students work in groups to write an anthem to honor the people of South America. Have them pick a familiar tune and write words to it.

Enrichment (challenging) Have students write a "What If" essay for this question: *What would the people of South America be like if Europeans had never gone there to explore and settle?*

SKILLS LESSON
pages 162–163

Lesson Theme Distinguishing fact from opinion means telling the difference between information that can be proved true and personal beliefs that cannot be proved true.

Lesson Objective
- Identify and apply a strategy for distinguishing facts from opinions.

PREPARE

Motivate Before students read the introductory paragraphs, begin a short discussion about a topic of immediate interest to them (class elections, a holiday, a sports event, a school dance). Write the words *fact* and *opinion* on the chalkboard. As students discuss the topic, write some of their comments under the appropriate headings.

Have students read the introductory paragraphs and define the terms *fact* and *opinion*. Write their definitions on the chalkboard. Ask students to give examples of *value judgments* and *reasoned opinions* and explain how the two differ. Write definitions for both terms on the chalkboard.

Set Purpose Tell students that in this lesson they will learn one way to distinguish fact from opinion and a value judgment from a reasoned opinion.

TEACH

Trying the Skill Have students read about life in the Amazon Basin and answer the questions that follow the passage. Tell students that if they have trouble answering the questions, they may refer to *Helping Yourself* on the next page.

Distinguishing Facts from Opinions

Key Vocabulary
value judgment
reasoned opinion

Have you ever read a story in which a detective solved a mystery by gathering the facts? If so, you know that a fact is information that can be proved to be true.

Statements of opinion, however, cannot be proved true. An opinion is a personal view or belief. There are two types of opinions. One type of a personal opinion is a **value judgment**. A value judgment tells how someone feels about something, such as "this is the best cookie I ever ate."

Sometimes an opinion is supported by evidence or reasons. "This is the best novel I have read because it has an exciting plot and interesting characters" is a **reasoned opinion**. The speaker or writer tells you the reasons on which the opinion is based.

It is important to distinguish among facts, value judgments, and reasoned opinions.

Trying the Skill

As you read this description of life in the Amazon Basin in Brazil, decide whether each sentence states a fact or an opinion.

> Life for the people living in the Amazon Basin is harsh and lonely. They find it difficult to grow food and to make a living from the forest. Their only contact with the outside world is with traders who stop at settlements along the rivers. More than 60 percent of these people, most of whom are part-Indian and part-Portuguese, cannot read. Their rate of infant mortality is high. I would rather live in a modern city than in the villages of the Amazon Basin.

1. What facts did you find?
2. What opinions did you find?
3. Which opinion was supported by reasons?

162

CURRICULUM CONNECTION

Art Have students design a poster advertising a product or service of their choice. Tell students to include at least two facts, one value judgment, and one reasoned opinion in their advertisement.

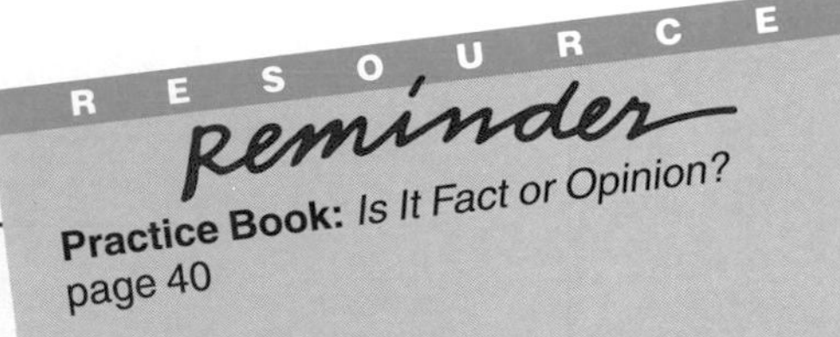

HELPING YOURSELF

The steps on the left show one way to distinguish between facts and opinions. The examples on the right show how these steps can be used to identify facts and opinions in the paragraph on the Amazon Basin.

One Way to Distinguish Between Facts and Opinions	Example
1. Recall the definitions of a fact, a reasoned opinion, and a value judgment.	A fact is something that can be checked and proved true. A reasoned opinion is a personal view or belief supported by evidence. A value judgment is a personal opinion about a subject.
2. Look for clues to statements of fact. Look for statements that can be proved to be true.	The percentage of a population that is literate and infant mortality rates are facts that can be checked.
3. Look for clues to value judgments. Clues such as "I think" and adjectives such as "best" signal statements of opinion.	"Harsh and lonely" and "I would rather live" are clues to the writer's opinion.
4. Look for clues to reasoned opinions. Look for words such as "because" and judgments supported by evidence.	Sentences 2 and 3 give evidence to support the opinion that life is "harsh and lonely."
5. Read each statement carefully to find clues to facts, value judgments, and reasoned opinions.	The first sentence is an opinion, supported by the next sentences, which are facts. The last sentence states a value judgment.

Applying the Skill

Read the following description of another South American country.

Bolivia is the most "Indian" of the countries in the Andes Mountains. Three fourths of the population are of almost pure Indian heritage. I saw Indian sheepherders on the high, remote plains. They were wrapped in dark ponchos. They stood guard over their flocks of sheep on cold, windy days. I believe their way of life is very difficult.

1. Which sentence states a fact?
   - **a.** I saw Indian sheepherders on the high, remote plains.
   - **b.** Bolivia is the most "Indian" of the countries in the Andes mountains.
   - **c.** I believe their way of life is very difficult.
2. What value judgments can you find in the passage?
   - **a.** They were wrapped in dark ponchos.
   - **b.** Three fourths of the population are of almost pure Indian heritage.
   - **c.** I believe their way of life is very difficult.
3. Which of the opinions in the passage are supported by reasons or evidence?

Reviewing the Skill

1. What is the difference between a fact and a value judgment?
2. What clue words can help you to distinguish facts from opinions?
3. Why is it important to be able to distinguish a fact from an opinion?

Thinking About Thinking *Ask:* What did you do to identify the facts? What clues helped you identify opinions? How did you distinguish between value judgments and reasoned opinions? What did you do first? Next? And so on. Write students' answers and the clues they used on the chalkboard.

Help Yourself Tell students that this section presents one way to distinguish facts from opinions. They may want to use all or some of the steps and word clues as guidelines. Have students compare the steps and clues on the chalkboard with those in *Helping Yourself.* Brainstorm other clues.

Applying the Skill Have students read the passage about Bolivia and answer the questions that follow. (See answers below.) Discuss with students the processes they used to identify the facts, value judgments, and reasoned opinions.

3 CLOSE

Reviewing the Skill Use students' answers to Question 1 to add to or revise the definitions written on the chalkboard. Have students work in small groups to list word clues that will help them to separate facts from opinions. Have a member from each group read the list aloud. End class discussion by asking students to tell when they might use this skill outside school (when shopping, settling an argument, voting, making a decision).

Independent Practice
Practice Book: page 40

ANSWERS TO SKILLS QUESTIONS

Applying the Skill

1. a
2. c
3. The first statement is a reasoned opinion because it is supported by the fact that three fourths of the population are of almost pure Indian heritage.

Reviewing the Skill

1. A fact can be proved true. A value judgment is a personal belief that cannot be proved true.
2. *I think* and adjectives such as *best*
3. Being able to distinguish between facts and opinions will help you to identify information that is accurate. You need accurate information to make good decisions.

LESSON 2
pages 164–167

Lesson Theme The developing economies of South America are based on limited farmland and attempts to develop a wider range of mining and manufacturing.

Lesson Objectives
- Describe the dilemma of development of the Amazon rain forest.
- Identify some of the industries on which the economies of South American countries depend.
- Explain the dangers in developing only one major resource in a nation.

PREPARE

Motivate Read the *Read Aloud* section to the class. Suggest that this sounds like the setting for a western town of the 1800s in the United States. Discuss students' ideas of what Brazil's frontier might be like.

Set Purpose Pose the *What You Know* question and record students' answers on the chalkboard. Have students keep the *What You Will Learn* question in mind as they read the lesson.

TEACH

Discussing the Search for Economic Opportunity Help students recognize the dilemma South America faces in developing the Amazon rain forest. Have them name the pros and cons of settling the Amazon rain forest. You may now wish to have students read the *Viewpoints* on pages 168–169.

LESSON 2

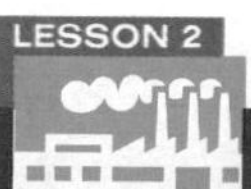

The Economy

READ TO LEARN

Key Vocabulary
per capita income

Key Places
Venezuela
Brasília

Read Aloud

With its simple wooden houses and horses tied to hitching posts, [this town] looks a lot like towns in the western United States 100 years ago. And well it might, for it is located on Brazil's frontier, the western Amazon Basin.

The government of Brazil is trying to get more people to move to the cleared land of the rain forest in the Amazon River Valley. The nation's leaders describe this area as "a land without people for a people without land." However, Indian groups already live in this land.

Read for Purpose

1. WHAT YOU KNOW: What are some of Latin America's natural resources?
2. WHAT YOU WILL LEARN: How are the nations of South America trying to develop their economies?

THE SEARCH FOR OPPORTUNITY

Like people all over Latin America, many South Americans are searching for better jobs and better opportunities. The desire for a better life has led thousands of people to the Amazon rain forest. Some of them want to "get rich quick." Others just want to have enough land to feed their families and improve their lives. Think of what you know about United States history. Why were these immigrants willing to leave their homes?

One Brazilian, Raimundo Pinho, has spent five years clearing 125 acres (50 ha) in the rain forest. He thinks his hard work will pay off. "Take my word for it," he says. "In five more years there will be a bus stop in front of my house. . . ."

Many people do not agree with Pinho. They say that the soil of the rain forest is poor and cannot be used for long. Others believe that cutting down the rain forest harms the world's environment by destroying plants and animals. You can read about this issue on pages 168–169.

COMMERCIAL AGRICULTURE AND RANCHING

The economy of South America is largely based on agriculture. Profits in agriculture come from cash crops that plantation owners sell to other countries. Ecuador, for example, sells more bananas than any other nation. Colombia and Brazil grow some of the world's finest coffee.

164 WHAT YOU KNOW: This question refers to information in Chapter 4, Lesson 2; petroleum, tin, copper, tropical fruits, coffee, sugar cane, tropical forests.

READING STRATEGY AND VOCABULARY DEVELOPMENT

Outlining Divide the class into ten groups. Assign two groups to each of the first five sections of the lesson. Have students preview and read the lesson. Then have each group develop a one- or two-sentence summary of their section. Have the groups that work on the same section compare and evaluate their summary statements. Have the class work together to create a summary of the entire lesson.

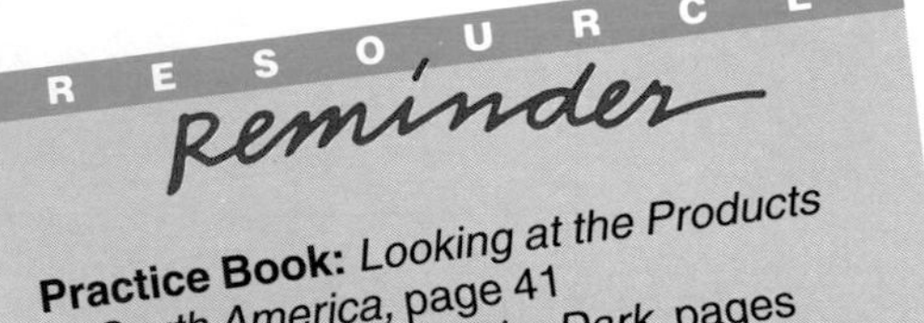

Practice Book: *Looking at the Products of South America,* page 41
▪ **Anthology:** *Child of the Dark,* pages 56–57; *Saving the Rain Forest,* page 53

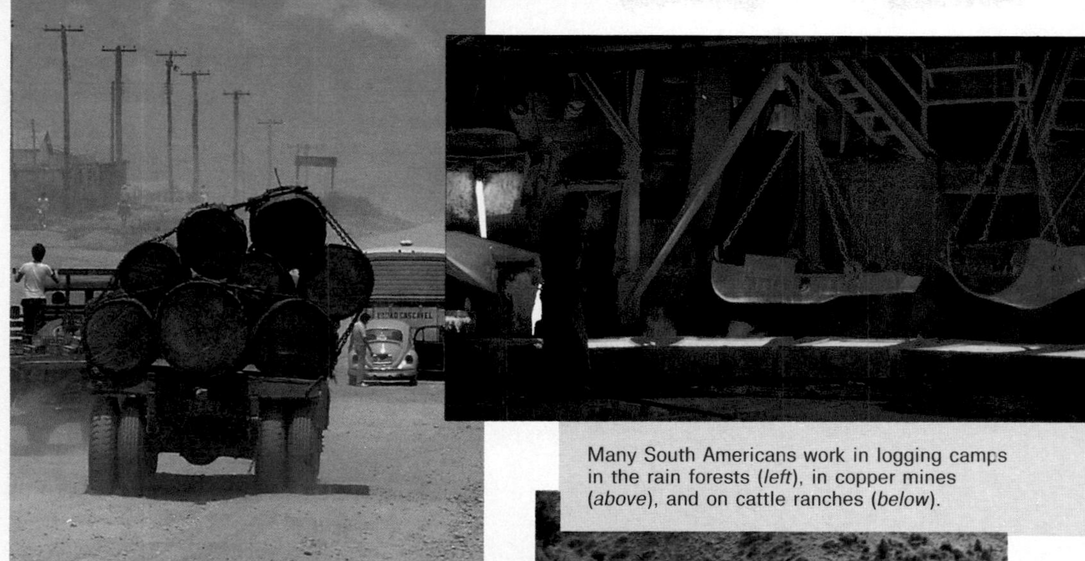

Many South Americans work in logging camps in the rain forests (*left*), in copper mines (*above*), and on cattle ranches (*below*).

South America is also a major producer of meat and wool. The Pampas and other plains areas are good for raising cattle, sheep, and other grazing animals. Wheat and cotton are also grown in these areas.

MINING AND MANUFACTURING

South America wants to develop more kinds of manufacturing businesses. Most of South America's manufacturers process, or treat, agricultural resources. For example, some businesses squeeze fruit for juice, while others make cheese. Colombia and Ecuador are leading food-processing nations. Argentina is a leader in meat packing and leather production.

South Americans want to use more of their own minerals to make products. This will give people jobs. Only about 20 percent of the workers in South America are in manufacturing and mining jobs.

Several South American countries have large mineral and fuel deposits. However, most of what is mined is sold to other countries. In Bolivia, for example, 90 percent of the money made by exports comes from tin. About 80 percent of Suriname's export income comes from bauxite. Copper brings in almost half of Chile's income. This situation is risky, as you will read.

VENEZUELA

Look at the map showing Venezuela on page 166. Venezuela is a nation that has used a major resource, petroleum, to help its economic development.

Venezuela was a leader in forming the Organization of Petroleum Exporting Countries (OPEC) in 1960. OPEC wanted

165

Looking at Commercial Agriculture and Ranching

Ask students:

- **What is the economy of South America based on?** (agricultural profits from cash crops grown on plantations and sold to other countries)
- **Which plantation crops are most successful in South America?** (bananas and coffee)
- **Which other South American agricultural products bring profits to economies there?** (cotton, wheat, meat, wool)

Understanding Mining and Manufacturing Stress to students that South American manufacturing is tied closely to the processing of agricultural products.

Ask students:

- **What kinds of manufacturing jobs do agricultural products provide?** (factory jobs such as squeezing fruit into juice, making cheese, packing meat, etc.)
- **What percentage of South American workers are in mining and manufacturing?** (about 20 percent)
- **Which countries of South America have large mineral or fuel deposits?** (Bolivia—tin; Suriname—bauxite; Chile—copper)
- *THINKING FURTHER:* **Why is it dangerous to a country's economy when a large percentage of that country's export income comes from minerals?** (a drop in world prices for minerals can lower the incomes of everyone in the country.)

CURRICULUM CONNECTION

Math Divide the class into three groups to each represent a different nation—Bolivia, Suriname, or Chile. Have students find in this lesson the percentage of income that their nation makes from exports. Have each group calculate and prepare a math problem to give the class. The problem should demonstrate what happens to income in their country if there is a 50 percent drop on the world market in the price of their main mineral export. Then have each group explain what happens to per capita income in their country when the price of their mineral export jumps 100 percent.

Multicultural Perspectives South America's rich deposits of precious metals have caused conflict ever since Spanish gold-hunters first arrived in the region during the 1500s. Today South American Indians continue to be at the center of conflict over their lands. More then 45,000 miners have invaded the lands of Brazil's Yanomami Indians, causing the destruction of hunting and fishing grounds and the introduction of deadly diseases. When police officers tried to remove the miners, some of them protested, "Who will feed our families?" and "The Amazon isn't only for the Indians." Ask students to discuss how each group could believe that they have a right to the land.

Talking About Venezuela Make sure students understand that changes in demand for a product on the world market can affect the whole economy of a nation that develops only one major resource.

Ask students:

- **What does OPEC mean?** (Organization of Petroleum Exporting Countries)
- **What was Venezuela's goal in helping to form OPEC?** (to work with other oil-rich nations to control the price and amount of oil produced around the world)
- **What unit of measure is used to show the average income for each person in a country?** (per capita income)

Examining Transportation Emphasize to students that a developed economy must have many forms of transportation to move goods.

Ask students:

- **What are the major methods of transportation in South America today?** (air, railroad)
- **What determines the location of modern systems of transportation and communication?** (the location of cities and industrial sites)
- *THINKING FURTHER:* **As economies develop, why would traffic on the Pan-American Highway tend to increase?** (As more goods are manufactured, they need to be moved; movement of goods provides jobs for more people who can then afford cars.)

EXTENDING MAP SKILLS

Direct students' attention to the petroleum map of Venezuela.

Ask students:

- **In which part of Venezuela are the oil pipelines?** (northern)
- **Are there more reserves in the Llanos or near Lake Maracaibo?** (near Lake Maracaibo)

to control the price and amount of petroleum produced around the world. After OPEC raised the price of oil, Venezuela became one of the richest nations in South America. Its yearly **per capita income**, or average income for each person, rose to about $3,000. This was one of the highest per capita incomes in Latin America.

During the 1980s, world oil prices fell and hurt Venezuela's economy. But by the 1990s, Venezuela once again had the fastest-growing economy in South America, followed by Chile.

Oil still makes up the greatest part of Venezuela's trade, but the country is also developing its natural gas, coal, steel, and aluminum resources.

Like other Latin American countries, Venezuela has debts it owes to other countries. Venezuelans hope that they can find the right mix of industries to keep the country's economy strong.

TRANSPORTATION

Because much of South America is rugged, dry, or thickly forested, most people live along the coasts. The continent's big cities are found here. These cities are joined by modern systems of travel and communication.

Efforts have been made to develop the interior. In 1960 Brazil built a new capital city, **Brasília**, inland. This city was to be the first step toward settling the central part of Brazil. Today more than a million

MAP SKILL: Venezuelan oil wells produce about 2 million barrels of oil a day. Several oil pipelines help to transport this oil to refineries or ports. Name two bodies of water within Venezuela that have pipelines near them.

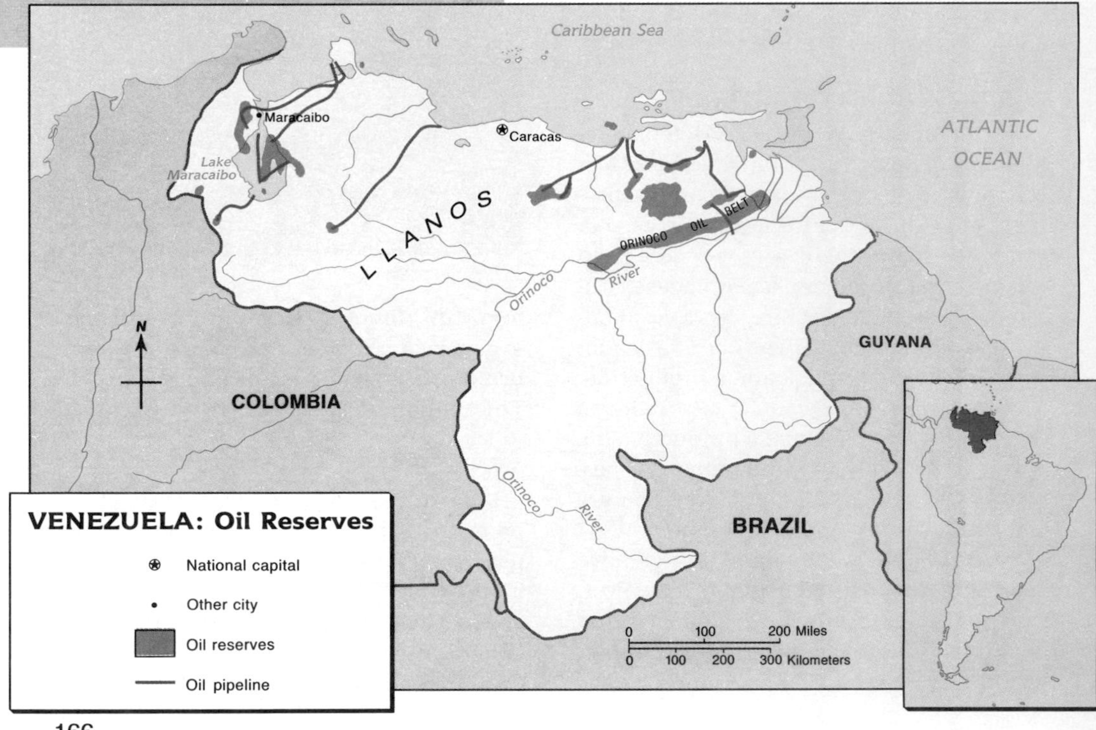

166 MAP SKILL: Lake Maracaibo, Orinoco River

FUNDAMENTAL THEMES OF GEOGRAPHY

Location The location of cities can determine how an economy develops. Cities include more than just the area within their boundaries—they serve a wider metropolitan area. The result is a need for movement of people, goods, and ideas through transportation and communication networks linking cities to suburbs and cities to cities. Have students analyze the location of South American cities on the political map on page 160. Have students discuss reasons that cities developed where they did and what natural barriers are preventing transportation between various cities. (You may also want students to refer to the map on page 108.)

South Americans depend upon many types of transportation. People use buses (*above*) and horses and carts (*left*) daily. Trains (*right*) connect most parts, even the most mountainous and densely forested areas, of the continent.

people live in Brasília. But few people have moved to the very dry area around the city. Hundreds of thousands of people living in the center of South America have never seen a railroad, ridden in a car, or used a telephone.

Airplanes and railroads are South America's major means of transportation. More and more, though, the Pan American Highway is making it easier for South Americans to reach more places by automobile. This highway begins in Mexico and continues south through much of Chile. As you read earlier, it also connects the east and west coasts of South America.

DEVELOPING ECONOMIES

South America has very little good farmland, but most people still farm small plots of land for a living. Throughout the continent new solutions are being tried to develop modern, strong economies.

Check Your Reading

1. What is *per capita income*?
2. Why are people settling in the Amazon rain forest?
3. How did Venezuela achieve one of the highest per capita incomes in South America?
4. THINKING SKILL: List three questions that you could ask to find out about the economy of a typical South American country.

THINKING SKILL: Asking Questions

167

Applying the Lesson Give students the outline map of South America. Have them locate and label the major cities, mineral deposits, and transportation links.

CLOSE

Summarizing Tell students they have learned that the countries of South America are trying to develop better economies. Have them list some of the ways the countries are doing this.

Evaluating Use these questions to assess students' understanding.

- **Where do most South Americans live?** (along the coasts)
- **What other products does Venezuela sell besides oil?** (steel and aluminum)
- **What sign is there that the location of Brasília in the center of the country has not been highly successful?** (Not many people have moved to the dry lands around that capital city.)

Answers to Check Your Reading

1. the average income for each person
2. search for better jobs and opportunities; seeking land of their own
3. by helping to form an organization (OPEC) that seeks to control the price and production of the world's petroleum, Venezuela's major natural resource
4. Possible questions include: Is it centrally planned or a free enterprise system? What is the per capita income? What are its major exports?

Independent Practice
Practice Book: page 41

MEETING INDIVIDUAL NEEDS

Reteaching (easy) Have students draw cartoon-style pictures to show the series of events that take place when a country sells export products at one price and then the price falls, ruining every other element of the economy.

Extension (average) Students should gather up-to-date information from newspapers, magazines, and television on the Amazon rain forest dilemma. Divide the class into two teams and have them prepare a debate on the question: "What is the best use of the land in the Amazon Basin today?"

Enrichment (challenging) Have students research gasohol production in Brazil and then ask them to write a report on its effects on that country's economy.

CHAPTER 7

CITIZENSHIP

Viewpoints

pages 168–169

Lesson Objective

- Analyze three points of view on the best way to develop the tropical rain forest of Brazil.

Identifying the Issue Help students to see that genuine differences of opinion can arise on this issue, even when people have the same goal of preserving the rain forest.

Suggested Questions

- ***Why is the rain forest environment so important?*** *(Rain forests help maintain the world's climates and also contain a huge variety of plants and animals.)*

Discussing Three Different Viewpoints Give students a few minutes to read the viewpoints on page 169.

OSMARINO RODRIGUES

Suggested Questions

- ***What does Rodrigues mean by "empty environmentalism"?*** *(environmentalism that speaks of nature while forgetting human beings)*
- ***According to Rodrigues, what is his contribution to the world environmental movement?*** *(that defense of nature and social justice are inseparable)*

MARCELLO DE ANDRADE

Suggested Questions

- ***What are some of the uses of the rain forest that de Andrade mentions?*** *(farmland, timber, ranching, and medicine)*
- **According to de Andrade, what portion of the world's medicines come from the rain forest?** *(one-quarter)*
- ***What does de Andrade believe we must do if we are to benefit from further discoveries in the rain forest?*** *(We must conserve the rain forest for future generations.)*

CITIZENSHIP VIEWPOINTS

The Iguaçú River flows through the forest in southern Brazil.

WHAT IS THE BEST WAY TO USE THE BRAZILIAN RAIN FOREST?

South America's rain forests are one of the world's most talked-about environments. Millions of trees in these forests help maintain Earth's climates in ways scientists are only beginning to understand. Rain forests are also important for their variety of plants and animals. Three-quarters of all species are found in rain forests. Many of the plants have medicinal value, and new species are being discovered daily.

Besides plants and animals, however, Brazil's rain forests are home to thousands of people who need to earn a living there. Loggers cut down trees to sell the wood for lumber. Farmers need to burn the forest to clear land to raise crops and cattle.

Unfortunately, any damage done to the forest is permanent. When a species becomes extinct, it is lost forever. The race is on to find ways to develop the rain forest that also preserve the environment. Osmarino Rodrigues believes the needs of local people are the most important issue. Marcelo de Andrade sees the rain forest as a vital source of medicines and resources. Beto Borges thinks development should vary.

Consider three viewpoints on this issue and then answer the questions that follow.

168

BACKGROUND INFORMATION

About the Rain Forest A tropical rain forest is made up of three layers: the canopy, the understory, and the forest floor. The canopy is made up of the tops of trees, many of which are over 200 feet tall. Most of the animals, such as birds, monkeys, frogs, and snakes, live in the canopy. The understory is made up of the younger trees and smaller plants that live under the canopy. The forest floor is almost bare, and is made up of rotting vegetation. Large animals, such as boars and jaguars, and many insects live on the forest floor.

South American rain forests are located near the equator, where the average temperature is about 80º year round. Rain forests receive between 160 and 400 inches of rain each year. The largest rain forest in the world is located in Brazil.

Three DIFFERENT Viewpoints

1 OSMARINO AMÂNCIO RODRIGUES
Rubber Tapper, Brasiléia, Acre, Western Amazon, Brazil
Excerpt from interview, 1996

We honor the commitment of those who . . . defend the rain forest. We don't want an empty environmentalism that speaks of nature while forgetting human beings; that speaks of defense of the forest while forgetting the peoples of the forest. This is our contribution to the world environmental movement: defense of nature and social justice are inseparable.

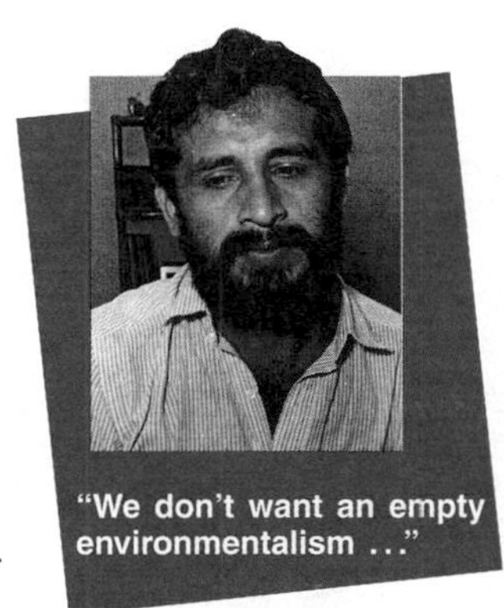

"We don't want an empty environmentalism . . ."

2 DR. MARCELO C. DE ANDRADE
International Development Specialist,
Rio de Janeiro, Brazil
Excerpt from interview, 1996

Rain forests should be used for more than farmland, timber, and ranching. For example, one-quarter of today's medicines come from plants in the rain forest and they earn billions of dollars each year. We can only continue to benefit from new discoveries such as these if the rain forest is conserved for future generations.

"We can only . . . benefit . . . if the rain forest is conserved . . ."

3 BETO BORGES
Brazil Program Director, Rainforest Action Network,
San Francisco, California
Excerpt from interview, 1996

We need to realize that the needs and values of people vary from group to group. Large-scale exploitation of natural resources does not help the people or the environment. Instead, we need to create an economy that takes into account long-term preservation of the rain forest, such as harvesting rain forest crops, medicinal plants, and rubber. Only this will preserve the cultures of the people and the environment.

"Large-scale exploitation of natural resources does not help the people or the environment."

BUILDING CITIZENSHIP

1. What is the viewpoint of each person?
2. In what ways are some of the viewpoints alike? In what ways are they different?
3. What other viewpoints might people have on this issue?

SHARING VIEWPOINTS

Discuss what you agree with or disagree with about these and other viewpoints. Discuss why you think each speaker might feel as he or she does. Then, as a class, write three statements that all of you can agree with about the best way to develop the Brazilian rain forest.

BETO BORGES

Suggested Questions

- ***Why does Borges believe that large-scale exploitation of natural resources is bad for the rain forest?*** *(Because it does not help the people or the environment.)*
- ***What does Borges believe is the proper goal of rain forest development?*** *(the preservation of indigenous cultures and the environment)*

EVALUATE
Answers to Citizenship Viewpoints

1. Rodrigues believes that the most important thing to take into account is the people who live in the rain forest. De Andrade believes that the rain forest can be used in many different ways, but it must be preserved. Borges believes there is no single answer to rain forest development, but that it must follow the needs and values of local people.
2. All three believe that the rain forest must be preserved. De Andrade supports a wider range of development, while Rodrigues and Borges support smaller-scale development.
3. Some people, such as farmers and ranchers, might support the destruction of parts of the rain forest. Others might support the large-scale extraction of resources such as timber and oil, which would do little to help local people.

Sharing Viewpoints Encourage students to recognize that these three speakers share the common goal of preserving the rain forest. Three agreed-on statements might be: **1.** We need to preserve the rain forest for future generations. **2.** We need to consider the lives of the people who live in the rain forest. **3.** We need to develop sustainable ways of supporting the rain forest economy.

Debating Viewpoints Discuss with students how a debate about the rain forest usually raises difficult questions about the environment and economics. Invite students to debate the issue of economic development versus environmental preservation.

CITIZENSHIP

Understanding Environmental Concerns Preservation of the rain forest is one of the most pressing concerns of environmentalists around the world. Encourage students to research on their own what is happening in rain forests in different parts of the world. The following word list will help them understand some of the important issues of the rain forest.

- **clear-cut** to cut down all the trees in a part of the forest
- **ecosystem** all the interacting living and non-living things in a particular environment or area
- **deforestation** the clearing of forest land
- **diversity** variety
- **hunter-gatherers** people who live by hunting, fishing, and gathering food in their environment
- **indigenous people** the original people who live in an area
- **sustainable development** using the environment in a way that it is not harmful and which can be sustained indefinitely

LESSON 3
pages 170–171

Lesson Theme Though most countries in South America are guaranteed a democratic government by their constitutions, dictatorial governments are common.

Lesson Objectives
- Define *caudillos*, *junta*, and *coup*.
- Explain the types of governments in South America.

PREPARE

Motivate Have the class read the *Read Aloud* section. Discuss students' ideas on the kinds of issues a *yaya* would decide.

Set Purpose Have students review the definition of a dictator. Discuss the *What You Will Learn* question.

TEACH

Identifying Caudillos Discuss with students the reasons that the people in the governments of newly formed countries had little experience in governing.

Understanding Rule by Dictatorship

Ask students:

- **What are three powers of a dictator?** (A dictator can stop government leaders from meeting, prevent laws from being carried out, and declare a state of emergency.)
- **What is a junta?** (a group of military officers that rules a country)
- *THINKING FURTHER:* **Under which form of rule, a dictator or a junta, do you think life is easier for the people of a country? Why?** (Students should give reasons for their answers.)

LESSON 3

The Government

READ TO LEARN

Key Vocabulary	**Key People**	**Key Places**
caudillo	Juan Perón	Argentina
junta		
coup		

Read Aloud

Yaya is someone who knows a lot. He is the oldest. He knows how to talk. Children learn from him. . . .

The villagers of Hualcan in the Peruvian Andes respect their *yaya*—their "father of fathers." Yayas are older people who once served in the village government. Many South American communities that depend upon the advice of such leaders are far from other communities, in the mountains or rain forests.

Read for Purpose

1. **WHAT YOU KNOW:** What is a dictator?
2. **WHAT YOU WILL LEARN:** Why has South America been troubled by frequent political change and social unrest?

CAUDILLOS

Most Latin American colonies gained their independence in the 1800s. However, few people in the new governments had experience governing large areas. This sometimes made it possible for local military leaders called **caudillos** (kou dē′ yōz) to gain great power. Some caudillos became so powerful that they were able to form their own armies. One such caudillo was the Argentine gaucho Juan Quiroga (kē rō′ gä), who was called *El Tigre*, meaning "the Tiger." Quiroga used fear and cruelty to control people.

RULE BY DICTATORSHIP

Today all the countries of South America except French Guiana have constitutions that require them to have democratic governments. French Guiana is an overseas area of France.

But in many countries, democracy exists only on paper. Instead, presidents rule as dictators. Sometimes these presidents stop government leaders from meeting. Sometimes, to prevent laws from being carried out, they declare national emergencies. In a state of emergency, the president rules with complete power.

In some countries the army and not the president plays the most important role. This situation occurs when the army is the only group in the nation that is well organized and has the power to bring about change. When an army assumes control, military leaders may choose to rule through a group of officers called a **junta** (hůn′ tə).

WHAT YOU KNOW: This question refers to information in Chapter 6, Lesson 2; a ruler who has total control over a country and usually rules by force.

READING STRATEGY AND VOCABULARY DEVELOPMENT

Summarizing Suggest to students that a television newscast is basically a summary of important news of the day. Have students preview and read this lesson, taking notes about important facts they might include in a news broadcast. Have them work in groups to develop a five-minute news summary on leadership in South America. After they have heard the newscasts, have students discuss the facts upon which each group focused and compare and contrast the points each group made.

RESOURCE *Reminder*

Practice Book: *A Look at the Dictatorship of Juan Perón*, page 42
Anthology: *A Tale of Disappearance*, pages 58–60
Outline Map: *South America*
Technology: *Adventures CD-ROM*
See page 157-B for activity.

Other times, military leaders do not rule directly, but through the president whom they control. Without orderly systems for changing governments, changes occur often. These changes may be violent.

A STRUGGLE FOR DEMOCRACY

For many years Argentina was ruled by a president who became a dictator. Juan Perón (pə rōn′) became the president of Argentina in 1946. He maintained power by creating labor unions, schools, and new industries to help Argentina's "shirtless ones." His wife, Eva Perón, helped him by encouraging workers to support the government's programs. Meanwhile, however, Perón became a dictator. He took control of the press, businesses, labor unions, and the army.

Juan Perón's enemies overthrew him in a coup (kü) in 1955. A coup is the sudden overthrow of a government. But after years of unrest, Perón was elected again in 1973. He died in 1974. For several years afterward, Argentina was ruled by dictators. They arrested and killed people without cause, and many people "disappeared."

Though many problems remain, Argentina, its neighbor Chile, and several other Latin American countries have recently made progress towards improving their economies and becoming more democratic. Other countries are still ruled by military dictators.

STRONG LEADERS, WEAK GOVERNMENTS

Almost all the countries of South America have constitutions that guarantee representative government. But for hundreds of years, these same countries have been plagued by dictatorships and military governments. This has caused unrest and lack of stability throughout the continent.

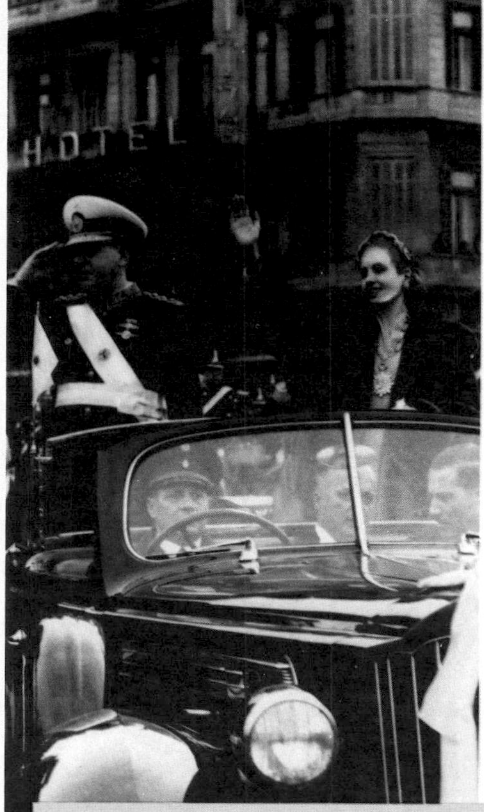

Argentina's President Juan Perón and Eva Perón rode through Buenos Aires in 1952 after he took the oath of office for a new presidential term.

Check Your Reading

1. What is the difference between a caudillo and a junta?
2. Why have many military leaders been able to gain control of national governments in South America?
3. What are some methods dictators use to stay in power in South America?
4. **THINKING SKILL:** From what you read about Juan Perón and his rule, what conclusions can you draw about the political life of Argentina?

THINKING SKILL: Drawing Conclusions

171

Discussing Perón of Argentina

Have students discuss what they may already know about Juan Perón or other dictators.

Ask students:

- **How did Perón gain great power as president?** (forming labor unions, building schools, starting new industries)
- **What is a coup?** (a sudden overthrow of a government)
- *THINKING FURTHER:* **Do you think Argentina was better off with Perón in or out of power?** (Students' answers may vary but may focus on the unrest that occurred when Perón was not in power.)

Applying the Lesson Have students research the type of rule in each of the countries of South America.

3 CLOSE

Summarizing Students have learned about the nondemocratic forms of government in South America. Have students make a chart comparing rule by caudillos, dictators, and juntas.

Evaluating Use the *Check Your Reading* questions (answers given below) to assess students' understanding.

Answers to Check Your Reading

1. A caudillo is rule by one person, whereas a junta consists of a group of leaders.
2. usually because the army is the only group in the nation that is well organized and can bring about change
3. declaring states of emergency; taking control of the press, businesses, labor unions, and the army
4. Students' answers should focus on the political instability of Argentina.

Independent Practice
Practice Book: page 42

MEETING INDIVIDUAL NEEDS

Reteaching (easy) Have students look through newspapers and magazines for articles about countries ruled by dictators or juntas. Then have them list three pros and three cons about each system.

Extension (average) Give each student the outline map of South America, which is found in the Teacher's Resource Center. Then have students identify on the map the type of government found in each country. Tell them to develop a key for their map.

Enrichment (challenging) Have students research a dictator or military leader from South America. Then have them prepare a brief report on the person, including any positive results of his rule.

LESSON 4
pages 172–173

Lesson Theme South Americans celebrate their heritage and share their culture through their literature, the arts, sports, and music.

Lesson Objective
- Describe the literature, music, arts, and sports of South America.

PREPARE

Motivate Read the *Read Aloud* section to the class. Discuss with the class how a language can be beautiful. Have students give examples of what makes them proud of the English language.

Set Purpose Review by having students answer the *What You Know* question. Tell students to look for the influences of South America's ethnic groups as they read this lesson.

TEACH

Talking About Literature Help students to identify the different themes in South American writings, including poverty, ethnic identity, climate, and history.

Ask students:

- **What helps South Americans enjoy stories that are imaginative and out of the ordinary?** (Their culture is rich in myths.)

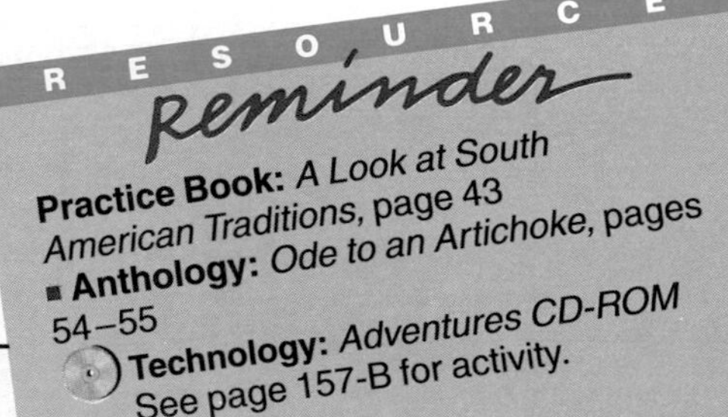
RESOURCE *Reminder*
Practice Book: *A Look at South American Traditions,* page 43
■ **Anthology:** *Ode to an Artichoke,* pages 54–55
Technology: *Adventures CD-ROM* See page 157-B for activity.

LESSON 4

Arts and Recreation

READ TO LEARN

Key People
Pablo Neruda
Gabriel García Márquez

Key Places
Rio de Janeiro

Read Aloud

It's a great language . . . we inherited from the [Spanish] conquerors. They carried everything off, [yet still] left us everything. They left us the words.

The above words were written by a Chilean poet. He tells of the pride that many South Americans have in their Spanish heritage, especially in their language.

Read for Purpose

1. **WHAT YOU KNOW:** What are some of the major ethnic groups of South America?
2. **WHAT YOU WILL LEARN:** How have South American arts been shaped by the continent's many ethnic groups?

LITERATURE

South America has many famous poets and novelists. They have told the stories of the continent's Indians, gauchos, and other peoples. Among the topics most often described are the problems of ethnic identity and poverty.

South America's writers also help people to understand what it is like to live in a tropical environment. The Chilean poet **Pablo Neruda**, for instance, describes the rain that often fell on the tin roof over his room as "the piano of my childhood." He also wrote about the rain forests.

South American authors are noted for their imaginative writing. Because they live in a land where many people believe in myths, South American writers feel comfortable writing about things that are out of the ordinary.

One South American novel that uses this style is *One Hundred Years of Solitude* by **Gabriel García Márquez** of Colombia. Many of his readers think that through the imaginary town of Macondo, the author tells the whole history of South America. In the novel, he mixes real life with events that are out of the ordinary. No one in Macondo finds it strange that it rains flowers one day or that for a time all the villagers lose their memories.

MUSIC AND CELEBRATIONS

South America's artistic tradition also includes music, dancing, and many different kinds of celebrations.

One of the best known examples of South American dance is the tango, the national dance of Argentina. A dramatic dance based on Spanish dances, the tango

 WHAT YOU KNOW: This question refers to information in Lesson 1; Indians; Spanish, Portuguese, French, Italians, English, and other Europeans; Africans.

READING STRATEGY AND VOCABULARY DEVELOPMENT

Summarizing Review the summarizing strategy. Have students preview the lesson before reading. Then have them choose one of the section heads, such as "Literature," and write a one-paragraph summary to share with the class. Review the summaries by having students evaluate them in terms of the number of important points that they include.

Many South Americans join Rio de Janeiro's Carnaval (*above*) and play or watch soccer. Argentina's soccer team (*left*), in blue and white, plays Trinidad's soccer team, in red uniforms.

is recognized internationally as a serious art form.

Another national dance, the samba of Brazil, has African roots. Every year in Rio de Janeiro, during a huge celebration known as Carnaval, different samba bands plan the parades. Band members decorate their own floats and gather dancers. The good times of Carnaval bring happiness to even the poorest people of Brazil and of many other South American countries. It is summed up in a recent Carnaval song: "You must find in imagination what you lack in your wallet."

SOCCER

South Americans are fans of many sports. Among the most popular sports are baseball, tennis, jai alai, and polo. Above all, though, South Americans love the game of soccer.

Soccer player João Nuñes de Oliveira (zhwou nün' yāz dā ol ə vâr' ə), known also as "Nuñes," says that Brazilian soccer is special.

> *When a Brazilian player gets hold of the ball, he does some wonderfully artistic and skillful things with it. He creates a special relationship between the man and the ball.*

ARTS AND SPORTS

Through literature, the arts, sports, and many other traditions, South Americans celebrate their heritage and share their culture with the world.

Check Your Reading

1. What is Carnaval?
2. Who is Gabriel García Márquez? What does he do?
3. Describe two South American dance forms.
4. **THINKING SKILL:** What do the photographs above tell you about the arts and recreation in South America?

THINKING SKILL: Observing

173

Discussing Music and Celebrations Emphasize the role that music and public celebrations have in giving the poorest South Americans a way to find enjoyment.

Ask students:

- **What are two dances of South America?** (the tango and the samba)
- **Why is the tango important in Argentina?** (It is the national dance and has been declared an international art form.)

Looking at Soccer Write the name João Nuñes de Oliveira on the chalkboard and ask students how many have ever heard of "Nuñes." Some may know of the Brazilian soccer star Pelé. Emphasize that soccer skills made these men world famous.

Applying the Lesson Have students write an imaginary story about a parade they attended during Carnaval. Have them include at least three new words from this lesson in the story.

3 CLOSE

Summarizing Students have learned that South Americans have given the world great cultural gifts in literature, arts, music, and sports. Have students list authors, musicians, and athletes from South America.

Evaluating Use the *Check Your Reading* questions (answers below) to assess students' understanding.

Answers to Check Your Reading

1. a huge national celebration
2. a Colombian writer of novels
3. The tango is a dramatic dance based on Spanish dances; the samba has African roots and is used in parades during Carnaval.
4. The people of South America are enthusiastic about sports and other recreational activities.

Independent Practice
Practice Book: page 43

MEETING INDIVIDUAL NEEDS

Reteaching (easy) Have students list all the South Americans named in this lesson. They should identify the work of each artist or athlete and draw a picture illustrating what they like about the work that interests them most.

Extension (average) Have students gather information about the New Orleans Mardi Gras and about Carnaval in South America. Have them write one paragraph about the ways they are the same and a second paragraph about the ways they differ.

Enrichment (challenging) Have students research the samba and the tango. Then have them draw a diagram showing the steps in each dance. Play tango and samba music so that students can hear the differences in their rhythms and sounds.

CHAPTER 7 REVIEW
pages 174–175

USING THE CHAPTER SUMMARY AND REVIEW

Cultural Geography These questions may be used for review.

- **Who were among the earliest people to live in South America?** (the Incas)
- **What is South America's economy based on?** (agriculture)
- **How are many of the countries of South America ruled?** (by dictators, juntas, or democracies)
- **Why is Carnaval important to the people of Brazil?** (Carnaval brings happiness for a time to even the poorest people of Brazil.)

Ideas to Remember

- **Which major ethnic groups settled South America?** (Indian, Spanish, Portuguese, African)
- **How are the nations of South America trying to develop their economies?** (by creating modern mining, manufacturing, and transportation systems)
- **Which South American country does not have a constitution requiring it to have a democratic government?** (French Guiana)
- **What is the national dance of Argentina?** (the tango)

Answers to Reviewing Vocabulary

1. junta
2. gaucho
3. per capita income
4. caudillo
5. coup

CHAPTER 7 • SUMMARY

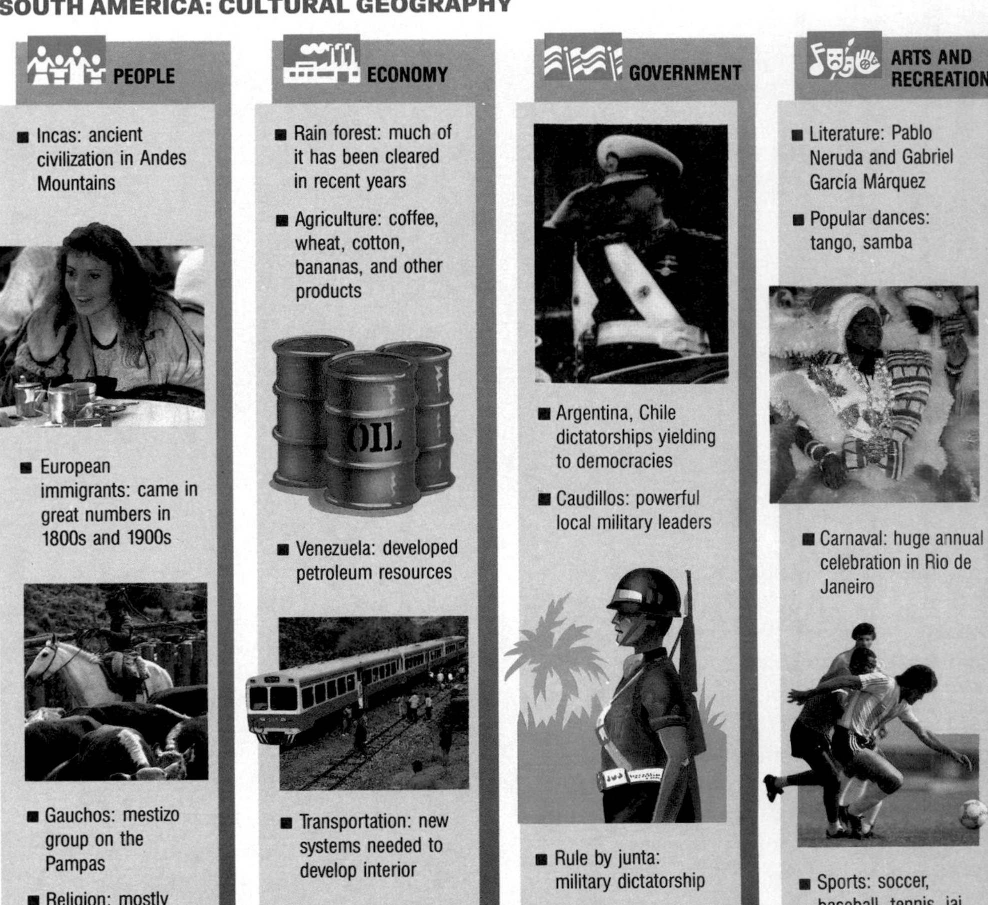

IDEAS TO REMEMBER

- Most of the people of South America are a blend of Indian, Spanish, Portuguese, and African ethnic groups.
- The nations of South America are trying to develop their economies by creating modern mining, manufacturing, and transportation systems.
- South American governments are marked by unrest.
- South American arts and recreational activities include literature, dances, Carnaval, and popular sports such as soccer.

174

ENRICHMENT ACTIVITY

Making Gaucho Neckerchiefs **Materials:** 36-inch unbleached muslin squares and permanent markers or 36-inch squares of old solid-color sheets and poster paints; pencils

1. Review with the class the picture of the gaucho on page 158 and the text on page 161. Point out that part of traditional gaucho clothing was a colorful scarf, worn around the neck. Neckerchiefs might be bright solid colors or fancy designs. Tell students that they will design and make their own gaucho neckerchiefs.
2. Tell students to work out designs, draw them on the cloth, and then fill in the colors their designs call for.
3. Discuss with students how practical items, like neckerchiefs, can become a symbolic part of traditional dress. Point out the similarities between gauchos' neckerchiefs and the bandannas worn by North American cowhands.

CHAPTER 7 • REVIEW

REVIEWING VOCABULARY

caudillo junta
coup per capita income
gaucho

Number a sheet of paper from 1 to 5. Beside each number write the word or term from the list above that best completes each sentence.

1. Control of the government by a ____, or small group of military officers, has been common in South America.
2. Similar to a cowboy of the American West, a ____ herds cattle on Argentina's Pampas.
3. The average yearly earnings per person, or ____, is generally low in the countries of South America.
4. In many countries of South America, inexperience in self-government led to harsh rule by a ____, a powerful local military leader.
5. Political instability in Latin America has often resulted in a ____, or sudden overthrow of a government.

REVIEWING FACTS

1. Which area of Brazil is being cleared for thousands of settlers who are looking for a better life?
2. Why did Venezuela's economy suffer during the 1980s?
3. Which South American leader became a dictator after becoming president of Argentina?
4. Why is it important for South American nations to develop orderly systems by which to change political leadership?
5. Which Argentine dance has become popular worldwide?
6. Why did Brazil build its new capital in the country's interior?
7. What is the dominant religion in South America?
8. What is the primary economic activity in South America?
9. Name five European countries that have contributed large numbers of immigrants to Argentina and Uruguay.
10. What are some topics often described by South American writers?

WRITING ABOUT MAIN IDEAS

1. **Writing a Summary:** Reread the description on page 171 of Juan Perón's rise to power in Argentina. Then write a summary of the events in Perón's political career.
2. **Writing About Perspectives:** If you were an Argentinian worker, why might you prefer to live under an elected leader instead of army rule? Write a letter in which you explain your position to a friend.

BUILDING SKILLS: DISTINGUISHING FACT FROM OPINION

1. Explain how a fact is different from an opinion. Write an example of each.
2. List some key words that indicate that an opinion is being expressed.
3. What are some steps you could take to distinguish a fact from an opinion?
4. When would it be helpful to be able to distinguish a fact from an opinion?

175

MAKING CONNECTIONS

Organizing Information Use the Semantic Map Graphic Organizer Transparency, writing in only the underlined headings. Ask students to fill in the map with important concepts about the cultural geography of South America. *Ask:* What factors make up the cultural geography of South America?

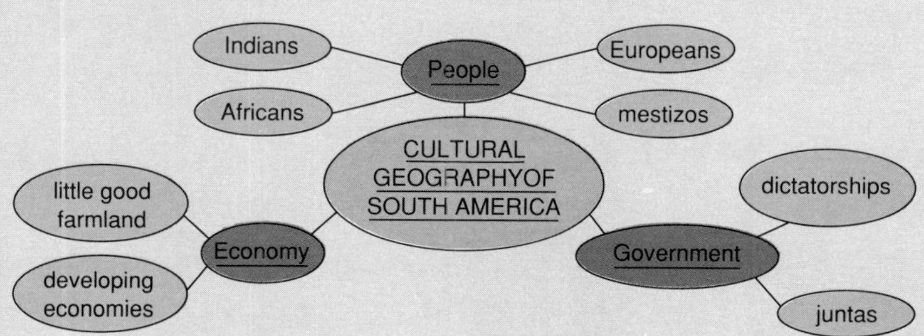

Answers to Reviewing Facts

1. Amazon rain forest
2. World oil prices fell.
3. Juan Perón
4. Through an orderly system, political change can be accomplished without unrest or a struggle for control.
5. the tango
6. as a first step toward settling the central part of Brazil
7. Roman Catholicism
8. agriculture
9. Italy, Spain, France, England, Germany
10. ethnic identity and poverty

Suggestions for Writing About Main Ideas

1. Students should include in their summaries his rise from junta member to president, his overthrow, and his reelection to the presidency.
2. Students' letters should compare the life of an average working person living in a country under military rule to that of life in a democracy.

Answers to Building Skills: Distinguishing Facts from Opinions

1. A fact can be proven to be true; statements of opinion cannot be proven to be true. Possible answers include: Fact—Brazil is in South America; opinion—South America is the best place to live.
2. *best, I think*
3. Look for clues to statements of fact; look for statements that can be proven to be true; look for clues to value judgments; look for clues to reasoned opinions.
4. when making a judgment about what you are reading

Chapter Review and Test
Practice Book: *Vocabulary Review,* page 44
Transparency: *Graphic Organizer*
Assessment Book: *Chapter 7 Test*

UNIT 2 REVIEW
pages 176–177

USING THE UNIT SUMMARY AND REVIEW

Physical Geography These questions may be used for review.

- **What are the three main river systems of South America?** (Amazon, Río de la Plata, Orinoco)
- **What are the three climate zones of the region?** (tierra caliente, tierra templada, tierra fría)
- **Which countries have large reserves of petroleum?** (Mexico and Venezuela)

Cultural Geography

- **When did Europeans first settle the region?** (in the 1500s)
- **What is needed to develop South America's interior?** (new transportation systems)
- **What types of governments are found in South America?** (rule by juntas, military dictatorships, representative democracies, communist dictatorships)
- **Which sports are popular in the region?** (soccer, baseball, jai alai, tennis, horseback riding)

UNIT 2 ▪ SUMMARY

LATIN AMERICA: PHYSICAL GEOGRAPHY

LANDFORMS

- High mountains (Andes) and vast river systems: Amazon, Río de la Plata, Orinoco

- Volcanoes: Popocatépetl
- Caribbean Islands: formed into archipelagos

CLIMATE

- Three climate zones:
  a) Tierra caliente ("hot land")
  b) Tierra templada ("temperate land")
  c) Tierra fría ("cold land")
- Largest rainy place in the world: Amazon River Valley
- Driest place in the world: Atacama Desert

NATURAL RESOURCES

- Gold, silver, tin, and other minerals
- Mexico and Venezuela: huge petroleum reserves
- Uneven distribution: some countries have many resources, some have few

LATIN AMERICA: CULTURAL GEOGRAPHY

PEOPLE

- First inhabitants were Indians: Mayas, Aztecs, and Incas had prominent ancient civilizations
- Europeans came, starting in the 1500s: Spanish, British, French, and Dutch
- Third and fourth streams of settlers: enslaved Africans and Asians
- Today: blend of Indian, European, and African people
- Religion: most people are Roman Catholics

ECONOMY

- Many countries have one-crop economies
- Mexico has rapidly growing population: Mexico City is world's largest metropolitan area
- South America: new transportation systems needed to develop the interior
- Crops: coffee, bananas, sugarcane, wheat, cotton, spices
- Brazilian rain forest: much of it has been cleared
- Venezuela: has developed petroleum resources

GOVERNMENT

- Return to democracy in Argentina
- Mexico: representative democracy, with strong rule by the president
- Cuba: communist dictatorship led by Fidel Castro
- Only a few European colonies left

ARTS AND RECREATION

- Many important painters, such as Diego Rivera and José Orozco
- Literature: famous writers such as Pablo Neruda and Gabriel Garcia Márquez
- Sports: soccer, baseball, jai alai, tennis, horseback riding
- Traditional crafts handed down from generation to generation

176

ENRICHMENT ACTIVITY

Creating a Picture Atlas **Materials:** construction paper, paints or markers, pens, yarn

1. If you had the class make a picture atlas of the United States and Canada for Unit 1, remind them of it and point out that it consists of illustrated maps bound together. Tell them that they are now going to make a picture atlas of Latin America.
2. Divide the class into five groups and assign each group one of the following: Mexico, Central America, Caribbean Islands, Northern South America, Southern South America.
3. Tell each group to draw illustrated maps of their areas on construction paper, showing important cities, rivers, landmarks, animals, occupations, products, and services. Tell them to use both the text and other books to find ideas. (National Geographic, *National Geographic Picture Atlas of Our World, 1993* is a good source.)
4. Have students make a cover for their atlas and bind it with yarn.
5. As mentioned on page 98, this activity may be combined with the activity at the end of Unit 1. If students decide to combine their atlases, have them make a "supercover"—Picture Atlas of the Western Hemisphere.

UNIT 2 • REVIEW

REVIEWING VOCABULARY

archipelago
coup
developing economy
dictator
junta
mestizo
metropolitan area
mural
per capita income
sect

Number a sheet of paper from 1 to 10. Beside each number write the word or term from the list above that matches the definition.

1. The average yearly income per person in a given country
2. A leader who assumes total control of a country, often by force
3. A large city with its surrounding towns and suburbs
4. Large work of art painted on building walls
5. The sudden overthrow of a government, often by army officers
6. A person of mixed Spanish and Indian ancestry
7. An island system such as the Caribbean Islands
8. Religious group other than mainstream religions
9. A country with very little industry and a strong dependence on agriculture
10. A type of military government that is often set up after a government is overthrown

WRITING ABOUT THE UNIT

1. **Writing an Explanation:** Look at the places in Latin America listed below. Which of them probably has the coldest climate? Explain why.
   a. a village in the Andes
   b. Brasília, the capital of Brazil
   c. San Juan, Puerto Rico
2. **Writing About Perspectives:** Write a dialogue between a Brazilian of African descent and one of Indian descent. Have them discuss whether the arrival of Europeans in the Americas was good or bad, in the long run.

ACTIVITIES

1. **Constructing a Bar Graph:** Make a bar graph to show the per capita income of five Latin American countries. After you have chosen five countries, look in encyclopedias or almanacs for the information you need to make the bar graph.
2. **Working Together to Research Volcanoes:** As a class, find out more information about the volcanoes of Latin America. Some members of the class may use the library to learn how volcanoes are formed, how and why they erupt, and how they become inactive. Other students may draw diagrams of the various volcanoes to illustrate the information.

LINKING PAST, PRESENT, AND FUTURE

For centuries the United States has focused its attention on the countries of Europe. Today many people believe that Latin America will soon replace Europe and Japan as the United States' main interest. What do you think of that opinion? Tell why you agree or disagree with it.

177

Answers to Reviewing Vocabulary

1. per capita income
2. dictator
3. metropolitan area
4. mural
5. coup
6. mestizo
7. archipelago
8. sect
9. developing economy
10. junta

Suggestions for Writing About the Unit

1. Students should answer: **a.** a village in the Andes. Their explanations should focus on the effect elevation has on temperature.
2. Students' dialogues should include an examination of the lives of Indians and Africans pre- and post-European conquest.

Suggestions for Activities

1. Students should use the most recent almanac or other source to find the most current per capita incomes for Latin America. You may wish to have students work in assigned groups to make sure all countries are researched.
2. You may wish to have a group of volunteers create a clay model of a volcano. Have them label the parts of the volcano.

Answers to Linking Past, Present, and Future Students should give reasons for their opinions. Some students may focus on economic, political, or social reasons.

PERFORMANCE ASSESSMENT

Demonstrating Understanding Remind students that at the beginning of the unit they were told they would have a chance to demonstrate what they have learned about Latin America by making a map. Before students begin, allow time for them to work in pairs studying the maps in their books and identifying the information from the unit they wish to include on their own maps. Have students work individually to make their maps. Ask them to draw their maps freehand without using any resources, including their textbooks. Suggest they use colored pencils to show the information they have chosen to include on their maps.

Remind students of the standards that will be applied to their maps, which were outlined in the Unit Opener on page 100. After students have completed their maps, have them compare these maps with the maps they made at the beginning of the unit. For additional performance assessment information, see page T42 in the *Assessment Book.*

For the Portfolio: Students' old and new maps should be included in their portfolios. Also include your anecdotal record or observational checklist.

UNIT 3 ORGANIZER

WESTERN EUROPE text pages 178–287

UNIT THEME

The relatively small region of Western Europe has 24 countries characterized by cultural diversity, democratic governments, and developed economies striving to unite in the 1990s.

UNIT RESOURCES

- Practice Book: pp. 45–78
- Anthology: Part 3
- Anthology Cassette
- Outline Maps: 1, 17–22
- Transparency Maps: 2, 9, 10, 11
- Unit 3 Poster
- Desk Maps
- Internet Project Handbook
- Geo Adventures Pad
- Pupil Edition on Cassette
- Transparency: Graphic Organizer
- **Technology:** *Videodisc/ Video Tape*
- **Technology:** *Adventures CD-ROM*
- Assessment Book, Chapter Tests: 8, 9, 10, 11, 12, 13

Internet CONNECTION

The Home Page at **http://www.mmhschool.com** and the **Internet Project Handbook** contain on-line student activities related to this unit.

UNIT PLANNING GUIDE

CHAPTER	SUGGESTED PACING	THEMES
8 PHYSICAL GEOGRAPHY OF WESTERN EUROPE pages 182–199	4 days	Located in the central latitudes of the Northern Hemisphere, Western Europe profits from a mild climate, rich soil, and navigable rivers.
9 THE BRITISH ISLES pages 200–215	6 days	The British Isles offer the world a great legacy of democratic rights in a parliamentary form.
10 FRANCE AND THE LOW COUNTRIES pages 216–231	6 days	The rich plains of France and the Low Countries promote swift transportation, specialized farming, and developed economies.
11 CENTRAL EUROPE pages 232–247	6 days	Central Europe is an industrial heartland united by language and religion.
12 COUNTRIES OF SOUTHERN EUROPE pages 248–269	7 days	Pride in an ancient cultural and religious heritage characterizes the countries of the Southern Europe.
13 SCANDINAVIA pages 270–285	6 days	Rugged Scandinavia and Finland have high standards of living and efficient governments.

UNIT PROJECTS

Writing a Diary Ask students to imagine they are traveling through one of the nations of Western Europe. They should write a diary entry about the land, people, economic activities, evidence of government, and arts and sports they see.

Oral Reports Have student pairs present interviews between a TV newscaster and a European worker on the European Union (EU).

Cooperative Learning: Making Cartoon Maps Have groups prepare large colorful maps showing the borders of the European nations. They should then attach diverse cartoons or sketches of people to characterize each nation.

Field Trip See a movie or a play that features life in Europe today. Afterward have students write three questions they have about Europe and then find answers to their questions in the library.

BULLETIN BOARD IDEAS

Making Your Own Bulletin Board Make a bulletin board display titled "Western Europe's Different Economies." Have students bring in relevant articles, illustrate them, and post their work in the appropriate section of the display. Ask volunteers to develop a section on the EU, including its history, new members, and future importance. Use the display in reviewing the unit on Western Europe.

Using the Unit Poster As an alternative to the bulletin board activity, display the Unit 3 Poster, which shows an enlarged version of the Unit Opener globe on pages 178–179.

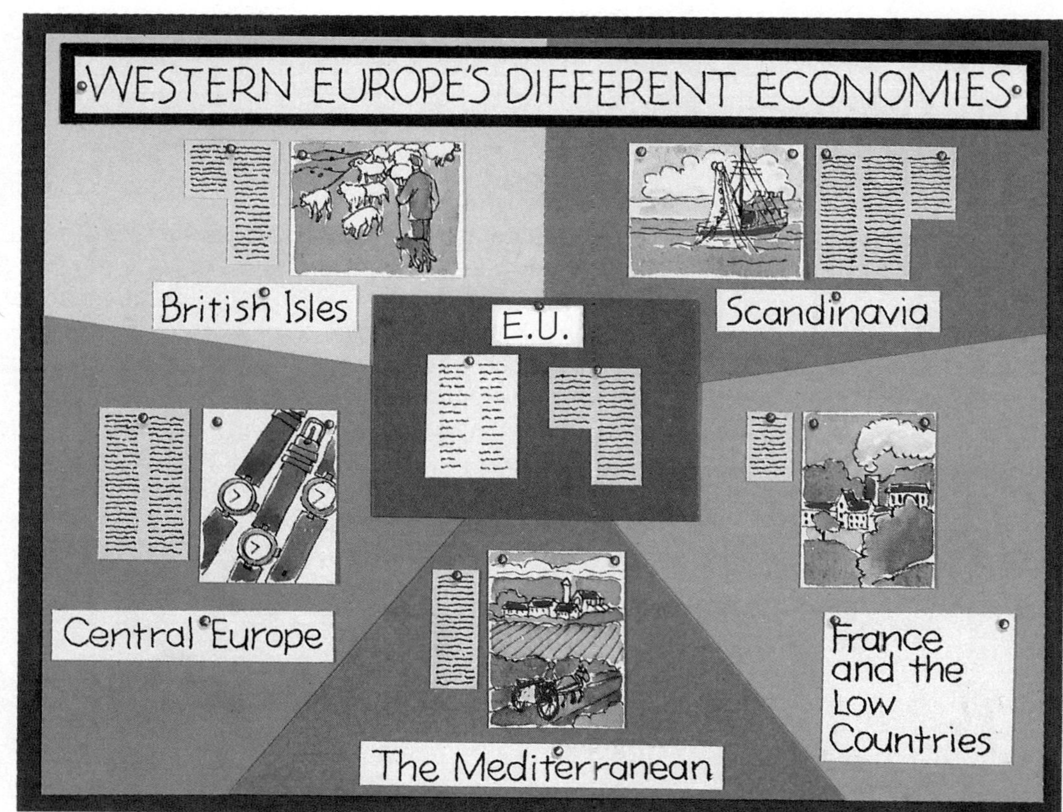

UNIT BIBLIOGRAPHY

For descriptions and additional resources, see the Annotated Bibliography beginning on page T-1 in the back of the book.

For the Teacher

Books

Biskup, Michael D., ed. *Europe.* San Diego, CA: Greenhaven Press, 1992.

Dunnan, Nancy. *One Europe.* Brookfield, Ct: Millbrook Press, 1992.

Read-Alouds

Vittorino, Domenico. *The Thread of Life: Twelve Old Italian Tales.* New York: Crown Publishers, Inc., 1995.

Williamson, Duncan. *Tales of the Seal People: Scottish Folk Tales.* New York: Interlink Books, 1992.

Technology Multimedia

■ *Europe.* Video. National Geographic. Toll Free: 1-800-368-2728.

France: Land and People. Video or Videodisc. Society For Visual Education. Toll Free: 1-800-829-1900.

Spain: Land and People. Video or Videodisc. Society For Visual Education. Toll Free: 1-800-829-1900.

Free Materials

For information on Britain, send to: British Information Services; Reference Section; 845 Third Avenue; New York, NY 10022.

For the Student

Dunford, Mick. *France.* New York: Thomson Learning, 1995. **(Average)**

Flint, David. *The United Kingdom.* Austin, TX: Steck-Vaughn, 1994. **(Average)**

Fradin, Dennis B. *The Netherlands.* Chicago, IL: Childrens Press, 1994. **(Average)**

Garrett, Dan. *Scandinavia.* Austin, TX: Steck-Vaughn, 1991. **(Average)**

Hollinger, Peggy. *Greece.* New York: The Bookwright Press, 1990. **(Easy)**

Osman, Karen. *The Italian Renaissance.* San Diego, CA: Lucent Books, 1996. **(Challenging)**

Pateman, Robert. *Belgium.* New York: Marshall Cavendish, 1995. **(Average)**

Stanley, Diane. *Bard of Avon: The Story of William Shakespeare.* New York: Morrow Jr. Books, 1992. **(Challenging)**

Symynkywicz, Jeffrey B. *Germany: United Again.* Columbus, OH: Silver Burdett Press, 1996. **(Challenging)**

■ National Geographic selection

UNIT 3
ORGANIZER

TEACHER EXCHANGE

Making and Playing Board Games

Thanks to:
Holli Kenley
Acacia Middle School
Hemet, California

Materials
index cards, art supplies, six colors of pencils or markers, dice, empty boxes

Instructions

1. Let students form groups to create a board game for each chapter in the unit.
2. Have group members use their books to develop 20 questions and answers for each of 6 categories, which may include vocabulary, geography, and text sections. Have students print the questions and answers on index cards and color code each card by category. Then have each group design a game board (see art below), playing pieces, and a storage box.
3. Explain that each player rolls a die to determine how many spaces to move in any direction. Other players ask a question from the color category upon which each player lands. If he or she answers correctly, the turn continues.
4. To win, a player must answer questions in each of the categories and land exactly in the hub. The opponents choose a category for the final question.
5. Have the groups exchange and play all of the games to review the unit.

Creating Travel Brochures

Thanks to:
DeLin DuBois
Cedar Hill Middle School
Cedar Hill, Texas

Materials
art supplies; travel magazines, brochures, newspaper articles; addresses of the closest tourism offices of European countries

Instructions

1. Ask groups of three or four students to each choose a major city in Western Europe for which they would like to design travel brochures.
2. Suggest to students that they can find information on such cities in the library, in travel articles, and at local travel agents. Students may also contact United States tourism offices of various countries.
3. Have each group construct an original travel brochure for its chosen city. Tell students that brochures should include information about the city's history, location, people, attractions, natural resources, industries, and traditions. They may add a slogan to sum up the attractions of their chosen city.
4. Let each group give a persuasive presentation to the class. Then ask students which cities they would most like to visit and the reasons therefor.

TECHNOLOGY CENTER

Enriching with Multimedia

RESOURCE: ***Internet Project Handbook***

Look at the ***Internet Project Handbook*** for student projects related to this unit or have students go on-line at http://www.mmhschool.com, Macmillan/McGraw-Hill's Home School page on the World Wide Web.

RESOURCE: ***Videodisc/Video Tape 3***

Enrich Unit 3 with the Videodisc *Renaissance* segment.

Search Frame 6339 Side B

SCHOOL-TO-HOME

Stamps of Nations

- Throughout this unit, students will have the opportunity to learn about the economies of the countries that make up Western Europe. They will also learn that three countries in this region produce stamps as their leading export. Discuss with students images and postal rates that appear on United States postage stamps. Then discuss images that might appear on stamps in the countries being studied.
- Provide each student with an oversized stamp consisting of a sheet of white drawing paper with pinked edges. Have students and their families design a stamp for a Western European country of their choice. They might also research true pictures on stamps from that country. Assemble a class "stamp collection" organized in a binder.

SECOND-LANGUAGE SUPPORT

While these activities are designed especially for students needing second-language support, they are meant to be shared by all students in the class.

Chapter 8, Lesson 2 ■ Physical Geography of Western Europe

Helping second-language students to understand cause-and-effect relationships in this lesson will improve their comprehension. List some effects, such as high precipitation and cold winters, and have pairs of students skim to find their causes.

Chapter 9, Lesson 3 ■ The British Isles

To explain the concept of *constitutional monarchy* to second-language students, conduct a guided reading of the section "Traditions of Rule." Have the class brainstorm a table: Differences Between the American and British Governments.

Chapter 10, Lesson 2 ■ France and the Low Countries

Working in committees to master sections of this economics lesson will help second-language students organize the large amount of information. Assign several groups of students particular sections on which to give oral/visual presentations.

Chapter 11, Lesson 2 ■ Central Europe

Ask groups of students to create a brochure advertising an industry described in the lesson.

Chapter 12, Lesson 2 ■ Countries of Southern Europe

Assign student committees sections of the lesson for group reading. Encourage better readers to help less proficient ones. Have committees create a semantic map or other visual aid about a particular industry.

Chapter 13, Lesson 3 ■ Scandinavia

To help students organize information, have groups prepare a review puzzle, word game, or some other fun way to review this lesson on government.

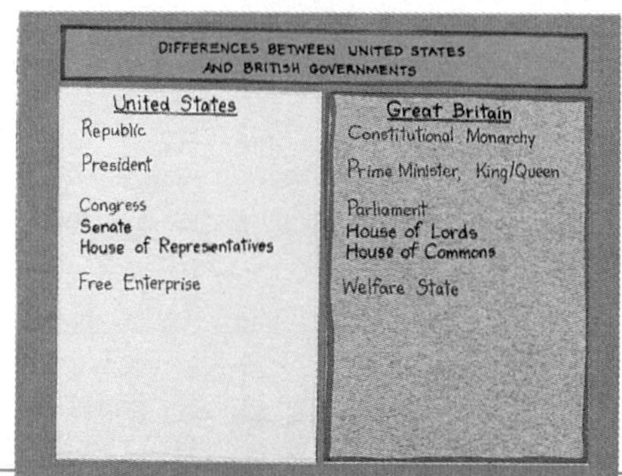

Chapter 9, Lesson 3

UNIT 3 ORGANIZER

UNIT 3

pages 178–287

USING THE UNIT OPENER

Introducing the Unit Have students look at the unit title and silently read the *Where We Are* section on the facing page.

Ask students:

- **What is this unit about?** (Western Europe)
- **Is most of Western Europe located in the Eastern Hemisphere or the Western Hemisphere?** (the Eastern Hemisphere)
- **Which five areas make up the region called Western Europe?** (the British Isles, France and the Low Countries, Central Europe, Southern Europe, Scandinavia)

EXTENDING MAP SKILLS

Help students to become aware of how observation of detail is an important focus in map reading.

Ask students:

- **What is striking about the shape of Europe?** (all the indentations, irregularities, and peninsulas around the coast of Western Europe as compared with other landmasses on this map, such as Africa)
- **Which mountain ranges stand out when you look at this map of Western Europe?** (two mountain ranges in Southern Europe and one mountain range in Scandinavia)
- **Which major bodies of water border Western Europe?** (Mediterranean Sea, Atlantic Ocean, North Sea, Arctic Ocean, Baltic Sea)

PHY • GEOGRAPHY • GEOGRAPHY

NORTH AMERICA
North Pole
ARCTIC OCEAN
Arctic Circle
Barents Sea
SCANDINAVIA
THE BRITISH ISLES
North Sea
Baltic Sea
ATLANTIC OCEAN
FRANCE AND THE LOW COUNTRIES
CENTRAL EUROPE
SOUTHERN EUROPE
ASIA
Black Sea
Caspian Sea
Mediterranean Sea
Tropic of Cancer
60°N
45°N
30°N
30°W
15°W
0°
AFRICA
15°N
INDIAN OCEAN
Equator
45°E
60°E
15°S
Tropic of Capricorn

178

ONGOING UNIT PROJECT

Planning for Assessment Tell students that in this unit they will learn about the geography and the culture of Western Europe. Say that when they finish the unit they will prepare a magazine about one of the regions. Encourage students to collect articles and pictures about Western Europe. Students will write their own articles and captions to accompany the pictures. For information on completing this unit project, see page 287.

Goal: Students' work should show that they understand the cultural diversity, democratic governments, and developed economies that are characteristic of Western Europe.

Signs of Success: Tell students that an adequate magazine would reflect the geography, economy, and culture of the region. An excellent magazine would also reflect the current government situation and regional current events.

Y • GEOGRAPHY • GEOGRAPHY • GEOGRAPHY • GEOGRAPHY • GEOGRAPHY • GEOGRA

WESTERN EUROPE

WHERE WE ARE

You have read about the regions of the Western Hemisphere. It is now time to journey to the Eastern Hemisphere, on the other side of the globe. You will start with Western Europe, a region that is small in size but, as you will read in the following chapters, of great importance.

As the map shows, Western Europe is divided into five areas—the British Isles, France and the Low Countries, Central Europe, Southern Europe, and Scandinavia. Let's look at the physical geography of this compact region and at the way of life of the people who live there today.

Continue the discussion.

Ask students:

- **In which hemispheres is Western Europe located?** (the Northern, Eastern, and Western hemispheres)
- **Which key line of longitude runs through Western Europe?** (0°, or the prime meridian)
- **Which Western European countries does the prime meridian cross?** (England, France, Spain)

Comparing Regions Have students refer back to the map in Unit 1 on pages 34 and 35 and to the one in Unit 2 on pages 100 and 101 and compare them with the map of Western Europe on pages 178 and 179. Ask students to write at least three sentences comparing the three regions shown on these maps. (Possible answers include: Western Europe is a much smaller region than the regions of the United States and Canada, and the Latin American region; Western Europe is a peninsula on the large landmass of Eurasia, but the other two regions each include a whole continent; Western Europe is mostly in the Eastern Hemisphere, and the other two regions are in the Western Hemisphere.)

5 FUNDAMENTAL THEMES OF GEOGRAPHY

Movement Have students study the map above to find places where ships would have to navigate narrow passages in order to move around Western Europe. (the English Channel between England and France; the Strait of Gibraltar between the Mediterranean Sea and the Atlantic Ocean) Tell students that the Strait of Gibraltar is a "choke point," a place where ships can be watched or fired upon from shore.

- In ancient times the high rocks on each side of this passage were called the "Pillars of Hercules."
- The British took the northern rock, the Rock of Gibraltar, located on the European side, from the Spanish in 1704.
- During the American Revolutionary War, the British withstood a four-year-long siege when the Spanish attempted to retake Gibraltar. High on the Rock of Gibraltar, the British won by firing hot cannonballs that made the Spanish ships catch fire.
- During World War II the British stationed on the Rock of Gibraltar guarded Allied supply lines in and out of the Mediterranean and continue to track ship movements today.
- Many important military movements took place on the English Channel. In 1066 Norman warriors crossed the channel from France to invade England. In 1944 the Allies crossed the channel to invade France.

Introducing the Table Have students skim the table on Western Europe and tell how many of the countries they have heard of and what they know about them.

EXTENDING TABLE SKILLS

Point out to students that tables such as this one give much information in a small space. They also allow comparisons to be made because of the information they include. Stress that drawing conclusions from numbers alone can be deceiving. Encourage students to think about the meaning behind the numbers.

Ask students:

- **How many Western European nations are represented in this table?** (24)
- **What general statement can you make about the languages that are spoken in Western Europe?** (Many countries have their own language.)
- **Which languages are most frequently spoken in the countries of Western Europe?** (German and French)
- **Which countries have German as a major language?** (Austria, Germany, Liechtenstein, Luxembourg, Switzerland)
- **Which countries have French as a major language?** (France, Luxembourg, Belgium, Monaco, Switzerland)
- **Which countries have English as a major language?** (Republic of Ireland, Malta, United Kingdom)
- **What other information should we compare before drawing the conclusion that more people speak German and French than any other languages in Western Europe?** (Possible answer: Countries vary in size of population, so we should add up the population figures for each set of countries to determine whether more people speak German, French, or English.)

AY • LIFE TODAY • LIFE TODAY • LIFE TODAY • LIFE TODAY • LIFE TODAY • LIFE TODAY • LIFE T

WESTERN EUROPE

ANDORRA
Capital ★ Andorra la Vella

Major languages: Catalan, French, and Spanish
Population: 64,000
Area: 174 sq mi; 450 sq km
Leading exports: tobacco products and furniture

AUSTRIA
Capital ★ Vienna

Major language: German
Population: 7.9 million
Area: 32,375 sq mi; 83,850 sq km
Leading exports: iron and steel products, and machinery

BELGIUM
Capital ★ Brussels

Major languages: Dutch and French
Population: 10.1 million
Area: 11,779 sq mi; 30,510 sq km
Leading exports: machinery, and iron and steel products

DENMARK
Capital ★ Copenhagen

Major language: Danish
Population: 5.2 million
Area: 16,629 sq mi; 43,070 sq km
Leading exports: food and machinery

FINLAND
Capital ★ Helsinki

Major languages: Finnish and Swedish
Population: 5.1 million
Area: 130,128 sq mi; 337,030 sq km
Leading exports: paper and machinery

FRANCE
Capital ★ Paris

Major language: French
Population: 57.8 million
Area: 211,209 sq mi; 547,030 sq km
Leading exports: machinery and manufactured goods

GERMANY
Capital ★ Berlin

Major language: German
Population: 81.1 million
Area: 137,803 sq mi; 356,910 sq km
Leading exports: machinery and manufactured goods

GREECE
Capital ★ Athens

Major language: Greek
Population: 10.6 million
Area: 50,942 sq mi; 131,940 sq km
Leading exports: fruits and vegetables, and textiles

ICELAND
Capital ★ Reykjavik

Major language: Icelandic
Population: 0.3 million
Area: 39,768 sq mi; 103,000 sq km
Leading export: fish

IRELAND
Capital ★ Dublin

Major languages: English and Irish
Population: 3.5 million
Area: 27,135 sq mi; 70,820 sq km
Leading exports: machinery and food

ITALY
Capital ★ Rome

Major language: Italian
Population: 58.1 million
Area: 116,305 sq mi; 301,230 sq km
Leading exports: machinery and manufactured goods

LIECHTENSTEIN
Capital ★ Vaduz

Major language: German
Population: 30,000
Area: 62 sq mi; 160 sq km
Leading export: stamps

180

BACKGROUND INFORMATION

Why Ministates Sell Stamps Because of their limited natural resources, three tiny countries in Western Europe make stamps their leading export. Have students find these countries in the table and list them on the chalkboard.

- Philatelists, or stamp collectors, visit these countries to get first editions and to trade stamps.
- Tourism is important to the economies of these countries.

Have students discuss the idea that human or cultural activities may be as valuable as material natural resources, such as minerals and energy sources. Ask them to think of other cultural activities that can bring economic gain to a country. (Britain's "export" of the Beatles, American rock groups on international tours, and so on)

TODAY • LIFE TODAY • LIFE TODAY • LIFE TODAY • LIFE TODAY • LIFE TODAY • LIFE TODAY • LIFE

LUXEMBOURG
Capital ★ Luxembourg
Major languages: Letzeburgesch, German, and French
Population: 0.4 million
Area: 998 sq mi; 2,586 sq km
Leading exports: iron and steel products

MALTA
Capital ★ Valletta
Major languages: Maltese and English
Population: 0.4 million
Area: 123 sq mi; 320 sq km
Leading exports: machinery and clothing

MONACO
Capital ★ Monaco
Major languages: French and Monégasque
Population: 31,000
Area: 0.7 sq mi; 1.9 sq km
Leading export: stamps

NETHERLANDS
Capital ★ Amsterdam
Major language: Dutch
Population: 15.4 million
Area: 14,405 sq mi; 37,310 sq km
Leading exports: machinery, chemicals, and manufactured goods

NORWAY
Capital ★ Oslo
Major language: Norwegian
Population: 4.3 million
Area: 125,182 sq mi; 324,220 sq km
Leading exports: oil and natural gas

PORTUGAL
Capital ★ Lisbon
Major language: Portuguese
Population: 10.5 million
Area: 35,552 sq mi; 92,080 sq km
Leading exports: machinery, manufactured goods, and timber

SAN MARINO
Capital ★ San Marino
Major language: Italian
Population: 24,000
Area: 23 sq mi; 60 sq km
Leading exports: stamps, lime, and wood

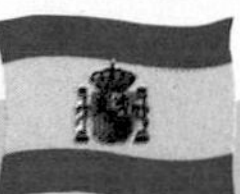

SPAIN
Capital ★ Madrid
Major languages: Spanish and Catalan
Population: 39.3 million
Area: 194,884 sq mi; 504,750 sq km
Leading exports: iron and steel products, and manufactured goods

SWEDEN
Capital ★ Stockholm
Major language: Swedish
Population: 8.8 million
Area: 173,730 sq mi; 449,960 sq km
Leading export: machinery

SWITZERLAND
Capital ★ Bern
Major languages: German, French, Italian, and Romansh
Population: 7.0 million
Area: 15,942 sq mi; 41,290 sq km
Leading exports: machinery and chemicals

UNITED KINGDOM
Capital ★ London
Major language: English
Population: 58.1 million
Area: 94,525 sq mi; 244,820 sq km
Leading exports: machinery and manufactured goods

VATICAN CITY
Capital ★ Vatican City
Major languages: Italian and Latin
Population: 821
Area: 0.17 sq mi; 0.44 sq km

181

Continue the discussion.

Ask students:

- **If you knew nothing about Western Europe, how would this table tell you that this is a region of highly developed industrial economies?** (The table shows that more than half of the nations sell machinery or iron and steel products as a leading export.)
- **What products are major exports of countries that do not have machinery or iron and steel products as a major export?** (stamps; fruits and vegetables; textiles; fish; oil; and natural gas)
- **Which country has the larger population, Sweden or the Netherlands?** (the Netherlands)
- **Which country is larger in area, Sweden or the Netherlands?** (Sweden)
- *THINKING FURTHER:* **What might one reason be that the smaller country has the larger population?** (Encourage students to think of reasons that the population of the Netherlands outnumbers that of Sweden: warmer climate, more land that is good for farming, more cities.)

CURRICULUM CONNECTION

Math The power of a nation can often be seen in its population. By using methods like ranking and classifying, we can get a better feeling for what the statistics of a region mean. Tell students to list the populations of the Western European countries in order, from largest to smallest.

Have students study their ranked lists of populations. Ask them what kind of groupings they see in the numbers. Have them suggest classes of number ranges. These are the obvious groupings that the numbers fall into.

- 55–75 million and above
- 10–55 million
- 3–10 million
- 300,000–500,000
- 20,000–65,000
- under 1,000 (only Vatican City)

Give students these groupings, and ask which one has only one country in it. (See list above.)

CHAPTER 8
ORGANIZER

PHYSICAL GEOGRAPHY OF WESTERN EUROPE

text pages 182–199

CHAPTER THEME

Located in the central latitudes of the Northern Hemisphere, Western Europe profits from a mild climate, rich soil, and navigable rivers.

CHAPTER OBJECTIVES

CONTENT

- Describe the main geographic features of Western Europe.
- Identify the five major peninsulas of Western Europe and name the countries found on each peninsula.
- Define *fjord* and name the country where most fjords are found.
- Explain how Western Europe's long coastline and good harbors have made the region a "world crossroads."
- Compare the average population density of Western Europe with that of the United States.
- Describe how the Gulf Stream and Atlantic winds influence the climate of Western Europe.
- Explain how the Alps and Pyrenees affect the climate of southern Europe.
- Describe the effects of acid rain on the forests of Western Europe.

SKILLS

Geography
- Interpret an elevation map of Western Europe.
- Analyze maps showing map projections and distortions.

Thinking
- Compare the landforms of the northern and southern regions of Western Europe.
- Ask focused questions about the climate of Scandinavia.

Reading and Writing
- Write a letter to a European pen pal asking about her or his country.

CITIZENSHIP VALUES

- Appreciate the value of geographic diversity.
- Appreciate the importance of free and open debate of public issues.

TEACHER OPTIONS

READING STRATEGY: Study Guide Strategies to help students read and remember the main ideas of the lesson.
Lesson 1: p. 183 Lesson 2: p. 192

MEETING INDIVIDUAL NEEDS Activities for reteaching, extension, and enrichment.
Lesson 1: p. 187 Lesson 2: p. 197
Geography Skills: p. 189

GEO ADVENTURES ACTIVITIES PAD Daily activities to assess students' understanding of geography skills.

CURRICULUM CONNECTION Activities to help integrate other subject areas with Social Studies.
Math: p. 186

PUPIL EDITION ON CASSETTE Language support for students who have difficulty reading or who will benefit from listening to the Pupil Edition on Cassette as they read.

SECOND-LANGUAGE SUPPORT Activities and suggestions for second-language learners.
Lesson 2: p. 15

CHAPTER PLANNING GUIDE

LESSON	SUGGESTED PACING	THEMES	TEACHER SUPPORT MATERIALS: TEACHER'S RESOURCE CENTER
1 LANDFORMS pages 183–187	1 day	Although they occupy a small region, the 24 Western European nations have a great variety of landforms.	Practice Book p. 45 Outline Map p. 17 **Technology:** *Adventures CD-ROM*
BUILDING GEOGRAPHY SKILLS Understanding Map Projections pages 188–191	1 day	Because all flat maps have at least one kind of distortion, care must be taken in choosing the right projection for a particular kind of use.	Practice Book p. 46 Transparency Map 10
2 CLIMATE AND RESOURCES pages 192–197	1 day	Western Europe benefits from a mild climate, rich soil, and navigable, ice-free rivers.	Practice Book p. 47 Outline Map p. 17 **Technology:** *Adventures CD-ROM*
CHAPTER SUMMARY AND REVIEW pages 198–199	1 day	Chapter content, skills, and vocabulary are reviewed and evaluated.	Practice Book p. 48 Transparency: Graphic Organizer Assessment Book, Chapter 8 Test

Technology CONNECTION

Lesson 1
ADVENTURES CD-ROM
Have students find some of Western Europe's highest mountain ranges in *Explore.*

Lesson 2
ADVENTURES CD-ROM
Enrich this lesson with the climographs available under *Charts,* in *Investigate.*

CHAPTER 8

pages 182–199

USING THE CHAPTER OPENER

Discussing the Photograph One of the striking things about this photograph is the contrast between the small Alpine village and its setting of majestic mountains. In spite of the possibility of winter storms and avalanches, the village looks very cozy and secure.

Ask students:

- **What do you think the villagers do for a living?** (farm, work in a nearby hotel)
- **Would you enjoy visiting this village?** (Encourage students to imagine visiting this village.)
- **What might you do there?** (ski, mountain climb, ice-skate, sightsee)
- **What structure do you usually picture dominating a European village?** (Students might suggest a castle.)
- **What do you think the bigger buildings in this village might be?** (Possible answers include rich people's houses, hotels.)
- *THINKING FURTHER:* **What does the presence of several hotels in such a small town suggest about the way the people of this area make a living?** (They serve tourists.)

Reading/Listening to the Primary Source Read the passage aloud. Tell students to list all the words or phrases in the reading that refer to Europe. (*mystery, challenge, puzzling, problem, temptation, delight*) Ask them how these words make them feel about studying this region.

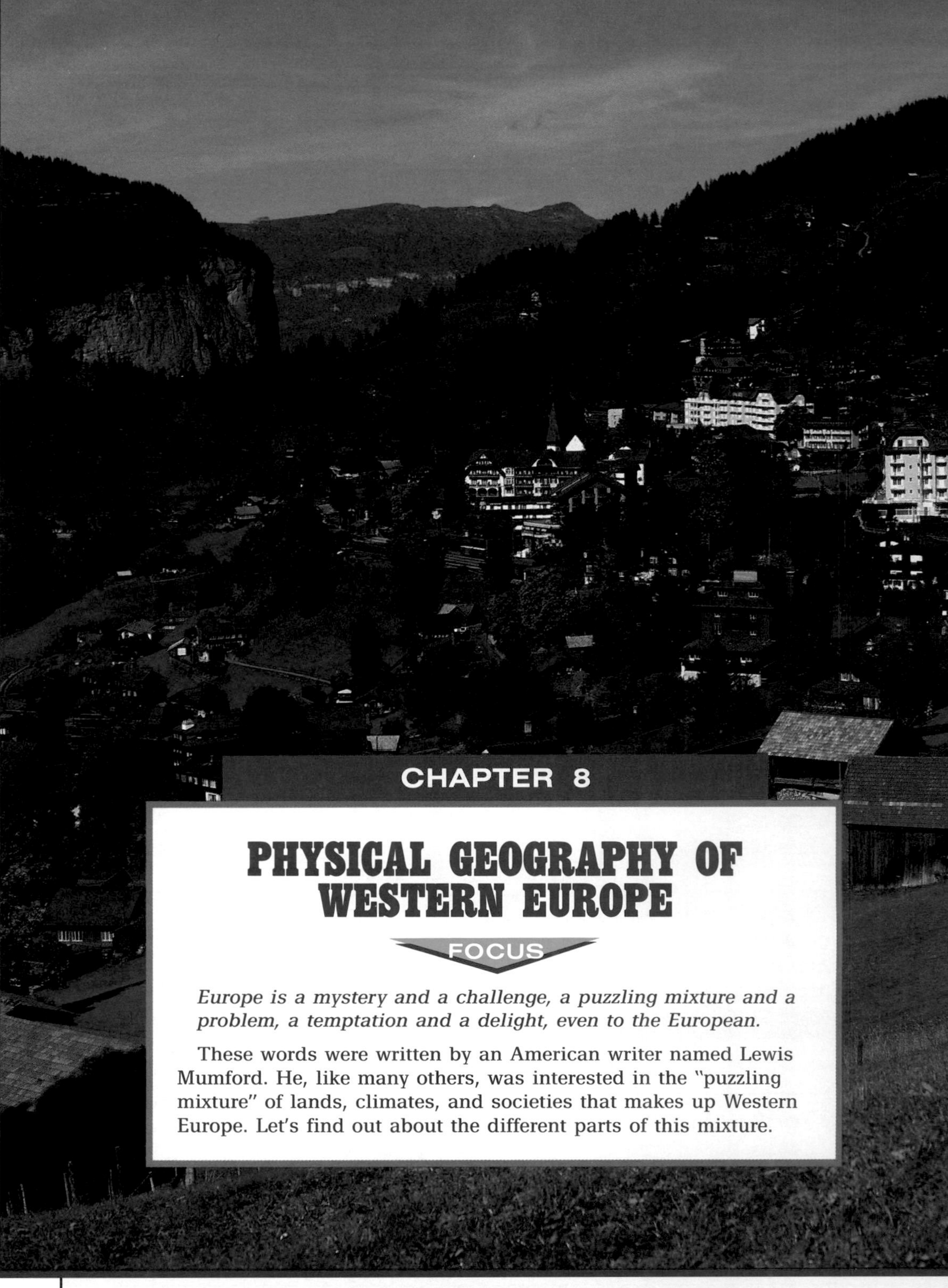

CHAPTER 8

PHYSICAL GEOGRAPHY OF WESTERN EUROPE

FOCUS

Europe is a mystery and a challenge, a puzzling mixture and a problem, a temptation and a delight, even to the European.

These words were written by an American writer named Lewis Mumford. He, like many others, was interested in the "puzzling mixture" of lands, climates, and societies that makes up Western Europe. Let's find out about the different parts of this mixture.

BACKGROUND INFORMATION

About the Photograph Commonly perceived as a quaint scene suitable for a picture postcard, the rural Alpine village is also evidence of the qualities of perseverance and carefulness that are necessary to farm such a rugged terrain.

- Although agriculture plays only a small part in Switzerland's total economic picture, the Swiss government considers it important enough to offer its citizens such inducements as higher prices for farm products in order to encourage them to remain on the land.
- Although Swiss farms are small (only about 30 percent are larger than 25 acres [10.13 ha]), they produce 60 percent of the nation's food. Their productivity is due to abundant rainfall and the Swiss farmers' efficient cultivation of the limited farmland.

LESSON 1

Landforms

READ TO LEARN

Key Vocabulary

fjord

Key Places

Scandinavian Peninsula
Jutland Peninsula
Iberian Peninsula
Italian Peninsula
Balkan Peninsula
British Isles
Low Countries

Read Aloud

On the opposite side of the ship, so near that a [person] could swim it, was Europe! I had no idea whether it was France, Belgium, England, Italy, or perhaps even one of the Scandinavian coasts, but it glistened in the dawn, and seemed so clean and peaceful. This was Europe and I, a child from a prairie state, was looking at it with my own eyes!

These words were written by a young American sailor as he first gazed at the continent of Europe. In this lesson you will learn that Europe is a land of great geographical variety, from tall mountains to flat farmlands, from sparkling blue lakes to rushing mountain streams. As you read on, try to imagine that you are seeing Europe for the first time "with your own eyes."

Read for Purpose

1. WHAT YOU KNOW: What are some of the major landforms of the earth?
2. WHAT YOU WILL LEARN: What are the main geographic features of Western Europe?

A SMALL REGION

Look at the map of Western Europe on page 626 of your Atlas. You can see that it is a small region. In fact, it is the smallest region that you will study in this book. It covers slightly more than 1,431,826 square miles (3,708,430 sq km). That means that it is less than half the size of the United States. But unlike the United States, Western Europe is divided into many different countries. As you read this lesson, think about how the geography of Western Europe might have contributed to the creation of so many nations.

THE SHAPE OF THE LAND

Many thousands of years ago, glaciers covered all of northwestern Europe. These thick sheets of ice inched slowly forward, crushing the land under their enormous weight. As the ice moved, it smoothed hills and mountains, polished rocks, and deepened valleys.

About 10,000 years ago the ice began to melt. As sunshine warmed the land, trees and grass grew and covered huge areas. Birds, animals, and fish moved into this new wilderness. So did people. As they settled every part of the continent, they

WHAT YOU KNOW: Students should respond with some of the earth's major types of landforms, such as mountains, plains, plateaus, and basins.

LESSON 1
pages 183–187

Lesson Theme Although they occupy a small region, the 24 European nations have a great variety of landforms.

Lesson Objectives

- Describe the shape and elevations of European lands.
- Understand how Europe's long coastline has helped it develop its economy.
- Describe Europe's population distribution.

PREPARE

Motivate Read the *Read Aloud* to the class. Ask students why they think the American sailor was so excited about seeing Europe. (perhaps because it's the source of much of our cultural heritage)

Set Purpose Use the *What You Know* question to start a discussion of landforms. Display the Wall Map of Western Europe and ask students to make up questions using the *What You Will Learn* question.

TEACH

Looking at a Small Region Tell students that Western Europe is the smallest of the regions covered in this book.

Ask students:

- **How big is Western Europe compared to the United States?** (less than half the size of the U.S.)

Discussing the Shape of the Land Remind students that the Arctic Islands and Scandinavia both have features formed by glaciers. Encourage them to remember what these are. (fjords)

READING STRATEGY AND VOCABULARY DEVELOPMENT

Study Guide Review note taking, outlining, and summarizing as methods of study. Show students how a Know-Want-Learn (KWL) guide can help them find their way through new material. Focus on the section "A Long Coastline." Using the first category, *What I Know*, elicit students' prior knowledge about lands that have easy access to the sea. Develop the category *What I Want to Know* by encouraging students to pose such questions as, "Why is a greater variety of cultures found in a coastal city than in an inland city?" After students have read the section, have them complete the process by filling in the last category, *What I Have Learned*. Point out how asking questions before reading the section has helped them read it more attentively.

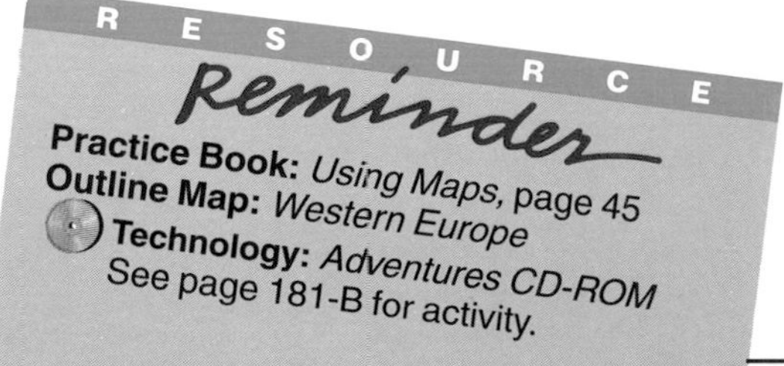

Looking at the Shape of the Land

Continue discussing the shape of the land.

Ask students:

- **What are the two main shapes of European landmasses?** (peninsulas and islands)

EXTENDING MAP SKILLS

Have students study the elevation map on this page.

Ask students:

- **Find the highest mountain in Western Europe and name the mountain range in which it is located.** (Mont Blanc; the Alps)
- **Which of the European mountain ranges are the highest?** (the Alps and the Pyrenees)
- **Where is the elevation generally higher, in northern or southern Europe?** (in southern Europe)
- **Which European island lies the farthest west in the Atlantic Ocean?** (Iceland)

Locating a Peninsula of Peninsulas

Have students use the map on this page to note Western Europe's location relative to the world's other major landmasses.

Ask students:

- **Of which continent is Europe a peninsula?** (Eurasia)
- **Which five large bodies of water surround the European peninsula?** (the Atlantic Ocean, the North Sea, the Baltic Sea, the Mediterranean Sea, the Arctic Ocean)
- **What advantage have these waterways given Europe?** (They have made the movement of people, goods, and ideas easier.)

MAP SKILL: Which is at a generally higher elevation, the United Kingdom or Spain?

learned how to use the resources of this large and lovely land.

The shape of the land of Western Europe can be divided into two main landforms: peninsulas and islands. Let's find out about each of them.

A PENINSULA OF PENINSULAS

If you look at the map above, you will see that most of Western Europe is a giant peninsula jutting out from a huge land area. Geographers call this large area Eurasia (ū rā′ zhə). As you might have guessed, the name *Eurasia* comes from combining the words *Europe* and *Asia*.

184

MAP SKILL: Spain

BACKGROUND INFORMATION

More About Continental Drift

- The shape of Europe was formed when the supercontinent Pangaea broke up. At first North America and Eurasia were one piece; later they split apart. The fact that coal beds running through the eastern United States match coal seams in Scotland is evidence that North America and Europe were once joined.
- The high elevations of the Alps and of the southern European volcanoes, such as Vesuvius and Mount Etna, are caused by the African Plate subducting under the Eurasian Plate and pushing up parts of Eurasia.
- The movement of the plates in the Mediterranean region is not fully understood. Earthquakes and volcanic eruptions frequently occur there.

To the west of Western Europe lies the Atlantic Ocean. Among the other large bodies of water that surround the continent are the Arctic Ocean, the North Sea, the Baltic Sea, and the Mediterranean Sea. Over the years Europeans have used these waterways as transportation routes to the rest of the world.

Not only is Western Europe itself a large peninsula, but it also contains many smaller peninsulas. Several long pieces of land jut out from the northern and southern sides of the continent. To the north the **Scandinavian Peninsula** is made up of Norway and Sweden. To the south is the much smaller **Jutland Peninsula**, which includes Denmark. Together, these two peninsulas are known as Scandinavia. Extending southward into the Mediterranean Sea are three other peninsulas. One of these, the **Iberian Peninsula**, contains the countries of Spain and Portugal.

Can you find the two other peninsulas on the map? First find the piece of land that is shaped like a long boot. This is called the **Italian Peninsula** because it contains the country of Italy.

Finally, east of Italy lies the **Balkan Peninsula**, on which lies the country of Greece. Some people think that Greece is shaped like a large hand. The pieces of land that extend from the mainland remind them of long fingers.

THE ISLANDS OF WESTERN EUROPE

Western Europe also includes many islands. Rising out of the Atlantic Ocean in the north is Iceland. To the south, and closer to the mainland, lie the **British Isles**. The English Channel cuts the British Isles off from the rest of Europe.

The Mediterranean Sea also contains several large islands. The three largest are Corsica, Sicily, and Sardinia.

A LONG COASTLINE

Because of its many peninsulas and islands, Western Europe has thousands of miles of coastline. Look at the map on the opposite page. Find France and the **Low Countries**—Belgium, the Netherlands, and Luxembourg. The coastline of three of these countries—France, Belgium, and the Netherlands—stretches for more than 600 miles (965 km).

In some parts of Europe, the coastline is rugged. For example, the western coast of

Many of the islands of Western Europe are located in the Mediterranean Sea. This one, Mykonos Island, is in Greece.

Exploring a Peninsula of Peninsulas
Continue discussing Europe as a complex of peninsulas.

Ask students:

- **Which two peninsulas make up Scandinavia?** (the Scandinavian and Jutland peninsulas)
- **Which three peninsulas extend into the Mediterranean Sea?** (Iberian, Italian, Balkan)
- *THINKING FURTHER:* **What is Europe's location in relation to the rest of Eurasia?** (It is on Eurasia's western coast.)

Identifying the Islands of Europe
Help students to understand that the clusters of islands off the European coastline are considered parts of Europe.

Ask students:

- **Which body of water separates the British Isles from Europe?** (the English Channel)
- **Identify the three largest islands in the Mediterranean Sea.** (Sicily, Corsica, and Sardinia)

Understanding a Long Coastline
Help students to understand the importance of a long coastline to a nation's trade and culture.

Ask students:

- **Identify the physical features that add length to Western Europe's coastline.** (peninsulas and islands)
- *THINKING FURTHER:* **Why do you think that Belgium, the Netherlands, and Luxembourg are called the Low Countries?** (Students will notice on the map on page 184 that most of the Low Countries are at or below sea level.)

FUNDAMENTAL THEMES OF GEOGRAPHY

Movement Europe's long coastline with many bays has made it easier for people, goods, and ideas to move through that continent. Have students research the imports and exports of France and Switzerland and then write reports explaining the differences in the two countries' patterns of trade.

Appreciating the Advantages of a Long Coastline Continue the discussion of Europe's coastline.

Ask students:

- **What is distinctive about the coast of Norway?** (It has fjords.)
- **What is the location of all the land of Europe in relation to the sea?** (No point lies more than 300 miles [480 km] from the sea.)
- **Name two factors that have made Europe a world crossroads.** (nearness to the sea; many bays that form naturally protected harbors)

EXTENDING MAP SKILLS

Have students study the population density map on this page.

Ask students:

- **How many European cities shown are located on a coast?** (11)
- **Where do most Europeans live?** (in or near the cities)

Talking About Population Help students to connect the information on the population density map with that in the text.

Ask students:

- **About what fraction of the European population is found in or near cities?** (three fourths)
- **Compare the population density of Western Europe with that of the United States.** (*U.S.:* 71 persons per square mile [27 per sq km]; *Europe*: 265 persons per square mile [102 per sq km])

Norway is cut by great bays and long **fjords** (fyôrdz). A fjord is a deep, narrow inlet of the sea between high cliffs.

Because of Western Europe's long coastline, most people do not live far from the sea. In fact, there is no spot within this entire region that is more than 300 miles (480 km) from a seacoast.

Many port cities have developed along the bays on Europe's coastline. These bays form naturally protected harbors where people can load and unload goods from ships easily.

MAP SKILL: Which is more heavily populated, Central Europe or Scandinavia?

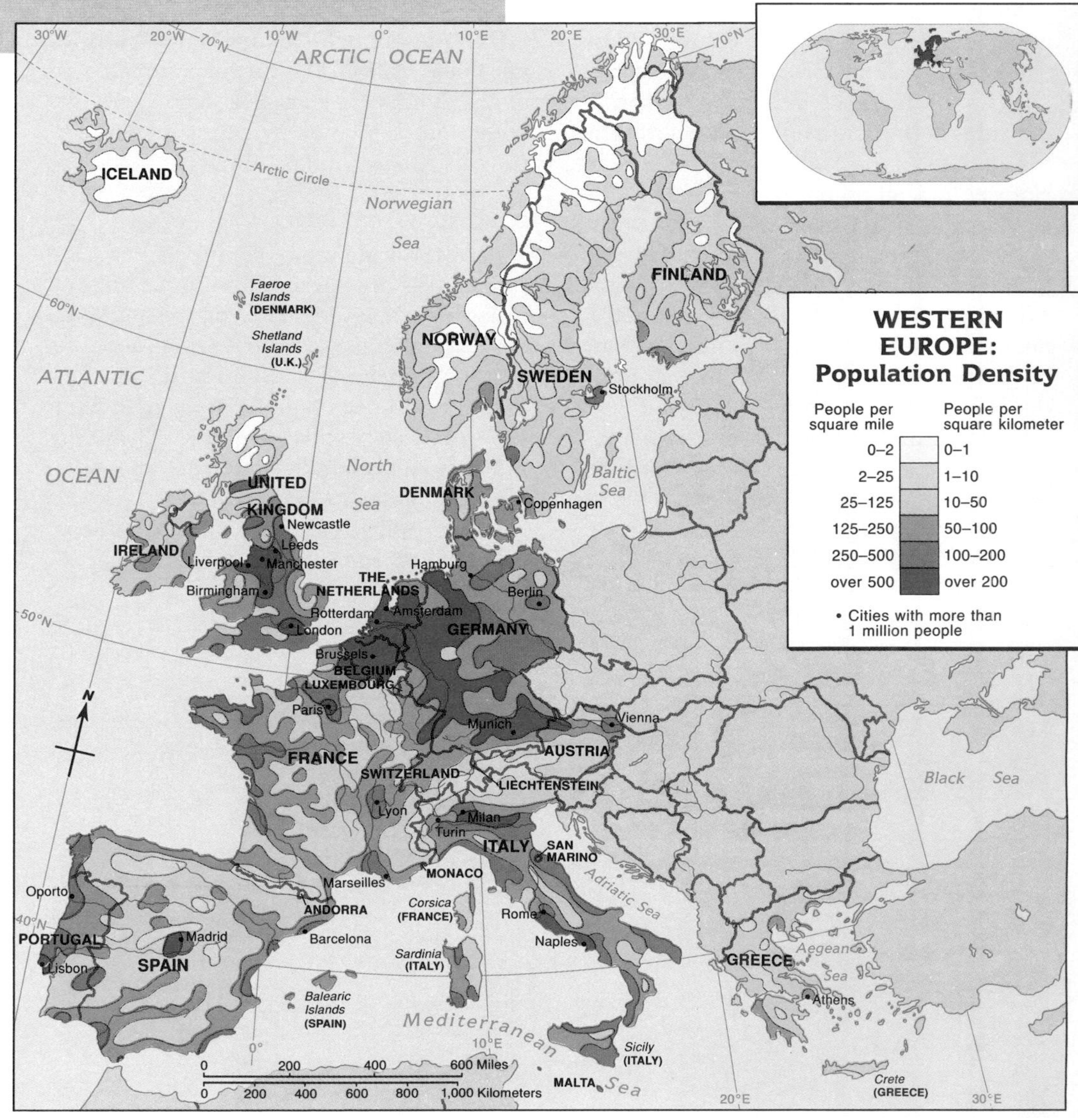

MAP SKILL: Central Europe

CURRICULUM CONNECTION

Math To make the meaning of "number of people per square mile" more concrete, have students make models showing the Western European and United States population densities as expressed by that phrase. Students will need markers that each represents a specific number of people, and two square sheets of paper to represent square miles in Western Europe and square miles in the United States. Once they have decided which sheet of paper will represent Western Europe and which the United States, they can place the appropriate number of markers in each to show that in Western Europe each square mile contains 265 people, while in the United States each square mile contains only 71 people. Ask students to divide the number of people per square mile in Western Europe by the number of people per square mile in the United States to discover the ratio between the two. (about 4 to 1) Display the models and discuss them with the class.

Because Western Europe has many good bays and harbors, and because it is so close to the sea, the region has become a world crossroads. Throughout their history, Western European people have used the sea to transport their products and their ideas all over the globe. At the same time, Western Europe has absorbed other products and ideas from many of the world's other cultures.

POPULATION

Although Western Europe is small in size, it has many people. Over 370 million people live in this compact region.

Look at the map on the opposite page. This map shows you where people live in Western Europe. The population density of this region is about 265 people per square mile (102 people per sq km). You read in Chapter 2 that the United States has a population density of about 71 persons per square mile (27 people per sq km). These figures should tell you that little land in Western Europe is uninhabited.

As you may have guessed, most of Western Europe's people live in urban areas. Almost three fourths of all Western Europeans live in or near cities.

Look again at the population density map. It shows the cities of Western Europe that have more than 1 million people living in them.

A LAND OF MANY WONDERS

You have read that Western Europe is a land of peninsulas and islands. Although it is a small region, it is divided into many countries by its mountains, rivers, and seas. Yet these same mountains, rivers, and seas have not created barriers between the different parts of the land. Over the years Western Europe has developed into a region where people can move, trade, and share ideas with ease.

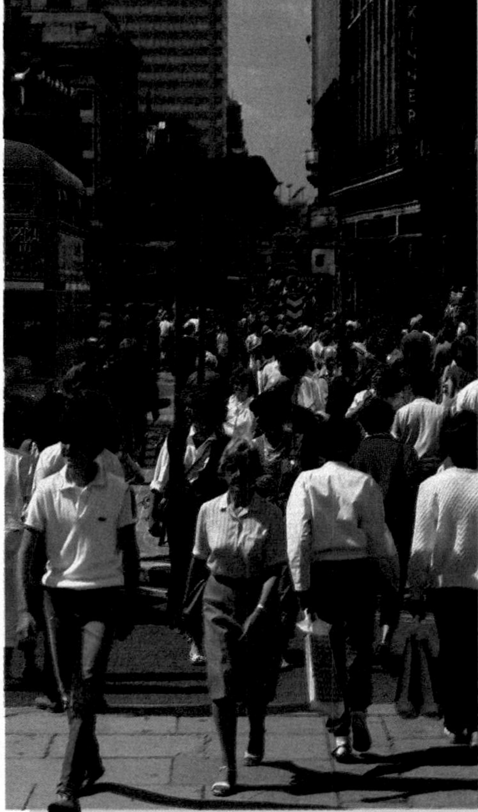

London is one of the most densely populated cities in Western Europe.

Check Your Reading

1. Name three peninsulas found in Western Europe.
2. What has the long coastline of Western Europe meant to the region throughout its history?
3. How would you describe the shape of the land that makes up the countries of Western Europe?
4. THINKING SKILL: Look at the map on page 184. Compare and contrast the elevations of France and Norway.

THINKING SKILL: Compare and Contrast

Applying the Lesson Give students the outline map of Europe (from the Teacher's Resource Center) and the following instructions: Find the political map of Europe in the *Atlas*. Using this map for reference, label the nations, the major bodies of water, and the mountain ranges of Western Europe. Keep the labeled outline maps handy for reference during your study of Unit 3.

3 CLOSE

Summarizing Students have learned about the variety of land shapes, the elevations, and the population distribution in Western Europe. Remind them that easy movement by water is available to most European countries in the region.

Evaluating Use these questions to assess students' understanding.

- **How would you describe the general shape of Western Europe?** (Possible answers include: "variously shaped peninsulas with islands sprinkled around the edges.")
- **What is the greatest advantage of Europe's long coastline?** (It allows easy movement of people, goods, and ideas.)
- **Where are there more people per square mile, in Western Europe or the United States?** (in Europe)

Answers to Check Your Reading

1. Jutland, Scandinavian, Italian, Iberian, Balkan
2. easy movement of people, goods, and ideas into and out of Europe
3. peninsulas and islands
4. Norway has more land above 1,500 feet (500 meters) while France has more land from 0 to 1,500 feet (0 to 500 meters).

Independent Practice
Practice Book: page 45

MEETING INDIVIDUAL NEEDS

Reteaching (easy) Have students draw a map of Europe from memory and then label the peninsulas and the four major bodies of water. Have them compare their maps to the *Atlas* map on page 627.

Extension (average) Have students compare the population density map on page 186 and the elevation map on page 184. Tell them to list the conclusions they draw from this comparison and then encourage them to discuss their conclusions.

Enrichment (challenging) Have students turn to the *Atlas* on page 622 and compare the map of the United States with the map of Western Europe on page 626. Remind them that the United States is one country, while Europe is divided into more than 24 countries. Ask them to write an article explaining the geographical reason for this difference.

SKILLS LESSON
pages 188–189

Lesson Theme Because all flat maps have some area of distortion, care must be taken in choosing the right projection for a particular kind of use.

Lesson Objectives
- Describe the kinds of distortion in map projections.
- Compare cylindrical and equal-area projections.

PREPARE

Motivate Have students look at the maps on these two pages and describe what is the same and what is different about them. Discuss which map looks more like a globe. If possible, project Transparency Map 10.

Set Purpose Tell students they will learn about some of the problems that mapmakers face when trying to show the round globe on a flat surface.

TEACH

Understanding Distortion and Projection Point out to students that all flat maps have some distortion.

Ask students:

- **What are some of the errors that can be found in different kinds of flat maps?** (errors in size, shape, distance, and/or direction)
- **Why have mapmakers developed so many different kinds of projections?** (They are constantly trying to find better and less distorted ways to show places on the earth on a flat map.)

BUILDING SKILLS
GEOGRAPHY SKILLS

Understanding Map Projections

Key Vocabulary
distortion
projection
cylindrical projection
equal-area projection

You can learn about the geographic features of Western Europe by looking at a globe. Because a globe is a sphere like the earth, it can show the earth accurately. All the countries that appear on the globe are in correct proportion to one another.

Distortion and Projection

Maps are less accurate representations of the earth than globes. Imagine trying to flatten a globe. You would have to cut or stretch some parts of the earth, causing **distortions**, or errors in size, shape, distance, and or direction.

Mapmakers solve the problem of distortion by using **projections**. A projection is a way of showing locations on the earth on a flat map. The people who make maps have developed many different kinds of projections.

Cylindrical Projection

One common type of map projection is called a **cylindrical projection**. On a cylindrical projection distances measured along the equator are correct because there is little distortion in the areas near the equator. Distortion increases as you move toward the poles.

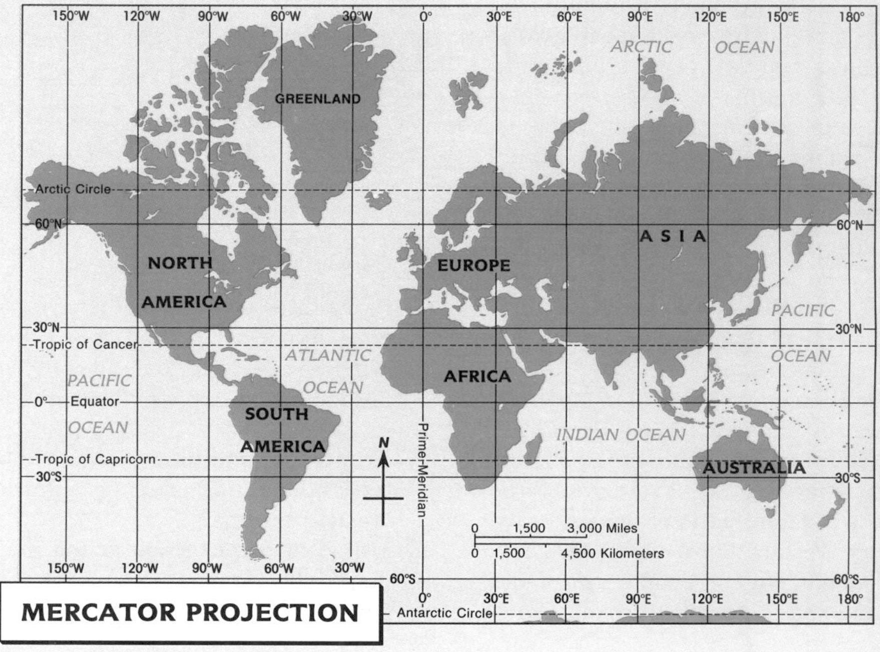

MERCATOR PROJECTION

188

BACKGROUND INFORMATION

Map Projections There are many types of map projections that a cartographer may use. It is important to know what kind of projection is used on a map in order to know what distortions exist. The following are some projections in use.

- *Miller Cylindrical*—sizes of areas are not as exaggerated as on a Mercator projection; shapes are shown inaccurately.
- *Lambert Equal Area*—shows accurate sizes and true shapes of land areas; distances are distorted increasingly as you go away from the center of the map.
- *Goode's Interrupted*—shows fairly accurate shapes and sizes of landmasses; distances are distorted across water.
- *Eckert*—shows correct sizes of landmasses; inaccurate shapes.

RESOURCE *Reminder*
Practice Book: *Understanding Map Projections*, page 46
Transparency Map: 10

ROBINSON PROJECTION

The Mercator projection on page 188 is an example of a cylindrical projection. Notice that the island of Greenland, which is actually much smaller than the continent of Africa, appears almost as large as Africa on the map. Remember that Greenland appears distorted in size because it is located near to the North Pole.

On cylindrical maps north is always directly toward the top of the map, east is to the right, west is to the left, and south is toward the bottom. Cylindrical projection is useful to navigators of ships, who use it to draw their ships' courses in straight lines.

Equal-area Projection

Another type of projection is called an **equal-area projection**. On equal-area maps sizes and shapes are shown fairly accurately, and distances are nearly correct. For these reasons, equal-area projections are useful when different places on the earth are compared.

The Robinson projection on this page is an example of an equal-area map. Find Greenland on this map and compare it to Africa. Notice that Greenland is shown as smaller than Africa.

On this Robinson projection only the lines of latitude are always drawn as straight lines. Other than the prime meridian, all the lines of longitude are curved. As a result, north is not always in a straight line to the top of the map.

Reviewing the Skill

1. What is a map projection? What is distortion?
2. Which kind of map would be most useful to someone who wants to compare the size of two continents?
3. Why is it useful to understand different kinds of map projections?

189

Identifying Cylindrical and Equal-Area Projections Stress that each projection is suited for a particular kind of use.

Ask students:

- **Which areas are accurate and which are distorted on a cylindrical projection?** (Distances along the equator are accurate and those toward the poles are distorted.)
- **For whom are Mercator projections the most useful?** (navigators of ships)
- **What is the best use for an equal-area projection?** (to compare different places on earth)
- **How is north represented on a cylindrical projection compared with on an equal-area projection?** (North is always toward the top of a cylindrical projection, whereas on an equal-area projection, it is not always toward the top of the map.)

Applying the Skill Ask students to compare Greenland and South America on the Mercator projection on page 188. (Greenland looks larger.) Then have students compare them on the Robinson projection on page 189. Have students estimate how many Greenlands would fit into South America on the Robinson projection. Discuss distortion in the two maps.

CLOSE

Summarizing Students should understand that the globe is the only true model of the earth and that flat maps are distorted. Have students make a chart comparing cylindrical and equal-area map projections.

Answers to Reviewing the Skill

1. A map projection is a way of showing a location on the earth on a flat map. Map distortions are errors in size, shape, distance, and/or direction on a flat map.
2. equal-area projection
3. to be able to use the right map for the right purpose

Independent Practice
Practice Book: page 46

MEETING INDIVIDUAL NEEDS

Reteaching (easy) Give each student a ball and a flat sheet of modeling clay. Have students work the modeling clay until it can be wrapped around the ball like a skin. Then have them engrave the shapes of the world's continents on the clay. Ask them to remove the clay in one piece and spread it out. Have students write a brief description of what happens to the continents when the clay is spread out flat.

Extension (average) Have students research these three types of map projections: Eckert, Good's Interrupted, and Lambert Equal Area. Have them make a chart showing the pros and cons of each.

Enrichment (challenging) Have students think about why most maps show Europe as the center of the world. Give students copies of the article "Reflections on the Gall-Peters' Projection" from the April/May 1987 issue of *Social Education* and ask them to summarize the article.

CHAPTER 8
CITIZENSHIP Viewpoints
pages 190–191

Lesson Objective

- Analyze and compare contrasting points of view on the future of nuclear power in Europe.

Identifying the Issue Help students to see that concerns about scientific knowledge, environmental safety, and economics affect attitudes towards nuclear power.

Suggested Question

- ***Why is the use of nuclear energy as a power source an issue in Europe today?*** *(Although nuclear power is widely used in Europe today, scientists and environmental activists disagree about its safety and environmental impact.)*

Discussing Three Different Viewpoints Have students read the viewpoints on page 191.

BAS BRUYNE

Suggested Question

- ***What is the "difficult choice" for Europeans according to Bruyne?*** *(While nuclear power is an energy source that is plentiful and does not rely on Middle East oil supplies, Bruyne believes it is not safe for humans or the environment.)*

PETER HOLT

Suggested Question

- **What does Holt say are benefits of nuclear power?** *(It reduces reliance on oil as a fuel source, reduces the risk of global warming, and causes less pollution than the burning of fossil fuels.)*

EMMY ROOS

Suggested Question

- ***Why does Roos believe many European nations will continue to rely heavily on nuclear power?*** *(They lack alternative energy sources.)*

CITIZENSHIP VIEWPOINTS

Steam escapes the cooling towers of this nuclear plant in Yorkshire, England.

WHAT IS THE FUTURE OF NUCLEAR POWER IN EUROPE?

Today nuclear power plants supply around one-third of Europe's electricity. The use of nuclear power varies though, from France, where it meets 75 percent of the nation's energy needs, to less than 10 percent in the Netherlands. Supporters of nuclear power, like Peter Holt, say that it is an abundant, reliable source of energy which does not cause air pollution, unlike such fossil fuels as coal, gas, and oil. Supporters also point out that reserves of oil, gas, and coal will not last forever.

Opponents of nuclear power, such as Bas Bruyne, point to its health hazards. A major accident in 1986 at a nuclear power plant in Chernobyl in the former Soviet Union made many Europeans fearful of building new nuclear plants. Nuclear waste remains radioactive and dangerous for thousands of years and cannot be destroyed. Such waste must be buried. Scientists continue to look for safer ways to dispose of radioactive waste, but some fear that accidents may yet occur. Emmy Roos and others feel that it is up to individual nations to decide whether to develop nuclear power. Consider three viewpoints on this issue and answer the questions that follow.

190

BACKGROUND INFORMATION

About Nuclear Power Scientists say that burning fossil fuels like coal, oil, and gas may lead to global warming, an increase in Earth's average temperature caused by the trapping of heat within the Earth's atmosphere as a result of the presence of large amounts of carbon dioxide, chlorofluorocarbons, and other substances in the atmosphere.

The Chernobyl nuclear power plant, located about 80 miles from Kiev in Ukraine, suffered a meltdown of its nuclear fuel. A radioactive cloud spread over most of Europe, contaminating crops and livestock.

The primary waste from nuclear power generation is the spent fuel from nuclear reactors. It is radioactive and some of its components remain radioactive and highly dangerous for many thousands of years.

Three DIFFERENT Viewpoints

1 BAS BRUYNE
Environmental activist, Netherlands
Excerpt from interview, 1996

Nuclear power poses a difficult choice for Europeans, between a secure form of electricity and enormous risks to human health and the environment. The accident at Chernobyl, the impossibility of dealing with all the radioactive waste nuclear power produces, and the increasing evidence that exposure to radioactivity poses long-term dangers suggest that nuclear power has no future in Europe.

"... nuclear power has no future in Europe."

2 PETER HOLT
Editor, Switzerland
Excerpt from interview, 1996

Nuclear power produces one third of Western Europe's electricity and helps protect against oil crises and against the global warming and air pollution that results from burning fossil fuels. Wind, sea wave, and sun energy can only make a small contribution. Water power resources are at their limits. So, nuclear energy should have a long-term future in Europe. Politically, however, a difficult decade lies ahead, because governments and the public act short-term.

"... nuclear energy should have a long-term future in Europe."

3 EMMY ROOS
Public Relations Specialist, Belgium
Excerpt from interview, 1996

Each European nation has its own energy policy. In some, such as France, nuclear power is very important, mainly because France lacks natural resources. In other countries, nuclear energy has little future, either because the country has its own gas, oil, or coal or because citizens strongly oppose building new plants. For half of European nations, nuclear energy is a significant energy resource and cannot be cast aside in energy policy.

"Each European nation has its own energy policy."

BUILDING CITIZENSHIP

1. What is the viewpoint of each person?
2. In what ways are some of the viewpoints alike? In what ways are they different?
3. What other viewpoints might people have on this issue?

SHARING VIEWPOINTS

Discuss what you agree with or disagree with about these viewpoints. Discuss why each speaker might feel as he or she does. As a class, write three statements that all of you can agree with about the future of nuclear power in Europe.

CITIZENSHIP

Using Current Events Concern over disposal of toxic waste and low level nuclear waste have led to opposition to nuclear power plants in the United States as well as Europe. Many people who favor the use of nuclear energy as a power source are nonetheless resistant to having power plants or waste products disposal sites in their communities. Writers have called this reaction the NIMBY (Not In My Backyard) effect. Check the national and local papers for any disputes over hazardous waste disposal and bring in clippings for class discussion and debate.

EVALUATE

Answers to Citizenship Viewpoints

1. Bruyne believes nuclear power has no future because it is unsafe and an environmental hazard. Holt says nuclear power's future in Europe is unclear in the short term because of public opposition to it, but is brighter in the long term. Roos says nuclear energy will be essential to about half of all European nations in the future, because they lack alternative energy resources.
2. Bruyne and Holt agree that nuclear power is a secure energy source and all three agree that some public opposition exists to building new nuclear power plants. Bruyne says nuclear power hurts the environment, while Holt says the effect is positive. Bruyne and Holt disagree on its future, while Roos takes a middle ground position.
3. Other viewpoints might include believing that new technologies are making nuclear plants and waste disposal safer, advocating outlawing nuclear power, or putting greater emphasis on reducing energy consumption and/or developing alternate energy sources.

Sharing Viewpoints Encourage students to express their own viewpoints and to identify the costs and benefits of nuclear energy. Have students decide whether benefits outweigh costs. Three statements the class might agree on include: **1.** Nuclear power has both risks and benefits. **2.** In some countries, opposition by citizens to nuclear power is strong. **3.** Scientific advances may someday change the way we think about nuclear power.

Debating Viewpoints As an extension, have students research and debate nuclear energy vs. fossil fuels or nuclear energy vs. such alternative energy sources as solar or geothermal power. Debate can focus on the availability, practicality, expense, and safety of each as a primary power source.

LESSON 2
pages 192–197

Lesson Theme Western Europe benefits from a mild climate, rich soil, and navigable, ice-free rivers.

Lesson Objectives
- Identify Western Europe's climates.
- Describe Western Europe's natural resources.
- Identify the advantages of Western Europe's waterways.

1 PREPARE

Motivate Ask students to keep their books closed, and read the first two sentences of the *Read Aloud* to them. Ask students to answer the question in the second sentence by making a list of the kinds of clothes they would pack. Read the rest of the *Read Aloud*, and tell students that they may want to change their lists at the end of the lesson.

Set Purpose Ask students the *What You Know* question and discuss their answers. Point out that the answers to the *What You Will Learn* question supplement the information about the effect of elevation on climate contained in the last lesson.

2 TEACH

Understanding Oceanic Climate Remind students that two places located in the same latitude do not always have similar climates, because factors other than latitude can affect the climate of a location.

Ask students:

- **What are two main influences on the climate most typical of Western Europe?** (the Gulf Stream and Europe's nearness to the ocean)

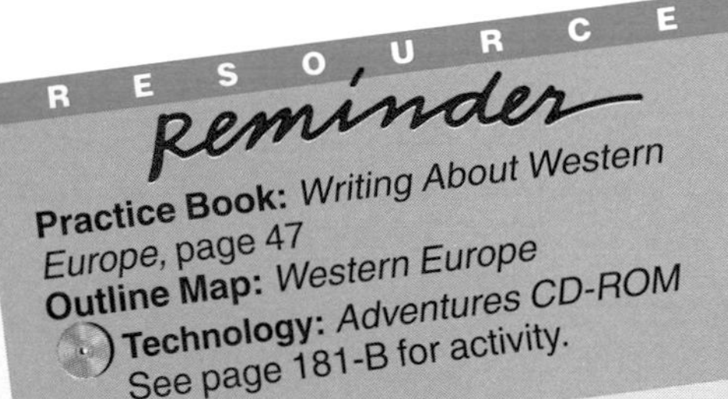
RESOURCE Reminder
Practice Book: *Writing About Western Europe, page 47*
Outline Map: *Western Europe*
Technology: *Adventures CD-ROM*
See page 181-B for activity.

LESSON 2

Climate and Resources

READ TO LEARN

Key Vocabulary	**Key Places**
Gulf Stream	Danube River
landlocked	Rhine River

Read Aloud

Imagine that you are planning a trip to Great Britain and Ireland this winter. What kinds of clothes would you pack? Looking at a globe, you might think that the weather in the British Isles would be about the same as it is in Canada. After all, London is in the same latitude as the southern shore of Hudson Bay. But, as you will see, you would be very surprised.

Read for Purpose

1. WHAT YOU KNOW: How would you describe the land of Western Europe?
2. WHAT YOU WILL LEARN: How does the climate vary in different parts of Western Europe?

AN OCEANIC CLIMATE

If you actually visited Great Britain and Ireland, you would find that the climate there is much warmer than Canada's. In January, London is about as warm as Washington, D.C., which is almost 900 miles (1,450 km) south of Canada's Hudson Bay.

The main reason for this difference in climate is a special "river" that flows in the Atlantic Ocean. It is called the **Gulf Stream**. The Gulf Stream brings warm water from the Gulf of Mexico to the Atlantic coast of Europe. The photograph on page 193 shows what the Gulf Stream looks like from miles above the earth.

Western Europe's climate is mild also because the ocean waters off its Atlantic coast heat up in summer and cool off in winter more slowly than the land does. In winter, winds blowing off the Atlantic Ocean warm coastal areas. In summer ocean breezes keep places near the coast cooler than the inland areas. Look at the climate map on page 194. In which areas do you think the climate is affected by ocean breezes? ✻

Ocean winds also bring plenty of rain to the coastal areas of Western Europe. Every year these areas get more than 20 inches (50 cm) of precipitation.

In the northern part of Western Europe, the moderating effect of the Gulf Stream and the Atlantic Ocean is not nearly as strong. As a result, the winters are long, cold, and snowy. In northern Sweden and most of Finland, the ground is covered with snow, and temperatures are very cold for several months of the year.

WHAT YOU KNOW: This question refers to material covered in Lesson 1; a land of peninsulas and islands.

✻ Most of the coastal areas indicated as "Mild winter, cool summer, wet" are warmed by ocean breezes.

READING STRATEGY AND VOCABULARY DEVELOPMENT

Study Guide Remind students that a Know-Want-Learn (KWL) guide can help them master new material. Review the process of using this strategy with "An Oceanic Climate." Beginning with the *What I Know* category, encourage students to describe a London winter as being foggy and without much snow. Develop the *What I Want to Know* category by first reminding them that London is in the same latitude as the southern shore of Hudson Bay, and then by encouraging them to question why it is colder in the Hudson Bay area than in London. After they have read "An Oceanic Climate," have them complete the last step, *What I Have Learned*, by answering the question. Divide the class into groups and have each group devise a similar KWL guide for each of the remaining sections in the lesson.

A completely different type of climate is found in the southern part of Western Europe. You can see from the climate map that Portugal, Spain, Greece, and Italy have mostly hot summers and mild winters. Two mountain ranges, the Alps and the Pyrenees, prevent Atlantic breezes from reaching this area. This explains why summers are mostly sunny and dry and winters are usually mild or even warm in Southern Europe. Every winter tourists from the rainy or snowy countries of northern Europe flock to Spain and Italy to enjoy the blue seas and warm, sandy beaches of these countries.

Although Western Europe has different climate regions, the weather in the region is generally temperate. Only in the farthest northern lands of Scandinavia is the winter bitterly cold.

Most of Western Europe also gets plenty of rainfall. The area around the Mediterranean Sea is one of the few areas of the region in which there is little rainfall during part of the year.

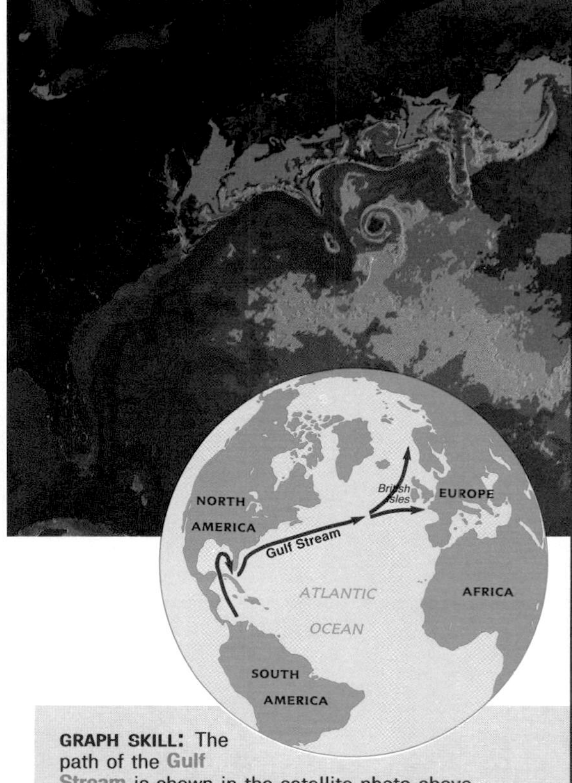

GRAPH SKILL: The path of the Gulf Stream is shown in the satellite photo above. Is London or Stockholm more strongly affected by the Gulf Stream?

AVERAGE MONTHLY TEMPERATURE IN LONDON, ENGLAND AND STOCKHOLM, SWEDEN

Degrees Fahrenheit: 0, 10, 20, 30, 40, 50, 60, 70, 80
Degrees Centigrade: −18, −12, −7, −1, 4, 10, 16, 21, 27
London
Stockholm
Jan. Feb. Mar. Apr. May June July Aug. Sept. Oct. Nov. Dec.
Month

GRAPH SKILL: London

Understanding Oceanic Climate

Continue the discussion of oceanic climate.

Ask students:

- **In which other area of Europe is the climate not greatly influenced by the Atlantic Ocean?** (the southern part of Western Europe)
- **Which word would you use as a general description of Europe's climate?** (*temperate*)

EXTENDING GRAPH SKILLS

Help students to recognize that temperature averages are important aids to understanding climate.

Ask students:

- **What does this graph show?** (the monthly average temperatures of two cities, London and Stockholm)
- **Which city has the highest average temperature? In which month?** (London; in June)
- **Is there any month in which the two cities have the same average temperature?** (July)
- **For how many more months does Stockholm have average temperatures under 40°F. (5°C)?** (5 months)

FUNDAMENTAL THEMES OF GEOGRAPHY

Location One of the greatest advantages of Western Europe's location is its position in the path of the Gulf Stream's flow.

- The source of the Gulf Stream, the Gulf of Mexico, has been likened to a huge teapot. The spout of the teapot points to the narrow Straits of Florida, through which its steam (the relatively hot Gulf Stream water) pours northward into the Atlantic. (The satellite image on page 193 shows this process clearly.)
- Gulf Stream winds enable palm trees to grow in southern England.
- Scientists fear that one of the ill effects of global warming will be the lessening, or even the stopping, of the Gulf Stream's flow.

EXTENDING MAP SKILLS

Emphasize to students that most of Western Europe has a temperate climate. Tell them to study the climate map on this page.

Ask students:

- **Where in Western Europe is the temperature least temperate?** (Iceland, northern Sweden, Norway, and Finland)
- **How would you describe the climate of most of Western Europe?** (temperate, oceanic)
- **In which part of Western Europe is the climate hot and dry in the summer and mild in the winter?** (the Southern European countries)
- *THINKING FURTHER:* **In which parts of Western Europe might the climate make it hard either to farm or to manufacture goods?** (mountaintop regions, northern Sweden, Norway, and Finland)

Discussing Natural Resources
Discuss with students why the landscape in Europe has a cared-for look compared with the wilderness areas in other parts of the world. Ask them to make up analogies illustrating the contrast between the European landscape and the landscape of a developing country. (Possible analogy: the cultivated gardens and grounds of someone's family home compared with a construction site.)

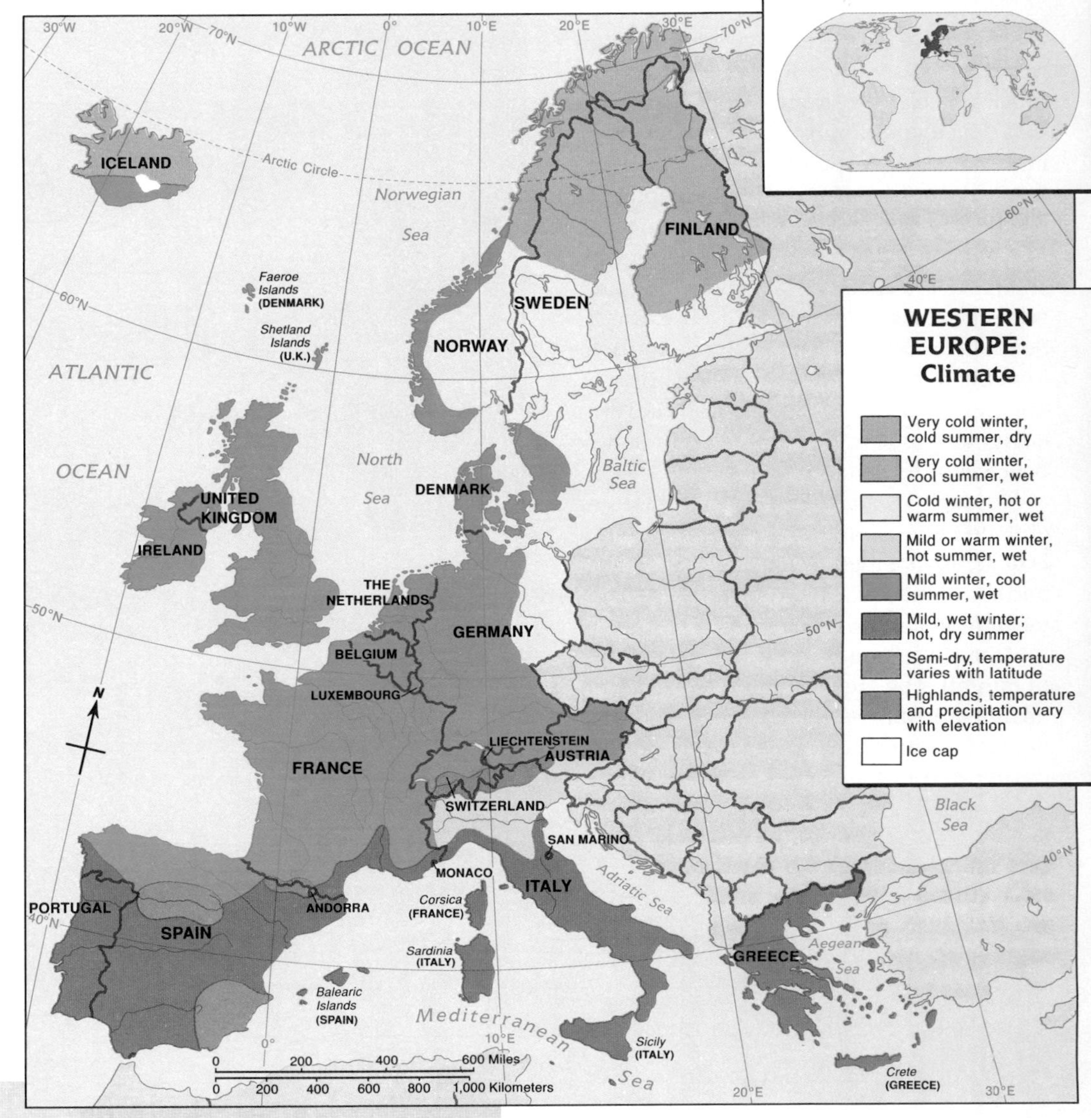

MAP SKILL: What type of climate covers most of the central part of Western Europe?

NATURAL RESOURCES

> *Under an ash-colored sky, the fields have been combed and rolled till they appear to have been finished with a pencil instead of a plough.*

The American poet Ralph Waldo Emerson wrote these words to describe the countryside of Great Britain. But they could have been written about many places in Western Europe. This region is rich in farmland and other natural resources. People have been using these resources for so many years that the landscape has a

194

MAP SKILL: "Mild winter, cool summer, wet"

BACKGROUND INFORMATION

Multicultural Perspectives Increasingly, the nations of Europe have perceived that pollution crosses borders and must be dealt with internationally. Western Europe's highly developed industries produce a great deal of air pollution. This pollution in turn produces acid rain. Germans call acid rain damage *waldsterben,* meaning "forest death." Forty-one percent of the spruce trees in Germany's Black Forest are diseased because of acid rain. Acid rain is also polluting lakes and destroying forests in Sweden and Denmark. Eastern Europe has even greater acid rain problems since it has few environmental laws. Schoolchildren there must wear face masks on acid rain "alert" days.

Air pollution, however, does not stay within the borders of the state that produced it. Winds carry pollution from as far away as Great Britain to Eastern Europe, where it falls as acid rain. Finland has become the victim of acid rain created by Russian industry. A massive forest in Poland has been destroyed largely because of pollutants created by Czech, German, and Polish power plants.

Ask students whether nations should be responsible for the pollution that is created within their boundaries. Have them suggest ways in which European nations could work together to solve their joint acid rain problems.

cared-for look that contrasts sharply with the areas of wilderness often found in other parts of the world.

FORESTS AND SOIL

Look around you. How many things do you see that are made of wood or paper? All these products come from an important natural resource—forests.

In the past, much of Western Europe was covered with dense forests. But over the years most of the trees were cut down to make room for farms. The wood was burned as fuel and used for buildings and furniture.

Today there are few large forests left in Western Europe. And the forests that remain are threatened not only by logging, but also by acid rain. As you may remember from Chapter 3, acid rain is rain mixed with chemicals from the burning of coal and other fuels. Much of the Black Forest, which was once a huge forest in Germany, has been destroyed by acid rain.

As the map on page 196 shows, Western Europe has ample rich soil for farming. About 25 percent of the soil is arable. In some countries, like the Netherlands, more than half the land can be farmed. Raising livestock is also an important economic activity throughout the region.

RIVERS AND OTHER WATERWAYS

You read in Lesson 1 that most countries in Western Europe have access to oceans and seas. The region is also fortunate in having several important inland rivers. Because of Western Europe's temperate climate, most rivers are open all year long. Ships can navigate in ice-free waters around most European ports.

Many of Western Europe's major cities, like London, Paris, and Rome, developed along the banks of rivers. Having good inland waterways has also meant that even the **landlocked** countries of Western Europe—Luxembourg, Switzerland, Austria, Andorra, and Liechtenstein—have ade-

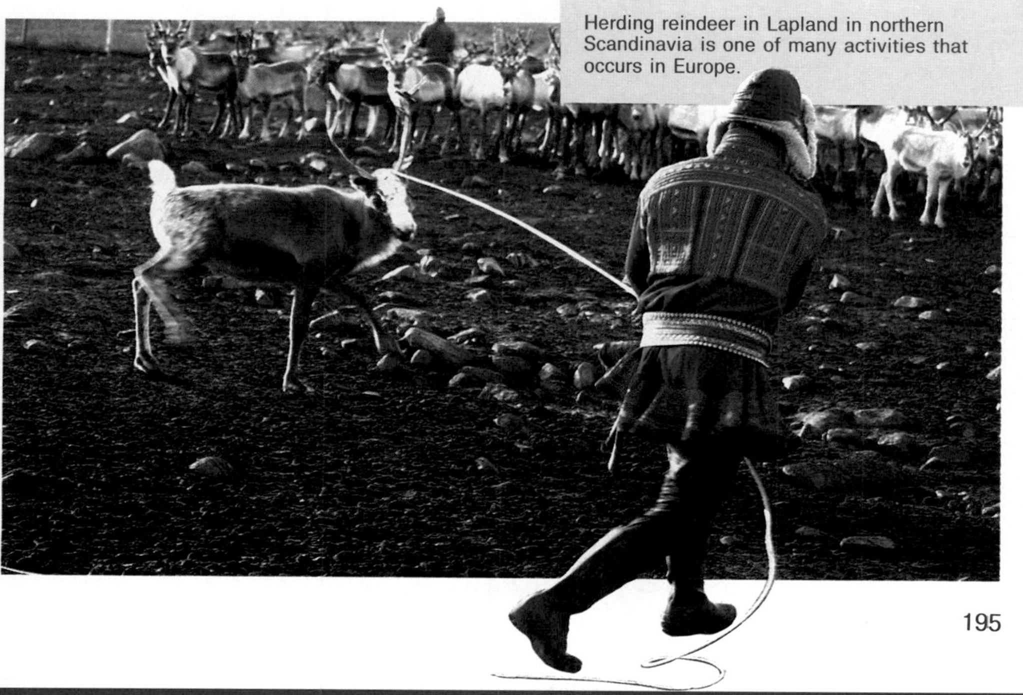

Herding reindeer in Lapland in northern Scandinavia is one of many activities that occurs in Europe.

195

Discussing Forests and Soils
Stress to students that Europe's soil and forests are carefully managed.

Ask students:

- **Name two agricultural activities that are important in Western Europe today.** (farming, livestock raising)
- **What percentage of the soil is arable?** (about 50 percent in Holland, about 25 percent in the rest of Europe)
- **Why are there few forests left today?** (They were cut down to make room for farmland and to be used for fuel, buildings, and furniture.)

Discussing Rivers and Waterways

Ask students:

- **How does Western Europe's climate affect the use of rivers?** (By keeping many rivers ice-free, it enables people and goods to move through Europe all year.)

BACKGROUND INFORMATION

The Rhine The Rhine River is important in at least three ways: culturally, commercially, and politically.

- The Rhine often figures in German art, music, and literature. In his opera *Das Rheingold* Richard Wagner chose the Rhine to represent the source of a power whose misuse destroys the peace and harmony of the world.
- The Rhine is commercially important because it is used to transport goods manufactured in Germany's industrial centers to the upper Rhine and to Dutch ports.
- Because the Rhine serves as both a trade route and a political boundary, the French and the Germans have, over the centuries, contested each other's right to control it. Following World War II, Rhine traffic was placed under international control.

Looking at Rivers and Waterways
Continue discussing Europe's rivers.

Ask students:

- **What is a landlocked country?** (a country completely surrounded by land)
- **Why don't the landlocked European nations suffer from the lack of a coast?** (They have navigable inland rivers that provide access to the sea.)
- **What two things do the Rhine and the Danube have in common?** (Both serve landlocked countries as outlets to the sea; both flow through several different countries.)
- **How do the Scandinavian nations use their short rivers?** (for hydroelectric power)
- *THINKING FURTHER:* **How might having the same river flow through their territories help neighboring nations? How might sharing the same river cause hostility among neighboring nations?** (It might encourage cultural and commercial ties between the different countries; it might cause the nations to fight over ownership of the river.)

EXTENDING MAP SKILLS

Have students study the land-use map on this page.

Ask students:

- **What is the major land use in Western Europe?** (farming and livestock raising)
- **Do you see any differences between land uses in northern and southern Europe?** (There are more manufacturing, mining, and forestry industries in northern Europe.)
- *THINKING FURTHER:* **Why do you think there is little economic activity in northern Norway?** (cold climate, few resources)

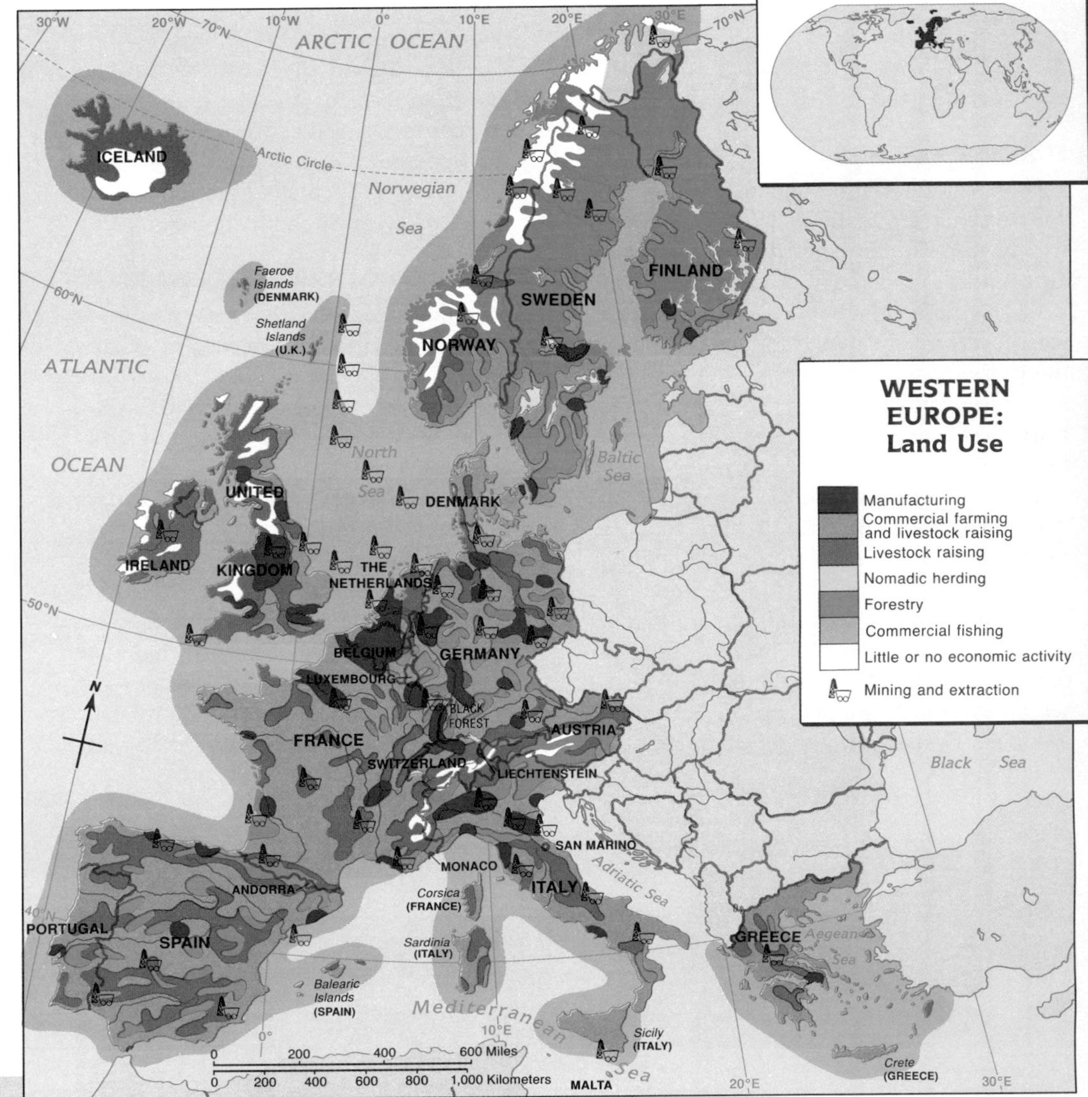

MAP SKILL: What is the major economic activity of Scandinavia?

quate transportation. A landlocked country is one that is entirely surrounded by land.

The longest river in Western Europe is the **Danube** (dan′ ūb) **River**. It flows for nearly 1,800 miles (2,900 km). That makes it slightly longer than the Rio Grande in the United States. The Danube flows from the Black Forest in Germany to the Black Sea in Romania. On its way it passes through seven countries in Western and Eastern Europe.

The **Rhine** (rīn) **River** is another important river in Western Europe. The Rhine is

196

MAP SKILL: forestry

BUILDING CITIZENSHIP

The Threat of Acid Rain Since Western Europe is highly developed, its air is polluted by the waste products of fuels burned in factories, power plants, cars, and homes. Its forests, especially the famous Black Forest in Germany, have been severely damaged by acid rain. Forests cover one third of Germany, provide 800,000 jobs, and produce $1.3 billion worth of lumber and pulp each year. They protect watersheds and stop erosion. To help students understand how some Europeans have reacted to *waldsterben,* or "forest death," have them research the European Green Party. Discuss the choices Europeans must make if they want to save the forests.

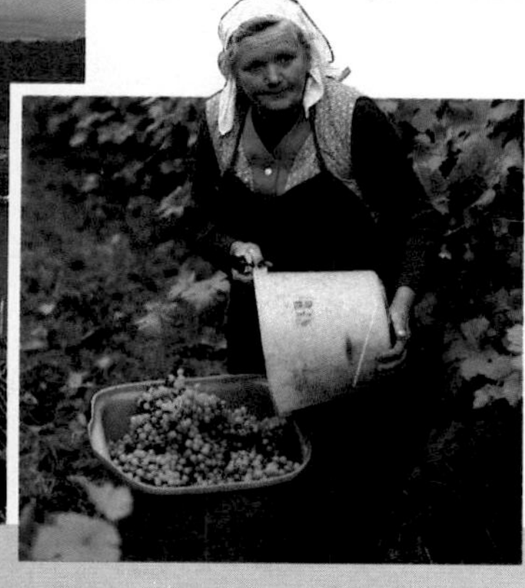

The Rhine River is a major transportation route and runs through some of the best farmland in Western Europe.

a large navigable river. That means it is wide and deep enough for ocean-going ships to use. More ships travel on the Rhine every year than on any other waterway in the world.

The Rhine begins in Switzerland, where it is fed by streams rushing down the slopes of the Alps. The Rhine then flows through the center of Western Europe and empties into the North Sea on the north coast of the Netherlands. The Rhine and its tributaries form a water highway that stretches from the heart of Western Europe to the North Sea.

The American poet Henry Wadsworth Longfellow described the Rhine this way:

> *O, the pride of the German heart is this noble river! And right it is; for of all the rivers of this beautiful earth there is none so beautiful as this.*

In the Scandinavian countries, the rivers are shorter and narrower than those in other parts of Western Europe. But Scandinavians have found ways to put these waterways to work. In the north, swift rivers have been dammed where they emerge from the mountains in order to make hydroelectricity. In Finland factories producing paper and pulp have been built near sources of hydroelectric power.

MILD CLIMATE, RICH SOIL

Western Europe is a land with many advantages. It has rich soil and a mild climate for growing crops. It has navigable rivers that are free from ice during the winter. And it has a central location that makes it accessible to all of the world.

In this chapter you learned that the countries of Western Europe mostly share these advantages. In the next five chapters you will learn what makes each country different. No traveler today would mistake London for Athens or confuse the Swiss countryside with that of Spain. The special character of the individual countries of Western Europe is one of the things that makes this region so interesting.

Check Your Reading

1. What problems threaten the forests of Western Europe today?
2. How does the Gulf Stream affect Western Europe's climate?
3. Why are rivers important to Western Europeans?
4. THINKING SKILL: What are three questions you could ask to find out about the climate of Scandinavia?

THINKING SKILL: Asking Questions

Applying the Lesson Have students review the lists of clothing they made at the beginning of Lesson 2. Discuss how they would change their lists now.

3 CLOSE

Summarizing Students have learned that the Gulf Stream warms Europe's climate and that Europe's rich environment favors many human activities.

Evaluating Use these questions to assess students' understanding.

- **Which two factors are responsible for Western Europe's temperate climate?** (the Gulf Stream; the fact that the waters of the Atlantic Ocean heat up in summer and cool off in winter more slowly than the land does and that the wind from the ocean brings to the land warm air in the winter and cool air in the summer)
- **What are two of Europe's most important resources?** (navigable rivers, rich soil)
- **What are two advantages of Europe's waterways?** (Most are navigable and ice-free all year long.)

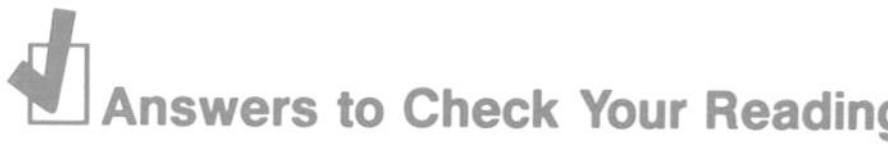

Answers to Check Your Reading

1. acid rain and logging practices such as cutting down trees without replacing them
2. It makes it warmer than other locations at the same latitude and is therefore favorable for farming.
3. They make travel easier and provide the manufacturing industries with a means of transporting their goods.
4. Possible questions include: How long is the growing season? What is the yearly temperature range and average temperature? During how many months are temperatures above freezing?

Independent Practice
Practice Book: page 47

MEETING INDIVIDUAL NEEDS

Reteaching (easy) Have students write one or two paragraphs answering the following question: "What would Europe be like if the Gulf Stream did not flow past it?"

Extension (average) Give students the outline map of Western Europe (available in the Teacher's Resource Center) and have them label the major rivers and cities. Then have pairs of students quiz each other in order to learn these place names.

Enrichment (challenging) Have each student write a proposal for steps that Europeans might take to solve their acid rain problem. Each proposal could include a budget that outlines where the funds to implement their plan would come from.

CHAPTER 8 REVIEW
pages 198–199

USING THE CHAPTER SUMMARY AND REVIEW

Physical Geography These questions may be used for review.

- **What are the five peninsulas of Western Europe?** (Scandinavian, Jutland, Iberian, Italian, Balkan)
- **What effect does the Gulf Stream have on the climate of Western Europe?** (It brings warm waters that help create a mild climate in coastal areas.)
- **What are the natural resources of Western Europe?** (forests, rich soil, waterways)

Ideas to Remember

- **What are the largest islands of Western Europe?** (the British Isles, Corsica, Sardinia, Sicily)
- **Describe the climate of Western Europe.** (temperate)

Answers to Reviewing Vocabulary

1. F
2. F
3. T
4. T
5. F

Answers to Reviewing Facts

1. peninsulas and islands
2. the name used for the large land area made up of Europe and Asia
3. Scandinavian, Jutland, Iberian, Italian, Balkan
4. Corsica, Sicily, Sardinia
5. a deep, narrow inlet of the sea between high cliffs; Norway
6. the Gulf Stream and ocean breezes off the Atlantic
7. They prevent Atlantic breezes from reaching the southern part of Western Europe, which causes mostly dry summers and mild winters.
8. Most were cut down.
9. one that is entirely surrounded by land; Luxembourg, Switzerland, Austria, Liechtenstein
10. Rhine and Danube; provide adequate transportation

CHAPTER 8 • SUMMARY

WESTERN EUROPE: PHYSICAL GEOGRAPHY

LANDFORMS

- Peninsulas: Scandinavian, Jutland, Italian, Balkan, Iberian

- Islands: British Isles, Greece, Corsica, Sardinia, Sicily
- Thousands of miles of coastline

CLIMATE

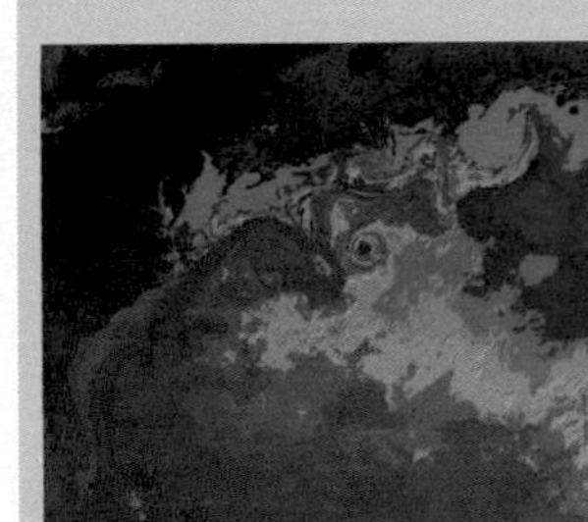

- Gulf Stream: brings warm waters that help create mild climate in coastal areas
- Ocean winds bring plenty of rainfall to most areas

- Northern part of the region: winters are long and cold
- Southern part: summers are sunny and dry, winters short and mild

NATURAL RESOURCES

- Forests: important resource, but few large ones are left

- Many long inland rivers and waterways, such as Danube and Rhine rivers

- Rich soil: used for farming and raising livestock

IDEAS TO REMEMBER

- Western Europe is made up of two main landforms: islands and peninsulas.
- Western Europe's climate is generally temperate, and its major resources include rich soil and long waterways.

198

ENRICHMENT ACTIVITY

Making a Puzzle Map of Europe **Materials:** large map of Europe, posterboard, paints or markers, pens, scissors

1. Paste or trace a large map of Europe on posterboard. Tell students that they are going to make a puzzle map that will help them locate the countries and landforms of Europe.
2. Divide the class into six groups and assign each group one area: (1) France, the Low Countries, and Central Europe (2) British Isles (3) Scandinavian Peninsula and Iceland (4) Iberian Peninsula and nearby islands (5) Italian Peninsula and nearby islands (6) Balkan Peninsula and nearby islands.
3. Have a member of each group cut out the assigned area from the large map. Then have the groups label and color the major countries and islands of their region. Mix all the finished pieces together.
4. Have each student put the pieces of the puzzle together.

CHAPTER 8 • REVIEW

REVIEWING VOCABULARY

Number a sheet of paper from 1 to 5. Read the definition of each underlined word. Beside each number write **T** if the definition is true and **F** if it is false.

1. The dense forests of Finland are called fjords.
2. Countries that are entirely surrounded by water are landlocked.
3. A fjord is a deep, narrow inlet of seawater between high cliffs.
4. Landlocked countries are entirely surrounded by land.
5. The fjords bring warm water from the Gulf of Mexico to Europe.

REVIEWING FACTS

1. What are the two main geographic features of Western Europe?
2. What does the term *Eurasia* mean?
3. Name the five major peninsulas of Western Europe.
4. Name three European islands in the Mediterranean Sea.
5. What is a fjord? In which country are most fjords found?
6. What two factors are responsible for the mild climate of Western Europe?
7. How do the Alps and the Pyrenees affect the climate in the southern part of Western Europe?
8. Why are there few large forests in Europe today?
9. What is a landlocked country? Name three countries in Western Europe that are landlocked.
10. Name the two largest rivers in Western Europe. How have rivers been used to help Europe's landlocked countries?

WRITING ABOUT MAIN IDEAS

1. **Writing a List:** Bodies of water are important resources in Western Europe. List the ways in which countries of Western Europe are affected by the Atlantic Ocean, the Danube River, and the Rhine River.
2. **Writing a Magazine Article:** Imagine that the Gulf Stream has suddenly shifted its course away from Western Europe. What do you think would happen to the people of the region? Write a magazine article describing the change and the efforts of Western Europeans to cope with it.
3. **Writing a Travel Log:** You have read that Europe is divided into many different countries. Imagine that you are taking a trip from Sweden to Greece. Name the countries and the bodies of water you would pass through or over on your trip.
4. **Writing About Perspectives:** Choose the country in Western Europe that you would most like to visit. Then write a letter to a pen pal in that country, asking questions about what life there is like.

BUILDING SKILLS: UNDERSTANDING MAP PROJECTIONS

1. What is meant by the term *distortion* as it relates to mapmaking?
2. What is a map projection?
3. How is a grid system useful in determining a map's distortion?
4. Why is it important to understand map projection and distortion?

199

Suggestions for Writing About Main Ideas

1. Atlantic Ocean—climate, transportation; Danube River—transportation; Rhine River—transportation
2. Students should describe how the resulting colder climate would affect all aspects of life and how Western Europeans would have to find new energy sources, new industries, and even new pastimes.
3. Possible answers include: the Baltic Sea, Denmark, West Germany, Austria, Italy, the Adriatic Sea.
4. Students may ask questions about climate, geography, places to visit, school life, and lifestyle.

Answers to Building Skills: Understanding Map Projections

1. errors in size, shape, distance, and/or direction
2. A projection is a way of showing locations on the earth on a flat map.
3. You can tell how a map is distorted by looking at the way its grid system is drawn. Different projections have different distortions.
4. so that you can tell if the size, shape, distance, and/or direction of an area are accurately drawn

Chapter Review and Test

Practice Book: *Vocabulary Review,* page 48
Transparency: *Graphic Organizer*
Assessment Book: *Chapter 8 Test*

MAKING CONNECTIONS

Supporting Main Ideas Use the Main Idea Map Graphic Organizer Transparency, labeling the chapter theme and the headings, which are underlined. Have students complete the diagram by filling it in with statements that show how each geographic feature named benefits Western Europe. *Ask:* How has geography benefited Western Europe?

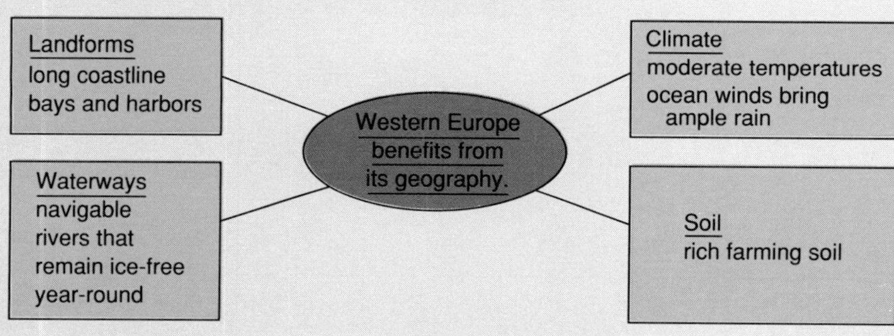

CHAPTER 9
ORGANIZER

THE BRITISH ISLES text pages 200–215

CHAPTER THEME The British Isles offer a great legacy of democratic rights in a parliamentary form that has been copied the world over.

CHAPTER OBJECTIVES

CONTENT

- Name the two parts that make up the United Kingdom and the three provinces that make up Great Britain.
- Name the two groups involved in the conflict in Northern Ireland and give reasons for the conflict.
- Recognize Great Britain as the home of the Industrial Revolution.
- Explain why the development of offshore oil and natural gas fields is important to the economy of Great Britain.
- Identify the Magna Carta and explain its importance in the development of political freedom.
- Define *constitutional monarchy* and contrast it with earlier absolute monarchies.
- Define *welfare state* and name the most far-reaching welfare state program in Great Britain.
- Describe the major literary and athletic traditions of the British Isles.

SKILLS

Geography
- Identify different time zones using a world time zone map.

Thinking
- Compare and contrast the governments of the British Isles and the United States.
- Distinguish between fact and opinion.

Reading and Writing
- Write a poem about England.

CITIZENSHIP VALUES

- Appreciate the contributions of British traditions and institutions to the growth of democracy worldwide.

TEACHER OPTIONS

READING STRATEGY: Text Structure Strategies to help students read and remember the main ideas of the lesson.

Lesson 1: p. 201 Lesson 3: p. 209
Lesson 2: p. 206 Lesson 4: p. 212

MEETING INDIVIDUAL NEEDS Activities for reteaching, extension, and enrichment.

Lesson 1: p. 203 Lesson 2: p. 208
Geography Skills: p. 205 Lesson 3: p. 211
Lesson 4: p. 213

GEO ADVENTURES ACTIVITIES PAD Daily activities to assess students' understanding of geography skills.

CURRICULUM CONNECTION Activities to help integrate other subject areas with Social Studies.

Science: p. 207

PUPIL EDITION ON CASSETTE Language support for students who have difficulty reading or who will benefit from listening to the Pupil Edition on Cassette as they read.

SECOND-LANGUAGE SUPPORT Activities and suggestions for second-language learners.

Lesson 3: p. 17

CHAPTER PLANNING GUIDE

LESSON	SUGGESTED PACING	THEMES	TEACHER SUPPORT MATERIALS: TEACHER'S RESOURCE CENTER
1 THE PEOPLE pages 201–203	1 day	Throughout much of their history, the British Isles have been a land of freedom and opportunity for many people.	Practice Book p. 49 **Technology:** *Adventures CD-ROM*
BUILDING GEOGRAPHY SKILLS Reading Time Zone Maps pages 204–205	1 day	The earth is divided into 24 time zones, one for each hour of the day. The day changes as you cross the International Date Line.	Practice Book p. 50 Transparency Map 9
2 THE ECONOMY pages 206–208	1 day	Although Great Britain was once the economic leader of the world, the British Isles today face economic problems such as limited resources and aging factories.	Practice Book p. 51 ■ Anthology pp. 86–87 **Technology:** *Adventures CD-ROM*
3 THE GOVERNMENT pages 209–211	1 day	A traditional respect for royalty, combined with modern democratic ideas, has inspired the basic principles of the British government.	Practice Book p. 52 **Technology:** *Adventures CD-ROM*
4 ARTS AND RECREATION pages 212–213	1 day	The two nations of the British Isles have given the world a rich cultural legacy.	Practice Book p. 53 ■ Anthology pp. 73–76, 81, 99–100
CHAPTER SUMMARY AND REVIEW pages 214–215	1 day	Chapter content, skills, and vocabulary are reviewed and evaluated.	Practice Book p. 54 Transparency: Graphic Organizer Assessment Book, Chapter 9 Test

Technology CONNECTION

Lesson 1
ADVENTURES CD-ROM
Have students *Travel* to and *Explore* the British Isles.

Lesson 2
ADVENTURES CD-ROM
Explore the map of Ireland.

Lesson 3
ADVENTURES CD-ROM
Students can find *Movies* and *Sounds* in *Investigate.*

CHAPTER 9
pages 200–215

USING THE CHAPTER OPENER

Discussing the Photograph Encourage students to guess what the woman in the picture is doing. If possible, play a tape or recording of bagpipe music. Have students speculate about the ways in which bagpipe music might have been useful in an isolated, mountainous country. (Because the sound carried so well, it might have been used as a means of communication.)

Ask students:

- **What is the nationality of the woman in the picture?** (Scottish)
- **What identifies the woman as a Scot?** (She is wearing a plaid outfit and playing a bagpipe.)

Reading/Listening to the Primary Source Read the passage under the picture to the class. Help students to understand that the reason they were able to guess the woman's nationality from her instrument and clothes is that on ceremonial occasions, Scots identify themselves with their country's history by playing the bagpipe and dressing in a special tartan, or plaid fabric. The tartan identifies the Scots as belonging to a particular clan, or group of people that share an ancestor.

Ask students:

- **Why do you think the headline says "Continent Isolated," rather than "Britain Isolated"?** (Encourage students to consider the national perspective implied by the headline.)

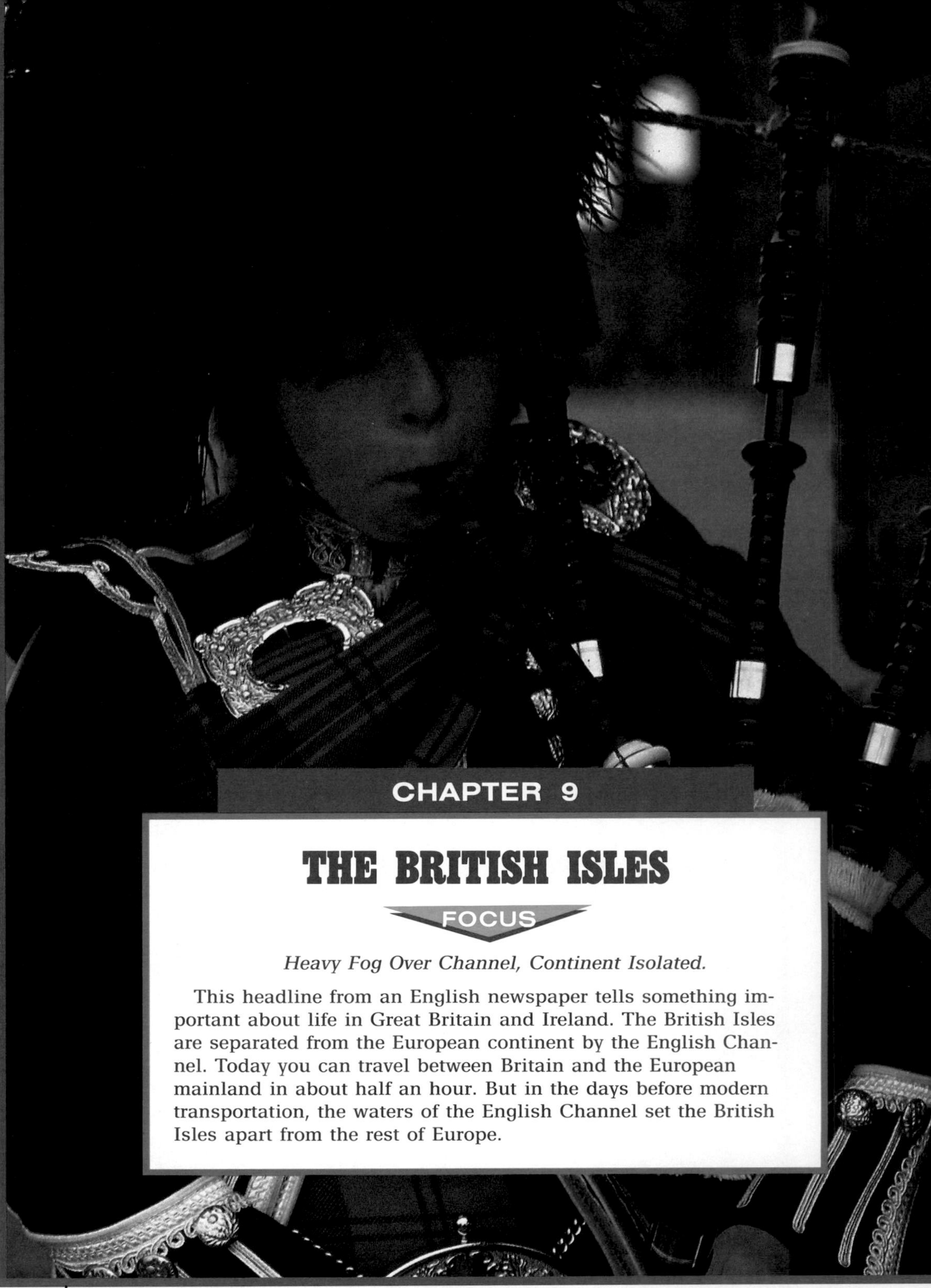

CHAPTER 9

THE BRITISH ISLES

FOCUS

Heavy Fog Over Channel, Continent Isolated.

This headline from an English newspaper tells something important about life in Great Britain and Ireland. The British Isles are separated from the European continent by the English Channel. Today you can travel between Britain and the European mainland in about half an hour. But in the days before modern transportation, the waters of the English Channel set the British Isles apart from the rest of Europe.

BACKGROUND INFORMATION

About the Highland Scots Since the Highland Scots live in an isolated, rather rugged, mountainous region, they have tended to preserve some very old customs.

- Many Highland Scots feel an attachment to their clan. A clan is a group of people who have descended from the same ancestor and who often share a surname. Each clan is headed by a chieftain and has its own particular pattern of tartan, or plaid. Ceremonial clothes, such as the famous skirtlike kilt, are made from material patterned with the clan's tartan.
- The Scots have many national dishes. Most people are familiar with their delicious shortbread and scones. Fewer people, perhaps, have tried haggis. Haggis is a pudding made of a sheep's heart, liver, and other organ meats. It is minced up with suet and oatmeal and then boiled in a sheep's stomach.
- Sir Walter Scott, one of Scotland's most famous writers, wrote many novels that depict life in eighteenth- and nineteenth-century Scotland. He portrayed all kinds of people, from wild Highland chieftains conspiring against the English king to peaceful farmers.

LESSON 1

The People

READ TO LEARN

Key People

William the Conqueror

Key Places

Great Britain
Ireland
Stonehenge
Northern Ireland

Read Aloud

Britain, long before the discovery of America, was the America of Europe, the farthest point west, where [people] were driven by invaders from the east; the land of the free, where refugees could find sanctuary [a place of protection], *and the hungry and disappointed could find hope.*

The author Anthony Glyn wrote these words to explain why so many people have come to the British Isles. Although these misty green islands are small in size and crowded in many places, they offer freedom and opportunity to people from all over the world.

Read for Purpose

1. WHAT YOU KNOW: Where are the British Isles located in relation to the rest of Western Europe?
2. WHAT YOU WILL LEARN: Which groups of people have settled in the British Isles?

ISLAND NATIONS

The British Isles are made up of two main islands. They are **Great Britain** and **Ireland**. Great Britain is made up of England, Scotland, and Wales. Several smaller islands in the North Sea and the Atlantic Ocean are also included in the British Isles.

The British Isles consist of two nations, the United Kingdom and the Republic of Ireland. The United Kingdom is made up of Great Britain and the northern part of Ireland. The people of the United Kingdom live mainly on the island of Great Britain, which includes England, Scotland, and Wales. The people of these areas are often referred to as the British.

WAVES OF SETTLERS

The British are a complex mixture of different peoples and cultures. To understand their story, we have to look back in time several thousand years.

Little is known about the first people who settled in the British Isles. They left no written records. Like the first Americans, they did not have a system of writing. The chief remains of their existence are a group of enormous gray stones called **Stonehenge**. The purpose of this huge

WHAT YOU KNOW: The British Isles are located off the western coast of Europe.

LESSON 1
pages 201–203

Lesson Theme Throughout much of their history, the British Isles have been a land of freedom and opportunity for many people.

Lesson Objectives

- Identify the groups that have settled in the British Isles.
- Explain why immigrants are still coming to Great Britain.
- Describe the problems in Northern Ireland.

PREPARE

Motivate Read the *Read Aloud* and ask students if they have ever heard of Robin Hood. Encourage them to make connections between the story about an outlaw band that protected poor people against tyrants and the idea of Britain as a place of refuge.

Set Purpose Pose the *What You Will Learn* question. Explain to students that they will read about the different settlers of the British Isles.

TEACH

Identifying Island Nations Tell students that the British Isles consist of two nations.

Ask students:

- **What are the two nations of the British Isles?** (the United Kingdom and the Republic of Ireland)

Understanding Waves of Settlers As they read the lesson, encourage students to track the order in which the different waves of settlers arrived in the British Isles.

READING STRATEGY AND VOCABULARY DEVELOPMENT

Text Structure Explain to students that some writers use chronological order to present their material as clearly as possible. Using the sections "Waves of Settlers" and "Modern Newcomers," demonstrate the use of chronological order as an organizational pattern. Point out the logic of using this pattern for writing historical material. Have students identify the dates, the specific periods of time, and the key words (such as *first, after, since, now, today*) that indicate the order of events. Have students make a time line using the information from "Waves of Settlers" and "Modern Newcomers."

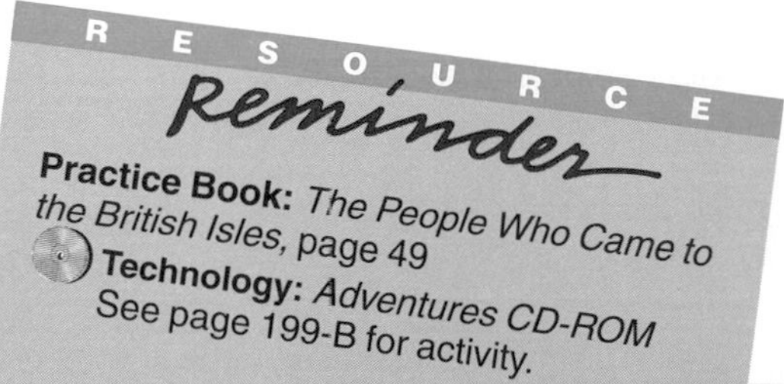

Practice Book: *The People Who Came to the British Isles*, page 49
Technology: *Adventures CD-ROM*
See page 199-B for activity.

Looking at Waves of Settlers Continue the discussion of the settlers of the British Isles.

Ask students:

- **What evidence of their culture did the earliest settlers of the British Isles leave behind?** (Stonehenge)
- **What skills did the Celts bring to the British Isles?** (farming, metalworking)
- **Why do you think the Romans built a wall across England?** (Possible answers include: for defense, to mark boundaries.)
- **Which group named England?** (the Anglo-Saxons)
- **From where did the Normans come?** (western France, or Normandy)

EXTENDING MAP SKILLS

Have students study the political map on this page.

Ask students:

- **Name the two nations of the British Isles and describe their locations in relation to one another.** (the United Kingdom and the Republic of Ireland; The Republic of Ireland is west of Great Britain; Great Britain is east of the Republic of Ireland; Northern Ireland, which is part of the United Kingdom, is northeast of the Republic of Ireland and west of Great Britain.)
- **Name the largest province of Great Britain.** (England)

Looking at Modern Newcomers Be sure students recognize that current immigrants to Britain come mainly from her former colonies to seek opportunities for a better life. Ask students to locate India, Pakistan, and the West Indies on the world map in the *Atlas* on pages 638–639.

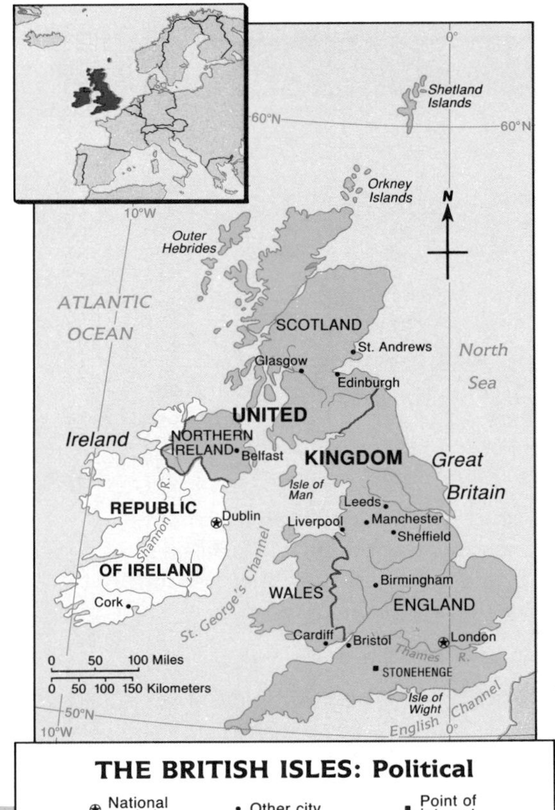

THE BRITISH ISLES: Political

⊛ National capital • Other city ▪ Point of interest

MAP SKILL: The United Kingdom and the Republic of Ireland make up the British Isles. What is the capital of the Republic of Ireland?

stone structure, which was built in southern England about 4,000 years ago, is still a mystery. Some historians think Stonehenge was built as a means to study the stars and the planets. Others think that it was for religious celebrations.

In the early history of the British Isles, the islands were invaded several times. After the builders of Stonehenge, the oldest known inhabitants of the British Isles were the Celts. They came from the mainland of Europe in about 800 B.C. Most Celts were either farmers or metalworkers.

In about A.D. 43 the Romans invaded the British Isles. By this time the Celts had spread throughout the islands. Within the next four years, the Romans gained control of most of Britain. They ruled this area for more than 400 years. Today the remains of a wall that the Romans built all the way across the northern part of England still exist.

When the Romans left Britain in around A.D. 450, the area was invaded by several groups of warriors from northern Europe. Together these people were known as Anglo-Saxons. They called the land they settled *Angleland*, or England. Over the years the Anglo-Saxons pushed the Celts north and west into Wales, Scotland, and Ireland. Find these on the map.

In 1066 the world of the Anglo-Saxons changed forever. A group of invaders led by **William the Conqueror** took over England. This group was called the Normans, because they came from the western part of France known as Normandy. They brought with them their own culture and their own language, French. Several centuries would pass before the Anglo-Saxon and French languages would blend together to form the English language that is spoken today.

MODERN NEWCOMERS

After 1066 no other group or nation invaded the British Isles. Since that time, however, millions of people have crossed the waters of the English Channel and settled in the British Isles. During the 1900s immigrants from outside Europe flooded into Great Britain. To these people, the British Isles represented opportunity. Here they could find land, work, and freedom.

Today more than 60 million people live in the British Isles. Great Britain is the fourth most crowded nation in the world. The largest groups of newcomers come

MAP SKILL: Dublin

BUILDING CITIZENSHIP

The Role of a Minority in a Democracy The situation in Northern Ireland illustrates how conflicts can arise between a powerful minority group (such as the Catholics in Northern Ireland) and a majority group (such as the Protestants in Northern Ireland). Have students: (1) find out more about the background of the British decision to deny Northern Ireland its independence; (2) bring in news clippings and articles about the current developments in this controversy; and (3) discuss and give examples of the importance of minorities in the United States today and how minority groups in the United States can affect political decisions.

The city of Dublin is the political, economic, and cultural center of Ireland.

from countries once ruled by Britain—India, Pakistan, and other parts of Asia, the West Indies and parts of Africa. Like earlier immigrants they come seeking freedom and opportunities for a better life.

TROUBLES IN NORTHERN IRELAND

The United Kingdom began as the small nation of England. As it grew more powerful, it took over Wales, Scotland, and Ireland. Today the people in each of these areas are proud of their separate customs. But different traditions have sometimes led to bloody conflicts.

For example, religious differences in Northern Ireland have torn that area apart. About 60 percent of the people living in Northern Ireland are Protestants. The rest are Roman Catholics.

After Britain gave southern Ireland its independence in 1921, Catholics in Northern Ireland hoped to join their southern neighbors in forming an Irish Republic. But their dream was never realized. Angry Protestants in Northern Ireland feared that such a union would leave them outnumbered by Catholics.

Since the 1960s British soldiers have been stationed in Northern Ireland. Violence has broken out repeatedly in the area. Thousands of people have been killed. Hope for peace came in 1993. The British announced that Northern Ireland would be free to choose whether or not to stay in the United Kingdom. But first the Irish Republican Army, the group committing much of the violence in Northern Ireland, had to abandon their violence.

TWO NATIONS, MANY PEOPLES

The British Isles consist of two countries with many groups of people. You have read how the Celts were the first people to come to the British Isles. They were followed by several other groups of invaders. Later, immigrants from other countries came to work in these island nations. Like newcomers before them, they saw the British Isles as a land of opportunity.

Check Your Reading

1. Which two main islands make up the British Isles?
2. What happened to the Celts who lived in the British Isles thousands of years in the past?
3. Why has Northern Ireland been a land of conflict?
4. THINKING SKILL: Beginning with the Celts, list in order the groups of people that have invaded the British Isles.

THINKING SKILL: Sequencing

Understanding Troubles in Northern Ireland

Ask students:

- **What is the reason for the conflict in Northern Ireland?** (The 40 percent of the population that is Catholic wants to be independent of Britain; the 60 percent that is Protestant fears the loss of its customs and religion if Northern Ireland were to break away from the United Kingdom.)

Applying the Lesson Have students write a paragraph comparing the ways in which the British and American cultures have been affected by having a population made up of many different groups of people. Help students to identify and describe how being aware of this mixed population gives us an important perspective on the American way of life.

3 CLOSE

Summarizing Students have read that the British Isles were settled by many different peoples and that its culture was formed by the blending of these peoples' cultures.

Evaluating Use the *Check Your Reading* questions (answers given below) to assess students' understanding.

Answers to Check Your Reading

1. Great Britain and Ireland
2. The Anglo-Saxons pushed them north and west into Scotland, Ireland, and Wales.
3. because of cultural and religious differences between Catholics and Protestants
4. Celts, Romans, Anglo-Saxons, Normans

Independent Practice
Practice Book: page 49

MEETING INDIVIDUAL NEEDS

Reteaching (easy) Have students make a vertical time line that begins 4,000 years ago, listing all the groups that settled in the British Isles and the changes those groups brought about.

Extension (average) Divide the class into two groups. Have one group research Stonehenge and the other research Hadrian's Wall. Have students in each group prepare and present a panel discussion on their subject.

Enrichment (challenging) Have students debate the issue: "Does the assertion of a minority group's interests strengthen or weaken a democracy?" Suggest that they consider these ideas: (1) democracy means the rule of the majority, and (2) a minority viewpoint can serve as part of the system of checks and balances that keeps a government democratic in spirit as well as in name.

SKILLS LESSON
pages 204–205

Lesson Theme The earth is divided into 24 time zones, one for each hour of the day. The day changes as you cross the International Date Line.

Lesson Objectives
- Explain the differences between time zones.
- Identify the International Date Line.
- Interpret a time zone map.

PREPARE

Motivate Shine a lamp on a globe to show students how half of the world has day when the other half has night. Position the globe so that "dawn" (the leading edge of the lighted hemisphere) is on the International Date Line. Slowly turn the globe counterclockwise so the class sees dawn travel through the 24 time zones around the earth, ending at the International Date Line. Ask students what happens when dawn, or the edge of the light, crosses the International Date Line. (It is the second day and a new date.)

Set Purpose Tell students that in this lesson they will learn how to use a time zone map and how to determine the date by using the International Date Line. If possible, project Transparency Map 9.

TEACH

Understanding Time and Space

Ask students:

- **Why is each time zone about 15° of longitude wide?** (The earth turns 360° in 24 hours; 360° divided by 24 hours equals 15° an hour.)
- **From which place are all time zones calculated?** (the prime meridian in Greenwich, England)

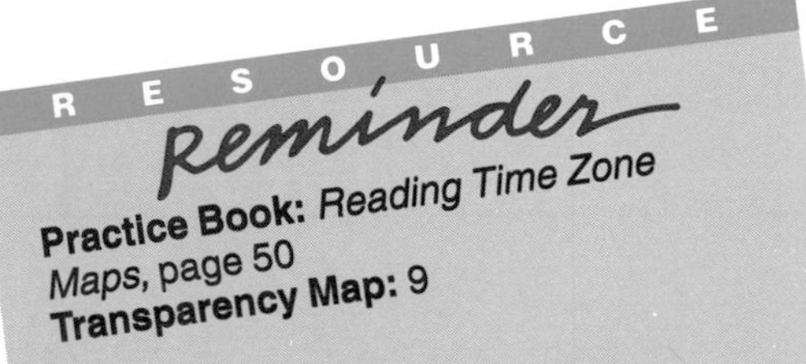

BUILDING SKILLS
GEOGRAPHY SKILLS

Reading Time Zone Maps

Key Vocabulary
time zone
International Date Line

When it is noon in London, England, it is 7:00 A.M. in Washington, D.C., and it is 2:00 P.M. in Cairo, Egypt. As you can see from the map below, the world is divided into 24 **time zones**, one for every 15° of longitude on a map or globe.

Time and Space

Why does time differ from place to place? As you know, the earth completes one rotation on its axis every 24 hours. Because the earth rotates 360° each day, it follows that in one hour it rotates 15°. This is the reason that each of the world's time zones is about 15° of longitude wide.

The time on which all time zones are based is located on the prime meridian in Greenwich, England. Find the prime meridian on the map. The times given at the top of the map show how the time changes as a person moves away from the prime meridian.

Because the earth rotates from west to east, the time in any zone east of you is always later than it is in your zone. As you move east, you add one hour for each time zone that you cross. The time in any zone west of you is always earlier than it is in your zone. As you move to the west, you subtract an hour for each time zone crossed.

For example, suppose it is 10:00 A.M. in Washington, D.C. To find the time in Houston, which is one time zone west of Washington, D.C., you subtract one hour.

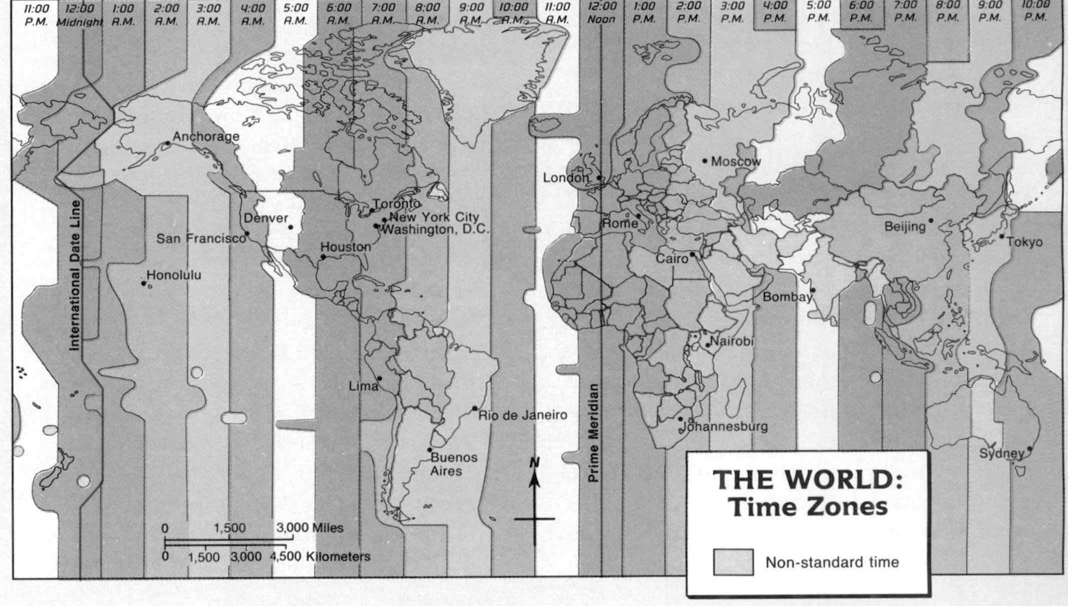

FUNDAMENTAL THEMES OF GEOGRAPHY

Movement The world is often referred to as a "global village" because distances seem to have been reduced by swift modern communications and transportation. The movement of people, goods, and ideas is affected by the different times of day around the world. In some cases the differences of day and night times are also significant. For instance, since on a given date when a New Yorker wakes at 7:00 A.M., the Tokyo Stock Exchange has already closed after a full day of trading, business decisions may be affected. Also, when important political events in other time zones of the world occur, the President of the United States may have to be awakened in the middle of the night to make decisions. Discuss with students their experiences with phone calls to different time zones or their experiences, if any, with the International Date Line.

Now find Lima on the map. When it is 7:00 P.M. in Lima, what time is it in Rio de Janeiro? Since Rio de Janeiro is two time zones east of Lima, you must add two hours to the time in Lima.

The International Date Line

Halfway around the world from the prime meridian is the International Date Line, located on the 180° meridian of longitude. The International Date Line is an imaginary line that marks the boundary between one day and the next. Because of the International Date Line, two different days always exist at the same time throughout the world.

At the International Date Line you gain or lose a day, depending on the direction in which you are traveling. For example, suppose you are on a ship which sails west across the International Date Line on Tuesday at 3:00 P.M. Your time would change one full day to Wednesday at 3:00 P.M. What do you think would happen if you crossed the International Date Line traveling east on Friday at 5:00 P.M.? You would go back one full day to Thursday at 5:00 P.M.

Look at the time zone map. You will see that the red line marking the International Date Line is not a straight line. It zigzags so that eastern Siberia and Russia are on the same side of the International Date Line. The line has also been redrawn so that it does not cross land areas. Similarly, time zones around the world zigzag to follow national boundaries or to prevent one city from having two different time zones.

Using the Time Zone Map

To understand how to use a time zone map, look at the map on page 204 and read the following examples.

A. When it is 7:00 A.M. Monday in Toronto, it is 3:00 A.M. Monday in Anchorage. (As the map shows, Anchorage is four time zones west of Toronto.)

B. When it is 9:00 P.M. Friday in Tokyo, it is 2:00 A.M. Thursday in Honolulu. (As the map shows, Honolulu is five time zones east of Tokyo, and the International Date Line was passed.)

C. When it is 10:00 P.M. Thursday in Sydney, it is 5:00 A.M. Wednesday in Denver. (As the map shows, Sydney is seven time zones west of Denver, and the International Date Line was passed.)

D. When it is 6:00 A.M. Tuesday in San Francisco, it is 12:00 P.M. Tuesday in Sydney. (Sydney is six time zones west of San Francisco, and both the midnight time zone and the International Date Line were passed.)

Reviewing the Skill

1. What is a time zone?
2. What is the prime meridian?
3. What is the International Date Line?
4. Why are the world's time zones about 15° of longitude wide?
5. If you were traveling through time zones from west to east, would you turn your clock ahead or back?
6. If it is noon in London, what time is it in Beijing? In Sydney? In Houston?
7. If it is 6:00 A.M. Monday in Moscow, what day and time is it in Lima?
8. If it is 5:00 P.M. Friday in San Francisco, what day and time is it in Bombay? In Tokyo?
9. What day and time will it be when you arrive in Denver, if your three-hour flight left New York on Wednesday at 4:00 P.M.?
10. Why is it important to know how to use a time zone map?

205

Discussing the International Date Line Help students understand that going west across the International Date Line adds a day and going east across it subtracts a day. Discuss the location of and zigzags in the International Date Line.

Applying the Skill Have students write a time and location on a sheet of paper. Have each student then choose one of the sheets and determine the current time and day in the zone they chose.

3 CLOSE

Summarizing Students have learned that there are 24 time zones and that movement across the International Date Line changes the date. Have students determine the number of time zones in the United States.

Answers to Reviewing the Skill

1. one of 24 longitudinal strips, each about 15° wide, that cover the globe
2. the 0° longitude line at Greenwich, England, from which all time zones are measured
3. the 180° meridian that marks the boundary between days
4. The earth turns 360° in 24 hours; 360° divided by 24 = 15°.
5. ahead
6. in Beijing—8:00 P.M.; in Sydney—10:00 P.M.; in Houston—6:00 A.M.
7. in Lima—10:00 P.M. Sunday
8. in Nairobi—4:00 A.M. Saturday; in Tokyo—10:00 A.M. Saturday
9. 5:00 P.M. Wednesday
10. It enables you to determine the time in different locations on the earth. You would use it when telephoning or traveling to far-off places.

Independent Practice
Practice Book: page 50

MEETING INDIVIDUAL NEEDS

Reteaching (easy) Have students work in pairs, using the maps of the world from the *Atlas* in the back of the book and the map on page 204. Have them quiz each other by picking city names and telling the time there at the time of the lesson.

Extension (average) Have students research the reasons for the American switch to daylight saving time each year. Have students debate whether or not daylight saving time should be used throughout the United States for the whole year.

Enrichment (challenging) Have students research and write a report on how the correct time is established in the United States and on new methods for keeping accurate time.

LESSON 2
pages 206–208

Lesson Theme Although Great Britain was once the economic leader of the world, the British Isles today face economic problems such as limited resources and aging factories.

Lesson Objectives
- Compare British and Irish industry and agriculture.
- Describe a mixed economy.
- Identify Great Britain's natural resources.

PREPARE

Motivate Tell students that before the Industrial Revolution, most people lived on farms or in villages. Read the *Read Aloud* to the class, and then ask students to guess what effects, besides those described by Dickens, the Industrial Revolution might have had on Great Britain.

Set Purpose Use the *What You Will Learn* question to challenge students to compare the British economy with the economies of the other regions they have studied so far.

TEACH

Looking at the Industrial Revolution Stress to students that one of the most important results of the Industrial Revolution was the increased speed with which goods were produced.

Ask students:

- **Compare the effect of the Industrial Revolution on Ireland with its effect on Great Britain.** (It developed at a slower pace in Ireland than it did in Great Britain.)

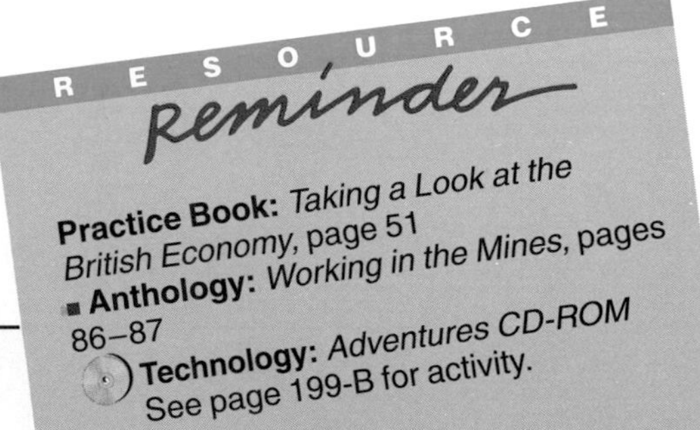

RESOURCE Reminder

Practice Book: *Taking a Look at the British Economy,* page 51
- **Anthology:** *Working in the Mines,* pages 86–87

Technology: *Adventures CD-ROM* See page 199-B for activity.

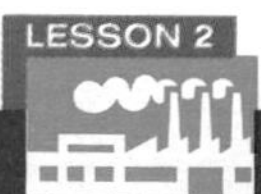

LESSON 2

The Economy

READ TO LEARN

Key Vocabulary

Industrial Revolution
nationalize
mixed economy

Read Aloud

It was a town of machinery and tall chimneys, out of which interminable [endless] *serpents of smoke trailed themselves for ever and ever. It had a . . . river that ran purple with ill-smelling dyes and vast piles of buildings . . . where the piston of the steam engine worked monotonously up and down like the head of an elephant in a state of melancholy madness.*

These words by the writer Charles Dickens describe the factory towns of England during the 1800s. In this lesson you will read how the British economy has changed since the days when English factories first filled the air with dark clouds of smoke.

Read for Purpose

1. WHAT YOU KNOW: Why have millions of immigrants moved to the British Isles?
2. WHAT YOU WILL LEARN: What economic challenges do the British face today?

THE INDUSTRIAL REVOLUTION

At the time when Charles Dickens was writing about factory towns in England, the country was in the middle of the **Industrial Revolution** of the 1800s. Jobs that were once done by hand were being done by machine. Products that once were made at home or in small workshops were being produced in factories. Machines helped factory workers to produce goods faster than ever before. In 1865 a shoe factory could turn out 300 pairs of machine-made shoes in a day. This was as many as a cobbler making shoes by hand could produce in an entire year.

The Industrial Revolution made Great Britain the economic leader of the world. Meanwhile, the Republic of Ireland was developing at a much slower pace. Ireland, which was a colony of Great Britain for hundreds of years, has few natural resources. Today the average income of the Irish is about half that of the British.

A MIXED ECONOMY

In the 1940s the British government took over large sections of industry. The government **nationalized** several businesses, including coal mines, gas and electric utilities, and railroads. To nationalize an

206 WHAT YOU KNOW: This question refers to material covered in Lesson 1; to find land, work, and freedom.

READING STRATEGY AND VOCABULARY DEVELOPMENT

Text Structure Remind students that writers choose the organizational pattern that they think will make their material as clear and easy to understand as possible. Point out that when writers discuss two different members of the same category (such as two countries), they often use comparison as an organizational pattern. Make a chart comparing the information given in this lesson about Great Britain and about the Republic of Ireland. Point out to students that in most sections of this lesson, the writer compares different aspects of Great Britain and the Republic of Ireland.

industry means to place it under the control or ownership of the government.

In recent years, however, many nationalized industries have been made private again. This means that today the United Kingdom has a **mixed economy**. A mixed economy is an economy consisting of a mixture of both private enterprises and government-run businesses.

The Republic of Ireland also has a mixed economy. The Irish government owns and operates the railroad and airline industries, and television and radio stations. Most other industries are controlled by private companies.

NEW RESOURCES

Things have changed in Great Britain since the days of the Industrial Revolution. The United Kingdom is no longer the world's leading industrial nation as it was in the 1800s. Today people in other countries are building new factories and setting up new businesses. They can produce goods more cheaply than the British because many British factories are outdated. But the British have recently discovered some valuable new resources.

During the 1960s huge oil and natural gas fields were found beneath the waters of the North Sea. When the price of oil increased dramatically in the 1970s, North Sea oil became very valuable. This pumped money into the British economy, which helped offset the loss of income from manufacturing industries.

FARMING

Every day John O'Leary tends the cows and sheep on his 22-acre (9-ha) farm in western Ireland. He adds to his income by cutting turf, or peat—the half-formed coal that the Irish dig out of the ground to burn as fuel. O'Leary is known as a *crofter*—a person who owns or rents a small farm.

Large platforms have been set up in the North Sea to get at valuable oil reserves far below the sea waters.

Understanding a Mixed Economy Be sure students understand that the present pattern of British nationalization was formed over time and that some of the industries nationalized in the 1940s have since been made private again.

Ask students:

- **What is nationalization?** (a system in which a nation's government controls or owns a company or an industry)
- **What is the role of nationalization in a mixed economy?** (In a mixed economy, some industries are government-owned, or nationalized, while others are privately owned.)

Looking at New Resources Help students to recognize that since Great Britain was one of the first nations to industrialize, its factories are older and less efficient than those of more recently industrialized countries.

Ask students:

- **Why has Great Britain lost the lead in industrial production?** (It has old-fashioned, inefficient factories.)
- **What and where are the valuable new British resources that were discovered in the 1960s?** (natural gas and oil in the North Sea)

Discussing Farming

Ask students:

- **What is a crofter?** (a farmer who owns or rents a small farm)

CURRICULUM CONNECTION

Science By developing an oil industry in the North Sea, Britain has brought high technology to a marine environment. Gigantic oil-rig platforms were embedded in the bottom of the sea. Often the oil rigs and other equipment cannot withstand the stresses of the ocean. Such breakdowns cause technological disasters in which people are injured and the ocean is polluted. Have students research two subjects—a food chain from the simplest organisms in the sea to humanity, and the effects of an oil spill on that food chain. Ask students to present their findings in two diagrams, one showing the food chain and one showing the effect of an oil spill on that food chain.

BACKGROUND INFORMATION

Multicultural Perspectives Britain's economic decline has been painful in many ways for its citizens. In 1987 Robert Chesshyre observed: *Britain has invented the television, the commercial computer, the jet engine, the video recorder—but now imported millions of pounds' worth of these items each week. We needed jobs . . . we essentially needed to start making things again. We still had [seeds] of the creativity of the first industrial revolution, most visible perhaps in the innovative street styles of London. . . . But . . . we were not going to fashion an economic miracle out of purple [mohawks].*

Ask students who they think has taken Britain's place as industrial leader of the world and why.

Comparing British and Irish Farming Continue the discussion of farming.

Ask students:

- **How does Great Britain's food production compare with the Republic of Ireland's?** (Great Britain does not produce enough food to feed its population; while Ireland does.)

Applying the Lesson Ask students to write a report on the current status of nationalization in Great Britain's economy. For information, have them write the Department of Trade and Industry, 1 Victoria St., London SW1H OET.

3 CLOSE

Summarizing Students have read about the industrial economy of Great Britain and the farm economy of the Republic of Ireland.

Evaluating Use the *Check Your Reading* questions (answers given below) to assess students' understanding.

Answers to Check Your Reading

1. a period during the 1800s when machine-made goods began to replace handmade goods and factories began to replace small workshops
2. It means that some of Great Britain's industries are government-owned (nationalized) and some are privately owned.
3. The farms in Ireland are small and old-fashioned, yet they produce almost enough food for the population. The farms in Great Britain are large and modern, yet they do not produce enough food for the population.
4. The Industrial Revolution occurred in the 1800s; nationalization of industries began in the 1940s; new resources in the form of oil and natural gas fields were found in the North Sea in the 1960s.

Independent Practice
Practice Book: page 51

The countryside of Ireland is dotted with small farms. At right, a man and a girl load turf they have cut for fuel onto a donkey.

The O'Leary family members are among those Irish workers who farm for a living. Like other crofters they grow potatoes and oats in addition to raising livestock. Today most Irish farms are smaller than 30 acres (12 ha). But they provide enough food to feed most of the people living in Ireland.

In Great Britain farming is different. Only about 2 percent of the people there are farmers. But most farms are large, modern, and efficient. Despite these farms' productivity, however, there is simply not enough farmland to feed Britain's large population. Every year the British import tons of food from countries around the world.

A WORLD LEADER

The Industrial Revolution made Great Britain a wealthy and powerful nation. Today Britain faces new economic problems. Because of its small size, its natural resources are limited. In addition, British factories now find it hard to compete against more modern factories in other countries. So the British now produce and sell fewer goods than in the past. The key to Britain's economic future may lie in resources buried under the North Sea.

Check Your Reading

1. What was the Industrial Revolution?
2. What does it mean to say that Great Britain has a mixed economy?
3. How is farming in Ireland different from farming in Great Britain?
4. **THINKING SKILL:** What is the correct order of the major events discussed in this lesson?

THINKING SKILL: Sequencing

208

MEETING INDIVIDUAL NEEDS

Reteaching (easy) Have students draw a series of "Before" and "After" pictures showing methods of British production before and after the Industrial Revolution.

Extension (average) Have students draw an organizational diagram for a mixed economy, using flow lines to show who makes investments in industries and where the profits go.

Enrichment (challenging) Have students research the nationalization pattern of Great Britain's industries today. Hold a class debate on this issue: "All nationalized British industries should be converted to private ownership."

The Government

READ TO LEARN

Key Vocabulary

Magna Carta
constitutional monarchy
welfare state

Key People

Margaret Thatcher

Read Aloud

Imagine that you are visiting London. It is autumn, and the leaves are turning bright shades of red and orange. Suddenly you see a stately procession winding through the streets. Soldiers in glittering uniforms escort a gilded horse-drawn coach. Why all the fuss? Because in that coach rides the queen of England.

Read for Purpose

1. WHAT YOU KNOW: What countries make up the British Isles?
2. WHAT YOU WILL LEARN: What are the important features of the governments of the British Isles?

TRADITIONS OF RULE

You read in Chapter 3 that Canada has a form of government called a parliamentary democracy. This kind of government is headed by a prime minister who rules through a national legislature. The system of parliamentary democracy began to be adopted by Canadians from the British during the 1700s.

The roots of British government go back hundreds of years. Early kings, such as William the Conqueror, whom you read about in Lesson 1, had great power. They could make laws, choose officials, and declare war or peace. Over the centuries, however, English thinking changed. Some people began to argue that all individual citizens had certain rights that ought to be protected.

Over time the British Parliament limited the power of the king and assumed more power. The rights and freedoms of each individual, argued Parliament leaders, were just as important as the powers of the king. In 1215 King John of Great Britain was forced to sign the **Magna Carta**, a document that limited the powers of the monarch. The Magna Carta is one of the most important documents in the history of the world.

Great Britain became the world's first **constitutional monarchy**. It is a monarchy because it is headed by a king or queen. It is constitutional because the monarch's powers are limited by a constitution that guarantees the rights of the people, especially the right to elect representatives to make laws.

Unlike the United States Constitution and most of the world's constitutions, the British constitution is not a single written document. Instead, it is made up of

WHAT YOU KNOW: This question refers to material in Lesson 1; the United Kingdom and the Republic of Ireland.

LESSON 3
pages 209–211

Lesson Theme A traditional respect for royalty combined with modern democratic ideas has inspired the basic principles of the British government.

Lesson Objectives
- Identify the Magna Carta.
- Describe Great Britain's constitutional monarchy.

PREPARE

Motivate Read the *Read Aloud* to the class. Ask students what the procession described here and the phrase "queen of England" suggest to them.

Set Purpose Answer the *What You Know* question to establish that this lesson will be about the United Kingdom. Tell students that the answers to the *What You Will Learn* question will be the most important facts they will learn about the British Isles.

TEACH

Discussing Traditions of Rule Help students to understand that a long, gradual process was begun when the Magna Carta, a document limiting the powers of the monarch, was signed. The belief that people should participate in their own government grew and led to the forming of the British Parliament.

READING STRATEGY AND VOCABULARY DEVELOPMENT

Text Structure Tell students that a fact is easier to remember when it is associated with an example. Have students read the section "Parliament and the Monarchy Today." Then, taking each paragraph in order, ask students to identify the fact given about the British government and the example that accompanies it. To start them off, identify the following fact: The House of Lords is the house of Parliament made up mainly of aristocrats. Then ask the class to find the example the paragraph gives of an aristocrat. Encourage students to find different organizational patterns in the other sections of this lesson. Help them to realize that the section "The British Influence" uses a comparison/contrast pattern. Have them list the similarities and differences between the governments of the United States and of Great Britain given in this section.

Understanding Parliament and the Monarchy Today Emphasize the unique role of the monarchy in unifying the British nation.

Ask students:

- **Who belongs to the House of Lords?** (The House of Lords has more than 1,000 members. Most are aristocrats holding titles from the queen. Others are judges or leaders of the Church of England.)
- **Describe the lower house of Parliament and its powers.** (The House of Commons, consisting of 650 elected members, passes all the country's laws.)
- **How is the prime minister chosen?** (He or she is the leader of the political party that has the most seats in Parliament.)
- **What role does the monarch play in Great Britain's constitutional monarchy?** (carries out many public functions, acts as a figurehead for the Commonwealth of Nations, inspires the loyalty of the British people)
- *THINKING FURTHER:* **Do you think the British monarch is a leader?** (One possible answer might be that the British monarch is a leader because he or she inspires the loyalty of the British people.)

Identifying British Influence Be sure students recognize that Great Britain is the source of powerful democratic ideas that still reverberate around the world.

Ask students:

- **What do some of the world's democracies have in common?** (Many were modeled on the British system.)

Defining New Approaches Point out that Great Britain has tried different philosophies of government. Help students to understand Great Britain's welfare state of the 1940s.

Ask students:

- **What was one of the programs designed during the 1940s to protect people "from the cradle to the grave"?** (the National Health Service)

Great Britain's royal family includes Queen Elizabeth (*left*), and Prince William (*right*).

important laws and charters adopted over many centuries. A charter is a formal written document, like the Magna Carta, issued by a government.

PARLIAMENT AND THE MONARCHY TODAY

The British Parliament consists of two parts called "houses." The upper house, known as the House of Lords, has more than 1,000 members. The House of Lords is made up largely of aristocrats who hold titles granted to them by English monarchs. The Duke of Kent, for example, is a member of the House of Lords. Some judges and leaders of the Church of England also belong to the House of Lords.

The lower house of Parliament is called the House of Commons. Its 650 members are elected by the British people. In the twentieth century the House of Commons has become more and more powerful. It now has the right to pass any measure into law. Now, unlike in the past, the House of Lords cannot interfere with any bills dealing with finances. Today few of its members play an active role in government.

The leader of the political party with the most seats in Parliament is the prime minister. The prime minister meets regularly with the cabinet, all of whom must be members of Parliament. Britain's legislative and executive branches of government are not separated.

In 1979 **Margaret Thatcher** became Britain's first woman prime minister. She was the first prime minister in more than 150 years who was elected for three consecutive terms. She resigned in 1990, to be replaced by John Major.

Under the British system of government, the monarch does not play a direct role in making policy. But the king or queen carries out many public functions. The monarch opens and closes Parliament, visits hospitals and factories, and represents Great Britain in foreign countries. The monarch also heads the Commonwealth of Nations. As you may remember from Chapter 3, the Commonwealth of Nations includes Great Britain and more than 40 other countries once ruled by the British.

Above all, the monarch inspires the loyalty of the British people. Today it costs

FUNDAMENTAL THEMES OF GEOGRAPHY

Movement The existence of the Commonwealth of Nations shows how the seafaring people of the British Isles, by sending forth explorers, armies, settlers, goods, and ideas all over the world, have spread their influence. Today, during the yearly meetings of the Commonwealth of Nations, ideas are exchanged and people move regularly among more than 40 member nations (many of which are former colonies).

the British over $40 million a year to maintain the "royals"—Queen Elizabeth and her family. But most British people believe that it is a good investment. "In laying out millions on the monarchy," explained one British woman, "the public is paying partly for a unique product—magic." An inhabitant of London put it more simply: "There's no one like her [the queen], that's all. We'd be lost without her."

The Republic of Ireland, like Great Britain has a parliament with two houses. But unlike Great Britain, Ireland does not have a monarch.

THE BRITISH INFLUENCE

As you have already read, democracies around the world have different forms of government. The United States, for example, is not headed by a hereditary ruler. Yet the world's democracies all have one thing in common: they are all modeled on the British system of government. The people who wrote the Declaration of Independence and the Constitution were familiar with British theories of government and documents like the Magna Carta. They were influenced by the long British tradition of respect for the individual rights and liberties of citizens.

NEW APPROACHES

During the 1940s the United Kingdom became a **welfare state**. Under this system, the government of the country took responsibility for the well-being of all its citizens. New programs aimed at protecting people "from the cradle to the grave" were established. The most far-reaching program was the National Health Service. The government provides free medical care to all British citizens.

Today some people say the health service is becoming too expensive. Others say that health care is worth the cost.

Margaret Thatcher became the first woman prime minister of Great Britain in 1979 and remained prime minister until 1990.

A LONG TRADITION

As you have seen, government in the British Isles is a complex system that tries to balance ancient traditions with modern concerns for the individual. The British are very proud of their government. One observer has noted:

> *The typical Englishman believes that his government is incomparably the best in the world. . . . He does not, of course, always agree with the course of policy pursued . . . but he is certain that the general form of government is well-nigh perfect.*

Check Your Reading

1. How has the role of the British monarch changed over the years?
2. Why is the House of Commons more powerful than the House of Lords?
3. Why is the British government called a constitutional monarchy?
4. THINKING SKILL: Compare and contrast the governments of Great Britain and the United States.

THINKING SKILL: Compare and Contrast

Applying the Lesson Have students discuss recent world events and bring in news clippings showing that belief in democracy is alive in many other countries.

CLOSE

Summarizing Students have read about some of the events and ideas that led to the development of Great Britain's parliamentary democracy, about its structure, and about its role as a model for other democracies.

Evaluating Use these questions to assess students' understanding.

- **What is the Magna Carta?** (a document, signed by King John in 1215, that limited the powers of the monarch)
- **What is one right guaranteed the people of Great Britain by their constitutional monarchy?** (Possible answers include: the right to elect representatives to make laws.)

Answers to Check Your Reading

1. from ruler to symbolic figurehead
2. It is elected by the people and has complete power over financial decisions.
3. It is headed by a queen or king who is limited by a constitution that protects citizens' rights.
4. They are both representative democracies; Great Britain has no single document that serves as a constitution and the United States has no monarch.

Independent Practice
Practice Book: page 52

MEETING INDIVIDUAL NEEDS

Reteaching (easy) Have students draw a diagram of the British Parliament. Have them label the House of Lords, the House of Commons, and the prime minister, and then list the powers of each.

Extension (average) Have students choose either Margaret Thatcher or Queen Elizabeth II and gather information about her life. Then have them write a short biography of the leader they chose.

Enrichment (challenging) Ask students to find out more about the history of the British National Health Service and to research current proposals for a national health care system in the United States. Then have them write an essay on "The Advantages and Disadvantages of a National Health Care System for the United States."

LESSON 4
pages 212–213

Lesson Theme The two nations of the British Isles have given the world a rich cultural legacy.

Lesson Objectives
- Describe sports in the British Isles.
- Identify the literary tradition of the British Isles.

PREPARE

Motivate Read the *Read Aloud* to the class. Ask the final question. Then, using students' answers, write two lists on the chalkboard, one of British and Irish sports and one of British and Irish books. Tell students that this lesson may give them new items for their lists.

Set Purpose Use students' answers to the *What You Know* question to review the variety of American sports. Tell students that the answers to the *What You Will Learn* question will provide a comparison of arts and sports in the British Isles and in the United States.

TEACH

Talking About Sports Help students to recognize the creativity displayed by the British in devising their sports.

Ask students:

- **Name three sports that were invented in Great Britain.** (cricket, soccer, golf)
- **What is the British attitude toward sportsmanship?** (They value good sportsmanship.)

LESSON 4

Arts and Recreation

READ TO LEARN

Key People

William Shakespeare

Read Aloud

It is late afternoon on a hot summer's day. On the village green in the center of town several people dressed in white pants and shirts are playing a game called cricket. Now and then spectators applaud or call out, "well played!" Soon it will be time for a tea break. After tea the two teams will return to the field and finish the game.

You have read that the British came up with many new ideas about government. But did you also know that they have had a great effect on the games played and the books read around the world?

Read for Purpose

1. WHAT YOU KNOW: What sports are popular in the United States?
2. WHAT YOU WILL LEARN: What are the literary and sporting traditions of the British Isles?

SPORTS

Cricket is just one of many sports enjoyed in the British Isles. The British people believe that good sportsmanship is important in all sports. A famous poem expresses this attitude:

For when the one Great Scorer comes
To write against your name.
He marks not that you won or lost,
But how you played the game.

Soccer, which is called "football" in the British Isles, is the most popular British spectator sport. It was invented in England and is enjoyed today in countries from Europe to South America.

Different sports are popular in different parts of the British Isles. In Scotland, for example, many people love to play golf. The game was invented there, and players all over the world follow the rules established by the Royal and Ancient Golf Club of St. Andrews in Scotland.

LITERARY TRADITIONS

Assassination, countless, gloomy, and *laughable*—do you know what these words have in common? All of them, and many more, were invented by the great English playwright William Shakespeare Whether or not you have yet read any of Shakespeare's plays, you are probably familiar with several characters in his plays. Do you know the sad stories of Romeo and Juliet, Hamlet, King Lear, and Macbeth?

English writers created many of the world's first novels. The fame of novelists and poets like Charlotte Brontë, Elizabeth Barrett Browning, Charles Dickens, and Thomas Hardy has spread around the

 WHAT YOU KNOW: Possible responses include: baseball, football, basketball, tennis, golf, and many other sports.

READING STRATEGY AND VOCABULARY DEVELOPMENT

Text Structure Review the organizational patterns covered in this chapter (chronological order, statement/example, comparison/contrast). Ask students which of these patterns is used in the sections "Sports" and "Literary Traditions." (statement/example) Ask them to list all the facts and accompanying examples given in these sections. Have students write a paragraph using the organizational pattern of comparison/contrast to discuss British and American sports.

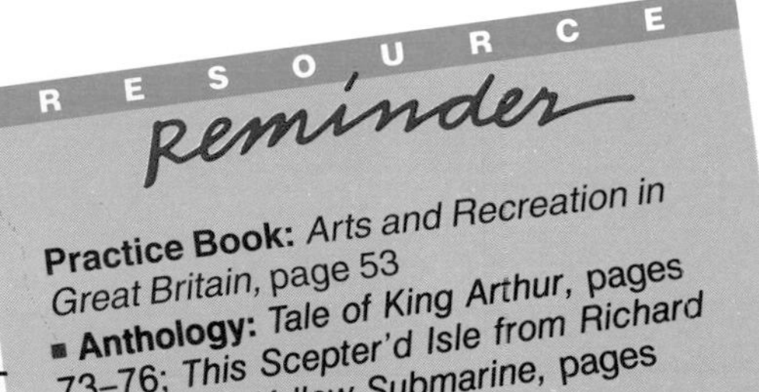

RESOURCE *Reminder*

Practice Book: *Arts and Recreation in Great Britain*, page 53
▪ **Anthology:** *Tale of King Arthur*, pages 73–76; *This Scepter'd Isle from Richard II*, page 81; *Yellow Submarine*, pages 99–100

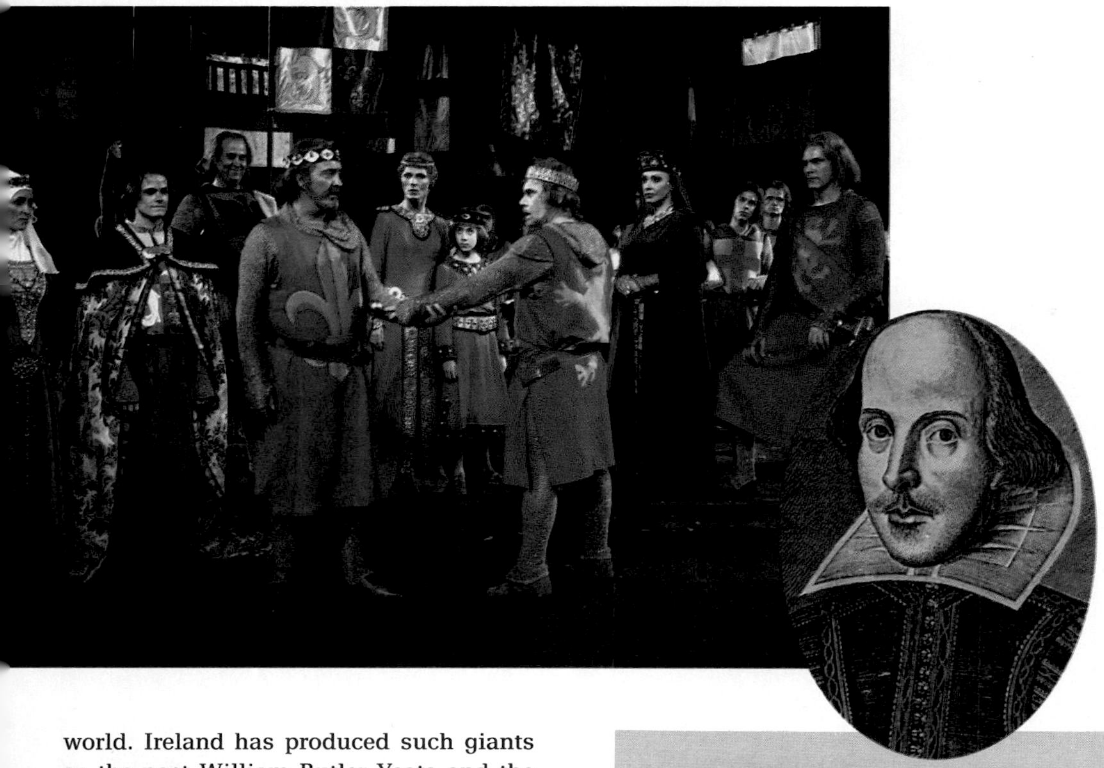

world. Ireland has produced such giants as the poet William Butler Yeats and the novelist James Joyce. The best-known Welsh poet of recent times is Dylan Thomas. And Scots like to memorize and recite the poems of the writer, Robert Burns.

THE INFLUENCE OF THE BRITISH

Although Great Britain and Ireland are small in size, the people living there have had a huge impact on the rest of the world. In addition to soccer and cricket, Britain has given the world many great works of literature. Britain also gave the world the English language. English is the main language of about 400 million people all over the world, and a second language for 600 million more. As you read the rest of this book, remember that it is written in English because of the wide influence of the people of the British Isles.

The plays of William Shakespeare (*inset*), such as this one, *King John*, are still produced all over the world.

Check Your Reading

1. Name some of the major writers who came from the British Isles.
2. Name three sports that are enjoyed by people in Great Britain and Ireland.
3. List two examples of the influence British literature and sports have had on the rest of the world.
4. THINKING SKILL: Is the following statement a fact or an opinion? Explain your answer. "The British [are] sport-mad. Whatever else may be going on in the world . . . [they] will prefer both to talk and to think about sport."

THINKING SKILL: Fact and Opinion

Identifying Literary Traditions Point out to students that British writers invented the novel and that William Shakespeare gave the world great plays and poetry and many new English words.

Discussing the Influence of the English Language Ask students to calculate how many people use English as a first or second language. (400 million + 600 million = 1 billion people) Discuss how this fact reveals the cultural impact of the British and Irish on the world.

Applying the Lesson Ask students to write a paragraph about the relationship between cricket and baseball.

3 CLOSE

Summarizing Students have read that the British and Irish have given the world a rich legacy of arts and sports.

Evaluating Use the *Check Your Reading* questions (answers given below) to assess students' understanding.

Answers to Check Your Reading

1. William Shakespeare, Charlotte Brontë, Elizabeth Barrett Browning, Charles Dickens, Thomas Hardy, William Butler Yeats, James Joyce, Dylan Thomas, Robert Burns
2. cricket, soccer, golf
3. They have had a huge impact. Worldwide soccer and golf tournaments are held. Over 1 billion people know English and are familiar with the great literary works of the British Isles.
4. It is an opinion. The value-laden description "sport-mad" is one clue to its being an opinion.

Independent Practice
Practice Book: page 53

MEETING INDIVIDUAL NEEDS

Reteaching (easy) Have students write a paragraph on the relationship between the British game of rugby and the North American game of football.

Extension (average) Have each student choose one of the writers mentioned in this lesson and find out more about her/his life. Then ask each student to write a skit about an incident in that person's life.

Enrichment (challenging) Have students learn more about how Shakespeare's plays were performed. Ask students to imagine that they lived in Shakespeare's time and have just attended one of his plays. Have them write a letter to a friend in France describing the performance and their opinion of Shakespeare as a playwright.

CHAPTER 9 REVIEW
pages 214–215

USING THE CHAPTER SUMMARY AND REVIEW

Cultural Geography These questions may be used for review.

- **Which groups of people invaded the British Isles?** (Possible answers include: the Romans and Anglo-Saxons.)
- **What kind of economy does the United Kingdom have?** (a mixed economy)
- **What is a constitutional monarchy?** (a government that is headed by a king or queen whose powers are limited by a constitution that guarantees the rights of the people)
- **Identify two sports that are popular in the British Isles?** (cricket and soccer)

Ideas to Remember

- **Where do most of today's immigrants to Great Britain come from?** (India, Pakistan, the West Indies)
- **What economic problems does Great Britain face today?** (outdated factories, competition from other countries that produce goods more cheaply than Great Britain does)
- **Who heads the government of Great Britain?** (the prime minister)
- **Who was William Shakespeare?** (a great English playwright)

Answers to Reviewing Vocabulary

1. Magna Carta
2. mixed economy
3. welfare state
4. Industrial Revolution
5. nationalize

Answers to Reviewing Facts

1. the United Kingdom and the Republic of Ireland
2. the English Channel
3. Normans; William the Conqueror
4. Protestants and Roman Catholics

CHAPTER 9 • SUMMARY

THE BRITISH ISLES: CULTURAL GEOGRAPHY

PEOPLE

- First People: Celts

- Anglo-Saxons invaded from northern Europe
- 1066: Norman invasion: William the Conqueror
- Today: many immigrants from Asia, West Indies, and Africa

- Northern Ireland: constant conflict during modern period

ECONOMY

- Industrial Revolution: made Britain world economic leader
- Mixed economy: private enterprise and government-run businesses

- 1960s: oil and natural gas discovered in North Sea

- Farming: small farms in Ireland, large farms in England

GOVERNMENT

- Parliamentary democracy and constitutional monarchy
- Parliament: House of Lords and House of Commons

- British influence: their form of democracy has spread all over the world
- Welfare state: government takes great responsibility for well-being of citizens

ARTS AND RECREATION

- Sports: cricket, rugby, and soccer

- Great literary tradition: William Shakespeare, Charlotte Brontë, Elizabeth Barrett Browning, Charles Dickens, and many more

IDEAS TO REMEMBER

- The people of the British Isles are a complex mixture of peoples and cultures.
- Though Great Britain was once an industrial leader, today the country faces economic problems.
- The government of Great Britain provides for both a parliamentary democracy and a constitutional monarchy; the Republic of Ireland has a parliamentary democracy.
- Arts and sports that originated in Great Britain are popular the world over.

214

ENRICHMENT ACTIVITY

Performing English Literature **Materials:** costumes or props

1. Review with the class the British literary traditions described on pages 212–213. Have them look in their anthologies for works by British writers. Then tell students that they are going to plan a presentation based on British writing.
2. Divide the class into groups and help each choose excerpts from a different writer. For example, from Shakespeare they might select Juliet's "Wherefore art thou" speech, or from Dickens' *A Tale of Two Cities,* the part beginning "It was the best of times. . . ." Suggest also Edward Lear's nonsense verses, perhaps from *The Jumblies.*
3. Help students to plan their presentations. Some selections will be suited to role playing, other selections to choral reading. Provide time for students to rehearse.
4. Have the groups perform their readings for each other.

CHAPTER 9 • REVIEW

REVIEWING VOCABULARY

Industrial Revolution
Magna Carta
mixed economy
nationalize
welfare state

Number a sheet of paper from 1 to 5. Beside each number write the word or term from the list above that best completes each sentence.

1. Because it set limits on royal power, the ____ became one of the greatest political documents of all time.
2. A ____ has both government-owned and privately owned businesses.
3. In a ____ the government takes responsibility for the well-being of its citizens by providing free health care and other services.
4. During the ____ machines began to be used to do many jobs that had once been done by hand.
5. To take government control of a business is to ____ it.

REVIEWING FACTS

1. Which two nations make up the British Isles?
2. Which body of water separates the British Isles from the European mainland?
3. Which powerful group conquered England in A.D. 1066? Who was its leader?
4. Which two religious groups are involved in the conflict in Northern Ireland?
5. What is a mixed economy? How has Great Britain changed its economy in recent years?
6. Why must Britain import thousands of tons of food each year?
7. How does a constitutional monarchy limit the power of a king or queen?
8. What are the main functions of the monarch in present-day Great Britain?
9. Describe the two houses of the British Parliament.
10. Which two sports now popular worldwide began in Great Britain?

WRITING ABOUT MAIN IDEAS

1. **Writing an Essay:** The quotation by a British writer at the beginning of the chapter suggests that Great Britain was "the America of Europe." Write an essay expressing agreement or disagreement with the writer's suggestion.
2. **Writing a Poem:** Write a poem about some aspect of England that you have read about or seen in an illustration.
3. **Writing About Perspectives:** Imagine that you live in Great Britain. Write a paragraph telling five things that make your country a place in which you are glad to live.

BUILDING SKILLS: READING A WORLD TIME ZONE MAP

1. If you are traveling, by how many hours should you adjust your watch for each time zone you cross?
2. What happens when you cross the International Date Line?
3. If you cross the International Date Line from east to west on a Sunday, what day does it become?
4. Why is it helpful to understand world time zones?

5. an economy consisting of a mixture of both private enterprises and government-run businesses; Many nationalized industries have become private again, and the British are developing new valuable resources.
6. There is not enough farmland to feed its large population.
7. It is limited by a constitution that guarantees the rights of the people, especially the right to elect representatives to make laws.
8. The monarch opens and closes Parliament, visits hospitals and factories, represents Great Britain in foreign countries, and heads the Commonwealth of Nations.
9. The House of Lords consists mainly of aristocrats who cannot interfere with any bills having to do with finances. The House of Commons is made up of elected members who have the right to pass any measure into law.
10. soccer and golf

Suggestions for Writing About Main Ideas

1. You may wish to divide the class into two groups. Have the groups debate whether or not Great Britain was "the America of Europe."
2. It may help the students to first brainstorm to come up with a list of things that they might want to write about.
3. Students should try to include a variety of types of things that British people might like about their country.

Answers to Building Skills: Reading a World Time-Zone Map

1. one hour
2. You gain or lose one day.
3. Monday
4. Possible answers include: It helps to know the time in places you might be dealing with.

Chapter Review and Test

Practice Book: *Vocabulary Review,* page 54
Transparency: *Graphic Organizer*
Assessment Book: *Chapter 9 Test*

MAKING CONNECTIONS

Organizing Information Use the Main Idea Map Graphic Organizer Transparency, and write in the five underlined labels. Have students review the chapter and fill in details relating to the topic. *Ask:* What contributions have the British Isles made to the world?

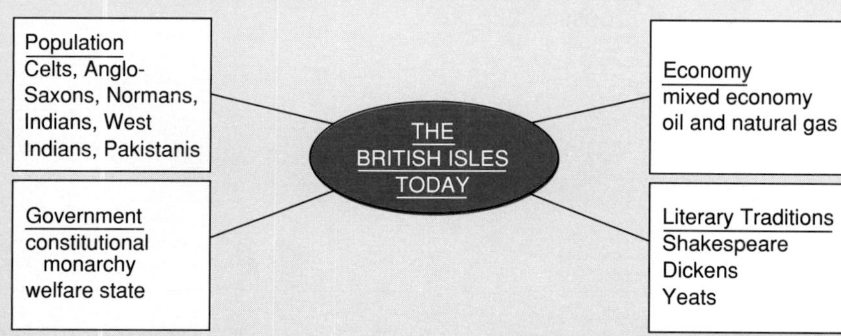

CHAPTER 10
ORGANIZER

FRANCE AND THE LOW COUNTRIES text pages 216–231

CHAPTER THEME The rich plains of France and the Low Countries promote swift transportation, specialized farming, and developed economies.

CHAPTER OBJECTIVES

CONTENT

- Name the countries that make up the Low Countries.
- Define *guest worker* and list the countries from which most French guest workers come.
- Name the two major groups of people in Belgium and indicate in what region each lives.
- List the major industries and services of France and the Low Countries.
- Define *dike* and explain why dikes have been essential to the Netherlands' survival.
- Define *European Union* and describe how the EU has helped the countries of Western Europe.
- Explain why the French constitution allows for a strong president.
- Contrast the monarchies of the Low Countries with the British monarchy.
- List the arts and sports that have developed in France and the Low Countries.

SKILLS

Geography
- Interpret a political map of France and the Low Countries.
- Use a map to identify land reclaimed from the sea in the Netherlands.
- Use maps at different scales.

Thinking
- Describe how geography has influenced the economies of France and the Low Countries.
- Identify alternatives in a particular historical situation.

Reading and Writing
- Write a summary about European unification.

CITIZENSHIP VALUES

- Appreciate that individuals can make a difference in society.
- Appreciate the role that language plays in shaping a people's identity and character.

TEACHER OPTIONS

READING STRATEGY: Note Taking and Outlining Strategies to help students read and remember the main ideas of the lesson.

Lesson 1: p. 217 Lesson 3: p. 226
Lesson 2: p. 221 Lesson 4: p. 228

MEETING INDIVIDUAL NEEDS Activities for reteaching, extension, and enrichment.

Lesson 1: p. 220 Lesson 3: p. 227
Lesson 2: p. 223 Lesson 4: p. 229
Geography Skills: p. 225

GEO ADVENTURES ACTIVITIES PAD Daily activities to assess students' understanding of geography skills.

CURRICULUM CONNECTION Activities to help integrate other subject areas with Social Studies.

Language Arts: p. 219 Math: p. 224

PUPIL EDITION ON CASSETTE Language support for students who have difficulty reading or who will benefit from listening to the Pupil Edition on Cassette as they read.

SECOND-LANGUAGE SUPPORT Activities and suggestions for second-language learners.

Lesson 2: p. 18

CHAPTER PLANNING GUIDE

LESSON	SUGGESTED PACING	THEMES	TEACHER SUPPORT MATERIALS: TEACHER'S RESOURCE CENTER
1 THE PEOPLE pages 217–220	1 day	Over the ages the fertile plains of France and the Low Countries have attracted many groups of people.	Practice Book p. 55 ■ Anthology p. 77 **Technology:** *Adventures CD-ROM*
2 THE ECONOMY pages 221–223	1 day	Farming, diversified products, and many service industries characterize the developed economies of France and the Low Countries.	Practice Book p. 56 **Technology:** *Adventures CD-ROM*
BUILDING GEOGRAPHY SKILLS Using Maps at Different Scales pages 224–225	1 day	A small-scale map is used to show a large area, and a large-scale map is used to show a small area in detail.	Practice Book p. 57 Transparency Map 11
3 THE GOVERNMENT pages 226–227	1 day	Both France and the Low Countries are representative democracies, but the French president has sweeping powers, and monarchs still reign in the Low Countries.	Practice Book p. 58 **Technology:** *Adventures CD-ROM*
4 ARTS AND RECREATION pages 228–229	1 day	France and the Low Countries enjoy a rich heritage of arts and sports.	Practice Book p. 59 ■ Anthology p. 85
CHAPTER SUMMARY AND REVIEW pages 230–231	1 day	Chapter content, skills, and vocabulary are reviewed and evaluated.	Practice Book p. 60 Transparency: Graphic Organizer Assessment Book, Chapter 10 Test

Technology CONNECTION

Lesson 1
ADVENTURES CD-ROM
In *Travel,* students can find maps of France, Belgium, the Netherlands, and Luxembourg.

Lesson 2
ADVENTURES CD-ROM
Explore Media and find out about some of the agricultural resources of these countries.

Lesson 3
ADVENTURES CD-ROM
Have students listen to "La Marseillaise" in *Investigate, Sounds, France.*

CHAPTER 10
pages 216–231

USING THE CHAPTER OPENER

Discussing the Photograph Point out to students that the policeman in this picture projects a different image from that of the Mountie in the picture on page 80. Encourage students to describe this policeman.

Ask students:

- **Do you think this policeman works in the city or in the country? Why?** (Most students will probably guess that this policeman works in the city because he seems to be directing traffic.)
- **How does the policeman's appearance compare to that of the Canadian Mountie?** (Possible answers include: His uniform, with its tie and white collar, looks more like a business suit than does the uniform of the Mountie.)

Reading/Listening to the Primary Source Read the passage under the picture to the class. Encourage students to imagine that the policeman works in Paris. Ask them what they know about Paris from movies, books, or travel.

Ask students:

- **How might a city reflect the desire of a nation's people to be the best and the first in everything?** (Since a nation's cities are its centers of business, politics, fashion, art, and scholarship, they are considered symbols of the success of the people of that nation in those areas.)
- *THINKING FURTHER:* **Why do you think the French people might be proud of Paris?** (Possible answers include: because Paris is an important center of culture; because Paris was the site where most of the important events of the French Revolution occurred, and because Paris is a beautiful city.)

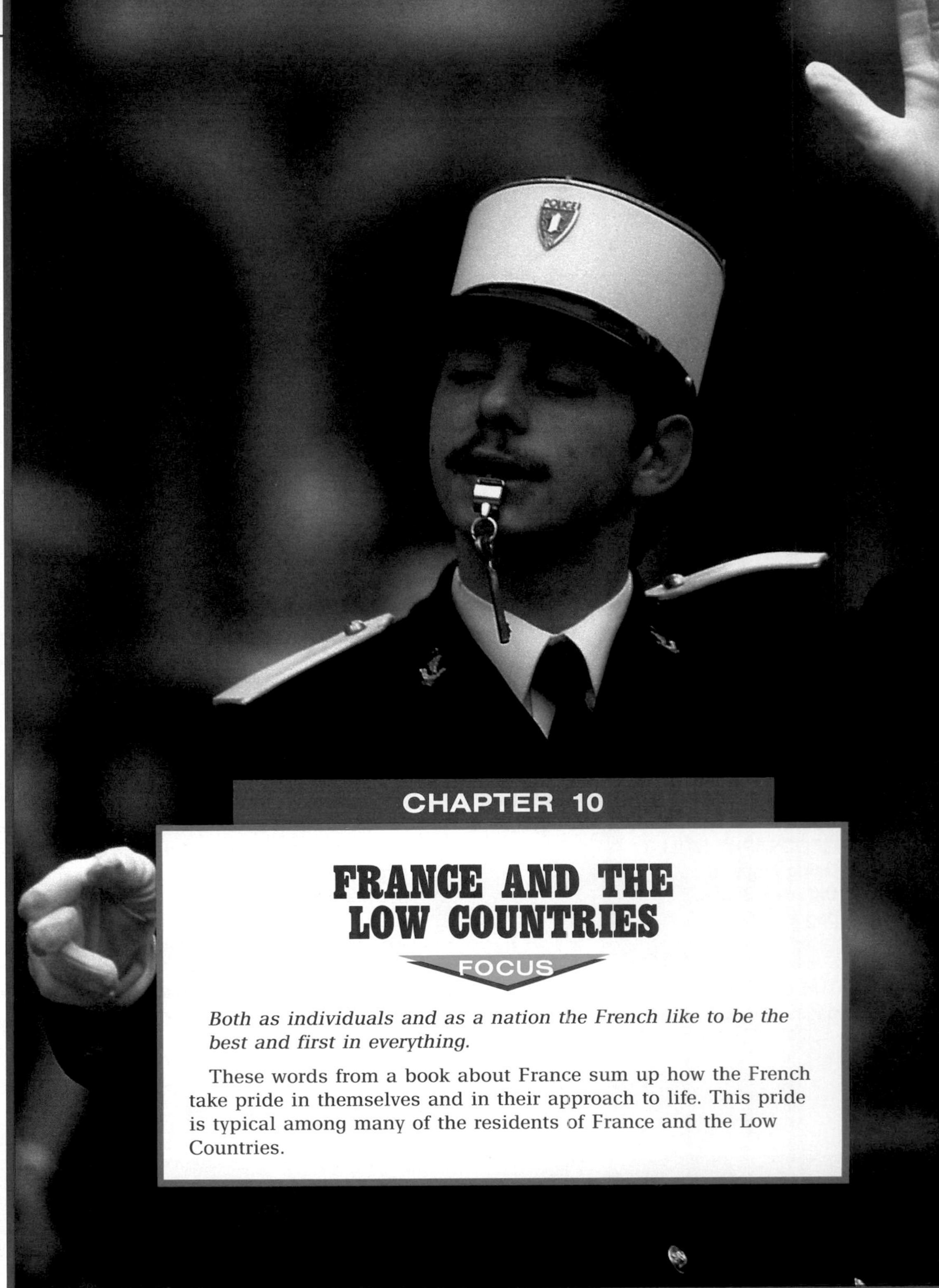

CHAPTER 10

FRANCE AND THE LOW COUNTRIES

FOCUS

Both as individuals and as a nation the French like to be the best and first in everything.

These words from a book about France sum up how the French take pride in themselves and in their approach to life. This pride is typical among many of the residents of France and the Low Countries.

BACKGROUND INFORMATION

About Paris Paris, the capital of France, is divided by the Seine River into three different sectors.

- The Île de la Cité, where the first settlement of Paris was established, contains some of France's most famous buildings, for example, the Conciergerie, where Queen Marie Antoinette was imprisoned before her execution, and the Cathedral of Nôtre Dame.
- The Right Bank is the commercial and industrial center of Paris. Here one can find the Place de la Bastille, where the Bastille once stood. The storming of the Bastille signaled the start of the French Revolution.
- The Left Bank has long represented France's intellectual and artistic life. Here is located the Sorbonne, the seat of the main faculty of letters of the University of Paris.

The People

READ TO LEARN

Key Vocabulary

guest worker

Key Places

Belgium
the Netherlands
Luxembourg

Read Aloud

Every yard of Europe has, at one time or another, belonged to some other nation, race, or clan; every foot has been fought for, given, or stolen.

The words above are especially true of France and the Low Countries. For thousands of years, other Europeans have envied these lands along the Atlantic Coast. In this lesson you will read how different groups of people have lived and worked in France and the Low Countries.

Read for Purpose

1. WHAT YOU KNOW: What are the Low Countries?
2. WHAT YOU WILL LEARN: Which groups of people have settled in France and the Low Countries?

AN ATTRACTIVE LAND

Can you guess the reason Belgium, the Netherlands, and Luxembourg are called the Low Countries? Their land is among the lowest-lying in all of Europe. For thousands of years, invading armies were attracted to these fertile lowlands. They were also attracted to the wide, navigable rivers and to the long flat coastlines that provided natural ports for trade. For these reasons, France and the Low Countries have been a crossroads of people for many centuries.

CELTS, FRANKS, AND OTHERS

On the walls of a cave at Lascaux, France, wonderful pictures show prehistoric animals. Stone Age hunters painted them about 20,000 years ago. Thousands of years later, new groups moved in from the north and south. Among them were the Celts, whom you read about in Chapter 9. In France one group of Celts were known as the Gauls. They called the land that they settled Gaul.

The Romans also took an interest in France, just as they did in Great Britain. In 58 B.C. Julius Caesar led a powerful Roman army into Gaul. After seven years of fighting, his soldiers conquered part of what is now France and the Low Countries.

Roman colonists spread their language—Latin — throughout much of southern

WHAT YOU KNOW: This question refers to material in Chapter 8, Lesson 1; Belgium, the Netherlands, and Luxembourg.

LESSON 1

pages 217–220

Lesson Theme Over the ages the fertile plains of France and the Low Countries have attracted many groups of people.

Lesson Objectives

- Describe the Low Countries.
- Describe the groups that have settled in France and the Low Countries.
- Explain the growth of the French language.

1 PREPARE

Motivate Read the *Read Aloud* section to students. Have them speculate on the meaning of the opening quotation.

Set Purpose Have a student answer the *What You Know* question. Refer students to the *Atlas* map of Western Europe and discuss the location of France and the Low Countries. Use the *What You Will Learn* question to challenge students to look for connections between what they know about the movement of settlers into the British Isles and what they will read about the movement of settlers into France and the Low Countries.

2 TEACH

Looking at an Attractive Land Help students to realize that the low, fertile land, navigable rivers, flat coast, and natural harbors of France and the Low Countries have attracted people to the region.

Discussing Celts, Franks, and Others Encourage students to track the order in which different groups of people came to France and the Low Countries over the ages.

READING STRATEGY AND VOCABULARY DEVELOPMENT

Note Taking and Outlining The purpose of this strategy is to help students recognize and record important information from a selection. Review the note-taking and outlining strategies introduced in Chapters 4 and 6 of Unit 2. As a review, you may wish to help students prepare their notes or outlines for the first section of this lesson. For this chapter have students record their notes and outlines in a notebook. In one column of the notebook have students record their notes, and in the second column have students record personal observations or opinions about what they have read.

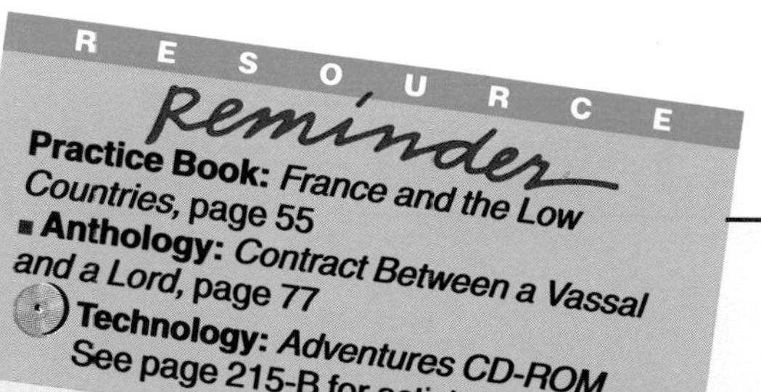
RESOURCE *Reminder*

Practice Book: *France and the Low Countries*, page 55

Anthology: *Contract Between a Vassal and a Lord*, page 77

Technology: *Adventures CD-ROM* See page 215-B for activity.

Following the Celts, Franks, and Others Continue the discussion.

Ask students:

- **Beginning 20,000 years ago, which groups of people moved into France and the Low Countries and what were the results of their movement?** (Stone Age hunters—cave paintings; Gauls—French language; Romans—Latin; Frisians—conquered the Celts of the Netherlands; Franks—France's name; Vikings—caused fortresses to be built)
- *THINKING FURTHER:* **Which groups of people moved into both the British Isles and France and the Low Countries?** (Celts, Vikings, Romans)

EXTENDING MAP SKILLS

Have students study the political map on this page.

Ask students:

- **What are the capitals of France and the three Low Countries?** (Paris, France; Brussels, Belgium; Amsterdam, the Netherlands; Luxembourg, Luxembourg)
- **Which countries border France and the Low Countries on the east?** (Germany, Italy, Switzerland)
- **Which countries border France on the south?** (Andorra and Spain)
- **What point of interest is located in southern France?** (Lascaux)
- **What geographic feature connects France and the Low Countries?** (a river)
- **Which cities are located on the Garonne River?** (Bordeaux and Toulouse)
- **Which country has the longest border with France and the Low Countries?** (Germany)

FRANCE AND THE LOW COUNTRIES: Political

⊛ National capital • Other city ▪ Point of interest

MAP SKILL: What body of water is located off the coast of Belgium and The Netherlands?

Europe. But people in Gaul had trouble pronouncing the Latin words correctly. They added new terms and phrases to the language until they created a brand new one, which became known as French.

As the power of the Romans weakened, warlike groups swept across many parts of Europe. One group, called the Frisians, conquered the Celts of the Netherlands. Another group called the Franks took control of what is today Belgium.

Soon, the kingdom of the Franks spread southward from Belgium. This kingdom became known as France. Under the powerful ruler Charlemagne, France became a Roman Catholic country. Great cathedrals like Notre Dame in Paris were built by hand, stone by stone.

Although the Franks ruled France for more than 400 years, they constantly had to fight off invaders from all sides. In the A.D. 800s, for example, ships from Scandinavia filled with warriors called the Vikings attacked settlements on the North Atlantic coast. Fortresses had to be built all over France to keep out invaders like the Vikings.

The Vikings were not the last people to invade France and the Low Countries. But until the 1900s no other group settled there in very large numbers. From the ninth century until the middle of the twentieth, the people of France and the Low Countries developed their own cultures.

FRANCE: A NATION OF INDIVIDUALISTS

Today each part of France has its own individual groups. In Bordeaux (bôr dō′), for example, some family names sound English. This is due to the fact that for 300 years Bordeaux was ruled by the English. Find the Bordeaux region on the map on this page.

People living in the rugged slopes of the Pyrenees Mountains speak Basque, a language unrelated to any other tongue. And the Bretons of Brittany came to France from across the English Channel. Many still speak an ancient Celtic language similar to languages in Wales and Ireland.

In recent years immigrants from many lands have added to France's diversity. Some newcomers, called **guest workers**, have moved to France in search of work. They come mostly from Southern Europe. Usually they cannot become citizens.

Another group of immigrants left Algeria and Morocco to live in France. These North African lands had been under French control for many years. After

MAP SKILL: the North Sea

BACKGROUND INFORMATION

Multicultural Perspectives People often think of France as having a single culture, yet in reality France is a multicultural nation.

- About one out of every 12 residents in France is either a recent immigrant or the descendant of an immigrant.
- Over half of France's immigrants, or more than 2.3 million people, have come from France's former African colonies: Algeria, Morocco, and Tunisia. Others have come from Italy, Portugal, Spain, and Vietnam.
- Islam is France's second-largest religion.
- Some of France's biggest celebrities were actually born in other countries. Designer Pierre Cardin and actor Yves Montand were born in Italy. Writer Albert Camus was born in Algeria.

Ask students what makes French people, French people.

The Eiffel Tower (*right*) is one of the popular landmarks of Paris, France. People in Paris enjoy gathering at sidewalk cafés (*left*).

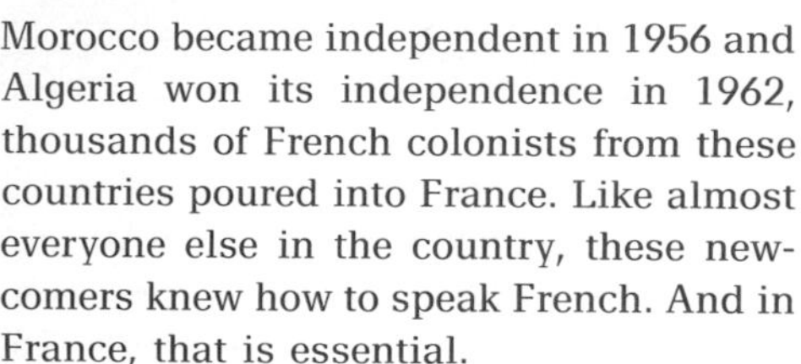

Morocco became independent in 1956 and Algeria won its independence in 1962, thousands of French colonists from these countries poured into France. Like almost everyone else in the country, these newcomers knew how to speak French. And in France, that is essential.

THE FRENCH LANGUAGE

The French consider their language to be a national treasure. In 1635 King Louis XIII of France founded the French Academy to write a dictionary of *bon usage* (good and proper use). To this day the Academy is still busy revising definitions and deciding on the correct use of the French language. Every three months the Academy publishes a list of new errors that creep into common use.

Today the French government tries to preserve the purity of the French language by preventing American phrases from being used. Road signs, menus, and other printed materials are constantly examined to root out French words that have been taken over from American phrases. Businesses can be fined for using terms like *le jogging* or *le compact disc.*

Today at least 122 million people speak French. It is one of the official languages of Belgium, Luxembourg, Switzerland, Canada, and 20 other countries. It is one of the six official languages of the United Nations.

THE LOWLANDERS

If language is the connecting thread in French life, it is the dividing wedge in nearby Belgium. Unlike Canada, which is a bilingual nation, Belgium is divided into language areas. In the southern part of Belgium are the Walloons. They speak French, and French is the official language of their area, called Wallonia. In the

Discussing France—A Nation of Individualists Help students to see the mix of languages that exists in France along with the official language, French. On the political map have students locate the regions in which other languages are in evidence.

Ask students:

- **How are guest workers increasing the diversity in France?** (They come from other nations and bring their cultures and languages to France.)
- **From which two former colonies did immigrants move to France after the colonies became independent?** (Algeria and Morocco)
- *THINKING FURTHER:* **What might happen to a country's language when newcomers settle there?** (Gradually, new words are added to the country's language.)

Talking About the French Language

Ask students:

- **What is the role of the French Academy?** (The Academy revises definitions, decides on the correct use of the French language, and publishes a list of new errors that are in common use.)
- **What is the official language of Belgium, Luxembourg, and Switzerland?** (French)

Looking at the Lowlanders

Ask students:

- **What is unique about the use of language in Belgium?** (Belgium is divided into language areas.)

CURRICULUM CONNECTION

Language Arts Have those students studying a foreign language report on any English-sounding words or English root words that they have found in their studies. Ask the class to brainstorm all the words they can think of that are used in spoken English, but which come from another language. On the chalkboard classify lists of words under the names of other languages; for example, French—*potpourri*; Spanish—*cafeteria*; German—*kindergarten*, and so on. Challenge students to make a board game using a world map and these word lists. Have students give a creative title to their game; for example, "Ethnic English."

Discussing the Lowlanders Continue discussing the Lowlanders.

Ask students:

- **What is a problem for the Dutch?** (The country is crowded, with 900 people per square mile, or 347.5 people per sq km.)

Applying the Lesson Have students make a chart comparing the people who settled in France and the Low Countries with those who settled in the British Isles.

3 CLOSE

Summarizing Students should understand that in the past waves of settlers moved into France and the Low Countries. Ask students why they think information about these groups is so important today.

Evaluating Use these questions to assess students' understanding.

- **Which countries are called the Low Countries?** (Belgium, the Netherlands, Luxembourg)
- **Which group conquered Gaul?** (the Romans)
- **With which group did the French language originate?** (the Gauls)

Answers to Check Your Reading

1. Celts, Gauls, Romans, Frisians, Franks, Vikings
2. Ancient Roman colonists spread Latin throughout Gaul, but people in Gaul had trouble pronouncing Latin words correctly. These people added new terms to the language until they created a new language known as French. Today the French people try to preserve the purity of their language.
3. French, Flemish Dutch, and German
4. They are similar in their history of conquering invaders. They are different because language connects the people of France, but Belgium is divided into language regions.

Independent Practice
Practice Book: page 55

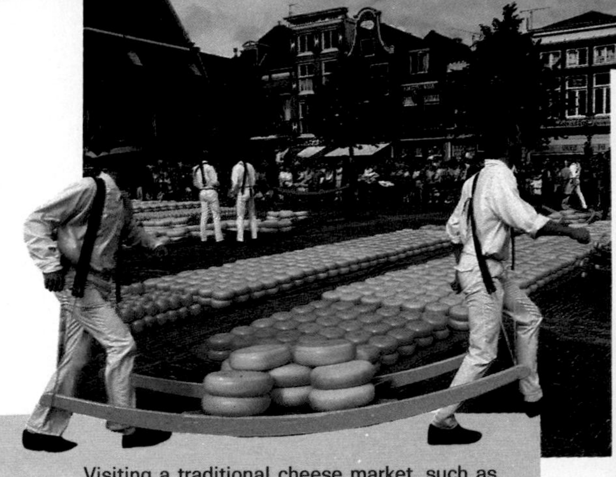

Visiting a traditional cheese market, such as this one in the Netherlands, is just one popular activity in the Low Countries.

north are the Flemings, who speak a form of Dutch known as Flemish. Dutch is the official language of this area, but many Flemings are bilingual. A small group of Belgians near the southeastern border speak German. The capital city of Belgium, Brussels, is bilingual.

Family ties are strong among the people of Belgium. Many Belgians rarely travel far from home. They prefer to spend time with their families than to travel overseas or to other European countries.

The people of the Netherlands do not have the language divisions that the Belgians do. But the Dutch have other problems. They live in a very crowded country. With more than 900 people per square mile (347.5 people per sq km), the Netherlands is one of the most densely populated countries in Western Europe.

A RICH LAND

The people who settled in France and the Low Countries found a rich land. As you have read, there was fertile soil on the coastal plain. The climate was mild most of the year. And navigable rivers made the area easy to reach.

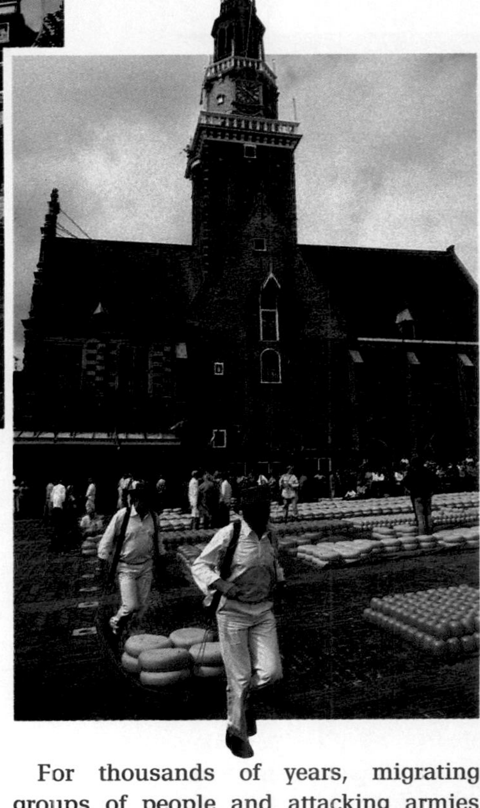

For thousands of years, migrating groups of people and attacking armies crisscrossed France and the Low Countries. Over the years the Celts, Gauls, Romans, and Vikings who lived here formed the different people of this region. Today immigrants from southern Europe and North Africa come to live and work in this prosperous part of the world.

Check Your Reading

1. Which groups of people have invaded France and the Low Countries in the past?
2. How was the French language created? How does it unite the people of France?
3. Which languages are commonly spoken in Belgium?
4. **THINKING SKILL:** How are the people of Belgium and France similar? How are they different?

THINKING SKILL: Compare and Contrast

220

MEETING INDIVIDUAL NEEDS

Reteaching (easy) Have students make a vertical time line showing the groups that invaded and settled in France and the Low Countries.

Extension (average) Have student groups research the Eurotunnel, which was built under the English Channel and opened in 1994. Assign these topics to the groups: "How the Tunnel Was Built"; "How the Tunnel Works"; "*Trains à Grande Vitesse* (TGVs, or Trains of Great Speed)." Have student groups present reports on their topics.

Enrichment (challenging) Have student groups research: "Viking Beliefs"; "Viking Settlements in Europe"; and "Viking Voyages in the Atlantic and Southern Europe." Then have the groups make an illustrated world map showing the movement of Vikings into Europe, into Southern Europe, and across the Atlantic into North America.

LESSON 2

The Economy

READ TO LEARN

Key Vocabulary

vineyard
canal
dike
polder
European Union

Read Aloud

France and the Low Countries have highly developed economies. They produce everything from tulips to supersonic jets. In this lesson you will read how these countries, individually and in cooperation with the rest of Western Europe, work to keep their economies strong.

Read for Purpose

1. WHAT YOU KNOW: What is a mixed economy?
2. WHAT YOU WILL LEARN: What makes the economies of France and the Low Countries strong?

FOOD AND FARMING PATTERNS

Although today less than 8 percent of the working people in France and the Low Countries are farmers, the countrysides are dotted with well-tended and highly productive farms. Most are small, family-owned businesses.

You might not think of flowers as a farm product, but the Dutch do. Dutch flowers and bulbs are exported all over the world. One of the world's largest flower markets is held at Aalsmeer, near Amsterdam. Aided by computers, farmers sell more than 12 million flowers and 1 million houseplants every day.

In France family farms often specialize in just one product. A small farm might grow only tiny green beans picked while they are young and tender. Or it might raise chickens for only the most demanding French chefs. In Normandy farmers are famous for their apples and pork. And in Bordeaux, hundreds of vineyards (vin′ yərdz) produce grapes for some of the finest wines in the world. A vineyard is an area used for growing grapes.

INDUSTRIAL POWER

Farming is only one small part of the economies of France and the Low Countries. These countries also have advanced technological industries.

Many French industries specialize in finely crafted goods, while others produce complicated electronic equipment. Several factories in southern France produce satellites, missiles, and sophisticated weapons. The Concorde jet is assembled in the French city of Toulouse.

The Netherlands has few mineral resources. So the Dutch have to import many resources, such as iron ore, from other countries. Later, skilled Dutch workers turn these resources into everything from ships, airplanes and trucks, to toys.

WHAT YOU KNOW: This question refers to material covered in Chapter 9, Lesson 2; an economy consisting of a mixture of private enterprises and government-run businesses.

LESSON 2
pages 221–223

Lesson Theme Farming, diversified products, and many service industries characterize the developed economies of France and the Low Countries.

Lesson Objectives

- Describe agriculture in France and the Low Countries.
- Explain the factors that support developed economies in France and the Low Countries.
- Explain the European Union.

PREPARE

Motivate Have students read the *Read Aloud* section. Tell students that they should try to discover what an economy needs in order to produce such a wide range of products.

Set Purpose Review with the class the *What You Know* question. Tell students to look for clues during their reading on how to define a strong economy.

TEACH

Looking at Food and Farming Patterns

Ask students:

- **How would you describe farms in France and the Low Countries?** (They raise specialized products on family-run farms.)

Understanding Industrial Power Help students to understand that a wide variety of factories and products make a strong economy. Discuss the industries of France.

READING STRATEGY AND VOCABULARY DEVELOPMENT

Note Taking and Outlining Have students work in groups to develop a compare/contrast outline for this lesson. Assign a group of students to each section of the lesson: "Food and Farming Patterns," "Industrial Power," "Services," "Trade and Transportation," and "The Common Market." In their outlines have students compare and contrast the economies of France and the Low Countries. When students have finished, help them to develop a class outline for the entire lesson. Then have students record the completed outline in their notebooks.

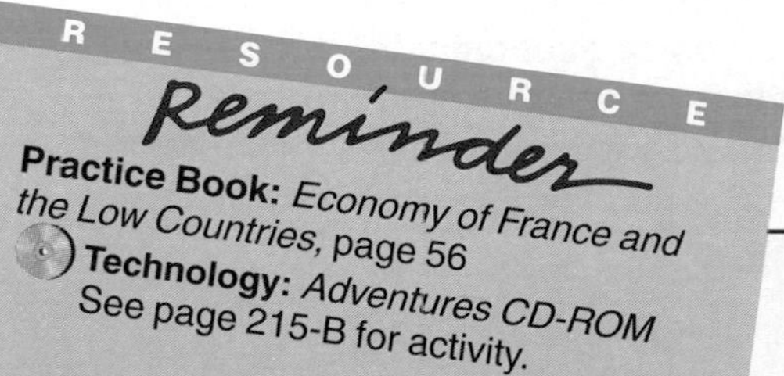

RESOURCE Reminder

Practice Book: *Economy of France and the Low Countries,* page 56

Technology: *Adventures CD-ROM* See page 215-B for activity.

EXTENDING MAP SKILLS

Have students study the Reclaimed Land map on this page.

Ask students:

- **What does the map title mean?** (The Netherlands has taken some of the sea floor for farming.)
- **What is the most important feature shown on this map for reclaiming land?** (the dam)
- **Where is the longest dam?** (in the north—the Barrier Dam)
- *THINKING FURTHER:* **What would be a rough estimate of the percentage of the Netherlands that has been reclaimed?** (more than 40 percent)

Understanding Services Stress to students that systems of services support an advanced economy. Have students list service industries.

Talking About Trade and Transportation

Ask students:

- **Which transportation systems are there in France and the Low Countries?** (roads, airlines, railroads, navigable rivers, canals)
- **How has water caused problems for the people of the Netherlands?** (by flooding and encroaching on the sea line)

Talking About the European Union

Mention to students that, in addition to linking European economies and infrastructure, the European Union also participates in social causes, such as scientific research and fighting cross-border crime.

Ask students:

- **What are tariffs and what are their effects?** (taxes on imports; make imported goods cost more so people buy fewer of them)
- *THINKING FURTHER:* **After centuries of economic independence, why are European nations now cooperating?** (They want to become a world economic power.)

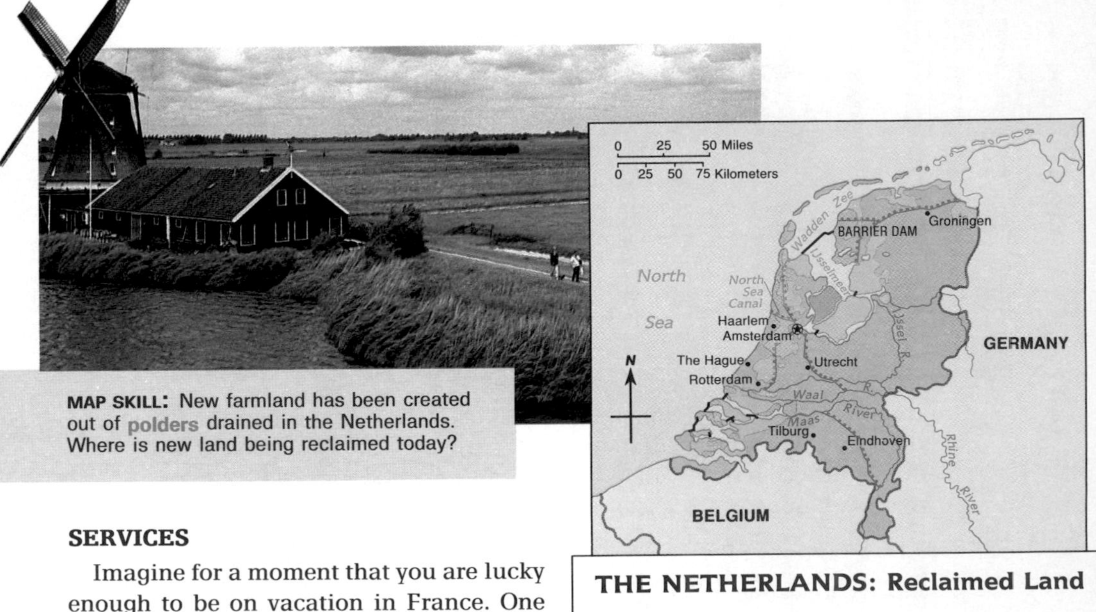

MAP SKILL: New farmland has been created out of **polders** drained in the Netherlands. Where is new land being reclaimed today?

THE NETHERLANDS: Reclaimed Land

Land reclaimed from the sea
Land being reclaimed from the sea
Canal
National capital
Other city
Dam

SERVICES

Imagine for a moment that you are lucky enough to be on vacation in France. One day you might visit the Riviera and enjoy its warm, sandy beaches. Or you might decide to go to Paris and wander through its ancient cathedrals and magnificent art museums. Or perhaps you'll spend an afternoon just relaxing in an outdoor café. France, as its citizens are proud to tell you, is a country "with everything."

Service industries, such as tourism, banking, and shipping, also play an important part in the economies of the Low Countries. For example, the city of Rotterdam, in the Netherlands, is the world's busiest port. Another Dutch city, Amsterdam, is an international banking center.

TRADE AND TRANSPORTATION

France and the Low Countries are fortunate in having excellent transportation networks. There are many roads, railroads, and airports. In addition, wide, navigable rivers flow from the heart of Western Europe, through the Low Countries, into the North Sea. For hundreds of years, these rivers have provided the region with great trade and transportation advantages.

The Dutch landscape is covered by a network of waterways. Where rivers did not connect people to each other, people built **canals**. A canal is a waterway that has been dug for boat travel. Unlike rivers, canals can be built to flow wherever people want them to.

But if water has been a friend to the Netherlands, it has also been a foe. For a thousand years the Dutch have had to invent ways to protect their land from the sea. First they built huge walls called **dikes** to keep the water back. Then they pumped out the sea water from inside the dikes, and used canals to drain the water from the low ground back into the North Sea. Look at the map above. It shows the lowland areas that have been reclaimed from the sea. They are called **polders**. "God created the earth," goes an old saying, "but the Dutch created Holland."

 MAP SKILL: in the IJsselmeer

FUNDAMENTAL THEMES OF GEOGRAPHY

Human-Environment Interaction Taming the sea has been the goal of the Dutch people for hundreds of years. By building dikes and drainage canals and by constant pumping of water, they have built a country with more than 40 percent of its land below sea level. Their intense effort and interaction with the environment continues. In 1987 the Dutch completed a project that provides a unique defense against North Sea storms. As part of the project, a flood barrier was put across a river estuary to protect the Zeeland Province. The barrier contains huge trapdoors that can be closed against North Sea storms to prevent disastrous floods like the one that took place in this location in 1953, killing 1,800 people.

THE EUROPEAN UNION

Western Europe, including France and the Low Countries, has been a center of world trade for hundreds of years. However, in the past the nations of this region often set up trade barriers against each other. They passed tariffs, or taxes on imports, to protect their own industries. Tariffs raise the price of imported goods, so people will buy fewer of them.

After World War II, some countries of Western Europe formed the European Economic Community to promote free trade and link transportation routes among themselves. That organization later became part of the **European Union**, or E.U. The members of the E.U., formerly called the European Community, are listed on the chart on this page.

The European Union changed the way France, the Low Countries, and the rest of Western Europe did business. It ended most trade barriers so that people and goods could move freely among its nations.

In the coming years the European Union will change even more. Member countries want to join together economically, so they work together much as the 50 states of the United States now do. Eventually, plans are to have one kind of currency (money) for all member countries and one European banking system, perhaps by the year 2000. Western Europeans hope that working together will make their region a world economic power in the years to come.

STRONG ECONOMIES

France and the Low Countries have developed economies that produce a wide variety of farm products and manufactured goods. Services play an important economic role in these countries.

The E.U. ended most trade barriers among its members, linking France and the Low Countries with Western Europe.

THE EUROPEAN UNION

Country	Currency	Year Joined
Austria	Schilling	1995
Belgium	Franc	1958
Denmark	Krone	1973
Finland	Markka	1995
France	Franc	1958
Germany	Mark	1958
Great Britain	Pound	1973
Greece	Drachma	1981
Ireland	Pound	1973
Italy	Lira	1958
Luxembourg	Franc	1958
The Netherlands	Guilder	1958
Portugal	Escudo	1986
Spain	Peseta	1986
Sweden	Krona	1995

CHART SKILL: Someday the countries of the European Union may all use the same currency. Who are the three newest members of the European Union?

Check Your Reading

1. How would you describe farming in France?
2. What have the Dutch done to reclaim their land from the sea?
3. Why was the European Union created?
4. THINKING SKILL: How has the geography of France and the Low Countries influenced the economies of the countries of this area?

CHART SKILL: Portugal and Spain
THINKING SKILL: Cause and Effect

223

EXTENDING CHART SKILLS

Review with students the countries that are part of the EU.

Ask students:

- **Which six countries first made up the EU?** (Belgium, the Netherlands, Luxembourg, France, West Germany, Italy)
- **How many countries now make up the EU?** (15)
- **Which country joined in 1981?** (Greece)

Applying the Lesson Have each student write a paragraph telling what factors contribute to the strong economies of France and the Low Countries today.

3 CLOSE

Summarizing Students have learned how France and the Low Countries have prospered and built strong economies. Ask students how the European Community might continue to help the people of this region.

Evaluating Use the *Check Your Reading* questions (answers given below) to assess students' understanding.

Answers to Check Your Reading

1. family farming with specialized products
2. built dams, dikes, and canals and used pumps to drain land below sea level
3. to promote free trade and improve transportation links in Europe
4. Flat land, good harbors, navigable rivers, and energy sources provide ideal conditions for building factories and for movement of products.

Independent Practice
Practice Book: page 56

MEETING INDIVIDUAL NEEDS

Reteaching (easy) Have students draw a picture on individual index cards to illustrate each word in the *Key Vocabulary*. Have students pair off to quiz each other using these cards.

Extension (average) Divide the class into two groups, one to research Amsterdam, the other to research Rotterdam. Then have each group prepare for a debate on the topic, "Amsterdam is the most important Dutch city."

Enrichment (challenging) Have students find out more about the EU's plans to unify Europe. Divide the class into three groups to role play the following scenes both before and after the EU's plan: (1) a farmer driving a truckload of cabbages from Germany to France; (2) a British citizen going through customs to enter Spain; (3) an Italian woman exchanging her money for American dollars at a bank in Italy.

SKILLS LESSON
pages 224–225

Lesson Theme A small-scale map is used to show a large area, and a large-scale map is used to show a small area in detail.

Lesson Objectives
- Compare small-scale maps and large-scale maps.
- Identify uses for maps at different scales.

PREPARE

Motivate Before beginning the lesson you may wish to project Transparency Map 11 on the screen for students to study. Ask students if they can find the Eiffel Tower on the small-scale map of France (Map A) on this page. Help them to conclude that details are not shown on small-scale maps.

Set Purpose Tell students that in this lesson they will learn the difference between small-scale and large-scale maps.

TEACH

Identifying Small-Scale Maps Have students read the scale for the map of France on this page.

Ask students:

- **Why is Map A called a small-scale map?** (It shows a large area in a fairly small space.)
- **How many miles does 1 inch represent on Map A?** (200 miles)
- **How many kilometers do 2.5 centimeters represent on Map A?** (about 320 kilometers)
- **How is this small-scale map helpful?** (It reveals many facts about France in relation to other countries.)

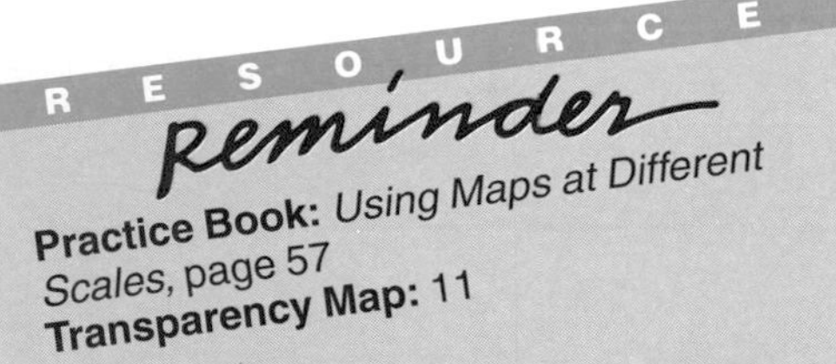

BUILDING SKILLS
GEOGRAPHY SKILLS

Using Maps at Different Scales

Key Vocabulary
small-scale map
large-scale map

As you know, maps can be used to show the world in many different ways. They can be used to show areas as large as the whole world or areas as small as a city block.

One important way in which maps differ is in scale. As you have seen, most of the maps in this book have a scale of miles and kilometers. The scale for a particular map tells how distance shown on that map translates into actual distance on the earth.

Maps can be drawn to many different scales. When mapmakers want to show a large area in a small space, they draw a **small-scale map**. For example, suppose you wanted to know how far Marseilles is from Paris. You would look on a small-scale map, such as **Map A**, that shows many of the important cities in France.

Small-scale Maps

Map A will help you understand what the term *small-scale map* means. On small-scale maps a very small unit of

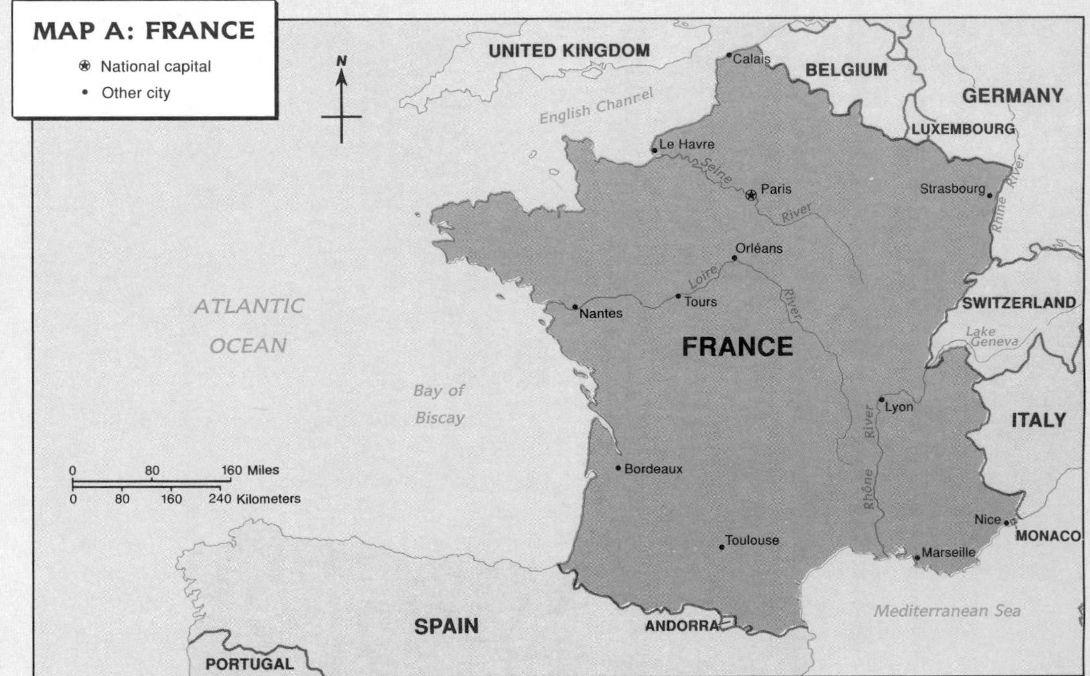

224

CURRICULUM CONNECTION

Math Have students set up a ratio based on the scale 1 millimeter = 200 miles, that is, 1/200. Have them use a ruler to measure a distance on Map A in millimeters and then use a formula, based on the ratio, to find the actual distance.

1/200 = measured distance ÷ actual distance, or actual distance = measured distance × 200

measure, such as 1 inch (2.54 cm), stands for a large distance, such as 500 miles (805 km). Small-scale maps usually show large areas in a fairly small space.

Looking at a small-scale map can be very helpful when you are studying about all the countries of Western Europe. **Map A** shows you the size and location of France in relation to the countries it borders. France is larger than any of the countries it borders. The map shows the location of major rivers and important cities in France.

Large-scale Maps

Suppose that you wanted more detailed information about a city, such as Paris, in France. This type of information can be shown on a large-scale map, such as **Map B** on this page. Compare the information shown on **Map A** with that shown on **Map B**. Notice the details about Paris that are found on **Map B**. For example, the map shows the names and locations of many streets in Paris. It also shows the location of some important points of interest, such as Notre Dame, the Louvre, and the Eiffel Tower.

Paris appears larger on **Map B** than it does on **Map A** because on a large-scale map, a unit of measure stands for a smaller distance than it does on a small-scale map. For example, on **Map B**, 1 inch (2.54 km) stands for 1.25 miles (2 km). Notice that the map of Paris is only about 3.75 miles (6 km) across, while the map of France is about 560 miles (900 km) across. Remember that even though maps are often drawn to different scales, real distances do not change.

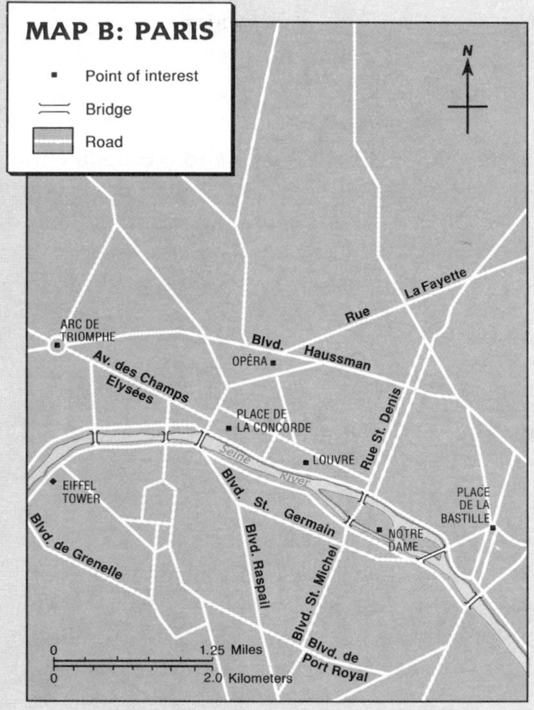

Reviewing the Skill

1. Which map, **Map A** or **Map B**, shows more details about Paris?
2. Which map, **Map A** or **Map B**, covers a larger area?
3. Which map, **Map A** or **Map B**, is drawn to a larger scale?
4. Look at the map on page 224. What river flows northwest into Le Havre? Now look at the map on this page. What river flows through the center of Paris?
5. How can using maps drawn to different scales be useful?

225

Analyzing Large-Scale Maps Have students locate on Map A the same area shown on Map B (Paris) and compare the details shown.

Ask students:

- **How many miles does 1 inch represent on Map B?** (1.5 miles)
- **Why is Map B called a large-scale map?** (It shows a limited area in a fairly large space.)
- **What is the advantage of Map B over Map A?** (Map B gives a more in-depth look at an area.)
- **What is the advantage of Map A over Map B?** (Map A shows the relationship of France to other countries.)

Applying the Skill Have students choose a unit of measure to make a scale bar. They should use it to measure and make a small-scale map of the classroom. With a different scale bar they should make a large-scale inset map of a section of the room containing bookshelves or cabinets.

CLOSE

Summarizing Students have compared large-scale and small-scale maps. Have students identify the maps in Chapter 10 as either small-scale or large-scale. Then have them explain why each map is drawn to that scale.

Answers to Reviewing the Skill

1. Map B
2. Map A
3. Map B
4. the Seine; the Seine
5. If maps are drawn at different scales, different size areas can be represented.

Independent Practice
Practice Book: page 57

MEETING INDIVIDUAL NEEDS

Reteaching (easy) Have students make a chart with the headings "Small-Scale Maps" and "Large-Scale Maps." Have them go through Unit 3 and list all the maps as large-scale or small-scale.

Extension (average) Have students make small-scale maps of their communities and include a large-scale inset map of the school grounds and school.

Enrichment (challenging) Have students choose a section of France or the Low Countries to map. They should do research to enable them to draw a small-scale map of France and the Low Countries as well as a companion large-scale map of a section of one of the countries, showing many details.

LESSON 3
pages 226–227

Lesson Theme Both France and the Low Countries are representative democracies, but the French president has sweeping powers, and monarchs still reign in the Low Countries.

Lesson Objectives
- Describe the French government.
- Describe the constitutional monarchies of the Low Countries.

PREPARE

Motivate Read the *Read Aloud* section to the class. Ask students if they know of any similar rallying cry from the American Revolution.

Set Purpose Use the *What You Know* question for review. Tell students to look for the contrasts that answer the *What You Will Learn* question.

TEACH

Talking About Governing France Stress to students the changes that have characterized the French government. Compare the roles of the president and the premier.

Looking at Three Monarchies

Ask students:

- **How do the people's views of the monarchs of the Low Countries differ from the people's views of the monarchy in Britain?** (The Dutch, especially, see a crown as representing too much power. The monarchs are less formal with their people.)
- *THINKING FURTHER:* **Which part of government oversees any powers that these monarchs might have?** (the two-house legislatures in each of these nations)

Practice Book: *Comparing Governments,* page 58

Technology: *Adventures CD-ROM* See page 215-B for activity.

The Government

READ TO LEARN

Key Vocabulary
premier

Key People
Charles de Gaulle

Read Aloud

Liberté! Égalité! Fraternité!

These three words, translated as "Liberty! Equality! Fraternity!" were the rallying cry of the French Revolution in 1789. That revolution marked the end of monarchy and the start of republican government in France. Since 1789 the ideas of the French Revolution have spread to almost every country in Western Europe.

Read for Purpose

1. WHAT YOU KNOW: What is a constitutional monarchy?
2. WHAT YOU WILL LEARN: What is the structure of the government of France? Of the governments of the Low Countries?

GOVERNING FRANCE

France has long had the reputation of being a difficult nation to govern. The country has many individual areas that do not always act together. "How can you govern a country that makes 265 kinds of cheeses?" the former French President Charles de Gaulle once joked.

The government of France has changed many times since the French Revolution. The country has been governed by kings, emperors, presidents, and elected national assemblies.

Unlike the United States, France has had several constitutions. "How can you live with the same old constitution for two centuries?" one French politician asked an American. "Don't you think it's good to freshen up now and then?"

The current French constitution, which was adopted in 1958, calls for a government named the Fifth Republic. The Fifth Republic has a strong president who is elected by the people for a seven-year term. The president makes the important decisions on matters of defense and foreign affairs. He or she has the authority to dismiss the elected National Assembly, thus bringing about new elections. The president also names the prime minister, who heads the day-to-day activities of the government. In France the prime minister is called the premier.

Why does the Fifth Republic give the president so much power? In the first four republics, the National Assembly argued so much that little was accomplished. Now the French support the idea of a strong national leader.

THREE MONARCHIES

Like Great Britain, the Netherlands, Belgium, and Luxembourg are constitutional monarchies. The head of state inherits his

WHAT YOU KNOW: This question refers to material covered in Chapter 9, Lesson 3; a government headed by a king or queen whose powers are limited by a constitution.

READING STRATEGY AND VOCABULARY DEVELOPMENT

Note Taking and Outlining The purpose of this lesson is to help students prepare notes. Students will then use their notes to prepare a debate on the topic of governments in France, the Low Countries, Great Britain, and the United States. Tell students to refer to their notes or their text to gather information on the governments of the United States and Great Britain. You may wish either to divide the class into four groups, one for each country or group of countries, in order to hold a class debate, or to assign one student in each group to a country, and then have each group conduct their own debate. Have students compare and contrast the governments, discuss the pros and cons of each government, or debate which government is better and why.

or her throne. King Baudouin of Belgium, Grand Duke Jean of Luxembourg, and Queen Beatrix of the Netherlands are mostly ceremonial rulers. Like Queen Elizabeth of Britain, they are symbols of their nations as a whole.

The people of the Low Countries treat their monarchs more casually than the British do. Dutch monarchs, for example, are not crowned. To the Dutch, crowns symbolize too much power. Members of the Dutch royal family live much like other people. They ride around town on bicycles just as everybody else does.

In each of the Low Countries, a two-house legislature not only passes laws but also makes most of the important decisions. In Belgium, for example, the king can appoint officials, declare war, and make treaties. But all of these actions must be approved by the Parliament.

REPRESENTATIVE GOVERNMENTS

France and the Low Countries all have representative governments. But, as you have read, there are some important differences in these governments. France's Fifth Republic gives wide powers to the president. The three Low Countries are all constitutional monarchies, and they have elected legislatures.

Check Your Reading

1. What do the governments of the Low Countries have in common?
2. How many republics has France had since the French Revolution?
3. How are the governments of France and the Low Countries similar?
4. **THINKING SKILL:** What alternatives did the people of France have to consider in deciding how much power to give their president?

THINKING SKILL: Decision Making

CITIZENSHIP MAKING A DIFFERENCE

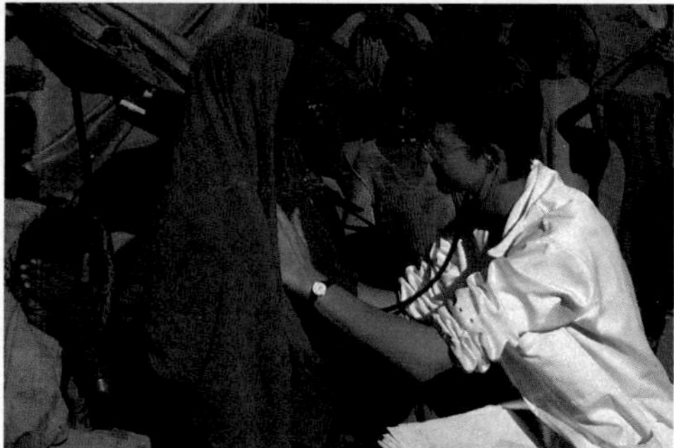

DOCTORS WITHOUT BORDERS

Every year disasters, such as earthquakes, hurricanes, and floods, strike all over the world. At such times huge numbers of people require immediate medical care. In 1971 five French medical doctors decided to form an organization to respond to emergencies throughout the world. Today when disasters strike, the group they formed, *Médecins Sans Frontières* (MSF), responds. *Médecins Sans Frontières* means "Doctors Without Borders."

When natural disasters like floods and volcanoes occur, the volunteers of MSF must be ready at a moment's notice. Their mission is to get to disaster scenes fast in order to save lives. They set up clinics, distribute medicines, and provide clean drinking water. The volunteers of MSF have brought their medical skills to people in more than 80 countries.

Depending upon the particular situation, MSF teams may live in an area for a few days, for several months, or for years at a time. Some of the teams build hospitals, some train doctors, and some work at controlling the spread of a disease.

The volunteers of MSF treat all people regardless of race, religion, or politics, and they do so free of charge. Their sole commitment is to save lives.

227

Applying the Lesson Divide the class into two groups. Have one group argue against rewriting a constitution and the other group argue for rewriting a constitution from time to time. Discuss with students the dangers to democracy in either course of action.

3 CLOSE

Summarizing Students should understand the many forms of representative democracy in Europe. Ask them to suggest ways to democratically govern a country with many individual regions like France.

Evaluating Use the *Check Your Reading* questions (answers given below) to assess students' understanding.

Answers to Check Your Reading

1. The governments are all constitutional monarchies with two-house legislatures.
2. five
3. All are representative governments.
4. whether to let the country drift or to accomplish something

Independent Practice
Practice Book: page 58

MEETING INDIVIDUAL NEEDS

Reteaching (easy) Have students make a three-column chart showing the roles and powers of the French president, premier, and National Assembly.

Extension (average) Have students research a monarch of the Low Countries. Ask them to imagine that they are citizens of that monarch's country and to write a letter to an imaginary pen pal in America describing how people feel about their monarch.

Enrichment (challenging) Have students read more about the French revolution of 1789. Then have each student write a diary account as a French revolutionary, telling what they felt when they first heard the shout "*Liberté! Egalité! Fraternité!*"

BUILDING CITIZENSHIP

Doctors Without Borders Discuss the role of Doctors Without Borders and why such a group is needed. Have students discuss the variety of skills these volunteers must have to do their jobs. Ask students how these volunteers demonstrate good cititizenship. Discuss volunteers who offer their skills and time, either in the students' community or at the national level, to organizations such as the Red Cross and why these people become volunteers. Then discuss ways in which students can offer aid to those in need.

LESSON 4
pages 228–229

Lesson Theme France and the Low Countries offer the world a rich heritage of arts and sports.

Lesson Objectives

- Describe the arts of France and the Low Countries.
- Describe the sports of France and the Low Countries.

PREPARE

Motivate Read the *Read Aloud* section to the class. Ask students to consider why wealthy people foster art, music, and literature.

Set Purpose Have students answer the *What You Know* question. Tell students that in this lesson they will learn the answer to the *What You Will Learn* question.

TEACH

Looking at a Rich Heritage of the Arts

Ask students:

- **Identify two terms describing some famous painters in France and the Low Countries.** (Old Masters and Impressionists)

Talking About Sports

Ask students:

- **What makes the Tour de France bike race unusual?** (It lasts three weeks, is 2,500 miles [4,023 km] long, and covers steep mountain passes.)
- *THINKING FURTHER:* **How does the Tour de France unify that nation?** (For three weeks French people watch the race on their televisions.)

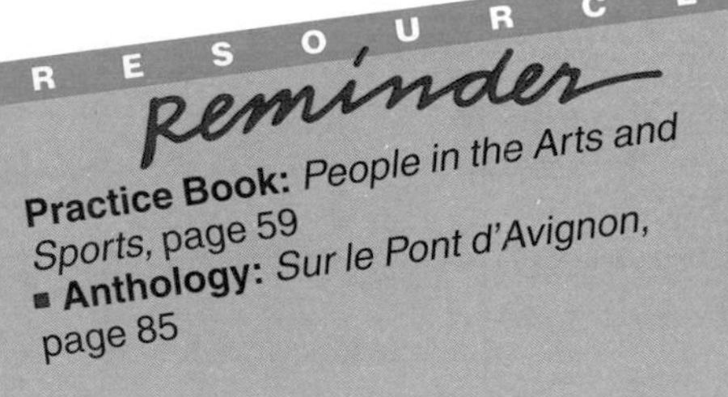

RESOURCE Reminder

Practice Book: *People in the Arts and Sports*, page 59

- **Anthology:** *Sur le Pont d'Avignon*, page 85

LESSON 4

Arts and Recreation

READ TO LEARN

Key Vocabulary

Impressionism
Tour de France

Key People

Jan van Eyck
Pieter Brueghel
Vincent van Gogh
Claude Monet
Edgar Degas

Read Aloud

Other cities are cities. Paris is a world.

This is what Emperor Charles V of France said about his country's capital city. In Paris and throughout France and the Low Countries, there is much to see and do. For thousands of years, the people of France and the Low Countries have had the time and wealth to create and support great works of art.

Read for Purpose

1. WHAT YOU KNOW: What kinds of sports are popular in the British Isles?
2. WHAT YOU WILL LEARN: Which arts and sports have developed in France and the Low Countries?

A RICH HERITAGE OF THE ARTS

As Great Britain is famous for its writers and playwrights, so France and the Low Countries are well known for their many fine painters.

From the 1300s to the 1600s, Europe produced many great painters known as the Old Masters. Several of these came from Flanders, an area in western Belgium. **Jan van Eyck** (yän′ van īk′) helped invent new ways to show light in paintings. Today Belgians looking at the paintings of **Pieter Brueghel** (pē′ tər broi′ gəl) can see how their ancestors lived 400 years in the past.

A famous Dutch painter, **Vincent van Gogh** (van gō), worked during the late 1800s. Van Gogh sold only one painting in his lifetime. But artistic tastes change. In 1988 a painting of sunflowers by Van Gogh sold for almost $40 million.

Van Gogh worked for a while in Paris, the center of the art world during the late nineteenth century. In this period, a style of painting known as **Impressionism** was developed by French artists like **Claude Monet** (mō nā′) and **Edgar Degas** (dā gä′). Impressionists did not paint scenes exactly as they appeared. They tried to capture the feeling of a place in a moment of time. The light-filled paintings of the Impressionists are among the world's most popular works of art.

 WHAT YOU KNOW: Possible answers include: soccer, cricket, and golf.

READING STRATEGY AND VOCABULARY DEVELOPMENT

Note Taking and Outlining The purpose of this lesson is to help students compare the arts and sports in France, the Low Countries, Great Britain, and the United States. After students have read this lesson and taken notes, have them prepare a chart like the one below. Under each heading have students list information about the four countries.

Country	Arts	Sports
France		
Low Countries		
Great Britain		
United States		

Horse races and the sporting life of Western Europe were popular subjects with Impressionist painter Edgar Degas.

BICYCLING AND OTHER SPORTS

The people of France and the Low Countries share a passion for bicycling. For three weeks every summer they are glued to their television sets to watch the famous Tour de France, a 2,500-mile (4,023-km) bicycle race that winds around the perimeter of France.

The colored jerseys of racers on the Tour de France help enthusiastic fans identify them. For example, the first-place cyclist on each day wears a yellow jersey. The rider who goes fastest on sprints up mountains gets to wear a polka-dotted shirt.

Eddy Merckx of Belgium has won the Tour de France five times. He says cycling is part of the Belgian way of life. "It would be very difficult to find a town or village here that doesn't have a bike race."

In France and the Low Countries, soccer is also a favorite sport—unless it happens to be ski season. Then people head for the Alps. Some ski runs in the Alps are so long that skiers need to ride up the mountain only once or twice a day.

ARTS AND SPORTS

France and the Low Countries have rich cultural traditions. As you have read, these countries have produced many great painters. Sports are also very popular. "I'm passionate about various kinds of sports," said one French citizen. "To keep fit, yes, but also because I enjoy the competition. That's the French way."

 **Check Your Reading**

1. What is Impressionism? How would you describe this style of painting?
2. What is the Tour de France?
3. Which sports are popular in France and the Low Countries?
4. THINKING SKILL: Classify the painters mentioned in this lesson into these two groups: The Old Masters and The Impressionists.

THINKING SKILL: Classifying

Applying the Lesson Have students prepare a three-column chart about France and the Low Countries with the headings "Old Masters," "Impressionists," and "Sports." Then have them affix pictures from magazines or other sources to illustrate each of the headings.

3 CLOSE

Summarizing Students have read about the paintings by artists from France and the Low Countries and about the sports that interest the people who live there. Ask students why Eddy Merckx is a hero to many people from this region.

Evaluating Use these questions to assess students' understanding.

- **What style of painting did artists like Claude Monet and Edgar Degas help develop?** (Impressionism)
- **Which bicycle race is famous in France?** (the Tour de France)

 **Answers to Check Your Reading**

1. paintings that are full of light and capture the feeling of the place painted; Accept all reasonable answers.
2. a bicycle race around the perimeter of France
3. cycling, skiing, soccer
4. *Old Masters*: Jan van Eyck, Pieter Brueghel; *Impressionists*: Claude Monet, Edgar Degas, Vincent van Gogh

Independent Practice
Practice Book: page 59

MEETING INDIVIDUAL NEEDS

Reteaching (easy) On individual index cards write the *Key People* and *Key Vocabulary* terms from the lesson. On separate cards write the definition or importance of each term or person. Distribute the cards in random order to the class. Have students try to match each of the *Key People* and *Key Vocabulary* terms with the appropriate "importance" or "definition" card.

Extension (average) Have students gather information about the Tour de France. Ask them to draw a map of the course and to write an imaginary TV interview with Eddy Merckx after he won the race.

Enrichment (challenging) Have students choose a painter that was known as an Old Master and one who painted in the Impressionist style. Have them research the painters' lives and works and then write a comparison essay about the two artists.

CHAPTER 10 REVIEW
pages 230–231

USING THE CHAPTER SUMMARY AND REVIEW

Cultural Geography These questions may be used for review.

- **How has language divided the people of Belgium?** (Language divides the country into separate areas.)
- **How are France and the Low Countries linked economically to the rest of Western Europe?** (They are members of the European Union)
- **Which countries have constitutional monarchies?** (the Low Countries)
- **What have these countries given to the art world?** (great painters and the impressionist style of painting)

Ideas to Remember

- **Which groups of people settled in France and the Low Countries?** (Celts, Gauls, Romans, Franks)
- **What does the European Union have to offer France and the Low Countries?** (It links France and the Low Countries with the rest of Western Europe and eliminates trade barriers within Western Europe.)
- **How many republics has France had?** (five)
- **Which sports event is the most popular in this region?** (the Tour de France)

Answers to Reviewing Vocabulary

1. True.
2. A vineyard is an area used for growing grapes.
3. True.
4. The premier of France directs the day-to-day activities of the government.
5. True.
6. True.

CHAPTER 10 • SUMMARY

FRANCE AND THE LOW COUNTRIES: CULTURAL GEOGRAPHY

PEOPLE

- Early settlers and conquerors: Celts, Gauls, Romans, Franks
- Guest workers: have come to France and Low Countries to work

- Language: ties French people together
- Belgium: divided into Walloons and Flemings

ECONOMY

- Highly developed economies

- Farming: small-scale, but highly productive

- Industry: highly developed, advanced technology
- Services: tourism, banking and shipping important in Low Countries
- European Union: helps link France and Low Countries with rest of Western Europe

GOVERNMENT

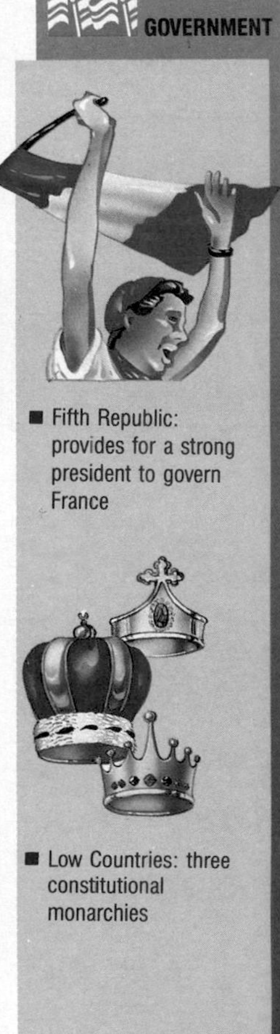

- Fifth Republic: provides for a strong president to govern France
- Low Countries: three constitutional monarchies

ARTS AND RECREATION

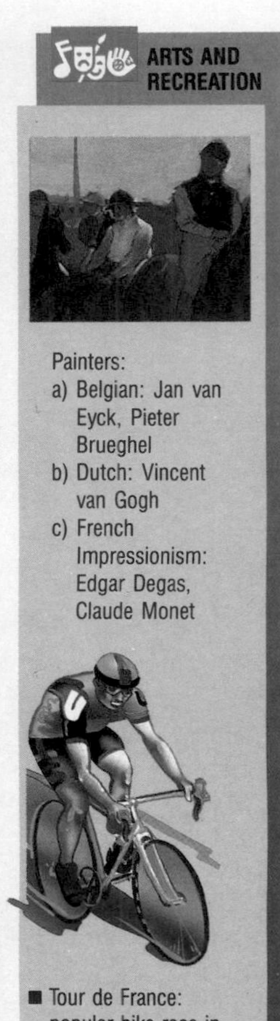

Painters:
a) Belgian: Jan van Eyck, Pieter Brueghel
b) Dutch: Vincent van Gogh
c) French Impressionism: Edgar Degas, Claude Monet

- Tour de France: popular bike race in France

IDEAS TO REMEMBER

- The people of France and the Low Countries are a mixture of Celts, Gauls, Romans, Franks, and other groups who settled in the area.
- France and the Low Countries have industrial economies and are linked to the rest of Western Europe by the European Union.
- France and the Low Countries all have representative governments, but France is a republic and the Low Countries are constitutional monarchies.
- The area is characterized by a rich artistic heritage (particularly painting) and a great interest in competitive sports such as bicycle racing.

230

ENRICHMENT ACTIVITY

Making a Cathedral Model **Materials:** shoeboxes, colored cellophane, cardboard, construction paper, paste, paints or markers

1. Review with students the information on page 218 that describes the great cathedrals of France. Tell students that they are going to make models of French cathedrals.
2. Divide the class into groups and have them do some additional research on cathedrals. Many encyclopedias show floor plans and photographs of the elaborate exteriors. Have each group choose a cathedral to use for their model. Tell students to plan a design together before they begin the model.
3. Students can use shoeboxes for the nave of the cathedral, and colored cellophane for stained-glass windows. Suggest that they attach cardboard spires and towers separately.
4. Have each group arrange a display for its cathedral.

CHAPTER 10 • REVIEW

REVIEWING VOCABULARY

Each of the following statements contains an underlined vocabulary word or term. Number a sheet of paper from 1 to 10. Beside each number write whether each of the following statements is true or false. If the statement is true, write "true." If it is false, rewrite the sentence using the vocabulary word or term correctly.

1. A polder is an area reclaimed from the sea so that it can be used as land for farming.
2. A vineyard is a farm where flowers grow on vines.
3. The Dutch have built and maintained dikes for hundreds of years in order to protect their land from the sea.
4. Like the powers of the British monarch, the powers of the French premier are limited to ceremonial and symbolic functions.
5. A vineyard is a place for growing grapes.
6. Canals, or waterways, are used to transport goods and people.
7. Guest workers are servants, maids, and cooks employed only by wealthy families in France.
8. The European Union was established to promote free trade and to link transportation routes among its member countries.
9. The Tour de France is a large-scale tourist group for visitors to France from many countries.
10. Impressionism is a style of painting in which objects are painted realistically, to look exactly as they do in real life.

REVIEWING FACTS

1. What are the names of the three Low Countries?
2. Why have the Low Countries and France attracted invaders throughout their history?
3. Why does the French constitution allow for a strong president with broad powers?
4. Who were the Old Masters?
5. Which city was the center of the art world in the late nineteenth century?

WRITING ABOUT MAIN IDEAS

1. **Writing an Explanation:** The Netherlands—a tiny, densely populated country with few natural resources—has one of the world's highest standards of living. Write a paragraph explaining why.
2. **Writing About Perspectives:** Imagine that you live in one of the Low Countries. Write a letter to the editor of your local newspaper expressing your opinion on whether Europe should be unified. Give reasons for your opinion.

BUILDING SKILLS: USING MAPS OF DIFFERENT SCALES

1. What are the differences between large-scale maps and small-scale maps?
2. Look at the map on page 225. How many miles does 1 inch represent on the map?
3. Which map on pages 224–225 shows a larger area—Map A or Map B?
4. Which map, A or B, uses a larger scale?
5. How can using maps of different scales be helpful?

231

7. Guest workers are people who move to a country in search of work.
8. True.
9. The *Tour de France* is a famous bicycle race that winds around the perimeter of France.
10. Impressionist paintings are light-filled paintings that capture the feeling of a place in a moment of time.

Answers to Reviewing Facts

1. Belgium, the Netherlands, Luxembourg
2. because of its fertile lowlands, wide navigable rivers, and long flat coastlines
3. Because the first four republics accomplished little, the French supported a strong national leader.
4. Great European painters from the 1300s to the 1600s, such as Jan van Eyck and Pieter Brueghel
5. Paris

Suggestions for Writing About Main Ideas

1. Students should note that the Netherlands has a developed economy that produces a wide range of goods, is an international banking center, has service industries, and has the world's busiest port—all of which create jobs for the people of the region.
2. Students' letters should give reasons for their opinions.

Answers to Building Skills: Using Maps of Different Scales

1. A large-scale map shows more detailed information than a small-scale map.
2. 1.25 miles
3. Map A
4. Map B
5. Different scales enable us to show a great deal of detail or a larger area with little detail.

Chapter Review and Test

Practice Book: *Vocabulary Review*, page 60
Transparency: *Graphic Organizer*
Assessment Book: *Chapter 10 Test*

MAKING CONNECTIONS

Supporting Main Ideas Use the Main Idea Map Graphic Organizer Transparency, writing in only the underlined items. Ask students to review the chapter and fill in the table with important ideas about France and the Low Countries, organizing the information from general to specific. *Ask:* Are France and the Low Countries more alike or different?

CULTURAL GEOGRAPHY OF FRANCE AND THE LOW COUNTRIES

People		Economy	Arts and Recreation		Government	
France	Low Countries	France & Low Countries	France	Low Countries	France	Low Countries
many early conquerors European and African immigrants	Walloons Flemings	developed, diversified good transportation networks Common Market members	Impressionists bicycle racing, soccer, skiing	Old Masters soccer and bicycling	representative democracy strong president	constitutional monarchy

CHAPTER 11
ORGANIZER

CENTRAL EUROPE text pages 232–247

CHAPTER THEME Central Europe is an industrial heartland united by language and religion.

CHAPTER OBJECTIVES

CONTENT

- Describe the roles that language and religion play in uniting the people of Central Europe.
- Define *dialect* and explain why having many dialects sometimes creates problems for German speakers.
- Explain why Germany was divided into two parts following World War II and how it came to be reunited.
- Identify the Ruhr Valley and explain why the cluster that the valley's cities form is called a megalopolis.
- Explain why no European country can solve its pollution problems by itself.
- Describe the structures of the governments of Germany, Switzerland, and Austria.
- Define *canton* and describe how it promotes a pure form of democracy.
- Explain how Switzerland's policy of neutrality has kept the country out of war.
- Describe how music is an important part of the artistic heritage of Central Europe.

SKILLS

Geography
- Use a political map to identify the countries and major cities of Central Europe.
- Use a map to give details about Germany's Ruhr Valley.

Thinking
- Predict historical outcomes based on changed conditions.
- Recognize bias.

Reading and Writing
- Write a letter about Central Europe.

CITIZENSHIP VALUES

- Appreciate the role that traits such as discipline and a willingness to work hard play in promoting prosperity.

TEACHER OPTIONS

READING STRATEGY: Using Semantic Clues
Strategies to help students read and remember the main ideas of the lesson.
Lesson 1: p. 233 Lesson 3: p. 240
Lesson 2: p. 237 Lesson 4: p. 244

MEETING INDIVIDUAL NEEDS Activities for reteaching, extension, and enrichment.
Lesson 1: p. 236 Lesson 3: p. 241
Lesson 2: p. 239 Lesson 4: p. 245

GEO ADVENTURES ACTIVITIES PAD Daily activities to assess students' understanding of geography skills.

CURRICULUM CONNECTION Activities to help integrate other subject areas with Social Studies.
Math: p. 234

PUPIL EDITION ON CASSETTE Language support for students who have difficulty reading or who will benefit from listening to the Pupil Edition on Cassette as they read.

SECOND-LANGUAGE SUPPORT Activities and suggestions for second-language learners.
Lesson 2: p. 20

CHAPTER PLANNING GUIDE

LESSON	SUGGESTED PACING	THEMES	TEACHER SUPPORT MATERIALS: TEACHER'S RESOURCE CENTER
1 THE PEOPLE pages 233–236	1 day	Switzerland, Austria, and newly reunited Germany make up Central Europe, a region united by language and religion and inhabited by a mainly urban population.	Practice Book p. 61 ■ Anthology pp. 90–93 Outline Map p. 20
2 THE ECONOMY pages 237–239	1 day	Since the destruction caused by World War II, Central Europe has developed prosperous, industrial economies, but the region does suffer from environmental problems.	Practice Book p. 62 **Technology:** *Adventures CD-ROM*
3 THE GOVERNMENT pages 240–241	1 day	Democracies characterize the governments of Central Europe today.	Practice Book p. 63 ■ Anthology pp. 88–89 **Technology:** *Adventures CD-ROM*
BUILDING THINKING SKILLS Recognizing Bias pages 242–243	1 day	Recognizing bias means identifying a one-sided or slanted presentation of information.	Practice Book p. 64
4 ARTS AND RECREATION pages 244–245	1 day	Music is a strong artistic focus in Central Europe, while festivals and outdoor recreation also enrich life there.	Practice Book p. 65 **Technology:** *Adventures CD-ROM*
CHAPTER SUMMARY AND REVIEW pages 246–247	1 day	Chapter content, skills, and vocabulary are reviewed and evaluated.	Practice Book p. 66 Transparency: Graphic Organizer Assessment Book, Chapter 11 Test

Technology CONNECTION

Lesson 2
ADVENTURES CD-ROM
Have students make a resources map of a country of their choice, using *Build* and *Paint* stamps.

Lesson 3
ADVENTURES CD-ROM
Students can find a movie about the Berlin Wall in *Investigate, Germany.*

Lesson 4
ADVENTURES CD-ROM
Have students make a list of key Austrian and German composers in the *Notebook.*

CHAPTER 11
pages 232–247

USING THE CHAPTER OPENER

Discussing the Photograph Help students to recognize that the man in the photograph is carving a case for the cuckoo clock, which is also shown in the picture. Encourage students to talk about any carving they may have done or about any experiences they may have had in taking a clock apart to see how it works.

Ask students:

- **What qualities must you develop to be good at carving?** (Students may suggest manual dexterity, imagination.)
- **What qualities must you develop to be able to put a clock together?** (Possible answers include: curiosity, mechanical ability.)
- *THINKING FURTHER:* **How would a combination of all these qualities help someone to survive in a harsh environment?** (Almost all these qualities might help someone avoid or overcome danger and hardship.)

Reading/Listening to the Primary Source Have students read the passage under the picture to themselves.

Ask students:

- **What might the "yonder mountains" be that Schiller talks about?** (The mention of Tell's Swiss citizenship might give students a clue that they are the Alps.)

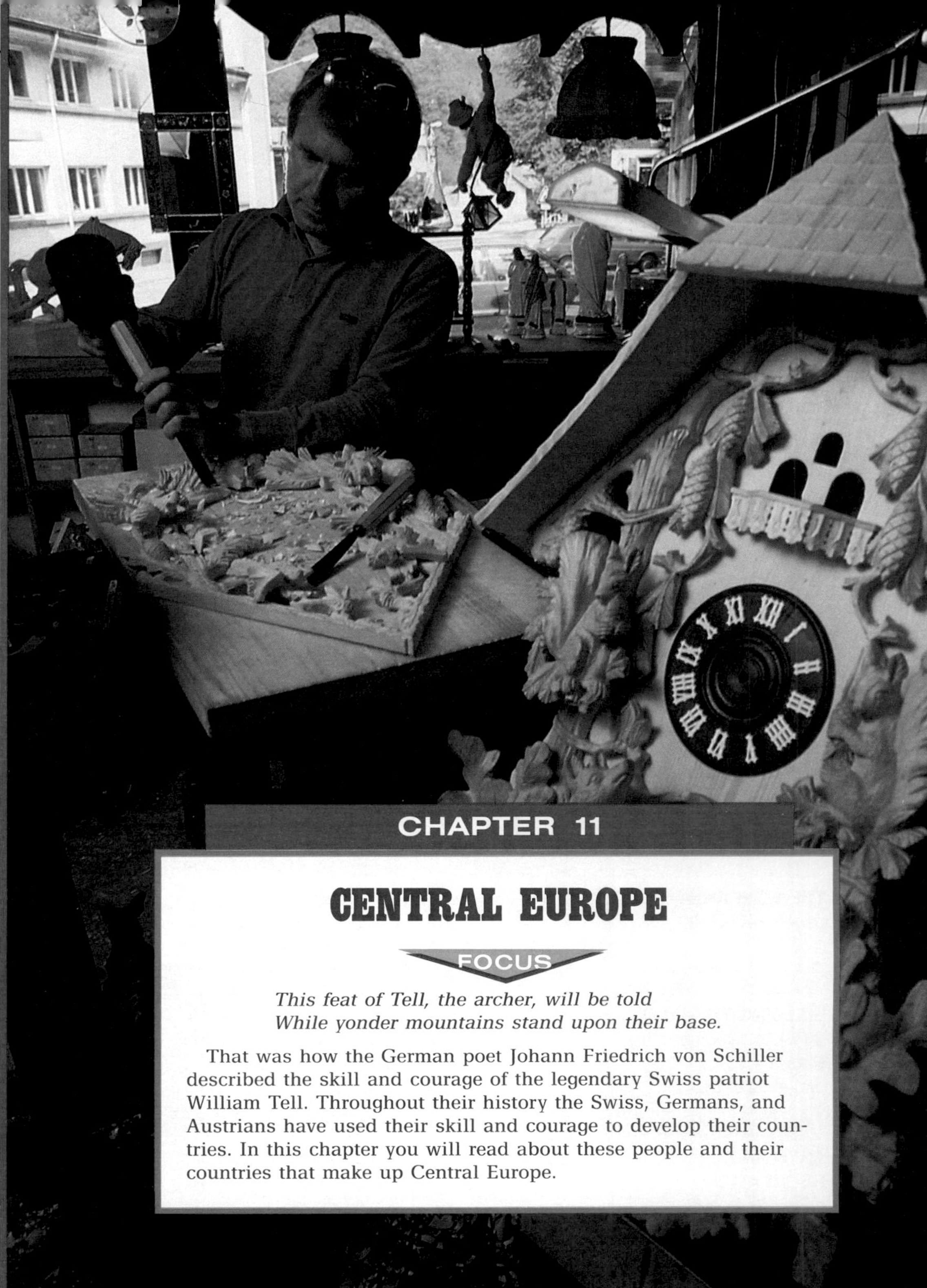

CHAPTER 11

CENTRAL EUROPE

FOCUS

This feat of Tell, the archer, will be told
While yonder mountains stand upon their base.

That was how the German poet Johann Friedrich von Schiller described the skill and courage of the legendary Swiss patriot William Tell. Throughout their history the Swiss, Germans, and Austrians have used their skill and courage to develop their countries. In this chapter you will read about these people and their countries that make up Central Europe.

BACKGROUND INFORMATION

About Manufacturing in Austria Like the Swiss, the Austrians have used ingenuity and engineering to develop their country. Austria's important industrial centers are the environs of Vienna and the provinces of Styria, Upper Austria, and Salzburg.

- Among the goods manufactured near Vienna are precision instruments, fine furniture, foodstuffs, textiles, and metal goods.
- Styria owes its prosperous lumber industry to its dense forests.
- Upper Austria supports some of Austria's newer industries. Besides maintaining a large nitrogen plant, the city of Linz in Upper Austria also supports a blast furnace and a steel assembly plant.
- Salzburg factories produce aluminum, machinery, scientific instruments, and chemicals.

LESSON 1

The People

READ TO LEARN

Key Vocabulary
reunification
dialect
Holocaust

Key People
Martin Luther

Key Places
Germany
Switzerland
Austria
Alps
Berlin
Vienna

Read Aloud

It is a very positive thing. . . . It overcomes a division that never represented the will of the people.

These words were spoken in 1990 by Peter Perbandt, a German businessperson who had fled from East Berlin four years before. He was talking about the end of a division that for 45 years had split Germany into two countries. In this lesson you will read about the people of Germany. You will learn how their country was split up and then brought together again. You will also read about the people of the two other countries—Austria and Switzerland—that together with Germany make up Central Europe.

Read for Purpose

1. WHAT YOU KNOW: How does language unify the people of France?
2. WHAT YOU WILL LEARN: What roles do language and religion play in unifying the people of Central Europe?

IN THE CENTER OF EUROPE

Central Europe is made up of Germany, Switzerland, Austria, and Liechtenstein. Germany is the largest country in Central Europe. It stretches from the shores of the North Sea south to the snow-covered Bavarian Alps. Many major rivers flow through Central Europe, but Germany is the only country with a coastline.

DIVIDED GERMANY

People have lived in present-day Germany for at least 50,000 years. Around 500 B.C. groups of Celtic people settled in Germany's forests and plains. About 500 years later, the Romans arrived. They built roads and fortresses and introduced their system of law. Hundreds of years after that the Huns, groups of warriors on horses, made their way from Asia into Germany.

Germany had more than 1,800 separate kingdoms whose people shared one language. In 1871 it finally became one nation.

Then, in 1945, after its defeat in World War II, Germany was divided again. The western part was controlled by Great Britain, France, and the United States. In 1949 it became the Federal Republic of Germany, known as West Germany. The same year, the eastern part, controlled by the

WHAT YOU KNOW: This question refers to material covered in Chapter 10, Lesson 1; the French people take great pride in their language and try to protect its purity.

LESSON 1
pages 233–236

Lesson Theme Switzerland, Austria, Liechtenstein, and newly reunited Germany make up Central Europe, a region united by language and religion and inhabited by a mainly urban population.

Lesson Objectives
- Describe how Germany came to be divided, then reunited.
- Identify the languages and religions of Central Europe.
- Describe Central Europe's cities and countryside.

1 PREPARE

Motivate Display the *Atlas* map of Western Europe. Ask students how difficult it would be to unify 1,800 separate kingdoms into one nation.

Set Purpose Present the *What You Know* question as one clue to the answer to how to unify a nation. Tell students to keep the *What You Will Learn* question in mind as they read.

2 TEACH

Looking at the Center of Europe

Ask students:

- **Which nations make up Central Europe?** (Germany, Switzerland, Austria, Liechtenstein)
- **Which is the largest?** (Germany)

Discussing a Divided Germany
Help students get a sense of Germany's complex development.

Ask students:

- **Which different groups settled Germany?** (Celts, Romans, Huns)
- **What caused Germany to be divided in 1945?** (defeat in World War II)

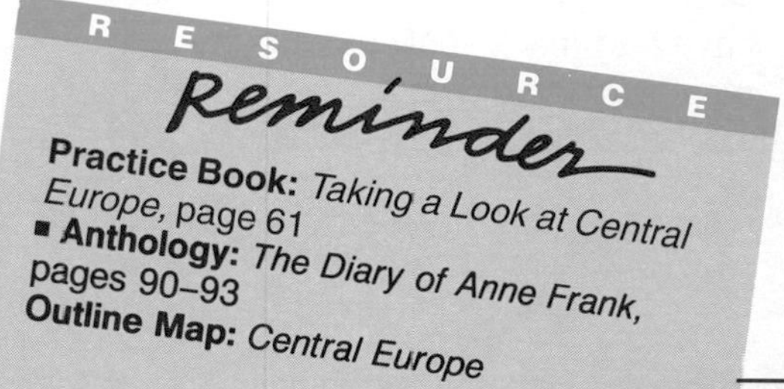

READING STRATEGY AND VOCABULARY DEVELOPMENT

Using Semantic Clues The purpose of this strategy is to point out the various clues that authors use to define words for the reader. Preview the lesson with students and brainstorm ways in which they might define the *Key Vocabulary* words. Although they will find these words in the *Glossary* or dictionary, also suggest that authors often provide clues to meaning directly in the text. Have students skim the text and find the *Key Vocabulary* words. Point out that two types of semantic clues are employed in this lesson: synonyms and the use of examples and facts to give a meaning. *Reunification* and *dialect* are each defined by a synonym, a word or phrase that has the same or nearly the same meaning as the unfamiliar term. *Holocaust* is defined by facts that clarify its meaning.

Looking at a Divided Germany

Continue the discussion.

Ask students:

- **How was Germany divided?** (Great Britain, France, and the U.S. took control of what became West Germany, and the Soviet Union took control of East Germany.)
- *THINKING FURTHER:* **Why do you suppose the Allies wanted to divide Germany?** (to weaken it so it could not make war again)

EXTENDING MAP SKILLS

Have students study the political map of Central Europe.

Ask students:

- **Which countries border Central Europe on the east?** (Poland, Czech Republic) **On the west?** (Belgium, Luxembourg, the Netherlands, France) **On the south?** (Italy) **On the north?** (Denmark)

Discussing a Reunited Country

Help students to understand the experience of reunification.

Ask students:

- **How had Soviet-controlled East Germany tried to keep its people from fleeing to the west?** (by building the Berlin Wall)
- **Why did people want to flee from East Germany to West Germany?** (They must have thought life was better there; they wanted democratic rather than communist rule.)
- **What did the people of East Germany finally do to get the life many of them wanted?** (They overthrew their Soviet-controlled government and tore down the Berlin Wall.)
- *THINKING FURTHER:* **How do you think the people felt as they tore down the Berlin Wall?** (They must have had many feelings, among them joy.)

CENTRAL EUROPE: Political

⊛ National capital • Other city

MAP SKILL: Central Europe includes Germany, Austria, Liechtenstein, and Switzerland. On which river is the capital of Austria located?

Soviet Union, became the German Democratic Republic, or East Germany. Barriers were built between the two areas.

The city of **Berlin**, the traditional capital of Germany, was also divided. West Berlin became part of West Germany, and East Berlin became part of East Germany.

West Germany was encouraged to become a democracy. East Germany and other countries of Eastern Europe became communist countries under the control of the Soviet Union. About 3 million people emigrated from East Germany to West Germany through Berlin.

In 1961, to keep people from moving to the west, the Soviet-controlled East German government built a huge wall to separate East and West Berlin. Many Germans longed for the Berlin Wall to topple and the barriers to come down so they would once again live in one country. Many people in East Germany tried to flee to West Germany by getting past the Berlin Wall and other barriers.

A REUNITED COUNTRY

By 1989 many people began to find new ways to get out of communist countries including East Germany. As a new spirit of freedom and democracy spread across Europe, the Soviet Union could no longer control East Germany. East Germans overthrew the Soviet-controlled government. Then, with the help of West Germans, they began to tear down the Berlin Wall. Germany was united again.

On October 3, 1990, 1 million people poured into Alexanderplatz, the main square of East Berlin. They came to celebrate **reunification** [rē ū nə fi kā′ shən], being united again. Look at the map on this page to see the present borders of Germany along with its Central European neighbors, Austria and Switzerland.

Reunification was a time for family reunions. Here is an account of one such reunion.

> *Over a 12-year period, three Grabowski children, a son and two daughters, had fled to the West. Their daughters, they explained, had risked arrest and prison by hiding illegally in the trunks of automobiles that carried them across the armed checkpoints that vanished with the Berlin Wall.*
>
> *"Now they can visit us freely, we can visit them," Mr. Grabowski said.*

LANGUAGE AND DIALECTS

People in Germany share the German language. So do most people in Switzerland and Austria. Yet not everyone who

MAP SKILL: the Danube River

CURRICULUM CONNECTION

Math As a result of the Crusades during the Middle Ages, trade increased throughout Europe. Old crossroads turned into marketplaces, and these marketplaces grew into towns and cities. Many German cities founded during the Middle Ages are today the largest cities in the country. Have students look up the dates when the cities shown on the map on this page were founded and have them group the cities by age. Ask students during which centuries most of Germany's largest cities were founded. Then have students look up the population of these cities today. Have them add these populations together and figure out what percentage of Germany's people live in major cities. Ask students to write a paragraph explaining their findings. Have them speculate on the impact ancient trading patterns have on where people live today. Ask them why understanding history helps us to better understand life today.

speaks German sounds the same. The official language of Germany is called High German, and all German schoolchildren learn to read and write High German. But there are many **dialects**, or local variations, of the language.

"Up here we have our own dialect, which we often use when we're with friends or members of the family," explains Hanna Bumann, a German who lives near the Baltic Sea. "It's almost totally different from standard [High] German."

German is also Austria's official language. But Switzerland has four national languages. About 70 percent of Swiss citizens speak German. Another 20 percent speak French. The language of the Swiss city Ticino (ti chē' nō), near Lake Lugano, is Italian. Some Swiss speak Romansh (rō mänsh'). This language comes from Latin. Despite differences in their languages, the Swiss people remain united.

RELIGION

Most Central Europeans practice some branch of Christianity. In Austria, 85 percent of the people are Roman Catholics. In Germany and Switzerland about half are Roman Catholics, and the other half Protestant.

Protestantism began in Germany in the 1500s after a young priest named **Martin Luther** "protested" against some actions taken by the Catholic Church. Luther and his followers broke away from the Roman Catholic Church and formed a new branch of Christianity called Protestantism.

Until World War II, many Jews lived in Germany and other countries of Central and Eastern Europe. But Adolf Hitler, the dictator of Germany, had more than 6 million Jewish men, women, and children in these countries put to death. This destruction of nearly half the world's Jewish population is called the **Holocaust**.

Martin Luther founded the Protestant movement in Germany in the 1500s. Today many people in Germany and throughout Central Europe are Protestants.

Discussing Language Help students grasp the role of the German language in unifying Central Europe.

Ask students:

- **What is the difference between a spoken and a written version of a language?** (Written language will be standard; spoken language may be more difficult to understand because of dialects.)
- **What are dialects?** (variations in how the same basic language is spoken)
- **How are Germany and Austria similar in language?** (German is the official language of both.)
- **How is language in Switzerland unique?** (The Swiss have four national languages: German, Italian, French, and Romansch.)
- *THINKING FURTHER:* **What do you suppose contributes to the fact that many dialects are spoken in Central Europe?** (the great size of the region coupled with geographical and historical barriers)

Looking at Religion Help students to realize that Christianity is the predominant religion in Central Europe and that an important branch of Christianity—Protestantism—was born in Germany.

Ask students:

- **What is the predominant religion in Austria?** (Roman Catholicism)
- **How do Germany and Switzerland compare in the religions practiced there?** (Both are half Roman Catholic and half Protestant.)
- **What happened to the Roman Catholic religion in the 1500s?** (Martin Luther protested some of the church's actions and broke away from it to form a new branch of Christianity—Protestantism.)
- **What was the Holocaust?** (the destruction of half the world's Jewish population—6 million in all)
- **How was Central Europe involved in the Holocaust?** (Most of the Holocaust victims came from Central Europe or from Eastern European nations occupied by German and Austrian soldiers.)

BACKGROUND INFORMATION

Multicultural Perspectives For 28 years the Berlin Wall was a universal symbol of the forced division of people along artificial boundaries. When this famous symbol came tumbling down in 1989, many people hoped that it signified the beginning of greater human unity everywhere. But symbols of division still exist throughout the world today.

- Since 1945 a deadly strip of land known as the "Demilitarized Zone" has divided Korea into two countries. (In 1992 there was the beginning of a reconciliation between South Korea and North Korea.)
- In Lebanon's capital city, a "no-man's land" called the Green Line divides Muslim West Beirut from Christian East Beirut.
- In some South African neighborhoods, white residents have built walls around their homes to keep out black neighbors.

Ask students to identify symbols of division in other parts of the world.

Discussing Cities and Open Spaces Encourage students to identify and describe the attractions of Central Europe's major cities.

Applying the Lesson Write *Germany, Austria,* and *Switzerland* on three separate pieces of paper. Let three students each choose a piece of paper, but tell them to keep their choice a secret. Tell them to imagine they live in these places and to describe to the class what they are like. Have the class guess the places.

3 CLOSE

Summarizing Students should understand that factors in their history have both united and divided the people of Central Europe. Ask students to identify and categorize these factors.

Evaluating Use the *Check Your Reading* questions (answers given below) to assess students' understanding.

Answers to Check Your Reading

1. Germany, Austria, Switzerland, Liechtenstein
2. The majority of people speak German and follow Christian faiths, either Catholic or Protestant.
3. that they are one nation once again
4. Mountains are a natural barrier that keep people from uniting.

Independent Practice
Practice Book: page 61

CITIES AND OPEN SPACES

Since the end of World War II, most Central Europeans have lived in cities and large towns. Yet huge areas are set aside for parks, farms, and forests. Berlin, the largest city in Central Europe, has over 50 square miles (130 sq km) of parks, forests, and lakes. There are even farms within the city limits.

Most German and Austrian cities were badly damaged in World War II, but many have been rebuilt. The mayor of Lübeck, a German city on the Baltic Sea, is proud that so many historic buildings have survived. "Only as a last resort," he said, "do we knock down a building. Preservation of our rich heritage is always uppermost in our minds."

Vienna's people believe no other city in the world can match this Austrian city for style and elegance. Vienna is the capital and cultural center of Austria. Splendid palaces dating back many hundreds of years are found throughout the city.

FOUR COUNTRIES

Central Europe is made up of Switzerland, Austria, Liechtenstein, and the newly reunited Germany. The German language and the Christian religion unite many people of this area. There are many large forests and farms in Central Europe, but most people live in large cities.

Check Your Reading

1. Which four countries make up Central Europe?
2. How do language and religion help to unite the people of Central Europe?
3. What does reunification mean for the people of Germany?
4. THINKING SKILL: What effect might the Alps have had in keeping Switzerland and Austria separate countries?

THINKING SKILL: Cause and Effect

CITIZENSHIP MAKING A DIFFERENCE

A NEW Award

Jakob von Uexkull (yä′ küp fôn ůk′ skəl) grew up in Hamburg, Germany, but his mother came from Sweden. Each year he and his mother listened to the announcement of the Nobel prizes from Sweden. These prizes honor writers, scientists, and humanitarians from all over the world.

Jakob knew that the Nobel prizes were very important, but he had another idea. He thought that people who try to solve world problems, such as pollution and poverty, should also be honored for their important work.

When he grew up, Jakob sold the stamp collection he had started when he was nine years old. With the money he received he decided to establish The Right Livelihood Awards. Jakob traveled all over the world looking for people who were trying to solve problems, such as cleaning up the environment and educating children.

Now the Right Livelihood Awards are announced in Sweden the day before the Nobel prize ceremonies. Since 1980 Jakob has awarded prizes to people from over 25 countries. The idea he had as a boy is today a reality.

MEETING INDIVIDUAL NEEDS

Reteaching (easy) Give students the outline map of Central Europe, which is found in the Teacher's Resource Center. First have them color and label the countries of Central Europe. Then have them label the neighboring countries, cities mentioned in this lesson, the North Sea, and the Baltic Sea.

Extension (average) Have students learn more about Martin Luther, and then have the class role-play his story.

Enrichment (challenging) Have students research the Huns and then write a paragraph about how their settlements affected the early development of Central Europe.

BUILDING CITIZENSHIP

A New Award Begin by discussing what students know about the Nobel prize and why it is awarded. Ask students what the Right Livelihood Award is and why it is important. Discuss the sacrifice that Von Uexkull made to create this award. Have students compare the two awards and decide which, if either, is more important and why. Have students research winners of the Right Livelihood Award and why they won the award.

LESSON 2

The Economy

READ TO LEARN

Key Vocabulary

standard of living
pollution

Key Places

Ruhr Valley
Basel

Read Aloud

It's very good, very hopeful. . . . Maybe things won't be rosy at first, but the future will be better.

These words were spoken by Doris Bruch (brükh), who lives in a town near Berlin, as she and her family celebrated the reunification of Germany. Although problems lie ahead for Doris and other former East Germans, she is optimistic about the future for her newly united country. Her confidence is common to the people of Central Europe.

Read for Purpose

1. WHAT YOU KNOW: What are the four countries of Central Europe?
2. WHAT YOU WILL LEARN: How have the countries of Central Europe developed strong economies?

COMMUNISM IN EAST GERMANY

After World War II East Germany built its economy under the system of communism. As you read in Chapter 6, under communism the government controls the entire economy.

Doris Bruch, whose words you just read, lives in Bernau (bûr' nō). East Germans like Doris worked hard and enjoyed the most advanced economy of communist Eastern Europe. Wages were low, yet Doris could afford many basic goods because the government kept prices low. The East German government also guaranteed everyone a job.

Most East Germans worked in mining, agriculture, and industry. The goods that they made were often of poor quality because many factories in East Germany were old and inefficient.

If Doris had owned a television set, she might have received programs from nearby West Berlin. She would have seen that West Germany's economy had become much more successful than the economy of East Germany.

Few people could have predicted West Germany's growth after World War II. Most factories had been destroyed. Bridges, canals, and roads lay in ruins. Yet, under the economic system of capitalism and with hard work, planning, and efficiency, West Germany was transformed into a prosperous nation within 20 years.

West German factories make a wide variety of products, from cars and computers to chemicals and steel. The farms of West Germany are efficient, often using advanced technology.

WHAT YOU KNOW: Germany, Austria, Switzerland, and Liechtenstein

LESSON 2
pages 237–239

Lesson Theme Since the destruction caused by World War II, Central Europe has developed prosperous, industrial economies, but the region does suffer from environmental problems.

Lesson Objectives

- Describe the problems involved in combining the economies of the two Germanies.
- Describe the economies and high standards of living of Switzerland and Austria.
- Describe the pollution problem in Central Europe.

PREPARE

Motivate Read the *Read Aloud* section to the class. Have students speculate on what kind of problems East Germans might face in a reunited Germany.

Set Purpose Use the *What You Know* question to get students to refocus on the nations under study. Tell students that as they read to seek answers to the *What You Will Learn* question, they will learn some of the secrets and some of the pitfalls of building a strong economy.

TEACH

Discussing Communism in East Germany Stress the inequality between the economies developed by East Germany and West Germany following World War II.

Ask students:

- **How would you compare the economies that developed in the two Germanies after the war?** (West Germany's was dramatically more efficient and prosperous, as East Germany could readily see.)

READING STRATEGY AND VOCABULARY DEVELOPMENT

Using Semantic Clues Point out to students that two semantic, or meaning, clues are used for *Key Vocabulary* terms in this lesson—synonyms and direct definition. Students learned about synonyms in Lesson 1. A direct definition is the definition of a term given directly when the word is introduced. Tell students that authors of content-area material often use a direct definition. Have students locate the *Key Vocabulary* terms in the lesson and determine which type of semantic clue is used. A direct definition is given for *standard of living. Pollution* is defined using a synonym.

EXTENDING MAP SKILLS

Have students study the Ruhr Valley map.

Ask students:

- **The Ruhr is a tributary of which major European river?** (the Rhine)
- *THINKING FURTHER:* **Why do you think it is an advantage for Ruhr factories to be on a river that flows into the Rhine?** (Factory products can be moved easily north or south to European nations or out to the North Sea to world markets.)

Discussing Combining Two Economies Help students realize just how far behind West Germany East Germany was.

Ask students:

- **What did East Germany have to change about its economy after reunification?** (It had to go from a communist to a capitalist system.)
- **Why was this so hard for East Germany?** (Because its factories were so inefficient, they couldn't compete in a capitalistic world; they had to close, putting many people out of work.)
- *THINKING FURTHER:* **Why do you suppose tensions might arise between the people of western and eastern Germany?** (Resentment can build up on both sides, with the westerners unhappy about the cost of rebuilding and easterners unhappy about the westerners telling them what to do.)

Looking at Switzerland and Austria

Ask students:

- **What is a standard of living?** (how well-off people are with the goods and services available to them)
- **With few natural resources to draw on, why does Switzerland have such a high standard of living?** (because the Swiss produce high-quality goods and services that people around the world want to buy)

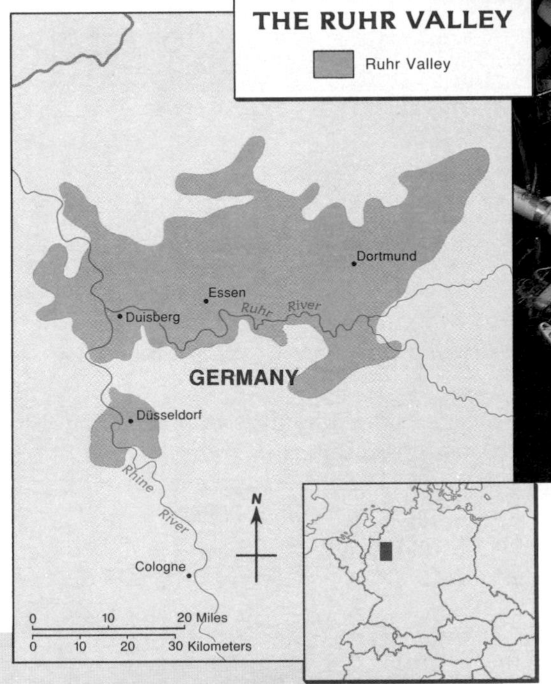

MAP SKILL: Auto-making is just one of the important industries of the Ruhr Valley. What are some important cities in this area?

The map on this page shows you the main cities along the **Ruhr Valley**, Europe's biggest industrial center. The Ruhr Valley is crowded with coal and iron mines, oil refineries, chemical plants, and heavy industries.

COMBINING TWO ECONOMIES

Through reunification, East Germany exchanged communism for capitalism. Now the people of what was once East Germany want to improve their lives, but conditions may get worse first.

Economic reunification is expensive for both western and eastern Germany. It will eventually cost Germany billions of dollars to help build the economy in the east. But it has already cost the former East Germany nearly half its jobs. Inefficient factories have been forced to close. Their goods cannot compete with goods from Western Europe.

SWITZERLAND AND AUSTRIA

Unlike Germany, Switzerland has few natural resources and little arable land. But the Swiss people have the highest **standard of living** in Europe. A country's standard of living is measured by the goods and services that its people have. A high standard of living offers people good medical care, decent housing, and the chance for an education and a good job.

The Swiss have worked hard for their prosperity. They pride themselves on making high-quality goods that include machinery, tools, and watches.

Tourists arrive to enjoy the majestic scenery or to ski down the snow-covered Swiss Alps. Since tourists are vital to the Swiss economy, the Swiss try hard to make them feel welcome.

Switzerland is a safe place to keep money. People all over the world keep their money in Swiss banks. Banking is an important part of the Swiss economy.

Today many people want to live and work in this prosperous, productive na-

MAP SKILL: Düsseldorf, Duisberg, Essen, Dortmund

BACKGROUND INFORMATION

The Marshall Plan To help war-torn nations of Europe rebuild their economies after World War II, United States Secretary of State George C. Marshall proposed a plan that would grant them financial aid. Congress enacted the plan and the offer of United States financial aid was made. The Soviet Union refused to accept such aid and forced the nations it occupied to decline as well. West Germany and Austria both accepted, and their march to prosperity began. (Switzerland, not having taken part in the war, was not eligible, but aid was not needed there.) East Germany was left to rebuild without the added boost of Marshall Plan aid.

Pollution has caused many problems in Central Europe, from killing fish to damaging outdoor statues.

tion. As a result Switzerland has many residents, guest workers, and visitors from other countries.

Like Switzerland, Austria has little arable land and few natural resources. Austria's massive snow-covered peaks, shimmering blue lakes, and thick green forests also attract many visitors. The income from tourism, along with industries such as steel and machinery, play a key part in Austria's economy.

PROBLEMS AND PROSPECTS

In 1986 a fire in a factory in Basel, Switzerland, sent clouds of foul-smelling smoke over the city. Deadly chemicals poured into the Rhine River. Many fish died. The chemical spill caused problems in areas far beyond Switzerland.

Pollution, or dirty and dangerous elements in the environment, is a serious problem in Central Europe. It is one price the area has paid for its factories. No country in Central Europe remains unaffected by its neighbors' problems. The air and rivers cross national borders. That means that countries need to cooperate to solve pollution problems.

A PROSPEROUS REGION

Central Europe is an industrial region with a high standard of living based on manufacturing, advanced technology, and service industries. While Switzerland and Austria have strong economies, reunited Germany faces economic challenges. Together, these countries must fight common problems such as air and water pollution.

Check Your Reading

1. How have the countries of Central Europe developed strong economies?
2. What impact did German reunification have on the country's economy?
3. Name three businesses that are important to Switzerland's economy.
4. THINKING SKILL: Before reunification, how was life in East Germany and West Germany similar? How was it different?

THINKING SKILL: Compare and Contrast

Discussing Problems and Prospects Call on students to define *pollution* and have them relate it to industrial production. Encourage them to explain why nations must cooperate if they are to solve pollution problems.

Applying the Lesson Have students research and chart the nations with the ten highest standards of living. Then ask how the standard of living of the United States compares with the others.

3 CLOSE

Summarizing Students should understand that Central Europe's developed economies are the industrial heart of Europe. Ask them to review the factors that support these strong economies.

Evaluating Use these questions to assess students' understanding.

- **Why has reunification brought Germany problems?** (The economy of former East Germany must be totally rebuilt, at great expense.)
- **What is the Ruhr Valley?** (Europe's biggest industrial center)
- **Which European country has the highest standard of living?** (Switzerland)
- **What price has Central Europe had to pay for its industrialization?** (pollution)

Answers to Check Your Reading

1. through hard work, efficiency, and quality
2. It cost the economy a great deal, both in money and jobs.
3. any three of the following: machinery, tools, watches, tourism, banking
4. Both were the most successful in their regions, but West Germany was by far the more efficient and prosperous.

Independent Practice
Practice Book: page 62

MEETING INDIVIDUAL NEEDS

Reteaching (easy) Have students imagine that they are in West Germany immediately following World War II. Ask them to write a list of five or six actions that will help their economy to recover.

Extension (average) Have students learn more about the 1986 Rhine River fish kill. Have them list the cooperative actions that the nations of Europe took to stop the spread of toxic chemicals in the river and to prevent future pollution.

Enrichment (challenging) Tell students to find up-to-date statistics on reunited Germany's economy. Have them also find the same statistics for East Germany and West Germany before reunification. They should record the comparative information in chart form and present it to the class.

LESSON 3
pages 240–241

Lesson Theme Democracies characterize the governments of Central Europe today.

Lesson Objectives
- Describe the governments of Germany and Austria.
- Explain the direct democracy of Switzerland's government.

PREPARE

Motivate Read the *Read Aloud* section to the class. Ask what momentous events caused such drastic changes in the size of the nations of Central Europe. (World Wars I and II) Discuss what was happening to the size of the United States at these times.

Set Purpose Ask the *What You Know* question and have a student draw on the chalkboard a rough diagram showing federalism. Read the *What You Will Learn* question along with the class and challenge students to think in terms of diagrams during this lesson.

TEACH

Looking at German Government

Ask students:

- **What is the Bundestag?** (Germany's two-house national legislature, elected by the people)
- **What is the role of the chancellor?** (Appointed by the Bundestag, the chancellor heads the government.)
- **What is the federal system of Germany?** (Political power is divided between the central government and 16 powerful states, called Lander.)

LESSON 3

The Government

READ TO LEARN

Key Vocabulary
chancellor
canton
neutral

Key Places
Bonn
Geneva

Read Aloud

At the beginning of World War I in 1914, Austria was the center of a huge empire called Austria-Hungary. Germany was a unified nation that stretched from the Low Countries to Russia.

The face of Central Europe has changed greatly since World War I. Today, Austria is a small republic. Germany has recently become a reunited country after having been divided into two countries. As you read this lesson, you will learn how some of these changes came about.

Read for Purpose

1. WHAT YOU KNOW: What is a federal system of government?
2. WHAT YOU WILL LEARN: What are the structures of the governments of Germany, Austria, and Switzerland?

ONE GERMAN GOVERNMENT

On July 1, 1990, East and West Germany united their economies. Three months later, they also united their governments. They dissolved East Germany's government and kept West Germany's form of government.

Now East Germans will have to relearn how to make choices in electing their leaders. Under communism, they did not have choices when they voted.

The united government of Germany has a two-house national legislature. It is called the Bundestag [bu̇n′ dəs täk]. German citizens elect representatives to the Bundestag but do not directly elect the heads of the government. Instead the two houses of the Bundestag elect a president as the country's head of state. The president performs ceremonial duties and, with the approval of the Bundestag, appoints a prime minister, called a **chancellor**. The chancellor is head of government.

Like many other democracies, Germany has a federal system of government. Political power is divided between a central government and 16 states—called *Lander*. The *Lander* have more power than states in the United States.

Before reunification, the Bundestag met in the city of **Bonn**. After reunification, Germans agreed to move their government to Berlin, which had been Germany's capital until the end of World War II. That means thousands of people and all their office files had to be moved. The move is expected to take at least ten years!

TWO OTHER DEMOCRACIES

Austria's government is similar to Germany's. A chancellor leads the government, while a president heads the nation.

WHAT YOU KNOW: This question refers to material covered in Chapter 2; a system of government in which power is divided between a national government and local governments.

READING STRATEGY AND VOCABULARY DEVELOPMENT

Using Semantic Clues Review with students the different types of semantic clues that they have learned about so far: synonyms, using examples and facts, and direct definition. Have students preview the lesson and read the *Key Vocabulary* terms and other unfamiliar words. Then have students predict the meanings of these terms. After students have read the lesson, ask them to find the *Key Vocabulary* terms and determine which type of semantic clue is used to define the meaning of each. Then have students check to see whether the meanings they predicted were correct.

Less than a year after East and West Germans celebrated the destruction of the Berlin Wall in 1989, they celebrated the reunification of their country.

Switzerland is made up of 26 **cantons**. A canton is a small political unit, like a state or province. A Swiss canton is one of the few places in the world where direct democracy is at work. Its citizens hold regular meetings to decide all local issues.

Switzerland has been a self-governing democracy since the 1500s—longer than any other nation in Europe. Yet Swiss women could not vote on a national level until 1971. Even then several cantons refused to allow women full political rights at the local level. It was not until 1991 that the last canton recognized the full political rights of women.

Switzerland has remained at peace for hundreds of years. Since 1815 the country has been officially **neutral**. This means that Switzerland refuses to take sides in wars or disputes. It was neutral in World Wars I and II.

Because of Switzerland's neutrality, the city of **Geneva** is the headquarters of about 200 world organizations. Among them is the International Red Cross.

MAINTAINING DEMOCRACIES

Austria, Switzerland, and the newly reunited Germany all have democratic governments. As you have read, each country has a legislature with elected representatives.

Check Your Reading

1. What became of the government of East Germany after reunification?
2. How are the governments of Germany, Austria, and Switzerland organized?
3. What are cantons? Describe how they are governed.
4. **THINKING SKILL:** How could you determine the accuracy of this statement: "Switzerland has been a self-governing democracy since the 1500s"?

THINKING SKILL: Evaluating Accuracy

241

Discussing Two Other Democracies

Ask students:

- **How is Austria's government like Germany's?** (A chancellor leads the government and a president heads the nation.)
- **What is the role of the cantons in Switzerland's government?** (They are the 26 small political units that are Switzerland's local governments.)
- **What are two characteristics of democracy in Switzerland?** (It is Europe's oldest self-governing democracy and a direct democracy.)

Applying the Lesson Have students make a two-column chart comparing the following for Germany and Switzerland: the forms of government, political units, and how citizens exercise their political power.

3 CLOSE

Summarize Students should understand that representative democracies govern in Central Europe. Ask them to give examples of democracy in action in these countries.

Evaluating Use the *Check Your Reading* questions (answers given below) to assess students' understanding.

Answers to Check Your Reading

1. It was dissolved.
2. They are organized in a federal system in which national government and local governments divide political power between themselves.
3. Cantons are Switzerland's "states"; citizens decide local issues in them by a direct vote.
4. by consulting a history of Switzerland or an encyclopedia entry on it

Independent Practice
Practice Book: page 63

MEETING INDIVIDUAL NEEDS

Reteaching (easy) Have students draw diagrams showing the organization of each of the governments of the three nations of Central Europe. Then have students exchange diagrams to quiz each other on their meanings.

Extension (average) Have students write a short sketch describing how each Central European government works.

Enrichment (challenging) Have each student find out about one of the international organizations headquartered in Geneva, Switzerland, and report to the class about the work of that organization.

SKILLS LESSON
pages 242–243

Lesson Theme Recognizing bias means identifying a one-sided or slanted presentation of information.

Lesson Objective
- Describe and apply a procedure for recognizing bias.

PREPARE

Motivate Have students discuss a music group, song, TV show or personality, sports event, or another subject about which they have strong opinions. As they talk, write some of the words they use to describe the subject on the chalkboard. Tell students that the words they use reveal their bias for or against the subject. Write the word *bias* on the chalkboard. Have students read the introductory paragraphs and define *bias*. Write the definition on the chalkboard.

Set Purpose Tell students that in this lesson they will learn how to recognize bias.

2 TEACH

Trying the Skill Have students read the comments by the German farmer. Tell them that if they have trouble answering the questions, they may refer to the *Helping Yourself* section on the next page.

Thinking About Thinking Ask several students to read their answers aloud. To help students identify the process they followed, ask: How did you determine whether the account was biased? What did you do first? Why? Next? Why? And so on. What clues did you look for? Write the steps and clues students cite on the chalkboard.

RESOURCE Reminder
Practice Book: *Identifying a Biased Statement*, page 64

Recognizing Bias

Key Vocabulary
bias

Imagine that you went to a rock concert that you really enjoyed. The next day you read a newspaper review. The reviewer wrote that he thought all rock musicians were amateurs and that all rock music was boring. He could not understand why the audience was so excited about the music.

The reviewer had decided in advance that he did not like any rock music. This kind of one-sided view is known as **bias**. A person can be biased for or against something. Recognizing bias will help you to determine the accuracy of information you hear or read.

Trying the Skill

Read the following comments made by a German farmer. He lives on land in northern Bavaria that has been farmed by his family for generations.

> Farming used to be a pleasant way of life around here, but now it's terrible. The price we get for our milk is outrageously low. The soil is thin and rocky. Our three sons have factory jobs. They never wanted to farm. We'd like to sell, but only a crazy person would buy this farm. Nobody wants to be a farmer. Soon there will be no farms left.

1. Does this account show any bias?
2. What did you do to determine if this account was biased?
3. Did you find any clues to bias in the account? What clues did you find?

BUILDING CITIZENSHIP

Looking at Editorials and Political Cartoons Bring in a selection of editorials and political cartoons from newspapers and magazines. Divide the class into groups and give each group an editorial and a cartoon to analyze. Have the students in each group work together to identify the bias in the editorial and in the political cartoon.

HELPING YOURSELF

The steps on the left will help you to recognize bias. The examples on the right show one way to apply these steps to the farmer's comments.

One Way to Recognize Bias	Example
1. Recall the definition of *bias*.	*Bias* is a one-sided or slanted presentation of information.
2. Recall clues to bias.	Clues to bias include: • loaded or emotionally charged words such as *massacre* or *fantastic*, • exaggerations, especially *always* or *never*, • presentation of only one side of an issue.
3. Examine the information presented, sentence by sentence, looking for clues.	*Outrageously low* and *crazy* are words loaded with emotional impact. "Soon there will be no farms left" is an exaggeration.
4. Ask yourself: Do the clues I find give a one-sided view or impression for or against something?	Only the negative side of farming is given. The farmer does not talk about the positive aspects of farming or the possibility of improvement in the future.
5. State the bias, if any.	The farmer shows a bias against farming in his area of Germany.

Applying the Skill

Read the two passages below. Each discusses the Black Forest in Germany. Which passage shows bias?

Passage A

The Black Forest has long been a favorite place for hikers in the summer and skiers in the winter. Now, however, the forest is showing the effects of air pollution. Acid rain has caused many trees to become diseased, and some have died. Steps are being taken to curb pollution, but these are costly steps, both in money and in jobs, since industry causes much of the pollution.

Passage B

I looked at the trees of the forest. Some were already dead. Others were dying, their needles yellow, their branches drooping wearily, their trunks stained. It was the saddest sight I have ever seen. Our highest priority must be to save this beautiful forest, no matter what it costs.

1. Which passage shows bias?
2. What are some clues that helped you to recognize the bias?
3. Describe the bias in your own words

Reviewing the Skill

1. What does the word *bias* mean?
2. What are some steps you can follow to recognize bias?
3. Name two clues that will help you to identify bias.
4. Give some examples of when you should be alert to bias.

243

Helping Yourself Point out that this feature presents a step-by-step approach for recognizing bias. Explain that there are other procedures they could also use. These steps are guidelines to which students can refer if they need help searching for bias. Have students compare the steps and clues on the chalkboard with those listed here to identify the useful ones.

Applying the Skill Have students read Passage A and Passage B and answer the questions that follow them. (See answers below.) Remind students that the steps outlined in *Helping Yourself* can help them with their answers.

CLOSE

Reviewing the Skill Use students' answers to Question 1 to add to or revise the definition of *bias* on the chalkboard. Use Questions 2 and 3 to elicit from students explanations in their own words of how to recognize bias. Then use these questions to elicit examples of when and why it is important to be alert to a writer's or a speaker's bias.

Independent Practice
Practice Book: page 64

ANSWERS TO SKILLS QUESTIONS

Applying the Skill

1. The second passage (b) is biased.
2. Some clues are: Use of exaggeration—*It was the saddest sight I have ever seen.* One-sidedness—no weighing of possible costs of saving the trees or mention of other national priorities.
3. The writer thinks that saving the Black Forest should be the highest national priority, regardless of cost.

Reviewing the Skill

1. Bias is a one-sided or slanted view.
2. Look for clues to bias, such as exaggerations and emotionally loaded words. Identify patterns in the presentation of information. State the bias, if any.
3. Emotionally charged words, such as "saddest sight," and presentation of only one side of an issue.
4. You should be alert to bias whenever you need accurate information.

LESSON 4
pages 244–245

Lesson Theme Music is a strong artistic focus in Central Europe, while festivals and outdoor recreation also enrich life there.

Lesson Objectives
- Explain the role of music in Central European life.
- Describe Central European festivals.
- Explain outdoor recreation in Central Europe.

PREPARE

Motivate Read the *Read Aloud* section to the class. Ask students to name other European musical compositions or musicians they know of.

Set Purpose Review the *What You Know* question to help students compare Central Europe with France and the Low Countries. Tell students to keep the *What You Will Learn* question in mind as they read this lesson.

TEACH

Discussing Music Yesterday and Today

Ask students:

- **What role does music play in the Central European way of life?** (Central Europe is the home of many famous musicians, music festivals, opera houses, concert halls, orchestras, and ballet and theater groups.)
- **In which places are some music festivals of Central Europe held to honor artists?** (Salzburg, Austria—Mozart; Bonn, Germany—Beethoven; Bayreuth, Germany—Wagner)

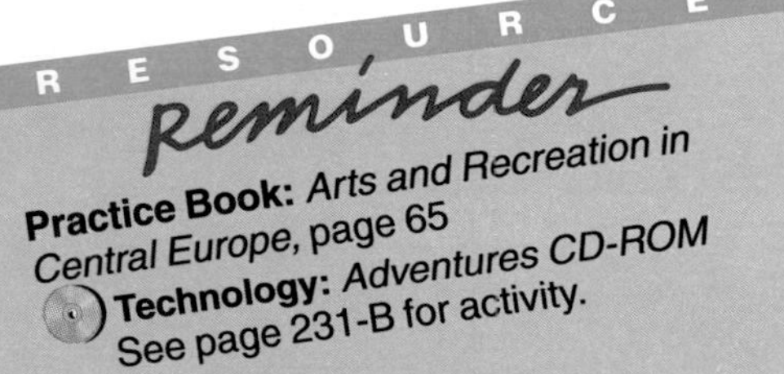

Practice Book: *Arts and Recreation in Central Europe,* page 65

Technology: *Adventures CD-ROM* See page 231-B for activity.

LESSON 4

Arts and Recreation

READ TO LEARN

Key People	**Key Places**
Johann Sebastian Bach	Munich
Ludwig van Beethoven	
Johannes Brahms	
Wolfgang Amadeus Mozart	

Read Aloud

On Christmas Eve in 1818, mice chewed through a church organ in an Austrian town. The organ would have provided the music for church services, and the villagers were upset. So the schoolmaster wrote music that could be played on a guitar. The priest wrote words to accompany the music. The song they composed, "Silent Night," became one of the most popular Christmas songs of all time. "Silent Night" is just one of many contributions that Central Europeans have made to the world of music.

Read for Purpose

1. **WHAT YOU KNOW:** What kinds of recreational activities are popular in France and the Low Countries?
2. **WHAT YOU WILL LEARN:** How is music an important part of the artistic heritage of Central Europe?

MUSIC YESTERDAY AND TODAY

Any list of great composers includes a large number of Germans and Austrians. You can start with the famous "3 Bs" of German music—Johann Sebastian Bach (bäk), Ludwig van Beethoven (bā′ tō vən), and Johannes Brahms (brämz). Then add still another name, Wolfgang Amadeus Mozart (mō′ tsärt), an Austrian.

Beethoven was born in 1770 in Germany. He moved to Vienna, Austria, in 1792 to study music. For hundreds of years, Vienna has been a center of opera and music. Mozart also worked in Vienna.

Today Central Europe celebrates its musical heritage through yearly music festivals. One of the biggest festivals is held every year at Mozart's birthplace, Salzburg, Austria. The city of Bonn, Germany, stages a Beethoven festival. And Bayreuth (bī roit′), Germany, hosts a third major music festival presenting operas by composer Richard Wagner.

Almost every major city in Central Europe has an opera house or a concert hall. But the people of Central Europe also enjoy their traditional songs and brass bands.

FESTIVALS AND CELEBRATIONS

Festivals of all kinds provide welcome breaks from work in Central Europe. Peo-

WHAT YOU KNOW: Possible answers include bicycle racing, soccer, and skiing.

244

READING STRATEGY AND VOCABULARY DEVELOPMENT

Using Semantic Clues The purpose of this exercise is to help students identify the type of semantic clue used to define unknown words. After students have read the lesson, have them find examples of semantic clues used in the text to define words. For example, *opera house* is defined by using the synonym *concert hall; breweries* has a direct definition; *festivals* is defined using examples. You may wish to have students practice writing sentences using the different types of semantic clues to define words.

Marching bands are just one part of the entertainment at festivals in Germany and the other countries of Central Europe.

ple listen to brass bands, dress in colorful costumes, and eat many kinds of delicious foods.

Every year about 6 million people attend a festival in Munich (mū' nik), Germany, known as *Oktoberfest*. This city-wide celebration marks the end of the growing season. Munich's many breweries—places where beer and ale are made—put up huge tents at the fair grounds. Some of the tents hold up to 7,000 people!

SPORTS AND LEISURE

Central Europeans love to participate in outdoor recreation. Hiking, rock climbing, skiing, ice skating, track, and bicycling are all very popular activities.

Switzerland's snow-capped Alps attract skiers from around the world. Many come to train for international competitions. The Swiss themselves—with their natural "home-field advantage"—are often winners in these events.

Before reunification, both East and West Germany were extremely successful in many international sports competitions. East Germany spent a great deal of effort developing outstanding athletes. For example, Katarina Witt won Olympic gold medals for figure skating in 1984 and 1988. Both East and West Germans won gold medals for team sports. Since then, German athletes have represented one country at the Olympics.

OLD TRADITIONS

Central Europe has produced many great musicians. Central Europeans have always strongly supported their musical, ballet, and theater groups. They also enjoy festivals, sports, and outdoor recreation.

Check Your Reading

1. Name four great German and Austrian composers who are part of the heritage of Central Europe.
2. What is *Oktoberfest*?
3. What are some activities that Central Europeans do in their spare time?
4. THINKING SKILL: Explain why the following statement is biased: "To people like me, who live in Vienna, there never was a musician as great as Mozart."

THINKING SKILL: Recognizing Bias

245

Talking About Festivals and Celebrations Help students to recognize that the hardworking people of Central Europe make time for fun and recreation. Discuss the reason for the *Oktoberfest*. Ask students if they know of any other people who celebrate the end of the growing season. (Pilgrims celebrated Thanksgiving; some African Americans celebrate *Kwaanza,* and so on.)

Looking at Outdoor Sports and Pleasures Stress to students the importance of participation in outdoor recreation in Central Europe.

Applying the Lesson Have students research the number of symphony orchestras, theaters, and opera houses in their state or area. Then have them write a paragraph titled "Why Classical Music and Drama Do or Do Not Need More Financial Support in Our State."

3 CLOSE

Summarizing Students have learned of the rich musical heritage and many outdoor activities of Central Europeans. Discuss why 6 million people attend the *Oktoberfest* each year.

Evaluating Use the *Check Your Reading* questions (answers given below) to assess students' understanding.

Answers to Check Your Reading

1. Bach, Beethoven, Brahms, Mozart
2. a festival celebrating the end of the growing season
3. going to concerts and festivals, hiking, climbing, skiing, skating, track, bicycling
4. The phrase "never was a musician as great as" can be seen as an exaggeration; with the millions of musicians the world has known, it is arguable who was the greatest of all.

Independent Practice
Practice Book: page 65

MEETING INDIVIDUAL NEEDS

Reteaching (easy) Have students draw pictures to show how music and outdoor recreation fit into the lives of Central Europeans.

Extension (average) Assign one of the five great musicians mentioned in this lesson to each of five student groups. Have them research his life and prepare a skit about one important event in his life. Then have each group write ten sentences about the ways in which the musician's life was different from the life of a music star today.

Enrichment (challenging) Have students listen to the music of the great composers they learned about in this lesson. Have students try to find out how the music of these composers has been used in modern times. (For example, many cartoons and commercials use their music.)

CHAPTER 11 REVIEW
pages 246–247

USING THE CHAPTER SUMMARY AND REVIEW

Cultural Geography These questions can be used for review.

- **Which groups of people invaded Central Europe?** (Celts, Romans, Huns)
- **How is a country's standard of living measured?** (by the goods and services that the people of that country have)
- **What is a federal system?** (a system of government in which political power is divided between national and local governments)
- **What type of sports are popular in Central Europe?** (outdoor sports)

Ideas to Remember

- **What unites the people of Central Europe?** (the German language and the Christian religion)
- **Why are the economies of the countries of Central Europe prosperous?** (These countries are highly industrialized, with manufacturing, advanced technology, and service industries.)
- **What type of government do the countries of Central Europe have?** (democratic)
- **What has Central Europe contributed to the world of music?** (many great composers)

Answers to Reviewing Vocabulary

1. dialect
2. reunification
3. canton
4. neutral
5. pollution

Answers to Reviewing Facts

1. Germany, Austria, Switzerland; German
2. There are many different dialects.

CHAPTER 11 • SUMMARY

CENTRAL EUROPE: CULTURAL GEOGRAPHY

PEOPLE

- Early peoples: Celts and Romans
- Today: People of a divided Germany have been reunited

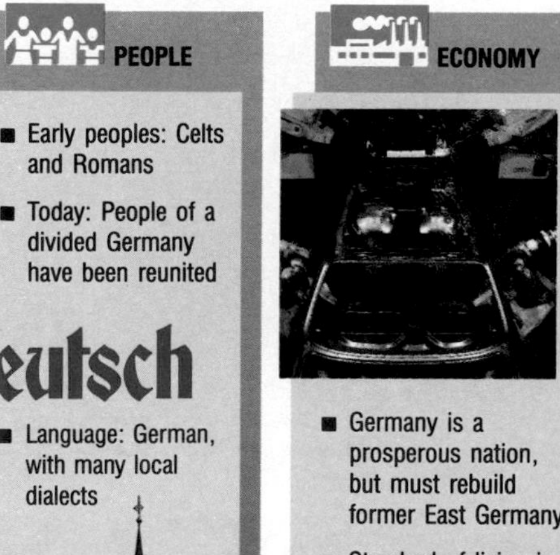

Deutsch

- Language: German, with many local dialects

- Religion: Christianity, about evenly divided between Catholics and Protestants

ECONOMY

- Germany is a prosperous nation, but must rebuild former East Germany
- Standard of living is high throughout area

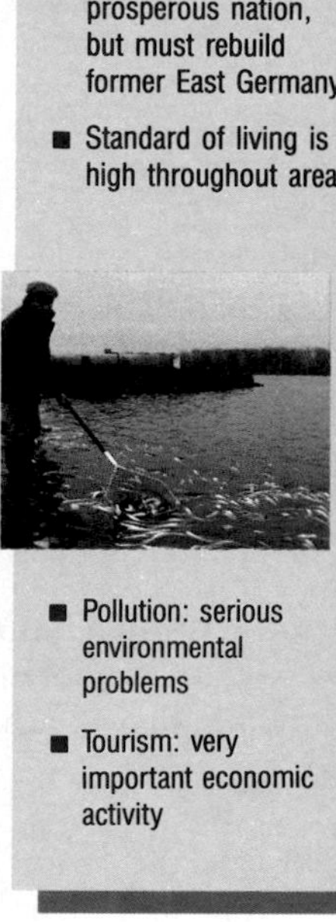

- Pollution: serious environmental problems
- Tourism: very important economic activity

GOVERNMENT

- Germany: parliamentary democracy, headed by a chancellor

- Federal system in Germany: power divided between national and local governments
- Switzerland: oldest working democratic government in Europe

ARTS AND RECREATION

- Many famous composers: Mozart, Bach, Brahms, Beethoven

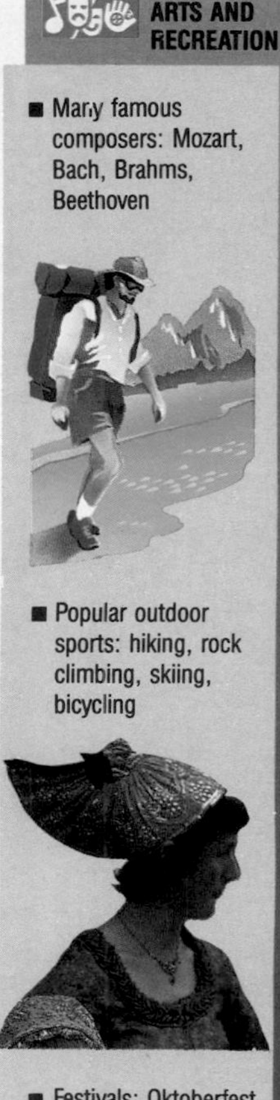

- Popular outdoor sports: hiking, rock climbing, skiing, bicycling
- Festivals: Oktoberfest

IDEAS TO REMEMBER

- The people of Central Europe are united by language and by the Christian religion.
- Central Europe is a highly industrialized and prosperous region.
- The countries of Central Europe have democratic governments with elected representatives and power divided between central and local governments.
- Central Europe has produced many great composers and musicians.

246

ENRICHMENT ACTIVITY

Creating Carnival Masks **Materials:** cardboard, felt, cloth scraps, yarn, glitter, feathers, paints or markers, glue, elastic, stapler

1. Tell the class that annual festivals or carnivals are a cultural tradition in many Central European cities. As part of some celebrations, people wear humorous masks of animal faces—for example, pigs with long eyelashes and red hair, or cows with blue eyes and long, blond hair. Tell students to imagine that they will be participating in such a celebration and that they are going to make actual masks to wear.
2. Have students work independently or in small groups. Have them design their masks on the cardboard and then cut out the faces, including holes for the eyes and nostrils. Tell students to decorate their masks with as many different materials as they like. When the masks are finished, have students staple a strip of elastic to both sides of each mask so that they can wear them.

CHAPTER 11 • REVIEW

REVIEWING VOCABULARY

canton pollution
dialect reunification
neutral

Number a sheet of paper from 1 to 5. Beside each number write the word from the list above that best matches the definition.

1. A local variation of speech, such as that found in the German regions of Central Europe
2. The bringing together of parts that had been separated
3. One of the areas, resembling a state or province, into which the country of Switzerland is divided
4. Not taking sides in a war or dispute
5. The act of making something dirty or dangerous, as with harmful wastes or chemicals

REVIEWING FACTS

1. Name the three largest countries of Central Europe. What is the main language of these countries?
2. Why do Germans sometimes have difficulty understanding each other even though they speak the same language?
3. What are the four national languages of Switzerland?
4. Why was Germany divided into two parts?
5. What is the name of Western Europe's greatest industrial region?
6. Which nation has Western Europe's highest standard of living?
7. Why is pollution a serious problem in Central Europe? Why can no one country solve the pollution problem by itself?
8. In Austria and Germany, what is the title of the person who runs the government?
9. Why has the city of Geneva, Switzerland, become the headquarters for many international organizations?
10. Which city has an annual festival in honor of the composer Wolfgang Amadeus Mozart? Of the composer Ludwig van Beethoven?

WRITING ABOUT MAIN IDEAS

1. **Writing an Essay:** Write an essay comparing the democracy of the United States with the "pure" democracy of the Swiss canton.
2. **Writing a Letter:** Imagine that you are visiting a town or city in Germany, Switzerland, or Austria. Write a letter to a friend at home describing the city or town—its people, environment, culture, and economy.
3. **Writing About Perspectives:** Imagine that you live in a Central European country and are concerned about pollution. Write a plan telling five things people could do to help curb pollution in your country.

BUILDING SKILLS: RECOGNIZING BIAS

1. What is the meaning of *bias*?
2. What are some of the clues that will help you to recognize bias?
3. Write a statement that expresses strong bias about a topic that interests you.
4. Why is it important to recognize an author's use of bias?

3. German, French, Italian, Romansh
4. The division of Germany was one of the results of World War II.
5. the Ruhr Valley
6. Switzerland
7. The area is highly industrialized; because the countries are so closely tied together economically and geographically.
8. the chancellor
9. because of Switzerland's neutrality
10. Salzburg, Austria; Bonn, Germany

Suggestions for Writing About Main Ideas

1. Students should compare who runs each country, how each leader is elected, and the length of each leader's term; the role of citizens; and the powers of local governments. You may wish to have students do more research about the Swiss government and then create a chart comparing the Swiss and American forms of government.
2. Students should try to stress what they think are the positive aspects of the country they chose.
3. Students' responses will probably fall into the following categories: recycling, developing processes that cut back on industrial pollution, and using pollution control devices on motor vehicles.

Answers to Building Skills: Recognizing Bias

1. a one-sided or slanted presentation of information
2. loaded or emotionally charged words; exaggerations; presentation of only one side of an issue
3. Accept all reasonable answers.
4. so that you can determine the accuracy of information

Chapter Review and Test
Practice Book: *Vocabulary Review,* page 66
Transparency: *Graphic Organizer*
Assessment Book: *Chapter 11 Test*

MAKING CONNECTIONS

Supporting the Main Idea Use the Main Idea Outline Graphic Organizer Transparency, writing in only the underlined items. Have students fill in other details about the people, economy, government, and arts of Central Europe. *Ask:* How have the rich natural resources of Central European countries affected their economies?

- Most of the people in Central Europe are city-dwellers, Christian, and speak German.
- Central Europe has a high standard of living.
- The countries of Central Europe have strong, highly developed economies.
- Central European countries have democratic governments.
- Central Europe has a strong musical heritage.
- Central Europeans enjoy outdoor recreation.

MAIN IDEA: A common cultural heritage, religion, and language, as well as prosperous economies, characterize the nations of Central Europe.

CHAPTER 12
ORGANIZER

COUNTRIES OF SOUTHERN EUROPE text pages 248–269

CHAPTER THEME

Pride in an ancient cultural and religious heritage characterizes the countries of Southern Europe.

CHAPTER OBJECTIVES

CONTENT

- Name the four major countries of Southern Europe.
- Describe the major achievements of two ancient Southern European civilizations.
- Identify the Roman Catholic and Greek Orthodox churches and explain how they differ.
- Describe economic challenges faced by Southern Europe today.
- Discuss tourism in Southern Europe and describe its positive and negative aspects.
- Describe how the governments of the Southern European countries are similar.
- Describe how Southern European countries have preserved their ancient traditions.

SKILLS

Geography
- Interpret a political map of Southern Europe.
- Use a map to give details about Vatican City.

Study and Research
- Interpret graphs and charts.

Thinking
- Make generalizations about the peoples and cultures of Southern Europe.
- Describe ways to find out whether facts presented in the text are true.

Reading and Writing
- Write an essay about a Southern European country.

CITIZENSHIP VALUES

- Appreciate the ability of people to establish democratic governments despite years of dictatorship.

TEACHER OPTIONS

READING STRATEGY: Summarizing Strategies to help students read and remember main ideas.
Lesson 1: p. 249
Lesson 2: p. 254
Lesson 3: p. 257
Lesson 4: p. 261
Legacy: p. 264

MEETING INDIVIDUAL NEEDS Activities for reteaching, extension, and enrichment.
Lesson 1: p. 252
Study and Research Skills: p. 253
Lesson 2: p. 256
Lesson 3: p. 260
Lesson 4: p. 263
Legacy: p. 267

GEO ADVENTURES ACTIVITIES PAD Daily activities to assess students' understanding of geography skills.

CURRICULUM CONNECTION Activities to help integrate other subject areas with Social Studies.
Language Arts: pp. 251, 259, 262
Music: p. 262

PUPIL EDITION ON CASSETTE Language support for students who have difficulty reading or who will benefit from listening to the Pupil Edition on Cassette as they read.

SECOND-LANGUAGE SUPPORT Activities and suggestions for second-language learners.
Lesson 2: p. 22

CHAPTER PLANNING GUIDE

LESSON	SUGGESTED PACING	THEMES	TEACHER SUPPORT MATERIALS: TEACHER'S RESOURCE CENTER
1 THE PEOPLE pages 249–252	1 day	Southern Europe has given the world a rich heritage, and the people are united today by a common language base, religion, way of life, and the Mediterranean Sea.	Practice Book p. 67 Outline Map p. 21
BUILDING STUDY AND RESEARCH SKILLS Reading Graphs and Charts page 253	1 day	Graphs and charts present detailed information in a visual form that is easily readable.	Practice Book p. 68
2 THE ECONOMY pages 254–256	1 day	Southern European countries are striving to develop their economies in the areas of manufacturing, farming, shipping, and tourism.	Practice Book p. 69
3 THE GOVERNMENT pages 257–260	1 day	The Southern European countries have representative democracies.	Practice Book p. 70 **Technology:** *Adventures CD-ROM*
4 ARTS AND RECREATION pages 261–263	1 day	Southern Europe has given the world a rich legacy of artistic achievements and religious traditions.	Practice Book p. 71 ■ Anthology pp. 68–72, 78–80 **Technology:** *Videodisc/Video Tape 3*
LEGACY The Palio pages 264–267	1 day	The Palio, a horse race held in Siena, Italy, is a traditional celebration of the city's heritage and its neighborhoods.	Outline Map p. 21
CHAPTER SUMMARY AND REVIEW pages 268–269	1 day	Chapter content, skills, and vocabulary are reviewed and evaluated.	Practice Book p. 72 Transparency: Graphic Organizer Assessment Book, Chapter 12 Test

Technology CONNECTION

Lesson 3
ADVENTURES CD-ROM
Investigate Symbols for Greece, Italy, Spain, and Portugal on the CD-ROM.

Lesson 4
VIDEODISC/VIDEO TAPE 3
Enrich this lesson with *The Renaissance,* Video Lesson 11.

Search Frame 6339 Side B

CHAPTER 12 ORGANIZER

CHAPTER 12
pages 248–269

USING THE CHAPTER OPENER

Discussing the Photograph Encourage students to imagine that they have just met the girl in the picture. Have them make a list of questions that they might ask her about her country.

Ask students:

- **What makes you think the girl is not wearing her everyday clothes?** (Possible answers include: Her clothes look like a costume from another era; they are too fancy for everyday wear.)
- **For what occasion do you think she is dressed?** (Possible answers include: for a play, a pageant, a national holiday.)
- **If you were to dress like one of your ancestors, what kind of clothes would you wear?** (Answers will vary depending on the students' ethnic backgrounds.)
- *THINKING FURTHER:* **Why do you think people sometimes like to dress like their ancestors?** (Students may suggest that it helps them to feel connected to their roots.)

Reading/Listening to the Primary Source Read the passage under the picture to the class. Have students make one list of the things that they would miss if they were away from their homes and another list of the things that they would miss if they were away from the United States.

Ask students:

- **Judging from what you know about Italy, what do you think Italians might miss most about their country?** (Possible answers include: the food, the climate, the old buildings, the people.)

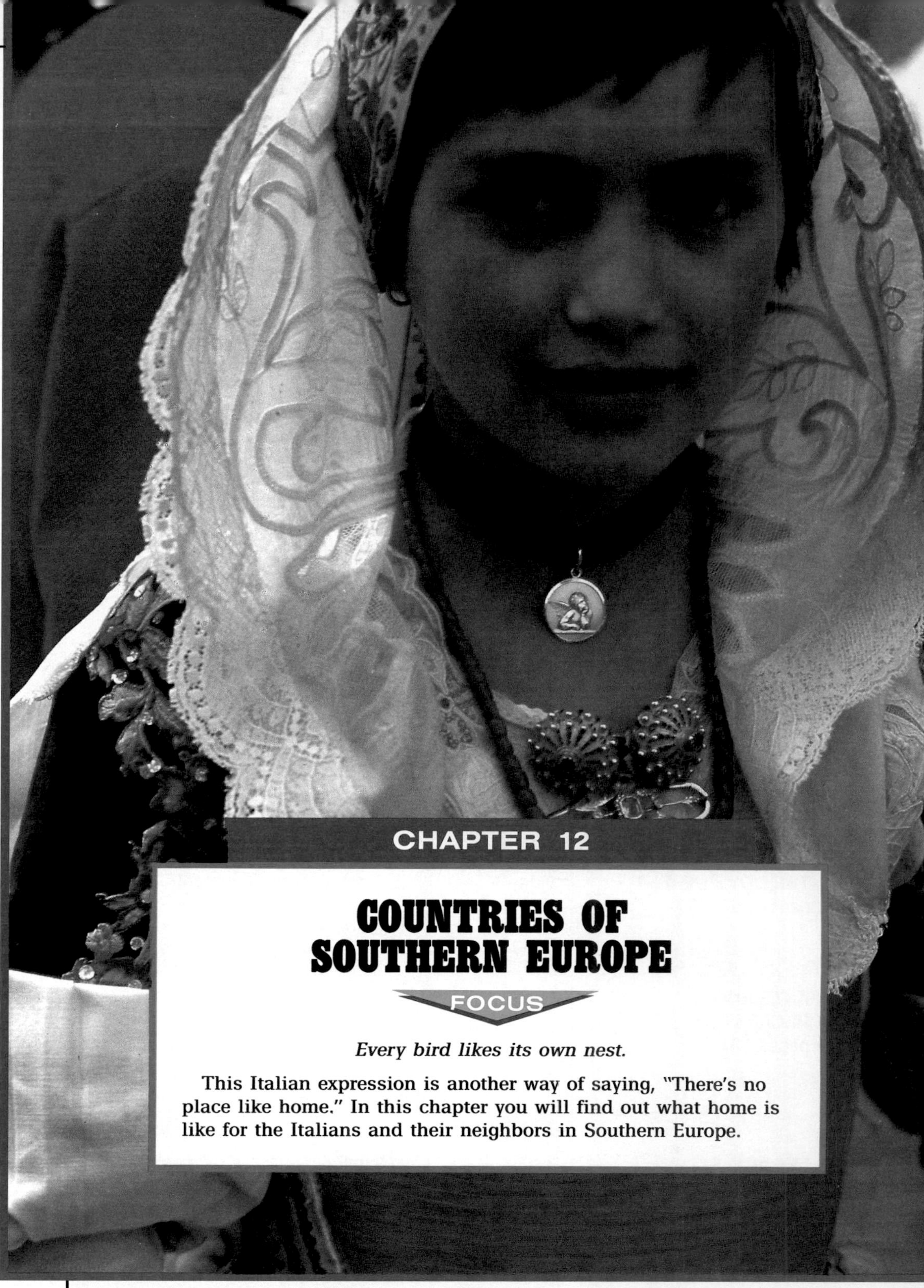

CHAPTER 12

COUNTRIES OF SOUTHERN EUROPE

FOCUS

Every bird likes its own nest.

This Italian expression is another way of saying, "There's no place like home." In this chapter you will find out what home is like for the Italians and their neighbors in Southern Europe.

BACKGROUND INFORMATION

About Venice Venice is so closely associated with the sea that it is called the "Queen of the Adriatic" and is often compared to the Roman goddess Venus, who was believed to have materialized from sea foam.

- Since the main thoroughfares of Venice are canals, people travel through the city in small steamers, gondolas (flat-bottomed boats with high prows), water buses, and small motorboats.
- Streets exist in Venice but are too narrow for automobiles. Pedestrian traffic is accommodated by narrow passages and small arched bridges that lead across the canals.

LESSON 1

The People

READ TO LEARN

Key Vocabulary

siesta

Key Places

Spain, Portugal, Italy, Greece, Vatican City, Athens

Read Aloud

Have you ever read about the ancient Greeks and the spread of their advanced civilization? Have you read about the Spanish and Portuguese who built large empires in the Amercias hundreds of years ago? Do you know what these people had in common? They all came from Southern Europe.

Read for Purpose

1. WHAT YOU KNOW: What peninsula contains the countries of Spain and Portugal?
2. WHAT YOU WILL LEARN: What do the people of Southern Europe have in common?

SETTLERS AND EXPLORERS

In the region we call Southern Europe are four large countries: **Spain**, **Portugal**, **Italy**, and **Greece**. Thousands of years ago, the people of this area began leaving their homes to explore faraway lands. Because much of this area is too rocky and steep for farming, many of its more adventurous sailors set sail in search of new lands to settle. The people of ancient Greece and Rome played an especially important role in the development of all of the region of Western Europe.

The ancient Greeks, for example, were among the first people to use shipping to import and export food. Early in Greek history the Greeks traveled to the plains north of the Black Sea and returned with wheat and animal hides. In return the Greeks exported wine to these areas.

Over the years the Greeks established trading posts around the Black Sea, along the shores of western Asia and northern Africa, and in far-off France. They also settled on the hundreds of islands that surround mainland Greece.

Like the Greeks, the Romans also spread their civilization throughout Europe. From their capital in Italy, the Romans ruled lands that stretched from North Africa to England and from Spain to Syria. The Mediterranean Sea became the center of a vast Roman Empire. In fact, during the Roman Empire the Romans called the Mediterranean Sea *Mare Nostrum*—the Latin words for "our sea."

Portugal and Spain were two of the great exploring nations of later times. In the 1400s and the 1500s, Spanish and Portuguese explorers discovered new trade

WHAT YOU KNOW: This question refers to material covered in Chapter 8, Lesson 1; the Iberian Peninsula.

LESSON 1
pages 249–252

Lesson Theme Southern Europe has given the world a rich heritage, and the people are united today by a common language base, religion, way of life, and the Mediterranean Sea.

Lesson Objectives
- Identify the countries of Southern Europe and the areas they explored.
- Identify the languages of Southern Europe.
- Describe the religions of Southern Europe.
- Describe the way of life of the Southern European people.

PREPARE

Motivate Read the *Read Aloud* section to the class. Ask students to answer the questions with information they know now. Ask students what other things they would like to find out about the people of Southern Europe.

Set Purpose Have students answer the *What You Know* question and locate the peninsula they name on a world map. Read the *What You Will Learn* question and tell students they will learn about things that unify the people of Southern Europe.

TEACH

Looking at Settlers and Explorers Help students to grasp the magnitude of the cultural contributions of the ancient Southern European people. Discuss the contributions of the Greeks, Romans, Portuguese, and Spanish to Western European civilization.

READING STRATEGY AND VOCABULARY DEVELOPMENT

Summarizing Review with students the purpose for summarizing that they learned in Chapter 7, as a way of paraphrasing important information in their own words to facilitate comprehension. Brainstorm with students the strategies that are useful for summarizing, such as scanning and skimming, note taking, outlining, and understanding patterns of organization. Suggest to students that the Thinking Skill question in *Check Your Reading* is really a summarizing question for which they use information from the text and their own background knowledge and judgment to arrive at an answer. Have students write and compare their answers to this question.

RESOURCE *Reminder*

Practice Book: *The Southern European Countries, page 67*
Outline Map: *Southern Europe*

EXTENDING MAP SKILLS

Have students study the political map on this page and identify the four countries of Southern Europe.

Ask students:

- **What is the capital of Spain?** (Madrid) **Of Portugal?** (Lisbon) **Of Italy?** (Rome) **Of Greece?** (Athens)
- **Which country of Southern Europe is most isolated from the rest of Europe, sharing only one border with another nation?** (Portugal)
- **Which country of Southern Europe extends farthest north?** (Italy)
- **Which is the only country of Southern Europe with no coast on the Mediterranean Sea?** (Portugal)
- **Which is the easternmost country in Southern Europe?** (Greece)
- **Which country of Southern Europe is closest to Africa?** (Spain)

THINKING FURTHER: **What physical characteristic do all the nations of Southern Europe share?** (All are on peninsulas.)

Discussing Language and Religion

Ask students:

- **Why are the languages spoken in Spain, Portugal, and Italy similar?** (All are languages based on Latin, which makes them sound very much alike.)
- **What other languages are spoken in Southern Europe?** (Greek, Catalan, Basque)
- **How does religion unify this region?** (Most people are Christians.)
- **What is the major religious difference between the people of Southern Europe?** (The western nations are Roman Catholic under the pope in Rome; Greece follows the Greek Orthodox religion under the archbishop of Athens.)

routes and explored the Americas. In Latin America they found huge amounts of gold and silver. Eventually Spain and Portugal controlled empires that reached from Latin America all the way to Asia.

Recently, people from Southern Europe have flocked to areas farther north in search of work. Today guest workers from Spain and Portugal hold a variety of jobs in other European countries. They send much of the money they earn back home to support their families.

LANGUAGE AND RELIGION

Each of the four Southern European countries has a different language. But if you were to listen to people speaking Portuguese, Spanish, and Italian, you would notice many similarities among these languages. The reason is that they all come from Latin, the language of the Roman Empire. Let's take the word *milk* as an example. It is *leite* in Portuguese, *leche* in Spanish, and *latte* in Italian.

In Greece the people speak a language that can be traced back thousands of years. Greek is written in a different alphabet from that of the other languages you have read about so far. Although many of the letters of the Greek alphabet sound similar to the letters of our Roman alphabet, they sometimes look very different. The letter *mu*, for example, begins with an "*m*" sound, but it looks like this: μ.

Two groups of people living in Spain speak languages all their own. The Catalans, who live in and around the city of Barcelona, speak a language that is a cross between Spanish and French. The Basques, who live in the Pyrenees mountains of northern Spain and southern France, have a language unlike any other in the world. Some people think that the Basque language is the oldest in Europe.

In religion as well as in language, Portugal, Spain, and Italy are similar. Most people in these three countries belong to the Roman Catholic Church. In Greece nearly

MAP SKILL: Many different countries border on the Mediterranean Sea. Which large Southern European country is not on the Mediterranean?

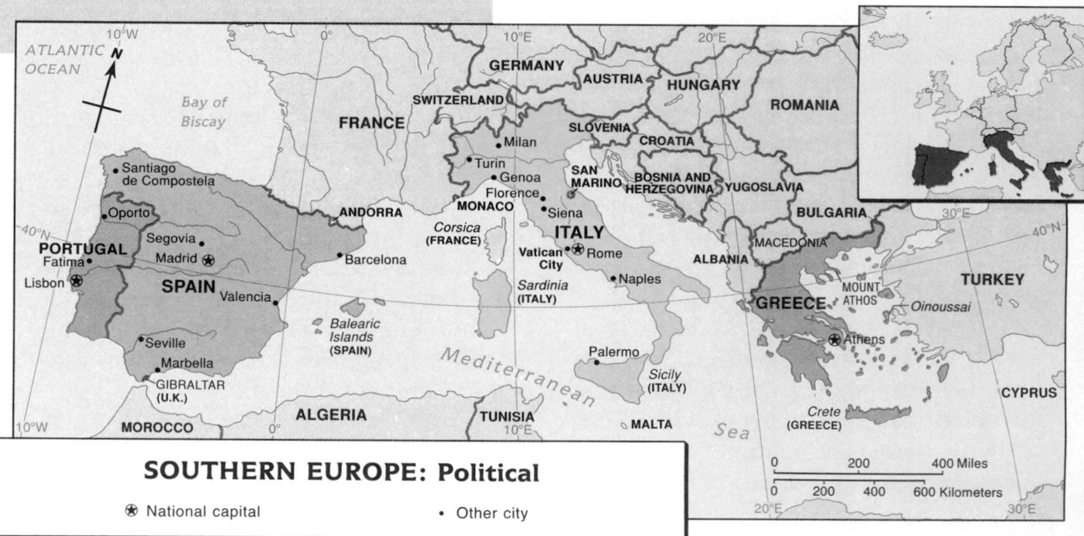

250 MAP SKILL: Portugal

5 FUNDAMENTAL THEMES OF GEOGRAPHY

Movement In the 1400s and 1500s Spanish and Portuguese ships, exploring dangerous and uncharted seas, changed tremendously the mental maps that Europeans had of the world. Have six student groups give oral reports on the voyages of the explorers listed below. Have students color on a large classroom world map the part of the world that their explorer charted (or alternatively, have five groups of students work on the Desk Maps of the world, found in the Teacher's Resource Center).

1415	Prince Henry the Navigator of Portugal
1488	Bartholomeu Dias of Portugal
1497–1499	Vasco da Gama of Portugal
1500	Pedro Álvares Cabral of Portugal
1492–1506	Christopher Columbus (Italian, but working for Spain)
1519–1522	Ferdinand Magellan (Portuguese, but working for Spain)

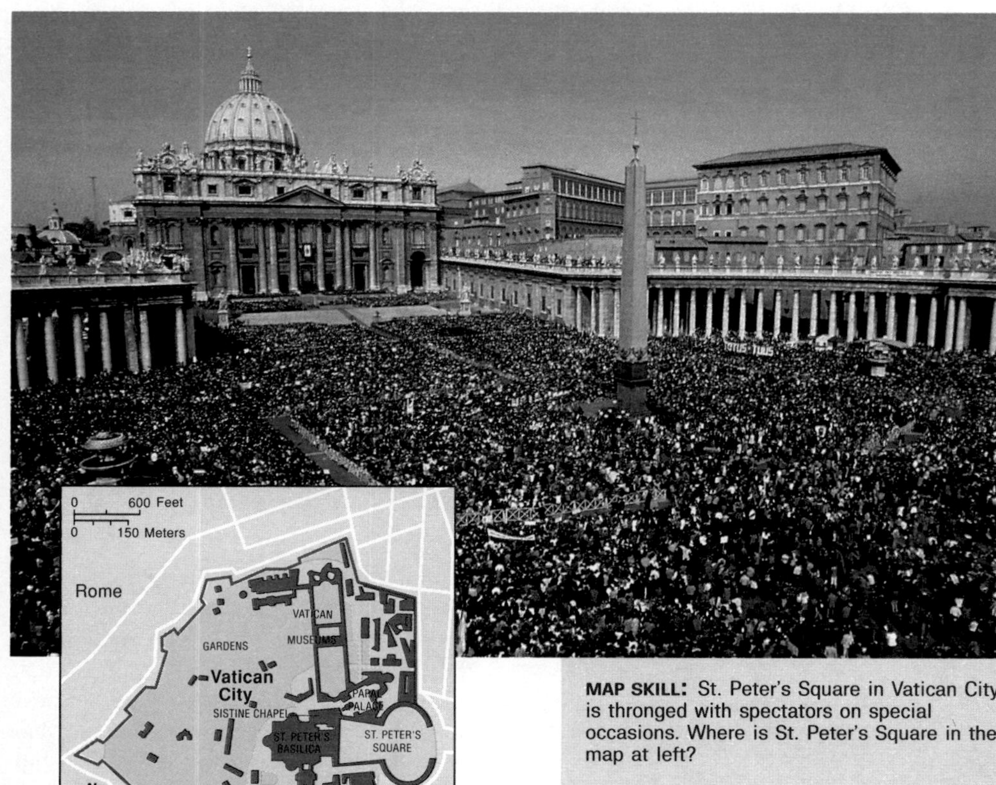

MAP SKILL: St. Peter's Square in Vatican City is thronged with spectators on special occasions. Where is St. Peter's Square in the map at left?

all the people belong to the Greek Orthodox Church.

Although the Roman Catholic and Greek Orthodox religions have much in common, there are several differences. For example, the leader of the Roman Catholic Church is the pope. The pope lives in **Vatican City**, shown on the map, a tiny independent state located within the city of Rome. Vatican City is the world headquarters of the Roman Catholic Church. The archbishop of Athens, not the pope, is the head of the Greek Orthodox Church. In addition, Greek Orthodox priests, unlike Roman Catholic priests, are permitted to marry.

PATTERNS OF LIVING

Imagine for a moment that you could spend a day living in Southern Europe. What do you think a typical day would be like? You might be surprised at some of the differences between the average day of a person living in Southern Europe and a typical day in your life.

Most working people in Southern Europe leave their jobs at 1:00 or 2:00 P.M. and return home for a large meal. A typical meal might consist of baked fish, stewed chicken, fruit, black coffee, and wine. The whole family spends a few hours together, enjoying their delicious meal.

In the middle of the afternoon, most people take a long nap, which is called a **siesta** in Spanish. People rest at this time

MAP SKILL: in the lower right corner of the map

Examining Language and Religion Continue the discussion by helping students to realize that Catholicism and the Greek Orthodox religion, rather than Protestantism, are the predominant forms of Christianity in the Southern European countries.

Discussing Patterns of Living Make sure students understand the relationship between the climate and midday sun of Southern Europe and the custom of stopping activity after a big noontime meal. Discuss students' reactions to the daily schedule of the people.

EXTENDING MAP SKILLS

Have students study the map of Vatican City.

Ask students:

- **What is the largest structure in Vatican City?** (St. Peter's Basilica)
- **In which direction would you travel to go from the Papal Palace to St. Peter's Square?** (south)
- **How wide and how long is Vatican City?** (approximately 3,300 feet, or 1,000 m, long and 2,550 feet, or 780 m, wide)

CURRICULUM CONNECTION

Language Arts Have students read more about the families of languages in the world. Ask each of them to find one more fact about the Catalan and Basque languages. List these facts in two columns on the chalkboard and have students discuss the facts. Then have students find and compare Portuguese, Spanish, and Italian words for: *school, family, boy, girl, mother,* and *father.* Encourage them to try to figure out the Latin root words within these words.

BACKGROUND INFORMATION

Description of Place Vatican City is a unique place on a very small plot of land.

- In 1929 it became an independent state and today exchanges ambassadors with other countries.
- One of the largest Christian churches in the world, St. Peter's Basilica, which contains the remains of the apostle Peter, is the pope's church. On certain occasions the pope stands on a papal palace balcony and blesses thousands of worshipers from all over the world in the huge piazza below.
- Since ancient days, colorfully dressed Swiss Guards have protected the pope and the Vatican.

Talking About Traffic and Smog Help students to see that pollution hurts not only people but also physical things.

Applying the Lesson Have students write a paragraph about whether or not they would like the two-part workday common in Southern European countries.

3 CLOSE

Summarizing Students have learned that life in Southern Europe has been influenced by the Mediterranean Sea. Ask students to list the advantages the sea gives the people of Southern Europe.

Evaluating Use these questions to assess students' understanding.

- **Which were the two great exploring nations from Southern Europe in the 1400s and 1500s?** (Spain and Portugal)
- **Which Southern European languages are based on Latin?** (Portuguese, Spanish, and Italian)
- **What are some differences between the Roman Catholic and Greek Orthodox churches?** (Greek Orthodox worshipers do not recognize the pope as supreme, and their priests can marry.)
- **Why do Southern Europeans often go north?** (to find work and send money back home)

1. Portugal, Spain, Italy, Greece
2. work until 1:00 P.M.; home for a big meal followed by nap or rest; back to work; home for a snack; dinner after 10:00 P.M.; bedtime after midnight
3. It is very populated and has four rush hours instead of two.
4. Since most people go home for lunch, they travel to and from work twice a day rather than once a day, creating more car exhaust and thus more pollution.

Independent Practice
Practice Book: page 67

Like children in the United States, children in Southern Europe use their free time for hobbies such as playing guitar.

because it is usually the hottest part of the day. After the siesta people return to work for several more hours.

Most children come home from school around 5:30 or 6:00 P.M. After a filling snack of cakes, pastries, and tea, they either do their homework or go out to play with friends. Several hours later, at around 10:00 or 11:00 P.M., it's time for supper. The family does not go to bed until after midnight.

TRAFFIC AND SMOG

Since most people in Southern Europe come home for lunch, they have to travel back and forth to work twice each day. "The only trouble with our two days in one," explains a Greek businessman, "is four rush hours instead of two." All this commuting creates a special problem in **Athens**, the Greek capital. Athens is home to half the country's 10 million people. Every day car exhaust fills the air. As a result, Athens is the most polluted city in Western Europe. Heavy smog not only endangers people's health, but it also damages the priceless buildings of ancient Athens, many of which still stand.

SHARED TRADITIONS

The people of Southern Europe have much in common. As you have read, they are alike in many ways. The sea has played an important role in each of their countries. The Latin-based languages that developed in Portugal, Spain, and Italy are very similar. Except for the Greeks, most people in the area are Roman Catholics. Finally, the people of Southern Europe lead similar daily lives.

Check Your Reading

1. Name the four major countries that are part of Southern Europe.
2. Describe an average day in Southern Europe.
3. Why does Athens have an air pollution problem?
4. THINKING SKILL: How does the lifestyle of people in Southern Europe help contribute to pollution problems in the area?

THINKING SKILL: Cause and Effect

252

MEETING INDIVIDUAL NEEDS

Reteaching (easy) On the outline map of Southern Europe, which can be found in the Teacher's Resource Center, have students label the countries, capitals, and peninsulas of Southern Europe. Tell them that it is important to include a key for this map.

Extension (average) Have students draw two clocks. One clock should show the daily schedule of a student in Southern Europe. The other clock should show the daily schedule of a student in America. Around the rim of each clock, have students draw pictures of student activities taking place at different times of the day.

Enrichment (challenging) Have each student write a diary entry as if he or she were a citizen of an island near Iberia who sees a Greek ship dock and wonders what cargo it is carrying.

BUILDING SKILLS
STUDY AND RESEARCH SKILLS

Reading Graphs and Charts

Key Vocabulary
graph
chart

Throughout this book you will often see graphs and charts as you study the people and places around the world. Graphs show numbers in picture form. Charts are used to organize more detailed information in a form that you can read easily.

Reading a Bar Graph
A bar graph is used to compare different amounts. Bar graphs have a horizontal axis that runs along the bottom of the graph and a vertical axis that runs up the side of the graph. The bar graph on this page uses bars to represent the populations of two cities in Mediterranean Europe. Which city had the smaller population in 1970?*

Reading a Chart
Charts are often used to show numbers and other, more detailed kinds of information. To read a chart, first look at the title, and then read the labels at the top of each column and along each row. The chart on this page shows the capital cities, the populations, and the people per square mile for two countries in Southern Europe.

Using Graphs and Charts
Notice that the graph and the chart on this page each presents information in a different way. For example, the graph shows at a glance which city had the larger population in 1960. The chart presents actual population figures more accurately than does the graph.

Would you use the chart or the graph to find out which city had the larger population in 1980? Which would you use to find the population of Italy, the graph or the chart?*

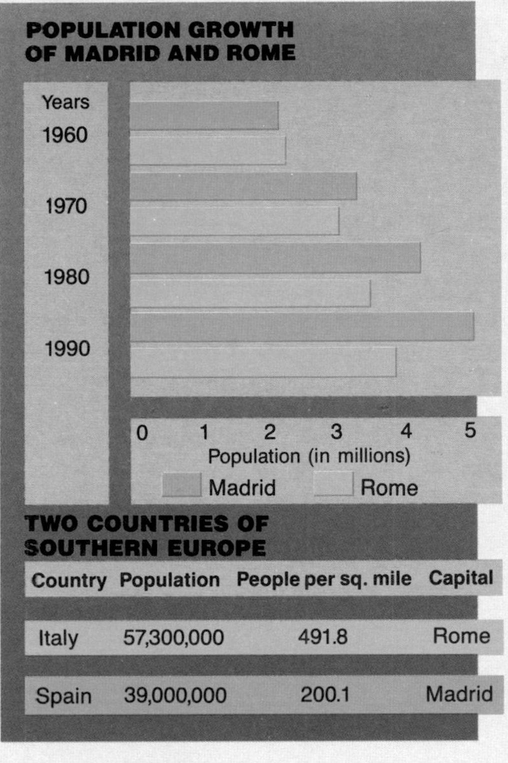

TWO COUNTRIES OF SOUTHERN EUROPE

Country	Population	People per sq. mile	Capital
Italy	57,300,000	491.8	Rome
Spain	39,000,000	200.1	Madrid

Reviewing the Skill
1. What is the population of Italy?
2. Which city had the larger population in 1980?
3. Which city's population is growing faster, Madrid or Rome?
4. Why is it useful to be able to use both graphs and charts?

*Rome

*the graph; the chart

253

SKILLS LESSON
page 253

Lesson Theme Graphs and charts present detailed information in a visual form that is easily readable.

Lesson Objective
- Compare charts and graphs.

PREPARE

Motivate Have students compare the graph and chart in this lesson. Ask them how each of them presents some of the same data in a different way.

Set Purpose Tell students that in this lesson they will learn when to use graphs and charts.

TEACH

Reading a Bar Graph and a Chart Discuss the difference between a graph and a chart. Contrast the different methods for reading a graph versus a chart.

Applying the Skill Ask students to make a list of topics about their school that can be shown better on a graph and those that can be shown better on a chart.

CLOSE

Summarizing Students should know that graphs are used for comparisons and that charts are used for detailed data. Have students graph and chart information about their school or class.

Answers to Reviewing the Skill
1. 57,300,000
2. Madrid
3. Madrid
4. Data can be read easily and quickly.

MEETING INDIVIDUAL NEEDS

Reteaching (easy) Have students go through their textbooks and list pages on which they find graphs or charts. Have them create graphs that compare the number of graphs to charts.

Extension (average) Give students facts about how many male and female staff members there are in the school. Help them make a bar graph comparing the number of male teachers, male administrators, and other male personnel with the number of female teachers, female administrators, and other female personnel.

Enrichment (challenging) Have each student choose a subject that interests him or her and make a bar graph and chart from statistics about that subject. After class presentation and discussion, display the array of graphs and charts.

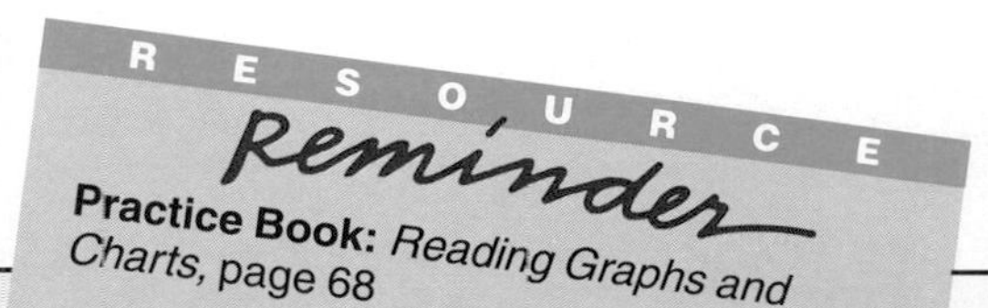

LESSON 2
pages 254–256

Lesson Theme Southern European countries are striving to develop their economies in the areas of manufacturing, farming, shipping, and tourism.

Lesson Objectives
- Describe the mix of manufacturing and farming in Southern European economies.
- Explain the special role of tourism and shipping in the Southern European countries.

1 PREPARE

Motivate Have a student read the *Read Aloud* section to the class. Discuss how manufacturing in Southern Europe differs from manufacturing in other countries.

Set Purpose Use the *What You Know* question to review what helps to develop an economy. Ask the *What You Will Learn* question to challenge students to find economic patterns that are different from those they have studied so far.

2 TEACH

Looking at Manufacturing and Trade Help students recognize the range of sizes in manufacturing businesses in Southern Europe and the importance of the EU.

Ask students:

- **What percent of Southern European workers are in manufacturing?** (40 percent)
- **What advantages does belonging to the EU give to these Southern European nations?** (It gives them access to northern European markets.)

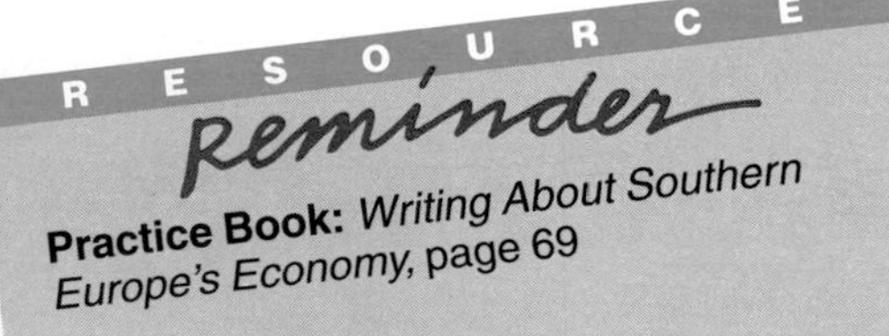

Practice Book: *Writing About Southern Europe's Economy, page 69*

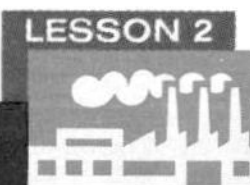

The Economy

READ TO LEARN

Key Places

Turin
Madrid
Marbella
Rome
Oinoussai

Read Aloud

The two Basile brothers, Gianni and Salvatore, own and manage a handbag factory in the Italian city of Naples. Housed in a small building, the factory has just ten employees—all of them relatives. The Basile's factory produces about 50 handbags a day and provides a good living for everyone who works there.

Many companies in Southern Europe are small family operations like that of the Basiles. In this lesson you will read about how the economies of the Southern European countries are different from those in other parts of Europe.

Read for Purpose

1. **WHAT YOU KNOW:** Why does Germany have such a strong economy?
2. **WHAT YOU WILL LEARN:** What economic challenges does Southern Europe face today?

MANUFACTURING AND TRADE

Today about 40 percent of the workers in Southern Europe have jobs in manufacturing. Important industries include food and beverage processing, textiles, and chemicals. Factories in Italy, Portugal, and Spain make handbags, shoes, and other small leather goods.

Not all the factories in Southern Europe are as small as the one owned by the Basile brothers. Fiat, the largest privately owned company in Italy, employs almost 60,000 workers. Every year more than 1 million cars roll off Fiat's assembly lines in **Turin**. Automobiles and trucks are also manufactured in factories in the Spanish city of **Madrid**. Workers there produce Ford and General Motors cars for sale throughout Europe.

All four of these countries are members of the European Union. Every year they buy products from and sell goods to other European countries, such as Germany, France, and the United Kingdom. Italy and Spain also trade extensively with the United States.

FARMING

In many parts of Southern Europe, the land is not good for growing crops. The soil is poor, and the rainfall is scanty. Yet today more than 22 percent of the working

WHAT YOU KNOW: This question refers to material in Chapter 11, Lesson 2; through hard work and planning, Germans created an efficient, modern, industrialized economy.

READING STRATEGY AND VOCABULARY DEVELOPMENT

Summarizing Tell students that the last section in each lesson is often a summary of the lesson content. After they have read the lesson, have students read and analyze the text under the heading "An Economic Struggle." Then have them scan the text to identify specific parts of the text mentioned in the summary. Discuss why certain facts are included in the summary while others are not. Have students work in groups to come up with their own summary. Compare the groups' summaries and discuss how students decided what should go into their group's summary.

Picking olives (*left*) and gathering hay (*right*) are only two of the important farm activities of Southern Europe.

people of this region are farmers. Many of them are too poor to buy machinery, fertilizers, and the types of seeds that would make their land as productive as possible.

Although all four of these countries ship oil and wine around the world, the main crops of the region are cereal grains, such as wheat and barley. Farmers also grow olives, citrus fruits, nuts, tobacco, and cotton. "Our oranges and tangerines are sweeter than those from other countries," explains one Portuguese farmer. "The high temperatures . . . allow the fruit to ripen earlier and at the same time develop a higher concentration of sugar."

TOURISM

In the 1940s the Spanish coastal town of Marbella was a small fishing village that had only a few paths down to the beach and about 10,000 inhabitants. Today it is a very different place. Huge hotels and apartment buildings line its busy streets. Boutiques sell everything from designer sunglasses to gleaming yachts. The population has grown and now includes 170,000 visitors. Every spring and summer, they come to enjoy the ocean beaches in this once quiet town.

Tourism has come to Marbella. The money spent by visitors at local hotels, restaurants, and stores has brought prosperity to many people in the area. Yet economic success has come at a high price: today Marbella is often crowded, noisy, and polluted.

Hundreds of towns like Marbella dot the Mediterranean shore. But, as any travel agent will tell you, the sea and the sand are not the only attractions of this area. In Greece and Italy visitors wander through such ancient remains as the Parthenon in Athens and the Forum in Rome. "Everywhere you go in Italy," noted one American tourist, "you look up in wonderment at the unequaled architecture of churches, cathedrals, palaces, and towers."

Understanding Farming Help students understand the problems faced by Southern European farmers.

Ask students:

- **What environmental conditions make farming difficult in Southern Europe?** (poor soil, scanty rainfall)
- **What percentage of the Southern European population are farmers?** (22 percent)
- **What are the main crops of this region?** (cereal grains, such as wheat and barley)
- **Identify one advantage of the hot, sunny Mediterranean climate.** (It helps the fruit to ripen earlier and develop a higher concentration of sugar.)

Talking About Tourism Help students understand why tourism is a mixed blessing.

Ask students:

- **What caused the increase in population in Marbella?** (tourism)
- **Why do you think some of the people of Marbella may be against tourists?** (They value the old days and are unhappy about the crowding, noise, and pollution the tourists cause.)

THINKING FURTHER: **Why would Americans in particular be impressed by the cathedrals and palaces of this region?** (Most of our buildings are less than 200 years old; in Southern Europe some buildings are thousands of years old.)

FUNDAMENTAL THEMES OF GEOGRAPHY

Region Lands around the Mediterranean Sea have such a distinct climate that they are a separate climate region from the rest of Europe. In fact, among the mild climates of the world, climatologists have made a separate category and named it "the Mediterranean climate." Lands in other places that have mild, rainy winters and hot, dry summers are said to have a Mediterranean climate. These climate areas are usually areas on the west coasts of continents between the 30° and 40° latitudes, both north and south of the equator.

- Plants must adapt to be able to live through the dry, hot summers in a Mediterranean climate region.
- Trees are short with thick bark and grow like a scrubby, dense forest; bushes and shrubs grow thick coverings and small leaves.
- With so much sunshine, farming can take place year-round if water can be brought to the land.

Have students suggest which crops grow best in this climate region. (cork, citrus fruits, nuts, tobacco, cotton, olives, grapes, irrigated rice, cereal grains)

Understanding Shipping Discuss the size of the Greek merchant fleet compared to the size of Greece.

Discussing Developing Economies Help students understand that economies in this region have not developed fully because of the climate, location, soils, and lack of technology.

Applying the Lesson Have students fill out a two-column chart on the advantages and disadvantages that Southern European nations with developing economies face.

3 CLOSE

Summarizing Students should understand that although there is a wide range of economic activities in the Southern European countries, these nations are hoping to develop further. Have students discuss ways in which these countries are improving their economies.

Evaluating Use these questions to assess students' understanding.

- **Do more people in Southern Europe work in manufacturing or farming?** (manufacturing)
- **Who controls the largest merchant fleet in the world?** (Greek shipowners)

Answers to Check Your Reading

1. poor soil, scant rainfall, not enough money for machinery, seeds, or fertilizer
2. sun, beaches, historic places
3. Southern European countries have a lower standard of living and are not as developed as Western European countries.
4. farming, manufacturing, shipping, tourism; From students' answers you can discuss whether they made choices based on the money a job provides or the pleasure they thought the job would bring.

Independent Practice
Practice Book: page 69

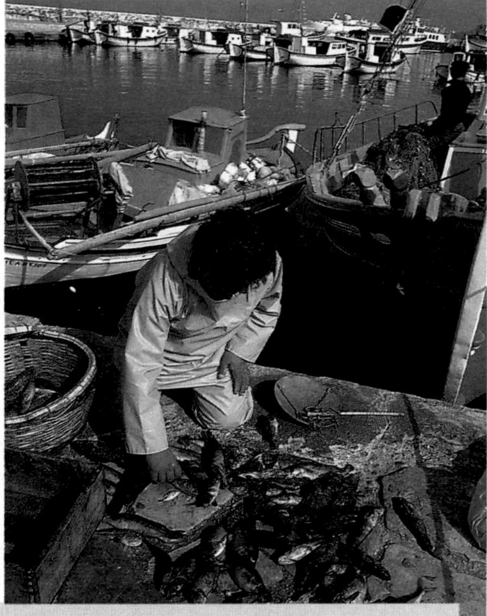

In Greece and the other countries of Southern Europe, fishing is still an important economic activity.

SHIPPING

Near the eastern end of the Mediterranean Sea lies a tiny Greek island called **Oinoussai** (ē nü′ sā). Less than 12 miles square (31 sq km), the island has a population of only about 400.

What makes Oinoussai special is that it is the home of 30 millionaire shipping families. Together, Greek shipowners control the largest merchant fleet in the world, a third of whose vessels come from this small island. One of the owners from Oinoussai is the richest shipper of all, Constantine Lemos, who is said to make 1 million dollars a day.

The sea is important to the economies of all the Southern European countries. Both Italy and Portugal have large merchant fleets. Fishing is a major industry throughout the area.

DEVELOPING ECONOMIES

Economically, the countries of Southern Europe have trouble keeping up with the rest of the European Union. Three of the four countries—Greece, Portugal, and Spain—are among Western Europe's poorest nations. They hope that closer ties with the European Union will bring greater investment and improving economies.

In recent years, much of the income in these nations has come from tourism. Another source of income has been money that Southern European guest workers have made in other countries and sent back to their own countries.

AN ECONOMIC STRUGGLE

As you have read, the people of Southern Europe are trying to develop the economic strengths of their region. Shipping and tourism are two of Southern Europe's successful industries. In addition, many of its people have manufacturing jobs, often in small family-owned businesses. And many other people work hard to get the most from this area's limited farmland.

Check Your Reading

1. What are some of the problems that farmers in Southern Europe face today?
2. Why do tourists choose to visit southern Europe?
3. How do the economies of the Southern European countries compare with those of countries in other parts of Western Europe?
4. **THINKING SKILL:** What kinds of jobs could you choose from if you lived in Southern Europe? Which job would you choose? Why?

THINKING SKILL: Decision Making

256

MEETING INDIVIDUAL NEEDS

Reteaching (easy) Have students write an editorial about tourism in Italy that might appear in the newspaper of an Italian town that is visited by many tourists.

Extension (average) Have students work in pairs to prepare a fictional interview with one of the Greek shipping millionaires on the island of Oinoussai. Tell students that each interview should explain how this owner feels he or she is helping to develop the economy of Southern Europe and what problems he or she sees in the shipping industry.

Enrichment (challenging) Have students work in groups to research trade and production figures for one of the Southern European nations and to compare these figures with those of other European countries. Have students present their findings in chart form.

LESSON 3

The Government

READ TO LEARN

Key Vocabulary	**Key People**	**Key Places**
coalition	Juan Carlos	Sicily
autonomy		Gibraltar
terrorism		

Read Aloud

On a bright spring morning in 1974, thousands of Portuguese soldiers and sailors overthrew their country's dictator. But instead of using bullets and bombs, they stuffed red carnations into the barrels of their guns. The troops paraded down the streets in triumph. Only a few shots were fired. Freedom had arrived in Portugal.

Although Portugal's "carnation revolution" was unusual, its earlier control by a dictator was not. At one time or another, all the countries of Southern Europe have been dictatorships. In addition, all of these countries have also once been controlled by monarchs. Yet today, as you will read, each country of Southern Europe has a democratic form of government that is responsible to the people it governs.

Read for Purpose

1. **WHAT YOU KNOW:** What do all of the governments of Western Europe that you have studied so far have in common?
2. **WHAT YOU WILL LEARN:** How are the governments of Southern Europe similar?

GREECE

As you may already know, the Greeks were the first people in the history of the world to develop a democratic system of government. In the days of ancient Greece, each Greek city ruled itself. Today there is one national government for the country.

Greece has a parliamentary democracy. Unlike legislatures in most other democracies, the Greek parliament has just one house, consisting of more than 200 members. The government is headed by a prime minister, who is usually the leader of the political party that has the most members in the parliament.

Greece also has a president, who is elected by the parliament. The president leads the armed forces and has the power to declare war and make treaties with other nations.

The central government of Greece oversees each of the country's local governments. There is one exception to this rule, however. That is the community of Mount Athos, which is completely self-governing. Mount Athos is a small peninsula jutting out from the Greek mainland, on which 1,400 monks live in 20 monasteries. Women cannot set foot on Mount Athos.

WHAT YOU KNOW: Students should be aware that all of the countries of Western Europe have elements of representative democracy in their governments.

LESSON 3

pages 257–260

Lesson Theme In spite of internal disputes, the countries of Southern Europe are representative democracies.

Lesson Objectives

- Describe the differences among the four large Southern European democracies.
- Explain the regional disputes in Spain and Italy.

PREPARE

Motivate Read the *Read Aloud* section to the class. Discuss with students other, similar incidents, for example, Chinese students demonstrating for political change and greeting soldiers with flowers in 1989.

Set Purpose Use the *What You Know* question to explore the degree of democracy in Western Europe. Use the *What You Will Learn* question to ask students if they think the governments are democratic.

TEACH

Looking at Greece Help students to understand that Greece was the original source of the concept of democracy.

Ask students:

- **How does the Greek Parliament differ from the United States Congress?** (It has only one house, with fewer members than Congress, and it elects the Greek president.)
- **How is the executive branch of the Greek government different from the executive branch of the United States government?** (The Greek government has two leaders, and the United States has one.)

READING STRATEGY AND VOCABULARY DEVELOPMENT

Summarizing The purpose of this lesson is to help students use what they know and what they learn about a topic to create a summary. Have students preview the lesson and then write down by section what they already know about the lesson. Then have students write a list of things they would like to learn by reading the lesson. After reading the lesson, students should write down what they learned. Have students use these notes to create a summary about the government of one particular Southern European country.

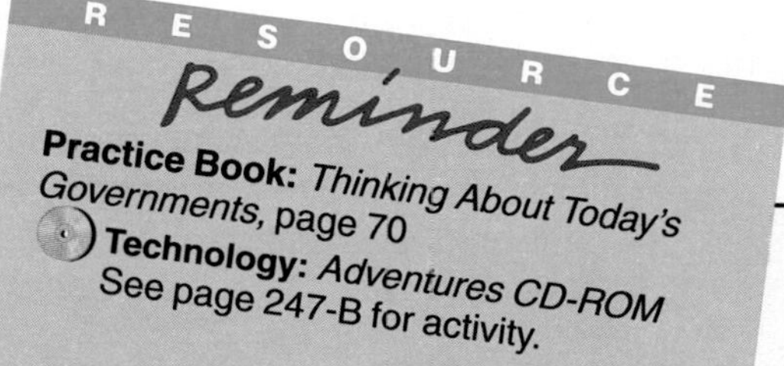

Talking About Italy Help students to see how valuable political compromise has been in helping Italy run its coalition governments. Ask why it is important to use compromise in many situations that arise in a democracy.

Ask students:

- **How do the powers of the two leaders in Italy compare?** (The president represents the nation but has few powers. The prime minister runs the country.)
- **Why has Italy had so many governments?** (No single party has ever been strong enough to gain control.)
- **What is the basis for the north-versus-south conflict in Italy?** (The north is industrial with high living standards; the south has poor land and little income.)

  THINKING FURTHER: **What else do you think the government of Italy can do to help ease the problem between the north and south?** (Students' answers should focus on ways to improve the economy of the south.)

Looking at Portugal Stress the belief in democracy and hope that is found in Portugal today.

Ask students:

- **How does the political instability in Portugal compare with that in Italy?** (Since World War II Italy has had over 40 governments; since 1974 Portugal has had 15 governments. Both countries expect to maintain a democratic form of government.)

ITALY

Like Greece, Italy is a parliamentary democracy. The parliament is made up of two houses—the Chamber of Deputies and the Senate. As in many other republics, a president serves as the head of state but has little political power. The real power is in the hands of the prime minister, who runs the country from day to day.

The government of Italy has been unstable for many years. Since World War II, Italy has had more than 40 different governments. No single political party has ever been strong enough to gain control. As a result, Italy has been ruled by a series of coalition governments. A coalition is a temporary union between different political parties that agree to work together for a common purpose.

One of the greatest difficulties faced by Italy's coalition governments has been a lack of national unity. Although the country has been united for more than 100 years, there are still huge differences between the north and the south. Most industry in Italy is located in the fertile north, around the cities of Milan and Turin. People there have a high standard of living.

In southern Italy and on the island of Sicily, however, the land is poor, as are many of the people. In the past, workers from the south have moved north in search of jobs. But they have often been unwelcome. Recently the Italian government has tried to improve the southern economy by bringing new industries there. As American journalist Flora Lewis explains, "Italians say the north produces the wealth and Rome spends it, mainly on the south."

PORTUGAL

As you have read at the beginning of this lesson, Portugal today is a democracy. But the Portuguese, like the Italians, have found political stability hard to achieve. Since the revolution in 1974, more than 15 national governments have come and gone in Portugal.

Under Portugal's current plan of government, executive power is shared by a president and a prime minister. The legislative branch of the government, like that of Greece, has only one house.

These posters are used to promote three of many different political parties in Italy.

BUILDING CITIZENSHIP

The Thread of Democracy It has taken a long time for democracy to reach Italy and Portugal. The word *democracy* comes from the Greek words *dēmos*, meaning "the people," and *kratos*, meaning "power." The idea that people should have a say in what happens in their own community began in the ancient Greek city-states. For this reason Greece is called "the birthplace of democracy."

- If you look at how democracy has moved through the history of the western world, you discover it runs like a thread, sometimes unseen, but reemerging in different places. The thread became very strong when the Declaration of Independence was written and when the United States Constitution shaped our government's recognition of citizens' power and rights. Abraham Lincoln described democracy best when he said, "of the people, by the people and for the people."
- Have students give recent examples of people asking for more democracy. Ask them to bring in newspaper accounts about issues of democratic rule.

The Portuguese people are proud of their country's democratic government. One member of parliament says: "Our parliamentary democracy must be defended. We can't go back to the years of darkness under a dictatorship again."

SPAIN

Like Portugal, Spain emerged from a long dictatorship to become a peaceful, democratic country. But Spain's government is somewhat different from the governments of the other Southern European countries. Spain is governed by an elected parliament, but it also has a monarch. In this respect Spain's government is like that of Great Britain.

In 1975 Prince Juan Carlos became King of Spain. He took over after the death of Francisco Franco, who had ruled the country as a dictator.

Under Franco's rule free elections and political parties had not been allowed in the country. When Juan Carlos came to power, the government of Spain was completely changed. First the Spanish people elected a new parliament. Then a new constitution was both written and approved in 1978. It established a parliamentary democracy with King Juan Carlos as head of the government.

Under the new constitution the legislative branch, called the Cortes, is divided into two houses. Most of the power is in the lower house, called the Congress of Deputies, which is made up of 350 members elected by the people. The upper house is called the Senate.

A NATION OF SEPARATE GROUPS

Spain, like Italy, has long been troubled by differences among areas. After Juan Carlos became king, one of his first acts was to lift a ban on traditional local languages and flags in Spain. Yet some groups of people, like the Catalans and the Basques, were still not satisfied. They wanted much more.

King Juan Carlos rules Spain under its new constitution written in 1978.

The Catalans live in an area called Catalonia in northeastern Spain that is cut off by mountains from the rest of the country. Catalonia has always been more closely tied to France than to Spain. Although the Catalans do not want complete independence, they do want full autonomy. Autonomy is the right to self-government. Today Catalonia has an elected regional assembly. In addition, all direction signs and advertising billboards in the area are in both Spanish and Catalan.

For thousands of years, the Basques have wanted to preserve their independence. You may remember from Lesson 1 that the Basques live in the rugged Pyrenees on the border between northern Spain and France. When democracy came to Spain, the Basques were granted autonomy. But despite the changes, many Basques are still separatists. They want to split their area off from both Spain and France and set up their own country.

259

Discussing Spain

Ask students:

- **How are the governments of Spain and Portugal similar and different?** (Both are now free from dictators; Spain has a monarch as head of the government, while Portugal has a president and a prime minister.)
- **What makes Spain's government different from those of the other Southern European countries?** (It has a monarch.)
- **What changes came about when Juan Carlos came to power?** (A new parliament was elected, a new constitution was approved, and a parliamentary democracy was established.)

Understanding a Nation of Separate Groups Help students to understand that while the Spanish government is unified, there are regional disputes over land and language. Compare the demands of the Catalans and the Basques.

Ask students:

- **What separates Catalonia from the rest of Spain?** (mountains)
- **What is autonomy?** (It is the right to self-government.)
- **Where do the Basques live?** (They live in the Pyrenees, on the border between northern Spain and France.)
- **What do the Basques want?** (They want to set up their own country.)

CURRICULUM CONNECTION

Language Arts Have students find the definition for *autonomy* in this book. Discuss with the class how autonomy is different from democracy. Have students find the dictionary definitions for the words *democracy*, *independence*, and *separatism.* Help students to see that there are different shades of meaning between independence and autonomy. Help them to understand the differences among the meanings. Ask students if they have read other words about government that are not clear to them. Take this opportunity to clear up definitions by using the dictionary and class discussion.

BACKGROUND INFORMATION

Multicultural Perspectives Catalans and Basques are largely self-governed, but they are still subjects of another country—Spain. People around the world in similar circumstances are pushing for change.

- Puerto Rico is a commonwealth of the United States and has control over matters of local government. Some Puerto Ricans want to become independent of the United States, while others want Puerto Rico to become the fifty-first state.
- China controls the once-sovereign state of Tibet, but many Tibetans want independence.
- Ask students what these regions may gain or lose by achieving independence.

Discussing Separate Groups
Continue discussing the problems in Spain, including the Catalan, the Basque, and the Gibraltar disputes.

EXTENDING DIAGRAM SKILLS

Have students study the diagram titled Parliamentary Government in Southern Europe. Make sure they understand that this is a generalized diagram and not a diagram of one specific country. Discuss how each group or leader is chosen.

Applying the Lesson Have students use the diagram on this page as a template for a government diagram for each of the four nations of Southern Europe.

CLOSE

Summarizing Students should understand that though Southern European governments may differ, they are all representative democracies. Ask them if they would change our government and in what ways.

Evaluating Use the *Check Your Reading* questions (answers given below) to assess students' understanding.

Answers to Check Your Reading

1. Juan Carlos became king. Parliament was elected by the people; a new constitution was written. A ban on local languages and flags was lifted.
2. instability; no strong political party; coalition governments; lack of unity between north and south
3. All are representative democracies.
4. Students should tell how to prove their chosen facts.

Independent Practice
Practice Book: page 70

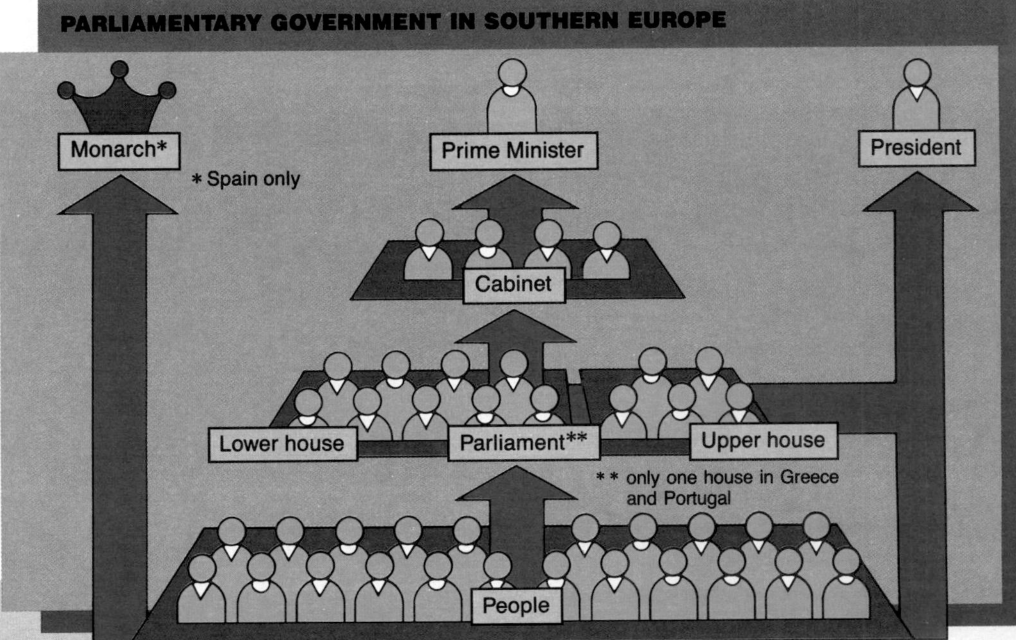

DIAGRAM SKILL: Which Southern European countries have a parliament with only one house?

In order to draw attention to their cause, some Basques have resorted to **terrorism**. Terrorism is the use of violence and the threat of violence, usually to gain political ends. Today the bombings and murders in the Basque areas still go on.

Another problem area for the Spanish government is **Gibraltar**. This rocky point at the southernmost tip of Spain has belonged to the British since the early 1700s. Now Spain wants the territory back. But the people of Gibraltar have voted to remain under British control.

FOUR DEMOCRACIES

As you have read, the governments of the four countries of Southern Europe are all democratic. The diagram above shows a typical government. Spain and Portugal are the youngest democracies in Southern Europe.

Many parts of the area have been torn apart by conflicts. In Italy differences between the north and the south remain strong. In Spain, the Catalans and Basques have long fought the country's national government. If these countries are to grow and prosper, they need to solve the internal conflicts they have with different groups of people.

Check Your Reading

1. In what ways did the government of Spain change in 1975?
2. What problems does Italy's government face today?
3. What do the governments of Southern European countries have in common?
4. **THINKING SKILL:** Find three statements of fact in the section of this lesson titled "Spain." How could you prove these statements are true?

260

DIAGRAM SKILL: Greece and Portugal

THINKING SKILL: Fact and Opinion

MEETING INDIVIDUAL NEEDS

Reteaching (easy) Have students imagine that they were Spaniards living in Spain after the dictator Franco was replaced by King Juan Carlos. Tell them to write a letter to a friend in the United States about their experiences in the past under Franco and their hopes for the future of their government.

Extension (average) Have students research the 1974 revolution in Portugal and illustrate each step with drawings.

Enrichment (challenging) Have students prepare a debate on economic issues between politicians from the north of Italy and politicians from the south of Italy.

LESSON 4

Arts and Recreation

READ TO LEARN

Key Vocabulary

Renaissance
pilgrimage

Key Places

Florence
Santiago de Compostela
Fátima

Read Aloud

Southern Europe has a rich artistic history that dates from the ancient Greek writers to the Italian painters of the Renaissance to the writers and painters of the present time. In this lesson you will read about this artistic heritage and about the festivals and celebrations that are so important to the people of Southern Europe today.

Read for Purpose

1. WHAT YOU KNOW: What are some things that the people of Southern Europe have in common?
2. WHAT YOU WILL LEARN: What are the popular arts and recreational activities of Southern Europe?

ARTISTIC ACHIEVEMENTS

The artistic heritage of Southern Europe stretches back thousands of years. The world's oldest dramas were written by the Greek poets Aeschylus (es′ kə ləs), Sophocles (sof′ ə klēz), and Euripides (ū rip′ ə dēz) in the 400s B.C. But these plays are still staged today in Greece and all over the world.

Few countries can match Italy's impressive achievements in the arts. During the 1300s and 1400s, a period of great activity in the arts began in the city of Florence. This was the Renaissance (ren′ ə säns), which means "rebirth." Artists of the Renaissance wanted to imitate nature and even improve on it. Their goal was to create an image of the ideal human being.

Today museums all over the world display works by such Italian painters of the Renaissance as Leonardo da Vinci and Raphael. Another great artist of the period was Michelangelo, whose works include both heroic statues and paintings. His paintings done on the ceiling of the Sistine Chapel in Vatican City are among his best-known works.

Other Renaissance painters include the Spaniard Diego Velázquez and El Greco, who was born in Crete but spent much of his life in Spain. In more recent times, Spain has produced such master artists as Pablo Picasso.

Some outstanding music has also been produced in Southern Europe. For example, opera was invented in Florence in about 1600, when several musician-poets began experimenting with dramas set to music. Later operas, such as those of Giuseppe Verdi and Giacomo Puccini thrill audiences around the world.

WHAT YOU KNOW: This question refers to material covered in Lesson 1. Possible answers include: most share Latin-based languages and most of the people are Roman Catholics.

LESSON 4
pages 261–263

Lesson Theme Southern Europe has given the world a rich legacy of artistic achievements and religious traditions.

Lesson Objectives

- Describe the artistic heritage of the Southern European people.
- Explain the role of religious celebrations in the life of Southern Europe.
- Explain how climate influences the daily amusements in the Southern European region.

PREPARE

Motivate Have students read the *Read Aloud* section. Ask them what art from the Southern European countries they are familiar with.

Set Purpose Use the *What You Know* question to tell students that these commonalities form the basis for many of the artistic achievements of the people in the Southern European region. Then ask the *What You Will Learn* question.

TEACH

Looking at Artistic Achievements Help students to understand that this region has produced masterpieces in all the arts.

Ask students:

- **What forms of artistic achievement came from this one area of Europe?** (Greek drama, Italian and Spanish painting and sculpture, Italian opera)

READING STRATEGY AND VOCABULARY DEVELOPMENT

Summarizing Suggest to students that summarizing is a tool used in many occupations. Discuss ways in which summarizing is used in the travel industry, notably in advertising. Have students look through various travel brochures. Have students read the lesson and then prepare a travel brochure, letter, poster, or some other form of advertisement that summarizes the information they learned in this lesson on arts and recreation in the Southern Europe.

RESOURCE *Reminder*

Practice Book: *The Heritage of Southern Europe*, page 71
- **Anthology:** *The Iliad*, pages 68–70; *The Aeneid*, pages 71–72; *Notebooks of Leonardo da Vinci*, pages 78–80

Technology: *Videodisc/Video Tape* See page 247-B for activity.

Discussing the Song Direct students' attention to the lyrics of the song "Oh, Caterina."
Discuss the lyrics with students. Have the class sing or recite the song. Tell students that this is an Italian folk song. Explain what a folk song is and then ask students if they know any folk songs.

Ask students:

- **Who is this song about?** (Caterina)
- **What is this song about?** (looking for Caterina so they can dance)
- **Do you think this is a festive song? Why?** (Yes; because it's about dancing.)

Tell students that songs are an important part of many festivals and celebrations. Discuss songs that students associate with festivals, holidays, and celebrations.

Talking About Festive Times Help students to recognize the role of religion in the Southern European lifestyle.

Ask students:

- **What role does religion play in the festive occasions of Southern European life?** (Most festivals are centered on religion.)

Discussing Everyday Amusements Stress to students the variety of outdoor activities that the constant sunshine of Southern Europe permits. Discuss the effect the variety of outdoor activities has on a city's atmosphere.

CURRICULUM CONNECTION

Music Have students decide on a holiday, festival, or celebration that is important to them. Then have students write lyrics for a song about their topic. Tell them that the lyrics could be about why their topic is important, what they like about it, when it occurs, or why it is celebrated. Have students write their lyrics to go with the music from another song or, if students are musically inclined, have them write their own music. Have students sing or recite their finished songs.

Language Arts People write songs for many reasons. Some songs are about history, religion, people, or regions, and some are just nonsense songs. Have students choose a folk song they like and research the topic or the musician who wrote the song. Have them report to the class what they have learned. Ask students to include a sample of the musician's work or the folk song that they have researched.

FESTIVE TIMES

People in all the Southern European countries observe major Christian holidays, such as Christmas and Easter. Traditional costumes are often worn during festivals and celebrations on these and other holidays. In Spain, for example, girls and women may wear lace headdresses that are called *mantillas*.

Among the special events that take place are **pilgrimages**, or journeys that people make to sacred places. In Spain, pilgrims have been going to **Santiago de Compostela**, in the northwest, for nearly a thousand years. Huge crowds of people gather on July 25, the feast day of Santiago (St. James). Santiago is the patron saint of Spain. A saint is a person who is honored after his or her death by Christians, for being a holy person worthy of deep love and respect.

In **Fátima**, a small town north of Lisbon, Portugal, a major site is the shrine of Our Lady of Fátima. On May 13, 1917, three children reported having a vision of Mary, the mother of Jesus, at Fátima. According to the children the vision reappeared on the thirteenth of each month until October. Today people come from all over the world to be in Fátima between May and October.

The most important holiday in Greece is Easter. It is usually celebrated a week or two later than in other Western European countries because the Greek Orthodox calendar is different.

On the night before Easter Sunday, people gather at their local church, carrying candles. At midnight the priest appears, dressed in scarlet and gold, and announces "Christ is risen!" Everyone in the crowd shouts back, "He is risen indeed." At this cry all eyes turn toward the sky, where fireworks explode overhead. On Easter day Greek Orthodox families gather to eat a large feast of roasted lamb.

EVERYDAY AMUSEMENTS

After a day's work, many people in Southern European countries enjoy relaxing at outdoor restaurants and cafés. In Greece only the men gather at the cafés, where they drink small cups of strong coffee and play a board game called backgammon. The women often meet at the local church.

Because Southern Europe has a mild, sunny climate, it is not surprising that its people tend to spend much of their leisure time outdoors. Many enjoy golf, cycling, and tennis. During the winter months crowds of people gather on the ski slopes of the Alps and the Pyrenees to ski. And legacies like the Palio races, which you will read about on pages 264–267, remain strong.

As in many other parts of the world, folk songs are an important part of the culture of Southern Europe. One of the most popular folk songs of Italy appears on page 262.

DISTINCTIVE TRADITIONS

The nations of Southern Europe have cultural traditions that go back hundreds of years. In this lesson you read that Greek poets wrote the world's first dramas and that Italy led the Western world in painting, sculpture and opera. You also read how people in these countries celebrate religious holidays that are centuries old.

Check Your Reading

1. What was the Renaissance?
2. Why is the town of Fátima important to many people?
3. What do people in Greece do to celebrate Easter?
4. **THINKING SKILL:** What three questions could you ask to learn more about the Renaissance?

THINKING SKILL: Asking Questions

263

Applying the Lesson Divide the class into four groups. Have each group plan part of a newspaper about arts and amusements in Southern Europe. Assign one of the following topics to each group: theater, painting and sculpture, music, and sports. Have each group write a news or feature article for the newspaper.

3 CLOSE

Summarizing Students should understand that artistic achievement has flowed for centuries from the creativity of Southern European people. Have students compare Southern European holidays and festivals to those celebrated in their area.

Evaluating Use these questions to assess students' understanding.

- **What is the name of the period of great activity in the arts that began in Florence?** (the Renaissance)
- **What effect does climate have on the daily amusements of the people of the Southern European region?** (Because the weather is warm, the people of this region tend to spend much leisure time outdoors.)

Answers to Check Your Reading

1. a period of great activity in the arts in Europe that began in the 1300s and 1400s
2. It is a place where visions of Mary were reported by children in 1917 and where a shrine is now located.
3. They gather at the church at midnight and celebrate with candlelight and fireworks.
4. Possible answers include: Which kinds of arts were involved? What was the ideal human being? What were the paintings of?

Independent Practice
Practice Book: page 71

MEETING INDIVIDUAL NEEDS

Reteaching (easy) Have students each make a chart with four columns headed "Drama," "Painting and Sculpture," "Music," and "Sports." Have them complete the charts with information from this lesson and then compare the charts.

Extension (average) Have students read more about the Renaissance and a great artist or a great artistic work from the Southern European region during that period. Then have students create their own work of art that is reminiscent of that time.

Enrichment (challenging) Have students research the subject of pilgrimages. Have them write an essay on the purpose of a pilgrimage, famous pilgrimages in history, or pilgrimages that still take place today.

LEGACY
pages 264–267

Lesson Theme The Palio, a horse race held in Siena, Italy, is a traditional celebration of the city's heritage and its neighborhoods.

Lesson Objectives
- Discuss the origins of the Palio.
- Explain the importance of the Palio to the people of Siena.
- Describe the rules of the Palio and the festivities that take place on race day.

1 PREPARE

Motivate Have students discuss why people take pride in the neighborhoods in which they live.

Set Purpose Focus students' attention with the following question. How do sporting events encourage people to respect one another? (Encourage students to share their feelings about the value of athletic competition.) Direct students to read the introductory section. Ask them to think about the concluding suggestion while they read the lesson.

2 TEACH

Understanding the Concept of Legacies Review the definition of a legacy. Then ask students how they think a sport or a sporting event can be a legacy. (Possible answers include: A sport can be a very old custom that is handed down from generation to generation, keeping part of a culture alive.)

Discussing a City of Neighborhoods Have students describe the neighborhoods in their community. You might explain that *contrade* is the plural for "neighborhoods" and that a single neighborhood is called a *contrada*.

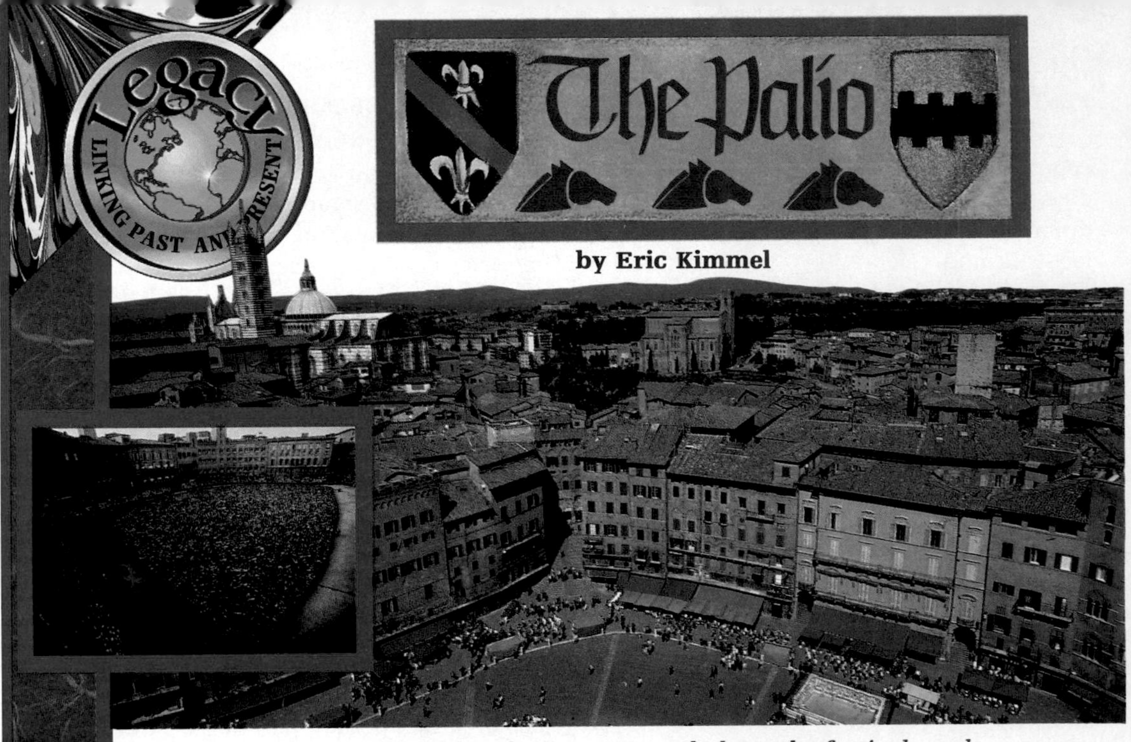

The Palio

by Eric Kimmel

In the last lesson, you read about the festivals and celebrations that play an important role in the culture of Mediterranean Europe. One of these celebrations, called the Palio (pä′ lē ō), takes place twice every summer in the Italian city of Siena (sē en′ ə). As you read, think about what makes this legacy special, and how it keeps Siena's history alive.

A CITY OF NEIGHBORHOODS

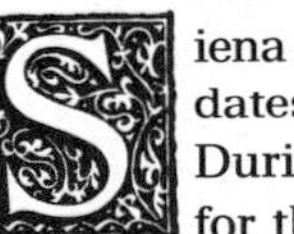

Siena is located in a hilly area of central Italy. This ancient city dates back to Roman times, when it was the site of a fortress. During the early years of the Renaissance, it became a center for the arts. Michelangelo, whom you read about in the last lesson, carved decorations for the city's Duomo (dwō′ mō), or cathedral. Other painters and sculptors helped to make Siena one of Italy's most beautiful cities.

Along with its beauty, Siena is also famous for its *contrade* (kon trä′ dā), or neighborhoods. The 17 contrade are very important. Each one has a name such as Shell, Tower, Forest, Eagle, or Goose. When two Sienese meet, they never fail to mention the names of their respective contrade. Why? The people in each neighborhood feel a tightly knit sense of community, as though they were members of a single family. They live together and work together. They may even go on vacations together!

READING STRATEGY AND VOCABULARY DEVELOPMENT

Summarizing Have students work together in small groups to summarize the lesson. Have them construct their summaries by turning each section title into a question. Then have the groups answer each question by listing at least two central details. The following example of a summary is based on the section titled "A City of Neighborhoods."

Why Is Siena Called a City of Neighborhoods?
1. The city has long been divided into 17 neighborhoods called contrade.
2. The people of each neighborhood feel a powerful sense of community.
3. The neighborhoods compete in one of Siena's most famous traditions, the Palio.

The Sienese are proud of their contrade. Often this pride encourages a friendly rivalry between the various neighborhoods. The Sienese long ago discovered an exciting way for these rivals to compete. This is the Palio.

THE PALIO

The Palio is a horse race held in the main square of the city. It was first run in July 1656 to celebrate a Christian religious holiday, the Feast of the Madonna of Provenzano. Over the years it also became a celebration of Siena's past and its rival contrade.

The rules have remained the same for more than three centuries. Each neighborhood is represented by a horse and jockey—a person who races horses as a profession. But this "battle of the neighborhoods" is no ordinary horse race. For one thing, the jockeys ride bareback, without a saddle. For another, the jockeys are allowed to strike out at each other with whips as they fight for position. And a horse can win the race even if its jockey falls off!

In this race, even the prize is unusual. The winner receives no money, no crown, no silver trophy. Instead he is presented with a special silk flag, painted with religious symbols. This flag has been the traditional prize since the 1600s. The winner usually hangs it in his neighborhood's church.

In fact, the Palio gets its name from this prize. The original meaning of the Italian word *palio* was "flag." For centuries the word has also been used to refer to the race itself.

Understanding a City of Neighborhoods Continue the discussion.

Ask students:

- **Why do you think the contrade are important to the people of Siena?** (Students' responses should reflect an understanding of how belonging to a contrada can give a person a sense of pride and "belonging.")

Discussing the Palio Remind students of the importance of religious festivals in Southern Europe. Refer students back to the discussion of this point in Lesson 4.

Ask students:

- **List three reasons why the Palio is a celebration.** (The Palio celebrates the Feast of the Madonna of Provenzano, Siena's past, and the contrade.)
- *THINKING FURTHER:* **Why do you think the prize for winning the Palio is a flag rather than a crown, money, or a trophy?** (Possible answers include: The flag represents the religious origins and significance of the Palio; since the flag is the traditional prize of the Palio, awarding the flag helps to keep the legacy alive; the goal of the race is neighborhood and civic pride, not profit.)

Discussing the Photographs Direct students' attention to the photographs at the top of this page.

Ask students:

- **What do you think the different flags in the photographs represent?** (Lead students to understand that the flags show symbols of the contrade.)

BACKGROUND INFORMATION

About the Photographs The large photograph on page 264 shows one end of the Piazza del Campo. The Duomo is visible in the background on the upper left. The inset shows a crowd of people gathered in the center of the Piazza del Campo to watch the Palio.

The Piazza del Campo is the largest open space in the city. Throughout Siena's history, people have traditionally gathered here for public meetings, speeches, and open-air markets. The canopies lining the edges of the piazza provide shade for cafés, which are the center of social life throughout Italy. Italians visit cafés to meet their friends, to read their daily newspapers, and to discuss politics, sports and other topics.

Sienese Art The Sienese School of Early Renaissance Painting is noted for its colorful, cheerful style. Some art historians believe that the bright pinks and golds of this style were intended to give hope to the Sienese people after the plague struck the city in the fourteenth century.

One of the most famous Sienese paintings is *The Crucifixion,* by Duccio (düt' chō), which shows the transition from Medieval to Renaissance art. Lorenzetti's painting entitled *Allegory of Good Government* is another Sienese masterpiece. In the Duomo, Pinturicchio (pint ə rē' kē ō) created a series of frescoes depicting the life of Pope Pius II, who was from Siena.

Discussing Preparations Point out to students that an event such as the Palio requires a great deal of preparation.

Ask students:

- **Why do you think the horses are chosen by lottery?** (to give each contrada a fair chance to win the Palio)
- *THINKING FURTHER:* **What three questions could you ask to learn more about the preparations for the Palio?** (Possible questions include: How much are the jockeys paid? How are talented jockeys persuaded to switch sides? Why are the horses blessed?)

Discussing the Photographs Direct students' attention to the photographs on this page.

Ask students:

- **What type of costumes do you think the two children are wearing?** (Renaissance costumes)

Discussing the Race Tell students that visitors from around the world come to watch the Palio.

Ask students:

- **How does the day of the race begin?** (There is another parade.)
- **How is the Palio different from most horse races?** (Possible answers include: The jockeys ride bareback; a horse can win without its jockey; the race takes place in the middle of the city.)
- *THINKING FURTHER:* **Why do you think that the Palio draws people from around the world?** (Although students' responses will vary, lead them to understand that the Palio is a unique and exciting legacy.)

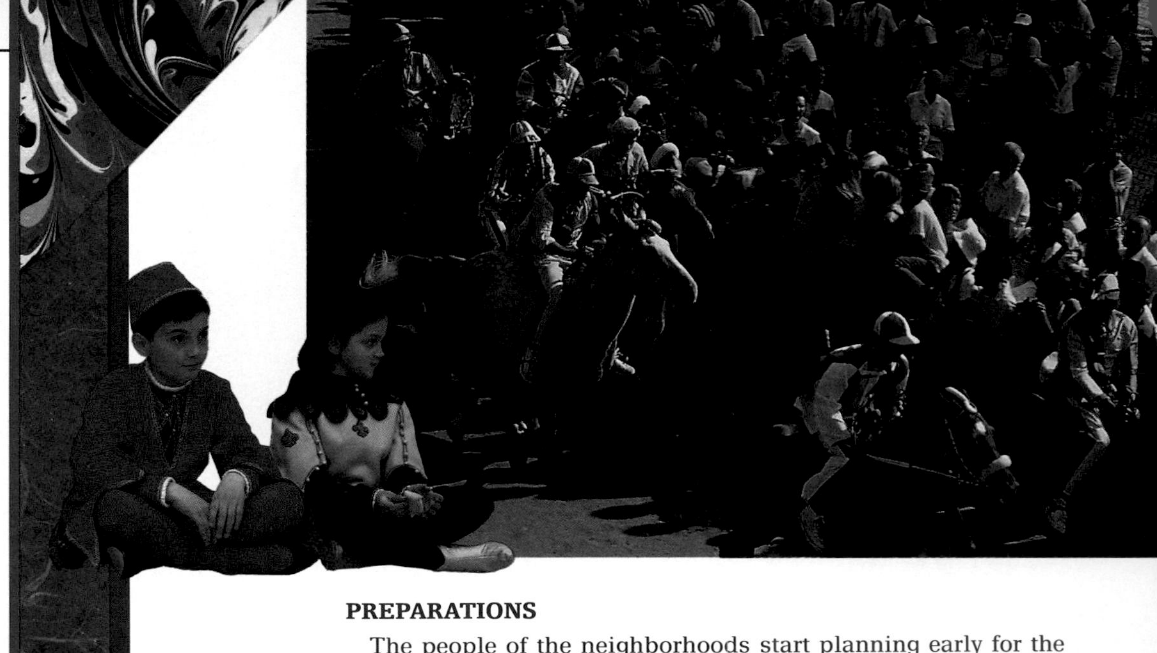

PREPARATIONS

The people of the neighborhoods start planning early for the Palio. Each contrada hires a jockey. Often rival neighborhoods try to persuade talented jockeys to switch sides. Horses, on the other hand, are chosen by lottery, and matching the horse and jockey can be a tricky process. If a neighborhood draws a horse with a good chance of winning, it may fire its jockey and hire a better one. If a neighborhood draws a poor horse but has already hired a good jockey, it may allow the jockey to ride for a different, friendly neighborhood.

Several events take place before the actual race. First the Palio opens with an elaborate parade. Representatives of each neighborhood dress in the Renaissance costumes of Siena's "golden age." Marching through the streets, carrying their neighborhood banners, they are followed by excited crowds of children and adults.

Next there are several days of trial races. These trials allow the horses and jockeys to get used to the narrow, curving course around the main square. After the last trial, all the horses are led into the neighborhood churches to be blessed for the race.

THE RACE BEGINS

Palio Day—the day of the race—begins with another parade. Some people march on foot. Others ride on horseback, dressed in armor and Renaissance clothing. An ox-drawn chariot follows, carrying the flag that the winner will receive.

266

BACKGROUND INFORMATION

Celebrating Carnevale The Palio is just one of many celebrations that help Italians to keep their legacies alive. Another such celebration is called *Carnevale* (kär nə vä' lā).

Carnevale is an ancient holiday. Its roots go back to ceremonies celebrating the coming of spring. Since spring arrives earlier in Europe than in the United States, Carnevale is held in February.

Several hundred years ago, this holiday was incorporated into the calendar of the Roman Catholic Church. Since then Carnevale has assumed a religious significance: It marks the period before Lent, during which people are encouraged to celebrate life and enjoy themselves. In some Italian towns and cities, Carnevale was also once the occasion for an unusual "masquerade." For just one day, peasants were allowed to rule the community, while kings and nobility played the role of peasants. Needless to say, everybody returned to their original roles at the end of the day.

Today Carnevale is celebrated all over Italy during a period of several days. In Venice people attend balls dressed up in elaborate costumes. They also wear beautiful, hand-painted masks, which are a trademark of the city. The Mardi Gras festival in New Orleans is a celebration of the same legacy.

Now it is time for the jockeys to mount their horses. Each jockey splashes water on his pants to make it easier to grip the horse's back. Then police search them thoroughly. Why? Jockeys are not allowed to carry anything but the official whip.

Mounted, the jockeys raise their whips in salute, and the judges assign them starting positions. The horses line up. The signal is given. They're off!

The crowd lets out a mighty roar. Each jockey immediately begins fighting for a good position. At the same time, he tries to block his rivals.

The crowd cheers wildly as the horses enter the third and final lap. As the front-runners near the dangerous San Martino curve, the horse from the Forest neighborhood stumbles. It knocks into the Shell horse, and the Eagle horse plows into both. Three horses are down!

The others surge ahead. Tower and Goose are in the lead. The jockeys lash at each other with whips as they round the Casato corner. Suddenly the jockey on Goose loses his balance and falls to the ground. But his riderless horse pulls ahead and thunders across the finish line. Goose has won!

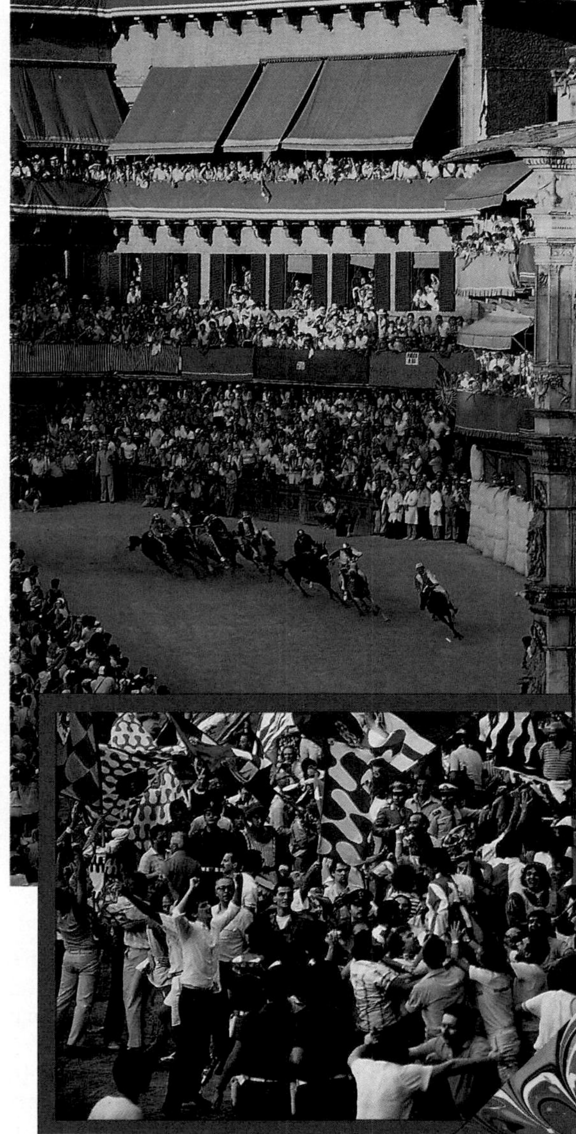

A LEGACY CONTINUES

That night there is feasting in the Goose neighborhood and its "allies" among the other contrade. The Tower neighborhood is quiet. But the losers can't feel too bad—after all, the Palio will be run next summer! In only months the crowds will gather again for this traditional celebration of Siena's past and present.

How does the legacy of the Palio keep Siena's history alive?

267

Talking About the Race Continue the discussion.

Ask students:

- **Would Goose have been the winner in an ordinary horse race?** (No, because in most races the horse cannot win if its jockey has fallen off.)

Discussing a Continuing Legacy Begin the discussion by asking students about their own reactions to victory and defeat in sports.

Ask students:

- **Compare and contrast the reactions of the Goose contrada to those of the Tower contrada.** (The Goose neighborhood enjoys a feast, along with its "allies." The Tower neighborhood is quiet, since it lost the Palio.)

Applying the Lesson Have students imagine that their own neighborhoods are going to compete in the Palio. Have each student draw an illustration for a banner that could represent his or her neighborhood.

3 CLOSE

Summarizing Students have learned about the Sienese legacy of the Palio. Have students list the different elements of the Palio and identify how these elements (races, religion, parades) are common to many cultures.

Evaluating Assess students' understanding of the lesson by asking them the question at the bottom of the pupil page. (Possible answer includes: The Palio keeps Siena's history alive by celebrating traditional aspects of Sienese culture, including religion, the Renaissance, and the contrade.)

MEETING INDIVIDUAL NEEDS

Reteaching (easy) Have students design and draw a poster for tourists based on one of the incidents described under the heading "The Race Begins."

Extension (average) Have students imagine that they have recently attended the Palio. Ask them to write a newspaper article about the event.

Enrichment (challenging) Have students research and write a report on a legacy of Italy not mentioned in this chapter.

CHAPTER 12 REVIEW
pages 268–269

USING THE CHAPTER SUMMARY AND REVIEW

Cultural Geography These questions may be used for review.

- **Which groups of people played an important role in the development of this region?** (Greeks and Romans)
- **What are the main agricultural products of Southern Europe?** (cereal grains, olive oil, wine)
- **What factors have caused regional conflicts in Italy and Spain?** (Italy—uneven distribution of industries between the north and the south; Spain—the demand for autonomy by the Catalans and independence for the Basques)
- **What was the Renaissance?** (a period of great artistic activity from the 1300s through the 1600s)

Ideas to Remember

- **What unites the people of Southern Europe?** (languages with a common base in Latin and the Roman Catholic and Greek Orthodox religions)
- **Which industries are important in Southern Europe?** (shipping, manufacturing, tourism)
- **What do the governments of Greece, Italy, and Portugal have in common?** (They are all governed by parliamentary democracies.)
- **Which Renaissance painters came from this region?** (Leonardo da Vinci, Raphael, Michelangelo, Diego Velázquez, El Greco)

Answers to Reviewing Vocabulary

1. coalition
2. Renaissance
3. siesta
4. terrorism
5. autonomy

Answers to Reviewing Facts

1. Spain, Portugal, Italy, Greece; the Mediterranean Sea

CHAPTER 12 SUMMARY

MEDITERRANEAN EUROPE: CULTURAL GEOGRAPHY

PEOPLE

- Greeks: used shipping to import and export food
- Romans: spread their civilization throughout Europe
- Spanish and Portuguese: discovered new trade routes
- Languages: different but based on Latin in three countries

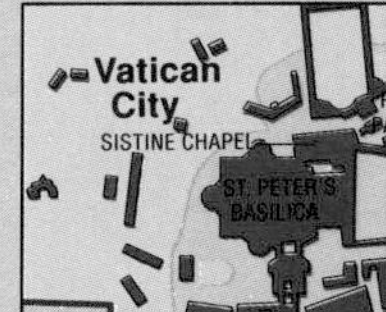

- Religions: Roman Catholic and Greek Orthodox

ECONOMY

- Industries: shipping, manufacturing, tourism

- Farming: cereal grains, olive oil, wine
- Standard of living: improving, but not as strong as other areas of Western Europe

GOVERNMENT

- Greece, Italy, and Portugal: parliamentary democracies

- Spain: constitutional monarchy
- Italy and Spain: plagued by regional conflicts

ARTS AND RECREATION

- Rich cultural heritage that stretches back thousands of years
- Renaissance: Italy: Leonardo da Vinci, Michelangelo

- Festivals: used to celebrate religious and other holidays
- Outdoor activities: golf, cycling, tennis, skiing, Palio races

IDEAS TO REMEMBER

- Most of the people of Southern Europe share a way of life that includes the Christian religion and three languages that are based on Latin.
- Industries such as shipping and tourism are helping to develop the economies of Southern Europe.
- Greece, Italy, and Portugal are governed by parliamentary democracies, while Spain is led by a constitutional monarchy.
- The region has a long cultural heritage and has produced many of the world's greatest writers, artists, and musicians.

268

ENRICHMENT ACTIVITY

Creating Mobiles **Materials:** construction paper, markers, glue, string, wooden rods, hangers

1. Ask students to identify some of the unique characteristics of Spain, Portugal, Italy, and Greece. Tell students that they are going to make mobiles that are representative of these countries.
2. Divide the class into four groups and assign one country to each group. Tell the groups to discuss their country and choose characteristics which would work well on a mobile.
3. Have students draw and cut out designs, attach them to string, and hang them from wooden dowels or hangers.
4. Hang the finished mobiles in the classroom for everyone to look at and enjoy.

CHAPTER 12 • REVIEW

REVIEWING VOCABULARY

autonomy
siesta
coalition
terrorism
Renaissance

Number a sheet of paper from 1 to 5. Beside each number write the word from the list above that best completes each sentence.

1. Since World War II, Italy has been run by a series of unstable ____ governments.
2. The ____ was a period of artistic flowering that began in Italy in the 1300s and 1400s and spread throughout Europe.
3. It is customary in Southern Europe to take a ____, or long nap, during the hottest part of the day.
4. Some separatist groups have tried to achieve independence through ____, a method of frightening people with the threat of violence.
5. Although they do not want to separate completely from Spain, the Catalans seek ____, or the right to govern themselves.

REVIEWING FACTS

1. Name the four major countries of Southern Europe. What body of water is important to three countries in this region?
2. Which two great ancient civilizations emerged from Southern Europe?
3. Why did the ancient Romans call the Mediterranean Sea *Mare Nostrum*, or "our sea"?
4. What is the name of the tiny state in Rome that is the home of the leader of the Roman Catholic Church?
5. Which region of Europe, northern or southern, has a greater percentage of people who are farmers?
6. Why is tourism a mixed blessing for towns like Marbella, Spain?
7. Name two factors that have heavily influenced Italian politics since World War II.
8. In which region are most Italian industries located?
9. How do the goals of the Catalans and the Basques differ?
10. What is a pilgrimage? Why are pilgrimages common in Southern European countries?

WRITING ABOUT MAIN IDEAS

1. **Writing a Paragraph:** Write a paragraph that discusses why the economies of Spain, Portugal, and Greece are sometimes called "developing economies."
2. **Writing a List:** List five sights in Southern Europe that you would like to see on a vacation to the region.
3. **Writing About Perspectives:** Imagine that you live in one of the countries of Southern Europe. Which country did you choose? Write a letter to a friend in the United States describing the different pace of life, the culture, and the physical environment of the country in which you live.

BUILDING SKILLS: READING GRAPHS AND CHARTS

1. What is the difference between a graph and a chart?
2. What do the labels on each axis tell you about the graph?
3. What kind of information does a chart give you?
4. When might it be useful to understand the difference between a graph and a chart?

269

2. Greek and Roman
3. This was the center of their vast empire.
4. Vatican City
5. southern
6. Although it improves the economy, tourism brings crowds, noise, and pollution.
7. lack of national unity, inability of any political party to gain control
8. the north
9. The Catalans want full autonomy, while the Basques want to set up their own country.
10. a journey that people make to sacred places; The people are very religious and value tradition.

Suggestions for Writing About Main Ideas

1. You may wish to have each student create a chart showing the type of economy of each country of Mediterranean Europe.
2. Students may wish to create a travel brochure for one of the sights they have listed.
3. You may want to have students take turns reading their letters aloud. Have the class try to identify the country being described in each letter.

Answers to Building Skills: Reading Graphs and Charts

1. Charts are used to show more detailed information than graphs can show.
2. the amounts that are being compared
3. numbers and more detailed kinds of information
4. You would want to use a chart when you need more detailed information about a topic.

Chapter Review and Test
Practice Book: *Vocabulary Review*, page 72
Transparency: *Graphic Organizer*
Assessment Book: *Chapter 12 Test*

MAKING CONNECTIONS

Organizing Information
Use the Main Idea Map Graphic Organizer Transparency, filling in the underlined headings. Tell students to fill in phrases about Southern Europe that relate to each heading. *Ask:* What are some common characteristics of the countries of Southern Europe?

SOUTHERN EUROPE

Economy
developing economies
limited farmlands
shipping and tourism important

People
Roman Catholic
Greek Orthodox
speak Latin-based languages

Government
representative democracies
constitutional monarchy
parliamentary democracies

Arts and Recreation
ancient Greek writers
Italian Renaissance artists
opera composers

CHAPTER 13 ORGANIZER

SCANDINAVIA text pages 270–285

CHAPTER THEME Peace-loving Scandinavia and Finland have high standards of living, efficient governments, and rugged environments.

CHAPTER OBJECTIVES

CONTENT

- Describe what the people of Scandinavia are like today.
- Identify Scandinavia and list the five countries and two territories it includes.
- Contrast the population density of Scandinavia with that of other parts of Europe.
- Describe how Scandinavian countries have developed diversified economies.
- Name the two traditional industries of Scandinavia.
- Define *cooperative* and name two types of cooperatives common throughout Scandinavia.
- Contrast the monarchies of Denmark, Norway, and Sweden with the British monarchy.
- Describe welfare state programs and benefits found throughout Scandinavia and relate these programs to the people's confidence in their government.
- Explain how Scandinavians' love of the land is reflected in their arts and recreation.
- Identify Eddas and sagas and relate them to the Scandinavian love of storytelling.

SKILLS

Geography
- Interpret a political map of Scandinavia.

Thinking
- Ask focused questions to find out whether a statement about Scandinavians is true.
- Determine a person's point of view.

Reading and Writing
- Write a profile of Scandinavian life.

CITIZENSHIP VALUES

- Appreciate a people's ability to achieve prosperity despite scarce resources.
- Appreciate the contributions of individuals to society.

TEACHER OPTIONS

READING STRATEGY: Monitoring Comprehension
Strategies to help students read and remember the main ideas of the lesson.
Lesson 1: p. 271 Lesson 3: p. 277
Lesson 2: p. 274 Lesson 4: p. 282

MEETING INDIVIDUAL NEEDS Activities for reteaching, extension, and enrichment.
Lesson 1: p. 273 Lesson 3: p. 278
Lesson 2: p. 276 Lesson 4: p. 283

GEO ADVENTURES ACTIVITIES PAD Daily activities to assess students' understanding of geography skills.

CURRICULUM CONNECTION Activities to help integrate other subject areas with Social Studies.
Science: p. 275

PUPIL EDITION ON CASSETTE Language support for students who have difficulty reading or who will benefit from listening to the Pupil Edition on Cassette as they read.

SECOND-LANGUAGE SUPPORT Activities and suggestions for second-language learners.
Lesson 3: p. 25

CHAPTER PLANNING GUIDE

LESSON	SUGGESTED PACING	THEMES	TEACHER SUPPORT MATERIALS: TEACHER'S RESOURCE CENTER
1 THE PEOPLE pages 271–273	1 day	The Scandinavians are bound by close family ties, a common language, and their adjustment to a rugged environment.	Practice Book p. 73 Outline Map p. 22 **Technology:** *Adventures CD-ROM*
2 THE ECONOMY pages 274–276	1 day	Scandinavian economies are diversified, enabling people to have a high standard of living in these countries.	Practice Book p. 74 Outline Map p. 22 **Technology:** *Adventures CD-ROM*
3 THE GOVERNMENT pages 277–279	1 day	The representative democracies of Scandinavia are generously supported by citizens expecting high standards of service from efficient governments.	Practice Book p. 75 **Technology:** *Adventures CD-ROM*
BUILDING THINKING SKILLS Determining Point of View pages 280–281	1 day	Determining a writer's or speaker's point of view helps you to understand how that person views or feels about something.	Practice Book p. 76
4 ARTS AND RECREATION pages 282–283	1 day	The rugged land and the hardy people of Scandinavia are celebrated in Scandinavian arts and recreation.	Practice Book p. 77 ■ Anthology pp. 66–67
CHAPTER SUMMARY AND REVIEW pages 284–285	1 day	Chapter content, skills, and vocabulary are reviewed and evaluated.	Practice Book p. 78 Transparency: Graphic Organizer Assessment Book, Chapter 13 Test

Technology CONNECTION

Lesson 1
ADVENTURES CD-ROM
Enrich this lesson using *Travel* and *Explore.*

Lesson 2
ADVENTURES CD-ROM
Investigate Sounds in Sweden.

Lesson 3
ADVENTURES CD-ROM
In *Explore,* use the *Measure* tool to consider the sizes of the Scandinavian countries.

CHAPTER 13

pages 270–285

USING THE CHAPTER OPENER

Discussing the Photograph Ask students to examine the photograph on this page. Encourage students to describe the clothes that the men are wearing. Most students will probably comment on the bright colors and fancy embroidery.

Ask students:

- **If you were to write a story about these men, in which historical period would you place them? Why?** (Possible answers include: the Middle Ages, an unspecified time in the remote past such as that in which fairy tales and folktales are set; because their clothes look like the clothes worn in the Middle Ages or like those depicted in illustrations of folktales.)
- **Would the climate of the country in which your characters live be hot or cold? Why?** (It would be cold; their clothes are too heavy for a hot climate.)

Reading/Listening to the Primary Source Ask a volunteer to read the passage under the picture to the class. Encourage them to think about how they might feel in the latter part of a long, cold winter.

Ask students:

- **In what ways do you think the people of Scandinavia cope with the low spirits that are often brought on by long, dark winters?** (Possible answers include: engage in cold weather sports; invent indoor games, stories, and other amusements to pass the time when they cannot go outdoors; keep their houses brightly lit, warm, and colorfully furnished; visit with or entertain friends frequently.)
- *THINKING FURTHER:* **What qualities might such activities develop in a group of people?** (Possible answers include: vigor, courage, imagination, hospitality.)

CHAPTER 13

SCANDINAVIA

FOCUS

Throughout Scandinavia at this time of year, the effect of the long daily periods of sunlight on people's behavior, temperament, and work habits is strikingly different. People, it seems, are like plants: they blossom in the sunlight.

You probably have felt the uplifting effects of spring yourself. The newspaper article from which these sentences come tells us that Scandinavians "think bright" under the spring sunlight. In this chapter you will learn about the ways of life that have developed in the north.

BACKGROUND INFORMATION

Multicultural Perspectives The two men in the picture live in Lapland, a bitterly cold area that lies mostly north of the Arctic Circle in Scandinavia. The following Lapp legend explains how the Lapps came to live in their homeland.

In the beginning Ibmel, the God of gods, created two brothers. They lived together in a land of mountain and marsh. . . . Then came the first snowstorm, threatening to bury the two men. One of them quickly made up his mind what to do. He found a cavern on the side of a mountain, and hid there till the storm was over. But his brother stayed where he was in the open, fighting grimly for survival. He won his battle. From him sprang the Lapps, choosing for their land the coldest on earth. But the one who sought shelter was the ancestor of the Men of the South.

Ask students what skills it would take to survive in such a harsh environment.

LESSON 1

The People

READ TO LEARN

Key Places

Norway Denmark Faeroe Islands
Sweden Finland Stockholm
Iceland Greenland Copenhagen

Read Aloud

Imagine what it would be like to stand outside in the middle of the night with the sky still light. Every year, because of the angle of the earth as it circles the sun, the sky is light in parts of Scandinavia. Every June this event is celebrated during a holiday called Midsummer Eve. In Helsinki, the capital of Finland, the sun is still shining brightly at 11:00 P.M. About two hours later dawn begins. At midnight the sky is still bright.

During winter the opposite happens. Some days the sun barely rises. To help keep their homes cheerful during the dark winter, Scandinavians decorate them with brilliant colors. This is just one of the many ways in which they make the most of what they have. In this lesson you will read how the Scandinavians, a proud, self-reliant people, live in their home in the far north.

Read for Purpose

1. WHAT YOU KNOW: Where is the Scandinavian Peninsula located?
2. WHAT YOU WILL LEARN: What ways of life do the people of Scandinavia share today?

LANDS OF THE NORTH

Before you read about how Scandinavians live, it is important to know where they live. As you may remember from Chapter 8, the Scandinavian Peninsula is one of the many peninsulas in Western Europe. It includes the countries of **Norway** and **Sweden**. The term *Scandinavia* is also used for a larger area. It includes **Iceland**, **Denmark**, and **Finland**. The Danish island of **Greenland**, which is the world's largest island, and the **Faeroe** (fâr' ō) **Islands** are also part of Scandinavia.

THE EARLY SCANDINAVIANS

Scandinavia is a rugged land, much of it mountainous or snow-covered. It has produced some of the most hardy, rugged, and self-reliant people in the world.

Hundreds of years ago the Scandinavians were a warlike people. In Chapter 10 you read about daring Scandinavian seafarers called Vikings who raided many European communities. But the Vikings were also skilled shipbuilders and traders. Sturdy Viking ships traveled as far away as North America.

WHAT YOU KNOW: This question refers to material covered in Chapter 8, Lesson 1; in the northern part of Western Europe.

LESSON 1
pages 271–273

Lesson Theme The Scandinavians are bound by close family ties, a common language, and their adjustment to a rugged environment.

Lesson Objectives
- Describe the location and lands of Scandinavia.
- Explain the differences between Scandinavians in the past and Scandinavians today.
- Describe Scandinavian languages and families.

PREPARE

Motivate Read the *Read Aloud* section to the class. Ask if any students have ever witnessed the midnight sun. Discuss how this pattern of day and night might affect daily life.

Set Purpose Have a student answer the *What You Know* question by locating Scandinavia on a wall map or on the map on page 272. Use the *What You Will Learn* question to explore any preconceived notions of Scandinavians that students might have.

TEACH

Talking About Lands of the North Discuss with the class the areas considered part of Scandinavia according to this lesson.

Understanding the Early Scandinavians Have each student tell one fact that they know about the Vikings. Discuss the complete reversal of attitudes toward war and fighting between today's Scandinavians and the Vikings of Scandinavia's past.

READING STRATEGY AND VOCABULARY DEVELOPMENT

Monitoring Comprehension The purpose of this strategy is to help students become more aware of what they are reading so that they can find sense and meaning from a text. Suggest to students that reading is an active process, one in which the reader must constantly try to make sense out of what he or she reads by asking questions about the content. Examples of these questions include: Does the information make sense? Do the facts agree with other materials I have read? Develop a strategy for students to use while reading. For example, as they are reading a section, tell students to remind themselves of what they know and to ask questions about what they are reading. Have students use this strategy or a similar strategy when they read this lesson.

EXTENDING MAP SKILLS

Have students study the political map of Scandinavia.

Ask students:

- **Which country has no countries along its borders?** (Iceland)
- **Which country is bordered by land only to the south?** (Denmark)
- **Which Scandinavian nations are on peninsulas of Europe?** (all of them except Iceland)
- **What are the capital cities of the countries of Scandinavia?** (Helsinki, Finland; Stockholm, Sweden; Oslo, Norway; Copenhagen, Denmark; Reykjavík, Iceland)

Understanding Similarities of Language

Ask students:

- **Why can Danes, Swedes, and Norwegians understand one another if they all speak different languages?** (Their languages all developed from one common language.)
- **How is Finnish different from other Scandinavian languages?** (The people of Finland are descended from people from Asia and therefore Finnish has a different language base.)

Discussing a Small Population

Speculate with students about the effects of cold climate, scarce resources, and a small population on an economy. Tell them to check their predictions in the next lesson.

Talking About Close-Knit Families

Ask students:

- **What travel tradition of the Scandinavians shows their devotion to family life?** (Their willingness to travel miles to attend family gatherings.)
- *THINKING FURTHER:* **In which part of the year would it be most comforting to be part of a family in Scandinavia?** (in the cold, dark days of winter)

MAP SKILL: Copenhagen is one of the most important cities in Scandinavia. Where is Copenhagen located?

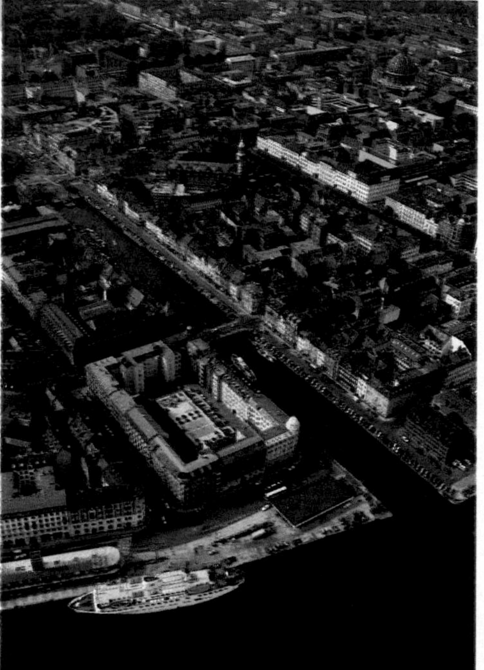

After the Viking period ended, Scandinavians turned their energies toward developing their own land. Today they work hard to make the most out of what their land has to offer.

SIMILARITIES OF LANGUAGE

What ties the Scandinavian people together? Their language does, for one thing. Most of the early settlers of Scandinavia spoke the same language. Over thousands of years, this one language has developed into different Scandinavian languages. But even today Danes, Swedes, and Norwegians can understand each other. Look at the table on the opposite page. It shows the similarity of the Scandinavian languages.

The languages of Finland are exceptions to this language similarity. One group of people in Finland, the Finns, are descended from people who probably came from Asia. They also speak an entirely different language. Look at the chart again to see the differences between the Finnish language and the other languages.

Another group of people in Finland—the Lapps—also speak their own language. The Lapps live in Lapland. As the map on this page shows, Lapland includes parts of northern Finland, Norway, and Sweden. The Lapp language is similar to Finnish.

A SMALL POPULATION

The Scandinavians are a people who have taken on many challenges, such as cold climate and scarce resources. Scandinavians have won a reputation as a people who get things done. Today their towns, governments, and businesses are known for the efficiency with which they are run. In the next two lessons you will read about the governments and economies of the Scandinavian countries.

MAP SKILL: in Denmark, in the southern part of Scandinavia

BUILDING CITIZENSHIP

The Value of Family Life People everywhere need their families for security, love and affection, and recognition. A strong family life within a nation gives strength to the whole country. Discuss with students what a nation gains from close-knit family support systems. (Families make sure the young are healthy and receive an education. They take care of the elderly and ill. Family life teaches people loyalty and appreciation for the lands in which they live.) Also, discuss the problems that can arise if a family cannot help its members. Have students consider what role, if any, they think the government of the nation should then have.

The size of the population helps Scandinavians get things done. The area has few people—its 23 million residents represent only about 6 percent of the total population of Western Europe. Most of the people live in or near cities. However, Scandinavian cities are both small and uncrowded. Stockholm, the capital of Sweden and the largest city in Scandinavia, has about 1.5 million people. By contrast, the cities of Paris, Vienna, and Rome each have more than 2 million people. London has more than 6 million residents.

CLOSE-KNIT FAMILIES

How do the Scandinavian people live? Let's look at one Scandinavian family.

Leise Abrahamson lives in a small city near Copenhagen, the capital of Denmark. She and her brother Neel often bicycle with their mother to do the food shopping. Their mother is a weaver. In the evening their father, an architect, sometimes reads to the family.

Leise's parents, like many others throughout Scandinavia, spend much of their spare time with their children. Family occasions are especially important. Relatives travel miles to attend graduations, weddings, or other family events. On birthdays—especially on the milestone birthdays that fall every 10 years—relatives and friends stop by. Such celebrations can be tiring, as visits may start as early as 7:30 in the morning!

LIVING IN THE NORTH

Scandinavians, as you have read, share a common heritage of efficiency and hard work. They are a peaceful people who make the most of their rugged land. Because they are few in number, Scandinavians make up a small percentage of the population of Western Europe. They are united by a common language and close-knit families. In the following lessons you will read about the economic, political, and social lives of these people of the North.

COMPARING WORDS IN SCANDINAVIAN LANGUAGES

	day	house	man
Danish	dag	hus	mand
Finnish	päivä	talo	mies
Icelandic	dagur	hús	mandur
Norwegian	dag	hus	mann
Swedish	dag	hus	man

CHART SKILL: The people of Scandinavia speak very similar languages. Which three languages use the same word for *day*?

Check Your Reading

1. Which countries and areas make up Scandinavia?
2. Where is Lapland located, and what group of people lives there?
3. What do the Scandinavian people have in common?
4. THINKING SKILL: In what ways are Scandinavians like people in other parts of Western Europe? In what ways are they different?

CHART SKILL: Danish, Norwegian, Swedish

THINKING SKILL: Compare and Contrast

273

EXTENDING CHART SKILLS

Have students study the Scandinavian Languages chart.

Ask students:

- **How many Scandinavian languages are shown?** (five)
- **Which column of words does not match as closely as the others?** (Finnish) **What does this tell us?** (The origin of Finnish is different.)

Applying the Lesson Have students write a paragraph describing three ways in which Scandinavia differs from Southern European countries and two ways in which it is the same.

CLOSE

Summarizing Students have read that the small population of Scandinavia gains strength from a common language base and family life. Discuss why family is important.

Evaluating Use these questions to assess students' understanding.

- **Which countries are on the Scandinavian Peninsula?** (Norway and Sweden)
- **Which country developed a language quite unlike those of the other Scandinavian countries?** (Finland)

Answers to Check Your Reading

1. Norway, Sweden, Iceland, Finland, Greenland, Denmark, the Faeroe Islands
2. in the northern part of Norway, Sweden, and Finland; the Lapps
3. language, family life, traditions
4. *Same:* they are bonded by language and customs; *different:* they have a small population, try to solve problems peacefully, have to adjust to a cold, dark land.

Independent Practice
Practice Book: page 73

MEETING INDIVIDUAL NEEDS

Reteaching (easy) Have students draw two pictures of family life in Scandinavia. Tell them to draw one picture showing family activities during the dark days with no sun above the horizon; tell them to draw a second picture showing the family celebrating Midsummer Eve.

Extension (average) Give students the outline map of Scandinavia, which can be found in the Teacher's Resource Center. Have them label the Scandinavian countries and their capital cities, the oceans and seas, and Lapland. Have students include a title and legend for the map.

Enrichment (challenging) Have students research and then create a chart of the national symbols of the Scandinavian countries.

LESSON 2
pages 274–276

Lesson Theme Scandinavian economies are diversified, enabling people to have a high standard of living in these countries.

Lesson Objectives
- Describe how Scandinavian economies are diversified.
- Explain the role of cooperatives in Scandinavia.

PREPARE

Motivate Read the *Read Aloud* section to students. Speculate with them as to how Scandinavians may have changed their dependence on forests and fish.

Set Purpose Use the *What You Know* question to list the resources Scandinavia has. Use the *What You Will Learn* question to challenge students to name items that show a diversified economy.

TEACH

Looking at a Norwegian Fishing Crew

Ask students:

- **Why do Norwegian fishing crews go to the Lofoten Islands?** (The islands are located in some of the richest fishing grounds in the world.)
- *THINKING FURTHER:* **What are the disadvantages and advantages of fishing at the Lofotens?** (Crews must go there in February for three months without their families, live in a dormitory, and work 16-hour days. The big advantage is the large amount of fish they take back to Norway.)

LESSON 2

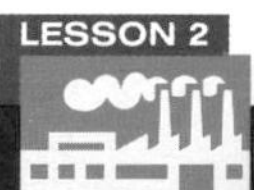

The Economy

READ TO LEARN

Key Vocabulary
diversified economy
cooperative

Key Places
Lofoten Islands

Read Aloud

The trouble is, we don't have any means of making the trees grow faster or persuading the herring to come back.

The Norwegian economist who spoke these words describes a problem that Scandinavians have had for many years—dependence on a few natural resources. In the past, Scandinavians relied on a few resources to earn a living. Today, however, things have changed.

Read for Purpose

1. WHAT YOU KNOW: What are natural resources?
2. WHAT YOU WILL LEARN: How have the Scandinavian countries developed diversified economies?

HAULING IN THE LINES

It's 2:30 A.M., and Edmund, Ole, and the rest of their Norwegian fishing crew are already out of bed. After breakfast they board their boat and chug out to the sea around the **Lofoten** (lō′ fōt ən) **Islands**. These islands are located in some of the richest fishing waters in the world.

When they reach the fishing grounds, the members of the crew haul in the three long lines they had dropped overboard a day or two earlier.

Each of these lines is 2 miles (3.2 km) long and baited with hundreds of mackerel. Now the three lines each have hundreds of cod caught on them.

Most crews like Edmund and Ole's come to the Lofotens for three months, beginning in February. This is a lonely stretch of time for the crews because they come without their families. Many crew members live in a large dormitory called a *fiskerheimen*, which means "home for fishers." The work is hard—16-hour days are common. But the large catches make the hard work worthwhile.

DEVELOPING NEW RESOURCES

Edmund and Ole play an important part in Norway's oldest and most important industry—fishing. The economies of Norway and Iceland have long been dependent on the sea. But lately these and other Scandinavian countries have found new resources to develop. In Iceland, for example, sheep have become a major resource.

Oil is another example of a new resource that has come to play a major role in the economies of the Scandinavian countries. Norway has Western Europe's largest

WHAT YOU KNOW: Students should be aware that natural resources are things found in nature that are useful to humans, such as water, air, and soil.

READING STRATEGY AND VOCABULARY DEVELOPMENT

Monitoring Comprehension Remind students that an important part of monitoring their comprehension of what they read is previewing the lesson and thinking about what they already know about the lesson before they read. Have students preview the lesson and develop three or four questions about it. As they read the lesson, remind them to monitor their comprehension so that they can answer the questions they have developed. The following are questions students may develop about the section titled "Developing New Resources."

What are the new resources of the area?
What were the old resources?
Where are the resources located?
Which country has the most varied resources?

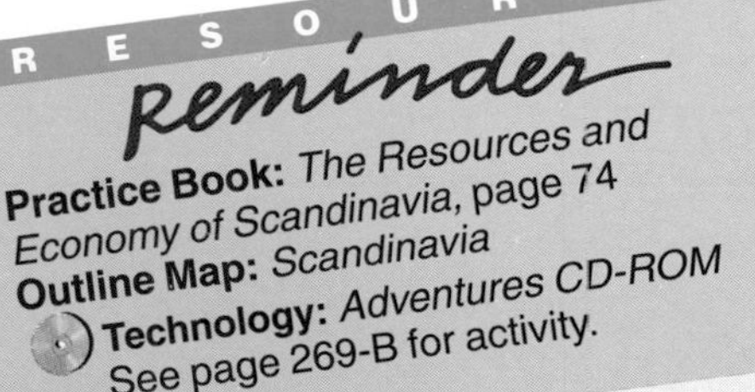
RESOURCE Reminder
Practice Book: *The Resources and Economy of Scandinavia,* page 74
Outline Map: *Scandinavia*
Technology: *Adventures CD-ROM*
See page 269-B for activity.

fields of offshore petroleum and natural gas. That country now plays an important part in the world oil market.

The economies of Finland and Sweden have been based on their huge forests for hundreds of years. These countries are two of the most heavily forested nations in Europe. About 70 percent of Finland is covered with forests.

Lumbering still plays a key role in the economies of Finland and Sweden. But today these countries also have highly developed manufacturing industries. Sweden, now the most industrialized country in Scandinavia, produces steel, automobiles, furniture, and other products. Finland produces clothing and chemicals.

Denmark, too, has made great strides. As one Dane says, "Denmark is a little country. We have no wood, no metals, nothing in the ground." But, he added, "We have fantastically good craftsmen." Today Denmark is renowned for its furniture, glassware, and toys.

Scandinavian factories are among the most efficient in the world. These factories were among the first to use robots. Many lumber camps and farms in the area are automated as well.

Because of their hard work in developing new resources, most Scandinavian countries have diversified economies. This means that they produce a wide range of goods. From automobiles and airplanes to processed wood and fish, Scandinavia's economies produce a wide range of products for world markets.

In the past most Scandinavians earned their living either by fishing, farming, or lumbering. This is no longer true. Today less than 8 percent of workers earn their living by farming, fishing, or lumbering. Instead, because of diversified economies, most workers have jobs in service industries, mining, or manufacturing.

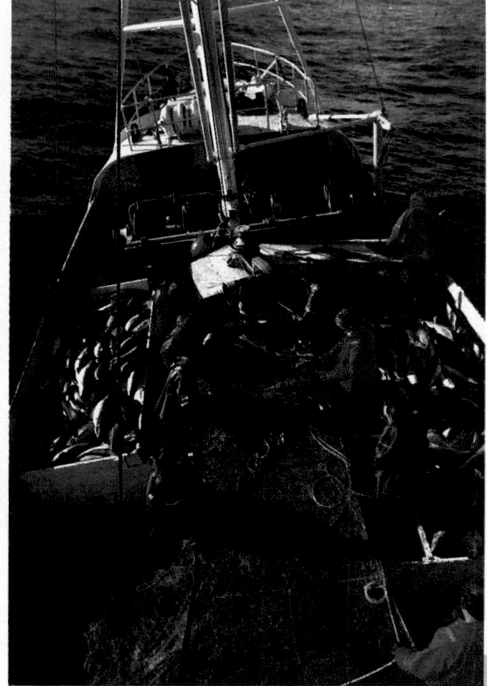

Fishing is now just one part of the diversified economies of Scandinavian countries.

PLANNING AND SHARING

How has Scandinavia developed such successful diversified economies? Government has played a large role. All five Scandinavian countries have mixed economies. As you read in Chapter 9, in a mixed economy the government owns some businesses while private companies own others. In most of Scandinavia, the telephone and electric power companies are owned and operated by the government. Governments control other large industries, such as the oil industry.

Scandinavians also work together in another way. Scandinavia is known for its many cooperatives. A cooperative is a business organization owned by its members. Denmark was a pioneer in the development of the agricultural cooperative,

275

Discussing the Development of New Resources Help students to contrast Scandinavia's old economic activities with the new.

Ask students:

- **What are the old and new economic activities of Norway?** (fishing; petroleum and natural gas) **Of Sweden?** (lumbering; manufacturing of steel, automobiles, furniture, and so on) **Of Finland?** (lumbering; manufacturing clothing and chemicals) **Of Denmark?** (fisheries; manufacturing furniture, glassware, and toys) **Of Iceland?** (fisheries; raising sheep)
- **What is distinctive about Norway's oil and natural gas resources?** (Norway has Western Europe's largest offshore petroleum and natural gas fields.)
- **What has Denmark substituted for physical resources?** (the skills of craftspeople in making excellent products)
- **What characterizes Scandinavian economic production today?** (efficient automated factories, farms, and lumber camps; use of robots; wide range of goods; most workers in services, mining, or factories, with only 8 percent of workers in farming, fishing, or lumbering)
- *THINKING FURTHER:* **How would Norway's oil and gas production help the economies of Scandinavia?** (by providing Scandinavian nations with convenient energy sources for running all kinds of factories)

Discussing a Planned Economy

Ask students:

- **What is a mixed economy?** (one in which government and business leaders work together)
- **What role does government play in most economies of Scandinavia?** (In many Scandinavian countries the government owns and operates telephone and electric power companies and controls petroleum and other large industries.)

CURRICULUM CONNECTION

Science Petroleum and natural gas are not abundant throughout Scandinavia. Most countries have to import oil and gas or find other energy sources. In Iceland geothermal energy is used. Geothermal energy is created when underground water is heated by the hot magma below the surface, creating hot springs and steamy geysers. This energy source enables Iceland to pipe hot water to cities to heat homes, office buildings, and factories. Using geothermal energy, greenhouses are kept warm and produce fruits, flowers, and vegetables that otherwise could never grow in this icy climate. Outdoor recreation, such as swimming in the hot springs, has also developed. Best of all, this energy source causes no pollution. Have students report on geothermal energy and other kinds of energy sources being used throughout the United States.

Looking at Planned Economies Continue to discuss the economies of Scandinavia.

Ask students:

- **What are some examples of international cooperation in Scandinavia?** (Trade flows freely; people move easily from one country to another; they share television programs and a commercial airline.)
- **What is the result of careful planning and cooperation among Scandinavian countries?** (Scandinavia has one of the highest standards of living in Western Europe.)

Applying the Lesson Have students chart the economic activities of Norway, Sweden, Finland, Denmark, and Iceland before and after economic diversification.

CLOSE

Summarizing Students have learned that careful planning and cooperation has helped to develop Scandinavian economies. Discuss problems these countries would have today if they had not diversified.

Evaluating Use these questions to assess students' understanding.

- **What kind of economies do most of the nations of Scandinavia have?** (diversified economies)
- **What kinds of cooperatives are there in Scandinavia?** (agricultural, retail, between nations)

Answers to Check Your Reading

1. fish and other sea products, petroleum and natural gas, forests
2. a business organization owned by its members; helps them buy supplies and market their products
3. Many different kinds of products are made.
4. What resources do they have? What products do they make? How much is left unused?

Independent Practice
Practice Book: page 74

Many people in Scandinavia buy consumer goods at retail **cooperatives** such as this one in Stockholm, Sweden.

which helps farmers buy supplies and market their products.

Retail cooperatives are also common in Scandinavia. Many food and department stores are owned by consumers. The consumers save money because items in the stores are sold at the same price that the store paid to purchase them.

Finally, Scandinavian nations cooperate with one other. Trade flows freely among the five countries, and it is easy for people to move from one country to another to find work. Scandinavians also share television programs as well as a commercial airline.

Cooperation and planning have enabled Scandinavia to have one of the highest standards of living in Western Europe. The area has virtually no city slums and few poor people. In Norway, the wealthiest country in Scandinavia, the average yearly per capita income is over $20,000, one of the highest incomes in the world.

276

SHARING THE GOOD LIFE

The countries of Scandinavia have developed diversified economies, and their people enjoy a high standard of living. As you have read, traditional industries such as fishing, farming, and lumbering are still important. However, fewer people today work in these areas than did people in the past. Scandinavia has prospered through government planning, cooperation, and the production of quality goods.

Check Your Reading

1. What are the main natural resources of Scandinavia?
2. What is a cooperative? How do cooperatives help their members?
3. What is the meaning of the following statement: "Scandinavia has diversified economies"?
4. **THINKING SKILL:** List three questions you could ask to find out whether or not the following statement is true: "Scandinavians make the most of what they have to work with."

THINKING SKILL: Asking Questions

MEETING INDIVIDUAL NEEDS

Reteaching (easy) Have students draw pictures on the outline map of Scandinavia, which can be found in the Teacher's Resource Center, to show the products from the diversified economies of Scandinavia.

Extension (average) Have students draw a diagram showing the three kinds of cooperation found in Scandinavia: (1) between government and business, (2) in cooperatives, and (3) between nations.

Enrichment (challenging) Divide the class into groups representing Norway, Sweden, Finland, Denmark, Iceland, Greenland, and the Faeroe Islands. Have each group find the latest production figures for economic activities in their country or territory. Have groups present this information to the class in poster or chart form. Discuss students' findings.

LESSON 3

The Government

READ TO LEARN

Key Vocabulary ombudsman

Key Places Thingvellir

Read Aloud

I would rather have a welfare state where people are not fully satisfied than the old world where people had no choice but to suffer.

This is how the Finnish author Vaino Linna explained why many Scandinavians want to keep the types of governments they have. In this lesson you will read about the welfare states of Scandinavia.

Read for Purpose

1. WHAT YOU KNOW: What is a welfare state?
2. WHAT YOU WILL LEARN: What beliefs about government are shared by the countries of Scandinavia?

DRIVERS CHANGE TO THE RIGHT

September 3, 1967, was a special day in Sweden. On that day all drivers switched from driving on the left-hand side of the road to driving on the right-hand side of the road. Swedes called it H-Day, from *hoger*, the Swedish word for "right."

Sweden made this change so that driving would be the same there as it is in most other Western European countries. Experts believed—rightly, as it turned out—that the number of accidents in Scandinavian countries would decrease if drivers did not have to change from one system of driving to another.

H-Day took four years of planning. It was very costly. Road signs and traffic lights had to be changed—almost 350,000 lights were changed in Stockholm alone. Buses had to be changed so that passengers could board from the right side instead of from the left side.

In spite of all these changes, H-Day went smoothly. This fact says a lot about how government works in Sweden and all of Scandinavia. The governments of Scandinavia are known for their efficiency. In all of the Scandinavian countries, people have put great trust in their governments. Citizens work hard to make government work well for them and to provide them with the services they need.

Although the governments of Scandinavia share a reputation for efficiency, they are not all the same. Let's look at the different kinds of government found in the countries of Scandinavia—three monarchies and two republics.

THREE MONARCHIES

Denmark, Norway, and Sweden, like many countries of Western Europe, are constitutional monarchies. As you may remember, this means they have both

WHAT YOU KNOW: This question refers to material covered in Chapter 9, Lesson 3; a country in which the government takes responsibility for the well-being of its citizens.

277

LESSON 3
pages 277–279

Lesson Theme The representative democracies of Scandinavia are generously supported by citizens expecting high standards of service from efficient governments.

Lesson Objectives
- Describe the forms of government in Scandinavia.
- Explain Scandinavian welfare programs.

PREPARE

Motivate Read the *Read Aloud* section to the class. Discuss what might make citizens dissatisfied with a welfare state. Ask students what Vaino Linna meant by, "the old world where people had no choice but to suffer."

Set Purpose Use the *What You Know* question to ask students if they have heard the term *welfare state* used by Americans in either a positive or a negative way. Have students keep the *What You Will Learn* question in mind as they read this lesson.

TEACH

Looking at H-Day in Sweden Discuss what H-day was, how it was to improve life in Sweden, and why it succeeded.

Discussing Three Monarchies Discuss with students their ideas on what a monarchy is and how this kind of government functions.

READING STRATEGY AND VOCABULARY DEVELOPMENT

Monitoring Comprehension Point out to students that monitoring their comprehension is helpful to use with other reading strategies. Discuss ways in which the strategy of summarizing could be aided by comprehension monitoring. Have students preview and read the lesson. Then have them prepare a summary that compares/contrasts the governments in Scandinavia with the government of another country or set of countries that they have studied in Western Europe. Summarize the lesson by having students discuss how monitoring comprehension helped them to acquire information for their summary.

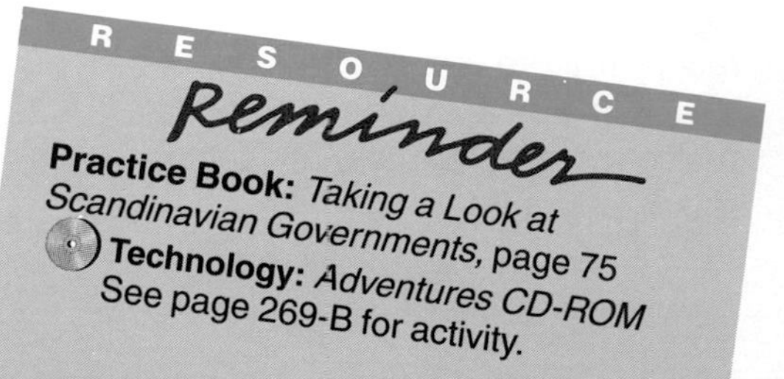

Looking at Three Monarchies Continue the discussion.

Ask students:

- **In what two ways do the constitutional monarchies of Denmark, Norway, and Sweden differ from Great Britain's government?** (They have one-house legislatures; their royalty are treated like ordinary citizens.)

Discussing Two Republics

Ask students:

- **Why is the Icelandic Parliament called the "Grandmother of Parliaments"?** (It is the world's oldest lawmaking body.)
- **How are Iceland and Finland alike? How are they different?** (Both are republics with a prime minister and a president. Finland had closer ties to the former Soviet Union than did Iceland.)

Understanding the Ombudsman

Ask students:

- **Why did Sweden develop the office of ombudsman?** (to receive citizens' complaints about government service or action, thus creating a more efficient government)
- **What actual powers does an ombudsman have?** (the power to persuade elected representatives)

Talking About Welfare States Help students to recognize the specific advantages of a welfare state and the disadvantage of high taxes.

Ask students:

- **What is a welfare state?** (one that ensures the well-being of its citizens through a variety of government programs)
- *THINKING FURTHER:* **What does the positive opinion Scandinavians have about their welfare states tell you about efficiency in their countries?** (It must be very high because people complain readily if there is a problem. However, if things are done well, people praise the program and are enthusiastic about it.)

elected representative governments and royal families.

Unlike Queen Elizabeth and the "royals" of the United Kingdom, Scandinavia's ruling families live simply and with little special treatment. They are treated just the same as other citizens of their countries.

Denmark, Norway, and Sweden all have one-house legislatures. In each country a prime minister is chosen from the parliament to head the executive branch of government. The prime minister, not the monarch, is the true head of the government.

TWO REPUBLICS

Many visitors to Iceland travel to a tiny southwestern settlement of **Thingvellir** (thēng′ vet lēr). There, overlooking a deep gorge, is the "law rock"—the place where Iceland's parliament used to meet. The Icelandic legislature, formed in the year 930, is the oldest working lawmaking body in the world. For this reason this legislature is sometimes called "the grandmother of parliaments."

Both Iceland and Finland are republics. They have both a prime minister and a president. Unlike Norway, Sweden, and Denmark, they do not have monarchs.

Finland is also different in another way. Unlike other countries in Scandinavia and the rest of Western Europe, Finland had close ties to the former Soviet Union. You will read more about the former Soviet Union in Unit 4. In the 1940s, after World War II, Finland and the Soviet Union signed a friendship treaty. Finland keeps up close relations with countries, like Russia, that were part of the Soviet Union.

THE OMBUDSMAN

Whatever form their governments take, Scandinavians demand that they perform well and respond to the needs of the people. Let's look at how one country—Sweden—has responded to this demand.

Almost 200 years ago Sweden created a special officer called the **ombudsman** (om′ budz mən). The ombudsman receives complaints from citizens who are not satisfied with a government service or action. Complaints may be about such things as the courts, the environment, or taxes.

The ombudsman cannot take legal action. But he or she informs government representatives about the problems and tries to persuade them to make changes. This, the Swedes say, gives people a close link to their elected representatives.

WELFARE STATES

At the beginning of this lesson, you read a quote about the Finnish welfare state. As you may remember from Chapter 9, a welfare state is one that ensures the well-being of its citizens through a variety of government programs. These include health care, unemployment insurance, child care, pensions, and various housing programs.

The countries of Scandinavia are some of the best-known welfare states in the

The welfare states of Scandinavia have many social programs for their people. In most countries medical care is free.

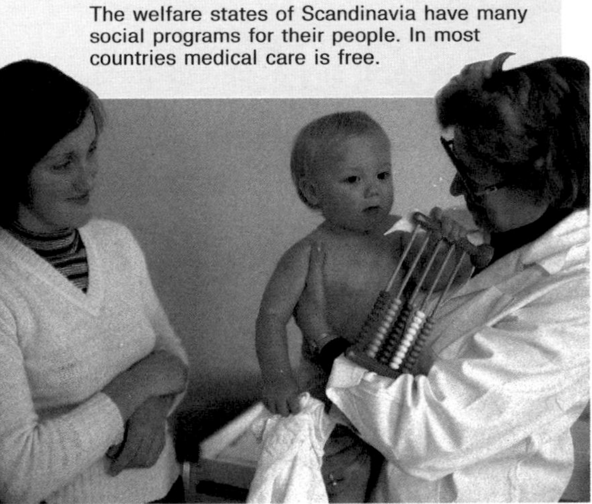

MEETING INDIVIDUAL NEEDS

Reteaching (easy) Have student groups discuss the role of a Swedish ombudsman and make a list of six appropriate problems that Swedish citizens could take to an ombudsman. Each group should perform a skit about a citizen presenting a concern to an ombudsman and the actions the ombudsman would then take.

Extension (average) Have students research the highest tax rate for citizens in the United States, Sweden, Norway, Denmark, and Finland. Have them make a bar graph to show the percentage of income that goes to the government and the percentage the citizens keep in each country.

Enrichment (challenging) Have students debate the pros and cons of living in a welfare state.

world. In Denmark, for instance, workers who are sick or out of a job receive about 90 percent of what they would normally earn. In Sweden parents can take up to 60 days off each year for every child under 12 who is ill. A new mother in Sweden can automatically take a year off at 90 percent of her salary. Most medical care is free or low-cost.

Of course, all of these social programs do not come without a price. Taxes in Scandinavia are very high. In Sweden, which has the highest taxes in the world, some people have to pay more than 75 percent of their earnings to the government.

But most people in Scandinavia would not have it any other way. They ask their governments to do a lot and to do it well. As one young Finnish worker says, "Being born in this country is like winning the lottery of life."

EFFICIENT GOVERNMENTS

Three of the Scandinavian governments are constitutional monarchies and two are republics. Also, as you have read, all five nations have efficient governments that provide necessary services for their citizens through far-reaching welfare programs. Such programs are costly and cause taxes to be high. But to the people of Scandinavia, the investment in their governments is worth the cost.

Check Your Reading

1. Why was H-Day important to the people of Sweden?
2. What is an ombudsman?
3. Why are the nations of Scandinavia called welfare states?
4. **THINKING SKILL:** Reread the Read Aloud passage on page 277. What is the author's bias about welfare states and countries that have them?

THINKING SKILL: Recognizing bias

CITIZENSHIP MAKING A DIFFERENCE

Ecological Development

For generations the people of the rural villages of Suomussalmi, Finland, had supported themselves by fishing, farming, and logging. However, as these industries modernized, fewer workers were needed and people began moving to the cities.

The people wanted to improve their economy, but they did not want to endanger their peaceful way of life. Kauko Heikurainen (kou' kō hā kə rān' ən) believed the economy could be developed without destroying the beauty of the villages. His idea was to apply new methods to traditional ways of using the land.

Under Kauko's leadership, the villagers started an experiment called "ecological development." Farmers learned how to grow crops without using harmful chemicals. Other villagers learned new methods of fishing and forestry.

The "ecovillages" experiment was a success. Today the farmers can barely meet the demand for their products. The many visitors who come to Suomussalmi to study the "ecovillages" have created a tourist industry. "When we started," Kauko remembers, "we were afraid these villages would die. Now we see they are healthy and thriving. We are eagerly planning for the future with great hope."

279

Applying the Lesson Have students list as many facts as possible explaining why the welfare state is popular in Scandinavia.

3 CLOSE

Summarizing Students have learned that Scandinavian citizens are well-served by the welfare programs of the three constitutional monarchies and two republics that exist in Scandinavia today. Have students discuss whether they would rather live in the United States or in a welfare state. Have them give reasons for their answers.

Evaluating Use these questions to assess students' understanding.

- **What are the differences between monarchies and republics in Scandinavia?** (Monarchies have prime ministers as heads of government, and powerless monarchs. Republics have prime ministers and presidents.)
- **What types of programs do welfare states offer?** (health care, pension, housing, child care, and unemployment insurance programs)

Answers to Check Your Reading

1. Everyone had to switch from driving on the left to driving on the right side of the road to help reduce traffic accidents.
2. a special officer who receives citizens' complaints and tries to get the government to make changes to improve things
3. Citizens pay high taxes so that their governments can ensure their well-being through many social programs.
4. very much in favor of them

Independent Practice
Practice Book: page 75

BUILDING CITIZENSHIP

Ecological Development Help students to understand ecological development. Ask students why Kauko developed this program and how the people in his community benefited from it. Have students discuss how people from other countries also benefited from Kauko's program. Help students to name industries that developed because of the desire to save the environment, such as solar energy and recycling industries. Have students think of ways an industry in their area could be developed without harming the environment.

SKILLS LESSON
pages 280–281

Lesson Theme Determining point of view involves identifying how a writer or speaker views or feels about a subject or issue.

Lesson Objective
- Explain and apply a procedure for determining point of view.

 PREPARE

Motivate Before students read the introductory paragraphs, ask them to recall a time when they saw a movie, read a book, or bought a CD that a friend recommended but they did not like. Point out that the friend's opinion and their opinion reflect different points of view about something. Have students read the introductory paragraphs. Discuss with students why it is important to recognize how a writer or speaker views something. (When you recognize a writer's or speaker's point of view, you are better able to evaluate the accuracy of the information presented.)

Set Purpose Tell students that in this lesson they will learn a strategy for determining point of view.

 TEACH

Trying the Skill Have students read the report about education in one of the Scandinavian countries and answer the questions that follow. Tell students to refer to the *Helping Yourself* section on the next page if they need assistance.

RESOURCE Reminder
Practice Book: *Recognizing Point of View*, page 76

Determining Point of View

Key Vocabulary
point of view

Last winter Karen thought rabbits were adorable, furry little animals. This summer Karen thinks rabbits are nasty, greedy pests. Karen changed her thinking because rabbits have eaten most of the vegetables she planted in her garden. She now has a different **point of view**. Point of view is the way a person looks at or feels about something.

It is important to determine people's point of view when they are speaking or writing. How a person feels about a subject often affects the accuracy of what he or she says. Someone who had an unhappy time at camp, for example, might tell you that going to camp is boring. You might really enjoy camp, but if you believe this camper's stories you might never go.

Trying the Skill
Read the following passage about education in one of the Scandinavian countries. As you read, think about how the writer feels about the subject.

> The most striking feature of Finnish education is the emphasis on learning foreign languages. In Finland all students must learn two foreign languages. Third-graders begin to study English, Russian, German, or French. Students begin to study a second foreign language in seventh grade.
>
> I believe the study of languages is just as important as the study of science or math. The world is growing smaller because of improved transportation and communication techniques. American schools should require all students to learn two foreign languages.

1. What is the writer's point of view about the study of foreign languages?
2. How did you determine the writer's point of view?

 **BUILDING CITIZENSHIP**

Looking for Point of View Have students look through current newspapers and magazines and select a review of a book, concert, movie, show, or television program. Have students describe the point of view of the reviewer and underline words in the review that are clues to the reviewer's feelings or beliefs.

HELPING YOURSELF

The steps on the left will help you to determine a writer's or speaker's point of view. The example on the right shows one way to apply these steps to the passage on Finnish education.

One Way to Determine Point of View	Example
1. Identify the subject or topic.	Foreign language study in Finland.
2. Identify statements of fact.	Students study English, Russian, German, or French in third grade and a second foreign language in seventh grade.
3. Identify value judgments and reasoned opinions.	Look for clues to how the writer feels or what the writer believes. For example, *I believe*, *just as important*, and *should* in the second paragraph.
4. Look for any biases the writer or speaker has. Identify information that was left out but could have been included, loaded words, and exaggerations.	Finns need to learn other languages because Finnish is not spoken in other countries. English, however, is spoken in many different countries. The writer states only one view about learning languages.
5. Describe the point of view from which the author writes. What is the writer for or against?	The author's point of view is that studying foreign languages is as important for Americans as it is for Finns.

Applying the Skill

Read the following passage describing one person's view of sports. Look for clues that will help you to determine the writer's point of view.

In the United States there are many professional sports teams. People go to football or baseball games or watch them on TV. In Norway we don't have any professional teams. We love sports of all kinds, but we like to "do it ourselves." We prefer to exercise and to have a good time playing sports rather than to watch others play. Winning is not the important thing. It's having a healthy body and enjoying some exercise.

1. Which is a statement of fact?
   - **a.** In Norway we don't have any professional teams.
   - **b.** Winning is not the important thing.
   - **c.** We prefer to exercise and have a good time playing sports rather than to watch others play.
2. What information is left out?
   - **a.** Americans enjoy playing sports.
   - **b.** There are professional teams in America.
   - **c.** Sports are very popular in Norway.
3. Which of the following do you think the writer would most enjoy: attending a soccer game or going skiing?

Reviewing the Skill

1. What does *point of view* mean?
2. Which five steps can you follow to recognize a person's point of view?
3. Where, outside of school, would it be useful to try to determine the point of view of a writer or a speaker?

281

Thinking About Thinking Ask several students to read their answers aloud. Guide students' responses to question 2 by asking: What did you do first? Why? What did you do next? Why? And so on. Record the steps cited in lists on the chalkboard.

Helping Yourself Compare students' lists to this section that presents a step-by-step procedure to which students can refer whenever they need help determining point of view. Have students identify the steps they consider the most useful.

Applying the Skill Tell students that they will now apply their skill in determining a writer's point of view. Have them read the passage about sports and answer the questions that follow it. (See answers below.) Help them to understand the process they used by having them complete a chart drawn on the chalkboard with these headings: "Subject," "Facts," "Words that Express Feelings," "Opinions," and "Facts Left Out."

CLOSE

Reviewing the Skill Discuss Question 1 with students. Have students work in small groups to come up with synonyms for *fact (truth, reality), opinion (belief, feeling),* and *bias (one-sidedness, prejudice).* Have them use the synonyms to explain the steps they would use to determine point of view. Use Question 3 as a starting point for students to cite examples of situations in which they would use the skill.

Independent Practice
Practice Book: page 76

ANSWERS TO SKILLS QUESTIONS

Applying the Skill

1. a
2. a
3. The writer enjoys participating in sports much more than being a spectator. He or she would rather go skiing, as would most Norwegians, according to the writer.

Reviewing the Skill

1. Point of view is the way a person looks at or feels about something.
2. Identify the subject or topic. Identify statements of fact. Identify statements of reasoned opinion. Identify any biases the person has. Identify information that was left out but could have been included.
3. Anytime you hear or read information about which you will make a decision or form an opinion, you should use the skill. You can use the skill while listening to TV news, settling an argument, listening to a political debate, or making a purchase.

LESSON 4
pages 282–283

Lesson Theme The rugged land and the hardy people of Scandinavia are celebrated in Scandinavian arts and recreation.

Lesson Objectives

- Explain various forms of Scandinavian literature.
- Describe recreational activities of Scandinavia.

PREPARE

Motivate Have students close their eyes as you read the *Read Aloud* quotation to them. Ask students what they feel this scene tells about Scandinavia.

Set Purpose Discuss the *What You Know* question. Tell students that the answer to the *What You Will Learn* question can be found in the lesson.

TEACH

Discussing Scandinavian Literature Have volunteers discuss any Scandinavian literature and authors with which they are familiar. Discuss the differences between eddas, sagas, and folktales.

Ask students:

- **Who are modern-day Scandinavian storytellers and what kinds of things have they written?** (*Selma Lagerlöf*—updated Swedish folktales; *Henrik Ibsen*—wrote plays about modern human problems; *Sigrid Undset*—wrote about Norwegian history and modern life)
- *THINKING FURTHER:* **Why are eddas and sagas especially important?** (They help to preserve Scandinavian history.)

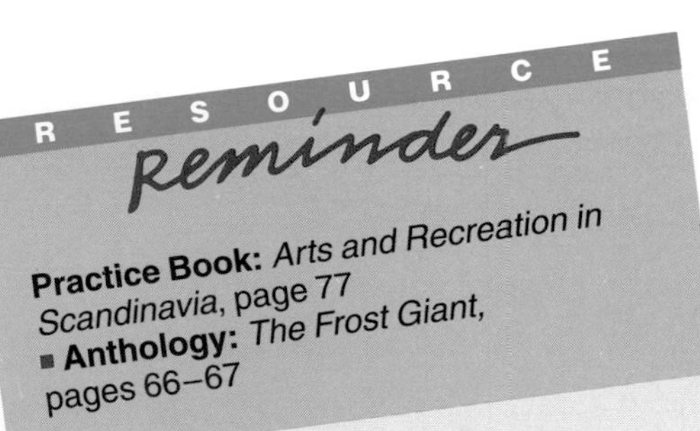

LESSON 4

Arts and Recreation

READ TO LEARN

Key Vocabulary

Edda
saga

Key People

Hans Christian Andersen
Selma Lagerlöf
Henrik Ibsen
Sigrid Undset

Read Aloud

The sea was all green to look at, and round there floated large icebergs. . . . She had seated herself on one of the largest, and all the ships made a wide circle in fear, away from the place where she was sitting and letting the wind set her long hair flying.

This was how the heroine of the story "The Little Mermaid" first saw the world above the ocean floor where she lived. In this tale by Hans Christian Andersen, the mermaid gave up her fish's tail and then her life to gain the love of a human prince. Today a bronze statue of the Little Mermaid sits on a rock in the harbor of Copenhagen, Denmark. Andersen's story, like so many other Scandinavian tales, celebrates the heroes and heroines of Scandinavia and the rugged land in which they live.

Read for Purpose

1. WHAT YOU KNOW: Which winter sports are popular in the United States?
2. WHAT YOU WILL LEARN: How do the arts and recreational activities of Scandinavia show the Scandinavians' love of their land and its people?

SCANDINAVIAN LITERATURE

Hans Christian Andersen is only one of many writers honored in Scandinavia. Scandinavian stories and poems date back hundreds of years. They describe many kinds of heroes—some larger than life, and some ordinary people.

The Vikings were among the earliest Scandinavian storytellers. They created long poems called **Eddas**. The Eddas tell stories about early Scandinavian gods, such as Woden, the chief god, and Thor, the god of thunder.

In Iceland a group of lengthy stories called **sagas** tell the history of that country. Most of the sagas tell about the deeds of kings and heroes. One saga tells how the explorer Leif Ericson reached North America in about the year 1000.

In the modern era Scandinavians have continued the storytelling tradition. **Selma Lagerlöf** (sel′ mä läg′ ər lôv) of Sweden updated the folktales she heard as a child. Other modern Scandinavian writers highlighted the daily lives of ordinary people. **Henrik Ibsen** of Norway wrote many plays

WHAT YOU KNOW: Possible responses include: skiing, skating, ice hockey.

READING STRATEGY AND VOCABULARY DEVELOPMENT

Monitoring Comprehension Review the *Thinking Skill* lesson on "Determining Point of View" on pages 280–281. Have students preview and then read Lesson 4, being careful to monitor their comprehension to focus on the different points of view expressed in the lesson. Tell students to make notes as they read. After they have finished reading, discuss the points of view that students found. Review with students how monitoring comprehension helped them to keep their minds on what they were looking for as they read.

Cross-country skiing is just one of the many popular outdoor sports of Scandinavia.

about the problems of contemporary people. Sigrid Undset (sig′ rē ůn′ set) of Norway wrote books that explored the history of her country as well as books that examined present-day life.

ENJOYING THE OUTDOORS

Scandinavians do not just write and tell stories about their land. They also explore the land themselves.

Many Scandinavians like being outdoors. Even the coldest of winters do not keep them inside. Many Scandinavians love to fish, sail, and hike. Even in the winter they fish through ice and swim outdoors in heated pools.

The favorite—and perhaps the oldest—winter sport in Scandinavia is skiing. Wooden skis about 6,000 years old have been found in Sweden and Finland.

Every year crowds of Scandinavians take to the ski slopes and fields just for fun. The largest cross-country ski meet in the world is held yearly in Dalarna, Sweden. There is even a ski meet in July at a glacier in western Norway.

People all over the world who exercise are grateful for a Finnish invention, the sauna (sô′ nə). A sauna is a kind of steam bath taken in a special wooden room. The steam cleans people's skin and relaxes their muscles.

A LOVE FOR THE LAND

Through their arts and recreational activities, Scandinavians celebrate their land and its people. Ancient works, such as the Eddas and sagas, and modern writings tell about the heroes, heroines, and ordinary people of these northern lands. When Scandinavians aren't reading about their countries, they are exploring them by skiing, sailing, swimming, hiking, and in many other ways.

Check Your Reading

1. What is the difference between an Edda and a saga?
2. What is the favorite winter sport in Scandinavia?
3. How do literature and the recreational activities of Scandinavia reflect a love for the land?
4. THINKING SKILL: Classify the people mentioned in this lesson into two or more groups. What do your groupings tell you about Scandinavians?

THINKING SKILL: Classifying

Talking About the Outdoors

Ask students:

- **Which winter activities of Scandinavians show their love of the land and the outdoors?** (ice fishing, ice boating, swimming outdoors in heated pools, skiing)
- **What special Finnish invention is enjoyed by Scandinavians and what is its purpose?** (the sauna; cleans the skin and relaxes the muscles)

Applying the Lesson Divide the class into six groups. Give each group one of the terms from *Key Vocabulary* or *Key People.* Have each group write a sentence using its word. Tell students that the sentence should show why the word is important in explaining the Scandinavians' love of their land and its people.

3 CLOSE

Summarizing Students have learned that Scandinavians shape their arts and recreational activities to honor their land and people. Discuss reasons that literature is important to Scandinavians.

Evaluating Use the *Check Your Reading* questions (answers given below) to assess students' understanding.

Answers to Check Your Reading

1. Eddas are Viking poems about early Scandinavian gods. Sagas are stories of the deeds of Icelandic kings and heroes.
2. skiing
3. Writings celebrate the land and its people. Recreational activities center on physical outdoor sports.
4. Possible answers include: writers and lovers of the outdoors; arts and recreation are important to them.

Independent Practice
Practice Book: page 77

MEETING INDIVIDUAL NEEDS

Reteaching (easy) Have students imagine that they are visiting Scandinavia in the winter. Have them write a letter to a friend in the United States describing winter sports that they have seen.

Extension (average) Have students try to write their own eddas, sagas, or folktales based on American history.

Enrichment (challenging) Give students the option of reading an edda or a saga. They should then present the story in a series of newspaper headlines to the rest of the class.

CHAPTER 13 REVIEW
pages 284–285

USING THE CHAPTER SUMMARY AND REVIEW

Cultural Geography These questions may be used for review.

- **What is challenging about the land and climate of Scandinavia?** (The land is rugged, mountainous, and mostly snow-covered, and the climate is cold.)
- **How do retail cooperatives help consumers save money?** (Items in stores are sold at the same prices that the stores paid to purchase them so that consumers are able to buy goods at low prices.)
- **Which two types of government do the countries of Scandinavia have?** (constitutional monarchy and republic)
- **What is the difference between a saga and an edda?** (An edda is a poem about early Scandinavian gods, and a saga is a long story about Scandinavia's history.)

Ideas to Remember

- **What do the people of Scandinavia have in common?** (similar languages and close-knit family traditions)
- **Which two things have helped the countries of Scandinavia develop a high standard of living?** (cooperation and planning)
- **What types of programs do welfare states provide for their citizens?** (health care, pensions, housing programs, unemployment insurance)
- **Which outdoor activities do the Scandinavians enjoy?** (fishing, sailing, hiking, skiing)

Answers to Reviewing Vocabulary

1. ombudsman
2. diversified economy
3. edda
4. cooperative
5. saga

CHAPTER 13 • SUMMARY

SCANDINAVIAN COUNTRIES: CULTURAL GEOGRAPHY

PEOPLE

- Peaceful, hard-working people live in or near small cities
- Challenges: cold climate and scarce resources
- Languages are very similar except in Finland
- Close-knit families typical in the area

ECONOMY

- Diversified economies produce a wide range of goods—autos, airplanes, furniture
- Cooperatives: workers organize together to produce and sell goods

- New resources being developed: petroleum, natural gas

GOVERNMENT

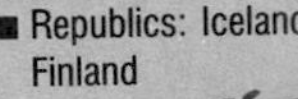

- Constitutional monarchies: Denmark, Sweden, Norway
- Republics: Iceland, Finland

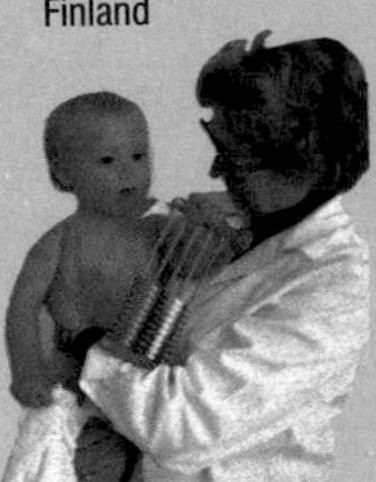

- Welfare states: many welfare programs, high taxes

ARTS AND RECREATION

- Rich storytelling tradition, from Viking poems, modern stories, and plays

- Popular outdoor activities: fishing, sailing, hiking, skiing

IDEAS TO REMEMBER

- The peaceful, hard-working Scandinavians are linked together by similar languages and close-knit family traditions.
- Cooperation and planning have been combined to make Scandinavia a region with a very high standard of living.
- The Scandinavian nations are run by efficient governments with far-reaching welfare programs.
- Scandinavians express their love for their land through their enjoyment of the outdoors.

284

ENRICHMENT ACTIVITY

Making Viking Arm-rings **Materials:** cardboard strips, paints, markers, pens, tape or stapler, illustrated books on Vikings

1. Review with students what they have learned about the Vikings in Chapters 10 and 13.
2. Tell students that Vikings often turned the gold and silver they took on their raids into beautifully crafted arm-rings. Explain that both men and women wore the arm-rings. For examples, refer students to the illustrations in books on Viking culture. Tell students that they will be designing and making their own arm-rings.
3. Have students draw their arm-ring designs on paper. Then have them color cardboard strips to appear either gold or silver. Next, have students draw or paint their final designs on the cardboard strips. Have students help each other to tape or staple their strips into rings to fit their arms.

CHAPTER 13 • REVIEW

REVIEWING VOCABULARY

cooperative
diversified economy
Edda
ombudsman
saga

Number a sheet of paper from 1 to 5. Beside each number write the word or term from the list above that best matches each definition.

1. A Swedish official who helps citizens to resolve problems involving governmental policies and actions
2. A type of economy that produces many different kinds of goods and services
3. A long poem that describes the deeds of Scandinavian gods and goddesses
4. A business organization owned and operated by its members
5. One of the group of long stories that tell the history of Iceland

REVIEWING FACTS

Number a sheet of paper from 1 to 10. Determine whether each statement is true or false. If the statement is true, write "true" next to the appropriate number. If the statement is false, rewrite it to make it true.

1. Scandinavian people live in a rugged land that has a cold climate.
2. People in Sweden and Finland speak the same language.
3. Stockholm, a typical Scandinavian capital, is overpopulated.
4. Family events and activities are especially important to Scandinavians.
5. Norway's most important industry is fishing.
6. Most Scandinavian countries have recently developed diversified economies.
7. The countries of Scandinavia cooperate and trade freely with one another.
8. The standard of living in Scandinavia is one of the lowest in the world.
9. The governments of Denmark, Norway, and Sweden are constitutional monarchies with royal families as well as elected representatives.
10. Taxes in Sweden are lower than in any other country.

WRITING ABOUT MAIN IDEAS

1. **Writing a List:** List five things you have read about Scandinavia that show that cooperation is an important principle among its people.
2. **Writing a Summary:** Reread the section in this chapter about H-Day in Sweden. Then write a summary of what happened on H-Day and why.
3. **Writing a Report:** Write a report about some aspect of Scandinavia. Topics might include a particular town, a group such as the people of Lapland, or a way of life such as that of the people who fish the waters near the Lofoten Islands.
4. **Writing About Perspectives:** Imagine that you lived in a Scandinavian country. Write a paragraph describing a day in the middle of winter, how you feel about having little sunlight, and what you do to deal with it.

BUILDING SKILLS: DETERMINING POINT OF VIEW

1. What is meant by the term *point of view*?
2. Name some steps you could take to determine an author's point of view.
3. Write a statement that expresses your point of view on a topic that interests you.
4. When would it be helpful to know how to identify an author's point of view?

285

Answers to Reviewing Facts

1. True.
2. The people in Finland speak a different language from that spoken in Sweden.
3. Stockholm, like other Scandinavian cities, is not overcrowded.
4.–7. True.
8. The standard of living in Scandinavia is one of the highest in Western Europe.
9. True.
10. Taxes in Sweden are the highest in the world.

Suggestions for Writing About Main Ideas

1. Possible answers include: agricultural cooperatives, retail cooperatives, trade cooperation among nations, helping family members, government and business leaders working together to develop the economy.
2. You may want to have students list the benefits and drawbacks that resulted from H-day.
3. Students might want to write the report from the point of view of an individual. For example, if writing about Lapland, they might write about a day in the life of a Lapland child as seen by that child.
4. Students' paragraphs should describe the effects long, dark winters might have on their daily moods.

Answers to Building Skills: Determining Point of View

1. the way a person looks at or feels about something
2. Identify the subject; identify the information included; identify words that are expressions of opinion.
3. Accept all reasonable answers.
4. How a person feels about a subject often affects the accuracy of what he or she says about it.

Chapter Review and Test

Practice Book: *Vocabulary Review,* page 78
Transparency: *Graphic Organizer*
Assessment Book: *Chapter 13 Test*

MAKING CONNECTIONS

Outlining Main Ideas Use the Outlining Chart Graphic Organizer Transparency, filling in the underlined main ideas from Lessons 1 and 2. Have students review the chapter, add the main ideas from Lessons 3 and 4 to the chart, and then fill in details to support each main idea. *Ask:* What is the main idea in this chapter?

Scandinavia

1. Unifying factors have helped the Scandinavians face many challenges. similar languages close-knit families	2. Diversified economies have created high living standards. fishing, farming, lumbering wide range of manufactured goods cooperation and planning
3. Representative democratic governments provide many services to citizens. welfare states with costly social programs highest taxes in the world	4. Arts and recreation honor the land and the people. tradition of storytelling from Eddas to modern times land explored by skiing, hiking, and other sports

UNIT 3 REVIEW
pages 286–287

USING THE UNIT SUMMARY AND REVIEW

Physical Geography These questions may be used for review.

- **What are the four peninsulas of the region?** (Scandinavian, Jutland, Italian, Balkan peninsulas)
- **How does the Gulf Stream affect the climate of the region?** (It brings warm waters that help to create mild climates in coastal areas.)
- **How much of the land in the region is suitable for farming?** (25 percent)

Cultural Geography

- **Who were the early inhabitants of the region?** (Celts, Gauls, Franks, Vikings, ancient Greeks and Romans)
- **What does the EU do?** (It links the countries of the region together.)
- **Which countries have constitutional monarchies?** (Great Britain, Low Countries, Spain, Denmark, Sweden, Norway)
- **In which area is storytelling an important tradition?** (Scandinavia)

Answers to Reviewing Vocabulary

1. True.
2. True.
3. A constitutional monarchy is a form of government in which a monarch's powers are limited by a constitution.

UNIT 3 • SUMMARY

WESTERN EUROPE: PHYSICAL GEOGRAPHY

LANDFORMS

- Peninsulas: Scandinavian, Jutland, Italian, Balkan

- Islands: British Isles, Greece, Corsica, Sardinia, Sicily
- Thousands of miles of coastline

CLIMATE

- Gulf Stream: brings warm waters that help create mild climate in coastal areas
- Northern part of the region: winters are long and cold
- Southern part: summers are sunny and dry, winters short and mild
- Ocean winds bring plenty of rainfall to most areas

NATURAL RESOURCES

- Forests: important resource, but few large ones are left
- Rich soil: about 25 percent of land is arable
- Many long inland rivers and waterways, such as Danube and Rhine

WESTERN EUROPE: CULTURAL GEOGRAPHY

PEOPLE

- Early peoples: Celts, Gauls, Franks, Vikings, ancient Greeks and Romans
- Language: ties some people together (such as French) and separates others (such as Flemings and Walloons in Belgium)
- Guest workers: come from Southern Europe to France, the Low Countries, and Central Europe
- Religion: mostly Christians (Roman Catholic, Protestant, Greek Orthodox)

ECONOMY

- Mixed economies common: private enterprise and government-run businesses
- European Union: links many countries of the region together
- Highly developed economies with advanced technology industries in many parts of the region
- Services: tourism, banking and shipping are all important
- Pollution: has caused serious environmental problems

GOVERNMENT

- Each country in the region has some form of democracy
- Great Britain has a constitutional monarchy with parliamentary democracy; British form of democracy is widespread
- Other constitutional monarchies: Low Countries, Spain, Denmark, Sweden, Norway
- Welfare states: government takes great responsibility for well-being of citizens; common in Scandinavia

ARTS AND RECREATION

- Great Britain: great literary tradition

- France and the Low Countries: many famous painters
- Central Europe: many famous composers
- Southern Europe: rich cultural heritage
- Scandinavia: rich storytelling tradition

286

ENRICHMENT ACTIVITY

Making a Class Scrapbook **Materials:** construction paper, paste, cardboard, yarn, markers, magazines

1. Tell students that they are going to make a scrapbook about Unit 3. Divide the class into five groups and assign each group a chapter from the unit. Tell each group to discuss topics to be included for their chapter. Suggest that students skim the chapter in their books for ideas.
2. For artwork have students draw some entries or use existing photographs and pictures from magazines and travel brochures. Have students write a caption for each entry. Tell each group to design an introductory page for its chapter.
3. When each group has finished with its chapter, assemble a book by binding all the chapters together. Have several students make a cover for the book and leave it on display for everyone to share.

UNIT 3 • REVIEW

REVIEWING VOCABULARY

Each of the following statements contains an underlined vocabulary word or term. Number a sheet of paper from 1 to 10. Beside each number write whether the statement is true or false. If it is false, rewrite it to make it true.

1. A neutral country is one that refuses to take sides in international disputes.
2. Fjords are long, narrow inlets of the sea, bordered by steep cliffs.
3. A constitutional monarchy is a form of government in which a monarch is given absolute power by a constitution.
4. Groups striving for autonomy seek stronger political ties with the national governments of their countries.
5. The Swiss canton is one of the most democratic political units in the world.
6. A diversified economy depends on only one or two industries to provide jobs and consumer goods.
7. Terrorism is the use or threat of violence to frighten people.
8. People who live in a welfare state receive little assistance from the government while they are sick or unemployed.
9. The coalition governments of Italy have generally tended to be unstable.
10. The French premier, elected by the people, makes defense and foreign affairs decisions.

WRITING ABOUT THE UNIT

1. **Writing an Essay:** The following events or movements that took place in Europe had enormous impact on the world: the Renaissance, the Industrial Revolution, communism, World War I, and World War II. Choose one of these events or movements and write an essay describing how it affected world history.
2. **Writing About Perspectives:** You have read about the diverse regions of Western Europe. Yet there is also much that unites the regions of Western Europe. Imagine that you are a citizen of Iceland. Write a paragraph describing ideas and attitudes that would link you to other Europeans.

ACTIVITIES

1. **Writing a Report:** Use magazines and newspapers to find an article that interests you about a country in Western Europe. Summarize the article in an oral report to the rest of the class.
2. **Working Together to Make a Bar Graph:** Use an almanac to find the population densities (average number of persons per square mile or square kilometer) for ten countries of Western Europe. Then make a bar graph to show the relative population densities of the countries.

LINKING PAST, PRESENT, AND FUTURE

For centuries the countries of Europe have shared common interests. Today some Europeans believe that these shared interests will be unified under a political group—the United States of Europe. Do you agree with this prediction? Do you believe such a union would have positive or negative consequences? Explain your answer.

4. Groups striving for autonomy want the right to self-government rather than complete control by the national governments of their countries.
5. True.
6. Diversified economies produce a wide range of goods.
7. True.
8. Welfare states ensure the well-being of their citizens through a variety of government programs, especially during periods in which citizens are sick or unemployed.
9. True.
10. The French premier, named by the president, heads the day-to-day activities of the government.

Suggestions for Writing About the Unit

1. Stress to students that their essays should include an explanation of the event or movement that they are writing about.
2. Students' paragraphs should list the similarities between the people of various European nations.

Suggestions for Activities

1. Students can categorize their articles and then create a bulletin board display of the articles.
2. Tell students to use the most recent almanac they have in order to find up-to-date statistics. For comparison they can include the population densities for Canada and the United States.

Answers to Linking Past, Present, and Future Students should specify the consequences that such a union would have on the countries of Europe as well as on the rest of the world. You may want to divide the class into two groups. One group can focus on the positive consequences of such a union and the other group can focus on the negative consequences.

PERFORMANCE ASSESSMENT

Demonstrating Understanding Explain to students that they will prepare magazines about Western Europe. Have students choose one of the five regions they studied in this unit. Suggest that students share the articles and pictures they have collected. Then have each student write articles or captions for pictures that will be included in his or her own magazine. Have students make a table of contents and a cover for their magazines. Remind them of the standards that will be applied to their magazines, which were outlined in the Unit Opener on page 178. For additional performance assessment information, see page TM43 in the *Assessment Book.*

For the Portfolio: Include the magazines and summaries in students' portfolios along with your anecdotal record or observational checklist.

UNIT 4 ORGANIZER

EASTERN EUROPE AND NORTHERN ASIA text pages 288–349

UNIT THEME

The nations of Eastern Europe and Northern Asia share a vast region where widespread changes in governments and economies are taking place at a rapid pace.

UNIT RESOURCES

- Practice Book: pp. 79–94
- Anthology: Part 3
- Anthology Cassette
- Outline Maps: 2, 3, 23–25
- Transparency Maps: 1, 1A
- Unit 4 Poster
- Desk Maps
- Internet Project Handbook
- Geo Adventures Pad
- Pupil Edition on Cassette
- Transparency: Graphic Organizer
- **Technology:** *Adventures CD-ROM*
- Assessment Book, Chapter Tests: 14, 15, 16

Internet CONNECTION

The Home Page at **http://www.mmhschool.com** and the **Internet Project Handbook** contain on-line student activities related to this unit.

UNIT PLANNING GUIDE

CHAPTER	SUGGESTED PACING	THEMES
14 PHYSICAL GEOGRAPHY OF EASTERN EUROPE AND NORTHERN ASIA pages 292–303	4 days	The region of Eastern Europe and Northern Asia is one of vast plains, dense forests, mineral-rich lands, and mountain ranges that stretch lengthwise for thousands of miles.
15 RUSSIA AND ITS NEIGHBORS pages 304–329	7 days	The end of the Soviet Union and the subsequent creation of 15 new countries has caused enormous changes in the lives of the peoples who live in this region.
16 EASTERN EUROPE pages 330–347	6 days	After breaking free from years of Soviet domination, Eastern European nations have emerged with a strong sense of ethnic and nationalistic pride.

UNIT PROJECTS

Writing a Poem Ask students to find a Russian poem and determine its theme. Have them each write a poem on the same theme based on their own life experiences.

Oral Reports Tell each student to pick a place of interest in Eastern Europe or Northern Asia. Have students find out about the special physical and human characteristics of their chosen places and write speeches as if they were those places and these places could talk. The title of each speech should be: "Why I Am a Special Place in ______."

Cooperative Learning: Preparing a Puppet Show Have four groups of students prepare puppets, scenery, and dialogue for each of four puppet shows discussing changes in this region from the point of view of a family, a group of farmers, a group of factory workers, and members at a Communist party meeting.

Field Trip Take the class to a museum or shop that displays Slavic crafts such as nesting dolls, lacquer ware, or Ukrainian Easter eggs. Before the field trip, have students write questions they might have about Slavic crafts. Encourage them to find the answers to their questions on their trip and/or in the library.

BULLETIN BOARD IDEAS

Making Your Own Bulletin Board Have students design a bulletin board display titled "Peoples of Eastern Europe and Northern Asia." Pairs of students should do research and then create and label drawings of many of the region's ethnic groups and traditions. Help students connect their work to the appropriate place on a map with a push pin and some string. Have each pair of students contribute to a discussion about the cultural diversity of the region.

Using the Unit Poster As an alternative to the bulletin board activity, display the Unit 4 Poster, which shows an enlarged version of the Unit Opener globe on pages 288–289.

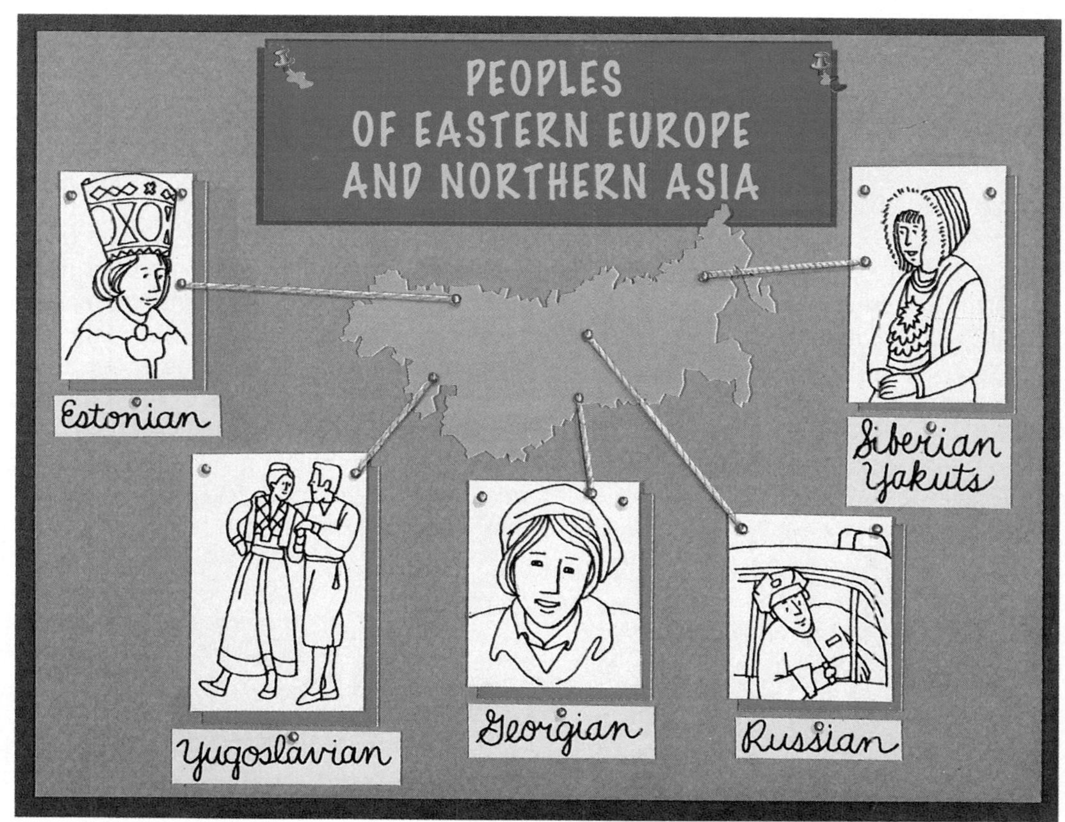

UNIT BIBLIOGRAPHY

For descriptions and additional resources, see the Annotated Bibliography beginning on page T-1 in the back of the book.

For the Teacher

Books

Harbor, Bernard. *The Conflict in Eastern Europe.* Columbus, OH: Silver Burdett Press, 1993.

Kort, Michael. *Russia: Nations in Transition.* New York: Facts On File, Inc., 1995.

Read-Alouds

Kuniczak, W. S. *The Glass Mountain: Twenty-six Ancient Polish Folk Tales and Fables.* New York: Hippocrene Books, 1992.

Philip, Neil. *Fairy Tales of Eastern Europe.* New York: Clarion Books, 1991.

Technology Multimedia

Czech Republic and Slovakia. Video. Society For Visual Education. Toll Free: 1-800-829-1900.

Moscow and Leningrad. Video. Knowledge Unlimited. Toll Free: 1-800-356-2303.

The Russian Federation: A Nation in Transition. Video. Society For Visual Education. Toll Free: 1-800-829-1900.

Free Materials

For information on Romania, send to: Romanian Cultural Center; 200 East 38 Street; New York, NY 10016.

For the Student

Bradley, John. *Russia: Building Democracy.* Austin, TX: Raintree Steck-Vaughn, 1996. **(Challenging)**

Buettner, Dan. *Sovietrek: A Journey By Bicycle Across Russia.* Minneapolis, MN: Lerner Publications Co., 1994. **(Average)**

Carran, Betty. *Romania.* Chicago, IL: Childrens Press, 1993. **(Average)**

Chicoine, Stephen, and Ashabranner, Brent. *Lithuania: The Nation That Would Be Free.* New York: Dutton Children's Books, 1995. **(Average)**

Filopovic, Zlata. *Zlata's Diary: A Child's Life in Sarajevo.* New York: Viking Press, 1994. **(Easy)**

Hintz, Martin. *Hungary.* Chicago, IL: Childrens Press, 1992. **(Average)**

Mayhew, James. *Koshka's Tales: Stories From Russia.* New York: Kingfisher Books, 1993. New York: Kingfisher Books, 1993. **(Average)**

Miller, Calvin Craig. *Boris Yeltsin: First President of Russia.* Greenboro, N.C.: Morgan Reynolds, Inc., 1994. **(Average)**

Strom, Yale. *A Tree Still Stands: Jewish Youth in Eastern Europe Today.* New York: Philomel Books, 1990. **(Average)**

Vnenchak, Dennis. *Lech Walesa and Poland.* New York: Franklin Watts, 1994. **(Challenging)**

UNIT 4
ORGANIZER

TEACHER EXCHANGE

Finding the Main Idea

Thanks to:
Carolyn Claiborne
South Middle School
Downey, California

Materials
drawing paper, colored pencils or crayons

Instructions
1. Have students try this activity to help them understand their reading.
2. After each student has chosen a portion of the text or other reading material, have students fold drawing paper into as many squares as there are paragraphs in their selections. Let students use as many pieces of paper as are necessary for the individual squares to be large enough for use in this activity.
3. Have students find the main idea of each paragraph and then write each main idea in a separate square of the folded paper.
4. Ask them to illustrate each main idea in the appropriate square.
5. Let students help each other find the main ideas. Then have each student share his or her work with the class.

Modeling a Cross Section of a Country

Thanks to:
Addie Alley
Beals Elementary School
Beals, Maine

Materials
plasticene in several colors, rulers, plastic wrap, large index cards, maps of Eastern Europe and Northern Asia that give elevations of landforms

Instructions
1. Tell students that they will make three-dimensional models of the cross section of an Eastern European or Northern Asian country.
2. Have each student use a map to choose a country and then decide upon a cross section to model. Ask each student to use a ruler to determine the exact cross section. Then on an index card write the geographic features, place names, landforms, scale, and lines of latitude and longitude found on or along the cross section.
3. Ask students to choose colors of plasticene to represent water, plains, mountains, and so on. Then have them make the plasticene pliable and shape the various landforms required for their cross sections.
4. Each student can then mount his or her cross section on plastic wrap and place it on the index card. Finally students should add color keys and titles.

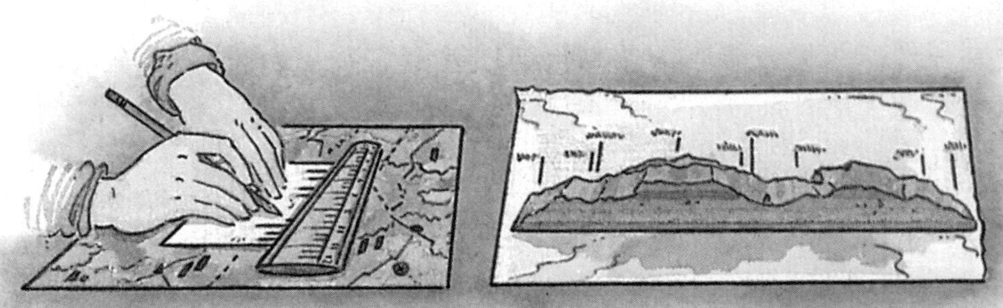

TECHNOLOGY CENTER

Enriching with Multimedia

RESOURCE: *Internet Project Handbook*

Look at the ***Internet Project Handbook*** for student projects related to this unit or have students go on-line at http://www.mmhschool.com, Macmillan/McGraw-Hill's Home School page on the World Wide Web.

RESOURCE: *Adventures CD-ROM*

Enrich Unit 4 with the *Build* and *Create* activities on the Adventures CD-ROM.

SCHOOL-TO-HOME

New Ideas and Recent Changes

- Throughout this unit, students will have the opportunity to learn about historic changes that have taken place in the countries of Eastern Europe and Northern Asia. Discuss with students the changes relating to government and the economy and their effects on countries or the region itself. Make students aware that this region is constantly changing, even today.
- Provide students with paper "bricks" cut from construction paper. Encourage students to work with their families to find clippings and photographs about one recent change in this region and to paste them on the bricks. Arrange the bricks in chronological order on a bulletin board to build a wall of change.

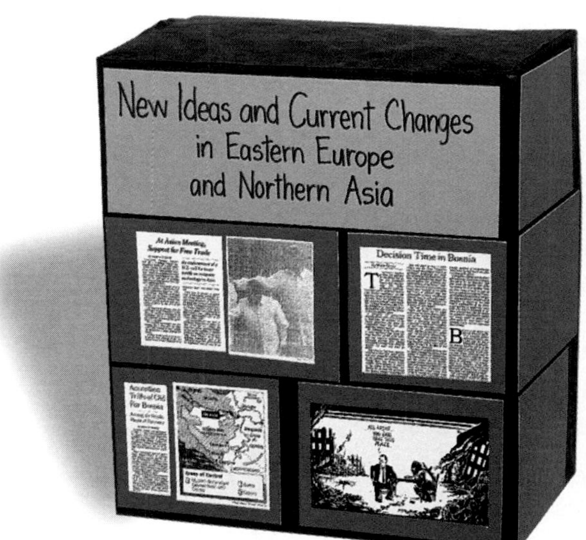

SECOND-LANGUAGE SUPPORT

While these activities are designed especially for students needing second-language support, they are meant to be shared by all students in the class.

Chapter 14, Lesson 2 ■ Physical Geography of Eastern Europe and Northern Asia

Previewing will help second-language students to better understand the material. Using the climate map on page 299, help students to identify climates and the region's two main climate zones.

Chapter 15, Lesson 3 ■ Russia and Its Neighbors

To aid comprehension after reading and discussing the lesson, have groups of students create a series of charts titled *Problems in Russia Before Communism, Problems with Communism in the Soviet Union,* and *Challenges Facing Russia and Its Neighbors Today.*

Chapter 16, Lesson 4 ■ Nations of Eastern Europe

Preview the lesson by discussing with students how nationalism can be expressed through arts and recreation. Play for students excerpts of music by Chopin, Dvorák, and Bartok and elicit reactions. Have students brainstorm ways that nationalism might also influence artists, writers, and athletes.

Chapter 16, Lesson 4

UNIT 4

pages 288–349

USING THE UNIT OPENER

Introducing the Unit Have students look at the unit title and read the *Where We Are* section on the facing page. Ask them to turn to the Table of Contents and read the chapter and lesson titles for this unit.

Ask students:

- **Which subjects are covered in this unit?** (From the Table of Contents and the *Where We Are* section, students should be able to give a complete outline of the topics covered in Unit 4.)
- **What is the main physical difference between this region and Western Europe?** (Western Europe is the smallest world region; Eastern Europe and Northern Asia is one of the largest, and it straddles two continents.)
- **Which two continents does this region straddle?** (Europe, Asia)
- **What is the largest country in this region?** (Russia)

EXTENDING MAP SKILLS

Make sure that students understand where the two continents of Europe and Asia are located. They should be able to locate the Ural Mountains as the dividing line between those two continents.

Ask students:

- **What is the area that extends across the dark purple area and includes part of the light purple up to the Ural Mountains called?** (Eastern Europe)
- **What is the area from the Ural Mountains west called?** (Northern Asia)
- **What nation straddles both areas?** (Russia)

ONGOING UNIT PROJECT

Planning for Assessment Tell students that in this unit they will be learning about Eastern Europe and Northern Asia. Explain that when they finish the unit, they will write a travel diary about an imaginary trip through this region. They will also draw the route of their trip on a map. Throughout the unit students should take notes to help them describe people and places along the way. For information on completing this unit project, see page 349.

Goal: Students' work should show an understanding of the physical and cultural geography of this region as well as the sweeping changes that are taking place there.

Signs of Success: Explain to students that an adequate travel diary should describe three or four places visited. An excellent travel diary would also provide a description of current political or cultural events.

HY • GEOGRAPHY • GEOGRAPHY • GEOGRAPHY • GEOGRAPHY • GEOGRAPHY • GEOGRA

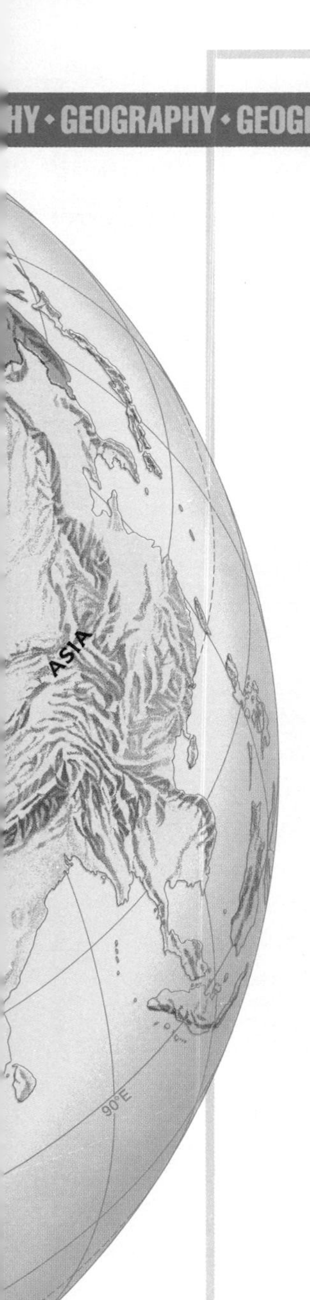

EASTERN EUROPE AND NORTHERN ASIA

WHERE WE ARE

In Unit 3 you read about tremendous changes that have taken place in Germany. The same forces that brought about the reunification of Germany have brought even greater changes to the region we call Eastern Europe and Northern Asia. The huge country known as the Soviet Union ceased to exist at the end of 1991. In its place there are now 15 independent countries. Seven other countries in this region were not part of the Soviet Union but were strongly influenced by Soviet policies.

The first chapter of this unit describes the region's physical geography. Chapter 15 discusses the countries that were once part of the Soviet Union. The map on these pages shows that area in light purple. The following chapter refers to the countries of Eastern Europe that were not part of the Soviet Union. The map shows that area in darker purple. You are about to read about a region of the world that is changing rapidly.

289

Continue the discussion.

Ask students:

- **What are the names of the seas that border this region?** (Baltic, Barents, Caspian, Black, Mediterranean)
- **Which ocean does not touch this region?** (Indian)
- *THINKING FURTHER:* **Which ocean seems to be the gateway to Russia? Why isn't it?** (the Arctic Ocean, which forms Russia's northern border; students should recall from their study of Canada that Arctic waters are frozen much of the year.)

Comparing Map Perspectives
Have students compare this map with the global maps at the beginning of the earlier units in this book. Tell them to look, in order, at the maps in Unit 1 (pages 34 and 35), Unit 2 (pages 100 and 101), and Unit 3 (pages 178 and 179). Ask them to explain how the map perspective changes from Unit 1 to Unit 4. (Students should be able to express ideas about the changing perspective of these global views and recognize that the globe is "turning" through this series of maps as we move from regions in the west to regions in the east.)

Discussing the Soviet Union Point out to the class that all of this region but the seven nations in the east were once part of the gigantic Soviet Union. Be sure that they recognize that this great monolith has now broken into 15 separate countries.

CURRICULUM CONNECTIONS

Language Arts Tell students that a mnemonic is a verbal device that uses the first letters of words in a saying as an aid for remembering a list of other words. Divide the class into groups and have students work on mnemonics to remember the names of the twelve countries in Eastern Europe: Albania, Bulgaria, the Czech Republic, Slovakia, Hungary, Poland, Romania, Yugoslavia, Slovenia, Croatia, Bosnia and Herzegovina, and Macedonia. Give this example: "*H*igh *Y*early *M*arks *C*ome *B*y *S*tudents *R*egularly *C*hecking *B*oth *S*pelling *A*nd *P*unctuation." Have groups trade mnemonics to see how well they work in helping students remember the list of countries.

Music Ask students if they know any Russian or Eastern European songs. (They may know the "Volga Boat Song" or the "Hungarian rhapsodies.") Explain that the "Volga Boat Song" was a song that boat haulers sang as they dragged boats upstream along the Volga riverbank. On every third beat or word all the haulers would pull together. Point out to students that it is in the key of A minor, which is a sad key.

Introducing the Table Explain to students that until the end of 1991 these pages would have contained only eight country tables. Ask them why they think the number of countries in the region has multiplied so much. (the breakup of the former Soviet Union into 15 separate countries)

EXTENDING TABLE SKILLS

Have students identify the countries in this table that were not once part of the Soviet Union—those that appear in darker purple on page 288: Albania, Bulgaria, the Czech Republic, Hungary, Poland, Romania, Slovakia, Yugoslavia, Slovenia, Croatia, Bosnia and Herzegovina, and Macedonia.

Ask students:

- **How many countries are in this region?** (27)
- **How many major languages are spoken in this region?** (27)
- **Which language is spoken in the largest number of countries?** (Russian)
- **Which is the largest of these countries in area?** (Russia) **The smallest?** (Slovenia)
- **What is the most common leading export?** (machinery)
- **What does this reveal about the level of industrialization of these nations?** (They produce a great many capital goods. This shows a developed industrial economic pattern.)

LIFE TODAY • LIFE TODAY • LIFE TODAY • LIFE TODAY

EASTERN EUROPE AND NORTHERN ASIA

ALBANIA
Capital ★ Tiranë
Major language: Albanian
Population: 3.4 million
Area: 11,100 sq mi; 28,750 sq km
Leading export: minerals

ARMENIA
Capital ★ Yerevan
Major language: Armenian
Population: 3.5 million
Area: 11,490 sq mi; 29,800 sq km
Leading exports: electronic parts and food items

AZERBAIJAN
Capital ★ Baku
Major languages: Azerbaijani, Russian, and Armenian
Population: 7.7 million
Area: 33,430 sq mi; 86,600 sq km
Leading exports: oil and textiles

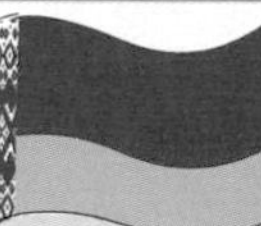

BELARUS
Capital ★ Minsk
Major languages: Belarusian and Russian
Population: 10.4 million
Area: 80,134 sq mi; 207,800 sq km
Leading exports: tractors and chemicals

BOSNIA AND HERZEGOVINA
Capital ★ Sarajevo
Major language: Serbo-Croatian
Population: 4.6 million
Area: 19,741 sq mi; 51,129 sq km

BULGARIA
Capital ★ Sofia
Major languages: Bulgarian and Turkish
Population: 8.8 million
Area: 42,822 sq mi; 110,910 sq km
Leading export: machinery

CROATIA
Capital ★ Zagreb
Major language: Croatian
Population: 4.7 million
Area: 21,829 sq mi; 56,538 sq km
Leading export: machinery

CZECH REPUBLIC
Capital ★ Prague
Major languages: Czech and Slovak
Population: 10.4 million
Area: 30,450 sq mi; 78,864 sq km
Leading exports: glassware, textiles, and machinery

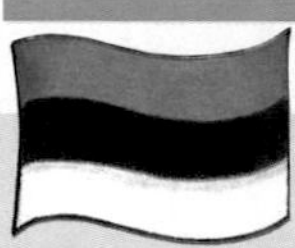

ESTONIA
Capital ★ Tallinn
Major languages: Estonian and Russian
Population: 1.6 million
Area: 17,413 sq mi; 45,100 sq km
Leading exports: agricultural and wood products and textiles

GEORGIA
Capital ★ Tbilisi
Major languages: Georgian and Russian
Population: 5.7 million
Area: 26,900 sq mi; 69,700 sq km
Leading exports: agricultural products and machinery

HUNGARY
Capital ★ Budapest
Major language: Hungarian
Population: 10.3 million
Area: 35,919 sq mi; 93,030 sq km
Leading exports: raw materials and chemicals

KAZAKHSTAN
Capital ★ Alma-Ata
Major languages: Kazakh and Russian
Population: 17.3 million
Area: 1,049,155 sq mi; 2,717,300 sq km
Leading exports: oil and food products

KYRGYZSTAN
Capital ★ Bishkek
Major languages: Kyrgyz, Russian, and Uzbek
Population: 4.7 million
Area: 76,640 sq mi; 198,500 sq km
Leading exports: metals and agricultural products

290

5 FUNDAMENTAL THEMES OF GEOGRAPHY

Movement The Danube River is the second longest waterway in Eastern Europe, after the Volga River. Its source is in the Black Forest of Germany, and it flows from west to east across Eastern Europe into the Black Sea.

- People have traveled on the Danube River for thousands of years bringing goods and ideas with them to the different countries through which the Danube flows.
- Its upper course runs from its source to Vienna, the capital of Austria.
- Its middle course runs from Vienna through Hungary to the borders of Yugoslavia and Romania.
- The lower course flows across the plain of Romania and Bulgaria.

LATVIA
Capital ★ Riga
Major languages: Latvian and Russian
Population: 2.7 million
Area: 24,595 sq mi; 63,700 sq km
Leading exports: metals and agricultural products

SLOVAKIA
Capital ★ Bratislava
Major languages: Slovak, Czech, and Hungarian
Population: 5.4 million
Area: 18,932 sq mi; 49,035 sq km
Leading exports: consumer goods, industrial products, and chemicals

LITHUANIA
Capital ★ Vilnius
Major languages: Lithuanian and Russian
Population: 3.8 million
Area: 25,170 sq mi; 65,200 sq km
Leading exports: machinery, food, and chemicals

SLOVENIA
Capital ★ Ljubljana
Major language: Slovenian
Population: 2.0 million
Area: 7,819 sq mi; 20,251 sq km
Leading exports: manufactured goods and aluminum

MACEDONIA
Capital ★ Skopje
Major language: Macedonian
Population: 2.2 million
Area: 9,928 sq mi; 25,713 sq km
Leading exports: manufactured goods and machinery

TAJIKISTAN
Capital ★ Dushanbe
Major languages: Tajik and Russian
Population: 6.0 million
Area: 55,240 sq mi; 143,100 sq km
Leading exports: aluminum and textiles

MOLDOVA
Capital ★ Kishinev
Major languages: Moldovan, Gagauz, and Russian
Population: 4.5 million
Area: 13,000 sq mi; 33,700 sq km
Leading exports: wine, fur, and clothing

TURKMENISTAN
Capital ★ Ashgabat
Major languages: Turkmen and Russian
Population: 4.0 million
Area: 186,400 sq mi; 488,100 sq km
Leading exports: gas, oil, and cotton

POLAND
Capital ★ Warsaw
Major language: Polish
Population: 38.2 million
Area: 120,726 sq mi; 312,680 sq km
Leading export: machinery

UKRAINE
Capital ★ Kiev
Major languages: Ukrainian and Russian
Population: 51.8 million
Area: 231,990 sq mi; 445,000 sq km
Leading exports: wheat, beets, and coal

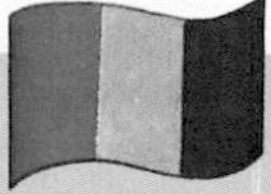

ROMANIA
Capital ★ Bucharest
Major language: Romanian
Population: 23.2 million
Area: 91,699 sq mi; 237,500 sq km
Leading exports: metals and machinery

UZBEKISTAN
Capital ★ Tashkent
Major languages: Uzbek and Russian
Population: 22.6 million
Area: 172,741 sq mi; 447,400 sq km
Leading export: cotton

RUSSIA
Capital ★ Moscow
Major language: Russian
Population: 149.6 million
Area: 6,592,813 sq mi; 17,075,000 sq km
Leading exports: raw materials and consumer goods

YUGOSLAVIA
Capital ★ Belgrade
Major languages: Serbo-Croatian, Slovene, and Macedonian
Population: 10.8 million
Area: 39,448 sq mi; 102,173 sq km
Leading export: machinery, food products, and textiles

Comparing Countries Converting the numbers in a table into written statements is an important step and skill in the practical use of a table. Help students to understand this vital connecting step in working with tables. Ask students to study the table on Eastern Europe and Northern Asia. Tell them to write at least two sentences about each of the types of information in the table and about the flags pictured in the table. Caution them that these sentences should sum up or compare and contrast all the information in one category; they should not focus upon only one country. Tell students that this collection of descriptive and comparative sentences, based on the information in the table, could be titled, "A Dynamic Geography of Eastern Europe and Northern Asia." (Possible statements include: "The languages of the region reflect the wide variety of ethnic groups there"; "Each country has its own unique language or languages"; "The smallest Eastern European country by area is Albania, and the largest is Russia"; and so on.)

BUILDING CITIZENSHIP

Current Events and Change Flags express a nation's idea of its identity. After the Soviet Union collapsed, most of its former republics continued to use pre-Soviet or republic flags for a while. But many began to design new flags. In 1991, first Croatia and then other republics of Yugoslavia declared their independence. Each of these has its own flag. Just as some groups want to separate from a larger political group, others want to unite. For example Moldova and Romania share a language. Some citizens of each have expressed a desire for union. The flags on this page reflect the geopolitical realities of Eastern Europe and Northern Asia in 1996. Encourage your students to do research on current flags and to use an outline map to draw the current borders of this region. Display their work on the bulletin board.

CHAPTER 14 ORGANIZER

PHYSICAL GEOGRAPHY OF EASTERN EUROPE AND NORTHERN ASIA text pages 292–303

CHAPTER THEME The region of Eastern Europe and Northern Asia is one of vast plains, dense forests, mineral-rich lands, and mountain ranges that stretch lengthwise for thousands of miles.

CHAPTER OBJECTIVES

CONTENT

- Describe the main physical features of Eastern Europe and Northern Asia.
- Identify Siberia and name the mountain range that separates Siberia from Eastern Europe.
- Explain why only a small percentage of the Russian people lives in Siberia.
- Explain why the Volga and Danube rivers are important to this region.
- Describe the major climates and natural resources of this region.
- Define *taiga* and *steppes* and list the key characteristics of these regions.
- Identify the countries of Central Asia and explain this region's historical importance.
- Contrast the amount of mineral reserves in Eastern Europe and countries of the former Soviet Union.

SKILLS

Geography
- Interpret an elevation map of Eastern Europe and Northern Asia.
- Compare the climate of Moscow with those of major cities in Eastern Europe and Northern Asia using a map.
- Analyze land use in Eastern Europe and Northern Asia using a map.

Study and Research
- Interpret climographs.

Thinking
- Ask focused questions about why people are exiled to Siberia.

Reading and Writing
- Write a letter describing this region's vastness, its diverse geography and climate.

CITIZENSHIP VALUES

- Appreciate the contributions of outstanding individuals to society.

TEACHER OPTIONS

READING STRATEGY: Question/Answer Relationships Strategies to help students read and remember the main ideas of the lesson.
Lesson 1: p. 293 Lesson 2: p. 298

MEETING INDIVIDUAL NEEDS Activities for reteaching, extension, and enrichment.
Lesson 1: p. 297 Study and Research
Lesson 2: p. 300 Skills: p. 301

GEO ADVENTURES ACTIVITIES PAD Daily activities to assess students' understanding of geography skills.

CURRICULUM CONNECTION Activities to help integrate other subject areas with Social Studies.
Science: p. 295 Math: p. 299
Language Arts: p. 295

PUPIL EDITION ON CASSETTE Language support for students who have difficulty reading or who will benefit from listening to the Pupil Edition on Cassette as they read.

SECOND-LANGUAGE SUPPORT Activities and suggestions for second-language learners.
Lesson 2: p. 26

CHAPTER PLANNING GUIDE

LESSON	SUGGESTED PACING	THEMES	TEACHER SUPPORT MATERIALS: TEACHER'S RESOURCE CENTER
1 LANDFORMS pages 293–297	1 day	The vast plains and difficult terrain that characterize Eastern Europe and Northern Asia make travel in this region difficult.	Practice Book p. 79 Outline Map p. 23 **Technology:** *Adventures CD-ROM*
2 CLIMATE AND RESOURCES pages 298–300	1 day	Temperate and cold climates dominate the rich farmlands and forests of Eastern Europe and Northern Asia.	Practice Book p. 80 Outline Map p. 23 **Technology:** *Adventures CD-ROM*
BUILDING STUDY AND RESEARCH SKILLS Reading Climographs page 301	1 day	A climograph shows the temperature and precipitation of a place over a period of time.	Practice Book p. 81
CHAPTER SUMMARY AND REVIEW pages 302–303	1 day	Chapter content, skills, and vocabulary are reviewed and evaluated.	Practice Book p. 82 Transparency: Graphic Organizer Assessment Book, Chapter 14 Test

Technology CONNECTION

Lesson 1
ADVENTURES CD-ROM
Explore the country maps and the continent maps of Asia and Europe.

Lesson 2
ADVENTURES CD-ROM
Have students *Investigate* climographs for a country of their choice under *Charts.*

CHAPTER 14

pages 292–303

USING THE CHAPTER OPENER

Discussing the Photograph Read the chapter title and point out to students the wintry beauty of the Russian landscape that they see in this photograph.

Ask students:

- **What do you think this photograph shows?** (Possible answers include: a Russian agricultural worker driving his wagon through a dense forest; that an old-fashioned way of life still exists in the rural areas of Russia; that winter is hard and long in Russia.)
- **What does the thickly wooded area tell you?** (Possible answers include: Russia contains many forests and that forests might be a valuable natural resource of the Eastern Europe and Northern Asia region.)

Reading/Listening to the Primary Source Have students continue to examine the photograph as you read the quotation and the passage to them.

Ask students:

- **Does this poem describe a harsh or a gentle landscape? Explain your answer.** (harsh; It refers to the cold, the wind, and the sea.)
- **Does the poet love his homeland without any misgivings? How do you know?** (No; he says his love is odd and without reason; it comes from his heart and not his head.)
- *THINKING FURTHER:* **Do you think it is possible for a person to love his or her country and still want to leave it? Why?** (Yes; to escape persecution or to seek a better economic life.)

Point out that the poem "My Country" was written in the early 1800s. Ask students if any of them have had ancestors who emigrated from Eastern Europe to the United States from the 1800s on. Have volunteers tell when and why their ancestors emigrated.

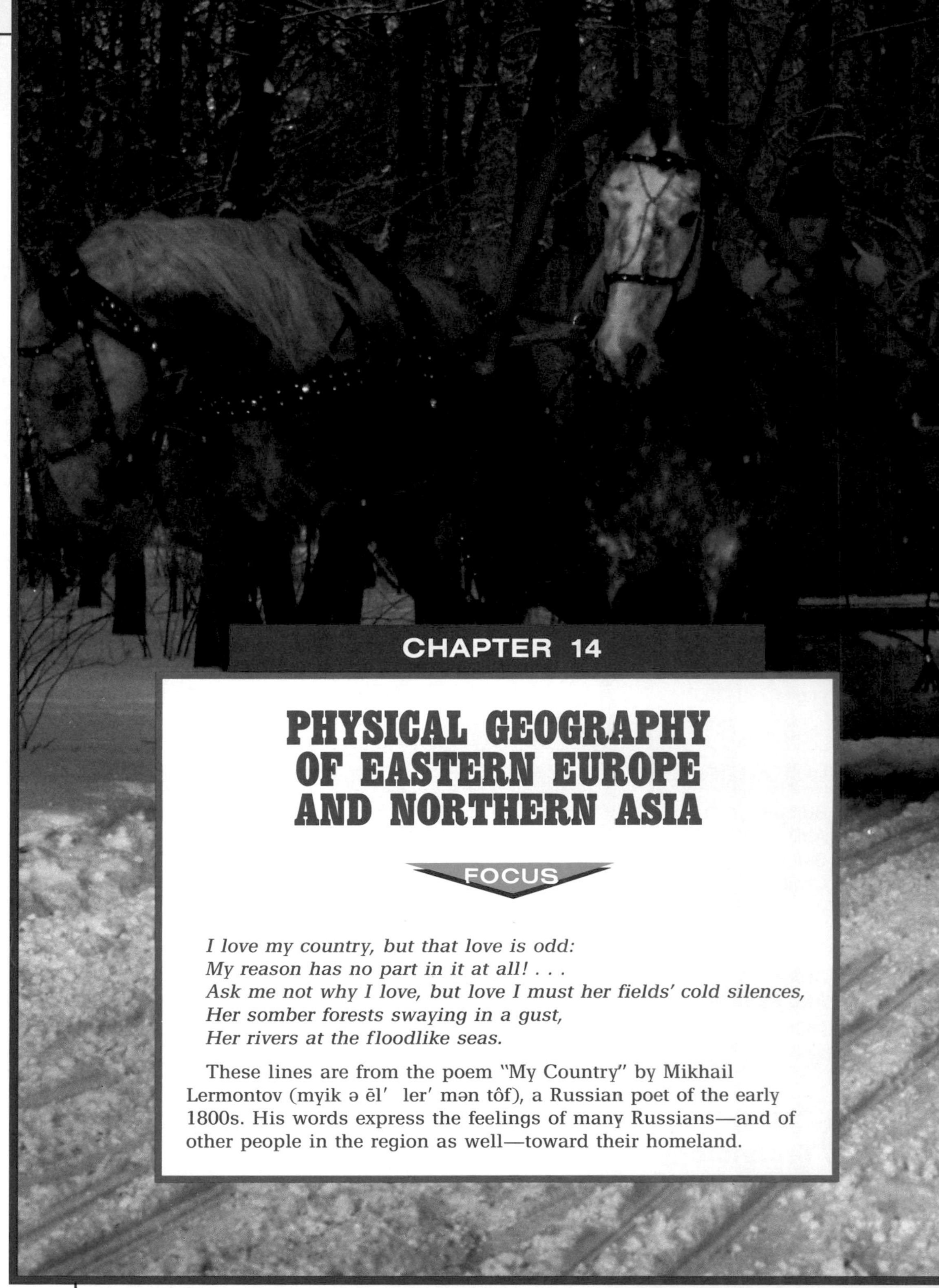

CHAPTER 14

PHYSICAL GEOGRAPHY OF EASTERN EUROPE AND NORTHERN ASIA

FOCUS

I love my country, but that love is odd:
My reason has no part in it at all! . . .
Ask me not why I love, but love I must her fields' cold silences,
Her somber forests swaying in a gust,
Her rivers at the floodlike seas.

These lines are from the poem "My Country" by Mikhail Lermontov (myik ə ēl′ ler′ mən tôf), a Russian poet of the early 1800s. His words express the feelings of many Russians—and of other people in the region as well—toward their homeland.

BACKGROUND INFORMATION

About the Photograph

- An immense zone of forest covers the northern half of Russia. The northern half of that zone contains a coniferous, or cone- bearing, forest called the taiga. The southern half has mixed forest.
- Trees of the taiga include pine, spruce, birch, and larch trees. The mixed forest contains elm, oak, maple, and ash trees.
- Among animals that inhabit the forests are moose, bear, lynx, sable, beaver, squirrel, and rabbit. The woodpecker and grouse are also common in the wooded areas.

Landforms

READ TO LEARN

Key Places

Eastern Europe, Northern Asia, Ural Mountains, Russia, Soviet Union, Caucasus Mountains, Siberia, Caspian Sea, Central Asia, Volga River, Danube River

Read Aloud

There is something solemn about crossing the [boundary] line the first time. Thousands of kilometers lie behind you. Ahead thousands of kilometers . . . stretch . . . endlessly before you. At a moment like this you have a physical sensation of your country's vastness.

This is how one journalist described the experience of crossing the Ural Mountains, which form the boundary line between the European and Asian parts of the region. The region is so vast that it spans two continents.

Read for Purpose

1. WHAT YOU KNOW: What is Eurasia?
2. WHAT YOU WILL LEARN: What are the main physical features of Eastern Europe and Northern Asia?

SPANNING TWO CONTINENTS

If you were to travel from east to west across the vast expanse that makes up the region of Eastern Europe and Northern Asia, you would cross more than half the world's time zones. When people in the eastern part of Northern Asia are waking up in the morning, people in the western part of Eastern Europe are eating their dinner or getting ready to go to sleep for the night.

As you read above, the Ural Mountains form the boundary between Europe and Asia. The Urals are not very high mountains. They rarely rise above 3,000 feet (900 m). Because they are so low, they never became a barrier for travelers.

MANY LANDFORMS AND CLIMATES

Cold, icy, forested—these words are often used to describe the land of Eastern Europe and Northern Asia. They are good descriptions because much of this region spans the northern part of the Eastern Hemisphere. A long northern coastline borders the frigid Arctic Ocean.

Dry and *dusty*—these words are also accurate descriptions because parts of the region reach as far south as 35°N latitude, which is the same latitude as northern Africa. In fact, almost any words you could think of to describe landforms and climates would fit some part of the region.

Russia, the largest country in the world, is spread over more than half the region.

WHAT YOU KNOW: the large landmass that includes Europe and Asia

LESSON 1
pages 293–297

Lesson Theme The vast plains and difficult terrain that characterize Eastern Europe and Northern Asia make travel in this region difficult.

Lesson Objectives
- Describe the landforms of Eastern Europe and Northern Asia.
- Describe the major rivers of the region.

PREPARE

Motivate Read the *Read Aloud* section to the class. Ask students if they have ever had a feeling like this about the spaciousness of a place.

Set Purpose Use the *What You Know* question to help students locate Europe and Asia on the world map in the Atlas. Have students predict answers to the *What You Will Learn* question after studying the wall map that shows the physical features of Eastern Europe and Northern Asia.

TEACH

Looking at Two Continents

Ask students:

- **What two continents does this region span?** (Europe and Asia)
- **How many of the world's time zones does it span?** (more than half of them)
- *THINKING FURTHER:* **What problems might arise for a country that crosses many time zones, like Russia?** (Students might mention communication and transportation problems.)

READING STRATEGY AND VOCABULARY DEVELOPMENT

Question/Answer Relationships Preview the lesson with students, directing their attention to the questions at the beginning and end of the lesson. Point out to them that it is important to know where to find answers to questions. Tell students that answers can come from a variety of sources. Answers can be directly stated in the text, they can be inferred from reading the text and then putting ideas together, or the answers may not be stated but instead may be based on the students' knowledge or personal experience. Help students identify the source of the answers to the questions in this lesson. For example, the answer to the *What You Know* question will come from students' prior knowledge.

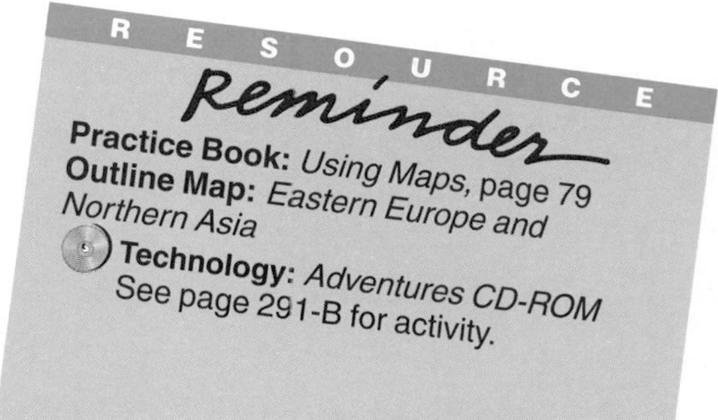
RESOURCE *Reminder*

Practice Book: *Using Maps, page 79*

Outline Map: *Eastern Europe and Northern Asia*

Technology: *Adventures CD-ROM* See page 291-B for activity.

Examining Landforms and Climates

Help students to realize that landforms and climates vary in this region.

Ask students:

- **Why is this region often described as being cold and icy? Dry and dusty?** (much of it spans the northern part of the Eastern hemisphere; parts reach as far south as 35°N latitude)
- **What is the largest country in the region?** (Russia)
- **How does it rank in size with other world nations?** (It is largest.)
- **What was Russia's relation to the Soviet Union?** (It was a major part of it until 1991, when the Soviet Union broke up into 15 countries.)

EXTENDING MAP SKILLS

Help students to recognize the patterns of plains and mountains on the elevation map.

Ask students:

- **Where is the lowest elevation in Russia?** (around the Caspian Sea)
- **In which part of this region are elevations generally higher?** (the southern part)
- **What is the predominant elevation in this region?** (0–700 feet, or 0–200 m)
- **Which landform separates part of Europe from the Middle East?** (the Caucasus Mountains)

Talking About Plains and Mountains

Ask students:

- **Where are the Caucasus Mountains located?** (in the southern part of Eastern Europe between the Black Sea and the Caspian Sea)

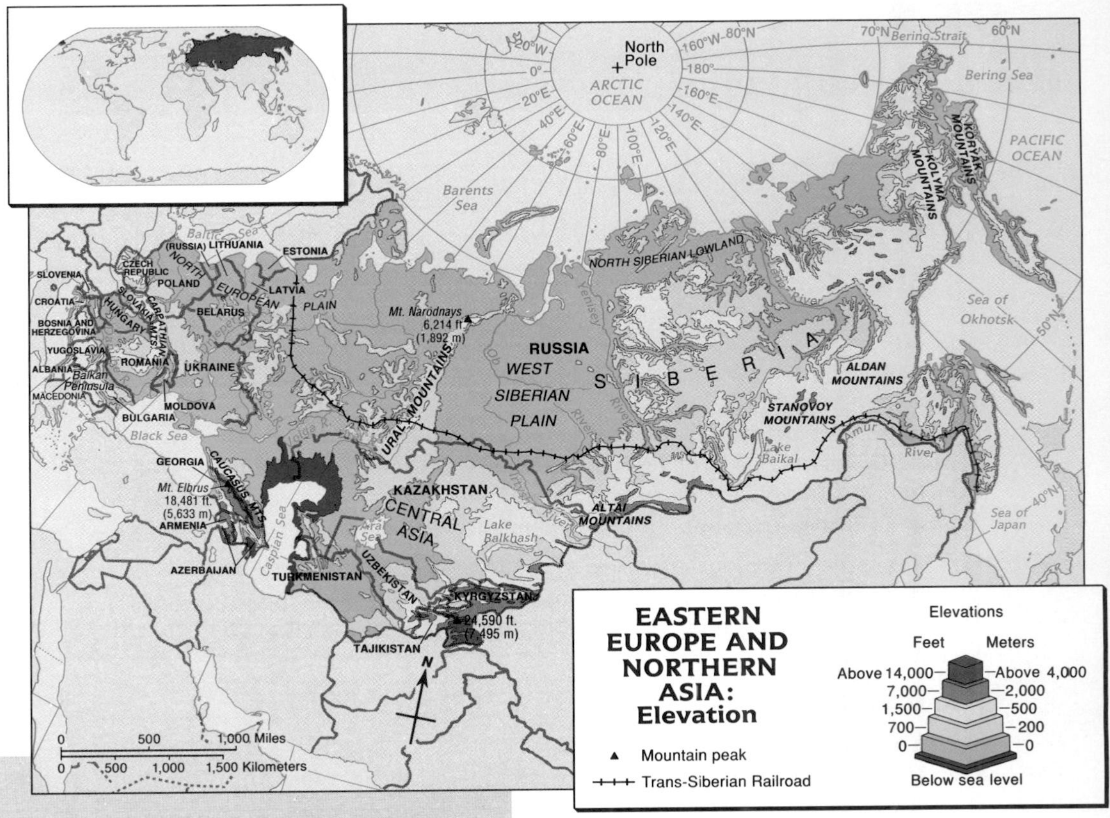

MAP SKILL: What is the area of lowest elevation in Eastern Europe and Northern Asia?

Until late 1991 Russia was part of an even larger country, the **Soviet Union**. But in 1991 the republics that made up the Soviet Union separated into 15 independent countries. You will read more about the former Soviet Union in Chapter 15.

To the west of the former Soviet Union are the countries that you will study in Chapter 16. These countries were dominated by the Soviet Union in the years following World War II. East Germany was also one of these countries, but as you read in Chapter 11, East Germany is now part of a united Germany. The Eastern European countries have also become fully independent.

PLAINS AND MOUNTAINS

Imagine an area of vast plains surrounded by mountains. Much of the land of Eastern Europe and Northern Asia is very flat. Find some of the plains and mountains on the map above.

Use the map above to locate the **Caucasus** (kô′ kə səs) **Mountains** in the southwestern part of the region. These mountains separate Europe from southwestern Asia. This area has had many severe earthquakes.

To the east of the Caucasus Mountains lie a series of other mountain ranges, which you can find on the map. These mountain ranges stretch eastward for thousands of miles, all the way to the shores of the Pacific Ocean.

MAP SKILL: the area around the Caspian Sea

BACKGROUND INFORMATION

About Eurasia Geologists view Europe and Asia as one continent known as Eurasia. They even consider Europe a western peninsula of Asia. On the other hand, because of the different historical patterns and ways of life in the two places, historians and political scientists view Europe and Asia as two continents separated by the Ural Mountains. Eurasia is the world's largest landmass, with an area of over 21 million square miles (nearly 55 million sq km), which covers 38 percent of the world's land area. Europe makes up 19 percent of the total, while Asia takes up the remaining 81 percent. Eurasia lies almost entirely in the northern hemisphere.

Farther west in Eastern Europe you will also find many mountain ranges. As you can see on the map on page 294, the Balkan Peninsula contains several mountain ranges. In fact, the name *Balkan* comes from the Turkish word meaning "mountain." Throughout history, the Balkan Peninsula has served as a crossroads for Europe, Asia, and Africa.

All of these mountain ranges form a great circle around a land of wide plains with few geographical barriers. In the past conquering armies often swept back and forth across these plains. Now people cross these plains to find jobs and homes.

The population of the region is mainly concentrated in the warmer western plains and plateaus. As the map on page 296 shows, Moscow, St. Petersburg (formerly called Leningrad), Budapest, Prague, Warsaw, and many other cities each have more than 1 million people. The region's major industrial centers and its most important rivers are also found mainly in the European part of the area.

SIBERIA

At the beginning of this lesson, you read a description by a journalist who made his way across the Ural Mountains. The Urals are an important dividing line between Europe and Siberia (sī bêr′ ē ə). Siberia is the name for a former political region made up of the entire Asian portion of Russia and a small part of land that now belongs to Kazakhstan (kä zäk stan′). Siberia extends across roughly three fourths of the entire region of Eastern Europe and Northern Asia. Siberia alone is larger than the entire United States.

The vast West Siberian Plain is the largest single area of level land on the surface of the earth. It has many marshes, or wetlands, that are frozen for up to eight months a year.

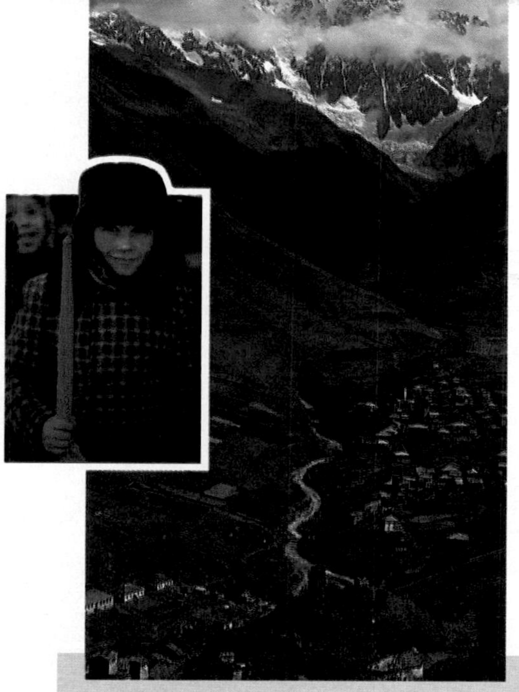

Climbing steep hills is an everyday activity in this Caucasus Mountain town.

For a long time Siberia was a very remote region. As one writer noted, Siberia was "a land of exiles, religious refugees, . . . and fugitive rebels." An exile is a person who is sent either out of the country or to a remote area because the government of that country thinks he or she is dangerous. The father of Nina Kosterina, a young student, was exiled to a camp in Siberia in 1937. Nina wrote in her diary that her father described the camp as being in a beautiful area, near a "wild canyon, [and] a cold . . . , rapid forest stream."

Nina Kosterina's diary, though, also helps to explain why few people escaped from Siberia. She wrote that one November her father's camp "was moved in a frost of −50°C (−58°F.) to another river that is not even on the map. Before pitching their tents, the exiles had to dig through a 1-meter-thick (3.2-ft) layer of snow."

295

Discussing Plains and Mountains Continue the discussion about plains and mountains.

Ask students:

- **Where did the name Balkan come from and what does it mean?** (from Turkish; It means "mountain.")
- **Why is the population of Eastern Europe and Northern Asia centered in the western part of the region?** (It's warmer and has important rivers, industrial centers, and large cities.)

Looking at Siberia Stress the size and extremes of Siberia. Point out Siberia on the map on page 294. Discuss its boundaries.

Ask students:

- **How large is Siberia?** (It makes up three fourths of the region of Eastern Europe and Northern Asia and is larger than the United States.)
- **What is noteworthy about the West Siberian Plain?** (It is the largest single area of level land on earth and is frozen for up to eight months a year.)
- **What is an exile?** (a person sent out of his or her country or to a remote area within the country by the government because that person is considered dangerous)
- *THINKING FURTHER:* **Why do you suppose Siberia was used for exiles?** (Its remote location and harsh climate helped to prevent escapes.)

5 FUNDAMENTAL THEMES OF GEOGRAPHY

Location Russia has the longest coastline of any nation. However, its relative location makes it nearly landlocked.

- The northern Arctic coastline of Russia is icebound almost all year. Some years the ocean stays frozen year-round.
- For trade to the West, Russia has only three outlets to the sea: (1) a long Black Sea route into the Mediterranean, (2) the port of St. Petersburg on the Baltic Sea that can freeze in winter, and (3) Murmansk, the only port on the Arctic coast that is free of ice year-round.

CURRICULUM CONNECTION

Science The Russian port of Murmansk on the Arctic coast is free of ice year-round. Have students research and report on why this port is ice-free.

Language Arts Because of its harsh climate and remoteness, Siberia has been used as a place of exile. Have students read about this region and those who have lived there in exile.

Examining Siberia Continue discussing Siberia.

Ask students:

- **Why is special technology needed today to live in Siberia?** (to defeat the cold and allow buildings to be built on ice)
- *THINKING FURTHER:* **How do you think people were able to live in Siberia in the past without modern technology?** (Students may suggest that people adapted to the harsh environment by wearing special clothing, by building special kinds of homes, and by other means.)

EXTENDING MAP SKILLS

Have students study the population density map.

Ask students:

- **Which part of the region is the most densely populated? The least populated?** (western; eastern)
- **What is the population density of Siberia?** (0–25 people per square mile, or 0–10 people per square km)
- **Which city has a population density of over 500 people per square mile (over 200 people per sq km)?** (Moscow)

Discussing Central Asia

Ask students:

- **Which landform characterizes Central Asia?** (huge stretches of dry lowland)
- **What causes the dry climate of Central Asia?** (mountains in the south block rain-bearing clouds)
- **What is the historical importance of Central Asia?** (It was the path for invaders from the East and the West and an important trade route with China.)

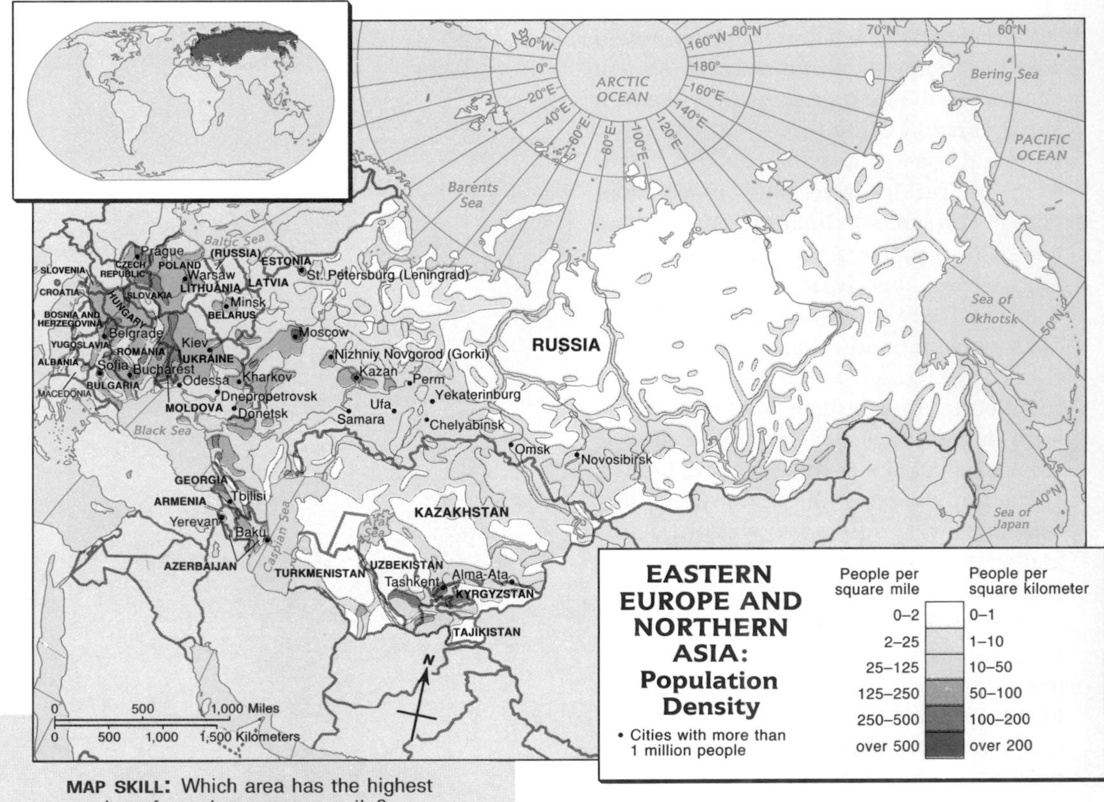

MAP SKILL: Which area has the highest number of people per square mile?

To live in Siberia today requires the use of special technology. In many places houses have to be built in such a way that they don't melt the permafrost under them. If the ice melts, the houses begin to sink.

Although there are many settlements in Siberia, only a small number of people live there. Look at the population density map above. It shows where most of the people in the region live.

CENTRAL ASIA

Find the **Caspian Sea** on the map above. To its east is a large, dry lowland that is part of **Central Asia**. Central Asia includes the countries of Kazakhstan, Uzbekistan (ůz bek′ i stän), Tajikistan (tä jik′ i stän), Turkmenistan (tûrk men′ i stän) and Kyrgyzstan (kîr giz′ stän). It continues into China and Mongolia.

High mountains form the southern border of Central Asia. Because these mountains block rain-bearing clouds that blow from the south, the climate of Central Asia is very dry. Hundreds of years ago, the "Silk Route," an important trade route between China and southwestern Asia, ran through this area. This route was also used by invaders from the east and the west.

LONG RIVERS

Travel between the widely separated areas of Eastern Europe and Northern Asia has always been difficult. Only after the Trans-Siberian Railroad was built in 1916

296

MAP SKILL: the area around the city of Moscow

FUNDAMENTAL THEMES OF GEOGRAPHY

Movement The sweeping plains of Eastern Europe and Northern Asia affected the movement of people and played a crucial role in the history of Europe and Asia. The plains were a burden to individuals who tried to travel long distances from one settlement or city to another. At the same time their openness allowed invading armies on horseback to claim huge areas of land.

- Throughout history, waves of invaders like the Huns, Magyars, Avars, and Mongols swept into Europe from the Asian plains.
- In 1271 Marco Polo was the first European to successfully cross the vast Central Asian plains. He took back to Europe news of the great riches of the East.

were the eastern and western parts of the region linked. Because severe cold breaks up the surfaces of roads, even today no major highway connects the east with the west.

In the past rivers were the most important transportation routes. Russia has some of the world's longest rivers, as you can see from the table on this page. Yet most of Russia's rivers do not provide good transportation routes. The reason for this is that no major rivers flow from east to west. Almost all Russia's rivers flow from south to north. Because these rivers are so far north, almost all of them are frozen solid for at least four months of each year. During the winter the sight of large sleds, snowmobiles, and even trucks traveling across the frozen rivers is common.

One of Russia's most important rivers is the Volga River, the longest river in Europe. The Volga, which is sometimes called the "Main Street" of Russia, flows 2,300 miles (3,680 km) through Russia before emptying into the Caspian Sea. The Volga is linked by canals to the Baltic Sea, the Don River, and the Black Sea.

The most heavily traveled river in Eastern Europe is the Danube River. It links many countries in Eastern Europe and Western Europe as well as the cities of Vienna, Budapest, and Belgrade.

AN IMMENSE REGION

The region of Eastern Europe and Northern Asia spans a large portion of two continents. Most of the population is concentrated in the European part of the region. The Asian part has two distinct areas—Siberia and Central Asia.

It is a region of vast plains with few geographic barriers, except in the south. Yet the great distances that stretch across these plains have traditionally made travel throughout the region difficult.

LONGEST RIVERS OF THE WORLD

River	Country	Length in Miles (Kilometers)
Nile	Egypt	4,100 (6,560)
Amazon	Brazil	4,000 (6,400)
Chang (Yangtze R.)	China	3,964 (6,342)
Mississippi-Missouri	United States	3,710 (5,936)
Ob	Russia	3,362 (5,379)
Huang (Yellow R.)	China	2,903 (4,644)
Congo	Zaire	2,900 (4,640)
Amur	Russia	2,744 (4,390)
Lena	Russia	2,734 (4,374)
Mackenzie	Canada	2,635 (4,216)
Mekong	China	2,600 (4,160)
Yenisey	Russia	2,543 (4,068)
Paraná	Brazil	2,485 (3,976)
Murray Darling	Australia	2,310 (3,718)
Volga	Russia	2,194 (3,531)

CHART SKILL: Which is Russia's third-longest river?

Check Your Reading

1. Which is the largest country in Eastern Europe and Northern Asia?
2. Why is Siberia's population density lower than other parts of the region?
3. Describe the region's major landforms.
4. **THINKING SKILL:** How are the landforms of Siberia and Central Asia alike? How are they different?

THINKING SKILL: Compare and Contrast
CHART SKILL: the Lena

Discussing Long Rivers

Ask students:

- **What is the major link between the western and eastern lands of this region today?** (the Trans-Siberian Railroad)

EXTENDING CHART SKILLS

After reviewing the chart of the longest rivers of the world on this page, have students tell how many of these rivers are in Russia. (five)

Applying the Lesson Give students a copy of the outline map of Eastern Europe and Northern Asia, found in the Teacher's Resource Center. Have them label: Eastern Europe, Siberia, Central Asia; the Ural and the Caucasus mountains; the Balkan Peninsula; and the Black and Caspian seas.

3 CLOSE

Summarizing Students have learned that Eastern Europe and Northern Asia comprise a plains region spanning a major portion of Europe and Asia. Have students describe the land of this region.

Evaluating Use the *Check Your Reading* questions (answers given below) to assess students' understanding.

Answers to Check Your Reading

1. Russia
2. Siberia is a remote region, most of which is frozen up to eight months a year.
3. open sweeping plains and southern mountains
4. Both are large regions with vast plains. Siberia is wet, cold, and frozen, while Central Asia is very dry.

Independent Practice
Practice Book: page 79

MEETING INDIVIDUAL NEEDS

Reteaching (easy) Give students a copy of the outline map of Eastern Europe and Northern Asia, found in the Teacher's Resource Center. Have them label and color the seven countries of Eastern Europe that became tied to the former Soviet Union after World War II.

Extension (average) Give students the outline map of Eastern Europe and Northern Asia and have them locate and label Russia and the other 14 countries that once made up the Soviet Union.

Enrichment (challenging) Divide the class into three groups. Have each group draw cross-sections of the elevations of Eastern Europe and Northern Asia along one of these parallels: 45°N, 50°N, 55°N.

LESSON 2
pages 298–300

Lesson Theme Temperate and cold climates dominate the rich farmlands and forests of Eastern Europe and Northern Asia.

Lesson Objectives
- Describe the climates found in Eastern Europe and Northern Asia.
- Describe the soil and vegetation of Eastern Europe and Northern Asia.
- Identify the mineral resources of Eastern Europe and Northern Asia.

 PREPARE

Motivate Read the *Read Aloud* section to the class. Discuss how the effects of cold climate could be reflected in folktales.

Set Purpose Discuss the *What You Know* question with the class. Remind students that answers to the *What You Will Learn* question can be found in the lesson.

 TEACH

Understanding Climate Help students to understand that there is a wide range of climates in this region.

Ask students:

- **Which two climate zones dominate Eastern Europe and Northern Asia?** (a zone of temperate climates covers most of Eastern Europe; a zone of short, cool summers and long, cold winters includes Siberia and the northern part of Eastern Europe)

LESSON 2

Climate and Resources

READ TO LEARN

Key Vocabulary

taiga steppes

Read Aloud

In one Eastern European folk tale a girl named Marushka is forced by her stepmother to search for violets, then for strawberries, and finally for apples in the dead of winter. Marushka is able to find all of these through the kindness of Great January, King of the Months. This powerful ruler then punishes Marushka's stepmother by sending her a blizzard.

The story of Marushka is a reminder that winter in many parts of Eastern Europe and Northern Asia is a serious matter. Snow, ice, and freezing temperatures are a reality for at least half the year.

Read for Purpose

1. WHAT YOU KNOW: How long does winter last where you live? How cold does it get during winter?
2. WHAT YOU WILL LEARN: What are the major climates and natural resources of Eastern Europe and Northern Asia?

CLIMATE

Many stories describe the climate of Siberia—its blizzards and freezing temperatures. Because of these stories, some people think all of Eastern Europe and Northern Asia has a harsh climate.

In fact, the region has several climates. However, as the climate map on page 299 shows, most of the region falls within two large climate zones. The first zone includes the western part of Northern Asia and all of Eastern Europe. This zone has different kinds of temperate climates, ranging from warm to hot summers and from mild to cold, snowy winters.

The second large climate zone is in Siberia and the northern part of Eastern Europe. It has short, cool summers and long, cold winters. Most of this zone is inland, far from large bodies of water that help make temperatures milder. The northern part of Russia is tundra and has an Arctic climate.

SOIL AND VEGETATION

In countries that have large plains—such as Poland and Hungary—people can farm more than 50 percent of the land. Even in more mountainous countries of Eastern Europe, such as Slovakia, the Czech Republic, and Romania, at least one third of the land can be cultivated.

Less than 20 percent of Russia's land is arable, mainly because of the cold climate of much of the country. Hardly anything can grow in the bleak northern tundra, where permafrost lies just below the earth's surface. Even south of the tundra,

WHAT YOU KNOW: Encourage students to think about what it is like to live through a long, cold winter.

READING STRATEGY AND VOCABULARY DEVELOPMENT

Question/Answer Relationships Review the strategy that students learned in Lesson 1 for finding answers to questions by identifying the source of the answers—directly stated in the text, inferred from the text, or based on prior knowledge or personal experience. Preview the lesson with students. Then have students work in groups to develop questions based on the headings in the lesson. After they read the lesson, have students answer the questions they developed and determine the source of their answers.

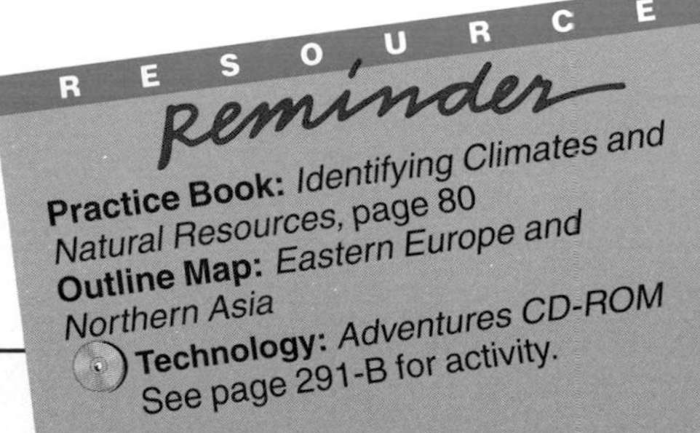

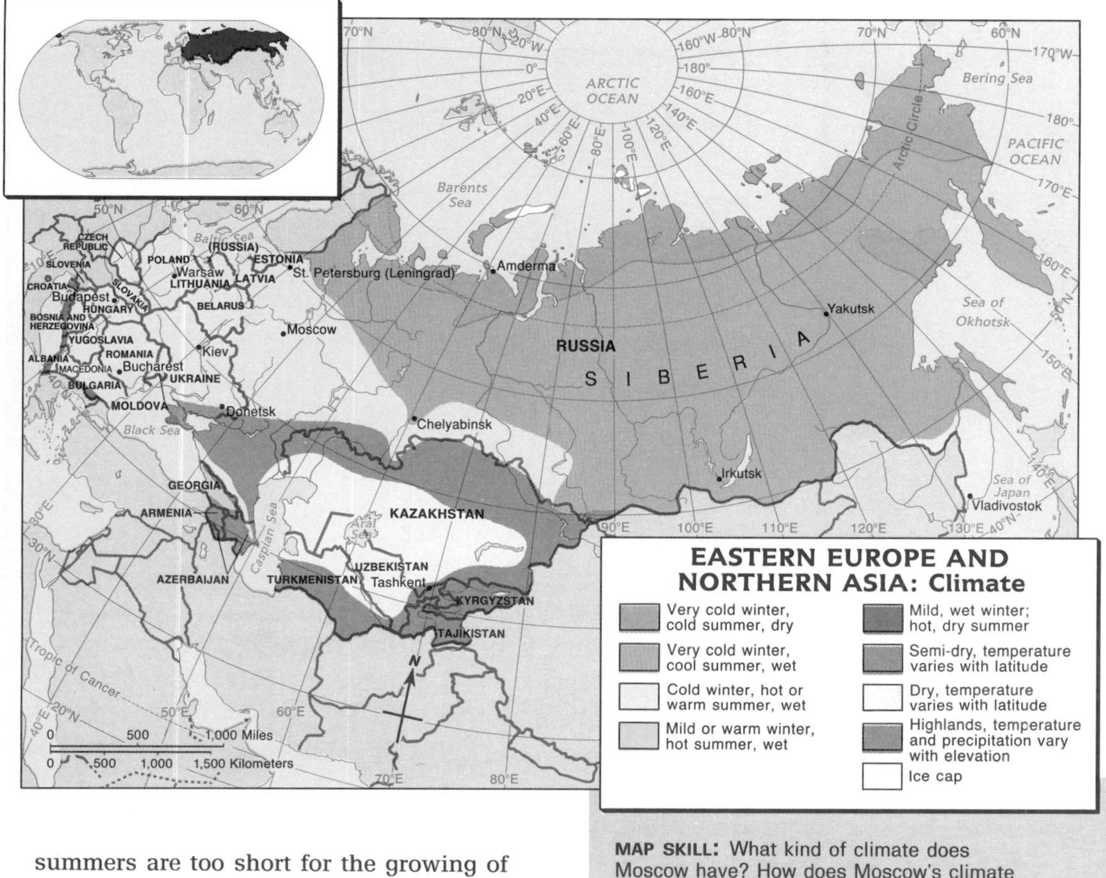

MAP SKILL: What kind of climate does Moscow have? How does Moscow's climate compare with the climates of the major cities in Eastern Europe?

summers are too short for the growing of many crops.

FORESTS AND GRASSLANDS

In addition to its farmland, Eastern Europe is heavily forested, with trees covering about one third of the land. Russia has a vast region of evergreen forests south of the tundra. It is called the taiga (tī′ gə), and it stretches all the way from Finland to the Pacific Ocean.

South of the taiga are the steppes (steps). Steppes are dry, grassy plains. These grasslands cover much of Russia, Ukraine, parts of Eastern Europe, as well as western Siberia. The steppes of Europe contain some of the world's richest soil.

In the 1950s the government of what was then the Soviet Union sent people to Northern Asia to cultivate the steppes. When the first settlers arrived, they found that cultivating the land was backbreaking work. One settler wrote:

> *Slowly, first one then another plow dug into the black soil, which cracked like a torn [canvas] all interlaced with strong roots. . . .*

But the pioneers refused to give up. As a result, the steppes of Northern Asia are a major grain-growing area today.

MINERALS

Russia is richer in minerals than all of its neighbors in Eastern Europe combined.

MAP SKILL: cold winter, hot or warm summer, wet; same climate

EXTENDING MAP SKILLS

Have students study the climate map.

Ask students:

- **What kind of climate is found in Tashkent?** (semidry)
- **Generally, where are the most temperate climates found?** (in Eastern Europe, western Russia and parts of Central Asia)
- **Where are the hot, dry climate areas?** (in Central Asia)
- **Where are the cold, dry climate areas?** (in northern Siberia)
- *THINKING FURTHER:* **Which climate area do you think is the easiest to live in? Why?** (Students should give reasons for their answers.)

Discussing Soil and Vegetation
Ask students to compare the percentages of land that can be farmed in (1) nations with large plains, like Poland and Hungary, (2) mountainous countries, like Slovakia and Romania, and (3) all of Russia.

Looking at Forests and Grasslands

Ask students:

- **Where is the taiga and what kind of vegetation grows there?** (south of the tundra from Finland to the Pacific; evergreen forests)
- **What are the steppes?** (dry, grassy plains)
- **Why are the steppes so valuable to this region?** (They are a major grain-growing area.)

CURRICULUM CONNECTION

Math By looking at the average annual temperature of a place, students can get an idea of what the climate of that place is like. Averaging is a key process for students to understand. Have students research the average monthly temperatures for both Bucharest, Romania, and Moscow, Russia. Then have them calculate the average annual temperature for each city. Help students to do this by telling them to add together the monthly temperatures for each city to get a total and then to divide the total by 12. Have students compare the average temperatures and explain what these numbers tell about the climate of these two cities.

BACKGROUND INFORMATION

Multicultural Perspectives Siberia is a diverse land made up of tundra, taiga, and steppes. Yet writer Maxim Gorky summarized most people's image of Siberia when he described it as "the land of chains and groans." For hundreds of years brutal government prisons and labor camps have been Siberia's unfortunate claim to fame. But many people fondly call Siberia home. Tanya Glushakova is a seventh-grader in the village of Naikhan. She says: "Our village is very beautiful, the nature around us is very rich. There are a lot of fish at our place. And in the forest there are a lot of mushrooms." Ask students why the two very different descriptions of Siberia can both be true.

Discussing Minerals Help students to realize the extent of Russian coal reserves. Have students compare the energy resources of Russia with nations that lie entirely in Eastern Europe.

EXTENDING MAP SKILLS

Ask students:

- **Where are the major farmlands of this region?** (Commercial farming and livestock raising cover a wide belt extending from Eastern Europe across southern Russia and Central Asia.)
- **Which parts of this region have little or no economic activity?** (the northlands and areas east of the Caspian Sea)

Applying the Lesson Have students write an essay on land use in the tundra, taiga, and steppes regions.

CLOSE

Summarizing Students have learned about the climate, soil, vegetation, and minerals of this region. Have students develop a chart comparing each of these characteristics in Eastern Europe and Northern Asia.

Evaluating Use the *Check Your Reading* questions (answers given below) to assess students' understanding.

Answers to Check Your Reading

1. temperate; short, cool summers and long, cold winters
2. The taiga has evergreen forests; the steppes are grassy plains.
3. Plowing the hard soil was backbreaking work.
4. clothing for spring and winter

Independent Practice
Practice Book: page 80

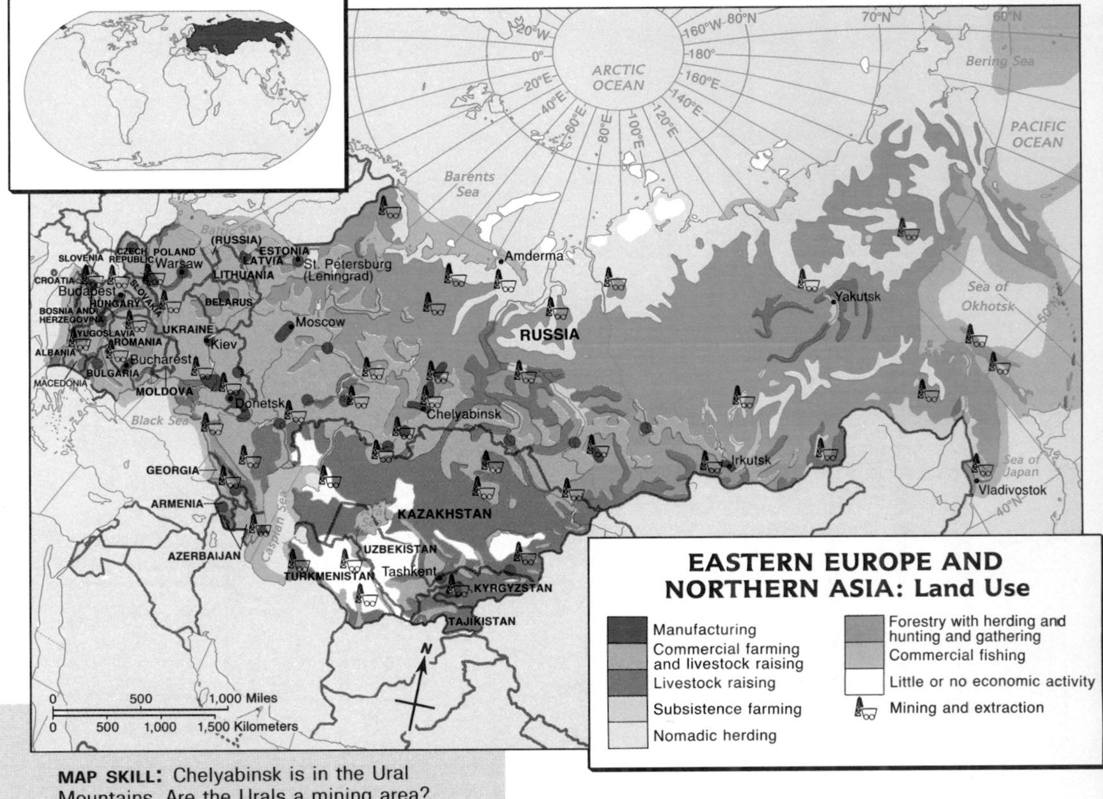

MAP SKILL: Chelyabinsk is in the Ural Mountains. Are the Urals a mining area?

Russia has about one third of all the coal in the world. It also has huge oil reserves in Siberia. The countries in the Caucasus Mountains and Central Asia also possess productive oil fields.

In general, the countries of Eastern Europe are not rich in minerals. There are some exceptions. Poland has large deposits of coal, while Romania is one of Eastern Europe's few oil-producing nations.

DIFFERENT CLIMATES AND RESOURCES

You have read that most of Eastern Europe and Northern Asia is located within two climate zones. You have also read that the land varies from fertile steppes to dry land. Russia has coal and oil reserves. Oil is also found in the Caucasus Mountains, Central Asia, and Romania. Poland has large deposits of coal.

Check Your Reading

1. List two major climate zones of Eastern Europe and Northern Asia.
2. What is the difference between the taiga and the steppes?
3. Why was it difficult to begin to cultivate the steppes of Northern Asia?
4. **THINKING SKILL:** Imagine that you plan to visit Moscow and then the Caspian Sea in March. Use the climate map on page 299 to decide what kind of clothing you might pack for your trip.

300

MAP SKILL: Yes. The map shows mining north and south of Chelyabinsk.

THINKING SKILL: Decision Making

MEETING INDIVIDUAL NEEDS

Reteaching (easy) Give students a copy of the outline map of Eastern Europe and Northern Asia found in the Teacher's Resource Center. Have them use different colors to color the tundra, taiga, and steppe regions. Have students include a map key.

Extension (average) Have students research the types of crops grown in the taiga, tundra, and steppes regions. Have them present their findings in chart form.

Enrichment (challenging) Have students find out more about Russian programs to cultivate the steppes. Ask them to write a paragraph comparing the steppes with the American prairies.

BUILDING SKILLS
STUDY AND RESEARCH SKILLS

Reading Climographs

Key Vocabulary
climograph

In this chapter, as well as throughout this book, you have seen climate maps of the world's regions. These maps tell a lot about the climate of a place. Another way to learn about the climate of a place is to look at a **climograph**. A climograph is a graph that shows information about the temperature and precipitation of a particular location over a period of time.

Parts of a Climograph

Climographs are useful because they give a picture of the weather in a particular place for each month of the year.

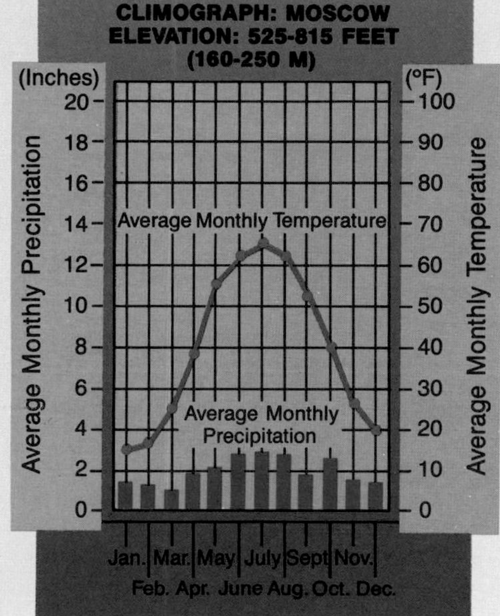

Notice that the climograph on this page includes two graphs—a bar graph and a line graph. The bar graph shows the average monthly precipitation in Moscow. The line graph shows the average monthly temperature in Moscow.

To read the climograph, first look at the title. The title tells you the location of the place whose climate is being described. What else does it tell you? Then read the labels on the sides and along the bottom of the graph. What do these labels tell you about the graph?*

Next look at the vertical bars along the bottom of the bar graph. The bars tell you the average precipitation during each month. Now look at the line on the line graph that shows the average temperature for each month. What is the average temperature in Moscow during May? Which is the driest month on average in the city?**

Reviewing the Skill

1. What does a climograph show?
2. Which is the coldest month of the year in Moscow?
3. During which months of the year are there more than 2 inches (5 cm) of rain in Moscow?
4. In which month of the year does the most rain fall in Moscow?
5. According to the climograph, would the precipitation in February be in the form of rain or snow?
6. In which month do you think it would be best to visit Moscow if you like mild, dry weather?
7. When might you find climographs especially helpful for understanding climate?

*the elevation of Moscow; that average monthly temperature and precipitation will be described

**about 55°F; March

301

SKILLS LESSON
page 301

Lesson Theme A climograph shows the temperature and precipitation of a place over a period of time.

Lesson Objective
- Identify and interpret the parts of a climograph.

PREPARE

Motivate Speculate with students about which month in Moscow, Russia, would have the warmest average temperature and which would have the coldest.

Set Purpose Tell students that they will learn to read a climograph.

TEACH

Reading the Parts of a Climograph Be sure that students understand what averaging is. Help them read the climograph on this page.

Applying the Skill Have students research the average monthly temperature and average monthly precipitation in their communities or state. Have them use this information to create a climograph.

CLOSE

Summarizing Students should realize that a climograph shows the yearly climate pattern of a place.

Answers to Reviewing the Skill

1. the average temperature and precipitation of a place over a period of time
2. January
3. May, June, July, August, October
4. July
5. snow
6. May or September
7. when comparing places or when planning a trip

MEETING INDIVIDUAL NEEDS

Reteaching (easy) Have students turn to the *Atlas* map on page 628 and find the latitude and longitude of Moscow, Russia. Then have them find the latitude and longitude of their communities. Discuss how the difference in latitude affects the climograph of each place.

Extension (average) Have students research and make a climograph for another city in the Eastern Europe and Northern Asia region. Then have them compare their climograph to the one for Moscow, shown on this page.

Enrichment (challenging) Have students do research to find climographs for a place in a tropical rain forest, a savanna, a desert, in temperate lands, the Antarctic, and the Arctic. Have them make posters to show the climograph differences visually.

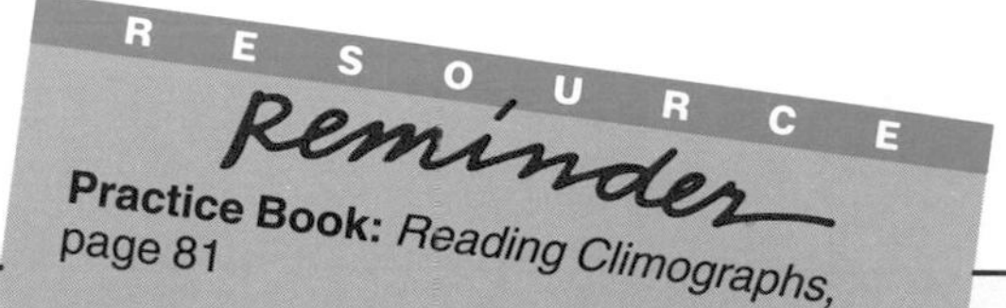

CHAPTER 14 REVIEW
pages 302–303

USING THE CHAPTER SUMMARY AND REVIEW

Physical Geography These questions may be used for review.

- **What are three distinct areas of this region?** (Siberia, Central Asia, Balkans)
- **What are the two main climate zones of the region?** (temperate and arctic)
- **In what part of this region is arable soil found?** (mainly in Eastern Europe and the steppes of Russia and the Ukraine)

Ideas to Remember

- **What kind of landform dominates this region?** (lowland plains)
- **Which area in this region is rich in minerals?** (Russia)

Answers to Reviewing Vocabulary

1. The steppes are regions of dry, grassy plains.
2. The taiga is a heavily forested region that stretches from Finland to the Pacific Ocean.
3. True.
4. True.
5. True.

CHAPTER 14 • SUMMARY

EASTERN EUROPE AND NORTHERN ASIA: PHYSICAL GEOGRAPHY

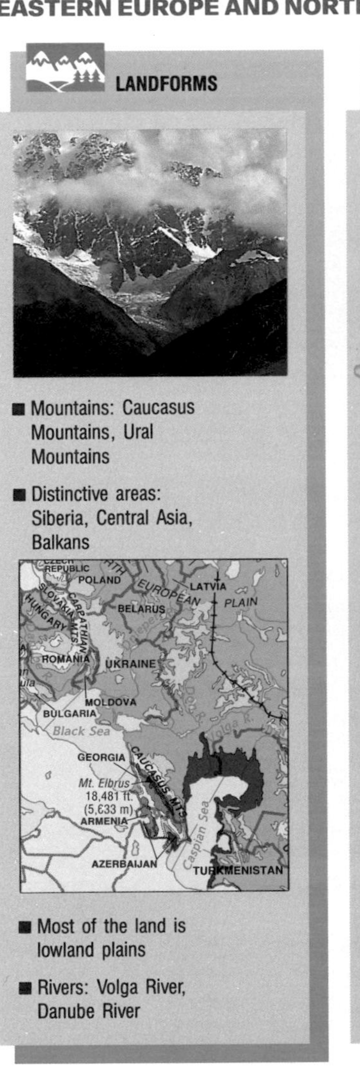

LANDFORMS

- Mountains: Caucasus Mountains, Ural Mountains
- Distinctive areas: Siberia, Central Asia, Balkans
- Most of the land is lowland plains
- Rivers: Volga River, Danube River

CLIMATE

- Mainly temperate and Arctic climates, with many extremes
- Temperate climates: mainly in Eastern Europe
- Arctic climate: northern Siberia and Northern Europe

NATURAL RESOURCES

- Arable soil: mainly in Eastern Europe and the steppes of Russia and Ukraine
- Eastern Europe and Russia are heavily forested
- The steppes of Russia and Ukraine are vast grasslands
- Minerals: coal, oil

IDEAS TO REMEMBER

- The region of Eastern Europe and Northern Asia spans two continents and is made up mainly of lowland plains.
- Russia has several climate zones and is richer in minerals than all of the Eastern European countries combined.

302

ENRICHMENT ACTIVITY

Making a Textured Map **Materials:** posterboard, felt tip pens, dry split-green peas, dry cereal, dry kidney beans, glue

1. Review with students the geography of Eastern Europe and Northern Asia. Tell them that they are going to make a map of the area which will help them to appreciate the variety of its geographic features and its vastness.
2. Have students draw a large outline map of Eastern Europe and Northern Asia on posterboard. Tell them to use a blue pen to draw important rivers, seas, and lakes. Tell them to also show the boundary between Eastern Europe and Northern Asia.
3. Have students spread glue on the plains area of the map. Then have them apply one of the dried foods to the glue. Repeat the process for the mountains and the lowlands.
4. Have students add a compass rose, a map legend, and a title.

CHAPTER 14 • REVIEW

REVIEWING VOCABULARY

Each of the following statements contains an underlined vocabulary word. Number a sheet of paper from 1 to 5. Beside each number, write whether the following statements are true or false. If a statement is true, write true. If a statement is false, rewrite the sentence using the vocabulary word correctly.

1. The steppes are regions of high mountains and heavily wooded foothills.
2. The taiga is a vast arctic plain where almost nothing grows and where a layer of permafrost lies just below the surface.
3. Russia is heavily forested by a vast region of evergreen called the taiga.
4. The steppes are dry, grassy plains covering vast areas of Russia, Ukraine, and parts of Eastern Europe.
5. The European part of the steppes contains some of the world's most fertile soil.

REVIEWING FACTS

1. Which mountain range divides Eastern Europe from Northern Asia? Which mountain range divides Eastern Europe from southwestern Asia?
2. In the region of Eastern Europe and Northern Asia, where is most of the population concentrated?
3. Why does only a small percentage of the region's population live in Siberia?
4. About what fraction of this region's area is in Russia?
5. Why do no major highways in this region link the east and west? How are the eastern and western parts linked?
6. What drawbacks make river transportation very difficult in Russia?
7. Why is Central Asia, the lowland south of Siberia, a dry area?
8. What is the main reason that while roughly 50 percent of Hungary's land is arable, only 20 percent of Russia's land can be farmed?
9. Which area of Northern Asia has been turned into a major grain-growing area in the past few decades?
10. Which two minerals are found in large quantities in Russia?

WRITING ABOUT MAIN IDEAS

1. **Writing an Explanation:** Look at the places listed below. Which of the choices in each pair probably has a colder climate? Explain why.
   a. a village in Siberia; the city of Moscow
   b. the city of St. Petersburg; a village in the Ural Mountains
2. **Writing a Paragraph:** Look at the climate map on page 299. What kind of climate would you be living in if you lived in St. Petersburg? Write a paragraph comparing the climate where you live with the climate in St. Petersburg.
3. **Writing About Perspectives:** Imagine that you are a member of a family that is riding the Trans-Siberian Railroad across Russia from Moscow to your new home in eastern Siberia. Write a letter to a friend describing the vastness of Russia's land, its diverse geography, and its climate.

BUILDING SKILLS: READING CLIMOGRAPHS

Look at the climograph on page 301 to answer the following questions.

1. What does a climograph show?
2. Which month of the year is the warmest in Moscow?
3. When might you find climographs especially helpful for your own use?

303

Answers to Reviewing Facts

1. the Ural Mountains; the Caucasus Mountains
2. on the warmer western plains and plateaus
3. The area is remote and has a severe climate.
4. three fourths
5. because severe cold breaks up the surfaces of roads; by the Trans-Siberian Railroad
6. No major rivers flow east to west, and even those that flow south to north are frozen solid at least four months a year.
7. High mountains that form its southern border block rain-bearing clouds from reaching it.
8. mainly because so much of Russia has such a cold climate and thus a short growing season
9. the steppes
10. coal, oil

Suggestions for Writing About Main Ideas

1. a. the village in Siberia, because Siberia has a harsh climate and Moscow has a temperate climate
   b. the village in the Ural Mountains, because this area is inland, away from large bodies of water that make the climate more temperate, as it is in St. Petersburg
2. Students would be living in a climate with cold winters, hot or warm summers, and abundant rain. Students should compare the climate they live in with the climate of St. Petersburg.
3. Students should include their feelings about the varied lands they are crossing.

Answers to Building Skills: Reading Climographs

1. A climograph shows the temperature and precipitation of a place over a period of time.
2. July
3. when comparing places or when planning a trip

MAKING CONNECTIONS

Recognizing Cause and Effect Use the Cause and Effect Chart Graphic Organizer Transparency, filling in only the underlined sentences. For Column 1, have students write three causes of the effect stated. For Column 2, have students write three effects of the cause stated. *Ask:* Why is travel so difficult from east to west in Northern Asia?

Causes	Effects
The distances stretching across the plains are enormous. No major highway or river runs from east to west in Northern Asia. Siberia, about 3/4 of the region, has many marshes and is frozen most of the year.	Travel in Eastern Europe and Northern Asia is difficult.
Temperate and cold climates dominate Northern Asia and Eastern Europe.	Little vegetation can grow in the northern tundra. Summers are too short for growing crops. The climate of the taiga supports a vast region of evergreen forests.

CHAPTER 15 ORGANIZER

RUSSIA AND ITS NEIGHBORS **text pages 304–329**

CHAPTER THEME

The end of the Soviet Union and the subsequent creation of 15 new countries has caused enormous changes in the lives of the peoples who live in this region.

CHAPTER OBJECTIVES

CONTENT

- Name the different countries and ethnic groups which were formerly part of the Soviet Union.
- Explain what a command economy is.
- Describe the Commonwealth of Independent States and explain its purpose.
- Define *perestroika* and describe its impact on the former Soviet Union.
- Explain the ideas of Karl Marx and how they were applied in the Soviet Union.
- Describe the Soviet Communist Party's importance in Soviet government and explain how it lost power.
- Describe how the Soviet Union broke up into 15 separate countries.
- Define *glasnost* and describe how this policy affected political and cultural life in the countries which were once part of the Soviet Union.

SKILLS

Geography
- Locate Russia and its neighbors using a map.

Thinking
- Identify the former Soviet government's point of view regarding religion.
- Analyze contrasting points of view concerning the change from a command economy to a market economy.
- Draw conclusions based on information presented.

Reading and Writing
- Write a letter from a Russian to a pen pal in the United States about the great changes in Russia.

CITIZENSHIP VALUES

- Appreciate the importance of hearing both sides of an issue.
- Appreciate the difficulty of making major changes in an economic system.

TEACHER OPTIONS

READING STRATEGY: SQ3R Study Guide Strategies to help students read and remember the main ideas of the lesson.

Lesson 1: p. 305
Legacy: p. 310
Lesson 2: p. 314
Lesson 3: p. 320
Lesson 4: p. 326

MEETING INDIVIDUAL NEEDS Activities for reteaching, extension, and enrichment.

Lesson 1: p. 309
Legacy: p. 313
Lesson 2: p. 317
Lesson 3: p. 323
Lesson 4: p. 327

GEO ADVENTURES ACTIVITIES PAD Daily activities to assess students' understanding of geography skills.

CURRICULUM CONNECTION Activities to help integrate other subject areas with Social Studies.

Math: pp. 312, 324

PUPIL EDITION ON CASSETTE Language support for students who have difficulty reading or who will benefit from listening to the Pupil Edition on Cassette as they read.

SECOND-LANGUAGE SUPPORT Activities and suggestions for second-language learners.

Lesson 3: p. 28

CHAPTER PLANNING GUIDE

LESSON	SUGGESTED PACING	THEMES	TEACHER SUPPORT MATERIALS: TEACHER'S RESOURCE CENTER
1 THE PEOPLE pages 305–309	1 day	Russia and its neighbors—the 15 countries that once made up the Soviet Union—are home to a large number of different ethnic groups.	Practice Book p. 83 **Technology:** *Adventures CD-ROM*
LEGACY Survival of Religion pages 310–313	1 day	Despite government opposition to religion, many Soviet citizens continued to practice their faiths. In the lands of the former Soviet Union, religion is flourishing today.	Practice Book p. 83
2 THE ECONOMY pages 314–319	1 day	The 15 separate countries the Soviet Union broke into in 1991 face major problems in converting their 1 Soviet command economy into mixed economies.	Practice Book p. 84 ■ Anthology pp. 97–98
3 THE GOVERNMENT pages 320–323	1 day	After nearly 75 years, the Soviet Union fragmented into 15 independent countries.	Practice Book p. 85 ■ Anthology pp. 97–98 **Technology:** *Adventures CD-ROM*
BUILDING THINKING SKILLS Drawing Conclusions pages 324–325	1 day	Drawing a conclusion involves pulling together related pieces of information so that they mean something.	Practice Book p. 86
4 ARTS AND RECREATION pages 326–327	1 day	With many former restrictions lifted, the arts flourish today in Russia and neighboring countries.	Practice Book p. 87 ■ Anthology p. 84 **Technology:** *Adventures CD-ROM*
CHAPTER SUMMARY AND REVIEW pages 328–329	1 day	Chapter content, skills, and vocabulary are reviewed and evaluated.	Practice Book p. 88 Transparency: Graphic Organizer Assessment Book, Chapter 15 Test

Technology CONNECTION

Lesson 1
ADVENTURES CD-ROM
Enrich this lesson using *Travel* and *Explore.*

Lesson 3
ADVENTURES CD-ROM
Enrich this lesson with Sounds and Movies in *Investigate, Russia.*

Lesson 4
ADVENTURES CD-ROM
Students can make a presentation on a selection of relevant countries in *Create.*

CHAPTER 15
pages 304–329

USING THE CHAPTER OPENER

Discussing the Photograph Help students understand that the Russian woman is in an open-air market.

Ask students:

- **What is your impression of the goods in the marketplace?** (Students may point out the abundance of vegetables for sale.)
- **What kind of expression does the woman in the photograph have?** (She has a serious expression.)
- *THINKING FURTHER:* **Do you think that this much food is always available in the markets of Russia and its neighbors?** (Help students understand that the former Soviet Union had to import some food and that, since the scant arable land is not equally distributed between the 15 nations which replaced it, food shortages could become a serious problem.)

Reading/Listening to the Primary Source Have a volunteer read the passage under the picture to the rest of the class.

Ask students:

- **In what ways might the Russian people interpret this praise?** (Possible answers include: Their leaders consider the Russian people important and think that it is as necessary to develop people's potential abilities as it is to develop other resources; their leaders expect them to be useful, loyal citizens.)
- *THINKING FURTHER:* **How does the idea expressed by the quotation compare with the idea expressed by John F. Kennedy when he said, "Ask not what your country can do for you; ask what you can do for your country"?** (This question is intended to stimulate a class discussion about the rights and responsibilities of citizenship.)

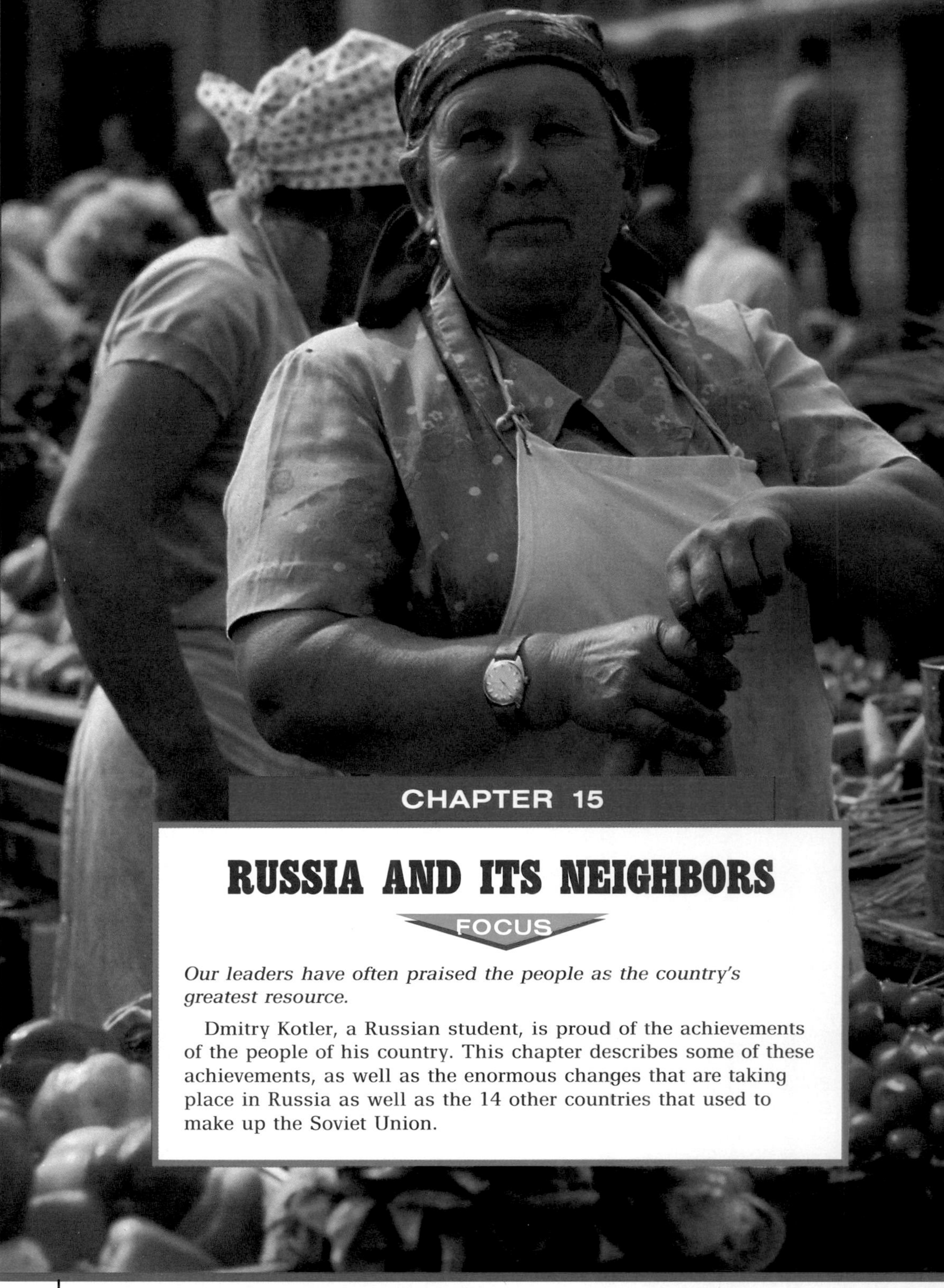

CHAPTER 15

RUSSIA AND ITS NEIGHBORS

FOCUS

Our leaders have often praised the people as the country's greatest resource.

Dmitry Kotler, a Russian student, is proud of the achievements of the people of his country. This chapter describes some of these achievements, as well as the enormous changes that are taking place in Russia as well as the 14 other countries that used to make up the Soviet Union.

BACKGROUND INFORMATION

About Education in Russia and Neighboring Countries One way in which nations help their people to develop is by the kind of education that they provide. Because of recent changes, aspects of the education system and of most other institutions are currently in flux.

- Many of the 15 new countries will probably substitute their own language for Russian as the primary language of education and their own majority culture for Russian culture.
- Education in the countries that were once part of the Soviet Union is free and compulsory through secondary school or, for nonacademic students, through technical and vocational schools.
- The educational system set up by the old Soviet Union aimed to produce a large number of engineers and scientists. Its schools have emphasized science, mathematics, and technical studies.

The People

READ TO LEARN

Key Vocabulary

Soviet

Key Places

Latvia
Lithuania
Estonia
Georgia
Armenia
Uzbekistan
Moscow
Azerbaijan

Read Aloud

The unity of the multinational Soviet people is as solid as a diamond.

History has proved Leonid Brezhnev, leader of the Soviet Union from 1964 to 1982, to be wrong in describing his country as solidly unified. In this lesson you will read about the different groups of people that live in Russia and the other 14 countries that until 1991 made up the Soviet Union. You will also learn about the enormous changes that have caused the unity among the countries, once "solid as a diamond," to crumble.

Read for Purpose

1. WHAT YOU KNOW: In which parts of Russia do most of its people live?
2. WHAT YOU WILL LEARN: What changes have been taking place in Russia and the other 14 countries that were once part of the Soviet Union?

A TIME OF CHANGE

In 1991 Latvia, Lithuania, and Estonia gained their independence from the Soviet Union. These three countries along the eastern shore of the Baltic Sea had been the last to become part of the Soviet Union. In 1991 they were the first to break away. Within a few months, the enormous country known as the Soviet Union ceased to exist. In its place were 15 separate, independent countries.

By far the largest of these countries is Russia. Even before the birth of the Soviet Union in 1917, Russia had dominated its neighbors and had conquered many of them throughout the centuries.

MANY ETHNIC GROUPS

The word Soviet describes people who lived in the former Soviet Union and their government. It does not describe an ethnic group. As you know, an ethnic group is made up of people who share a common language, history, and customs. More than 150 different ethnic groups lived in the Soviet Union. Some of these groups are huge. The Russians, with about 145 million people, are the largest. The smallest group has only about 500 people.

While the Soviet Union existed, some people in other countries mistakenly called all Soviet people *Russians*. That practice annoyed many non-Russians.

WHAT YOU KNOW: This question refers to information given in Chapter 14, Lesson 1; the European part of Russia.

LESSON 1
pages 305–309

Lesson Theme Russia and neighboring countries—the 15 countries that once made up the Soviet Union—are home to a large number of different ethnic groups.

Lesson Objectives

- Describe the ethnic groups who live in Russia and neighboring countries.
- Explain the role of religion, family, and education in these countries.

1 PREPARE

Motivate Read the *Read Aloud* section to the class. Have students discuss how the end of national unity might affect the peoples of the former Soviet Union.

Set Purpose Use the *What You Know* question to review population density patterns of Russia. Tell students that they will read about how diverse the populations of Russia and its neighbors are.

2 TEACH

Understanding a Time of Change Help students understand how significant the end of the Soviet Union was for the whole world.

Ask students:

- **What were the first three nations to gain their freedom in the Soviet Union?** (Latvia, Lithuania, Estonia)
- **How many countries did the Soviet Union become?** (15)

Identifying Many Ethnic Groups Review the term *ethnic group* with the class.

Ask students:

- **To what did the term *Soviet* refer?** (all the people of the Soviet Union)

READING STRATEGY AND VOCABULARY DEVELOPMENT

SQ3R Study Guide Review the concept that students learned in Chapter 8 of using a study guide to organize information in a lesson. Introduce students to another way of organizing information for study—the SQ3R study guide. Explain that there are five steps in this method—Survey, Question, Read, Recite, Review. First students *survey*, or preview, the lesson. Next they develop *questions* about the lesson by turning headings into questions. Then they *read* to find the answers to their questions. In the next step, *recite*, they say the answers quietly to themselves. Finally they *review* the answers and summarize their major findings. Have students follow the SQ3R study guide for this lesson. You may wish to help students get started by doing the first two steps with them.

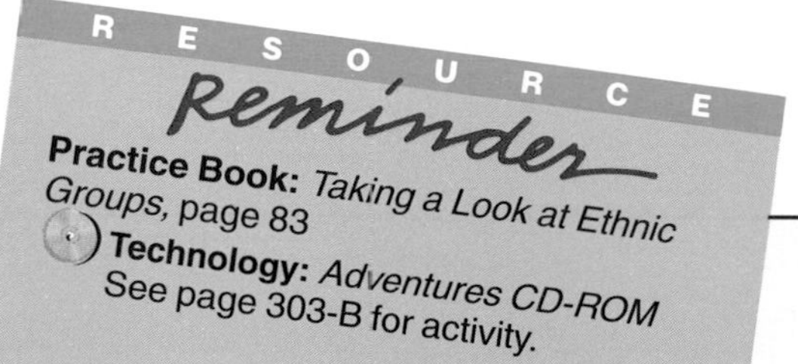

Looking at Ethnic Groups Continue discussing the ethnic groups and countries that once were part of the Soviet Union.

Ask students:

- **What larger group makes up nearly 75 percent of the population of Russia and its neighbors?** (Slavs)
- **Which three ethnic groups are part of this group?** (Russians, Ukrainians, Belarusians)
- **What two ethnic groups live in the Caucasus Mountain region?** (Georgians and Armenians)
- **What are two ethnic groups who live in central Asia?** (Uzbeks, Kazakhs, or Tajiks)
- **What ethnic group is related to the Inuit of North America?** (the Chukchi)

EXTENDING MAP SKILLS

Have students study the political map of Russia and its neighbors.

Ask students:

- **Which is the largest country in this group?** (Russia)
- **Which three of Russia's neighbors border the Baltic Sea?** (Latvia, Lithuania, Estonia)
- **Which two of Russia's neighbors border the Black Sea?** (Ukraine, Georgia)
- **Which three of Russia's neighbors border the Caspian Sea?** (Azerbaijan, Kazahkstan, Turkmenistan)
- **Which three of Russia's neighbors border Afghanistan?** (Turkmenistan, Uzbekistan, Tajikistan)
- **Which three nations of the former Soviet Union border Kyrgyzstan?** (Tajikistan, Uzbekistan, Kazahkstan)
- **Which country surrounds Moldova on three sides?** (Ukraine)

Russians are part of a larger group of people called *Slavs*. Two other ethnic groups, the Ukrainians and Belarusians (bel ə růs′ ənz), are also Slavs. Together these three Slavic groups make up nearly 75 percent of the population of present-day Russia and its neighboring countries. Even though they are all Slavs, Russians, Ukrainians, and Belarusians consider themselves to be very different from one another.

MAP SKILL: In 1991 the people of Estonia celebrated their independence from the Soviet Union. On which body of water is Estonia located?

In addition to the Slavic groups, many other ethnic groups live in the region. Georgians and Armenians, for example, live in the Caucasus Mountain region. Each of these groups has its own distinctive language and culture. Find **Georgia** and **Armenia** on the map on this page.

The Uzbeks make up the third largest ethnic group after the Russians and Ukrainians. Uzbeks, Kazakhs (kä zäks′), and Tajiks (tä jiks′) are a few of the ethnic groups of Central Asia. Use the map below to locate the five countries of Central Asia—**Uzbekistan**, Tajikistan, Kazakhstan, Turkmenistan, and Kyrgyzstan.

306

MAP SKILL: the Baltic Sea

BACKGROUND INFORMATION

Multicultural Perspectives Throughout the Cold War many Americans and their Western allies referred to all Soviet citizens as "Russians," a label which at the time was practically a synonym for "the enemy." Few realized that the Soviet Union was home to over 100 different ethnic groups, and fewer still realized that some of those groups also looked upon "Russians" as "the enemy." The Soviet Union was built upon the foundations of the old Russian Empire, and that empire had been created by conquering neighboring peoples. So when these conquered peoples—Uzbeks, Lithuanians, Azerbaijanis, and others—won their freedom from Moscow in 1991, they had great cause to celebrate. Today the republics of the former Soviet Union and that nation's former enemies have all established new relations with Russia. Ask students how people's images of Russia throughout the world have changed.

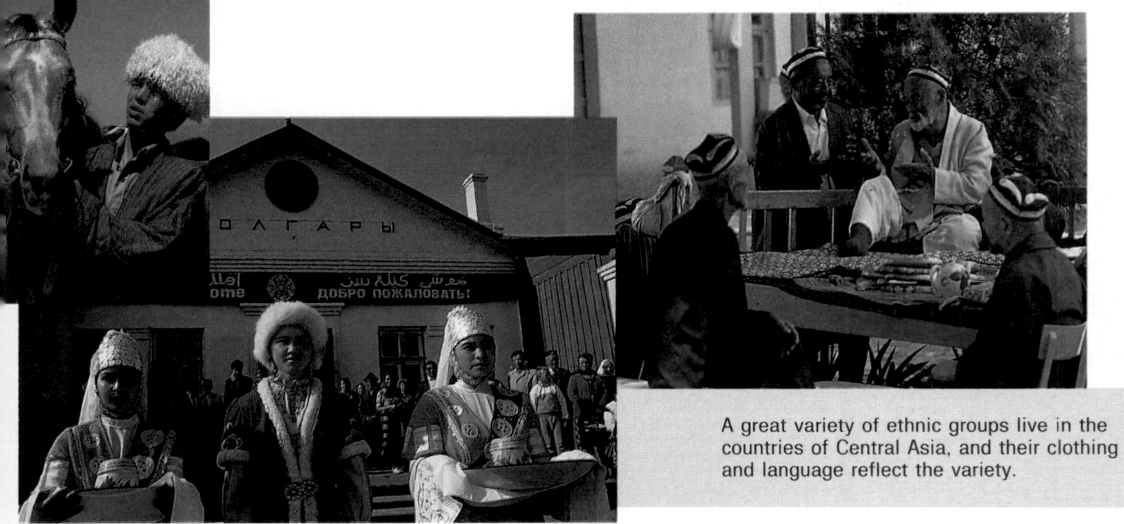

A great variety of ethnic groups live in the countries of Central Asia, and their clothing and language reflect the variety.

Farther east in northeastern Siberia live the Chukchi (chuk′ chē). This ethnic group is related to the Inuit of North America.

INDEPENDENT COUNTRIES

As you know, Russia is the largest country of this region. Russia's capital city, **Moscow**, was also the capital of the Soviet Union. You have read that Russia dominated many of its neighbors. Today people are wondering whether Russia will continue to dominate its neighbors.

Many Russians also live in the countries that were once part of the Soviet Union. In the past the rulers of Russia and the Soviet government sent Russians to fill jobs throughout the region. Often Russians had the best jobs, and other people objected.

While the Soviet Union existed, it was divided into 15 republics. Today each of those republics is a separate country. Each country is known by the name of its major ethnic group. However, within each country there are many people who do not belong to the main ethnic group. Many groups live side by side peacefully, but others have long histories as enemies.

One such rivalry exists between Armenians and Azerbaijanis. Many Armenians live in **Azerbaijan** (äz ər bī jän′), and some Azerbaijanis live in Armenia. Find these countries on the map on page 306. Armenians and Azerbaijanis speak different languages and practice different religions. Armed fights have often occurred between the two groups. While they were part of the Soviet Union, the Soviet government sent troops to the area to keep the peace.

RELIGION

During the more than 70-year period that the Soviet Union existed, its Communist government made it very difficult for people to practice their religion. Soviet leaders feared that any form of religion could endanger the communist government because some religious leaders had been powerful under previous governments. Soviet leaders wanted people to be loyal only to the government, not to their religious groups.

Houses of worship were closed. Some were kept as museums or public buildings. Others were allowed to fall apart.

In spite of years of discouraging religion, the Soviet leaders never destroyed it.

307

Discussing Independent Countries Help students to see a very real problem that the former republics of the Soviet Union face as they make their way independently.

Ask students:

- **Of the 15 countries that once made up the Soviet Union, which was the dominant one?** (Russia)
- **How did Russia show this dominance?** (The Soviet Union was ruled from Russia—from the capital at Moscow; Russians moved into neighboring republics and took the best jobs, often to the annoyance of the major ethnic groups in the republics.)
- **What problems have arisen among ethnic groups in the republics?** (Sometimes their differences—in culture and history—have made them rivals and bitter enemies, as in the case of Armenians in Azerbaijan and Azerbaijanis in Armenia.)
- *THINKING FURTHER:* **What clues do these facts give to problems that Russia and its neighbors are likely to face in the future?** (Students should recognize that the potential for civil wars and other conflicts exists in the region.)

Looking at Religion Help students to recognize the tenacity with which many people in the region held onto their religious beliefs in spite of Soviet attempts to destroy such feeling.

Ask students:

- **How did the Soviet government treat religion? Why?** (It discouraged religion; the government saw religion as a threat to communism.)
- **What actions did the government take to stamp out religion?** (It closed the houses of worship and put some into the service of the government.)

BACKGROUND INFORMATION

Changing Times As a new era dawned following the breakup of the Soviet Union, there were signs of unrest within newly independent countries and dissension among them.

- In Georgia the freely elected president was attacked and driven out by military factions that accused him of having become a dictator.
- In Kazakhstan, where Russians and Ukrainians together outnumbered the Kazakhs, the government feared that the Russians would secede and make part of Kazakhstan into Russian territory.
- Muslim populations of Central Asian countries suspected that the Russians, Ukrainians, and Belarusians were uniting to form a Slavic coalition that would dominate the region.
- Have groups of students do research to provide information on the current political situation in the 15 newly independent countries.

Discussing Religion Continue discussing religion in the newly independent nations.

Ask students:

- **What are the major religions practiced in Russia and its neighbors?** (Orthodox faiths, Protestant faiths, Roman Catholicism, Islam, and Judaism)
- *THINKING FURTHER:* **Why do you think so many people continued to follow religious beliefs, despite years of government opposition?** (Students may mention the strong faith and conviction many people feel in their religion.)

Looking at the Family Help students to recognize that family life is at the center of life in the region.

Ask students:

- **How does family size differ in urban and rural areas in the region? Why?** (In cities, families tend to be smaller, due to limited living space; in more rural areas they tend to be larger, at least in part because of more living space.)
- **What is distinctive about women in the work force in this region?** (About 85 percent of the women of working age work; 75 percent of all the doctors are women.)
- **Who cares for the children while the parents work?** (state-run day-care centers or live-in grandmothers)
- **What are the disadvantages for working women in the region?** (Women do most of the shopping and housekeeping, even if they hold jobs. They must spend many hours waiting in lines to buy food and other goods.)

You will read more about the survival of religious legacies on pages 310–313.

Many Russians belong to the Russian Orthodox Church. Ukraine and Georgia each has its own Orthodox church. Like the Greek Orthodox Church, which you read about in Chapter 12, these Orthodox churches are Christian churches that are not headed by the Roman Catholic pope in Rome. Each of the Orthodox churches has its own leader.

Most Estonians and Latvians are Protestant. The majority of Lithuanians are Roman Catholic. Armenia has its own Christian church that separated from the Roman Catholic Church and the Orthodox churches hundreds of years ago.

Followers of Islam form the largest non-Christian religious group in the region. You will read more about this religion in Chapter 18.

Jews have lived throughout the region for centuries. Even before the Soviet Union was created Jews were often treated harshly. Some Jews emigrated to Israel and the United States. Today Jews, like other religious groups, are free to worship as they choose.

Most women hold full-time jobs. Many work in factories such as this textile factory in Tajikistan employing 10,000 workers.

THE FAMILY

When the whole family is together, the soul is in place.

These are the words of an old Russian proverb, or saying. In the major cities, where apartments are tiny and hard to find, families tend to be small and close-knit. In Siberia and Central Asia, where more space is available, families are also close, but they tend to be somewhat larger than in the cities.

Whether families are large or small, both men and women usually work outside the home. About 85 percent of all women of working age have jobs outside the home. This is a higher percentage than in any other industrialized region. Women hold many different kinds of jobs, from construction worker to judge. Almost 75 percent of all the region's doctors are women. There are more female engineers in the countries of this region than in any other region of the world.

Some families have a live-in *babushka*, or grandmother, to look after the children while the parents work. But most children of preschool age are cared for in day-care centers run by the government.

Life is hard for working mothers in the region, as it is everywhere. After a full day at their jobs, women do most of the shopping and housekeeping. There are few supermarkets. Shopping often means waiting for hours in long lines to buy food and other goods. When shoppers reach the front of the line, they often find that there is very little left to buy.

EDUCATION

"Give me a generation to train the children," wrote one Soviet leader, "and the seed I sow [plant] will never be uprooted." Soviet leaders saw education as a way to teach children about communism as well as to train them for jobs and professions.

BACKGROUND INFORMATION

The Russian Orthodox Church When the Christian Church in the Mediterranean region split into east-west branches, the eastern, or orthodox, branch developed into two state religions—the Greek Orthodox Church and the Russian Orthodox Church. In Chapter 12 students read about the Greek Orthodox Church.

- The icons of the Russian Orthodox Church are known and valued the world over as eloquent symbols of mysticism and compassion.
- Russian Orthodox churches have distinctive onion-shaped dome steeples.
- The Russian Orthodox Church helped the tsars of early Russia control the peasants. This is one reason that these churches were destroyed or closed after the 1917 Revolution.

This farm family in Georgia shares a traditional breakfast of meat, cucumbers, scallions, and bread.

Before the Soviet Union was formed, only a small percentage of children in the region attended school. The creation of the Soviet Union changed that. Schooling became free and available to everyone in the country. All children went to school until they were at least 15 years old.

In the Soviet Union children of all ethnic groups studied Russian. Many studied their own languages as well. Students throughout the country learned the same subjects. Their textbooks were produced by the Soviet government. Until the late 1980s, Soviet textbooks did not mention events in the country's history that might reflect badly on its communist leaders.

Now that there is no Soviet Union, the schools remain. But the system of education has changed because it no longer trains students in communism. Education in the region may vary from country to country because each of the 15 countries must design and operate its own school system.

A REGION OF MANY PEOPLE

Russia is a huge land with many different ethnic groups. Its neighboring countries also have a great variety of ethnic groups. Russians outnumber all the other ethnic groups in the region. As you have read, each group in the 15 countries follows its own customs and traditions.

For years the Soviet government kept a tight control over its people, but changes began to take place. In 1991, the Soviet republics became independent countries. In the next two lessons, you will read more about how these countries have been changing.

Check Your Reading

1. How many countries are in the region?
2. Which ethnic group is the largest in the region?
3. How did the Soviet government change the availability of education?
4. THINKING SKILL: What was the Soviet government's point of view regarding religion?

THINKING SKILL: Point of View

Talking About Education Encourage students to understand the similarities and differences between education there and here.

Ask students:

- **What was the aim of Soviet education?** (to train people about communism and for jobs and professions)
- **How did the Soviet government change the number of people educated?** (It broadened it greatly, from very few to almost everyone age 15 or younger.)
- **How has education changed since the breakup of the Soviet Union?** (There is no longer training in communism and there is more variety.)

Applying the Lesson Have students prepare a four-column chart with the headings "Ethnic Groups," "Religion," "The Family," and "Education." Have students use this lesson to complete the chart.

3 CLOSE

Summarizing Students have read that there are 150 ethnic groups in the countries that once made up the Soviet Union. Have students name as many of the countries as they can before consulting a map.

Evaluating Use the *Check Your Reading* questions (answers given below) to assess students' understanding.

Answers to Check Your Reading

1. 15
2. Russian
3. The government broadened education widely, making it free and mandating that everyone must attend school until at least age 15.
4. The Soviet government felt religion was dangerous to the survival of communism and must therefore be discouraged.

Independent Practice
Practice Book: page 83

MEETING INDIVIDUAL NEEDS

Reteaching (easy) Have students write one or two paragraphs about what might happen if women in the independent countries of the former Soviet Union were no longer members of the work force.

Extension (average) Have students choose one of the ethnic groups they read about in this lesson. Have them write a paragraph describing the role of the ethnic group in the history of the region since 1917.

Enrichment (challenging) Have students research the Russian education system. Ask each student to write a short sketch about a day in the life of a Russian student as compared with their own school day.

LEGACY
pages 310–313

Lesson Theme Despite government opposition to religion, many Soviet citizens continued to practice their faiths. Today, religion is flourishing in the lands of the former Soviet Union.

Lesson Objectives

- Describe how religious worship was suppressed in the Soviet Union.
- Explain how various groups continued to worship despite government opposition.

1 PREPARE

Motivate Have students discuss how and why the First Amendment of the United States Constitution forbids Congress from interfering with the practice of religion.

Set Purpose Focus students' attention with the following question. Why should people be allowed to practice religion freely? (Encourage students to share their feelings about religious freedom.) Direct students to read the introductory section. Ask them to think about the concluding suggestion as they read the lesson.

2 TEACH

Understanding the Concept of Legacies Ask students why they think that religious practice is a legacy. (Possible answers include: because the customs associated with religious practice spring from beliefs that are both ancient and powerfully alive.)

Discussing a War on Religion Have students discuss why a government might want to suppress religious practice.

SURVIVAL of RELIGION

by Blake Eskin

In the last lesson you read that the Soviet Union broke up into 15 independent countries in 1991. Until then many ethnic groups were ruled by the Soviet government. Each of these groups has its own distinctive customs. In many cases, these groups also have religious traditions that are centuries old. However, until recently, the communist government of the Soviet Union opposed all religious practices. In this lesson you will read about how these legacies survived despite the government's opposition. As you read, think about how religion and its survival can be important to a culture.

A WAR ON RELIGION

As you know, the communist leaders of the 1917 revolution tried to abolish religion in their country. They insisted that the existence of many different religious groups would divide the Soviet Union. Using this argument, the government closed most houses of worship. The few that remained open were converted to museums. The government also tried to replace traditional religious holidays with newly invented holidays such as the Anniversary of the Revolution.

The Soviet government also refused to allow people to write or read books about religion. In response, people began printing such books in secret. This custom was called *samizdat* (säm′ ēz dät), which means "self-publishing." In many cases, people were sent to prison or were executed for possessing samizdat literature or illegal printing presses. Still, these homemade books continued to circulate among friends and relatives. Samizdat was a method of struggle shared by many faiths. But just as each religious group in the Soviet Union had its own history, each group also had its own way of keeping religious traditions alive.

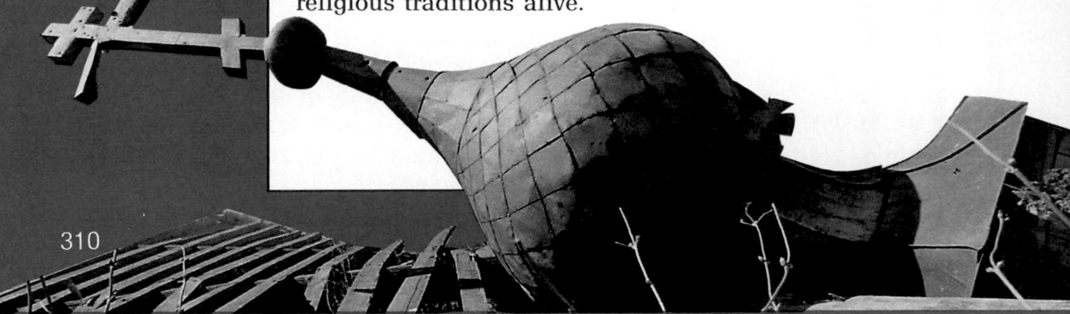

310

READING STRATEGY AND VOCABULARY DEVELOPMENT

SQ3R Study Guide Review with the class the five steps of the SQ3R study guide: *survey, question, read, recite, review.* Call on students to explain each step. Then have students create a model of this study guide and record their model on the chalkboard. Relate the different steps to one another. To get the students started, you may work with the material on this page in the section "A War on Religion." The *survey* step previews this section and suggests that students will learn about the efforts of the former Soviet government to suppress religion. The *question* may be, "How did religion come under attack?" Then students *read* the section and *recite* by answering their question and discussing it. Finally, they *review* what they have learned by writing a few important facts that they have learned about the former Soviet government's opposition to religion.

THE SURVIVAL OF CHRISTIANITY

The people of what was once the Soviet Union practice many different kinds of Christianity, including Roman Catholicism and Protestantism. However, the oldest and largest Christian church in the region is the Russian Orthodox Church.

The Orthodox Church originally developed in Byzantium (bə zant' ē əm)—the ancient name for the modern-day city of Istanbul. According to tradition, a Russian noble named Prince Vladimir of Kiev decided to convert to Orthodox Christianity in A.D. 988. His conversion had a major impact on his country's history. Many Russians—including Russia's rulers—became Orthodox Christians. Churches in the Byzantine style, with high ceilings and onion-shaped domes, began appearing throughout Russia. Inside, worshipers prayed in front of icons. An icon is a painting of a saint or religious leader. Many Russians also hung icons on the walls of their houses and worshiped at home.

Russian Orthodoxy enjoyed the support of Russian governments for hundreds of years. After 1917, however, Orthodox Christians were subject to the same oppression as other groups in the Soviet Union. Most churches were boarded up. Others were converted to museums, warehouses, and even factories. The government asked people to stop praying to icons and to remove them from their houses.

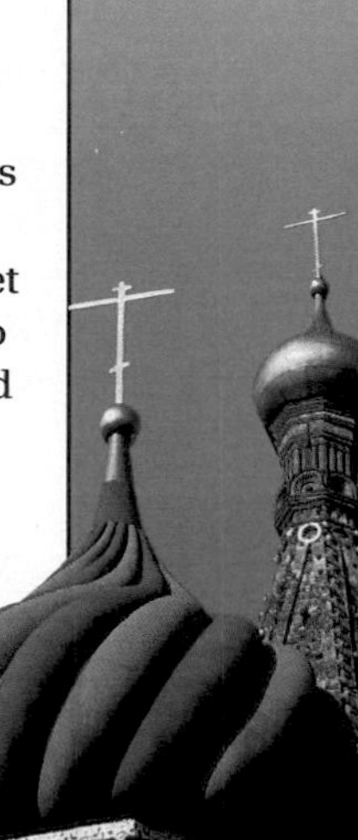

Under these conditions, the churches themselves began to decay and fall apart. Still, millions of Orthodox Christians continued to worship in their own homes. In this way the church struggled and survived. Proof of this survival was evident in 1988, when Orthodox Christians celebrated the one-thousandth anniversary of Prince Vladimir's conversion. In many parts of the country, churches and religious schools were restored and reopened. The icons that many people had been hiding in their homes were now openly and proudly displayed on their walls.

Talking About a War on Religion Continue the discussion, focusing on why people resisted the government.

Ask students:

- **Name one reason that Soviet leaders gave for their opposition to religion.** (They claimed that the existence of many different religious groups would divide the country.)
- **Why do you think that many people practiced religion despite government opposition?** (Student responses should reflect an understanding of the importance of religious practice.)

Discussing the Survival of Christianity Have students look at the photographs on pages 310–311 after they have read this section. Identify the clergyman on page 311 as an Orthodox Christian priest. Then have students use the information contained in this section to help them identify and describe the photographs.

Ask students:

- **Where did the Russian Orthodox Church originally develop?** (Byzantium)
- **Why do you think that Christianity managed to survive in the Soviet Union?** (Possible answers include: There was a long tradition of Christian worship; people found ways around the ban by worshiping at home.)

BACKGROUND INFORMATION

Multicultural Perspectives Although the freedom to practice religion is flourishing today in the countries that once formed the Soviet Union, in other countries this freedom remains severely limited. In China, for instance, the Communist Party continues to exert strict control over religious practice.

- According to the Chinese Constitution, religious freedom is guaranteed only as long as it does not interfere with the Communist Party or with the government. Religious reading materials and tapes from abroad must be authorized by the government.
- Religions practiced in China include Christianity, Islam, and Buddhism. The fastest-growing religion in China today is Christianity. Because of Christianity's associations with the West, the Chinese government is particularly concerned with this trend. Beginning in 1989 the government expanded an anti-Christian campaign to counteract what it perceived as a growing threat. China's current population of Christians consists of up to 60 million people—about 5 percent of the country's total population of 1,203,097,268.

Have students discuss the reasons that the leaders of the Chinese Communist Party would want to control religious practice.

Discussing the Survival of Islam As they read, have students think about both the historical and geographical contexts of Islam in the former Soviet Union.

Ask students:

- **What *historical* fact might help explain why Muslims of the Caucasus and Central Asia were able to resist Soviet opposition to Islam?** (Muslims have lived in these areas for over 1,200 years and have succeeded in preserving their traditions despite centuries of foreign rule.)
- *THINKING FURTHER:* **What *geographical* fact might help to explain why Muslims of the Caucasus and Central Asia were able to resist Soviet opposition to Islam?** (Direct students' attention to the *Atlas* maps of Eastern Europe and Northern Asia on pages 628–629. Locate Moscow, and remind students that this city was the center of the Soviet government. Then locate the lands of the Caucasus and Central Asia. Explain that because of the great distance between these areas and the center of government, Soviet officials may have been less effective in enforcing government policies.)

THE SURVIVAL OF ISLAM

Followers of Islam, who are called Muslims, have lived in the Caucasus and Central Asian areas of what was the Soviet Union for over 1,200 years. They have succeeded in preserving their traditions through centuries of foreign rule. When the Soviet government tried to restrict their customs, they found ways to adapt them to the new political situation.

For example, Muslims are commanded to make a pilgrimage to their holy city of Mecca in Saudi Arabia. But for many years, the Soviet government allowed no more than 20 Soviet Muslims to make this pilgrimage each year. Khadzhi Adil Zeinalov (käd′ zhē ä dēl′ zā′ nə lov), the head of a mosque in Baku, Azerbaijan, summed up the problem this way:

> *You know, to a Muslim, there are ten sacred things one must do, and among them [is] . . . going to Mecca, if health and finances permit. Here we have always had to add "and if the Government allows."*

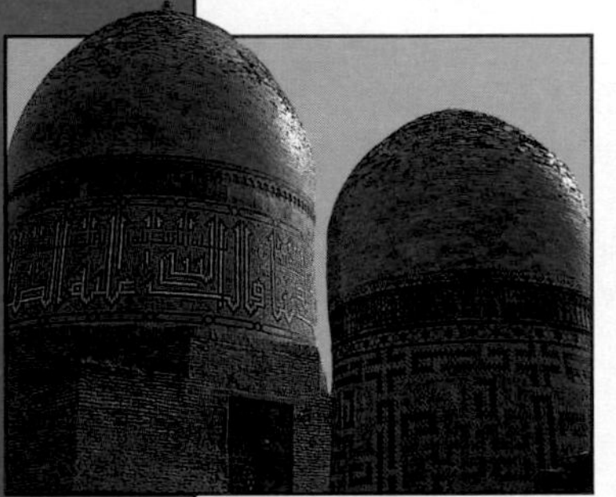

How could Soviet Muslims make this required pilgrimage? For many years, their solution was to visit other places called *mazars*, which means "holy tombs." One such mazar is the Shah-i-zind tomb in the city of Samarkand, in Uzbekistan. This tomb is the burial site of Kusam-bin-Abbas, who brought Islam to Uzbekistan centuries ago. Thousands of Soviet Muslims made pilgrimages to Shah-i-zind every year.

More recently, the persistence of this tradition was officially acknowledged by the government. In April 1990 Soviet officials announced that special airline flights to Mecca would be arranged for Soviet Muslims. Zeinalov was elated by this good news. "For us, this announcement is a gift," he said. "It is like we are celebrating a holiday."

312

CURRICULUM CONNECTION

Math Have students work in small groups to conduct research about the various religions practiced today in Russia and its neighbors. Have each group choose one neighboring country and present its research in the form of a pie chart. The pie chart should break down the various religious populations by percentage, including "Atheists" as one category. When the charts are completed, have the groups compare their results.

BACKGROUND INFORMATION

Multicultural Perspectives In 1992 Mikhail Gorbachev described how his country's treatment of religion had changed during the 1980s:

> *One of perestroika's especially important contributions . . . was the passing of a law on freedom of religion. We restored the rights of the Russian Orthodox Church which had suffered greatly in the years of Stalinism. At the same time, we also acknowledged the role of other religions—and nearly all the world's religions are to be found in our country.*

After reading this quote aloud, ask students to discuss which of the world's religions can be found in their community, state, and nation.

THE SURVIVAL OF JUDAISM

As you read in Lesson 1, Jewish people living in the Soviet Union were treated harshly for many years. But like the Christians and Muslims, the Jews fought to preserve their religious legacies. One such tradition is the study of the Torah and other Jewish holy books written in Hebrew. After 1917 the Soviet government refused to allow Jews to study Hebrew books. It also made sure that the Hebrew language was not taught in any state-run schools.

Many people broke these rules. For example, a Soviet Jew named Josif Begun (bā′ gün) secretly taught himself Hebrew and decided that he wanted to study the Torah. Since it was a crime to undertake such study in the Soviet Union, Begun asked permission to emigrate. Government officials refused his request. They also punished Begun by making sure he lost his job.

However, Begun refused to give up. To support himself and to help keep Jewish legacies alive, he began teaching Hebrew. On several occasions he was arrested, and spent a total of eight years in prison. He was finally allowed to immigrate to Israel in 1988, where he now pursues the Jewish tradition of study.

Although the Soviet Union has ceased to exist, many Jews fear continued persecution. Thousands have recently immigrated to Israel, the United States, and other countries. But many remain, looking for signs of hope. One such sign came in 1990, when a visiting American rabbi named Arthur Schneier led a Jewish prayer service in the Kremlin, the headquarters of the Soviet government! "It was very, very moving, the fact that we were obviously chanting and singing Hebrew prayers," said Schneier. "And they echoed throughout the Kremlin."

A PROMISING FUTURE

The independent governments of Russia and its neighbors now permit the practice of religion. Millions of young people have begun reclaiming ancient customs. By attending religious schools or quizzing their grandparents about religious practice, they are demonstrating how these traditions have survived, changed, and once again flourished.

Why did people struggle to keep their religious legacies alive in spite of government oppression?

Discussing the Survival of Judaism Help students to identify the photograph of Josif Begun on this page.

Ask students:

- **Why do you think that the Soviet government did not allow Hebrew to be taught in state-run schools?** (Since Hebrew is needed to study Jewish holy books, the banning of Hebrew instruction was an effective way to suppress Jewish religious traditions.)
- **Why was it "moving" that Hebrew prayers were recited in the Kremlin?** (Until recently the Kremlin, as the former headquarters of the Soviet government, was instrumental in suppressing Judaism.)

Exploring a Promising Future Emphasize to students that religious practice is no longer forbidden in what was once the Soviet Union.

Ask students:

- **Why do you think that young people of Russia and its neighbors are particularly interested in reclaiming traditional religious customs?** (Possible answers include: Open religious practice is something new for young people there, and it is a way for them to reclaim a past that was denied to them during the years of Soviet rule.)

Applying the Lesson Ask students to write a paragraph that describes the difficulties once faced by Soviet Christians, Muslims, and Jews.

3 CLOSE

Summarizing Students have read about the endurance of religious faith in the Soviet Union despite government opposition. Have students discuss why religion is an important legacy for many different groups.

Evaluating Assess students' understanding of the lesson by asking them the question at the bottom of the pupil page. (Students' responses should reflect an understanding of the importance of religion to cultures throughout the world.)

MEETING INDIVIDUAL NEEDS

Reteaching (easy) Have students make a drawing based on one of the illustrations contained in this lesson. Then have students accompany their illustrations with a paragraph that describes what they have depicted.

Extension (average) Have students conduct research in order to write a report on the history of either Christianity, Islam, or Judaism. The report should include some information about how this particular faith was practiced in the former Soviet Union.

Enrichment (challenging) Divide the class into two groups. Have one group imagine that they are Soviet citizens who have just been granted religious freedom. Have the other group imagine that they are journalists, and ask them to interview members of the first group in front of the class.

LESSON 2
pages 314–317

Lesson Theme The 15 separate countries the Soviet Union broke into in 1991 face major problems in converting their one Soviet command economy into mixed economies.

Lesson Objectives
- Explain the failings of the Soviet command economy.
- Describe how the new nations are attempting to change their economies.
- Explain what the Commonwealth of Independent States is.

PREPARE

Motivate Read the *Read Aloud* section to the class. Discuss what is wrong with a system that can produce goods but cannot distribute them properly, a basic problem in the region under study.

Set Purpose Use the *What You Know* question to review. Ask the *What You Will Learn* question and tell students that as they read the lesson, they should list the ways the countries are trying to change their economies.

TEACH

Discussing the End of an Economic System Help students to recognize the wrenching and far-reaching change that the collapse of an economic system brings on.

Ask students:

- **How did the Soviet economic system work?** (All economic decisions were made by government officials in Moscow, who had to be obeyed.)
- **How did the breakup of the Soviet Union change this?** (The new countries have to find ways to make their own economic decisions.)

Practice Book: *Economies of Russia and Its Neighbors*, page 84
- **Anthology:** *Farewell Speech*, pages 97–98

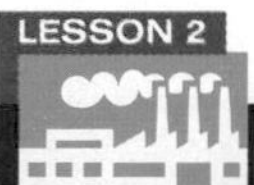

The Economy

READ TO LEARN

Key Vocabulary

command economy
capital goods
consumer goods
reform
perestroika
Commonwealth of Independent States

Key People

Mikhail Gorbachev
Boris Yeltsin

Read Aloud

This country produces 24 percent of all the world's milk and now we produce machines that can package all that milk efficiently and safely. But still, there's no milk in the stores.

These words were spoken by Alexander Panchenko, a manager of a factory that manufactured milk cartons. Shortages of basic goods such as milk were common in the Soviet Union. When Russia and its neighbors became independent, these shortages continued. But now these countries are free to work out new ways of organizing their economies.

Read for Purpose

1. WHAT YOU KNOW: How does a free-enterprise economic system work?
2. WHAT YOU WILL LEARN: How are the countries of the region trying to change their economies?

AN ECONOMIC SYSTEM ENDS

Imagine this. You live in a family in which the head of the family makes all the economic decisions. These include which businesses to begin, who will do which jobs, what products the business will produce, and how much each person will be paid. You as an individual cannot go into business for yourself and set your own prices. Suddenly the head of the family disappears. Family members now must make all the decisions that the head of the family once made. But family members have no experience in making decisions.

The situation described above is similar to what happened when the communist government of the Soviet Union ceased to exist and 15 separate countries had to work out their own economies. Until 1991 Soviet government officials in Moscow had made the decisions about where to build factories, what and how much to produce, how much to charge for products, and how much to pay workers.

Now these countries have to build new economies using what they can from the old Soviet Union. They must decide how much to cooperate with each other and with other countries. To understand the changes that must be made, you must first understand the old system.

 WHAT YOU KNOW: Students should recall that in a free-enterprise system individuals, not the government, make most economic decisions.

READING STRATEGY AND VOCABULARY DEVELOPMENT

SQ3R Study Guide Review the SQ3R study guide students learned in Lesson 1—Survey, Question, Read, Recite, Review. Ask students to name other strategies they have learned that can be incorporated into the SQ3R method. Discuss such strategies as previewing (Chapter 5), developing questions (Chapter 2), monitoring comprehension (Chapter 13), note taking (Chapter 4), and summarizing (Chapter 7). Have students work in pairs to incorporate these strategies into the SQ3R study guide. Discuss students' questions and answers.

A COMMAND ECONOMY

The Soviet economy was not working. Although it provided jobs for Soviet citizens, the economy did not produce enough of the goods and services that the people needed and wanted.

From 1917 until the late 1980s, Soviet citizens lived under the communist system of a **command economy**. In a command economy, the government makes most of the economic decisions. The government owns and operates land, factories, banks, and businesses. Everything from coal mines to taxicabs is owned and operated by the government.

Planners who worked for the Soviet government decided how many businesses needed to be established. They decided what goods would be manufactured, and they set all prices and wages. Often only one factory in the entire Soviet Union made a particular product.

For many years Soviet planners concentrated on producing **capital goods**. These are products that are used by industries to make other products. Soviet factories turned out huge quantities of capital goods, such as heavy machinery, tractors, trucks, and chemicals. But they failed to produce enough **consumer goods**, such as stoves, refrigerators, clothing, and furniture. Consumer goods satisfy people's needs and wants. Often the Soviet people simply did without them.

Workers did not have to worry about losing their jobs. In fact, the Soviet government guaranteed everybody a job. Keeping a job and getting paid had nothing to do with how good a job a worker did, so workers were not motivated to work hard. Most consumer goods were very scarce. Goods were bought and workers were paid even if the quality of the goods they produced was poor. As a result, the Soviet economy suffered.

This truck factory on the Kama River, west of the Ural Mountains, has been a major supplier of tractors for the region.

CHANGING THE ECONOMY

In 1985, **Mikhail Gorbachev** (mik ə ēl′ gôr′ bə chôf) became the head of the Soviet Union. Gorbachev wanted to **reform** the entire economy. To *reform* means "to make a change for the better."

Gorbachev called his plan of reforms **perestroika** (per ə stroi′ kə), or "restructuring." He hoped to reform the Soviet Union's economy by taking decision making out of the hands of the government officials. He wanted to give greater control to managers of factories and businesses. Workers who produced more would earn more.

Perestroika did not take place quickly enough for most Soviet citizens. Consumer

Looking at a Command Economy Help students to discover what was wrong with the Soviet economic system.

Ask students:

- **How does a command economy operate?** (The government owns all business and industry and government officials make all economic plans and decisions.)
- **What kind of goods did Soviet planners concentrate on producing?** (capital goods—products that were used by industries to make other products)
- **What effect did the emphasis on producing capital goods have on the people of the Soviet Union?** (They had to go without many consumer goods—not enough products like refrigerators were made for everyone who wanted them.)
- **What employment policy did the Soviet economic system practice?** (Everyone was guaranteed a job and pay.)
- **What is the advantage of such a policy?** (Nobody has to be unemployed.) **What are the disadvantages?** (Without motivation to work hard, some workers work poorly, which produces poor quality products and weakens the economy.)
- *THINKING FURTHER:* **Why might people be unhappy and dissatisfied living under a command economy like the one the Soviet Union had?** (People might resent having no power to make decisions that affect them deeply; they may resent having to sacrifice their own needs and wants indefinitely because the government orders it; they may be unhappy that good work is not more highly rewarded than bad work or no work at all.)

Discussing the Changing Economy

Ask students:

- **What was perestroika?** (an attempt by Mikhail Gorbachev to transfer economic decisions from government officials to producers and to reward good work)

BUILDING CITIZENSHIP

Current Events and Economics While the Soviet Union existed, its 15 republics had a single command economy controlled by the planners in Moscow. Mikhail Gorbachev's plans for perestroika were economic as well as political. But the Soviet economic planners did not want to lose their power, and Gorbachev had difficulty designing a restructured economy. Boris Yeltsin, after becoming president of the Russian republic, announced that price controls would be removed in Russia. This move led to a removal of price controls throughout the region, but the former republics found that it was easier to create political independence than economic independence. Many citizens had trouble dealing with the effects of the changing economy. Refer students to the *Viewpoints* on pages 318–319. Have students bring in news articles that describe economic problems and solutions in the 15 countries that had been Soviet republics.

Looking at Many Problems

Ask students:

- **How did Boris Yeltsin come to power?** (In June 1991, he was elected president of the Russian republic.)
- **What did he want to do to the economic system of Russia?** (He wanted to toss out the command economy and replace it with a free-enterprise system—and do it faster than Mikhail Gorbachev.)
- **What steps did he take to accomplish this goal?** (He initiated a kind of "shock therapy" by lifting all the controls on prices, previously set by the government.)
- **What was the immediate effect of this plan on consumers?** (Many found that they could not afford to buy what they needed because their salaries had not gone up.)
- *THINKING FURTHER:* **What do you think Yeltsin hoped this plan would accomplish?** (Students may suggest that he hoped that sellers would produce more because they could get higher prices for their goods. This would make more goods available on the market.)

Understanding Separate Economies Stress the difficulties of fragmentation that the new economies faced.

Ask students:

- **Why was it necessary for the Soviet economy to break up into 15 different economies?** (because the Soviet Union had divided into 15 independent countries.)
- **What problems did they face?** (how to divide and assign ownership of factories, how to generate and divide electric power, how to pay pensions earned under the Soviet system)

goods were still hard to find, and their quality was still poor.

MANY PROBLEMS TO SOLVE

In June 1991 an historic election took place in the Soviet Union. **Boris Yeltsin** was elected as the president of the Russian republic. Yeltsin was chosen from five candidates in the first free presidential election in Russia's history. Yeltsin wanted to abandon the communist command economy in favor of a capitalist free-enterprise system. He wanted to proceed at a much faster pace than that set by Gorbachev in the rest of the Soviet Union.

Yeltsin wanted to plunge the Russian republic into a kind of "shock therapy." The plan he supported was to lift all controls on prices for most foods and other goods. For years the government had set prices for meat, cooking oil, gasoline, and hundreds of other items. Yeltsin wanted prices to be determined by what buyers were willing to pay and what sellers were willing to be paid.

Yeltsin put his "shock therapy" plan into effect in Russia at the end of 1991. Prices shot up overnight. Some foods cost three or four times what they cost the day before. Meat was often ten times more expensive. Many people became angry because their salaries had not been raised, and they could not afford to buy necessary foods.

Once Russia removed price controls, other countries in the region also raised prices. Otherwise people from Russia would have crossed national borders to buy goods at lower prices. That would have created shortages outside of Russia.

CREATING SEPARATE ECONOMIES

When Russia and its neighbors became independent countries, they realized that they were all connected by a single economic system. Many problems had to be solved and many questions had to be answered.

All 15 republics had used the ruble as their money. The independent countries had to decide whether to continue using rubles or to create their own currency. The Soviet Union had owned all the factories. The countries had to decide how to divide

There have been frequent shortages of food in stores and outdoor markets in Moscow.

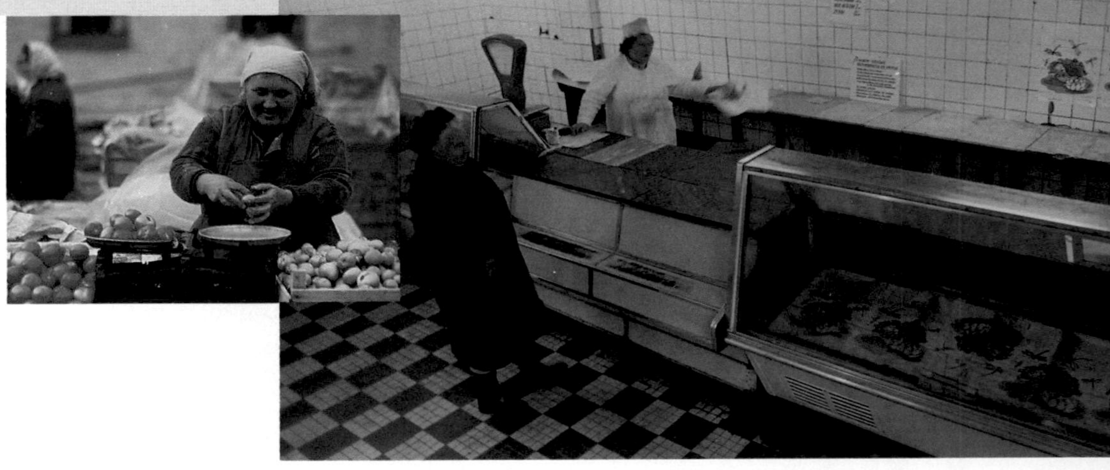

316

CURRICULUM CONNECTION

Math Use the situation of prices soaring more quickly than salaries to give students practice in working with percentages. Assign them such problems as the following:

- Prices rise by 80 percent. How much of a raise would a worker earning 300 rubles a month need to be able to afford goods now? (80 percent x 300 rubles = 240 rubles)
- Prices rise by 300 percent. What salary would a worker who originally made 400 rubles a month have to make to keep up with this rise? (300 percent x 400 rubles = 1,200 rubles)
- A worker making 500 rubles a month gets a raise to 750 rubles. How much of a percentage raise in prices could she now afford? (750 rubles minus 500 rubles = 250 rubles, which is a 50 percent raise, making it possible to afford a 50 percent rise in prices)

Farmers in Ukraine grow a great deal of wheat. In Georgia, sheep-raising is an important economic activity.

the factories among themselves. Each country also had to decide who would now own the factories—the governments of the countries or private companies. They had to decide how the countries that had no plants for generating electric power could get a fair share of electricity. The countries also had to work out how to guarantee people the pensions and other benefits they had earned as citizens of the Soviet Union.

These were only a few of the economic problems that 15 countries had to solve. They needed a way to work together to solve them.

A NEW FORM OF UNION

Most of the countries realized that they could not solve their problems without cooperating. Some leaders suggested that they begin a new form of cooperation. They called the new organization they began in 1991 the **Commonwealth of Independent States**, or C.I.S.

Like the European Union, or E.U., which you read about in Chapter 10, the Commonwealth of Independent States offered a way to join the economies of a group of countries. The countries would remain independent, but they could link their economies.

The task of the C.I.S. was different from that of the E.U. The E.U. began with economies that were not strongly connected and worked to connect them. The C.I.S. began with a single economic system and tried to find ways to separate it while keeping some of the links.

LOOKING TO THE FUTURE

The economic system that existed in the Soviet Union underwent great changes even before the country ceased to exist. What had been a command economy is gradually changing to a mixed economy or a free-enterprise system. Each country must choose its own way.

Check Your Reading

1. What is a command economy?
2. What are capital goods and consumer goods?
3. Describe some economic problems that the newly independent countries had to solve.
4. THINKING SKILL: How could you check the accuracy of this statement, "This country produces 24 percent of all the world's milk."

THINKING SKILL: Accuracy of Information

317

Discussing a New Form of Union

Ask students:

- **What is the C.I.S.?** (the Commonwealth of Independent States)
- **What is its aim?** (to give the newly independent countries a way to cooperate economically)

Applying the Lesson Have students imagine that they are citizens of Russia or one of its neighbors. Ask them to write a paragraph in which they tell whether they approve or disapprove of Boris Yeltsin's reforms and explain why.

CLOSE

Summarizing Students have learned that in 1991 the Soviet Union broke up and that the countries that had been part of the Soviet Union have had to establish their own separate economies. Have students predict how successful they might be and why.

Evaluating Use these questions to assess students' understanding.

- **What did the Soviet economy fail to do?** (It could not produce enough for its people.)
- **Why did some of the newly independent countries feel the need to found the C.I.S.?** (to allow economic cooperation with their neighbors)

Answers to Check Your Reading

1. an economy in which government officials make most of the important economic decisions
2. capital goods—products that are used by industries to make other products; consumer goods—goods that satify people's needs and wants
3. ownership, division of utilities, how to pay debts, fast-rising prices, shortages
4. check other sources of information

Independent Practice
Practice Book: page 84

MEETING INDIVIDUAL NEEDS

Reteaching (easy) Have students create a before-and-after chart contrasting the economic system of the Soviet Union with that of Russia and its neighbors.

Extension (average) Have students prepare an on-the-spot newscast in which economists and citizens of Russia or one of its neighbors discuss the economic changes they are undergoing.

Enrichment (challenging) Have students write an essay in which they trace the breakup of the Soviet Union's command economy into 15 separate economies from Mikhail Gorbachev's plan for perestroika to the present.

CHAPTER 15

CITIZENSHIP Viewpoints

pages 318–319

Lesson Objective
- Compare and contrast points of view on how Russia should solve its current economic problems.

Identifying the Issue Help students to see that the complex economic challenges Russia faces can be viewed from many perspectives.

Suggested Question
- ***Why might there be differences of opinion about how Russia should improve its economy?*** *(The Russians interviewed have each had different experiences dealing with Russia's economy since the collapse of the USSR.)*

Discussing Three Different Viewpoints Have students read the viewpoints on page 319.

NATASHA PETROVA

Suggested Question
- ***What is her solution to the problem of corruption?*** *(Pay government officials higher salaries so they will take pride in their work and won't be tempted to accept bribes.)*

EMMA VAINIKHOVITCH

Suggested Question
- ***What role does Vainikhovitch say government should play in Russia's economy?*** *(The central government should play a very limited role and reduce regulations that discourage the growth of private businesses. Local governments should work closely with private citizens to encourage growth of the market economy.)*

CITIZENSHIP VIEWPOINTS

The Central Market in Yekaterinburg, Russia offers fresh food—and long lines—for those willing to wait.

HOW SHOULD RUSSIA SOLVE ITS ECONOMIC PROBLEMS?

In the 1990s Russia began the difficult process of moving from a communist command economy to an open, free market economy. The collapse of the centrally-planned economy resulted in great hardship for many Russians. Workers have seen prices rise and their government jobs disappear.

Some, mostly older, Russians long to return to what they believe to be the safety and stability of communist rule and decision making by government planners. The 1996 election of Boris Yeltsin as president of Russia, however, showed that most Russians do not want to go back to a planned economy. Yet opinion is divided over the best way to solve Russia's economic problems. Some, like Natasha Petrova, blame Russia's current economic downturn on corruption in government. Others, like Emma Vainikhovitch, favor the growth of private businesses. Still others, like Slava Wlassoff, believe that Russia's economy will not improve until the government encourages more of Russia's newly-rich private business owners to invest in rebuilding the Russian economy. Read and consider three viewpoints on the Russian economy and answer the questions that follow.

318

BACKGROUND INFORMATION

About Russia's Economic Concerns
- Under Boris Yeltsin's leadership the government has sold off most of its small enterprises, such as shops, restaurants, and other service-oriented businesses. Privatization of larger factories has been hindered by the difficulties of deciding the value of these industries.
- Some factories are so outdated or in such a state of disrepair that private buyers may never be found.
- As unprofitable state-run factories have been shut down, unemployment has soared.
- Russia has also faced serious inflation. In January 1992 the Yeltsin government lifted price controls on a variety of items. Within eight months, the price of bread was fifty times higher. Wages have not kept pace with rising prices.

Three **DIFFERENT** Viewpoints

"The major problem ... is corruption ..."

1 NATASHA PETROVA
Office manager, Novisibirsk, Russia
Excerpt from interview, 1996

The major problem facing Russia today is corruption in government. The money that is given at the top is not getting to the local level. Government workers are poorly paid, so they are lured into taking bribes. No business can be done without paying bribes. If government officials were paid more, they would be proud of working for the state. People would respect them and they would be more honest.

"All industries should be privatized."

2 EMMA VAINIKHOVITCH
Retired teacher, St. Petersburg, Russia
Excerpt from interview, 1996

The Russian economy must be free of regulations coming from the top. The central government should not interfere or put any pressure on local governments. Each local area should fix its own problems through the free market economy. All industries should be privatized. Russians need to be free to travel and to say what they think. Russia will thrive in the future if it keeps to the same course as now. Russians must be patient.

3 SLAVA A. WLASSOFF
Chemist, Academgorodok, Russia
Excerpt from interview, 1996

"We need a strong government ..."

Russians need to have confidence in their economy. Our country now has many rich people. For young people who want to start private businesses, this is a time of opportunity. We need a strong government that can guarantee that money put into banks is safe and will encourage the rich to use their money to develop Russia's natural resources and industry.

BUILDING CITIZENSHIP

1. What is the viewpoint of each person?
2. In what ways are some of the viewpoints alike? In what ways are they different? What might be the reasons each speaker has this perspective on Russia's economic problems?
3. What other viewpoints might people have on this issue?

SHARING VIEWPOINTS

Discuss what you agree with or disagree with about these and other viewpoints. Think about the ways these views might change as the Russian economy improves or if it weakens further. Then write three statements that all of you can agree with about solving Russia's economic problems.

319

SLAVA WLASSOFF

Suggested Question

- ***Why does Wlassoff call this a "time of opportunity" for young people?*** *(Russians can now start their own businesses; formerly all enterprises were run by the state.)*

EVALUATE

Answers to Citizenship Viewpoints

1. Petrova says an end to government corruption is the answer to Russia's economic problems. Vainikhovitch favors increasing privatization of industry and decreasing regulation by the central government. Wlassoff says the money and business skills of wealthy Russians are needed to develop the nation's industry and natural resources.
2. All are concerned with the role of the central government in the new Russia. None want to return to a centrally-planned economy. Vainikhovitch wants the central government to reduce its role in economic life, while Wlassoff wants it to take a more active role in creating a climate for investment. Each person's occupation might have influenced his or her opinion.
3. Other viewpoints might favor a return to a centrally-planned economy, a faster pace towards a free market economy, or encouraging investments by foreign corporations in Russia.

Sharing Viewpoints Encourage students to express their own viewpoints and speculate on how Russian viewpoints might change as the economy changes. Three statements the class might agree on include: **1.** The present economic system needs to be improved. **2.** The actions of government influence the economy. **3.** The economy can be improved.

Debating Viewpoints As an extension, have students debate the merits of each proposed solution to Russia's economic problems, considering feasibility, the difficulties of implementation, and potential economic impact.

CITIZENSHIP

Using Current Events In Russia, economic concerns are closely linked to politics and changes in government. For most of this century, real power in Russia was held by the Communist party. Since the breakup of the USSR, efforts in Russia to move toward a market economy and continue on a path toward economic reform have been led by those outside the Communist party. Reform has moved forward or stalled depending upon the strength of the country's political leadership. Discuss with students the reasons why economic and political life are so connected. Then call for student volunteers to research Russia's current economic situation, looking at whether Russia's economic outlook is improving or worsening and at how politics is influencing its current economic policy.

LESSON 3
pages 320–323

Lesson Theme After nearly 75 years of Communist rule, the Soviet Union fragmented into 15 independent countries.

Lesson Objectives
- Explain how Communist government worked in the Soviet Union.
- Describe how the Communist Party lost power in the Soviet Union.
- Describe the political problems that the new nations face.

PREPARE

Motivate Read the *Read Aloud* section to the class. Ask students why the present is both a happy and a sad time in the newly independent nations.

Set Purpose Ask the *What You Know* question to review the dramatic economic changes in Russia and its neighbors. Ask the *What You Will Learn* question and tell students that they will learn about the political changes going on there.

TEACH

Discussing Changing Governments

Ask students:

- **What was the result of the breakup of the Soviet Union?** (The 15 Soviet republics declared their independence and formed their own governments.)
- *THINKING FURTHER:* **Why do you think that map and textbook makers were affected by events in the Soviet Union?** (Students may suggest that the Soviet Union was such a large and important country and changes occurred so fast that maps and textbooks would require enormous changes very quickly.)

RESOURCE Reminder

Practice Book: *Using a Map*, page 85
■ **Anthology:** *Farewell Speech*, pages 97–98
Technology: *Adventures CD-ROM*
See page 303-B for activity.

LESSON 3

The Government

READ TO LEARN

Key Places
Kremlin
Ukraine
Belarus
Minsk
Kazakhstan

Key People
Karl Marx
Lenin

Read Aloud

People have a free soul now. It's a hard time but nevertheless a happy time. The free spirit compensates [makes up] *for the deficiencies* [shortages] *in food, and so forth. The process of democracy is a living organism. It has just been born. It has to grow.*

These words capture the optimism of Vladimir Tikhonov. He was a Soviet citizen who was excited by the changes that had begun to take place in the Soviet Union even before the 15 countries became independent. Now even greater changes are taking place.

Read for Purpose

1. **WHAT YOU KNOW:** How have the economic systems of Russia and its neighbors been changing?
2. **WHAT YOU WILL LEARN:** What changes took place in the governments of Russia and its neighboring countries after the Soviet Union collapsed?

CHANGING GOVERNMENTS

During 1991, change was taking place so rapidly in the Soviet Union that map makers and textbook writers had difficulty keeping up. At the beginning of the year there was a country called the Soviet Union. It was made up of 15 republics that were all part of one nation. By the end of the year there was no country called the Soviet Union. One after another, each of the 15 republics had declared that it was independent. Maps had to be redrawn and textbooks had to be rewritten.

In this lesson you will learn about how those countries and their people began adapting to the change. You will learn more about the Commonwealth of Independent States. Above all you will learn that the breakup of the Soviet Union was only the start of many changes.

ABANDONING THE SOVIET SYSTEM

Even before the end of the Soviet Union many leaders had decided to try to introduce democracy. The communist system of the Soviet Union had been based on ideas of government described by a German thinker and writer named Karl Marx.

In the 1800s Marx described an idea of social organization in which all property is owned in common. He called this system communism. In a communist nation,

320 WHAT YOU KNOW: This question refers to information given in the previous lesson; a command economy is being exchanged for free-enterprise systems.

READING STRATEGY AND VOCABULARY DEVELOPMENT

SQ3R Study Guide Be sure students are aware of the different approaches they can use to study. Review the KWL guide students learned in Chapter 8. Divide the class into four groups to study this lesson—two groups using the KWL study guide approach and two groups using the SQ3R approach. After the groups have completed their study guides, discuss the questions and answers that each group came up with. Then encourage students to discuss the advantages and disadvantages of each study approach.

the government also runs the nation's economy. Marx believed that, eventually, there would be no need for government because everyone's needs would be met. Then true communism would be established and everyone would be treated equally. The Soviet Union was the first country to apply some of Marx's ideas.

As you know, the United States and many other countries have a free-enterprise system, one in which individuals, called capitalists, own property and make economic decisions. Marx believed that capitalists kept workers poor in order to maintain their own power. Sooner or later, he said, the workers would revolt against the rich. Then people would be equal, and property would be commonly owned.

In the early 1900s Vladimir Ilyich Ulyanov, better known as Lenin, came to believe that Marx's ideas could be used in Russia. Lenin believed that the revolution against the wealthy should be led by a few strong leaders. In 1917 Lenin selected a group of people to help him guide the Russian Revolution. This group later became the core of the Communist party.

In 1917, the old Russian government fell apart as a result of the Russian Revolution. Lenin and the Communist party came to power. Lenin argued that the Communists should seize all private property and control it for the benefit of the people. The Communists controlled the government, and the government took full control of the nation's economy.

Pictures of Lenin, the founder of the Soviet Union, were displayed throughout the country.

COMMUNISM IN THE SOVIET UNION

Communism in the Soviet Union did put an end to most private property. The government seized the ownership of most farms and factories. Almost all workers worked for the government.

Yet all workers were not equal. Government officials received better apartments and more money and benefits than ordinary workers. Athletes, ballet dancers, and a few other people also had better standards of living than ordinary workers.

The Soviet Union's constitution stated that all citizens had the right to a job, vacation, and free education, as well as to freedom of speech, press, assembly, and religion. But the Soviet government failed to guarantee these freedoms for individuals. Thus, many people, especially writers and scientists, found their freedoms denied. Many people who disagreed with the government were forced to live in Siberia or were sent to jail.

In 1989 the Soviet constitution was amended to provide greater protection for the freedom of individuals. However, many people were still unhappy because the constitution still did not provide adequate protection for certain freedoms.

THE COMMUNIST PARTY

Between 1917 and 1990 the Communist party was the "leading and guiding force of Soviet society." By law, it was the only political party allowed. For many years all

Looking at the Abandonment of the Soviet System

Ask students:

- **What was Karl Marx's goal for society?** (a society where everyone would be equal and all property would be commonly owned)
- **Why was Lenin important in Soviet history?** (He led the Russian Revolution and his followers became the core of the Communist party.)
- **What effect did Lenin's ideas have on the political and economic system of the Soviet Union?** (The Communists controlled the government and the government controlled politics and the economy.)

Discussing Communism in the Soviet Union Help students to recognize how different the Communist Soviet system was from a democratic free-enterprise system.

Ask students:

- **What did the Communist party do concerning ownership of property in the Soviet Union?** (It put an end to it and made most farms and factories the property of the government.)
- **Were all people equal under the Soviet system?** (No, government officials and prominent people had an above-average standard of living.)
- **What rights did the Soviet Union's constitution promise all citizens?** (a job, a free education, and basic personal freedoms)
- **Were these rights always available to citizens?** (No, freedom of speech, press, assembly, and religion were not enforced, and those who tried to claim them were often punished.)
- *THINKING FURTHER:* **Do you think that communism in the Soviet Union resembled the idea of society described by Karl Marx? Why or why not?** (Students who agree may point to government operation of the economy; those who disagree may mention the inequality in the Soviet Union.)

BUILDING CITIZENSHIP

The Role of Political Parties Political parties are not mentioned in the United States Constitution. They formed over time as a practical system for candidates to gain support in the American electoral process. They were a way to gather people who had similar ideas about government. In contrast, until 1990 the Soviet Communist party was defined by the Soviet Constitution as the only party permitted to direct the Soviet government. Have students gather more facts about these two different party systems, one current and one now historic. Then have them create a comparison chart of the party systems in the United States and the old Soviet Union. The chart should contrast the differences in becoming a member, financing party activities, and the parties' roles in each country.

Looking at the Communist Party Students should understand the formerly unique importance of the Communist party in Soviet life.

Ask students:

- **What major change did the Communist party undergo in the Soviet Union in 1990?** (It lost its place as the only party when parties that held other views were allowed to emerge.)

Discussing a Historic Election Help students understand how great a change the election was for Soviet citizens.

Ask students:

- **What happened to many Communist party candidates?** (They were voted out of office.)
- **What happened to Communist party membership?** (Many Communists resigned from the party.)
- *THINKING FURTHER:* **What do you suppose the Communists wanted to gain from their coup?** (to regain the power they had lost and put the old government back in power)

Looking at Struggles for Power Help students to recognize the suddenness with which events moved in the Soviet Union, following the coup.

Ask students:

- **What problems did the governments of the new nations have?** (what to do about the army and navy, about nuclear weapons, about who owned the Kremlin and other Soviet government offices)

Boris Yeltsin, president of Russia, stood on a tank to defy a communist group that tried to stop the move to democracy.

the real power for ruling the Soviet Union was in the hands of the Communist Party. The party controlled the government and the economy.

A HISTORIC ELECTION

In March 1989, for the first time since the Communists came to power in 1917, the people of the Soviet Union were given a choice of candidates in a national election. Previously, only approved Communist party candidates had been on the ballot.

Throughout the country members of the Communist party were voted out of office. Even party leaders who ran unopposed lost because they failed to win 50 percent of the vote. Voters had simply crossed their names off the ballots.

By the end of 1991 the Communist party had lost all its power. Many Communists had lost elections. Other former Communists had declared that they no longer belonged to the party.

In August 1991 some government officials who were unhappy about the Communist party's loss of power tried to stage a coup, a sudden seizing of the government. Russian President Boris Yeltsin defied the coup leaders, and the coup failed. Mikhail Gorbachev rapidly lost power.

STRUGGLES FOR POWER

After all the republics had become independent countries, Gorbachev found that he was head of a country that did not exist. His job had disappeared.

The 15 new countries faced problems of government similar to those they faced with the economy. For example, they had to decide which country would be in charge of the army and navy. Several countries said that the portion of the army or navy stationed in their country belonged to them. But soldiers and sailors wanted to serve in their own country's forces. The Soviet Union had many nuclear weapons. Which country would keep them? Or should they all be destroyed?

Moscow, the capital of Russia, had also been the capital of the Soviet Union. After independence, Russia claimed all buildings in the **Kremlin**, the Soviet government offices. On December 25, 1991, the Russian flag was raised over the Kremlin.

CONTINUED UNREST

The three Slavic countries of Russia, **Ukraine**, and **Belarus** began the Commonwealth of Independent States (C.I.S.). They chose **Minsk**, the capital of Belarus, to be the headquarters of the C.I.S.

BUILDING CITIZENSHIP

Current Events and Government The Commonwealth of Independent States was formed in 1991. At that time it included all of the countries that had been republics of the Soviet Union, except for Latvia, Lithuania, and Estonia. Georgia joined the C.I.S. in 1993. The member countries do not agree about the C.I.S.'s role in many areas. The organization's original plans were to have C.I.S. members share a unified currency, control the nuclear weapons that had belonged to the Soviet Union, and to command the army and navy. Nevertheless, some C.I.S. members, in particular Ukraine, have begun to build up their own national military forces and to print their own currency. Most of the member countries see the C.I.S. as a cooperative body for assisting with trade relations and economic issues. Yet because of past history, many members of the C.I.S. fear the organization will inevitably be dominated by Russia and become the instrument through which Russia could once again dominate its neighbors. The goals and perhaps even the membership of the C.I.S. may change over time. Have students use newspapers and magazines to learn more about the current status and membership of the C.I.S. Then have them create a map with symbols to indicate any ways in which member countries have chosen to be independent in matters such as currency.

MAP SKILL: The Commonwealth of Independent States was established in 1991 at a meeting in Alma-Ata. In which country is Alma-Ata located?

Kazakhstan was the first non-Slavic nation to join. The C.I.S. is a plan of economic and governmental relations.

Russia, too, has had problems. Immediately after being elected president in 1991, Yeltsin faced many economic and political challenges. These difficulties caused some parliamentary leaders who had been communists to try to stop Russia's move to democracy. In 1996, a renewed Communist party ran a candidate against Yeltsin in national elections. Although the communists received some votes, most Russians voted to re-elect Yeltsin and continue on the path of democracy.

THEN AND NOW

The Soviet Union has ceased to exist, and 15 independent countries have taken its place. The Communist party, which ruled the Soviet Union for about 70 years, has lost its power. Economic, political, and ethnic unrest have troubled Russia and its neighbors in the 1990s.

Check Your Reading

1. Describe the theory of communism.
2. Who was Lenin?
3. What changes have taken place in Russia and its neighboring countries?
4. **THINKING SKILL:** What questions could you ask to find out what changes are still taking place in this region?

THINKING SKILL: Asking Questions
MAP SKILL: Kazakhstan

EXTENDING MAP SKILLS

After students examine the map on this page, have them identify the three nations that were part of the Soviet Union but are not part of the Commonwealth of Independent States. (Estonia, Latvia, Lithuania)

Applying the Lesson Have students collect newspaper articles describing current happenings in the 15 nations that were once the Soviet Union. Have students paste them in a scrapbook and write a paragraph explaining each article in their own words.

3 CLOSE

Summarizing Students have just read about a major political transformation. Have students discuss how far-reaching the transformation is, for the nations involved and for the rest of the world.

Evaluating Use the *Check Your Reading* questions (answers given below) to assess students' understanding.

Answers to Check Your Reading

1. After rising up against capitalists, workers would own all property in common.
2. Vladimir Ilyich Ulyanov, the main leader of the Russian Revolution
3. They have gone from being part of the Soviet Union to becoming 15 independent nations.
4. Questions might include the following: What has been done about ownership of property—who owns what? What has happened with jobs—are there still enough for everyone? How has the military situation been resolved? Has one nation, like Russia, come to dominate the others?

Independent Practice
Practice Book: page 85

MEETING INDIVDUAL NEEDS

Reteaching (easy) Have students draw a flow chart that shows the progression of government in Russia from the Revolution of 1917 to the present.

Extension (average) Ask students to role-play a conversation among young citizens of Russia in which they discuss their reactions to the changes their country is undergoing.

Enrichment (challenging) Discuss with students the transition in government from 13 American colonies under British rule to 13 united states. Then have them write an essay that compares it to the transition in government from one unified Soviet nation to 15 separate and independent nations.

SKILLS LESSON
pages 324–325

Lesson Theme Drawing a conclusion involves pulling together related pieces of information so that they mean something.

Lesson Objective
- Identify and apply the steps that lead to drawing a conclusion.

PREPARE

Motivate Before students read the introductory paragraph, write the term *drawing a conclusion* on the chalkboard. Ask students to give examples of some conclusions they have drawn recently. (I didn't understand the material in this lesson. I will have to get help to get a good mark on the quiz.) Ask students for other words that mean the same as *conclude*. (*decide, determine, figure, deduce*) Have students read the introductory paragraph and explain the meaning of the term *drawing a conclusion.* Discuss the reasons that some conclusions are easier to draw than others.

Set Purpose Tell students that in this lesson they will learn how to draw conclusions.

TEACH

Trying the Skill Have students read the facts about shopping in Russia. Tell students that if they have trouble answering the questions, they may refer to the *Helping Yourself* section on the next page.

Thinking About Thinking Have several volunteers read their answers. Guide discussion of Question 2 by asking: What did you do first? Why? Next? Why? And so on. List students' steps on the chalkboard.

Drawing Conclusions

When you draw a conclusion, you put facts together so that they mean something to you. Suppose you walk into your backyard just in time to see a raccoon disappearing into the bushes. The garbage pail is overturned, with its lid removed and garbage spread out on the lawn. You would probably conclude that the raccoon had knocked over the pail, opened the lid, and started to eat some garbage. You could tell what had happened even though you had not seen it happen.

Trying the Skill

Read the facts listed below. Think about what the facts mean. State a conclusion based on the facts.

- The average shopper in Russia spends 14 hours a week standing in shopping lines.
- Because most consumer goods, even ordinary ones like toothpaste, are often unavailable, shoppers rush to join a line even when they don't know what is for sale.
- In most Russian stores making a purchase requires waiting in three lines: one line to select the item, a second line to pay for it, and a third line to pick up the item purchased.

1. What conclusion did you draw?
2. What did you do to draw your conclusion?

324

CURRICULUM CONNECTION

Math Point out that solving math problems involves drawing conclusions. Tell students that to solve a math problem, they must ask: What information have I been given? How do all the pieces of information relate to each other and to solving the problem? Do I have enough information to solve the problem? What conclusion (or answer) can I reach from the information? Is my conclusion reasonable?

HELPING YOURSELF

The steps on the left will help you to draw conclusions. The example on the right shows one way to apply these steps to the facts about Russian shoppers.

One Way to Draw Conclusions	Example
1. Identify the topic or subject.	The subject is consumer shopping in Russia.
2. Read the information given.	In this step you quickly read the information to get a general sense of the facts.
3. Look for ideas that are common to all the pieces of information.	Each piece of information is about Russian shoppers waiting in line.
4. Write a sentence stating how the subjects or ideas common to all the pieces of information relate to one another. This is your conclusion.	One conclusion that you might draw is that shopping in Russia is difficult and time-consuming.

Applying the Skill

Now apply what you have learned by drawing a conclusion from the following pieces of information.

- In Kazakhstan, the Kazakhs make up only 36 percent of the population. Russians and Ukrainians together make up the largest ethnic groups there, with about 50 percent of the population.
- Most Kazakh familes have five or six children. The Russian and Ukrainian families usually have two or three.
- The Kazakh population is likely to increase at two or three times the rate of the Russian and Ukrainian populations for the foreseeable future.

1. What is the topic of the information given above?
   a. Infant deaths among the people of Kazakhstan
   b. Population figures for some groups in Kazakhstan
   c. Ethnic groups in Kazakhstan

2. What patterns do you see in this information?
   a. Birthrates are the same for both the Kazakhs and the Russians and Ukrainians in Kazakhstan.
   b. Birthrates are increasing faster for Kazakhs than for Russians and Ukrainians.
   c. Birthrates are declining among Kazakhs, Russians, and Ukrainians.

3. Write a sentence that states a conclusion you can draw from the information given above.

Reviewing the Skill

1. Tell in your own words what it means to draw a conclusion.
2. List some steps you can follow to help you to draw conclusions.
3. Name some occasions when you find it necessary or useful to draw conclusions in school.

Helping Yourself Remind students that this section presents one procedure people use to draw conclusions. Tell students to read each step carefully and notice how the example applies to each step. Have students compare the steps listed on the chalkboard to those listed here to identify the most useful series of steps for drawing conclusions.

Applying the Skill Have students apply the skill to the list of facts on this page and answer the questions that follow. Remind them that they may refer to the steps outlined in *Helping Yourself* and also to the steps listed on the chalkboard.

3 CLOSE

Reviewing the Skill Use students' answers to Question 1 to add to or revise the definition and synonyms listed on the chalkboard. Use Questions 2 and 3 to elicit from students explanations in their own words of how to draw conclusions. End class discussion by having students cite situations outside school in which they might use this skill.

Independent Practice
Practice Book: page 86

ANSWERS TO SKILLS QUESTIONS

Applying the Skill
1. b
2. b
3. In the future less than one half of the Kazakh population is likely to consist of Russians and Ukrainians. In the future an increasing percentage of the population of Kazakhstan will consist of Kazakhs.

Reviewing the Skill
1. Drawing a conclusion means pulling together related pieces of information so that they mean something.
2. Identify the topic of the information given. Look for common ideas in all the information. Write a sentence telling how the ideas are related to one another and connected to the topic.
3. Drawing a conclusion gives meaning to information presented in class, in a textbook, in an assembly, or during extracurricular activities.

LESSON 4
pages 326–327

Lesson Theme With many former restrictions lifted, the arts flourish today in Russia and neighboring countries.

Lesson Objectives
- Describe the literature and music of Russia and neighboring countries.
- Explain how government control of the arts has lessened in the region.
- Describe recreation there.

PREPARE

Motivate Read the *Read Aloud* section to the class. Ask students to speculate about how government controls might limit the arts. (For example, government officials might prohibit art which criticizes the government.)

Set Purpose Use the *What You Know* question to get students to focus on the lack of free speech under the old Soviet government. Use the *What You Will Learn* question to encourage students to speculate on what the changes might be.

TEACH

Looking at Literature and Music
Call on students to identify and discuss the giants of Russia's literature and music.

Discussing Government and the Arts

Ask students:

- **How have conditions changed for artists in Russia and its neighbors?** (Beginning with glasnost, the government has considerably relaxed its controls over what artists produce.)

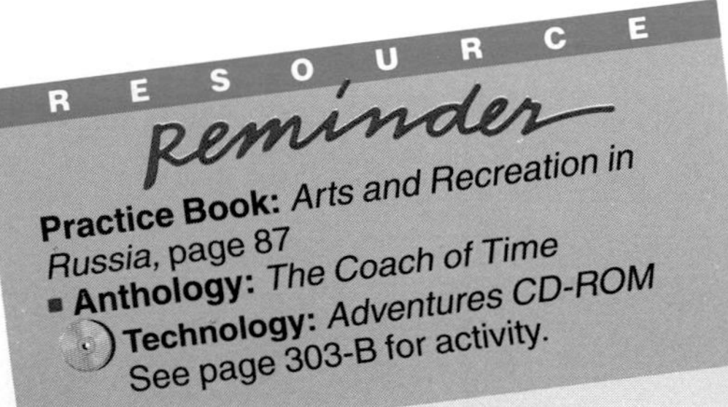
RESOURCE *Reminder*
Practice Book: *Arts and Recreation in Russia*, page 87
- **Anthology:** *The Coach of Time*
- **Technology:** *Adventures CD-ROM* See page 303-B for activity.

LESSON 4

Arts and Recreation

READ TO LEARN

Key Vocabulary
censor
glasnost

Key People
Alexander Pushkin
Feodor Dostoyevsky
Leo Tolstoy
Peter Ilyich Tchaikovsky
Boris Pasternak
Alexander Solzhenitsyn

Read Aloud

For many years the Soviet government strictly controlled the right to print newspapers and to produce art such as poetry. Today the glorious tradition of arts, long held captive by the government of the Soviet Union, is being returned to the people of Russia and its neighbors.

Read for Purpose

1. WHAT YOU KNOW: What had been the Soviet government's attitude toward the rights of its citizens?
2. WHAT YOU WILL LEARN: What changes are taking place for the region's artists and athletes?

LITERATURE, PAST AND PRESENT

For many years Russian literature astounded the world with the richness of its prose and poetry. The poet and story writer **Alexander Pushkin**, who wrote in the 1800s, is called the father of Russian literature. He was followed by great novelists, such as **Feodor Dostoyevsky** (fyō dôr dos tə yef′ skē) and **Leo Tolstoy**.

Russian writers have written about everything from the beauty of the Russian countryside to the tragedy of unhappy love. During the time of the Soviet Union some writers' works opposed the government. They were not allowed to publish in the Soviet Union, but some writings were passed around secretly.

Not all of the great literature of the region has been produced by Russians. Many other ethnic groups have their own literature. For example, Georgia has a long history of beautiful poetry and songs. Unfortunately, few people outside of Georgia can read the Georgian language and little has been translated.

MUSIC

Among the many famous Russian composers, several wrote music especially for the ballet. One of the best known of these composers is **Peter Ilyich Tchaikovsky** (il′ yich chī kof′ skē). About 100 years ago he wrote the music for the famous ballet *The Nutcracker*. Adults and children around the world have delighted in the tale of a magical nutcracker that comes alive.

GOVERNMENT AND THE ARTS

Writers and other artists were supported and controlled by the Soviet government. Government-approved artists often received training and jobs that allowed them

326 WHAT YOU KNOW: The Soviet government did not permit its citizens to exercise many of the rights provided in the Soviet Union's constitution.

READING STRATEGY AND VOCABULARY DEVELOPMENT

SQ3R Study Guide Use the SQ3R approach to gather information for a class discussion on arts and recreation in Russia and its neighbors. Have students use the SQ3R approach independently to study this lesson. The class discussion could focus on literature, music, and the role of government in the arts in the Soviet Union of the past and the 15 newly independent nations of the present. You might also wish to have students compare the role of the old Soviet government with the role of the United States government in the arts.

to concentrate on their work. But works of art that criticized the government or its leaders were censored. To censor is to prevent something from being made public.

Until the 1980s control of what was written and published in the Soviet Union was strict. But well-known Soviet writers were able to publish censored works in other countries. When writer Boris Pasternak was awarded the Nobel Prize for literature in 1958, the Soviet government forced him to turn it down. Alexander Solzhenitsyn (sol zhə nēt′ sən), who wrote about life in Soviet labor camps, lost his citizenship and was sent into exile.

In the 1980s Mikhail Gorbachev introduced a new policy known as glasnost, or "openness." For the first time since the Russian Revolution, state controls over the press were outlawed. As a result, there was an explosion of free speech. Soviet citizens gained the freedom to see plays and read literature that had been banned for more than 60 years. As one writer said:

> *Even if [glasnost] were to end today, what has already been accomplished in the past three years will go down in the history of Russian literature.*

Glasnost had an effect on music as well. Until 1986 all rock music had been carefully controlled by a government agency. Today anyone can listen to their favorite rock groups.

SPORTS AND LEISURE

Television shows and movies are also very popular in Russia and its neighbors. Another favorite pastime is the game of chess. Chess players from Russia and its neighboring countries have won many international chess competitions.

Even when the weather is cold, people like to be outdoors. On even the coldest days both children and adults enjoy skating, skiing, hiking, and sledding.

Russia's Kirov Ballet is world famous for the skill and grace of its dancers.

For many years talented young Soviet athletes received special training in sports academies. The academies prepared these athletes for international events such as the Olympics. As a result, Soviet athletes won many Olympic medals.

NEW FREEDOMS

As you have read, the people of this region have made many contributions to literature and music. Government control of the arts has ended, and artists now enjoy a greater variety of free expression.

Check Your Reading

1. Name three major Russian writers.
2. What effect did glasnost have on the arts?
3. What do people in the region do to relax?
4. THINKING SKILL: What were the effects of the Soviet Union's decision to censor many of its artists?

THINKING SKILL: Cause and Effect

327

Looking at Sports and Leisure

Ask students:

- **What game is a favorite pastime in Russia and its neighbors?** (chess)
- **What helped the Soviet Union win many Olympic medals?** (It had special training academies for its athletes.)

Applying the Lesson Have students make a photo collage of arts and recreation in Russia and its neighbors.

3 CLOSE

Summarizing Students have read that Russia and its neighbors have produced a brilliant body of artistic work that is appreciated throughout the world. They have also read that artists there had to contend with censorship by the Soviet government. Have students discuss how censorship eased beginning with glasnost.

Evaluating Use these questions to assess students' understanding.

- **Identify the composer of *The Nutcracker.*** (Tchaikovsky)
- **How did glasnost affect the press and music?** (It eased press controls and freed rock and roll groups to perform.)
- **Identify three sports popular in Russia and its neighbors.** (skating, skiing, sledding)

Answers to Check Your Reading

1. Any three of the following: Pushkin, Dostoyevsky, Tolstoy, Pasternak, Solzhenitsyn
2. It freed people to see plays and read literature that had been banned.
3. watch television and movies, play chess, skate, ski, hike, sled
4. It severely limited what all artists could present to the public, and some artists were imprisoned unjustly.

Independent Practice
Practice Book: page 87

MEETING INDIVIDUAL NEEDS

Reteaching (easy) Have students find information about a writer, musician, or chess champion from Russia or its neighbors. Then have them use the information to write an imaginary television interview with the person.

Extension (average) Have students draw a series of before-and-after cartoons showing the life of writers or musicians during the period of government censorship and after the policy of glasnost began.

Enrichment (challenging) Tell students that ballet is especially important in Russia and Ukraine. Have students report on ballet companies in these countries and any others in the former Soviet Union. Students may bring in records or videotapes of ballet performances to share with the class.

CHAPTER 15 REVIEW
pages 328–329

USING THE CHAPTER SUMMARY AND REVIEW

Cultural Geography These questions may be used for review.

- **Why was the Soviet Union officially atheistic?** (When they formed the government in 1917, the Soviet leaders believed any form of religion would endanger the communist government.)
- **What effect did perestroika have on the Soviet Union?** (This new system of reform led to more open policies, which in turn led to the complete restructuring and ultimate demise of the Soviet Union.)
- **What system did Karl Marx originate? What was its theory?** (communism; a new theory of social organization in which all property is owned in common)
- **What are some of the arts for which this region is known?** (literature, ballet, music)

Ideas to Remember

- **What is the largest ethnic group in this region?** (the Slavs)
- **What is a planned economy?** (one in which the government owns and operates everything)
- **What is the purpose of the Commonwealth of Independent States?** (to foster economic relations among the newly independent nations)
- **Which sports do Russians enjoy?** (skating, skiing, hiking, sledding)

Answers to Reviewing Vocabulary

1. censor
2. command economy
3. capital goods
4. reform
5. consumer goods

CHAPTER 15 • SUMMARY

RUSSIA AND ITS NEIGHBORS: CULTURAL GEOGRAPHY

PEOPLE

- The Slavs are the largest of the more than 150 ethnic groups in the region
- The Soviet Union was officially atheistic

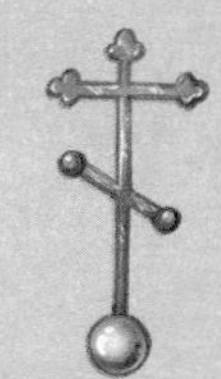

- Religions: Eastern Orthodox, Islam, Roman Catholicism, Judaism

- Soviet families are close-knit
- Education is highly valued

ECONOMY

- The Soviet government owned most land, most factories, and most banks
- Perestroika, or economic restructuring began to introduce capitalism
- Each newly independent country has its own economic system

- A change to a free-enterprise system has caused hardships

GOVERNMENT

- Soviet system: communism developed by Karl Marx and shaped by Lenin, the founder of the Soviet state
- The real power in the Soviet Union was the Communist party

- 15 former republics are now independent countries
- Some newly independent countries formed the Commonwealth of Independent States to cooperate on mutual interests

ARTS AND RECREATION

- Famous writers: Tolstoy, Dostoyevsky, Pushkin, Pasternak, Solzhenitsyn

- The Russian ballet is world famous
- Tchaikovsky wrote the music for The Nutcracker ballet
- Many ethnic groups have their own traditions of arts

- Many people enjoy television, movies, skating, skiing, hiking, and sledding

IDEAS TO REMEMBER

- The Slavs belong to the largest of more than 150 ethnic groups in Russia and its neighboring countries.
- The Soviet Union had a planned economy, but most newly independent countries in the region have encouraged free enterprise.
- The 15 independent countries have established new governments and are also trying to cooperate with one another.
- The region has produced many famous writers and composers, and its people enjoy a variety of sports.

ENRICHMENT ACTIVITY

Organizing a Political Campaign **Materials:** posterboard, cardboard, tape, safety pins, paper, markers, scissors

1. Remind students that the citizens of Northern Asian countries are not accustomed to free elections. Tell the class to imagine they are going to provide assistance to the citizens of these countries by helping them to organize a political campaign.
2. Divide the class into groups and have each group plan its campaign. Members should produce a government office and a candidate who is running for that office. Have students choose (or make up) several controversial issues and decide their candidate's position on these issues.
3. Tell students to write a campaign plan. Have them make posters and campaign buttons, and choose or write a campaign song.

CHAPTER 15 • REVIEW

REVIEWING VOCABULARY

capital goods
consumer goods
censor
reform
command economy

Number a sheet of paper from 1 to 5. Beside each number write the word or term from the above list that best completes the sentence.

1. To prevent works of art it disliked from being made public, the Soviet government acted to ____ them.
2. In a ____, the government makes most economic decisions for a country.
3. Products, like heavy machinery, tractors, and trucks, that industries make for use by other industries are called ____.
4. To make a change for the better in something is to ____ it.
5. Products like stoves, refrigerators, clothing, and furniture that satisfy people's needs and wants, are called ____.

REVIEWING FACTS

1. Which three countries were the first to gain independence from the Soviet Union in 1991?
2. To which larger ethnic group do Russians, Ukrainians, and Belarusians all belong?
3. What are the five countries of Central Asia?
4. Name three major religions practiced by the people of Russia and neighboring countries.
5. Toward what kind of economic system have Russia and its neighbors been trying to move?
6. What does *perestroika* mean? Which leader of the Soviet Union introduced it?
7. How did Boris Yeltsin's "shock therapy" affect prices in Russia and neighboring countries?
8. Who was the leader who helped to bring the Communist Party to power and establish the Soviet Union in 1917?
9. Why was the Commonwealth of Independent States established? What were some its first economic goals and challenges?
10. What was glasnost and what effect did it have on the arts in the former Soviet Union?

WRITING ABOUT MAIN IDEAS

1. **Writing a List:** Write a list of statements about the many ethnic groups that live in Russia and its neighboring countries.
2. **Writing a Paragraph:** "Gorbachev opened a volcano, and I don't think he realized the lava was so deep," stated a candidate in the 1989 Soviet elections. What do you think the writer meant? Write a paragraph giving facts that support the quotation.
3. **Writing About Perspectives:** Imagine that you and your family are Russians who are undergoing the challenge of living with a new economic system in your country. Write a letter to a pen pal in the United States explaining what changes you are going through and what you hope for in the future.

BUILDING SKILLS: DRAWING CONCLUSIONS

1. What does it mean to draw a conclusion?
2. List some of the steps you could follow to draw conclusions.
3. Why is it important that you be able to draw conclusions?

329

Answers to Reviewing Facts

1. Latvia, Lithuania, Estonia
2. Slavs
3. Kazakhstan, Kyrgyzstan, Tajikistan, Turkmenistan, Uzbekistan
4. Russian Orthodoxy, Protestant groups, Roman Catholicism, Islam, Judaism
5. a free-enterprise system
6. an attempt to restructure the Soviet economy by taking economic decision making out of the hands of government officials; Mikhail Gorbachev
7. It drove them up sharply overnight.
8. Lenin
9. to provide a means of economic and political cooperation between the countries which had been part of the Soviet Union; to maintain important economic links between the member nations
10. an effort toward openness by removing government controls on the press and arts; It created an explosion of free speech.

Suggestions for Writing About Main Ideas

1. Students' lists should contain names of various ethnic groups, reference to their large number, and mention of their many different languages, religions, and other cultural traits.
2. Students' answers should focus on broad and unexpected consequences of Gorbachev's actions, eventually leading to the dissolution of the Soviet Union.
3. Students' letters should reflect the hardships of fast-rising prices, shortages, and general uncertainty; they should also reflect the hope that eventually better conditions will emerge.

Answers to Building Skills: Drawing Conclusions

1. to put facts together so that they mean something to you
2. Identify the topic or subject; read the information given; look for ideas that are common to all the pieces of information; draw a conclusion.
3. so you can act on information or be able to put facts together meaningfully

MAKING CONNECTIONS

Organizing Information Use the Main Idea Map Graphic Organizer Transparency, filling in only the underlined headings. Have students review the chapter for other headings (religion, education) and add them to the diagram. Ask students to fill in important details for each heading. *Ask:* Since 1991 what freedoms have people gained in the countries that once formed the Soviet Union?

RUSSIA AND ITS NEIGHBORS

People: ethnic diversity (Slavs, non-Slavs); many religions

Changing Economy: developing free-enterprise system; 15 separate economies

Government Organization: 15 independent republics; Commonwealth of Independent States

The Arts: glasnost; Russian literature (Tolstoy, Pushkin)

CHAPTER 16
ORGANIZER

NATIONS OF EASTERN EUROPE text pages 330–347

CHAPTER THEME After breaking free from years of Soviet domination, Eastern European nations have emerged with a strong sense of ethnic and national pride.

CHAPTER OBJECTIVES

CONTENT

- Identify the main ethnic groups and major religions in Eastern Europe.
- Define *satellite* and name the five Eastern European countries that were satellites of the Soviet Union from World War II to the late 1980s.
- Compare a command economy, a mixed economy, and a free market economy.
- Explain the importance of mining, manufacturing, and agriculture to Eastern European industry
- Identify the Warsaw Pact and compare it with NATO in Western Europe.
- Identify Lech Walesa and describe his role in the Solidarity movement in Poland.
- Explain what is distinctive about Eastern European arts and leisure activities.

SKILLS

Geography
- Locate specific countries in Eastern Europe and identify their spatial relationships using a map.
- Identify land use in Eastern Europe by using maps.

Study and Research
- Interpret mileage charts.

Thinking
- Predict what effect lack of Soviet domination will have on Eastern Europe.
- Compare and contrast a planned economy with a free enterprise economy.
- Distinguish fact from opinion.

Reading and Writing
- Write a paragraph about the responsibilities their new freedom will bring to the nations of Eastern Europe.

CITIZENSHIP VALUES

- Appreciate the relationship between lack of political freedom and economic stagnation.

TEACHER OPTIONS

READING STRATEGY: Text Structure Strategies to help students read and remember the main ideas of the lesson.

Lesson 1: p. 331 Lesson 3: p. 339
Lesson 2: p. 335 Lesson 4: p. 343

MEETING INDIVIDUAL NEEDS Activities for reteaching, extension, and enrichment.

Lesson 1: p. 334 Lesson 4: p. 344
Lesson 2: p. 338 Study and Research
Lesson 3: p. 342 Skills: p. 345

GEO ADVENTURES ACTIVITIES PAD Daily activities to assess students' understanding of geography skills.

CURRICULUM CONNECTION Activities to help integrate other subject areas with Social Studies.

Language Arts:
p. 333

PUPIL EDITION ON CASSETTE Language support for students who have difficulty reading or who will benefit from listening to the Pupil Edition on Cassette as they read.

SECOND-LANGUAGE SUPPORT Activities and suggestions for second-language learners.

Lesson 4: p. 30

CHAPTER PLANNING GUIDE

LESSON	SUGGESTED PACING	THEMES	TEACHER SUPPORT MATERIALS: TEACHER'S RESOURCE CENTER
1 THE PEOPLE pages 331–334	1 day	After years of Soviet domination, Eastern European countries have emerged with a growing spirit of nationalism and with their many ethnic and religious groups proudly intact.	Practice Book p. 89 Outline Map p. 25
2 THE ECONOMY pages 335–338	1 day	European countries are making the difficult transition from command to free market economies.	Practice Book p. 90 **Technology:** *Adventures CD-ROM*
3 THE GOVERNMENT pages 339–342	1 day	Now freed of Soviet control, the countries of Eastern Europe are working to develop new, more democratic governments.	Practice Book p. 91 ■ Anthology pp. 95–96 **Technology:** *Adventures CD-ROM*
4 ARTS AND RECREATION pages 343–344	1 day	The arts and recreational activities of the Eastern European peoples often reflect national pride.	Practice Book p. 92 ■ Anthology pp. 95–96 **Technology:** *Adventures CD-ROM*
BUILDING STUDY AND RESEARCH SKILLS Reading a Newspaper page 345	1 day	The parts of a newspaper and the parts of a news article serve different purposes.	Practice Book p. 93 Outline Map p. 2 Desk Maps
CHAPTER SUMMARY AND REVIEW pages 346–347	1 day	Chapter content, skills, and vocabulary are reviewed and evaluated.	Practice Book p. 94 Transparency: Graphic Organizer Assessment Book, Chapter 16 Test

Technology CONNECTION

Lesson 2
ADVENTURES CD-ROM
Have students make a personalized map of an Eastern European country of their choice, using *Build* and *Paint.*

Lesson 3
ADVENTURES CD-ROM
Students can look at flags for their Eastern European country of choice in *Investigate, Symbols.*

Lesson 4
ADVENTURES CD-ROM
Using the Notebook, have students make notes on the Key People of Eastern Europe taught in this lesson.

CHAPTER 16
pages 330–347

USING THE CHAPTER OPENER

Discussing the Photograph Tell students that in this photograph a small child is seen standing with a group of elderly women. All are in traditional Eastern European dress. Help students to understand that the child's youth sets her apart from the women, while her dress links her to them.

Ask students:

- **Why do you think these people are dressed in their national clothing?** (Possible answers include: They are celebrating a national holiday.)
- **Name some examples of traditional American dress.** (Possible answers include: cowboy, Pilgrim, and Native American clothing.)
- *THINKING FURTHER:* **Why do you think some immigrants to the United States dress in the clothing of their native lands for parades?** (This question is intended to help students realize that wearing national dress can bring out feelings of unity with traditional qualities and values.)

Reading/Listening to the Primary Source Read the passage aloud. Ask students how this quotation is related to the photograph. Point out that the little girl, as she celebrates a holiday or festival by dressing in traditional national clothing, or probably feels that being Czech or Slovakian is special.

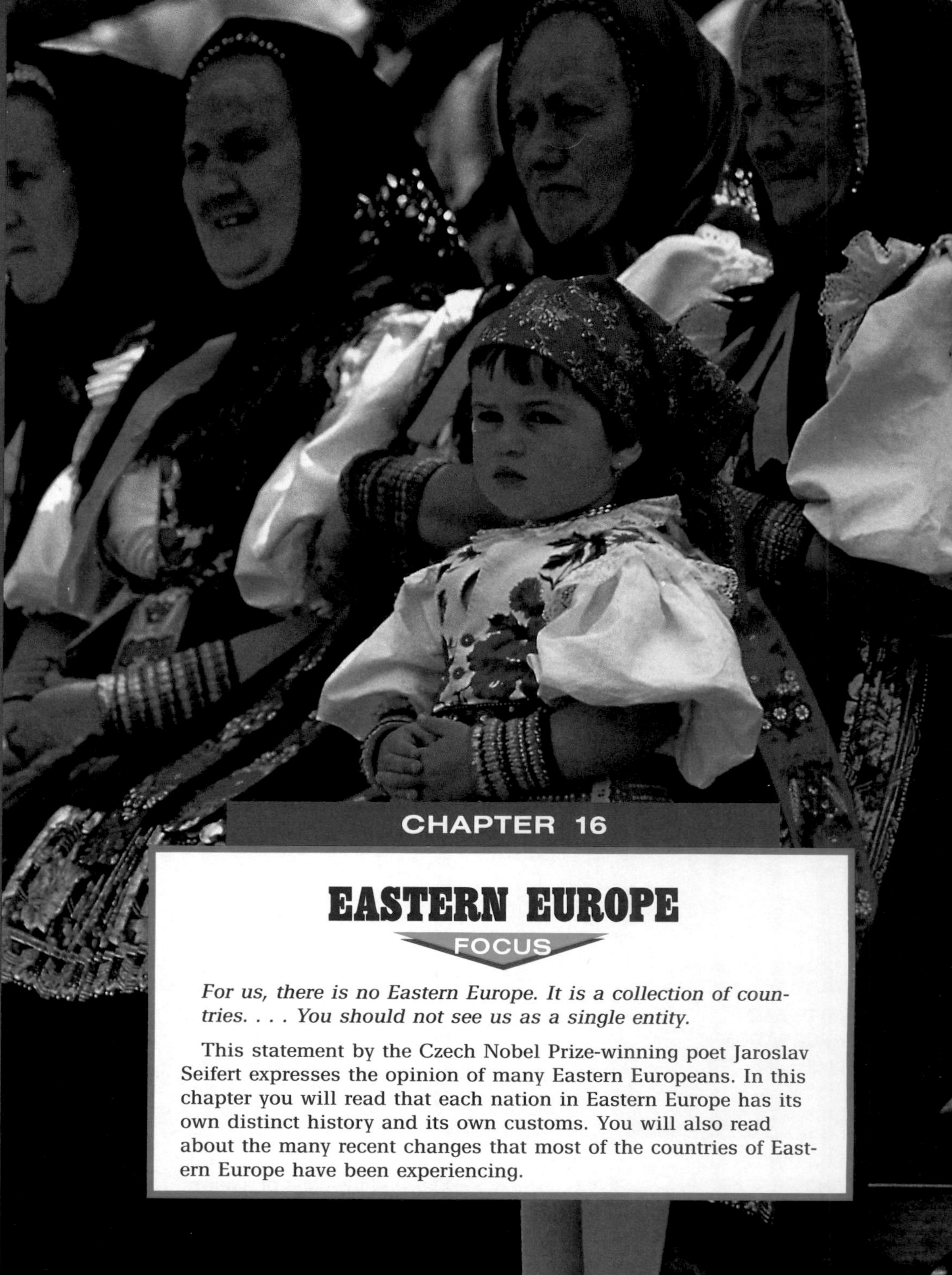

CHAPTER 16

EASTERN EUROPE

FOCUS

For us, there is no Eastern Europe. It is a collection of countries. . . . You should not see us as a single entity.

This statement by the Czech Nobel Prize-winning poet Jaroslav Seifert expresses the opinion of many Eastern Europeans. In this chapter you will read that each nation in Eastern Europe has its own distinct history and its own customs. You will also read about the many recent changes that most of the countries of Eastern Europe have been experiencing.

BACKGROUND INFORMATION

About the former Czechoslovakia The former Czechoslovakia was inhabited mainly by two peoples—the Czechs and the Slovaks.

- Czechoslovakia was under Communist rule from 1948 to 1989.
- In 1968 the people's resistance to Czechoslovakia's repressive measures brought about a period of liberalization called the "Prague Spring," which lasted until a Soviet invasion crushed the regime.
- In late 1989 popular, nonviolent protests forced the Communist government to give up its monopoly of power.
- When Vaclav Havel, the leader of the Civic Forum, became president, he made the office more powerful than it had been before.
- In January 1993, Czechoslovakia split into two countries: the Czech Republic and Slovakia. Vaclav Havel became President of the Czech Republic.

The People

READ TO LEARN

Key Vocabulary

satellite
nationalism
Cyrillic

Key Places

Poland
Czechoslovakia
Hungary
Bulgaria
Romania
Albania
Yugoslavia

Read Aloud

For the first time in my life, I feel proud singing the national anthem.

These are the words of Andrea Ernyeiova, a 16-year-old student from the Czech Republic. Across much of Eastern Europe, people are rediscovering their national pride after years of domination by the Soviet Union.

Read for Purpose

1. WHAT YOU KNOW: How do the ethnic groups of Russia and its neighbors contribute to the cultures of their countries?
2. WHAT YOU WILL LEARN: How do the ethnic groups of Eastern Europe contribute to the cultures of their countries?

SATELLITES NO MORE

Great changes took place in Eastern Europe in 1989. Beginning with **Poland**, five countries freed themselves from Communist rule and became independent of the Soviet Union.

Until 1989 Poland, the former country of **Czechoslovakia**, **Hungary**, **Bulgaria**, and **Romania** were called **satellites** of the Soviet Union. Like planets, they all "revolved" around the same "sun"—the Soviet Union. After World War II the Soviet Union kept tight control of these countries. The former country of East Germany was also a satellite nation.

The Soviet Union placed severe limits on people's freedom in the satellite countries. In Hungary in 1956, and in Czechoslovakia in 1968, the people rose up against their Soviet-controlled governments to demand more freedom. Both times the Soviet army moved in to crush the uprisings.

In the late 1980s the Soviet Union could no longer control the demand for freedom that the people of the satellite countries expressed. By 1989 all the satellite countries had broken free.

Two other Eastern European countries had not been Soviet satellites. **Albania** and the former country of **Yugoslavia** had cut their ties with the Soviet Union many decades ago. Although both were communist nations, they were very different from each other. Albania had strict rules about what its people could do, where they could go, and even what they could wear. In Yugoslavia people often enjoyed greater freedom than people in the Soviet Union.

WHAT YOU KNOW: This question refers to information given in Chapter 15, Lesson 1; many ethnic groups provide a variety of people, customs, and interests.

LESSON 1
pages 331–334

Lesson Theme After years of Soviet domination, Eastern European countries have emerged with a growing spirit of nationalism and with their many ethnic and religious groups proudly intact.

Lesson Objectives

- Explain what the relationship was between the Soviet Union and Eastern Europe and the change it has undergone.
- Identify the ethnic groups of Eastern Europe.
- Identify the different languages and religions of Eastern Europeans.
- Describe the ways of life of Eastern Europeans.

PREPARE

Motivate Read the *Read Aloud* section to the class. Ask students what it tells them about how Eastern Europeans view themselves. Help them to understand the Eastern European peoples' fierce sense of being separate peoples and nations.

Set Purpose Tell students that they will be reading about the different groups of people who live in seven Eastern European countries.

TEACH

Understanding Eastern Europe's Change Help students to understand Eastern Europe's dramatic change—pre- and post-Soviet.

Ask students:

- **What was several Eastern European nations' status in relation to the Soviet Union?** (satellites controlled by it)
- **How did this change?** (They freed themselves of Soviet control.)

READING STRATEGY AND VOCABULARY DEVELOPMENT

Text Structure Remind students that in order to make material easier to understand and remember, writers use such patterns of text structure as cause-and-effect, chronological order, statement-example, and comparison/contrast. Tell students that the following words can help them to identify the patterns being used: *because* and *as a result of* identify the cause-and-effect pattern; *first* or *next* identify the chronological-order pattern; *for example* or *for instance* identifies the statement-example pattern; and *similar to*, *unlike*, or *yet*, the comparison/contrast pattern. Have students scan the section in this lesson titled "Many Ethnic Groups." Ask them to pick out the phrases that identify the patterns of text structure used in it. Help students to see that since two key phrases are *for instance* and *yet*, two patterns are being used—statement-example and contrast.

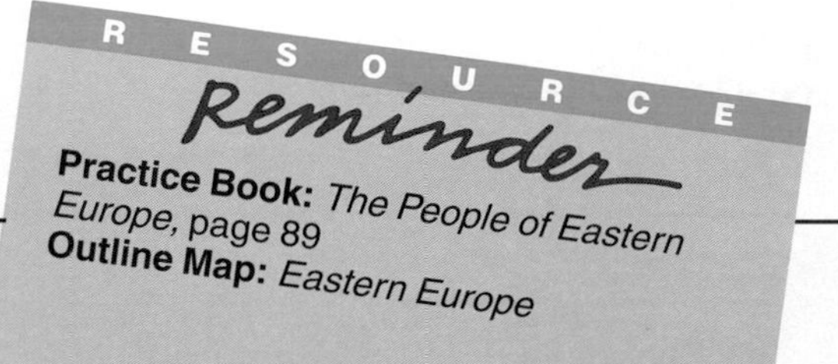

EXTENDING MAP SKILLS

On the map, point out that the former Yugoslavia is now split into five countries. The Czech Republic and Slovakia make up the former Czechoslovakia.

Ask students:

- **Which Eastern European countries border Austria?** (Slovakia, the Czech Republic, Hungary, Slovenia, Croatia)
- **Which Eastern European countries are not landlocked?** (Yugoslavia, Albania, Romania, Bulgaria, Poland)

Discussing Many Ethnic Groups

Stress the strong nationalism and ethnic pride that mark Eastern Europe.

Ask students:

- **What is nationalism?** (a strong love of one's country)
- **From which people are most of Eastern Europe's ethnic groups descended?** (the Slavs)
- **Are Hungarians Slavic people?** (No, they are descendants of an Asian people called Magyars.)
- **What ethnic groups predominate in Slovakia and the Czech Republic?** (Czechs, Slovaks)
- **How have strong feelings of nationalism among ethnic groups of Yugoslavia affected that country?** (Various group's strong love and pride in themselves have brought on rivalries among them.)
- **Who are the Gypsies and how did they get their name?** (non-Slavic wanderers of Eastern Europe; their name came from the belief that they came from Egypt.)
- *THINKING FURTHER:* **How might strong feelings of nationalism and ethnic pride strengthen a nation? How might they weaken it?** (Students should be able to see that such feelings help to unify people and give them national goals while they can also divide people and make them rivals.)

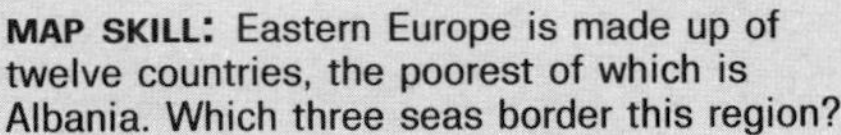

MAP SKILL: Eastern Europe is made up of twelve countries, the poorest of which is Albania. Which three seas border this region?

MANY ETHNIC GROUPS

Eastern Europeans are known for their **nationalism**, or a strong love of one's country. In fact, Eastern Europe consists of many ethnic groups, each one proud of its heritage. The map on this page shows you the countries in which they live.

Many ethnic groups in Eastern Europe are descended from Slavs who migrated into the area about 1,500 years ago from lands to the east of the area where they now live. Large Slavic groups live in many countries of Eastern Europe.

Poland, Hungary, and Albania each have a majority population of one ethnic group and small minorities of other groups. The Hungarians are not Slavs. They descended from people called *Magyars* who came from the east 1,000 years ago.

Other Eastern European countries are home to more than one large ethnic group. The former Czechoslovakia, for instance, had roughly 10 million Czechs and nearly 4 million Slovaks. Both the Czechs and the Slovaks cling to their own identities. That was one reason why Czechoslovakia was split into two nations—Slovakia and the Czech Republic—at the beginning of 1993.

Several major ethnic groups lived in former Yugoslavia. Many of these people lived in their own republic in Yugoslavia and spoke their own language. After the Soviet Union ended in 1991, the republics began to declare their independence. By 1992 Yugoslavia had split into five countries: Slovenia, Croatia, Bosnia and Herzegovina, Yugoslavia, and Macedonia.

That same year, a bitter civil war broke out among the Serbs, Croats, and Muslims in Bosnia and Herzegovina. World leaders tried to end the war, but it was fueled by strong feelings of nationalism. Despite common Slavic roots, the Serbs and the Croats maintain a fierce rivalry. There are also rivalries between Slavic and non-

332 MAP SKILL: the Baltic Sea, Black Sea, and Adriatic Sea

BACKGROUND INFORMATION

Multicultural Perspectives In the late 1980s and early 1990s the forces of nationalism transformed the map of Eastern Europe in a series of events that stirred the hearts of people around the world. But at what point can nationalism actually become a negative rather than a positive force? In 1991 ethnic rivalry began to tear apart Yugoslavia. By 1992 the country had split into five separate republics, one still called Yugoslavia. The others are Bosnia and Herzegovina, Croatia, Macedonia, and Slovenia. Since the breakup, ethnic conflicts have continued to tear at the region, especially in Bosnia, where Serbs, who are Orthodox Christians, fought with the Muslim-controlled government. Thousands lost their homes and lives in this civil war until a tenuous peace was established in 1995. Ask students to identify positive and negative aspects of nationalism.

Slavic groups, such as the Christian Serbs and the Muslim Bosnians.

The Gypsies are another non-Slavic ethnic group in Eastern Europe. These wandering people once earned a living mainly by mending pots and pans, telling fortunes, and trading horses. Believing that these people originated in Egypt, Europeans called them Gypsies. However, the Gypsies probably came to Europe from India. Gypsies call themselves the *Rom* and their language, *Romany.*

LANGUAGES

According to an often quoted Czech proverb, "As long as the language lives, the nation is not dead." Each Eastern European ethnic group takes pride in its language, knowing that language helps to preserve people's ethnic identity.

Most Eastern European languages are Slavic in origin. These related languages contain many similar words. For example, the word *please* is *prosím* (pro' sēm) in Czech and *prosze* (pro' shē) in Polish.

As the chart on this page shows, Eastern European languages are written in several different alphabets. Usually the alphabet is Roman, which is used in English, or **Cyrillic** (sə ril' ik), which is used in Russian. Some languages were once written in the Greek and Arabic alphabets. The alphabet for a language may contribute to feelings of belonging to a group. For example, Serbians and Croatians speak the same language, called Serbo-Croatian, but Croatians use the Roman alphabet, and Serbians use Cyrillic.

RELIGION

Christians have lived in Eastern Europe for over 1,000 years. The Eastern Orthodox Church and the Roman Catholic Church are the two largest religious groups in the region. Muslims have lived in Eastern Europe for over 500 years. Until the end of World War I, many Eastern European countries were ruled by the Muslims of the Ottoman Empire.

While under the influence of the Soviet Union, most Eastern European governments tried to discourage the practice of religion. Yet religious feelings ran so high in Eastern Europe that the governments often had no choice but to allow the people to follow their faith. As Eastern Europe broke away from the Soviet Union, people gained more religious freedom.

In parts of Eastern Europe, religion is a very strong force that binds people together. Nearly all Poles are Roman Catholics. The importance of the Roman Catho-

LANGUAGES OF EASTERN EUROPE

Language	Language Family	Alphabet
Albanian	separate branch of Indo-European	Roman
Bulgarian	Slavic	Cyrillic
Croatian	Slavic	Roman
Czech	Slavic	Roman
Hungarian (Magyar)	Finno-Ugric	Roman
Macedonian	Slavic	Cyrillic
Montenegrin	Slavic (Serbian)	Cyrillic
Polish	Slavic	Roman
Romanian	Romance	Roman
Serbian	Slavic	Cyrillic
Slovak	Slavic	Roman
Slovene	Slavic	Roman

CHART SKILL: The chart shows many of the languages spoken in Eastern Europe. Which of these languages are not Slavic?

CHART SKILL: Albanian, Hungarian, Romanian

Looking at Languages Help students understand that language helps people preserve their ethnic identity.

Ask students:

- **What is the basic language from which most Eastern European languages originated?** (Slavic)
- **How do the alphabets in which Eastern European languages are written differ?** (Some are written in the Roman alphabet—the one English uses—and some are written in the Cyrillic alphabet.)

Discussing Religion Help students to understand the history of religion in this region.

Ask students:

- **What are the three major religious groups of Eastern Europe?** (Eastern Orthodox, Roman Catholicism, and Islam)
- **When Soviet influence was strong, how did Eastern European governments deal with religion?** (They tried to discourage practice of it.)
- **How successful were they?** (Not very, since religious belief remains strong.)

EXTENDING CHART SKILLS

Have students study the chart on this page.

Ask students:

- **What two pieces of information does this chart give about each of the Eastern European languages?** (the family of languages it belongs to and the alphabet it uses)
- **Which alphabet is the more widely used?** (Roman, accounting for 8 of the 12)
- **Which are the languages that use the Cyrillic alphabet?** (Bulgarian, Macedonian, Montenegrin, Serbian)

CURRICULUM CONNECTION

Language Arts Cyril and Methodius were monks from Byzantium, or the Eastern Roman Empire centered in present-day Greece, Turkey, and the lower Balkans. The monks were called to Moravia in what is now the Czech Republic in A.D. 863. They taught Christianity to the people in their own Slavic language and adapted the Greek alphabet to the Slavic language. By dint of this cultural interchange, the missionaries converted the people of Moravia, Slovakia, and Bohemia to the Christian faith. Have students research and give oral reports to the class about the use of the alphabet that these monks designed.

Looking at Religion Continue the discussion.

Ask students:

- **How did the Holocaust affect one religious group in Eastern Europe?** (Millions of Jews were killed.)

Discussing Ways of Life Encourage students to supply words and phrases to describe urban families (small, crowded, working at city jobs) and to describe rural families (larger, less crowded, more traditional, working at farming).

Applying the Lesson Have students use the outline map of Eastern Europe, located in the Teacher's Resource Center, to make a picture map of the people of Eastern Europe. Have them draw or paste pictures of people in traditional dress on the map.

3 CLOSE

Summarizing Students have read that Eastern Europe consists of countries with many different ethnic groups. They have also read that these countries have thrown off Soviet control.

Evaluating Use the *Check Your Reading* questions (answers given below) to assess students' understanding.

Answers to Check Your Reading

1. They were tied as closely to the Soviet Union as satellites revolving around a sun.
2. It has helped them maintain their ethnic identities despite decades of Soviet control.
3. It's a means of preserving their culture.
4. Possible responses include the following: Is there something in their history that explains it? Are there cultural traits that encourage nationalism?

Independent Practice
Practice Book: page 89

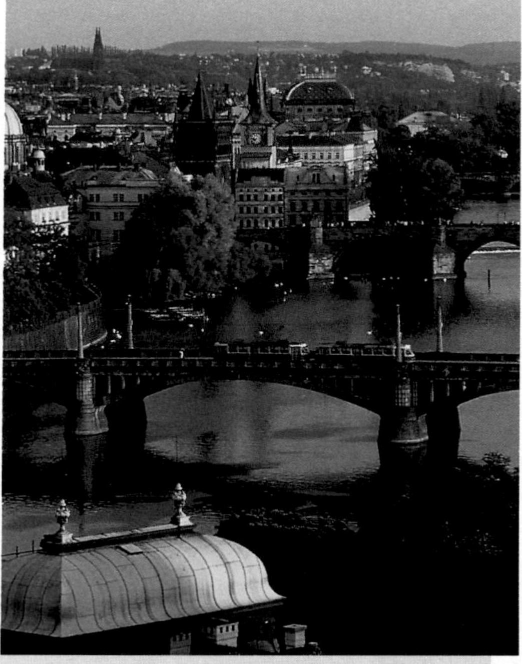

Prague, the capital of the Czech Republic, is considered by many to be one of the most beautiful cities in Eastern Europe.

lic Church was made clear in 1978 when one of its leaders, Karol Wojtyla (voi ti' wə) became Pope John Paul II. The Roman Catholic Church in Poland also helped to lead the country to independence from the Soviet Union.

Eastern Europe once had a large Jewish population. During World War II, 3 million Jews in Poland alone died in concentration camps. As a result of the Holocaust, few Jews live in Eastern Europe today.

WAYS OF LIFE

Many Eastern European families are small. Most families have just one or two children. Both men and women typically work outside the home.

About half of all Eastern Europeans live in or near cities. Many Eastern European cities have preserved many of their traditional buildings. In Prague, the capital of the Czech Republic, ancient churches with gold-topped spires stand side by side with lovingly restored buildings from before the turn of the century. Most cities contain both traditional and modern buildings.

Housing shortages are common. People often crowd together in small apartments. The three members of the Novak family of Hungary, for example, live in two city rooms. According to Peter Novak:

> *Even in a family as close and loving as ours, everyone has to be very patient so that we can live together in such a small, crowded place.*

Modern ways of life have reached rural areas. Yet traditional ways of life are also preserved. In rural areas, families tend to be larger, and farming is a way of life.

ETHNIC HERITAGE

As you have read, the different ethnic groups of Eastern Europe are proud of their heritage. Despite decades of Soviet control, the various ethnic and religious groups maintained their identity. Today a spirit of nationalism is sweeping through the region. This spirit has served to unite certain countries and to tear others apart.

Check Your Reading

1. Why were some countries called "satellites" of the Soviet Union?
2. Why is nationalism important to the people of Eastern Europe?
3. How does language affect people's sense of belonging in Eastern Europe?
4. **THINKING SKILL:** What are two questions you might ask to learn more about why nationalism is so strong in Eastern Europe?

THINKING SKILL: Asking Questions

334

MEETING INDIVIDUAL NEEDS

Reteaching (easy) Give students the outline map of Eastern Europe, found in the Teacher's Resource Center. Have them color and then cut out the seven Eastern European nations. Have students reassemble the map and label each country by name.

Extension (average) Have students research one of the ethnic groups of Eastern Europe. Then have them give an oral report on their findings. Ask students to use a map of Eastern Europe and show where the group lives today.

Enrichment (challenging) Have students research the role played by the Catholic Church in the political changes that began in Poland in 1989. Have students list the actions taken by the Church in response to each action taken by the members of Solidarity.

The Economy

READ TO LEARN

 **Key Vocabulary**

quota

 **Read Aloud**

I have courage. Every day is exciting.

These are the words of Malgorzata Zuch, who runs a small business in Poland. Malgorzata is one of many people who are bringing new energy to Poland's economy. After Soviet control ended, the economic condition of many Eastern European countries changed almost overnight. As a result, new laws and attitudes are developing as people adjust to changing business needs. Some Eastern European economies are changing at a dizzying pace, while economic change in other countries is slower.

 **Read for Purpose**

1. WHAT YOU KNOW: What changes are taking place in the economies of Russia and its neighbors?
2. WHAT YOU WILL LEARN: What changes are taking place in the economies of the countries of Eastern Europe?

CHANGING THE SYSTEM

Until the late 1980s the Soviet Union controlled nearly all economic matters in the satellite countries. The Soviet Union maintained communist systems in these countries. A Soviet-controlled trade group set **quotas**, or fixed amounts, for the types of goods that each Eastern European country could produce and sell. There were also quotas that required each country to buy a certain amount of goods. Hungary, for example, may have had to buy a set amount of steel from the Soviet Union and sell a set number of buses to the Soviet Union.

Today the former satellite countries are pursuing independent economic paths. Some countries, such as Poland, have taken great strides by making a complete change to a free-market system. Other countries are experimenting with a mixed economy.

ALBANIA AND YUGOSLAVIA

As you read in Lesson 1, both Yugoslavia and Albania broke their ties with the Soviet Union several decades ago. Yugoslavia followed an economic path that was much freer than that of the Soviet Union and the satellite countries. Trade with the West was encouraged. Workers had the power to own and manage their industries. A Croatian leader noted, "Here workers feel they participate, that the decisions are in their own hands."

In Albania the government has had almost total control over the nation's economy. Albania's government hoped that in

WHAT YOU KNOW: This question refers to information given in Chapter 15, Lesson 2; the economies are trying to shift from communist to free-enterprise systems.

LESSON 2
pages 335–338

Lesson Theme Most Eastern European countries are making the difficult transition from command to free market economies.

Lesson Objectives

- Identify the changes that Eastern European economies are making.
- Describe mining, manufacturing, and agriculture in Eastern European countries.

PREPARE

Motivate Read the *Read Aloud* section to the class. Have students discuss the energy and enthusiasm that Malgorzata Zuch brings to her new business opportunity and why these traits are necessary to economic success.

Set Purpose Use the *What You Know* question to review with students the difficulties involved in making sweeping economic changes.

TEACH

Examining Changes in Albania and Yugoslavia Help students to understand how important a country's economic system is to its success as a nation.

Ask students:

- **How has the end of Soviet control changed Eastern European economies?** (It has freed them to experiment with different economic systems.)
- **Why were Albania and Yugoslavia free to experiment economically before their neighbors?** (They broke away from Soviet control decades ago.)

READING STRATEGY AND VOCABULARY DEVELOPMENT

Text Structure Remind students that statement-example is the most frequently used pattern of text structure because it can be used with almost any of the other patterns. Point out that using an example to clarify a statement is like showing a picture of something as you talk about it. Discuss with students how chronological order helps make material easier to learn by putting facts in the correct order. Have students read the section titled "Agriculture" in this lesson and ask them to pick out the key phrases that help them to identify the main pattern of text structure in that section. Help them to see that the main pattern of text structure is chronological order. Encourage students to find the other structures used in this same section. (statement-example and comparison/contrast)

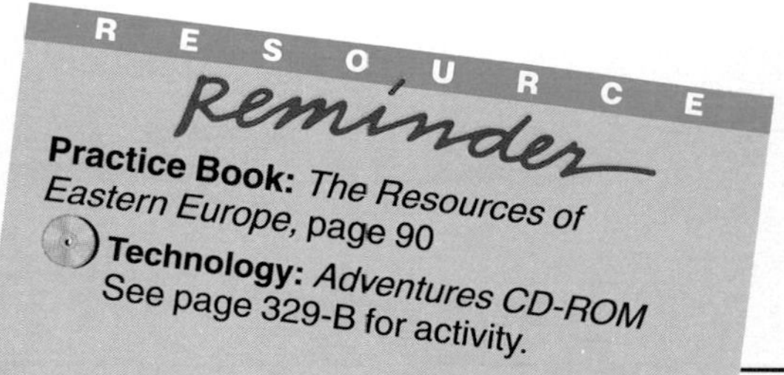

Discussing Industry and Resources Help students to identify the industries that are important to Eastern European economies.

Ask students:

- **How would you rate the importance of mining and manufacturing in Eastern Europe?** (Since it employs a full one third of all workers there, it must be rated as very important to economic life.)
- **How were the factories owned and run under Soviet influence?** (They were state-owned and state-run.)
- **How is this now changing?** (Many factories are now going into private ownership, thus removed from government control.)
- *THINKING FURTHER:* **Why do you suppose small businesses are better able to make changes than large businesses?** (Encourage students to see how resistant to change large bureaucracies can be, whereas a small entrepreneur is likely to try something new and to make and implement decisions quickly.)

Looking at Agriculture Discuss with students the changes taking place in Eastern European agriculture.

Ask students:

- **Name some agricultural products of the Eastern European countries.** (grain, potatoes, sugar beets, livestock)
- **How did Soviet control change farming in Eastern Europe?** (It took farms out of private hands and turned them into state-run and collective farms.)
- **How is this now changing?** (Private ownership is returning, though large state-run farms will probably continue to operate for some time.)

Among Eastern Europe's many large factories are this textile factory in Hungary (*above*) and this aircraft factory in Yugoslavia (*below*).

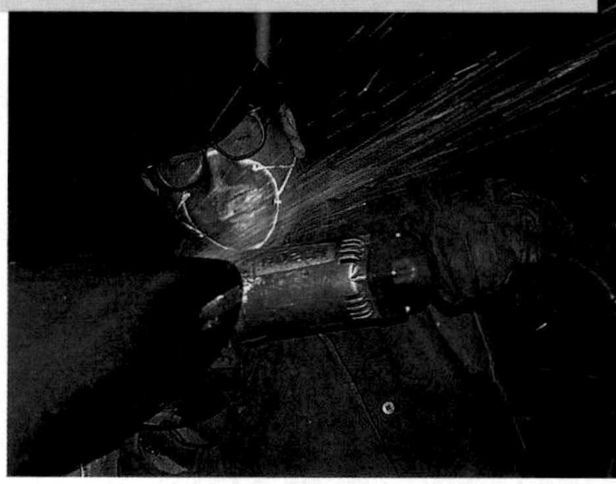

this way Albania would become entirely self-sufficient. However, as Albanian industry and agriculture suffered, the country slowly began to trade with other countries. It remains to be seen whether Albania will expand its trade or whether it will emphasize production from within.

INDUSTRY AND RESOURCES

About one third of the workers in Eastern Europe have jobs in mining and manufacturing. High-quality coal is mined in Poland, and various other mineral resources are mined in Yugoslavia. Look at the map on page 337 to see the areas where mining and manufacturing take place in Eastern Europe.

Given the satellite countries' former ties to the Soviet Union, it is not surprising that Eastern Europe, as did the Soviet Union, has several factories that are huge. It is also not surprising that for many years these countries produced more capital goods than consumer goods.

Many state-run enterprises are being transformed from state ownership to private ownership. In the process, factories are being modernized in order to produce goods that will be competitive with goods produced in other countries.

The transition from a controlled economy to a free-market economy has been difficult. Tough decisions determine how much of a product to manufacture and where the products should be sold. The larger the enterprise, the harder it is to make these decisions. For the time being, small businesses will probably lead the transition to a free-enterprise system.

AGRICULTURE

Until the 1950s Eastern Europe was mainly an agricultural area. The top map on page 337 shows that much of Eastern Europe contains major farming areas. Today many of the workers in Eastern Europe still have jobs in agriculture. Eastern European agricultural products include grain, potatoes, sugar beets, and livestock. Regional specialties abound, one of which is paprika, a type of red pepper that Hungarians use to spice many dishes.

In the late spring a valley in the Balkan Mountains of Bulgaria blossoms with millions of roses. The roses are grown for one purpose—to make perfume. The perfume is produced from rose oil. Rose oil is expensive to make because 3 tons (2.7 metric t) of rose petals produce only

BUILDING CITIZENSHIP

Current Events and Economics Unlike the countries of the former Soviet Union, which started out with a single economy, each country of Eastern Europe had its own economy, none of which were identical. Poland, Hungary, Yugoslavia, and to some extent Czechoslovakia, each had some elements of a free-market economy within a command economic system. Romania, Bulgaria, and Albania were more tightly controlled by government planners. In fact, Albania had been taken on an economic path more like China's than like that of the Soviet Union. As Yugoslavia has been disrupted by independence movements, its economy has fallen apart. Encourage students to bring in newspaper and magazine articles about the economic situation in these countries. Then ask the students to use these articles to write their own updates on the economies of Eastern Europe.

about 1 quart (0.95 l) of oil. Hundreds of workers are needed to pick the roses by hand. They start work at 4:00 A.M. and quit at sunrise because the sunlight causes the rose oil to evaporate. Bulgaria is the world's leading producer of rose oil. Much of the oil is exported to other nations.

Under the influence of the Soviet Union, most farmers in Eastern Europe were encouraged to work on collectives or state farms. On collectives, land is owned by a group of farmers who work together and share the earnings. State farms are owned and operated by the government.

Private ownership of small farms is now common. Even under Soviet control, many farmers were allowed to own their own small plots of land. For the time being, many agricultural products are produced by large farms that are run by the government. As with factories, the people of Eastern Europe are slowly working to transfer the ownership of certain agricultural enterprises to private hands.

PRIVATE ENTERPRISE

While under Soviet control, limited private ownership was allowed in Hungary and Poland. After gaining control of their economies, these countries had a head start in leading other Eastern European nations toward private ownership and a free-market system. In Bulgaria and Romania, the move toward private ownership has been slower.

You had read in Lesson 1 that Czechoslovakia split into two countries because of ethnic differences. It also separated because western Czechoslovakia, now the Czech Republic, wanted to tie itself closer to Western Europe. Eastern Czechoslovakia, now Slovakia, wanted to make economic changes more slowly. To prevent unrest, Czechoslovakia's leaders decided to divide the nation into two countries.

EASTERN EUROPE: Agriculture

Major farming area

EASTERN EUROPE: Coal and Petroleum

Coal Petroleum

EASTERN EUROPE: Manufacturing

Major manufacturing area

MAP SKILL: According to the maps, does Eastern Europe have more farming, mining, or manufacturing areas?

MAP SKILL: farming

EXTENDING MAP SKILLS

Have students study and compare the three maps on this page.

Ask students:

- **Based on the top map on this page, how would you rate Eastern Europe as an agricultural region?** (Students should rate it very high: green, which designates major farming areas, predominates on the map and is found in all of the Eastern European countries.)
- **In which Eastern European country are most of the petroleum mining areas located?** (Romania)
- **Which country has the most coal reserves?** (Poland)
- *THINKING FURTHER:* **Judging from these maps, why might you assume that Eastern Europeans should have a fairly good standard of living?** (They have some of the elements that contribute to strong economies—agriculture, manufacturing, and power sources.)

Discussing Private Enterprise Help students to get a sense of why some Eastern European nations have a better chance for economic success than others.

Ask students:

- **In what important respect did Hungary and Poland differ from their other neighbors living under Soviet control?** (They were allowed some private ownership.)
- **How did this give them a head start toward a market economy?** (They had some experience and practice in running a private economy.)

How did the Czech Republic increase its chances for free market growth? (By making closer ties with Western Europe.)

5 FUNDAMENTAL THEMES OF GEOGRAPHY

Regions Before World War II Poland, Czechoslovakia, Hungary, Romania, Yugoslavia, Bulgaria, and Albania were considered part of Europe. After World War II when they came under Soviet domination, they were perceived in the light of their political and economic rather than their physical characteristics and were grouped together under one name—Communist East Europe. This method of identification became less useful in the late 1980s when the countries of Eastern Europe began to rebel against their communist governments and freed themselves of Soviet control. Remind students of Jaroslav Seifert's objection (quoted on page 330) to having the various Eastern European countries designated as Eastern Europe. Discuss with students the ways in which the events of the late 1980s and beyond changed our view of these countries as a region unified by its political affiliations.

Applying the Lesson Have students bring in news clippings about recent changes in the economies of Eastern Europe. Discuss reasons for these changes.

CLOSE

Summarizing Students have read about how Eastern European countries have freed themselves from Soviet control and are making efforts to transform their command economies to free market economies.

Evaluating Use the *Check Your Reading* questions (answers given below) to assess students' understanding.

Answers to Check Your Reading

1. grain, potatoes, sugar beets, livestock
2. a fixed amount of something, for example, how much of a particular type of good a satellite could produce or sell under Soviet trade rules
3. They have rebelled against their own Communist leaders, freed themselves from Soviet control, and begun converting from command economies to market economies.
4. Under free enterprise individuals decide what they will produce; in planned economies the government decides. Under free enterprise individuals choose the markets they will aim for; in planned economies the government chooses.

Independent Practice
Practice Book: page 90

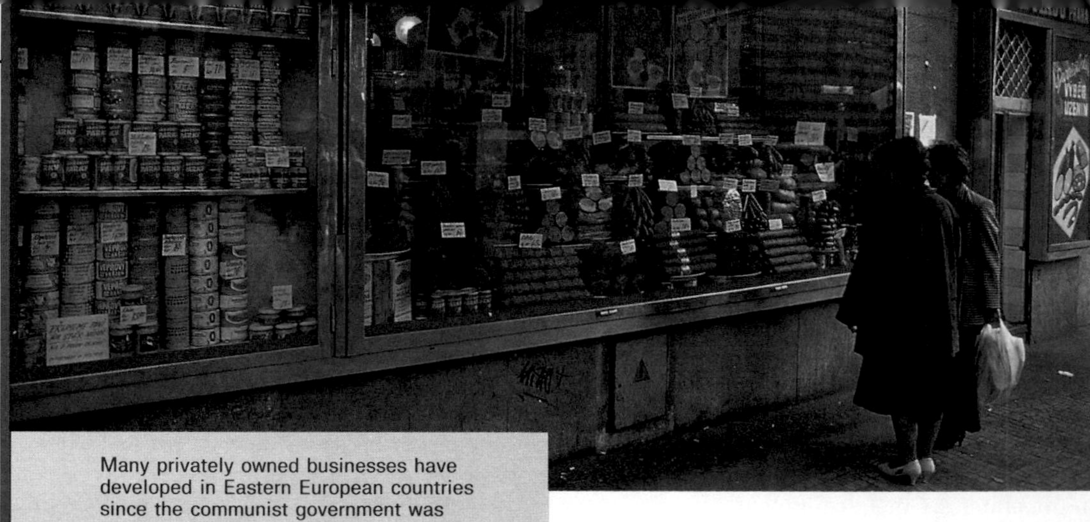

Many privately owned businesses have developed in Eastern European countries since the communist government was overthrown.

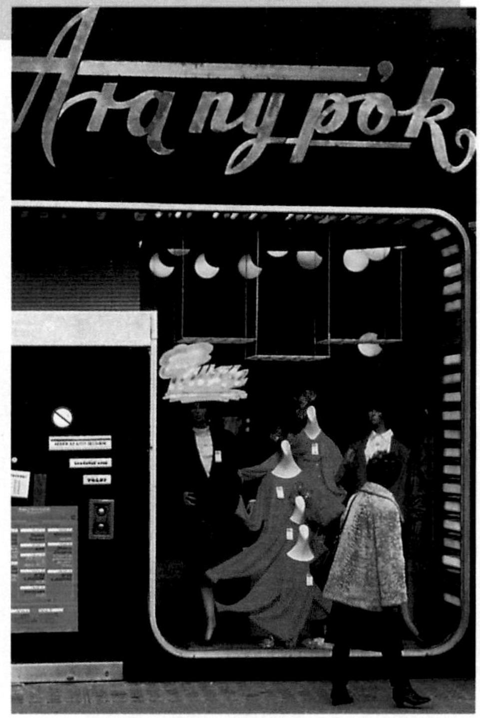

One Hungarian factory worker, Gyula Balogh, has embraced free enterprise by selling herbal teas. With a growing business, he is succeeding in a way that had been impossible. "Ten or 20 years ago," he says, "I never could have done all this."

LIVING WITH ECONOMIC CHANGE

You have read that in the past the Soviet Union controlled the economies of most of Eastern Europe. These economies were based on central planning and featured collective farms and industries that produced capital goods.

Today many of the countries of Eastern Europe are making the transition from a command to a free-market economy. Some countries have made more progress than others. Given the difficulty of the transition, much work remains to be done.

Check Your Reading

1. List the agricultural products that are produced in Eastern Europe.
2. What is a quota?
3. How have the economies of the former satellite countries of Eastern Europe changed in recent times?
4. **THINKING SKILL:** Compare and contrast a controlled economy and a free-enterprise economy. List at least two ways in which they are different.

THINKING SKILL: Compare and Contrast

MEETING INDIVIDUAL NEEDS

Reteaching (easy) Ask students to write one general statement about the economy of each of the seven Eastern European countries.

Extension (average) Divide the class into seven groups. Have each group research the economy of an Eastern European nation and then report orally on that nation's progress toward a freer economic system.

Enrichment (challenging) Have students do research and prepare a circle graph showing the percentage of Eastern European workers in agriculture, the percentage in mining and manufacturing, and the percentage in other industries.

LESSON 3

The Government

READ TO LEARN

Key Vocabulary

buffer zone
Warsaw Pact

Key People

Vaclav Havel
Lech Walesa

Read Aloud

From a democracy to a dictatorship, sometimes you need a day, . . . from a dictatorship to a democracy, the way is very much longer.

These are the words of Romania's former prime minister, Petre Roman, who led his country after a revolution. In the following lesson you will read that many of the countries of Eastern Europe suddenly broke away from the influence of the Soviet government. You will also read about how these countries are learning to govern themselves.

Read for Purpose

1. WHAT YOU KNOW: How are Eastern European countries changing their economies?
2. WHAT YOU WILL LEARN: How have Eastern European countries been changing their governments since 1989?

A NEW FREEDOM

I learned in prison that everything is possible, so perhaps I should not be amazed. But I am.

These were the words of Vaclav Havel (väk' lav häv' el) as he reflected on the sudden changes that took place in Eastern Europe in 1989. Havel is a playwright who helped lead the opposition to Soviet control over the government of Czechoslovakia. Havel has been a firm believer in freedom for his people. His outspoken views on freedom led him to be jailed several times by the communist government. Yet Havel's spirit remained unbroken.

In 1989 the people of Czechoslovakia rallied around Havel in demanding freedom from Soviet control. Similar demands were made by the people of Hungary, Bulgaria, Poland, and Romania. One by one the Soviet-backed governments in each country fell. These revolutions were accomplished with little violence, except for Romania where several hundred people died and the former communist leader was quickly executed. In Czechoslovakia Vaclav Havel was elected as the country's president. He became the president of the Czech Republic in 1993.

With the removal of the communist governments in the former satellite countries, many Eastern Europeans enjoyed a fresh breath of freedom. Soon, however, it became clear that the new freedom had brought with it a new set of responsibilities.

WHAT YOU KNOW: In the previous chapter students learned that some Eastern European economies have been moving to free-enterprise systems.

LESSON 3
pages 339–342

Lesson Theme Now freed of Soviet control, the countries of Eastern Europe are working to develop new, more democratic governments.

Lesson Objectives
- Tell how Eastern European countries threw off Soviet control.
- Explain Eastern Europe's former role as a buffer zone.
- Describe ways in which Eastern European countries are working toward political change.

1 PREPARE

Read the *Read Aloud* section to the class. Have students try to imagine both the joy and the fear that a sudden break for freedom must have aroused in Eastern Europeans.

Set Purpose Discuss the *What You Know* and *What You Will Learn* questions with students.

2 TEACH

Talking About a New Freedom Help students to appreciate that greater freedom means greater responsibilities.

Ask students:

- **Why was Vaclav Havel of Czechoslovakia imprisoned?** (because he wanted freedom for his people—a crime to his country's communist government)

READING STRATEGY AND VOCABULARY DEVELOPMENT

Text Structure Review with the students the cause-and-effect pattern of text structure. Have them read the section in this lesson titled "An End to the Warsaw Pact." After students have read the first paragraph, ask them what caused the leaders of the Soviet Union to decide their country needed protection. ("Because the land of the Soviet Union had fought two major wars with Germany within 30 years . . .") Point out that the key word here is *because*. Go on to tell them that the second paragraph also contains a cause and effect, though it is not signaled with *because*. Ask students to read this paragraph and identify it. ("The Warsaw Pact formally came to an end . . . Troops from the Soviet Union began to leave . . .")

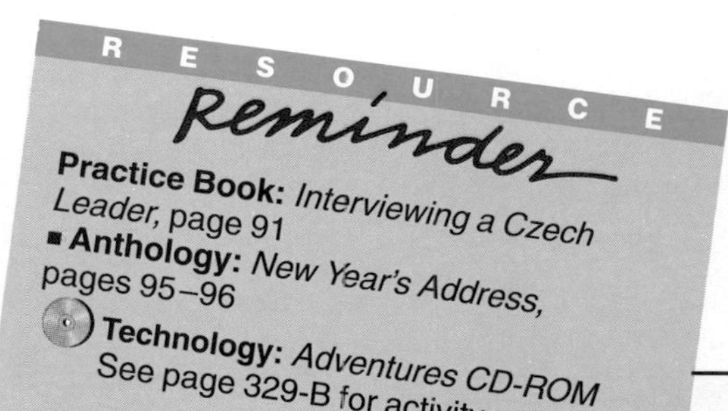

RESOURCE Reminder

Practice Book: *Interviewing a Czech Leader*, page 91

Anthology: *New Year's Address*, pages 95–96

Technology: *Adventures CD-ROM* See page 329-B for activity.

Examining a New Freedom Continue the discussion.

Ask students:

- **What were the responsibilities brought on by freedom?** (setting up the new governments, writing new laws, selecting new leaders—in short, the responsibilities that come with self-government)
- *THINKING FURTHER:* **Why is it fair to say that freedom brings both privileges and obligations?** (Freedom brings with it individual human rights but it also demands that citizens take responsibility for running their government and protecting their freedom.)

Discussing an End to the Warsaw Pact Help students to understand that the Soviet Union made Eastern European nations into a buffer zone to protect itself from possible invasion from the west.

Ask students:

- **What is a buffer zone?** (a region between two hostile powers)
- **How did the Warsaw Pact help the Soviet Union to maintain Eastern Europe as a buffer zone?** (As a military alliance of the Soviet Union and several Eastern European countries, it granted the Soviet Union the legal right to station its troops in Eastern Europe.)
- *THINKING FURTHER:* **What advantage do you suppose the Soviet Union hoped to gain from keeping Eastern Europe as a well-armed buffer zone?** (If war came from the west, Eastern Europe would be the first battle zone. Armed forces would have to fight their way through that region before they could reach Soviet soil.)

Decisions had to be made as to what kind of government to establish. New constitutions and new laws had to be written. New leaders had to be chosen, and people had to decide what to do with their former leaders. After years of living under the influence of the Soviet Union, people had to learn how to live in a democracy in which they could rule themselves.

AN END TO THE WARSAW PACT

At the end of World War II, the Soviet Union extended its sphere of influence to include Eastern Europe, partly to protect itself. Because the land of the Soviet Union and Germany had fought two major wars within 30 years, the Soviets decided to make Eastern Europe a **buffer zone**, or a region between hostile powers. However, unlike many buffer zones, Eastern Europe was not expected to remain neutral, but to be friendly to the Soviet Union.

The buffer-zone countries of Eastern Europe were joined to the Soviet Union by a military alliance called the **Warsaw Pact**. The Warsaw Pact included East Germany and all of the other countries of Eastern Europe except Yugoslavia and Albania. As part of the pact, the Soviet Union was allowed to station troops in Eastern Europe. The Warsaw Pact formally came to an end on July 1, 1991. Troops from the Soviet Union began to leave Eastern Europe.

After Hungary overthrew its communist leaders, voters chose a new government in a democratic election.

340

BACKGROUND INFORMATION

NATO and the Warsaw Pact For 35 years, these two giant military alliances eyed each other suspiciously across Europe.

- NATO, or the North Atlantic Treaty Organization, was established in 1949 as the United States, Canada, and 10 Western European nations joined together to deter potential Soviet aggression in Europe. Later, other nations joined.
- One week after West Germany joined NATO in 1955, the Soviet Union established the Warsaw Pact. Albania, originally a member, withdrew in the 1960s. In 1985, Warsaw Pact members renewed their agreement for another 20 years, an agreement that became a dead letter as Eastern Europe broke away from Soviet control.
- In a supreme irony, in its final year of existence, the Soviet Union voiced an interest in joining NATO.

Lech Walesa (*left*), a former leader of Poland's Solidarity union, and Vaclav Havel (*right*), a Czech playwright, each became president of his country.

NEW POLITICAL PARTIES

In working to throw off the influence of the Soviet Union, the countries of Eastern Europe began to form new political parties. One of the earliest "new" parties in Eastern Europe developed in Poland. Under the leadership of **Lech Walesa** (lek vä len' sə), an independent workers' union called Solidarity was organized in 1980. In the beginning, the union was broken up by the government, but after years of struggle Solidarity won the right to form a political party in 1989. During the elections that followed, the party won. A Solidarity candidate explained:

> *In 1981 they first legalized us, then crushed us. . . . We fear that the same thing can happen again. So we are creating democratic institutions to make it less likely.*

In 1990 Lech Walesa was elected as Poland's president. Upon his election, Walesa declared, "since we defeated the system without one gunshot or one drop of blood, we can dare to build a new system."

The Czech Republic and Hungary are also daring to build new systems. These countries have avidly embraced the right to form new political parties and to hold elections for government leaders.

CHANGING ATTITUDES

Eastern European attitudes about the limits on their freedom have changed greatly over the last few years. Until recently many people might have agreed with this quotation from a factory worker.

> *Why waste time worrying about how to change something that cannot be changed? . . . We prefer to keep quiet and have a reasonably comfortable life.*

Today the Czech Republic, Poland, and Hungary are well on their way to abolish-

Discussing New Political Parties
Open the discussion of political parties in Eastern Europe with a review of the role political parties play.

Ask students:

- **What are political parties? What are the two major political parties in the United States?** (groups of people who come together with the aim of gaining political power, for example, by running candidates for government office; the Democratic party and the Republican party)
- **When did political parties begin to emerge in the Soviet satellites of Eastern Europe?** (when the people began to rebel against Soviet control)
- **What role did Lech Walesa play in the rise of political parties in Eastern Europe?** (He led an independent worker's union—Solidarity—in Poland that later emerged as a political party and helped elect him president of Poland.)
- **How are the Czech Republic and Hungary's aims like Walesa's for Poland?** (They too are trying to create more democratic governments.)

Examining Changing Attitudes

Ask students:

- **How would you describe the attitude of the Eastern European factory worker quoted here?** (resigned to his fate and willing to take the road of least resistance)

FUNDAMENTAL THEMES OF GEOGRAPHY

Movement In the 1980s it became clear that ideas from the democratic countries had taken hold in Eastern Europe and the Soviet Union. People began to discuss openly the adoption of such elements of the free enterprise system as private property, profit incentives, and open competition. Changes to make elections more democratic actually took place. Discuss with students the fact that throughout history ideas have brought about change. Have them make a vertical time line of the key events in the emergence of Poland's Solidarity movement.

Discussing Changing Attitudes Continue the discussion and encourage students to suggest the kinds of attitudes Eastern Europeans will need if they are to achieve democratic government.

Applying the Lesson Have students write a paragraph contrasting Lech Walesa's outlook with the quoted factory worker's.

3 CLOSE

Summarizing Students have read that until the late 1980s, Eastern Europe was dominated by the Soviet Union. They have also read that since that time Eastern Europe has thrown off Soviet domination and has begun moving in a new political direction, generally toward greater democracy.

Evaluating Use the *Check Your Reading* questions (answers given below) to assess students' understanding.

Answers to Check Your Reading

1. a region between two hostile powers
2. They need to establish new governments, write new laws, and choose new leaders.
3. It gave them a means of protection against invasion from the west.
4. It is a fact that the government crushed Solidarity in 1981; the worker's fear that it will happen again is an opinion.

Independent Practice
Practice Book: page 91

ing the limits to freedom that they had experienced under Soviet control. Yet in other countries the road to freedom has been rocky.

Though free of the Soviet influence, the new governments of Romania and Bulgaria continue to restrict their people's freedom. Albania has allowed increased freedom as well, but many restrictions are still in effect. The move toward freedom and democracy in these countries may take some time.

George Karasimeonov, a professor at Sofia University in Bulgaria, made the following observation about democracy in his country.

> *We have experienced the birth of democracy, but democracy has not yet created its own institutions and traditions.*

A TIME OF CHANGE

Eastern Europe came under the control of the Soviet Union after World War II and remained under its influence until 1990. With the end of the Warsaw Pact, several of the newly independent countries of Eastern Europe began to move toward freedom and democracy. For other Eastern European countries, freedom and democracy will take a longer time to achieve. Each country of Eastern Europe will have to create its own democratic institutions.

Check Your Reading

1. What is a buffer zone?
2. Describe the new responsibilities that need to be met by countries of Eastern Europe that are pursuing democracy.
3. Why was the Warsaw Pact important to the Soviet Union?
4. THINKING SKILL: Reread the quote on page 341 by the Solidarity candidate. How does it express both a fact and an opinion? How do you know?

 THINKING SKILL: Fact and Opinion

CITIZENSHIP MAKING A DIFFERENCE

Speaking OUT

Adam Michnik was born in 1946, the year the Soviets seized control of Poland. While he was growing up, he did not know what it was like to live in a free country. But at the age of 15, Adam did know that he disliked the way the government treated the people of Poland. He began to speak publicly against the government—something that many people did not dare to do.

During the 1970s Poland was ruled by a military government. Some of the people in Poland began to talk about a violent revolution against the government. By this time Adam was known for his opposition to the government. But Adam preferred to avoid violence. He instead suggested that the Polish people work to create a better society on their own, without force.

In 1976 Michnik organized KOR, a group that gave medical, financial, and legal help to Polish workers. Some of the workers had been fired, beaten, or jailed by the Polish government. Encouraged by the example of KOR, people all over the country began to form groups of workers, consumers, and environmentalists. They started to behave as if they were free, even though they faced the risk of being punished by the government.

Because of his work with KOR, Adam Michnik became known as one of the "Fathers of Solidarity." He has helped to unite the people of Poland in building a more caring society.

MEETING INDIVIDUAL NEEDS

Reteaching (easy) Have students read about NATO and then make a T-chart comparing the Warsaw Pact nations with the NATO nations. Compare what has happened to each.

Extension (average) Have students research Lech Walesa and write an essay about the stages in his political career.

Enrichment (challenging) Have students choose an Eastern European country and a Western European country and do research on their governments in recent years. Have them write a comparison of the two.

BUILDING CITIZENSHIP

Making a Difference: Adam Michnik Refer students to the feature about Adam Michnik on this page, then ask them these questions.

- *What was the important action taken by Adam Michnik?* (He founded the KOR to give medical, financial, and legal help to Polish workers harmed by the government.)
- *How did Adam show good citizenship?* (He encouraged others to behave as if they were free.)
- *Have you ever done anything like this in your community? Do you know anyone who has?* (Encourage students to consider those people who give aid to refugees, and so on.)

Arts and Recreation

READ TO LEARN

Key People

Frédéric Chopin
Anton Dvořák
Béla Bartók
Constantin Brancusi
Czeslaw Milosz
Karel Čapek
Franz Kafka

Read Aloud

As you have read, Eastern Europeans have strong feelings of nationalism. Eastern Europeans often express their love for their countries through their art.

Read for Purpose

1. WHAT YOU KNOW: In what ways besides voting can you show your love of country?
2. WHAT YOU WILL LEARN: What is distinctive about Eastern European art and leisure activities?

MUSIC AND ART

Over the years music has served as a major outlet for feelings of nationalism. For example, have you ever heard of the composer Frédéric Chopin (frā dā rĕk shō′ pan)? His name in Polish was Frydederyk Szopen. Chopin was one of the first composers to use themes from Eastern European folk music. Chopin loved Poland so much that when he died in France in 1849, soil from his homeland was sprinkled on his grave.

Other Eastern European composers were also influenced by their love of their homelands. For example, the musician Anton Dvořák (an′ tōn dvôr′ zhäk), who lived from 1841 to 1904, was inspired by the melodies of his native Bohemia (now the Czech Republic). The Hungarian composer Béla Bartók (bā′ lä bär′ täk) produced haunting music that was influenced by folk music of his native country.

The Romanian sculptor Constantin Brancusi (kôn stän tēn′ bran kü′ sē) has created sleek works of sculpture in smooth metal and stone. His work has had a strong influence on abstract art of the twentieth century.

WRITING ABOUT FREEDOM

During the years of Soviet control, several Eastern European writers addressed issues of personal and political freedom. They created works that kept spirits alive and paved the way for freedom.

In 1980 the Polish poet and essay writer Czeslaw Milosz (chez′ lō mē lôsh) won the Nobel Prize in literature. His poems, written both in Poland and abroad, express his deep love for his homeland, Poland, which at the time was not free.

Vaclav Havel, about whom you read in the last lesson, is a playwright whose

WHAT YOU KNOW: Students may suggest many ways, such as respecting its laws, working for peaceful improvements, and protecting the environment.

LESSON 4
pages 343–344

Lesson Theme The arts and recreational activities of the Eastern European peoples often reflect national pride.

Lesson Objectives

- Describe the role of nationalism in Eastern European arts and sports.
- Identify the works of Eastern European writers.
- Explain the Eastern European emphasis on athletic achievement.

1 PREPARE

Motivate Read the *Read Aloud* section to the class. Ask students if they can think of any American works of art that reflect a love for the United States.

Set Purpose Tell students that they are about to learn some ways in which the Eastern Europeans express love for their countries.

2 TEACH

Discussing Music, Art, and Literature Help students to understand how political issues can be addressed through art.

Ask students:

- **What did Chopin, Dvořák, and Bartók all use in their music that reflected their love of country?** (themes from the folk music of their lands)
- **What did writers Milosz and Havel contribute to their native lands?** (writings that reflected love of their countries and served as inspirations for political change)

READING STRATEGY AND VOCABULARY DEVELOPMENT

Text Structure Remind students that knowing patterns of text structure can help them understand new material. Demonstrate the following method of using text structure. Read the section titled "Music and Art" aloud and identify the key phrase *example*. Then tell students that the phrase *for example* indicates that the writer may be using a statement-example pattern. Next tell students that you are going to identify some statements that are followed by examples. Point out that the writer follows the statement "Over the years, music has served as a major outlet for feelings of nationalism" by giving Chopin, Dvořák, and Bartók as examples of Eastern European composers who expressed love of their countries in their music. Have students practice this procedure using the section in this lesson titled "Writing About Freedom."

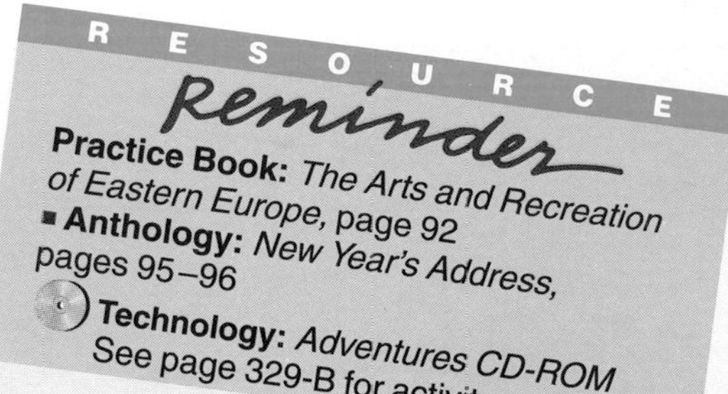

RESOURCE *Reminder*

Practice Book: *The Arts and Recreation of Eastern Europe*, page 92
Anthology: *New Year's Address*, pages 95–96
Technology: *Adventures CD-ROM* See page 329-B for activity.

Looking at Excellence in Sports Encourage students to identify reasons why Eastern Europeans have been so successful in the Olympics (being spotted early and receiving special sports training).

Applying the Lesson Have students imagine themselves as citizens of one of the Eastern European nations. Have them write a diary entry expressing their hopes for their country.

CLOSE

Summarizing Students have read about some of the ways that Eastern European people express their nationalistic feelings in music, writing, and sports.

Evaluating Use these questions to assess students' understanding.

- **How did Chopin express nationalism in his musical compositions?** (by using themes from Eastern European folk music in his works)
- **Identify one Czech playwright whose works have been banned by the Communist government.** (Vaclav Havel)
- **How have Eastern European countries encouraged athletic excellence?** (making sports training a high priority; looking for talented youngsters and giving them special training)

Answers to Check Your Reading

1. Karel Capek introduced it in his play.
2. by using themes from the folk music of their native lands
3. Their talents have been noticed early, and they have received extra training.
4. Students may comment that with communist government organization and support now gone, expensive sports training programs may be lost.

Independent Practice
Practice Book: page 92

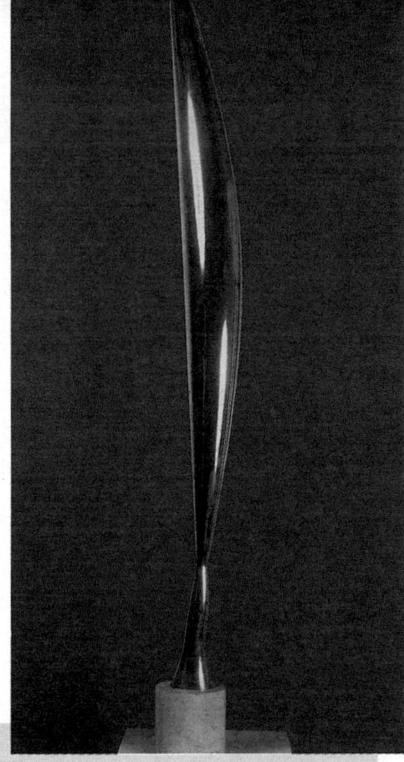

The work of Constantin Brancusi, a Romanian sculptor, has influenced many artists around the world. This sculpture, called Bird in Space, is one of his most famous works.

works were written in defiance of the communist government of Czechoslovakia. As a result, he was imprisoned several times and his plays were banned. Today, Havel's plays are freely performed and, as you have read, he became the president of Czechoslovakia. When that country split in 1993, Havel became the president of the Czech Republic.

Several Eastern European writers have described what can happen to people who find themselves in frightening circumstances. The Czech **Karel Capek** (kä rel chä pek), for example, introduced the word *robot* in his play *R.U.R.*, which is about what happens when technology gets out of control.

Another Czech, **Franz Kafka**, wrote about people who find themselves in circumstances that they do not understand. His short stories and novels were often about the difficulties that people face in a world that does not seem to make sense.

EXCELLENCE IN SPORTS

If you had watched the Olympics on television in the past, you may well have seen Romanian gymnasts, Czechoslovakian hockey players, and the Yugoslavian soccer team. Over the years the Olympic teams fielded by the countries of Eastern Europe have enjoyed remarkable success.

While under Soviet control, the Eastern European countries placed a great deal of emphasis on sports. Within the schools, sports training was given a high priority. As in the Soviet Union, talented athletes are recognized early in their lives and given special training. Athletes from Eastern Europe will no doubt continue to excel.

PRIDE IN ONE'S COUNTRY

As you have read, nationalism is a strong creative force among Eastern Europe's musicians, writers, and other artists. Many of them have taken themes from their homelands and integrated them into their work. Nationalism has also been evident in the region's competitive sports.

Check Your Reading

1. What is the origin of the word *robot?*
2. How have Eastern European composers shown their love of their homelands in their music?
3. Why have Eastern European athletes excelled in sports?
4. THINKING SKILL: The countries of Eastern Europe are no longer satellites of the Soviet Union. What effect do you think this fact will have on the Eastern Europeans' pursuit of sports?

THINKING SKILL: Cause and Effect

MEETING INDIVIDUAL NEEDS

Reteaching (easy) Play the music of Chopin, Dvořák, and Bartók for the class. Ask students to try to identify the folk themes in the music. Then have them write a paragraph describing how the folk themes made them feel.

Extension (average) Have students research an Eastern European Olympic athlete and then write a fan letter to that athlete. Tell students that their letters should express their appreciation of how hard the athlete has trained.

Enrichment (challenging) Have students review the material concerning Vaclav Havel on pages 339 and 343–344. Then ask each of them to use it as a source of ideas to write a play about Havel and other young Czechs plotting to overthrow their repressive government.

BUILDING SKILLS
STUDY AND RESEARCH SKILLS

Reading a Newspaper

Key Vocabulary

news article	editor
feature article	headline
editorial	dateline

You have read about Eastern Europe in this chapter. But new events are taking place there every day. You can learn more about them by reading a newspaper.

The Parts of a Newspaper

All newspapers contain several different forms of information. They usually begin with news articles. A news article is a story about an important event that has just taken place. News articles can be about important local, national, or international events.

Inside the newspaper you will usually find feature articles and editorials. A feature article is a detailed report on a person, an issue, or an event. An editorial is an article in which the editors, or the people who run the newspaper, give their opinion on an important issue.

Parts of a News Article

News articles are an important source of information. Look at the news article on this page. Can you find the headline? It is printed in large type across the top of the story to catch your attention.

Each news article usually also has a dateline. The dateline tells when and where the story was written. Find the dateline in the story on this page.

In the first paragraph of a news article, the reporter tries to get the reader interested in the story. The reporter also answers some important questions: *Who* was involved in the story? *What* happened? *When* did the event take place? *Where* did it occur? These points are called the *Who, What, When,* and *Where* of the story.

Walesa Asked to Lead New Government

WARSAW, August 17—Solidarity leader Lech Walesa was asked today to form a cabinet and to lead a new government in Poland.

Legislators from Solidarity and two smaller political parties met and agreed to propose that General Wojciech Jaruzelski (voi′ chek yär ü zel′ skē), Poland's Communist president, allow Walesa to form a cabinet and govern the country as its premier. The legislators said that Walesa "is capable of forming a government of national responsibility in which there can be represented all the political forces of our country that have decided to act for political and economic reforms."

Walesa said he had not made a final decision on whether or not he would accept the proposal.

Reviewing the Skill

1. What three types of articles can be found in a newspaper?
2. What is the difference between a news article and an editorial?
3. What are the *Who, What, When,* and *Where* of the story on this page?
4. Why is it important to understand how to read newspapers?

345

SKILLS LESSON
page 345

Lesson Theme The parts of a newspaper and the parts of a news article serve different purposes.

Lesson Objective
- Describe the parts of a newspaper and the parts of a news article.

1 PREPARE

Motivate Ask students how many of them read newspapers, which section they read first, and why.

Set Purpose Tell students they will learn how newspapers and news articles are organized.

2 TEACH

Discussing Newspapers Discuss why news articles are separate from features and editorials. Explain the reasons for a headline and a dateline. Discuss the purpose of the four *W* questions.

Applying the Skill Have students find a news article about an Eastern European nation and list the headline, dateline, and questions that the article answers.

3 CLOSE

Summarizing Students have read about the parts of a newspaper and about a news article. Discuss why news articles are so important.

Answers to Reviewing the Skill

1. news, features, editorials
2. facts versus opinions
3. Lech Walesa, legislators from Solidarity; a meeting and a proposal; August 17; Warsaw
4. to be an informed citizen

MEETING INDIVIDUAL NEEDS

Reteaching (easy) Ask students to read the first page of a newspaper in order to list the headlines and datelines and to see how the *Who, What, When,* and *Where* questions were dealt with in each news article.

Extension (average) Divide the class into two groups to compare the extent of the news coverage of two different newspapers. Give each group an outline map of the world, found in the Teacher's Resource Center. (Alternatively, 12 groups of students may use the desk maps of the world to compare five newspapers.) Have students plot on the maps, in different colors for each newspaper, all the places that appear in datelines in the two newspapers.

Enrichment (challenging) Divide the class into three groups to design and write a newspaper about Eastern Europe. The groups should plan and write the news, features, and editorial sections.

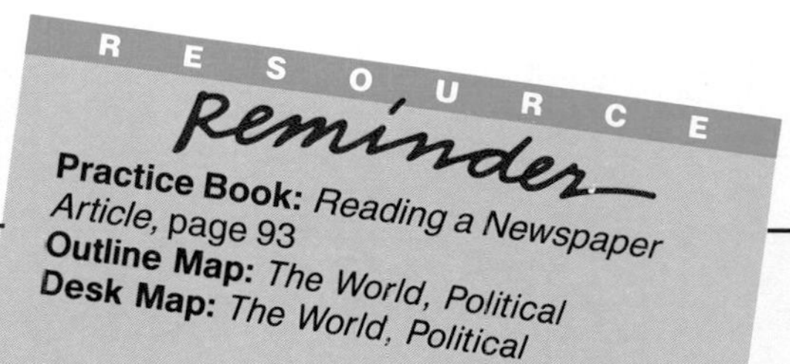

CHAPTER 16 REVIEW
pages 346–347

USING THE CHAPTER SUMMARY AND REVIEW

Cultural Geography These questions may be used for review.

- **What are the two main religions of Eastern Europe?** (Christianity and Islam)
- **What are the three most important industries in Eastern Europe?** (mining, manufacturing, and agriculture)
- **Which area was once used as a buffer zone between Western Europe and the Soviet Union?** (Eastern Europe)
- **What is nationalism?** (a strong love of one's country)

Ideas to Remember

- **Most Eastern Europeans are descended from what ethnic group?** (Slavs)
- **What economic transition are many Eastern European countries currently in the process of making?** (controlled economy to free market economy)
- **What type of government did these nations have between World War II and 1990?** (communist)
- **What is an important factor in the arts and sports of Eastern Europe?** (nationalism)

Answers to Reviewing Vocabulary

1. Warsaw Pact
2. satellite
3. quota
4. buffer zone
5. Cyrillic

CHAPTER 16 • SUMMARY

EASTERN EUROPE: CULTURAL GEOGRAPHY

PEOPLE

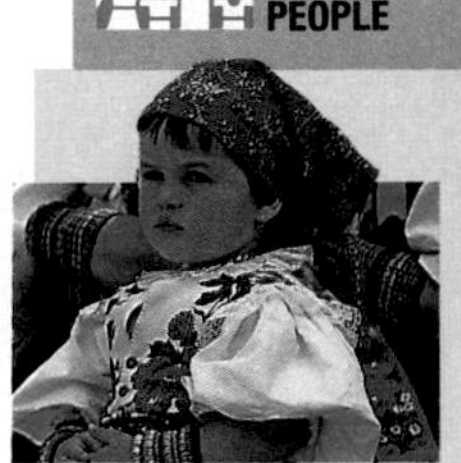

- Ethnic groups: many Slavic groups, Gypsies
- Religions: Christianity, Roman Catholicism (and Eastern Orthodox) Islam
- Families tend to be small

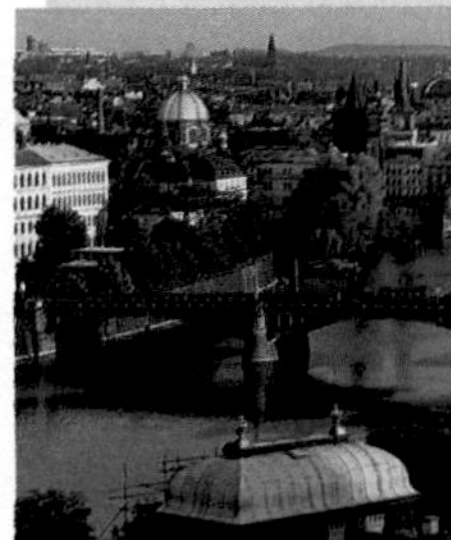

- 55% of people live near cities

ECONOMY

- Most Eastern Europe countries are now encouraging free enterprise
- Agriculture: collective farms and state farms are gradually being replaced with private farms

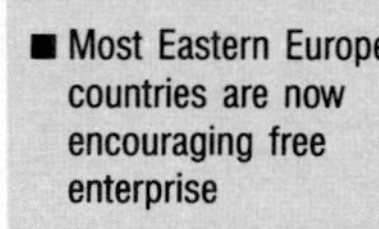

- Workers: 1/4 are in agriculture; 1/3 are in mining and manufacturing

- Products: coal, petroleum, perfume made from roses

GOVERNMENT

- Had been a buffer zone between Western Europe and the Soviet Union
- All but Albania and former Yugoslavia were tied to Soviet Union by Warsaw Pact, which ended in 1991
- The Communist party was the major party until the late 1980s

- Poland's Solidarity Union won a majority in 1989 elections
- Many countries are encouraging democracy

ARTS AND RECREATION

- Major characteristic: nationalistic themes

- Famous composers: Frédéric Chopin, Anton Dvorák
- Well known writers: Czeslaw Milosz, Vaclav Havel
- Famous sculptor: Constantin Brancusi

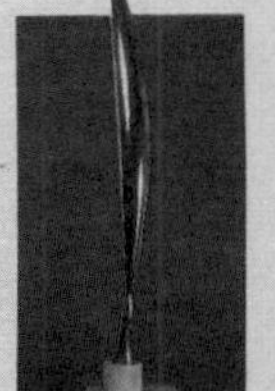

- Popular sports: tennis, track, gymnastics, ice skating

IDEAS TO REMEMBER

- Eastern Europe has many ethnic groups, most of whom are Slavic in origin.
- The area's planned economies are being replaced by free-enterprise systems.
- The area was long a buffer zone in which most nations were tied to the Soviet Union but many of these countries have recently held free elections.
- Nationalism is important in the arts and in the sports of Eastern Europe.

346

ENRICHMENT ACTIVITY

Making Bumper Stickers **Materials:** construction paper, paints, markers, and pens

1. Tell students that although families in Eastern Europe might have to wait five years to buy a small car, many people do own cars. Tell students that they are going to design bumper stickers for those cars.
2. Discuss with students some familiar slogans from bumper stickers. Then discuss the problems of Eastern Europeans that have been described in Chapter 16. Divide the class into seven groups, one for each Eastern European country.
3. Tell each group to research relevant issues pertaining to its country and to produce two or more bumper stickers addressing these issues.
4. Have each group share its bumper stickers with the class.

CHAPTER 16 • REVIEW

REVIEWING VOCABULARY

buffer zone
Cyrillic
quota
satellite
Warsaw Pact

Number a sheet of paper from 1 to 5. Beside each number write the word or term from the above list that best matches the definition.

1. A military alliance that joined most countries of Eastern Europe with the former Soviet Union until 1991
2. A country that is controlled or dominated by another, more powerful country
3. A fixed amount allotted to or expected from a country, state, or person
4. An area that lies between two hostile powers
5. The alphabet that is used by some Eastern European languages, like Russian and Serbian

REVIEWING FACTS

1. Which five Eastern European countries were long-time satellites of the Soviet? Which two Eastern European countries were not controlled by the Soviet Union?
2. What do all the countries of Eastern Europe have in common?
3. What is nationalism? What are some of its effects in Eastern Europe?
4. How did the Holocaust affect the size of the Jewish population in Eastern Europe?
5. What kinds of farm ownership can be found in Eastern Europe?
6. What gave Poland and Hungary a head start in developing free market systems? Which two Eastern European countries are finding it more difficult to begin free market systems?
7. Why did the Soviet Union want to create a buffer zone in Eastern Europe?
8. How did Lech Walesa help to establish one of Eastern Europe's earliest "new" political parties in Poland?
9. Who is Vaclav Havel and how has he helped his country on the road to democracy?
10. What Romanian sculptor influenced the work of many modern artists?

WRITING ABOUT MAIN IDEAS

1. **Writing an Explanation:** Read the Read Aloud quote on page 339 concerning democracy and dictatorship. Write an explanation of why you think it takes longer to go from dictatorship to democracy than the other way around.
2. **Writing a Paragraph:** The people of Eastern Europe are learning that their new freedom brings with it a new set of responsibilities. Write a paragraph in which you explain why this is so.
3. **Writing About Perspectives:** Imagine that you are a farmer working on a large government-run farm and that you are given the opportunity to begin your own small agricultural enterprise. Write a journal entry in which you debate whether or not to make this change.

BUILDING SKILLS: READING A NEWSPAPER

1. What types of articles can be found in a newspaper?
2. What kind of information would you find in a news article?
3. What kind of information would you find in an editorial?
4. Why is it important to read newspapers?

347

Answers to Reviewing Facts

1. Bulgaria, former Czechoslovakia, Hungary, Poland, Romania; Albania, Yugoslavia
2. Slavic
3. a strong love for one's country; It has encouraged both unity and rivalry among different ethnic groups and has had a large impact on the arts.
4. It virtually wiped it out; few Jews still live in Eastern Europe.
5. State farms are run by the government, collective farms are owned by groups of farmers who work them together, and private farms are owned and worked by individual farmers.
6. Some private ownership was allowed there; Bulgaria and Romania
7. After fighting two world wars against Germany, the land of the Soviet Union wanted to protect itself from the West.
8. He led an early union movement called Solidarity, which became a political party.
9. a Czechoslovakian playwright who worked to free his country from Soviet domination and was elected its president
10. Constantin Brancusi

Suggestions for Writing About Main Ideas

1. Students' answers should reflect the idea that a dictator can take power quickly, but that setting up a democracy is a time-consuming process.
2. Students' paragraphs should show that freedom has to be maintained with participation.
3. Students' responses should reflect an understanding of the concept of nationalism and how it can move a person to do great things.

Answers to Building Skills: Reading a Newspaper

1. news articles, feature articles, and editorials
2. A news article answers the questions *Who? What? When?* and *Where?*
3. An editorial gives someone's opinion on an important issue.
4. in order to be an informed citizen

MAKING CONNECTIONS

Supporting Main Ideas Use the Main Idea Chart Graphic Organizer Transparency, writing in only the underlined copy from Lesson 1. Have students add details that support the main idea. Have students review Lessons 2–4. Then have them write main ideas and details for those lessons. *Ask:* How has life changed in Eastern Europe in recent years?

MAIN IDEAS	DETAILS
Many ethnic groups live in Eastern Europe.	Slavs, Slovaks, Czechs, Serbs, Croats, and Gypsies.
Many different languages are spoken.	Polish, Czech, Serbo-Croatian
Economies are changing rapidly.	Poland–free market; Albania–attempting self-sufficiency; private ownership; private enterprise
Eastern European governments are independent of the Soviet Union.	Independent countries moving toward freedom and democracy
Nationalism is a strong force in Eastern Europe.	Many artists and athletes express nationalism in their work; nationalism causes problems in some countries.

UNIT 4 REVIEW
pages 348–349

USING THE UNIT SUMMARY AND REVIEW

Physical Geography These questions may be used for review.

- **What are the major mountains and rivers in the region?** (Caucasus and Ural mountains; Volga, Danube, and Don rivers)
- **What are the two major climates of the region?** (temperate and arctic)
- **In which areas is farming dominant?** (Eastern Europe and the steppes of Russia)

Cultural Geography

- **What are the major religions of the region?** (Eastern Orthodox, Islam, Roman Catholicism, and Judaism)
- **What economic changes are the countries of this region in the process of making?** (from command economies to free-enterprise economies)
- **What system of government is replacing Communism in many countries of this region?** (Many countries have been moving towards democracy.)
- **Which famous composers came from Eastern Europe?** (Chopin, Dvořák, Bartók)

UNIT 4 • SUMMARY

EASTERN EUROPE AND NORTHERN ASIA: PHYSICAL GEOGRAPHY

- Mountains: Caucasus Mountains, Ural Mountains
- Distinctive areas: Siberia, Central Asia, Balkans
- Most of the land is lowland plains
- Rivers: Volga River, Danube River

- Temperate climates: mainly in Eastern Europe and the western part of Northern Asia
- Arctic climate: Siberia

- Arable soil: mainly in Eastern Europe and the steppes of Russia and Ukraine
- Eastern Europe and Russia are heavily forested
- The steppes of Russia and Ukraine are vast grasslands
- Minerals: coal, oil

EASTERN EUROPE AND NORTHERN ASIA: CULTURAL GEOGRAPHY

- The region has more than 150 ethnic groups; Slavs are the largest
- Religions: Eastern Orthodox, Islam, Roman Catholicism, Muslim

- Under the communist system, the government owned most land, banks, and factories
- The command economies are trying to change to free-enterprise economies
- Each country is now free to establish its own economic system
- Each country must determine how to convert huge government-run farms to private farms
- The change from command economies has caused hardship

- The country that was the Soviet Union is now broken up into 15 independent countries
- The Communist party has lost its power to control the governments of these countries
- The Warsaw Pact, which tied Eastern Europe to the Soviet Union, ended in 1991
- Many countries held their first democratic elections between 1989 and 1991

- Famous writers: Tolstoy, Dostoyevsky, Pushkin, Pasternak, Solzhenitsyn, Milosz
- Famous composers: Tchaikovsky, Chopin, Dvorák

- The region has some of the best-trained and most successful athletes in the world

348

ENRICHMENT ACTIVITY

Producing Slide Shows **Materials:** posterboard, paints or markers

1. Tell students to imagine that they have been hired by a travel agency to attract tourists to the countries of Northern Asia and Eastern Europe. The agency has asked them to produce a slide show.
2. Divide the class into four groups—two for Eastern Europe and two for Northern Asia. Have the groups do additional research on their areas. Tell students to look for interesting and attractive images for the "slides." Remind them of the many dramatic geographical features (Siberia, Caspian Sea, Ural Mountains) in the two areas. Also have them look for images of interesting cultural events and landmarks. Have the groups divide the tasks for drawing the slides and writing a script for the show.
3. Arrange for each group to present its slide show to the class.

UNIT 4 • REVIEW

REVIEWING VOCABULARY

Each of the following statements contains an underlined vocabulary word or term. Number a sheet of paper from 1 to 10. Beside each number write whether the statement is true or false. If a statement is true, write true. If it is false, rewrite the sentence using the vocabulary word correctly.

1. In a command economy, the government makes most economic decisions.
2. To censor is to prevent something from being made public.
3. Capital goods are products that are used to produce other products.
4. A buffer zone is an area that lies between two hostile powers.
5. The word Soviet has the same meaning as "Russian."
6. The Warsaw Pact was a way to join the economies of several Eastern European countries to the economy of the Soviet Union.
7. Perestroika refers to attempts at economic reforms in the Soviet Union.
8. Glasnost describes the attempts made to limit freedom in the Soviet Union.
9. Nationalism is a purely political movement found only in Eastern Europe.
10. The steppes are dry, treeless, grassy plains that cover much of Russia, Ukraine, and parts of Eastern Europe.

WRITING ABOUT THE UNIT

1. **Writing a Tall Tale:** You have read about the cold and harsh climate of Siberia. Write a tall tale telling how Siberia's environment and climate were formed.
2. **Writing About Perspectives:** Write a dialogue between an elderly Russian who accepted and lived under communism all his life and a young Russian who supports a change to democratic rule. Have each discuss which is better for Russia.

ACTIVITIES

1. **Constructing a Bar Graph:** Construct a bar graph showing the populations of the following countries: Albania, Bulgaria, Slovakia, Hungary, Kazakhstan, Poland, Romania, Russia, Ukraine, and Uzbekistan. Use Unit 4 opening pages 290–291 to find the information you need.
2. **Producing Progress Reports:** You have read about ways that both the Eastern European countries and the countries that once made up the Soviet Union have been trying to strengthen their individual political and economic systems. Work together in groups, each dealing with a different country, to produce progress reports on each. Look in newspapers and magazines to find the information you need.

LINKING PAST, PRESENT, AND FUTURE

Imagine it is the year 2017—the one-hundredth anniversary of the Bolshevik Revolution that transformed Russia into the world's first communist state. Describe what has happened to communism in Russia since it was first established in 1917.

349

Answers to Reviewing Vocabulary

1. True.
2. True.
3. True.
4. True.
5. The word "Soviet" refers to anything having to do with the former Soviet Union, while Russian refers to the Russian ethnic group or the country of Russia.
6. The Warsaw Pact was a military alliance between the Soviet Union and several Eastern European countries.
7. True.
8. *Glasnost* describes attempts by Mikhail Gorbachev to loosen state controls over the press, the theater, literature, and other cultural activities in the Soviet Union.
9. Nationalism is a strong love of one's country.
10. True.

Suggestions for Writing About the Unit

1. Have students share their tall tales with the rest of the class.
2. Students might contrast the attitude of the elderly Russian with that of the younger Russian.

Suggestions for Activities

1. The bar graphs students create should help them recognize how overwhelmingly larger Russia is than its neighbors.
2. This activity lends itself to a cooperative learning approach. There will be more information reported on some countries than on others, but encourage students to catch up with as many countries as possible.

Suggestions for Linking Past, Present, and Future Students should trace the progression of private ownership of property to government ownership of property. They should compare Marx's original theory of people sharing ownership of property with the actual economic reality of Soviet government control —a reality which is giving way, once again, to private ownership.

PERFORMANCE ASSESSMENT

Demonstrating Understanding Remind students that at the beginning of the unit they were told that they would be writing a travel diary and drawing the route of their trip on a map. Tell students that they can use their books as well as news articles and other references to complete this activity. Encourage students who have chosen similar trips to work together. Have students write their diaries and draw their maps independently. Remind them of the standards that will be applied to their diaries and maps, which were outlined in the Unit Opener on page 288. For additional performance assessment information, see page TM44 in the *Assessment Book.*

For the Portfolio: Include students' travel diaries and maps in their portfolios. Also include your anecdotal record or observational checklist.

UNIT 5
ORGANIZER

THE MIDDLE EAST AND NORTH AFRICA text pages 350–407

UNIT THEME

Life for the majority of people in the Middle East and North Africa is guided by the principles of Islam, shaped by economies based on agriculture and oil, and centered in the cities and irrigated areas of the region.

UNIT RESOURCES

- Practice Book: pp. 7–22
- Anthology: Parts 4 and 5
- Anthology Cassette
- Outline Maps: 1, 26–28
- Transparency Maps: 2, 12, 13
- Unit 5 Poster
- Desk Maps
- Internet Project Handbook
- Geo Adventures Pad
- Pupil Edition on Cassette
- Transparency: Graphic Organizer
- **Technology:** *Videodisc/ Video Tape 1*
- **Technology:** *Adventures CD-ROM*
- Assessment Book, Chapter Tests: 17, 18, 19

Internet CONNECTION

The Home Page at **http://www.mmhschool.com** and the **Internet Project Handbook** contain on-line student activities related to this unit.

UNIT PLANNING GUIDE

CHAPTER	SUGGESTED PACING	THEMES
17 PHYSICAL GEOGRAPHY OF THE MIDDLE EAST AND NORTH AFRICA pages 354–367	4 days	Although much of the land in the Middle East and North Africa is desert, most of the region's people live in cities and towns along riverbanks, seacoasts, and irrigated areas.
18 THE MIDDLE EAST pages 368–385	6 days	Life in the Middle East is shaped by powerful leaders, economies based on agriculture or oil, religion, and a strong sense of family and ethnic identity.
19 NORTH AFRICA pages 386–405	7 days	Water and oil control the economic development of the newly independent Islamic nations of North Africa.

UNIT PROJECTS

Writing a Short Story Ask students to write short stories in which they are engaged in the discovery of oil in a Middle Eastern or North African nation. Tell students that each story should have a setting, several characters, and a plot.

Oral Reports Have students report on the ways in which the region of the Middle East and North Africa has historically served as an important crossroads of people and cultures—from ancient to modern times. To avoid repetition assign each student a specific period in history.

Cooperative Learning: Researching Current Events Have student groups work together to research and produce colored maps of news-making spots in the Middle East and North Africa today. They should collect news articles to support their choice of places illustrated on their maps.

Field Trip Arrange a class trip to a mosque or to a Muslim cultural center or exhibit. After the visit have students prepare and fill in a T-chart comparing Islamic law and practices with those of another religion.

BULLETIN BOARD IDEAS

Making Your Own Bulletin Board Ask the class to use the text and other references as aids in drawing pictures of physical and cultural features of North Africa and the Middle East. Encourage students to summarize the significance of their subjects in their own words on index cards. Assemble the artwork and index cards and display on a bulletin board titled "North Africa and the Middle East."

Using the Unit Poster As an alternative to the bulletin board activity, display the Unit 5 Poster, which shows an enlarged version of the Unit Opener globe on pages 350–351.

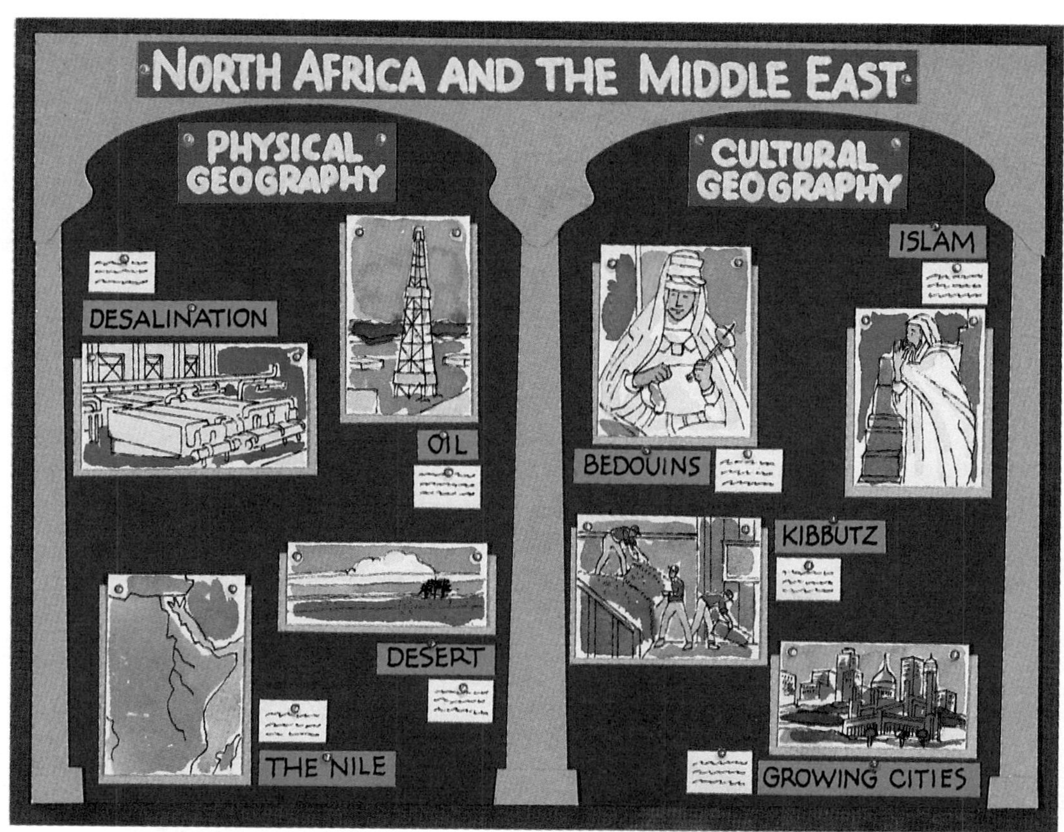

UNIT BIBLIOGRAPHY

For description and additional references, see the Annotated Bibliography beginning on page T-1 in the back of the book.

For the Teacher

Books

Franck, Irene M., and David M. Brownstone. *Across Africa and Arabia.* New York: Facts On File, 1991.

Ross, Stewart: *Causes and Consequences of the Arab-Israeli Conflict.* Austin, TX: Raintree Steck-Vaughn, 1995.

Read-Alouds

Lattimore, Deborah Nourse. *Arabian Nights: Three Tales.* New York: HarperCollins Publishers, 1995.

Walker, Barbara. *A Retelling of Turkish Folktales.* Hamden, CT: The Shoe String Press, 1988.

Technology Multimedia

Africa Series. (3 Videos) Society for Visual Education. Toll free: 1-800-829-1900.

Geography Search. (software, Macintosh or Windows) #SEAGSRM3A. Tom Snyder Productions, Watertown, MA 02172. Toll free: 1-800-342-0236.

The Middle East. (3 Videos) Society for Visual Education. Toll free: 1-800-829-1900.

Free Materials

For a poster about oil in Saudi Arabia, send to: Aramco World; Special Requests, P.O. Box 2106; Houston, TX 77252-2106.

■ Books excerpted in the Anthology

For the Student

■ Al Hoad, Abdul Latif. *We Live in Saudi Arabia.* New York: The Bookwright Press, 1987. **(Easy)**

Altman, Linda Jacobs. *Life on an Israeli Kibbutz.* San Diego, CA: Lucent Books, Inc., 1996. **(Average)**

■ Ashabranner, Brent. *Gavriel and Jamal: Two Boys of Jerusalem.* New York: Dodd, Mead & Co., 1984. **(Easy)**

Cohen, Barbara. *The Secret Grove.* New York: Union of Hebrew Congregations, 1985. **(Average)**

Harkonen, Reijo. *The Children of Egypt.* Minneapolis, MN: Carolrhoda, 1991. **(Average)**

Hassig, Susan M. *Iraq.* New York: Marshall Cavendish, 1993. **(Challenging)**

King, John. *Bedouin.* Austin, TX: Raintree Steck-Vaughn, 1993. **(Average)**

MacMillan, Diane M. *Ramadan and Id al-Fitr.* Hillside, NJ: Enslow Publishers Inc., 1994. **(Easy)**

Schami, Rafik. *A Hand Full of Stars.* Translated by Rika Lesser. New York: Dutton Publishing Co., 1990. **(Challenging)**

Scoones, Simon. *The Sahara and Its People.* New York: Thomson Learning, 1993. **(Average)**

Spencer, William. *The Land and People of Turkey.* New York: J. B. Lippincott, 1990. **(Challenging)**

UNIT 5 ORGANIZER
IDEAS FOR ACTIVE LEARNING

TEACHER EXCHANGE

Cartoon Carnival

Thanks to:
Henry Harvey
Riverside Middle School
Fort Worth, Texas

long unlined paper, pencils, colored markers

Instructions

1. Ask the class to read or watch news stories to become more informed about the geography, people, and current events of North Africa and the Middle East. Have them share facts or news items during their study of the unit.
2. Have students each select a topic, such as a current event, person, political organization, or a place about which they are informed.
3. Ask each student to design a cartoon strip of three frames to illustrate some aspects of his or her chosen topic. The cartoons can be serious or entertaining. Have each student title his or her cartoon strip.
4. Display the cartoons together on a bulletin board so that the entire class can enjoy all of them.

Graphing Enlargements of Maps

Thanks to:
Lillie McGuire
Covert Elementary School
Covert, Michigan

Materials

copies of outline maps to be enlarged, rulers, pencils, 1″ graph paper (or paper marked off in 1″ squares), colored pencils

Instructions

1. Tell students that they will learn how to use graph paper to make enlargements of maps. Some students may have already used this technique in art classes.
2. Have students use rulers to draw a 1/4″ grid over the map sections that they wish to enlarge. Tell them to number the 1/4″ squares in order, being careful not to cover up the outlines and features on the map.
3. On the paper with the 1″ squares, have students number the squares in the same sequence as they did on the 1/4″ grid.
4. Have students look carefully at one square at a time and copy the map lines and features from each 1/4″ square to the corresponding 1″ square. Allow students to color their finished maps.

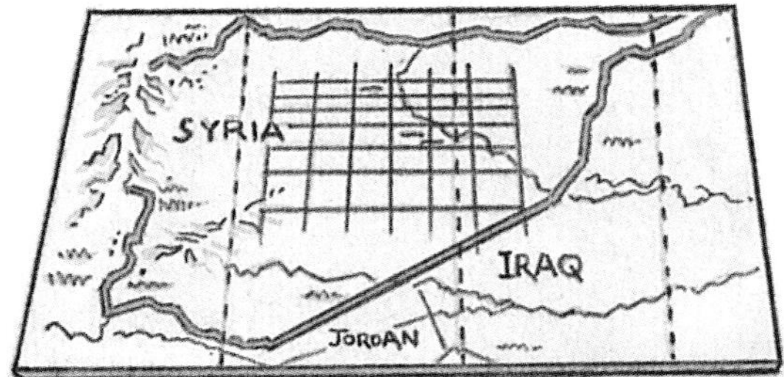

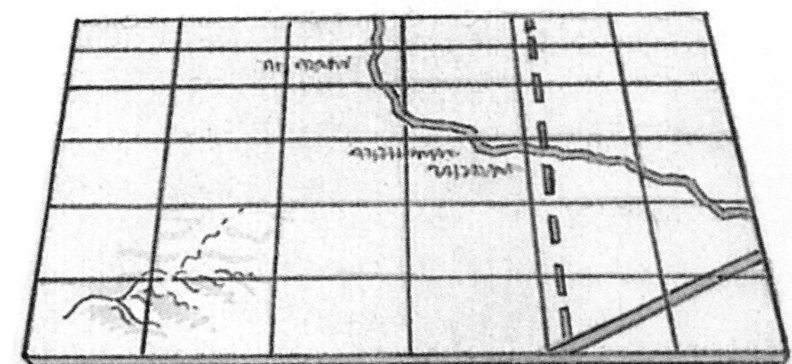

TECHNOLOGY CENTER

Enriching with Multimedia

RESOURCE: *Internet Project Handbook*

Look at the ***Internet Project Handbook*** for student projects related to this unit or have students go on-line at http://www.mmhschool.com, Macmillan/McGraw-Hill's Home School page on the World Wide Web.

RESOURCE: *Videodisc/Video Tape 1*

Enrich Unit 5 with the Videodisc *Middle East Today* segment.

Search Frame 22739 Side A

SCHOOL-TO-HOME

Economic Contrasts

- Throughout this unit, students will have the opportunity to learn about the economies of the Middle East and North Africa. Help students to recognize that oil and water have been key components of economies in this region. Have students in class create a chart of the different kinds of jobs found in this region and how those jobs are linked to natural resources in the area.
- Students and their families can work together to create a similar chart of jobs in their own area, using newspapers and classified ads.

SECOND-LANGUAGE SUPPORT

While these activities are designed especially for students needing second-language support, they are meant to be shared by all students in the class.

Chapter 17, Lesson 2 ■ Physical Geography of the Middle East and North Africa

Help second-language students use prior knowledge to better comprehend what they read. Prior to reading the lesson, have students list what they know about deserts; then have them create shoebox dioramas depicting desert life.

Chapter 18, Lesson 2 ■ The Middle East

A categorizing activity will help students needing second-language support to organize information. After students have read the lesson, create two semantic maps on the chalkboard with the words *Traditional* and *Modern* in the centers. Brainstorm with the class a list of things in the Middle East that can become spokes on each of the maps.

Chapter 19, Lesson 4 ■ North Africa

Students may have difficulty understanding Islamic influence on the arts. Have pairs of students map an imaginary pilgrimage to Mecca from anywhere in North Africa. Then ask them to use art supplies and magazine pictures to create a mural or series of pictures illustrating their journey.

Chapter 19, Lesson 4

UNIT 5

pages 350–407

USING THE UNIT OPENER

Introducing the Unit Have students look at the unit title and silently read the *Where We Are* section on the facing page.

Ask students:

- **Which areas make up this region?** (the southwestern part of Asia, the northern part of Africa, and a small piece of Europe)
- **How has this region been important in the history of the world?** (It has been a crossroads for the movement of people and cultures for thousands of years; some of the world's earliest known civilizations began in this region; and three of the world's great religions arose there and spread to other parts of the world.)

ONGOING UNIT PROJECT

Planning for Assessment Tell students that in this unit they will be learning about the geography and people of North Africa and the Middle East. Explain to them that when they finish the unit they will have an opportunity to demonstrate what they have learned by contributing to a museum display. Students' contributions will consist of dioramas (and corresponding written explanations) that depict scenes from this region. As students read the unit, they should think about the scene they would like to depict. For information on completing this unit project, see page 407.

Goal: Students' work should show they understand that the Middle East and North Africa is a region of geographical and cultural contrasts.

Signs of Success: Assure students that they will not be assessed on their artistic ability. Tell them that an adequate diorama should accurately depict the geography and people of a region in this part of the world, and an adequate explanation should describe the scene in the diorama. An excellent diorama would also depict an important aspect of cultural or economic life in the region, and an excellent explanation would contain background information about the scene and its importance in the economic or cultural life of the people in this region.

EXTENDING MAP SKILLS

Stress to students the importance of the relative location of the Middle East and North Africa as a crossroads for human migrations. Have them study the map.

Ask students:

- **What can you say about the shape of the Middle East and North Africa compared with the shapes of other regions we have studied so far?** (Accept all reasonable answers. Possible answers include: It has the most complicated shape of the regions studied so far; it would be the hardest to draw from memory.)
- **Which landform in this region has the most distinctive shape?** (the peninsula labeled "The Middle East")
- **Using the map on page 356, name the peninsula.** (the Arabian Peninsula)
- **What physical features in this region are shown on this map?** (mountains on the northwest coast of North Africa and in the northeast, the northwest, and the southeast of the Middle East; one long river with a delta in Africa; two long rivers draining into the Persian Gulf in the Middle East)
- **Which bodies of water surround this region?** (Atlantic Ocean, Mediterranean Sea, Black Sea, Caspian Sea, Persian Gulf, Arabian Sea, Indian Ocean, Gulf of Aden, Red Sea)
- *THINKING FURTHER:* **Why have the waters around the Middle East become so important to North Americans?** (Tankers that bring oil from the Middle East to the United States must navigate these waters.)

GEOGRAPHY • GEOGRAPHY • GEOGRAPHY • GEOGRAPHY • GEOGRAPHY • GEOGRA

THE MIDDLE EAST AND NORTH AFRICA

WHERE WE ARE

Now and throughout the past, three great continents—Asia, Africa, and Europe—have been linked by the region described in this unit. Many different groups of people have lived in and traveled through this region, making it a crossroads of peoples and cultures. Three of the world's great religions arose here and spread to other parts of the world. This region is known as the Middle East and North Africa.

As the map shows, the Middle East and North Africa covers the southwestern part of Asia and the northern part of Africa. Some of the world's earliest known civilizations developed in this region. Now you will read about the people who make this region their home today. Turn the page to continue your journey through the world around us.

351

FUNDAMENTAL THEMES OF GEOGRAPHY

Location The relative location of this region between three continents, Europe, Asia, and Africa, makes it a vital crossroads.

Movement Two natural waterways and one man-made canal allow the movement of people and goods through this complex region.

- The Dardanelles, the Sea of Marmara, and the Bosporus provide passages from the Mediterranean Sea to the Black Sea through Turkey and divide Europe from Asia.
- The Strait of Gibraltar provides a passage from the Mediterranean Sea into the Atlantic Ocean and divides Africa from Europe.
- The Suez Canal provides a passage from the Mediterranean Sea into the Red Sea and divides Africa from Asia.

Introducing the Table Have students study the table on these two pages. Since the class has probably already worked with the tables from prior units, have them take the lead in suggesting questions to use in understanding this table.

EXTENDING TABLE SKILLS

Stress to students that the questions they suggest for reading this table for meaning should be comparative and logical.

Ask students:

- **Which key questions would you ask to gain a deeper understanding of what the facts in this table mean?** (Students should apply the kinds of "questions that help make tables more meaningful" that they learned to formulate in Unit 2 on page 104. The following are examples of questions they might suggest.)
- **What question can you ask to learn the most important fact to be drawn from these figures?** (What is the number of nations in this region? answer: 20)
- **What is the most striking piece of information given by this table?** (Arabic is spoken in the overwhelming majority of countries in this region—that is 17 out of 20.)

LIFE TODAY • LIFE TODAY • LIFE TODAY • LIFE TODAY • LIFE TODAY • LIFE TODAY • LIFE TODAY •

THE MIDDLE EAST AND NORTH AFRICA

ALGERIA
Capital ★ Algiers
Major languages: Arabic, Berber, and French
Population: 27.9 million
Area: 919,592 sq mi; 2,381,740 sq km
Leading exports: oil and natural gas

BAHRAIN
Capital ★ Manama
Major language: Arabic
Population: 0.6 million
Area: 239 sq mi; 620 sq km
Leading export: oil

CYPRUS
Capital ★ Nicosia
Major languages: Greek and Turkish
Population: 0.7 million
Area: 3,571 sq mi; 9,250 sq km
Leading exports: clothing, fruit and potatoes

EGYPT
Capital ★ Cairo
Major language: Arabic
Population: 60.8 million
Area: 386,661 sq mi; 1,001,450 sq km
Leading export: oil

IRAN
Capital ★ Tehran
Major languages: Farsi, Azerbaijani, and Kurdish
Population: 65.6 million
Area: 636,294 sq mi; 1,648,000 sq km
Leading export: oil

IRAQ
Capital ★ Baghdad
Major languages: Arabic and Kurdish
Population: 19.9 million
Area: 167,923 sq mi; 434,920 sq km
Leading export: oil

ISRAEL
Capital ★ Jerusalem
Major languages: Hebrew and Arabic
Population: 5.1 million
Area: 8,091 sq mi; 20,770 sq km
Leading exports: diamonds and machinery

JORDAN
Capital ★ Amman
Major language: Arabic
Population: 4.0 million
Area: 35,475 sq mi; 91,880 sq km
Leading exports: phosphates and agricultural products

KUWAIT
Capital ★ Kuwait
Major language: Arabic
Population: 1.8 million
Area: 6,880 sq mi; 17,820 sq km
Leading export: oil

LEBANON
Capital ★ Beirut
Major languages: Arabic and French
Population: 3.6 million
Area: 4,015 sq mi; 10,400 sq km
Leading exports: jewelry, clothing, and metal products

LIBYA
Capital ★ Tripoli
Major language: Arabic
Population: 5.1 million
Area: 679,360 sq mi; 1,759,540 sq km
Leading export: oil

352

BACKGROUND INFORMATION

Israel's Diamonds Diamonds make us think of glistening jewelry. However, they have an equally important use in cutting and abrasive tools. When used for these purposes, they are called industrial diamonds. Industrial diamond production is an important Israeli industry.

- The hardest of all minerals, diamonds can only be ground and polished by diamond dust.
- Imperfect diamonds and small fragments that can't be cut as gems are crushed to powder and used in drills and abrasive instruments.
- Most of Israel's industrial diamond production is exported to the United States.

FUNDAMENTAL THEMES OF GEOGRAPHY

Place Istanbul, Turkey, is the only city located on two continents.

Physical Characteristics

- On the European side a 5-mile- (8 km-) deep harbor, the Golden Horn, serves the city. Two bridges span from Europe to Asia.

Human Characteristics

- The diversity of Istanbul's cultures is shown by buildings such as Hagia Sophia, once the most important church in Christendom, the magnificent Blue Mosque, and Topkapi Palace.

LIFE TODAY • LIFE TODAY • LIFE TODAY • LIFE TODAY • LIFE TODAY • LIFE TODAY • LIFE TODAY

MOROCCO
Capital ★ Rabat
Major languages: Arabic, Berber, and French
Population: 28.6 million
Area: 172,413 sq mi; 446,550 sq km
Leading exports: food and phosphates

TUNISIA
Capital ★ Tunis
Major languages: Arabic and French
Population: 8.7 million
Area: 63,170 sq mi; 163,610 sq km
Leading export: oil

OMAN
Capital ★ Muscat
Major language: Arabic
Population: 1.7 million
Area: 82,013 sq mi; 212,460 sq km
Leading export: oil

TURKEY
Capital ★ Ankara
Major languages: Turkish and Kurdish
Population: 62.1 million
Area: 301,383 sq mi; 780,580 sq km
Leading exports: textiles and food

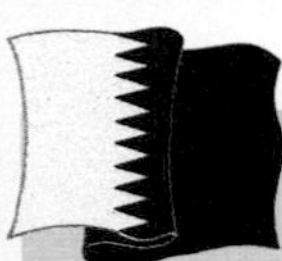

QATAR
Capital ★ Doha
Major languages: Arabic and English
Population: 0.5 million
Area: 4,247 sq mi; 11,000 sq km
Leading export: oil

UNITED ARAB EMIRATES
Capital ★ Abu Dhabi
Major language: Arabic
Population: 2.8 million
Area: 32,278 sq mi; 83,600 sq km
Leading export: oil

SAUDI ARABIA
Capital ★ Riyadh
Major language: Arabic
Population: 18.2 million
Area: 829,997 sq mi; 2,149,690 sq km
Leading export: oil

YEMEN
Capital ★ San'a
Major language: Arabic
Population: 11.1 million
Area: 203,850 sq mi; 527,970 sq km
Leading exports: oil and coffee

SYRIA
Capital ★ Damascus
Major languages: Arabic and Kurdish
Population: 14.9 million
Area: 71,498 sq mi; 185,180 sq km
Leading exports: oil and textiles

353

Continue the discussion. You may want to fill in the gaps in students' questions with the following.

Ask students:

- **In which countries are more than two major languages spoken?** (Algeria and Iran)
- **Which is the largest nation by population in this region?** (Iran)
- **Which nation ranks closely behind Iran in population?** (Turkey)
- **Which two nations have the smallest populations in this region?** (Bahrain, Qatar)
- **Which is the largest country in area?** (Algeria)
- **What are the leading exports from the nations of this region?** (oil, natural gas, fruit and vegetables, cotton, hides, phosphates, diamonds, textiles)
- **What is the most common leading export in this region?** (oil)
- **Which countries do not export oil?** (Cyprus, Israel, Jordan, Lebanon, Morocco, Turkey)
- *THINKING FURTHER:* **What conclusion might you draw from the fact that the majority of the nations in this region have oil as their leading export?** (This is a rich region. Challenge students to check the accuracy of their conclusions as they study this unit.)

FUNDAMENTAL THEMES OF GEOGRAPHY

Human-Environment Interactions One of the most colossal human-environment interactions of the nineteenth century was the building of the Suez Canal.

- It is a 100-mile- (160-km-) long artificial waterway that connects Port Said on the Mediterranean with Suez on the Red Sea.
- At first it was dug by hand, but it was finished with machinery.
- Europe's oceangoing ships can avoid going around the whole continent of Africa on their way to South and East Asia by crossing the isthmus between Africa and Asia via this canal.

CHAPTER 17 ORGANIZER

PHYSICAL GEOGRAPHY OF THE MIDDLE EAST AND NORTH AFRICA text pages 354–367

CHAPTER THEME

Because much of the land in the Middle East and North Africa is desert, and water is a limited resource, most of the region's people live in cities and towns along riverbanks, seacoasts, and irrigated areas.

CHAPTER OBJECTIVES

CONTENT

- Describe the main physical features of the Middle East and North Africa.
- Explain why many geographers consider the Middle East and North Africa to be an important crossroads.
- Identify the Fertile Crescent and name the two most important rivers in this region.
- Explain why irrigation is essential to farming in this region.
- Identify the climates of the desert, the Mediterranean coast, and the Iranian Plateau.
- Explain why Egypt is called the "gift of the Nile."
- Locate the major oil-producing region of the Middle East and name four countries there.

SKILLS

Geography
- Interpret an elevation map of the Middle East and North Africa.
- Use a population density map.
- Use a climate map to identify different climate regions.
- Read contour maps.

Study and Research
- Interpret a diagram showing desert surfaces.

Thinking
- Predict the impact that a discovery of vast oil reserves in North America would have on the Middle East.

Reading and Writing
- Write a myth describing the origin of the great deserts of the Middle East and North Africa.

CITIZENSHIP VALUES

- Appreciate the ability of people to develop complex cultures in harsh environments.

TEACHER OPTIONS

READING STRATEGY: Note Taking Strategies to help students read and remember the main ideas of the lesson.

Lesson 1: p. 355 Lesson 2: p. 362

MEETING INDIVIDUAL NEEDS Activities for reteaching, extension, and enrichment.

Lesson 1: p. 359 Lesson 2: p. 365
Geography Skills: p. 361

GEO ADVENTURES ACTIVITIES PAD Daily activities to assess students' understanding of geography skills.

CURRICULUM CONNECTION Activities to help integrate other subject areas with Social Studies.

Science: pp. 358, 360

PUPIL EDITION ON CASSETTE Language support for students who have difficulty reading or who will benefit from listening to the Pupil Edition on Cassette as they read.

SECOND-LANGUAGE SUPPORT Activities and suggestions for second-language learners.

Lesson 2: p. 349-D

CHAPTER PLANNING GUIDE

LESSON	SUGGESTED PACING	THEMES	TEACHER SUPPORT MATERIALS: TEACHER'S RESOURCE CENTER
1 LANDFORMS pages 355–359	1 day	The main physical features of the Middle East and North Africa are peninsulas, deserts, mountains, seas and river valleys.	Practice Book p. 95 ■ Anthology pp. 104–105, 107–109, 158 Outline Map p. 26 **Technology:** *Videodisc/Video Tape 1*
BUILDING GEOGRAPHY SKILLS Reading Contour Maps pages 360–361	1 day	Contour maps help us to picture the shape of the land.	Practice Book p. 96 Transparency Map 12
2 CLIMATE AND RESOURCES pages 362–365	1 day	The two key resources of the Middle East and North Africa are water, which is used for irrigation, and petroleum, the profits from which help to develop the region's economies.	Practice Book p. 97 Outline Map p. 26 **Technology:** *Adventures CD-ROM*
CHAPTER SUMMARY AND REVIEW pages 366–367	1 day	Chapter content, skills, and vocabulary are reviewed and evaluated.	Practice Book p. 98 Transparency: Graphic Organizer Assessment Book, Chapter 17 Test

Technology CONNECTION

Lesson 1
ADVENTURES CD-ROM
Enrich Lesson 1 using *Travel* and *Explore.*

Lesson 2
VIDEODISC/VIDEO TAPE 1
Enrich Lesson 2 with Video Lesson 5, *The Middle East Today.*

Search Frame 22739 Side A

CHAPTER 17
pages 354–367

USING THE CHAPTER OPENER

Discussing the Photograph Tell students that in this photograph a man is seen riding a donkey near a cluster of trees growing out of the sand. Point out how small and dark the figures of the man and his animal appear against the vast stretch of desert and in the glare of the sun. Ask students to imagine how they would feel if they found themselves in such a setting.

Ask students:

- **What kind of trees are in the picture?** (palm trees)
- **Where in the United States do palm trees grow?** (Possible answers include: in California; in Miami Beach; in the South near the ocean.)
- **What do these places in the United States have in common with the place in the picture?** (hot climate, sandy soil)
- *THINKING FURTHER:* **What is the difference between these places in the United States and the place in the picture?** (The places in the United States have more water than the place in the picture.)

Reading/Listening to the Primary Source Have students read the passage. Encourage them to name and then express their feelings for places in which the physical environment is overwhelming and majestic. Ask them how they think the man in the photograph feels about the desert and to explain their answer.

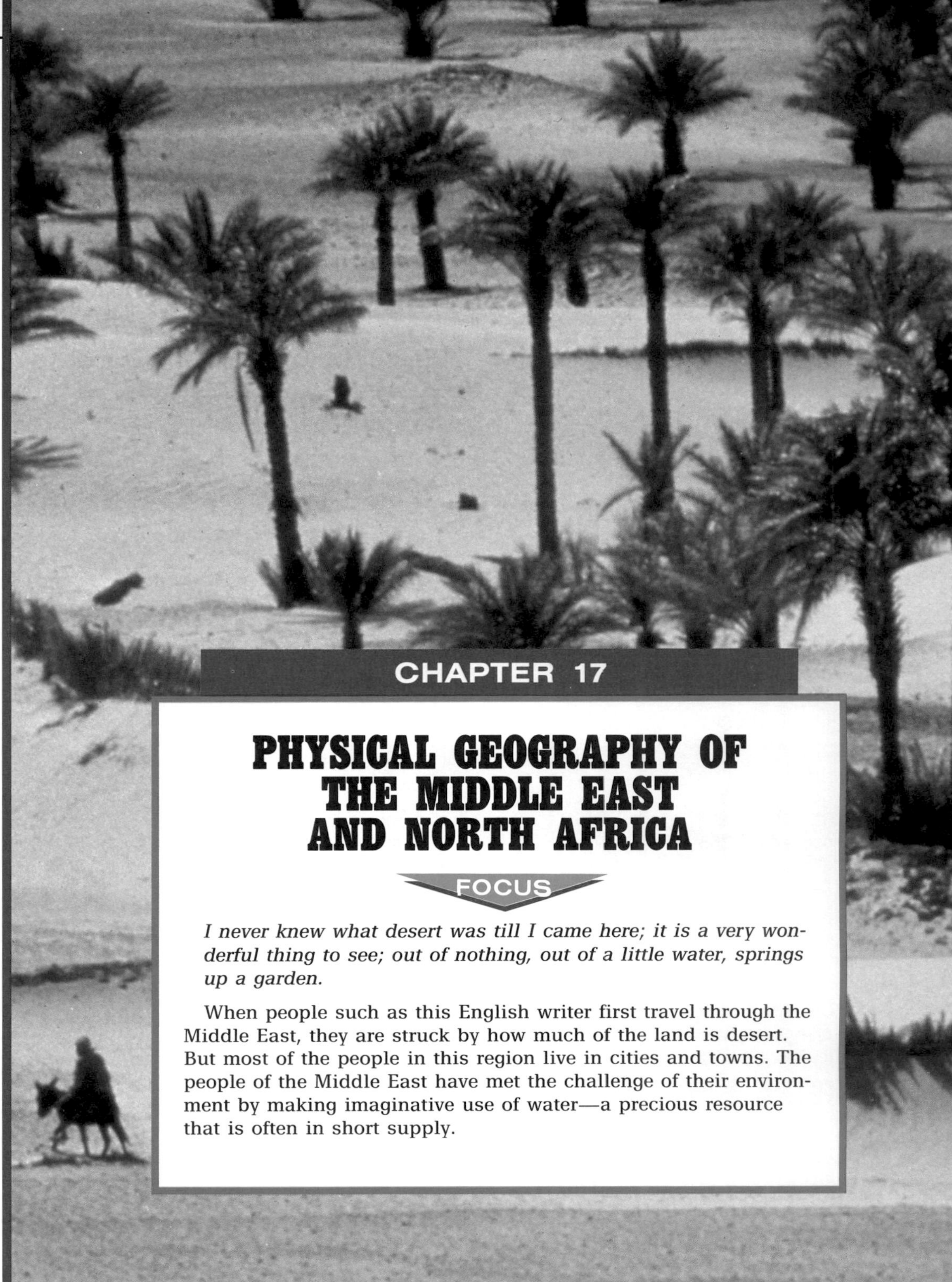

CHAPTER 17

PHYSICAL GEOGRAPHY OF THE MIDDLE EAST AND NORTH AFRICA

FOCUS

I never knew what desert was till I came here; it is a very wonderful thing to see; out of nothing, out of a little water, springs up a garden.

When people such as this English writer first travel through the Middle East, they are struck by how much of the land is desert. But most of the people in this region live in cities and towns. The people of the Middle East have met the challenge of their environment by making imaginative use of water—a precious resource that is often in short supply.

BACKGROUND INFORMATION

Multicultural Perspectives There are many myths about the Middle East and North Africa and the people who live there, and those myths often center around the region's most prominent landscape—its deserts. Movies and other sources often suggest that most people in the region live in the desert and ride camels, or ride about in luxury cars under the shadow of gleaming oil wells. Yet writer David Lamb has been quick to point out: "The great majority of Arabs, in fact, have never slept in a tent, ridden a camel or even seen an oil rig." Most people in the region live in cities, and most are poor. Yet the vision of nomads riding in the desert is a powerful image even to local residents, for it symbolizes a romantic sense of freedom that has all but disappeared in modern societies. Ask students whether Americans have similarly romantic notions about geographic regions in their country and the lifestyles those regions once supported.

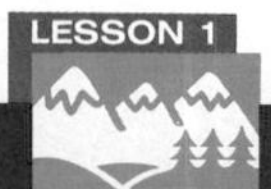

Landforms

READ TO LEARN

Key Vocabulary

desert
oasis
irrigation

Key Places

Sinai Peninsula
Arabian Peninsula
Anatolia
Sahara
Nile River
Tigris River
Euphrates River

Read Aloud

Two of the world's earliest civilizations—ancient Egypt and ancient Sumer—began in North Africa and the Middle East. The people of these ancient societies invented farming, the wheel, and writing. They invented many new forms of technology, and they traveled and traded throughout the Middle East and North Africa. Later, people in the Middle East and North Africa founded three of the world's great religions—Judaism, Christianity, and Islam. In order to understand the people of this historic region better, it is important to begin by learning about the land.

Read for Purpose

1. **WHAT YOU KNOW:** What is a crossroads?
2. **WHAT YOU WILL LEARN:** What are the main physical features of the Middle East and North Africa?

A CROSSROADS

The region of the Middle East and North Africa is considered to be one of the world's most important crossroads. The main reason for this is that the region spans two continents, Asia and Africa. These two continents are connected by a land bridge called the Sinai Peninsula. They also share with Europe a coastline along the Mediterranean Sea. Find the Sinai Peninsula and the Mediterranean Sea on the map on page 356. In what ways do you think the Sinai Peninsula and the Mediterranean Sea may have helped to make this region a major crossroads? ✻

Even in ancient times traders and explorers used the currents of the Mediterranean Sea to carry them from shore to shore in the Middle East and North Africa. For example, more than 3,500 years ago North African traders from Egypt sailed along Asia's Mediterranean coast.

Similarly, many different groups from Asia migrated into North Africa across the Sinai Peninsula. For example, the ancient Hebrews made the journey after a drought destroyed their crops. You have read in previous chapters that when different cultures meet, ideas are often exchanged. Because this is what has happened in the Middle East and North Africa, many geographers consider this region to be an important crossroads.

WHAT YOU KNOW: a place where roads meet
✻ They made it easy to travel between places in Africa and Asia (the two continents that meet here) and Europe.

LESSON 1
pages 355–359

Lesson Theme The main physical features of the Middle East and North Africa are peninsulas, deserts, mountains, seas, and river valleys.

Lesson Objectives

- Explain why the region of the Middle East and North Africa is considered a world crossroads.
- Describe the Saharan landscape.
- Explain how the population density of the Middle East and North Africa is related to its water sources.

PREPARE

Motivate Have a student read the *Read Aloud* section to the class. Then ask students to name everyday things we use that would not exist if the wheel had not been invented.

Set Purpose Tell students that they are about to read a description of the physical features of the Middle East and North Africa. Display the corresponding *Atlas* map of this region so that students can refer to it throughout the lesson.

TEACH

Looking at a Crossroads Help students to understand that people, goods, and ideas moved into this region from both Asia and Africa.

Ask students:

- **Name two physical features that have helped make this region a crossroads.** (Sinai Peninsula, Mediterranean Sea)
- **Name one group of people that came into North Africa across the Sinai Peninsula.** (the ancient Hebrews)

READING STRATEGY AND VOCABULARY DEVELOPMENT

Note Taking Remind students that taking notes on what they read can help them learn new material more easily. Encourage them to see that this strategy helps them to select and concentrate on the most important items of information in their reading. Remind them that they will understand and remember the material better if they put the information into their own words. Have students preview Chapter 17 and take notes, using the lesson headings to organize their notes.

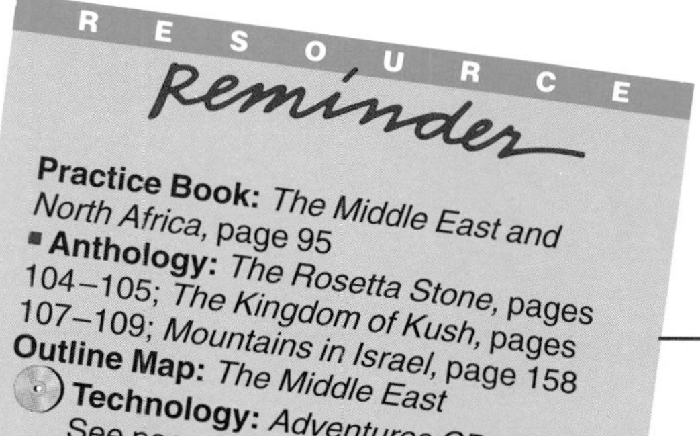

RESOURCE Reminder

Practice Book: *The Middle East and North Africa*, page 95
Anthology: *The Rosetta Stone*, pages 104–105; *The Kingdom of Kush*, pages 107–109; *Mountains in Israel*, page 158
Outline Map: *The Middle East*
Technology: *Adventures CD-ROM*
See page 353-B.

Exploring Important Peninsulas
Have students locate all the places mentioned in this section on the map on this page.

Ask students:

- **Name three of the region's important peninsulas.** (Sinai, Anatolia, Arabian)
- **Why does Anatolia have a special place in history?** (Many of the world's first villages may have been built there.)

EXTENDING MAP SKILLS

Have students study the elevation map on this page.

Ask students:

- **Name two of the highest mountain ranges in the Middle East and North Africa.** (Zagros Mountains, Atlas Mountains)
- **Name two plateaus in this region.** (Ahaggar, Iranian)
- **What elevation is the most common throughout the Middle East and North Africa?** (1,500 to 7,000 feet, or 500 to 2,000 m)

Looking at a Region of Contrasts
In order to help students form an image of the size of the Sahara Desert, ask them to imagine the United States as a vast stretch of sand.

Ask students:

- **Why is this area described as a region of contrasts?** (It has some of the driest land on earth, but it also has some of the most fertile farming valleys.)
- **What is this region's average annual rainfall?** (less than 10 inches, or 25 cm)
- **Describe a desert.** (a dry, sandy, or rocky region that receives very little rainfall)

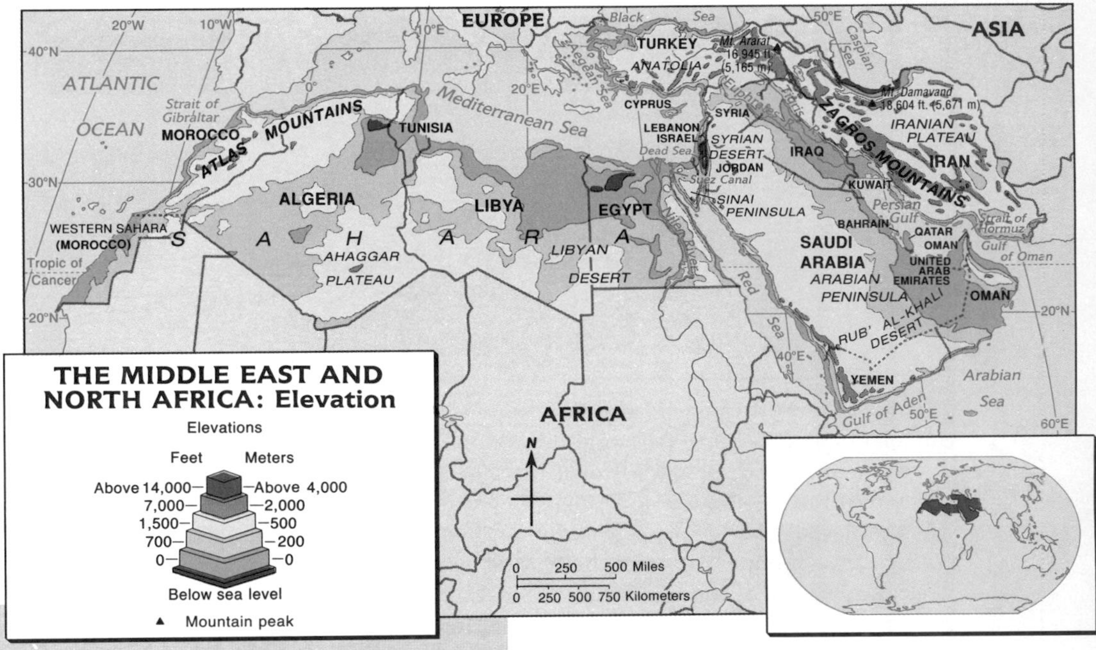

MAP SKILL: The Suez Canal (*below*) is between the Red and Mediterranean seas. In which country is the Suez Canal located?

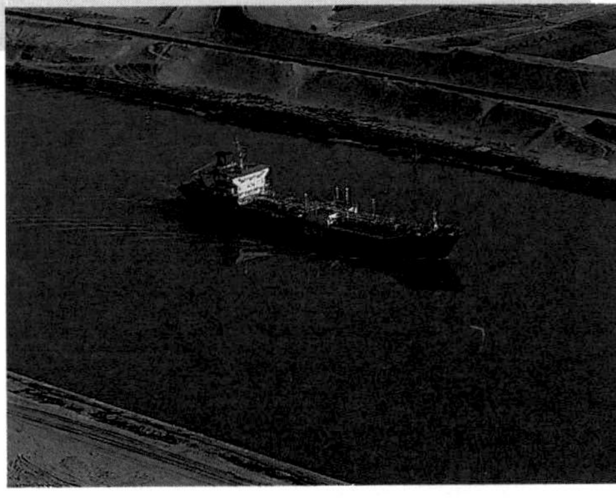

IMPORTANT PENINSULAS

In addition to the Sinai Peninsula, the region of the Middle East and North Africa also has two larger peninsulas. Find the **Arabian Peninsula** on the map above. As you can see, it is separated from Africa by the Red Sea and from the rest of Asia by the Persian Gulf.

In the northern part of the Middle East, you will find a peninsula called **Anatolia**. Geographers often call this peninsula Asia Minor. Anatolia has a special place in history. According to archaeologists, many of the world's first villages were built on this peninsula.

A REGION OF CONTRASTS

This region has some of the driest land on earth. But it also has some of the most fertile farming valleys. Rich farmlands are even found close to **deserts**. A desert is a dry, sandy, or rocky region that receives very little rainfall. Very few people live in deserts.

The deserts of the Middle East and North Africa exist because a vast area of the region receives little rainfall. Many parts of this region receive an average of less than 10 inches (25.4 cm) of annual rainfall.

356

MAP SKILL: Egypt

FUNDAMENTAL THEMES OF GEOGRAPHY

Place The surface of the Dead Sea is the lowest point on earth. It is 1,299 feet (396 m) below sea level. Have students check the encyclopedia for more information about the Dead Sea and its surrounding area. Have them make a two-column list of the physical and human characteristics of the sea and its environment.

Movement Ask students to note any information this unit gives about movement in the Middle East and North Africa. Have them make three columns with the headings "People," "Goods," and "Ideas." Then have students record in the appropriate column every reference to movement that they find in their reading.

The world's largest desert, the Sahara, is located in North Africa. You can find the Sahara on the Atlas map on page 631. The word *Sahara* comes from the Arabic word for "wilderness."

You might think that the landscape of a desert is all the same. But desert landscapes vary from place to place. Some parts of the Sahara look like great oceans of sand dunes. Dunes, as you may know, are mounds or ridges of sand formed by wind. Other parts of the Sahara have a gray, rocky surface. Little vegetation grows in any part of the desert, except after a rare rainstorm, when even flowers have been known to bloom suddenly. Use the diagram below to compare some of the different kinds of desert landscapes.

Most of the region's area is covered by desert, but the desert is not where most of the people live. Most people live along the narrow river valleys or on the seacoasts. Others live in the highlands or mountains, especially in Turkey, Syria, Iraq, and Iran.

DESERT DWELLERS

Only a small percentage of the region's people live in the deserts. Those who do need special skills to live there. The Bedouins (bed′ ü inz) are one group that has developed the skills to survive in the desert. *Bedouin* is an Arabic word meaning "desert dweller." Many Bedouins tend herds of sheep and goats. However, the camel is their most important animal.

Camels are well suited to desert life. They can walk for many days without drinking, carry heavy loads, and exist on

DIAGRAM SKILL: The desert contains many different types of landforms. Which form has an oasis nearby? Which form was created by the flow of old rivers?

DIAGRAM SKILL: hammada; wadi

Exploring a Region of Contrasts Continue the discussion about the region's landscapes.

Ask students:

- **Give two examples of the varied landscape of the Sahara Desert.** (Some parts look like great oceans of sand dunes, while other parts have a gray, rocky surface.)
- **From which language does the name "Sahara" come?** (Arabic) **What does it mean?** ("wilderness")

EXTENDING DIAGRAM SKILLS

Have students study the diagram on this page and help them to recognize the different types of desert surfaces.

Ask students:

- **Name the desert surface characterized by stretches of shifting sand dunes.** (*erg*)
- **Name and describe the desert surface surrounding oases.** (*hammada*—worn-down rock platform)
- **What had the surface called *wadi* been before it became a desert surface?** (a riverbed)
- **Describe the desert surface named *reg*.** (plains covered with sand and gravel)

Understanding Desert Dwellers Help students to realize that the Bedouins have developed special skills as a means of surviving in the desert.

Ask students:

- **Name three domestic animals important to the Bedouins.** (sheep, goats, camels)
- **In which ways are camels well suited to desert life?** (They can walk for many days without drinking, carry heavy loads, and exist on sparse vegetation.)

BACKGROUND INFORMATION

About the Arabs The Arabs' role as traders helped them to spread their language and religion throughout the Middle East and North Africa.

- Between 1200 and 1000 B.C. the Arabs domesticated the camel. Because camels can go for long distances without water, Arab merchants began to use them to carry goods across the desert. Gradually the Arabs established overland routes through the southern and western coasts to Syria and the Mediterranean Sea; these routes bypassed the old Persian Gulf routes.
- By extending the trade routes inland into North Africa, the Arabs transformed the small oasis villages that served their caravans into cities.

Learning About Desert Dwellers
Continue the discussion about the Bedouins.

Ask students:

- **How do the Bedouins use camels to survive in the desert?** (They use camels for transportation, drink camels' milk, make tents out of camel skins, and make many other useful products out of camel hair and skin.)
- **Which physical feature of the desert makes it possible for the Bedouins to survive?** (the oasis)
- **Name a Middle Eastern city that began as an oasis.** (Riyadh)

Looking at Fertile Farmlands
Help students to understand that most of the people of this region are *not* desert dwellers; most live beside rivers and seacoasts.

Ask students:

- **What is the population of the Middle East and North Africa?** (more than 200 million people)
- **State two important facts about the Nile River.** (Ninety-five percent of Egypt's population lives beside it. It's the longest river in the world.)
- **What is irrigation?** (the watering of dry lands by means of streams, canals, or pipes)
- *THINKING FURTHER:* **Why do you think an important population center has formed in the Nile River Valley?** (because the Nile River provides water for farming, drinking, washing, and so on)

EXTENDING MAP SKILLS

Have students study the population density map on this page.

Ask students:

- **Identify the reason for the location of the areas of highest population density.** (nearness to rivers or seacoasts)
- **Which area has more than 500 people per square mile?** (the Nile River Valley)

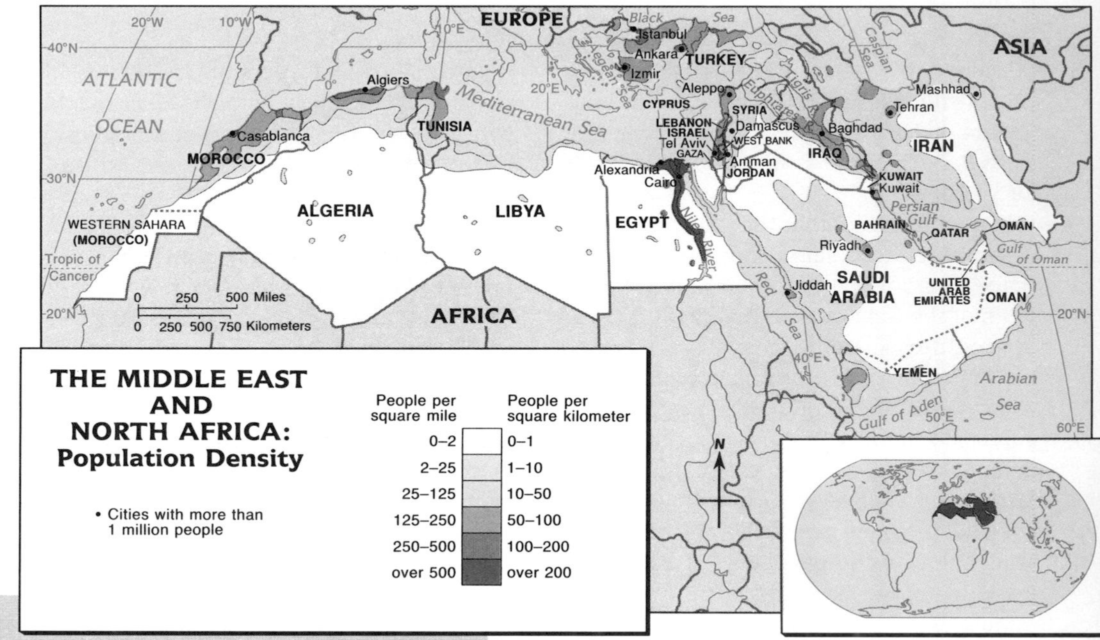

MAP SKILL: Which areas have the greatest population? Are most of them near water?

sparse vegetation. The Bedouins depend on their camels. They drink the camels' milk and they make tents out of camel skins. They also use camel hair and skin to make many useful products.

These animals can survive without food and water for many days because the humps on their backs store fat, which the camels burn for energy when they must go without food. The kind of camel found in the Middle East and North Africa is a single-humped beast, called a dromedary. Another variety of camel is the Bactrian camel, which has two humps. It is found in Central Asia.

Desert dwellers carry their food with them as they travel across the desert. When they need new supplies, they stop at an **oasis** to find food and water. An oasis is a green, fertile spot in the desert that has a water supply. Many oases have developed into large towns or cities. For example, Riyadh (rē yäd'), the capital of Saudi Arabia, began as an oasis.

FERTILE FARMLANDS

More than 200 million people live in the Middle East and North Africa. As you can see from the map above, most of the region's people live along its narrow river valleys or on its seacoasts. For example, more than 95 percent of Egypt's 60 million people live along the banks of the **Nile River**, the world's longest river. From an airplane the Nile River Valley looks like a long, thin green ribbon on a vast brown blanket. The Nile River Valley is one of the earth's most densely populated areas.

Along the river valleys of the Middle East and North Africa, **irrigation** helps to make farming possible. Irrigation is the watering of dry land by means of streams, canals, or pipes. Irrigation was invented by this region's first farmers more than 8,000 years ago. Today farmers still use

358

MAP SKILL: areas along the Nile River Valley and near major cities; Yes

CURRICULUM CONNECTION

Science Divide the class into two groups, one to research desert vegetation and the other to research features of the desert that have been formed by water.

- Ask the first group to prepare a discussion on how plants adapt to dry conditions. Encourage them to draw on their own experiences growing cacti or other desert plants as examples.
- Ask the second group to prepare a discussion on how water flows in the desert. Have them draw the following diagrams to be used as illustrations: a cross section of an oasis showing how water flows under it; the different stages in the formation of the Nile River delta; and the different phases in the life of an intermittent desert stream.

irrigation to provide the water to grow their crops. You will read more about irrigation in the Middle East and North Africa in the following chapters of this unit.

As the map on page 358 shows, important centers of population have also formed around other rivers in this region. In the Middle East, the **Tigris River** and the **Euphrates** (ū frā′ tēz) **River** flow through a rich river-valley region that some geographers call the Fertile Crescent because of its crescentlike shape.

Parts of the Fertile Crescent are watered by irrigation. Other areas rely upon a string of oases. These oases are sustained by the Tigris, the Euphrates, and the other rivers that flow through this area. Sumer, one of the world's earliest civilizations, developed in the Fertile Crescent.

OTHER FARMLANDS

Not all parts of the Middle East and North Africa depend on irrigation for farming. Along the coast of North Africa, some areas get enough rainfall for farms. In fact, for part of its history, the coastal farming areas of North Africa provided southern Europe with much of its wheat and other farm products.

Some areas depend on a combination of rainfall and irrigation to supply enough water for farming. The highlands of Turkey, Syria, and Iran often get enough rain for crops, but additional irrigation can guarantee a supply of water.

VARIED ENVIRONMENTS

In this lesson you have been introduced to the physical geography of the Middle East and North Africa. You have learned that large parts of the region are covered by deserts. However, most of the region's people live in areas in which rivers provide one of the region's most important resources—water.

Irrigation has helped create fertile farmland in Jordan. Along the Nile River, the desert is next to fertile fields (*above*), and people live on the desert to save farmland.

Check Your Reading

1. What land bridge connects the Middle East and North Africa?
2. Name the world's largest desert and describe a desert environment.
3. Use the map on page 358 to identify three very densely populated parts of the Middle East and North Africa.
4. **THINKING SKILL:** Based on your reading of the section "Fertile Farmlands" in this lesson, what conclusions can you draw about the Nile River Valley?

THINKING SKILL: Drawing Conclusions

359

Examining Other Farmlands Help students to understand that not all areas of the Middle East and North Africa depend on irrigation for farming.

- **Which areas of this region get enough rain for crops?** (the highlands of Turkey, Syria, and Iran)

Applying the Lesson Provide students with the outline map of the Middle East and North Africa (from the Teacher's Resource Center). Ask them to label mountains, deserts, plateaus, bodies of water, and countries. Have them use these maps as references as they study this unit.

3 CLOSE

Summarizing Students have read about this region's physical geography, its desert dwellers, and its population centers.

Evaluating Use these questions to assess students' understanding.

- **How does the Sinai Peninsula help to make the Middle East and North Africa a world crossroads?** (It forms a bridge across which people and goods can move between Asia and Africa.)
- **Near which physical features are the major cities of this region found?** (rivers, oases, seacoasts)

Answers to Check Your Reading

1. Sinai Peninsula
2. Sahara; few plants, temperature regularly more than 100°F. (38°C)
3. Nile River Valley; coastal areas along the Atlantic Ocean and the Mediterranean, Aegean, and Black seas; central Iraq in the valley where the Tigris and Euphrates rivers flow
4. It is a long, narrow strip that is densely populated and extremely fertile.

Independent Practice
Practice Book: page 95

MEETING INDIVIDUAL NEEDS

Reteaching (easy) Have students write the terms for the physical features of the region of the Middle East and North Africa on flashcards. Have students pair off and take turns matching a name with each physical feature; for example, desert—Sahara.

Extension (average) Ask students to imagine that they live in one of the regions' desert areas. Have them write three pages of a diary entry describing things about their lives that they enjoy.

Enrichment (challenging) Divide the class into five groups and have them research the Fertile Crescent. Have each group use one of the themes of geography as its focus for studying that region. Have each group make charts with which to illustrate their findings.

SKILLS LESSON
pages 360–361

Lesson Theme Contour maps help us to picture the shape of the land.

Lesson Objective
- Interpret a contour map.

PREPARE

Motivate You may want to project Transparency Map 12 on the screen for students to study. Have students read the introduction. Then have them list the ways we can depict the earth with maps such as: a pictorial or 3-D map that looks like a photograph; a side view called a cross section or profile; and a plane view, or bird's-eye view, from overhead. Tell students to imagine that they are flying over the land. Explain that the contour map shown in Diagram B is a way of picturing what they would see. Discuss how it is like a road map in that it is a bird's-eye view of land. Compare how the lines on Diagram B differ from the lines on a road map. (Road map lines show locations of human-built roads, and contour map lines show the physical shape of the land.)

Set Purpose Tell the students that they will interpret contour lines to determine the shape of the land surface that the lines represent.

TEACH

Interpreting Contour Maps Stress that most maps are used to measure distances from point to point. However, contour maps measure distances perpendicular to the surface of the sea.

Ask students:

- **What kind of walk would you have along a contour line?** (absolutely flat)

BUILDING SKILLS
GEOGRAPHY SKILLS

Reading Contour Maps

Key Vocabulary

contour map
relief
contour line
contour interval

The geography of the Middle East and North Africa is varied, ranging from the extremes of vast, flat deserts to rugged mountain peaks. Today we can refer to maps to find the exact locations of these landforms. But imagine the difficulties before accurate maps were available.

Long ago people did not know the extent of a desert's vastness or the height of a mountain. As you know, cartographers, or the people who make maps, now can represent actual distances and elevations on the maps they draw.

In this book you have seen a number of elevation maps that use different colors to represent the height of land above sea level. In this lesson you will find out about another way cartographers show elevation on a map.

Meters
1,600
1,200
800
400
0
(Sea level)

DIAGRAM A

CYPRUS: Contour Lines

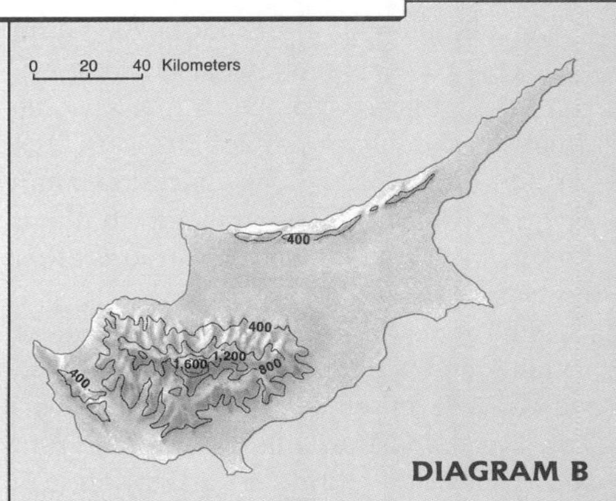

DIAGRAM B

Contour Maps

The elevation and features of a place can be shown on a **contour map**. *Contour* means "shape." Contour maps help us to picture the shape of the earth's surface. These kinds of maps represent the actual elevation of an area.

Contour maps show landforms and use lines or colors to show different elevations. A **contour line** on a map connects areas that have the same elevation. As you know from reading the maps in this book, elevation is given in either feet or meters. If you were to walk along an area represented by a contour line, you would not go up or down. You would remain at the same elevation.

Using the Diagrams

Diagram A on this page will help you to understand contour lines. It shows a model of Cyprus, an island in the Mediterranean Sea. This diagram illustrates how

360

CURRICULUM CONNECTION

Science Seeing vertical contour intervals as horizontal contour lines is a difficult spatial understanding. Use the following materials to perform a "vertical-to-horizontal" demonstration: a plastic dishpan with "sea level" written on the inside of the bottom; a ruler; three water-filled jugs; a dark crayon; a sheet of Plexiglas to cover the pan; a rock that fits inside the pan; and a transparency. Have students look down into the pan as you work on the floor. Place the rock in the pan and have a student hold the ruler vertically in the pan. Pour water into the pan until it reaches 1 inch (25.4 mm) on the ruler. Mark the water level all around the rock with the crayon. Keep pouring water carefully into the pan, marking 2 inches (50.8 mm), 3 inches (76.2 mm), etc., until the water covers the rock. Put the Plexiglas on top of the pan, with the transparency on top of the Plexiglas. Draw the lines seen on the rock below onto the transparency. Display the rock and map together.

RESOURCE *Reminder*
Practice Book: *Reading Contour Maps,* page 96
Transparency Map: 12

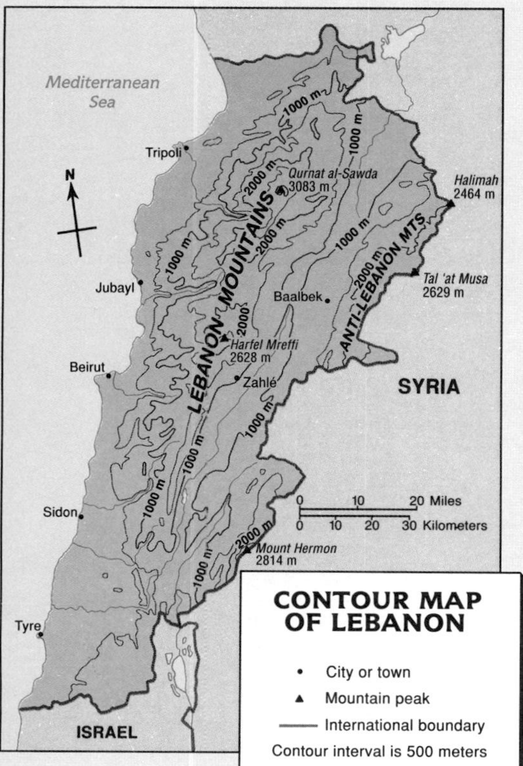

the island can be cut into layers by using horizontal sheets that intersect the land. Note the elevation of each sheet. Imagine that you can push the sheets completely through the model, line them up directly above one another, and trace the outline of each "cut" on the sheet below it. If you took each outline in turn and positioned it correctly over a piece of paper, you would have a simple contour map of Cyprus as shown in **Diagram B**.

If you now compare **Diagram A** with **Diagram B**, you will see that the contour lines reflect the shape of the land. The closed, somewhat circular lines of **Diagram B** show the varied elevations of Cyprus.

Contour Maps Show Relief

When you look at a contour map, you see the relief of an area. Relief is variation in elevation. Rugged mountains with great variation in elevation have high relief. But flat plains with little variation in elevation have low relief.

Cartographers show relief on a map by the spacing of contour lines. For example, widely spaced contour lines mean that the land is flat or gently sloping. A steep slope, or mountainside, is shown by lines that are drawn close together. The contour map of Lebanon on this page shows low relief in the coastal areas and high relief in the mountains.

When reading contour maps, it is important to check first the contour interval of the map. This is the difference in elevation between any two contour lines. The contour interval, which may vary from map to map, is usually shown in the legend. Look at the map of Lebanon. You can see that the contour interval is 500 meters.

Reviewing the Skill

1. What is a contour line? A contour interval?
2. What is the contour interval on the map of Lebanon on this page?
3. According to the map of Lebanon, Tripoli is located how many meters below the highest peak in the Lebanon Mountains?
4. How do contour maps help you to picture the elevation of the land?

361

Using the Diagrams Be sure students understand that contour lines connect all the points on a map that have the same elevation, as shown in Diagram B. Help them to see the connection between Diagram A and Diagram B.

Ask students:

- **What elevations are shown on Diagram A?** (sea level to 1,600 m) **On Diagram B?** (sea level to 1,600 m)

Using Contour Maps to Show Relief Emphasize that the first information to look for on a contour map is its contour interval.

Ask students:

- **What are two ways to find the contour interval of a map?** (in the legend or by subtracting the numbers for any two consecutive lines)
- **How does the pattern of lines on a contour map show relief?** (Lines far apart mean flat land, while lines close together show steep relief.)

Applying the Skill Have students write their own lists of questions about contour maps and the diagrams shown in this lesson. Then have them trade lists and answer the questions.

CLOSE

Summarizing Students have learned to interpret contour lines and contour intervals.

Answers to Reviewing the Skill

1. line connecting areas of the same elevation; difference in elevation between any two contour lines on the same map
2. 500 meters
3. 3,083 meters
4. Their patterns of lines tell you where high and low relief are located.

Independent Practice
Practice Book: page 96

MEETING INDIVIDUAL NEEDS

Reteaching (easy) Have student groups find a relief map of a Middle Eastern or North African country and make a clay or plaster model of the country from the map.

Extension (average) Have students compare the Middle East and North Africa elevation map on page 356 in this chapter with the contour maps in the *Building Skills* lesson. Have them write a paragraph explaining how an elevation map is different from a contour map.

Enrichment (challenging) Have students draw a rough contour map of the school grounds. If the relief is too uniform, extend the assignment to a local area with high and low relief.

LESSON 2
pages 362–365

Lesson Theme The two key resources of the Middle East and North Africa are water, which is used for irrigation, and petroleum, the profits from which help to develop the region's economies.

Lesson Objectives

- Describe the climate of the Middle East and North Africa.
- Identify the irrigation methods used in the Middle East and North Africa.
- Describe the petroleum reserves of the Middle East and North Africa.

PREPARE

Motivate Read the *Read Aloud* section to the class. Discuss why the king was disappointed with the results of American drilling.

Set Purpose Ask the *What You Know* question to stimulate a discussion on the importance of water for survival. Tell students they will learn why water and oil are important resources in the Middle East and North Africa.

TEACH

Discussing Sharp Contrasts in Climate

Ask students:

- **What does *arid* mean?** ("dry")
- **State two important facts about the climate of the Middle East and North Africa.** (It's the hottest and most arid region in the world.)

LESSON 2

Climate and Resources

READ TO LEARN

Key Vocabulary	Key Places
arid	Plateau of Iran
aquifer	Zagros Mountains
qanat	Atlas Mountains
petroleum	Persian Gulf

Read Aloud

In the 1930s an American oil company asked King Ibn Saud of Saudi Arabia for permission to drill wells to test for oil in his desert kingdom. When the company struck oil, the king is said to have been disappointed. He had hoped the drillers would find water.

Oil has brought great wealth to Saudi Arabia and much of the Middle East. Yet the need for fresh water in these dry lands is more urgent today than ever. Populations are growing fast, creating a greater demand for water.

Read for Purpose

1. WHAT YOU KNOW: Has your community ever had to conserve water? What did people do to use less water?
2. WHAT YOU WILL LEARN: Why are water and oil key resources in the Middle East and North Africa?

SHARP CONTRASTS IN CLIMATE

You read in Lesson 1 that the region of the Middle East and North Africa has vast deserts and fertile farmland. Some of this region's deserts are the most **arid**, or dry, places in the world. They also are among the hottest places in the world. The world's record for high temperature is 136°F. (58°C), and it was recorded at Al-'Aziziyah (al az ē zē' yä), in the Libyan Desert. Due to the high temperature in this region, any rain that falls evaporates quickly.

"Between 11:00 A.M. and 3:30 P.M. even the camels lie down," wrote Wayne Eastep, a writer who lived in Saudi Arabia one summer. "The desert baked. We seemed immersed in a [glowing] furnace." He also noted that his thermometer burst one day when the temperature reached 125°F. (52°C).

Yet other parts of the region are mild and wet, or even cold and snowy. As the map on page 363 shows, people who live along the Mediterranean coast from Morocco to Turkey enjoy a climate that is hot and dry in summer and mild and wet in winter, with 30 inches (75 cm) or more of rainfall a year.

As you move inland from the coast, the climates are more arid. In the higher ele-

WHAT YOU KNOW: Students should be encouraged to think about the various ways communities have saved water, such as limiting the amount used to water gardens, to wash automobiles, and to take showers and baths.

READING STRATEGY AND VOCABULARY DEVELOPMENT

Note Taking Have students make up questions based on the headings of Lesson 2. Tell students that answering these questions can help them select the most important ideas for their notes. Demonstrate this strategy by using the first heading, "Sharp Contrasts in Climate," to form the question "What are the sharp contrasts in climate?" Point out that the main idea of the section is summed up in the answer "It is very dry and hot in some of the region's deserts, yet other parts of the region are mild and wet, or even cold and snowy." Have students finish the lesson by themselves. Collect students' questions and answers, and choose some to use as a guide for class discussion.

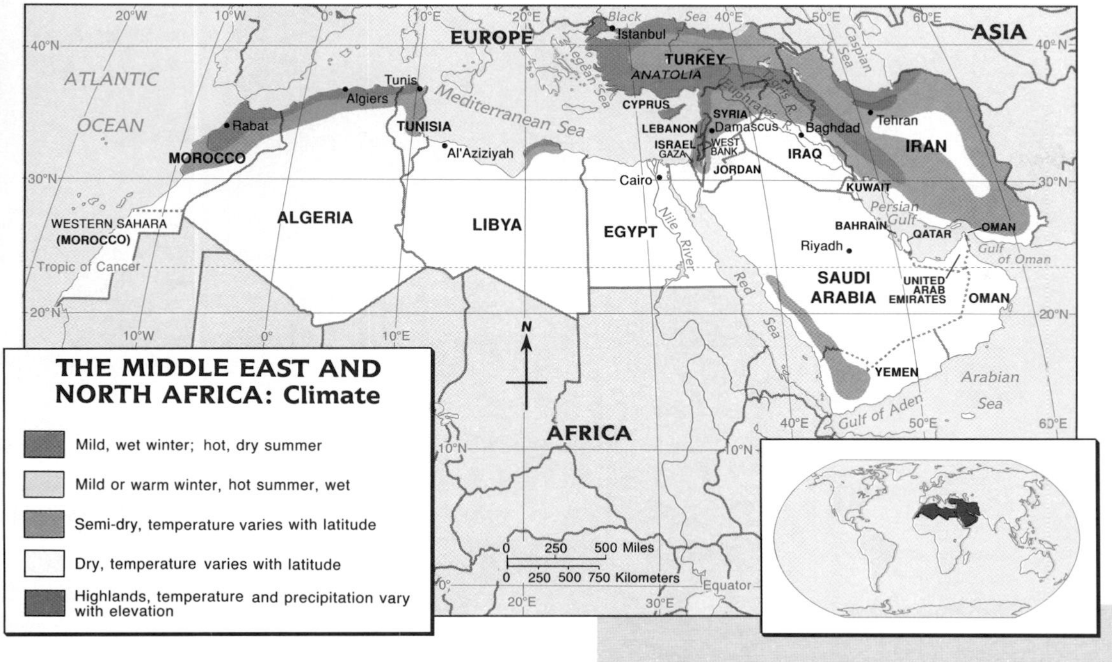

MAP SKILL: In which type of climate do you think farming would be most difficult in North Africa and the Middle East?

vations of Anatolia and the **Plateau of Iran**, the weather is like that of Wyoming or Colorado. Summers are hot, while winters are long and cold. You can find the Plateau of Iran on the Atlas map on page 631. Enough snow covers the mountains north of Tehran, Iran, in winter to create good conditions for skiing.

WATER—A PRECIOUS RESOURCE

According to an ancient legend, a prince once lived in an African kingdom near Lake Victoria. Enemies threatened his life and forced him to flee. The prince ran northward. As he fled from his enemies, his sword trailed behind him. Wherever it touched the ground, the earth opened and poured forth water to protect him. When he reached the Mediterranean Sea, the prince disappeared. But the river that sprang up behind him remained. It is called the Nile.

The Nile River has been so vital that the people of Egypt call their country the "gift of the Nile." The river provides Egyptians with 85 percent of the water they use.

As you read in Lesson 1, irrigation from rivers such as the Nile, the Tigris, and the Euphrates helps make farming possible throughout the region. According to one Egyptian farmer, irrigation "helps the farmer harness the water to his advantage."

Not all water for irrigation comes from rivers. For example, **aquifers** are important sources of water in some areas. An aquifer is an underground layer of rock that holds water or carries water to springs or wells.

In Iran, for example, people have built underground tunnels called **qanats** (kä′ nats). The water that runs through the qanats comes from the **Zagros Mountains** in southwestern Iran. Some qanats are 40 miles (64 km) long, and a few extend as far as 300 feet (91 m) underground.

MAP SKILL: the dry, or desert, climate that exists in almost every country of the region

EXTENDING MAP SKILLS

Have students study the climate map on this page.

Ask students:

- **What is the most typical climate for the Middle East and North Africa?** (dry; Temperature varies with latitude.)
- **In which areas do you find mild, wet winters and hot, dry summers?** (along the Mediterranean coast in Morocco and Algeria; along the northern Mediterranean coast of Tunisia, the coasts of Israel, Lebanon, and Syria; along the Mediterranean, Aegean, and Black Sea coasts in Turkey)
- **Name the climate with mild, wet winters and hot, dry summers.** (Mediterranean climate)

Discussing Water—A Precious Resource Help students to understand that irrigation is essential to farming in most of the Middle East and North Africa.

Ask students:

- **Why do the Egyptians call the Nile a "gift"?** (It provides 85 percent of Egypt's water; its floods bring rich soil to fertilize the fields.)
- **Name an ancient Iranian irrigation device.** (qanat)

BACKGROUND INFORMATION

The Aswan High Dam and the Nile River Today In 1960 the Egyptians, aided by other countries, began building the Aswan High Dam in order to gain control of some of the Nile River's untapped power. Since its completion in 1970, the dam has brought about many changes—both good and bad.

- The positive changes include the production of electricity for farms and industry and the irrigation of millions of acres of once-dry land.
- The negative changes include reducing the flooding that brought the mud to fertilize the farmers' fields and slowing the flow that had formerly reduced the number of disease-causing organisms in the water.

Talking About Water Continue the discussion about water.

Ask students:

- **From where do the qanats bring the water?** (from the Zagros Mountains in southwestern Iran)
- *THINKING FURTHER:* **Why is it an advantage to have the qanats underground?** (There is less evaporation of water.)

EXTENDING MAP SKILLS

Have students study the land use map on this page.

Ask students:

- **Which has more petroleum reserves, North Africa or the Middle East?** (the Middle East)
- **Where are the largest commercial farming areas of this region generally located?** (along the coasts and rivers)

Looking at Using the Land Stress to students that even though fertile, well-watered land is scarce in this region, there are areas with arable farmland and enough rainfall to support forests.

Ask students:

- **How is the arable land distributed among this region's countries?** (unevenly)
- **Name the areas with arable, well-watered land.** (Lebanon, the Nile Delta, Yemen)

Discussing a Wealth of Oil Help students to understand the variety of ways in which the oil-rich nations use their wealth.

Ask students:

- **What are some of the ways in which oil-rich kingdoms have used their wealth?** (built schools, roads, and hospitals to improve the lives of the country's citizens)

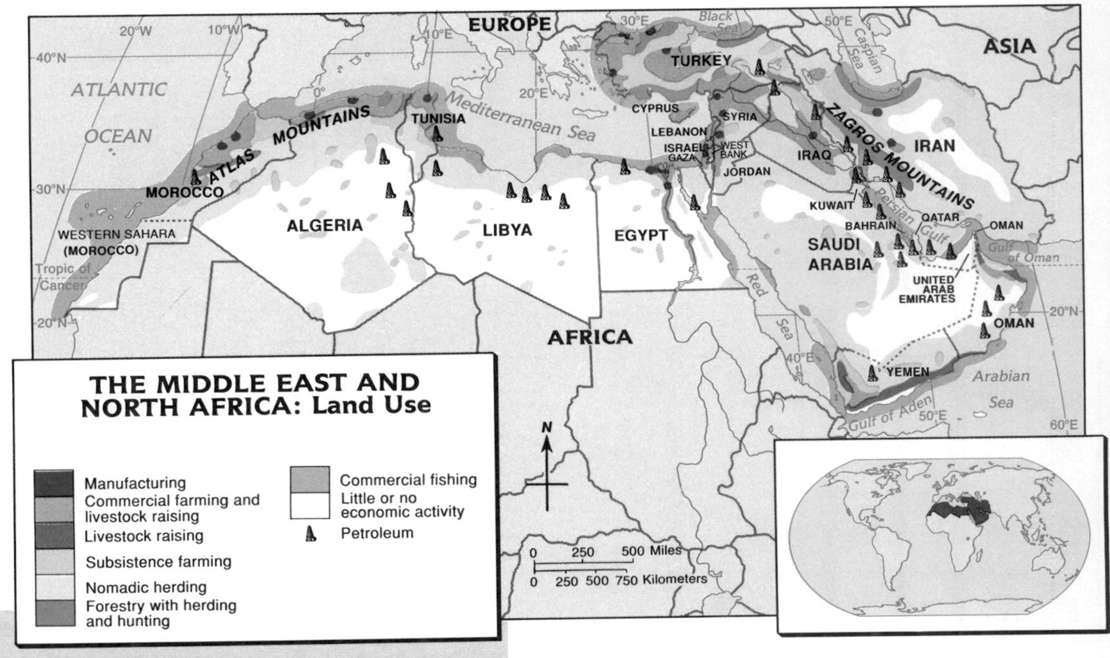

MAP SKILL: Why do you think many parts of this region have little or no economic activity?

The first qanats were dug more than 2,000 years ago in Persia (the old name for Iran). About 50,000 qanats still provide water to 75 percent of Iran's farms. Since qanats are underground, the water cannot evaporate, as it can from an open canal.

USING THE LAND

Fertile, well-watered land is scarce in the region of the Middle East and North Africa. About 10 percent of the land is farmed today. The distribution of the arable farmland that does exist is very uneven. For example, Turkey and Iran have large areas of fertile land, while in Saudi Arabia only 1 percent of the land can be farmed. Less than 4 percent of Egypt's land is used for farming. Yet Egyptian farmers along the Nile River can grow two or more crops on the same field each year. Scientists have tried to increase the cultivatable land in Egypt with irrigation, but the desert soil is too salty for farming.

Fertile land with enough natural moisture to grow crops is found only in a few other areas. They include Lebanon, the Nile Delta, and Yemen, which gets abundant yearly rains from the Indian Ocean.

On the slopes of the **Atlas Mountains** of North Africa, enough rain falls to support forests of cork, oak, and evergreen trees. Northern Iran also has major forests along the Caspian Sea. Look at the map above to find other forested areas.

A WEALTH OF OIL

The discovery of **petroleum**, or oil, in the 1930s has greatly affected the Middle East and North Africa. The rulers of the oil kingdoms in this region are among the world's richest people. These rulers use some of the oil wealth to build schools, roads, and hospitals to improve the lives of their countries' citizens.

 MAP SKILL: because many parts of the region are hot and dry and have few people in them

BUILDING CITIZENSHIP

How Should a Country Use Its Wealth? Tell students that before the discovery of oil in the 1930s, many of the Middle Eastern oil kingdoms were extremely poor. Divide the class into groups and assign one of these kingdoms to each group. Have the groups research the conditions in these countries before and after the discovery of oil. Then have students prepare a skit dramatizing the ways in which the leaders of the countries that they researched have used their new wealth. Discuss with students the various ways in which the money might have been used to benefit each nation as a whole.

The Middle East produces nearly one third of the petroleum in the world today. An even larger share—two thirds—of the earth's known oil reserves is found in the Middle East. Reserves are supplies of a resource that are available for future use.

Most of the Middle East's oil is located beneath the lands bordering the **Persian Gulf**. Saudi Arabia alone has about one fourth of the world's known oil reserves. Tiny Kuwait had another 15 to 20 percent, but Iraq set Kuwait's oil fields on fire in a war in 1990, and Kuwait lost huge amounts of petroleum. Iraq and Iran are also oil giants.

Libya is the largest oil-producing country in North Africa. This makes Libya the richest nation in North Africa.

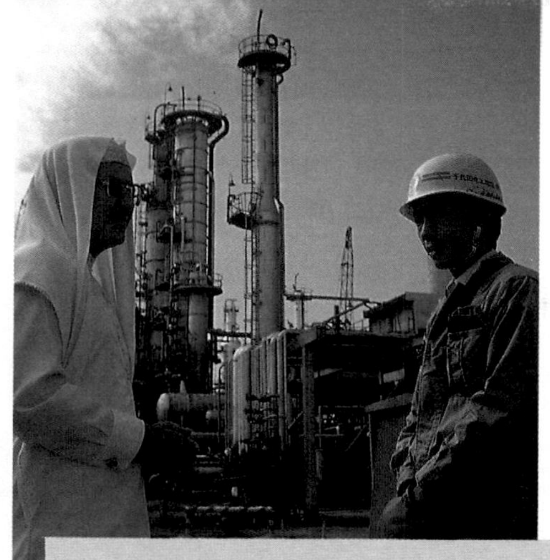

Many countries have invested in the oil-rich Middle East and North Africa. Japan gets nearly all of its oil supply from the region.

USING PETROLEUM

A Saudi Arabian leader once said that petroleum was too valuable to burn. But today, petroleum's greatest value is as a fuel. The Saudis and Kuwaitis are trying to find more ways to use their greatest resource. Petroleum is already used to make plastics and fertilizer. It is also used in other, more surprising ways.

For example, in its fight to prevent the sand dunes of the Sahara from covering valuable farmland, Libya planted 400 million trees. Each tree was first sprayed with oil. The sticky oil held the shifting sands against the trees, stopping the dunes from moving over farmland.

So much oil lies beneath Saudi Arabia and Kuwait that these countries rarely bother to save the natural gas that is often discovered with petroleum. By contrast, Iran, which has the world's second-largest supply of natural gas, has built pipelines that send this resource to markets in neighboring countries. Other than oil and natural gas, the Middle East and North Africa have few natural resources.

WATER AND OIL

As you have read, the Middle East and North Africa is a hot, dry region. Because water is scarce, the rivers and aquifers provide water for irrigation. Most farmers in the region depend heavily on irrigation. If more water were available for irrigation, more than the 10 percent of the land now being farmed could be used for crops.

The discovery of oil in the 1930s has transformed the region and brought great wealth to some of its countries. The nations bordering the Persian Gulf have two thirds of the world's known oil reserves.

Check Your Reading

1. What is an oil reserve?
2. What are qanats?
3. Are water and oil key resources in this region for the same reason? Explain your answer.
4. THINKING SKILL: In what ways do you think the countries of the Middle East would be affected if large new oil reserves were found in North America?

THINKING SKILL: Drawing Conclusions

Talking About Oil Wealth Continue the discussion of oil kingdoms.

Ask students:

- **What portion of the world's petroleum is produced in the Middle East?** (nearly one third)

Talking About Petroleum Use Help students to appreciate some of the ingenious uses of petroleum.

Applying the Lesson Have students draw a large outline map of the Middle East and North Africa on butcher paper. Then have them paste pictures from magazine illustrations of the climate and resources in each of the Middle Eastern and North African countries.

CLOSE

Summarizing Students have read that since water and other natural resources are scarce in this region, its economy depends mostly on oil production and farm products made possible by irrigation.

Evaluating Use these questions to assess students' understanding.

- **Describe the climate contrasts of the Middle East and North Africa.** (The climate ranges from hot and dry to mild and wet, or even cold and snowy.)
- **Name and describe Iran's irrigation device.** (qanat—underground tunnel that prevents evaporation)

Answers to Check Your Reading

1. a supply of oil available for future use
2. underground irrigation tunnels
3. No; water because it is scarce; oil because it is abundant.
4. They might become poorer and less powerful.

Independent Practice
Practice Book: page 97

MEETING INDIVIDUAL NEEDS

Reteaching (easy) Have students use each word from the *Key Vocabulary* and *Key Places* to write eight facts from the lesson.

Extension (average) Have students list all the ways this region is different from other regions in the world. Have them illustrate such striking features as the Sahara, the oil fields, the deserts, and rich farmland in a large mural or collage.

Enrichment (challenging) Have three student groups research the following topics: how to dig a qanat; how solar power is being used in the desert; and how a desalinization plant works. Ask them to present their findings in the form of a TV special.

CHAPTER 17 REVIEW
pages 366–367

USING THE CHAPTER SUMMARY AND REVIEW

Physical Geography These questions may be used for review.

- **Which two continents are connected by the Sinai Peninsula?** (Asia and Africa)
- **What type of climate can be found on the Iranian Plateau?** (hot summers; long, cold winters)
- **Which resources are scarce in this region? Which are abundant?** (water and arable land; oil and natural gas)

Ideas to Remember

- **Why is the Middle East considered a crossroads of people and cultures?** (Three great continents —Africa, Asia, and Europe—are linked by this region; it is the birthplace of three of the world's great religions and some of the world's earliest known civilizations.)
- **How is the Middle East and North Africa a region of physical contrasts?** (It has some of the driest land on earth, but it also has some of the most fertile farming valleys.)
- **Where do most of the people of this region live?** (along the narrow river valleys or on the seacoasts)
- **Why is oil such an important resource of the Middle East and North Africa?** (Oil, an extremely valuable product, is the region's major export; it produces nearly one third of the world's petroleum and contains two thirds of the earth's known oil reserves.)

CHAPTER 17 • SUMMARY

MIDDLE EAST AND NORTH AFRICA: PHYSICAL GEOGRAPHY

LANDFORMS

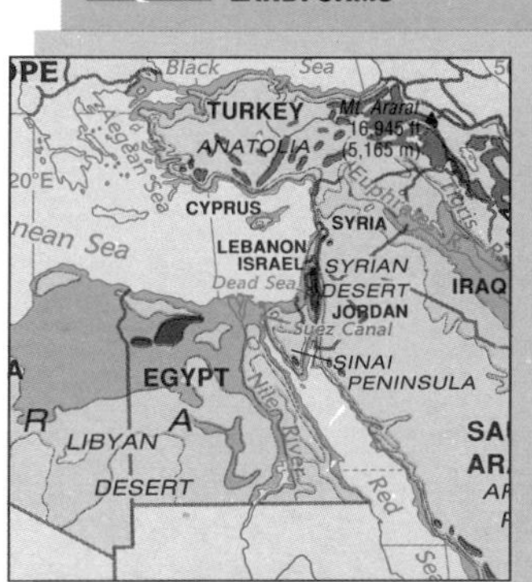

- Peninsulas: Sinai Peninsula, Arabian Peninsula, Anatolian Peninsula

- Deserts: Sahara, Syrian, Rub-al-Khali
- Fertile river valleys: Nile River Valley, Tigris River Valley, Euphrates River Valley
- Mountains: Zagros Mountains, Atlas Mountains, Lebanon Mountains

CLIMATE

- Arid climate: hot and dry in deserts
- Mild climate: warm and wet along Mediterranean coast
- Cold climate: long, cold winters in Anatolia and Plateau of Iran

NATURAL RESOURCES

- Fertile land in Lebanon; the Nile Delta; and parts of Yemen, North Africa, Iran, and Turkey
- Forests in Atlas Mountains, northern Iran, and Turkey
- Abundant resources: oil, natural gas, phosphates

- The Middle East produces one third of the world's supply of oil

IDEAS TO REMEMBER

- The region has vast deserts and also fertile, irrigated farmland.
- Although the region has some of the hottest and driest places in the world, it also has warm, wet sections and some areas with cold winters.
- Oil and natural gas, which are abundant in the region, have brought great wealth to the countries that have them.

366

ENRICHMENT ACTIVITY

Creating an Oasis **Materials:** Large cardboard box bottoms, sand, mirror, flat stones, modeling clay, cardboard tubes from hangers, construction paper, paints or markers, tape

1. Remind students that they have learned that many Middle Eastern cities, such as Riyadh, the capital of Saudi Arabia, began as oases. Tell students that they are going to create a model of an oasis.
2. Divide the class into groups, and have each group make an oasis using the following steps as a guide.
   - First overturn the box bottom to serve as a base.
   - Use the mirror as a small spring-fed pond, and cover the rest of the base with sand.
   - Use the tubes, colored brown, for palm tree bases, and cut out construction paper palm fronds, colored green, for their tops.
   - Model buildings and people with clay.
3. Have the groups assemble their models, inserting trees in holes in the base and distributing buildings and people around the oasis.

CHAPTER 17 ▪ REVIEW

REVIEWING VOCABULARY

aquifer oasis
arid petroleum
irrigation

Number a sheet of paper from 1 to 5. Beside each number write the word or term that best completes the sentence.

1. An ____ is a layer of rock that holds large amounts of underground water.
2. ____, another word for oil, has brought great wealth to several nations in the Middle East and North Africa.
3. Some cities grew up around an ____, or a fertile and well-watered spot in the desert.
4. Because they are so dry, deserts are often called ____ regions.
5. ____, or bringing water to dry land, has made farming possible in many desert regions.

REVIEWING FACTS

1. Why is the Middle East and North Africa often called a crossroads?
2. Name three major peninsulas in the Middle East and North Africa. Which peninsula is also called Asia Minor?
3. Describe ways in which people have used the camel to help them survive in the desert.
4. Where do most people live in the Middle East and North Africa? What percentage of Egypt's population lives along the Nile River?
5. What is the Fertile Crescent? What was the earliest civilization to develop in this region?
6. Which climate in the Middle East and North Africa is the mildest? What are the characteristics of this climate?
7. Name two regions in the Middle East in which the climate is similar to that of the American West.
8. Why have the people of Iran built huge qanats underground?
9. What fraction of the world's oil production comes from the Middle East?
10. Which country in North Africa has the largest oil supply?

WRITING ABOUT MAIN IDEAS

1. **Writing a Paragraph:** Even though Kuwait and Saudi Arabia are desert countries with almost no farmland, they are among the world's wealthiest nations. Write a paragraph explaining why.
2. **Writing a Myth:** You read about an ancient African myth describing the origin of the Nile River. Write your own myth describing the origin of the great deserts of the Middle East and North Africa.
3. **Writing About Perspectives:** Imagine that you live in a country that is rich in petroleum. First, decide whether you are a ruler or an ordinary citizen. Then write a paragraph that explains your plan for using the money made from selling oil to benefit the people of your country and perhaps other people in the world.

BUILDING SKILLS: READING CONTOUR MAPS

1. What is the purpose of a contour map?
2. Which type of landform would be shown by lines drawn very close together? Very far apart?
3. When do you think you might find contour maps useful?

Answers to Reviewing Vocabulary

1. aquifer
2. petroleum
3. oasis
4. arid
5. irrigation

Answers to Reviewing Facts

1. The region spans two continents, and many groups migrated from Asia into North Africa.
2. Sinai, Arabian, Anatolia; Anatolia
3. Camels are used for transportation and food, camel skin is used to make tents, and camel hair and skin are used for other products.
4. Most people live in the region's narrow river valleys or along its seacoast; 95 percent.
5. It is a rich river valley; Sumer.
6. Mediterranean climate; hot, dry summers and mild, wet winters
7. Anatolia and the Iranian Plateau
8. Qanats are used to irrigate crops, bring water to villages, and prevent water from evaporating.
9. one third
10. Libya

Suggestions for Writing About Main Ideas

1. Students should focus on the great petroleum reserves in these countries.
2. Students' myths should include the creation of the Sahara.
3. Students' plans should include concrete examples of the ways in which they would use their petroleum profits for philanthropic purposes.

Answers to Building Skills: Reading Contour Maps

1. Contour maps help us to picture the shape of the earth's surface.
2. a steep slope or mountainside; flat or gently sloping land
3. Possible answers include: when planning for a trip to a place; when looking for a building site.

MAKING CONNECTIONS

Organizing Information Display the Semantic Map Graphic Organizer Transparency, filling in only the underlined main topics. Then have students fill in information relating to each topic, moving from the general to the specific. *Ask:* What can be said generally of the geography of the Middle East and North Africa?

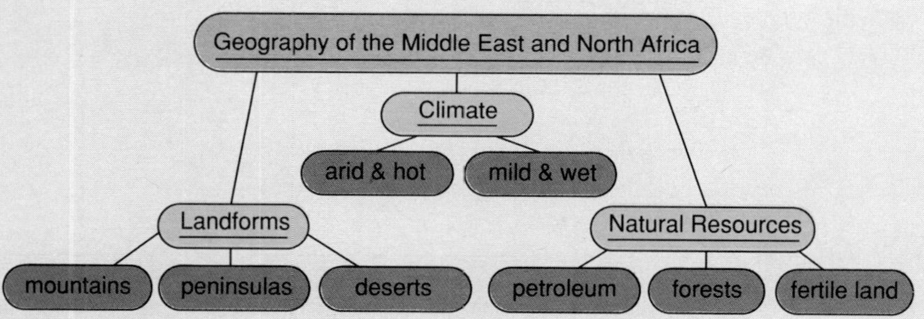

CHAPTER 18
ORGANIZER

THE MIDDLE EAST text pages 368–385

CHAPTER THEME Life in the Middle East is shaped by powerful leaders, economies based on agriculture or oil, religion, and a strong sense of family and ethnic identity.

CHAPTER OBJECTIVES

CONTENT

- Describe how religion affects the lives of the people of the Middle East.
- Identify the Arabs and describe their importance to the culture of the Middle East
- Identify the non-Arab Muslim peoples of the Middle East.
- Identity the non-Muslim peoples of the Middle East.
- Describe how the discovery of oil changed the economies of Middle Eastern countries.
- Explain how Islamic law has influenced the legal systems of Middle Eastern countries.
- Describe the origins of the conflict between the Palestinians and Israel.
- Describe how Middle Eastern arts and sports are a blend of the old and the new.

SKILLS

Geography
- Identify Middle Eastern ethnic groups by using a map.
- Locate Israel and its neighbors on a map.

Study and Research
- Interpret a graph showing world oil production.
- Identify OPEC nations on a chart.

Thinking
- Ask focused questions about the development of the nation of Israel.
- Compare and contrast absolute rule with democratic rule.

Reading and Writing
- Write a list of questions with which to interview a resident of the Middle East.

CITIZENSHIP VALUES

- Appreciate the ability of the individual to have an impact on society.
- Appreciate the importance of religion in shaping people's attitudes and ways of life.

TEACHER OPTIONS

READING STRATEGY: Outlining Strategies to help students read and remember the main ideas of the lesson.

Lesson 1: p. 369 Lesson 3: p. 377
Lesson 2: p. 373 Lesson 4: p. 382

MEETING INDIVIDUAL NEEDS Activities for reteaching, extension, and enrichment.

Lesson 1: p. 372 Geography Skills: p. 381
Lesson 2: p. 376 Lesson 4: p. 383
Lesson 3: p. 379

GEO ADVENTURES ACTIVITIES PAD Daily activities to assess students' understanding of geography skills.

CURRICULUM CONNECTION Activities to help integrate other subject areas with Social Studies.

Math: p. 374 Music: p. 378
Language Arts: p. 378 Science: p. 380

PUPIL EDITION ON CASSETTE Language support for students who have difficulty reading or who will benefit from listening to the Pupil Edition on Cassette as they read.

SECOND-LANGUAGE SUPPORT Activities and suggestions for second-language learners.

Lesson 2: p. 349-D

CHAPTER PLANNING GUIDE

LESSON	SUGGESTED PACING	THEMES	TEACHER SUPPORT MATERIALS: TEACHER'S RESOURCE CENTER
1 THE PEOPLE pages 369–372	1 day	The three major ethnic groups in the Middle East are Arabs, Persians, and Turks, and the major religion is Islam, followed by Christianity and Judaism.	Practice Book p. 99 ■ Anthology pp. 144–145, 148–149, 154, 163 **Technology:** *Videodisc/Video Tape 1*
2 THE ECONOMY pages 373–376	1 day	There are dramatic contrasts between the economies of the different Middle Eastern nations and the lifestyles of those nations' inhabitants.	Practice Book p. 100 Desk Maps **Technology:** *Videodisc/Video Tape 1*
3 THE GOVERNMENT pages 377–379	1 day	Many of the Middle Eastern nations are led by powerful leaders, ruled by religious laws, and involved in longstanding disputes.	Practice Book p. 101 ■ Anthology pp. 146–147, 159–161, 162 **Technology:** *Videodisc/Video Tape 1*
BUILDING GEOGRAPHY SKILLS Comparing Maps pages 380–381	1 day	Comparing maps with different themes provides more information than one map can give.	Practice Book p. 102 Transparency Map 13
4 ARTS AND RECREATION pages 382–383	1 day	The arts of the Middle East include poetry, storytelling, calligraphy, and design; sports include both modern and ancient games.	Practice Book p. 103 ■ Anthology pp. 155–157
CHAPTER SUMMARY AND REVIEW pages 384–385	1 day	Chapter content, skills, and vocabulary are reviewed and evaluated.	Practice Book p. 104 Transparency: Graphic Organizer Assessment Book, Chapter 18 Test

Technology CONNECTION

Lesson 1
VIDEODISC/VIDEO TAPE 1
Enrich Lesson 1 with a segment from Video Lesson 5, *The Middle East Today.*

Search 22740, Play To 24882 Side A

Lesson 2
VIDEODISC/VIDEO TAPE 1
Enrich Lesson 2 with a segment from Video Lesson 5, *The Middle East Today.*

Search 24883, Play To 25741 Side A

Lesson 3
VIDEODISC/VIDEO TAPE 1
Enrich Lesson 3 with a segment from Video Lesson 5, *The Middle East Today.*

Search 25742, Play To 27913 Side A

CHAPTER 18
pages 368–385

USING THE CHAPTER OPENER

Discussing the Photograph Have students read the passage under the picture. Then ask them why they think this picture was chosen to illustrate the ideas in the passage.

Ask students:

- **Which books do we usually associate with religion?** (Possible answers include: the Bible, the Torah, the Koran.)
- **Why do you think the picture shows an elderly man?** (This question is designed to focus students' thinking on the importance of the role of older people in keeping cultural traditions alive and to prepare them for learning about the respect that Muslims show for older family members.)
- *THINKING FURTHER:* **Why do you think this picture was chosen to introduce a chapter on the Middle East?** (Possible answers include: By showing someone who looks absorbed in reading and is perhaps praying, the picture illustrates that religion is important to people in the Middle East.)

Reading/Listening to the Primary Source Have students read the opening quotation and the paragraph that follows. Ask them to think about what it would be like to start their day in this manner.

Ask students:

- **Name some things that practitioners of other religions do to call people to pray or worship.** (ringing church bells, singing hymns and other songs of worship, sending notices through the mail, displaying information about services on signs outside or on the hour of worship.)

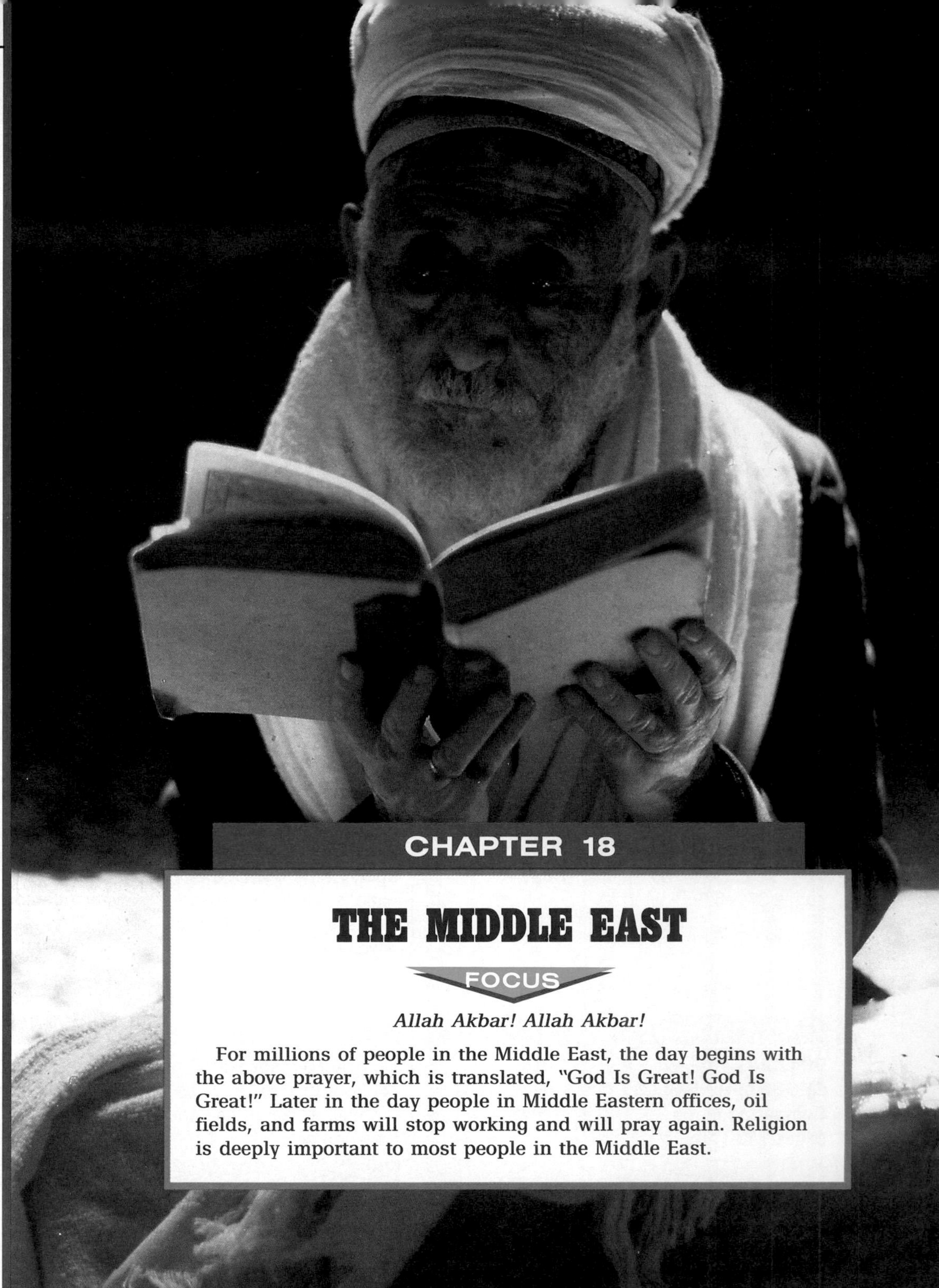

CHAPTER 18

THE MIDDLE EAST

FOCUS

Allah Akbar! Allah Akbar!

For millions of people in the Middle East, the day begins with the above prayer, which is translated, "God Is Great! God Is Great!" Later in the day people in Middle Eastern offices, oil fields, and farms will stop working and will pray again. Religion is deeply important to most people in the Middle East.

BACKGROUND INFORMATION

The Koran

Muslims consider the Koran to be the word of God as revealed to the prophet Muhammad.

- Generally speaking, the Koran contains the history of Muhammad's search for God, as well as the principles of the Islamic creed, its duties, and its prohibitions. It is the foundation for Islam's social law.
- Principles basic to the Islamic creed are the belief in one God, the belief in a series of prophets—Adam, Noah, Abraham, Moses, Jesus, and Muhammad—the belief in a Day of Judgment, and the belief in God's mysterious will.
- The Koran's definition of moral behavior stresses respect for parents, charity, and hospitality.

LESSON 1

The People

READ TO LEARN

Key Vocabulary
Islam
hajj

Key People
Muhammad

Key Places
Israel

Read Aloud

Prince Sultan Salman al-Saud is a grandson of the founder of Saudi Arabia. He is also the first Middle Eastern astronaut. On his space flight aboard the United States space shuttle *Discovery* in 1985, the prince launched a communications satellite owned by Middle Eastern countries. His life aboard the shuttle was busy. But, he said, "I still had time to read the Koran [the holy book of the Muslims] in space from beginning to end. I am more proud of that than all my other achievements."

Read for Purpose

1. WHAT YOU KNOW: Where do most people of the Middle East live?
2. WHAT YOU WILL LEARN: What role does religion play in the lives of the people of the Middle East?

THE MIDDLE EASTERN CROSSROADS

What is the Middle East? It is the southwestern part of the continent of Asia. It begins in the northwest with Turkey and continues south and east to the Arabian Peninsula and Iran. Europeans called it the "Middle East" because the region is located in the "middle" of the land area between Europe and the area Europeans call the "Far East," which means China and its neighbors.

As you read in Chapter 17, the Middle East is one of the world's great crossroads. People and ideas from Asia, Africa, and Europe have long mingled in the Middle East. The alphabet that is used in the West, as well as the Western way of writing numbers, began here. The Middle East is also the birthplace of three of the world's great religions—Judaism, Christianity, and **Islam**. You will read about Islam in this chapter.

ARABS, THE MAIN CULTURE GROUP

Although the Middle East has hundreds of ethnic groups, the Arabs are the largest group. The Arab culture and language are important in many countries of the Middle East. Two large non-Arab groups who live in the region are the Persians and the Turks.

The first Arabs lived in the Arabian Peninsula. The language they spoke was called Arabic. Today the term Arab also

WHAT YOU KNOW: This question refers to material in Chapter 17, Lesson 1; along the region's narrow river valleys or on its seacoasts.

LESSON 1
pages 369–372

Lesson Theme The three major ethnic groups in the Middle East are Arabs, Persians, and Turks, and the major religion is Islam, followed by Christianity and Judaism.

Lesson Objectives
- Identify the ethnic origins of today's Arabs.
- Identify the beliefs of Islam.
- Describe the other cultures and ethnic groups of the Middle East.

PREPARE

Motivate Read the *Read Aloud* section to the class. Discuss why Prince al-Saud was proud of reading the whole Koran while he was in space.

Set Purpose Tell students they will learn about the role that religion plays in Middle Eastern culture.

TEACH

Reviewing the Concept of the Middle Eastern Crossroads Stress that important ideas have been exchanged and developed in the Middle East.

Ask students:

- **Which two cultural tools came from the Middle East?** (Western alphabet, Western numbers)
- **Which three religions originated in the Middle East?** (Judaism, Christianity, Islam)

Learning about Arab Culture Tell students that the Arab culture and language are important in many countries of the Middle East.

- **Where did the first Arabs live?** (the Arabian Peninsula)

READING STRATEGY AND VOCABULARY DEVELOPMENT

Outlining Semantic mapping can serve as a bridge between jotting down ideas about a subject and organizing those ideas into an outline. An example of how the beginning of such a map might look is given below.

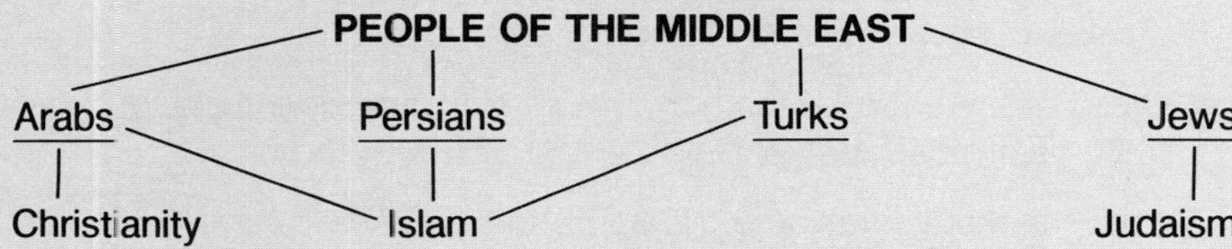

Ask students to make an outline of this chapter, using the Semantic Map as a guide. Help students to understand that Arabs, Persians, Turks, and Jews should be the outline headings, and that Islam, Christianity, and Judaism should be the subheadings.

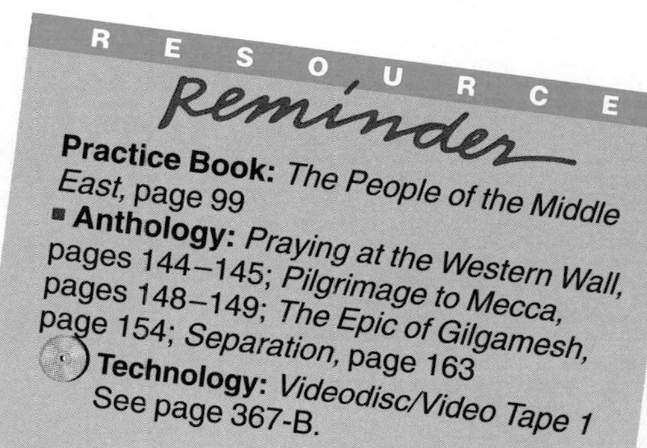

RESOURCE Reminder

Practice Book: *The People of the Middle East*, page 99

Anthology: *Praying at the Western Wall*, pages 144–145; *Pilgrimage to Mecca*, pages 148–149; *The Epic of Gilgamesh*, page 154; *Separation*, page 163

Technology: *Videodisc/Video Tape 1*

See page 367-B.

Talking About Arab Culture
Continue the discussion.

Ask students:

- **To whom does the term Arabic refer?** (people who speak Arabic and share a common culture)
- **By what factors are Arabs united?** (their language, customs, and, to a great extent, their religion)

EXTENDING MAP SKILLS

Have students study the political map of the Middle East on this page.

Ask students:

- **Which Middle Eastern countries border on Israel?** (Egypt, Lebanon, Syria, and Jordan)
- **Which Middle Eastern countries border on Iran?** (Turkey and Iraq)

Tracing the Beginnings of Islam
Help students to understand that Islam is practiced throughout the Middle East.

Ask students:

- **What does the word *Islam* mean?** ("submission, or surrender, to the will of God")
- **Identify the people who practice Islam.** (Muslims)
- **What did the Muslims do after Muhammad's death?** (spread their culture and religion throughout the Middle East and North Africa "in the name of Allah")

Exploring Islamic Beliefs Stress to students that all Muslims hold common beliefs and traditions.

Ask students:

- **List the "five pillars of Islam."** (the *hajj;* belief in one god; prayer five times a day; the giving of alms; and fasting during the holy month of Ramadan)

includes most people who speak Arabic and share a common culture. They live throughout the Middle East and North Africa and in many other parts of the world.

Most Arabs live in cities and towns. Some, such as the Bedouins, live in deserts, but even many former nomads have moved to settled communities.

Arabs are united by their language and by many customs. Even more important, most Arabs are united by their religion.

THE BEGINNINGS OF ISLAM

Until the sixth century, the small group of Arab people worshiped many different gods. Then an Arab merchant named **Muhammad** (mu̇ ham′ əd) began to teach that there was only one *Allah*, the Arabic word for "God." Muhammad said that he was God's messenger. Muhammad's teachings about Allah were the foundation of the religion of Islam. The word ***Islam*** means "submission, or surrender, to the will of God." People who follow Islam are called Muslims (muz′ limz).

Muhammad died in A.D. 632. After that, people who had been inspired by his preaching left their homeland on the Arabian Peninsula. Their goal, they explained, was to spread the religion of Islam "in the name of Allah." They spread their religion throughout the Middle East and North Africa. Within 100 years after Muhammad's death, Islam had spread westward to Spain and other parts of southern Europe and as far east as India and southern Asia. Islam also spread southward into other parts of Africa.

Today Islam is the second largest religion in the world. There are now more than 1 billion Muslims in the world.

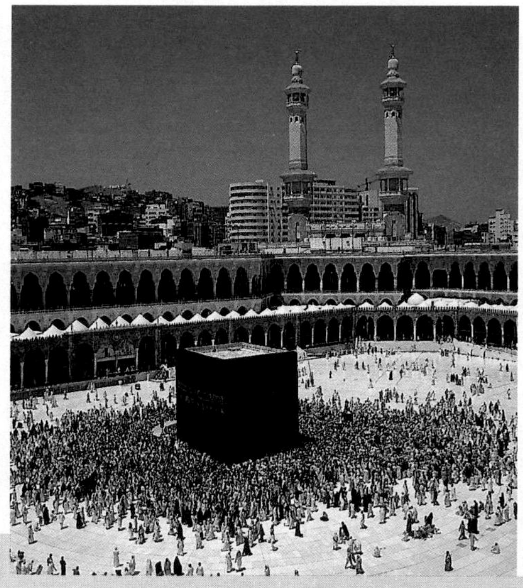

MAP SKILL: All Muslims turn to Mecca to pray five times a day. In which country is Mecca located?

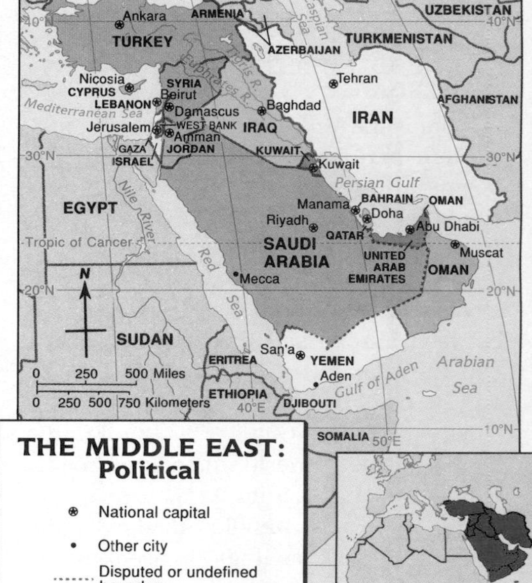

370

MAP SKILL: Saudi Arabia

BACKGROUND INFORMATION

Making a Hajj Every Muslim man and woman hopes to make a *hajj*, or pilgrimage to Mecca, the birthplace of Muhammad, once in his or her lifetime.

- The Muslim religion requires a person to make this pilgrimage only if he or she is physically and financially able to do so.
- Within 5 miles (8 km) of the holy city, the Muslim pilgrim changes into a white seamless robe, leaving the feet and head bare.
- Among the many rituals the pilgrim performs in Mecca are visiting the sacred mosque, kissing a sacred stone that is said to have turned black from the tears of repentant sinners, and circling the Kaaba (the building that contains the stone) seven times.
- After performing the required rites, the pilgrim puts on his or her usual clothes and goes north to Medina to visit Muhammad's tomb.

ISLAMIC BELIEFS

No matter where they live, all Muslims hold certain beliefs. "I suppose the high spot of my life was performing the **hajj** in the company of my son," says one Saudi Arabian. The *hajj* is the name Muslims give to the pilgrimage they make to the city of Mecca, the birthplace of Muhammad. A pilgrimage, as you may remember, is a trip to a religious shrine or holy place. As one Muslim says:

> *This pilgrimage is one of the "five pillars of Islam," the other four being the belief in one God; prayer five times a day; the giving of alms* [charity]*; and fasting during the holy month of Ramadan.*

NON-ARAB MUSLIM PEOPLE

Some Muslim people in the Middle East are not Arabs. Find Turkey on the map on this page. Turkey is a Muslim nation, but most of its people are not Arab.

The Turks probably originated in Central Asia and moved westward. Most of them converted to Islam some time after the Arabs became Muslims. In the past, great Turkish empires have ruled large parts of Europe, the Middle East, and North Africa. Although most Turks share the Muslim religion, their customs and languages are different from Arab customs and language.

The Persian people are not Arabs either. Most people in Iran descend from the people of ancient Persia. They speak a language called *Farsi*, or Persian. Like the Turks, the Persians are Muslims but have their own language and customs.

Another Muslim group, the Kurds, live mostly in the mountainous areas of Turkey, Iran, Iraq, Syria, and Armenia. Their language is related to Persian, but their customs are different from those of most Persians. For a long time, Kurds have wanted their own country, but the countries in which they live oppose Kurdish independence.

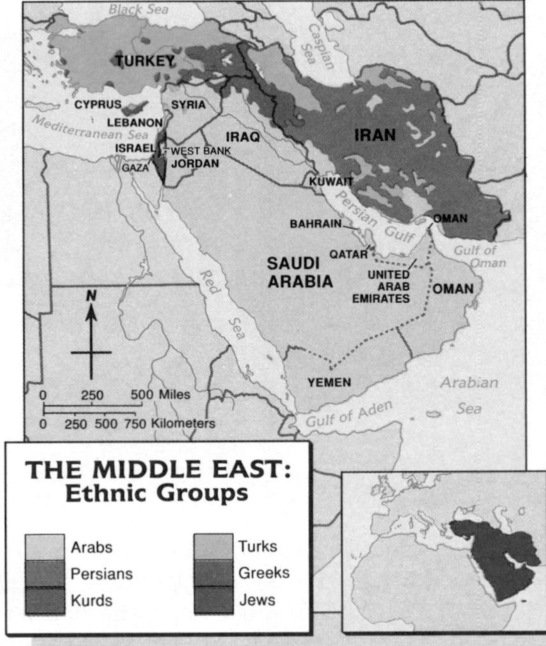

MAP SKILL: Arabs live in most of the countries in the Middle East. In which countries of the Middle East do most non-Arab groups live?

NON-MUSLIM PEOPLES

Some people in the Middle East are neither Muslims nor Arabs. Many of the people in Cyprus and Lebanon are Christians. Some are Christian Arabs. The majority of the people in **Israel** are Jews.

Israel was founded in 1948 as a homeland for Jewish people from all over the world. Jews had lived in Israel, which was part of a region called Palestine, and in other parts of the Middle East since ancient times. But until after World War II, they did not have their own country.

During the 1930s and 1940s, many Jews fled persecution in Europe and made their way to Palestine. They fled because of the

MAP SKILL: Turkey, Iran, Cyprus, and Israel

Looking at Non-Arab Muslim People Stress to students that not all Muslim people in the Middle East are Arabs.

Ask students:

- **Identify three non-Arab Muslim groups.** (Turks, Persians, and Kurds)
- **How do the Turks and Persians differ from the Arabs?** (Although they share the Muslim religion, their customs and languages are different from those of the Arabs.)

Identifying Non-Muslim Peoples Make sure that students understand that not all people in the Middle East practice Islam.

Ask students:

- **Which Middle Eastern people are non-Muslim, and where do many of them live?** (*Christians*—Cyprus and Lebanon; *Jews*—Israel)

EXTENDING MAP SKILLS

Have students study the map about ethnic groups on this page.

Ask students:

- **Which are the two smallest ethnic areas shown on the map?** (the areas in which the Greeks and Jews are located)

Learning About Women in the Middle East Stress to students that women's roles in society vary from country to country within the region.

Ask students:

- **Generally speaking, how are the roles of Middle Eastern women different from those of the United States and Western Europe?** (In many Middle Eastern countries, women and men are expected to live apart more often.)

BACKGROUND INFORMATION

Multicultural Perspectives Although the sight of women wearing veils and garments that completely cover the body has long been associated with the Middle East, in reality, women's modes of dress vary greatly from country to country and individual to individual. Even though the wearing of Western clothes has become a mark of greater freedom for some Muslim women, others prefer traditional garments. For these women traditional dress is a symbol of independence and freedom from Western influences. According to some Muslim women, the advantages of wearing traditional clothes include the freedom to go out in public without attracting unwelcome attention, and protection from dust, heat, and flies. Ask students what various modes of dress symbolize in their own communities.

Understanding Women in the Middle East Continue the discussion.

Ask students:

- **How do the lives of women in Saudi Arabia differ from the lives of women in Turkey?** (Women in Saudi Arabia follow strict rules; for example, they may not drive automobiles. Women in Turkey have few rules that limit their conduct.)
- **What are some examples of jobs held by Middle Eastern women?** (doctors, lawyers, teachers)

Applying the Lesson Have students make a chart of Middle Eastern religions and ethnic groups.

3 CLOSE

Summarizing Students have read that the Arab Muslims are the largest ethnic group in the Middle East and that smaller ethnic groups inhabit Iraq, Iran, Cyprus, Lebanon, Turkey, and Israel.

Evaluating Use these questions to assess students' understanding.

- **Identify the main culture group in the Middle East.** (Arabs)
- **What are the two large non-Arab Muslim groups in the region?** (Persians and Turks)
- **Identify the two major non-Muslim groups in the region.** (Christians and Jews)

Answers to Check Your Reading

1. The Europeans thought it was between Europe and the Far East.
2. five Islamic duties
3. Prayers are said five times a day, and fasting is done every day during the holy month of Ramadan.
4. When was Israel founded? How did the Holocaust contribute to the founding of Israel? How did the Jews get permission to found it?

Independent Practice
Practice Book: page 99

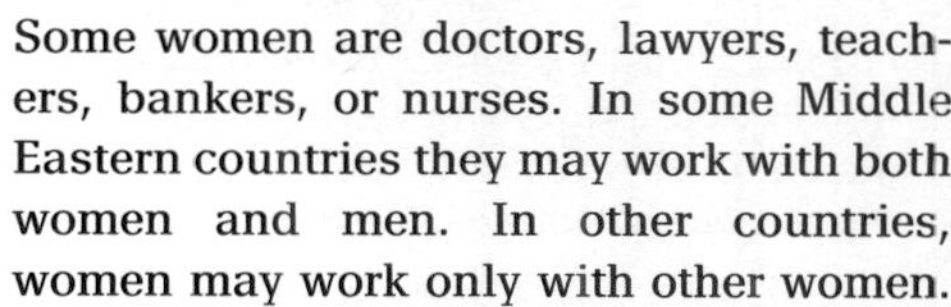

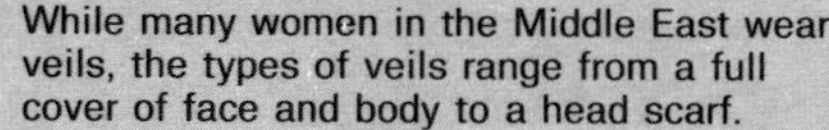

While many women in the Middle East wear veils, the types of veils range from a full cover of face and body to a head scarf.

Holocaust in Germany and other countries of Europe. The Jews in Palestine joined small groups of other Jews who had left Europe earlier to live in what they believed to be their historic homeland. Since Israel became a country, Jews from many continents have left their countries to live in Israel. In the following lessons you will read more about Israel and its relations with Arab countries.

WOMEN IN THE MIDDLE EAST

In many countries of the Middle East, men and women are expected to live apart more than they do in the United States or Western Europe. However, the idea of separate lives varies from country to country and even in regions of a country.

Some countries, such as Saudi Arabia, have very strict rules about what women may or may not do. For example, women are not allowed to drive automobiles, and they are not allowed to shop in some stores. Other countries, like Turkey, make few rules to limit what women may or may not do.

Women in all countries of the Middle East may work at jobs outside their homes. Some women are doctors, lawyers, teachers, bankers, or nurses. In some Middle Eastern countries they may work with both women and men. In other countries, women may work only with other women.

Women in some Muslim countries are expected to veil their faces when they leave their homes. But while women in Iran have had to wear full coverings since 1979, women in many other Muslim countries wear smaller veils or even head scarves and sunglasses.

ARAB AND NON-ARAB COUNTRIES

As you have read, religion is very important throughout the Middle East. Most of the nations of this area have largely Arab populations. In these lands and in Iran and Turkey, people organize their lives around the Islamic religion. In Israel, the majority of the people practice the Jewish religion.

Check Your Reading

1. How did the Middle East get its name?
2. What are the "five pillars of Islam"?
3. In what ways does religion affect the daily lives of the Islamic people of the Middle East?
4. **THINKING SKILL:** List three questions you could ask to find out more about how the country of Israel developed.

THINKING SKILL: Asking Questions

MEETING INDIVIDUAL NEEDS

Reteaching (easy) Have students draw a mural showing a Muslim as he or she follows the rules laid down by the "five pillars of Islam" (mentioned on page 370).

Extension (average) Have students identify the "Eight *M*'s of Islam": Muslim, Muhammad, Medina, Mecca, mosque, minaret, mullah, and muezzin. Have them make a poster showing the relationships among these people and places.

Enrichment (challenging) Ask students to select one of the following topics: "Prince Sultan Salman al-Saud's Career as an Astronaut," "Bedouin Oil Riches," or "The Kurdish Independence Movement." Have students research these topics and then write essays describing how the events covered by their chosen topic indicate political or social change in the Middle East.

LESSON 2

The Economy

READ TO LEARN

Key Vocabulary

bazaar
labor-intensive
moshav
kibbutz

Key Places

Bahrain

Read Aloud

For months in 1932, a small group of workers had been drilling through rock and pockets of tar on the sandy island of Bahrain in the Persian Gulf. Finally, on a June day, their drills struck oil. With a mighty rumble, a black torrent of oil burst upward before raining down on the jubilant crew. Bahrain—a small island of pearl divers and traders—soon became one of the world's richest countries.

Read for Purpose

1. WHAT YOU KNOW: Name three countries in the Middle East.
2. WHAT YOU WILL LEARN: How has the discovery of oil changed the economies of many of the countries in the Middle East?

MONEY MADE FROM OIL

"Bahrain lies in just the right time zone for international trading," says Bachir Barbir, a banker in the island country. He buys and sells stocks on the stock exchanges of the world. Barbir explains:

That is why we work 12 hours a day, from 8 A.M. until 8 P.M., Bahrain time. Our day begins before the Tokyo and Singapore [stock] markets close, and we keep going . . . until after New York opens.

Mr. Barbir works for one of the more than 170 banks in Bahrain. You might wonder how such a small country has come to be a world banking center. The answer, as you read above, is oil money. Bahrain is the financial center of the countries around the Persian Gulf.

The contrast between Bahrain now and Bahrain 60 years ago is dramatic. The Bahrain oil discovery you read about above was not the first oil struck in the Middle East. Petroleum had already been found in Iran earlier in the 1900s. But the discovery in Bahrain began the era of large-scale development.

This development increased rapidly after the founding of the Organization of Petroleum Exporting Countries, or OPEC, in 1960. The Middle Eastern countries that helped to found OPEC agreed to work together to sell their oil. By doing so, they were able to raise the price of oil.

The richest oil-producing countries of the Middle East are located on the Arabian Peninsula. Kuwait, Qatar, and the United Arab Emirates have some of the world's highest per capita incomes. In Qatar, for example, the average yearly income per person is about $25,000. This is about the same average yearly income per person as

WHAT YOU KNOW: You may wish to refer students to the map on page 370 to identify the countries.

LESSON 2
pages 373–376

Lesson Theme There are dramatic contrasts between the economies of the different Middle Eastern nations and the lifestyles of those nations' inhabitants.

Lesson Objectives
- Describe the effect that the discovery of oil had on the economies of some nations.
- Describe the contrasts between old and new ways of life in the Middle East.
- Identify the different methods of farming used by the people of the Middle East.

PREPARE

Motivate Read the *Read Aloud* section to the class. Ask students to imagine that they have suddenly become very rich. Ask them to discuss how they would use the money.

Set Purpose Display the political *Atlas* map of the Middle East and North Africa. Tell students that they are going to read about the ways in which the discovery of oil has affected the countries shown on the map.

TEACH

Discussing Money Made from Oil Help students to understand that the distribution of oil reserves among the Middle Eastern countries is uneven.

Ask students:

- **For what purpose was OPEC founded?** (to help the oil-producing countries get a fairer price for oil)

READING STRATEGY AND VOCABULARY DEVELOPMENT

Outlining Ask the class to preview this lesson. Then divide the class into groups containing three students each. Ask them to make skeleton outlines of this lesson by using general terms to describe each topic. Help them to begin by telling them that this lesson's title, "The Economy," can serve as the title of the outline. Ask students to volunteer ideas that might help them to develop the topic of the economy. Help them select an idea that is meaningful and is also general enough to be used as the first heading. Two possibilities might be "Different Types of Economies" and "The Industries of an Economy." After the groups have finished the skeleton outlines, ask them to exchange papers. Then have them refer to the lesson and write in specific terms on another group's outline. For example, have them change the outline's title from "The Economy" to "The Economy of the Middle East."

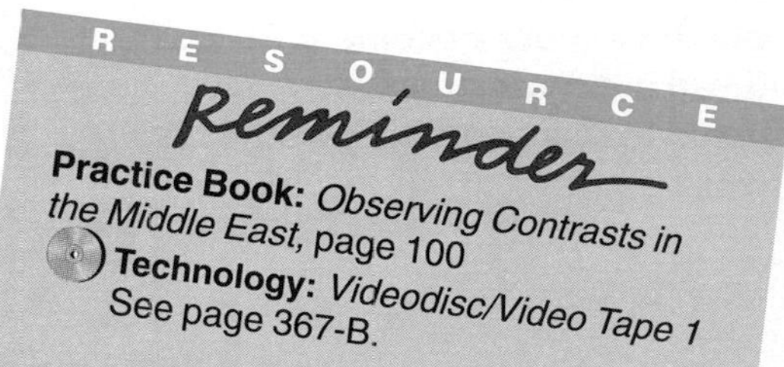

Talking About Money and Oil Continue the discussion about oil reserves.

Ask students:

- **Identify four Middle Eastern countries that have very low per capita incomes.** (Yemen, Lebanon, Jordan, and Turkey)
- **Why are these countries so poor?** (They have few petroleum reserves or other natural resources.)
- *THINKING FURTHER:* **Why are the Middle Eastern nations that have few oil reserves poor?** (The Middle Eastern region has few natural resources besides oil.)

EXTENDING GRAPH SKILLS

Have students study the circle graph and chart on this page.

Ask students:

- **According to the circle graph, what portion of oil production takes place in the Middle East and North Africa?** (34.5 percent)
- **According to the chart, how many more barrels of oil does Saudi Arabia produce annually than Iran?** (1,674,620,000)

Discussing Workers from Many Countries Help students to understand that oil-rich nations often bring in additional workers from other countries.

Ask students:

- **Why do the oil-rich nations of the Middle East hire guest workers?** (to help them build schools, airports, highways, ports, hospitals, and factories)
- *THINKING FURTHER:* **Why do you think the oil-producing countries such as Kuwait do not let the guest workers become citizens?** (Lead a discussion in which students realize and discuss the implications of this critical issue.)

WORLD OIL PRODUCTION

Sub-Saharan Africa 5.2%
Western Europe 7.6%
Australia and New Zealand 1%
Southern and Eastern Asia 9.8%
Middle East and North Africa 34.5%
Latin America 12%
United States and Canada 14.6%
Eastern Europe and Northern Asia 15.3%

OPEC OIL PRODUCTION-1995

Country	Barrels of oil annually
Saudia Arabia	3,004,315,000
Iran	1,329,695,000
Venezuela	1,003,750,000
United Arab Emirates	830,010,000
Kuwait	750,805,000
Nigeria	740,220,000
Indonesia	555,895,000
Libya	507,350,000
Algeria	436,905,000
Iraq	202,575,000
Qatar	176,295,000
Gabon	122,640,000

GRAPH/CHART SKILL: How does the Middle East and North Africa's oil production compare with that of other regions? Which country produces the most oil?

United States. Look at the chart and graph above. They show that the oil-rich countries of the Middle East produce a large part of the world's oil.

Other than oil, however, the Middle East has few natural resources. Therefore, nations in this area that are without oil are usually poor. For example, Yemen, Lebanon, and Jordan have little oil. They are among those countries with the world's lowest per-capita incomes. Turkey also has little oil. While its per-capita income is not as low as those of Yemen, Lebanon, and Jordan, it is lower than those of its oil-rich neighbors. Nearly 2 million Turkish citizens have left their homeland to find work in Europe, the Middle East, and North Africa.

WORKERS FROM MANY COUNTRIES

The wealthy countries of the Middle East have used some of their money to build modern schools, airports, highways, ports, hospitals, and factories. These nations often need to hire guest workers from other countries. Some guest workers come from other countries in the Middle East. Others come from Asia and Africa.

These guest workers are welcome to come and work, but they may not be allowed to become citizens. As one Jordanian who lived in Kuwait explained:

> *My son was born here but will never be a citizen. An uncle worked a lifetime in Kuwait. When he retired, they gave him a week to leave the country.*

Guest workers usually send money home to their own countries. Often this money makes it possible for their families to survive.

THE EFFECTS OF A WAR

In August 1990 Iraq invaded Kuwait. After asking Iraq to withdraw, the United States and other countries sent troops to the Persian Gulf area to drive the Iraqis out of Kuwait. War broke out in January 1991. In less than two months Iraq was defeated. During the war Iraq blew up hundreds of Kuwait's oil fields causing long-lasting fires that polluted the air and

GRAPH/CHART SKILL: The Middle East and North Africa produces more oil than any other region. Saudi Arabia produces the most oil.

CURRICULUM CONNECTION

Math Have students look up the population and the total annual income of their state. Have them divide the number of state residents into the amount representing the total annual state income to find yearly per capita income. Then have them use the same method to find the yearly per capita incomes of at least two Middle Eastern nations. Ask students to compare the per capita incomes of these two Middle Eastern nations. Then have them compare and discuss the differences in per capita income for the Middle Eastern nations and their own state.

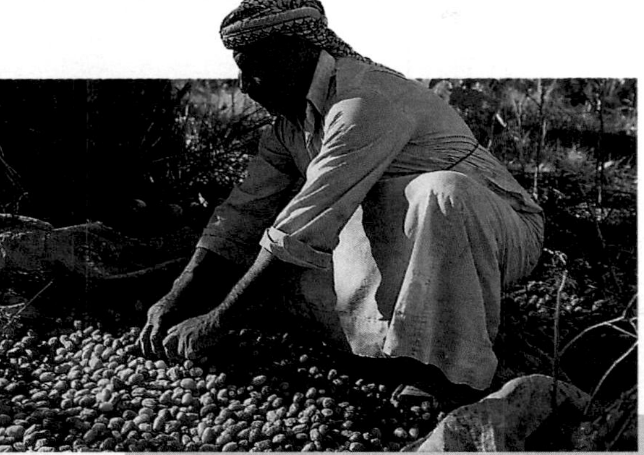

The fruit of the date palm tree is a favorite food in the Middle East. The trees also provide sugar, oil, and fiber for weaving.

stopped much of Kuwait's oil production. Then fighting broke out in Iraq between the Kurds and the Iraqi government.

As a result of the war, nearly 5 million people were forced to leave the Middle Eastern countries where they lived and worked. Many departing guest workers lost both the money and their savings.

COMMERCE

Despite the changes brought about by oil, most of the people in the Middle East earn their livings in traditional ways—mainly by commerce, or trade, and farming the land.

Hundreds of years ago caravans traveled long distances to large trading centers such as Baghdad in Iraq, Damascus in Syria, and Istanbul in Turkey. Today trucks and railroads have replaced most of the caravans in the Middle East. But at city **bazaars**, or outdoor markets, some of the same products that were traded long ago are still traded today. Textiles and fine carpets made in Iran and Turkey are exchanged for farm products. Farm products are in high demand because, as you read in the last chapter, much of the soil in the Middle East is not good for farming.

FARMING METHODS

In those parts of the Middle East where the land can be farmed, many farms continue to employ **labor-intensive** methods. That is, they use people rather than machinery to do the work. On labor-intensive farms whole families work in the fields.

Some farmers, however, make use of the latest technology. For example, some farmers on the Arabian Peninsula now get water from huge plants that turn salt water from the sea into fresh water.

One Saudi Arabian farmer tells how his family created a farm in the desert near the city of Riyadh. They used both traditional and modern methods to make the farm a success. First they planted rows of fast-growing tamarisk trees to act as windbreaks. Next the family planted date palms. Date palms grow well in the dry climate and are sources of fruit, sugar, oil, and fiber. After drilling deep water wells, the family also was able to grow alfalfa and vegetables. Funds to drill the deep water wells were provided by the Saudi Arabian government from its petroleum profits.

375

Understanding the Effects of a War Help students to realize the devastating effects that the war in the Persian Gulf had on the people of that region.

Ask students:

- **What are some of the ways in which Kuwait was affected by the war?** (Hundreds of Kuwait's oil fields were blown up, causing pollution and stopping oil production.)
- **What happened to many guest workers as a result of the war?** (They were forced to leave the countries where they lived and worked, often losing both their earnings and their savings.)

Looking at Commerce Help students to recognize that most Middle Eastern people earn their living by trade and farming.

Ask students:

- **Give a synonym for the word *commerce*.** (*trade*)
- **How did the Middle Eastern traders of the past transport their goods?** (by caravans)
- **How are city bazaars a link to the past?** (Items traded long ago, such as textiles and fine carpets, are still traded today.)

Analyzing Farming Methods Help students to recognize that the people of the Middle East use both traditional and modern methods of farming.

Ask students:

- **Explain the meaning of labor-intensive farming methods.** (the use of people rather than machinery to do the work)
- **Identify and describe a modern method of acquiring water that is used by Arab farmers.** (desalinization, or changing sea water into fresh water)

FUNDAMENTAL THEMES OF GEOGRAPHY

Human-Environment Interaction It has been said that the Israeli farmers have "made the desert bloom."

- They have done this by using technology to solve the crucial problem of bringing water to desert areas.
- One such place, the Negev Desert, is located in the southern part of Israel. By constructing pipelines and making tunnels and canals, the Israelis have moved water from the Sea of Galilee, a freshwater lake situated in the north of Israel, to farms in the Negev Desert.
- Today apples, avocados, grapes, bananas, peaches, citrus fruits, tomatoes, potatoes, and wheat grow in what had once been one of Israel's most barren places.

Discussing Agriculture in Israel Stress to students that Israel has a highly developed economy that does not depend on oil.

Applying the Lesson Have students write an essay comparing the economy of Israel with that of Bahrain.

3 CLOSE

Summarizing Students have read that some Middle Eastern nations have developed economies and others have economies based on traditional forms of trade and farming.

Evaluating Use these questions to assess students' understanding.

- **Compare Bahrain's economy before and after the discovery of its oil fields.** (*before*—poor and traditional; *after*—rich and highly developed)
- **Give an example of the contrast between the old and the new in the Middle East.** (farmers that use both traditional methods—such as planting trees to act as windbreaks—and modern methods—such as drilling deep water wells)
- **Identify a modern method of acquiring water used on Middle Eastern farms.** (desalinization of seawater)

Answers to Check Your Reading

1. It is their only major natural resource.
2. Nearly 5 million people were forced to leave the countries where they lived and worked.
3. Traditional farming and trading practices occur along with modern methods.
4. the availability of water, which kinds of produce can grow in the soil of the area, the availability of technology for modern farming techniques

Independent Practice
Practice Book: page 100

People on each Israeli **kibbutz** own and work the land in common. Children on a kibbutz share the work of taking care of animals.

AGRICULTURE IN ISRAEL

In one Middle Eastern country, Israel, modern methods of farming are extensively used. When Israel was created in 1948, it lacked raw materials, energy resources, and industries. Jewish immigrants from Europe and other parts of the world worked hard to make their new country a success. They also received economic aid from the United States and Europe. Today Israel has a highly developed economy.

To farm their harsh land, the early settlers of Israel developed two special kinds of farms. One is the **moshav** (mō shäv′), a cooperative farm. Under the moshav system, each farm family owns its own land but sells its produce through the moshav.

The other kind of Israeli farm community is the **kibbutz** (ki bu̇ts′), or collective farm. Members of a kibbutz own and work the land in common. They eat together in communal dining halls. About one third of Israel's farmers cooperate in their work either on a moshav or a kibbutz.

Sometimes a kibbutz also produces manufactured goods. One kibbutz, for instance, makes drip irrigation systems. In these systems water is trickled to the roots of plants. That way no water is wasted by evaporation in the dry air.

THE TRADITIONAL AND THE MODERN

Most of the people of the Middle East earn their living in traditional ways, like farming and commerce. Yet, as you read in this lesson, money from oil has changed the economies of some of the countries of this area. In these countries money from oil is used to build schools, highways, factories, and power plants. As a result very modern ways of life exist along with very traditional ones.

Check Your Reading

1. Why is oil so important to some nations in the Middle East?
2. How did the war in the Persian Gulf affect the people of the Middle East?
3. How are the economies of the Middle East a mix of the traditional and the modern?
4. THINKING SKILL: If you were deciding whether or not to start a farm in the Middle East, what important facts would you need to know to help you make your decision?

THINKING SKILL: Decision Making

MEETING INDIVIDUAL NEEDS

Reteaching (easy) Have students write sentences using all the words from *Key Vocabulary* and *Key Places*. Then have them draw a picture that illustrates each term and use the sentences as captions.

Extension (average) Ask the class to act out a skit portraying a bazaar at which both American tourists and Middle Easterners are present. Have them contrast the items that the Middle Easterners and the Americans choose to buy as well as their bargaining techniques.

Enrichment (challenging) Have students do research on the flow of foreign workers into the Middle East. Ask them to draw a chart showing the workers' countries of origin and their destinations. You may have students trace this flow on the Desk Map of the world (found in the Teacher's Resource Center).

LESSON 3

The Government

READ TO LEARN

Key Vocabulary

absolute ruler
sharia
Islamic Republic

Key People

Qaboos bin Saud
Yitzhak Rabin
Yasir Arafat

Read Aloud

This behavior is against the will of Allah.

This statement was made in 1991 by Sheik Ibn Baz, a Saudi Arabian religious leader. He was criticizing some other Islamic leaders for opposing Saudi Arabia's education system, especially the education of women.

Like other countries in the Middle East, Saudi Arabia has many people who want their country's laws to be based on a strict interpretation of the Koran. Other people in these countries also want laws to follow the Koran but are concerned that some religious leaders interpret the Koran too strictly and keep their countries from being part of the modern world.

Read for Purpose

1. WHAT YOU KNOW: Who makes the laws in your community?
2. WHAT YOU WILL LEARN: What kinds of government are most common in the Middle East?

ABSOLUTE RULE

During the 1950s the nation of Oman was led by a ruler called Sultan Said. The sultan was determined to keep the nation as it had been for hundreds of years. He succeeded in keeping most Western influences out of Oman. He banned Western medicine and education and refused to allow people to wear Western clothes, ride bicycles, and even to wear eyeglasses.

However, the Sultan did send his son, **Qaboos bin Saud**, to England to be educated. By the time Qaboos returned to Oman, oil had been discovered there. When Sultan Said refused to use the country's new wealth to modernize it, his son led a peaceful revolt against his father and became sultan.

Less than 20 years later, Oman has almost 500 schools and many hospitals. The changes in the country came about because one person wanted them. Oman has no constitution and no elections. Sultan Qaboos is an **absolute ruler**, one with complete power whose authority cannot be challenged.

Most of the Middle East's rulers with traditional titles, such as *sultan* or *emir*, have been absolute rulers. In some of these countries, attempts are being made to make the rule less absolute. Jordan's king,

WHAT YOU KNOW: Students should be encouraged to think about the kind of community they live in and the kind of legislature it has; legislatures may include town councils, county boards, and city councils.

377

LESSON 3
pages 377–379

Lesson Theme Many of the Middle Eastern nations are led by powerful leaders, ruled by religious laws, and involved in longstanding disputes.

Lesson Objectives
- Describe the governments of the Middle East.
- Describe the relationship of government and religion in the Middle East.
- Explain the reasons for the conflicts over territory and religion in the Middle East.

PREPARE

Motivate Read the *Read Aloud* section to the class. Ask students if they can connect the information in this passage to news items about conflicts between different groups in their own town or city.

Set Purpose Tell students that they are going to read about some of the governments in the Middle East.

TEACH

Understanding Absolute Rule

Ask students:

- **Define the term *absolute ruler.*** (one whose authority cannot be challenged)
- **Which Middle Eastern nations still have absolute rulers?** (Kuwait, Bahrain, Qatar, Saudi Arabia, and the United Arab Emirates)

READING STRATEGY AND VOCABULARY DEVELOPMENT

Outlining Because this lesson describes Middle Eastern governments with different forms but similar practices, some students may be confused about the correct categories for these governments when outlining the lesson. To help students visualize a situation in which a government with an absolute ruler can have democratic traditions and yet belong in a different category from a government with an elected leader, draw a Venn diagram, (see below). Let A be a set of governments with an absolute ruler; let B be a set of governments with an elected leader; let C be a set of governments with democratic traditions.

Ⓐ (C Ⓑ)

Suggest to students that they draw a similar diagram when outlining the part of this lesson dealing with different types of governments whose laws are based on religious rules.

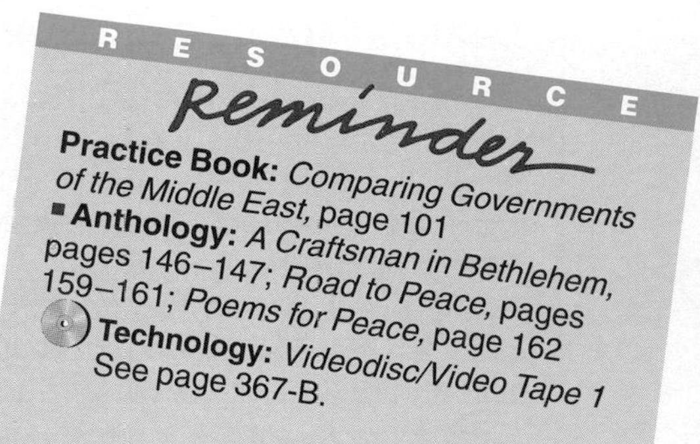

EXTENDING MAP SKILLS

Have students study the map of Israel on this page.

Ask students:

- **Which country disputes the boundary of the Gaza Strip with Israel?** (Egypt)
- **Which country disputes the boundary of the Golan Heights with Israel?** (Syria)
- **Which areas are occupied by Israel?** (Gaza Strip, West Bank, Golan Heights)

Understanding Government and Religion Help students to understand the role that religion plays in government in the Middle East.

Ask students:

- **What is an Islamic republic?** (a nation ruled by *sharia,* or Islamic law)
- **Which religious laws are basic to the Israeli government?** (the laws of Judaism)
- **Which Middle Eastern countries have a democratic form of government?** (Israel has a parliamentary system, and Turkey is a republic.)
- *THINKING FURTHER:* **Why do you think democratic governments are scarce in the Middle East?** (Democratic systems might conflict with Middle Eastern traditions of absolute rule and religious law.)

who is officially a constitutional monarch, is no longer exercising absolute authority. Since the war in the Persian Gulf ended, Kuwait has been pressured to allow more democracy. Yet Kuwait, Bahrain, Qatar, Saudi Arabia, and the United Arab Emirates still have absolute rulers.

GOVERNMENT AND RELIGION

Turkey, a Muslim country, has had a democratic form of government since it became a republic in 1923. Most governments in the Middle East, however, rely on Islamic law, or **sharia**, to govern them fully or partially. Some governments in the Middle East have constitutions that combine sharia and western law. Others rely entirely on sharia.

In 1979 the people of Iran overthrew the Shah, their ruler, and then declared Iran to be an **Islamic republic**, a nation ruled by sharia. In Iran there is not a sharp difference between religious laws and state laws. Religious leaders make up a majority of Iran's parliament and play an important role in its government.

Saudi Arabia, which is ruled by a king, is also heavily influenced by Islamic religious leaders. In addition to regular police, Saudi Arabia has a religious police force. They patrol to see that religious laws are enforced. These include laws that forbid alcohol and drugs as well as laws that do not permit women to drive.

In Israel Judaism plays a special role. Israel has no official constitution, and the government is influenced by Jewish law. Every Jew in the world has the legal right to enter Israel and become a citizen. Israel is also a democracy.

Israel has a parliamentary system of government. The Jewish, Christian, and Muslim citizens of Israel all enjoy the right to vote and to practice their religions. However, many Palestinian Arabs living in areas that Israel had occupied after wars have not had the same rights as Israeli citizens. One such area is the West Bank. Find the West Bank on the map on this page. It is the home of a large number of Palestinians.

HISTORY OF CONFLICT

Often different groups in the Middle East claim the same homeland. One serious conflict involves Israel and the Palestinians. As you have read, Israel was formerly part of a region called Palestine.

MAP SKILL: Besides the West Bank, what other areas have been occupied by Israel?

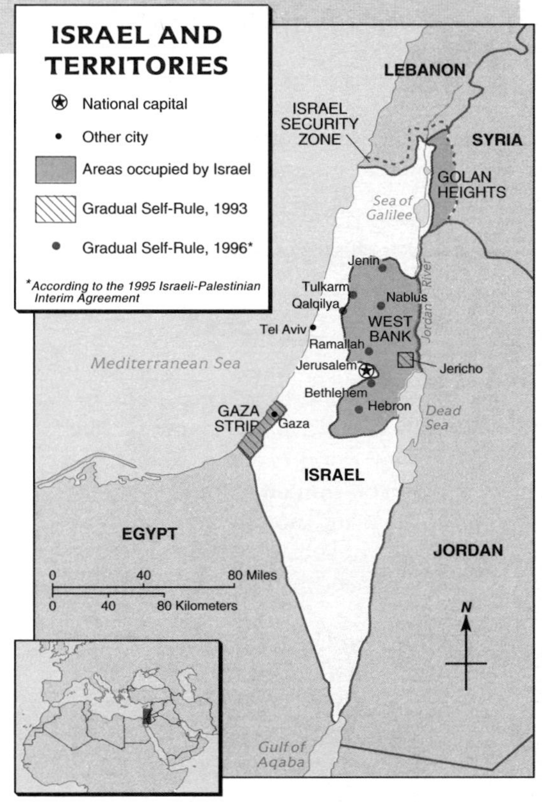

378 **MAP SKILL:** the Golan Heights, the Gaza Strip

CURRICULUM CONNECTION

Language Arts Have students do research on the conflict between the Israelis and the Palestinians. Ask students to list all the issues in this conflict that they think are important. Then ask the class to vote on which one of these issues they would like to debate. Divide the class into two groups and have the groups draw lots to decide which will represent the Israeli position and which will represent the Palestinian position. Emphasize to students the importance of understanding the position of someone with whom they do not agree.

BUILDING CITIZENSHIP

Current Events Have students bring in news clippings relating to important issues in the Middle East. Ask students to share their news items by reading them aloud to the rest of the group. Then ask students to decide as a group whether each news item reflects conflict or cooperation. On the *Atlas* political map of the Middle East, have students identify each area of conflict and cooperation.

Palestinians are Arabs who have traditionally lived in this region. The Palestinians along with the Muslim countries of the region opposed the creation of Israel in 1948. They thought that Palestine should be an Arab homeland. As a result, Israel's neighbors attacked Israel several times. In 1967 Israel gained control of the West Bank, Golan Heights, and some other areas. Palestinians and Arab countries demanded that these lands be returned.

A large step toward peace was taken in 1993. Yitzhak Rabin, the prime minister of Israel, and Yasir Arafat, the Palestinian leader, shook hands after a peace agreement was signed in Washington, D.C. They also agreed to a timetable for self-rule in the West Bank and Gaza Strip. The two leaders signed a further agreement in 1995, as shown on the map on page 378.

However, as the 1995 Israeli-Palestinian agreement was about to take effect, Yitzhak Rabin was assassinated by a Jewish Israeli opposed to the peace process. To assassinate means to kill for political reasons. The process of gradual Palestinian self-rule continued. Palestinians were allowed to hold their own elections in January, 1996, and Yasir Arafat was elected the Palestinian leader. Benjamin Netanyahu was elected as Israel's next Prime Minister. Continued tensions between Israel and the Palestinians have slowed the process of self-rule.

Check Your Reading

1. What is an absolute ruler?
2. What role does *sharia* play in some Middle Eastern nations?
3. What kinds of government are most common in the Middle East?
4. **THINKING SKILL:** Compare and contrast absolute rule with democratic rule.

THINKING SKILL: Compare and Contrast

CITIZENSHIP MAKING A DIFFERENCE

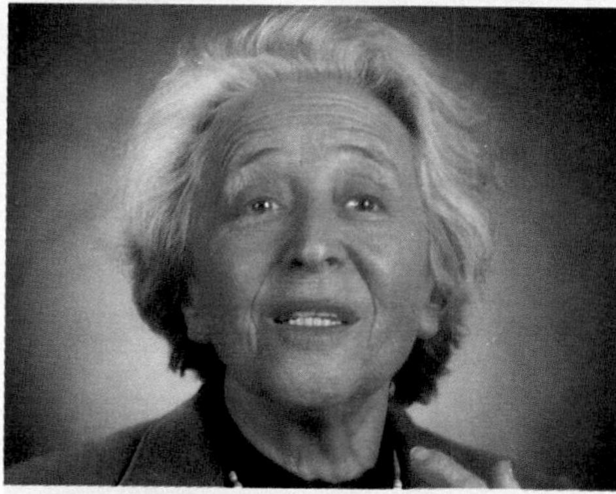

LIFELINE For The Old

Myriam Mendilow, who lived in Jerusalem, noticed that more and more elderly people were wandering the streets and that some of them were asking passersby for money. Myriam discovered that many of these lonely people felt that they had outlived their usefulness.

Myriam decided to help these people to find meaningful work. She founded a workshop, called Lifeline for the Old, to train the elderly to bind books. Myriam convinced elderly people that joining the workshop would help to restore their self-respect. They learned that saying no to Myriam was not easy. When they protested she told them, "If a person has just one finger, I'll put that finger to work."

Today Lifeline for the Old is an active center for young people with disabilities as well as the elderly. Together they have found dignity in a shared activity.

Although Myriam died in 1989, the workshop she started continues to flourish, a lasting monument to her many years as its director. Today it still serves elderly and young people with disabilities, but has also expanded to meet the needs of the many new immigrants who have come to Israel from the countries of the former Soviet Union and Ethiopia.

379

Discussing a History of Conflict Help students to understand the serious conflict between the Palestinians and the Israelis and the ways in which greater cooperation can benefit the countries of the Middle East.

Applying the Lesson Have students make a chart listing the countries of the Middle East and their corresponding systems of government.

3 CLOSE

Summarizing Students have read about the strong centralized leadership and state religions of the Middle Eastern countries and of the religious and boundary disputes in the region.

Evaluating Use the *Check Your Reading* questions (answers given below) to assess students' understanding.

Answers to Check Your Reading

1. one with complete power
2. acts as the basis for their government
3. governments that rely on Islamic law, or *sharia*
4. under absolute rule, an individual does not have the power to challenge the ruler's authority; whereas under democratic rule, an individual may take part in the governing process.

Independent Practice
Practice Book: page 101

MEETING INDIVIDUAL NEEDS

Reteaching (easy) Have students write a paragraph describing what they think it might be like to live in a Middle Eastern country governed by absolute rule.

Extension (average) Have students research and write an essay about the Israeli-Palestinian conflict. Have them include information on the 1993 peace talks between Israel and its Arab neighbors.

Enrichment (challenging) Have students write a newspaper editorial contrasting the role of religion in the government of the United States with its role in the governments of the Middle East.

BUILDING CITIZENSHIP

Myriam Mendilow: Lifeline for the Old

- *What important action did Myriam Mendilow perform?* (She founded a workshop to train the elderly to do useful work.)
- *How did Myriam show good citizenship?* (She gave her own time to help the elderly find meaning in life through worthwhile work.)
- *Do you know anyone who has done something to help the elderly in your community?* (Possible answers include: volunteers at a home for the elderly or in a nursing home.)

SKILLS LESSON
pages 380–381

Lesson Theme Comparing maps with different themes provides more information than one map can give.

Lesson Objective
- Compare and draw conclusions from a study of two maps.

PREPARE

Motivate Ask students what kind of map they would choose if they could have only one map to use in the next unit of study. Point out to those who choose a political map that they will learn very little about the physical characteristics of the area; advise those who choose a physical map that they will learn very little about the locations of places and the borders of countries.

Set Purpose You may want to project Transparency Map 13, which shows two temperature maps, on the screen. Tell students that in this lesson they will learn the advantages of using more than one map at a time.

TEACH

Analyzing How to Compare Temperature Maps Help students to understand that averages, seasonal differences, and location are important in comparing temperature maps.

Ask students:

- **What two variables are most important in comparing the two maps of Egypt on this page?** (time of year and location)

BUILDING SKILLS
GEOGRAPHY SKILLS

Comparing Maps

While reading about the Middle East, you were often referred to maps for specific information. For example, a political map provides a general picture of an area, showing the locations of countries and their capitals. A population-density map shows the distribution of people within a given area.

Sometimes information is best described by showing two or more different maps of the same area. Then these maps can be compared and conclusions can be drawn from the comparison. When you compare maps, you can acquire information that either map alone might not provide. In this lesson you can compare similar maps to find new information and draw conclusions.

Comparing Temperature Maps

Look at the two maps of Egypt on this page. On both maps the average temperature in Egypt is shown. Notice that **Map A** shows temperatures in January while **Map B** shows temperatures in July. **Map A** shows how the average January temperature varies in Egypt. **Map B** shows the variation in average July temperature.

By comparing **Map A** with **Map B**, you see that it is hotter in Egypt in July than it is in January. You can also see that in general there is a greater difference between January and July temperatures in southern Egypt than in northern Egypt. What is the average January temperature in Cairo? What is the average July temperature in the city?*

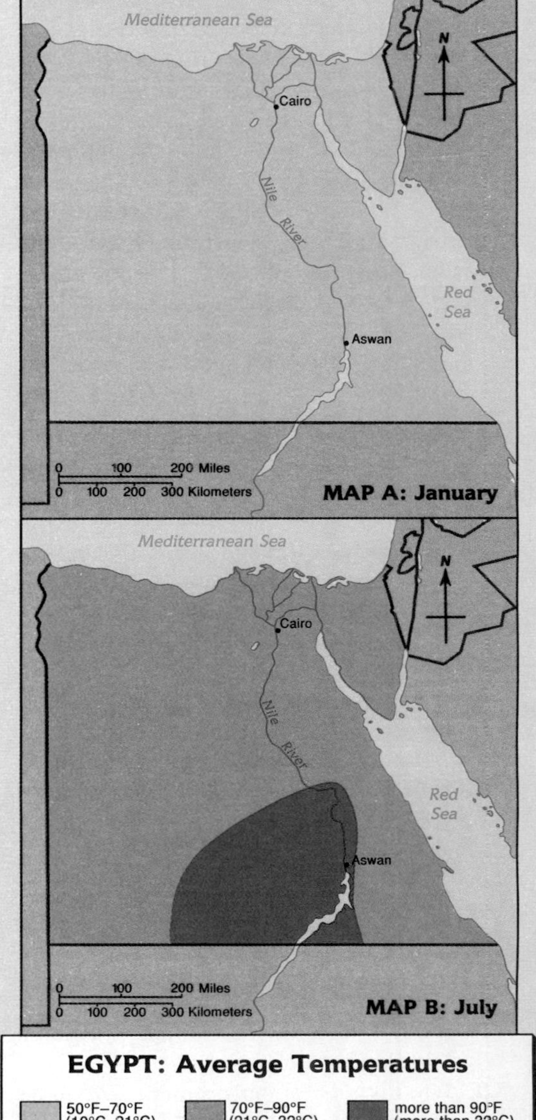

*The average January temperature is 50°–70°F. (10°–21°C.); the average July temperature is 70°–90°F. (21°–32°C.).

380

CURRICULUM CONNECTION

Science Tell students that maps are important to scientists as well as geographers. Have students investigate the kinds of maps that meteorologists would use in determining the weather in a region. Have them collect samples of these maps and demonstrate how they would be used by meteorologists.

RESOURCE *Reminder*

Practice Book: *Comparing Maps,* page 102
Transparency Map: 13

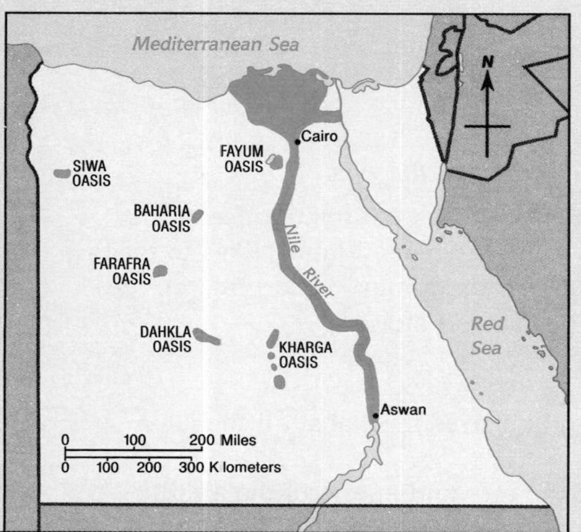

MAP C EGYPT: Important Oases

Oasis — Color shows extent of irrigated land.

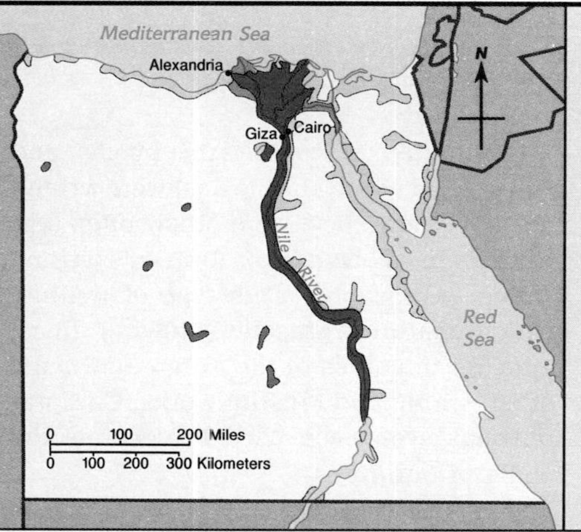

MAP D EGYPT: Population Density

People per square mile 0 2 25 125 250 500

People per square kilometer 0 1 10 50 100 200

• Cities with more than 1 million people

Comparing Other Maps

Comparing maps can help you to understand relationships or to draw conclusions. Look at **Map C** and **Map D** on this page. The titles of these maps tell you that the maps have different subjects. **Map C** shows the location of oases in Egypt. You can see that the color green represents the location of oases on the map.

Map D shows the population density of Egypt. Look at the legend to see which color represents each population category. Which color represents the greatest number of people per square mile? Which color represents the lowest number of people per square mile? In which areas of Egypt is the population density greatest?*

Now compare **Map C** with **Map D**. Are the most densely populated areas near oases? Which areas of Egypt are the least densely populated? Are these areas located near oases? By using the maps, what conclusions can you draw about the relationship between population density and the location of oases in Egypt?**

Reviewing the Skill

1. What is the purpose of comparing maps?
2. During which month are temperatures lower in Cairo than in Aswan?
3. Which city is cooler in July, Cairo or Aswan?
4. Which area in Egypt is the most densely populated?
5. What is the relationship between oases and population in Egypt?
6. Why is it helpful to understand how to compare maps?

*orange; yellow; along the Nile River and in selected other spots in the interior of the country

**Yes; the areas away from the Nile; no. In Egypt, the population tends to be high near oases.

Discussing Comparing Other Maps Help students to recognize that they need to be thoroughly familiar with how to read legends and symbols on maps in order to compare maps and draw conclusions.

Ask students:

- **Why is it important to know the titles of maps being compared?** (Titles give you the basic subject matter being compared.)
- **Why would you compare maps of different themes?** (to see relationships that allow you to draw a conclusion or conclusions about the subjects of the maps)

Applying the Skill Divide the class into groups and have each group pick two maps from this book. Ask students to compare the two maps and write down their conclusions. Have them present their conclusions to the class.

 CLOSE

Summarizing Students have analyzed maps with different themes in order to draw conclusions. Have students tell whether a comparison of Map A or B with Map C or D would be worthwhile and have them explain their answers.

Answers to Reviewing the Skill

1. to draw conclusions from an analysis of the maps
2. Temperatures are lower in Cairo than in Aswan during July.
3. Cairo
4. along the Nile River
5. There is a greater settlement of population near oases.
6. It enables you to get information you cannot get from using only one map.

Independent Practice
Practice Book: page 102

MEETING INDIVIDUAL NEEDS

Reteaching (easy) Have students look through this book and list pairs of maps they might like to compare, along with a sentence telling why. Then have students compare one pair of maps and write a paragraph about their conclusions.

Extension (average) Have students collect as many maps as possible of their community. Display these in the classroom and have students present an oral comparison of two of them.

Enrichment (challenging) Have students research the average temperatures in your state for January and July and create two temperature maps. Have students draw conclusions from the maps.

LESSON 4
pages 382–383

Lesson Theme The arts of the Middle East include poetry, storytelling, calligraphy, and design; sports include both modern and ancient games.

Lesson Objectives
- Explain why the spoken word is important in Middle Eastern storytelling and poetry.
- Explain how Islamic law has influenced Middle Eastern painting and drawing.
- Describe Middle Eastern sports.

PREPARE

Motivate Read the *Read Aloud* section to the class. Ask students if they enjoy hearing poetry or stories recited or told.

Set Purpose Use the *What You Know* question to prepare students to understand that Arab culture and the Islamic religion have a great influence on Middle Eastern arts.

TEACH

Tracing the Written and Spoken Word Help students to understand the importance of the oral tradition of the Middle East.

Ask students:

- **Which artistic skill has always been important to the people of the Middle East?** (storytelling)
- *THINKING FURTHER:* **Why did the oral tradition of storytelling develop in the Middle East?** (Because few people could read hundreds of years ago, they had to rely on stories and poems that were passed on by word of mouth.)

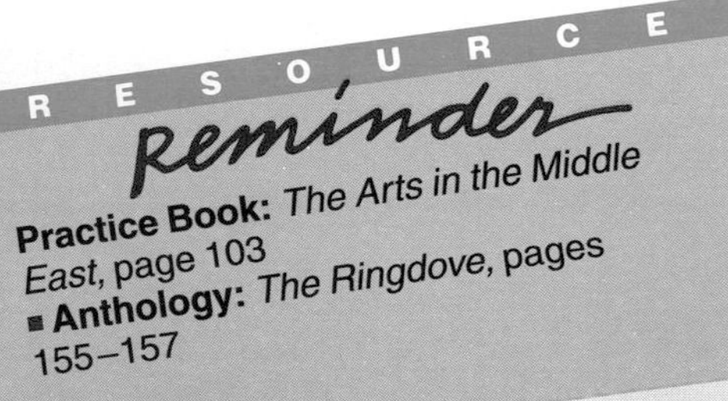

LESSON 4

Arts and Recreation

READ TO LEARN

Key Vocabulary

calligraphy

Read Aloud

Baghdad is, for me, a city full of the spirits of the past.

This is how Iraqi poet Khalil Khoury explains the importance of his home city to his work. As he works on new poems, Khoury likes to recite them aloud to his family. When he does this, Khoury is carrying on the Middle Eastern tradition of spoken poetry and stories.

Read for Purpose

1. WHAT YOU KNOW: Which ethnic group lives in almost all the countries of the Middle East?
2. WHAT YOU WILL LEARN: How are the arts and sports of the Middle East a blend of the traditional and the modern?

THE WRITTEN AND SPOKEN WORD

People like Khalil Khoury have been sharing their poems and stories for centuries in the Middle East. The importance of the skill of storytelling is highlighted in the Middle East's most famous collection of tales, the *Arabian Nights*. In these tales a ruler tells his new wife, Scheherazade (shə hâr ə zäd′), that she will be put to death if she fails to amuse him. So each night, to save her life, she tells a story. Her stories are so interesting that each day the ruler puts off giving the death order.

Hundreds of years ago few people could read. So storytellers memorized poetry and stories. Early tales from the Middle East were passed on by word of mouth. Poems about heroes and famous events became favorites. As one writer explained:

> *The Arabian poet was regarded as one gifted with knowledge beyond ordinary humans, and . . . began to assume many roles, including that of leader, . . . teacher, and priest.*

Eventually, of course, the poems and stories told in the Middle East were written down. When they were, they often appeared in a beautiful form of writing called calligraphy. This type of writing, which features graceful, flowing lines, appears in copies of the Koran and many other Arabic and Muslim works. Calligraphy has even been used to decorate the walls of buildings.

DETAILS IN DESIGN

The Islamic religion has had and continues to have a great effect on the arts of the Middle East. Islam discourages the painting of pictures of humans and animals in public buildings such as mosques in order to keep people from praying to

382 WHAT YOU KNOW: This question refers to material in Chapter 18, Lesson 1; Arabs.

READING STRATEGY AND VOCABULARY DEVELOPMENT

Outlining Have the class preview this lesson. Help students to make an outline of this lesson, using the chapter title "Arts and Recreation" as the topic. Have students use the section titles as the headings for the outline. Have students fill in the explanatory details by themselves. Suggest to students that they save this outline and use it as a study guide for a future examination.

idols. To avoid portraying images of living beings, many Muslim artists turned to and perfected the art of design. The finest, most elaborate designs decorate mosques.

Yet there is also a rich history of Muslim artists portraying people and animals in their famous miniature paintings.

Designs like those on mosques also appear on carpets. The carpets of the Middle East are both works of beauty and useful objects.

OLD AND NEW ENTERTAINMENTS

In the Middle East, as in other parts of the world, popular pastimes keep old traditions alive. Today training and racing camels has become a sport. Most of the riders are boys ten years old or younger.

"The races keep alive one of our most important traditions," says Sheik Abdul Aziz of Sharjah, a small Middle Eastern kingdom. In Sharjah, camel races take place every other Friday in winter.

Many sports and pastimes are thousands of years old. Men in the Middle East have competed in wrestling since their ancestors learned it from the Greeks thousands of years ago.

Falconry is also popular among men of the Middle East. Falconry is the practice of raising and training hawk-like birds called falcons. Men use these birds for hunting.

Sports from other parts of the world are also popular, especially soccer. Women have their own sports clubs at which they enjoy swimming, tennis, volleyball, and other athletics.

ARTS AND LEISURE

The spoken and written word are considered forms of art in the Middle East. As you have read, poetry and storytelling are especially popular. Because Islam discourages showing the human figure and animals, most artists paint beautiful designs based on flowers or trees or geometric shapes. Camel races and soccer are two of the many leisure activities popular in the Middle East. Sports and recreational activities in the area combine old and new pastimes.

Middle Eastern art often includes examples of calligraphy, a beautiful form of writing.

Check Your Reading

1. Why were storytellers held in such high regard by the ancient Arabs?
2. What is calligraphy?
3. Name two traditional Middle Eastern pastimes.
4. **THINKING SKILL:** Is the following statement from this lesson a fact or an opinion: "The Islamic religion has had and continues to have a great effect on the arts of the Middle East."? Why?

THINKING SKILL: Fact and Opinion

383

Looking at Details in Design Encourage students to discuss the difference between a representational drawing and a design.

Ask students:

- **What are two types of art in which Middle Eastern artists specialize?** (Middle Eastern artists are known for their beautiful, elaborate designs and their famous miniature paintings.)
- *THINKING FURTHER:* **Why does Islam discourage the portrayal of living beings?** (to prevent people from praying to idols)

Discussing Old and New Entertainments Help students to understand that recreational activities in the Middle East are rooted in both modern and ancient pastimes.

Applying the Lesson Have students choose one subject from this lesson that they would like to know more about. Have them list the steps they would take to find out about that subject.

CLOSE

Summarize Students have read that Middle Eastern literature and art have been influenced by Islamic law. They have also read that both old and new sports are enjoyed in this region.

Evaluating Use the *Check Your Reading* questions (answers given below) to assess students' understanding.

Answers to Check Your Reading

1. Storytellers both entertained and taught.
2. graceful, flowing writing
3. camel races, wrestling, falconry
4. Fact; Middle Eastern art shows evidence of Islamic influence.

Independent Practice
Practice Book: page 103

MEETING INDIVIDUAL NEEDS

Reteaching (easy) Have students cooperate in making a mural entitled "Arts and Recreation in the Middle East" on a long piece of butcher paper.

Extension (average) Have students read a Middle Eastern story, such as a tale from the *Arabian Nights Entertainment*, or a poem by Omar Khayyam. Ask them to write out their favorite part of the poem or story in their best, most decorative handwriting.

Enrichment (challenging) Have students read the story "Aladdin and His Wonderful Lamp" from the *Arabian Nights Entertainment*. Then ask two students to each retell the story to the class in his or her own words. Have the class note any differences in the style in which the two students tell the story.

CHAPTER 18 REVIEW
pages 384–385

USING THE CHAPTER SUMMARY AND REVIEW

Cultural Geography These questions may be used for review.

- **Which groups of people are non-Arab Muslims?** (Persians, Turks, and Kurds)
- **Which resource is important to the economy of many Persian Gulf nations?** (oil)
- **On what are the laws of some Arab countries based?** (Islamic law, or *sharia*)
- **What is a popular traditional sport of the people of the Middle East?** (camel racing)

Ideas to Remember

- **Which religion do most of the people of the Middle East practice?** (Islam)
- **What are the main ways in which the people in this region earn a living?** (commerce and farming)
- **What kind of rulers do many countries in the region have?** (absolute rulers)
- **What is calligraphy?** (a beautiful form of writing)

Answers to Reviewing Vocabulary

1. bazaar
2. hajj
3. kibbutz
4. absolute ruler
5. Islam
6. calligraphy
7. Islamic republic
8. labor-intensive
9. sharia
10. moshav

CHAPTER 18 ▪ SUMMARY

MIDDLE EAST: CULTURAL GEOGRAPHY

PEOPLE

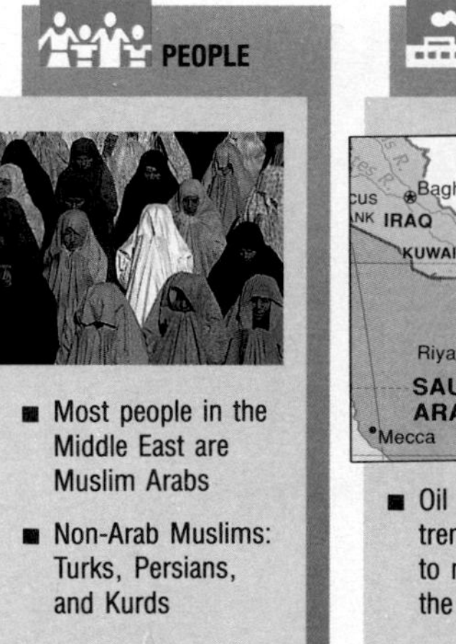

- Most people in the Middle East are Muslim Arabs
- Non-Arab Muslims: Turks, Persians, and Kurds
- Non-Muslim groups: Jewish people of Israel, Christians, especially in Cyprus and Lebanon
- In Muslim countries Islam is an important influence

ECONOMY

- Oil has brought tremendous wealth to many nations on the Persian Gulf

- Labor force: farmers, traders, guest workers
- Farming methods: irrigation important, labor-intensive, modern as well as traditional farming

GOVERNMENT

- Absolute rulers and laws based on Islam
- Democracies: Israel, Turkey

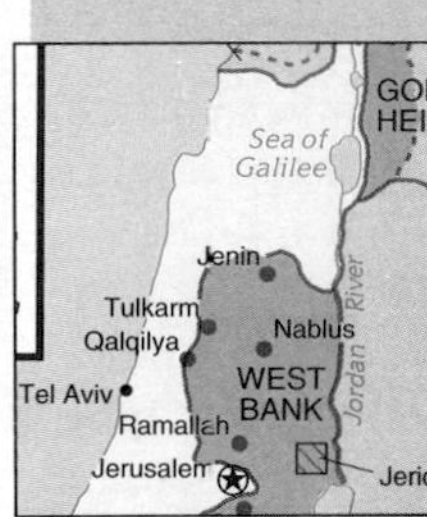

- Israel has a parliamentary system of government
- Religious disputes cause conflict in many countries of the Middle East

ARTS AND RECREATION

- Storytellers are highly regarded

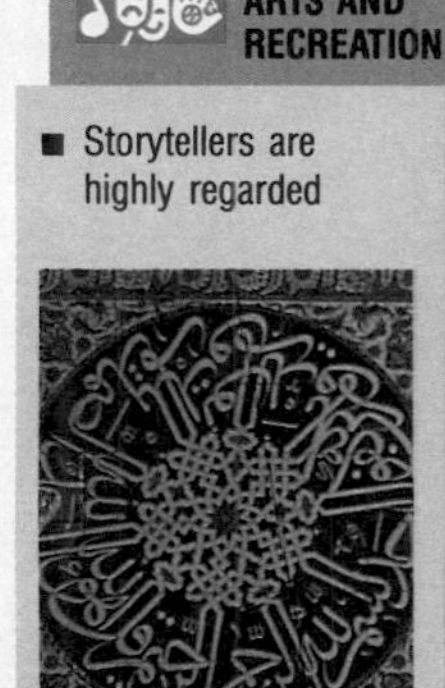

- Muslim artists are famous for their calligraphy

- Camel racing is a popular traditional sport

IDEAS TO REMEMBER

- Most people in the Middle East are Muslim Arabs.
- Commerce and farming are the main ways of earning a living, although oil has brought wealth to some countries.
- Some governments of the area have absolute rulers as well as laws that are based on Islam; some governments are democratic.
- Storytelling, calligraphy, carpet making, camel racing, and falconry have long been popular in the Middle East.

384

ENRICHMENT ACTIVITY

Designing an Arabesque Rug **Materials:** construction paper, pens and pencils, paints or markers

1. Review with the class pages 382–383 about Islamic influences on design. Point out to students that Middle Eastern carpets and rugs are known for their beauty and workmanship. Explain to students that one style of design is called arabesque (''like or from the Arabs''), and if possible, show them an example of it that appears with the word in a dictionary. Discuss the definition—''a design that uses flower, foliage, or fruit and sometimes animal and figural outlines to produce an intricate pattern of interlaced lines.'' Have students design their own arabesque rugs.
2. Have students work out their designs with ordinary paper and pencil. Then have them transfer their designs to construction paper and use paint or markers to draw in striking colors.

CHAPTER 18 • REVIEW

REVIEWING VOCABULARY

absolute ruler	Islamic Republic
bazaar	kibbutz
calligraphy	labor-intensive
hajj	moshav
Islam	sharia

Number a sheet of paper from 1 to 10. Beside each number write the word or term from the above list that best matches the definition.

1. An outdoor market that has been the center of Middle Eastern economic life for hundreds of years
2. The pilgrimage Muslims make to the city of Mecca
3. A kind of collective farm in Israel on which people share the work
4. A leader who has complete authority over his subjects
5. A world religion based on the teachings of Muhammad
6. A writing style that features beautiful, graceful lines
7. A nation ruled by sharia
8. A type of production that is based on human strength instead of machinery
9. A set of Islamic rules based on the Koran
10. A cooperative Israeli farm system under which each family owns its own land

REVIEWING FACTS

1. Name two non-Arab Muslim nations in the Middle East. In which Middle Eastern country is Judaism the main religion?
2. Why did many Jews leave Europe and move to Palestine in the 1930s and 1940s?
3. Why are Middle Eastern nations that do not have oil generally poor?
4. How did the war in the Persian Gulf affect guest workers in the Middle East?
5. Why are many works of art in Muslim countries more likely to portray designs rather than people or animals?

WRITING ABOUT MAIN IDEAS

1. **Writing a Paragraph:** "In the Middle East traditional ways of life exist alongside very modern ones." In a paragraph, explain why this is so and list the benefits of each way of living.
2. **Preparing an Interview:** Imagine that you are planning to interview someone in the Middle East. Whom would you interview? Make a list of five questions that you would ask.
3. **Writing About Perspectives:** Imagine that you are the son or daughter of guest workers and you were born in the Middle Eastern country in which your parents work. Write a diary entry about your feelings when it is time to leave the country in which you have lived all your life and return to a country you do not know.

BUILDING SKILLS: COMPARING MAPS

1. What is the purpose of comparing maps?
2. Look at the maps on pages 380 and 381. Which city is warmer in July, Cairo or Aswan?
3. Why is it useful to understand how to compare maps?

Answers to Reviewing Facts

1. Iran and Turkey; Israel
2. Millions of Jews sought refuge from persecution and the Holocaust.
3. Middle Eastern nations without oil are generally poor because they have few natural resources.
4. Nearly 5 million people had to leave the countries where they lived and worked.
5. To prevent people from praying to idols, Muslim artists portray designs rather than living beings in art.

Suggestions for Writing About Main Ideas

1. Students may point out ancient religious influences as a reason for traditional lifeways which keep alive rich cultural heritages; oil income and foreign interaction account for standard-of-living benefits of modernization.
2. Students' interview questions should include the five journalism "Ws"—who, what, where, why, and when.
3. In order to help them write their diary entries, students should think about what it would be like to leave their school, home, or country.

Answers to Building Skills: Comparing Maps

1. to draw conclusions from an analysis of the maps
2. Aswan
3. It enables you to get information you cannot get from using only one map.

MAKING CONNECTIONS

Supporting Main Ideas Use the Main Idea Table Graphic Organizer Transparency, writing in only the underlined main idea and four topic headings. Have students fill in the "legs" of the table with information that supports each subject. Have them fill in details by listing specific examples in the table "feet." *Ask:* What are some of the cultural factors which shape life in the Middle East?

MAIN IDEA: Life in the Middle East is shaped by religion, contrasting economies, powerful leaders, and cultural traditions.			
People	Economy	Government	Arts and Recreation
The main culture group in the Middle East is united by language, customs, and religion.	Oil-producing countries have a high standard of living; countries with no oil are often poor.	Many governments have absolute rulers as well as laws based on Islam.	Poetry and storytelling are popular arts in the Middle East.
Arabs (Islam, Arabic)	Kuwait, Qatar, United Arab Emirates, Yemen, Lebanon, Jordan	Sultan of Oman sharia	*Arabian Nights*

CHAPTER 19
ORGANIZER

NORTH AFRICA text pages 386–405

CHAPTER THEME

Water and oil control the economic development of the newly independent Islamic nations of North Africa.

CHAPTER OBJECTIVES

CONTENT

- List the major reasons for and the effects of population growth in North Africa.
- Explain why many Muslims believe that Western culture threatens their way of life.
- Explain why water and oil are so important to the economies of North Africa.
- Explain why most North African countries must import much of the food they consume.
- Describe the problems that independence brought to many North African countries.
- Outline the various forms of government in North Africa.
- Describe the consequences of Anwar Sadat's peace treaty with Israel.
- List three major sources of conflict in North Africa.
- Explain how Islam influences the leisure activities of North Africa.

SKILLS

Geography
- Interpret a political map of North Africa.
- Use a map to locate major oil reserves in North Africa.

Study and Research
- Interpret a diagram of a typical home in North Africa.

Thinking
- Draw conclusions about life in North Africa based on information in the text.
- Assess a statement for bias.

Reading and Writing
- Write a travel brochure about a trip through North Africa.

CITIZENSHIP VALUES

- Appreciate the importance of leaders who take risks to achieve positive change.

TEACHER OPTIONS

READING STRATEGY: Summarizing Strategies to help students read and remember the main ideas of the lesson.

Lesson 1: p. 387 Lesson 3: 398
Lesson 2: p. 391 Lesson 4: 402
Legacy: p. 394

MEETING INDIVIDUAL NEEDS Activities for reteaching, extension, and enrichment.

Lesson 1: p. 390 Lesson 3: 399
Lesson 2: p. 393 Lesson 4: 403
Legacy: p. 397

GEO ADVENTURES ACTIVITIES PAD Daily activities to assess students' understanding of geography skills.

CURRICULUM CONNECTION Activities to help integrate other subject areas with Social Studies.

Art: p. 389

PUPIL EDITION ON CASSETTE Language support for students who have difficulty reading or who will benefit from listening to the Pupil Edition on Cassette as they read.

SECOND-LANGUAGE SUPPORT Activities and suggestions for second-language learners.

Lesson 4: p. 349-D

CHAPTER PLANNING GUIDE

LESSON	SUGGESTED PACING	THEMES	TEACHER SUPPORT MATERIALS: TEACHER'S RESOURCE CENTER
1 THE PEOPLE pages 387–390	1 day	People in the Islamic lands of North Africa face problems caused by a rapidly rising population.	Practice Book p. 105 Anthology p. 106 Technology: Adventures CD-ROM
2 THE ECONOMY pages 391–393	1 day	Water and oil resources control the economies of North African nations.	Practice Book p. 106 Technology: Videodisc/Video Tape 1
LEGACY Egyptian Boatbuilding: An Ancient Tradition pages 394–397	1 day	Boatbuilding is a legacy that goes back thousands of years.	Outline Map p. 28
3 THE GOVERNMENT pages 398–399	1 day	After gaining independence from the European powers, the nations of North Africa developed a variety of governments, usually dominated by one strong ruler.	Practice Book p. 107 Outline Map p. 28 Technology: Adventures CD-ROM
BUILDING THINKING SKILLS Asking Questions pages 400–401	1 day	Asking good questions will help you get the information you need.	Practice Book p. 108
4 ARTS AND RECREATION pages 402–403	1 day	Traditional themes are reflected in the arts and leisure activities of North Africa.	Practice Book p. 109
CHAPTER SUMMARY AND REVIEW pages 404–405	1 day	Chapter content, skills, and vocabulary are reviewed and evaluated.	Practice Book p. 110 Transparency: Graphic Organizer Assessment Book, Chapter 19 Test

Technology CONNECTION

Lesson 1
ADVENTURE CD-ROM
Enrich Lesson 1 by having students *Travel* to Egypt on the CD-ROM.

Lesson 2
VIDEODISC/VIDEO TAPE 1
Enrich Lesson 2 with a segment from Video Lesson 3, *Africa Today.*

Search 11444, Play To 12178 Side A

Lesson 3
ADVENTURE CD-ROM
Enrich Lesson 3 by having students *Travel* to and *Explore* Algeria.

CHAPTER 19
pages 386–405

USING THE CHAPTER OPENER

Discussing the Photograph Have students study the photograph and read the chapter title.

Ask students:

- **What does the photograph show?** (a smiling, teenage girl dressed in traditional clothes and holding a black lamb)
- **What conclusions can you draw about this girl from the photograph?** (Possible answers include: She wears a head covering, so the sun may be strong and the climate, hot. Her ease with the black lamb suggests that she works with animals, possibly as a herder.)
- *THINKING FURTHER:* **The girl's smile suggests that she likes her life. What reasons can you think of to account for her happiness?** (perhaps a family life that gives her a sense of roots and belonging, or a love of animals and the outdoors that helps her to enjoy her work.)

Reading/Listening to the Primary Source Read aloud the quotation and the passage that follows. Explain to students that the girl in the photograph is a Bedouin and that many Bedouins are herders of sheep and goats.

Ask students:

- **What does the Arabic word *Bedouin* mean?** (desert dweller)
- *THINKING FURTHER:* **What difficulties do you imagine a Bedouin herder might face due to the environment?** (Possible answers include: drought, loss of animals due to diseases and harsh conditions, desert sandstorms, extreme temperatures)

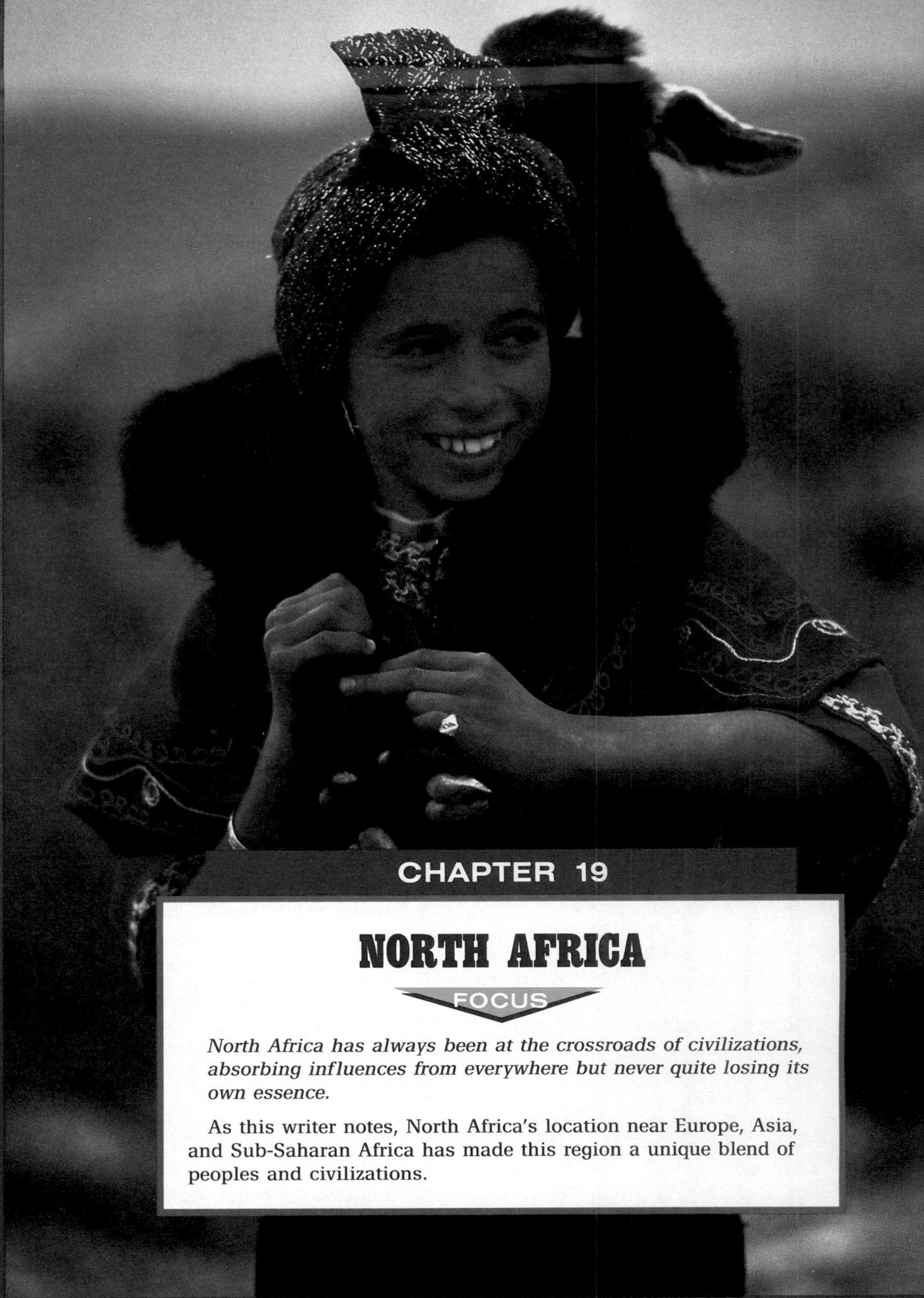

CHAPTER 19

NORTH AFRICA

FOCUS

North Africa has always been at the crossroads of civilizations, absorbing influences from everywhere but never quite losing its own essence.

As this writer notes, North Africa's location near Europe, Asia, and Sub-Saharan Africa has made this region a unique blend of peoples and civilizations.

BACKGROUND INFORMATION

About the Photograph

- The Bedouins, who tend to be herders, live in clans, or groups of related families. In time of danger several clans band together to form a tribe under the supervision of a leader called a sheik.
- In their travels these herders form camps by erecting black tents, which they carry with them. To protect themselves from sand, dust, and extreme temperatures, they often wear long cloaks with hoods called burnooses.
- At oases, where they seek water and pasture for their herds of camels, sheep, horses, and goats, the Bedouins trade meat, animal hides, and milk for the vegetable produce of farmers.
- Many former Bedouin herders now work for oil companies.

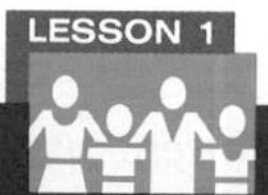

LESSON 1

The People

READ TO LEARN

Key Vocabulary	Key Places
muezzin	Marrakesh Cairo

Read Aloud

To outsiders the name of Egypt's capital is Cairo. But Egyptians often call the city *Misr* (mis′ rə), which means "big city" or "home." When Egyptians say, "I am going to Misr," they are heading for Cairo, whether it is their home or not. Today about 11 million people live in this sprawling city, and its population is growing by almost 1,000 people a day. Cairo is just one place in North Africa in which the population is growing quickly. In this lesson you will read how the countries of North Africa have tried to deal with their rapidly increasing populations.

Read for Purpose

1. WHAT YOU KNOW: Which type of landscape covers much of North Africa?
2. WHAT YOU WILL LEARN: What challenges do the people of North Africa face today?

PEOPLE AND LANGUAGES

When an American writer walked through **Marrakesh** (mar ə kesh′), Morocco, he was amazed at what he saw.

> *Never have I seen so much diversity in one place, like a great party with a thousand guests. Many men wore djellabas, ankle-length robes of brown, white, or gray, with turbans or crocheted skullcaps. . . . Women in flowing caftans, often sheltered by their special form of invisibility, the veil, moved with graceful dignity among them.*

Some of the people shopping in the market at Marrakesh were Berbers, descendants of the first known group of people to live in North Africa. Today the Berbers, a tall, light-skinned people, live mostly in the mountains of southern Morocco and Algeria. One group of Berbers are Tuareg (twä′ reg) nomads who live in the desert. They stand out in a crowd of North Africans because the Tuareg men, not the women, wear veils.

Since the days of the ancient Berbers, many other groups have entered and spread out over North Africa. The Greeks, Persians, Romans, and Turks have all invaded Egypt and its neighbors. But no group has had as much impact on North Africa as the Arabs have had. In A.D. 640 a small army of Arab warriors conquered much of the area. Wherever they went, they spread their language and their religion. Soon most of the people in North Africa were speaking Arabic and following the rules of Islam.

WHAT YOU KNOW: This question refers to information in Chapter 17, Lesson 1; desert.

LESSON 1
pages 387–390

Lesson Theme People in the Islamic lands of North Africa face problems caused by a rapidly rising population.

Lesson Objectives
- Identify the problems caused by population growth in North Africa.
- Describe Muslim family life in North Africa.
- Identify the conflicts that arise from Islamic laws versus modern ways.

1 PREPARE

Motivate Read the *Read Aloud* section to the class. Remind students of the problems caused by overpopulation in Mexico City. Discuss with the class whether or not there are similar problems in Cairo.

Set Purpose Display the *Atlas* map showing the physical features of the Middle East and North Africa. Use the *What You Know* question to establish the limits that the desert sets on expansion of human settlements. Tell students to make a list of answers to the *What You Will Learn* question as they read the lesson.

2 TEACH

Identifying People and Languages

Ask students:

- **Who are the Berbers?** (descendants of the first known group of people to live in North Africa)
- **Which group has had the greatest impact on North Africa?** (the Arabs)

READING STRATEGY AND VOCABULARY DEVELOPMENT

Summarizing Review with students the summarizing strategy that they learned in Chapter 7. Tell students that for this lesson they will keep a journal in which they summarize the important facts. Have students preview the lesson. Then have them develop an outline using the section headings. Students can then turn their outlines into summaries. Some students may enjoy writing their journal in the first person as if they were traveling in the area. If you wish, have students also keep a journal for the rest of the chapter.

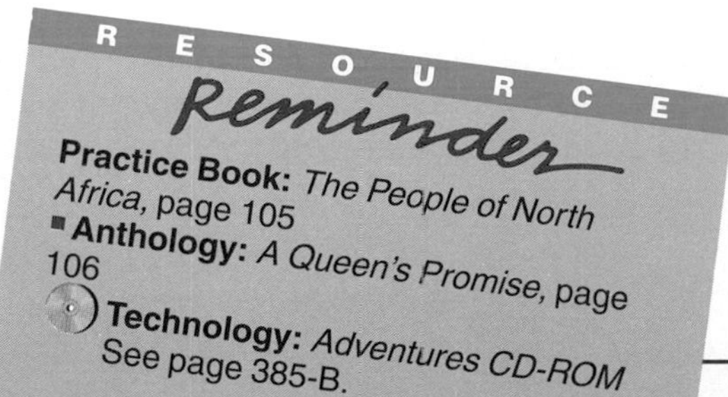
RESOURCE Reminder

Practice Book: *The People of North Africa,* page 105
Anthology: *A Queen's Promise,* page 106
Technology: *Adventures CD-ROM*
See page 385-B.

Studying People and Languages
Continue the discussion.

Ask students:

- **What are two of the languages spoken in North Africa?** (Arabic and Berber)
- *THINKING FURTHER:* **Why has Berber continued to be used when many other spoken languages have given way to Arabic?** (Berber people have been in North Africa the longest and live in an isolated location.)

Discussing Growing Populations

Ask students:

- **What are two causes of Cairo's overpopulation?** (a high birth rate and a lowered death rate as a result of improved health care)
- **Which areas of daily life are most affected by the growing population in this region?** (housing space, schools, sewers, amount of available farmland)
- *THINKING FURTHER:* **Why might the cost of food be so high in North Africa?** (There is a lack of arable land, leading to food shortages, high prices, and the need to import expensive food.)

EXTENDING MAP SKILLS

Have students study the political map of North Africa on this page.

Ask students:

- **How many nations are in North Africa?** (five)
- **Which capital cities are on the Mediterranean Sea?** (Tunis, Tripoli, Algiers)
- **Which North African nation is closest to Europe?** (Morocco)
- **Which North African nation is closest to the Middle East?** (Egypt)
- *THINKING FURTHER:* **What pattern is there in the location of major North African cities?** (They are close to or on the coast.)

One group of people who resisted the Arabs were the Berbers. The Berbers had lived in North Africa for thousands of years before the invasion of the Arabs. Although most Berbers became Muslims, for many years they did not learn to speak Arabic. They continued to use their own language, known as Berber.

GROWING POPULATIONS

Cairo, the capital of Egypt, is an example of the huge, growing cities of North Africa. Its population of about 11 million people is increasing by almost 1,000 people a day. Cairo has the largest population of any city in North Africa, and is thirteenth overall in the world.

Because Cairo is growing so rapidly, it does not have enough running water, sewers, schools, or housing for its people. Although Cairo's wealthy citizens live in elegant buildings away from the center of the city, in many poor neighborhoods eight or nine people often share a single room.

Explosive population growth is a major problem throughout North Africa. For example, every ten months Egypt has another 1 million people to feed, house, and educate. Part of the reason for the sharp rise in population is good news. As a result of improved health care, North Africans now live longer than they did.

Schools in North Africa share the same problems with schools in North America or other areas whenever there is a rapid increase in the number of schoolchildren. Many students go to school in shifts. They attend classes for half a day—some from 7:00 to 11:30 in the morning and others from 1:30 to 4:00 in the afternoon. Classes with 45 to 60 students are not unusual.

Housing is also a problem. Tens of thousands of people live in Cairo's cemeteries.

MAP SKILL: All the capital cities of North Africa are port cities. Which capital is on the Atlantic Ocean? Which is on the Nile River?

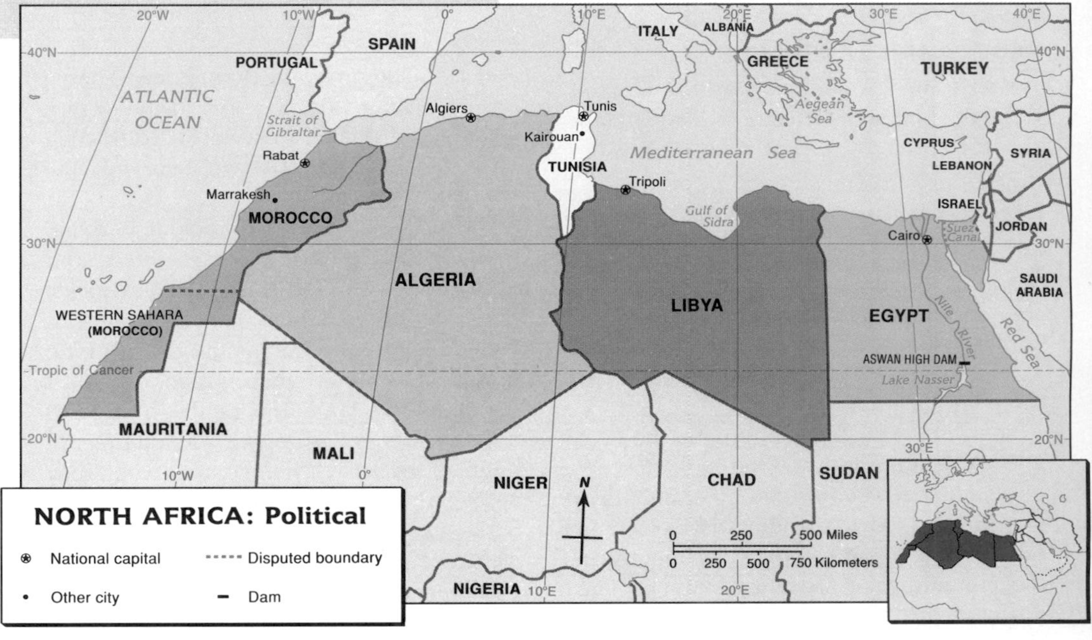

MAP SKILL: Rabat; Cairo

BACKGROUND INFORMATION

Education in North Africa North African countries are trying to increase their literacy rate, or the number of people that can read and write.

- About 48 percent of Egyptians over the age of 15 are literate, compared to the United States where 96 percent of those over 15 can read and write.
- One problem North African nations face is the lack of jobs for those who have college educations.

They camp in the ancient tombs because they cannot find any better place in which to live. Many people have trouble finding work and getting enough food.

You read in Chapter 17 that North Africa has little arable farmland. Since there are so many people to feed, it is not surprising that food shortages are common. Egypt's president has warned that if the country's population growth does not slow down, "We will have terrible famine, unemployment, and terrorism." Since the 1970s, riots over the high cost of food have shaken cities in Morocco, Algeria, and Tunisia as well as in Egypt.

THE FAMILY

Extended families are common among the Muslims of North Africa. In a typical Muslim North African family the bride moves in with her husband's family. Large extended families often share the same household. For example, a Moroccan teenager named Mokhtar lives in a house built hundreds of years ago by his Berber ancestors. His grandfather is the head of the family. An aunt and uncle and their children also live in the house.

High, windowless walls surround most North African houses to give families privacy. Unlike the houses in many suburban neighborhoods of the United States, North African houses have no backyards. Instead homes are built around courtyards.

Although Islamic law allows a man to have four wives if he can support them equally, few Muslim men have more than one wife. Many Muslim nations now make it illegal to have more than one wife. In 1980 Egypt passed a law that allowed a woman to divorce her husband if he took a second wife. Other Muslim countries have similar laws. Many Muslims object. They argue that governments should not interfere with sharia, or the laws of Islam.

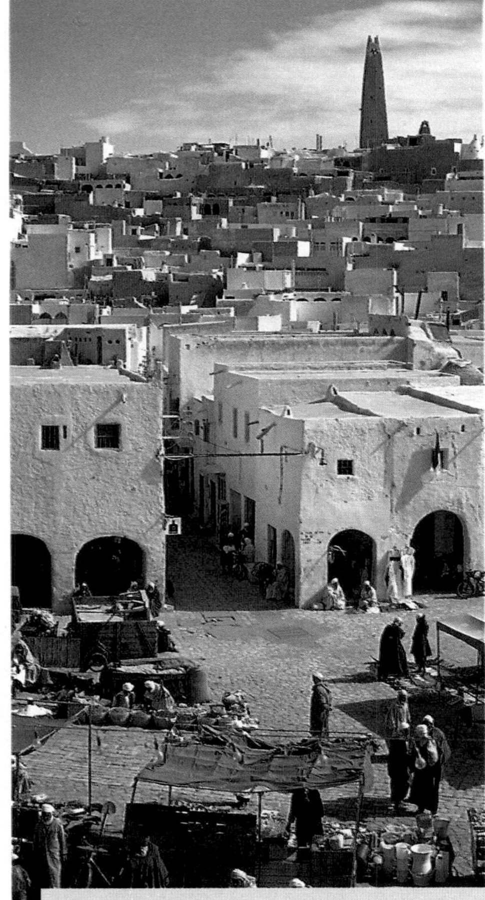

High walls surround the homes of many of North Africa's families.

ISLAMIC INFLUENCES

Hajji Ammar Baccar is not a young man. Yet 5 times a day he climbs 101 steps to the top of a minaret, or tower, that rises above the main mosque of the town of Kairouan (kâr wän'), Tunisia. From the top of the minaret, he calls out the Muslim chant "Allah u Akbar!"

Hajji Ammar Baccar is a **muezzin** (mü ez' ən), a crier who announces each of the five times a day when Muslims are sup-

Studying the Family Help students to recognize the role of extended families in North Africa and the passing on of houses from one generation to the next.

Ask students:

- **In North Africa how does marriage affect the size of a Muslim family?** (The bride moves in with the groom's family.)
- **What advantage do you think there might be to the style of house with an enclosed courtyard in North Africa?** (It provides privacy.)
- **What divorce law did Egypt pass in 1980?** (a law that allowed a woman to divorce her husband if he took more than one wife)
- **Even though other Muslim countries have passed similar divorce laws, why do many Muslims object to these new laws?** (They argue that governments should not interfere with Islamic law, which allows a man to have as many as four wives if he can support them equally.)

Understanding Islamic Influences Emphasize that Muslim law dominates daily life in North Africa.

Ask students:

- **What does a muezzin do?** (calls Muslims to prayer five times a day)

CURRICULUM CONNECTION

Art The Islamic religion has had a strong influence on North African art. Have students collect pictures of European art found in cathedrals and examples of North African art found in mosques. Display these pictures in class and ask students to write a paragraph describing the major differences between the two kinds of art.

Art Have students research what a North African neighborhood looks like. Then have each student make a model of a typical neighborhood. Their models should include homes, stores, a mosque, and vegetation. Have students display and compare the different models.

Analyzing Influences from Other Lands Discuss the influences that the French and English have had on North Africa. Suggest that North Africans are still reacting to changes brought about by European influences.

Applying the Lesson Have students review the lesson and make two lists about daily life in North Africa. One list should give all the traditional ways of life, and the other list should give modern influences.

CLOSE

Summarizing Students have read about the problems of overpopulation and the problems of traditional Islamic ways versus modern influences. Have students give examples of the effects of each problem.

Evaluating Use these questions to assess students' understanding.

- **What problems does Egypt's president fear might result if population growth does not slow down?** (famine, unemployment, terrorism)
- **What type of family life is common in North Africa?** (extended families)
- **How do influences from other lands cause conflict in North African countries?** (North African nations are torn between traditional Islamic ways and modern culture.)

Answers to Check Your Reading

1. the first people to live in North Africa
2. a decreasing death rate and the Islamic emphasis on large families
3. It shapes the way they live, work, and play, and influences government, education, and customs.
4. Students' answers may be about the conflicts between the traditional and the modern and/or the changes brought about by Western culture.

Independent Practice
Practice Book: page 105

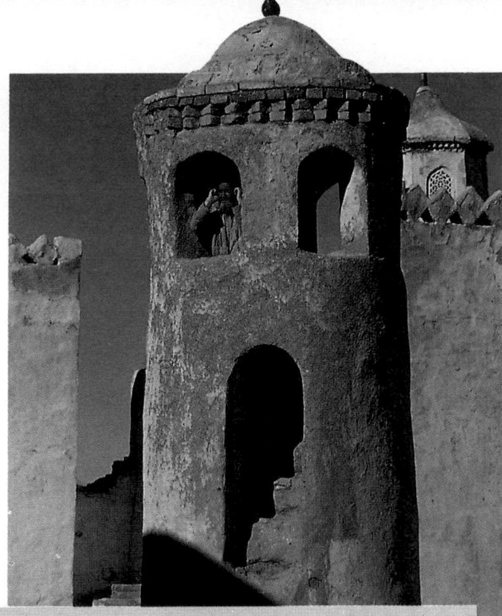

For centuries Muslim **muezzins**, or public criers, have climbed to the tops of minarets to announce the time of prayers.

stop whatever they are doing and pray. These times are at dawn, at noon, in the afternoon, at sunset, and at night. In cities where the human voice cannot be heard over the roar of traffic, tape-recorded calls to prayer are broadcast over loudspeakers.

Nine out of ten people in North Africa are Muslims. Islam shapes the way they live, work, and play. Islam also has a strong effect on the government, education, and customs of North Africa.

INFLUENCES FROM OTHER LANDS

Between 1830 and 1900 France and Great Britain won control of much of North Africa. In Egypt the British introduced their language, their books, and their ideas of government. In Algeria, Morocco, and Tunisia, which were colonized by France, the French language and customs were introduced. Today English and French are still widely used in North Africa as second languages.

In 1912 Italy made Libya a colony and ruled it until the end of World War II. Then France and Britain ruled Libya until 1952. As a result, Libya has several different European influences.

All the countries of North Africa are now independent. Yet some of the people in these countries are not happy. They want to cut all ties to their European past and return to a stricter form of Muslim life. For example, some Egyptian Muslim leaders urge the government to make all Egyptians obey Islamic laws. They say the changes are needed to stop "the invasion of Egypt by modern culture."

The question of how much Western culture should be borrowed and retained sparks bitter quarrels in North Africa, as it does in the Middle East. Many of the people in North Africa want to return to stricter Islamic ways.

GROWTH AND CONFLICT

In this lesson you have read that the people of North Africa share several problems caused by a rapidly growing population. Most of the cities in the area are overcrowded, and many countries do not grow enough food to feed their people. You have also read that most of the people in North Africa are Arabs who practice the Islamic religion. In the following lessons you will learn more about these people and how Islam affects North Africa.

Check Your Reading

1. Who are the Berbers?
2. Why has North Africa's population been growing so rapidly?
3. How does Islam affect the lives of the people of North Africa?
4. **THINKING SKILL:** Based on your reading of this lesson, what can you conclude about life in North Africa?

THINKING SKILL: Drawing Conclusions

390

MEETING INDIVIDUAL NEEDS

Reteaching (easy) Have students draw a scene showing a muezzin calling worshipers to prayer. Students should include and label the following: mosque, minaret, muezzin, and people praying as they kneel facing Mecca.

Extension (average) Have students make a list of Islamic influences on the government, education, and customs of North Africa.

Enrichment (challenging) Have students choose a North African city to research. Then have them write a report on the effects that population growth and modern influences have had on the city in the last few decades. Students should conclude their reports by predicting the future of the city in the year 2050.

LESSON 2

The Economy

READ TO LEARN

 **Key Vocabulary**

fellahin

 **Read Aloud**

"This is the best place on earth," says Ahmed, an Egyptian farmer in the Nile Delta. The Nile Delta, between Cairo and the Mediterranean Sea in Egypt, is one of the most fertile areas on the earth. "Truly Allah has blessed us," says Ahmed. "Soil, water, sun—we can grow everything!"

As you know, much of North Africa is desert. Little rain falls, and very little of the land is suitable for farming. Therefore, millions of people live crowded together in places like the Nile Delta. Like everyone else in North Africa, they know how important water is to the future of their country.

Read for Purpose

1. WHAT YOU KNOW: What major problem faces the people of North Africa today?
2. WHAT YOU WILL LEARN: Why are water and oil so important to the economies of the countries of North Africa?

FARMERS AND FOOD SHORTAGES

Although only a tiny part of North Africa can be farmed, most of the people work on the land. More than one third of Egypt's people are fellahin (fel ə hēn'), or farmers. Most of them raise crops on small plots, using labor-intensive methods.

Ezzat, an Egyptian boy, lives on his grandfather's farm south of Cairo. When his grandfather dies, the 2.5-acre (1.0-ha) farm will be divided four ways among Ezzat's father and his three uncles. Even now the farm does not produce enough food to feed everyone who lives on it. Although Ezzat's grandfather and one uncle are farmers, his father is a camel driver. Another uncle works in a factory, and the third uncle is looking for a job.

Many North African children never go to high school. Instead they stay home to work on family farms. By the time he was 12 years old, Mokhtar, the Moroccan teenager whom you read about in the last lesson, had to quit school. Like Ezzat he was needed to work on his grandfather's farm. Today Mokhtar's jobs include hauling water from irrigation ditches to the fields and keeping irrigation ditches in good repair. During the walnut harvest he climbs the trees to collect the nuts.

Of the five countries of North Africa, only Morocco once grew enough to feed its people. It even exported nuts, fruits, and vegetables. But a severe drought and a plague of insects hurt Morocco's agriculture in the 1980s. As a result, Morocco had to import food.

WHAT YOU KNOW: This question refers to material in Lesson 1; rapid population growth in the area.

LESSON 2
pages 391–393

Lesson Theme Water and oil resources control the economies of North African nations.

Lesson Objectives

- Describe irrigation in North Africa.
- Describe the oil industry in North Africa.

PREPARE

Motivate Read the *Read Aloud* section to the class. Discuss why a delta is fertile and whether the reason explains why Ahmed is such a satisfied farmer.

Set Purpose Ask students to identify the connection between the answers to the *What You Know* question and the *What You Will Learn* question.

TEACH

Understanding Farmers and Food Shortages Discuss how land is divided among family members.

- **What is the meaning of fellahin?** (farmers)
- **What fraction of the Egyptian population farms for a living?** (more than one third)
- **What is one reason why many North African children do not go to high school?** (They stay home to work on family farms.)
- **Which is the only North African country that, until recently, grew enough food to feed its people?** (Morocco)

READING STRATEGY AND VOCABULARY DEVELOPMENT

Summarizing You may wish to have students continue to keep a journal summarizing important facts or you may have them write a newscast as a summary of the lesson. Help students to see that a television newscast is actually a summary of important information. Tell students that they will prepare a newscast on the economy of North Africa. Have them begin by previewing the lesson. Then have them make notes of important information that should be covered and prepare questions that should be answered by the newscast. Have students work in small groups to prepare their summary newscasts. Let them discuss the facts that each group focused on and compare and contrast the points that each group made.

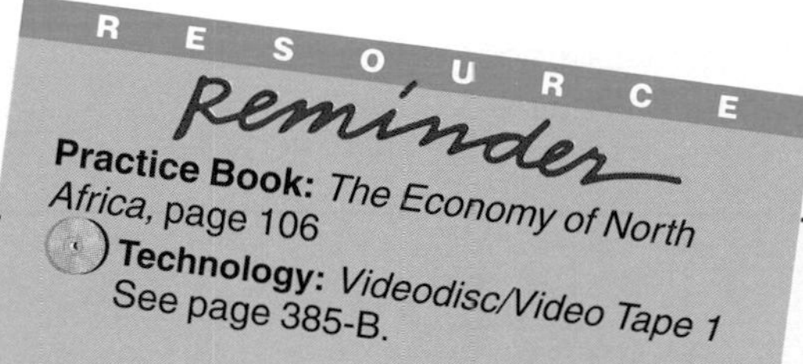

Discussing Farmers and Food Shortages Continue the discussion.

Ask students:

- **Why is there less land available for farming today?** (The land is being used for roads and housing.)
- **What seems to be the best long-range solution to the problem of feeding North Africa's people?** (finding ways to bring water to desert lands)

Assessing Irrigation

Ask students:

- **How were the Nile floodwaters a help to Egyptian fellahin before the Aswan High Dam was built?** (Floodwaters irrigated their fields and deposited rich soil.)
- **What advantages for Egypt resulted from the Aswan High Dam?** (30 percent more irrigated land; electric power; even flow of water each year; three crops per year instead of one)
- **What is one disadvantage of the Aswan High Dam?** (no silt deposits, so expensive artificial fertilizers must be used)
- *THINKING FURTHER:* **Why are experts uncertain if the benefits of the Aswan High Dam outweigh its harmful effects?** (The dam has provided for more irrigated farmland, but all the harmful effects may not have been seen as yet.)

Locating Oil and Other Industries Discuss the effects that oil discoveries have had on the developing economies of North Africa.

Ask students:

- **What effect has the discovery of oil had upon the Libyan economy?** (People get higher wages; the nation is richer than other North African nations.)
- **Which North African countries produce oil and natural gas?** (Libya and Algeria)
- **How has oil helped Egypt's economy?** (It helped Egypt develop from a one-crop economy to the second-largest industrialized nation in Africa.)

The other four North African nations usually have to buy food from different parts of the world. Egypt imports almost half of the food its people eat. The daily bill for food imported into Cairo alone is $10 million. Farms in Algeria can produce only one third of the food that the country needs. The rest must be imported.

Every year the countries of North Africa have to produce more and more food for their growing populations. Yet as the number of people increases, usable farmland is disappearing. Some farmland is being taken over to build new roads and houses. So North Africans have had to find ways of bringing water to remote lands so that they can be farmed. For example, after Egypt's giant Aswan High Dam was built, 30 percent more land could be farmed.

IRRIGATION—NEW AND OLD

For thousands of years, the Nile River regularly overflowed its banks each year in late summer. Egyptian fellahin relied on the flooding river to irrigate their fields. The floodwaters also brought silt, a fine clay that spread over the land and made it much more fertile.

Today the Nile no longer overflows its banks. The Aswan High Dam stops the river's annual floods by storing the water behind huge walls. Then the water is released steadily throughout the year and carried to the fields by canals.

Although the Aswan High Dam provides much-needed water and is also used to create electric power, it has created some problems. The land is now poorer because the rich silt that used to come with the flood waters has stopped. Expensive artificial fertilizers must instead be used. Over 25 years after the completion of the dam, experts are not certain whether its effects are helpful or harmful.

OIL AND OTHER INDUSTRIES

Unlike Egypt, Libya has no great river. The country is nearly all desert. Yet Libyans are more prosperous than most North Africans. Oil has transformed Libya from a poor desert country into a rich land. Today workers in a Libyan oil field earn more in one month than they earned in a year working as farmers. Oil and a small population keep Libya prosperous.

Libya and Algeria are major oil and natural gas producers. Tunisia, Egypt, and Morocco produce some oil, but they do not have the large reserves of their neighbors.

The Aswan High Dam (*left*) provides a steady supply of water for many Egyptians. Now some farmers can grow as many as three crops a year. Farm animals (*right*) make some farming less labor-intensive.

BACKGROUND INFORMATION

More About the Aswan High Dam Unexpected results have arisen from the building of the Aswan High Dam.

- The healthfulness of the water has been affected. Slow river flow means that parasites and disease organisms proliferate in the river water, infecting more people than before.
- Fish species in the Mediterranean are endangered because of the change in the water flow of the Nile.
- In some places either the water table is so high or salt residues from irrigation are so high that farming is becoming a problem.

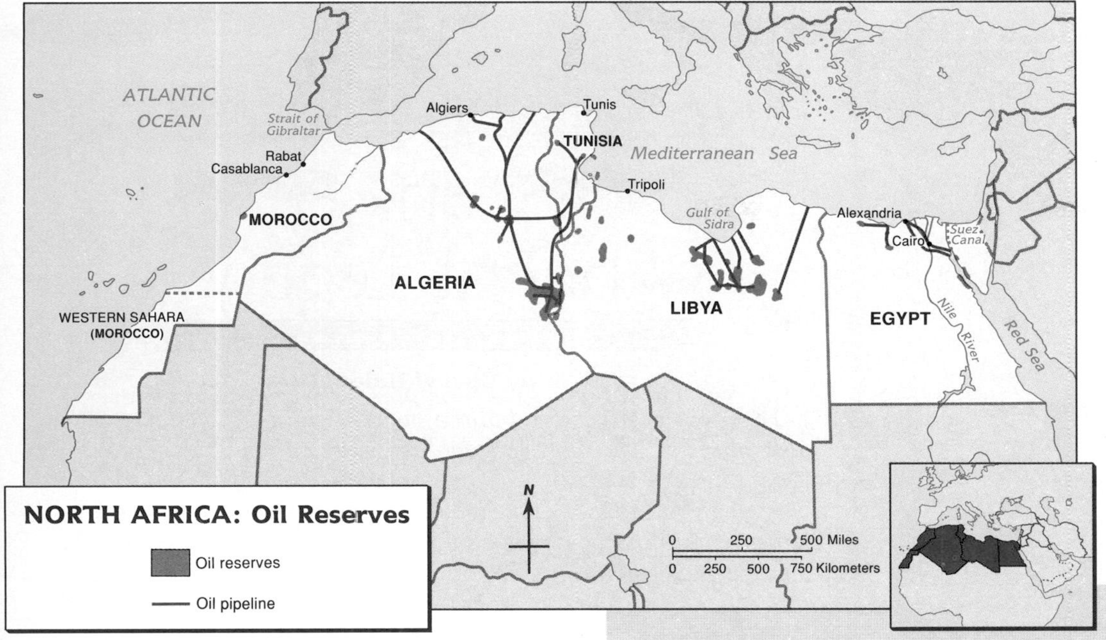

MAP SKILL: Oil reserves in North Africa have raised the standard of living of its people. Which countries have the most reserves?

Even having small oil reserves, though, can be a great help to a country. For example, Egypt today produces just enough oil so that it does not have to import any from foreign countries. This is an advantage for a country that is trying to develop its industries. Until recently the economy of Egypt was based on the production of just one crop—cotton. Now Egypt is the second-largest industrialized nation in Africa, after South Africa. It has some heavy industries, such as iron and steel manufacturing, and some light industries, such as textile manufacturing.

WATER AND OIL

When the nations of the Middle East and North Africa gained their independence after World War II, they were all poor, undeveloped lands. They have come a long way since that time.

In this lesson you have read how much North Africa depends on two important resources—water and oil. People in North Africa, like people everywhere, need water to live. But to North African countries, having oil is almost as important because it brings in badly-needed money from foreign countries. The economic future of North Africa depends heavily on how the people of this region use their water and oil resources.

Check Your Reading

1. What are *fellahin*?
2. How has the Aswan High Dam helped Egypt? What problems has it caused?
3. How does the future of North Africa depend on water and oil?
4. **THINKING SKILL:** Do you think that the quotation in the Read Aloud section on page 391 is biased? Why or why not?

MAP SKILL: Algeria and Libya

THINKING SKILL: Recognizing Bias

393

EXTENDING MAP SKILLS

Have students study the oil reserves map on this page.

Ask students:

- **Which country in North Africa has the least amount of oil reserves?** (Morocco)
- **Which two cities in Egypt are connected by an oil pipeline?** (Alexandria and Cairo)
- *THINKING FURTHER:* **Why do most of the pipelines run south to north?** (to take oil to the Mediterranean Sea for export)

Applying the Lesson Have students list the advantages and disadvantages of the Aswan High Dam.

CLOSE

Summarizing Students have learned how water and oil affect the economies of North African nations. Ask students to explain whether oil or water is the more important resource.

Evaluating Have students write a paragraph describing the connections among overpopulation, water, and oil in North Africa.

Answers to Check Your Reading

1. Egyptian farmers
2. It provides electric power, 30 percent more irrigated land, steady water flow, and three crops a year. There is a loss of topsoil deposits.
3. Water provides food for survival; oil brings money for development and a higher living standard.
4. Students might suggest that use of the word *best* makes it biased.

Independent Practice
Practice Book: page 106

MEETING INDIVIDUAL NEEDS

Reteaching (easy) Have students research the Aswan High Dam to find out how electricity and water from the dam reach the villages and the fields. Have students present their findings in diagram form.

Extension (average) Have students research and list the ways in which the oil industry has benefited the people of Libya.

Enrichment (challenging) Ask students to look up the meaning of the term *gross national product.* Have students research the gross national product of each North African nation and rank each nation in a list from the highest to the lowest gross national product. Then have each student write an essay explaining why the countries rank as they do.

LEGACY
pages 394–397

Lesson Theme Boat building is an Egyptian legacy that goes back thousands of years and is characterized by remarkable technological innovations such as the sail.

Lesson Objectives
- Describe the discovery of the boat of the pharaoh Khufu.
- Identify Egyptian advances in boat-building technology.
- Discuss the voyages to Punt and Lebanon and the huge capacity of ancient Egyptian ships.
- Describe a trip on a Nile sailboat today.

1 PREPARE

Motivate Have students describe experiences they have had on boats. Ask them to think about what makes a boat seaworthy.

Set Purpose Focus students' attention with the following question. Why are many cities located on rivers? Have students read the introduction. Ask them to think about the concluding suggestion while they read the rest of the lesson.

2 TEACH

Understanding the Concept of Legacies Ask students why they think a boat-building legacy developed in ancient Egypt. (Egyptians lived along the Nile and relied on the river for travel and food.)

Discussing an Amazing Discovery Help students to understand that archaeological discoveries are important to our understanding of the past.

Ask students:

- **What was Kamal el-Mallakh looking for?** (two pits containing buried boats)

Egyptian Boat Building an Ancient Legacy

by Cheryl Haldane

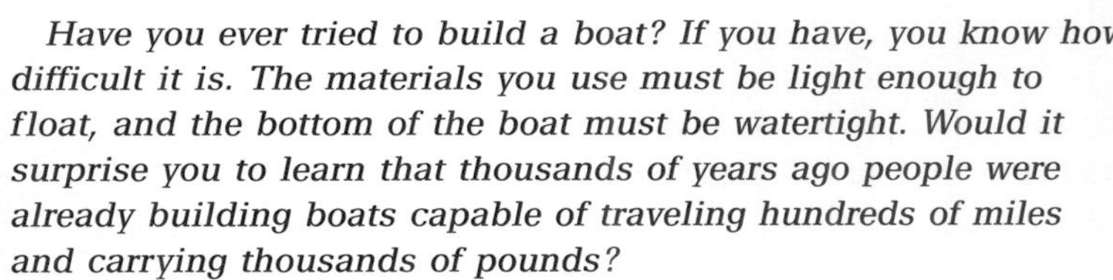

Have you ever tried to build a boat? If you have, you know how difficult it is. The materials you use must be light enough to float, and the bottom of the boat must be watertight. Would it surprise you to learn that thousands of years ago people were already building boats capable of traveling hundreds of miles and carrying thousands of pounds?

As you read in Lesson 2, people have been living along the Nile River, the "superhighway of Egypt," for thousands of years. We will never know when they first tied together bundles of papyrus plant stems to build boats. But we do know that boat building and sailing became important traditions in Egypt. Egyptians today still sail the Nile's waters, and they see some of the same sights their ancestors saw more than 5,000 years ago. As you read this lesson, think about why advances in boat building have played such an important role in human history.

AN AMAZING DISCOVERY

In 1954 a young Egyptian archaeologist was at work beside the huge pyramids just outside of Cairo. His name was Kamal el-Mallakh (kə′ mol el′ mə′ lokh) and he was directing the removal of a pile of sand and rubble next to an ancient wall. El-Mallakh suspected that under the sand and rubble were two pits containing buried boats.

Weeks later, el-Mallakh chiseled a hole in a huge stone his workers had uncovered. After he cut deeper and deeper through the stone, el-Mallakh finally was able to peer into the darkness of one of the pits. At first he could not see a thing, but a sweet smell began to fill his nose. It was the smell of cedar wood. El-Mallakh says that smell made him sure a boat was in the pit. With a little more work, what a boat el-Mallakh discovered.

394

READING STRATEGY AND VOCABULARY DEVELOPMENT

Summarizing Review with students the importance of summarizing important facts. After they have read the lesson, have students create a journal that might have been written by Kamal el-Mallakh during his work recovering the Khufu boat. As in Lesson 1, students may enjoy writing their journals in the first person. Tell students that their journals should include a summary of the information in this lesson. Remind students that the information contained in each journal should be organized chronologically or thematically.

THE KHUFU BOAT

Imagine you are a child in ancient Egypt. You are kneeling to draw water from the Nile in a large pottery jar. When you look up, the beautiful boat you see in the photo at right is gliding past. This boat is towed by another boat, and it is steered by oars held by royal servants of Khufu (kü′ fü), a ruler the ancient Egyptians considered their living god.

Today the boat discovered by Kamal el-Mallakh majestically fills a museum next to the Great Pyramid of Khufu. The boat was built in about 2550 B.C. and is more than 140 feet (43 m) long. That's almost half the length of a football field! Built of cedar wood planks, the Khufu boat makes people catch their breath when they see it. Although at least 4,500 years old, it looks as if it could float on the Nile today.

Khufu's boat is an example of the advanced technology of ancient Egypt. In the diagram on the right you can see how the planks of the hull were sewed together by ropes made from grass. No nails were used. Only the ropes laced back and forth across it and small pieces of wood called tenons kept the hull fastened together.

Khufu Hull

tenons

One of the boat's most remarkable features was its "air-conditioned" cabin. Water was poured onto grass mats laid on a frame above the cabin's roof. As the breeze moved air around and under the mats, the water slowly evaporated and cooled the cabin. As you have read, temperatures in North Africa have been recorded as high as 136°F. (58°C). Imagine how nice it must have felt to sit in the air-conditioned cabin on a hot summer day.

395

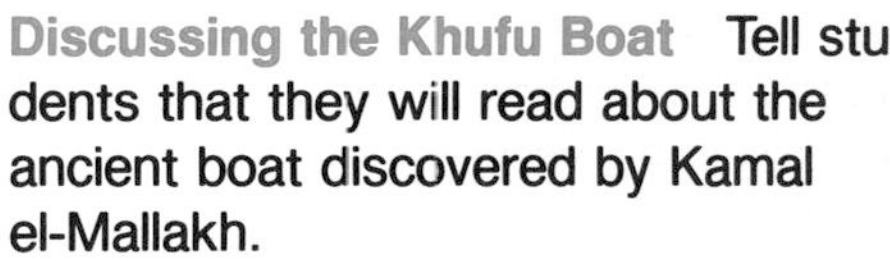

Discussing the Khufu Boat Tell students that they will read about the ancient boat discovered by Kamal el-Mallakh.

Ask students:

- **About how long is the Khufu boat?** (about half the length of a football field)
- **How is the Khufu boat an example of the advanced technology of ancient Egypt?** (The hull was beautifully constructed even though nails had not yet been invented; the boat had an "air-conditioned" cabin.)
- *THINKING FURTHER:* **How did the use of grass mats create the effect of air-conditioning?** (Water was poured on the mats. As the breeze moved air around the mats, the water evaporated and cooled the cabin.)

EXTENDING DIAGRAM SKILLS

Direct students' attention to the diagram on this page.

Ask students:

- **What does this diagram show?** (how the hull of Khufu's boat was held together)
- **What are tenons?** (small pieces of wood that help to hold the planks of the hull together)
- **How are the planks of the hull held together?** (by the tenons and grass ropes threaded through the planks to "sew" them together)

BACKGROUND INFORMATION

About the Great Pyramid of Khufu The Khufu boat was buried next to the pyramid built as the tomb of the pharaoh Khufu (called Cheops by the Greeks). Khufu lived around 2600 B.C. Little is known about his life, but historians believe that only a powerful ruler could have built such a huge tomb. The pyramid contains more than 2 million stone blocks averaging 2.5 tons (2.3 metric t) each. It was originally 481 feet (147 m) tall and its base covers 13 acres (5 ha). Although no one knows how long it took to build the pyramid, historians believe that 100,000 people may have been involved in its construction.

Multicultural Perspectives Although most people think of Egypt when pyramids are mentioned, many large pyramids also are found in the Western Hemisphere. Over a 2,000 year period from about 1200 B.C. to A.D. 900, hundreds of pyramids were erected in present-day Mexico, Honduras, and Guatemala. Unlike the Egyptian pyramids, many of these structures had flat tops and served as large platforms for temples. In general, the pyramids of Mexico and Central America are less tall than the Egyptian pyramids, but some of them are far larger. The 210-foot (64-m) tall pyramid at Cholua, in Mexico, covers more than 30 acres (12 ha). Ask students why they think pyramids were built by so many people in different parts of the world.

Discussing the First Sail Help students to understand how technology spreads from its point of origin to nearby areas. You may wish to refer to the Wall Maps of the Middle East and North Africa.

Ask students:

- **How did sailboats change the way people traveled?** (They allowed people to journey farther and faster on ships than they ever had before.)
- *THINKING FURTHER:* **How do you think that the technology of the sail may have passed from ancient Egyptians to the Phoenicians and the ancient Greeks?** (Other cultures may have recognized the benefits of Egyptian sailing ships and learned the technology.)

Discussing Great Voyages Make sure students understand the genius of ancient Egyptian boat builders.

Ask students:

- **How do historians today know that Egyptian boats were able to carry tremendous loads?** (Ancient wall paintings show large ships loaded with huge stone monuments.)
- *THINKING FURTHER:* **How do you think that Egyptian boats were able to carry such heavy loads?** (Possible answers include: because they were so strong and so well constructed.)

Building a boat like Khufu's 4,500 years ago was a lot like building a spacecraft today. The best materials and the finest craftworkers were used, and the result was tremendously expensive. The cedar wood came from Lebanon, which was a long journey away by sea. The Egyptians had to trade treasured goods such as gold, perfumes, exotic feathers, and animal skins for the cedar. Then they towed large rafts of cedar logs across the eastern Mediterranean Sea and along the Nile.

THE FIRST SAIL

Early Egyptian advances in boat-building technology influenced the way that boats were built in other parts of the world. It is possible that the sailboat was first developed in Egypt, although we do not know for sure. We do know that the oldest picture of a sailboat comes from the side of an ancient Egyptian vase. The invention of the sail changed the way people traveled. The sail allowed ships to journey farther and faster than they ever had before. The sail may have been one of the inventions the ancient Egyptians passed on to later civilizations around the Mediterranean Sea, such as the ancient Greeks and the Phoenicians.

GREAT VOYAGES

Ancient wall paintings tell us much about how boats were used in ancient Egypt. Some paintings show large ships loaded with cattle and grain, part of expeditions to distant lands such as Punt, which was located in what is now Ethiopia and Somalia. Perhaps the most incredible feat of ancient Egyptian boats was their ability to move gigantic stone monuments from quarries in the south of Egypt to temples farther north. One wall carving, which is drawn below, shows a boat carrying two needle-shaped monuments end to end. The boat would have been built much like the Khufu vessel, with thick planks fastened together with wood and rope. We know that

396

BACKGROUND INFORMATION

About the Khufu Boats In 1985, 31 years after the first Khufu boat was discovered, an international team of scientists confirmed Kamal el-Mallakh's suspicion. A second ship lies in the other underground chamber beside the Pyramid of Khufu. Historians and archaeologists have debated the purpose of these two marvelous ships. Most believe that Khufu, who was entombed in the pyramid that bears his name, intended the boats for his use in the afterlife. Often everything a pharaoh was thought to need in the afterlife was buried with him, or nearby.

In their discovery of the second Khufu boat in 1985, archaeologists made use of space-age technology. In order not to disturb the ship or the chamber's air, which they hoped to analyze, the scientists first determined the best location for drilling. A profile of the pit was obtained with the use of ground-penetrating radar. Then the team drilled the hole an inch at a time, removing stone powder with a vacuum after each stage. Later a camera probe that was only 3 inches (80 mm) in diameter was inserted into the chamber. It was finally decided to leave the boat sealed in its chamber for future archaeologists to excavate.

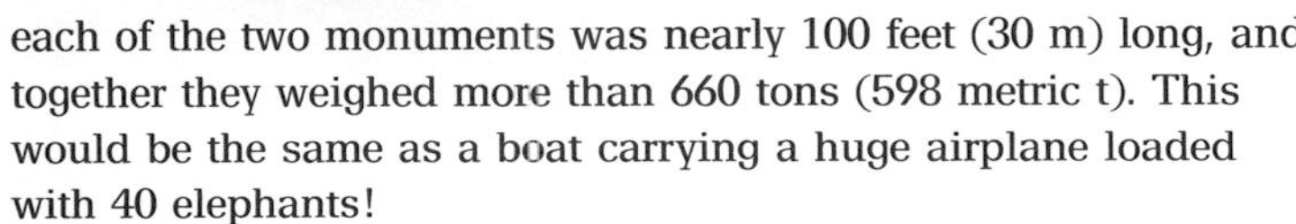

each of the two monuments was nearly 100 feet (30 m) long, and together they weighed more than 660 tons (598 metric t). This would be the same as a boat carrying a huge airplane loaded with 40 elephants!

LIFE ON THE RIVER TODAY

If you visited Egypt today, you would see some of the same sights a student might have seen in ancient Egypt. Large boats still sail the Nile carrying people, as well as cargoes of bricks, pottery jars, animals, and stone. Of course, today most Egyptians live in modern cities like Cairo, but some families still live on small boats and fish in the Nile. The life-giving river irrigates nearby fields, creating a narrow band of lush green growth in the desert sands.

Picture yourself sailing on the Nile. You are in a small sailboat called a felucca (fə lü' kə), which is not that different from boats that have sailed the Nile for ages. You smell the earthy scent of the river, and if you only close your eyes, a cool breeze can transport you to another time. The mast creaks as the sail strains against it, and the captain sings softly to himself about the beauty of the river.

Now, like a modern Egyptian, drink your hibiscus tea and eat some honeyed bread. Remember that your river trip is the result of a boat-building legacy that goes back thousands of years.

Why did boat building become an important legacy in ancient Egypt and elsewhere?

397

Discussing Life on the River Today Ask students to discuss what they know about Egypt today. Make sure they understand that most Egyptians live in Cairo, a huge modern city.

Ask students:

- **Why is the Nile called a "life-giving" river?** (because it allows people to plant fields and grow crops in a very dry region)

Applying the Lesson Have students write a paragraph comparing other advances in transportation to the development of the sail. Students may wish to focus on twentieth-century advances such as the automobile and the airplane.

3 CLOSE

Summarizing Students have read about the legacy of boat building and that Egyptian technology influenced boat building in other parts of the world.

Evaluating Ask students the question at the bottom of the pupil page. (Possible answers include: because boats, particularly sailboats, provide an efficient way to travel; because many people live near rivers, seas, or oceans.)

MEETING INDIVIDUAL NEEDS

Reteaching (easy) Have students imagine that they are accompanying Kamal el-Mallakh on his archaeological dig. Have them write several paragraphs describing how he might have felt upon the discovery of the Khufu boat.

Extension (average) Ask students to find pictures of modern sailboats. Have them draw or clip pictures of the boats for a classroom display. Each picture should have a label comparing it to the Khufu boat.

Enrichment (challenging) Have students do further research on ancient Egypt. They may wish to focus on how the pyramids were built, the tombs of pharaohs such as Tutankhamen, or ancient Egyptian beliefs about the afterlife. After they are done, have students present reports to the class sharing what they have learned.

LESSON 3
pages 398–399

Lesson Theme After gaining independence from the European powers, the nations of North Africa developed a variety of governments, usually dominated by one strong ruler.

Lesson Objectives
- Explain the effects of foreign rule on North Africa.
- Describe North Africa's patterns of government.
- Explain the conflicts in North Africa today.

PREPARE

Motivate Read the *Read Aloud* section to the class. Discuss with students the ways in which the Algerian Revolution was the same as and different from the American Revolution.

Set Purpose Use the *What You Know* question to establish the similarities among the governments of the Middle East and those of North Africa. Ask students how the answers to the *What You Will Learn* question can be compared with the problems that the United States faced after gaining independence.

Summarizing the Effects of Foreign Rule Discuss colonialism.

Ask students:

- **What was one benefit Algeria received from the French? What was the negative side of this benefit?** (The French introduced many technological improvements; colonialism and the fact that Algerians did not share the wealth.)

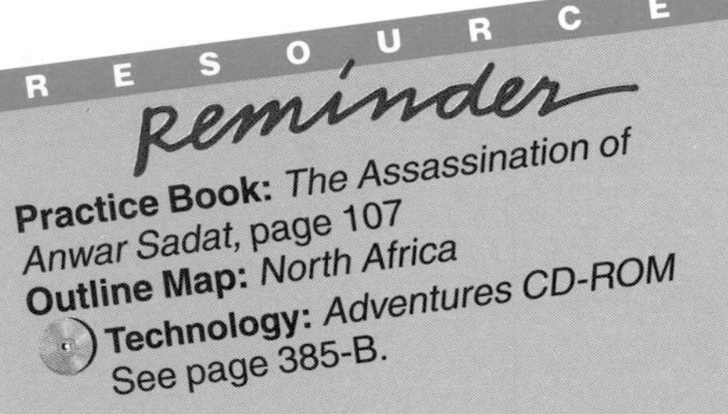

Practice Book: *The Assassination of Anwar Sadat*, page 107
Outline Map: *North Africa*
Technology: *Adventures CD-ROM*
See page 385-B.

LESSON 3

The Government

READ TO LEARN

Key Vocabulary	**Key Places**
colonialism	Algeria

Read Aloud

In 1954 a revolt against French rule began in Algeria. First there were scattered attacks on police stations and other government buildings. Soon rebels armed with old rifles and homemade explosives were fighting a well-equipped French army of 500,000 soldiers.

At least one half million Algerians died in the eight-year war that followed. But when the shooting finally stopped, Algeria had won its independence. Although the new nation faced great challenges ahead, its people were proud and hopeful.

Read for Purpose

1. WHAT YOU KNOW: What kind of governments are common in the Middle East?
2. WHAT YOU WILL LEARN: What problems did many of the countries of North Africa face after gaining their independence?

EFFECTS OF FOREIGN RULE

At the beginning of this century, all of North Africa was ruled by European nations. Great Britain controlled Egypt (as you read in Lesson 1). France ruled Tunisia and **Algeria**, and Italy ruled Libya. Morocco was split into two colonies, one ruled by France and one by Spain.

During more than 130 years of colonial rule in Algeria, the French introduced many improvements, such as modern irrigation systems and good railroads. Yet most Algerians received few of the benefits. Europeans owned the best land and most of the businesses. They also held the highest-paying jobs.

Most Algerians resented **colonialism**. Colonialism is the control of a country as a colony by another country. Resentment against colonialism led to revolutions like the one described above.

PATTERNS OF GOVERNMENT

No two governments in North Africa are exactly alike, but they all follow similar patterns. Morocco is a kingdom, and the other countries are republics. Yet they all have strong central rule by one leader.

King Hassan II of Morocco has a great deal of political power. He can suspend the legislature and can issue rules and regulations that have the force of law. At the same time King Hassan has worked hard to modernize Morocco. One of his first official acts was to issue a constitution giving equal rights to all citizens.

WHAT YOU KNOW: This question refers to information in Chapter 18, Lesson 3; governments with absolute or powerful rulers.

READING STRATEGY AND VOCABULARY DEVELOPMENT

Summarizing Reinforce the idea that a summary is a way of identifying and organizing important information. Have students review the summarizing strategy. For this lesson have students create pamphlets that summarize the governments of North Africa. To do this students should first preview the lesson and make a list of questions that will be answered in the pamphlet. Have students include the similarities and differences among North African governments and those of other countries they have studied.

The president of Egypt is another North African ruler with a great deal of power. Egypt's president can dissolve the legislature of his country. He can also order people to be imprisoned without trial.

In most of the countries of North Africa, single political parties hold great power. For example, in Libya only one political party is permitted. Algeria also had a government that permitted only one political party. But in 1991, Algeria let candidates from other parties run in the national election. More than half the candidates elected wanted a strict Islamic Republic.

Before 1978 Egypt was also a one-party government. Now several small opposition parties hold seats in the Egyptian legislature. However, the Arab Socialist Union, the political party that has governed Egypt for more than 40 years, is still in control.

CONFLICT AND PEACE

North Africa has long been a land of conflict. Egypt, for example, had a longstanding conflict with Israel. As you have read, since 1948 Israel has fought several bitter wars against Egypt and other Arab countries.

In 1979 President Anwar Sadat of Egypt broke with his Arab neighbors and made peace with Israel. After 30 years of war he signed a peace treaty that stated that Israel had a right to exist.

Because no other Arab nation would accept the new peace treaty, Sadat's decision isolated Egypt from the Arab world. Even some Egyptians were upset by the treaty. In 1981 a small group of Egyptian terrorists assassinated Sadat.

At the time, other Arab nations disagreed with Sadat, but Egypt ended up gaining from the treaty. It regained land that it had lost in the Sinai peninsula, and it gained a certain amount of security from destructive wars.

Anwar Sadat (*left*) of Egypt and Menachem Begin of Israel discuss peace in 1979.

All the governments of North Africa are faced with conflicts. People disagree about how to interpret the laws of Islam. Most of all, they disagree about how governments should deal with rapid population growth and limited resources.

AN UNCERTAIN FUTURE

The countries of North Africa have a troubled past but hope for a better future. You have read that after they won their independence, they all set up new governments. Today the countries' leaders vary from kings to presidents. These leaders have the responsibility of trying to keep their countries at peace in the years ahead.

Check Your Reading

1. Which European nations controlled North Africa during the 1900s?
2. What problems did the newly independent countries of North Africa face?
3. Why was President Sadat of Egypt assassinated?
4. THINKING SKILL: Governments change, sometimes very quickly. How could you determine if the information in this lesson is still accurate?

THINKING SKILL: Evaluating Accuracy

Looking at Patterns of Government

Ask students:

- **How do the powers of the king of Morocco differ from those of the kings in Europe?** (The king of Morocco has more powers. He can suspend legislatures and issue rules and regulations.)
- **How do political parties in the countries of North Africa and in the United States differ?** (Many North African countries have only one party, whereas the United States has several.)

Exploring Conflict and Peace Discuss the three major disagreements in North Africa today: the Arab-Israeli conflict; the interpretation of the laws of Islam; the ways of dealing with population growth and limited resources.

Applying the Lesson Have students make a list of the pros and cons of having strong central rule by one leader.

3 CLOSE

Summarizing Students have learned that the types of leaders in North Africa vary from kings to presidents. Ask students how practices formed under colonial rule might influence the governments of North Africa today.

Evaluating Use the *Check Your Reading* questions (answers given below) to assess students' understanding.

Answers to Check Your Reading

1. Great Britain, France, Italy, Spain
2. having to set up new governments, sometimes in postwar circumstances
3. land and who it belongs to
4. by using fast-breaking new sources, such as newspapers, newsmagazines, and newsbroadcasts

Independent Practice
Practice Book: page 107

MEETING INDIVIDUAL NEEDS

Reteaching (easy) Have students make a chart showing the leaders of the countries of North Africa.

Extension (average) Have students research the story of the Algerian Revolution and make a time line of its key events. Have them write a paragraph comparing these events with key events of the American Revolution.

Enrichment (challenging) Have students choose a country of North Africa. Then have them research that country and make a list of the powers held by its leader. Have students write the information for each country on the outline map of North Africa (found in the Teacher's Resource Center).

SKILLS Lesson
pages 400–401

Lesson Theme Asking good questions involves generating questions that will get you the information you need to know.

Lesson Objective
- Identify one way to ask good questions and apply the procedure to selected topics.

PREPARE

Motivate Before students read the introductory paragraphs, ask them if they have ever wanted to ask a question but did not do so. Then ask them to explain why not. Have volunteers give examples from their own experiences of how they learned something as a result of asking questions (such as, asking for directions). Then ask them how they knew which questions to ask. Have students read the introductory paragraphs and describe a "good" question.

Set Purpose Tell students that in this lesson they will learn how to ask good questions.

TEACH

Trying the Skill Have students read the paragraph and answer the questions that follow it. Tell students that if they have trouble completing the assignment, they may refer to the *Helping Yourself* section on the next page.

Thinking About Thinking Focus on Question 1. *Ask:* What did you do first? Why? Next? Why? and so on. Which words did you use to begin your questions? Why? Write several lists of the steps and words cited on the chalkboard. Brainstorm other question starters and discuss the kinds of information they would produce.

RESOURCE Reminder
Practice Book: *Asking the Right Questions,* page 108

BUILDING SKILLS
THINKING SKILLS

Asking Questions

Imagine that your teacher has divided your class into groups. The teacher tells each group to research and prepare an oral report on one country of North Africa. The reports are due in one week, and each report should last for no longer than ten minutes. Then the teacher asks, "Are there any questions?"

What questions would you ask? How did you know which questions to ask? Questions help you to learn what you want to know. The more skilled you are at asking questions, the easier it will be for you to get the information you need.

Trying the Skill

You have read that nine out of ten people in North Africa are Muslims, and that Islam shapes the way they live, work, and play. Suppose you want to know more about the religion of Islam. List three questions that would help you to get this information.

1. How did you come up with your questions?
2. What information would the answers to your questions provide?

400

BUILDING CITIZENSHIP

Asking Questions as a Citizen Point out to students that asking good questions can help people to become better citizens. For example, in order to know which candidate to support in an election, voters need to ask questions about the candidates and about their stands on different issues. Ask students for other situations in which citizens need to ask good questions in order to make informed decisions.

HELPING YOURSELF

The steps on the left will help you to ask questions to learn what you want to know. The example on the right shows one way to use these steps to learn more about the Islamic religion.

One Way to Ask Questions	Example
1. Identify the topic or subject.	The topic is the religion of Islam.
2. Determine what you want to know about the topic.	Do you want to learn facts or to evaluate the accuracy of information?
3. Brainstorm questions that will help you. • To find factual information, ask *who*, *what*, *where*, *when*, and *how*. • To find the meaning or importance of a topic or event, ask *why* or "What conclusions can I draw?" • To evaluate information, ask questions to distinguish fact from opinion, or to identify bias or point of view.	Asking "What are the main beliefs of Islam?" will help you to gather facts. Asking "Why is a pilgrimage to Mecca so important to Muslims?" will help you to understand the importance of this event. Asking "What information is not included?" can help you to determine a writer's bias or point of view.
4. Review your questions to be sure they focus on what you want to know. Cross out those that are not helpful.	A question such as "What is the population of Mecca?" will not help you to learn about Muslim beliefs.
5. Arrange the remaining questions in order, from the easiest to the most difficult.	The easiest questions are usually ones that ask for facts. The facts will help you to answer the more difficult questions.
6. Ask and then answer your questions.	Asking questions will help you to find the information you need.

Applying the Skill

Morocco was once a colony of France. Suppose you wanted to learn about how Morocco became an independent country.

1. Which question would probably be the easiest to answer?
   a. When did Morocco declare its independence from France?
   b. Why did the French want to control Morocco?
   c. How did the events of World War II affect French control of Morocco?
2. For which of the following would you need to ask questions to identify the writer's point of view?
   a. an encyclopedia chart on Morocco
   b. the French governor-general's account of Morocco's struggle for independence
   c. a textbook time line of the history of North Africa
3. What are some questions you would ask to learn how Morocco became an independent country?

Reviewing the Skill

1. Name four steps you can follow to ask good questions.
2. Why is it important for you to ask your own questions?

Helping Yourself Point out that this section outlines a procedure for generating good questions. Explain that there may be other procedures but that these guidelines should prove to be helpful to most students. Have students compare the lists of steps and question starters on the chalkboard to those listed in *Helping Yourself* and draw up a composite list for future reference.

Applying the Skill Tell students that they will now use what they have learned to generate a new set of questions. Have them read about Morocco and answer the questions that follow. Remind them to refer to the steps and question starters outlined on the chalkboard and in *Helping Yourself* if they need assistance. Have students read pages 398–399 to find answers to their questions.

CLOSE

Reviewing the Skill Have students read their answers to Question 1 aloud. Use these answers as a starting point for students to explain why knowing how to ask good questions is an important skill and to cite situations outside school in which they might find the skill helpful.

Independent Practice

Practice Book: page 108

ANSWERS TO SKILLS QUESTIONS

Applying the Skill

1. a
2. b
3. When did Morocco become independent? Who were the leaders of the independence movement? Why did France grant Morocco independence?

Reviewing the Skill

1. (a) Determine what you want to know. (b) List your questions, using question starters that will help you to find out this information. (c) Cross out questions that are not helpful. (d) Arrange questions from the easiest to the most difficult.
2. If you do not ask questions, you will learn only what someone else wants you to know.

LESSON 4
pages 402–403

Lesson Theme Traditional themes are reflected in the arts and in the leisure activities of North Africa.

Lesson Objectives
- Describe the traditional art and literature of North Africa.
- Explain the role of religious holidays in North African life.

PREPARE

Motivate Have students close their eyes while you read the *Read Aloud* section to them. Ask students to visualize the scene as you read. Ask how this vision compares with noisy, busy city scenes they have witnessed.

Set Purpose Use the *What You Know* question to review ways in which religious holidays can bring people together in a richer social life. Have students keep the *What You Will Learn* question in mind as they read this lesson.

TEACH

Discussing Traditions in Art and Literature Help students to recognize Islamic influences on folk art and literature in North Africa.

Ask students:

- **How is folk art shown on Muslim homes?** (by wall paintings of pilgrimages done in a style that is 4,000 years old)
- **What are two favorite themes of North African artists?** (the importance of keeping Islamic traditions alive in a constantly changing world; the way in which modern influences and traditional values challenge one another.)

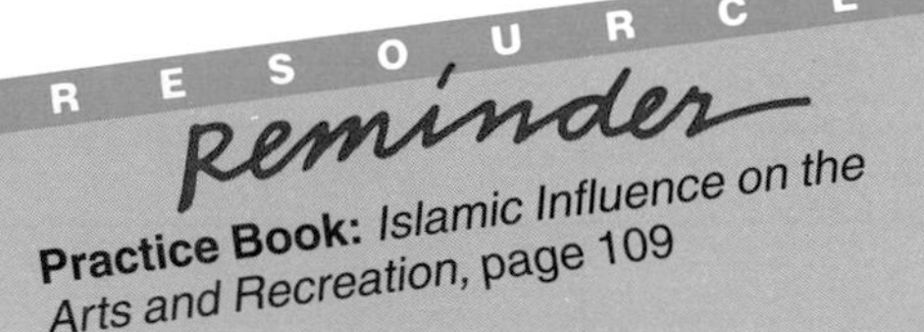

Practice Book: *Islamic Influence on the Arts and Recreation*, page 109

LESSON 4

Arts and Recreation

READ TO LEARN

Key Vocabulary

Ramadan

Read Aloud

Jemaa el Fna—the Assembly of the Dead. What a strange name for a place that is so alive, the noisy, vibrant center of the dusty oasis city of Marrakesh. The broad plaza pulsed day and night, week in and week out, with the beat of drums, the whine and wail of flutes, the twang of three-string instruments—mixed with shouts, singing, and amplified readings from the Koran.

Visitors to Marrakesh, Morocco, have always been fascinated by the bazaar held in the city's big market square. Like so many other things in North Africa, the bazaar in Marrakesh is also influenced by the rules of Islam.

Read for Purpose

1. **WHAT YOU KNOW:** What are some religious holidays that are celebrated in Western Europe?
2. **WHAT YOU WILL LEARN:** How do the arts of North Africa reflect both traditional and modern styles?

TRADITIONS IN ART AND LITERATURE

In a typical North African bazaar, like the one in Marrakesh, you can see metalworkers hammering copper, silver, and other metals just as their ancestors did for hundreds of years. Most of the designs are traditional. North Africans take pride in making things the way their ancestors did.

The arts of North Africa are related to those of the Middle East. For example, Moroccan rugs and Turkish carpets are similar in design.

Egypt has its own artistic traditions. For more than 5,000 years artists in Egypt have created fine wall paintings, elegant jewelry, and other works of art. Many modern Egyptian artists use traditional themes in their work. Like other North Africans they see no reason to believe that "modern" art is better than traditional art.

Let's look at an example. As you know, the Koran commands Muslims to make a *hajj*, or pilgrimage, to the holy city of Mecca at least once in a lifetime. After an Egyptian family makes this important journey, they may paint pictures of the pilgrimage on the outside of their house. On the walls you might see drawings of the airplanes and taxis they took, as well as the places they visited along the way to Mecca.

If you look closely at the pictures, you would notice that people's heads and feet

WHAT YOU KNOW: This question refers to information in Unit 3; Christmas, Easter, and feast days of the saints.

READING STRATEGY AND VOCABULARY DEVELOPMENT

Summarizing If you do not want to have students continue the journal entries begun in Lesson 1, have students develop a summary of festival days of the region. Students' summaries can reflect what they might see on different festival days and can include a bazaar. After students have finished, review their summaries aloud, comparing and contrasting the points that everyone in the class included. You may wish to prepare a chart of those points that everyone found important.

are drawn in profile while their bodies are drawn facing forward. This is the style that ancient Egyptians painted in 4000 years ago.

Islam influences the arts and literature of North Africa, just as it affects many other aspects of life in the area. Egyptian poets, novelists, and playwrights are widely read throughout the Arabic-speaking world. One of their favorite themes is the importance of keeping Islamic traditions alive in a constantly changing world. This idea appears in stories, poems, plays, and many television programs.

Another popular theme with artists is the way modern influences and traditional values challenge one another. Much of the art in North Africa today deals with modern influences on the people of the region. Many artists try to strike a balance between the modern and the traditional.

RELIGIOUS HOLIDAYS

Religious holidays are the most important days of the year for Muslims. Presents are exchanged on Muhammad's birthday, just as they are exchanged by Christians on Christmas.

For those who practice Islam, Ramadan is the most holy month of the year. Like Muslims in other parts of the world, Muslims in North Africa are not supposed to eat, drink, or smoke during the daytime for the entire month of Ramadan. At night they get together for special meals and celebrations. Ramadan is a time of daytime fasting and nighttime feasting. It is also a time of spiritual renewal for Muslims.

As you know, the Koran requires Muslims to pray five times a day. During each of these times, television programming in North Africa is interrupted to allow Muslims time to pray. In countries like Libya, where Islam is followed very strictly, television is regulated by the rules of Islam.

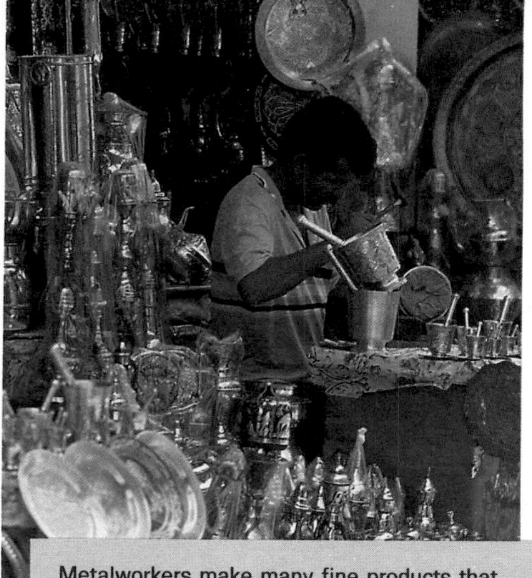

Metalworkers make many fine products that are sold at North African bazaars.

TIES TO THE PAST

As you have read, the arts of North Africans are strongly influenced by Islam. In fact Islamic law plays a large part in nearly every aspect of everyday life. Religious holidays are the most important days of the year for Muslims in North Africa.

Many different kinds of entertainment can be found in the great squares and bazaars of North Africa's cities. As you read at the beginning of this lesson, these "noisy, vibrant" places are filled with the music, arts, and crafts of North Africa.

Check Your Reading

1. What happens at the bazaar in the city of Marrakesh?
2. What happens during the Muslim month of Ramadan?
3. How do the arts of North Africa reflect both traditional and modern concerns?
4. THINKING SKILL: Compare and contrast the role of religion in the lives of the people of North Africa and the people of Western Europe.

THINKING SKILL: Compare and Contrast

Understanding Religious Holidays

Ask students:

- **What meaning do the sacrifices and fasting required during Ramadan have for the Muslims?** (They bring spiritual renewal.)
- **How is television viewing affected by Islam?** (Programs are interrupted for prayer; in some countries television is regulated by Islamic laws.)

Applying the Lesson Have students discuss the role of religious holidays in Muslim life.

3 CLOSE

Summarizing Students have read that Islam strongly influences the arts and recreation of North Africa. Discuss the ways that religion reinforces the traditional arts and leisure activities of the North African nations.

Evaluating Use these questions to assess students' understanding.

- **What kind of metalwork is a traditional North African art form?** (hammered copper, silver, and other metals)
- **What kind of days are the most important days for Muslims?** (religious holidays)
- **Where do the music and the arts and crafts of North Africa blend into one social scene?** (in the great squares and bazaars)

Answers to Check Your Reading

1. There is music, art, crafts, and readings from the Koran.
2. Muslims do not eat, drink, or smoke during daytime hours.
3. Many North African artists make a point of striking a balance between the modern and the traditional in their work.
4. In both, religious holidays are valued, but there is mandatory daily prayer in North Africa.

Independent Practice
Practice Book: page 109

MEETING INDIVIDUAL NEEDS

Reteaching (easy) Have students choose an interesting event or trip that they have experienced. Have them draw the events in the style of ancient Egyptian art. Have students try to interpret the events in one another's drawings.

Extension (average) Have students find more information about Ramadan. Then have them write a description of the month of Ramadan from the point of view of a devout Muslim, explaining such details as how the onset of night is determined.

Enrichment (challenging) Divide the class into three groups to find out more about the activities in North African bazaars—for example, bargaining or the performance of music. Provide each group with a large piece of paper on which to depict three different activities of a typical bazaar. Put the pieces together and display the mural with an appropriate title.

CHAPTER 19 REVIEW

pages 404–405

USING THE CHAPTER SUMMARY AND REVIEW

Cultural Geography These questions may be used for review.

- **What problems has overpopulation caused?** (overcrowding, food shortages, unemployment)
- **Which North African nation is self-sufficient in producing food for its people?** (Morocco)
- **Which European nations once ruled in North Africa?** (Great Britain, France, Spain, Italy)
- **What is a popular theme in North African art?** (the importance of keeping Islamic traditions alive)

Ideas to Remember

- **What are the major ethnic groups in North Africa?** (Berbers, Arabs)
- **What is the key to successful economic development in North Africa?** (wise use of water and oil)
- **What governments are found in North Africa?** (one constitutional monarchy, four republics)
- **Which crafts are popular in North Africa?** (metalworking, carpet making, jewelry making, and others related to the Middle East)

Answers to Reviewing Vocabulary

1. True.
2. Colonialism is the total control of a country by another country.
3. True.
4. The fellahin are Egyptian farmers.
5. A *muezzin* calls Muslims to prayer five times a day.

Answers to Reviewing Facts

1. the Arabs
2. not enough running water, sewers, schools, and housing; riots over the high cost of food
3. growing populations; disappearing usable farmland
4. Libya and Algeria
5. improvements such as irrigation and railroads; The best land, most businesses, and highest-paying jobs were held by Europeans.

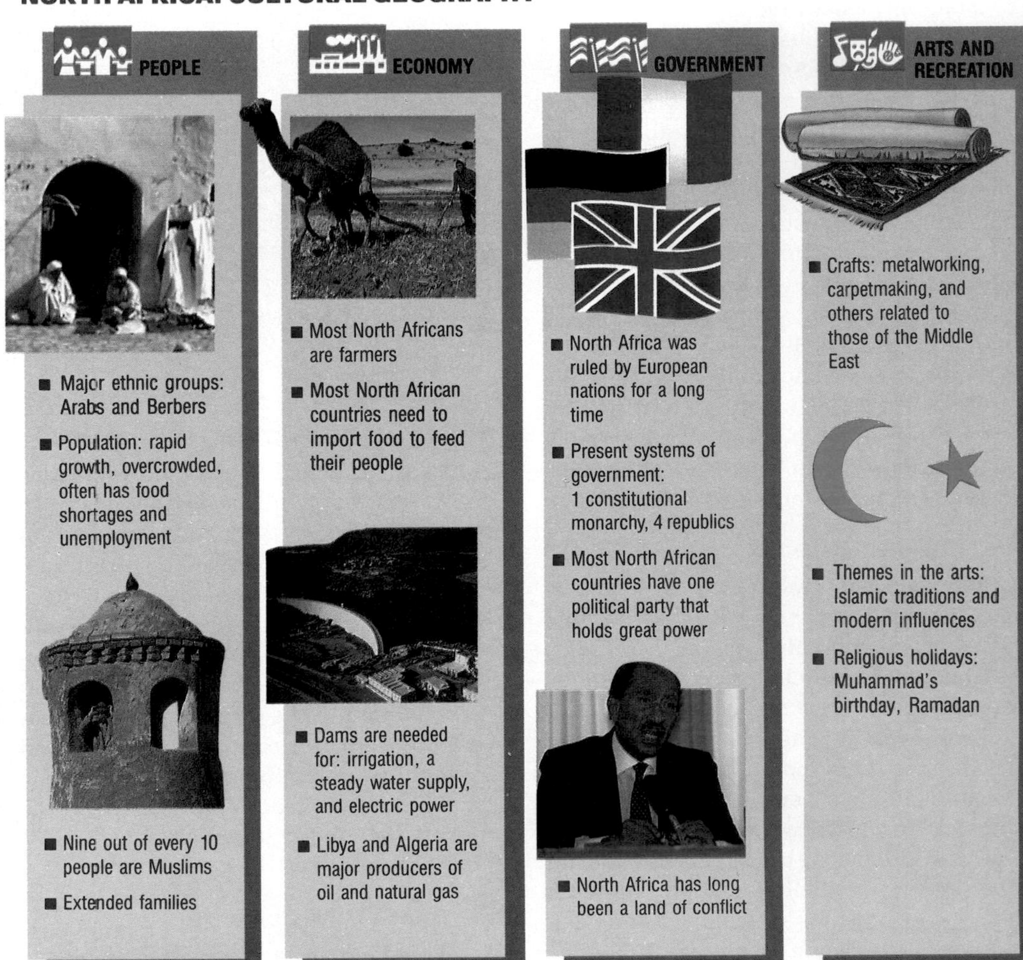

IDEAS TO REMEMBER

- The people of North Africa are mostly Arab, Berber, and Muslim.
- The wise use of water and oil is the key to successful economic development in North Africa.
- Formerly European colonies, the governments of North Africa now include one constitutional monarchy and four republics.
- Many arts and leisure activities in the area are similar to those in the Middle East.

404

ENRICHMENT ACTIVITY

Creating a Bazaar **Materials:** dates, oranges, spices, aluminum foil, cloth, paper plates, plastic cups, clothes, water heater, teapot, teacups, tea, lemon, sugar

1. Remind the class that bazaars have existed for hundreds of years in some countries in the Middle East and North Africa, and have them review text pages 374–375 and 402. Tell students that they are going to create their own version of a bazaar.
2. Divide the class into groups. Put one group in charge of gathering and displaying foods and goods that might be sold in a bazaar. Have another group set up a tea stand. Another group might fashion "copper and silver" plates and vessels like the ones on page 403 by wrapping foil around plates and cups. If the class designed rugs, as suggested on page 384, include them.
3. Have students display their offerings and "buy and sell" them.

CHAPTER 19 • REVIEW

REVIEWING VOCABULARY

Each of the following statements contains an underlined vocabulary word. Number a sheet of paper from 1 to 5. Beside each number write whether the following statements are true or false. If the statement is true, write **T**. If the statement is false, rewrite the sentence using the vocabulary word correctly.

1. A muezzin is a crier in the Islamic world who calls Muslims to prayer.
2. Because it involved only control of the government, colonialism had little effect on the countries of North Africa.
3. During the month of Ramadan, Muslims are not supposed to eat, drink, or smoke during the daytime.
4. The fellahin are a class of merchants and businesspeople who live in North Africa's large urban centers.
5. A muezzin is a pilgrimage to the holy city of Mecca.

REVIEWING FACTS

1. Which group of conquerors has had the most lasting impact on the culture of North Africa?
2. List three effects of the exploding population in the Middle East.
3. What are the two main reasons that most North African countries have difficulty feeding their people?
4. Which countries in North Africa produce the most oil and natural gas?
5. What were some of the effects of French colonialism on Algeria?
6. How does Morocco's constitutional monarchy differ from constitutional monarchies in Europe?
7. Why is Ramadan an important month for Muslims? How do Muslims observe Ramadan?
8. Why did the peace treaty with Israel isolate Egypt from the Arab world?
9. Why did terrorists assassinate Egyptian president Anwar Sadat?
10. Name one example of how religion influences popular art in Egypt.

WRITING ABOUT MAIN IDEAS

1. **Writing a Travel Brochure:** Imagine a journey that begins in Casablanca, Morocco, passes through each country of North Africa, and ends in Mecca, Saudi Arabia. Write a travel brochure for such a trip.
2. **Writing a List:** Write a list of some of the social and political effects of population growth in the countries of North Africa. You may wish to obtain additional information from encyclopedias, newspapers, and magazines.
3. **Writing About Perspectives:** Imagine that you are a Muslim observing Ramadan in North Africa. Write a journal entry describing your day and your feelings about the holiday.

BUILDING SKILLS: ASKING QUESTIONS

1. What does it mean to understand how to ask good questions?
2. What are some steps that could help you to ask good questions?
3. Why is it important to come up with your own questions?
4. Write five questions you might ask to learn more about North Africa.
5. Why is it useful to understand how to ask good questions?

6. Unlike the figureheads of Europe, Morocco's king can suspend the legislature and can issue rules and regulations that have the force of law.
7. They consider it the most holy month of the year; they do not eat, drink, or smoke during the day for the entire month.
8. because no other Arab nation would accept the peace treaty
9. They believed they had removed a ruler who had failed to follow the rules of Islam.
10. After making a pilgrimage Egyptians sometimes paint a picture of the journey on the outside of their houses.

Suggestions for Writing About Main Ideas

1. Students should include information on each country of North Africa in their brochures. You may want to have them include illustrations to accompany their copy.
2. You may wish to have students work in groups and have each group focus on a different country.
3. Students should use their knowledge of the Muslim way of life to describe the importance of this holiday.

Answers to Building Skills: Asking Questions

1. to be able to ask the right questions to get the information you need
2. To find factual information ask: *Who? What? Where? When?* and *How?*; to find the meaning or importance of a topic or an event, ask *Why?* or *What conclusions can I draw?*; to evaluate information ask questions to distinguish fact from opinion, or to identify bias or point of view.
3. Questions help you to learn what you want to know.
4. Possible questions include: Which areas border North Africa? Why are most people Muslim? Why do most people still follow Muslim beliefs? Why are some areas heavily populated? Why do the Bedouins live in the deserts?
5. Good questions enable you to get the information you need.

MAKING CONNECTIONS

Identifying Cause and Effect Display the Cause and Effect Chart Graphic Organizer Transparency, writing in only the underlined titles and phrases. Ask students to review the chapter, fill in the missing causes or effects, and then brainstorm other cause-and-effect relationships to add. *Ask:* What factors have great influence on life in North Africa today?

Causes	Effects
explosive population growth	overcrowded conditions, food shortages
building of Aswan High Dam	provided electric power, made land less fertile
colonial rule	revolutions and independence

UNIT 5 REVIEW
pages 406–407

USING THE UNIT SUMMARY AND REVIEW

Physical Geography These questions may be used for review.

- **What are the three fertile river valleys in the region?** (the Nile, Tigris, and Euphrates river valleys)
- **In general, what type of climate does the region have?** (arid)
- **Which areas have fertile land with adequate rainfall?** (the coast of North Africa; the highlands of Turkey, Syria, and Iran)

Cultural Geography

- **Of which ethnic and religious background are most people in North Africa?** (Muslim Arabs)
- **What types of farming methods are used in the region?** (labor-intensive; modern technology)
- **What are two causes of conflict in the region?** (religious and boundary disputes)
- **Why were storytellers highly regarded in the region?** (Storytellers were the only ones who could entertain people with stories because early tales were not written down.)

UNIT 5 • SUMMARY

THE MIDDLE EAST AND NORTH AFRICA: PHYSICAL GEOGRAPHY

LANDFORMS

- Peninsulas: Sinai Peninsula, Arabian Peninsula, Anatolia Peninsula

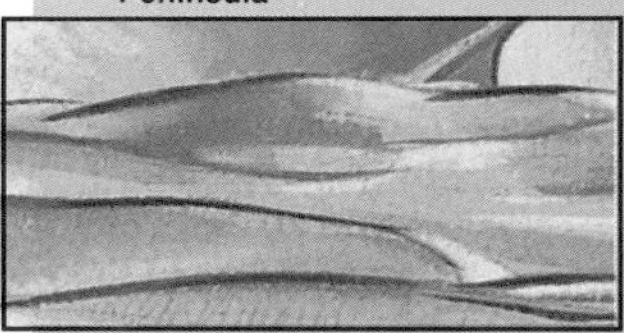

- Deserts: Sahara
- Fertile river valleys: Nile River Valley, Tigris River Valley, Euphrates River Valley

CLIMATE

- Arid climate: dry

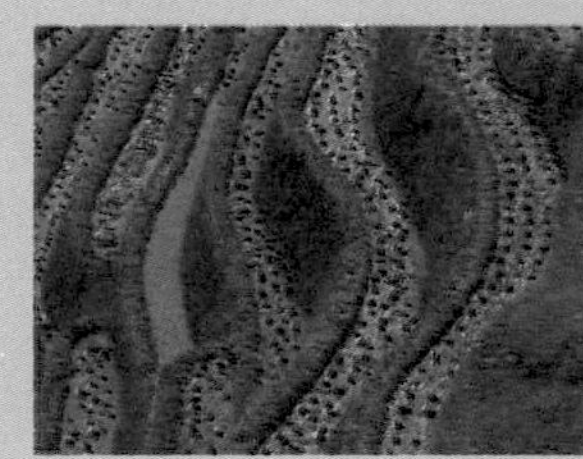

- Temperatures: hot except the Mediterranean coast, Iranian Plateau, and Anatolia, where winters may be long and cold

NATURAL RESOURCES

- Scarce resources: water, arable land
- Fertile land with adequate rainfall is found in Lebanon, the Nile delta, and Yemen
- Forests grow in Atlas Mountains and northern Iran
- Abundant resources: oil and natural gas
- The Middle East produces one third of the world's supply of oil

THE MIDDLE EAST AND NORTH AFRICA: CULTURAL GEOGRAPHY

PEOPLE

- Most people are Muslim Arabs; Turks, Persians, and Kurds are non-Arab Muslims; non-Muslim groups include Jewish people of Israel and Christians
- Among traditional Muslims women and men lead separate lives
- Major ethnic groups of North Africa: Arabs and Berbers
- Population: rapid growth, has led to overcrowding, often has caused food shortages and unemployment

ECONOMY

- Oil has brought tremendous wealth to many nations on the Persian Gulf, and to Libya and Algeria
- Farming methods: labor-intensive, modern in Israel and some other regions

- Dams are needed for irrigation, a steady water supply, and electric power

GOVERNMENT

- Absolute rulers and laws based on Islam are common
- Israel has a parliamentary system
- Some countries are ruled by Islamic law; others combine Islamic law with constitutional law
- Efforts have been made to resolve disputes between some Arab countries and Israel
- North Africa was long ruled by European nations
- Most North African countries have one political party that holds great power

ARTS AND RECREATION

- Storytellers are highly regarded in the region
- Beautiful calligraphy is used for Arabic and Muslim writings

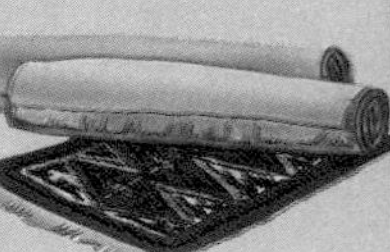

- Crafts: metalworking, carpetmaking, and others
- Themes in the arts: Islamic traditions and modern influences

406

ENRICHMENT ACTIVITY

Designing Postage Stamps **Materials:** construction paper, paints or markers Note: If any of your students are stamp collectors, encourage them to bring in foreign stamps from their collections to show the class.

1. Discuss postage stamps with the class—what their purpose is, what kinds of information they carry (name of issuing nation, cost), what kinds of things they picture, what they tell about the issuing nation. Tell the class that they are going to design postage stamps for the countries they have just studied.
2. Divide the class into five groups, and assign each group one of the North African countries—Algeria, Egypt, Libya, Morocco, Tunisia. Tell the groups to find their nation in the chart on pages 352–353 and to do some further encyclopedia research.
3. Tell each group to design two stamps that its country might issue. Have them present their stamps to the class, explain why they designed them as they did, and make a bulletin board display.

UNIT 5 • REVIEW

REVIEWING VOCABULARY

bazaar	irrigation
colonialism	kibbutz
desert	labor-intensive
fellahin	qanat
Islam	sharia

Number a sheet of paper from 1 to 10. Beside each number write the word or term from the above list that best completes the sentence.

1. The legal systems of most Middle Eastern countries are based on ____.
2. After many years of ____, Algerians revolted against French rule.
3. A ____ is an outdoor marketplace.
4. Farming in most of the Middle East would be impossible without ____.
5. Founded by Muhammad, ____ is the dominant religion of the Middle East and North Africa.
6. Water from a large underground tunnel called a ____ is used to irrigate many farms in Iran.
7. The ____ are a class of Middle Eastern farmers who work small plots of land.
8. Members of an Israeli ____ own and farm the land together.
9. Methods of production that are slower and less efficient than production by machines are called ____.
10. A ____ is a dry, sandy, or rocky region that receives very little rainfall.

WRITING ABOUT THE UNIT

1. **Writing an Essay:** The Middle East is the birthplace of three world religions—Judaism, Christianity, and Islam. It is also the site of nearly constant religious conflict. Write an essay supporting an end to conflict based on the beliefs these three religions hold in common.
2. **Writing About Perspectives:** Imagine that you are the Middle Eastern astronaut who traveled aboard the space shuttle *Discovery* in 1985. You look down on earth and see that the spacecraft is over your country, Saudi Arabia. Describe your feelings in a poem.

ACTIVITIES

1. **Constructing a Bar Graph:** Show the oil production of the world's ten largest oil-producing countries by drawing a bar graph. Use the figures given in the chart on page 374.
2. **Working Together to Make a Scrapbook:** With a group of classmates, gather articles from newspapers and magazines about a current issue in the Middle East or North Africa. Use the articles to make a scrapbook for the rest of the class.

LINKING PAST, PRESENT, AND FUTURE

Do you believe the Islamic world will be able to preserve its culture and modernize at the same time? What adjustments will have to be made? Will those changes be smooth or will they be accompanied by violence and conflict? In what way do you think Islam will have changed by the year 2025?

407

Answers to Reviewing Vocabulary

1. *sharia*
2. colonialism
3. bazaar
4. irrigation
5. Islam
6. qanat
7. fellahin
8. kibbutz
9. labor-intensive
10. desert

Suggestions for Writing About the Unit

1. You may wish to review the beliefs on which these three religions are based before students begin to write. Have students share their essays with the rest of the class.
2. Students' poems will probably focus on the awe or beauty of the situation.

Suggestions for Activities

1. Review with students how to construct a bar graph. Be sure the amounts they draw are accurate.
2. This activity lends itself to a cooperative learning approach. You may wish to have each group focus on a different issue or different country.

Suggestions for Linking Past, Present, and Future In answering these questions, students will have to deal with the conflict between traditional ways and modern ways. They should use their knowledge of the history and current events of the Islamic world when answering these questions.

PERFORMANCE ASSESSMENT

Demonstrating Understanding Remind students that at the beginning of the unit they were told they would contribute to a museum display of dioramas depicting scenes from the Middle East and North Africa. Tell students they may use their books and other resource materials to complete this activity. Have students who wish to create similar scenes work together. Suggest they begin by sketching the scene they have chosen to depict on a sheet of paper. If possible, provide materials for the dioramas, such as large cardboard boxes, clay, construction paper, paint, pipe cleaners, sand, glue, and craft sticks. Have students write explanations for their dioramas individually. Remind them of the standards that will be applied to their contributions, which were outlined in the Unit Opener on page 350. After the dioramas and explanations are complete, enlist students' help in assembling the exhibit. For additional performance assessment information, see page TM45 in the *Assessment Book.*

For the Portfolio: Include photographs of students' dioramas, if available, and students' written explanations in their portfolios. Also include your anecdotal record or observational checklist.

UNIT 6
ORGANIZER

SUB-SAHARAN AFRICA text pages 408–485

UNIT THEME

Sub-Saharan Africa, a major portion of the world's most tropical continent, is a region with a very old and rich past, political and social problems caused by post-colonialism, and, with the exception of South Africa, economies that are largely agricultural.

UNIT RESOURCES

- Practice Book: pp. 111–132
- Anthology: Part 4
- Anthology Cassette
- Outline Maps: 1, 29–32
- Unit 6 Poster
- Desk Maps
- Internet Project Handbook
- Geo Adventures Pad
- Pupil Edition on Cassette
- Transparency: Graphic Organizer
- **Technology:** *Videodisc/ Video Tape 1*
- **Technology:** *Adventures CD-ROM*
- Assessment Book, Chapter Tests: 20, 21, 22, 23

Internet CONNECTION

The Home Page at **http://www.mmhschool.com** and the **Internet Project Handbook** contain on-line student activities related to this unit.

UNIT PLANNING GUIDE

CHAPTER	SUGGESTED PACING	THEMES
20 PHYSICAL GEOGRAPHY OF SUB-SAHARAN AFRICA pages 414–425	4 days	Trade winds dominate the climate over Sub-Saharan Africa's wide variety of dramatic landforms and water bodies.
21 WEST AFRICA pages 426–447	7 days	In West Africa, African ways, Islam, and European influences shape the lives of a mix of people and make national unity a challenge.
22 EAST AND EQUATORIAL AFRICA pages 448–465	6 days	Herding, farming, and fishing are the key livelihoods in East and Equatorial Africa, where economic development has faltered because of drought, poor transportation, and lack of funds.
23 NATIONS OF SOUTHERN AFRICA pages 466–483	6 days	In striking contrast to the rest of Sub-Saharan Africa, Southern Africa is dominated by white South Africa and its highly developed economy.

UNIT PROJECTS

Writing a Letter from a Tourist Ask students to imagine that they have toured one subregion of Sub-Saharan Africa for a month. Have them write a letter home to a friend about their African experiences. Encourage them to describe the people, languages, methods of transportation, food, and recreational activities they have encountered.

Oral Reports Take the class to the library to find books about Africa. Have each student read one and give an oral report focusing on how their reading helped them to understand African culture better.

Cooperative Learning: Planning a Safari Divide the class into four groups and have each plan a safari through Sub-Saharan Africa. They should show their route on a wall map and each member should describe why the group chose one place or activity on their itinerary.

Field Trip Arrange a visit to a museum or cultural center with an African exhibit. Before the trip have students write three questions about Sub-Saharan Africa to which they would like answers. After the trip have each student present their questions and answers to the class.

BULLETIN BOARD IDEAS

Making Your Own Bulletin Board Have three teams of students explore human-environment interaction in Sub-Saharan Africa. Suggest that students illustrate a variety of environments, African peoples, and ways in which people adapt to or change their environments. Create a colorful bulletin board titled "Geography of Sub-Saharan Africa."

Using the Unit Poster As an alternative to the bulletin board activity, display the Unit 6 Poster, which shows an enlarged version of the Unit Opener globe on pages 408–409.

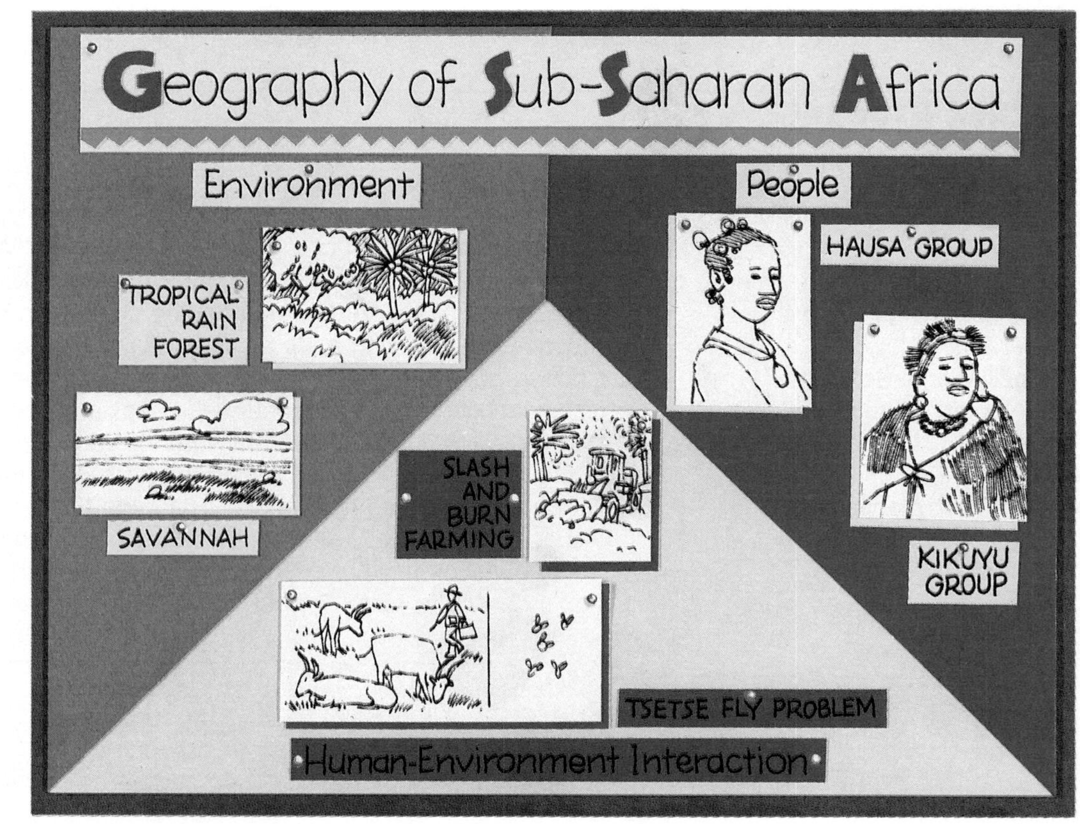

UNIT BIBLIOGRAPHY

For description and additional references, see the Annotated Bibliography beginning on page T-1 in the back of the book.

For the Teacher

Books

Ibazebo, Isimene. *Exploration Into Africa.* Columbus, OH: Silver Burdett Press, 1995.

Paton, Jonathan. *The Land and People of South Africa.* New York: J. B. Lippincott, 1990.

Read-Alouds

Fairman, Tony, reteller. *Bury My Bones, But Keep My Words: African Tales for Retelling.* New York: Henry Holt & Co., 1991.

Larungu, Ruth. *Myths and Legends from Ghana for African-American Cultures.* Mogadore, OH: Telcraft Books, 1992.

Technology Multimedia

Africa Trail. CD-ROM. MECC. Toll Free: 1-800-215-0368.

Sub-Saharan Africa: The Land. (4 Videos) Society for Visual Education. Toll Free: 1-800-829-1900.

Free Materials

For a free loan of a video called "The Africans: A Clash of Cultures," send to: Church World Service, Film Library, 28606 Phillips Street, P.O. Box 968, Elkhart, Indiana 46515.

For the Student

Brandenburg, Jim. *Sand and Fog: Adventures in Southern Africa.* New York: Walker and Company, 1994. **(Average)**

Chiasson, John. *African Journey.* New York: Bradbury Press, 1987. **(Challenging)**

Courlander, Harold, and George Herzog. *The Cow-Tail Switch and Other West African Stories.* New York: Henry Holt & Co., 1986. **(Average)**

Gordon, Sheila. *The Middle of Somewhere: A Story of South Africa.* New York: Orchard Books, 1990. **(Average)**

Hughes, Libby. *Nelson Mandela: Voice of Freedom.* Dillon Press, 1992. **(Average)**

Middleton, Nick. *Southern Africa.* Austin, TX: Raintree Steck-Vaughn, 1995. **(Average)**

Mollel, Tololwa M. *The Orphan Boy: A Masai Story.* New York: Clarion Books, 1990. **(Easy)**

Onyefulu, Ifeoma. *Ogbo: Sharing Life in an African Village.* San Diego, CA: Harcourt Brace & Company, 1996. **(Easy)**

Pratt, Paula Bryant. *The End of Apartheid in South Africa.* San Diego, CA: Lucent Books, 1995. **(Challenging)**

IDEAS FOR ACTIVE LEARNING

TEACHER EXCHANGE

Playing "What's the Question?"

Thanks to:
Vicki Sherrod
Stigall Middle School
Humboldt, Tennessee

Materials
poster board, manila paper

Instructions
1. Have students construct a poster board to play "What's the Question?"
2. Have students cut out and attach 25 manila pockets to the poster board in 5 equal rows. Ask a student to label the pockets in the top row 10 points and those in the following rows 20, 30, 40, and 50 points, respectively.
3. Choose five students to write a topic heading above each column.
4. Have each of the five students write answers to questions for each topic, so that there are a total of five answers for each topic. Place the easiest answers in the pockets in the top row and the hardest in the bottom row.
5. Divide the class into five groups. Have the first group select a topic and point value. Read the answer in the pocket aloud. If the first group gives an appropriate question for that answer, the group wins the points. If not, another group has a chance to give the right question and win the points.

WHAT'S THE QUESTION???

Geography	People	Culture	Economy	Government	SCORE Team	
10	10	10	10	10	A	60
20	20	20	20	20	B	40
30	30	30	30	30	C	110
40	40	40	40	40	D	50
50	50	50	50	50	E	80

Making Relief Maps

Thanks to:
Jo Anne Rathvon
Cascade Elementary School
Marysville, Washington

Materials
heavy cardboard, flour, salt, cold water, spoon, mixing container, tempera paint, elevation maps of the African continent and countries

Instructions
1. Tell students that they will make relief maps showing the physical features of the African continent or of individual countries.
2. Have students draw on cardboard the shapes of the areas they wish to map.
3. Mix flour and salt using the proportion 2 cups flour to 1 cup salt. Add cold water and stir until the mixture has the consistency of mayonnaise.
4. Place portions of the mixture within the boundaries of the cardboard maps. Students may then press and spread the mixture to fill their outlines, covering all areas with 1/8" thickness. Using the elevation maps for reference, students should build up the regions of higher elevation.
5. When the maps are dry, have students paint the elevation ranges in different colors and paint or write keys to the elevations.

TECHNOLOGY CENTER

Enriching with Multimedia

RESOURCE: ***Internet Project Handbook***

Look at the ***Internet Project Handbook*** for student projects related to this unit or have students go on-line at http://www.mmhschool.com, Macmillan/McGraw-Hill's Home School page on the World Wide Web.

RESOURCE: ***Adventures CD-ROM***

Enrich Unit 6 with the *Travel* and *Media* activities on the Adventures CD-ROM.

SCHOOL-TO-HOME

Preserving Legacies

- Throughout this unit, students will have the opportunity to learn about the cultures of Sub-Saharan Africa. After studying each region, discuss with students the ways in which traditional African practices and beliefs are preserved. Help students construct a semantic map to organize these legacies. As an alternative to drawing rings or boxes, have students draw outline maps of the regions in which they write the legacies.
- Encourage students to share their semantic maps with family members. Suggest that students draw an outline map of the United States or of their state. With family members, have them identify and add legacies they preserve at home or in their communities.

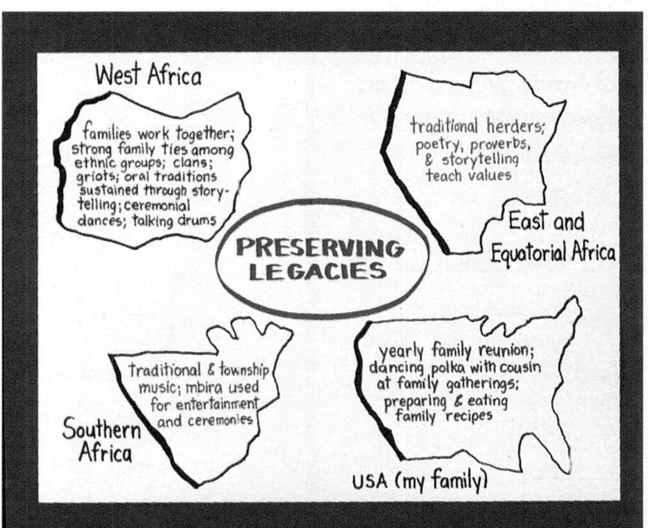

SECOND-LANGUAGE SUPPORT

While these activities are designed especially for students needing second-language support, they are meant to be shared by all students in the class.

Chapter 20, Lesson 1 ■ Physical Geography of Sub-Saharan Africa

To help second-language students remember vocabulary and place names, group students into three- or four-member teams and ask each team to define the *Key Vocabulary* and *Key Places.* Have teams exchange and check each others' definitions.

Chapter 21, Lesson 1 ■ West Africa

As an organizational activity, have the class brainstorm and create a semantic map of cultural influences in West Africa. Detail traditional, Muslim, and European influences.

Chapter 22, Lesson 4 ■ East and Equatorial Africa

Provide a basis for second-language students to understand the importance of cultural legacies. Encourage students to identify traditional poems, songs, or stories from their native cultures.

Chapter 23, Lesson 3 ■ Nations of Southern Africa

Highlight the diversity of Southern African governments: assign groups of students the following countries for post-reading research: Mozambique, Zimbabwe, Botswana, Madagascar, Swaziland, Lesotho, and South Africa. Have each group present an oral report on what they've learned.

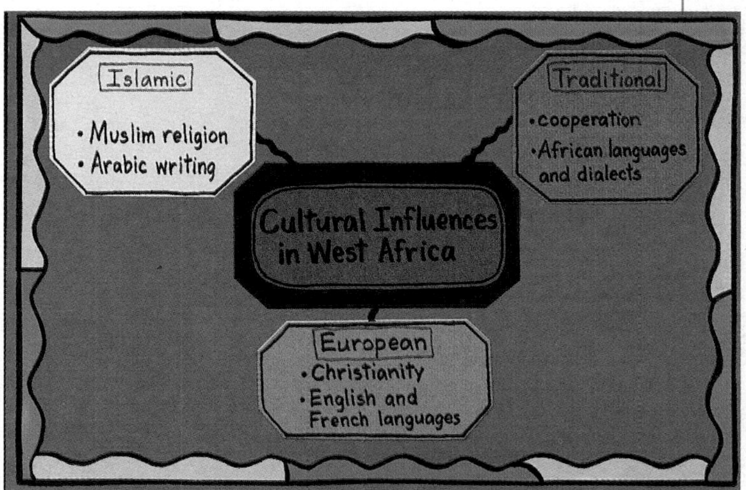

Chapter 21, Lesson 1

UNIT 6

pages 408–485

USING THE UNIT OPENER

Introducing the Unit Have students look at the unit title and silently read the *Where We Are* section on the facing page.

Ask students:

- **What is the unit title?** (''Sub-Saharan Africa'')
- **Which three areas make up Sub-Saharan Africa?** (West Africa, East and Equatorial Africa, Southern Africa)
- **What kinds of lands will you find here?** (They range from harsh deserts to tropical rain forests.)

EXTENDING MAP SKILLS

Help students recognize in which direction they are moving on the globe to get to Sub-Saharan Africa from the Middle East and North Africa. Encourage them to compare and to relate Sub-Saharan Africa to the last region they studied.

Ask students:

- **In which direction would you move to go from the last region we studied to Sub-Saharan Africa?** (Students should realize that they would move southwest or south.)
- **Compare the three areas of Sub-Saharan Africa and tell which looks largest.** (East and Equatorial Africa)
- **Where is the equator in relation to Sub-Saharan Africa?** (The equator runs through the center of the region—through East and Equatorial Africa.)
- *THINKING FURTHER:* **Locate the Tropic of Cancer and Tropic of Capricorn, and study their relative locations in terms of this region. What conclusion can you make about this region compared with all the others studied so far?** (It has more tropical land.)

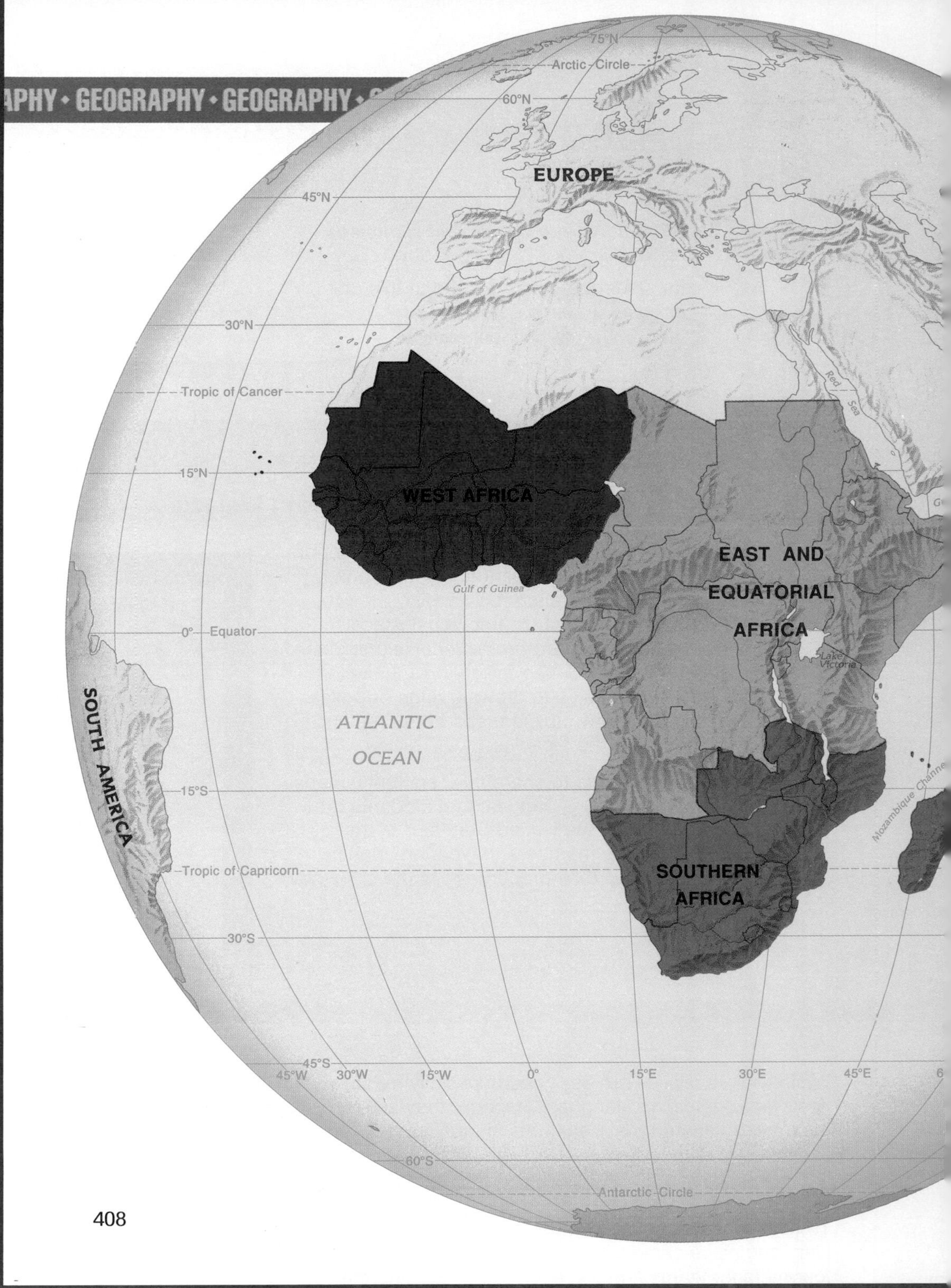

ONGOING UNIT PROJECT

Planning for Assessment Tell students that in this unit they will learn about the people, culture, and geography of Sub-Saharan Africa. Explain that at the end of the unit they will participate in a fair. Suggest that students participate by making maps, tools, clothing, food, or artwork. Each student should write a description of his or her project. Near the end of the unit set a date for the fair. For information on completing this unit project, see page 485.

Goal: Students' work should show that they understand and appreciate the richness and diversity of Sub-Saharan culture.

Signs of Success: Tell students that an adequate contribution should include a display object or demonstration and a written description of it. An excellent contribution would also include an explanation of why the object or demonstration is important to the people in this part of the world.

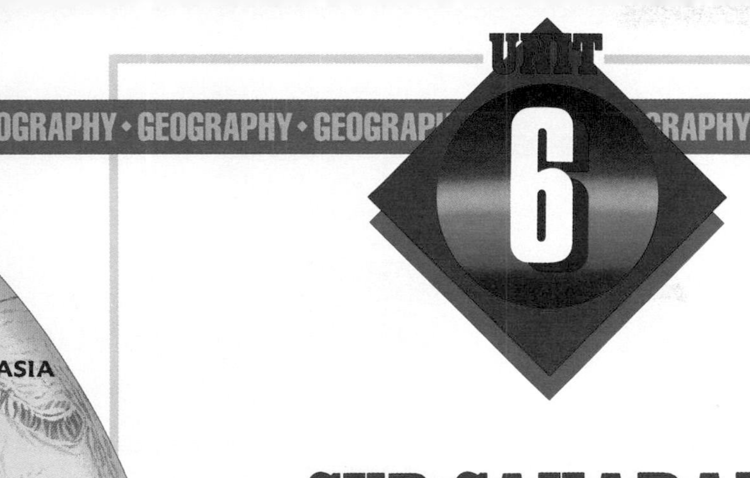

SUB-SAHARAN AFRICA

WHERE WE ARE

In the last unit you read about the vast Sahara, the desert that covers much of Northern Africa. Now your journey through the world takes you south of the Sahara to the region with the largest number of countries that have become independent during the past 50 years. This region is known as Sub-Saharan Africa.

Sub-Saharan Africa is divided into three areas: West Africa, East and Equatorial Africa, and Southern Africa. Find these areas on the map. They contain all kinds of land, from harsh deserts to tropical rain forests. As you read about these lands and their peoples, think again about the region in which you live and the others you have studied in this book. How is Sub-Saharan Africa similar to these regions? How is it different?

409

Expressing Relative Locations Tell students that they can learn how to express relative location with this map of Sub-Saharan Africa. Have students write sentences that describe the relative locations of the three areas of Sub-Saharan Africa. (examples: "West Africa is located on the western hump of Africa that juts into the Atlantic Ocean"; "East and Equatorial Africa forms the central length and width, or the core, of Africa"; "Southern Africa includes the whole southern tip of the continent of Africa.")

Identifying Physical Patterns on the Land Students also should be encouraged to look for physical patterns on the map. Tell them to put a finger on the mountains of Sub-Saharan Africa and trace them around the continent. They should be able to see a rough circle of continuous higher elevation around the edge of the southern mass of the continent. Tell them that this pattern will be important to remember when they study the elevation of Africa later. Direct their attention to the sizes of the countries of Sub-Saharan Africa, and ask if they see any pattern as to where the largest countries are. (With the exception of the one large central country of Zaire, the countries with the largest expanses on this map are all along the edge of the Sahara on the northern border of Sub-Saharan Africa.) Ask students if they have any explanation as to why these nations would be so large. (More marginal desert land is needed in order to produce a livelihood for the people. Europeans drew the countries' boundaries when they founded colonies in Africa and made huge countries out of the desert wastelands.) Alert them to remember these patterns and the questions these patterns raise when reading the lessons about Sub-Saharan Africa that follow in this unit.

BACKGROUND INFORMATION

Madagascar The fourth-largest island in the world, Madagascar, was once connected to the continent of Africa.

- People from the Malay Peninsula migrated to Madagascar in prehistoric times. Later Africans and Arabs moved to the island from the west, and their cultures combined with that of the earlier settlers.
- Because of Madagascar's isolation, its fauna has developed in unique ways. The aye-aye, which is distantly related to the lemur, is peculiar to the island. This animal's most striking trait is its long, flexible middle finger, which it uses as an all-purpose tool. A great, wingless bird larger than the ostrich also once lived in Madagascar. As evidence of its existence, it has left behind the largest bird's egg ever found, which is 12.5 x 9.5 inches (32 x 24 cm).

EXTENDING TABLE SKILLS

So far, students have worked verbally with the pattern for analysis of a table suggested in Unit 2. By now they should be able to name the questions to ask to gain meaning from a table. Help them to list the subject matter of these questions on the chalkboard. Be sure to include:

1. subject of table
2. types of information given
3. total number of items
4. common things
5. unique things
6. comparisons and contrasts
7. ranking subjects according to the sizes of their areas or populations
8. special sizes or numbers

Have students use the list that they have just made to create a worksheet of questions to help them learn about the tables on Sub-Saharan Africa. (Remind students that the tables cover four pages of the book.) Tell students to make up a separate answer sheet and then to exchange their worksheets with one another. Ask students not only to answer each other's questions but also to write a critique of each other's questions. The critique should tell the author of the worksheet what was good about the questions and what might be done to make them better. After each student has read the critique of his or her worksheet, have him or her mark the wrong answers and hand the corrected sheet back to the student who answered the questions.

LIFE TODAY • LIFE TODAY • LIFE TODAY • LIFE TODAY • LIFE TODAY • LIFE TODAY

SUB-SAHARAN AFRICA

ANGOLA
Capital ★ Luanda
Major languages: Portuguese and Ovimbundo
Population: 9.8 million
Area: 481,352 sq mi; 1,246,700 sq km
Leading exports: oil and coffee

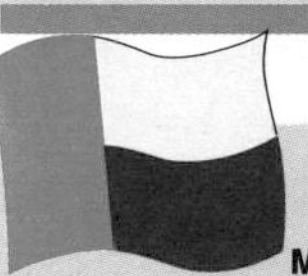

BENIN
Capital ★ Porto-Novo
Major languages: French and Fon
Population: 5.3 million
Area: 43,483 sq mi; 112,620 sq km
Leading exports: fuels and coffee

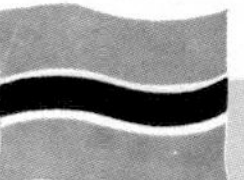

BOTSWANA
Capital ★ Gaborone
Major languages: English and Setswana
Population: 1.4 million
Area: 231,803 sq mi; 600,370 sq km
Leading exports: diamonds and cattle

BURKINA FASO
Capital ★ Ouagadougou
Major language: French
Population: 10.1 million
Area: 105,869 sq mi; 274,200 sq km
Leading exports: cotton and manufactured goods

BURUNDI
Capital ★ Bujumbura
Major languages: Kirundi and French
Population: 6.1 million
Area: 10,745 sq mi; 27,830 sq km
Leading export: coffee

CAMEROON
Capital ★ Yaoundé
Major languages: English and French
Population: 13.1 million
Area: 183,568 sq mi; 475,440 sq km
Leading exports: oil, coffee, and cocoa

CAPE VERDE
Capital ★ Praia
Major languages: Portuguese and Crioulo
Population: 0.4 million
Area: 1,556 sq mi; 4,030 sq km
Leading exports: fish and bananas

CENTRAL AFRICAN REPUBLIC
Capital ★ Bangui
Major languages: French and Sango
Population: 3.1 million
Area: 237,362 sq mi; 622,980 sq km
Leading exports: coffee, diamonds, and timber

CHAD
Capital ★ N'Djamena
Major languages: French and Arabic
Population: 5.5 million
Area: 495,754 sq mi; 1,284,000 sq km
Leading export: cotton

COMOROS
Capital ★ Moroni
Major languages: French, Arabic, and Comoran
Population: 0.5 million
Area: 838 sq mi; 2,170 sq km
Leading export: vanilla

CONGO
Capital ★ Brazzaville
Major language: French
Population: 2.4 million
Area: 132,047 sq mi; 342,000 sq km
Leading export: oil

CÔTE D'IVOIRE (Ivory Coast)
Capital ★ Yamoussoukro
Major language: French
Population: 14.3 million
Area: 124,502 sq mi; 322,460 sq km
Leading exports: cocoa, coffee, and fuels

410

BACKGROUND INFORMATION

The African Continent Over 200 million years ago the continents of South America, Antarctica, Australia, India, and Africa were all joined together in one giant landmass. This landmass was called Gondwanaland, after a place in India where proof of its existence was found.

- When Gondwanaland split apart 200 million years ago, South America, Antarctica, Australia, and India drifted to their present locations, leaving a piece of high land that later tilted over and became the continent known today as Africa.
- The fact that Africa is a remnant from which land has been torn away explains why its coasts have either narrow plains or steep cliffs.
- The tilting of Africa caused enormous north-south cracks in the continent along which the land dropped, forming the Great Rift Valley. Many of the other breaks in the earth filled with water and became the great lakes along the rift.

LIFE TODAY • LIFE TODAY • LIFE TODAY • LIFE TODAY • LIFE TODAY • LIFE TODAY • LIFE TODAY

DJIBOUTI
Capital ★ Djibouti

Major languages: Arabic and French
Population: 0.4 million
Area: 8,494 sq mi; 22,000 sq km
Leading exports: hides and skins

EQUATORIAL GUINEA
Capital ★ Malabo

Major language: Spanish
Population: 0.4 million
Area: 10,830 sq mi; 28,050 sq km
Leading exports: cocoa and coffee

ERITREA
Capital ★ Asmara

Major languages: Tigrinya and Arabic
Population: 3.2 million
Area: 42,842 sq mi; 121,320 sq km
Leading exports: salt, leather, and textiles

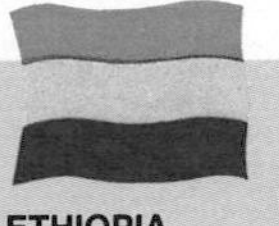

ETHIOPIA
Capital ★ Addis Ababa

Major language: Amharic
Population: 54.9 million
Area: 435,607 sq mi; 1,128,221 sq km
Leading export: coffee

GABON
Capital ★ Libreville

Major languages: French and Fang
Population: 1.1 million
Area: 103,348 sq mi; 267,670 sq km
Leading export: oil

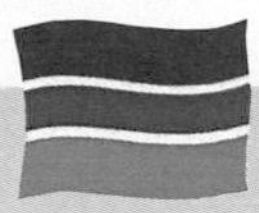

GAMBIA
Capital ★ Banjul

Major languages: English and Mandinka
Population: 1.0 million
Area: 4,363 sq mi; 11,300 sq km
Leading export: peanut products

GHANA
Capital ★ Accra

Major language: English
Population: 17.2 million
Area: 92,101 sq mi; 238,540 sq km
Leading exports: cocoa and gold

GUINEA
Capital ★ Conakry

Major languages: French, Sausou, and Manika
Population: 6.4 million
Area: 94,927 sq mi; 245,860 sq km
Leading export: bauxite

GUINEA-BISSAU
Capital ★ Bissau

Major languages: Portuguese and Crioulo
Population: 1.7 million
Area: 13,946 sq mi; 36,120 sq km
Leading export: peanut products

KENYA
Capital ★ Nairobi

Major languages: English and Kiswahili
Population: 28.2 million
Area: 224,962 sq mi; 582,650 sq km
Leading exports: coffee and tea

LESOTHO
Capital ★ Maseru

Major languages: Sesotho and English
Population: 1.9 million
Area: 11,718 sq mi; 30,350 sq km
Leading exports: manufactured goods and wool

LIBERIA
Capital ★ Monrovia

Major language: English
Population: 2.9 million
Area: 43,000 sq mi; 111,370 sq km
Leading exports: iron ore and rubber

Identifying Historic Name Changes
Explain to students that the study of Sub-Saharan Africa is complicated for two reasons: (1) This region has many more nations in it than any other region in this book; (2) Many nations in Africa are former colonies, and there have been many changes in their names since they became independent. Warn students that if they try to look up names of countries in this unit, they should recognize that there may be more than one name for each country or city. Some examples of the most recent name changes are: Gold Coast to Ghana; the Belgian Congo, or the Democratic Republic of the Congo, to Zaire; Portuguese Guinea to Guinea-Bissau; and Ivory Coast to Côte d'Ivoire.

BACKGROUND INFORMATION

From Africa to North America Peanuts have become an important food source both for people and livestock in the United States.

- In Africa peanuts are called "groundnuts" or "goobers"; they came to the United States with Africans who were brought here as slaves.
- As the peanut plant grows, its flowers wither and sink into the ground, where their seeds mature. In Africa the seeds are eaten as fresh vegetables; to be eaten as nuts, they must be dried slowly and roasted.
- In the southern United States peanut plants are fed to livestock, and pigs are put into the fields to uproot and eat the seeds.

George Washington Carver Born into slavery, George Washington Carver worked his way through school and college to become a botanist.

- While doing agricultural research to help the South and other African Americans, he conducted experiments and taught at Tuskegee Institute in Alabama.
- He persuaded farmers to plant peanuts and sweet potatoes instead of soil-depleting cotton; then he found new uses for these soil-enrichers.
- From peanuts he made more than 300 products including flour, ink, dyes, soap, wood stains, insulating board, and synthetic substitutes for butter, cheese, milk, and coffee.

EXTENDING TABLE SKILLS

To help students explore further the table on Sub-Saharan Africa, divide the class into two groups. Have the groups compete in drawing up questions of comparison based on the information presented in this table. Give them some sample questions, such as: How many bilingual nations are there in Sub-Saharan Africa as compared with unilingual nations? How many countries have agricultural products as their leading export as compared with countries whose leading export is a mineral or minerals? How many nations have populations of less than 1 million as compared with nations that have populations of over 1 million? and so on.

Have each group present their questions to the opposing group using a time limit like 30 seconds to answer each question and to gain a point.

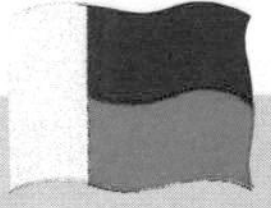

MADAGASCAR
Capital ★ Antananarivo
Major languages: French and Malagasy
Population: 13.4 million
Area: 226,656 sq mi; 587,040 sq km
Leading exports: coffee, vanilla, and sugar

MALAWI
Capital ★ Lilongwe
Major languages: English and Chichewa
Population: 9.7 million
Area: 45,745 sq mi; 118,480 sq km
Leading exports: tobacco, sugar, and tea

MALI
Capital ★ Bamako
Major languages: Bambara and French
Population: 9.1 million
Area: 478,765 sq mi; 1,240,000 sq km
Leading exports: cotton and livestock

MAURITANIA
Capital ★ Nouakchott
Major languages: Arabic and French
Population: 2.2 million
Area: 397,954 sq mi; 1,030,700 sq km
Leading exports: iron ore and fish

MAURITIUS
Capital ★ Port Louis
Major languages: English, Creole, and French
Population: 1.1 million
Area: 718 sq mi; 1,860 sq km
Leading export: sugar

MOZAMBIQUE
Capital ★ Maputo
Major language: Portuguese
Population: 17.3 million
Area: 309,495 sq mi; 801,590 sq km
Leading exports: shrimp, cashew nuts, and sugar

NAMIBIA
Capital ★ Windhoek
Major languages: English, Afrikaans, and German
Population: 1.6 million
Area: 318,259 sq mi; 824,290 sq km
Leading exports: diamonds, uranium, and livestock

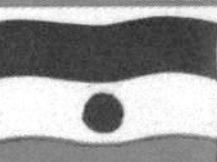

NIGER
Capital ★ Niamey
Major languages: French and Hausa
Population: 9.0 million
Area: 489,190 sq mi; 1,267,000 sq km
Leading export: uranium

NIGERIA
Capital ★ Abuja
Major languages: English, Hausa, Yoruba, and Ibo
Population: 98.1 million
Area: 356,669 sq mi; 923,770 sq km
Leading exports: oil, cocoa, and rubber

RWANDA
Capital ★ Kigali
Major languages: Kinyarwanda and French
Population: 8.4 million
Area: 10,170 sq mi; 26,340 sq km
Leading exports: coffee and tea

SÃO TOMÉ and PRÍNCIPE
Capital ★ São Tomé
Major language: Portuguese
Population: 0.1 million
Area: 371 sq mi; 960 sq km
Leading export: cocoa

SENEGAL
Capital ★ Dakar
Major languages: French and Wolof
Population: 8.7 million
Area: 75,749 sq mi; 196,190 sq km
Leading exports: fuels, fish, and chemicals

BACKGROUND INFORMATION

Uranium Pitchblende is the name of the ore from which uranium, a radioactive substance, can be extracted; the mine tailings are very dangerous because they are radioactive.

- Nuclear energy plants are fueled by radioactive materials derived from uranium, as are atomic and hydrogen bombs.
- The radium available from uranium is used for many medical purposes today. It is also used in industrial radiography, especially for the inspection of metal castings by X rays.
- The uranium exported by Niger goes to France to help fuel the nuclear energy plants there.

CURRICULUM CONNECTION

Art Discuss with the class why nations have flags. (to have a symbol of their country that they can honor) Have students study the flags of Sub-Saharan Africa in the table and note the colors and designs. Discuss why they think many of the designs are so similar. Divide the class into three groups to design a flag for your school. Tell the groups to discuss first which symbols should represent your school. Have the class vote for the best flag design.

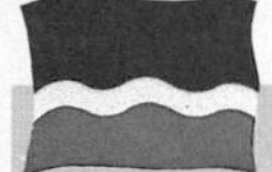

SEYCHELLES
Capital ★ Victoria
Major languages: Creole, English, and French
Population: 0.1 million
Area: 171 sq mi; 443 sq km
Leading exports: fish and cinnamon

SIERRA LEONE
Capital ★ Freetown
Major languages: English, Mende, and Temne
Population: 4.6 million
Area: 27,699 sq mi; 71,740 sq km
Leading exports: rutile, diamonds, and bauxite

SOMALIA
Capital ★ Mogadishu
Major languages: Somali and Arabic
Population: 6.7 million
Area: 246,201 sq mi; 637,660 sq km
Leading exports: bananas and bauxite

SOUTH AFRICA
Capitals ★ Pretoria, Cape Town and Bloemfontein
Major languages: Afrikaans, English, Zulu, Xhosa, and Sesotho
Population: 43.9 million
Area: 471,445 sq mi; 1,221,040 sq km
Leading exports: gold, coal, and minerals

SUDAN
Capital ★ Khartoum
Major language: Arabic
Population: 25.9 million
Area: 967,496 sq mi; 2,505,810 sq km
Leading export: cotton

SWAZILAND
Capital ★ Mbabane
Major languages: siSwati and English
Population: 0.8 million
Area: 6,703 sq mi; 17,360 sq km
Leading exports: food, sugar, and wood products

TANZANIA
Capital ★ Dar es Salaam
Major languages: Swahili and English
Population: 27.9 million
Area: 364,900 sq mi; 945,090 sq km
Leading exports: coffee and cotton

TOGO
Capital ★ Lomé
Major languages: French, Kabiye, and Ewe
Population: 4.3 million
Area: 21,927 sq mi; 56,790 sq km
Leading export: phosphates

UGANDA
Capital ★ Kampala
Major languages: English and Luganda
Population: 19.1 million
Area: 91,135 sq mi; 236,040 sq km
Leading export: coffee

ZAIRE
Capital ★ Kinshasa
Major languages: French, Kiswahili, and Kiluba
Population: 42.7 million
Area: 905,565 sq mi; 2,345,410 sq km
Leading export: copper

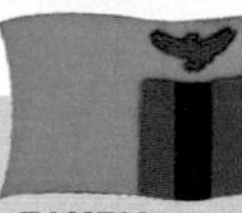

ZAMBIA
Capital ★ Lusaka
Major languages: English, Nyanja, and Bamba
Population: 9.2 million
Area: 290,583 sq mi; 752,610 sq km
Leading export: copper

ZIMBABWE
Capital ★ Harare
Major languages: English, Chishona, and Sindebele
Population: 10.1 million
Area: 150,803 sq mi; 390,580 sq km
Leading exports: tobacco and gold

Making a Card Game from a Table In the first units of this book, students were given practice in asking questions to help them learn a process for grasping the meaning of a table. Then they were asked to make a worksheet of their own from the key questions or approaches. Now students should know the key ways to find meaning in a table. They should be encouraged to manipulate a table as often as possible as a basis for games, competitions, and computer applications.

Divide the class into four groups and have each group make a pack of 47 cards, with each card having information about one country on it. Have each group design a game using the pack of cards and write out the directions so others can play. Have the groups exchange the decks of cards and try each other's games.

Making a Computer Database from a Table If your school has computers for student use, or if you have a computer in the classroom, students could be assigned to key in the information about each country. Computer programs that sort and rank numbers could be applied to the Sub-Saharan database to sort and list records by the information categories in the table.

Students with advanced computer experience could produce graphic charts illustrating the relative sizes of land areas, and circle or bar graphs listing the percent of population and land area for each country. Encourage these students to design visuals from these tables and to be as creative as possible using the computer software available to them. If computers are not available, have students create graphic charts on their own.

FUNDAMENTAL THEMES OF GEOGRAPHY

Human-Environment Interaction In 1886 the city of Johannesburg arose as a result of the discovery of gold ore in a rich vein on the Witwatersrand Reef, or "The Rand."

- Tunnels were dug deep below the streets of Johannesburg before the mines were exhausted there.
- This gold vein, dubbed the Golden Arc, swings south into the Orange Free State. Running at an average of 4,000 feet (1,219 m) deep, the vein is less than 1 foot (.3 m) thick.
- The miners work and live in difficult conditions, and large areas of dormitory-like living quarters have been built for the miners to live in because their homes are far away in the black homelands.

CHAPTER 20 ORGANIZER

PHYSICAL GEOGRAPHY OF SUB-SAHARAN AFRICA

text pages 414–425

CHAPTER THEME

Trade winds dominate the climate over Sub-Saharan Africa's wide variety of dramatic landforms and bodies of water.

CHAPTER OBJECTIVES

CONTENT

- Describe the major physical features of Sub-Saharan Africa.
- Define *rift valley* and describe the main characteristics of Africa's Great Rift Valley.
- Define *escarpment* and describe the impact escarpments have on river transportation.
- Describe the two major economic activities in the savanna region of Africa.
- Describe the climate and list the chief natural resources of Sub-Saharan Africa.
- Identify the trade winds and describe their impact on the climate of Sub-Saharan Africa.
- Describe the impact that years of drought have had on people in Africa's savanna.
- Explain how the tsetse fly has affected health in large regions of Sub-Saharan Africa.
- Explain why the nations of Sub-Saharan Africa have not harnessed their water resources to make electricity.

SKILLS

Geography
- Identify different regions of elevation in Sub-Saharan Africa by using an elevation map.
- Interpret a population density map of Sub-Saharan Africa.
- Interpret a land use map of Sub-Saharan Africa.
- Read distribution maps.

Thinking
- Classify a series of terms into two different geographic categories.
- Predict which resources will be developed in the future in Sub-Saharan Africa.

Reading and Writing
- Write a travel article about Sub-Saharan Africa.

CITIZENSHIP VALUES

- Appreciate the importance of geographical diversity.

TEACHER OPTIONS

READING STRATEGY: Adjusting Reading Rate
Strategies to help students read and remember the main ideas of the lesson.
Lesson 1: p. 415 Lesson 2: p. 420

MEETING INDIVIDUAL NEEDS Activities for reteaching, extension, and enrichment.
Lesson 1: p. 418 Lesson 2: p. 423
Study and Research Skills: p. 419

GEO ADVENTURES ACTIVITIES PAD Daily activities to assess students' understanding of geography skills.

CURRICULUM CONNECTION Activities to help integrate other subject areas with Social Studies.
Earth Science: p. 417 Life Science: p. 417

PUPIL EDITION ON CASSETTE Language support for students who have difficulty reading or who will benefit from listening to the Pupil Edition on Cassette as they read.

SECOND-LANGUAGE SUPPORT Activities and suggestions for second-language learners.

Lesson 1: p. 407-D

CHAPTER PLANNING GUIDE

LESSON	SUGGESTED PACING	THEMES	TEACHER SUPPORT MATERIALS: TEACHER'S RESOURCE CENTER
1 LANDFORMS pages 415–418	1 day	Sub-Saharan Africa has a variety of environments that differ greatly in climate, vegetation, and landforms.	Practice Book p. 111 Outline Map p. 29 **Technology:** *Adventures CD-ROM*
BUILDING STUDY AND RESEARCH SKILLS Reading a Mileage Chart page 419	1 day	Mileage charts tell the distance between two places.	Practice Book p. 112
2 CLIMATE AND RESOURCES pages 420–423	1 day	Sub-Saharan Africa's economic growth depends on solving agricultural problems and on developing mineral and water resources.	Practice Book p. 113 **Technology:** *Adventures CD-ROM*
CHAPTER SUMMARY AND REVIEW pages 424–425	1 day	Chapter content, skills, and vocabulary are reviewed and evaluated.	Practice Book p. 114 Transparency: Graphic Organizer Assessment Book, Chapter 20 Test

Technology CONNECTION

Lesson 1
ADVENTURES CD-ROM
Enrich Lesson 1 by having students make their own map of Africa in *Build,* using *Paint* to mark the Sub-Saharan region.

Lesson 2
ADVENTURES CD-ROM
Enrich Lesson 2 with the climographs in *Investigate, Charts.*

CHAPTER 20

pages 414–425

USING THE CHAPTER OPENER

Discussing the Photograph Use the photograph to help students to realize how the houses they see here relate to the climate and the terrain of Sub-Saharan Africa.

Ask students:

- **What do you think this photograph shows?** (Possible answers include: a village that is home to some people living in Africa; a group of houses built to withstand a tropical climate.)
- **From what materials do you think these houses are built?** (leaves, grasses, the bark of trees)
- **Why do you think the houses are constructed from these materials?** (Students might suggest that in a tropical climate houses built of leaves and grasses allow free circulation of air.)
- *THINKING FURTHER:* **How do you think that people in this village earn their livelihood?** (probably from some form of agriculture)

Reading/Listening to the Primary Source Have students study the photograph as you read the quotation and the opening passage to them. Ask them to locate Gambia on the map on page 428.

Ask students:

- **How do most Africans feel about the land on which they build their homes?** (They feel that the land gives them life, in return for which they must treasure it.)

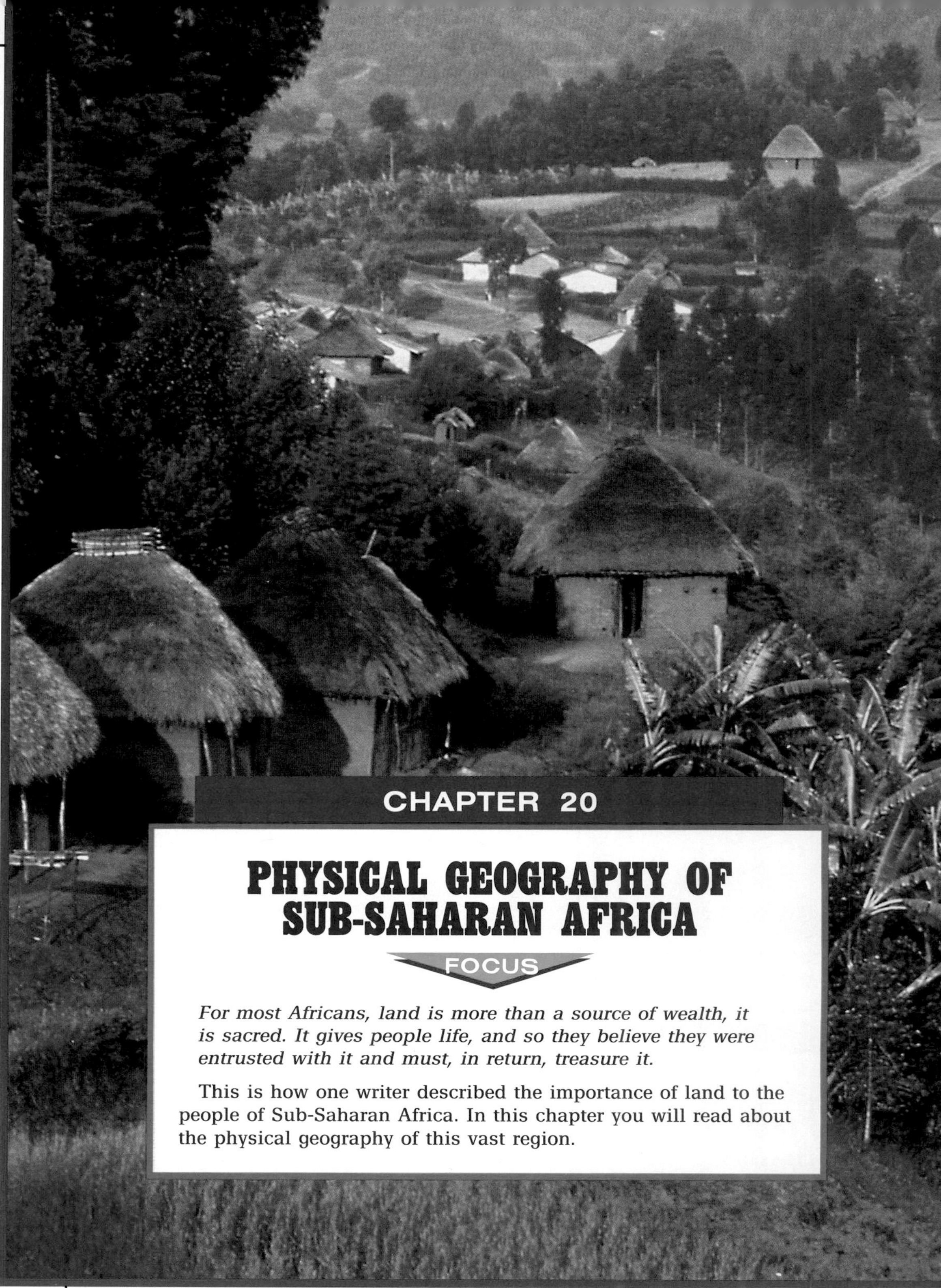

CHAPTER 20

PHYSICAL GEOGRAPHY OF SUB-SAHARAN AFRICA

FOCUS

For most Africans, land is more than a source of wealth, it is sacred. It gives people life, and so they believe they were entrusted with it and must, in return, treasure it.

This is how one writer described the importance of land to the people of Sub-Saharan Africa. In this chapter you will read about the physical geography of this vast region.

BACKGROUND INFORMATION

About African Cities Although most Africans live in small farm villages, more and more of them are moving to cities.

- The trend toward urbanization began to rise in the early 1960s when most African countries gained their independence. One reason for this trend is that an increasing number of Africans who had received high school and university educations left their farm villages to find suitable employment.
- Urban Africans remain in close communication with their rural friends and relatives. Because of this interchange the cultural and political ideas born in the city spread rapidly to the villages.
- Urban Africans from the same village or family group form clubs and other associations into which they take newcomers to help them adjust to city life.

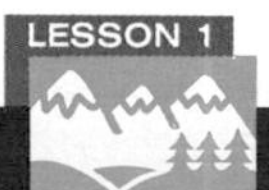

LESSON 1

Landforms

READ TO LEARN

Key Vocabulary

basin
rift valley
escarpment
savanna

Key Places

West Africa
East and Equatorial Africa
Southern Africa
Great Rift Valley
Sahel

Read Aloud

According to an ancient African legend, two angry bulls once fought a fierce battle. They pawed and stamped with such rage that they smashed mountains into powdery dirt. Their hoofs churned up giant clouds of red dust that covered the entire land of West Africa.

In this lesson you will read about the red clay landscape of West Africa. You will also read about vast grasslands and thick, green forests in other parts of Sub-Saharan Africa. As you will discover, this is a region of great variety.

Read for Purpose

1. WHAT YOU KNOW: How would you describe the physical geography of North Africa?
2. WHAT YOU WILL LEARN: What are the major physical features of Sub-Saharan Africa?

SOUTH OF THE SAHARA

Did you know that Africa is the world's second-largest continent? You began to learn about Africa when you read about North Africa in Unit 5. You may recall that the world's largest desert, the Sahara, extends across North Africa from the Atlantic Ocean to the Red Sea. You may also recall that geographers link North Africa together culturally with the area known as the Middle East.

In this unit you will read about Sub-Saharan Africa. This region extends southward from the Sahara and includes most of Africa.

If you look at the map of the region of Sub-Saharan Africa in the Unit Opener on pages 408–409, you can see that this region includes about three fourths of the continent of Africa. Note also that Madagascar, a large island in the Indian Ocean, is included in this region. Within Sub-Saharan Africa there are great extremes of climate, vegetation, and landforms. Although people have created special ways to live in the different environments of this region, some parts of it are so harsh that few people try to live there.

West Africa, East and Equatorial Africa, and Southern Africa are the three areas

WHAT YOU KNOW: Possible responses include: deserts, fertile river valleys, and oases.

415

LESSON 1
pages 415–418

Lesson Theme Sub-Saharan Africa has a variety of environments that differ greatly in climate, vegetation, and landforms.

Lesson Objectives

- Describe the physical features of Sub-Saharan Africa.
- Compare the elevations and kinds of vegetation in this region's different environments.

PREPARE

Motivate Read the *Read Aloud* section to the class. Ask students if they have ever seen red soil.

Set Purpose Use the *What You Know* question to ask students what features of North Africa might extend into Sub-Saharan Africa. Tell students that the answer to the *What You Will Learn* question will include more physical features than are found only in North Africa. Point out the physical *Atlas* map of Sub-Saharan Africa so that students may refer to it throughout the lesson.

TEACH

Introducing the Area South of the Sahara Help students to realize the size and complexity of Sub-Saharan Africa.

Ask students:

- **How does Africa's size compare with that of the other continents?** (It is the second-largest continent.)
- **What are the three parts of Sub-Saharan Africa?** (West Africa, East and Equatorial Africa, Southern Africa)

READING STRATEGY AND VOCABULARY DEVELOPMENT

Adjusting Reading Rate Review with students the importance of varying their reading rate according to their purpose for reading. Have students preview Lesson 1 of this chapter by scanning the section headings, the words from the *Key Vocabulary*, and the sentences that begin and end each paragraph. Then ask students how their purpose affected their rate of reading. (Since the purpose was to identify the important ideas in the lesson, the reading rate was rapid.) Next have students read the section titled "South of the Sahara." Point out that since this section is a general introduction to the lesson, it should be read quickly for the topics that will be explained more fully in subsequent sections. Ask students to read the rest of the lesson by themselves. Have them note whether they read each section quickly or slowly and give reasons for their rate of reading.

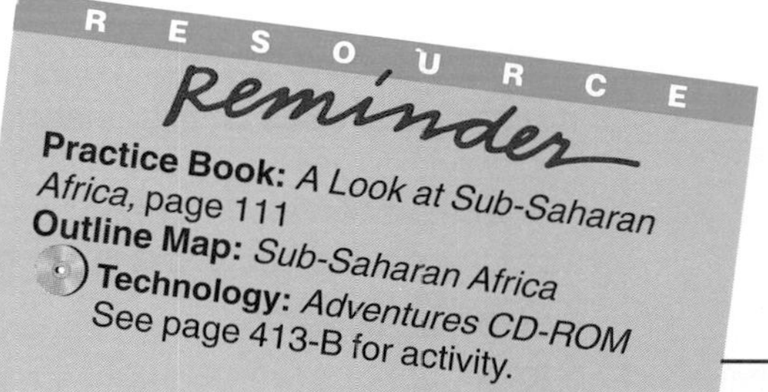

RESOURCE Reminder

Practice Book: *A Look at Sub-Saharan Africa*, page 111
Outline Map: *Sub-Saharan Africa*
Technology: *Adventures CD-ROM*
See page 413-B for activity.

EXTENDING MAP SKILLS

Have students study the elevation map on this page.

Ask students:

- **What is the most common elevation in Southern Africa?** (1,500–7,000 feet, or 500–2,000 m)
- **What is the most common elevation in West Africa?** (700 feet, or 200 m)
- **Where are the highest mountains in Sub-Saharan Africa?** (East Africa)

EXTENDING MAP SKILLS

Have students study the vegetation map on this page.

Ask students:

- **What is the most common vegetation zone in Sub-Saharan Africa?** (the savanna)
- **Which deserts other than the Sahara are labeled on the elevation map?** (the Kalahari, the Namib)
- **What is distinctive about the location of the Sahel?** (It lies between the Sahara and the savanna areas of this region.)
- **Compare the two maps. At which elevation is most of the equatorial rain forest of Sub-Saharan Africa located?** (0–1,500 feet, or 0–500 m)

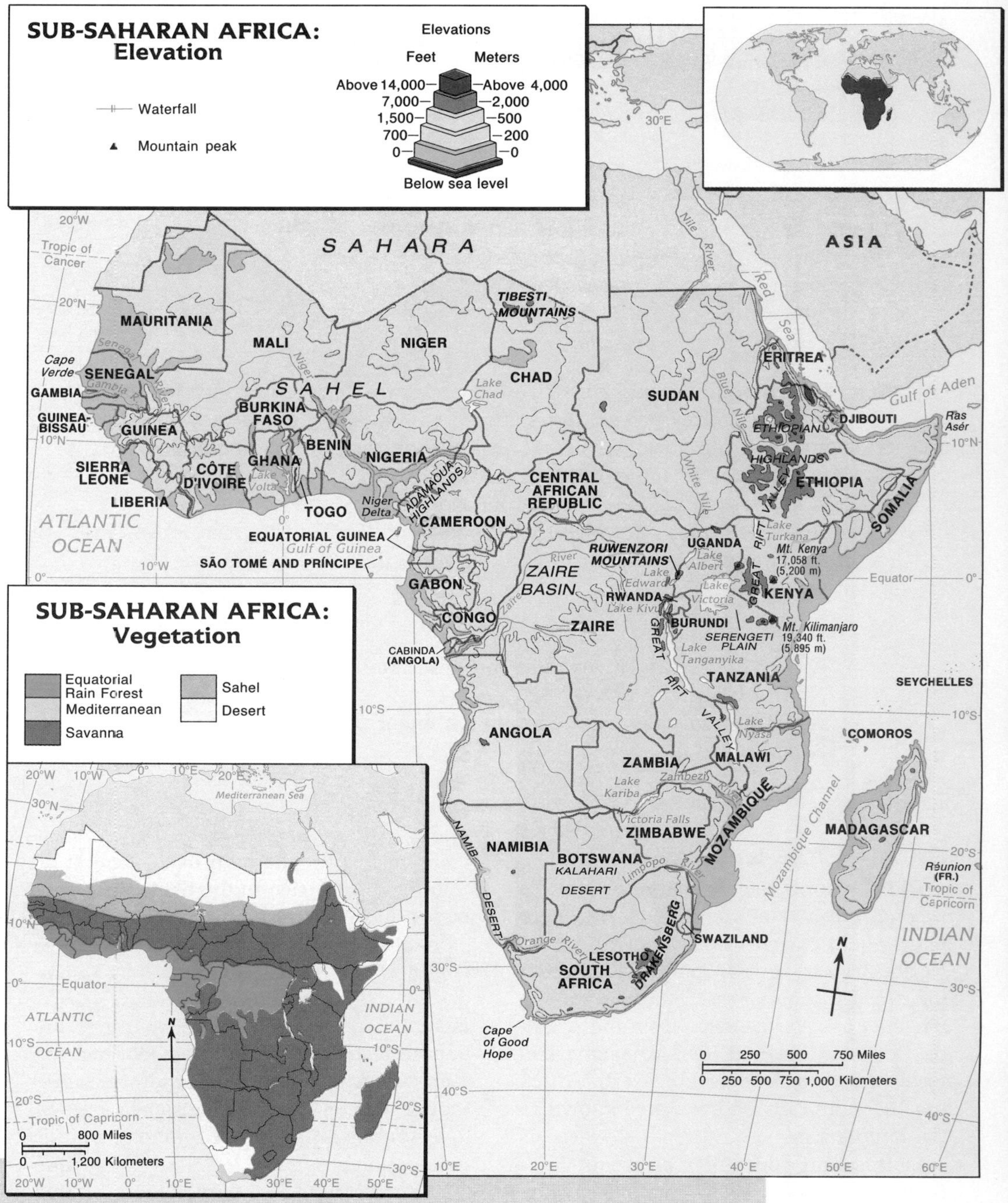

SUB-SAHARAN AFRICA: Elevation

Elevations: Feet / Meters — Above 14,000 / Above 4,000; 7,000 / 2,000; 1,500 / 500; 700 / 200; 0 / 0; Below sea level

Waterfall; Mountain peak

SUB-SAHARAN AFRICA: Vegetation

Equatorial Rain Forest; Mediterranean; Savanna; Sahel; Desert

MAP SKILL: Most of Sub-Saharan Africa's land is at low elevations. What is the region's largest area of high elevation? What type of vegetation is found in the Zaire Basin?

MAP SKILL: the Ethiopian Highlands; equatorial rain forest

BACKGROUND INFORMATION

Multicultural Perspectives People around the world have demonstrated their ties to their land by naming it. During Africa's colonization many local names were replaced by European names.

- In the late 1880s British financier Cecil Rhodes oversaw the takeover of land controlled by the Shona and Ndebele peoples. In 1895 the land became a British colony named Rhodesia in his honor.
- In 1878 Belgium's King Leopold II hired an explorer to set up his own personal colony on land controlled by the Kongo and other peoples. In 1885 Leopold II named his new colony "the Congo Free State."

As Africans began winning their independence, European names were changed to African names.

- In 1980 the newly independent country of Rhodesia was renamed Zimbabwe, which means "house of stone" in Shona. In about A.D. 1000 the Shona had built a great city of stone called Zimbabwe.
- In a 1971 "authenticity" campaign designed to break all ties with colonialism, Congo's President Mobuto changed his country's name to Zaire. In the Kikongo language, *zaire* means "the river that swallows all rivers" and refers to the mighty river that flows through the heart of Zaire. Ask students how names can reflect the history of places.

that make up Sub-Saharan Africa. Find those areas on the Unit Opener map. More than 435 million people live in the more than 45 large and small countries that make up these areas.

A VAST PLATEAU

As the map on page 416 shows, much of Sub-Saharan Africa rises no higher than 7,000 feet (2,000 m) above sea level. There are lowlands along the coasts and rivers, and there is a great plateau that stretches the length of the region. As the map shows, this plateau is broken in East Africa by an area of highlands. The highest mountains of Africa, Mount Kilimanjaro (kil ə mən jär′ ō) and Mount Kenya, are found in this region. Both of these towering mountains are volcanoes that are no longer active.

In addition to plateaus, there are huge basins in Sub-Saharan Africa. As you may know, a basin is a large, bowl-shaped dip in the land. Rivers flow into basins from surrounding highlands. The huge Zaire (zä îr′) Basin is sometimes called "The Heart of Africa." It is a place of dense rain forests, swamps, and winding rivers. Where is the Zaire Basin on the map?✻

THE GREAT RIFT VALLEY

The most dramatic landforms in Sub-Saharan Africa are a series of huge north-south cracks in the land called rift valleys. A rift valley is a narrow valley with steep sides that was formed millions of years ago by cracks in the earth's crust. One large area of rift valleys in Sub-Saharan Africa is the Great Rift Valley. This area starts in Mozambique at Lake Nyasa (also called Lake Malawi) and is made up of several systems of rift valleys. North of Lake Nyasa, the western part of the Great Rift Valley bends to the west of Lake Victoria and includes Lake Tanganyika (tan gən yē′ kə), Lake Kivu, Lake Edward, and Lake Albert.

✻In the west-central part of Sub-Saharan Africa

In Zimbabwe, the Zambezi River plunges over an escarpment to form "The Smoke That Thunders," Victoria Falls.

Another system of rift valleys branches to the east of Lake Victoria toward Lake Rudolf, forming the eastern belt of the Great Rift Valley. Still farther north a system of rift valleys cuts through the highlands of Ethiopia and forms the Red Sea.

RIVERS AND ESCARPMENTS

While many people in Sub-Saharan Africa live in the Great Rift Valley, others are clustered along great rivers and their tributaries. Did you know that the Nile River has its source in Sub-Saharan Africa? The Nile, Zaire, and Niger rivers are Africa's longest rivers. They descend from Africa's vast plateau, forming rapids and waterfalls. In fact many African rivers fall over escarpments. An escarpment is a steep cliff at the edge of a plateau.

For example, the Zambezi River plunges 350 feet (100 m) at Victoria Falls in Zimbabwe (zim bäb′ wē). People who live near the falls call it "The Smoke That Thunders" because the thundering Zambezi River crashes over an escarpment and constantly sprays water into the air.

Identifying a Vast Plateau As they read the text, have students locate the Sub-Saharan African central plateau on the elevation map on page 416.

Ask students:

- **How does the land along the coasts and rivers contrast with the land in the center of this region?** (Plains are found along the coasts and rivers; a vast plateau is found inland.)
- **What are Mount Kenya and Mount Kilimanjaro?** (inactive volcanoes)
- **Which place is known as the "Heart of Africa"?** (the Zaire Basin)
- *THINKING FURTHER:* **Why do you think that the Zaire Basin has rain forests and swamps?** (It has rain forests because the moisture from the rivers that flow into the basin, combined with the equatorial heat, create good conditions for their growth. It has swamps because of its abundance of water and because of its location in an area lower than the surrounding areas.)

Understanding the Great Rift Valley Help students to understand that the Great Rift Valley is the result of movements in the earth's crust that occurred millions of years ago.

Ask students:

- **What is a rift valley?** (a narrow valley with steep sides formed by cracks in the earth's crust)

Looking at Rivers and Escarpments Point out to students that, as in other regions of the world, Africans live clustered along rivers and other sources of water.

Ask students:

- **What are the longest rivers of Africa?** (the Nile, Zaire, and Niger rivers)
- **What is an escarpment?** (a steep cliff at the edge of a plateau)

CURRICULUM CONNECTION

Earth Science In terms of geologic time, the Great Rift Valley was formed fairly recently. Ask students to research and prepare written reports on the various changes that geologists predict for the shape of Africa. For example, some geologists predict that the Great Rift Valley will become a sea and that East Africa will separate from the rest of the continent and drift into the Indian Ocean.

Life Science The plants of the savanna have evolved special features that are suitable for that region's two-season year. Have students research and write a report on one of the following topics: "How the Baobab Tree Adapts"; "The Relationship Between Fire and Seeds"; "The Advantages of Long Roots for the Grasses"; "Seed Dispersal Techniques"; "How Thorns and Narrow Leaves Help a Plant Survive in a Dry Climate."

EXTENDING MAP SKILLS

Tell students to study the population density map on this page.

Ask students:

- **Which two population densities are most common in Sub-Saharan Africa?** (0–2 people per square mile, or 0–1 people per sq km; 2–25 people per square mile, or 1–10 people per sq km)

Comparing the Sahel, the Savanna, and the Rain Forest Help students to see the contrasts between these vegetation zones.

Applying the Lesson Give students the outline map of Sub-Saharan Africa, which can be found in the Teacher's Resource Center. Have them label the three vegetation zones, the three longest rivers, the Great Rift Valley, the Sahel, the savanna, and the Zaire Basin.

3 CLOSE

Summarizing Students have read that this region has a variety of environments, that most of its people live near water, and that most of its farming is done on the savanna.

Evaluating Use the *Check Your Reading* questions (answers given below) to assess students' understanding.

Answers to Check Your Reading

1. narrow valleys with sharp sides formed from cracks in the earth
2. a steep cliff at the edge of a plateau
3. The Sahel is more desertlike than the savanna.
4. *landforms:* basin, escarpment, rift valley; *vegetation zones:* rain forest, Sahel, savanna; These terms suggest the variety of environments in this region.

Independent Practice
Practice Book: page 111

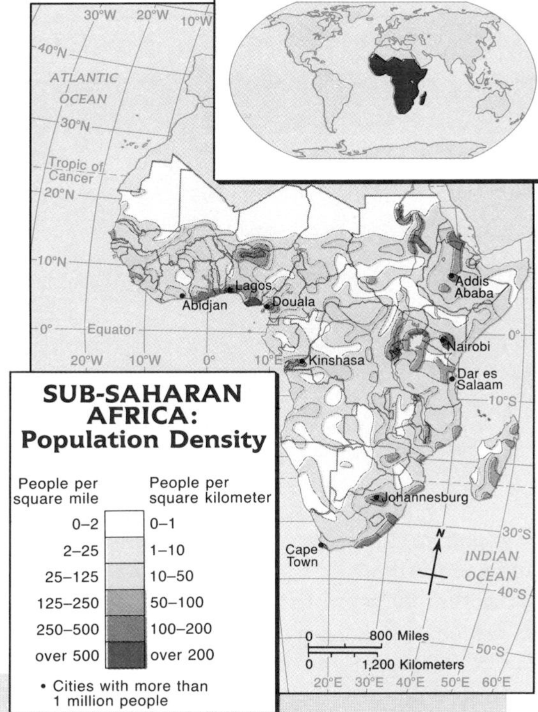

MAP SKILL: Which are the two southernmost cities in Sub-Saharan Africa shown above?

Because they are dramatic and beautiful, waterfalls throughout the world often attract tourists. But waterfalls present a constant challenge to the people who live near them. Huge waterfalls make rivers useless for boat traffic. The great number of escarpments in Sub-Saharan Africa means that there are few navigable rivers.

SAHEL, SAVANNA, AND RAIN FOREST

Just south of the Sahara is a mostly dry area of grasslands known as the **Sahel** (sä' hel). *Sahel* is an Arabic word meaning "border" or "shore." As you might have guessed, this vegetation zone got its name because it borders the Sahara. Parts of the Sahel are dry and dusty. The dusty red clay of West Africa that you read about in the lesson opener is found in the Sahel.

In addition to the Sahel, Sub-Saharan Africa is famous for two other special zones of vegetation. The largest zone is known as the **savanna**. A savanna is a broad grassland containing scattered trees and shrubs. The savanna covers more than one fourth of the African continent. It is the major farming and livestock-grazing area of Sub-Saharan Africa. Most of the large animals for which Africa is famous—such as lions, elephants, and giraffes—live on the savanna.

The other important vegetation zone in Sub-Saharan Africa is the tropical rain forest. The rain forest forms a curving belt that begins in West Africa and loops south to include all of the Zaire Basin. It rains almost every day in the rain forest, and temperatures are always high.

THE LAND SOUTH OF THE SAHARA

As you have read, Sub-Saharan Africa is a large region, and its people live in a variety of environments. Note from the map on this page that most of the people live near bodies of water. Plateaus, rift valleys, river basins, escarpments, and waterfalls are all found in Sub-Saharan Africa.

Check Your Reading

1. Describe the Great Rift Valley.
2. What is an escarpment?
3. What is the difference between the Sahel and the savanna?
4. **THINKING SKILL:** Classify the terms below into at least two categories. Explain what this information tells about Sub-Saharan Africa.

basin	*rain forest*	*Sahel*
escarpment	*rift valley*	*savanna*

 MAP SKILL: Johannesburg and Cape Town

THINKING SKILL: Classifying

MEETING INDIVIDUAL NEEDS

Reteaching (easy) Give students the outline map of Sub-Saharan Africa, which can be found in the Teacher's Resource Center, and ask them to mark the three vegetation zones in different colors. Have students tell what percentage of Africa each zone covers.

Extension (average) Divide the class into three groups and have each research one of these rivers: the Niger, the Zaire, or the Zambezi. Have each group present its findings in the form of a diary kept by a tourist traveling the full length of the river.

Enrichment (challenging) Divide the class into four groups and have each research one of these topics: "The Zaire Basin"; "The Great Rift Valley"; "The Source of the Nile"; "Wildlife on the Savanna." Have each group present its findings as a TV news team giving an on-the-spot report.

BUILDING SKILLS
STUDY AND RESEARCH SKILLS

Reading a Mileage Chart

Key Vocabulary
mileage chart

Suppose you wanted to know how far it is from Lagos, Nigeria, to Nairobi, Kenya. You might refer to a map, using its scale bar to measure the distance between these two cities. But you could use a mileage chart instead. A mileage chart is a table that shows distances between specific places. Some mileage charts show distances by air while others show distances by road, train, or water.

How to Read a Mileage Chart

Look at the mileage chart on this page. First, read the title of the chart. It tells you that the chart shows distances between 5 cities in Sub-Saharan Africa. The title also tells whether the distances are by air or by land. Next, read the labels on the horizontal and vertical axes on the chart. The labels on the horizontal axis list some of the cities in Sub-Saharan Africa in alphabetical order. The labels on the vertical axis list the same 5 cities, also in alphabetical order.

Suppose you want to find the distance between Kampala and Nairobi. Find Kampala on the horizontal axis and place your right index finger on it. Now find Nairobi on the vertical axis, and put your left index finger on it. Move both fingers, one across the chart and one down, until they meet. You have found the distance between the two cities. What is it?✻

Have you noticed that there is a blank space in each row on the chart? You will find that the blank space is where each city listed on the vertical axis meets the same city on the horizontal axis. Of course, there is no distance between a city and itself, so this area of the chart is left blank.

✻414 miles

MILEAGE CHART
FIVE AFRICAN CITIES

Road Distance in Miles	Jinja	Kampala	Mombasa	Nairobi	Tanga
Jinja		50	668	364	764
Kampala	50		718	414	814
Mombasa	668	718		304	96
Nairobi	364	414	304		401
Tanga	764	814	96	401	

Reviewing the Skill

1. What is the purpose of using a mileage chart?
2. How far is it from Mombasa to Nairobi? From Jinja to Mombasa?
3. Which trip would be longer—traveling from Jinja to Nairobi or from Mombasa to Nairobi?
4. If you were to travel from Jinja to Nairobi to Mombasa by car, how many miles would you drive?
5. Why is it useful to understand how to read mileage charts?

419

SKILLS LESSON
page 419

Lesson Theme Mileage charts tell the distance between two places.

Lesson Objective
- Read a mileage chart.

 PREPARE

Motivate Have the class choose two cities from the elevation map on page 416. Using the scale bar, list the distances between the two cities by air, road, and water in comparative columns. Discuss why each is a different distance.

Set Purpose Tell the class that they will learn how to read a mileage chart.

 TEACH

Practicing How to Read a Mileage Chart Ask the class if the chart on this page gives air or land distances. (land distances) Name pairs of cities and ask students to read the mileage between each pair.

Applying the Lesson Have the class construct a chart of landmarks in their town, using city blocks or miles as the measure.

 CLOSE

Summarizing Students have learned how to read a mileage chart. Ask why each row on the mileage chart has a blank space.

Answers to Reviewing the Skill

1. to find the distance between two cities
2. 304 miles; 668 miles
3. from Jinja to Nairobi
4. 668 miles
5. to know comparative distances by air, land, or water in order to plan travel; saves time during trips

MEETING INDIVIDUAL NEEDS

Reteaching (easy) Have students work in pairs. Have students give their partners the names of pairs of cities. From the chart on this page, have them read the road mileage between the cities in each of their pairs.

Extension (average) Have students use the elevation map on page 416 and its scale bar, to convert the road mileage chart on this page into an air mileage chart by measuring in straight lines from city to city.

Enrichment (challenging) Have students research and report to the class on all the places they have found mileage charts, such as in travel books, and on what kinds of charts they have found. From this information, have students determine whether air, road, train, or water mileage charts are most available to the general public.

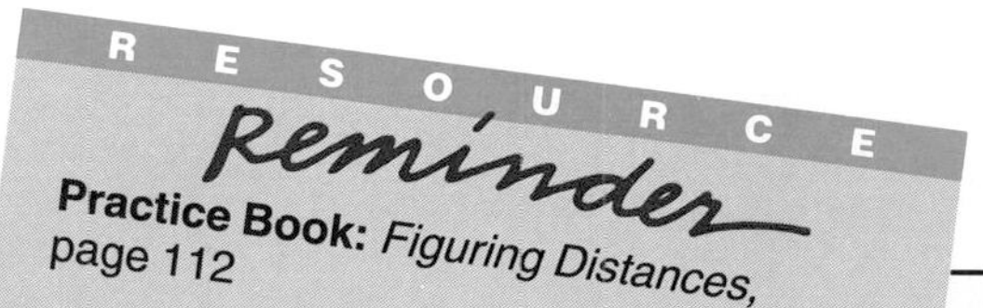

Practice Book: *Figuring Distances,* page 112

LESSON 2
pages 420–423

Lesson Theme Sub-Saharan Africa's economic growth depends on solving agricultural problems and on developing mineral and water resources.

Lesson Objectives
- Describe the climates of Sub-Saharan Africa.
- Identify the problems caused by disease-bearing insects.
- Identify Sub-Saharan Africa's potential resources.

PREPARE

Motivate Read the *Read Aloud* section to the class. Ask students why they think this lesson begins with a passage discussing the scarcity of water.

Set Purpose Ask the *What You Know* question to review the effect of latitude on climate. Ask the *What You Will Learn* question and encourage students to speculate about the climates and natural resources of this region.

TEACH

Looking at the Tropics

Ask students:

- **What are three major facts about the climates in Sub-Saharan Africa?** (warm all year; often dry; great differences between daytime and nighttime temperatures)

LESSON 2

Climate and Resources

READ TO LEARN

Key Vocabulary
trade winds
drought
harmattan

Key Places
Kano

Read Aloud

In southwestern Niger there is a type of antelope called an addax that rarely needs to drink water. This is just as well, because most of this region gets only a few inches of rain each year. Some of the scarce water collects in rock pools that attract many kinds of wildlife. Ostriches, baboons, cheetahs, gazelles, and other animals live in this arid climate.

Read for Purpose

1. WHAT YOU KNOW: What kind of climate would you expect lands located at the equator to have?
2. WHAT YOU WILL LEARN: What are the climates of Sub-Saharan Africa? What are the region's chief natural resources?

THE TROPICS

Africa has more tropical land than any other continent. More than 90 percent of Sub-Saharan Africa lies between the Tropic of Cancer and the Tropic of Capricorn. As you can see from the map on the opposite page, the equator slices through the middle of this region.

Except for its mountainous regions, all of Sub-Saharan Africa is warm or hot all year. There is not much difference between the summer and winter temperatures. However, there is often a great difference between daytime temperatures and nighttime temperatures, especially in the deserts. The variation can be as much as 60°F. (15°C). The highest temperatures in Sub-Saharan Africa occur near the Sahara and in the desert of Somalia, along the Indian Ocean.

Rainfall varies throughout Sub-Saharan Africa. As the map on page 421 shows, rain is scarce in about three fourths of Africa. Many places get enough rain for part of the year. For several months after, they swelter under the tropical sun.

For example, the region around **Kano**, in northern Nigeria, gets about the same amount of rain every year as does Chicago, Illinois. Yet Chicago is green with trees, grass, and shrubs because moisture is available year-round. Farmers in the areas around Chicago can grow many kinds of crops. In the area around Kano, the rain comes all at once. Then, in the long dry season, plants turn brown. Few crops can grow because of the long dry spell.

WINDS

Sub-Saharan Africa's seasonal patterns of rainy and dry seasons are caused by winds. Sailors called some of these winds **trade winds** because they determined which way trading ships could sail.

WHAT YOU KNOW: Students should be aware that areas near the equator usually have hot, warm climates because they receive the most direct rays of the sun.

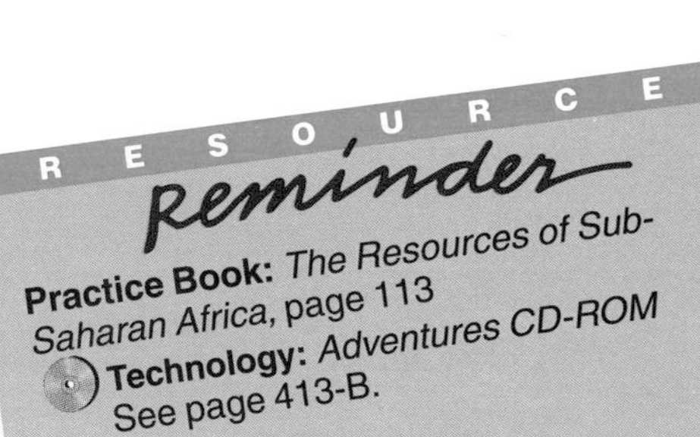

READING STRATEGY AND VOCABULARY DEVELOPMENT

Adjusting Reading Rate Have students practice two different reading rates—rapid reading, or scanning, and slow, careful reading. Ask students to scan Lesson 2 of this chapter for the most important ideas in each section. Remind them that the section headings and the first and last paragraphs of each section usually contain the main ideas. Ask them to write these ideas in the form of questions. For example, they might reword the main idea of the section titled "The Tropics" in the following way: "How does the fact that Sub-Saharan Africa has more tropical land than any other region affect its climate?" After students have scanned the lesson and written the questions, have them reread the lesson slowly to answer the questions. Suggest to students that rereading material in order to answer specific questions is an effective way to study for a test.

In Sub-Saharan Africa trade winds blow from the Atlantic Ocean, carrying moist ocean air into West Africa. As the winds rise over the escarpments at the edge of the plateau, they drop moisture as heavy rain. This is the reason that rain forests start just inland from the west coast.

A second kind of wind picks up dry, dusty air from the Sahara and carries it to Sub-Saharan Africa. This hot, dry wind, called the **harmattan** (här mə tan′), creates a hot, dry season especially in the northwestern part of Sub-Saharan Africa.

Some years the winds shift, resulting in no rainy season in the savannas. Since 1970 the rains have failed several times. **Drought**, or a lack of rain over a long period, has caused plants and crops to die. The results for the people have been disastrous. Millions of people in Ethiopia, Chad, Niger, Mali, Burkina Faso, Somalia, and Senegal have died of hunger-related illnesses after their crops and animals died. More than 240 million Africans live in these areas that have suffered droughts.

INSECTS AND DISEASE

Drought is only one problem that changing trade winds can cause. Another problem is diseases. Mosquitoes and other tropical insects spread malaria, yellow fever, and other illnesses.

One tropical insect, the tsetse (tset′ sē) fly, carries a disease known as sleeping sickness. The tsetse fly also infects cattle, horses, sheep, camels, and other livestock with another disease called nagana. It is usually fatal.

Tsetse flies breed in hot climates that have plenty of rain. They cluster on the banks of streams and rivers. Unfortunately 38 countries in Sub-Saharan Africa have just the right conditions for tsetse flies to thrive. At least 50 million people live in the tsetse-fly area of Sub-Saharan Africa.

MAP SKILL: a strip along the northern edge of the region and a small area in Southern Africa

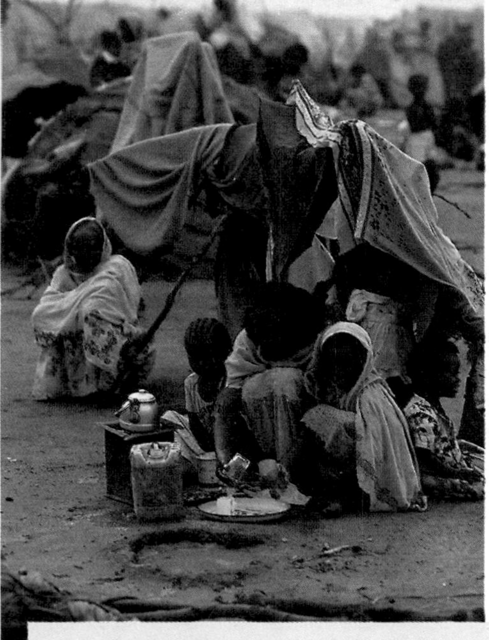

MAP SKILL: Hundreds of millions of people in Sub-Saharan Africa have experienced **drought**, or extremely dry conditions. Which parts of the region are always dry?

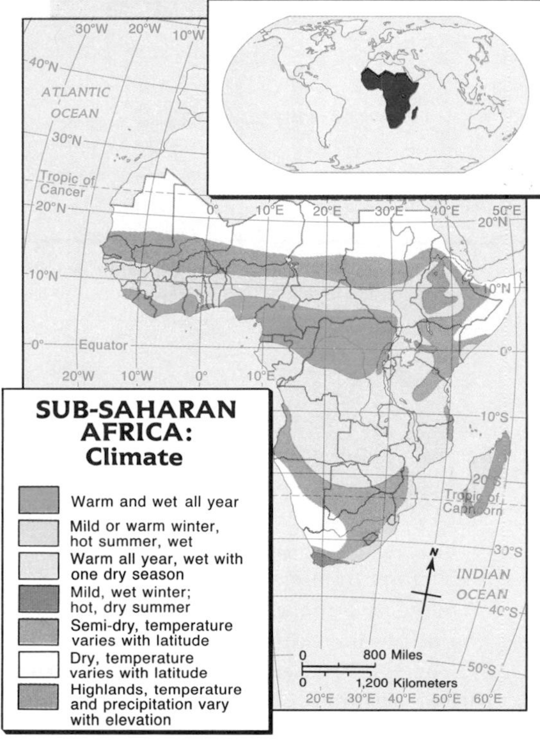

421

Analyzing Winds Help students to understand that the failure of the winds to bring rain causes drought in Sub-Saharan Africa.

Ask students:

- **Why were the seasonal winds in this region named trade winds?** (They determined which way trading ships could sail.)
- **How do the trade winds from the Atlantic bring rain to West Africa?** (They bring moist ocean air, which falls on this area as rain when the winds rise over the bordering escarpments.)
- **How many people have been affected by droughts in Sub-Saharan Africa since 1970?** (240 million)

EXTENDING MAP SKILLS

Have students study the climate map on this page.

Ask students:

- **What is the predominant climate in Sub-Saharan Africa?** (warm all year, wet with one dry season)
- **What kind of climate is found in the middle western area of Sub-Saharan Africa?** (warm and wet all year)
- *THINKING FURTHER:* **Why do you think the climate in this area is wet all year long?** (The area is directly in the path of the trade winds.)

Understanding Insects and Disease Help students to understand how disease-bearing insects affect agriculture in this region.

Ask students:

- **Which two diseases are caused by the tsetse fly? Whom or what do the diseases affect?** (nagana—affects livestock; sleeping sickness—affects humans)
- **How many countries and people are affected by the tsetse fly?** (38 nations; 50 million people)

BACKGROUND INFORMATION

Desertification and Drought The Sahel, which borders Africa's savanna, is merging into the Sahara Desert.

- Since 1970 the lack of rain in the Sahel has speeded up the desertification process, or the process by which land becomes arid or desert. Scientists warn us that within 50 years deserts may cover as much as 45 percent of Africa instead of the 20 percent that they cover today.
- Because goats are hardier than cattle, some farmers have begun to raise goats. Unfortunately this measure only increases desertification, for these animals strip the land of its moisture-holding grass by eating the grass, including the root.
- Some farmers have begun to plant fast-growing trees as a barrier against the invading desert.

Talking About Insects and Disease Continue the discussion.

Ask students:

- **Why is nagana an agricultural problem?** (It kills farm animals.)
- **Why are large areas of the savanna useless for grazing?** (The tsetse fly breeds in large areas of the savanna.)
- *THINKING FURTHER:* **How does drought make prevention of nagana difficult?** (When the grasslands uninfected by the tsetse fly dry up, the farmers have to let their animals graze in the infected areas.)

EXTENDING MAP SKILLS

Have students study the land use map on this page.

Ask students:

- **In which parts of Sub-Saharan Africa does most of the nomadic herding occur?** (in the northern and southern parts)
- **What are the most important economic activities in Sub-Saharan Africa?** (livestock raising, nomadic herding, forestry, mining, fishing)
- *THINKING FURTHER:* **Why do you think such large areas in the northern part of Sub-Saharan Africa support little or no economic activity?** (The northern part is mainly desert.)

Discussing Agriculture Help students to see that farming in Sub-Saharan Africa occurs mainly on the tropical coast and on the savanna.

Ask students:

- **Which products besides cacao come from the African rain forest?** (coffee, rubber, palm oil, timber)
- **In what ways does the savanna serve as a support to important Sub-Saharan African resources?** (as a grazing area for livestock and as a habitat for this region's wildlife)

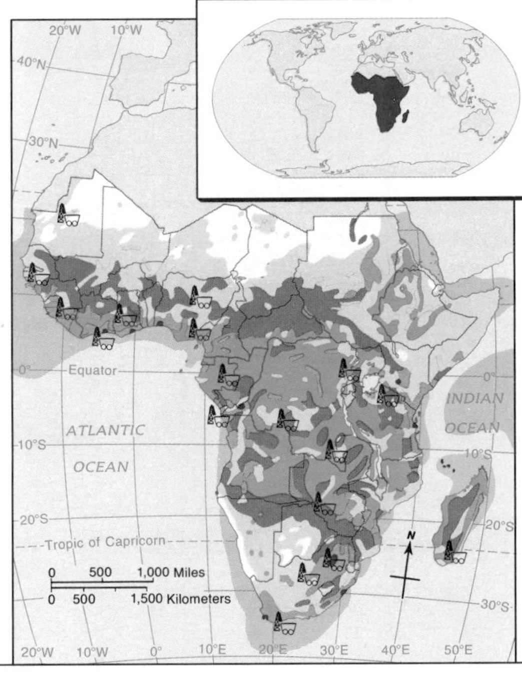

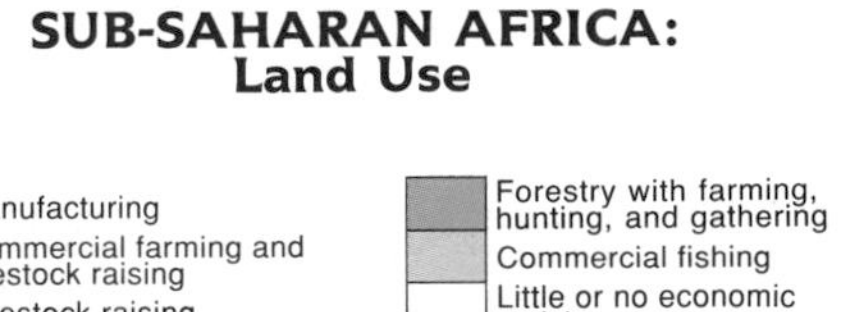

MAP SKILL: Much of Sub-Saharan Africa is rich in minerals. In which part of the region does the least amount of mining take place?

In the tsetse-fly area people cannot keep horses, oxen, camels, or cattle alive. Therefore they have no work animals. Since the people are also usually too poor to buy farm machinery, they must tend their crops by hand.

On the savanna, where herding cattle is a way of life for many people, the tsetse-fly area acts as an invisible wall. Much of the African savanna could support more humans if tsetse flies did not breed there. Herders like the Masai (mä sī′) of East Africa have been very careful to keep their cattle out of the tsetse-fly area. But in recent years, because drought has scorched their traditional lands, some Masai have had to drive their cattle into the danger zone in search of food.

Fortunately some Masai have received help from veterinarians and scientists who are working on the tsetse-fly problem. Governments and health groups are also working hard to find ways to control tropical insects. If killers like tsetse flies can be controlled, Africans can make greater use of the Sub-Saharan region's agricultural resources.

AGRICULTURE

In 1879 a blacksmith named Tete Kwashi (tē tē kwä′ shē) returned to his village in Ghana with seeds from a tree he had seen on an island off the west coast of Africa. Tete Kwashi tended the seedlings that sprouted from the reddish-brown seeds. Five years later he harvested his first cacao (kə ka′ ō) crop.

Today cacao is the most important crop in both Ghana and in the nearby Côte d'Ivoire. Flavoring for the chocolate ice cream or candy you eat may have come from African trees.

Cacao trees grow only in the tropics. They need at least 50 inches (130 cm) of rain a year and hot weather. The tropical coast of West Africa has just the right conditions for growing cacao.

Cacao is by no means the only successful crop of Sub-Saharan Africa. In addition to cacao, the rain forest provides coffee, rubber, palm oil, and other products. Timber from such trees as mahogany, teak, ebony, cedar, and walnut is also a major resource of the rain forest of Sub-Saharan Africa.

MAP SKILL: the northern part of Sub-Saharan Africa

BUILDING CITIZENSHIP

Conserving a Natural Resource Because Africa's magnificent animals attract tourists, they are important natural resources in a practical, as well as in an aesthetic or scientific, sense. Unfortunately many species are in danger of becoming extinct. Have students write to Secretary-General, Unep/CITES Secretariat, 6 Rue du Maupas, Case Postale 78, 1000 Lausanne 9, Switzerland, for information about programs for protecting endangered species in Africa. Ask students to "adopt" one of these species (which might be chosen by vote), and then have them form committees to prepare proposals for saving this animal. Have them bring in magazine and newspaper clippings that report on this animal's fate. You might want to encourage students to organize drives for raising money to help those groups whose conservation programs they support.

The savanna is an important grazing area for livestock. In areas that have enough rain, residents can raise grain crops like millet or corn. The migrating wildlife of the savanna is also a resource. Tourists come from all over the world to see a variety of African wildlife in their natural settings.

A WEALTH OF MINERALS

Sub-Saharan Africa is a storehouse of minerals. Copper, iron, gold, uranium, manganese and many other minerals have been found in the region. And many parts of Sub-Saharan Africa have not as yet been fully explored for their minerals.

Look at the map on page 422. You can see that mining takes place all over Sub-Saharan Africa. Zaire is a center of copper mining. South Africa, the richest country in the region, mines gold, diamonds, uranium, and other scarce resources. Nigeria, in West Africa, has valuable petroleum.

WATER RESOURCES

In the last lesson you read that waterfalls can make rivers useless for transportation. But those same waterfalls can be used to create hydroelectric power. Although Africa has many rivers that could be harnessed to make electricity, most of its countries are too poor to spend the large amounts of money needed to build power dams. Only recently have dams been built. For example, a huge dam on the Zaire River provides the power to run Zaire's mines.

Rivers can be used over and over as an energy resource. Unlike oil or coal, this resource is not gone after one use. Africa's rivers, like its mineral treasures, hold great promise for the continent's future.

A CONTINENT OF CONTRASTS

You have read that trade winds help shape the climate patterns and economy of Sub-Saharan Africa. You have also read that Sub-Saharan Africa is a region of untapped resources. As agricultural problems are solved and mineral and water resources are developed, the economic growth of the region should increase.

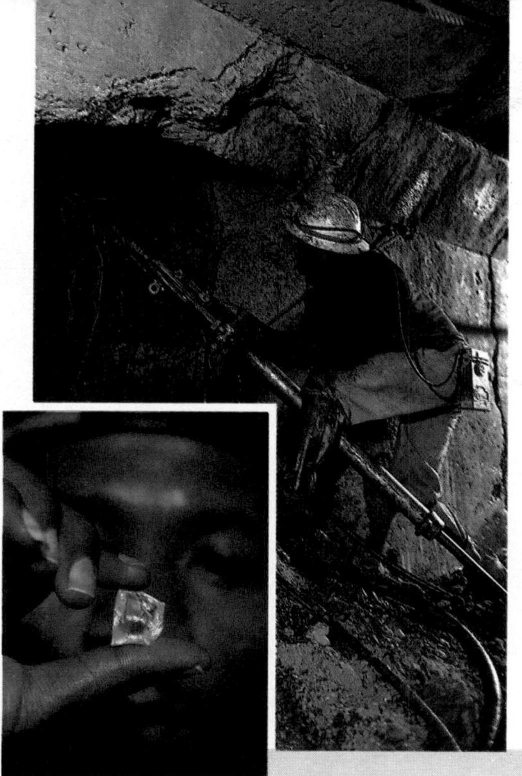

Diamonds (*inset*) are a major mineral resource of South Africa.

Check Your Reading

1. What is a drought?
2. How do the trade winds affect Sub-Saharan Africa's climate?
3. What are some of the important agricultural resources of Sub-Saharan Africa?
4. THINKING SKILL: Which resources do you think will be developed in Sub-Saharan Africa in the future? Why?

THINKING SKILL: Predicting

423

Discussing Mineral and Water Resources

Ask students:

- **In what way are the utilization of Sub-Saharan Africa's waterfalls and the mining of its mineral resources connected?** (If dams are built to harness the power of the waterfalls, the resulting hydroelectricity can be used to run mines.)

Applying the Lesson Have students make a chart listing the resources of Sub-Saharan Africa and the problems in developing them.

3 CLOSE

Summarizing Students have learned that the economic growth of Sub-Saharan Africa depends on the development of its water and mineral resources and the solution of its agricultural problems.

Evaluating Use these questions to assess students' understanding.

- **What kind of climate does the savanna area have?** (warm with one wet and one dry season)
- **Which disease does the tsetse fly cause in cattle?** (nagana)
- **Which two resources have Africans not yet fully developed?** (minerals, rivers)

Answers to Check Your Reading

1. a lack of rain over a long period of time
2. The failure of these winds causes drought.
3. grain crops, grazing areas, rubber, cacao, coffee, palm oil, timber
4. Possible answers include: Dams will be built with money lent by richer nations, whose leaders could then invest in the mines operated by the resulting hydroelectric power.

Independent Practice
Practice Book: page 113

MEETING INDIVIDUAL NEEDS

Reteaching (easy) Ask students to review the lesson and write three statements about precipitation in Sub-Saharan Africa. Then have them develop these sentences into a paragraph about the importance of rainfall in this region.

Extension (average) Have students find out more about the causes of drought in the Sahel in the 1980s and in the 1990s. Ask them to write one paragraph discussing the causes of this drought and another paragraph discussing scientists' predictions about future droughts in the Sahel.

Enrichment (challenging) Ask students to research the causes of famine in Africa and to then write an essay discussing the effects of colonial and modern agricultural practices, war, desertification, and drought on the Sahel food supply.

CHAPTER 20 REVIEW
pages 424–425

USING THE CHAPTER SUMMARY AND REVIEW

Physical Geography These questions may be used for review.

- **What are the three vegetation zones of Sub-Saharan Africa?** (Sahel, savanna, rain forest)
- **What is the climate of Sub-Saharan Africa like?** (mostly tropical with high temperatures all year, rainfall scarce in most parts; Trade winds cause rainy and dry seasons.)
- **Which resource of the region provides electric power?** (waterfalls)

Ideas to Remember

- **What are three landforms of the region?** (plateaus, basins, rift valleys)
- **What are the resources of Sub-Saharan Africa?** (tropical crops, migrating wildlife, mineral resources, waterfalls that can be harnessed to provide hydroelectric power)

Answers to Reviewing Vocabulary

1. savanna
2. basin
3. rift valleys
4. trade winds
5. escarpments

CHAPTER 20 • SUMMARY

SUB-SAHARAN AFRICA: PHYSICAL GEOGRAPHY

LANDFORMS

- Highest mountains: Mount Kilimanjaro, Mount Kenya
- Most of Sub-Saharan Africa is a great plateau

- Special features: Zaire Basin, Great Rift Valley, waterfalls
- Rivers: Nile, Zaire, Niger, Zambezi

- Vegetation zones: Sahel, savanna, rain forest

CLIMATE

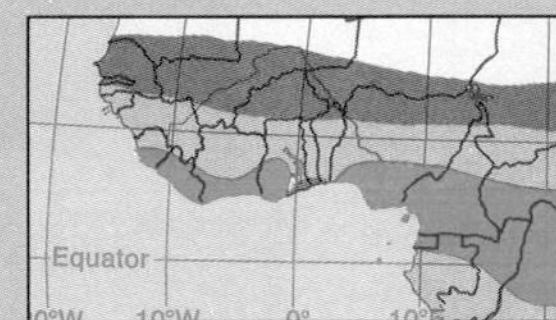

- Mostly tropical, with high temperatures all year
- Rainfall is scarce in about three fourths of the continent

- Trade winds cause rainy and dry seasons
- Tropical diseases include malaria, yellow fever, sleeping sickness

NATURAL RESOURCES

- Tropical crops: cacao, coffee, rubber, palm oil, timber

- Large wildlife preserves attract tourists

- Rich in minerals: copper, iron, gold, uranium, manganese, diamonds
- Many waterfalls that can be harnessed to provide hydroelectric power

IDEAS TO REMEMBER

- The region's plateaus, basins, and rift valleys are covered mainly by savannas and rain forests.
- Most of Sub-Saharan Africa has a tropical climate and its resources include tropical crops, migrating wildlife, and mineral resources.

424

ENRICHMENT ACTIVITY

Making Environmental Models **Materials:** cardboard box bottoms for use as bases, colored tissue paper, construction paper, twigs, reddish powder, modeling clay, crayons, tempera paints, brushes, glue, wire

1. Review with the class the text material on the Sahel, savanna, and rain forests found on page 418. Tell students that they are going to make vegetation models that simulate these three major Sub-Saharan environments.
2. Divide the class into three groups and assign each group one of the three areas. Encourage students to do further research to find more information on the plants and animals in each of their areas.
3. Have students make the models. Encourage them to use the materials provided as freely and creatively as possible. For example, they might use red powder for the Sahel's dry red clay, twigs, green paper leaves, and fronds for the rainforests, shredded green paper for grass, and crumbled paper for shrubs. Suggest to students that they use clay to make models of the animals found in their area. Some students might want to use crayons or paints to develop contrast in the vegetation colors.
4. When students have completed their models have each group make an attractive label for their area. Then have each group arrange a display to share with the rest of the class.

CHAPTER 20 • REVIEW

REVIEWING VOCABULARY

basin
escarpments
rift valleys
savanna
trade winds

Number a sheet of paper from 1 to 5. Beside each number write the word or term from the above list that best matches the definition.

1. A vast region of grasslands in Africa that is similar to prairies in the United States
2. A large bowl-shaped depression named for Zaire in central Africa
3. Low-lying areas bordered by high cliffs that extend through much of the African continent
4. Air currents that strongly influence cycles of rain and drought in Sub-Saharan Africa
5. Steep cliffs that form the boundaries of many of Sub-Saharan Africa's great plateaus

REVIEWING FACTS

1. What is Sub-Saharan Africa? Name its three main regions.
2. What is the Great Rift Valley? Why has this region attracted people throughout history?
3. What is the relationship between escarpments and the lack of navigable rivers in Africa?
4. What is the Sahel? What are two of the main features of this region?
5. Which region of Sub-Saharan Africa is most famous for wildlife?
6. Which vegetation zone is characterized by rain and dense vegetation? In which two African regions is most of this zone located?
7. Name three characteristics of the climate of Sub-Saharan Africa.
8. What effect has drought had on the people of Sub-Saharan Africa?
9. In what way has cacao helped the economies of Ghana and Côte d'Ivoire?
10. What factor has prevented Sub-Saharan nations from developing hydroelectric power?

WRITING ABOUT MAIN IDEAS

1. **Writing a Paragraph:** Write a paragraph describing some of the ways in which the tsetse fly affects the economy of Sub-Saharan Africa.
2. **Writing an Editorial:** Write an editorial about famine in Sub-Saharan Africa.
3. **Writing About Perspectives:** Imagine that you are an African journalist who is traveling from the northern to the southern part of Sub-Saharan Africa. Write a travel article in which you describe the three natural features that you find the most interesting.

BUILDING SKILLS: READING A MILEAGE CHART

1. What is the purpose of using a mileage chart?
2. Look at the mileage chart on page 419. How far is it from Jinja to Kampala?
3. Which trip would be longer—traveling from Tanga to Jinja or from Tanga to Nairobi?
4. Why is it useful to understand how to read mileage charts?

Answers to Reviewing Facts

1. the region that extends southward from the Sahara and includes most of Africa; West Africa, East and Equatorial Africa, Southern Africa
2. a large area of rift valleys in Sub-Saharan Africa; Many waterfalls in this area attract tourists.
3. Many of Africa's rivers fall over escarpments, making the rivers useless for boat traffic.
4. An area of mostly dry grasslands that borders the Sahara; dry and dusty.
5. savanna
6. tropical rain forest; West Africa and the Zaire Basin
7. hot, dry, windy
8. Millions have died of hunger-related illnesses after their crops and animals died.
9. It is the most important crop in both areas.
10. These nations are too poor to spend money on dams.

Suggestions for Writing About Main Ideas

1. Students should focus on the fact that the tsetse fly kills off most livestock, forcing farmers to tend crops by hand since work animals are unavailable.
2. Have students present their editorials to the class. You may wish to have students discuss ways to relieve the famine.
3. Students' journals should include a description of the land, climate, vegetation, and people. Be sure that they identify the areas through which they are traveling.

Answers to Building Skills: Reading a Mileage Chart

1. to determine the distance between places
2. 50 miles (80 km)
3. from Tanga to Jinja
4. to compare distances by air, land, or water for planning travel

Chapter Review and Test

Practice Book: *Vocabulary Review,* page 114
Transparency: *Graphic Organizer*
Assessment Book: *Chapter 20 Test*

MAKING CONNECTIONS

Classifying and Concluding Display the Classification Chart Graphic Organizer Transparency, writing in only the underlined headings. Have students brainstorm geographic features to include in the chart, and classify the features into four groups. *Ask:* What conclusions can you draw about the physical geography of Sub-Saharan Africa?

TOPIC: PHYSICAL GEOGRAPHY OF SUB-SAHARAN AFRICA			
Geographic Features: tropical, savanna, rift valley, waterfalls, minerals, basin, rain forest, trade winds, plateau			
Landforms	Vegetation	Climate	Resources
plateau basin rift valley	rain forest savanna	trade winds tropical	minerals waterfalls

CHAPTER 21 ORGANIZER

WEST AFRICA text pages 426–447

CHAPTER THEME

In West Africa African ways, Islam, and European influences shape the lives of a mix of peoples and make national unity a challenge.

CHAPTER OBJECTIVES

CONTENT

- Describe the three major influences that have helped to shape West African culture.
- Recognize that West African society is made up of hundreds of ethnic groups.
- Explain why West African culture evolved strict rules for cooperation among people.
- Identify the major occupations of the people of West Africa.
- Define *clan* and explain the importance of clans to the structure of West African society.
- Describe the different kinds of economies found in West Africa.
- Define *desertification* and describe its causes.
- Contrast subsistence farming with cash crop farming.
- Identify the traditional forms of government in West Africa.
- Explain how West African leaders justify one-party government in their countries.
- Describe the ways that West Africans make the arts part of their everyday lives.

SKILLS

Geography
- Interpret a political map of West Africa.

Study and Research
- Interpret a diagram describing shifting cultivation in West Africa.

Thinking
- Ask focused questions about colonial influences in West Africa.
- Distinguish facts from opinions.

Reading and Writing
- Write a proposal for stopping the desertification of the Sahel.

CITIZENSHIP VALUES

- Appreciate the positive and negative aspects of the existence of many different ethnic groups in a country.

TEACHER OPTIONS

READING STRATEGY: Question/Answer Relationships Strategies to help students read and remember the main ideas of the lesson.

Lesson 1: p. 427 Lesson 4: p. 440
Lesson 2: p. 432 Legacy: p. 442
Lesson 3: p. 435

MEETING INDIVIDUAL NEEDS Activities for reteaching, extension, and enrichment.

Lesson 1: p. 431 Lesson 4: p. 441
Lesson 2: p. 434 Legacy: p. 445
Lesson 3: p. 438

GEO ADVENTURES ACTIVITIES PAD Daily activities to assess students' understanding of geography skills.

CURRICULUM CONNECTION Activities to help integrate other subject areas with Social Studies.

Language Arts: pp. 429, 436 Art: p. 436
Music: p. 430

PUPIL EDITION ON CASSETTE Language support for students who have difficulty reading or who will benefit from listening to the Pupil Edition on Cassette as they read.

SECOND-LANGUAGE SUPPORT Activities and suggestions for second-language learners.

Lesson 1: p. 407-D

CHAPTER PLANNING GUIDE

LESSON	SUGGESTED PACING	THEMES	TEACHER SUPPORT MATERIALS: TEACHER'S RESOURCE CENTER
1 THE PEOPLE pages 427–431	1 day	Three major influences—traditional African cultures, Islam, and European colonialism—have shaped the way of life of the peoples of West Africa.	Practice Book p. 115 ■ Anthology pp. 114–115
2 THE ECONOMY pages 432–434	1 day	Subsistence farming and cash crop farming dominate the developing economies in West Africa.	Practice Book p. 116 ■ Anthology pp. 126–127 Technology: Adventures CD-ROM
3 THE GOVERNMENT pages 435–438	1 day	National unity is the goal of both democratic and dictatorial West African governments.	Practice Book p. 117 ■ Anthology pp. 110–111, 112–113, 124–125 Outline Map p. 30 Technology: Adventures CD-ROM
BUILDING THINKING SKILLS Distinguishing Facts from Opinions: Review page 439	1 day	In order to decide if information you hear or read is accurate, you need to separate facts from opinions.	Practice Book p. 118
4 ARTS AND RECREATION pages 440–441	1 day	Art, music, and dance are all a part of West African daily life.	Practice Book p. 119 ■ Anthology pp. 102–103, 129–130, 131–133, 141–142 Desk Maps Technology: Adventures CD-ROM
LEGACY A Storytelling Legacy pages 442–445	1 day	The storytelling griots have preserved West African history for centuries.	■ Anthology pp. 102–103, 129–130, 131–133, 141–142
CHAPTER SUMMARY AND REVIEW pages 446–447	1 day	Chapter content, skills, and vocabulary are reviewed and evaluated.	Practice Book p. 120 Transparency: Graphic Organizer Assessment Book, Chapter 21 Test

Technology CONNECTION

Lesson 2
ADVENTURES CD-ROM
Enrich Lesson 2 by having students make a presentation on a selection of West African countries in *Create*.

Lesson 3
ADVENTURES CD-ROM
Enrich Lesson 3 by having students *Travel* to The Gambia.

Lesson 4
ADVENTURES CD-ROM
Enrich Lesson 4 by having students *Investigate Sounds* to hear an example of the West African Ewe language.

CHAPTER 21
pages 426–447

USING THE CHAPTER OPENER

Discussing the Photograph Have students look at the picture and read the chapter title. Help them to speculate about the mood of the three young people pictured.

Ask students:

- **In what kind of climate do you think these three people live? Explain your answer.** (a hot climate; because they are dressed in light clothing and the girl in the center is wearing a straw hat against the sun; because the chapter title tells their location)
- **How would you describe the mood of these young people? Their relationship?** (Two of them seem to be happy and pleased with their existence; the person on the right is serious, but not unhappy. Their grouping shows their closeness, either because of a family relationship or friendship.)

Reading/Listening to the Primary Source Have students continue to look at the photograph as you read the quotation and the passage that follows.

Ask students:

- **What are two features of the West African country of Gambia?** (its natural beauty and the peaceful way in which many varied groups of people are able to live together)
- **How does the ability of different ethnic groups to live and work together help to improve the quality of life for all?** (When people are able to live and work together in peace, they can use all their energy to solve problems and improve the standard of living.)
- *THINKING FURTHER:* **How does the country of Gambia remind you of the United States?** (The United States is a country that finds its strength in a population drawn from many different ethnic and racial backgrounds.)

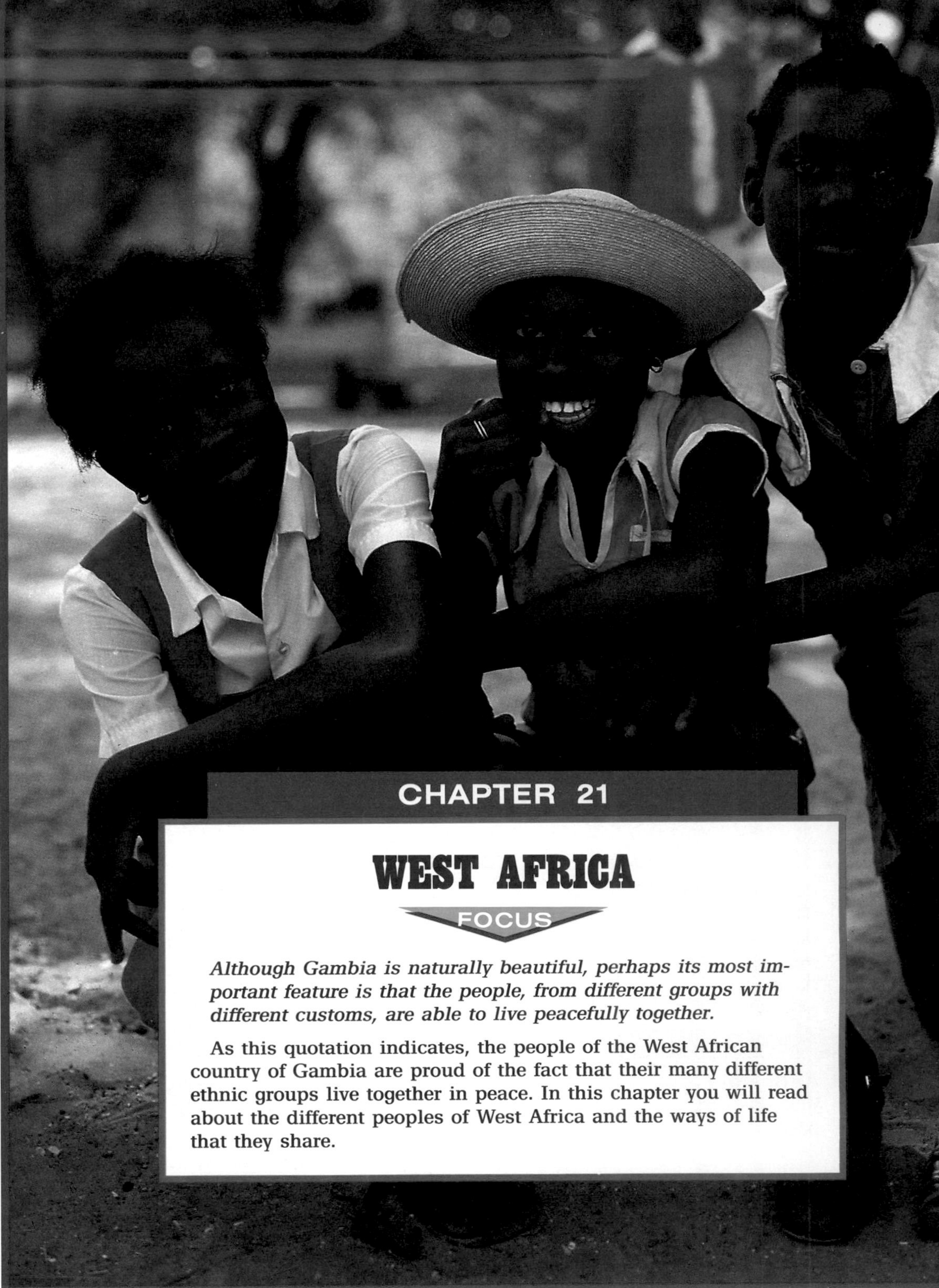

CHAPTER 21

WEST AFRICA

FOCUS

Although Gambia is naturally beautiful, perhaps its most important feature is that the people, from different groups with different customs, are able to live peacefully together.

As this quotation indicates, the people of the West African country of Gambia are proud of the fact that their many different ethnic groups live together in peace. In this chapter you will read about the different peoples of West Africa and the ways of life that they share.

BACKGROUND INFORMATION

About the Photograph

- Gambia, a West African nation situated on the Atlantic Ocean, has an area of 4,363 square miles (11,300 sq km). The country consists of a strip of land about 200 miles (320 km) long and about 20 miles (32 km) wide, on both sides of the Gambia River.
- The climate of Gambia is tropical, with a rainy season from June to October.
- Most of the people of Gambia make their living by farming and fishing.
- Gambia gained its independence from the United Kingdom in 1965 and became a republic in 1970. It is a member of the Commonwealth of Nations.

LESSON 1

The People

READ TO LEARN

Key Vocabulary

clan

Read Aloud

Once, oh small children round my knee, there were no stories on earth to hear. All the stories belonged to Nyame, the Sky God. He kept them in a golden box next to his royal stool.

That is the way that one West African story about the origin of stories begins. Some West African stories are about forest creatures. Others are about families and their histories. As you will learn in this lesson, family history is very important to the people of West Africa.

Read for Purpose

1. WHAT YOU KNOW: What are the three parts of Sub-Saharan Africa?
2. WHAT YOU WILL LEARN: What three major influences have helped to shape West African culture?

THE NATIONS OF WEST AFRICA

West Africa has a long history. Hundreds of years ago many powerful black African kingdoms flourished along its rivers. By A.D. 400 the kingdom of Ghana was a rich trading center. Historians believe that great amounts of gold, ivory, and prized woods were bought and sold in the busy marketplaces of ancient Ghana.

Today West Africa is made up of 16 modern nations. They range in size from tiny Gambia to Nigeria, Africa's largest country. Many of these nations are located along the coasts of the Atlantic Ocean and the Gulf of Guinea. West Africa is the most densely populated area of Sub-Saharan Africa.

Did you know that most nations of West Africa have been independent only since the 1960s? Before that time, every country except Liberia was a colony of a European power. However, it is important to realize that even though West Africa is a land of newly independent nations, the cultures of the West African people are very old and rooted in a rich past.

A BLEND OF CULTURES

The cultures of West Africa have had three major influences: first, traditional African practices and beliefs; second, the religion of Islam; and third, European colonialism and Christianity. These influences became uniquely West African.

WHAT YOU KNOW: This question refers to information in Chapter 20, Lesson 1; West Africa, East and Equatorial Africa, Southern Africa

LESSON 1

pages 427–431

Lesson Theme Three major influences—traditional African cultures, Islam, and European colonialism—have shaped the way of life of the peoples of West Africa.

Lesson Objectives

- Describe the three major influences on West African culture.
- Describe West African ethnic groups, clans, and languages.

1 PREPARE

Motivate Read the *Read Aloud* section to the class. Stress that without the strong tradition of storytelling in his family, Haley would not have been able to trace his ancestry.

Set Purpose Use the *What You Know* question to have students identify the three parts of Sub-Saharan Africa. Have students keep the *What You Will Learn* question in mind as they read the lesson. Display the political *Atlas* map of Sub-Saharan Africa so that students can study the nations of West Africa.

2 TEACH

Introducing the Nations of West Africa

Ask students:

- **What kind of governments did the people of ancient West Africa have?** (monarchies)

Identifying Cultures Discuss the three major influences on West African culture.

READING STRATEGY AND VOCABULARY DEVELOPMENT

Question/Answer Relationships The purpose of this strategy is for students to understand the importance of identifying sources of answers to questions. Review with students the question/answer strategy introduced in Chapter 14. Have students identify the sources of the answers to the questions in this lesson. Answers may be stated in the text, inferred, or based on a student's personal experience. Discuss students' answers.

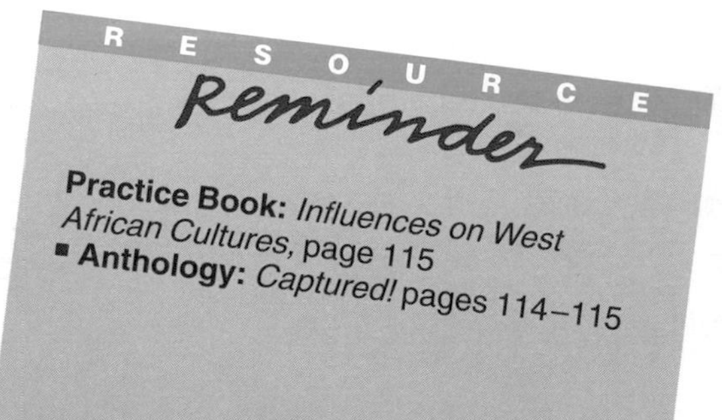

RESOURCE *Reminder*

Practice Book: *Influences on West African Cultures,* page 115

- **Anthology:** *Captured!* pages 114–115

Understanding a Blend of Cultures Continue the discussion, helping students to recognize that each period of West African history added influences to its culture.

Ask students:

- **Why was the African tradition of cooperation necessary?** (so families in harsh lands could survive)
- **How did Islam influence West African culture?** (Those people who were Muslim learned Arabic to read the Koran, and Islamic scholars taught the children of the rulers about early African kingdoms.)
- **How important is Islam in West Africa today?** (It is the major religion in most of the region.)
- **For what time period were West African nations ruled by colonial powers?** (from the 1500s to about 1960)
- **What is one important effect that the colonial period had on West African culture?** (English, French, and Portuguese languages bind nations together today.)

EXTENDING MAP SKILLS

Have students study the political map of West Africa.

Ask students:

- **What are the names of the landlocked nations in West Africa?** (Niger, Mali, Burkina Faso)
- **What is the northernmost country of West Africa?** (Mauritania)
- **How is the country of Cape Verde different from the other nations of West Africa?** (It is an island nation.)
- **Accra is the capital of which country?** (Ghana)
- **What is the capital of Liberia?** (Monrovia)
- *THINKING FURTHER:* **Where are the capitals of most West African nations located? Why?** (on the coast for transport, trade)

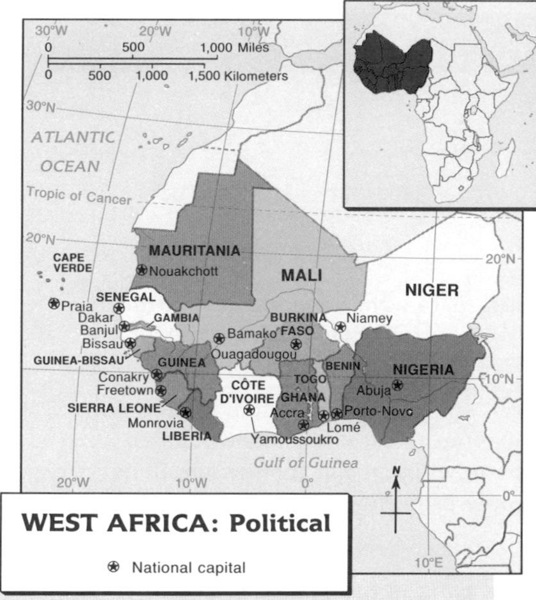

MAP SKILL: West Africa is made up of many different countries, large and small. Which large country is located in the northeastern part of the area?

Traditional customs and beliefs are rooted in the rich, ancient past of West Africa. Long ago West Africans developed strict rules for working together so that families in the harsh lands south of the Sahara could survive. Cooperation became more important than success for individuals in the area.

As you may know, the religion of Islam reached West Africa more than a thousand years ago when Arab and Berber traders brought Muslim ideas across the Sahara. As groups of West Africans adopted Islam, they learned Arabic in order to read the Koran, the sacred book of Islam. Islamic scholars taught the children of the rulers of early African kingdoms. Today Islam is the major religion in most of West Africa. Nigeria has about 60 million Muslims, more than any other country in Africa.

The third major influence on the cultures of the people of West Africa was European colonialism and the Christian religion. Europeans reached West Africa in the 1500s. Most West African countries, as you have read, were ruled as colonies for many years by European powers. After the Europeans left about 1960, their languages remained. Today the most frequently spoken European languages are English, French, and Portuguese. Many black West Africans speak one of these languages in addition to the language of their particular ethnic group. In Nigeria, for example, the members of the Hausa, the Ibo, and the Fulani ethnic groups each speak their own language. However, they all use English as a common language. As you can see on the chart on pages 410–413, the official language of many West African nations is English or French.

MANY ETHNIC GROUPS

> *They are young. When they come back to us, they bring motorcycles, bicycles, and radios. These are things they buy just for themselves. In Dogon culture things are acquired for use by the whole family.*

Boua Diabate (bü' ə dē ə ba' tē) is a member of the Dogon ethnic group of West Africa. In recent years drought has scorched the Dogon homelands in the Sahel, south of the Sahara. Hundreds of Dogon people have moved to other parts of West Africa in search of food, and so Boua worries about the survival of his culture. Like most West African ethnic groups, family bonds are very strong among the Dogon people.

The Dogon are just one small group in West Africa's patchwork of peoples, cultures, and nations. Hundreds of ethnic groups each have their own customs and special way of life. Family ties are very strong among West Africa's ethnic groups.

428

MAP SKILL: Niger

FUNDAMENTAL THEMES OF GEOGRAPHY

Movement Ancient West African kingdoms traded goods such as gold, salt, and food. These kingdoms on the Niger River declined drastically after the slave trade began to spread through West Africa to the Americas. The slave trade affected all of Africa as vast numbers of people were moved from the continent. Very conservative estimates are that 36 million Africans were involved and that for every African who arrived in the Americas, 3 had died from the slave raids, wars, or the march to the sea, or had died at the coast or on board ship. African historians believe the numbers involved were more like 60 to 70 million people, and that 10 died for every 1 who got to the Americas.

The many different ethnic groups of West Africa have developed ways of life to fit the lands they live in. The Fulani and the Tuaregs of the arid savanna herded goats, camels, and cattle. The Ibo and other ethnic groups in the south have had the benefit of richer soil and more rain. They have made their homes in permanent villages as farmers and fishing people. A few groups, like the Yoruba, have traditionally worked as traders and merchants.

There are many different ethnic groups in West Africa. The people in these ethnic groups live in both villages (*bottom*) and large cities such as Lagos, Nigeria (*top*).

MANY LANGUAGES

Because there are so many different ethnic groups in West Africa, there are also many different West African languages. This is typical throughout Africa. Between 800 and 1,000 languages are spoken on the African continent. Varying dialects are spoken in different villages. As you read in Chapter 11, a dialect is a variation of a language spoken by a particular group. In Nigeria alone, more than 250 different dialects are spoken.

Most people in the southern part of West Africa speak a dialect of a group of languages known as the Niger-Congo languages. The majority of these people are black Africans. In the northern part of West Africa, there are many different mixes of black, Berber, and Arab people. Most of these people speak languages related to Berber or Arabic.

Identifying Many Ethnic Groups Help students to recognize the conflict between traditional West African ethnic values and modern ways.

Ask students:

- **How do traditional Dogon values conflict with the activities of their young?** (Traditionally material things are shared by the whole Dogon family; today the young buy things for their own use.)
- **How do West African droughts threaten traditions?** (People must move away to find food, thus threatening the survival of ethnic cultures.)
- **What is important to most West African ethnic groups?** (family ties)
- **Which ethnic groups are herders?** (the Fulani and the Tuaregs)
- **In which area of West Africa are most ethnic groups farmers?** (the south)

Analyzing Languages Stress the extremely large number of West African languages and dialects and their relationship to the large number of ethnic groups.

Ask students:

- **How many languages are spoken in Africa today?** (800–1,000)
- **How do West African languages differ between the south and the north?** (The people in the south speak Niger-Congo languages; the people in the north speak languages related to Berber or Arabic.)
- *THINKING FURTHER:* **How do people from different parts of West Africa communicate when they trade?** (Most use a common colonial language like English, French, or Portuguese.)

CURRICULUM CONNECTION

Language Arts Students have learned that there are hundreds of languages spoken in West Africa. Have each student choose a country in West Africa and research the number and names of the languages spoken there. Then have the class combine the information they have gathered to create a chart of West African languages.

Discussing Many Religions Explain to students that a variety of religions are practiced throughout West Africa.

Ask students:

- **Which religions are practiced in West Africa?** (traditional religions that developed long before the arrival of Muslims or Christians; Islam; and Christianity)

Understanding Mixed Loyalties Talk with students about the reasons the loyalties of many West Africans are divided. Ask them to think of similar examples in their own lives.

- **What is a clan?** (a group of families descended from the same ancestor)
- **Why is it difficult for many West Africans to feel a loyalty to their countries?** (Many Africans already have a very strong sense of loyalty to their clan or ethnic group; in addition, Europeans, not Africans, created the borders of these newly established nations—borders that often have little to do with where different groups live.)
- **What is a recent occurrence involving the issue of West African nationalism?** (Some people have begun to form feelings of national loyalty.)
- *THINKING FURTHER:* **Why is it hard for a country to survive without a sense of national unity?** (Students may say that a country is not just land—it is an idea; for a country to survive, it must be an idea that people believe in.)

MANY RELIGIONS

The three major influences on West Africa have left a legacy of different religions in the region. Many West Africans practice traditional religions that developed long before the Muslims or Christians arrived. In Burkina Faso, Côte d'Ivoire, Guinea-Bissau, Liberia, and Togo, more than half the people follow various traditional religions.

Many countries today are mainly Muslim. Mauritania, for example, describes itself as an Islamic Republic. Nearly all of its people are Muslim. Gambia, Mali, Niger, and Senegal also have populations that are mostly Muslim.

Only Cape Verde has a population that is mostly Christian. The people of Cape Verde are descended from Portuguese colonists and Africans who were enslaved. The Portuguese colonists brought Roman Catholicism, which remains the chief religion of Cape Verde.

In Nigeria, most members of an ethnic group practice the same religion. The Hausa, Fulani, and Kanuri people, who live mostly in northern Nigeria, are mainly Muslim. Christianity is the major religion of the Ibo and other groups that live mostly in southern Nigeria.

Usually a country's leaders belong to the largest religious group in the nation, but sometimes they do not. In Côte d'Ivoire, for example, about 20 percent of the people are Christian, about 20 percent are Muslim, and the rest practice traditional religions. Yet the Christian leaders of Côte d'Ivoire decided to build a great Roman Catholic cathedral in its capital, Yamoussoukro. It is the largest Roman Catholic cathedral in the world. Côte d'Ivoire's leaders hope that the cathedral will attract many tourists and visitors.

Our Lady of Peace in Côte d'Ivoire is the largest Roman Catholic cathedral in the world.

CURRICULUM CONNECTION

Music Recordings of West African songs can be found in most record stores or in the public library. These songs may be used to give students some feel for the outlook on life of the West African peoples. The Liberian folk song "Take Time in Life" presents a universal wisdom about how humans should pace their lives. The song "Ev'rybody Loves Saturday Night" is from Sierra Leone. This song is probably familiar to most students in the class. If you wish, have the class sing the song. Find out how many students had heard the song before and how many had thought it was from an industrialized nation of the West. Discuss the message of the song that can apply to working people everywhere.

MIXED LOYALTIES

The newly independent countries of West Africa have found it difficult to encourage people to feel a loyalty to the country. Many Africans have a strong sense of loyalty to their ethnic group. Some have a feeling of loyalty to their religious group. Africans are also loyal to their **clan**. A clan is a group of families who are descended from one ancestor.

Members of a clan share a common religion and set of values. Being part of a clan gives Africans a sense of belonging.

There is an important reason that many Africans feel stronger loyalties to their ethnic group or to their clan than to their nation. Africans did not create all the borders of their countries. The borders of most African nations were established mainly by the European colonial nations. Often the borders have little to do with where different groups live.

In the years since the countries of West Africa gained independence, some people have begun to develop a new feeling of belonging to a country. Without this feeling, it is hard for a country, especially a new country, to survive.

PEOPLES AND CULTURES

West Africa is a patchwork of peoples and cultures. The region's people are a mixture of black African, Berber, and Arab. They speak many different languages and dialects and belong to hundreds of ethnic groups.

As you have read, three different influences have strongly shaped the West African way of life. The first are customs and traditional beliefs rooted in the rich history of West Africa.

The second influence on West Africa was Islam, which was brought to the area more than a thousand years ago. Today Islam is the major religion in West Africa.

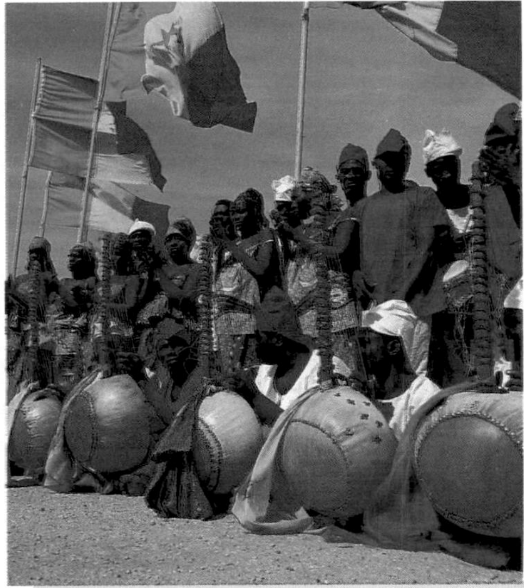

Traditional ways of life are followed in many parts of West Africa. This crowd is attending a Senegalese government rally at which traditional instruments are played.

Finally, the people of West Africa have also been strongly influenced by European colonialism and Christianity. European languages are still spoken in many of the West African countries. Recently some African countries have begun to form feelings of national loyalty.

Check Your Reading

1. Why do many West Africans speak French or English?
2. What three influences have shaped the way of life of the people of the countries of West Africa?
3. What are some groups that claim the loyalties of many people of West Africa?
4. THINKING SKILL: List two questions you could ask to learn more about European colonial influences in West Africa. Then provide the answer to one of the questions.

THINKING SKILL: Asking Questions

Applying the Lesson Have students complete a three-column chart that outlines the three major influences on the culture of West Africa.

CLOSE

Summarizing Students have learned that a mixture of cultural influences and peoples have shaped West African life. Have students review the roles of ethnic groups, languages, and clans in West African life.

Evaluating Use these questions to assess students' understanding.

- **What are the three major influences on West African culture?** (traditional African practices and beliefs, the religion of Islam, European colonialism)
- **How do colonial languages serve West Africa today?** (as unifying common languages)
- **What is the most strongly valued tradition in West Africa?** (family ties)
- **How are family groups defined?** (by the line of descent of people in a clan)

Answers to Check Your Reading

1. France and England were early colonizers of West Africa, and using the colonial languages makes it easier for different ethnic groups to communicate today.
2. traditional African practices and beliefs, Islam, European colonialism
3. ethnic groups, religious groups, clans
4. Possible questions include: For how long was West Africa colonized? (about 460 years) Which European nations colonized West Africa? (England, France, Portugal)

Independent Practice
Practice Book: page 115

MEETING INDIVIDUAL NEEDS

Reteaching (easy) Have students do research and create a chart showing the year each nation of West Africa became independent.

Extension (average) Have students do research on the effect of recent droughts on the culture of the Dogon ethnic group of West Africa. Divide the class into four groups and ask each group to hold a panel discussion on one aspect of the Dogon's lives that has been affected by the drought—for example, where they live, how they earn a living, their traditions, or their family ties.

Enrichment (challenging) Have students read the last three chapters of *Roots*, paying special attention to the role of the African griot and to Alex Haley's reference to his method of research. Then have them write an essay titled, "The Most Amazing Thing About Alex Haley's Book, *Roots*."

LESSON 2
pages 432–434

Lesson Theme Subsistence farming and cash crop farming dominate the developing economies in West Africa.

Lesson Objectives
- Describe desertification.
- Identify the types of shifting cultivation.
- Describe the new industries in West Africa.

PREPARE

Motivate Have volunteers read the *Read Aloud* section aloud. Discuss with students the role that factories play in processing farm products and in promoting industrial development.

Set Purpose Use the *What You Know* question to have students make a class list of community and state businesses that can be compared later with the businesses found in West Africa. Have students predict answers to the *What You Will Learn* question.

TEACH

Looking at the Growing Desert
Help students to realize that desertification has multiple causes from both natural and human effects.

Ask students:

- **What are the two main effects from drought in the Sahel?** (reduced farm production, desertification)

LESSON 2

The Economy

READ TO LEARN

Key Vocabulary
desertification
shifting cultivation
slash-and-burn farming

Key Places
Côte d'Ivoire
Senegal
Nigeria

Read Aloud

Louise Able lives in a cacao-growing village in Côte d'Ivoire. As you know, the beans of the cacao plant are used to make chocolate. How, then, can it be possible that Louise has tasted chocolate only twice in her life? The answer is that the cacao beans must be processed before they can be used to make chocolate. Côte d'Ivoire does not have the kind of factories that can turn cacao beans into a chocolate bar. However, as you will read in this lesson, new industrial growth is changing West Africa.

Read for Purpose

1. WHAT YOU KNOW: What types of businesses are important to the economy of your community and your state?
2. WHAT YOU WILL LEARN: What kinds of economies are found in West Africa?

THE GROWING DESERT

As it is in places all over the world, farming is an important economic activity in West Africa. But in much of this area, farming is becoming more and more difficult because of drought conditions.

As you read in Chapter 20, a dry grassland called the Sahel borders the Sahara to the south. For those nations of West Africa that are located in the Sahel, less rainfall than usual is dangerous. The farming economy of these nations depends on the little rain they already receive. In recent years, however, the rains over the Sahel have failed. As you can imagine, this has created many problems.

The droughts have not just reduced farm production, they have changed the landscape of the Sahel. Desertification, or the expansion of a desert, has crept southward from the Sahara. Desertification is caused by drought coupled with too much grazing by animals and by the cutting down of trees and bushes for firewood. The soil blows away because there is nothing to hold it. If desertification cannot be halted, the Sahel may become part of the Sahara.

SHIFTING CULTIVATION

South of the Sahel lies the savanna. In the savanna parts of West Africa continuing east to Sudan and the Indian Ocean coast, rain provides sufficient moisture for crops and animals. Far more people live in the savanna than in the Sahel.

432 WHAT YOU KNOW: Students should be encouraged to think about the variety of economic activities that take place in their community and their state.

READING STRATEGY AND VOCABULARY DEVELOPMENT

Question/Answer Relationships Preview the lesson with students. Then divide the class into groups and have each group develop questions about the lesson. You might want to instruct students to use the lesson headings as a guide for their questions. After the questions have been written, have the groups exchange lists and answer the questions. Have students provide both the answer to each question and the source of the answer (stated in the text, inferred, or based on personal experience).

RESOURCE Reminder
Practice Book: *Some Methods of Farming in West Africa,* page 116
Anthology: *In the Streets of Accra,* pages 126–127
Technology: *Adventures CD-ROM*
See page 425-B.

However, in much of the savanna, the soil is not fertile enough to bear crops every year. People have therefore developed a plan of shifting cultivation. Shifting cultivation allows some fields to rest, lying unplanted, while crops are planted on other fields. While a field is resting, it becomes covered with new grass which helps to restore the soil's precious nutrients. In some areas of the savanna, villagers allow fields to remain unplanted for many years. Other villagers will move their entire village to a place where the fields have not been used for a long time.

Shifting cultivation often depends on slash-and-burn farming. In this type of farming, people first clear a field by cutting down trees and stumps, as you can see in the top drawing. Next they burn the brush. The burning creates ashes that enrich the soil. Finally the people plant crops, such as millet, peanuts, and yams.

Often the farmers use the soil wisely by rotating, or changing, the crops they grow in a field. Each crop uses up different minerals in the soil. If millet is planted in a field one year, peanuts may be planted there the next year. In the third year the field may be planted with a starchy root plant called cassava or manioc. This crop can survive drought, but it uses up minerals in the soil quickly.

The policy of shifting cultivation requires a lot of land. Recently, in order to produce enough food for more people, many villagers have been forced to shorten the rest periods of a large number of their fields. As the fields are replanted again and again, the soil wears out and produces smaller and smaller crops.

CASH CROPS

Most West Africans are subsistence farmers who grow only enough food for their families. Families work together to

SLASH-AND-BURN FARMING

1. Trees and brush are slashed to the ground.

2. The land is burned.

3. Crops are planted.

DIAGRAM SKILL: How is the land prepared in the slash-and-burn farming system?

DIAGRAM SKILL: First trees and brush are slashed, then the land is burned.

Analyzing Shifting Cultivation Emphasize that unplanted land regains important nutrients.

Ask students:

- **Where do most people in West Africa live?** (in the Sudanese savanna and along the Atlantic coast)
- **What is the problem with the soil in the savanna?** (It's not fertile enough to produce crops every year.)
- **What is shifting cultivation?** (allowing some fields to remain unplanted while crops are planted in other fields)
- **How is shifting cultivation done in the tropical rain forest?** (Farmers plant the same field year after year, but they vary the kind of crop they plant.)
- **What are the disadvantages to shifting cultivation?** (In areas with limited land, farmers must shorten the rest periods of their fields; as a result, the soil loses its nutrients and produces smaller and smaller crops.)

EXTENDING DIAGRAM SKILLS

Have students study the diagram on this page.

Ask students:

- **What is the first step in this farming method?** (Trees and brush are slashed to the ground.)
- *THINKING FURTHER:* **Why is the land burned?** (Burning creates ashes that enrich the soil.)

Discussing Cash Crops Help students to understand the value of subsistence farming and of cash crops.

Ask students:

- **What helps subsistence farming in West Africa?** (shifting cultivation)

BUILDING CITIZENSHIP

Hunger The security of a nation depends upon the strength of its people. Proper nutrition, especially for the young, contributes to a healthy work force. In West Africa six nations face malnutrition problems from Sahel droughts. Discuss the Dust Bowl and Great Depression of the 1930s, when regions of the United States had food supply problems, and the problem of hunger in the country today. Have students research methods of fighting hunger, such as food distribution, granary storage, ways of speeding food to areas of drought, predicting weather trends, developing new seed strains, and using biotechnology.

Talking About Cash Crops Continue the discussion.

Ask students:

- **Which important cash crops are grown in West Africa?** (coffee, cacao, bananas, peanuts)

Identifying New Industrial Growth Help students contrast the former colonial economies with the economies of West Africa today.

Ask students:

- **Why was there little industrial development in West Africa during the colonial period?** (Raw materials were shipped out.)
- **Which West African nations are building mills and factories to process cash crops?** (Ghana, Nigeria, Ivory Coast)
- **What new industries does West Africa have?** (processing minerals and oil)

Applying the Lesson Have students write a paragraph titled "The Strengths and Weaknesses of West African Economies."

3 CLOSE

Summarizing Students have learned that West African economies have traditional farming with some new industries. Have students discuss why cash crops are a risk to an economy.

Evaluating Use the *Check Your Reading* questions (answers given below) to assess students' understanding.

Answers to Check Your Reading

1. drought, overgrazing, cutting down trees and bushes
2. It has led to many problems, such as desertification and lowered food production.
3. Subsistence farming; cash crops based on cacao and peanuts; developing industrial economies
4. a food drain yet a potential work force

Independent Practice
Practice Book: page 116

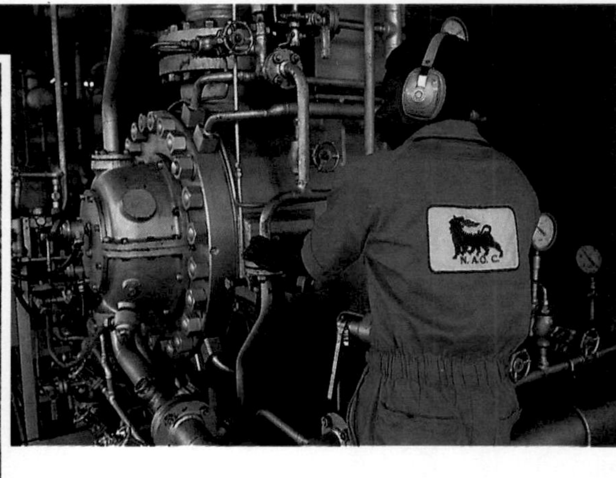

Jobs in West Africa range from traditional farming to modern manufacturing.

grow their food, often sharing fields. Subsistence farmers eat most of what they grow, but some subsistence farmers grow enough produce to sell small amounts in local markets. Women often are in charge of the business of selling farm products in these markets.

However, growing cacao, peanuts, and other cash crops is a very important part of the economies of West Africa's coastal nations. As you may remember, a cash crop is a plant or plant product raised to make money. The prosperous economy of **Côte d'Ivoire** is based on cash crops such as coffee, cacao, and bananas. The entire economy of **Senegal** rises or falls with the price that customers pay for peanuts in world markets.

GROWING INDUSTRIES AND CITIES

Most West Africans live in farming communities, and the economies of this region rely heavily on agriculture. However, industries are developing, and cities are growing. West Africa now has 5 cities with more than 1 million people each.

African countries want to sell more than raw materials. **Nigeria**, Ghana, and Côte d'Ivoire are building mills and factories to process their crops.

Minerals also play an important new role in West Africa. For example, the discovery of oil in Nigeria has provided work in the oil industry for thousands of Nigerians. When people move to take jobs in oil fields or in offices in cities, they leave their old ways of life.

A DEVELOPING AREA

Most West African economies are still in the early stages of development. As you have read, many people are subsistence farmers or use shifting cultivation to produce cash crops. Others find work in the developing industries of West Africa.

Check Your Reading

1. What has caused desertification?
2. How has the drought in the Sahel affected the rest of West Africa?
3. What kinds of economies are found in West Africa?
4. THINKING SKILL: What effect has the growing population of West Africa had on its economy?

THINKING SKILL: Cause and Effect

434

MEETING INDIVIDUAL NEEDS

Reteaching (easy) Have students write three short paragraphs describing how the three *Key Vocabulary* words are related and how the concepts they name are important in the economies of West Africa.

Extension (average) Have students find out more about the production of one of the cash crops in West Africa. Ask them to create a poster showing the fluctuation of profits from that crop over a number of years. Have them explain to the class how the fluctuation affected the countries producing that crop.

Enrichment (challenging) Have students find out more about a growing industry in West Africa and write a brief essay about it. Have them tell how the new industry has helped or hurt the people of the nation.

LESSON 3

The Government

READ TO LEARN

Key Vocabulary oba

Key Places Benin, Gambia

Read Aloud

For the Gambia, our homeland,
We strive and work and pray,
That all may live in unity,
Freedom, and peace each day.

These words are taken from the national anthem of Gambia. As you read earlier, Gambia's people are proud of the fact that they "live in unity." This country's small population has six main ethnic groups. Larger West African nations have hundreds of different ethnic groups. In this lesson you will read about how the nations of West Africa strive to unify their people.

Read for Purpose

1. WHAT YOU KNOW: For about how long have the nations of West Africa been independent?
2. WHAT YOU WILL LEARN: What special problems face the governments of West Africa's nations?

DIFFERENT TRADITIONS

When the English created the colony that is now the nation of Nigeria, they brought together people who governed themselves by very different customs. The Yoruba people were used to obeying kings. The Hausa and Fulani were loyal to Muslim rulers who had great authority over their lives. In sharp contrast, millions of Ibo in the tropical south were used to running their villages democratically.

The Ibo system used a village council of older men to talk over problems and make decisions. These men were called elders. In the council every elder had an equal voice. Other men in the village could also attend the meetings of the council and speak. This tradition of democratic village councils is common in West Africa.

In the past, African women, who have always been important at home and in the marketplace, took little part in government. This tradition is changing slowly. One Muslim woman asked her husband for permission to run for a state council in Nigeria. She won and became the only woman on a council of 350 people.

TRADITIONAL RULERS

West Africa also has a long tradition of rule by kings. In the north these rulers are known as emirs, as they are in some areas

WHAT YOU KNOW: This question refers to information in Lesson 1; for about the last 30 years.

LESSON 3
pages 435–438

Lesson Theme National unity is the goal of both democratic and dictatorial West African governments.

Lesson Objectives

- Describe the traditional governments in West Africa.
- Explain the problems that remain from colonial rule in West Africa.
- Explain the West African argument for one-party government.

PREPARE

Motivate Read the *Read Aloud* question to the class. Discuss the idea of unity and the difficulties of staying unified experienced by any nation with people of differing ethnic groups.

Set Purpose Ask the *What You Will Learn* question to begin a discussion on the problems of young nations.

TEACH

Understanding Different Traditions

Ask students:

- **Before the arrival of the British, what kinds of leaders governed the people in the area that is now Nigeria?** (kings, Muslim rulers, elders in democratic village councils)
- **How has the traditional role of women in government changed?** (Their role, limited by tradition, is expanding.)

Discussing Traditional Rulers Help students to understand the importance of traditional rulers in West African life.

READING STRATEGY AND VOCABULARY DEVELOPMENT

Question/Answer Relationships Tell students that questions can be used as a way to compare and contrast information. Have students work in groups to compare and contrast the governments of West Africa with those of other countries. Assign each group a country they have already studied. Then have each group develop questions that require compare/contrast answers. Have the class discuss the answers to the questions.

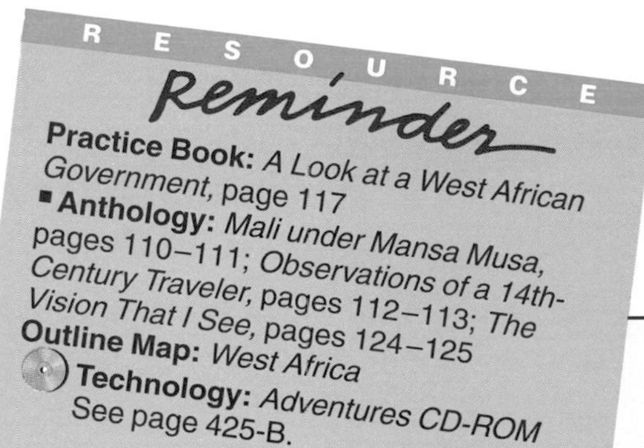

Looking at Traditional Rulers
Continue the discussion about the traditional leaders of West Africa.

Ask students:

- **What are the two traditional names for rulers in West Africa?** (emir, oba)
- **How has the role of the emir and the oba changed?** (They were once absolute rulers and now they are citizens subject to the government.)
- **Where are traditional rulers most powerful?** (in their own section of the country)
- **With whom does the oba often meet to discuss the people's needs?** (council of chiefs)
- **What is the purpose of a Nigerian *durbar*?** (to show respect to the emir with an old salute of loyalty)
- **Why do you think traditional West African rulers are treated with such great respect?** (They are a living link to past traditions, and they represent the ability of West African peoples to govern their own communities despite the history of colonialism.)

Traditional councils are still important in modern Nigeria. They continue to make important decisions for their villages.

of the Middle East and North Africa. In other parts of West Africa, a ruler is known as an oba. According to one Egyptian visitor to Benin:

> *It is the oba who is mighty. Though his attendants wear ivory, the oba is decorated in gold.*

In the past many emirs and obas were absolute rulers who made decisions for the people in their villages. Today, there are still traditional rulers in West Africa, and many of them are still important. But now most work with the government systems of their nations.

Traditional rulers are most powerful in their own section of a country. An oba may hold a meeting of a council of chiefs in the walled courtyard of his home and discuss present-day concerns. At one such meeting, the council discussed ways to use the country's oil wealth wisely. Local chiefs gave their opinions in turn. One chief summed up what he believed were the most urgent needs: electricity, good drinking water, and medical care for the people of his village.

Traditional rulers are often treated with great respect. Old and new ways blend when the people of the Katsina region of Nigeria gather to honor their emir. Such a gathering is called a *durbar* and includes a horseback ceremony to honor the emir. Wearing flowing robes, riders gallop forward, swords flashing, to within a few feet of the emir. Abruptly, the riders pull up on the reins and the horses stop. The riders raise their right hands in clenched fists, an old salute of loyalty to the emir.

At a modern durbar, an elderly Nigerian man explained that his people have given respect to traditional rulers for many hundreds of years. "You can be a doctor or lawyer in Lagos, but out of respect you come home to ride in the durbar." When the durbar ends, some of the people who attended board jet airplanes to fly home to their regular lives in the city.

CURRICULUM CONNECTION

Art Have students research additional information about a *durbar.* Tell them to look through books for pictures and descriptions of what a *durbar* includes. Then have them draw a picture of how they visualize a *durbar* of today.

Language Arts Have students choose a West African country and research one of its early rulers, such as Mansa Mūsā of Mali. After students have read books about the ruler they chose, have them give an oral presentation to the class telling what impressed them most about the ruler.

THE LEGACY OF COLONIALISM

When West African countries became independent, they found themselves with oddly drawn boundary lines. These borders had been set by the European countries that ruled African colonies. Many modern African countries include ethnic groups that are ancient enemies. Other boundaries have separated people who might have formed one country.

Gambia, for example, might easily join with Senegal, which surrounds it. The two nations remain separate because the former British colony of Gambia is an English-speaking country while the people of Senegal speak French. Senegal was once a French colony.

Newly independent countries have also had to find a way to blend governments influenced by Europe with traditional African systems. Often a national government and traditional rulers have disagreed about how to govern the country.

MODERN NATIONS

After they gained their independence, most West African nations had representative governments, but few of them were truly democratic. Nearly all of them have had either one-party systems or military governments. For a while, only Senegal and Gambia allowed more than one party.

Political parties in West Africa, like those in other regions of Africa often form along ethnic group lines. Some West African leaders argued that because of these ethnic-political ties, many political parties would slow down the task of unifying their country. The leaders claimed that one-party governments were the glue holding together countries with different groups.

The "glue" often came unstuck. Rebellions and overthrown governments have been common. In one nine-year period, the government of Benin was overthrown five

West Africa's rulers have included traditional monarchs (*above*) and modern military leaders, such as Ibrahim Babangida of Nigeria (*below*).

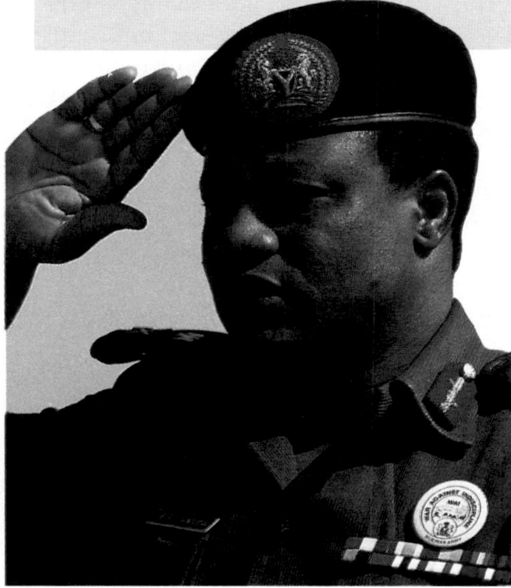

Looking at the Legacy of Colonialism Help students to understand the political effects of European colonial boundaries on West Africa today.

Ask students:

- **What problem often interferes with the cooperative work that would benefit West African nations?** (Often a national government and traditional rulers disagree about how to govern a country.)
- **How have the boundary lines drawn arbitrarily by the Europeans caused problems today?** (Ancient enemies often live within one nation.)

Understanding Modern Nations Help students to understand the problems that modern West African nations face in trying to combine traditional and modern rule. You may want to explain that President Babangida, shown in the bottom photograph, was a military dictator who promised free elections. He was overthrown in a military coup after elections that he tried to control were held in Nigeria.

Ask students:

- **What are the most common types of government in West Africa?** (one-party rule or military government)
- **What was the argument given by some West African leaders for the one-party system?** (Because political parties often formed along ethnic group lines, too many political parties might slow down the task of unifying the country.)
- **What are some steps that West African governments have taken recently to encourage democratic rule?** (Benin held a national conference in 1991; Mali and several other nations began to try to put an end to one-party rule and military governments.)

BACKGROUND INFORMATION

Multicultural Perspectives Africa's nationalist movement of the 1950s and 1960s began in West Africa—yet independence failed to bring democracy to most of that region. Nigerian writer Chinua Achebe described the bitter disappointment of that time.

The nationalist movement in British West Africa after the Second World War brought about a mental revolution which began to reconcile us to ourselves. It suddenly seemed that we too might have a story to tell. "Rule Britannia!" to which we had marched so unself-consciously on Empire Day now stuck in our throats. . . . But things happen very fast in Africa. I had hardly begun to bask in the sunshine of reconciliation when a new cloud appeared, a new estrangement. Political independence had come. The nationalist leader of yesterday . . . had become the not so attractive party boss.

Ask students to describe the "new cloud" identified by Achebe.

Discussing Modern Nations Continue to discuss the dilemmas of postcolonial West African nations. Point out that building national unity and establishing democracies are two of the great challenges facing these nations.

Applying the Lesson Give students the outline map of West Africa, found in the Teacher's Resource Center. Have them color West African nations one of three colors according to each country's type of government: military, democratic legislative, or traditional absolute ruler.

3 CLOSE

Summarizing Students have learned that West African nations want national unity and have many different types of government. Ask students to list the advantages and disadvantages of one-party governments.

Evaluating Use the *Check Your Reading* questions (answers given below) to assess students' understanding.

Answers to Check Your Reading

1. *oba, emir*
2. They were drawn up by Europeans without regard to pre-existing ethnic and cultural patterns.
3. lack of national unity; unstable governments
4. Opinion; the speaker is guessing at effects of political parties.

Independent Practice
Practice Book: page 117

times. In Nigeria a military government overthrew the democratically elected leaders in 1983. Elections controlled by the military government were held in 1993, but were followed by a military coup.

Leaders who are in power often rely on censorship of newspapers and television. Censorship, as you have read, means limiting what may be published or broadcast. To some extent, most African governments have censored the information that their people receive.

In the 1990s several West African nations began to try to put an end to one-party rule and military governments. Benin held a national conference in 1991 to encourage democracy. Mali also joined in the call for democratic rule. Many West African nations are working to combine the best of traditional and modern rule.

CHANGING GOVERNMENTS

West African countries have competing forms of government. Many nations have a strong tradition of local councils. They also have a modern history of strong central governments under one party or leader. As you have read, building national unity and establishing democracies are two great challenges facing many West African governments.

Check Your Reading

1. Name two titles of traditional rulers in West Africa.
2. Why are many boundaries of West African nations oddly drawn?
3. What are some problems facing the governments of West Africa?
4. THINKING SKILL: Is the following a statement of fact or opinion? "Having many political parties will surely slow the process of unifying our land." Explain your answer.

438 THINKING SKILL: Fact and Opinion

CITIZENSHIP MAKING A DIFFERENCE

REVIVING A TRADITION

Bernard Ledea Ouedraogo (wā drä' gō) lives in Burkina Faso, West Africa. In 1960, when his country gained independence, Bernard decided to revive a tradition his people had lost under many years of European rule.

During the days of the ancient Mossi Empire, men and women had worked together to plant and harvest crops. Cooperation was an important and respected tradition. Bernard persuaded the farmers in his village to work together instead of independently. They planted crops and harvested them during the rainy season.

During the long dry season Bernard organized the villagers to work on community projects. They dug wells, planted gardens and woodlots, and built mills and storehouses for grain. Bernard called the group *Naam*, a word from the Mossi language that means "agricultural cooperative."

Bernard also helped people in other villages to form Naam groups. In Somiaga the villagers dug and hauled rock with which to build a huge dam. A woman who worked on the project described her work as "throwing stones at the drought."

Now there are over 3,000 Naam groups in Burkina Faso. Bernard continues to visit the villages, where he helps communities to work together in the Mossi tradition.

MEETING INDIVIDUAL NEEDS

Reteaching (easy) Have students use each of the section headings in this lesson to write a sentence describing the key ideas of the paragraphs in each section.

Extension (average) Have students do research to find the type of government in each nation of West Africa. Have students present their findings in chart form.

Enrichment (challenging) Have students research recent elections in West Africa and write an essay titled "Issues Facing West African Governments Today."

BUILDING CITIZENSHIP

Making a Difference Review the meaning of a tradition with students and have them discuss various traditions with which they are familiar. Ask students what was important about the tradition that Bernard Ouedraogo revived. Point out that there are many examples of people cooperating here in America. Students may mention these communal acts: the early American barnraisings still done by the Amish people; people working together to meet a disaster, such as placing sandbags on the banks of a flooding river; and people working together to build homes for the poor. Discuss ways in which students cooperate at home, in school, and in the community.

BUILDING SKILLS
THINKING SKILLS

Distinguishing Facts from Opinions: Review

A statement of a fact is information that can be proved to be true. An opinion is a personal view or belief, and cannot be proved to be true. Another name for a personal opinion is a value judgment. If an opinion is supported by evidence or reasons, it is called a reasoned opinion.

HELPING YOURSELF

Here is one way to distinguish between facts and opinions.

1. Recall the definitions of a fact, a reasoned opinion, and a value judgment.
2. Look for clues to statements of fact. Look for statements that can be proved to be true.
3. Look for clues to value judgments. Look for words such as *I think*, *should*, or *best*.
4. Look for clues to reasoned opinions, such as evidence or reasons supporting an opinion.
5. Read each statement carefully to find these clues.

Applying the Skill

As you read the account below, identify statements of fact and opinion.

I believe the traditional way of life of the Dogon people in Mali is doomed. The Dogon have been among the best farmers in Africa. Their little mud storehouses were usually filled with crops. But now, because of the drought, there is much less water for farming. Nomads have moved south to camp in the fields of the Dogon. Some of the Dogon have gone to cities to look for work. Others are dying from hunger and disease. Attempts to aid the Dogon have been a complete failure. What is happening is a tragedy.

1. What facts can you find in this passage?
2. What opinions can you find?
3. Which of these opinions are supported by reasons or evidence?

Reviewing the Skill

1. How does a fact differ from an opinion?
2. What are some steps to follow to distinguish facts from opinions?
3. What are some situations outside of school when you might find it useful to distinguish between fact and opinion?

SKILLS LESSON
page 439

Lesson Theme Distinguishing facts from opinions involves separating personal beliefs from statements that can be proved to be true.

Lesson Objective

- Identify and apply steps for distinguishing facts from opinions.

PREPARE

Motivate Before students begin reading this section, ask them to recall the process they learned for distinguishing facts from opinions in Chapter 7. Write the steps and clues cited on the chalkboard and have the class compare the list with the steps outlined in *Helping Yourself*.

TEACH

Applying the Skill Tell students that they will now have a chance to apply the skill. Have students read the passage and answer the questions that follow it. (See answers below.) Remind them to refer to *Helping Yourself* and the steps listed on the chalkboard if they need assistance.

Thinking About Thinking Discuss with students the different procedures and clues they found most useful for distinguishing fact from opinion.

CLOSE

Reviewing the Skill Have students give examples of other situations in which they might find it useful to apply the skill.

ANSWERS TO SKILLS QUESTIONS

Applying the Skill

1. *Facts:* Because of the drought, there is much less water for farming. Nomads have moved south to camp in the fields of the Dogon. Some of the Dogon have gone to cities to look for work.
2. *Opinions:* I believe the traditional way of life of the Dogon in Mali is doomed. The Dogon have been among the best farmers in Africa. Attempts to aid the Dogon have been a complete failure. What is happening is a tragedy.
3. The first two opinions are supported by data.

Reviewing the Skill

1. A fact can be proven true, an opinion cannot.
2. Look for clues to facts and clues to opinions such as *I think*.
3. when buying something, when listening to someone's account of an incident, when voting

Practice Book: *Distinguishing Fact from Opinion,* page 118

LESSON 4
pages 440–441

Lesson Theme Art, music, and dance are all an important part of West African daily life.

Lesson Objectives
- Explain the importance of the oral tradition in West Africa.
- Describe West African music and dance.
- Explain the role of masks in West Africa.

PREPARE

Motivate Read the *Read Aloud* section to the class. Discuss the reasons for the tradition of storytelling in West Africa.

Set Purpose Discuss the *What You Know* question. Have students predict answers to the *What You Will Learn* question. Discuss students' predictions after they have read the lesson.

TEACH

Understanding the Oral Tradition Help students to understand the role that oral storytelling has in maintaining the histories of the West African peoples. Discuss why the stories were not written down.

Ask students:

- **What is oral tradition?** (spoken history and literature passed down from person to person)
- **What are West African storytellers called?** (griots, or "praise singers")
- **Identify some well-known African poets and writers.** (Leopold Senghor, Birago Diop, Wole Soyinka)

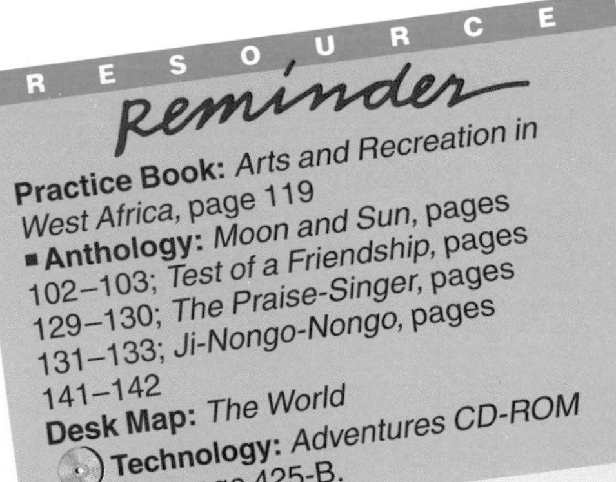
RESOURCE *Reminder*
Practice Book: *Arts and Recreation in West Africa,* page 119
▪ **Anthology:** *Moon and Sun,* pages 102–103; *Test of a Friendship,* pages 129–130; *The Praise-Singer,* pages 131–133; *Ji-Nongo-Nongo,* pages 141–142
Desk Map: *The World*
Technology: *Adventures CD-ROM*
See page 425-B.

LESSON 4

Arts and Recreation

READ TO LEARN

Key Vocabulary
oral tradition
talking drums
griot

Key People
Léopold Senghor
Wole Soyinka

Read Aloud

Mouse may seem small and unimportant, yet she goes all places, and sees all things. Long ago she wove [created] *story children from all that she saw. During a quarrel . . . all the story children ran outside. They never returned, and to this day they travel all over the world.*

According to this ancient Nigerian legend, Mouse, through the creation of magical beings called "story children," brought stories into the world. As you will read in this lesson, stories and other arts such as music, dance, and sculpture are an important part of daily life in West Africa.

Read for Purpose

1. WHAT YOU KNOW: What are some popular stories and folktales of the United States?
2. WHAT YOU WILL LEARN: In what ways do West Africans make the arts part of their everyday lives?

THE ORAL TRADITION

West African tales are rich with humor, wisdom, and mischief. These tales originated hundreds of years ago when Africa did not have written languages. So the stories were spoken, but not written down. History and literature that is spoken, rather than written, and passed down from person to person is called **oral tradition**.

Since early African history, stories and poems were not written. Storytellers told them aloud to people in the villages. The stories were passed from generation to generation. Much of West Africa's history is preserved in its oral tradition.

The most famous West African storytellers are the **griots** (grē′ ōz), who are the "praise singers" and historians of many groups. You will read more about the griot legacy on pages 442–445.

Today there are also many well-known African poets and writers. **Léopold Senghor**, a poet from Senegal, also served as Senegal's president for many years. Birago Diop, whose poem you can read on page 441, is also from Senegal. In 1986 the Nigerian writer **Wole Soyinka** (sō ying′ ka) became the first African to win a Nobel Prize for literature.

MUSIC AND DANCE

In West Africa skillful dancers and musicians are highly respected. Ceremonial dances mark the main events of human life, such as birth, death, marriage, and

WHAT YOU KNOW: Students should respond with the names of popular American folktales, such as those of Paul Bunyan, Rip Van Winkle, and Johnny Appleseed.

READING STRATEGY AND VOCABULARY DEVELOPMENT

Question/Answer Relationships To review either the lesson or the entire chapter, have students develop questions and answers. Divide the class into groups. Assign each group a section of the lesson or chapter from which to develop questions and answers. Have the groups put each question on one side of an index card and the answer on the other side. Then shuffle the cards together or categorize them. Ask students to pretend that they are on a TV game show, and have them play a game in which they must supply questions when presented with answers. You may redivide the class to play the game or choose three students to play while the rest of the class acts as the audience.

even a successful hunt. Dances also mark the seasons of the farming year.

The main musical instrument in West Africa and throughout the African continent is the drum. In some areas there are large orchestras made up only of drums. Talking drums can be made to imitate the sound of human speech. By using these drums, people can send messages over long distances. Some West African languages use different tones to give the words different meanings. A master of the talking drum can produce these tones.

THE MEANING OF MASKS

In many parts of Africa dances and music for important ceremonies are performed by people in masks. These masks are large and elaborately decorated with wood, feathers, leather, and shells.

The masks are much more than decoration. They are believed to have great power. Among traditional West African groups, masks are a way of calling gods and spirits to speak to humans. When a mask is well made, it is believed to take on the spirits of ancestors.

Most West African masks are made mainly of wood, but metal, clay, and ivory are also used. Nigerian artists made bronze masks as early as A.D. 1000.

THE LEGACY OF AFRICAN ART

West Africans make art, music, and dance a part of their daily lives. As you have read, the oral tradition, poetry, music, and dance have helped to preserve the history of West Africa.

AN AFRICAN POEM

Listen more to things
Than to words that are said.
The water's voice sings
And the flame cries
And the wind that brings
The woods to sighs
Is the breathing of the dead.

Those who are dead have never gone
away.
They are in the shadows darkening
around,
They are in the shadows fading
into day,
The dead are not under the ground.
They are in the trees that quiver,
They are in the woods that weep,
They are in the waters of the rivers,
They are in the waters that sleep.
They are in the crowds, they are in the
homestead.
The dead are never dead. . . .

Those who are dead have never gone
away.
They are at the breast of the wife.
They are in the child's cry of dismay
And the firebrand bursting into life.
The dead are not under the ground.
They are in the fire that burns low
They are in the grass with tears to
shed,
In the rock where whining winds blow
They are in the forest, they are in the
homestead.
The dead are never dead. —Birago Diop

Poems are important in West Africa. This poem expresses the belief that the spirits of the dead are in living things.

Check Your Reading

1. How was history passed down among the early people of West Africa?
2. What is the main musical instrument used in West Africa?
3. When are ceremonial dances performed in West Africa?
4. THINKING SKILL: Why do you think the instruments and skill for playing the talking drums were developed?

THINKING SKILL: Cause and Effect

Introducing Music and Dance

Ask students:

- **How is dance part of everyday life in West Africa?** (Ceremonial dances are done to celebrate birth, death, marriage, successful hunts, and seasons.)

Discussing the Meaning of Masks

Ask students:

- **Why are masks important in West Africa?** (They are believed to be a way of calling the gods and spirits to speak to humans.)

Applying the Lesson Have students draw pictures to illustrate each of the *Key Vocabulary* words. Then have students make a very large collage to hang on the classroom wall.

3 CLOSE

Summarizing In West Africa art, music, and dance are woven into the daily life of the people. Ask students to compare the use of art, music, and dance in their lives with the use of the arts in the lives of West Africans.

Evaluating Use these questions to assess students' understanding.

- **Why are West African tales important?** (They tell the history of the people.)
- **What object is used to call gods and spirits?** (a mask)

Answers to Check Your Reading

1. by storytellers (griots)
2. the drum
3. for all important life events
4. Possible answer includes: With no written language, messages could be sent easily by drumbeat.

Independent Practice
Practice Book: page 119

MEETING INDIVIDUAL NEEDS

Reteaching (easy) Have students choose one West African art form that they like and give a presentation in which they describe how that art form would be used in West African daily life.

Extension (average) Have 12 groups of students use the Desk Maps of the world (found in the Teacher's Resource Center) as a background for a comparison chart for West Africa and the United States titled "Art in Our Daily Lives." Have students make columns for stories, art, music, and dance.

Enrichment (challenging) Have students research how masks were made in West Africa. Then have them create their own paper masks.

LEGACY
pages 442–445

Lesson Theme The storytelling griots have preserved West African history for centuries. Today elements of the oral tradition originated by griots endure in West Africa and among some African Americans in the United States.

Lesson Objectives
- Describe the traditional role of the griot in West Africa.
- Explain the survival of the storytelling legacy in West Africa and the United States.

1 PREPARE

Motivate Ask students to describe the ways in which families preserve their past. Examples might include having family dinners or singing songs on special occasions.

Set Purpose Focus students' attention with the following question. How is storytelling important to you? (Have students share their feelings about the value of storytelling.) Tell students to read the introduction. Ask them to think about the concluding suggestion while they read the rest of the lesson.

2 TEACH

Understanding the Concept of Legacies Ask students how storytelling can be a legacy. (Stories are handed down from generation to generation; they may communicate beliefs and ideas about ways of life.)

Discussing Oral History You may wish first to review the countries of West Africa on the *Atlas* map.

Ask students:

- **How does storytelling play a role in the lives of people in West Africa?** (Storytelling is an oral tradition shared by the many cultures

ms 300 p 442

serves the history and legacies of the people of West Africa.)

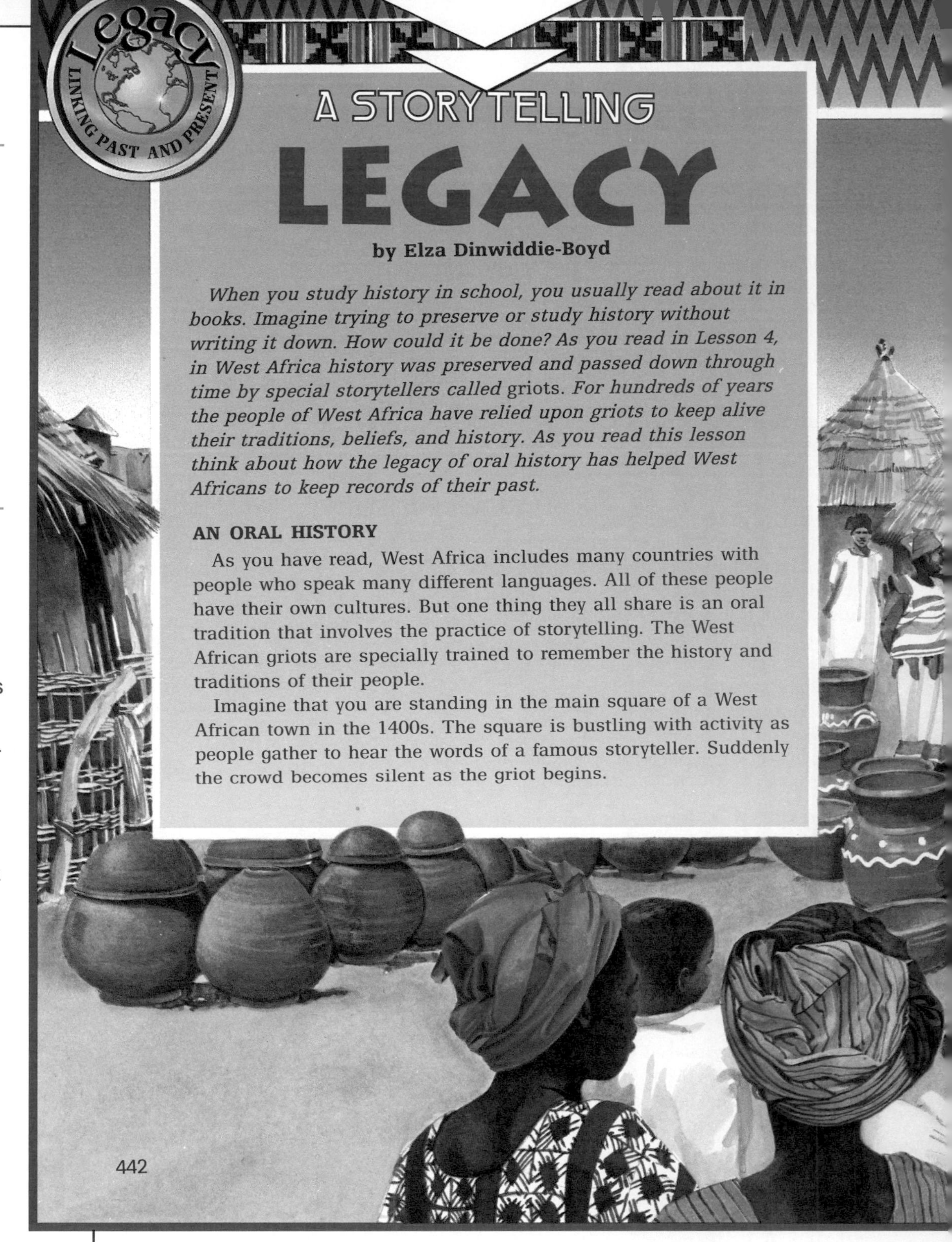

A STORYTELLING LEGACY

by Elza Dinwiddie-Boyd

When you study history in school, you usually read about it in books. Imagine trying to preserve or study history without writing it down. How could it be done? As you read in Lesson 4, in West Africa history was preserved and passed down through time by special storytellers called griots. *For hundreds of years the people of West Africa have relied upon griots to keep alive their traditions, beliefs, and history. As you read this lesson think about how the legacy of oral history has helped West Africans to keep records of their past.*

AN ORAL HISTORY

As you have read, West Africa includes many countries with people who speak many different languages. All of these people have their own cultures. But one thing they all share is an oral tradition that involves the practice of storytelling. The West African griots are specially trained to remember the history and traditions of their people.

Imagine that you are standing in the main square of a West African town in the 1400s. The square is bustling with activity as people gather to hear the words of a famous storyteller. Suddenly the crowd becomes silent as the griot begins.

442

READING STRATEGY AND VOCABULARY DEVELOPMENT

Question/Answer Relationships Remind students that the purpose of this strategy is to understand the importance of identifying sources of answers to questions. Tell students that another approach to this strategy is to develop a set of questions based on the text in order to master the material. Have students brainstorm clue words and phrases that could be used in forming questions for this lesson. For example, the word *griot* might give rise to the questions "What is a griot?" and "How are griots important in West Africa?" Have students use the question-asking strategy to develop a set of questions based on this lesson. Then have students identify whether the answers are stated in the text, inferred, or based on a student's personal experience.

RESOURCE Reminder

- **Anthology:** *Moon and Sun,* pages 102–103; *Test of a Friendship,* pages 129–130; *The Praise-Singer,* pages 131–133; *Ji-Nongo-Nongo,* pages 141–142

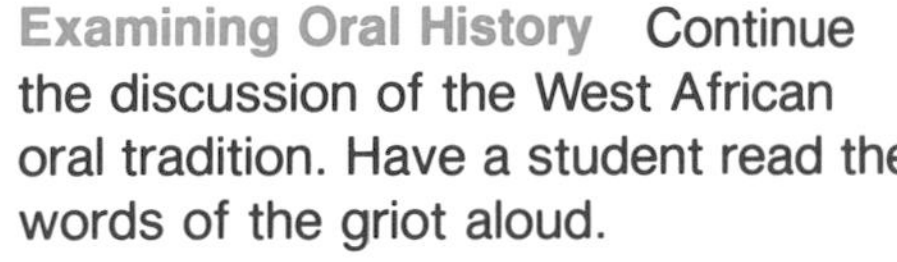

I am a griot. It is I, Mamoudou Kouyaté [ma mü' dü kü' yo tā], *son of griots, master in the art of* [storytelling].

I teach kings the history of their ancestors so that the lives of the ancients might serve them as an example, for the world is old, but the future springs from the past.

My word is pure and free of all untruth; it is the word of my father; it is the word of my father's father. I will give you my father's words just as I received them; royal griots do not know what lying is.

Listen to my word, you who want to know; by my mouth you will learn the history of [our people].

REMEMBERING HISTORY

How does a person become a griot? As you have read, the ideas of clan and family are very important to West Africans. To become a griot a person must be the son or daughter of a griot. Most griots are male, but occasionally a woman can be a griot. Griots begin learning their craft as children. Griot parents teach their children to remember centuries of history. It is not easy. Reciting oral history can take days. Memorizing thousands of stories and historical facts that have added up over many centuries requires fantastic memory skills. It also requires many years of practice.

Examining Oral History Continue the discussion of the West African oral tradition. Have a student read the words of the griot aloud.

Ask students:

- **Why do you think that griots were important to West African kings?** (Griots taught the history of the kings' ancestors; griots taught the kings their ancestors' principles of governing.)

Remembering History Have students discuss the standard path of training that a historian in the United States must follow. Tell them that historians spend many years in school but start at a later age than griots.

Ask students:

- **What are the qualifications necessary to become a griot?** (son or daughter of a griot; good memorization and speaking skills)
- *THINKING FURTHER:* **How are griots similar to typical historians from the United States? How are they different?** (*similar:* learn history; utilize memory; practice for years; *different:* Historians rely on writing and research, whereas a griot relies on memory; historians do not necessarily begin training at an early age.)

BACKGROUND INFORMATION

Multicultural Perspectives The following is from "The Role of the Griot," by a Senegalese griot named D'jimo Kouyate.

> *When you are away from your ancestral land and lack the necessary cultural information, you become "lost" by concept. The color of the skin remains the same but the concept, the knowledge of Africa, is gone. The traditional names and roles in society, everything that belonged to us by birthright, was taken away from most of us.*
>
> *This is known as "the painful period." In order to get back what was ours, information and knowledge about African society and culture must be learned now. This the griot gives to all who need it.*

Have students discuss this passage, focusing on how griots can help African Americans to preserve or recover traditions.

Discussing Talking Books Have students predict what the term *talking book* means before they read this section.

Ask students:

- **Why do you think that people generously cared for griots?** (because the information that griots possessed was valuable)
- **Why might griots be thought of as talking books?** (because they preserve memories like a history book does)
- **Why do you think that griots sometimes wear costumes and masks?** (Students may suggest that costumes and masks are used to represent historical characters and thus aid in the storytelling process.)
- *THINKING FURTHER:* **How might the use of music be helpful to a griot?** (Lead students to understand that the use of lyrics coupled with rhythm can be an effective way of remembering information.)

Learning History Through Griots Discuss with students whether they know when their ancestors arrived in the United States.

Ask students:

- **Why do you think that Alex Haley was interested in finding out about his roots?** (Encourage students to discuss why people are interested in finding out about their ancestry.)

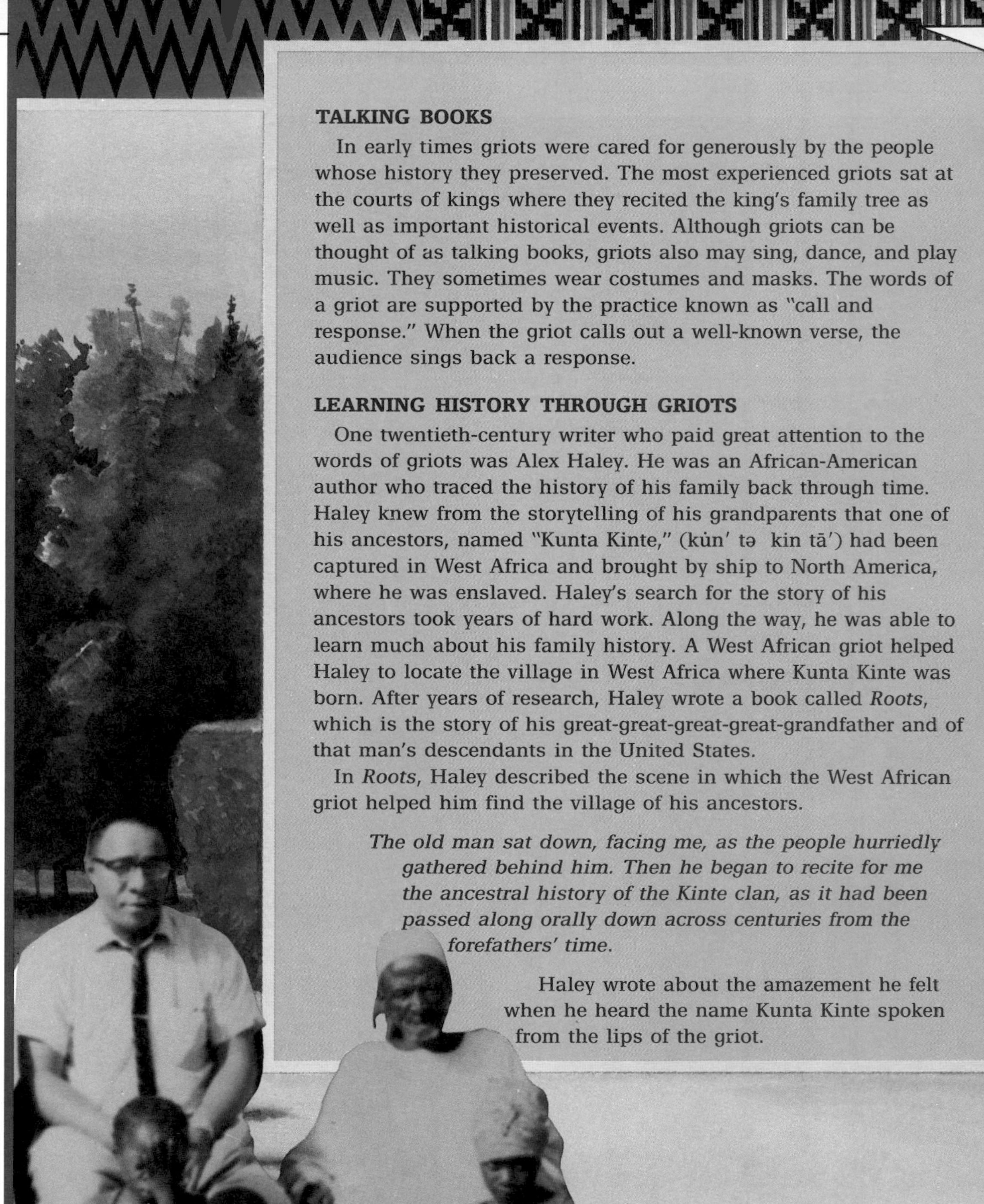

TALKING BOOKS

In early times griots were cared for generously by the people whose history they preserved. The most experienced griots sat at the courts of kings where they recited the king's family tree as well as important historical events. Although griots can be thought of as talking books, griots also may sing, dance, and play music. They sometimes wear costumes and masks. The words of a griot are supported by the practice known as "call and response." When the griot calls out a well-known verse, the audience sings back a response.

LEARNING HISTORY THROUGH GRIOTS

One twentieth-century writer who paid great attention to the words of griots was Alex Haley. He was an African-American author who traced the history of his family back through time. Haley knew from the storytelling of his grandparents that one of his ancestors, named "Kunta Kinte," (kủn' tə kin tā') had been captured in West Africa and brought by ship to North America, where he was enslaved. Haley's search for the story of his ancestors took years of hard work. Along the way, he was able to learn much about his family history. A West African griot helped Haley to locate the village in West Africa where Kunta Kinte was born. After years of research, Haley wrote a book called *Roots*, which is the story of his great-great-great-great-grandfather and of that man's descendants in the United States.

In *Roots*, Haley described the scene in which the West African griot helped him find the village of his ancestors.

> *The old man sat down, facing me, as the people hurriedly gathered behind him. Then he began to recite for me the ancestral history of the Kinte clan, as it had been passed along orally down across centuries from the forefathers' time.*

Haley wrote about the amazement he felt when he heard the name Kunta Kinte spoken from the lips of the griot.

BACKGROUND INFORMATION

West African Sayings and Proverbs Like storytelling, sayings and proverbs also preserve beliefs and ideas of West African cultures. The following are traditional proverbs told by the Hausa of West Africa.

> *A stone in the water does not comprehend how parched the hill is.*
>
> *It is not the eye which understands, but the mind.*
>
> *Lack of knowledge is darker than the night.*
>
> *The man who is carried on another man's back does not appreciate how far off the town is.*
>
> *Faults are like a hill: You stand on your own and talk about those of other people.*
>
> *One does not need to measure to know that a horse's bridle is too large for a hen's mouth.*

Ask students to discuss the meaning of each of these sayings. Ask them to discuss the meanings of any other proverbs with which they are familiar.

I sat as if I were carved of stone. My blood seemed to have congealed [hardened]. *This man whose lifetime had been in this back-country African village had no way in the world to know that he had just echoed what I had heard all through my boyhood years on my grandma's front porch in Henning, Tennessee . . . of an African who always had insisted that his name was "Kin-tay"; who had called a guitar a "ko," and a river within the state of Virginia, "Kamby Bolongo"; and who had been kidnaped into slavery while not far from his village, chopping wood, to make himself a drum.*

GRIOTS TODAY

The spread of European-style educational systems has reduced greatly the number of griots in West Africa. In the twentieth century some griots have become teachers, university professors, and historians. These scholars and writers have played an important role in creating a written record of what their ancestors recited and chanted. Some modern griots earn their livings by performing at weddings, births, and celebrations of many kinds.

The West African legacy of oral history remains strong on at least two continents—Africa and North America. Enslaved Africans brought their memories, history, and the practice of "call and response" to America. Today it is not uncommon for an elderly African American to recite the memories handed down by his or her great-grandparents. In fact, this is exactly how Alex Haley first heard the stories about his ancestors. On the African continent the griots have preserved the memories of their elders. The methods and the memories of the griots have survived over the ages to be passed on to new generations in Africa and in North America.

How is the legacy of oral history important in West Africa and the United States?

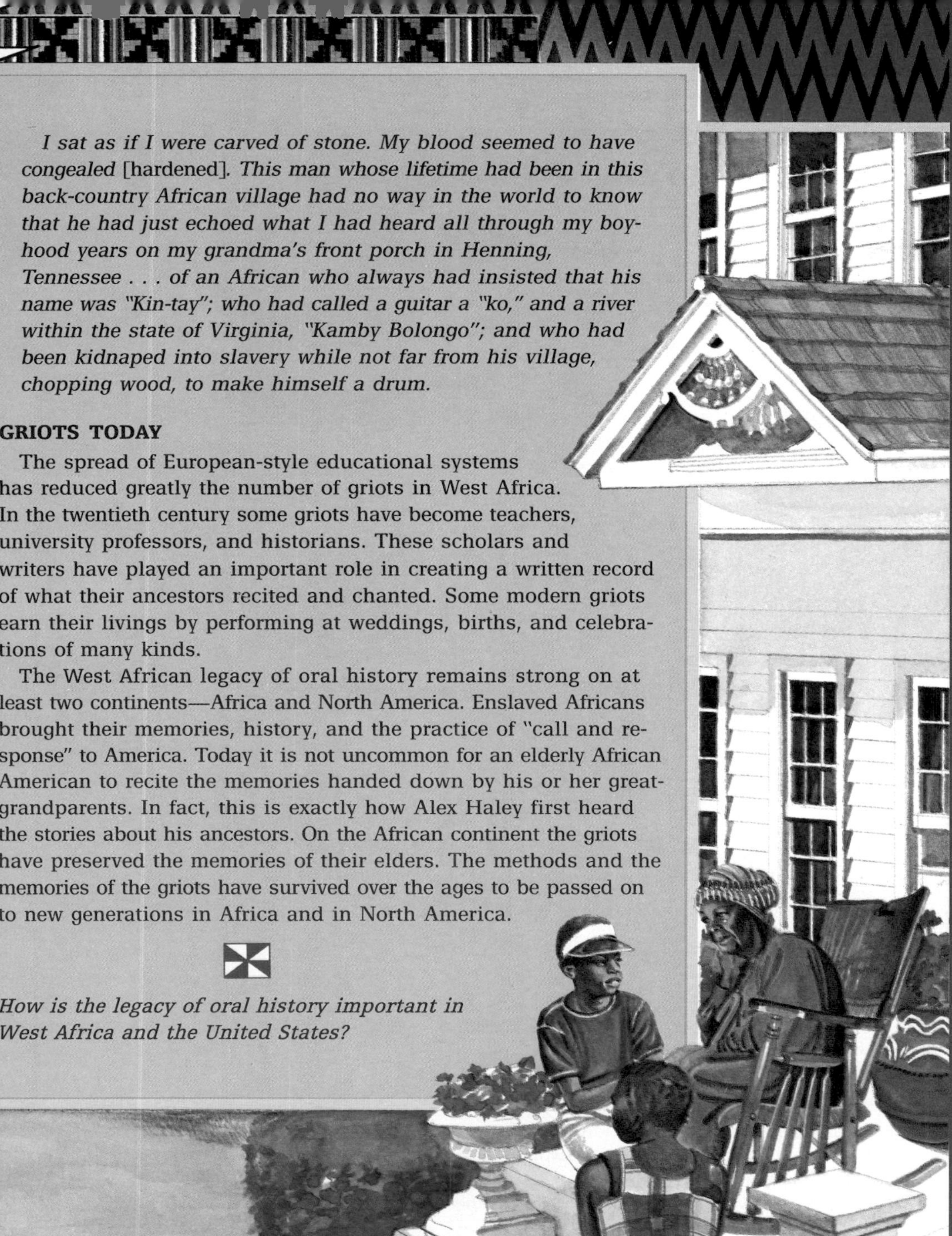

445

Discovering History Through Griots Continue the discussion of Haley's search for his roots. Have a student read the excerpts aloud.

Ask students:

- **Where did Alex Haley first hear about Kunta Kinte?** (on his grandmother's front porch in Henning, Tennessee)

Discussing Griots Today Ask students to discuss how the use of written historical records might change the role of griots in West Africa.

Ask students:

- **Why do you think that some griots have become teachers and historians?** (Possible answers include: These are professions in which people teach others and preserve knowledge and legacies.)
- **Why do you think that some griots still perform at weddings, births, and other celebrations?** (Students may suggest that griots help to lend a traditional tone to these events.)
- **List three similarities between the West African and African-American legacies of oral history.** (Possible answers include: Both preserve memories, history, and the practice of "call and response.")

Applying the Lesson Encourage students to write and to try to memorize a paragraph about their family history.

3 CLOSE

Summarizing Students have read about the oral tradition of West Africa and its continuing influence in Africa and the United States.

Evaluating Assess students' understanding of the lesson by asking them the question at the bottom of the pupil page. (Possible answer includes: oral history in West Africa and the United States helps people to remember their ancestors and helps to keep their legacies and beliefs alive.)

MEETING INDIVIDUAL NEEDS

Reteaching (easy) Ask students to write one generalization for each section heading in the lesson. For each generalization, ask them to scan the section and write two supporting details.

Extension (average) Have students select and memorize part of a story and recite it to the rest of the class.

Enrichment (challenging) Have students read part of Alex Haley's book, *Roots.* Then have them present to the class a summary of what they have read. You may wish to have students focus on Haley's encounter with the griot in Chapter 120.

CHAPTER 21 REVIEW
pages 446–447

USING THE CHAPTER SUMMARY AND REVIEW

Cultural Geography

- **What is the most densely populated part of Sub-Saharan Africa?** (West Africa)
- **What are the four main cash crops of the region?** (cacao, peanuts, coffee, bananas)
- **Which types of traditional government are common in West Africa?** (monarchies with absolute rulers, Islamic systems, democratic village councils)
- **What are griots?** (storytellers)

Ideas to Remember

- **What are three cultural influences on the people of West Africa?** (traditional African customs, Islam, European colonialism)
- **On what two types of agriculture are the economies of West Africa dependent?** (subsistence farming and growing cash crops)
- **Why is national unity a problem for the countries of West Africa?** (because of conflicting loyalties and different types of government)
- **How do the people of West Africa preserve their community life and history?** (through oral tradition, music, dance, and art)

Answers to Reviewing Vocabulary

1. An oba is a ruler of West Africa.
2. True.
3. True.
4. True.
5. Oral tradition is the passing down of history and literature by the spoken word.

CHAPTER 21 • SUMMARY

NATIONS OF WEST AFRICA: CULTURAL GEOGRAPHY

PEOPLE

- Most densely populated part of Sub-Saharan Africa

- Cultural influences: traditional practices and beliefs, Islam, and Christianity

- Many ethnic groups and languages
- Clans provide a deep sense of belonging

ECONOMY

- Expanding desert caused by increasing drought and overgrazing in the Sahel

- Agriculture: both subsistence farming and cash crops

- Cash crops: cacao, peanuts, coffee bananas
- Industrial facilities: mills, food-processing plants, oil wells and refineries in Nigeria

GOVERNMENT

- Nations include several political traditions

- Traditional local governments and fairly new national governments
- National problems include longstanding ethnic enmities and conflicting loyalties
- Some countries are trying to end one-party rule and move toward democracy

ARTS AND RECREATION

- Griots preserve West Africa's rich oral tradition
- Talking drums are means of celebration and of communication
- Decorated masks are used in religious ceremonies to call on gods and spirits
- Present-day writers in many countries are well known throughout the world

IDEAS TO REMEMBER

- The ethnic groups and clans of West Africa have been influenced by traditional African customs, Islam, and European colonialism and Christianity.
- Economies depend mainly on two types of agriculture: subsistence farming and the growing of cash crops.
- National unity has been hard to achieve because of conflicting loyalties and different types of government.
- West Africa's oral tradition, music, dance, and art enrich and preserve community life and history.

446

ENRICHMENT ACTIVITY

Making Sculpture **Materials:** modeling clay

1. Tell students that they will make sculpture in the style of West African art.
2. Refer the class to the text material on African masks on page 441. Explain that West African sculpture, including masks, is admired around the world.
3. Have students refer to encyclopedia entries under "African Art." These entries often show examples such as Nok sculptures from northern Nigeria, art from the kingdom of Benin, and works by the Dan and related peoples of Liberia, Sierra Leone, and Côte d'Ivoire.
4. Have students choose a particular West African culture and design their sculpture in the artistic style of that culture.
5. Have students label and display their sculptures.

CHAPTER 21 • REVIEW

REVIEWING VOCABULARY

Each of the following statements contains an underlined vocabulary word or term. Number a sheet of paper from 1 to 5. Beside each number write whether the following statements are true or false. If the statement is true, write true. If it is false, rewrite the sentence using the underlined vocabulary word correctly.

1. An oba is a traditional West African musical instrument that is often used in religious ceremonies.
2. Shifting cultivation is a method of farming in which certain fields are allowed to "rest" between plantings.
3. Griots preserve the stories and history of their people.
4. Desertification, or the expansion of desert, is the result of both natural processes and human activities.
5. Oral tradition involves regular public readings of works of poetry, histories, and other printed materials.

REVIEWING FACTS

1. Why is West Africa called a blend of cultures?
2. Which West African groups are herders? Traders and merchants?
3. What is subsistence farming? Why are cash crops important to the economies of West Africa?
4. How do national boundaries created by colonial powers contribute to conflict and instability in West African countries?
5. In what ways do masks serve religious purposes in West Africa?

WRITING ABOUT MAIN IDEAS

1. **Writing a Paragraph:** You have read that West Africans feel loyal to their families and clans. Write a paragraph describing the importance of clans in West African life.
2. **Writing a Letter:** Imagine you are visiting the savanna in West Africa. Write a letter to a friend describing the farming methods of shifting cultivation and slash-and-burn farming.
3. **Writing an Outline:** Write an outline of the various forms of art, music, and dance that West Africans use to express themselves.
4. **Writing About Perspectives:** Imagine that you are a West African trying to stop the desertification of the Sahel. Write a plan for bringing about change. Discuss at least two changes you would like to make. Why do you think that people might be willing or unwilling to follow your suggestions?

BUILDING SKILLS: DISTINGUISHING FACTS FROM OPINIONS

1. What is a fact? What is an opinion? Write an example of each.
2. What are some steps you could take to identify a fact and an opinion?
3. Why is it important to be able to distinguish between facts and opinions?

Answers to Reviewing Facts

1. It has been influenced by traditional African customs, Islam, and European colonialism.
2. Fulani and Tuaregs; Yoruba
3. growing only enough food to meet the needs of one's family; Many economies are dependent on the cash crops they grow.
4. The lands within the boundaries drawn by colonial powers include people who are ancient enemies.
5. It is believed that the masks are a way of calling spirits to speak to humans, and can take on the spirits of ancestors.

Suggestions for Writing About Main Ideas

1. Students should focus on the sense of belonging that a clan gives a person and how one's life revolves around the clan.
2. Students should describe each method and tell how they complement one another.
3. You may wish to have the class as a whole select the main ideas for the outline headings and then have each student fill in the supporting details on his/her own.
4. Students' plans should list their suggestions, along with the pros and cons of each.

Answers to Building Skills: Distinguishing Facts from Opinions

1. information that can be proved to be true; a personal view or belief that cannot be proved to be true; Accept all reasonable responses.
2. Recall the definition of a fact, an opinion, and a value judgment; look for clues to statements of fact; look for clues to value judgments; look for clues to reasoned opinions; read each statement carefully to find these clues.
3. to be able to make reasoned conclusions about what you read

MAKING CONNECTIONS

Classifying and Concluding Display the Main Idea Map Graphic Organizer Transparency, filling in only the underlined labels. Have students review the chapter and fill in each box with the appropriate items for each topic. *Ask:* What characteristics of West African culture make national unity hard to achieve?

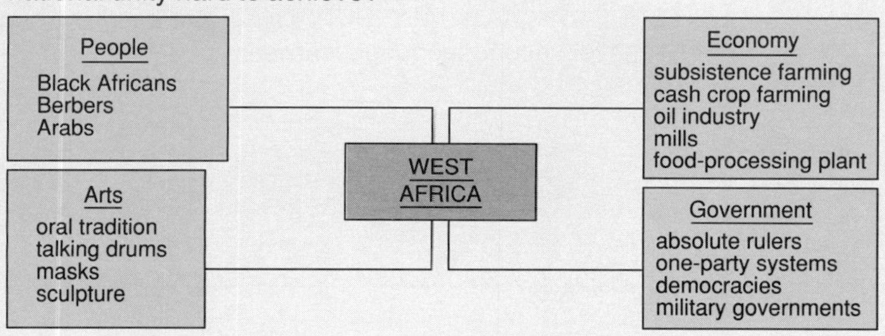

Chapter Review and Test

Practice Book: *Vocabulary Review,* page 120
Transparency: *Graphic Organizer*
Assessment Book: *Chapter 21 Test*

CHAPTER 22 ORGANIZER

EAST AND EQUATORIAL AFRICA text pages 448–465

CHAPTER THEME Herding, farming, and fishing are the key livelihoods in East and Equatorial Africa, where economic development has been slowed by drought, poor transportation, and lack of funds.

CHAPTER OBJECTIVES

CONTENT

- Identify the groups of people that settled in East and Equatorial Africa and explain how their languages and cultures developed.
- Describe how the lands in which the East and Equatorial Africans live shape the way they earn their living.
- Define *famine* and explain how it has affected such countries as Ethiopia and Sudan.
- Explain why governments in this region are urging their people to grow more cash crops.
- Explain why most countries in East and Equatorial Africa have one-party governments.
- Explain the relationship between economic and political problems in East and Equatorial Africa.
- Describe the cultural and economic effects of European colonialism on this region.
- Describe the importance of poems, stories, and other forms of spoken language in East and Equatorial Africa.

SKILLS

Geography
- Interpret a political map of East and Equatorial Africa.

Study and Research
- Use a chart to trace the growth of independence in East and Equatorial Africa.
- Make a graph from a chart.

Thinking
- Compare and contrast the people of East and Equatorial Africa with the people of West Africa.
- Locate statements of fact in the text.

Reading and Writing
- Write a description of a new business venture in East and Equatorial Africa.

CITIZENSHIP VALUES

- Appreciate the importance of political stability.

TEACHER OPTIONS

READING STRATEGY: Study Guide Strategies to help students read and remember the main ideas of the lesson.

Lesson 1: p. 449 Lesson 3: p. 458
Lesson 2: p. 453 Lesson 4: p. 461

MEETING INDIVIDUAL NEEDS Activities for reteaching, extension, and enrichment.

Lesson 1: p. 452 Lesson 4: p. 462
Lesson 2: p. 455 Study and Research
Lesson 3: p. 460 Skills: p. 463

GEO ADVENTURES ACTIVITIES PAD Daily activities to assess students' understanding of geography skills.

CURRICULUM CONNECTION Activities to help integrate other subject areas with Social Studies.

Art: p. 450

PUPIL EDITION ON CASSETTE Language support for students who have difficulty reading or who will benefit from listening to the Pupil Edition on Cassette as they read.

SECOND-LANGUAGE SUPPORT Activities and suggestions for second-language learners.

CHAPTER PLANNING GUIDE

LESSON	SUGGESTED PACING	THEMES	TEACHER SUPPORT MATERIALS: TEACHER'S RESOURCE CENTER
1 THE PEOPLE pages 449–452	1 day	The great variety of ethnic groups in East and Equatorial Africa developed out of thousands of years of migration, trade, and colonialism.	Practice Book p. 121 Outline Map p. 31 Technology: Adventures CD-ROM
2 THE ECONOMY pages 453–457	1 day	Traditional occupations dominate the developing economies of East and Equatorial Africa.	Practice Book p. 122 ■ Anthology pp. 135–136 Outline Map p. 31 Technology: Adventures CD-ROM
3 THE GOVERNMENT pages 458–460	1 day	One-party systems, or dictatorships, characterize the mostly unstable governments of East and Equatorial Africa.	Practice Book p. 123 ■ Anthology pp. 116–117, 118–119, 120–123 Technology: Adventures CD-ROM
4 ARTS AND RECREATION pages 461–462	1 day	Ethnic traditions are preserved and learned in East and Equatorial Africa through proverbs, stories, and poetry.	Practice Book p. 124 ■ Anthology pp. 134, 141–142
BUILDING STUDY AND RESEARCH SKILLS Making a Graph from a Chart page 463	1 day	Trends can be seen when statistics in chart form are converted into a line graph.	Practice Book p. 125
CHAPTER SUMMARY AND REVIEW pages 464–465	1 day	Chapter content, skills, and vocabulary are reviewed and evaluated.	Practice Book p. 126 Transparency: Graphic Organizer Assessment Book, Chapter 22 Test

Technology CONNECTION

Lesson 1
ADVENTURES CD-ROM
Enrich Lesson 1 by having students *Travel* to Zaire.

Lesson 2
ADVENTURES CD-ROM
Enrich Lesson 2 by having students look at Pictures in *Investigate, Media,* taking notes in the *Notebook.*

Lesson 3
ADVENTURES CD-ROM
Enrich Lesson 3 by having students *Explore* Kenya.

CHAPTER 22
pages 448–465

USING THE CHAPTER OPENER

Discussing the Photograph Tell students that this is a photograph of a Masai woman. The Masai live in Kenya and Tanzania in East Africa. Ask students what they notice about the way in which the woman is dressed. (Students may comment on the colorful beadwork and the way it is used on the headband, earrings, and necklaces.) Tell students that this is the way Masai women traditionally dress.

Ask students:

- **What are some of the ways in which girls and women use jewelry and other decoration in our society?** (Accept various answers that show the variety of kinds of female personal adornment, including makeup, hair tints, and so on.)
- **Why do you think the Masai women dress the way that they do?** (Accept various answers, such as: to show off their handiwork; because it is the traditional way of dressing; and so on.)
- *THINKING FURTHER:* **How can the way people dress help to express their unity as a group?** (Dressing in a similar fashion is one way in which people identify themselves as members of a distinct group.)

Reading/Listening to the Primary Source Note that chants, mottoes, passwords, prayers, and so on are other ways in which people create unity. Have a student give the meaning of the term *Harambee!* Then ask the class to recite the word *Harambee!* together, in a reasonably loud voice.

Ask students:

- **What other cheers, chants, prayers, or mottoes do you know that help people create a feeling of unity?** (Accept various answers. You might wish to point out that the motto of the United States, *E Pluribus Unum* [''Out of Many One''], is also a call for unity.)

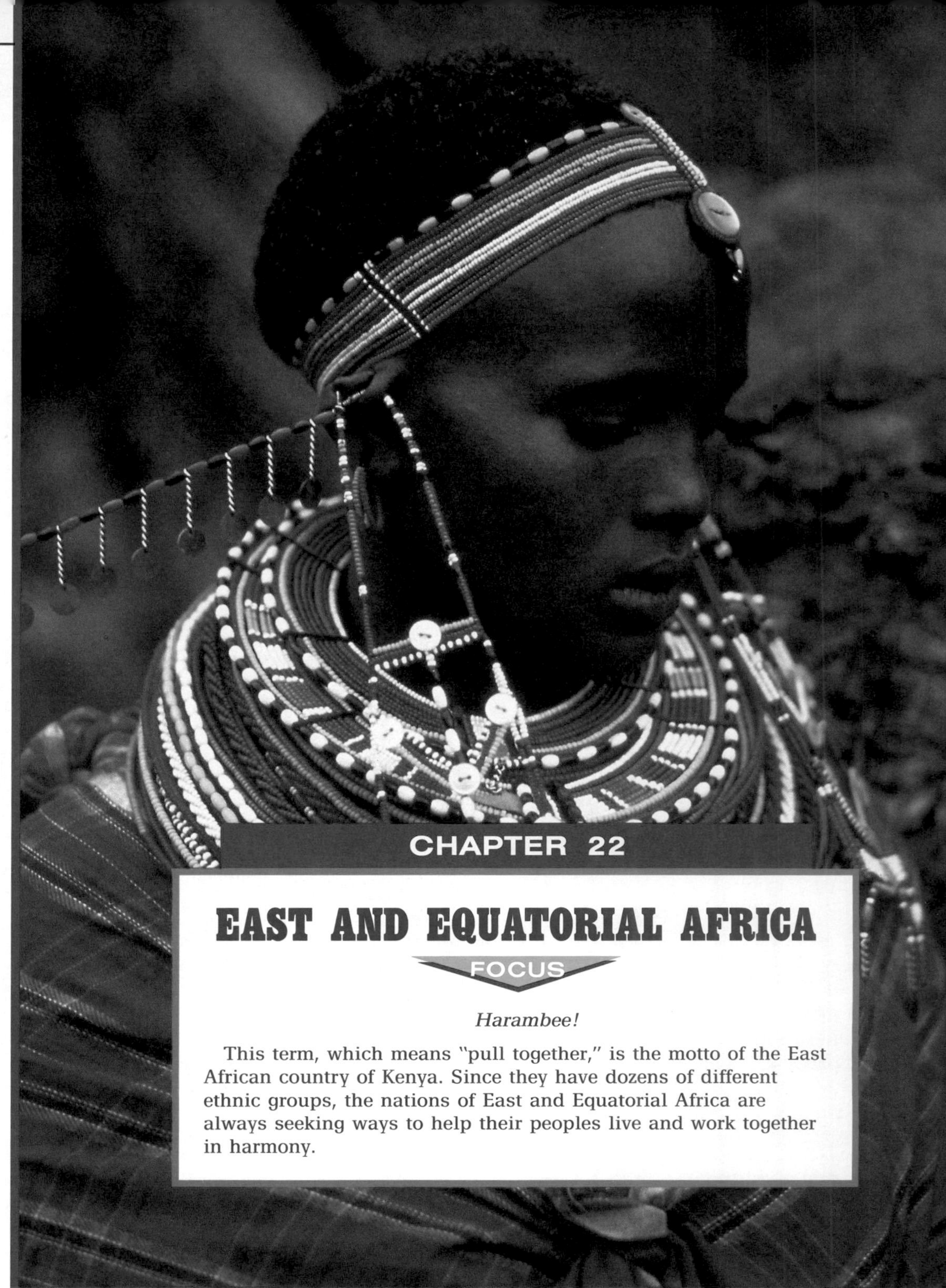

CHAPTER 22

EAST AND EQUATORIAL AFRICA

FOCUS

Harambee!

This term, which means "pull together," is the motto of the East African country of Kenya. Since they have dozens of different ethnic groups, the nations of East and Equatorial Africa are always seeking ways to help their peoples live and work together in harmony.

BACKGROUND INFORMATION

The Swahili Language Language can also be a powerful unifying force among people. Swahili is the most common language of East and Equatorial Africa.

- Swahili is the official language of Tanzania and Kenya and is widely understood in Uganda, Burundi, and eastern Zaire.
- Swahili is the primary language of trade, having originally been developed from local dialects by Arab traders.
- Literature in Swahili goes back to the eighteenth century. It has flourished since the mid-nineteenth century, when missionaries introduced the Roman alphabet.
- Like English, Swahili has several dialects. The standard form of the language is the dialect spoken in Zanzibar.

LESSON 1

The People

READ TO LEARN

Key Vocabulary

migration
Swahili

Key Places

Zaire

Read Aloud

Less than a hundred years ago, Nairobi, Kenya, was little more than a quiet watering spot for cattle. In fact, in the language of the Masai people who named it, *Nairobi* means "The Place of Cool Waters."

Today "The Place of Cool Waters" is a jam-packed city. On the streets you will still see some Masai people, but you will also find people from many other ethnic groups. Some are African, some are Asian, some are Middle Eastern, and some are European. In this lesson you will read about the many different ethnic groups who have made their home in East and Equatorial Africa.

Read for Purpose

1. WHAT YOU KNOW: What causes people to move to new places? What do they hope to find?
2. WHAT YOU WILL LEARN: What groups of people settled in East and Equatorial Africa, and how did their languages and cultures develop?

THE NATIONS OF EAST AND EQUATORIAL AFRICA

East and Equatorial Africa is one of the important divisions of Sub-Saharan Africa. In the last chapter you read about West Africa. Now you will learn about the lands near the equator and in the east of Africa.

East and Equatorial Africa is a vast area, larger than the continental United States. It includes ten countries in East Africa: Burundi, Djibouti (ji bü′ tē), Ethiopia, Kenya, Rwanda (rü än′ də), Eritrea, Somalia, Sudan, Tanzania, and Uganda. The region also includes ten countries in Equatorial Africa: Angola, Cameroon, Central African Republic, Chad, Congo, Equatorial Guinea, Gabon, São Tomé and Príncipe (soun tü mā′ and prēn′ si pā), Seychelles (sā shel′), and Zaire.

THE BANTU MIGRATION

Hundreds of ethnic groups share the lands of East and Equatorial Africa. In Sudan alone there are more than 500 groups. Zaire has more than 200 ethnic groups. The ancestors of these people came to East and Equatorial Africa over thousands of years.

About 2,500 years ago a great migration began in and around what is today the country of Cameroon. A migration is a movement of groups of people into new lands. The group of people who migrated

WHAT YOU KNOW: Students should be encouraged to think about the different reasons that people move, such as to change jobs or to try to improve their quality of life.

LESSON 1
pages 449–452

Lesson Theme The great variety of ethnic groups in East and Equatorial Africa developed from thousands of years of migration, trade, and colonialism.

Lesson Objectives

- Describe the migrations into East and Equatorial Africa.
- Identify the languages and ethnic groups of East and Equatorial Africa today.

PREPARE

Motivate Read the *Read Aloud* section to the class. Compare this description of city growth with the growth of other cities studied so far, such as Mexico City. Ask students to speculate about why there are so many different ethnic groups in Nairobi.

Set Purpose Use the *What You Know* question to continue the discussion about Nairobi's growth. Ask the *What You Will Learn* question to encourage students to seek information about the stages in the growth of East and Equatorial African culture.

TEACH

Introducing the Nations of East and Equatorial Africa After students read this section, help them identify each nation on the map on page 450.

Discussing the Bantu Migration Identify the Bantus as an early group of people that migrated to Cameroon. Locate Cameroon on the map on page 450. Discuss the meaning of *migration*.

READING STRATEGY AND VOCABULARY DEVELOPMENT

Study Guide The purpose of this strategy is to help students to understand that there are many strategies they can use to summarize and organize lesson information. Review the two types of study guides already taught: the KWL Guide (Chapter 8) and the SQ3R Study Guide (Chapter I5). Tell students that a chart can also be used as a study guide. Have students use one of these three strategies to study this lesson. Explain to students who wish to use the chart approach that lesson headings can be used as headings for their charts. As they read the lesson, they can fill in important information under each chart heading. Have students review and compare their charts after they have read the lesson.

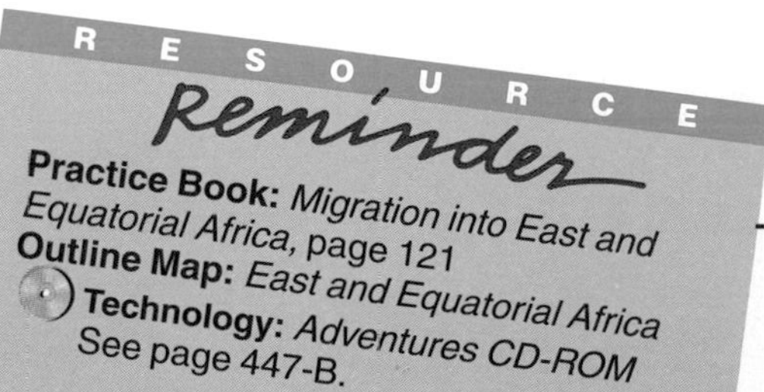
RESOURCE Reminder

Practice Book: *Migration into East and Equatorial Africa*, page 121
Outline Map: *East and Equatorial Africa*
Technology: *Adventures CD-ROM*
See page 447-B.

Tracing the Bantu Migration Continue to discuss the migration of the Bantus. Help students to understand how far back in time the background of the Bantu people reaches and how long migration takes.

Ask students:

- **When did the Bantu migration begin, how long did it last, and where did the people go?** (It began 2,500 years ago. For over 2,000 years the Bantus moved from Cameroon to the Zaire Basin and out into East and Equatorial Africa.)
- **What are the results of that migration today?** (over 400 Bantu languages; largest ethnic groups in the region are Bantu)
- **What are the largest Bantu ethnic groups and where are they located?** (Kikuyu in Kenya and Baganda in Uganda)

EXTENDING MAP SKILLS

Have students study the political map on this page.

Ask students:

- **What are the two largest countries of this region?** (Sudan and Zaire)
- **Which four countries are completely landlocked?** (Central African Republic, Uganda, Rwanda, Burundi, Chad)
- **What are the smallest countries in this region?** (Djibouti, Burundi, Uganda, Rwanda, Equatorial Guinea, São Tomé and Príncipe, Seychelles)
- **Which countries border the Red Sea?** (Ethiopia, Eritrea, Sudan, Djibouti)
- **Which countries border West Africa?** (Chad, Cameroon)
- **Through which countries does the equator pass?** (São Tomé and Príncipe, Gabon, Congo, Zaire, Uganda, Kenya, Somalia)

EAST AND EQUATORIAL AFRICA: Political

⊛ National capital

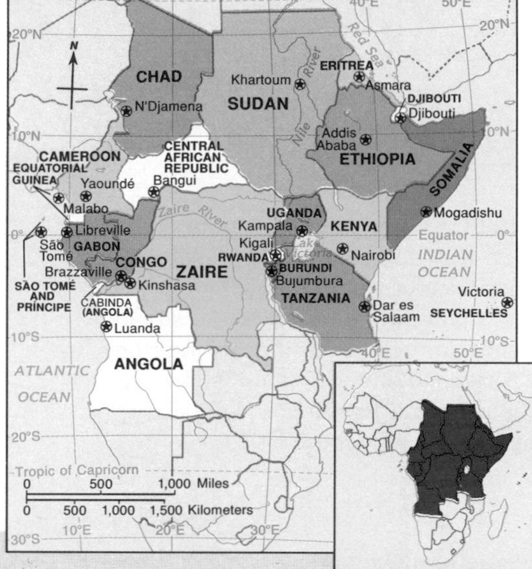

MAP SKILL: Which important river flows through Sudan?

were known as the Bantu. The word *Bantu* means "people." It is used to describe the groups of people that speak the Bantu languages.

The Bantu migration proceeded south and east from Cameroon into Equatorial Africa. In time the Zaire Basin became the center of Bantu kingdoms. Find Zaire on the map on this page. From the Zaire Basin, Bantu people later fanned out into new lands in East and Equatorial Africa.

The Bantu migration was a slow process. In fact, it lasted more than 2,000 years! Over this long period of time the Bantu languages and Bantu customs changed. Today there are about 400 different Bantu languages. Bantu-speaking people form the largest ethnic groups in Equatorial Africa and the southern part of East Africa. Among the largest Bantu ethnic groups are the Kikuyu of Kenya and the Baganda of Uganda.

MUSLIM SETTLEMENTS

The Bantu were by no means the only people to migrate into East and Equatorial Africa. Look at the map on this page. Notice how close the country of Djibouti is to the Arabian Peninsula. Also notice that the Nile River runs through the heart of Sudan. It should come as no surprise to learn that the countries of East Africa are strongly influenced by the cultures of the Middle East and North Africa.

In about A.D. 650, Muslim traders began to set up trading posts on the east coast of Africa. Dar es Salaam, now the capital city of Tanzania, was founded by Arabs. Merchants came to this city from as far away as India and Indonesia to buy ivory, gold, and slaves. Some merchants stayed and founded other trade settlements on the coast of Africa.

Muslim traders brought the Arabic language and the religion of Islam to the East African coast. Traders also introduced important food crops, such as yams, coconuts, and bananas. Farmers started planting these crops throughout much of East and Equatorial Africa.

OTHER MIGRATIONS

Many other groups migrated within East and Equatorial Africa. A group known as the Kushites migrated south from Ethiopia into the fertile plateaus of the present-day countries of Uganda, Kenya, and Tanzania. The Kushites were skilled farmers.

Another group of people migrated south from the valley of the Nile River in what is now the country of Sudan. These people knew how to grow grain and keep livestock alive in very dry climates. They were called Nilotes, because they came from

MAP SKILL: the Nile River

CURRICULUM CONNECTION

Art Help students to understand that since works of art reflect the experiences, customs, and beliefs of the culture in which the artist who produced them lives, we can discover much about that culture by studying its art. Have students research the art of an East and Equatorial African group and write reports on how its sculptures and paintings illustrate its history and life style. For example, students may wish to report on the Ethiopians and the way in which their art has been influenced by Christianity and by their country's nearness to the Middle East. Or students may report on the Pygmies of Zaire whose wandering life, uncluttered by possessions, is reflected in singing and dancing rather than in carvings and metalwork.

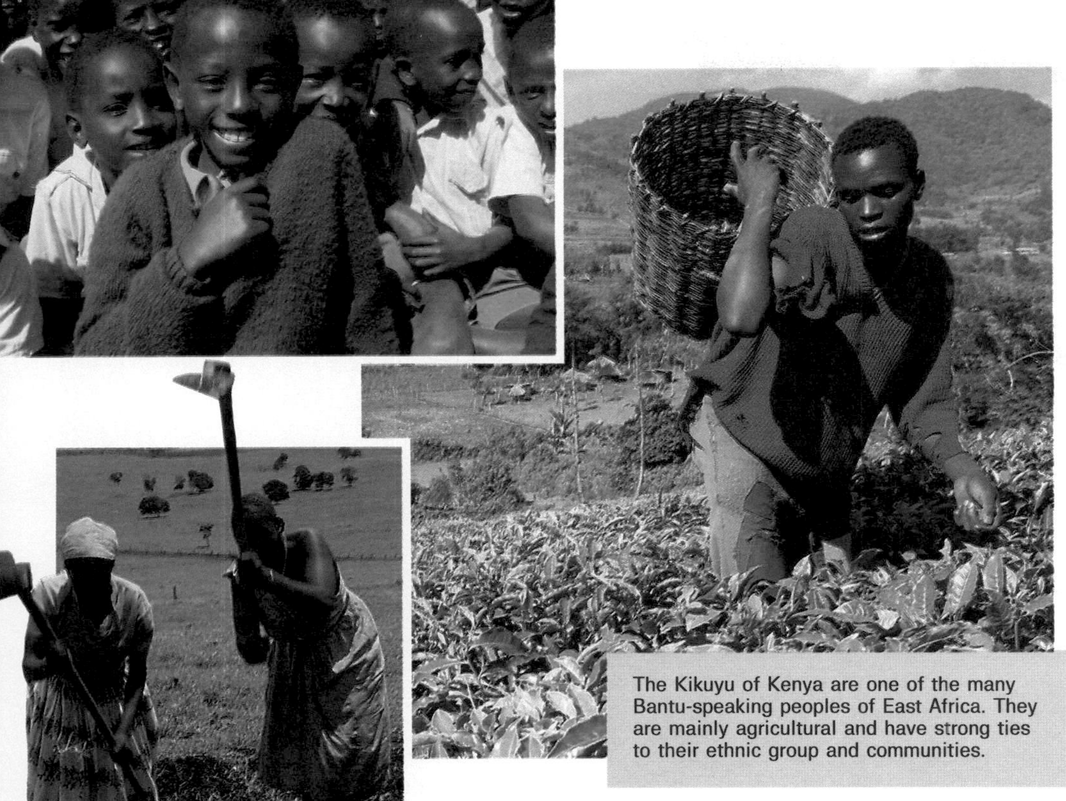

The Kikuyu of Kenya are one of the many Bantu-speaking peoples of East Africa. They are mainly agricultural and have strong ties to their ethnic group and communities.

lands near the Nile River. The Nilotes roamed all over the dry lands of East and Equatorial Africa.

Of course not everyone in East and Equatorial Africa chose to migrate somewhere else. There are people in Ethiopia today who can trace their ancestry back to a thriving civilization of Biblical times. And some Kushite peoples have been in the northern part of Sudan since the days of the Egyptian empire. In the fourth century A.D., Christianity began to spread from Egypt to Ethiopia. By 600 most Ethiopians had become Christians.

In the 1400s and 1500s Europeans came in great numbers to many parts of Africa, including East and Equatorial Africa. Some Europeans came to trade and others came to settle. They brought their languages with them and converted many East and Equatorial Africans outside Ethiopia to Christianity. Eventually European colonies were established in the area and Europeans soon ruled all of East and Equatorial Africa except Ethiopia.

MANY PEOPLE, MANY LANGUAGES

As a result of migrating, trading, and colonialism, ethnic groups tended to blend together. Many present-day East and Equatorial Africans are mixtures of several groups. Their ancestors might be a mix of Bantus, Kushites, and Nilotes. As was true in West Africa, the blend of peoples led to the development of many new languages.

Locating Muslim Settlements Help students to identify the routes that Muslims took into this region.

Ask students:

- **Which routes did Muslims take into East and Equatorial Africa?** (south up the Nile River through Sudan and down the east coast of Africa)
- **What important Muslim action took place in about A.D. 650?** (They set up trading posts on Africa's east coast.)
- **What did Muslims bring to East Africa?** (the Arabic language, the religion of Islam, and traders who brought foods such as yams, coconuts, bananas)

Identifying Other Migrations

Ask students:

- **What migrations took place within East and Equatorial Africa?** (Ethiopian Kushites moved south into present-day Uganda, Kenya, and Tanzania; Nilotes moved south from the Nile River into Sudan.)
- **Which skills did these groups bring to the region?** (farming, herding skills)
- **What did the Europeans bring to East and Equatorial Africa?** (European languages, customs, colonization)
- **What was the only part of East and Equatorial Africa that did not become a European colony?** (Ethiopia)
- **In what two ways was Ethiopia different from the rest of East and Equatorial Africa?** (adopted Christianity more than 1,400 years ago; never a European colony)

Looking at Peoples and Languages

Ask students:

- **What kinds of movement created the mixtures of peoples in East and Equatorial Africa today?** (migrations, trade, colonialism)
- **What was a natural result of the mixing of many peoples?** (Many languages developed.)

BACKGROUND INFORMATION

The Changing World of the Masai Another group in the region is the Masai. When the British colonized the land that is now Kenya, the way of life of the Masai was threatened. The Masai refused to adopt British ways. As cattle herders, the Masai have always needed wide grazing lands. Today they have been forced to change because Kenya's land must support a growing population and must also provide wilderness reserves to protect the remaining species of Africa's once rich wildlife.

- The Masai count their riches in the number of cattle they own. During World War II they provided beef for the Allied armies.
- The Masai wear distinctive red cloth and are famous for their skill with slender spears. Masai boys traditionally had to spear-kill a lion to be initiated into manhood. With few lions left in the wild today, this test of courage is now rare.

Discussing Many People, Many Languages Continue to discuss the people and languages of the region.

Ask students:

- **A blend of which languages make up Swahili?** (Bantu, Arabic, Portuguese, English, and others)
- **Which languages are widely spoken in much of the region?** (Swahili, English, French)

Applying the Lesson Have students draw a map of East and Equatorial Africa. Then ask them to choose three ethnic groups of the region and use different colors to show each group's place of origin, migration route, destination, and skills.

3 CLOSE

Summarizing East and Equatorial Africa is a rich mixture of ethnic groups and languages resulting from major migrations of many peoples. Ask students to map the migrations of the Bantus, Kushites, and Nilotes on the outline map of East and Equatorial Africa, which is found in the Teacher's Resource Center.

Evaluating Use the *Check Your Reading* questions (answers given below) to assess students' understanding.

Answers to Check Your Reading

1. the largest ethnic group in East and Equatorial Africa
2. Muslims moved into the region.
3. Muslim traders crossed over from the Arabian Peninsula to Djibouti and then went south; Kushites moved south from Ethiopia to what are today Uganda, Kenya, and Tanzania; Nilotes moved south from the Nile Valley to the dry lands of the region.
4. similar because they are a blend of peoples; different origins and different African languages

Independent Practice
Practice Book: page 121

European colonialism had a strong influence on the development of East and Equatorial Africa. This Christian church was established during the colonial period and many people still worship there today.

One of the most common languages in East and Equatorial Africa is **Swahili**. It contains Bantu words along with elements of the Arabic and Portuguese languages. Swahili is still changing and acquiring words from other languages. For example, the Swahili word for bicycle, *baisikeli*, comes from English.

Today Swahili is widely spoken in East Africa. In much of the region, English and French are also spoken. Both were introduced during the colonial period.

A BLEND OF ETHNIC GROUPS

In this lesson you have read the story of how East and Equatorial Africa's ethnic groups developed. Many people in this area are descended from Bantus who migrated into the region over the course of more than 2,000 years. Other groups came from the Nile River Valley and the Middle East. Finally Europeans arrived in the 1400s and 1500s, bringing their own languages, religion, and customs.

Today East and Equatorial Africa has hundreds of different ethnic groups. They speak many different languages. Swahili is one of the most common, but English and French are also widely used.

Check Your Reading

1. Who are the Bantu-speaking people?
2. Why were some people in East Africa influenced by the cultures of the Middle East and North Africa?
3. List three groups of people who came to East and Equatorial Africa, and name the routes they took to get there.
4. **THINKING SKILL:** In what ways are the people of East and Equatorial Africa similar to West Africans? In what ways are they different?

THINKING SKILL: Compare and Contrast

452

MEETING INDIVIDUAL NEEDS

Reteaching (easy) Have students skim the lesson to list all the ethnic groups mentioned. Then have them write a sentence about each group.

Extension (average) Have students choose a nation in East and Equatorial Africa to find out what ethnic groups live there today. Have them write a descriptive statement about the contributions of the ethnic groups to that country.

Enrichment (challenging) Divide the class into three groups to research the stories of migration of the Nilotes and Kushites and the history of the Ethiopian people. Have each group role play for the class an important scene from their group's past.

LESSON 2

The Economy

READ TO LEARN

Key Vocabulary

famine
barter
malnutrition

Read Aloud

Tied to the trunks [of trees] is a scaffolding of poles from which big baskets are hung to catch the fish coming down in the roaring force of water. Wagenya men work like acrobats along the poles. . . .

This is how a visitor described Wagenya fishermen catching fish at a series of waterfalls along the Zaire River. The Wagenya people have been fishing in this way for hundreds of years. To catch fish, they have to cooperate. In East and Equatorial Africa, whether people are subsistence farmers, herders, or fishers, they typically work closely together to get the most out of their land and water.

Read for Purpose

1. WHAT YOU KNOW: How would you describe the people of East and Equatorial Africa?
2. WHAT YOU WILL LEARN: How do the lands in which the East and Equatorial Africans live shape the way they earn their livings?

TRADITIONAL HERDERS

It is hard for non-Africans to understand the importance of cattle to the people of East and Equatorial Africa. Cattle are not just sources of food. They are a status symbol—a sign of a person's wealth and importance. Some of the Luo people, who live along the shores of Lake Victoria, may leave to work in cities—but only long enough to earn money to buy cattle.

Many people in East and Equatorial Africa are nomadic herders of cattle. They move back and forth across the savanna areas of Sudan, Ethiopia, Djibouti, Somalia, and Kenya. When the land becomes too dry in one area, they move across the savanna to another place.

DROUGHT AND FAMINE

Even in the best times the savanna is often harsh and dry. In many parts of the savanna, water and vegetation are scarce. There are many droughts.

Droughts have led to famine and great misery for many people in East and Equatorial Africa. Famine is the widespread and extreme shortage of food. Droughts and famine have caused millions of deaths in Sub-Saharan Africa. Many people here also suffer from malnutrition, a condition that occurs when people have too little food or too little of the right kinds of food. Ethiopia, Somalia, and Sudan have been particularly hard hit by famine and malnutrition in recent times.

WHAT YOU KNOW: This question refers to information in Lesson 1; responses should note that there are many different ethnic groups and that the people are descended from various migrating groups.

LESSON 2
pages 453–455

Lesson Theme Traditional occupations dominate the developing economies of East and Equatorial Africa.

Lesson Objectives

- Describe herding, farming, and fishing in this region.
- Describe industrial development in East and Equatorial Africa.
- Explain the economic problems and the potential for development of the economies in this region.

1 PREPARE

Motivate As you read the *Read Aloud* quotation to the class, have students think of the skills these workers used. Discuss with students how important it is for people to cooperate.

Set Purpose Review the *What You Know* question. Then ask the *What You Will Learn* question. Tell students to look for connections between the land and occupations in this lesson.

2 TEACH

Understanding Traditional Herders

Ask students:

- **Why are cattle especially valued in East and Equatorial Africa?** (They are both status symbols and food.)

Analyzing Drought and Famine

Ask students:

- **What is famine?** (widespread and extreme shortage of food)
- **Which two Sub-Saharan African nations have been hit the hardest by famine?** (Sudan and Ethiopia)

READING STRATEGY AND VOCABULARY DEVELOPMENT

Study Guide Have students develop a chart to use as a study guide. Tell students that sometimes something visual like a chart makes it easier to remember information. Have students use the lesson headings as headings for their charts. Then have them read the lesson and complete the chart. A sample chart appears below.

Traditional Herders	Drought and Famine
1. Cattle are a status symbol and a source of food.	1. Due to droughts famine is widespread.
2. Many people are nomadic herders of cattle.	2. Ethiopia and Sudan have been hardest hit.

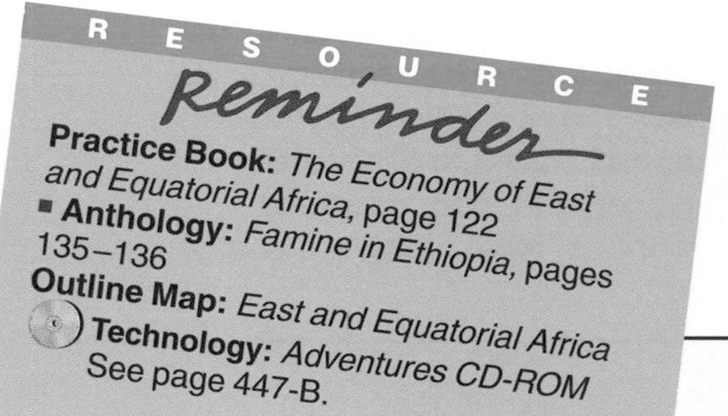
RESOURCE Reminder

Practice Book: *The Economy of East and Equatorial Africa*, page 122
▪ **Anthology:** *Famine in Ethiopia*, pages 135–136
Outline Map: *East and Equatorial Africa*
Technology: *Adventures CD-ROM*
See page 447-B.

Discussing Farming Peoples Help students to realize how subsistence farming and community ownership of land dominate agriculture in this region.

Ask students:

- **How does barter help subsistence farmers?** (If they do not grow something, farmers can swap for it.)
- **What kinds of cash crops are encouraged by governments in this region?** (coffee, tea, sugarcane, cotton, sisal)
- **Where land is owned by a clan, why is an outsider not allowed to buy any land?** (It is owned both by those alive now and those yet to be born.)
- *THINKING FURTHER:* **Why are East and Equatorial Africans unconcerned about their lack of individual ownership of land?** (They know that in order to get the most out of the land, a group must work closely together on it.)

Discussing Industrial Development

Ask students:

- **What major problems hinder industrial development in this region?** (lack of investment money, poor transportation)
- **Which industries in general are doing well?** (lumbering, iron and manganese mining, copper mining)
- **Which resources are waiting to be developed?** (petroleum, gold, diamonds, iron, silver, tin, aluminum)

Looking at Economic Problems Explain the relationship between lack of industrial development and lack of money.

Ask students:

- **How does the lack of industry affect the standard of living in this region?** (It keeps it very low.)
- **What costly steps need to be taken to promote economic development in this region?** (better transportation, more electric power, and more educated workers, all of which are costly)

The sisal plant is harvested and dried before being twisted into rope or twine.

FARMING PEOPLES

The southern part of East and Equatorial Africa gets more rainfall than the dry savannas to the north. In the southern areas most people work as farmers.

Most people are subsistence farmers, raising only enough to feed themselves. If they do not raise something they need, they **barter**, or swap, for it.

The governments of East and Equatorial Africa have urged people to grow more cash crops, such as coffee, tea, sugarcane, cotton, and sisal. Leaves of the sisal plant are used to make rope and twine.

In many farming villages individuals and families do not own land. In traditional Kikuyu villages of Kenya, for example, village land belongs to the clan. Those yet to be born have the same right to use the land as those presently alive. Therefore, no one may sell a field to an outsider since it belongs to a future Kikuyu.

In many villages farms are owned jointly, either by an extended family or by members of the village. Whole villages may join together to borrow money to buy equipment or seed. Community ownership of land is widespread in East and Equatorial Africa. Families and communities work closely together to get the most out of their land. This is how one Ugandan woman described her life on a farm.

> *Our old clan forest extends for 28 miles* [45 km]. *We raise cotton, millet, maize, simsim* [a seed for cooking oil], *cassava, peanuts, and all our own fruit and garden vegetables. My four sisters and I, my brother, my late mother, my present stepmother, my father, and some of his brothers, all worked in the fields. . . .*

INDUSTRIAL DEVELOPMENT

Generally, the countries of East and Equatorial Africa are not industrially well developed. Lack of money to invest in industry and poor transportation are major problems in the area.

There are some exceptions. Lumbering is very important in Congo and in Gabon, which also has very rich iron and manganese deposits. Zaire has developed rich copper mines and is one of the world's largest producers of that metal. On the whole, however, although countries have deposits of valuable resources such as petroleum, gold, diamonds, iron, silver, tin, and aluminum, these resources have yet to be developed.

FACING ECONOMIC PROBLEMS

The standard of living of the people of East and Equatorial tends to be low. The countries of this area have low per capita

BACKGROUND INFORMATION

Multicultural Perspectives A growing number of young people throughout Africa are leaving their families' farms and taking jobs in cities. While the money jobs generate can mean help for families at home, the migration of sons and daughters also means more work for their parents. In his novel *Petals of Blood*, Kenyan writer Ngugi wa Thiong'o describes the changes in the life of an old farmer named Njuguna.

The land seemed not to yield much and there was now no virgin soil to escape to as in those days before colonialism. His sons had gone away to European farms or to the big towns. Daughters he had none. . . . So, Njuguna, like the other peasants in all the huts scattered about Ilmorog Country, had to be contented with small acreage, poor implements and with his own small family labour. But he kept on hoping.

Ask students in what other ways migration would change village life.

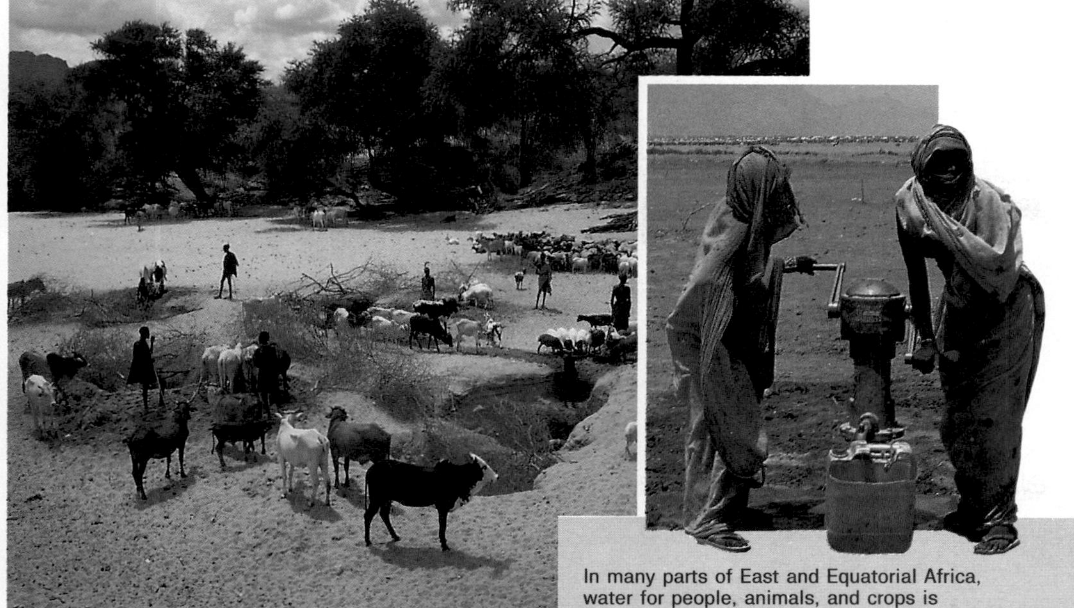

In many parts of East and Equatorial Africa, water for people, animals, and crops is scarce.

incomes. The per capita income in Zaire, for example, is about $150 per year. As you have read, per capita income is the average income for each person in a country.

To become more developed economically, the countries of East and Equatorial Africa need to take several costly steps all at once. All the countries need better transportation systems and more dams to produce hydroelectric power. They also need more educated workers. Most people agree on these needs. The problem is finding the money to pay for it all. Most countries of East and Equatorial Africa are deeply in debt.

TRADITION AND DEVELOPMENT

At least three out of four people of East and Equatorial Africa make their living by herding, farming, or fishing. In this lesson you have read about the way of life of some of the people in these traditional kinds of occupations.

You have also read that the economies of the countries of East and Equatorial Africa are still developing. Mineral resources are slowly being tapped. Drought, lack of money for investment, and poor transportation systems have slowed the economic development of this area.

Check Your Reading

1. Where is herding most common in East and Equatorial Africa?
2. What kind of land ownership is common in this area?
3. What are some of the problems slowing the economic development of East and Equatorial Africa?
4. **THINKING SKILL:** What are some alternatives by which East and Equatorial Africans could develop their economies over the next 20 years? Which do you think they will choose? Why?

THINKING SKILL: Predicting

Applying the Lesson Have students complete a chart showing the positive and negative factors for economic change in East and Equatorial Africa.

3 CLOSE

Summarizing Students have learned that the economies of East and Equatorial Africa are built around herding, farming, and fishing, with potential future economic growth provided by the development of mineral resources. Discuss what it means to a region to have three out of four people in traditional occupations.

Evaluating Use these questions to assess students' understanding.

- **Which traditional occupations are dominant in East and Equatorial Africa?** (farming, herding, fishing)
- **Which industries are doing well in the region?** (lumbering; iron, manganese, and copper mining)
- **What is needed to make the needed improvements to the economy?** (money)

Answers to Check Your Reading

1. the savanna areas of Sudan, Ethiopia, Djibouti, Somalia, and Kenya
2. clan ownership
3. little money, poor transportation
4. Possible answers include: producing more cash crops, building dams, mining. Students should give reasons for their answers.

Independent Practice
Practice Book: page 122

MEETING INDIVIDUAL NEEDS

Reteaching (easy) Give students an outline map of East and Equatorial Africa, found in the Teacher's Resource Center, and information about the location of mineral resources in Africa. Have them label the resources on the map with symbols that show resources now being used and resources still to be developed.

Extension (average) Have students research lumbering or copper mining in this region. Have them write a report on the past, present, and future of the industry they chose. Tell them to include a time line of the industry's development.

Enrichment (challenging) Have students find statistics on the standard of living in each East and Equatorial African nation over the past ten years. Have them create posters that identify and explain changes revealed by these statistics.

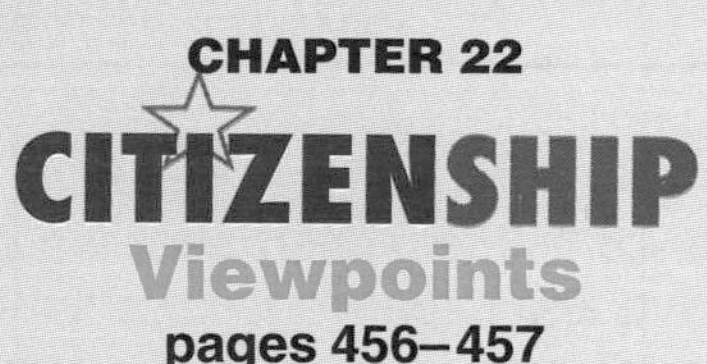

Lesson Objective

- Analyze three points of view on land use in East Africa.

Identifying the Issue Help students to see that environmental and economic concerns must often be balanced in making land-use decisions.

Suggested Question

- ***Why is land use an issue that can cause conflict in East Africa?*** *(Land has multiple uses. In East Africa supporters of tourism and environmental preservation want to put the land to different uses than do farmers and herders.)*

Discussing Three Different Viewpoints Give students a few minutes to read the viewpoints on page 457.

NDYAKIRA AMOOTI

Suggested Questions

- ***Why does Amooti consider land a key natural resource for the economies of East African countries?*** *(Five major economic activities rely on it: farming, fishing, tourism, mining, and herding.)*
- ***Why does he say there is "no choice but to protect the environment"?*** *(If the environment is not protected, East Africans will face even greater hardships through loss of economic opportunities.)*

ALEX DIANG'A

Suggested Questions

- ***According to Diang'a, what is the only way to encourage people to protect animals?*** *(The only way is to make sure they benefit economically from doing so.)*
- ***How can East Africans benefit from protecting wildlife?*** *(Tourists come to the region to see the wildlife, making tourism a major economic activity.)*

CITIZENSHIP VIEWPOINTS

Mt. Kilimanjaro, in Tanzania near the Kenya border, rises majestically over the savanna.

HOW SHOULD LAND BE USED IN EAST AFRICA?

Every year Kenya and Uganda attract thousands of tourists from around the world. East Africa draws these visitors with the promise of remarkable, "up-close" views of elephants, lions, zebras, giraffes, and other wildlife. Tourism is a major industry and wildlife is the main attraction. Some East African animals live in national parks and game reserves. However, in Kenya, for example, over two-thirds of wild animals inhabit range land outside the public preserves.

Competition for land between people and animals is growing. Range lands are also home to traditional farmers who have seen drought, overgrazing, and the growth of cities reduce land available for cultivation. Farmers often see wildlife as destructive, since animals ramble through fields at night eating and trampling crops.

Some people, like Ndyakira Amooti, believe that wildlife must be preserved. Others, like Gitobu Imnyara, say human needs should take priority over other land uses. Alex Diang'a and others are searching for ways to preserve the environment that will also benefit people. Consider three viewpoints on this issue and answer the questions that follow.

456

BACKGROUND INFORMATION

About East African Wildlife In East Africa, national governments have created huge national parks to serve as wildlife sanctuaries. Many parks cover thousands of square miles.

Over the past twenty years, wildlife in Kenya has declined by almost one-third. Wildlife has been greatly reduced throughout Africa as a result of overhunting and poaching and because large areas of natural habitats are now used for farming.

In areas such as Kenya, where a shortage of land for herders and farmers exists, citizens view the parks as depriving people of land and livelihood. In 1996 Kenyan wildlife officials began working with Masai farmers and herders on the creation of a for-profit game sanctuary near the Amboseli National Park. It will be the first community game reserve run by local people. Its profits will go directly to the 840 Masai families living in the area.

Three DIFFERENT Viewpoints

1 **NDYAKIRA AMOOTI**
Journalist, Kampala, Uganda
Excerpt from interview, 1996

The economies of East African countries rely heavily on one natural resource—land. Farming, fishing, tourism, mining, and herding all depend on careful land use. One threat to the environment is overuse of land to meet human needs. What used to be great herds of animal wildlife are disappearing. We have no choice but to protect the natural environment because degrading it will make the economic hardships people already face much worse.

"... no choice but to protect the natural environment ..."

2 **ALEX DIANG'A**
Government worker, Nairobi, Kenya
Excerpt from interview, 1996

Ways must be found for people and animals to share the land. The only way to stop the threat to wildlife is to insure that people gain from protecting them. Tourism brings in more dollars and other foreign currency than any other activity. We need to find ways for the farmers and herders who must share the land with animals to also share in the profits of tourism. Then they will have a reason to preserve the environment.

"Ways must be found for people and animals to share the land."

3 **GITOBU IMANYARA**
Lawyer, Nairobi, Kenya
Excerpt from interview, 1996

People's needs must come first. Game reserves should be maintained for tourists but if the result is the destruction of the way of life of a people, then we must think again and devise a policy that considers their true needs. The Masai have based their way of life on moving from place to place. Now they are confined to a small area in part because the government is concerned with setting aside land for wildlife. We should not alienate a people's way of life for short-term gains in tourist revenue.

"People's needs must come first."

BUILDING CITIZENSHIP

1. What is the viewpoint of each person?
2. In what ways are some of the viewpoints alike? In what ways are they different? Which speaker do you think makes the strongest argument?
3. What other viewpoints might people have on this issue?

SHARING VIEWPOINTS

Discuss reasons why some people may be more concerned about land conservation and wildlife protection while others are more concerned about human needs. Identify two or three issues related to land use and preservation of the environment that all three people could agree on.

GITOBU IMANYARA

Suggested Questions

- ***What goal is more important to Imanyara than environmental preservation?*** *(Protecting the culture and livelihood of people is more important to him.)*
- ***According to Imanyara, how has the Kenyan government's emphasis on game parks affected the Masai people?*** *(He believes it has hurt them by preventing them from practicing their traditional nomadic way of life.)*

EVALUATE

Answers to Citizenship Viewpoints

1. Amooti believes environmental protection should have highest priority. Diang'a believes the needs of animals and humans must be balanced, while Imanyara believes human needs must come first.
2. All agree that protecting the environment is necessary. However, Amooti believes failure to protect the environment will make the economic situation worse, while Imanyara argues that the cost to people of environmental protection may be too high. Diang'a believes that protecting the environment will benefit people. Answers will vary about the strongest argument.
3. Other viewpoints might include allowing the herders and wildlife to share certain reserves or giving people affected by land-use decisions greater say in those decisions.

Sharing Viewpoints Three agreed-upon statements might include: **1.** Tourism is important to the economies of East African countries. **2.** There is a threat to wildlife in East Africa. **3.** Both humans and animals are affected by land-use decisions.

Debating Viewpoints As an extension activity, have students debate how public lands should be used in East Africa, given the economic challenges these nations face, the threat to wildlife of failing to protect the environment, and the impact of land-use decisions on traditional herding and farming peoples.

CITIZENSHIP

Understanding Environmental Concerns The Masai people have always been a cattle-herding people. Their lives have been shaped by their constant movement in search of water and grazing lands for their animals. Although today many Masai have become farmers and lead a more settled existence, in drier areas livestock is still moved seasonally to find new pastures for the animals. Call for student volunteers to do some research on the way of life of the Masai and other nomadic herding peoples in East Africa. Have students report to the class on the impact of game park creation and preservation on the lifestyles of these peoples. Have students discuss what might be done to balance the needs of the Masai with concerns about tourism and wildlife protection.

LESSON 3
pages 458–460

Lesson Theme One-party systems, or dictatorships, characterize the mostly unstable governments of East and Equatorial Africa.

Lesson Objectives
- Describe the role of colonialism in this region.
- Describe one-party rule in this region.

PREPARE

Motivate Read the *Read Aloud* section to the class. Discuss with students the definition of a prophecy.

Set Purpose Display the *Atlas* map of Sub-Saharan Africa so that students can study the political divisions of this region. Use the *What You Know* question to have students consider how long many of the nations of this region have existed. Use the *What You Will Learn* question to discuss the pros and cons of diversity of opinion.

TEACH

Looking at the Lessons of Colonialism

Ask students:

- **Why is colonialism such an important influence on this region?** (Every nation but one was a European colony; the colonial powers introduced their languages and customs to the region.)
- **What injustices did colonies in this region suffer?** (Europeans took the best farmland and mineral resources.)

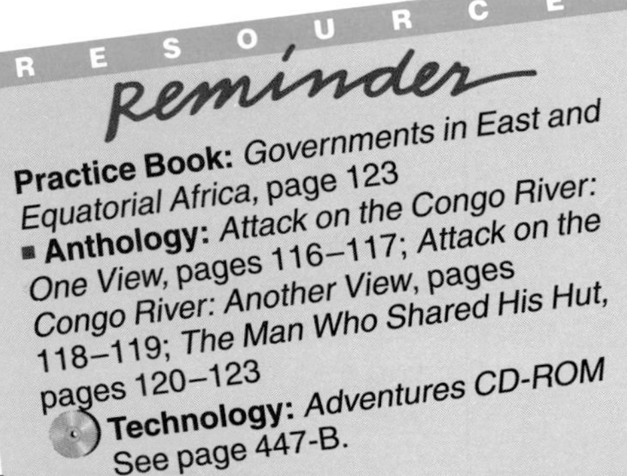

RESOURCE *Reminder*

Practice Book: Governments in East and Equatorial Africa, page 123
- **Anthology:** Attack on the Congo River: One View, pages 116–117; Attack on the Congo River: Another View, pages 118–119; The Man Who Shared His Hut, pages 120–123

Technology: Adventures CD-ROM
See page 447-B.

LESSON 3

The Government

READ TO LEARN

Key Vocabulary	Key People	Key Places
civil war	Jomo Kenyatta	Kenya

Read Aloud

In the nineteenth century a Kikuyu medicine man in Kenya had a terrifying vision. He warned his people that pale strangers carrying firesticks would soon come to their land, and that they would be followed by a fire-belching iron snake with as many legs as a centipede.

Not long afterward, white European settlers with guns appeared in Kenya. Later they built a railroad from Mombasa on the Indian Ocean to Lake Victoria. It was the first of many "iron snakes" in Kenya. The "pale strangers" had taken over.

Read for Purpose

1. **WHAT YOU KNOW:** When did most of the countries of West Africa gain their independence from European nations?
2. **WHAT YOU WILL LEARN:** Why have many countries in East and Equatorial Africa had one-party governments?

LESSONS OF COLONIALISM

In 1938 **Jomo Kenyatta**, a young Kikuyu, told the above story in a book called *Facing Mount Kenya*. When Kenyatta wrote this book, **Kenya** was a British colony. After Kenya won its independence in 1963, Kenyatta became its first president.

The legacy of European colonialism is strong in East and Equatorial Africa. Every country of Equatorial Africa was once a colony of a European nation. In East Africa only Ethiopia remained an independent nation. Belgium, Germany, Italy, Great Britain, France, and Portugal all held colonies. The chart on page 459 gives the dates that each of these countries gained its independence.

As you read in Lesson 1, the European colonial powers introduced their languages and their religion to East and Equatorial Africa while they governed the area. Europeans also took the best farmlands and mineral resources. For example, the English passed a law that no African could own land in the fertile lands of Kenya and Tanzania known as the White Highlands. Suddenly, only white people could farm what had been the Kikuyus' most fertile fields.

INDEPENDENT NATIONS

Today the countries of East and Equatorial Africa are independent of European rule. Look again at the chart. During what

 WHAT YOU KNOW: This question refers to information in Chapter 21, Lesson 1; during the 1960s.

READING STRATEGY AND VOCABULARY DEVELOPMENT

Study Guide Review the KWL guide (What I Know, What I Want to Know, What I Learned) that students read about in Chapter 8. Since students have read about the governments of many other nations, the KWL guide may be very useful for studying this lesson. It should be easy for them to fill in the first two parts of the guide. Have students compare their completed guides.

period did the countries of East and Equatorial Africa win their independence? ✻

Leaders like Jomo Kenyatta knew that independence was only the first step in creating stable, lasting governments. The young nations of the region are still trying to pull together and help themselves.

Many of the new countries have been torn apart by **civil wars** and uprisings. A civil war is a war between people of the same country. Somalia, Ethiopia, Angola, Zaire, Burundi, and Sudan have all had major civil wars and unrest. Although there have been brief periods of peace, violence and civil war continue in many of these poor, war-torn nations.

ONE-PARTY RULE

After they gained independence, the countries of East and Equatorial Africa faced great challenges. Most needed new schools and transportation systems. Often the economies of the countries could not support these badly needed projects.

Many citizens thought that their new governments could work instant miracles. When miracles did not occur, leaders were forced from office in coups. Coups have been very common in the region.

Most East and Equatorial African leaders believe that stable government is more important than guaranteeing democratic rights to their people. The governments of this area have had one-party systems or dictatorships. In most elections only one candidate's name is listed on the ballot. Power has usually changed only when a leader died or was overthrown in a coup. However changes are coming to this region. In 1990 Zaire ended a 20-year ban on multiple political parties. Other countries in the region are also moving to end one-party rule.

Many people in East and Equatorial Africa believe that things will change only as

✻the decade of the 1960s

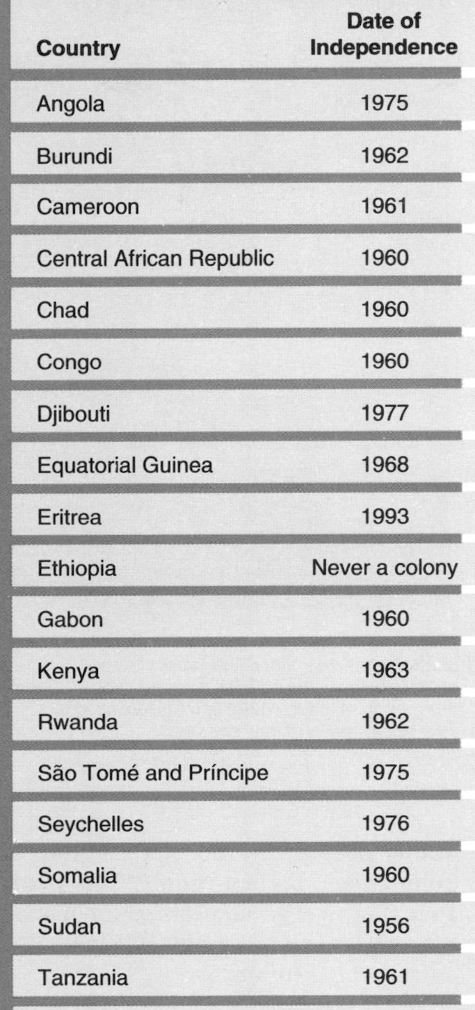

INDEPENDENCE IN EAST AND EQUATORIAL AFRICA

Country	Date of Independence
Angola	1975
Burundi	1962
Cameroon	1961
Central African Republic	1960
Chad	1960
Congo	1960
Djibouti	1977
Equatorial Guinea	1968
Eritrea	1993
Ethiopia	Never a colony
Gabon	1960
Kenya	1963
Rwanda	1962
São Tomé and Príncipe	1975
Seychelles	1976
Somalia	1960
Sudan	1956
Tanzania	1961
Uganda	1962
Zaire	1960

CHART SKILL: Jomo Kenyatta (*top*) was a leader of the independence movement in Kenya. When did Kenya win its independence?

CHART SKILL: 1963

EXTENDING CHART SKILLS

Have students study the chart on this page.

Ask students:

- **What information does this chart show?** (the dates that the nations of East and Equatorial Africa became independent)
- **What is the oldest nation on this chart? Why is it the oldest?** (Ethiopia; it was never a colony and actually dates back thousands of years.)
- **Why are the nations of this region called "young"?** (With the exception of Ethiopia, all are less than 35 years old.)
- **Which nation is the youngest?** (Eritrea)
- *THINKING FURTHER:* **In what year did the most nations become independent?** (1960)

Introducing Independent Nations Stress that independence did not bring the expected peace to East and Equatorial Africa.

Ask students:

- **What is civil war?** (war between people of the same country)
- **Which nations of East and Equatorial Africa have had civil wars since becoming independent?** (Ethiopia, Angola, Zaire, Burundi, Sudan, Somalia)

Discussing One-Party Rule Help students to understand that Africans have hope for the future in spite of their present unstable governments.

Ask students:

- **Why were coups common after African nations became independent?** (The people thought improvements would come quickly and became disappointed with their leaders.)
- **When does government power usually change in this region?** (when a leader dies or is overthrown in a coup)

BACKGROUND INFORMATION

Jomo Kenyatta A pattern developed during the dissolving of the European colonies in East and Equatorial Africa. Often the most effective African leaders were jailed, but when independence was achieved, they were released and became leaders of the new nations. Jomo Kenyatta was kept in jail for nine years by the British for allegedly leading the Mau Mau terrorist uprisings against British rule.

- Kenyatta became the first prime minister of Kenya when it gained independence in 1963. He became president in 1964 and held that position until his death in 1978.
- A member of the Kikuyu people, Kenyatta received a modern education in Britain.
- As president of Kenya, he strove to provide equal opportunities for all Kenyans, black and white.

Looking at One-Party Rule Continue the discussion of governments in this region.

Ask students:

- **Why do Africans in this region have hope for more democratic governments in the future?** (They hope that the next generation, having grown up free of colonialism, will be able to govern themselves better than the earlier generations have done.)

Applying the Lesson Have students discuss the idea expressed on pages 461–462 that East and Equatorial African nations will have more democratic governments "only when young people who are not familiar with colonialism grow up."

3 CLOSE

Summarizing Students have learned that former colonies in Africa's East and Equatorial region remain unstable in governing themselves. Discuss with students how new schools might help to change the governments of these nations.

Evaluating Have students review the headings in this lesson and write explanations of how each topic contributes to the understanding of the governments of East and Equatorial Africa.

Answers to Check Your Reading

1. first president of Kenya
2. The people became dissatisfied with the slow pace of change.
3. strong central government with one-party system
4. Possible answer: One-party systems will continue to dominate this region.

Independent Practice
Practice Book: page 123

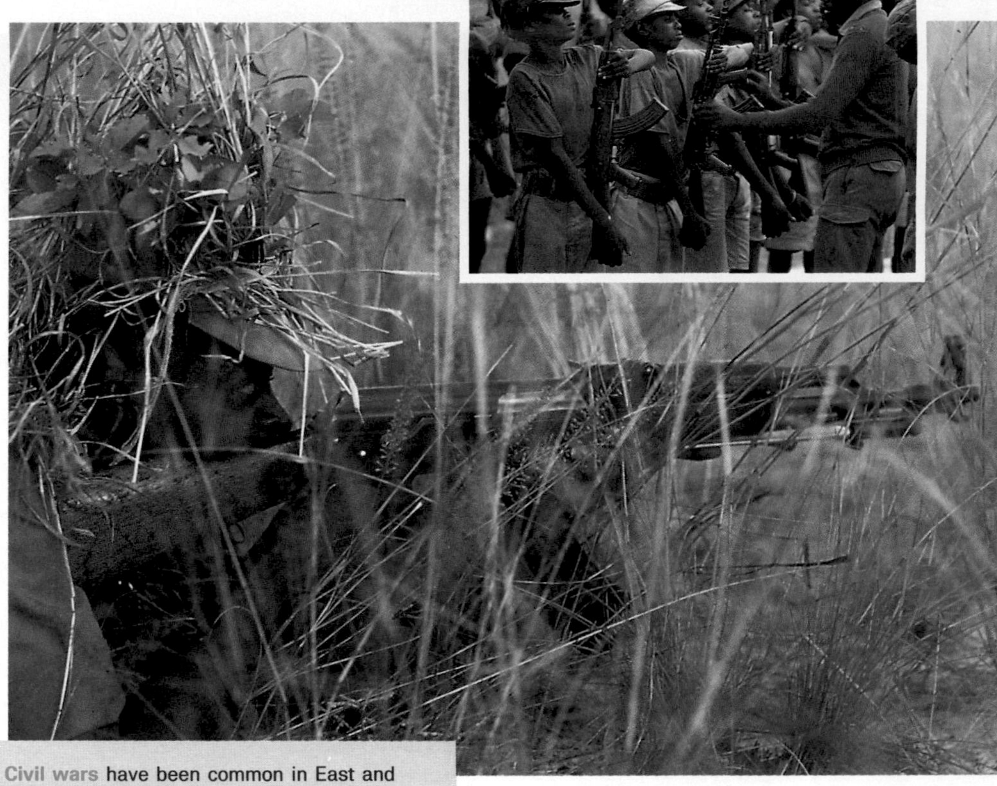

Civil wars have been common in East and Equatorial Africa since the independence movements started. These soldiers were training in Angola, where a long-lasting civil war upset much of the country.

young people who are not familiar with colonialism become adults. They think that this new generation of independent citizens will be better able to govern themselves in the future.

UNSTABLE GOVERNMENTS

You have read that all of the countries of East and Equatorial Africa except Ethiopia were once ruled by colonial powers. Without recent traditions and experience of self-rule, many governments of this area have been unstable. Some governments are trying to change one-party systems or dictatorships. But civil wars and coups still take place.

Check Your Reading

1. Who was Jomo Kenyatta?
2. Why have many governments been overthrown in many of the countries of East and Equatorial Africa?
3. How would you describe a typical government in East and Equatorial Africa today?
4. THINKING SKILL: Tell what conclusions you can draw from the following statement: "Many East and Equatorial African leaders believe that stable government is more important than guaranteeing democratic rights to their people."

THINKING SKILL: Drawing Conclusions

460

MEETING INDIVIDUAL NEEDS

Reteaching (easy) Have students research the type of government in each of the countries in the region. Then have them create a chart showing the type of government and current leader for each nation.

Extension (average) Have students choose one nation and find out more about the history of its change in status from colony to independent country. Ask them to prepare a panel discussion on the problems that still remain in the political scene of that nation.

Enrichment (challenging) Have students research the Mau Mau uprising. Ask them to write reports on the movement.

LESSON 4

Arts and Recreation

READ TO LEARN

Key Vocabulary

proverb

Read Aloud

The stars are hearing, the earth is hearing. The people are hearing—all is well, good, sweet. Then laugh, laugh, laugh.

When the Pokot people of East Africa say good-bye, each person repeats this old blessing. Spoken language is one of the most important arts in East and Equatorial Africa.

Read for Purpose

1. WHAT YOU KNOW: What is an example of a saying or proverb that is popular in the United States?
2. WHAT YOU WILL LEARN: How are poems, stories, and other forms of spoken language important in East and Equatorial Africa?

PROVERBS

Most of the groups in East and Equatorial Africa have a rich store of proverbs. A proverb is a short, popular saying that illustrates a truth. The Luyia people, who live by the Great Lakes of East Africa, warn: "Don't laugh at a distant boat being tossed by the waves. Your relative may be in it." This proverb not only warns people against laughing at the misfortune of others, but also shows the strong loyalty to family that the Luyia people feel.

The following are Swahili proverbs from Zanzibar. What do you think is the meaning of each, and what are some of the values expressed?

Ability is wealth.

He who does not listen to an elder's advice comes to grief.

Blood is thicker than water.

A bad brother is far better than no brother.

To stumble is not to fall down but to go forward.

Do not forget what it is to be a sailor because you became a captain.

When elephants fight, the reeds get hurt.

STORYTELLING

Ethnic groups in East and Equatorial Africa did not have systems of writing until outsiders brought them. As you have read, in groups without writing systems, storytellers serve as important teachers, historians, and entertainers.

Storytelling sessions are among the favorite recreational activities of East and Equatorial African people. Stories are often combined with music and dance. Listeners know most of the stories and join in by clapping and singing.

WHAT YOU KNOW: Some examples of popular proverbs in the United States are: "A penny saved is a penny earned" and "He who laughs last laughs best."

LESSON 4
pages 461–462

Lesson Theme Ethnic traditions are preserved and learned in East and Equatorial Africa through proverbs, stories, and poetry.

Lesson Objectives
- Describe the role of proverbs in East and Equatorial Africa.
- Describe the poetry and storytelling traditions of this region.

1 PREPARE

Motivate Read the *Read Aloud* section to the class. Ask students if they know of any good-bye blessings. Discuss with students the reasons that the Pokot people value laughter. Have students discuss the saying "Laughter is the best medicine."

Set Purpose Use the *What You Know* question to continue class contributions about proverbs. Ask the *What You Will Learn* question and challenge students to compare the use of poems, stories, and spoken language in our society with their use in African life.

2 TEACH

Identifying Proverbs Stress the universality of proverbs. Discuss the proverbs on this page.

Ask students:

- **What is a proverb?** (a short, popular saying that illustrates a truth)

Discussing Storytelling

Ask students:

- **Without a written language, how is history preserved and passed on?** (by storytellers)

READING STRATEGY AND VOCABULARY DEVELOPMENT

Study Guide Give students a choice of guides to use for this lesson: KWL, SQ3R, or a chart. Review any of the guides that they choose to use. Discuss reasons for students' choices of study guides and the pros and cons of each guide. When students have completed their guides, discuss the lesson with them.

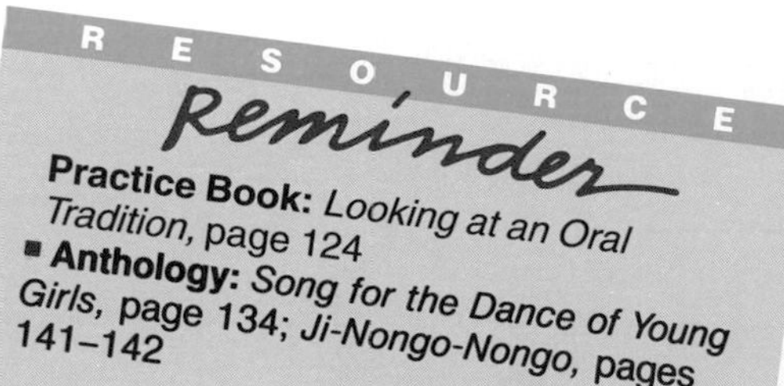

RESOURCE *Reminder*

Practice Book: *Looking at an Oral Tradition,* page 124
■ **Anthology:** *Song for the Dance of Young Girls,* page 134; *Ji-Nongo-Nongo,* pages 141–142

Looking at Poetry

Ask students:

- **What is expressed by poetry?** (human feelings, dreams, hopes, and fears)
- **Why are Bantu poets so valued?** (They tell poems that reflect the wisdom and history of their people.)

Applying the Lesson Have students discuss the role of stories, proverbs, and poetry in the lives of the people of this region.

3 CLOSE

Summarizing Students have learned that proverbs, stories, and poetry have great power to teach and entertain in East and Equatorial Africa. Ask students which form of spoken language they think the people of the region would learn the most from. Have them explain their answer.

Evaluating Use the *Check Your Reading* questions (answers given below) to assess students' understanding.

Answers to Check Your Reading

1. a short, popular saying that illustrates a truth
2. the wisdom and history of the Bantu people
3. They teach, inform, and entertain.
4. Possible answers include: The Luyia people live by the Great Lakes of East Africa; African stories are often combined with music and dance; listeners join in the storytelling in East Africa. Students' answers should be based on the facts presented in the lesson.

Independent Practice
Practice Book: page 124

Cloth for sale in the East African country of Kenya portrays a gathering of people. Above the cloth are handmade necklaces.

As people gather to hear tales, they gain a strong sense of belonging to a particular group. Stories also help children to understand their place in the world and allow them to feel proud of their past. Through tales and songs, storytellers educate young people in the values and traditions of their ethnic groups.

POETRY

Throughout East and Equatorial Africa, poetry is a major way of expressing feelings, dreams, hopes, and fears. Poetry occupies a special place in everyday life. A Swahili newspaper in Tanzania features a "Poems to the Editor" section next to "Letters to the Editor." The poems are about anything from personal problems to the cost of food.

Among Bantu-speaking people, poets receive a special place of honor. Like the West African griots you read about in Chapter 21, Bantu poets memorize and recite poems that reflect the wisdom of their people. A skilled Bantu poet can talk for several days about ancient Bantu kingdoms. Bantu poets in Rwanda recite epic poems that tell of the great deeds of their ancestors.

TRADITIONAL ARTS

People in East and Equatorial Africa learn the traditions of their ethnic group through proverbs, stories, and poetry. As you have read, young people in traditional villages learn by watching and listening.

Check Your Reading

1. What is a proverb?
2. About which subjects do Bantu poets often recite poems?
3. What special role do proverbs, stories, and poems play in the lives of the people of East and Equatorial Africa?
4. **THINKING SKILL:** Write three statements of fact from this lesson. What can you conclude about East and Equatorial Africa based on these facts?

THINKING SKILL: Fact and Opinion

462

MEETING INDIVIDUAL NEEDS

Reteaching (easy) Have students write the definitions for *stories, proverbs,* and *poetry* and bring in examples of each to read to the class. Have students compare them with the African story on page 440, the African proverbs on page 461, and the African poem on page 441.

Extension (average) Have students go to the library and find an African story to read. Then have them tell about the story and explain its meaning to the class. Have the class discuss similar stories from our society.

Enrichment (challenging) Have students read a translation of a Bantu epic poem. Discuss with them the most important features of the poem's style, then have students write a poem about a school event imitating the Bantu epic style. Encourage them to recite their poems as if they were Bantu poets.

BUILDING SKILLS
STUDY AND RESEARCH SKILLS

Making a Graph from a Chart

Key Vocabulary
line graph

In this book information is presented in many different forms. You have already seen that one of these forms is a chart. The chart on this page shows the populations of two cities in East and Equatorial Africa from 1960 to 1990.

Drawing a Line Graph

The same information presented in a chart might also be presented in a different way on a line graph. In this lesson you will read about making a line graph to show the information that appears in the chart on this page.

First, copy a grid like the one below the chart. Next, write a title for the graph. Label the vertical axis "Population (in millions)." Number the vertical axis beginning with 0. Then number each line up to 3 million. Next, label the horizontal axis, "Year." Use each line on the horizontal axis to represent a decade, starting at 1960 and ending at 1990.

To make a population graph of Kinshasa, follow the vertical line labeled 1960 until it reaches halfway between 0 and 1 million. Mark this place with a dot to show that in 1960 the population of Kinshasa was approximately 500,000 (half a million) people. Next, follow the vertical line for 1970 until you reach 1.25 million. Place a dot one quarter of the way between 1 and 2 million. Continue to mark dots at the correct number for all years up to 1990. When you have marked all the dots for Kinshasa, connect the dots with straight lines.

POPULATION PATTERN OF TWO AFRICAN CITIES

	Kinshasa, Zaire	Nairobi, Kenya
1960	500,000	265,000
1970	1,250,000	500,000
1980	2,200,000	800,000
1990	3,000,000	1,700,000

Population (in millions)
3
2
1
0
1960 1970 1980 1990
Year

Use a different color to plot the graph for Nairobi. When you have finished plotting the graph for both cities, you will see the direction of population growth at a glance. The line graph also shows the differences in population growth between the two cities.

Reviewing the Skill

1. What does a line graph show?
2. Why must the vertical and horizontal axes of a line graph be labeled?
3. Which city, Kinshasa or Nairobi, had the larger population in 1960?
4. Why is it important to understand how to make a graph from a chart?

SKILLS LESSON
page 463

Lesson Theme Trends can be seen when statistics in chart form are converted into a line graph.

Lesson Objective
- Draw a line graph using the information from a chart.

1 PREPARE

Motivate Have students read the introduction and study the chart to find out about Kinshasa and Nairobi.

Set Purpose Tell students that they will learn how to change the form of the statistics in this chart so that they can see trends, or changes over time, more clearly.

2 TEACH

Drawing a Line Graph With students' help, list the direction of and differences in population growth between the two cities shown on the line graph.

Applying the Lesson Have students chart the weekly class attendance for boys and girls for a month and then make a line graph using the information on the chart. Discuss the results.

3 CLOSE

Summarizing Students have learned to draw a line graph using information from a chart. Have them suggest other school information to show by chart and graph.

Answers to Reviewing the Skill
1. trends over time
2. to plot two kinds of information
3. Kinshasa
4. to see the direction of change

MEETING INDIVIDUAL NEEDS

Reteaching (easy) Give students charts showing the growth of population in their town or city and in the capital of their state. Have them each make a line graph using this information.

Extension (average) Have students find all the charts in this book and determine which ones could be turned into line graphs. Have them make graphs from any appropriate charts.

Enrichment (challenging) Have students choose four cities in Africa, find their population-growth statistics for at least a 50-year period, and chart them. Then students should make a line graph and write statements explaining what the graph tells about direction of population growth and differences in population growth in these four cities.

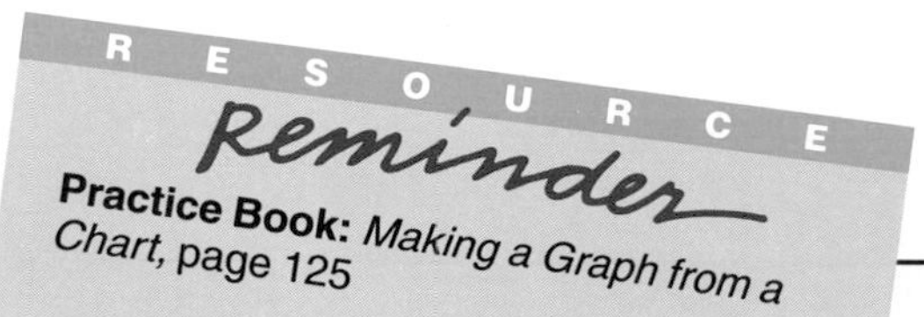
RESOURCE Reminder
Practice Book: *Making a Graph from a Chart*, page 125

CHAPTER 22 REVIEW

pages 464–465

USING THE CHAPTER SUMMARY AND REVIEW

Cultural Geography These questions may be used for review.

- **Name the four major groups that migrated to this region.** (Bantu, Muslim traders, Kushites, Europeans)
- **What does this region need to improve economically?** (better transportation, more hydroelectric power, educated workers, industry)
- **Which nation was never a European colony?** (Ethiopia)
- **What are three forms of traditional art from the region?** (proverbs, storytelling, and poetry)

Ideas to Remember

- **Why does this region have a variety of peoples, cultures, and languages?** (because of several large migrations)
- **What are the main economic activities in the region?** (herding, farming, fishing)
- **With what problems have the governments in the region had to deal?** (civil wars and uprisings)
- **What do proverbs, stories, and poetry teach?** (values and history)

Answers to Reviewing Vocabulary

1. migration
2. proverbs
3. barter
4. malnutrition
5. famine

Answers to Reviewing Facts

1. the Bantu tribe; During the course of a 2,000-year-long migration they spread their language and customs throughout the region.
2. trade settlements, the Arabic language, Islam, new food crops
3. It contains Bantu words along with elements of the Arabic and Portuguese languages.

CHAPTER 22 • SUMMARY

EAST AND EQUATORIAL AFRICA: CULTURAL GEOGRAPHY

PEOPLE

- People: hundreds of ethnic groups, many ethnic mixtures
- Bantu–speaking people are the largest ethnic groups

- Swahili—a common language of the area—combines Bantu, Arabic, and Portuguese
- Migrations: Bantu, Muslim traders, Kushites, European settlers

ECONOMY

- Cattle: source of food, a sign of a person's wealth and importance
- Main economic activities: herding, subsistence farming, fishing
- Export products: coffee, tea, sugar, cotton, sisal, copper, lumber, iron, manganese

- Economic needs: better transportation; more hydroelectric power, educated workers, industry

GOVERNMENT

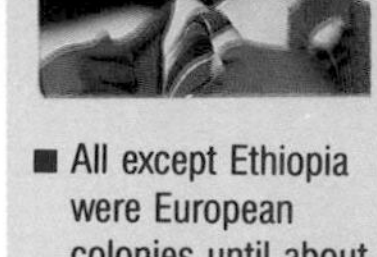

- All except Ethiopia were European colonies until about 30 years ago

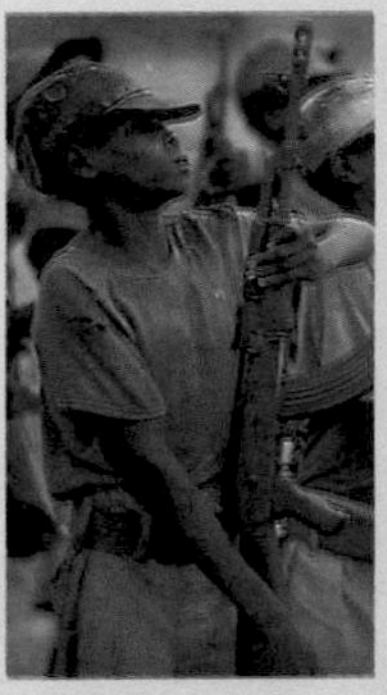

- Civil wars and uprisings have been common
- Many are trying to end one-party systems or dictatorships

ARTS AND RECREATION

- Traditional arts include proverbs, storytelling, and poetry
- Literature reflects the wisdom of the people
- Through songs and tales, storytellers teach values and traditions

IDEAS TO REMEMBER

- Several large migrations have caused East and Equatorial Africa to have a variety of peoples, cultures, and languages.
- Herding, farming, and fishing are the major important ways of earning a living.
- Since their independence in the 1960s, most of the area's governments have suffered from civil wars and coups, but many are trying to change.
- Proverbs, stories, and poetry both entertain and teach important values, customs, and history.

ENRICHMENT ACTIVITY

Making Wildlife Posters **Materials:** posterboard, pens, paints or markers

1. Refer students to the *Viewpoints* on pages 456–457, "How Should Land Be Used in East Africa?" Briefly review the controversy over wildlife reserves with students. Encourage students to take one side or another in the controversy.
2. Tell students that they will make posters supporting the side of the controversy that they have chosen.
3. Have students write a slogan that expresses their position on the issue. Then have students design a poster based on the slogan. (Try to have pictures of the wildlife available for reference.)
4. When the posters are finished, have students display them in the classroom.

CHAPTER 22 • REVIEW

REVIEWING VOCABULARY

barter
famine
malnutrition
migration
proverb

Number a sheet of paper from 1 to 5. Beside each number write the word or term from the above list that best completes the sentence.

1. ____ is the movement of large groups of people into new lands.
2. Popular throughout Africa, ____ are short sayings that illustrate important truths.
3. Instead of purchasing something, many Africans ____, or exchange, one good for another.
4. ____ is a condition that occurs when people have too little food or not enough of the right kinds of food.
5. Drought and overgrazing have resulted in ____, or severe food shortages, in large parts of Africa.

REVIEWING FACTS

1. Which ancient African tribe had the greatest impact on the culture of East and Equatorial Africa? How did they achieve this impact?
2. Name three contributions of Muslim traders to East and Equatorial Africa.
3. How does the Swahili language reflect the blend of cultures in East and Equatorial Africa?
4. Why are many herders in the savanna region nomadic?
5. Why do governments in East and Equatorial Africa encourage farmers to raise such crops as cotton and coffee?
6. How does land ownership in East and Equatorial Africa differ from land ownership in the United States?
7. Name four major reasons that explain why most countries in East and Equatorial Africa remain poor despite abundant resources.
8. Name two ways in which European nations affected the countries of East and Equatorial Africa.
9. Why do the governments of most countries in East and Equatorial Africa practice one-party rule?
10. How does the custom of storytelling strengthen the community in East and Equatorial Africa?

WRITING ABOUT MAIN IDEAS

1. **Writing an Editorial:** Write an editorial titled: "More Democracy, Not Less, Is Needed to Solve the Problems of East and Equatorial Africa."
2. **Writing a Proverb:** The groups in East and Equatorial Africa have a rich store of proverbs. Write your own proverb that illustrates some basic truth about life.
3. **Writing About Perspectives:** Pretend you live in a country in East and Equatorial Africa and want to start a small business. What kind of business could you start that would use both the region's resources and have customers? Write a paragraph explaining your plan.

BUILDING SKILLS: MAKING A GRAPH FROM A CHART

1. How is a graph different from a chart?
2. Look at the chart on page 463. Which city, Kinshasa or Nairobi, had the larger population in 1980?
3. Which labels would you use on a graph showing the same information as the chart on page 463?
4. Why is it helpful to understand how to make a graph from a chart?

465

4. because they have to move their herds across the savanna as the land becomes too dry
5. These are cash crops that their economies need.
6. Unlike in the United States, in East and Equatorial Africa individuals do not own land—clans and villages do.
7. They need better transportation systems, more dams, more educated workers, and more industries.
8. They introduced their languages and customs.
9. Most leaders of the countries believe that stable government is more important than guaranteeing democratic rights to their people.
10. Storytelling unites people by giving them a strong sense of belonging to a particular group, helps them understand their place in the world, and allows them to feel proud of their past.

Suggestions for Writing About Main Ideas

1. You may wish to have students form groups to debate whether more democracy or less democracy is needed in the region.
2. Before students begin, review what a proverb is and, if possible, read some proverbs aloud. Have students present their proverbs to the class.
3. Have students think about the needs of the region's people as well as the availability of the necessary resources.

Answers to Building Skills: Making a Graph from a Chart

1. A graph helps you to compare information more easily.
2. Kinshasha
3. label for vertical axis: "population (in millions)"; label for horizontal axis: "year"
4. Graphs can help clarify information found in a chart.

Chapter Review and Test

Practice Book: *Vocabulary Review,* page 126
Transparency: *Graphic Organizer*
Assessment Book: *Chapter 22 Test*

MAKING CONNECTIONS

Recognizing Cause and Effect Display the Cause and Effect Chart Graphic Organizer Transparency, filling in only the underlined headings and sentences. For Column 1, have students write causes for the effects stated. For Column 2, have students write effects for the causes stated. *Ask:* What are some of the factors that contribute to problems in this region of the world?

LIFE IN EAST AND EQUATORIAL AFRICA TODAY	
Causes	Effects
migrations	blend of ethnic groups
post-colonialism	unstable governments, civil wars
little money, poor transportation	slow industrial industrial development
community ownership and families working together on land	successful farming

CHAPTER 23
ORGANIZER

NATIONS OF SOUTHERN AFRICA text pages 466–483

CHAPTER THEME

In striking contrast to the rest of Sub-Saharan Africa, Southern Africa is dominated by one country—white South Africa with its highly developed economy.

CHAPTER OBJECTIVES

CONTENT

- Describe how the different ethnic groups of Southern Africa live together today.
- Explain how the Bushmen came to live in the Kalahari Desert.
- Identify the Afrikaners and describe their origins.
- Define *apartheid* and describe its effects on South African society.
- Contrast the economy of South Africa with the economies of most of the countries of Southern Africa.
- Explain how Zambia's reliance on one product has hurt its economy.
- Describe the major forms of government in Southern Africa.
- Explain why most of the countries in Southern Africa had one-party political systems.
- Explain what is unique about the government of Botswana.
- Describe how black South Africans were able to resist apartheid.
- Explain why most countries do not recognize the black homelands of South Africa.
- Describe some of the popular arts and sports in Southern Africa.

SKILLS

Geography
- Interpret a political map of Southern Africa.
- Locate minerals in Southern Africa using maps.

Thinking
- Compare and contrast the economies of South Africa and Zambia.
- Classify the countries of Southern Africa according to their type of political system.

Reading and Writing
- Write an essay about political change in Southern Africa.

CITIZENSHIP VALUES

- Appreciate the contributions of individuals to the well-being of society.
- Appreciate the negative impact of racial prejudice on a society.

TEACHER OPTIONS

READING STRATEGY: Vocabulary Development Strategies to help students read and remember the main ideas of the lesson.

Lesson 1: p. 467 Lesson 3: p. 474
Lesson 2: p. 471 Lesson 4: p. 479

MEETING INDIVIDUAL NEEDS Activities for reteaching, extension, and enrichment.

Lesson 1: p. 470 Lesson 3: p. 476
Lesson 2: p. 473 Lesson 4: p. 481

GEO ADVENTURES ACTIVITIES PAD Daily activities to assess students' understanding of geography skills.

CURRICULUM CONNECTION Activities to help integrate other subject areas with Social Studies.

Music: p. 480

PUPIL EDITION ON CASSETTE Language support for students who have difficulty reading or who will benefit from listening to the Pupil Edition on Cassette as they read.

SECOND-LANGUAGE SUPPORT Activities and suggestions for second-language learners.

Lesson 3: p. 407-D

CHAPTER PLANNING GUIDE

LESSON	SUGGESTED PACING	THEMES	TEACHER SUPPORT MATERIALS: TEACHER'S RESOURCE CENTER
1 THE PEOPLE pages 467–470	1 day	Black ethnic groups make up the overwhelming majority of people in Southern Africa, but whites still have great influence on the area.	Practice Book p. 127 Outline Map p. 32 Desk Maps **Technology:** *Adventures CD-ROM*
2 THE ECONOMY pages 471–473	1 day	Most of the nations of Southern Africa have developing economies that contrast with the highly developed industrial economy of the country of South Africa.	Practice Book p. 128 Outline Map p. 32 **Technology:** *Adventures CD-ROM*
3 THE GOVERNMENT pages 474–477	1 day	While many countries in Southern Africa have made progress towards democracy, some governments are still restrictive.	Practice Book p. 129 ■ Anthology pp. 137–138, 139–140 Outline Map p. 32 **Technology:** *Videodisc/Video Tape 1*
BUILDING THINKING SKILLS Recognizing Bias: Review page 478	1 day	Recognizing bias means identifying a one-sided or slanted presentation of information.	Practice Book p. 130
4 ARTS AND RECREATION pages 479–481	1 day	The arts and sports in Southern Africa have a variety of origins.	Practice Book p. 131 ■ Anthology p. 128
CHAPTER SUMMARY AND REVIEW pages 482–483	1 day	Chapter content, skills, and vocabulary are reviewed and evaluated.	Practice Book p. 132 Transparency: Graphic Organizer Assessment Book, Chapter 23 Test

Technology CONNECTION

Lesson 1
ADVENTURES CD-ROM
Enrich Lesson 1 by having students *Travel* to and *Explore* South Africa.

Lesson 2
ADVENTURES CD-ROM
Enrich Lesson 2 by having students make their own presentations about South Africa in *Create.*

Lesson 3
VIDEODISC/VIDEO TAPE 1
Enrich Lesson 3 with a segment of Video Lesson 3, *Africa Today.*

Search 13656, Play To 16177 Side A

CHAPTER 23
pages 466–483

USING THE CHAPTER OPENER

Discussing the Photograph Ask students to pretend that the picture on this page is a snapshot of their pen pal.

Ask students:

- **What are three questions that you might ask this boy about his country?** (Answers may include: What is the climate like in your country?What kind of schools are there? Do a lot of people live in your country?)

Reading/Listening to the Primary Source Read the passage under the picture to the class.

Ask students:

- **What is the definition of the word *resilient*?** (Have students look up this word in the dictionary, whether or not they think they know the meaning.)
- **What does the word mean in this quotation?** (an ability to recover from a misfortune or change)
- **Why do you think the people of South Africa must be resilient?** (to meet challenges)

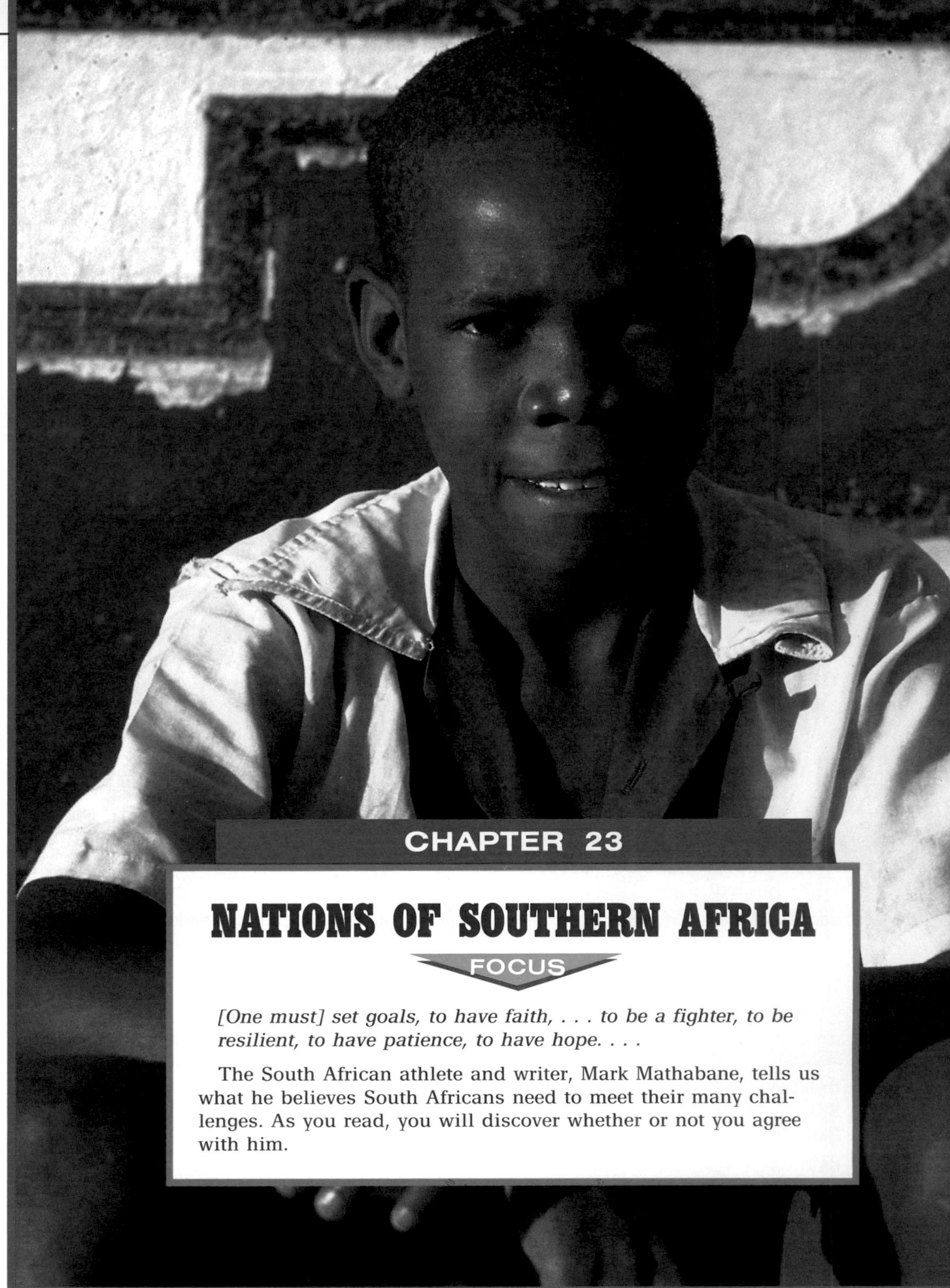

CHAPTER 23

NATIONS OF SOUTHERN AFRICA

FOCUS

[One must] set goals, to have faith, . . . to be a fighter, to be resilient, to have patience, to have hope. . . .

The South African athlete and writer, Mark Mathabane, tells us what he believes South Africans need to meet their many challenges. As you read, you will discover whether or not you agree with him.

BACKGROUND INFORMATION

About a South African Theatrical Performance One way in which South African blacks show their resilience is by their creative energy.

- A recent example of this energy is the musical *Sarafina!* This show was performed largely by a group of South African schoolchildren, few of whom had previous acting experience. They were selected by Mgongeni Ngoma, the show's director, principal actor, and cocomposer.
- Hugh Masakela, the well-known South African trumpet player and bandleader, contributed several songs. Among the songs in *Sarafina!* that suggest its uplifting spirit are "Freedom Is Coming Tomorrow" and "Give Us Power."
- The show was first performed in Johannesburg, South Africa. It then traveled to the United States, where it ran on Broadway for over a year. *Sarafina!* has toured widely in the United States, further spreading the spirit of South Africa's black children.

LESSON 1

The People

READ TO LEARN

Key Vocabulary

apartheid

Key Places

South Africa Kalahari Desert

Read Aloud

Yes, this is a good land. Everyone who has come here, from the first blacks to the earliest whites, has found it so. Can we work together to keep it so? That is our test.

These are the words of a store owner in the city of Harare, Zimbabwe. The "test" he speaks of—having whites and blacks live together in peace—is faced by all of the countries of Southern Africa.

Read for Purpose

1. WHAT YOU KNOW: Think of some news articles you have read or some television shows you have seen about South Africa. What were these articles or programs about?
2. WHAT YOU WILL LEARN: What changes are taking place in the way in which different ethnic groups of Southern Africa live today?

A RICH LAND

Southern Africa is rich in mineral resources, such as gold, copper, diamonds, and coal. The climate of the area is warm and inviting, especially on the southern tip. Much of the region is at high altitudes, so there are few disease-spreading insects. These factors have combined to draw many groups of people to the region.

There are several nations in the region of Southern Africa. Yet the country of South Africa is so rich and powerful that it dominates most of its neighbors. These include Botswana, Lesotho, Madagascar and other islands, Malawi, Mozambique, Namibia, Swaziland, Zimbabwe, and Zambia.

Many ethnic groups have fought for and are still fighting for control of these lands. Let's learn about the major ethnic groups.

BUSHMEN AND BANTUS

A people known as the Bushmen have been living in Southern Africa longer than any other peoples. Hundreds of years ago Bushmen had lived throughout the continent of Africa. Bushmen cave paintings have been found as far north as Ethiopia.

Until recently most Bushmen lived in the Kalahari (kä lə här′ ē) Desert of Botswana and Namibia. Find this area on the map on page 468. Most people would starve to death in this harsh land. Bushmen are skilled at tracking animals and finding food and water. Today many Bushmen live on farms and in towns.

Between 500 and 800 years ago, Bantu peoples migrated to the lands of the Bushmen. This movement was part of the great Bantu migration you read about in Chapter 22. The Bantu drove the Bushmen from

WHAT YOU KNOW: Students should be aware that many news articles and programs about South Africa deal with the country's racial policies, which they will read about in this lesson.

LESSON 1
pages 467–470

Lesson Theme Although black ethnic groups make up the overwhelming majority of people in Southern Africa, the whites who rule South Africa have the greatest influence on the area.

Lesson Objectives
- Describe the lifestyles of the Bushmen and the Bantu ethnic groups of Southern Africa.
- Identify the groups of European ancestry in this area.
- Describe racial separation in South Africa.

1 PREPARE

Motivate Read the *Read Aloud* section to the class. Have students identify and discuss the problems faced by all the countries of Southern Africa.

Set Purpose Ask the *What You Know* question to explore what students know about the social and political problems of racial separation in this region. Ask for possible answers to the *What You Will Learn* question.

2 TEACH

Introducing a Rich Land

Ask students:

- **What has drawn many people to this region?** (rich mineral resources, warm climate, highlands free of disease-spreading insects)

Looking at the Bushmen and the Bantus Focus on the Bushmen's ancient roots in this area.

READING STRATEGY AND VOCABULARY DEVELOPMENT

Vocabulary Development In Chapter 11 students read about the different context clues that authors use for defining words. They are direct definitions, synonyms, and examples. Have students skim the lesson to locate the *Key Vocabulary* words. Then have them read to find the definitions of the words and to identify the type of context clues that were used.

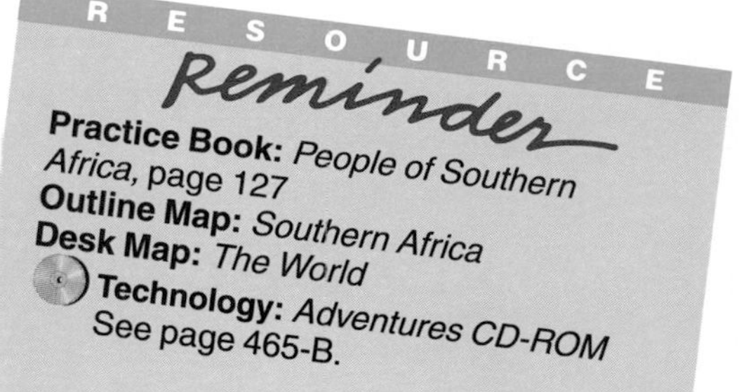

Practice Book: *People of Southern Africa*, page 127
Outline Map: *Southern Africa*
Desk Map: *The World*
Technology: *Adventures CD-ROM*
See page 465-B.

Comparing the Bushmen and the Bantus Continue the discussion.

Ask students:

- **What drove the Bushmen into the Kalahari Desert?** (the migration of the Bantus)
- **To which ethnic group do the majority of the people in Southern Africa belong?** (the Bantus)
- **How has Bantu life changed?** (Many younger Bantus no longer live in the traditional clan-village way. One third of Southern Africa's Bantus now live in cities.)

EXTENDING MAP SKILLS

Have students study the political map of Southern Africa.

Ask students:

- **What does the inset map tell about the relative location of this part of the region?** (It covers the whole southern tip of Africa.)
- **How many nations make up Southern Africa?** (12)
- **What is the latitudinal range of Southern Africa?** (about 11°S to 35°S)
- **What is the easternmost country in the region?** (Mauritius)
- **To which country does Réunion belong?** (France)
- **Moroni is the capital of which country?** (Comoros)
- **Which countries border South Africa?** (Namibia, Botswana, Zimbabwe, Mozambique, Lesotho, Swaziland)
- *THINKING FURTHER:* **What is unusual about the location of Lesotho and Swaziland?** (They are surrounded by the country of South Africa.)

MAP SKILL: There are many Bantu ethnic groups living in Southern Africa. Here, a group of people called the Hereros gathers at a rally in Namibia. They wear traditional clothing. Where is Namibia on the map of Southern Africa below?

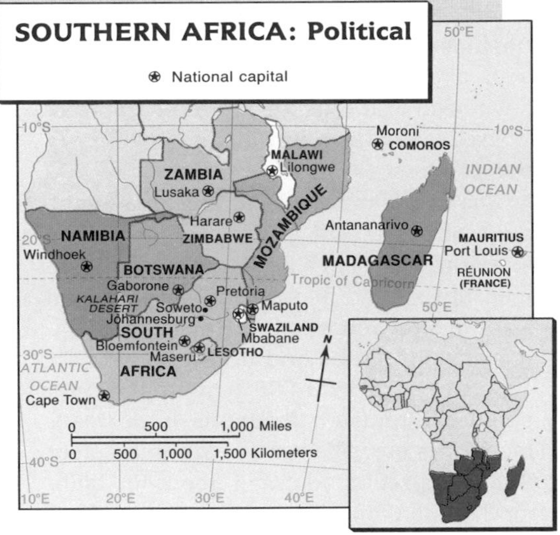

the savanna areas of Southern Africa into the Kalahari Desert.

Today the majority of people in Southern Africa are of Bantu descent. Some of them still live in a traditional way. Extended families are grouped into clans, and these clans live in small villages.

Millions of younger Africans, however, have given up the old ways of living. About one third of Southern Africa's people live in cities. These cities include Johannesburg, Pretoria, and Cape Town in South Africa, and Harare in Zimbabwe. Most of these city dwellers still have parents or grandparents who live in traditional African villages.

EUROPEAN GROUPS

As you have read in this unit, the European influence is strong throughout

MAP SKILL: in the western part of Southern Africa

BACKGROUND INFORMATION

Multicultural Perspectives For thousands of years the Basarwa have lived as hunters and gatherers in the Kalahari Desert. Today, however, the government of Botswana is working to remove the Basarwa from their homeland. Leaders say that removal is necessary in order to protect the Kalahari's endangered wildlife. They also say that life in a new reserve is in many ways an improvement for the Basarwa because they have access to government social services there. But a Basarwa chief named Manta who already lives in the new reserve feels differently.

People are sick and we just had two deaths. We only get free meal [grain] from the Government to eat. We can't get much meat. Some people do a little hunting but I don't because I am too old.

Ask students to name ways in which the Basarwa's inability to hunt and gather might change their lives and the way they see themselves.

Sub-Saharan Africa. Southern Africa is no exception.

Dutch settlers arrived on the southern tip of Africa in 1652. They were sent to set up a supply station for European merchant ships traveling between India and Indonesia, and Western Europe. Look at the world map in the Atlas on pages 638–639. Why do you think the southern tip of Africa would be an important location for ships sailing to and from Europe? *

The settlers set up a new colony called Cape Colony. More settlers came to the new colony not only from the Netherlands, but from Germany and France as well. As a result of this mixture of groups, a new language was created that contains Dutch, German, and French words. This language is called *Afrikaans*. It also includes many words from Bantu languages.

People of Dutch, German, and French ancestry who speak Afrikaans are called Afrikaners, or Boers. They are the largest group of whites in South Africa.

In 1795 the British took over Cape Colony. Thousands of Boers, not wanting to live under English rule, left the colony. They traveled north over the Drakensberg Mountains and the Orange River and formed two republics, the Transvaal and the Orange Free State. Both are now part of South Africa.

The areas that the Boers claimed for the two republics had large Bantu populations. Years of war between the Bantus and the Boers followed. Later, the Boers fought the British for control of these areas, which were rich in minerals. In more recent times the descendants of these two European groups made up less than 20 percent of South Africa's population, yet they ruled a country that was more than 70 percent black. This situation caused bitter conflicts.

Black South Africans have had to live in areas with few modern conveniences (*left*). Protests (*right*) eventually led to the end of apartheid laws.

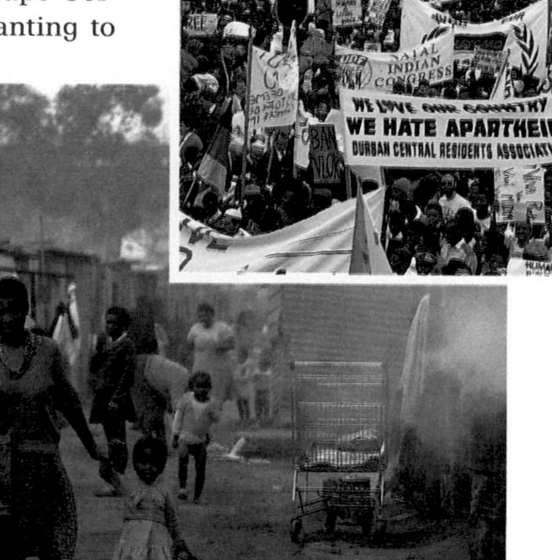

* because ships would have to travel around Southern Africa to get from Europe to India and Indonesia

469

Identifying European Groups

Ask students:

- **Why did Dutch settlers go to the southern tip of Africa in 1652?** (to set up a supply station for European sea traders)
- **What was the settlement called?** (Cape Colony)
- **Which other Europeans went to the new colony?** (the Germans and the French)
- **What resulted from this mixture of peoples?** (a new group of people called Afrikaners, or Boers, who were of Dutch, French, and German ancestry and who spoke a new language called Afrikaans)
- **Why is this group important today?** (It is the largest group of whites in South Africa.)
- **Which group of Europeans took over Cape Colony in 1795?** (the British)
- **What were the results of the British takeover?** (Many Boers moved north and founded two new republics, the Transvaal and the Orange Free State. Today both are part of South Africa.)
- **Which groups did the Boers fight for these new lands?** (the Bantus and then the British)
- *THINKING FURTHER:* **Do you think that the reason the Bantus wanted the land was different from the reason the British wanted it?** (Students might point out that the Bantus wanted the land because it was their ancestral home and they needed it to live on, while the British might have wanted the land to develop its resources.)

Discussing the Photographs Have students study the photographs. Discuss the meaning of the term *apartheid* and the effects that the system has had on the blacks of South Africa. Compare this policy with the policy of racial separation that existed in the southern part of the United States prior to the 1970s.

5 FUNDAMENTAL THEMES OF GEOGRAPHY

Movement The greatest movement of people on earth has been the migration of the human species to every part of the world. Much evidence points to Africa as the birthplace of humans. At least five great migrations filled the other continents, except Antarctica, with people. Divide the class into 12 groups to study and report on the following migrations: (1) movement throughout Africa and across the Middle East into the great plains of China; (2) movement into Europe by way of the Caucasus Mountains; (3) movement out of China and Siberia to North and South America; (4) forced migration of Africans from West Africa to North and South America; (5) immigration of peoples from all over the world to North America. In addition, each group of students may trace one of these migration routes on the Desk Map of the world, found in the Teacher's Resource Center.

Discussing Racial Separation

Ask students:

- **What was apartheid?** (a system that kept racial groups separate)
- *THINKING FURTHER:* **How is Zimbabwe different from South Africa?** (Zimbabwe is controlled by blacks and is trying to encourage blacks and whites to live in peace.)

Applying the Lesson Have students write two paragraphs telling about the daily life of a black South African and of a black Zimbabwean.

CLOSE

Summarizing Students have read about the ethnic groups of Southern Africa. Ask students to point out on a map the location of the ethnic groups that they have studied in this lesson.

Evaluating Use these questions to assess students' understanding.

- **Why did the Bushmen move to the Kalahari Desert?** (The Bantus forced them off their lands.)
- **What does the word *apartheid* mean?** (apartness or separateness)
- **How has Zimbabwe been different from South Africa?** (Zimbabwe has not separated black and white citizens.)

Answers to Check Your Reading

1. Kalahari Desert
2. people of Dutch, German, and French ancestry, who speak Afrikaans
3. Laws separate people by their color or race.
4. Possible answers include: They were kept apart, given the lowest-paying jobs, are poor and uneducated; they feel that the government was unjust.

Independent Practice
Practice Book: page 127

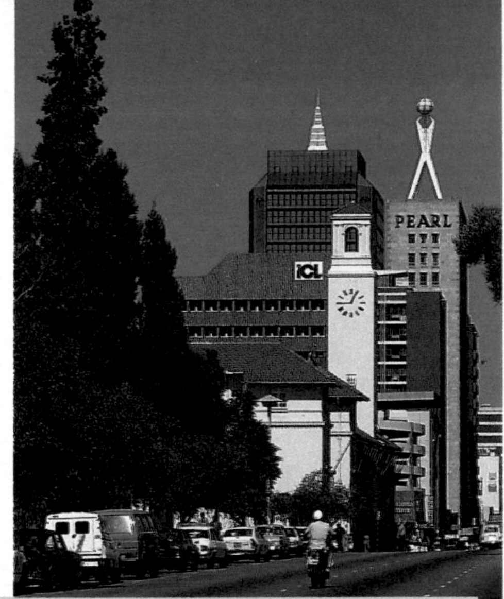

Blacks and whites live and work together in Harare, Zimbabwe.

RACIAL SEPARATION

From 1948 to 1991, South Africa's laws separated people by race and color. The country recognized four main racial groups: whites, blacks, "coloured," and Asian. People labeled coloured have both black and white, and sometimes Asian, ancestors. Most of them live in Cape Province and speak Afrikaans. Most Asians are descendants of immigrants from India.

The term for South Africa's system of separating racial groups is **apartheid** (ə pär′ tīd), from an Afrikaans word meaning "separateness" or "apartness." Under apartheid laws each of the four racial groups in South Africa had to live in its own area and attend segregated schools.

These rules left most blacks in South Africa poor. Often families were separated for long periods of time while some family members worked in cities. Many black South Africans lived without water, electricity, or good housing. Most of them had no hope of improving their lives as long as apartheid rules continued.

In 1991, the South African government announced plans to change some of its apartheid laws. Some schools and other public places became integrated. The total end of apartheid was announced in 1993. In 1994, South Africa held the first democratic elections in which all South Africans could vote.

Neighboring Zimbabwe also has a majority of blacks and a minority of whites. The black majority has governed Zimbabwe since 1980. Zimbabwe's leaders have worked hard to create a country in which black people and white people can live and work together in peace. As one way to promote understanding among different groups, the Zimbabwe government makes students study other people's languages. Most classes in Zimbabwe's schools are taught in English. However, every student also has to study the languages of the two main Bantu groups of Zimbabwe—Shona and Ndebele.

A MIX OF PEOPLES

In this lesson you have read about some of the different ethnic groups of Southern Africa. A majority of the people of Southern Africa are Bantu-speaking peoples. A small population of Bushmen live in or near the Kalahari Desert. Until recently South Africa was the only country in Sub-Saharan Africa that was ruled by a minority racial group. In the following lessons you will read more about Southern Africa.

Check Your Reading

1. Where do most of the Bushmen live?
2. Who are the Afrikaners?
3. Describe the system of apartheid.
4. THINKING SKILL: What effects did apartheid have on black people in South Africa?

THINKING SKILL: Cause and Effect

MEETING INDIVIDUAL NEEDS

Reteaching (easy) On an outline map of Southern Africa, found in the Teacher's Resource Center, have students label the countries and capitals of Southern Africa.

Extension (average) Have students role-play the story of European settlement in South Africa. Assign students various roles, including those of the Bantus, sea traders, Dutch, Germans, French, and British.

Enrichment (challenging) Ask students to research the Boer War. Then have them write essays discussing the causes of that war and its repercussions.

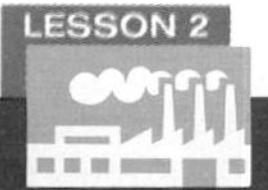

LESSON 2

The Economy

READ TO LEARN

Key Vocabulary

township
veld

Key Places

Johannesburg
Soweto
Zambia
Harare

Read Aloud

When Botswana gained its independence in 1966, it was one of the least developed countries on earth. There were few paved roads and not one public high school. Today Botswana is an economic success story. How did it happen? It started with three new diamond mines. To open the mines, Botswana needed help. South African companies gave money to build the mines, in return for part of the profits. South African companies also own part of Botswana's new nickel and copper mines.

All of the economies of the countries of Southern Africa are influenced by South Africa. South Africa has a strong, industrialized economy. Most of the rest of the area, as you will read, is still developing.

Read for Purpose

1. WHAT YOU KNOW: What valuable resources are found in Southern Africa?
2. WHAT YOU WILL LEARN: How does the economy of South Africa contrast with the economies of most countries of Southern Africa?

SOUTH AFRICA'S DIVERSIFIED ECONOMY

Why is South Africa's economy relatively strong? One reason is that it is diversified. A diversified economy, as you have read, is one that produces a wide range of goods and services. South Africa is a land of farms, mines, and advanced industries.

South Africa has vast mineral resources. It is the world's largest supplier of gold and one of the main sources of diamonds. Look at the maps on page 472. Which other lands have gold and diamonds?✻

South Africa also has chrome, which is scarce elsewhere. Coal, iron, platinum, and uranium are part of its mineral wealth.

Both blacks and whites work in South Africa's mines, but they are still not treated equally. White miners still earn more than black miners earn.

South Africa also has highly developed industries, particularly in the processing of metals. The Witwatersrand area around Johannesburg is South Africa's industrial center. Less than 100 years old, Johannesburg looks like industrial cities in the United States, such as Cleveland or Pittsburgh. Johannesburg is South Africa's largest city. Soweto has even more residents than Johannesburg, but it is called a township, not a city. In South Africa a township is a racially segregated urban

WHAT YOU KNOW: This question refers to material in Lesson 1; Southern Africa is rich in mineral resources, such as gold, copper, diamonds, and coal.
✻Gold: Zambia, Botswana Diamonds: Botswana, Namibia, Lesotho

LESSON 2
pages 471–473

Lesson Theme Most of the nations of Southern Africa have developing economies that contrast with the highly developed industrial economy of the country of South Africa.

Lesson Objectives
- Describe South Africa's diversified economy.
- Explain the effects of segregation on black workers in South Africa.
- Identify the mineral resources of South Africa.
- Describe the relationship of the other economies of Southern Africa to the economy of South Africa.

1 PREPARE

Motivate Read the *Read Aloud* section to the class. Point out to students that money is needed to start a business. Discuss places where a country might turn for money.

Set Purpose Ask the *What You Know* question to review the resources that form the base of South Africa's economy. Have students predict answers to the *What You Will Learn* question.

2 TEACH

Analyzing South Africa's Economy

Ask students:

- **What is a diversified economy?** (one that produces a wide range of goods and services)
- **Why is mining so important in South Africa?** (because it has vast mineral resources)
- **What advantage do white miners have in South Africa?** (They earn more than black miners earn.)

READING STRATEGY AND VOCABULARY DEVELOPMENT

Vocabulary Development Have students categorize this lesson's unfamiliar terms in chart form. The terms should be listed by type of industry, such as mining and agriculture. For example, under mining students may list any term related to mining: *chrome, processing, industrial center,* and *export.* Then have students define the terms. If any of the vocabulary terms have multiple meanings, have students check the *Glossary* in the back of the book or a dictionary for additional definitions. Then have students write the terms in sentences, using context clues to define each of the meanings.

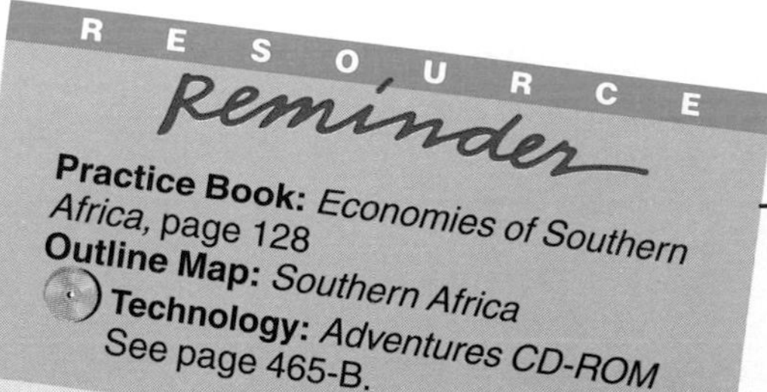

Looking at South Africa's Economy Continue the discussion, focusing on South Africa's success in agriculture.

Discussing Poverty

Ask students:

- **Why did 87 percent of South Africa's land belong to white people?** (The law set aside this amount for white people.)
- **What was one disadvantage for blacks in not being able to live in the same areas as white people?** (Since most jobs were in white areas, many blacks had to work far from home.)
- **What has happened since South Africa's separation laws were changed?** (Black South Africans have begun moving to formerly white areas.)

EXTENDING MAP SKILLS

Have students compare the three maps on this page.

Ask students:

- **Which nations have diamonds?** (Namibia, South Africa, Botswana, Lesotho)
- **Which nations of Southern Africa have none of the five minerals shown on these three maps?** (Madagascar, Malawi, Comoros, Mauritius, Mozambique)
- **Which minerals are found in South Africa?** (diamonds, gold, coal, iron, copper)

Looking at Economies in a Giant's Shadow

Ask students:

- **What has kept the economy of Zambia weak?** (reliance on copper, and insufficient money)
- **What has kept many Southern African nations from economic development?** (effects of wars)
- **Why do women do much of Zimbabwe's farming?** (Men work away from home in industries or mines.)

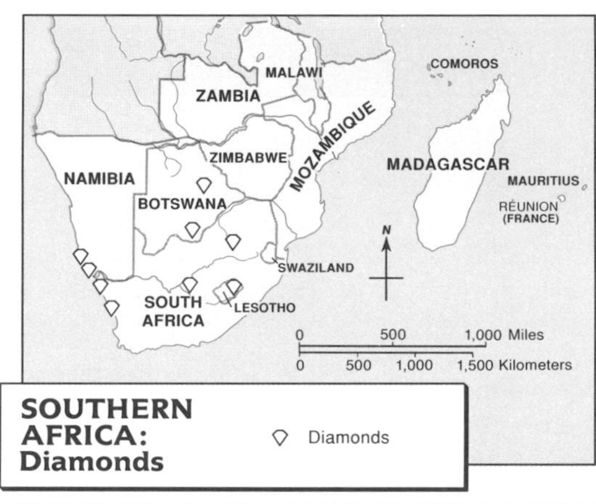

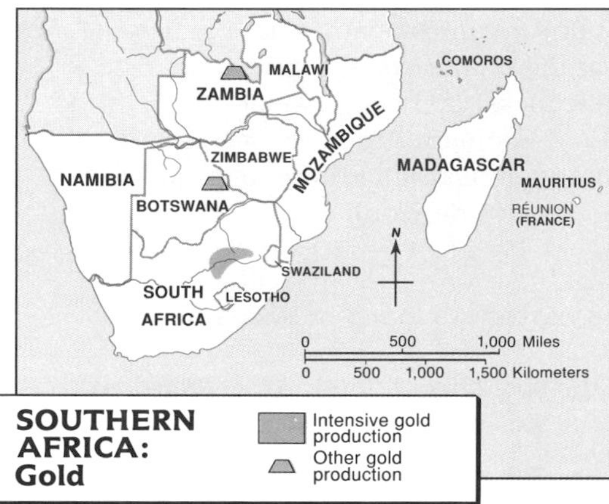

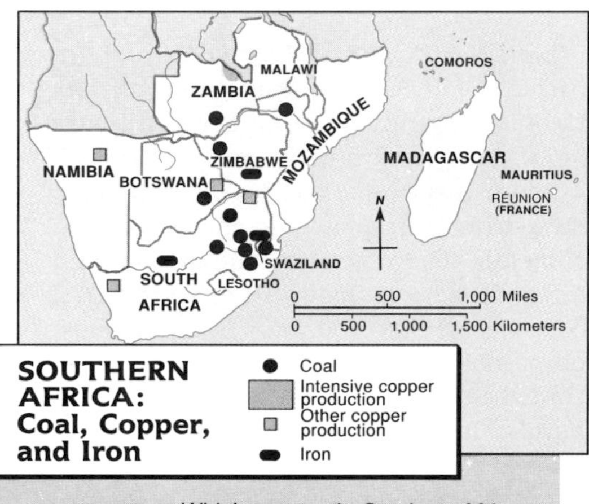

MAP SKILL: Which country in Southern Africa has intensive gold production?

area located just outside a city. About 30 percent of South Africa's blacks live in townships. In recent years, however, South African cities have become more racially integrated.

South Africa is also an important agricultural nation, even though much of the country's land is not good for growing crops. A vast, dry, treeless plateau called the **veld** covers much of South Africa. Most crops need irrigation in order to grow on the veld.

Despite poor land and lack of water, South African farmers raise a wide variety of products, ranging from sheep for wool to grapes and tea. In fact, South Africa raises enough food to export.

POVERTY

South Africa's economy is developed, but many of its people do not live well. Apartheid separated groups of people, and whites had an unfair advantage. By law, 87 percent of South Africa's land was set aside for white people even though whites made up less than 20 percent of the population. Blacks were allowed to work in cities set aside for whites, but blacks were not permitted to live in them. These land laws were ended in 1990.

Since most jobs in South Africa have been in areas reserved for whites, millions of black people have had to work far from their homes. Others have had to live in temporary quarters and go home only once a week, or even less often.

Now that laws have changed, some blacks are moving into areas that were once reserved for whites. Yet more than three million South Africans continue to live in squatters' towns. A squatter is someone who lives without permission on land he or she does not own. Many squatters' towns in South Africa have no running water, sewers, or electricity.

472

MAP SKILL: South Africa

BUILDING CITIZENSHIP

Segregation Under apartheid written law separates people. South Africa had thus legally decreed segregation of its people. Ask students if the United States ever had written legal segregation. (Before the 1954 Supreme Court decision *Brown v. the Board of Education of Topeka*, black children had to attend separate schools in some states. In some states people were legally segregated in other ways before the Civil Rights Act of 1964. The Supreme Court struck down other segregation laws in the 1960s.) Ask students to name ways in which African Americans were segregated, such as on trains, buses, beaches, and in restaurants. Discuss whether there is still segregation of people by color in our country. Segregation is not legal in the United States. However, there is separation, often based on prejudice.

IN A GIANT'S SHADOW

South Africa is the economic giant of Southern Africa. Most of South Africa's neighbors have concentrated on agriculture or mining and have bought many manufactured goods from South Africa. Selling raw materials and buying more expensive finished goods has left neighboring countries with weak economies.

Zambia has one fourth of the world's copper, and copper and copper products make up nine tenths of Zambia's exports. But copper is less valuable than it once was, and Zambia's reliance on one export product has caused its economy to suffer.

Development of agriculture has been uneven in Zambia. The country has abundant arable farmland, but much of it is still used for subsistence farming. Zambia does not have enough money to develop many goods and services that it needs.

In other parts of Southern Africa, years of war have wrecked normal living and working patterns. In Mozambique, for example, a long war combined with a drought have caused widespread famine, malnutrition, and death.

In Zimbabwe almost 80 percent of the people farm for a living. Zimbabweans raise crops and livestock on farms. Women do most of the farming, partly because many of the men are away working in cities or in mines. Racial segregation has been abolished in Zimbabwe. In its capital, **Harare**, black and white Zimbabweans live and work together.

As you read on page 471, Botswana's mines are being developed with money from South Africa.

AN ECONOMIC CONTRAST

As you have read, South Africa's economy contrasts with the economies of other countries in Southern Africa. South Africa has a highly developed industrial economy in which blacks and whites do not share equally in the wealth. The other countries in the area are still developing. With time and effort, South Africa may narrow the huge economic gap between its people. In the other countries of Southern Africa, economic growth is likely to come gradually as industries expand, farming is modernized, and peace is established.

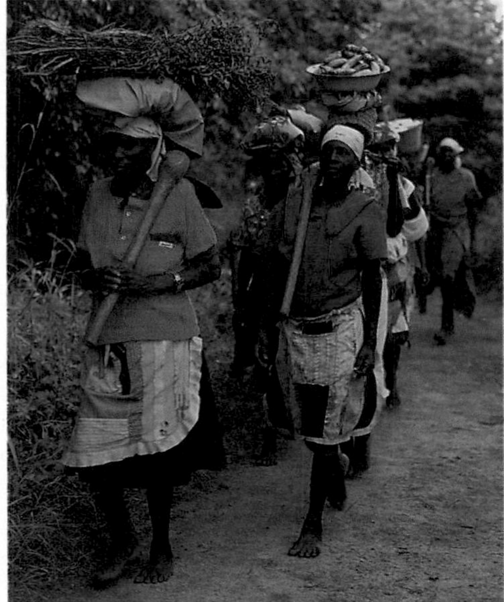

These women are among the almost 80 percent of Zimbabweans who farm for a living.

Check Your Reading

1. What are some of South Africa's most valuable minerals?
2. How did apartheid affect the economy of South Africa?
3. How quickly has industry developed in different countries of Southern Africa?
4. THINKING SKILL: Compare and contrast the economies of South Africa and Zambia.

THINKING SKILL: Compare and Contrast

473

Applying the Lesson Give students an outline map of Southern Africa, found in the Teacher's Resource Center. Have them design a color key for three different levels of economic development and then color the nations according to the key. Discuss why South Africa is the only nation with a fully developed economy.

3 CLOSE

Summarizing Students have learned of the sharp contrast between the economy of South Africa and the economies of other nations in this area. Have the class list ways in which apartheid added to this economic contrast.

Evaluating Use these questions to assess students' understanding.

- **What is the relationship between Johannesburg and Soweto?** (Soweto is a black township that provides cheap labor for white Johannesburg.)
- **What is the veld?** (South Africa's dry, treeless plateau)
- **Which country has one fourth of the world's copper?** (Zambia)

Answers to Check Your Reading

1. gold, diamonds, chrome, coal, tin, copper, iron
2. South Africa has a highly developed economy, but blacks and whites do not share equally in the wealth; there is a lower pay scale for blacks.
3. Industry has developed at uneven rates, quickly in South Africa, more slowly in other countries.
4. South Africa's economy is highly developed. Zambia lags in farming, and copper makes up nine tenths of its exports.

Independent Practice
Practice Book: page 128

MEETING INDIVIDUAL NEEDS

Reteaching (easy) Ask students to write a paragraph describing two reasons that South Africa has a developed economy and two reasons that the economies of other Southern African nations are not yet fully developed.

Extension (average) Have students write a paragraph contrasting the effects apartheid has had on the economic conditions of black workers and white workers in South Africa.

Enrichment (challenging) Have students research the economic sanctions that other nations imposed on South Africa because of apartheid. Then have them write two paragraphs giving arguments for and against such economic sanctions.

LESSON 3
pages 474–477

Lesson Theme While many countries in Southern Africa have made progress towards democracy, many governments in the region are still restrictive.

Lesson Objectives
- Describe the forms of government in Southern Africa.
- Explain the effects of apartheid on South Africa's government.

PREPARE

Motivate Read the *Read Aloud* section to the class. Ask students if they know of ways in which people in Western democracies have a chance to share their opinions. (New England town meetings, Hyde Park Corner speeches in London) Discuss whether or not "freedom squares" would work in the United States.

Set Purpose Ask the *What You Know* question to assess how well students have understood the system of apartheid, which they read about in Lesson 2. Use the *What You Will Learn* question to speculate with students whether or not the governments in this region will differ from those in Sub-Saharan Africa.

TEACH

Identifying Forms of Government Stress to students that most nations in Southern Africa have only recently become independent and are seeking to establish government systems that work well.

Ask students:

- **What three characteristics are, or were, shared by most governments in Southern Africa?** (newly independent, parliamentary, ruled by one person or had a one-party system)

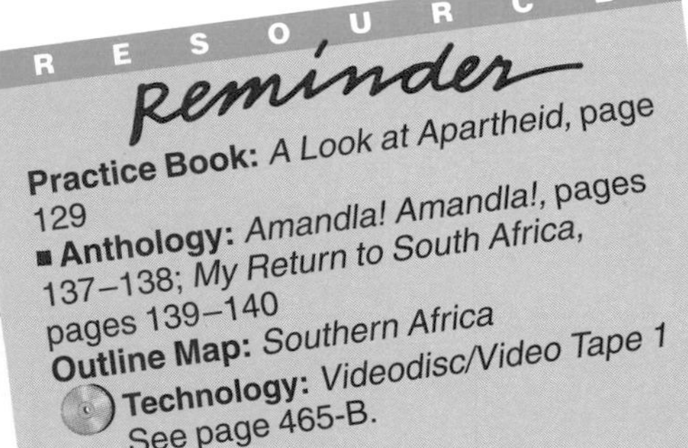

The Government

READ TO LEARN

Key Vocabulary
sanctions

Key People
Desmond Tutu
Nelson Mandela

Read Aloud

In the villages and towns of Botswana, citizens have special places called "freedom squares." All over the country, people meet in these squares to debate issues about government. Politicians in the capital city of Gaborone make a point of showing up at the squares to talk and listen. "We haven't learned democracy from America or England," says the country's Vice President, Peter Mmusi. "It is inborn."

Read for Purpose

1. WHAT YOU KNOW: What is apartheid?
2. WHAT YOU WILL LEARN: What are the major forms of government in Southern Africa?

FORMS OF GOVERNMENT

Many governments in Southern Africa are based on Great Britain's system of government. As you read in Chapter 9, Great Britain has a parliamentary form of government. In a parliamentary system the leader of the political party that wins the most votes in an election becomes prime minister. The prime minister heads the government. Botswana, Mauritius, Namibia, South Africa, Zambia, and Zimbabwe are all republics with parliamentary systems of government.

As in the rest of Sub-Saharan Africa, most of the countries of Southern Africa have won their independence from European control only recently. They are still trying to find systems of government that work well for their people.

Independence did not always mean democracy. Soon after independence, most countries of Southern Africa had one-party systems. Often such parties were headed by a leader whom the people regarded as the "father of the nation," the person who had led the independence movement.

A "SECOND REVOLUTION"

In the early 1990s many countries began a change some people call a "second revolution." This revolution was a move away from one-party government to a multiparty system.

For example, in Zambia, Kenneth Kaunda had led the government since 1964, when the country became independent. In 1991 he was voted out of office when voters were given a choice. As one Zambian woman said, "It's a good idea to have many people, then you let people choose the leader they want."

474 WHAT YOU KNOW: This question refers to information in Lesson 1; the system of racial separation in South Africa.

READING STRATEGY AND VOCABULARY DEVELOPMENT

Vocabulary Development Students have learned many vocabulary terms that have to do with government. Have students skim through the lessons on government they have studied so far and list the words they already know and understand along with the definition of each. (Among the words that students might list are: *party, ruler, system, democratic,* and *representational*.) Have students review these terms before reading the lesson. Then have them skim this lesson to see how many of these terms appear. After they have read the lesson, have students add any new terms, along with their definitions, that relate to government (for example, the word *sanctions*).

Many countries in the region are moving toward greater democracy. Botswana, Madagascar, Mauritius, and Namibia have multiparty systems, and Mozambique is moving in this direction. In 1994, after 30 years of single-party rule, Malawi adopted a new constitution and held multi-party elections.

But some countries have not become more democratic. Lesotho, which began as a constitutional monarchy, has been ruled by military officers since the army seized power there in 1986.

A SOUTHERN AFRICAN KINGDOM

Swaziland is a monarchy ruled by King Mswati (em swä' tē) III, who in 1986 at the age of 18 became the world's youngest monarch. His rule combines traditional customs that Bantu chiefs have followed for centuries with modern government practices.

The king rules with a parliament, and he chooses some of its members. He also settles questions about property ownership and other disputes. These are things that Bantu chiefs have done for centuries.

YEARS OF APARTHEID

You have read that South Africa has several political parties and a parliamentary form of government modeled on Great Britain's system. Yet blacks, who are the majority of South Africans, were not allowed to vote.

When South Africa became independent from Great Britain in 1961, the country's white minority controlled the government. White people had a privileged position that they did not want to lose. In 1948 they enacted apartheid laws that kept people who were not considered white from voting and from serving in any important government jobs. The apartheid laws also kept blacks, coloureds, and Asians in the poorest jobs, schools, and neighborhoods.

Events in other countries have affected South Africa. Most countries of Sub-Saharan Africa became independent in the 1960s. Black people in the United States began to win a long struggle for equal rights including the right to vote in the parts of the country where voting had been denied them. South Africa's government found it increasingly difficult to find support for the idea that rule by a small minority was acceptable.

Other nations criticized South Africa's policies. So in 1976, the South African government created the first of ten black "homelands" within its borders. Each homeland had its own flag, capital, and official language. But each homeland had very little land and few resources for the needs of the people. The homelands were

South African police sometimes reacted violently to anti-apartheid protests.

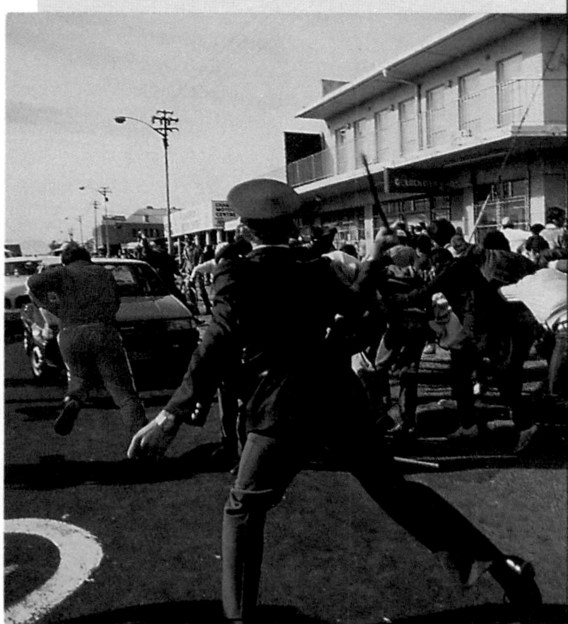

Analyzing a Second Revolution
Continue the discussion.

Ask students:

- **Which countries have multiparty systems or have moved in that direction?** (Zambia, Botswana, Madagascar, Malawi, Mauritius, Namibia, and Mozambique)

Introducing a Southern African Kingdom

Ask students:

- **What is ancient about Swaziland's monarchy? What is new?** (The king's role in settling disputes is traditional; having the youngest king in the world and a parliament are both new.)

Understanding the Years of Apartheid

Ask students:

- **What did the white population of South Africa do to keep their privileged position?** (They passed laws to keep people not considered white from voting or holding important government jobs.)
- **What effect did the apartheid laws have on South Africa's non-white population?** (They were kept in the poorest jobs, neighborhoods, and schools.)
- **How did the government of South Africa react to foreign criticism?** (It created "homelands" for South Africa's black population.)
- **How are the homelands like countries?** (They have flags, capitals, and official languages.)
- *THINKING FURTHER:* **Why do you think that independence for Sub-Saharan African nations and greater rights for African Americans put pressure on South Africa?** (All these events meant greater power and respect for people of African descent.)

 **FUNDAMENTAL THEMES OF GEOGRAPHY**

Place Most places in the world develop their physical and human characteristics over a long period of time as humans adapt to the various environments in those places. The black homelands were less than 50 years old when the constitution unveiled in 1993 disclosed plans to abolish the homelands and divide South Africa into provinces. Have students research the physical and human characteristics of the South African homelands and write an essay titled "Were the Black Homelands 'Artificial' Countries?" Help students to find answers to these questions: What is the ratio of blacks to whites in South Africa (including those blacks in the homelands)? Which natural resources were found in the homelands? What prevented the homelands from becoming truly independent of South Africa? How were the homelands similar to and different from the reservations of Native Americans?

Looking at Apartheid Continue the discussion.

Ask students:

- **What methods did the South African government use to stop black resistance to apartheid?** (declared a state of emergency in order to jail thousands, censored the news)
- **What are sanctions?** (actions taken by nations against a country to get that country to change)

Discussing Change in South Africa

Ask students:

- **What helped to change the system of apartheid?** (sanctions against South Africa, efforts of South African blacks)
- **What approach to apartheid did Desmond Tutu urge South African blacks to use?** (nonviolent resistance)
- **How were Desmond Tutu's efforts to end apartheid honored?** (He was awarded the 1984 Nobel Peace Prize.)
- **What did the African National Congress believe was necessary to end apartheid?** (armed conflict)
- **Who is Nelson Mandela?** (A leader of the ANC who was jailed for 27 years for opposing apartheid; elected president in 1994.)
- **What changes occurred in South Africa in 1990?** (state of emergency ended, many apartheid laws repealed, black South Africans permitted to own land in formerly white areas)

said to be independent and ruled by governments made up largely of traditional chiefs.

Most blacks opposed this plan, saying it did not offer true self-rule. They continued to demand full and equal rights in an undivided South Africa. Other nations refused to recognize the homelands as independent countries. Yet South Africa forced more than 3 million people to move into the already crowded homelands.

South Africa's blacks continued to fight for years against apartheid. In response, the South African government declared a state of emergency in 1986. The state of emergency permitted the government to jail more than 20,000 people without any trial. The government also controlled the press.

To protest apartheid many other countries, including the United States, passed **sanctions** against South Africa. Sanctions are actions taken against a country by other countries to try to bring about change. For example, other countries would not buy or sell goods to South Africa. They would not allow South Africa's athletes to compete in most world sports events because many South African teams were racially segregated.

Nelson Mandela, a leader of the ANC, greets crowds in triumph after his release from imprisonment. Mandela was elected president of South Africa in 1994.

CHANGE IN SOUTH AFRICA

Sanctions against South Africa did help to change the system of apartheid. Even more important, South Africa's blacks made great efforts to change the system. Their struggle was supported by many coloureds and Asians as well as a small but significant number of whites.

Desmond Tutu, a black archbishop in South Africa's Anglican Church, was one of the most important leaders in the fight against apartheid. Tutu urged South Africa's blacks to resist unfair laws without violence. Their methods included boycotts, demonstrations, and hunger strikes. In 1984 Archbishop Tutu won the Nobel Peace Prize for his efforts to end apartheid without violence.

Other groups in South Africa believed that violence was necessary to end apartheid. The African National Congress (ANC), took part in armed conflict. **Nelson Mandela**, a leader of the ANC, was jailed for 27 years after being convicted of treason for opposing apartheid laws. Another black group, Inkatha, opposed both the white government leaders and the ANC.

BUILDING CITIZENSHIP

Current Events and Change Opening up the political process to permit all people to take part can be a slow and painful process. Black people in South Africa struggled a long time for equal rights. In 1992 white South Africans voted for the *principle* of putting an end to white minority rule. But how that change would be made, how long it would take to implement, and who would take part in the decision still had to be worked out. Have students write predictions of future changes in South Africa. Post the list on the bulletin board. Have students bring in news articles to add to the display and to use in checking their predictions.

MEETING INDIVIDUAL NEEDS

Reteaching (easy) On the outline map of Southern Africa, found in the Teacher's Resource Center, have students label the form of government in each country of Southern Africa.

Extension (average) Have students present a report, done in the style of a TV special, showing the differences between the governments of Botswana and South Africa.

Enrichment (challenging) Have students research the lives of Desmond Tutu and Nelson Mandela. They should report on how the activities of these men aid or detract from the black civil rights movement in South Africa.

By 1990, under the pressure of black resistance and foreign sanctions, South Africa's government began to give in. The state of emergency was declared over, and many apartheid laws were repealed. People no longer had to list their race on government papers. Black people were allowed to own land in areas that were formerly reserved for whites.

A major change for the future was announced in 1993. Late in that year black and white leaders reached agreement on a new constitution to grant equal rights to blacks. Black citizens finally gained the right to vote for their country's leaders.
In the national election that followed, in 1994, South Africans elected former political prisoner Nelson Mandela as their new president.

CHANGING GOVERNMENTS

You have read that the countries of Southern Africa have different kinds of political systems and that many systems are changing. A "second revolution" is bringing greater democracy to many countries that had one-party governments.
South Africa is trying to improve living and working conditions for the black people who make up 70 percent of its population.

Check Your Reading

1. What was once the most common form of government in Southern Africa?
2. What changes are taking place in the governments of some countries in the region?
3. What has happened to South Africa's system of apartheid?
4. THINKING SKILL: Classify all the countries mentioned in this lesson into three or more groups according to their systems of government. What generalization could you make about the governments of Southern Africa?

CITIZENSHIP MAKING A DIFFERENCE

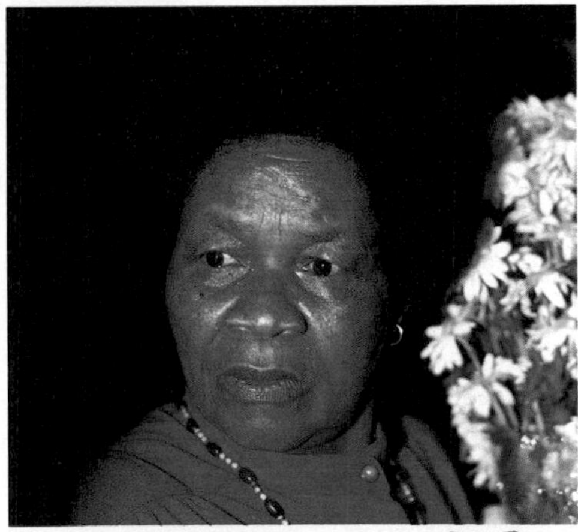

FIGHTING FOR RIGHTS

Albertina Sisulu, a black nurse from Soweto, South Africa, protested against the restrictions that were imposed by the white minority government on the black people of South Africa. Albertina was jailed several times for her nonviolent resistance to apartheid.

From 1964 to 1983 Albertina lived under a government ban. A banned person was not allowed to leave the area where he or she lived without police permission. Banned people could not talk to reporters, leave their homes after dark, or attend any gathering of more than two people. For 19 years Albertina could leave her house only to go to work. She raised six children alone because her husband, Walter, was imprisoned for his anti-apartheid activities.

In 1994, after South Africa's first-ever multiracial elections, Albertina Sisulu was elected to the South African Parliament as a member of the African National Congress Party (ANC). Today, two of Mrs. Sisulu's children serve in parliament along with her, while her husband, Walter Sisulu, is Deputy President of the ANC, the country's majority party.

Applying the Lesson Have students compare the struggle of black South Africans against the apartheid system with the struggle of African Americans for equal rights.

3 CLOSE

Summarizing Students have learned that the governments of Southern Africa resemble those in the rest of Sub-Saharan Africa. Ask students to explain the exceptions, such as South Africa's former apartheid government, the monarchy of Swaziland, and Botswana's multiparty, multiracial government.

Evaluating Have each student write a paragraph about the effect of apartheid on the governments in this area.

Answers to Check Your Reading

1. a one-party system
2. Many countries are moving towards multiparty democracy.
3. South Africa finally ended apartheid in 1993.
4. *monarchy:* Swaziland; *republics with parliaments:* Botswana, Mauritius, Namibia, Zimbabwe, South Africa, Zambia; *multiparty systems:* Botswana, Namibia, Madagascar, Mauritius; *military rule:* Lesotho; *one-man rule:* Malawi; Southern Africa has many types of governments, some of which are democratic and some of which are not.

Independent Practice
Practice Book: page 129

BUILDING CITIZENSHIP

Fighting for Rights Have students read the feature before you discuss Albertina Sisulu. Discuss why Albertina Sisulu was jailed. Explain to students that it was common for a person who spoke out against the government in South Africa to be jailed. Discuss other political prisoners in South Africa. Nelson Mandela, for example, was in prison from the late 1950s to 1990.

Ask students if they think Albertina is a good citizen. Have students discuss whether or not Albertina's protests and years of being banned have had any positive results. Compare Albertina's belief in nonviolent resistance to the beliefs of Gandhi and Dr. Martin Luther King, Jr. Ask students when they think it would be proper to protest an action by a government or a school administration. Have them relate the steps they would take in their protest.

SKILLS LESSON
page 478

Lesson Theme Recognizing bias means identifying a one-sided or slanted presentation of information.

Lesson Objective
- Explain and apply a procedure for recognizing bias.

PREPARE

Motivate Before students begin reading this section, ask them to define the term *bias* and to recall the steps and clues they learned to recognize bias in Chapter 11. Write the steps and clues cited on the chalkboard and compare them with those listed in *Helping Yourself.*

TEACH

Applying the Skill Have students read the two accounts and answer the questions that follow them. (See answers below.)

Thinking About Thinking Ask students to describe the processes they used to recognize bias in as much detail as possible. Have students identify the steps and clues they consider the most useful and give reasons for their choices.

CLOSE

Reviewing the Skill Encourage students to explain in their own words how to recognize bias and to identify situations outside school in which they might use this skill.

Practice Book: *Recognizing Bias,* page 130

Recognizing Bias: Review

Suppose you read a movie review in your school newspaper. The review is so positive that you go to see the movie the following weekend. However, you do not like the film at all. Later you discover that the writer is a fan of the movie's director.

An account that is one-sided often shows bias. It may be exaggerated and filled with emotionally charged words. If you can recognize bias, you will not easily accept a biased account as being true and accurate.

HELPING YOURSELF
One way to recognize bias is to:

1. Recall the definition of *bias*.
2. Recall clues to bias such as exaggerations, emotionally charged words, and a slanted presentation of an issue.
3. Examine the information presented, looking for clues.
4. Ask yourself: Do the clues I have found give a one-sided view for or against something?
5. State the bias, if any.

Applying the Skill

Read the following accounts of a past event in South Africa. Then answer the questions that follow.

A. Police in Cape Town used tear gas to break up a student demonstration near a mainly white university yesterday. More than 2,000 students carrying posters were lined up along a highway to demonstrate their support of a nationwide anti-apartheid campaign.

B. Brutal police action crushed a student anti-apartheid demonstration today. Students who were peacefully parading with posters near the university were attacked without warning. Police savagely fired tear gas and rubber bullets into the crowd of young people. Hundreds of girls and boys ran weeping from the scene.

1. Which account shows bias?
2. What are some clues that alerted you to the bias?
3. Describe the bias in your own words.

Reviewing the Skill

1. What does the word *bias* mean?
2. What are some clues that help you to recognize bias?
3. Why is it important for you to be alert to bias in visual, spoken, or written accounts?

478

ANSWERS TO SKILLS QUESTIONS

Applying the Skill
1. Passage B
2. Words that serve as clues to bias are: *brutal*, *crushed*, *attacked without warning*, *savagely*. They are used to describe the police action, while the students are described as defenseless young people.
3. The writer of Passage B is biased against the police and in favor of the students.

Reviewing the Skill
1. a slanted presentation of information
2. Look for exaggerations, loaded words, as well as a one-sided presentation.
3. Recognizing bias will help you to determine the accuracy of information you are given.

LESSON 4

Arts and Recreation

READ TO LEARN

Key Vocabulary

mbira

Read Aloud

A traditional house of the Ndebele people of South Africa has a thatched roof and walls painted with bright geometric shapes. Bold reds, greens, yellows, and blues seem to burst out of their black outlines.

As in the rest of Sub-Saharan Africa, the arts are woven into everyday life in Southern Africa. In this lesson, you will read about some of these arts and about some of the popular sports of Southern Africa.

Read for Purpose

1. WHAT YOU KNOW: Have you ever heard music from Africa? How does it compare with other kinds of music you have heard?
2. WHAT YOU WILL LEARN: What are some of the popular arts and sports of Southern Africa?

TOWNSHIP MUSIC

Music can be very competitive in South Africa. In black townships, choral groups hold contests with one another. Singers make beautiful melodies and also dance and make people laugh. Groups are judged for their wit as well as for their sound. The song on page 480 is traditional Zulu music.

One of the best known choral groups is Ladysmith Black Mambazo. Through their own recordings and their work with Paul Simon, an American singer and songwriter, they introduced the sounds of South Africa to people in the United States and other parts of the world.

Black South Africans call the kind of songs sung by Ladysmith Black Mambazo "township music." It was born in the all-black townships at the edges of industrial cities. People in these townships created the music by mixing traditional African music with Christian hymns and popular American and British songs they heard on the radio. This combination proved to be very popular not only in Africa, but also in the United States and Great Britain.

TRADITIONAL MUSIC

Some Southern African groups play and sing traditional music. One group, Amampondo, uses only instruments invented in Africa. One of the main instruments used by Amampondo is the **mbira** (em bîr ə), a finger piano. It is made of metal or bamboo strips tied to a wood bowl. Like some other African instruments, the mbira can "talk," meaning that it can be used to imitate the human voice. Traditionally the mbira is not just for entertainment. The Shona people of Zimbabwe, for example, play mbiras to call the spirits during healing ceremonies.

WHAT YOU KNOW: Students should be aware that much of the music that is popular all over the world today comes from African rhythms.

LESSON 4
pages 479–481

Lesson Theme The arts and sports in Southern Africa have a variety of origins.

Lesson Objectives
- Describe township music and traditional music of Southern Africa.
- Identify the sports that are played in this region.

1 PREPARE

Motivate Read the *Read Aloud* section to the class. Discuss what other kinds of artwork and which sports students think are popular in Southern Africa.

Set Purpose Use the *What You Know* question to discover how many students understand that African rhythms are now common throughout the world. Ask the *What You Will Learn* question and have students speculate about possible answers.

2 TEACH

Introducing Township Music Help students to recognize that in addition to singing, choral groups in South Africa are rated on their dancing and on their wit.

Ask students:

- **What is township music?** (a mix of traditional music with popular American and British music)
- **Which American singer worked with Ladysmith Black Mambazo?** (Paul Simon)

Understanding Traditional Music Help students to recognize the role of traditional music in the everyday lives of Southern Africans. Discuss how an mbira is used today.

READING STRATEGY AND VOCABULARY DEVELOPMENT

Vocabulary Development Have students compile an arts and recreation word book. Begin by having students skim similar lessons they have already read to locate pertinent terms. Have them list each word and its definition along with the country being studied when the term was introduced. Then have students skim this lesson to add any additional terms. Ask students to note how many times a particular word has been used and the country or countries being discussed. What conclusions can they draw about these vocabulary terms?

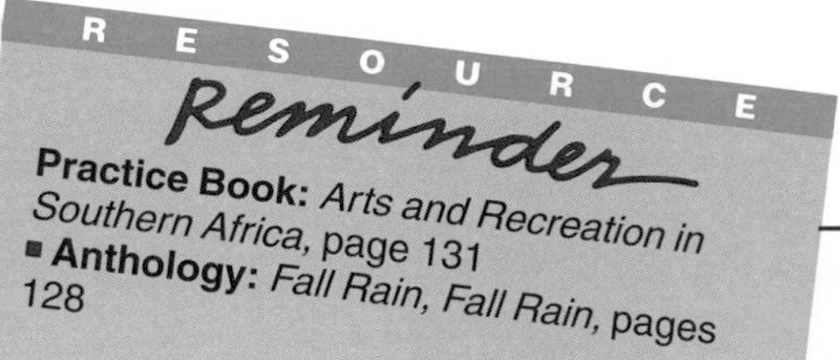
RESOURCE Reminder

Practice Book: *Arts and Recreation in Southern Africa*, page 131
- **Anthology:** *Fall Rain, Fall Rain*, pages 128

Discussing the Song Have students read the lyrics to the song "The Trees Bend" on the bottom of the page. Identify it as a traditional Zulu folk song. Have students give their interpretation of the lyrics of the song. Have volunteers try to read the Zulu version of the song. You may wish to have the class try to sing the song in English or Zulu.

Ask students:

- **Which part of the natural world is being honored in this song?** (trees)
- **Which other songs or poems do you know that praise trees?** (Possible answers include: Joyce Kilmer's "Trees" and "Oh Christmas Tree," the American version of "O Tannenbaum.")

Discussing Sports

Ask students:

- **Which sports from Great Britain are popular in Southern Africa?** (golf, soccer, rugby, cricket, tennis)
- **Where do the young play soccer in this area?** (in empty lots)
- **How did South Africa's apartheid laws affect its sports teams?** (Black and white South Africans could not play on the same team.)
- **Why did the International Olympic Committee end its 21-year ban on South African teams?** (South Africa promised to end segregation in sports.)

CURRICULUM CONNECTION

Music The role that spirits play in nature has a powerful meaning for people who live close to the land. The arts of Southern Africa provide a way for people to communicate with and honor nature. Ask if any student musicians can play or sing the traditional Zulu folk song on this page. Have students identify other songs that deal with nature.

BACKGROUND INFORMATION

More About Sports and Apartheid The banning of South African sports teams from international events may have been more successful than economic sanctions in influencing white South Africans to rethink apartheid.

- In 1970 South Africa was barred from competing in the 1972 Olympics, in the Davis Cup tennis tournament, and in international track and field events for two years.
- In the United States, Arthur Ashe and Harry Belafonte lead a group called Artists and Athletes Against Apartheid.

South Africa's Ladysmith Black Mombazo has performed with American singer Paul Simon.

SPORTS

Music, of course, is not the only popular recreational activity in Southern Africa. People like to play and watch many different kinds of sports.

Many of the popular sports came from Great Britain. The English brought soccer, rugby (the English form of football), cricket, golf, and tennis to Southern Africa. In just about any country of the area, young people play soccer in empty lots.

Sports are very important to people in South Africa. For many years apartheid laws kept blacks and whites from playing on the same teams in South Africa. To protest this policy, many international sports competitions, such as the Olympics, imposed a sanction against South Africa refusing to let its athletes participate. In 1991, after South Africa promised to end segregation in sports, the International Olympic Committee removed its 21-year ban on letting South Africans compete in the Olympics.

MUSIC AND SPORTS

The popular recreational activities of Southern Africa come from many different sources. As you have read, township music is a combination of African, British, and American forms. Other kinds of popular music are completely African in origin. A traditional African folk song of the Zulu people is found on page 480. Finally, some sports, such as soccer and tennis, come directly from Europe.

Check Your Reading

1. What is township music?
2. How have sanctions helped to change segregation in sports?
3. What are some of the popular arts and sports of Southern Africa?
4. **THINKING SKILL:** Based on this lesson, what conclusions can you draw about music in Southern Africa?

THINKING SKILL: Drawing Conclusions

Applying the Lesson Have students read the entertainment and sports sections of newspapers and magazines for several weeks and bring in articles about Southern African entertainment groups and sports teams to post in the classroom.

CLOSE

Summarizing Students have learned that arts and sports in Southern Africa are international in scope. Discuss what makes them Southern African and what makes them international.

Evaluating Have each student write an essay titled, "How Arts and Sports Contribute to the Culture of Southern Africa."

Answers to Check Your Reading

1. It is a blend of American and British popular songs with traditional African music that is composed by blacks in the townships near industrial cities.
2. South Africa ended segregation in its sports teams as a result of sanctions.
3. township and traditional music, rugby, cricket, golf, soccer, tennis
4. It is integrated into both the traditional and modern lives of Southern Africans.

Independent Practice
Practice Book: page 131

MEETING INDIVIDUAL NEEDS

Reteaching (easy)

Extension (average) Have students listen to some examples of township music. (Examples of this music can be found in most public libraries.) Then ask students to write reviews of the CDs or tapes that they heard.

Enrichment (challenging) Divide the class into five groups. Tell each group to focus on one of the following sports in South Africa: soccer, rugby, cricket, golf, and tennis. Then have each group write and illustrate a booklet on how apartheid affected their sport.

CHAPTER 23 REVIEW
pages 482–483

USING THE CHAPTER SUMMARY AND REVIEW

Cultural Geography These questions may be used for review.

- **Which group of people and which country are dominant in the region?** (descendants of European settlers, South Africa)
- **Which country has a diversified economy?** (South Africa)
- **Which country has a monarchy?** (Swaziland)
- **Name a traditional instrument of the region.** (mbira)

Ideas to Remember

- **Which ethnic group is the largest in the region?** (Bantus)
- **Which nation in the region affects the economies of its neighbors?** (South Africa)
- **Which country followed the system of apartheid?** (South Africa)
- **What influences the music and sports of the region?** (traditional and European ways)

Answers to Reviewing Vocabulary

1. veld
2. apartheid
3. sanctions
4. mbira
5. township

Answers to Reviewing Facts

1. The Bantus pushed them into this area.
2. The Boers left the colony and created the Transvaal and the Orange Free State.
3. white, black, colored, Asian
4. It is diversified, has vast mineral resources, and has highly developed industries.
5. Whites were paid more, allowed to live on better lands, and did not share the wealth equally with blacks.

CHAPTER 23 ▪ SUMMARY

NATIONS OF SOUTHERN AFRICA: CULTURAL GEOGRAPHY

PEOPLE

- South Africa—dominant country of the area

- Bushmen were earliest settlers, followed by Bantus, the largest group
- European settlers became most powerful group and include Afrikaners, or Boers, and British
- Apartheid kept racial groups separate

ECONOMY

- Diversified economy exists in South Africa, which has mineral resources
- White workers earned more than black workers
- Agriculture: irrigated farming in South Africa; subsistence farming; communal farming
- Many workers migrate to South Africa
- Botswana has a rapid growth rate

GOVERNMENT

- Main type: parliamentary

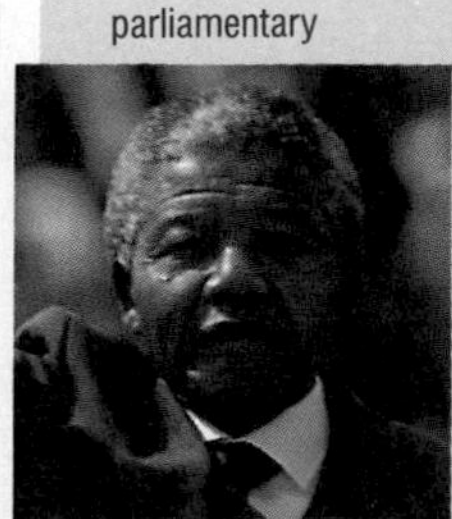

- Monarchy: Swaziland
- Many countries are changing from one-party to multiparty systems

- South Africa has ended its apartheid laws

ARTS AND RECREATION

- Diverse types of music: township music, traditional
- Traditional instruments—such as the mbira—used for entertainment and in religious ceremonies
- Popular sports: soccer, rugby, cricket
- Segregation in team sports has ended in South Africa

IDEAS TO REMEMBER

- Ethnic groups in Southern Africa include Bushmen, Bantu (the largest group), and the white minority.
- South Africa's economy affects the economies of its neighbors.
- Systems of government include many parliamentary governments, democracies, long-time heads of government, and one kingdom. South Africa's government has been forced to move away from the system of apartheid.
- Music and sports include traditional and European influences.

ENRICHMENT ACTIVITY

Playing an African Game **Materials:** a beanbag and a long rope
Note: This game is for 20 or fewer players. It should be played in an open area, such as a gym or out of doors.

1. Tie the rope around the beanbag.
2. Tell the class that they are going to learn to play a game that is very popular in Sub-Saharan Africa. It is called "Jumping the Beanbag." Young people play it for fun and to increase skills in jumping and timing.
3. Describe the rules. One player who is "It" stands at the center of a circle formed by the other players. "It" swings the roped beanbag in a circle just above the ground. The players in the circle must jump over the beanbag. If players fail to jump in time, they are out of the game.
4. The last player to remain in the circle wins.

CHAPTER 23 • REVIEW

REVIEWING VOCABULARY

apartheid township
mbira veld
sanctions

Number a sheet of paper from 1 to 5. Beside each number write the word from the above list that best matches the definition.

1. A dry plateau that covers much of South Africa
2. Afrikaans word that means "separateness" and refers to South Africa's former system of racial separation
3. Actions taken to pressure a country to change its policies
4. A musical instrument that can imitate the human voice
5. An area in South Africa in which black people were forced to live under apartheid

REVIEWING FACTS

1. How did the Bushmen come to live in the Kalahari Desert?
2. How did the Boers respond when the British seized control of Cape Colony in 1795?
3. Into which four racial groups did the South African government classify its people?
4. Name three reasons that explain why South Africa has the most powerful economy in the region.
5. What economic benefits did South African whites gain from the system of apartheid?
6. Name three economic effects that apartheid had on blacks in South Africa.
7. How does Zambia's reliance on one product damage its economy?
8. Which South African country is ruled by a king?
9. Why were the black homelands in South Africa not recognized by the international community?
10. Why is the mbira popular in Southern Africa?

WRITING ABOUT MAIN IDEAS

1. **Writing a List:** Write a list of five or more reasons that explain why living in South Africa was very difficult for black people.
2. **Writing a Letter to the Editor:** Write a letter to the editor explaining your position for or against sanctions against South Africa.
3. **Writing a Journal Entry:** Imagine you are visiting South Africa. Write a journal entry describing the expressions of art and music you observe.
4. **Writing About Perspectives:** Imagine that you live in a country of Southern Africa that has had one ruler since independence. Now for the first time, voters have elected a new ruler. Write an essay telling what you hope will happen and what you worry might happen when the change in government takes place.

BUILDING SKILLS: RECOGNIZING BIAS

1. Define what is meant by *bias*. Give an example.
2. List several steps you might take to recognize bias.
3. Why is it important to recognize bias?

6. They were paid less than whites, they had to travel far to work, and they could not live in white neighborhoods.
7. Since copper is not as valuable as it once was, Zambia's economy has suffered.
8. Swaziland
9. Most countries believed that the homelands are not truly independent and treat them as part of South Africa.
10. It is a traditional instrument that is used by some groups of people to call the spirits during healing ceremonies.

Suggestions for Writing About Main Ideas

1. Possible answers include: They were paid less, they had to live far from their work, they were denied the right to live in some areas, many were forced to live in squatter towns, and they were not treated as equals.
2. Students should state the reason that they are for or against sanctions and what form the sanctions should take.
3. Have students share their opinions on the art and music of the area with the rest of the class.
4. Have students choose a specific country which still has, or recently had, one-person rule.

Answers to Building Skills: Recognizing Bias

1. a one-sided view about something; A possible example: Television is bad and no one should watch anything on television.
2. Recall the definition of bias; recall clues to bias; examine the information presented to look for clues; ask if the clues are one-sided; state bias if any.
3. It will help you to determine the accuracy of information that you hear or read.

Chapter Review Test
Practice Book: *Vocabulary Review,* page 132
Transparency: *Graphic Organizer*

MAKING CONNECTIONS

Comparing and Concluding Display the Matrix Chart Graphic Organizer Transparency, filling in only the underlined labels. Have students complete the chart with examples from the chapter. *Ask:* How is South Africa similar to other Southern African nations?

	OTHER NATIONS OF SOUTHERN AFRICA	SOUTH AFRICA
People	descendants of Bantu, Bushmen (Botswana)	descendants of Bantu, Afrikaners, British
Government	parliamentary, one-party, multi-party, monarchy	parliamentary, multi-party system, moving away from apartheid
Economy	developing	developed, diversified
Music	traditional music	township music

UNIT 6 REVIEW

pages 484–485

USING THE UNIT SUMMARY AND REVIEW

Physical Geography These questions may be used for review.

- **What type of landform is dominant in Sub-Saharan Africa?** (plateau)
- **How do trade winds affect the climate of the region?** (The trade winds that blow from the Atlantic Ocean bring rainy seasons; those that blow from the Sahara Desert bring dry seasons.)
- **Which minerals are found in Sub-Saharan Africa?** (copper, iron, gold, uranium, manganese, diamonds)

Cultural Geography

- **Which ethnic group is one of the largest in the region?** (Bantu)
- **What are the effects of drought and overgrazing on the land?** (The desert is expanding.)
- **What were almost all of Sub-Saharan Africa's countries about 30 years ago?** (European colonies)
- **Which modern form of music is popular in this region?** (traditional and township music)

UNIT 6 • SUMMARY

SUB-SAHARAN AFRICA: PHYSICAL GEOGRAPHY

LANDFORMS

- Highest mountains: Mount Kilimanjaro, Mount Kenya
- Most of Sub-Saharan Africa is a great plateau
- Special features: Zaire Basin, Great Rift Valley, waterfalls
- Rivers: Nile, Zaire, Niger, Zambezi are among the most important
- Vegetation zones: Sahel, savanna, rain forest

CLIMATE

- Mostly tropical, with high temperatures all year
- Rainfall is scarce in about three fourths of the continent

- Trade winds cause rainy and dry seasons

NATURAL RESOURCES

- Tropical crops: cacao, coffee, rubber, palm oil, timber
- Wildlife preserves attract tourists
- Rich in minerals: copper, iron, gold, uranium, manganese, diamonds
- Many waterfalls that can be harnessed to provide hydroelectric power

SUB-SAHARAN AFRICA: CULTURAL GEOGRAPHY

PEOPLE

- Three cultural influences: traditional beliefs, Islam, and European colonialism and Christianity
- Hundreds of ethnic groups and many languages: Bantus are one of the largest groups
- South Africa has ended apartheid system that kept racial groups separate

ECONOMY

- Expanding desert caused by drought and overgrazing
- Agriculture: mainly shifting cultivation, slash-and-burn farming
- Economic needs: better transportation; more hydroelectric power, better-educated workers, more industry
- Industrial facilities are still being developed: mills, food-processing plants, oil wells and refineries in Nigeria
- South Africa has a diversified economy

GOVERNMENT

- Many nations have parliamentary systems
- Some nations have one-party rule; others are becoming more democratic
- Almost all countries were European colonies until about 30 years ago
- Under apartheid system, blacks forced to live in Bantu "homelands," lacked rights

ARTS AND RECREATION

- Traditional arts include proverbs, poetry; rich oral tradition
- Music: traditional instruments; modern forms of music like township music are also popular
- Traditional religious ceremonies: decorated masks are used to call on gods

484

ENRICHMENT ACTIVITY

Playing "Where in Time and Place in Africa Am I?"

1. Tell the class that they are going to play a quiz game called "Where in Time and Place in Africa Am I?"
2. Explain the game by giving the following example: One team presents a clue such as, "I have had to live my life under the system of apartheid. Where in time and place in Africa am I?" The opposing team would answer: in South Africa before 1993.
3. Divide the class into an even number of four- or five-member teams. Tell each team to do the following: Choose someone to write down the clues; review the information in Unit 6 to write five clues; and choose a team name.
4. Arrange the teams in pairs and choose one of the pairs to give the first clue. Students should share turns giving clues. Each team scores one point for a correct answer. The team in each pair with the most points wins.
5. After the game have a few students rewrite the clues and their answers using markers and construction paper. Then display the clues to create an attractive unit review.

UNIT 6 • REVIEW

REVIEWING VOCABULARY

apartheid	migration
civil war	oral tradition
desertification	rift valleys
drought	sanctions
harmattan	savanna

Number a sheet of paper from 1 to 10. Beside each number write the word or term from the above list that best completes the sentence.

1. In Africa drought and overgrazing have contributed to the expansion of dry land in a process known as ____.
2. ____ explains why Bantu culture spread from Cameroon throughout East and Equatorial Africa.
3. ____ separated the races and kept the white minority in power.
4. A major farming and grazing region, the ____ is a broad grassland covering much of Sub-Saharan Africa.
5. The ____ is a wind that blows from the Sahara over western Africa.
6. Beginning as cracks in the earth, ____ are steep-sided lowlands that extend through much of eastern Africa.
7. Common in Sub-Saharan Africa, ____ is armed conflict between two or more groups within the same country.
8. ____ are actions taken by one country to force change within another country.
9. In West Africa history and literature were preserved through ____ instead of through written language.
10. A ____ is a long period without adequate rain.

WRITING ABOUT THE UNIT

1. **Writing a Paragraph:** Write a paragraph explaining why European languages are often used as the official languages of Sub-Saharan Africa.
2. **Writing Questions for an Interview:** Write a list of questions for an interview with the leader of a country in Sub-Saharan Africa. Focus your questions on political issues and democracy versus one-party rule.
3. **Writing About Perspectives:** You have read how Tanzanians write "poems to the editor" that address issues of concern. Imagine that you live in Sub-Saharan Africa. Write a poem to the editor dealing with an issue that would be important to you.

ACTIVITIES

1. **Working Together to Tell a Story:** Choose a well-known folktale or legend to share with your classmates. Assume the role of a griot and ask other members of the class to be your audience. Tell the story and encourage the rest of the class to respond in the call-and-response technique.
2. **Gathering Information About an Issue in Sub-Saharan Africa:** Choose an important political, economic, or social issue affecting Sub-Saharan Africa. Gather articles about the issue from newspapers and magazines. Then present the information in an oral report to the rest of the class.

LINKING PAST, PRESENT, AND FUTURE

Ancient hatreds, the legacy of colonialism, and decades of misrule have made Sub-Saharan Africa a poor and strife-torn region. What changes would you make to establish political stability and prosperity for Africans?

Answers to Reviewing Vocabulary

1. desertification
2. migration
3. apartheid
4. savanna
5. harmattan
6. rift valleys
7. civil war
8. sanctions
9. oral tradition
10. drought

Suggestions for Writing About the Unit

1. Students should mention the large number of African languages and dialects and the role that European colonies played in introducing European languages to the region.
2. You may wish to have students work in groups to make a list of questions and then have them role-play the questions and answers.
3. Before students begin their poems, be sure that they have decided on a specific issue to write about. Have volunteers read their poems aloud.

Suggestions for Activities

1. Review with students what a griot is and what the call-and-response technique is. Have students read the story once before the class participates in the call and response.
2. You may wish to have students also prepare bulletin boards on the issues they have chosen. Then have the class review the bulletin boards before the oral reports are given so that they can prepare questions to ask the speakers.

Suggestions for Linking Past, Present, and Future You may want to divide the class into three groups for this activity. One group can focus on political changes, another on economic changes, and the last on social changes. Then have the groups share their ideas.

PERFORMANCE ASSESSMENT

Demonstrating Understanding Remind students of the fair they were told about at the beginning of the unit. Encourage students who wish to make similar kinds of projects to work together in small groups. Suggest that they share and divide responsibilities among them. However, have students complete the written part of their contributions independently. Remind them of the standards that will be applied to their contributions, which were outlined in the Unit Opener on page 408. During the fair provide students with time to visit the other exhibits. For additional performance assessment information, see page TM46 in the *Assessment Book.*

For the Portfolio: Include students' summaries and written explanations in their portfolios. Also include photographs, if available, and your anecdotal record or observational checklist.

UNIT 7
ORGANIZER

SOUTHERN AND EASTERN ASIA text pages 486–577

UNIT THEME

The region of Southern and Eastern Asia has some of the oldest cultures, most populated countries, and most varied governments and economies of any world region.

UNIT RESOURCES

- Practice Book: pp. 133–158
- Anthology: Part 5
- Anthology Cassette
- Outline Maps: 2, 33–37
- Transparency Maps: 1, 1A, 14
- Unit 7 Poster
- Desk Maps
- Internet Project Handbook
- Geo Adventures Pad
- Pupil Edition on Cassette
- Transparency: Graphic Organizer
- **Technology:** *Videodisc/ Video Tape 2*
- **Technology:** *Adventures CD-ROM*
- Assessment Book, Chapter Tests: 24, 25, 26, 27, 28

Internet CONNECTION

The Home Page at **http://www.mmhschool.com** and the **Internet Project Handbook** contain on-line student activities related to this unit.

UNIT PLANNING GUIDE

CHAPTER	SUGGESTED PACING	THEMES
24 PHYSICAL GEOGRAPHY OF SOUTHERN AND EASTERN ASIA pages 490–503	4 days	High mountain ranges affect the tropical to temperate climate patterns of Southern and Eastern Asia; great river systems provide energy, but natural resources are distributed unevenly.
25 NATIONS OF SOUTH ASIA pages 504–523	6 days	In the densely populated nations of South Asia, British colonial influence first instilled democratic ideals and industrialization is rising.
26 CHINA AND ITS NEIGHBORS pages 524–539	6 days	Ancient religious and family values are blended with communism in China and with private enterprise in some neighboring nations.
27 JAPAN pages 540–559	7 days	Mixing traditional and modern ways, Japan's hardworking people maintain democracy and strong economic growth.
28 SOUTHEAST ASIA pages 560–575	6 days	A cultural crossroads, Southeast Asia has a rural population and varied governments.

UNIT PROJECTS

Writing an Essay Have students research and write essays comparing the six great religions of Southern and Eastern Asia. Discuss with the class why first-time Western visitors to this region of Asia find exposure to the "philosophy of the East" a jolting experience that often contrasts with their outlook on life.

Oral Reports Have each student choose a nation in this region and report on it. Students should apply the five fundamental themes of geography: location, place, human-environment interaction, movement, and region.

Cooperative Learning: Designing a Book Divide the class into five groups and assign each team a chapter from this unit. Have each team put together an illustrated booklet showing the main ideas in each lesson.

Field Trip Find a factory in your area where students can be given a tour, or visit a business in an Asian community or one run by Asians. Have the class prepare questions to ask their host about the business's relations with the Far East in terms of possible competition, trade, or materials and manufacturing.

BULLETIN BOARD IDEAS

Making Your Own Bulletin Board Prepare a bulletin board display called, "Population Pressure in Southern and Eastern Asia." Ask small groups of students to contribute posters on the subject, including brief reports and supporting charts, graphs, or pictures. Help to map the reports appropriately and have each group summarize its work for the class.

Using the Unit Poster As an alternative to the bulletin board activity, display the Unit 7 Poster, which shows an enlarged version of the Unit Opener globe on pages 486–487.

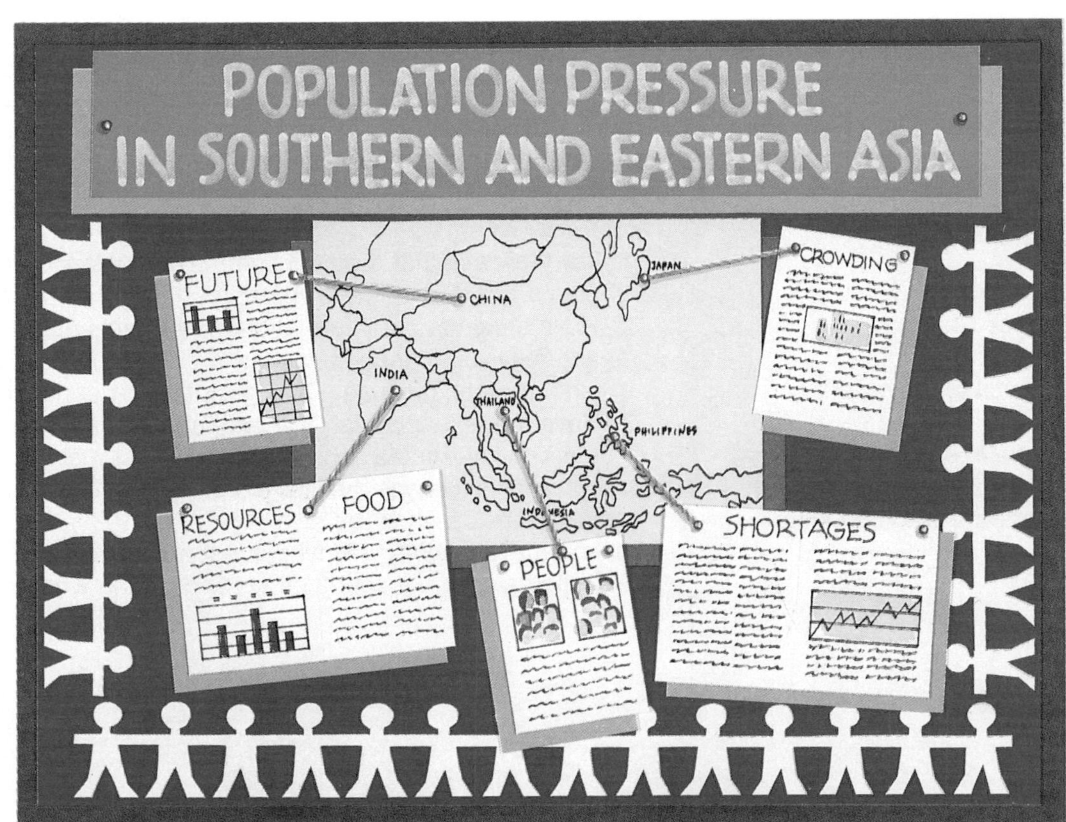

UNIT BIBLIOGRAPHY

For descriptions and additional resources, see the Annotated Bibliography beginning on page T-1 in the back of the book.

For the Teacher

Books

Langone, John. *In the Shogun's Shadow: Understanding a Changing Japan.* Boston, MA: Little, Brown and Co., 1994.

Tao, Wang. *Exploring Into China.* Columbus, OH: Silver Burdett Press, 1995.

Read-Alouds

Conger, David, reteller. *Many Lands, Many Stories.* Rutland, VT: Charles E. Tuttle, 1987.

Ness, Caroline, reteller. *The Ocean of Story: Fairy Tales from India.* New York: Lothrop, Lee & Shepard Books, 1993.

Technology Multimedia

Geography Search. (software, Macintosh or Windows) #SEAGSRM3A. Tom Snyder Productions, Watertown, MA 02172. Toll free: 1-800-342-0236.

■ *Japan.* (Videocassette). National Geographic Society. Toll Free: 1-800-368-2728.

Free Materials

For a fact sheet on the countries in Southeast Asia, send to: Center for Southeast Asian Studies; University of Wisconsin-Madison, 4115 Helen C. White Hall, 600 North Park Street, Madison, Wisconsin 53706.

For the Student

Choi, Sook Nyul. *Year of Impossible Goodbyes.* Boston, MA: Houghton Mifflin, 1991. **(Average)**

Clifford, Mary. *The Land and People of Afghanistan.* New York: J. B. Lippincott, 1989. **(Challenging)**

Davis, James E., and Sharryl Davis Hawke. *Tokyo.* Milwaukee, WI: Raintree Publishing, 1990. **(Average)**

Finck, Lila, and John P. Hayes. *Jawaharlal Nehru.* New York: Chelsea House Publishers, 1987. **(Challenging)**

Fisher, Leonard Everett. *Gandhi.* New York: Atheneum, 1995. **(Average)**

Fraser, Mary Ann. *On Top of the World: The Conquest of Mt. Everest.* New York: Henry Holt & Co., 1991. **(Easy)**

Goedecke, Christopher J., and Rosmarie Hausherr. *The Wind Warrior: The Training of a Karate Champion.* New York: Four Winds Press, 1992. **(Easy)**

■ Huynh Quang Nhuong. *The Land I Lost: Adventures of a Boy in Vietnam.* New York: Harper & Row, 1982. **(Average)**

Rigg, Jonathan. *Southeast Asia.* Austin, TX: Raintree Steck-Vaughn, 1995. **(Average)**

Weston, Mark. *The Land and People of Pakistan.* New York: J. B. Lippincott, 1992. **(Challenging)**

■ Book excerpted in the Anthology

■ National Geographic selection

IDEAS FOR ACTIVE LEARNING

TEACHER EXCHANGE

Fantasy Travel

Thanks to:
Joyce Shupper
Hillside School
Montclair, New Jersey

Materials
maps, travel brochures, and posters of Asian countries

Instructions
1. Tell the class that they will use their knowledge of maps and other cultures to plan a trip to one of the Asian countries they are studying.
2. Have students get information from travel agents, guidebooks, library resources, and relatives or friends who have traveled in Asia. Students should research the land, climate, language, and customs of their countries.
3. Have students plan fantasy trips about what they would like to see and do. Ask them to investigate accommodations, meal plans, air and land transportation, currency exchange, health and passport concerns, and the time and cost of taking their fantasy trips.
4. You may also wish to invite guest speakers, such as people who have lived in or visited any of the countries studied, airline workers, and travel agents.

Playing "Classroom Contest"

Thanks to:
Carolyn Reeder
North Central School
Hanlontown, Iowa

Materials
two desk bells, chalk and chalkboard for scoring

Instructions
1. Tell students they will play a review game based on a popular TV program.
2. Place two desk bells in the front of the room.
3. Divide the class into two teams, each with a name, such as Stars or Stripes.
4. Appoint five students to write and ask questions about the unit.
5. Have one contestant from each team go to the front of the room. Each tries to beat the other in ringing the bell first to answer the question.
6. If the student who rings first answers correctly, one point is scored for his or her team. If the answer is incorrect, the opponent may answer and score.
7. After each question the next contestants should step forward.
8. The team with the most points at the end of the game wins.

TECHNOLOGY CENTER

Enriching with Multimedia

RESOURCE: ***Internet Project Handbook***

Look at the ***Internet Project Handbook*** for student projects related to this unit or have students go on-line at http://www.mmhschool.com, Macmillan/McGraw-Hill's Home School page on the World Wide Web.

RESOURCE: ***Videodisc/Video Tape 2***

Enrich Unit 7 with the Videodisc *China Today* segment.

Search 48074, Play To 50471 Side A

SCHOOL-TO-HOME

Cultures and Beliefs

- Throughout this unit, students will have the opportunity to learn about the establishment of different religions in both Southern and Eastern Asia, including Christianity, Islam, Hinduism, Sikhism, Confucianism, Daoism, and Buddhism. Discuss with students the cultures in which each religion originated, and how each system of belief has influenced the lives of people in these regions. Assist students in writing summaries which outline the principles of each religion.
- Encourage students to share their summaries with family members. Working together, students and their families can research and add to one or more of the summaries and assemble a booklet. Encourage students to share their finished booklets with the class.

SECOND-LANGUAGE SUPPORT

While these activities are designed especially for students needing second-language support, they are meant to be shared by all students in the class.

Chapter 24, Lesson 1 ■ Physical Geography of Southern and Eastern Asia

To help second-language students remember place names, group students into teams and ask each to create a map showing *Key Places* and other geographical features of the region.

Chapter 25, Lesson 4 ■ Nations of South Asia

Make South Asian arts and recreation more meaningful to students: assign different aspects of South Asian culture, such as architecture or yoga, to each of several teams. Have teams do extra research and visually present a report to the class.

Chapter 26, Lesson 3 ■ China and Its Neighbors

Help students organize the various governments presented in the lesson by assigning one country to each of several teams. Each team should prepare a brief outline of their county's government to share.

Chapter 27, Lesson 2 ■ Japan

Reinforce lesson concepts by discussing and creating a class collage of products made in Japan.

Chapter 28, Lesson 2 ■ Southeast Asia

Pairs of students can choose one nation in Southeast Asia to focus on. Ask them to create brochures advertising their nation's businesses.

Chapter 27, Lesson 2

UNIT 7

pages 486–577

USING THE UNIT OPENER

Introducing the Unit Have students look at the unit title and silently read the *Where We Are* section on the facing page.

Ask students:

- **Why is Southern and Eastern Asia one of the most important regions of the world today?** (It has over 3 billion people.)
- **Which lands does this region encompass?** (India, Afghanistan, Pakistan, China, Japan, North Korea, South Korea, Bangladesh, Taiwan, Mongolia, Myanmar, Laos, Malaysia, Bhutan, Nepal, Thailand, Cambodia, Vietnam, Brunei, Singapore, Philippines, Maldives, Indonesia, and Sri Lanka)

EXTENDING MAP SKILLS

Help students to recognize the great variety of land shapes that comprise Southern and Eastern Asia.

Ask students:

- **What are the three areas that make up Southern and Eastern Asia today?** (South Asia, East Asia, and Southeast Asia)
- **What makes this region's shape even more complicated than the irregular pattern of the region of the Middle East and North Africa?** (the variety of island groups in the region)

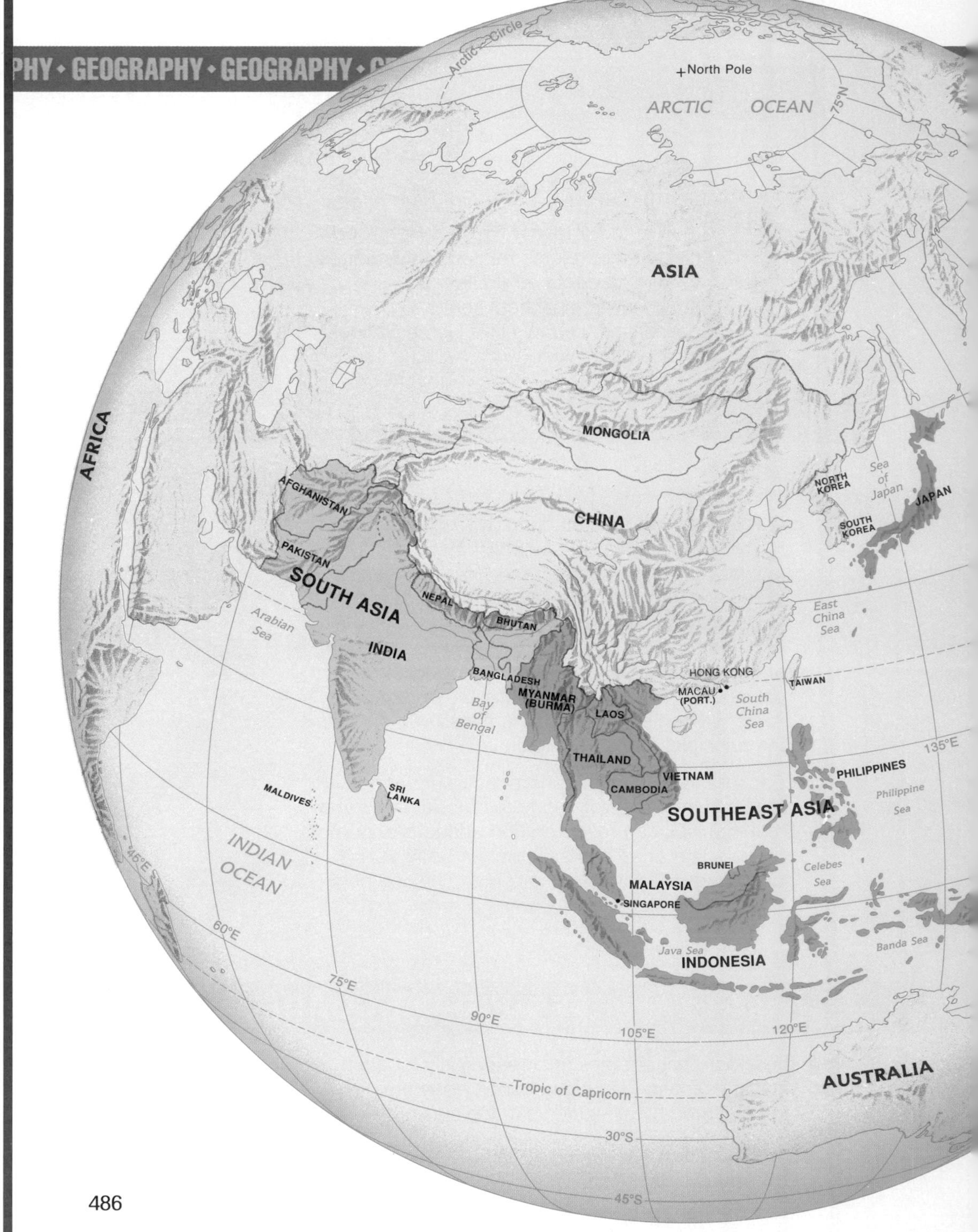

GEOGRAPHY • GEOGRAPHY • GEOGRAPHY

North Pole
ARCTIC OCEAN
Arctic Circle
75°N
ASIA
AFRICA
MONGOLIA
CHINA
NORTH KOREA
SOUTH KOREA
Sea of Japan
JAPAN
AFGHANISTAN
PAKISTAN
SOUTH ASIA
NEPAL
BHUTAN
INDIA
Arabian Sea
East China Sea
BANGLADESH
Bay of Bengal
MYANMAR (BURMA)
HONG KONG
MACAU (PORT.)
TAIWAN
South China Sea
LAOS
THAILAND
VIETNAM
CAMBODIA
PHILIPPINES
Philippine Sea
135°E
MALDIVES
SRI LANKA
SOUTHEAST ASIA
INDIAN OCEAN
BRUNEI
MALAYSIA
SINGAPORE
Celebes Sea
45°E
60°E
75°E
Java Sea
INDONESIA
Banda Sea
90°E
105°E
120°E
Tropic of Capricorn
AUSTRALIA
30°S
45°S

486

ONGOING UNIT PROJECT

Planning for Assessment Explain to students that in this unit they will be learning about the land and people of Southern and Eastern Asia. Explain to them that when they finish the unit, they will have an opportunity to demonstrate what they have learned by writing and performing skits in which people from different countries or parts of Southern and Eastern Asia meet and exchange ideas. Tell students that they will be working in pairs or groups. As students read the unit, they should think about ideas the characters in their skits might talk about and which characters they would like to play. For information on completing this unit project, see page 577.

Goal: Students' work should show they understand the extent of cultural and historical diversity among the countries of Southern and Eastern Asia.

Signs of Success: Assure students that they will not be assessed on their acting ability, but rather on the information the characters in their skits exchange. Explain that the characters in an adequate skit should share ideas about the geography, climate, and natural resources in the part of the world in which they live. In an excellent skit the characters would also exchange ideas about cultural similarities and differences, including ideas about the arts and recreation, language, writing and religion.

SOUTHERN AND EASTERN ASIA

WHERE WE ARE

As you have read, the world around us is made up of many different nations, cultures, religions, and ideas. In this unit you will read about Southern and Eastern Asia, a region that is home to more than 3 billion people.

As the map shows, Southern and Eastern Asia stretches from India, Afghanistan, and Pakistan across China to Japan and to North and South Korea. As you read about this region, think about its people and the different economic, political, and social systems they have developed. Then you will understand why Southern and Eastern Asia is one of the most important regions of the world today.

487

Continue the discussion.

Ask students:

- **Name the six main islands or island groups that lie off the coasts of Southern and Eastern Asia.** (Sri Lanka, Indonesia, the Philippines, Taiwan, Japan, and Maldives)
- **Other than islands, what is the main physical feature shown on the map of this region?** (the mass of mountains in south-central Asia)
- **Where are the major river systems on this map?** (in northern India, through Southeast Asia, and through central and eastern China)
- **Which oceans surround Southern and Eastern Asia?** (Indian and Pacific oceans)
- **Which other bodies of water border this region?** (Arabian Sea, Bay of Bengal, Philippine Sea, Celebes Sea, Banda Sea, Java Sea, South China Sea, East China Sea, Sea of Japan)
- **What other observations can you make about what you see on this map of Southern and Eastern Asia?** (This open-ended question is intended to help you to see which students can observe maps carefully and which students need help with map work.)

FUNDAMENTAL THEMES OF GEOGRAPHY

Movement One of the most dramatic movements of the continents that ride on the earth's crustal plates took place when India and Australia split off from Africa about 65 million years ago.

- Over millions of years, the chunk of land now known as the Indian subcontinent separated from Australia. It turned in the Indian Ocean, headed northeast, and crashed into Eurasia, pushing up the highest land on earth.
- The "crash" is not over; India is still pushing under Eurasia and lifting even higher the mountain peaks of the Pamirs, which are called "The Roof of the World." Other South Asian ranges are also being lifted higher, such as the Himalayas, where Mount Everest is located.

EXTENDING TABLE SKILLS

Stress to students that they should now be able to ask questions that will help them to get meaning from the information given by a table. (See Unit 2 page 104.)

Ask students:

- **How many nations make up the region of Southern and Eastern Asia?** (24)
- **How many different major languages are spoken in this region?** (28)
- **Which country in this region has the largest area?** (China)
- **Which country in this region has the largest population?** (China)
- **Which country in this region has both the smallest area and the smallest population?** (Maldives)
- *THINKING FURTHER:* **What key comparisons can you make between North Korea and South Korea?** (North Korea is larger in area. South Korea has a larger population. North Korea exports minerals; South Korea exports machinery and manufactured goods.)

LIFE TODAY • LIFE TODAY • LIFE TODAY • LIFE TODAY • LIFE TODAY • LIFE TODAY • LIFE TODAY

SOUTHERN AND EASTERN ASIA

AFGHANISTAN
Capital ★ Kabul
Major languages: Pashtu and Afghan Persian
Population: 16.9 million
Area: 251,773 sq mi; 647,500 sq km
Leading exports: natural gas, fruit, and carpets

INDIA
Capital ★ New Delhi
Major languages: Hindi and English
Population: 919.9 million
Area: 1,269,342 sq mi; 3,287,590 sq km
Leading exports: gems, clothing, and machinery

BANGLADESH
Capital ★ Dhaka
Major language: Bengali
Population: 125.1 million
Area: 55,599 sq mi; 144,000 sq km
Leading exports: textiles and jute

INDONESIA
Capital ★ Jakarta
Major languages: Bahasa Indonesia and Javanese
Population: 200.4 million
Area: 741,098 sq mi; 1,919,440 sq km
Leading exports: oil and natural gas

BHUTAN
Capital ★ Thimphu
Major language: Dzonkha
Population: 0.7 million
Area: 18,147 sq mi; 47,000 sq km
Leading export: cement

JAPAN
Capital ★ Tokyo
Major language: Japanese
Population: 125.1 million
Area: 145,883 sq mi; 377,835 sq km
Leading export: machinery

BRUNEI
Capital ★ Bandar Seri Begawan
Major language: Malay
Population: 0.3 million
Area: 2,228 sq mi; 5,770 sq km
Leading export: oil

KOREA, NORTH
Capital ★ P'yongyang
Major language: Korean
Population: 23.1 million
Area: 46,541 sq mi; 120,540 sq km
Leading export: minerals

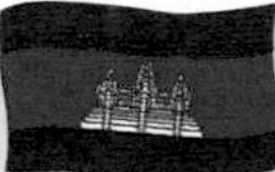

CAMBODIA
Capital ★ Phnom Penh
Major language: Khmer
Population: 10.3 million
Area: 69,900 sq mi; 181,040 sq km
Leading export: rubber

KOREA, SOUTH
Capital ★ Seoul
Major language: Korean
Population: 45.6 million
Area: 38,023 sq mi; 98,480 sq km
Leading exports: machinery and manufactured goods

CHINA
Capital ★ Beijing (Peking)
Major language: Chinese
Population: 1,190.4 million
Area: 3,705,396 sq mi; 9,596,960 sq km
Leading export: manufactured goods

LAOS
Capital ★ Vientiane
Major languages: Lao and French
Population: 4.7 million
Area: 91,429 sq mi; 236,800 sq km
Leading exports: food and timber

488

BACKGROUND INFORMATION

Jute Rope and coarse fabrics like burlap are made from the strong plant fiber called jute.

- Jute plants must be sown every year and grow from 5 to 10 feet (1.5 to 3.04 m) high.
- The fiber is separated from the stalk by a process called retting. Stalks are put under water until the fibers separate. Bark, roots, and dirt are picked out by hand. Stalks are squeezed to remove water and hung in the sun to dry.
- Jute is grown in Bangladesh, where the climate is ideal for its growth. Although people in other places have tried to grow this plant, cheap production in Bangladesh has slowed competition.

"Cracking" Oil One of Singapore's leading exports is petroleum products. This does not mean there are oil wells in Singapore, but rather that oil is imported and processed in modern refineries.

- A test-tube miracle took place when chemists and engineers learned how to "crack" oil by putting it under tremendous heat and pressure to break down heavier molecules of petroleum into lighter molecules of gasoline and other by-products.
- As a result of this complex distilling process, petroleum yields materials for making the following products: nylon, plastics, styrofoam, cosmetics, medicine, tires, ink, polyester, paint, kerosene, and asphalt.

LIFE TODAY • LIFE TODAY • LIFE TODAY • LIFE TODAY • LIFE TODAY • LIFE TODAY • LIFE TODAY

MALAYSIA
Capital ★ Kuala Lumpur
Major languages: Bahasa Malaysia, English, and Chinese
Population: 19.3 million
Area: 127,317 sq mi; 329,750 sq km
Leading exports: machinery and rubber

MALDIVES
Capital ★ Malé
Major language: Divehi
Population: 0.2 million
Area: 116 sq mi; 300 sq km
Leading exports: fish and clothing

MONGOLIA
Capital ★ Ulaanbaatar
Major language: Khalkha Mongolian
Population: 2.4 million
Area: 604,248 sq mi; 1,565,000 sq km
Leading exports: copper and livestock

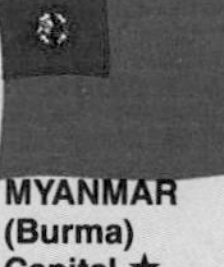

MYANMAR (Burma)
Capital ★ Yangon (Rangoon)
Major language: Burmese
Population: 44.3 million
Area: 261,217 sq mi; 676,550 sq km
Leading exports: rice and timber

NEPAL
Capital ★ Kathmandu
Major language: Nepali
Population: 21.0 million
Area: 54,363 sq mi; 140,800 sq km
Leading exports: food products and manufactured goods

PAKISTAN
Capital ★ Islamabad
Major languages: Urdu, Punjabi, and English
Population: 128.9 million
Area: 310,402 sq mi; 803,940 sq km
Leading exports: cotton products, clothing, and rice

PHILIPPINES
Capital ★ Manila
Major languages: Filipino, Tagalog, and English
Population: 69.8 million
Area: 115,830 sq mi; 300,000 sq km
Leading exports: food, copra, and minerals

SINGAPORE
Capital ★ Singapore
Major languages: Chinese, English, Malay, and Tamil
Population: 2.9 million
Area: 224 sq mi; 580 sq km
Leading exports: machinery and petroleum products

SRI LANKA (Ceylon)
Capital ★ Colombo
Major languages: Sinhala, Tamil, and English
Population: 18.1 million
Area: 25,332 sq mi; 65,610 sq km
Leading export: tea

TAIWAN (Formosa)
Capital ★ Taipei
Major language: Chinese
Population: 21.3 million
Area: 13,892 sq mi; 35,980 sq km
Leading exports: machinery, plastics, and textiles

THAILAND
Capital ★ Bangkok
Major language: Thai
Population: 59.9 million
Area: 198,456 sq mi; 514,000 sq km
Leading exports: food and machinery

VIETNAM
Capital ★ Hanoi
Major language: Vietnamese
Population: 73.1 million
Area: 127,243 sq mi; 329,560 sq km
Leading exports: oil and agricultural products

Relating Information in the Table to the *Atlas* Map Point out that each nation of Southern and Eastern Asia has its own character. Location is an important factor in the development of a country's characteristics. Have students choose a country listed on this page and then find it on the *Atlas* map on pages 638–639. On the same *Atlas* map have students find the approximate location of the state in which they live. Ask them to tell which lies farther north—the country they chose or the state they live in. Have students select a number of different countries and compare the latitude of each with that of their own state. Then have students write a short paragraph telling what they have learned about the location of their state compared with the locations of most countries of Southern and Eastern Asia.

Using a Table with Speed and Accuracy Divide the class into two teams to compete in reading this table with speed and accuracy. Prepare a series of questions that require students to read and analyze the tables on pages 488 and 489. (You may want to use the questions on page 488.) Have the teams answer the questions. Keep score to find out which team can use the table more accurately and quickly.

CURRICULUM CONNECTION

Math Discuss with the class the ways in which the number of people per square mile affects the human characteristics of a place. List responses on the chalkboard and have students copy the list.

Give students this formula for finding the number of people per square mile or square kilometer: number of square miles, or square kilometers, divided by the total number of people. Ask students to determine which country of this region is the most densely populated and which is the second most densely populated. (Singapore and Bangladesh) Tell students to use the map on pages 486–487 and the tables on pages 488 and 489 to write three sentences that compare these two countries.

BACKGROUND INFORMATION

Rubber The leading export of Cambodia and one of the leading exports of Malaysia is rubber.

- Four hundred years ago Spanish explorers in South America saw Indians playing some games with a ball made from latex, a gum from a tropical tree. The English scientist Joseph Priestley saw that latex rubbed out pencil marks and gave it the name "rubber."
- Rubber plantations were developed to control the quality of rubber production, but some people believe that one way to save the Amazon rain forest is to support the gathering of wild natural rubber instead of clearing the land for plantations.

CHAPTER 24
ORGANIZER

PHYSICAL GEOGRAPHY OF SOUTHERN AND EASTERN ASIA text pages 490–503

CHAPTER THEME

High mountain ranges affect the tropical-to-temperate-climate patterns of Southern and Eastern Asia; great river systems provide potential energy, but natural resources are distributed unevenly.

CHAPTER OBJECTIVES

CONTENT

- Describe how high mountains affect the region of Southern and Eastern Asia.
- Name the two largest island groups of Asia.
- Explain the importance of the Huang River to Chinese civilization.
- Locate the source and mouth of the Mekong River.
- Name the three great rivers of the Indian subcontinent.
- Explain why land and water are precious in Asia.
- Define *monsoon* and explain the importance of monsoons to Southern and Eastern Asia.
- Define *terraces* and explain how this method of farming increases food production.

SKILLS

Geography
- Use a map to locate different regions of elevation in Southern and Eastern Asia.
- Interpret a population density map of Southern and Eastern Asia.
- Use a climate map to locate different climate regions in Asia.
- Identify great-circle routes on a map.

Thinking
- Ask focused questions about the major landforms of Asia.
- Determine cause-and-effect relationships.

Reading and Writing
- Write a travel narrative about Asia.

CITIZENSHIP VALUES

- Appreciate how physical features shape the ways of life of a region.

TEACHER OPTIONS

READING STRATEGY: Using Prior Knowledge
Strategies to help students read and remember the main ideas of the lesson.
Lesson 1: p. 491 Lesson 2: p. 498

MEETING INDIVIDUAL NEEDS Activities for reteaching, extension, and enrichment.
Lesson 1: p. 495 Lesson 2: p. 501
Geography Skills: p. 497

GEO ADVENTURES ACTIVITIES PAD Daily activities to assess students' understanding of geography skills.

CURRICULUM CONNECTION Activities to help integrate other subject areas with Social Studies.
Art: p. 493

PUPIL EDITION ON CASSETTE Language support for students who have difficulty reading or who will benefit from listening to the Pupil Edition on Cassette as they read.

SECOND-LANGUAGE SUPPORT Activities and suggestions for second-language learners.
Lesson 1: p. 485-D

CHAPTER PLANNING GUIDE

LESSON	SUGGESTED PACING	THEMES	TEACHER SUPPORT MATERIALS: TEACHER'S RESOURCE CENTER
1 LANDFORMS pages 491–495	1 day	The region of Southern and Eastern Asia is characterized by high mountains, deserts, fertile river valleys, and lowlands.	Practice Book p. 133 **Technology:** *Adventures CD-ROM*
BUILDING GEOGRAPHY SKILLS Understanding Great-Circle Routes pages 496–497	1 day	Great-circle routes provide the shortest distance between any two points on earth.	Practice Book p. 134 Outline Map p. 2 Transparency Map 14 Desk Maps
2 CLIMATE AND RESOURCES pages 498–501	1 day	The region of Southern and Eastern Asia has a variety of climates and has limited resources that are unevenly distributed.	Practice Book p. 135 **Technology:** *Adventures CD-ROM*
CHAPTER SUMMARY AND REVIEW pages 502–503	1 day	Chapter content, skills, and vocabulary are reviewed and evaluated.	Practice Book p. 136 Transparency: Graphic Organizer Assessment Book, Chapter 24 Test

Technology CONNECTION

Lesson 1
ADVENTURES CD-ROM
Enrich Lesson 1 by having students find the major rivers on the maps of China and India in *Travel.*

Lesson 2
ADVENTURES CD-ROM
Enrich Lesson 2 by having students refer to the climographs for each country in *Investigate, Charts.*

CHAPTER 24
pages 490–503

USING THE CHAPTER OPENER

Discussing the Photograph Tell students that this is a photograph of a part of southern China near the city of Guilin, an area that is known for its spectacular scenery. Ask students if they find any unusual features in the photograph. (Students may note the many steep peaks that rise from the flat valley.) Tell students that this area is popular with tourists because of its striking beauty.

Ask students:

- **What signs of human activity do you see in the photograph?** (Students may note signs of farming, such as cultivated fields.)
- **How do we know that the area is a fertile one?** (All of the flat land seems to be cultivated, and even the steep hills are covered with vegetation.)
- *THINKING FURTHER:* **What conclusions can you draw from the fact that all of the available land is cultivated?** (Either there must be a large population that requires a lot of food, or there must not be very much flat land available for growing crops.)

Reading/Listening to the Primary Source Ask students to imagine a typical day in the life of a farmer who cultivates some of these fields. Then have a student read aloud the words to the folk song.

Ask students:

- **How can we tell that the fields in the picture, like the fields described by the farmer, are probably plowed by hand or with animals rather than by machines?** (The fields are small. If they were plowed by machines, the fields would probably be much larger.)

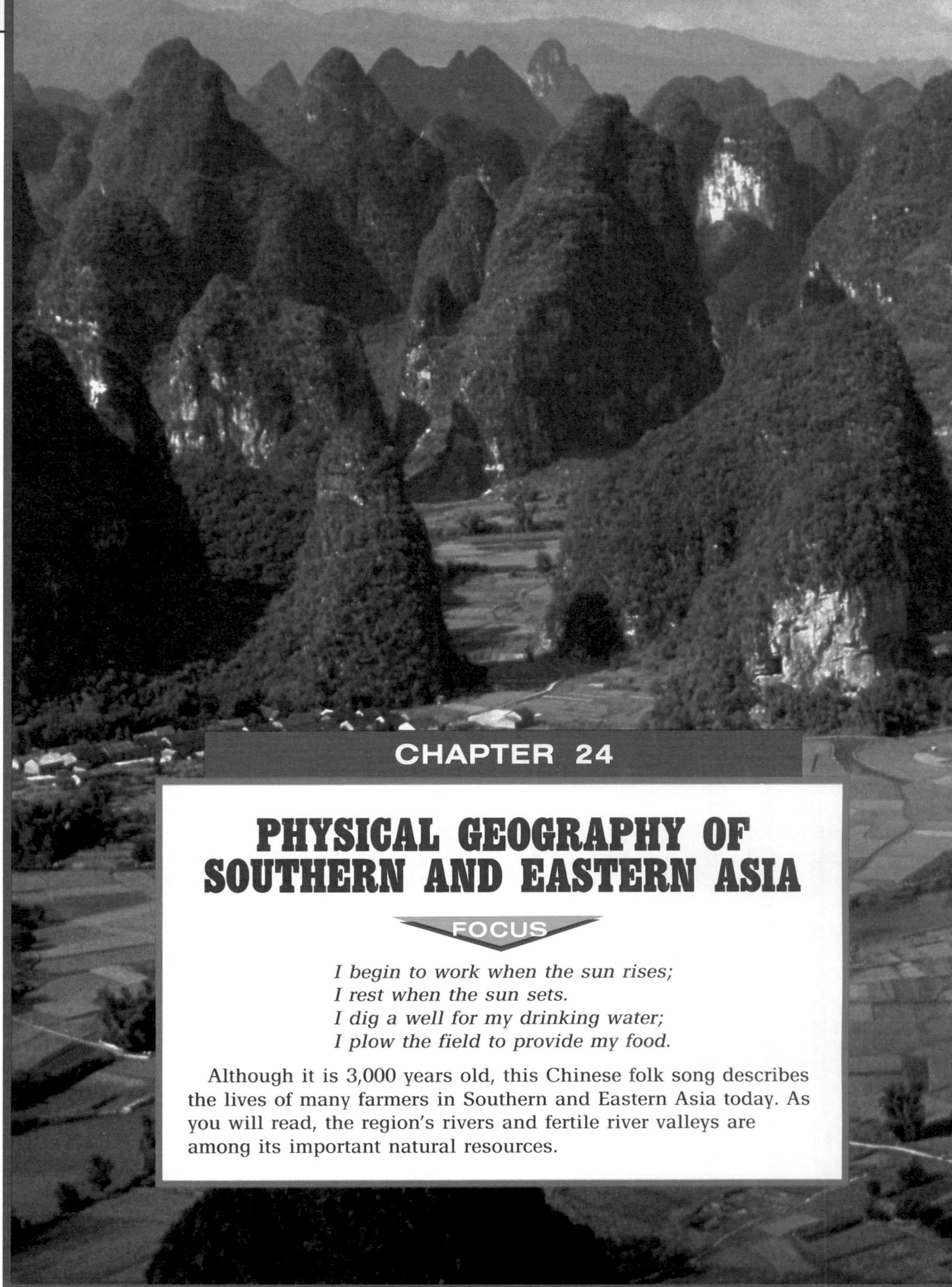

CHAPTER 24

PHYSICAL GEOGRAPHY OF SOUTHERN AND EASTERN ASIA

FOCUS

I begin to work when the sun rises;
I rest when the sun sets.
I dig a well for my drinking water;
I plow the field to provide my food.

Although it is 3,000 years old, this Chinese folk song describes the lives of many farmers in Southern and Eastern Asia today. As you will read, the region's rivers and fertile river valleys are among its important natural resources.

BACKGROUND INFORMATION

Characteristics of Southern China The area around Guilin, which is located about 225 miles (362 km) northwest of Guangzhou, has many characteristics common to southern China.

- *Physical Features:* mountainous, with most land 1,000–2,000 feet (305–610 m) in elevation, interspersed with higher peaks of 2,000–5,000 feet (610–1,525 m), with valleys, and with a western plateau of 5,000–10,000 feet (1,525–3,050 m).
- *Precipitation:* 60–80 inches (1,500–2,000 mm) along the western and central coasts; 40–60 inches (1,000–1,500 mm) along the eastern coast and in the interior.
- *Climate:* humid, subtropical; hot summer and cool winter.
- *Growing Season:* On average, 300–360 days each year are frost free.

LESSON 1

Landforms

READ TO LEARN

Key Vocabulary	Key Places	
subcontinent	Gobi	Chang River
loess	Mount Everest	Mekong River
alluvial soil	Himalayas	Ganges River
	North China Plain	Indus River
	Huang River	Brahmaputra River

Read Aloud

A hundred mountains
echoed in the jeweled eyes
of a dragonfly. . . .

This poem was written a little over 200 years ago by the famous Japanese poet, Issa. With a few words it describes mountains reflected again and again in the many shiny eyes of a dragonfly. In this chapter you will read about the many high mountains of Southern and Eastern Asia, as well as its other landforms.

Read for Purpose

1. WHAT YOU KNOW: Which parts of Asia have you already learned about in this book?
2. WHAT YOU WILL LEARN: How do the high mountains of Asia affect the rivers and lowlands of South, East, and Southeast Asia?

LAND OF CONTRASTS

The continent of Asia is vast. Larger than North America and South America combined, Asia makes up almost one third of the earth's land. However, in this unit you will read about only part of Asia—the region of Southern and Eastern Asia. About half of Asia's countries are located in this region.

Asia is the only continent that has a **subcontinent**, a large landmass that is smaller than a continent. Turn to the map on page 492 and look at the southern coast of Asia. You will find a large triangular peninsula there. This peninsula is called the subcontinent of India. The subcontinent includes the countries of India, Pakistan, Bangladesh, Bhutan, and Nepal.

Besides the subcontinent, Southern and Eastern Asia has many distinctive features, several of which contrast greatly with one another. One of the best ways to see these features would be to fly over the land. For example, if you were flying north over India, you would see hundreds of miles of ice-capped mountains at India's northern border. After the mountains end, you would fly over high plateaus and never spot a house or any other sign of human life. The **Gobi** and Takla Makan

WHAT YOU KNOW: Middle East, Northern Asia

491

LESSON 1
pages 491–495

Lesson Theme The region of Southern and Eastern Asia is characterized by high mountains, deserts, fertile river valleys, and lowlands.

Lesson Objectives

- Identify the main landforms of Southern and Eastern Asia.
- Explain how mountain ranges affect life in this region.
- Identify the important rivers of this region and describe how they affect the land.

PREPARE

Motivate Read the *Read Aloud* section to the class and ask students to imagine what the poet has described.

Set Purpose Use the *What You Know* question to review geographic information about other parts of Asia. Use the *What You Will Learn* question to discuss what effect these almost impassable mountains might have on a land and its people. Point out the *Atlas* map showing the physical features of this region so that students might refer to it throughout the lesson.

TEACH

Examining a Land of Contrasts Help students to envision the region's different landforms.

Ask students:

- **What is the subcontinent of Asia?** (a large, triangular peninsula jutting off Asia's southern coast)
- **What land feature separates the Indian subcontinent from the rest of Asia?** (the mountain chain that includes the Hindu Kush and the Himalayas)

READING STRATEGY AND VOCABULARY DEVELOPMENT

Using Prior Knowledge The purpose of this strategy is to remind students of the importance of recalling what they know about a topic before they begin to read and as they are reading. Help students to assess their background knowledge while they preview this lesson. Students have attained prior knowledge of landforms from reading previous chapters. Remind them of what they know when they read such headings as "Effect of the Mountains." Have them recall effects of mountains in other countries and on other continents. Have students continue previewing, focusing on using prior knowledge.

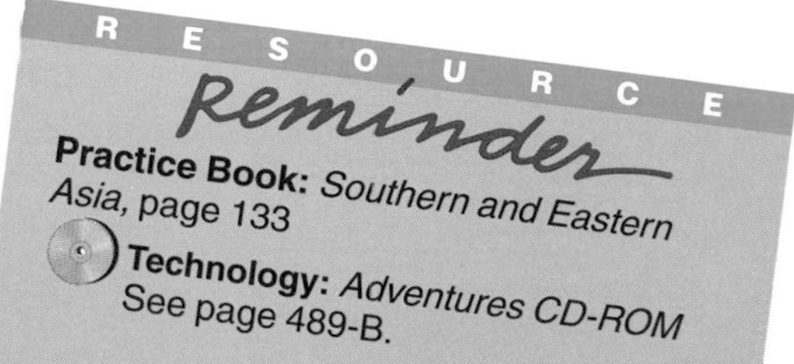

Looking at Asia's Features Continue describing the fictional airplane ride over Asia.

Ask students:

- **What would you see if you were flying over the eastern coast of Asia?** (lowland river valleys and islands)

EXTENDING MAP SKILLS

Use the map on this page to enrich and reinforce students' understanding of the geography of Southern and Eastern Asia. Help students to identify the countries in this region.

Ask students:

- **Which areas of Asia are at the lowest elevations?** (the valleys of the Indus, and Ganges, Irrawaddy, and Mekong rivers and the coastal lowlands)
- **In which countries are the highest mountain ranges found?** (Nepal, Bhutan, China, India)

Looking at Asia's Islands Help students to recognize the islands and archipelagos that form some of Asia's countries.

Ask students:

- **How were many of Asia's islands formed?** (by volcanic action)
- **What are two of the largest countries made up of island groups in Southern and Eastern Asia?** (Indonesia and the Philippines)
- *THINKING FURTHER:* **What problems might a government face when governing a country that is made up of thousands of islands?** (A government might have difficulty controlling outer areas.)

deserts, which are located here, are among the driest places on earth. The writer Ross Terrill calls the Gobi, "utterly barren, an unrelieved ginger [colored] waste, baking in the sun."

If you were then to turn and fly east toward the coast, you would see that the land changes greatly. Instead of an empty landscape, you would see densely populated lowland river valleys and thousands of crowded islands. For instance, the island of Taiwan has over 1,500 people per square mile (over 600 per sq km). The view of the islands is very dramatic. You might spot a bright light. This light could mark an active volcano forming a new mountain on an island.

THOUSANDS OF ISLANDS

Many of the islands off Asia's southeastern shore were formed by volcanoes. Some of these islands are very large. If you look at the map below, you can see that several Asian nations are also made up of archipelagoes, or groups of islands. The largest island groups are Indonesia, which has more than 13,500 islands, and the Philippines, which has more than 7,000 islands. Wide seas separate these densely populated archipelagoes.

THE WORLD'S HIGHEST MOUNTAINS

Although Southern and Eastern Asia has many distinctive features, its high mountain ranges are the major physical feature. These huge barriers separate countries and areas within the region.

MAP SKILL: In and near which Asian countries are the Himalayas located?

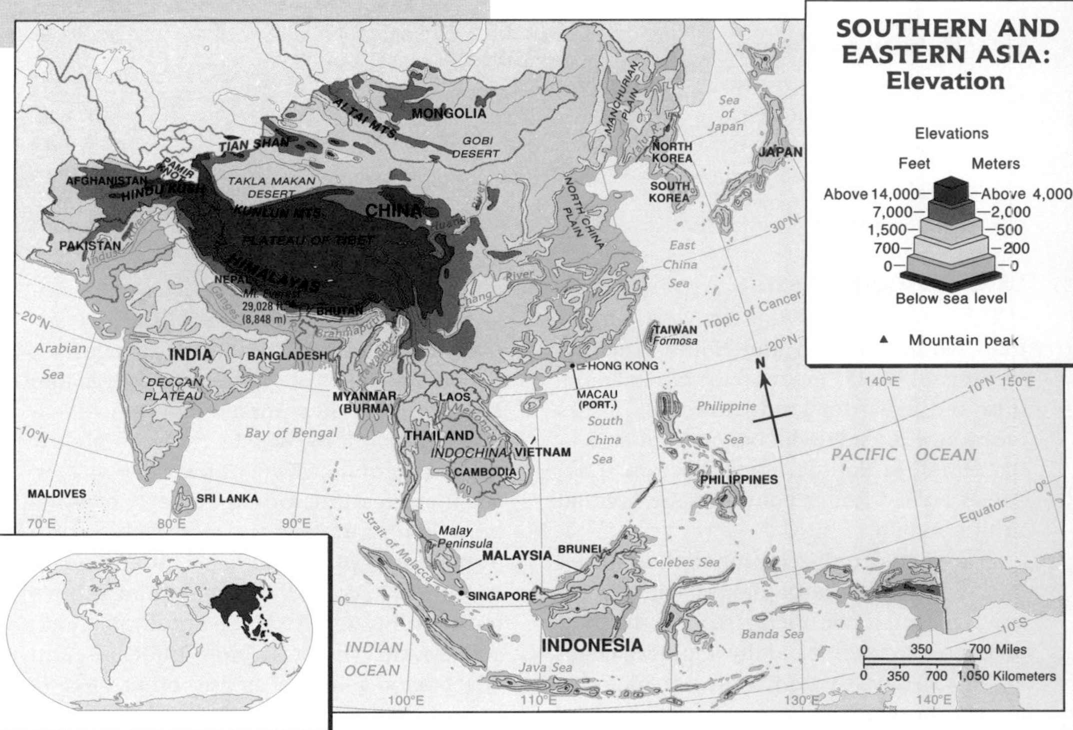

492 **MAP SKILL:** Nepal, Bhutan, India, and China

BACKGROUND INFORMATION

The Gobi Desert One of the world's largest deserts, the Gobi is about 500,000 square miles (1,295,000 sq km) in area. It covers the southeastern part of Mongolia and extends into northern China. The Gobi Desert lies on a high plateau; its surface consists mostly of rock and sand.

- The Gobi is inhabited by only a few groups of people who herd sheep and cattle on the grasslands that fringe the desert.
- Visitors can cross the desert either on one of the many caravan routes or by railroad. The railroad runs from China to Ulan Bator, the capital of Mongolia.
- In the 1920s a scientific expedition headed by an American, Roy Chapman Andrews, found important fossils in the Gobi, including fossilized dinosaur eggs, the first ever discovered.

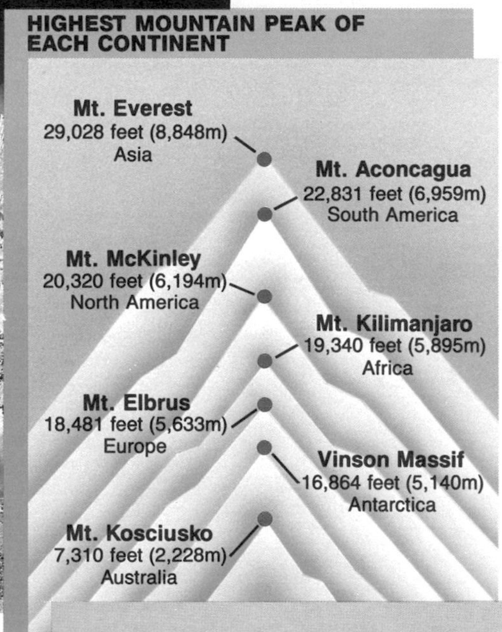

DIAGRAM SKILL: Mount Everest (*left*) is in the Himalayas. How much higher is Mount Everest than South America's highest peak?

These high mountains also affect climate and the fertility of the soil throughout Southern and Eastern Asia.

Nowhere on earth are there higher mountains than those in Asia, as you can see on the diagram on this page. These mountains have long been a challenge to climbers. It was not until 1953 that a New Zealand climber and his Nepalese guide chipped their way up cliffs of ice more than 5 miles (9 km) above sea level in Nepal. Edmund Hillary and Tenzing Norgay were the first to reach the peak of **Mount Everest**, the world's highest mountain at 29,028 feet (8,848 m). Hillary described the breathtaking view from the top of the mountain.

> *[W]herever we looked, icy peaks and somber gorges lay beneath us like a relief map. Perhaps the view was most spectacular to the east, for here the giants Makalu and Kanchenjunga dominated the horizon and gave some idea of the vast scale of the Himalayas. The . . . Himalayas stretched hundreds of miles in a tangled mass of peaks, glaciers, and valleys.*

Around Mount Everest are a dozen other peaks in the **Himalayas** that are almost as high. The Himalayas and nearby ranges form the heart of Asia. Long ago, natural forces deep within the earth thrust this land high above the rest of the continent. People call this high area "The Roof of the World." At the center of the "roof" are the Pamirs (pə mîrz'), a mountain range where several other mountain ranges meet to form a knot called the "Pamir Knot." Now look at the elevation map on page 492. Notice that China, Afghanistan, Pakistan, and Tajikistan meet in this area.

From the Pamirs other mountains reach outward like crooked spokes in a lopsided wheel. For example, the Altai and Tian Shan mountains stretch across northwest China. South of these mountains, the Kunlun Mountains split China into northern and southern China.

DIAGRAM SKILL: 6,197 feet (1889 m)

493

Discussing the World's Highest Mountains Have students use the map on the previous page to locate places named in this section.

Ask students:

- **What is the name and location of the highest mountain in the world?** (Mount Everest in the Himalayas)
- **What is "The Roof of the World"?** (the Himalayas and nearby peaks and ranges)
- **Where is the center of The Roof of the World, and what are its "spokes"?** (Pamir Knot is the center; the Altai, Tian Shan, and Kunlun mountains are the spokes.)
- **Which countries meet in the Pamir Knot area?** (Tajikistan, China, Afghanistan, Pakistan)

EXTENDING DIAGRAM SKILLS

Have students use the diagram to compare the heights of each continent's highest mountain peak.

Ask students:

- **Which is the highest mountain peak?** (Mount Everest)
- **On which continent is it located?** (Asia)
- **Which continent has the lowest mountain peak listed? What is it?** (Australia; Mount Kosciusko)

BACKGROUND INFORMATION

The Challenge of Mount Everest Before the conquest of Mount Everest, 11 major expeditions had attempted to reach its peak.

- Sir John Hunt, who led the successful British expedition of 1953, gave "at least half" the credit to an unsuccessful Swiss expedition that had preceded his. This team gave the British team advice and maps and left markers for them to follow. Improved oxygen equipment had also enabled the British to adjust better to the thin air of the high altitude. On May 29, 1953, Edmund Hillary and Tenzing Norgay reached the top and conquered the highest mountain in the world.

CURRICULUM CONNECTION

Art Have students work in groups to draw and paint a mural showing the contrasting landscapes of Southern and Eastern Asia. Suggest to them that they use the descriptions on pages 491–492 as guides.

EXTENDING MAP SKILLS

Have students study the population map on this page.

Ask students:

- **Which areas are the most populated?** (India, eastern and northeastern China)
- **What is the population density at the southern tip of India?** (250–500 people per square mile, or 100–200 people per sq km)

Discussing Effects of the Mountains Help students to understand how the mountains affect life in this region.

Ask students:

- **How do the mountains isolate many parts of Southern and Eastern Asia?** (They make travel extremely difficult, thereby reinforcing the separation of areas and countries in the region.)
- **Why is population sparse in the interior, high mountainous regions?** (The climate is very cold and dry; farming is difficult.)
- **Why did deserts form north of the mountains?** (The mountains block rain-bearing winds from the south.)
- **How do the winds in the high plateaus affect the North China Plain?** (As the winds cross Mongolia, they carry dry soil, called loess, to the plains of North China.)

Talking About River Valleys Help students use the map on page 492 to identify the major rivers of the region.

Ask students:

- **What are the great rivers in this region, and where are they located?** (Huang and Chang rivers in China; the Mekong River, through China and into Vietnam; the Ganges, Indus, and Brahmaputra rivers in India)
- **What are the sources of all these rivers?** (the Plateau of Tibet and mountain ranges east of the plateau)

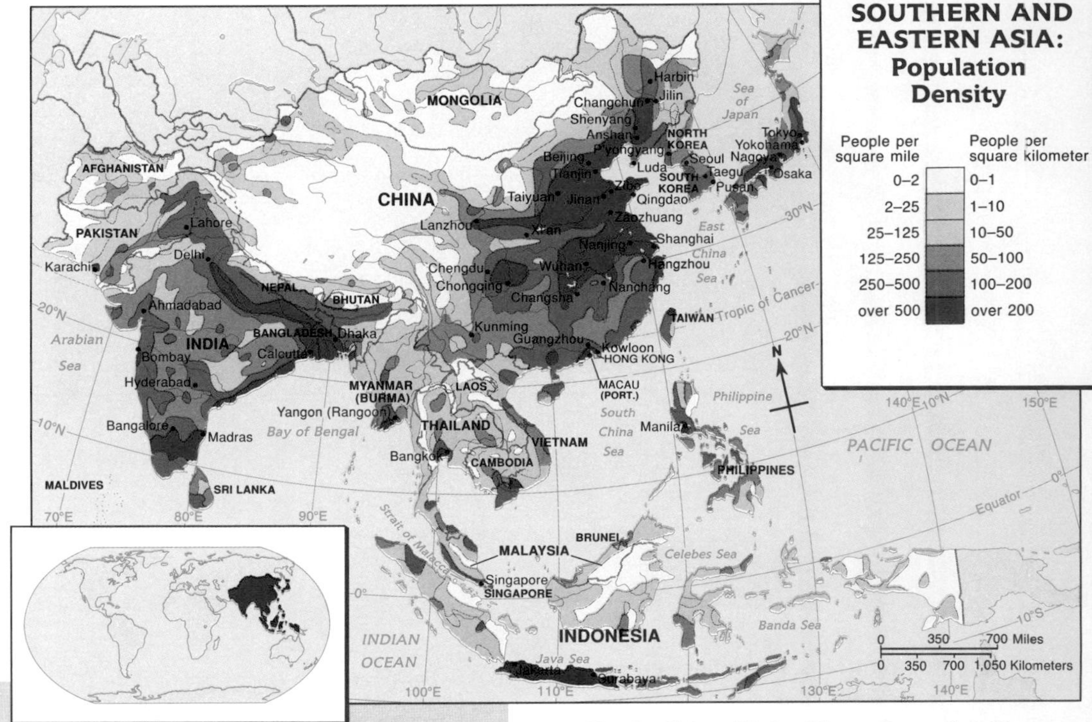

MAP SKILL: India has more than 900 million people. Which parts of India have the lowest population densities?

EFFECT OF THE MOUNTAINS

Mountains divide and isolate many parts of Southern and Eastern Asia. Look at the map on page 492 again. How many countries in this part of Asia have mountains on their borders? *

Mountains make travel or farming difficult in many countries of the region. Also, where the land is too high, people cannot live in comfort. The climate in these areas is too cold and dry.

Asia's mountains affect the land in one other way. In the high plateaus of Tibet, Mongolia, and western China, dry winds howl across a bleak, arid landscape. As the winds cross Mongolia, they lift bits of dry soil into the air and carry them to the North China Plain. There the soil drifts to the ground, creating a yellowish topsoil known as loess (les). This soil is very fertile and is refertilized each year.

The mountains also block rain-bearing winds blowing from the south. Therefore, north of the mountains and the Plateau of Tibet, Asia has several deserts. The Gobi and the Takla Makan, and other arid areas are located there.

RIVER VALLEYS

As the land slopes away from the highlands at the heart of Asia, it lowers to the sea in hills and plateaus before reaching the plains. Some of these lower areas are among the most fertile and crowded places on earth. They are the valleys of the great rivers that carry soil and water down from "The Roof of the World." Look at the population-density map above. Which areas have the highest population density? * *

494

*ten

MAP SKILL: northeastern, northwestern, and extreme western India

* *near rivers and the sea

BACKGROUND INFORMATION

People of the Deserts The Gobi Desert has cold winters and hot summers. Farming is difficult there. Because the desert has sparse vegetation, the Mongolian herders of the Gobi Desert move about in search of pasture for their animals.

- During the winter some desert dwellers still live in round, tentlike shelters made of fur or felt, called yurts. The yurts permit them to keep warm during the severest weather.
- At oases they trade horses, hides, and wool for such things as tea, tobacco, and utensils.
- The Mongolians are excellent horse trainers. They raise sheep and horses, and a few own oxen and camels.
- Their food consists mainly of milk, cheese, and mutton.

Each spring melting mountain ice renews the major rivers of the region. Two of China's rivers, the **Huang River**, (or Yellow River) and the **Chang River** (Yangtze) start in the mountains east of the Plateau of Tibet. As the rivers flow downhill toward the sea, they cut through the plains and often flood them.

Thousands of years ago China's first civilization began along the Huang River in the North China Plain. People learned to farm the rich **alluvial** (ə lü′ vē əl) **soil**, or soil deposited by the river as it flows. The Huang River is nicknamed "China's Sorrow" because it has often raged out of control, flooding crops and homes. Today dams along the river help to prevent floods and also provide power.

The Chang is China's longest river and the third longest in the world. The word *chang* means "long" in Chinese.

A third great river of the region also starts in the Plateau of Tibet. This river, the **Mekong River**, flows south through China into the area called Southeast Asia. You will read more about Southeast Asia in Chapter 28. The river deposits alluvial soil over a large valley, then winds south through tropical rain forests to enter the sea near Ho Chi Minh City, Vietnam.

Other great rivers also flow out of the Plateau of Tibet. Look at the Indian subcontinent on the map on page 492. In the north you will see three long rivers—the **Ganges** (gan′ jēz) **River**, **Indus River**, and **Brahmaputra River**. They flow across plateaus and plains and through fertile deltas to empty into the sea. These three rivers often flood, leaving behind some of the fertile soil they carry.

THE PATTERN OF THE LAND

As you can see, Southern and Eastern Asia has a pattern of high mountains and great river valleys. This pattern explains why some parts of the region are crowded and others have few or no people. The mountains also have isolated some of the region's peoples from one another. As a result, their cultures have developed with few outside influences. You will read about some of these cultures in the next few chapters.

Strangely shaped rocks and lush green fields line the Li River in southern China.

Check Your Reading

1. What is "The Roof of the World"? Which parts of Southern and Eastern Asia does it separate?
2. Why is the Huang River called "China's Sorrow"?
3. Where do many of the region's major rivers originate?
4. **THINKING SKILL:** List two questions you could ask to help you learn more about the major landforms of Asia.

THINKING SKILL: Asking Questions

Discussing River Valleys Continue the discussion of the great rivers of this region. Discuss how the rivers both help and hurt the people.

Applying the Lesson Have students list some major geographic features of Asia and, next to each, list a similar feature in the United States. For example, next to the Himalayas, they might list the Rockies or the Sierras.

3 CLOSE

Summarizing Students have learned about the geographic features that help and hinder human settlement in Southern and Eastern Asia. Have students choose a place in this region where they might like to live and give reasons for their choices.

Evaluating Use these questions to assess students' understanding.

- **What are two contrasting landforms of this region?** (high mountains and fertile river lowlands)
- **What are the major physical features of this region?** (high mountains, plateaus, river valleys, deserts)
- **How do the mountain ranges and rivers affect food production?** (Mountains are sources of rivers, which carry soil that fertilizes the lowlands; mountain winds carry soil that enriches the plains.)

Answers to Check Your Reading

1. Himalayas and nearby ranges; India and Nepal from China, parts of Afghanistan from Pakistan
2. Its many floods cause damage.
3. the Himalayas and high Tibetan plateaus
4. Possible questions include: Are there high areas? Are there fertile areas? What is the climate like?

Independent Practice
Practice Book: page 133

MEETING INDIVIDUAL NEEDS

Reteaching (easy) Have students make colorful posters inviting tourists to visit Southern and Eastern Asia. Tell students to describe the distinctive land and water features that a tourist might wish to see.

Extension (average) Ask students to imagine that they are traveling on one of the great rivers of Asia. Have them write a description of what they would see, beginning in the highest mountain range and ending when they reach the sea.

Enrichment (challenging) Have students research the many attempts to scale Mount Everest, the people involved, and the results of each attempt. Suggest to students that they use primary source material wherever possible. You may wish to have them make a large wall drawing of the mountain on which they show the various heights reached by the major expeditions.

SKILLS LESSON
pages 496–497

Lesson Theme Great-circle routes provide the shortest distance between any two points on earth.

Lesson Objective
- Locate great-circle routes.

PREPARE

Motivate You may wish to project Transparency Map 14 on the screen for students to study, if possible. Have them read the opening two paragraphs of the lesson on this page. Then have them find the mentioned great circles on a globe.

Set Purpose Tell the class that in this lesson they will learn how navigators find the shortest distance between two points.

TEACH

Exploring Great-Circle Routes
Have the class work with the string exercise described in the text.

Ask students:

- **What is a great-circle route?** (a route that follows a great circle between places)
- **Who benefits from using great-circle routes? How?** (navigators of ships and airplanes; By finding the shortest routes, they save time and fuel.)

BUILDING SKILLS
GEOGRAPHY SKILLS

Understanding Great-Circle Routes

Key Vocabulary
great circle
great-circle route

You have read that the equator divides the earth into equal halves, the Northern Hemisphere and the Southern Hemisphere. The equator is also called a **great circle**. A great circle is any circle that divides the earth into equal halves. Great circles are the largest circles that can be drawn along the earth.

Another great circle is formed by the 0° line of longitude and the 180° line of longitude. It divides the earth into the Eastern Hemisphere and the Western Hemisphere. Every line of longitude and the line of longitude opposite it make up a great circle. The diagram on this page shows how great circles divide the earth in half. Look at the diagram to identify the four hemispheres formed by the two great circles.

WESTERN HEMISPHERE | EASTERN HEMISPHERE
180°
NORTHERN HEMISPHERE
Equator 0°
SOUTHERN HEMISPHERE
0°
WESTERN HEMISPHERE | EASTERN HEMISPHERE

MAP A
TWO GREAT-CIRCLES
+ North Pole
— Great-Circle

Great-Circle Routes

You may recall having read that the easiest way to find true distances is by using a globe. The shortest, most direct route between any two places on the earth lies along a great circle. Such a route is called a **great-circle route**.

Ship and airplane navigators need to know the shortest routes from one place to another. You can understand why navigators of ships and planes use great-circle routes.

A simple exercise will help you to understand great circles and great-circle routes. All you need is a piece of string and a globe. Wrap the string tightly around the globe along the equator. Mark the distance on the string with a pen. Now wrap the string tightly around the globe in any other direction. If the distance is the same as that of the equator, you have found another great circle. Any route that is along a great circle is a great-circle route.

Suppose you want to find the great-circle route between Los Angeles and Tokyo. Hold the string against the globe so that is passes through the dots for both cities and pull it tight. The string now shows the great-circle route, or shortest distance, between Los Angeles and Tokyo.

496

BACKGROUND INFORMATION

More About Great-Circle Routes

- Technically, the great circles formed by the same lines of longitude are really great near-circles. Because the earth is slightly flattened at the poles, these circles are really somewhat ellipsoid.
- To follow a great-circle route ships must constantly change compass bearings, so special charts have been developed that show the compass directions as straight lines linked together. When followed, these lines approximate the great-circle route.
- Great circles are important in a number of fields beyond ship and air travel. Radio beacons follow great circles, and great-circle directions are important in seismology and in satellite and intercontinental ballistic missile tracking.

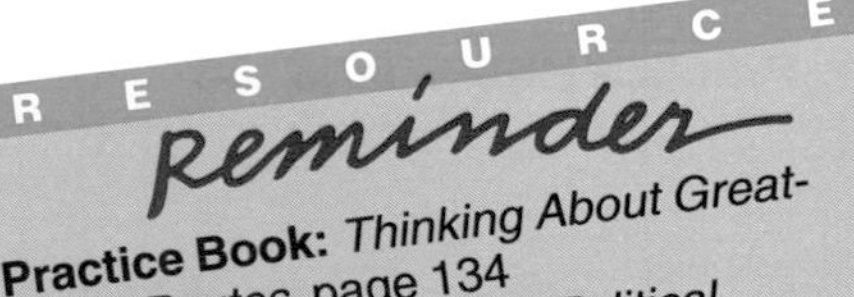

Practice Book: *Thinking About Great-Circle Routes*, page 134
Outline Map: *The World, Political*
Transparency Map: 14
Desk Map: *The World*

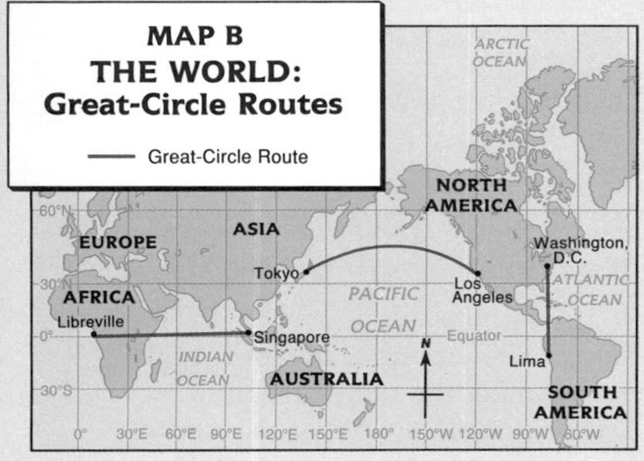

MAP B
THE WORLD:
Great-Circle Routes

—— Great-Circle Route

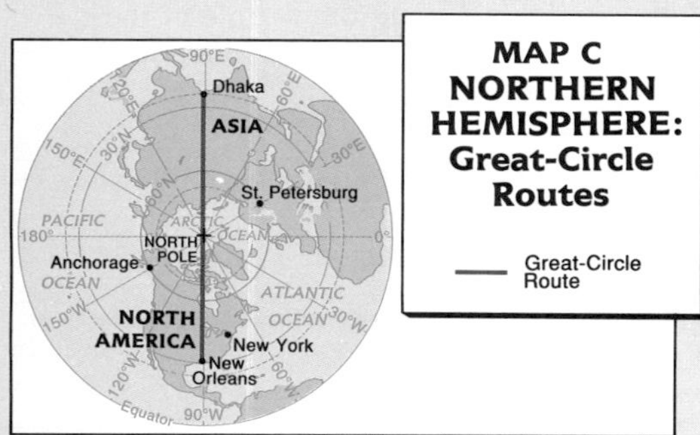

MAP C
NORTHERN HEMISPHERE:
Great-Circle Routes

—— Great-Circle Route

Using a Great-Circle Route Work

On maps great-circle routes may appear as either straight lines or curved lines, depending on the map projection. Find the great-circle route between Los Angeles and Tokyo on **Map B**. Is it a straight or curved line?✻

On the map a straight east-west line appears to be the shortest distance between Los Angeles and Tokyo. The great-circle route appears to be longer. However, the distance along the straight line is nearly 5,800 miles (9,332 km). The real distance along the great-circle route is about 5,430 miles (8,737 km).

On **Map B** all lines of latitude and longitude are shown as straight lines. As you know, every line of longitude is part of a great circle. The equator (0° latitude) is the only line of latitude that is a great circle. On this map, great-circle routes between places on the equator or on the same line of longitude appear as straight lines. Other great-circle routes appear as curved lines. For example, a navigator flying a plane from Lima to Washington, D.C., on the great-circle route would fly directly north throughout the entire trip. On the great-circle flight from Los Angeles to Tokyo, however, a plane would travel northwest at the beginning of the trip, west during the middle of the trip, and southwest at the end of the trip.

Navigators use special maps on which the great-circle routes appear as straight lines. **Map C** is such a special map for great-circle routes passing over the North Pole. To fly the great-circle route from Dhaka to New Orleans, a plane would first travel directly north to the North Pole, then directly south along 90°W to New Orleans.

Reviewing the Skill

1. What is a great circle? What is a great-circle route?
2. Which line of latitude is a great circle? Why is it that no other line of latitude is a great circle?
3. What line of longitude, together with 150°E, makes up a great circle?
4. On **Map B** would the great-circle route between Los Angeles and Washington, D.C., appear as a straight line or as a curved line?
5. In which direction would a plane flying the great-circle route from Singapore to Libreville travel at the beginning of the trip? During the middle of the trip?
6. Why are great-circle routes useful?

✻a curved line

Using a Great-Circle Route Work through the text and encourage students to trace the routes mentioned on Maps A and B on the maps themselves and also on a globe.

Ask students:

- **On Map B, why can some great-circle routes be shown as straight lines while others must be shown as curved?** (Any route that does not follow the equator or the same line of longitude must be shown curved on a flat surface.)
- **Judging from what is shown on Map C, in which direction would one fly from Anchorage to St. Petersburg?** (north and then south)

Applying the Lesson Have students imagine that they can take a trip to any faraway place they wish. Have them plot the great-circle route from their nearest international airport to their chosen spot and name places they will pass on the way.

3 CLOSE

Summarizing Students have learned that great-circle routes are the shortest distances between any two points on earth. Have them demonstrate on a globe why this is true.

Answers to Reviewing the Skill

1. any circle that divides the earth into equal halves; a route that follows this circle between places
2. the equator; No other line of latitude divides the earth into equal halves.
3. 30° W
4. curved line
5. west, west
6. because they are the shortest routes between points

Independent Practice
Practice Book: page 134

MEETING INDIVIDUAL NEEDS

Reteaching (easy) Have students choose two cities that are on different continents. On a globe, have students use a string to find the great-circle route between the two cities and list the places near which the route passes. Then have students exchange their cities with a partner, who will repeat the exercise.

Extension (average) Have students choose two cities as suggested in Reteaching, find the great-circle route between them on a globe, and then draw that route on an outline map of the world that can be found in the Teacher's Resource Center, or alternatively, have 12 groups of students use the Desk Maps of the world (also in the TRC).

Enrichment (challenging) Have students follow the suggestion in Reteaching. In addition, have them write a list of instructions telling a pilot the route to follow, the directions in which to fly, the longitudes and latitudes to cross, and the landmarks to look for on the way.

LESSON 2
pages 498–501

Lesson Theme Southern and Eastern Asia has a variety of climates and has limited resources that are unevenly distributed.

Lesson Objectives
- Describe the climates of the region.
- Identify the resources of the region.

PREPARE

Motivate Have students read the *Read Aloud* passage. Help students to realize why rain is so important to the people of Southern Asia.

Set Purpose Use the *What You Know* question to have students recall the results of heavy tropical rains in other parts of the world. Have students suggest possible answers to the *What You Will Learn* question.

TEACH

Discussing Tropical Climates

Ask students:

- **What are two places in Southern and Eastern Asia that have hot, rainy climates?** (the Philippines, Singapore)

Discussing Monsoons

Ask students:

- **What are monsoons?** (seasonal winds that bring rain in summer and cool weather in winter)
- **What do monsoons from the southwest bring?** (ocean moisture and heavy rain)
- **What negative results do monsoons from the southwest bring?** (heavy floods)

LESSON 2

Climate and Resources

READ TO LEARN

Key Vocabulary

monsoons terraces

Read Aloud

The clouds advance like . . . elephants, enormous and full of rain. They come forward as kings among tumultuous armies; their flags are lightning, the thunder is their drum. . . .

The Indian poet Kālidāsa (käl′ ē däs′ ə) wrote these words over 1,500 years ago to describe the first dramatic signs of the rainy season in India. People throughout Southern Asia still wait eagerly for the start of the life-giving rains. If the rains fail to appear, so do the crops. When that happens, hunger and famine follow quickly among the people of the crowded lands of this area.

Read for Purpose

1. WHAT YOU KNOW: In what other parts of the world do soaking rains pour down every day for long periods of time?
2. WHAT YOU WILL LEARN: Why are land and water precious in Asia?

TROPICAL CLIMATES

The climates of Southern and Eastern Asia are as varied as the landforms of the region. Northern China has long, cold winters and one growing season. The Philippines and Singapore, on the equator, are almost always hot and rainy. The warm temperatures and plentiful rain allow farmers in the tropical part of the region to grow three crops a year.

Not all of tropical Asia has the same climate. Parts of southern Asia, such as India, are hot and dry for much of the year. Other parts may be soaked with cooling rains during some seasons. These areas have three seasons a year. A winter rainy season is followed by a fiercely hot, dry season. Then a summer rainy season usually follows.

MONSOONS

The region's heavy rains are brought by strong seasonal winds called monsoons (mon sünz′). In winter, monsoons from the north bring cooler weather. As you can see from the climate map on page 499, summer monsoons blowing from the southwest carry ocean moisture. Summer monsoons dump heavy rains in a wide arc from India on the west to Southeast Asia and southeast China on the east. These rains can fall so steadily that they cause heavy flooding. For example, in Cherrapunji, a city in the northeastern part of India, as much as 41 inches (104 cm) of rain may fall in a single day.

The rains also can come suddenly. One visitor to India recalls a year when the rains were very late.

WHAT YOU KNOW: This question refers to information in Chapter 4, Lesson 2, and Chapter 20, Lesson 2; tropical areas of Central America, South America, and Africa.

READING STRATEGY AND VOCABULARY DEVELOPMENT

Using Prior Knowledge As students preview this lesson, have them concentrate on the questions at the beginning and end of the lesson. Have them use the *What You Know* question to recall other countries that have heavy rainfall. Then have them predict the answers to the *What You Will Learn* questions based on this previous knowledge. For instance, they may hypothesize that if rain is so eagerly awaited in India, there must be long stretches of time when it does not rain. Have students preview the questions at the end of the lesson, calling on their background knowledge to predict answers. After students have read the lesson, ask them to discuss any changes in their answers. Then have them discuss how their background knowledge influenced the first set of answers that they gave.

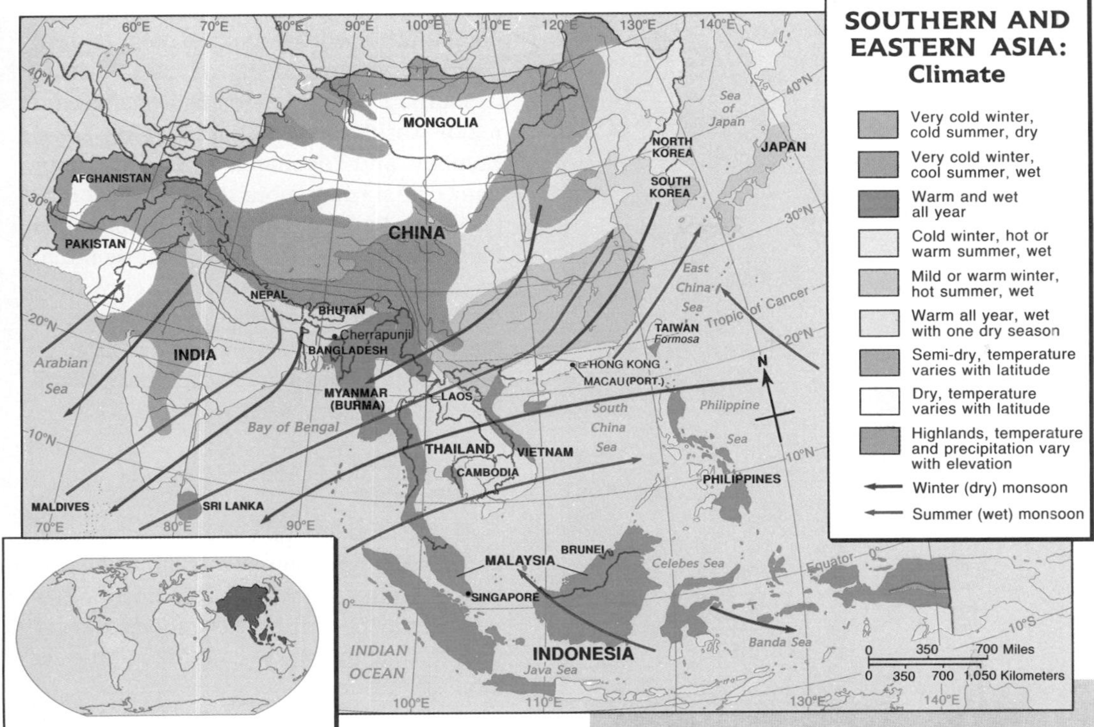

MAP SKILL: Few countries in Southern and Eastern Asia have areas with dry or semidry climates. Name the countries that do.

I remember on the first of July . . . passing over the causeway that spanned [a dried-up waterway]. How absurdly large [the causeway] looked in that sun-scorched land . . .!
At midday . . . there was a change . . .
a damp feeling of softness in the air. . . .
A strong wind blew toward us. . . .
There was the roar of close thunder, and suddenly the rain came down in bucket-loads. . . . When the fury of the storm had passed away, we went toward the railway station. We only got halfway; the causeway had disappeared under a raging torrent of dark muddy water.

HIGH-ELEVATION AND DESERT CLIMATES

To the north of the tropics, Southern and Eastern Asia has two main types of climate: high elevation and desert. Since much of the central part of Asia is at high elevations, the climate is far colder than you might expect at such latitudes. The Plateau of Tibet is nearly 2 miles (3.2 km) high and very cold. It also is very dry because the Himalayas and other mountains block most rain from this area. Mongolia, Tibet, and western China have mostly high-elevation climates.

In the steppes and deserts of Mongolia and western China, people once made their livings by moving about to graze their sheep, camels, cattle, or horses. Today one herder says, "We still raise herds of cattle, horses, and sheep, but now we have modern veterinary services. We still live in felt tents, but we have brick houses for the winter." Many people in this area also work in cities and towns in shops, factories, and in service industries.

MAP SKILL: China, Mongolia, India, Pakistan, and Afghanistan

499

Understanding Monsoons Continue discussing the effects of sudden, heavy rainfalls.

Ask students:

- **According to the description of the monsoon, what was the first sign of change?** (a damp feeling in the air)
- **Which words from the description foretell the coming of the monsoon?** ("A strong wind blew toward us.")
- *THINKING FURTHER:* **How do you think the people feel when the monsoon season approaches?** (They probably want it for the life-giving water it brings but also fear it for the damage it causes.)

EXTENDING MAP SKILLS

Have students study the climate map.

Ask students:

- **What type of climate does Hong Kong have?** (warm all year, wet with one dry season)
- **Which country does the map show as having only one climate? What climate?** (North Korea; cold winter, hot or warm summer, wet)
- **Which country has a predominantly semidry climate with temperatures that vary with latitude?** (Afghanistan)
- **From which direction do the Indian summer monsoons come?** (the southwest)

Discussing High-Elevation and Desert Climates

Ask students:

- **What are the two types of climates north of the tropics in Asia?** (high-elevation and desert)
- **Why is the climate of the central part of Asia cold?** (because of the high elevation)
- **What was once the main occupation of the Mongolian people?** (herding)

BUILDING CITIZENSHIP

Helping Others The people of the United States do not have to worry about damages caused by monsoon floods, but we have had other natural disasters. Encourage students to recall major hurricanes, floods, tornadoes, or earthquakes that have struck any part of the United States in the last few years. Ask them to think about the things that good citizens might do to help if a disaster struck their community. Ask students what kinds of emergency resources are available in their community and how people can prepare in advance for natural disasters. Have students find out how the federal government and state and local agencies help citizens during and after a disaster. Discuss with students the ways in which private organizations, such as the Red Cross, United Way, Salvation Army, Girl Scouts, and Boy Scouts, help the victims.

Discussing Temperate Climates Make sure students understand the meaning of the term *temperate climates.*

Ask students:

- **In which region of the United States do we have temperate climates?** (the eastern United States)
- **Which countries in Southern and Eastern Asia have temperate climates?** (Japan, North Korea, South Korea, China, Taiwan)

Discussing Water Resources Help students to understand the importance of the region's waterways and seaports.

Ask students:

- **How are Southern and Eastern Asia's waterways important to the economy of the region?** (They provide a means of transportation for people and goods, they are a source of income for fishers and boat workers.)
- **What are three important seaports in this region?** (Yokohama, Hong Kong, Bombay)

Discussing Agricultural and Mineral Resources Help students to recognize that, despite a shortage of arable land, most people in many countries of this region are farmers.

Ask students:

- **What does the term *arable land* mean?** (land suitable for farming)
- **Is there much arable land in this region?** (No; it is scarce.)
- **What is the main occupation of many of the people in this region?** (farming)
- **How, with so little arable land, do so many of Southeast Asia's people farm?** (They make the most of their farmland. For example, they carve terraces into hills and plant crops there.)
- **What are the main farm products of the region?** (rice, wheat, millet, maize, sweet potatoes, cotton)

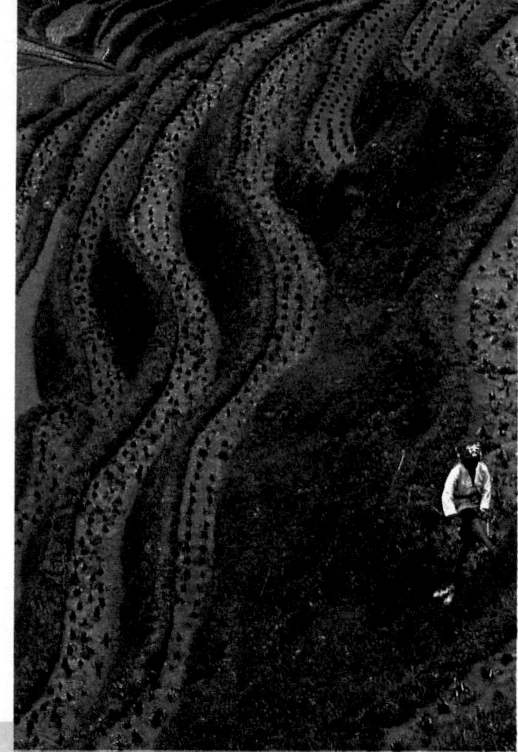

Much of southern China near Vietnam is hilly. Farmers grow rice and other crops in terraces built in the hillsides.

TEMPERATE CLIMATES

Find Japan, North Korea, South Korea, and China on the map on page 499. Most or all of these countries are north of the Tropic of Cancer, which is the southern border of the temperate zone. All four nations have mainly temperate climates. This means that these countries have four seasons similar to those of the eastern United States.

WATER RESOURCES

The region's great rivers are a major resource for its countries. China and India have thousands of miles of navigable rivers and canals. China's longest waterway, the Chang River, allows people to ship goods from far inland to the great eastern port city of Shanghai.

Southern and Eastern Asia has several major world ports, including Hong Kong, Bombay, and Yokohama. In fact the continent of Asia has more than 80,000 miles (129,000 km) of coastline. It also has many large seas. It is no wonder then that so many people make their living by fishing or working on boats or on docks. In many Asian countries people also farm, or raise fish and other marine animals, in the lakes, rivers, and seas.

AGRICULTURAL AND MINERAL RESOURCES

Arable land, or soil suitable for farming, is scarce in the region. Only about 11 percent of China's land and 15 percent of Japan's land is arable. Nevertheless, most people in many of the countries of the region are farmers.

Farmers have found ways to make the most of their scarce farmland. For centuries, the Chinese and Filipinos have carved big steps, or terraces, into hillsides. Then they plant crops, such as rice, on the flat steps.

Southeast Asia has the richest farmland on the continent. Almost everywhere farmers can be seen working ankle-deep in the waters of flooded rice fields. Rice, Asia's most important crop, thrives in such wet climates.

Crops like wheat grow well in the loess of the North China Plain. There farmers like Ki Quanping (kē' chwän ping') are "in the fields by 5:00 every morning. At midday I shelter from the heat, which gets up to 33°C (92°F.) in the shade, but then I'm back in the fields until dark." Among plentiful products are wheat, millet, maize, sweet potatoes, and cotton.

Despite its size, Southern and Eastern Asia lacks a generous share of the world's

500

FUNDAMENTAL THEMES OF GEOGRAPHY

Human-Environment Interaction In Southeast Asia the farmers have learned to utilize every bit of land they own. They cultivate their plots to the very edges, even far up the sides of mountains. Every inch of arable land must be used to grow food for the family.

- Each seed is planted, one by one, in a seed bed.
- When the seeds sprout, farmers pull them up and flood the entire field with water.
- Every member of the family, from the oldest to the youngest, works from dawn to dusk, planting the seedlings in the water-filled paddies.

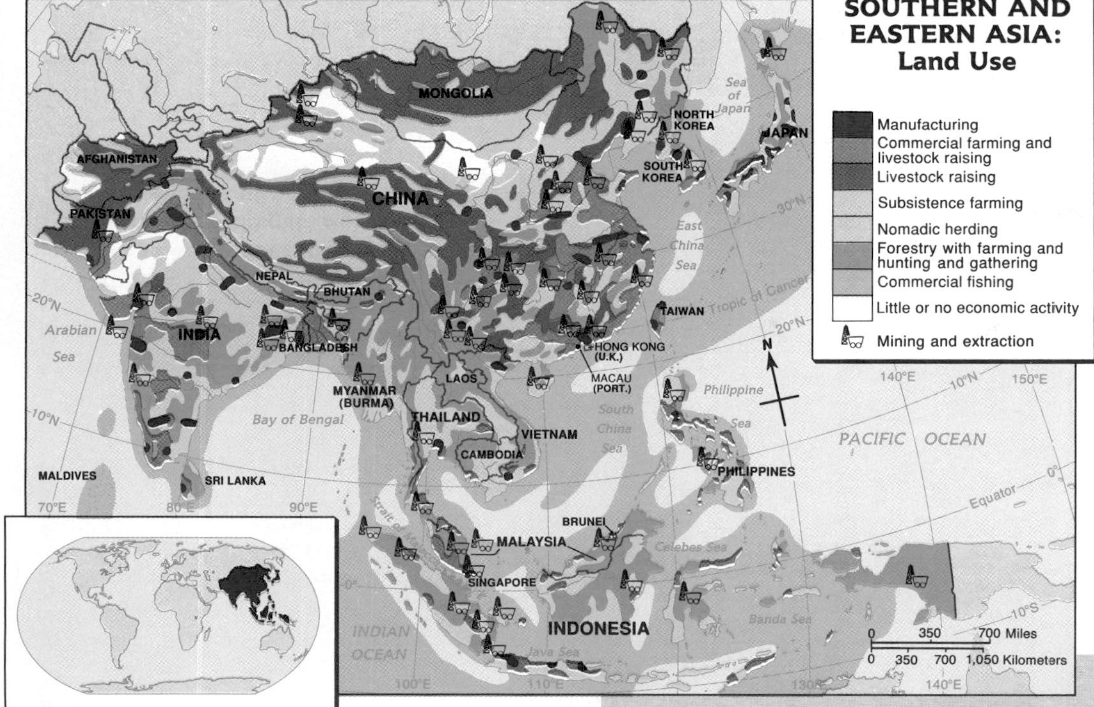

MAP SKILL: Which countries of the region have considerable commercial farming?

minerals. Look at the land-use map above. One of the areas with rich natural resources is Southeast Asia, which has large reserves of petroleum. India, China, and several other countries have iron and coal deposits. Which countries have considerable mining?*

MANY CLIMATES, LIMITED RESOURCES

Southern and Eastern Asia has a variety of climates. The entire tropical part of the region is affected by monsoons. Since rains carried by the monsoons are blocked by the high mountains between Southern and Eastern Asia, land north of the mountains is dry. Most of the people who live in this area herd animals for a living.

The region has little arable land, yet large numbers of people are farmers. Mineral and energy resources are distributed unevenly. Some rivers are used for transportation and some for irrigation. In the next four chapters you will read about how these countries use their resources.

Check Your Reading

1. What are the major climates of Southern and Eastern Asia?
2. How do monsoons help the farmers of Southern and Eastern Asia?
3. Which resources are scarce in Southern and Eastern Asia?
4. THINKING SKILL: What effects do the mountains at the heart of Southern and Eastern Asia have on the climate of the region?

MAP SKILL: Japan, China, India, the Philippines

*China, Indonesia, India, and Malaysia

THINKING SKILL: Cause and Effect

EXTENDING MAP SKILLS

Ask students:

- **Which countries do not engage in mining and extraction?** (Mongolia, Afghanistan, Nepal, Bhutan, Laos, Vietnam, Cambodia, Taiwan, Sri Lanka)
- **Which countries have areas of little or no economic activity?** (Mongolia, China, Afghanistan, India)

Applying the Lesson Ask students to select a part of Asia they would like to visit. Have them write a short paragraph telling what kind of weather they might find there.

3 CLOSE

Summarizing Students have read that this region has a variety of climates. Have students identify the different climates of this region.

Evaluating Use these questions to assess students' understanding.

- **What climates are found in the Philippines, the Plateau of Tibet, and South Korea?** (Philippines: tropical; Plateau of Tibet: dry and cold; South Korea: temperate)
- **How are water resources used in China and India?** (China and India use their rivers for navigation, shipping, and irrigation, and their coastal waters for fishing.)

Answers to Check Your Reading

1. tropical, dry and cold, desert, temperate
2. provide rain for their crops
3. minerals and arable land
4. They block the rain, creating desert areas.

Independent Practice
Practice Book: page 135

MEETING INDIVIDUAL NEEDS

Reteaching (easy) Ask students to list the different climates in Southern and Eastern Asia. Next to each climate have them list the names of the countries in this region where this climate can be found. Tell students to use the map on page 499 for help.

Extension (average) Have students find several descriptive passages about monsoons in books of fiction or in reference works, such as encyclopedias. Ask students to copy these passages and to note the source of each. Then have students read the passages aloud to the class.

Enrichment (challenging) Have students do research to find the five leading petroleum-producing countries of the world. Have them compare the production of petroleum in Southeast Asia with that of the world leaders.

CHAPTER 24 REVIEW
pages 502–503

USING THE CHAPTER SUMMARY AND REVIEW

Physical Geography These questions may be used for review.

- **What are the major mountains in the region?** (Himalayas, Pamirs, Altai, Tian Shan, Kunlun)
- **What types of climate does the region have?** (temperate, dry and semidry, highland, and tropical)
- **Why are rivers important to the region?** (for transportation and for seaports)

Ideas to Remember

- **What are three major landforms found in the region?** (mountains, deserts, archipelagoes)
- **Which part of the region is rich in natural resources?** (Southeast Asia)

Answers to Reviewing Vocabulary

1. subcontinent
2. terraces
3. alluvial soil
4. monsoons
5. loess

Answers to Reviewing Facts

1. Mount Everest; Himalayas
2. the place where several mountain ranges meet to form a knot; Tajikistan, China, Afghanistan, and Pakistan
3. The mountains block rain-bearing winds; the Gobi, the Takla Makan.

CHAPTER 24 • SUMMARY

SOUTHERN AND EASTERN ASIA: PHYSICAL GEOGRAPHY

LANDFORMS

- Mountains: Himalayas, Pamirs, Altai, Tian Shan, Kunlun
- Deserts: Gobi, Takla Makan, Tarim Basin
- Archipelagoes: Philippines, Indonesia

- Mount Everest is the world's highest mountain
- Major rivers: Huang, Chang, Mekong, Ganges, Indus, Brahmaputra

CLIMATE

- Temperate climates: northern India, northern and eastern East Asia
- Dry and semidry climates: central China, western South Asia

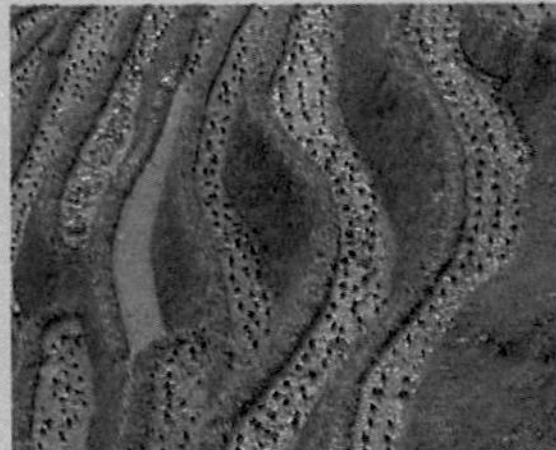

- Highland climates: southwestern China, northern South Asia
- Tropical climates: southern South Asia, Sri Lanka, Maldives, Southeast Asia

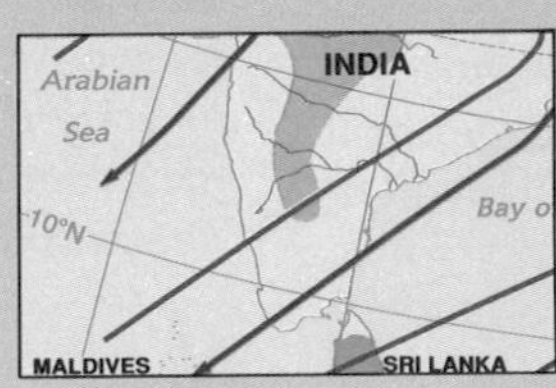

- Monsoons cause both rainy and dry seasons

NATURAL RESOURCES

- Rivers are important for transportation
- Major seaports: Hong Kong, Bombay, Yokohama
- Richest farmland is in Southeast Asia

- Few mineral resources, except in Southeast Asia, which has abundant petroleum

IDEAS TO REMEMBER

- Southern and Eastern Asia has many dramatic landforms, including the world's largest mountains, the driest deserts, and giant archipelagoes.
- The region has a variety of climates, with the most prosperous countries located in the temperate zone, but few areas except for Southeast Asia are rich in natural resources.

502

ENRICHMENT ACTIVITY

Creating a Songfest **Materials:** drums, tambourines, or other musical instruments

1. Remind the class of the song "America," which celebrates geographic features of the United States—for example, "purple mountains' majesty about the fruited plain." Tell them that they are going to make up their own songs that will celebrate geographic features of Southern and Eastern Asia.
2. Divide the class into groups and have each group compose their songs. Tell them to review the chapter for geographic features they might describe, and encourage them to pick simple, familiar melodies to set their lyrics to. For example, they might use "This Land Is Your Land" (whose lyrics and melody are given on page 71), or current pop or rap hits.
3. Have the groups perform their songs in a class songfest.

CHAPTER 24 ▪ REVIEW

REVIEWING VOCABULARY

alluvial soil subcontinent
loess terraces
monsoons

Number a sheet of paper from 1 to 5. Beside each number, write the word or term from the above list that best matches the definition.

1. The triangular landmass jutting from southern Asia into the Indian Ocean is the world's only example of this type of landform.
2. Consisting of "steps" carved into the hillside, people in eastern Asia have used this method of increasing scarce farmland for centuries.
3. This term refers to rich soils deposited by rivers.
4. These seasonal winds bring heavy rains in an arc from India and Southeast Asia to Hong Kong and southeast China.
5. This fertile soil in the North China Plain starts out as dust from Mongolia that is carried by winds.

REVIEWING FACTS

1. What is the name of the world's highest mountain? In which mountain range is this mountain found?
2. What is the "Pamir Knot"? Which four countries meet in this region?
3. What explains the presence of deserts in central Asia? What are the names of two of these deserts?
4. Along which river did China's first civilization arise? Name the three great rivers of the Indian subcontinent.
5. How do high elevations affect the climate in Mongolia and western China?
6. How has life changed for people in the steppes and deserts of Mongolia and western China?
7. In which climate zone are Asia's most prosperous countries found?
8. How do farmers in Asia create farms on steep hillsides?
9. Name three major world ports in Asia. In which countries are these ports found?
10. What is Asia's most important crop? In which region are Asia's richest farmlands found?

WRITING ABOUT MAIN IDEAS

1. **Writing a Journal Entry:** Imagine that you are Edmund Hillary. You have just reached the summit of the world's highest mountain. Write a journal entry recording your impressions.
2. **Writing a Travel Narrative:** Write a travel narrative of a journey down the Mekong River, from its source in the mountains of Tibet to its mouth in the South China Sea.
3. **Writing About Perspectives:** Imagine that you live in one of the Asian countries that experience monsoons. Write an eyewitness account describing the arrival of the first of the summer monsoons.

BUILDING SKILLS: UNDERSTANDING GREAT-CIRCLE ROUTES

1. What is a great circle? A great-circle route?
2. Why do ships and planes often follow great-circle routes?
3. Which is the only line of latitude that is a great circle? Explain.
4. What line of longitude, together with 0°, makes up a great circle?

4. Huang River; Ganges, Indus, and Brahmaputra rivers
5. The climate is cold and dry.
6. Many people who once made their living by moving about to graze animals now have modern veterinary services and live in brick houses during the winter. Some work in cities and towns in shops, in factories, and in service industries.
7. temperate zone
8. They carve big steps, or terraces, into hillsides.
9. Hong Kong, Bombay, Yokohama; Hong Kong, India, Japan
10. rice; Southeast Asia

Suggestions for Writing About Main Ideas

1. Students' journal entries should show excitement and awe.
2. Students' travelogues should describe the climate and geography of the surrounding area.
3. Each student should write his or her account as an eyewitness.

Answers to Building Skills: Understanding Great-Circle Routes

1. any circle that divides the earth into equal halves; the shortest, most direct route between any two places on the earth
2. They are often the shortest routes.
3. the equator; It is the only line of latitude that divides the earth in half.
4. 180°

Chapter Review and Test
Practice Book: *Vocabulary Review,* page 136
Transparency: *Graphic Organizer*
Assessment Book: *Chapter 24 Test*

MAKING CONNECTIONS

Organizing Information Display the Semantic Web Graphic Organizer Transparency, labeling the underlined headings. Have students brainstorm other topics to add to the map (bodies of water, land use, size). Then have students review the chapter to fill in information relating to each topic, moving from the general to the specific. *Ask:* What physical characteristics make Southern and Eastern Asia a unique region?

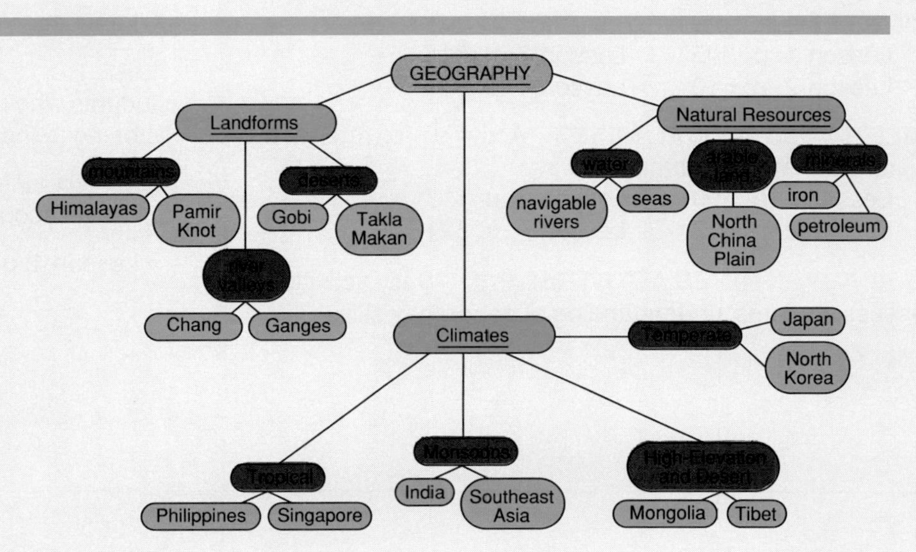

CHAPTER 25
ORGANIZER

NATIONS OF SOUTH ASIA text pages 504–523

CHAPTER THEME

The most densely populated places on earth are the eight nonaligned nations of South Asia, where British colonial influence originally instilled democratic ideals and industrialization is on the rise.

CHAPTER OBJECTIVES

CONTENT

- Describe the ways that religion shapes the lives of the people of South Asia.
- Define *caste* and describe the main features of the caste system in India.
- Explain how high population density affects South Asia's ability to feed itself.
- Describe the impact of the Green Revolution on agriculture in South Asia.
- Explain the importance of cottage industries to the economies of South Asia.
- Explain why many people are leaving the countryside for large cities in South Asia.
- Describe the types of governments that are found in South Asia.
- Describe the political impact of British rule on the countries of South Asia.
- Describe the effects of the independence movement led by Gandhi on South Asia.
- Explain the origins and consequences of the religious conflict in India and Sri Lanka.
- Describe ways in which traditional and modern ideas have influenced the arts and recreation in South Asia.

SKILLS

Geography
- Interpret a political map of South Asia.

Thinking
- Ask focused questions about the impact of religion on South Asia.
- Compare and contrast work in a cottage industry with work in a small factory.
- Determine point of view.

Reading and Writing
- Write a report about India.

CITIZENSHIP VALUES

- Appreciate both the positive and negative impact of religion on a culture.
- Appreciate the unique quality of the independence movement led by Mohandas Gandhi.

TEACHER OPTIONS

READING STRATEGY: Previewing and Predicting Strategies to help students read and remember the main ideas of the lesson.

Lesson 1: p. 505 Lesson 3: p. 514
Lesson 2: p. 510 Lesson 4: p. 519

MEETING INDIVIDUAL NEEDS Activities for reteaching, extension, and enrichment.

Lesson 1: p. 509 Lesson 3: p. 517
Lesson 2: p. 513 Lesson 4: p. 521

GEO ADVENTURES ACTIVITIES PAD Daily activities to assess students' understanding of geography skills.

CURRICULUM CONNECTION Activities to help integrate other subject areas with Social Studies.

Language Arts: p. 515

PUPIL EDITION ON CASSETTE Language support for students who have difficulty reading or who will benefit from listening to the Pupil Edition on Cassette as they read.

SECOND-LANGUAGE SUPPORT Activities and suggestions for second-language learners.

Lesson 4: p. 485-D

CHAPTER PLANNING GUIDE

LESSON	SUGGESTED PACING	THEMES	TEACHER SUPPORT MATERIALS: TEACHER'S RESOURCE CENTER
1 THE PEOPLE pages 505–509	1 day	The lives of the people of South Asia are greatly affected by their religious and family traditions.	Practice Book p. 137 ■ Anthology pp. 150–151 **Technology:** *Videodisc/Video Tape 2*
2 THE ECONOMY pages 510–513	1 day	The nations of South Asia are rich in natural resources, but they must deal with famine and malnutrition.	Practice Book p. 137
3 THE GOVERNMENT pages 514–517	1 day	Today the governments of South Asia include representative democracies, constitutional monarchies, and military dictatorships.	Practice Book p. 138 ■ Anthology pp. 165–166 **Technology:** *Adventures CD-ROM*
BUILDING THINKING SKILLS Determining Point of View: Review page 518	1 day	Point of view is the way a person feels about or sees something.	Practice Book p. 139
4 ARTS AND RECREATION pages 519–521	1 day	The arts and recreation of South Asia are a blend of the traditional and the modern.	Practice Book p. 140 ■ Anthology pp. 155–157, 164 **Technology:** *Adventures CD-ROM*
CHAPTER SUMMARY AND REVIEW pages 522–523	1 day	Chapter content, skills, and vocabulary are reviewed and evaluated.	Practice Book p. 141 Transparency: Graphic Organizer Assessment Book, Chapter 25 Test

Technology CONNECTION

Lesson 1
VIDEODISC/VIDEO TAPE 2
Enrich Lesson 1 with Video Lesson 7, *India Today.*

Search Frame 33733 Side A

Lesson 3
ADVENTURES CD-ROM
Enrich Lesson 3 by having students find the movie on Mahatma Gandhi in *Investigate.*

Lesson 4
ADVENTURES CD-ROM
Enrich Lesson 4 by having students *Investigate* the Taj Mahal in the Media section.

CHAPTER 25
pages 504–523

USING THE CHAPTER OPENER

Discussing the Photograph Have students study the photograph and read the chapter title. Help them to identify the nationality of the women.

Ask students:

- **What kind of clothing are these women wearing?** (saris, the traditional dress of Indian women)
- **When do you think that this photograph was made?** (After a discussion, lead students to conclude that the photograph is a recent one and that many women in modern-day India still wear the traditional sari.)
- *THINKING FURTHER:* **Do you think that wearing traditional dress prevents women from having a responsible role in society?** (After students discuss the question, tell them that Indira Gandhi, who was the prime minister of India, always wore the traditional sari.)

Reading/Listening to the Primary Source Read the quotation to the class. Then ask a student to read aloud the passage that follows.

Ask students:

- **What is an important tradition in India?** (hospitality)
- **Why do you suppose that Amita Vohtra Sarin says that "life is seldom lonely in India"?** (Possible answers include: Hospitality is an important Indian tradition.)

Ask students what they know about India and about other nations of South Asia from books, magazines, motion pictures, and television programs. Have them share what they know. Tell students that they can compare this knowledge with the information that they will gather from this chapter.

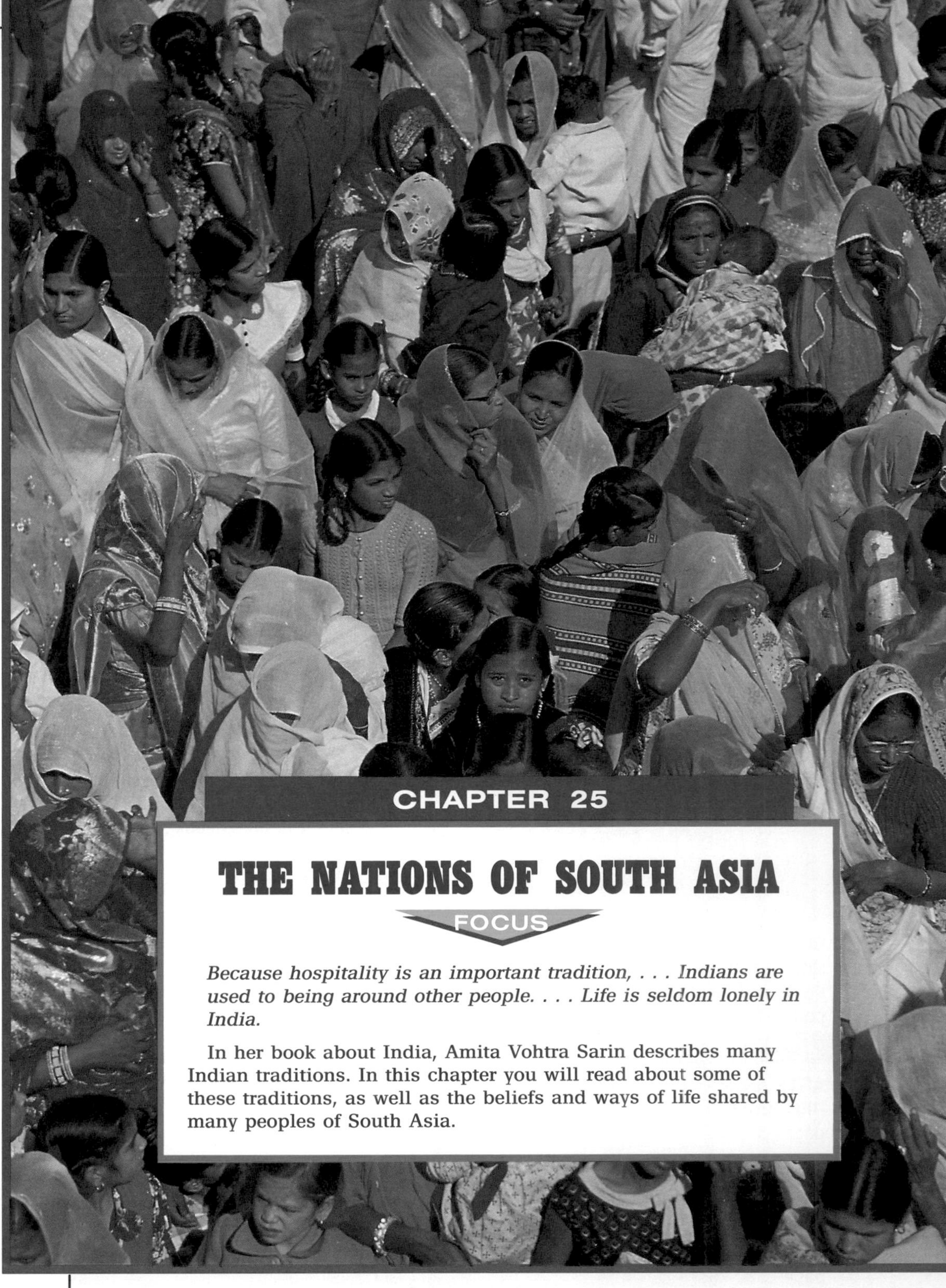

CHAPTER 25

THE NATIONS OF SOUTH ASIA

FOCUS

Because hospitality is an important tradition, . . . Indians are used to being around other people. . . . Life is seldom lonely in India.

In her book about India, Amita Vohtra Sarin describes many Indian traditions. In this chapter you will read about some of these traditions, as well as the beliefs and ways of life shared by many peoples of South Asia.

BACKGROUND INFORMATION

About Traditional Dress in India

- A sari is made by wrapping a long piece of silk or cotton cloth around the body to form a long skirt and by bringing one end up in front and over the shoulder to form the top.
- Most women in the north of India veil themselves, but in the south the practice is confined to Muslim women.
- Among high Hindu castes, or classes, women are subordinate to men. A woman is expected to be an obedient wife, a dutiful daughter-in-law, and a devoted mother. A dowry, or money or property paid by a woman's family on the occasion of her marriage, is common in India. A high-caste Hindu woman may not divorce her husband (although he may divorce her), and a widow may not remarry.

LESSON 1

The People

READ TO LEARN

Key Vocabulary
Hinduism
caste
Brahmans
Sikhism

Key People
Mohandas Gandhi
Benazir Bhutto

Key Places
South Asia
Bangladesh
India
Pakistan
Sri Lanka

Read Aloud

Each time we visited a different part of India it seemed we were visiting a new land. The language, the food, the clothes were all so different.

The speaker, a 17-year-old Indian student named Sanjay Kaul, is describing field trips he had taken in his own country with his school. As you will read, South Asia is an area in which many of its peoples have remained deeply attached to their traditions, especially those of family and religion.

Read for Purpose

1. WHAT YOU KNOW: Which regions have you studied that have religious traditions that are over a thousand years old?
2. WHAT YOU WILL LEARN: In what ways does religion shape the lives of the people of South Asia?

AN ANCIENT PATCHWORK OF CULTURES

South Asia is formed by the subcontinent of India and its neighbors. The area includes eight countries: Afghanistan, Bangladesh, Bhutan, India, Maldives, Nepal, Pakistan, and Sri Lanka (also known by the island's name of Ceylon).

The subcontinent is the home of some of the world's earliest civilizations. Buried beneath the plains of the Indus River valley are the ruins of cities more than 4,000 years old. The people who formed these civilizations came from many places. Some had developed unique cultures in the area. Others were invaders who struggled into the warm subcontinent through the icy mountain passes on South Asia's northwest border. Each group had its own religious beliefs, customs, and languages. They made South Asia a patchwork of many cultures.

From the 1700s until World War II, the British either ruled or influenced the countries of South Asia. You will read more about the British influence in Lesson 3.

HINDUISM

The Aryans (âr′ ē ənz), one of the first groups to invade the subcontinent, came through the mountain passes about 3,500 years ago. The legends and customs they

WHAT YOU KNOW: This refers to information in Chapter 5, Lesson 1, Chapters 9 to 12, 15, 18, and 19; Latin America, Western Europe, Eastern Europe and Northern Asia, Middle East and North Africa.

LESSON 1
pages 505–509

Lesson Theme The lives of the people of South Asia are greatly affected by their religious and family traditions.

Lesson Objectives
- Identify the countries of South Asia.
- Identify the major religions of South Asia.
- Explain how tradition and religion influence Indian life.

PREPARE

Motivate Have a student read the *Read Aloud* section to the class. Ask students if they think Sanjay Kaul's impressions would be the same if he traveled through different parts of the United States.

Set Purpose Review the answers to the *What You Know* question. Then have students read the *What You Will Learn* question. Tell students that in this lesson they will learn about another area of the world where religion plays a dominant role in people's lives.

TEACH

Discussing Ancient Cultures Display the political *Atlas* Map of Southern and Eastern Asia. Have students identify the countries of South Asia. Help students to understand that people of many cultures formed South Asia.

Ask students:

- **What is meant by "a patchwork of cultures"?** (Each group that came to this area brought its own culture, beliefs, and so on.)

Describing Hinduism Discuss who the Aryans were.

READING STRATEGY AND VOCABULARY DEVELOPMENT

Previewing and Predicting Remind students of the importance of previewing and predicting as helpful strategies to improve reading comprehension. Have students scan the lesson title and the vocabulary. Remind them to call upon what they know, both about the meaning of the *Key Vocabulary* terms and their knowledge of this textbook's organization, to predict what this lesson will be about. Have students use their knowledge of other countries with strong religious traditions to predict answers to the *What You Will Learn* question. Then have them use the headings to preview the rest of the lesson. Remind students to think about what they already know as they scan the *Check Your Reading* questions. After reading the lesson, have students evaluate their predictions.

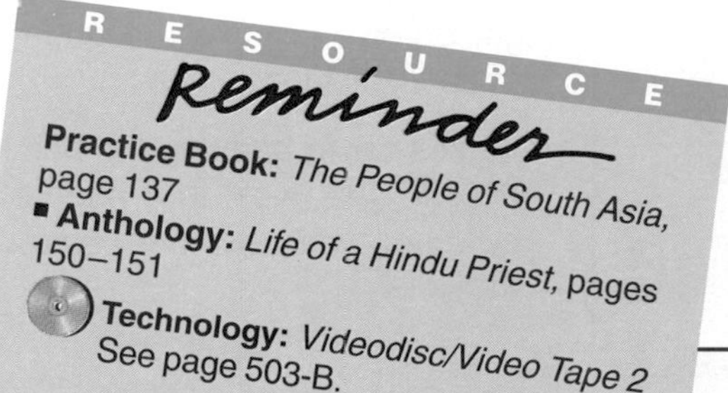

RESOURCE *Reminder*

Practice Book: *The People of South Asia,* page 137

Anthology: *Life of a Hindu Priest,* pages 150–151

Technology: *Videodisc/Video Tape 2* See page 503-B.

Discussing Hinduism Continue discussing the Hindu religion.

Ask students:

- **What is the connection between the Aryans and Hinduism?** (Hinduism developed out of the legends and customs of the Aryans.)
- **What does Hinduism teach?** (There is one universal spirit, which appears in the form of many gods; all life is holy; all living things have souls.)
- **Where do Hindus worship?** (At family shrines, at home, in temples, or at the Ganges.)
- **Why don't Hindus eat meat from cows?** (because they have a special respect for the lives of cows)

EXTENDING MAP SKILLS

Have students study the political map of South Asia.

Ask students:

- **What is the capital of India?** (New Delhi)
- **Which countries border Nepal?** (China and India)
- **Which are the two southernmost nations of South Asia?** (Sri Lanka, Maldives)
- **Which South Asian countries border the Bay of Bengal?** (India, Bangladesh, Sri Lanka)

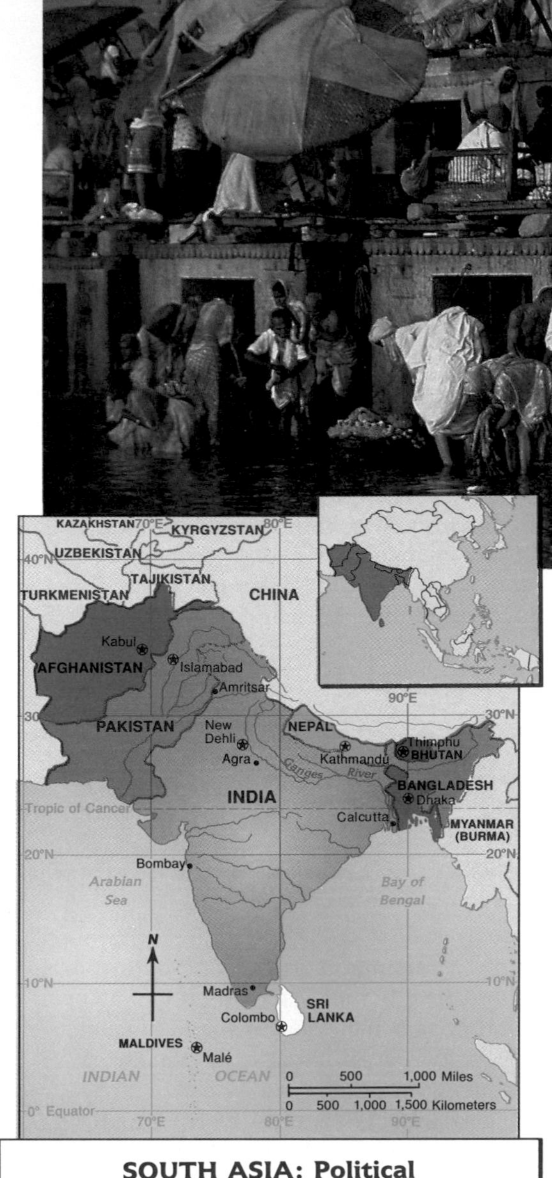

MAP SKILL: The Ganges River (*above*), which is holy to the Hindus, is India's longest river, at 1,600 miles (2,560 km). Which cities are near the Ganges?

brought later grew into the religion of **Hinduism** (hin′ dü iz əm). Today Hinduism is the major religion of South Asia. The nations of South Asia are shown on the map on this page. In India Hindus make up 80 percent of the population.

Hinduism teaches that there is one great spirit in the universe, but this spirit can appear in the form of different gods. These gods can be worshiped in different ways—in temples, at family shrines at home, or at the Ganges River. The Ganges is holy to all Hindus, and people come from all over South Asia to bathe in its waters.

To Hindus all life is holy and all living things have souls. Hindus have a special respect for cows. No Hindu will eat meat from a cow, and Hindus won't harm cows that wander through streets or villages.

THE CASTE SYSTEM

One important way in which Hinduism affects the lives of South Asians is to divide them into **castes**. Castes are social groups that are ranked from highest to lowest. Hindus believe that a person is

MAP SKILL: Calcutta, Agra, New Delhi, Dhaka

FUNDAMENTAL THEMES OF GEOGRAPHY

Human-Environment Interactions Many places are sacred to the Hindus. The rich and the very poor make pilgrimages to sacred places. Sometimes whole villages go on a pilgrimage together. The Ganges River is holy to all Hindus.

- Hindus try to bathe in the holy Ganges River at least once in their lives; they hope that this may help them be reborn into a better caste or position in life after they die.
- On the shore of the Ganges is the city of Varanasi (Benares). Hundreds of temples line the river, and funeral pyres burn day and night. Because of their belief in reincarnation, or rebirth, Hindus do not fear death but want to finish their life as free from sin as possible. Thus they want to be cremated in Varanasi and have their ashes scattered over the Ganges.
- If a person cannot be cremated in Varanasi, relatives may carry the ashes of the deceased from distant parts of India or other parts of the world in order to scatter the ashes in the sacred Ganges.

born again after death. Depending on the way the person lived, rebirth may return the person into a higher or lower caste or as an animal.

In ancient India people belonged to one of four main castes. These were the **Brahmans**, or priests; the warriors; the merchants and farmers; and the servants. Over time these castes were divided into more than 3,000 castes.

Below the caste system was a group called the "untouchables." What does the word tell you about the way untouchables were treated? For centuries untouchables were forced to live apart, avoided by other Hindus. They were not even allowed to draw water from a village well. The untouchables did the jobs that no caste members would do, such as cleaning streets and collecting garbage.

Caste affects what people eat and where they live. When caste rules are strictly followed, people marry only someone from the same caste. Rarely do people leave the caste into which they were born.

Some Hindus have tried to change the caste system. **Mohandas Gandhi**, the leader of India's independence movement, tried to improve the lives of the untouchables. Gandhi called these people *harijans* (här i jänz′), meaning "children of God." Gandhi also appeared in public with *harijans*. Since 1950, Indian law has forbidden citizens from discriminating against *harijans*, but some Hindus find it hard to change.

In large cities, where people of all castes work together, caste has become less important than it was. However, it remains an important part of South Asian life.

OTHER RELIGIOUS GROUPS

Islam came to South Asia many centuries after Hinduism. Today three South Asian nations, Afghanistan, Pakistan, and Bangladesh, have populations that are almost completely Muslim, meaning that the people follow Islam. India also has more than 90 million Muslims. Most of India's Muslim citizens live in the northern part of the country.

Religious differences have caused much conflict in South Asia. In 1947 conflict between Hindus and Muslims in India led to the creation of Pakistan, a separate Muslim country. However, forming the new country did not completely end the tension between the two groups.

Another religion, **Sikhism** (sēk′ iz əm), is a blending of Hinduism and Islam. Founded in the late 1400s, Sikhism is today a separate religion combining some elements of Hinduism and Islam. You will read about the tension between Sikhs and Hindus in Lesson 3.

Mohandas Gandhi was both the political leader and the spiritual leader of India for more than 25 years.

Looking at the Caste System Help students to understand that the caste system, which evolved from Hinduism, influences every part of a Hindu's life.

Ask students:

- **What are castes?** (social groups that identify people according to the occupation of their ancestors)
- **What were the four castes of ancient India?** (Brahmans, or priests; warriors; merchants and farmers; servants)
- **What do Hindus believe happens to them when they die?** (They believe they are reborn into a higher or lower caste, or even as untouchables or animals, depending on how they lived in their previous lives.)
- **What is an untouchable?** (Someone below the caste system who does jobs no other caste would do, lives apart, and is avoided by other Hindus.)
- **In what ways does the caste system determine people's lives?** (It affects what jobs they have, where they live, what they eat, with whom they can associate, and whom they can marry.)
- *THINKING FURTHER:* **Why do you think Gandhi referred to the untouchables as *harijans* ("children of God")?** (perhaps to remind others that the untouchables had been created by God like everyone else)

Discussing Other Religions in South Asia Develop the concept that strongly held religious beliefs can lead to conflict.

Ask students:

- **Which three nations of South Asia are mostly Muslim?** (Afghanistan, Pakistan, and Bangladesh)
- **What circumstance led to the creation of Pakistan?** (conflict between Hindus and Muslims in India)
- **Which religion is a blend of Hinduism and Islamic elements?** (Sikhism)

BACKGROUND INFORMATION

More About Gandhi Mohandas Gandhi worked to achieve brotherhood and equality for all men and women. He strove to gain independence from Britain, eliminate hatred between Muslims and Hindus, and to end the curse of "untouchability." He hoped to achieve these goals not by violence or physical strength but through the use of civil disobedience and nonviolence.

- Civil disobedience does not mean only refusing to obey unjust laws. It also means taking full responsibility and paying the penalty for one's beliefs and actions. Gandhi and his followers willingly spent much time in jail.
- Gandhi believed that nonviolence was mightier than weapons.
- His methods and philosophy have influenced political activists throughout the world.

Identifying Other Religions Continue the discussion.

Ask students:

- **Where did Buddhism begin?** (in India)
- **Where do most of South Asia's Buddhists live?** (in Nepal, Bhutan, and other Himalayan areas, and in Sri Lanka)
- **Why are most of the Christian communities located along the coasts of India?** (because European influence has been strongest there)

EXTENDING GRAPH SKILLS

Ask students:

- **Which religion has the most followers in India? The fewest?** Hinduism; Christianity and Sikhism
- **What percentage of Indians practice the Christian religion?** (2 percent)
- **Are there more followers of Islam or of Sikhism in India?** (Islam)

Discussing the Languages of South Asia

Ask students:

- **How many different languages and dialects are spoken in India?** (several hundred)
- **Which language is spoken by more Indians than any other?** (Hindi)

Examining Family Structure

Ask students:

- **What are some of the strengths of an extended family?** (care for the aged, help with work)
- **Which marriage custom do most Muslim and Hindu families have in common?** (arranging their children's marriages)

As the graph on this page shows, India has too few Buddhists for Buddhism to be listed as a major religion. You will read about Buddhism in Chapter 26. Although Buddhism began in India, it has not kept as many followers there as it did in East Asia. In South Asia most Buddhists are in Nepal, Bhutan, and other Himalayan areas. Buddhism is also the majority religion in Sri Lanka. Tension between Buddhists and the Hindu minority in Sri Lanka burst into violence in 1988, with some Hindus demanding their own state. Christians are found mainly along India's coasts, where European influence has been strong.

LANGUAGES OF SOUTH ASIA

Even the languages of South Asia have been shaped by religion. The one language spoken by more Indians than any other is Hindi. It evolved from Sanskrit, an ancient language of South Asia still used in Hindu sacred books. Closely related to Hindi is Urdu, the official language of Pakistan and 1 of the 16 official languages of India. Most Sikhs speak Punjabi, the language of the Indian state of Punjab and of Sikh holy writings.

India has hundreds of other languages and dialects. The fact that no one of these languages and dialects is spoken by every Indian helps to explain why today many educated Indians can speak English. In

GRAPH SKILL: One Indian religious group, the Hindus, considers cows sacred and allows them to roam freely (*below, right*). How many Indians are Hindus? The Ladakh (*below*) are among the few Buddhist groups in India.

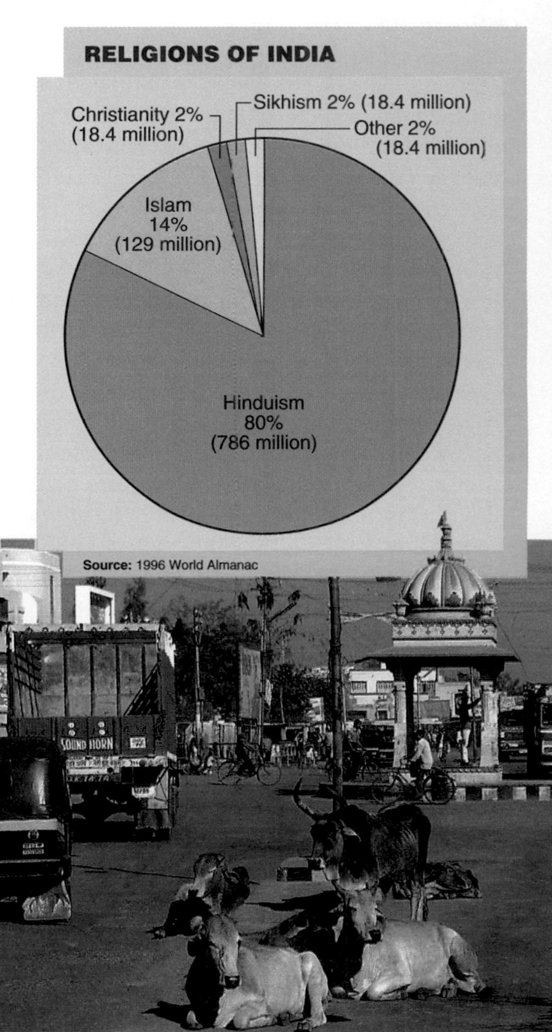

GRAPH SKILL: 713 million

BACKGROUND INFORMATION

More About Religion in South Asia The following table shows the religions of the people of South Asia by country. The figures are estimated, taken from the *1996 World Almanac*.

Afghanistan	Sunni Muslim 84%, Shia Muslim 15%
Bangladesh	Sunni Muslim 83%, Hindu 16%
Bhutan	Buddhist 75%, Hindu 25%
India	Hindu 80%, Sunni Muslim 14%, Christian 2%, Sikh 2%
Maldives	Sunni Muslim
Nepal	Hindu 90%, Buddhist 5, Muslim 3%
Pakistan	Sunni Muslim 77%, Shia Muslim 20%, Ahmadi 3%
Sri Lanka	Buddhist 69%, Hindu 15%, Christian 8%, Sunni Muslim 8%

the years Great Britain ruled the area, many Indians and other groups learned English in school. Although the government recently made Hindi the main official language, many Indians still use English.

THE FAMILY

Most South Asians live in villages. A bride often moves in with her husband's extended family. That includes his parents, uncles, brothers, their children, and unmarried sisters. The extended family provides many hands to do the farm work. It also provides aging parents someone to live with and to care for them.

No matter what religious group they belong to, many South Asian families arrange marriages for young people. These families believe that parents know what is best for their children. In the past, newlyweds often met each other for the first time at their wedding. Today, future mates usually meet before the wedding.

In cities young people sometimes arrange their own marriages, often for love. Or they may advertise for a spouse in newspapers. The ads usually mention caste, as well as their education and their occupation.

Women are expected to marry. Benazir Bhutto (bü' tō), the prime minister of Pakistan (1988–1990, 1993–1996), married a man chosen by her relatives after she decided to run for office. She first met him five days before they became engaged. "For me, there was no other choice," she said. It was either "no marriage or an arranged marriage."

THE FORCE OF TRADITION

The eight countries of South Asia have many different peoples and customs. Much of this variety stems from one source—a deep attachment to traditional ways of life.

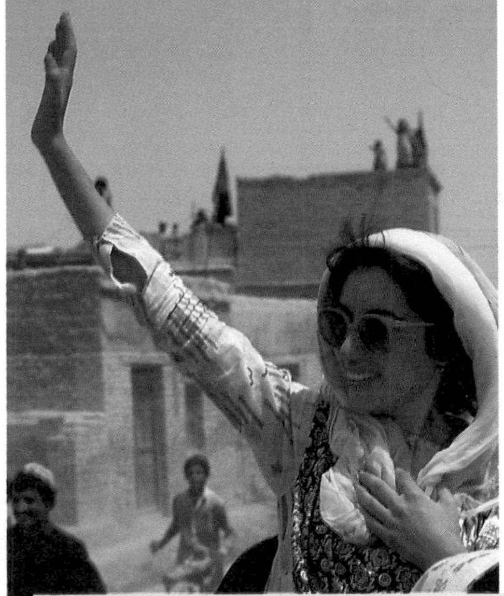

Wearing traditional dress, Benazir Bhutto crossed Pakistan several times in her campaign to become prime minister in 1988.

Hinduism and Islam are among the major religions that influence daily life in South Asia. The clothes people wear, the food they eat—and sometimes even the jobs they have—may be the result of traditions that stretch back for hundreds of years. As you read on, you will learn more about life in South Asia.

Check Your Reading

1. What are the major religions of South Asia?
2. How does religion shape life in India?
3. List some aspects of a Hindu's life that are influenced by the caste system. Explain why this influence may be weaker in cities.
4. **THINKING SKILL:** Classify into two or more groups the ways of life affected by South Asia's religions.

THINKING SKILL: Classifying

509

Applying the Lesson Ask students to imagine they are living in India today. Have half the class write a paragraph arguing against the tradition of living in an extended family group. Have the other half of the class think about the advantages of living in an extended family and write a paragraph defending this tradition.

3 CLOSE

Summarizing Students have learned that the people of South Asia have a variety of strong traditions that have been shaped by religion and family. Help students review the religions and languages of South Asia.

Evaluating Use these questions to assess students' understanding.

- **Why is South Asia called "a patchwork of cultures"?** (Many groups of people settled there, each with its own religious beliefs, customs, and language.)
- **What are some important beliefs of Hinduism?** (There is one universal spirit, which can appear in many forms; all life is holy; the caste system.)
- **What are two South Asian family traditions?** (living in extended family groups, arranged marriages)

Answers to Check Your Reading

1. Hinduism, Islam, Sikhism, Buddhism, and Christianity
2. It affects the clothes, food, languages, and jobs of the people.
3. Possible answers include: where they live, whom they marry, what jobs they have. People of all castes work together in offices and factories.
4. social: the caste system; cultural: languages

Independent Practice
Practice Book: page 137

MEETING INDIVIDUAL NEEDS

Reteaching (easy) Have students refer to the text and look carefully at all the pictures in the lesson. Tell them to write a paragraph about each picture, telling who the people are, what they are doing, and what each picture shows about Indian life.

Extension (average) Assign each student a particular period of time in Gandhi's life. Have them research that period and report their findings to the class.

Enrichment (challenging) Have students look through newspapers and magazines to find articles about one of the South Asian countries. Ask students to prepare a bulletin board display of the current news items about their chosen country.

LESSON 2
pages 510–513

Lesson Theme The nations of South Asia are rich in natural resources, but providing for their large populations is difficult.

Lesson Objectives
- Describe some of the effects of overpopulation in South Asia.
- Explain what South Asian farmers are doing to produce more food.
- Describe various ways in which South Asian countries are trying to meet their economic needs.

PREPARE

Motivate Have students read the *Read Aloud* section. Ask them to focus on the image of "the cruel sky." Discuss the unpredictability of nature and what it means to those whose survival depends on the food they grow.

Set Purpose Read the *What You Know* question aloud and encourage students to think about differences between urban and rural life. Review with students what they know about the land and climate of South Asia, and ask them to predict answers to the *What You Will Learn* question.

TEACH

Discussing a Large Population Help students to understand why, despite its natural resources, there is so much famine in South Asia.

Ask students:

- **What is one reason that there is a constant food shortage in South Asia?** (The population is too large for the supply of food.)

RESOURCE *Reminder*

Practice Book: *The People of South Asia*, page 137

LESSON 2

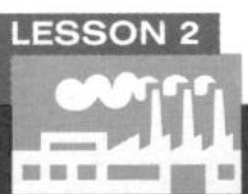

The Economy

READ TO LEARN

Key Vocabulary	**Key Places**
Green Revolution	Calcutta
cottage industry	Bombay

Read Aloud

That year the rains failed. A week went by, two. We stared at the cruel sky—calm, blue, indifferent to our need. We threw ourselves on the earth and we prayed. . . . But no rain came. . . .

The person who spoke these words, a woman in southern India, lost her land when the monsoon failed to bring rain in the 1950s. She and her husband then moved to a city to find work. In this lesson you will read about the ways in which people earn a living in South Asia.

Read for Purpose

1. WHAT YOU KNOW: In what ways might people's lives change when they move from a farm village to a large city?
2. WHAT YOU WILL LEARN: In what ways do the land and climate of South Asia shape the ways in which people earn their livings?

FEEDING A LARGE POPULATION

South Asia is rich in natural resources. It has many fertile valleys with plenty of water and a long growing season. There are many mineral deposits. Yet in spite of this abundance, many South Asians are poor. How can this poverty in the midst of abundance be explained?

One explanation is that South Asia has one of the highest population densities on earth. For example, the United States has about 71 people per square mile (about 27 per sq km), and Bangladesh has more than 2,000 people per square mile (more than 800 per sq km).

Bangladesh is one of the most densely populated countries in the world, and it cannot grow enough food to feed all its people. Most people of Bangladesh live under the constant threat of famine and malnutrition. In Chapter 21 you read about the ways in which these problems affect people in Sub-Saharan Africa.

CONTROLLING THE WATER SUPPLY

To end famine and malnutrition, South Asia's farmers have begun programs to produce more food. One such program is aimed at creating a steady supply of water. As you read in Chapter 24, South Asia does not have a regular supply of water. Although most of the subcontinent receives plenty of rain, almost all of it falls during the few months of the summer

WHAT YOU KNOW: Encourage students to think about differences in urban and rural life, such as in earning a living, housing, and social life.

READING STRATEGY AND VOCABULARY DEVELOPMENT

Previewing and Predicting As students preview this lesson, have them focus on the *Key Vocabulary* words *famine* and *malnutrition.* Make sure students understand the meaning of the words. Have them read the *What You Will Learn* question. Ask students to think of other countries they have studied and how the land and the climate of those countries influence the ways in which people earn their living. Have students use this prior knowledge to make predictions about what they will learn in this lesson. Have students turn the lesson headings into questions and then predict the answers. For example, "Feeding a Large Population" would become "How Does South Asia Feed Its Large Population?" After students have predicted their answers, have them read the section under each heading and discuss the accuracy of their predictions. Then ask them to revise their answers as necessary.

South Asia's rapidly growing population causes many of its cities to be crowded.

monsoon. The rest of the year is almost completely dry. Also, when the rains do come, they are often followed by floods that wash away crops and houses.

No one can tame the wild monsoon, but South Asians are learning to control its effects. Engineers build ditches and high walls to contain floods. They put up dams on the rivers to harness the power of rushing water. Most important, they build reservoirs and irrigation canals to water the fields all year long.

Pakistan needs irrigation for a different reason than India does. Find Pakistan on the Atlas map on page 634. Because the country is located north of the monsoon zone, it receives little rain. Pakistani farmers rely on the Indus River system for water. Each year Pakistan builds more canals and cultivates more areas.

THE GREEN REVOLUTION

In addition to irrigation, some South Asian farmers plant new types of crops and use new farming techniques that result in larger harvests. These changes are known as the **Green Revolution** because the new techniques produce leafier plants that make the fields look greener.

One of these crops is a new type of rice, South Asia's basic food. Since this new kind of rice grows more quickly than ordinary rice, farmers can now plant more than one crop per year. Some parts of Bangladesh have three rice harvests.

Another new crop is "miracle wheat," grown in areas that are too dry and cool for rice. This new type of wheat is more resistant to many crop diseases than are older types of wheat. Raja Gohar Masud, a farmer in northern Pakistan, says that the land produced very little when he was young. But farmers "have increased production now by using tractors and fertilizers, and also by planting a new [type of] wheat. . . ." Such methods have helped Pakistan to more than double its wheat production since 1967.

Discussing the Water Supply Help students to understand the importance of water control to this region's food supply.

Ask students:

- **Why is the creation of a steady water supply important?** (to irrigate crops, to provide water for human and animal use)
- **What problem do the monsoons cause?** (Monsoon rains are followed by floods that wash away crops and houses.)
- **How do the South Asians try to control the effects of the monsoons?** (They build ditches and high walls to contain the floods as well as canals and reservoirs to provide water throughout the year.)
- **What water problem does Pakistan have, and how is it being solved?** (Pakistan is a dry land. Canals are being built to bring water from the Indus River so that more land can be cultivated.)

Discussing the Green Revolution Help students to realize that improved farming methods have greatly increased South Asia's food supply.

Ask students:

- **What is the Green Revolution?** (the use of modern farming techniques and the introduction of new kinds of crops)
- **How did the Green Revolution get its name?** (The new techniques produce leafier plants that make the fields look greener.)
- **Which two crops have been introduced by the Green Revolution?** (a new type of rice and "miracle wheat")
- **Why is the new type of wheat called miracle wheat?** (it can grow in places that are too dry and cool for rice and has a high resistance to many crop diseases.)
- **What have modern farming and miracle wheat done for the food supply of Pakistan?** (more than doubled its wheat production)

BACKGROUND INFORMATION

Multicultural Perspectives As is the case in many developing nations, India's "Green Revolution," with its new machinery and new techniques, has transformed life in farming communities throughout the country. Some observers question whether the social upheaval that often accompanies modernization carries too high a price tag. Indian author V.S. Naipaul shares this view. "The agricultural practices which I saw [as a child] are totally extinct today. . . . [M]y grandfather would take about 40 people as labourers, give them sickles, and they would go out to the fields at about four in the morning to avoid the heat. . . . It was sort of a celebration, this harvesting. . . . Now it is impossible to see this sight in any village. . . . I think the adoption of machinery has changed attitudes and life."

Ask students about the debates in their own communities concerning the advantages and disadvantages of technology.

Examining Farm Life Help students to understand how most farmers in South Asia live.

Ask students:

- **What is subsistence farming?** (growing only enough food for one's own family)
- **Why are most farms in South Asia very small?** (An old custom dictates that when a father dies, his farm is divided among all his sons.)
- *THINKING FURTHER:* **How can subsistence farmers get food if their crops fail?** (Use this question to help students realize that there are few alternatives for these people other than starvation or leaving their land.)

Discussing the Photographs Refer to the photographs on this page. Have students compare South Asia's traditional farming methods with those of modern agriculture.

Examining Industry in the Home

Ask students:

- **What are cottage industries?** (manufacturing that takes place in people's homes)
- **What are some of the products made in Indian cottage industries?** (handicrafts, jewelry, textiles, carpets)

Looking at Industrial India Help students to realize that India is becoming more industrialized. Discuss the products that are produced in India.

Discussing Economic Challenges Make sure that students understand why cities in South Asia are so crowded.

Ask students:

- **Why do people leave their villages to go to cities?** (to seek job opportunities)
- **What conditions do they often find in the cities?** (overcrowding, not enough housing or jobs)

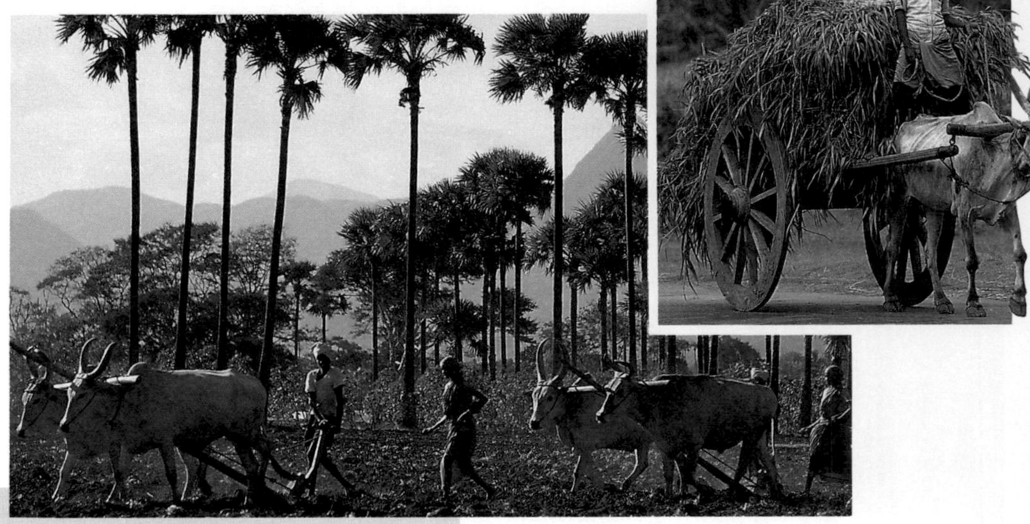

Many farmers in South Asia use traditional methods to plant (*above*), harvest, and transport their crops (*right*).

FARM VILLAGES

Many of the new crops and farming techniques are used on bigger farms. However, about 75 percent of South Asians live in small farm villages. Here "women still carry pots of drinking water on their hips. . . ." writes an Indian poet about village life.

Old customs also shape village economies. For example, when an Indian farmer dies, the fields are divided among his sons. In each generation the land is divided again, leaving most farmers with very small plots. The size of the average Indian farm is only about 2 acres (0.8 ha). In the United States the average farm measures about 456 acres (185 ha), although many people have larger or smaller farms.

The farmers working these tiny fields are mostly subsistence farmers, who grow food only for family use. They have little money to spend on modern farm machinery, insecticides, or fertilizers. However, several governments have started programs to help poor farmers to take part in the Green Revolution.

INDUSTRY IN THE HOME

When you think of industry, you are likely to imagine huge factories with hundreds of workers. That type of industry can be found in South Asia, but manufacturing often takes place in people's homes. These small manufacturers, or **cottage industries**, provide millions of jobs and produce the fine crafted goods for which South Asia has long been known.

The major products from handicrafts include gold and silver jewelry, textiles, and carpets. Have you heard of the luxurious soft wool known as cashmere? It comes originally from the state of Kashmir in northern India.

INDUSTRIAL INDIA

All the countries of South Asia are developing nations, even India, which has many industries. In the hills just outside **Calcutta**, miners extract coal and iron ore from underground deposits. Nearby fac-

512

BUILDING CITIZENSHIP

Solving Economic Problems Ask students to pretend that they live in a small Indian village with no major industries to provide jobs for them and their neighbors. Have students volunteer solutions to this problem. (Possible suggestions might include establishing cottage industries or inviting a large industry to move into the community.) Have students select a specific Indian village (for example, one just outside Calcutta) and do research to see which solution proposed above might work in that area. When students have chosen a proposal for a solution to the problems of the area, assign them to committees, each designed to deal with a different aspect of the solution. For example, if the solution is to attract a large industry into the area, one committee might think of ways to make the area attractive to that business, while another committee might consider measures to reduce such negative effects of industry as pollution.

tories turn iron into steel, which is then shipped elsewhere to be processed.

Calcutta is also home to the jute industry. The tough fibers of this plant, which is grown mostly in Bangladesh, are used to make rope and burlap bags.

In and around Bombay are numerous textile mills. India also produces automobiles, bicycles, chemicals, computer components, and electronic parts.

ECONOMIC CHALLENGES

India and Pakistan are making major progress in manufacturing. The rest of the area, though, has few factories. Nepal's economy is based on agriculture and tourism. People from all over the world go there to see the majestic Himalayas. Sri Lanka relies heavily on plantations where rubber and tea are grown for export. Afghanistan and Bhutan are isolated mountain lands where herding is the chief occupation.

Every year steady streams of farmers and cottage workers leave the villages of South Asia to seek job opportunities in the large cities. As a result, large cities have grown even larger. Bombay's population, for instance, grew from 1.5 million people in 1941 to almost 13 million in 1991.

Unfortunately many villagers do not find the jobs or homes they seek. Many residents of South Asia's cities live on the streets. Despite their growing wealth, most large cities cannot create housing or jobs fast enough for the rapidly increasing numbers of people.

DEVELOPING SOUTH ASIA'S ECONOMIES

South Asia has some of the most densely populated places on earth. As a result, malnutrition and famine remain constant threats although the area has abundant natural resources. New methods of irrigation and the Green Revolution are producing more food.

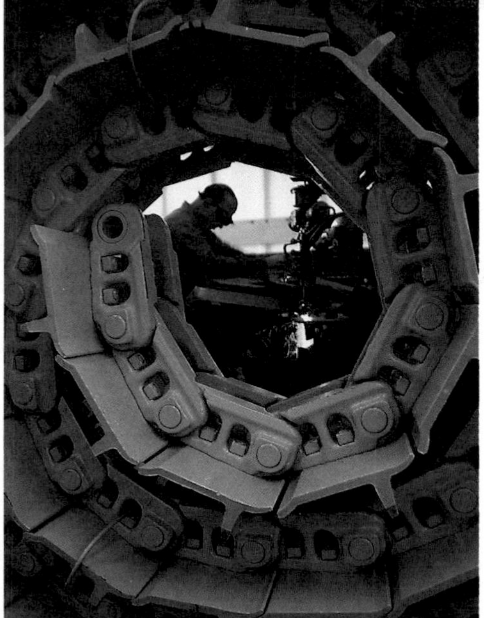

Among India's factories are tractor plants like this one. After they are manufactured, tractors and parts are shipped around the world.

India and Pakistan are the most industrialized countries of South Asia, with many large factories as well as cottage industries. Every year thousands of farmers leave their homes to seek better job opportunities in the cities.

Check Your Reading

1. Why is population density a problem in a country like Bangladesh?
2. How have South Asians begun to control their water supplies?
3. If India is becoming more industrially developed, why does it have trouble feeding its people?
4. THINKING SKILL: In what ways might working in a cottage industry be similar to working in a small factory? How might it be different?

THINKING SKILL: Compare and Contrast

Applying the Lesson Discuss some of the problems of large cities in the United States. Ask students to write a paragraph comparing these problems with those of large South Asian cities. Discuss the improvements that could benefit both American and South Asian cities.

3 CLOSE

Summarizing Students have learned that in this region, despite improved farming methods and water control, food shortages still exist. Discuss students' ideas on how to avoid food shortages.

Evaluating Use these questions to assess students' understanding.

- **What is being done to increase the food supply in South Asia?** (controlling the water supply, using new farming techniques)
- **Where do most of the people of South Asia live and what is their occupation?** (in small villages; farming)
- **How is industry in India both helping and hurting the people?** (It provides jobs for many people; it causes overcrowding in the cities.)

Answers to Check Your Reading

1. It cannot produce enough food for the large population.
2. by building ditches and walls to control floods, dams to use water power, and reservoirs and canals to irrigate farmland
3. The population is very high.
4. Like small factory workers, cottage industry workers know each other, do much of the work by hand, and deal directly with the boss or manager. Unlike small factory workers, cottage industry workers work and live in the same place and belong to the same family.

Independent Practice
Practice Book: page 137

MEETING INDIVIDUAL NEEDS

Reteaching (easy) Have students draw a picture of how farmland might have looked before the Green Revolution and one of how that same farmland might look after. Have them write a paragraph on what caused the difference in the land's appearance.

Extension (average) Have students pretend that they are young South Asians who have left their rural homes and families to find work in a large industrial city. Have them pick a South Asian city and research the conditions there. Ask students to write a letter home describing what they see and how they feel about living in the city.

Enrichment (challenging) Have students work in groups to construct models of dams, reservoirs, and irrigation canals. When the models are completed, have students show them to the class and demonstrate how the models work.

LESSON 3
pages 514–517

Lesson Theme Today the governments of South Asia include representative democracies, constitutional monarchies, and military dictatorships.

Lesson Objectives
- Explain the British legacy and how it has influenced the countries of this region.
- Identify the major events and people in the political history of modern India.
- Identify the types of South Asian governments.

 PREPARE

Motivate Have students read the quotation in the *Read Aloud* section. Ask them what they think Gandhi meant by "not at the expense of others." Discuss whether they think any political leaders today might have such a caring and generous world view.

Set Purpose Use the *What You Know* question to point out that in a democracy, the people need to make their own decisions. Have students predict answers to the *What You Will Learn* question.

 TEACH

Recognizing the British Legacy
Be sure students understand the term *legacy.*

Ask students:

- **Which country influenced or controlled all of South Asia before 1947?** (Great Britain)
- **What was an important British legacy in South Asia?** (the democratic ideal that people can govern themselves through elected representatives)

LESSON 3

The Government

READ TO LEARN

Key Vocabulary	Key People	Key Places
partition	Mohammed Ali Jinnah	Bhutan
nonaligned nations	Indira Gandhi	Nepal
	Jawaharlal Nehru	Afghanistan

Read Aloud

We want freedom for our country, but not at the expense of others.

The great Indian leader Mohandas Gandhi spoke these words before World War II, when South Asia was part of the British Empire. Gandhi hoped to unite all of South Asia into one independent nation. There the many peoples of the area could live together in peace and equality. As you will read, South Asia did gain independence, but not in the way Gandhi had hoped.

Read for Purpose

1. WHAT YOU KNOW: Would you find it easy to make your own decisions if someone else had always made decisions for you?
2. WHAT YOU WILL LEARN: What types of governments are found in the countries of South Asia?

THE BRITISH LEGACY

The governments of the countries of South Asia vary from democracies to dictatorships. Despite their differences, the countries of South Asia have one thing in common. At one time they were all under the control or influence of Great Britain.

European merchants first entered South Asia in the 1500s. Eventually the British gained control of the local governments. By the middle 1800s the British had made the subcontinent a British colony.

The years of British rule have left their mark on South Asian life. Perhaps the most important British legacy has been the democratic ideal that the people can govern themselves through their elected representatives.

INDEPENDENCE AND PARTITION

Britain contributed to India's independence movement in another way. Starting about 100 years ago, many young Indians went to study in Great Britain. There they learned about democracy and their rights as British citizens. The Indians realized that they did not enjoy equal rights with the British in their home country, India.

One Indian who studied law in London was Mohandas Gandhi. When he returned to India in 1915, Gandhi began a campaign for justice that soon became a fight for independence. Gandhi's fight was unusual because it was fought without violence. He urged peaceful protests against British power. His movement gained the support of much of the world and earned

 WHAT YOU KNOW: Encourage students to think of decisions they now make that were made by parents or teachers not too long ago.

READING STRATEGY AND VOCABULARY DEVELOPMENT

Previewing and Predicting Since students have read about various forms of government in previous chapters, have them make two lists, one of topics that they predict will be covered in this lesson and one of questions that are related to these topics. The first list might include the following topics: "Past and Present Government Leaders," "Dates When the Countries Were Established," and "Political Factions Within the Countries." The second list might include: "What Forms of Government Do the South Asian Countries Have?" "Why Were the Different Countries Established?" "How Did the Governments of These Countries Evolve?" "What Problems Did the Countries Have Early in Their History?" "What Problems Do the Countries Have Today?" After students have read this lesson, have them edit and revise both lists, then answer the questions in the second list.

Prime Minister Indira Gandhi (*inset*) became increasingly undemocratic in the late 1970s.

him the nickname *Mahatma*, which is Hindi for "great soul."

By 1947 the British had agreed to grant India independence, but bitter tensions divided the people. Muslims realized that an independent India would be ruled by a Hindu majority. Many Muslims wanted to live under Islamic law in their own land.

Mohammed Ali Jinnah (jin' ä) led a Muslim group that wanted to establish its own country. At last everyone agreed to a **partition**, or division, of British India. In 1947 two countries, India and Pakistan, were formed.

After partition many Muslims left India for Pakistan, while Hindus fled Pakistan for India. Violent fights broke out between Hindus and Muslims on the roads and in railroad cars. At least half a million people died. Some Hindus were angry about the partition. One Hindu extremist murdered Gandhi in 1948.

TROUBLED PAKISTAN

Muslim Pakistan was originally two separate sections divided by almost 1,000 miles (1,600 km) of Indian land. Find Pakistan and Bangladesh in the Atlas on page 634. Pakistan was West Pakistan and Bangladesh was East Pakistan.

The people of both Pakistans were mostly Muslim. But they had different languages, economic resources, and ways of life. These differences led to civil war in 1971. With India's help, East Pakistan won its independence and became the nation of Bangladesh.

THE WORLD'S LARGEST DEMOCRACY

India has a huge population—more than 900 million people. Only China has more people, as you will read in Chapter 26. The size of its population causes India sometimes to be called "the world's largest democracy." Most of the electorate goes to the polls to vote. Many go to support local parties and issues.

515

Discussing Independence and Partition Explain to students the meaning of the word *partition* as it is used in this lesson. Help students to understand Gandhi's great contribution to India's independence.

Ask students:

- **Who was Mohandas Gandhi?** (a great leader in India's struggle for independence)
- **What tactics did Gandhi use in his fight for India's independence?** (nonviolent action and peaceful protest)
- **Why was India partitioned in 1947?** (Religious tensions divided the people; Muslims feared domination by Hindus.)
- **Which countries were formed as a result of the partition?** (India and Pakistan)
- **What happened to Gandhi?** (He was murdered by a Hindu extremist in 1948.)
- *THINKING FURTHER:* **Mohandas Gandhi is considered to be one of the greatest people of this century. What made Gandhi so special?** (Help students to realize that he was a philosopher and teacher—a person of great humanity who lived humbly and preached nonviolence and respect for all life.)

Explaining Pakistan's Troubles Help students to understand reasons for the partition of Pakistan.

Ask students:

- **Why was the nation of Bangladesh created?** (Although the people of both parts of Pakistan were Muslim, they differed greatly in language and economic resources. These differences led to a civil war.)

Identifying the World's Largest Democracy Help students to understand just how large India's population is.

CURRICULUM CONNECTION

Language Arts Most libraries have books about Gandhi's ideas and philosophical beliefs. (See, for example, *The Words of Gandhi* selected by Richard Attenborough and *The Essential Gandhi* by Louis Fischer.) Have students look through one book about Gandhi and choose a quotation of Gandhi's that they particularly admire. Tell them to think about the quotation to be sure they understand its meaning. Suggest to students that they practice reading the quotation aloud at home. Then have students read their quotation to the class and explain its meaning. Ask students to try to imagine the situation Gandhi was in when he spoke these words. Have students speculate about the people to whom he might have been speaking, the question to which he might have been responding, and so on.

Discussing the World's Largest Democracy Continue discussing democracy in India. Help students to understand the democratic structure of India's government.

Ask students:

- **How is India ruled?** (by a prime minister and a parliament)
- **Where did India get its system of government?** (It borrowed the idea from the British.)
- **How were state borders determined?** (When possible, borders were drawn to include members of mainly one ethnic or religious group.)
- **How are India's states and territories governed at the local level?** (They have local self-government.)
- **Why did the Sikhs rebel against the central government of India?** (They felt that their religious rights were not respected.)
- **What did the Sikhs want?** (to have their own country)
- **Who was Jawaharlal Nehru?** (India's first prime minister)
- **Name two other prime ministers of India.** (Indira Gandhi and Rajiv Gandhi)

Discussing Other Governments Review the meanings of the terms *dictatorship* and *monarchy*.

Ask students:

- **What are the forms of government in Pakistan, Bangladesh, Sri Lanka, Bhutan, and Nepal?** (Bangladesh has a military government; Sri Lanka and Pakistan are democracies; Bhutan and Nepal are constitutional monarchies.)
- **Why did troops from the Soviet Union enter Afghanistan?** (to help keep the socialist government in power)
- *THINKING FURTHER:* **Why do you think there is so much fighting in South Asia?** (Point out that much of the fighting is due to religious and ethnic differences.)

In 1984 Sikhs demonstrated for rights in New Delhi, the capital (*left*). Unrest spread to Amritsar (*right*), the Sikh headquarters.

India borrowed ideas for government from Britain and the United States. The Indian Parliament meets in New Delhi. The head of the party that wins the most votes becomes the prime minister. India also has a supreme court modeled on that of the United States.

India has 25 states and several territories. Wherever possible, state borders were drawn to include mainly members of one ethnic or religious group. This allows India's peoples to govern themselves at the local level. But it does not prevent conflict from happening.

For example, the northern state of Punjab has more than 10 million Sikhs. Some Sikhs feel that India's central government does not respect their religious and economic rights. They want the Sikhs to form their own country. A number of Sikhs began a terrorist campaign to gain their ends. One attack, in 1984, resulted in the death of India's Prime Minister **Indira Gandhi**. For the second time in less than 40 years, India had lost a leader to religious violence.

Indira Gandhi was the daughter of **Jawaharlal Nehru** (jə wä′ hər läl nā′ rü), India's first prime minister and the leader who helped shape modern India. According to Nehru, he "was no believer in kings and princes." Indira Gandhi also believed in democracy. But when India's economic and political problems began to increase in the late 1970s, she took on almost dictatorial powers. After Indira Gandhi's death in 1984, India remained a democracy. Her son, Rajiv Gandhi, was prime minister until 1989. He too was assassinated while campaigning for re-election in 1991.

OTHER GOVERNMENTS

In Bangladesh the government is under the control of army officers. A mili-

516

BACKGROUND INFORMATION

More about Nehru Jawaharlal Nehru (1889–1964) was a close associate of Gandhi in the struggle for independence. When independence was won in 1947, Nehru became India's first prime minister.

- Nehru studied in England. When he returned to India he practiced law and joined the independence movement. Nehru was often jailed for his political activities.
- The political, economic, and social policies that Nehru established as prime minister still influence many of India's policies today.
- Nehru's only daughter, Indira Gandhi, later became prime minister. In spite of her name, which she acquired through marriage, she is not related to Mohandas Gandhi.

tary government was also in power in Pakistan until 1988 when free elections were held. Benazir Bhutto, whom you read about in Lesson 1, was the first prime minister chosen under the new laws and the first woman to govern a Muslim country.

Another South Asian country with a democratic system is the island nation of Sri Lanka. There, struggles between the Buddhist Sinhalese, the major group of people on the island, and the Hindu Tamils threaten the nation's stability.

The Himalayan nations of **Bhutan** and **Nepal** are among the world's few remaining monarchies. Like Great Britain, these two countries also have representative governments. In each country, a king rules with the help of advisers and an elected assembly. The two nations look to India for economic support, military protection, and guidance in foreign affairs.

In **Afghanistan** a revolution toppled the king from his throne in 1973. A second revolution in 1978 brought a socialist group to power. When other Afghans rebelled, troops from what was then the Soviet Union crossed the border to keep Afghanistan's socialist government in power. Soviet troops left Afghanistan in 1989, unable to claim victory. Since then, the country has been torn by civil war, as Islamic rebel groups struggle for control.

INDEPENDENT SOUTH ASIA

To preserve their independence, the nations of South Asia banded together with other small countries in a worldwide movement of **nonaligned nations**. These were developing countries that did not want to take sides in the struggles between the United States and its allies and the Soviet Union and its allies. "We in India," said Prime Minister Nehru in 1953, "follow a foreign policy . . . of nonalignment with any power bloc."

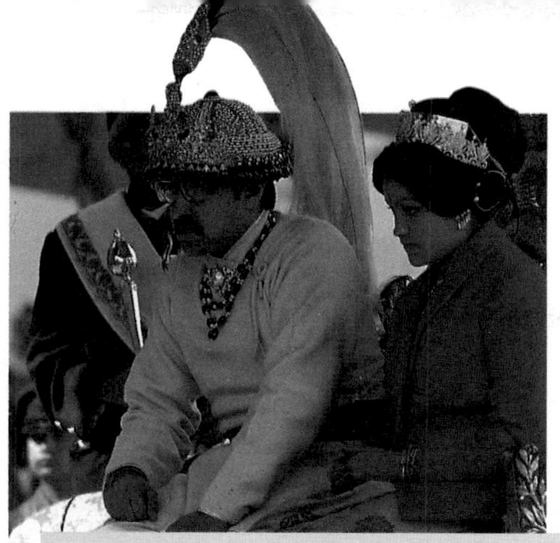

King Birendra and Queen Aisswarya of Nepal hold a public audience in the capital.

CHALLENGES OF DEMOCRACY

Until 1947, when India and Pakistan became independent countries, all of South Asia was under either British rule or influence. From the British, South Asians inherited a belief in democracy and independence. However, the new countries often differed on such matters as religion and political systems. Today South Asia's governments include representative democracies, monarchies, and dictatorships.

Check Your Reading

1. Name three nations that were once part of the British colony of India.
2. What kinds of governments are found in the countries of South Asia? Which countries have borrowed British ideas of government?
3. In what ways do you think being nonaligned helped countries preserve their independence?
4. **THINKING SKILL:** Reread the information about Nepal and Bhutan on this page. From this information, what conclusion can you draw about the independence of these two countries?

THINKING SKILL: Drawing Conclusions

Looking at Independent South Asia Help students to understand nonalignment.

Ask students:

- **What are nonaligned countries?** (They are developing countries that did not want to take sides in the struggles between the world's superpowers.)
- *THINKING FURTHER:* **Why are they nonaligned?** (to preserve their independence)

Applying the Lesson Have students discuss Dr. Martin Luther King, Jr., and his political ideals. Point out that King was a great admirer of Gandhi. Ask students to list similarities in the lives and philosophies of these men.

3 CLOSE

Summarizing Students have read about the British legacy in South Asia, about Indian independence, and about the governments of this region. Have students review the type of government in each South Asian country.

Evaluating Use these questions to assess students' understanding.

- **Who was Mohandas Gandhi?** (a great leader in India's fight for independence, who preached respect for all life)
- **Who was Jawaharlal Nehru?** (the first prime minister of India)
- **Which country provided India with a model for its system of government?** (Great Britain)

Answers to Check Your Reading

1. India, Pakistan, Bangladesh
2. democracies, dictatorships, monarchies; India, Sri Lanka, Pakistan
3. By not taking sides, they were less influenced by the superpowers.
4. They are somewhat dependent on India.

Independent Practice
Practice Book: page 138

MEETING INDIVIDUAL NEEDS

Reteaching (easy) Ask students to bring in newspaper and magazine articles and pictures about the people of modern South Asia. Give students a large sheet of tagboard on which to make a collage of the pictures and articles.

Extension (average) Have students research important events in India's history. Then have them create a time line of India's history from its colonial status to modern times.

Enrichment (challenging) Remind students that in the last lesson the metaphor "a patchwork" was used to describe the many cultures of South Asia. Also remind students that the United States is often called a "melting pot." Ask students to write an essay in which they use these metaphors to point out important political and cultural differences between the two areas.

SKILLS LESSON
page 518

Lesson Theme Determining point of view involves identifying the position from which a person views a subject or issue.

Lesson Objective
- Describe and apply a procedure for determining point of view.

 PREPARE

Motivate Write the term *point of view* on the chalkboard. Ask students to define the term and to recall the steps they took to determine point of view in Chapter 13. Write the steps on the chalkboard.

 TEACH

Applying the Skill Have students read the passage and answer the questions that follow it. (See answers below.)

Thinking About Thinking Ask several students to explain the procedures and clues they used to determine the writer's point of view. Help the class draw up a composite list of the most useful steps and clues.

 CLOSE

Reviewing the Skill Use students' answers to reinforce their knowledge of how to determine point of view and to relate the skill to situations outside the classroom.

RESOURCE Reminder
Practice Book: Recognizing Point of View, page 139

BUILDING SKILLS
THINKING SKILLS

Determining Point of View: Review

Wendy's family recently moved from the city to a house in the country. On the first day in the country Wendy was delighted to see a family of deer on the lawn behind the house. At school Wendy told her classmates about the deer. She was surprised when they said that deer are a nuisance because they eat shrubbery, flowers, and vegetables in the garden.

Point of view is the way a person looks at or feels about something. How a person feels about something can affect the accuracy of what he or she says.

HELPING YOURSELF
The procedure below shows one way to determine point of view.

1. Identify the subject or topic.
2. Identify statements of fact and opinion.
3. Identify information that was left out but could have been included.
4. Identify any biases the writer has.
5. Describe the point of view from which the author writes. Is the writer for or against something?

Applying the Skill
Read the following passage about rail travel in India. Look for clues that will help you to determine the writer's point of view.

The Indian railway system provides service throughout the country. Every visitor to India should take a long train trip. This is the best way to experience the Indian way of life: its beauty, its excitement, and its frustrations. Even though monkeys change the signals, floods wash away the tracks, and cows fall asleep on the tracks, somehow the trains keep running.

1. Which sentences in the above paragraph are statements of fact?
2. Which sentences in the above paragraph are statements of opinion?
3. What biases, if any, does the writer of the paragraph have?
4. What do you think is the writer's point of view?

Reviewing the Skill
1. What is the meaning of the phrase *point of view*?
2. What are some steps you can take to determine a writer or speaker's point of view?
3. Where, outside of school, would it be useful to try to determine the point of view of a writer or a speaker?

518

ANSWERS TO SKILLS QUESTIONS

Applying the Skill
1. first and last sentences
2. second and third sentences
3. The writer is biased in favor of rail travel.
4. The writer believes all visitors to India should take a long train trip because it is the best way to experience the Indian way of life.

Reviewing the Skill
1. how a person looks at or feels about something
2. (a) Identify the topic. (b) Identify statements of fact, value judgments, and reasoned opinions. (c) Identify information that was left out but could have been included. (d) Identify any biases the writer has.
3. at a meeting or during a debate, at home when you are watching TV news, on the playground when you are settling an argument

LESSON 4

Arts and Recreation

READ TO LEARN

Key Vocabulary

Vedas
yoga

Read Aloud

According to the Hindu holy book, the Ramayana, the god Vishnu once came to earth as the prince Rama. Rama was the ideal Hindu. Even while he was in exile, he remained a loyal son, a lover of all living things, and a devoted husband. So greatly was Rama loved that when Rama's wife, Sita, was kidnapped and carried away to an island, the monkeys built a bridge across the ocean to rescue her.

Throughout South Asia stories about Prince Rama are shown frequently on television and in the movies and are told in many forms. Religion plays an important role in the arts and recreation of the area.

Read for Purpose

1. WHAT YOU KNOW: What are some movies or television programs that you have seen dealing with religious themes?
2. WHAT YOU WILL LEARN: In what ways have both traditional and modern ideas influenced the arts and recreation of South Asia?

A LIVING HINDU TRADITION

The above story of Rama belongs to an epic that is more than 2,000 years old. Even older is the collection of Hindu religious writings known as the Vedas (vā' dəz). The Vedas are a part of the culture found throughout South Asia.

Hindu tales are told through traditional drama, dance, and song. Traveling troupes of actors bring Hindu tales to the villages. "Villagers will watch . . . all night, for as long as 12 hours at a time," wrote one visitor. Audiences know the stories so well that they sometimes yell out an actor's lines before the actor can speak them.

Traditional dances remain popular in both villages and cities. For example, in Nepal's capital city of Kathmandu a dancer paints his face blue because the color identifies the Hindu god Vishnu. People in the audience follow the story because they know the specific meaning of each of the dancer's steps and gestures.

ART AND ARCHITECTURE

South Asians like to create things that are beautiful as well as meaningful and useful in everyday life. For example, Hindus decorate everything, from clothes to statues. Carpenters carve religious designs on roof beams as they build houses. In some villages women paint rice-powder designs on doors to honor Hindu gods.

WHAT YOU KNOW: Encourage students to think about movies and television programs that deal with real religious figures and events.

LESSON 4
pages 519–521

Lesson Theme The arts and recreation of South Asia are a blend of the traditional and the modern.

Lesson Objectives

- Explain how traditional Hindu tales are kept alive.
- Identify traditional kinds of architecture.
- Identify some Western forms of art and recreation adopted by the people of South Asia and some South Asian forms adopted by people in the West.

1 PREPARE

Motivate Have students read the *Read Aloud* section about Vishnu. Ask them to name the characteristics of the ideal Hindu mentioned in this passage and to compare them with the characteristics of one of the heroes of our culture. Discuss how the heroes personify the values of each culture.

Set Purpose Use the *What You Know* question to discuss how religion has influenced Western arts. Read the *What You Will Learn* question and tell students they will discover the various ways in which both traditional and modern ideas have influenced the arts and recreation of South Asia.

2 TEACH

Discussing Tales from Hindu Tradition Help students to understand that much of South Asia's performing arts have religious origins. Discuss what the Vedas are.

Understanding Art and Architecture Stress that South Asians like their buildings to be not only useful but also beautiful.

READING STRATEGY AND VOCABULARY DEVELOPMENT

Previewing and Predicting After previewing and reading this lesson, students may enjoy preparing a videotape of or role-playing a situation that depicts sports and leisure activities in South Asia. Have students research how sports, such as badminton, or activities, such as chess, are played, and how they developed. Students can either construct or gather props. Have students present a brief history of each sport or activity. Then have volunteers take turns enacting the game or activity. If students are videotaping, you may wish to have them review the arts and recreation lessons from previous units and make videotapes of class presentations based on the material covered in these earlier lessons.

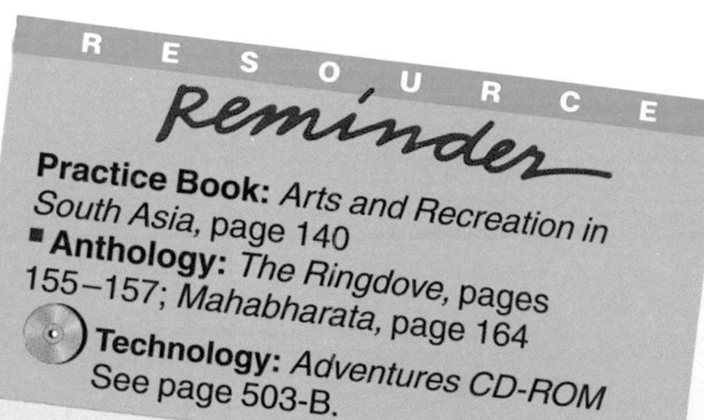
RESOURCE Reminder

Practice Book: *Arts and Recreation in South Asia*, page 140

Anthology: *The Ringdove*, pages 155–157; *Mahabharata*, page 164

Technology: *Adventures CD-ROM* See page 503-B.

Looking at Art and Architecture Continue discussing the art and architecture of South Asia.

Ask students:

- **What do many examples of Hindu carving depict?** (gods and scenes from the Vedas)
- **What kinds of monuments to their gods do Hindus and Buddhists build?** (shrines and temples)

Discussing Muslim Influence

Ask students:

- **What is the Taj Mahal?** (a memorial tomb that a Muslim ruler built for his wife in the 1600s)
- **What does Mohammad Husain do?** (He grinds precious stones into colorful chips and shapes them to decorate boxes and table tops. Explain mosaics to students.)

Looking at the Photograph Have students examine the picture at the top of the page. Discuss why the Taj Mahal is considered by many people to be the most beautiful building in the world.

Discussing Religious Holidays Help students to understand that many Hindu religious holidays are festive. Compare the customs of the Hindu holiday of *Holi* with the festive holidays of other religious traditions.

Looking at Cultural Exchange

Ask students:

- **Which British game is enjoyed in South Asia?** (cricket)
- **What forms of South Asian recreation are popular in the United States and elsewhere in the West?** (yoga, polo, badminton, chess)

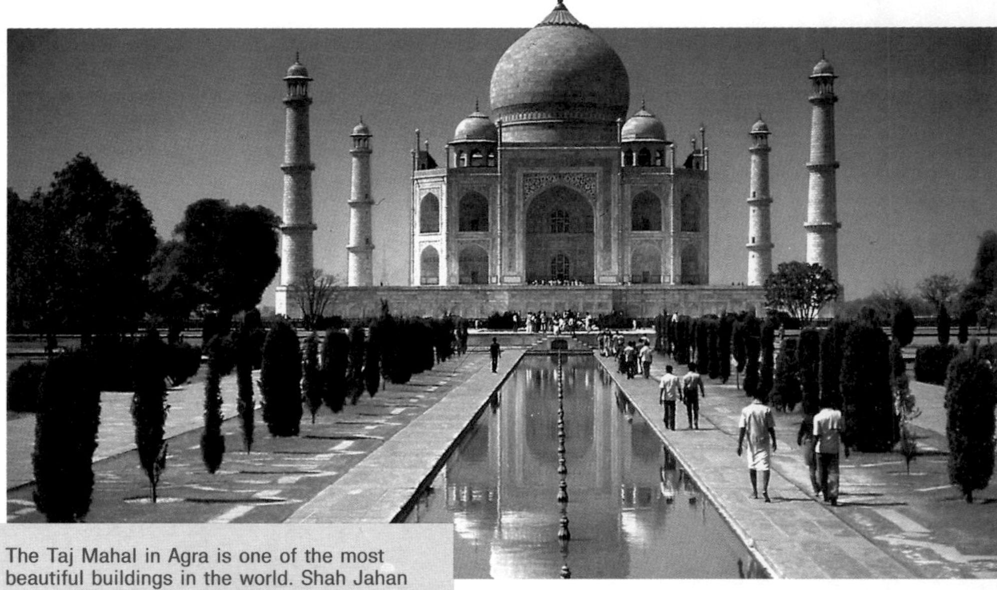

The Taj Mahal in Agra is one of the most beautiful buildings in the world. Shah Jahan and his wife Mumtaz Mahal are buried there.

Each of South Asia's major religious groups has built magnificent monuments to their gods. Usually every inch of the outside of a Hindu temple is carved and decorated. The carvings illustrate scenes from the Vedas and show many gods.

Buddhist shrines, some of which are more than 1,500 years old, are found in many parts of South Asia. Other Buddhist structures are the sturdy monasteries clinging to the steep Himalayan slopes of Bhutan and Nepal.

MUSLIM INFLUENCE

In Agra, India, Mohammad Husain (hü sän') grinds precious stones into colorful chips. With a hand-turned grinding wheel, he shapes bits of turquoise and other stones into tiny pieces to decorate boxes and tabletops. Husain says his craft has changed little over hundreds of years. His ancestors, he believes, helped decorate the building that has become India's most famous architectural symbol, the Taj Mahal (täzh' mə häl').

The Taj Mahal was built in the 1600s as the tomb of the wife of the ruler, Shah Jahan. Because he was Muslim, the Taj Mahal is Islamic in design. The tomb is spectacular, with mosaics, domes and slender columns, beautiful gardens, and a large reflecting pool in front. There are no human images because their use in art is discouraged by Islam.

RELIGIOUS HOLIDAYS

South Asia observes many religious holidays. One recent month of March, three American college students were bicycling through Bombay. They noticed that the streets and houses were splashed with purple, red, and pink. As the students rounded a corner, a group of young men threw balloons at them. The balloons burst and the students were drenched with purple dye.

The Americans were "victims" of the prank-filled Hindu festival called *Holi*. It's

520

BACKGROUND INFORMATION

More About the Taj Mahal Located in Agra, a city in northern India, the Taj Mahal is often called "the most beautiful building in the world." It was built by a Mogul emperor as a memorial for his beloved wife, who was known as "Taj Mahal," meaning "The Crown of the Palace."

- The building is set in a formal garden and is reflected in a sunken pool. Its marble walls are inlaid with jewels and semiprecious stones.
- For 17 years 20,000 workers labored to build the Taj Mahal (1631–1648).
- It stands on a marble platform that is 315 feet (96 m) square.
- Light enters through carved screens to illuminate the interior.
- Ninety-nine different names for God are engraved on the walls, as well as many verses of the Koran.

a day of mischief, when Hindus fling differently colored dyes at everyone and everything in sight.

Holi is only one of many religious celebrations. Each religious community has its own holidays, and cities have their own local celebrations.

CULTURAL EXCHANGE

Many of the area's newer forms of art and recreation have entered South Asia through contact with the British. For example, the English game of cricket has become a favorite sport in India.

Even more popular in India are movies. The film industry is the world's largest, producing hundreds of movies every year. Filmmakers have discovered that movies provide a way for Indians to explore problems of ethnic and religious conflict.

Although India has imported such activities as cricket and filmmaking, it also has given much of its culture to the world. One example is the ancient Hindu practice of **yoga**—a way of training both body and mind through exercise and meditation. Yoga has become popular in the United States and other countries of the world.

The game Indians call *poona* crossed the ocean and was renamed badminton by a British earl. Polo, a sport played on horseback, comes from India. Chess, one of the world's greatest games of skill, originated in India at least 2,500 years ago. One ruler liked the game so much he had huge squares painted on the ground. People stood on the squares of this huge chessboard waiting for him to call out moves.

LIVING WITH PAST AND PRESENT

South Asia combines past traditions with modern ideas. As you have read, ancient tales remain popular and are retold in many forms. Some people have adopted customs from outside the region. Buildings throughout the area reflect the traditions of Islam, Buddhism, Hinduism, and other religions. Yoga has spread from India to many parts of the world. Arts and crafts, and even sports and festivals, keep alive the traditions of the people of South Asia.

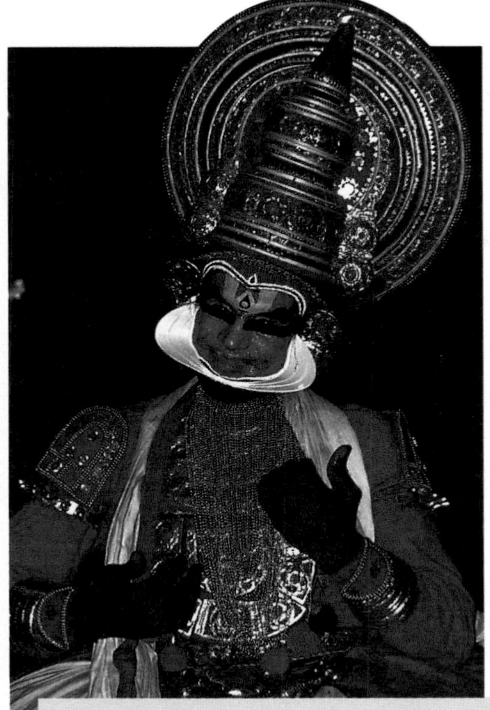

Costumed dancers use special movements to act out Hindu and other religious tales.

Check Your Reading

1. How do South Asians use both modern and old ways to retell tales?
2. What is the Taj Mahal?
3. Give examples of the cultural exchange between South Asia and Great Britain.
4. **THINKING SKILL:** Based on what you read about Prince Rama on page 519, what can you conclude about the qualities Hindus admire in people?

THINKING SKILL: Drawing Conclusions

Applying the Lesson Have students make lists of things they would like to see if they were visiting South Asia, and have them explain their choices.

3 CLOSE

Summarizing Students have learned about South Asian ancient tales that are retold through the performing arts, about traditional architecture, and about recreational activities that originated in South Asia. Have students discuss the similarities and differences between South Asian culture and their own culture.

Evaluating Use these questions to assess students' understanding.

- **How is religious tradition kept alive in South Asia?** (through the visual and performing arts, architecture, observance of religious holidays and festivals)
- **What kinds of religious buildings would you expect to see if you visited South Asia?** (Hindu temples, Buddhist shrines and monasteries, mosques, churches)
- **What are three activities found in the United States that come from South Asia?** (yoga, chess, badminton)

Answers to Check Your Reading

1. Hindus use film, television, drama, music, dance, and decorative arts to retell stories from the Vedas.
2. The Taj Mahal is a tomb built in the 1600s by the Muslim ruler of India for his wife.
3. India has adopted parliamentary democracy and cricket from the British. India has given yoga, polo, badminton, and chess to Britain.
4. Possible answers include: loyalty to parents and spouse, a loving attitude toward all living things.

Independent Practice
Practice Book: page 140

MEETING INDIVIDUAL NEEDS

Reteaching (easy) Ask students to prepare a travel folder inviting visitors to come to South Asia. Remind students to describe such features as religious celebrations and famous buildings. Have students illustrate the folder with their own drawings, or have them collect pictures from magazines or brochures.

Extension (average) Have students select a tale from the Vedas. Ask them to dramatize the story and to act it out for their classmates. These stories are retold in many books about India.

Enrichment (challenging) Have students collect pictures of different examples of Islamic and Hindu art and architecture. Then have them describe the differences between Islamic and Hindu art and architecture.

CHAPTER 25 REVIEW
pages 522–523

USING THE CHAPTER SUMMARY AND REVIEW

Cultural Geography

- **What is the majority religion of India?** (Hinduism)
- **What is the Green Revolution?** (new farming techniques that produce new crops and larger harvests)
- **What role did Great Britain play in South Asia?** (It once had influence in all of South Asia.)
- **Which famous building in the region is Muslim in design?** (the Taj Mahal)

Ideas to Remember

- **How are the region's religious and cultural traditions reflected?** (through language and customs)
- **What type of economy do most countries in South Asia have?** (a developing economy)
- **What types of governments are found in the region?** (democracies, monarchies, dictatorships)
- **What has influenced South Asian arts and recreation?** (religious traditions and British ways)

Answers to Reviewing Vocabulary

1. True.
2. True.
3. In ancient India the Brahmans were the priests.
4. Yoga began in India but has become popular in the United States.
5. True.
6. True.
7. Sikhism is a blending of Hinduism and Islam.
8. The countries of India and Pakistan were created after the partition of British India.
9. Nonaligned nations are developing countries that did not want to take sides in the struggles among the superpowers.
10. Hinduism teaches that the one great spirit in the universe can appear as different gods and that people are born into various social groups.

CHAPTER 25 ▪ SUMMARY

SOUTH ASIA: CULTURAL GEOGRAPHY

PEOPLE

- Religion is an important part of South Asian culture

Hinduism 80% (786 million)

- About 80 percent of India's people are Hindus
- Muslims live mainly in Pakistan, Bangladesh, and northern India
- South Asia has many languages and dialects

- Force of tradition remains strong

ECONOMY

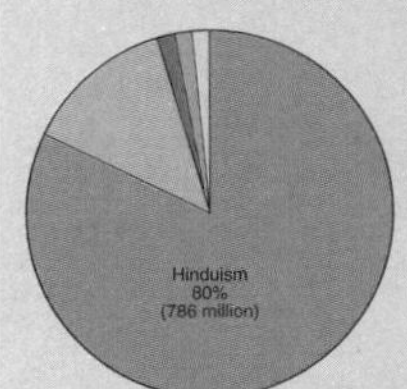

- Population grows faster than ability of nations to provide food and jobs
- Green Revolution, with new technology and stronger, more rapidly growing grains, has doubled production of some crops
- Cottage industries produce: jewelry, textiles, carpets

- Other industries: mining, steel, jute, textiles

GOVERNMENT

- All of South Asia was once under the influence of Great Britain

- Religious differences cause conflict
- Religious conflicts led to creation of India and Pakistan

- India is the world's largest democracy
- Other types of government: military dictatorships, constitutional monarchies

ARTS AND RECREATION

- Arts and recreation strongly influenced by religious traditions
- Area has many temples and shrines

- India's Taj Mahal, Muslim in design, is one of the world's most beautiful buildings
- Cricket and other British sports are popular
- Favorite Indian pastimes: yoga, chess, badminton, and polo

IDEAS TO REMEMBER

- Many languages and customs in South Asia reflect religious and cultural traditions.
- Most countries in South Asia are densely populated and have developing economies in which the majority of workers are farmers.
- South Asia today has many types of government—representative democracies, monarchies, and dictatorships.
- South Asian arts and recreation is a mixture of traditional themes and practices with more recent British influences.

522

ENRICHMENT ACTIVITY

Decorating Boxes **Materials:** small cardboard or wood boxes, colored stones, beads, glitter, sequins, brightly colored paper, glue

1. Refer the class to the description of the popular Indian craft of decorating boxes and table tops on page 520. Tell them that they are going to create similar decorated boxes.
2. Have students work together in groups to create their versions of Indian decorated boxes, sharing available materials and discussing possible design techniques. For example, students might use colored paper as a base, arrange materials in geometric patterns, or punctuate their designs with sequins.
3. Have the class choose their favorites from among the decorated boxes and then arrange them in a classroom display.

CHAPTER 25 • REVIEW

REVIEWING VOCABULARY

Each of the following statements contains an underlined vocabulary word or term. Number a sheet of paper from 1 to 10. Beside each number write whether the following statements are true or false. If the statement is true, write true. If it is false, rewrite the sentence using the vocabulary word correctly.

1. Common in South Asia, cottage industry is the small-scale production of goods that takes place inside people's homes.
2. Although they have weakened in recent times, castes, or rigid social classes, are found in parts of South Asia.
3. In ancient India the Brahmans were members of the servant class and belonged to one of the lowest castes.
4. Yoga began in the United States but has become popular in India.
5. Vedas are ancient Hindu religious stories and are still a source of art, entertainment, and worship.
6. The Green Revolution resulted in more production of food crops.
7. Sikhism is a branch of Islam whose beliefs are identical to those of Muslims in other countries.
8. The partition, or division, of British India created the countries of East Pakistan and West Pakistan.
9. Nonaligned nations are developing countries that had close military and economic ties to one of the superpowers.
10. Hinduism teaches that there is only one god and that all people are equal.

REVIEWING FACTS

1. Which eight countries make up the region of South Asia?
2. Why does English continue to be spoken by large numbers of people in India?
3. What is the Green Revolution?
4. What changes have affected the government of Afghanistan since 1973?
5. What is yoga? From which religious tradition does yoga come?

WRITING ABOUT MAIN IDEAS

1. **Writing a Paragraph:** Write a paragraph contrasting the way in which India gained independence with struggles for independence in other countries. Discuss Mohandas Gandhi's role in this struggle.
2. **Writing a Report:** You have read how religious conflict is the source of much unrest in the Middle East. Write a report about religious conflict in South Asia and the impact this unrest has had on South Asian countries.
3. **Writing About Perspectives:** Write an essay giving your opinion of the following statement: "The Green Revolution may fail if the population continues to grow unchecked in South Asia."

BUILDING SKILLS: DETERMINING POINT OF VIEW

1. What does it mean to determine an author's point of view?
2. List at least four steps you could take to recognize a point of view.
3. Why is it important to be able to determine an author's point of view?
4. Locate a statement in the text that expresses a person's point of view. Describe what that point of view is.

523

Answers to Reviewing Facts

1. Afghanistan, Bangladesh, Bhutan, India, Maldives, Nepal, Pakistan, Sri Lanka
2. Since English was taught in the schools throughout India, it was spoken by more educated Indians than were most of the languages native to India. Because of its general use, many Indians found it convenient to continue speaking English after the departure of the British.
3. new farming techniques that produce new crops
4. A second revolution in 1978 brought a socialist group to power. The Soviet Union invaded in 1978 to protect this government from a new rebellion but began to withdraw after 1989.
5. a way of training both body and mind through exercise and meditation; Hinduism

Suggestions for Writing About Main Ideas

1. Students should mention the role of Great Britain, colonialism, education, and nonviolent protests.
2. You may want students to present their reports in the form of a magazine article.
3. Students should understand that they may agree or disagree with the statement, or just discuss it.

Answers to Building Skills: Determining Point of View

1. to determine the way a person looks at or feels about something
2. Identify the subject; identify statements of fact and opinion; identify information that was left out but could have been included; identify the writer's biases.
3. A person's point of view, or how the person feels about something, can affect the accuracy of what he or she says.
4. Students will probably choose one of the quotes used in the chapter.

Chapter Review and Test

Practice Book: *Vocabulary Review,* page 141
Transparency: *Graphic Organizer*
Assessment Book: *Chapter 25 Test*

MAKING CONNECTIONS

Supporting Main Ideas Display the Main Idea Table Graphic Organizer Transparency, filling in only the underlined words. Have students fill in the "legs" of the table with ideas about each subject. Have them fill in details by listing specific examples in the table "feet." Then have students use the information to write a main idea. *Ask:* What are some examples of contrasts in the cultural geography of South Asia?

MAIN IDEA: South Asia is a region of cultural contrasts.

People	Economy	Government	Arts and Recreation
Each group that settled in South Asia brought its own religious beliefs.	Many South Asian nations have trouble feeding their populations.	South Asia today has many types of government.	The arts of South Asia are a blend of the traditional and the modern.
Hinduism, Islam, Sikhism, Christianity	high population density, famine, malnutrition	democracies, monarchies, dictatorships	the Vedas, temples, shrines, yoga

CHAPTER 26
ORGANIZER

CHINA AND ITS NEIGHBORS text pages 524–539

CHAPTER THEME

Ancient religious and family values are blended with communism in China, North Korea, and Mongolia, and with private enterprise in neighboring nations.

CHAPTER OBJECTIVES

CONTENT

- Describe the ways in which the cultures of East Asia are similar today.
- Identify Confucianism, Daoism, and Buddhism and describe how these belief systems have influenced the culture of East Asia.
- Describe how most people in East Asia earn their living.
- Outline the changes that Deng Xiaoping introduced into the communist system in China.
- Explain why even limited economic freedom threatens the "iron rice bowl" mentality in China.
- Compare the East Asian countries that have communist economies with those countries that have economies based on free enterprise.
- Describe the different kinds of governments of the countries of East Asia.
- Outline the events leading to the Communist victory in China and the creation of a Nationalist government in Taiwan.
- Describe the types of arts and recreation popular in East Asia today.
- Identify socialist realism and explain how it serves the needs of communist governments.

SKILLS

Geography
- Interpret a political map of East Asia.

Study and Research
- Read political cartoons.

Thinking
- Contrast the Chinese writing system with the Western alphabet.
- Ask focused questions about private enterprise in China.

Reading and Writing
- Write a paragraph about the changes that have occurred in the Pacific Rim.

CITIZENSHIP VALUES

- Appreciate the relationship between economic freedom and prosperity.

TEACHER OPTIONS

READING STRATEGY: Study Guide Strategies to help students read and remember the main ideas of the lesson.

Lesson 1: p. 525 Lesson 3: p. 532
Lesson 2: p. 529 Lesson 4: p. 536

MEETING INDIVIDUAL NEEDS Activities for reteaching, extension, and enrichment.

Lesson 1: p. 528 Study and Research
Lesson 2: p. 531 Skills: p. 535
Lesson 3: p. 534 Lesson 4: p. 537

GEO ADVENTURES ACTIVITIES PAD Daily activities to assess students' understanding of geography skills.

CURRICULUM CONNECTION Activities to help integrate other subject areas with Social Studies.

Language Arts: p. 533

PUPIL EDITION ON CASSETTE Language support for students who have difficulty reading or who will benefit from listening to the Pupil Edition on Cassette as they read.

SECOND-LANGUAGE SUPPORT Activities and suggestions for second-language learners.

Lesson 3: p. 485-D

CHAPTER PLANNING GUIDE

LESSON	SUGGESTED PACING	THEMES	TEACHER SUPPORT MATERIALS: TEACHER'S RESOURCE CENTER
1 THE PEOPLE pages 525–528	1 day	Chinese culture is a blend of traditional ways and communism.	Practice Book p. 142 ■ Anthology pp. 152–153, 167, 168–170
2 THE ECONOMY pages 529–531	1 day	Private enterprise has solved some problems and caused others in East Asia's economies.	Practice Book p. 143 Outline Map p. 35 **Technology:** *Adventures CD-ROM*
3 THE GOVERNMENT pages 532–534	1 day	There are both democratic and communist governments in East Asia.	Practice Book p. 144 ■ Anthology p. 171 Outline Map p. 35 **Technology:** *Videodisc/Video Tape 2*
BUILDING STUDY AND RESEARCH SKILLS Reading Political Cartoons page 535	1 day	Political cartoons use symbols to express a point of view about political events.	Practice Book p. 145
4 ARTS AND RECREATION pages 536–537	1 day	There is a blend of new socialist realism and old traditions in the arts and recreation of the countries of East Asia.	Practice Book p. 146 ■ Anthology pp. 179–180 **Technology:** *Adventures CD-ROM*
CHAPTER SUMMARY AND REVIEW pages 538–539	1 day	Chapter content, skills, and vocabulary are reviewed and evaluated.	Practice Book p. 147 Transparency: Graphic Organizer Assessment Book, Chapter 26 Test

Technology CONNECTION

Lesson 2
ADVENTURES CD-ROM
Enrich Lesson 2 by having students *Compare* the size of China to some of its neighboring Asian countries.

Lesson 3
VIDEODISC/VIDEO TAPE 2
Enrich Lesson 3 with Video Lesson 9 Segment 2, *China Today.*

Search 48074, Play To 50471 Side A

Lesson 4
ADVENTURES CD-ROM
Enrich Lesson 4 by having students listen to language samples in *Sounds, China/Korea.*

CHAPTER 26
pages 524–539

USING THE CHAPTER OPENER

Discussing the Photograph Have students study the photograph while they read the chapter title.

Ask students:

- **How might you describe the person who is pictured here?** (young, of Chinese origin, dressed in modern clothes)
- **What do you think she does? Why do you think so?** (She probably goes to school in a town or city; because she is not dressed for work or farm life and most children in China go to school)

Reading/Listening to the Primary Source Have students continue to examine the photograph as you read the passage aloud.

Ask students:

- **What is the enormous task that China faces?** (the task of building a modern nation)
- **What is one of the biggest problems that China must solve?** (feeding, housing, and employing its huge population of more than 1 billion people—one fifth of the world's population)
- *THINKING FURTHER:* **How can a large population be both an advantage and a disadvantage?** (A large population provides a labor force to accomplish great tasks. On the other hand, a large population needs to be fed, clothed, housed, and educated and can drain a country's resources.)

Mention to the class the Chinese cultural traditions of respect for the elderly and of extended families in which parents and grandparents are cared for in their old age. Discuss how these traditions might clash with the needs of a modern nation.

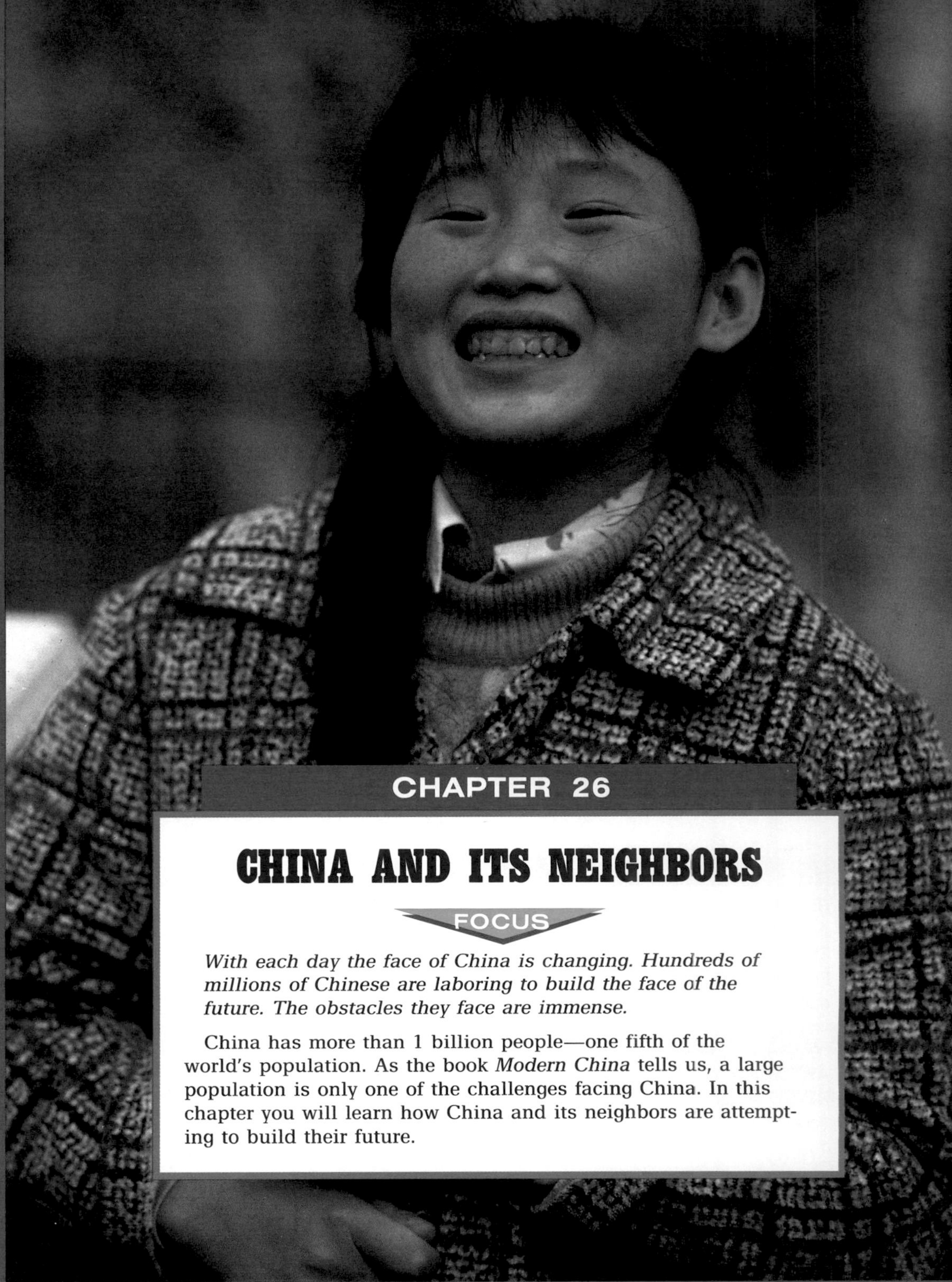

CHAPTER 26

CHINA AND ITS NEIGHBORS

FOCUS

With each day the face of China is changing. Hundreds of millions of Chinese are laboring to build the face of the future. The obstacles they face are immense.

China has more than 1 billion people—one fifth of the world's population. As the book *Modern China* tells us, a large population is only one of the challenges facing China. In this chapter you will learn how China and its neighbors are attempting to build their future.

BACKGROUND INFORMATION

About the Chinese People

- The people of China belong to many different ethnic groups. The largest group is that of the Han Chinese, but there are more than 50 minority groups.
- The non-Chinese population of mainland China is concentrated in the southwestern provinces. Some of these minority groups are related to the people of Thailand. All of them are culturally distinct from the Han Chinese.
- Other important minorities are located in the autonomous regions of China. The Manchus form an important cultural group in Manchuria. Tibetans are a majority of the population of Tibet. Uighurs and other Turkic people live in Xinjiang. Mongolians live mainly in Inner Mongolia and Xinjiang.

LESSON 1

The People

READ TO LEARN

Key Vocabulary
Confucianism
Daoism
Buddhism
pinyin

Key People
Mao Zedong
Confucius
Laozi
Siddhartha Gautama

Key Places
East Asia
Beijing

Read Aloud

Just 80 years ago, any common person who made his way into China's Imperial Palace—the "Forbidden City"—was immediately dragged out again and beheaded. Today 140,000 sightseers a week wander through the palace.

The person describing this change is Sun Jue (sůn′ jü′ ə). He works at the Palace Museum located in Beijing, the capital city of China. The building he mentions used to be the home of China's emperor. Today the palace is the home of art treasures that Mr. Sun calls the "reminders of China's cultural history."

Read for Purpose

1. WHAT YOU KNOW: What revolutions have you read about that completely changed a country's way of life?
2. WHAT YOU WILL LEARN: What ways of life do the people of East Asia continue to share despite their political differences?

EAST ASIA

Life is changing throughout East Asia. East Asia includes China and nearby areas that share many parts of China's culture. As you can see from the map on page 526, these nearby areas are the countries of Mongolia, North Korea, South Korea, Taiwan, and the British colony of Hong Kong. North and South Korea were once one country. Hong Kong is scheduled to become part of China in 1997.

For many centuries China has influenced the ways of life of the peoples in the surrounding areas. Once a great empire, China is today the largest country in East Asia. Its area of 3.8 million square miles (9.8 million sq km) makes China the third-largest country in the world, after Russia and Canada.

CHINA'S BREAK WITH THE PAST

Life changed in almost every way in China after 1949. That was the year the Communist forces under the leadership of Mao Zedong (mou′ dze dung′) won control of China in a civil war. At that time, most Chinese people were poor and a few very rich people held most of the country's wealth.

LESSON 1
pages 525–528

Lesson Theme Chinese culture is a blend of traditional ways and communism.

Lesson Objectives
- Identify communism as the main reason for the changes in Chinese life.
- Describe the ways Confucianism, Daoism, and Buddhism have influenced East Asia.

1 PREPARE

Motivate Read the opening passage aloud to the class. Point out the drastic changes in policy that have occurred over the last 80 years. Ask students to speculate on what could have caused the changes.

Set Purpose Have the class use the *What You Know* question to discuss any revolutions with which they are familiar. Use the *What You Will Learn* question to discuss the similarities and differences in the ways of life of the various East Asian groups.

2 TEACH

Identifying East Asian Countries Display the political *Atlas* Map of Southern and Eastern Asia. Have students identify the countries that compose East Asia. Discuss the vast size of China.

Discussing China's Break with the Past

Ask students:

- **Who led the Communist forces to victory in 1949?** (Mao Zedong)

READING STRATEGY AND VOCABULARY DEVELOPMENT

Study Guide Have students develop a journal for the nation of China. Students may find it helpful to use study guides in order to identify important information to include in their journals. Since this lesson deals with the changes in tradition and government that have occurred over a specific period of time, have students construct a time line as a means of selecting the most important of these changes. Use 1949 as a focal point since the communist government of China was established in that year. Help students to identify the key points of China's early history—the many inventions, the teachings of Confucius, and the development of Buddhism and Daoism. Then guide them in identifying the major changes since 1949, including the recent practice of free enterprise.

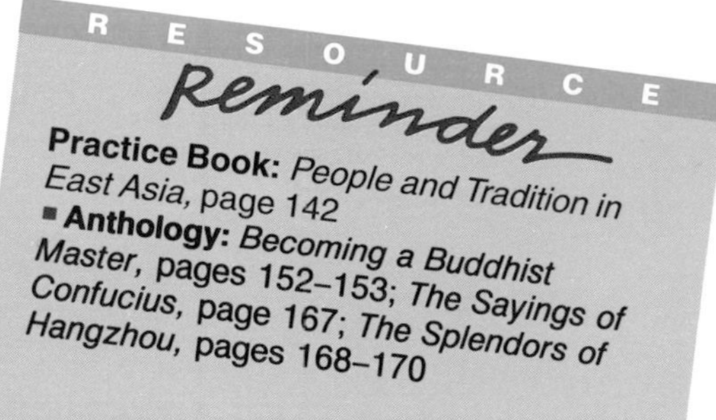

Practice Book: *People and Tradition in East Asia,* page 142
▪ **Anthology:** *Becoming a Buddhist Master,* pages 152–153; *The Sayings of Confucius,* page 167; *The Splendors of Hangzhou,* pages 168–170

Discussing the Change in China
Continue the discussion.

Ask students:

- **What did the Communist leaders want for the Chinese people?** (They wanted them to be equal to one another.)
- **How has China changed since the Communist victory?** (Fewer people are poor, and there are more schools and factories.)
- **Why are the Chinese proud?** (The Chinese civilization is very old, and the Chinese invented many things that are still used today.)
- **What are some of the items invented by the Chinese?** (silk, paper, the technique of printing)

EXTENDING MAP SKILLS

Help students to identify the neighboring countries of China.

Ask students:

- **Which East Asian country is an island?** (Taiwan)
- **Which countries are on a peninsula?** (North Korea, South Korea)
- **Which East Asian country is to the north of China?** (Mongolia)
- **What is the capital of Mongolia?** (Ulaanbaatar)
- **Is the capital of China in the eastern, western, or southern part of the country?** (eastern)
- **Which countries are on the boundary of Russia?** (China, Mongolia, and North Korea)

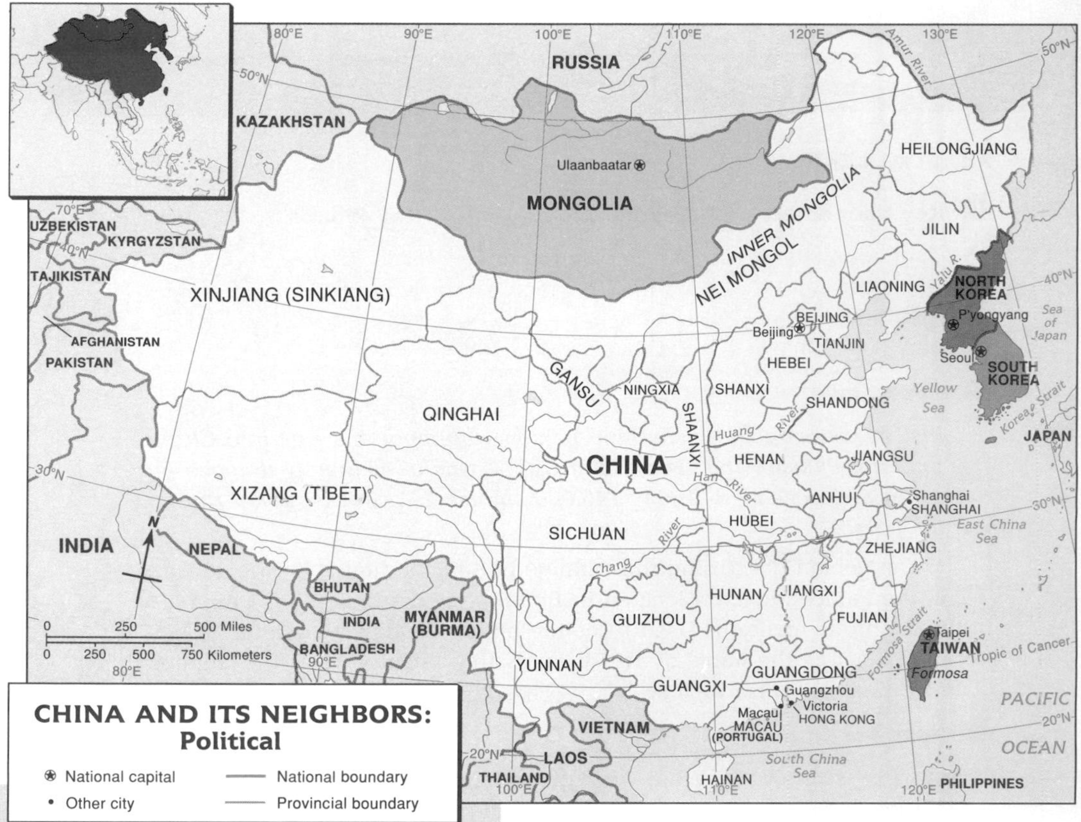

CHINA AND ITS NEIGHBORS: Political

⊛ National capital • Other city — National boundary — Provincial boundary

MAP SKILL: China is so large it shares a border with many countries. What country is on China's north-central border?

The new Communist rulers wanted to make all people in China equal. They gave most of the rich people's land to poor farmers. The Communists experimented with new ways of organizing farms and factories and tried to teach everyone to read and write. They wanted to get rid of many ancient traditions and values and to replace them with Communist beliefs.

Have the Communists succeeded in changing China? The answer is yes, in many ways. If you were to visit China you would see fewer poor people and more schools and factories than there were at the end of World War II.

As in the past, the present-day people of China are proud to be Chinese. This sense of pride reflects their long and impressive history. Over the centuries Chinese civilization invented silk, paper, printing, and many other things. China also maintained centuries of peace and prosperity for its people.

EAST ASIA'S TRADITIONAL VALUES

Family loyalty helped to shape the cultures of China and its neighbors. In East Asia the idea of honoring one's parents goes back at least 2,500 years to the time of Kongfuzi, China's great philosopher and teacher. Kongfuzi is known outside Asia as **Confucius** (kən fū′ shəs).

MAP SKILL: Mongolia

BACKGROUND INFORMATION

China in Relation to the World China is the third-largest country in the world. It is 3,000 miles (4,827 km) wide from east to west, and 2,500 miles (4,022 km) long from north to south. The mainland has 3.7 million square miles (9.6 million sq km), while Taiwan has 13,892 square miles (35,980 sq km).

- China has the largest population in the world. About one fifth of the world's people live in China.
- The highest plateau region in the world is the Plateau of Tibet in the southwest part of China. Its average elevation is approximately 16,000 feet (4,877 m) above sea level.
- The Himalayas, on China's border with India and Nepal, include Mount Everest, the highest mountain in the world.

Many East Asian statues and paintings honor Confucius (*right*) and Buddha (*left*).

The teachings of Confucius, known as **Confucianism**, are a set of rules for behavior. Confucius taught that family members have responsibilities to one another. In the same way, people and their rulers have responsibilities to each other. Confucius also taught respect for learning because he believed that knowledge can bring human beings closer to perfection.

Confucianism remains a strong influence on life in Taiwan, Hong Kong, and South Korea. In those countries, family loyalty and respect for elders are important values.

After the Communists took power in China and North Korea, they tried to replace family loyalty with loyalty to the state. But the breaking of family ties went against tradition and met with only limited success. In China today, many staunch Communists still keep the traditions of honoring their parents in many different ways.

FAMILY SIZE

In the past most East Asian families lived close to their relatives. Relatives might live in the same house or near one another in the village.

Large families are traditional, and many East Asian couples would like to have several children. But most of the governments throughout East Asia are trying to slow the rapid growth of their large populations.

In China especially, the size of the population is overwhelming. China's 1 billion people make its population four times as large as that of the United States. The Chinese government has made an effort to slow population growth by passing laws that encourage families to have only one child. These measures have slowed down the increase in population somewhat, but population growth is still a serious problem for China.

DAOISM AND BUDDHISM

In addition to Confucianism, two systems of belief have helped to shape life in East Asia. They are **Daoism** (dou′ iz əm) and **Buddhism** (bůd′ iz əm). Daoism teaches that people should accept calmly whatever fate brings. Buddhism teaches that human suffering is caused by selfishness or the desire for things.

Daoism may have been started by a teacher named **Laozi** (lou′ dzu′), who lived about the same time as Confucius. When things have gone wrong, have you

527

Discussing Traditional Values Help students to identify Confucius and the ways in which his teachings still influence Chinese life.

Ask students:

- **What are some of the main teachings of Confucius?** (family members, like people and their rulers, have responsibilities to each other; respect for learning; respect for elders)
- **Were the Communists successful in replacing family loyalty with loyalty to the state?** (only partly)
- *THINKING FURTHER:* **Why might loyalty to the state be important in a communist form of government?** (The government wants the people to follow the rules without questioning them.)

Discussing Family Size

Ask students:

- **Why does the government want to slow down population growth?** (The country is already overcrowded.)
- **How is the government trying to do this?** (It is trying to limit the number of children per family to one.)

Discussing the Photographs Have students refer to the illustrations of Buddha and Confucius. Discuss why people would want statues and paintings of Buddha and Confucius in their homes.

Distinguishing Between Daoism and Buddhism Help students to distinguish between the two crucial belief systems.

Ask students:

- **What is one important Daoist teaching?** (that people should accept their fate calmly)
- **What is one important Buddhist teaching?** (that human suffering is caused by selfishness)

BACKGROUND INFORMATION

Confucius Confucius was born in 551 B.C. and died in 479 B.C. It is believed that he was raised by his mother after his father died and that his family was very poor.

- Confucius was married at the age of 19. He had one son and two daughters.
- Confucius believed that the ruling classes should aim for a perfect society by using exemplary behavior that the lower classes would imitate.
- The sayings of Confucius are collected in a volume called the *Lun Yu*, or *Analects*.

Discussing Language and Writing Stress that written Chinese is the same throughout the country, but the many spoken dialects make it difficult for Chinese people from different areas to speak to one another.

EXTENDING CHART SKILLS

Ask students:

- **When did Chinese words look most like pictures?** (before 1500 B.C.)

Applying the Lesson Have students discuss ways in which the important influences of religion and family loyalty might conflict with communist teachings.

CLOSE

Summarizing In this lesson students have learned about traditional Chinese life and how communism has brought about changes in lifestyle.

Evaluating Use the *Check Your Reading* questions (answers given below) to assess students' understanding.

Answers to Check Your Reading

1. to make all people equal
2. a set of rules for behavior, developed by Confucius
3. a belief system developed by Laozi, emphasizing calm acceptance
4. The Chinese system uses characters to represent ideas, while English combines letters that symbolize individual sounds to make words.

Independent Practice
Practice Book: page 142

ever heard someone say, "Well, that's the way life is"? That thought is somewhat like a Daoist. *Dao* means "the way." Daoists believe that people should leave things alone and not try to change them. Over the centuries Daoism slowly changed into a religion.

Another belief system, Buddhism, was begun by the Indian prince **Siddhartha Gautama** (si där′ tə gô′ tə mə). He believed that the way to overcome suffering is to get rid of selfish desires. Instead of seeking worldly gains, Siddhartha said that people should concentrate on forming good thoughts and good behavior. Siddhartha came to be called the Buddha, which means the "enlightened one."

The Communist governments of East Asia discourage Buddhism and Daoism. The Communist government leaders believe that all religions are old-fashioned and unscientific. Yet Buddhism and Daoism remain important religions in East Asia.

LANGUAGE AND WRITING

Being able to write helped the Chinese to communicate and to unite into an empire. The Chinese also introduced their way of writing to their neighbors. The Mongolians and Koreans now have their own systems of writing.

Wherever they live, the people of China can read the same books because written Chinese is the same throughout the country. However, Chinese from different parts of the nation may not be able to understand one another's spoken language. In addition to different languages, China has many dialects. The official dialect is based on that of **Beijing**, the capital.

Chinese writing is not based on an alphabet which represents different sounds, as is English. Chinese writing is based on characters, which represent ideas. The Chinese government recently developed a new system of using our alphabet to write Chinese sounds. This system is called **pinyin**. For example, you may have seen the capital city of China written *Peking*. In pinyin it is now written *Beijing*.

CHART SKILL: When did pictures of words begin to look like characters?

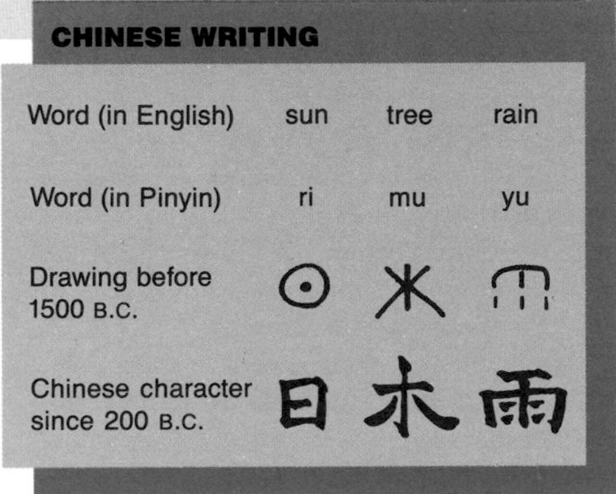

CHART SKILL: since 200 B.C.

TRADITION, FAMILY, AND LANGUAGE

As you have read, Confucianism, Daoism, and Buddhism have been important belief systems in East Asia. Family loyalty is an important value which has endured in Communist as well as non-Communist countries. The Chinese system of writing has helped to unify their country.

Check Your Reading

1. Why did China's Communist rulers want the Chinese people to break with their past?
2. What is Confucianism?
3. What is Daoism?
4. **THINKING SKILL:** How is the Chinese system of writing different from the alphabet you use?

THINKING SKILL: Compare and Contrast

MEETING INDIVIDUAL NEEDS

Reteaching (easy) Have students list the main teachings of Confucianism, Daoism, and Buddhism.

Extension (average) Have students find books on the Chinese writing system and/or photos and illustrations of the system. Make a bulletin board display with appropriate English translations.

Enrichment (challenging) Have students research and prepare a brief report on the life of Confucius, Laozi, or Siddhartha Gautama.

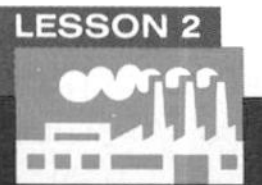

LESSON 2

The Economy

READ TO LEARN

Key Vocabulary
aquaculture
iron rice bowl
Pacific Rim

Key People
Deng Xiaoping

Key Places
Hong Kong
Taiwan
South Korea

Read Aloud

I was a farmer like everyone else. Nobody had their own land at that time.

Yin Yengcheng (yung' chung'), who spoke these words, borrowed money to start his own orchard in China in 1978. The Communist government had decided to allow some people to have private plots of land. A few years later Yin's orchard earned a profit, but the village committee would not permit Yin to dig the irrigation pond he needed to increase the size of this orchard. Why? A newspaper article said Yin was the victim of the "red-eyed disease"—jealousy.

In this lesson you will learn why East Asia's economies are changing, some faster than others, and why changes may cause disagreements.

Read for Purpose

1. WHAT YOU KNOW: What is the major difference between a communist economic system and capitalism?
2. WHAT YOU WILL LEARN: In what ways do most people in East Asia earn their living?

SCARCE LAND

As you read in Lesson 1, in the past many Chinese had been poor, but under the Communists life slowly improved. China's government took over all land and businesses. Like the government of the Soviet Union at that time, China's government made economic decisions for the entire country. The government was also strict about keeping everyone economically equal. It became a serious crime to make a profit or run a private business.

Then in the late 1970s the government discovered that the population was growing faster than the country's ability to grow food. The government tried to find ways to feed 1 billion people and to slow the growth of the population. That is why it urges families to have only one child, as you read in Lesson 1.

Unfortunately, the country's resources are limited. As you read in Chapter 24, good land is scarce in China. Only about 11 percent of China's land is suitable for farming, and the Chinese are already using every available bit of land. In addition China does not have enough money to buy all the food it needs.

WHAT YOU KNOW: In a communist system the state owns the property and makes economic decisions; under capitalism citizens own property and make economic decisions.

LESSON 2
pages 529–531

Lesson Theme Private enterprise has solved some problems and caused others in East Asia's economies.

Lesson Objectives
- Identify the reasons for the growth of private enterprise.
- Describe the problems that developed as a result of the economic changes.

1 PREPARE

Motivate Have a student read the opening passage aloud. Discuss why Yin was a victim of jealousy.

Set Purpose Have the class use the *What You Know* question to compare and contrast capitalism and communism. Use the *What You Will Learn* question to encourage discussion of the major occupations held by people in East Asia.

2 TEACH

Understanding the Scarcity of Arable Land Have students read to find out the effects of scarce land and a large population on China's economy.

Ask students:

- **How did the government make everyone equal?** (It took over all of the land, made all economic decisions, and restricted private enterprise.)
- **Why did the government fail in its attempts to feed the people?** (The population grew faster than the country was able to grow food, there was not much good farmland, and there was not enough money to buy additional food.)

READING STRATEGY AND VOCABULARY DEVELOPMENT

Study Guide Have students add to their journals by creating a cause-effect chart. Have them chart the successes and failures of the communist and capitalist economies in China. An example is charted below.

CAUSE	EFFECT
population growth	government unable to feed all
people wanted several children	government's failure to slow population growth
scarcity of good land	food shortage

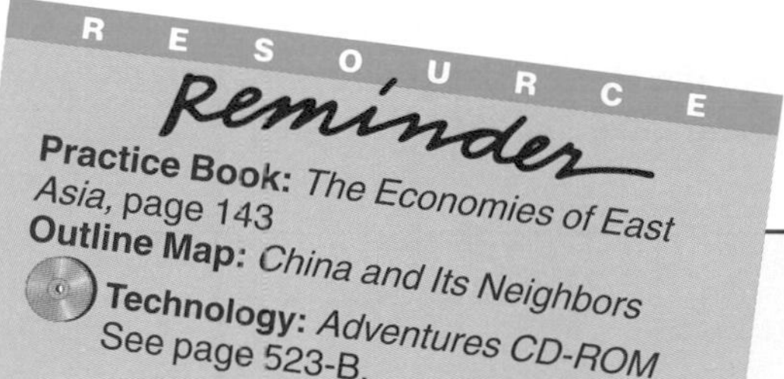

Understanding Land Scarcity Continue the discussion.

Ask students:

- **What did the government do to solve the food problem?** (It started collective farms, tried to grow crops on dry land, raised more cattle, dug ponds to raise fish, and allowed limited private enterprise.)

Discussing Private Enterprise Help students to understand why the changes in policy toward private enterprise were successful.

Ask students:

- **What kinds of businesses were started?** (small businesses such as knitting, repairing bicycles and farm machinery)
- **Why was the private fan company more successful than the government-run company?** (The private company had foreign money available and was located in a more business-oriented area than the one in which the government-run company was located.)

Understanding the Problems in Changing the System

Ask students:

- **Who are some of the people who dislike free enterprise?** (Those who gained their jobs as a result of their political beliefs rather than their skills.)
- **What problems has free enterprise caused?** (uneven distribution of goods, higher prices)

Explaining Economic Miracles Stress that hard work and education made many private enterprises successful in Hong Kong, Taiwan, and South Korea.

Ask students:

- **Why are some Pacific Rim Countries called "economic miracles?"** (because they have increased their business and trade so much)
- **How has their success affected the "miracle" countries of the Pacific Rim?** (Rising standards of living have increased wages.)

Experts looked for new ways to solve China's food problem. The government started collective farms like those the Soviet Union had. Farmers tried to grow crops on dry land and to raise more cattle in outlying areas. In addition many Chinese dug ponds in order to raise fish. **Aquaculture** (ak′ wə kul chər), or fish farming, is an important source of food throughout East Asia. However, China still needed to have more food.

In the late 1970s China's leader, **Deng Xiaoping** (dung′ shou′ ping′), decided to allow a limited amount of private enterprise in China. Some farmers were allowed to work small plots for themselves and to sell their goods at open markets for a profit.

THE SPREAD OF PRIVATE ENTERPRISE

China's new economic program was successful. Villages and towns permitted people to start businesses in their free time. For example, in a small building near the fields, a dozen women might be knitting sweaters for sale or a group might be repairing bicycles and farm machinery for a fee.

Within a few years some Chinese businesses began to take greater risks, often using foreign money and techniques. Many of the private enterprises started in the coastal provinces where people have long been traders. For example, in southern Guangdong Province a small town began its own electric fan company in 1987. Money for the machinery came from a company in **Hong Kong**. The factory's approximately 2,000 workers produce about 5 million fans a year, which are sold through the company in Hong Kong for a large profit.

In contrast to the fan factory is a giant state-owned computer factory in Hunan Province. Its workers produce only about 5,000 units a year because of frequent shortages of parts and money. The people of Hunan live inland where change is slower. Some Hunanese, who are more traditional in outlook, do not place much value on business as a way to earn a living. Thus they keep prices low and do not compete vigorously for business.

This farmer is winnowing rice, or separating the grain from the husks. Rice is a major crop of East Asia.

PROBLEMS IN CHANGING THE SYSTEM

Complaints have led the government of China to tighten its control over private enterprises. Some people have much to gain by slowing the program of private enterprise. They include people who gained their jobs as a result of their political beliefs rather than their skills. In these instances factory heads may know little about the type of work that is done in the factory. Also, in the past workers were paid whether or not they worked. This sys-

BUILDING CITIZENSHIP

Using Current Events In most countries the economy is a political issue, but this is especially the case in China.

China depends on foreign investment for the development of many of its private industries. The spread of private enterprise in the early 1980s meant that large numbers of Chinese citizens came into contact with foreigners and foreign ideas. This made some cautious Chinese leaders very unhappy, and they tried to block some of the economic reforms. This in turn helped inspire popular protests (see Lesson 3 of this chapter). When the government violently suppressed the protests, foreign investment diminished and the value of Chinese currency dropped.

Have students look for articles on the current economic situation in China. Have them prepare oral or written reports about what effects this may be having on Chinese politics.

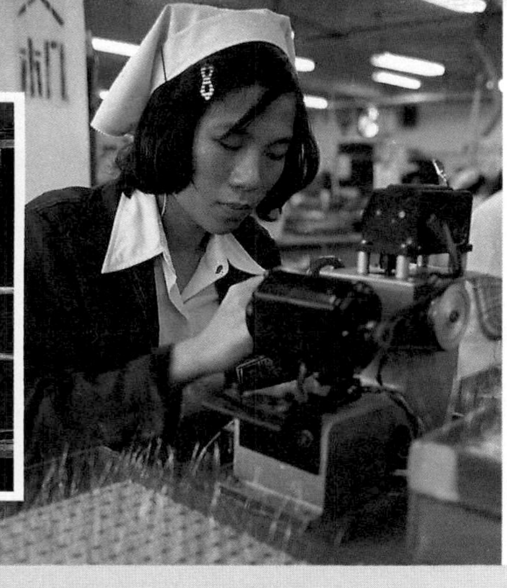

Among East Asia's growing industries are shipbuilding in South Korea (*left*) and electronics in Taiwan (*right*).

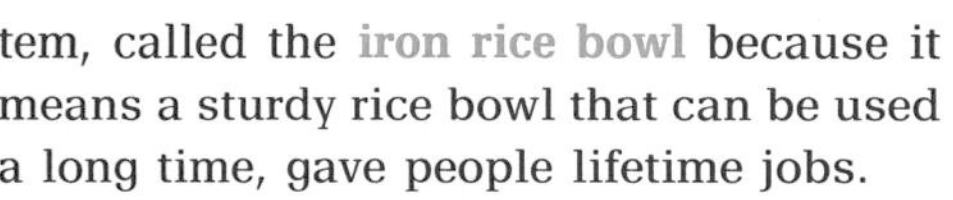

tem, called the iron rice bowl because it means a sturdy rice bowl that can be used a long time, gave people lifetime jobs.

Still other Chinese worry about the problems that free enterprise has caused. Some parts of China now have too many goods, while other parts have severe shortages. Many prices have risen steeply. These are only a few of China's problems.

THE PACIFIC RIM

With the exception of Mongolia, China and its East Asian neighbors are among the more than 30 countries of the Pacific Rim. This term refers to all the countries that border the Pacific Ocean. The United States, Canada, and Mexico are Pacific Rim countries. So are Australia, New Zealand, and the countries on the western coasts of Central and South America.

Trade among these countries has grown rapidly. Some of the Pacific Rim countries in Asia have increased their business and trade so much that they are called "economic miracles." Because their workers' wages were low, Hong Kong, Taiwan, and South Korea produced goods more cheaply than other countries. Rising standards of living have increased wages in the "miracle" countries, but this has not diminished their trade.

CONTRASTING ECONOMIES

You have read that in 1949, China's new Communist government started programs to make everyone economically equal. When China's population began to grow faster than the nation's ability to feed its people, its leaders looked for new solutions. One answer was limited private enterprise. Pacific Rim countries Taiwan and South Korea, along with the colony of Hong Kong, have become "economic miracles" by rapidly increasing trade.

Check Your Reading

1. Why did China's government decide to allow limited private enterprise?
2. Give two reasons that the government decided to slow the spread of private enterprise in China.
3. Why do you think Taiwan, Hong Kong, and South Korea are called "economic miracles"?
4. THINKING SKILL: List three questions you would ask to find out whether a business in China is privately run.

THINKING SKILL: Asking Questions

531

Applying the Lesson Have students make a list of the problems facing East Asia and the solutions that have been tried so far.

Summarizing Students have learned that there is great economic upheaval in East Asia. Private enterprise has alleviated some problems and caused others. Discuss reasons for the economic success of Hong Kong, Taiwan, and South Korea.

Evaluating Use these questions to assess students' understanding.

- **What major economic problems does China face today?** (still growing population, shortages, rising prices)
- **Why is private enterprise one possible solution?** (People take more responsibility for their work and produce more.)

1. The government thought private enterprise might help to solve some of the economic problems.
2. There was an uneven distribution of goods and higher prices.
3. They increased their trade and business a great deal by producing goods more cheaply than other countries.
4. Possible questions include: Who pays your salary? Are you in business for yourself? What kind of work do you do?

Independent Practice
Practice Book: page 143

MEETING INDIVIDUAL NEEDS

Reteaching (easy) Have students discuss possible solutions to the shortage of food in China.

Extension (average) Have students examine product labels and make a chart of items that they find are made in China, Hong Kong, and Taiwan. Have them list these items on an outline map of the region, found in the Teacher's Resource Center.

Enrichment (challenging) For cooperative learning divide the class into research teams. Assign each team a country or colony (mainland China, Taiwan, Hong Kong, South Korea). Have each team research current economic conditions and policies of their assigned country or colony and give a report to the class.

LESSON 3
pages 532–534

Lesson Theme There are both democratic and communist governments in East Asia.

Lesson Objectives
- Identify the various forms of government in East Asia.
- Discuss the similarities and differences among the governments.

PREPARE

Motivate Have a student read the opening passage aloud to the class. Remind students how many communist governments lost power in the 1980s and 1990s. Ask students how communist leaders in China might feel about this.

Set Purpose Discuss any knowledge students already have about the role of the Communist Party in the former Soviet Union. Have students think about the *What You Will Learn* question as they read the lesson.

TEACH

Understanding a Divided China

Ask students:

- **What types of governments do the two Chinas have?** (Communist government for mainland China and a non-Communist government for the Nationalist island of Taiwan)
- **What led to these two separate governments?** (two internal wars)
- *THINKING FURTHER:* **What does Mao Zedong's quote "China has stood up" mean?** (Perhaps he meant that since the people were willing to fight, or stand up, for what they believed, they were capable of helping China take its place among the other nations of the world.)

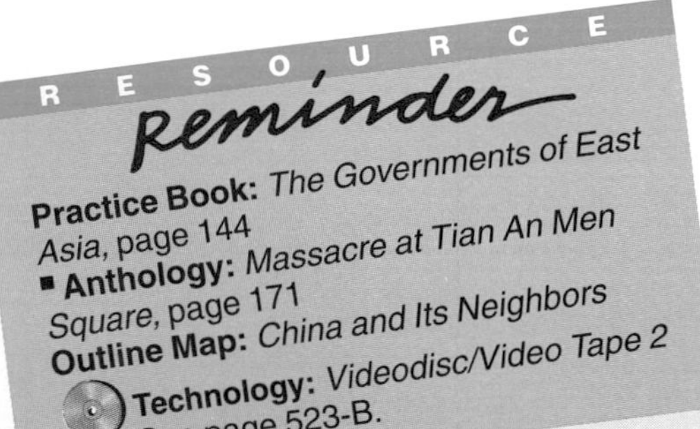

RESOURCE *Reminder*

Practice Book: *The Governments of East Asia*, page 144

▪ **Anthology:** *Massacre at Tian An Men Square*, page 171

Outline Map: *China and Its Neighbors*

Technology: *Videodisc/Video Tape 2*

See page 523-B.

LESSON 3

The Government

READ TO LEARN

Key Vocabulary

autonomous region

Read Aloud

The glorious history of the People's Republic of China of the past 42 years has proved and will continue to prove that no difficulty can crush or cow the Chinese people. . . . No tempests [disturbances] *will shake their determination to move along the path of building socialism under the leadership of the Communist Party of China.*

These words were spoken by Prime Minister Li Peng in 1991 as he declared that his country would keep a communist government even after the former Soviet Union and the countries of Eastern Europe had ended their commitment to communism.

Read for Purpose

1. WHAT YOU KNOW: What was the role of the Communist party in Eastern Europe and the former Soviet Union?
2. WHAT YOU WILL LEARN: What kinds of governments do the countries of East Asia have?

A DIVIDED CHINA

Two internal wars led to the present systems of government in China and Taiwan. The first was a brief revolt that broke out as the emperor's government began to fall apart. The victorious rebels established a republic in 1912.

In the 1920s a civil war began between the Communists and the Nationalists, who had taken control of the government. The Communists won in 1949. Mao Zedong declared that "China has stood up" and was on the road to greatness.

The Nationalists retreated to the island of Taiwan, which had been part of China. Vowing to return to the mainland one day, they formed a non-Communist government-in-exile on Taiwan. They called their government the Republic of China. Until 1971, the United Nations recognized Taiwan's government as the "official China." Taiwan's government is headed by a president and a national assembly. Until 1986, only one political party was allowed.

GOVERNING CHINA

On the mainland the Communists faced a difficult task. In 1949 they had nearly a half billion people to govern, more than any other country at that time. China, renamed the People's Republic of China, was divided into 21 provinces and 5 **autonomous regions**. The autonomous regions are self-governing areas that are supervised by the central government in Beijing, the capital.

WHAT YOU KNOW: The Communist party once had a monopoly of power in Eastern Europe and the former Soviet Union.

READING STRATEGY AND VOCABULARY DEVELOPMENT

Study Guide Have students continue developing a study guide. They should focus on the changing face of East Asian governments. Divide the class into research groups. Assign each group to research the government of one country (Taiwan, mainland China, Hong Kong, Mongolia, North Korea, and South Korea). Each group should also prepare a one-page study outline to distribute to the class. The group researching China should emphasize the student movement of 1989 and compare it to the current status of citizen participation. The group researching Hong Kong should emphasize the success of its free enterprise system under British control.

A peaceful demonstration for more rights became violent when troops fired upon crowds in Beijing's Tiananmen Square in 1989.

Most of China's minority groups live in autonomous regions in the sparsely populated north and west. Together, they make up about 5 percent of China's population. One area, Tibet, had been an independent country, but China attacked it and made it an autonomous region in 1950.

The army has remained a powerful force throughout East Asia. In China soldiers have many roles. They may act as police, guides, or even physical laborers. One soldier, Liu Yongshe (lyü′ yông′ shûr′), says that such "activities not only benefit the people but also remind us that we belong to the people."

The Chinese army played a critical role in 1989. When thousands of students gathered in Beijing to demand more political rights, some of the troops at first refused to break up the crowds because the soldiers considered themselves part of the people. More troops were brought in from other parts of China, and they used force to end the protest. Many students were killed and imprisoned at this time.

ONE-PARTY GOVERNMENT

Officially the head of China's government is the premier. However, the country's real leader is the head of the Communist party. The Chinese Communist party is the only political party allowed in China. Most government officials are members of the Communist party.

China's Communist party and government resemble two pyramids. At the bottom of the party's pyramid are the small Communist cells found in all neighborhoods. At the top of the pyramid is the Central Committee of the Communist Party Congress. The chairman of the Central Committee is the head of the entire party.

In government smaller groups elect people to represent them in larger groups. The largest group is the National People's Congress, the national legislature. It has more than 3,500 members and meets once a year in Beijing. The congress chooses the State Council, which is headed by the premier.

HONG KONG

China claims a number of the areas around it. One of them is Hong Kong. Until 1842 Hong Kong was a relatively unknown island on the southeastern coast of China. In that year the British won from China the

533

Discussing How to Govern China Point out that governing half a billion people required organization and much supervision.

Ask students:

- **How is the country divided for governing?** (There are 21 provinces and 5 autonomous regions that are supervised by the central government.)
- **Where do most of China's ethnic minorities live?** (in the autonomous regions)
- *THINKING FURTHER:* **Why is the army so important in the governing process?** (Possible answers include: to enforce government policy, to keep the multitude of people under control.)

Discussing One-Party Government Help students to understand how the governments of China and the former Soviet Union were similar.

Ask students:

- **Who is the real head of China's government?** (the head of the Communist party)
- **Which group is at the bottom of the party's pyramid?** (the small Communist cells found in all neighborhoods)
- **Which group is at the top of the pyramid?** (the Central Committee of the Communist Party Congress)
- **What is the role of the National People's Congress?** (It chooses the State Council.)

Visiting Hong Kong Explain to students that the government of Hong Kong will be changing. Have them speculate on the final form it may take.

Ask students:

- **Where is Hong Kong?** (off the southeastern coast of China)

CURRICULUM CONNECTION

Language Arts Have students read *China Homecoming* by Jean Fritz. After they have read this book, have students make a list of questions that they might ask someone returning to his or her native country after a long absence. If possible, have students use these questions to interview such a person.

Looking at Hong Kong Continue the discussion, focusing on the importance of Hong Kong as a major center of world trade.

Discussing Inner and Outer Mongolia and North and South Korea Ask students why these areas may be important to China. Discuss the similarities and differences between the two Koreas and the two Mongolias.

Applying the Lesson Have students write essays describing some of the changes, if any, in Hong Kong.

CLOSE

Summarizing Students have learned about the Communist and non-Communist governments in East Asia.

Evaluating Use these questions to assess students' understanding.

- **Which countries have a Communist government?** (mainland China, North Korea)
- **How will the political status of Hong Kong change in 1997?** (Hong Kong will be returned to China.)

Answers to Check Your Reading

1. The Chinese army has many roles; soldiers may act as police, guides, or even physical laborers.
2. Hong Kong has been owned by the British government and China.
3. The Communist troops held the northern part of Korea during World War II.
4. After the second civil war, the defeated Nationalists retreated to Taiwan and formed a non-Communist government-in-exile there.

Independent Practice
Practice Book: page 144

right to use Hong Kong as a port. In 1898 the British invaded the mainland and forced the Chinese to cede, or legally give them, all of this area as a British colony for 99 years.

Hong Kong has grown into an important center of world trade and finance. Those who live there have considerable personal freedom. But the governor is appointed by the British government, and there are no elected officials.

Many people have wondered what will happen to Hong Kong when the 99-year lease runs out in 1997. The British have agreed to return the colony to China. Also, the Chinese government has said it would allow Hong Kong to keep its free-market economy. However, some people in Hong Kong cautiously feel that "only the future will tell what will really happen."

MONGOLIA AND KOREA

The homeland of the Mongols was divided into two areas in China: Inner Mongolia and Outer Mongolia. Inner Mongolia remained part of China. But Outer Mongolia gained its independence in 1911. A few years later it became the Mongolian People's Republic with a Communist government and ties to the Soviet Union. When the Soviet Union ended in 1991, Mongolia began to become more democratic.

Like the Chinese on the mainland and Taiwan, the Koreans also have different kinds of government. After World War II Communist troops held the northern part of Korea and formed a Communist system of government. North Korea became the Democratic People's Republic of Korea. South Korea became the Republic of Korea. Most of South Korea's presidents have been military leaders. By 1988 the country, strengthened by economic success, felt less threatened by North Korea, and it held free elections. North and South Korea are members of the United Nations.

Skyscrapers line the deep, sheltered harbor of Victoria on Hong Kong Island.

CONTRASTING SYSTEMS OF GOVERNMENT

You have read that China and North Korea have governments in which the Communist party makes all important decisions. Taiwan and South Korea have republican forms of government. Democracy has been increasing in Taiwan and South Korea. Hong Kong is a British colony that will be returned to China in 1997.

Check Your Reading

1. What role does the army play in China?
2. Explain why Hong Kong is not an independent country.
3. Why did Korea become divided into two countries?
4. **THINKING SKILL:** What caused Taiwan to have a different type of government from that of mainland China?

THINKING SKILL: Cause and Effect

MEETING INDIVIDUAL NEEDS

Reteaching (easy) Have students do research to find the locations of the 5 autonomous regions and the 21 provinces of China. On the outline map *China and Its Neighbors* found in the Teacher's Resource Center, have students label the various regions.

Extension (average) Have students draw a pyramid on a piece of drawing paper. Then have them fill in the various parts of the Communist party's organization.

Enrichment (challenging) Have students read an account of the life of Mao Zedong and write a report on the way his life affected the history of China.

BUILDING SKILLS
STUDY AND RESEARCH SKILLS

Reading Political Cartoons

Key Vocabulary
political cartoon
symbol

A cartoon is a drawing that is supposed to make you laugh. Cartoonists draw cartoons to express themselves and amuse others. You can find cartoons in comic books as well as in newspapers and magazines. One kind of cartoon is a political cartoon.

A political cartoon is a drawing that focuses attention on important issues and tries to influence public opinion. A cartoon can help you to understand political events. Political cartoonists use visual humor to express their views on an issue. In this lesson you will read about how political cartoonists share their point of view.

Recognizing Symbols

Political cartoonists often use symbols as a way to express their ideas. A symbol is a person, an animal, or an object that stands for something beyond itself. For example, a picture of a dove is a symbol of peace. Uncle Sam is a symbol of the United States. Can you think of other symbols for our country? They include the Liberty Bell and the Statue of Liberty.

During the 1800s a cartoonist named Thomas Nast created two symbols that are still used today. He drew an elephant to represent the Republican party and a donkey to stand for the Democratic party. When you look at a political cartoon, look at all the people, animals, and objects in the drawing. To understand a cartoon that uses symbols, you need to understand what each symbol stands for.

Interpreting a Political Cartoon

Look at the cartoon on this page. A Canadian drew this cartoon about the Chinese government's use of violence to prevent democratic change. The cartoonist has used dominoes to stand for governments of countries. The Eastern European dominoes have fallen over because of democratic change, but the Chinese domino has been propped up with guns. What point do you think the cartoonist is making?*

Reviewing the Skill

1. What is a political cartoon?
2. Why do cartoonists use symbols?
3. What symbols can you identify in the cartoon on this page?
4. Do you think the cartoonist approved of what China was doing? Why or why not?
5. Why is it important to be able to understand political cartoons?

*China has used military force to keep democratic change from taking place.

SKILLS LESSON
page 535

Lesson Theme Political cartoons use symbols to express a point of view about political events.

Lesson Objective
- Analyze a political cartoon.

1 PREPARE

Motivate Pass out several political cartoons from a local paper and challenge students to tell what point each is making.

Set Purpose Tell the class that they will learn how to analyze such cartoons.

2 TEACH

Discussing Political Cartoons Help students to recognize the need for simplicity and visual impact in a political cartoon. Review the symbols used in political cartoons.

Applying the Lesson Have students identify the symbols used in political cartoons and explain what the symbols stand for.

3 CLOSE

Summarizing Have students explain the importance of political cartoons.

Answers to Reviewing the Skill

1. a drawing that expresses a political point of view
2. to convey ideas concisely
3. fallen dominoes for countries that have become more democratic, the guns for violent resistance to democratic change
4. Have students support their opinions with explanations based on the cartoon and what they know about China.
5. to be able to understand political events

MEETING INDIVIDUAL NEEDS

Reteaching (easy) Have students find two political cartoons on their own. Have them paste each on a piece of paper, on which they identify the symbols and explain the message of each.

Extension (average) Instruct each student to locate a political cartoon that he or she finds interesting. Ask students to imagine that they want to share the cartoon with a friend elsewhere in the country. Have them each write a letter to the friend to accompany the cartoon, explaining its symbols and its point of view and describing their personal reactions to it.

Enrichment (challenging) Have students think about political events —local, national, or international. Then have them choose an event and create their own cartoon to express their point of view about the event.

LESSON 4
pages 536–537

Lesson Theme There is a blend of new socialist realism and old tradition in the arts and recreation of the countries of East Asia.

Lesson Objectives
- Define *socialist realism.*
- Describe the traditional and modern arts and sports of East Asia.

PREPARE

Motivate Discuss the influence that literature, such as that represented in the opening passage, might have on daily life.

Set Purpose Have the class make a list of the sports and art forms they enjoy. Tell them they will be reading to find the answer to the *What You Will Learn* question.

TEACH

Understanding the Breaks with Tradition

Ask students:

- **How did Chinese art change after 1949?** (The nature scenes in paintings were replaced with views of people working.)
- *THINKING FURTHER:* **Why is socialist realism in art important to the Communist government?** (Possible answers include: It encourages the people to change old traditions; serves to reinforce communist principles.)

Discussing Traditions Help students to understand that some traditional crafts still flourish alongside the newer styles.

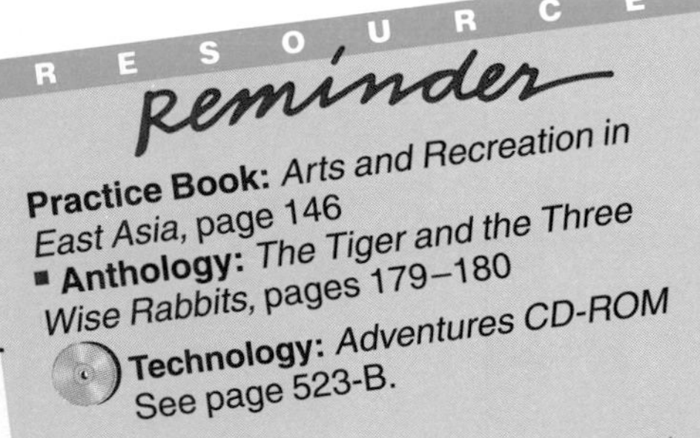
RESOURCE Reminder
Practice Book: Arts and Recreation in East Asia, page 146
- **Anthology:** *The Tiger and the Three Wise Rabbits,* pages 179–180

Technology: Adventures CD-ROM
See page 523-B.

LESSON 4

Arts and Recreation

READ TO LEARN

Key Vocabulary

socialist realism
martial arts

Read Aloud

The wise delight in water; the good delight in mountains. The wise move; the good are still. The wise find happiness; the good achieve long life.

The Chinese landscape has inspired the country's poets, painters, and thinkers throughout its history. In the above quote, Confucius explained that mountains and water are not just part of the landscape. They also bring out deep feelings about the proper way to live.

Read to Learn

1. **WHAT YOU KNOW:** Which traditional American sports do you enjoy?
2. **WHAT YOU WILL LEARN:** Which arts and recreation are popular in East Asia today?

BREAKING WITH TRADITION

Before 1949 the arts in China, Korea, and Japan shared some of the same themes and techniques. For example, they shared the same kinds of landscape painting, nature poems, and use of ink and watercolor for painting.

After 1949 China's new leaders said that the arts must "serve the people." In painting, landscapes and other traditional themes had to be replaced by true-to-life views of working people or heroes performing great deeds for the nation. This form of art is called **socialist realism**. Its purpose is to use the "tremendous energy of the masses" to bring about change. Mongolia and North Korea also make use of socialist realism. Look at the left photograph on page 537. It shows a modern Chinese ballet that is performed today.

KEEPING TRADITIONS ALIVE

Western artistic styles and ideas are increasingly popular in Hong Kong, Taiwan, and South Korea. However, traditional arts and crafts continue to thrive. "Window flowers," which are colorful paper cutouts of birds, animals, and flowers, are often hung in windows for good luck. Some people earn their livings at the crafts they learned as children. For example, Kam Wang makes paper dragons in Hong Kong, as his father did in China before 1949.

My father brought our art with him from China. We make lions' heads, dragons, and Chinese lanterns. These objects are used by people to celebrate events in their history or folklore.

Kam's biggest job is making dragon costumes for parades. On holidays, such as the Chinese New Year, many people climb

WHAT YOU KNOW: Encourage students to think of sports that have long been popular in the United States, such as baseball and football.

READING STRATEGY AND VOCABULARY DEVELOPMENT

Study Guide Have students continue their study guide strategy for China. For this lesson ask them to research books, magazines, and movies that show the arts and culture of China. Have them collect articles about China and samples of artwork. Then have them create a group scrapbook and/or class display of items. Try to display artwork from the traditional and socialist realism periods so that students can compare and contrast the two.

In China, socialist realism, has become the main influence in art, dance, and literature.

under the bamboo-and-paper dragon costume and weave and dance through the streets. This holiday falls between January 21 and February 19.

SPORTS AND PHYSICAL FITNESS

Among the international sports that are popular in East Asia are swimming, tennis, and running. In China Mao Zedong wanted to end the low value that China's educated classes placed on physical activity. Therefore, he urged people to exercise.

Early in the morning in parks and open spaces, dozens of Chinese move silently in slow, flowing body movements. They are doing taiji quan (tī′ jē′ chü än′). This form of exercise is sometimes called shadowboxing because people seem to be fighting an unseen enemy.

Martial arts have become very popular. These ancient forms of hand-to-hand combat are methods of self-defense. The best-known martial arts are kung fu of China, karate of Japan, and tae kwan do (tī′ kwän′ dō′) of Korea. These martial arts are practiced to improve physical and mental skills.

ARTS THAT SERVE THE PEOPLE

After the Communists came to power in 1949, Chinese arts were made to "serve the people." The new socialist realist art of China, North Korea, and Mongolia praised workers and heroes of the people. In another break with tradition, China urged its people to exercise and take part in sports. In non-Communist parts of East Asia, both traditional and modern arts continue to flourish.

Check Your Reading

1. Why was the form of art known as socialist realism introduced into China?
2. Name some traditional arts and crafts that are practiced in Hong Kong, Taiwan, and South Korea.
3. List at least three forms of East Asian martial arts.
4. **THINKING SKILL:** What would you do to check the accuracy of what Kam Wang said on page 536?

THINKING SKILL: Determining Accuracy

Enjoying Sports Help students to contrast the low degree of importance that had traditionally been placed on sports and exercise with the modern emphasis on both.

Applying the Lesson Have students compare the traditional arts and crafts of East Asia with those of the United States. Discuss the role of the arts in society.

CLOSE

Summarizing Students have learned that the arts and physical fitness are considered to be important in modern East Asia. Discuss the changes that the Communists have brought to the arts and sports of East Asia.

Evaluating Use these questions to assess students' understanding.

- **How is socialist realism different from traditional art?** (Socialist realism represents working people and national heroes, while traditional art dealt with nature.)
- **How is the modern attitude toward sports different from the traditional?** (The modern attitude places more emphasis on sports and physical fitness.)

Answers to Check Your Reading

1. to serve the people and bring about change
2. window flowers, paper dragons, dragon costumes
3. kung fu, karate, taiji quan, tae kwan do
4. identify the source of the information; research how Chinese celebrate their history and folklore

Independent Practice
Practice Book: page 146

MEETING INDIVIDUAL NEEDS

Reteaching (easy) Help students to understand the differences between traditional and socialist realist art. Have students draw two pictures. The first should be a nature scene. The second should be representative of the socialist realist style. The pictures could depict students studying, people working in a field, or people exercising. Display the finished products.

Extension (average) Have students research one of the martial arts. Then have them prepare a short oral report about the one they chose or demonstrate a few movements to the class.

Enrichment (challenging) Have students research and report on traditional arts and crafts of East Asia. Have them include pictures of the arts and crafts they included in their report.

CHAPTER 26 REVIEW

pages 538–539

USING THE CHAPTER SUMMARY AND REVIEW

Cultural Geography These questions may be used for review.

- **The civilization of which country influenced most of the countries in this region?** (China)
- **Who makes major economic decisions in China?** (the government)
- **Why is the government of Taiwan separate from that of mainland China?** (because of civil war between Communists and Nationalists)
- **What is socialist realism?** (art that serves the masses)

Ideas to Remember

- **What are the major belief systems in East Asia?** (Confucianism, Daoism, Buddhism)
- **Which countries and colony of the region are newly industrialized?** (Hong Kong, Taiwan, South Korea)
- **Which are the Communist countries in the region?** (China and North Korea)
- **What did socialist realism replace?** (traditional arts)

Answers to Reviewing Vocabulary

1. autonomous regions
2. martial arts
3. Confucianism
4. aquaculture
5. Pacific Rim
6. Daoism
7. iron rice bowl
8. socialist realism
9. pinyin
10. Buddhism

Answers to Reviewing Facts

1. China, Mongolia, North Korea, South Korea, Taiwan, Hong Kong; China
2. symbols used in Chinese writing that represent ideas; spelling of Chinese words has changed
3. the coastal provinces; inland

CHAPTER 26 • SUMMARY

CHINA AND ITS NEIGHBORS: CULTURAL GEOGRAPHY

PEOPLE

- China's early civilization influenced the cultures of its neighbors

- Major beliefs: Confucianism, Buddhism, and Daoism
- Confucianism taught importance of family loyalty, education, and social harmony
- Communism has changed ways of life in China, Mongolia, and North Korea, but not totally
- Chinese language is written with characters instead of an alphabet

ECONOMY

- Under China's Communist system, the government makes major economic decisions for the whole country

- The capitalist economies of Hong Kong, Taiwan, and South Korea are called "economic miracles"

- China has more than 1 billion people

GOVERNMENT

- Civil war between Communists and Nationalists led to a communist China and a separate government in Taiwan
- China and North Korea: Communist parties are strong
- Taiwan, South Korea: representative democracies under strong leaders

- Hong Kong: rule by British until 1997, when the colony will be returned to China

ARTS AND RECREATION

- Landscape painting and use of ink and watercolor are popular among traditional artists
- Communists replaced much traditional art with socialist realism, art that serves the masses

- Popular East Asian recreations: swimming, table tennis, martial arts

IDEAS TO REMEMBER

- Confucianism, Daoism, and Buddhism remain important beliefs in East Asia, although Communist influence has been strong.
- China has government-run businesses with limited private enterprise, while Hong Kong, Taiwan, and South Korea are newly industrialized.
- China and North Korea are Communist; Taiwan, South Korea, and Mongolia are republics; and Hong Kong will return to China in 1997.
- In the Communist countries of East Asia, many traditional arts have been replaced by socialist realism; elsewhere traditional forms flourish.

538

ENRICHMENT ACTIVITY

Designing Porcelain **Materials:** large white paper plates, pens, paints or markers, pictures of Chinese porcelain, cardboard

1. Point out to the class that the Chinese have been making high quality pottery for about 5,000 years and were the first to discover how to make porcelain. Try to have available for the class some pictures of typical Chinese porcelain designs, for example, from the Yuan, Ming, and Qing dynasties, which often feature dragon, flower, or fruit motifs. Tell students that they are going to make up their own designs using Chinese motifs.
2. Distribute the paper plates, but tell the class to make their design first on a separate piece of paper. Then have them transfer their design to the paper plate, drawing in its outlines and then coloring it in with paints or markers.
3. Have students display their completed plates on cardboard stands.

CHAPTER 26 • REVIEW

REVIEWING VOCABULARY

aquaculture	iron rice bowl
autonomous regions	martial arts
Buddhism	Pacific Rim
Confucianism	pinyin
Daoism	socialist realism

Number a sheet of paper from 1 to 10. Beside each number write the word or term from the above list that best completes the sentence.

1. China's five ____ are self-governing areas that report to Beijing.
2. The ____ are ancient forms of combat used today for self defense.
3. ____ teaches a system of responsibility between family members, government, and people.
4. ____ is a method of raising fish in ponds people have made.
5. All of the East Asian nations except Mongolia are among the more than 30 countries of the ____.
6. ____ is a philosophy that emphasizes accepting the natural flow of life.
7. The ____ system guaranteed lifetime employment to every Chinese person.
8. ____ is a form of art that often portrays people performing heroic deeds on behalf of the "masses."
9. The modern system of writing Chinese words in our alphabet is called ____.
10. ____ teaches that to avoid suffering, one must get rid of one's selfish desires.

REVIEWING FACTS

1. What are the names of the five countries and one British colony of East Asia? Which of these countries is the largest?
2. What are Chinese characters? How has pinyin changed the way Chinese words are written in our alphabet?
3. In which part of China is private enterprise most developed? In which part is it least developed?
4. How is the Chinese Communist party different from political parties in the West?
5. How does socialist realism differ from traditional forms of art in East Asia?

WRITING ABOUT MAIN IDEAS

1. **Writing a Paragraph:** You have read that one of the main goals of the Chinese Communists was "to make all people in China equal." Write a paragraph discussing to what extent that goal has been achieved.
2. **Writing Lists:** In the past, under the iron rice bowl system, all Chinese people were paid whether or not they worked. Write two lists, one of advantages and one of disadvantages of such a system.
3. **Writing About Perspectives:** Many people in the Pacific Rim have experienced great changes in their standard of living. Imagine that you live in one of the Asian Pacific Rim countries. Write about how the changing economy has changed your life in both pleasant and unpleasant ways.

BUILDING SKILLS: READING POLITICAL CARTOONS

1. What is a political cartoon?
2. Why do cartoonists use symbols?
3. Look at the political cartoon on page 535. What do you think the cartoonist is trying to say?
4. Why is it important to be able to understand political cartoons?

539

4. The Chinese Communist party controls the government and is the only party allowed; western political parties compete with other legal parties in elections.
5. Socialist realism shows true-to-life views of working people or heroes performing great deeds for the nation, while traditional forms of art show such themes as landscapes.

Suggestions for Writing About Main Ideas

1. Students' answers should mention that the achievement of that goal has been retarded by the current trend toward limited private enterprise. They should also note that in spite of the food shortage that caused this trend, the number of poor people in China has decreased under Communism.
2. Possible answers include: *advantages*—everyone gets paid, has a job, has money to buy basic needs; *disadvantages*—a person does not get paid more for producing more or better goods, inferior goods are produced, people get jobs for their political beliefs, not their skills.
3. Students may wish to write about an "economic miracle" country or about China.

Answers to Building Skills: Reading Political Cartoons

1. a drawing that focuses attention on an important issue and tries to influence public opinion
2. as a way to express their ideas
3. Accept all reasonable answers. Students should explain what symbols are used and what they mean.
4. so you can understand the cartoonists' views on the issues represented in their drawings

Chapter Review and Test
Practice Book: *Vocabulary Review,* page 147
Transparency: *Graphic Organizer*
Assessment Book: *Chapter 26 Test*

MAKING CONNECTIONS

Organizing Information Display the Main Idea Map Graphic Organizer Transparency, filling in only the underlined text. Ask students to review the chapter and add the themes of Lessons 3 and 4, providing supporting details. Have students write the main idea of the chapter in the center of the map. *Ask:* In what ways is East Asia a region of contrasts?

Center: China and its neighbor combine old and new values with communism and private enterprise.

- Chinese culture is a blend of traditional ways and communism. — communism, Confucianism, Daoism, Buddhism
- There are democratic and Communist governments in East Asia. — Communist: China, North Korea, Mongolia; increasing democracy: Taiwan, South Korea
- Private enterprise solved and created problems. — high prices, uneven distribution, rapid industrialization
- There is a blend of socialist realism and old traditions. — art to "serve the people"; traditional crafts

CHAPTER 27
ORGANIZER

JAPAN text pages 540–559

CHAPTER THEME Mixing traditional and modern ways, Japan's hardworking, homogeneous people maintain a democracy and produce miraculous economic growth and production.

CHAPTER OBJECTIVES

CONTENT

- Explain why Japan developed a culture distinct from that of the rest of East Asia.
- Explain why Japan is called a homogeneous society.
- Identify Shintoism and describe how the Japanese blend the ideas of Shintoism with those of Buddhism and Confucianism.
- List the factors that helped create Japan's economic miracle.
- Explain the significance of the martial arts in Japanese society.
- Contrast Japanese schools with those in the United States.
- Describe how the Japanese government is a mixture of the old and new.
- Name two unusual provisions in the Japanese constitution and explain their origin.
- Describe the relationship between government and business in Japan.
- Explain how the people of Japan combine the old and new in their arts and leisure.
- Contrast Japanese and Western attitudes toward art.

SKILLS

Geography
- Interpret a political map of Japan.

Study and Research
- Use a line graph to measure the growth of Japanese exports.

Thinking
- Compare and contrast the economies of Japan and China.

Reading and Writing
- Write a haiku poem about Japan.
- Write an eyewitness memoir.

CITIZENSHIP VALUES

- Appreciate the need to hear both sides of an issue.
- Appreciate the role that discipline and respect for education play in a nation's prosperity.

TEACHER OPTIONS

READING STRATEGY: Summarizing Strategies to help students read and remember the main ideas of the lesson.

Lesson 1: p. 541 — Lesson 4: p. 552
Lesson 2: p. 545 — Legacy: p. 554
Lesson 3: p. 550

MEETING INDIVIDUAL NEEDS Activities for reteaching, extension, and enrichment.

Lesson 1: p. 543 — Lesson 3: p. 551
Writing Skills: p. 544 — Lesson 4: p. 553
Lesson 2: p. 547 — Legacy: p. 557

GEO ADVENTURES ACTIVITIES PAD Daily activities to assess students' understanding of geography skills.

CURRICULUM CONNECTION Activities to help integrate other subject areas with Social Studies.

Math p. 546

PUPIL EDITION ON CASSETTE Language support for students who have difficulty reading or who will benefit from listening to the Pupil Edition on Cassette as they read.

SECOND-LANGUAGE SUPPORT Activities and suggestions for second-language learners.

Lesson 2: p. 485-D

CHAPTER PLANNING GUIDE

LESSON	SUGGESTED PACING	THEMES	
1 THE PEOPLE pages 541–543	1 day	The people of Japan are a homogeneous group who place great emphasis on duty to country and family.	Practice Book p. 148 Outline Map p. 36 **Technology:** *Adventures CD-ROM*
BUILDING WRITING SKILLS Writing a Summary page 544	1 day	Writing a summary helps in organizing and recalling the material that was read.	Practice Book p. 149
2 THE ECONOMY pages 545–549	1 day	Japan has a highly prosperous economy, due to the diligence of the people, excellent standards of quality control, and the high skill level of the workers.	Practice Book p. 150 **Technology:** *Adventures CD-ROM*
3 THE GOVERNMENT pages 550–551	1 day	The government of Japan contains elements of both ancient Japanese traditions and modern democratic ways.	Practice Book p. 151 ■ Anthology pp. 174, 175–176, 177–178
4 ARTS AND RECREATION pages 552–553	1 day	The Japanese emphasize the beauty of nature and believe that art should be part of everyday life.	Practice Book p. 152 ■ Anthology pp. 172–173 **Technology:** *Adventures CD-ROM*
LEGACY Martial Arts—More Than Just Fighting pages 554–557	1 day	The legacy of martial arts reflects many parts of Japanese history and culture.	Outline Map p. 36
CHAPTER SUMMARY AND REVIEW pages 558–559	1 dav	Chapter content, skills, and vocabulary are reviewed and evaluated.	Practice Book p. 153 Transparency: Graphic Organizer Assessment Book, Chapter 27 Test

Technology CONNECTION

Lesson 1
ADVENTURES CD-ROM
Enrich Lesson 1 by having students *Travel* to and *Explore* Japan.

Lesson 2
ADVENTURES CD-ROM
Enrich Lesson 2 by having students *Investigate* movies in *Explore.*

Lesson 4
ADVENTURES CD-ROM
Enrich Lesson 4 by having students make their own multimedia presentations on Japan, in *Create.*

CHAPTER 27
pages 540–559

USING THE CHAPTER OPENER

Discussing the Photograph Have students study the photograph and read the chapter title. Help them to focus on the dress worn by the girls in the picture.

Ask students:

- **What can you tell about the Japanese girls in the photograph?** (They are all dressed alike in sailor-type outfits, and they are all about the same age.)
- **Why do you think they are dressed this way?** (Students may guess that the girls are probably a class from a Japanese school.)
- *THINKING FURTHER:* **Do you think that Japanese children dress this way all the time?** (No, these children will probably change into other clothes when school is over. Explain that not all Japanese schools have special uniforms, and that many schools in other countries also use uniforms. School uniforms are thought by some to encourage cooperation and unity.)

Reading/Listening to the Primary Source Have students study the picture as you read aloud the quotation and the passage that follows.

Ask students:

- **What belief is basic to the attitudes of Japanese toward one another?** (that cooperation and harmony help them to accomplish their goals)
- *THINKING FURTHER:* **How might this belief affect people on a daily basis?** (Possible answers include: Cooperation of workers can result in a better product in a shorter time. Cooperation means good manners and respect for others, and, therefore, a more pleasant way of life.)

CHAPTER 27

JAPAN

FOCUS

Cooperation and harmony help us work together on things we consider most important.

This quote by a Japanese worker expresses an important Japanese attitude. In this chapter you will learn about many of the beliefs and customs that have made the Japanese way of life a unique one.

BACKGROUND INFORMATION

About Japanese Customs

- Many traditional Japanese customs have been replaced by Western ways. The most extensive changes have occurred in the big cities and have had the greatest effect on Japanese youth.
- Most Japanese now wear Western clothing, but they may wear the traditional kimono on ceremonial occasions.
- The Japanese observe rigid rules of etiquette and social behavior.
- After World War II, Japanese women were put on a somewhat more equal footing with Japanese men and given increased opportunities for education and for employment outside the home.

LESSON 1

The People

READ TO LEARN

Key Vocabulary

homogeneous
samurai
Shinto

Key Places

Tokyo

Read Aloud

Use every moment of every day without wasting it.

Tsuneko Tashiro, a Japanese schoolteacher, lives by the saying above. Although it is her own personal saying, it could well be a motto describing the Japanese people. By working very hard for long hours, the Japanese have turned Japan into a bustling, thriving land. In this lesson you will read about the ways of life that made this possible.

Read for Purpose

1. **WHAT YOU KNOW:** What are Confucianism and Buddhism?
2. **WHAT YOU WILL LEARN:** What distinct ways of life have the people of Japan developed?

AN ISLAND NATION

You read in Chapter 24 that Japan is a group of islands off the eastern coast of China. Japan has hundreds of islands, but most people live on four main islands. They are: the largest island Honshu (hon' shü), Shikoku (shi kō' kü), Kyushu (kū' shü), and the least populated one of the four—Hokkaido (ho kī' dō).

Japan's island location kept it safe from invaders. Yet the Japanese were close enough to their Asian neighbors to borrow new ideas and ways of living. During the 600s and 700s the Japanese began to eat with chopsticks and write with Chinese characters. They read about the teachings of Confucius and adopted the Buddhist religion from Korean and Chinese monks.

The Portuguese arrived in Japan in the 1500s. At first the Japanese welcomed these and other Europeans. However, fearing that foreign missionaries and traders were gaining too much power in Japan, the country's leaders tried to cut the islands off from the rest of the world. In 1638 the government passed a law forbidding all Japanese citizens from building large ships or going on long voyages. All foreigners, except the Dutch, were also expelled from the country. This closed-door policy lasted until 1853, when Commodore Matthew Perry of the United States Navy sailed into Tokyo Bay and demanded that Japan open its ports to other nations of the world.

Japanese culture continued to develop during this period of isolation. Some ideas from China, Korea, and the West were studied and adopted into the Japanese culture. As you will read, the Japanese balanced new and traditional ways of life.

WHAT YOU KNOW: two systems of belief that shaped the culture of China and its neighbors

LESSON 1
pages 541–543

Lesson Theme The Japanese, who consider themselves a homogeneous people, place great emphasis on duty to country and family.

Lesson Objectives
- Understand the characteristics that make the Japanese consider themselves a homogeneous group.
- Describe the importance of loyalty and duty in the Japanese culture.

PREPARE

Motivate Have a student read the *Read Aloud* section to the class. Have students discuss how the quotation could be applied to their own lives.

Set Purpose Use the *What You Know* question to review the key beliefs of Confucianism and Buddhism.

TEACH

Exploring an Island Nation Have students locate Japan on the political *Atlas* Map of Southern and Eastern Asia. Help students to understand the earlier closed door policy in Japan and the effect it had on the country's development.

Ask students:

- **How was the Japanese culture influenced by the rest of East Asia?** (The Japanese were influenced by ideas about religion, ways of living, and writing from other East Asian countries.)
- *THINKING FURTHER:* **How could its location keep Japan safe from invaders?** (Students may recognize that an island is hard to attack.)

READING STRATEGY AND VOCABULARY DEVELOPMENT

Summarizing Review the summarizing strategy that students studied in Chapter 7. Have students use their summarizing skills to give a presentation of the lesson based on television news shows such as "20/20" or "48 Hours." Tell students to begin by keeping a written summary of each section of the lesson. They should write the key points of the lesson in a news format and answer the five *W* questions (*W*ho, *W*hat, *W*hen, *W*here, *W*hy). You may wish to divide the class into small groups and have each group refine one section of their summary for the final presentation.

RESOURCE Reminder

Practice Book: *The People of Japan,* page 148

Outline Map: *Japan*

Technology: *Adventures CD-ROM*

See page 539-B.

Learning About the People Help students to understand the characteristics that most Japanese people have in common.

Ask students:

- **What are the characteristics that make the Japanese consider themselves a homogeneous group?** (same ethnic group, language, history, values)
- **Which religions do the Japanese follow?** (Shinto, Buddhism, Confucianism)
- *THINKING FURTHER:* **What has enabled the Japanese to seem homogeneous?** (Possible answers include: their island location and the closed door policy that kept them isolated.)

Discussing Group Membership Help students to compare and contrast Japanese and Western values and to understand the Japanese emphasis on group membership.

Ask students:

- **How is society thought of in the Japanese culture?** (It is more important than the individual.)
- **How does this thinking differ from that of our country?** (We place more emphasis on the individual.)

Appreciating Manners, Duty, Loyalty Discuss the importance of manners and respect in the Japanese way of life.

Ask students:

- **Why do the Japanese people treat each other so respectfully?** (They believe that everyone has a position in society and that agreement is important.)
- **How did the samurai influence the Japanese culture?** (Their values were adopted by others and evolved into the Japanese sense of duty and loyalty.)

THE PEOPLE AND THEIR BELIEFS

Would you say that most people in your country look and act as you do? Some Japanese would answer yes. The Japanese consider themselves to be a **homogeneous** group. That is, their appearances and behavior are somewhat similar. Almost all Japanese belong to the same ethnic group. They speak the same language, share the same history, and have similar values.

If you were to ask Japanese people about their religion, many would say that they are not very religious. Then they would probably tell you that they take part in both **Shinto** (shin′ tō) and Buddhist celebrations. Shinto is the oldest of Japan's religions. Shinto followers believe that spirits, or *kami* (kä′ mē), dwell in all things in nature, such as mountains, trees, streams, lakes, and rocks.

Most people in Japan are Shinto, Buddhist, and Confucian—all at once. They accept Confucian ideas of an orderly society and duty to family and country. Yet they also like the peaceful beliefs of Buddhism. They combine many beliefs into an outlook on life that is uniquely Japanese.

MEMBERS OF THE GROUP

Some of the values that have developed in Japan are very different from those in Europe or the United States. For example, unlike most Westerners, many Japanese believe that society is more important than any one person. They see themselves as members of a group that makes gains together, rather than as unique individuals striving to get ahead.

At an early age children in Japan are taught loyalty and respect for the common good. They learn that it is important to get along with the group. "A nail that sticks out," goes an old Japanese saying, "must be hammered down."

MANNERS, DUTY, AND LOYALTY

In a land where agreement among people is so important, there is a deep respect for authority and order. Both family members and schoolteachers teach children that everyone has a certain position in society. As a result, some people think the

The *Matsuri* Festival (*right*), celebrating the founding of the city of Kyoto, is a popular Shinto festival. Japanese Children's Day (*left*) is an official holiday.

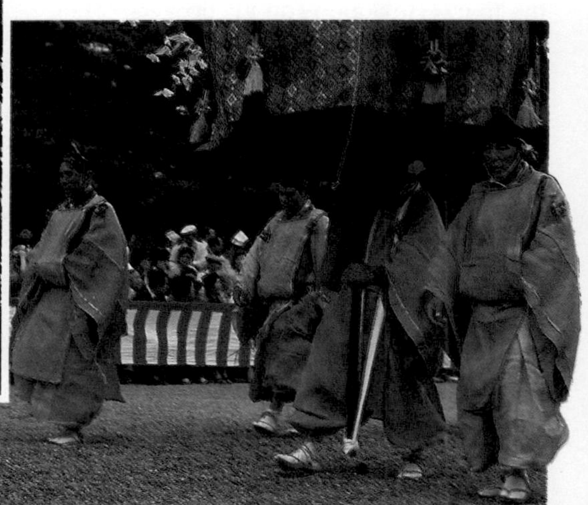

542

BACKGROUND INFORMATION

The Shinto Religion Shinto is the original religion of Japan. It dates back to prehistoric times. Shinto includes the worship of spirits and the royal ancestors.

- The term *Kami* is used to mean any god or spirit, as well as things in nature.
- A *torii* is a gateway that stands at the front of the worship sites.
- Many homes contain a small shrine where family members worship their ancestors. Neighborhoods often contain shrines to a favorite god, and these shrines are carried through the neighborhood once a year.

Japanese may be the most polite people in the world. Students bow to teachers, employees bow to their bosses, and friends bow to one another.

Over the centuries the Japanese have worked out a thousand rules of correct behavior. Responsibilities have become very important in this system. People are taught that they have special duties to their families and their leaders.

The idea that every person owes a debt to his or her family is an important part of Japanese culture. To fail to do one's duty causes a person to "lose face." The whole family is shamed and disgraced when one member fails to do his or her duty.

How did such traditions begin? For hundreds of years warriors called samurai (sam′ ů rī) ruled Japan. Samurai were taught to feel a great sense of duty to their families, their rulers, and to their country. Over the years these values have been passed on to other groups.

TOKYO, A CROWDED CITY

Tokyo, the capital of Japan, has one of the largest populations of any city in the world. Together with other nearby cities, Tokyo is part of a megalopolis. You may recall that a megalopolis is an area with so many cities close together that they seem to form one large city.

Most of this megalopolis is densely populated. Often the trains that people ride to work are so crowded that railroad employees have to push people into the cars to make them fit. Because so many other people drive automobiles, traffic jams are a common problem in Tokyo.

A SEPARATE PEOPLE

As the political map on this page shows, Japan stands apart from East Asia. In this lesson you have read how the Japanese developed a distinctive culture. The people of Japan are a mostly homogeneous group whose members share the same basic beliefs, cultural values, and manners. As one Japanese writer explained, "Only when everybody acts the same do individual differences become clear."

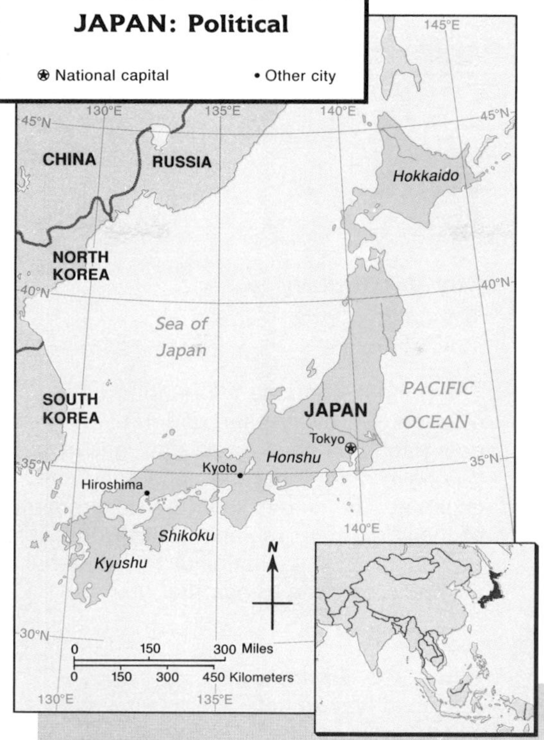

MAP SKILL: On which Japanese island is the city of Kyoto located?

Check Your Reading

1. Why did the Japanese develop a culture that was different from those of the rest of Asia?
2. What are some types of belief that many Japanese share?
3. Why is Japan considered to be a nation of "team players"?
4. **THINKING SKILL:** State one fact and two opinions that you read about in this lesson.

MAP SKILL: Honshu
THINKING SKILL: Fact and Opinion

EXTENDING MAP SKILLS

Have students study the map of Japan.

Ask students:

- **What are the main islands of Japan?** (Hokkaido, Honshu, Shikoku, Kyushu)
- **On which island is the capital of Japan?** (Honshu)
- **Which island is closest to Russia?** (Hokkaido)

Applying the Lesson Have students list the characteristics that make the Japanese seem like a homogeneous group and then compare the homogeneous population of Japan with the multiethnic population of the United States.

❸ CLOSE

Summarizing Students have learned that the Japanese people consider themselves a homogeneous group with a culture based on loyalty and duty to the group and to one's family.

Evaluating Use the *Check Your Reading* questions (answers given below) to assess students' understanding.

Answers to Check Your Reading

1. because they were isolated from the other countries
2. Many Japanese share belief in Shinto, Buddhist, and Confucian ideas.
3. The emphasis is on the good of society over the good of the individual.
4. *fact:* "Japan is a group of islands off the eastern coast of China;" *opinion:* "The Japanese may be the most polite people in the world;" "Society is more important than any one person."

Independent Practice
Practice Book: page 148

MEETING INDIVIDUAL NEEDS

Reteaching (easy) On an outline map of Japan found in the Teacher's Resource Center, have students label the major islands of Japan. Have them research the largest city on each island and indicate the cities on the map.

Extension (average) Have students make a chart to compare and contrast Japanese and Western values. Then have students write a short point/counterpoint paper based on their chart. You might wish to have them use the *Viewpoints* on pages 190–191 as a model.

Enrichment (challenging) Have students research Japanese family life. They should find out what the responsibilities of different family members are to each other, and what the family members' responsibilities are outside the home. Then have students prepare a short oral report on what they have learned.

SKILLS LESSON
page 544

Lesson Theme Writing a summary helps in organizing and recalling the material that was read.

Lesson Objective
- Learn how to write a summary.

 PREPARE

Motivate Tell students to close their books and then make a list of all the main ideas in Lesson 1, which was just completed. Have them compare lists to see which ideas they missed.

Set Purpose Tell the class that in this lesson they will learn how to organize and record main ideas for easier recall.

 TEACH

Discussing Summaries

Ask students:

- **Why are topic sentences important in writing a summary?** (They carry the main ideas.)
- **How do short and long summaries differ?** (*short*—carries only main ideas; *long*—includes details)

Applying the Skill Have students develop a class summary of the main ideas in this skills lesson.

 CLOSE

Summarizing Review the two kinds of summaries.

Answers to Reviewing the Skill

Summaries should include the ideas that the traveler to Japan was surprised by the behavior of some children and that the children were collecting insects.

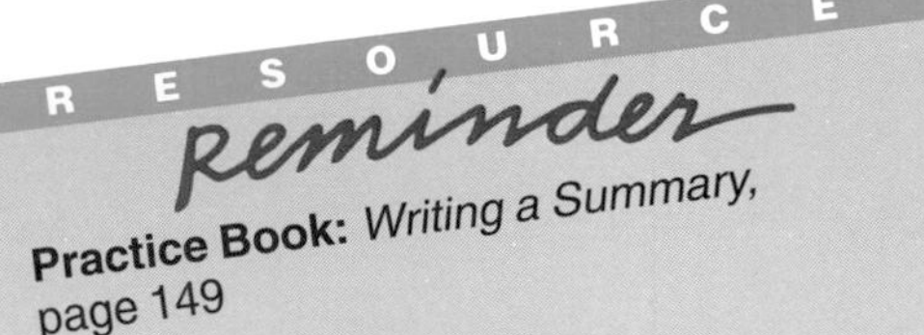

Writing a Summary

Key Vocabulary
summary
topic sentence

This book contains information on many subjects. On every page and in every paragraph you have found different facts. You have read about the geography, the economy, the culture, and the government of many different regions in the world. Sometimes it is a challenge to remember all the interesting things that you are reading about.

What Is a Summary?

A good way to help you to remember what you have read is to write a short **summary**. A summary briefly states the main ideas contained in a piece of writing. Writing a summary helps you to sort out the most important information.

To prepare for writing a summary look for the **topic sentences**, or the sentences that contain the main ideas. First, read through the entire selection and write down the topic sentences. Often a topic sentence is the first sentence in a paragraph. However, it may also be in the middle or at the end of a paragraph. Notice that the rest of the sentences give supporting details.

When you write a short summary, you will be concerned only with main ideas. In a longer summary, you might want to include some important details.

Summarizing the Lesson

To write a summary of Lesson 1, which is about the Japanese people, first read through the whole lesson. It will help to pay close attention to the bold headings within the lesson. Headings help you to figure out what each section is about. Headings also provide an outline of the main ideas of the lesson.

For example, the second heading in Lesson 1 tells you that one of the main ideas in your summary will have to do with the people and their beliefs. You can find it on page 542. Write down the most important ideas in each section.

As you read each section, ask yourself these questions: "What is the main idea of this paragraph? Which are supporting details?" When you have finished, write a summary using your own words.

Reviewing the Skill

Read the paragraph below. Then write a summary of the article in two or three sentences.

> **Not long after my arrival [in Japan], I was surprised again by the odd behavior of some Japanese children. They had boxes or jars in one hand, and with the other they were trying to catch some invisible creature. Then I heard the sound of the cicada [an insect] and I realized what they were after. Then, too, I caught my first glimpse of one, held between the thumb and forefinger of a boy. He held it with a mixture of tenderness and unconcern, before putting it in his box with the rest of his crawling collection.**

MEETING INDIVIDUAL NEEDS

Reteaching (easy) Have students refer to Lesson 1 of Chapter 26, pages 525–528, on the people of China, and list the main ideas in each section, using the headings as hints to those main ideas.

Extension (average) Have students choose any lesson that they have already studied in the text and make an outline of it, including at least one main idea and two supporting details for each section. Then have them write a summary of the lesson based on this outline.

Enrichment (challenging) Have students choose a famous person who interests them. Then have them read about that person in an encyclopedia. Tell them to outline the article and write a summary based on their outline.

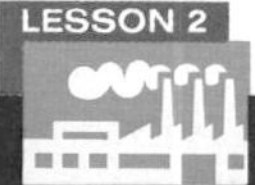

LESSON 2

The Economy

READ TO LEARN

Key People

Akio Morita

Read Aloud

A Japanese businessman named Akio Morita visited West Germany in the early 1950s. He often stopped to buy ice cream in a small neighborhood shop. One day a waiter told him that the decorative little umbrella stuck in his ice cream came from Japan.

As Morita looked around the ice cream shop, he noticed that the only items with a "Made in Japan" label were the paper umbrellas. He believed that Japan could export better products than the one he saw.

At the time Akio Morita headed a small Japanese company named Sony. Today Sony is a huge electronics company, and Japan is the second-largest industrial power in the world. In this lesson you will read how this dramatic change came about.

Read for Purpose

1. WHAT YOU KNOW: Which Japanese goods have you bought most recently?
2. WHAT YOU WILL LEARN: What factors helped create Japan's recent economic miracle?

JAPAN'S ECONOMIC MIRACLE

You read in Chapter 11 that many German factories were destroyed at the end of World War II. The same was true in Japan. Most of Japan's cities were shattered by American bombs, including two atomic bombs that were dropped on the cities of Hiroshima and Nagasaki.

Japan built itself into a major industrial power in the years following the war. Today Japanese businesses produce goods and services that make up about 11 percent of the world's economic output. Only the United States produces more. Japanese products now include everything from calculators, computers, videocassette players, and microchips to motorcycles, automobiles, and grand pianos, not just the paper umbrellas you read about at the beginning of this lesson.

The growth of Japan from a ruined land into a modern, prosperous nation has been called a miracle. What makes this development so remarkable is that Japan has very few natural resources. Every year the country must buy most of its oil, iron ore, copper, and lumber from overseas. "We are very different from the rest of the world," explained one Japanese businessperson. "Our only natural resource is the hard work of our people."

WHAT YOU KNOW: Encourage students to name goods and brands for which Japan is famous.

545

LESSON 2
pages 545–547

Lesson Theme Japan has a highly prosperous economy, due to the diligence of the people, excellent standards of quality control, and high skill level of the workers.

Lesson Objectives

- Describe the transition from ruined land to economic miracle.
- Identify the standards of quality control.
- Discuss the Japanese approach to educating the country's work force.

1 PREPARE

Motivate Read the *Read Aloud* section to the class. Encourage students to use their knowledge of Japan to tell how Morita's observation in the 1950s differs from what it might be today.

Set Purpose Use the *What You Know* question to discuss the various goods that are made in Japan. Pose the *What You Will Learn* question and tell students to read the lesson for the answer.

2 TEACH

Understanding Japan's Economic Miracle Help students to appreciate Japan's recovery after World War II.

Ask students:

- **What was Japan like after World War II?** (economically and physically ruined)
- **What is Japan's natural resource?** (the hard work of its people)

READING STRATEGY AND VOCABULARY DEVELOPMENT

Summarizing Remind students that the last section of each lesson is a summary of the lesson content. Have students analyze the summary of this lesson. Then have them scan the lesson to identify the specific parts of the text mentioned in the summary. Have students work in groups or individually to create their own summaries. Discuss any differences between students' summaries and the text summary. Have students explain how they decided what material to include in their summaries.

Discussing Quality and Technology Use examples to help students understand the concept of quality control. Japan produces high quality, reliable products that are in demand worldwide.

Ask students:

- **Why do the Japanese want to work efficiently?** (They want to make the finest products without wasting time or effort.)
- **How did the Japanese adapt the technologies of other countries?** (They observed the ways of others, thought of ways to improve upon what they had seen, and initiated the improvements.)
- *THINKING FURTHER:* **Why is replacing out-of-date equipment important?** (It keeps industry working as efficiently as possible.)

EXTENDING GRAPH SKILLS

Use the graph to analyze the value of Japan's exports.

Ask students:

- **In which year did Japan export $175 billion worth of goods?** (1985)
- **In which year did Japan export the most goods?** (1993)
- **Have Japan's exports increased or decreased since 1980?** (increased)

Describing Skilled Workers Use the text to extend students' appreciation of the education and training systems in Japan.

Ask students:

- **What is school like in Japan?** (All children go for 9 years, then those who qualify go to high school and college. Curriculum is rigorous.)
- **What do employers offer their workers?** (extensive training, additional education for some, recreational facilities)

QUALITY AND TECHNOLOGY

Many things help to explain the success, shown on the graph on this page. One is the demand for excellence. When asked why Sony can sell so much in the United States, **Akio Morita** replied that there are many reasons. But the first three reasons are "quality, quality, and quality."

When they do a job, the Japanese try to do it efficiently and artistically. That means not wasting time or effort while making the finest products possible. One Japanese writer explained:

> *[W]atching a Japanese assembly line is like watching a ballet performance; every body movement has been worked out to achieve the most efficiency. . . . Everything is calculated to allow the worker to accomplish the most amount of work in one continuous movement.*

Another reason for Japan's economic success has been its ability to adapt the technologies of other countries. After World War II hundreds of Japanese businesspeople came to the United States to observe America's best factories. Then they returned home to improve Japan's industries based upon what they had seen.

The Japanese have been careful since then to replace old or out-of-date equipment so that their industries work efficiently.

One kind of technology that the Japanese have used effectively is robots that perform various jobs in factories. Many Japanese factories have installed computer-controlled machines that do some jobs faster and better than a human could. Japan also builds robots to export to other countries.

By 1980 Japan had become the leading producer of automobiles in the world. Japan has also become a world leader in the manufacture of iron, steel, chemicals, and electronic equipment like computers and radios.

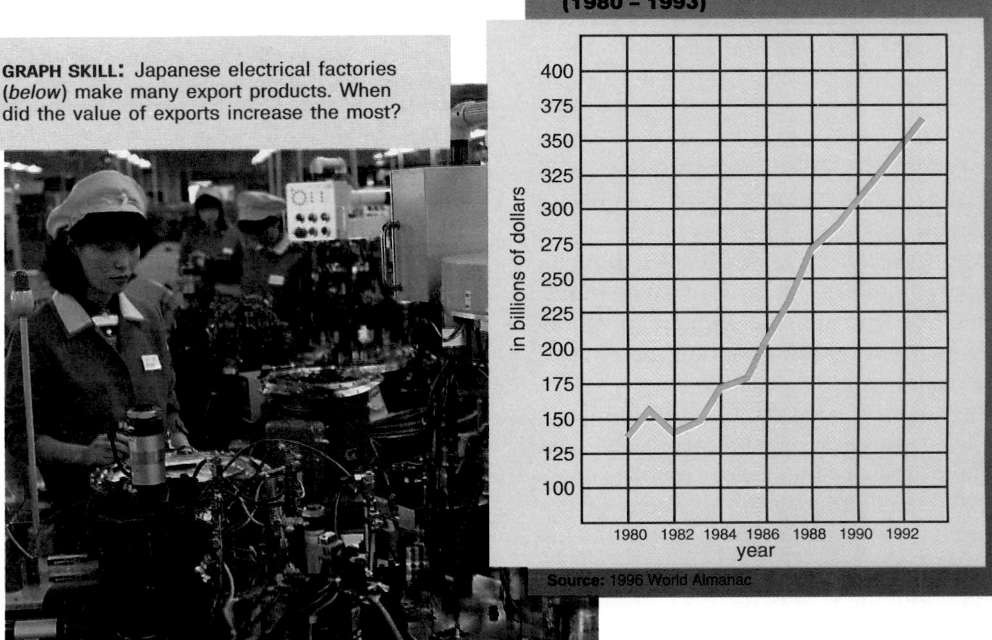

GRAPH SKILL: Japanese electrical factories (*below*) make many export products. When did the value of exports increase the most?

546

GRAPH SKILL: accept any answer from 1985 to 1988

CURRICULUM CONNECTION

Math The computer, one of the electronic products that the Japanese excel at producing, is becoming more and more important as a tool for the home, office, and classroom. Many people use this machine without knowing how it works. Tell students that an important first step in understanding the computer is to learn the terms used to explain its processes. Have students look up and write down the definitions for the following terms: analog, digital, microchip, byte, and binary system. Ask the seventh grade mathematics teacher to explain to the class why the binary numbers system forms the basis for a computer's ability to do arithmetic.

LOYAL, SKILLED WORKERS

An industrial economy needs highly skilled, educated workers. Japan has plenty of them. In Japan all children must go to school for nine years. After junior high school, students take exams that determine which high school they will attend. It is not uncommon for students to spend nearly every waking hour either doing regular homework or studying for the exams. Still, 94 percent of Japan's teenagers enter high school and almost all of them graduate.

Getting into one of the best universities in Japan means passing the most difficult exams of all. Throughout the country, students attend private "cram schools" in addition to regular schools to help them pass these tests with high marks. In some cases students must pass an exam to get into cram school.

If a person goes to work for a large company in Japan, he or she receives extensive training. Many businesses even send employees to foreign universities for additional education.

Large companies find that it pays to spend time and money training workers because few people in these companies change jobs. Once they are hired, workers are part of the company family. Many people expect to work their whole lives for just one company.

In some businesses the workday begins with group exercise and company songs and slogans. Large companies have gyms, swimming pools, and other recreational facilities for their workers. Such training and group activities have made the Japanese work force both highly skilled and loyal. "All of us, every one of us in Japan," one worker said, "believe that the rise or fall of our organization rests on the individual shoulders of each one of us." Each individual is important to the team.

Japanese students study hard to acquire good handwriting. The people in this picture have entered a writing contest.

A STRONG ECONOMY

As you have read, Japan is the second-largest industrial power in the world. After World War II the country turned to technology and quality to modernize its industries. Japan's success also rests with its workers. They are educated, hard working, eager, and reliable.

Check Your Reading

1. Name three factors that contributed to Japan's economic success.
2. What do many Japanese students attend besides regular school?
3. How do Japanese companies maintain worker loyalty?
4. **THINKING SKILL:** From your reading of the lesson, what three factors would you select to explain Japan's economic success? Explain your choice.

THINKING SKILL: Observing

Applying the Lesson Have students compare and contrast the Japanese educational and work systems with those of the United States.

3 CLOSE

Summarizing Students have learned that Japan has become an economically strong nation. Discuss the reasons for Japan's economic success.

Evaluating Use these questions to assess students' understanding.

- **What are the characteristics of many Japanese workers?** (hard-working, loyal, productive, efficient, well-educated)
- **How did the Japanese rebuild their industry after World War II?** (They observed U.S. industries and adapted and improved on what they learned at home.)
- **Why do Japanese companies spend so much money training their workers?** (Few workers change jobs, it creates a loyal work force.)

Answers to Check Your Reading

1. quality control, research, trained workers
2. private "cram schools" to help them pass the tough exams
3. They provide extensive training, additional education for some, and recreational facilities.
4. Possible answers include: observing other countries' ways, maintaining quality, and conducting careful research on ways to improve products. Students should explain how the factors they chose have contributed to Japan's economic success.

Independent Practice
Practice Book: page 150

MEETING INDIVIDUAL NEEDS

Reteaching (easy) Have students participate in an assembly line process to accomplish a task, such as doing an art project or making peanut butter sandwiches. Then have them discuss ways to improve the process.

Extension (average) Have students compile a list of items that are made in Japan. Then have them find or draw pictures of the items to make a class bulletin board of Japanese products.

Enrichment (challenging) Have students research Japan's rise from a ruined country after World War II to an economic success today. Have them list the steps in Japan's economic recovery.

CHAPTER 27

CITIZENSHIP
Viewpoints
pages 548–549

Lesson Objective

- Analyze three points of view on Japan's trade policies.

Identifying the Issue Help students see that differences of opinion arise on issues, such as trade, which involve people from different cultures.

Suggested Question

- ***Which countries have the two largest economies in the world today?*** *(The U.S. and Japan)*

Discussing Three Different Viewpoints Have students read the viewpoints on page 549.

MISAKI NAKANO

Suggested Question

- ***What does Nakano cite as one of the effects of Japanese companies moving jobs and companies overseas?*** *(Japanese workers are losing their jobs.)*

MARJORY E. SEARING

Suggested Question

- ***According to Searing, why is the United States unable to sell some of its excellent products in Japan?*** *(Because Japan does not let the United States do so.)*

LEO SHINOZAKI

Suggested Questions

- ***According to Shinozaki, are Japan's trade policies unfair?*** *(They are not as unfair as Americans are led to believe.)*
- ***According to Shinozaki, what is one reason why American companies sell few cars in Japan?*** *(Most American cars sold in Japan have the steering wheel on the left, which makes driving difficult and dangerous on Japanese roads.)*

CITIZENSHIP VIEWPOINTS

Thousands of cars await loading for export on the docks of Shimizu Port, Japan.

HOW FAIR ARE JAPAN'S TRADE POLICIES?

Today the economy of Japan is the second-largest in the world, exceeded only by that of the United States. Every year, Japan exports more than $300 billion worth of goods around the world. Perhaps you have a Japanese-made radio, or maybe your family drives a Japanese car. In fact, the United States imports more goods from Japan than from any other country except Canada. The United States also exports many products to Japan. However, since Japan exports to the United States much more than it imports, there is a trade imbalance. A trade imbalance is the difference between the value of the goods a country exports and the value of the goods the country imports.

The trade imbalance between the United States and Japan has caused disagreements between the two countries. Marjory Searing believes that Japan does not always play fair in international trade. Leo Shinozaki, on the other hand, argues that Japan's trade laws are fair and that United States companies do not work hard enough to sell their goods in Japan. Misaki Nakano offers a different view entirely. She thinks that Japan's trade policies hurt Japanese consumers and workers. Consider these three viewpoints on the issue and then answer the questions that follow.

548

BACKGROUND INFORMATION

- Disagreements on trade between Japan and the United States go all the way back to the 1850s, when the United States wanted to open the port of Tokyo (then called Edo) for use as a stopover point for American trading ships on their way to mainland Asia. In 1854, Commodore Matthew Perry sailed eight United States Navy ships to Japan and forced the Japanese to open their country to trade.
- After World War II, Japan's industrial base was rebuilt with the assistance of the United States. By the 1970s, however, the economic phenomenon known as the "Japanese Miracle" began to threaten many American industries, most notably automobiles and electronics. For example, in 1964 the U.S. imported 16,000 cars from Japan. By 1979 that number was 100 times greater, or 1,600,000. By the mid-1990s, however, the trade imbalance between Japan and the United States had begun to shrink again, in part due to the exchange rate between the dollar and the yen.

Three DIFFERENT Viewpoints

1 MISAKI NAKANO
Company Secretary, Kyoto, Japan
Excerpt from interview, 1996

Because the Japanese economy is stronger, prices have gone down. However, Japanese companies have been busy becoming more competitive and are moving many jobs and factories overseas. This means Japanese workers are losing their jobs. Also, companies don't pass along the benefits of free trade. Japanese consumers still pay higher prices for goods and services.

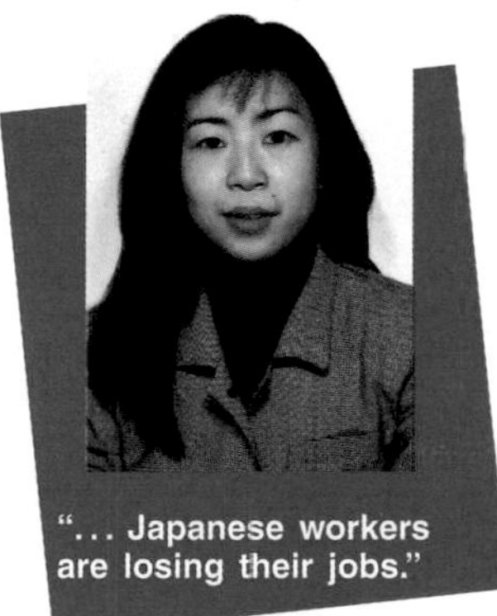
"... Japanese workers are losing their jobs."

2 MARJORY E. SEARING
Deputy Assistant Secretary for Japan, U.S. Department of Commerce, Washington, D.C. Excerpt from interview, 1996

It is important that Japan play by the same rules as everyone else. The United States has the most open market of any major country. We let Japan sell its cars, its TVs, its video games, and its other products in the U.S. without restriction. We have lots of excellent products that we want to sell in Japan, but Japan does not always let us do so. Japan should not be afraid to let our companies compete with theirs in Japan.

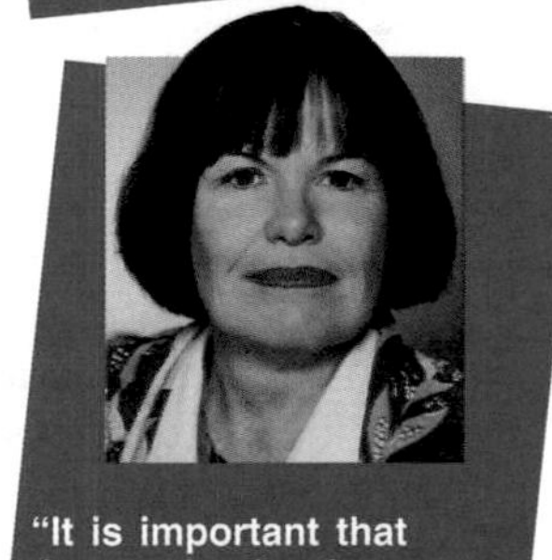
"It is important that Japan play by the same rules as everyone else."

3 LEO SHINOZAKI
Director, Japan Federation of Economic Organizations, Tokyo, Japan
Excerpt from interview, 1996

Japan's trade policies are not as unfair as Americans are led to believe. For example, the United States restricts imports of sugar and beef. Yet Americans complain that Japan does not buy rice from the U.S. Also, Americans tend to think that whatever sells in the U.S. must sell elsewhere. In Japan, people drive on the left-hand side. Meanwhile, American car companies have complained that very few Japanese buy American cars with the steering wheel on the left, which makes driving both difficult and dangerous in Japan.

"Japan's trade policies are not as unfair as Americans are led to believe."

BUILDING CITIZENSHIP

1. What is the viewpoint of each person? How does each support his or her views?
2. In what ways are the viewpoints alike? In what ways are they different?
3. What other viewpoints might people have on this issue? How might people in other countries feel about this issue?

SHARING VIEWPOINTS

Discuss what you agree or disagree with about each of these viewpoints. Discuss why you think each speaker might feel as he or she did. Then, as a class, write a statement that all of you can agree with on this issue.

EVALUATE
Answers to Citizenship Viewpoints

1. Nakano believes that Japan's trade policies have strengthened Japan's economy, but that companies haven't passed along enough benefits to Japanese consumers. Searing believes Japan does not always play fair in trade issues. Shinozaki claims that all countries, including the United States, have unfair trade policies.
2. The three speakers approach the issue very differently. Nakano is most concerned with the effect of trade on Japanese consumers. Searing and Shinozaki strongly disagree about the fairness of Japanese trade policies.
3. A Japanese rice farmer might feel that Japan's trade policies that restrict the importing of rice are a good idea. An American rice farmer might be angry that the Japanese do not buy any American rice. An American consumer might like the idea that America's policies allow inexpensive and well-made Japanese products to be sold in the United States.

Sharing Viewpoints Encourage students to link the viewpoints with the nationalities and situations of the speakers. Three statements on which the speakers might all agree include: **1.** Trade is a good thing for both the United States and Japan. **2.** No country has trade policies that are completely open. **3.** Good trade policies should benefit both countries.

Debating Viewpoints Discuss with students how expressing ideas in a debate can help to clarify the issues and sometimes lead to compromise. As an extension, have students research a particular area of trade dispute between the United States and Japan, such as automobiles or agricultural products, and report back to the class in the form of a debate.

CITIZENSHIP

Understanding Government As trade becomes an increasingly important part of the economies of all nations, the laws and regulations that control it become more complicated. In 1993, 117 countries signed the General Agreement on Tariffs and Trade (GATT), that heralded a new era of world trade. This agreement sets new trade laws that include:

- Creating the World Trade Organization (WTO) to settle disputes between countries.
- Cutting tariffs on many manufactured products by more than one-third.
- Protecting intellectual property, such as software and music CDs, of inventors and entertainers.

Ask students to research in recent newspapers how the United States is currently involved with GATT, such as trying to resolve trade disputes with Japan through the WTO. Have them report back to the class with their findings.

LESSON 3
pages 550–551

Lesson Theme The government of Japan contains elements of both ancient Japanese traditions and modern democratic ways.

Lesson Objectives
- Describe the role of the emperor.
- Identify similarities between Japan's government and the governments of the United States and Great Britain.
- Discuss the role of MITI.

PREPARE

Motivate Have a student read the *Read Aloud* passage to the class. Encourage students to use their prior knowledge to compare the role of Japan's emperor with that of Great Britain's queen.

Set Purpose Ask the *What You Know* question to review the definition of a constitutional monarchy. Have students read the lesson to find the answer to the *What You Will Learn* question.

TEACH

Describing the Emperor's Role
Help students to understand that while the emperor does not rule the country, he is an important link between traditional elements of government and modern government.

Ask students:

- **What does the emperor do?** (greets visitors, attends ceremonies)

Understanding the Japanese Constitution Discuss ways in which the Japanese Constitution is like the United States Constitution. Point out the unique features of the Japanese Constitution.

RESOURCE

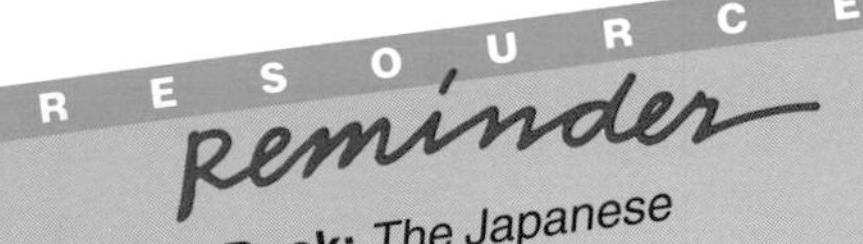

Practice Book: *The Japanese Government,* page 151
■ **Anthology:** *Attack on Pearl Harbor,* page 174; *When the Atomic Bomb Fell,* pages 175–176; *Governing Japan Today,* pages 177–178

LESSON 3

The Government

READ TO LEARN

Key Vocabulary
Diet

Key People
Akihito

Read Aloud

On January 1, 1946, Japan's Emperor Hirohito told his people that he did not rule by divine right. His power came from the will of the people, he said, not from God.

Today the Japanese honor their emperor as a symbol of the country. The present emperor, the son of Hirohito, is the one hundred twenty-fifth member of his family to act as emperor of Japan. The family has been serving the country for more than 1,500 years. Think about how long this time is and the great store of tradition it suggests. As you read this lesson, you will see how Japan's government successfully blends a very old monarchy with present-day democracy.

Read for Purpose

1. **WHAT YOU KNOW:** What is a constitutional monarchy?
2. **WHAT YOU WILL LEARN:** How is the Japanese government organized?

ROLE OF THE EMPEROR

For centuries emperors in Japan held no real power. Government leaders and military chiefs ran the nation. The emperor was important to his people mainly as a symbol of the past and of the nation's accomplishments. After World War II, Japan officially became a constitutional monarchy. In 1989, Akihito became emperor after his father, Hirohito, died.

Emperor Akihito remains a symbol of the country today. He presides at ceremonies and greets important visitors. By continuing to live in Tokyo's Imperial Palace, the emperor also serves as a reminder to his people of the strong link between Japan's traditional government and the newer democratic government that was formed after World War II.

THE JAPANESE CONSTITUTION

At the end of World War II, the United States forced Japan to accept a new kind of government. It ordered a group of Americans and Japanese to write a constitution forming a democracy for Japan.

In many ways the Japanese Constitution of 1947 resembles the Constitution of the United States. It guarantees free speech and a free press. Japan is one of the few countries in East Asia that permits its citizens to speak out against the government without fear of punishment.

The Japanese constitution has some unique features. It states that "the Japanese people forever renounce war as a sovereign right of the nation and the threat or use of force as a means of settling international disputes." A sovereign right is a na-

WHAT YOU KNOW: This question refers to information in Chapter 9, Lesson 3; a government headed by a monarch whose powers are limited by a constitution.

READING STRATEGY AND VOCABULARY DEVELOPMENT

Summarizing Demonstrate to students how to organize a summary of this lesson by making a chart showing the changes in the form of government in Japan since World War II. A sample chart showing two items of this information follows.

CHANGES IN JAPAN'S GOVERNMENT

	Before World War II	After World War II
Ruler	emperor, military chiefs	prime minister, Diet
Type	monarchy	constitutional monarchy

tion's right to act independently. Japan's defense force is not used outside of the country.

THE DIET

Japan's government is also different from that of the United States in other ways. For example, although a democracy, Japan has a parliamentary system of government, much like that of Great Britain. Its legislature, called the Diet, makes all laws for the country. As in Great Britain, the leader of the majority party in the legislature becomes prime minister, or the leader of the government. The prime minister selects a cabinet to give advice.

Until 1989 all Japanese prime ministers and top government officials had been men. In that year two women joined the cabinet. Although their constitution gives women equal rights, the Japanese by custom have not encouraged women to become political leaders.

GOVERNMENT AND BUSINESS

Since the 1950s the government of Japan has actively supported business. The main government agency dealing with foreign trade is the Ministry of International Trade and Industry (MITI). After World War II MITI took the lead in urging Japanese industries to modernize.

MITI doesn't just collect facts and give suggestions. It pushes and prods businesses to follow its advice. In addition MITI helps companies obtain bank loans and contributes money for research. One example of MITI's leadership and support over the last 30 years is the help it has given to make the country's electronics industry a world leader.

A CONSTITUTIONAL MONARCHY

The government of Japan is a mixture of the traditional and modern. In this lesson you have read that the country blends ancient Japanese traditions in a Western-style democracy. At the end of World War II, the government of Japan was completely changed. It adopted a constitution that made the country a parliamentary democracy headed by the emperor. Unlike most of East Asia, Japan has free elections, free speech, and a free press.

Among the important duties of Emperor Akihito and Empress Michiko of Japan is making goodwill visits to other nations.

Check Your Reading

1. How did the government of Japan change after World War II?
2. Name two unique features of Japan's present constitution.
3. How does the government help business in Japan?
4. **THINKING SKILL:** Classify the provisions of Japan's constitution into two groups. Explain your classification.

THINKING SKILL: Classifying

551

Understanding the Diet

Ask students:

- **What is the role of the Diet in the Japanese government?** (It makes the laws.)
- *THINKING FURTHER:* **What and who would be the United States equivalent to the Diet and the prime minister?** (Congress and the President)

Discussing Government and Business

Ask students:

- **What does MITI do?** (It encourages companies to follow its advice and encourages research.)

Applying the Lesson Have students discuss the changes in Japan's government after World War II.

3 CLOSE

Summarizing Students have learned that the government of Japan is a constitutional monarchy that supports free enterprise. Discuss the ways in which Japan's government differs from other East Asian governments.

Evaluating Use the *Check Your Reading* questions (answers given below) to assess students' understanding.

Answers to Check Your Reading

1. It became a constitutional monarchy and adopted a constitution resembling the Constitution of the U.S.
2. It renounces war and the use of force for settling disputes.
3. MITI gives money and suggestions. It collects information.
4. *provisions like those of the United States:* permits freedom of speech and press; *provisions unlike those of the United States:* renounces war and the use of force for settling disputes; shows the Japanese and U.S. constitutions to be both alike and unalike

Independent Practice
Practice Book: page 151

MEETING INDIVIDUAL NEEDS

Reteaching (easy) Have students research the role of Japan's emperor before and after World War II. Have them list the changes in the emperor's role.

Extension (average) Both India and Japan have democratic governments. Have students write an essay comparing and contrasting the political situations in India and Japan. Be sure students recognize that the homogeneity of Japan's population makes the political situation of that country more stable.

Enrichment (challenging) Have students create a chart that compares the governments of all the East Asian countries. Discuss the similarities and differences among them.

LESSON 4
pages 552–553

Lesson Theme The Japanese emphasize the beauty of nature and believe that art should be part of everyday life.

Lesson Objectives
- List ways that art is incorporated into daily life.
- Identify traditional and modern sports of Japan.

PREPARE

Motivate Read the *Read Aloud* section to the class. Encourage a discussion of haiku and other art forms. Have volunteers try to write their own haikus.

Set Purpose Use the *What You Know* question to review Chinese art. Pose the *What You Will Learn* question and have students read the lesson to find the answer.

TEACH

Discussing Art as a Way of Life Encourage students to appreciate the importance of art in Japanese life.

Ask students:

- **How do the Japanese "catch the moment"?** (They fill their lives with beauty.)
- **What is calligraphy?** (an ancient form of beautiful writing)
- **What form of beauty is found in most Japanese homes?** (flower arrangements)

LESSON 4

Arts and Recreation

READ TO LEARN

Key Vocabulary

sumo wrestling

Read Aloud

Midnight full of stars . . .
dim cherry-petals float on
rice-paddy waters

A famous Japanese poet named Buson wrote these lines over 200 years ago. They are an example of the country's most popular form of poetry, haiku (hī′ kü). Like other types of Japanese art, haiku look simple but are difficult to create. Each short poem reflects a respect for the marvels of nature as well as for traditional forms of art.

Read for Purpose

1. WHAT YOU KNOW: What kind of painting was popular in China?
2. WHAT YOU WILL LEARN: How do the people of Japan combine traditional and new styles in their arts and leisure activities?

ART AS A WAY OF LIFE

In the poem above, Buson sketches a picture of the delicate cherry blossom, a flower admired by the ancient samurai warriors. The cherry blossom not only signals the coming of spring, it also reminds us that nature's beauty is fleeting. To enjoy the flower, a person must stop and look now, before the blossom withers and dies.

The Japanese have long valued "catching the moment." They fill their everyday lives with as much beauty as possible. For example, traditional Japanese food is served in a way that makes it look as good as it tastes, with colors and shapes chosen to balance one another. In school students study both writing and the ancient art of calligraphy, or beautiful writing. Because the Japanese believe that the way in which a person writes is important, students study calligraphy from third grade through ninth grade.

In their homes the Japanese try to make room for beauty in many detailed ways. Few homes are without a tasteful display of flowers. A Japanese flower arrangement does not use big bunches of many blossoms. Instead it has only a few parts. One might be a twisted branch or a cluster of leaves. The art of flower arranging has been handed down from generation to generation by the Japanese.

The people of Japan also love to be outdoors surrounded by beautiful flowers and trees. In a nation where living space is scarce, small spaces are used for gardens.

 WHAT YOU KNOW: This question refers to information in Chapter 26, Lesson 4; landscape painting.

READING STRATEGY AND VOCABULARY DEVELOPMENT

Summarizing Continue emphasizing to students the importance of using their own words when summarizing. Have students read and summarize this lesson. Then have students work in groups and use their summaries to create a travelogue depicting the various arts and leisure activities. Some students may wish to create a narrative, perhaps an interview between a tour guide and a prospective tourist, instead of a travelogue. Others may wish to create pictures to go with their narrative descriptions.

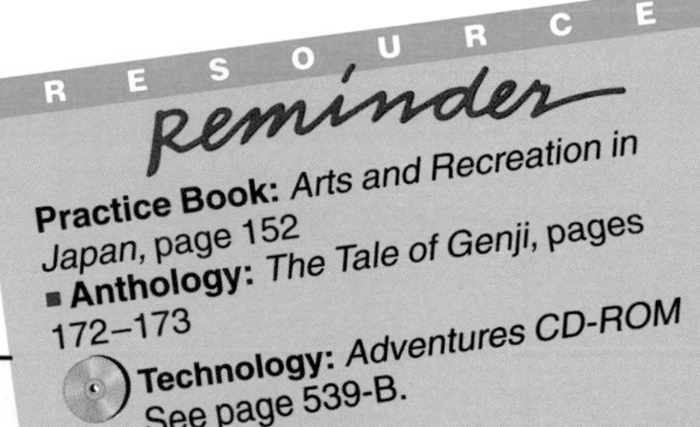

In some of the most famous Japanese gardens, rocks are an important part of the design. For example, large stones may be surrounded by rounded pebbles that have been raked to resemble waves or other kinds of designs.

TRADITIONAL SPORTS

In sports as in art, the Japanese try to preserve and cherish their past. Yasuhiro Yamashita (yä sü hē′ rō yä mä shē′ tə) is an athlete who practices a traditional sport called judo. Judo and karate are two kinds of martial arts, or methods of unarmed fighting similar to those you read about in China. Judo uses balance and weight to knock over opponents. Karate uses blows struck with the hands and feet. You will read more about the martial arts legacy in the lesson on pages 554–557.

To perform another of Japan's traditional sports, sumo wrestling, a person should weigh about 300 pounds (136 kg). In sumo wrestling two enormously strong players try to force each other to touch the ground with any part of the body other than the feet. However, sumo wrestlers may not pull hair, kick, or punch their opponents during the match.

BASEBALL AND GOLF

While the Japanese love traditional sports, they have also adopted sports from other countries. Among the most popular of these are baseball, golf, and skiing. The Japanese adopted baseball from the United States in 1873.

Golf is a Western sport that has become popular in Japan more recently. But in a country where level land is scarce, it is very costly to play. People in Tokyo have spent up to $900,000 to buy a membership in a golf club. Even as members, they may have to call weeks ahead for a starting time because courses are heavily booked.

Grand champion Wajima stands in a traditional pose of Japan's sumo wrestlers

TRADITIONAL AND MODERN

Japan's traditional arts are still popular. Haiku poetry is hundreds of years old. As you have read, the Japanese believe that art should be part of everyday life. Thus flower arranging, calligraphy, and gardening are practiced.

Today the Japanese enjoy such traditional sports as karate and sumo wrestling along with baseball, golf, and other Western sports.

 **Check Your Reading**

1. Name two ways that the Japanese include art in their everyday lives.
2. How might a Japanese person combine a haiku with the art of calligraphy?
3. What is sumo wrestling?
4. THINKING SKILL: In what ways might Japanese flower arrangements be different today from those of the past? In what ways might they be the same?

THINKING SKILL: Compare and Contrast

553

Describing Traditional Sports Help students to understand that karate, judo, and sumo wrestling are important not only as sports but also as links to the past.

Discussing Baseball and Golf Discuss the modern sports that interest the Japanese.

Applying the Lesson Discuss the attitude of the Japanese toward art and sports compared to the attitude of Americans.

 CLOSE

Summarizing Students have learned that arts and sports are an integral part of Japanese life. The people seek beauty and a reminder of their traditions in both. Review the arts and sports of Japan.

Evaluating Use these questions to assess students' understanding.

- **What are the traditional and nontraditional sports found in Japan?** (Judo, karate, and sumo wrestling are traditional. Baseball, skiing, and golf are nontraditional.)
- **What is special about calligraphy?** (It is traditional and beautiful.)
- **What are two ways in which art is incorporated into daily life in Japan?** (food serving, flower arranging)

Answers to Check Your Reading

1. flower arranging, food serving
2. Write a haiku poem in calligraphy.
3. Two wrestlers try to force each other to touch the ground using any part of the body except the feet.
4. There may be new strains of flowers, new materials for vases, or the use of synthetic flowers. The arrangements might be similar to ones done hundreds of years ago.

Independent Practice
Practice Book: page 152

MEETING INDIVIDUAL NEEDS

Reteaching (easy) Have students research origami. Then have them collect samples for display or try to create their own origami pieces.

Extension (average) Have students research Japanese flower arranging or food arranging. Then have students attempt either art form. Display their works.

Enrichment (challenging) Tell students that baseball is enjoyed as much in Japan as it is in the United States. Have them research the similarities and differences between the American and Japanese versions of this sport. Students may present their findings in chart form.

LEGACY
pages 554–557

Lesson Theme The legacy of martial arts reflects many aspects of Japanese history and culture. Drawing on these various sources, martial arts teach not only self-defense but also discipline and honor.

Lesson Objectives
- Describe some of the types of martial arts that are practiced in Japan.
- Describe the historic and cultural roots of various martial arts.
- Explain the way in which martial arts stress speed, grace, and inner control.

1 PREPARE

Motivate Ask students to list their favorite sports. Have them discuss why they enjoy watching or participating in these sports.

Set Purpose Focus students' attention with the following question. How can sports be used to train both the mind and the body? (Student responses should reflect the idea that sports require concentration, discipline, and strategy, along with physical prowess.) Have students read the introduction. Ask them to think about the concluding suggestion while they read the rest of the lesson.

2 TEACH

Understanding the Concept of Legacies Ask students why they think that art forms can be legacies. (Possible answer includes: Many art forms are handed down from generation to generation and are an important part of culture.)

Discussing a Martial Arts Class Have students discuss after-school activities in which they participate.

Ask students:

- **List the benefits of learning a martial art.** (the ability to defend oneself; exercise; self-improvement through training and self-control)

MARTIAL ARTS: *More Than Just Fighting*

by Diana Reische

You just read about how the people of Japan have adopted several sports from other countries, such as baseball and golf. You also read about sports that date from earlier periods in Japan's history, such as sumo wrestling and karate. As you read this lesson, think about the legacy of the martial (mär′ shəl) arts and their significance to Japanese culture.

LEARNING A MARTIAL ART

Classes are over for the day at your Japanese school, but you do not leave the building. Instead you hurry to the gym, where your after-school club is meeting. You and the other club members are there to practice one of Japan's traditional martial arts. A martial art is a system of fighting and exercise that stresses self-defense. The goal of such a system is not just winning, but improving yourself through training and self-control.

When your teacher arrives, you bow courteously. So do the other students. Why? Courtesy and discipline are part of learning any martial art. "If you do not master yourself," your teacher always says, "you cannot hope to improve."

A JUDO CLUB

Your club practices judo. This modern sport grew out of an older, rougher

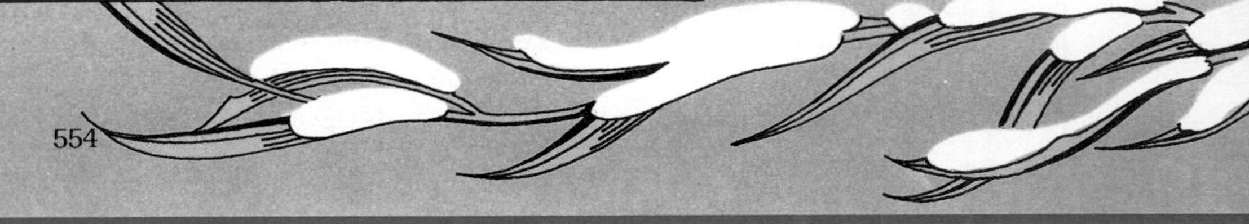

554

READING STRATEGY AND VOCABULARY DEVELOPMENT

Summarizing Review the summarizing strategy. Have students preview the lesson before reading it. Then divide the class into five groups. Have each group develop a summary of one of the five sections of this lesson. Then have the class work together to present a coherent summary of the entire lesson.

Japanese martial art called jujitsu (jü jit' sü). Jujitsu is a system of hand-to-hand fighting that includes kicks, throws, and other dangerous moves. How did judo emerge from this rough-and-tumble style?

It was invented by a man named Jigoro Kano (kä'nō) in the late 1800s. As a boy, Kano was sickly, and his parents sent him to study with jujitsu masters to make him stronger. Kano became an expert in this style of fighting. However, as an adult and educator, he wanted to develop a less dangerous sport that could be taught to schoolchildren. Kano called this new martial art *judo*, which means "the gentle or flexible way."

Kano borrowed many moves from jujitsu for his new sport, but he left out the chops and strikes that could seriously harm someone. No hitting, striking, or kicking was allowed. And as its name suggests, judo encouraged a flexible form of fighting. This flexibility has been compared to that of a willow branch heavy with snow. Because the branch bends, it saves itself from breaking under the snow's weight. Yet the branch is not weak. A judo expert learns to use the force of an attacker *against* the attacker: to bend with that force, rather than being broken by it.

Jigoro Kano invented the art of judo.

A WAY TO IMPROVEMENT

The word judo ends in *do*, which means "path" or "way" in Japanese. When you study judo you learn much more than how to defend yourself. You follow a specific training "path" toward improving yourself. Jigoro Kano set down precise moves for every judo fall, throw, lock, or hold.

Yet Japanese martial arts consist of much more than simply learning moves. For inner control, the training draws on a special form of Buddhism, which you read about in Chapter 26. For calming the mind, it draws on yoga, the Hindu method of exercise and meditation that you read about in Chapter 25. And for its code of honor, martial arts training draws on Japan's samurai past.

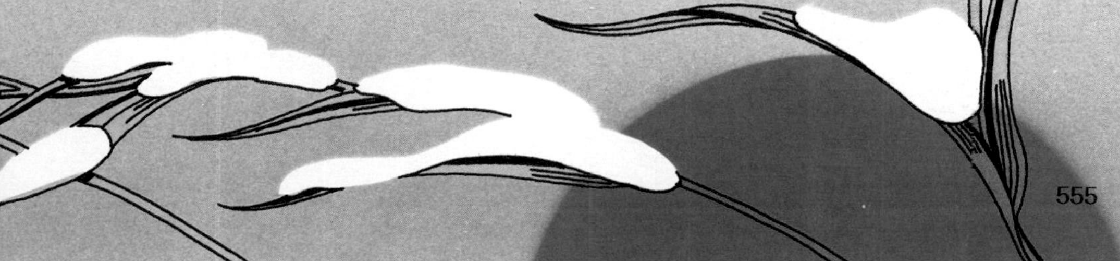

Discussing a Judo Club Have students discuss the measures used to improve the safety of the sports in which they participate.

Ask students:

- **Why is judo especially suited for schoolchildren?** (Possible answers include: Judo is less dangerous than other forms of the martial arts.)
- **How can judo be used effectively by a weaker person against a stronger attacker?** (Judo allows the weaker person to use the strength of the attacker against the attacker.)
- *THINKING FURTHER:* **How are judo and jujitsu similar? How are they different?** (*similarities:* Both are martial arts; certain moves are similar; *differences:* Judo does not teach the jujitsu chops and strikes that could harm someone; judo does not allow the types of hitting, striking, or kicking used in jujitsu.)

Exploring a Way to Improvement Have students discuss the ways in which sports strengthen both the mind and the body.

Ask students:

- **What roles do Buddhism and Hindu yoga play in learning judo?** (Judo is partly a method of spiritual training that strengthens the mind as well as the body. Therefore, Buddhism is used to teach inner control and Hindu yoga is used to calm the mind.)

BACKGROUND INFORMATION

Multicultural Perspectives Just as the Japanese have enthusiastically adopted foreign sports such as baseball and golf, the martial arts have attained considerable popularity in the United States. People in this country received their first exposure to judo and jujitsu when people from Japan began immigrating to the United States in the late 1800s and the early 1900s. However, it was not until after World War II that people from the United States began to practice the martial arts. Large numbers of soldiers began studying these traditions during the postwar occupation of Japan. A number of these soldiers opened martial arts schools upon their return to the United States and invited Japanese teachers to direct them. Soon people all over the United States were learning judo and jujitsu. Others studied karate, aikido (ī kē' dō), which is a combination of jujitsu and Chinese boxing, and kendo (ken' dō), which is a type of swordplay. After the Korean War in 1953, soldiers from the United States brought back Korean karate techniques as well. Today thousands of American children study martial arts in order to learn discipline and gain bodily strength. Adults are also attracted to the martial arts, often with a stress on self-defense as well as mental training.

Ask students to name other examples of sports legacies that have crossed national and cultural boundaries.

Discussing the Samurai Legacy Make sure that students can point out the location of Japan on the political *Atlas* Map of Southern and Eastern Asia.

Ask students:

- **How does the teacher's encouragement to fight with "honor and style" echo samurai values?** (The samurai code of honor did not allow fighting that relied on dirty tricks or dishonesty.)
- *THINKING FURTHER:* **How are the use of the naginata and the martial art of judo similar? How are they different?** (*similar:* Both are used to help a weak fighter fend off a more powerful attacker; *different:* Judo does not use weapons.)

Discussing the Photograph Direct students' attention to the photograph at the bottom of this page.

Ask students:

- **Describe what is shown in the photograph.** (two women fighting with the naginata)
- *THINKING FURTHER:* **How does the photograph show both modern and traditional aspects of the use of the naginata?** (*modern:* The naginata does not have a blade; the women are wearing sparring helmets; *traditional:* The women are also wearing traditional dress; the use of the naginata dates from the time of the samurai.)

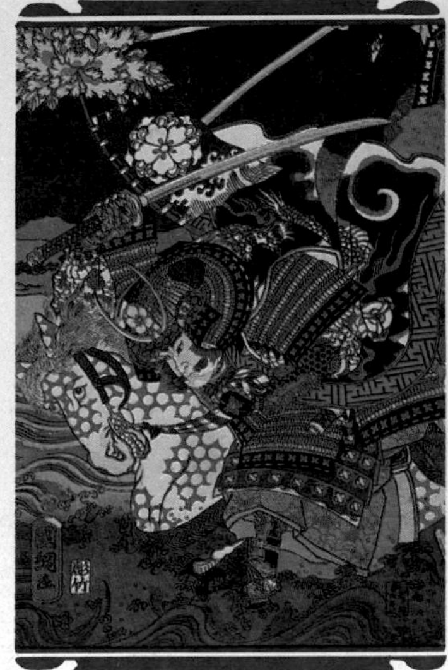

THE SAMURAI LEGACY

You have already read about the samurai—the great warriors who ruled Japan centuries ago. Their code of honor still influences every Japanese martial art. A samurai was forbidden to win a fight by using dirty tricks or dishonesty. When a modern-day martial arts teacher tells a classroom of students to always perform "with honor and style," the teacher is echoing samurai values.

Women, too, formed part of the samurai tradition. While warriors were away fighting, Japanese women sometimes had to defend themselves from roving bandits. The women trained with weapons that the warriors had left at home because they were too difficult to carry on horseback. One of these was called the *naginata* (nä gē nä' tä). This weapon consisted of a long wooden shaft with a blade on one end and an iron knob on the other. A woman skilled in using the naginata might fight off a more powerful attacker using a short sword.

Fighting with a naginata remains a popular sport with Japanese women today. In the modern sport, however, the emphasis is on speed and grace, and instead of a blade, the modern weapon contains nothing more dangerous than a curved bamboo tip.

556

BACKGROUND INFORMATION

More About the Martial Arts In addition to judo, jujitsu, naginata, and karate, other martial arts that are studied in East Asia include Chinese boxing, aikido, and kendo.

- Chinese boxing is taught in several styles. Some, such as Shaolin kung fu, stress external strength, utilizing many extremely intricate moves. On the other hand, a style such as tai chi chuan (tī' chē' chü' an) stresses internal strength. Tai chi uses a minimum amount of strength to absorb an attacker's blow, while simultaneously delivering a counterblow.
- The Japanese martial art of aikido utilizes some of the techniques of both Chinese boxing and jujitsu. With an emphasis on circular movement, participants seek to topple opponents through the use of wrist and arm techniques. Once on the ground, the opponent is immobilized with joint-locks. Like judo, aikido uses the force of the attacker against the attacker.
- Kendo is a Japanese martial art that grew out of an earlier tradition of swordplay. Participants wear protective garments to guard against blows to the head, chest, and hands. The object is to score points by striking target areas with a springy bamboo sword called a shinai (shin' ī).

KARATE

While judo, naginata, and many other arts of self-defense emerged from Japan's warrior traditions, one popular martial art came from outside Japan. In the 1600s the Japanese ruled the island of Okinawa (ō kə nä' wə). Since the Japanese rulers did not allow the Okinawans to carry weapons, the islanders needed to develop a way to protect themselves.

Their solution was to borrow a Chinese fighting style. In China monks often had to defend themselves from bandits. However, they had no wish to carry weapons. For this purpose, a group of monks invented a fighting style called "temple boxing," which involved only the use of bare hands. The Okinawans modified this Chinese style of weaponless fighting into karate, which means "empty hand."

Karate remained an Okinawan art for many years. In the early 1900s, however, a karate expert named Gichin Funakoshi (fü nə kō' shē) was invited to demonstrate this martial art at the Japanese emperor's palace. The slim, small-boned Funakoshi, who was only 5′1″ (1.52 m), won match after match against much bigger opponents. His fame spread, and when he opened a karate school in Tokyo, students from all over Japan came to attend.

Since then, karate has become popular all over the world. There may be a karate school in your city or town. Many different styles of this sport have developed over the years. Yet Funakoshi's words still sum up the ideals of karate and other Japanese martial arts:

As a mirror's polished surface reflects whatever stands before it and a quiet valley carries even small sounds, so must the student of karate render his mind empty of selfishness and wickedness in an effort to react appropriately toward anything he may encounter.

How do martial arts such as judo, naginata, and karate combine old and new aspects of Japanese culture?

557

Discussing Karate Ask students if they have ever watched or participated in a karate class. Tell them that martial arts such as judo and karate are popular in the United States.

Ask students:

- **Why do you think that the word *karate*, which means "empty hand," is an appropriate name for this martial art?** (because karate uses only the bare hand and does not use weapons)
- *THINKING FURTHER:* **List the characteristics of the martial arts that are described by Funakoshi's words.** (Possible characteristics include: samurai tradition forbidding dishonesty; focus on self-control; calmness of mind based on Buddhist principles; flexibility.)

Applying the Lesson Have the class discuss the similarities and differences between each of the martial arts described in this lesson.

3 CLOSE

Summarizing Students have learned about the origins and practices of the Japanese legacy of the martial arts. Have students list the historic origin of each of the martial arts described in this lesson.

Evaluating Assess students' understanding of the lesson by asking them the question at the bottom of the pupil page. (Student responses may note that today the martial arts are popular sports that preserve centuries-old customs and values.)

MEETING INDIVIDUAL NEEDS

Reteaching (easy) Have students list each of the martial arts described in this lesson. Then have them make a chart detailing two characteristics of each martial art they have identified.

Extension (average) Have students conduct research to learn some of the "moves" associated with a particular martial art. Have students explain the moves to the rest of the class.

Enrichment (challenging) Have students conduct research in order to write a short essay about a martial art that is not discussed in this lesson. Encourage students to provide a description of the origin of the martial art, as well as a summary of the martial art's basic principles. Students may want to use the Outline Map of Japan, found in the Teacher's Resource Center, as part of their report.

CHAPTER 27 REVIEW
pages 558–559

USING THE CHAPTER SUMMARY AND REVIEW

Cultural Geography These questions may be used for review.

- **What values do the Japanese find important?** (respect for authority and order, duty to family and rulers)
- **What is Japan's most important natural resource?** (hard-working people)
- **What type of government does Japan have?** (constitutional monarchy)
- **What are three popular traditional arts in Japan?** (haiku, calligraphy, flower arranging)

Ideas to Remember

- **What do the people of Japan share?** (common beliefs, values, and customs)
- **Why has Japan become a successful industrial nation?** (because of its hard-working, well-educated, loyal workers)
- **Why is the emperor of Japan important?** (He is the symbol of the country.)
- **What are some of the modern forms of recreation of the Japanese?** (baseball, golf, skiing)

Answers to Reviewing Vocabulary

1. Shinto
2. sumo wrestling
3. samurai
4. homogeneous
5. Diet

Answers to Reviewing Facts

1. chopsticks, Chinese characters, the Buddhist religion, and teachings of Confucius
2. The samurai tradition of duty to family, rulers, and country has been passed on and has become part of the present culture.
3. bowing, being members of a group rather than individuals striving to get ahead

CHAPTER 27 • SUMMARY

JAPAN: CULTURAL GEOGRAPHY

PEOPLE

- Japan has a nearly homogeneous population

- Many Japanese believe in Shinto, Confucianism, and Buddhism
- The group is considered to be more important than the individual
- Important values: respect for authority and order, duty to family and rulers

ECONOMY

- Japan is the second most productive industrial power in the world
- Few natural resources except for the hard work of its people

- Reasons for economic success: efficiency, quality control, ability to adapt foreign technologies, extensive research to improve products, skilled and loyal workers

GOVERNMENT

- Emperor: an important symbol of the country

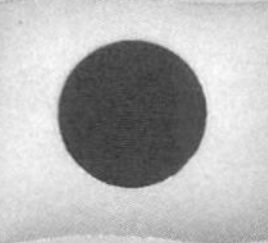

- The constitution guarantees the rights of citizens; prohibits the formation of armed forces, except a defensive force
- Parliamentary system includes the Diet (legislature)
- Government supports business

ARTS AND RECREATION

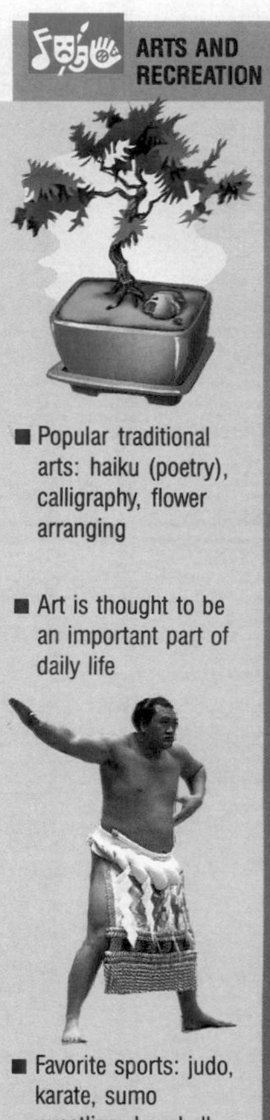

- Popular traditional arts: haiku (poetry), calligraphy, flower arranging
- Art is thought to be an important part of daily life
- Favorite sports: judo, karate, sumo wrestling, baseball, golf

IDEAS TO REMEMBER

- Many of the members of Japan's homogeneous population share common beliefs, values, and customs.
- Japan has become the second-largest industrial nation in the world with the help of its hard-working, well-educated, loyal workers.
- Japan is a constitutional democracy in which the emperor serves as a symbol of the country.
- Traditional arts and sports, such as haiku and sumo wrestling, exist side by side with adopted recreations, such as golf and baseball.

558

ENRICHMENT ACTIVITY

Creating Calligraphy Scrolls **Materials:** samples of Japanese writing, long strips of paper, markers or brushes and ink, wooden rods, string

1. Refer the class to the photograph on page 547. Explain that the picture shows a calligraphy contest in which children write on scrolls. Tell the class that they are going to hold their own calligraphy contest of Japanese character writing.
2. Encourage the class to study the Japanese characters. Try to have other examples of Japanese writing available. Have them copy Japanese characters and write them vertically on their scrolls as the Japanese do.
3. Have students display their scrolls on wooden rods and hang them with string around the classroom.

CHAPTER 27 • REVIEW

REVIEWING VOCABULARY

Diet
homogeneous
samurai
Shinto
sumo wrestling

Number a sheet of paper from 1 to 5. Beside each number write the word or term from the above list that best matches the definition.

1. A Japanese religious belief that spirits dwell in nature
2. A sport in which participants try to force each other to touch the ground
3. Japanese warriors who were taught to feel a great sense of duty
4. A word that applies to people who share many of the same characteristics
5. The legislative body that makes all national laws in Japan

REVIEWING FACTS

1. Name four things that the Japanese borrowed from their Asian neighbors.
2. How has the samurai tradition influenced Japanese culture?
3. Name two ways in which the Japanese express their sense of loyalty and respect for the common good.
4. What percentage of total world output is contributed by Japan? Which country is ahead of Japan in industrial production?
5. How did Japan's electronic industry become first in the world?
6. Why is education an important part of Japan's economic success?
7. How does the Japanese sense of loyalty help companies in Japan?
8. How was democracy forced on Japan?
9. Why have few Japanese women achieved high positions in government despite the equality given to women in the constitution?
10. How does the Japanese attitude toward art differ from that of Americans and Europeans?

WRITING ABOUT MAIN IDEAS

1. **Writing a Paragraph:** You have read that Japan's homogeneous society is one of the country's key characteristics. Write a paragraph comparing Japanese society with American society.
2. **Writing a Poem:** Haiku is a short, vivid, 3-line poem containing only 17 syllables that often deals with some aspect of nature. Write a haiku that expresses something that is important to you.
3. **Writing About Perspectives:** Imagine that you are away from home, enrolled away in a "cram school." Write a letter to your parents describing your experiences at the school.

BUILDING SKILLS: WRITING A SUMMARY

1. What is a summary?
2. What is a topic sentence?
3. Read Lesson 2 in this chapter. Find 5 topic sentences in the lesson.
4. Use the topic sentences to help you to write a summary of Lesson 2.
5. When might it be helpful to know how to write a summary.

4. 11 percent; the United States
5. through quality, efficiency, adapting technologies of other countries, and research
6. An industrial economy like Japan's needs skilled, educated workers.
7. Few people change jobs; they are eager, reliable, and hard-working.
8. It was forced on them by the United States after Japan's defeat in World War II.
9. Japanese custom has not encouraged women to become political leaders.
10. The Japanese make room for beauty and art in their everyday lives.

Suggestions for Writing About Main Ideas

1. Students should note the great mixture of cultures, religions, values, and beliefs in the United States compared to Japan's homogeneous society.
2. Have volunteers share their haikus with the rest of the class.
3. Students should note the long hours and hard work expected of them in a "cram school."

Answers to Building Skills: Writing a Summary

1. a brief statement of main ideas contained in a piece of writing
2. a sentence that expresses the main idea
3. Possible answers include: first sentences of paragraphs 2, 3, 5, 6, 8, and 10.
4. Students' summaries should be similar to the summary under "A Strong Economy." Accept all reasonable answers.
5. when you want to sort out the most important information

Chapter Review and Test
Practice Book: *Vocabulary Review,* page 153
Transparency: *Graphic Organizer*
Assessment Book: *Chapter 27 Test*

MAKING CONNECTIONS

Identifying Main Ideas Display the Main Idea Diagram Graphic Organizer Transparency, writing in only one underlined detail. Have the class review the chapter to fill in other details about the people, economy, government, and arts of Japan. Then ask students to "add up" the details to write a main idea statement. *Ask:* What features make the Japanese culture so distinctive?

Japan's mostly homogeneous population shares basic values.
+
Japan is a parliamentary democracy headed by an emperor.
+
The Japanese enjoy both traditional and modern sports.
=
Main Idea: Japan today is a balance of traditional and modern.

CHAPTER 28
ORGANIZER

SOUTHEAST ASIA text pages 560–575

CHAPTER THEME A cultural crossroads with few pockets of strong economic growth, Southeast Asia has a rural population with a wide variety of governments.

CHAPTER OBJECTIVES

CONTENT

- Explain why Southeast Asia has always been a great crossroads.
- Describe the impact of Chinese and Indian civilizations on Southeast Asian culture.
- Describe the impact of European colonialism on Southeast Asia.
- Name products of Southeast Asia that are essential to countries elsewhere in the world.
- Describe the effects of population growth in some Southeast Asian countries.
- Explain why it has been difficult for the nations of Southeast Asia to achieve peace.
- Outline the events leading to the overthrow of the Marcos dictatorship in the Philippines.
- Define *authoritarian government* and explain why it is common in Southeast Asia.
- Describe the ways that religion has influenced the arts and leisure in Southeast Asia.

SKILLS

Geography
- Interpret a political map of Southeast Asia.
- Interpret a map showing the distribution of the major religions in Southeast Asia.

Study and Research
- Analyze a cartogram showing per capita income in Southeast Asia.
- Interpret a diagram showing the process of growing rice in a paddy.

Thinking
- Ask focused questions about the people of Southeast Asia.
- Contrast democracy and authoritarian government.
- Draw conclusions based on information presented.

Reading and Writing
- Write a narrative about political events in Southeast Asia.

CITIZENSHIP VALUES

- Appreciate both positive and negative aspects of great ethnic diversity.
- Appreciate the importance of peace in the creation of just and prosperous societies.

TEACHER OPTIONS

READING STRATEGY: Vocabulary Development
Strategies to help students read and remember the main ideas of the lesson.

Lesson 1: p. 561 Lesson 3: p. 568
Lesson 2: p. 565 Lesson 4: p. 572

MEETING INDIVIDUAL NEEDS Activities for reteaching, extension, and enrichment.

Lesson 1: p. 564 Lesson 3: p. 570
Lesson 2: p. 567 Lesson 4: p. 573

GEO ADVENTURES ACTIVITIES PAD Daily activities to assess students' understanding of geography skills.

CURRICULUM CONNECTION Activities to help integrate other subject areas with Social Studies.

Language Arts: p. 566 Science: p. 566

PUPIL EDITION ON CASSETTE Language support for students who have difficulty reading or who will benefit from listening to the Pupil Edition on Cassette as they read.

SECOND-LANGUAGE SUPPORT Activities and suggestions for second-language learners.

Lesson 2: p. 485-D

CHAPTER PLANNING GUIDE

LESSON	SUGGESTED PACING	THEMES	TEACHER SUPPORT MATERIALS: TEACHER'S RESOURCE CENTER
1 THE PEOPLE pages 561–564	1 day	Because of its location, Southeast Asia has been influenced by many Asian and European groups.	Practice Book p. 154 ■ Anthology pp. 152–153 Outline Map p. 37
2 THE ECONOMY pages 565–567	1 day	Farming, mining, and forestry form the basis for Southeast Asia's economy. Some of the nations are prospering, while others are developing slowly.	Practice Book p. 155 ■ Anthology pp. 182–185 Outline Map p. 37 **Technology:** *Adventures CD-ROM*
3 THE GOVERNMENT pages 568–570	1 day	Southeast Asia has a variety of governments that cope with various social and economic problems.	Practice Book p. 155 ■ Anthology pp. 186–188, 189–190 Outline Map p. 37
BUILDING THINKING SKILLS Drawing Conclusions: Review page 571	1 day	Drawing conclusions involves pulling together related pieces of information so that they mean something.	Practice Book p. 156
4 ARTS AND RECREATION pages 572–573	1 day	The arts and recreation of Southeast Asia are influenced by religion and are a blend of modern and traditional forms.	Practice Book p. 157 ■ Anthology p. 181 **Technology:** *Adventures CD-ROM*
CHAPTER SUMMARY AND REVIEW pages 574–575	1 day	Chapter content, skills, and vocabulary are reviewed and evaluated.	Practice Book p. 158 Transparency: Graphic Organizer Assessment Book, Chapter 28 Test

Technology CONNECTION

Lesson 2
ADVENTURES CD-ROM
Enrich Lesson 2 by having students make their own customized maps of Malaysia using *Build* and *Paint.*

Lesson 4
ADVENTURES CD-ROM
Enrich Lesson 4 by having students *Travel* to Bali, making notes in the *Notebook* about what they see.

CHAPTER 28
pages 560–575

USING THE CHAPTER OPENER

Discussing the Photograph Have students read the chapter title and study the photograph.

Ask students:

- **What do you notice about the boys in this photograph?** (They all have shaved heads and are wearing a special kind of robe.)
- **Do you think that most people in Southeast Asia dress in this fashion? Why?** (Probably not; These boys appear to belong to a group that may be set apart from the rest of society.)

Reading/Listening to the Primary Source Read the quotation aloud. Then ask a student to read the passage that follows.

Ask students:

- **What is the way of life of the boys in the photograph?** (They are Buddhist monks.)
- **How is life changing in Southeast Asia?** (People in this part of the world are learning to balance respect for tradition with the need to adapt to the modern world.)
- *THINKING FURTHER:* **What does the fact that these monks are young boys tell you about the future importance of tradition in Southeast Asia?** (Most students will probably conclude that tradition will continue to be important in Southeast Asia. Even if these boys become westernized, their early training will still be an important part of them.)

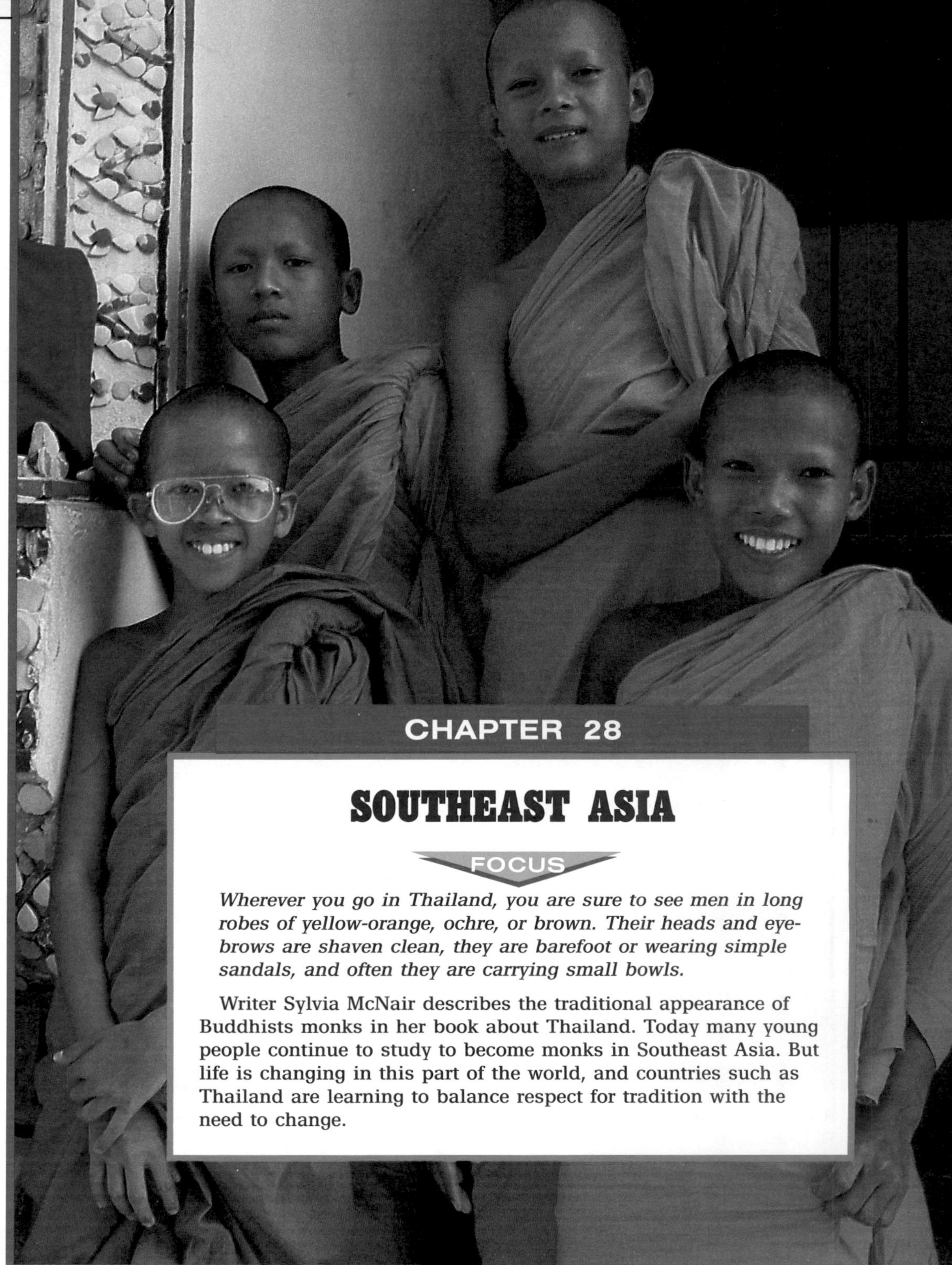

CHAPTER 28

SOUTHEAST ASIA

FOCUS

Wherever you go in Thailand, you are sure to see men in long robes of yellow-orange, ochre, or brown. Their heads and eyebrows are shaven clean, they are barefoot or wearing simple sandals, and often they are carrying small bowls.

Writer Sylvia McNair describes the traditional appearance of Buddhists monks in her book about Thailand. Today many young people continue to study to become monks in Southeast Asia. But life is changing in this part of the world, and countries such as Thailand are learning to balance respect for tradition with the need to change.

BACKGROUND INFORMATION

About the Thai People The boys in the photograph will not necessarily be monks for life. In Thailand it is an important part of a young man's religious training to spend a period of his youth serving as a monk.

- If they do return home, they will probably live in small villages along a river or canal, and their houses will be set on stilts to protect them from floods.
- Their diet will be healthy—rice, fish, and vegetables. If they are like the average Thai farmer, they will have enough to eat. Poverty is not common in Thailand except in infrequent years of drought.
- Any rice not consumed by their families will be sold to buy animals, tools, and meat.

LESSON 1

The People

READ TO LEARN

Key Places

Southeast Asia   Jakarta

Read Aloud

Tsang Su Yin (dzäng′ sü′ yin′) works for a newspaper in Singapore. Like many of the people who live in this small Southeast Asian country, she was born elsewhere.

"My mother came from the Malay Peninsula," she explains. She also says that during World War II, when the Japanese army invaded the peninsula, her family fled south to India.

"In Bombay, in India," continues Tsang Su Yin, "Mom met and married Dad, who had arrived earlier from Hong Kong. My brother was born in Bombay, and so was I."

Many of the people of Southeast Asia have been forced to relocate at various times. In this lesson you will read about these people, as well as their ways of life.

Read for Purpose

1. **WHAT YOU KNOW:** How did Japan's separation from mainland Asia influence its people and their culture?
2. **WHAT YOU WILL LEARN:** Why has Southeast Asia always been a great crossroads?

CROSSROADS OF SOUTHERN AND EASTERN ASIA

Like the Middle East, Southeast Asia is one of the great crossroads of the world. Southeast Asia separates India and China and stretches about 3,800 miles (6,114 km) from the western border of Myanmar (formerly known as Burma) southeast through Irian Jaya, the western part of the island of New Guinea. It is made up mostly of peninsulas and archipelagoes and includes ten countries: Brunei, Myanmar, Cambodia (formerly known as Kampuchea), Indonesia, Laos, Malaysia, the Philippines, Singapore, Thailand (formerly called Siam), and Vietnam.

THE FIRST SETTLERS IN SOUTHEAST ASIA

Southeast Asia has many different peoples and ways of life. Over thousands of years people and ideas have been introduced there from nearby places.

Given the area's location, it is not surprising that the greatest influences have come from China and India. The first settlers came to Southeast Asia many thousands of years ago during the Ice Age. They were related to the early peoples of Australia and the Pacific.

The next group to arrive were the Malays. They came from Southwest China about 2,500 years ago. These skilled sail-

WHAT YOU KNOW: Japan's separation kept its people safe from invaders while the Japanese developed a unique culture.

LESSON 1
pages 561–564

Lesson Theme Because of its location, Southeast Asia has been influenced by many Asian and European groups.

Lesson Objectives

- Identify the influences of various countries on Southeast Asia.
- Describe the two major religions of the area.
- Discuss the importance of cooperation among Southeast Asians.

PREPARE

Motivate Have a volunteer read the *Read Aloud* section to the class. Discuss the ways that a multiethnic society might differ from a homogeneous society.

Set Purpose Pose the *What You Know* question asking students to name some characteristics of Japanese society caused by Japan's separation. At the end of the lesson compare these answers with what you have learned about Southeast Asian societies. Have students read the lesson to answer the *What You Will Learn* question.

TEACH

Discussing Southeast Asia as a Crossroads and Its First Settlers

Ask students:

- **Name one factor that makes Southeast Asia one of the crossroads of the world.** (It is located between China and India.)
- **Who were the first settlers of the region?** (relatives of the people of Australia and the Pacific)
- **Which countries had the greatest influence on the area?** (China and India)

READING STRATEGY AND VOCABULARY DEVELOPMENT

Vocabulary Development Have students compile a vocabulary book containing all of the *Key Vocabulary* terms for the entire chapter. They may also include other terms with which they are unfamiliar or of which they are unsure. Review with students the ways that authors use different context clues to define unfamiliar terms. For each word have students write the definition and a sentence that uses context clues to define the term. You may wish to have students illustrate the words or find magazine pictures that go with them. Discuss possible formats for the book, such as alphabetical order or arrangement by lessons or lesson headings.

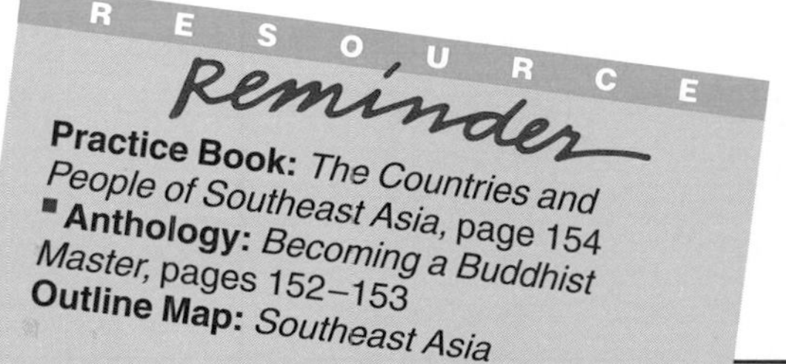

RESOURCE Reminder

Practice Book: *The Countries and People of Southeast Asia,* page 154

Anthology: *Becoming a Buddhist Master,* pages 152–153

Outline Map: *Southeast Asia*

EXTENDING MAP SKILLS

Have students use the map to locate the positions of the countries of Southeast Asia relative to China and India.

Ask students:

- **Where is the Celebes Sea?** (between Indonesia and the Philippines)
- **Which country is the smallest?** (Singapore)
- **Which countries separate Vietnam from Thailand?** (Laos and Cambodia)
- **Which countries would you cross if you traveled from Malaysia to India by land?** (Thailand and Myanmar, or Burma)
- **On which island is the capital of Indonesia?** (Java)
- **Of which country is Sumatra a part?** (Indonesia)
- **Through which Southeast Asian country does the equator pass?** (Indonesia)

Discussing Nearby Influences Assist students in listing the many groups who settled in Southeast Asia.

Ask students:

- **How did the different settlers influence the area?** (They brought their languages, systems of government, writing systems, and farming techniques.)
- **Discussing European Influences**

Ask students:

- **When did Europeans arrive in the area?** (in the early 1500s)
- **Why did Europeans come to Southeast Asia?** (in search of spices)
- **Which country was not controlled by Europeans?** (Thailand)

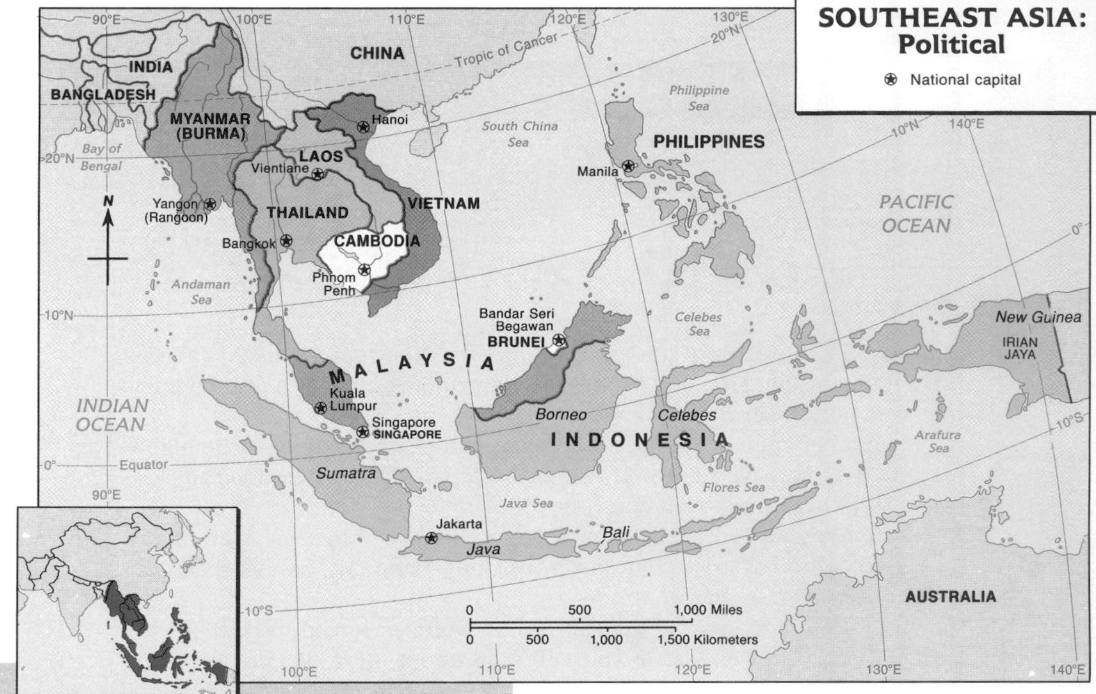

MAP SKILL: What is the capital of Thailand? The children shown here live in the mountains of Vietnam.

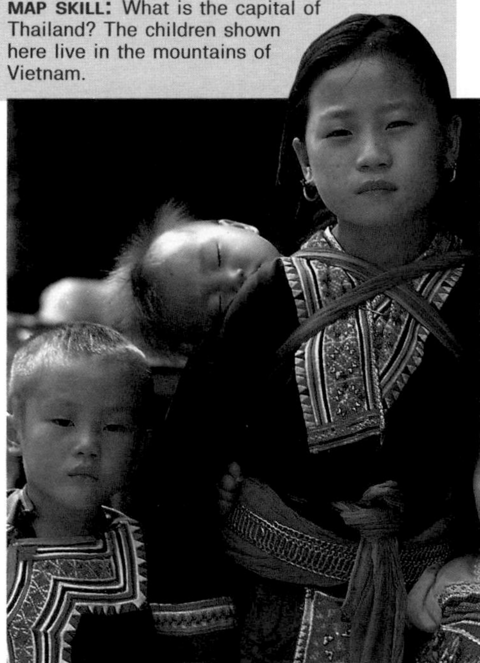

ors used the Southeast Asian seas, shown on the map above, as a great sea route.

NEARBY INFLUENCES

The Malays moved farther south when later settlers arrived from China and India. Some people, such as the Vietnamese from southeastern China, brought Chinese ideas and ways of life to Southeast Asia. For example, the Vietnamese wrote with Chinese characters and had adopted the Chinese system of government. The ancestors of the people of Myanmar, Thailand, and Laos, also came from southern China.

During this time merchants from India settled in Burma and the Malay Peninsula. There they introduced soil irrigation and the building of harbors.

Eventually the largest and strongest ethnic groups lived along the river deltas and other lowlands. Small ethnic groups lived in the hills.

562

MAP SKILL: Bangkok

BACKGROUND INFORMATION

Cities in Southeast Asia Southeast Asia boasts several major cities that are highly populated.

- *Bangkok, Thailand*—Located at the delta of the Chao Phraya River, Bangkok is Thailand's capital and largest city. The population of Bangkok is over 5.5 million.
- *Hanoi, Vietnam*—Located near the junction of the Red River and the South China Sea, this capital has over 2 million people.
- *Ho Chi Minh City, Vietnam*—Formerly Saigon, this city has 4.2 million people and lies near the Mekong River delta.
- *Manila, the Philippines*—The capital of the Philippines has a natural harbor and lies on both sides of the Pasig River. It has well over 1 million inhabitants.

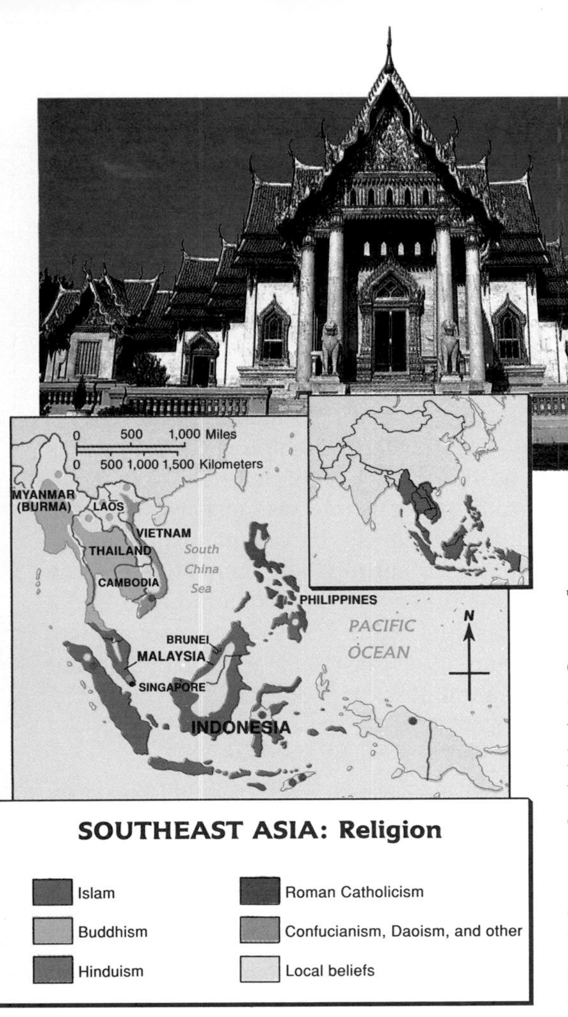

MAP SKILL: Which countries have many Buddhists? The building (*left*) and guardian statue (*right*) are part of an ancient palace complex in Bangkok.

EUROPEAN INFLUENCES

Europeans arrived in the early 1500s. They came in search of spices but stayed to build colonies. In time every country in the area except Thailand was controlled by Europeans—the Portuguese, British, Dutch, Spanish, and French.

Traces of colonialism are still seen in the area. For example, the capital of Indonesia, **Jakarta** has canals like those in Amsterdam in the Netherlands. The Spanish introduced Roman Catholicism to the Philippines. Today 85 percent of Filipinos are Roman Catholics.

THE CONTINUING MIGRATION

During the past 100 years great numbers of Indians and Chinese have migrated to Southeast Asia. As a result, 55 percent of the people who live in Malaysia today are Malays. One third are Chinese, and one tenth are Indian. Nearly every large Southeast Asian city has a large Chinese or Indian population.

The mixing of different peoples has caused hundreds of different languages to be used. Tsang Su Yin, about whom you read at the beginning of the lesson, works for an English-language newspaper in Singapore. But English is only one of the four official languages in Singapore. The others are Chinese, Malay, and an Indian language called Tamil. One hundred different languages are used in Myanmar, and Indonesia has as many as 365 languages—one for every day in the year.

RELIGION

It is impossible to travel far in mainland Southeast Asia without seeing Buddhist monks and temples. More than 1,500 years ago, monks and merchants began spreading Buddhism from India to this region. Today Buddhism is the major religion of

MAP SKILL: Myanmar, Thailand, Cambodia, Laos

Discussing European Influences Continue the discussion.

Ask students:

- **What European influences are still present?** (Catholicism, canals)
- *THINKING FURTHER:* **What other European influences may still be felt?** (Possible answers include: language, architecture, holidays, foods, customs.)

Understanding the Continuing Immigration Help students to understand the influence that continuing migration has had on the population.

Ask students:

- **Identify the four official languages in Singapore.** (English, Chinese, Malay, Tamil)
- *THINKING FURTHER:* **Why do you think people immigrated to Southeast Asia during the past 100 years?** (Possible answers include: wars, overcrowded conditions at home, a promise of a better life.)

EXTENDING MAP SKILLS

Have students study the map of Southeast Asian religions.

Ask students:

- **Which religion is most prevalent in Thailand?** (Buddhism)
- **In which countries can followers of Islam be found?** (Malaysia, Indonesia, Brunei, Thailand, Singapore, Philippines)
- **In which countries can followers of Roman Catholicism be found?** (the Philippines, Vietnam, Indonesia)

Discussing Religion Help students to understand the influences of Buddhism and Islam in the area.

BACKGROUND INFORMATION

Multicultural Perspectives Southeast Asia's religious diversity tells a great deal about the history of the region.

- Most of the countries on the mainland of Southeast Asia are largely Buddhist nations. That is because the cultures of India and China greatly influenced life in the region for centuries.
- The island nations of Malaysia, Brunei, and Indonesia are largely Muslim. That is because Muslim traders from India and the Middle East established roots and influence in the islands during the 1300s.
- Islam continues to be a powerful force on the southern Philippine island of Mindanao, even though the majority of the nation is Roman Catholic. Muslims on Mindanao resisted Spanish rule for hundreds of years because Spain was a Christian nation.

Ask students about religious diversity in the United States.

Studying Religion Continue the discussion.

Ask students:

- **In which countries is Buddhism a major religion?** (Myanmar, Thailand, Laos, Cambodia, Vietnam)
- **Which religion did the Arab traders bring?** (Islam)

Understanding the Importance of Cooperation

Ask students:

- **Give an example of how extended families in Southeast Asia work together.** (If someone's home is destroyed by flood, neighbors will help build a new one.)

Applying the Lesson Have students list the different groups that settled in Southeast Asia and the areas in which they settled.

CLOSE

Summarizing Students have learned that Southeast Asia has long been a crossroads of people and ideas. Discuss the effects that other cultures have had on life in Southeast Asia.

Evaluating Use the *Check Your Reading* questions (answers given below) to assess students' understanding.

Answers to Check Your Reading

1. Its position as a crossroads has caused many people to travel through and to settle there.
2. Buddhism, Islam, Confucianism, Daoism, Christianity, Hinduism
3. The Europeans came to look for spices and then stayed and built colonies.
4. The villagers would probably make building the center a cooperative venture.

Independent Practice
Practice Book: page 154

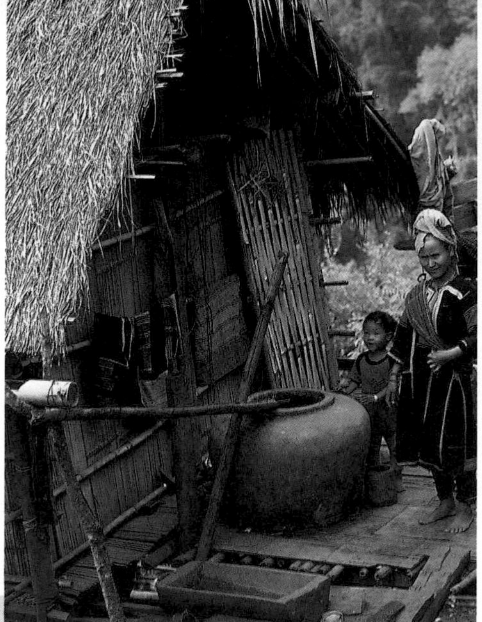

Like these people of northern Thailand, many rural Southeast Asians live in groups of homes built from wood and bamboo.

Myanmar, Thailand, Cambodia, and Laos.

The region's second major religion, Islam, was brought to the coastal towns of Southeast Asia by Indian and Arab traders in the 1300s. During the next two centuries, Islam spread from the Malay Peninsula to the islands of Southeast Asia. Islam is the official religion of Indonesia and Malaysia.

Many Southeast Asians maintain a variety of traditional beliefs that have evolved over thousands of years. These beliefs include the worshiping of spirits thought to exist in nature—in trees, animals, winds, and rivers. Other Southeast Asians, such as the Vietnamese, have been influenced by Confucianism and Daoism. Many Indonesians on the island of Bali are Hindus.

THE IMPORTANCE OF COOPERATION

Most Southeast Asian families are extended families, and family loyalties are strong. Within the family women hold respected positions. In some places in the area women inherit the property and manage the family income.

No matter which ethnic group they belong to, most Southeast Asians are concerned about the well-being of others. For example, in Indonesia if someone's house washes away in a mud slide, the family doesn't have to ask for aid. They know that neighbors will help them rebuild.

This custom of helping one another is an important part of Southeast Asian culture. Today people work closely together to build schools, roads, and irrigation canals. An entire village may help a young man find a wife or a young woman find a husband. By working in cooperation, many Southeast Asians are helping their communities to modernize.

A CULTURAL CROSSROADS

Because of its location, Southeast Asia has long been a great crossroads. You have read how people, ideas, and ways of life from nearby areas moved to Southeast Asia. The Hindu and Buddhist religions were brought from India. Islam was introduced by Indian and Arab traders. Later, during the colonial period, Southeast Asia came under the influence of different groups of Europeans.

Check Your Reading

1. Why does Southeast Asia have so many different ethnic groups?
2. Which major religions have spread to Southeast Asia?
3. Why did the Europeans come to Southeast Asia?
4. **THINKING SKILL:** From what you read about Southeast Asia, what would most likely happen if villagers decided they needed a community center?

THINKING SKILL: Predicting

564

MEETING INDIVIDUAL NEEDS

Reteaching (easy) Give students the outline map of Southeast Asia, found in the Teacher's Resource Center. Then have them label the countries, capitals, and major bodies of water.

Extension (average) Have students research a country that was once under colonial rule. Have them prepare a report on what life was like for the people under colonial rule. They should include the ways that the colonial rulers helped and hurt the country.

Enrichment (challenging) Have students use old maps and atlases to research the former names and boundaries of the countries of Southeast Asia. On the outline map of Southeast Asia, found in the Teacher's Resource Center, have students identify the old and new names of the countries.

LESSON 2

The Economy

READ TO LEARN

Key Vocabulary

gross national product (GNP)
paddy

Key Places

Singapore
Malaysia
Brunei

Read Aloud

Have you ever heard of the "Four Little Tigers"? The name refers to four Asian places—three countries and one colony—that have strong industrial economies. Three of the "Little Tigers" are located in East Asia. They are Hong Kong, South Korea, and Taiwan. The fourth tiger is located in Southeast Asia. It is the tiny island of Singapore.

In this lesson you will read about the economy of Singapore as well as the economies of other Southeast Asian countries. In the future there may be more "Little Tigers" in the Pacific Rim of Southeast Asia.

Read for Purpose

1. WHAT YOU KNOW: Why does Japan have one of the strongest economies today?
2. WHAT YOU WILL LEARN: Why are the economies of some Southeast Asian countries booming while others are developing slowly?

BOOMING ECONOMIES

You might wonder how a nation as small as Singapore can have an economy with so much influence. About the size of Chicago in the United States, Singapore is a major financial, industrial, and communications center. It also has the world's second-busiest port, after the city of Rotterdam in the Netherlands.

One reason for Singapore's economic success is its location. You can see from the Atlas map on page 634 that this tiny island is located halfway between India and China. Goods coming from East Asia and other parts of Southeast Asia enter Singapore on their way to Europe, Africa, and the United States.

Located next to Singapore is the area's third-richest country, Malaysia. Malaysia is rich in natural resources. In addition to farm and forest products, it has petroleum and natural gas. Malaysia is also a major exporter of tin.

The sultanate of Brunei is the richest country in Southeast Asia. Its large deposits of oil make Brunei's 300,000 people among the wealthiest in the world. The average yearly income per person is almost $15,000.

Thailand, Indonesia, and the Philippines are not as industrialized as the Four Little Tigers. However, these three countries have natural resources similar to Malaysia's. Their economies are making

WHAT YOU KNOW: This question refers to information in Chapter 27, Lesson 2; hard work, demand for excellence, efficiency.

LESSON 2
pages 565–567

Lesson Theme Farming, mining, and forestry form the basis for Southeast Asia's economy. Some of the nations are prospering, while others are developing slowly.

Lesson Objectives

- Compare and contrast the various economies of Southeast Asia.
- List the reasons for the economic problems of Southeast Asia.
- Describe the various types of agriculture of Southeast Asia.

1 PREPARE

Motivate Read the *Read Aloud* section to the class. Discuss the meaning of the term *The Four Little Tigers*.

Set Purpose Ask the *What You Know* question. Have students make predictions about the *What You Will Learn* question.

2 TEACH

Discussing Booming Economies Point out to students that the sea route between India and China is a major thoroughfare.

Ask students:

- **How does Singapore's location help its economy?** (It is on a major sea route between India and China. Goods from all over the world enter its harbor.)
- **What are some of Malaysia's resources?** (tin, petroleum, natural gas, farm and forest products)
- **Why is Brunei so rich?** (It has large deposits of oil.)

READING STRATEGY AND VOCABULARY DEVELOPMENT

Vocabulary Development Review with students how using the *Key Vocabulary* terms can help them to develop purpose-setting questions for the lesson. Have students generate group questions to be used for discussion of the lesson. Remind students to use the five *W* questions (*W*ho, *W*hat, *W*hen, *W*here, *W*hy), and the *H* question (*H*ow). Assign pairs of students to use the section headings to develop additional questions. Have students write each question on a separate index card. Use the questions to guide the reading. After students have finished reading, the questions may be used to review the material.

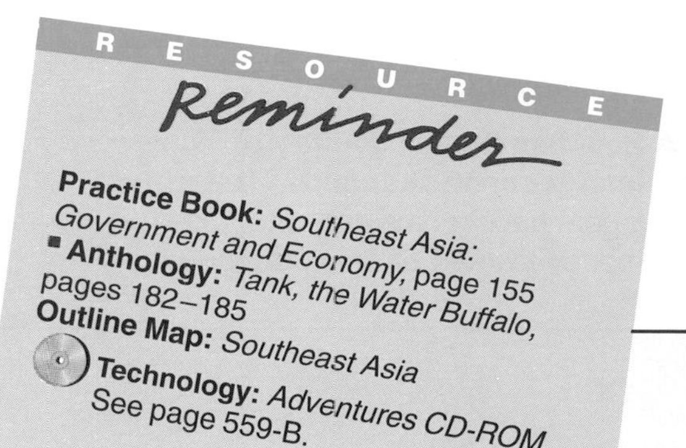

Looking at Booming Economies Continue the discussion.

Ask students:

- **What resources does Southeast Asia have in great quantities?** (rubber, copper, tin)
- **What is the money from oil and natural gas sales used for?** (to finance industrialization)

EXTENDING GRAPH SKILLS

Help students to read the cartogram. Explain that the size of each country is proportional to its gross national product. Tell students that the GNP is the value of the total amounts of goods and services produced by a country during a year.

Ask students:

- **Which country has the highest GNP?** (Japan)
- **Which country has the higher GNP, Taiwan or China?** (China)
- **Which country has the lower GNP, the Philippines or South Korea?** (the Philippines)

Reviewing the War Ask students what they know about the Vietnam War.

Ask students:

- **How have the economies of Vietnam, Laos, and Cambodia been affected by war?** (War has caused the educated people to flee, leaving fewer skilled workers to keep the economy running.)
- **What kind of economies do Vietnam, Laos, and Cambodia have now?** (communist)
- **What are the causes of Myanmar's economic problems?** (civil unrest, debt, poor planning)

Understanding Changing Ways of Life

Ask students:

- **How has the hill country of Thailand recently changed?** (The villagers have radios and often use money instead of only bartering.)

gains, and foreign companies have increased their trade with these countries.

Singapore, Malaysia, Brunei, Thailand, Indonesia, and the Philippines are working to create a free-trade area to lower tariffs on each other's goods. They plan to invite other Asian nations to join them.

The cartogram on this page shows the **gross national products (GNPs)** of countries of the region. The GNP is the value of the total goods and services produced by a country during a year. A special kind of map, a cartogram, enables us to compare facts about countries. On the cartogram below, sizes of countries represent their GNPs rather than true area and shape. The cartogram shows the way in which one country's GNP compares with others.

Southeast Asia is rich in resources. It produces more than 80 percent of the world's natural rubber and more than 60 percent of its copper and tin. Money from the sale of these resources and from oil and natural gas is being used to finance industrialization in Southeast Asia.

IMPOVERISHED BY WAR

Unlike the countries you have just read about, Vietnam, Laos, and Cambodia are very poor. Since the end of World War II, they each have been torn apart by a series of terrible wars, which you will read about in Lesson 3. These wars caused hundreds of thousands of educated people to flee to safer countries. The resulting lack of skilled workers has weakened these countries.

Laos and Vietnam have communist economies that were modeled after that of the former Soviet Union. Each government controls its economy and decides what and how much to produce.

Myanmar is also a poor country. However, its economic problems have not been caused by war, but by civil unrest, poor planning, and harmful economic policies.

MAP SKILL: Helping Indonesia's GNP to rise are large factories such as this helicopter factory (*right*). Does Laos, Singapore, or Indonesia have the highest GNP?

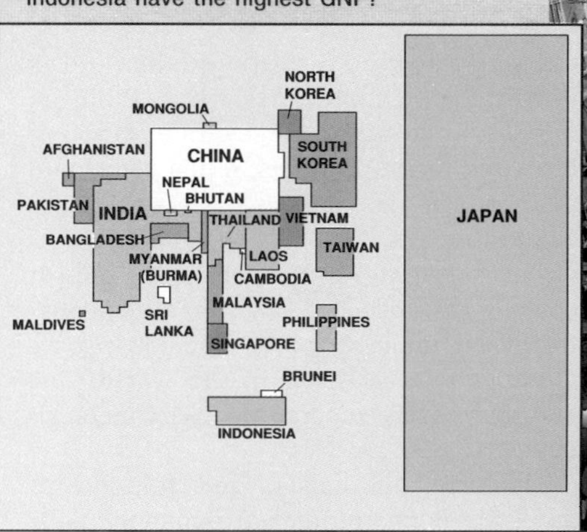

CARTOGRAM: Gross National Product of Southern and Eastern Asia

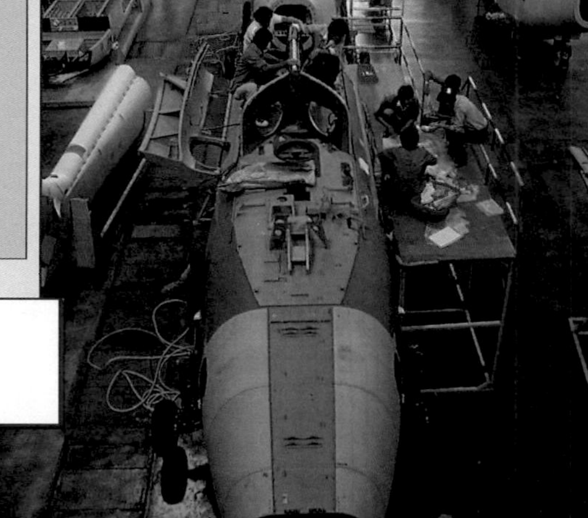

566

MAP SKILL: Indonesia

CURRICULUM CONNECTION

Language Arts Many books have been written about the Vietnam War, including such topics as life in Vietnam during and after the war, the effects of the Vietnam War, and the role of the United States in the war. Have students read part of one such book and prepare a short oral report on the material they read.

Science Rubber is an important export of Southeast Asia. Have students research how rubber is harvested and processed and the products that are made from rubber. Then have them create a flowchart showing the path of rubber from the forest to the store.

CHANGING WAYS OF LIFE

Some parts of Southeast Asia are changing more slowly. Not so long ago, a visitor described the hill country of Thailand as a place "that has been completely bypassed by time." But now people in even the most remote villages have radios and tape players. Village people now use money instead of relying entirely on barter, and they also pay taxes.

About four out of five people in Southeast Asia live in rural areas. Many of them work small farms. Farming areas are becoming crowded. In the past there was enough land for the children of farmers. Today, however, many of the children of farmers have left the farm areas to move to the cities where they work to earn money, often in the newly established industries. As a result, cities such as Yangon (formerly Rangoon), in Myanmar, Jakarta in Indonesia, and Manila in the Philippines have become very crowded. Even smaller towns and cities are growing rapidly as people who used to live on farms move into them.

PADDY RICE AND PLANTATIONS

Farmers in the lowlands of Southeast Asia plant rice in fields called paddies. First, tiny seedlings are grown in seedbeds and then moved by hand from the seedbeds to the flooded paddy fields. Paddy rice, or wet rice as it is often called, has a higher yield per acre than any other kind of grain.

The lowlands also have large plantations. Most of them are owned by a few families and companies. Although the plantations were started by Europeans, most of them today are controlled by Southeast Asians. Plantation crops are exported. Among the region's major exports are tea, rubber, coffee, bamboo, and sugarcane.

RICH LANDS AND POOR LANDS

The economies of the countries of Southeast Asia are based mainly on farming, mining, and forestry. Singapore has a booming economy, and Brunei and Malaysia are industrializing rapidly. Others, however, have been slower to develop. It will be years before Vietnam, Laos, and Cambodia can fully recover from the devastating effects of the wars in Southeast Asia.

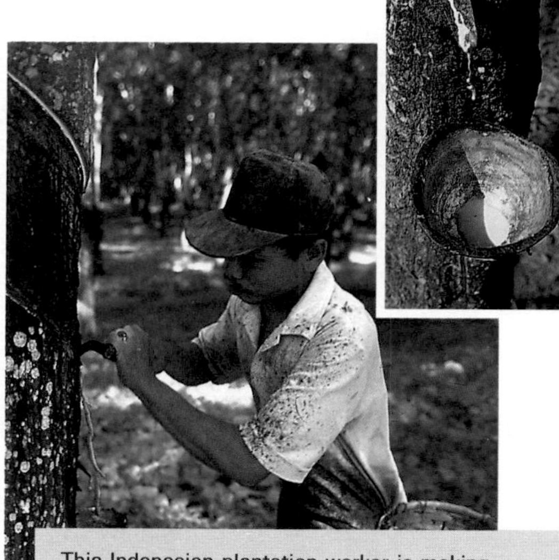

This Indonesian plantation worker is making cuts in rubber trees to get at the latex.

Check Your Reading

1. Why does Singapore have such a strong economy?
2. Why are Vietnam, Laos, and Cambodia economically poor countries?
3. Name three natural resources found in Southeast Asia that are essential to countries all over the world.
4. **THINKING SKILL:** Compare and contrast the countries in this region with booming economies and those with poorer economies.

THINKING SKILL: Compare and Contrast

567

Discussing Changing Ways of Life Continue the discussion.

Ask students:

- **Do most Southeast Asians live in the cities?** (No, most Southeast Asians live in rural areas.)
- **How is crowding in farming areas affecting Southeast Asia's cities and towns?** (Former farmers are moving into the cities, causing them to grow rapidly.)

Discussing Rice Paddies and Plantations

Ask students:

- **Why is wet rice a good crop to grow in Southeast Asia?** (A lot can be grown in a small space.)
- **Which crops are grown on the plantations?** (tea, rubber trees, coffee, bamboo, sugarcane)

Applying the Lesson Have students compare the problems of Southeast Asia (crowded cities, uneven industrialization, destructive wars) with other regions of the world.

3 CLOSE

Summarizing Students have learned that the economies of the countries of Southeast Asia vary from very wealthy to poor.

Evaluating Use the *Check Your Reading* questions (answers given below) to assess students' understanding.

Answers to Check Your Reading

1. It is a major link between China and India. Ships traveling in either direction go through, making Singapore a major commercial center.
2. War has damaged their economies.
3. oil, rubber, natural gas
4. Those with booming economies are wealthy from trade and exploitation of natural resources; poor countries have been hurt by wars and other problems.

Independent Practice
Practice Book: page 155

MEETING INDIVIDUAL NEEDS

Reteaching (easy) Have students use the cartogram on page 566 to list the countries of Southeast Asia in order, from the country with the highest GNP to the country with the lowest GNP.

Extension (average) Distribute outline maps of Southeast Asia, found in the Teacher's Resource Center. Have students make a product map of the area. Tell them to use symbols for the products and to include a map key.

Enrichment (challenging) Have students look in newspapers and magazines to find articles about the economy of Southeast Asia. Then have them make a scrapbook or bulletin board display of the articles. Tell them to try to find positive as well as negative articles. Discuss the problems and solutions presented in the articles.

LESSON 3
pages 568–570

Lesson Theme Southeast Asia has a variety of governments that must cope with social and economic problems.

Lesson Objectives
- Identify the various forms of government in Southeast Asia.
- Discuss the difficulties that Southeast Asia has encountered in maintaining peace.

 PREPARE

Motivate Have a student read the *Read Aloud* section to the class. Ask students what they know about Ferdinand Marcos, Corazon Aquino, and the Philippine government.

Set Purpose Have students answer the *What You Know* question. Ask for possible answers to the *What You Will Learn* question. Tell students to read the lesson to learn about the governments of Southeast Asia.

 TEACH

Understanding Philippine Democracy Help students to appreciate the great strides towards democracy taken in the Philippines.

Ask students:

- **What did the people do to ensure a fair election?** (They formed human chains around the ballot boxes.)
- *THINKING FURTHER:* **What do the actions of the people tell you about them?** (Possible answers include: they wanted democracy, they believed in Aquino, they wanted Marcos out.)

LESSON 3

The Government

READ TO LEARN

Key Vocabulary	Key People	Key Places
Vietnam War	Corazon Aquino	Philippines

Read Aloud

I am not embarrased to tell you that I believe in miracles.

In 1986 many people around the world agreed with the speaker, Corazon Aquino. With little political experience, she had just become the president of the Philippines. In this lesson you will discover why this election was so remarkable in the history of Southeast Asia.

Read for Purpose

1. WHAT YOU KNOW: What are the two main types of government of the countries in East Asia?
2. WHAT YOU WILL LEARN: Why has it been difficult for the nations of Southeast Asia to achieve peace and stability?

DEMOCRACY IN THE PHILIPPINES

The newspaper stories coming from the Philippines in 1986 seemed too amazing to be true. This Southeast Asian country had been ruled by President Ferdinand Marcos, who had been charged with having a corrupt government. In 1986 Corazon Aquino ran against him for the presidency of the Philippines.

During the election the Marcos government had sent troops into most communities to destroy ballot boxes and votes that had been cast for Aquino. The National Assembly of the Philippines then declared Marcos the winner. In response thousands of Filipinos accused the Marcos government of election fraud and formed human chains around the ballot boxes. Soldiers put down their guns and joined the protesters. Faced with such protests, Marcos and his followers were forced to flee the country. Marcos went to Hawaii, where he died in 1989. Meanwhile, Corazon Aquino became the president of the Philippines. Aquino was popular with the people, but there were groups loyal to Marcos that continued to oppose her.

AUTHORITARIAN TRADITIONS

Throughout Southeast Asia the 1986 presidential election in the Philippines offered an example of political hope. Since the end of World War II, most of the countries in Southeast Asia have been run by governments with only one political party. Although these governments vary from communist dictatorships to constitutional monarchies, they have one thing in common: They are run by powerful leaders who make their own rules.

Southeast Asia has a long history of rule by kings or other powerful leaders. People

WHAT YOU KNOW: Communist governments, Western-style republics

READING STRATEGY AND VOCABULARY DEVELOPMENT

Vocabulary Development Review the idea that words with multiple meanings rely on context for definition. Have students skim the lesson for examples of such words. Some words with multiple meanings are: *party, run, word,* and *land.* Tell students that these words can be found in the sections titled "Authoritarian Traditions" and "Different Governments." Discuss the various meanings of the words, using context clues and the dictionary. Have students enter these words in their vocabulary books. You may wish to ask those students having difficulty to rewrite each sentence containing a word with multiple meanings using a synonym in its place.

RESOURCE *Reminder*

Practice Book: *Southeast Asia: Government and Economy,* page 155
Anthology: *The War Years in Vietnam,* pages 186–188; *Life in a Cambodian "Reeducation" Camp,* pages 189–190
Outline Map: *Southeast Asia*

In 1986 Corazon Aquino (*right, center*) campaigned hard against Ferdinand Marcos (*left*) for the presidency of the Philippines.

made decisions for their villages but had no say in higher levels of government. Moreover, before World War II, nearly all of Southeast Asia had been controlled by Europeans. Only Thailand had avoided European rule and was able to continue governing itself.

For these reasons, most Southeast Asian countries lacked experience in governing themselves when they gained independence after World War II. Where democracy exists, it is fragile. Corazon Aquino almost lost power to military rebels many times before leaving office in 1992.

DIFFERENT GOVERNMENTS

Today the people of the countries of Southeast Asia are trying to work out ways to govern their lands successfully. They hope to preserve traditional ways of life and attitudes while introducing modern ideas. Thailand has a constitutional monarchy, and its government is among the most stable in the area.

Two other Southeast Asian countries have also remained monarchies. Brunei's leader is a sultan, a muslim title for ruler. As an absolute monarch, his word is law in Brunei. Malaysia, however, has an unusual kind of constitutional monarchy. It has a parliamentary system in which the ruler is the country's leading sultan. He is chosen by the nine sultans who head the nine states of Malaysia. The sultan's most important role is as the religious leader of Malaysia's Muslim people.

Indonesia and Myanmar are both republics ruled by military leaders. Singapore has a parliamentary system of government, with a president as head of the country and a prime minister as head of government. Laos and Vietnam have communist governments. Cambodia is a constitutional monarchy.

SOCIAL UNREST

In many places in Southeast Asia, social stability has been rare. One reason has been that old quarrels among the area's ethnic groups have caused much unrest. For example, in Malaysia many of the poorer rural people are Malays, while the wealthier city dwellers and business leaders are Chinese. Recent programs that put government in the hands of the Malays have been criticized by the Chinese as unfair. In Myanmar the Karen ethnic group is fighting bitterly to form their own country.

569

Discussing Authoritarian Traditions
Help students to understand the significance of the one-party system.

Ask students:

- **What are two forms of government in this area?** (communist dictatorships and constitutional monarchies; Those forms of government are often one-party systems.)
- **Why was democracy a difficult concept for the people?** (They were not used to governing themselves because they were ruled by kings, dictators, or European powers.)
- *THINKING FURTHER:* **Why was the 1986 election in the Philippines a symbol of hope?** (It showed that democracy was possible.)

Discussing Different Governments
Help students to understand the ways that Southeast Asian countries are blending traditional and modern forms of government.

Ask students:

- **Which countries are monarchies?** (Thailand, Brunei, Malaysia)
- **What is unusual about Malaysia's monarchy?** (It is a constitutional monarchy with a parliamentary system in which the ruler is the country's leading sultan.)
- **Which countries are republics?** (Indonesia and Myanmar)
- **Which countries have a Communist government?** (Laos and Vietnam)

Understanding Social Problems
Discuss the ethnic and economic problems that led to quarreling in the different countries.

Ask students:

- **What are some of Malaysia's problems?** (Many poor people are Malays, while many rich people are Chinese. The Chinese think that the government programs to help the Malays are unfair.)
- **Why is the Karen group dissatisfied?** (They want their own country.)

BACKGROUND INFORMATION

More About Southeast Asian Governments

- In 1980 Thailand passed a law giving women the right to be monarchs. Previously only men could attain the monarchy. The name *Thailand* in Thai is *Muang Thai*. It means "The Land of the Free."
- Women in the Philippines are allowed to vote and hold office. This is unusual for Southeast Asia.

Describing the Years of War

Ask students:

- **How did the Vietnam War affect the area?** (Many people were killed, and many others fled from the area. In Vietnam great distrust exists between the people of the north and those of the south.)

Applying the Lesson Have the class hold a panel discussion on which form or forms of Southeast Asian governments are most likely to become democratic.

3 CLOSE

Summarizing Students have studied the various types of government in Southeast Asia.

Evaluating Use these questions to assess students' understanding.

- **What do most Southeast Asian governments have in common?** (Most of these governments are run by powerful rulers who make their own rules.)
- **Describe the beginning of the Vietnam War.** (It began as a civil war in South Vietnam between communists and government troops.)

Answers to Check Your Reading

1. The Philippines is a democracy.
2. wars, no experience with democracy, gaps in standards of living, lack of trust among different ethnic groups, many years of control by European powers
3. Possible answers include: poverty, lack of skilled workers, lack of trust among ethnic groups.
4. constitutional monarchy/monarchy—Thailand, Malaysia, Brunei; democracy—the Philippines, Singapore; republics ruled by military leaders—Indonesia, Myanmar; communist—Vietnam, Laos, Cambodia.

Independent Practice
Practice Book: page 155

Over 30 years of war has caused millions of people to become refugees in Southeast Asia.

Unrest is also caused by the great gaps in the standards of living between the rich and the poor in some parts of Southeast Asia. While a few families are very wealthy, most people have little or no land or money. One of the most serious problems faced by Corazon Aquino in the Philippines has been finding a way in which to deal with communist rebels. The rebels have gained support among the nation's many poor plantation workers.

YEARS OF WAR

Much of Southeast Asia is deeply scarred by years of war. The longest and most damaging was the Vietnam War, which the United States joined in the early 1960s and withdrew from in 1973. The Vietnam War began as a civil war in South Vietnam between Vietnamese communists and the government troops. After the United States became more deeply involved in the conflict, war also was waged in Laos and Cambodia.

In 1975, two years after the United States withdrew, Communist North Vietnamese took control of all of Vietnam. The North Vietnamese had also been supplying arms to Communist rebels in neighboring Cambodia for a civil war there.

After Communists gained control of Cambodia in 1975, they began a reign of terror in the country that lasted more than three years. Many Cambodians were murdered or died of starvation. Differences between the two Communist governments caused Vietnam to invade Cambodia in 1979. Millions of Cambodians were forced from their homes.

It is believed that perhaps as many as 3 million people have died in Cambodia since the 1970s. In neighboring Vietnam there is still great distrust between the people of the north and those of the south.

MANY KINDS OF GOVERNMENT

The governments of the countries of Southeast Asia range from a republic in the Philippines to an absolute monarchy in Brunei. You have read that most of these governments have one powerful group or leader in control. Most people have few individual rights or freedoms. Social and economic problems make it difficult to set up stable governments. As a result, the future of Southeast Asia remains uncertain.

Check Your Reading

1. How does the government of the Philippines differ from most of its neighbors?
2. Why have some countries in Southeast Asia had difficulty in establishing stable governments?
3. Name three problems that many countries of Southeast Asia face today.
4. THINKING SKILL: Classify Southeast Asia's governments into two or three groups. Give each group a title.

THINKING SKILL: Classifying

570

MEETING INDIVIDUAL NEEDS

Reteaching (easy) On the outline map of Southeast Asia, found in the Teacher's Resource Center, have students label the countries of Southeast Asia. Under the name of each country, have students write the type of government that country has.

Extension (average) Have students scan newspapers and news magazines to find articles about the governments of Southeast Asia. Then display the articles by country on a class bulletin board.

Enrichment (challenging) Divide the class into groups. Have each group research a different phase of the Vietnam War (early stages, escalation, U.S. withdrawal). Have groups present oral reports in the form of a documentary.

BUILDING SKILLS
THINKING SKILLS

Drawing Conclusions: Review

Suppose you and your family arrive home after spending the weekend away. While you are unpacking your suitcase you notice that the time on your electric alarm clock does not agree with the time on your wristwatch. When you go to the refrigerator for a glass of milk you notice a sour smell coming from the milk carton. Now you draw the conclusion that while you were away the electricity was off in your house.

When you draw a conclusion, you put facts together to arrive at a statement of meaning. A conclusion tells how pieces of information relate, or connect, to one another.

HELPING YOURSELF
Here is one way to draw conclusions.

1. Identify the topic of the information.
2. Examine the information given.
3. Look for ideas or subjects that are common to all the pieces of information.
4. Draw a conclusion stating how the subjects or ideas common to all pieces of information relate, or link, to one another.

Applying the Skill

Read the following pieces of information. Then answer the questions below.

- In 1970 the Kingdom of Cambodia became the Khmer Republic.
- In 1975 the Khmer Republic became Democratic Kampuchea.
- In 1979 Democratic Kampuchea became the People's Republic of Kampuchea.
- In 1989 the People's Republic of Kampuchea became the State of Cambodia.

1. What is the topic of the information given above?
   a. the politics of the People's Republic of Kampuchea
   b. the people of Kampuchea
   c. the history of Cambodia's name
2. What subjects or ideas are common to all the pieces of information?
3. What is one conclusion you can draw from the above information?

Reviewing the Skill

1. What is the meaning of the phrase *draw a conclusion*?
2. Describe four steps that will help you to draw conclusions.
3. In which subjects, other than social studies, do you often find it necessary to draw conclusions? Give an example.

571

SKILLS LESSON
page 571

Lesson Theme Drawing a conclusion involves pulling together related pieces of information so that they mean something.

Lesson Objective
- Identify and apply the steps that lead to drawing a conclusion.

1 PREPARE

Motivate Before students read the introductory paragraphs, ask them to recall the steps they took to draw conclusions in Chapter 15. Write the steps on the chalkboard and have the class compare these steps with those listed in *Helping Yourself*.

2 TEACH

Helping Yourself Point out to students that the strategy outlined here is one they may use or adapt any time they need to apply the skill.

Applying the Skill Have students read the information and answer the questions that follow it. (See answers below.) Have students explain in their own words how they went about drawing a conclusion.

3 CLOSE

Reviewing the Skill Encourage students to compare strategies they use to draw conclusions and to describe situations in and out of school in which they might use the skill.

ANSWERS TO SKILLS QUESTIONS

Applying the Skill

1. c
2. The subjects common to all the pieces of information are date, name of country, and kind of government.
3. One possible conclusion is that over the past 20 years, Cambodia has often changed its name and government.

Reviewing the Skill

1. to give meaning to several different pieces of information
2. (a) Identify the topic of the information. (b) Examine the information. (c) Look for ideas or subjects common to the pieces of information. (d) State how the pieces of information relate to each other.
3. You draw conclusions in all subject areas: for example, in English, after reading a novel or a poem, or in science, after conducting an experiment.

RESOURCE *Reminder*
Practice Book: *Drawing Conclusions,* page 156

LESSON 4
pages 572–573

Lesson Theme The arts and recreation of Southeast Asia are influenced by religion and are a blend of modern and traditional forms.

Lesson Objectives
- Discuss the ways that religion has influenced the arts and recreation of the area.
- Identify shadow plays, a gamelan, and Thai boxing.

PREPARE

Motivate Read the *Read Aloud* section to the class. Discuss the significance of the religious festivals. Have students locate Bali on the political *Atlas* map of Southern and Eastern Asia, or on the map on page 562.

Set Purpose Use the *What You Know* question to prompt a discussion of the significance of religious festivals in other countries. Pose the *What You Will Learn* question and ask students to predict answers based on their prior knowledge. Have them read the lesson to check the accuracy of their predictions.

TEACH

Describing Festivals Discuss the significance of farming as a festival theme.

Ask students:

- **How did religion influence the Thai rice festival?** (After the festival the boys became temporary monks.)
- *THINKING FURTHER:* **Why do so many of the festivals center around farming?** (Possible answers include: importance of food, ancient beliefs that the gods or spirits controlled the growth of the crops.)

LESSON 4

Arts and Recreation

READ TO LEARN

Key Vocabulary
meditate
shadow play
gamelan

Key Places
Indonesia
Java

Read Aloud

On the island of Bali a religious year is 210 days long. Each temple on the island holds a religious festival once a year. Since there are hundreds of temples, there are festivals on Bali on most days. These festivals give the Balinese many opportunities to wear traditional costumes, hear traditional music, and watch traditional plays and dances.

In this lesson you will read about some of the ways in which Southeast Asians enjoy leisure time.

Read for Purpose

1. **WHAT YOU KNOW:** What other areas of the world have numerous religious festivals?
2. **WHAT YOU WILL LEARN:** In what ways has religion influenced the arts and recreational activities of Southeast Asia?

FESTIVALS FOR EVERY SEASON

Many of the oldest festivals in Southeast Asia have to do with farming. Festivals mark the cycle of planting, transplanting, and harvesting rice. In April or May people ask a god or gods to help their newly planted crops. At other festivals people pray or give thanks for rain.

In Thailand Buddhist boys become temporary monks at a rice festival. This festival takes place at the time the seedlings are transplanted from seedbeds to the flooded paddy fields. After the festival the boys go to monasteries to live, pray, and work together for a few months. The boys also spend a period of time **meditating**, or thinking deeply, while they are at the Buddhist monastaries.

SHADOW PLAYS AND MUSIC

When a child in **Indonesia** spends the evening watching a **shadow play**, he or she isn't just being entertained. Puppets are used to act out well-known stories by casting shadows. The leather puppets in the plays are called *wayang* (wā' āng), which means "shadow." The puppets are held up behind a cloth screen that is stretched between two bamboo poles. A light behind the screen casts the shadows.

These puppet dramas are part of the education of most Indonesian children. Shadow plays are used to teach moral and religious values. Most tell the stories of ancient Hindu rulers, gods, and heroes.

An important part of every shadow play is the music, which is performed by a

572

WHAT YOU KNOW: Latin America, Southern Europe, South Asia, Japan

READING STRATEGY AND VOCABULARY DEVELOPMENT

Vocabulary Development Creating puzzles is a good way for students to practice writing definitions. Students may enjoy making up different types of puzzles as a way to review the vocabulary terms they learned in this chapter. Possible word puzzles include word search and crossword puzzles. Students can use the vocabulary books they have made as an aid in creating their puzzles. Distribute copies of the various puzzles to the class to solve, or have students trade puzzles.

In Indonesian shadow plays, light shining on a puppet (*left*) casts a shadow such as the one shown on the right.

gamelan (gam′ ə lan). A gamelan is an orchestra of drums, gongs, bells, chimes, cymbals, and xylophones made of bamboo and metal. A gamelan orchestra has no conductor. The drums set the pace, and the other players join in. Traditionally music was not written down, but taught by a master musician to a student.

In recent years the government of Indonesia has been trying to get people to move from Java, a large island that is extremely crowded, to islands that have fewer people. As soon as a new village is built, the people start saving money to support a village gamelan. The Indonesians believe that a village without a gamelan can't have a proper festival.

SPORTS AND RECREATION

Among the favorite sports in Southeast Asia are badminton and basketball. As in Japan, many traditional sports are also very popular. One is Thai boxing. Boxing in Thailand is a different sport from boxing that is practiced in the United States. Thai boxers wear gloves and trade punches, but they also use their elbows and knees and make lightning-fast kicks.

The waters off Southeast Asia's islands and peninsulas have some of the world's best underwater viewing. In addition to this activity, snorkeling, scuba diving, and water sports of all kinds are popular with tourists from around the world.

LOCAL TRADITIONS

Religion plays an important part in the arts and recreation of Southeast Asia. As you have read, festivals are held throughout the year in the area. Traditional art forms, such as shadow plays and gamelans, are still favorite forms of entertainment. Performed at festivals, they help to keep alive local traditions. Both traditional and modern sports are popular.

Check Your Reading

1. Give two examples of the ways in which religion has influenced the arts in Southeast Asia.
2. What is a shadow play? What does it teach the children of Indonesia?
3. Why do you think gamelans are popular throughout Southeast Asia?
4. THINKING SKILL: Based on this lesson, what conclusions can you make about the recreation of the people of Southeast Asia?

THINKING SKILL: Drawing Conclusions

Enjoying Shadow Plays Help students to understand that shadow plays are used as educational tools.

Ask students:

- **What kinds of stories are used for shadow plays?** (stories about Hindu gods, rulers, heroes)

Looking at Sports and Recreation

Ask students:

- **Which traditional sport is enjoyed in Thailand?** (Thai boxing)
- **Which modern sports are enjoyed in Thailand?** (badminton, basketball)

Applying the Lesson Have students discuss similarities and differences in the arts and recreational pastimes of Southeast Asia and the other Asian countries discussed in this unit.

3 CLOSE

Summarizing Students have learned that the arts and recreation of Southeast Asia are a blend of modern and traditional forms and that religious themes are interwoven in both.

Answers to Check Your Reading

1. religious festivals with costumes, music, plays, and dances are held almost every day in some places; shadow plays teach religious values and tell stories of Hindu rulers, gods, and heroes
2. a play with puppets whose shadows are lit up behind a cloth screen; A shadow play teaches moral and religious values.
3. Since a gamelan is played by a group without a leader, it may appeal to the cooperative, community-oriented spirit of the Southeast Asian people.
4. It takes the form of religious festivals and sports.

Independent Practice
Practice Book: page 157

MEETING INDIVIDUAL NEEDS

Reteaching (easy) Have students research one of the festivals of Southeast Asia. Have them report to the class on the purpose of the festival and on the way that it is celebrated. Then have students draw illustrations of the festival.

Extension (average) Have students do more research on traditional Southeast Asian music such as gamelan, Balinese vocal music, and Thai music. If possible, students should incorporate recordings borrowed from a library into a report on their research.

Enrichment (challenging) Have students make a chart comparing the arts and recreation of the countries of Southeast Asia with those of the other Asian countries they have studied. Then have them discuss the similarities and differences.

CHAPTER 28 REVIEW
pages 574–575

USING THE CHAPTER SUMMARY AND REVIEW

Cultural Geography These questions may be used for review.

- **What are the major religions of the region?** (Buddhism, Islam)
- **What are the major resources of this region?** (rubber, copper, tin, oil, natural gas)
- **What types of governments do these nations have?** (republics, parliamentary systems, monarchies, communist)
- **What is one way in which important religious values are taught in Southeast Asia?** (through the arts)

Ideas to Remember

- **The cultures of Southeast Asia were influenced by the ideas and ways of which countries?** (China, India, the countries of Europe, the countries of the Middle East)
- **Why are some countries in the region not developing rapidly?** (because of the effects of years of war)
- **What type of rule is found in most Southeast Asian countries?** (rule by one powerful group or leader)
- **What has influenced the arts and recreation of Southeast Asia?** (religious traditions)

Answers to Reviewing Vocabulary

1. paddy
2. gross national product
3. meditate
4. shadow play
5. gamelan

Answers to Reviewing Facts

1. China and India
2. Myanmar, Thailand, Cambodia, Laos
3. Portugal, Britain, Spain, France, the Netherlands
4. Singapore, Malaysia, Brunei; Vietnam, Laos, Cambodia

CHAPTER 28 ▪ SUMMARY

SOUTHEAST ASIA: CULTURAL GEOGRAPHY

PEOPLE

- The cultures of Southeast Asia were influenced by those of China, India, and Europe
- Southeast Asia has hundreds of languages
- Major religions: Buddhism, Islam

- Values: family loyalty, cooperation, concern for well-being of others

ECONOMY

CHINA, SOUTH KOREA, NEPAL, BHUTAN, THAILAND, VIETNAM, TAIWAN, [MY]ANMAR ([B]URMA), LAOS, CAMBODIA, [S]RI [L]ANKA, MALAYSIA, PHILIPPINES

- Booming economies: Singapore (trade), Brunei (oil)
- Major resources: rubber, copper, tin, oil, natural gas
- Years of war and civil unrest have caused poverty in: Cambodia, Laos, Vietnam, Myanmar

- Agriculture: small farms, paddies, and plantations (in lowlands)

GOVERNMENT

- Tradition of authoritarian rule
- Only Thailand was never a European colony
- Monarchies: Thailand, Brunei, Malaysia, Cambodia

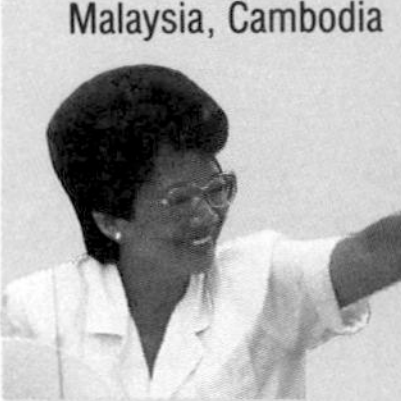

- Republics: Philippines, Indonesia, Myanmar; parliamentary system: Singapore; Communist: Laos, Vietnam

- The area has many refugees

ARTS AND RECREATION

- Arts are used to teach important religious values in Southeast Asia

- Religious festivals and shadow plays are popular traditional practices
- Gamelan: traditional orchestra in Indonesia
- Popular sports: badminton, basketball, Thai boxing

IDEAS TO REMEMBER

- Southeast Asia is a cultural crossroads, combining ideas and ways of life from southern China, India, the Middle East, and Europe.
- Some countries in Southeast Asia are rapidly developing, while others suffer the effects of years of war.
- Most Southeast Asian countries are ruled by one powerful group or leader and have found it difficult to form stable governments.
- Religious traditions influence the art and recreation of Southeast Asia.

574

ENRICHMENT ACTIVITY

Making Indonesian Shadow Puppets **Materials:** thin cardboard, paper fasteners, tape, markers, 1/4 inch dowels or sticks, a table lamp, a sheet, pennies

1. Tell students that they are going to make shadow puppets and put on a shadow play of their own. Refer students to pages 572–573.
2. Have the class make a puppet for each character in a simple story they all know, such as *Jack and the Beanstalk.*
3. Have students draw and decorate the parts of the puppets' bodies on cardboard with the heads and trunks connected and cut them out. Join the limbs to the bodies with the paper fasteners. Attach a long dowel to the puppet, supporting the head and body. Attach dowels to the puppets' hands with tape and let the legs, taped with pennies, swing freely. Hang the sheet up in front of the lamp and make shadows on it by holding the puppets in between.

CHAPTER 28 • REVIEW

REVIEWING VOCABULARY

gamelan
gross national product
meditate
paddy
shadow play

Number a sheet of paper from 1 to 5. Beside each number write the word or term that best matches the definition.

1. A field where rice is grown
2. The total amount of goods and services produced in a country during a year
3. To think deeply about important matters
4. Puppet drama that is part of the education of Indonesian children
5. An Indonesian orchestra that plays music

REVIEWING FACTS

1. Which two Eastern civilizations have had the greatest impact on Southeast Asia?
2. In which Southeast Asian countries is Buddhism the dominant religion?
3. Which five European countries established colonies in Southeast Asia?
4. What are the names of the three wealthiest countries in Southeast Asia? The three poorest?
5. What effect has population growth had on the rural economy of Southeast Asia?
6. Name four exports from plantations in Southeast Asia.
7. Who became president of the Philippines in 1986?
8. Which country in Southeast Asia avoided European rule?
9. How has the gap between the rich and the poor strengthened communist rebel movements in the Philippines?
10. How does a gamelan orchestra differ from an orchestra in the United States?

WRITING ABOUT MAIN IDEAS

1. **Writing an Essay:** Using Singapore as an example, write an essay with the title: "A Country Doesn't Have to Be Big to Be Prosperous."
2. **Writing a Narrative:** Write a narrative of the events leading up to the overthrow of Ferdinand Marcos in the Philippines and the coming to power of Corazon Aquino.
3. **Writing a List:** You have read that Southeast Asia has many natural resources. Yet it also contains some of the world's poorest countries. Write a list of reasons explaining this paradox.
4. **Writing About Perspectives:** What would it be like to have to flee from your country and start a new life where the language and customs are different? Imagine that you had to leave your country in Southeast Asia. Write a paragraph describing some of the ways in which you would have to change your life.

BUILDING SKILLS: DRAWING CONCLUSIONS

1. What does it mean to "draw a conclusion"?
2. Explain the process involved in drawing a conclusion.
3. Why is the ability to draw conclusions important?

575

5. The growing population has caused crowding in some rural areas and has forced many people to move to cities.
6. tea, coffee, rubber, bamboo, sugarcane
7. Corazon Aquino
8. Thailand
9. The rebels have gained support among the nation's poor plantation workers.
10. It has no conductor; music is not written down; it consists of drums, gongs, bells, chimes, cymbals, and xylophones.

Suggestions for Writing About Main Ideas

1. Students should note the importance of location in Singapore's success.
2. You may want students to write their narratives as though they were eyewitnesses to the events.
3. To stimulate students' recall of this chapter, have them brainstorm as many of the items for the list as possible before rereading the chapter.
4. Students should think about which countries they are fleeing from and to, what sort of life they had in their native lands, and how they will live in their new homes.

Answers to Building Skills: Drawing Conclusions

1. to put facts together to arrive at a statement of meaning
2. Identify the topic of the information; examine the information; look for ideas or subjects that are common to all the pieces of information; draw a conclusion stating how the subject or ideas common to all pieces of information relate to one another.
3. Drawing conclusions helps you to relate how pieces of information are connected to one another.

MAKING CONNECTIONS

Identifying Cause and Effect Display the Cause and Effect Diagram Graphic Organizer Transparency. Write in only the underlined copy. Have students fill in the missing causes and effects. Then have students create similar diagrams illustrating other cause-and-effect relationships described in the chapter. *Ask:* How has geography affected the culture of Southeast Asia?

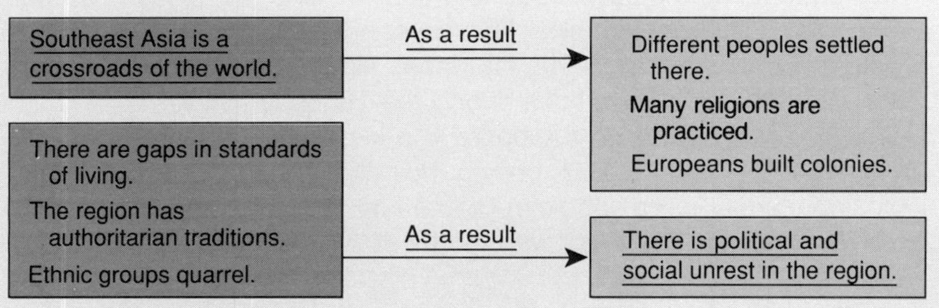

Chapter Review and Test
Practice Book: *Vocabulary Review,* page 158
Transparency: *Graphic Organizer,*
Assessment Book: *Chapter 28 Test*

UNIT 7 REVIEW
pages 576–577

USING THE UNIT SUMMARY AND REVIEW

Physical Geography These questions may be used for review.

- **What are the major deserts of the region?** (Gobi, Takla Makan, Tarim Basin)
- **What type of climate is common in Southeast Asia?** (tropical climate)
- **Where are the region's richest farmlands?** (in Southeast Asia)

Cultural Geography

- **Which values are important to the Japanese?** (respect for authority and order, duty to family and rulers)
- **What economic system does Hong Kong have?** (capitalist)
- **What type of government does the largest country in the region have?** (communist)
- **What is the greatest influence on the arts and recreation of the region?** (religious traditions)

UNIT 7 • SUMMARY

SOUTHERN AND EASTERN ASIA: PHYSICAL GEOGRAPHY

LANDFORMS

- Mount Everest is the world's highest mountain
- Deserts: Gobi, Takla Makan, Tarim Basin
- Archipelagoes: Phillippines, Indonesia
- Major rivers: Huang, Chang, Mekong, Ganges, Indus, Brahmaputra

CLIMATE

- Temperate climates: northern India, northern and eastern East Asia
- Dry and semi-dry climates: central China, western South Asia
- Highland climates: southwestern China, northern South Asia
- Tropical climates: southern South Asia, Sri Lanka, Maldives, Southeast Asia
- Monsoons cause both rainy and dry seasons

NATURAL RESOURCES

- Rivers are important for transportation
- Major seaports: Hong Kong, Bombay, Yokohama
- Richest farmland is in Southeast Asia
- Few mineral resources, except in Southeast Asia, which has abundant petroleum

SOUTHERN AND EASTERN ASIA: CULTURAL GEOGRAPHY

PEOPLE

- Religions: Hinduism, Buddhism, Islam, Confucianism, Daoism, Shinto
- Communism has changed ways of life in China, Mongolia, North Korea, Vietnam, Cambodia, and Laos
- Japanese values: respect for authority and order, duty to family and rulers

ECONOMY

- Population often grows faster than ability of nations to provide for people
- Under China's Communist system, the government owns most of the land
- The capitalist economies of Hong Kong, Taiwan and South Korea are called "economic miracles"
- Japan is the second most productive industrial power in world
- Years of war have caused poverty in Cambodia, Laos, Vietnam, Myanmar

GOVERNMENT

- Many different kinds of government in the region, from India (world's largest democracy) to China (huge independent communist power)
- Other types of governments: military dictatorships, monarchies
- Japan: parliamentary system includes the Diet (legislature)
- Tradition of authoritarian rule in Southeast Asia

ARTS AND RECREATION

- Arts and recreation strongly influenced by religious traditions; India's Taj Mahal is one of the world's most beautiful buildings
- Popular traditional arts: painting, poetry, flower arranging
- Popular East Asian recreations: chess, swimming, tennis, martial arts, baseball, golf

ENRICHMENT ACTIVITY

Playing "Where in Time and Place in Asia Am I?"

1. This game is based on "Where in Time and Place in Africa Am I?" which was described as a unit activity on page 484.
2. Divide the class into four teams and have each team choose a name for itself. Tell each team to use the information in Unit 7 to make up five statements that give clues to a specific time and place in South and East Asia. For example, "I have just built a beautiful tomb for my wife in Agra; it is called the Taj Mahal. Where in time and place in Asia am I?" Answer: In India during the 1600s.
3. List the team names on the board and keep score under them.
4. Have the teams take turns posing their clues one by one to the opposing teams. Score one point for the first team to come up with the correct answer. The team with the most points wins.

UNIT 7 • REVIEW

REVIEWING VOCABULARY

Buddhism	monsoons
castes	nonaligned nations
Confucianism	samurai
cottage industry	Shinto
Diet	socialist realism

Number a sheet of paper from 1 to 10. Beside each number write the word or term from the above list that best completes the sentence.

1. ____, a major religion of Asia, teaches that one must give up selfish desires in order to overcome suffering.
2. ____ is a form of art that often shows people at work on farms or in factories.
3. ____ are rigid social classes that define a way of life for people in India.
4. ____ are seasonal winds that have a great influence on the climate of Southern and Eastern Asia.
5. The ____ is Japan's national legislature.
6. Japanese ____ were taught to feel a great sense of duty to their country.
7. ____ emphasizes respect for others and the performance of one's duty.
8. By not joining a particular power bloc, ____ tried to avoid being drawn into great power rivalries.
9. ____ is a type of small-scale production that makes up a large percentage of India's total output.
10. ____ is the oldest of Japan's religions.

WRITING ABOUT THE UNIT

1. **Writing an Essay:** Write an essay contrasting the methods that Mao Zedong and Mohandas Gandhi used to achieve sweeping changes in their countries.
2. **Writing a Scenario:** A scenario is a brief description, similar to a news story, of an event or condition. The story is often a projection based on current trends. Write a scenario for an Asian country or region for the year 2010.
3. **Writing About Perspectives:** If you were living in a poor country in Asia, what would you do to try to improve the economy? In writing your answer to this question, tell how your solution would affect different groups of people in the country.

ACTIVITIES

1. **Constructing a Collage:** Locate pictures and photographs of Asia in magazines and travel brochures. Construct a collage to show how the modern and the traditional mix in this continent.
2. **Working Together to Create a Dialogue Between Members of Different Religions:** Work together to role-play a dialogue between a member of an Eastern religion, such as Buddhism, and a member of a Western religion, such as Christianity. In your dialogue highlight similarities and differences between the religions.

LINKING PAST, PRESENT, AND FUTURE

Many people believe that countries in Asia, such as Taiwan, South Korea, and Japan are becoming more powerful economically. Do you think this area will surpass the West as the world's foremost economic power?

577

Answers to Reviewing Vocabulary

1. Buddhism
2. socialist realism
3. castes
4. monsoons
5. Diet
6. samurai
7. Confucianism
8. nonaligned nations
9. cottage industry
10. Shinto

Suggestions for Writing About the Unit

1. Students should contrast the violent and nonviolent methods used.
2. You may want to have students work in groups to develop their scenarios. Have volunteers read their scenarios to the class.
3. Students should select a particular country and use what they know about that country in their answer. They should try to keep in mind how the beliefs of a person from their country could affect their choice of solutions.

Suggestions for Activities

1. You may want to divide the class into three groups, one dealing with the modern aspects, one with the traditional aspects, and another with a combination of the two.
2. This activity lends itself to a cooperative learning approach. Divide the class into groups. Assign different religions to each group so that a balanced presentation will be made. Have the groups role-play their dialogues for the rest of the class.

Suggestions for Linking Past, Present, and Future Students who agree may mention the growing economic power of the area and the current stagnant growth in the West. Others may feel that the growth of Asia is only temporary and that the West, having been economically developed longer, will once again dominate.

PERFORMANCE ASSESSMENT

Demonstrating Understanding Tell students that now that they have read about the land and people of Southern and Eastern Asia, they will write and perform skits in which people from different parts of the region meet and exchange ideas. Divide the class into groups of four to write and rehearse their skits. Suggest that group members work individually or in pairs for researching and drafting parts of the script. Have group members work together to develop the final script. Encourage them to make and use costumes and artifacts for their skits. Remind students of the standards that will be applied to their skits, which were outlined on page 486. For additional performance assessment information see page TM47 in the *Assessment Book.*

For the Portfolio: Include students' scripts and the video or audiocassette tape, if available, in the portfolios. Also include your anecdotal record or observational checklist.

UNIT 8 ORGANIZER

THE PACIFIC text pages 578–615

UNIT THEME

The mostly tropical and semitropical Pacific region includes two unique continents, Australia and Antarctica, as well as an immense expanse of water dotted with islands generally limited in natural resources.

UNIT RESOURCES

- Practice Book: pp. 159–168
- Anthology: Part 6
- Anthology Cassette
- Outline Maps: 1, 38
- Transparency Maps: 2, 15
- Unit 8 Poster
- Internet Project Handbook
- Geo Adventures Pad
- Pupil Edition on Cassette
- Transparency: Graphic Organizer
- **Technology:** *Videodisc/Video Tape 2*
- **Technology:** *Adventures CD-ROM*
- Assessment Book, Chapter Tests: 29, 30

Internet CONNECTION

The Home Page at **http://www.mmhschool.com** and the **Internet Project Handbook** contain on-line student activities related to this unit.

UNIT PLANNING GUIDE

CHAPTER	SUGGESTED PACING	THEMES
29 PHYSICAL GEOGRAPHY OF THE PACIFIC pages 582–595	4 days	With seasons that are the reverse of those of the Northern Hemisphere, the Pacific region includes the dry, mineral-rich Australian outback, a polar icecap, coral atolls, volcanoes, islands with few natural resources, and the ocean.
30 NATIONS OF THE PACIFIC pages 596–613	7 days	Ancient traditions are mixed with new ones in the varied governments, economies, and lifestyles of the Pacific nations.

UNIT PROJECTS

Writing a Dialogue Remind students that a dialogue is a conversation between two or more people. Suggest that students write a dialogue between themselves and a Pacific island chief in which they seek information about the island lifestyle, ways of making a living, and the chief's views on the role of government.

Oral Reports Have students choose books to read about life in the Pacific region. (Two histories are Thor Heyerdahl's *Kon Tiki* and the first two chapters of James Michener's *Hawaii*.) Ask them to give oral reports about how the reading helped them to understand the Pacific region.

Cooperative Learning: Creative Mapping Have groups research early maps used in the Pacific region, such as stick/stone maps. Have the groups brainstorm ways that they could map the Pacific region, choose one method, and produce a map. Encourage students to create examples of "junk cartography" in which everything from Styrofoam worms to macaroni is used.

Field Trip Visit a museum with an exhibit on early Pacific peoples or a collection of Pacific artifacts. Have students make a list of contributions to our culture from the Pacific region, including, for example, surfing and water-skiing.

BULLETIN BOARD IDEAS

Making Your Own Bulletin Board Help students to create a bulletin board called "Pacific Traditions." Have students write and illustrate index card reports about Pacific cultures. Encourage students to consider and to discuss the oldest and the most recently established traditions of the region.

Using the Unit Poster As an alternative to the bulletin board activity, display the Unit 8 Poster, which shows an enlarged version of the Unit Opener globe on pages 578–579.

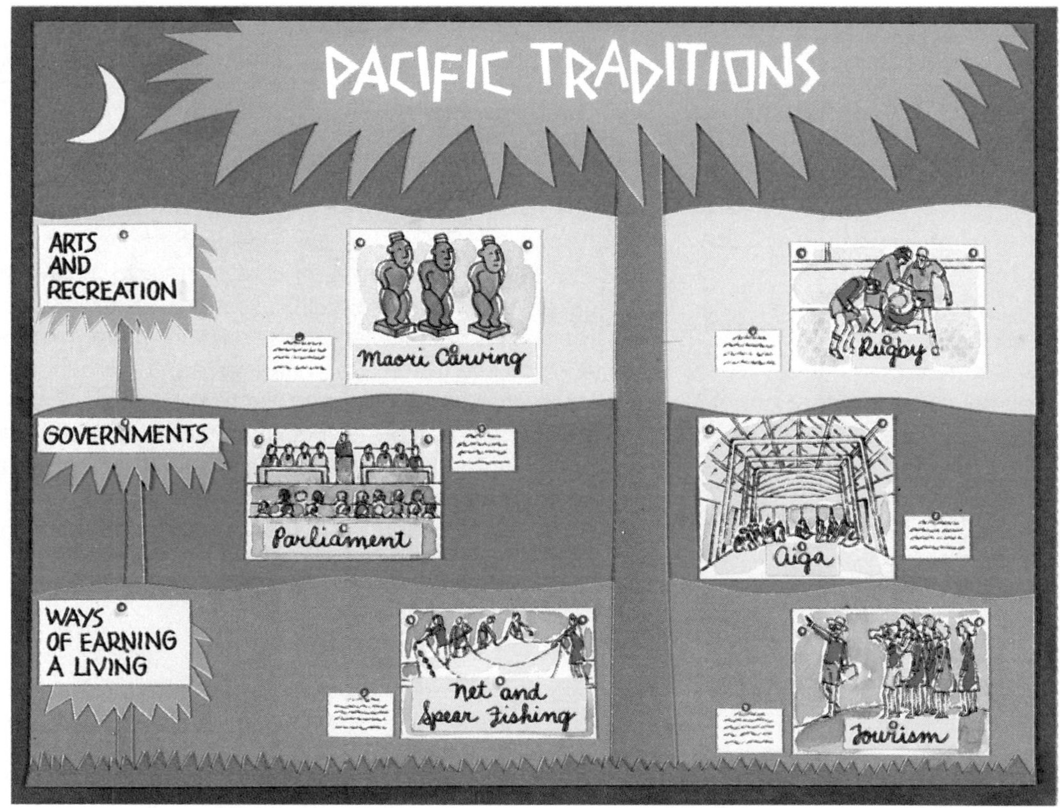

UNIT BIBLIOGRAPHY

For descriptions and additional resources, see the Annotated Bibliography beginning on page T-1 in the back of the book.

For the Teacher

Books

■ Harrell, Mary Ann. *Surprising Lands Down Under.* Washington, D.C.: National Geographic Society, 1989.

Ross, Stewart. *Causes and Consequences of the Rise of Japan and the Pacific Rim.* New York: Austin, TX: Raintree Steck-Vaughn, 1996.

Read-Alouds

Morgan, Sally. *The Flying Emu: And Other Australian Stories.* New York: Alfred A. Knopf, 1992.

Oodgeroo. *Dreamtime: Aboriginal Stories.* New York: Lothrop, Lee & Shepard Books, 1993.

Technology Multimedia

■ *Antarctica.* (Video) National Geographic. Toll Free: 1-800-368-2728.

■ *Australia.* (Video) An exploration of Australia's cities, farms, desert outback, and rain forest. National Geographic. Toll Free: 1-800-368-2728.

Free Materials

For a 96-page booklet about New Zealand, send to: New Zealand Embassy; 37 Observatory Circle, N.W; Washington, D.C. 20008.

For the Student

■ Conway, Jill Ker. *The Road From Coorain.* New York: Random House, Inc., 1989. **(Challenging)**

The Cousteau Society. *An Adventure in New Zealand.* New York: Simon & Schuster Books, 1992. **(Average)**

Darien-Smith, Kate, and David Lowe. *The Australian Outback and Its People.* New York: Thomson Learning Publishing, 1995. **(Average)**

Hereniko, Vilsoni, and Patricia Hereniko. *South Pacific Islanders.* Vero Beach, FL: Rourke Publications, 1987. **(Average)**

Kanawa, Kirite. *Land of the Long White Cloud: Maori Myths, Tales, and Legends.* New York: Arcade Publishing, 1989. **(Average)**

Nile, Richard. *Australian Aborigines.* Austin, TX: Raintree Steck-Vaughn, 1993. **(Average)**

Pringle, Lawrence. *Antarctica: The Last Unspoiled Continent.* New York: Simon & Schuster Books, 1992. **(Average)**

Reynolds, Jan. *Down Under: Vanishing Cultures.* New York: Harcourt Brace Jovanovich, 1992. **(Easy)**

Vyner, Sue. *Swim for Cover: Adventure on the Coral Reef.* New York: Crown Publishers, 1995. **(Easy)**

■ Book excerpted in the Anthology
■ National Geographic selection

UNIT 8 ORGANIZER
IDEAS FOR ACTIVE LEARNING

TEACHER EXCHANGE

Traditional Cultures of the Pacific

Thanks to:
Fred Ketchum
Seymour Elementary School
Payson, Illinois

Materials
Necessary materials depend upon students' choices of projects.

Instructions

1. Ask students to do research reports and accompanying projects about ways of life among traditional cultures of the Pacific. Students may be interested in the food, clothing, shelter, tools, religion, governments, and traditions of peoples such as the Maori, Samoans, or Australian aborigines.
2. Have students work on projects by finding, drawing, or constructing objects that illustrate their reports. For example, they could bring in models of villages and boats, drawings of village life, maps showing the area inhabited by a tribe, or even samples of food, clothing, and tools.
3. Allow each student to make a brief presentation of his or her report and project to the class.

Designing the Perfect Country

Thanks to:
Dorothy Clinton
St. Louis Elementary School
St. Louis, Oklahoma

Materials
white paper or poster board

Instructions

1. After the class has studied a variety of other countries, including their economic systems and governments, ask students to design the perfect country.
2. Tell students that they should first consider and list the features that any country needs, such as natural resources, waterways, transportation, government, laws, towns and cities, and so on.
3. Tell students that the design of their country should include the best possible geography and the best possible political and economic systems.
4. Have students support their concepts of what makes a country perfect. They should show an understanding of the needs of a country to be at the same time self-sufficient and able to interact with other countries.

TECHNOLOGY CENTER

Enriching with Multimedia

RESOURCE: *Internet Project Handbook*

Look at the ***Internet Project Handbook*** for student projects related to this unit or have students go on-line at http://www.mmhschool.com, Macmillan/McGraw-Hill's Home School page on the World Wide Web.

RESOURCE: *Adventures CD-ROM*

Enrich Unit 8 with the *Investigate* and *Create* activities on the Adventures CD-ROM.

SCHOOL-TO-HOME

Discover the Pacific

- Throughout this unit, students will have the opportunity to learn about the geography of the Pacific and both traditional and modern governments, economies, and lifestyles. Students will also discover that tourism is the main source of income on many Pacific islands. With this in mind, help students to generate a list of headings they could use in a travel brochure for Australia, Oceania, or New Zealand.
- Students and their families can select an area in the Pacific that they would most like to visit, and then design a brochure for that place. Invite students to write a descriptive paragraph under each heading and to draw or add appropriate pictures. Encourage students to share their brochures with the class.

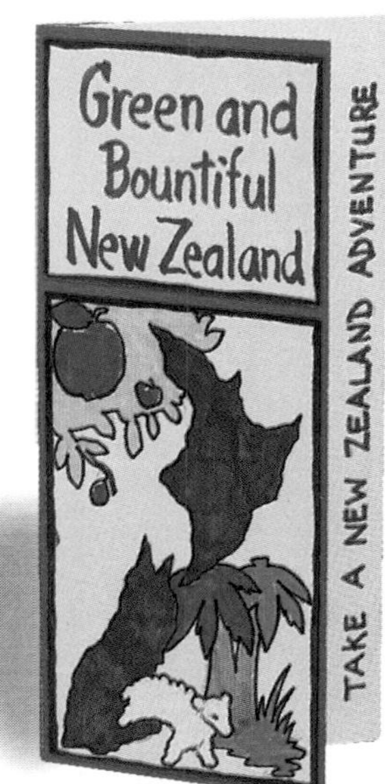

SECOND-LANGUAGE SUPPORT

While these activities are designed especially for students needing second-language support, they are meant to be shared by all students in the class.

Chapter 29, Lesson 2 ■ Physical Geography of the Pacific

A brief writing activity will help students internalize what they've read. Ask pairs or small heterogeneous groups of students to review the lesson and list aspects of the Pacific region's climate and resources. Have each team create a travel brochure or television commercial for one part of the Pacific.

Chapter 30, Lesson 2 ■ Nations of the Pacific

Ask pairs of students to choose one industry of the Pacific and construct a poster illustrating that industry. Students may include on their posters a brief paragraph about their chosen industry and the economy of the region.

Chapter 29, Lesson 2

UNIT 8

pages 578–615

USING THE UNIT OPENER

Introducing the Unit Display the Unit 8 Poster. Have students look at the unit title and silently read the *Where We Are* section on the facing page.

Ask students:

- **Which two continents make up much of the Pacific region?** (Australia and Antarctica)
- **What two other facts about this region are revealed in the *Where We Are* section?** (It is vast in size and has thousands of small islands.)

EXTENDING MAP SKILLS

Tell students that the patterns of islands that make up this region are not clear-cut.

Ask students:

- **What makes the shape of this region quite different from the shapes of other regions you have studied in this book?** (It is made up of mostly water and islands.)
- **What are the two most easily recognized shapes on the map of this region?** (Australia and Antarctica)

578

ONGOING UNIT PROJECT

Planning for Assessment Explain to students that in this unit they will learn about the people and geography of Australia, Antarctica, and the islands of the Pacific. They will have an opportunity to demonstrate what they have learned by taking part in an imaginary television quiz show in which they ask and answer questions about the people and places of the Pacific. As students read the unit, they should take notes on the questions they would like to ask and answer. For information on completing this unit project, see page 615.

Goal: Students' work should show an understanding of the differences in physical and cultural geography of the countries that make up the Pacific region.

Signs of Success: Assure students that they will have ample time to prepare both the questions and answers before the show. Tell students to make sure their questions are clear and concise. Explain to students that an adequate quiz show should include general questions on the environment, people, and culture of the region. An excellent quiz show would include more detailed questions about landforms, climate, natural resources, and the history of the region's various peoples (including their governments, economies, and art forms).

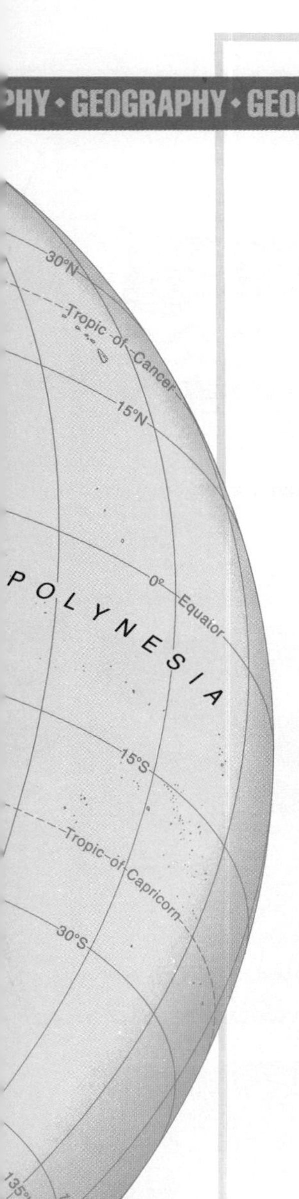

GEOGRAPHY • GEOGRAPHY • GEOGRAPHY • GEOGRAPHY • GEOGRAPHY • GEOGRAPHY

THE PACIFIC

WHERE WE ARE

In your journey through the world around us, you have seen almost all of the world's continents, from North and South America to Europe, Asia, and Africa. But there are two continents that you have not yet studied. Can you guess which ones they are?

If you guessed Australia and Antarctica, you're right. These two continents make up much of the region known as the Pacific. As you can see from the map, this is a vast region, made up not only of these two continents, but also of thousands of small islands. What makes this region different from all the others you have studied? In the following chapters you will find out.

579

Identifying the Patterns of Island Nations in the Pacific Region Have students study the map on these two pages to find the patterns of islands that make up Polynesia, Micronesia, and Melanesia. Give students an outline map of the Pacific region from the Teacher's Resource Center. Tell students to refer to the map on pages 578–579 as they draw the boundaries of Polynesia, Micronesia, and Melanesia on the outline map. Then have students color and label the area of ocean enclosed by the boundaries. Have students color and label Australia and Antarctica and draw a key explaining the colors. Students should use their map as a reference as they study this unit, adding key place names that they learn in each lesson.

5 FUNDAMENTAL THEMES OF GEOGRAPHY

Movement Scientists believe that Australia, Antarctica, Africa, and India were once one huge landmass, which they have named Gondwanaland.

- There are several pieces of evidence for this theory. Bones of a sheep-sized animal called a Lystrosaurus have been found in Africa, India, Australia, and Antarctica. Since this animal would have been incapable of swimming the long distances that separate these four places, the discovery of its bones in all of these places suggests that they were once one landmass. Further evidence for this theory is provided by the discovery in Antarctica of remains of tropical forests like those in Africa and India.

BACKGROUND INFORMATION

Ring of Fire Under the Pacific region are two of the earth's great crustal plates. Australia and Antarctica ride on one. The other encircles the huge Pacific Ocean basin and is the larger plate.

- This larger plate, which is called the Pacific plate, lies under the floor of the Pacific Ocean. It is also known as the Ring of Fire.
- The majority of the earth's 516 active volcanoes are located around the edges of the Pacific plate. Many of the most active are on the islands of the Pacific region.
- The Pacific plate is moving northwest at about the same rate as human fingernails grow.

Introducing the Pacific Table Explain to students that the Pacific region is immense, but, as this table shows, only 13 nations are located in this region.

Ask students:

- **Which is the only country in this region in which English is not a major language?** (Nauru)
- **How many of the 13 nations in this region have more than 1 million people? Which nations are they?** (three; Australia, New Zealand, Papua New Guinea)
- **Which is the largest nation in the Pacific region in both population and land area?** (Australia)
- **Which is the smallest country in the Pacific region in both population and land area?** (Nauru)
- **As you look at the leading exports of the nations of the Pacific region, what can you conclude about the development of the economies of this region?** (Only three export minerals; all the rest export foodstuffs. There are probably few developed economies in this region.)
- *THINKING FURTHER:* **Why is Antarctica not represented on this table when the map shows that it is part of this region?** (It is not owned by a single nation and has neither permanent residents nor citizens. It is under international control, with several nations claiming parts of it.)

THE PACIFIC

KIRIBATI
Capital ★ Tarawa

Major languages: Gilbertese and English
Population: 77,853
Area: 277 sq mi; 717 sq km
Leading export: fish

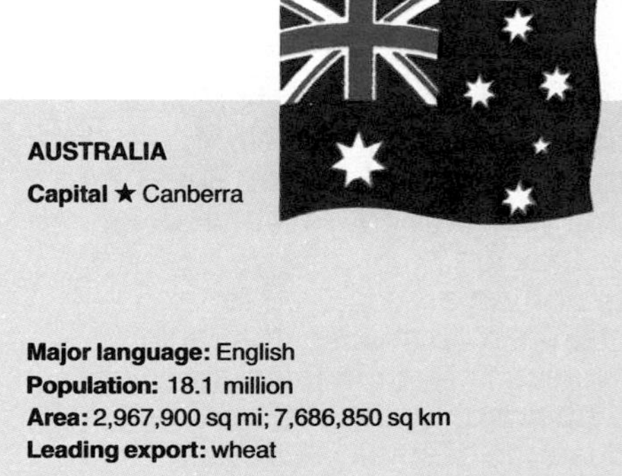

AUSTRALIA
Capital ★ Canberra

Major language: English
Population: 18.1 million
Area: 2,967,900 sq mi; 7,686,850 sq km
Leading export: wheat

MARSHALL ISLANDS
Capital ★ Majuro

Major language: English
Population: 54,031
Area: 70 sq mi; 181.3 sq km
Leading exports: agricultural products and handicrafts

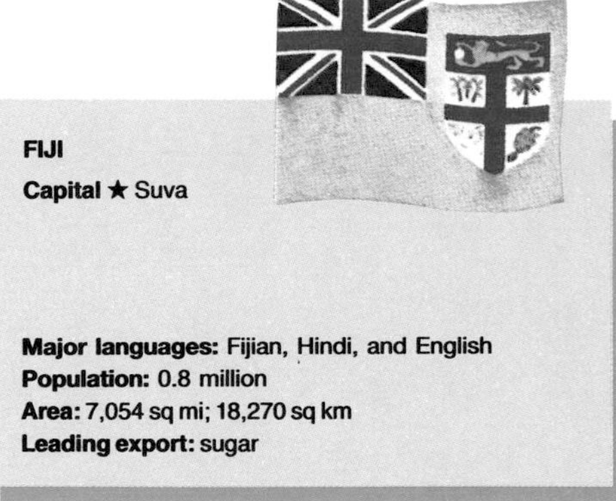

FIJI
Capital ★ Suva

Major languages: Fijian, Hindi, and English
Population: 0.8 million
Area: 7,054 sq mi; 18,270 sq km
Leading export: sugar

MICRONESIA
FEDERATED STATES OF
Capital ★ Palikir

Major languages: English, Trukese, Yapese, and Kosrean
Population: .1 million
Area: 270 sq mi; 700 sq km
Leading export: copra

5 FUNDAMENTAL THEMES OF GEOGRAPHY

Movement The Hawaiian Islands were formed by a hot spot, or a plume, near the center of the Pacific plate. It is from this hot spot that magma from inside the earth continually oozes or erupts as lava to form volcanoes or to build up areas of land.

- The Pacific plate is so huge that the Hawaiian hotspot near its center may act as a relief valve, letting off the pressure of the magma below.

Movement of the Pacific Plate The arrangement of the Hawaiian Islands provides evidence that the Pacific plate has moved toward the northwest over millions of years.

- The oldest islands in this group are located in the northwest. Each island was formed by the lava that erupted as the plate moved over the hot spot. As the plate moved on, it carried the island with it, leaving space on the ocean floor for the lava, still escaping from the hot spot, to form a new island.
- At present, the big island of Hawaii is over the hot spot. Kilauea, the largest active crater in the world, demonstrates that the hot spot is beneath this island by regularly releasing lava. As the big island of Hawaii is carried farther to the northwest by the plate, the lava released from the hot spot will form another island.

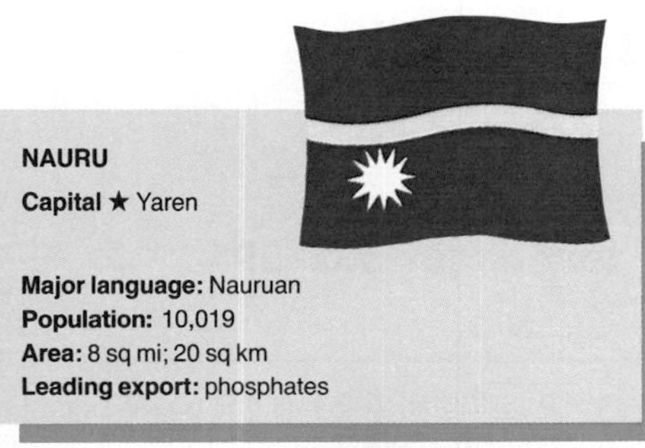

NAURU
Capital ★ Yaren

Major language: Nauruan
Population: 10,019
Area: 8 sq mi; 20 sq km
Leading export: phosphates

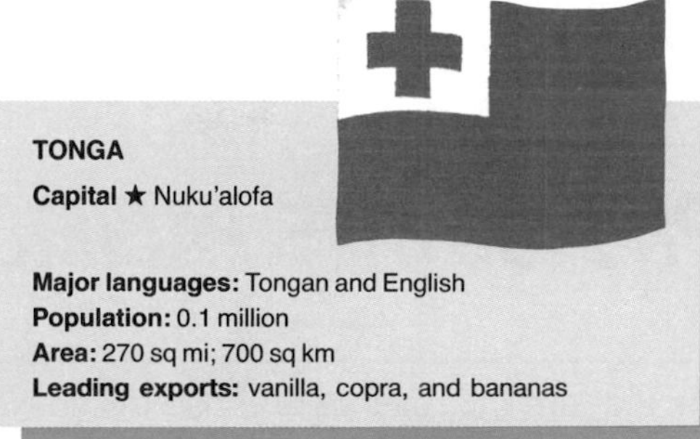

TONGA
Capital ★ Nuku'alofa

Major languages: Tongan and English
Population: 0.1 million
Area: 270 sq mi; 700 sq km
Leading exports: vanilla, copra, and bananas

NEW ZEALAND
Capital ★ Wellington

Major languages: English and Maori
Population: 3.4 million
Area: 103,738 sq mi; 268,680 sq km
Leading exports: lamb and wool

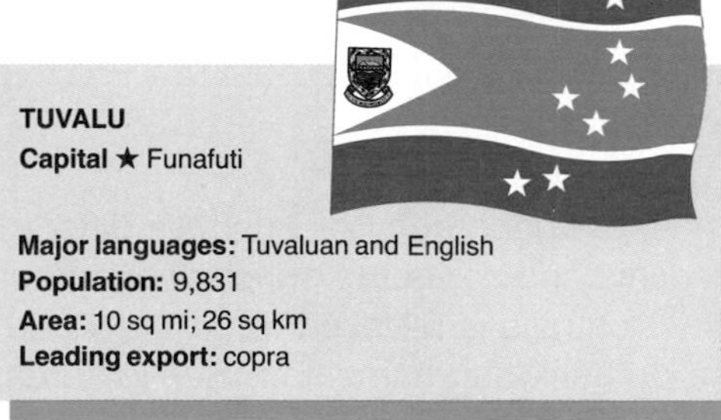

TUVALU
Capital ★ Funafuti

Major languages: Tuvaluan and English
Population: 9,831
Area: 10 sq mi; 26 sq km
Leading export: copra

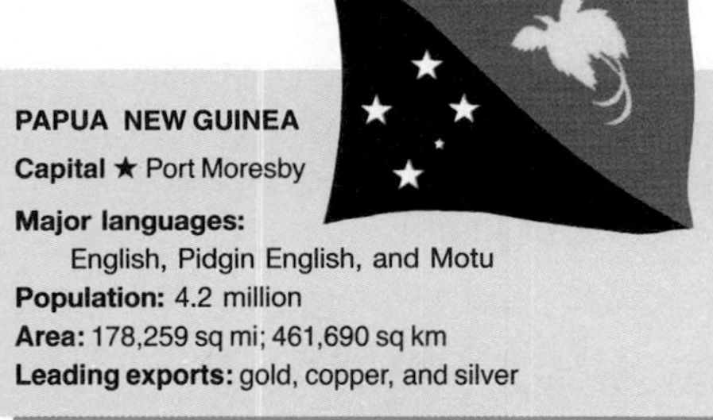

PAPUA NEW GUINEA
Capital ★ Port Moresby
Major languages:
English, Pidgin English, and Motu
Population: 4.2 million
Area: 178,259 sq mi; 461,690 sq km
Leading exports: gold, copper, and silver

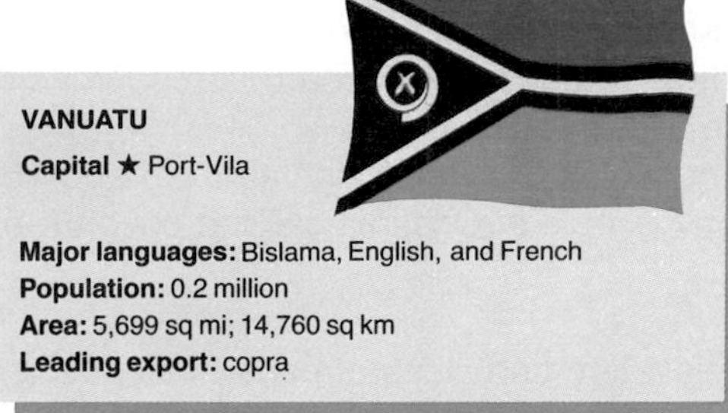

VANUATU
Capital ★ Port-Vila

Major languages: Bislama, English, and French
Population: 0.2 million
Area: 5,699 sq mi; 14,760 sq km
Leading export: copra

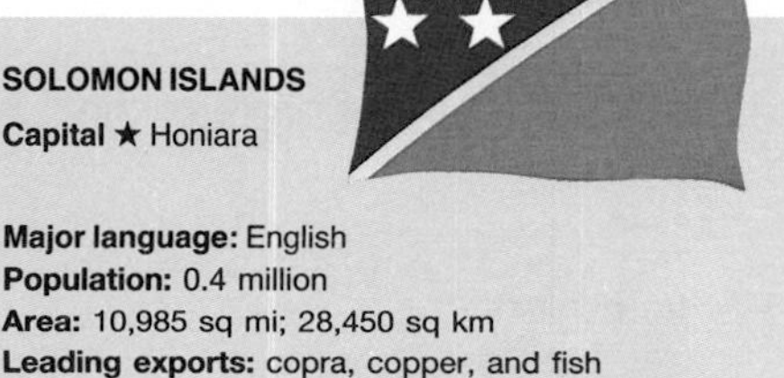

SOLOMON ISLANDS
Capital ★ Honiara

Major language: English
Population: 0.4 million
Area: 10,985 sq mi; 28,450 sq km
Leading exports: copra, copper, and fish

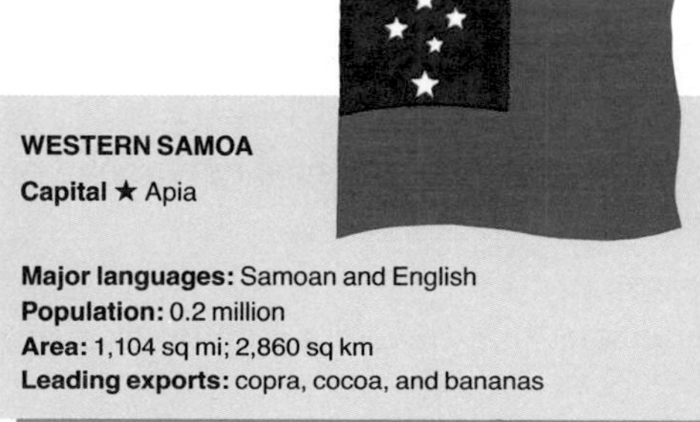

WESTERN SAMOA
Capital ★ Apia

Major languages: Samoan and English
Population: 0.2 million
Area: 1,104 sq mi; 2,860 sq km
Leading exports: copra, cocoa, and bananas

Identifying Physical Characteristics of a Nation from a Table Challenge students to draw conclusions about the nations of the Pacific Region from the information in the table. Ask students what tentative conclusions they might draw from the data in this table if they were looking for clues about what the nations in a region were like. (The small size of some of these nations might indicate that they are islands. Exports of coconut and sugar show that the nations are tropical.)

Ranking to Find Population Categories Tell students to make a list in which they first rank the nations by population. Then they should group the nations into ranges or categories. Next have students write a paragraph explaining why they think there are such wide ranges of population in this region.

CURRICULUM CONNECTION

Language Arts The names of the countries in the Pacific region may not be familiar to many students. Have students research the correct pronunciation for and the meanings of the names of each country. Then help students to practice pronouncing the names as they locate the countries on a map. Have students write a short essay explaining why some of the countries (at least four) were named as they were.

FUNDAMENTAL THEMES OF GEOGRAPHY

Place Both the physical and the human characteristics of Antarctica are influenced by its frigid climate.

Physical Characteristics

- The ice cap that covers this continent is 2 miles (3.2 km) thick in some places.

Human Characteristics

- No humans live in Antarctica permanently, but scientists from many nations spend periods of time in a research station at the South Pole.

CHAPTER 29
ORGANIZER

PHYSICAL GEOGRAPHY OF THE PACIFIC

text pages 582–595

CHAPTER THEME

With seasons that are the reverse of those of the Northern Hemisphere, the Pacific region includes the dry, mineral-rich Australian outback, a polar icecap, coral atolls, volcanoes, islands with few natural resources, and the ocean.

CHAPTER OBJECTIVES

CONTENT

- Describe how the geography of Australia differs from that of the rest of the region.
- Identify Oceania and name the principal geographic feature in this region.
- Explain why Australia is believed to be the world's oldest continent.
- Identify the outback and name its major features.
- Identify the Great Barrier Reef and describe how it was formed.
- Name the two major types of Pacific islands.
- Describe key features of Antarctica.
- Describe how the climate and natural resources of the Pacific affect the way of life of the people of the region.
- Describe how New Zealand benefits from abundant water resources and cool weather.
- Explain why people in Oceania call the coconut palm the "Tree of Life."

SKILLS

Geography
- Interpret elevation and climate maps of Australia and New Zealand.
- Use a map to identify regions of differing population density in Australia and New Zealand.
- Read a map of the ocean floor.

Thinking
- Compare and contrast the physical geography of Australia with that of other parts of the Pacific region.

Reading and Writing
- Write observations that travelers might make about the Pacific region.

CITIZENSHIP VALUES

- Appreciate the role that individual citizens play in bringing about social change.

TEACHER OPTIONS

READING STRATEGY: Comprehension Monitoring
Strategies to help students read and remember the main ideas of the lesson.
Lesson 1: p. 583   Lesson 2: p. 590

MEETING INDIVIDUAL NEEDS Activities for reteaching, extension, and enrichment.
Lesson 1: p. 587   Lesson 2: p. 593
Geography Skills: p. 589

GEO ADVENTURES ACTIVITIES PAD Daily activities to assess students' understanding of geography skills.

CURRICULUM CONNECTION Activities to help integrate other subject areas with Social Studies.
Language Arts: p. 585

PUPIL EDITION ON CASSETTE Language support for students who have difficulty reading or who will benefit from listening to the Pupil Edition on Cassette as they read.

SECOND-LANGUAGE SUPPORT Activities and suggestions for second-language learners.

Lesson 2: p. 577-D

CHAPTER PLANNING GUIDE

LESSON	SUGGESTED PACING	THEMES	TEACHER SUPPORT MATERIALS: TEACHER'S RESOURCE CENTER
1 LANDFORMS pages 583–587	1 day	Geographically isolated and scattered over a vast expanse of the Pacific, Australia, Oceania, and Antarctica have sharply contrasting natural features.	Practice Book p. 159 ■ Anthology pp. 192–193, 204–207 **Technology:** *Adventures CD-ROM*
BUILDING GEOGRAPHY SKILLS Reading Maps of the Ocean Floor pages 588–589	1 day	Satellite photos and contour maps reveal ocean floor features.	Practice Book p. 160 Outline Map p. 1 Transparency Map 15
2 CLIMATE AND RESOURCES pages 590–593	1 day	Spread out over a vast region, Australia and Oceania vary greatly in climate and resources.	Practice Book p. 161 ■ Anthology pp. 198–199 **Technology:** *Adventures CD-ROM*
CHAPTER SUMMARY AND REVIEW pages 594–595	1 day	Chapter content, skills, and vocabulary are reviewed and evaluated.	Practice Book p. 162 Transparency: Graphic Organizer Assessment Book, Chapter 29 Test

Technology CONNECTION

Lesson 1
ADVENTURES CD-ROM
Enrich Lesson 1 by having students make maps of Australia showing Shading in *Build.*

Lesson 2
ADVENTURES CD-ROM
Enrich Lesson 2 by having students look at country climographs in *Investigate, Charts.*

CHAPTER 29
pages 582–595

USING THE CHAPTER OPENER

Discussing the Photograph Have the class study the photograph and read the chapter title.

Ask students:

- **What are you looking at in this photograph?** (an airplane flying above the sea)
- **What seems to lie near the surface of the sea?** (Some students may recognize a coral reef.)
- **What sea do you think this is?** (from the chapter title, the Pacific Ocean)
- **What kind of plane is shown?** (a seaplane)
- *THINKING FURTHER:* **Why might this be a popular means of transport in this region?** (Students should infer that there must be much water to cross in a region named for an ocean.)

Reading/Listening to the Primary Source Read the opening passage to the class.

Ask students:

- **What are the writers saying about the lands of the Pacific region?** (They are far apart and isolated from the rest of the world, and they can be both lovely and lonely.)
- **How do such descriptions make you feel about this region?** (Students may feel that the region is beautiful and sparsely populated.)
- *THINKING FURTHER:* **What do you already know about Australia, New Zealand, and the other islands of the South Pacific?** (Encourage students to draw on what they have seen in the movies or on television or on what they have read. Have them pool their knowledge and organize their ideas to create a description of each of the three areas. Then have them tell what other information they might look for to fill out their descriptions.)

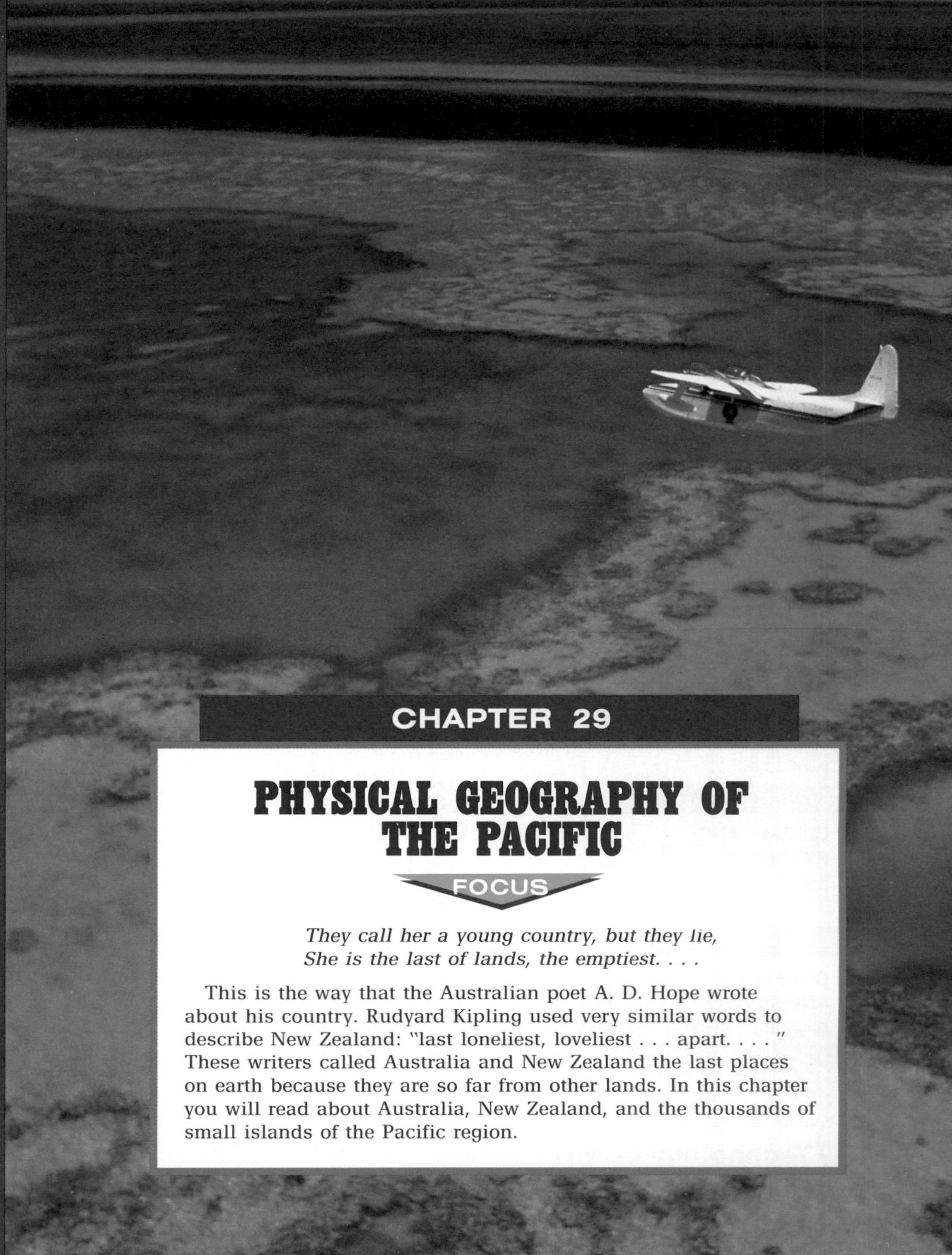

CHAPTER 29

PHYSICAL GEOGRAPHY OF THE PACIFIC

FOCUS

They call her a young country, but they lie,
She is the last of lands, the emptiest. . . .

This is the way that the Australian poet A. D. Hope wrote about his country. Rudyard Kipling used very similar words to describe New Zealand: "last loneliest, loveliest . . . apart. . . ." These writers called Australia and New Zealand the last places on earth because they are so far from other lands. In this chapter you will read about Australia, New Zealand, and the thousands of small islands of the Pacific region.

BACKGROUND INFORMATION

About the Photograph

- The seaplane shown here is flying over the Great Barrier Reef, off the northeastern coast of Australia.
- Seaplanes are perhaps more widely used in the Pacific region than anywhere else in the world. They are used mainly for island hopping.
- This seaplane may be one of the many that take day trippers from Cairns or Mackay in Queensland to the Great Barrier Reef and drop them off to scuba dive or snorkel and to explore its natural wonders. More than 20 offshore resorts accommodate visitors who wish to stay longer.

Landforms

READ TO LEARN

Key Vocabulary
outback
atoll
iceberg

Key Places
Australia
Oceania
Great Barrier Reef
Polynesia
Micronesia
Melanesia

Read Aloud

The lands of the Pacific region vary greatly, but they have one important feature in common. Wide expanses of ocean surround them all. Thousands of years ago, the first explorers of the Pacific must have had enormous confidence. They sailed into the empty spaces of the Pacific with no guarantee of finding anything. In the end, after sailing huge distances in small, open boats, they found islands that no human had ever seen before.

Read for Purpose

1. WHAT YOU KNOW: If you could live in any area, which geographic features would you choose to live near? Mountains? The seashore? Rivers? Why would you choose these features?
2. WHAT YOU WILL LEARN: In what ways does the geography of Australia differ from that of the rest of the Pacific region?

AN ISOLATED REGION

Australia is the world's smallest continent. It is about the same size as the United States, not including Alaska. The small continent of Australia is like an enormous island, with 23,000 miles (37,000 km) of coastline.

The rest of the Pacific region is made up of islands. There are large islands, such as New Zealand, but there are also thousands of small islands that dot the Pacific Ocean. All of the islands of the Pacific are known collectively as Oceania.

The Pacific region is made up mostly of water, with very little land. It includes only 3.3 million square miles (8.5 million sq km) of land—less than 6 percent of the earth's land surface. This land is scattered over a vast ocean. On a map most of the islands may appear to be close together, but in fact they are very far apart. Australia and New Zealand are more than 1,000 miles (1,609 km) apart. Because of such vast distances, various ways of life have developed in distinct ways in the Pacific.

AUSTRALIA

Winds and rain have scraped, sanded, and washed the surface of Australia for millions of years. They have worn the land down to make it the flattest, lowest continent on earth. There are no volcanoes or rugged new mountains on the continent. Australia is not only the smallest, but also the oldest continent.

Most Australians live on the coastal rim

WHAT YOU KNOW: In their responses students should state their reasons for choosing certain geographic features over others.

583

LESSON 1
583–587

Lesson Theme Geographically isolated and scattered over a vast expanse of the Pacific, Australia, Oceania, and Antarctica have sharply contrasting natural features.

Lesson Objectives
- Describe Australia's land features.
- Identify Oceania's three island groups and describe their features.
- Describe Antarctica.

1 PREPARE

Motivate Read the *Read Aloud* passage to the class.

Set Purpose Pose the *What You Know* question and give students time to identify features they favor. Display the *Atlas* map of Australia and New Zealand so that students can see which of these features can be found in the Pacific region. Have students read the lesson to answer the *What You Will Learn* question.

2 TEACH

Locating an Isolated Region

Ask students:

- **What two areas make up the Pacific region?** (Australia and Oceania)
- *THINKING FURTHER:* **Why is *isolated* a good word to describe this region?** (The region is composed of islands at great distances from one another and from the rest of the world.)

READING STRATEGY AND VOCABULARY DEVELOPMENT

Comprehension Monitoring Review with students how important it is to monitor what they read. Tell students that they should be active in their reading by constantly asking questions about the material. For example, they might ask themselves: Does this seem reasonable? Does it agree or disagree with the facts as I know them? Have students preview the lesson. Give them a model of questions to use to monitor their reading. Prepare questions for a section from the lesson, such as "The Outback" on pages 584–585. Questions might include: What is this saying about the outback? (that it is huge and dry and sparsely populated) What gives me the idea that it is sparsely populated? (the lack of roads, the use of airplanes as common transportation) Does this agree with what I know about the outback? (Yes, I've seen films that show this.) Then have students read other paragraphs to practice monitoring their comprehension.

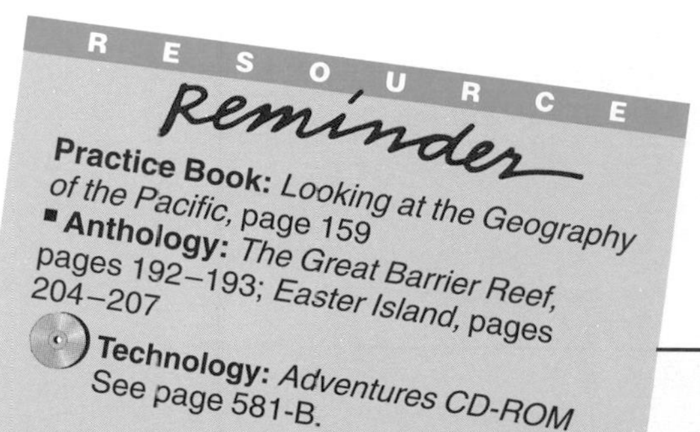

Looking at Australia Discuss the shape and size of Australia.

Ask students:

- **In which part of Australia do most of the people live?** (along the coastal rim)
- **Why is the eastern coastal rim the most populous?** (It is a narrow, fertile strip.)
- **What role does the Great Dividing Range play in Australia's river system?** (Most of its rivers start here.)
- **What is the major river system of Australia?** (the Murray River with its tributaries)

EXTENDING MAP SKILLS

Refer the class to the elevation map on this page.

Ask students:

- **Where in this region is the elevation the highest?** (in the Southern Alps of New Zealand's South Island)
- **Where is the elevation the lowest?** (in portions of Australia's interior and along coastal areas)
- **What is the highest point in New Zealand?** (Mount Cook)
- **Which waterway separates the two islands of New Zealand?** (Cook Strait)

Exploring the Outback

Ask students:

- **How would you describe the outback?** (vast area, arid rocky land, lightly populated, long distances between inhabited spots)
- *THINKING FURTHER:* **Why do you suppose the outback is much less populated than the eastern coastal rim?** (Students should recognize the role that fertile soil and nearness to water play in the size of population.)

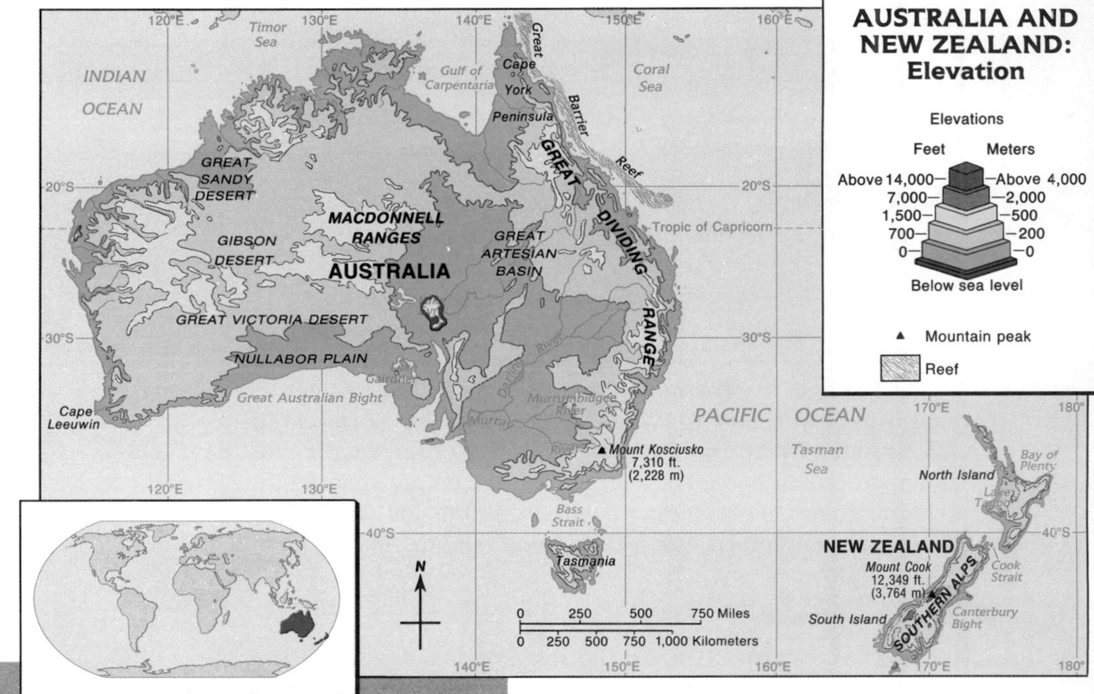

MAP SKILL: What area of high elevation lies along Australia's east coast? Name a mountain peak in this area.

of their land. Inland there are three main regions: the huge Western Plateau, the Central Plains (or Central Eastern Lowlands), and the Eastern Highlands.

All the large cities of Australia, except Perth, are on the east coast. It is like the east coast of the United States, a narrow, fertile strip with an ocean on one side and low mountains to the west.

Not far inland a system of low mountains, hills, and highlands parallels the east coast. This area is the Great Dividing Range. Part of it looks blue when viewed from a distance. The color comes from the eucalyptus (ū kə lip′ təs), or gum trees, that cover the Blue Mountains. Sunlight glints off the oily leaves of the trees, making a blue haze.

As the map above shows, most of Australia's major rivers begin in the Great Dividing Range in the northeast. The Murray River and its branches, especially the Darling River, form the continent's major river system. Find the Murray River on the map above. Australia has few other rivers.

THE OUTBACK

You have read that Perth is the only large city in Australia that is not on the east coast. Separating Perth from other cities is the huge, arid area Australians call the **outback**. There wasn't even a paved road between Perth and Adelaide until 1976. An Australian writer has said of the outback:

> *It is a hard land, even today. Times change, but the Australian heartland never does. . . . Most of it lies as it has for countless millennia* [thousands of years], *sunk in a coma of ancient waterlessness.*

584 MAP SKILL: the Great Dividing Range; Mount Kosciusko

5 FUNDAMENTAL THEMES OF GEOGRAPHY

Region Most of the islands in the region of Oceania fall within the "Ring of Fire," or the belt that rims the Pacific Plate. The Pacific Plate is the most dynamic of the earth's plates.

- Within the Ring of Fire, about 1 million earthquakes occur each year, more than three fourths of the world's total.
- Most of the world's volcanoes are also found along this belt. Volcanoes are formed when pressurized, rising magma breaks through the earth's crust and spews forth.
- Many additional volcanoes are found far within the belt. The volcanoes of the Hawaiian Islands of Polynesia are examples.

In some parts of the outback huge outcroppings of red rock rise out of the flat land. They are old rocks that were too strong to erode. One of them, Ayers Rock, is 1.5 miles (2.4 km) long.

In the outback, where there are few roads or gas stations, Australians use airplanes for everyday transportation. They run errands and visit friends by plane. Even their ambulances are airplanes.

THE GREAT BARRIER REEF

Australia contains not only a famous dry area, but also an underwater wonderland. Just off the northeast coast of Australia lies the Great Barrier Reef. A reef is a ridge of rocks near the surface of a sea.

The Great Barrier Reef is as large as the British Isles, yet it is comprised of tiny sea creatures called polyps. These little creatures live in huge colonies in the sea, and when they die, coral reefs are built up from their skeletons. The reefs keep growing as living polyps attach themselves to the coral skeletons.

The water temperature of the Great Barrier Reef never falls below 68°F. (18°C), and the water has very little dirt in it. The conditions of the Great Barrier Reef resemble a gigantic outdoor aquarium. Some 1,500 kinds of fish live amid its coral.

PACIFIC ISLANDS

Like the Great Barrier Reef, many of the islands of Oceania are made of coral. Some of them are called atolls. Atolls are doughnut-shaped coral reefs looped around an area of still, warm water. Most atolls are formed by coral buildup on the rims of sunken volcano craters.

Low coral islands lack fertile soil. Only a few plants can grow on such islands, so they cannot support many people. The people of Oceania bring soil from other islands to grow plants on some atolls.

Red-orange Ayers Rock rises out of the flat Australian outback. Ayers Rock is one of the most popular attractions among tourists visiting Australia.

Other Pacific islands are actually the tops of mountains that start below the sea. These mountains are part of the great mountain chains that circle the world. They just happen to be located mostly underwater.

Some of the islands that are part of these mountain chains rise far above sea level. They have varied landscapes of mountains, rivers, and valleys. Many of them are also volcanic. The lava that comes from the volcanoes forms fertile soil, so volcanic islands have many kinds of vegetation. They can support more people than can atolls.

POLYNESIA, MICRONESIA, AND MELANESIA

The islands of Oceania can be sorted into three main groups. The name of each group tells something about its islands. Polynesia means "many islands," but the name makes most people think of a warm, sunny climate, palm trees, and

Investigating the Great Barrier Reef Have students locate the Great Barrier Reef on the map on the facing page.

Ask students:

- **Where does this reef lie in relation to Australia?** (off the northeastern coast)
- **What is a reef?** (a ridge of rocks near the sea's surface)
- **How is a reef formed?** (by the accumulation of the skeletons of polyps and by living polyps attaching themselves to the skeletons)
- *THINKING FURTHER:* **Do you think that the Great Barrier Reef is as large as it will ever be?** (Help students to recognize that because the reef is formed by living polyps, it will grow as long as the polyps continue to attach themselves to it.)

Understanding the Making of the Pacific Islands Encourage students to draw diagrams to illustrate their answers concerning the building process by which the Pacific islands are formed.

Ask students:

- **What is an atoll and how are most atolls formed?** (a doughnut-shaped coral reef; Most are formed by coral buildup on the rim of a sunken volcano crater.)
- **How are other Pacific islands formed?** (Others are formed by underwater mountain ranges that rise above the sea surface.)
- **Which of these two kinds of islands is better able to support people and why?** (the kind of island formed by mountains, because of more varied landscapes and fertile soil)

Discussing Polynesia, Micronesia, and Melanesia Have students note the similarities among these three names. Ask students what they know about the area.

- **What do all of these words have in common?** (The ending *nesia*—tell students that this is from the Greek word for "islands.")

CURRICULUM CONNECTION

Language Arts Have students choose a place that they might like to visit in Australia, New Zealand, or one of the Pacific islands. Have them write about their visit in a series of diary entries. As students read through each lesson in this unit, encourage them to include details on the landforms, climate, resources, people, economy, government, and arts and recreation of the place they choose.

Differentiating Island Groups Continue discussing Polynesia, Micronesia, and Melanesia.

Ask students:

- **The islands of which island group are spread over the greatest distance?** (Polynesia)
- **Which island group contains more than 2,000 tiny islands?** (Micronesia)
- **Which are the "black islands"?** (Melanesia)
- **Of which island group are Hawaii, Tahiti, and American Samoa a part?** (Polynesia)
- **Of which island group are Fiji, the Solomons, and Papua New Guinea a part?** (Melanesia)

Exploring New Zealand

Ask students:

- **Why can New Zealand be called an island nation?** (because it is a nation made up mainly of two islands, North Island and South Island)
- *THINKING FURTHER:* **Why might New Zealand be an exciting place to visit?** (Encourage students to identify its many dramatic natural beauties and the activities made possible by these natural features, such as swimming, surfing, and mountain climbing.)

EXTENDING MAP SKILLS

Refer students to the map on this page.

Ask students:

- **What are the most densely populated areas of Australia and New Zealand?** (Australia's east coast, New Zealand's North Island)
- *THINKING FURTHER:* **What characteristic might account for these areas' large populations?** (Students should infer that these areas have natural resources, among them arable land, to support large populations.)

sandy beaches. Polynesia includes Tahiti, American Samoa, and, far to the east, Easter Island. Hawaii, the westernmost state of the United States, is located within the area of Polynesia. The map on pages 638–639 of the Atlas shows the location of many Pacific islands.

Polynesia is spread over a huge stretch of ocean, which covers 15 million square miles (39 million sq km). The isolation of all the islands in this area, as well as their small size, has limited their economic development.

Can you guess the size of the islands of **Micronesia** from the name? *Micronesia* means "tiny islands." Micronesia contains more than 2,000 islands. Most of these islands are atolls.

Melanesia means "black islands," a name given to the islands possibly because of the dark vegetation of their hillsides. Melanesia lies south of the equator, west of Polynesia, and northeast of Australia. Fiji and the Solomon Islands are part of Melanesia.

Papua New Guinea, the eastern half of the island of New Guinea, is the largest country in Melanesia. It has a rugged, mountainous terrain. Heavy rainfall in the mountains collects in streams that cross swamps and forests.

NEW ZEALAND

There is one large Pacific island country that you have not yet read about—New Zealand. New Zealand has everything from mountains and waterfalls to seashores and hot springs. In this land, which is about the size of Colorado, peo-

MAP SKILL: How would you describe the population density of Australia and New Zealand compared to other regions?

AUSTRALIA AND NEW ZEALAND: Population Density

People per square mile	People per square kilometer
0–2	0–1
2–25	1–10
25–125	10–50
125–250	50–100
250–500	100–200
over 500	over 200

INDIAN OCEAN · Timor Sea · Gulf of Carpentaria · Coral Sea · Tropic of Capricorn · AUSTRALIA · Brisbane · Perth · Great Australian Bight · Sydney · Melbourne · PACIFIC OCEAN · Tasman Sea · NEW ZEALAND

0 250 500 750 Miles · 0 250 500 750 1,000 Kilometers

586 MAP SKILL: Australia and New Zealand have lower population densities than most of the other regions.

BUILDING CITIZENSHIP

Oceania and American History Many of the islands of Oceania were battlegrounds for the American military during World War II. Ask volunteers to research and report to the class on the topics below. If possible, have students interview veterans of the war in the Pacific.

- The Battle of the Coral Sea
- The Battle of Midway
- The Battle of Guadalcanal in the Solomon Islands
- The Solomons Campaign
- The New Guinea Campaign
- The fight for Saipan and Guam in the Mariana Islands

ple are never more than 80 miles (129 km) from the coast. As the map on page 586 shows, much of New Zealand's population is along its coastlines.

The coastlines have one magnificent area of scenery after another. Mountainsides plunge straight down to the sea. Glaciers have scraped out mountain lakes, coastal fjords, and deep harbors. The city of Auckland, located at the base of a long peninsula, has not one, but two very fine harbors.

New Zealand has two main islands, North Island and South Island. South Island is larger than North Island and has a major mountain range, the Southern Alps. Mount Cook, New Zealand's highest peak, offers a very rare sight—snow in the Pacific region.

THE SOUTHERNMOST CONTINENT

Before leaving the Pacific region, we need to take a look at a continent that you have not yet read about in this book—Antarctica. This continent at the South Pole is in total contrast to the tropical and subtropical islands of the Pacific. All but 2 percent of its land is covered permanently with a thick cap of ice that spreads beyond the land. Ice shelves extend far into the surrounding ocean.

In 1987 part of one ice shelf in Antarctica broke off to become an iceberg that is larger than the state of Delaware. Icebergs are large bodies of ice that have broken away from glaciers. A scientist said of this iceberg:

> *If you could somehow transport it to California and melt it, it would supply all the water needs of Los Angeles for the next 675 years.*

If all the ice in Antarctica were to melt, the world's oceans would rise at least 160 feet (50 m). In some places, the ice pack is 2 miles (3.2 km) thick.

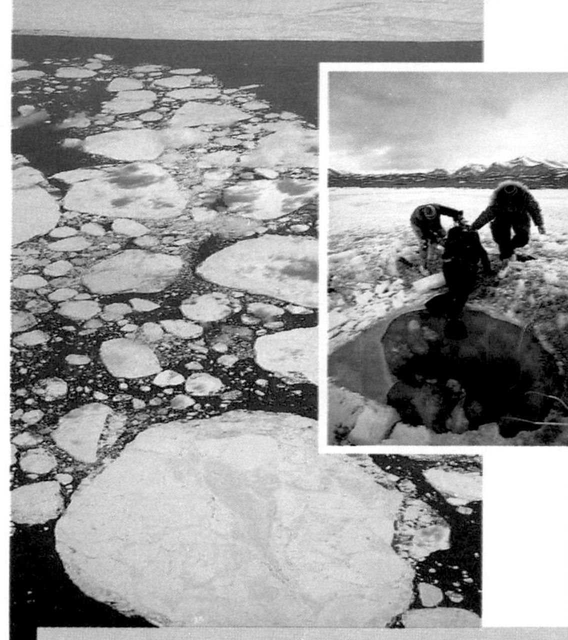

Explorers have visited many parts of the frozen continent of Antarctica.

CONTINENTS AND ISLANDS

In this lesson you have read that the land area of the Pacific region consists of two continents, Australia and Antarctica, and many large and small islands. These islands are divided into three groups: Polynesia, Micronesia, and Melanesia. In the next lesson you will read about the region's climate and resources.

Check Your Reading

1. Of the seven continents, which is the smallest?
2. What are Polynesia, Micronesia, and Melanesia?
3. Describe the physical geography of Antarctica.
4. **THINKING SKILL:** Compare and contrast Australia's physical geography with that of other parts of the Pacific region.

THINKING SKILL: Compare and Contrast

Talking About the Southernmost Continent

Ask students:

- **What covers the land of this continent?** (a thick icecap)
- *THINKING FURTHER:* **Why is so much of this continent covered with ice?** (because it is at a pole, the coldest place on earth)

Applying the Lesson Have students review the geographic features of the region and tell which ones most closely resemble features in their own area.

3 CLOSE

Summarizing Students have learned that Australia, Antarctica, and Oceania are spread out over a vast area.

Evaluating Use these questions to assess students' understanding.

- **How does the physical geography of Papua New Guinea differ from that of Australia's outback?** (Papua New Guinea has rugged mountains, heavy rains, swamps, and forests while Australia's outback is a flat, rocky, dry area.)
- **How does the physical geography of New Zealand differ from that of Antarctica?** (New Zealand has mountains, waterfalls, and hot springs. Antarctica has only one striking physical feature—a thick layer of ice.)

Answers to Check Your Reading

1. Australia
2. They are three island groups in the South Pacific that make up Oceania.
3. a continent almost entirely covered with thick ice, which extends far into the surrounding ocean
4. Australia is large and has a varied terrain; other parts of the region are smaller and have less varied terrains.

Independent Practice
Practice Book: page 159

MEETING INDIVIDUAL NEEDS

Reteaching (easy) Have students collect pictures of scenes from Australia, Oceania, and Antarctica and make a bulletin board display titled, "Down Under—Lands of Contrast."

Extension (average) Have students choose a place in this region and ask them to imagine that they are visiting that place. Have them use an encyclopedia or travel books to research the place they have chosen. Then have students write a letter to a friend and describe the geographic features they have seen on their visit.

Enrichment (challenging) Divide the class into six groups and assign each group one of the following: Antarctica, Australia, New Zealand, a Polynesian island, a Melanesian island, and a Micronesian island. Have each group research the topography of their subject and then make a topographical model of it in clay.

SKILLS LESSON
pages 588–589

Lesson Theme Satellite photos and contour maps reveal ocean floor features.

Lesson Objective

- Interpret a photograph and maps in order to visualize the surface of the ocean floor.

 PREPARE

Motivate You may wish to project Transparency Map 15, and have students tell what they see. Ask them how this map differs from maps that they usually see. Point out the total reversal—here the land areas are blank, and it is the ocean area that is mapped topographically.

Set Purpose Tell the class that in this lesson they will see how the surface of the ocean floor resembles the surface of land areas.

 TEACH

Discovering Ocean Floor Features
Refer the class to the picture on this page. Tell them that the light areas that look like mountain ranges are just that, and the long dark strips off the coasts of Asia and Australia are deep trenches lined with mountains.

Ask students:

- **In which oceans are mountain ranges especially prevalent?** (the North Atlantic, the Indian Ocean, the waters between South America and Antarctica, the western and northern Pacific)

BUILDING SKILLS
GEOGRAPHY SKILLS

Reading Maps of the Ocean Floor

Earth is sometimes called the water planet. The reason that this name is used for the earth is that much of it—about 71 percent of the planet's surface—is covered by water!

The ocean is a major factor in the geography of the Pacific. As you have read, this region includes a lot of water. To understand more about its geography, then, it is helpful to be able to read the special photographs and maps showing details of the ocean floor. The ocean floor is the part of the earth's crust that lies below sea level. Have you ever wondered what the ocean floors look like? You may be surprised to learn that the ocean floor has many different features.

Maps of the earth's land areas are the most common kinds of maps. Less common are maps of the ocean floor. Until about 60 years ago, it was thought that the ocean floor was a nearly flat plain. Scientists have discovered, however, that the different parts of the ocean's floor are extremely varied.

Ocean Floor Features

The surface of the ocean floor is just as varied as the surface of the earth above sea level. Mountain ranges, basins, plains, ridges, canyons, and valleys are all found there. You can see such features in the special photograph below. Called a Seasat photograph, it shows the roughness of the ocean floor.

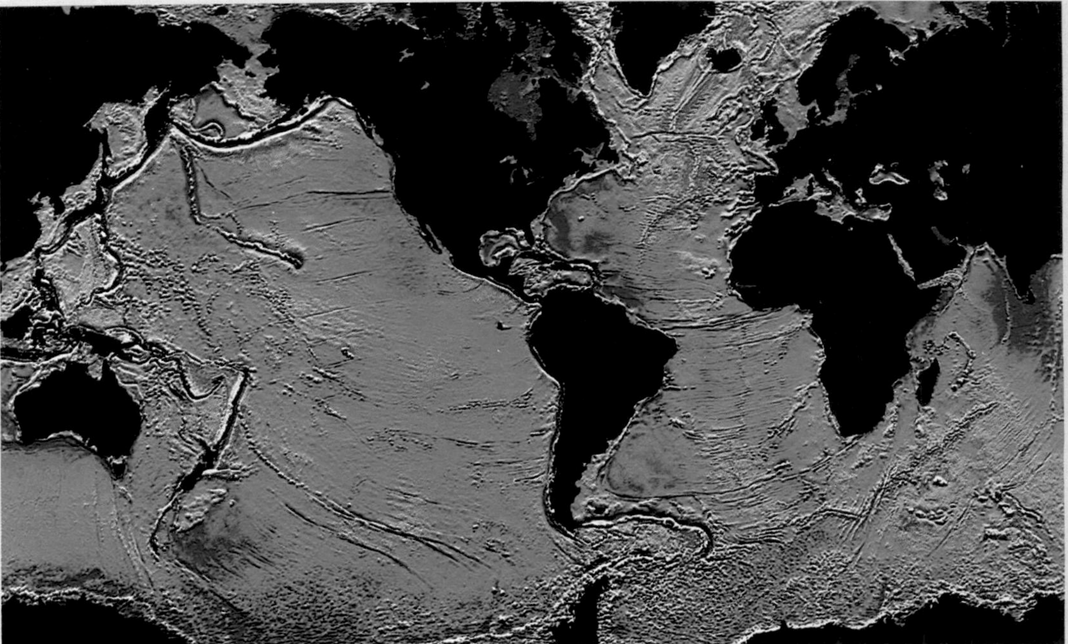

BACKGROUND INFORMATION

More About the Ocean Floor

- Running west from North America, down the Asian coast, and across and down near Australia is the world's longest trench. It forms the northern and western border of the Pacific Plate. Different areas of this trench have their own names—for example, the Aleutian Trench, the New Guinea Trench, and the Tonga Trench. One area, the Mariana Trench, is believed to be the deepest on earth, at 38,000 feet (11,515 m). This makes it deeper than Mount Everest is tall.
- The ridge that appears so clearly in the North Atlantic actually runs all the way south through the South Atlantic and is called the Mid-Atlantic Ridge. It marks the meeting of the American Plate on the west with the Eurasian and African plates on the east.

RESOURCE *Reminder*
Practice Book: *Using Maps of the Ocean Floor*, page 160
Outline Map: *The World*
Transparency Map: 15

Using Seasat photographs, such as the one on page 588, scientists have been able to make more accurate maps of the ocean floor. The photograph was taken by a satellite in space. If you look closely you can see the deep trenches, or valleys, of the ocean floor. Trenches are the deepest parts of the ocean floor. Look at the photograph and find the trenches that run in the Pacific Ocean near Asia and Australia. You can also see the many ranges of hills that lie across the ocean floor in the Pacific region and other parts of the world.

Contour Maps

Elevation and features of the ocean floor are shown by contour maps. As you read in Chapter 7, contour maps outline landforms with lines or different colors showing different elevations. You may recall that these lines are called contour lines. A contour line on a map connects areas of the same elevation.

As you may recall, contour lines that are drawn close together mean that the land is very steep. Contour lines show height both above sea level and below sea level on land maps. On sea maps contour lines show height only below sea level. As shown on **Diagram A** on this page, the measurement of the depth below sea level in meters or feet is preceded by a minus sign (−).

Map A and **Map B** also show Fin Island. Note that both maps are contour maps. What is the difference between **Map A** and **Map B**? As you can see, the contour lines shown on **Map A** show land above sea level. The contour lines shown on **Map B** show land below sea level. What is the contour interval on these maps? You may recall that contour intervals are the differences in elevation between the contour lines. As shown on both of the maps, the contour interval is 20 meters.

FIN ISLAND: Contour Lines

DIAGRAM A

Fin Island
60'
40'
20'
0' (Sea Level)
-20'
-40'
-60'
-80'

MAP A

Fin Island
X
60'
40'
20'
0' (Sea Level)

MAP B

Y
Fin Island
0' (Sea Level)
-20'
-40'
-60'
-80'

Reviewing the Skill

1. What is one difference between a physical map and a contour map?
2. Compare a contour line and a contour interval.
3. Look at the Seasat photograph and name the deepest parts of the Pacific.
4. If you wished to have a picnic and to take a swim, and then an easy climb to the highest point on Fin Island, which map would you use to choose the best site? Explain the reason for your choice.
5. On maps **A** and **B**, what is the difference in elevation between points **X** and **Y**?
6. How do maps of the ocean floor help you to better understand the earth's surface?

589

Discussing Contour Maps Review the *Building Skills: Reading Contour Maps* on pages 360–361.

Ask students:

- **What does a contour line show?** (It shows the elevation of an area.)
- **What three levels of elevation does Diagram A show?** (height above sea level, sea level, and depth below sea level)
- **How is elevation shown on Diagram A?** (Height above sea level is shown in feet, depth below sea level is shown with a minus sign, and sea level is shown with a zero.)

Applying the Lesson Have students brainstorm the uses of an ocean floor map.

3 CLOSE

Summarizing Students have learned that the surface of the ocean floor resembles land surfaces. Ask them to explain how modern technology has helped us to learn about the ocean floor.

Answers to Reviewing the Skill

1. A physical map uses colors and shading and a contour map uses contour lines.
2. A contour line connects points of equal elevation and a contour interval shows the difference in elevation between adjacent contour lines.
3. the trenches
4. For a picnic and a climb, Map A shows a wide beach along the western shore and a gentle slope along the southeastern shore; for swimming, Map B shows water of equal depth on all sides of the island.
5. 60 feet, from 40 feet on X to −20 feet on Y
6. They enable us to see how varied the ocean floor is and how similar the earth's surface is above and below water.

Independent Practice

Practice Book: page 160

MEETING INDIVIDUAL NEEDS

Reteaching (easy) Have students draw a contour map showing an underwater mountain that rises 10,000 feet from the ocean floor to sea level and 2,000 feet above sea level.

Extension (average) The tectonic activity of the earth's plates has great influence in creating surface contours. Have students do research on plate tectonics. Then on an outline map of the world found in the Teacher's Resource Center, have them outline the earth's major plates.

Enrichment (challenging) Divide the class into six groups and assign each group one of the following types of tectonic activity—spreading, subduction, collision, faulting, accretion, and hot spots. Have each group research its subject and prepare a presentation to the class, using illustrations to show how tectonic activity affects the surface of the ocean floor.

LESSON 2
pages 590–593

Lesson Theme Spread out over a vast region, Australia and Oceania vary greatly in climate and resources.

Lesson Objectives
- Describe the climates of Australia and Oceania.
- Identify the variety of natural resources across the region.

PREPARE

Motivate As you read the *Read Aloud* quotation, have students close their eyes and picture the contrasting scenes. Ask them to think about how different life might be in each of these scenes.

Set Purpose Use the *What You Know* question to help students review how good climate contributes to comfort, abundant crops, and attracting tourists. Use the *What You Will Learn* question to help students to focus on how good climate and other resources encourage development and how the lack of such resources can impede development.

TEACH

Discussing Climate Have students locate Australia on a globe. Next ask them to move their fingers up from Australia and across the equator to their own area, to emphasize the term *down under* and the concept of reversal of seasons.

LESSON 2

Climate and Resources

READ TO LEARN

Key Vocabulary	**Key Places**
typhoon	Queensland
copra	Papua New Guinea
	Samoa

Read Aloud

Like much of the rest of Australia, the place suffers from earth-cracking droughts, blistering heat, surging brown floods and explosive brushfires. Such land forms its people—and draws them together.

This is the way that one writer described part of Queensland, Australia. Most places in the Pacific region have a wet climate, but Australia often bakes under cloudless skies. For instance, the city of Sydney has about 340 days of sunshine a year. By contrast rain falls year-round on the green islands of the rest of Oceania.

Read for Purpose

1. **WHAT YOU KNOW:** Why can a good climate be considered a resource?
2. **WHAT YOU WILL LEARN:** How do the climate and natural resources of the Pacific affect the way of life of the people of the region?

CLIMATE "DOWN UNDER"

If you were lucky enough to vacation in New Zealand or Australia, you'd find that the seasons are the reverse of what you are used to. In the lands of the Southern Hemisphere, "down under" the equator, winter starts in June. Summer runs from December to February.

Climates within Australia also are different from what you might expect. **Queensland**, on the north coast, is hotter and drier than places on the south coast. This is because Queensland is located nearer the equator.

CLIMATE IN OCEANIA

In Chapter 8 you read that lands near large bodies of water have milder climates than do lands far from water. Oceans affect the climate. In lands near large bodies of water, temperatures don't rise or fall as much because water absorbs and holds both heat and cold. Oceans make winters warmer and summers cooler.

The climate of New Zealand and the other islands of Oceania is greatly affected by both the Pacific Ocean and by wind currents. For example, Samoa is in the tropics, yet it is much cooler than land at the same latitude in Africa. Moist ocean breezes cool the Pacific islands.

Usually islanders welcome the ocean breezes. Yet some ocean winds are dangerous. Powerful windstorms called **typhoons** strike this region two or three times a year. Typhoons are whirling tropical hurri-

 WHAT YOU KNOW: Students should be aware that tourists like to visit places with good climates, so climate can be a strong economic resource.

READING STRATEGY AND VOCABULARY DEVELOPMENT

Comprehension Monitoring Duplicate sections of the lesson and pass them out to the class. Have students read the sections and place check marks where they have questions or where they think of something they already know about the topic. After they have read the complete lesson, have them compare the places they checked. Point out to the class that everyone monitors a reading selection differently, depending upon each person's knowledge and experience.

RESOURCE *Reminder*

Practice Book: *Products of Australia and the Pacific Islands*, page 161

Anthology: *The Road From Coorain*, pages 198–199

Technology: *Adventures CD-ROM* See page 581-B.

canes. In a typhoon very high winds churn around a center of low air pressure.

THE "LUCKY COUNTRY"

Australia has been called the "Lucky Country." It is an uncrowded land with abundant natural resources.

As you have read, the outback is one of the least settled areas of Australia. Ranchers in the outback graze livestock on vast landholdings. They need about 40 acres (16 ha) of land to graze one head of sheep because the land is so dry that little vegetation grows. Peter Cannon says that the 600,000-acre (243,000-ha) ranch he manages in the outback is not large—the one "next door" is nearly 2 million acres (800,000 ha)! It's no wonder some Australian ranches, which are called stations, make Texas ranches seem small.

Land for ranching is by no means Australia's only natural resource. Look at the land use map on page 592. It shows that mining is a major industry in Australia. People who want to earn money in mining must leave the coastal areas and head inland. Drilling for oil and mining Australia's bauxite, diamonds, iron, copper, lead, silver, and zinc are all done on the country's inland deserts.

In addition to these minerals, Australia has many other natural resources. Although there are few rivers that can be used to create electric power, Australia has many other energy sources. There is abundant coal, oil, and natural gas. Australia also has large amounts of uranium, which is used in creating nuclear power.

GREEN AND BOUNTIFUL NEW ZEALAND

Water is a major resource for New Zealand. The country gets plenty of rain, and there is abundant water for electric power. The high rainfall in New Zealand also encourages the growth of forests. About one fourth of the country is covered with large forests.

New Zealand has both good soil and a variety of climates. Farmers can grow fruits that need cooler climates, like apples. They can also raise fruits that need subtropical warmth. The cool highlands of New Zealand that you see on the map above are perfect for sheep raising.

THE TROPICAL ISLANDS

In the islands of Oceania near the equator, it would not be possible to raise sheep.

AUSTRALIA AND NEW ZEALAND: Climate

- Warm and wet all year
- Mild or warm winter, hot summer, wet
- Warm all year, wet with one dry season
- Mild winter, cool summer, wet
- Mild, wet winter; hot, dry summer
- Semi-dry, temperature varies with latitude
- Dry, temperature varies with latitude
- Highlands, temperature and precipitation vary with elevation

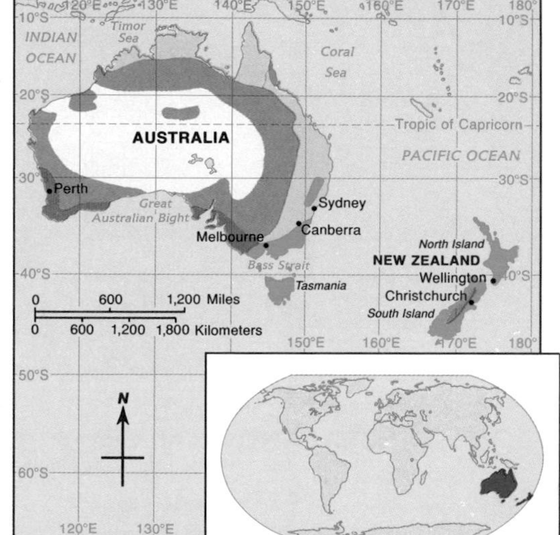

MAP SKILL: How does the climate on the eastern coast of Australia differ from the climate in the interior of the country?

MAP SKILL: eastern coast—"mild or warm winter, hot summer, wet"; interior—"dry, temperature varies"

591

Understanding the Climate of Oceania

Ask students:

- **What affects the climate of New Zealand?** (the Pacific Ocean and wind currents)
- **Why does Australia's interior have harsher climates than Oceania?** (It does not benefit from the tempering effects of having the ocean nearby, as islands do.)

EXTENDING MAP SKILLS

Refer the class to the climate map on this page.

Ask students:

- **Where in Australia is the climate the driest?** (in the interior)
- **Where in Australia and New Zealand is farming likely to be best? Why?** (along Australia's east coast and through much of New Zealand because of mild and moist climates)

Talking About the "Lucky Country" Help students to see how resources create jobs and wealth.

Ask students:

- **Why is Australia's outback a resource?** (Because it is so vast, it can be used for ranching.)
- **Which other industries do natural resources support in Australia?** (the petroleum, metal, diamond, and energy-production industries)

Exploring New Zealand

Ask students:

- **How does the climate enrich New Zealand with resources?** (Plenty of rainfall feeds the rivers, which can be harnessed to generate electricity, and contributes to the growth of forests and to good agriculture.)

Looking at the Tropical Islands Discuss the relationship between the term *tropical* and nearness to the equator.

BACKGROUND INFORMATION

Multicultural Perspectives In the 1500s Portuguese and Spanish sailors became the first Europeans to explore present-day Australia. On European maps the continent was soon labeled "Terra Australis Incognita," which means "Unknown Southern Land" in Latin. At the time, however, there were as many as 300,000 people living on the "unknown" land. Aborigines had their own names for the diverse geographic features of their land. For example, they called a distinctive bluff overlooking a harbor "Boree," which means "enduring one." Later on, English settlers named that harbor "Sydney Harbor," after a lord in England. Ask students how names can reflect people's values and their relation to others around them.

Discussing the Tropical Islands Discuss why the beauty of the islands is a resource.

EXTENDING MAP SKILLS

Refer students to the map on this page.

Ask students:

- **Where is the major manufacturing carried on?** (in the cities along Australia's southeastern coast)
- **What are the major land uses in New Zealand?** (forestry and livestock raising)
- **Where does livestock raising predominate?** (in the Australian outback)

Discussing Island Resources

Ask students:

- **Which other industries can some of these islands support? Why?** (Those with mineral resources can support mining; those with rich soil from lava can support forestry and agriculture.)
- **What sometimes stands in the way of the development of island resources?** (rugged terrain and very thick rain forests)

Discovering the Tree of Life Help students to understand the traditional importance of the coconut tree to island life.

Ask students:

- **How many different uses can you name for the coconut tree?** (food, drink, wood for building, fronds for thatching and weaving, copra for export)
- *THINKING FURTHER:* **How is the coconut tree of Oceania like the buffalo of the American plains long ago?** (Help students to understand that each provides or provided for many basic needs of a people—the coconut tree for the Pacific islanders and the buffalo for the Plains Indians of the past.)

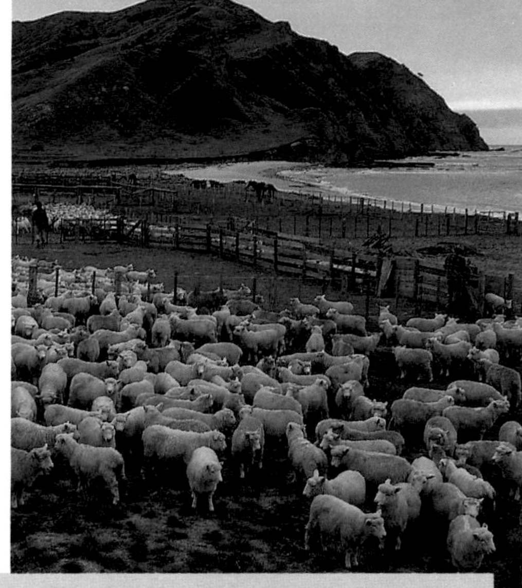

MAP SKILL: Sheep are raised in many parts of Australia and New Zealand. According to the map, what is the most common economic activity in these two countries?

AUSTRALIA AND NEW ZEALAND: Land Use

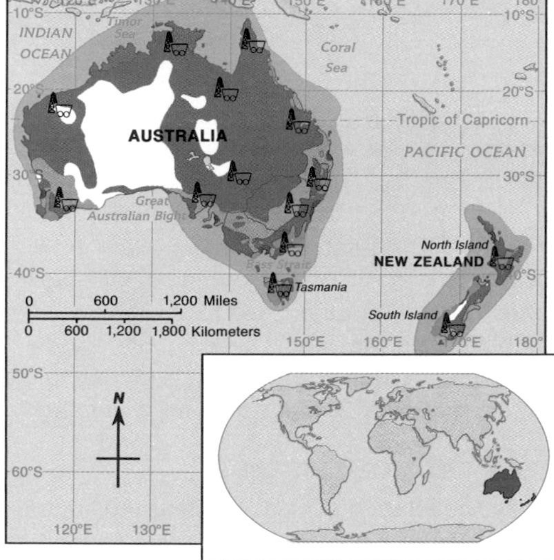

592 MAP SKILL: Livestock raising

Sheep could not survive the hot monsoon climate of places like Papua New Guinea.

There are thousands of islands in Oceania, and no two are exactly alike. Some have few natural resources. Other larger island countries, like Papua New Guinea, have some mineral resources. Yet the beauty of the islands is itself a resource, for it draws many tourists. Many years ago one visitor to the island of Samoa wrote home:

> *There's only one thing on earth as beautiful, and that's Samoa by moonlight. . . . You lie on a mat in a cool Samoan hut, and look on the white sand under the high palms and a gentle sea, and the black line of the reef a mile out, and the moonlight over everything, floods and floods of it. . . .*

OTHER ISLAND RESOURCES

As you have read, volcanoes are active on some of the Pacific islands. Though volcanoes are dangerous when they erupt, they yield a valuable resource. Volcanic ash and lava wear down into rich soil. The volcanic islands are the most fertile of Oceania. Many of them are covered with dense rain forests.

Island countries such as Papua New Guinea also have many more mineral resources than the smaller coral islands. Papua New Guinea has the most varied resources of any of the Pacific islands. It has deposits of copper, gold, and silver, as well as good farmland. Yet the land is so rugged that most resources have not yet been developed.

THE TREE OF LIFE

You have read that the sandy coral soil of many of the Pacific Islands is not good for farming. But one plant that will grow in this soil is the coconut palm tree. People in the island countries of the Pacific call it the "Tree of Life."

5 FUNDAMENTAL THEMES OF GEOGRAPHY

Place In the Pacific region harsh and lush environments can occur at the same latitude. For example, as 24°S runs across the globe, it crosses both the Gibson Desert of west central Australia and Pitcairn Island of Polynesia. Yet two more different geographies can hardly be imagined. The hot sun beats down unrelentingly on the trackless surface of small stones and pebbles on the Gibson Desert. Here, less than 5 inches (12.7 cm) of rain falls all year. No air stirs because this desert lies outside the path of the general wind direction, and temperatures routinely reach 130°F. (54°C) in summer. On the other hand, Pitcairn is a tropical paradise, recognized as such by the infamous mutineers of *H.M.S. Bounty*, who made it their permanent home. There they could luxuriate in its mild temperatures, ranging from 75°F. (24°C) in summer to 66°F. (19°C) in winter. Fertile soil is abundant and 80 inches (203 cm) of rain falls annually, so tropical fruits and roots grow readily.

Islanders use the "meat" inside the coconut to flavor fish and to make cakes and puddings. People who live on tiny coral islands that do not have rivers often drink the milk inside the coconut instead of water.

The hardwood trunks of the coconut palms are used for the beams of houses and the masts of boats. The fronds, or leaves, of the palm trees are used to thatch roofs. They are also woven into mats, baskets, and hats.

Today an important coconut product for export is copra, the dried meat of a coconut. Crushed copra yields an oil used in the making of margarine, soap, shampoo, cosmetics, and other products.

PACIFIC CLIMATES AND RESOURCES

You have read that since the Pacific region is in the Southern Hemisphere, the seasons are reversed from the way they are in our part of the world. Most of the region is tropical or semitropical, with plenty of rain year-round. Australia, however, is mostly dry, except on its coastal rim.

Natural resources are unevenly spread in the region. Australia has abundant minerals, including major energy sources. New Zealand has excellent agricultural resources, as well as a variety of climates. Most islands of Oceania have limited natural resources.

Check Your Reading

1. How does the Pacific Ocean affect the climate of Oceania?
2. What are the important mineral resources of Australia?
3. How do the region's climate and natural resources affect how people live?
4. **THINKING SKILL:** What conclusion can you draw from the quote on page 592?

THINKING SKILL: Drawing Conclusions

CITIZENSHIP MAKING A DIFFERENCE

In 1979 John Seed was living on a farm in New South Wales, Australia, when he learned that the nearby rain forest was going to be cut down by loggers. At one time forests had nearly covered the Australian continent. Now only a small percentage of the forested acres remained.

John decided to do something about the planned logging. First he met with state and national politicians. Then he organized people in his community by writing petitions and demonstrating at the logging sites. The protest grew in size and strength until finally the state government stopped the logging.

Since then John has taken his campaign to the national level. Because of his efforts, preservation of the rain forests in Tasmania and Queensland were important issues in the national elections of 1983 and 1987. The people of Australia voted into office a prime minister who supported conservation of the rain forests. In 1987 the federal government announced that more than 2 million acres (809,400 ha) of rain forest would be permanently protected.

Today John travels all over the world, helping people to understand the role of the rain forests in maintaining the future of our planet.

593

Applying the Lesson Have students identify the major industries of Australia and Oceania and compare them to the industries in their own area.

3 CLOSE

Summarizing Students have learned that climate and resources vary widely both within Australia and among the islands of Oceania—from very dry to very wet and from rich in resources to limited in resources. Have students write a paragraph in which they contrast the Australian outback with Papua New Guinea.

Evaluating Use these questions to assess students' understanding.

- **What affects the climate of the islands of Oceania?** (the Pacific Ocean and wind currents)
- **How can an island of great beauty compete economically with an island with mineral resources?** (The beauty can attract tourism.)

Answers to Check Your Reading

1. It tempers it, making winters warmer and summers cooler.
2. oil, bauxite, diamonds, iron, copper, lead, silver, zinc
3. They help to determine how people make a living and the types of products they export.
4. Students will probably conclude that Samoa is a tropical paradise, open to sky and sea.

Independent Practice
Practice Book: page 161

MEETING INDIVIDUAL NEEDS

Reteaching (easy) Have students make a chart titled, "Australia—the Lucky Country" in which they list and illustrate resources that make Australia lucky.

Extension (average) Have students do research about the coconut. Have them make a chart listing all the products that come from the coconut palm tree.

Enrichment (challenging) Divide the class into six groups and assign each group one of the following: Nauru or Republic of the Marshall Islands in Micronesia, Fiji or Vanuatu in Melanesia, and Western Samoa or Tonga in Polynesia. Have students do research to prepare maps of their locales.

BUILDING CITIZENSHIP

Conserving the Rain Forests Begin by reviewing with students what they know about the Amazon rain forest and about its conservation. Students may be surprised to learn that there are rain forests in Australia. Discuss why some people believe rain forests should be saved. Divide the class into two groups to debate the issue of conservation. Ask what things could be done to conserve the rain forests. Encourage students to identify preservation efforts in their area that they might support.

CHAPTER 29 REVIEW

pages 594–595

USING THE CHAPTER SUMMARY AND REVIEW

Physical Geography These questions may be used for review.

- **What are the three main island groups of Oceania?** (Polynesia, Micronesia, Melanesia)
- **What effect does the ocean have on climates in this region?** (The ocean moderates climate.)
- **What are the natural resources of Australia? Of New Zealand?** (abundant land, bauxite, iron, silver, coal, oil, natural gas, uranium; water, forests, good soil)

Ideas to Remember

- **Which two continents are in the Pacific region?** (Australia and Antarctica)
- **What is the dominant climate in the region?** (tropical)

Answers to Reviewing Vocabulary

1. typhoon
2. outback
3. atoll
4. copra
5. iceberg

CHAPTER 29 • SUMMARY

THE PACIFIC: PHYSICAL GEOGRAPHY

LANDFORMS

- Continents: Australia (world's smallest) and Antarctica
- Islands of Oceania: New Zealand; thousands of small islands
- Australia has three main areas: Western Plateau, Central Plains (or Central Eastern Lowlands); Eastern Highlands

- Island groups of Oceania: Polynesia, Micronesia, Melanesia
- Antarctica: huge frozen continent

CLIMATE

- Australia mostly dry; others get plenty of rain
- Ocean moderates climates

- Typhoons: tropical hurricanes that strike 2-3 times a year

NATURAL RESOURCES

- Australia: abundant land for ranching; minerals such as bauxite, iron, silver, coal, oil, natural gas, uranium
- New Zealand: water, forests, good soil

- Tropical islands: natural beauty
- Coconut: the "Tree of Life" for island countries

IDEAS TO REMEMBER

- The Pacific region is made up of numerous islands and two continents—Australia and Antarctica.
- Most of the islands of the Pacific have tropical climates and limited resources; Australia and New Zealand are exceptions.

594

ENRICHMENT ACTIVITY

Creating Crossword and Hidden-word Puzzles **Materials:** paper, rulers, pencils, pens

1. Review with the class a variety of examples of both crossword and hidden-word puzzles—their formats, the type of information they contain, and the tasks that the solver must accomplish. Tell students that they are going to construct their own crossword and hidden-word puzzles, using terms that are related to the physical and cultural geography of the Pacific region. (Assure those students who do not feel comfortable with word puzzles that they will receive help from their classmates and that a quick review of the chapter will help them to construct and solve the puzzles.)
2. Divide the class into six groups. Tell three groups to create crossword puzzles and the other three to create hidden-word puzzles. Encourage them to review the chapter for subject matter to include, paying particular attention to vocabulary terms and place names. Then have them draw up their puzzles, following the examples they have reviewed. Tell students to use at least ten terms.
3. Pair each crossword group with a hidden-word group and tell them to exchange puzzles. How quickly can each group solve the other's puzzle? (Remember, though, that the hidden-word puzzles will probably take longer to solve because they call for more tasks.)

CHAPTER 29 • REVIEW

REVIEWING VOCABULARY

atoll
copra
iceberg
outback
typhoon

Number a sheet of paper from 1 to 5. Beside each number write the word or term from the above list that best matches the definition.

1. Whirling tropical storms that strike the region of Oceania several times each year
2. The vast, dry interior region of Australia in which few people live
3. Coral islands that encircle a small, warm body of water
4. Dried meat of the coconut used for export
5. Floating "islands of ice" that often form when ice packs break up

REVIEWING FACTS

1. What is the general name for the islands of the Pacific Ocean? What are the names of the two largest landmasses in this region?
2. What are the names of Australia's three main regions? Where are most of Australia's large cities located?
3. What is the Great Barrier Reef? How did the reef form?
4. What are the two main types of islands in Oceania? Which of these has the most fertile soil?
5. Which American state is part of Polynesia?
6. What are the names of the two main islands of New Zealand? What is the name of the mountain range on the southern island?
7. Why is the northern coast of Australia hotter and drier than the southern coast?
8. What are the two most important industries of the Australian outback?
9. Name the economic benefits that New Zealand enjoys because of its abundant water resources and cool climate.
10. Why is the coconut palm tree called the "tree of life" in Oceania?

WRITING ABOUT MAIN IDEAS

1. **Writing a Travel Brochure:** Write a travel brochure describing places to visit in Australia's outback, such as the great stations or the red rock outcroppings.
2. **Writing a Survival Manual:** Write a survival manual for people who are shipwrecked on a small, deserted island in the Pacific.
3. **Writing About Perspectives:** Imagine that you have just completed a long stay in New Zealand and have visited many towns and scenic places. Write a paragraph of your observations describing New Zealand's land and people.

BUILDING SKILLS: READING MAPS OF THE OCEAN FLOOR

1. Compare the surface of the ocean floor with the surface of the earth above sea level.
2. Name one kind of map used to show the surface of the ocean floor.
3. How do contour maps of the ocean floor differ from contour maps of land above sea level?
4. Who might find maps of the ocean floor useful?

595

Answers to Reviewing Facts

1. Oceania; Australia and Antarctica
2. Western Plateau, Central Plains, Eastern Highlands; on the east coast
3. a ridge of rocks near the surface of the sea just off the northeast coast of Australia; As polyps die, coral reefs are built up from their skeletons; the reefs continue to grow as living polyps attach themselves to the skeletons.
4. atolls, tops of mountains or volcanoes; volcanoes
5. Hawaii
6. North Island and South Island; the Southern Alps
7. It is closer to the equator.
8. ranching and mining
9. large forests, good farming, sheep raising
10. It is used to meet many basic needs—food, housing, clothing. It is also used for making soap, shampoo, margarine, and other products.

Suggestions for Writing About Main Ideas

1. Students' brochures should describe the land and the climate. You may want to have students collect pictures for their brochures.
2. Before students begin their manuals, suggest that they first list the things they would need to survive.
3. Have volunteers read their observations aloud.

Answers to Building Skills: Reading Maps of the Ocean Floor

1. Students should note the varied surfaces found both above and below sea level.
2. contour
3. One shows land above sea level, and the other shows land below sea level.
4. Possible answers include: oceanographers, divers, salvage crews, geologists.

Chapter Review and Test

Practice Book: *Vocabulary Review, page 162*
Transparency: *Graphic Organizer*
Assessment Book: *Chapter 29 Test*

MAKING CONNECTIONS

Comparing and Contrasting Display the Matrix Chart Graphic Organizer Transparency, filling in only the underlined copy. Have students use the information in their texts to fill in the geographic features of the Pacific region. *Ask:* How does Australia differ from Oceania? Have students use the completed chart to draw a conclusion about the physical geography of the Pacific.

	Physical Features	Climate	Natural Resources
Australia	lowlands, Great Barrier Reef, outback	hot, dry	land for ranching, minerals, energy sources
Oceania	atolls, mountains	moderate, wet, typhoons	volcanic soil, natural beauty
New Zealand	mountains, glaciers	cool highland, sub-tropical	agricultural resources
Conclusion: The region has a variety of landscapes, climates, and resources.			

CHAPTER 30
ORGANIZER

NATIONS OF THE PACIFIC text pages 596–613

CHAPTER THEME Ancient traditions are mixed with new ones in the varied governments, economies, and lifestyles of the Pacific nations.

CHAPTER OBJECTIVES

CONTENT

- Identify the first groups of people to live in the lands of the Pacific.
- Define *clan* and describe the importance of clans to the people of Melanesia.
- Describe how Australia was first settled by Europeans.
- Describe the economic challenges faced today by the people of the Pacific.
- Explain why Australia has a high standard of living.
- Contrast the economies of the Pacific islands with the economy of Australia.
- Describe how traditional values and customs are reflected in the governments of many Pacific islands.
- Describe how Australia combines Great Britain's parliamentary system with the federal system of the United States.
- Explain how the Maoris are represented in New Zealand's parliamentary system.
- Describe how the people of the Pacific blend traditional and modern forms of art.

SKILLS

Geography
- Interpret a political map of the Pacific.

Thinking
- Draw conclusions about how people of the Pacific islands lived before the arrival of Europeans.
- Compare and contrast the governments of Great Britain and Australia.

Reading and Writing
- Write about the varied perspectives of different Pacific peoples.

CITIZENSHIP VALUES

- Appreciate the importance of finding ways for traditional and modern cultures to live together peacefully.

TEACHER OPTIONS

READING STRATEGY: Mapping Strategies to help students read and remember the main ideas of the lesson.

Lesson 1: p. 597 Lesson 4: p. 606
Lesson 2: p. 600 Legacy: p. 608
Lesson 3: p. 603

MEETING INDIVIDUAL NEEDS Activities for reteaching, extension, and enrichment.

Lesson 1: p. 599 Lesson 4: p. 607
Lesson 2: p. 601 Legacy: p. 611
Lesson 3: p. 605

GEO ADVENTURES ACTIVITIES PAD Daily activities to assess students' understanding of geography skills.

CURRICULUM CONNECTION Activities to help integrate other subject areas with Social Studies.

Art: p. 598

PUPIL EDITION ON CASSETTE Language support for students who have difficulty reading or who will benefit from listening to the Pupil Edition on Cassette as they read.

SECOND-LANGUAGE SUPPORT Activities and suggestions for second-language learners.

Lesson 2: p. 577-D

CHAPTER PLANNING GUIDE

LESSON	SUGGESTED PACING	THEMES	TEACHER SUPPORT MATERIALS: TEACHER'S RESOURCE CENTER
1 THE PEOPLE pages 597–599	1 day	The first wave of people to live in Australia and Oceania probably came from Asia; the second came from Europe.	Practice Book p. 163 ■ Anthology pp. 194–195, 196–197, 200–201 Outline Map p. 38 Desk Maps
2 THE ECONOMY pages 600–601	1 day	Economies in the Pacific region range from highly developed in Australia to somewhat less developed in New Zealand to traditional in the remaining islands of the region.	Practice Book p. 164 Outline Map p. 38 **Technology:** *Adventures CD-ROM*
BUILDING THINKING SKILLS Decision Making: Review page 602	1 day	Decision making means choosing from among many options to attain a goal.	Practice Book p. 165
3 THE GOVERNMENT pages 603–605	1 day	The governments of the Pacific region generally follow principles of Western democracy, which are combined with traditional values on some of the islands.	Practice Book p. 166 ■ Anthology pp. 202–203
4 ARTS AND RECREATION pages 606–607	1 day	Traditional and modern arts, as well as sports, thrive in the Pacific region.	Practice Book p. 167 **Technology:** *Adventures CD-ROM*
LEGACY Aborigine Painting pages 608–611	1 day	The traditional way of life of Australia's Aborigines has changed greatly.	■ Anthology pp. 194–195, 196–197
CHAPTER SUMMARY AND REVIEW pages 612–613	1 day	Chapter content, skills, and vocabulary are reviewed and evaluated.	Practice Book p. 168 Transparency: Graphic Organizer Assessment Book, Chapter 30 Test

Technology CONNECTION

Lesson 2

ADVENTURES CD-ROM

Enrich Lesson 2 by having students assemble their own presentations on Australia or New Zealand in *Create.*

Lesson 4

ADVENTURES CD-ROM

Enrich Lesson 4 by having students *Investigate Sounds, New Zealand.*

CHAPTER 30
pages 596–613

USING THE CHAPTER OPENER

Discussing the Photograph Encourage the class to study the details of the picture and to read the chapter title.

Ask students:

- **In which nation of the Pacific would you guess this photograph was taken?** (New Zealand, judging from the name on the shirt)
- **How would you describe the young man in the picture?** (happy, friendly, enjoying what he is doing)
- **What is the young man riding?** (a motorcycle)

Encourage the class to speculate on what he might be doing besides riding a motorcycle.

Reading/Listening to the Primary Source Have a student read the passage to the rest of the class.

Ask students:

- **How well do you think this quote fits the picture?** (Students will probably think the quote describes the picture accurately.)
- **What is the "great outdoors" shown here?** (The sheep seem to indicate that it is a sheep ranch.)
- *THINKING FURTHER:* **Why might working on a ranch encourage friendliness and treating others as equals?** (Help the class to recognize that hard work like that required on a sheep ranch calls for cooperation. When people work cooperatively, they learn to like and respect each other.)

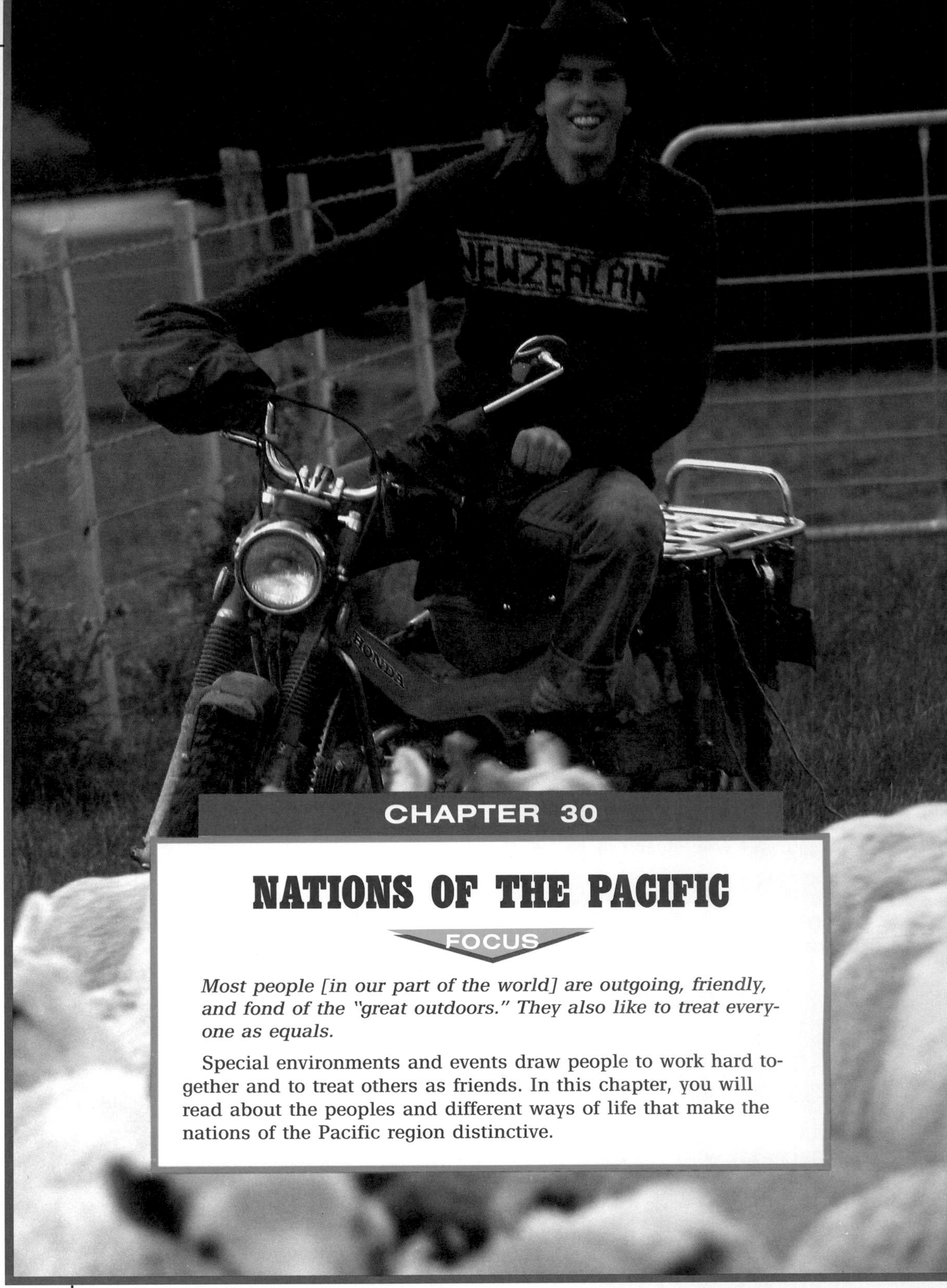

CHAPTER 30

NATIONS OF THE PACIFIC

FOCUS

Most people [in our part of the world] are outgoing, friendly, and fond of the "great outdoors." They also like to treat everyone as equals.

Special environments and events draw people to work hard together and to treat others as friends. In this chapter, you will read about the peoples and different ways of life that make the nations of the Pacific region distinctive.

BACKGROUND INFORMATION

About the Photograph

- The young man is "sheep mustering," or sheep herding, on a station at Hastings, on New Zealand's North Island.
- Motorcycles have replaced horses on most of the ranches in New Zealand and Australia because of the enormous size of the sheep stations—4,000 acres (1,619 ha) is common.
- The motorcycles have many advantages over horses—they can cover more ground more quickly, they don't get tired, and many of the station hands (mostly young men) prefer riding them to riding horses.

Multicultural Perspectives Although the islands of the Pacific region are not large, geographically speaking, the people who live on them have great pride in their island homes. Women on Rongelap Island sing this song to visitors:

Now you're here on Rongelap you'll find it the best place
Rongelap is in the Marshall Islands, though the waves try to wash it away
I'll praise you to the heavens, Rongelap
For there is no place like you
You're my land, my home sweet home.

Ask students what songs they sing to express pride in their nation or community.

LESSON 1

The People

READ TO LEARN

Key Places

Tahiti

Read Aloud

I felt as though I had been transported to the Garden of Eden. Everywhere we found hospitality, peace . . . and every appearance of happiness. What a country! What a people!

The French navigator Louis-Antoine de Bougainville wrote this glowing description after seeing the island of Tahiti for the first time. Yet his words could have been written about any of the Pacific islands. In this lesson you will read about the groups of people who live in this "Garden of Eden."

Read for Purpose

1. WHAT YOU KNOW: What is the name for the thousands of islands that dot the Pacific Ocean?
2. WHAT YOU WILL LEARN: Who were the first groups of people to live in the lands of the Pacific?

AUSTRALIA'S ABORIGINES

The first settlers of the Pacific region came in several groups over a long period of time.

Historians believe that the earliest known Australians came from Asia more than 50,000 years ago. English explorers called these people *aborigines* (ab ə rij′ ə nēz), which means "the first people to live in a place." The aborigines call themselves the *Koori* (kü′ rē). This name comes from one of their words for human.

For thousands of years the aborigines survived by hunting, fishing, and gathering wild seeds, nuts, and fruits. They made tools of stone, wood, or shell.

When the first Europeans arrived in Australia in 1788, there were about 300,000 aborigines living there. Many were attacked and killed by the European explorers. Others died from diseases that came to the continent with the newcomers.

In spite of the hardships, however, the aborigine culture survived. Today some aborigines live in Australia's busy cities. Others choose to live in the outback, trying to continue the ways of their ancestors.

MELANESIANS AND MICRONESIANS

After the aborigines, another wave of settlers sailed across the Pacific and landed on the islands of Melanesia. You can see from the map on page 598 that Melanesia is located north and east of Australia. The rugged land in most of this area separated groups of Melanesians

WHAT YOU KNOW: This question refers to material in Chapter 29, Lesson 1; Oceania

LESSON 1
pages 597–599

Lesson Theme The first wave of people to live in Australia and Oceania probably came from Asia; the second came from Europe.

Lesson Objectives

- Identify the Aborigines, Melanesians, Micronesians, and Polynesians and describe their ways of life.
- Describe the European immigrants to the South Pacific.

1 PREPARE

Motivate Have a volunteer read the *Read Aloud* quotation. Ask the class to describe what Bougainville must have seen, based on what they learned in Chapter 29.

Set Purpose Have students answer the *What You Know* question. Ask them to tell who the first people to live in our country were. Then use the *What You Will Learn* question to alert students to look for parallels in the settling of the Pacific.

2 TEACH

Investigating Australia's Aborigines

Ask students:

- **How did life change for the Aborigines when the Europeans arrived?** (Their lives became harder than before; some were killed by the Europeans; some died from diseases brought by the Europeans.)

READING STRATEGY AND VOCABULARY DEVELOPMENT

Mapping The purpose of this strategy is to help students understand that techniques of mapping, or using graphic organizers, are good ways to remind ourselves of important information. Go over such mapping techniques as outlining, semantic maps, time lines, and charts. Tell students that in this lesson they will read about five groups of people who first settled the Pacific region. Have students design a simple chart in which they identify and describe these people. For example, students might make two columns. The first column would have the heading "Name of Group" and would list the names of the five different groups of people who settled the Pacific region; the second column would have the heading "Important Facts" and would list an important fact about each group. Direct students to fill in the chart as they read.

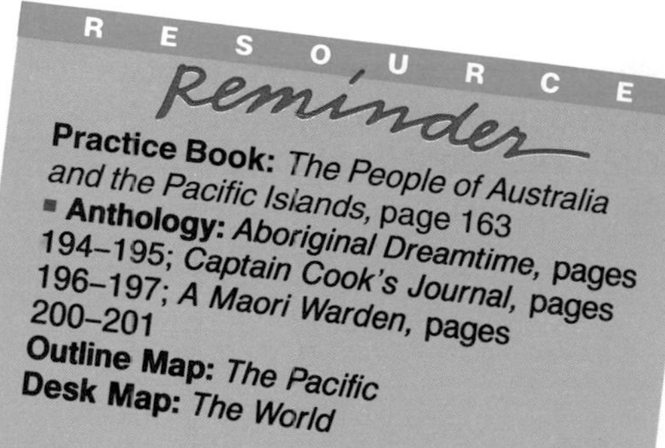

Discussing Micronesians and Melanesians

Ask students:

- **Why did different groups of Melanesians develop their own languages and customs?** (Rugged land separated groups of Melanesians.)
- **How does the Melanesian extended family differ from others you have read about?** (Men and women live in separate houses.)

EXTENDING MAP SKILLS

Refer the class to the map on this page.

Ask students:

- **What evidence do you find here that the islanders, especially the Polynesians, were great sailors?** (The distances between the islands that they settled indicate that they were good sailors.)
- **Which is the northernmost group of islands in this region?** (the Northern Mariana Islands)
- **Which Polynesian country is on the largest island in Melanesia?** (Papua New Guinea)
- **What does this map show you about the political organization of the islands of Oceania?** (Many are organized into island nations.)

Looking at the Polynesians

Ask students:

- **What special talents did the Polynesians display?** (They were experts at sailing and shipbuilding.)
- **Where did the Polynesians first settle in the Pacific?** (Samoa and Tahiti)
- **Why might the Polynesians have moved on to other places?** (overcrowding, shortage of food, wars between clans)

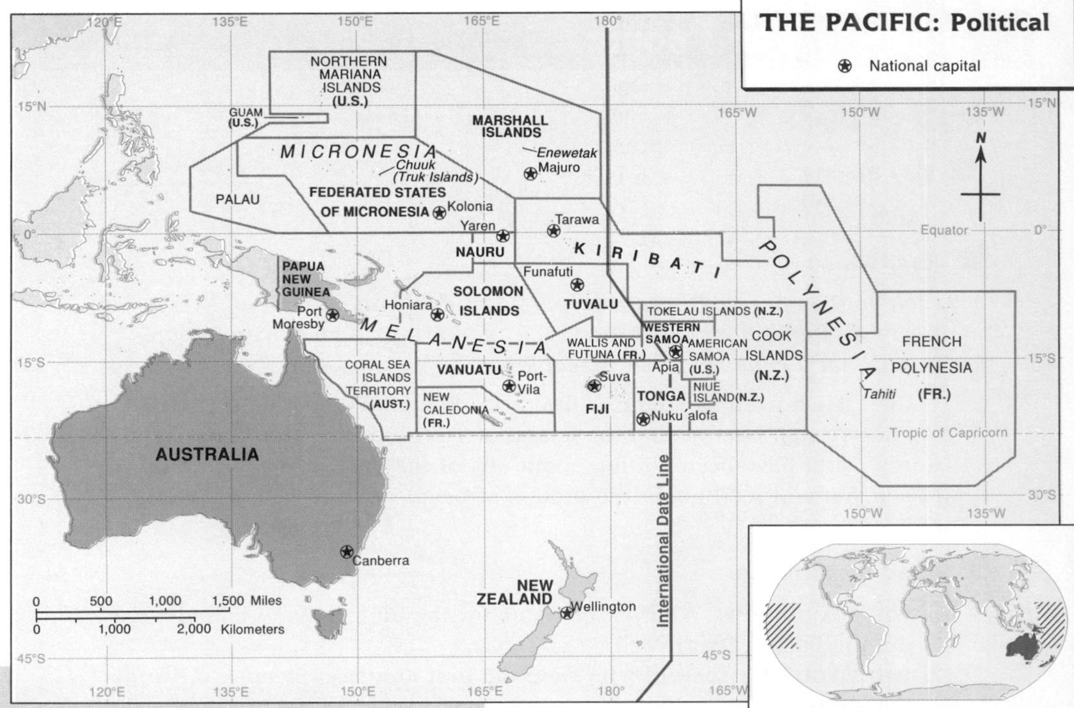

MAP SKILL: The thousands of islands of the Pacific are divided into various groups. Which of the groups of islands are part of Australia?

from their neighbors. Different groups of people spoke their own languages and followed their own customs.

Life was often difficult in tropical Melanesia. Mosquitoes spread malaria and other diseases. In some of the swampy areas there were no stones to use for making houses or tools.

In the cooler highlands, however, life was less difficult. Many Melanesians learned to farm. They grew such crops as sweet potatoes, bananas, and a starchy root called taro.

Traditional ways are still followed in the rural areas of Melanesia. Unlike in many parts of the West, life is centered around the clan, or extended family group. Men and women live in separate houses. Even today Melanesian women may not enter the houses that are shared by the men of the clan.

The people who settled in Micronesia developed a culture similar to that of their Pacific neighbors. Like the Melanesians, the Micronesians are trying to save some of their old ways in a world that is constantly changing.

THE POLYNESIANS: SAILORS AND SETTLERS

A new group of settlers reached the Pacific islands about 4,000 years ago. The Polynesians have been called "Vikings of the Sunrise" because they were expert in both sailing and shipbuilding. Without compasses they paddled canoes for amazing distances across the world's largest

MAP SKILL: Coral Sea Islands Territory

598

CURRICULUM CONNECTION

Art Tell students that "dreaming" or the special kind of time that myths and rituals express is an important concept for Australian Aborigines. This "time" is somewhat like the "time" that people with a European-based culture refer to when they begin a story with the words "Once upon a time." Ask students to research and report on Aborigine art forms, such as pictures, dances, and stories, that have developed from this concept. Encourage them to draw their own illustrations for their reports.

ocean. When they landed on the islands of Samoa and Tahiti, they were amazed by the beauty of the land. Polynesian legends describe these islands as places "where there was plenty of everything for everyone and nobody had to be either poor or rich." Not surprisingly, the sailors decided to stay in their newly found paradise.

Once they were settled, the Polynesians had little or no contact with outsiders. After hundreds of years, however, groups of Polynesians sailed off to find new homes. Some settled in the islands of Hawaii in the north. Other groups, like the Maoris (mä ôr' ēz), sailed south to settle New Zealand. Many of the Maori people, like the aborigines of Australia, still live according to their traditional culture.

You might wonder why some people chose to leave such wonderful places as Samoa or Tahiti for a risky voyage across the Pacific. Some historians think that these islands had become overcrowded and that food was in short supply. They also suggest that wars between rival clans drove some of the islanders away.

ARRIVAL OF THE EUROPEANS

During the 1500s European ships began crossing the Pacific. One by one the Pacific islands were claimed by European explorers. Each group brought new ways of living to places that had been unchanged for hundreds of years.

The first British settlers arrived in Australia in 1788 on 11 large ships. They were mostly convicts who had been in prison in England. The British government hoped to empty its crowded jails by sending prisoners to Australia.

Later, immigrants arrived from England, Scotland, and Ireland, not as criminals, but as free people. They came because Australia and New Zealand offered land, work, and adventure.

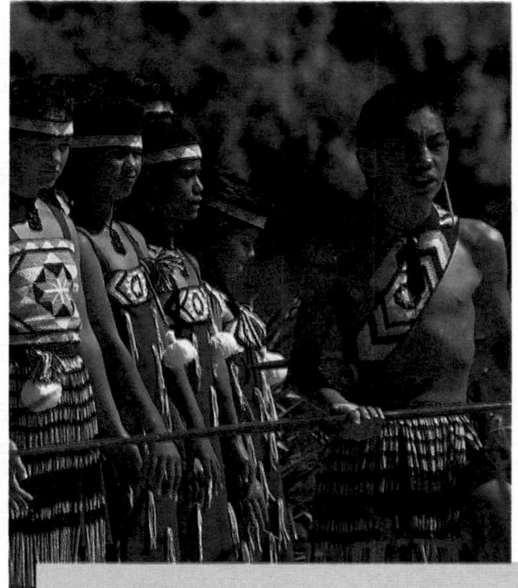

These Maoris from the North Island are getting ready to compete in a boat race.

THE PEOPLE OF THE PACIFIC

Australia and the Pacific islands were settled by several waves of newcomers. As you have read, the first people arrived in the region thousands of years ago. Later, European colonists and landholders changed the traditional way of life of the people of the Pacific Islands. Today, because of satellites, jet planes, and television, the Pacific is no longer such a faraway place.

Check Your Reading

1. Who were the first people to live in Australia?
2. How would you describe the lives of the early settlers of Melanesia?
3. Why did some Polynesians leave Samoa and Tahiti?
4. THINKING SKILL: Based on this lesson, what conclusions can you draw about the people of the Pacific islands?

THINKING SKILL: Drawing Conclusions

Discussing the European Arrival

Ask students:

- **When did Europeans first begin to arrive in the Pacific?** (during the 1500s)
- **How did they affect the region?** (They settled there and brought their own ways and technology.)
- *THINKING FURTHER:* **In what ways do you think life changed for the islanders as a result of the Europeans' arrival?** (loss of life, loss of land, change in ways people made a living, end of isolation)

Applying the Lesson Have students make a chart that identifies similarities between how the Australia/Oceania areas were settled and how the United States was settled.

CLOSE

Summarizing Students have learned how successive waves of immigrants settled the Pacific region and how each acted upon the environment and developed its traditional culture. Have students speculate about the way that isolation affected these cultures.

Evaluating Use the *Check Your Reading* questions (answers given below) to assess students' understanding.

Answers to Check Your Reading

1. aborigines
2. Possible answers include: difficult because of the rugged land and diseases; traditional.
3. Historians suggest that overcrowding and shortages of food and/or wars between rival clans drove some Polynesians from these islands.
4. Students will probably focus on the people's adventurousness, their practicality, and their ability to adapt to their environment.

Independent Practice

Practice Book: page 163

MEETING INDIVIDUAL NEEDS

Reteaching (easy) Have students review the groups of people they read about in this lesson. Ask them to choose one group and to imagine themselves a part of that group. Have them list three things that made them choose this group.

Extension (average) The convict settlement of Australia is a fascinating page in history. Have students do research and write a report on one aspect—crimes for which the convicts were sent there, the journey from the British Isles, work that convicts had to do once they got there, or what the convicts' future was once they "did their time."

Enrichment (challenging) On the outline map of the region, which is found in the Teacher's Resource Center, have students map the waves of settlers to the region. Or alternatively, have 12 groups of students work on the Desk Maps of the world.

LESSON 2
pages 600–601

Lesson Theme Economies in the Pacific region range from highly developed in Australia to somewhat less developed in New Zealand to traditional in the remaining islands of the region.

Lesson Objective
- State the differences between the economies of Australia and those of Oceania.

PREPARE

Motivate As you read the *Read Aloud* passage to the class, ask students to picture the isolated towns along the railway and try to feel what the railroad must mean to the lives of people along the way.

Set Purpose Use the *What You Know* question to remind the class of what a relatively short time Europeans have been in the area. Have students read the lesson to answer the *What You Will Learn* question.

TEACH

Discussing the Australian Economy

Ask students:

- **What are Australia's major industries?** (farming, ranching, mining, manufacturing, and services like banking and law)
- **With what commodities does Australia supply the world in large amounts?** (wool, iron ore, copper, nickel, aluminum)

Looking at a Land of Farms Discuss the importance of wool to New Zealand's economy.

RESOURCE *Reminder*

Practice Book: *Economies: Australia and Pacific Islands*, page 164
Outline Map: *The Pacific*
Technology: *Adventures CD-ROM* See page 595-B.

LESSON 2

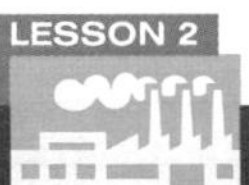

The Economy

READ TO LEARN

Key Vocabulary
station

Key Places
Melbourne
New Zealand

Read Aloud

Once a week the "Tea and Sugar" train stops in Rawlinna, a place that appears to be a speck on the map of the Nullarbor Plain, a bleak, unpopulated plateau that cuts Western Australia off from the east. The "Tea and Sugar" links tiny communities made up mostly of railroad workers to the outside world. It is one way that Australians have overcome the problems of distance and isolation in building their economy. As you will read, other countries of the Pacific face similar challenges.

Read for Purpose

1. WHAT YOU KNOW: When did Europeans first explore the Pacific?
2. WHAT YOU WILL LEARN: What economic challenges do the people of the Pacific face today?

THE AUSTRALIAN ECONOMY

Like the United States, Australia has a developed economy that includes a mixture of farming, mining, manufacturing, and service industries. Today over 85 percent of the country's people live in urban areas. In the many skyscrapers of big cities like Sydney and Melbourne, people earn their living in such areas as banking, insurance, law, and medicine.

Only 6 percent of Australians work on farms or stations, which are huge sheep ranches. Yet farm exports like wool help to keep the country's standard of living high. Every year millions of sheep are loaded onto ships that haul them to markets around the world. Australian sheep supply the world with more than one third of the wool used for clothing.

You read in Chapter 29 that Australia is a land of abundant minerals. Australia leads the world in the production of iron ore. It also ranks among the top producers of copper, nickel, and aluminum.

A LAND OF FARMS

New Zealand is neither as prosperous nor as industrialized as Australia. Farming and ranching is still the most important part of the country's economy. For every person living in New Zealand, there are at least 20 sheep.

New Zealand is the world's largest exporter of wool. You may own a sweater or jacket made with wool from sheep on a New Zealand sheep station. New Zealand also exports lamb, beef, and such dairy products as butter and cheese.

Because of its variety of climates, New Zealand has almost every kind of farm. In

WHAT YOU KNOW: This question refers to information in Lesson 1; during the 1500s.

READING STRATEGY AND VOCABULARY DEVELOPMENT

Mapping Tell students that they will create a graphic organizer for the information in this lesson. Ask students to create a chart showing the economies of Australia, New Zealand, and other Pacific islands. A partially completed sample is given below.

Country	Type of Economy	Industries	Exports
Australia	developed	farming, mining, manufacturing, service	wool, copper, nickel, iron ore, aluminum
New Zealand			
Pacific Islands			

Sydney, Australia, is a modern, industrialized city. The famous Sydney Opera House (*right*) is a center for many of the arts.

addition to cattle and sheep stations and dairy farms, there are large orchards in which apples, pears, and nectarines are grown. Some farmers also raise flowers to sell overseas. On the Canterbury Plains, one of the few flat areas in New Zealand, farmers grow wheat and other grains.

ISLAND ECONOMIES

On many of the Pacific islands, tourism is the main source of income. In the days before jet planes, the South Pacific seemed liked an exotic, faraway land. Today, however, people can travel by plane and within hours be on a tropical beach.

Despite money from tourism, however, the economies of most of the Pacific islands are still developing. In Papua New Guinea, for example, farming, fishing, and forestry are the main sources of income.

The island of Tonga also has a developing economy. It exports mostly bananas and copra, the dried meat of coconuts. Yet Tonga's imports greatly outnumber its exports. The government of Tonga hopes that money brought in by tourism will help make up the difference.

THE PACIFIC ISLANDS AT WORK

As you have read, the Pacific region has a variety of economic systems. Australia has a developed economy based on farming, mining, manufacturing, and service industries. New Zealand's economy, based on farming and ranching, is less developed. The remaining Pacific islands have traditional economies.

Check Your Reading

1. Why does Australia have a high standard of living?
2. What products does New Zealand sell to countries around the world?
3. Describe the economy of a typical Pacific island country.
4. THINKING SKILL: List some of the goods produced in Australia and in the other nations of the Pacific. Now group the goods. What do your groups tell you about the economies of this region?

THINKING SKILL: Classifying

Looking at Farms Continue the discussion.

Ask students:

- **How does New Zealand's economy differ from Australia's?** (less developed, with farming and ranching most important)
- **What are the major exports of New Zealand?** (wool, lamb, beef, dairy products)

Discussing the Island Economies

Ask students:

- **What is the major industry of the Pacific islands?** (tourism)
- **Which products do various islands sell to the world?** (farm, fish, and forestry products, and bananas and copra)

Applying the Lesson Have students choose from amont the tourist, farming, fishing, ranching, manufacturing, and service industries and imagine that they earn their living in one of them. Have them write a letter to a friend describing their work.

Summarizing Students have learned about the varied economies of the Pacific region. Ask why transportation is so crucial to further development in the region.

Evaluating Use the *Check Your Reading* questions (answers given below) to assess students' understanding.

Answers to Check Your Reading

1. because it has a highly developed economy based on rich resources
2. wool, lamb, beef, dairy products, fruits, flowers, grains
3. a traditional economy probably relying on tourism for most of its income, but also exporting products like bananas and copra
4. Students' responses should note that the greater the variety of goods produced, the more highly developed the economy.

Independent Practice
Practice Book: page 164

MEETING INDIVIDUAL NEEDS

Reteaching (easy) Have students draw or collect pictures of people at work in the Pacific region. Have them label their pictures and use them to create a bulletin board display titled, "The Economies of the Pacific Region."

Extension (average) Tell students to pretend that they have been hired by a nation or an island of the Pacific region to prepare a brochure that will attract people to invest in its economy. The brochures they create should combine pictures and text describing possibilites for the success of various businesses.

Enrichment (challenging) Have students use the outline map of the region, found in the Teacher's Resource Center, to create a resource map for the Pacific region.

SKILLS LESSON
page 602

Lesson Theme Decision making involves choosing the best option from among many to attain a goal.

Lesson Objective
- Identify and apply a process that leads to sound decision making.

PREPARE

Motivate Before students read the introductory paragraphs, ask them to describe a decision that they have recently made and the decision-making process they used. List the steps they cite on the chalkboard and have the class compare them with those listed in *Helping Yourself*.

TEACH

Helping Yourself Point out to students that these steps are the same ones they learned in Chapter 2. Remind students that they may use the steps as guidelines when they need to apply a decision-making strategy.

Applying the Skill Have students read the case study and answer the questions that follow it. (See answers below.)

Thinking About Thinking Have students name the steps they followed to reach their decisions and to compare them to ones in *Helping Yourself* and on the chalkboard. Discuss with the class which steps should be included in all decision-making processes.

CLOSE

Reviewing the Skill Ask students to tell what they can do in the future to become better decision makers.

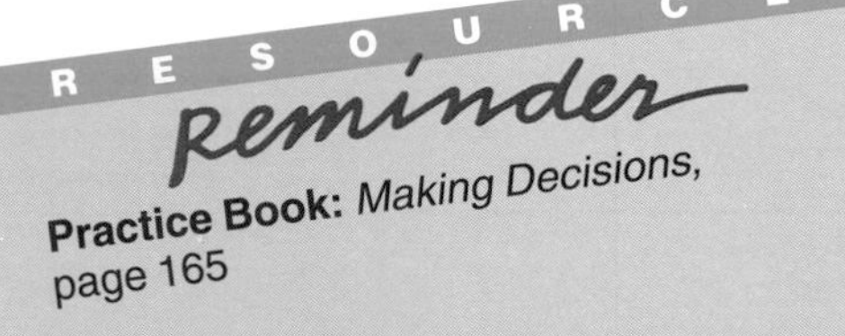
RESOURCE *Reminder*
Practice Book: *Making Decisions,* page 165

BUILDING SKILLS
THINKING SKILLS

Decision Making: Review

Each day you make many decisions. Some decisions are small, such as which clothes you are going to wear. Other decisions are more important, such as whether or not to join a particular team at school.

When you make a decision, you select from among a number of alternatives, or options, one that will help you to achieve a goal or goals. If you are clear about your goal and carefully evaluate all possible alternatives, you will be more likely to make good decisions.

HELPING YOURSELF
One way to make a decision is to:

1. Identify and clearly define the goal(s) you wish to achieve.
2. Identify all possible options by which you can achieve your goal(s).
3. Predict the likely consequences, both immediate and long range, of each option.
4. Evaluate each consequence by determining whether it will benefit or harm you or others.
5. Choose the best option.

Applying the Skill

Read the example below. Then answer the questions that follow.

Imagine that your teacher has assigned a research project on which students can work together in pairs or in small groups. This project is a good opportunity for you to improve your social studies grade. Your two best friends ask you to work with them. A classmate who has just moved into your neighborhood also asks you to work with her. This new classmate is one of the smartest and most creative students in your school. You must decide with whom you want to work. Your teacher will ask about your plans soon, so you must make your decision.

1. What is your goal?
2. What are your options?
3. What might the consequences be of each option?
4. Which option would you choose? Why?

Reviewing the Skill

1. List some steps you can follow to make a good decision.
2. When you make a decision, why should you have a clear understanding of your goal(s)?
3. Why should you think of as many options as possible before making a decision?

ANSWERS TO SKILLS QUESTIONS

Applying the Skill
1. The goal is to improve your social studies grade.
2. You can work with your best friends or the new classmate.
3. If you work with your best friends, you will keep their friendship, have fun, and possibly get a good grade. If you work with the new classmate, you improve your chances of getting a good grade, but risk hurting your friends.
4. Answers will vary since the decision depends on personal values.

Reviewing the Skill
1. Identify your goal(s), options for reaching the goal(s), and likely consequences of each option.
2. to give you a framework against which to identify and evaluate all possible options
3. If you limit your options, you may overlook better choices.

LESSON 3

The Government

READ TO LEARN

Key Vocabulary

trust territory

Key Places

Canberra
Northern Territory
Guam

Read Aloud

When the Queen of England visits Australia, she is not an outsider because she is also the head of state of the land "down under." Although it is an independent nation, Australia is also part of the British Commonwealth of Nations and, like Canada, recognizes the British monarch as its leader. The same is true of New Zealand, Papua New Guinea, and Fiji. These countries were once English colonies. When they gained their independence, they kept some of their ties to Great Britain.

In recent years many other nations of the Pacific have gained their independence. As you will read, the governments that these nations have established combine traditional island values with Western principles of democracy and justice.

Read for Purpose

1. WHAT YOU KNOW: What do many of the governments of Southeast Asia have in common?
2. WHAT YOU WILL LEARN: On what principles are the governments of the nations of the Pacific based?

GOVERNING AUSTRALIA

Australia's government was shaped by hundreds of years of British rule of the country. Like the British government, the Australian government values the rights and liberties of its people. Like the people of the United States, Australians saw the advantages of a federal system of government for their country.

The government of Australia is a democratic monarchy. Australia's legislature is a parliament, like Great Britain's. The government is headed by a prime minister, who is the leader of the political party with the most seats in the parliament.

Australia has six large states: New South Wales, Victoria, Queensland, South Australia, Western Australia, and Tasmania. There are also two territories that are run by the federal government. They are Canberra, which is the nation's capital, and the Northern Territory. Recently much of the Northern Territory was set aside for aborigines.

Australians have long been strong believers in democracy and equality. Australia was the first nation to allow every adult male to vote, and one of the first to allow women to vote. Australia also introduced the use of secret ballots in elections.

WHAT YOU KNOW: This question refers to material in Chapter 28, Lesson 3; many of the governments have dictatorial, one-party rule.

LESSON 3
pages 603–605

Lesson Theme The governments of the Pacific region generally follow principles of Western democracy, which are combined with traditional values on some of the islands.

Lesson Objectives

- Describe the governments of Australia and New Zealand.
- Describe the different kinds of governments in the Pacific islands.

PREPARE

Motivate Have a student read the *Read Aloud* passage and have the class review what independence meant to our country—how we needed to set up a new government utilizing some of the best principles of the old government.

Set Purpose Discuss the *What You Know* question. Then ask students to predict answers to the *What You Will Learn* question. Have students review their answers at the end of the lesson.

TEACH

Discussing Australia's Government As students discuss this form of government, have them make a simple diagram to illustrate it.

Ask students:

- **What is the name of the legislative body in Australia's government?** (parliament)
- **How is its executive chosen?** (The prime minister is the leader of the party with the most seats in parliament.)
- **What breakthroughs did Australia make in democratic government?** (full adult male suffrage, early female suffrage, secret ballot)

READING STRATEGY AND VOCABULARY DEVELOPMENT

Mapping Have students use outlining as their graphic organizer for this lesson. Show them a model outline and go through it to analyze how the parts show the order and importance of ideas. Then tell students to preview the lesson and to note how each heading can become an outline entry. Work through the first section with students and then have them continue the outline as they read the lesson. (A partial example is shown below.)

A. Governing Australia
  1. The government is a democratic monarchy.
    a. A parliament is the legislative body.
    b. A prime minister is the chief executive.
  2. Australia is a federation.
    a. It has six large states.
    b. It has two territories, one for Aborigines.

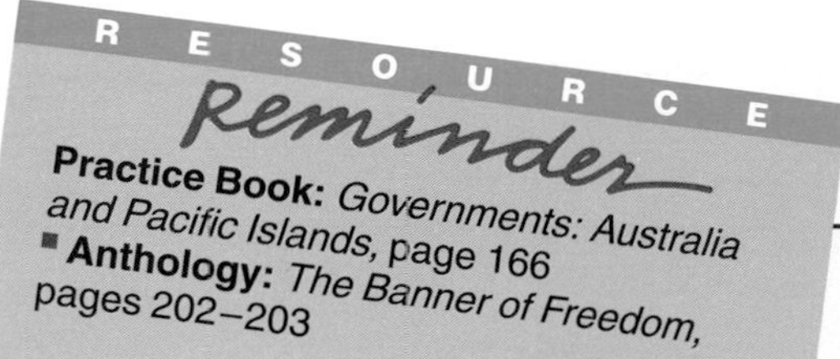

RESOURCE Reminder

Practice Book: *Governments: Australia and Pacific Islands,* page 166
■ **Anthology:** *The Banner of Freedom,* pages 202–203

Talking About Australia's Government Continue the discussion.

Ask students:

- **In what ways are Australia's government and our government like and unlike each other?** (*like*—both are federal systems, democratic; *unlike*—Australia has a parliament and prime minister with queen as monarch, instead of congress and President.)

Discussing New Zealand and the Pacific Islands

Ask students:

- **How is New Zealand's government similar to Australia's?** (Both are parliamentary and belong to the British Commonwealth.)
- **How is a trust territory governed?** (It is under the control of another country until judged ready to govern itself.)
- *THINKING FURTHER:* **When Guam becomes independent, do you think its government is likely to be parliamentary? Why or why not?** (Probably not, since its history is American rather than British; help students to recognize the strong influence of colonial rule.)

Exploring Island Traditions of Government Focus discussion on the strong influence of tradition.

Ask students:

- **How were many of the Pacific islands governed traditionally?** (by chiefs)
- **How have Pacific islands combined the new with the old in their modern governments?** (by adopting elected legislatures while still retaining chiefs in governmental roles such as advisers and council members)
- *THINKING FURTHER:* **Why do you suppose that the Pacific islands have combined the new and old in their governments?** (Help students to recognize that they probably want to preserve their traditional ways while enjoying democratic ways.)

Today all major democracies use secret ballots so that people cannot be frightened into voting a particular way. Australians believe that voting is so important that anyone who does not vote must pay a fine.

NEW ZEALAND AND THE PACIFIC ISLANDS

New Zealand also has a parliamentary system of government, with elected representatives in its legislature and a prime minister. Like Australia, New Zealand is a member of the British Commonwealth of Nations.

Until recently many Pacific island countries were controlled by European powers. Since most island nations had very few people, they were easily taken over by more powerful countries. For example, Palau, in Micronesia, was ruled first by Spain, followed by Germany, then Japan, and finally New Zealand.

After World War II the United Nations decided to make Palau a **trust territory**. A trust territory's government is controlled decides the trust territory is ready to govern itself. Palau became an independent nation in 1994.

Some Pacific islands, such as **Guam** (gwäm), are still trust territories of the United States. The United States has naval bases on some of these islands.

ISLAND TRADITIONS OF GOVERNMENT

The governments of most Pacific island nations are a mixture of ancient customs and Western principles of democracy. For thousands of years most islanders lived in villages that were headed by several chiefs. The chiefs ran not only the village government, but the economy as well.

Many island nations include chiefs in their present systems of government. For example, Vanuatu has an elected legislature and a council of chiefs. The council advises the government on how to save many of their traditional ways. Similarly, Tonga is a kingdom ruled by a monarch and a council. Half of the council are nobles, while the other half are elected by the people of Tonga.

The United States has large navy bases on the islands of Midway (*right*) and Guam.

604

BUILDING CITIZENSHIP

New Nations and Good Citizenship New nations are regularly emerging in Oceania as island groups end colonial rule and declare their independence. Have class members imagine that they are members of a commission that is supposed to design a program to train people in newly independent nations to be active participants in their governments as well as contributors to their communities. Have students identify the behaviors they think their program should stress and have them suggest ways to convince the people of the importance of their participation in the government of their country.

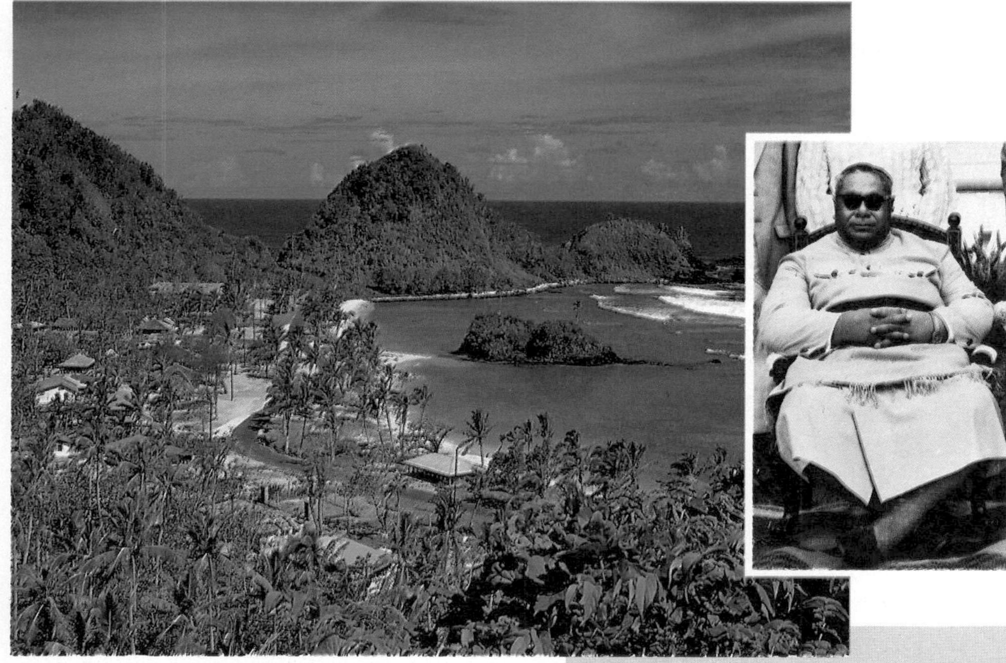

Beautiful and isolated, many of the islands of the Pacific have rulers whose families date back for hundreds of years. For example, King Tupou IV of Tonga comes from a royal line of rulers that is 1,000 years old.

Polynesians traditionally lived in large family clans known as *aigas*. An *aiga* might have several chiefs and hundreds of members. From the chiefs the *aiga* chose one person as *matai*, or high chief.

This system of government is still used in Samoa. The *matai* is in charge of the *aiga's* communal land and sits on the village council. In Western Samoa only *matai* have the right to vote for government officials to represent them.

GOVERNMENT IN THE PACIFIC

There are many forms of government in the Pacific region. But, as you have read, most of these nations have representative assemblies. Australia, New Zealand, Papua New Guinea, and Fiji are part of the British Commonwealth of Nations. Although the British monarch is the head of state, each country elects its own prime minister and parliament.

In many of the island nations of the rest of the Pacific, most governments are a mixture of old and new. Together, traditional island chiefs and government officials try to solve each country's problems.

Check Your Reading

1. What system of government is used in Australia today?
2. Name two democratic practices that are followed in Australia.
3. How does Western Samoa combine the new and the old in its government?
4. **THINKING SKILL:** How are the governments of Great Britain and Australia similar? How are they different?

THINKING SKILL: Compare and Contrast

605

Applying the Lesson Have students imagine that they live in a trust territory that is about to become independent. Have them create a system of government for the newly independent nation.

3 CLOSE

Summarizing Students have learned that Australia and New Zealand have closely followed Western principles of government while many Pacific islands have tempered these principles with traditional ways. Have the class speculate on the causes of this difference. (If necessary, remind students of how the new settlers nearly completely displaced the aborigines and Maoris.)

Evaluating Use these questions to assess students' understanding.

- **How can you tell that Australia has a federal system of government?** (It is made up of six states and two territories.)
- **Why might some islanders want chiefs to continue to play a role in government?** (possibly because of love of tradition or respect for chiefs' knowledge and position)

Answers to Check Your Reading

1. a democratic monarchy with a parliamentary system
2. right to vote for all adults, secret ballot
3. It has an elected government, but only the chiefs can vote for its government officials.
4. Both are parliamentary systems with a prime minister as head of government; only Australia fines people who do not vote.

Independent Practice
Practice Book: page 166

MEETING INDIVIDUAL NEEDS

Reteaching (easy) Have students make a two-column chart. In the first column have them list characteristics of the governments of Australia and New Zealand. In the second column have them list characteristics of the Pacific island governments that make use of traditions.

Extension (average) Have students imagine that they live under a government in the Pacific region that combines traditions with Western principles of democracy. Have them write a letter to a pen pal in the United States in which they describe their government and what they like about it.

Enrichment (challenging) Ask students to choose one of the nations of Oceania. Have them do research on their nation and write a report telling who its colonial rulers were, how and when independence was achieved, and what form of government it has.

LESSON 4
pages 606–607

Lesson Theme Traditional and modern arts and sports thrive in the Pacific region.

Lesson Objectives
- Describe the traditional arts of Pacific peoples.
- Identify modern arts and sports popular in the Pacific region.

PREPARE

Motivate Read the *Read Aloud* passage and have the class discuss how the arts and sports enrich their own lives. Encourage students to think about how people across the world are similarly enriched.

Set Purpose To answer the *What You Know* question, students should identify and describe examples of the arts enjoyed by people in their own community and tell whether they were created long ago (for example, classical music) or are newly made. Use the *What You Will Learn* question to help students focus their reading on discovering how the Pacific region also blends old and new.

TEACH

Talking About Traditional and Modern Arts

Ask students:

- **What are this region's major traditional arts?** (carving, designing tattoos, chanting)
- **Why do Maoris and other Pacific peoples want to keep these arts?** (They do not want to lose their connection to the past.)
- **Which more modern arts thrive in the Pacific region?** (new architecture, opera, movies, pop singing)

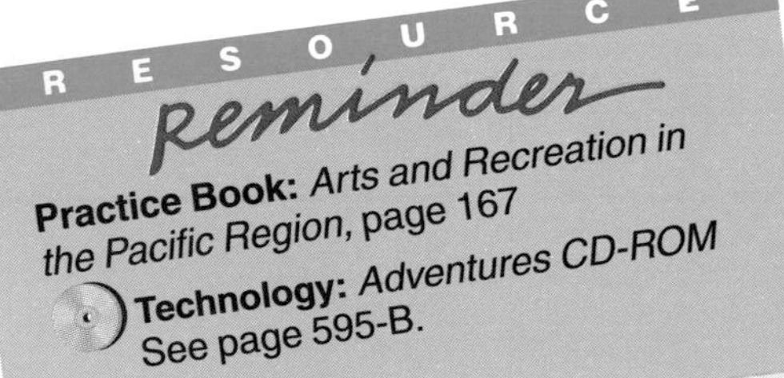

RESOURCE *Reminder*

Practice Book: *Arts and Recreation in the Pacific Region*, page 167

Technology: *Adventures CD-ROM* See page 595-B.

LESSON 4

Arts and Recreation

READ TO LEARN

Key Places

Sydney

Read Aloud

If you visited the Pacific region, you would see that its people make use of traditional designs on weapons, boats, and even as tattoos. As you will read, in the Pacific the arts are a part of daily life.

Read for Purpose

1. WHAT YOU KNOW: How are the arts a part of daily life in the United States?
2. WHAT YOU WILL LEARN: How do the people of the Pacific blend traditional and modern forms of art?

TRADITIONAL ARTS

In the days before European explorers arrived in the Pacific region, warriors in opposing clans danced and chanted before they went into battle. You can imagine how they sounded by watching a Samoan canoe race today. Two dozen young men in a single canoe yell fierce chants to the beat of drums as they bend over their oars. The boats seem to fly over the water.

Some chants tell the history of families. Wi Huata (wē hü ä′ tä) is an Episcopal priest in New Zealand. He is also a Maori who can tell the history of 50 generations of his family in a chant. To help recall the chant, he moves his fingers across a spear carved with his family's history.

Keeping their cultural identity alive is very important to the Maori and other Pacific peoples. The Aborigines of Australia have a legacy of ancient art that you can read about on pages 608–611. Traditional art connects Pacific peoples to the past.

ENJOYING THE MODERN ARTS

At the center of the spectacular harbor in Sydney is a building like no other in the world. It looks like a flock of great white birds with their wings extended, ready to soar over the water. This building is the Sydney Opera House. It was planned to be an eye-catching building. Australians hoped to show outsiders that they not only appreciate the fine arts, but that they can also create beautiful architecture.

Several Australians have become world-famous opera stars, like Joan Sutherland. The country has also produced many other world-famous entertainers. From movie stars such as Paul Hogan and Mel Gibson, to singers such as Olivia Newton John, Australian entertainers are recognized all over the world today.

SPORTS

In the warm climate of the Pacific region, outdoor sports are available year-

WHAT YOU KNOW: Students should be aware that people in the United States enjoy such activities as visiting museums, attending concerts, engaging in hobbies and joining amateur groups.

READING STRATEGY AND VOCABULARY DEVELOPMENT

Mapping Have students preview the lesson and decide which form of graphic organizer would be the best choice for taking notes on the information. You may want to have them work in groups to preview, read, and prepare their organizers. Have them share the information in their organizers at the end of the lesson.

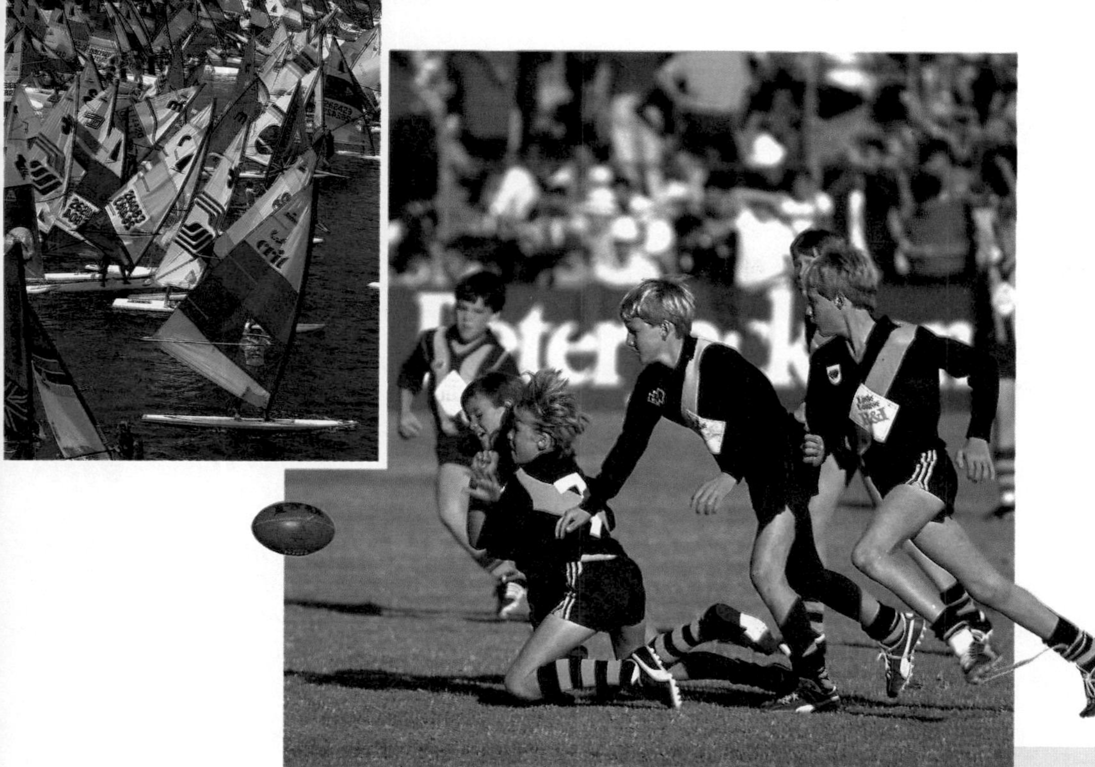

Australian children play a game of football, a game that is similar to rugby. Wind surfing is also a popular sport in the Pacific.

round. In Australia, for example, it seems as if everyone hikes, swims, surfs, or plays tennis or golf. Australians like to watch sports, but they will almost always say, "I'd rather give it a go myself."

There's no question about the most popular sport in New Zealand. "Kiwis," as New Zealanders are sometimes called, love to play rugby. As you have read, the game of rugby is much like American football. In addition to rugby players, New Zealand has also produced world-class distance runners and mountain climbers.

PACIFIC ARTS AND SPORTS

The arts and leisure of the Pacific region are a mixture of ancient and modern. On the same island you can enjoy a new movie or hear a family's history through a traditional chant.

As you have read, sports are enormously popular in this region of sunny days and warm temperatures. From sailing and swimming to golfing and hiking, the people of the Pacific love to be outdoors.

Check Your Reading

1. How do some New Zealanders try to preserve their past?
2. How is the Sydney Opera House unique?
3. What are some popular outdoor activities in the Pacific region?
4. **THINKING SKILL:** What effect do you think the climate of the Pacific has had on the development of the popular sports of the region?

THINKING SKILL: Cause and Effect

Discussing Sports

Ask students:

- **Which sports are particularly popular in the Pacific region?** (hiking, running, surfing, swimming, mountain climbing, tennis, golf, rugby)
- **Why is the region so good for these sports?** (warm climate, water all around, mountains)

Applying the Lesson Have students review the arts and sports that thrive in the Pacific region and then have them write a paragraph telling which one they would enjoy most and giving reasons for their choice.

3 CLOSE

Summarizing Students have learned that arts and sports are an important part of the daily life of people of the Pacific region. Have them list examples of these sports on the chalkboard and then categorize them as traditional or modern.

Evaluating Use these questions to assess students' understanding.

- **Which traditional art is popular in New Zealand?** (chants about history)
- **Do you think climate affects the sports of the region? How?** (Yes. Many of these sports could not be enjoyed in cold weather.)

Answers to Check Your Reading

1. They continue to memorize ancient chants and to read carvings.
2. because of its architecture
3. hiking, running, mountain climbing, swimming, surfing, tennis, golf, rugby
4. Its warmth all year round and its ocean breezes would encourage outdoor pursuits.

Independent Practice
Practice Book: page 167

MEETING INDIVIDUAL NEEDS

Reteaching (easy) Have students cut out pictures from newspapers, magazines, and travel brochures to make their own booklets entitled "Recreation in the Pacific Region."

Extension (average) Divide the class into groups and have each group make up a chant in which they describe events that happened during the school year. Encourage them to use rhyme for easier recall, and have each group perform its chant for the class.

Enrichment (challenging) Divide the class into groups to research a traditional art, modern art, professional sport, or amateur sport of the region. Then have each group prepare a presentation for the class as part of a "Pacific Region Fair."

Lesson Theme The traditional way of life of Australia's Aborigines has changed greatly. Yet some Aborigine artists keep their culture alive by continuing to paint in the traditional ways of their ancestors.

Lesson Objectives
- Describe the work of a traditional Aborigine artist.
- Explain why traditional Aborigine painting is meaningful to modern Aborigine artists.
- Describe some of the ways in which Aborigines continue to learn about their heritage.

1 PREPARE

Motivate Have students look at the illustrations on these pages. Ask them to identify some of the animals they see.

Set Purpose Focus students' attention with the following question. Why do people value the arts and crafts made by their ancestors? (They are reminders of their heritage.) Have students read the introduction. Ask them to think about the concluding suggestion while they read the rest of the lesson.

2 TEACH

Understanding the Concept of Legacies Ask students why art forms can be legacies. (They are handed down from generation to generation. They communicate beliefs and ideas.)

Discussing an Aborigine Artist at Work Tell students that Bluey Ilkirr's paintings communicate beliefs about the Aborigine past.

Ask students:

- **What does Bluey Ilkirr do before he starts painting?** (He strips off a piece of bark, flattens it, and scrapes it clean.)

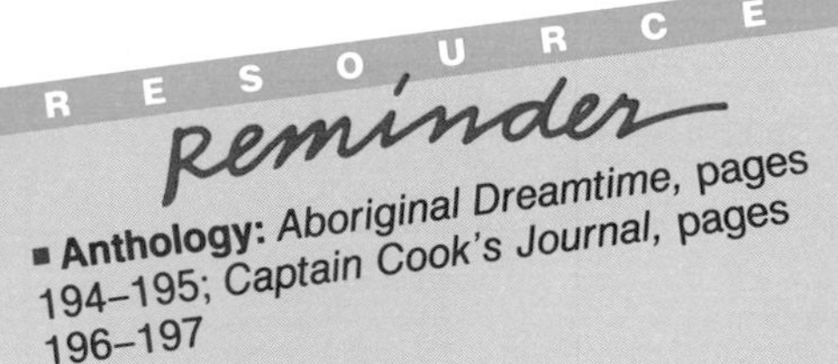

RESOURCE *Reminder*
- **Anthology:** Aboriginal Dreamtime, pages 194–195; Captain Cook's Journal, pages 196–197

Legacy — LINKING PAST AND PRESENT

ABORIGINE PAINTING

by Carrie Evento

As you read in Chapter 29, the first people to live in Australia were the Aborigines. The Aborigine way of life has changed greatly. Despite change, Aborigines are holding on to many of their legacies. Some Aborigine artists continue to paint in the traditional ways of their ancestors. Many of these modern artists paint on the bark of trees and on rock walls just as Aborigines who lived long before them did. With their paintings, Aborigine artists keep an important part of their culture alive. As you read, think about why traditional ways of painting are so important to Aborigine artists.

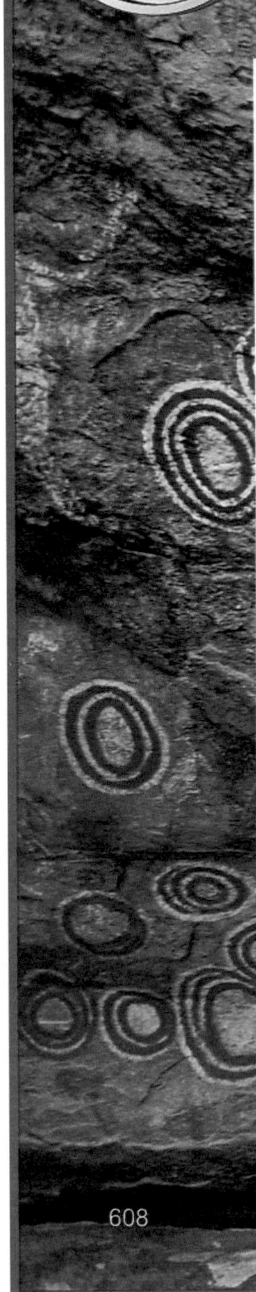

AN ABORIGINE ARTIST AT WORK

Bluey Ilkirr, an Aborigine artist, props a long forked branch against the tall trunk of a stringybark tree. With an ax in one hand, he climbs up the branch until he is next to the tree trunk, about 20 feet (6 m) above the ground. Ilkirr reaches up and wedges the blade of the ax under the bark. Pulling down, he removes a large strip of bark in one piece from the tree.

Ilkirr spends weeks preparing the strip of bark for painting. He weighs it down with stones to make it flat and scrapes it clean.

608

READING STRATEGY AND VOCABULARY DEVELOPMENT

Mapping As in Lesson 4, have students preview the lesson and decide which form of graphic organizer would be the best choice for taking notes on the information. You may want to have students work in groups of two or three to preview, read, and prepare their organizers. At the end of the lesson, have them share the information in their organizers and compare the techniques used by different groups.

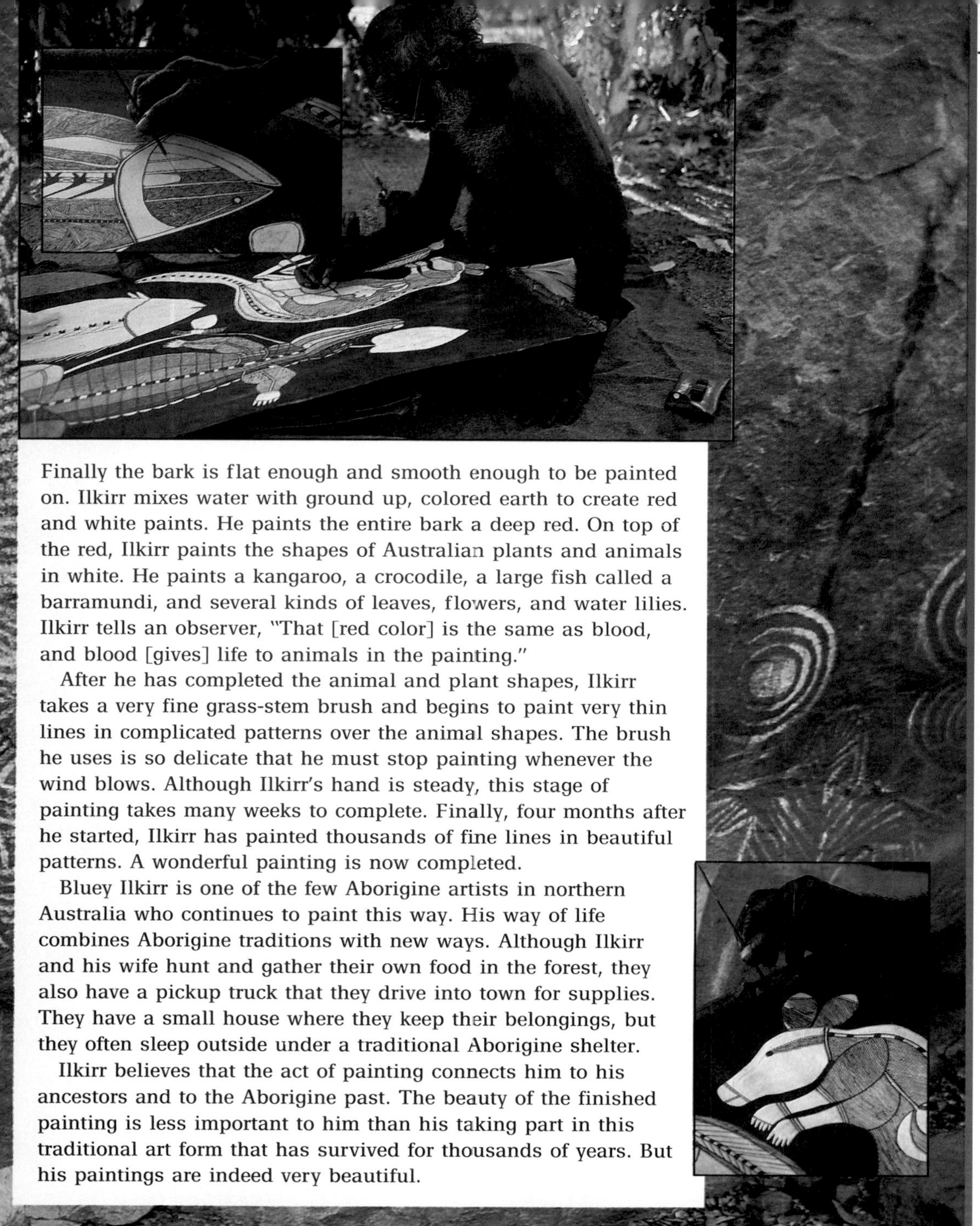

Finally the bark is flat enough and smooth enough to be painted on. Ilkirr mixes water with ground up, colored earth to create red and white paints. He paints the entire bark a deep red. On top of the red, Ilkirr paints the shapes of Australian plants and animals in white. He paints a kangaroo, a crocodile, a large fish called a barramundi, and several kinds of leaves, flowers, and water lilies. Ilkirr tells an observer, "That [red color] is the same as blood, and blood [gives] life to animals in the painting."

After he has completed the animal and plant shapes, Ilkirr takes a very fine grass-stem brush and begins to paint very thin lines in complicated patterns over the animal shapes. The brush he uses is so delicate that he must stop painting whenever the wind blows. Although Ilkirr's hand is steady, this stage of painting takes many weeks to complete. Finally, four months after he started, Ilkirr has painted thousands of fine lines in beautiful patterns. A wonderful painting is now completed.

Bluey Ilkirr is one of the few Aborigine artists in northern Australia who continues to paint this way. His way of life combines Aborigine traditions with new ways. Although Ilkirr and his wife hunt and gather their own food in the forest, they also have a pickup truck that they drive into town for supplies. They have a small house where they keep their belongings, but they often sleep outside under a traditional Aborigine shelter.

Ilkirr believes that the act of painting connects him to his ancestors and to the Aborigine past. The beauty of the finished painting is less important to him than his taking part in this traditional art form that has survived for thousands of years. But his paintings are indeed very beautiful.

Examining an Aborigine Artist at Work Continue the discussion. Tell students that people all over the world have begun to appreciate Aborigine paintings.

Ask students:

- **How does Bluey Ilkirr make the paints that he uses?** (He mixes water with ground-up earth.)
- **How does Ilkirr's lifestyle combine Aborigine tradition with modern ways of life?** (Although Ilkirr and his wife continue to live by hunting and gathering, they also own a truck that they drive into town to get supplies.)
- **Why does Ilkirr want to paint in the same way as his ancestors?** (He believes that by painting in the traditional style he is connected to his ancestors and to the Aborigine past.)
- *THINKING FURTHER:* **Why do Bluey Ilkirr and his wife continue to hunt and gather their food and to sleep in a traditional shelter?** (Lead students to understand that modern ways of life are not necessarily more desirable than traditional ways. Ilkirr and his wife prefer to live according to the traditions that they learned from their parents.)

BACKGROUND INFORMATION

Multicultural Perspectives In many ways the recent history of Australia's Aborigines has been similar to that of Native Americans. Both groups lost their lands and experienced a drastic reduction in population as a result of European colonization. When the British first came to Australia in the late 1700s, the Aborigine population was about 350,000. The British considered the Aborigines to be inferior, and they wanted to take the Aborigine lands. Thousands of Aborigines were killed during fights with the British. Even more died after they were exposed to diseases brought from Europe.

It was not until the 1960s that all Aborigines were considered citizens of Australia. Today there are only about 160,000 Aborigines in that country. Less than half of this group is considered to be full-blooded Aborigine. Many Aborigine legacies have ceased as Aborigines lost their traditional lands and were forced to move to cities. The legacies that have been kept alive, such as painting, are often continued by only a small number of people.

Ask students why the recent history of Australian Aborigines might make Aborigine painters even more committed to keeping their legacies alive.

Discussing the Dreamtime Help students to understand that different cultures have different beliefs about their origins.

Ask students:

- **What is the Dreamtime?** (According to Aborigine belief, it is a period in the past during which everything in nature was created.)
- **According to Aborigine belief, what happened to the creator spirits after they finished their work?** (They made themselves part of the land.)
- **Who do the Gagudju believe made the earliest paintings at Kakadu?** (the creator spirits)
- *THINKING FURTHER:* **Can you think of other examples of people creating stories to explain the existence of things they see in the natural world?** (Lead students to realize that people all over the world have created stories to explain things in nature that they did not understand. An example is the ancient Greek belief that the god Apollo carried the sun in his chariot across the sky.)

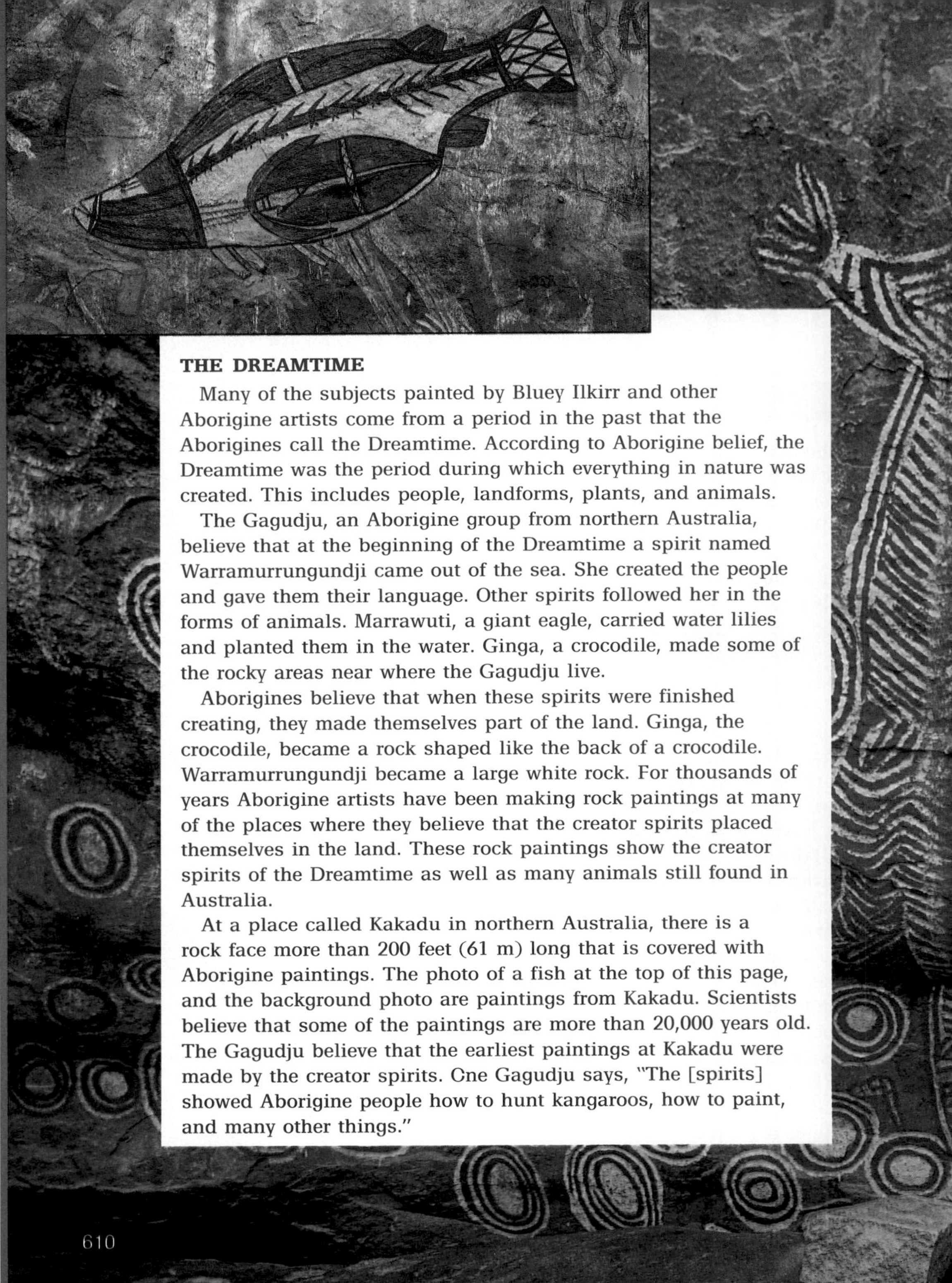

THE DREAMTIME

Many of the subjects painted by Bluey Ilkirr and other Aborigine artists come from a period in the past that the Aborigines call the Dreamtime. According to Aborigine belief, the Dreamtime was the period during which everything in nature was created. This includes people, landforms, plants, and animals.

The Gagudju, an Aborigine group from northern Australia, believe that at the beginning of the Dreamtime a spirit named Warramurrungundji came out of the sea. She created the people and gave them their language. Other spirits followed her in the forms of animals. Marrawuti, a giant eagle, carried water lilies and planted them in the water. Ginga, a crocodile, made some of the rocky areas near where the Gagudju live.

Aborigines believe that when these spirits were finished creating, they made themselves part of the land. Ginga, the crocodile, became a rock shaped like the back of a crocodile. Warramurrungundji became a large white rock. For thousands of years Aborigine artists have been making rock paintings at many of the places where they believe that the creator spirits placed themselves in the land. These rock paintings show the creator spirits of the Dreamtime as well as many animals still found in Australia.

At a place called Kakadu in northern Australia, there is a rock face more than 200 feet (61 m) long that is covered with Aborigine paintings. The photo of a fish at the top of this page, and the background photo are paintings from Kakadu. Scientists believe that some of the paintings are more than 20,000 years old. The Gagudju believe that the earliest paintings at Kakadu were made by the creator spirits. One Gagudju says, "The [spirits] showed Aborigine people how to hunt kangaroos, how to paint, and many other things."

BACKGROUND INFORMATION

More About Aborigines Today To a certain extent all Aborigines have adopted modern ways of life. Some Aborigines make a living by selling traditional artwork or crafts. However, some small groups still choose to live apart from Australia's urban society. Several Aborigine groups have managed to regain control of portions of their traditional lands. The Australian government provides Aborigines with schooling and limited economic assistance. Many Aborigines are continuing the struggle to maintain their legacies and to raise their standard of living. At the same time they must overcome the attitudes that remain from the long period of oppression.

About Aborigine Arts Just as Aborigines have a traditional style of painting, they also have traditional songs. Most are made up of short verses that are combined in long storytelling cycles. A song about a journey, for example, might tell of a traveler's thirst, the sharp stones that hurt his feet, the wild honey he found, and the spirits he encountered. The most popular musical instrument is the *didjeridu*, an end-blown wood or bamboo pipe that is 4–7 feet (1–2 m) long. Other traditional instruments are clapping sticks and rattles made from nuts or shells.

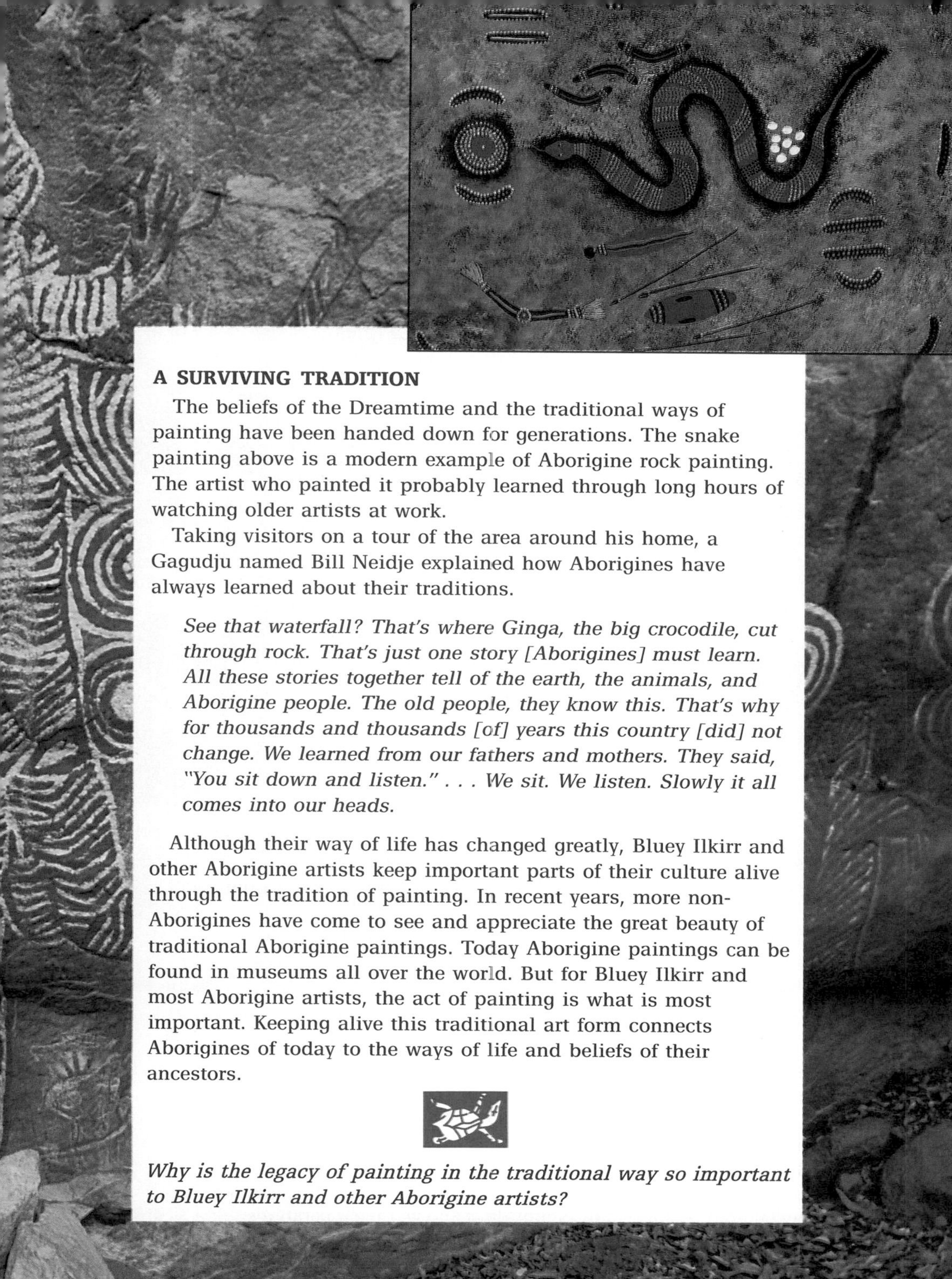

A SURVIVING TRADITION

The beliefs of the Dreamtime and the traditional ways of painting have been handed down for generations. The snake painting above is a modern example of Aborigine rock painting. The artist who painted it probably learned through long hours of watching older artists at work.

Taking visitors on a tour of the area around his home, a Gagudju named Bill Neidje explained how Aborigines have always learned about their traditions.

> *See that waterfall? That's where Ginga, the big crocodile, cut through rock. That's just one story [Aborigines] must learn. All these stories together tell of the earth, the animals, and Aborigine people. The old people, they know this. That's why for thousands and thousands [of] years this country [did] not change. We learned from our fathers and mothers. They said, "You sit down and listen." . . . We sit. We listen. Slowly it all comes into our heads.*

Although their way of life has changed greatly, Bluey Ilkirr and other Aborigine artists keep important parts of their culture alive through the tradition of painting. In recent years, more non-Aborigines have come to see and appreciate the great beauty of traditional Aborigine paintings. Today Aborigine paintings can be found in museums all over the world. But for Bluey Ilkirr and most Aborigine artists, the act of painting is what is most important. Keeping alive this traditional art form connects Aborigines of today to the ways of life and beliefs of their ancestors.

Why is the legacy of painting in the traditional way so important to Bluey Ilkirr and other Aborigine artists?

Discussing a Surviving Tradition Have a student read aloud the words of Bill Neidje.

Ask students:

- **How do Aborigine children learn about their past?** (They listen to stories told by their parents and grandparents.)

Applying the Lesson Have students look at the snake painting on this page. Point out that the snake appears to be laying eggs. Ask students to discuss what they think the painting may be communicating. (Students should understand that the subjects of Aborigine paintings are things that are important in the spiritual and everyday lives of Aborigines.)

3 CLOSE

Summarizing Students have read about the traditional painting style of Bluey Ilkirr and other Aborigine artists. They have learned why these artists feel it is important to keep their art alive.

Evaluating Assess students' understanding of the lesson by asking them the question at the bottom of the pupil page. (Possible answer includes: because these artists want to preserve their heritage.)

MEETING INDIVIDUAL NEEDS

Reteaching (easy) Have students imagine that they are Aborigine artists. Have them write a paragraph explaining why they want to follow the traditional painting style of their ancestors.

Extension (average) Have students research another aspect of Aborigine life or art. Body painting and hunting techniques are possible topics. Ask students to present to the class a report summarizing what they have learned.

Enrichment (challenging) Have students use paper and markers or crayons to make a painting in the traditional Aborigine style. Have them follow the steps described in the text on page 609.

CHAPTER 30 REVIEW
pages 612–613

USING THE CHAPTER SUMMARY AND REVIEW

Physical Geography These questions may be used for review.

- **Who were the original inhabitants of Australia?** (the Aborigines)
- **What are the two major industries in Australia? In New Zealand?** (sheep ranching, mining; farming, ranching)
- **What are the four British Commonwealth countries in the region?** (Australia, New Zealand, Papua New Guinea, Fiji)
- **What is one example of tradition in the arts?** (chants that retell histories of clans)

Ideas to Remember

- **Why did the people of Australia and the Pacific islands develop distinct cultures?** (because of their isolation from the outside world)
- **Which two countries have the most developed economies in the region?** (Australia and New Zealand)
- **What are three forms of government in the region?** (parliamentary, monarchy, a mix of traditional and modern)
- **Why are outdoor sports popular in the region?** (because of sunny days and warm temperatures)

Answers to Reviewing Vocabulary

1. True.
2. True.
3. True.
4. True.
5. Trust territories are controlled by another country until that country decides the trust territory is ready to govern itself.

Answers to Reviewing Facts

1. Many were killed or died from diseases that the Europeans brought.

CHAPTER 30 • SUMMARY

NATIONS OF THE PACIFIC: CULTURAL GEOGRAPHY

PEOPLE

- Australian Aborigines: original inhabitants; some live traditional life today
- Micronesians and Melanesians: farmers; extended family groups or clans

- Polynesians: expert sailors and shipbuilders; settled Tahiti, Samoa, Hawaii, New Zealand
- Europeans: first arrived in 1500s; first settled in Australia in 1788; introduced English language and customs

ECONOMY

- Australia: developed economy; urban, with large cities like Sydney and Melbourne

- Australian sheep ranching provides one third of world's wool; mining is also a major industry
- New Zealand: farming and ranching; world's largest wool exporter
- Islands: tourism key source of income; developing economies; subsistence farming

GOVERNMENT

- British Commonwealth countries: Australia, New Zealand, Papua New Guinea, Fiji

- Australia: democratic monarchy; parliamentary system; country made up of six states and two territories
- Trust territories: temporarily controlled by outside country; for example, Guam
- Many islands have traditional governments with village chiefs

ARTS AND RECREATION

- Traditional culture: chants retell histories of clans

- Australia has produced world-famous entertainers in opera, movies, popular music

- Outdoor sports are popular

IDEAS TO REMEMBER

- People who settled in Australia and the Pacific islands developed distinct cultures because of their isolation from the outside world.
- Australia and New Zealand have the most developed economies in the region; in the Pacific island countries tourism is important.
- Among the forms of government in the Pacific are parliamentary systems, monarchies, and mixtures of traditional and modern governments.
- Arts and recreation in the Pacific combine the old and new, while outdoor sports are popular because of the sunny days and warm temperatures.

612

ENRICHMENT ACTIVITY

Making Polynesian Boat Models **Materials:** Styrofoam blocks, craft sticks, milk cartons, string, cloth for sails, scissors

1. Review with the class the material on Polynesian sailing and boatbuilding on pages 598–599. Tell students that they are going to build models of traditional Polynesian vessels.
2. Divide the class into groups and assign half of them catamarans and the other half outrigger canoes. Have students utilize encyclopedias and the services of the school librarian to research and find pictures of their vessels.
3. Have students make their models by carving catamaran hulls out of Styrofoam blocks, making catamaran platforms out of craft sticks, carving canoes out of milk cartons, using craft sticks for canoe outrigger and oars, and cutting sails from cloth.

CHAPTER 30 • REVIEW

REVIEWING VOCABULARY

Each of the following statements contains an underlined vocabulary word or term. Number a sheet of paper from 1 to 5. Beside each number write whether the following statements are true or false. If the statement is true, write "true." If it is false, rewrite the sentence using the vocabulary word correctly.

1. Stations are huge cattle ranches in New Zealand and Australia.
2. Although a trust territory does not belong to an outside power, its government is controlled by a foreign country.
3. Only 6 percent of Australians work on farms or stations.
4. Several Pacific islands, such as Guam, are trust territories of the United States.
5. Trust territories are controlled by another country until the trust territory decides to govern itself.

REVIEWING FACTS

1. Describe two effects that European settlement had on Australia's aborigines.
2. What effect did Melanesia's rugged landscape have on the region's culture?
3. Describe two features of traditional culture that are still maintained in rural Melanesia.
4. Why have the ancient Polynesians often been compared to the Vikings?
5. Who were the first British settlers in Australia? When did these settlers arrive?
6. Why is Australia's economy called a developed economy?
7. Name two things that are similar about the governments of Australia and the United States.
8. How are the governments of New Zealand and Australia similar?
9. What are *aigas*? What are *matais*? On which Polynesian island are these institutions still found?
10. What does a Samoan canoe race have in common with traditional warfare in the Pacific islands?

WRITING ABOUT MAIN IDEAS

1. **Writing a Legend:** You read about a Polynesian legend describing the "paradise" of Tahiti. Write a legend describing the arrival of Europeans in Australia from the standpoint of the aborigines.
2. **Writing a Proposal:** A proposal is a document that makes recommendations to create, improve, or change something. Write a proposal entitled "A Plan for Developing the Economies of the Pacific Islands."
3. **Writing a Report:** Write a report about the status of both the aborigines in Australia and the Maoris in New Zealand. You may wish to use encyclopedias, magazines, and newspapers to supplement the information presented in the text.
4. **Writing About Perspectives:** Imagine a conversation between two New Zealanders: one of Maori ancestry, the other of European ancestry. Write something each might tell the other about the important traditions of his or her people.

BUILDING SKILLS: DECISION MAKING

1. Use your own words to define *decision making*.
2. List the steps you might follow in making a sound decision.
3. Why is it important to know how to make decisions?

613

2. Different languages and customs developed.
3. Life is centered around the clan or extended family group, and men and women live in separate houses.
4. They were expert sailors and shipbuilders.
5. mostly convicts; in 1788
6. because it is a mixture of farming, ranching, mining, manufacturing, and service industries
7. federal system of government, secret ballots
8. parliamentary systems, both headed by a prime minister
9. large family clans; high chiefs; Samoa
10. During canoe races Samoans chant as they once did going into battle.

Suggestions for Writing About Main Ideas

1. Students should focus on how the Europeans upset the lives of the aborigines.
2. You may want to have students work in groups to develop their proposals.
3. Have students take turns presenting their reports. Discuss the similarities and differences between students' reports.
4. You may want to have students work in pairs and present their conversation as a dramatic dialogue.

Answers to Building Skills: Decision Making

1. Possible answers include: selecting from among a number of alternatives or options one that will help you achieve your goal.
2. Identify and clearly define the goal you wish to achieve; identify all possible options; predict the likely consequences; evaluate each consequence; choose the best option.
3. to help you in achieving success and happiness

Chapter Review and Test

Practice Book: *Vocabulary Review,* page 168
Transparency: *Graphic Organizer*
Assessment Book: *Chapter 30 Test*

MAKING CONNECTIONS

Organizing Information Have students create their own graphic organizer for this chapter or display the Semantic Map Graphic Organizer Transparency, filling in only the chapter title, or underlined copy. Have students fill in the main topics covered in the chapter and important details relating to each topic. *Ask:* What conclusion(s) can you draw about the governments, economies, and cultures of the Pacific nations? (varied; blend of the traditional and modern)

Nations of the Pacific

Economy
Australia: developed
Islands: tourism, farming

Government
British Commonwealth, trust territories, traditional

Culture
traditional, football, rugby

People
Aborigines, Polynesians, Europeans

UNIT 8 REVIEW
pages 614–615

USING THE UNIT SUMMARY AND REVIEW

Physical Geography These questions may be used for review.

- **Which landmasses make up this region?** (the continents of Australia and Antarctica and the islands that make up Oceania)
- **How does the ocean affect the climate of the region?** (The ocean moderates the climate.)
- **What is the "Tree of Life" and in which countries is it important?** (the coconut; the island countries)

Cultural Geography

- **Where did Europeans first settle in this region?** (Australia)
- **What is the main source of income in the islands?** (tourism)
- **What are two examples of trust territories in the region?** (Palau and Guam)
- **What type of sports are popular in the region?** (outdoor sports)

UNIT 8 • SUMMARY

THE PACIFIC: PHYSICAL GEOGRAPHY

LANDFORMS

- Two large continents (Australia and Antarctica), thousands of islands (Oceania)
- Antarctica: huge frozen continent

CLIMATE

- Australia mostly dry; others get plenty of rain
- Ocean moderates climates

- Typhoons: tropical hurricanes that strike 2-3 times a year

NATURAL RESOURCES

- Australia: abundant land for ranching; minerals such as bauxite, iron, silver, coal, oil, natural gas, uranium
- New Zealand: water, forests, good soil
- Tropical islands: natural beauty
- Coconut: the "Tree of Life" for island countries

THE PACIFIC: CULTURAL GEOGRAPHY

PEOPLE

- Original inhabitants and early settlers: Australian aborigines, Melanesians, Micronesians, Polynesians
- Europeans: first arrived in 1500s; first settled in Australia in 1788; introduced English language and customs

ECONOMY

- Australia: developed economy; urban, with large cities like Sydney and Melbourne

- Sheep ranching: major industry in Australia and New Zealand
- Islands: tourism key source of income; developing economies; subsistence farming

GOVERNMENT

- British Commonwealth countries: Australia, New Zealand, Papua New Guinea, Fiji
- Trust territories: temporarily controlled by outside country; for example, Palau, Guam
- Many islands have traditional governments with village chiefs

ARTS AND RECREATION

- Traditional culture: chants retell histories of clans
- Australia has produced world-famous entertainers in opera, movies, popular music

- Outdoor sports are popular

614

ENRICHMENT ACTIVITY

Creating a Newsmagazine **Materials:** construction paper, pictures from magazines or travel brochures, paste, pens, paints or markers, hole puncher, string

1. Tell the class that they are going to create a newsmagazine called "Pacific Report." The magazine's purpose is to keep Pacific nations in touch with one another and to communicate that information to the rest of the world.
2. Divide the class into groups. Make one the editorial and production group. Assign each of the other groups one or two of the Pacific nations listed on pages 580–581. Tell each group to do research both in encyclopedias and in current news publications to find material for a magazine article about their nation(s). Have students write and illustrate their articles.
3. Meanwhile, the editorial and production group should be designing and producing a cover and making up a few ads that might appear in such a magazine. When this group receives the stories from the other groups, its members should assemble and bind the edition.

UNIT 8 • REVIEW

REVIEWING VOCABULARY

atoll
trust territory
copra
typhoon
outback

Number a sheet of paper from 1 to 5. Beside each number write the word or term from the above list that best completes the sentence.

1. Consisting of the dried meat of the coconut, ____ is a major export product for many Pacific islands.
2. The government of a ____ is controlled by another country until that country feels the land is ready for self-government.
3. A whirling tropical hurricane, or ____, strikes Oceania several times a year.
4. A doughnut-shaped coral reef, or ____, may have formed on the rim of a submerged volcano in Oceania.
5. The ____ is an arid, desolate region in the interior of Australia where few people live.

WRITING ABOUT THE UNIT

1. **Writing a Paragraph:** You read that Australia is the oldest continent. Write a paragraph that describes the evidence for this idea.
2. **Writing a Letter:** Imagine that you are a scientist stationed in Antarctica. In a letter to a friend, write your observations about the frozen continent.
3. **Writing About Perspectives:** Imagine that you are the leader of the first group of Polynesians to land on the island of Tahiti. Write a diary entry describing your new island home.

ACTIVITIES

1. **Working Together to Construct a Regional Data Chart:** Work together to construct a chart showing data for Australia, New Zealand, and the United States. The three countries should be listed at the left of the chart. At the top of the chart, from left to right, the following categories should appear: area (in square miles and kilometers); population; population density (number of persons per square mile/square kilometer); GNP (gross national product); and per capita income (expressed in dollars). Use almanacs to obtain this information.
2. **Presenting an Oral Report:** Use juvenile nonfiction books and encyclopedias to research coral reef formation. Present your findings in an oral report to the rest of the class.

LINKING PAST, PRESENT, AND FUTURE

Some of the things that have attracted countless newcomers to Oceania, from ancient Polynesian seafarers to modern tourists, are the mild climate, abundant food, and natural beauty of the islands. Many of these islands are now struggling to develop their resources to meet the needs of growing populations. Do you think that Oceania will be able to remain a "paradise" in the face of such change? What will islands like Samoa and Tahiti be like in the twenty-first century?

615

Answers to Reviewing Vocabulary

1. copra
2. trust territory
3. typhoon
4. atolls
5. outback

Suggestions for Writing About the Unit

1. You may wish to have students do additional research before they write their paragraphs.
2. Students might focus on their feelings about this isolated region as well as on the climate and geography of the continent.
3. Students should discuss the geography and climate of the region and perhaps how the group will manage in their new home.

Suggestions for Activities

1. Students should use the most current almanacs to obtain the information they need. You may wish to display students' charts in the classroom.
2. This activity lends itself to a cooperative learning approach. Have students take turns presenting their oral reports. Students may include information on how a reef is formed and what kinds of animal life depend on reefs.

Suggestions for Linking Past, Present, and Future Students who think that Oceania will remain a paradise might focus on the positive role of tourism in the area. Those who disagree may focus on the problems that tourism might bring to the region, such as pollution.

PERFORMANCE ASSESSMENT

Demonstrating Understanding Remind students that they were told at the beginning of the unit that they would have a chance to demonstrate what they have learned by taking part in a television quiz show. Have students work in groups of four or five. Suggest that the members of each group work together to write 40 questions about the Pacific. Have students write each question on one side of a 3x5 card. Then have students work individually or in pairs to find and write the answer to each question on the reverse side of the card. Allow time for students to study and practice answering the questions. Remind them of the standards that will be applied to their questions, which were outlined in the Unit Opener on page 578. Call on volunteer observers to act as game show hosts, reading either the questions or answers on the 3x5 cards while you keep track of the contestants' responses on tally sheets. For additional performance assessment information, see page TM48 in the *Assessment Book.*

For the Portfolio: Include students' 3x5 cards in their portfolios as well as your participation tally sheets. Also include your anecdotal record or observational checklist.

CONCLUSION
pages 616–618

Lesson Theme A healthy earth depends upon people and countries cooperating and working together to protect our vital natural resources.

Lesson Objectives
- Identify the cooperation needed in the twenty-first century.
- Describe citizenship responsibilities in the future.

1 PREPARE

Motivate Have students imagine that they are on the satellite taking the photographs from which this map was made. Ask them if they think they will experience space travel during their lifetime. (It is predicted that many people in the twenty-first century will travel in space.)

Set Purpose Tell students it is now time to put together all the regions that they have studied in this book in order to see the world as a whole.

2 TEACH

Looking at the Whole World Have students ponder the question, "What have you learned about our world?" Divide the class into groups to brainstorm and list the things they know about the world as a whole. (Possible answers include: all the continents, all the oceans, the eight culture regions, how people everywhere are the same and how they are different, how economies are tied together by world trade, how governments follow international laws, and how arts, leisure activities, and sports unify people the world over.)

RESOURCE Reminder
Outline Map: *The World*
Transparency Maps: 1–3.

Conclusion

In this book you have studied the planet earth, from the farthest northern reaches of Canada to the outback of Australia. You have seen how people interact in the world's eight regions: the United States and Canada, Latin America, Western Europe, Eastern Europe and Northern Asia, the Middle East and North Africa, Sub-Saharan Africa, Southern and Eastern Asia, and the Pacific. What have you learned about our world?

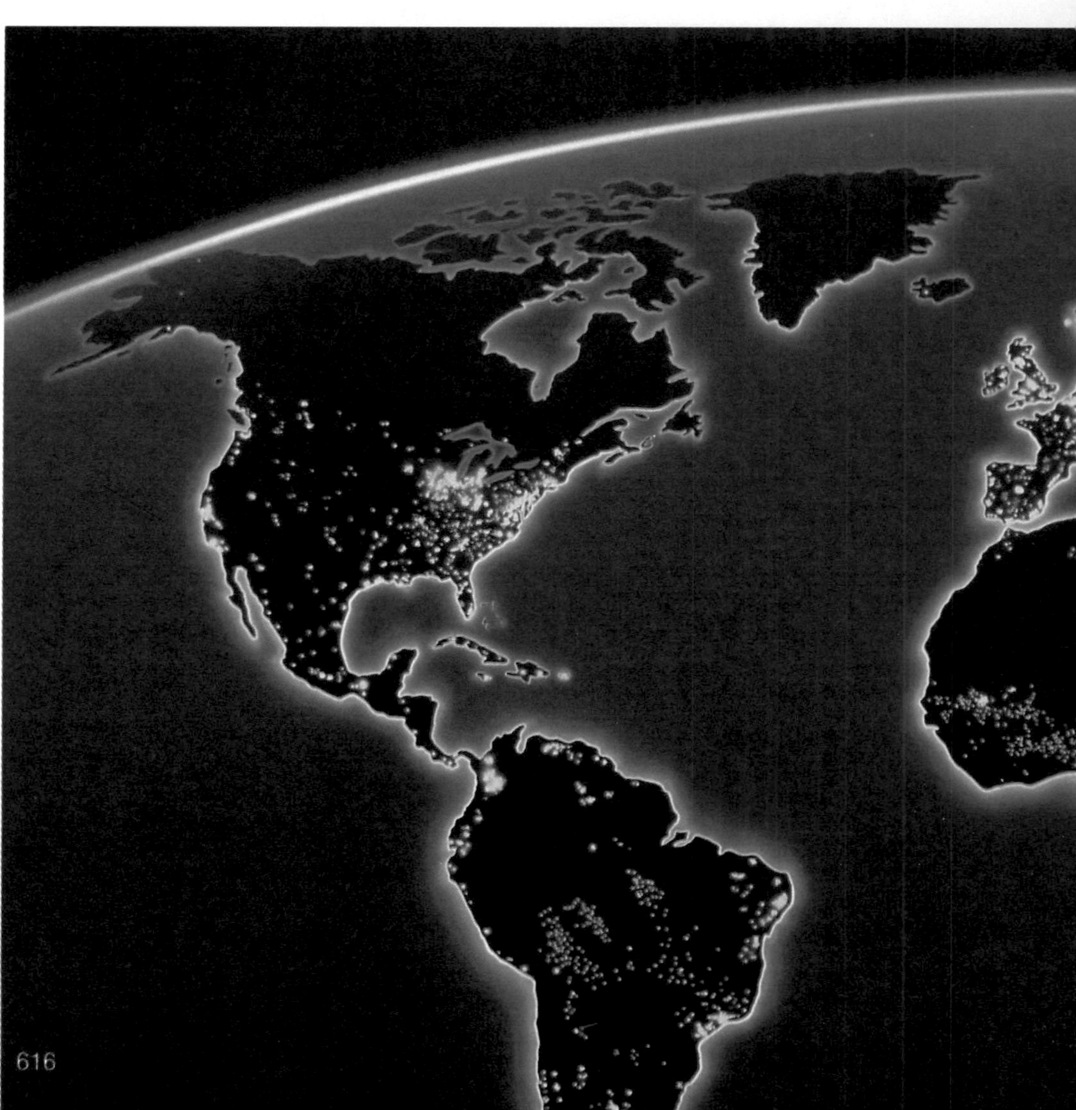

616

5 FUNDAMENTAL THEMES OF GEOGRAPHY

Human-Environment Interaction During the 1980s people became more conscious of environmental issues. In 1989 *Time* magazine did a cover story on the "Planet of the Year" instead of the "Man of the Year" and named the "Endangered Earth" as the featured planet. There was concern about the negative results of human-environment interaction over the entire earth. Economists and environmentalists who had disagreed for many years began to talk together about the endangered earth systems. Out of this cooperation came a new concept. It is known as "sustainable economic development," "sustainable growth," or a "sustainable earth." This new concept means that humans will try to make wiser use of the earth's resources, thus promoting economic growth that does less damage to the environment through policies such as recycling. Discuss students' ideas on ways to make wiser use of the earth's resources.

THE EARTH AT NIGHT

Look at the map on this page. It shows what the earth looks like at night, based on satellite photographs. The bright yellow spots on the map are sources of light. Most are from urban areas but some come from other sources, such as fires used in slash-and-burn farming. The bright lights around Japan are from huge floodlights used by fishing fleets to attract squid.

As you look at the map, think about what you have read in this book. Can you see how some of the important concepts you have learned are shown on the map?

Look at the eastern United States and Western Europe. Their dense population is shown by the tight grouping of bright lights. Similarly, you can see by the lights that most of Canada's people live along its southern border with the United States.

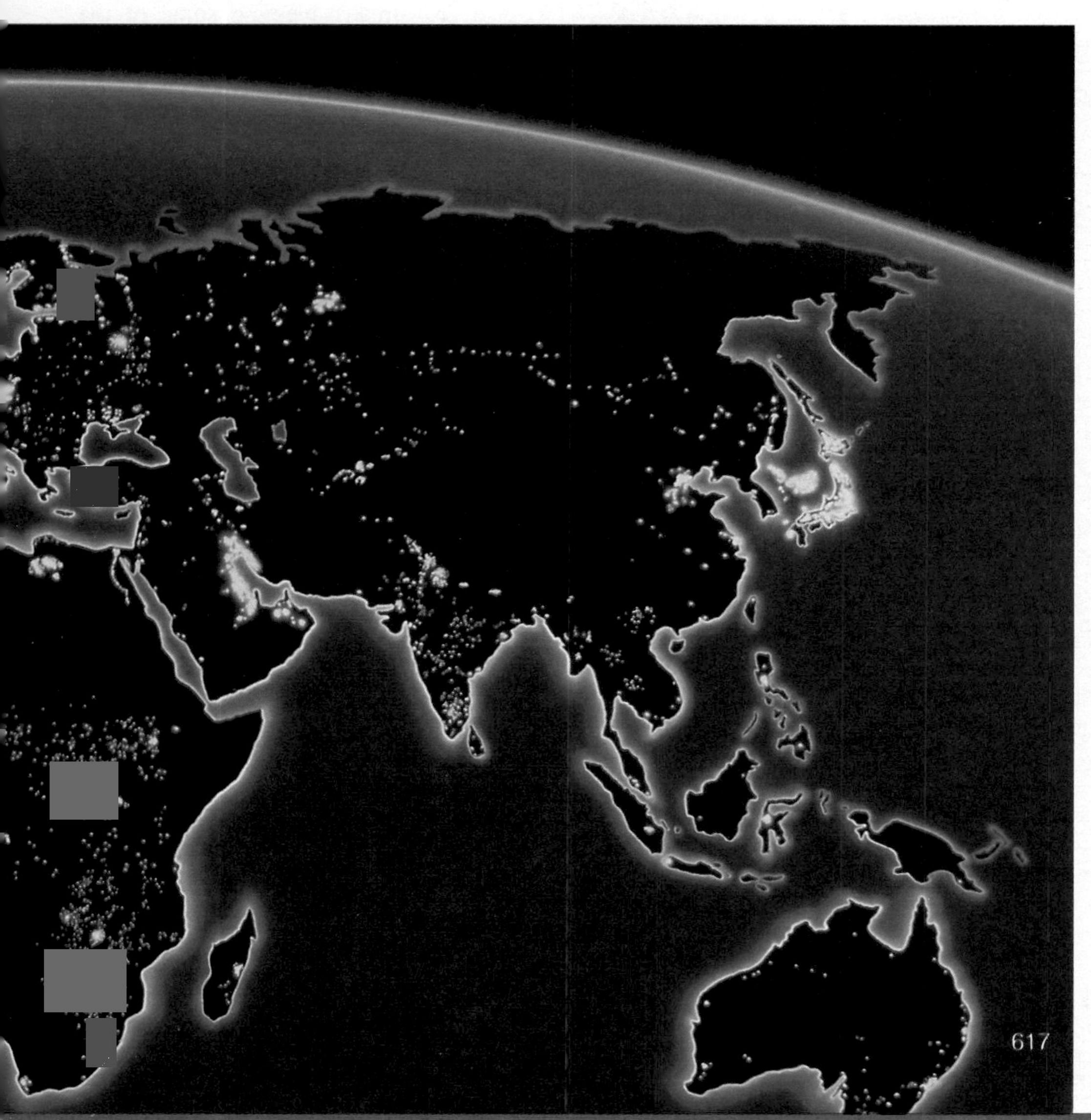

617

Analyzing the Earth at Night Help students to locate the following on the map on pages 616–617: fires from slash-and-burn farming in the Amazon Basin; squid-fishing boat lights in the Sea of Japan to the west of Japan; the megalopolises on the northeastern and southwestern coasts of the United States, along the southern edge of the Great Lakes in the United States, in southern England, in the Ruhr Valley between France and Germany, and in Japan; lights along Canada's southern border with the United States.

EXTENDING MAP SKILLS

Have students study the map on pages 616–617.

Ask students:

- **What makes this map so dramatic?** (its color scheme showing night lights and the curve of the earth's horizon)
- *THINKING FURTHER:* **What do you think causes the brightest splotches of light along the Persian Gulf and in North Africa, Venezuela, Eastern Europe, Nigeria, and Northern Asia?** (These are oil fields in which the natural gas that comes up with the oil is burned away into the air as gigantic flares that burn continuously.)

BACKGROUND INFORMATION

More About the "Map" A mosaic image was made from many satellite photographs of the earth that were taken at night; then this "map" was created from that mosaic image.

- The band of lights across the southern border of the Sahara Desert in the Sahel represents the seasonal grassland fires burning there.
- Ask students to locate the two nations that look as if they are almost totally illuminated and to tell how they are the same and how they are different. (Japan and the United Kingdom are both island nations, but one is in Asia and the other is in Europe.)

CURRICULUM CONNECTION

Math On page 23 students studied a circle graph showing the land surface on earth. In the Curriculum Connection section on that page students were asked to design and complete a chart of the percentages of arable land on each continent. Their charts should now be complete. Have students compare the percentages of the earth's land surface under the column headings on their chart with the arable land in each region. Use this chart to discuss whether or not we can keep producing enough food to feed the world. Suggest that the amount of arable land may limit future food production.

Discussing Working Together and the Future Ask students to give examples of how people worldwide are cooperating.

Applying the Lesson Divide the class into groups. Have them read the final quotation on this page and brainstorm a list of actions they could take to help planet earth.

3 CLOSE

Summarizing Students have learned that views of regions from space have helped people to realize that international cooperation is necessary to save our endangered earth. Discuss ways this cooperation might be accomplished.

Evaluating Have students write an essay titled "The Most Important Things I Learned This Year."

The children of today will become the workers and leaders of tomorrow.

Can you find the Nile River Valley? As you may remember, it is in the northeastern part of Africa, near the Arabian Peninsula. You can follow the outline of the river on the map by the lights from the many towns along its banks. In contrast, look at the vast dark expanses of the Sahara, home to so few people.

In Unit 4 you read about how the Trans-Siberian Railroad links the remote parts of Russia. Can you find the railroad on this map? It is indicated by the lights of the cities and villages along its route.

In Unit 2 you read about the pros and cons of the effort to develop Brazil's rain forest. Many of the lights shown in South America are from forest fires that have been set to clear the rain forest.

These are just some of the things this map shows about life on our planet. As you study the map further, think about other ways in which it reflects what you have learned about the world.

WORKING TOGETHER

As we move toward the twenty-first century we on planet earth face many great challenges. You have read about some of them, such as the acid rain that threatens to kill forests in the United States, Canada, and Western Europe. At times it may seem that these problems are too big to be solved. Is there a future for our planet? Yes, if the people of the earth work together to guarantee it.

We are already meeting some of the challenges, such as population growth. Although the world's population is growing quickly, food production is growing even faster. If we can keep producing food at this pace, we will be able to feed a world population of more than 10 billion people 100 years from now!

THE FUTURE

Right now people from all over the world are working together in ways that you probably cannot even imagine. American, Canadian, Russian, Italian, Norwegian, and Chinese scientists are exploring Antarctica and measuring the far-reaching effects of air pollution. UNICEF—the United Nations Children's Fund—is working to house, feed, and clothe nearly 1 billion children in more than 100 countries. And in cities and towns all over our country, people are organizing efforts to recycle important natural resources such as aluminum. Recycling programs enable us to use natural resources over and over again.

In the future it will be your responsibility to make sure that these efforts continue. As one scientist has noted:

> *Our ability to look back on ourselves from outer space symbolizes the unique perspective we have on our environment. . . . With this knowledge comes a responsibility . . . to manage the human use of planet earth.*

 GRAPH SKILL: 2.1 percent

MEETING INDIVIDUAL NEEDS

Reteaching (easy) Have a class discussion about how world regions are tied together like a global village. Then have students write a paragraph giving reasons that the United States needs to cooperate with other countries.

Extension (average) Have students create posters on ways that countries can cooperate to make the twenty-first century better than the twentieth.

Enrichment (challenging) Divide the class into five groups to research and report on these world topics: the economics of a "global village"; global warming versus a new Ice Age; natural hazards; technological hazards; "sustainable economic growth."

REFERENCE SECTION

619

Atlas

An atlas is a collection of maps. An atlas can be a book or a separate section within a book. This Atlas is a separate section with maps to help you study the history and geography presented in this book.

MAP BUILDER

The World: Land Use and Population

The map on the facing page is a special kind of map. Each transparent overlay shows a different aspect of the world's population and different types of land use. You can see where in the world different land uses dominate and how these relate to population. You can also compare population densities around the world and see which areas contain the greatest concentrations of people. Start by lifting all of the transparent overlays and observe the base map of the world's continents and oceans. Then cover the base map with the first overlay to study the land use shown. Does your area fall into this category?

Allow the second overlay to cover the first and consider these land uses. What land uses are now show? Finally, let down the third overlay and compare population densities around the world. Which areas of the world are the most densely populated? In which areas do the fewest people live?

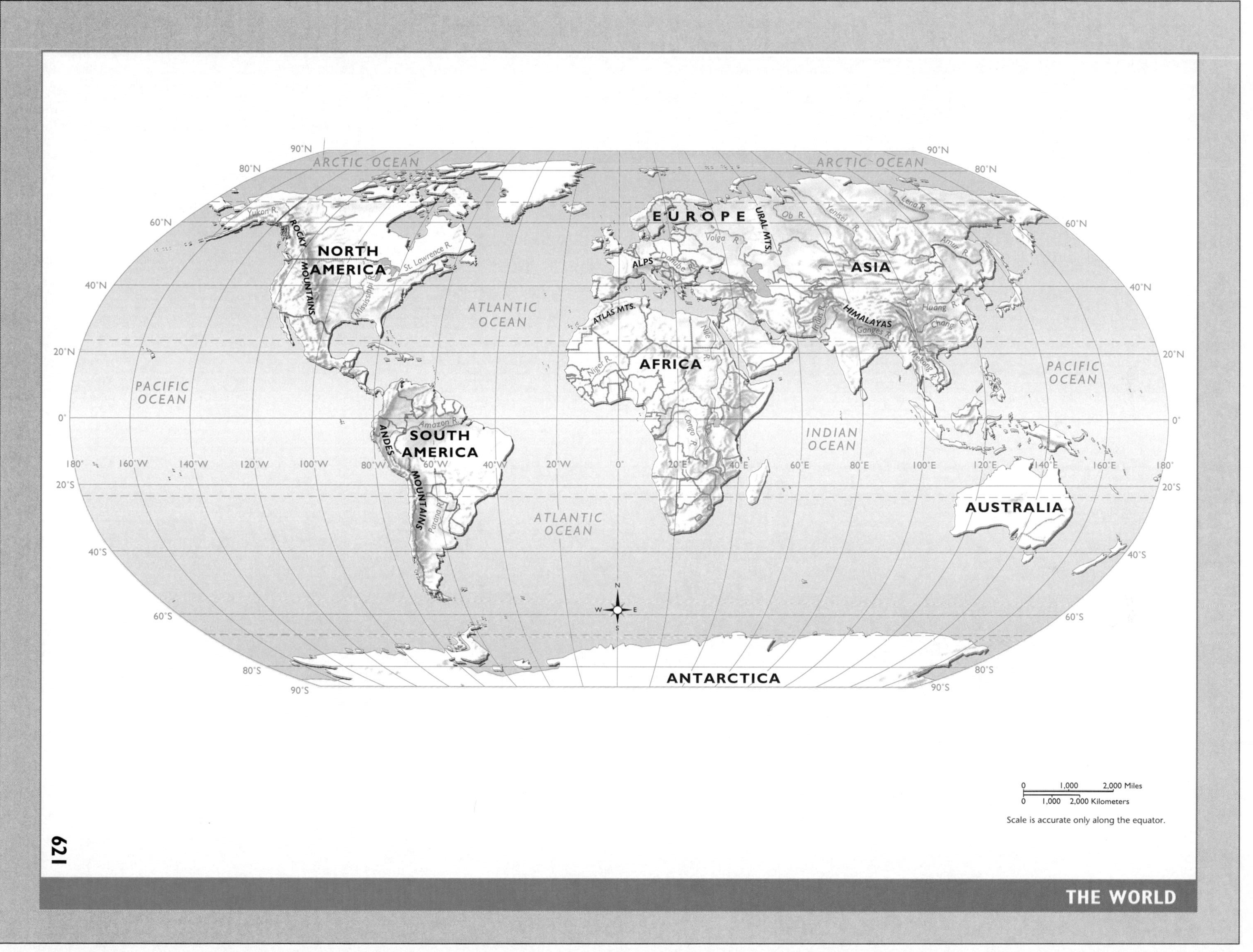

THE WORLD
ARCTIC OCEAN
ARCTIC OCEAN
NORTH AMERICA
ROCKY MOUNTAINS
Yukon R.
Mississippi R.
St. Lawrence R.
ATLANTIC OCEAN
PACIFIC OCEAN
SOUTH AMERICA
ANDES MOUNTAINS
Amazon R.
Parana R.
EUROPE
ALPS
Danube R.
Volga R.
URAL MTS.
Ob R.
Yenisei R.
Lena R.
Amur R.
ASIA
HIMALAYAS
Indus R.
Ganges R.
Huang R.
Chang R.
Mekong R.
AFRICA
ATLAS MTS.
Niger R.
Nile R.
Congo R.
ATLANTIC OCEAN
INDIAN OCEAN
PACIFIC OCEAN
AUSTRALIA
ANTARCTICA
N
S
E
W
90°N
80°N
60°N
40°N
20°N
0°
20°S
40°S
60°S
80°S
90°S
180°
160°W
140°W
120°W
100°W
80°W
60°W
40°W
20°W
0°
20°E
40°E
60°E
80°E
100°E
120°E
140°E
160°E
180°
0 1,000 2,000 Miles
0 1,000 2,000 Kilometers
Scale is accurate only along the equator.

621

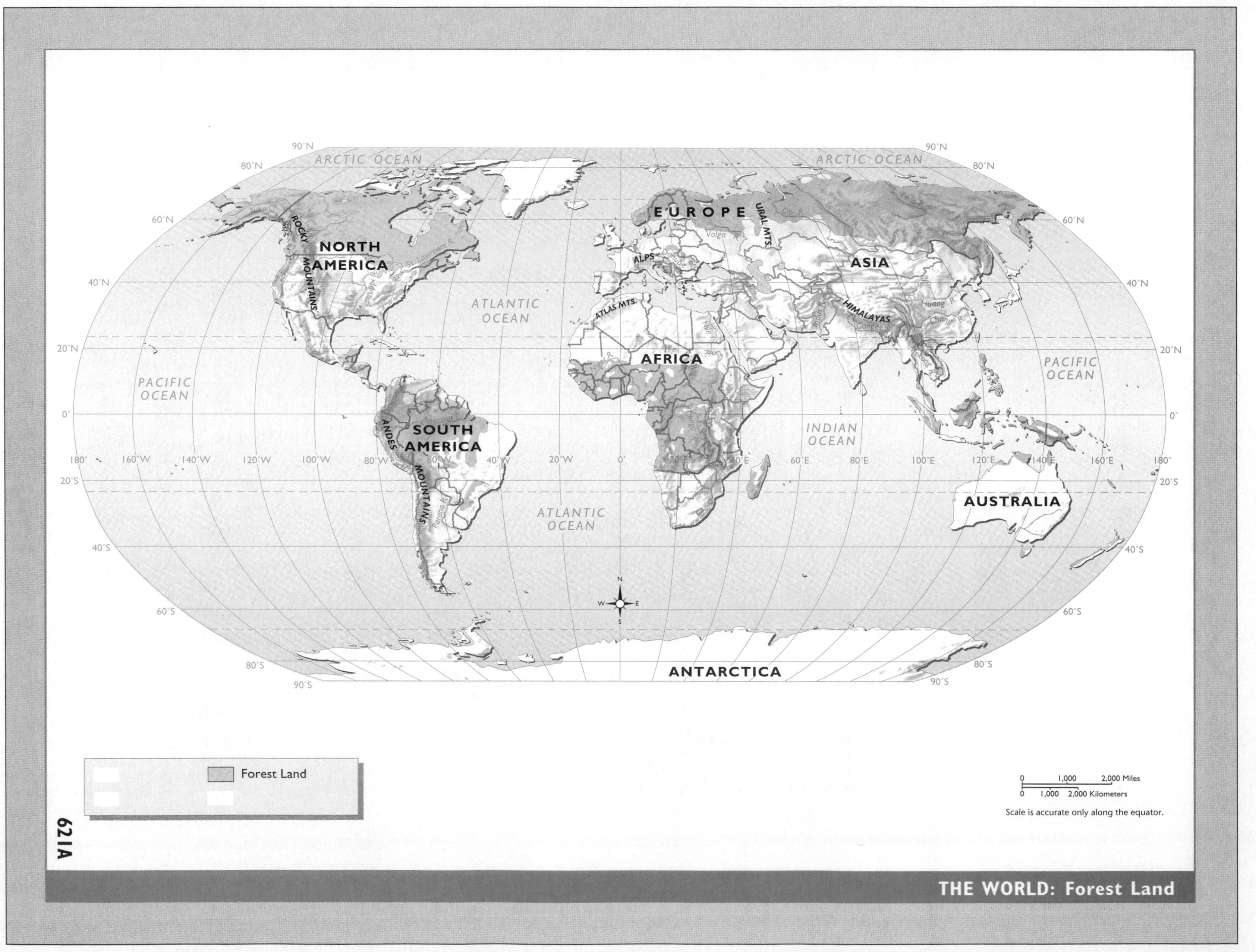
THE WORLD: Forest Land
ARCTIC OCEAN
PACIFIC OCEAN
ATLANTIC OCEAN
INDIAN OCEAN
NORTH AMERICA
SOUTH AMERICA
EUROPE
ASIA
AFRICA
AUSTRALIA
ANTARCTICA
ROCKY MOUNTAINS
ANDES MOUNTAINS
ALPS
ATLAS MTS.
URAL MTS.
HIMALAYAS
Forest Land
0 1,000 2,000 Miles
0 1,000 2,000 Kilometers
Scale is accurate only along the equator.
621A

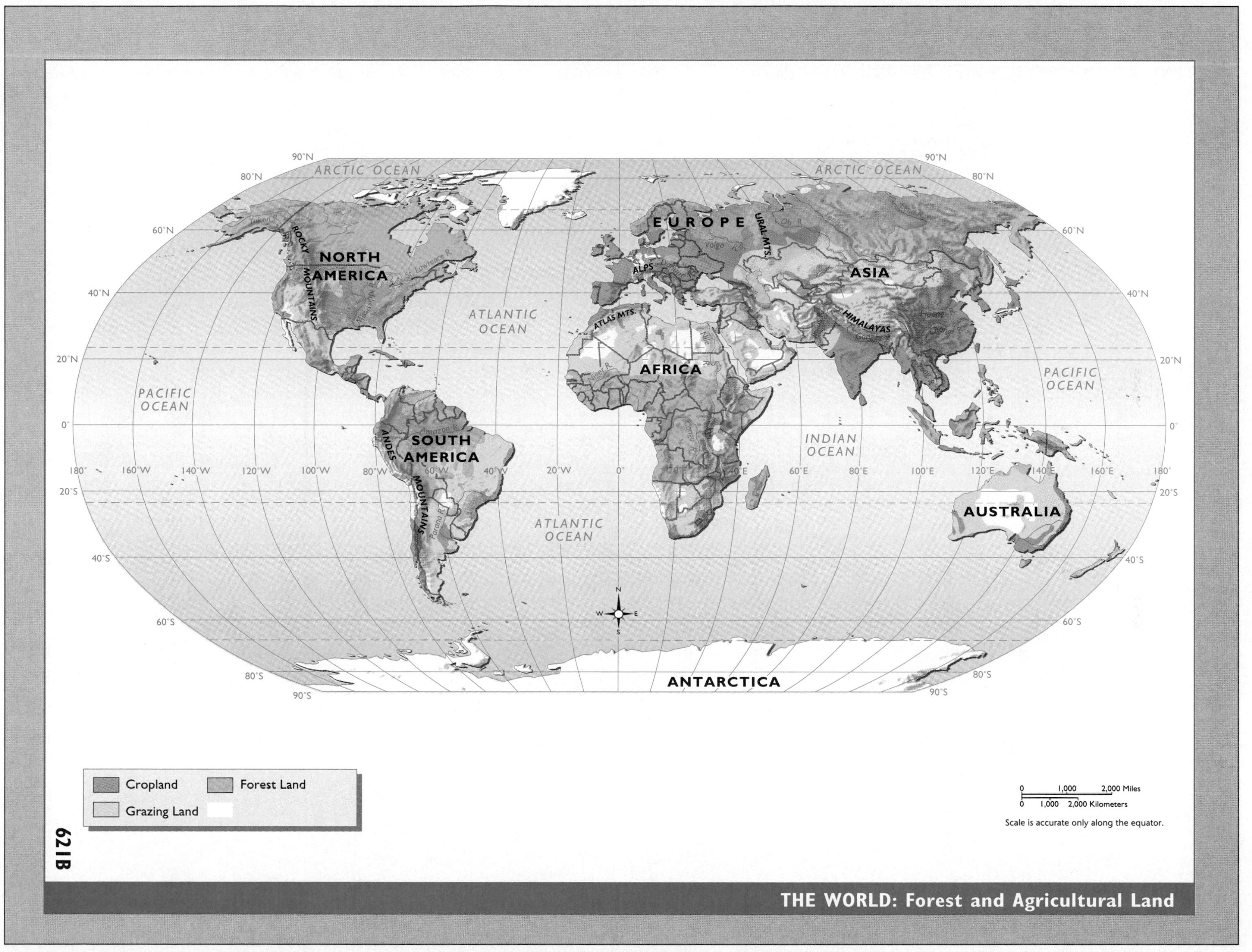

THE WORLD: Forest and Agricultural Land

621B

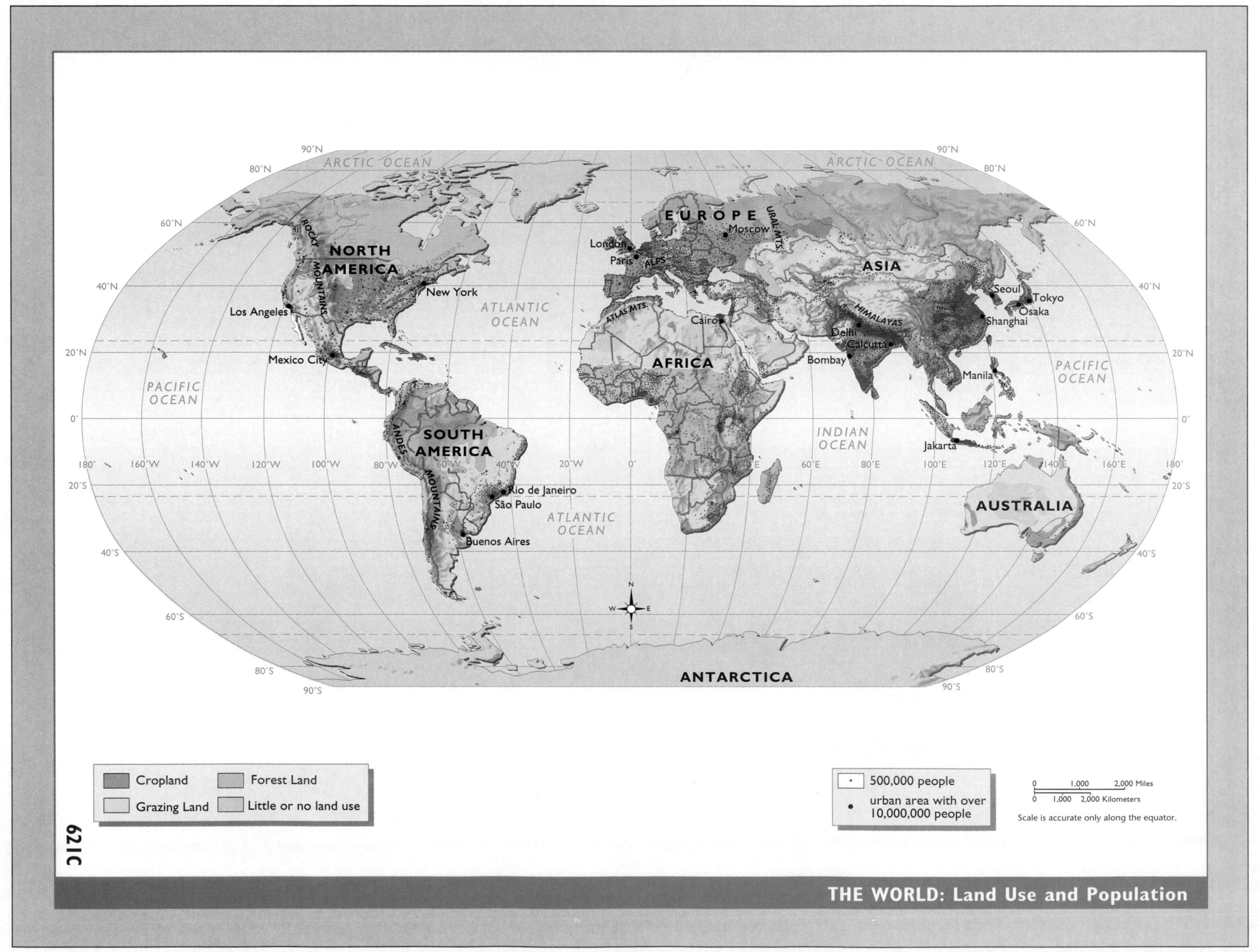
THE WORLD: Land Use and Population
ARCTIC OCEAN
PACIFIC OCEAN
ATLANTIC OCEAN
INDIAN OCEAN
NORTH AMERICA
SOUTH AMERICA
EUROPE
ASIA
AFRICA
AUSTRALIA
ANTARCTICA
ROCKY MOUNTAINS
ANDES MOUNTAINS
ALPS
URAL MTS.
ATLAS MTS.
HIMALAYAS
Los Angeles
Mexico City
New York
Rio de Janeiro
São Paulo
Buenos Aires
London
Paris
Moscow
Cairo
Delhi
Calcutta
Bombay
Seoul
Tokyo
Osaka
Shanghai
Manila
Jakarta
Cropland
Forest Land
Grazing Land
Little or no land use
500,000 people
urban area with over 10,000,000 people
0 1,000 2,000 Miles
0 1,000 2,000 Kilometers
Scale is accurate only along the equator.

621C

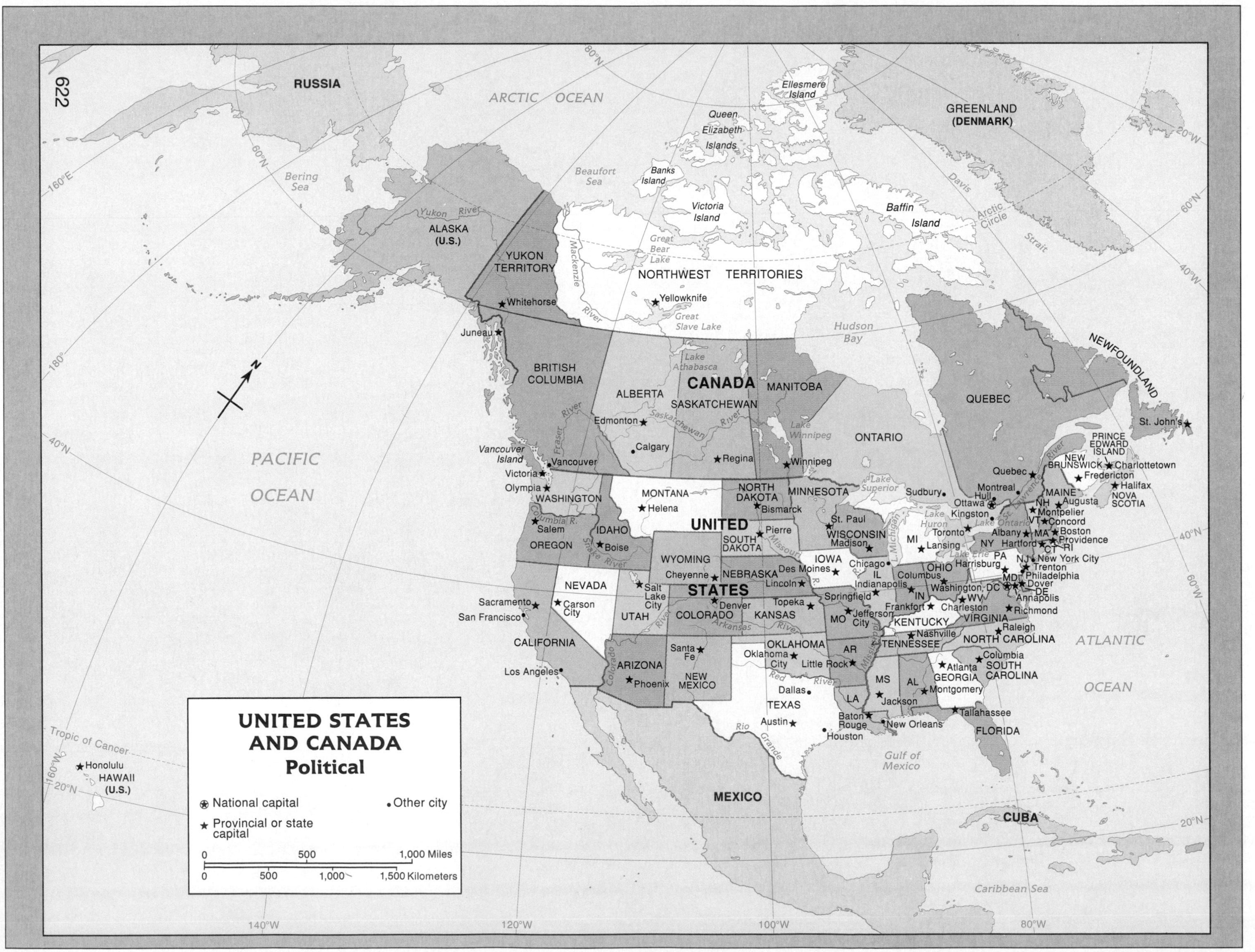

UNITED STATES AND CANADA
Political
National capital
Other city
Provincial or state capital
0 500 1,000 Miles
0 500 1,000 1,500 Kilometers
622
RUSSIA
ARCTIC OCEAN
GREENLAND (DENMARK)
ALASKA (U.S.)
YUKON TERRITORY
NORTHWEST TERRITORIES
BRITISH COLUMBIA
ALBERTA
SASKATCHEWAN
MANITOBA
CANADA
ONTARIO
QUEBEC
NEWFOUNDLAND
PACIFIC OCEAN
UNITED STATES
ATLANTIC OCEAN
MEXICO
CUBA
HAWAII (U.S.)
Hudson Bay
Gulf of Mexico
Caribbean Sea

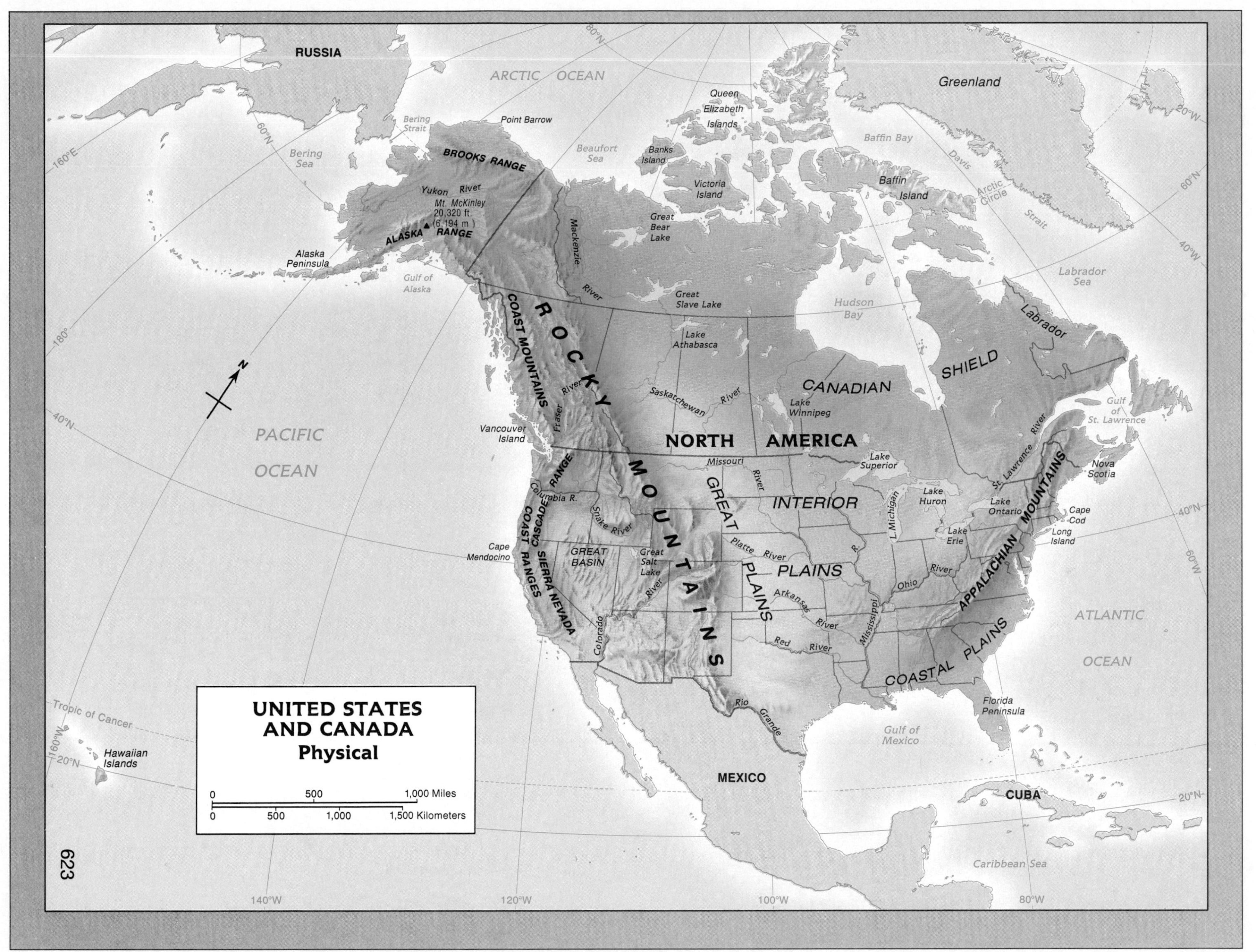

UNITED STATES
AND CANADA
Physical
0 500 1,000 Miles
0 500 1,000 1,500 Kilometers
RUSSIA
ARCTIC OCEAN
Greenland
Queen Elizabeth Islands
Point Barrow
Bering Strait
Bering Sea
Beaufort Sea
Banks Island
Victoria Island
Baffin Bay
Davis Strait
Arctic Circle
Baffin Island
BROOKS RANGE
Yukon River
Mt. McKinley 20,320 ft. (6,194 m.)
ALASKA RANGE
Alaska Peninsula
Gulf of Alaska
Great Bear Lake
Mackenzie River
Great Slave Lake
Labrador Sea
Hudson Bay
Labrador
ROCKY MOUNTAINS
COAST MOUNTAINS
Lake Athabasca
SHIELD
CANADIAN
Saskatchewan River
Lake Winnipeg
Fraser River
Gulf of St. Lawrence
PACIFIC OCEAN
Vancouver Island
NORTH AMERICA
Lake Superior
St. Lawrence River
Nova Scotia
Missouri River
CASCADE RANGE
Columbia R.
GREAT PLAINS
INTERIOR PLAINS
Lake Huron
L. Michigan
Lake Ontario
APPALACHIAN MOUNTAINS
Cape Cod
Long Island
Snake River
Lake Erie
Cape Mendocino
COAST RANGES
SIERRA NEVADA
GREAT BASIN
Great Salt Lake
Platte River
Ohio River
Colorado River
Arkansas River
Mississippi
ATLANTIC OCEAN
Red River
COASTAL PLAINS
Tropic of Cancer
Hawaiian Islands
Rio Grande
Florida Peninsula
Gulf of Mexico
MEXICO
CUBA
Caribbean Sea
N
160°E
180°
160°W
140°W
120°W
100°W
80°W
60°W
40°W
20°W
20°N
40°N
60°N
80°N
623

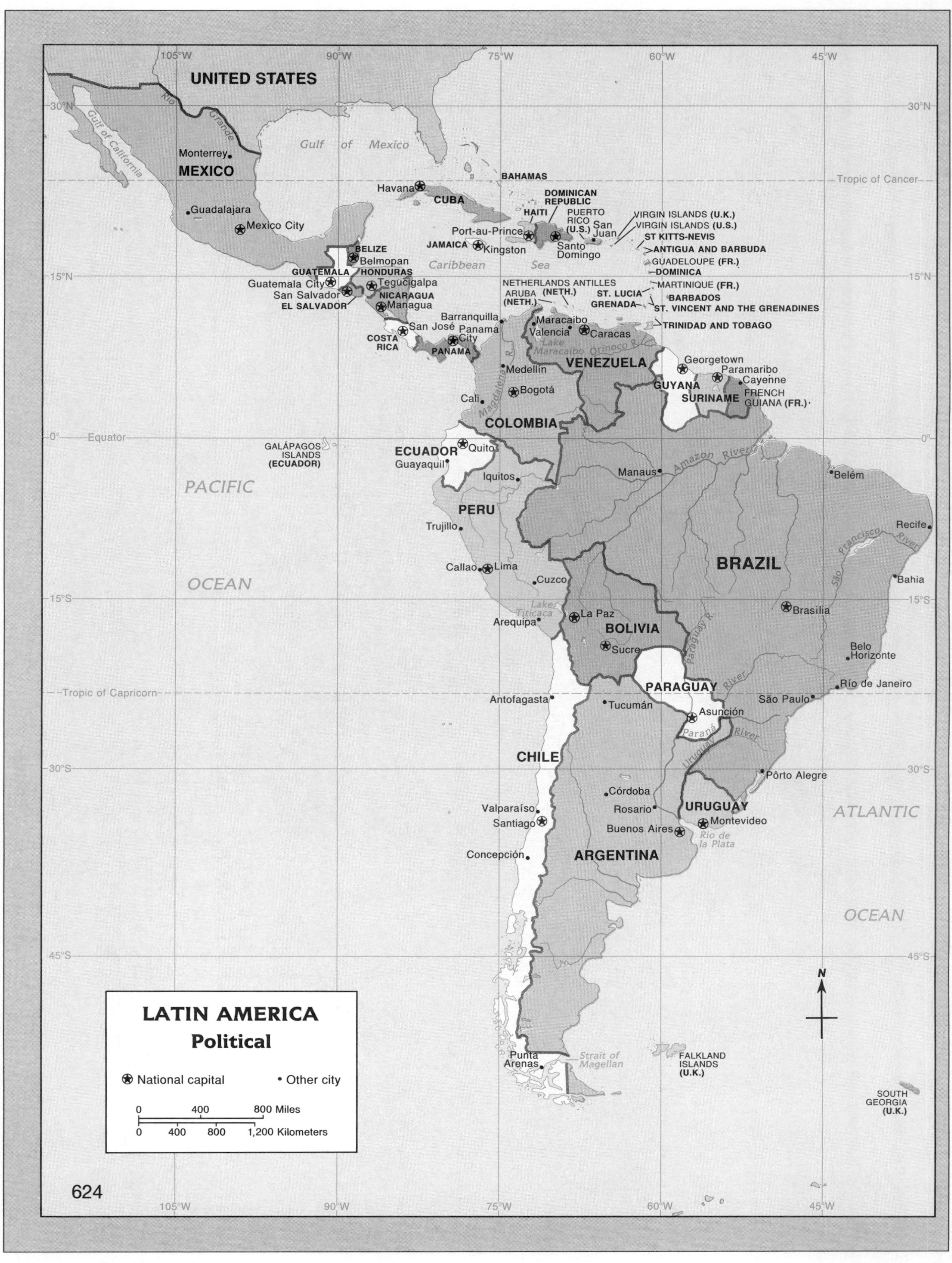

LATIN AMERICA
Political
National capital
Other city
0 400 800 Miles
0 400 800 1,200 Kilometers
UNITED STATES
MEXICO
Monterrey
Guadalajara
Mexico City
Gulf of California
Rio Grande
Gulf of Mexico
Tropic of Cancer
BAHAMAS
CUBA
Havana
DOMINICAN REPUBLIC
HAITI
Port-au-Prince
Santo Domingo
PUERTO RICO (U.S.)
San Juan
JAMAICA
Kingston
VIRGIN ISLANDS (U.K.)
VIRGIN ISLANDS (U.S.)
ST KITTS-NEVIS
ANTIGUA AND BARBUDA
GUADELOUPE (FR.)
DOMINICA
MARTINIQUE (FR.)
ST. LUCIA
BARBADOS
GRENADA
ST. VINCENT AND THE GRENADINES
TRINIDAD AND TOBAGO
NETHERLANDS ANTILLES (NETH.)
ARUBA (NETH.)
Caribbean Sea
BELIZE
Belmopan
GUATEMALA
Guatemala City
HONDURAS
Tegucigalpa
San Salvador
EL SALVADOR
NICARAGUA
Managua
COSTA RICA
San José
PANAMA
Panama City
Barranquilla
Maracaibo
Lake Maracaibo
Valencia
Caracas
Orinoco R.
VENEZUELA
Georgetown
GUYANA
Paramaribo
SURINAME
Cayenne
FRENCH GUIANA (FR.)
Medellín
Bogotá
Cali
Magdalena R.
COLOMBIA
Equator
GALÁPAGOS ISLANDS (ECUADOR)
ECUADOR
Quito
Guayaquil
PACIFIC OCEAN
Iquitos
PERU
Trujillo
Callao
Lima
Cuzco
Lake Titicaca
Arequipa
Manaus
Amazon River
Belém
Recife
São Francisco River
BRAZIL
Bahia
Brasília
Belo Horizonte
Rio de Janeiro
São Paulo
Paraguay R.
La Paz
BOLIVIA
Sucre
PARAGUAY
Asunción
Paraná River
Uruguay River
Tropic of Capricorn
Antofagasta
Tucumán
CHILE
Pôrto Alegre
Córdoba
Rosario
Valparaíso
Santiago
Buenos Aires
URUGUAY
Montevideo
Río de la Plata
ATLANTIC OCEAN
Concepción
ARGENTINA
Punta Arenas
Strait of Magellan
FALKLAND ISLANDS (U.K.)
SOUTH GEORGIA (U.K.)
N
105°W
90°W
75°W
60°W
45°W
30°N
15°N
0°
15°S
30°S
45°S
624

LATIN AMERICA
Physical
0 400 800 Miles
0 400 800 1,200 Kilometers
NORTH
AMERICA
SIERRA MADRE OCCIDENTAL
SIERRA MADRE ORIENTAL
Gulf of California
Baja California
Gulf of Mexico
Tropic of Cancer
Cuba
Greater Antilles
Hispaniola
Yucatán Peninsula
Caribbean Sea
Lesser Antilles
CENTRAL AMERICA
Lake Nicaragua
Isthmus of Panama
Guajira Peninsula
Lake Maracaibo
Gulf of Panama
Orinoco R.
GUIANA HIGHLANDS
LLANOS
Cauca River
Magdalena R.
Equator
Galápagos Islands
Japurá
Rio Negro
River
AMAZON
BASIN
Amazon River
Marajó Island
Cape São Roque
Gulf of Guayaquil
Marañon R.
Aguja Point
PACIFIC
OCEAN
ANDES MOUNTAINS
Ucayali
Purus
Madeira R.
Tapajós R.
Xingu River
Tocantins
Parnaíba River
São Francisco River
SOUTH
MATO GROSSO PLATEAU
AMERICA
Araguaia
BRAZILIAN
HIGHLANDS
Lake Titicaca
Lake Poopó
Paraguay R.
GRAN CHACO
Pilcomayo River
Tropic of Capricorn
ATACAMA DESERT
ANDES
Salado River
Paraná River
Uruguay
Mt. Aconcagua 22,834 ft. (6,960 m)
MOUNTAINS
PAMPAS
Rio de la Plata
ATLANTIC
OCEAN
Blanca Bay
San Matías Gulf
Chiloé Island
PATAGONIA
Gulf of San Jorge
Strait of Magellan
Tierra del Fuego
Cape Horn
Falkland Islands
South Georgia
N
105°W
90°W
75°W
60°W
45°W
30°N
15°N
0°
15°S
30°S
45°S
625

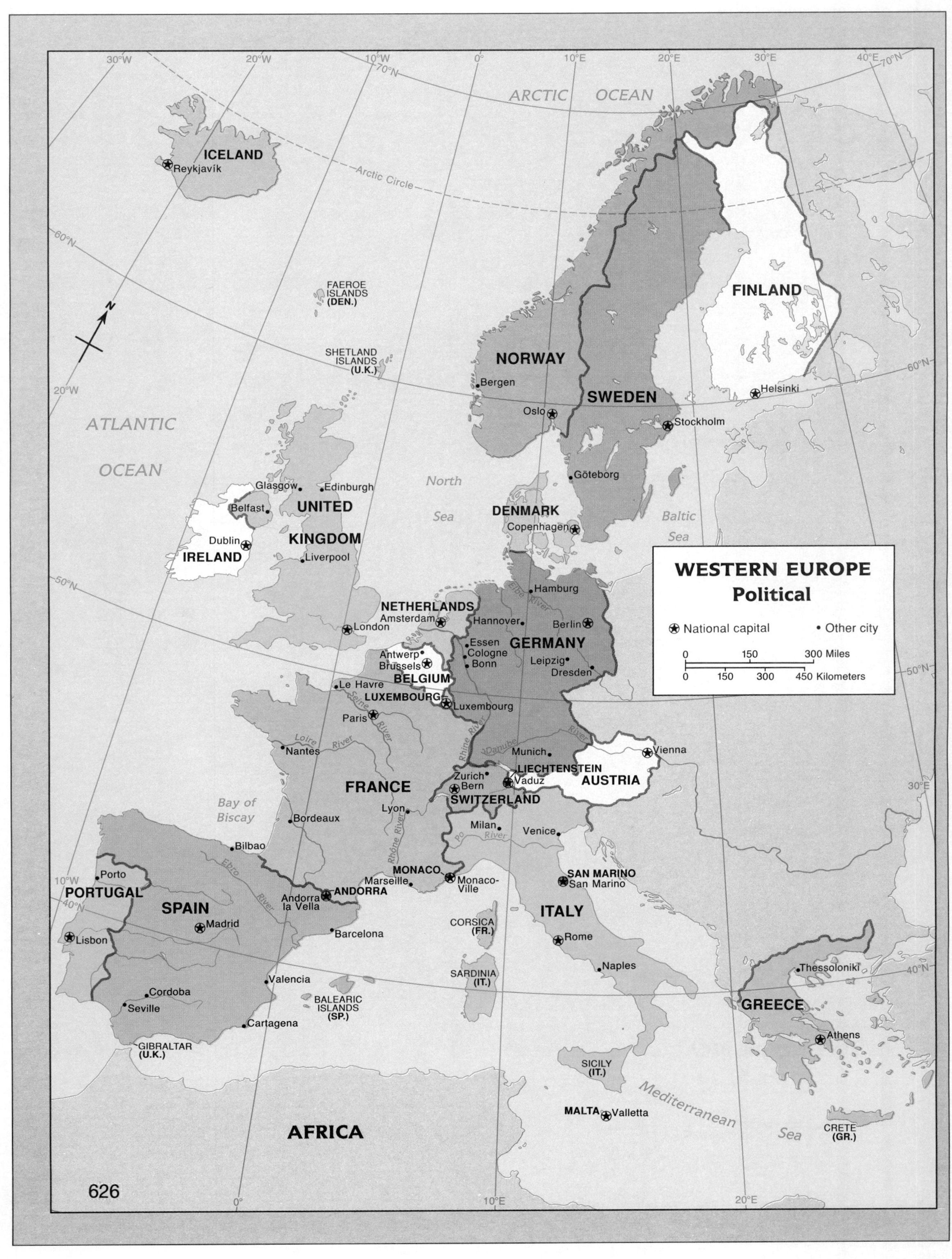

WESTERN EUROPE
Political
National capital
Other city
0 150 300 Miles
0 150 300 450 Kilometers
ARCTIC OCEAN
Arctic Circle
ICELAND
Reykjavík
FAEROE ISLANDS (DEN.)
SHETLAND ISLANDS (U.K.)
ATLANTIC OCEAN
NORWAY
Bergen
Oslo
SWEDEN
Stockholm
Göteborg
FINLAND
Helsinki
North Sea
Baltic Sea
DENMARK
Copenhagen
UNITED KINGDOM
Glasgow
Edinburgh
Belfast
Liverpool
London
IRELAND
Dublin
NETHERLANDS
Amsterdam
Antwerp
Brussels
BELGIUM
LUXEMBOURG
Luxembourg
GERMANY
Hamburg
Hannover
Berlin
Essen
Cologne
Bonn
Leipzig
Dresden
Munich
Elbe River
Rhine River
Danube River
LIECHTENSTEIN
Vaduz
AUSTRIA
Vienna
SWITZERLAND
Zurich
Bern
FRANCE
Le Havre
Paris
Nantes
Lyon
Bordeaux
Marseille
Seine River
Loire River
Rhône River
Bay of Biscay
MONACO
Monaco-Ville
ANDORRA
Andorra la Vella
SPAIN
Bilbao
Madrid
Barcelona
Valencia
Cordoba
Seville
Cartagena
Ebro River
PORTUGAL
Porto
Lisbon
GIBRALTAR (U.K.)
BALEARIC ISLANDS (SP.)
CORSICA (FR.)
SARDINIA (IT.)
ITALY
Milan
Po River
Venice
SAN MARINO
San Marino
Rome
Naples
SICILY (IT.)
MALTA
Valletta
GREECE
Thessoloniki
Athens
CRETE (GR.)
Mediterranean Sea
AFRICA
626

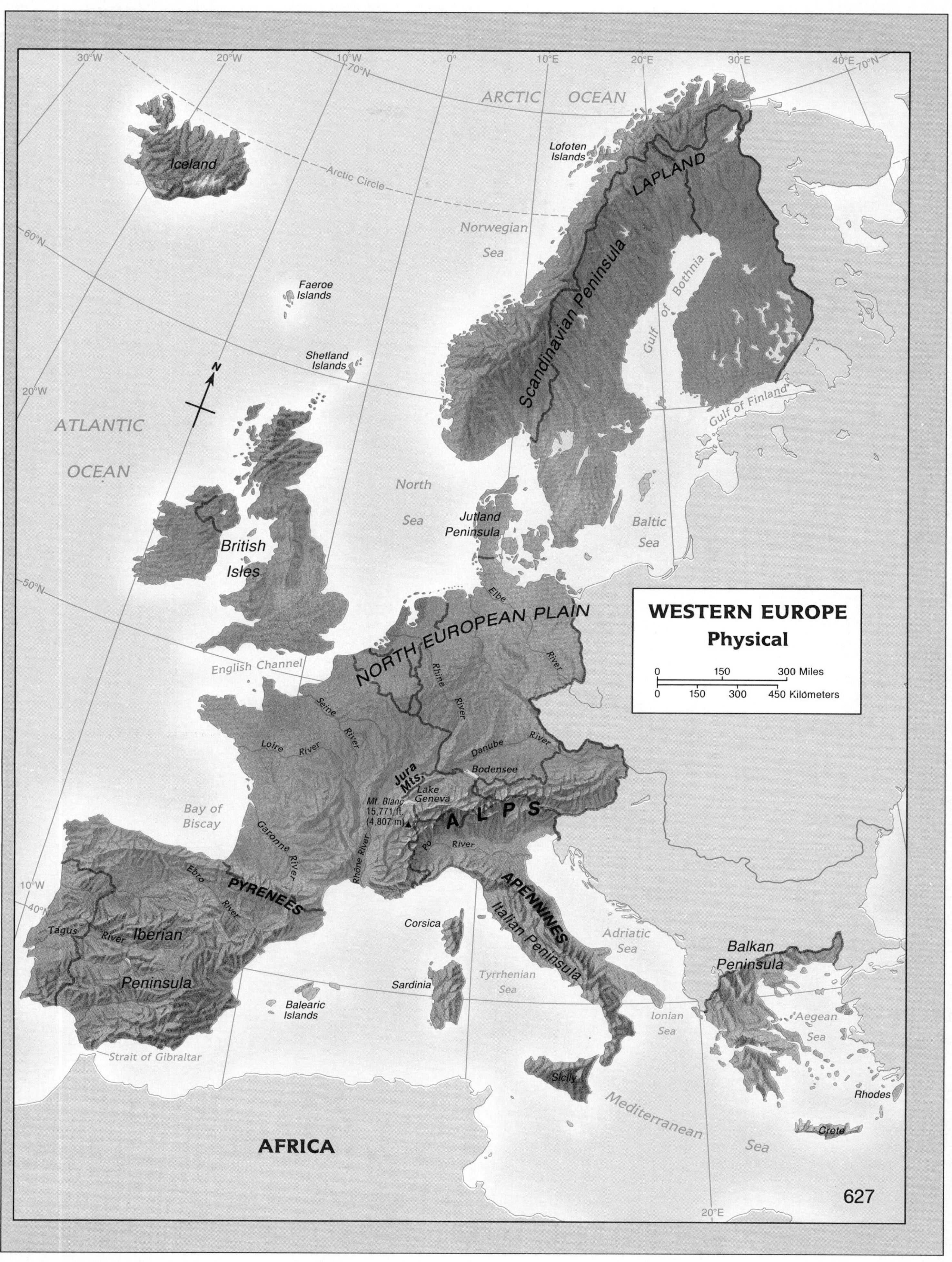
WESTERN EUROPE
Physical
0 150 300 Miles
0 150 300 450 Kilometers
ARCTIC OCEAN
ATLANTIC OCEAN
Iceland
Arctic Circle
Lofoten Islands
LAPLAND
Norwegian Sea
Faeroe Islands
Shetland Islands
Scandinavian Peninsula
Gulf of Bothnia
Gulf of Finland
North Sea
Jutland Peninsula
Baltic Sea
British Isles
NORTH EUROPEAN PLAIN
Elbe River
English Channel
Rhine River
Seine River
Loire River
Danube River
Bodensee
Jura Mts.
Lake Geneva
Mt. Blanc 15,771 ft. (4,807 m)
ALPS
Bay of Biscay
Garonne River
Rhône River
Po River
Ebro River
PYRENEES
APENNINES
Italian Peninsula
Adriatic Sea
Balkan Peninsula
Tagus River
Iberian Peninsula
Corsica
Sardinia
Tyrrhenian Sea
Balearic Islands
Ionian Sea
Aegean Sea
Rhodes
Strait of Gibraltar
Sicily
Mediterranean Sea
Crete
AFRICA
627

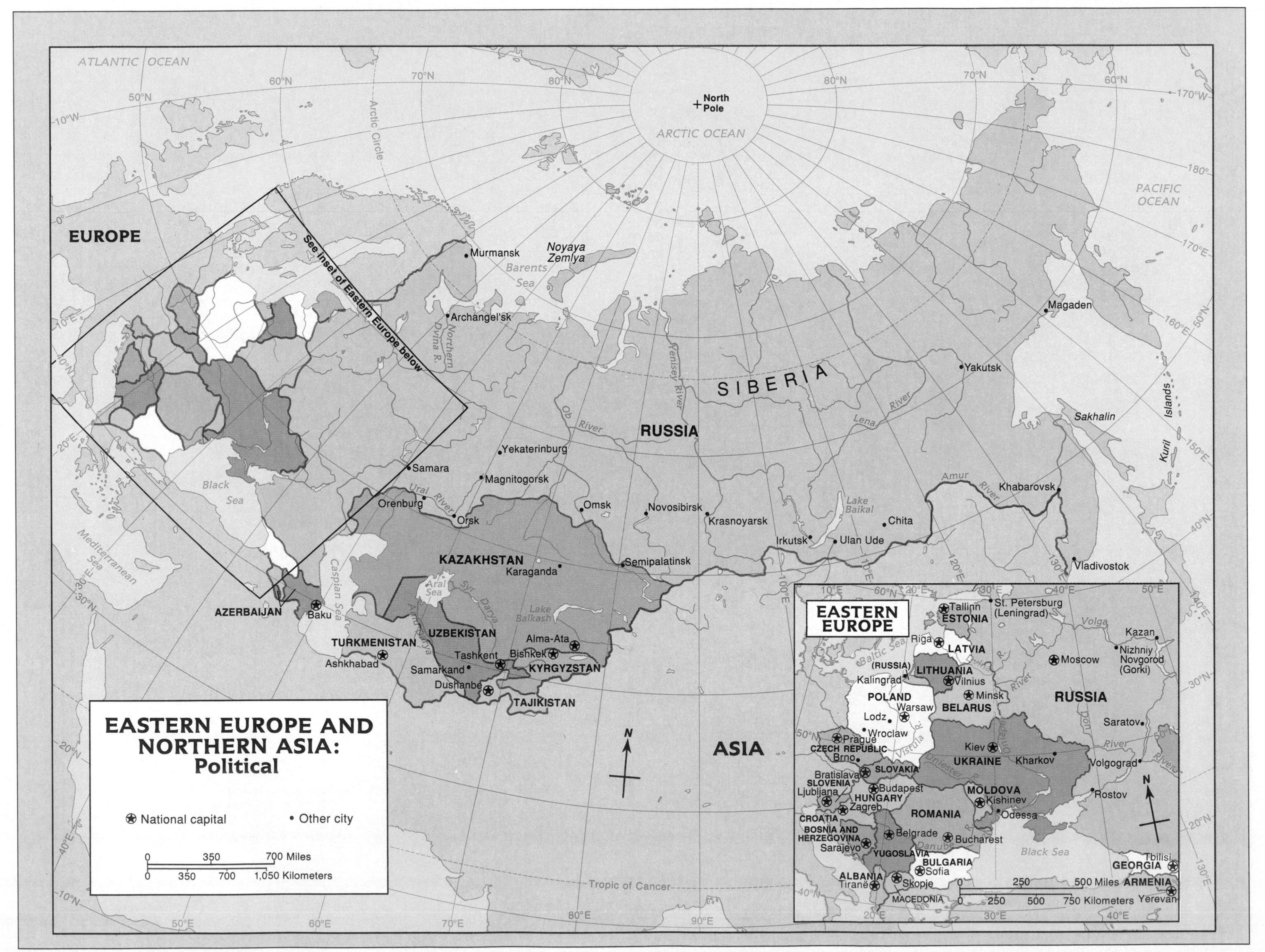
EASTERN EUROPE AND NORTHERN ASIA: Political
National capital
Other city
0 350 700 Miles
0 350 700 1,050 Kilometers
EUROPE
ASIA
RUSSIA
SIBERIA
ARCTIC OCEAN
North Pole
ATLANTIC OCEAN
PACIFIC OCEAN
Arctic Circle
Tropic of Cancer
See inset of Eastern Europe below
Black Sea
Mediterranean Sea
Caspian Sea
Aral Sea
Lake Balkash
Lake Baikal
Barents Sea
Noyaya Zemlya
Sakhalin
Kuril Islands
Yenisey River
Ob River
Lena River
Amur River
Ural River
Syr Darya
Amu Darya
Northern Dvina R.
KAZAKHSTAN
UZBEKISTAN
TURKMENISTAN
KYRGYZSTAN
TAJIKISTAN
AZERBAIJAN
Murmansk
Archangel'sk
Samara
Orenburg
Orsk
Magnitogorsk
Yekaterinburg
Omsk
Novosibirsk
Semipalatinsk
Krasnoyarsk
Irkutsk
Ulan Ude
Chita
Yakutsk
Magaden
Khabarovsk
Vladivostok
Karaganda
Alma-Ata
Bishkek
Tashkent
Samarkand
Dushanbe
Ashkhabad
Baku
EASTERN EUROPE
ESTONIA
LATVIA
LITHUANIA
BELARUS
(RUSSIA)
POLAND
CZECH REPUBLIC
SLOVAKIA
HUNGARY
SLOVENIA
CROATIA
BOSNIA AND HERZEGOVINA
YUGOSLAVIA
ALBANIA
MACEDONIA
BULGARIA
ROMANIA
MOLDOVA
UKRAINE
RUSSIA
GEORGIA
ARMENIA
Tallinn
Riga
Vilnius
Minsk
Kaliningrad
Warsaw
Lodz
Wroclaw
Prague
Brno
Bratislava
Budapest
Ljubljana
Zagreb
Sarajevo
Belgrade
Tiranë
Skopje
Sofia
Bucharest
Kishinev
Odessa
Kiev
Kharkov
St. Petersburg (Leningrad)
Moscow
Nizhniy Novgorod (Gorki)
Kazan
Saratov
Volgograd
Rostov
Tbilisi
Yerevan
Volga
Don River
Dnieper R.
Dniester R.
Danube
Vistula R.
Baltic Sea
Black Sea
0 250 500 Miles
0 250 500 750 Kilometers

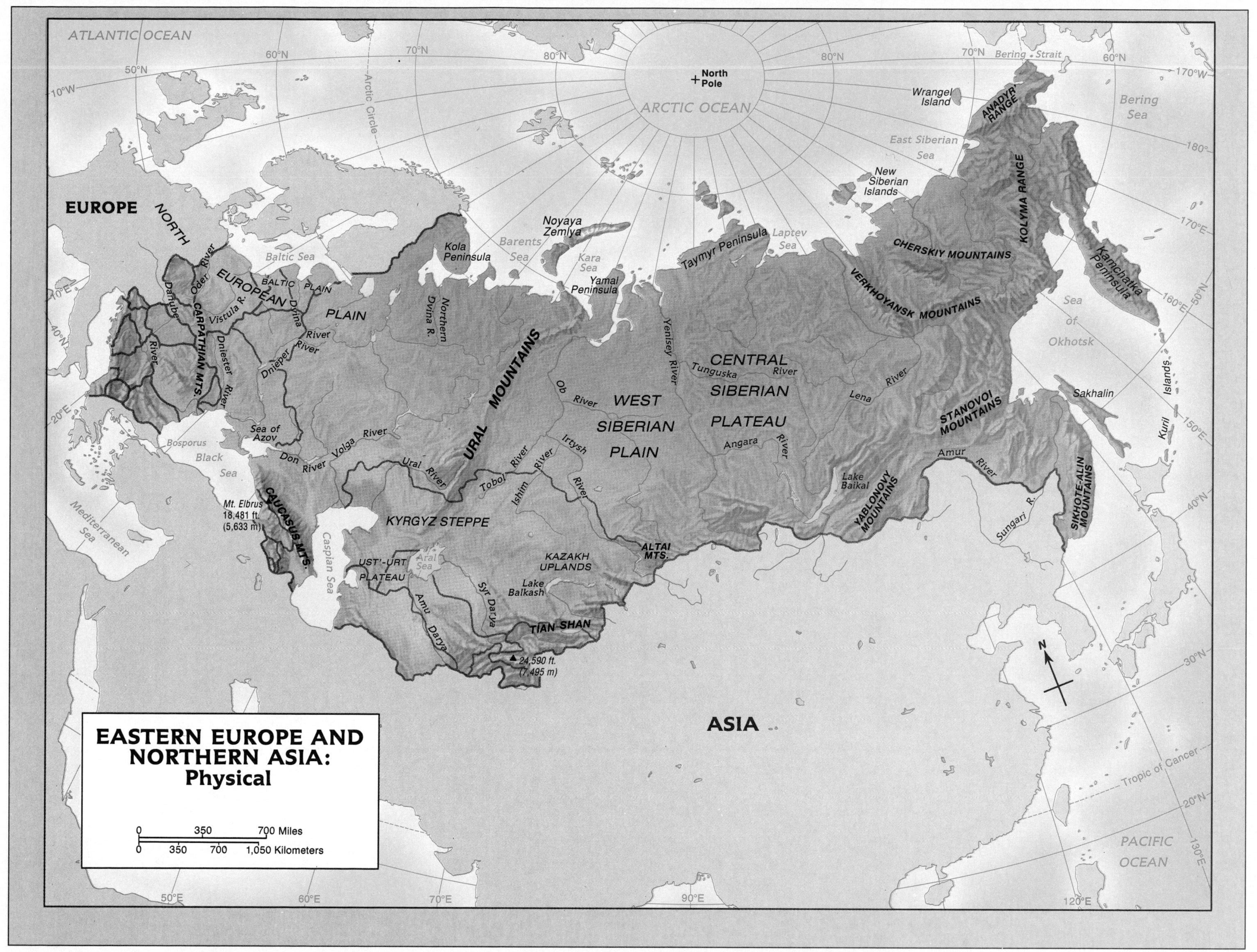

EASTERN EUROPE AND NORTHERN ASIA: Physical
0 350 700 Miles
0 350 700 1,050 Kilometers
EUROPE
ASIA
ATLANTIC OCEAN
ARCTIC OCEAN
PACIFIC OCEAN
North Pole
NORTH EUROPEAN PLAIN
BALTIC PLAIN
CARPATHIAN MTS.
CAUCASUS MTS.
Mt. Elbrus 18,481 ft. (5,633 m)
URAL MOUNTAINS
KYRGYZ STEPPE
UST'-URT PLATEAU
KAZAKH UPLANDS
TIAN SHAN
24,590 ft. (7,495 m)
ALTAI MTS.
WEST SIBERIAN PLAIN
CENTRAL SIBERIAN PLATEAU
VERKHOYANSK MOUNTAINS
CHERSKIY MOUNTAINS
KOLYMA RANGE
ANADYR RANGE
STANOVOI MOUNTAINS
YABLONOVY MOUNTAINS
SIKHOTE-ALIN MOUNTAINS
Kola Peninsula
Yamal Peninsula
Taymyr Peninsula
Kamchatka Peninsula
Noyaya Zemlya
New Siberian Islands
Wrangel Island
Sakhalin
Kuril Islands
Barents Sea
Kara Sea
Laptev Sea
East Siberian Sea
Bering Strait
Bering Sea
Sea of Okhotsk
Baltic Sea
Black Sea
Sea of Azov
Caspian Sea
Aral Sea
Mediterranean Sea
Bosporus
Lake Baikal
Lake Balkash
Northern Dvina R.
Dvina River
Dnieper River
Dniester River
Vistula R.
Oder River
Danube River
Don River
Volga River
Ural River
Tobol River
Ishim River
Irtysh River
Ob River
Yenisey River
Tunguska River
Angara River
Lena River
Amur River
Sungari R.
Syr Darya
Amu Darya
Arctic Circle
Tropic of Cancer
N

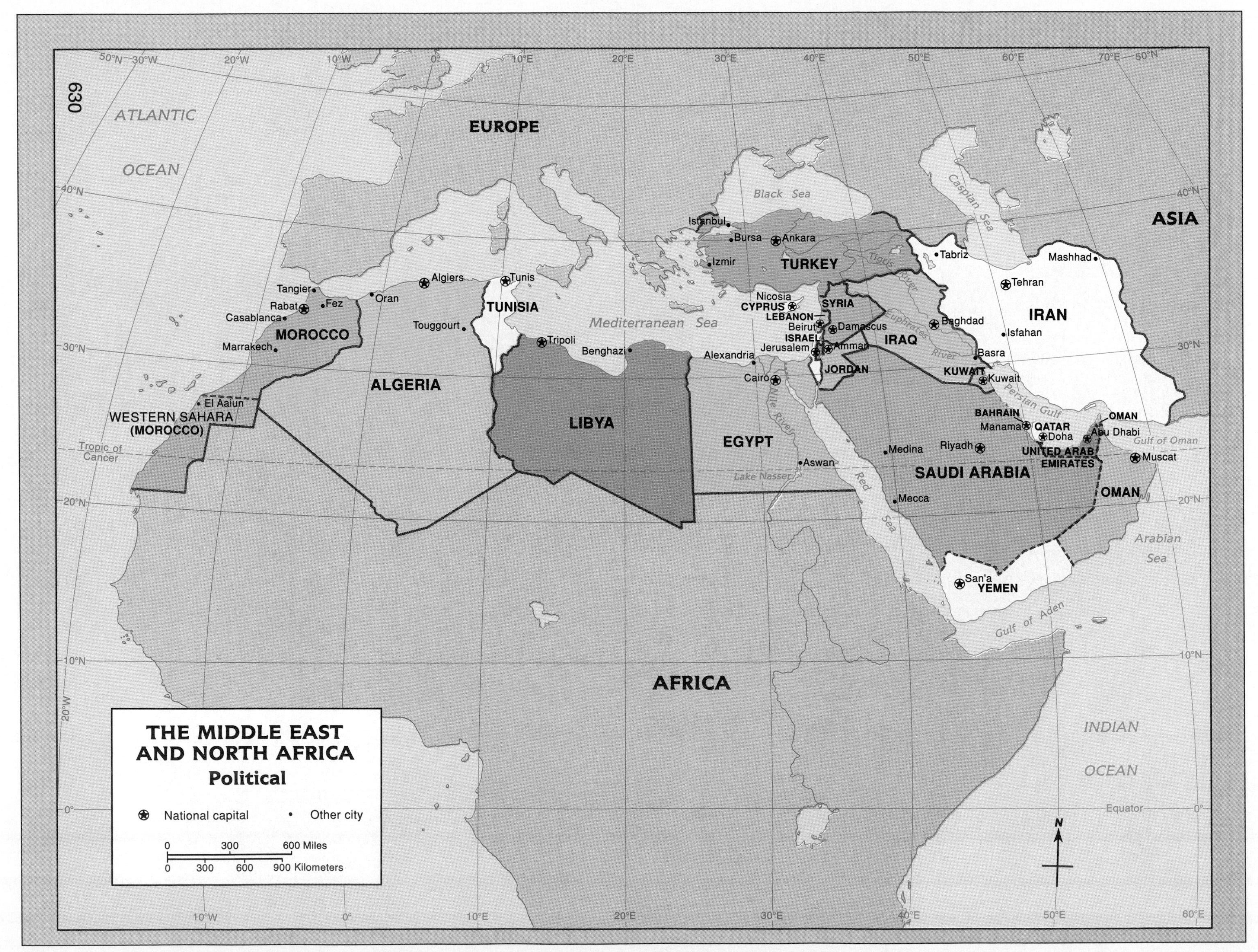
630
THE MIDDLE EAST AND NORTH AFRICA
Political
National capital
Other city
0 300 600 Miles
0 300 600 900 Kilometers
ATLANTIC OCEAN
EUROPE
ASIA
AFRICA
INDIAN OCEAN
Mediterranean Sea
Black Sea
Caspian Sea
Red Sea
Persian Gulf
Gulf of Oman
Gulf of Aden
Arabian Sea
Lake Nasser
Nile River
Tigris River
Euphrates River
Tropic of Cancer
Equator
MOROCCO
WESTERN SAHARA (MOROCCO)
ALGERIA
TUNISIA
LIBYA
EGYPT
TURKEY
CYPRUS
SYRIA
LEBANON
ISRAEL
JORDAN
IRAQ
IRAN
KUWAIT
SAUDI ARABIA
BAHRAIN
QATAR
UNITED ARAB EMIRATES
OMAN
YEMEN
Tangier
Rabat
Fez
Casablanca
Marrakech
El Aaiun
Oran
Algiers
Touggourt
Tunis
Tripoli
Benghazi
Alexandria
Cairo
Aswan
Istanbul
Bursa
Izmir
Ankara
Nicosia
Beirut
Damascus
Jerusalem
Amman
Baghdad
Basra
Kuwait
Tabriz
Tehran
Isfahan
Mashhad
Manama
Doha
Abu Dhabi
Muscat
Riyadh
Medina
Mecca
San'a
N
50°N
40°N
30°N
20°N
10°N
0°
30°W
20°W
10°W
0°
10°E
20°E
30°E
40°E
50°E
60°E
70°E

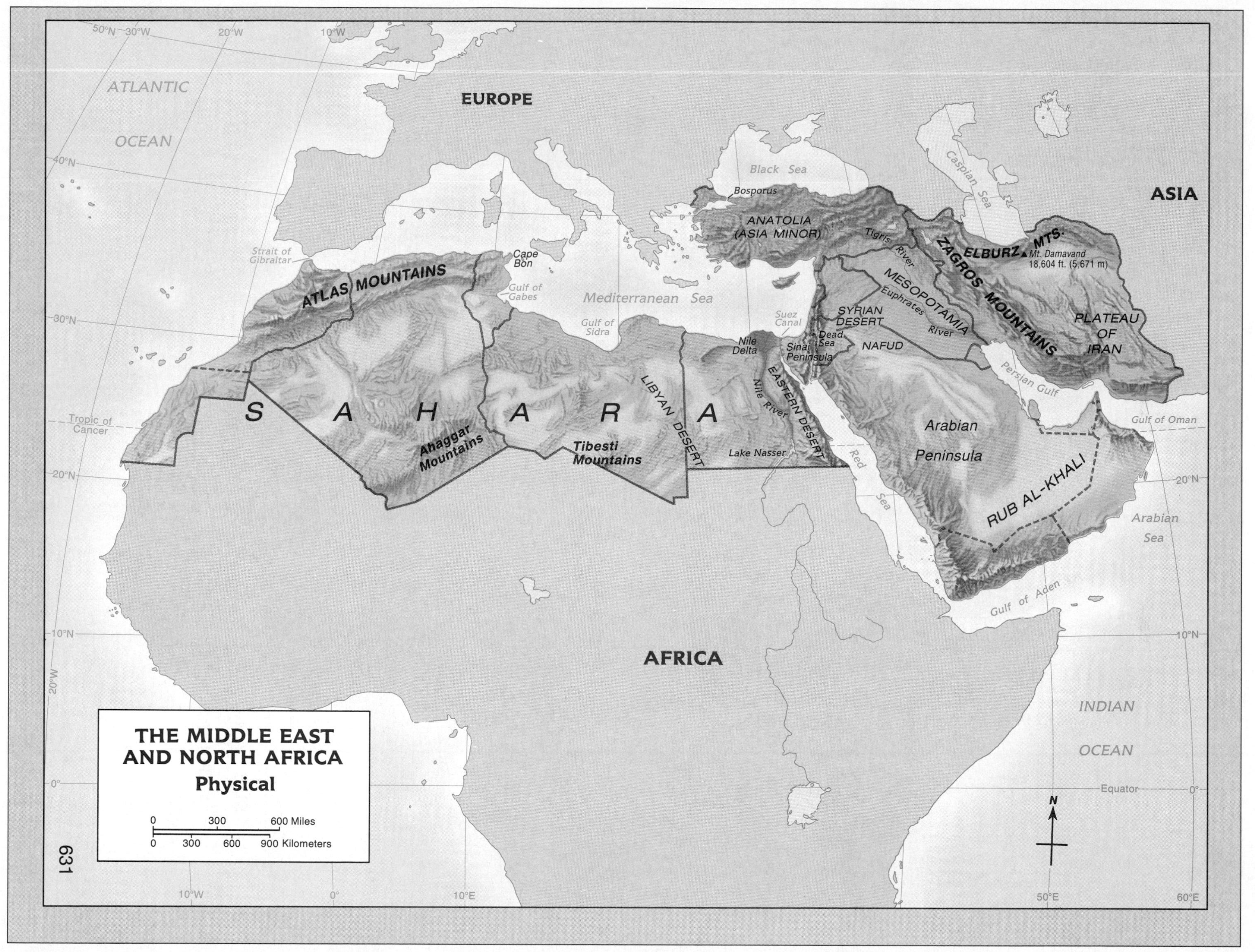
THE MIDDLE EAST AND NORTH AFRICA
Physical
0 300 600 Miles
0 300 600 900 Kilometers
EUROPE
ASIA
AFRICA
ATLANTIC OCEAN
INDIAN OCEAN
Black Sea
Bosporus
Caspian Sea
ANATOLIA (ASIA MINOR)
Tigris River
Euphrates River
MESOPOTAMIA
ELBURZ MTS.
Mt. Damavand 18,604 ft. (5,671 m)
ZAGROS MOUNTAINS
PLATEAU OF IRAN
Persian Gulf
Gulf of Oman
Arabian Sea
Gulf of Aden
SYRIAN DESERT
NAFUD
Dead Sea
Sinai Peninsula
Suez Canal
Nile Delta
Nile River
EASTERN DESERT
Lake Nasser
Red Sea
Arabian Peninsula
RUB AL-KHALI
Mediterranean Sea
Gulf of Sidra
Gulf of Gabes
Cape Bon
Strait of Gibraltar
ATLAS MOUNTAINS
S A H A R A
Ahaggar Mountains
Tibesti Mountains
LIBYAN DESERT
Tropic of Cancer
Equator
50°N
40°N
30°N
20°N
10°N
0°
30°W
20°W
10°W
0°
10°E
50°E
60°E
N
631

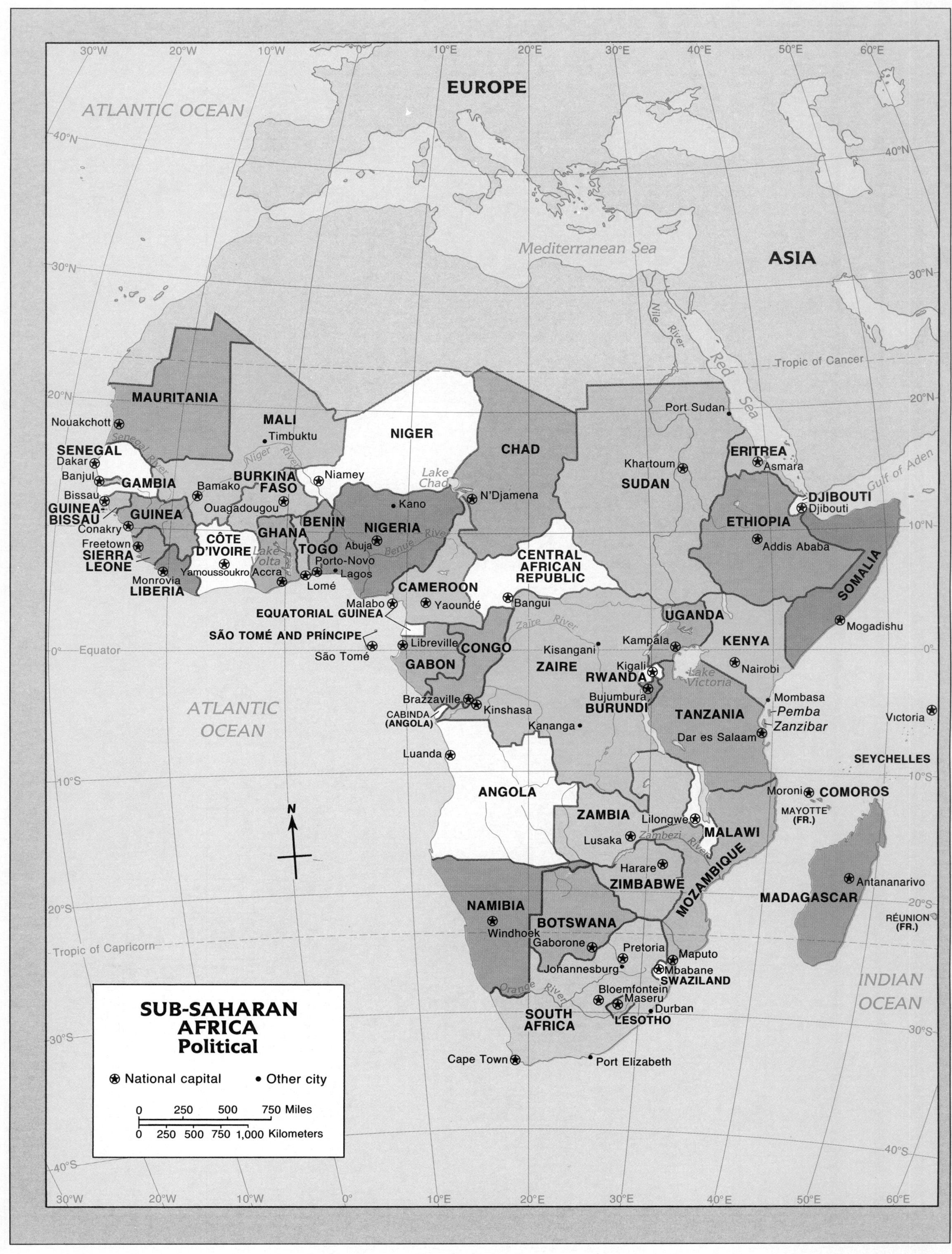

SUB-SAHARAN AFRICA Political
National capital
Other city
0 250 500 750 Miles
0 250 500 750 1,000 Kilometers
EUROPE
ASIA
ATLANTIC OCEAN
Mediterranean Sea
INDIAN OCEAN
MAURITANIA
Nouakchott
SENEGAL
Dakar
Banjul
GAMBIA
Bissau
GUINEA-BISSAU
GUINEA
Conakry
Freetown
SIERRA LEONE
Monrovia
LIBERIA
MALI
Timbuktu
Bamako
BURKINA FASO
Ouagadougou
CÔTE D'IVOIRE
Yamoussoukro
GHANA
Accra
TOGO
Lomé
BENIN
Porto-Novo
Lagos
NIGER
Niamey
NIGERIA
Kano
Abuja
CHAD
N'Djamena
Lake Chad
SUDAN
Khartoum
Port Sudan
ERITREA
Asmara
DJIBOUTI
Djibouti
ETHIOPIA
Addis Ababa
SOMALIA
Mogadishu
CENTRAL AFRICAN REPUBLIC
Bangui
CAMEROON
Yaoundé
Malabo
EQUATORIAL GUINEA
SÃO TOMÉ AND PRÍNCIPE
São Tomé
Libreville
GABON
CONGO
Brazzaville
Kinshasa
CABINDA (ANGOLA)
ZAIRE
Kisangani
Kananga
UGANDA
Kampala
KENYA
Nairobi
Mombasa
RWANDA
Kigali
BURUNDI
Bujumbura
TANZANIA
Dar es Salaam
Pemba
Zanzibar
Lake Victoria
SEYCHELLES
Victoria
COMOROS
Moroni
MAYOTTE (FR.)
ANGOLA
Luanda
ZAMBIA
Lusaka
Lilongwe
MALAWI
Harare
ZIMBABWE
MOZAMBIQUE
Maputo
MADAGASCAR
Antananarivo
RÉUNION (FR.)
NAMIBIA
Windhoek
BOTSWANA
Gaborone
Pretoria
Johannesburg
Mbabane
SWAZILAND
Bloemfontein
Maseru
LESOTHO
Durban
SOUTH AFRICA
Cape Town
Port Elizabeth
Senegal River
Niger River
Lake Volta
Benue River
Zaire River
Zambezi River
Orange River
Nile River
Red Sea
Gulf of Aden
Tropic of Cancer
Tropic of Capricorn
Equator
N

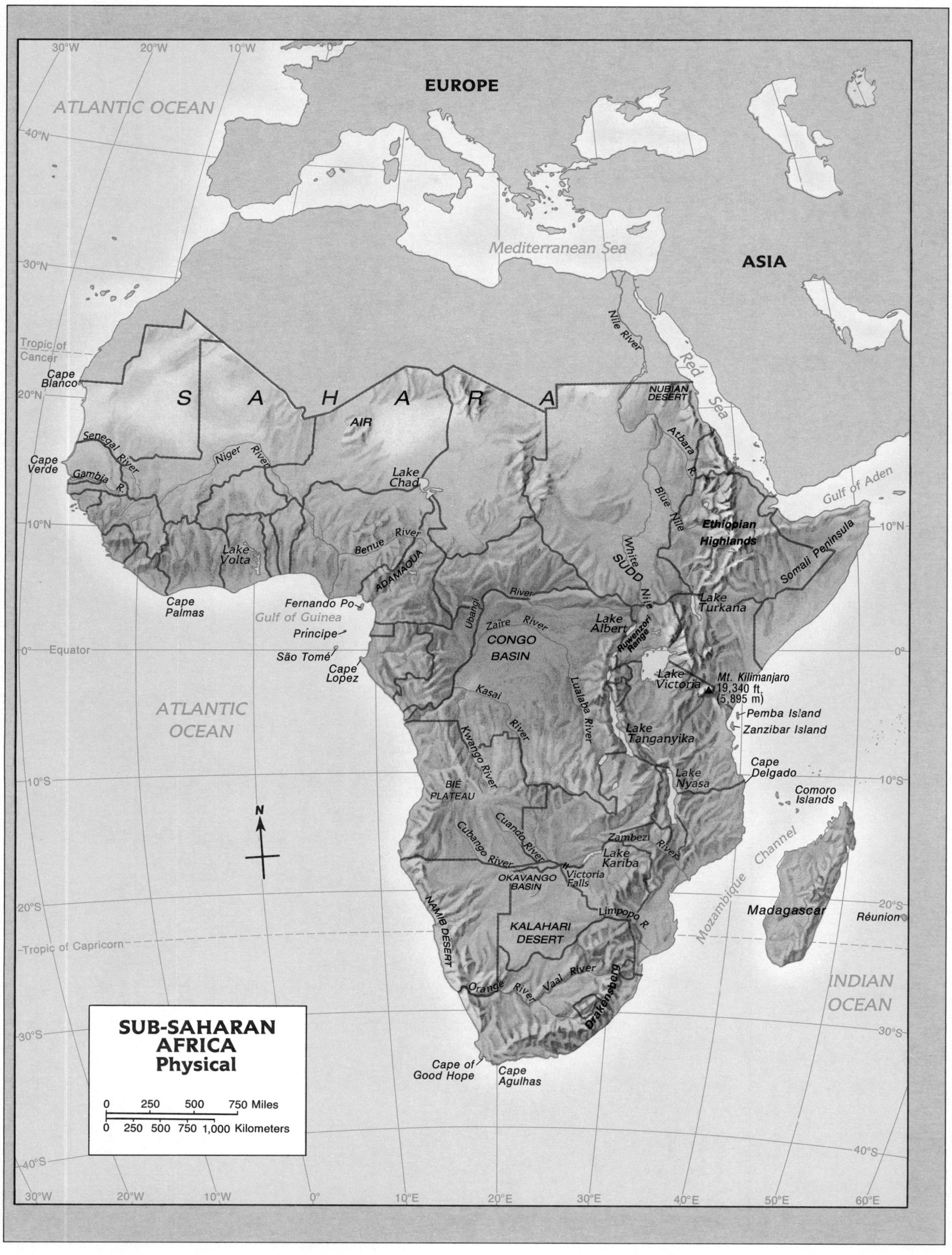
SUB-SAHARAN
AFRICA
Physical
0 250 500 750 Miles
0 250 500 750 1,000 Kilometers
EUROPE
ASIA
ATLANTIC OCEAN
Mediterranean Sea
Red Sea
Gulf of Aden
Tropic of Cancer
Cape Blanco
S A H A R A
AIR
NUBIAN DESERT
Nile River
Atbara R.
Blue Nile
White Nile
SUDD
Ethiopian Highlands
Somali Peninsula
Senegal River
Niger River
Gambia R.
Cape Verde
Lake Chad
Lake Volta
Benue River
ADAMAOUA
Cape Palmas
Fernando Po
Gulf of Guinea
Principe
São Tomé
Cape Lopez
Equator
Ubangi
River
Zaïre River
CONGO BASIN
Lake Albert
Ruwenzori Range
Lake Turkana
Lake Victoria
Mt. Kilimanjaro 19,340 ft. (5,895 m)
Pemba Island
Zanzibar Island
ATLANTIC OCEAN
Kasai River
Lualaba River
Lake Tanganyika
Kwango River
BIE PLATEAU
Lake Nyasa
Cape Delgado
Comoro Islands
N
Cuando River
Cubango River
Zambezi River
Lake Kariba
Victoria Falls
OKAVANGO BASIN
Mozambique Channel
Madagascar
Réunion
NAMIB DESERT
Limpopo R.
KALAHARI DESERT
Tropic of Capricorn
Orange River
Vaal River
Drakensberg
INDIAN OCEAN
Cape of Good Hope
Cape Agulhas
30°W
20°W
10°W
0°
10°E
20°E
30°E
40°E
50°E
60°E
40°N
30°N
20°N
10°N
0°
10°S
20°S
30°S
40°S

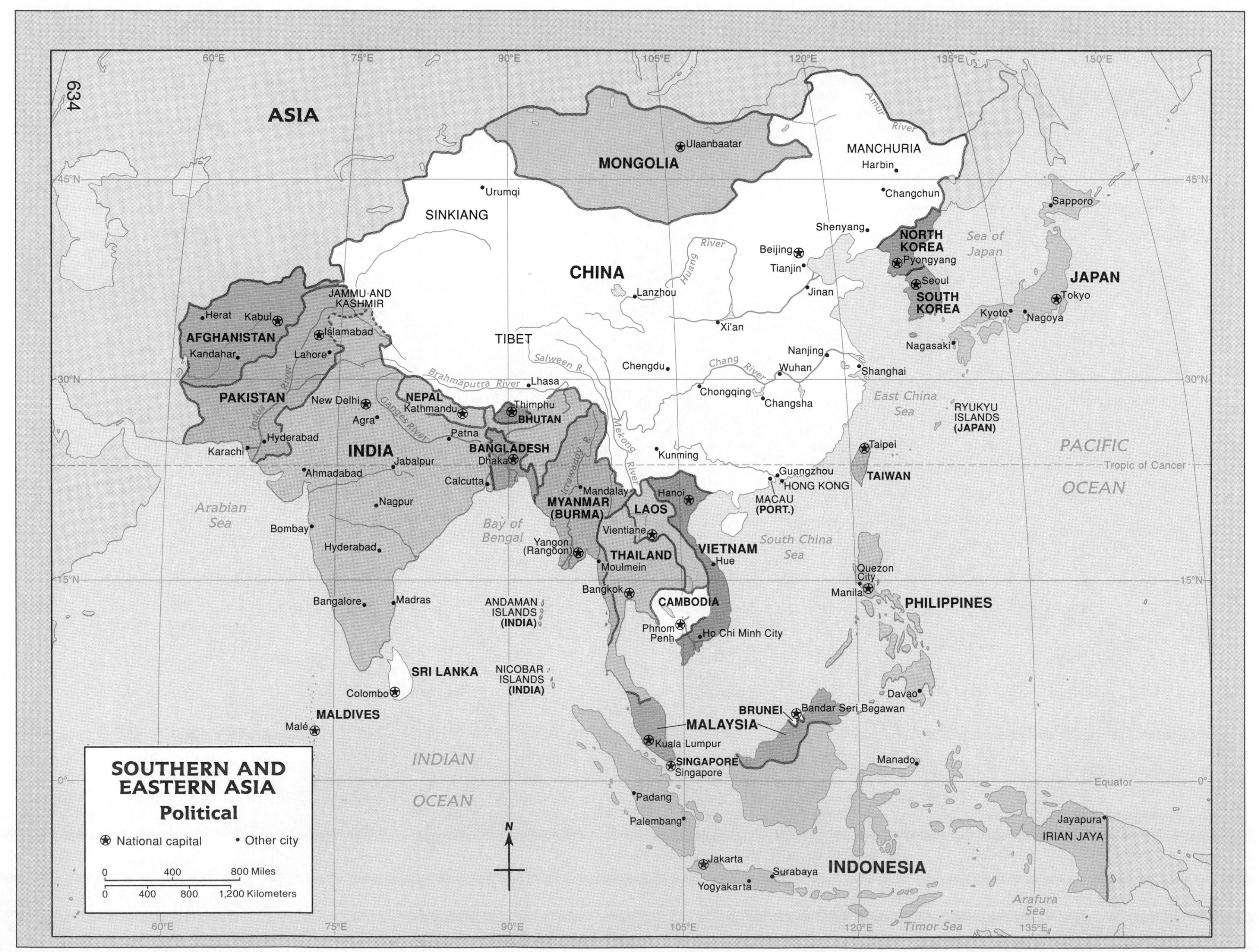
634
ASIA
SOUTHERN AND EASTERN ASIA
Political
National capital
Other city
0
400
800 Miles
0
400
800
1,200 Kilometers
MONGOLIA
Ulaanbaatar
CHINA
SINKIANG
Urumqi
TIBET
Lhasa
MANCHURIA
Harbin
Changchun
Shenyang
Beijing
Tianjin
Jinan
Lanzhou
Xi'an
Chengdu
Nanjing
Wuhan
Shanghai
Chongqing
Changsha
Kunming
Guangzhou
HONG KONG
MACAU
(PORT.)
Huang
River
Chang
River
Salween R.
Mekong
River
Brahmaputra River
Amur
River
NORTH
KOREA
Pyongyang
Seoul
SOUTH
KOREA
JAPAN
Sapporo
Tokyo
Kyoto
Nagoya
Nagasaki
Sea of
Japan
East China
Sea
RYUKYU
ISLANDS
(JAPAN)
Taipei
TAIWAN
PACIFIC
OCEAN
Tropic of Cancer
AFGHANISTAN
Herat
Kabul
Kandahar
JAMMU AND
KASHMIR
Islamabad
Lahore
PAKISTAN
Indus
River
Hyderabad
Karachi
INDIA
New Delhi
Agra
Ganges River
Jabalpur
Ahmadabad
Nagpur
Bombay
Hyderabad
Bangalore
Madras
Calcutta
Patna
NEPAL
Kathmandu
Thimphu
BHUTAN
BANGLADESH
Dhaka
Arabian
Sea
Bay of
Bengal
SRI LANKA
Colombo
MALDIVES
Malé
ANDAMAN
ISLANDS
(INDIA)
NICOBAR
ISLANDS
(INDIA)
INDIAN
OCEAN
MYANMAR
(BURMA)
Mandalay
Irrawaddy R.
Yangon
(Rangoon)
Moulmein
LAOS
Vientiane
Hanoi
THAILAND
Bangkok
VIETNAM
Hue
CAMBODIA
Phnom
Penh
Ho Chi Minh City
South China
Sea
PHILIPPINES
Quezon
City
Manila
Davao
BRUNEI
Bandar Seri Begawan
MALAYSIA
Kuala Lumpur
SINGAPORE
Singapore
INDONESIA
Padang
Palembang
Jakarta
Yogyakarta
Surabaya
Manado
Jayapura
IRIAN JAYA
Arafura
Sea
Timor Sea
Equator
N
60°E
75°E
90°E
105°E
120°E
135°E
150°E
45°N
30°N
15°N
0°

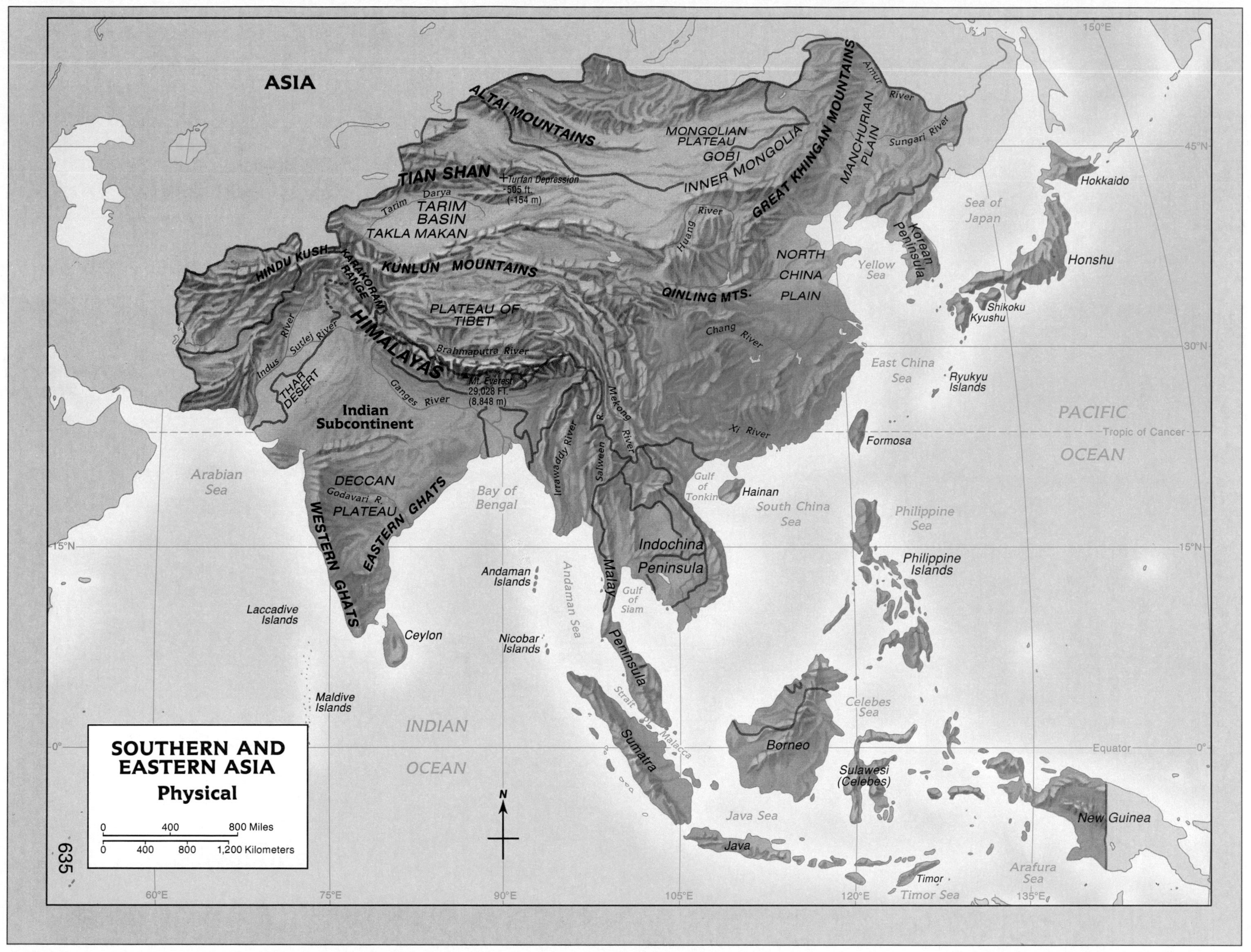
SOUTHERN AND EASTERN ASIA
Physical
0 400 800 Miles
0 400 800 1,200 Kilometers
ASIA
ALTAI MOUNTAINS
MONGOLIAN PLATEAU
GOBI
INNER MONGOLIA
GREAT KHINGAN MOUNTAINS
MANCHURIAN PLAIN
Amur River
Sungari River
TIAN SHAN
Turfan Depression -505 ft. (-154 m)
Tarim Darya
TARIM BASIN
TAKLA MAKAN
HINDU KUSH
KARAKORAM RANGE
KUNLUN MOUNTAINS
PLATEAU OF TIBET
HIMALAYAS
Brahmaputra River
Mt. Everest 29,028 FT. (8,848 m)
Huang River
QINLING MTS.
NORTH CHINA PLAIN
Chang River
Xi River
Indus River
Sutlej River
THAR DESERT
Ganges River
Indian Subcontinent
DECCAN PLATEAU
Godavari R.
WESTERN GHATS
EASTERN GHATS
Arabian Sea
Bay of Bengal
Irrawaddy River
Salween R.
Mekong River
Korean Peninsula
Yellow Sea
Sea of Japan
Hokkaido
Honshu
Shikoku
Kyushu
East China Sea
Ryukyu Islands
PACIFIC OCEAN
Tropic of Cancer
Formosa
Gulf of Tonkin
Hainan
South China Sea
Philippine Sea
Philippine Islands
Indochina Peninsula
Malay Peninsula
Gulf of Siam
Andaman Islands
Andaman Sea
Nicobar Islands
Laccadive Islands
Ceylon
Maldive Islands
INDIAN OCEAN
Strait of Malacca
Sumatra
Borneo
Celebes Sea
Sulawesi (Celebes)
Equator
Java Sea
Java
New Guinea
Timor
Timor Sea
Arafura Sea
N
150°E
45°N
30°N
15°N
0°
60°E
75°E
90°E
105°E
120°E
135°E
635

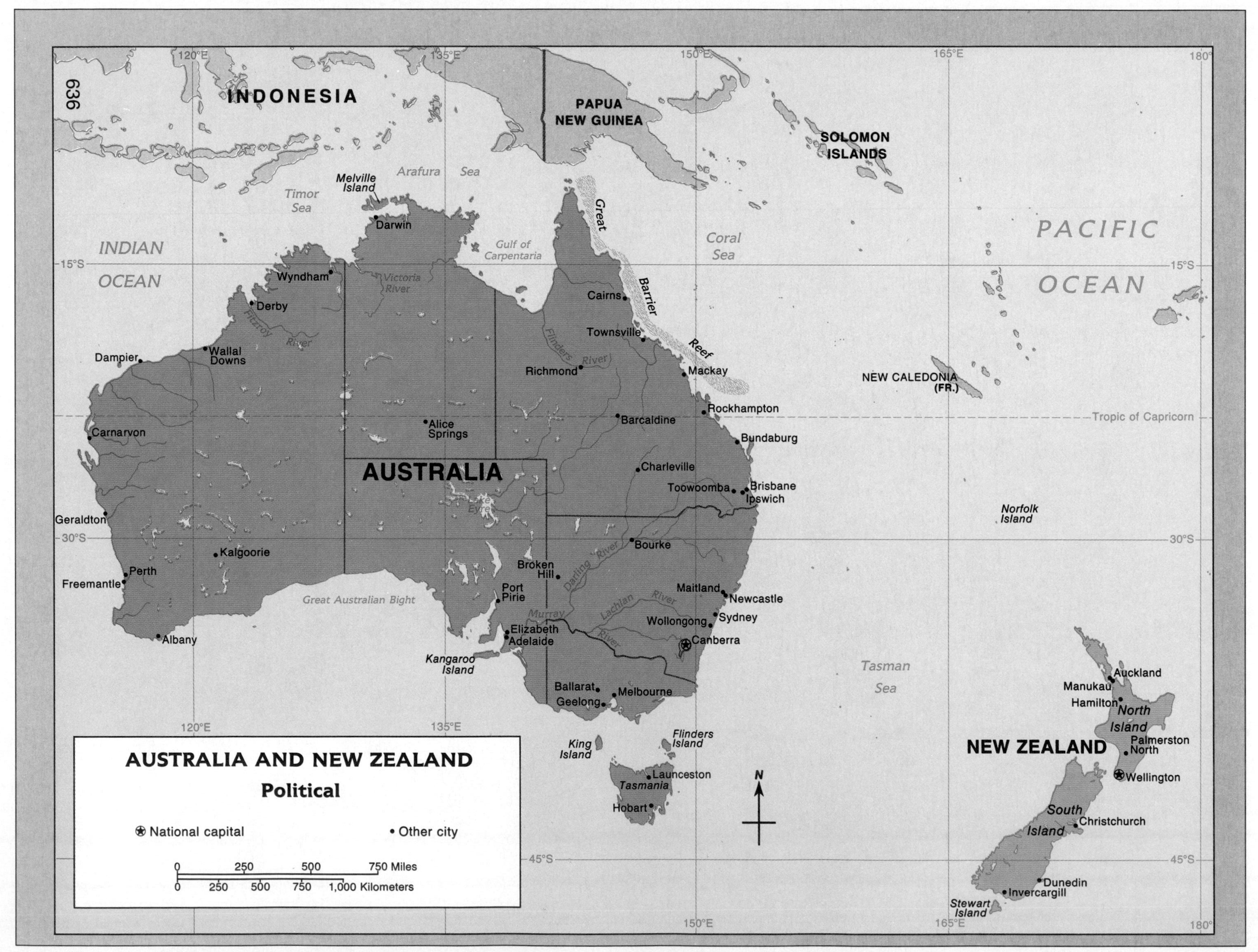

636
INDONESIA
PAPUA NEW GUINEA
SOLOMON ISLANDS
PACIFIC OCEAN
INDIAN OCEAN
Timor Sea
Arafura Sea
Melville Island
Gulf of Carpentaria
Coral Sea
Great Barrier Reef
NEW CALEDONIA (FR.)
Tropic of Capricorn
AUSTRALIA
Darwin
Wyndham
Derby
Fitzroy River
Victoria River
Wallal Downs
Dampier
Carnarvon
Geraldton
Perth
Freemantle
Kalgoorie
Albany
Alice Springs
Lake Eyre
Great Australian Bight
Kangaroo Island
Port Pirie
Elizabeth
Adelaide
Broken Hill
Darling River
Lachlan River
Murray River
Cairns
Townsville
Flinders River
Richmond
Mackay
Rockhampton
Barcaldine
Bundaburg
Charleville
Toowoomba
Brisbane
Ipswich
Bourke
Maitland
Newcastle
Sydney
Wollongong
Canberra
Ballarat
Geelong
Melbourne
King Island
Flinders Island
Launceston
Tasmania
Hobart
Norfolk Island
Tasman Sea
NEW ZEALAND
Auckland
Manukau
Hamilton
North Island
Palmerston North
Wellington
South Island
Christchurch
Dunedin
Invercargill
Stewart Island
120°E
135°E
150°E
165°E
180°
15°S
30°S
45°S
AUSTRALIA AND NEW ZEALAND
Political
National capital
Other city
0 250 500 750 Miles
0 250 500 750 1,000 Kilometers

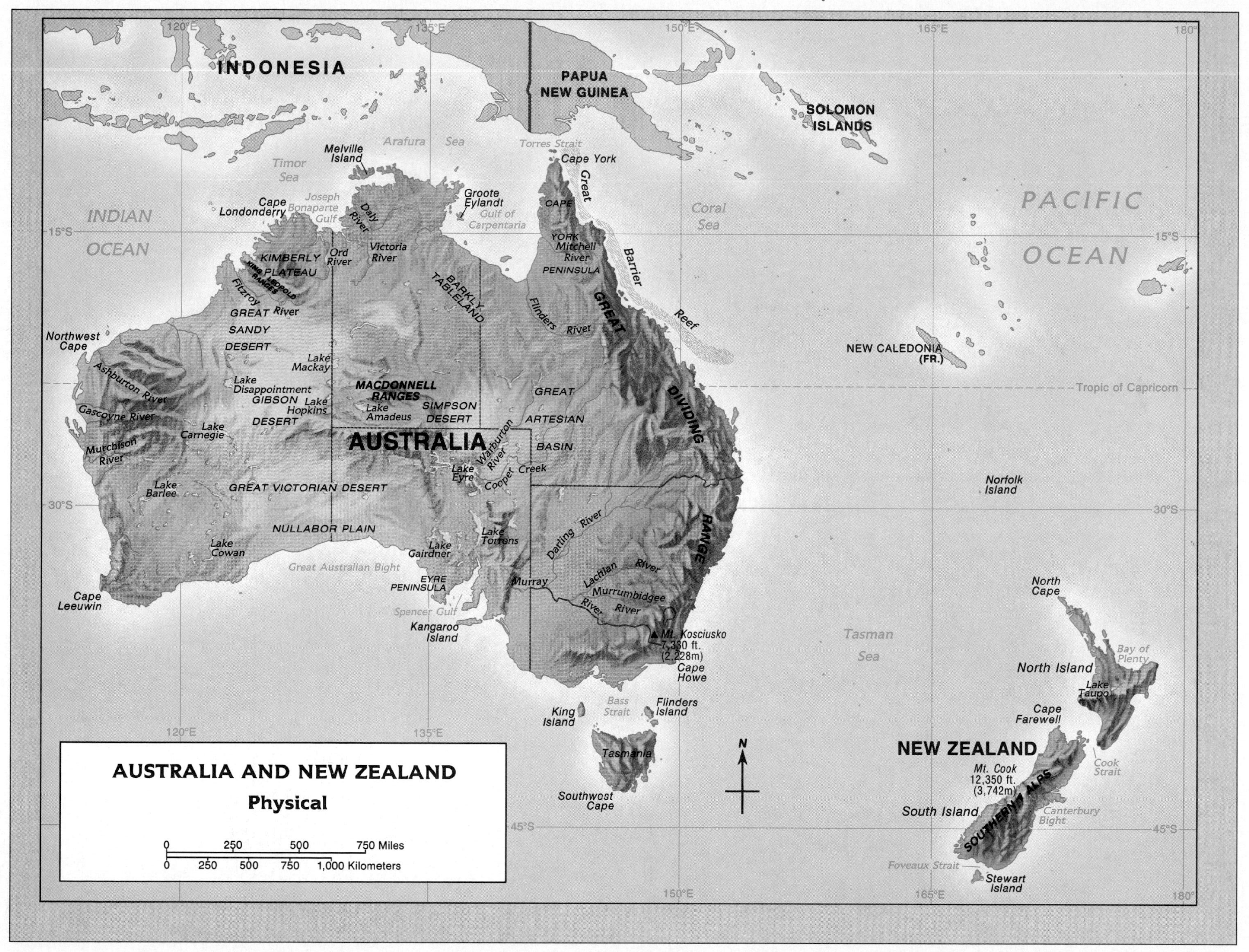

AUSTRALIA AND NEW ZEALAND
Physical
0 250 500 750 Miles
0 250 500 750 1,000 Kilometers
INDONESIA
PAPUA NEW GUINEA
SOLOMON ISLANDS
PACIFIC OCEAN
INDIAN OCEAN
Timor Sea
Arafura Sea
Torres Strait
Coral Sea
Melville Island
Cape York
Cape Londonderry
Joseph Bonaparte Gulf
Groote Eylandt
Gulf of Carpentaria
Daly River
Victoria River
Ord River
KIMBERLY PLATEAU
KING LEOPOLD RANGES
Fitzroy River
GREAT SANDY DESERT
CAPE YORK PENINSULA
Mitchell River
Great Barrier Reef
BARKLY TABLELAND
Flinders River
GREAT DIVIDING RANGE
Northwest Cape
Ashburton River
Gascoyne River
Murchison River
Lake Mackay
Lake Disappointment
GIBSON DESERT
Lake Hopkins
MACDONNELL RANGES
Lake Amadeus
SIMPSON DESERT
GREAT ARTESIAN BASIN
AUSTRALIA
Lake Carnegie
Warburton River
Lake Eyre
Cooper Creek
Lake Barlee
GREAT VICTORIAN DESERT
NEW CALEDONIA (FR.)
Tropic of Capricorn
Norfolk Island
NULLARBOR PLAIN
Lake Torrens
Darling River
Lake Cowan
Lake Gairdner
Great Australian Bight
EYRE PENINSULA
Murray
Lachlan River
Murrumbidgee River
River
Cape Leeuwin
Spencer Gulf
Kangaroo Island
Mt. Kosciusko 7,310 ft. (2,228m)
Cape Howe
Tasman Sea
North Cape
Bay of Plenty
North Island
Lake Taupo
King Island
Bass Strait
Flinders Island
Cape Farewell
Tasmania
N
NEW ZEALAND
Cook Strait
Mt. Cook 12,350 ft. (3,742m)
Southwest Cape
SOUTHERN ALPS
South Island
Canterbury Bight
Foveaux Strait
Stewart Island
120°E
135°E
150°E
165°E
180°
15°S
30°S
45°S

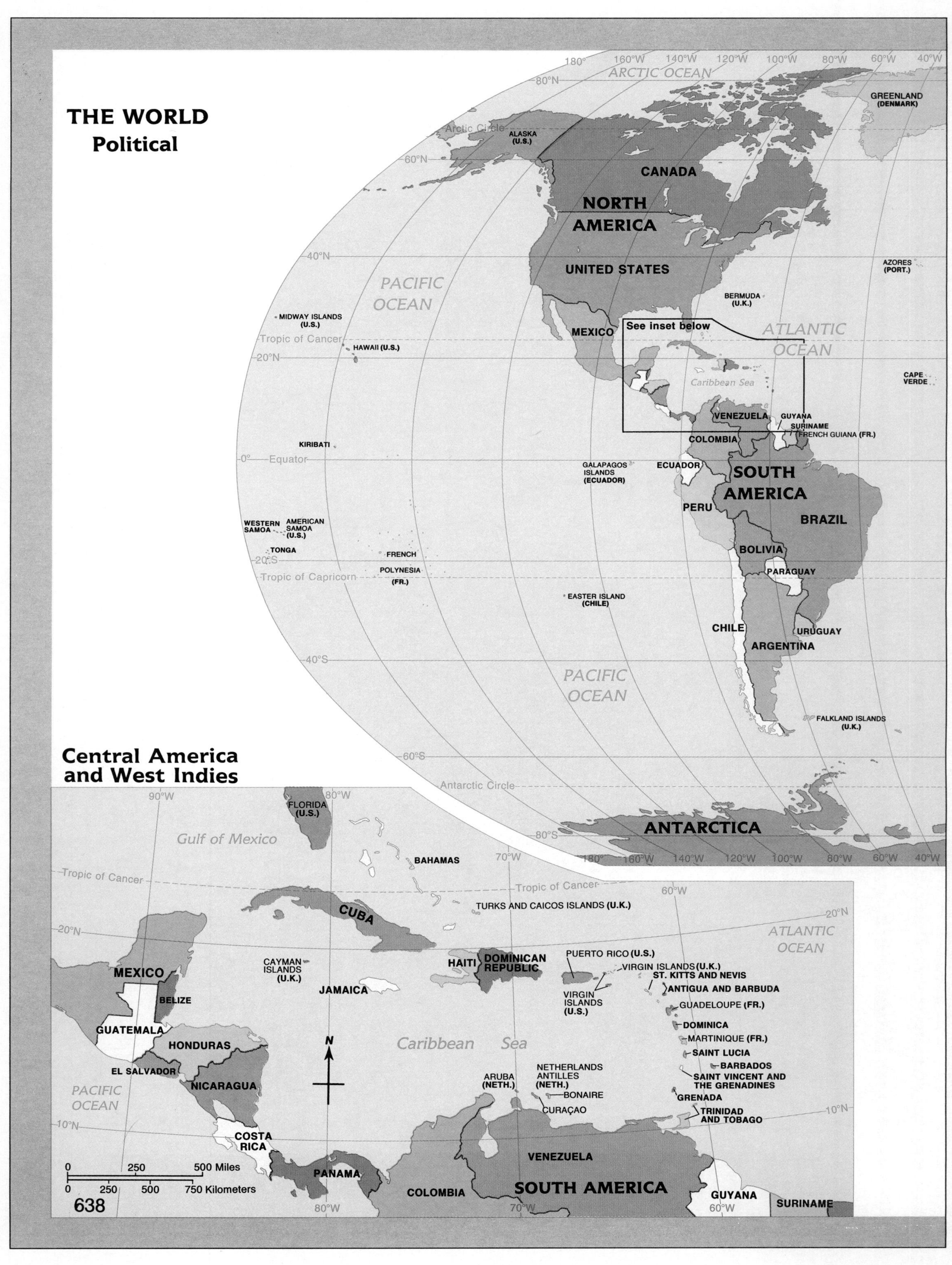
THE WORLD
Political
ARCTIC OCEAN
Arctic Circle
ALASKA (U.S.)
GREENLAND (DENMARK)
CANADA
NORTH AMERICA
UNITED STATES
AZORES (PORT.)
PACIFIC OCEAN
BERMUDA (U.K.)
MIDWAY ISLANDS (U.S.)
Tropic of Cancer
HAWAII (U.S.)
MEXICO
See inset below
ATLANTIC OCEAN
Caribbean Sea
CAPE VERDE
VENEZUELA
GUYANA
SURINAME
FRENCH GUIANA (FR.)
COLOMBIA
KIRIBATI
Equator
GALAPAGOS ISLANDS (ECUADOR)
ECUADOR
SOUTH AMERICA
PERU
BRAZIL
WESTERN SAMOA
AMERICAN SAMOA (U.S.)
TONGA
FRENCH POLYNESIA (FR.)
BOLIVIA
PARAGUAY
Tropic of Capricorn
EASTER ISLAND (CHILE)
CHILE
URUGUAY
ARGENTINA
PACIFIC OCEAN
FALKLAND ISLANDS (U.K.)
Antarctic Circle
ANTARCTICA
Central America and West Indies
FLORIDA (U.S.)
Gulf of Mexico
BAHAMAS
Tropic of Cancer
TURKS AND CAICOS ISLANDS (U.K.)
CUBA
ATLANTIC OCEAN
CAYMAN ISLANDS (U.K.)
HAITI
DOMINICAN REPUBLIC
PUERTO RICO (U.S.)
VIRGIN ISLANDS (U.K.)
ST. KITTS AND NEVIS
MEXICO
JAMAICA
ANTIGUA AND BARBUDA
BELIZE
VIRGIN ISLANDS (U.S.)
GUADELOUPE (FR.)
DOMINICA
GUATEMALA
MARTINIQUE (FR.)
HONDURAS
Caribbean Sea
SAINT LUCIA
BARBADOS
EL SALVADOR
NETHERLANDS ANTILLES (NETH.)
ARUBA (NETH.)
SAINT VINCENT AND THE GRENADINES
NICARAGUA
BONAIRE
PACIFIC OCEAN
CURAÇAO
GRENADA
TRINIDAD AND TOBAGO
COSTA RICA
VENEZUELA
0 250 500 Miles
0 250 500 750 Kilometers
PANAMA
COLOMBIA
SOUTH AMERICA
GUYANA
SURINAME
638

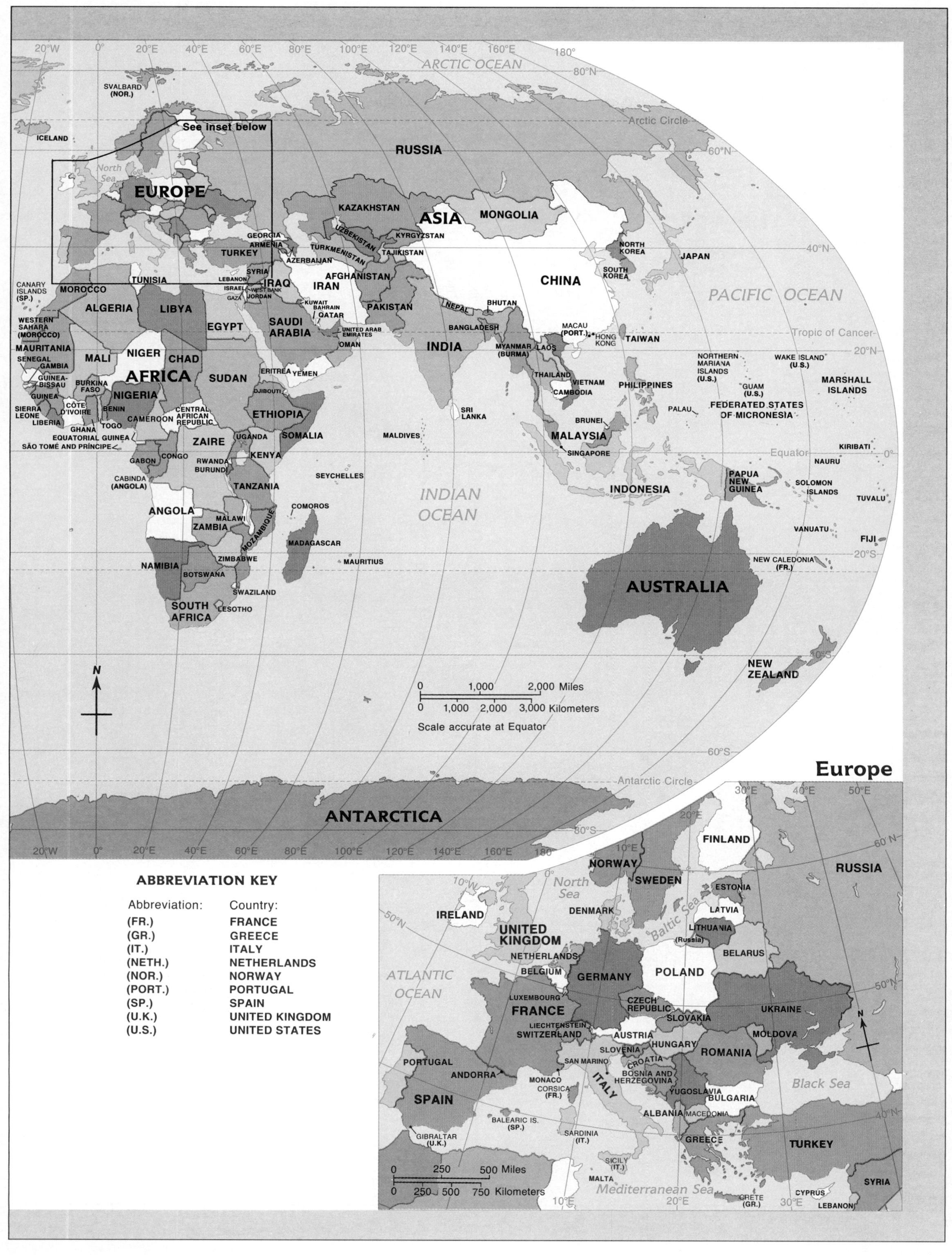
ARCTIC OCEAN
Arctic Circle
SVALBARD (NOR.)
ICELAND
See inset below
North Sea
EUROPE
RUSSIA
KAZAKHSTAN
ASIA
MONGOLIA
GEORGIA
ARMENIA
AZERBAIJAN
TURKEY
UZBEKISTAN
KYRGYZSTAN
TURKMENISTAN
TAJIKISTAN
AFGHANISTAN
NORTH KOREA
SOUTH KOREA
JAPAN
CHINA
PACIFIC OCEAN
Tropic of Cancer
CANARY ISLANDS (SP.)
MOROCCO
TUNISIA
SYRIA
LEBANON
ISRAEL
WEST BANK
GAZA
JORDAN
IRAQ
IRAN
KUWAIT
BAHRAIN
QATAR
PAKISTAN
NEPAL
BHUTAN
BANGLADESH
MACAU (PORT.)
HONG KONG
TAIWAN
ALGERIA
LIBYA
EGYPT
SAUDI ARABIA
UNITED ARAB EMIRATES
OMAN
INDIA
MYANMAR (BURMA)
LAOS
WESTERN SAHARA (MOROCCO)
MAURITANIA
SENEGAL
GAMBIA
MALI
NIGER
CHAD
SUDAN
ERITREA
YEMEN
THAILAND
VIETNAM
CAMBODIA
PHILIPPINES
NORTHERN MARIANA ISLANDS (U.S.)
GUAM (U.S.)
WAKE ISLAND (U.S.)
MARSHALL ISLANDS
AFRICA
GUINEA-BISSAU
GUINEA
BURKINA FASO
NIGERIA
DJIBOUTI
SIERRA LEONE
LIBERIA
CÔTE D'IVOIRE
GHANA
TOGO
BENIN
CAMEROON
CENTRAL AFRICAN REPUBLIC
ETHIOPIA
SRI LANKA
PALAU
FEDERATED STATES OF MICRONESIA
BRUNEI
MALAYSIA
SINGAPORE
EQUATORIAL GUINEA
SÃO TOMÉ AND PRÍNCIPE
ZAIRE
UGANDA
SOMALIA
MALDIVES
KIRIBATI
Equator
NAURU
GABON
CONGO
RWANDA
BURUNDI
KENYA
SEYCHELLES
PAPUA NEW GUINEA
SOLOMON ISLANDS
CABINDA (ANGOLA)
TANZANIA
INDIAN OCEAN
INDONESIA
TUVALU
COMOROS
ANGOLA
MALAWI
ZAMBIA
MOZAMBIQUE
VANUATU
FIJI
MADAGASCAR
NAMIBIA
ZIMBABWE
MAURITIUS
NEW CALEDONIA (FR.)
BOTSWANA
AUSTRALIA
SWAZILAND
SOUTH AFRICA
LESOTHO
NEW ZEALAND
N
0 1,000 2,000 Miles
0 1,000 2,000 3,000 Kilometers
Scale accurate at Equator
Antarctic Circle
ANTARCTICA
20°W 0° 20°E 40°E 60°E 80°E 100°E 120°E 140°E 160°E 180°
80°N 60°N 40°N 20°N 0° 20°S 40°S 60°S 80°S
ABBREVIATION KEY
Abbreviation: Country:
(FR.) FRANCE
(GR.) GREECE
(IT.) ITALY
(NETH.) NETHERLANDS
(NOR.) NORWAY
(PORT.) PORTUGAL
(SP.) SPAIN
(U.K.) UNITED KINGDOM
(U.S.) UNITED STATES
Europe
FINLAND
RUSSIA
NORWAY
SWEDEN
ESTONIA
North Sea
IRELAND
DENMARK
LATVIA
Baltic Sea
LITHUANIA
(Russia)
UNITED KINGDOM
NETHERLANDS
BELARUS
POLAND
BELGIUM
GERMANY
ATLANTIC OCEAN
LUXEMBOURG
CZECH REPUBLIC
UKRAINE
FRANCE
SLOVAKIA
LIECHTENSTEIN
SWITZERLAND
AUSTRIA
MOLDOVA
HUNGARY
SLOVENIA
ROMANIA
CROATIA
SAN MARINO
BOSNIA AND HERZEGOVINA
PORTUGAL
ANDORRA
MONACO
ITALY
CORSICA (FR.)
YUGOSLAVIA
Black Sea
BULGARIA
SPAIN
ALBANIA
MACEDONIA
BALEARIC IS. (SP.)
GIBRALTAR (U.K.)
SARDINIA (IT.)
GREECE
TURKEY
SICILY (IT.)
MALTA
Mediterranean Sea
CRETE (GR.)
CYPRUS
SYRIA
LEBANON
0 250 500 Miles
0 250 500 750 Kilometers
10°W 10°E 20°E 30°E 40°E 50°E
60°N 50°N 40°N

THE WORLD
Physical

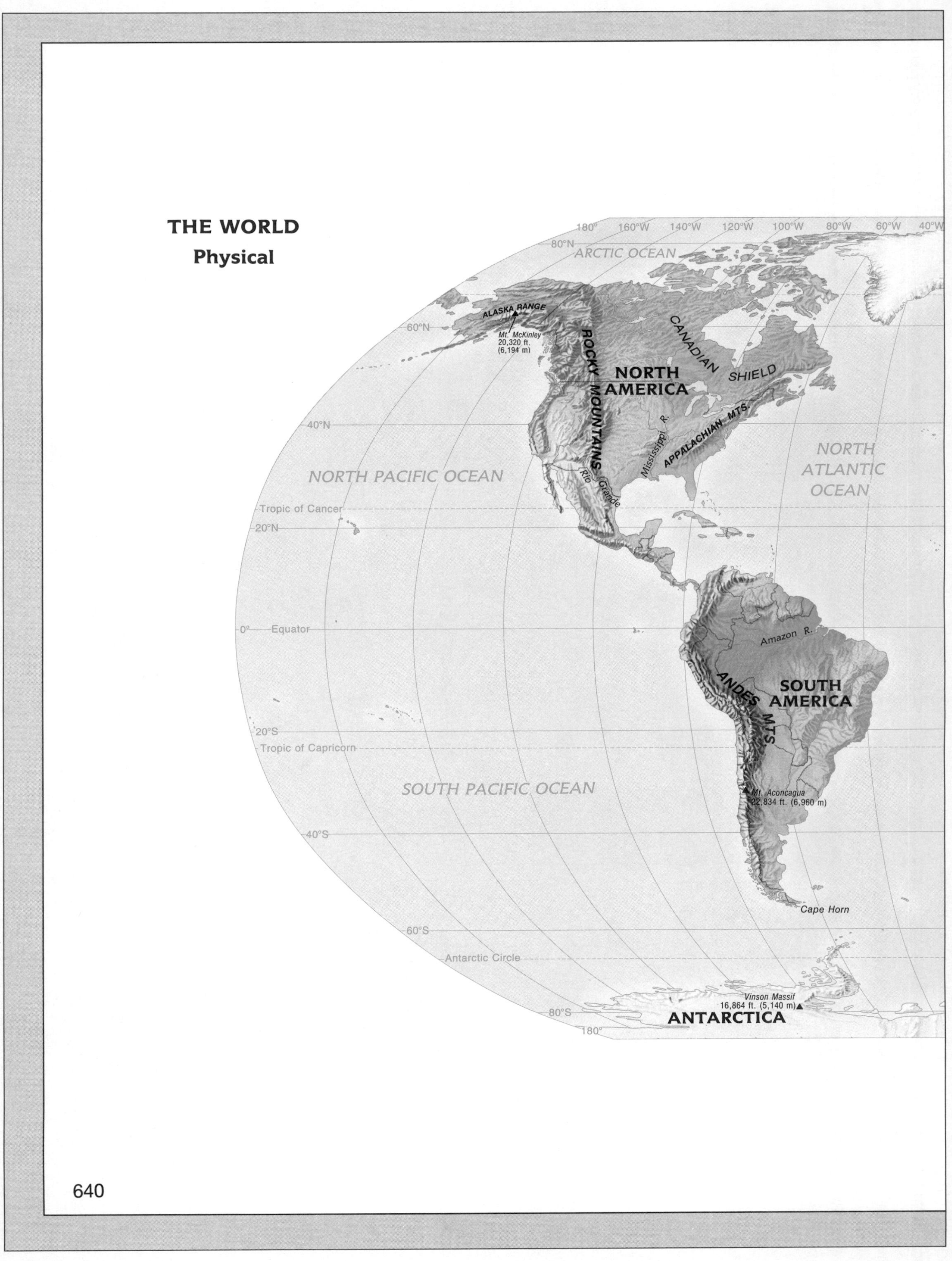

640

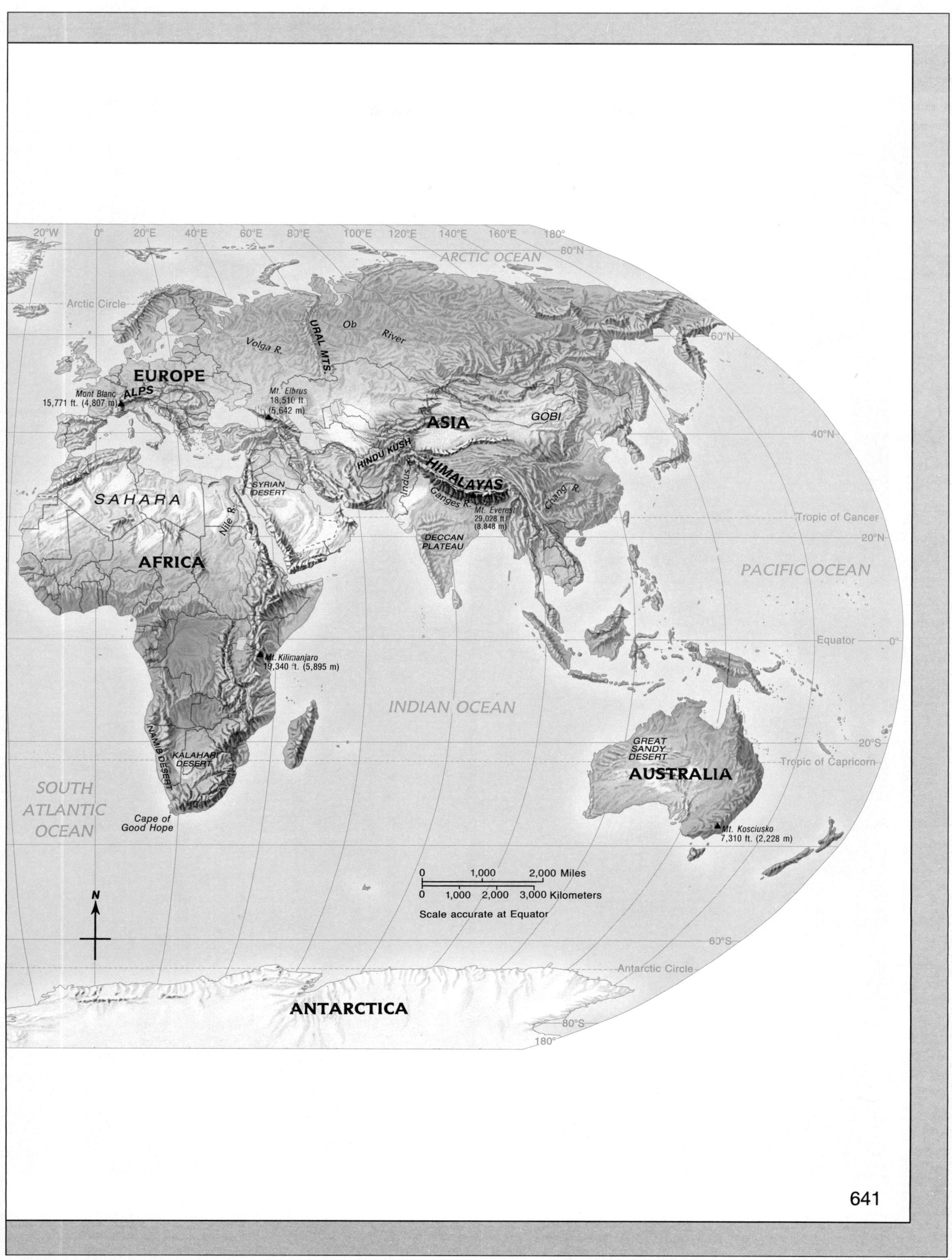
20°W
0°
20°E
40°E
60°E
80°E
100°E
120°E
140°E
160°E
180°
80°N
ARCTIC OCEAN
Arctic Circle
60°N
40°N
Tropic of Cancer
20°N
Equator
0°
20°S
Tropic of Capricorn
60°S
Antarctic Circle
80°S
180°
Ob
River
Volga R.
URAL MTS.
EUROPE
Mont Blanc
15,771 ft. (4,807 m)
ALPS
Mt. Elbrus
18,510 ft.
(5,642 m)
ASIA
GOBI
HINDU KUSH
HIMALAYAS
Indus R.
Ganges R.
Mt. Everest
29,028 ft.
(8,848 m)
Chang R.
SYRIAN DESERT
SAHARA
Nile R.
DECCAN PLATEAU
AFRICA
PACIFIC OCEAN
Mt. Kilimanjaro
19,340 ft. (5,895 m)
INDIAN OCEAN
NAMIB DESERT
KALAHARI DESERT
GREAT SANDY DESERT
AUSTRALIA
SOUTH ATLANTIC OCEAN
Cape of Good Hope
Mt. Kosciusko
7,310 ft. (2,228 m)
0 1,000 2,000 Miles
0 1,000 2,000 3,000 Kilometers
Scale accurate at Equator
N
ANTARCTICA

641

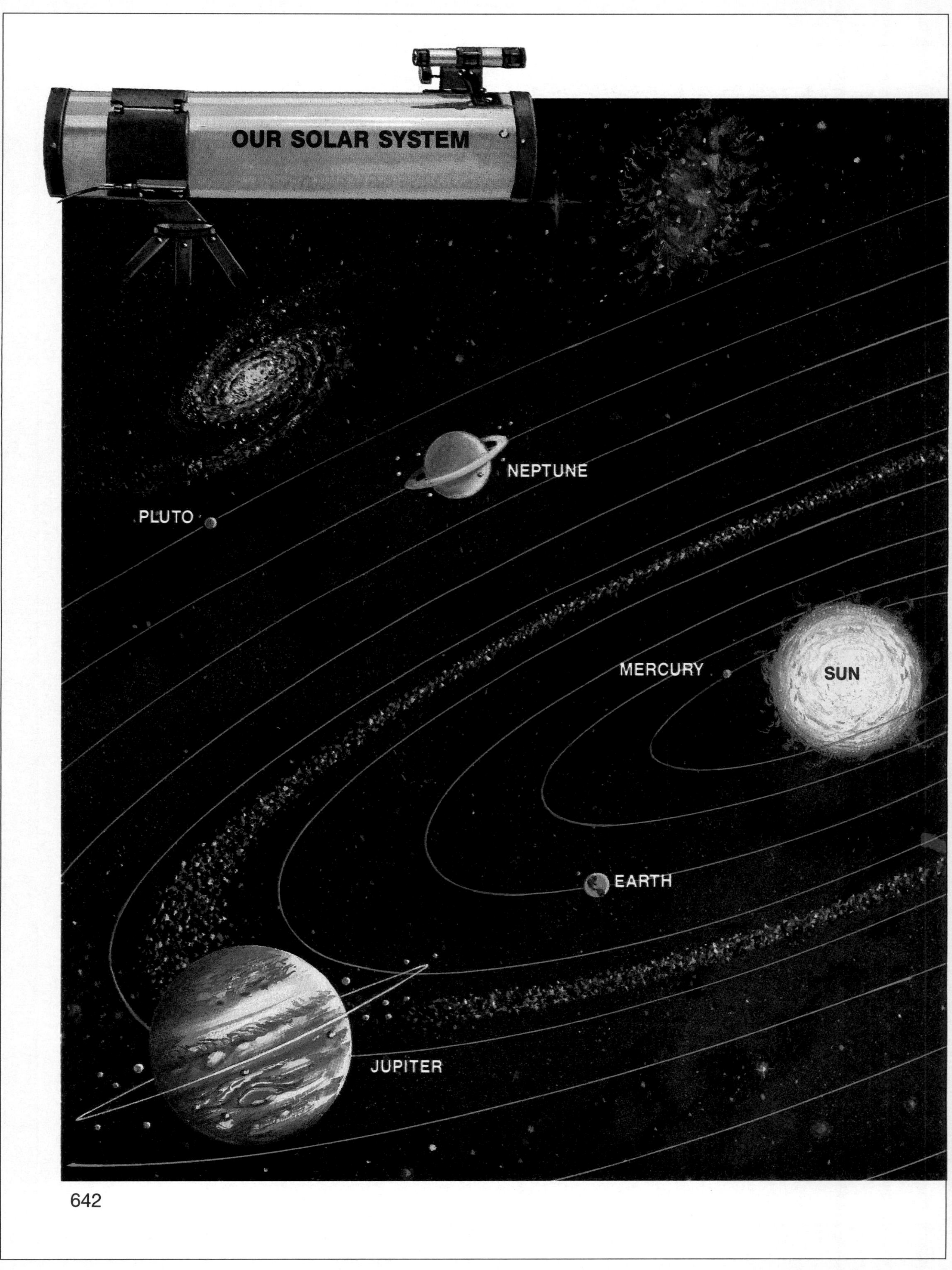

OUR SOLAR SYSTEM
NEPTUNE
PLUTO
MERCURY
SUN
EARTH
JUPITER
642

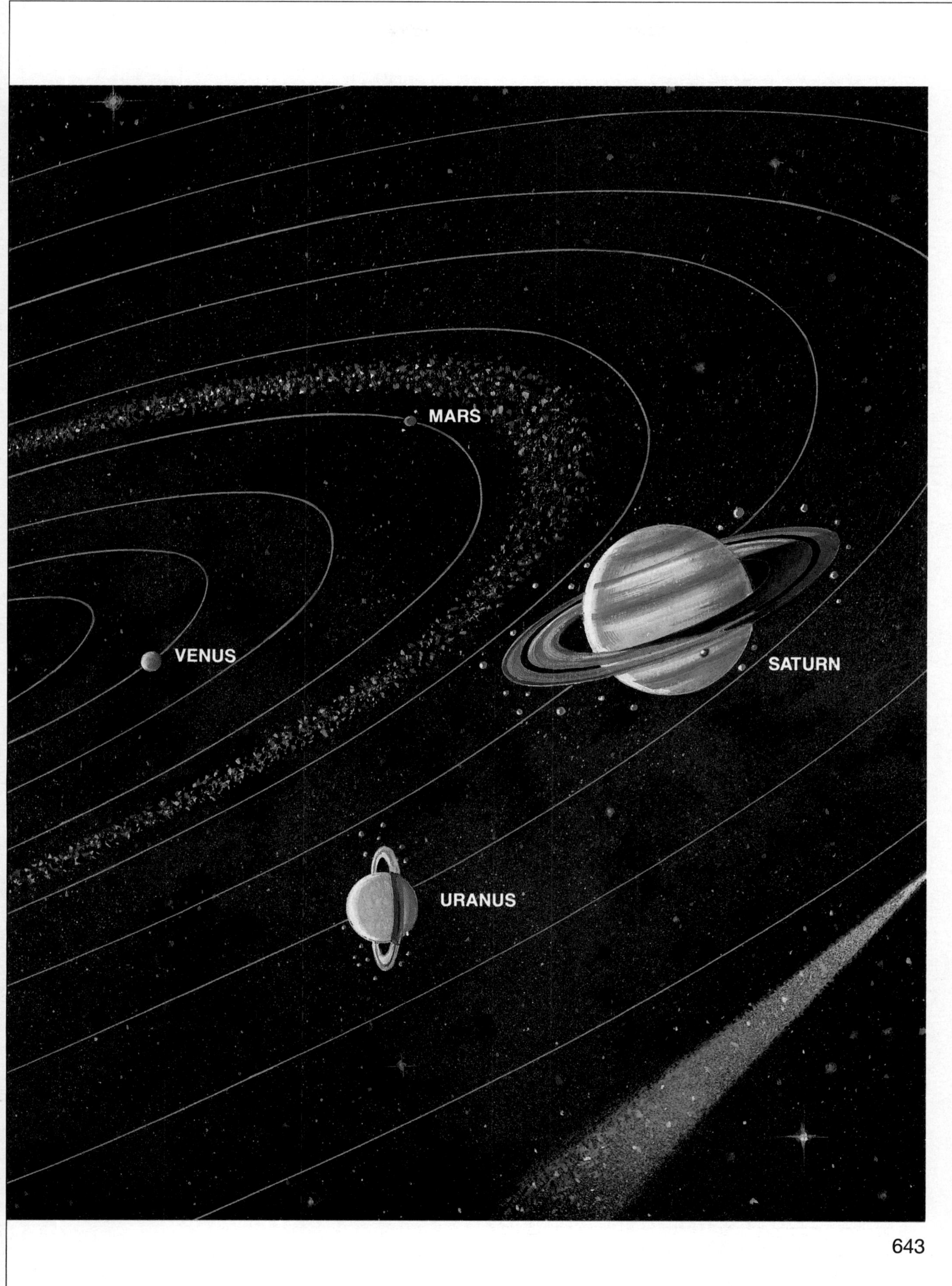
MARS
VENUS
SATURN
URANUS

DICTIONARY OF GEOGRAPHIC TERMS

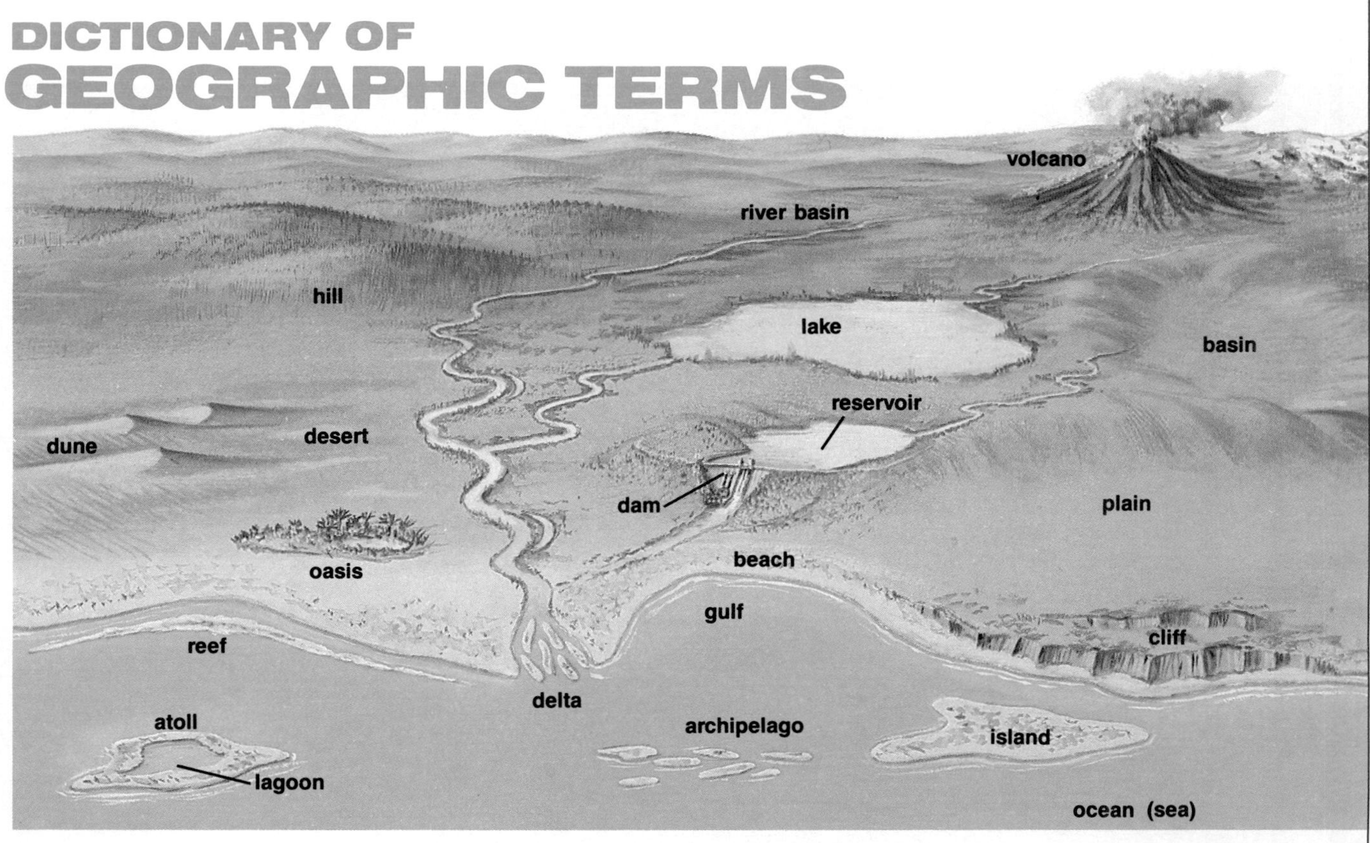

archipelago (ar kə pel i gō) A large group or chain of islands.

atoll (at′ ôl) A ring-shaped coral island or string of islands, surrounding a lagoon.

basin (bā′ sin) An area of low-lying land surrounded by higher land. *See also* **river basin.**

bay (bā) Part of an ocean, sea, or lake, that extends into the land. A bay is usually smaller than a gulf.

beach (bēch) The gently sloping shore of an ocean or other body of water, especially that part covered by sand or pebbles.

butte (būt) A small, flat-topped hill. A butte is smaller than a plateau or a mesa.

canal (kə nal′) A waterway built to carry water for navigation or irrigation. Navigation canals usually connect two other bodies of water.

canyon (kan′ yən) A deep, narrow valley with steep sides.

cape (kāp) A projecting part of a coastline that extends into an ocean, sea, gulf, bay, or lake.

cliff (klif) A high, steep face of rock or earth.

coast (kōst) Land along an ocean or sea.

dam (dam) A wall built across a river to hold back the flowing water.

delta (del′ tə) Land formed at the mouth of a river by deposits of silt, sand, and pebbles.

desert (dez′ ərt) A very dry area where few plants grow.

dune (dün) A mound, hill, or ridge of sand that is heaped up by the wind.

fjord (fyôrd) A deep, narrow inlet of the sea between high, steep cliffs.

foothills (fu̇t′ hilz) A hilly area at the base of a mountain range.

glacier (glā′ shər) A large sheet of ice that moves slowly over some land surface or down a valley.

gulf (gulf) Part of an ocean or sea that extends into the land. A gulf is usually larger than a bay.

harbor (här′ bər) A protected place along a shore where ships can safely anchor.

hill (hil) A rounded, raised landform, not as high as a mountain.

island (ī′ lənd) A body of land completely surrounded by water.

isthmus (is′ məs) A narrow strip of land bordered by water, that connects two larger bodies of land.

lagoon (lə gün′) A shallow body of water partly or completely enclosed within an atoll; a shallow body of sea water partly cut off from the sea by a narrow strip of land.

lake (lāk) A body of water completely surrounded by land.

644

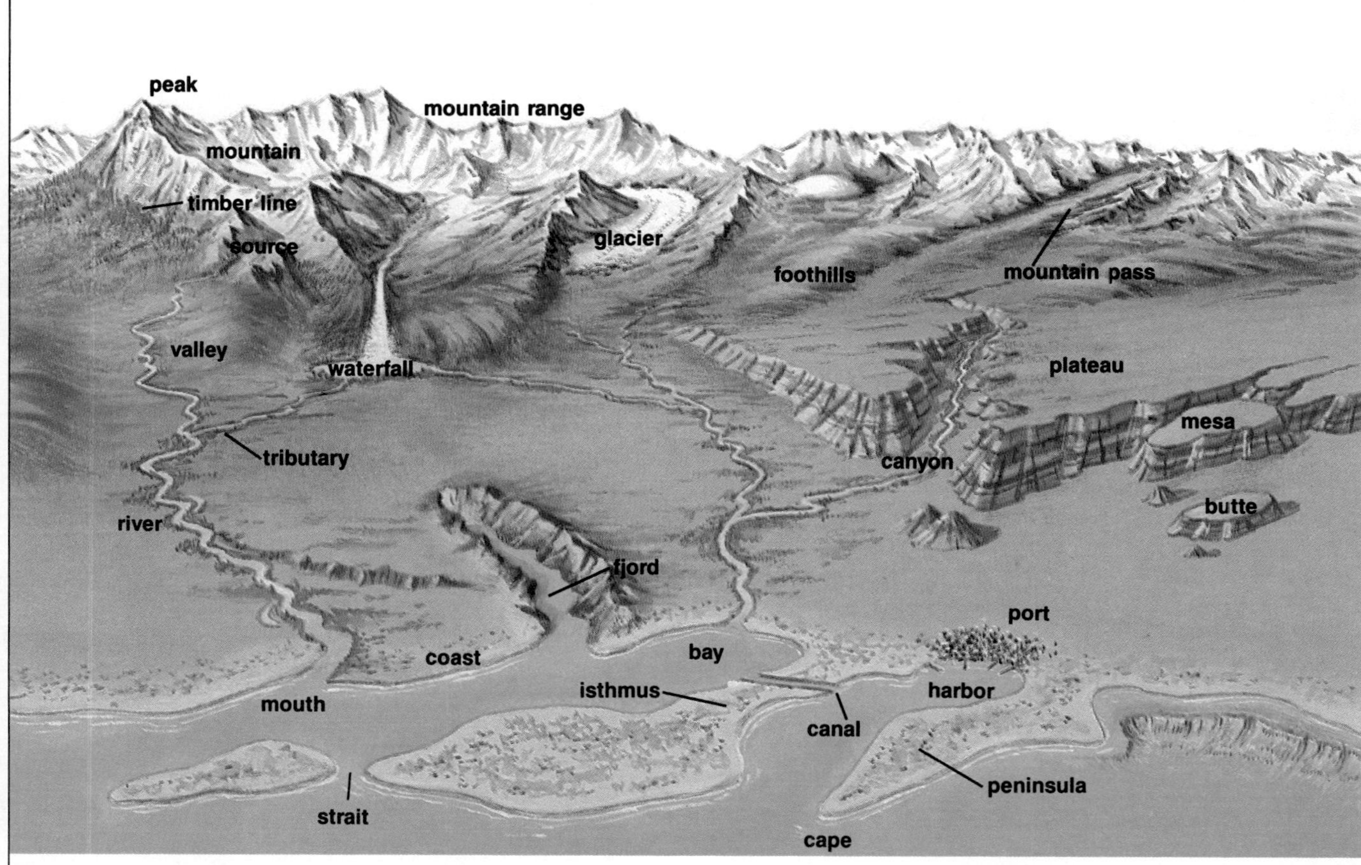

mesa (mā′ sə) A high, flat landform rising steeply above the surrounding land. A mesa is smaller than a plateau and larger than a butte.

mountain (mount′ ən) A high, rounded or pointed landform with steep sides, higher than a hill.

mountain pass (mount′ ən pas) An opening or gap through a mountain range.

mountain range (mount′ ən rānj) A row or chain of mountains.

mouth (mouth) The place where a river empties into another body of water.

oasis (ō ā′ sis) A place in the desert made fertile by a steady supply of water.

ocean (ō′ shən) One of the earth's four largest bodies of water. The four oceans are really a single connected body of salt water that covers about three fourths of the earth's surface.

peak (pēk) The pointed top of a mountain or hill.

peninsula (pə nin′ sə lə) A body of land nearly surrounded by water.

plain (plān) A large area of flat or nearly flat land.

plateau (pla tō′) A high, flat landform that rises steeply above the surrounding land. A plateau is larger than a mesa and a butte.

port (pôrt) A place where ships load and unload goods.

reef (rēf) A ridge of sand, rock, or coral that lies at or near the surface of a sea.

reservoir (rez′ ər vwär) A natural or artificial lake used to store water.

river (riv′ ər) A large stream of water that flows across the land and usually empties into a lake, ocean, or other river.

river basin (riv′ ər bā′ sin) All the land drained by a river and its tributaries.

sea (sē) A large body of water partly or entirely surrounded by land; another word for *ocean*.

source (sôrs) The place where a river or stream begins.

strait (strāt) A narrow waterway or channel connecting two larger bodies of water.

timber line (tim′ bər līn) An imaginary line on mountains, above which trees do not grow.

tributary (trib′ yə ter ē) A river or stream that flows into a larger river or stream.

valley (val′ ē) An area of low land between hills or mountains.

volcano (vol kā′ nō) An opening in the earth through which lava, rock, gases, and ash are forced out.

waterfall (wô′ tər fôl) A flow of water falling from a high place to a lower place.

645

GAZETTEER

This Gazetteer is a geographical dictionary that will help you to pronounce and locate the places discussed in this book. Latitude and longitude are given for cities and some other places. The page number tells you where each place appears on a map.

PRONUNCIATION KEY

a	cap	êr	clear	oi	coin	ü	moon
ā	cake	hw	where	ôr	fork	ū	cute
ä	father	i	bib	ou	cow	ûr	term
är	car	ī	kite	sh	show	ə	about, taken,
âr	dare	ng	song	th	thin		pencil, apron,
ch	chain	o	top	th	those		helpful
e	hen	ō	rope	u	sun	ər	letter, dollar,
ē	me	ô	saw	u̇	book		doctor

A

Abuja (ä bü′ zhä) The capital of Nigeria since 1991; 8°N, 7°E. (p. 428)

Afghanistan (af gan′ ə stan) A country in South Asia. (p. 486)

Africa (af′ ri kə) The world's second-largest continent. It lies south of Europe between the Atlantic and Indian oceans. (p. 5)

Albania (al bā′ nē ə) A country in southeastern Europe on the Adriatic Sea. (p. 294)

Algeria (al jêr′ ē ə) A country in western North Africa. (p. 356)

Alps (alps) A major European mountain system, extending in an arc from the Mediterranean coast east to the Balkan Peninsula. (p. 184)

Altai (al′ tī) A mountain range of Asia, extending from the south-central part of Russia east into western Mongolia. (p. 492)

Amazon River (am′ ə zon riv′ ər) The longest river in South America and the second-longest river in the world. It flows from the Andes across Brazil into the Atlantic Ocean. (p. 108)

Amsterdam (am′ stər dam) The capital and largest city of the Netherlands, in the west-central part of the country; 52°N, 4°E. (p. 222)

Anatolia (an ə tō′ lē ə) A peninsula in western Asia, bordered by the Black and Mediterranean seas. It is also known as Asia Minor. (p. 356)

Andes Mountains (an′ dēz moun′ tənz) A major mountain system stretching along the west coast of South America. They form the longest mountain chain in the world. (p. 108)

Antarctica (ant ärk′ ti kə) The fifth-largest continent. Ice-covered, it surrounds the South Pole and lies mainly within the Antarctic Circle. (p. 5)

Appalachian Highlands (ap ə lā′ chē ən hī′ ləndz) The hills and low mountains that stretch along much of the east coast of North America. (p. 40)

Arabian Peninsula (ə rā′ bē ən pə nin′ sə lə) A large peninsula in southwestern Asia. (p. 356)

Arctic Islands (ärk′ tik ī′ ləndz) Islands lying in the Arctic Ocean north of North America. (p. 40)

Arctic Ocean (ärk′ tik ō′ shən) The world's smallest ocean. It surrounds the North Pole and lies north of the Arctic Circle. (p. 5)

Argentina (är jən tē′ nə) A country in southern South America. (p. 108)

Armenia (är mē′ nē ə) A country in Eastern Europe. Armenia was a republic of the Soviet Union from 1936 until 1991, when it became independent. (p. 306)

Asia (ā′ zhə) The largest continent, bounded on the west by Europe, on the east by the Pacific Ocean, and on the south by the Indian Ocean. (p. 5)

Asia Minor (ā′ zhə mī′ nər) A peninsula in western Asia, bordered by the Mediterranean and Black seas. It is also known as Anatolia. (p. 356)

Atacama Desert (ä tə kä′ mə dez′ ərt) A cold desert that extends along the Pacific Coast of South America from southern Peru to central Chile. (p. 108)

Athens (ath′ ənz) The capital and largest city of Greece. It was once the most important and powerful city of ancient Greece; 38°N, 24°E. (p. 186)

Atlantic Coastal Plain (at lan′ tik kōs təl plān) The low land plain extending along the east coast of the United States. (p. 40)

Atlantic Ocean (at lan′ tik ō′ shən) The second-largest ocean. It separates North America and South America from Europe and Africa. (p. 5)

Atlas Mountains (at′ ləs moun′ tənz) A mountain range extending along the northwestern coast of Africa. (p. 356)

Australia (ôs trāl′ yə) The world's smallest continent, bounded by the Indian and Pacific oceans. (p. 5)

Austria (ôs′ trē ə) A country lying mainly in the Alps of Central Europe. (p. 184)

Azerbaijan (ä zər bī jän′) A country in the Caucasus Mountain region of Eastern Europe. Azerbaijan was a republic of the Soviet Union from 1939 until 1991, when it became independent. (p. 306)

B

Bahrain (bä rān′) An island country off the Arabian Peninsula in the Persian Gulf; a world center for oil and banking. (p. 356)

Balkan Peninsula (bôl′ kən pə nin′ sə lə) A large peninsula in southern Europe bounded by the Black, Aegean, and Adriatic seas. (p. 184)

Baltic Sea (bôl′ tik sē) An inland sea in northern Europe. (p. 178)

Bangladesh (bang glə desh′) A country in eastern South Asia, on the Bay of Bengal. (p. 486)

Barbados (bär bā′ dōs) An island country, part of the Lesser Antilles group in the Caribbean Islands. (p. 142)

Basel (bä′ zəl) An important commercial city on the Rhine River in northwestern Switzerland; 48°N, 8°E. (p. 234)

Beijing (bā jing′) The capital of the People's Republic of China in the northeastern part of the country. It was formerly called Peking; 40°N, 116°E. (p. 494)

Belarus (be lä rüs′) A country in Eastern Europe. Belarus was a republic of the Soviet Union from 1922 until 1991, when it became independent. (p. 306)

Belgium (bel′ jəm) A country in the Low Countries of Western Europe, on the North Sea. (p. 184)

Belize (be lēz′) A country on the northeastern coast of Central America, on the Caribbean Sea. (p. 142)

Benin (be nēn′) A country on the Gulf of Guinea in West Africa. (p. 416)

Berlin (bər lin′) The capital of Germany, located in the northeastern part of the country; 52°N, 13°E. (p. 186)

Bhutan (bü tän′) A country in eastern South Asia, on the border between India and China. (p. 486)

Black Sea (blak sē) An inland sea between Europe and Asia. (p. 178)

Bohemia (bō hē′ mē ə) A historic region and ancient kingdom in western Czech Republic (p. 343)

Bombay (bom bā′) The largest city and chief port of India, on the west coast; 19°N, 73°E. (p. 494)

Bonn (bon) The capital city of the former West German state; 50°N, 7°E. (p. 234)

Bosnia and Herzegovina (boz′ nē ə and hûrt sə gō vē′ nə) A republic in the central part of Yugoslavia that became independent in 1991. (p. 332)

Brahmaputra River (brä mə pü′ trə riv′ ər) A major river of southern Asia, flowing south from Tibet into the Bay of Bengal. (p. 492)

Brasília (brə zēl′ yə) The capital of Brazil in the east-central part of the country; 16°S, 48°W. (p. 110)

British Isles (brit′ ish īlz) A group of islands off the western coast of Europe, made up of Great Britain, Ireland, and some small islands. (p. 178)

Brittany (brit′ ə nē) A historic region in northwestern France, between the English Channel and the Bay of Biscay. (p. 218)

Brunei (brü nī′) A country on the northern coast of the island of Borneo in Southeast Asia. (p. 486)

Bucharest (bü kə rest) The capital and largest city of Romania, in the south-central part of the country; 44°N, 26°E. (p. 296)

Bulgaria (bul gâr′ ē ə) A country in Eastern Europe, on the Black Sea coast of the Balkan Peninsula. (p. 294)

C

Cairo (kī′ rō) The capital and largest city of Egypt, in the northeastern part of the country on the Nile River; 30°N, 31°E. (p. 358)

Calcutta (kal kut′ ə) A port city in northeastern India, on the Bay of Bengal; 23°N, 88°E. (p. 494)

Canadian Shield (kə nā′ dē ən shēld) The plains and hills that surround Hudson Bay and cover about half of Canada. (p. 40)

Canberra (kan ber′ ə) The capital of Australia in the southeastern part of the country; 35°S, 149°E. (p. 591)

Cape Town (kāp toun) A port city on the southwestern coast of South Africa; 34°S, 18°E. (p. 468)

Caribbean Islands (kar ə bē′ ən ī′ ləndz) Islands of the Caribbean Sea, also known as the West Indies. They are made up of the Greater Antilles, the Lesser Antilles, and the Bahamas. (p. 100)

Caspian Sea (kas′ pē ən sē) The largest inland body of water in the world, located in south-central Asia. (p. 294)

Catalonia (kat ə lō nē ə) A historic region and former principality in northeastern Spain, bordered by France to the north and the Mediterranean Sea to the east. (p. 259)

Caucasus Mountains (kô′ kə səs moun′ tənz) A mountain range that forms part of the southern boundary between Europe and Asia. (p. 294)

Central America (sen′ trəl ə mer′ i kə) The part of North America lying south of Mexico and north of South America. (p. 142)

647

Central Asia (sen′ trəl ā′ zhə) A large, dry area in the central parts of Asia including the countries of Kazakhstan, Kyrgyzstan, Tajikistan, Turkmenistan, Uzbekistan, China, and Mongolia. (p. 294)

Central Europe (sen′ trəl yůr′ əp) Part of Western Europe including West Germany, Switzerland, and Austria. (p. 178)

Central Plateau (sen′ trəl pla tō′) A large plateau in central Mexico. (p. 108)

Chaco (chä′ kō) A dry, lowland area of South America covering much of Paraguay, eastern Bolivia, and northern Argentina. (p. 108)

Chang River (chäng riv′ ər) The longest river in China, flowing from Tibet east into the East China Sea. It is also known as the Chang Jiang and the Yangtze River. (p. 492)

China (chī′ nə) A country in East Asia. (p. 486)

Coastal Plains (kōs′ təl plānz) The lowland plains of the United States lying along the Atlantic Coast (Atlantic Coastal Plain) and the Gulf of Mexico coast (Gulf Coastal Plain). (p. 40)

Continental Divide (kon tə nən′ təl di vīd′) An imaginary line formed by the peaks of the Rocky Mountains in North America. It separates the rivers flowing eastward across the land from those flowing westward across it. (p. 40)

Copenhagen (kō′ pən hā gən) The capital and largest city of Denmark, located on a small island off the southwestern coast of Sweden; 56°N, 12°E. (p. 188)

Corsica (kôr′ si kə) A French Island in the Mediterranean Sea, south of France. (p. 184)

Costa Rica (kos′ tə rē′ kə) A country in Central America where the population is mainly of Spanish descent. (p. 108)

Côte d'Ivoire (kōt dē vwär′) A country in West Africa, on the Gulf of Guinea. (p. 416)

Croatia (krō ā′ shə) A country in Eastern Europe. It was a republic in northern Yugoslavia until it became independent in 1991. (p. 332).

Cuba (kū′ bə) An island country, part of the Greater Antilles group in the Caribbean Islands. (p. 108)

Czechoslovakia (Chek ə slə vä′ kē ə) A country in Eastern Europe that split into two countries, the Czech Republic and Slovakia, in 1993. (p. 294)

D

Danube River (dan′ ūb riv′ ər) The second-longest river of Europe. It flows from southern Germany east into the Black Sea. (p. 184)

Denmark (den′ märk) A country in Scandinavia, in Western Europe, with coasts on the North Sea and the Baltic Sea. (p. 184)

Dnieper River (nē′ pər riv′ ər) River flowing through Eastern Europe into the Black Sea. (p. 294)

Dominican Republic (də min′ i kən rə pub′ lik) A country in the Caribbean Sea, on the eastern part of the island of Hispaniola in the Greater Antilles. (p. 108)

Drakensberg Mountains (drä′ kənz bûrg moun′ tənz) Mountain range in southeastern Africa. (p. 417)

E

East Africa (ēst af′ ri kə) An area in Africa stretching along the east coast from Egypt south to Mozambique. (p. 408)

East and Equatorial Africa (ēst and ē kwə tôr′ ē əl af′ ri kə) Part of Sub-Saharan Africa stretching from the Sahara Desert south to Mozambique, Zimbabwe, and Namibia. (p 408)

East Asia (ēst ā′ zhə) The part of Asia that includes China, Japan, Mongolia, North Korea, South Korea, Taiwan, and Hong Kong. (p. 486)

Eastern Europe (ēs′ tərn yůr′ əp) The part of Europe that lies between Western Europe and Northern Asia. (pp. 288–289)

Eastern Hemisphere (ēs′ tərn hem′ i sfêr) The half of the world that lies east of 0° longitude and includes Europe, Asia, Africa, and Australia. (p. 6)

Edmonton (ed′ mən tən) The capital and largest city of Alberta, Canada; 54°N, 114°W. (p. 82)

Elbe River (el′ bə riv′ ər) A river flowing from Central Europe into the North Sea. (p. 184)

England (ing′ glənd) The largest political division of the United Kingdom. England is located in the southern part of the island of Great Britain. (p. 202)

English Channel (ing′ glish chan′ əl) A narrow body of water between the island of Great Britain and northwestern Europe. (p. 194)

Equatorial Africa (ē kwə tôr′ ē əl af′ ri kə) The part of Sub-Saharan Africa that lies along the equator in the central part of the continent. (p. 408)

Eritrea (êr ə trē′ ə) A country of East Africa that was part of Ethiopia from 1952 to 1993. (p. 416)

Estonia (es tō′ nē ə) A country on the Baltic Sea in northern Europe. It was a republic of the Soviet Union from 1940 until its independence in 1991. (p. 306)

Euphrates River (ū frā′ tēz riv′ ər) A river in the Middle East flowing from Turkey to Iraq, where it joins the Tigris River to empty into the Persian Gulf. (p. 356)

Eurasia (yů rā′ zhə) The large landmass on which Europe and Asia are located. (p. 5)

Europe (yůr′ əp) The sixth-largest continent. It lies between the Atlantic Ocean and Asia, from which it is separated by the Ural and Caucasus mountains. (p. 5)

F

Faeroe Islands (fâr′ ō ī′ ləndz) A group of Danish islands in the North Atlantic Ocean, lying between Iceland and the Shetland Islands. (p. 184)

Fátima (fat′ ə mə) A village and pilgrimage center in central Portugal; 40°N, 10°E. (p. 250)

Fertile Crescent (fûr′ təl kres′ ənt) A fertile, crescent-shaped area of the Middle East. It was the site of several early civilizations. (p. 359)

GAZETTEER

Finland (fin′ lənd) A country in Scandinavia, in Western Europe, between the Scandinavian Peninsula and Russia. (p. 184)

Flanders (flan′ dərz) A historic region in west-central Western Europe, comprising parts of present-day Belgium, France, and the Netherlands. (p. 228)

Florence (flôr′ əns) A city in central Italy that became a great center of art and ideas during the Renaissance; 44°N, 11°E. (p. 250)

Formosa (fôr mō′ sə) The former name for Taiwan, an island off the southeast coast of China. (p. 486)

French Guiana (french gē an′ ə) An overseas department of France, on the northeastern coast of South America. (p. 108)

G

Gambia (gam′ bē ə) An English-speaking country on the Atlantic coast of West Africa, totally surrounded by French-speaking Senegal. (p. 416)

Ganges River (gan′ jēz riv′ ər) A river in northern India and Bangladesh, flowing from the Himalayas into the Bay of Bengal. (p. 492)

Geneva (jə nē′ və) A city in southwestern Switzerland; 46°N, 6°E. (p. 234)

Georgia (jôr′ jə) A country in the Caucasus Mountain region of Eastern Europe. Georgia was a republic of the Soviet Union from 1936 until 1991, when it became independent. (p. 306)

Germany (jûr′ mə nē) A country in Central Europe with coasts on the North Sea and the Baltic Sea. From the end of World War II until 1990, Germany was split into East Germany and West Germany. (p. 184)

Gibraltar (ji brôl′ tər) A British crown colony near the southern tip of Spain; 36°N, 5°W. (p. 250)

Gobi (gō′ bē) A large desert in Central Asia. (p. 492)

Grand Canyon (grand kan′ yən) A wide, deep canyon on the Colorado River in the western part of the United States; 36°N, 112°W. (p. 40)

Great Barrier Reef (grāt bar′ ē ər rēf) The largest barrier reef in the world, lying off the northeastern coast of Australia. (p. 584)

Great Dividing Range (grāt di vīd′ ing rānj) Highlands extending along the eastern coast of Australia. (p. 584)

Great Britain (grāt brit′ ən) One of the British Isles, in Western Europe. Great Britain is part of the United Kingdom, and contains the provinces of England, Scotland, and Wales. (p. 202)

Great Lakes (grāt lāks) Five large freshwater lakes lying along the border between Canada and the United States. They are Lake Superior, Lake Huron, Lake Michigan, Lake Erie, and Lake Ontario. (p. 40)

Great Plains (grāt plānz) The western, nearly treeless part of the Interior Plains of North America. (p. 40)

Great Rift Valley (grāt rift val′ ē) A series of valleys in eastern Africa extending from the Red Sea south to Mozambique. (p. 416)

Greater Antilles (grā′ tər an til′ ēz) The islands, excluding the Bahamas, making up the western part of the West Indies, or Caribbean Islands. (p. 108)

Greece (grēs) A country in the eastern part of Southern Europe. (p. 184)

Greenland (grēn′ lənd) The largest island in the world, located off the northeast coast of North America. It is part of Denmark. (p. 188)

Guam (gwäm) An island in the western part of the Pacific Ocean. Guam is a trust territory of the United States. (p. 621)

Guatemala (gwä tə mä′ lə) A country in Central America. (p. 108)

Gulf Coastal Plain (gulf kōs′ təl plān) The low-lying plain that borders the Gulf of Mexico. (p. 40)

Gulf of Guinea (gulf əv gin′ ē) A large arm of the Atlantic Ocean on the coast of west-central Africa. (p. 416)

Gulf of Mexico (gulf əv mek′ si kō) An arm of the Atlantic Ocean lying between the United States and Mexico. (p. 40)

Gulf Stream (gulf strēm) A special "river" that flows in the Atlantic Ocean. It brings warm water from the Gulf of Mexico to the Atlantic coast of Europe. (p. 193)

H

Haiti (hā′ tē) A country in the Caribbean Islands, on the western part of the island of Hispaniola in the Greater Antilles. (p. 108)

Harare (hə rär′ ā) The capital and largest city of Zimbabwe; 18°S, 31°E. (p. 468)

Helsinki (hel′ sing kē) The capital and largest city of Finland, located in the southern part of the country; 60°N, 24°E. (p. 272)

Himalayas (him ə lā′ əz) The world's highest mountain system, forming part of the northern boundary of the Indian subcontinent. (p. 492)

Hiroshima (hêr ə shē′ mə) A port city in southwestern Japan on the island of Honshu. In 1945 it was the first city to be devastated by an atomic bomb; 34°N, 132°E. (p. 543)

Hokkaido (ho kī′ dō) The northernmost and second-largest island of Japan. (p. 543)

a cap; **ā** cake; **ä** father; **är** car; **âr** dare; **ch** chain; **e** hen; **ē** me; **êr** clear; **hw** where; **i** bib; **ī** kite; **ng** song; **o** top; **ō** rope; **ô** saw; **oi** coin; **ôr** fork; **ou** cow; **sh** show; **th** thin; **th** those; **u** sun; **ů** book; **ü** moon; **ū** cute; **ûr** term; **ə** about, taken, pencil, apron, helpful; **ər** letter, dollar, doctor

649

Hong Kong (hong′ kong′) A British crown colony off the southeastern coast of China. It will return to Chinese control after 1997; 22°N, 115°E. (p. 486)

Honshu (hon′ shü) The largest island of Japan. (p. 543)

Huang He (hwäng′ hù) A large river that flows across north China. It is also known as the Huang River and the Yellow River. (p. 492)

Hungary (hung′ gə rē) A country in Eastern Europe. (p. 294)

I

Iberian Peninsula (ī bêr′ ē ən pə nin′ sə lə) A large peninsula of southwestern Europe that includes Spain and Portugal. (p. 184)

Iceland (īs′ lənd) An island country in the northern Atlantic Ocean. (p. 184)

India (in′ dē ə) A country in South Asia. (p. 486)

Indian Ocean (in′ dē ən ō shən) The third-largest ocean. It lies south of Asia between Australia and Africa. (p. 5)

Indonesia (in də nē′ zhə) A country in Southeast Asia, located in the Malay Archipelago. (p. 486)

Indus River (in′ dəs riv′ ər) A river in South Asia, flowing from Tibet into the Arabian Sea. (p. 492)

Interior Plains (in têr′ ē ər plānz) Plains covering much of the central part of North America. (p. 40)

International Date Line (in tər nash′ ən əl dāt līn) An imaginary line running approximately along the line of longitude at 180°, in the middle of the Pacific Ocean, marking the time boundary between one day and the next. (p. 204)

Ireland (īr′ lənd) One of the British Isles, in Western Europe. Ireland contains the Republic of Ireland and the province of Northern Ireland, which is part of the United Kingdom. (p. 184)

Israel (iz′ rā əl) A country in the Middle East, lying between the Mediterranean Sea and the Jordan River, founded in 1948 as a Jewish homeland. (p. 356)

Italian Peninsula (i tal′ yən pə nin′ sə lə) A long peninsula in Southern Europe on which Italy is located. (p. 184)

Italy (it′ ə lē) A country in Southern Europe. Italy includes the Italian Peninsula and the islands of Sardinia and Sicily. (p. 184)

J

Jakarta (jə kär′ tə) The capital and largest city of Indonesia. It is a major seaport on the island of Java; 6°S, 107°E. (p. 494)

Java (jä′ və) A large island of Indonesia, in the Malay Archipelago. (p. 562)

Jerusalem (jə rü′ sə ləm) The capital of Israel and a holy city for Jews, Christians, and Muslims; 31°N, 31°E. (p. 370)

Johannesburg (jō han′ əs bûrg) An important industrial city in northeastern South Africa; 26°S, 29°E. (p. 418)

Jordan River (jôr′ dən riv′ ər) A river in the Middle East, flowing between Jordan and the West Bank into the Dead Sea. (p. 378)

Jutland Peninsula (jut′ lənd pə nin′ sə lə) A peninsula in the northern part of Western Europe that is located between the North and Baltic seas. (p. 184)

K

Kalahari Desert (käl ə här′ ē dez′ ərt) A large desert in southern Africa. (p. 416)

Kano (kä′ nō) A city in north-central Nigeria; 12°N, 9°E. (p. 634)

Kazakhstan (kä zäk stän′) A country in Central Asia. Kazakhstan was a republic of the Soviet Union from 1936 until 1991, when it became independent. (p. 306)

Kenya (ken′ yə) A country in East Africa. (p. 416)

Kiev (kē′ ev) The capital and largest city of Ukraine; 50°N, 30°E. (p. 296)

Kremlin (krem′ lin) The buildings that are the seat of government for Russia and were the seat of government for the Soviet Union. (p. 322)

Kunlun Mountains (kùn′ lùn′ moun′ tənz) A mountain chain in western China. (p. 492)

Kyrgyzstan (kêr′ giz stän) A country in Central Asia. Kyrgyzstan was a republic of the Soviet Union from 1936 until 1991, when it became independent. (p. 306)

Kyushu (kū′ shü) The third-largest island of Japan, the southernmost of the four largest islands. (p. 513)

L

Lake Lugano (lāk lü gä′ nō) A lake on the border between Switzerland and Italy; 46°N, 9°E. (p. 234)

Lake Titicaca (lāk tit i kä′ kə) The largest lake in South America and the highest navigable lake in the world. It is located in the Andes on the border of Peru and Bolivia; 16°S, 71°W. (p. 108)

Lake Victoria (lāk vik tôr′ ē ə) The largest lake in Africa, located in the east-central part of the continent. (p. 408)

Lapland (lap′ land) A region in northern Europe that includes northern Norway, Sweden, and Finland, and northwestern Russia. (p. 272)

Latin America (lat′ in ə mer′ i kə) The parts of the Western Hemisphere where Spanish and Portuguese are widely spoken. The region includes Mexico and Central America, South America, and the Caribbean Islands. (p. 31)

Latvia (lat′ vē ə) A country on the Baltic Sea in northern Europe. Latvia was a republic of the Soviet Union from 1940 until 1991, when it became independent. (p. 306)

Lesser Antilles (les′ ər an til′ ēz) The islands, excluding the Bahamas, making up the eastern part of the West Indies, or Caribbean Islands. (p. 108)

GAZETTEER

650

Lithuania (lith ü ā′ nē ə) A country on the Baltic Sea in northern Europe. Lithuania was a republic of the Soviet Union from 1940 until 1991, when it became independent. (p. 306)

Lofoten Islands (lō′ fōt ən ī′ ləndz) Island group of Norway, off the northwestern coast of Norway. (p. 272)

London (lun′ dən) The capital of the United Kingdom. London is located in southeastern England on the Thames River; 52°N, 0°longitude. (p. 12)

Low Countries (lō kun′ trēz) An area in the west-central part of Western Europe that is made up of the Netherlands, Belgium, and Luxembourg. (p. 218)

Luxembourg (luk′ səm bûrg) One of the Low Countries in Western Europe. (p. 184)

M

Macedonia (mas ə do′ nyə) A country in Eastern Europe. It was a republic in the southern part of Yugoslavia until it became independent in 1991. (p. 332)

Madrid (mə drid′) The capital and largest city of Spain, located in the central part of the country; 40°N, 4°W. (p. 186)

Malay Peninsula (mā′ lā pə nin′ sə lə) A long, narrow peninsula extending from Southeast Asia into the Indian Ocean. (p. 492)

Malaysia (mə lā′ zhə) A country in Southeast Asia, located partly on the Malay Peninsula and partly on the island of Borneo. (p. 486)

Marbella (mär bā′ yä) A popular vacation town in southern Spain; 37°N, 5°W. (p. 250)

Marrakesh (mar ə kesh′) A city in the central part of Morocco; 32°N, 8°W. (p. 388)

Mecca (mek′ ə) A city in western Saudi Arabia. Mecca was the birthplace of Muhammad and is the holiest city of Islam; 21°N, 40°E. (p. 370)

Mediterranean Sea (med i tə rā′ nē ən sē) A large, nearly landlocked arm of the Atlantic Ocean lying between Europe, Asia, and Africa. (p. 178)

Mekong River (mā′ kong riv′ ər) A river in Southeast Asia, flowing from western China southeast into the South China Sea. (p. 492)

Melanesia (mel′ ə nē′ zhə) One of three main divisions of the Pacific islands. Melanesia lies south of Micronesia and west of Polynesia. (p. 578)

Melbourne (mel′ bərn) A port city in southeastern Australia; 38°S, 145°E. (p. 586)

Mexico (mek′ si kō) A Latin American country in North America. (p. 122)

Mexico City (mek′ si kō sit′ ē) The capital and largest city of Mexico; 19°N, 99°W. (p. 110)

Micronesia (mī krə nē′ zhə) One of three main divisions of the Pacific islands. Micronesia is located north of Melanesia and west of Polynesia. (p. 578)

Middle East (mid′ əl ēst) The southwestern part of Asia that stretches from Turkey to Iran. (p. 350)

Minsk (minsk) The capital city of Belarus. Minsk is also the headquarters of the Commonwealth of Independent States; 53°N, 27°E. (p. 296)

Mississippi River (mis ə sip′ ē riv′ ər) The longest river in North America and the fourth longest river in the world. It flows south across the interior United States into the Gulf of Mexico. (p.40)

Moldova (mol dō′ və) A country in Eastern Europe. Moldova was a republic of the Soviet Union from 1940 until 1991, when it became independent. (p. 306)

Mongolia (mong gō′ lē ə) A vast area in east-central Asia, extending from northern China to Siberia and including Inner Mongolia and the country of Mongolia. (p. 492)

Montenegro (mon tə neg′ rō) A republic in the southern part of Yugoslavia. (p.332)

Moscow (mos′ kou) The capital and largest city of Russia. 56°N, 38°E. (p. 296)

Mount Aconcagua (mount ak ən kä′ gwə) The highest mountain in South America, located in the Andes Mountains between Argentina and Chile at 22,834 feet (6,960 m); 33°S, 70°W. (p. 108)

Mount Athos (mount ath′ os) A small peninsula in northeastern Greece on which several monasteries are located. (p. 250)

Mount Cook (mount ku̇k) The highest mountain in New Zealand, in the central part of the Southern Alps on South Island. Its elevation is 12,349 feet. (3,764 m); 44°S, 170°E. (p. 584)

Mount Everest (mount ev′ ər əst) The highest mountain in the world. It is located in the Himalayas on the border between Nepal and Tibet at 29,028 feet (8,848 m); 33°N, 87°E. (p. 492)

Mount Kilimanjaro (mount kil ə mən jär′ ō)) The highest mountain in Africa, located in northern Tanzania at 19,340 feet (5,895 m); 3°S, 37°E. (p. 416)

Mount McKinley (mount mə kin′ lē) The highest mountain in North America, located in south-central Alaska at 20,320 feet (6,194 m); 63°N, 151°W. (p. 40)

Munich (mū′ nik) A city in southern Germany; 48°N, 11°E. (p. 234)

a cap; **ā** cake; **ä** father; **är** car; **âr** dare; **ch** chain; **e** hen; **ē** me; **êr** clear; **hw** where; **i** bib; **ī** kite; **ng** song; **o** top; **ō** rope; **ô** saw; **oi** coin; **ôr** fork; **ou** cow; **sh** show; **th** thin; **th** those; **u** sun; **u̇** book; **ü** moon; **ū** cute; **ûr** term; **ə** about, taken, pencil, apron, helpful; **ər** letter, dollar, doctor

GAZETTEER

N

Nepal (nə pôl′) A country in South Asia, located on the southern slopes of the Himalayas. (p. 486)

Netherlands, the (neth′ ər ləndz) One of the Low Countries in Western Europe, on the North Sea. (p. 184)

Netherlands Antilles (neth′ ər ləndz an til′ ēz) Dutch islands lying off the coast of Venezuela that are part of the Lesser Antilles of the Caribbean Islands. (p. 108)

New Brunswick (nü brunz′ wik) A province in eastern Canada. (p. 82)

New Zealand (nü zē′ lənd) An island country in the southern Pacific. (p. 578)

Niger River (nī′ jər riv′ ər) A river in West Africa, flowing from the Sierra Leone-Guinea border into the Gulf of Guinea. (p. 416)

Nigeria (nī jêr′ ē ə) A country on the Gulf of Guinea in West Africa. (p. 416)

Nile River (nīl riv′ ər) The world's longest river, flowing from east-central Africa north into the Mediterranean Sea. (p. 356)

Normandy (nôr′ mən dē) A historic region in northwest France, bordering the English Channel. (p. 218)

North Africa (nôrth af′ rik ə) Region consisting of the Muslim countries of Africa lying along the Mediterranean coast. (p. 350)

North America (nôrth ə mer′ ik ə) The world's third-largest continent, lying between the Pacific and Atlantic oceans. (p. 5)

North China Plain (nôrth chī′ nə plān) A large fertile plain lying north of the Qin Ling Mountains in eastern China. (p. 492)

North Island (nôrth ī′ lənd) The smaller and more northerly of the two main islands of New Zealand. (p. 584)

North Pole (nôrth pōl) The northernmost point on the earth; the northern end of the earth's axis, at 90°N. (p. 6)

North Sea (nôrth sē) A large arm of the Atlantic Ocean, between Great Britain and mainland Europe. (p. 184)

Northern Asia (nôr′ thərn ā′ zhə) The part of Asia east of the Ural Mountains and the Caspian Sea. (p. 294)

Northern Ireland (nôr′ thərn īr′ lənd) A province of the United Kingdom located in the northeastern part of Ireland. (p. 202)

Norway (nôr′ wā) A country in Western Europe, located in the western part of the Scandinavian Peninsula. (p. 184)

O

Oceania (ō shē an′ ē ə) Islands of the Pacific Ocean including Polynesia, Melanesia, Micronesia, and many other islands. Australia and New Zealand are sometimes considered part of Oceania. (p. 598)

Oinoussai (ē nü′ sā) A small Greek island in the Aegean Sea, lying near the Turkish coast; 39°N, 26°E. (p. 250)

Orinoco River (ôr ə nō′ kō riv′ ər) A large river of northwestern South America that flows into the Atlantic Ocean. (p. 108)

Ottawa (ot′ ə wə) Canada's capital, located in the province of Ontario in the southeastern part of the country. (p. 82)

P

Pacific Mountains (pə sif′ ik moun′ tənz) A mountain system in the United States and Canada that lies between the Pacific Ocean and the Rocky Mountains. (p. 40)

Pacific Ocean (pə sif′ ik ō′ shən) The world's largest body of water, lying between Asia and Australia on the west and North America and South America on the east. (p. 5)

Pakistan (pak′ ə stan) A country in South Asia, on the Arabian Sea. (p. 486)

Palestine (pal′ ə stīn) A historical area in the Middle East, lying between the Mediterranean Sea and the Jordan River. It was the homeland of the Jews in biblical times and a British protectorate that became the nations of Israel and Jordan. (p. 372)

Pamirs (pä mêrz′) A mountain region of Asia bordering Afghanistan, Tajikistan, Pakistan, and China. Several mountain ranges meet here to form the "Pamir Knot." (p.492)

Pampas (päm′ pəz) Grass-covered plains of South America that cover much of central Argentina and parts of Uruguay. (p. 108)

Panama (pa′ nə mä) A country of Central America, between the Atlantic and Pacific Oceans. (p. 108)

Panama Canal (pan′ ə mä kə nal′) A ship canal across the Isthmus of Panama connecting the Atlantic and Pacific oceans. (p. 151)

Panama Canal Zone (pan′ ə mä kə nal′ zōn) A strip of land on both sides of the Panama Canal that, from 1903 to 1978, was a United States territory. Panama controls most of the Canal Zone and will gain complete control of it in the year 2000. (p. 151)

Papua New Guinea (pap′ ù ə nü gin′ ē) A country in the Pacific, located on the eastern part of the island of New Guinea and several nearby islands. (p. 578)

Paris (par′ is) The capital city of France and one of Western Europe's great cultural centers; 49°N, 2°E. (p. 186)

Patagonia (pat′ ə gō′ nē ə) The southern part of Argentina. (p. 108)

Persian Gulf (pûr′ zhən gulf) A body of water located between the Arabian Peninsula and Iran. (p. 356)

Philippines (fil′ ə pēnz) A country located on an archipelago in Southeast Asia, separated from the mainland by the South China Sea. (p. 486)

652

Plateau of Iran (pla tō′ əv i ran′) A plateau located in the northeastern part of Iran, in the Middle East. (p. 356)

Plateau of Tibet (pla tō′ əv ti bet′) A high, dry plateau in southwestern China, north of the Himalayas. (p. 492)

Poland (pō lənd) A country in Eastern Europe, on the Baltic Sea. (p. 332)

Polynesia (pol ə nē′ zhə) One of the three main island groups of Oceania in the Pacific Ocean. (p. 579)

Popocatépetl (pō pō kä tā′ pə təl) A volcano in southern Mexico, near Mexico City; 19°N, 99°W. (p. 108)

Portugal (pôr′ chə gəl) A country in Southern Europe, in the western part of the Iberian Peninsula. (p. 184)

Puerto Rico (pwer′ tō rē′ kō) An island in the Greater Antilles of the West Indies. It is a commonwealth of the United States. (p. 108)

Pyrenees (pir′ ə nēz) A mountain range in the southwestern part of Western Europe, extending from the Bay of Biscay to the Mediterranean Sea. (p. 184)

Q

Quebec (kwi bek′) The capital city of the province of Quebec in eastern Canada; 46°N, 71°W. (p. 82)

Queensland (kwēnz′ lənd) A state of Australia, in the northeastern part of the country. (p. 590)

R

Red Sea (red sē) A narrow sea located between the Arabian Peninsula and northeastern Africa. (p. 350)

Rhine River (rīn riv′ ər) A river in Western Europe that flows from eastern Switzerland into the North Sea. (p. 184)

Rio de Janeiro (rē′ ō dā zhə nâr′ ō) A large port city in southeastern Brazil; 23°S, 43°W. (p. 110)

Río de la Plata (rē′ ō dā lä plä′ tə) A river system in east-central South America. It is actually the mouth of the Paraná and Uruguay rivers and their main tributaries and empties into the Atlantic Ocean. (p. 108)

Riviera (riv ē âr ə) A narrow strip of land along the Mediterranean coasts of France, Monaco, and Italy, famous as a vacation spot. (p. 222)

Riyadh (rē yäd′) The capital and largest city of Saudi Arabia, located in the central part of the country; 25°N, 47°E. (p. 358)

Rocky Mountains (rok′ ē moun′ tənz) The high, rugged mountains that stretch along the western part of North America from Alaska south to New Mexico. (p. 40)

Romania (rō mā′ nē ə) A country in Eastern Europe, on the Black Sea coast of the Balkan Peninsula. (p. 294)

Rome (rōm) The capital and largest city of Italy, located on the Tiber River in the central part of the country; 42°N, 13°E. (p. 186)

Rotterdam (rot′ ər dam) A city in the southwestern Netherlands and the busiest port in the world; 51°N, 4°E. (p. 186)

Ruhr Valley (ru̇r val′ ē) The valley of the Ruhr River, a major tributary of the Rhine River in northwestern Germany. (p. 238)

Russia (rush′ ə) A country in Eastern Europe and Northern Asia. Russia was a republic of the Soviet Union from 1922 until 1991, when it became independent. (p. 306)

S

Sahara (sə har′ ə) The largest desert in the world, covering much of northern Africa. (p. 623)

Sahel (sä′ hel) A dry grassland that stretches across Africa just south of the Sahara Desert. (p. 416)

Samoa (sə mō′ ə) An archipelago in Polynesia, about halfway between New Zealand and Hawaii. (p. 598)

San Francisco (san frən sis′ kō) A port city in west-central California, on the Pacific Ocean; 38°N, 122°W. (p. 43)

San Pedro de Macorís (san pā′ drō dā mä kō rēs′) A city in the southeastern Dominican Republic; 19°S, 69°W. (p. 142)

Santiago de Compostela (sän′ tē ä′ gō də kom pō stel′ ä) A pilgrimage center in northwestern Spain; 43°N, 9°W. (p. 250)

Sardinia (sär din′ ē ə) An Italian island in the Mediterranean Sea, west of the Italian Peninsula. (p. 184)

Scandinavia (skan də nā′ vē ə) Area in northwestern Europe including the countries of Norway, Sweden, Denmark, and their dependents. Iceland and Finland are also considered part of Scandinavia. (p. 178)

Scandinavian Peninsula (skan də nā′ vē an pə nin′ sə lə) A large peninsula in the northern part of Western Europe. (p. 184)

Senegal (sen i gôl′) A country on the Atlantic coast of West Africa. (p. 416)

Serbia (sûr′ bē ə) A republic in the western part of Yugoslavia. (p. 332)

Shikoku (shi kō′ kü) The smallest of the four main islands of Japan. (p. 543)

a cap; ā cake; ä father; är car; âr dare; ch chain; e hen; ē me; êr clear; hw where; i bib; ī kite; ng song; o top; ō rope; ô saw; oi coin; ôr fork; ou cow; sh show; th thin; <u>th</u> those; u sun; u̇ book; ü moon; ū cute; ûr term; ə about, taken, pencil, apron, helpful; ər letter, dollar, doctor

GAZETTEER

653

Siberia (sī bêr′ ē ə) A vast region in Russia lying between the Ural Mountains and the Pacific Ocean. It includes the Asian part of Russia. (p. 294)

Sicily (sis′ ə lē) An Italian island in the Mediterranean Sea off the southwestern tip of Italy. (p. 184)

Siena (sē en′ ə) A city in central Italy; 43°N, 11°E. (p. 264)

Sinai Peninsula (sī′ nī pə nin′ sə lə) A small peninsula in northeastern Egypt, bordered by the Mediterranean Sea on the north and the Red Sea on the south. It is a bridge between Asia and Africa. (p. 356)

Singapore (sing′ ə pôr) An island country in Southeast Aisa off the southern tip of the Malay Peninsula. (p. 486)

Slovenia (slō vēn′ ē ə) A country in Eastern Europe. It was a republic in northwestern Yugoslavia until it became independent in 1991. (p. 332)

South Africa (south af′ ri kə) A country in Southern Africa. (p. 416)

South America (south ə mer′ i kə) The world's fourth-largest continent. It lies between the Pacific and Atlantic oceans. (p. 160)

South Asia (south ā′ zhə) The part of Asia made up of the Indian subcontinent and nearby lands. (p. 486)

South Korea (south kə rē′ ə) A country in Eastern Asia, occupying the southern part of the Korean Peninsula. (p. 486)

Southeast Asia (south ēst′ ā′ zhə) The part of Asia lying between South Asia and East Asia. (p. 486)

Southern Africa (suth′ ərn af′ ri kə) The part of Sub-Saharan Africa that is south of East and Equatorial Africa. It is the southernmost part of the continent. (p. 408)

Southern Europe (suth′ ərn yůr′ əp) The countries of the southern part of Western Europe. (p. 350)

South Island (south ī′ lənd) The larger and more southerly of the two main islands of New Zealand. (p. 584)

South Pole (south pōl) The southernmost point of the earth; the southern end of the earth's axis, at 90°S. (p. 6)

Soviet Union (sō′ vē et ūn′ yən) A former country of Eastern Europe and Northern Asia. The Soviet Union existed from 1922 until 1991, when it was replaced by 15 independent countries. (pp. 288–289)

Soweto (sə wā′ tō) A black township in South Africa, near Johannesburg; 26°S, 27°E. (p. 471)

Spain (spān) A country in Southern Europe, on the Iberian Peninsula. (p. 184)

Sri Lanka (srē läng′ kə) An island country in South Asia, off the southern tip of India. (p. 486)

St. Lawrence Seaway (sānt lôr′ əns sē′ wā) The St. Lawrence River and its system of dams, locks, and canals that connect the Great Lakes with the Gulf of St. Lawrence. This waterway allows large ships to travel between interior North America and the Atlantic Ocean. (p. 49)

Stockholm (stok′ hōm) The capital and largest city of Sweden, located on the eastern coast; 59°N, 18°E. (p. 272)

Sub-Saharan Africa (sub′ sə har′ ən af′ ri kə) The part of Africa lying south of the Sahara. (p. 31)

Sweden (swē′ dən) A country in Western Europe, located in the eastern part of the Scandinavian Peninsula. (p. 184)

Switzerland (switz′ ər lənd) A country in Central Europe. (p. 184)

Sydney (sid′ nē) The largest city and chief port of Australia, on the eastern coast of the country; 34°S, 151°E. (p. 586)

T

Tahiti (tə hē′ tē) The largest of the Society Islands, located in French Polynesia, midway between Australia and South America; 18°S, 150°W. (p. 598)

Taiwan (tī wän′) An island off the southeastern coast of China, between the Formosa Strait and the Philippine Sea. It is also known as Formosa. (p. 486)

Tajikistan (tä jik′ i stän) A country in Central Asia. Tajikistan was a republic of the Soviet Union from 1929 until 1991, when it became independent. (p. 306)

Takla Makan (täk′ lə mə kän′) A large desert in northwestern China. (p. 492)

Tarim Basin (dä′ rem′ bā′ sin) A dry region in northwestern China, lying between the Tian Shan and the Kunlun Mountains. (p. 637)

Tenochtitlán (te nôch tē tlän′) Capital of the Aztecs. It was located where Mexico City stands today. (p. 120)

Thingvellir (theng′ vet lêr) A small settlement and plain in southwestern Iceland, about 25 miles (40 km) east of Reykjavik; 64°N, 21°W. (p. 272)

Tian Shan (tē än′ shän′) A mountain system of central Asia, extending from Kyrgyzstan into western China. (p. 492)

Tibet (ti bet′) An autonomous region in southwestern China, north of the Himalayas. (p. 526)

Tigris River (tī′ gris riv′ ər) A river in southwestern Asia, flowing from eastern Turkey to southeastern Iraq, where it joins the Euphrates River to empty into the Persian Gulf. (p. 356)

Tokyo (tō′ kyō) The capital and largest city of Japan, in the east-central part of the island of Honshu; 36°N, 140°E. (p. 494)

Tropic of Cancer (trop′ ik əv kan′ sər) An imaginary line around the earth at latitude 23° 27′N. (p. 25)

Tropic of Capricorn (trop′ ik əv kap′ ri kôrn) An imaginary line around the earth that is at latitude 23° 27′S. (p. 25)

Turin (tůr′in) A city in northwestern Italy, an important automobile-manufacturing center; 45°N, 8°E. (p. 186)

Turkmenistan (tûrk men′ i stän) A country in Central Asia. Turkmenistan was a republic of the Soviet Union from 1929 until 1991, when it became independent. (p. 306)

GAZETTEER

654

U

Ukraine (ū krān′) A country in Eastern Europe. Ukraine was a republic of the Soviet Union from 1922 until 1991, when it became independent. (p. 306)

Ural Mountains (yůr′ əl moun′ tənz) A mountain system traditionally forming part of the boundary between Europe and Asia. (p. 294)

Uruguay (yůr′ ə gwā) A country on the southeastern coast of South America. (p. 108)

Uzbekistan (ůz bek′ i stan) A country in Central Asia. Ukraine was a republic of the Soviet Union from 1924 until 1991, when it became independent. (p. 306)

V

Vatican City (vat′ i kən sit′ ē) An independent state within the city of Rome. It is the world headquarters of the Roman Catholic Church; 42°N, 12°E. (p. 250)

Venezuela (ven ə zwā′ lə) A country in the northern part of South America, on the Caribbean Sea. (p. 108)

Victoria Falls (vik′ tôr ē ə fôlz) A spectacular waterfall in Southern Africa, on the Zambezi River between Zimbabwe and Zambia; 18°S, 26°E. (p. 416)

Vienna (vē en′ ə) The capital and largest city of Austria, on the Danube River in the northeastern part of the country; 48°N, 16°E. (p. 186)

Virgin Islands (vûr′ jin ī′ ləndz) A group of islands in the West Indies, divided politically between the United States and Great Britain; 18°N, 64°W. (p. 142)

Volga River (vôl′ gə riv′ ər) The longest river in Europe, located in Russia. It flows from the Ural Mountains into the Caspian Sea. (p. 294)

W

West Africa (west af′ ri kə) The part of Sub-Saharan Africa that makes up the southern part of the continent's northwestern "bulge." (p. 408)

West Bank (west bangk) An area in the Middle East, west of the Jordan River. It has been occupied by Israel since 1967. (p. 378)

Western Europe (wes′ tərn yůr′ əp) The countries that make up the western part of Europe. (p. 31)

Western Hemisphere (wes′ tərn hem′ i sfêr) The half of the world that lies west of the prime meridian and includes North America and South America. (p. 6)

West Indies (west in′ dēz) Islands in and around the Caribbean Sea, also known as the Caribbean Islands. They are made up of the Greater Antilles, the Lesser Antilles, and the Bahamas. (p. 142)

West Siberian Plain (west si bêr′ ē ən plān) A vast plain, one of the largest flat areas in the world, located in Siberia. (p. 294)

Witwatersrand (wit wôt′ ərz rand) An area in South Africa noted for its rich deposits of gold and other minerals. Several industrial cities, including Johannesburg, are located there. (p. 471)

Y

Yucatán Peninsula (ū kə tän′ pə nin′ sə lə) A peninsula in southeastern Mexico and northeastern Central America that juts between the Gulf of Mexico and the Caribbean Sea. (p. 108)

Yugoslavia (ū gō slä′ vē ə) A country in Eastern Europe, on the eastern shore of the Adriatic. (p. 294)

Z

Zagros Mountains (zag′ rəs moun′ tənz) A mountain range in western Iran. (p. 356)

Zaire (zä êr′) A country in Equatorial Africa. (p. 416)

Zambia (zam′ bē ə) A country in Southern Africa. (p. 416)

Zanzibar (zan′ zə bär) An island in the Indian Ocean, off the coast of Africa, that is part of Tanzania; 6°S, 40°E. (p. 635)

a cap; **ā** cake; **ä** father; **är** car; **âr** dare; **ch** chain; **e** hen; **ē** me; **êr** clear; **hw** where; **i** bib; **ī** kite; **ng** song; **o** top; **ō** rope; **ô** saw; **oi** coin; **ôr** fork; **ou** cow; **sh** show; **th** thin; **th** those; **u** sun; **ů** book; **ü** moon; **ū** cute; **ûr** term; **ə** about, taken, pencil, apron, helpful; **ər** letter, dollar, doctor

GAZETTEER

655

GLOSSARY

This Glossary will help you to pronounce and understand the meanings of the Key Vocabulary in this book. The page number at the end of the definition tells where the word first appears.

PRONUNCIATION KEY

a	cap	êr	clear	oi	coin	ü	moon
ā	cake	hw	where	ôr	fork	ū	cute
ä	father	i	bib	ou	cow	ûr	term
är	car	ī	kite	sh	show	ə	about, taken, pencil, apron, helpful
âr	dare	ng	song	th	thin		
ch	chain	o	top	th	those		
e	hen	ō	rope	u	sun	ər	letter, dollar, doctor
ē	me	ô	saw	u̇	book		

A

absolute ruler (ab′ sə lüt rü′ lər) A ruler with complete power whose authority cannot be questioned. (p. 377)

acid rain (as′ id rān′) Rain mixed with chemicals from the burning of coal and other fuels. Acid rain pollutes waterways and kills wildlife and trees. (p. 88)

alluvial soil (ə lü′ vē əl soil) Soil deposited by a river as it flows. (p. 495)

almanac (ôl′ mə nak) A reference book that contains up-to-date facts on many subjects. (p. 89)

altiplano (äl ti plän′ ō) A high, cold, flat area between two mountain ranges in Bolivia and Peru. (p. 109)

apartheid (ə pär′ tīd) A system used in South Africa to separate people of different races by law. (p. 470)

aquaculture (ak′ wə kul chər) Fish farming. (p. 530)

aquifer (ak′ wə fər) An underground layer of rock, sand, or gravel that holds water or carries it to springs or wells. (p. 363)

arable (ar′ ə bəl) Good for farming. (p. 47)

archipelago (är kə pel′ i gō) An island group, such as the West Indies. (p. 109)

arid (ar′ id) Dry. (p. 362)

atlas (at′ ləs) A reference book that contains a variety of maps and information about places in the world. (p. 89)

atoll (at′ ôl) A doughnut-shaped coral reef looped around an area of still, warm water. (p. 585)

autonomous region (ô ton′ ə məs rē′ jən) An area within a country, such as China, that is self-governing but supervised by the central government. (p. 532)

autonomy (ô ton′ ə mē) The right to self-government. (p. 259)

B

barter (bär′ tər) To swap. (p. 454)

basin (bā′ sin) A large, bowl-shaped dip in the land. (p. 417)

bazaar (bə zär′) An outdoor market. (p. 375)

bias (bī′ əs) A tendency to favor one point of view over another. (p. 242)

Brahmans (brä′ mənz) The priestly caste in the Hindu caste system. (p. 507)

Buddhism (bu̇d′ iz əm) A system of belief in Asia that teaches that suffering is caused by selfishness. (p. 527)

buffer zone (buf′ ər zōn) A region between two hostile powers. (p. 340)

C

cabinet (kab′ ə nit) Members of a government, either a parliament or an executive branch, who help run the government by giving advice and helping to carry out the laws. (p. 91)

call and response (kôl and ri spons′) A traditional African way of telling a story in which the storyteller calls out part of a well-known story and the listeners call out or sing out a response. (p. 443)

calligraphy (kə lig′ rə fē) A beautiful form of writing that features graceful, flowing lines. (p. 382)

calypso (kə lip′ sō) A style of music developed in the Caribbean by enslaved Africans who sang while they worked. (p. 154)

campesino (kam pə sē′ nō) Village farmer in Mexico. (p. 124)

canal (kə nal′) A waterway that is dug to provide a water route for travel or irrigation. (p. 222)

656

canton (kan′ tən) A small political unit in Switzerland, similar to a state or province. (p. 241)

capital goods (kap′ i təl gu̇dz) Products that are used by industries to make other goods. (p. 315)

capitalism (kap′ i tə liz əm) An economic system in which businesses are owned by individuals rather than by the government. (p. 62)

cardinal directions (kär′ də nəl di rek′ shənz) The four primary directions: north, south, east, and west. (p. 7)

caste (kast) A social group among the Hindus that identifies a person according to the occupation of his or her ancestors. (p. 506)

caudillo (kou dē′ yō) In South America, a local military leader who gained power in his local area after the country gained its independence. (p. 170)

censor (sen′ sər) To examine something to decide if it may be made public. (p. 327)

chancellor (chan′ sə lər) Title of the prime minister in Germany. (p. 240)

chart (chärt) An organized way of presenting information in rows and columns. (p. 253)

checks and balances (cheks and bal′ əns əz) The system by which each branch of government limits the power of the others. (p. 67)

civil war (siv′ əl wôr) A war between people of the same country. (p. 459)

civilization (siv ə lə zā′ shən) A culture in which learning and government reach high levels. (p. 119)

clan (klan) A group of families who are descended from the same ancestor. (p. 431)

climate (klī′ mit) The kind of weather a place has over a long period of time. (p. 23)

climograph (klī′ mə graf) A graph that shows information about the temperature and precipitation in a particular location over a period of time. (p. 301)

coalition (kō ə lish′ ən) A temporary union between different political parties that agree to work together for a common purpose. (p. 258)

colonialism (kə lō′ nē ə liz əm) The control of a country as a colony by another country. (p. 398)

command economy (kə mand′ i kon′ ə mē) An economic system in which the government makes and organizes most economic decisions. (p. 315)

commercial farming (kə mûr′ shəl fär′ ming) A type of farming where crops are grown for sale. (p. 124)

commonwealth (kom′ ən welth) A self-governing territory, such as Puerto Rico. (p. 150)

Commonwealth of Independent States (kom′ ən welth əv in di pen′ dənt stāts) An organization formed in 1991 by some of the countries that had been members of the Soviet Union to foster cooperation in economic and governmental concerns. (p. 317)

Commonwealth of Nations (kom′ ən welth əv nā′ shənz) A group of independent nations once ruled by Great Britain; they consider the British monarch to be the head of their governments. (p. 92)

communism (kom′ yə niz əm) The system developed by Karl Marx in the 1800s in which all property is owned in common. (p. 147)

Confucianism (kən fū′ shə niz əm) The teachings of Confucius, including the importance of honoring one's parents, of being honest, respecting others, working hard, and acquiring learning. (p. 527)

constitutional monarchy (kon sti tü′ shən əl mon′ ər kē) A government headed by a king or queen, in which the monarch's powers are limited by a constitution that guarantees the people's rights. (p. 209)

consumer goods (kən sü′ mər gu̇dz) Products bought by individuals for personal use. (p. 315)

continent (kon′ tə nənt) A large body of land, separated or nearly separated from another by water. (p. 5)

Continental Divide (kon tə nen′ təl di vīd′) An imaginary line in the Rocky Mountains that separates rivers flowing east from those flowing west. (p. 42)

contour interval (kon′ tür in′ tər vəl) The difference in elevation between two contour lines on a contour map. (p. 361)

contour line (kon′ tür līn) A line on a contour map that connects areas of the same elevation. (p. 360)

contour map (kon′ tür map) A map that shows the elevation and landforms of a place. (p. 360)

cooperative (kō op′ ər ə tiv) A business organization owned by its members. (p. 275)

copra (kō′ prə) The dried meat of a coconut. (p. 593)

cottage industry (kot′ ij in′ də strē) Manufacturing on a small scale that takes place in people's homes. (p. 512)

coup (kü) A sudden seizing or overthrowing of a government. (p. 171)

culture (kul′ chər) The way of life of a group of people, including their beliefs, customs, rules, and ways of relating to each other. (p. 28)

cultural geography (kul′ chər əl jē og′ rə fē) The study of people and their ways of life. (p. 28)

custom (kus′ təm) A practice from the past that people continue to observe. (p. 29)

cylindrical projection (sə lin′ dri kəl prə jek′ shən) A type of map projection in which distances measured along the equator are correct, but become more distorted as they near the poles. (p. 188)

Cyrillic (sə ril′ ik) Relating to the alphabet used for the languages of Russian, Ukrainian, Bulgarian, and certain other mostly Slavic languages. (p. 333)

D

Daoism (dou′ iz əm) A system of belief, formulated in Asia, that teaches that people should accept their fate calmly. (p. 527)

dateline (dāt′ līn) The words at the beginning of a news article that tell when and where the story was written. (p. 345)

democracy (di mok′ rə sē) A government in which decisions are made by the citizens. (p. 66)

desert (dez′ ərt) A dry, sandy region with very little plant or animal life. (p. 356)

desertification (di zûrt′ i fi kā′ shən) The expansion of a desert. (p. 432)

developed economy (di vel′ əpt i kon′ ə mē) An economy that has many different economic activities. (p. 64)

developing economy (di vel′ ə ping i kon′ ə mē) An economy that is only partly industrialized. (p. 124)

dialect (dī′ ə lekt) A local variation of a language. (p. 235)

dictator (dik′ tā tər) A ruler who has total control over a country and usually rules by force. (p. 147)

dictionary (dik′ shə ner ē) A reference book that gives meanings of words and tells how to pronounce them. (p. 89)

Diet (dī′ it) The national legislature in Japan. (p. 551)

dike (dīk) A huge wall used to keep back the sea. (p. 222)

discrimination (di skrim ə nā′ shən) The unfair treatment of a person or a group of people by another person or group. (p. 58)

distortion (di stôr′ shən) The shrinking, stretching, and changes in shape of places that results when a globe is represented on the flat surface of a map. (p. 188)

distribution map (dis′ trə bū shən map) A map that shows how such things as population, rainfall, language, and religion are distributed in parts of the world. (p. 13)

diversified economy (di vûr′ sə fīd i kon′ ə mē) An economy in which a wide range of goods are produced. (p. 275)

drought (drout) A lack of rain over a long period of time. (p. 421)

E

Edda (ed′ ə) A long Viking poem about the early Scandinavian gods. (p. 282)

editor (ed′ i tər) One of the people who runs a newspaper. (p. 345)

editorial (ed i tôr′ ē əl) An article in which the people who run a newspaper give their opinion on an important issue. (p. 345)

elevation (el ə vā′ shən) Height above sea level. (p. 25)

encyclopedia (en sī klə pē′ dē ə) A reference book that contains information about many subjects written in the form of articles. (p. 89)

environment (en vī′ rən mənt) All the surroundings of a place, including the land and water, weather patterns, and plants and animals that live there. (p. 22)

equal-area projection (ē′ kwəl âr′ ē ə prə jek′ shən) A type of map projection good for comparing different places on the earth because sizes and shapes are shown fairly accurately and distances are nearly correct. (p. 189)

equator (i kwā tər) The imaginary line that divides the earth halfway between the North Pole and the South Pole. (p. 6)

erosion (i rō′ zhən) The gradual wearing down of the earth's surface by water or wind. (p. 41)

escarpment (e skärp′ mənt) A steep cliff at the edge of a plateau. (p. 417)

ethnic group (eth′ nik grüp) A group of people who share a language, history, or place of origin. (p. 29)

European Union (yůr ə pē′ ən ūn′ yən) An organization of western European nations formed after World War II to promote free trade and to link transportation routes among themselves; also known as the European Community. (p. 223)

executive branch (eg zek′ yə tiv branch) The branch of the government that carries out the laws. (p. 68)

export (eks′ pôrt) Any item sold to another nation. (p. 64)

extended family (ek stend′ əd fam′ ə lē) A family that contains, in addition to parents and their children, other relatives, such as cousins, aunts, uncles, and grandparents. (p. 122)

F

famine (fam′ in) A widespread and severe shortage of food. (p. 453)

feature article (fē′ chər är′ ti kəl) In a newspaper, a detailed report on a person, an issue, or an event. (p. 345)

federal system (fed′ ər əl sis′ təm) The division of power between the national and local governments. (p. 67)

fellahin (fel ə hēn′) Farmers in Arab countries. (p. 391)

fjord (fyôrd) A deep narrow inlet of the sea between high cliffs. (p. 186)

fossil fuel (fos′ əl fū′ əl) Fuel that is made from the remains of plants and animals that died thousands of years ago and is found underground. Examples are coal, petroleum, and natural gas. (p. 27)

free enterprise (frē en′ tər prīz) In a capitalist economy, the freedom to own property and run a business largely free of government control. (p. 62)

freedom of expression (fre′ dəm əv ek spresh′ ən) The freedom to express all aspects of an individual's life. (p. 70)

G

gamelan (gam′ ə lan) An Indonesian orchestra of drums, gongs, bells, chimes, cymbals, and xylophones, in which there is no conductor. (p. 573)

gaucho (gou′ chō) A cowhand in South America who herds cattle on the Pampas. (p. 161)

geography (jē og′ rə fē) The study of the earth's landforms, its plants and animals, its climates, and the relationship of people to their natural environment. (p. 6)

glasnost (glas′ nōst) A policy of "openness" in the former Soviet Union. (p. 327)

GLOSSARY

658

global grid (glō bəl grid) The lines of latitude and longitude on a map or globe. (p. 51)

graph (graf) A type of diagram that shows numbers in picture form, such as a bar graph. (p. 253)

great circle (grāt sûr′ kəl) Any circle that divides the earth into equal halves. (p. 496)

great-circle route (grāt sûr kəl rüt) A route between two places that falls along a great circle. (p. 496)

Green Revolution (grēn rev ə lü′ shən) New farming techniques used in South Asia and elsewhere that produce larger harvests. (p. 511)

grid map (grid map) A map that is divided into squares identified by letter and number to help people locate places or points of interest. (p. 13)

griot (grē′ ō) A traditional storyteller or "praise singer" in West Africa. (p. 440)

gross national product (grōs nash′ ən əl prod′ əkt) The total value of all goods and services that a nation produces each year. (p. 566)

guest worker (gest wûr kər) A person who moves to another country to find work and who is usually not permitted to become a citizen of the other country. (p. 218)

Gulf Stream (gulf strēm) A special "river" that flows in the Atlantic Ocean, bringing warm water from the Gulf of Mexico to the Atlantic coast of Europe. (p. 192)

H

hajj (häj) The pilgrimage that every Muslim is supposed to make at least once to Mecca, the birthplace of Muhammad. (p. 370)

harmattan (här mə tan′) A seasonal wind that carries dry, dusty air from the Sahara to Sub-Saharan Africa. (p. 421)

headline (hed′ līn) Words printed in large type across the top of a newspaper article to catch the reader's attention. (p. 345)

hemisphere (hem′ i sfêr) Half of the earth. The Northern and Southern hemispheres are divided by the equator, and the Eastern and Western hemispheres by the prime meridian. (p. 5)

high latitudes (hī lat′ i tüdz) The lands around the North and South poles, with the earth's coldest temperatures. (p. 115)

Hinduism (hin′ dü iz əm) The oldest and widest-spread religion in South Asia. (p. 506)

Holocaust (hol′ ə kôst) The killing of more than 6 million Jewish people by German and its allies during World War II (1939–1945). (p.235)

homogeneous (hō mə jē′ nē əs) Similar; of the same kind. (p. 542)

hydroelectric power (hī drō i lek′ trik pou′ ər) Electricity that is produced by the force of rapidly moving water, as at a waterfall or dam. (p. 49)

I

iceberg (īs′ bûrg) A large body of ice that has broken away from a glacier. (p. 587)

icon (ī′ kon) A painting of a saint or a religious leader. (p. 311)

immigrant (im′ i grənt) A person who moves to a country other than the one where he or she was born. (p. 56)

import (im′ pôrt) An item brought in from another country. (p. 64)

Impressionism (im presh′ ə niz əm) A style of painting started in France in the late 1800s, in which artists tried to capture the feeling of a place during one moment in time. (p. 228)

Industrial Revolution (in dus′ trē əl rev ə lü′ shən) In Western Europe, the gradual changeover from homemade goods to the production of goods by machine in factories. The changeover was so sweeping that it is considered a revolution. (p. 206)

intermediate directions (in tər mē′ dē it di rek′ shənz) The directions halfway between the cardinal directions: northeast, northwest, southeast, and southwest. (p. 7)

International Date Line (in tər nash′ ə nəl dāt līn) An imaginary line located halfway around the world from the prime meridian. It marks the end of one day and the beginning of the next. (p. 205)

iron rice bowl (ī′ ərn rīs bōl) A system of employment in China under which people expect to be guaranteed jobs for life. (p. 531)

irrigation (ir i gā′ shən) The watering of dry land with the use of streams, canals, or pipes. (p. 358)

Islam (is′ lam) One of the world's great religions, founded by Muhammad. (p. 369)

Islamic republic (is lam′ ik ri pub′ lik) A nation that is governed by the religious laws of Islam. (p. 378)

J

judicial branch (jü dish′ əl branch) The branch of the government that interprets the laws. (p. 68)

junta (hün′ tə) A group of army officers who rule a country after the army takes control. (p. 170)

a cap; **ā** cake; **ä** father; **är** car; **âr** dare; **ch** chain; **e** hen; **ē** me; **êr** clear; **hw** where; **i** bib; **ī** kite; **ng** song; **o** top; **ō** rope; **ô** saw; **oi** coin; **ôr** fork; **ou** cow; **sh** show; **th** thin; **th** those; **u** sun; **ù** book; **ü** moon; **ū** cute; **ûr** term; **ə** about, taken, pencil, apron, helpful; **ər** letter, dollar, doctor

659

K

kibbutz (ki bu̇ts′) A collective farm in Israel, where the members own and work the land together. (p. 376)

L

labor-intensive (lā′ bər in ten′ siv) A term that describes a situation in which people, rather than machines, do the work. (p. 375)

landform (land′ fôrm) A physical feature of a place. (p. 23)

landform map (land′ fôrm map) A physical map that shows how the earth's surface varies from place to place. (p. 11)

landlocked (land′ lokt′) Entirely surrounded by land. (p. 195)

large-scale map (lärj skāl map) A map that shows detailed information about a place because the map includes only a small area. (p. 225)

latitude (lat′ i tüd) Line on a map or globe that extends east and west and shows distance from the equator. (p. 50)

legislative branch (lej′ is lā tiv branch) The branch of the government that makes the laws and decides how much money the government can spend. (p. 68)

line graph (līn graf) A type of graph that uses a line to show changes in the amount of something over time. (p. 463)

loess (les) A yellowish soil that is very fertile. (p. 494)

longitude (lon′ ji tüd) A measure of the distance east or west from the prime meridian. (p. 50)

low latitudes (lō lat′ i tüdz) Areas located near the equator that have generally hot temperatures. (p. 115)

M

Magna Carta (mag′ nə kär′ tə) A document signed by King John of Great Britain in 1215 that limited the powers of the monarch. (p. 209)

malnutrition (mal nü trish′ ən) A condition caused by a lack of food or of the right kinds of food. (p. 453)

map key (map kē) The guide that appears on a map to explain what its symbols stand for. (p. 9)

martial arts (mär′ shəl ärts) Forms of self defense and exercise, such as karate and kung fu, that are based on ancient Asian methods of hand-to-hand combat. (p. 537)

Maroon (mə rün′) In Jamaica, a descendant of slaves who escaped from the Spanish to set up an independent community. (p. 143)

mbira (em bêr′ ə) A South African finger piano. (p. 479)

meditate (med′ i tāt) To think deeply. (p. 572)

megalopolis (meg ə lop′ ə lis) A region that is so crowded with cities and suburbs that it appears to be one large city. (p. 59)

meridian (mə rid′ ē ən) A line of longitude. (p. 50)

mestizo (mes tē′ zō) A person of mixed Indian and Spanish ancestry. (p. 120)

metropolitan area (met rə pol′ i tən âr′ ē ə) A large city and its surrounding suburbs and towns. (p. 123)

middle latitudes (mid′ əl lat′ i tüdz) Areas farther from the equator than the low latitudes, with generally cooler temperatures and changing seasons. (p. 115)

migration (mī grā′ shən) A movement of a group of people into new lands. (p. 449)

mileage chart (mī′ lij chärt) A table that shows distances between specific places. (p. 419)

mixed economy (mikst i kon′ ə mē) An economy that has both private enterprises and government-run businesses. (p. 207)

monarchy (mon′ ər kē) Any government headed by a hereditary ruler, such as a king or queen. (p. 92)

monsoons (mon sünz′) Seasonal winds that bring heavy rainstorms or hot, dry weather. (p. 498)

mosaic (mō zā′ ik) A pattern or picture made up of many small pieces of stone or glass. (p. 81)

moshav (mō shäv′) A cooperative farm in Israel, in which each farmer owns his or her own land but sells produce through the cooperative. (p. 376)

muezzin (mü ez′ in) The crier who calls Muslims to prayer five times each day. (p. 389)

mural (myu̇r′ əl) A work of art on a wall. (p. 131)

N

NAFTA (naf′ tä) North American Free Trade Agreement that went into effect in 1994. (p. 88)

nationalism (nash′ ə nə liz əm) A strong love for and pride in one's country or ethnic group. (p. 332)

nationalize (nash′ ə nə līz) To place an industry under the control or ownership of the government. (p. 206)

natural resources (nach′ ər əl rē′ sôrs əz) Materials in nature that people use, such as soil. (p. 25)

neutral (nü′ trəl) Refusing to take sides in a war or dispute. (p. 241)

news article (nüz är′ ti kəl) In a newspaper, a story about an event that has just taken place. (p. 345)

nonaligned nations (non ə līnd′ nā′ shənz) Developing countries that do not take sides in the struggles between the world's superpowers. (p. 517)

O

oasis (ō ā′ sis) A green, fertile, well-watered spot in a desert. (p. 358)

oba (ō′ bə) A traditional ruler in some West African areas. (p. 436)

ombudsman (om′ bədz mən) A government official in Sweden, whose job is to hear people's complaints about a government service or action, to inform government representatives of the complaints, and to push for action. (p. 278)

one-crop economy (wun′ krop′ i kon′ ə mē) An economy that depends on a single crop for income. (p. 145)

660

oral tradition (ôr′ əl trə dish′ ən) History and literature that is spoken and passed down from person to person. (p. 440)

outback (out′ bak) A huge, arid area in central Australia where few people live. (p. 584)

P

Pacific Rim (pə sif′ ik rim) All the countries that border on the Pacific Ocean, including many countries of Asia, North America, and South America, as well as Australia and New Zealand. (p. 531)

paddy (pad′ ē) A type of field in which wet rice is grown. (p. 567)

parallel (par′ ə lel) A line of latitude on a map or globe. (p. 50)

parliamentary democracy (pär lə men′ tə rē di mok′ rə sē) A country with a representative national legislature called a parliament. (p. 91)

partition (pär tish′ ən) A division, as in the division of British India into India and Pakistan. (p. 515)

per capita income (pər kap′ i tə in′ kum) The amount of income each person would have if the country's total income were divided equally among all its people. (p. 166)

perestroika (pâr əs trô i kə) In the former Soviet Union and Eastern Europe, a plan for economic restructuring, including reducing the amount of government control over businesses. (p. 315)

permafrost (pûr′ mə frôst) In Arctic lands, a layer of soil that is permanently frozen, found below a thin layer of topsoil. (p. 44)

petrochemical (pet rō kem′ i kəl) A chemical, such as ammonia or benzene, that is made from petroleum. (p. 124)

petroleum (pə trō′ lē əm) Oil. (p. 364)

physical geography (fiz′ i kəl jē og′ rə fē) The study of the earth's surface, the climate, plant and animal life, and other factors that affect the earth. (p. 22)

physical map (fiz′ i kəl map) A map that shows the earth's natural features, such as continents, oceans, mountains, and deserts. (p. 10)

pilgrimage (pil′ grə mij) Journey to a sacred place. (p. 263)

pinyin (pin′ yin′) Presently, the official method of writing Chinese words in English. (p. 528)

plantation (plan tā′ shən) A large farm that grows crops for sale. (p. 145)

point of view (point əv vū) The way a person looks at or feels about something. (p. 280)

polar climate (pō′ lər klī′ mit) A type of climate found in the areas around the North and South poles, where the weather is generally cold. (p. 25)

polder (pōl′ dər) A lowland area reclaimed from the sea in the Netherlands. (p. 222)

political cartoon (pə lit′ i kəl kär tün′) A drawing that focuses attention on an important issue and tries to influence public opinion. (p. 535)

political map (pə lit′ i kəl map) A map that shows political divisions such as countries and states as well as cities. (p. 10)

pollution (pə lü′ shən) Dirty and unpure elements in the environment. (p. 239)

population density (pop yə lā′ shən den′ si tē) The number of people per square mile or square kilometer in a given land area. (p. 43)

prejudice (prej′ ə dis) An unfavorable opinion that is formed unfairly about a group of people without knowing all the facts. (p. 58)

premier (pri mêr′) The title given to the prime minister in France and some other countries. (p. 226)

prime meridian (prīm mə rid′ ē ən) The starting line for measuring longitude. (p. 6, 50)

prime minister (prīm min′ ə stər) The leader of the political party that has the majority of members in a parliament. (p. 91)

projection (prə jek′ shən) A way of showing locations on the earth on a flat map. (p. 188)

proverb (prov′ ərb) A short, popular saying that illustrates a truth. (p. 461)

province (prov′ ins) A self-governing area within a nation, similar to a state in the United States. (p. 82)

Q

qanat (kä′ nât) In Iran, underground tunnels for carrying water from the mountains to irrigate land. (p. 363)

quota (kwō′ tə) A fixed amount as for buying or producing goods. (p. 335)

R

rain forest (rān′ fôr′ ist) A dense tropical forest in a region with high annual rainfall. (p. 113)

Ramadan (ram ə dän′) The ninth month of the Muslim year, a month in which Muslims fast from sunrise to sunset. (p. 403)

reasoned opinion (rē′ zənd ə pin′ yən) A type of opinion based on evidence or reasons. (p. 162)

a cap; ā cake; ä father; är car; âr dare; ch chain; e hen; ē me; êr clear; hw where; i bib; ī kite; ng song; o top; ō rope; ô saw; oi coin; ôr fork; ou cow; sh show; th thin; th̲ those; u sun; ů book; ü moon; ū cute; ûr term; ə about, taken, pencil, apron, helpful; ər letter, dollar, doctor

reference (ref′ ər əns) Having to do with information to be referred to, as in a reference book; reference books include dictionaries and almanacs. (p. 89)

reform (ri fôrm′) To make a change for the better. (p. 315)

reggae (reg′ ā) A style of music that began in Jamaica and combines elements of rock 'n' roll, blues, and calypso. (p. 154)

region (rē′ jən) A large area with common features that set it apart from other areas. (p. 7)

relief (ri lēf′) A variation in elevation. (p. 361)

Renaissance (ren ə säns′) A period of rebirth in Europe during the 1300s and 1400s that included great activity in the arts. (p. 261)

republic (ri pub′ lik) A government in which voters elect officials to represent them. (p. 66)

reunification (rē ū nə fi kā′ shən) The act of uniting again or the results of that act. (p. 234)

rift valley (rift val′ ē) A narrow valley with steep sides formed millions of years ago by cracks in the earth's crust. (p. 417)

river system (riv′ ər sis′ təm) The land drained by a river and its tributaries; also known as a river basin. (p. 109)

Roman Catholicism (rō′ mən kə thol′ ə siz əm) The branch of the Christian religion that is under the authority of the pope in Rome. (p. 83)

S

saga (sä′ gə) A long story first told by people in Iceland about their early kings and heroes. (p. 282)

samizdat (säm′ ēz dät) A system of publishing and distributing censored or unapproved literature secretly in the former Soviet Union. (p. 310)

samurai (sam′ ù rī) A member of a class of warriors who once ruled Japan. (p. 543)

sanctions (sangk′ shənz) Actions taken against a country by other countries to try to get that country to change. (p. 475)

satellite (sat′ ə līt) One of several countries in Eastern Europe that were closely tied to the former Soviet Union. (p. 331)

savanna (sə van′ ə) A broad grassland containing scattered trees and shrubs. (p. 418)

scale (skāl) The measurement used to indicate the proportion that distances on a map have to the real distances they represent. (p. 7)

sect (sekt) A religious group that is outside the mainstream of large, organized religions. (p. 144)

separatism (sep′ ər ə tiz əm) A movement to break away from a nation or province. (p. 83)

shadow play (shad′ ō plā) A type of entertainment in Indonesia in which puppets are used to act out well-known stories and to teach moral and religious values. (p. 572)

sharia (shə rē′ ə) Islamic law, based on the Koran as interpreted by Muslim scholars. (p. 378)

shifting cultivation (shift′ ing kul tə vā′ shən) A method used in farming in which a field periodically is not planted so new grasses can grow and replace nutrients in the soil. (p. 433)

Shinto (shin′ tō) Japanese religion which teaches that spirits dwell in all things in nature. (p. 542)

siesta (sē es′ tə) A long afternoon nap, commonly taken by people in Southern European lands. (p. 251)

Sikhism (sēk′ iz əm) A religion blending Hinduism and Islam, founded in the 1400s. (p. 507)

slash-and-burn farming (slash and bûrn fär′ ming) A type of farming where a field is cleared of its trees and stumps and then the brush is burned, creating ash which enriches the soil. (p. 433)

small-scale map (smôl skāl map) A map that shows a large area in a small space. (p. 224)

socialist realism (sō′ shə list rē′ ə liz əm) A form of art practiced in communist countries which shows true-to-life scenes and heroes of the country performing great deeds. (p. 536)

Soviet (sō′ vē et) Referring to people, customs, the government, or the country of the former Soviet Union. (p. 305)

standard of living (stan′ dərd əv liv′ ing) A measure of the amount of goods and services available to the people in a country. (p. 238)

station (stā′ shən) A ranch for raising sheep or cattle in Australia or New Zealand. (p. 600)

steppes (steps) Dry, grassy plains, found south of the taiga in Russia, Ukraine, and parts of Eastern Europe. (p. 299)

subcontinent (sub kon′ tə nənt) A large landmass that is smaller than a continent. (p. 491)

subsistence farming (sub sis′ təns fär′ ming) A type of farming in which the farmer raises only enough food to feed his or her own family. (p. 124)

summary (sum′ ə rē) A brief statement that tells the main ideas contained in a piece of writing. (p. 544)

sumo wrestling (sü′ mō res′ ling) Traditional Japanese sport in which two large, very strong men try to force each other to touch the ground with any part of their body except their feet. (p. 553)

Swahili (swä hē′ lē) A common language in East and Equatorial Africa, containing Bantu words and elements of Portuguese and Arabic. (p. 452)

symbol (sim′ bəl) A person, an animal, or an object that stands for something beyond itself. Symbols are often used in political cartoons. (p. 9, 535)

T

taiga (tī′ gə) In Russia, a vast region of evergreen trees, south of the tundra. (p. 299)

talking drums (tô′ king drumz) Traditional African drums that can be made to imitate the sound of human speech. (p. 441)

tariff (tar′ if) A tax on imports. (p. 88)

GLOSSARY

662

technology (tek nol′ ə jē) The methods, tools, and machinery that are used to meet human needs. (p. 64)

temperate climate (tem′ pər it klī′ mit) A type of climate found in the areas that are farther from the equator than the tropics, where there are changing seasons and mild weather that is neither too hot nor too cold. (pp. 25, 45)

terraces (ter′ is əz) Large steps carved into hillsides to allow planting. (p. 500)

terrorism (ter′ ə riz əm) The use of violence and the threat of violence, usually to gain political ends. (p. 260)

timberline (tim′ bər līn) The elevation above which trees cannot grow because of the cold climate. (p. 47)

time zone (tīm zōn) One of the 24 areas into which the earth is divided to compensate for the earth's rotation of 15° per hour. (p. 204)

topic sentence (top′ ik sen′ təns) One of the sentences that contains the main ideas in a piece of writing. (p. 544)

Tour de France (tür′ də frans′) A 2,500-mile (4,023-km) bicycle race that winds around the perimeter of France. (p. 229)

township (toun′ ship) In South Africa, a segregated area in which blacks live and, despite its size, is not officially considered a city. (p. 471)

trade winds (trād windz) Winds that cause seasonal patterns of rainy and dry seasons. (p. 420)

tropical climate (trop′ i kəl klī′ mit) A type of climate found in the areas just north and south of the equator, where the weather is usually hot. (p. 25)

trust territory (trust ter′ i tôr ē) An area that an outside country controls until it decides the trust territory is ready to govern itself. (p. 604)

typhoon (tī fün′) A whirling tropical hurricane. (p. 590)

V

value judgment (val′ ū juj′ mənt) A type of opinion based on a person's judgment about the worth or value of something. (p. 162)

Vedas (vā′ dəz) A collection of Hindu religious writings. (p. 519)

vegetation (vej i tā′ shən) Plant life. (p. 26)

veld (velt) A vast, dry, treeless plateau that covers much of South Africa. (p. 472)

Vietnam War (vē et näm′ wôr) A war that began as a civil war in Vietnam in the 1950s and that eventually spread into Laos and Cambodia. (p. 570)

vineyard (vin′ yərd) An area used for growing grapes. (p. 221)

W

Warsaw Pact (wôr′ sô pakt) A military alliance that bound the nations of Eastern Europe to the Soviet Union until 1991. (p. 340)

welfare state (wel′ fâr stāt) A country in which the government takes responsibility for the well-being of all its citizens. (p. 211)

Y

yoga (yō′ gə) A Hindu way of training both body and mind through exercise and meditation. (p. 521)

a cap; ā cake; ä father; är car; âr dare; ch chain; e hen; ē me; êr clear; hw where; i bib; ī kite; ng song; o top; ō rope; ô saw; oi coin; ôr fork; ou cow; sh show; th thin; th those; u sun; ů book; ü moon; ū cute; ûr term; ə about, taken, pencil, apron, helpful; ər letter, dollar, doctor

663

INDEX

Page references in italic type that follow an *m* indicate maps. Those following a *p* indicate photographs, artwork, or charts.

INDEX

664

INDEX

665

INDEX

667

INDEX

668

INDEX

670

INDEX

672

673

INDEX

CREDITS

MAPS: R.R. Donnelley and Sons Company Cartographic Services

CHARTS AND GRAPHS: Tom Cardamone Associates, Inc.

ILLUSTRATION CREDITS: **Alex Bloch** pp. 34, 554–557; **Allan Eitzen** pp. 60, 126, 162, 242; **Howard S. Friedman** pp. 16–17, 113, 116 (center, top), 357, 640–641; **Ignacio Gomez** p. 89; **Gershom Griffith** pp. 400, 433, 480; **Joe LeMonnier** pp. 74–77; **Maria Pia Marrella** pp. 264–267; **Leonard Morris** p. 140; **Ann Neumann** pp. 52, 96, 98, 116, 138, 156, 174, 176, 198, 214, 230, 246, 268, 284, 286, 302, 328, 346, 348, 366, 384, 404, 406, 424, 446, 464, 482, 484, 502, 538, 558, 576, 594, 614; **Hima Pamoedjo** pp. 42, 71, 120, 279, 345, 441, 544; **Rodica Prato** p. 262; **Larry Raymond** pp. 442–445; **Blanche Sims** pp. 280, 324; **Joel Snyder** pp. 394–397.

PHOTOGRAPHY CREDITS All photographs are by Macmillan/McGraw-Hill School Division (MMSD) except as noted below.

i: John Riley/Folio, Inc. **Table of Contents:** iii: t. Hans Wendler/The Image Bank; m. Miami Herald Cross/Black Star; b. Dilip Mehtal/ Contact Press Images/Woodfin Camp & Associates. iv: t. Robert Frerck/Odyssey Productions t.m. Luis Villota/The Stock Market; b.m. Leonar Morris; b. Robert Frerck/Woodfin Camp & Associates. v: t. Tibor Bognar/The Stock Market; t.m. R. Steedman/The Stock Market; m.m. Sepp Seitz/Woodfin Camp & Associates; b.m. Bob Krist/Black Star; b. Viesti Associates. vi: t. Marcello Bertinetti/Photo Researchers, Inc.; t.m. Paolo Koch/Photo Researchers, Inc.; b.m. Sovfoto/Tass; b. John Eastcott/Yva Momatiuk/Woodfin Camp & Associates. vii: t. Thomas Hopker/The Image Bank; t.m. R. & S. Michaud/Woodfin Camp & Associates; m.m. Geoff Juckes/The Stock Market; b.m. James Sugar/Black Star; b. Pedrocoll/The Stock Market; viii: t. Bertrand/Explorer Photo Researchers, Inc.; t.m. Robert Frerck/ Odyssey Productions; m. Fong Siu Nang/The Image Bank; b.m. Tardos Camesi/The Stock Exchange; b. Wolfgang Kaehler. ix: t. Harvey Lloyd/The Stock Market; t.m. Wolfgang Kaehler; b.m. Lindsay Hebberd/Woodfin Camp & Associates; b. Robert Frerck/Odyssey Productions. **Chapter 1:** 4: Nancy Sheehan. 14: NASA. 18: l. Ken Sakamoto/Black Star; r. Roger Miller/The Image Bank. 20: Eddie Hironaka/The Image Bank. 21: t.l. Mike Yamashita/Woodfin Camp & Associates; b.l. Kate Bader; m. Wolfgang Kaehler; t.r. Alberto Rossi/ The Image Bank; b.r. Terry Madison/The Image Bank. 25: Rick Ridgeway/Adventure Photo. 27: t.l. Breck Kent; m. Breck Kent; t.r. Brian Peterson/The Stock Market; b.r. Breck Kent; b.l. Breck Kent. 29: Robert Frerck/Odyssey Productions. 32: t.l. NASA; b.l. Eddie Hironaka/The Image Bank; m. Rick Ridgeway/Adventure Photo; t.r. Robert Frerck/Odyssey Productions. 36: t.r. Pete Saloutos/The Stock Market; b.l. Karl Hentz/The Image Bank; m. Bob Thomason/Tony Stone Worldwide; b.r. Steve Elmore/The Stock Market; t.l. Charles Krebs/The Stock Market. 37: b.l. Grant Faint/The Image Bank; b.r. Nick Nicholson/The Image Bank; t.r. Stuart Dee/The Image Bank; t.l. Michelle Burgess/The Stock Market; m. Susan McCartney/Photo Researchers, Inc. 38: Hans Wendler/The Image Bank. 41: t. Dan Routh/The Stock Market; b. David Muench Photography. 42: Annie Griffiths/ Woodfin Camp & Associates. 44: l. John Eastcott, Yva Momatiuk/Woodfin Camp & Associates; r. John Eastcott, Yva Momatiuk/Woodfin Camp & Associates. 47: l. Bill Ross/Westlight/ Woodfin Camp & Associates; r. Chris Sorenson/The Stock Market. 52: t.l. Annie Griffiths/Woodfin Camp & Associates; b.r. Chris Sorenson/The Stock Market. **Chapter 2:** 54: Miami Herald Cross/Black Star. 56: t. Viesti Associates; b. Jeff Dunn/The Picture Cube; c. Bob Daemmrich/ Stock Boston. 57: David Barnes/The Stock Market; Steve Proehl/The Image Bank. 63: l. Courtesy: Junior Achievement/Tom Hollyman; m. Leif Skoogfors/Woodfin Camp & Associates; r. Michael A. Keller/The Stock Market. 64: Al Satterwhite/The Image Bank. 67: Linda Schaefer/ Black Star. 69: Courtesy of Matthew Rothman. 72: l. Adam J. Stoltman/Duomo; m. Steven E. Sutton/Duomo; r. Adam J. Stoltman/ Duomo. 73: l. Steve Satushek/The Image Bank; r. Jonathon Blair/ Woodfin Camp & Associates. 74: Steve McCutcheon. 76: Jeff Schultz/ Alaska Stock Images; b. Jeff Schultz/Alaska Stock Images. 77: t. Jeff Schultz/Alaska Stock Images. 78: t.l. Miami Herald Cross/Black Star; b.l. Bob Daemmrich/Stock Boston; b.m.l. Al Satterwhite/The Image Bank; t.r. Adam J. Stoltman/Duomo; b.r. Steve Satushek/The Image Bank. **Chapter 3:** 80: Dilip Mehta/Contact Press Image/Woodfin Camp & Associates. 83: Robert Frerck/Odyssey Productions. 84: l. Doug Wilson/Black Star; m. J.P. Laffont/SYGMA; t.r. Ken Ross/Viesti Associates; b.r. Timothy Eagan/Woodfin Camp & Associates. 87: (both) Cominco, Ltd. 91: l. Bob Anderson/Masterfile; r. Robert Frerck/ Woodfin Camp & Associates; l. Tim Graham/SYGMA. 94: t.l. Focus on Sports; t.r. D.S. Henderson/The Image Bank; b. Porterfield Chickering/Photo Researchers, Inc. 95: DC Productions/The Image Bank. 96: t.l. Stuart Dee/The Image Bank; m.l. Doug Wilson/Black Star; b.l. Ken Ross/Viesti Associates; m.m.l. Cominco, Ltd; m.m.r. Robert Frerck/Woodfin Camp & Associates; t.r. Susan McCartney/ Photo Researchers, Inc.; b.r. Focus on Sports. 98: Steve Satushek/ The Image Bank. **Chapter 4:** 106: Robert Frerck/Odyssey Productions. 109: Kal Muller/Woodfin Camp & Associates. 110: Claus C. Meyer/Black Star. 112: Loren McIntyre. 114: t.l. Claus C. Meyer/ Black Star; b.l. Kal Muller/Woodfin Camp & Associates; m: Claus C. Meyer/Black Star; r. Randy Taylor/SYGMA. **Chapter 5:** 118: Luis Villota/The Stock Market. 120: t.l. Steven D. Elmore/The Stock Market; b.l. Robert Frerck/Odyssey Productions; t.r. Robert Frerck/ Odyssey Productions. 121: t. Nik Wheeler/Black Star; b. Robert Frerck/Odyssey Productions. 124: Robert Frerck/Odyssey Productions. 125: t. Robert Frerck/Odyssey Productions; b. Randy Taylor/SYGMA. 129: t. Keith Dannemiller/Black Star; m. S. Dorantes/ SYGMA; b. Cindy Karp/Black Star. 130: t. & b. OAS (Organization of American States). 132: t. Robert Frerck/Odyssey Productions; b. Robert Frerck/Odyssey Productions. 133: Courtesy of Maria Teresa Pomar. 134–135: t. The Detroit Institute of Arts. 135: b. Nathanial Tarn/Photo Researchers, Inc. 136: Cameramann, Int'l. 137: t. James Hackett/Leo deWys; (inset) Dirk Bakker, Chief Photographer/The Detroit Institute of Arts. 138: t.l. Robert Frerck/Odyssey Productions; b.l. Nik Wheeler/Black Star; l.m.t. Robert Frerck/Odyssey Productions; r.m.t. S. Dorantes/SYGMA; b.m.t. Keith Dannemiller/Black Star; t.r. Robert Frerck/Odyssey Productions; b.r. Robert Frerck/Odyssey Productions. **Chapter 6:** 143: Robert Frerck/Odyssey Productions. 144: t. Andrew Holbrooke/Black Star; b. Dan Miller/Woodfin Camp & Associates. 147: Tibor Bognar/The Stock Market. 150: t. UPI/Bettman Newsphotos; b. K. Dannemiller/Black Star. 151: Harvey Lloyd/The Stock Market. 152: top (inset) David Hamilton/The Image Bank; b. (inset) D.C. Promotions/The Image Bank; Robert Frerck/Woodfin Camp & Associates. 153: t. Eric Neurath/Stock Boston; b. David Madison/Duomo. 155: t.l. Dale Ware, Ph.D./D.D.B. Stock Photo; t.r. Judy Leeta/Shooting Star; b. David Madison/Duomo. 156: t.l. Dan Miller/Woodfin Camp & Associates; b.l. Andrew Holbrooke/Black Star; b.l.m. Tibor Bognar/The Stock Market; t.r.c. K. Dannemiller/Black Star; t.r. Eric Neurath/Black Star; b.r. David Madison/Duomo. **Chapter 7:** 158: Robert Frerck/Woodfin Camp & Associates. 161: l. Robert Frerck/Woodfin Camp & Associates; r. Alan Reininger/Woodfin Camp & Associates. 165: t.l. Claus C. Meyer/Black Star; t.r. Luis Padilla/The Image Bank; b. Arturo A. Wesley/Black Star. 167: t.r. Robert Frerck/ Odyssey Productions; l. Wolfgang Kaehler; b.r. Robert Frerck/ Odyssey Productions. 168: l. Claus Meyer/Black Star; r. Loren McIntyre. 171: UPI/Bettmann Newsphotos. 173: l. Dan Helms/Duomo; r. Claus Meyer/Black Star. 174: t.l. Robert Frerck/Odyssey Productions; b.l. Arturo A. Wesley/Black Star; c.l. Robert Frerck/ Odyssey Productions; m. UPI/Bettmann Newsphotos; b.r. Dan Helms/ Duomo; t.r. Claus C. Meyer/Black Star. 176: Kal Muller/Woodfin Camp & Associates. **Chapter 8:** 182: Tibor Bognar/The Stock Market. 185: Chuck O'Rear/Westlight/Woodfin Camp & Associates. 187: Ira Block/The Image Bank. 190: M. Philippot/SYGMA. 193: O. Brown, R. Evans & M. Carle/University of Miami Rosensteil School of Marine & Atmospheric Sound. 195: Farrell Grehan/Photo Researchers, Inc. 197: l. Gary Cralle/The Image Bank; r. Michael Pasdzior/The Image Bank. 198: l. Chuck O'Rear/Westlight/Woodfin Camp & Associates; m.t. O. Brown, R. Evans & M. Carle/University of Miami Rosensteil School of Marine & Atmospheric Sound; t.r. Michael Pasdzior/The Image Bank; b.r. Farrell Grehan/Photo Researchers, Inc. **Chapter 9:** 200: R. Steedman/The Stock Market. 203: Madere/The Image Bank. 207: t. Stuart Franklin/SYGMA. b. Stuart Franklin/SYGMA. 208: top Tom Bean/DRK Photo Photo; b. (inset) D'Lynn Waldron/The Image Bank. 210: l. Her Majesty Queen Elizabeth; m. Universal Pictorial Press, London/Photoreporters; r. David Jones/Press Association LTD. 211: Peter Turnley/Black Star. 213: l. Martha Swope/Assoc.; r. The Folger Shakespeare Library/Washington, D.C. 214: t.l. R. Steedman/The Stock Market; m.l.t. Stuart Franklin/SYGMA; m.l.b. D'Lynn Waldron/The Image Bank; m.r.t. Universal Pictorial Press Photo, London/Photoreporters; r.b. The Folger Shakespeare Library, Washington, D.C. **Chapter 10:** 216: Sepp Seitz/Woodfin Camp & Associates. 219: l. Thomas Craig/Black Star; r. J. Messerschmidt/The Stock Market. 220: l. Bob Krist/Black Star: r.

Waldron/The Image Bank; m.r.t. Universal Pictorial Press Photo, London/Photoreporters; r.b. The Folger Shakespeare Library, Washington, D.C. **Chapter 10:** 216: Sepp Seitz/Woodfin Camp & Associates. 219: l. Thomas Craig/Black Star; r. J. Messerschmidt/The Stock Market. 220: l. Bob Krist/Black Star; r. Bob Krist/Black Star. 222: Bob Krist/Black Star. 227: Courtesy MST. 229: Giraudon/Art Resource. 230: l. Thomas Craig/Black Star; l.m.t. Bob Krist/Black Star. r.t. Giraudon/Art Resource. **Chapter 11:** 232: Bob Krist/Black Star. 235: l. (inset) The Granger Collection; r. J. Messerschmidt/The Stock Market. 236: Courtesy of Jacob Von Vexkull. 238: Henning Cristoph/Black Star. 239: l. H.P. Merten/The Stock Market; m. J. Gardin/SYGMA; r. (inset) Pete Turnley/Black Star. 241: r. Anthony Suau/Black Star; l. (inset) Ralph Rieth/SIPA Press. 245: l. Adam Woolfit/Woodfin Camp & Associates; r. Bob Krist/Black Star. 246: l. J. Messerschmidt/The Stock Market; l.t.m. Henning Christopher/Black Star; l.b.m. Anthony Suau/Black Star; t.r.m. Ralph Rieth/SIPA Press; b.r. Adam Woolfit/Woodfin Camp & Associates. **Chapter 12:** 248: Viesti Associates. 251: Giansanti/SYGMA. 252: Robert Frerck/ Odyssey Productions. 255: l. Hans Wolf/The Image Bank; r. Nedra Westwater/Black Star. 256: Pamela J. Zilly/The Image Bank. 258: Photoreporters. 259: Universal Pictorial Press Photo, London/ Photoreporters. 264: t. Doug Armond/Tony Stone Worldwide; (inset) Richard Kalvar/Magnum. 265: t.l. Joe Viesti Associates; t.r. Joe Viesti Associates; b. Nima Tallah Weinberger/Superstock. 266: l. Nima Tallah Weinberger/Superstock; r. Richard Kalvar/Magnum. 267: t. Lane Steward/Sports Illustrated © Time, Inc.; b. Richard Kalvar/ Magnum. 268: t.m.l. Pamela J. Zilly/The Image Bank; b.m.l. Nedra Westwater/Black Star; m.r. Universal Pictorial Press Photo, London/ Photoreporters. **Chapter 13:** 270: Marcello Bertinetti/Photo Researchers, Inc. 272: Thomas Nebbia/Woodfin Camp & Associates. 275: Bob Krist/Black Star. 276: Jan Halaska/Photo Researchers, Inc. 278: Diego Goldberg/SYGMA. 279: Courtesy: Kauko Heikurainen. 283: Teeje Rakke/The Image Bank. 284: t.l. Thomas Nebbia/Woodfin Camp & Associates; b.l. Marcello Bertinetti/Photo Researchers, Inc.; r.m.b. Diego Goldberg/SYGMA; b.r. Terje Rakkel/The Image Bank. 286: t.l. Chuck O'Rear/Westlight/Woodfin Camp & Associates; b.r. Giraudon/Art Resource. **Chapter 14:** 292: Paolo Koch/Photo Researchers, Inc. 295: (inset) Bryan Alexander/Black Star; r. Serguei Fedorov/Woodfin Camp & Associates. 302: Serguei Fedorov/Woodfin Camp & Associates. **Chapter 15:** 304: J. Messerschmidt/Leo de Wys. 306: Bob Stern/The Image Works. 307: m. Basile Grigoriev/SIPA Press; t.l. Novosti/Gamma Liaison; t.r. M. Givannanangeli/Gamma Liaison. 308: l. (inset) Bryan Alexander/Black Star; r. Serguei Fedorov/ Woodfin Camp & Associates. 309: Stephanie Maze/Woodfin Camp & Associates. 310: Sovfoto/Eastfoto. 311: b.r. Dallas & John Heaton/ Westlight; l. J. Langevin/SYGMA; t.r. Bob Saler and Paolo Koch/ Photo Researchers, Inc.. 312: t. Sovfoto/Eastfoto; b. Christopher Rennie/Robert Harding Picture Library. 313: t. East News/SIPA Press; b. SHONE/SIPA Press. 315: (inset) Claus Meyer/Black Star; l. Howard Sochurek/Woodfin Camp & Associates. 316: l. Frank Siteman/ The Picture Cube; r. Reuters/Bettmann Archive. 317: l. Joe Traver/ Gamma Liaison; Gaye Hilsenrath/The Picture Cube. 318: Anatoly Sapronenko/A.F.P. Photo. 321: Alain Keler/SYGMA. 322: EAST NEWS/SIPA Press. 327: Bob Krist/Black Star. 328: b.l. Stephanie Maze/Woodfin Camp & Associates; t.m.l. Howard Sochurek/Woodfin Camp & Associates; b.m.l. SYGMA; t.r. Bob Krist/Black Star. **Chapter 16:** 330: John Eastcott, Eva Momatiuk/Woodfin Camp & Associates. 332: Nicholas Jallot/Cosmos/Woodfin Camp & Assoc. 334: Steve Dunwell/The Image Bank. 336: t. C. Niedentahl/Black Star; b. Tom Sobolik/Black Star. 338: t. V. Garbutt/Camera Press London/Globe Photos; b. Chris Niedenthal/Black Star. 340: b. Julienne/SIPA Press; t. (inset) P. Habans/SYGMA. 341: l. Chip Hires/Gamma Liaison; r. Y. Karsh/Woodfin Camp & Assoc. 342: Courtesy: Adam Michnik. 344: Giraudon/Art Resources, Inc.; © 1992 ARS N.Y. ADAGP, Paris; 346: t.l. John Eastcott, Eva Momatiuk/Woodfin Camp & Associates; b.l. Steve Dunwell/The Image Bank; t.m.l. Tom Sobolik/Black Star; b.m.l. V. Garbutt/Camera Press London/Globe Photos; t.m.r. Julienne/SIPA Press; b.r. Giraudon/Art Resources © 1992 ARS N.Y. ADAGP, Paris. 348: John Eastcott, Eva Momatiuk/Woodfin Camp & Associates. **Chapter 17:** 354: Thomas Hopker/The Image Bank. 356: Guido Alberto Rossi/The Image Bank. 359: t. Farrell Grehan/Photo Researchers, Inc.; b. Peter Paz/The Image Bank. 365: Nogues/ SYGMA. 366: l. L. Girard/Photo Researchers, Inc.; r. Nogues/ SYGMA. **Chapter 18:** 368: R. & S. Michaud/Woodfin Camp & Associates. 370: Robert Azzi/Woodfin Camp & Associates. 372: l. David Austen/Stock Boston; m. Don Smetzer/Tony Stone Worldwide, Ltd.; r. © Aubert/Keystone/Paris/Picture Group 375: l. Fred Mayer/ Woodfin Camp & Associates; r. Anthony Suau/Black Star. 376: Guido Alberto Rossi/The Image Bank. 379: Courtesy: Photo: David Ottenstein. 383: R. & S. Michaud/Woodfin Camp & Associates. 384: t.l. Michael Coyne/The Image Bank; t.r. Rus Michaud/Woodfin Camp & Associates. **Chapter 19:** 386: Geoff Juckes/The Stock Market. 389: Mario Fantin/Photo Researchers, Inc. 390: R. &. S. Michaud/Woodfin Camp & Associates. 392: l. Minosa/Scorpio/SYGMA; r. George Holton/Photo Researchers, Inc. 394: t.l. Dallas & John Heaton/Stock Boston. 394–395: b.r. & b.l. Bill Gallery/Stock Boston. 395: t. David W. Hamilton/The Image Bank. 397: t.r. Richard Steedman/The Stock Market; b.l. Luis Villota/The Stock Market. 399: Alain Keler/SYGMA. 403: Mahauxo Photography/The Image Bank. 404: t.l. Marion Fantin/ Photo Researchers, Inc.; b.l. R. & S. Michaud/Woodfin Camp & Associates; t.m.l. George Holton/Photo Researchers, Inc.; b.m.l. Mimosa/Scorpio/SYGMA; b.m.r. Alain Keler/SYGMA. 406: Mimoso/ Scorpio/SYGMA. **Chapter 20:** 414: James Sugar/Black Star. 417: Gregory G. Dimijan/Photo Researchers, Inc. 421: Peter Turnley/Black Star. 423: t. Fred Ward/Black Star; b. (inset) William Campbell/ SYGMA. 424: t.l. George G. Dimijan/Photo Researchers, Inc.; b.l. James Sugar/Black Star; m. Peter Turnley/Black Star; r. Fred Ward/ Black Star. **Chapter 21:** 426: Pedrocoll/The Stock Market. 429: t. M. Bertinetti/Photo Researchers, Inc.; b. Marco & Evelyn Bernheim/ Woodfin Camp & Associates. 430: Gideon Mendel/Magnum. 431: George Holton/Photo Researchers, Inc. 434: l. Marco & Evelyn Bernheim/Woodfin Camp & Associates; r. M. Bertinetti/Photo Researchers, Inc. 436: Lawrence Manning/Woodfin Camp & Associates. 437: t. Gerald Buthard/Cosmos/Woodfin Camp & Associates; b. Louise Gubb/JB Pictures. 438: Courtesy Bernard Ledea Ouedradeo. 441: Lawrence Manning/Woodfin Camp & Associates. 444: Schomberg Center for Research in Black Culture. 446: b.m.l. Marc & Evelyn Bernheim/Woodfin Camp & Associates; t.m.r. Gerald Buthard/Cosmos/Woodfin Camp & Associates; b.m.r. Lawrence Manning/Woodfin Camp & Associates; b.r. Lawrence Manning/Woodfin Camp & Associates. **Chapter 22:** 448: Bertrand/ Explorer/Photo Researchers, Inc. 451: t.l. & r. Robert Frerck/Odyssey Productions; b.l. Marc & Evelyn Bernheim/Woodfin Camp & Associates. 452: Marc & Evelyn Bernheim/Woodfin Camp & Associates. 454: t. Lynn McLaren/The Picture Cube; b. (inset) Kal Muller/Woodfin Camp & Associates. 455: l. Victor Englebert/Photo Researchers, Inc.; r. Richard Hoffman/SYGMA. 456: Stephen J. Kreaseman/DRK Photo Photo. 459: Marc & Evelyn Bernheim/Woodfin Camp & Associates. 460: r. SYGMA. 462: Lisl Dennis/The Image Bank. 464: t.l. Bertrand Explorer/Photo Researchers, Inc.; t.m.l. Victor Englebert/Photo Researchers, Inc.; t.m.r. Marc & Evelyn Bernheim/ Woodfin Camp & Associates; b.m.r. SYGMA. **Chapter 23:** 466: Robert Frerck/Odyssey Productions. 468: M. Courtney-Clark/Photo Researchers, Inc. 469: b. Peter Magubane/Gamma Liaison; t. Gideon Mendel/Magnum. 470: Guido Alberto Rossi/The Image Bank. 473: Alon Reininger/Contact/Woodfin Camp & Associates. 475: Bernard Bisson/SYGMA. 476: Peter Turnley/Black Star. 477: Courtesy of A. Sisulu. 481: Peter Magubane/Gamma Liaison. 482: l. m. Courtney Clark/Photo Researchers, Inc.; t.m.r. Peter Turnley/Black Star; b.m.r. Selwyn Tait/Black Star; t.r. Peter Magubane/Gamma Liaison. 484: l.b. R. & S. Michaud/Woodfin Camp & Associates; t.m. Peter Turnley/ Black Star. **Chapter 24:** 490: Fon Siu Nang/The Image Bank. 493: Robert Frerck/Odyssey Productions. 495: Terry Madison/The Image Bank. 500: Claus Meyer/Black Star. 502: m. Claus Meyer/Black Star; l. Robert Frerck/Odyssey Productions; t.r. Tom Sobolik/Black Star. **Chapter 25:** 504: George Holton/Photo Researchers, Inc. 506: Robert Frerck/Odyssey Productions. 507: l. AP/Wide World. 508: l. Antoinette Jongen/Black Star; r. Wolfgang Kaehler. 509: Peter Charlesworth/JB Pictures. 511: Joe Viesti. 512: l. Mathias Oppersdorff/ Photo Researchers, Inc.; r. (inset) Mark. N. Boulton/Photo Researchers, Inc. 513: Jahangir Gazohk/Woodfin Camp & Associates. 515: t. Baldev/SYGMA; (inset) UPI-Bettmann Newsphoto. 516: l. S. Franklin/SYGMA; r. Baldev/SYGMA. 517: J.P. Laffont/SYGMA. 520: Steve Elmore. 521: Gary Halpern/Black Star. 522: b.l. George Holton/ Photo Researchers, Inc.; t.m.l. Joe Viesti; b.m.l. Jahangir Gazohk/ Woodfin Camp & Associates; t.m.r. S. Franklin/SYGMA; t.r. Gary Halpern/Black Star; b.r. Steve Elmore. **Chapter 26:** 524: Jerry Cooke/ Photo Researchers, Inc. 527: l. Lee Day/Black Star; r. The Granger Collection. 530: Doug Wilson/Black Star. 531: l. Anthony Suan/Black Star; r. J.P. Laffont/SYGMA. 533: l. Bill Pierie/SYGMA; r. J.P. Laffont/ SYGMA. 534: Steve Leonard/Black Star. 535: Raeside, Times-Colorist, Victoria, B.C. 537: t.l. The Granger Collection; t.r. Johan Elbers/International Stock Photo. 538: l. The Granger Collection; t.m.l. J.P. Laffont/SYGMA; b.m.l. Bill Pierce/SYGMA; b.m.r. Steve Leonard/ Black Star. **Chapter 27:** 540: Ken Straiton/The Stock Market. 542: b.l. Sekai Bunka Photo; l. Ken Rossi/Viesti Associates; r. Lindsay Hebberd/Woodfin Camp & Associates. 546: Claude Charlier/Black Star. 547: Claude Charlier/ANA/Viesti Associates. 548: l. (inset) J.P.

676

Laffont/SYGMA; r. Steve Dunwell/The Image Bank. 551: NOVA/SYGMA. 553: John Launois/Black Star. 554: SALMOIRAGHI/The Stock Market. 555: Courtesy: Martial Arts Supply Co. 556: t. Orion Press; b. Kyoto News Service. 557: David Madison. 558: b.l. Ken Straiton/The Stock Market; t.l. Sekai Bunka Photo; l.m. Claude Charlier/Black Star; r.m. NOVA/SYGMA; r. John Launois/Black Star. **Chapter 28:** 560: Wolfgang Kaehler. 562: Lindsay Hebbard/Woodfin Camp & Associates. 563: l. Wolfgang Kaehler; r. Wolfgang Kaehler. 564: Lindsay Hebbard/Woodfin Camp & Associates. 566: Chuck O'Rear/Woodfin Camp & Associates. 567: r. (inset) Wolfgang Kaehler; l. Wolfgang Kaehler. 569: (inset) Ken Sakamoto/Black Star; r. Christopher Morris/Black Star. 570: Chauvel/SYGMA. 573: l. Mike Yamashita/Woodfin Camp & Associates; r. (inset) Hans Hoffer/APA Woodfin Camp & Associates. 574: t.l. Wolfgang Kaehler; b.l. Lindsay Hebberd/Woodfin Camp & Associates; b.m.l. Wolfgang Kaehler; t.m.r. Christopher Morris/Black Star; b.m.r. Cauvel/SYGMA; r. Hans Hoffer/APA/Woodfin Camp & Associates. 576: t. Robert Frerck/Odyssey Productions; b. George Holton/Photo Researchers. **Chapter 29:** 582: Lindsay Hebberd/Woodfin Camp & Associates. 585: Peter Vorlicek/The Stock Market. 587: l. Lynn Johnson/Black Star; r. (inset) Lynn Johnson/Black Star. 592: Eastcott/Momatiuk/Woodfin Camp & Associates. 593: David J. Cross. 594: l. Lindsay Hebberd/Woodfin Camp & Associates; t.m. Peter Vorlicek/The Stock Market. **Chapter 30:** 596: George Holton/Photo Researchers, Inc.; Robert Frerck/Odyssey Productions. 599: Joe Viesti. 601: Harvey Lloyd/The Stock Market. 604: U.S. Navy. 605: l. Morton Beebe/The Image Bank; r. (inset) AP/Wide World. 607: l. (inset) David Moore/Black Star; r. P. Robert Gravey/Black Star. 608: t.l. George Holton/Photo Researchers, Inc.; t.r. Claudia Parks/The Stock Market; b. Belinda Wright. 608–609; David Hancock. 609: Belinda Wright; 610: Belinda Wright. 609–610; David Hancock. 611: t. Ken Ross/Viesti Associates. 612: l. Joe Viesti; l.m. Eastcott/Momatiuk/Woodfin Camp & Associates; t.r. Harvey Lloyd/The Stock Market; b.r. P. Robert Gravey/Black Star. 614: t.l. Lindsay Hebberd/Woodfin Camp & Associates; b.l. Joe Viesti; b.m.l. Eastcott/Momatiuk/Woodfin Camp & Associates; b.r. P. Robert Gravey/Black Star. 616–617: From: "Managing Planet Earth" © 1989 by Scientific American, Inc. George V. Kelvin, all rights reserved.

ADDITIONAL PHOTOGRAPHY CREDITS

Cover: background: © Erich Schrempp/Photo Researchers, Inc.; globe: © WorldSat International/Science Source; 4: b.l. Jeff Greenberg /Photo Researchers, Inc.; b.r. William Franklin; 5: t.r. Robb Kendrick; b.l. Anthony Howarth/International Stock Photo; b.r. Michael S. Yamashita; 4-5: Elizabeth Wolf; 16: Frank La Bua/Liaison International; 17: t. Kasyan Bartlett; m.t. Peter Seaward/Tony Stone Worldwide; m.b. Harald Sund/The Image Bank; b.r. Alan Cave/D. Donne Bryant Stock Photos; 18: t.l. Pete Saloutos/The Stock Market; b.l. B & C Alexander/Photo Researchers, Inc.; 19: t.l. James Balog/Black Star; b.l. Bill Brooks/Masterfile; b.r. Elizabeth Wolf; 18-19: Kenneth Garrett; 20: b.l. William Albert Allard; b.r. Robert W. Madden; 21: t.l. Georg Gerster; b.l. Richard Steedman/The Stock Market; b.r. Elizabeth Wolf; 20-21: Thomas Ernsting,/Bilderberg; 84: Brice Flynn/Stock Boston; 85: t. Lucien Bouchard; m. Marcel Hamelin; b. Pamela Paul; 92: t.l. Jayne Fincher/Gamma Liaison; 129: m. Stephen Ferry/Gamma Liaison; 152: Josi Azel/Aurora; 153: t. Christon Archer; m. Rosita Jara; b. Ninoska Perez-Castellón; 168: Donald Nausbaum/Tony Stone Worldwide; 169: t. Carlos Carlvaho/Amanaka'a Amazon Network Archives; m. Marcello De Andrade; b. Beto Borges; 173: t.r. Remi Benali/Gamma Liaison; 190: Colin Raw/Tony Stone Worldwide; 191: t. Bas Bruyne; m. Peter Holt; b. Emmy Roos; 210: t.r. Ian Jones/Gamma Liaison; 318: Adam Tauner/Comstock; 319: t. Natasha Petrova; m. Emma Vainikhovitch;b. Slava A.Wlassoff; 450: Robert Fried/Stock Boston; 456:t. Comstock; 457: t. Ndyakira Amooti; m. Alex Diang'a; b. Gitobu Imanyara; 548: t. Raga/The Stock Market; 549: t. Misaki Nakano; m. Marjorie E. Searing; b. Leo Shinozaki; 618: t.l. MMSD.

ACKNOWLEDGMENTS, continued from page ii

The New York Times, May 8, 1989. Copyright © 1989 by the New York Times Company. Reprinted by permission. Excerpt from "In Kenya, Man and Beast Compete for Free Land" by Sheila Rule from *The New York Times,* August 2, 1987. Copyright © 1987 by The New York Times Company. Reprinted by permission. Excerpt from "Alumnus Football" from THE FINAL ANSWER AND OTHER POEMS BY GRANTLAND RICE, selected by John Kieren. Excerpt from "Bye-bye" from THE MAGIC ORANGE TREE AND OTHER HAITIAN FOLKTALES by Diane Wolkstein. Copyright © 1978. Reprinted by permission of Alfred A. Knopf, Inc. "A hundred mountains . . ." from MORE CRICKET SONGS, Japanese Haiku, translated by Harry Behn. Copyright © 1971 by Harry Behn. All Rights Reserved. Reprinted by permission of Marian Reiner. "This Land Is Your Land," words and music by Woody Guthrie. TRO- © Copyright 1956 (renewed), 1958 (renewed), and 1970 Ludlow Music, Inc., New York, NY. Used by permission. Excerpt from an article from *L'Express,* Paris. Published in *World Press Review,* 200 Madison Ave., New York, NY 10016. Used by permission. Excerpts reproduced from WE LIVE IN MEXICO by Carlos Somonte with the kind permission of Wayland (Publishers) Limited, 61 Western Road, Hove, East Sussex BN3 1JD, England. Excerpts reproduced from WE LIVE IN CANADA by Jack Brickenden with the kind permission of Wayland (Publishers) Limited, 61 Western Road, Hove, East Sussex BN3 1JD, England. Time-Life Books for excerpt from WILD ALASKA by Dale Brown. Copyright © 1972, 1973 Time-Life Books. Reprinted with permission. Excerpt from MARTIAL ARTS: A COMPLETE ILLUSTRATED HISTORY by Michael Finn. Copyright © 1988 by The Overlook Press. Reprinted with permission. Excerpt from "The First Australians" by Stanley Breeder, from *National Geographic,* February 1988. Copyright 1988 by The National Geographic Society. Reprinted with permission. "Oh Caterina!" Translation and versification by M. R. de Saettone and Augustus D. Zanzig. From SONGS TO KEEP. Used by permission of World Around Songs. "The Trees Bend" from AFRICAN SONGS, published by World Around Songs. "My Country" by Mikhail Lermontov from TWO CENTURIES OF RUSSIAN VERSE, edited by Avrahm Yarmolinsky. Used by permission of the Estate of Avrahm Yarmolinsky. "An African Poem" by Birago Diop was first published as "Souffles" in LEURRES ET LUEURS (Presence Africaine, Paris, 1960) and also appears as "Breath" in A BOOK OF AFRICAN VERSE edited by Reed and Wake (London: Heinemann Educational Books Ltd., 1964). Reprinted by permission. Excerpt from "Politics After the Coup" interview with Roy Medvedev in NEW LEFT REVIEW, Sept./Oct. 1991. Reprinted with permission. Random House, Inc. for excerpt from WINDOW OF OPPORTUNITY by Graham Allison and Grigory Yavlinsky. Copyright © 1991. Reprinted by permission of the publisher.

ANNOTATED BIBLIOGRAPHY

■ Books excerpted in the Anthology
■ National Geographic selection

UNIT 1

For the Teacher

Books

Gordon, Patricia, and Reed C. Snow. *Kids Learn America: Bringing Geography to Life With People, Places, and History.* Charlotte, VT: Williamson Publishing Company, 1992. Suggestions for activities and projects which will familiarize students with information on regions, cities, and states in the United States.

Wartik, Nancy. *The French Canadians.* New York: Chelsea House Publishers, 1989. An examination of the history, culture, and achievements of the French Canadian people.

Read-Alouds

Cohn, Amy, ed. *From Sea to Shining Sea: A Treasury of American Folklore and Folk Songs.* New York: Scholastic Inc., 1993. Myths, songs, poems, and stories all combine to celebrate America.

Martin, Eve. *Tales of the Far North.* New York: Dial Press, 1987. Twelve Canadian tales depict the folklore that originated in France and England.

Technology Multimedia

Canada: Land of Diversity. 2 Videos. A description of Canada's natural resources, culture, and people. Society For Visual Education. Toll Free: 1-800-829-1900.

■ *STV North America.* Interactive Videodisc. Students can explore the different regions of North America. National Geographic. Toll Free: 1-800-541-5513.

■ *ZipZapMap! Canada.* Students learn about Canada's main geographic features and have fun locating them on the map. National Geographic. Toll Free: 1-800-368-2728.

■ *ZipZapMap! USA.* A fast-paced geography game that entertains students while they learn. National Geographic. Toll Free: 1-800-368-2728.

Free Materials

For information on the Province of Ontario, send to: Management Board Secretariat; Citizens' Inquiry Bureau; Room zm1-52; MacDonald Block; 900 Bay Street; Toronto, Ontario, Canada. M7A IN3.

For the Student

■ Carlson, Natalie Savage. *The Talking Cat and Other Stories of French Canada.* New York: Harper & Row Publishers, Inc., 1952. A collection of folktales passed down from the French settlers of Canada. **(Average)**

Harrison, Ted. *O Canada.* New York: Ticknor and Fields, 1993. An artist's portrayal of Canada's provinces and territories; in paintings and descriptive text. **(Easy)**

Hicks, Roger. *The Big Book of America: A Young Person's Guide to the United States of America.* Philadelphia, PA: Running Press, 1994. A combination of facts, maps, and colorful illustrations; providing good reference material. **(Average)**

Kalman, Bobbie. *Canada: The Culture.* New York: Crabtree Publishing Company, 1993. A brief description of the music, dance, theater, and traditions that make up Canada's culture. **(Easy)**

Kalman, Bobbie. *Canada: The People.* New York: Crabtree Publishing Company, 1993. The background and heritage of Canada's diversified population are briefly described. **(Easy)**

Katz, William Loren. *A History of Multicultural America: The Great Migrations 1800s–1912.* Austin, TX: Raintree Steck-Vaughn, 1993. A description of immigration in the United States in the late nineteenth and early twentieth centuries. **(Challenging)**

LeVert, Suzanne. *Northwest Territories.* New York: Chelsea House Publishers, 1992. A brief introduction to the land, history, and people of Canada's Northwest Territories; with colorful photographs. **(Easy)**

O'Dell, Scott. *Black Star, Bright Dawn.* Boston, Houghton Mifflin, 1988. A young Inuit girl takes her father's place in Alaska's Iditarod dogsled race. **(Average)**

■ Wilder, Laura Ingalls. *On the Way Home: The Diary of a Trip from South Dakota to Mansfield, Missouri, in 1894.* New York: Harper & Row, Publishers, 1962. A diary by the well-known author of The Little House series describes her life on the plains during the late nineteenth century. **(Challenging)**

UNIT 2

For the Teacher

Books

Machado, Ana Marie. *Exploration Into Latin America.* Columbus, OH: Silver Burdett Press, 1996. The historical background of the countries that make up Latin America is discussed, along with the impact of modern civilization on the region.

Morrison, Marion. *Central America.* Austin, TX: Raintree Steck-Vaughn, 1993. The history, geography, economy, culture, and daily life of the countries that make up Central America.

Read-Alouds

Carlson, Lori M., and Cynthia L. Ventura, ed. *Where Angels Glide at Dawn: New Stories From Latin America.* New York: J. B. Lippincott, 1993. A collection of stories that reflect the culture and traditions of Latin America.

Turenne Des Pres, Francois. *Children of Yayoute.* New York: Universe Publishing, 1994. Traditional Haitian folk tales of African origin are retold as the author remembers them from his own childhood.

Technology Multimedia

The Amazon Trail. CD-ROM. Students can explore the Amazon River and travel back in time. MECC. Toll Free: 1-800-215-0368.

Central America and the West Indies. 5 Videos. The history, geography, economy, and people of Central America and the West Indies. Society For Visual Education. Toll Free: 1-800-829-1900.

■ *Mexico.* Video. A geographic and cultural view of life in Mexico's cities and on its farms. National Geographic. Toll Free: 1-800-368-2728.

■ *South America.* Video. A geographic tour of South America's physical features, from the Andes Mountains to the Argentine plains. National Geographic. Toll Free: 1-800-368-2728.

ANNOTATED BIBLIOGRAPHY

Free Materials

For information on the Panama Canal, send to: Panama Canal Commission; Office of Public Affairs; Unit 2300; APO, AA 34011-2300.

For the Student

- ■ Ada, Alma Flor. *The Gold Coin.* New York, Atheneum, 1991. A Central American folktale about a young man who attempts to steal a gold coin from an elderly woman, and then learns a lesson in generosity. **(Average)**
- Ancona, George. *The Piñata Maker/El Piñatero.* San Diego, CA: Harcourt Brace, 1994. A colorful photo-essay describing how a craftsman from southern Mexico makes piñatas for fiestas. **(Easy)**
- Bachelis, Faren Maree. *The Central Americans.* New York: Chelsea House Publishers, 1990. A discussion of the history, culture, and religion of the people who live in Central America. **(Average)**
- Lewis, Richard. *All of You Was Singing.* New York: Atheneum, 1991. An Aztec myth that explains how music came to Earth. **(Average)**
- ■ Montejo, Victor. *The Bird Who Cleans the World and Other Mayan Fables.* Willimantic, CT: Curbstone Press, 1991. A collection of fables and stories that the author heard while growing up in Guatemala. **(Average)**
- Robb, Patricia. *We Live in Brazil.* New York: The Bookwright Press, 1985. Twenty-six people of various occupations describe the way they live in Brazil. **(Easy)**
- Stein, R. Conrad. *Mexico.* Chicago, IL: Childrens Press, 1992. Students get a complete picture of Mexico through a description of the country's geography, history, government, economy, and people. **(Challenging)**

UNIT 3

For the Teacher

Books

Biskup, Michael D., ed. *Europe.* San Diego, CA: Greenhaven Press, 1992. A detailed reference on Europe, using primary sources to help examine political and economic issues.

Dunnan, Nancy. *One Europe.* Brookfield, CT: The Millbrook Press, 1992. Political, economic, and social issues in Europe are examined through maps, charts, and full-color photos.

Read-Alouds

Vittorino, Domenico. *The Thread of Life: Twelve Old Italian Tales.* New York: Crown Publishers, Inc., 1995. Italian fairy tales are retold by the author who remembers them from his own childhood.

Williamson, Duncan. *Tales of the Seal People: Scottish Folk Tales.* New York: Interlink Books, 1992. A collection of stories that were passed down by Scottish fisherman and travelers.

Technology Multimedia

- ■ *Europe.* Video. A journey through Europe, focusing on the landscapes and physical features. National Geographic. Toll Free: 1-800-368-2728.
- *France: Land and People.* Video or Videodisc. An overview of the land and people of France. Society For Visual Education. Toll Free: 1-800-829-1900.
- *Spain: Land and People.* Video or Videodisc. Students are familiarized with Spain's geographic features and the culture of each region in Spain. Society For Visual Education. Toll Free: 1-800-829-1900.

Free Materials

For information on Britain, send to: British Information Services; Reference Section; 845 Third Avenue; New York, NY 10022.

For the Student

Dunford, Mick. *France.* New York: Thomson Learning, 1995. An overview of the land, industry, people, and daily life in France. **(Average)**

Flint, David. *The United Kingdom.* Austin, TX: Steck-Vaughn, 1994. A brief description of the geography, industry, people, and daily life in Great Britain and Northern Ireland. **(Average)**

Fradin, Dennis B. *The Netherlands.* Chicago, IL: Childrens Press, 1994. The history, geography, people, and culture of the Netherlands are described in detail and shown in colorful photographs. **(Average)**

Garrett, Dan. *Scandinavia.* Austin, TX: Steck-Vaughn, 1991. An overview of the history, geography, economy, culture, and people of Norway, Denmark, Sweden, Finland, and Iceland. **(Average)**

Hollinger, Peggy. *Greece.* New York: The Bookwright Press, 1990. An introduction to the land, history, religions, and culture of Greece. **(Easy)**

Osman, Karen. *The Italian Renaissance.* San Diego, CA: Lucent Books, 1996. A comprehensive study of the Renaissance period in Italy and its impact on the rest of the world. **(Challenging)**

Pateman, Robert. *Belgium.* New York: Marshall Cavendish, 1995. An introduction to the geography, history, government, culture, and people of Belgium. **(Average)**

Stanley, Diane. *Bard of Avon: The Story of William Shakespeare.* New York: Morrow Jr. Books, 1992. A beautifully illustrated biography of England's most famous dramatist and poet. **(Challenging)**

Symynkywicz, Jeffrey B. *Germany: United Again.* Columbus, OH: Silver Burdett Press, 1996. A recounting of the reunification of East and West Germany and the challenges the German people face in modern Germany. **(Challenging)**

UNIT 4

For the Teacher

Books

Harbor, Bernard. *The Conflict in Eastern Europe.* Columbus, OH: Silver Burdett Press, 1993. An examination of the economy, religions, and political issues surrounding the countries in Eastern Europe.

Kort, Michael. *Russia: Nations in Transition.* New York: Facts On File, Inc., 1995. An examination of the history, social conditions, political, and economic changes that have occurred in Russia.

Read-Alouds

Kuniczak, W. S. *The Glass Mountain: Twenty-six Ancient Polish Folk Tales and Fables.* New York: Hippocrene Books, 1992. Tales from Poland are gathered for retelling.

Philip, Neil. *Fairy Tales of Eastern Europe.* New York: Clarion Books, 1991. A collection of folklore representative of Eastern European culture.

Technology Multimedia

Czech Republic and Slovakia. Video. Two teenage cousins guide students through the Czech Republic and Slovakia. Society For Visual Education. Toll Free: 1-800-829-1900.

Moscow and Leningrad. Video. Students are taken on a tour while they learn about the culture, people, and history of these two important cities. Knowledge Unlimited. Toll Free: 1-800-356-2303.

The Russian Federation: A Nation in Transition. Video. A description of life in the modern-day Russian Federation and neighboring Ukraine. Society For Visual Education. Toll Free: 1-800-829-1900.

Free Materials

For information on Romania, send to: Romanian Cultural Center; 200 East 38 Street; New York, NY 10016.

For the Student

Bradley, John. *Russia: Building Democracy.* Austin, TX: Raintree Steck-Vaughn, 1996. Russia's recent political, economic, and social changes presented in newspaper format, with dramatic photos. **(Challenging)**

Buettner, Dan. *Sovietrek: A Journey By Bicycle Across Russia.* Minneapolis, MN: Lerner Publications Co., 1994. The fascinating story of four cyclists, two from Siberia and two from America, and how they traveled across Russia in 1990. **(Average)**

Carran, Betty. *Romania.* Chicago, IL: Childrens Press, 1993. An introduction to the land, history, government, culture, and people of Romania; with colorful photos. **(Average)**

Chicoine, Stephen, and Brent Ashabranner. *Lithuania: The Nation That Would Be Free.* New York: Dutton Children's Books, 1995. A glance at Lithuania's struggle to restore democracy after communist rule. **(Average)**

Filopovic, Zlata. *Zlata's Diary: A Child's Life in Sarajevo.* New York: Viking Press, 1994. The moving account of a ten-year-old girl's daily life during the war in Sarajevo. **(Easy)**

Hintz, Martin. *Hungary.* Chicago, IL: Childrens Press, 1992. A description of Hungary's geography, history, economy, people, and culture. **(Average)**

Mayhew, James. *Koshka's Tales: Stories From Russia.* New York: Kingfisher Books, 1993. A collection of famous fables from Russia, accompanied by beautiful illustrations. **(Average)**

Miller, Calvin Craig. *Boris Yeltsin: First President of Russia.* Greenboro, N.C.: Morgan Reynolds, Inc., 1994. The story of Boris Yeltsin from childhood, and the events that led to his leadership and presidency. **(Average)**

Strom, Yale. *A Tree Still Stands: Jewish Youth in Eastern Europe Today.* New York: Philomel Books, 1990. A group of children, descendants of Holocaust survivors, describe in interviews what their lives have been like. **(Average)**

Vnenchak, Dennis. *Lech Walesa and Poland.* New York: Franklin Watts, 1994. The role of Lech Walesa in Poland's history is examined. **(Challenging)**

UNIT 5

For the Teacher

Books

Franck, Irene M., and David M. Brownstone. *Across Africa and Arabia.* New York: Facts On File, Inc., 1991. The events that led to the development of important trade and travel routes in Africa and Arabia is traced.

Ross, Stewart: *Causes and Consequences of the Arab-Israeli Conflict.* Austin, TX: Raintree Steck-Vaughn, 1995. An in-depth discussion of the contributing factors that led to the Arab-Israeli conflicts and the events that followed, accompanied by maps, photographs, and primary sources.

Read-Alouds

Lattimore, Deborah Nourse. *Arabian Nights: Three Tales.* New York: HarperCollins Publishers, 1995. Stunning illustrations accompany these exciting, classic, adventure tales of sultans, caravans, and jewels.

Walker, Barbara. *A Retelling of Turkish Folktales.* Hamden, CT: The Shoe String Press, 1988. A collection of Turkish folktales; particularly suitable for reading aloud.

Technology Multimedia

Africa Series. 3 Videos. A detailed look at the history, geography, culture, and lifestyles in the different regions of Africa. Society for Visual Education. Toll Free:1-800-829-1900.

Geography Search. (software, Macintosh or Windows) #SEAGSRM3A. Geography activities. Tom Snyder Productions, Watertown, MA 02172. Toll Free: 1-800-342-0236.

The Middle East. 3 Videos. The history, geography, people, and culture of the countries of the Middle East are all featured in this series. Society for Visual Education. Toll Free: 1-800-829-1900.

Free Materials

For a poster about oil in Saudi Arabia, send to: Aramco World; Special Requests, P.O. Box 2106; Houston, TX, 77252-2106.

For the Student

- Al Hoad, Abdul Latif. *We Live in Saudi Arabia.* New York: The Bookwright Press, 1987. Twenty-six people of varied occupations discuss what it is like to live and work in Saudi Arabia. **(Easy)**
- Ashabranner, Brent. *Gavriel and Jamal: Two Boys of Jerusalem.* New York: Dodd, Mead & Co., 1984. The story of two young boys growing up in Jerusalem—one Jewish and the other Palestinian. **(Easy)**

Cohen, Barbara. *The Secret Grove.* New York: Union of Hebrew Congregations, 1985. A short novel about how two boys, one Israeli and one Jordanian, make a secret pact in an effort to overcome their families' prejudices. **(Average)**

Foster, Leila Merrell. *Saudi Arabia.* Chicago, IL: Childrens Press, 1994. A thorough exploration of the largest country on the Arabian Peninsula. **(Average)**

Harkonen, Reijo. *The Children of Egypt.* Minneapolis, MN: Carolrhoda, 1991. A beautiful photo-essay showing children engaged in daily activities in present-day Egypt. **(Average)**

Hassig, Susan M. *Iraq.* New York: Marshall Cavendish, 1993. Iraq's geography, history, government, economy, and people are examined in detail. **(Challenging)**

King, John. *Bedouin.* Austin, TX: Raintree Steck-Vaughn, 1993. A description of the Bedouin way of life and the threats to its future. **(Average)**

Long, Cathryn J. *The Middle East in Search of Peace.* Brookfield, CT: The Millbrook Press, 1994. An examination of the Arab-Israeli conflict; its origin, and the hope for future peace. **(Average)**

ANNOTATED BIBLIOGRAPHY

MacMillan, Diane M. *Ramadan and Id al-Fitr.* Hillside, NJ: Enslow Publishers Inc., 1994. Islamic customs and beliefs are explained in a clear and concise style. **(Easy)**

Sabuda, Robert, reteller. *Arthur and the Sword.* New York: Atheneum Books, 1995. In this well-illustrated story from the Arabian Nights, young Arthur proves himself to be the rightful heir to the throne. **(Easy)**

Schami, Rafik. *A Hand Full of Stars.* Translated by Rita Lesser. New York: Dutton Publishing Co., 1990. The compelling story of a 14-year-old boy living in Damascus, Syria under an authoritarian regime; written in diary style. **(Challenging)**

Scoones, Simon. *The Sahara and Its People.* New York: Thomson Learning, 1993. A fascinating, informative glimpse of the hottest and largest desert in the world; with colorful photographs. **(Average)**

Spencer, William. *The Land and People of Turkey.* New York: J. B. Lippincott, 1990. A comprehensive examination of Turkey's history, geography, government, economy, and people. **(Challenging)**

UNIT 6

For the Teacher

Books

Ibazebo, Isimene. *Exploration Into Africa.* Columbus, OH: Silver Burdett Press, 1995. A discussion of the history of Africa, and the impact of modern civilization there.

Paton, Jonathan. *The Land and People of South Africa.* New York: J. B. Lippincott, 1990. An in-depth presentation of South Africa's geography, history, government, economy, and people.

Read-Alouds

Fairman, Tony, reteller. *Bury My Bones, But Keep My Words: African Tales for Retelling.* New York: Henry Holt and Co., 1991. A gathering of traditional and contemporary stories from Africa; especially suited for reading aloud.

Larungu, Ruth. *Myths and Legends from Ghana for African-American Cultures.* Mogadore, OH: Telcraft Books, 1992. Stories that have been gathered from the folklore of the Ashanti and Hausa peoples of western Africa.

Technology Multimedia

Africa Trail. CD-ROM. An interactive program that enables students to experience the sights and sounds of a bicycle trip in Africa. MECC. Toll Free: 1-800-215-0368.

Sub-Saharan Africa: The Land. 4 Videos. Students can travel through southern Africa and learn about the geography, natural resources, and other aspects of life in this region. Society for Visual Education. Toll Free: 1-800-829-1900.

Free Materials

For a free rental of a video called "The Africans: A Clash of Cultures," send to: Church World Service; Film Library; 28606 Phillips Street; P.O. Box 968; Elkhart, Indiana 46515.

For the Student

Brandenburg, Jim. *Sand and Fog: Adventures in Southern Africa.* New York: Walker and Company, 1994. An exploration of Namibia and the Namib desert area; accompanied by beautiful photographs. **(Average)**

Chiasson, John. *African Journey.* New York: Bradbury Press, 1987. A glimpse at how nature dictates the way of life for the people who live in six different regions of Africa; with dramatic, colorful photographs. **(Challenging)**

Courlander, Harold, and George Herzog. *The Cow-Tail Switch and Other West African Stories.* New York: Henry Holt & Co., 1986. Stories gathered by the authors while on expeditions in western Africa. **(Average)**

Gordon, Sheila. *The Middle of Somewhere: A Story of South Africa.* New York: Orchard Books, 1990. A young girl and her family, living under the rules of apartheid, are evicted from their village. **(Average)**

Hughes, Libby. *Nelson Mandela: Voice of Freedom.* Dillon Press, 1992. A biography of Nelson Mandela, written by a woman who lived in South Africa for ten years. **(Average)**

Middleton, Nick. *Southern Africa.* Austin, TX: Raintree Steck-Vaughn, 1995. The seven countries of southern Africa are described in detail and accompanied by colorful photographs, charts, flags, and fact boxes. **(Average)**

Mollel, Tololwa M. *The Orphan Boy: A Massai Story.* New York: Clarion Books, 1990. A beautifully illustrated story that originated in the Great Rift Valley of Kenya and Tanzania, telling how the planet came to be. **(Easy)**

Onyefulu, Ifeoma. *Ogbo: Sharing Life in an African Village.* San Diego, CA: Harcourt Brace & Company, 1996. A young girl explains the traditions and culture of her small village in Nigeria; in a colorful photo-essay format. **(Easy)**

Pratt, Paula Bryant. *The End of Apartheid in South Africa.* San Diego, CA: Lucent Books, 1995. The history of apartheid in South Africa is traced from beginning to end. **(Challenging)**

UNIT 7

For the Teacher

Books

Langone, John. *In the Shogun's Shadow: Understanding a Changing Japan.* Boston, MA: Little, Brown and Co., 1994. A glimpse into present-day Japan, plus significant information about Japan's history and culture that challenges many misconceptions.

Tao, Wang. *Exploring Into China.* Columbus, OH: Silver Burdett Press, 1995. A comprehensive look into China's history, from prehistory to the development of modern civilization.

Read-Alouds

Conger, David, reteller. *Many Lands, Many Stories.* Rutland, VT: Charles E. Tuttle, 1987. Fifteen tales have been gathered for retelling, depicting the cultures of five countries in Asia.

Ness, Caroline, reteller. *The Ocean of Story: Fairy Tales from India.* New York: Lothrop, Lee & Shepard Books, 1993. A collection of 19 stories gathered by the author while traveling and studying in India.

Technology Multimedia

Geography Search. (software, Macintosh or Windows) #SEAGSRM3A. Geography activities. Tom Snyder Productions, Watertown, MA 02172. Toll Free: 1-800-342-0236.

History and Culture of China. CD-ROM. Students travel through the regions of China and learn about its history, geography, people, and customs. Society for Visual Education. Toll Free: 1-800-829-1900.

- *Japan*. Video. Students tour the villages and cities of Japan as they learn about that nation's geography, people, and culture. National Geographic. Toll Free: 1-800-368-2728.

Free Materials

For a fact sheet on the countries in Southeast Asia, send to: Center for Southeast Asian Studies; University of Wisconsin-Madison; 4115 Helen C. White Hall; 600 North Park Street; Madison, Wisconsin 53706.

For the Student

Blumberg, Rhoda. *Commodore Perry in the Land of the Shogun*. New York: Lothrop, Lee & Shepard Books, 1985. A well-researched account of how Commodore Matthew Perry opened Japan to world trade. **(Challenging)**

Choi, Sook Nyul. *Year of Impossible Goodbyes*. Boston, MA: Houghton Mifflin, 1991. An autobiographical novel about a ten-year-old girl who, with her mother and brother, escape war-torn North Korea to meet her father in South Korea. **(Average)**

Clifford, Mary. *The Land and People of Afghanistan*. New York: J. B. Lippincott, 1989. A detailed discussion of Afghanistan's geography, history, government, economy, and people. **(Challenging)**

Davis, James E. and Sharryl Davis Hawke. *Tokyo*. Milwaukee, WI: Raintree Publishing, 1990. Tokyo's history, industries, culture, and people are shown in color photographs and described. **(Average)**

Finck, Lila, and John P. Hayes. *Jawaharlal Nehru*. New York: Chelsea House Publishers, 1987. A biography of Prime Minister Nehru, and the role he played in obtaining India's independence through nonviolent means. **(Challenging)**

Fisher, Leonard Everett. *Gandhi*. New York: Atheneum, 1995. Acrylic paintings accompany the life of Mohandas Gandhi. **(Average)**

Fraser, Mary Ann. *On Top of the World: The Conquest of Mt. Everest*. New York: Henry Holt & Co., 1991. The story of the two men who were the first to reach the summit of Mt. Everest. **(Easy)**

Goedecke, Christopher J. and Rosmarie Hausherr. *The Wind Warrior: The Training of a Karate Champion*. New York: Four Winds Press, 1992. A photo essay about the training techniques a thirteen-year-old boy undergoes to become a karate champion. **(Easy)**

Hermes, Jules. *The Children of India*. Minneapolis, MN: Carolrhoda Books, Inc. 1993. An attractive photo essay showing the daily lives of India's children and the variety of social levels that exist in India. **(Average)**

Major, John S. *The Land and People of China*. New York: J. B. Lippincott, 1989. A detailed description of China's geography, history, government, culture, and people. **(Challenging)**

- Huynh Quang Nhoung. *The Land I Lost: Adventures of a Boy in Vietnam*. New York: Harper & Row, 1982. Personal reminisces of the author's youth on the central highlands of Vietnam. **(Average)**

Rigg, Jonathan. *Southeast Asia*. Austin, TX: Raintree Steck-Vaughn, 1995. A concise, yet comprehensive presentation of the countries that make up Southeast Asia; accompanied by colorful photographs, charts, graphs, and maps. **(Average)**

Weston, Mark. *The Land and People of Pakistan*. New York: J. B. Lippincott, 1992. An in-depth description of Pakistan's geography, history, economy, government, and culture. **(Challenging)**

UNIT 8

For the Teacher

Books

- Harrell, Mary Ann. *Surprising Lands Down Under*. Washington, D.C.: National Geographic Society, 1989. A beautiful photographic journey through ancient forests, the Great Barrier Reef, the outback, and various cultures.

Ross, Stewart. *Causes and Consequences of the Rise of Japan and the Pacific Rim*. Austin, TX: Raintree Steck-Vaughn, 1996. An examination of the economic growth and the affects of Westernization on the countries in these Eastern regions.

Read-Alouds

Morgan, Sally. *The Flying Emu and Other Australian Stories*. New York: Alfred A. Knopf, 1992. A collection of twenty Australian tales that explain how the world began and what followed.

Oodgeroo. *Dreamtime: Aboriginal Stories*. New York: Lothrop, Lee & Shepard Books, 1993. A combination of Aboriginal folklore and stories from the author's childhood, based on Aboriginal beliefs.

Technology Multimedia

- *Antarctica*. Video. Students tour the world's harshest continent and its unique inhabitants. National Geographic. Toll Free: 1-800-368-2728.
- *Australia*. Video. An exploration of Australia's cities, farms, desert outback, and rain forests. National Geographic. Toll Free: 1-800-368-2728.

Free Materials

For a 96-page booklet about New Zealand, send to: New Zealand Embassy; 37 Observatory Circle, N.W; Washington, D.C. 20008.

For the Student

- Conway, Jill Ker. *The Road From Coorain*. New York: Random House, Inc., 1989. A description of the author's childhood on a sheep farm in the grasslands of Australia. **(Challenging)**

The Cousteau Society. *An Adventure in New Zealand*. New York: Simon & Schuster Books, 1992. Rare photographs accompany a journey through New Zealand's landscape, where unique creatures and cultures exist. **(Average)**

Darien-Smith, Kate, and David Lowe. *The Australian Outback and Its People*. New York: Thomson Learning Publishing, 1995. The challenge of living in this very dry region is discussed. **(Average)**

Hereniko, Vilsoni, and Patricia Hereniko. *South Pacific Islanders*. Vero Beach, FL: Rourke Publications, 1987. The history, culture, and people, and lifestyles in the South Pacific islands are vividly described and illustrated. **(Average)**

Kanawa, Kirite. *Land of the Long White Cloud: Maori Myths, Tales, and Legends*. New York: Arcade Publishing, 1989. A collection of legends from the Maori tribes and from the author's own childhood in New Zealand. **(Average)**

Lepthien, Emilie U. *Australia*. Chicago, IL: Childrens Press, 1994. A description of Australia's history, geography, industries, cultures, and aspects of modern life. **(Average)**

Nile, Richard. *Australian Aborigines*. Austin, TX: Raintree Steck-Vaughn, 1993. A description of the ancient culture of the Australian Aborigines and their struggle to keep their land, beliefs, and lifestyles. **(Average)**

ANNOTATED BIBLIOGRAPHY

Pringle, Lawrence. *Anarctica: The Last Unspoiled Continent.* New York: Simon & Schuster Books, 1992. A description of Antarctica's geography, history, climate, and wildlife, written by an award-winning science author and beautifully photographed. **(Average)**

Reynolds, Jan. *Down Under: Vanishing Cultures.* New York: Harcourt Brace Jovanovich, 1992. A detailed presentation of the Tiwi tribe, aborigines who live on a small island off the coast of Australia. **(Easy)**

Vyner, Sue. *Swim for Cover: Adventure on the Coral Reef.* New York: Crown Publishers, 1995. Sea life is described and well-illustrated in this attractive photo essay about the Great Barrier Reef. **(Easy)**

Wilson, Barbara. *Acacia Terrace.* New York: Scholastic Inc. 1990. The history of Acacia Terrace, Australia, is traced from the 1860s through World War II through the experiences of one family. **(Easy)**

Name Use with pages 6–15

Using Globes

Use the picture of the globe below to complete the activities on this page. For help, you can refer to pages 6–15 in your textbook.

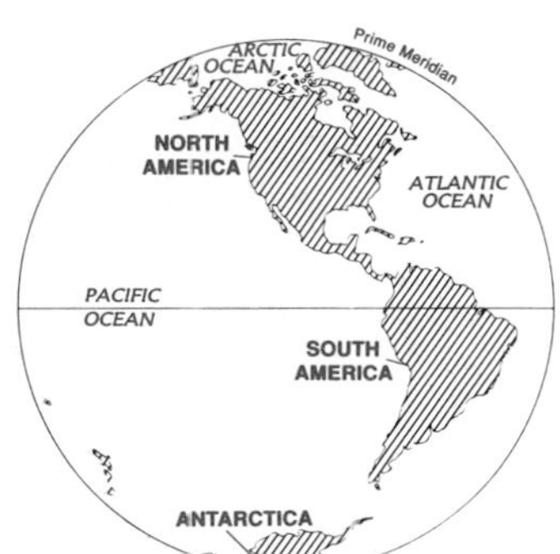

1. Underline the name of the hemisphere shown on the globe.
   a. Northern
   b. Southern
   c. Eastern
   d. Western

2. Underline the name of each continent in this hemisphere. Then label the continents on the globe.
   a. North America
   b. Antarctica
   c. South America
   d. Europe
   e. Asia
   f. Africa

3. Underline the name of the continent that is entirely in the Northern Hemisphere.
   a. South America
   b. Africa
   c. North America
   d. Asia

4. Underline the name of the imaginary line that separates the Eastern Hemisphere from the Western Hemisphere. Then find it on the globe and label it.
   a. prime meridian
   b. equator

5. Underline the name of each ocean in this hemisphere. Then label the oceans on the globe.
   a. Atlantic Ocean
   b. Pacific Ocean
   c. Arctic Ocean
   d. Indian Ocean

6. Underline the name of the ocean that is entirely in the Northern Hemisphere.
   a. Atlantic Ocean
   b. Pacific Ocean
   c. Arctic Ocean
   d. Indian Ocean

Name Use with pages 6–15

Distance and Direction on a Map

Use the map of Madagascar and the map scale below to answer the questions. For help, you can refer to pages 6–15 in your textbook.

1. If you were traveling from Toamasina to Antsiranana, in which direction would you be traveling?
   north

2. About how many miles is it from Toamasina to Maroantsetra?
   about 190 miles

3. Suppose you wanted to go from Antananarivo to Morondava. In which direction would you be traveling?
   southwest

4. About how many kilometers is it from Antananarivo to Morondava?
   about 450 kilometers

5. About how many miles long is the island of Madagascar?
   about 1,000 miles long

6. About how many kilometers is it from Morombe to the Indian Ocean by the shortest route?
   about 500 kilometers

7. About how many miles long is Isalo National Park?
   about 50 miles

8. In which part of Madagascar is Isalo National Park located?
   northern southern eastern western

Name Use with pages 6–15

Using Map Symbols

Study the map of Japan and the map key below. Then put an X next to each sentence that makes a true statement according to the information on the map. For help, you can refer to pages 6–15 in your textbook.

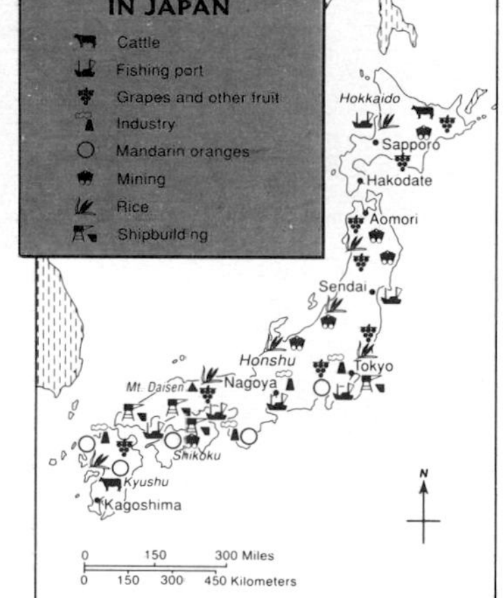

_____ 1. The major economic activity near the city of Sendai is shipbuilding.

__X__ 2. Most of Japan's industry is located on the island of Honshu.

_____ 3. Fruit production is the only economic activity on the island of Kyushu.

__X__ 4. Mt. Daisen is northeast of the city of Kagoshima.

__X__ 5. Sapporo is about 150 miles north of Aomori.

_____ 6. The main cattle raising areas are on the islands of Hokkaido in the south and Kyushu in the north.

__X__ 7. The two main crops grown on the island of Hokkaido are fruits and rice.

__X__ 8. Mandarin oranges are grown mostly in the southern half of Japan.

_____ 9. This map could help you figure out the locations of the most popular tourist attractions in Japan.

__X__ 10. This map helps you to understand where most of Japan's major economic activities are located.

Name Use with pages 6–15

Using Map Symbols

Put and **X** next to each question you can answer based on information on the map. Then use the space provided to answer each question you marked with an X. For help, you can refer to pages 6–15 in your textbook.

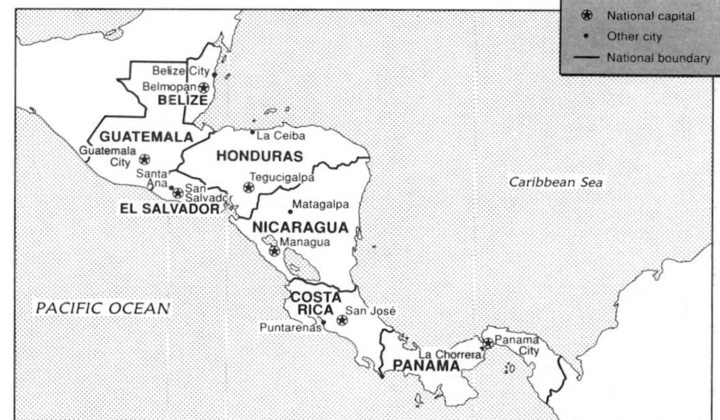

_____ 1. Which country has no mountains, hills, or plateaus? _____

_____ 2. Which country has the most people per square mile? _____

__X__ 3. What is the capital of Nicaragua? **Managua**

__X__ 4. Which countries border Costa Rica? **Panama and Nicaragua**

_____ 5. Which country is the most mountainous? _____

__X__ 6. How many countries make up Central America? **seven**

_____ 7. What crops are grown in Honduras? _____

_____ 8. What is the average temperature in San Salvador for the month of July? _____

Name _______________ Use with pages 6–15

Touring Paris

Use the map of Paris below to complete the activities on this page. For help, you can refer to pages 6–15 in your textbook.

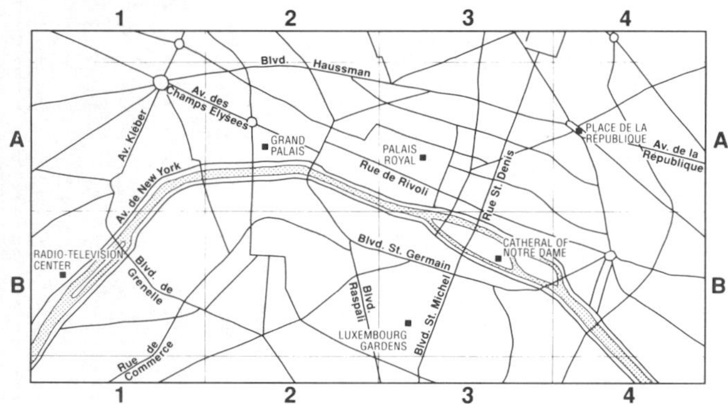

1. Suppose you and your family were planning a trip to Paris. Listed below are the places you intend to visit. Find and circle each place on the map. Then write the number and letter of the square in which it is shown on the map.

Cathedral of Notre Dame: **B–3** Grand Palais: **A–2**

Radio-Television Center: **B–1** Luxembourg Gardens: **B–3**

Place de la Republique: **A–4** Palais Royal: **A–3**

2. Use the map to plan a visit to each place in Paris listed above. Use a colored pencil to draw a line on the map showing the route you would take. Your route should require as little travel as possible. Then, in the space provided, list the places you would visit in the order shown on your route.

Stop 1: _______________ Stop 4: _______________

Stop 2: _______________ Stop 5: _______________

Stop 3: _______________ Stop 6: _______________

Answers will vary but should follow a logical order based on the student's starting point.

Name _______________ Use with pages 6–15

Using a Distribution Map

Draw a line under the word or phrase that best completes each sentence. For help, you can refer to pages 6–15 in your textbook.

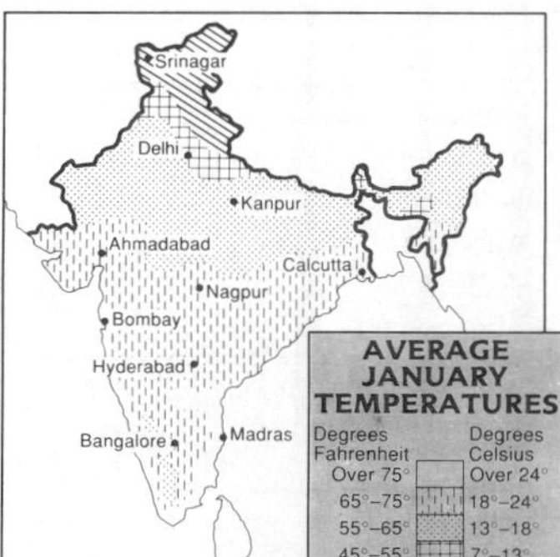

1. The kind of map on this page is called a ______ map.
   a. political
   b. distribution
   c. physical

2. The map key on this page shows different ______ categories.
   a. population
   b. temperature
   c. precipitation

3. According to the map, the city of Srinagar has an average January temperature of ______.
   a. below 45°F.
   b. 45°F. to 55°F.
   c. over 24°C

4. According to the map, it is colder in ______ than in Calcutta during January.
   a. Madras
   b. Hyderabad
   c. Delhi

5. According to the map, the coolest part of India during January is in the ______ part of the country.
   a. far northern
   b. southern
   c. southeastern

6. According to the map, the southeastern coast of India has an average January temperature of ______.
   a. over 24°C
   b. 13°C to 18°C
   c. below 7°C

7. According to the map, the average January temperature in Kanpur is ______ the average January temperature in your community.
   a. higher than
   b. lower than
   c. about the same as

8. The symbol for temperatures between 65°F. and 75°F. is ______.
   a. [symbol] b. [symbol] c. [symbol]

Name _______________ Use with pages 38–44

Using Maps

Use the map on this page to complete the activities below. For help, you can refer to pages 38–44 in your textbook.

1. Locate and label the following regions of the United States and Canada.

   Pacific Mountains Coastal Plains Arctic Islands
   Appalachian Highlands Interior Plains Rocky Mountains
   Canadian Shield

2. Name and describe the region of the United States in which you live.
   Student responses should accurately describe the region in which they live.

3. Name and describe the region you would most like to visit.
   Responses will vary but should demonstrate a knowledge of the geography of the region selected by the student.

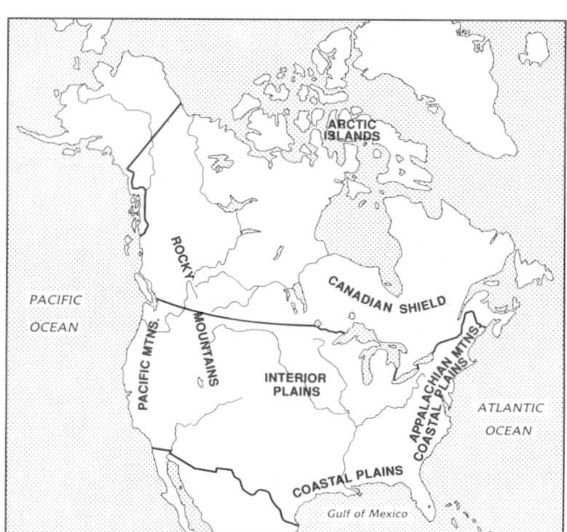

Name _______________ Use with pages 45–49

Resources of the United States and Canada

Study the table on this page. Then answer the questions below. For help, you can refer to pages 45–49 in your textbook.

PRODUCTS FROM NORTH AMERICAN RESOURCES

Products	United States	Canada
most important crops 	corn, soybeans, wheat	barley, oats, wheat
most valuable mineral products	petroleum, natural gas, coal	petroleum, natural gas, uranium, zinc
amount of lumber produced each year	37,153,000,000 board feet	21,136,000,000 board feet
percent of electricity from hydroelectric power	5 percent	70 percent

1. a. According to the table, which crop is an important product in both countries?
   wheat

   b. What natural resource makes an abundance of this crop possible?
   rich, arable soil

2. a. According to the table, which country produces more lumber per year?
   the United States

   b. What natural resource makes this product possible?
   trees, forests

3. Which two mineral products are valuable to both the United States and Canada?
   petroleum
   natural gas

4. Which country uses hydroelectric power as its main source of electricity?
   Canada

5. What are three reasons that the United States and Canada are lands of abundance?
   many natural resources
   temperate climate
   sufficient precipitation

Name ______ **Use with pages 50–51**

Using Latitude and Longitude

Chen and his family took a trip around the world. In the chart at the bottom of the page are the latitudes and longitudes near ten of the cities they visited. Put a dot on the map to show the approximate location of each city. Then label the city according to the letter in the chart. Finally, connect the dots with a line to show the route that Chen and his family took. For help, you can refer to pages 50–51 in your textbook.

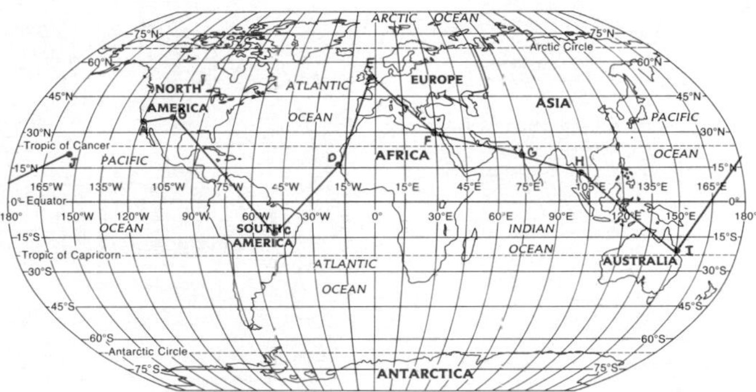

Los Angeles, California	35°N, 118°W	A
Denver, Colorado	40°N, 105°W	B
Brasília, Brazil	16°S, 48°W	C
Dakar, Senegal	15°N, 16°W	D
London, England	52°N, 0°	E
Cairo, Egypt	30°N, 30°E	F
Bombay, India	19°N, 73°E	G
Bangkok, Thailand	13°N, 100°E	H
Sydney, Australia	27°S, 150°E	I
Honolulu, Hawaii	20°N, 155°W	J

Name ______ **Use with pages 52–53**

Using New Words

Find each of the terms in the box hidden among the letters that follow. Draw a circle around each term you find. The words may be read forward, backward, up, down, or diagonally. For help, you can refer to the lessons in Chapter 1 in your textbook.

hydroelectric power	permafrost	erosion	population density
Continental Divide	temperate	arable	timberline

T E M P E R A T E D S N M N E T V O X L E K A P
C S E C Q A E L O E D W Q K C Q S T R P M N E S
A N I S H Y D R O E L E C T R I C P O W E R O A
C O P Z D T U S P D L E Q C X O E J I U M L R L
D I B P S N O E N I L R E B M I T E G A F R R E
J S E D O K T R K B R O P D V T Z A F R M E L U
P O P U L A T I O N D E N S I T Y R S I F B I K
A R T U R O Q E J K L S T R D Q O C O Z A M L O
D E N L M D T U S V E W N E T S O X L R E I A P
O E D I V I D L A T N E N I T N O C A N T O R K

Write each circled term in the space next to its definition.

Continental Divide 1. an imaginary line that separates rivers flowing eastward and westward across the land

erosion 2. the gradual wearing down of the earth's surface by water and wind

temperate 3. neither too hot nor too cold

timberline 4. the elevation above which trees cannot grow

arable 5. good for farming

population density 6. people per square mile in a given land area

permafrost 7. a layer of soil that is permanently frozen

hydroelectric power 8. electricity generated by the force of rapidly moving water

Name ______ **Use with pages 55–59**

A Look at Ethnic Groups

Read what Sadie Frowne wrote upon arriving in the United States in 1902. Then answer the questions. For help, you can refer to pages 55–59 in your textbook.

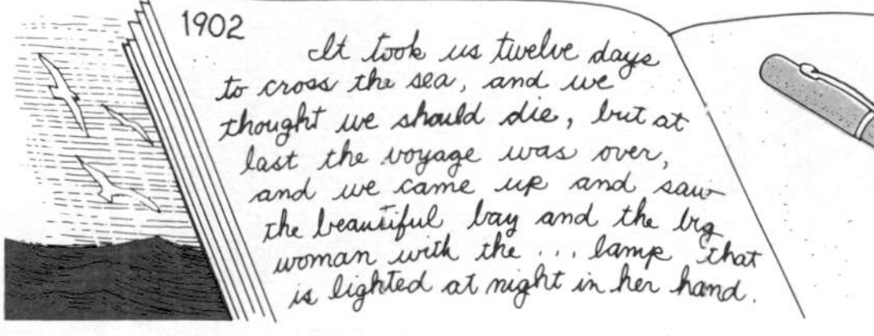

1. Sadie Frowne mentioned a "big woman with the . . . lamp." To whom or what was she referring? **the Statue of Liberty**
2. Sadie Frowne was one of the many Europeans who came to the United States in 1902. From which European countries have many immigrants come to the United States?
   Germany, Italy, Great Britain, Ireland, Austria
3. How has the pattern of immigration changed since the early 1900s?
   Today the largest groups of immigrants come from Asia and Latin America.
4. Why have people continued to immigrate to the United States?
   People continue to immigrate to the United States in order to find economic, religious, and political freedom.
5. What are two problems that most ethnic groups have faced at some time in their history? **prejudice** **discrimination**
6. How have members of ethnic groups been protected against these problems?
   Laws have been passed to protect people against unfair treatment in jobs, housing, transportation, education, and other areas of life.

Name ______ **Use with pages 60–61**

Immigrating to the United States

Mr. and Mrs. Slavin want to move to the United States. In the conversation below they are trying to decide how best to make the move. Read the conversation. Then answer the questions that follow. For help, you can refer to pages 60–61 in your textbook.

"We could save enough money to move the entire family all at once," said Mr. Slavin. "But that would take a long time. And we would still need more money to get started in the United States."

"Another way would be to wait until the children have grown up," said Mrs. Slavin. "Then we could move to the United States by ourselves. The children could follow if they wanted to. But that would be many years from now. And besides, I want the children to have the advantages of growing up in the United States."

"Perhaps it would be best if I went to the United States by myself and sent for you and the children later," said Mr. Slavin. "I could get a good job and find a place to live. Then in a year or two you and the children could come. When you arrive, everything would be ready. We would miss each other, but in the end we would all be together in our new country. What do you think?"

1. According to the conversation, what was Mr. and Mrs. Slavin's goal?
   a. to take a vacation in the United States
   b. <u>to move their family to the United States</u>
   c. to save money
   d. to get an education
2. Which three of the following alternatives did Mr. and Mrs. Slavin consider?
   a. <u>Have the entire family move together.</u>
   b. Have everyone in the family but Mr. Slavin move.
   c. <u>Wait until the children grow up before moving.</u>
   d. <u>Have Mr. Slavin move first and send for the family later.</u>
3. How do you think Mrs. Slavin answered the question that Mr. Slavin asked at the end of their conversation? Explain why you think she answered the way she did.
   Answers may vary but student responses should reflect an analysis of the outcome of the alternative they selected to determine its benefits and drawbacks.

Name ______ Use with pages 62–65

Earning a Living in the United States

Use the table below to answer the first three questions on this page. For help, you can refer to pages 62–65 in your textbook.

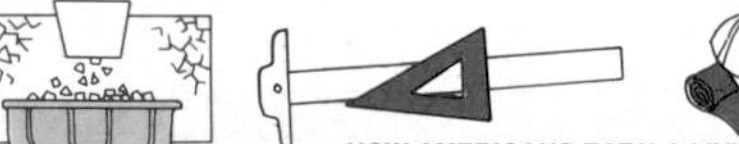

HOW AMERICANS EARN A LIVING (1995)

Type of Job	Number of Workers	Percentage of Workers
Services	43,953,000	35.0%
Trade	26,071,000	20.9%
Manufacturing / Mining	21,120,000	17.0%
Transportion / Communications	8,709,000	7.0%
Finance / Real Estate	7,983,000	6.3%
Construction	7,668,000	6.0%
Government	5,957,000	4.8%
Agriculture	3,440,000	3.0%

U.S. Bureau of Labor Statistics

1. According to the table, in which type of job do most people work?
   service jobs

   What percent of the people in the United States have these types of jobs?
   35 percent

2. In which type of job do the fewest people work?
   mining

3. About how many people have jobs in agriculture?
   about 3,440,000 people

4. If you worked in a factory, what type of job would you have?
   a manufacturing job

   About how many people in the United States have these types of jobs?
   about 21,120,000 people

5. What kind of economic system does the United States have?
   capitalist system

   What is an important part of this system?
   free enterprise

Name ______ Use with pages 66–69

The Federal Government

Use the pictures on the right to complete the activities on this page. For help, you can refer to pages 66–69 in your textbook.

1. a. Draw a line to the picture that shows the branch of federal government that makes the laws of the nation.
   b. Which two houses make up this branch?
   the House of Representatives
   the Senate

2. a. Draw a line to the picture that shows the branch of government that is responsible for carrying out the laws of the United States.
   b. What is the title of the person who heads this branch of government?
   the President

3. a. Draw a line to the picture that shows the branch of government that interprets the nation's laws.
   b. What court is at the head of this branch of government?
   the Supreme Court

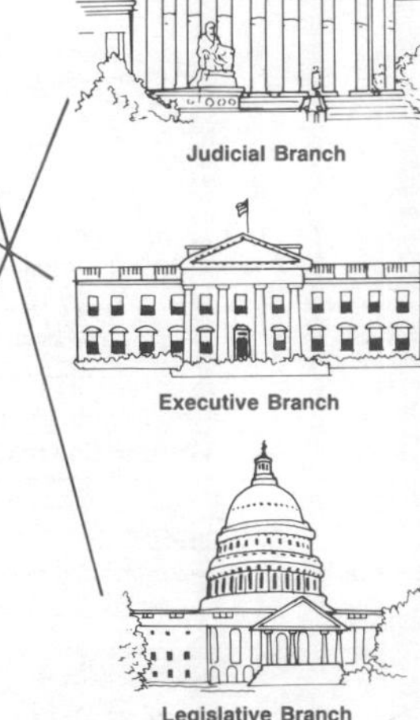

Judicial Branch

Executive Branch

Legislative Branch

4. How is a system of checks and balances built into the system of federal government in the United States? **Student responses should indicate an understanding of how each branch of government limits the powers of the other branches.**

5. How are state governments organized? **Each state has an executive branch headed by a governor, a judicial branch, and a legislative branch.**

Name ______ Use with pages 70–73

Freedom and the Arts

Use the pictures to answer the questions on this page. For help, you can refer to pages 70–73 in your textbook.

1. Which freedom are these artists exercising?
   freedom of expression

2. How has this freedom affected the arts in the United States?
   Freedom of expression has made the arts in the United States well known throughout the world. Because of this freedom, artists from many nations come to the United States to study and work.

3. Suppose you could participate in one of the events illustrated above. Which one would you choose? **Responses will vary depending upon individual interests.**

4. Which freedom would you be exercising when you choose? **freedom of choice**

5. Do you think freedom of expression and freedom of choice are important? Explain your ideas. **Responses may vary but should demonstrate an understanding of how these freedoms contribute to a rich and varied life in the United States.**

Name ______ Use with pages 78–79

Using New Words

Write the letter of the term that matches each description below. For help, you can refer to the lessons in Chapter 2 in your textbook.

a. freedom of expression	f. free enterprise	k. capitalism	p. republic
b. checks and balances	g. judicial branch	l. technology	q. export
c. legislative branch	h. discrimination	m. prejudice	r. import
d. developed economy	i. federal system	n. immigrants	
e. executive branch	j. megalopolis	o. democracy	

m 1. an unfavorable opinion of a group that is formed unfairly
c 2. the branch of goverment that makes the nation's laws
h 3. the unfair treatment of a person or group by another person or group
j 4. an area of cities and suburbs that is so crowded it looks like one vast city
g 5. the branch of government that interprets the nation's laws
k 6. an economic system in which businesses are owned by individuals or groups rather than by the government
n 7. people who move to a country other than the one where they were born
f 8. the freedom to own property and run a business free of government control
q 9. any item sold to another nation
d 10. an economy that has many different economic activities
l 11. the methods, tools, and machinery used to meet human needs
o 12. a government in which decisions are made by citizens
p 13. a democracy where voters elect officials to represent them in government
r 14. an item bought from another nation
b 15. a government system where each branch limits the powers of the others
i 16. a system of government that divides power between the national government and local governments
e 17. the branch of government responsible for carrying out the laws
a 18. the freedom to express any idea or opinion

Name Use with pages 81–83

Thinking About Canadian Culture

Read the following statements carefully. If a statement is true, write **True** after it. If a statement is false, write **False** after it. Then, in the space provided, write the reasons for your answers. For help, you can refer to pages 81–83 in your textbook.

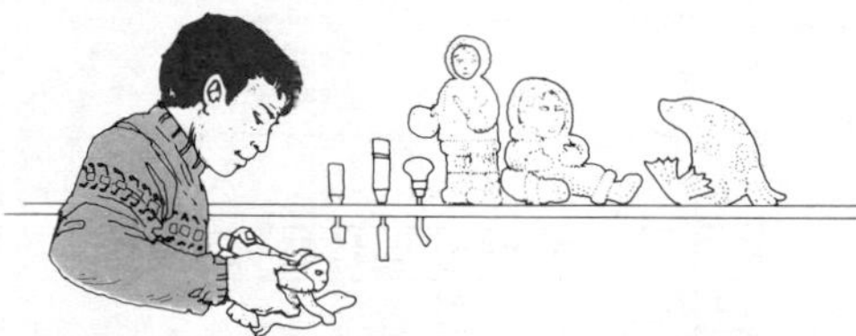

1. The picture above shows an Inuit making a traditional soapstone sculpture. The Inuit were one of the first peoples to settle in the land that is now called Canada.
True. The Inuit came from Asia to the land that is now called Canada about 6,000 years ago.
2. Today the Inuit are the largest cultural group in Canada.
False. Today British Canadians are the largest cultural group in Canada.
3. Because Canada was colonized mainly by people from Great Britain, its official language is English. **False. Canada was colonized mainly by people from both Great Britain and France. For this reason Canada has two official languages, English and French.**
4. In the 1960s some French Canadians wanted to break away from Canada.
True. They felt they had to break away from Canada in order to preserve their culture.
5. Some Canadians worry that the United States may be a threat to their way of life.
True. The United States has great influence in Canada because most Canadians live close to the United States–Canadian border.

Name Use with pages 86–88

Writing About Canada's Economy

A letter like the one below might have been written by a miner at the Polaris Mine. Read the letter. Then complete the following exercises. For help, you can refer to pages 86–88 in your textbook.

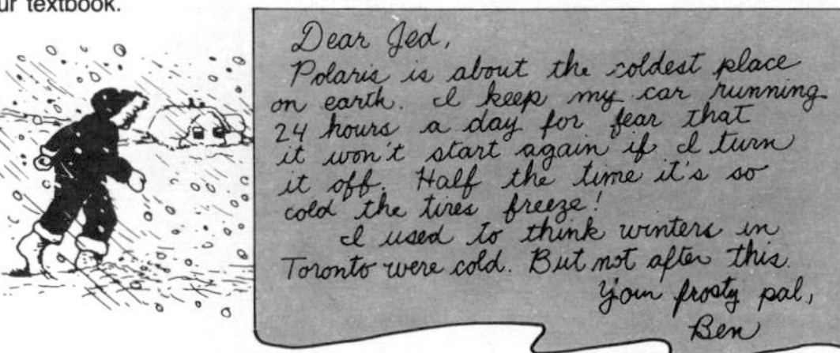

Dear Jed,
Polaris is about the coldest place on earth. I keep my car running 24 hours a day for fear that it won't start again if I turn it off. Half the time it's so cold the tires freeze!
I used to think winters in Toronto were cold. But not after this.
Your frosty pal,
Ben

1. What is the writer describing?
the climate at the Polaris Mine
2. Why is it so cold at Polaris?
because it is located north of the Arctic Circle
3. Because of its location, the Polaris Mine is expensive to run. Why is it profitable?
because the mine produces high-quality ore
4. Besides iron ore, what are two other minerals that help make mining Canada's most important industry?
nickel, lead, zinc, fossil fuels
5. List two other natural resources important for Canada's economy.
a. **From its huge forests, Canada produces newsprint.**
b. **Canada's rich farmland produces wheat.**
6. a. What is acid rain and how is it harmful to the environment?
Acid rain is rain mixed with chemicals. It pollutes waterways, killing fish and other water life, and damages trees and buildings.
b. How might the problem of acid rain strain relations between Canada and the United States?
A great deal of the acid rain in Canada comes from factories in the United States.

Name Use with page 89

Finding Information in a Library

Suppose you are writing a report about Canada. You need to check some facts in the library. Draw a line from the information you want to the picture that shows where you might find it. In the space provided, give a reason for your answer. For help, you can refer to page 89 in your textbook.

1. You want to check the location of each of Canada's provinces.
An atlas shows the location of places on a map.
2. You need to find out what the word *separatism* means and how to spell it.
A dictionary provides the meanings and spellings of words.
3. You want to check the most recent population figures for Canada's largest cities.
An almanac provides up-to-date facts on many subjects.

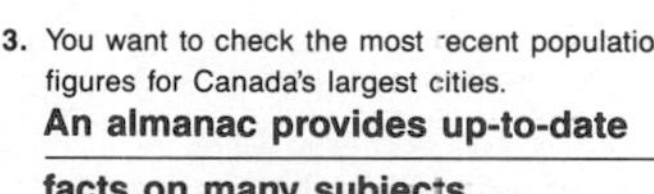

4. You need to find some information about Canada's economy.
An encyclopedia has articles on many useful subjects.
5. You need to find a book on the Inuit.
A card catalog tells where books in the library are located.

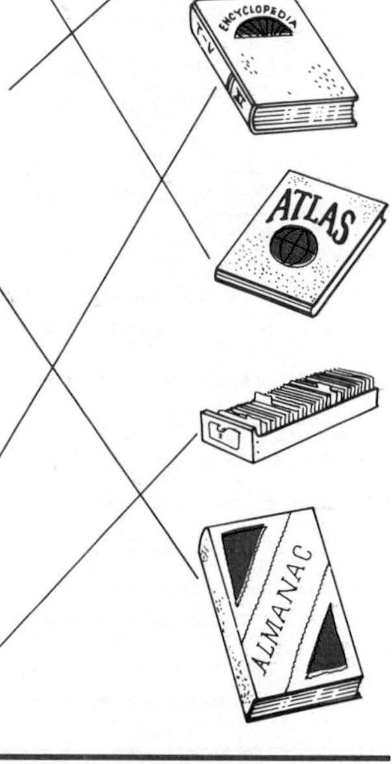

Name Use with pages 90–92

A Look at Canada's Government

Complete the activities below. For help, you can refer to pages 90–92 in your textbook.

1. The picture shows Queen Elizabeth II of Great Britain signing the Constitution Act, which gave Canada full independence from British rule. In what year did the signing take place?
1982
2. What role does the British monarch play in Canada's government today?
The British monarch is head of the government in name only.
3. In the picture the man looking on is former Prime Minister Pierre Trudeau of Canada. What part does the prime minister play in the national government of Canada?
The prime minister is the leader of Canada's national government.
4. Which branches of the Canadian government does the prime minister head?
the executive branch and the legislative branch
5. What is Canada's national legislative branch called? **parliament**
6. What two houses make up the Canadian legislative branch?
the House of Commons and the Senate
7. How are these two houses different? **The House of Commons is elected by the people. The Senate is appointed by the governor general.**
8. What must the Canadian prime minister do if he or she loses support of the majority of the members of Parliament? **resign**

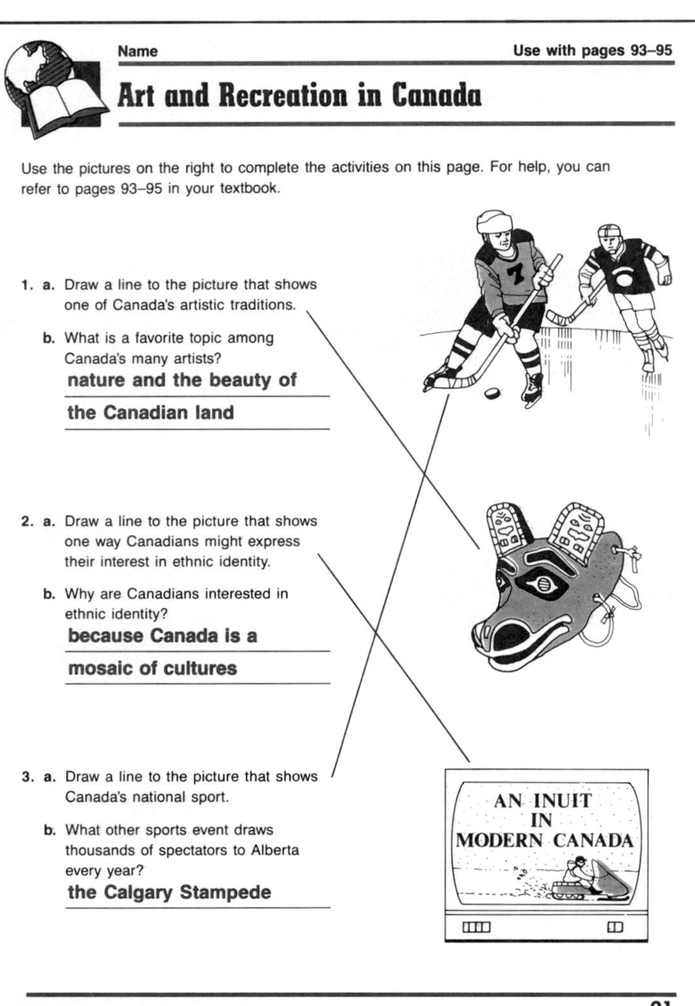

Name Use with pages 93–95

Art and Recreation in Canada

Use the pictures on the right to complete the activities on this page. For help, you can refer to pages 93–95 in your textbook.

1. a. Draw a line to the picture that shows one of Canada's artistic traditions.
   b. What is a favorite topic among Canada's many artists?
   nature and the beauty of the Canadian land

2. a. Draw a line to the picture that shows one way Canadians might express their interest in ethnic identity.
   b. Why are Canadians interested in ethnic identity?
   because Canada is a mosaic of cultures

3. a. Draw a line to the picture that shows Canada's national sport.
   b. What other sports event draws thousands of spectators to Alberta every year?
   the Calgary Stampede

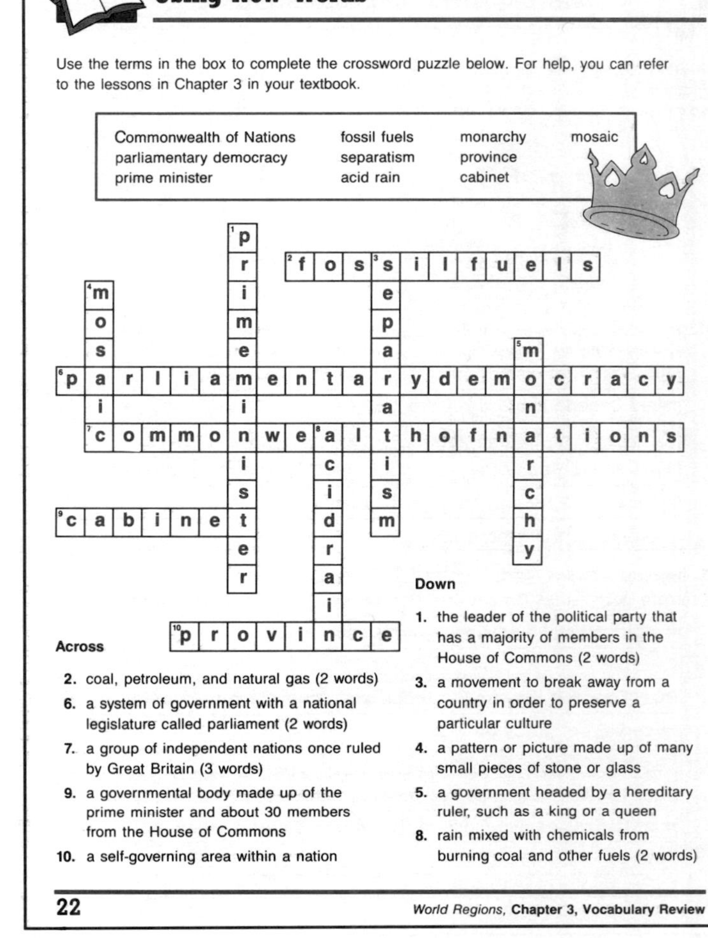

Name Use with pages 96–97

Using New Words

Use the terms in the box to complete the crossword puzzle below. For help, you can refer to the lessons in Chapter 3 in your textbook.

Commonwealth of Nations	fossil fuels	monarchy	mosaic
parliamentary democracy	separatism	province	
prime minister	acid rain	cabinet	

Across

2. coal, petroleum, and natural gas (2 words)
6. a system of government with a national legislature called parliament (2 words)
7. a group of independent nations once ruled by Great Britain (3 words)
9. a governmental body made up of the prime minister and about 30 members from the House of Commons
10. a self-governing area within a nation

Down

1. the leader of the political party that has a majority of members in the House of Commons (2 words)
3. a movement to break away from a country in order to preserve a particular culture
4. a pattern or picture made up of many small pieces of stone or glass
5. a government headed by a hereditary ruler, such as a king or a queen
8. rain mixed with chemicals from burning coal and other fuels (2 words)

Name Use with pages 107–110

Using Maps

Use the map on this page to complete the activities below. For help, you can refer to pages 107–110 in your textbook.

1. a. Locate and label the following land areas.
   Central America
   Caribbean Islands
   South America
   Mexico
   b. Which region do these land areas form?
   Latin America

2. a. Locate and label the following rivers. Then trace each river and its tributaries in blue.
   Amazon Orinoco
   Paraná Paraguay
   b. Which of these rivers forms one of the world's largest river systems?
   the Amazon

MEXICO
CARIBBEAN ISLANDS
CENTRAL AMERICA
SOUTH AMERICA
Orinoco R.
Amazon River
Lake Titicaca
ANDES MOUNTAINS
Paraguay
Paraná
blue
brown

3. a. Locate and label the Andes mountains. Then color them brown.
   b. How would you describe the climate in these mountains?
   It is hot during the day and very cold at night.

4. a. Locate and label Lake Titicaca.
   b. What is the area around Lake Titicaca called?
   the altiplano

Name Use with pages 111–114

Climate and Resources in Latin America

Use the picture to answer the first question below. Then answer the following questions. For help, you can refer to pages 111–114 in your textbook.

1. In which of Latin America's three climate zones would you find snow-capped mountain peaks?
   the tierra fría

2. What are Latin America's other two mountain climate zones called? What kind of climate does each have?
   name **tierra caliente**
   climate **hot all year**
   name **tierra templada**
   climate **temperate, mild**

Mount Aconcagua

3. Why is it surprising that Latin America's mountainous areas have three climate zones? **because most of Latin America is in the tropics**

4. What two places in Latin America hold world records for rainfall?
   a. World's driest place: **the Atacama Desert in Chile**
   b. World's largest rainy area: **the Amazon River Valley**

5. What natural resource is found in the rain forest of the Amazon River Valley?
   many kinds of trees

6. What are three other important natural resources found in Latin America?
   Possible answers: iron ore, petroleum, gold, silver, tin, emeralds

7. Why are many of these resources said to be "nature's jealously hidden treasures"?
   because many of them are difficult to find

Name Use with page 115

Relating Latitude, Elevation, and Climate

The following statements are based on information in the chart. Read the statements carefully. If a statement is true, write **True** after it. If a statement is false, write **False** after it. Then, in the space provided, write the reasons for your answer. For help, you can refer to page 115 in your textbook.

City and Country	Latitude	Approximate Elevation (ft.)
Mexico City, Mexico	21°N	7,500
Pueblo, Mexico	21°N	7,500
Bogotá, Colombia	5°N	8,500
Buenaventura, Colombia	5°N	500
Quito, Ecuador	equator	15,500
Guayaquil, Ecuador	2°S	sea level

1. You would expect the climate of Mexico City and Pueblo to be similar.
True. Both cities are at about the same latitude and elevation.
2. Despite the fact that Bogotá is near the equator, you would expect it to have a cold climate. **True. Although Bogotá is near the equator, it is at a high elevation, approximately 8,500 feet.**
3. Because Quito and Guayaquil are both near the equator, you would expect them to have hot climates. **False. Quito is at a very high elevation and would have a cold climate. Guayaquil is at a very low elevation and would have a hot climate.**
4. If you were planning to visit Mexico City and then Bogotá, you would expect to encounter cool climates in both cities. **True. Both are at high elevation and would have cool climates.**
5. The climates of Bogotá and Buenaventura are quite different from each other. **True. Although both cities are at the same latitude, Bogotá is at a much higher elevation and would thus have a much cooler climate.**

Name Use with pages 116–117

Using New Words

Put an **X** next to each statement that gives correct information about the term in boldface type. For help, you can refer to the lessons in Chapter 4 in your textbook.

1. archipelago

X a. An archipelago is a group of islands.
X b. The Caribbean archipelagos are part of Latin America's mountain system.
___ c. Latin America's mountain system is known as an archipelago.
X d. The Caribbean Islands are made up of small archipelagos.

2. rain forest

___ a. Much of North America is covered by rain forest.
X b. A rain forest is a dense tropical forest.
X c. Most of Latin America's trees grow in the rain forest of the Amazon River Valley.
___ d. The rain forests of Latin America are located in the climate zone known as tierra fría.

3. altiplano

___ a. The Andes mountains are sometimes called the altiplano.
X b. The altiplano is a high, cold, flat area between two mountain ranges in Bolivia and Peru.
X c. Many people live in the altiplano area of the Andes mountains.
X d. Lake Titicaca is on the altiplano.

4. river system

X a. A river system is the land drained by a major river and its tributaries.
___ b. South America doesn't have any large river systems.
X c. The Amazon is one of the world's greatest river systems.
___ d. The Andean altiplano is Latin America's second-largest river system.

Name Use with pages 119–122

The Origins of Mexico's Culture

Answer the following questions. For help, you can refer to pages 119–122 in your textbook.

1. The picture above shows the ancient city of Tenochtitlán. Who built the city and where did they build it? **Tenochtitlán was built by the Mexica (whom the Spanish called the Aztecs) where Mexico City stands today.**
2. The Spanish explorer Hernando Cortés thought Tenochtitlán was "the most beautiful city in the world." If he felt this way, why did he destroy it? **Cortés and his followers destroyed Tenochtitlán in order to defeat the Aztecs gathered there.**
3. How did the Spanish conquest of Mexico change the culture and way of life of its people? **The way of life of Mexico's people became a mixture of Spanish and Indian cultures.**
4. What is the ancestry of the Mexican people today? **About 55 percent of the people are mestizos. Another 29 percent are of pure Indian descent. Most of the remaining people are of Spanish ancestry.**
5. Why are most present-day Mexicans Roman Catholic? **The Spanish who conquered Mexico were Roman Catholic. They converted many of the Indians to their religion.**

Name Use with pages 123–125

A Look at Mexico's Economy

Use the graph below to answer the first two questions on this page. Then answer the following questions. For help, you can refer to pages 123–125 in your textbook.

HOW PEOPLE EARN A LIVING IN MEXICO (1995)

Commerce, restaurants, and hotels 15%
Construction 11%
Manufacturing Industries 11%
Mining 1%
Agriculture, forestry, and fishing 26%
Finance 2%
Health, social, and personal services 29%
Transportation and communications 5%

1. a. According to the graph, what percent of Mexicans work in the agriculture, forestry, and fishing industries? **26 percent**
   b. What two types of farming take place in Mexico? **subsistence farming** **commercial farming**
2. a. According to the graph, what percent of Mexicans work in manufacturing industries? **11 percent**
   b. In which city is most of Mexico's industry located? **Mexico City**
3. What is one reason that Mexico is only partly industrialized? **The ores mined in Mexico were not used to develop the nation's businesses and factories but went instead to other countries.**
4. How did the discovery of large petroleum deposits in Mexico in the 1970s affect Mexico's economy? **The discovery of oil created new industries, such as the petrochemical industry.**
5. How has Mexico's population affected the country's economic growth? **Mexico's population is growing faster than the nation's ability to provide jobs for everyone. As a result, its economic growth has slowed.**

Name Use with pages 126–127

Is It Accurate?

The paragraph below is from a book titled *Mexico From Montezuma to NAFTA, Chiapas, and Beyond.* The book was published in 1996. Read the paragraph. Then answer the questions that follow. For help, you can refer to pages 126–127 in your textbook.

> In addition to the diversity of its land and the nature of its climates, Mexico has much to offer in natural resources. Lush forests occupy vast regions of the country. Trees of great stature, age, and variety, such as pine and oak, populate the national parks set aside by the government to preserve these valuable resources. Minerals are yet another extremely important Mexican resource. As far back as the conquistadores, Mexico's mineral deposits have been of great interest to other countries. Today, Mexico is still a leading producer of silver.
>
> *by Jaime Suchlicki, leading scholar and author of several books on Latin America and Professor of History at the University of Miami.*

1. What is the source of the information above? **A book titled *Mexico From Montezuma to NAFTA, Chiapas, and Beyond***
2. Is the author an expert or well-informed on the topic? How do you know? **Yes. Jaime Sulchecki is a scholar, author, and professor.**
3. Does the author have anything to gain by giving inaccurate information on the topic?
   yes (no)
4. Is the information current? How do you know? **The information is probably current because the book was written only a few years ago.**
5. What are two sources you might check to determine the accuracy of the information? **Answers may vary, but should identify sources appropriate to the topic, such as world almanacs, encyclopedias, and newspapers.**
6. Do you think the information is probably accurate? How can you tell? **The information is probably accurate because it is from a good source, written by an expert on the topic, and is reasonably recent.**

Name Use with pages 128–130

Mexico's Government

Use the terms in the box to complete the diagram of Mexico's government. Then answer the questions that follow. For help, you can refer to pages 128–130 in your textbook.

Chamber of Deputies Senate Supreme Court President

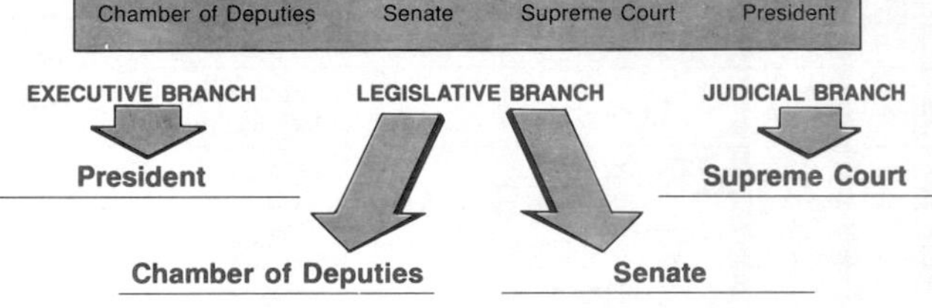

1. According to its constitution, what kind of government does Mexico have? **a representative democracy**
2. What are two powers that the President of Mexico has that the President of the United States does not have? **The president of Mexico can remove local officials from office and change laws with the approval of the Senate.**
3. For what is the Chamber of Deputies responsible? **The Chamber of Deputies passes laws and is responsible for elections.**
4. For what is the Senate responsible? **The Senate approves or disapproves treaties and presidential appointments.**
5. Why was only one strong political party, the PRI, formed in Mexico? **It was formed to include many interests and to prevent different groups from clashing and causing unrest.**
6. Why do critics of the PRI feel it is time for a change? **They believe it is time to make the government more directly responsible to the people and to allow parties to air their differences in public.**

Name Use with pages 131–133

Art, Culture, and Recreation in Mexico

The pictures below show two features of Mexican culture. Write a caption for each picture. Explain what is shown and how the picture illustrates the combining of Indian and Spanish cultures. Then answer the question that follows. For help, you can refer to pages 131–133 in your textbook.

1. **The game of jai alai shown in the picture had its origins in traditional Indian culture. The game is still one of the most popular sports in Mexico.**

2. **Murals like the one in the picture explore mestizo heritage. The simple lines and bold colors capture the spirit of Mexico's past sufferings and hopes for the future.**

3. How and why has the Mexican government supported traditional Mexican crafts? **The Mexican government has supported traditional Mexican crafts by giving craftsworkers awards and by helping them export their best works. By so doing, Mexico hopes to maintain its traditions, give people income, and produce goods for export.**

Name Use with pages 138–139

Using New Words

Write the letter of the term that matches each definition. For help, you can refer to the lessons in Chapter 5 in your textbook.

a. subsistence farming	e. mestizo	h. petrochemical
b. developing economy	f. mural	i. civilization
c. commercial farming	g. extended family	j. campesino
d. metropolitan area		

j 1. a Mexican village farmer with a small plot of land and a very low income
h 2. a chemical that is made from petroleum
i 3. a culture that has developed systems of government, religion, and learning
a 4. farming in which just enough food is grown to feed the families of the farmers
f 5. a work of art on a building wall
e 6. a Mexican of mixed Indian and Spanish ancestry
g 7. a family that contains, in addition to parents and their children, other family members
c 8. large-scale farming in which crops are sold and exported
b 9. a national economy that is only partly industrialized
d 10. an area that includes a large city and its surrounding suburbs and towns

Name Use with pages 141–144

The Origins of Latin American Cultures

Use the pictures on the right to complete the activities on this page. For help, you can refer to pages 141–144 in your textbook.

1. a. Draw a line to the picture that shows something made by the first people to live in Central America.
   b. Which three areas in Central America did these people settle?
   Guatemala
   Belize
   western Honduras

Enslaved Africans brought to the Caribbean Islands

2. a. Draw a line to the picture that shows the second stream of people to come to Central America and the Caribbean.
   b. Which four European countries gained control of the Caribbean Islands?
   England **France**
   Spain **Netherlands**

Spanish settlers landing on a Caribbean island

3. a. Draw a line to the picture that shows the third stream of people to come to Latin America.
   b. Why did these people come to Central America and the Caribbean Islands?
   They were brought against their will and forced to work on plantations.

Mayan sculpture

4. What makes each of the Caribbean Islands unique? **the combination of historical events, customs, and different ethnic groups**

Name Use with pages 145–147

ECONOMY: Central America and the Caribbean

Use the bar graph below to complete the exercises on this page. For help, you can refer to pages 145–147 in your textbook.

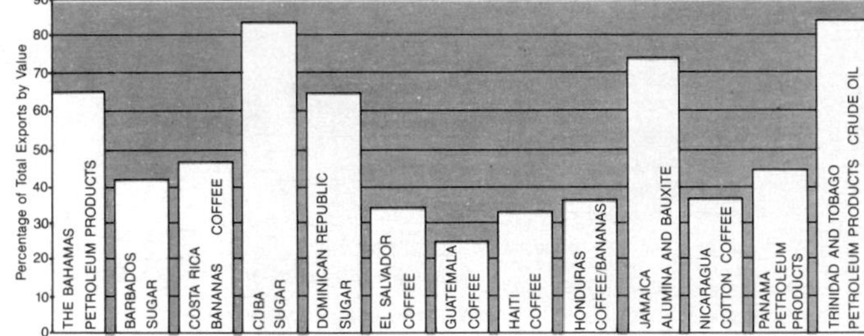

1. List the countries that export mineral products.
   the Bahamas **Jamaica**
   Panama **Trinidad and Tobago**
2. List the countries that export mainly agricultural products. Put an * next to those countries that depend heavily on a single crop.
   ***Barbados** **Costa Rica** ***Cuba**
   ***Dominican Republic** ***El Salvador** ***Guatemala**
   ***Haiti** **Honduras** **Nicaragua**
3. Why is it risky for a nation to depend heavily on one crop for its income?
   If world prices for that crop fall, or if a natural disaster that affects that crop strikes, the nation will lose the income from the crop.
4. Why are most manufacturing jobs in Central America and the Caribbean countries related to agricultural products instead of mineral products?
   Many of the nations in this part of the world do not have coal or other minerals needed for manufacturing.

Name Use with page 148

The Pan-American Highway

The map below shows the Pan-American Highway system. Study the map. Then answer the questions that follow. For help, you can refer to page 148 in your textbook.

1. According to the map, at which three cities in the United States does the Pan-American Highway begin?
   Laredo
   El Paso
   Eagle Pass
2. To which major city do each of these routes lead?
   Mexico City
3. If you traveled on the Pan-American Highway from Mexico City to Managua, Nicaragua, which three major cities would you pass through?
   Guatemala City
   San Salvador
   Tegucigalpa
4. Trace one route you could take from Managua to Brasília in red. Trace a second route you could take in blue. **Routes will vary, but should indicate the student's understanding of the map symbols for cities and roads.**
5. Why is the Pan-American Highway system of great importance to the economies of Latin America and South America? **It provides routes for the transportation of raw materials, agricultural products, and other goods.**

Name Use with pages 149–151

GOVERNMENT: Central America and the Caribbean

Complete the map by writing phrases from the box in the spaces provided on the map. Each space should have a separate phrase. For help, you can refer to pages 149–151 in your textbook.

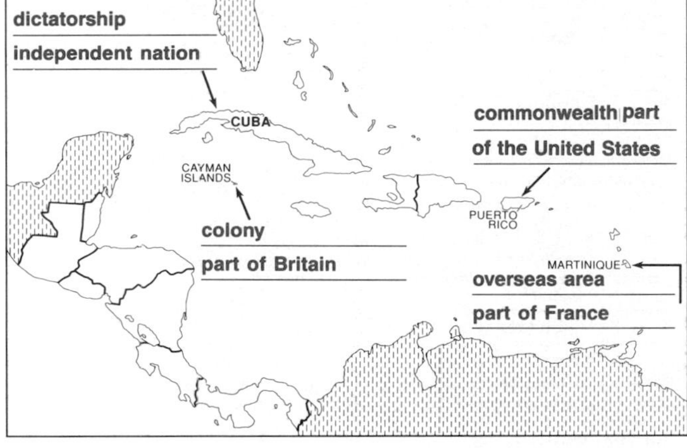

Why does the United States closely watch the events that take place in the Caribbean?
because the area is very near to its borders; the United States has possessions in the region; the United States has an interest in the Panama Canal

Name | Use with pages 154–155

Arts and Recreation in Latin America

Use the pictures below to complete the activities on this page. For help, you can refer to pages 154–155 in your textbook.

1. a. What kind of musical instrument are the people in the picture playing? **steel drums**

   b. On which Caribbean Island was this musical instrument developed? **Trinidad**

   c. What kind of music are the musicians probably playing? **calypso**

   d. What is the origin of calypso music? **Calypso was started in the Caribbean by enslaved Africans who sang while they worked.**

2. a. Which popular sport is being played in the picture? **baseball**

   b. In which Caribbean and Central American nations is this sport played most frequently? **Nicaragua, Cuba, Dominican Republic**

   c. What is remarkable about the Dominican Republic's contribution to this sport?

   Over 200 Dominicans play on major and minor league teams in the United States.

   d. What other sport is a favorite in this part of the world? **soccer**

Name | Use with pages 148–149

Using New Words

Use the code to spell the words in the left column. Then write the number of each word next to its definition in the right column. For help, you can refer to the lessons in Chapter 6 of your textbook.

CODE

a = 26	g = 23	m = 20	s = 17	y = 14
b = 1	h = 4	n = 7	t = 10	z = 13
c = 25	i = 22	o = 19	u = 16	
d = 2	j = 5	p = 8	v = 11	
e = 24	k = 21	q = 18	w = 15	
f = 3	l = 6	r = 9	x = 12	

1. 20 26 9 19 19 7 **maroon**
2. 25 26 6 14 8 17 19 **calypso**
3. 25 19 20 20 19 7 15 24 26 6 10 4 **commonwealth**
4. 17 24 25 10 **sect**
5. 2 22 25 10 26 10 19 9 **dictator**
6. 8 6 26 7 10 26 10 22 19 7 **plantation**
7. 19 7 24-25 9 19 8 24 25 19 7 19 20 14 **one-crop economy**

2 a. a style of music developed in the Caribbean by African slaves

1 b. a descendant of enslaved Africans who escaped from the Spanish in the Caribbean

4 c. a religious group that is outside the mainstream of large, organized religion

5 d. a ruler who has total control over a country

6 e. a large farm that grows crops for sale

3 f. a self-governing territory

7 g. an economy that depends on a single crop for income

Name | Use with pages 159–161

Some Ethnic Groups in South America

Use the map to complete the activities on this page. For help, you can refer to pages 159–161 in your textbook.

1. Shade and list the two countries in which much of the population is European or of European ancestry. **Argentina, Uruguay**

2. Put a star in and list each of the three countries whose population includes many Indians. **Bolivia, Peru, Ecuador**

3. Outline and list each of the four countries in which the population consists mainly of mestizos. **Paraguay, Venezuela, Ecuador, Chile**

4. Name and briefly describe South America's best-known mestizo group. **The gauchos of Argentina are cowhands who roam the pampas herding cattle.**

5. Briefly explain how the ethnic mix of South America affects its culture. **Student responses will vary but should indicate an understanding of how the different groups' ways of life have formed the cultures of present-day South America.**

Name | Use with pages 162–163

Is It Fact or Opinion?

You might read statements similar to the ones below in an article about the Incas. Decide if each statement is a fact, a value judgment, or a reasoned opinion. Circle your choice. Then explain your answer. For help, you can refer to pages 162–163 in your textbook.

1. The Incas are the most interesting people to have lived in South America.
   fact — (value judgment) — reasoned opinion
   explanation: **making a judgment about the worth or quality of something**

2. By the middle of the 1400s, the Incan empire had expanded to occupy more than 2,500 miles (4,200 km) along the western coast of South America.
   (fact) — value judgment — reasoned opinion
   explanation: **information that can be proved**

3. The Incas built a vast network of roads to link the provinces of their large empire.
   (fact) — value judgment — reasoned opinion
   explanation: **information that can be proven**

4. The Incan people must have been very creative since they made so many beautiful works of art.
   fact — value judgment — (reasoned opinion)
   explanation: **an opinion supported by evidence or reasons**

5. Because so much of the private and public lives of the Incas revolved around religious practices, priests and other religious leaders must have had great authority.
   fact — value judgment — (reasoned opinion)
   explanation: **an opinion supported by evidence or reasons**

6. Today the Incan ruins are the most interesting things to see in Peru.
   fact — (value judgment) — reasoned opinion
   explanation: **making a judgment about the worth or quality of something**

Name Use with pages 164–167

Looking at the Products of South America

Use the pictures below to complete the activities on this page. For help, you can refer to pages 164–167 in your textbook.

1. a. Which South American country is the leading exporter of this product?
   Ecuador

   b. What cash crop is grown in Colombia and Brazil?
   coffee

2. a. In which part of South America might these animals be raised?
   the pampas

   b. What two crops are also grown in this area?
   cotton **wheat**

3. a. From which South American country might these leather goods have come?
   Argentina

   b. What do most South American manufacturers process?
   Most South American manufacturers process, or treat, agricultural products.

4. a. Which South American country used this major resource to help its economic development?
   Venezuela

   b. Why was basing its economy on this one product risky?
   When world oil prices fell, Venezuela's economy was hurt.

Name Use with pages 170–171

A Look at the Dictatorship of Juan Perón

The headline and article below are from *The New York Times*, September 20, 1955. Read the article and answer the questions that follow. For help, you can refer to pages 170–171 in your textbook.

PERÓN'S REGIME IS OVERTHROWN; JUNTA WILL MEET WITH REBELS; CROWDS HAIL FALL OF DICTATOR

BUENOS AIRES, Tuesday, Sept. 20–The Government of President Juan D. Perón fell last night.

A four-man junta of army generals assumed command of the forces that had fought unsuccessfully to keep General Perón in power. He had been master of Argentina since Oct. 17, 1945, and its President for nine years. . . .

The junta quickly entered into negotiations to end the four-day civil war. Army and Navy units had joined in the rebellion and forced the resignation of the President, the Cabinet and other authorities. . . .

There was no news about the whereabouts of President Perón tonight. Some reports had him in . . . the Paraguayan Embassy in Buenos Aires.

1. According to the article, who was Juan Perón and what happened to him?
   Juan Perón was president of Argentina, and he was overthrown by army generals.

2. According to the headline, how did Argentinians feel about the fall of Perón's dictatorship?
   They were glad Perón's dictatorship had ended.

3. According to the article, how long had Perón been president of Argentina?
   almost ten years

4. How did Perón maintain power in Argentina?
   by creating labor unions, schools, and new industries

5. At the same time Eva Perón encouraged workers to give money to government programs, what did Juan Perón do?
   He took control of the press, businesses, labor unions, and the army.

6. Who ruled Argentina after Perón's death?
   dictators

Name Use with pages 172–173

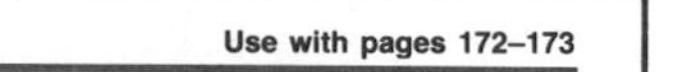

A Look at South American Traditions

Use the pictures on the right to complete the activities on this page. For help, you can refer to pages 172–173 in your textbook.

1. a. Draw a line to the picture that shows one of South America's famous poets.

   b. What are some of the topics most often described by South American poets?
   ethnic identity, environment, and poverty

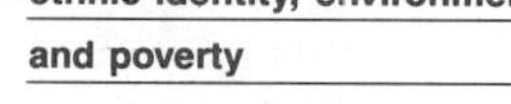

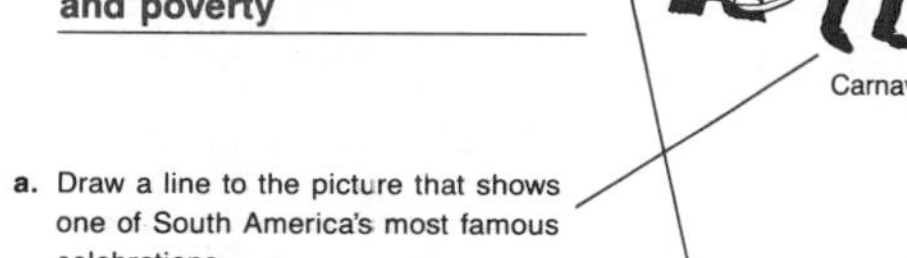

Carnaval in Rio de Janeiro

2. a. Draw a line to the picture that shows one of South America's most famous celebrations.

   b. What national dance is featured at this celebration?
   the samba

   c. What is the origin of this dance?
   It has African roots.

João Nuñes de Oliveira

3. a. Draw a line to the picture that shows one of South America's most famous soccer players.

   b. What are some other popular sports in South America?
   baseball, tennis, polo, jai alai

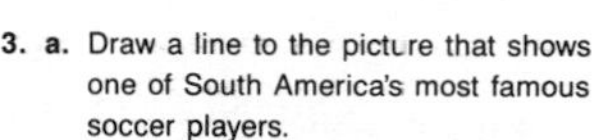

Pablo Neruda

Name Use with pages 174–175

Using New Words

Complete each of the exercises below. For help, you can refer to the lessons in Chapter 7 in your textbook.

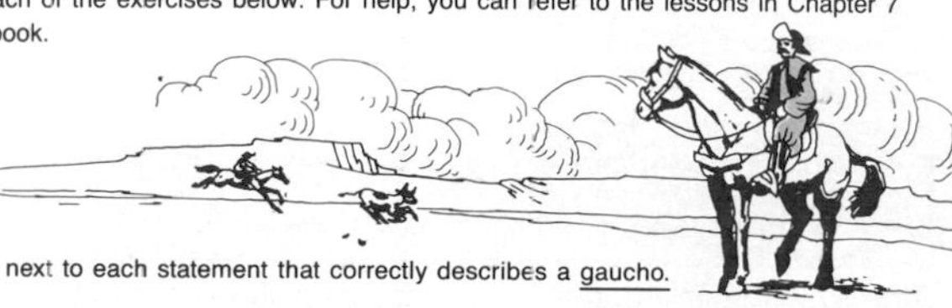

1. Put an **X** next to each statement that correctly describes a gaucho.
   - **X** a. A gaucho is a member of one of South America's best-known mestizo groups.
   - **X** b. A gaucho is a cowhand who roams the pampas herding cattle.
   - ____ c. A gaucho is a farmer who lives high in the Andes.

2. Put an **X** next to each statement that correctly describes a caudillo.
   - ____ a. A caudillo is a South American mestizo group.
   - **X** b. A caudillo is a local South American military leader.
   - **X** c. A caudillo may become powerful enough to form an army.

3. Put an **X** next to each statement that correctly describes junta.
   - **X** a. A junta is a group of military officers that run a country.
   - ____ b. Junta is the name of a South American dictator.
   - ____ c. A junta is a South American farmer.

4. Put an **X** next to each statement that correctly uses the word coup.
   - **X** a. A coup is the sudden overthrow of a government.
   - **X** b. Enemies of Juan Perón overthrew him in a coup.
   - ____ c. Perón's wife helped him by forming a coup.

5. Put an **X** next to each statement that correctly uses the term per capita income.
   - **X** a. The average yearly income for each person in a country is called per capita income.
   - ____ b. Taxes are called per capita income in some countries.
   - **X** c. Venezuela's per capita income rose when oil was discovered there.

Name Use with pages 183–187

Using Maps

Use the map on this page to complete the activities below. For help, you can refer to pages 183–187 and the atlas on page 629 in your textbook.

1. Locate and label the following bodies of water.
   Atlantic Ocean
   English Channel
   Mediterranean Sea
   North Sea
   Baltic Sea
2. Locate and label the following peninsulas. Then color each one as indicated.
   a. Jutland Peninsula—brown
   b. Scandinavian Peninsula—red
   c. Italian Peninsula—green
   d. Balkan Peninsula—blue
   e. Iberian Peninsula—yellow
3. Locate and label the following islands.
   British Isles
   Sardinia
   Corsica
   Sicily
4. List the countries that make up the Low Countries. Then color this area orange.
   Netherlands Belgium Luxembourg
5. Why is Western Europe called "a land of peninsulas and islands"?
   because the shape of the land can be divided into peninsulas and islands

Name Use with pages 188–189

Understanding Map Projections

The map below is called a Robinson projection. Put an **X** next to each sentence that makes a true statement about the map. For help, you can refer to pages 188–189 in your textbook.

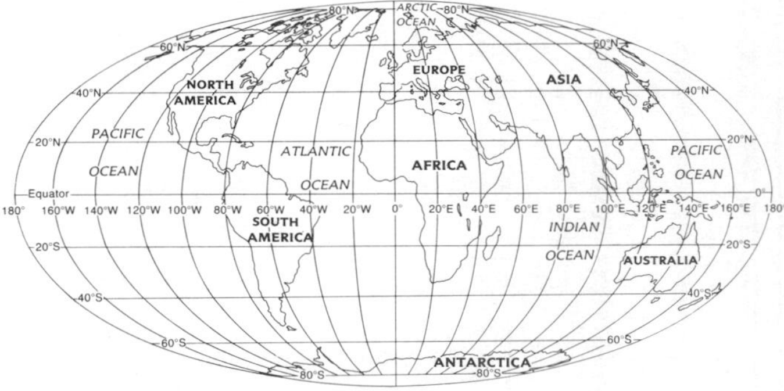

X 1. The map above is an example of an equal-area projection.

___ 2. As you move toward the poles on this map, distances and shapes become distorted.

___ 3. This kind of map is useful to navigators of ships because they can use it to draw their ships' courses in straight lines.

X 4. The projection of this map shows sizes and shapes of continents fairly accurately, and distances are nearly correct.

X 5. The projection of this map is useful for comparing different places on the earth.

___ 6. North is always directly toward the top of this map.

___ 7. A Mercator projection would show the shapes of the continents more accurately than they are shown on this map.

X 8. On this map all the lines of longitude are curved except the prime meridian.

Name Use with pages 192–197

Writing About Western Europe

Use the space provided to answer the questions in each box. Arrange your answers in paragraphs. Your paragraphs will be a summary of important ideas from the lesson. For help, you can refer to pages 192–197 in your textbook.

- Which factors cause the mild climate of the Atlantic coast of Europe?
- What kind of climate does the northern part of Western Europe have? Why?
- What kind of climate does the southern part of Western Europe have? Why?

The Gulf Stream brings warm water from the Gulf of Mexico to the Atlantic coast of Europe. These ocean waters heat up in summer and cool off in winter more slowly than the land does, creating a mild climate. In the northern part of Western Europe, the moderating effect of the Gulf Stream and the Atlantic Ocean are not nearly as strong. As a result, the winters are long, cold, and snowy. Two mountain ranges in the southern part of Western Europe, the Alps and the Pyrenees, prevent Atlantic breezes from reaching this area. This makes the summers mostly sunny and dry. The winters are usually mild or even warm.

- What happened to most of the forests that once covered Western Europe?
- What threatens the forests that are left?
- What makes Western Europe a good region for growing crops?
- Why are Western Europe's rivers and waterways important?

Many of the forests that once covered Western Europe were cut down to make room for farms. Today the forests that remain are threatened by logging and by acid rain. Western Europe's mild climate and rich soil make it a good region for growing crops. Its rivers and waterways provide transportation and shipping routes for even the landlocked countries of Luxembourg, Switzerland, and Austria.

Name Use with pages 198–199

Using New Words

Complete each of the activities below. For help, you can refer to the lessons in Chapter 8 in your textbook.

1. Put an **X** next to each statement that correctly uses the word *landlocked*.
   ___ **a.** A landlocked country is one that is surrounded by water on three sides.
   X **b.** A landlocked country is one that is entirely surrounded by land.
   X **c.** Luxembourg, Switzerland, and Austria are the three landlocked countries of Western Europe.
   ___ **d.** Good inland waterways are of little use to a landlocked country.
   ___ **e.** Great Britain is a landlocked country.
   X **f.** The Rhine River begins in the landlocked country of Switzerland.
2. Put an **X** next to each statement that correctly uses the word *fjord*.
   X **a.** A fjord is a deep, narrow inlet of the sea between high cliffs.
   X **b.** The western coast of Norway is a good place to see a fjord.
   ___ **c.** A fjord is a large lake formed by retreating glaciers.
   ___ **d.** The landlocked countries of Western Europe are good places to see a fjord.
   ___ **e.** A fjord is often located far from the sea.
   X **f.** A fjord must be located along the coast of a country.
3. Write a sentence containing both the words *fjord* and *landlocked*.
   Example sentence: You will never see a fjord in a landlocked country.

Name Use with pages 201–203

The People Who Came to the British Isles

Use the sentences in the box to complete the time line. Then answer the questions that follow. For help, you can refer to pages 201–203 in your textbook.

Stonehenge was built.
The Celts came to the British Isles.
The Romans invaded the British Isles.
The Anglo-Saxons invaded Britain.
The Normans invaded England.

Stonehenge was built. 2000 B.C.
Celts came to British Isles. 800 B.C.
Romans invaded British Isles. A.D. 43
Anglo-Saxons invaded Britain. 450
Normans invaded England. 1066

2000 | 1500 | 1000 | 500 | 500 | 1000 | 1500 | 2000
B.C. ← → A.D.

1. Who built Stonehenge? **the first people to settle the British Isles**
2. According to the time line, about how long after Stonehenge was built did the Celts invade the British Isles? **about 1,200 years**
3. About how long were the Celts in the British Isles before the Romans invaded? **about 850 years**
4. Who were the Anglo-Saxons? **warriors from northern Europe who invaded Britain**
5. Where did the Normans come from? **the western part of France known as Normandy**
6. Today where do the largest groups of newcomers to Great Britain come from? **from India, Pakistan, West Indies—countries once ruled by Britain**

Name Use with pages 204–205

Reading Time Zone Maps

Use the time zone map below to complete the sentences. For help, you can refer to pages 204–205 in your textbook.

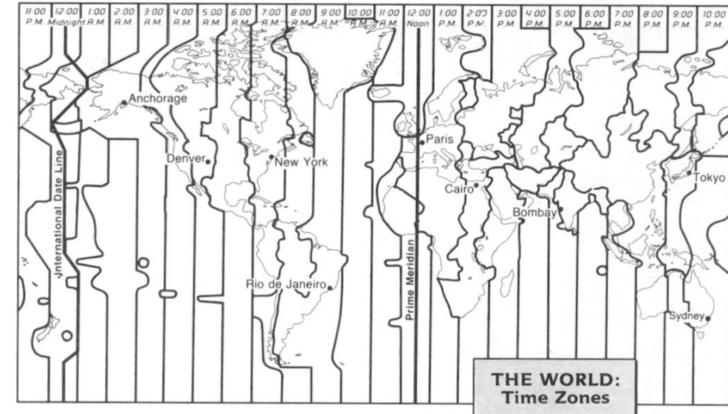

1. The line that marks the boundary between one day and the next is called the **International Date Line**.
2. If you travel east across this line, today becomes **yesterday**.
3. If you travel west across this line, today becomes **tomorrow**.
4. If you were traveling east from New York to Bombay, you would pass through **ten** time zones.
5. When it is noon on Monday in Paris, it is **4:00 A.M.** on **Monday** in Denver.
6. When it is 6:00 A.M. on Wednesday in Anchorage, it is **1:00 A.M.** on **Thursday** in Sydney.

Name Use with pages 206–208

Taking a Look at the British Economy

Answer the following questions. For help, you can refer to pages 206–208 in your textbook.

1. The picture above shows the inside of a British factory during the Industrial Revolution. How did factories like this change the way things were produced? **Jobs that were once done by hand were now done by machine. Products that once were made at home or in small workshops were now produced in factories like this one.**
2. How did the economies of Great Britain and the Republic of Ireland differ during the Industrial Revolution? **The Industrial Revolution made Great Britain the economic leader of the world. The economy of the Republic of Ireland developed at a much slower pace.**
3. How has the economy of Great Britain changed since the days of the Industrial Revolution? **Great Britain is no longer the world's leading industrial People in other countries can produce goods more cheaply than the British can.**
4. What economic problems does Britain face today? **Its natural resources are limited. In addition, British factories now find it hard to compete against the more modern factories in other countries.**
5. Which newly discovered natural resources in Great Britain are likely to be the key to Britain's economic future? **oil and natural gas**

Name Use with pages 209–211

The Government of Great Britain

Answer the questions below. For help, you can refer to pages 209–211 in your textbook.

1. The picture shows King John of England signing the Magna Carta. In which year did the signing take place? **1215**
2. What was the Magna Carta? **a document, or charter, limiting the power of Britain's monarch**
3. What role does the monarch play in Britain's government today? **The monarch carries out many public functions but does not play a direct role in making public policy.**
4. How does the British constitution differ from most other constitutions in the world today? **The British constitution is not a single written document. Instead, it consists of important laws and charters adopted over many centuries.**
5. What are the names of the two houses that make up the British Parliament? **House of Lords** **House of Commons**
6. What is the title of the person who heads the Parliament? **prime minister**
7. Who becomes the prime minister? **the leader of the political party with the most seats in Parliament**
8. How has the British system of government influenced other democracies in the world? **Many of the world's democracies are modeled after it.**

Name Use with pages 212–213

Arts and Recreation in Great Britain

Use the names of people and sports in the box to answer the map questions below. Then answer the following question. For help, you can refer to pages 212–213 in your textbook.

William Shakespeare	James Joyce	Robert Burns
Dylan Thomas	soccer	golf

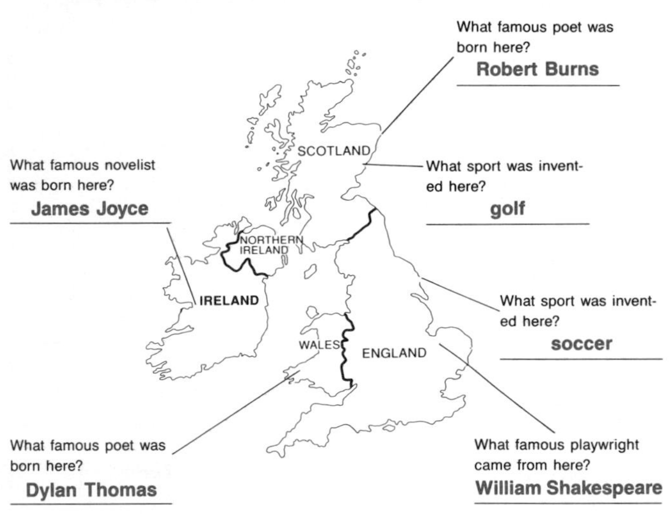

What famous poet was born here? **Robert Burns**

What famous novelist was born here? **James Joyce**

What sport was invented here? **golf**

What sport was invented here? **soccer**

What famous poet was born here? **Dylan Thomas**

What famous playwright came from here? **William Shakespeare**

What are three ways in which the great writers of Britain and Ireland have influenced the world? **They helped to invent the novel. They wrote many great plays, poems, and novels. They gave the world the English language.**

Name Use with pages 214–215

Using New Words

Choose a term from the box to answer each question. Some terms may be used more than once. For help, you can refer to the lessons in Chapter 9 in your textbook.

constitutional monarchy	welfare state
Industrial Revolution	nationalize
mixed economy	Magna Carta

1. Which term describes the government of Great Britain? **constitutional monarchy**
2. Which term would you use to refer to the period in the 1800s when factories began manufacturing most products? **Industrial Revolution**
3. Which term would you use to refer to the practice of placing industries under the control of government? **nationalize**
4. What is the name of the document that limited the powers of the British monarchy? **Magna Carta**
5. Which term describes the economy of the United Kingdom? **mixed economy**
6. Which term would you use to describe a country that takes the responsibility for the well-being of all its citizens? **welfare state**
7. Which term would you use to refer to an economy consisting of both private enterprise and government-run businesses? **mixed economy**
8. Which term would you use to describe a government that has both a monarch and a constitution? **constitutional monarchy**

Name Use with pages 217–220

France and the Low Countries

Follow the directions to do the exercises below. For help, you can refer to pages 217–220 in your textbook.

1. List three groups of people who invaded the region shown on the map between 58 B.C. and A.D. 900.
   Possible answers: Celts, Franks, Romans, Vikings
2. Shade the region of the map where you might hear an ancient Celtic language spoken today.
   Brittany
3. Put a star in the region where you might hear English-sounding names. **Bordeaux**
   How did such names come about here? **for 300 years Bordeaux was ruled by the English**
4. Put a triangle in the area where people speak Basque. **Pyrenees**
5. Belgians speak three different languages. What are they?
   French **Dutch (Flemish)** **German**
6. Why do you think so many different languages are spoken in the region of France and the Low Countries? **Student responses may vary but should demonstrate an understanding of how the invasion of this region by many different people resulted in many different languages being spoken.**

Name Use with pages 221–223

Economies of France and Low Countries

Imagine that you took a trip through France and the Low Countries. Here are some of the photographs you put in your scrapbook. Complete the captions below the pictures. For help, you can refer to pages 221–223 in your textbook.

I saw many fields like these in the **Netherlands**. Dutch **flowers** and **bulbs** are exported all over the world. At the world's largest flower market at Aalsmeer, farmers sell more than **12 million** flowers every day.

I spotted this ship in one of the Low Countries. Wide, navigable **rivers** flow from the heart of **Western Europe**, through this region, into the **North Sea**. The transportation network also consists of many **roads**, **railroads**, and **airports**.

I spent several afternoons just relaxing in this **outdoor café** in the city of **Paris**. **Service** industries such as tourism play an important part in the **economies** of France and the **Low Countries**.

This supersonic jet was assembled in **France**. Several cities in southern France also produce **satellites**, **missiles**, and sophisticated **weapons**.

Name _______________ Use with pages 224–225

Using Maps with Different Scales

Use the maps below to answer the questions that follow. For help, you can refer to pages 224–225 in your textbook.

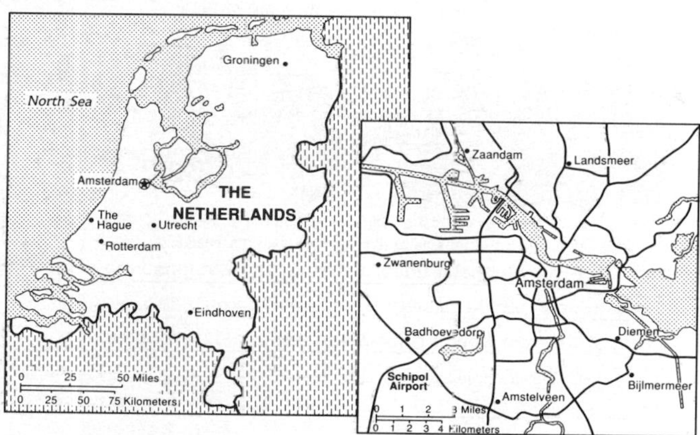

1. Which country does the small-scale map show?
   the Netherlands
2. What is the scale on the large-scale map?
   ¾ inch = 3 miles
3. Which part of the small-scale map is shown on the large-scale map?
   the area around Amsterdam
4. What is the scale on the small-scale map?
   1 inch = 50 miles
5. What does the large-scale map show that the small-scale map does not show?
   It shows more detail of the area around Amsterdam. It shows more cities and towns.
6. Suppose you were planning a vacation in a part of the Netherlands near Amsterdam. Which map would be more helpful? Why?
   The large-scale map would be more helpful because it provides more detailed information about the area.

Name _______________ Use with pages 226–227

Comparing Governments

Draw a line under the word or phrase that best completes each sentence. For help, you can refer to pages 226–227 in your textbook.

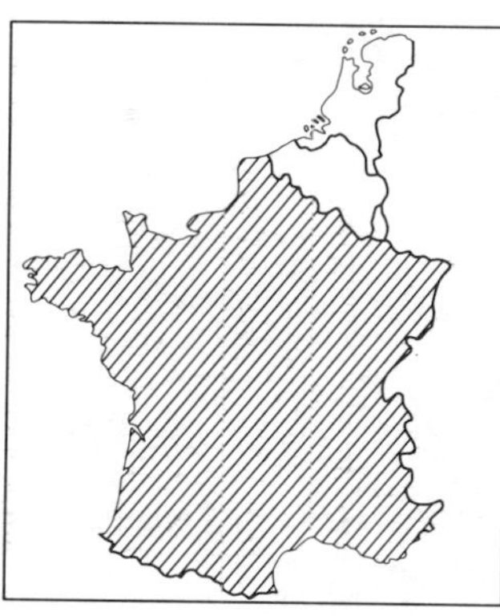

1. The current government of this country is called ______.
   a. a constitutional monarchy
   b. <u>the Fifth Republic</u>
   c. a dictatorship
2. This country's government is headed by a ______.
   a. monarch
   b. dictator
   c. <u>president</u>
3. In this country most of the important decisions are made by the ______.
   a. <u>president</u>
   b. National Assembly
   c. king or queen
4. The governments of these countries are all ______.
   a. <u>constitutional monarchies</u>
   b. republics
   c. dictatorships
5. The head of state in each of these countries is a ______.
   a. <u>monarch</u>
   b. dictator
   c. president
6. In these countries most of the important decisions are made by the ______.
   a. president
   b. <u>parliament</u>
   c. king or queen

Name _______________ Use with pages 228–229

People in the Arts and in Sports

Each picture below shows a person who has contributed to the arts or sports of France and the Low Countries. Draw a line from each picture to its correct description. Then complete each description with the correct word or words. For help, you can refer to pages 228–229 in your textbook.

1. 

2. 

3. 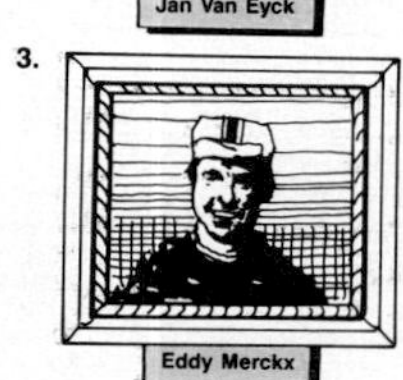

4. 

He is one of the Belgian painters who helped to invent new ways to show light in paintings. He is known as one of the **Old Masters**.

He is a Dutch painter who lived during the late 1800s. In 1988 his painting of **sunflowers** sold for almost $40 million.

He is a famous French painter of the late nineteenth century. He helped to develop a style of painting known as **impressionism**.

He has been a Belgian contender in the Tour de France. He has won this famous bicycle race **five** times.

Name _______________ Use with pages 230–231

Using New Words

Use the words in the box to complete the crossword puzzle below. For help, you can refer to the lessons in Chapter 10 of your textbook.

Tour de France	vineyard	polder
Impressionism		canal
guest worker	premier	dike

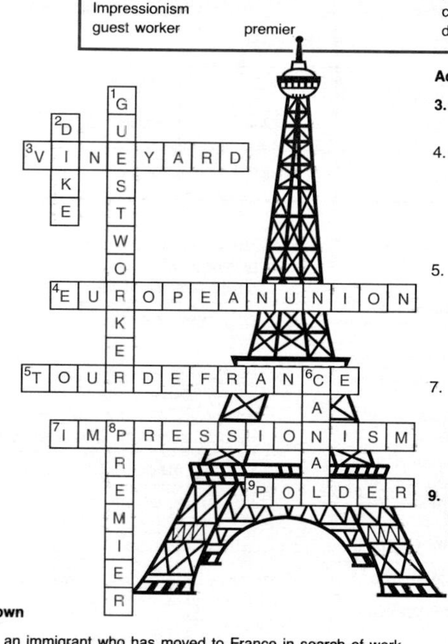

Across

3. an area used for growing grapes
4. a group of European countries that ended trade barriers with one another
5. a 2,500 mile (4,023 km) bicycle race that winds around the perimeter of France
7. a light filled style of painting that tries to capture the feeling of a place in a moment of time
9. a lowland area of the Netherlands that has been reclaimed from the sea

Down

1. an immigrant who has moved to France in search of work
2. a huge wall built to keep water away from the land
6. a waterway that is dug for boat travel
8. what the prime minister is called in France

Name — Use with pages 233–236

Taking a Look at Central Europe

Follow the directions and answer the questions below. For help, you can refer to pages 233–236 in your textbook.

1. Locate and label the following countries on the map.
   Germany
   Switzerland
   Austria
2. Locate the Alps and color them green.
3. a. Locate and label the largest city in Central Europe. **Berlin**
   b. Why was this city once a divided city? **because, until 1989, half was in West Germany and half in East Germany; the Berlin Wall separated them.**

Berlin
GERMANY
Vienna
AUSTRIA
SWITZERLAND
ALPS
green

4. How and when did reunification come about in Germany?
   Germany became reunified in 1990 after a movement for democracy swept through Europe; East Germans overthrew their government.
5. a. Locate and label the capital of Austria.
   Vienna
   b. Do most Austrians live in cities, such as the capital, or in rural areas?
   in cities and large towns
6. What two characteristics are common for most people of Central Europe?
   the German language; the Christian religion

Name — Use with pages 237–239

Thinking About Central Europe's Economy

Read the following statements carefully. If a statement is true, write **True** after it. If a statement is false, write **False** after it. Then, in the space provided, write the reasons for your answer. For help, you can refer to pages 237–239 in your textbook.

1. The picture above shows what most of Germany looked like at the end of World War II. The German people were never able to recover from such devastation.
   False. The East Germans under communism developed the most advanced economy in Eastern Europe and, in only 20 years, West Germany changed from a ruined land into a prosperous nation.
2. Since 1990 the Germans have found it easy to bring their two economies back together.
   False. It will cost billions of dollars and it has already cost nearly half the jobs in eastern Germany.
3. Today Germany's Ruhr Valley is Europe's biggest industrial center.
   True. Today the Ruhr Valley is crowded with coal and iron mines, oil refineries, chemical plants, and heavy industries.
4. The Swiss and Austrian peoples have low standards of living because their countries have few natural resources and little arable land.
   False. Despite few resources and little arable land, Switzerland has the highest standard of living in Europe, and Austria's economy benefits from tourism and industry.
5. Air and water pollution are a serious problem for the countries of Central Europe.
   True. Pollution is one price the region has had to pay for industrialization.

Name — Use with pages 240–241

The Governments of Central Europe

Use the table to answer questions 1 to 4. Then answer the question that follows. For help, you can refer to pages 240–241 in your textbook.

CENTRAL EUROPEAN GOVERNMENTS

Part of Government	Germany	Austria	Switzerland
two-house legislature	Bundestag	Nationalrat	Federal Assembly
head of state	president	president	president
head of government	chancellor	chancellor	Federal Council
local division of government	lander	province	canton

1. According to the table, how are the Bundestag, Nationalrat, and Federal Assembly similar?
   They are all two-house legislatures.
2. What is the head of state in each of the countries called?
   the president
3. What is the difference between the head of government in Switzerland and the head of government in Austria and Germany?
   A Federal Council, which is a group, heads the government in Switzerland. A chancellor heads the government in Germany and Austria.
4. a. How are lander, provinces, and cantons alike?
   They are all local divisions of government.
   b. In which country is pure democracy at work in its local division of government? Describe how it works.
   In Switzerland. Citizens hold regular meetings to make decisions on all local issues.
5. Why is the city of Geneva, Switzerland, the headquarters of many world organizations?
   because Switzerland is officially a neutral country

Name — Use with pages 242–243

Identifying a Biased Statement

Read each of the passages. Then follow the directions and answer the questions. For help, you can refer to pages 242–243 in your textbook.

Passage A

The Ruhr Valley is one of the largest industrial centers in Europe. Production from the region's factories has helped to make Germany one of the leading industrial nations of the world. But not without a price. The Ruhr is also one of the most polluted areas in Europe. Germany is taking steps to curb the pollution, but it will take time, money, and a serious commitment to solve the problem without seriously damaging Germany's economy.

Passage B

A heavy blanket of smog hangs over the entire Ruhr Valley. It is one of the most horrifying sights you can imagine. The greedy corporations responsible for the pollution care only about profits, not about the health of the nation's people. The German government must put an end to this national disgrace. Pollution generated by the region's industries must be stopped at once, no matter what the cost.

1. Recall the definition of bias. Write it here. **Bias is a one-sided, or slanted, presentation of information.**
2. Underline any loaded or emotionally charged words or phrases in either passage. Underline any words or phrases that are exaggerations.
3. Which passage presents only one side of the issue? passage A **(passage B)**
4. Which passage presents a one-sided view or impression about the pollution problem in the Ruhr Valley? passage A  **(passage B)**
5. Which passage do you think is a biased statement? passage A 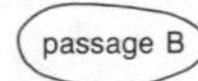 **(passage B)**
6. State the bias. **The writer of passage B shows a bias for immediately ending the pollution problem in the Ruhr Valley without considering the impact on the nation's economy.**

Name Use with pages 244–245

Arts and Recreation in Central Europe

Use the pictures on the right to complete the exercises below. For help, you can refer to pages 244–245 in your textbook.

1. a. Draw a line to the picture that shows one way Central Europe celebrates its musical heritage.

   b. Who are three well-known composers from Central Europe whose music is celebrated in this way?

   Mozart

   Beethoven

   Wagner

2. a. Draw a line to the picture that shows one way Central Europeans enjoy the outdoors.

   b. What are three other popular outdoor sports in Central Europe?

   rock climbing

   skiing

   bicycling

3. a. Draw a line to the picture that shows one way Central Europeans celebrate the harvest

   b. What are some of the things people do at festivals?

   People listen to brass bands, dress in colorful costumes, and eat delicious foods.

Name Use with pages 246–247

Using New Words

Follow the directions to find each hidden term. Then write the definition of the term on the line below the letters. For help, you can refer to the lessons in Chapter 11 in your textbook.

1. Cross out the letters b, o, r, s, u

   s d u i b a o l e r c t **dialect**

   local variation of a language

2. Cross out the letters d, g, i, s

   d c s h i a n i c e g l l o r **chancellor**

   what the head of government in Germany and Austria is called

3. Cross out the letters b, i, o, s

   s n b e o s u t i r a i l **neutral**

   refusing to take sides in any dispute

4. Cross out the letters a, c, k, r, s

   s p o a l l c u r a t i c o k n s **pollution**

   dirty and impure elements in the environment

5. Cross out the letters d, g, i, m

   i h g o l d o c d a u s m t **Holocaust**

   the killing of more than 6 million Jewish people by Germany and its allies during World War II

6. Cross out the letters b, k, d, h, l

   r l e u d n i f k i c h a t i b o n **reunification**

   being united again

7. Cross out the letters d, h, k, s, u

   s c a d n s t h o n k u **canton**

   a small political unit, like a state or province

Name Use with pages 249–252

The Southern European Countries

Answer the questions and complete the activities below. For help, you can refer to pages 249–252 in your textbook.

1. On the map below locate and label the following countries.

   Italy

   Spain

   Greece

   Portugal

2. What is this region called?

   Southern Europe

3. On the map below locate and label the following cities.

   Barcelona

   Rome

   Athens

4. From which of these cities did the ancient Romans once rule?

   Rome

5. On the map below shade in the countries where most of the people belong to the Roman Catholic Church. List them below.

   Spain, Portugal, Italy

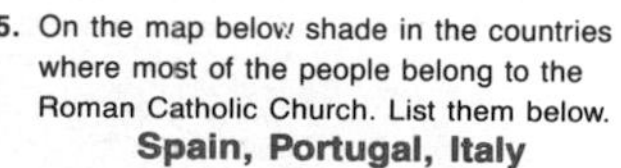

6. To which religion do most of the people in the remaining country belong?

   the Greek Orthodox Church

7. Outline each of the three countries where languages based on Latin are spoken. List them below.

   Spain

   Italy

   Portugal

8. Which Southern European country has a language that is written in a different alphabet from those of the other three?

   Greece

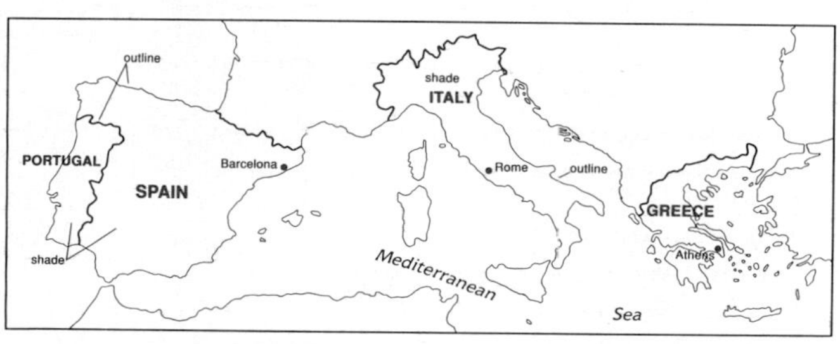

Name Use with page 253

Reading Graphs and Charts

Study the bar graph and the chart below. Then answer the questions that follow. For help, you can refer to page 253 in your textbook.

1. a. What does the bar graph show?

   areas of the four main countries of Southern Europe

   b. What does the horizontal axis of the graph show?

   the name of each country

   c. What does the vertical axis show?

   the area of each country

   d. According to the graph, which Southern European country has the largest area?

   Spain

AREA OF THE FOUR MAIN COUNTRIES OF SOUTHERN EUROPE

Source: World Almanac, 1989

2. a. According to the title, what does the chart show?

   the population and area of the four main countries of Southern Europe

   b. According to the chart, which country has the smallest area?

   Portugal

   c. Does this country also have the smallest population? If not, which country does?

   No. Greece has the smallest population.

POPULATION AND AREA OF THE FOUR MAIN COUNTRIES OF SOUTHERN EUROPE (1995)

Country	Population	Area (sq. mi.)
Greece	10,565,000	50,942
Italy	58,138,000	116,305
Portugal	10,524,000	35,552
Spain	39,303,000	194,884

3. If you wanted to compare information at a glance, would you use a chart or a bar graph? Circle your answer.

   chart **(bar graph)**

4. If you wanted to know actual figures, would you look at a chart or a bar graph? Circle your answer.

   (chart) bar graph

Name | Use with pages 254–256

Writing About Southern Europe's Economy

The travel brochure below tells about some of the things you might see and do in Southern Europe. Complete the brochure by filling in the blanks. For help, you can refer to pages 254–256 in your textbook.

Explore the Wonders of Southern Europe

Bask in the sun along the beautiful **Mediterranean** shore. Take a side trip to the village of Marbella on the **Spanish** coast. While in Athens, wander through the ancient remains of the **Parthenon**. Explore the ancient Forum on your visit to **Rome**. Everywhere you go you will see the splendid architecture of **churches**, **cathedrals**, **palaces**, and **towers.**

As you travel through the countryside, you will pass by the small farms that grow some of the sweetest **oranges** and **tangerines** in the world. Other crops produced in the region include **wheat**, **barley**, **nuts**, and **cotton**.

In **Turin** you can take a tour of the **Fiat** assembly lines. Every year more than one **million** cars are assembled here. Some of the finest leather goods in the world are made in factories in **Italy**, **Portugal**, and **Spain**.

If you arrived in Southern Europe by ship, the ship you were on may have been built by one of the shipping **families** that make the Greek island of **Oinoussai** their home. Greek shipowners control the largest **merchant** **fleet** in the world.

Name | Use with pages 257–260

Thinking About Today's Governments

Answer the questions below. For help, you can refer to pages 257–260 in your textbook.

1. a. What kind of government does this country have?
   parliamentary democracy
   b. How many houses does parliament have? Circle the answer.
   (one) two
   c. What is the head of government called?
   the prime minister

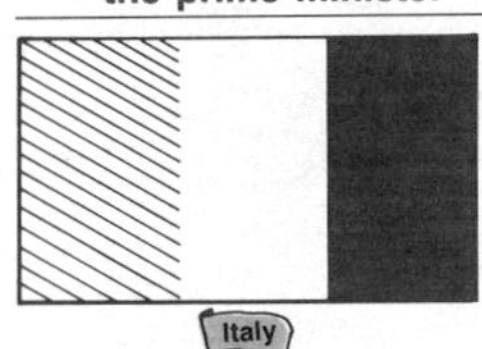

2. a. What kind of government does this country have?
   parliamentary democracy
   b. How many houses does parliament have? Circle the answer.
   one (two)
   c. Who runs the government from day to day?
   the prime minister

3. a. What kind of government does this country have?
   parliamentary democracy
   b. How many houses does parliament have? Circle the answer.
   (one) two
   c. Who shares executive power?
   president, prime minister

4. a. What kind of government does this country have?
   parliamentary democracy
   b. How many houses does parliament have? Circle the answer.
   one (two)
   c. Who is head of state?
   a monarch

Name | Use with pages 261–263

The Heritage of Southern Europe

Use the maps on the right to complete the activities below. For help, you can refer to pages 261–263 in your textbook.

1. a. Draw a line to the map of the country where the world's oldest dramas were written.
   b. What are the names of three poets who wrote these plays?
   Aeschylus
   Euripides
   Sophocles

2. a. Draw a line to the map of the country where the Renaissance began.
   b. What was the goal of the artists of this period?
   to create an image of the ideal human being
   c. Which Renaissance artist painted the inside of the Sistine Chapel?
   Michelangelo

3. a. Draw a line to the map of the country in which famous pilgrimages have been made for almost 2,000 years.
   b. What does this pilgrimage celebrate?
   the feast day of Santiago, the patron saint of Spain

ITALY

GREECE

SPAIN

Name | Use with pages 268–269

Learning New Words

Look at the box containing the Morse Code. The Morse Code uses dots and dashes to stand for the letters of the alphabet. Use the code to figure out the words that follow. For help, you can refer to the lessons in Chapter 12 in your textbook.

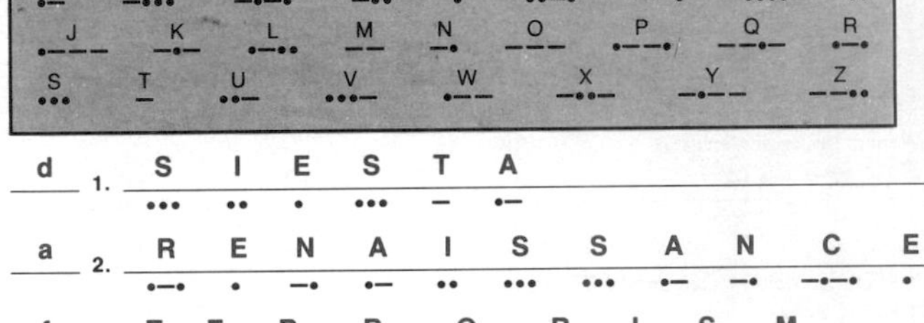

d 1. S I E S T A
a 2. R E N A I S S A N C E
f 3. T E R R O R I S M
c 4. A U T O N O M Y
b 5. C O A L I T I O N
e 6. P I L G R I M A G E

Match the definitions below with the words above. Write the letter of each definition on the line before the appropriate word.

a. a period of great activity in the arts beginning in the 1300s and 1400s
b. a temporary union between different political parties that agree to work together for a common purpose
c. the right of self-government
d. a period of rest taken during the middle of the afternoon
e. a journey that people make to a sacred place
f. the use of violence and the threat of violence to frighten people

Name Use with pages 271–273

The People of Scandinavia

Look at the picture and bar graph, then answer the questions. For help, you can refer to pages 271–273 in your textbook.

1. The picture shows a Viking warrior. Who were the Vikings?
   The Vikings were seafarers who lived in Scandinavia hundreds of years ago.

2. How do the people of Scandinavia today differ from their Viking ancestors?
   The Vikings were warlike seafarers. Today, the Scandinavians work at developing their own land and resources.

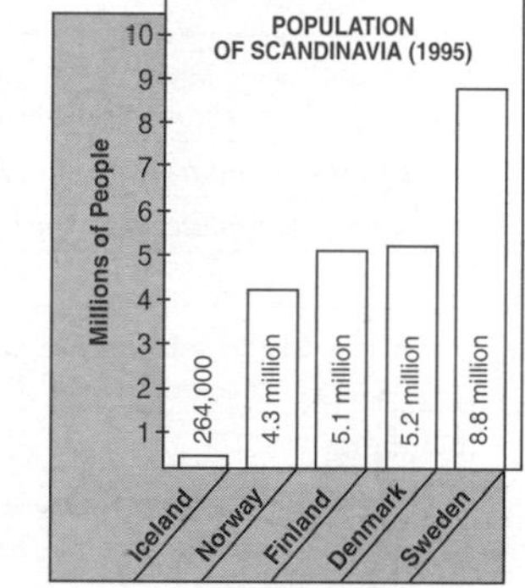

3. According to the graph, which Scandinavian country has the smallest population?
   Iceland

4. Which has the largest population?
   Sweden

5. How is the size of Scandinavia's population an advantage?
   Scandinavia's small population helps the Scandinavians get things done efficiently.

6. What ties the Scandinavian people together? **Most Scandinavians are tied together by languages and close-knit families.**

Name Use with pages 274–276

The Resources and Economy of Scandinavia

Use the map to complete the first five activities. Then answer the questions that follow. For help, you can refer to pages 274–276 in your textbook.

1. Draw a fish on the two countries where the fishing industry has played an important role in the economy.
   Norway, Iceland

2. Draw an oil barrel on the country that has Western Europe's largest fields of offshore oil and natural gas.
   Norway

3. Draw a tree on the two countries that have for hundreds of years based their economies on their huge forests.
   Finland, Sweden

4. Draw a factory on the country that is the most industrialized nation in Scandinavia.
   Sweden

5. Draw a chair on the country that is renowned for its furniture, glassware, and toys.
   Denmark

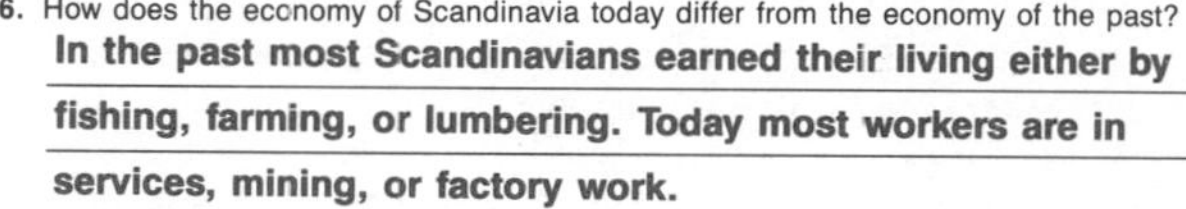

6. How does the economy of Scandinavia today differ from the economy of the past?
   In the past most Scandinavians earned their living either by fishing, farming, or lumbering. Today most workers are in services, mining, or factory work.

7. Why have the economies of the Scandinavian countries prospered?
   The Scandinavian economies have prospered because of cooperation between government and business, farming cooperatives, and cooperation among the different Scandinavian countries.

Name Use with pages 277–279

Taking a Look at Scandinavian Governments

Answer the questions below. For help, you can refer to pages 277–279 in your textbook.

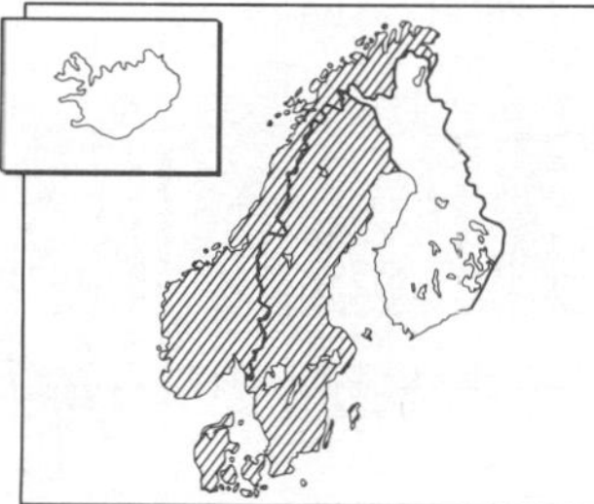

1. What form of government do these countries have?
   constitutional monarchies

2. How many houses make up the legislature in each of these countries?
   one

3. Who elects the head of the executive branch of government?
   the parliament

4. What is the head of government called?
   the prime minister

5. What form of government do these countries have?
   republics

6. How do the governments of these countries differ from those of Sweden, Norway, and Denmark?
   They each have a president, but neither has a monarch.

7. How are the governments of these countries like those of Sweden, Norway, and Denmark?
   They each have a parliament and a prime minister.

8. Why are the taxes in the Scandinavian countries so high? **Because the governments provide necessary services for their citizens through far-reaching welfare programs.**

Name Use with pages 280–281

Recognizing Point of View

Read the passages below. Then read the questions that follow and underline the answer to each question. For help, you can refer to pages 280–281 in your textbook.

The Swedish welfare state has come close to creating the ideal society. For example, just about everyone enjoys free medical service. The government loans newly married couples money for home furnishings. Every employed person is guaranteed a four-week vacation with pay. Swedes who lose their jobs receive generous unemployment benefits. After retirement most Swedes receive substantial retirement pensions. Sweden's welfare system takes the worry out of living.

1. Which of the following statements is a fact?
   a. The Swedish welfare system has come close to creating an ideal society.
   b. Just about everyone receives free medical service.
   c. Sweden's welfare system takes the worry out of living.

2. What information does the writer leave out?
   a. The Swedes pay the highest taxes in the world.
   b. After retirement, most Swedes receive substantial retirement pensions.
   c. Most Swedes receive free medical services.

3. What is the writer's point of view?
   The Swedish welfare system is good for its citizens.

The Swedish welfare state looks good on paper, but the price is too high. Sweden's tax rates are the highest in the world. Some people have to pay more than 75 percent of their earnings to the government. Many people believe that individuals should have the right to spend their money and plan for the future in the way they see fit. In my opinion the welfare state takes too much power from the people and places it in the hands of the government.

4. Which of the following statements is a fact?
   a. The Swedish welfare state looks good on paper, but the price is too high.
   b. Sweden's tax rates are the highest in the world.
   c. People have the right to spend their money and plan for the future in the way they see fit.

5. What information does the writer leave out?
   a. The Swedish government ensures the well-being of its citizens.
   b. Sweden's taxes are the highest in the world.
   c. Sweden's welfare state is very expensive.

6. What is the writer's point of view?
   The welfare state takes too much power from the people.

Name | Use with pages 282–283

Arts and Recreation in Scandinavia

Complete the activities below. For help, you can refer to pages 282–283 in your textbook. The excerpt below is from the poem entitled "Voluspa" on page 1, *Poems of the Elder Edda,* translated by Patricia Terry. Copyright © 1990 by the University of Pennsylvania Press. Reprinted by permission of Patricia Terry and the publisher.

Then all the gods
Met to give judgment,
The holy gods
Took counsel together;
They named night
and the waning moon,
They gave names
To morning and midday,
Afternoon and evening,
Ordered time by years.

1. The verse above is from an ancient **Edda.** What were Eddas and what did they tell about? **Eddas were long poems created by the Vikings. They told stories about early Scandinavian gods.**

2. What are the ancient **sagas** of Iceland and what do they tell about? **The sagas of Iceland are a long group of stories that tell about the history of that country.**

3. List three modern Scandinavian writers who have carried on this long tradition of storytelling. Tell what each wrote about.

WRITER	WROTE ABOUT
Henrik Ibsen	**wrote plays about the problems of contemporary men and women**
Selma Lagerlöf	**updated the folktales she heard as a child**
Sigrid Undset	**explored the history of her country and examined contemporary life**

Name | Use with pages 284–285

Thinking About New Words

Answer each question in the space provided. For help, you can refer to the lessons in Chapter 13 in your textbook.

1. What is a **diversified economy**? **A diversified economy is one that produces a wide range of goods.**

   Why do most Scandinavian countries now have diversified economies? **Skill, hard work in developing new resources, and modern factories have enabled most Scandinavian countries to now have diversified economies.**

2. Almost 200 years ago, Sweden created a special officer called an **ombudsman**. What does an ombudsman do? **An ombudsman receives complaints by citizens who are not satisfied with a government service or action. He or she informs government representatives about the problem and tries to persuade them to make changes.**

3. What is the difference between a Viking **Edda** and an Icelandic **saga**? What does each tell about? **A Viking Edda is a long poem that tells about the early Scandinavian gods. An Icelandic saga is a long story that tells about the history of that country.**

4. If you lived in Scandinavia, you might do business through a **cooperative**. What is a cooperative? **A cooperative is a business organization owned by its members.**

   How does a retail cooperative help consumers? **Retail cooperatives are owned by consumers. The consumers save money because items in the stores are sold at the cost the store paid to purchase them.**

Name | Use with pages 293–297

Using Maps

Use the map on this page to complete the exercises below. For help, you can refer to pages 293–297 in your textbook.

1. Locate and label the Ural Mountains. These mountains mark the boundary between which two continents? **Europe and Asia**

2. Locate and label these rivers. Then trace the rivers in blue.
   Volga River   Danube River

3. Locate and label the West Siberian Plain. What feature of its environment would make the West Siberian Plain an unpleasant place to live? **the fact that it is frozen for most of the year**

4. Locate and label Central Asia. Color the area brown. Why is Central Asia so dry? **because the mountains to its south block the rain-bearing clouds that would bring rain**

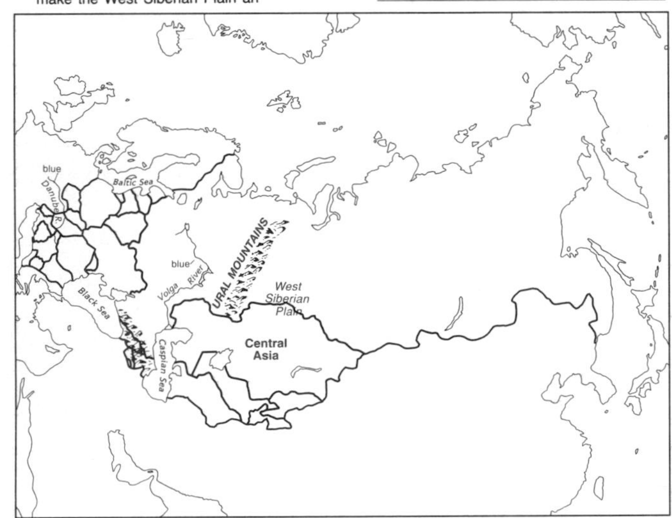

Name | Use with pages 298–300

Identifying Climates and Natural Resources

Study the pictures at the right. On the line beneath each picture write the letter of the place or places from the column at the left where you might find this scene. You may use a letter more than once or not at all. For help, you can refer to pages 298–300 in your textbook.

a. Romania
b. Siberia
c. steppes
d. Poland
e. taiga
f. Ukraine
g. Russia

evergreen forest: a, b, d, e, g

snowy landscape: a, b, d, f, g

wheat fields: c, f, g

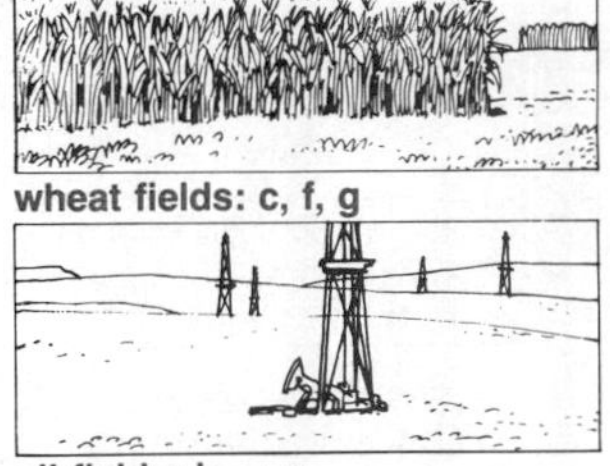

oil fields: b, a, g

Describe the two climate zones in Eastern Europe and Northern Asia.
Eastern Europe and the western part of Northern Asia have temperate climates with warm to hot summers and mild to cold winters. In Siberia and northern Eastern Europe the climate consists of short, cool summers and long, cold winters.

Name Use with page 301

Reading Climographs

Study the climograph below. Then answer the questions. For help, you can refer to page 301 in your textbook.

1. a. What does the bar graph of the climograph show?
average monthly precipitation in St. Petersburg

b. What does the line graph show?
average monthly temperature of St. Petersburg

AVERAGE PRECIPITATION AND TEMPERATURES IN ST. PETERSBURG

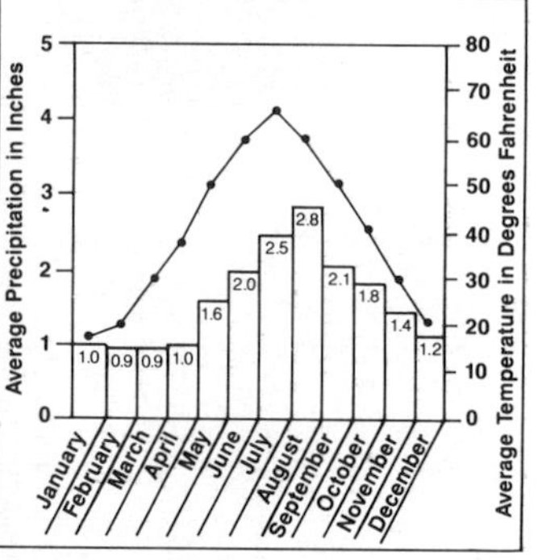

2. a. During which month is there the most precipitation?
August

b. What is the average temperature during this month?
60°

3. a. During which two months is there the least precipitation?
February and March

b. Which of the two months is generally cooler?
February

4. a. Suppose you were to visit St. Petersburg in July. How would you describe the weather?
warm and rainy

b. During which month do you think St. Petersburg has the most favorable weather? Why?
Answers should include information about the temperature and precipitation in the month selected.

Name Use with pages 302–303

Thinking About New Words

Put an **X** next to each statement that gives correct information about the word in boldface type. Then complete the activity that follows. For help, you can refer to the lessons in Chapter 14 in your textbook.

1. steppes

X **a.** Steppes are dry, treeless, grassy plains south of the taiga.
___ **b.** Steppes are vast regions of evergreen forests south of the tundra.
X **c.** Steppes cover much of Russia, Ukraine, and parts of Eastern Europe.
X **d.** The steppes of Europe contain some of the world's finest soil.
___ **e.** The steppes stretch all the way from Finland to the Pacific Ocean.
X **f.** Today the steppes of Northern Asia are a major grain-growing area.

2. taiga

___ **a.** The Eastern European countries are covered mostly by taiga.
X **b.** The taiga is a vast region of evergreen forests located south of the tundra.
___ **c.** The taiga is a dry, treeless, grassy plain located south of the steppes.
___ **d.** The taiga is one of the richest farming areas in the world.
X **e.** The taiga stretches all the way from Finland to the Pacific Ocean.
X **f.** Russia's vast regions of evergreen forests are located in the taiga.

Use the words *taiga* and *steppes* in a single sentence.
Example sentence: The taiga is a heavily forested region while the steppes are dry, treeless, grassy plains.

Name Use with pages 305–309

Taking a Look at Ethnic Groups

Read the following statements carefully. If a statement is true, write **True** after it. If a statement is false, write **False** after it. Then, in the space provided, write the reasons for your answer. For help, you can refer to pages 305–309 in your textbook.

1. Russia is part of a large country called the Soviet Union.
False. In late 1991 the Soviet Union ceased to exist. Russia and the other republics of the Soviet Union are now independent countries.

2. The largest ethnic groups in the region are the Uzbeks and Kazakhs.
False. The Russians, Ukrainians, and Belarusians make up nearly three fourths of the population in the region.

3. The people of Russia and its neighboring countires are now free to worship as they please.
True. Since the end of the Soviet Union, the governments in this region no longer discourage religion. There are Christians, Muslims, and Jews in the region.

4. In Russia women make up an important part of the work force.
True. About 85 percent of women of working age have jobs outside the home.

5. Even though there is no longer a Soviet Union in the region, education has changed little.
False. The schools are still there, but each government will run the schools as they choose. There is no longer a Soviet government requiring children to learn to believe in communism.

Name Use with pages 314–317

Economies of Russia and Its Neighbors

The headlines below might have been written about the economies of Russia and its neighbors. Answer the questions about each headline. For help, you can refer to pages 314–317 in your textbook.

Command Economy Slows Down

a. What is a command economy? an economy in which the government makes most of the decisions

b. What problems did people in the Soviet Union face under their command economy?
There were not enough consumer goods produced; workers were not motivated to do well in their work since they would be paid anyway; quality was often poor.

Gorbachev Seeks Change

a. What did Gorbachev call his plan of reforms? perestroika

b. How was Boris Yeltsin's plan different? Yeltsin's plan would have brought changes much more quickly; he wanted to shock the economy into the free-enterprise system

Commonwealth of Independent States Faces Many Challenges

a. In about what year would this headline have been written? 1991

b. Why was the Commonwealth of Independent States set up?
to help Russia and its neighbors link their economies in ways that would be helpful to make the transition from communism

c. What were three economic challenges faced by the C.I.S.?
Who would own the factories? How would electricity be shared? What would become of pensions owed people from jobs done in the former Soviet Union?

Name Use with pages 320–323

Using a Map

Use the map to complete the activities below. For help, you can refer to pages 320–323 in your textbook.

1. Which country took over the Kremlin, the Soviet Union's government offices in Moscow? **Russia**
   Label the country and color it green.
2. In which country are C.I.S. headquarters located? **Belarus**
   Label it and color it brown.
3. The C.I.S. was started by Russia, Belarus, and **Ukraine**.
   Label the third country and color it purple.
4. Which was the first non-Slavic country to join the C.I.S.? **Kazakhstan**
   Label it and color it yellow.
5. Label at least three other countries on the map.
6. What ideas of Lenin's were practiced in the Soviet Union until 1989?
   The government ran most economic affairs. The Communist Party controlled the government.

Name Use with pages 324–325

Drawing Conclusions

Put an **X** next to each conclusion you can draw from information in each of the boxes. For help, you can refer to pages 324–325 in your textbook.

- Whatever the size of the Russian family, both the men and the women usually work.
- About 85 percent of all Russian women of working age have jobs outside the home.
- Russian women hold many different kinds of jobs, from street cleaner to judge.
- About 75 percent of all Russian physicians are women.

_____ **a.** As many women as men work in Russia.

_____ **b.** Women have all the important jobs in Russia.

X **c.** In Russia most women of working age have jobs.

X **d.** Women are an important part of the Russian work force.

- Before the Soviet Union became 15 independent countries, the government controlled almost all economic and government decisions.
- Today 15 independent countries are each working to create mixed or free-enterprise economies.
- The C.I.S., set up in 1991, is a loose organization of most of the countries that used to be bound together by the Soviet Union.
- Leaders in each of the 15 countries were elected by their people.

X **a.** Enormous changes have come to the economies and governments of Russia and its neighbors.

_____ **b.** The people of the former Soviet Union are glad they now have their own countries.

_____ **c.** The 15 countries of the former Soviet Union are working together to solve their problems.

_____ **d.** Russia, through the C.I.S., still dominates its neighbors.

Name Use with pages 326–327

Arts and Recreation in Russia

Label each picture with a phrase from the box. Then answer the questions that follow. For help, you can refer to pages 326–327 in your textbook.

the father of Russian literature	won Nobel Prize for Literature in the 1950s
great Russian novelist of the 1800s	composed *The Nutcracker*

composed *The Nutcracker*

great Russian novelist of the 1800s

won Nobel Prize for Literature in 1950s

the father of Russian literature

1. In the past, what effect did the Soviet government have on the arts?
   Student responses may vary but should demonstrate an understanding of how strict government control of the arts was.
2. How did Mikhail Gorbachev's policy of glasnost affect the arts in the Soviet Union in the late 1980s? **Student responses may vary but should indicate that glasnost brought about less government control of the arts.**

Name Use with pages 328–329

Thinking About New Words

Write the letter of the term that matches each definition below. For help, you can refer to the lessons in Chapter 15 in your textbook.

a. Soviet	**d.** command economy	**g.** censor
b. consumer goods	**e.** perestroika	**h.** glasnost
c. capital goods	**f.** reform	
i. Commonwealth of Independent States		

e 1. the name of Mikhail Gorbachev's plan for economic reform in the Soviet Union

a 2. the name for people who lived in the former Soviet Union

g 3. to prevent something from being published

c 4. products that are used by other industries rather than by individuals

h 5. the name of Mikhail Gorbachev's policy of openness

d 6. a system in which the government makes most economic decisions

b 7. products, such as stoves, refrigerators, and clothes, that are used by individuals

i 8. an organization formed to promote cooperation among the countries that were once part of the Soviet Union

f 9. to make a change for the better

Name ______ Use with pages 331–334

The People of Eastern Europe

Czechoslovakia split into the Czech Republic and Slovakia in 1993. The charts on this page show you which of Czechoslovakia's ethnic groups now live in the Czech Republic and in Slovakia. Use the graphs to answer the questions on this page. For help, refer to pages 331–334 in your textbook.

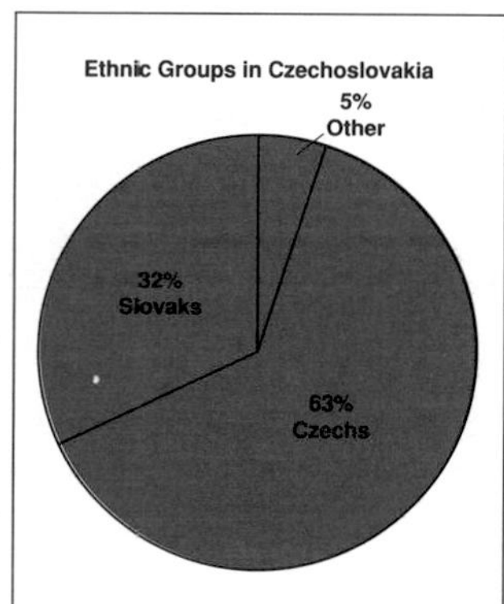

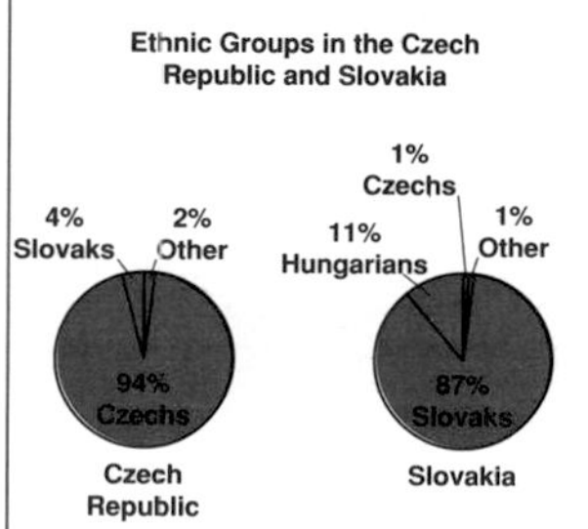

1. According to the top graph, which is the largest ethnic group in Czechoslovakia?
   Czechs
2. According to the top graph, which was the smaller ethnic group in Czechoslovakia?
   Slovaks
3. Which is the largest ethnic group in the Czech Republic?
   Czechs
4. What percentage of Slovakia's population are the Slovaks?
   87 percent
5. Using the map on page 332, discuss why you think more Hungarians live in Slovakia than in the Czech Republic.
   It is easier for Hungarians to reach Slovakia to the north.
6. Until the late 1980s how did the governments in Eastern European countries treat religion?
   They tried to discourage it.

Name ______ Use with pages 335–338

The Resources of Eastern Europe

Use the map to complete the activities. Then answer the questions that follow. For help, you can refer to pages 335–338 in your textbook.

1. Draw a piece of coal in the country where high-quality coal is mined.
   Students should identify Poland.
2. Draw a spice jar in the country where paprika is a specialty.
   Students should identify Hungary.
3. Draw a rose where rose petals are a specialty.
   What are the rose petals used for?
   Students should identify Bulgaria; to make perfume.
4. Draw a symbol for money in three countries where real progress is being made toward changing to a free market system.
   Students should identify Poland, Hungary, and the Czech Republic.
5. How was agriculture organized while Eastern European countries were satellites of the Soviet Union?
   in collectives, where the government owned all the farms and people worked in groups together to farm a certain area
6. In one sentence, state the main idea of Lesson 2.
   Enormous changes have come to the economies of the countries in Eastern Europe.

Name ______ Use with pages 339–342

Interviewing a Czech Leader

Suppose you had a chance to interview Vaclav Havel, who had been the first president of Czechoslovakia before becoming the president of the Czech Republic. You might ask him questions similar to those below. Use the space provided to write the answers you think Mr. Havel might give. For help, you can refer to pages 339–342 in your textbook.

Interviewer: What were some of the important events in your life before you were elected president of Czechoslovakia?

Mr. Havel: **I wrote plays, was sent to jail for opposing government, and rallied people in opposition to Soviet control**

Interviewer: What was the main change that resulted from the fall of the communist government in your country?

Mr. Havel: **The people now have freedom to make decisions about their lives.**

Interviewer: Have democracy and freedom come to all the countries in Eastern Europe?

Mr. Havel: **not equally; for example, the Czech Republic, Poland, and Hungary allow more freedom than does Bulgaria.**

Interviewer: What was the Warsaw Pact? What happened when it ended?

Mr. Havel: **The Warsaw Pact was a military alliance among the Soviet Union and its satellites; when it ended the Soviets began pulling their troops out of the countries in Eastern Europe.**

Interviewer: Was the change to freedom and democracy in neighboring countries always peaceful?

Mr. Havel: **No, in Romania several hundred people were killed and the former leader was executed.**

Name ______ Use with pages 343–344

The Arts and Recreation of Eastern Europe

Answer the questions below. For help, you can refer to pages 343–344 in your textbook.

1. Look at the picture. From which Eastern European country did this composer come?
   Poland
2. What did this composer use as themes for much of his music?
   Eastern European folk music
3. Which other Eastern European composer was inspired by the music of his homeland?
   Anton Dvořák, Béla Bartók

SUMMER OLYMPIC MEDAL TOTALS FOR SELECTED EASTERN EUROPEAN COUNTRIES

1988			1992			1996		
Country	Total	Rank	Country	Total	Rank	Country	Total	Rank
Bulgaria	35	5th	Hungary	30	6th	Hungary	21	12th
Romania	24	8th	Poland	19	14th	Romania	20	13th
Hungary	23	10th	Romania	18	16th	Poland	17	15th
Poland	16	12th	Bulgaria	16	17th	Bulgaria	15	17th

The chart gives information about how athletes from the four main Eastern European countries did in the last three Summer Olympic games. Use the chart to answer these questions.

4. In the 1988 Summer Olympics, which Eastern European countries finished among the top ten medal winners? In 1996?
   Bulgaria, Romania, and Hungary; none
5. What was the main reason for the success of athletes of these countries?
   There was a national emphasis on sports.
6. How might the political changes since 1989 have affected the performance of Eastern European countries in the Olympic games?
   While the countries still value success in sports, changing economic conditions have made it difficult to support sports in the same way.

Name Use with page 345

Reading a Newspaper Article

In June 1991 Soviet troops withdrew from Hungary. The paragraphs below might have appeared in a newspaper article describing the event. Label the headline and dateline. Then answer the questions. For help, you can refer to page 345 in your textbook.

headline

dateline

SOVIET TROOPS
LEAVE HUNGARY

Budapest, June 30—The last Soviet troops pulled out of Hungary this month, ending almost 47 years of occupation. The pullout followed months of dizzying changes in Hungary, where the first multi-party elections were held last October.

Reaction to the Soviet pullout was positive. One university student remarked, "Finally we are free to run our own lives, without interference from outside forces."

Soviet troops had been stationed in Hungary since 1956, when they were called in to crush an anti-Soviet uprising in the country.

1. The article might have appeared on page one of a newspaper. What kind of article is it?
   news article
2. What is the article about?
   the pullout of Soviet troops from Hungary after a 47-year occupation
3. Where did the event take place?
   Budapest
4. When did the event take place?
   the month ending June 30
5. In which kind of article might you read an editor's opinion about the pullout of Soviet troops?
   an editorial

Name Use with pages 346–347

Thinking About New Words

Use the code to figure out the words and write each word under its code in the left column. Then write the number of each word next to its meaning in the right column. For help, you can refer to the lessons in Chapter 16 in your textbook.

CODE

z=a	w=g	t=m	q=s	n=y
13=b	10=h	7=n	4=t	1=z
y=c	v=i	s=o	p=u	
12=d	9=j	6=p	3=v	
x=e	u=k	r=q	o=w	
11=f	8=l	5=r	2=x	

1. 7 z 4 v s 7 z 8 v q t
   nationalism
2. q z 4 x 8 8 v 4 x
   satellite
3. y n 5 v 8 8 v y
   Cyrillic
4. r p s 4 z
   quota
5. o z 5 q z o 6 z y 4
   Warsaw Pact
6. 13 p 11 11 x 5 1 s 7 x
   buffer zone

3 a. the alphabet used by the Russian language

6 b. a region between two hostile powers

4 c. a limit on the type and amount of a product that can be sold or produced

1 d. a strong love of one's country or ethnic group

2 e. a country that "revolved" around the Soviet Union

5 f. a military alliance of the Soviet Union and its satellites that ended in 1991

Name Use with pages 355–359

The Middle East and North Africa

Use the map on this page to complete the activities below. For help, you can refer to pages 355–359 in your textbook.

1. a. Locate and label the following peninsulas.
   Sinai Peninsula Anatolia
   Arabian Peninsula
   b. Which peninsula connects the continents of Africa and Asia?
   Sinai Peninsula
2. a. Locate and label the Sahara Desert. Then color it brown.
   b. What group has developed the special skills needed to survive in the desert?
   The Bedouins (desert dwellers)
3. Locate and label the following bodies of water.
   Mediterranean Sea Red Sea
   Persian Gulf
4. a. Locate and label the following rivers. Then trace the rivers in blue.
   Nile River Tigris River
   Euphrates River
   b. Why are the areas along these rivers densely populated?
   because they provide fertile soil and water for irrigation
5. a. Locate and label the following cities.
   Riyadh Jerusalem
   b. Which of these cities grew up around a desert oasis?
   Riyadh

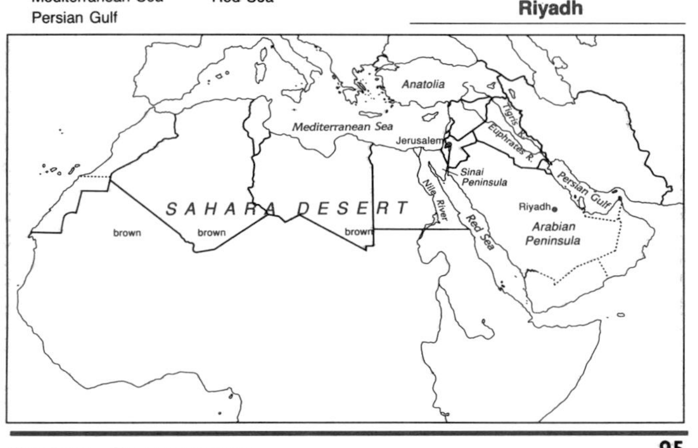

Name Use with pages 360–361

Reading Contour Maps

Use the contour map of Cyprus below to answer the questions. For help, you can refer to pages 360–361 in your textbook.

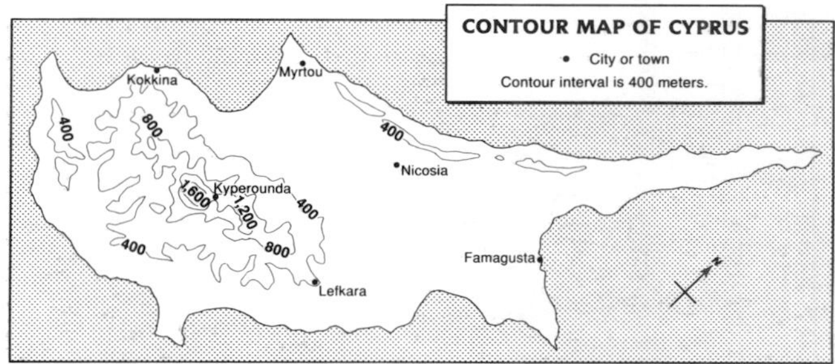

1. What is the elevation of Lefkara?
   about 400 meters above sea level
   How do you know?
   Lefkara is within the 400-meter contour line
2. Is the land around Kyperounda steep or level?
   steep
   How do you know?
   the contour lines are close together
3. List the cities on the map whose elevation is between sea level and 400 meters.
   Kokkina, Myrtou, Nicosia, Famagusta
4. Which part of Cyprus is more level, the western part or the eastern part?
   the eastern part
   How do you know?
   by the pattern and spacing of the contour lines

Name   Use with pages 362–365

Looking at Natural Resources

The bar graph below shows the major oil-producing countries in the Middle East and North Africa. Use the graph to answer the first three questions on this page. Then answer the following questions. For help, you can refer to pages 362–365 in your textbook.

SELECTED OPEC OIL PRODUCTION (1995)

Country	Oil Production (millions of barrels)
Iraq	203
Libya	507
Kuwait	751
United Arab Emirates	830
Iran	1,329
Saudi Arabia	3,004

Scale: 250 500 750 1000 1250 1500 1750 2000 2250 2500 2750 3000 — Oil Production (millions of barrels)

1. According to the graph, which country produces the most oil in the Middle East?
   Saudi Arabia
2. What are three other Middle Eastern countries shown on the graph? List them according to the amount of oil they produce.
   Iran   **Iraq**   **Kuwait**
3. Which North African country is shown on the graph?
   Libya
4. Where does most of the Middle East's oil lie? **Most of the Middle East's oil lie beneath the lands bordering on the Persian Gulf.**
5. About which percent of the petroleum used in the world today comes from the Middle East? **about one third**
6. Which natural resource would many people in the Middle East and North Africa consider more valuable than oil? Why? **Water.**
   In this arid region water is so scarce that farmers rely upon rivers for irrigation. Little of the land can be farmed.

Name   Use with pages 366–367

Thinking About New Words

Each of the words listed in the box below is hidden among the letters that follow. Draw a circle around each word you find. The words may be read forward, backward, up, down, or diagonally. For help, you can refer to the lessons in Chapter 17 in your textbook.

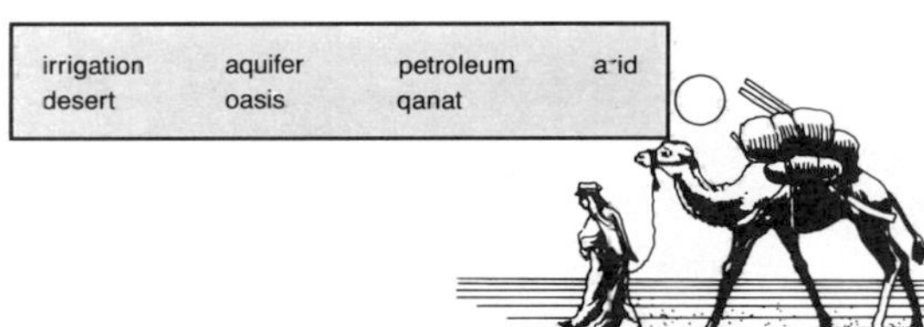

L U T S S Q P R E F U G E E T P H M L K I O C A

T B N O I T A G I R R I D I O Z C Y D C F J P W

D K T A S B A Z R M R E F I U Q A M T Q E T Q R

F D C Q A Y Z E A T R N P R O B T Y R A R S D E

C A R A O N O U E L B S C K D Z T R E K N J L K

I T O P Q J R S K C L P E I C K N B E E K A M O

C E I W C K E A H P E T R O L E U M H S E L Q Y

E T A D R D M S D P N A N M T E V X O E E J A D

U A O Q S O E Z L T W U E C A Z B K M E Q D E N

T Z A K S E D U D Z H N Y F E U R D I W S L A O

Write each circled word in the space next to its definition.

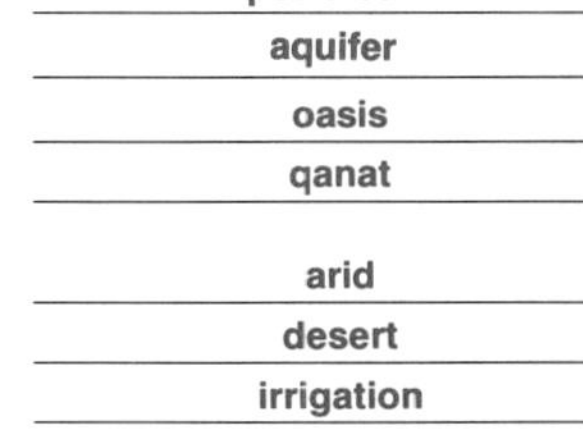

petroleum 1. oil

aquifer 2. an underground layer of rock that holds or carries water

oasis 3. a green, fertile, well-watered spot in a desert

qanat 4. massive underground tunnels built in Iran to carry water

arid 5. very dry

desert 6. a dry, sandy region with very little plant life

irrigation 7. the watering of dry land by means of streams, canals, or pipes

Name   Use with pages 369–372

The People of the Middle East

Review the picture on this page. Then answer the questions below. For help, you can refer to pages 369–372 in your textbook.

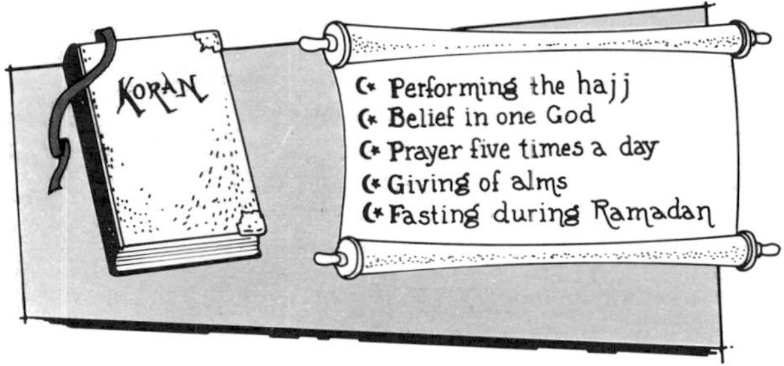

1. The religious book and the list of beliefs show above form the basis of the major religion in the Middle East. What is the name of that religion?
   Islam
2. What is the list of beliefs called?
   the five pillars of Islam
3. How was this religion spread throughout the Middle East?
   The followers of Muhammad carried Islam from the Arabian Peninsula throughout the Middle East.
4. What are two Middle Eastern countries where most of the people are Muslims, but are not Arab?
   Turkey
   Iran
5. What are some special rules that apply to women in Saudi Arabia?
   In Saudi Arabia, women cannot drive cars or shop in some stores.
6. What are two Middle Eastern countries where many of the people are Christians?
   Cyprus
   Lebanon
7. In which Middle Eastern country are most of the people Jewish?
   Israel
8. What role does religion play in the lives of most people in the Middle East?
   Responses should indicate that the lives of most of the people are organized around religion.

Name   Use with pages 373–376

Observing Contrasts in the Middle East

Use the pictures on the right to complete the activities on this page. For help, you can refer to pages 373–376 in your textbook.

1. a. Draw a line to the picture that shows the product that is most important to the economies of many Middle Eastern countries.
   b. Which Middle Eastern country has a highly developed economy without dependence on this product?
   Israel

Israeli Kibbutz

2. a. Draw a line to the picture that shows a modern way of farming in the Middle East.
   b. By contrast, what kinds of methods are used on many traditional farms in the Middle East?
   labor-intensive methods

Pollution

3. a. Draw a line to the picture that shows one effect of the war in the Persian Gulf.
   b. What effect did this action have on the environment and on Kuwait's oil production?
   The fires polluted the air and stopped much of Kuwait's oil production.

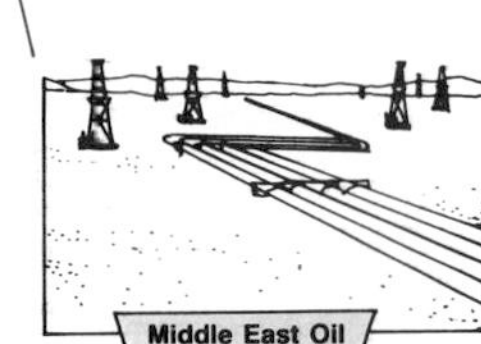

Middle East Oil

4. How is the economy of the Middle East both modern and traditional?
   Most of the people of the Middle East earn their living in the traditional ways of commerce and farming. Yet, money from oil has changed the economies of some of the countries of this region.

Name | Use with pages 377–379

Comparing Governments of the Middle East

Draw a line under the word or phrase that best completes each sentence. For help, you can refer to pages 377–379 in your textbook.

1. The man pictured above is the ______ of Oman.
   a. premier
   b. president
   c. absolute ruler
2. Oman has no constitution and ______.
   a. no elections
   b. no strong leaders
   c. no tradition of democracy
3. Turkey, a Muslim country, has a ______ form of government.
   a. democratic
   b. weak
   c. religious
4. The governments of most Muslim countries are based on ______ law.
   a. Jewish
   b. Christian
   c. Islamic
5. The man pictured above was the ______ of Israel.
   a. prime minister
   b. president
   c. absolute ruler
6. Israel has a ______ government.
   a. strong, centralized
   b. weak, federal
   c. parliamentary
7. The government of Israel is influenced by ______ law.
   a. Jewish
   b. Christian
   c. Muslim
8. The citizens of Israel have democratic rights and ______.
   a. free elections
   b. an absolute ruler
   c. no religious freedom

Name | Use with pages 380–381

Comparing Maps

Use the maps of Egypt below to answer the questions that follow. For help, you can refer to pages 380–381 in your textbook.

MAP A
Distribution of Farm Products

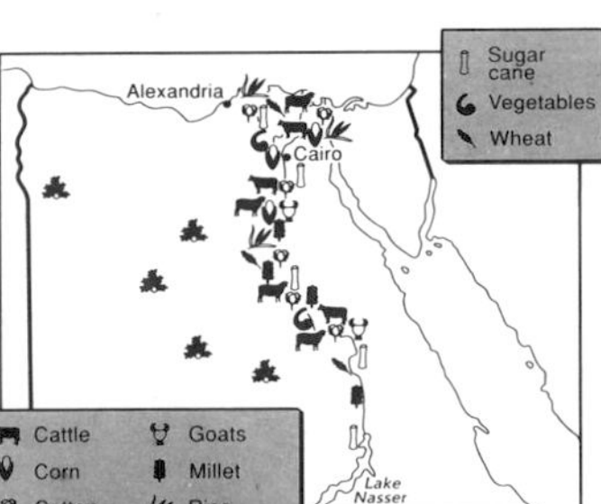

MAP B
Major Oases

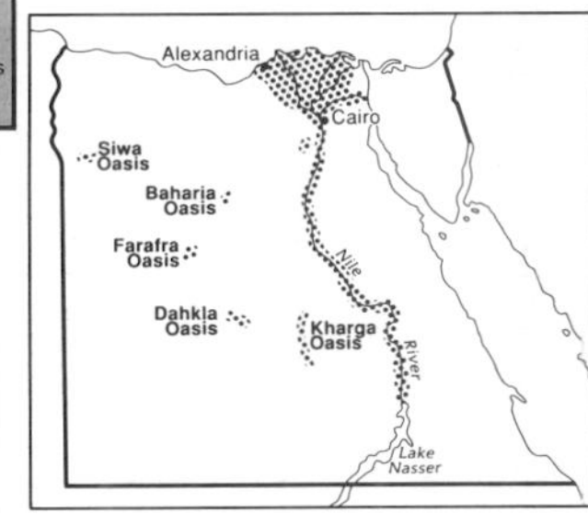

1. What do the two maps show?
   Map A: distribution of farm products in Egypt
   Map B: major oases in Egypt
2. According to Map A, what are three crops grown in the region of the Nile Delta? sugar cane, corn, wheat, rice, cotton, vegetables
3. What two kinds of farm animals are raised in this area? cattle and sheep
4. What is the only crop grown away from the Nile River? dates
5. Compare Map A with Map B. What two factors seem to determine where farm products are grown in Egypt? the Nile River; the location of oases
6. What farm product is grown around Egypt's major oases? dates

Name | Use with pages 382–383

The Arts in the Middle East

Use the pictures below to complete the activities on this page. For help, you can refer to pages 382–383 in your textbook.

1. a. What is the form of writing in this picture called? calligraphy
   b. What is one collection of Middle Eastern tales that may have been recorded in this form of writing? Arabian Nights
   c. Where might you see writing like this today? in the Koran and other Arabic and Muslim works and as decoration on the walls of buildings

2. a. Along with intricate designs, what else do you see in this picture of an Islamic mosaic? trees, clouds, flowers
   b. Why aren't animals and people depicted in most Islamic art? Islam discourages showing animals and humans in order to prevent people from praying to idols.
   c. Where might you see some of the finest Islamic designs today? on mosques and carpets

Name | Use with pages 384–385

Thinking About New Words

Write the letter of the term in the box that matches each description below. For help, you can refer to the lessons in Chapter 18 in your textbook.

a. labor-intensive	e. kibbutz	i. moshav
b. absolute ruler	f. bazaar	j. Islam
c. calligraphy	g. Islamic republic	
d. hajj	h. sharia	

d 1. the Arabic word for the pilgrimage that Muslims make to the city of Mecca
j 2. a religion based on the teachings of Muhammad
c 3. a type of Arabic writing that features graceful, flowing lines
g 4. the term for a nation ruled by Islamic law
a 5. using many people rather than machinery to do work
i 6. an Israeli cooperative farm
b 7. one with complete power whose authority cannot be challenged
f 8. an outdoor market
h 9. Islamic law
e 10. an Israeli collective farm

Name Use with pages 387–390

The People of North Africa

The graph below shows Egypt's population in the past and what the population is likely to be in the future. Review the graph and then answer the questions that follow. For help, you can refer to pages 387–390 in your textbook.

EGYPT'S POPULATION GROWTH (*projected figures)

Population (millions): 10, 20, 30, 40, 50, 60, 70, 80, 90, 100, 110

Year: 1975, 1980, 1985, 1990, 1995, 2000*, 2005*, 2010*, 2015*, 2020*, 2025*

1976 (36.6); 1988 (50.3); 1990 (52.7); 1995 (60.8); 2000 (67.2); 2025 (109.8)

1. According to the graph, what has been happening to Egypt's population?
   It has been growing at a rapid rate.

2. What does the graph show will happen to Egypt's population in the future?
   It will continue to grow rapidly.

3. What are some of the problems that the people of North Africa share because of the rapidly growing population?
   Most of the cities are overcrowded, and food shortages are common.

4. How has improved health care influenced the explosive growth of North Africa's population?
   North Africans are now living longer than they did before.

5. In which ways does Islam affect the people of North Africa?
   Islam shapes the way the people live, work, and play. It also has a strong effect on the government, education, and customs of North Africa.

6. How do many people in North Africa feel about influences from European cultures?
   They want to cut all ties to their European past and return to a stricter form of Muslim life.

Name Use with pages 391–393

The Economy of North Africa

Complete the map by writing the phrases from the box in the spaces provided on the map. Each space should have a separate phrase. Then answer the questions that follow. For help, you can refer to pages 391–393 in your textbook.

grew enough food for its people until the 1980s
major oil producing countries
second-largest industrialized nation in Africa
Aswan High Dam provides water for irrigation

grew enough food for its people until the 1980s

second-largest industrialized nation in Africa

MOROCCO
TUNISIA
ALGERIA
LIBYA
EGYPT
WESTERN SAHARA
Nile River

major oil-producing countries

Aswan High Dam provides water for irrigation

1. Why must most of the countries of North Africa import food? **Responses may vary but should demonstrate an understanding that there is little usable farmland in North Africa and that as the population increases, this land is also being used for other things such as housing, business, and roads.**

2. On what does the economic future of North Africa depend? **the way the people of the region use their water and oil resources**

Name Use with pages 398–399

The Assassination of Anwar Sadat

The headlines and articles below are from the October 7, 1981, issue of *The New York Times*. Read the headlines and articles and then answer the questions that follow. For help, you can refer to pages 398–399 in your textbook.

SADAT ASSASSINATED AT ARMY PARADE AS MEN AMID RANKS FIRE INTO STANDS; VICE PRESIDENT AFFIRMS 'ALL TREATIES'

Israel Stunned and Anxious; Few Arab Nations Mourning

WORRY IN JERUSALEM

JERUSALEM, Oct. 6—Israel, which had such a high stake in the survival of President Anwar el-Sadat, reacted with stunned anxiety today to the assassination in Cairo.

A fear for the peace treaty between Egypt and Israel dominated all emotions.

JUBILATION IN BEIRUT

BEIRUT, Lebanon, Oct. 6—There was no mourning in most of the Arab world today for President Anwar el-Sadat of Egypt, whose separate peace with Israel had led to his isolation.

Public jubilation was reported in the streets of Syria, Iraq, and Libya. . . .

1. According to the articles, who was Sadat and what happened to him?
   Sadat was the president of Egypt and was assassinated while he watched an army parade.

2. According to the articles, how did many of the Arab countries feel about what happened to Sadat? **There was no mourning in most of the Arab World. Syria, Libya, and Iraq were jubilant.**

3. According to the articles, what had isolated Sadat from the other Arab countries?
   He had signed a separate peace treaty with Israel.

4. According to the articles, why was Israel worried about the assassination?
   Israel was afraid something might happen to the peace treaty it had signed with Egypt.

Name Use with pages 400–401

Asking the Right Questions

Use the picture and caption below to complete the activity that follows. For help, you can refer to pages 400–401 in your textbook.

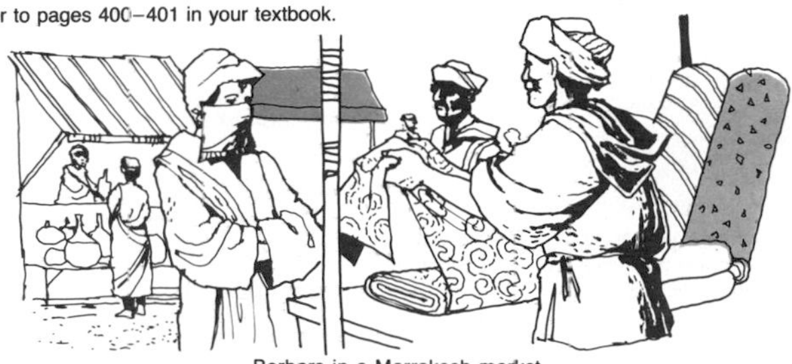

Berbers in a Marrakesh market.

Suppose a friend of yours had recently returned from a trip to Morocco. As you looked through his photographs of the trip, you came across the one shown above. You knew nothing about the Berbers except what was written under the picture. Yet you became interested in them as a topic of study. Place an X next to each question that would help you to learn more about the topic.

X a. Who are the Berbers?
X b. Where did the Berbers come from?
___ c. What kinds of things can you buy in a Marrakesh market?
X d. Why were Berbers in a Marrakesh market?
___ e. In which part of Africa is Morocco?
X f. How and where do most Berbers live?
___ g. What is the population of Morocco?
X h. How long have there been Berbers in Morocco, and are there Berbers in other parts of the world?
X i. Why is the woman in the picture wearing a veil?
X j. What are some Berber customs and religious practices?
___ k. What is the major religion of the people of North Africa?
___ l. Who are the people that operate the markets in Marrakesh?

Name Use with pages 402–403

Islamic Influence on the Arts and Recreation

Briefly explain how Islam influences each of the activities shown below. For help, you can refer to pages 402–403 in your textbook.

ARTISTIC AND RECREATIONAL ACTIVITIES	ISLAMIC INFLUENCE
	Paintings are often traditional with religious themes. Wall paintings of pilgrimages are a very popular form of North African folk art.
	One of the favorite themes is the importance of keeping Islamic traditions alive in a constantly changing world.
	Religious holidays are the most important days of the year for Muslims. Presents are exchanged on Muhammad's birthday. The holy month of Ramadan is observed.
	Television programming in North Africa is interrupted to allow Muslims time to pray.

Name Use with pages 404–405

Using New Words

Use the code in the box to figure out each word. For help, you can refer to the lessons in Chapter 19 in your textbook.

CODE

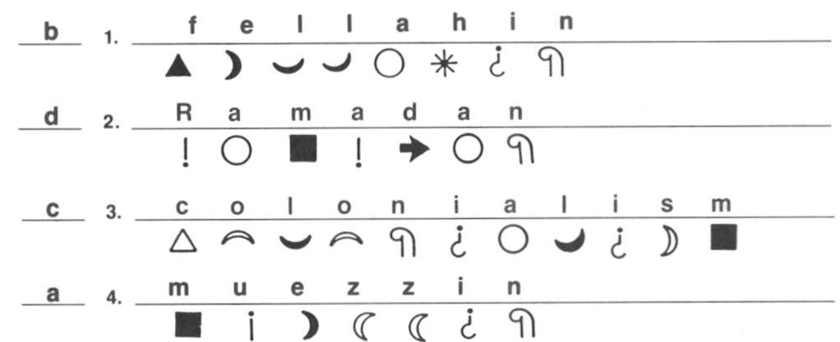

b 1. f e l l a h i n

d 2. R a m a d a n

c 3. c o l o n i a l i s m

a 4. m u e z z i n

In the space before each decoded word above, write the letter of each definition it matches.

a. a crier who announces each of the five times every day when Muslims are supposed to pray

b. an Egyptian farmer

c. the control of a country as a colony by another country

d. the most holy month of the Muslim year

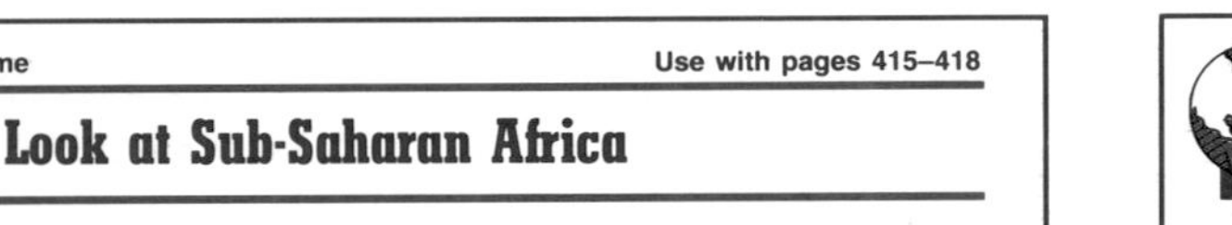

Name Use with pages 415–418

A Look at Sub-Saharan Africa

Read the directions and complete the map activities below. For help, you can refer to pages 415–418 in your textbook.

1. Locate and label the following regions of Sub-Saharan Africa. Then color each region as indicated.
   a. West Africa—brown
   b. East and Equatorial Africa—green
   c. Southern Africa—orange
2. Locate and label the following landforms.
   Mount Kilimanjaro Mount Kenya
   Zaire Basin Ethiopian Highlands
3. Locate and label Madagascar.
4. Locate and label the Great Rift Valley. Then color it red.
5. Locate and label the following bodies of water. Color the lake and trace the rivers in blue.
   Lake Victoria Niger River
   Zaire River Nile River

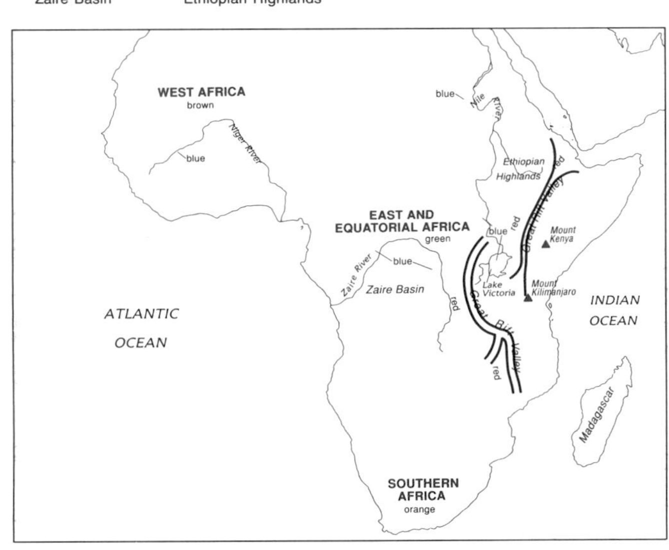

Name Use with page 419

Figuring Distances

Study the chart below. Then answer the questions that follow. For help, you can refer to page 419 in your textbook.

Road Distances in Miles	Jinga	Kampala	Mombasa	Nairobi	Tanga
Jinga		50	668	364	764
Kampala	50		718	414	814
Mombasa	668	718		304	96
Nairobi	364	414	304		401
Tanga	764	814	96	401	

1. What is the chart above called?
   a mileage chart
2. For what purpose is this kind of chart used?
   finding the distances between cities
3. How far is it from Kampala to Nairobi?
   414 miles
4. Would you travel farther going from Kampala to Nairobi or going from Nairobi to Jinga?
   going from Kampala to Nairobi
5. Using a car, which trip could you most likely take in a day—from Nairobi to Jinga or from Mombasa to Tanga?
   from Mombasa to Tanga
6. If you traveled by car from Jinga to Nairobi, on to Tanga, and then on to Mombasa, how many miles would you drive?
   861 miles
7. Are the distances you found on the chart by land or by air? How do you know?
   They are by land because a label on the chart says they are "road distances."
8. How could you use a map to find the same information that you found on the chart?
   You could use the scale bar on a map to measure the distances between cities.

Name Use with pages 420–423

The Resources of Sub-Saharan Africa

Read the following statements carefully. If a statement is true, write **True** in the space provided. If a statement is false, write **False** after it. Then write the reason for your answer. For help, you can refer to pages 420–423 in your textbook.

1. The picture above shows a herd of migrating animals at a drinking hole on the African savanna. Migrating wildlife is an important resource in Sub-Saharan Africa.
   True. Tourists come from all over the world to see African wildlife in its natural setting.
2. The entire African savanna is densely populated. **False. About one fourth of the savanna has very few people because the tsetse fly breeds there.**
3. In some areas of the savanna, people can raise grain crops. **True. In areas of the savanna that have enough rain, residents can raise crops like millet or corn.**
4. The rain forest of Sub-Saharan Africa provides many products and natural resources.
   True. The rain forest provides coffee, rubber, palm oil, and other products. Timber from such trees as mahogany, teak, ebony, cedar, and walnut is also a major resource of the rain forest.
5. Sub-Saharan Africa has very few mineral resources. **False. Sub-Saharan Africa is a storehouse of minerals. Copper, iron, gold, uranium, diamonds, manganese and many other minerals have been found in the region.**

Name Use with pages 424–425

Thinking About New Words

Answer each question in the space provided. For help, you can refer to the lessons in Chapter 20 in your textbook.

1. What is a **rift valley**? **A rift valley is a narrow valley with steep sides formed millions of years ago by cracks in the earth's crust.**

   What is the name of the large area of rift valleys in Sub-Saharan Africa?
   the Great Rift Valley
2. What is an **escarpment**? **An escarpment is a steep cliff at the edge of**

   What happens when a river flows over an escarpment? **A river flowing over an escarpment creates a waterfall.**
3. Why did sailors refer to the winds of Sub-Saharan Africa as **trade winds**?
   The winds determined which way trading ships could sail.
4. What is the **harmattan** and how does it affect the climate in Sub-Saharan Africa?
   The harmattan is a wind that carries dry, dusty air from the Sahara to Sub-Saharan Africa, where it creates a hot, dry season.
5. What is a **savanna** and how much of the African continent is covered by it?
   A savanna is a broad grassland containing scattered trees and shrubs. The savanna covers more than one fourth of Africa.
6. What is a **basin**? **A basin is a large, bowl-shaped dip in the land.**

   Why is the huge Zaire Basin sometimes called "The Heart of Africa"?
   because this place of dense rain forests, swamps, and winding rivers is at the center of Africa
7. What is a **drought**, and how have droughts affected many of the people of Africa?
   A drought is a lack of rain over a period of time. Millions of Africans have died because of droughts.

Name Use with pages 427–431

Influences on West African Cultures

Study the picture and answer the questions below. For help, you can refer to pages 427–431 in your textbook.

1. The picture above shows what a mosque might have looked like in West Africa hundreds of years ago. How and when did Islam reach this part of Africa?
   Islam reached West Africa more than 1,000 years ago when Arab and Berber traders brought Muslim ideas across the Sahara from North Africa.
2. How has the religion of Islam influenced the cultures of West Africa today?
   Today Islam is the major religion in most of West Africa.
3. a. What happened in the 1500s that had a major influence on West African cultures?
   Europeans reached West Africa in the 1500s and began to establish colonies.

   b. What was the result of this event? **For many years most West African countries were ruled as colonies by European powers.**

   c. How has this influenced the cultures of West Africa today? **Today the most frequently spoken European languages are English, French, and Portuguese. Many black West Africans speak one of these languages in addition to the language of their particular ethnic group.**
4. How did the tradition of cooperation develop in West African cultures? How important is this tradition? **Long ago West Africans developed strict rules for working together so that families could survive in their harsh lands. Cooperation became more important than individual success.**

Name Use with pages 432–434

Some Methods of Farming in West Africa

Follow the directions to answer the questions below. For help, you can refer to pages 432–434 in your textbook.

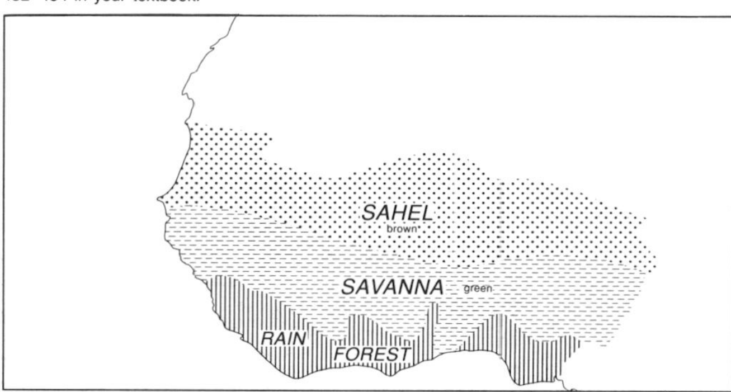

1. a. On the map above locate the region where desertification is occurring. Then color it brown.

   b. Why is desertification increasing?
   Drought, too much grazing, and the cutting down of trees and bushes leaves nothing to hold the soil and it blows away.

   c. What may happen to this region if desertification continues?
   The Sahel may become part of the Sahara.
2. a. On the map above locate the region where people practice shifting cultivation. Then color it green.

   b. What are two ways in which shifting cultivation is practiced?
   allowing some fields to rest
   slash-and-burn farming

   c. What is required for shifting cultivation to be successful?
   a lot of land
3. What are four crops produced by shifting cultivation in West Africa?
   millet **cassava** **yams** **peanuts**

Name Use with pages 435–438

A Look at a West African Government

Study the table and answer the questions below. For help, you can refer to pages 435–438 in your textbook.

FACTS ABOUT GAMBIA

Population: 959,000 (est. 1995)
Official Language: English
Major Religions: 90% Islam, 10% Christian and traditional
Ethnic Groups: Mandingo (41%), Fulani (14%), Wolof (13%), Serahuli (10%), Jola (8%), Other (14%)
Independence Day: February 18, 1965
Type of Government: Republic
Head of State: President elected to a five-year term
Major Political Parties: People's Progressive party, United party, National Convention party

1. a. According to the table, what kind of government does Gambia have?
   a republic
   b. What kinds of governments do most other West African countries have?
   either one-party systems or military governments
2. What is the Head of State of Gambia called?
   the president
3. How does a person become Head of State in Gambia?
   He or she is elected.
4. a. According to the table, how many major ethnic groups are in Gambia?
   five
   b. What challenge do so many ethnic groups present to the governments of West Africa?
   building national unity
5. How many major political parties does Gambia have?
   three
6. In your opinion, is Gambia more or less democratic than most other West African countries? Give a reason for your answer.
   Responses may vary, but students should indicate that Gambia, unlike most West African countries, has regular elections and several political parties.

Name Use with page 439

Distinguishing Fact from Opinion

Read the selection below. Then follow the directions and answer the questions. For help, you can refer to page 439 in your textbook.

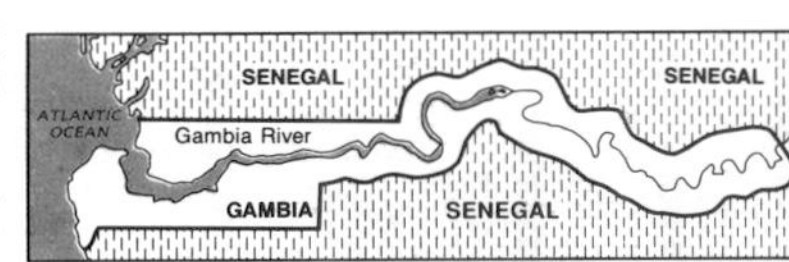

Gambia is the smallest independent country in Africa. I've always thought that the shape of Gambia is unusual. It is about 200 miles long but only from 10 to 40 miles wide. As it winds its way into the continent of Africa, it is surrounded by the country of Senegal. The entire length of Gambia follows the Gambia River, which is the major means of transportation through its interior. Gambia is planning to build a bridge and dam complex so that the river can be used for irrigation. I feel the dam will greatly benefit the Gambian people. It should allow them to grow more crops along the river's banks. In 1982 Gambia and Senegal established an organization for mutual cooperation. I believe this is one of the best things the two countries could have done.

1. Underline the sentences in the selection that state facts.
2. List two reasoned opinions stated in the selection. Then list the evidence the author gives to support each opinion.
   reasoned opinion: **I've always thought that the shape of Gambia is unusual.**
   supporting evidence: **It is about 200 miles long but only from 10 to 40 miles wide.**
   reasoned opinion: **I feel the dam will benefit the Gambian people.**
   supporting evidence: **It should allow them to grow more crops along the river's banks.**
3. Which reasoned opinion is supported by the map of Gambia?
   I've always thought that the shape of Gambia is unusual.

Name Use with pages 440–441

Arts and Recreation in West Africa

Use the pictures on the right to complete the exercises below. For help, you can refer to pages 440–441 in your textbook.

1. a. Draw a line to the picture that shows West Africa's oral tradition.
   b. Who are the most famous West African storytellers?
   the griots
   c. What role do they play in many groups?
   They are the praise singers and historians.
2. a. Draw a line to the picture that shows how many West Africans mark the main events in human life.
   b. What is the main musical instrument used for these events?
   the drum
3. a. Draw a line to the picture that shows how West Africans traditionally called the gods and spirits to talk to humans.
   b. What materials may be used in the making of West African masks?
   Wood, metal, clay, ivory, feathers, leather, shells, and many other materials.

Name Use with pages 446–447

Thinking About New Words

Choose a term from the box to answer each question. For help, you can refer to the lessons in Chapter 21 in your textbook.

slash-and-burn farming	lineage	desertification
shifting cultivation	clan	oral tradition
griot	oba	talking drums

1. Which term refers to a West African storyteller? **griot**
2. Which term refers to a West African ruler? **oba**
3. Which term describes a way of farming that involves clearing the land by burning? **slash-and-burn farming**
4. Which term describes literature and history that are passed down from person to person by the spoken word? **oral tradition**
5. Which term would you use to refer to drums that imitate the sound of human speech? **talking drums**
6. Which term describes a group of families that are descended from the same ancestor? **clan**
7. Which term would you use to refer to a kind of farming that allows some fields to rest while others are planted? **shifting cultivation**
8. Which term best describes what is happening to the Sahel of West Africa? **desertification**
9. Which term would you use to refer to a line of direct descent from an ancestor? **lineage**

Name Use with pages 449–452

Migration into East and Equatorial Africa

The chart below lists some of the major groups of people that migrated throughout East and Equatorial Africa. Read the list of groups. Then complete the chart by filling in the columns. For help, you can refer to pages 449–452 in your textbook.

MIGRATION INTO EAST AND EQUATORIAL AFRICA

Migrating Group	Area of Migration	Influence and Skills
Bantus	The Bantus migrated south and east from Cameroon on the west coast southeast into Equatorial Africa. In time the Zaire Basin became the center of Bantu kingdoms.	Bantu-speaking people form the largest ethnic groups in Equatorial Africa and the southern part of East Africa.
Arab Muslims	Muslim traders set up trading posts on the East Coast of Africa. Dar es Salaam, Tanzania, was founded by Arabs.	Arab Muslims introduced the Arabic language and the religion of Islam. They also introduced important food crops.
Kushites	The Kushites migrated south from Ethiopia into the fertile plateaus of the present-day countries of Uganda, Kenya, and Tanzania.	The Kushites were skilled farmers.
Nilotes	The Nilotes migrated south from the Nile River Valley into present-day Sudan. They roamed over the dry lands of East and Equatorial Africa.	The Nilotes knew how to grow grains and keep livestock alive in very dry climates.
Europeans	During colonial days, Europeans ruled most of East and Equatorial Africa.	They introduced European languages and customs.

Name Use with pages 453–455

The Economy of East and Equatorial Africa

Read the following statements carefully. If a statement is true, write **True** after it. If a statement is false, write **False** after it. Then, in the space provided, write the reasons for your answer. For help, you can refer to pages 453–455 in your textbook.

1. The picture above shows the tradition of cattle herding among the people of East and Equatorial Africa. To these people, cattle are much more than just a source of food. **True. Cattle are not just a source of food. They are a status symbol—a sign of a person's wealth and importance.**
2. Many of the people in East and Equatorial Africa are nomadic herders of cattle, moving their herds from one area to another. **True. They move their herds back and forth across the savanna area of Sudan, Ethiopia, Djibouti, Somalia, and Kenya.**
3. The area of cattle herding has plenty of rainfall and an abundance of vegetation for grazing. **False. Even in the best of times the savanna is often harsh and dry. It is not quite a desert, yet water and vegetation are scarce in many parts of the savanna.**
4. In the southern areas, the people farm land that is usually owned by wealthy individuals. **False. Most people are subsistence farmers, and land may be owned by the clan, an extended family, or members of the village.**
5. To become more developed economically, the countries of East and Equatorial Africa need to take several costly steps all at once. **True. All the countries need better transportation systems and more dams to produce hydro-electric power. They also need more educated workers.**

Name Use with pages 458–460

Governments in East and Equatorial Africa

Use the lines below the box to answer the questions in the box. Write your answers as complete sentences and arrange them in paragraphs. When you finish, you should have a brief summary of the typical government in the area, as well as a requirement for change. For help, you can refer to pages 458–460 in your textbook.

- How do most East and Equatorial African leaders feel about democratic rights for their people?
- What kinds of governments have the countries of this region had?
- How many candidates are on the ballot in most elections?
- How has power usually changed hands in these countries?
- What changes are coming to this region?
- What do many people think must happen before the governments of East and Equatorial Africa will change?
- Why do these people think future governments will be better?

Most East and Equatorial African leaders feel that forming stable governments is more important than guaranteeing democratic rights to their people. The governments of this area have had one-party systems or dictatorships. In most elections only one candidate is on the ballot. Power has usually changed only when a leader died or was overthrown in a coup. However, the countries in the region are moving to end one-party rule. Many people in East and Equatorial Africa believe that things will change only when young people who are not familiar with colonialism become adults. They think that this new generation of independent citizens will be better able to govern themselves.

Name Use with pages 461–462

Looking at an Oral Tradition

The song, saying, and proverb below are from the oral tradition of the people of East and Equatorial Africa. On the lines provided, briefly explain what each means to you. For help, you can refer to pages 461–462 in your textbook.

In the time when Dendid created all things,
He created the sun,
And the sun is born, and dies, and comes again.
He created the moon,
And the moon is born, and dies, and comes again;
He created the stars,
And the stars are born, and die, and come again;
He created man,
And man is born, and dies, and does not come again.

–Old Dinka Chant

Answers should indicate an understanding of the song's references to the cycles of nature and the finality of death.

Somewhere the Sky touches the Earth,
and the name of that place is the End.

–A Kamba Saying

To stumble is not to fall down but
to go forward.

–A Swahili Proverb

Responses will vary but should suggest that for the Kamba, the world ends somewhere out there where the sky touches the earth.

Responses will vary but should indicate that the proverb suggests people can learn from their mistakes.

Name Use with page 463

Making a Graph from a Chart

Make a line graph from the information in the chart. Use a different color for each point on your graph. Then use your graph to answer the questions that follow. For help, you can refer to page 463 in your textbook.

POPULATIONS OF TWO AFRICAN CITIES (*projected)

City	Population in Millions				
	1980	1985	1990	1995	2000*
Lagos, Nigeria	4.4	5.8	7.7	10.3	13.4
Casablanca, Morocco	2.2	2.7	3.2	3.4	3.7

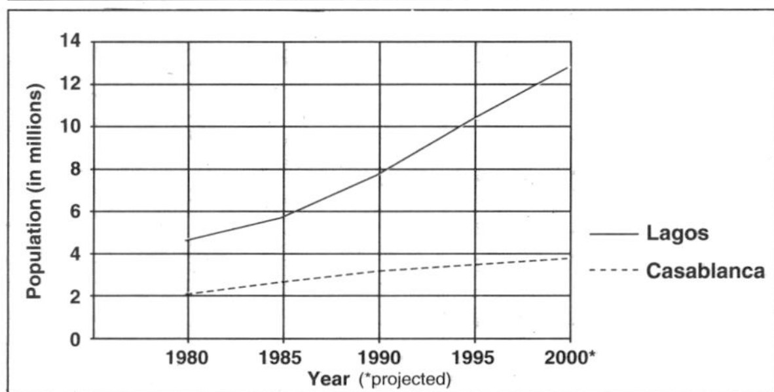

1. Has the population of each city decreased or increased since 1980? decreased (increased)
2. Which city had the smaller population in 1980? (Casablanca) Lagos
3. Which city's population grew faster between 1980 and 1995? Casablanca (Lagos) How can you tell? **The slope of the line is steeper.**
4. How many times larger will the population of Lagos be than that of Casablanca in 2000? **three**
5. Is it easier to compare the population growth of the two cities in the graph or in the chart? Give a reason for your answer. **in the graph because you can see the change of population growth at a glance**

Name Use with pages 464–465

Thinking About New Words

Each of the terms listed in the box below is hidden among the letters that follow. Draw a circle around each term you find. The words may be read forward, backward, up, down, or diagonally. For help, you can refer to the lessons in Chapter 22 in your textbook.

migration	Swahili	famine	malnutrition
civil war	proverb	barter	

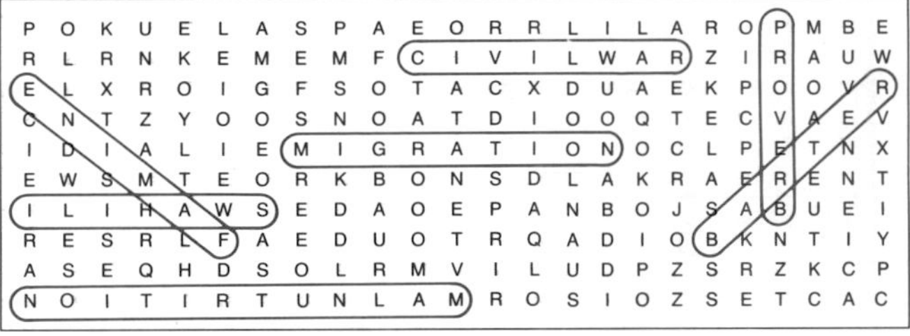

Write each circled word in the space next to its definition.

civil war 1. a war between people of the same country

migration 2. a movement of groups of people into new lands

proverb 3. a short, popular saying that illustrates a truth

malnutrition 4. a condition that occurs when people have too little food

famine 5. the widespread and extreme shortage of food

Swahili 6. one of the most common languages in East and Equatorial Africa

barter 7. to swap one thing for another

Name Use with pages 467–470

The People of Southern Africa

Follow the directions and answer the questions that follow. For help, you can refer to pages 467–470 in your textbook.

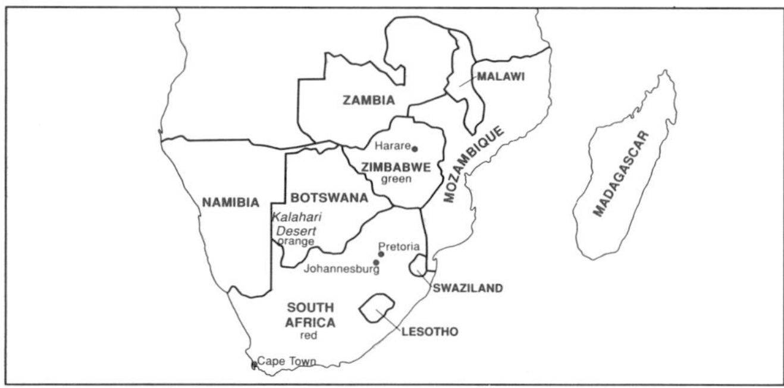

1. On the map above, locate and label the countries of Southern Africa.

Botswana	Lesotho
Madagascar	Malawi
Mozambique	Namibia
Swaziland	Zimbabwe
South Africa	Zambia

2. On the map above, locate and label the area where most Bushmen lived until recently. Then color the area orange. **Kalahari Desert of Botswana**
3. a. From what group are the majority of people in Southern Africa descended? **the Bantu**

   b. When did this group migrate into the lands of the Bushmen? **between 500 and 800 years ago**
4. a. Locate the only country in Southern Africa in which a white minority ruled until 1993. Then color the country red.

   b. How were different racial groups treated in this country? **Until recently, apartheid kept people separated from each other.**
5. a. Locate a country that was ruled by its white minority until 1980. Then color it green.

   b. What is one way this country tries to promote understanding between its different ethnic groups? **Students study the languages of people who belong to other ethnic groups.**

Name Use with pages 471–473

The Economies of Southern Africa

Answer the questions below. For help, you can refer to pages 471–473 in your textbook.

AVERAGE YEARLY INCOMES IN SOME SOUTH AFRICAN COUNTRIES (1994)

Country	Average Income per Year (U.S. dollars)
Mozambique	$115
Zambia	$380
Zimbabwe	$545
Botswana	$2,450
South Africa	$2,800

0 400 800 1200 1600 2000 2400 2800 3200

Average Income per Year (U.S. dollars)

1. The graph shows the average amount of money that people in the countries of Southern Africa earn in a year. In which of these countries do people earn the least amount of money? **Mozambique**
2. What two factors have contributed to this low per capita income? **civil war** **famine**
3. In which country shown on the graph do whites and blacks work equally and peacefully together? **Zimbabwe**
4. How do most people make a living in this country? **from farming**
5. According to the graph, in which country do people have the highest income? **South Africa**
6. What two mineral resources does this country have in vast abundance? **gold and diamonds**
7. Which country shown on the graph is a net exporter of food? **South Africa**
8. Which country shown on the graph has one fourth of the world's copper? **Zambia**

Name **Use with pages 474–477**

A Look at Apartheid

The graph below shows the categories of races in South Africa. After studying the graph, complete the activities that follow. For help, you can refer to pages 474–477 in your textbook.

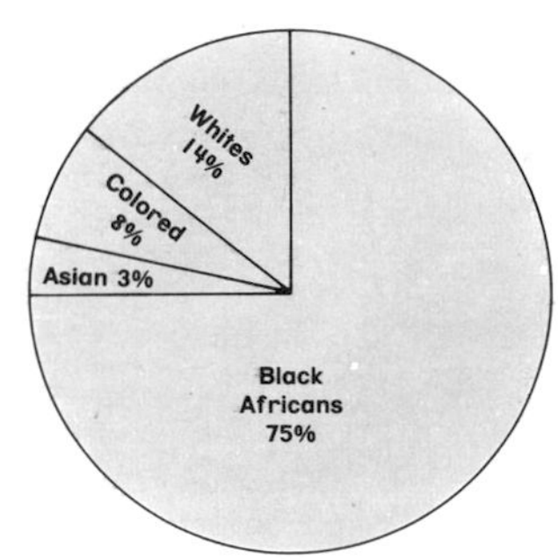

1. How many racial categories had been created by the South African system of apartheid?
   four
2. Which category is the largest?
   black Africans
3. Which racial category controlled the South African government until 1993?
   whites

   About what percentage of the population does this category make up?
   14 percent
4. What did many countries and international organizations do to protest the apartheid system? Give an example. **They passed sanctions against South Africa. For example, other nations did not allow South African athletes to compete in most world sports events because the majority of South African teams were separated by race.**

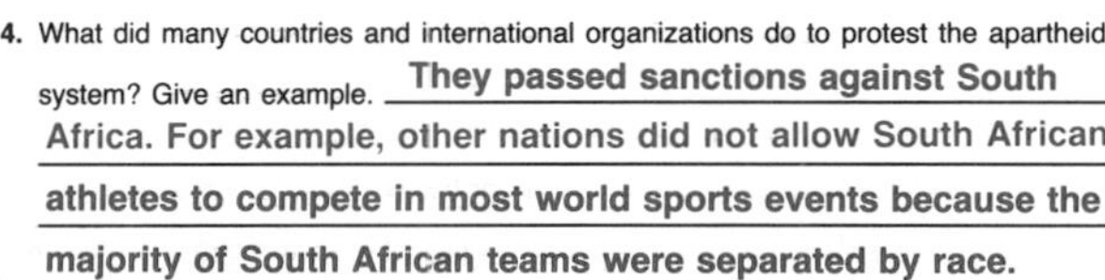

5. What changes happened in South Africa in 1993 and 1994? How did these changes affect the groups on this chart?
   Free elections were held, and Nelson Mandela was elected president. Blacks, Colored, and Asians gained rights and freedom.

Name **Use with page 478**

Recognizing Bias

Read the accounts below of the "state of emergency" declared by the South African government in 1986. These accounts describe some of the most extreme actions taken by the white minority government before the end of its rule in 1993. Then complete the activities that follow. For help, you can refer to page 478 in your textbook.

ACCOUNT A

In response to recent anti-apartheid demonstrations and protests, the South African government has placed the country under a state of emergency. The state of emergency gives the government the power to arrest and hold people without charge. The government has also limited news reporting and expelled journalists from several foreign countries. The government has taken these steps because it believes that excessive news coverage only makes the matter worse.

ACCOUNT B

In response to recent anti-apartheid demonstrations, the repressive white government of South Africa has assumed dictatorial power by placing the country under a state of emergency. Under the state of emergency the government has jailed tens of thousands of peaceful demonstrators and terrorized their leaders. It has also suppressed reporting of the protests and expelled any foreign journalists daring to report what is really happening.

1. Which account do you think shows bias? **Account B**
2. What are some clues that alerted you to the bias? **Answer may vary, but student responses should identify phrases such as "repressive white government," "assumed dictatorial power," "terrorized leaders," "suppressed reporting," and "daring to report what is really happening" as examples.**
3. Describe the bias in your own words. **Answers may vary, but student responses should indicate that the bias is against the South African government or in favor of the anti-apartheid demonstrators.**

Name **Use with pages 479–481**

Arts and Recreation in Southern Africa

You might see the announcements on this page in almost any Southern African country. Read each one. Then answer the questions. For help, you can refer to pages 479–481 in your textbook.

Ladysmith Black Mambazo

Enjoy the sound of South Africa as performed by this popular group.

1. a. What is the music called that is performed by the group in the top announcement?
   township music

   b. How was this music created?
   by mixing traditional African music with popular American and British songs heard on the radio

AMAMPONDO

The traditional instruments of Southern Africa as you've never heard them before.

2. a. What kinds of instruments does the group in the middle announcement use?
   They use only instruments invented in Africa.

   b. What is the main instrument used by this group called?
   a mbira

South Africa Reenters World Competition.

3. a. Who introduced the popular sport in this bottom announcement to Africa?
   the British

   b. What group ended its 21-year ban against competition by South African athletes in 1991?
   the International Olympic Committee

Name **Use with pages 482–483**

Learning New Words

Look at the box containing the Morse Code. The Morse Code uses dots and dashes to stand for the letters of the alphabet. Use the code to figure out the words and write each word on the lines provided. For help, you can refer to the lesson in Chapter 23 in your textbook.

A	B	C	D	E	F	G	H	I
•—	—•••	—•—•	—••	•	••—•	——•	••••	••
J	K	L	M	N	O	P	Q	R
•———	—•—	•—••	——	—•	———	•——•	——•—	•—•
S	T	U	V	W	X	Y	Z	
•••	—	••—	•••—	•——	—••—	—•——	——••	

c 1. **S A N C T I O N S**
••• •— —• —•—• — •• ——— —• •••

d 2. **V E L D**
•••— • •—•• —••

a 3. **T O W N S H I P**
— ——— •—— —• ••• •••• •• •——•

e 4. **M B I R A**
—— —••• •• •—• •—

b 5. **A P A R T H E I D**
•— •——• •— •—• — •••• • •• —••

Match the definitions below with the words above. Write the letter of each definition in the space before the appropriate word.

a. a racially segregated urban area in South Africa
b. the system used in South Africa for keeping racial groups separated
c. actions taken against a country by other nations to try to get the country to change
d. the vast, dry, treeless plateau that covers much of South Africa
e. an African finger piano made of metal or bamboo strips tied to a wood bowl

Name Use with pages 491–495

Southern and Eastern Asia

Use the map and follow the directions to complete the activities below. For help, you can refer to pages 491–495 in your textbook.

1. Locate and label the subcontinent of India.
2. Color the area of the Gobi and Takla Makan deserts brown.
3. Draw a red circle around the Indonesian archipelago.
4. Draw a green circle around the Philippine archipelago.
5. Locate and label the following rivers.
   Huang River Chang River
   Ganges River Mekong River
   Indus River
6. Locate and label the Pamir Knot.
7. Color the area of the North China Plain and the Tibetan Plateau orange.

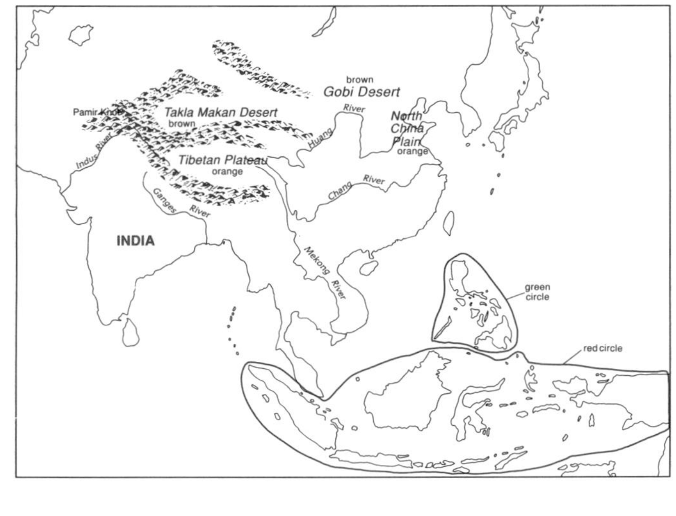

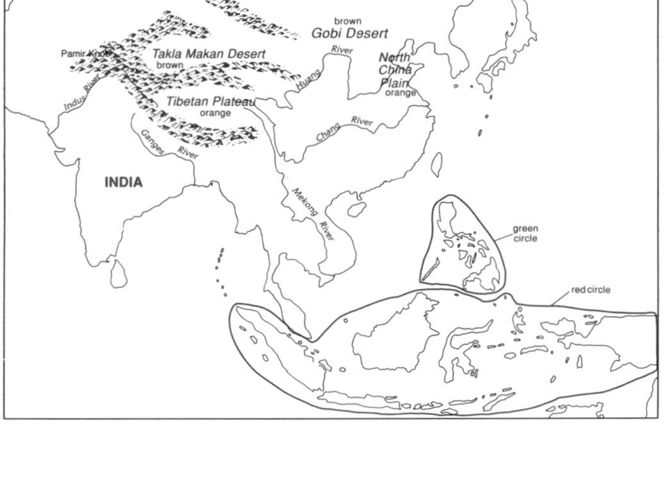

Name Use with pages 496–497

Thinking About Great-Circle Routes

Use the maps to answer the questions and complete the activities that follow. For help, you can refer to pages 496–497 in your textbook.

MAP A 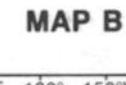 **MAP B**

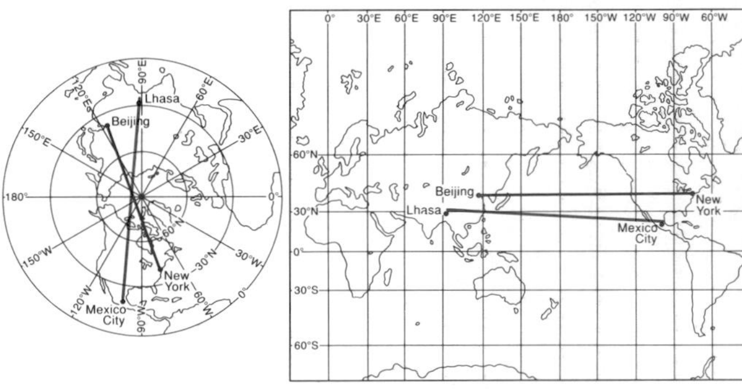

Circle the correct answer to each question.

1. Which map shows a great-circle route between New York and Beijing? **(Map A)** Map B
2. Which map shows the shortest route between New York and Beijing? **(Map A)** Map B
3. Draw a straight line from Mexico City to Lhasa on each map. Suppose this line shows your route of travel. Which map shows the longer route? Map A **(Map B)**
4. What kind of line would show a great-circle route between Mexico City and Lhasa on Map B? **(curved)** straight

Name Use with pages 498–501

Climate in Southern and Eastern Asia

Study the maps and answer the questions. For help, you can refer to pages 498–501 in your textbook.

1.

1. a. What kind of climate does most of this part of Asia have?
   tropical
   b. What is the major seasonal feature of this region?
   the monsoons

2.

2. a. What kind of climate does this part of Asia have?
   cold and dry
   b. Why is this region cold and dry?
   It is cold because it is located at high elevations. It is dry because the mountains block most of the rain.

3.

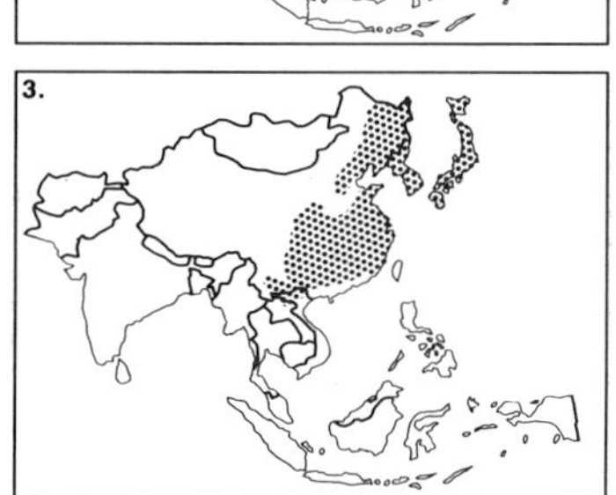

3. a. What is the major climate in this part of Asia?
   temperate
   b. How is this climate like the climate in the eastern part of United States?
   It has four seasons like the eastern United States.

Name Use with pages 502–503

Using New Words

Each of the terms listed in the box below is hidden among the letters that follow. Draw a circle around each term you find. The words may be read forward, backward, up, down, or diagonally. For help, you can refer to the lessons in Chapter 24 in your textbook.

subcontinent	monsoons	loess
alluvial soil	terraces	

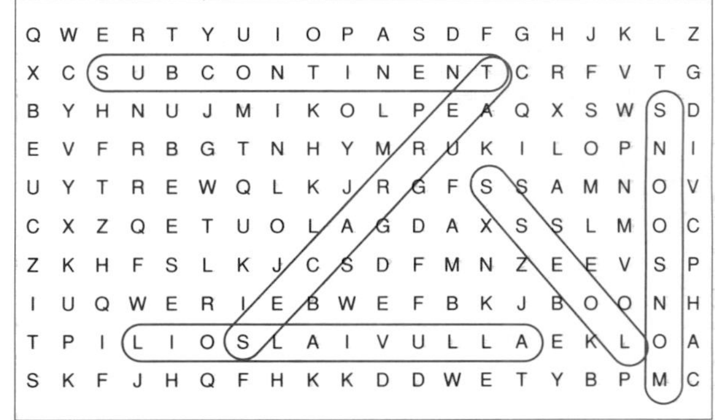

Write each circled word in the space next to its definition.

monsoons 1. heavy rains brought on by seasonal winds
terraces 2. large steps that have been carved into hillsides for the raising of crops
alluvial soil 3. soil deposited by a river as it flows
loess 4. yellowish, fertile soil that has been deposited by the wind
subcontinent 5. a large landmass that is smaller than a continent

Name Use with pages 505–513

The People of South Asia

Study the table. Then answer the questions that follow. For help, you can refer to pages 505–513 in your textbook.

THE PEOPLE AND RELIGIONS OF SOUTH ASIA (1995)

Country	Major Religion	Population Density	Major Occupation Percentage of Workers
Afghanistan	Islam	67/ per sq. mi.	68% farming/10% industry
Bangladesh	Islam	2,184/ per sq. mi.	74% farming/11% industry
Bhutan	Buddhism	39/ per sq. mi.	95% farming
India	Hinduism	752/ per sq. mi.	70% farming/19% industry
Maldives	Islam	2,191/ per sq. mi.	80% fishing and farming
Nepal	Hinduism	370/ per sq. mi.	91% farming
Pakistan	Islam	379/ per sq. mi.	53% farming/10% industry
Sri Lanka	Buddhism	714/ per sq. mi.	46% farming/27% industry

source: *World Almanac, 1989*

1. According to the table, what are the three major religions in South Asia?
   Hinduism
   Buddhism
   Islam
2. How did religious differences contribute to the formation of Pakistan?
   Conflict between Hindus and Muslims in India led to the partition of India and creation of Pakistan.
3. According to the table, what is the major occupation of South Asians?
   farming
4. According to the table, which South Asian country has the highest population density?
   Maldives
5. How has a high population density contributed to a low standard of living for many South Asians?
   Having so many people makes it hard for a country to grow enough food for everyone.
6. What is being done to ease the problems of famine and malnutrition in South Asia?
   New irrigation systems are being built, and new kinds of crops are being raised.

Name Use with pages 514–517

The Governments of South Asia

Complete the map by writing phrases from the box in the spaces provided on the map. Each space should have a separate phrase. For help, you can refer to pages 514–517 in your textbook.

torn by civil war
an Islamic country
a threatened island democracy
among the world's last monarchies
gained independence with India's help
the world's largest democracy

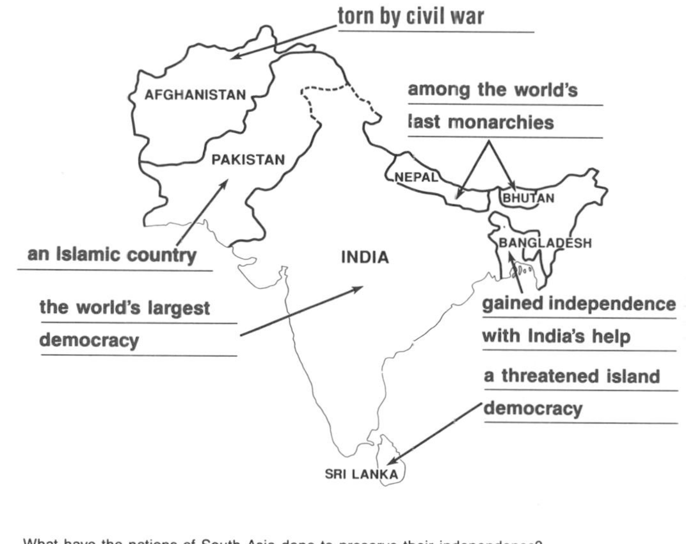

What have the nations of South Asia done to preserve their independence?
They have banded together with other small countries in a worldwide movement of nonaligned nations.

Name Use with page 518

Determining Point of View

Read the selection to complete the activities that follow. For help, you can refer to page 518 in your textbook.

Anyone visiting India should put the city of Agra at the top of his or her list of things to do and places to see. Agra is one of India's oldest cities and is famous for the Taj Mahal. The Taj Mahal may be the most beautiful building in the world. It was built in the 1600s by Emperor Shah Jahan as a memorial to his wife. The city of Agra is also famous for its gold lace and inlaid mosaics that are made mostly by hand. A visit to Agra is the best way to introduce yourself to the history, life, and customs of India.

1. List three sentences from the selection that are statements of fact.
   a. **Agra is one of India's oldest cities and is famous for the Taj Mahal.**
   b. **It was built in the 1600s by the Emperor Shah Jahan as a memorial to his wife.**
   c. **The city is also famous for its gold lace and inlaid mosaics that are made mostly by hand.**
2. List three sentences that are statements of opinion.
   a. **Anyone visiting India should put the city of Agra at the top of his or her list of things to do and places to see.**
   b. **The Taj Mahal may be the most beautiful building in the world.**
   c. **A visit to Agra is the best way to introduce yourself to the history, life, and customs of India.**
3. What is the writer's point of view? **Agra is one of the first places a visitor to India should see.**

Name Use with pages 519–521

Arts and Recreation in South Asia

Study the pictures. Then follow the directions to answer the questions that follow. For help, you can refer to pages 519–521 in your textbook.

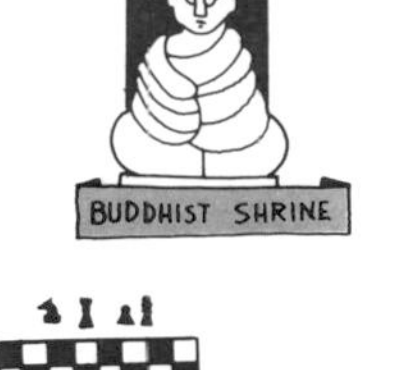

1. Circle the pictures that represent things from Indian culture that have spread to other parts of the world.
   yoga, badminton, polo, chess
2. Shade the picture that represents Islamic influence in art and architecture.
   Taj Mahal
3. Draw a triangle around the picture that represents Buddhist influence in art and architecture.
   Buddhist shrine
4. Put an X on the picture that represents a popular recreational activity imported from Britain.
   cricket
5. Draw a box around the picture that represents the telling of Hindu tales.
   Vedas
6. What plays a major role in the arts and recreation of South Asia?
   religion
7. What is meant by a cultural exchange between South Asia and other parts of the world?
   South Asia has imported some things from other cultures and has given much of its culture to other parts of the world.

Name ______ **Use with pages 522–523**

Using New Words

Use the words in the box to complete the puzzle below. For help, you can refer to the lessons in Chapter 25 in your textbook.

nonaligned nations	Hinduism	Vedas
Green Revolution	Brahmans	yoga
cottage industry	Sikhism	
partition	caste	

		1 G														
2 p	a	r	t	i	t	i	o	n			3 y					
		e									o					
		e						4 v			g			5 C		
6 n	o	n	a	l	i	g	n	e	d	n	a	t	i	o	n	s
		R						d						t		
		e						a						t		
		v						s						a		
		o												g		
		l												e		
		u			7 S									l		
8 B		t			i									n		
r		i			k									d		
a		o			h									u		
9 H	i	n	d	u	i	s	m							s		
m					s						10 c	a	s	t	e	
a					m									r		
n														y		
s																

Across

2. division
6. countries that do not want to take sides in the struggles between the world's superpowers
9. the religion that grew out of the legends and customs of the Aryans
10. a social group that identifies people according to the occupation of their ancestors

Down

1. changes in South Asian farming techniques that have resulted in larger harvests
3. a way of training body and mind through exercise and meditation
4. a collection of Hindu writings
5. manufacturing that takes place inside people's homes
7. a religion combining some elements of Hinduism and Islam
8. the priestly caste of ancient India

Name ______ **Use with pages 525–528**

People and Tradition in East Asia

Follow the directions to complete the activities below. For help, you can refer to pages 525–528 in your textbook.

1. a. Draw a line to the picture of the person who helped to establish the tradition of family loyalty in China.
   b. After the communists took power, with what did they try to replace family loyalty?
   loyalty to the state
2. a. Draw a line to the picture of the person who is believed to have been the founder of Daoism in East Asia.
   b. What does Daoism teach?
   People should accept their fate calmly.
3. a. Draw a line to the picture of the person who began Buddhism.
   b. What did this person come to be called?
   Buddha
   c. What does Buddhism teach?
   Suffering is caused by desire and selfishness.
4. a. Draw a line to the picture that shows the person who wanted China to break with the past.
   b. What system of government did he establish in China?
   communism

Siddhartha Gautama

Mao Zedong

Confucius

Laozi

Name ______ **Use with pages 529–531**

The Economies of East Asia

The headlines below might have been written about the economies of East Asia. Answer the questions about each headline. For help, you can refer to pages 529–531 in your textbook.

CHINA LOOSENS GRIP ON PRIVATE ENTERPRISE

a. During which years would this headline have been written? **in the late 1970s**

b. Why did China's leaders decide to allow limited private enterprise?
Answers may vary but should indicate that China's leaders believed that limited free enterprise would help solve China's food problem.

c. Was China's new economic program successful? Explain your answer.
The program was successful. More food and other goods were produced and sold on the open market.

CHINA SLOWS CHANGE TO PRIVATE ENTERPRISE

a. During which years would this headline have been written? **in the late 1980s**

b. List two problems that caused the government of China to tighten its control over private enterprise.
Under private enterprise some parts of China had too many goods, while other areas had severe shortages. Many prices had risen steeply.

ms 713 page 143 **EAST ASIA WORKS ECONOMIC MIRACLES**

a. Which areas of East Asia would this headline describe?
Hong Kong, Taiwan, South Korea

b. Why did these areas produce goods more cheaply than other countries?
because their workers' wages were low

c. How did the people in these regions make their economies successful?
by rapidly increasing their trade with other countries

Name ______ **Use with pages 532–534**

The Governments of East Asia

Look at the map and follow the directions to answer the questions below. For help, you can refer to pages 532–534 in your textbook.

1. Put an **X** on the countries that have communist governments.
   China, Mongolia, North Korea
2. Shade the countries that have republican forms of governments.
   South Korea, Taiwan
3. Circle the area that was a colony until 1997. What change happened?
   Hong Kong
   It was returned to China.
4. What led to the present systems of government in China and Taiwan?
   civil wars
5. What led to the present systems of government in North Korea and South Korea?
   After World War II communist troops held the northern part of Korea. South Korea was occupied by American troops.

MONGOLIA X

NORTH KOREA

SOUTH KOREA

shade

X CHINA

shade

TAIWAN

HONG KONG

Name Use with page 535

Reading Political Cartoons

The political cartoon below might have appeared in a newspaper during the time of the Korean War. Study the cartoon. Then answer the questions that follow. For help, you can refer to page 535 in your textbook.

1. What is the political cartoon about? **the Korean War**
2. What are four symbols in the cartoon? What do they stand for?
   a. **Uncle Sam is a symbol for United States forces and democracy.**
   b. **The Asian soldier is a symbol for communist forces.**
   c. **The torn shape of Korea is a symbol of the division of the country into North and South Korea.**
   d. **The trampled people is a symbol for the casualties of war.**
3. What point do you think the cartoonist was trying to make in the cartoon?
   Answers may vary, but student responses should indicate that the cartoon depicts the Korean War as a struggle between opposing forces with little regard for the people of the country.

Name Use with pages 536–537

Arts and Recreation in East Asia

Study the pictures and answer the questions that follow. For help, you can refer to pages 536–537 in your textbook.

1. What is the form of art called that is represented by the Chinese painting above?
   socialist realism
2. What is the purpose of this form of art?
   to use the "tremendous energy of the masses" to bring about change
3. In painting, what did this form of art replace?
   landscapes and other traditional themes
4. In which parts of East Asia do traditional arts and crafts continue to thrive?
   Hong Kong, Taiwan, and South Korea
5. What is the popular form of Chinese exercise called that is shown in the picture above?
   taiji quan
6. Why did Mao Zedong urge people to exercise?
   He wanted to end the low esteem in which China's educated classes held physical activity.
7. What are three forms of the martial arts that are popular throughout East Asia?
   kung fu
   tae kwan do
   karate
8. What are two crafts that are still practiced throughout East Asia?
   paper cutouts
   paper dragons

Name Use with pages 538–539

Using New Words

Write the letter of the term that matches each description below. For help, you can refer to the lessons in Chapter 26 in your textbook.

a. autonomous region	e. Confucianism	i. Daoism
b. socialist realism	f. aquaculture	j. pinyin
c. iron rice bowl	g. Pacific Rim	
d. martial arts	h. Buddhism	

e 1. the teachings of Confucius
j 2. a new way of spelling Chinese words
a 3. a self-governing area in China that is supervised by the central government in Beijing
f 4. fish farming
c 5. part of an economic policy in China where people are paid whether or not they work
g 6. all the countries that border the Pacific Ocean
h 7. a system of belief that teaches that suffering is caused by selfishness
b 8. a form of art that depicts true-to-life views of working people or heroes performing great deeds for the nation
d 9. ancient forms of hand-to-hand combat
i 10. a system of belief that teaches that people should accept their fate calmly

Name Use with pages 541–543

The People of Japan

Study the illustration, and then answer the questions that follow. For help, you can refer to pages 541–543 in your textbook.

1. The picture at the right shows a samurai who may have lived in Japan one thousand years ago. Who were the samurai?
   The samurai were warriors that once ruled Japan.
2. What Japanese traditions were passed down by the Samurai?
   a sense of duty and honor to one's family, leaders, and country

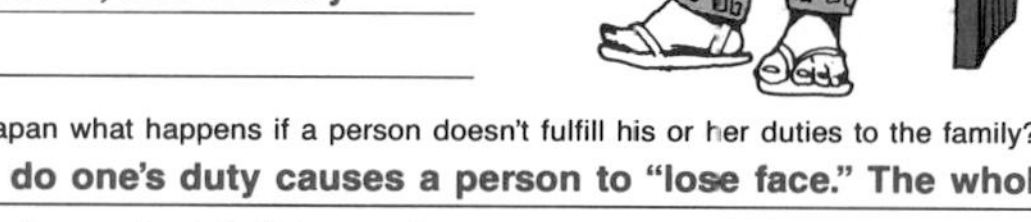

3. In today's Japan what happens if a person doesn't fulfill his or her duties to the family?
   To fail to do one's duty causes a person to "lose face." The whole family is shamed and disgraced.
4. Why are politeness and good manners important aspects of Japanese culture?
   The Japanese have deep respect for authority and order and believe that everyone has a certain position in society.
5. How does the Japanese view of society and the individual differ from the Western view?
   The Japanese believe that society is more important than any one person. They see themselves as members of a group, rather than as unique individuals striving to get ahead.
6. Why do you think the Japanese developed such a distinctive culture?
   Answers may vary but should indicate an understanding of the impact that Japan's isolation had on the development of Japanese traditions.

Name Use with page 544

Writing a Summary

Read the selection below. Then complete the activities that follow. For help, you can refer to page 544 in your textbook.

Samurai warriors were part of a privileged military class that ruled Japan from the twelfth to the nineteenth centuries. They pledged total loyalty to their feudal lords and defended their masters' territories. At the top of the samurai class was the shogun. He was the greatest of all feudal lords. Though shoguns were appointed by the emperor, it was the shoguns themselves who were the real rulers of Japan.

The samurai warrior was an awesome fighting machine. He was highly skilled in the use of the bow and sword. To protect himself he wore an elegant but very effective suit of armor. It was designed to provide freedom of movement while offering maximum protection. Because it was lightweight and flexible, it was unmatched by any other armor in the world.

The sword symbolized all that was important to a samurai warrior. In his hands it was a fearful weapon that had required strict training to master. The sword also stood for the samurai code of honor, bravery, and respect. All disagreements and problems were resolved by the sword, and the warrior lived and died by its laws. Strict rules were observed. For example, it was an offense to touch or step over another man's weapon. To lay your own sword on the floor and kick it in someone's direction was a challenge to the death.

1. Underline the topic sentence in each of the paragraphs.
2. Write a summary of the selection in three or four sentences.
   Samurai warriors were part of a privileged military class that ruled Japan from the twelfth to the nineteenth centuries. They pledged total loyalty to their feudal lords and protected their masters' territories. A samurai warrior was an awesome fighting machine. His sword symbolized all that was important to him.

Name Use with pages 545–547

Interviewing Akio Morita

Suppose you could interview Akio Morita. You might ask him questions similar to the ones below. Use the space to write the answers you think he might give. For help, you can refer to pages 545–547 in your textbook.

Interviewer: Japan has experienced remarkable growth since World War II. Yet, your country has very few natural resources. What made this growth possible?

Morita: The hard work of the Japanese people has made it possible. We demand excellence and efficiency of ourselves. We have also been able to adapt and improve upon the technologies of other countries. And we have continued to improve our manufacturing technology. For example we now use computer-controlled robots in many factories.

Interviewer: What are some of the products made by Japanese companies?

Morita: We produce everything from calculators and microchips to motorcycles and grand pianos.

Interviewer: What is it like to work in a Japanese company?

Morita: Workers receive extensive training after they are hired. They are made to feel as if they are part of the company family. In some businesses the workday begins with group exercises and company songs. Large companies may have recreational facilities for their workers.

Interviewer: Suppose you could give advice to the children of Japan. What would you tell them?

Morita: An industrial economy needs skilled, educated workers. I would advise the children of Japan to study hard in school so they could qualify for one of our best high schools.

Name Use with pages 550–551

The Japanese Government

The diagram below shows the organization of the Japanese government. Study the diagram and then answer the questions on this page. For help, you can refer to pages 550–551 in your textbook.

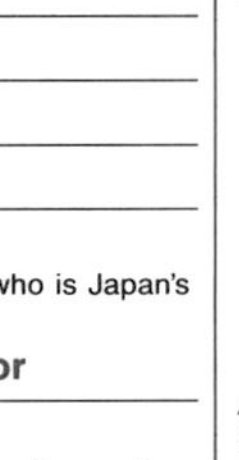

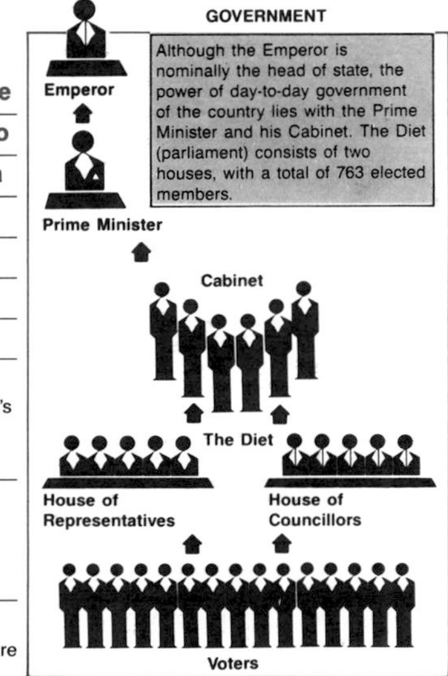

1. How did Japan's current form of government come about?
   At the end of World War II, the United States forced Japan to write a constitution forming a democracy.
2. According to the diagram, who is Japan's head of state?
   the emperor
3. Which person shown on the diagram is the head of the government?
   the prime minister
4. According to the diagram, from where are members of the cabinet selected?
   the Diet

   Who selects them?
   the prime minister
5. According to the diagram, what two Houses make up the Diet?
   House of Representatives
   House of Councillors
6. How are members of the Diet selected?
   They are elected by the voters.
7. What other country's government that you have studied is like that of Japan?
   Great Britain, Canada or other parliamentary systems

Name Use with pages 552–553

Arts and Recreation in Japan

Use the terms in the box to label each picture according to the artistic or recreational activity it represents. Then answer the question that follows. For help, you can refer to pages 552–553 in your textbook.

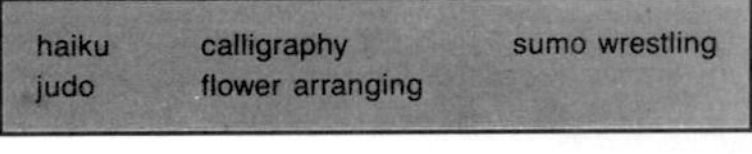

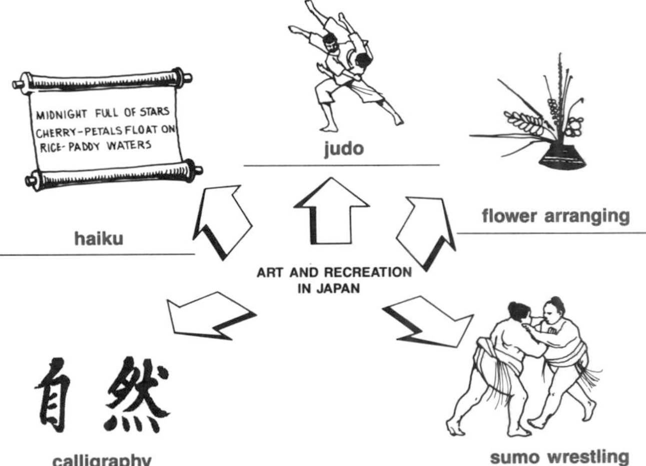

Why are flower arranging, gardening, and calligraphy among admired art forms in Japan?
The Japanese believe that art should be part of everyday life, not something for special times and places. Thus flower arranging, calligraphy, and gardening are highly admired art forms.

Name — Use with pages 558–559

Using New Words

Follow the directions to find each hidden term. Then, write the definition on the line below the letters. For help, you can refer to the lessons in Chapter 27 in your textbook.

1. Cross out the letters d, t, m, z, s **calligraphy**

   c ~~d~~ a ~~t~~ l l ~~m~~ i ~~z~~ g ~~s~~ r ~~d~~ a ~~t~~ p ~~m~~ h y

   the art of beautiful writing

2. Cross out the letters a, g, m, r, y **Shinto**

   ~~a~~ ~~g~~ s ~~r~~ h ~~y~~ ~~g~~ i n ~~a~~ ~~g~~ t ~~r~~ o ~~m~~

   the oldest of Japan's religions

3. Cross out the letters a, c, j, k, y, x **sumo wrestling**

   ~~c~~ ~~a~~ s ~~k~~ u ~~j~~ ~~a~~ m o ~~y~~ w ~~a~~ ~~c~~ r e ~~k~~ s t ~~c~~ ~~a~~ l i ~~x~~ n g

   one of Japan's traditional sports

4. Cross out the letters c, g, o, r, u, w **Diet**

   ~~w~~ ~~o~~ d ~~g~~ ~~r~~ i ~~c~~ e ~~u~~ ~~r~~ ~~g~~ t

   the Japanese legislature

5. Cross out the letters b, d, e, h, t **samurai**

   s ~~e~~ ~~b~~ a ~~t~~ ~~e~~ m ~~h~~ u r ~~d~~ a i ~~t~~

   warriors who ruled Japan thousands of years ago

6. Cross out the letters d, i, p, r, w **homogeneous**

   h ~~i~~ ~~p~~ o m ~~i~~ o ~~w~~ ~~i~~ g e n ~~r~~ e ~~i~~ o ~~d~~ u ~~i~~ s

   to look and act in a similar way

Name — Use with pages 561–564

The Countries and People of Southeast Asia

Use the map and follow the directions to complete the activities below. For help, you can refer to pages 561–564 in your textbook.

1. Locate and label the countries that make up Southeast Asia. List them below.

   Philippines **Laos**
   Indonesia **Brunei**
   Singapore **Cambodia**
   Malaysia **Myanmar**
   Thailand **Vietnam**

2. Locate the country that was settled by people from southwest China about 2,500 years ago. Then color it brown.

   Malaysia

3. Shade the other countries that were settled by people from southern China.

   Vietnam, Myanmar, Thailand, Laos

4. Draw a circle around the country in which the Dutch built canals.

   Indonesia

5. Draw a rectangle around the country into which the Spanish introduced the Roman Catholic religion.

   Philippines

6. From which two Asian countries have people immigrated to Southeast Asia during the last 100 years?

   China **India**

7. What are the two major religions in Southeast Asia today? List them below.

   Buddhism
   Islam

MYANMAR shade
LAOS shade
THAILAND shade
South China Sea
VIETNAM
rectangle
PHILIPPINES
PACIFIC OCEAN
circle
CAMBODIA
BRUNEI
MALAYSIA brown
SINGAPORE
INDIAN OCEAN
INDONESIA
circle

Name — Use with pages 565–570

Southeast Asia: Government and Economy

Use the terms and phrases in the box to complete the chart below. You will need to use some terms and phrases more than once. For help, you can refer to pages 565–570 in your textbook.

- constitutional monarchy
- republic ruled by military leaders
- republic headed by a president
- communist
- absolute monarchy
- parliamentary system
- richest country in the region
- financial and industrial center
- making economic gains with the help of foreign companies
- poor economy due to war
- third-richest country in the region
- poor economy due to poor planning, debt, and civil unrest

THE GOVERNMENTS AND ECONOMIES OF SOUTHEAST ASIA

Country	Type of Government	Condition of Economy
Philippines	republic headed by a president	making economic gains with the help of foreign countries
Singapore	parliamentary system	financial and industrial center
Brunei	absolute monarchy	richest country in the region
Malaysia	constitutional monarchy	third-richest country in the region
Indonesia	republic ruled by military leaders	making economic gains with the help of foreign countries
Laos	communist	poor economy due to war
Myanmar	republic ruled by military leaders	poor economy due to poor planning, debt, and civil unrest
Cambodia	communist	poor economy due to war
Thailand	constitutional monarchy	making economic gains with the help of foreign countries
Vietnam	communist	poor economy due to war

Name — Use with page 571

Drawing Conclusions

Read the article below. Then put an **X** next to each conclusion you can draw from the article. For help, you can refer to page 571 in your textbook.

During the Philippine elections of 1986, the Marcos government sent troops into most communities to destroy ballot boxes and votes that had been cast for Corazon Aquino. But the people of the Philippines formed human chains around the ballot boxes to protect them. Large crowds filled the streets, blocking the movement of military tanks. Soldiers put down their guns and joined the masses. Faced with such massive protests, Marcos and his followers were forced to flee the country, and Corazon Aquino became the president.

X 1. Ferdinand Marcos and Corazon Aquino were political opponents.

___ 2. Corazon Aquino disliked Marcos and his family.

X 3. Corazon Aquino had the support of the majority of the Philippine people.

X 4. The Philippine people were tired of the government of Ferdinand Marcos.

___ 5. No one supported the Marcos government.

___ 6. Marcos's high-level military generals gave their support to Aquino.

X 7. Marcos feared losing the 1986 presidential election.

X 8. Marcos did almost everything he could to keep Aquino from winning the election.

___ 9. Corazon Aquino had run for president in the previous election.

___ 10. The Philippine people based their decisions on debates between Marcos and Aquino.

Name Use with pages 572–573

Arts and Recreation in Southeast Asia

Follow the directions to complete the activities below. For help, you can refer to pages 572–573 in your textbook.

1. a. Draw a line to the picture that shows a popular sport in Southeast Asia.
   b. In which country did this sport originate?
   Thailand
   c. How is this sport different in Asia than it is in the United States?
   In Asia boxers use their elbows and knees and make lightening-fast kicks.

Gamelan

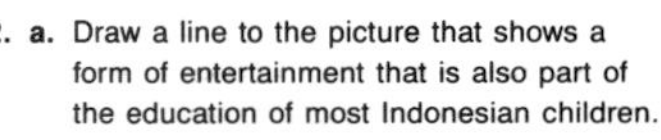

2. a. Draw a line to the picture that shows a form of entertainment that is also part of the education of most Indonesian children.
   b. What kinds of stories are depicted this way?
   stories of ancient Hindu rulers, gods, and heros

Thai Boxing

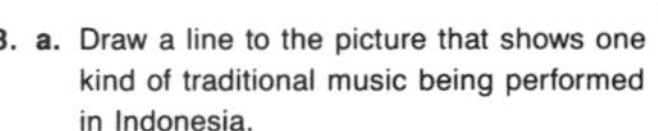

3. a. Draw a line to the picture that shows one kind of traditional music being performed in Indonesia.
   b. Why does almost every village in Indonesia have this kind of orchestra?
   because the people feel that without a gamelan a village can't have a proper festival

Shadow Plays

Name Use with pages 574–575

Learning New Words

Each of the words listed in the box below are hidden among the letters that follow. Draw a circle around each word you find. The words may be read forward, backward, up, down, or diagonally. For help, you can refer to the lessons in Chapter 28 in your textbook.

meditate
Vietnam War
shadow play
gross national product
paddy
gamelan

A G Y E D I M T R A B C K H I K L M H P C K C Q
H I A B R O E D V T Z N C A Z P O M A Y A L A M
S I L M K U D L A L B X E A T R O K M D A Y O S
U I P M E E I S L K E F V R S L E O M D K G E D
K W W M S L T I W S O L A E A E D N O A S N O M
G O O P S O A M E N U I E Q L K A N Z P E N S A
A D D V I E T N A M W A R E O W E Q R K O A K Q
D A A K D A E T J R X Q O A K L E U I S Y E D S
S H H E E K O T E S R X A S L O B A E A C T S O
T S S E T C U D O R P L A N O I T A N S S O R G

Write each circled word in the space next to its definition.

Vietnam War 1. The longest and most damaging war in Southeast Asia
gamelan 2. An Indonesian orchestra
meditate 3. Think deeply
gross national product 4. The total amount of goods and services produced in a country during a year
shadow play 5. A form of entertainment in which puppets are used to act out well-known stories by casting shadows
paddy 6. Flooded field where rice is grown

Name Use with pages 583–587

Looking at the Geography of the Pacific

The map below shows how the Pacific Islands are divided into three main groups. Study the map. Then complete the activities on this page. For help, you can refer to pages 583–587 in your textbook.

1. Collectively, what are the Pacific Islands called that are shown on the map?
   Oceania
2. Locate and label the area known as Polynesia. Then color the area green.
3. Locate and label the area known as Micronesia. Then color the area red.
4. Locate and label the area known as Melanesia. Then color the area brown.
5. Locate and label the island country known as New Zealand. Color North Island yellow. Color South Island orange.
6. Locate and label the world's smallest and oldest continent. **Australia**
7. Which three main inland regions make up this continent?
   the Western Plateau
   the Central Plains
   the Eastern Highlands
8. What large underwater area can be found off the northeast coast of this continent?
   the Great Barrier Reef

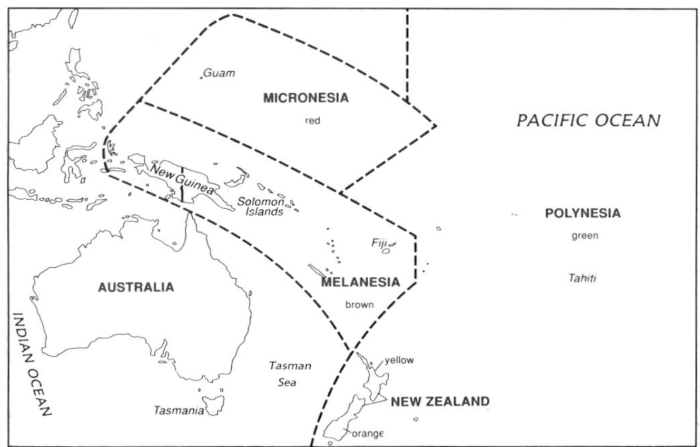

Name Use with pages 588–589

Using Maps of the Ocean Floor

The map below shows the floor of the South Pacific Ocean around the continent of Australia. Use the map to answer the questions. For help, you can refer to pages 588–589 in your textbook.

1. Is the map above a relief map or a contour map? How do you know?
   It is a relief map. It shows the features of the ocean floor without using contour lines.
2. What is the name of the mountain range that runs across the ocean floor south of Australia?
   the Southeast Indian Ridge
3. Which feature curves around the Fiji Plateau?
   the New Hebrides Trench
4. How far below sea level is the floor of the Tasman Basin?
   17,381 feet (5,267 m)
5. Would ocean ridges or ocean basins be further below sea level? Explain your answer.
   basins because they are flat areas on the ocean floor. Ridges are mountains that rise above the ocean floor.
6. How do scientists show elevations and features of the ocean floor more accurately than they are shown on the map above?
   by making contour maps

Name ______ Use with pages 590–593

Products of Australia and the Pacific Islands

Circle the pictures that represent products from Australia. Draw a box around the pictures that represent products from New Zealand. Draw a triangle around the picture that represents an important natural resource found on many of Oceania's tropical islands. Then answer the questions that follow. For help, you can refer to pages 590–593 in your textbook.

1. Why is Australia called the "Lucky Country"?
   It is an uncrowded land with abundant natural resources.
2. What are two minerals mined in Australia that are not shown in the picture?
   bauxite, iron, copper, lead, zinc
3. Why do the ranches in Australia have to be so large?
   Because of the dry land and sparse vegetation it requires a lot of land to graze livestock.
4. What are two major natural resources that New Zealand has that are not shown in the picture?
   water
   forests
5. Why can a variety of fruits be grown by New Zealand farmers?
   New Zealand has both good soil and a variety of climates.
6. Why do the people of Oceania's tropical islands call the coconut palm the "Tree of Life"?
   It grows in poor soil and has many uses.

Name ______ Use with pages 594–595

Using New Words

Use the code in the box to figure out each word. Then write the word on the line above its code. For help, you can refer to the lessons in Chapter 29 in your textbook.

CODE

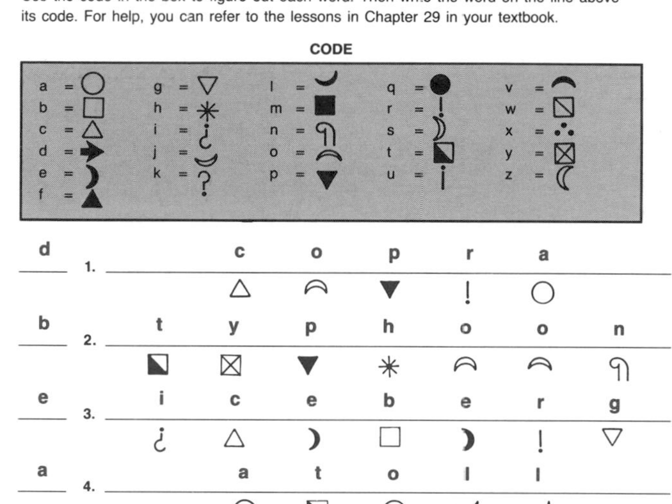

c 5. **o u t b a c k**

Write the letter of each of the following definitions in the space before the above word that it matches.

a. a doughnut-shaped coral reef looped around an area of still, warm water
b. a whirling tropical hurricane of the Pacific
c. a huge, arid area of Australia
d. the dried meat of a coconut
e. a large body of ice that has broken away from a glacier

Name ______ Use with pages 597–599

The People of Australia and the Pacific Islands

The words below were written by Louis-Antoine de Bougainville. Read what he wrote. Then answer the questions. For help, you can refer to pages 597–599 in your textbook.

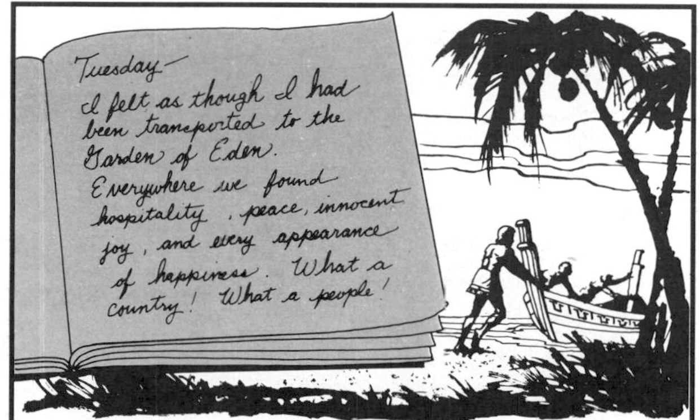

1. What island was de Bougainville writing about?
   Tahiti
2. Who were the people he mentions?
   Tahitians, one group of Polynesians
3. Why have these people been called the "Vikings of the Sunrise"?
   because they were expert in both sailing and shipbuilding
4. Which group of these people sailed south to settle New Zealand?
   the Maori
5. Which group of people were the first to settle in Australia?
   the Aborigines
6. How were these people treated by the early European explorers?
   Many were attacked and killed.
7. Why did many European immigrants come to New Zealand and Australia?
   because Australia and New Zealand offered land, work, and adventure

Name ______ Use with pages 600–601

ECONOMIES: Australia and Pacific Islands

Study the graphs. Then answer the questions. For help, you can refer to pages 600–601 in your textbook.

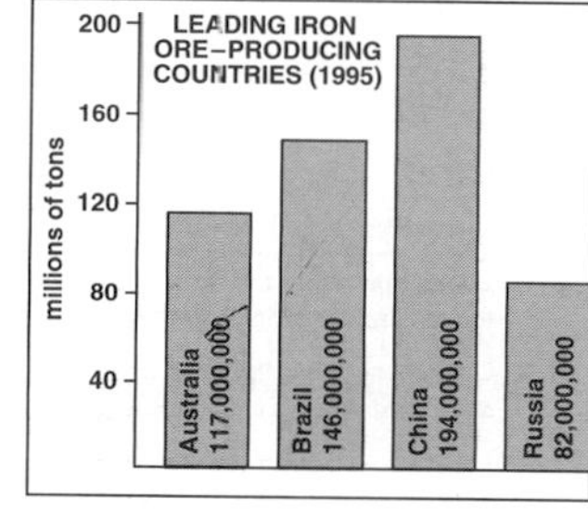

1. a. According to the bar graph on the right, which South Pacific country is one of the leading iron-ore producers in the world?
   Australia
   b. This country is a top producer of what other three mineral resources?
   copper
   nickel
   aluminum
   c. This country's developed economy includes a mixture of what economic activities?
   farming, mining, manufacturing, and service industries

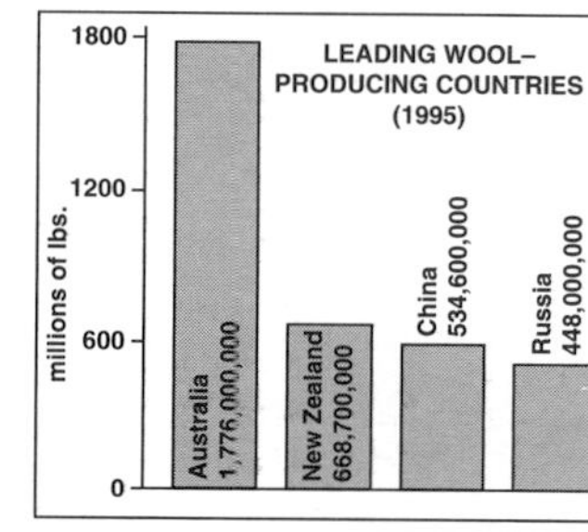

2. a. According to the graph on the right, which two Pacific countries are leading producers of wool?
   Australia
   New Zealand
   b. Which of these countries is the largest exporter of wool?
   New Zealand
   c. What is the most important part of this country's economy?
   farming and ranching
3. a. What is the main source of income for the many Pacific Islands not shown in the graphs? **tourism**
   b. How do the economies of these islands differ from the economies of New Zealand and Australia? **Most of the Pacific Islands have developing economies. New Zealand and Australia have developed economies.**

Name | Use with page 602

Making Decisions

Sonia's teacher has given the class three choices for a field trip. Tomorrow they will vote on where the class will go. Read how Sonia decided which trip to vote for. Then answer the questions. For help, you can refer to page 602 in your textbook.

I know that I want to go to the place where I can learn the most. The first choice is going to the botanical gardens. I could learn about many different kinds of plants and it's nearby. But I've already been there several times.

Our second choice is going to the Metropolitan Museum. They have many different kinds of exhibits including some on Pacific cultures. We are learning about the people of the Pacific Islands in our social studies class. The only problem is that it takes about two hours to get to the museum. We would have to leave early in the morning.

Our third choice is taking a tour of the historic district of our town. That sounds like fun, but it's fall and it may be cold. Besides, I have been to the district several times with my family, and I already know quite a lot about the history of our area.

The more I think about it, the better the museum sounds. I can learn about something I am studying in class, and there are lots of other things to see and do, too.

1. What decision did Sonia have to make? **She had to decide which field trip to vote for.**
2. What was her goal? **to go to a place where she could learn the most**
3. Which trip did Sonia finally decide to vote for? **the museum**
4. Which two things didn't Sonia consider as she thought about her decision? Put an **X** next to each one.
   - **X** a. Each trip would cost a different amount of money.
   - ____ b. Her social studies class is studying the people of the Pacific Islands.
   - ____ c. She has been to the historical district of her town several times with her family.
   - **X** d. A long trip might not leave much time at the museum.

Name | Use with pages 603–605

GOVERNMENTS: Australia and Pacific Islands

Complete the map by writing phrases from the box in the spaces provided on the map. Each space should have only one phrase, but you may use a phrase more than once. Then answer the question that follows. For help, you can refer to pages 603–605 in your textbook.

- parliamentary system of government
- trust territory of the United States
- elected legislature and a council of chiefs
- ruled by a monarch and a council
- only matai can vote for government officials

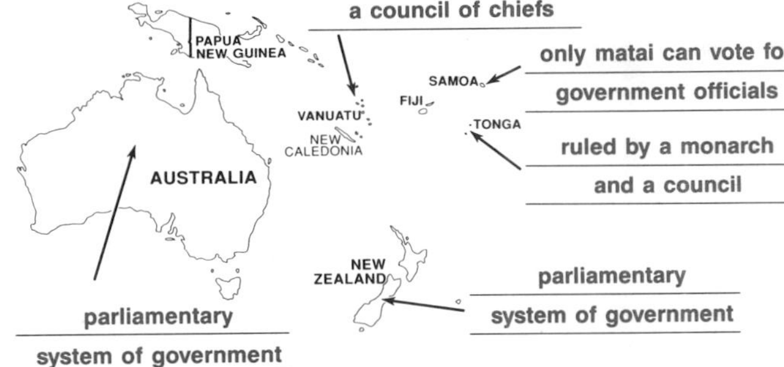

How would you describe the many forms of government in the Pacific region? **Most have representative assemblies. Australia, New Zealand, Papua New Guinea, and Fiji belong to the British Commonwealth of Nations. In most of the rest of the island nations, traditional island chiefs and elected government officials form the governments.**

Name | Use with pages 606–607

Arts and Recreation in the Pacific Region

Follow the directions to complete the activities below. For help, you can refer to pages 606–607 in your textbook.

1. a. Draw a line to the picture that shows one way the Samoans keep their cultural identity alive.
   b. What happens as warriors bend over their oars? **They yell out chants to the beat of drums.**
   c. What are some of the chants about? **the history of families**
2. a. Draw a line to the picture that shows where Australians enjoy performances of the fine arts.
   b. What did the Australians hope to show outsiders by building this structure? **They not only appreciate the fine arts, but they also create world-class architecture.**
3. a. Draw a line to the picture that shows the most popular sport in New Zealand.
   b. What are two other popular New Zealand sports? **long-distance running** / **mountain climbing**

Sydney Opera House

Rugby

Samoan Canoe

Name | Use with pages 612–613

Using New Words

Complete each of the activities below. For help, you can refer to the lessons in Chapter 30 in your textbook.

1. Put an **X** next to each statement that correctly describes a *trust territory*.
   - ____ a. A trust territory controls its own government.
   - **X** b. A trust territory does not belong to an outside power.
   - **X** c. The government of a trust territory is controlled by another country until that country decides the trust territory is ready to govern itself.
   - ____ d. A trust territory is a kind of economic system.
   - ____ e. An outside power controls the government of a trust territory permanently.
   - **X** f. Guam is a trust territory of the United States.
2. Put an **X** next to each statement that is true about *stations*.
   - **X** a. Stations are huge ranches where sheep and cattle are raised.
   - **X** b. Much of the world's wool is made from sheep on New Zealand stations.
   - ____ c. Sheep stations are the only kind of farm found in New Zealand.
   - ____ d. Stations are large fruit orchards in Australia and New Zealand.
   - **X** e. Only 6 percent of Australians work on farms or stations.
   - ____ f. Stations are a form of government in the Pacific islands.